CONTEMPORARY DRAMATISTS

Contemporary Writers of the English Language

Contemporary Poets
Contemporary Novelists
  (including short story writers)
Contemporary Dramatists
Contemporary Literary Critics
Contemporary World Writers

CONTEMPORARY DRAMATISTS

FIFTH EDITION

PREFACE TO THE THIRD EDITION
RUBY COHN

PREFACE TO THE FIFTH EDITION
MICHAEL BILLINGTON

EDITOR
K. A. BERNEY

St J

St James Press

London   Washington, DC   Detroit

FOR

COLIN NAYLOR

1944–1992

CONTENTS

PREFACE
to the third edition

This volume contains well over three hundred entries for contemporary dramatists writing in English, thousands of miles apart. It might seem then that English drama is alive and well, but for that to be true, audiences should embrace drama. Do they? I have seen estimates ranging from one per cent of the population (of America) to five per cent (of England) who *ever* attend the theatre, but *regular* attendance thins down to decimals of decimals. Will these dramatists continue to write for a diminishing audience?

How different from the burgeoning drama of the Elizabethans. And yet Burbage and Henslowe may also have worried about theatre attendance. No language seems to sport more than one great age of drama, and other periods of English language drama have looked pale by contrast with the Elizabethan. In later times English theatre came to be a fabulous invalid, enjoying its several prognoses, diagnoses, and forecasts of doom. Such a forecast is again appropriate today, not because our contemporary drama is less skillful than that of any age since the Elizabethan, nor less plentiful. But because our drama, like that of no other period, has to survive in the noxious atmosphere of the mass media. Playwrights can defy the media, sidestep them, try to ignore them, or, as more often happens, use dramatic form as an entrée into the media, notably films and television.

In English-speaking countries, with their meagre theatre subsidies and their major technical resources, drama abounds on film and television. (Dublin's Abbey Theatre in 1922 became the first nationally subsidized theatre in the English language, whereas the subsidized Comédie Française dates from 1680.) If today's writer is inadequately nurtured by theatre or publisher, he can turn to the media. But few media graduates have contributed significant dramas to live theatre. Mass media drama tends to appeal to the most facile reactions of an audience, and yet the techniques of the media can broaden the palette of the stage playwright. Since writing the Preface to the first edition of *Contemporary Dramatists*, I have become aware of media writers who return sporadically but significantly to the stage and of Heathcote Williams's *AC/DC* which grounds a frenzied strength in the weaknesses of a media civilization. The theatre has always drawn upon other arts, crafts, and technologies, and it may arrive at a *modus vivendi* with the media.

Perhaps the *drama* is dying in the form we have known for some four hundred years—a fairly inflexible prompt copy which is eventually printed. However, the *theatre* today—with or without promptbook—must recognize its uniqueness in that live actors play before live audiences. Each actor has a single instrument, the body that includes the voice. And for all the experimentation with non-verbal sounds, the voice has recourse to words, which are the province of the dramatist.

English drama is coeval with the printing press, and response to drama has for centuries been cumulative, as a reader-spectator travels from stage to page and, all the more receptive, to stage again. This itinerary may be less frequent for today's spectators. Contemporary stage dialogue may include primitive non-verbal sounds and electronic post-verbal devices, but new dramas of verbal distinction are nevertheless being written and played. As long as that continues, in the full awareness of live theatre as a minority art, drama will endure.

Prognosis pronounced, whom do we actually have in a volume on contemporary dramatists writing in English? Since "contemporary" has been defined (for this volume) as biologically alive, we find curious neighbors. Some dramatists have spent successful years appealing to middle-class entertainment-seekers; others have tried to entertain while supporting worthy causes or baring social problems. As has been true for four hundred years, certain plays were written to provide scope for the special talents of a particular actor. None of this sounds contemporary in an age when we take it for granted that we will fly faster than sound.

I have seen many, many plays, and many kinds of plays in nearly forty years of theatre-going. It seems only yesterday that I saw *The Iceman Cometh* in a production advised by Eugene O'Neill. (It was actually 1946.) Or *The Apple Cart*, crackling wittily, only shortly after Bernard Shaw's witticisms had ceased to crackle. (It was actually 1953.) But yesterday is far away in contemporary theatre, so that Shaw and O'Neill belong to another age and another theatre language. And since this is true of master-playwrights, it is all the truer for their lesser colleagues. Even living playwrights are dead in today's theatre: a windy would-be Elizabethan, a once angry young man turned surly, a once fragile young lyricist turned coy, a reacher for tragedy resigned to routine comedy, or various squatters in the Abbey Theatre which nearly exploded under the impact of three different meteors. Such dramatists are less contemporary than Euripides or Shakespeare, not to mention John Whiting and Joe Orton, who died in mid-career. For there is no necessary convergence between biological and artistic life. I hope all playwrights live to be a hundred, but I cannot help exclaiming at some of the entries in this volume: "Is he still alive?"!

Since mid-century, we have seen specimens of English language theatre labelled epic, angry, kitchen sink, absurd, ridiculous, radical, third world, puppet, guerrilla, fact, nude, improvisational, perspectivist, alternative—all soon exploited by the mass media. It is small wonder that many of the contemporary dramatists in this volume seem either uncontemporary or undramatic, regardless of chronology or biology.

To shift abruptly to a positive note, we have among contemporary dramatists one giant, Samuel Beckett, who writes sometimes in English, sometimes in French, always in his own distinctive dramatic idiom. Beckett's plays are enduring masterpieces. They are also a terminus to the Western dramatic tradition, dissecting the parts of a play so that they can never again articulate innocently. Through the tension of play, Beckett probes the bases of Western culture—faith, reason, friendship, family. Through the skills of play, Beckett summarizes human action—word and pause, gesture and stillness, motion rising from emotion. Beckett's most celebrated play, *Waiting for Godot*, is striking in its stage presence. As Brecht called attention to the theatre, Beckett calls attention to the play as play. Often pitched as polar opposites, Brecht and Beckett both reacted against the dominant illusionist drama of their time and ours, so that it is no longer so dominant. In spite of their differences, Beckett resembles Brecht in precision of language at the textural level, and in integration of verbal rhythms into an original scenic whole.

Relentlessly digging his own way, Beckett has inspired two English-language playwrights, one on each side of the Atlantic, Harold Pinter and Edward Albee. From Beckett both younger dramatists have learned to convey the presence of stage action, without before or after, exposition or resolution. Pinter capitalizes on the unverifiability of a past, and Albee fits the past obliquely into the stage present. Both playwrights create the stage present through carefully crafted dialogue. Their characters speak in stylized patterns that draw upon colloquial phrases of contemporary speech. Unlike the realists with whom they are sometimes confused, they use repetition and cross-talk to probe beneath or beyond surface reality.

In their rejection of realism, other contemporary dramatists resemble Pinter and Albee. Since no stage designer can compete with the camera in photographic fidelity to surface appearance, many contemporary dramatists don't ask them to try. Departures from realism can be as diversified as John Arden's Brechtian songs in *The Ballygombeen Bequest*, Edward Bond's Ghost in *Lear*, the penitential geometry of Kenneth H. Brown's *The Brig*, the seasonal symbolism of Ed Bullins's *In the Wine Time*, the eternal sparring in María Irene Fornés's *Tango Palace*, the opportunity for improvisation in Paul Foster's *Tom Paine*, the drug metaphor in Jack Gelber's *The Connection*, the mythic dimension in Amiri Baraka's *Dutchman*, the documentary absurdism of James Saunders's *Next Time I'll Sing to You*, the stretch toward Artaud in Peter Shaffer's *The Royal Hunt of the Sun*, the manic rock monologues of Sam Shepard's *The Tooth of Crime*, the tribal magic of Derek Walcott's *Dream on Monkey Mountain*, the play organically within the play in Patrick White's *The Ham Funeral*. I am not saying that these plays are of equal quality, but I am saying that forays into non-realistic modes provide richer possibilities of theatricalizing the profundities of contemporary experience.

Provided that audiences come to see the plays.

—RUBY COHN (1982)

PREFACE
to the fifth edition

Drama is an obstinate, if beleaguered, survivor. By all the laws of logic it should be tottering into its grave killed off by mounting production costs, the media explosion, massive competition for public attention. Yet, as the nearly 100 new entrants to the fifth edition of this volume testify, the urge to create plays remains irrepressible. There seems to be a fundamental need to tell stories, explore moral dilemmas, bear witness to great events or simply make sense of an increasingly chaotic world. Even perhaps to make money: one of the entrants to this volume told me that, by her reckoning, there are half-a-dozen millionaire playwrights in Britain alone.

For all that, playwriting has, over the last decade, become an increasingly hazardous occupation. The first threat comes from the sanctification of the musical as the holy altar of theatre. Travel to any major theatrical city in the world and you will find that a floating combination of hit musicals by Andrew Lloyd-Webber or the Boublil-Schönberg team is sure to be playing: they are as inescapable as fast food joints or American hotel chains. But instead of sneering at *Cats* or moaning about *Les Misérables*, one should perhaps ask why it is that musicals are gradually supplanting drama, for many people, as the central theatrical experience. My own answer is that they offer, apart from the obvious attractions of melody, colour and spectacle, some kind of transcendent experience. We go to the theatre seeking entertainment, enlightment and ecstasy; but the last of these is a quality that drama—with a few notable exceptions such as Brian Friel's *Dancing at Lughnasa* or Tony Kushner's *Angels in America*—has lately forgotten how to supply.

Playwriting is under threat from other factors. An obvious one is the insatiate appetite of the cormorant media. In the English-speaking world theatre is increasingly used as a nursery of talent by the film and television industries which often devour writers before they have had a chance to develop. Obviously film and television are valuable in that they help to keep writers off the breadline; and shrewd, mature talents like Harold Pinter and David Mamet bring the same verbal precision and technical craft to the screen as to the stage. The real problem is that television, especially, picks up young dramatists promiscuously and reduces them to the status of dialogue-writers leaving them ill-equipped to handle the structural complexities of drama.

Another threat to playwrights is the perceptible cultural shift away from the present towards the past. It may be less true in America, Australia and New Zealand or Africa. But certainly in Britain there is a feeling that new writing is no longer as sexy as it once was: that the smart, chic thing to do is to discover a neglected foreign classic from another century. It is partly a result of a gradual shift from a writers' to a directors' theatre and a realization by young directors that they can make their mark by offering a conceptual vision of a dead author rather than by serving a living writer. It is also tied up with a post-modernist belief that old texts exist to be re-invented, re-interpreted, even re-structured. This has a gamey whiff of excitement very different from that of teasing out the meaning of a new play with the writer sitting next to you in the rehearsal room.

And yet—particularly when I survey the list of new entrants to this volume—it strikes me that drama is anything but dead. For a start it is good to see that the old Anglo-American hegemony is being increasingly challenged. Obviously those two countries, because of history and tradition, dominate the scene; and they have lately produced some exciting new dramatists such as the morally exploratory Jon Robin Baitz or the alertly self-referential Martin Crimp. But a lot of the energy in recent years has been coming from other quarters. Ireland leaps to mind with writers like Frank McGuinness and Billy Roche adding to the existing achievements of dramatists such as Brian Friel and Tom Murphy. But what exactly is it about Irish writers that gives them such global popularity? My own thesis is that, whether they are Protestant or Catholic, hail from North or South, they still deal with themes that have a universal, mythic resonance; the power of motherhood, the tenacity of land, the pathos of exile, the inescapable imprint of religion. Intriguingly, the things that unite Ireland seem even greater than those that divide it.

But other countries are also using drama as a means of self-definition. Australian colleagues tell me that their late-1960's theatrical Renaissance—triggered partly by increased funding and partly by a need, in the light of the Vietnam experience, to discover a national identity—is tapering off. Yet frequent visits have convinced me Australia still has an exploratory new drama exemplified by works like Michael Gow's *Away*, which uses the structure of *A Midsummer*

Night's Dream to describe the country's entry into global maturity, and Hannie Rayson's *Hotel Sorrento* which argues that writers flourish best in their native soul. And in South Africa writers like Percy Mtwa, Mbongeni Ngema and Barney Simon, linked by their association with Johannesburg's Market Theatre, have all deployed drama as a means not just of raising consciousness but of exploring national identity.

Drama is not just being enriched geographically. It is also heading in new directions formally. This is almost inevitable in the age of television, mass advertising, pop videos. Given that we are used to receiving and absorbing information so much more quickly, the traditional theatrical structure of exposition, crisis, dénouement is bound to come in for a shake up. To put it crudely, plays are becoming much shorter or much longer; and this in itself is a reflection of theatre's increasing division into the powerfully intimate or the expansively epic. On the one hand dramatists are discovering, not least in America, that they can pack into a single 90-minute act a particularly violent, intense, emotional experience. On the other hand, they are realising that there is a renewed interest in narrative and that audiences today have a craving for inordinate, complex stories that take a long time to unravel. In classic theatre, we have seen it time and again with the popularity of productions like the Royal Shakespeare Company's *Nicholas Nickleby*, Mnouchkine's *Les Atrides*, Brook's *The Mahabharata*. Now living writers, such as David Hare with his epic trilogy on the state of Britain or Tony Kushner with *Angels in America*, are realising that long plays give you a chance to handle a multiplicity of themes and to depict the gradations of time. I suspect this is the way all theatre is heading: either towards brief, powerful experiences in small spaces or towards day-long rituals in big public places.

The key question is whether drama is also heading in new directions thematically. One school of thought argues, quite ferociously, that it has to: that the drama of political and social commentary is dead partly because audiences are bored with it and partly because, in this day and age, there are no visible Utopias to hand. We need, runs the cry, a drama that reflects the fragmented, discontinuous, essentially private nature of modern experience. Well maybe. But my antennae tell me that the opposite is true: that, if drama is to retain any hold on the attention of the public, it has to deal with the momentous issues that confront us at the end of the 20th century.

That is not simply a rhetorical phrase: already it is possible to identify some of the issues that are bound to dominate drama in the 1990's. One obviously is AIDS which, especially in the United States, has already yielded a substantial body of dramatic literature: what is heartening is that we have now moved from the slightly sentimental, consciousness-raising plays to works that relate this epidemic to prevailing moral attitudes and even treat it from a blackly comic standpoint.

A second key issue, particularly relevant to post-totalitarian societies, is our attitude to the past: whether it is right to seek revenge for criminal wrongs or to erase the memory of suffering. It is a subject that comes up time and time again in relation to the Nazi concentration camps (Peter Flannery's *Singer*), South American dictatorships (Ariel Dorfman's *Death and the Maiden*), South African apartheid (Athol Fugard's *Playland*), and European Communism (Howard Brenton's *Berlin Bertie*). It is also a theme that throws up endless moral dilemmas. Should revenge be a legal or an individual act? By exercising forgiveness, do we cancel out the past? And how do we draw the line between punishment and vindictiveness? As more and more evidence of past iniquities comes to light, I suspect this will emerge as the major issue of our time.

But is it the business of drama to engage with public events? All one can say is that, historically, it has always done so. The *Lysistrata* of Aristophanes was both about the madness engulfing Greece because of the drawn-out war with Sparta and about the exclusively male domination of public life. Shakespeare's history plays are about the continuing tension between order and chaos. And there is a whole stream of plays from Shaw's *Saint Joan* to Brecht's *Galileo* about the conflict between the conscience of the individual and the authority of the state. If art is a response to life, then that response inevitably includes events in the public arena.

All of this, of course, begs the question raised by Ruby Cohn in an earlier preface to this volume: is there still an audience that embraces drama? I suspect there is, even though that audience is clearly changing. Arthur Miller told me recently that when he started writing plays in the 1940's he assumed, idealistically, that he was addressing the whole nation: now he knows that he is speaking to a select handful. My own hunch is that, in the commercial theatre in all countries, there is a limited number of people prepared to pay high prices to see straight plays. But I still believe there is an audience in the subsidised venues, the studio spaces, the regional theatres everywhere that has a hunger for drama. Everything is related to ability to pay. In Hungary a theatre ticket costs no more than a bowl of soup. In Peter Brook's Paris theatre, the

Bouffes du Nord, a ticket costs the same as a decent bottle of wine. Result: never an empty seat. It is only when ticket prices reach unrealistic proportions that people start to question the value of a night at the theatre. In my experience, the appetite for drama still exists if only because people need some affirmation of their existence. The challenge for the future lies not just in keeping the plays coming—450 dramatists listed in this volume will see to that—but finally in ensuring that drama is affordable, available, and accessible to all.

—MICHAEL BILLINGTON (1993)

EDITOR'S NOTE

Contemporary Dramatists contains entries on living English-language writers for the stage. Entrants from previous editions not included in this volume are listed within the text with a reference to the most recent edition of *Contemporary Dramatists* that contains an entry on them.

The selection of writers included in this book is based on the recommendations of the advisers listed on page xvii, a number of whom have helped with all five editions.

The entry for each writer consists of a biography, a complete list of produced and/or published plays and all other separately published books, and a signed essay. In addition, entrants were invited to comment on their work.

Original British and United States editions of all books have been listed; other editions are listed only if they are first editions. Details for a play first published in a magazine or anthology are not given if the play has been published later as separate book or in a collection of the author; an acting edition of a play is not listed unless there is no trade edition. Librettos are listed among the plays. The first production, first productions in both Britain and the United States, as well as first productions in London and New York are listed. Reprints and revivals are not listed unless a revision of text or a change of title is involved. As a rule all books written about the entrant are listed in the Critical Studies section; the reviews and essays listed have been recommended by the entrant.

We would like to thank the entrants and contributors for their patience and cooperation in helping us compile this book.

ADVISERS

Arthur H. Ballet
Martin Banham
Michael Benedikt
Eric Bentley
C.W.E. Bigsby
Michael Billington
Herbert Blau
John Bowen
Katharine Brisbane
Constance Brissenden
Alasdair Cameron
Richard Christiansen
Harold Clurman
Ruby Cohn
John Robert Colombo
Albert Cook
Patricia Cooke
Robert W. Corrigan
Tish Dace
W.A. Darlington
John Elsom
Richard Gilman
Anthony Graham-White
Otis L. Guernsey, Jr.
Carole Hayman
Ronald Hayman

Nick Hern
Stanley Kauffmann
Veronica Kelly
Naseem Khan
Laurence Kitchin
Richard Kostelanetz
Frank Marcus
E.A. Markham
Bonnie Marranca
Howard McNaughton
Benedict Nightingale
Richard Schechner
Joel Schechter
Alan Schneider
Michael T. Smith
John Spurling
Alan Strachan
J.L. Styan
Howard Taubman
John Russell Taylor
J.C. Trewin
Darwin T. Turner
Irving Wardle
Gerald Weales
Ross Wetzsteon
B.A. Young

CONTRIBUTORS

Elizabeth Adams
Addell Austin Anderson
Frances Rademacher Anderson
Gary Anderson
Thomas Apple
Arthur H. Ballet
Carol Banks
Clive Barker
Judith E. Barlow
Gene A. Barnett
Joss Bennathan
Eugene Benson
Linda Ben-Zvi
Gerald M. Berkowitz
Michael Bertin
C.W.E. Bigsby
Michael Billington
Walter Bode
John Bowen
Gaynor F. Bradish
Katharine Brisbane
Constance Brissenden
John Russell Brown
Joseph Bruchac
John Bull
Jarka M. Burian
Alasdair Cameron
Susan Carlson
Bernard Carragher

Ned Chaillet
D.D.C. Chambers
Bill Coco
Ruby Cohn
Clare Colvin
Judy Cooke
Patricia Cooke
Richard Corballis
Tish Dace
W.A. Darlington
Terence Dawson
Elin Diamond
Reid Douglas
Tony Dunn
Arnold Edinborough
Jane Edwardes
John Elsom
Mark W. Estrin
John V. Falconieri
Michael Feingold
Peter Fitzpatrick
Leonard Fleischer
Richard Fotheringham
Leah D. Frank
Melvin J. Friedman
Helen Gilbert
Reid Gilbert
Lizbeth Goodman
Lois Gordon

Martin Gottfried
Anthony Graham-White
Steve Grant
Frances Gray
Prabhu S. Guptara
Paul J.A. Hadfield
Jonathan Hammond
James Hansford
Ronald Hayman
Dick Higgins
Errol Hill
Foster Hirsch
Harold Hobson
William M. Hoffman
Jorge A. Huerta
Christopher Innes
Esiaba Irobi
John Istel
C. Lee Jenner
Veronica Kelly
David E. Kemp
Burton S. Kendle
Liliane Kerjan
Helene Keyssar
Bruce King
H. Gustav Klaus
Richard Kostelanetz
John G. Kuhn
Bernd-Peter Lange
Paul Lawley
Michael T. Leech
Matthew Lloyd
Felicia Hardison Londré
Glenn Loney
James MacDonald
James Magruder
Frank Marcus
E.A. Markham
Thomas B. Markus
John Martin
John McCallum
Thomas J. McCormack
Paul McGillick
Arthur E. McGuinness
Howard McNaughton
Walter J. Meserve
Geoffrey Milne

Louis D. Mitchell
Tony Mitchell
Christian H. Moe
Christopher Murray
Paul Nadler
Benedict Nightingale
Olu Obafemi
Garry O'Connor
Marion O'Connor
Osita Okagbue
John O'Leary
Judy Lee Oliva
M. Elizabeth Osborn
Eric Overmyer
Malcolm Page
Dorothy Parker
Roxana Petzold
Rosemary Pountney
Henry Raynor
Leslie du S. Read
John M. Reilly
Sandra L. Richards
James Roose-Evans
Geoff Sadler
Arthur Sainer
Ellen Schiff
Adrienne Scullion
Elaine Shragge
Michael Sidnell
Christopher Smith
Michael T. Smith
A. Richard Sogliuzzo
Sandra Souchotte
John Spurling
Carol Simpson Stern
Alan Strachan
J.L. Styan
Alrene Sykes
John Thomson
Peter Thomson
Joanne Tompkins
Darwin T. Turner
Elaine Turner
Michelene Wandor
Daniel J. Watermeier
Gerald Weales
B.A. Young

CONTEMPORARY
DRAMATISTS

Michael Abbensetts
George Abbott
Paul Ableman
Dannie Abse
Ama Ata Aidoo
JoAnne Akalaitis
Edward Albee
William Alfred
Ted Allan
Robert Anderson
John Antrobus
Douglas Archibald
John Arden
George Axelrod
Alan Ayckbourn

Thomas Babe
Jon Robin Baitz
Janis Balodis
Amiri Baraka
Howard Barker
Peter Barnes
Neil Bartlett
Alan Bennett
Eric Bentley
Steven Berkoff
Barry Bermange
Kenneth Bernard
Stephen Bill
George Birimisa
Alan Bleasdale
Lee Blessing
Eric Bogosian
Carol Bolt
Robert Bolt
Chris Bond
Edward Bond
John Bowen
Howard Brenton
Lee Breuer
John Broughton
Kenneth H. Brown
Ed Bullins
John Burrows
Charles Busch
Alexander Buzo
John Byrne

David Campton
Denis Cannan
Lewis John Carlino
Lonnie Carter
Jim Cartwright
David Caute
Alice Childress
Frank Chin
Caryl Churchill
Brian Clark
John Pepper Clark
John Clifford
Darrah Cloud
Rick Cluchey
Barry Collins
Constance S. Congdon
Stewart Conn
Michael Cook
Ray Cooney

Ron Cowen
Richard Crane
David Cregan
Martin Crimp
Michael Cristofer
Beverley Cross

Sarah Daniels
Nick Darke
Robertson Davies
Jack Davis
Ossie Davis
Phillip Hayes Dean
Nick Dear
Alma De Groen
Shelagh Delaney
Keith Dewhurst
Barry Dickins
Steven Dietz
Charles Dizenzo
J.P. Donleavy
Rosalyn Drexler
Martin Duberman
Maureen Duffy
Nell Dunn
Christopher Durang
Charles Dyer

R. Sarif Easmon
Francis Ebejer
David Edgar
Obi B. Egbuna
Lonne Elder III
Ron Elisha
Barry England
Nick Enright
Marcella Evaristi
Stanley Eveling

Jules Feiffer
David Fennario
Lawrence Ferlinghetti
Harvey Fierstein
Peter Flannery
Horton Foote
Richard Foreman
María Irene Fornés
James Forsyth
Paul Foster
Mario Fratti
Michael Frayn
David Freeman
David French
Bruce Jay Friedman
Brian Friel
Terence Frisby
Christopher Fry
Athol Fugard
Charles Fuller
George Furth

Frank Gagliano
Tom Gallacher
Herb Gardner
Shirley Gee
Larry Gelbart
Jack Gelber

Jonathan Gems
Pam Gems
William Gibson
Peter Gill
Frank D. Gilroy
John Godber
James Goldman
Steve Gooch
Charles Gordone
Clem Gorman
Philip Kan Gotanda
Michael Gow
Ronald Gow
Jack Gray
John Gray
Simon Gray
Spalding Gray
Richard Greenberg
David Greenspan
Trevor Griffiths
John Grillo
John Guare
A.R. Gurney, Jr.

Oliver Hailey
Wilson John Haire
John Hale
Roger Hall
Willis Hall
David Halliwell
Christopher Hampton
William Hanley
Chris Hannan
John Harding
David Hare
Richard Harris
Tony Harrison
Ronald Harwood
Michael Hastings
William Hauptman
Allan Havis
Tom Hendry
Beth Henley
James Ene Henshaw
John Herbert
James Leo Herlihy
Dorothy Hewett
Jack Hibberd
Errol Hill
Robert Hivnor
Stuart Hoar
William M. Hoffman
Joan Holden
Margaret Hollingsworth
Robert Holman
John Hopkins
Israel Horovitz
Debbie Horsfield
Roger Howard
Donald Howarth
Tina Howe
Dusty Hughes
Ron Hutchinson
David Henry Hwang

Albert Innaurato
Debbie Isitt

Stephen Jeffreys
Ann Jellicoe
Len Jenkin
Terry Johnson
Keith Johnstone

Lee Kalcheim
Garson Kanin
Girish Karnad
John B. Keane
Charlotte Keatley
Barrie Keeffe
Tom Kempinski
Adrienne Kennedy
Wendy Kesselman
Thomas Kilroy
Kenneth Koch
Harry Kondoleon
Arthur Kopit
Bernard Kops
H.M. Koutoukas
Ruth Krauss
Hanif Kureishi
Tony Kushner

Kevin Laffan
David Lan
Arthur Laurents
Bryony Lavery
Ray Lawler
Jerome Lawrence
Robert E. Lee
Mike Leigh
Hugh Leonard
Doris Lessing
Deborah Levy
Romulus Linney
Henry Livings
Liz Lochhead
Stephen Lowe
Craig Lucas
Doug Lucie
Ken Ludwig
Peter Luke
Tes Lyssiotis

Sharman MacDonald
Eduardo Machado
Jackson Mac Low
Yulisa Amadu Maddy
David Mamet
Matsemela Manaka
Wolf Mankowitz
Emily Mann
Maishe Maponya
Tony Marchant
Frank Marcus
William Mastrosimone
Ray Mathew
Mustapha Matura
Eugene McCabe
Anthony McCarten
Michael McClure
Greg McGee
John McGrath
Tom McGrath
Frank McGuinness

Clare McIntyre
James McLure
Terrence McNally
Murray Mednick
Mark Medoff
Leonard Melfi
Ronald Millar
Arthur Miller
Jason Miller
Susan Miller
Ron Milner
Anthony Minghella
Adrian Mitchell
Julian Mitchell
Loften Mitchell
M.J. Molloy
Mavor Moore
Daniel Mornin
Bill Morrison
John Mortimer
Tad Mosel
Gregory Motton
David Mowat
Percy Mtwa
Rona Munro
Iris Murdoch
Tom Murphy
John Murrell
Joseph Musaphia

Richard Nelson
G.F. Newman
Mbongeni Ngema
Ngugi wa Thiong'o
Peter Nichols
Lewis Nkosi
John Ford Noonan
Marsha Norman
Louis Nowra

Mary O'Malley
Michael O'Neill
Vincent O'Sullivan
Wale Ogunyemi
John Osborne
Femi Osofisan
Eric Overmyer
Alun Owen
Rochelle Owens
Martin Owusu
OyamO

Louise Page
Suzan-Lori Parks
John Patrick
Robert Patrick
Caryl Phillips
John Pielmeier
David Pinner
Winsome Pinnock
Harold Pinter
Alan Plater
Stephen Poliakoff
Sharon Pollock
Bernard Pomerance
Dennis Potter
David Pownall

David Rabe
Peter Ransley
Hannie Rayson
James Reaney
Dennis J. Reardon
Barry Reckord
Keith Reddin
Christina Reid
Renée
Trevor D. Rhone
Ronald Ribman
Jack Richardson
Anne Ridler
Erika Ritter
Billy Roche
John Romeril
Ola Rotimi
David Rudkin
John Ruganda
Willy Russell

Arthur Sainer
Milcha Sánchez-Scott
James A. Saunders
Joan M. Schenkar
James Schevill
Murray Schisgal
Jeremy Seabrook
David Selbourne
Stephen Sewell
Alan Seymour
Anthony Shaffer
Peter Shaffer
Ntozake Shange
John Patrick Shanley
Wallace Shawn
Jill Shearer
Sam Shepard
Martin Sherman
Stuart Sherman
Barney Simon
Neil Simon
Beverley Simons
N.F. Simpson
Stephen Sinclair
Bernard Slade
Michael T. Smith
Zulu Sofola
Bode Sowande
Wole Soyinka
Johnny Speight
Colin Spencer
John Spurling
David Starkweather
Barrie Stavis
John Steppling
Tom Stoppard
David Storey
Mike Stott
Karen Sunde
Efua Sutherland

George Tabori
Ted Tally
Ronald Tavel
Megan Terry
Peter Terson

Steve Tesich
Judith Thompson
Sue Townsend
William Trevor
Tsegaye Gabre-Medhin

Alfred Uhry
Peter Ustinov

Luis Valdez
Jean-Claude van Itallie
Gore Vidal
Paula Vogel

Derek Walcott
George F. Walker
Joseph A. Walker
Michelene Wandor
Douglas Turner Ward
Wendy Wasserstein
Keith Waterhouse
Arnold Weinstein
Michael Weller
Mac Wellman
Timberlake Wertenbaker
Arnold Wesker

Richard Wesley
Peter Whelan
Edgar Nkosi White
John White
Ted Whitehead
Hugh Whitemore
Christopher Wilkinson
Heathcote Williams
Nigel Williams
David Williamson
Ted Willis
August Wilson
Doric Wilson
Lanford Wilson
Robert M. Wilson
Snoo Wilson
George C. Wolfe
Charles Wood
Nicholas Wright
Olwen Wymark

Susan Yankowitz

Paul Zindel

Writers not included in this volume who appear in previous editions.
(See listing within the text for reference to appropriate edition.)

Rodney Ackland
Jane Arden
Robert Ardrey
W.H. Auden

Enid Bagnold
James Baldwin
Djuna Barnes
James K. Baxter
Samuel Beckett
S.N. Behrman
Saul Bellow
Bridget Boland
Julie Bovasso
Brigid Brophy
Abe Burrows

Mary Chase
Paddy Chayefsky
Agatha Christie
Laurence Collinson
Marc Connelly
Noël Coward
Mart Crowley
Allen Curnow
Jackie Curtis

Joe DeGraft
Nigel Dennis
Andrea Dunbar
Ronald Duncan
Lawrence Durrell

Clive Exton
Tom Eyen

Paul Goodman
Paul Green
Graham Greene
Walter Greenwood

James Hanley
Don Harron
John Hawkes
Joseph Heller
Lillian Hellman
William Douglas Home

William Inge
Christopher Isherwood

Errol John

George Kelly
Peter Kenna
Sidney Kingsley

John Howard Lawson
Benn W. Levy
Robert Lord
Robert Lowell
Charles Ludlam
James Broom Lynne

Roger MacDougall
Archibald MacLeish
Albert Maltz
Bruce Mason
Elaine May
David Mercer
Arthur Lister Murphy

Bill Naughton
Frank Norman
Elliot Nugent

Lawrence Osgood

Stewart Parker
S.J. Perelman
Miguel Piñero
Hal Porter
J.B. Priestley

Terence Rattigan
Kenneth Rexroth
George Ryga

Howard Sackler
William Saroyan
Dore Schary
Irwin Shaw
Robert Shaw
R.C. Sherriff
Dodie Smith

William Snyder
Douglas Stewart

Cecil P. Taylor
Gwyn Thomas
Mervyn Thompson
Ben Travers
David Turner

Kurt Vonnegut, Jr.

Nancy Walter
Fred Watson
Leonard Webb
Jerome Weidman
Hugh Wheeler
Patrick White
Thornton Wilder
Emlyn Williams
Tennessee Williams

A

ABBENSETTS, Michael. British. Born in British Guiana (now Guyana), 8 June 1938; became British citizen, 1974. Educated at Queen's College, Guyana, 1952–56; Stanstead College, Quebec; Sir George Williams University, Montreal, 1960–61. Security attendant, Tower of London, 1963–67; staff member, Sir John Soane Museum, London, 1968–71. Resident playwright, Royal Court Theatre, London, 1974; visiting professor of drama, Carnegie Mellon University, Pittsburgh, 1981. Recipient: George Devine award, 1973; Arts Council bursary, 1977; Afro-Caribbean award, 1979. Address: c/o Heinemann Educational Books Ltd., Halley Court, Jordan Hill, Oxford OX2 8EJ, England.

<small>PUBLICATIONS</small>

Plays

Sweet Talk (produced London, 1973; New York, 1974). London, Eyre Methuen, 1976.
Alterations (produced London and New York, 1978; revised version produced London, 1985).
Samba (produced London, 1980). London, Eyre Methuen, 1980.
In the Mood (produced London, 1981).
Outlaw (produced Leicester and London, 1983).
El Dorado (produced London, 1984).
Living Together (includes *Royston's Day*, *The Street Party*). Oxford, Heinemann, 1988.

Radio Plays: *Home Again*, 1975; *The Sunny Side of the Street*, 1977; *Brothers of the Sword*, 1978; *The Fast Lane*, 1980; *The Dark Horse*, 1981; *Summer Passions*, 1985.

Television Plays: *The Museum Attendant*, 1973; *Inner City Blues*, 1975; *Crime and Passion*, 1976; *Black Christmas*, 1977; *Roadrunner*, 1977; *Empire Road* series, 1977, 1979; *Easy Money*, 1982; *Big George Is Dead*, 1987.

Novel

Empire Road (novelization of television series). London, Panther, 1979.

*

Critical Study: "Taking Race for Granted" by Margaret Walters, in *New Society* (London), 16 November 1978.

Michael Abbensetts comments:
(1982) I once read something a black American playwright had written: he said his plays could not be understood by a white person. That is not the way I feel about my plays. It seems to me that if a play is good enough it should have something to say to everybody, once they are prepared to look for that something. However, having said that, I would like to add that I would never want to write a play that a black audience did not like, no matter how popular it was with a white audience. When my stage play *Alterations* was praised by critics of the *Sunday Times* and the *Financial Times*, it made me feel very pleased, but I was equally pleased that the reviewer in the *Jamaica Gleaner* liked the play as well.

Which brings me to the question I am sometimes asked. Why do I write so much for television? First, BBC-TV pays me well—okay, *reasonably* well—and second, my TV plays are bound to reach a larger black audience than my stage plays ever do.

Yet originally I had never even thought of writing for the theatre. Originally I wanted to be a novelist. Then while I was at university in Canada I saw a version of Osborne's *Look Back in Anger*, and suddenly I knew what I wanted to be—a playwright. So then I came to England. Other West Indians were coming to the UK to find jobs, I came here to find theatre. I'd read of a place called the Royal Court Theatre, and I vowed to myself to get one of my plays on there, even though, at that time, I hadn't even written a single play. Yet in time I did get a play on at the Royal Court, and I was made resident dramatist at the Court. A lot has happened to me since those first, heady days at the Royal Court Theatre.

*　*　*

The majority of black British playwrights emerged in the 1970's. Michael Abbensetts is quite simply the best of these. His first work to be widely noticed, a 1973 television play *The Museum Attendant*, struck the two notes that characterize all of his output. First, it worked out a tragic situation within a broad tradition of comedy; the humour arises primarily from incongruity, though there are fine instances of verbal felicity and wit. In the juxtaposition of tragedy and comedy Abbensetts goes back to English Renaissance drama, though the more immediate mentor is probably Albee. Second, his work stood out because it was practically the first time that television drama had shown an accurate slice of immigrant life. A whole generation of television sitcoms (*Love Thy Neighbour* and *Mixed Blessings* were then the latest) had taken race as their main, if not sole, theme. With their appalling racialist jokes, shown on the dubious grounds of "therapeutic value," these plays were deeply upsetting to many people. *The Fosters*, the only previous all-black comedy series, was welcomed by black people but showed its American origins too clearly to be more than an aperitif. *Gangsters*, another television series, also with racialist jokes and in an American blood-and-thunder movie tradition, was more controversial. Condemned as "vicious and vacuous," it was also praised for "somehow managing to suggest more of the corruption and reasons for racial tension than a score of more balanced and realistic programmes." It did not, however, affect the convention of cardboard blacks who were a "problem," or were pawns in arguments about British politics —e.g., in the automatic coupling of racism and fascism. Generally, blacks in plays were just plain stupid, as in *Curry*

1

and Chips or *Till Death Us Do Part*. At best, the presence of blacks on television consoled a liberal conscience.

Abbensetts's achievement in presenting a black viewpoint on black life in Britain allowed his characters to emerge as fully human beings for the very first time in the history of British performing media. He provides an honest picture of the diversity of black people, with individuals as sincere, muddled, feckless, wicked, or wonderful as might come from any other group. In contrast to the work of otherwise fine black playwrights such as Mustapha Matura, Abbensetts's work is free from defensive clowning.

Abbensetts has said that *Black Christmas* constitutes his claim to be taken seriously as a writer. In it a West Indian family under the peculiar strains of life in Britain holds together only by sheer will; Abbensetts can be seen, then, as working also in a tradition of domestic drama, though "domestic" needs to be understood in its extended Third World rather than nuclear Western sense. The concentrated impact of the concerns of *Black Christmas* was spun out into two series called *Empire Road*. Slicker if slighter than the single play, this established Abbensetts with the public. In the second series, especially, he was able to match his writing to the personality and strength of the actors. *D.I.V.O.R.C.E.*, the seventh episode of the second series, is generally considered the best; and in its most praised section two of the characters, now drunk, reminisce about their life in Britain, and especially those experiences that are traumatic or hideous. Abbensetts often presents middle-aged characters haunted by memory, a device that enables him to add irony and bite to his plays. In *D.I.V.O.R.C.E.* that haunted hinterland of memory has a rich dramatic impact that itself comes to haunt viewers.

It is, however, the stage play *Alterations* that is Abbensetts's best complete work. Walker, a West Indian tailor, is desperately racing against the clock, trying to alter an immense number of trousers to sizes suitable for export to Japan: if he can finish this work, he will earn enough money in time to pay the deposit and begin to realize a life-long ambition of having his own shop. The pressures created by the situation impose a series of alterations in the lives, attitudes, and expectations of all the characters in the play: Walker himself, Horace and Buster, who intermittently help and hinder Walker, and Walker's discarded wife Darlene, to whom he is still attached in a strange West Indian way. All of Abbensetts's plays are, to a certain extent, parables. Though he tends to pack too much into his stage plays, they seem generally to be better constructed than his television plays.

His best television play is *Big George Is Dead*. At Big George's funeral Tony appears, having returned prosperous from Tobago, to repay the money he owes his former friend Boogie. For old times' sake, Tony and Boogie decide to relive their glorious past: back in the swinging sixties Boogie, Tony, and Big George were three black desperadoes calling themselves "the wild bunch." Identities forged on the frontline of Soho nightlife are tested in a London that now has punks, muggers, drug dealers. As the night wears on, the two become more and more immersed in the tragic sense of loss in their lives—particularly Tony, whose girlfriend married Boogie when Tony was forced to disappear to Tobago. Tony's son has been adopted by Boogie, and no-one wants the boy to realize the truth. Here is an understated, atmospheric play, finely testifying to Abbensetts's reluctant cleavage from his earlier comic mode, making it possible for him richly to explore the muted tragedies of everyday people, everyday lives.

Abbensetts was criticized earlier, by black and white activists, for his lack of political commitment. Over the years it has become clear that he does have a political vision, though it is not of course rendered in terms of British political allegiances. He has a larger vision of immigrant groups as incipiently one community, an all-embracing refuge which strengthens black people to tackle the problems presented by the alien white man's world in which they live. But Abbensetts also portrays the actualities of the relations between the different immigrant groups, as well as between generations, and raises the question of where this community is headed.

—Prabhu S. Guptara

ABBOTT, George (Francis). American. Born in Forestville, New York, 25 June 1889. Educated at Hamburg High School, New York; Rochester University, Rochester, New York, B.A. 1911; Harvard University, Cambridge, Massachusetts, 1912–13. Married 1) Ednah Levis in 1914 (died 1930), one daughter; 2) Mary Sinclair in 1946 (marriage dissolved 1951); 3) Joy Moana Valderrama in 1983. Founder, with Philip Dunning, Abbott–Dunning Inc., 1931–34. Recipient: Boston *Globe* award, 1912; Donaldson award, for directing, 1946, 1948, 1953, 1955; Tony award, 1955, 1956, 1960, and for directing, 1960, 1963, Special Tony, 1987; Pulitzer prize, 1960; New York Drama Critics Circle award, 1960; Lawrence Langner award, 1976; City of New York Handel medallion, 1976; Kennedy Center award, 1983. D.H.: Rochester University, 1961; H.H.D.: University of Miami, 1974. Address: 1270 Avenue of the Americas, New York, New York 10020, U.S.A.

PUBLICATIONS

Plays

The Head of the Family (produced Cambridge, Massachusetts, 1912).
Man in the Manhole (produced Boston, 1912).
The Fall Guy, with James Gleason (produced Milwaukee, 1924; New York, 1925; London, 1926). New York, French, 1928.
A Holy Terror: A None-Too-Serious Drama, with Winchell Smith (produced New York, 1925). New York, French, 1926.
Love 'em and Leave 'em, with John V.A. Weaver (also director: produced New York, 1926). New York, French, 1926.
Cowboy Crazy, with Pearl Franklin (produced New York, 1926).
Broadway, with Philip Dunning (also director: produced New York and London, 1926). New York, Doran, 1927.
Four Walls, with Dana Burnet (also director: produced New York, 1927). New York, French, 1928.
Coquette, with Ann Preston Bridgers (also director: produced New York, 1927; London, 1929). New York, Longman, 1928.
Ringside, with Edward A. Paramore, Jr., and Hyatt Daab (also director: produced New York, 1928).

Those We Love, with S.K. Lauren (also director: produced New York, 1930).

Lilly Turner, with Philip Dunning (also director: produced New York, 1932).

Heat Lightning, with Leon Abrams (also director: produced New York, 1933).

Ladies' Money (also director: produced New York, 1934).

Page Miss Glory (also director: produced New York, 1934).

Three Men on a Horse, with John Cecil Holm (also director: produced New York, 1935; London, 1936). New York, French, 1935.

On Your Toes, music and lyrics by Richard Rodgers and Lorenz Hart (also director: produced New York, 1936; London, 1937; revised version produced New York, 1983; London, 1984).

Sweet River, adaptation of the novel *Uncle Tom's Cabin* by Harriet Beecher Stowe (also director: produced New York, 1936).

The Boys from Syracuse, music and lyrics by Richard Rodgers and Lorenz Hart, adaptation of *A Comedy of Errors* by Shakespeare (also director: produced New York, 1938; London, 1963).

Best Foot Forward, with John Cecil Holm (also director: produced New York, 1941).

Beat the Band, with George Marion, Jr. (also director: produced New York, 1942).

Where's Charley?, music and lyrics by Frank Loesser, adaptation of the play *Charley's Aunt* by Brandon Thomas (also director: produced New York, 1948; London, 1958). London, French, 1965.

A Tree Grows in Brooklyn, with Betty Smith, adaptation of the novel by Smith (also director: produced New York, 1951).

The Pajama Game, with Richard Bissell, music by Richard Adler and Jerry Ross, adaptation of the novel *7½ Cents* by Bissell (also co-director: produced New York, 1954; London, 1955). New York, Random House, and London, Williamson Music, 1954.

Damn Yankees, with Douglass Wallop, music by Richard Adler and Jerry Ross, adaptation of the novel *The Year the Yankees Lost the Pennant* by Wallop (also director: produced New York, 1955; London, 1957). New York, Random House, 1956.

New Girl in Town, music and lyrics by Bob Merrill, adaptation of the play *Anna Christie* by Eugene O'Neill (also director: produced New York, 1957). New York, Random House, 1958.

Fiorello!, with Jerome Weidman, lyrics by Sheldon Harnick, music by Jerry Bock (also director: produced New York, 1959; Bristol and London, 1962). New York, Random House, 1960.

Tenderloin, with Jerome Weidman, lyrics by Sheldon Harnick, music by Jerry Bock, adaptation of the work by Samuel Hopkins Adams (also director: produced New York, 1960). New York, Random House, 1961.

Flora, The Red Menace, with Robert Russell, music by John Kander, lyrics by Fred Ebb (also director: produced New York, 1965).

Anya, with Guy Bolton, music and lyrics by Robert Wright and George Forrest, adaptation of the play *Anastasia* by Marcelle Maurette and Bolton (also director: produced New York, 1965).

Music Is, music by George Adler, lyrics by Will Holt, adaptation of *Twelfth Night* by Shakespeare (also director: produced Seattle and New York, 1976).

Tropicana, music by Robert Nassif, lyrics by Nassif and Peter Napolitano (also director: produced New York, 1985).

Frankie, music by Joseph Turin, lyrics by Gloria Nissenson, adaptation of *Frankenstein* by Mary Shelley (also co-director, with Donald Saddler: produced New York, 1989).

Screenplays: *The Saturday Night Kid*, with others, 1929; *Why Bring That Up?*, with others, 1929; *Half-Way to Heaven*, with Gerald Geraghty, 1929; *All Quiet on the Western Front*, with Dell Andrews and Maxwell Anderson, 1930; *The Sea God*, 1930; *Manslaughter*, 1930; *Stolen Heaven*, 1931; *Secrets of a Secretary*, with Dwight Taylor, 1931; *The Pajama Game*, with Richard Bissell, 1957; *Damn Yankees (What Lola Wants)*, 1958.

Novels

Broadway (novelization of stage play), with Philip Dunning. New York, Doran, 1927; London, Hutchinson, 1928.

Tryout. Chicago, Playboy Press, 1979.

Other

Mister Abbott (autobiography). New York, Random House, 1963.

*

Theatrical Activities:

Director: **Plays**—most of his own plays, and *Lightnin'* by Winchell Smith and Frank Bacon, New York, 1918; *Chicago* by Maurice Watkins, New York, 1927; *Spread Eagle* by George S. Brooks and Walter S. Lister, New York, 1927; *Bless You, Sister* by John Meehan and Robert Riskin, New York, 1927; *Gentlemen of the Press* by Ward Morehouse, New York, 1928; *Jarnegan* by Charles Beahen and Garrett Fort, New York, 1928; *Poppa* by Bella and Sam Spewack, New York, 1928; *Louder, Please* by Norman Krasna, New York, 1931; *The Great Magoo* by Ben Hecht and Gene Fowler, New York, 1932; *Twentieth Century* by Ben Hecht and Charles MacArthur, New York, 1932, 1971; *The Drums Begin* by Howard Irving Young, New York, 1933; *John Brown* by Ronald Gow, New York, 1934; *Kill That Story* by Harry Madden and Philip Dunning, New York, 1934; *Small Miracle* by Norman Krasna, New York, 1934; *Jumbo* by Richard Rodgers and Lorenz Hart, New York, 1935; *Boy Meets Girl* by Bella and Sam Spewack, New York, 1935; *Brother Rat* by John Monks, Jr., and Fred F. Finklehoffe, New York, 1936; *Room Service* by John Murray and Allen Boretz, New York, 1937; *Angel Island* by Bernie Angus, New York, 1937; *Brown Sugar* by Bernie Angus, New York, 1937; *All That Glitters* by John Baragwanath and Kenneth Simpson, New York, 1938; *What a Life* by Clifford Goldsmith, New York, 1938; *You Never Know* by Cole Porter, New York, 1938; *The Primrose Path* by Robert Buckner and Walter Hart, New York, 1939; *Mrs. O'Brien Entertains* by Harry Madden, New York, 1939; *Too Many Girls* by George Marion, Jr., New York, 1939; *Ring Two* by Gladys Harlbut, New York, 1939; *The White-Haired Boy* by Charles Martin and Beatrice Kaufman, Boston, 1939; *The Unconquered* by Ayn Rand, New York, 1940; *Goodbye in the Night* by Jerome Mayer, New York, 1940; *Pal Joey* by John O'Hara, music by Richard Rodgers, lyrics by Lorenz Hart, New York, 1940; *Sweet Charity*, by Irving Brecher and Manuel Seff, New York, 1942; *Kiss and Tell* by F. Hugh Herbert, New York, 1943; *Get Away Old Man* by William Saroyan, New York, 1943; *A Highland Fling* by J.L. Galloway, New York, 1944; *Snafu* by Louis Solomon and Harold Buchman, New York, 1944; *On the Town* by Betty Comden and Adolph Green,

New York, 1944; *Mr. Cooper's Left Hand* by Clifford Goldsmith, Boston, 1945; *Billion Dollar Baby* by Betty Comden and Adolph Green, New York, 1945; *One Shoe Off* by Mark Reed, New Haven, Connecticut, 1946; *Beggar's Holiday* by John La Touche (restaged), New York, 1946; *It Takes Two* by Virginia Faulkner and Sana Suesse, New York, 1947; *Barefoot Boy with Cheek* by Max Shulman, New York, 1947; *High Button Shoes* by Stephen Longstreet, music and lyrics by Jule Styne and Sammy Kahn, New York, 1947; *Look Ma, I'm Dancin'* by Jerome Lawrence and Robert E. Lee, music by Hugh Martin, New York, 1948; *Mrs. Gibbons' Boys* by Will Glickman and Joseph Stein, New York, 1949; *Tickets Please* (revue; restaged and rewritten), New York, 1950; *Call Me Madam* by Howard Lindsay and Russel Crouse, music and lyrics by Irving Berlin, New York, 1950; *Out of This World* by Dwight Taylor and Reginald Lawrence (restaged), New York, 1950; *The Number* by Arthur Carter, New York, 1951; *In Any Language* by Edmund Beloin and Harry Garson, New York, 1952; *Wonderful Town* by Joseph Fields and Jerome Chodorov, music by Leonard Bernstein, lyrics by Betty Comden and Adolph Green, New York, 1953; *Me and Juliet* by Richard Rodgers and Oscar Hammerstein II, New York, 1953; *Drink to Me Only* by Abram S. Ginnes and Ira Wallach, New York, 1958; *Once upon a Mattress* by Jay Thompson and others, New York, 1959; *Take Her, She's Mine* by Phoebe and Henry Ephron, New York, 1961; *A Call on Kuprin* by Jerome Lawrence and Robert E. Lee, New York, 1961; *A Funny Thing Happened on the Way to the Forum* by Burt Shevelove and Larry Gelbart, music and lyrics by Stephen Sondheim, New York, 1962, London, 1963; *Never Too Late* by Sumner Arthur Long, New York, 1962, London, 1963; *Fade Out—Fade In* by Betty Comden and Adolph Green, music by Jule Styne, New York, 1964; *Help Stamp Out Marriage* by Keith Waterhouse and Willis Hall, New York, 1966; *Agatha Sue, I Love You* by Abe Einhorn, New York, 1966; *How Now, Dow Jones* by Max Shulman, New York, 1967; *The Education of Hyman Kaplan* by Benjamin Zavin, New York, 1969; *The Fig Leaves Are Falling* by Allan Sherman, New York, 1969; *Norman Is That You* by Ron Clark and Sam Bobrick, New York, 1970; *Winning Isn't Everything* by Lee Kalcheim, New York, 1978. **Films**—*The Carnival Man*, 1929; *The Bishop's Candlesticks*, 1929; *Why Bring That Up?*, 1929; *Half-Way to Heaven*, 1929; *The Sea God*, 1930; *Manslaughter*, 1930; *Stolen Heaven*, 1931; *Secrets of a Secretary*, 1931; *My Sin*, 1931; *The Cheat*, 1931; *Too Many Girls*, 1940; *Kiss and Tell*, 1945; *The Pajama Game* (co-director, with Stanley Donen), 1957; *Damn Yankees* (co-director, with Stanley Donen), 1958. **Television**—*U.S. Royal Showcase*, 1952.

Actor: **Plays**—"Babe" Merrill in *The Misleading Lady* by Charles Goddard and Paul Dickey, New York, 1913; in *The Queen's Enemies* by Lord Dunsany, New York, 1916; Henry Allen in *Daddies* by John L. Hobble, New York, 1918; Sylvester Cross in *The Broken Wing* by Charles Goddard and Paul Dickey, New York, 1920; in *Dulcy* by Marc Connelly and George S. Kaufman, toured, 1921; Texas in *Zander the Great* by Salisbury Field, New York, 1923; Sverre Peterson in *White Desert* by Maxwell Anderson, New York, 1923; Sid Hunt in *Hell-Bent fer Heaven* by Hatcher Hughes, New York, 1924; Steve Tuttle in *Lazybones* by Owen Davis, New York, 1924; Dynamite Jim in *Processional* by John Howard Lawson, New York, 1925; Dirk Yancey in *A Holy Terror*, New York, 1925; in *Cowboy Crazy*, New York, 1926; Frederick Williston in *Those We Love*, New York, 1930; title role in *John Brown* by Ronald Gow, New York, 1934; Mr. Antrobus in *The Skin of Our Teeth* by Thornton Wilder, New York, 1955.

*   *   *

George Abbott called his autobiography *Mister Abbott*, but *Mister Broadway* would have been more apt. Abbott notes: "From 1935 to this time [1963] I have, with the exception of a week or two, always had at least one play running on Broadway." Accepting without question the hit/flop mentality of the Broadway marketplace, Abbott is a professional showman whose canon is altogether undisturbed by the least suggestion of intellect. The Abbott production is a good show, a farce, a melodrama, a musical comedy; briskly paced, it is geared for the big laugh, the big climax, and its light-fingered, high-stepping rhythm naturally does not translate well to the library.

The Abbott play comes wrapped in two basic packages: the racy, slangy comedies and melodramas of the 1920's and 1930's, and the musical comedies of the 1940's and 1950's. In both kinds of plays, the colorful details of a milieu or particular way of life offer the appeal. Abbott's plots (Abbott almost always works with a collaborator) are neither especially compelling nor well constructed. The "gimmick" is the milieu: the politics in *Fiorello!*, baseball in *Damn Yankees*, factory routine in *The Pajama Game*, the red-light district in *Tenderloin*. Sports, politics, the working class: the Abbott musical takes for its field of action a significant aspect of American life, only to reinforce popular myths of Americana. Relentlessly unexploratory, an Abbott show is indebted almost exclusively to the conventions of Broadway folklore. Entertainments like *The Pajama Game* and *Fiorello!* introduce a spurious kind of rebellious hero—a gal who wants the workers to get a raise, a mayor who tries to buck the compromises and corruptions of the political machine. But reinforcing rather than countering cliché, the shows ultimately leave the status quo unruffled. On the stage, aided by the music, and by the charm and élan of Abbott direction, the weaknesses of the books are camouflaged; on the page, unadorned, the plays are dreary, devoid not only of "ideas" but of spirit as well.

Abbott's earlier collaborations are much more flavorful. *Broadway*, a melodrama that combines prohibition, gang warfare, and the clichés of the backstage musical, is a lively and engaging portrait of an era. The earthy dialogue captures the lingo of the gangster and the entertainer; the slang has its own peculiar kind of melody, and the story—murder and retribution—is comfortably situated against the prohibition nightclub setting. *Three Men on a Horse* does for bookies what *Broadway* does for hoods: gives them the status of popular myth. This time the genre is farce rather than melodrama, but the same perky, accurate yet subtly stylized dialogue prevails. In less successful, but equally "contemporary" plays like *The Fall Guy* and *Love 'em and Leave 'em*, Abbott and his collaborators regard from the same sly angle other scenes of the 1920's. The fall guy goes wrong with some hoods, is caught and reprimanded, and returns chastened to his long-suffering wife. *Love 'em and Leave 'em* is a harsh portrait of a dame on the make; she'll go out with the highest bidder, the one who can give her the most diamonds and furs. Her schemes of self-advancement are set against the problems of the tenants of a working-class rooming house. The plays seem quaint today, but these glimpses into an America of the past retain their undignified comic and melodramatic energy. Artifacts of popular culture, the plays record the values and the aspirations and the setbacks and the sins of various character types of a turbulent and appealing era.

A shrewd practical man of the theatre, Abbott has given Broadway audiences what they have wanted to see, and he has entertained them more often, and over a longer period of time, than any other professional in the history of the American theatre. That is revealing if not an especially happy statistic.

—Foster Hirsch

————

ABLEMAN, Paul. British. Born in Leeds, Yorkshire, 13 June 1927; brought up in New York. Educated at King's College, University of London. Military service: 3 years. Married; one son. Agent: Peters, Fraser, and Dunlop Group, 503/4 The Chambers, Chelsea Harbour, Lots Road, London SW10 0XF. Address: 36 Duncan House, Fellows Road, London N.W.3, England.

PUBLICATIONS

Plays

Even His Enemy, with Gertrude Macauley (as *Letters to a Lady*, produced London, 1951). London, French, 1948.
Help! (revue; produced London, 1963).
One Hand Clapping (revue; produced Edinburgh, 1964).
Dialogues (produced London, 1965).
Green Julia (produced Edinburgh and London, 1965; Washington, D.C., 1968; New York, 1972). London, Methuen, and New York, Grove Press, 1966.
Tests (sketches). London, Methuen, 1966.
Emily and Heathcliff (produced London, 1967).
Blue Comedy, Madly in Love, Hank's Night (produced London, 1968). London, Methuen, 1968; *Madly in Love* published in *Modern Short Comedies from Broadway and London*, edited by Stanley Richards, New York, Random House, 1969.
The Black General, adaptation of *Othello* by Shakespeare (produced London, 1969).
And Hum Our Sword (produced London, 1973).
Little Hopping Robin (produced London, 1973).
The Visitor (produced London, 1974).
Windsor All-Sorts (produced London, 1977).

Radio Play: *The Infant*, 1974.

Television Plays: *Barlowe of the Car Park*, 1961; *That Woman Is Wrecking Our Marriage*, 1969; *Visits from a Stranger*, 1970; *The Catch in a Cold*, 1970; *The Wrong 'Un*, from a work by Michael Brett, 1983; *Love Song*, from a novel by Jeffrey Archer, 1985; *A Killing on the Exchange* series, 1987.

Novels

I Hear Voices. Paris, Olympia Press, 1957; London, New English Library, 1966.
As Near as I Can Get. London, Spearman, 1962.
Vac. London, Gollancz, 1968.
The Twilight of the Vilp. London, Gollancz, 1969.
Tornado Pratt. London, Gollancz, 1977.
Shoestring (novelization of television play). London, BBC Publications, 1979.
Porridge (novelization of screenplay). London, Pan, 1979.
Shoestring's Finest Hour. London, BBC Publications, 1980.

County Hall (novelization of television series). London, BBC Publications, 1981.
Hi-De-Hi (novelization of television series). London, BBC Publications, 1983.
A Killing on the Exchange (novelization of television series). London, Grafton, 1987.
Dad's Army (novelization of the television series by Jimmy Perry and David Croft). London, BBC Publications, 1989.

Verse

Bits: Some Prose Poems. London, Latimer Press, 1969.

Other

The Mouth and Oral Sex. London, Running Man Press, 1969; as *The Mouth*, London, Sphere, 1972; as *The Sensuous Mouth*, New York, Ace, 1972.
Anatomy of Nakedness. London, Orbis, 1982; as *The Banished Body*, London, Sphere, 1984.
The Doomed Rebellion. London, Zomba, 1983.

Translator, with Veronica Hall, *Egypt*, by Simonne Lacourture. London, Vista, 1963.

*   *   *

Paul Ableman's dramatic output so far is small, but striking, both for the unpretentious wit of its dialogue and for the moral concern implicit in its characterization and plot. One central concern would seem to be the difficulty of reconciling sexual fulfilment with good conscience and consideration for others. Certainly this is so in *Green Julia*, probably his most impressive piece to date, and as thoughtful a study of the hypocrisies of male sexuality as the modern theatre has produced.

There are only two characters onstage, Jake and Bob: the Julia of the title remains offstage throughout, a presence constantly invoked by them and, by the end of the play, a substantial one. Jake is leaving England, probably for a long time, and feels a faint guilt about Julia, the erratic, self-absorbed but generous divorcée he has made his mistress. Gradually, it becomes clear that he wants Bob, his best friend, to take her off his mind by taking her over. But Bob, who is the more morally pretentious of the two, affects both to despise her ("the most depraved old whore in Southern England") and to have a woman of his own. Not only will he reject the idea, he appears to resent it; and the verbal games the two men constantly play with each other (in which they imitate army officers, psychiatrists, university professors, anything capable of easy parody) become increasingly hostile. It is no longer possible to continue camouflaging their true feelings in such a way. Bob comes right out with: "What is your relationship with Julia? You never treat her, never help her or worry about her, hardly ever think about her except on the odd evenings when you happen to feel randy and she's available." This is clearly true; and yet, as we also gradually discover, Bob's stance is a fraud. He is inexperienced, anxious for sexual discovery, and likely to prove as unscrupulous as Jake in achieving it. The curtain falls on the arrival of Julia, who is evidently destined to be exploited by others until what promises to be a raddled and lonely old age.

By the end, the contrast between the jocular, harmless manner of these very ordinary young men and the callousness of their intentions is unmissable, and makes the play more than the light comedy it has at times pretended to be. With Ableman's other pieces on the same theme, however, there is no question of pretence. Both *Hank's Night* and *Madly in Love* leave a less bitter aftertaste, presumably because in each case mutual consent replaces exploitation and the tone can therefore remain good-humoured and amused. In *Madly in Love* an eccentric poet poses as a psychiatrist in the hope of losing his virginity by seducing a girl whose quirk is to obey every order she is given: the irony is that the shock of being told "make love to me" cures her, whereupon she freely gives herself to him in gratitude for his help. In *Hank's Night* two couples try to persuade themselves and each other to start an orgy, and fail lamentably until they gave up the attempt, whereupon the thing actually happens, spontaneously and unselfconsciously. The moral of both plays, and perhaps also of *Green Julia*, may be that those who do not seek to manipulate others and bend them to their will may receive something the more satisfying for being offered freely and without constraint. In the most unpretentious way, Ableman's work is a criticism of the earnestness and anxiety that attaches to sex nowadays, with so many people regarding it, not as a means of cementing genuine relationships or even as a form of enjoyment, but as a mere proof of personal adequacy.

All these pieces are naturalistic, or nearly so: Ableman has also written some 50 surrealist sketches under the general title of *Tests*, some of which have been performed in *One Hand Clapping* and other revues, and most of which prove to have little more to offer than verbal invention and a vague aura of "absurdism." One speech, typical both in the apparent arbitrariness of its language and in its facetiousness, reads: "A mammal of an estuary saluted a kindly laundryman. With a yelp the match teetered. Pickle all laundrymen. Toast archipelagos as if to pronounce renounce." A few "tests" do, however, seem to have a subject, notably *Johnson*, a parody of military conventions, *She's Dead*, in which two characters parrot cliché responses to violence and death, and *Another Lovely Day*, in which the speakers seek to fox each other by shifting their names and personae. However he develops as a dramatist (and since the 1970's he has applied himself more to the novel), it seems clear that Ableman is strongest when he is handling material that, at least to some extent, engages him as a moralist.

—Benedict Nightingale

ABSE, Dannie. British. Born in Cardiff, Glamorgan, 22 September 1923. Educated at Marlborough Road Elementary School, Cardiff; St. Illtyd's College, Cardiff; University of South Wales and Monmouthshire, Cardiff; King's College, London; Westminster Hospital, London; qualified as physician 1950, M.R.C.S., L.R.C.P. Served in the Royal Air Force, 1951–54: squadron leader. Married Joan Mercer in 1951; one son and two daughters. Specialist in charge of the chest clinic, Central London Medical Establishment 1954–89. Senior Fellow in Humanities, Princeton University, New Jersey, 1973–74. Editor, *Poetry and Poverty* magazine, London, 1949–54. President, Poetry Society 1978–92. Recipient: Foyle award, 1960; Welsh Arts Council award, 1971, 1987, for play, 1980; Cholmondeley award, 1985. D. Litt.: University of Wales, Cardiff, 1989. Fellow, Royal Society of Literature, 1983. Agent: Anthony Sheil Associates, 43 Doughty Street, London WC1N 2LF. Address: 85 Hodford Road, London NW11 8NH, England;

or, Green Hollows, Craig-yr-Eos Road, Ogmore-by-Sea, Glamorgan, South Wales.

PUBLICATIONS

Plays

Fire in Heaven (produced London, 1948). London, Hutchinson, 1956; revised version, as *Is the House Shut?* (produced London, 1964); revised version, as *In the Cage*, in *Three Questor Plays*, 1967.
Hands Around the Wall (produced London, 1950).
House of Cowards (produced London, 1960). Included in *Three Questor Plays*, 1967; in *Twelve Great Plays*, edited by Leonard F. Dean, New York, Harcourt Brace, 1970; revised version, in *The View from Row G*, 1990.
The Eccentric (produced London, 1961). London, Evans, 1961.
Gone (produced London, 1962). Included in *Three Questor Plays*, 1967; revised version, as *Gone in January* (produced Edinburgh, 1977; London, 1978), in *Madog* (Pontypridd, Glamorgan), 1981.
The Courting of Essie Glass (as *The Joker*, produced London, 1962; revised version, as *The Courting of Essie Glass*, broadcast 1975). Included in *Miscellany One*, 1981.
Three Questor Plays. Lowestoft, Suffolk, Scorpion Press, 1967.
The Dogs of Pavlov (produced London, 1969; New York, 1974). London, Vallentine Mitchell, 1973.
Funland (produced London, 1975).
Pythagoras (produced Birmingham, 1976; London, 1980). London, Hutchinson, 1979. As *Pythagoras Smith* in *The View from Row G*, 1990.
The View from Row G (includes *House of Cowards*, *The Dogs of Pavlov*, and *Pythagoras Smith*). Bridgend, Glamorgan, Seren, 1990.

Radio Plays: *Conform or Die*, 1957; *No Telegrams, No Thunder*, 1962; *You Can't Say Hello to Anybody*, 1964; *A Small Explosion*, 1964; *The Courting of Essie Glass*, 1975.

Novels

Ash on a Young Man's Sleeve. London, Hutchinson, 1954; New York, Criterion, 1955.
Some Corner of an English Field. London, Hutchinson, 1956; New York, Criterion, 1957.
O. Jones, O. Jones. London, Hutchinson, 1970.
There Was a Young Man from Cardiff. London, Hutchinson, 1991.

Verse

After Every Green Thing. London, Hutchinson, 1948.
Walking under Water. London, Hutchinson, 1952.
Tenants of the House: Poems 1951–1956. London, Hutchinson, 1957; New York, Criterion, 1959.
Poems, Golders Green. London, Hutchinson, 1962.
Dannie Abse: A Selection. London, Studio Vista, 1963.
A Small Desperation. London, Hutchinson, 1968.
Demo. Frensham, Surrey, Sceptre Press, 1969.
Selected Poems. London, Hutchinson, and New York, Oxford University Press, 1970.
Funland: A Poem in Nine Parts. London, Portland University Library, 1971.

Corgi Modern Poets in Focus 4, with others, edited by Jeremy Robson. London, Corgi, 1972.

Funland and Other Poems. London, Hutchinson, and New York, Oxford University Press, 1973.

Lunchtime. London, Poem-of-the-Month Club, 1974.

Penguin Modern Poets 26, with D.J. Enright and Michael Longley. London, Penguin, 1975.

Collected Poems 1948–1976. London, Hutchinson, and Pittsburgh, University of Pittsburgh Press, 1977.

Way Out in the Centre. London, Hutchinson, 1981; as *One-Legged on Ice*, Athens, University of Georgia Press, 1983.

Ask the Bloody Horse. London, Hutchinson, 1986; as *Sky in Narrow Streets*, in *Quarterly Review of Literature Poetry Series* (Princeton, New Jersey), 28, 1987.

White Coat, Purple Coat: Collected Poems 1948–1988. London, Hutchinson, 1989; New York, Persea, 1991.

Remembrance of Crimes Past. London, Hutchinson, 1990; New York, Persea, 1992.

Recordings: *Poets of Wales*, Argo, 1972; *The Poetry of Dannie Abse*, McGraw Hill, n.d.; *Dannie Abse*, Canto, 1984.

Other

Medicine on Trial. London, Aldus, 1968; New York, Crown, 1969.

A Poet in the Family (autobiography). London, Hutchinson, 1974.

Miscellany One. Bridgend, Glamorgan, Poetry Wales Press, 1981.

A Strong Dose of Myself (essays). London, Hutchinson, 1983.

Under the Influence Of (lecture). Cardiff, University College of Wales, 1984(?).

Journals from the Ant Heap. London, Hutchinson, 1986.

Editor, with Elizabeth Jennings and Stephen Spender, *New Poems 1956*. London, Joseph, 1956.

Editor, with Howard Sergeant, *Mavericks*. London, Editions Poetry and Poverty, 1957.

Editor, *European Verse*. London, Studio Vista, 1964.

Editor, *Corgi Modern Poets in Focus 1, 3, 5*. London, Corgi, 1971–73.

Editor, *Thirteen Poets*. London, Poetry Book Society, 1973.

Editor, *Poetry Dimension 2–5: The Best of the Poetry Year*. London, Robson, 1974–78; New York, St. Martin's Press, 1976–79; *The Best of the Poetry Year 6–7*, Robson, and Totowa, New Jersey, Rowman and Littlefield, 1979–80.

Editor, *Poetry Supplement, Christmas 1975*. London, Poetry Book Society, 1975.

Editor, *My Medical School*. London, Robson, 1978.

Editor, *Wales in Verse*. London, Secker and Warburg, 1983.

Editor, *Doctors and Patients*. Oxford, Oxford University Press, 1984.

Editor, with Joan Abse, *Voices in the Gallery*. London, Tate Gallery Publications, 1986.

Editor, with Joan Abse, *The Music Lover's Literary Companion*. London, Robson, 1988.

Editor, *The Hutchinson Book of Post-War British Poets*. London, Hutchinson, 1989.

*

Manuscript Collection: National Library of Wales, Aberystwyth, Dyfed.

Critical Studies: interviews in *Jewish Quarterly* (London), Winter 1962–63, *Flame* (Wivenhoe, Essex), March 1967, *Anglo-Welsh Review* (Tenby), Spring 1975, *The Guardian* (London), 31 January 1978, *Good Housekeeping* (London), May 1981, *The Times* (London), 28 February 1983, and *Sunday Times Magazine* (London), 22 May 1983; "Doctor and Magus in the Work of Dannie Abse" by Daniel Hoffman, in *Literature and Medicine* (Albany, New York), 3, 1984; *Dannie Abse* by Tony Curtis, Cardiff, University of Wales Press, 1985.

Dannie Abse comments:

Of a very early play of mine T.S. Eliot kindly remarked it was good for the stage and for the study. He was wrong. That play, alas, was not good for either; but I hope in later years some of my plays have earned Eliot's encomium. Anybody interested in my plays will find the three I'm most pleased with in a paperback, *The View from Row G*.

* * *

Dannie Abse's work explores the conflicting elements of the human psyche, showing man at war with his own self-destructive urges. As a practising doctor and a Jew, he sees clearly the limitations of the known, and the frightening depths of the subconscious, the irrational tyranny and subservience that underlie the apparent normality of the world. As one who wears both the white coat of the physician, and the magician's purple cloak, he remains wary of the system, and its threat to the individual. Abse sees in institutionalized obedience a force that reduces men and women to objects, detecting in the manipulation of medical experiments those same dark impulses that led to the gas ovens of Auschwitz and Belsen. Memory of the Nazi holocaust colours his writing, recalled in his plays with their potent themes of choice, delusion, the assertion and denial of self, and unquestioning obedience to evil.

Abse is a poet first and foremost and his earliest venture into drama was a verse play, *Fire in Heaven*. Set in an occupied country, it depicts the terrible choice placed before the main character, Christian, who is ordered to kill his family, or have the entire village massacred. After a painful struggle with his conscience, Christian murders his family. The appalling nature of the decision, and the horror of the killing itself, are ably—and shockingly—evoked by the author, although *Fire in Heaven* seems at times to be more akin to poetry than drama. Abse later rewrote it in two prose versions where the contrast is less stark, the occupying soldiers and their commander shown not as monsters, but as human beings caught in a fearful dilemma. Even so, some aspects of the work fail to satisfy completely, with Christian's character over-idealized, and an excess of dialogue betraying the story's poetic origins.

Choice and illusion also feature in *House of Cowards*, a drama based on Abse's poem "Meeting." It centres on the expected visit of the Speaker to a drab, uninteresting town whose inhabitants see him as the answer to their prayers. Eager at his promised coming, they recreate his image in their minds to fit their own requirements. But the Speaker, like Beckett's Godot, does not arrive, although expected the following day. Abse's story bears too close a resemblance to that of Beckett, while his everyday treatment of a symbolic theme renders the work less than effective.

Far better is *The Dogs of Pavlov*, where Abse continues his investigation of choice, and submission to evil. Taking his theme from an actual psychological experiment, he presents a horrifying picture of outwardly normal people only too easily persuaded to inflict pain on their fellows in the interests of "science." The fraught love relationship between Kurt and

Sally, whom Abse casts in the roles of victim and torturer, gives pointed emphasis to their situation, while clothing the horror in human terms. The fact that the "pain" is simulated, and the experiment a sham, does nothing to dispel its sinister implications. Abse views the godlike power of the doctors, their arbitary manipulation of their subjects, as directly linked with the Nazi "experiments" and the concentration camps. Sally's final outburst, begging for death in the "electric chair," is a cry of anguish from a dehumanised victim whose own worst instincts have been realized. Abse displays assurance in the interplay and speech patterns of his characters, and in his use of the stage. *The Dogs of Pavlov* shows human beings operating to destructive effect inside the sheaths of their own illusory ideals.

Similar themes are explored in *Pythagoras*, perhaps Abse's finest play so far. The scene is set in a mental hospital, where a power struggle takes place between the superintendent and an eccentric patient whose individuality constitutes a challenge to his authority. A former stage magician, Pythagoras sees himself as a reincarnation of the Greek sage, whose knowledge combined science, medicine, and religious magic, disciplines whose segregation is embodied in Dr. Aquillus, the superintendent. In the course of the play Pythagoras adopts the persona of his rival, and in one amusing but significant scene a reporter mistakes him for the superintendent and Pythagoras promptly "recreates" Dr. Aquillus as a psychopath. The play is derived from Abse's poem *Funland*, in which Pythagoras dies after a bungled rebellion by the inmates. Here there is a more profound and striking denouement, with Pythagoras collapsing at the moment of confrontation, and recuperating as a "normal" person, shorn of his individuality and powers. Deluded or not, his "fall" is tragic, a triumph of white-coated order over intuitive creation. Abse expands the theme with consummate skill, putting over his dark message with sharp exchanges of dialogue and frequent gems of humour. Here the symbolic and the natural fit together without strain, though their revelation is often bleak, as in the utterance of the patient being "demonstrated" to the medical students: "Yes, I am dead, and this is hell."

Pythagoras is matched on a smaller scale by some of Abse's shorter works. This is true of *Gone*, a one-act play whose basis is a prevented attempt at suicide. Similarly, *The Eccentric*, another one-acter, presents the idea of self-assertion through eccentricity, showing in the figure of the shopkeeper Goldstein a man fulfilled through his idiosyncrasies. His apparent stupidity in refusing to sell customers what they want is revealed as a principle of self-denial and as an ennobling act. "God doesn't say yes to everything," Goldstein tells his young protégé. "Maybe that's what makes a man." Though slight, *The Eccentric* is a poised, appealing work, whose deeper meanings are expressed in clear, individualised speech.

As the descendant of a persecuted race, Abse evokes the horrors of the past. As a writer and healer, he links them to the tyrannies of our own time. His plays, though secondary to his poetic works, sound a warning note that we ignore at our peril.

—Geoff Sadler

————

ACKLAND, Rodney. British. 1908–1991.
See 4th edition, 1988.

————

AIDOO, (Christina) Ama Ata. Ghanaian. Born in Abeadzi Kyiakor in 1942. Educated at the University of Ghana, Legon (Institute of African Studies fellowship), B.A. (honours) 1964; Stanford University, California. Lecturer in English, University of Cape Coast, Ghana, 1970–82; PNDC Secretary (Minister) for Education, 1982–83; writer-in-residence, University of Richmond, Virginia, 1989. Recipient: Fulbright scholarship, 1988. Address: P.O. Box 4930, Harare, Zimbabwe.

PUBLICATIONS

Plays

The Dilemma of a Ghost (produced Legon, 1964; Pittsburgh, 1988). Accra, Longman, 1965; New York, Macmillan, 1971.
Anowa (produced London, 1991). London, Longman, and New York, Humanities Press, 1970.

Novels

Our Sister Killjoy; or, Reflections from a Black-eyed Squint. London, Longman, 1977; New York, NOK, 1979.
Changes—A Love Story. London, Women's Press, 1991.

Short Stories

No Sweetness Here. London, Longman, 1970; New York, Doubleday, 1971.
The Eagle and the Chickens and Other Stories. Enugu, Nigeria, Tana Press, 1986.

Verse

Someone Talking to Sometime. Harare, College Press, 1985.
Birds and Other Poems. Harare, College Press, 1987.

Other

Dancing Out Doubts. Enugu, Nigeria, NOK, 1982.

*

Critical Studies: *Ama Ata Aidoo: The Dilemma of a Ghost* (study guide) by Jane W. Grant, London, Longman, 1980; *Women Writers in Black Africa* by Lloyd Brown, Westport, Connecticut, Greenwood, 1981; *Ngambika: Studies of Women in African Literature* edited by Carole Boyce Davies and Anne Adams Greaves, Trenton, New Jersey, Africa World Press, 1986; *Diverse Voices: Essays on Twentieth-Century Women Writers in English* edited by Harriet Devine Jump, London, Harvester Wheatsheaf, 1991.

* * *

Ama Ata Aidoo's two plays focus upon women's relationship to traditional values; in both plays the husband—the central male character—is ineffectual and unwilling to comprehend the effect of his actions or inaction on his wife.

A stock situation in African drama is the conflict between the modern ideas of the "been-to"—the man who has been to Europe for his education—and the traditions of his community. The title of Aidoo's first play, *The Dilemma of a Ghost*, comes from a song that we hear children singing, which the university graduate Ato loved as a child and which he now sees as symbolizing his position:

> One early morning,
> When the moon was up
> Shining as the sun,
> I went to Elmina Junction
> And there and there,
> I saw a wretched ghost
> Going up and down
> Singing to himself
> > "Shall I go
> > To Cape Coast,
> > Or to Elmina
> > I don't know,
> > I can't tell.
> > I don't know,
> > I can't tell."

The title character of Aidoo's other play, *Anowa*, who has followed her own will in defiance of her community's expectations, also refers to herself as a ghost. The metaphor points to the isolation and strain felt by someone who has set himself or herself apart from the life and values of the community.

African playwrights have tended to identify with the "been-to," but in *The Dilemma of a Ghost* Ato is almost unbelievably callow. He has not told his family that while in America he married. Nor does he explain, when they are concerned about his wife's infertility—not even when they come to subject her to curative herbal massage—that he has insisted upon using contraception. Nor, it seems, has he prepared his wife Eulalie in any way for the attitudes she will encounter in his home village.

The other twist on the dramatic norm is that he has married not a white but a black woman—someone who is, to his family's horror, the descendant of slaves. She, too, is a rather unsympathetic figure, filled with false suppositions about "native" life and increasingly given to drinking too much.

Given such a central couple (and the not altogether believable Americanisms that Eulalie is given), the vitality of the play lies in the women of Ato's village, in his mother and sister and in the two neighbouring women who act as chorus. It is from their perspective that the marriage and its conflicts are seen:

> My people have a lusty desire
> To see the tender skin
> On top of a child's scalp
> Rise and fall with human life.
> Your machines, my stranger-girl,
> Cannot go on an errand
> They have no hands to dress you
> when you are dead . . .

It is the compassion of Ato's mother that in the end leads her to rebuke her son and draw his wife into the family.

In Aidoo's second play, *Anowa* is a beautiful but willful girl whose mother resists the vocation of priestess that others foresee for her daughter. For her part, Anowa refuses the suitors of her parents' choice, marries a man the community considers a good-for-nothing, and leaves her village forever. With her aid, her husband Kofi prospers in trade with the British, but Anowa, driven by some inner vision, refuses the perquisites and leisure that her husband and (as in her earlier play) a choral pair take for granted. Finally, after a quarrel in which Anowa guesses the priest told Kofi that she has destroyed his manhood and that he half-believes her to be a witch, he shoots himself, and she drowns herself.

Remarkably, by comparison with many other African plays, the historical events of the late 19th century are relegated to the background. The British, for example, are represented only by a picture of Queen Victoria hanging in Kofi's house. There is some suggestion that in her sensitivity to "the common pain and the general wrong," and especially in her acute discomfort with the institution of slavery, Anowa represents Africa. But more intensely felt and conveyed is the misery of her personal situation: self-exile from her community, childlessness, and profound alienation from her husband's way of life. Aidoo uses the historical setting to present freshly the call for a more liberated role for women. Anowa says, "I hear in other lands a woman is nothing. And they let her know this from the day of her birth. But here, O my spirit mother, they let a girl grow up as she pleases until she is married. And then she is like any woman anywhere: in order for her man to be a man, she must not think, she must not talk." But Aidoo avoids the overt didacticism of some other African plays on women's roles by placing her central character in another century where her attitudes appear eccentric.

Ama Ata Aidoo's plays are individual, wry, sometimes poetic, and—in the case of *The Dilemma of a Ghost*—humorous. They deal with important themes, but these are secondary to the particular characters who are comfortable in or alienated from the community at the heart of the plays.

—Anthony Graham-White

———

AKALAITIS, JoAnne. American. Born in Chicago, Illinois, 29 June 1937. Educated at the University of Chicago, B.A. in philosophy 1960. Married Philip Glass (divorced); one daughter. Presented work and taught playwriting throughout North America, Europe, Australia, Nicaragua, Israel, and Japan. Co-founder of Mabou Mines, New York, 1970, and performer, designer, and director, 1970–90; playwright-in-residence, Mark Taper Forum, Los Angeles, 1984–85; artistic associate, Joseph Papp Public Theater, New York, 1990–91; since 1991 artistic director, New York Shakespeare Festival. Recipient: Obie award, 1976, 1977, 1979, 1984; Guggenheim fellowship, 1981; Rosemund Gilder award, 1981; Drama Desk award, 1983; Rockefeller grant, 1984. Agent: Flora Roberts, 157 West 57th Street, New York, New York 10019. Address: c/o New York Shakespeare Festival, 425 Lafayette Street, New York, New York 10003, U.S.A.

PUBLICATIONS

Plays

Southern Exposure (produced New York, 1979).
Dead End Kids: A History of Nuclear Power, music by David Byrne (produced New York, 1980).
Green Card (produced Los Angeles, 1986; New York, 1988). New York, Broadway Play Publishing, 1991.
The Voyage of the Beagle, (opera), music by Jon Gibson (produced New London, Connecticut, 1986).

Screenplay: *Dead End Kids: A History of Nuclear Power*, 1986.

*

Theatrical Activities:
Director: **Plays**—all her own plays; *Cascando* by Samuel Beckett, New York, 1976; *Dressed Like an Egg*, based on the writings of Colette, New York, 1977; *Request Concert* by Franz Xaver Kroetz, New York, 1981; *Red and Blue* by Michael Hurson, New York, 1982; *Through the Leaves* by Franz Xaver Kroetz, New York, 1984; *The Photographer* by Philip Glass, New York, 1984; *Endgame* by Samuel Beckett, Cambridge, Massachussetts, 1985; *Help Wanted* by Franz Xaver Kroetz, New York, 1986; *The Balcony* by Jean Genet, Cambridge, Massachusetts; *American Notes* by Len Jenkin, New York, 1988; *Leon & Lena (and Lenz)* by George Büchner, Minneapolis, 1989; *The Screens* by Jean Genet, Minneapolis, 1989; *Cymbeline* by Shakespeare, New York, 1989; *'Tis Pity She's a Whore* by John Ford, Chicago, 1990, and New York, 1992; *Henry IV, Parts One and Two* by Shakespeare, New York, 1991; *Prisoner of Love* by Jean Genet, New York, 1992; *Woyzeck* by Georg Büchner, New York, 1992. **Film**—*Dead End Kids*, 1986.
Actor: **Plays**—Role in *Dressed Like an Egg*, New York, 1977; *The Shaggy Dog Animation* by Lee Breuer, New York, 1977; *Dark Ride* by Len Jenkin, New York, 1981.

* * *

The title "avant-gardist" has stuck with JoAnne Akalaitis since she co-founded Mabou Mines. More anathema than blessing, it has prompted prejudice and a fundamental misunderstanding of her work. But Akalaitis is interested in the vicissitudes of human nature, a complex pursuit that requires her to delve deeply. Consequently, the theater of JoAnne Akalaitis has frequently been called "impenetrable," or "intimidating." Less interested in effect, she probes for cause: how does a noble quest become corrupt? (*Dead End Kids*; *The Voyage of the Beagle*); wherefore man's inhumanity to man? (*Green Card*). To do this, Akalaitis writes (and directs) with the focus on key links within the chain of events. Identified, the links are then viewed through a microscope. In much the same way that her physicists in *Dead End Kids* probe for the quintessence of an inanimate element, Akalaitis contemplates the cognizant animal.

One could take such a comparison further and say that, in a sense, to experience Akalaitis's theater is to sit in at the atomic level. At first sight, it appears chaotic: it is consuming, frenetic, kinetic, volatile, and often unforgiving. She eschews plot and narrative, alternately flashing, and contrasting, theory and practice. Dubious of rhetoric, she renders dialogue almost secondary in the process. The preservation of temporal and spatial continuity does not always accurately reflect cause and effect, and when it does not, Akalaitis arranges her own chronology. Not satisfied with actors simply reading dialogue and making the occasional gesture, she synthesizes a variety of media. Thus choreographer, composer, and photographer are as integral to the play as the text. Her atomic stage is rich in both image and language, and explicitly reflects the intensity of everyday life. The result is an almost successful transmogrification of theater, forming what critics have referred to as a "gestalt"—the creation of an environment where it is impossible to distill any element from the play without radically altering the work.

Akalaitis's concern with the shortcomings of language is perhaps best reflected in *Green Card*, a rapid-fire montage of music, slides, songs, dance, words, and film. It is a caustic satire concerning superficial values, bringing face-to-face the Haves (citizens of the United States) and Have Nots (refugees seeking asylum in the States). The play demonstrates how language is a trap and how its subscribers are too easily held captive. Immigrants struggle to understand the subtleties of the English language. "Learn English! Learn English!" native speakers of Vietnamese, Yiddish, Spanish, Russian, Chinese are warned or be faced with ignorance and confusion—even death. Yet when they resolve to do so, what they learn is that they have not been adequately prepared to comprehend it. For example, when a student asks for an explanation of the "REAL difference between 'I was writing' and 'I have written',", the response is an impatient: "'I was writing' is the imperfect tense while 'I have written' is the present perfect tense." Not quite sure what to make of this answer, the student denigrates herself (acknowledging the inferiority of her race) until the evening school teacher responds grandly: "The imperfect tense refers to what WAS, while the present perfect tense refers to what HAS BEEN."

To obtain a green card, that precious document promising a life with dignity and reward to thousands of refugees, characters must compete on The Green Card Show, the "game you have to play if you want to stay." Mocking the consumer culture, Akalaitis transforms Ellis Island into a TV game show set complete with canned applause and neon lights. If they win, the prize, of course, is permission to stay in the country; to lose however, is to "get sent back to where they belong." Akalaitis pummels characters and audience with idioms, building to a frenzy: what is the difference between "burn up," "burn down," "burnt out"; how does one get "carried away" without movement; how do Zan and Rich "pull off" a joke—what is being removed and from where? Her questions are ambiguous and mischievous enough to confuse a native American-English speaker:

Q: What is the most contemporary use of the expression to TURN ONE ON or to TURN ONE OFF?

a: Pretty women certainly TURN Charlie ON?

b: Some of the Great Renaissance painters TURN me ON but some of the modern ones TURN me OFF.

c. Minimalist post-modern performance art of the 1980's is a real TURN OFF for me.

Finally, language becomes more than just a trap—a prison and a kind of torture as an immigrant is grilled by officials to reveal his history and recent whereabouts. With search lights flashing across her stage and whistles at ear-piercing decibels, Akalaitis's immigration officials weed out the sick and undesirable and begin the examinations at break-neck speed. Struggling to keep up and misunderstanding the occasional trick question, the applicant begins blurting out responses half in English, half in Spanish.

This adroit manipulation of the traditional dramatic form is perhaps best experienced in *Dead End Kids*. Akalaitis has referred to this as an "impassioned repudiation of nuclear ineptitude." In context, it is a history of science (specifically, physics) beginning with 15th-century alchemists and ending in the present with the careless and devastating misuse of nuclear power. *Dead End Kids* is concerned with how, in spite of the best intentions, the human journey for knowledge is doomed. Released from its narrative, the play shifts into a whirling multimedia extravaganza. Switching to variety show format (circa 1962) our host and hostess primp and pose and gloss over any potentially distressing news items. Scenes change, and time shifts. Our hostess daydreams and the magic potions of an alchemist bubble forth. Another shift: suddenly, we are at a science fair where a young pupil and his perky teacher announce "This is the H bomb." Producing ingredients and parts from a bag, we are informed: "It's a question of design, not ingredients." "Be careful," our older guide counsels, "it would be such a pity to have even the tiniest explosion." Slides of Hiroshima and Nagasaki remind us just what sort of pity. "Splllllaaaaat! Nagasaki" reiterates Akalaitis. We witness explosion after explosion. Flash: a scene has changed; fragments fall and form new vignettes. She is as much an alchemist as the mysterious cloaked characters who mix potions and recite spells. The alchemist strives in vain to turn base metals into gold, while Akalaitis separates the elements of drama and recombines them to produce a strikingly original theater.

—Roxana Petzold

* * *

ALBEE, Edward (Franklin, III). American. Born in Virginia, 12 March 1928; adopted as an infant. Educated at Rye County Day School, Lawrenceville, New Jersey, 1940–43; Valley Forge Military Academy, Pennsylvania, 1943–44; Choate School, Connecticut, 1944–46; Trinity College, Hartford, Connecticut, 1946–47; Columbia University, New York, 1949. Served in the United States Army. Radio writer, WNYC, office boy, Warwick and Legler, record salesman, Bloomingdale's, book salesman, G. Schirmer, counterman, Manhattan Towers Hotel, messenger, Western Union, 1955–58, all in New York; producer, with Richard Barr and Clinton Wilder, Barr/Wilder/Albee Playwrights Unit, later Albarwild Theatre Arts, and Albar Productions, New York. Founder, William Flanagan Centre for Creative Persons, Montauk, Long Island, New York, 1971, and Edward Albee Foundation, 1978. U.S. cultural exchange visitor to the U.S.S.R., 1963. Co-director, Vivian Beaumont Theater, New York, 1981; resident playwright, Atlantic Center for the Arts, New Smyrna Beach, Florida, 1982; Regents' professor of drama, University of California at Irvine, 1983–85. Recipient: Berlin Festival award, 1959, 1961; Vernon Rice award, 1960; Obie award, 1960; Argentine Critics award, 1961; Lola D'Annunzio award, 1961; New York Drama Critics Circle award, 1964; Outer Circle award, 1964; London *Evening Standard* award, 1964; Tony award, 1964; Margo Jones award, 1965; Pulitzer prize, 1967, 1975; American Academy gold medal, 1980; Brandeis University Creative Arts award, 1983, 1984. D. Litt.: Emerson College, Boston, 1967; Litt.D.: Trinity College, 1974. Member, American Academy, 1966; member, Theater Hall of Fame, 1985. Agent: William Morris Agency, 1350 Avenue of the Americas, New York, New York 10019. Address: 14 Harrison Street, New York, New York 10013, U.S.A.

Publications

Plays

The Zoo Story (produced Berlin, 1959; New York and London, 1960). Included in *The Zoo Story, The Death of Bessie Smith, The Sandbox*, 1960.
The Death of Bessie Smith (produced Berlin, 1960; New York and London, 1961). Included in *The Zoo Story, The Death of Bessie Smith, The Sandbox*, 1960.
The Sandbox (produced New York, 1960). Included in *The Zoo Story, The Death of Bessie Smith, The Sandbox*, 1960.
The Zoo Story, The Death of Bessie Smith, The Sandbox:

Three Plays. New York, Coward McCann, 1960; as *The Zoo Story and Other Plays* (includes *The American Dream*), London, Cape, 1962.
Fam and Yam (produced Westport, Connecticut, and New York, 1960). New York, Dramatists Play Service, 1961.
The American Dream (produced New York and London, 1961). New York, Coward McCann, 1961; London, French, 1962.
Bartleby, with James Hinton, Jr., music by William Flanagan, adaptation of the story by Melville (produced New York, 1961).
Who's Afraid of Virginia Woolf? (produced New York, 1962; London, 1964). New York, Atheneum, 1962; London, Cape, 1964.
The Ballad of the Sad Café, adaptation of the story by Carson McCullers (produced New York, 1963; Worcester, 1969). New York and Boston, Atheneum-Houghton Mifflin, 1963; London, Cape, 1965.
Tiny Alice (produced New York, 1964; London, 1970). New York, Atheneum, 1965; London, Cape, 1966.
Malcolm, adaptation of the novel by James Purdy (produced New York, 1966). New York, Atheneum, 1966; London, Cape-Secker and Warburg, 1967.
A Delicate Balance (produced New York, 1966; London, 1969). New York, Atheneum, 1966; London, Cape, 1968.
Breakfast at Tiffany's, music by Bob Merrill, adaptation of the story by Truman Capote (produced Philadelphia, 1966).
Everything in the Garden, adaptation of the play by Giles Cooper (produced New York, 1967). New York, Atheneum, 1968.
Box and Quotations from Chairman Mao Tse-tung (as *Box-Mao-Box*, produced Buffalo, 1968; as *Box and Quotations from Chairman Mao Tse-tung*, produced New York, 1968). New York, Atheneum, 1969; London, Cape, 1970.
All Over (produced New York, 1971; London, 1972). New York, Atheneum, 1971; London, Cape, 1972.
Seascape (also director: produced New York, 1975; Kingston on Thames, Surrey, 1980). New York, Atheneum, 1975; London, Cape, 1976.
Counting the Ways (produced London, 1976; also director: produced Hartford, Connecticut, 1977). Included in *Two Plays*, 1977.
Listening (broadcast 1976; also director: produced Hartford, Connecticut, 1977; Coventry, 1977; New York, 1979). Included in *Two Plays*, 1977.
Two Plays. New York, Atheneum, 1977.
The Lady from Dubuque (produced New York, 1980). New York, Atheneum, 1980.
Lolita, adaptation of the novel by Vladimir Nabokov (produced Boston and New York, 1981). New York, Dramatists Play Service, 1984.
Plays:
 1. *The Zoo Story, The Death of Bessie Smith, The Sandbox, The American Dream.* New York, Coward McCann, 1981.
 2. *Tiny Alice, A Delicate Balance, Box and Quotations from Chairman Mao Tse-tung.* New York, Atheneum, 1982.
 3. *Seascape, Counting the Ways, Listening, All Over.* New York, Atheneum, 1982.
 4. *Everything in the Garden, Malcolm, The Ballad of the Sad Café.* New York, Atheneum, 1982.
The Man Who Had Three Arms (also director: produced Miami, 1982; New York, 1983; Edinburgh, 1989).

Envy, in *Faustus in Hell* (produced Princeton, New Jersey, 1985).

Screenplay: *A Delicate Balance*, 1976.

Radio Play: *Listening*, 1976 (UK).

Novel

Straight Through the Night. New York, Soho, 1989.

Other

Conversations with Edward Albee, edited by Philip C. Kolin. Jackson, University Press of Mississippi, 1988.

*

Bibliography: *Edward Albee at Home and Abroad: A Bibliography 1958-June 1968* by Richard E. Amacher and Margaret Rule, New York, AMS Press, 1970; *Edward Albee: An Annotated Bibliography 1968–1977* by Charles Lee Green, New York, AMS Press, 1980; *Edward Albee: A Bibliography* by Richard Tyce, Metuchen, New Jersey, Scarecrow, 1986.

Critical Studies: *Tradition and Renewal* by Gilbert Debusscher, translated by Anne D. Williams, Brussels, American Studies Center, 1967; *Edward Albee* by Richard E. Amacher, New York, Twayne, 1969, revised edition, 1982; *Edward Albee* by Ruby Cohn, Minneapolis, University of Minesota Press, 1969; *Edward Albee: Playwright in Protest* by Michael E. Rutenberg, New York, Drama Book Specialists, 1969; *Albee* by C.W.E Bigsby, Edinburgh, Oliver and Boyd, 1969, New York, Chip's Bookshop, 1978, and *Edward Albee: A Collection of Critical Essays* edited by Bigsby, Englewood Cliffs, New Jersey, Prentice Hall, 1975; *Edward Albee* by Ronald Hayman, London, Heinemann, 1971, New York, Ungar, 1973; *From Tension to Tonic: The Plays of Edward Albee* by Anne Paolucci, Carbondale, Southern Illinois University Press, 1972; *Edward Albee: The Poet of Loss* by Anita M. Stenz, The Hague, Mouton, 1978; *Who's Afraid of Edward Albee?* by Foster Hirsch, Berkeley, California, Creative Arts, 1978; *Edward Albee: An Interview and Essays* edited by Julian N. Wasserman, Houston, University of St. Thomas, 1983; *Edward Albee* by Gerald McCarthy, London, Macmillan, 1987; *Edward Albee: The Playwright of Quest* by C. P. Singh, Delhi, Mittal Publications, 1987; "Pure and Simple: the Recent Plays of Edward Albee" by Liliane Kerjan, in *New Essays on American Drama* edited by G. Debusscher, Amsterdam, Rodopi, 1989.

Theatrical Activities:
Director: several of his own plays.
Actor: Radio Play—Voice in *Listening*, 1988.

* * *

At the dawn of the 1960's Edward Albee introduced a humorous self-definition on stage with FAM, the "Famous American playwright," and YAM, the "Young American playwright," thus forecasting his exemplary career. Regarded as avant-garde when his first play, *The Zoo Story*, was produced in West Berlin on a double bill with Beckett's *Krapp's Last Tape*, he rocketed to fame when his director Alan Schneider decided to present *Who's Afraid of Virginia Woolf?* on Broadway.

Albee's beginnings established him as a master of language

and absurd humour, with a fine ear for idiom and rhythm, a compassionate voice appealing for communication between ethnic communities as in *The Death of Bessie Smith*, between generations as in *The American Dream* or *The Sandbox*, or again between the dominant segments of society and the hipsters, the drop-outs and the solitary dreamers as in *The Zoo Story*. For three decades, *The Zoo Story* has remained a favourite and a classic in university festivals and café-theatres of the western world because of its intensity, its spiritual dénouement, and above all its ultimate confrontation with the Other. Will Jerry change the world having changed one man, Peter, his neighbour on a bench in Central Park? In *Who's Afraid of Virginia Woolf?* will George and Martha—named after the Washingtons—be able to face the future without inventing new lies in order to survive? The question mark in the title sets Albee's tone: an incessant double-game of truth and illusion, of success and failure, of transgression and regression. The evaluation of ideological choices, the recognition of sterility sound all the more acute as it takes place on a New England campus, thus emphasizing the responsibility of academics in the intellectual and social debate of the nation.

As always, Albee tosses questions to the audience, refusing to give easy answers, demanding stringency and honesty. He places his characters—the middle-aged bourgeoisie, as a rule—in a *huis-clos* ("closed doors," in other words, no exit) where they are confronted with loss (*The American Dream*), with death (*All Over*, *The Lady from Dubuque*), with moral dilemmas (*A Delicate Balance*), with their conceptions of God (*Tiny Alice*). As always he denounces betrayals, vices born of leisure among the idle rich, comfortable clichés.

Albee has been presented as the saviour of the American theater, coming forth in a period of void, evolving from Off-Broadway to Broadway, experimenting in every direction, blending the surreal, the poetic, the hermetic into a naturalistic tradition, committing himself to serious articulation of the existential questions of our time. He also flirts with vaudeville (*Counting the Ways*), science fiction (*Seascape*), adaptations, film scripts, libretti: every dramatic form has spurred his curiosity. An admirer of Tennessee Williams, he captures the pulse and the tensions inherent in our conflicting desires and transposes them into flamboyant symphonies or subtle interrelated chamber-music pieces (*Box and Quotations from Chairman Mao Tse-Tung*, *The Sandbox*, *The American Dream*).

The years have brought a sense of the essentials: Albee has described *The Lady from Dubuque* as "perfectly straightforward and clear." Indeed, since it is terminal cancer. But the two-act drama about three interwoven suburban couples suddenly visited by the elegant and motherly lady and her black companion is also a ritual of compassion with games of comfort, not of pain. *Listening*, commissioned as radio-play, explores "the sound of an idea" and once more the failure to communicate within a strange triangle: a cook, a nurse, and a patient mix blurred memories and fatal refusals.

Press critics have too often considered *Who's Afraid of Virginia Woolf?* as Albee's main contribution to American drama and misjudged his later ventures. The play, which has been performed around the world and popularized through its film version, belongs undoubtedly to the classic repertory of the century, thanks to its organic integration of allegory, brilliant wit, and grotesque parody: no one will forget the psychic violence, the internal turmoil, the shared fantasies, and final compassion. But Albee's overwhelming presence covers more ground and nurtures a broader ambition: to keep characters and audiences off-balance, impelling a slow internal transformation of the dramatic medium.

For Edward Albee, writing is an act of optimism. Born inside the trade, like Eugene O'Neill, he remains a radical. Wealthy by birth and after the colossal success of *Woolf*, which gave him the economic leeway not to have "to go around writing *The Son of Virginia Woolf*," his aim is to continue to take chances in the theatre and create his own style.

—Liliane Kerjan

ALFRED, William. American. Born in New York City, 16 August 1922. Educated at Brooklyn College, B.A. 1948; Harvard University, Cambridge, Massachusetts, M.A. 1949, Ph.D. 1954. Served in the United States Army, 1943–46. Associate editor, *American Poet*, Brooklyn, 1942–44. Instructor, 1954–57, assistant professor, 1957–59, associate professor, 1959–63, and since 1963 professor of English, Harvard University. Recipient: Brooklyn College Literary Association award, 1953; Amy Lowell traveling poetry scholarship, 1956; Brandeis University Creative Arts award, 1960; American Academy grant, 1965. Address: 31 Athens Street, Cambridge, Massachusetts 02138, U.S.A.

PUBLICATIONS

Plays

The Annunciation Rosary. Matawan, New Jersey, Sower Press, 1948.
Agamemnon (produced Cambridge, Massachusetts, 1953). New York, Knopf, 1954.
Hogan's Goat (produced New York, 1965). New York, Farrar Straus, 1966; revised version, as *Cry for Us All*, with Albert Marre, music by Mitch Leigh (produced New York, 1970).
The Curse of an Aching Heart, music by Claibe Richardson (produced Chicago, 1979; New York, 1982). New York, French, 1983.
Holy Saturday (produced Boston, 1980). Published in *Canto* (Andover, Massachusetts), vol. 3 no. 1, 1979–80.

Other

Editor, with others, *Complete Prose Works of John Milton 1*. New Haven, Connecticut, Yale University Press, 1953; London, Oxford University Press, 1954.

Translator, *Beowulf*, in *Medieval Epics*. New York, Modern Library, 1963.

*

Manuscript Collections: Houghton Library, Harvard University, Cambridge, Massachusetts; Brooklyn College Library.

William Alfred comments:
I write plays because I love people the way dog-lovers love dogs, indiscriminately, and want to capture as many as I can in all their baffled splendor.

* * *

"It is a fearful thing to love what death can touch." These words are uttered by Cassandra in poet-playwright William Alfred's blank verse version of the tragedy of Agamemnon. Yet they come not from Homer nor Aeschylus; they were found on an ancient Vermont gravestone. The desperate sense of irremediable loss, both restrained and simple in this phrasing, is typical of Alfred's best dialogue in his *Agamemnon*. It is at once economic, poetic, and dramatically effective. In reading or in playing, one does not have the vaguely disquieting feeling that Alfred's characters are speaking English translations of Sophocles or Anouilh. They are all too human, which at times diminishes the magnitude of the tragic experience, especially when the dramatic diction tries to evoke a kind of realism. Cassandra says to Agamemnon on the voyage back from Troy: "A penny for your thoughts." Had she said "drachma" instead, it would still be jarring.

Central to Alfred's idea of the events is Agamemnon's guilty concealment of the true manner of his daughter Iphigenia's death at Aulis. On ship-board, he has the tongue cut from a man who dares to utter the truth. He keeps it from Cassandra, who divines it. Clytemnestra has been told her daughter died of fever, but her oldest adviser actually saw the ritual slaying. Her co-regents have said nothing of this, anxious to preserve order in the kingdom. Aegisthus, in an awkward situation he'd like to escape from, feels used. The action moves back and forth from the palace to Agamemnon's ship, as the moment of reunion approaches. When Clytemnestra finally discovers the truth, she goes down to the courtyard to receive—and to murder—her husband and Cassandra. This action is heard from offstage by her advisers—and the audience.

It's curious that Alfred observes this nicety of the Attic Greek theatre—scenes of horror offstage—when he is much more Shakespearean in his alternation of locales and inter-cutting of developing plotlines. He certainly makes thoughtful use of the soliloquy, but there are moments in the play when poetic ruminations detract from the potential power of the approaching confrontation by further foreshadowing it or by delaying it needlessly. Part of the problem is that Alfred is a poet first and a playwright second. That he is also a distinguished academic lends strength to his resources in rhetoric and cultural allusion, but this may have made him less spontaneous as a dramatist.

Periodically, there comes a fervent cry for the "return of poetry to the theatre," as though the victory of prose on stage were some kind of debasing of the drama. T.S. Eliot—who later said he'd learned playwriting at the public's expense—and Christopher Fry were hailed in the 1940's as new champions of the verse drama. The danger to the theatre in such cyclic surgings of desire for poetry on stage is that poetry-lovers and their favorite poets—encouraged to write for the theatre—will be more interested in images and devices than in characterisation and dramatic structure. When Alfred's tragic tale of ambition and deceit in *fin de siècle* Brooklyn, *Hogan's Goat*, was initially produced by the American Place Theatre which then specialized in staging works by poets and novelists, it was praised for its poetic virtues.

What made *Hogan's Goat* interesting to audiences, beyond its lilting Brooklyn Irish diction and homely but arresting images, was, however, its strong plot and vivid characters. As in *Agamemnon*, Alfred's tragic hero, Matthew Stanton, has concealed a terrible truth from his young wife. His vaunting political ambitions are brought low with the threat of blackmail, and he kills his wife in a frenzy when she tries to leave him, having learned their marriage isn't legal, that he was the kept man of a powerful woman whom he abandoned cruelly. There is power in the conflicts; complexity in the characters. Alfred's dialogue captures the idioms and rhythms of the Brooklyn Irish in the 1890's. *Hogan's Goat* recreates a bygone era in New York City's ethnic and political history in a vividly dramatic way. Best of all for ordinary audiences, the flow of Irish speech—heightened though it often is—is seldom perceived as poetry, but rather as passionate diction.

The critical and popular acceptance of *Hogan's Goat* led to a Broadway musical version, *Cry for Us All*, which failed. The essential failure was not in Alfred's drama, but in Albert Marre's notion that, with music by Mitch Leigh, this might be another Broadway hit like *Man of La Mancha*, also produced by Marre. As with the disappointing musical *Zorba!*, *Hogan's Goat* should have been an opera.

This disappointment didn't deter Alfred from offering Broadway in 1982 a charming suite of explorations among the Brooklyn Irish and their friends, *The Curse of an Aching Heart*. Subtitled "An Evening's Comedy," it is also a verse play, with some appealing songs by Alfred and music by Claibe Richardson. But the work failed to win a critical majority or a long run. Nonetheless, it remains a wryly and comically honest evocation of growing up in the big city in the 1920's and after. Its link with *Hogan's Goat* is its revelation of the hopes and defeats of descendants of figures noted in the earlier drama. It is not a sequential narrative; with a Prologue (1942) which looks backward, five one-act plays are offered, showing various stages in the lives of Frances Anna Duffy Walsh, her uncle Jo Jo, and their neighbors, friends, and lovers. The five minidramas are: *Friday Night Dreams Come True—1923*; *Clothes Make the Woman—1925*; *The Curse of an Aching Heart—1927*; *All Saints, All Souls—1935*; and *Holy Saturday—1942*. (The last play has been published and produced separately as well as *en suite*.) When Jo Jo inadvertently lets Fran know he is strongly attracted to her—even as he rages against her boyfriends, it shocks her. Until the end of the plays, when he's old and helpless and a healing occurs between them, she refuses to speak to him. These plays are not only an effective exercise in nostalgia, recreating games, folklore, values, prejudices, and style of the 1920's, 1930's, and 1940's, but they are also moving accounts of human strivings for contact and affection.

—Glenn Loney

ALLAN, Ted. Canadian. Born Alan Herman in Montreal, Quebec, 25 January 1916. Educated at Baron Byng High School, Montreal. Served in the International Brigade during the Spanish Civil War: colonel. Married Kate Schwartz in 1939 (divorced 1966); one daughter and one son. Store clerk, 1933–34; Montreal correspondent, Toronto *Daily Worker*, 1935; radio, television, and film actor; lived in London for nearly 30 years, now lives in Toronto and Los Angeles. Recipient: Canada Council grant, 1956, 1970, Senior Arts grant, 1974, and travel grant, 1974; Berlin Film Festival Golden Bear, 1985; Stephen Leacock award, for fiction, 1985. Agent: Linda Butler, 31–501 Yonge Street, Toronto M4Y 1Y4, Canada.

PUBLICATIONS

Plays

The Money Makers (produced Toronto, 1954; as *The Ghost Writers*, produced London, 1955).
Legend of Pepito, adaptation of a story by B. Traven (produced London, 1955).
Double Image, with Roger MacDougall, based on a story by Roy Vickers (produced London, 1956). London, French, 1957.
The Secret of the World (produced London, 1962).
Oh What a Lovely War, with the Theatre Workshop (produced London and New York, 1964). London, Methuen, 1965.
Chu Chem: A Zen Buddhist-Hebrew Musical, music and lyrics by Mitch Leigh, Jack Haines, and Jack Wohl (produced Philadelphia, 1966; New York, 1988).
My Sister's Keeper (as *I've Seen You Cut Lemons*, produced London, 1969; revised version, as *My Sister's Keeper*, produced Lennoxville, Quebec, 1974; New York, 1979). Toronto, University of Toronto Press, 1976.
Love Streams, and The Third Day Comes (produced Los Angeles, 1984).
Lies My Father Told Me (produced New York, 1986). Toronto, Playwrights, 1984.

Screenplays: *1001 Arabian Nights*, with others, 1959; *The Webster Boy*, with Leo Marks, 1962; *Fuse*, 1970; *Them Damned Canadians*, 1973; *Lies My Father Told Me*, 1975; *Love Streams*, with John Cassavetes, 1984; *Bethune: The Making of a Hero*, 1990.

Radio Plays: *Canadian Mental Health* series, 1953; *Coloured Buttons*, 1958; *The Good Son*, 1969.

Television Plays: *Willie the Squowse*, 1954; *Go Fall in Love*, 1955; *Early to Braden* series, 1957–58; *Legend of Paradiso*, 1960; *Flowers at My Feet*, 1968.

Novels

This Time a Better Earth. London, Heinemann, and New York, Morrow, 1939.
Quest for Pajaro (as Edward Maxwell). London, Heinemann, 1957.
Chu Chem: A Zen Buddhist-Hebrew Novel. Montreal, Editions Quebec, 1973.
Lies My Father Told Me (novelization of screenplay; as Norman Allan). New York, New American Library, 1975.
Love Is a Long Shot. Toronto, McClelland and Stewart, 1984; London, Hale, 1986.

Short Stories

Don't You Know Anybody Else? Family Stories. Toronto, McClelland and Stewart, 1985.

Other

The Scalpel, The Sword: The Story of Dr. Norman Bethune, with Sydney Gordon. Boston, Little Brown, 1952; London, Hale, 1954; revised edition, New York, Monthly Review Press, 1973.
Willie the Squowse (for children). Toronto, McClelland and Stewart, and London, Cape, 1977; New York, Hastings House, 1978.

Ted Allan comments:

(1977) I find it difficult to appraise my work. At some moments I think they are the most underestimated plays of the 20th century. At other moments I think they all need to be rewritten.

They have been praised and damned but have not attained the fame I sought for them, with the exception of *Oh What a Lovely War*. But here my pleasure is mixed, for the director-producer threw out my main plot, kept my peripheral scenes, rewriting most of them, took my name off the play in England, and gave writing credits to a few hundred people, to indicate that nobody *wrote* it. I consider my original version a theatrical tour de force and hope to get it produced one day under a new title: *Smith and Schmidt*, directed by someone who will do it as I wrote it.

Outside of *Gog and Magog*, which began life as *Double Image*, and which ran for a year in London and almost five years in Paris, none of my plays ever achieved commercial success.

The Secret of the World (my major opus), which told the story of three generations of a Montreal family (the head of which goes mad), did get wild critical hosannas from most of London's critics, but was panned by Canadian critics when it was performed at Lennoxville in 1976.

I've Seen You Cut Lemons probed the problem of alleged insanity in those we, the so-called normal, like to call abnormal. It was cruelly savaged by most of London's critics. That sent me brooding for a few years and to writing screenplays. I will return to playwriting next year, after I finish a new screenplay, which will provide me with the wherewithal to write for the theatre.

I consider *Chu Chem* the happiest of my plays although it died an untimely death after six performances in Philadelphia. I keep hoping it will one day get the kind of imaginative production it needs. (We had an elderly and beloved lead who couldn't remember his lines. The poor man died soon after the play did.)

My wildest fantasy is called *Willie the Squowse*, which nobody wants to produce, although it's been done on both radio and television. I have a horrible feeling that my plays will start getting produced all over the world to be acclaimed with noisy popularity after I am dead. If that is the price I must pay to get my plays produced, I agree. I have decided to die before I am ninety. This is a concession, for I had planned to live to a hundred. When I finally go, I will let you know.

(1988) I'm finding it easier to appraise my work now that I have rewritten *The Secret of the World* for the thousandth time. With the off-Broadway production of *Lies My Father Told Me* and a scheduled production of *Willie the Squowse* I feel less neglected.

*   *   *

With his high octane forcefulness and his formidable technical expertise, Ted Allan is a playwright who has been undeservedly neglected in the London theatre since *The Secret of the World* was produced at Stratford East in 1962. His two-hander *I've Seen You Cut Lemons* is a far more interesting piece of theatrical writing than William Gibson's *Two for the Seesaw*, for instance, a two-character play which enjoyed considerable success.

The Secret of the World is rather like a Canadian *Death of a Salesman*, with the life of the central family set in a context of direct involvement in union politics during and after the upheaval caused by Khrushchev's revelations about Stalin.

Chris Alexander (or Sam Alexander as he became at Stratford East) is an idealistic union leader who fails to get re-elected when he breaks with the Communist Party, and, from being successful, busy and well-liked, declines further into loneliness, ineffectuality, and near-madness. He is too honest to take advantage of an opportunity to get big money from a bus company in settlement of an accident claim, and hopes instead to make a fortune out of a crackpot invention—cufflinks joined by elastic, so that shirts can be put on without unfastening them.

The play's emotional brew is a very rich one. The interlocking emotional problems of Chris's father, wife, son, daughter, and brother-in-law are all boiled up together, and the resulting soup would possibly be more digestible with a little more comedy and a little less meat. But there is an admirable sureness of touch in creating theatrical effects, even if this is done without letting the characters be conscious enough of their own theatricality. The old father is rather like a Montreal version of Ibsen's Old Ekdal. But the decline of Chris is powerfully plotted, and, even when it is too obvious that Allan is trying to tug at the audience's heartstrings, the tugs are not usually fumbled.

In family plays especially, an over-rich emotional mixture is often due to the presence of too much autobiographical material and too much residue of the guilt that family pressures create. The suspicion one has that Allan is drawing directly on his own experience is strengthened when we see how much Sarah in *I've Seen You Cut Lemons* resembles Susan in *The Secret of the World* and when we hear her recalling incidents we actually saw in the earlier play—the mother, for instance, shouting "I believe in God, I believe in God! Atheists. Communists," outside the door of a room in her house where the Young Communist League was holding a meeting.

I've Seen You Cut Lemons is a more controlled, more economical play, which succeeds in sustaining tension all through the action by focusing on different aspects and different phases of a semi-incestuous brother-sister relationship. The action is set in the London bachelor flat of a Canadian university lecturer. His sister is a few years younger than he is. Like Susan, Sarah is a painter but she blames the relationship with her brother for her partially deliberate failure to make more use of her talent, which they both regard as a very considerable one.

They both have children from broken marriages. As the action starts he is on the point of taking his son to Corsica for a holiday, when she arrives unexpectedly, discharged early from the hospital. He lets her stay in the flat, judging her mental health to be sufficiently restored to stand up to a period of loneliness. Later, of course, he will regret this. When he returns she tries harder and harder to monopolise his life, untruthfully informing his girlfriend (who is also called Susan) that they are having an incestuous relationship, and going all out to convince him that this is what he really wants as much as she does. Allan's dialogue measures up well to the difficult task of registering her oscillations between lucidity and hallucination, and it even convinces us that she could play on her brother's guilt feelings cleverly enough to make him believe that her sanity could be fully and permanently restored if only he would devote a month of his life to looking after her. The play ends touchingly as she voluntarily goes back to hospital and he emerges from the purgatory of their time together a wiser man than he was before.

Allan has also written prolifically for the screen and television, and he collaborated with Roger MacDougall on the stage play *Double Image*. He has also written *Chu Chem*, which he describes as a Zen Buddhist-Hebrew Musical Comedy. It owes as much to Brecht as to Zen Buddhism, and the ingredients do not quite jell, but there are some very amusing moments. The most inspired theatrical image is a seesaw with buckets attached to either end. A rock is put into one, and the villagers have to "balance the budget" by putting jewels and gold into the other.

—Ronald Hayman

———

ANDERSON, Robert (Woodruff). American. Born in New York City, 28 April 1917. Educated at Phillips Exeter Academy, Exeter, New Hampshire, 1931–35; Harvard University, Cambridge, Massachusetts, 1935–42, A.B. (magna cum laude) 1939, M.A. 1940. Served in the United States Naval Reserve, 1942–46: lieutenant; Bronze Star. Married 1) Phyllis Stohl in 1940 (died 1956); 2) the actress Teresa Wright in 1959 (divorced 1978). Actor, South Shore Players, Cohasset, Massachusetts, summers 1937 and 1938. Assistant in English, Harvard University, 1939–42; teacher, Erskine School, Boston, 1941; teacher of playwriting, American Theatre Wing, New York, 1946–51, and Actors Studio, New York, 1955–56; member of the faculty, Salzburg Seminar in American Studies, 1968; writer-in-residence, University of North Carolina, Chapel Hill, 1969, and University of Iowa Writers Workshop, Iowa City, 1976, Member of the Playwrights Producing Company, 1953–60; president, New Dramatists Committee, 1955–56, and Dramatists Guild, 1971–73; member of the Board of Governors, American Playwrights Theatre, 1963–79. Since 1965 member of the Council, and since 1980 vice-president, Authors League of America. Recipient: National Theatre Conference prize, 1945; Rockefeller fellowship, 1946; Writers Guild of America award, for screenplay, 1970; ACE award, for television, 1991. Member, Theater Hall of Fame, 1980. Agent: Mitch Douglas, International Creative Management, 40 West 57th Street, New York, New York 10019. Address: Roxbury, Connecticut 06783, U.S.A.

PUBLICATIONS

Plays

Hour Town, music and lyrics by Anderson (produced Cambridge, Massachusetts, 1938).
Come Marching Home (produced Iowa City, 1945; New York, 1946).
The Eden Rose (produced Ridgefield, Connecticut, 1949).
Sketches in *Dance Me a Song* (produced New York, 1950).
Love Revisited (produced Westport, Connecticut, 1951).
All Summer Long, adaptation of the novel *A Wreath and a Curse* by Donald Wetzel (produced Washington, D.C., 1952; New York, 1954). New York, French, 1955.
Tea and Sympathy (produced New Haven, Connecticut, and New York, 1953; London, 1957). New York, Random House, 1953; London, Heinemann, 1957.
Silent Night, Lonely Night (produced New Haven, Connecticut, and New York, 1959). New York, Random House, 1960.
The Days Between (produced Dallas, 1965; New York, 1979). New York, Random House, 1965.
You Know I Can't Hear You When the Water's Running

(produced New York, 1967; London, 1968). New York, Random House, 1967.
I Never Sang for My Father (produced Philadelphia, 1967; New York, 1968; London, 1970). New York, Random House, 1968; screenplay published, New York, New American Library, 1970.
Solitaire/Double Solitaire (produced New Haven, Connecticut, Edinburgh, and New York, 1971). New York, Random House, 1972.
Free and Clear (produced New Haven, Connecticut, 1983).
The Last Act Is a Solo (televised 1991). New York, French, 1991.

Screenplays: *Tea and Sympathy*, 1956; *Until They Sail*, 1957; *The Nun's Story*, 1959; *The Sand Pebbles*, 1966; *I Never Sang for My Father*, 1970.

Radio and Television Plays: *David Copperfield*, *Oliver Twist*, *Vanity Fair*, *The Glass Menagerie*, *Trilby*, *The Old Lady Shows Her Medals*, *The Petrified Forest*, *The Scarlet Pimpernel*, *A Farewell to Arms*, *Summer and Smoke*, *Arrowsmith*, and other adaptations, 1946–52; *The Patricia Neal Story*, 1980; *The Last Act Is a Solo*, 1991; *Absolute Strangers*, 1991.

Novels

After. New York, Random House, and London, Barrie and Jenkins, 1973.
Getting Up and Going Home. New York, Simon and Schuster, 1978.

Other

Co-editor, *Elements of Literature* (anthology). New York, Holt Rinehart, 6 vols., 1988.

*

Bibliography: *The Apprenticeship of Robert Anderson* by David Ayers, unpublished dissertation, Columbus, Ohio State University, 1969.

Manuscript Collection: Harvard University Theatre Collection, Cambridge, Massachusetts.

Critical Studies: *Life among the Playwrights* by John F. Wharton, New York, Quadrangle, 1974; *Playwrights Talk about Playwriting* edited by Lewis Funke, Chicago, Dramatic Publishing Company, 1975; *Robert Anderson* by Thomas Adler, Boston, Twayne, 1978; "A Dramatist's Inner Space," in *Dramatists Guild Quarterly* (New York), Spring 1979; *The Strands Entwined* by Samuel Bernstein, Boston, Northeastern University Press, 1980; *Represented by Audrey Wood* by Audrey Wood and Max Wilk, New York, Doubleday, 1981.

Robert Anderson comments:
(1973) It is difficult and dangerous for a writer to talk about his own work. He should move on to whatever he is impelled to write about next without looking back and trying to analyze his work. Recently I read a doctoral thesis written about me and my plays. In many ways I wish I hadn't read it. I don't think it is wise for a writer to think about his "continuing themes" and recurring attitudes.
When I was near the end of writing *Tea and Sympathy*, my first wife begged me to tell her something of the subject of my

new play. (I never discuss my work with anyone while I am writing.) I gave in and simply told her it took place in a boys' school. She said, "Oh, my God, not another play about a boys' school!" This almost stopped me. At that moment I hadn't been consciously aware that I had written other (unproduced) work with a boys' school background. I simply knew that I wanted to write that play. My wife's making me aware that I had worked that vein before almost stopped me from finishing the play.

People sometimes say, "Why don't you write about something besides marriage?" Strangely, it is only after I have finished a play that I am aware that I have written again about marriage. Each time I start a play, I certainly don't have the feeling that I am going over old ground. I feel I have something new and different nagging at me to be written. I do not consciously say, "This is my theme. I have done it reasonably well before. Let's try it again."

And these "plays about marriage" are seldom just that. *Solitaire/Double Solitaire* was not about marriage in the present and in the future, as some critics described it. It was about the loneliness of being alone and the loneliness of marriage. *The Days Between* was not about an academic marriage on the rocks but about a man who was ruining his life and his marriage by being unable to live the ordinary, unexciting days of life, "the days between." Marriage is often the arena of the plays, but not always the real subject matter.

As a matter of fact, the plays are rarely "about" what critics say they are about. *Tea and Sympathy* has always been described as "a play about homosexuality." In effect, it has nothing to do with homosexuality. It has to do with an unjust charge of homosexuality and what follows such a charge. It has to do with responsibility, which must extend beyond giving tea and sympathy; it has to do again with loneliness; it has to do with questioning some popular definitions of manliness; and, most important, it has to do with judgment by prejudice . . . and a great deal more, I hope.

You Know I Can't Hear You When the Water's Running was said to be "about" sex. The plays were told in terms of sex, but they were not about sex. As Elia Kazan said when he first read the manuscript, "They're about the same things as your other plays except this time it came out funny and sad." They are very sad plays. As Walter Kerr said of them, "Laugh only when it hurts."

I seem to have written largely about the family, or rather to have used the family as the arena. By and large English critics feel that American playwrights rather overwork this area of concern. Still, our three finest plays are, probably, *The Glass Menagerie*, *Death of a Salesman*, and *Long Day's Journey into Night*. I am glad that Williams, Miller, and O'Neill didn't scare when and if someone said to them, "not another play about the family!"

I have been amused that I have sometimes been considered a "commercial" playwright. I am amused because each of my plays has had an enormous struggle to get on. Nobody has thought of them as "commercial" till after they were successful. *Tea and Sympathy* was turned down by almost every producer and was on its way back into my files when the Playwrights Company optioned it and started me on my career. *You Know I Can't Hear You When the Water's Running* was turned down by everyone until two new producers "who didn't know any better" took a chance on it. I waited something like seven years before someone "took a chance" on *I Never Sang for My Father*. I think I can't be blamed for being amused when I hear myself described as "commercial," especially inasmuch as three of my plays have premiered in very non-commercial regional theatres, one opened Off-Broadway, and one launched The American

Playwrights Theatre, a project which seeks to get the plays of "established" playwrights into the regional and college theatres rather than into Broadway theatres.

At various times in my youth I wanted to be an actor and a poet. I acted in college and summer theatres, and I was elected Harvard Class Poet on graduation. I think it is only natural that with these two "bents" I should end up a playwright, because in playwriting one finds the same kind of compression and essentialization one finds in poetry. Poems and plays are both the tips of icebergs.

Finally, I admire form. I took a course at Harvard with Robert Frost. One evening he was asked why he didn't write free verse. He replied, "I don't like playing tennis with the net down." I think that a great deal of the excitement in the theatre comes from using the limitations of the theatre creatively. Most plays, when they are adapted as movies, "opened up," lose their effectiveness, because part of their attraction was the way the playwright had found intensity and a creative impulse in dealing with the limitations of the theatre. Compare the play and the film of *Our Town*. I believe that form can be challenged, changed, stretched. But some kind of form seems to me of the essence of theatre.

I would wish that a person coming on my plays for the first time would not have any preconceived idea as to what they are "about." Each reader or spectator is a new collaborator, and he will, in a sense, write his own play and arrive at his own meanings, based on his own experience of life.

(1988) It has never been easier to get a play done someplace. It has never been more difficult to get a play done where a playwright can earn enough money to write the next play. Many years ago I wrote something which has been endlessly quoted and is still true: "You can make a killing in the theatre but not a living." If I had not been able to write movies and television from time to time, I could not have continued as a playwright. Most playwrights I know are moonlighters. When *Tea and Sympathy* was done in 1953, it cost forty thousand dollars to produce, with Elia Kazan, Jo Mielziner, and Deborah Kerr, all superb and expensive talents. I am told that my six character new play, *The Kissing Was Always the Best*, will probably cost close to a million dollars to produce on Broadway. I try not to think about this.

* * *

Robert Anderson first received limited recognition as a playwright in 1945 when his play *Come Marching Home* was awarded first prize in a National Theatre Conference contest. This was followed five years later by *Love Revisited* which was performed at the Westport County Playhouse. But it was Alan Schneider's Washington Arena production of *All Summer Long* that really marked his emergence as a writer of genuine power and considerable subtlety. Though it was not particularly well received when it eventually reached Broadway two years later, the success of *Tea and Sympathy* had by then established Anderson's reputation as a skilful and impressive playwright.

All Summer Long is a sensitive if somewhat portentously symbolic play about the loss of illusions and the inevitable dissolution of beauty, love, and innocence. The family, which is the focus for this elegy on human weakness, live beside a river which is slowly eroding the bank under their home—a none-too-subtle image of the collapse of genuine feeling within the family itself. Willie, the youngest boy, is on the verge of adolescence and his brother Don, a college sports star crippled in a motor accident, tries to protect him from his own emerging sexuality and from the cynicism and bitterness of the rest of the family, though ironically Don is unable to come to terms with the change in his own life. Anderson piles on the agony, with parents who no longer care for each other or their children, and a girl who tries to produce an abortion by throwing herself on an electrified fence. Though Willie and Don spend the summer trying to build a wall to hold out the threatening floodwaters, the forces of nature can no more be controlled on this level than they can in the lives of individuals growing more self-centered and lonely as they grow older. The play ends as the house collapses—an obvious image of the family itself which has long since disintegrated in human terms.

Though he has never since relied on such a melodramatic climax Anderson's work is never entirely free of a certain dramatic overstatement. In *All Summer Long* Don is not only a crippled sports star, itself something of a cliché, but the accident which caused his injury had been a result of his father's inadequacy. Similarly, in a later play, *Silent Night, Lonely Night*, a child dies because her mother is at that very moment preoccupied with reading a letter which reveals her husband's adultery. Her subsequent plunge into insanity is, perhaps, understandable, but serves to create a melodramatic setting for what is otherwise a subtle examination of human need. Nowhere, however, does Anderson control this tendency better than in what remains his best play, *Tea and Sympathy*, though even here there is a certain lack of subtlety in his portrait of a callous father and a weak and therefore vindictive schoolmaster who may well share the very sexual deviancy which he denounces in others.

Tea and Sympathy was Anderson's Broadway debut and earned him a deserved reputation for confronting delicate and even contentious issues with courage and effect—a reputation which he himself was to parody in his later *You Know I Can't Hear You When the Water's Running*. The play is concerned with the plight of a 17-year-old boy in a New England boarding school who is accused of being homosexual. Unsure of himself and tormented by his fellow pupils, he turns to his housemaster's wife, whom he loves with adolescent passion and anguish. Horrified by her husband's inhumanity and genuinely concerned for the fate of the young boy, she finally allows him to make love to her—the only way she can see him regaining his sexual self-confidence and his faith in other people. The boy's father, long since divorced, has never offered his son the slightest affection while his housemaster punishes the boy for his own suppressed fears. As a perceptive indictment of the witch-hunt the play was produced at a particularly appropriate moment, the height of the McCarthy era. But it is a great deal more than this and despite the rather casual psychological assumptions which underlie the portraits of both father and housemaster the play was a perceptive comment on the failure of compassion in a society which demanded conformity as the price of acceptance.

Anderson's next play, *Silent Night, Lonely Night*, again dealt with the anguish of those who are deprived of the affection and understanding of those who should be closest to them. Katherine, temporarily separated from a husband whom she has just discovered to be unfaithful, finds herself alone in a New England inn on Christmas Eve. Upset and lonely she dines with another guest whose wife is in a nearby mental hospital—driven there by his own infidelity. For this one night they manage to overcome their sense of guilt and self-concern in order to offer one another the momentary consolation of true compassion. The simple symmetry of the structure underlines the justice of those who see Anderson primarily as a constructor of well-made plays, but despite this and despite the melodramatic nature of the man's personal history the play remains a delicate study which compares well with Anderson's earlier work.

His next production, four one-act comedies presented under the title *You Know I Can't Hear You When the Water's Running*, was not staged until eight years later. Lightweight sketches which partly depend on and partly satirize the new vogue for sexual explictness, they show little of his earlier sensitivity or skill. The same nostalgic regret for the decay of love and the passing of youth is manifested in two of the plays, "The Footsteps of Doves" and "I'll Be Home for Christmas," but now it becomes the subject of rather tasteless jokes. The spectacle of Anderson mocking his earlier convictions is not an altogether attractive one, for the humour of the plays derives from precisely that cynical worldly-wise detachment which he had previously seen as the enemy of the human spirit. When he briefly comes close to a moment of true pathos, in "I'll Be Home for Christmas," the integrity of the scene is lost in the sophisticated banter of the rest of the play.

I Never Sang for My Father does little to redeem the weakness of this composite play. Centering on the almost neurotic need of a son to win the love of a bitter and virtually senile father, it reveals not only the terrifying gaps which can open up between those who should be drawn to one another by all the ties of natural affection and concern, but also the desperate absence of love in a world full of people who choose to shelter and exile themselves in the fragile shell of their own personalities. Yet, despite the emotive nature of his subject, Anderson fails, in the last resort, to establish the tension which he creates as anything more than a pathological study—a compassionate and detailed examination of individuals who, despite the familiarity of their situations, remain case studies rather than evocative projections of a universal state.

In some respects Anderson suggests comparison with dramatists like William Inge, Carson McCullers, and Tennessee Williams. Like them he has chosen to describe the plight of those whose romantic dreams founder on the harsh realities of modern life. Emotionally scarred and sexually vulnerable, his protagonists try to find their way in a world which frightens and dismays them. In *All Summer Long* and *Tea and Sympathy* the central figure, appropriately enough, is an adolescent—for the boy confronting sexuality and cruelty for the first time serves to emphasise simultaneously the ideals of youth and the cynicism and disillusionment of middle age. For Anderson this contrast constitutes the key to individual anguish and the mainspring of a pathos which he seems to regard as the truest expression of human experience. Clearly this is the stuff of which nostalgia and sentimentality are made and his work is open to both charges. Where Tennessee Williams balances his regret for the destruction of the innocent and the romantic with a grudging regard for the "Promethians" who dominate their surroundings, Anderson offers only a romantic regret that things cannot be other than they are. Where Inge and McCullers see the growth away from innocence into experience as a painful but necessary human process, Anderson tends to see it as the first stage in the extinction of genuine feeling and human compassion. If some people can sustain their innocence into maturity they do so, in his world it seems, only at the cost of their ability to act. It is a paradox which he is content to identify rather than examine with the kind of subtlety which Williams had brought to *The Glass Menagerie* and *Orpheus Descending*.

—C.W.E. Bigsby

ANTROBUS, John. British. Born in Woolwich, London, 2 July 1933. Educated at Bishop Wordsworth Grammar School, Salisbury, Wiltshire; Selhurst Grammar School, Croydon, Surrey; King Edward VII Nautical College; Royal Military Academy, Sandhurst, Camberley, Surrey. Served in the British Army, East Surrey Regiment, 1952–55. Married Margaret McCormick in 1958 (divorced 1980); two sons and one daughter. Apprentice deck officer, Merchant Navy, 1950–52; supply teacher and waiter, 1953–54. Since 1955 freelance writer. Recipient: George Devine award, 1970; Writers Guild award, 1971; Arts Council bursary, 1973, 1976, 1980, 1982; Banff Television Festival award, 1987. Lives in London. Agent: Pat White, Rogers, Coleridge, and White, 20 Powis Mews, London W11 1JN, England.

PUBLICATIONS

Plays

The Bed-Sitting Room, with Spike Milligan (also co-director: produced London, 1963). Walton on Thames, Surrey, Hobbs, 1970; revised version, as *The Bed-Sitting Room 2* (also director: produced London, 1983).
Royal Commission Review (produced London, 1964).
You'll Come to Love Your Sperm Test (also director: produced Edinburgh and London, 1965). Published in *New Writers 4*, London, Calder and Boyars, 1965.
Cane of Honour (produced London, 1965).
The Missing Links (televised 1965; produced London, 1977). Included in *Why Bournemouth? and Other Plays*, 1970.
Trixie and Baba (produced London, 1968). London, Calder and Boyars, 1969.
Why Bournemouth? (produced London, 1968). Included in *Why Bournemouth? and Other Plays*, 1970.
Captain Oates' Left Sock (produced London, 1969). London, French, 1974.
An Evening with John Antrobus (produced London, 1969).
Why Bournemouth? and Other Plays. London, Calder and Boyars, 1970.
An Apple a Day (televised 1971; produced London, 1974). Included in *Why Bournemouth? and Other Plays*, 1970.
Stranger in a Cafeteria, in *Christmas Present* (produced Edinburgh, 1971).
The Looneys (produced Edinburgh, 1971; London, 1974).
Crete and Sergeant Pepper (produced London, 1972).
The Dinosaurs, and Certain Humiliations (produced Edinburgh, 1973; London, 1974).
The Illegal Immigrant (produced London, 1974).
Mrs. Grabowski's Academy (produced London, 1975).
They Sleep Together (produced Leicester, 1976).
Sketches in *City Delights* (revue; produced Oxford, 1978; London, 1980).
Jonah (also director: produced Cambridge, 1979).
Hitler in Liverpool, One Orange for the Baby, Up in the Hide (produced London, 1980). London, Calder, and New York, Riverrun Press, 1983.
When Did You Last See Your Trousers?, with Ray Galton, adaptation of a story by Galton and Alan Simpson (produced Mold, Clwyd, 1986; London, 1987). London, French, 1988.

Screenplays: *Carry on Sergeant*, with Norman Hudis, 1958; *Idol on Parade*, 1959; *Jazzboat*, with Ken Hughes, 1960; *The Wrong Arm of the Law*, with others, 1962; *The Big Job*, with Talbot Rothwell, 1965; *The Bed-Sitting Room*, with Charles Wood, 1969.

Radio Writing: *Idiot Weekly* and *The Goon Show* series; *Brandy, Brandy*, 1972; *LMF (Lack of Moral Fibre)*, 1976; *Haute Cuisine*, 1977; *The Lie*, 1978; *In a Dry Place*, 1986; *Looneys*, 1987; *The Milligan Papers* series, 1987.

Television Writing: *Idiot Weekly* series; *A Show Called Fred* series; *The Army Game* series; *Bootsie and Snudge* series; for Eric Sykes, Arthur Haynes, Frankie Howerd, Jimmy Wheeler shows; *Lenny the Lion Show*, 1957; *Variety Inc. Show*, 1957; *For the Children Show*, 1957; *Early to Braden* series, 1957; *The April 8th Show (Seven Days Early)*, 1958; *The Deadly Game of Chess*, 1958; *The Missing Links*, 1965; *An Apple a Day*, 1971; *Don't Feed the Fish*, 1971; *Marty Feldman Show*, 1972; *A Milligan for All Seasons*, with Spike Milligan, 1974; episode in *Too Close for Comfort*, 1984 (USA); *The Last Laugh Before T.V. AM*, with Spike Milligan, 1985; *Room at the Bottom* series, with Ray Galton, 1986 and 1987; *Alfred Hitchcock Presents*, 1987 (USA).

Other (for children)

The Boy with Illuminated Measles. London, Robson, 1978.
Help! I Am a Prisoner in a Toothpaste Factory. London, Robson, 1978.
Ronnie and the Haunted Rolls Royce. London, Robson, 1982.
Ronnie and the Great Knitted Robbery. London, Robson, 1982.
Pirates, with Mike Wallis. London, Carnival, 1990.
Polo Time, with Mike Wallis. London, Carnival, 1990.
Spooky Time, with Mike Wallis. London, Carnival, 1990.
Picnic, with Mike Wallis. London, Carnival, 1990.
Ronnie and the High Rise. London, Robson, 1992.
Ronnie and the Flying Fitted Carpet. London, Robson, 1992.

*

Manuscript Collection: Mugar Memorial Library, Boston University.

Theatrical Activities:
Director: **Plays**—*The Bed-Sitting Room* (co-director, with Spike Milligan), London, 1963; *You'll Come to Love Your Sperm Test*, Edinburgh and London, 1965; *Savages* by Christopher Hampton, Aalsburg, Denmark, 1973; *Jonah*, Oxford, 1979; *One Orange for the Baby*, London, 1980; *The Bed-Sitting Room 2*, London, 1983.
Actor: **Plays**—*You'll Come to Love Your Sperm Test*, Edinburgh and London, 1965; *An Evening with John Antrobus*, London, 1969; Glendenning in *The Contractor* by David Storey, London, 1970; *Hitler in Liverpool*, London, 1980. **Film**—*Raising the Wind (Roommates)*, 1961; *Carry on Columbus*, 1992. **Radio**—*The Missing Links*, 1986. **Television**—*A Milligan for All Seasons*, 1974; *Squaring the Circle* by Tom Stoppard, 1986.

*   *   *

John Antrobus wrote his first play, *The Bed-Sitting Room*, with Spike Milligan; and though Antrobus's range has broadened, all his work has retained characteristics which are as well examined through this first play as through any other.
World War III, apparently caused by a "Nuclear Misunderstanding," mutates Lord Fortnum of Alamein into the bed-sitting room of the title. His doctor moves into the premises instead of curing his patient, a trendy vicar in a Victorian bathing costume performs a marriage service by reading from *Lady Chatterley's Lover*, and Harold Wilson becomes a par-

rot. It is a surrealist mock-heroic fable, then, a shell-distorted mirror to an absurd society. The Milligan element is clearly crucial; like that of *The Goon Show*, its humour may or may not be tasteful, and its vaudeville cross-talk moves from brilliant lunacy to dead trivialities. It remains hilarious— indeed it must be one of the funniest plays to come out of modern England—and it cocktails gentleness with blasphemy, pathos, beauty, desperation, and innocent reverence. The exuberance of the play gives way to tenderness in the scene at the end in which a mother cries, "Give me back my baby." But Goonishness is a fraught context for simple or naive sincerity, especially where it leads to immediate wish-fulfilment. Muddling through the ineptitude of the protagonists and the play is a strong moral concern addressed to the perennially urgent question of human survival. The play's satire, directed against politicians, vicars, advertising men, and all other regulators of modern man, is clearly rooted in Britain—as is its refusal to take itself seriously.

Ambivalences and tensions are rife in all of Antrobus's plays, and it is unclear whether these result from mere self-indulgence or from a lack of critical sense. At its worst, Antrobus's indiscipline leads to monotony, flabbiness, and garrulity; at his best Antrobus bids fair to rival Pinter; and usually, in spite of his lack of clarity and faults of his dramatic structure, Antrobus manages to be profoundly disturbing and stimulating. From a formal or technical point of view, his best work has been for radio. He is among the half dozen radio dramatists who manage to produce work which both understands and exploits the distinctive nature of radio as a medium. Antrobus is best known, however, for his work on television where both *The Army Game* and *Bootsie and Snudge* have acquired immortality.

His Christian conversion, though a conversion to Jesus rather than to dogma or denomination, seemed out of character to observers who could only see in his work brilliant if anarchic satire of the Establishment. Lying just under that hard and polished surface has been a concern, usually expressed through irony, with the deepest issues of our time: the problems posed by the "advances" of science, the nature of militarism, whether anything differentiates normalcy from madness, pretence and honesty in human relationships, the wolfish and sheepish character of such religion as is tolerated (or connived at) by those in cultural and political power. However, his conversion seems to have had no discernible effect on his work—or is the relatively conservative form of *Crete and Sergeant Pepper* part of a search for a new synthesis that is as yet only partly evident? If Antrobus can find a structure for his pyrotechnic fluidity, and grow the body of his work from that inner womb or heart which is clearly sensitive to moral and even spiritual issues, we may find his genius properly revealed instead of the individual, energetic, and zany playwright whom we have seen so far.

—Prabhu S. Guptara

ARCHIBALD, (Rupert) Douglas. Citizen of Trinidad and Tobago. Born in Port-of-Spain, 25 April 1919. Educated at Queen's Royal College, Port-of-Spain, 1928–35; McGill University, Montreal, Bachelor of Engineering (Civil) 1946. Served in the 2nd Battalion, Trinidad Light Infantry, 1938–40: sergeant; in the Canadian Army Reserve, 1943–45: 2nd lieutenant. Married Maureen Wedderburn Berry in 1953; one daughter and one son. Student engineer, Trinidad Government Railways, 1935–41; riot policeman, 1937, and platoon commander, 1940–41, Trinidad Special Police; assistant maintenance engineer, Trinidad Government Railways, 1946–48; in private practice as a consulting civil engineer, 1949–63 and 1969–83; editor, *Progress* magazine, 1952; member of the Editorial Board, *Clarion* newspaper, 1954–56; general manager, Trinidad and Tobago Telephone Service, 1963–68, and managing director, Trinidad and Tobago Company Ltd., 1968–69; chair of the Railway Board, Trinidad, 1963–65; chair of the Central Water Distribution Authority, Trinidad and Tobago, 1964–65; vice-chair of the Public Transport Service Corporation, Trinidad and Tobago, 1965–67; director, Trinidad Engineering and Research Ltd., 1970–83. Tutor in creative writing, University of the West Indies, St. Augustine, Trinidad, 1971, 1973, 1975. Founding member, later vice-president and president, Readers and Writers Guild of Trinidad and Tobago, 1948–54; since 1953, life member, Engineering Institute of Canada; founding member, 1958, later vice-president and president, and fellow, 1974, Association of Professional Engineers of Trinidad and Tobago; president, Historical Society of Trinidad and Tobago, 1967–80. Recipient: Theatre Guild award, 1962. Address: 7 Stephens Road, Maraval, Trinidad and Tobago.

PUBLICATIONS

Plays

Junction Village (produced Port-of-Spain, 1954; London, 1955). Mona, University of the West Indies, 1958.
Anne-Marie (produced Port-of-Spain, 1958; London, 1976). St. Augustine, Trinidad, University of the West Indies, 1967.
The Bamboo Clump (produced Port-of-Spain, 1962). Mona, University of the West Indies, 1967.
The Rose Slip (produced Port-of-Spain, 1962). Mona, University of the West Indies, 1967.
Old Maid's Tale (produced Port-of-Spain, 1965). Mona, University of the West Indies, 1966.
Island Tide (produced San Fernando, Trinidad). Mona, University of the West Indies, 1972.
Defeat with Honour. Mona, University of the West Indies, 1977.
Back of Beyond (produced Port-of-Spain, 1984).

Radio Plays: *That Family Next Door* series and *Island Tide* series, 1973.

Television Play: *My Good Friend Justice*, 1974.

Novel

Isidore and the Turtle. St. Augustine, University of the West Indies, 1977.

Other

Tobago, "Melancholy Isle". Port-of-Spain, Westindiana, 1987.

*   *   *

Douglas Archibald is concerned with the decay of rural society in Trinidad. We see something of the old bourgeois order in *Anne-Marie*, set on an estate 50 miles from Port-of-Spain towards the end of the last century. Here, James Fanshawe and his Spanish-descended neighbour, Pedro Meijas, bemoan the fact that they are not the men their fathers were. Their estates are being run down, they have no male heirs and if they make their housekeepers pregnant, it is not to perpetuate the old line. *Old Maid's Tale* is a sentimental extension of this world where "Aunt Hetty," last of the Macdougals, brings romantic young lovers together over tea and cucumber sandwiches, recalling the lovers of her own youth—who exist only in her imagination.

Men in this society abdicate responsibility, and this is also the basic fact of life in the village, cut off equally from the town and from the plantation. In *The Bamboo Clump* the hypochondriac Charles Mackenzie is master of the house in name only. He has ignored his family, neglected his 30-acre cocoa estate, and done little in the last five years but sit on a bench in his garden. As a result, his son Dennis, like every other West Indian youth unable to emigrate, adopts supposedly United States dress (this was before Black Power!) and drifts towards trouble with the police. His daughter Drina is an intolerable prude and is being trained for her projected schoolteacher's career by the usual caricature spinster. When she fails her exams, there seems no way to stop Li Fat (the middleaged Chinese shopkeeper from whom they'd been getting credit) claiming her as his wife. To stop the rot, Charles finally (and improbably) asserts himself.

But the men are fighting a losing battle, In *Junction Village* the matriarchal society has arrived. The action centres round the household of Grannie Gombo who, past 90, is apparently dying. The neighbours (including Bobo and Lizzy, also in their 90's) gather for the wake, but are on their guard as Grannie has tried this trick before. As they wait, the granddaughters discuss Grannie's money, and Bobo relives the many conquests of his youth—counting Granny and Lizzy among them. Bobo is now treated as a harmless nuisance, but when he echoes the dying cry of all the other nonagenarian men, from Baba in *Anne-Marie* to Bucket in *The Rose Slip*, we are genuinely disturbed. Archibald shows us that their fear isn't only of a cold bath and the poor house, but of the loneliness and loss of power and respect which afflict the old. And they abound in these villages. Bobo reflects that

> dere was a time w'en Ah wus strong, an' me arm wus like iron. Den pipple use to fear me an' Ah use ter walk in an' out a whey Ah did want. . . . Ah had moh bed dan one to sleep in dose days. Now me strenk gorn. One day it leave me sudden, jus' like dat an' dey begin to push me aroun' an aroun'. Dese days me bones hurtin' me somet'ing bad and me t'roat always dryin' up. . . .

This is unsettling, also, because there seems so little compensating vitality among the youth. In the fishing village of *Island Tide* the three generation family of Mr. Paps, his son Copy Cat, and his grandson Uncle Look Up, suggests a sort of evolution in reverse—somewhat like R.S. Thomas's hill farmers. Of the two young men in *Junction Village*, one is a fool addicted to long words, and the other is a violent lout who hides under the dying woman's bed to escape detection from the police—there is energy here but ill-directed. However, there is comic relief as Grannie Gombo returns to life and demands food. There's nothing like this to lighten the drudgery of the city dwellers in *The Rose Slip*. Men, young and old, have been reduced to children; the women are harassed by their landlord, and in spite of their prayer meetings, can't feed their children. There is no relief in sight.

Archibald's social concern is serious enough. The plays suggest that a lack of paternal grip in all its forms leads to

disintegration. But there is a certain old-fashioned view of social order in that things are measured against the loss of past certainties rather than explored for their present potential. It is a determinism which eschews experiment, and is reflected at its worst in the characterization. The caricatures —of the spinster, the black Englishman, the druggist using long words, etc.—work beautifully; but when in play after play, *individuals* fail to break through this "type casting" either of their aspirations or of their diction, the result is an overall complacency that confirms old prejudices.

—E.A. Markham

————

ARDEN, Jane. British.
See 3rd edition, 1982.

————

ARDEN, John. British. Born in Barnsley, Yorkshire, 26 October 1930. Educated at schools in Barnsley; Sedbergh School, Yorkshire, 1944–48; King's College, Cambridge, 1950–53, B.A. in architecture 1953; Edinburgh College of Art, 1953–55, diploma in architecture 1955. Served in the British Army Intelligence Corps, 1949–50: lance-corporal. Married the actress Margaretta Ruth D'Arcy in 1957; five sons (one deceased). Architectural assistant, London, 1955–57; full-time writer from 1958. Fellow in playwriting, Bristol University, 1959–60; visiting lecturer in politics and drama, New York University, 1967; Regents' lecturer, University of California, Davis, 1973; writer-in-residence, University of New England, Armidale, New South Wales, 1975. Founder, Committee of 100 anti-nuclear group, 1961; chair *Peace News* pacifist weekly, London, 1966–70; co-founder, Corrandulla Arts and Entertainment, County Galway, Ireland, 1973; founding member, Theatre Writers' Group (now Theatre Writers' Union), 1975. Recipient: BBC Northern Region prize, 1957; Encyclopaedia Britannica prize, 1959; *Evening Standard* award, 1960; Trieste Festival award, 1961; Vernon Rice award, 1966; John Whiting award, 1973; PEN Macmillan Silver Pen award, 1992. Lives in Galway. Agent: Casarotto Ramsay Ltd., National House, 60–66 Wardour Street, London W1V 3HP, England.

PUBLICATIONS

Plays

All Fall Down (produced Edinburgh, 1955).
The Waters of Babylon (produced London, 1957; New York, 1965). Included in *Three Plays*, 1964.
When Is a Door Not a Door? (produced London, 1958). Included in *Soldier, Soldier and Other Plays*, 1967.
Live Like Pigs (produced London, 1958; New York, 1965). Published in *New English Dramatists 3*, London, Penguin, 1961; in *Three Plays*, 1964.
Serjeant Musgrave's Dance: An Unhistorical Parable (produced London, 1959; San Francisco, 1961; New York, 1966). London, Methuen, 1960; New York, Grove Press, 1962; revised version (produced London, 1972).

The Happy Haven, with Margaretta D'Arcy (produced Bristol and London, 1960; Kingston, Rhode Island, 1963; New York, 1967).   Published in *New English Dramatists 4*, London, Penguin, 1962; in *Three Plays*, 1964.

Soldier, Soldier (televised 1960).   Included in *Soldier, Soldier and Other Plays*, 1967.

The Business of Good Government: A Christmas Play, with Margaretta D'Arcy (also co-director: as *A Christmas Play*, produced Brent Knoll, Somerset, 1960; New York, 1970; as *The Business of Good Government*, produced London, 1978).   London, Methuen, 1963; New York, Grove Press, 1967.

Wet Fish (televised 1961).   Included in *Soldier, Soldier and Other Plays*, 1967.

The Workhouse Donkey: A Vulgar Melodrama (produced Chichester, 1963).   London, Methuen, 1964; New York, Grove Press, 1967.

Ironhand, adaptation of a play by Goethe (produced Bristol, 1963).   London, Methuen, 1965.

Armstrong's Last Goodnight: An Exercise in Diplomacy (produced Glasgow, 1964; London, 1965; Boston, 1966).   London, Methuen, 1965; New York, Grove Press, 1966.

Ars Longa, Vita Brevis (for children), with Margaretta D'Arcy (produced London, 1964).   Published in *Eight Plays 1*, edited by Malcolm Stuart Fellows, London, Cassell, 1965.

Three Plays. London, Penguin, 1964; New York, Grove Press, 1966.

Play Without Words (produced Glasgow, 1965).

Fidelio, adaptation of a libretto by Joseph Sonnleithner and Friedrich Treitschke, music by Beethoven (produced London, 1965).

Left-Handed Liberty: A Play about Magna Carta (produced London, 1965; Boston, 1968).   London, Methuen, 1965; New York, Grove Press, 1966.

Friday's Hiding, with Margaretta D'Arcy (produced Edinburgh, 1966).   Included in *Soldier, Soldier and Other Plays*, 1967.

The Royal Pardon; or, The Soldier Who Became an Actor (for children), with Margaretta D'Arcy (also co-director: produced Beaford, Devon, 1966; London, 1967).   London, Methuen, 1967.

Soldier, Soldier and Other Plays. London, Methuen, 1967.

The True History of Squire Jonathan and His Unfortunate Treasure (produced London, 1968; New York, 1974).   Included in *Two Autobiographical Plays*, 1971.

The Hero Rises Up: A Romantic Melodrama, with Margaretta D'Arcy (also co-director: produced London, 1968).   London, Methuen, 1969.

The Soldier's Tale, adaptation of a libretto by Ramuz, music by Stravinsky (produced Bath, 1968).

Harold Muggins Is a Martyr, with Margaretta D'Arcy and the Cartoon Archetypical Slogan Theatre (produced London, 1968).

The Bagman; or, The Impromptu of Muswell Hill (broadcast 1970).   Included in *Two Autobiographical Plays*, 1971.

Two Autobiographical Plays. London, Methuen, 1971.

Two Hundred Years of Labour History, with Margaretta D'Arcy (produced London, 1971).

Granny Welfare and the Wolf, with Margaretta D'Arcy and Roger Smith (produced London, 1971).

My Old Man's a Tory, with Margaretta D'Arcy (produced London, 1971).

Rudi Dutschke Must Stay, with Margaretta D'Arcy (produced London, 1971).

The Ballygombeen Bequest, with Margaretta D'Arcy (produced Belfast and London, 1972; New York, 1976).

Published in *Scripts 9* (New York), September 1972; revised version, as *The Little Gray Home in the West: An Anglo-Irish Melodrama* (produced Birmingham, 1982), London, Pluto Press, 1982.

The Island of the Mighty: A Play on a Traditional British Theme, with Margaretta D'Arcy (produced London, 1972; section produced, as *Handful of Watercress*, New York, 1976).   London, Eyre Methuen, 1974; in *Performance* (New York), 1974.

The Devil and the Parish Pump, with Margaretta D'Arcy (produced Galway, 1974).

The Crown Strike Play, with Margaretta D'Arcy (produced Galway, 1974).

The Non-Stop Connolly Show: A Dramatic Cycle of Continuous Struggle in Six Parts, with Margaretta D'Arcy (also co-director: produced Dublin, 1975; London, 1976).   London, Pluto Press, 5 vols., 1977–78; 1 vol. edition, London, Methuen, 1986.

Sean O'Scrudu, with Margaretta D'Arcy (produced Galway, 1976).

The Mongrel Fox, with Margaretta D'Arcy (produced Galway, 1976).

No Room at the Inn, with Margaretta D'Arcy (produced Galway, 1976).

Silence, with Margaretta D'Arcy (produced Galway, 1977).

Mary's Name, with Margaretta D'Arcy (produced Galway, 1977).

Blow-in Chorus for Liam Cosgrave, with Margaretta D'Arcy (produced Galway, 1977).

Plays 1 (includes *Serjeant Musgrave's Dance*, *The Workhouse Donkey*, *Armstrong's Last Goodnight*). London, Eyre Methuen, 1977; New York, Grove Press, 1978.

Vandaleur's Folly: An Anglo-Irish Melodrama, with Margaretta D'Arcy (also co-director: produced Lancaster, 1978).   London, Eyre Methuen, 1981.

Pearl: A Play about a Play Within the Play (broadcast 1978).   London, Eyre Methuen, 1979.

The Old Man Sleeps Alone (broadcast 1982).   Published in *Best Radio Plays of 1982*, London, Methuen, 1983.

The Mother, with Margaretta D'Arcy, adaptation of a play by Brecht (produced London, 1984).

The Making of Muswell Hill, with Margaretta D'Arcy (produced London, 1984).

Whose Is the Kingdom?, with Margaretta D'Arcy (broadcast 1988).   London, Methuen, 1988.

Radio Plays: *The Life of Man*, 1956; *The Bagman*, 1970; *Keep These People Moving!* (for children), with Margaretta D'Arcy, 1972; *Pearl*, 1978; *To Put It Frankly*, 1979; *Don Quixote*, from the novel by Cervantes, 1980; *The Winking Goose* (documentary), 1982; *Garland for a Hoar Head*, 1982; *The Old Man Sleeps Alone*, 1982; *The Manchester Enthusiasts*, with Margaretta D'Arcy, 1984; *Whose Is the Kingdom?*, with Margaretta D'Arcy, 1988.

Television Plays: *Soldier, Soldier*, 1960; *Wet Fish*, 1961; *Sean O'Casey: Portrait of a Rebel* (documentary), with Margaretta D'Arcy, 1973 (Ireland).

Novels

Silence among the Weapons: Some Events at the Time of the Failure of a Republic. London, Methuen, 1982; as *Vox Pop: Last Days of the Roman Republic*, New York, Harcourt Brace, 1983.

Books of Bale: A Fiction of History. London, Methuen, 1988.

Short Stories

Cogs Tyrannic. London, Methuen, 1991.

Other

To Present the Pretence: Essays on the Theatre and Its Public. London, Eyre Methuen, 1977; New York, Holmes and Meier, 1979.
Awkward Corners: Essays, Papers, Fragments, with Margaretta D'Arcy. London, Methuen, 1988.

*

Critical Studies: *John Arden* by Ronald Hayman, London, Heinemann, 1968, New York, Ungar, 1972; *Theatre Language: A Study of Arden, Osborne, Pinter, and Wesker* by John Russell Brown, London, Allen Lane, and New York, Taplinger, 1972; *John Arden* by Simon Trussler, New York, Columbia University Press, 1973; *John Arden* by Glenda Leeming, London, Longman, 1974; *Arden: A Study of His Plays* by Albert Hunt, London, Eyre Methuen, 1974; *Anger and Detachment: A Study of Arden, Osborne, and Pinter* by Michael Anderson, London, Pitman, 1976; *John Arden* by Frances Gray, London, Macmillan, and New York, Grove Press, 1982; *John Arden* by Malcolm Page, Boston, Twayne, 1984, and *Arden on File* edited by Page, London, Methuen, 1985.

Theatrical Activities:
Director, with Margaretta D'Arcy: several of his own plays.
Actor: **Plays**—Wise Man in *A Christmas Play*, Brent Knoll, Somerset, 1960; Constable in *The Royal Pardon*, Beaford, Devon, 1966; Mr. Muggins in *Harold Muggins Is a Martyr*, London, 1968.

John Arden comments:
(1977) At the present time the gap between the playwright and the active life of the theatre seems as wide as it has ever been: and it shows no sign of closing. Figures such as the director and the scenic designer, whose relevance to good dramatic writing is at best marginal, have increased their power and influence in no small measure during the past few years: and they stand ominously between playwright and actors, inhibiting proper communication. The *content* of new plays is obscured and neutralized by over-emphasis on aesthetic theatrical *form*. The dependence of the dramatic art upon subsidies from public funds has given rise to a bureaucratic intransigence on the part of directors, who are too often administrators as well, and are becoming less and less inclined to take the necessary risks demanded by adventurous and expanding experiment. The problem is similar to that faced by Ben Jonson in the 1620's, when he struck out against the dominance of Inigo Jones as designer-director of court entertainment, and lost his battle. The result of Jones's victory was the securing by the monarchy of the complete allegiance of the theatrical profession, followed by the closure of the theatres during the Cromwellian revolution. The playwrights, as a trade-grouping, never again recaptured the position of artistic strength and poetic potency which they had attained at the beginning of the 17th century. To forestall an equivalent disaster today, the modern dramatists must attempt two apparently contradictory tasks. 1) They must abandon their solitary status and learn to combine together to secure conditions-of-work and artistic control over the products of their imagination. 2) They must be prepared to combine not only with their fellows, but also with *actors*. It is not enough

for the occasional author to *direct*; playwrights should be members of theatrical troupes, and take part in all aspects of production. In order to achieve goal 2), goal 1) must first be arrived at. The authors together must establish the importance of their written work as an essential *internal* element of the theatre, and then, individually, they must become absorbed into the theatre themselves as co-workers.

I am aware that these requirements go against all current trends. But the current trends are running towards the complete death of the modern drama. Remember, Shakespeare and Molière regarded themselves as men of the theatre rather than *literary* figures: and I believe it to be no accident that their works remain unequalled in the Western tradition.

* * *

A glance at John Arden's bibliography suggests that the entire opus of his work rests in his collaboration with his wife, Margaretta D'Arcy, for they have together produced a wealth of plays for both stage and radio, and Arden himself has not written for the stage for nearly 20 years. However, his handful of plays are generally acknowledged, by both critics and contemporaries, to be seminal to the modern British theatre, arguably classics within the lifetime of their author.

Arden's plays break through the confinements of realism by using open staging; broad, poetic language; characters bordering on caricature; complex visual imagery; active social settings; and an appropriation of traditional "popular" forms, like music-hall and medieval theatre, to dramatise the interactive effects of concepts, ideas, and social organisation on social, personal, and political life.

The scope and complexity of the plays, however, have often given rise to critical confusion, arguably owing to the very elements that have led to their acclaim, for change in form necessarily signals changes in perspective and concern. Thus, "realist" readings of a non-realist play will invariably cause confusion and misunderstanding. Bemusement over Arden's plays seem to stem from the assumption that whatever the form of the work, a play will inevitably boil down to an elaboration of human emotion, eliciting sympathy for the individual and taking a clear, simple literal moral stance, especially if it deals with social and moral issues.

For example, critics became focused on deciding whether *Serjeant Musgrave's Dance* was "pro" pacifism. A more inclusive view of the play, however, renders the question irrelevant. The play patently is not promoting war. No argument is proposed to polarise pacifism against war-mongering; rather, pacifism serves as the context, not the content of the play. That is, the play assumes its audience finds war, per se, undesirable, and this premise establishes the terms by which the relationship between means and ends may be dramatised.

Since on the whole we will agree that war is, generally, undesirable, we will also agree that Musgrave's aim to put an end to all war is commendable. Assuming that the audience is in accordance with Musgrave's purpose, the play turns our attention from his intentions to his actions: from his desired goal, which we share, to the means by which he pursues it; means which, in turn, produce their own ends contradictory to his original goal. Hence, through Musgrave we experience the process by which even the finest of intentions becomes corrupted by the means employed for its accomplishment, and we are called to assess the terms of their validity.

Our introduction to Musgrave through the effect he has on others prepares us to look towards action and consequence rather than explanation, to judge by effect rather than rationale. His soldiers prepare us for a man to admire: organised, commanding, demanding respect. His uniform and his confident manner suggest qualities our society admires: order, organisation, "God-fearing," and, above all, logic and reason. Alas, these are the very qualities which drive him to his horrifying conclusion. When Musgrave—steeped in simple fundamental religious belief, a soldier's training and discipline, a life of careful order and authority, and, especially, a total faith in logical thought—is confronted with the horrible chaos of war (to which he has devoted his life), he inevitably uses the only means he has to create a plan to annihilate war. His solution is neat, ordered, completely logical, and has, in his eyes, the blessing of God. His intentions are good; the result is destructive and insane. Musgrave's insight that the source of war lies with ordinary people who let their husbands and sons become cannon fodder has a certain validity, but his plan for eliminating war is both unacceptable and futile.

The opposition set up in *Serjeant Musgrave's Dance* is not between war and peace but between social ideals of order, organisation, and logic in contrast to the "messy scribbling" of day-to-day existence; the erratic demands of emotion and need. The extreme opposite to Musgrave is the Bargee, an unattractive picture of daily survival unhampered by principle or design. Near Musgrave, the Mayor and Parson organize fumblingly for their own ends. In the middle, the women and the miners with their needs, passions, and inconsistencies, their morals based more on experience than ideals. The play provides an analysis of the social precepts of order and reason as they are superimposed on the chaos of ordinary life.

Serjeant Musgrave's Dance also challenges the realist premises that good intentions mitigate behavior and that reason can solve all human problems, by calling "reason" into question. Annie's importance, for example, is not that she will sleep with any man but that her act of lovemaking is an act of revivification. Arden neither promotes nor condemns promiscuity, but contrasts the effect of Annie's actions with the imposed purity of Musgrave's orderliness.

Arden's vision is essentially anarchic. Ideals of organisation and reason distort human life. War itself is the result of order imposed on human existence. The entrance of the Dragoons to restore "order" and save us all from Musgrave may bring some relief, but it also brings an inescapable sense of failure.

The playwright's organization subverts the audience's preconception of order. Arden's use of the open stage, his ballads and heightened language, his frequent placing of more than one character at the centre of the action are devices to turn attention away from personalisation and simple moralising towards an examination of the practical functioning of these moral precepts in the social context. In *The Workhouse Donkey*, for example, it is fruitless to complain that none of the politicians is blameless. "Misgoverned," says Sweetman, "Oh, it's not exactly misgoverned. It's just the wrong lot are the governers, that's all." The play assumes that power corrupts. The difference between Labour and Tory is not corruptibility, but the form their corruption takes and to what end. The involvement of Feng, the incorruptible policeman, in this cosily untidy world takes us into an examination of the consequences of obsessive morality imposed on an imperfect world. As Arden says, Feng's absolute integrity causes infinitely more damage than Butterthwaite's bumbling dishonesty could ever manage. Feng lacks warmth and compassion for the catch-as-catch-can bustle of ordinary life. Butterthwaite's warmth and human failings endear us to him despite his imperfections. Assuming a world of general imperfection, Arden attempts to turn attention away from abstract ideals of simplistic morality and towards the effect of these ideals when they are put into practice without regard for the fundamental anarchy of daily living.

Arden's theatrical devices distance the audience from the characters so they might be seen as active members of working societies. No better or worse than others, these societies run, as by implication all do, on moral precepts that have both weaknesses and strengths. When one of these little worlds is confronted by another which does not share its assumptions, the characters find themselves in extreme situations which threaten these social preconceptions. The consequences and effects of these actions dramatize the complex relationships between the individual and society, between social ideals and their practical application, between means and end.

Live Like Pigs can be read as a confrontation between two ways of living, acceptable enough in themselves, but mutually destructive in confrontation. This pattern is most richly and tragically elaborated in *Armstrong's Last Goodnight*. Through Lindsay and Armstrong, the weaknesses and inner workings of their societies are set in relief. Neither Armstrong nor Lindsay is a villain. Each is the perfect representative of his society, but their worlds are different, with different ways of ordering and interpreting life, different moral concepts, different ideals. Both can enlist our sympathy: Armstrong, leader in an individualist world of action; Lindsay, spokesman for the King in an integrated world of reason. Each society, in its own terms, is perfectly viable. However, they are entirely incompatible.

Though both live in Scotland, Lindsay and Armstrong inhabit realities so different they can hardly speak to each other. The way each sees and evaluates the world excludes the world of the other. (When Lindsay tells Armstrong's wife he has come from the King, she answers "What King would that be?" Even such a simple concept as "King" is not shared.) The play's scenes are juxtaposed to emphasize the misinterpretations and incompatibilities. The use of the stage itself—with James's court on one side and Armstrong's castle on the other—presents a visual image of the distance between the two worlds. Clothing imagery eleborates the social symbols of value and role and marks the opposing experiences of the characters. It is not that one is right and one wrong, but rather that each, though wholly consistent within itself, is incompatible with the other. Yet, Lindsay's quest is to integrate the two.

The moral precepts that have been the strengths of each society are shown to also be their weaknesses as they are forced to the surface in the confrontation. Armstrong's dashing individualism leads him to his death. Lindsay's belief in reason is destroyed as his reasonable, organised society destroys Armstrong and the world he represents. We are not asked to judge the moral precepts informing these worlds so much as to wonder at the fact that despite their opposing orders and moralities, they resort to the same exact manner of dealing with threats—Wamphrey and Armstrong are executed on the same tree, victims of the same kind of treachery. Attention is turned from the superficialities of abstract moral judgement to the exacting examination of the execution of moral ideals in an imperfect world.

Arden's formal changes in his plays demand a shift from simplistic moralising to dramatic investigation, a transfer from idealised expectations and easy judgements to responsible application and political analysis that transcends the simple taking of sides.

Since his disengagement with the conventional theatre, Arden has collaborated with Margaretta D'Arcy on a host of works for both theatre and radio, hard-hitting, energetic pieces which overtly draw on "popular" theatre forms— music-hall, melodrama, living theatre. Directly confronting socio-political issues, their most salient quality is their expression of community. The plays not only confront community issues but are often the product of community cooperation. Thus, both form and content reflect the socio-political commitments of their collaborators.

Arden has also written radio plays which make full use of the vast canvas offered by the medium and continue his unblinkered investigation of socio-political dynamics including, unsurprisingly, the question of the artist's function in his society.

—Elaine Turner

––––––––

ARDREY, Robert. American. 1908–1980.
See 2nd edition, 1977.

––––––––

AUDEN, W(ystan) H(ugh). American. 1907–1973.
See 1st edition, 1973.

––––––––

AXELROD, George. American. Born in New York City, 9 June 1922. Served in the United States Army Signal Corps during World War II. Married 1) Gloria Washburn in 1942 (divorced 1954), two sons; 2) Joan Stanton in 1954, one daughter. Film director and producer. Recipient: Writers Guild of America West award, for screenplay, 1962. Agent: Irving Paul Lazar Agency, 211 South Beverly Drive, Beverly Hills, California 90212, U.S.A.

PUBLICATIONS

Plays

Sketches, with Max Wilk, in *Small Wonder* (produced New York, 1948).
The Seven Year Itch: A Romantic Comedy (produced New York, 1952; London, 1953). New York, Random House, 1953; London, Heinemann, 1954.
Will Success Spoil Rock Hunter? (also director: produced New York, 1955). New York, Random House, 1956.
Goodbye Charlie (also director: produced New York, 1959). New York, French, 1959.
Souvenir, with Peter Viertel (produced Los Angeles, 1975).

Screenplays: *Phffft!*, 1954; *The Seven Year Itch*, with Billy Wilder, 1955; *Bus Stop*, 1956; *Rally 'round the Flag, Boys* (uncredited), 1958; *Breakfast at Tiffany's*, 1961; *The Manchurian Candidate*, 1962; *Paris When It Sizzles*, 1963; *How to Murder Your Wife*, 1964; *Lord Love a Duck*, with Larry H. Johnson, 1966; *The Secret Life of an American Wife*,

1968; *The Lady Vanishes*, 1979; *The Holcroft Covenant*, with Edward Anhalt and John Hopkins, 1982.

Radio Writer: *Midnight in Manhattan* program, 1940; material for *Grand Old Opry*, 1950–52.

Television Writer: for *Celebrity Time*, 1950.

Night Club Writer: *All about Love*, New York, 1951.

Novels

Beggar's Choice. New York, Howell Soskin, 1947; as *Hobson's Choice*, London, Elek, 1951.
Blackmailer. New York, Fawcett, 1952; London, Fawcett, 1959.
Where Am I Now—When I Need Me? New York, Viking Press, and London, Deutsch, 1971.

*

Theatrical Activities:
Director: **Plays**—*Will Success Spoil Rock Hunter?*, New York, 1955; *Once More, With Feeling* by Harry Kurnitz, New York, 1958; *Goodbye Charlie*, New York, 1959; *The Star-Spangled Girl* by Neil Simon, New York, 1966. **Films**—*Lord Love a Duck*, 1966; *The Secret Life of an American Wife*, 1968.

* * *

The playwriting career of George Axelrod well illustrates that dramatist of particular wit and imagination who manages to create marketable products for Broadway tastes and, for a brief period, enjoys the fame and fortune that successful commercial comedy brings. His brief period was the decade of the 1950's. *The Seven Year Itch* ran nearly three years in New York, with 1,141 performances and *Will Success Spoil Rock Hunter?* lasted a year and had 444 performances. Prior to his first success he had learned his trade writing for radio and television. Since this decade of playwriting he has had some success as a director, effectively directing such plays as Neil Simon's *The Star-Spangled Girl* for an audience acceptance that he was no longer able to reach as a dramatist.

In the history of American comic drama Axelrod might be mentioned as the author of two plays which say something about American tastes and attitudes during that post-World War II decade when audiences enjoyed a semi-sophisticated joke along with a semi-realistic view of themselves. Although the period for this enjoyment continued under the aegis of Neil Simon, Axelrod's imagination for such playwriting dried up. A later novel, *Where Am I Now—When I Need Me?*, is an artless attempt to capitalize on current free expression in writing as well as a kind of pathetic admission. In the span of theatre history in America the decade of the 1950's will be considered undistinguished and Axelrod's contribution will be measured, if at all, as an instance of conscious yet effective technique on the Broadway scale of carefully analysed entertainment.

Axelrod's success as a dramatist came with his ability to write clever, simply structured comedy that seemed a bit outrageous or naughty at first but was generally acceptable and comforting. Liberal circles have labelled him a writer of right-wing comedy in which right-wing morality always triumphs and have considered his success a disturbing feature of American comedy. Such observations have their place in history, but it is nonetheless true that such conservative comedy has a rich reputation in American comedy and for a decade Axelrod's polished and carefully tailored plays were the most imaginative of these slim pieces of professionally manufactured theatre. His plays satisfied an audience's needs. *The Seven Year Itch* tells of a New York businessman, Richard Shermans, who combines a humorous reluctance and eagerness as he spends a night with a girl after his wife has left the hot city for the summer months. *Will Success Spoil Rock Hunter?* toys with the Faustus theme as George MacCawley sells his soul ten percent at a time for fame, fortune and certain pleasures. But Axelrod always emphasized a definite, if sometimes late, morality. Richard is funny because his reluctance, his ineptness, and his remorse contrast hilariously with his view of himself as a seducer. At the final curtain a likeable hero emerges from an educational experience; even the girl, who slept with him because he could not be serious with her, begins to think that marriage should be worth a try. George also eats his cake and has it to enjoy. His fantasies are dramatically fulfilled, and he does not lose his soul. In this manner Axelrod presented safe, conservative entertainment that would run for at least a year. A few years later it is out of date, and with another generation it has lost most of its appeal.

Technically, Axelrod used the accepted devices of unpretentious comic entertainment. Verbal and visual jokes were a major part of a play's success with an audience. Perhaps that is why Axelrod has since substituted directing for playwriting. Topicality in the jokes was as much a part of a play's success as it was an appeal to snobbishness in the audiences. There are numerous local references to New York, and names were dropped in almost every scene. Obviously, Axelrod studied his audiences, considering them knowledgeable but not overly bright. Certain gags in *Will Success Spoil Rock Hunter?*—the positioning of the "Scarlet Letter" on a scantily clad model and the impossibility of making love in the sand— are repeated, and the staircase in *The Seven Year Itch*, described as giving "the joint a kind of Jean-Paul Sartre quality," is further explained as having "no exit." In *The Seven Year Itch* Axelrod enlivened his presentation with dramatic devices such as fantasy sequences, flashbacks, and soliloquies. Throughout all of his plays, ridiculing, making witty comments, and satirizing man and his society are standard ploys for humor. But Axelrod is neither innovator nor reformer, merely a professional entertainer. He satirized the usual things—the movies, psychiatrists, rental-novel sex, certain kinds of decadence, and so on. He had nothing to say to any thoughtful person, and he scarcely took himself seriously, suggesting as he did a thorough and comfortable acceptance of all that he ridiculed in his plays. John Gassner referred to his work as "imaginative fluff," and as such it has appeal for certain theatre audiences at certain times.

—Walter J. Meserve

———

AYCKBOURN, Alan. British. Born in London, 12 April 1939. Educated at Haileybury, Hertford, 1952–56. Married Christine Roland in 1959; two sons. Stage manager and actor, Donald Wolfit's company, in Edinburgh, Worthing, Leatherhead, Scarborough, and Oxford, 1956–57; actor and stage manager, Stephen Joseph Theatre-in-the-Round, Scarborough, Yorkshire, 1957–62; associate director, Victoria Theatre, Stoke-on-Trent, Staffordshire, 1962–64; drama producer, BBC Radio, Leeds, 1964–70. Since 1970 artistic

director, Stephen Joseph Theatre-in-the-Round; associate director, National Theatre, London, 1986–88; professor of contemporary theatre, Oxford University, 1991–92. Recipient: *Evening Standard* award, 1973, 1974, 1977, 1985, 1987, 1989, 1990; Olivier award, 1985; *Plays and Players* award, 1987. D.Litt.: University of Hull, Yorkshire, 1981; University of Keele, Staffordshire, 1987; University of Leeds, 1987. C.B.E. (Commander, Order of the British Empire), 1987. Agent: Casarotto Ramsay Ltd., National House, 60–66 Wardour Street, London WIV 3HP, England.

PUBLICATIONS

Plays

The Square Cat (as Roland Allen) (produced Scarborough, 1959).
Love after All (as Roland Allen) (produced Scarborough, 1959).
Dad's Tale (for children; as Roland Allen) (produced Scarborough, 1960).
Standing Room Only (as Roland Allen) (also director: produced Scarborough, 1961).
Xmas v. Mastermind (produced Stoke-on-Trent, 1962).
Mr. Whatnot (also director: produced Stoke-on-Trent, 1963; revised version produced London, 1964).
Relatively Speaking (as *Meet My Father*, produced Scarborough, 1965; as *Relatively Speaking*, produced London, 1967; New York, 1984). London, Evans, and New York, French, 1968.
The Sparrow (also director: produced Scarborough, 1967).
How the Other Half Loves (also director: produced Scarborough, 1969; London, 1970; New York, 1971). London, Evans, and New York, French, 1972.
Countdown, in *We Who Are about to . . .*, later called *Mixed Doubles* (produced London, 1969). London, Methuen, 1970.
Ernie's Incredible Illucinations (for children; produced London, 1971). London, French, 1969; in *The Best Short Plays 1979*, edited by Stanley Richards, Radnor, Pennsylvania, Chilton, 1979.
The Story So Far (also director: produced Scarborough, 1970; revised version, as *Me Times Me Times Me*, produced Leicester, 1971; revised version, as *Family Circles*, produced Richmond, Surrey, 1978).
Time and Time Again (also director: produced Scarborough, 1971; London, 1972). London, French, 1973.
Absurd Person Singular (also director: produced Scarborough, 1972; London, 1973; New York, 1974). Included in *Three Plays*, 1977.
Mother Figure, in *Mixed Blessings* (produced Horsham, Sussex, 1973).
The Norman Conquests: Table Manners, Living Together, Round and Round the Garden (also director: produced Scarborough, 1973; London, 1974; Los Angeles and New York, 1975). London, Chatto and Windus, 1975; New York, Grove Press, 1979.
Absent Friends (also director: produced Scarborough, 1974; London, 1975; New Haven, Connecticut, 1977; New York, 1991). Included in *Three Plays*, 1977.
Confusions: Mother Figure, Drinking Companion, Between Mouthfuls, Gosforth's Fête, A Talk in the Park (also director: produced Scarborough, 1974; London, 1976). London, French, 1977.
Jeeves, music by Andrew Lloyd Webber, adaptation of works by P.G. Wodehouse (produced London, 1975).
Bedroom Farce (also director: produced Scarborough, 1975;

London, 1977; New York, 1979). Included in *Three Plays*, 1977.

Just Between Ourselves (also director: produced Scarborough, 1976; London, 1977; Princeton, New Jersey, 1981). Included in *Joking Apart, Ten Times Table, Just Between Ourselves*, 1979.

Three Plays. London, Chatto and Windus, 1977; New York, Grove Press, 1979.

Ten Times Table (also director: produced Scarborough, 1977; London, 1978; Cleveland, 1983). Included in *Joking Apart, Ten Times Table, Just Between Ourselves*, 1979.

Joking Apart (also director: produced Scarborough, 1978; London, 1979). Included in *Joking Apart, Ten Times Table, Just Between Ourselves*, 1979.

Men on Women on Men, music by Paul Todd (produced Scarborough, 1978).

Joking Apart, Ten Times Table, Just Between Ourselves. London, Chatto and Windus, 1979; augmented edition, as *Joking Apart and Other Plays* (includes *Sisterly Feelings*), London, Penguin, 1982.

Sisterly Feelings (also director: produced Scarborough, 1979; London, 1980). With *Taking Steps*, London, Chatto and Windus, 1981.

Taking Steps (also director: produced Scarborough, 1979; London, 1980; Houston, 1983; New York, 1986). With *Sisterly Feelings*, London, Chatto and Windus, 1981.

Suburban Strains, music by Paul Todd (also director: produced Scarborough, 1980; London, 1981). London, French, 1982.

First Course, music by Paul Todd (also director: produced Scarborough, 1980).

Second Helping, music by Paul Todd (also director: produced Scarborough, 1980).

Season's Greetings (also director: produced Scarborough and London, 1980; revised version, also director: produced London, 1982; Berkeley, California, 1983; New York, 1985). London, French, 1982.

Way Upstream (also director: produced Scarborough, 1981; London, 1982). London, French, 1983.

Making Tracks, music by Paul Todd (also director: produced Scarborough, 1981; London, 1983).

Me, Myself, and I, music by Paul Todd (also director: produced Scarborough, 1981). London, French, 1989.

Intimate Exchanges (also director: produced Scarborough, 1982; London, 1984). London, French, 2 vols., 1985.

A Trip to Scarborough, adaptation of the play by Sheridan (also director: produced Scarborough, 1982).

Incidental Music (produced Scarborough, 1983).

It Could Be Any One of Us (also director: produced Scarborough, 1983).

The Seven Deadly Virtues, music by Paul Todd (also director: produced Scarborough, 1984).

A Cut in the Rates (televised 1984). London, French, 1991.

The Westwoods (also director: produced Scarborough, 1984; London, 1987).

A Game of Golf (produced London, 1984).

A Chorus of Disapproval (also director: produced Scarborough, 1984; London, 1985; New York, 1988). London, Faber, 1986.

Woman in Mind (also director: produced Scarborough, 1985; London, 1986; New York, 1988). London, Faber, 1986.

Boy Meets Girl, music by Paul Todd (also director: produced Scarborough, 1985).

Girl Meets Boy, music by Paul Todd (also director: produced Scarborough, 1985).

Mere Soup Songs, music by Paul Todd (also director: produced Scarborough and London, 1986).

Tons of Money, adaptation of the farce by Will Evans and Valentine (also director: produced London, 1986). London, French, 1986.

A Small Family Business (also director: produced London, 1987; New York, 1992). London, French, 1988.

Henceforward (also director: produced Scarborough, 1987; London, 1988; Los Angeles, 1991). London, Faber, 1988.

Vaudeville (produced Scarborough, 1988).

Mr. A's Amazing Maze Plays (for children) (also director: produced Scarborough, 1988). London, Faber, 1989.

Man of the Moment (also director: produced Scarborough, 1988, London 1990). London, Faber, 1990.

The Revengers' Comedies (also director: produced Scarborough, 1989; London 1991). London, Faber, 1991.

Invisible Friends (for children) (also director: produced Scarborough, 1989; London 1991). London, Faber, 1991.

Body Language (also director: produced Scarborough, 1990).

This Is Where We Came In (for children) (also director: produced Scarborough, 1990).

Callis to 5 (for children) (also director: produced Scarborough, 1990).

My Very Own Story (for children) (also director: produced Scarborough, 1991).

Wildest Dreams (also director: produced Scarborough, 1991).

Time of My Life (also director: produced Scarborough, 1992).

Between the Lines, music by Paul Todd (produced London, 1992).

Dreams From a Summer House, music by John Pattison (produced Scarborough, 1992).

Television Plays: *Service Not Included* (*Masquerade* series), 1974; *A Cut in the Rates*, 1984.

Other

Conversations with Ayckbourn, with Ian Watson. London, Macdonald, 1981.

*

Critical Studies: *Theatre in the Round* by Stephen Joseph, London, Barrie and Rockliff, 1967; *The Second Wave* by John Russell Taylor, London, Methuen, and New York, Hill and Wang, 1971; *Post-War British Theatre* by John Elsom, London, Routledge, 1976, revised edition, 1979; *The New British Drama* by Oleg Kerensky, London, Hamish Hamilton, 1977, New York, Taplinger, 1979; *Alan Ayckbourn* by Michael Billington, London, Macmillan, 1983, New York, Grove Press, 1984, revised edition, London, Macmillan, 1990; *File on Ayckbourn*, edited by Malcolm Page, London, Methuen, 1989; *Alan Ayckbourn: A Casebook* by Bernard F. Dukore, New York, Garland, 1991.

Theatrical Activities:
Director: **Plays**—numerous productions at Victoria Theatre, Stoke-on-Trent, and Stephen Joseph Theatre, Scarborough, including *Miss Julie* by Strindberg, *Pygmalion* by Shaw, *A Man for All Seasons* by Robert Bolt, *Patriotic Bunting* and *Tishoo* by Brian Thompson, *Time and the Conways* by J. B. Priestley, *The Crucible* by Arthur Miller, *The Seagull* by Chekhov, *Thark* and *Rookery Nook* by Ben Travers, and many of his own plays; National Theatre, London: *Way Upstream*, 1982, *A Chorus of Disapproval*, 1985, *Tons of Money* by Will Evans and Valentine, 1986, *A View from the Bridge* by Arthur Miller, 1987, *A Small Family Business*, 1987, *'Tis Pity She's a Whore* by John Ford, 1988, and *The*

Haunt of Mr. Fossett by Stephen Mallatratt, 1988. **Radio**—more than 100 productions, Leeds, 1964–70, and subsequently.

Actor: **Plays**—roles with Stephen Joseph's touring company: The Cook in *Little Brother, Little Sister* by David Campton, Newcastle-under-Lyme, 1961; Victoria Theatre, Stoke-on-Trent: Fred in *The Birds and the Wellwishers* and Robert in *An Awkward Number* by William Norfolk, Aston in *The Caretaker*, James in *The Collection*, and Ben in *The Dumb Waiter*, by Harold Pinter, title role in *O'Flaherty, V.C.* by G. B. Shaw, Roderick Usher in *Usher* by David Campton, Bill Starbuck in *The Rainmaker* by N. Richard Nash, The Crimson Gollywog in *Xmas v. Mastermind*, The Count in *The Rehearsal* by Anouilh, Vladimir in *Waiting for Godot* by Beckett, Thomas More in *A Man for All Seasons* by Robert Bolt, Jordan in *The Rainbow Machine* and Anderson in *Ted's Cathedral* by Alan Plater, Jerry Ryan in *Two for the Seesaw* by William Gibson, Mr. Manningham in *Gaslight* by Patrick Hamilton, The Interrogator in *The Prisoner* by Bridget Boland, and A Jew and Martin del Bosco in *The Jew of Malta* by Marlowe, 1962–64.

* * *

In the early part of Alan Ayckbourn's career, discussion often turned on his method of playwriting, announcing a title and then, three or four days before rehearsals were due to start, shutting himself away to write. Ayckbourn responded by stressing that he was only a dramatist once a year, occasionally twice, and was primarily a director, of the Stephen Joseph Theatre-in-the-Round in Scarborough. (He cleverly, and uniquely, appeared in print, presenting his view of his writings, in *Conversations with Ayckbourn*, ahead of any books of criticism.)

Ayckbourn's early plays, such as *Relatively Speaking* and *Time and Time Again*, are polished and amusing. (As Ayckbourn's titles rarely point unmistakeably to the content, distinguishing between the plays is initially difficult.) His distinctive ingenuity is first shown in *How the Other Half Loves*, in which a couple attend two different dinner parties, on different days, at the same time. *Absurd Person Singular* has its three scenes on three consecutive Christmas Eves, in three different kitchens, featuring the same three married couples: a fastidious tidiness. *The Norman Conquests* is a trilogy about the events of one weekend; it shows what is happening in a dining-room, sitting-room, and garden. The plays are designed to make sense in any order, or indeed if only one is seen. *Bedroom Farce* somehow steers eight people into three onstage bedrooms. *Sisterly Feelings* has alternative second and third acts (the choice of which is to be played determined by tossing a coin at the end of Acts 1 and 2) leading to the same fourth act. *Taking Steps* is set on different floors of a three-storey house, but "really" there is only one floor. In *It Could Be Any One of Us* Ayckbourn essays the comedy thriller, with five different endings convicting each of the suspects. *Intimate Exchanges* has two first acts, four second acts, eight third acts, and 16 fourth acts. Each episode concludes with a choice, and Ayckbourn has written the scenes for both choices. Further, the time between acts is always five days, then five weeks and finally five years, and the fourth acts are all in a churchyard, variously following weddings, christenings, funerals, and Harvest Festivals. To make his task even harder, the whole is for one actor and one actress, playing two or three parts in every version.

Ayckbourn's first attempt to write, in his phrase, "a truly hilarious dark play" is *Absurd Person Singular*. In the middle act a woman attempts suicide by several methods, while a stream of kind visitors fail to see her misery and instead clean her oven and mend her light. The comic-sinister ending has an obnoxious man dictatorially imposing party games on a group who want nothing to do with him. In *Absent Friends*, Ayckbourn's most restrained and sombre work, five people gather for a Saturday afternoon tea party to cheer Colin, whom they have not seen for some years and whose fiancée drowned two months before. Colin proves to be cheerful, which exposes the unhappiness of the rest.

Just Between Ourselves was Ayckbourn's first "Winter Play," written for January production when "the pressure that had always been on me to produce a play suited primarily to a holiday audience was no longer there." In this work he shows how a well-meaning husband drives his wife to insanity through relentless cheerfulness and optimism. The second scene ends with a disastrous tea party at which everyone tries not to focus on the forgotten birthday cake and the likelihood of accidents by the tense wife. In the extraordinary climax of the third scene, wildly funny and deeply tragic, the wife goes insane. While her husband has become entangled inside the car with the steering-wheel, seat belts, and a neighbouring woman, to whom he is demonstrating it, his wife quarrels with her mother-in-law and pursues her with a roaring electric drill. The car horn "blasts loudly and continuously," then a birthday cake is carried in and lights are switched on "bathing the scene in a glorious technicolour." Four months later the wife is seen again, sitting silent in the garden in January. Throughout this chilling scene she stares out blankly, speechless, motionless, as grim an image as any in Beckett.

Joking Apart sets its four scenes on special occasions: Guy Fawkes Night, Boxing Day, an 18th-birthday party. The scenes are four years apart, so the seven characters are seen over 12 years, from their twenties to their thirties. *Joking Apart* studies winners and losers, a likeable, generous, hospitable couple (who, significantly, have never bothered to get married) and their circle. Ayckbourn illuminates the sadness intrinsic to the way the world has born winners, and the less obvious fact that other people shrink through contrasting themselves with the winners. Similar emotional bleakness, and the same misgivings about the married state, are found in *The Story So Far* and *Season's Greetings*.

Two plays represent changes of direction. *Way Upstream* is about three couples struggling with a cabin cruiser on a week's river trip. As their journey is to Armageddon Bridge, allegory is intended: the decent, unassertive moderates (perhaps Social Democrats) eventually realise they must fight authoritarianism, capitalism, and the idle rich. *Woman in Mind* extends what has been called Comedy of Pain. Hit on the head by a garden rake, a concussed wife copes with her unsympathetic family and fantasizes an ideal family as well—which may not be as delightful as it seems. As her husband is a vicar, Ayckbourn is alluding to the failings of religion, with central themes of dislocation and unfulfilled existences.

The darker vision, of society and of individuals, has dominated in the plays from 1986 on. Ayckbourn's recent plays for children (or for families) have been described as "Stoppard for tots," playful approaches to reality and the illusion of theatre. Michael Billington in 1974 tried to place Ayckbourn as "a left-wing writer using a right-wing form; even if there is nothing strident, obvious or noisy about his socialism, it is none the less apparent that he has a real detestation for the money-grubber, the status-seeker and the get-rich-quicker." Martin Bronstein emphasises the feminism: "He's the only contemporary playwright who shows the real plight of the average woman in today's world."

Ayckbourn himself has never admitted to such intentions; instead he speaks of examining "the Chekhovian field, exploring attitudes to death, loneliness, etc.—themes not generally dealt with in comedy." All Ayckbourn's work is amusing and ingenious; his greatest moments are those that combine laughs and true seriousness about the human condition—or at least the present condition of the English middle classes.

—Malcolm Page

B

BABE, Thomas. American. Born in Buffalo, New York, 13 March 1941. Educated at high school in Rochester, New York; Harvard University, Cambridge, Massachusetts, B.A. 1963 (Phi Beta Kappa), graduate work, 1965–68; St. Catharine's College, Cambridge (Marshall scholar, 1963–65), B.A. 1965; Yale University School of Law, New Haven, Connecticut, J. D. 1972. Married Susan Bramhall in 1967 (divorced 1976), one daughter. Operated the Summer Players, Agassiz Theatre, Cambridge, Massachusetts, with Timothy S. Mayer, 1966–68; speechwriter for John Lindsay, Mayor of New York City, 1968–69. Recipient: CBS-Yale fellowship; Guggenheim fellowship, 1977; Rockefeller grant, 1978; National Endowment for the Arts fellowship, 1983. Agent: Agency for the Performing Arts, 888 Seventh Avenue, New York, New York 10016. Address: 103 Hoyt Street, Darien, Connecticut 06820, U.S.A.

PUBLICATIONS

Plays

Kid Champion, music by Jim Steinman (produced New York, 1974). New York, Dramatists Play Service, 1980.
Mojo Candy (produced New Haven, Connecticut, 1975).
Rebel Women (produced New York, 1976). New York, Dramatists Play Service, 1977.
Billy Irish (produced New York, 1977). New York, Dramatists Play Service, 1982.
Great Solo Town (produced New Haven, Connecticut, 1977). New York, Dramatists Play Service, 1981.
A Prayer for My Daughter (produced New York, 1977; London, 1978). New York, French, 1977.
Fathers and Sons (produced New York, 1978). New York, Dramatists Play Service, 1980.
Taken in Marriage (produced New York, 1979). New York, Dramatists Play Service, 1979.
Daniel Boone (for children; produced on tour, 1979).
Salt Lake City Skyline (produced New York, 1980). New York, Dramatists Play Service, 1980.
Kathleen (produced New York, 1980; revised version, as *Home Again, Kathleen*, produced Baltimore, 1981; New York, 1983).
The Wild Duck, adaption of a play by Ibsen, translated by Erik J. Friis (produced New York, 1981).
Buried Inside Extra (produced New York and London, 1983). New York, Dramatists Play Service, and London, Methuen, 1983.
Planet Fires (produced Rochester, New York, 1985). New York, Dramatists Play Service, 1987.
Carrying School Children (produced New York, 1987).
A Hero of Our Time (produced New York, 1988).
Demon Wine (produced Los Angeles, 1989). New York, Dramatists Play Service, 1989.
Down in the Dumps (produced Costa Mesa, California, 1989).

Casino Paradise, with Arnold Weinstein, music by William Bolcom (produced Philadelphia, 1990).
Junk Bonds (produced Denver, 1991). Los Angeles, Prima Facie, 1991.
Great Day in the Morning (produced Costa Mesa, California, 1992).

Screenplays: *The Sun Gods*, with Mike Wadleigh, 1978; *The Vacancy*, 1979; *Kid Champion*, 1979; *Lincoln and the War Within*, 1991; *Junk Bonds*, 1991.

Radio Plays: *Hot Dogs and Soda Pop*, 1980; *The Volunteer Fireman*, 1981; *One for the Record*, 1986.

Ballet Scenarios: *When We Were Very Young*, music by John Simon, New York, 1980; *Twyla Tharp and Dancers*, 1980.

*

Manuscript Collection: Harvard University Theatre Collection, Cambridge, Massachusetts.

Theatrical Activities:
Director: **Plays**—*Two Small Bodies* by Neal Bell, New York, 1977; *Justice* by Terry Curtis Fox, New York, 1979; *Marmalade Skies* by M. Z. Ribalow, New York, 1983; *The Pornographer's Daughter* by Terry Curtis Fox, Chicago, 1984; *Life and Limb* by Keith Reddin, New York, 1985; *Voices in the Head* by Neal Bell, New York, 1986; *Finnegan's Funeral Parlor and Ice Cream Shoppe* by Robert Kerr, New York, 1989; *A Night with Doris* by Stephanie Brown, 1989; *Sleeping Dogs* by Neal Bell, New York, 1989; *Limbo Tales* by Len Jenkin, New York, 1990.

Thomas Babe comments:

(1982) My position as an American playwright has been realized in the tension between a longing for eternal verities and my perverse desire, like any writer who thinks he's worth his salt, to complicate things. I've gotten in a lot of critical trouble on my native turf, most of which I've tried to weather, because when you push at the edges of things that people really care about, you find the breaking point. This is not to say what I've written is best; only to mention that the theater, in bad money times, has become more conservative in its choices as the funding has dried up while ticket prices go on rising. I've never gotten a prize, and I don't expect one, but I would love to continue to work. And that is all the impetus behind what I've done—that, and a few bucks for the bills. There is a myth that has been promulgated about the suffering of American playwrights; it is neither true nor fair to their ability to survive. I most suspect that the ability to survive is what's behind the best work done by my contemporaries in the last decade, and nearly every one of them has upped the ante every time out.

*   *   *

A Prayer for My Daughter insists that social and political corruption depend upon *co*-existing individual corruption and that personal corruption depends upon *pre*-existing social and political corruption. With this play Thomas Babe presents a pervasive, depressing, and compelling drama of post-Watergate, post-fall-of-Saigon America. We witness one complex crime "committed" by the four principals, hear of a murder, and hear finally of a suicide. We cannot imagine an end to the extreme behavior of Kelly and Jack (the cops) and Sean and Jimmy (the crooks) because the law-keepers and the law-breakers seem to have exchanged equally meaningless roles and to have annihilated the rules of law and morality and the law of nature. Such men exist in symbiosis; the terrors of blind selfishness permeate their common membrane and generate a composite "cop-crook" which becomes the dominant creature in the environment. When the play closes, the sentiment of the old stand-by song "You are my sunshine"—sung intermittently by Jack throughout—becomes the lyric voiceover for Kelly's silent prayer "for [his] daughter" and it carries a terrible weight of meaning. Kelly and Jack function as the legal equivalent of Sean and Jimmy, whose end-product is two deaths, four killers, six victims.

The condition "daughter" renders all male-male and male-female relations radically and dangerously ill-defined, especially to the "daughters" themselves. Babe introduces the notion that man is partly composed of woman and therefore the struggle between men and women cannot be separated from the struggle within men. So long as human nature is misunderstood by the powerful, power will be destructive. Kelly's daughter kills herself with considerably less effect on Kelly than the elderly woman's murder which Sean and Jimmy are arrested for. And, although Sean and Jimmy seem at first to care for each other and to be more capable of caring than Kelly and Jack, neither has any loyalty, being perfectly ready to sell each other out when the moment comes. The love for *his* daughter which Jimmy expresses in Act II makes his being Sean's "daughter" strangely plausible, a plausibility reinforced when he becomes briefly Kelly's "daughter," whose vulnerability to Jimmy's "daughterliness" seems equally homosexual and paternal. The tenderness each realizes in the other, however, does nothing to mitigate the nasty course of their encounter; just as Kelly's initial "fatherly" concern for Margie does nothing to mitigate her despair—or ours. Law and love seem less compatible than love and crime but love seems overwhelmed by both partners. Love is negated by partnerships of lawful and unlawful crime and by a partnership ordinarily thought above the law, the "natural" partnership of father and daughter. All power in this play, from the enforcement of the statutes to the beginnings of self-discovery, acts to make things worse.

Buried Inside Extra is a comic reverie on faith and duty with the absurd threat (taken seriously) of an A-bomb blast from within the *Times-Record* building on the morning of the paper's last edition; the sketchy love of the editor for the hard-nosed women's page editor; the "pill and placebo" love Jake gives his wife over the telephone; the epidemic of compromising, lying, and unfaithfulness in the name of "twenty-five cents of the best writing that can be written in the full knowledge that the writing will be thrown out the next day." These reporters are driven to provide the public with a substitute for experience; those who "have weak hearts . . . and don't drink . . . [and] only fuck about twice a year" are promised an "everything" defined as "true facts, clear impressions, informed guesses. . . . We will make our readers wear *our* shoes during the long night." Babe's "newsies" possess little wisdom, little sympathy, little contentment, and little self-esteem. Their already moribund paper will be defunct after this "extra" edition to cover the atom bomb scare. This newsroom can only generate stories from within itself; Liz's hiding (and hidden) father, Culhane (also a reporter), himself manufactures the bomb and phones the threat in because he knows that such news will cause Jake to print an extra edition. It's a way of prolonging life which Babe would have us consider to be the *modus operandi* of the press. Their own lives confused and conflicted, media people seek to clarify the lives of others by purveying the news, even if the clarity is fleeting and untrustworthy, even if the news moves society into yet more obscurity tomorrow, even if the headline proclaims and the columns elaborate a non-event. When all stories are taken at face-value and textualized as news, the distinction between true and false knowledge cannot function.

The edge to *Buried Inside* lies along the blade joining realism to parody. The *real* atom bombs exploded decades ago over Nagasaki and Hiroshima and reporters like these covered the story and made us *a* story, not *the* story. Babe uses Culhane's bomb as a device to explode any remaining fragments of trust in newspapers as truth-bearing instruments. Indeed, any trust in communication or in truth per se doesn't carry as far as Jake and Liz's choral, terminal "Write, you bastards." They know that everything beyond the headline article won't be read and won't be considered significant; that news will be "buried inside extra." This last edition will reconstruct events which might have led to *their* being "buried inside extra." Their willingness to make news out of themselves, to make reality conform to autobiography, at once represents the news business and business as usual in the 1970's.

With *Junk Bonds* Babe offers a comparatively unfocused and largely unaccountable play, especially since the stronger *Demon Wine* was produced not long before. Pressing questions of personal morality are paramount in each but substantial characters and a dynamic plot work only in *Demon Wine* in which the parallel but opposing *educations sentimentales* of an auto parts salesman and a mobster's son are experienced. It turns out that the child of organized crime embodies honor, the child of the people, dishonor; power breeds authenticity, powerlessness, a dangerous inauthenticity. The laying-out of full dilemmas seems to elicit Babe's strongest writing.

—Thomas Apple

———

BAGNOLD, Enid. British. 1962–1981.
See 2nd edition, 1977.

———

BAITZ, Jon Robin. American. Born in 1964 in California. Lived in Brazil, South Africa, and the United States. Playwright-in-residence, New York Stage and Film Company, 1989; currently co-artistic director, Naked Angels, New York. Recipient: Playwrights Horizons Revson fellowship, 1987; Rockefeller fellowship; New York *Newsday* Oppenheimer award, 1987; Playwrights U.S.A. award, 1988;

Humanitas award, 1990. Agent: George Lane, William Morris Agency, 1350 Avenue of the Americas, New York, New York 10019, U.S.A.

PUBLICATIONS

Plays

Mizlansky/Zilinsky (produced Los Angeles, 1985).
The Film Society (produced Los Angeles, 1987; New York and London, 1988). New York, Theatre Communications Group, 1987.
Dutch Landscape (produced Los Angeles, 1989).
The End of the Day (produced Seattle, 1990; New York and London, 1992).
The Substance of Fire (produced New York, 1992).

Television Play: *Three Hotels*, 1990.

* * *

Before his writing career was 10 years old, Jon Robin Baitz was already perceived as many things. First, he was that rarity, a Hollywood playwright concentrating on the stage when every waiter in town had pretensions to being a screenwriter. When his second play appeared, a sophisticated and knowledgeable piece about apartheid, he was seen as South African. He was still well under 25. When that was followed by a disastrous new play at Los Angeles's Mark Taper Forum, he abandoned California for New York where his reputation became a cosmopolitan one.

Not all his audience was aware of it, but he was cosmopolitan from the first. His California credentials seemed impeccable, from his birth in Beverly Hills to studies at Beverly Hills High School. It was the time in between that gave him his international perspective.

As the son of an executive for Carnation Milk, Baitz spent most of his boyhood travelling, from Brazil to South Africa with spells in Israel, Holland, and England, before returning to California. His earliest plays were reports from the vastly different front lines of Hollywood and South Africa.

His first substantial play, *Mizlansky/Zilinsky*, was propelled by dialogue that possessed the same earthy vigour as David Mamet's *Glengarry Glen Ross*, a point noted by several critics. There are similarities, most surprisingly in the authorial distance from characters who are allowed to present themselves sympathetically despite a catalogue of obvious flaws. Then, too, like the real estate salesmen in Mamet's play, Baitz's characters Mizlansky and Zilinsky are dealmakers: cynical, independent producers in the backwaters of Hollywood who have moved on from financing movies to creating tax shelters. If they make a record of children's Bible stories, they can guarantee it will fail.

But Baitz's individuality is also apparent and the play, produced when he was just 21, revealed his gifts of observation and empathy. In sharp, disjointed scenes—described by the Los Angeles *Times* as a "little like listening to the Nixon tapes"—he allowed his people to reveal their character as they themselves judged it. Mizlansky, in particular, signing checks while facing bankruptcy and prison, must be taken on his own terms while his morally quibbling partner Zilinsky finds that confession to the Internal Revenue does not cleanse his soul.

For a dramatist beginning his career in Hollywood, such a clear-sighted view of the movie business could only be an advantage.

His second play, *The Film Society*, appeared to secure his reputation. He used his experience as a pupil in South Africa to create an all-white prep-school, like his own, that served as an apparently benign model of the country's white society sealed off from the black majority culture. Through the character of a teacher, Jonathan Balton, who founds a film society in the school, Baitz dynamically illustrates the feebleness of neutrality. The effort to ignore the explosive realities of apartheid by projecting flickering images of western civilization on the wall is doomed by the actuality of South Africa's real society, where the pent-up force of the subjugated black majority constantly threatens to explode.

The play was seen in New York and at London's Hampstead Theatre, and attracted the interest of Hollywood filmmakers. For a time, Baitz was the hottest dramatic talent produced by Los Angeles. With unusual and commendable loyalty, Baitz continued to write for the stage, but his next play, *Dutch Landscape*, was a famously unhappy experience for the playwright and his distinguished director, Gordon Davidson.

Perhaps prematurely, it attempted to confront his family life, compacting three continents' worth of experience into a muddled portrait of his relationship with his parents. Autobiographical conflict was partly buried by an uncomfortable return to the theme of apartheid and the undigested nature of the piece drew vitriolic reviews.

His subsequent departure for New York proved a canny move. The confidence in his work that had been damaged by *Dutch Landscape* was restored, and the strength that all his plays showed in portraying older men was reaffirmed when he created the character of a New York publisher resisting pressures to sell out.

The Substance of Fire was the play which finally gave Baitz his all-important New York credibility, earning him comparisons with Shakespeare, Chekhov, and Edward Albee. In the way of New York theatrical success nowadays, even Off-Broadway, it also brought him Hollywood deals ranging from commissions for adaptations to original screenplays which he would also direct. By the age of 29, Baitz was ready to put into practice the lessons of *Mizlansky/Zilinsky*.

—Ned Chaillet

———

BALDWIN, James (Arthur). American. 1924–1987. See 4th edition, 1988.

———

BALODIS, Janis (Maris). Australian. Born in Tully, Queensland, 21 September 1950. Educated at Townsville College of Advanced Education, Queensland, teaching diploma 1970; James Cook University, Townsville, 1973; East 15 Acting School, Loughton, Essex, 1976–77. Married Pauline Walsh in 1982; one son and one daughter. Primary school teacher, Tully, 1971, and Bambaroo, 1972, Queensland; assistant stage manager, Queensland Theatre Company, Brisbane, 1974; civil servant, Brisbane, 1975; teacher and director, East 15 Acting School, 1977–79. From 1979 freelance writer, Sydney. Since 1988 associate director, Melbourne Theatre Company; chair, Australian National Playwrights' Centre, 1990–92. Recipient: Australia Literature Board grant, 1981, 1983, and fellowship, 1985, 1987; Victorian Premier's award, 1986. Agent: Hilary Linstead and Associates, Suite 302, Easts Tower, 9–13 Bronte Road, Bondi Junction, New South Wales 2022. Address: c/o The Melbourne Theatre Company, G.P.O.2622W, Melbourne, Victoria 3000, Australia.

PUBLICATIONS

Plays

Backyard (produced Sydney, 1980).
Happily Never After (produced Brisbane, 1982).
Beginning of the End (produced Darwin, 1982).
Summerland (produced Brisbane, 1984).
Too Young for Ghosts (produced Melbourne, 1985). Sydney, Currency Press, 1985.
Wet and Dry (produced Darwin, 1986). Sydney, Currency Press, 1991.
Heart for the Future (produced Melbourne, 1989).

Television Play: *A Step in the Right Direction*, 1981.

*

Critical Studies: interview with Rudi Krausman, in *Aspect: Art and Literature*, 1985; "Projecting the Inner World onto an Existing Landscape" (interview with Veronica Kelly), in *Australasian Drama Studies* (St. Lucia), no.17, October 1990.

*   *   *

Janis Balodis was brought up in rural North Queensland, the Australian son of Latvian parents, and he is distinguished from his fellow Australian playwrights on both counts: he is the first child of that generation of European displaced persons who came to Australia under the postwar immigration scheme to reach the front rank of our theatre writers; and he is the first Queenslander of his generation to do so. His background is that of a frontier society and his plays, not surprisingly, are inhabited by men and women cut off from their origins who cling together for self-preservation and irrationally engage with a mutual destiny which they variously attempt to oppose or assimilate.

This theme is present in two minor allegorical works with local political overtones, *Happily Never After* and *Summerland*, both written for the TN Company in Brisbane. In the first a group of characters from the tales of the Brothers Grimm gather to rewrite their stories more favourably; but are murdered severally in plots of self-interest. In the second, Sinbad the Sailor is narrator of a tale of a beggar transformed into a millionaire by learning to love himself. First he cheats and defrauds his way to power, then by experience he comes to terms with the good and the bad within himself. But the sense of deracination, of malevolent intervention in the laws of man and nature, is more significantly present in the three plays upon which Balodis's reputation rests: *Backyard*, *Too Young for Ghosts*, and *Wet and Dry*.

The setting of *Backyard* is a shabby house in a small Queensland country town. The inhabitants are Pencil, a sugar-mill worker, his wife Merlene, and her sister Dorothy; their relationship is based largely on long familiarity and fear of change. Merlene regularly leaves home, but never town, and when she goes Pencil takes Dorothy to bed. This betrayal comes to light when Dorothy becomes pregnant; and the play ends in a distorted, half-comic violence. Central to the theme is Sandshoeboots, an elderly backyard abortionist who sees herself as the instrument of a vengeful female God. On her first entrance she presents Pencil with the corpse of a pigeon she claims he shot; and the body follows the action like a talisman, becoming at one point an image of the aborted foetus. Written in a dense regional vernacular, the play shares with the early plays of Sam Shepard its portrayal of an inbred community.

Backyard is a chamber work; Balodis's next play, *Too Young for Ghosts*, advances the dual theme of destiny and survival onto an epic scale. A group of refugees gather in a Stuttgart camp in 1947 to decide their future. One man has become a black marketeer, one has returned from the front, grossly deformed by injuries; the third is his wife's lover. The women have been surviving as best they can, mainly on the spoils from American GIs. Later we find the group in a tin shed in North Queensland, working out their two-year government bond as cane-cutters. Their struggles with labour, loneliness, and the intractable language, climate, and culture are counterpointed with the colonial explorations of the German explorer Ludwig Leichhardt, who died in 1848 while attempting to cross northern Australia. The setting is an open stage and the structure complex and inventive: the action moves back and forward in time on an emotional pendulum while the actors perform in rotation the roles of the immigrants and the explorers. *Too Young for Ghosts* is a dense, demanding play with the inevitable thrust of tragedy.

Balodis's next stage play, probably his finest to date, makes an unexpected leap into comedy of manners. *Wet and Dry*, as the name implies, is a play of contrasts, using the language of comedy to hold emotion at bay while it examines the plight of urban men and women at war with nature—displaced persons in the urban middle class.

Pam and George are in their thirties. He is an estate agent, she a nurse; they have been unable to conceive a child. George is cynical, alienated: he buries himself in his work. When his young brother Alex comes to stay—an honest, disingenuous type of country worker—Pam decides that he will father her baby. Alex flees to Darwin, sets up with a pragmatic older woman and funds her hysterectomy. But finally Pam and Alex get together in a tropical storm and the result is a son with which both men now find they must—painfully—come to terms. Bisecting the play is a cyclone fence (another intervention in nature) which from scene to scene keeps at bay rabbits, neighbours, and the would-be suicides at Sydney's famous landmark, the Gap. The title refers in the first instance to the two seasons of tropical Australia and the opposing poles of north and south, bush and city; but more significantly it refers to the parallel struggle between nature and "civilisation" in which the characters are engaged. *Wet and Dry* is one of the finest examples of a particularly indigenous form of urban comedy in which the characters batten down with tight, elegant, ironic dialogue emotions, natural disasters, and an ungovernable country to which white Australians are only now becoming reconciled.

Heart for the Future, his most complex work to date, combines live performance and video to examine again the shifting boundaries of reality and consciousness, the pressures of the past upon the present, and the post-modern preoccupation with image and visual fictions masquerading as fact. Helen is a marathon runner attempting to cross the Nullarbor Plain when her reflections upon the death of her mother and other pressures lead to a breakdown and she disappears. She joins a couple living in a bunker at Maralinga, the desert site of British nuclear bomb testing in the 1950's, which rendered the land uninhabitable. Meanwhile, the television producer broadcasting her run has replaced her onscreen by a double, an actress who in due course becomes Helen in a soap opera. The process of revising her life as fiction in this way leads Helen back to sanity.

Balodis's most recent project has been to write a trilogy on the life of the *Too Young for Ghosts* immigrants.

—Katharine Brisbane

BARAKA, Amiri. American. Born Everett LeRoi Jones in Newark, New Jersey, 7 October 1934; took name Amiri Baraka in 1968. Educated at Central Avenue School, and Barringer High School, Newark; Rutgers University, Newark, New Jersey, 1951–52; Howard University, Washington, D.C., 1953–54, B.A. in English 1954. Served in the United States Air Force, 1954–57. Married 1) Hettie Roberta Cohen in 1958 (divorced 1965), two daughters; 2) Sylvia Robinson (now Amina Baraka) in 1967, five children; also two stepdaughters and two other daughters. Teacher, New School for Social Research, New York, 1961–64, and summers, 1977–79, State University of New York, Buffalo, Summer 1964, and Columbia University, New York, 1964 and Spring 1980; visiting professor, San Francisco State College, 1966–67, Yale University, New Haven, Connecticut, 1977–78, and George Washington University, Washington, D.C., 1978–79. Assistant professor, 1980–82, associate professor, 1983–84, and since 1985 professor of Africana studies, State University of New York, Stony Brook. Founder, *Yugen* magazine and Totem Press, New York, 1958–62; editor, with Diane di Prima, *Floating Bear* magazine, New York, 1961–63; founding director, Black Arts Repertory Theatre, Harlem, New York, 1964–66. Since 1966 founding director, Spirit House, Newark; involved in Newark politics: member of the United Brothers, 1967, and Committee for Unified Newark, 1969–75; chair, Congress of Afrikan People, 1972–75. Recipient: Whitney fellowship, 1961; Obie award, 1964; Guggenheim fellowship, 1965; Yoruba Academy fellowship, 1965; National Endowment for the Arts grant, 1966, award, 1981; Dakar Festival prize, 1966; Rockefeller grant, 1981; Before Columbus Foundation award, 1984; American Book award, 1984. D.H.L.: Malcolm X College, Chicago, 1972. Member, Black Academy of Arts and Letters. Address: Department of Africana studies, State University of New York, Stony Brook, New York 11794–4340, U.S.A.

PUBLICATIONS (earlier works as LeRoi Jones)

Plays

A Good Girl Is Hard to Find (produced Montclair, New Jersey, 1958; New York, 1965).
Dante (produced New York, 1961; as *The 8th Ditch*, produced New York, 1964). Included in *The System of Dante's Hell*, 1965.
The Toilet (produced New York, 1964). With *The Baptism*, New York, Grove Press, 1967.
Dutchman (produced New York, 1964; London, 1967).

With *The Slave*, New York, Morrow, 1964; London, Faber, 1965.
The Slave (produced New York, 1964; London, 1972). With *Dutchman*, New York, Morrow, 1964; London, Faber, 1965.
The Baptism (produced New York, 1964; London, 1971). With *The Toilet*, New York, Grove Press, 1967.
Jello (produced New York, 1965). Chicago, Third World Press, 1970.
Experimental Death Unit #1 (also director: produced New York, 1965). Included in *Four Black Revolutionary Plays*, 1969.
A Black Mass (also director: produced Newark, 1966). Included in *Four Black Revolutionary Plays*, 1969.
Arm Yrself or Harm Yrself (produced Newark, 1967). Newark, Jihad, 1967.
Slave Ship: A Historical Pageant (produced Newark, 1967; New York, 1969). Newark, Jihad, 1967.
Madheart (also director: produced San Francisco, 1967). Included in *Four Black Revolutionary Plays*, 1969.
Great Goodness of Life (A Coon Show) (also director: produced Newark, 1967; New York, 1969). Included in *Four Black Revolutionary Plays*, 1969.
Home on the Range (produced Newark and New York, 1968). Published in *Drama Review* (New York), Summer 1968.
Police, published in *Drama Review* (New York), Summer 1968.
The Death of Malcolm X, in *New Plays from the Black Theatre*, edited by Ed Bullins. New York, Bantam, 1969.
Rockgroup, published in *Cricket*, December 1969.
Four Black Revolutionary Plays. Indianapolis, Bobbs Merrill, 1969; London, Calder and Boyars, 1971.
Insurrection (produced New York, 1969).
Junkies Are Full of (SHHH . . .), and *Bloodrites* (produced Newark, 1970). Published in *Black Drama Anthology*, edited by Woodie King and Ron Milner, New York, New American Library, 1971.
BA-RA-KA, in *Spontaneous Combustion: Eight New American Plays*, edited by Rochelle Owens. New York, Winter House, 1972.
Black Power Chant, published in *Drama Review* (New York), December 1972.
Columbia the Gem of the Ocean (produced Washington, D.C., 1973).
A Recent Killing (produced New York, 1973).
The New Ark's a Moverin (produced Newark, 1974).
The Sidnee Poet Heroical (also director: produced New York, 1975). New York, Reed, 1979.
S-1 (also director: produced New York, 1976). Included in *The Motion of History and Other Plays*, 1978.
America More or Less, with Frank Chin and Leslie Marmon Silko, music by Tony Greco, lyrics by Arnold Weinstein (produced San Francisco, 1976).
The Motion of History (also director: produced New York, 1977). Included in *The Motion of History and Other Plays*, 1978.
The Motion of History and Other Plays (includes *S-1* and *Slave Ship*). New York, Morrow, 1978.
What was the Relationship of the Lone Ranger to the Means of Production? (produced New York, 1979).
At the Dim'crackr Convention (produced New York, 1980).
Boy and Tarzan Appear in a Clearing (produced New York, 1981).
Weimar 2 (produced New York, 1981).
Money: A Jazz Opera, with George Gruntz, music by Gruntz (produced New York, 1982).

Primitive World, music by David Murray (produced New York, 1984).

Screenplays: *Dutchman*, 1967; *Black Spring*, 1967; *A Fable*, 1971; *Supercoon*, 1971.

Novel

The System of Dante's Hell. New York, Grove Press, 1965; London, MacGibbon and Kee, 1966.

Short Stories

Tales. New York, Grove Press, 1967; London, MacGibbon and Kee, 1969.

Verse

April 13. New Haven, Connecticut, Penny Poems, 1959.
Spring and Soforth. New Haven, Connecticut, Penny Poems, 1960.
Preface to a Twenty Volume Suicide Note. New York, Totem-Corinth, 1961.
The Disguise. Privately printed, 1961.
The Dead Lecturer. New York, Grove Press, 1964.
Black Art. Newark, Jihad, 1966.
A Poem for Black Hearts. Detroit, Broadside Press, 1967.
Black Magic: Collected Poetry 1961–1967. Indianapolis, Bobbs Merrill, 1969.
It's Nation Time. Chicago, Third World Press, 1970.
In Our Terribleness: Some Elements and Meaning in Black Style, with Fundi (Billy Abernathy). Indianapolis, Bobbs Merrill, 1970.
Spirit Reach. Newark, Jihad, 1972.
Afrikan Revolution. Newark, Jihad, 1973.
Hard Facts. Newark, Peoples War, 1976.
Selected Poetry. New York, Morrow, 1979.
AM/TRAK. New York, Phoenix Book Shop, 1979.
Spring Song. Privately printed, 1979.
Reggae or Not! Bowling Green, New York, Contact Two, 1981.
Thoughts for You! Nashville, Winston Derek, 1984.

Other

Cuba Libre. New York, Fair Play for Cuba Committee, 1961.
Blues People: Negro Music in White America. New York, Morrow, 1963; London, MacGibbon and Kee, 1965.
Home: Social Essays. New York, Morrow, 1966; London, MacGibbon and Kee, 1968.
Black Music. New York, Morrow, 1968; London, MacGibbon and Kee, 1969.
Trippin': A Need for Change, with Larry Neal and A.B. Spellman. Newark, Cricket, 1969(?).
A Black Value System. Newark, Jihad, 1970.
Gary and Miami: Before and After. Newark, Jihad, n.d.
Raise Race Rays Raze: Essays since 1965. New York, Random House, 1971.
Strategy and Tactics of a Pan African Nationalist Party. Newark, National Involvement, 1971.
Beginning of National Movement. Newark, Jihad, 1972.
Kawaida Studies: The New Nationalism. Chicago, Third World Press, 1972.
National Liberation and Politics. Newark, Congress of Afrikan People, 1974.
Crisis in Boston!!!! Newark, Vita Wa Watu-People's War Publishing, 1974.

Afrikan Free School. Newark, Jihad, 1974.
Toward Ideological Clarity. Newark, Congress of Afrikan People, 1974.
The Creation of the New Ark. Washington, D.C., Howard University Press, 1975.
Selected Plays and Prose. New York, Morrow, 1979.
The Autobiography of LeRoi Jones/Amiri Baraka. New York, Freundlich, 1983.
Daggers and Javelins: Essays 1974–1979. New York, Morrow, 1984.
The Artist and Social Responsibility. N.p., Unity, 1986.
The Music: Reflections on Jazz and Blues, with Amina Baraka. New York, Morrow, 1987.

Editor, *Four Young Lady Poets*. New York, Totem-Corinth, 1962.
Editor, *The Moderns: New Fiction in America*. New York, Corinth, 1963; London, MacGibbon and Kee, 1965.
Editor, with Larry Neal, *Black Fire: An Anthology of Afro-American Writing*. New York, Morrow, 1968.
Editor, *African Congress: A Documentary of the First Modern Pan-African Congress*. New York, Morrow, 1972.
Editor, with Diane di Prima, *The Floating Bear: A Newsletter, Numbers 1–37*. La Jolla, California, Laurence McGilvery, 1974.
Editor, with Amina Baraka, *Confirmation: An Anthology of African American Women*. New York, Morrow, 1983.

*

Bibliography: *LeRoi Jones (Imamu Amiri Baraka): A Checklist of Works by and about Him* by Letitia Dace, London, Nether Press, 1971; *Ten Modern American Playwrights* by Kimball King, New York, Garland, 1982.

Manuscript Collections: Howard University, Washington, D.C.; Beinecke Library, Yale University, New Haven, Connecticut; Lilly Library, Indiana University, Bloomington; University of Connecticut, Storrs; George Arents Research Library, Syracuse University, New York.

Critical Studies: *From LeRoi Jones to Amiri Baraka: The Literary Works* by Theodore Hudson, Durham, North Carolina, Duke University Press, 1973; *Baraka: The Renegade and the Mask* by Kimberly W. Benston, New Haven, Connecticut, Yale University Press, 1976, and *Imamu Amiri Baraka (LeRoi Jones): A Collection of Critical Essays* edited by Benston, Englewood Cliffs, New Jersey, Prentice Hall, 1978; *Amiri Baraka/LeRoi Jones: The Quest for a Populist Modernism* by Werner Sollors, New York, Columbia University Press, 1978; *Amiri Baraka* by Lloyd W. Brown, Boston, Twayne, 1980; *To Raise, Destroy, and Create: The Poetry, Drama, and Fiction of Imamu Amiri Baraka (LeRoi Jones)* by Henry C. Lacey, Troy, New York, Whitston, 1981; *Theatre and Nationalism: Wole Soyinka and LeRoi Jones* by Alain Ricard, Ife-Ife, Nigeria, University of Ife Press, 1983; *Amiri Baraka: The Kaleidoscopic Torch* edited by James B. Gwynne, New York, Steppingstones Press, 1985; *The Poetry and Poetics of Amiri Baraka: The Jazz Aesthetic* by William J. Harris, Columbia, University of Missouri Press, 1985.

Theatrical Activities:
Director: several of his own plays.

Amiri Baraka comments:
     My work changes as I change in a changing world.

*   *   *

In March 1964 when three one-act plays at different Off-Broadway locales introduced Amiri Baraka (LeRoi Jones) to city audiences, black theatre in America knew it had found a compelling voice summoning black playwrights to a new and urgent mission.

The first of these plays, *The 8th Ditch*, closed by action of civic authorities after a few days. Its fate foretold the play-wright's continuing quarrel with officialdom. His second play, *The Baptism*, with its deliberate satire of subjects held sacred and taboo, served notice of Baraka's determination ruthlessly to strip the hypocritical masks that society wears to protect its vested interests. But it was in his third play and first professional production, *Dutchman*, that Baraka found his authentic voice to delineate a clearly perceived mission. That mission is nothing less than the cultural liberation of the black man in white America.

Dutchman, hailed by critic Clayton Riley as "the finest short play ever written in this country," spoke lucidly to black Americans of the savage destruction of their cultural identity should they continue to imitate or to flirt with an alien, though dominant, white lifestyle. White establishment critics praised Baraka's "fierce and blazing talent"; the *Village Voice* awarded *Dutchman* an Obie as the best American play of the season.

Baraka's next professional production consisted of two plays. *The Slave*, a two-act drama, and *The Toilet*, another one-acter, staged at the St. Mark's Playhouse in December 1964. *The Slave*, although it purports to speak of a coming race war between black and white and is called by Baraka "a fable," is frankly autobiographical in intent. Walker Vessels, a tall, thin Negro leader of a black army, enters the home where his former white wife, their two children, and her second husband are living together, apparently quite happily. The husband is a white liberal-minded professor who had taught Vessels in college. After a long, excoriating harangue in which he renounces his former life, Vessels shoots the white man, watches with indifference as his ex-wife is hit by a falling beam, and departs as shells from his black revolutionary forces demolish the house while the cries of children in an upstairs room mingle with the boom of guns and the shriek of falling debris. *The Toilet*, a curious work of teenage brutality and homosexual love set in a school lavatory, hints at the possibility of black and white coming together at some future time after the black man has earned his manhood and self-respect by defeating the white.

These two revolutionary plays were followed by an even more lurid and propagandistic work when *Experimental Death Unit #1* was staged at the St. Mark's Playhouse in New York in March 1965. In this short play Baraka concentrates on a night-time encounter between two white homosexuals and a black whore in a seamy section of the city. The climax occurs when a death unit of marching black militants enters and executes the three degenerates. The men are beheaded and their heads stuck on pikes at the head of the procession. The black liberation army, Baraka seems to say, has a duty to rid society not only of the oppressor but also of the collaborator. Black skin does not save one from the due penalty for betraying the revolution.

Writing of this second group of plays, white critics who a few months ago had hailed the rising star of playwright Baraka were now confounded. He had rejected the blandishments of popular (white) success held out to him and had become, to them, a bitter dramatist and violent propagandist preaching race hatred in virulent terms. Their attitude in the main confirmed Baraka's suspicions that the white culture would allow nothing but what it approved of to have credence and value.

A month after the production of *Experimental Death Unit #1*, Baraka imitated the actions of his fictitious character, Walker Vessels, by breaking with his past life. He left his white wife and two children, moved to Harlem, and founded the Black Arts Repertory Theatre School. The aim of the school was to train and showcase black theatrical talent, as well as teach classes in remedial reading and mathematics. It lasted for only a short time.

In a forum on Black Theatre held at the Gate Theatre, New York, in 1969, Baraka articulated the philosophic premise of the black arts movement, giving credit to Ron Karenga of San Francisco for having helped in its formulation. Black art, he affirmed, is collective, functional, and committed since it derives from the collective experience of black people, it serves a necessary function in the lives of black people (as opposed to the useless artifacts of most white art that adorn museums), and is committed to revolutionary change.

The short-lived Harlem-based theatre produced only one new play by Baraka: *Jello*, a hard-hitting satire on the once popular Jack Benny radio program advertising this product. The play, rejected by at least one established publisher because of its attack on a well-known stage personality, was performed on the streets of Harlem by the Black Arts Group. The straightforward plot casts Rochester, Benny's chauffeur and stereotype black handyman, as a militant who demands and gets full redress for years of subservience and oppression. In this play Baraka is less interested in attacking the white man than in erasing the myth of black inferiority which decades of white-controlled entertainment have helped to perpetuate. From this point Baraka was more conscious of addressing a black audience in his plays. His main characters were black, and whitey became either the symbolic beast whose ritualistic death is necessary for the emergence of black consciousness and nationhood, or else whitey will be pilloried mercilessly as completely irrelevant to the black struggle. Baraka declared:

> The artist must represent the will, the soul of the black community. [His art] must represent the national spirit and the national will. . . . We don't talk about theatre down here, or theatre up there as an idle jest but because it is necessary to pump live blood back into our community.

When the Black Arts Repertory Theatre closed in 1966, Baraka returned to his native Newark in New Jersey and formed the Spirit House Movers, a group of non-professional actors who performed his plays as well as the plays of other black writers.

In January 1969 Baraka formed the Committee for Unified Newark dedicated to the creation of a new value system for the Afro-American community. Aspects of this new system of values are evidenced in the wearing of traditional African dress, the speaking of Swahili language as much as English, the rejection of Christianity as a Western religion that has helped to enslave the minds of black people and the adoption of the Kawaida faith in its stead, and finally the assumption of Arabic names in place of existing Christian names. Jones became a minister of Kawaida faith and adopted his new name of Amiri Baraka prefixed by the title Imamu (Swahili for Spiritual Leader).

Baraka's work continues to dwell on themes of black liberation and the need to create a new black sensibility by alerting audiences to the reality of their lives in a country dominated by a culture that Baraka passionately believes to be alien and hostile to blacks. The urgent need to root out white ways from the hearts and minds of black people is constantly reiterated. White error is seen in *A Black Mass* as the substitution of thought for feeling, as a curiosity for anti-life. In *Home on the Range* the white family speaks a gibberish of unintelligible sounds and gazes glasseyed at the television box like robots of the computer society they have created. The devils in *Bloodrites* eat of the host and chant a litany of love immediately after attempting to shoot blacks in a glaring indictment of the hypocrisy of Christianity.

Baraka graphically dramatizes the problem by personifying the evil white lifestyle in the form of a devil or beast that must be slain if blacks are to gain their freedom. In *A Black Mass*, a play based on an Islamic fable, one of a trio of magicians persists in creating a wild white beast that he believes he can tame through love. The beast goes on a rampage and destroys everything in sight, including the magicians. *Madheart* has a Devil Lady who keeps a mother and sister of the Black Man in thrall, worshipping whiteness. In *Bloodrites*, whites are gun-toting devils that masquerade as artists, musicians, and hipsters to seduce blacks struggling towards spiritual reconstruction.

Baraka has been accused of preaching race hatred and violence as a way of life. In 1967 he was given the maximum sentence of three years in prison by a county judge for possession of revolvers during the Newark riots, a conviction that was condemned as victimization by the American Council of Civil Liberties and was later overturned by a higher court. It is true that violence permeates his plays, that Baraka seems to revel in bloodletting, but the intensity of his feeling and the power of his language have the effect of lifting violence to the level of a holy war against evil forces of supernatural potency. When the Devil Lady in *Madheart* boasts that she can never die, the Black Man responds "you will die only when I kill you" whereupon he stabs her several times, impales her with a stake and arrows, abuses her, stomps on her dead face, and finally drops her body into a deep pit from which smoke and light shoot up. Such needless overkill can only be understood in terms of magic and ritual.

Ritual, in fact, is the crucible that helps to transform the melodramatic incident in Baraka's plays into significant drama. Clay, the young black hounded by the vampire Lula in a subway train in *Dutchman*, realizes that the murder of a white is the only cure for the black man's neuroses, but he is too ingrained in white middle-class values to perform the rite that will liberate him. He dies as a result. Not so Walker Vessels in *The Slave*. When he shoots Easley, the white liberal professor, the latter's last words are "Ritual drama, like I said, ritual drama." Similarly, when Court Royal, the weak-kneed assimilationist in *Great Goodness of Life* is forced to shoot his militant son, this too is a rite that must be performed, "a rite to show that you would be guilty, but for the cleansing rite." In keeping with his philosophy that black theatre must be functional, Baraka has sought to make his plays identify with his audiences in form as well as content. Thus, *Bloodrites* calls for the sacrifice of a chicken whose blood is sprinkled into the audience. In *Police* the white cops are required to eat chunks of flesh from the body of the black policeman who has killed a member of his race and is forced by the black community to commit suicide. Such ritualistic acts reinforce the magical dimension of the struggle in which black people are engaged.

A second medium of identification is language. Baraka, the poet and littérateur, deliberately reaches for the vernacular and idiom of the urban black to pound home his message. *The Slave* is a fine example of the way in which college-educated Walker Vessels rejects the elegant but alienating discourse of which he is capable for the unifying language of the ghetto. The language in *Police* is pruned and compressed to a single drumbeat, with the syncopation and lyricism associated with

that pervasive black musical instrument. The process of creating a new and appropriate language for black drama is pushed further in *Slave Ship* where the narrative element relies heavily on action and music rather than language, and where Yoruba instead of English is used in the first part of the production.

Finally, in his capacity as Spiritual Leader, Baraka uses the stage as a pulpit from which he exhorts his audiences to carry his message for revolutionary thinking and action into their daily lives. The Black Man in *Madheart* urges the audience to "think about themselves and about their lives when they leave this happening." A concluding narration in *A Black Mass* reminds the audience that the beasts are still loose in the world and must be found and slain. *Junkies* begins with an address by an Italian dope dealer who informs the audience that he succeeds by getting "niggers to peddle dope." The audience at *Police* are expected to leap on stage at one point of the play and join the characters in demanding vengeance on the black cop who shot and killed a black brother.

Baraka's theatre is blatantly agit-prop drama exalted to an elemental plane. Apart from *Slave Ship* the structure of his plays remains conventional but the dynamic of message, the boldness of conception, and the lyricism of language give his dramas a fierceness on the stage that defies complacency. Critics may praise or damn him, but Baraka is no longer writing for critical acclaim.

—Errol Hill

BARKER, Howard. British. Born in London, 28 June 1946. Educated at Battersea Grammar School, London, 1958–64; Sussex University, Brighton, 1964–68, M.A. in history 1968. Married Sandra Law in 1972; one son. Resident dramatist, Open Space Theatre, London, 1974–75, and since 1988, the Wrestling School, London. Recipient: Arts Council bursary, 1971; Sony award, Society of Authors award, and Italia prize, all for radio play, 1985. Agent: Judy Daish Associates, 83 Eastbourne Mews, London W2 6LQ, England.

PUBLICATIONS

Plays

Cheek (produced London, 1970). Published in *New Short Plays 3*, London, Eyre Methuen, 1972.
No One Was Saved (produced London, 1971).
Edward: The Final Days (produced London, 1971).
Faceache (produced London, 1971).
Alpha Alpha (produced London, 1972).
Private Parts (produced Edinburgh, 1972).
Skipper, and My Sister and I (produced London, 1973).
Rule Britannia (produced London, 1973).
Bang (produced London, 1973).
Claw (produced London, 1975; New York, 1976). With *Stripwell*, London, Calder, 1977.
Stripwell (produced London, 1975). With *Claw*, London, Calder, 1977.
Wax (produced Edinburgh and London, 1976).
Aces High (screenplay). London, Futura, 1976.
Fair Slaughter (produced London, 1977). London, Calder,

1978; with *Crimes in Hot Countries*, New York, Riverrun Press, 1985.

That Good Between Us (produced London, 1977). With *Credentials of a Sympathizer*, London, Calder, 1980; New York, Riverrun Press, 1981.

The Love of a Good Man (produced Sheffield, 1978; revised version produced Oxford and London, 1980). With *All Bleeding*, London, Calder, 1980; New York, Riverrun Press, 1981.

The Hang of the Gaol (produced London, 1978). With *Heaven*, London, Calder, 1982.

The Loud Boy's Life (produced London, 1980). Included in *Two Plays for the Right*, 1982.

Birth on a Hard Shoulder (produced Stockholm, 1980). Included in *Two Plays for the Right*, 1982.

No End of Blame: Scenes of Overcoming (produced Oxford, London, and New York, 1981). London, Calder, 1981; New York, Riverrun Press, 1982.

The Poor Man's Friend (produced Bridport, Dorset, 1981).

Two Plays for the Right. London, Calder, and New York, Riverrun Press, 1982.

Victory: Choices in Reaction (produced London, 1983). London, Calder, and New York, Riverrun Press, 1983.

A Passion in Six Days (produced Sheffield, 1983). With *Downchild*, London, Calder, and New York, Riverrun Press, 1985.

The Power of the Dog (produced Brentford, Middlesex, 1984; London, 1985). London, Calder, and New York, Riverrun Press, 1985.

Don't Exaggerate (produced London, 1984). London, Calder, 1985; New York, Riverrun Press, 1986.

Scenes from an Execution (broadcast 1984; produced London, 1990). With *The Castle*, London, Calder, 1985; New York, Riverrun Press, 1986.

Crimes in Hot Countries (produced London, 1985). With *Fair Slaughter*, London, Calder, 1984; New York, Riverrun Press, 1985.

Downchild (produced London, 1985). With *A Passion in Six Days*, London, Calder, and New York, Riverrun Press, 1985.

The Castle (produced London, 1985). With *Scenes from an Execution*, London, Calder, 1985; New York, Riverrun Press, 1986.

Pity in History (televised 1985; produced Edinburgh, 1986). With *Women Beware Women*, New York, Riverrun Press, 1987.

Women Beware Women, adaptation of the play by Thomas Middleton (produced London, 1986; New York, 1987). London, Calder, 1986; with *Pity in History*, New York, Riverrun Press, 1988; London, Calder, 1988.

The Last Supper (produced London, 1988). London, Calder, and New York, Riverrun Press, 1988.

The Bite of the Night (produced London, 1988). London, Calder, and New York, Riverrun Press, 1988.

The Possibilities (10 plays) (produced London, 1988). London, Calder, and New York, Riverrun Press, 1988.

Golgo (produced Leicester, 1989; London 1990). With *Seven Lears*, London, Calder, and New York, Riverrun Press, 1990.

Seven Lears (produced Sheffield, 1989; London, 1990). With *Golgo*, London, Calder, and New York, Riverrun Press, 1990.

The Europeans. With *Judith*, London, Calder, and New York, Riverrun Press, 1990.

Judith. With *The Europeans*, London, Calder, and New York, Riverrun Press, 1990.

Collected Plays 1 (includes *Claw, No End of Blame, Scenes from an Execution, The Castle, Victory*). London, Calder, 1990; New York, Riverrun Press, 1990.

Screenplays: *Made*, 1972; *Rape of Tamar*, 1973; *Aces High*, 1976.

Radio Plays: *One Afternoon on the North Face of the 63rd Level of the Pyramid of Cheops the Great*, 1970; *Henry V in Two Parts*, 1971; *Herman, with Millie and Mick*, 1972; *Scenes from an Execution*, 1984; *The Early Hours of a Reviled Man*, 1990; *A Hard Heart*, 1992.

Television Plays: *Cows*, 1972; *The Chauffeur and the Lady*, 1972; *Mutinies*, 1974; *Pity in History*, 1985.

Verse

The Breath of the Crowd. London, Calder, 1986; New York, Riverrun Press, 1987.

Gary the Thief/Gary Upright. London, Calder, 1987; New York, Riverrun Press, 1988.

Lullabies for the Impatient. London, Calder, 1989.

The Ascent of Monte Grappa. London, Calder, and New York, Riverrun Press, 1991.

Other

Arguments for a Theatre (essays). London, Calder, 1989.

*

Critical Studies: *The New British Drama* by Oleg Kerensky, London, Hamish Hamilton, 1977, New York, Taplinger, 1979; *Stages in the Revolution* by Catherine Itzin, London, Eyre Methuen, 1980; *Dreams and Deconstructions* edited by Sandy Craig, Ambergate, Derbyshire, Amber Lane Press, 1980; "Howard Barker Issue" of *Gambit* (London), vol. 11, no. 41, 1984; *Howard Barker: An Expository Study of His Poetry and Drama, 1969–1987* by David Ian Rabey, London, Macmillan, 1989.

Theatrical Activities:
Director: **Play**—*Don't Exaggerate*, Edinburgh, 1986.

* * *

Having provided the high point of contemporary, radical theatre in the mid-1980's with a trilogy of plays (*Scenes from an Execution, Downchild, The Castle*) for the Royal Shakespeare Company at the small Pit theatre in London, Howard Barker has continued to excoriate the pieties of art, sex, and politics in a series of dramatic works whose intransigence and theatrical inventiveness still appal the managements of our main subsidised theatres. No Barker play has yet been main stage at either the National Theatre or the RSC. Actors, however, recognise his talent and an actors' company, The Wrestling School, was founded in 1988 exclusively to perform Barker. By 1992 it had five productions to its credit. Other theatres, such as the Almeida and Greenwich (both in London), Sheffield, and Leicester, have hosted Barker's extensive output. BBC-Radio 3 has recently broadcast his characterisation of Céline as a splenetic doctor wandering the wastelands of Paris by night (*The Early Hours of a Reviled Man*), and his libretto for Nigel Osborne's music to an opera on Goya.

There is always a war on in Barker's plays and it is perhaps his emphasis on struggle, pain, and treachery that affronts, and affrights, the rational humanism of theatre directors. *The Possibilities*, an evening of 10 short pieces, delights in cruel and abrupt reversals of lives and ideologies and proposes that all history is contemporary. In the eighth piece, Judith, after beheading Holofernes, is lauded as the heroine of Israel. A patriot comes to persuade her to leave her retreat and return in triumph to Jerusalem. Judith grows hot again as she recalls sex with Holofernes; when the patriot is caustic about deriving private pleasure from state business, Judith's knife comes out again and slashes off the patriot's hand. Desire, as in so many Barker plays, tramples across politics. In the seventh piece a typist refuses to submit her body and her clothes to the dowdy dictates of puritanical feminism. In the third piece a young whore, while constructing herself through underwear, shoes, and a red dress, argues with an old, despairing, female Stalinist that the zig-zags of history show as well in the seams of falling stockings as in the sagas of liquidations, show-trials, and barricades. She, too, in servicing the Party *nomenklatura*, is a revolutionary. In another piece a torturer turns on a young admirer and kills him because the young man lacked the courage to move from flattering his elder to usurping his position. The old, with Barker, maintain their position through cunning, not traditional respect. *Only Some Can Take the Strain* satirises the position of the specialist bookseller in an era of populism. He remains so loyal to his stock that he refuses to sell any of his books, arguing that their knowledge will be misused in a time of censorship. The piece contains the most bitterly accurate exchange of the collection. "I'm from the Ministry of Education," says the censor. "There's no such thing," replies the bookseller.

The education of a king is the theme of *Seven Lears*, Barker's imaginative "version" of Shakespeare's original. Barker's Lear, trying desperately to be a good king in the midst of war and intrigue, shuttles between his lover Prudentia and his wife Clarissa, Prudentia's daughter. Prudentia bolsters Lear with her endless desire for him, Clarissa reassures him with her clarity of motive and her leadership in war. Lear veers wildly between conscience and cruelty. The gaol, a collective of the unjustly imprisoned, is always at hand to remind him of the poor, but he orders merciless slaughter after a battle. He confers the dukedom of Gloucester on a beggar, but orders his most able minister to become his Fool and sanctions the execution of Prudentia at the prompting of Clarissa. Building on an old legend, Barker has Lear attempt to fly, but he only causes the death of a boy whom he was very fond of. He tries to drown Cordelia in a vat of gin and finishes playing chess with Kent, whom he hates. His desire for truth and honesty have caused only mayhem and unhappiness.

The war continues in *A Hard Heart* where a Greek city is under siege and its queen, Praxis, appeals to the architect Riddler to save them. Riddler, like Clarissa in *Seven Lears*, is arrogant, imperious, and a rationalist. By the play's end she will have been, in some measure, humbled by Seemore, a man of the streets who challenges her self-sufficient coldness and, in a parody of the Pluto and Proserpine myth, tries to drag her into the sewers to escape and be reborn. But Riddler's descent does not signal a subtle misogyny by Barker. Riddler has been stage-centre throughout the play, with a series of daring schemes to fool the enemy. They fail, not through her stupidity, but through the treachery of her son, Attila, the only person she loves and whom, through special pleading, she has preserved from military service and starvation. No Barker characters are immune from the upheaval of passion into their ordered lives. Their hubris is that they imagine they are.

In *The Europeans*, male and female are equally matched.

The Viennese siege of 1684 has been lifted. The Turks have been repulsed from Europe and the Emperor and his court have returned to hail Vienna's military commander, Starhemberg. But Starhemberg refuses honours. He is searching for another self, one that can love, and he finds it with Katrin. She has undergone the extreme suffering that, for Barker's typology, alone can create a character of knowledge and equality. She has been raped by the Turks and her breasts cut off, but she is in the line of Barker's clear-eyed, crisp-talking women. She insists on a public examination of her body by the city's leading doctors and wants a mass distribution of prints of her disfigurement around the city. The birth of the product of the rape, a girl named Concilia by the mocking Emperor, takes place in full public view. Katrin is in love with language and holds onto it even at moments of extreme stress: "Sometimes I find a flow and then the words go—torrent—cascade—cascade again. I used that word just now! I like that word now I have discovered it. I shall use it, probably ad nauseam, cascading!" But in the climatic scene three of Act II she and Starhemberg are largely silent. Both naked, they sit at a distance and gaze at one another in a shuttered room. Their bodies are imperfect but their endurance has been equal, as are their minds. This is not propaganda for safe sex, but rather a brief equilibrium between lust and intelligence which could only be envisaged after extensive experience of thwarted passion and defeated reason. The shutters are opened by Katrin's sister Susannah whose exasperated desire for the corrupt priest Orphuls has been blocked by his wilful celibacy. In the final scene Concilia is given to the Turks so there will be no false harmony between East and West. Katrin and Starhemberg, without children to distract them, finally kiss. The new Europe will be produced by war-weary adults.

—Tony Dunn

BARNES, Djuna (Chappell). American. 1892–1982. See 3rd edition, 1982.

BARNES, Peter. British. Born in London, 10 January 1931. Educated at Stroud Grammar School, Gloucestershire. Served in the Royal Air Force, 1949–50. Married Charlotte Beck in 1958. Worked for the London County Council, 1948 and 1950–53; critic, *Films and Filming*, London, 1954; story editor, Warwick Films, 1956. Recipient: John Whiting award, 1969; *Evening Standard* award, 1969; Olivier award, 1985; Royal Television Society award, 1989. Agent: Casarotto Ramsay Ltd., National House, 60–66 Wardour Street, London W1V 3HP. Address: 7 Archery Close, Connaught Street, London W2 2BE, England.

PUBLICATIONS

Plays

The Time of the Barracudas (produced San Francisco, 1963).
Sclerosis (produced Edinburgh and London, 1965).
The Ruling Class: A Baroque Comedy (produced Nottingham, 1968; London, 1969; Washington, D.C., 1971). London, Heinemann, and New York, Grove Press, 1969.

Leonardo's Last Supper, and Noonday Demons (produced London, 1969; *Noonday Demons* produced Los Angeles, 1977). London, Heinemann, 1970.

Lulu, adaptation of plays by Frank Wedekind, translated by Charlotte Beck (also co-director: produced Nottingham and London, 1970). London, Heinemann, 1971.

The Alchemist, with Trevor Nunn, adaptation of the play by Jonson (produced Nottingham and London, 1970; revised version produced Stratford-on-Avon and London, 1977).

The Devil Is an Ass, adaptation of the play by Jonson (also co-director: produced Nottingham, 1973; revised version produced Edinburgh, 1976).

The Bewitched (produced London, 1974). London, Heinemann, 1974.

The Frontiers of Farce, adaptation of the plays *The Purging* by Feydeau and *The Singer* by Wedekind (also director: produced London, 1976; *The Purging* produced New York, 1980). London, Heinemann, 1977.

For All Those Who Get Despondent (cabaret), adaptation of works by Brecht and Wedekind (also director: produced London, 1976; revised version, as *The Two Hangmen: Brecht and Wedekind*, broadcast 1978).

Antonio, adaptation of the plays *Antonio and Mellida* and *Antonio's Revenge* by Marston (broadcast 1977; also co-director: produced Nottingham, 1979).

Laughter! (produced London, 1978). London, Heinemann, 1978.

The Devil Himself (revue), adaptation of a play by Wedekind, music by Carl Davis and Stephen Deutsch (also director: produced London, 1980).

Barnes' People: Seven Monologues (broadcast 1981). Included in *Collected Plays*, 1981.

Collected Plays (includes *The Ruling Class, Leonardo's Last Supper, Noonday Demons, The Bewitched, Laughter!, Barnes' People*). London, Heinemann, 1981; as *Plays: One*, London, Methuen, 1989.

Somersaults (revue; also director: produced Leicester, 1981).

Barnes' People II: Seven Duologues (broadcast 1984). London, Heinemann, 1984.

Red Noses (produced London, 1985; Chicago, 1987). London, Faber, 1985.

Scenes from a Marriage, adaptation of a play by Feydeau (produced London, 1986).

The Real Long John Silver and Other Plays: Barnes' People III (as *Barnes' People III*, broadcast 1986). London, Faber, 1986.

The Real Long John Silver (produced London, 1989). Included in *The Real Long John Silver and Other Plays*, 1986.

Nobody Here But Us Chickens (televised 1989). With *Revolutionary Witness*, London, Methuen, 1989.

Revolutionary Witness (televised 1989). With *Nobody Here But Us Chickens*, London, Methuen, 1989.

The Spirit of Man (includes *A Hand Witch of the Second Stage, From Sleep and Shadow, The Night of the Simhat Torah*) (televised 1989; produced London, 1991). With *More Barnes' People*, London, Methuen, 1990.

More Barnes' People (broadcast 1989–90). With *The Spirit of Man*, London, Methuen, 1990.

Sunsets and Glories (produced Leeds, 1990). London, Methuen, 1990.

Tango at the End of Winter, adaptation of the play by Kunio Shimizu (produced London, 1991).

Screenplays: *Violent Moment*, 1959; *The White Trap*, 1959; *Breakout*, 1959; *The Professionals*, 1960; *Off-Beat*, 1961; *Ring of Spies* (*Ring of Treason*), with Frank Launder, 1963;

Not with My Wife You Don't, with others, 1966; *The Ruling Class*, 1972; *Enchanted April*, 1991.

Radio Plays: *My Ben Jonson*, 1973; *Eastward Ho!*, from the play by Jonson, Chapman, and Marston, 1973; *Antonio*, 1977; *The Two Hangmen: Brecht and Wedekind*, 1978; *A Chaste Maid in Cheapside*, from the play by Middleton, 1979; *Eulogy on Baldness*, from a work by Synesius of Cyrene, 1980; *For the Conveyance of Oysters*, from a work by Gorky, 1981; *The Soldier's Fortune*, from the play by Thomas Otway, 1981; *The Atheist*, from the play by Thomas Otway, 1981; *Barnes' People*, 1981; *The Singer*, from a work by Wedekind, 1981; *The Magician*, from a work by Gorky, 1982; *The Dutch Courtesan*, from the play by Marston, 1982; *A Mad World, My Masters*, from the play by Middleton, 1983; *Barnes' People II*, 1984; *The Primrose Path*, from a play by Feydeau, 1984; *A Trick to Catch the Old One*, from the play by Middleton, 1985; *The Old Law*, from the play by Middleton and Rowley, 1986; *Woman of Paris*, from a work by Henri Becque, 1986; *Barnes' People III*, 1986; *No End to Dreaming*, 1987; *The Magnetic Lady*, from the play by Jonson, 1987; *More Barnes' People* (series of monologues), 1989–90; *Billy and Me*, 1990; *Madame Zenobia*, 1990; *Slaughterman*, 1990; *The Road to Strome*, 1990; *Losing Myself*, 1990; *A True Born Englishman*, 1990; *Houdini's Heir*, 1991.

Television Plays: *The Man with a Feather in His Hat*, 1960; *Revolutionary Witness*, 1989; *Nobody Here But Us Chickens*, 1989; *More Than a Touch of Zen*, 1989; *Not as Bad as They Seem*, 1989; *The Spirit of Man*, 1990; *Bye Bye Columbus*, 1992.

*

Critical Studies: *The Theatre of Peter Barnes* by Bernard F. Dukore, London, Heinemann, 1981; *Landmarks of Modern British Drama: The Plays of the Sixties* edited by Roger Cornish and Violet Ketels, London, Methuen, 1986; *New Theatre Quarterly* (Cambridge), no.21, 1990; *The Gothic Impulse* by Marybeth Inveso, Ann Arbor, University of Michigan Research Press, 1991.

Theatrical Activities:
Director: **Plays**—several of his own plays; *Bartholomew Fair* by Jonson, London, 1978 and 1987. **Film**—*Leonardo's Last Supper*, 1977. **Television**—*Nobody Here But Us Chickens*, 1989; *The Spirit of Man*, 1990; *Bye Bye Columbus*, 1992.

Peter Barnes quotes from his programme note for *The Ruling Class*, 1968:

The aim is to create, by means of soliloquy, rhetoric, formalized ritual, slapstick, songs, and dances, a comic theatre of contrasting moods and opposites, where everything is simultaneously tragic and ridiculous. And we hope never to consent to the deadly servitude of naturalism or lose our hunger for true size, weight, and texture.

* * *

Peter Barnes is one of the most consistently exciting and inventive of contemporary playwrights, a savage satirist and a glorious free-booter of past theatrical styles. Some of the more obvious influences are discernible in the adaptations of work by Marston, Jonson, and Wedekind—and in particular a magnificent version of Wedekind's *Lulu* plays. He is as implacably opposed to the dominant theatrical mode of naturalism as he is to the perpetuation of the status quo in the world in which he writes. His chief weapon is comedy, but a comedy always on the verge of nightmare. He first came to prominence with *The Ruling Class* in 1968—a play in which the delusion of the latest in a long line of insane Earls of Gurney that he is Christ serves as a perfectly reasonable representation of the continued appropriation of power by a self-perpetuating ruling-class.

The play—the plot of which concerns the efforts of the Earl's relations to get a male heir from him before having him certified—is a free-wheeling farcical broadside on ruling-class excesses. However, a pervading sense of disgust at the way things are is never balanced by any suggestion of a way out of the impasse. The only character who might seriously threaten the perpetuation of the old order is the butler, an ill-defined revolutionary completely unable to leave the world of privilege he would destroy despite the acquisition of a substantial inheritance from the previous Earl. And this fascination with the ostensible object of attack is something that he shares with the play itself. For all its venom Barnes seemed at this juncture unable to do more than pick away at the scab.

Subsequently the humour would be increasingly less cosy and the visions of society far bleaker. His plays were to offer an excess of blood, vomit, and excrement, guaranteed to offend the conventional West End audience (as is clearly intended), without ever offering the kind of positive analysis that might appeal to a more politically engaged audience. His work thus falls between the two extremes of contemporary theatre, and as a result he has quite unfairly continued to struggle for productions. Indeed, it took him seven years to realise the 1985 production of *Red Noses*.

After *The Ruling Class* Barnes moved away from an albeit fantasy version of the contemporary world; and his later plays offer a series of nightmare visions of climactic moments of earlier "civilisation" inhabited by characters who speak a variety of inventive and historically unlocatable languages in ways which make the link between present crisis and past roots something never less than urgent and disturbing. In *Leonardo's Last Supper*, the great artist regains consciousness in a filthy charnel-house where he has been carried having been prematurely declared dead. His joy at his resurrection, and at the further works of genius he will now be able to leave the world, is not shared by the wretched family. They had seen their contract for the burial of the famous man as a way to worldly fame and success, and they simply carry on with the arrangements, having first ensured a real corpse by plunging Leonardo head first into a bucket of excrement, urine, and vomit. The wonders of the Renaissance mean nothing to this self-dependent family unit and the working model of the basic precepts of capitalist enterprise that they provide acts also as a demonstration of the way in which all that is represented by the aspirations of such as Leonardo is built on the usually mute sufferings of other such socially insignificant people.

In *The Bewitched* Barnes turned to a key moment in modern European history, the problems over the succession to the grotesquely inbred Philip IV of Spain. The effect of the transference of power on the lives of the powerless throughout Europe is heightened dramatically by the Court's own total lack of concern for them, all interest being centered on explanations of, and attempts to rectify, the ruler's impotence. It is a world in which spiritual salvation is sought for in the torture chamber and in the *auto-da-fé*, as the political fate of Europe is decided by the crazy attempts of the institutions of church and state to create a rightful heir from the seed of an impotent and degenerate imbecile. The central metaphor

that links a mad incapacity with political power is here used to far more telling effect, and the result is one of the most thrillingly disturbing plays of the modern period.

In *Laughter!* Barnes was to push the process a stage further with a series of carefully prepared theatrical shocks. Part One takes us back to another account of the insanity of rule, this time in the court of Ivan the Terrible. Terrifyingly comic though it is, it leaves the audience quite unready for what is to follow. Part Two opens in an office which is dominated by an eight-foot-high stretch of filing cabinets and in which a poster of Hitler is prominent on the wall. As the dialogue develops, the audience is invited to laugh as the bureaucrats fight for power and status amongst themselves, even as it becomes increasingly apparent that the office is responsible for organising the finer details of the extermination programme at Auschwitz Concentration Camp.

And then the wall of filing cabinets opens to reveal an interior of gassed corpses being violently stripped of valuables by a Sanitation Squad in gas-masks—the dry statistics of the files are suddenly metamorphosed in a grotesque masque of death. The audience is forced to confront the reality behind the language of a petty officialdom that carries out the insane demands of its rulers without questioning or ever properly looking at what it is that is being administered. That Barnes should then finish his play with an epilogue in which two Jewish stand-up comedians go through their paces at the concentration camp Christmas concert is evidence of a writer who is prepared to tread a more dangerous tightrope than any of his contemporaries.

With *Red Noses* he moved back into more distant history, continuing his exploration of the potential of laughter as a weapon against oppression. In the midst of a plague-torn Europe a group of self-appointed, and papally sanctioned Red Noses take on the role of theatrical clowns—acting out their parts on a politically repressive stage. They form an alliance with other more politically active groups in response to Barnes's own question: "Can we ever get laughter from comedy which doesn't accept the miseries of life but actually helps to change them? . . . Laughter linked with revolution might be the best of both worlds." But by the end of this remarkable play the passing of the plague is accompanied by the inevitable restoration of the old order of church and state.

The question that Barnes raises ever more urgently about the ability of the writer to affect change remains an open one, which makes his continuing problems in finding theatres to take his work the more depressing, and in itself provides a reason for his continual use of past history as a source for his plots; a desire to write about the problems of the individual at odds with a corrupt society, confronted by the worry that by the time his plays are produced any obviously contemporary references will have become dated. It was thus both peculiarly appropriate and very much to be welcomed that Britain's newest theatre, the West Yorkshire Playhouse in Leeds, should have opened in June 1990 with Barnes's *Sunsets and Glories*—his latest trip back through time. For the first time the playwright presents the figure of a truly good man, the 13th-century Pope Celestine IV, and his struggles. The play is "about a man who was a saint, became pope, and because he was good, was bad for the job . . . the only pope ever voted out of office." The humour is as black as ever, and Barnes continues magnificently to write as he wants, rather than bowing to the economically diminishing demands of the theatre of the new monetarist age for small-cast, small-scale domestic drama. If the National Theatre's title is to be taken seriously it is to be hoped that before too long the idea of offering this, one of the most important contemporary playwrights, a full season of his work—both old and new—is suggested. As it is, his lack of regular productions is nothing short of a national disgrace.

—John Bull

————

BARTLETT, Neil. British. Born in Hitchin, Hertfordshire, in 1958. Educated at Magdalen College, Oxford, 1979–81, B.A. in English literature 1981. Founder member, 1982 Theatre Company, London, 1982–84; staff member, Consenting Adults in Public, London, 1983, September in the Pink (London Lesbian and Gay Arts Festival), London, 1983, and International Aids Day, London, 1986; director, Théâtre de Complicité, London, 1985; M.C. for National Review of Live Art, London, Nottingham, and Glasgow, 1985–90; founder member, 1988, and since 1988 director, writer and performer, Gloria, London. Recipient: Perrier award, 1985; *Time Out*/Dance Umbrella award, 1989; Writers Guild of Great Britain award, 1991; *Time Out* award, 1992. Agent: Gloria, 16 Chenies Street, London WC1E 7EX, England.

PUBLICATIONS

Plays

Dressing Up (produced London, 1983).
Pornography (produced London, 1984).
The Magic Flute, adaptation of the opera by Mozart (produced London, 1985).
A Vision of Love Revealed in Sleep, 1 (produced London, 1986).
Lady Audley's Secret, adaptation of the novel by Mary E. Braddon (produced London, 1988).
Le Misanthrope, adaptation of the play by Molière (produced Edinburgh, 1988; London, 1989; Chicago, 1989). Bath, Absolute Classics, 1990.
A Vision of Love Revealed in Sleep, 2 (produced London, 1989).
A Vision of Love Revealed in Sleep, 3 (produced London, 1990). Published in *Gay Plays 3*, edited by Michael Wilcox, London, Methuen, 1990.
The School for Wives, adaptation of the play by Molière (produced Derby, 1990; Washington, D.C., 1992). Bath, Absolute Classics, 1990.
Bérénice, adaptation of the play by Jean Racine (produced London, 1990). Bath, Absolute Classics, 1990.
Sarrasine, adaptation of the story by Honoré de Balzac (produced Edinburgh, 1990; London, 1990; New York, 1991).
Let Them Call It Jazz, adaptation of the story by Jean Rhys (produced London, 1991).
A Judgement in Stone, adaptation of the novel by Ruth Rendell, music by Nicolas Bloomfield (produced London, 1992).

Screenplay: *Now That It's Morning*, 1992.

Television Plays: *That's What Friends Are For*, 1988; *That's How Strong My Love Is*, 1989.

Video: *Where Is Love*, 1988; *Pedagogue* with Stuart Marshall, 1988.

Novel

Ready to Catch Him Should He Fall. London, Serpent's Tail, 1990; New York, Dutton, 1991.

Short Stories

The Ten Commandments. London, Serpent's Tail, 1992.

Other

Who Was That Man? A Present for Mr. Oscar Wilde. London, Serpent's Tail, 1988.

*

Theatrical Activities:
Director: **Plays**—all his own plays; *More Bigger Snacks Now* by Théâtre de Complicité, London, 1985; *The Avenging Woman*, Riga, Australia, 1991; *Twelfth Night*, Chicago, 1992; *The Game of Love and Chance*, Poole, 1992.
Actor: **Plays**—role in *Pornography*, London, 1984; Robert Audley in *Lady Audley's Secret*, London, 1988. **Television**—roles in all his own television plays. **Video**—roles in all his videos.

Neil Bartlett comments:
I do not consider my work "playwriting" because my performance work has its professional roots in collectively devised small-scale work, physical theatre, and performance art. I regard script as the documentation rather than origin of performance. I regard all my work as gay theatre whether it is solo performance, music theatre, or the re-invention of classic texts. I characteristically write, direct, light, and design all my pieces. I have been particularly influenced by my collaborations with: Banuta Rubess in Toronto and Riga; painter Robin Whitmore; vaudevillian Bette Bourne; and my colleagues in Gloria, producer, Simon Mellor, choreographer, Leah Hausman, and composer, Nicolas Bloomfield. I am particularly influenced by the unique traditions of British gay theatre in musicals, pub drag, pantomime, and contemporary activism. My favourite performer is Ethyl Eichelberger, my favourite play Racine's *Athalie*. My ambition is to produce a commercial pantomime, a classical tragedy, and a spectacular revue in the same season, in the same building, and with the same company.

* * *

Although he has, as yet, completed only a few original dramatic texts, with them Neil Bartlett has established himself as one of the most interesting new writers for the theatre working in Britain. Perversely, he has earned this reputation precisely because he recognises the limitations of the dramatist within the theatre. It is his involvement with all aspects of a production which marks him out as unique. He acts, directs, designs, and stage manages shows with equal aplomb and always in the service of the performance as a complete work of art.

Bartlett draws his inspiration from many different forms of theatre, from opera to performance art. Fortunately though, he does not make the mistake of so many performance artists of reacting against the dominance of text-based theatre by devaluing the text. Bartlett loves the sound and the sensuality of words, but seeks to present them with as much help as he can, shrouding them in beautiful music, illuminating them with startling visual images. His is also a theatre of immediate and erotic impact and he revels in ornate Victorian theatres, lavish costumes, and shock. Much of this shock comes from his foregrounding of his gay sexuality. "I'm queer, I'm here, get used to it," is the message audiences have to accept before they can begin to appreciate Bartlett's work.

But Bartlett is, above all, the most fastidious of theatre artists and will constantly rework a play until he is satisfied with it, accepting the challenge of recreating a work for different venues and reshaping it until it seems to have been created as a site-specific piece of theatre. Yet though his plays are feasts for the eyes, the ears, and the mind, they are accessible, controlled, and immaculate works of art with a backbone of political steel. It is this mixture of challenging politics and aesthetics which won him his reputation in fringe theatre and which allowed him to move over into mainstream theatre.

After university and involvement as actor and director with the 1982 Theatre Company (where he made a memorable Cleopatra in a little black frock), Bartlett's first piece, *Dressing Up*, was presented in 1983 in London as part of a lesbian and gay festival called "September in the Pink." It was on the same bill as the first play about AIDS presented in Britain, Louise Kelly's *Antibody*. *Dressing Up* was a piece of postmodern theatre created before the term became fashionable. Weaving together fragments from the lives of gay men in London from 17th to the 19th centuries, the piece was played out before a rack of costumes which mingled leather and lace, crinolines and codpieces. Mixing historical research about the lives of gay men in London, it was claimed by Bartlett to be "a polemic guide to the splendours of the male body." Underlying the whole piece was a serious political purpose which might best, but rather drearily, be described as reclaiming history, and which revealed Bartlett as the marble fist in the gold lamé glove. The second part of *Dressing Up* was a series of reflections on the work and the words of the novelist Edmund White—an act of homage from disciple to master and one in which AIDS was touched upon at a time when it was hardly known in Britain.

Bartlett's next original piece was *Pornography*, created for the Institute of Contemporary Arts. This was, in part, a collective creation using monologues woven around the personal memories of the actors in the piece, a device he was later to use to devastating effect in the reworked version for drag queens and lavish set of *A Vision of Love Revealed in Sleep*. *Pornography* played with ideas of narrative, with memory, and with theatre. It introduced a touch of red plush theatricality into the rather grim confines of the Institute of Contemporary Arts, but at the heart of the piece were human stories of love and betrayal, raw and shocking, but delivered with such total honesty as to render them utterly compelling. *Pornography* began an association between Bartlett and the ICA which led to him producing a version of *The Magic Flute* for them. His gloss on Mozart's opera was his first step in what seems to have been his assured progress towards creating the all-embracing work of theatre which exploits all that the stage has to offer to create that one ultimate performance.

Bartlett's interest in the hidden history of gay men, also evident in his much-praised book of meditations on Oscar Wilde *Who Was that Man?*, was used to overwhelming theatrical effect in his first one-man show *A Vision of Love Revealed in Sleep*. Commissioned first by Nikki Milican for the Midland Group in Nottingham, it has since been staged on the ornate Edwardian staircase of the old Battersea Town Hall, in a Docklands warehouse, in studio theatres, and in the later incarnation mentioned above, as a large-scale theatre piece expanded to include a chorus of lavishly-costumed drag queens.

A Vision of Love is based round the life of the Victorian painter and poet Simeon Solomon whose blossoming career was destroyed when he was prosecuted for gross indecency. Bartlett draws parallels between his life and Solomon's and takes the audience through a series of variations on this theme. The play demonstrated Bartlett's combined virtuosity in writing and performing, and he gained some notoriety from performing in the nude, in order, he says, to prevent audiences from wasting time wondering whether he would take his clothes off. But while audiences cannot fail to appreciate the skill with which Bartlett performs in his chosen environment—floating candles in the warehouse, luminous murals in the studio theatres—his paralleling of the 19th century and now prevents the piece from ever becoming a cosy bio-pic. His chilling evocation of what it meant to be a gay man in a 1980's London threatened by AIDS and by queer-bashing made *A Vision of Love* as thought-provoking as it was entertaining.

This skilful mixture of history, comment upon history, and unnerving immediacy—for example the endless repetition of "young man, if you want to be happy, be careful," with its social and sexual message—was also a feature of *Sarrasine*, Bartlett's reworking of Balzac, which introduced the audience to a world of baroque intrigue amongst cardinals and castrati and used four actors and singers to evoke the murky interface between the glittering aristocracy and the infinitely more exciting underworld of 18th-century Rome. The piece is dominated by the figure of La Zambinella who when the play begins is over 200 years old. La Zambinella is kept alive, like a vampire, by the devotion of continuing generations to the perfection of his voice. Through this unlikely figure, a tale of love and murder is woven which in Bartlett's hands fused music hall and music theatre, exploring obsession, the human need for art and admiration, and the similarity in response of the connoisseur to 17th-century opera and the man in the pub to a raunchy drag number. Bartlett also gave the play a political subtext which explored the erotic attraction of art and the sinister undercurrents of our worship of the artists who fulfill our sexual fantasies.

Although he is a prolific writer, much of his stage work has been in translations from Molière and Racine and in adaptations of novels as diverse as *Lady Audley's Secret* and Ruth Rendell's *A Judgement in Stone*, as well as a story by Jean Rhys. Few other theatre practitioners manage to combine so successfully pleasure and politics, intellectual excitement and eroticism. Yet, as Bartlett would be the first to admit, although he may explore the heavens he is always rooted on the stage—preferably in an elaborate Edwardian Matcham theatre.

—Alasdair Cameron

BAXTER, James K(eir). New Zealander. 1926–1972. See 1st edition, 1973.

BECKETT, Samuel (Barclay). Irish. 1906–1989. See 4th edition, 1988.

BEHRMAN, S(amuel) N(athaniel). American. 1893–1973.
See 1st edition, 1973.

––––––––––

BEKEDEREMO, J.P. Clark. See **CLARK**, **John Pepper**.

––––––––––

BELLOW, Saul. American. Born in 1915.
See 3rd edition, 1982.

––––––––––

BENNETT, Alan. British. Born in Leeds, Yorkshire, 9 May
1934. Educated at Leeds Modern School, 1946–52; Exeter
College, Oxford, 1954–57 (Open Scholar in History), B.A.
(honours) 1957. National Service: Joint Services School for
Linguists, Cambridge and Bodmin. Temporary junior lecturer in history, Magdalen College, Oxford, 1960–62.
Recipient: *Evening Standard* award, 1961, 1968, 1971, 1985
(for screenplay); Tony award, 1963; Guild of Television
Producers award, 1967; Broadcasting Press Guild award, for
television play 1984, 1991; Royal Television Society award,
1984, 1986; Olivier award, 1990. D. Litt.: University of
Leeds, 1990. Honorary Fellow, Exeter College, Oxford,
1987. Agent: Peters, Fraser, and Dunlop Group, 503/4 The
Chambers, Chelsea Harbour, Lots Road, London SW10
0XF, England.

PUBLICATIONS

Plays

Beyond the Fringe, with others (produced Edinburgh, 1960;
London, 1961; New York, 1962). London, Souvenir
Press, and New York, Random House, 1963.
Forty Years On (produced Manchester and London, 1968).
London, Faber, 1969.
Sing a Rude Song (additional material), book by Caryl
Brahms and Ned Sherrin, music by Ron Grainer (produced
London, 1969).
Getting On (produced Brighton and London, 1971).
London, Faber, 1972.
Habeas Corpus (produced Oxford and London, 1973; New
York, 1975). London, Faber, 1973.
The Old Country (produced Oxford and London, 1977).
London, Faber, 1978.
Office Suite (includes *Green Forms*, televised as *Doris and
Doreen*, 1978, and *A Visit from Miss Prothero*, televised
1978; produced London, 1987). London, Faber, 1981.
Enjoy (produced London, 1980). London, Faber, 1980.
Objects of Affection and Other Plays for Television (includes
Objects of Affection: Our Winnie, A Woman of No

Importance, Rolling Home, Marks, and *Say Something
Happened*; and *A Day Out, Intensive Care, An Englishman
Abroad*). London, BBC Publications, 1982.
Single Spies London, Faber, 1989; with *Talking Heads*, New
York, Summit, 1990.
  An Englishman Abroad (televised 1983; also director: pro-
  duced London, 1988).
  A Question of Attribution (produced London, 1988).
A Private Function (screenplay). London, Faber, 1984.
Forty Years On, Getting On, Habeas Corpus. London, Faber,
1985.
The Writer in Disguise (television plays; includes *Me, I'm
Afraid of Virginia Woolf*; *Afternoon Off*; *One Fine Day*;
All Day on the Sands; *The Old Crowd*; and an essay).
London, Faber, 1985.
Kafka's Dick (produced London, 1986). Included in *Two
Kafka Plays*, London, Faber, 1987.
The Insurance Man (televised 1986). Included in *Two Kafka
Plays*, London, Faber, 1987.
Prick Up Your Ears (screenplay). London, Faber, 1987.
Talking Heads (includes *A Chip in the Sugar, Bed Among the
Lentils, A Lady of Letters, Her Big Chance, Soldiering On,
A Cream Cracker Under the Settee*) (televised 1987; pro-
duced London, 1992). London, BBC Publications, 1987;
with *Single Spies*, New York, Summit, 1990.
*Single Spies and Talking Heads: Two Plays and Six
Monologues.* New York, Summit, 1990.
The Wind in the Willows (produced London, 1990).
London, Faber, 1991.
Forty Years On and Other Plays (includes *Getting On, Habeas
Corpus, Enjoy*). London, Faber, 1991.
The Madness of George III (produced London, 1991).
London, Faber, 1992.

Screenplays: *A Private Function*, 1984; *Prick Up Your Ears*,
1987.

Radio Plays: *Uncle Clarence* (a talk) 1986; *The Lady in the
Van*, 1990.

Television Plays: *On the Margin* series, 1966; *A Day Out*,
1972; *Sunset Across the Bay*, 1975; *A Little Outing*, 1977; *A
Visit from Miss Prothero*, 1978; *Me, I'm Afraid of Virginia
Woolf*, 1978; *Doris and Doreen*, 1978; *The Old Crowd*, 1979;
Afternoon Off, 1979; *One Fine Day*, 1979; *All Day on the
Sands*, 1979; *Intensive Care*, 1982; *Objects of Affection* (5
plays), 1982; *An Englishman Abroad*, 1983; *The Insurance
Man*, 1986; *Talking Heads* (6 monologues), 1987; *102
Boulevard Haussmann*, 1990; *A Question of Attribution*,
1991.

*

Critical Study: *Beyond the Fringe . . . and Beyond: A Critical
Biography of Alan Bennett, Peter Cook, Jonathan Miller, and
Dudley Moore* by Roland Bergan, London, Virgin, 1990.

Theatrical Activities:
Director: **Plays**—*An Englishman Abroad*, London, 1988.
Actor: **Plays**—in *Better Late* (revue), Edinburgh, 1959; in
Beyond the Fringe, Edinburgh, 1960, London, 1961, and New
York, 1962; Archbishop of Canterbury in *The Blood of the
Bambergs* by John Osborne, London, 1962; Reverend Sloley-
Jones in *A Cuckoo in the Nest* by Ben Travers, London, 1964;
Tempest in *Forty Years On*, London, 1968; Mrs. Swabb in
Habeas Corpus, London, 1974; role in *Down Cemetery Road:
The Landscape of Philip Larkin*, London, 1987; Tailor in *An*

Englishman Abroad, London, 1988; Anthony Blunt in *A Question of Attribution*, London, 1988. **Films**—*Long Shot*, 1980; *The Secret Policeman's Ball*, 1986. **Radio**—in *The Great Jowett* by Graham Greene, 1980; *Dragon* by Don Haworth, 1982; Machiavelli in *Better Halves* by Christopher Hope, 1988. **Television**—Augustus Hare in *Famous Gossips*, 1965; in *The Drinking Party*, 1965; in *Alice in Wonderland*, 1966; in *On the Margin*, 1966; Denis Midgley in *Intensive Care*, 1982; Shallow in *The Merry Wives of Windsor*, 1982; Housemaster in *Breaking Up*, 1986; narrator of *Man and Music*, 1986; in *Fortunes of War*, 1987; narrator of *Dinner at Noon* (*By-Line* series), 1988; in *A Chip in the Sugar*, 1988.

* * *

. . . when we play language games, we do so rather in order to find out what game it is we are playing.
— *Beyond the Fringe*

Whatever their ostensible themes, Alan Bennett's plays ultimately dramatize man's desire to define himself and his world through teasingly inadequate language, whether folk adages, government jargon, pronouncements from TV experts, or misapplied quotations from the "Greats." The resulting parodies simultaneously mock and honor the impulse to erect linguistic defenses in a frightening world. Bennett's comedy generally respects his characters, from aspiring intellectuals to northern ladies for whom "conversation is a conspiracy." But some recent works, like the TV plays collected as *The Writer in Disguise*, do not always resist the temptation to condescend: "Still our eldest girl's a manicurist and we've got a son in West Germany, so we haven't done too badly." Bennett's increasing reliance on scatological humor, which reduces some characters to animals with pretensions to dignity, creates some easy laughs. When focusing on professional writers like Kafka in later plays or Joe Orton in the film *Prick Up Your Ears*, Bennett sometimes overworks the audience's smug recognition of verbal and thematic allusions to these authors. Such distractions threaten to overwhelm his serious aims.

In *Beyond the Fringe* both Bennett's monologues and sketches with Peter Cook, Jonathan Miller, and Dudley Moore focus on the game cliché, which trivializes the supposedly serious, yet suggests that even inane values are better than none. A supposed lecture by the Duke of Edinburgh illustrates the precariousness of metaphorical language as well as an underlying desire for decency: "This business of international politics is a game. . . . It's a hard game, it's a rough game . . . sometimes, alas, it's a dirty game, but the point about a game, surely, is that there's no need to take it seriously. . . ." Other *Fringe* sketches brilliantly question the limits of discourse: a prison governor rebukes a condemned man who rejects an analogy between capital punishment and public school caning, "Come along, now, you're playing with words." Just as this semantic comedy foreshadows later plays like Hampton's *The Philanthropist* and Stoppard's *Jumpers*, "Aftermyth," a *Fringe* sketch on Britain during the Blitz, seems the spiritual parent of the many parodies of wartime England during the early 1970's. Bennett illuminates both the hilarious perversion of political rhetoric and the profound need to find attractive equivalents for painful reality.

The Headmaster in *Forty Years On*, an ingenious play-within-a-play focusing on the annual performance by the boys and faculty of Albion School, indulges in similar rhetoric: "The more observant among you will have noticed that one of Bombardier Tiffin's legs was not his own. The other one, God bless him, was lost in the Great War. Some people lost other things, less tangible perhaps than legs, but no less worthwhile

—they lost illusions, they lost hope, they lost faith. . . ." *Forty Years On* organizes a series of skits, similar in tone to "Aftermyth," on the cultural and political life of 20th-century England. Wicked portraits of culture heroes like Virginia Woolf and T.E. Lawrence are both outrageously unfair and deadly accurate. The best sketch is the Wilde pastiche in which Lady Dundowne, played by one of the masters in drag, advises her nephew to marry his spinster mother: "the arrangement seems so tidy that I am surprised it does not happen more often in society"—a perfect spoof of the archetypal Wilde plot and wit. "But then all women dress like their mothers, that is their tragedy. No man ever does. That is his," a parody of Wildean paradox, resonates with additional meaning from the elaborate pattern of homosexual allusion in the play; in this representative public school world, witty hyperbole equals literal statement. Bennett exposes the simultaneous idiocy and seductiveness of language on all levels, from the folk-wisdom of a nanny to the devious rhetoric of Chamberlain, while the rude singing of the rugby team both undercuts and elevates the idealized game metaphor of the school anthem. Though only the Headmaster emerges as a character, the cast of stereotypes is suitable for what is essentially a comic allegory of English life.

Getting On, an ambitious Chekhovian comedy, involves a fortyish Labour MP, George Oliver, whose nostalgia for stability ("What we crave in life is order") and linguistic skill link him with the Headmaster. His precarious illusion of order depends on an innocence of the sexual and political realities of his world: his son by a first marriage, his young second wife, and a Conservative homosexual MP form a strange triangle; his West Indian constituent who claimed that neighbors were poisoning her dog is not mad, as he had believed. Reality seems too complex for his categorizing, analytical mind, and, despite his belief in logic and language, he concludes, after a hilariously unsuccessful attempt to order a taxi, "Words fail me." Though continually confronted with proof of the pointlessness of work, George persists with established values (his only radical action, from an English viewpoint, is throwing a bucket of water at a dog that perpetually fouls his doorstep). Yet, as the punning title suggests, the ultimate reward for hard work is aging and death.

Habeas Corpus, which focuses on a sadly lecherous, aging GP in Hove, somewhat uneasily balances a well-made farce plot with Bennett's verbal comedy, more elegiac than ever amid a frenzy of trouserless men, missed assignations, and a spinster with an artificial bust. The wit, frequently obsessed with the decline of England or of individual Englishmen, often slows down the crucial pacing of the farce, which, in turn, sometimes undercuts the impact of Bennett's parodies. The wistful tone of the comedy is apparent in the doctor's lament for his lacerated sensibility: "They parade before me bodies the color of tripe and the texture of junket. Is this the image of God, this sagging parcel of vanilla blancmange hoisted day after day on to the consulting table? Is this the precious envelope of the soul?" Though such disillusionment does not stop his pursuit of a nubile young patient, his later reference to "the long littleness of life" as he prepares to examine her attests to the general elegiac note of the play. This mood derives partly from the songs and verses, like those in Auden's verse plays, that allow characters to comment directly to the audience, as the action stops: "So if you get your heart's desire,/Your longings come to pass,/Remember in each other's beds,/It isn't going to last." The resulting vaudeville atmosphere, however effective, softens the hard lines of the farce, a form that Bennett wisely abandoned in the plays that followed.

The Old Country, another comic elegy on the continuing decline of England, initially puzzles the viewer with its tricky setting, a country house outside Moscow in which a British defector, Hilary, and his wife, Bron, have tried to recreate the England he betrayed. A visit from Hilary's sister and her husband, Duff, ostensibly in Russia to lecture on Forster, brings the offer of a return to an England Hilary will no longer recognize. Hilary and Duff, former Oxbridge men like Bennett, conduct a typical loving yet satirical analysis of Forster *dicta* like "Only connect."

In the debate over the desirability of return, when Bron asks where in England they could leave their doors unlocked for long periods, her sister-in-law replies, "Wiltshire once. Not any more. There are muggers in Malmesbury." Hilary attempts a more balanced assessment of the overall situation: "No Gamages. No Pontins. No more trains from Kemble to Cirencester. No Lyons. On the other hand I read of the Renaissance of the small bakery; country breweries revive. Better bread, better beer. They come from Florence to shop in Marks and Spencer. It is not an easy decision." But Bron angrily rejects this supposed objectivity as another instance of his ability to argue both sides simultaneously. Certainly Hilary does seem the archetypal Bennett verbal juggler as he tries to define the English response to experience with a complex litany of familiar allusions: "Irony is inescapable. We're conceived in irony. We float in it from the womb. It's the amniotic fluid. It's the silver sea. It's the waters at their priestlike task washing away guilt and purpose and responsibility. Joking but not joking. Caring but not caring. Serious but not serious." *The Old Country*, Bennett's most successful play since *Forty Years On*, dramatizes the dangerous moral and political consequences of this semantic playfulness.

Green Forms, one of two television plays collected as *Office Suite*, satirizes the attempts of government workers to define the unknown with comforting jargon. Perplexed by the computerization of the system and the expendability of employees and whole offices, the workers display typical linguistic resourcefulness: "Southport is being wound down. . . . Wound down. Wound up. Phased out anyway. I hope she hasn't been made . . . you know. . . . Well . . . redundant. I wouldn't like to think she's been made redundant; she was very nicely spoken." *A Visit from Miss Prothero*, the second one-acter, abounds in cozy malice as a retired bureaucrat gradually realizes the worthlessness of his life's work. In his world, gossip masquerades as folk-wisdom (Miss Prothero comments on an associate's eczema: "The doctor thinks it's nerves. I think it's those tights. Man-made fibers don't do for everybody. I pay if I wear crimplene").

Enjoy depicts a typical northern family, the son a transsexual social worker, the daughter a prostitute ("She's exceptional. You won't find girls like Linda stood on every street corner"), while the parents await the demolition of their home and speculate on their future residence: "It's a maisonette. They're built more on the human scale. That's the latest thing now, the human scale." Unfortunately, no authentic unifying tone emerges from the play's blend of folk comedy, parody, and satire on deranged social planners. That the old life with its family betrayals and vulgarities does not merit preservation, except as an historical curiosity, weakens concern for the fates of the couple, though there are affecting moments.

The Writer in Disguise, a collection of plays Bennett wrote for television, is uneven in quality and sometimes relies on a familiar mixture of nostalgia for, and broad satire of British seaside life (*All Day on the Sand*, *Afternoon Off*) but does reveal his ability to write for film and videotape as well as the stage. The best of the collection, *Me, I'm Afraid of Virginia Woolf*, develops Bennett's ambiguous views of Woolf and of high culture in general and mocks the futility of "further education" through the career of a literature teacher. As is frequent with Bennett, the best lines are not necessarily those that reinforce the key themes but primarily display his impressive wit, as when the protagonist attempts to explain unorthodox sex to his mother: "Having tea in Marshall and Snelgrove's isn't lesbianism."

A series of monologues, *Talking Heads*, further displays Bennett's skill at conveying character through speech. Aside from the strained and clichéd *Her Big Chance*, these monologues magically fuse pathos with their comedy and generate sympathy even for upper-class ladies in decline (*Soldiering On*). The strongest is *Bed Among the Lentils*, a showcase for Maggie Smith as the alcoholic wife of a vicar saved by an affair with a Pakistani shopkeeper. Though it never quite transcends the stereotypes of warring female parishioners ("If you think squash is a competitive activity, try flower arrangement") and sexually adroit third-worlders, the monologue brilliantly balances its compassion for the trapped wife with a satire of Christian values.

Single Spies, a program of one-acters, raises disturbing questions about patriotism and personal integrity in terms reminiscent of E.M. Forster, whose life seems of obsessive interest in a number of Bennett works. *An Englishman Abroad* derives from actress Coral Browne's encounter with Guy Burgess in Moscow, and *A Question of Attribution* wittily analyzes ethics and loyalties through conversations between Anthony Blunt, the "4th man," and Elizabeth II ("I was talking about art. I'm not sure that she was.") The play more than satisfies the uneasy anticipation created by the promise of a royal portrait: "If I am doing nothing, I like to be doing nothing to some purpose. That is what leisure means." With its Wildean echoes, the dialogue balances mockery of narrowness with insight into an impossible role. These two plays, while clearly sympathetic to their protagonists, differentiate interestingly between the physically and emotionally unkempt Burgess, and the colder, more controlled, provocatively ambiguous Blunt, for whom espionage may have been merely an elaborate game enabling him to savor his intellectual superiority to his compatriots. *Single Spies* reveals Bennett's increasing interest in biographical drama, a tendency evident in early works with references to the private lives of T.E. Lawrence or Forster and culminating in the plays on Kafka and George III.

The Insurance Man, written for television, wittily attempts to reconcile Kafka's career as both an insurance executive and partner in an asbestos factory with the view of the universe conveyed by his fiction. Kafka's concern for a laborer, Franz, suffering from a work-related malady, leads him to offer Franz a job in the factory. The bitter comedy of Bennett's version of Kafka's world ("Just because you're the injured party, it doesn't mean you are not the guilty party.") ingeniously reveals a system in which even well-meaning officials like Kafka are doomed to intensify human suffering.

Less successful is *Kafka's Dick*, which traces Kafka's antiauthoritarian themes to his relationship with his father. The play is long for what it accomplishes, brilliant in some set pieces, but more a series of vaudeville skits than a coherent work. The Kafka who returns to life to learn that his writings have not been destroyed as he wished tries futilely to balance posthumous fame and the attendant loss of privacy (the title allusion especially disturbs him) and rivalry with writers like Proust: "My room was noisy. It was next door to my parents. When I was trying to write I had to listen to them having sexual intercourse. I'm the one who needed the cork-lined room. And he's the greatest writer of the twentieth century. O God."

Even more ambitious is *The Madness of George III*. Bennett's earlier portrait of Elizabeth II demonstrated an ability to get inside the skin of unexpected characters, though George III's bad press makes him a special challenge. Bennett skillfully weaves in necessary exposition: "Pitt was on our side then. Now he has stitched himself into the flag and passed himself off as the spirit of the nation and the Tories as the collective virtue of England. . . ." though such speeches lack the force of parallel passages in Shakespeare's histories. Bennett's emphasis on scatological humor seems appropriate in an analysis of George's unfortunate physical symptoms, some of which result from the uninformed arrogance of his physicians and all of which reinforce his humanity, a humanity that seems especially vulnerable since his most private functions become matters of public interest and debate. Inviting comparison with such examples of royal madness as Lear and Caligula, George never approaches their tragic dimensions, despite Bennett's reference to "tragic hero" in the preface. Bennett's king is too limited intellectually and spiritually for tragic stature, and the audience's continual awareness of his unpleasant symptoms establishes him primarily as a physical man, a Job without the spiritual capacity. Bennett also errs in introducing long passages from Shakespeare's play, which, though touching in their picture of Lear's regeneration, underscore the limitations of Bennett's psychology and language. The curtailing of George's mad speeches, which Bennett justifies in the preface, tends to minimize any sense of the king's mental and emotional complexity; it is difficult to know whether Bennett might have transcended his talent for making jokes about doctors and politicians and presented a figure of real stature. Just as the copious prefaces and production notes for this play and others suggest another Shaw, so does Bennett's gift for debunking history: the portrait of a loquacious Burke who bored his auditors is especially amusing. Despite some problems, this play represents real development for Bennett in its attempt to define a character in the context of a complex society, when the character is a ruler and the society is that of 18th-century English politics.

Bennett's ability to subordinate his verbal flourishes to some larger purpose is evident in his film scripts *Prick Up Your Ears* and *A Private Function*. In fact, the former unnecessarily downplays Joe Orton's genius with language in order to highlight more cinematic material about his sexual antics, and thus Orton's core, the rich talent that justified the biography, seems missing, though the film has some brilliant episodes. Less ambitious, *A Private Function* succeeds in its treatment of the social hierarchy in a postwar northern town, as a chiropodist and his wife try to overcome class barriers and an unfair system of rationing with the help of an illegal pig for a dinner honoring the newly-wed Princess Elizabeth. The polished dialogue and comic atmosphere suggest Chaucer's fabliaux, and Bennett's signature scatological humor seems exactly right in a work involving a pig, a chiropodist, a butcher, and a bizarre farm family. Like Bennett's best comedy the film creates a believable social world, and the dialogue reaffirms his status as England's pre-eminent comic dramatist. Impressively prolific and apparently eager to expand his thematic range, Bennett has, through a long career, continued to fulfill the dazzling promise of his early work.

—Burton S. Kendle

————

BENTLEY, Eric (Russell). American. Born in Bolton, Lancashire, England, 14 September 1916; moved to the United States, 1939; became citizen, 1948. Educated at Bolton School; Oxford University, B.A. 1938, B.Lit. 1939; Yale University, New Haven, Connecticut, Ph.D. 1941. Married 1) Maja Tschernjakow (marriage dissolved); 2) Joanne Davis in 1953; twin sons. Teacher, Black Mountain College, North Carolina, 1942–44, and University of Minnesota, Minneapolis, 1944–48; Brander Matthews professor of dramatic literature, Columbia University, New York, 1952–69; freelance writer, 1970–73; Katharine Cornell professor of theatre, State University of New York, Buffalo, 1974–82. Professor of comparative literature, University of Maryland, College Park, 1982–89. Charles Eliot Norton professor of poetry, Harvard University, Cambridge, Massachusetts, 1960–61; Fulbright professor, Belgrade, 1980. Drama critic, *New Republic*, New York, 1952–56. Recipient: Guggenheim fellowship, 1948; Rockefeller grant, 1949; American Academy grant, 1953; Longview award, for criticism, 1961; Ford grant, 1964; George Jean Nathan award, for criticism, 1967; CBS fellowship, 1976; Obie award, 1978; Theater Festival gold medal, 1985. D.F.A.: University of Wisconsin, Madison, 1975; Litt.D.: University of East Anglia, Norwich, 1979. Member, American Academy of Arts and Sciences, 1969. Agent: Jack Tantleff, 375 Greenwich Street, Suite 700, New York, New York 10013; or, Joy Westendarp, International Copyright Bureau, 22A Aubrey House, Maida Avenue, London W2 1TQ, England. Address: 194 Riverside Drive, Apartment 4-E, New York, New York 10025, U.S.A.

PUBLICATIONS

Plays

A Time to Die, and A Time to Live: Two Short Plays, adaptations of plays by Euripides and Sophocles (as *Commitments*, produced New York, 1967). New York, Grove Press, 1967.
Sketches in *DMZ Revue* (produced New York, 1968).
The Red White and Black, music by Brad Burg (produced New York, 1970). Published in *Liberation* (New York), May 1971.
Are You Now or Have You Ever Been: The Investigation of Show-Business by the Un-American Activities Committee 1947–1958 (produced New Haven, Connecticut, 1972; New York, 1973; Birmingham, 1976; London, 1977). New York, Harper, 1972.
The Recantation of Galileo Galilei: Scenes from History Perhaps (produced Detroit, 1973). New York, Harper, 1972.
Expletive Deleted (produced New York, 1974). Published in *Win* (New York), 6 June 1974.
From the Memoirs of Pontius Pilate (produced Buffalo and New York, 1976). Included in *Rallying Cries*, 1977.
Rallying Cries: Three Plays (includes *Are You Now or Have You Ever Been*, *The Recantation of Galileo Galilei*, *From the Memoirs of Pontius Pilate*). Washington, D.C., New Republic Books, 1977; as *Are You Now or Have You Ever Been and Other Plays*, New York, Grove Press, 1981.
The Kleist Variations: Three Plays. Baton Rouge, Louisiana, Oracle Press, 1982.
    1. *Wannsee* (produced Buffalo, 1978).
    2. *The Fall of the Amazons* (produced Buffalo, 1979).
    3. *Concord* (produced Buffalo, 1982).
Larry Parks' Day in Court (produced New York, 1979).
Lord Alfred's Lover (produced Gainesville, Florida, 1979).

Toronto, Personal Library, 1981; in *Monstrous Martyrdoms*, 1985.

Monstrous Martyrdoms: Three Plays (includes *Lord Alfred's Lover*, *H for Hamlet*, *German Requiem*). Buffalo, Prometheus, 1985.

Round Two. Published in *Gay Plays: Four*, edited by Michael Wilcox, London, Methuen, 1990.

Other

A Century of Hero-Worship: A Study of the Idea of Heroism in Carlyle and Nietzsche, with Notes on Other Hero-Worshipers of Modern Times. Philadelphia, Lippincott, 1944; as *The Cult of the Superman*, London, Hale, 1947.

The Playwright as Thinker: A Study of Drama in Modern Times. New York, Reynal, 1946; as *The Modern Theatre: A Study of Dramatists and the Drama*, London, Hale, 1948.

Bernard Shaw: A Reconsideration. New York, New Directions, 1947; London, Hale, 1950; revised edition as *Bernard Shaw 1856–1950*, New Directions, 1957; as *Bernard Shaw*, London, Methuen, 1967.

In Search of Theater. New York, Knopf, 1953; London, Dobson, 1954.

The Dramatic Event: An American Chronicle. New York, Horizon Press, and London, Dobson, 1954.

What Is Theatre? A Query in Chronicle Form. New York, Horizon Press, 1956; London, Dobson, 1957.

The Life of the Drama. New York, Atheneum, 1964; London, Methuen, 1965.

The Theatre of Commitment and Other Essays on Drama in Our Society. New York, Atheneum, 1967; London, Methuen, 1968.

What Is Theatre? Incorporating "The Dramatic Event" and Other Reviews 1944–1967. New York, Atheneum, 1968; London, Methuen, 1969.

Theatre of War: Comments on 32 Occasions. New York, Viking Press, and London, Eyre Methuen, 1972.

The Brecht Commentaries 1943–1980. New York, Grove Press, and London, Eyre Methuen, 1981.

The Pirandello Commentaries. Lincoln, University of Nebraska Department of Modern Languages and Literatures, 1985.

The Brecht Memoir. New York, Performing Arts Journal Publications, 1986.

Thinking about the Playwright: Comments from Four Decades. Evanston, Illinois, Northwestern University Press, 1987.

Editor, *The Importance of "Scrutiny": Selections from "Scrutiny," A Quarterly Review, 1932–1948*. New York, G.W. Stewart, 1948.

Editor and Part Translator, *From the Modern Repertory*. Denver, University of Denver Press, series 1 and 2, 1949–52; Bloomington, Indiana University Press, series 3, 1956.

Editor, *The Play: A Critical Anthology*. New York, Prentice Hall, 1951.

Editor, *Shaw on Music*. New York, Doubleday, 1955.

Editor and Part Translator, *The Modern Theatre*. New York, Doubleday, 6 vols., 1955–60.

Editor and Part Translator, *The Classic Theatre*. New York, Doubleday, 4 vols., 1958–61.

Editor and Translator, *Let's Get a Divorce! and Other Plays*. New York, Hill and Wang, 1958.

Editor and Part Translator, *Works of Bertolt Brecht*. New York, Grove Press, 1961–.

Editor and Part Translator, *The Genius of the Italian Theatre*. New York, New American Library, 1964.

Editor, *The Storm over "The Deputy."* New York, Grove Press, 1964.

Editor, *Songs of Bertolt Brecht and Hanns Eisler. . . .* New York, Oak, 1966.

Editor, *The Theory of the Modern Stage: An Introduction to Modern Theatre and Drama*. London, Penguin, 1968.

Editor and Part Translator, *The Great Playwrights: Twenty-Five Plays with Comments by Critics and Scholars*. New York, Doubleday, 2 vols., 1970.

Editor, *Thirty Years of Treason: Excerpts from Hearings before the House Committee on Un-American Activities 1938–1968*. New York, Viking Press, 1971.

Editor and Translator, *Dramatic Repertoire*. New York, Applause, 1985–.

Translator, *The Private Life of the Master Race*, by Brecht. New York, James Laughlin, 1944.

Translator, *Parables for the Theatre: The Good Woman of Setzuan, and The Caucasian Chalk Circle*, by Brecht. Minneapolis, University of Minnesota Press, 1948; revised edition, University of Minnesota Press, and London, Oxford University Press, 1965.

Translator, with others, *Naked Masks: Five Plays*, by Pirandello. New York, Dutton, 1952.

Translator, *Orpheus in the Underworld* (libretto), by Hector Crémieux and Ludovic Halévy. New York, Program Publishing Company, 1956.

Translator, *The Wire Harp*, by Wolf Biermann. New York, Harcourt Brace, 1968.

Recordings (Folkways): *Bentley on Brecht*, Riverside, 1963; *Brecht Before the Un-American Activities Committee*, 1963; *A Man's a Man*, Spoken Arts, 1963; *Songs of Hanns Eisler*, 1965; *The Elephant Calf/Dear Old Democracy*, 1967; *Bentley on Biermann*, 1968; *Eric Bentley Sings The Queen of 42nd Street*, 1974.

*

Manuscript Collection: Boston University Library.

Critical Study: *The Play and Its Critic: Essays for Eric Bentley* edited by Michael Bertin, Lanham, University Press of America, 1986.

Theatrical Activities:
Director: **Plays**—*Sweeney Agonistes* by T.S. Eliot, Salzburg, 1949; *Him* by e.e. cummings, Salzburg, 1950; *The House of Bernarda Alba* by García Lorca, Dublin, 1950; *The Iceman Cometh* (co-director) by Eugene O'Neill, Zurich, 1950; *Purgatory* by W.B. Yeats, and *Riders to the Sea* and *The Shadow of the Glen* by J.M. Synge, U.S. tour, 1951; *The Good Woman of Setzuan* by Brecht, New York, 1956.

(1988) Eric Bentley quotes from an interview with Jerome Clegg:

> Clegg: Why on earth did you have to write a play? For you are nothing if not critical.
> Bentley: Maybe the impulse was to write a counter-play.
> Clegg: Counter to what?
> Bentley: A (good) performance of the Anouilh Antigone —in its integrity, not in the Galantiere adaptation-distortion—had riled me. So I had to write a "correct" Antigone; set Anouilh straight. The same with Brecht.
> Clegg: Meaning?
> Bentley: He made such absurd demands upon his people. What else could Mother Courage have done?

Clegg: Galileo?

Bentley: Brecht wilfully chose to misunderstand him. The recantation could not possibly be taken as a betrayal of Marxism.

Clegg: So it was historical correctness you were after? Oh, you and your scholarly background!

Bentley: Rubbish. There would be no possible "historical correctness" for Antigone. It is a human correctness that interests me. Telling a story more honestly—truer to *our* time, if you will, not necessarily truer to some other time.

Clegg: Someone had called your dramatic works "no nonsense plays."

Bentley: Can one tell the Jesus story without nonsense? There would be no precedents.

Clegg: The New Testament nonsense?

Bentley: A very over-rated book.

Clegg: "Better than the New Testament"—is that a good description of your Jesus-Pilate play?

Bentley: I hope so. Shaw spoke of himself as "better than Shakespeare" with something like that in mind.

Clegg: He also put a question mark after the phrase.

Bentley: As I do.

Clegg: What was your first play? I want to know how all this got started.

Bentley: Which is the wickedest of all your wicked questions.

Clegg: Answer it.

Bentley: My first play wasn't a play of mine at all, it was other people's plays.

Clegg: Especially Bertolt Brecht's.

Bentley: Actually, my first-play-that-was-really-someone-else's-play was not a Brecht, it was a Meilhac and Halévy.

Clegg: Who dey?

Bentley: Jacques Offenbach. The first time I launched out on my own was when I re-did the libretto to Offenbach's *Orpheus* for the New York City Opera Company.

Clegg: Everyone loved it.

Bentley: The press hated it. Except the communist paper.

Clegg: So you took up the Commie cause in *Are You Now or Have You Ever Been*?

Bentley: Well, that was some centuries later, and it wasn't the commie cause.

Clegg: But you do champion causes. What came next?

Bentley: *Lord Alfred's Lover*?

Clegg: Exactly. Your gay liberation play.

Bentley: Touché.

Clegg: After which I lose you. No causes but lots of Heinrich von Kleist.

Bentley: My three Kleist Variations. In which lots of Kleist got thrown overboard—and not all causes were forgotten . . .

Clegg: No?

Bentley: No! Didn't you interview me on this point, and isn't your interview the preface to *The Kleist Variations*, published sometime, somewhere?

Clegg: Is it? Oh, yes. What's your latest?

Bentley: Another gay item.

Clegg: But prompted by a non-gay item, Schnitzler's *Reigen*? *La Ronde*?

Bentley: Transposed to the 1970's and New York. *Round Two*.

* * *

The majority of Eric Bentley's plays are history plays, dealing with historical figures who have either attained the status of myth, or who are on the verge of entering the popular imagination. Bentley consequently is free to work upon our assumptions about his characters, and he usually works towards a radical point: the shoring-up of individual identity against the inroads of institutional power, be it of the church or the state.

He is a Shavian dramatist in that, not only does language matter, but his talent makes it central to his plays. He may rely upon a stage-grouping, he may use every available stage nuance; in the end, it is the pure dialectic of impassioned speech that gives his plays their force.

He is Shavian as well in the less obvious sense of writing plays against the stage, the stage being but the reflection of our melodramatic lives. Against the commonly held belief that our enemies are evil personified and that ours is a kill-or-be-killed world, he will grant the antagonist an argument and create a scene in which both sides are right from their own perspective. His plays are thus historical tragedies, not mere spectacles of put-upon humanity.

We can see all of these ingredients at work in his early play *The Recantation of Galileo Galilei*, his response to the *Galileo* of Bertolt Brecht. A close comparison of the two makes for fascinating reading. If Brecht writes inspired science fiction, with a cast of inquisitors who are mostly clowns, Bentley carries the conviction of political reality, his play building to the climax of the trial which Brecht necessarily avoids. Brecht's *Galileo* may be the greater play, its epic scope, easy manner, and fine touch of folk wisdom bearing the marks of genius. Nevertheless, Bentley's mastery of the issues, his sense of the argument, and his scene of contention create a trial that is the best set-piece since Shaw's *Saint Joan*.

As for the protagonists: if Brecht's appetitive man ends in cynicism and despair, of this false confession before the threat of torture becoming his true confession of self-hatred for having caved in, Bentley reverses the human dilemma, making his Galileo lie for the greater good. This refined man is a naïve intellectual headed for a rude awakening, but an awakening nevertheless. The cynicism of Brecht's protagonist is shifted in Bentley's play to the shoulders of a real antagonist, the Jesuit scientist and priest, Scheiner.

If Bentley's Galileo is an ideological man who fights for the ideal, his Oscar Wilde, by contrast, fights for the right to be himself. The description nicely fits the title of the play, *Lord Alfred's Lover*, which implies, of course, that Wilde is not yet established as himself. The playwright's masterstroke is to "tell" the story of the trials through the expedient of the aging Bosie's confession to a priest; he thereby not only wins sympathy for Bosie, but also subverts the intentions of those who would praise Wilde at Bosie's expense (the adulation of Wilde when carried to an extreme sounding suspiciously like gay-bashing, the Bosies of the world be damned!). By joining the two fates, Bentley encompasses the scope of the homosexual journey, which begins with Bosie, the man who never made peace with himself, and ends with Wilde, the man who did but at a cost.

Since the conventional audience reads the title for their definition of Wilde, Bentley establishes Wilde against their reading. The notorious homosexual is their creation, his notoriety being their contribution to the case. They would prefer the portrait of a self-destructive man, which absolves them of guilt. They get instead, the portrait of their victim, which does not.

Of course it is rash of Bentley to suggest that the gay Prime Minister Rosebery actively conspired against Wilde, but this is a mere quibble given the fine scene he creates for them at

Reading Gaol. Threatened by association with Wilde, influential homosexuals may have helped to bring him down; in any case, while we can argue that their "imaginary conversation" never took place, we can also imagine it as taking place every day in the minds of people who are forced into acting against themselves.

In a totally different key is a series of plays collectively known as *The Kleist Variations*. Contemporary readings of the plays of Heinrich von Kleist, they reveal the earlier playwright in a more metaphysical vein. To Kleist's astounding vision, Bentley offers the challenge of a whole new world of sexual politics, political hatreds, and apocalyptic fears.

Concord, the variation of Kleist's *Broken Jug*, is typical of the three plays. Set in Puritan New England during the early days of the Republic, it turns the tables on a sexual bounder and makes him the victim of Puritan hatred (read: "family values") instead. A "monstrous martyrdom" comically turned, it exposes the same hypocrisy that hit Wilde and Galileo, while it inspires the same hope.

—Michael Bertin

BERKOFF, Steven. British. Born in Stepney, London, 3 August 1937. Educated at schools in Stepney; Hackney Downs Grammar School, London; Webber-Douglas Academy of Dramatic Art, London, 1958–59; École Jacques Lecoq, Paris, 1965. Married Shelley Lee in 1976. Actor in repertory in Nottingham, Liverpool, Coventry, and at Citizens' Theatre Glasgow, for six years. Since 1973 founding director, London Theatre Group. Recipient: Los Angeles Drama Critics Circle award, for directing, 1983. Agent: Joanna Marston, Rosica Colin Ltd., 1 Clareville Grove Mews, London SW7 5AH, England.

PUBLICATIONS

Plays

In the Penal Colony, adaptation of a story by Kafka (produced London, 1968). Included in *The Trial, Metamorphosis, In the Penal Colony: Three Theatre Adaptations from Franz Kafka*, 1988.
Metamorphosis, adaptation of a story by Kafka (produced London, 1968; Los Angeles, 1982; New York, 1989). With *The Trial*, Ambergate, Derbyshire, Amber Lane Press, 1981.
The Trial, adaptation of a novel by Kafka (produced in the Netherlands, 1971; London, 1973). With *Metamorphosis*, Ambergate, Derbyshire, Amber Lane Press, 1981.
Agamemnon, adaptation of a play by Aeschylus (produced London, 1971; revised version produced London, 1976). Included in *East, Agamemnon, The Fall of the House of Usher*, 1977.
Knock at the Manor Gate, adaptation of a story by Kafka (produced Falmer, Sussex, and London, 1972).
Miss Julie Versus Expressionism, adaptation of a play by Strindberg (produced London, 1973).
Lunch (as *Mr. Prufrock's Songs*, produced London, 1974; revised version, as *Lunch*, produced London, 1981). Included in *West, Lunch, Harry's Christmas*, 1985.

The Fall of the House of Usher, adaptation of the story by Poe (produced Edinburgh, 1974; London, 1975). Included in *East, Agamemnon, The Fall of the House of Usher*, 1977.
East (produced Edinburgh and London, 1975). Included in *East, Agamemnon, The Fall of the House of Usher*, 1977.
East, Agamemnon, The Fall of the House of Usher. London, Calder, 1977; New York, Riverrun Press, 1982.
Greek (produced London, 1980; Los Angeles, 1982; New York, 1983). With *Decadence*, London, Calder, 1982; New York, Riverrun Press, 1983.
West (produced London, 1980). Included in *West, Lunch, Harry's Christmas*, 1985.
Decadence (produced London, 1981). With *Greek*, London, Calder, 1982; New York, Riverrun Press, 1983.
Harry's Christmas (produced London, 1985). Included in *West, Lunch, Harry's Christmas*, 1985.
The Tell-Tale Heart, adaptation of the story by Poe (produced London, 1985).
West, Lunch, Harry's Christmas. London, Faber, and New York, Grove Press, 1985.
Kvetch (produced Los Angeles, 1986; New York, 1987; Edinburgh and London, 1991). With *Acapulco*, London, Faber, 1986; New York, Grove Press, 1987.
Sink the Belgrano! (produced London, 1986). With *Massage*, London, Faber, 1987.
Acapulco (produced Los Angeles, 1986; London, 1992). With *Kvetch*, London, Faber, 1986; New York, Grove Press, 1987.
The Trial, Metamorphosis, In the Penal Colony: Three Theatre Adaptations from Franz Kafka. Oxford, Amber Lane, 1988.
Decadence and Other Plays (includes *East, West, Greek*). London, Faber, 1989.

Short Stories

Gross Intrusion and Other Stories. London, Calder, and Dallas, Riverrun Press, 1979.

Other

Steven Berkoff's America. London, Hutchinson, 1988.
A Prisoner in Rio. London, Hutchinson, 1989.
I Am Hamlet. London, Faber, 1989; New York, Grove Press, 1990.
Theatre of Steven Berkoff. London, Methuen, 1992.

*

Theatrical Activities:
Director: **Plays**—all his own plays; *Macbeth*, London, 1970; *The Zoo Story* by Edward Albee, Newcastle upon Tyne, 1973; *Coriolanus*, New York, 1988; *Salome* by Oscar Wilde, Dublin, 1988, Edinburgh, 1989, London 1989, Australia and Japan, 1992.
Actor: **Plays**—most of his own plays; Gentleman Caller in *The Glass Menagerie* by Tennessee Williams, London, 1971; title role in *Hamlet*, London, 1980; Herod in *Salome* by Oscar Wilde, Dublin, 1988, Edinburgh and London, 1989, Australia and Japan, 1992. **Films**—*A Clockwork Orange*, 1971; *Barry Lyndon*, 1975; *The Passenger*, 1975; *Joseph Andrews*, 1977; *McVicar*, 1980; *Outland*, 1981; *Octopussy*, 1983; *Beverly Hills Cop*, 1984; *Rambo: First Blood, Part II*, 1985; *Revolution*, 1985; *Absolute Beginners*, 1986; *Under the Cherry Moon*, 1986; *The Krays*, 1990. **Television**—*Charlie Was a Rich Man*, 1981; *Sins*, 1987; *War and Remembrance*, 1990; *Tell-Tale*

Heart, 1991; *Silent Night*, adaptation of *Harry's Christmas*, 1991.

* * *

Through his appearances in three of Hollywood's most successful motion pictures—*Octopussy*, *Beverly Hills Cop*, and *Rambo*—Steven Berkoff became one of the cinema's favourite villains. For those who knew Berkoff through his stage work in Britain and Los Angeles it was an unexpected transformation, as unlikely for a theatrical outsider as his subsequent embrace by Britain's National Theatre.

Long before the films were made, Berkoff had established his own dedicated following, an audience primed to admire the violent flow of his language as a dramatist and the physicality of his theatrical style. Where realism struggled to represent the inarticulacy of ordinary life, Berkoff gave his characters pages of poetic diatribe driven by profane imagery and obscene rhyme. He combined the street language of London's East End with Shakespearean grandiloquence. His visual images shared the urgent violence of his language, through the threatening presence of motorcycles and muscular actors in leather and denim.

His debt to classical theatre in his original plays was made clear by his productions of classics, ranging from Aeschylus to Shakespeare, and his adaptations of Kafka and Edgar Allan Poe. But his originality was also poured in great measure into those plays. In Berkoff's *Agamemnon*, for instance, the arrival of the watchman at the beginning of the play required an actor to exhaust himself on a quarter-mile run before the play began, collapsing onto the stage with his message. When a chorus is required, in his original work or in his production of a classic, it is as organic as any of the leading characters.

Reassuringly for those who cherished his iconoclasm, Berkoff reinvested much of his Hollywood earnings in stage projects that remained faithful to his chosen theatrical prophets. Very early in his career he chose some difficult masters, admiring, for instance, the discipline and formal skills of Bertolt Brecht as playwright and director, and noting with particular interest the way in which Brecht was able to develop his technique and beliefs through his own company, the Berliner Ensemble. That was a lesson he applied when he formed his own company, the London Theatre Group, where a Berkoff school of acting and presentation was carefully developed.

His next master was Antonin Artaud. All Berkoff's theatrical work demonstrates Artaud's dedication to using the theatre as a visceral art, drawing its energy from "the lower echelons of the body," from sexual and primal urges which can unleash profound feelings in actor and spectator. He once described his relationship with Artaud in clearly sexual terms when he said, "since I started with Artaud I've never flirted with anyone else."

Like the Living Theatre of Julian Beck and Judith Malina, however, and rather unlike Artaud, he has found in the primal physicality of his theatre a means of expressing political ideas. His disgust at Britain's conduct during the Falklands War in 1982 was dramatized in his play *Sink the Belgrano!*, a diatribe in punk-Shakespearean verse. The play made no concessions to the sensibilities of his admirers who knew him only for his film work. He scourged the audience with typically violent language, and, as in his earliest work, demanded of his actors extreme physical acts, portraying the dying sailors of the Argentinian battleship Belgrano in screams and formalized agony while his indictment of the British government was expressed through coarse poetry and coarse comedy, burlesquing the conventions of polite society.

Having demonstrated with *Sink the Belgrano!* that success would not soften his theatre, Berkoff consolidated the achievements of his earlier plays. His adaptation of Kafka's *Metamorphosis*, originally tailored to his own athletic performance as the man who is transformed into a giant insect, has proved exceptionally durable and has been staged by Berkoff in several languages, including a notable French production starring Roman Polanski. That adaptation has paved the way for his particular use of the human body and voice as the prime elements in his productions, powerfully demonstrating his concern for the expression of text through physical images which imprint themselves on the audience's memory. Visionary as his adaptations might be, however (his use of Poe is nightmarish in the extreme), it is the original writing which has proved most influential.

East, the play in which he first gave a violent representation to his vision of London life, has become a model for younger playwrights seeking to escape the limits of conversational drama. In that play he first mingled a Cockney corruption of Elizabethan-styled verse with sexual and aggressive prose speeches. Structured as a story of growing up in London's East End, with fights and fornication as major themes, the extreme imagery frequently grew into lyrical fantasias. "If I write a bit rationally, I know I fail. For instance, when I talk about a motorbike in *East*, it has to be the best, the shiniest. When I talk about a phallus, it is the largest. . . . Everything has to be extreme." The extreme view of London working-class life continued with the sequel, *West*, a few years later.

His whole vision of drama is one of extremes, demonstrated again in his North London reworking of the *Oedipus Tyrannus* of Sophocles which he called *Greek*. "In *Greek* every speech is an extreme feeling; of tenderness, of passion, of hate." Typically, despite the extremity of feeling when his hero, Eddie, discovers he has married his mother, Berkoff dispenses with the tragic ending and lets Eddie continue as her husband. Love, wherever you find it, is something worth keeping. It is by borrowing such themes as the Oedipus story and submitting them to his own vision that Berkoff achieves much of his intensity.

Decadence was his first full-scale assault on the ruling classes, though his distaste for middle-class values was earlier evident in his comically vulgar portrayal of the insect's family in *Metamorphosis*. Gluttony and the buggery of public schools were indulgences ideally suited to gross physical imagery, and the coarse poetry he provided for his couple in evening dress was potently expressed by the man as if the words were vomit. The theatricality of the play was enhanced by his demand that the same actors portray a complementary working-class couple, hopelessly in awe of decadence.

In *Harry's Christmas* Berkoff supplied a bitter corrective to the holiday spirit with his one-man play about a man whose loneliness leads him each year to recycle the few Christmas cards he has ever collected. Like his other work, the play was designed for sharp physical interpretations of the world rather than representations, and despite his work in Hollywood, his plays are still intended to tap the full potentiality of actors and clear away the trivial routines and reenactments of ordinary activity. With the use of his dialogue and monologues, "acting becomes a compulsive medium because I can touch primeval forces and release them—madness and maybe enlightenment." Occasionally, he finds an inspiration for such expression in existing sources, such as his internationally successful version of Oscar Wilde's *Salome*, first produced for Dublin's Gate Theatre.

His Hollywood and other American experiences have been absorbed into his writing, both dramatically and in prose, notably in his published imaginative "screenplay" *A Prisoner in Rio* and the plays *Kvetch* and *Acapulco*. The latter, in particular, demonstrates Hollywood's vulnerability to individuals such as Berkoff. In the process of turning him into a star, it allowed him to bear close-range witness to the moviemaking megalomania of actors such as Sylvester Stallone in *Rambo*. Those experiences have been digested with customary bile to become the harsher entertainment of a Berkoff play.

—Ned Chaillet

BERMANGE, Barry. British. Born in London, 7 November 1933. Educated at an art school in Essex, 1947–52. National service, 1952–54. Married Maurine Jewel Bright in 1961. Assistant designer, Perth Repertory Company, Scotland, 1955; actor and assistant stage manager, Swansea Repertory Company, 1956. Recipient: Arts Council bursary, 1964; Ohio State University award, 1967; German Critics award, 1968; Karl Sczuka prize (Germany), 1981, 1987. Address: 35 Alexandra Park Road, London N10 2DD, England.

PUBLICATIONS

Plays

No Quarter (broadcast 1962; produced London, 1964). Included in *No Quarter and The Interview*, 1969.
Nathan and Tabileth (broadcast 1962; produced Edinburgh and London, 1967). With *Oldenberg*, London, Methuen, 1967.
The Cloud (produced London, 1964).
Four Inventions (includes *The Dreams, Amor Dei, The After-Life, The Evenings of Certain Lives*) (broadcast 1964–65; produced London, 1969).
Oldenberg (televised 1967; produced Edinburgh and London, 1967). With *Nathan and Tabileth*, London, Methuen, 1967.
The Interview (televised 1968; produced London, 1969). Included in *No Quarter and The Interview*, 1969.
Invasion (televised 1969). Included in *No Quarter and The Interview*, 1969.
No Quarter and The Interview (includes *Invasion*). London, Methuen, 1969.
Scenes from Family Life (televised 1969; produced Leatherhead, Surrey, 1974). Published in *Collection: Literature for the Seventies*, edited by Gerald and Nancy S. Messner, Boston, Heath, 1972.
Warcries (broadcast 1981; produced Donaueschingen, 1981).
The Soldiers (broadcast 1985; produced Frankfurt-am-Main, 1985).
The Dreams, Warcries, Klänge am Mikrophon (produced Kassel, 1987).

Radio Plays: *The Voice of the Peanut*, 1960; *Never Forget a Face*, 1961; *No Quarter*, 1962; *A Glass of Lemonade*, 1962; *Nathan and Tabileth*, 1962; *The Imposters* series, 1962; *Four Inventions*, 1964–65; *The Mortification*, 1964; *The Detour*, 1964; *Paths of Glory*, from the novel by Humphrey Cobb, 1965; *Letters of a Portuguese Nun*, 1966; *As a Man Grows Older*, 1967; *Neues vom Krieg*, 1969 (Germany); *S.O.S.*, 1977

(Netherlands), 1978 (UK); *Social Welfare*, 1979; *Warcries*, 1981 (Germany); *English Speaking People*, 1981 (Germany); *Scenario*, 1981 (Netherlands); *Four Inventions (Reconstruction 1)*, 1983 (Netherlands); *Klänge am Mikrophon*, 1985 (Germany); *The Soldiers*, 1985 (Germany); *Testament*, 1985 (Germany); *Le Désir*, 1986 (Germany); *Radioville*, 1987 (Germany); *Der gelbe Klang*, 1987 (Germany); *Annulamento*, 1987 (Germany); *4-Channels*, 1989 (Germany); *Big City Nightwork*, 1990 (Germany); *Cielo y Tierra*, 1991 (Germany).

Television Plays: *Oldenberg*, 1967; *The Interview*, 1968; *Tramp*, 1968 (Germany); *Invasion*, 1969; *Scenes from Family Life*, 1969; *International*, 1976; *Stars*, 1976.

*

Critical Studies: "Amor Dei" by Peter Faecke, in *Neues Hörspiel: Essays, Analysen, Gespräche* edited by Klaus Schöning, Frankfurt-am-Main, Suhrkamp, 1970; *Das englische "Radioplay" seit 1945: Typen, Themen, und Formen*, Berlin, Schmidt, 1978, *Barry Bermange: Eine Beschreibung seines Buhnen-, Funk-, und Fernsehdramatischen Werken*, Tubingen, Narr, 1986, and *Ut Pictura/Musica Poesis: Radiokom-position von Barry Bermange*, Giessen, Hoffman, 1986, all by Horst Priessnitz; "Warcries" in *Kirche und Rundfunk 82*, 24 October 1981.

Theatrical Activities:
Director: most of his own plays.

* * *

The most remarkable characteristic of Barry Bermange's style as a dramatist is his ability to convey a powerful, universal theme with the utmost economy of means. His early plays (originally written for the stage) were first produced on radio, a medium ideally suited to capture the full evocativeness of the language, the symbolic power of the stories and the graceful accuracy of each carefully calculated effect. Indeed a live audience sometimes seems to disturb the precise timing on which his plays depend: there is too little room for laughter or any other spontaneous reaction. Bermange has sometimes been compared to Beckett and Ionesco: and his plots are occasionally reminiscent of the Theatre of the Absurd. In *No Quarter*, for example, a fat man and a quiet man seek lodging in a mysterious collapsing hotel: and eventually huddle together in a dark upper storey room, hoping that nothing will happen to them if they stay quite still. But Bermange's dialogue, unlike Ionesco's, rarely exploits for its own sake. His images do not carry the logic-shattering irrelevace of Dadaism. The plain meaning of *No Quarter* is also too apparent: the fat man and the quiet man represent two recognizable human reactions to the fear that their world is disintegrating. Nor is Bermange an iconoclastic writer. The collapsing hotel is not symbolic, say, of religion falling apart. Unlike the writers of the Absurd, Bermange does not delight in pointing out the nonsense of cherished institutions: nor are his stories tantalizingly ridiculous. He doesn't attempt to give a pleasing *frisson* to the rational mind by rubbing it up the wrong way. The themes of his plays are usually coherent and indeed logical, although they may contain many ambiguities. Bermange is a writer who defies easy categorizing simply because he chooses each technique carefully to express most directly his underlying themes. His plays can be absurdist: they can be naturalistic: they can even include carefully manoeuvred "happenings." But the styles have always been selected for their appropriateness, not from any *a priori* assumptions about Theatre or Dramatic Art.

In the same way he chooses his different styles with care, so Bermange distils each effect to its essential elements. Like Marguerite Duras, he sometimes presents an apparently small incident observed in precise detail: and separates it from all the surrounding life until it exists in a significant isolation. In *The Interview* eight men wait in an outer office, before being interviewed for a job. The audience never learns what the job is or who is finally selected. The play is solely concerned with the applicants' reactions to each other: and the small details—one man reading a newspaper, another looking at a picture—manage to convey an almost intolerable atmosphere of suspicion and rivalry. In *Nathan and Tabileth*, an elderly couple feed the pigeons in the park, return home and spend the evening by the fire. They are visited by a young man, Bernie, who says he is their grandson, although they do not recognize him, and who talks of relatives they have forgotten. When Bernie leaves, the couple go to bed: and "darkness comes." Bermange manages to capture in the rambling repetitive dialogue and in the intense short soliloquies the shifting concentration of the old. Certain details—the hired boats on the lake, the pigeons, and the glowing fire—emerge in sharp focus: others slide into a grey and closing background. The timing of the play is calculated to break up the normal pace of events: the old people do not think consecutively and the audience is not allowed to do so. Sometimes they ramble on about the past: sometimes they try to cope with the present, with the breaking of a plate, with a scratched hand. No other contemporary play—with the possible exception of Beckett's *Happy Days*—conveys with such agonizing plausibility the experience of old age.

The Interview and *Nathan and Tabileth* are both basically naturalistic plays: the observable details have been carefully selected and arranged to provide a particular impact—but these details are convincing on the level of external reality. In *Oldenberg*, however, Bermange caricatures the main characters. A man and a woman decide to let a room in their house. The tenant is a stranger, Oldenberg, whom they have never even met. At first they make considerable efforts to furnish the room comfortably: but then the possibility occurs to them that their tenant may not be *English*. In a fit of xenophobia, they destroy and desecrate the room they have so carefully prepared. But the stranger when he arrives is English—and blind. *Oldenberg* is an allegory about the way in which people long for change but are afraid of the unfamiliar—of invasion. By using some of the techniques of Absurdist writers, Bermange heightens the contradictory emotions caused by the intrusions of visitors.

But perhaps Bermange's most extraordinary achievement was to compile four "sound inventions," originally for radio, but which were afterwards presented at the Institute of Contemporary Arts in London—through loudspeakers in a darkened auditorium. The inventions were recorded extracts of interviews with ordinary men and women—about their dreams, their reflections on old age, their beliefs or scepticisms about God and the After-life. The speeches were carefully edited into short revealing phrases, "orchestrated" with electronic music and finally presented as totally original music-drama works. In these inventions, Bermange's remarkable gifts for ordering sound effectively—both ordinary speech patterns and electronic effects—were allied to themes which could scarcely have been expressed effectively any other way. He invented a new form of radio and theatrical experience: and the only possible contemporary parallel would be with Berio's music-drama for Italian radio. With equal ingenuity, Bermange also wrote an improvisatory work

for television, *Invasion*, where a dinner party is gradually submerged by the images of Vietnam, flickering across a television screen. Bermange's inventiveness, his assurance in handling different styles and media, and the powerful intensity of his chosen themes have won him a unique position among British dramatists. No other writer can rival him for controlled daring and insight into the potentialities of experimental drama.

—John Elsom

BERNARD, Kenneth. American. Born in Brooklyn, New York, 7 May 1930. Educated at City College of New York, B.A. 1953; Columbia University, New York, M.A. 1956, Ph.D. 1962. Served in the United States Army, 1953–55: private. Married Elaine Reiss in 1952; two sons and one daughter. Instructor, 1959–62, assistant professor, 1962–66, associate professor, 1967–70, and since 1971 professor of English, Long Island University, Brooklyn. Advisory editor, 1973–75, assistant editor, 1976–78, and since 1979 fiction editor, *Confrontation*, Brooklyn. Vice-president, New York Theatre Strategy, 1972–79. Recipient: Rockefeller grant, 1971, 1975; Guggenheim fellowship, 1972; Creative Artists Public Service grant, 1973, 1976; National Endowment for the Arts grant, for fiction, 1977; Arvon poetry prize, 1980. Address: 800 Riverside Drive, New York, New York 10032, U.S.A.

PUBLICATIONS

Plays

The Moke-Eater (produced New York, 1968). Included in *Night Club and Other Plays*, 1971.
The Lovers, published in *Trace* (London), May 1969; in *Night Club and Other Plays*, 1971.
Marko's: A Vegetarian Fantasy, published in *Massachusetts Review* (Amherst), Summer 1969.
Night Club (produced New York, 1970). Included in *Night Club and Other Plays*, 1971.
The Monkeys of the Organ Grinder (produced New Brunswick, New Jersey, and New York, 1970). Included in *Night Club and Other Plays*, 1971.
The Unknown Chinaman (produced Omaha, 1971). Published in *Playwrights for Tomorrow 10*, edited by Arthur H. Ballet, Minneapolis, University of Minnesota Press, 1973.
Night Club and Other Plays (includes *The Moke-Eater, The Lovers, Mary Jane, The Monkeys of the Organ Grinder, The Giants in the Earth*). New York, Winter House, 1971.
Mary Jane (also director: produced New York, 1973). Included in *Night Club and Other Plays*, 1971.
Goodbye, Dan Bailey, published in *Drama and Theatre* (Fredonia, New York), Spring 1971.
The Magic Show of Dr. Ma-Gico (produced New York, 1973). Published in *Theatre of the Ridiculous*, edited by Bonnie Marranca and Gautam Dasgupta, New York, Performing Arts Journal Publications, 1979.
How We Danced While We Burned (produced Yellow Springs, Ohio, 1974). With *La Justice; or, The Cock That Crew*, Santa Maria, California, Asylum Arts, 1990.

King Humpy (produced New York, 1975). Published in *2Plus2* (Lausanne, Switzerland), 1985.

The Sensuous Ape, published in *Penthouse* (New York), September 1975.

The Sixty Minute Queer Show, music by John Braden (produced New York, 1977).

La Justice; or, The Cock That Crew, music by John Braden (produced New York, 1979). With *How We Danced While We Burned*, Santa Maria, California, Asylum Arts, 1990.

La Fin du Cirque (produced New York, 1984). Published in *Grand Street* (New York), 1982.

The Panel (produced New York, 1984).

Play with an Ending; or, Columbus Discovers the World (produced New York, 1984).

We Should . . . (A Lie) (produced New York, 1992).

Short Stories

Two Stories. Mount Horeb, Wisconsin, Perishable Press, 1973.

The Maldive Chronicles. New York, Performing Arts Journal Publications, 1987.

From the District File. Boulder, Colorado, Fiction Collective 2, 1992.

*

Manuscript Collections: Lincoln Center Library of the Performing Arts, New York; University of Minnesota, Minneapolis.

Critical Studies: introduction by Michael Feingold to *Night Club and Other Plays*, 1971; "A Collaboration: Kenneth Bernard and John Vaccaro" by Gerald Rabkin, in *Performing Arts Journal* (New York), Spring-Summer 1978; *The Original Theatre of New York* by Stefan Brecht, Frankfurt am Main, Suhrkamp, 1978; *Contemporary American Dramatists 1960–1980* by Ruby Cohn, London, Macmillan, and New York, Grove Press, 1982; *The Darkness We Carry: The Drama of the Holocaust* by Robert Skloot, Madison, University of Wisconsin Press, 1988; article by Rosette LaMont in *Stages* (Norwood, New Jersey), 1992.

Theatrical Activities:
Director: **Play**—*Mary Jane*, New York, 1973.

Kenneth Bernard comments:

I like to think of my plays as metaphors, closer to poetic technique (the coherence of dream) than to rational discourse. I am not interested in traditional plot or character development. My plays build a metaphor; when the metaphor is complete, the play is complete. Within that context things and people do happen. I would hope the appeal of my plays is initially to the emotions only, not the head, and that they are received as spectacle and a kind of gorgeous (albeit frightening) entertainment. The characters in my plays can often be played by either men or women (e.g., *The Moke-Eater*, *Night Club*): only a living presence is necessary, one who reflects the character component in the play rather than any aspect of non-stage individuality: they are instruments to be played upon, not ego-minded careerists: they must "disappear" on stage. More important than technique, etc., are passion and flexibility. The defects of this preference are offset by strong directorial control: each play in effect becomes a training program. My plays use music, dance, poetry, rhetoric, film, sounds and voices of all kinds, costume, color, make-up,

noise, irrationality, and existing rituals to give shape (e.g., the auction, the magic show). The audience must be authentically pulled into the play in spite of itself. It must not *care* what it all means because it is enjoying itself and feels itself involved in a dramatic flow. What remains with the audience is a totality, the metaphor, from which ideas may spring—not ideas from which it has (with difficulty) to recreate the dramatic experience.

*   *   *

Kenneth Bernard's major plays have been produced mainly by the Play-House of the Ridiculous, under John Vaccaro's direction. This collaboration provides the best avenue of approach to an understanding of Bernard's plays. The "Ridiculous" style, with its shrilly pitched, frenzied extravagance, its compulsively and explicitly sexual interpretation of every action, the elaborate makeup and costumes that lend confusion to the antics of transvestites of both sexes, the general aura of bleakness and violence that adds despair to even the company's most optimistic productions—that style is a reasonable physicalization of the world Kenneth Bernard evokes.

The two interlocking themes of Bernard's drama are cruelty and entertainment. His characters are perpetually threatening each other with tortures, mutilations, particularly painful modes of execution, and these vicissitudes are constantly placed in a theatrical "frame" of some sort, as intended for the amusement of a group, or of the torture-master, or of the audience itself, implicated by its silent consent to the proceedings. In Bernard's first full-length work, *The Moke-Eater*, the setting is a prototypical American small town, the hero the stock figure of a traveling salesman, desperately ingenuous and jaunty, who suddenly finds himself, when his car breaks down, confronting the sinister, inarticulate townspeople and their malevolent boss, Alec. Alec alternately cajoles and bullies the salesman into submitting to a humiliating series of charades, nightmarish parodies of small-town hospitality, climaxing in his realization that he is trapped when he drives off in the repaired auto, only to have it break down outside the next town . . . which turns out to be exactly the same town he has just left. (In the Ridiculous production, an additional frisson was added to the salesman's re-entrance by having the townspeople, at this point, attack and eviscerate him—a fate which Alec describes earlier in the play as having been inflicted on a previous visitor.)

Later plays by Bernard present the spectacle of cruelty with the torturer, rather than the victim, as protagonist. *Night Club* displays Western civilization as a hideous, inept cabaret show, controlled by an androgynous master of ceremonies named Bubi, who, like Alec in *The Moke-Eater*, cajoles and bullies both audience and performers into humiliating themselves. In fact, the theatre audience first sees the company performing the show as a parody of itself: the grotesque nightclub acts all emerge out of the "audience," which meanwhile cheers, catcalls, attacks the club's one waitress, and generally behaves boorishly. The acts themselves include a ventriloquist (male) trapped in a virulent love-hate relationship with his dummy (female), who spouts obscenities; a juggler (recalling the "Destructive Desmond" of Auden and Isherwood's *The Dog Beneath the Skin*) who throws valuable antiques into the air and declines to catch them; an impersonator, obsessed with his own virility, whose imitations veer from a sex-starved southern belle to a sadistic Nazi; and "The Grand Kabuki Theatre of America," which lends the patina of Japanese ceremoniousness to a vulgar soap-opera-like story about a pregnant college girl. Eventually, the nightclub show culminates, at Bubi's behest, in mass copulation by the "audience," accompanied by the William Tell Overture; for a climax, the one member of the audience who declines to perform is summarily dragged onstage and decapitated, while he repeatedly screams, "The menu says there's no cover charge!" In a similar vein, Bernard's *The Magic Show of Dr. Ma-Gico* is a series of violent encounters, more courtly in tone but just as unpleasant, based on fairy-tale and romance themes. (A maiden, to test her lover's fidelity, transforms herself into a diseased old crone and forces him to make love to her; a king is challenged to pick up a book without dropping his robe, orb, and scepter; in both cases the man fails.) *Auction* (unproduced) is a surreal, aleatory version of a rural livestock auction, whose items include a pig-woman and an invalid who sells off his vital organs one by one. The world-picture contained in these plays is essentially that of a continuous nightmare, and while the surface action and language change (Bernard's language is exceptionally varied in texture, going from the loftiest politeness to the most degraded abuse), the emotional thrust of the material is constantly the same: towards revealing the sheer ludicrous horror of existence. In his collaboration with the Play-House of the Ridiculous, Bernard has carried the Artaudian project of raising and exorcizing the audience's demons about as far as it is likely to get through the theatrical metaphor.

—Michael Feingold

BILL, Stephen. British. Born in Birmingham, 16 January 1948. Educated at Handsworth and Hales Owen grammar schools, 1952–67; Royal Academy of Dramatic Art, London, 1968–70. Married Sheila Kelley in 1971; one son and one daughter. Commis chef, Norfolk Hotel, Birmingham, 1966; ward orderly, Romsley Sanatorium, Romsley, Worcestershire, 1967–68; grave digger, Hales Owen Council, 1967; civil servant in tax office, Birmingham, 1968; writer-in-residence, Crucible Theatre, Sheffield, 1977–78. Recipient: Thames Television award, 1977; John Whiting award, 1979; London *Evening Standard* award, 1987; *Plays and Players* award, 1987; *Drama* award, 1987; Writers Guild of Great Britain award, 1991. Agent: Judy Daish Associates, 83 Eastbourne Mews, London W2 6LQ, England.

PUBLICATIONS

Plays

Girl Talk (produced Sheffield, 1978; London, 1982).
Squeakers and Strags (produced Sheffield, 1978).
Final Wave (produced Sheffield, 1979).
The Old Order (produced Birmingham, 1979).
Piggy-Back Rider (produced Birmingham, 1981).
The Bottom Drawer (produced Oxford, 1982).
Naked in the Bull Ring (produced Birmingham, 1985).
Over the Bar (produced Derby, 1985).
Crossing the Line (produced Darlaston, West Midlands, 1987).
Curtains (produced London, 1987). London, Faber, 1988.
Heartlanders, with David Edgar and Anne Devlin (produced Birmingham, 1989). London, Hern, 1989.

Over a Barrel (produced Watford, 1990).
Stitched Up (produced Bolton, 1990).
The Antigone Project (produced Solihull, 1992).

Radio Play: *Worshipping the Ground*, 1988.

Television Plays: *Lyndsey*, 1980; *House Warming*, 1983; *Eh Brian, It's a Whopper* series, 1984; *Marjorie and the Preacher Man*, with Jim Broadbent, 1987; *Broke*, 1991.

*

Theatrical activities:
Actor: **Plays**—in repertory theatres and in London including: *The Silent Majority* by Mike Leigh, London, 1974; *Blood Sports* by David Edgar, London, 1975; *Blisters* by Sheila Kelley and Sarah Pia Anderson, London, 1976. **Film**—*Prick Up Your Ears*, 1987. **Television**—*Nuts in May* by Mike Leigh, 1976; *Spend, Spend, Spend* by Jack Rosenthal, 1977; *Stepping Out* by Sheila Kelley and Sarah Pia Anderson, 1977; *Days at the Beach* by Malcolm Mowbray, 1978.

Stephen Bill comments:
I feel like I am just a storyteller giving voice to the characters and situations that I have come across in everyday life. A voice to "ordinary" people whose stories I don't feel are normally told. I grew up in Handsworth, Birmingham. My father went from school into his father's small badge enamelling business in the jewellery quarter. They only employed women enamellers because they "couldn't pay enough to employ men." My mother died when I was about four and we never argued at home. I only mention these odd facts because everything I write relates back to upbringing. To pitting one set of values against another. To having the arguments in public that we didn't know how to have in private.
My theatre work falls into two categories: 1) intimate, character-based dramas; 2) broader, community based theatre. The character-based work often explores the values we hold in common—or don't. It looks at how "ordinary" people cope when placed in extraordinary situations. It tries to make sense of, or celebrate, the contradictions. My experience in community-based theatre stems from my time as resident writer at the Crucible Theatre, Sheffield. I worked with their Theatre Vanguard Company which toured the whole of South Yorkshire. The plays I wrote for them were specific to the area and were for specific audiences—children, teenagers, handicapped groups etc. This strand of my work continued with: 2nd City Theatre Company, Theatre Foundry—the touring company for the Black Country; the *Heartlanders* project—a community play for Birmingham's centenary, co-written with Anne Devlin and David Edgar, with a cast of over a hundred local people; and in 1992 with *The Antigone Project* for the Royal Shakespeare Company. This is a retelling of the Sophocles play, *Antigone*, by 26 young people in the Chelmsley Wood area of Solihull. The story we tell will be out of their experience and will be in a language that is real to them.

* * *

Stephen Bill was an actor before he was a dramatist, and his first plays were written as a member of a company: he was resident writer at the Sheffield Crucible Theatre. He applied himself diligently to his job as a community playwright, researching issues and turning them into drama. His early plays are above average but conventional theatre-in-education about pigeons, delinquent teenagers, and the generation gap, mainly based in South Yorkshire. One, *Final Wave*, is atypical of all Bill's other work, using folk song and folk ritual, set on the remote island of St. Kilda, most of the action taking place in the 18th century, and the characters frequently speaking Gaelic. No other Bill characters speak any foreign language. Though they are rooted in the past, it is a past which goes no further back than World War II, they are geographically located no further south than Birmingham, no further north than Doncaster, and they speak in the authentic voices of the British working class and petit bourgeoisie.

During the time at Sheffield, Bill's own voice was confident but not noticeably individual. Real Bill began with his three plays for the Birmingham Repertory Company, *The Old Order*, *Piggy-Back Rider*, and *Naked in the Bull Ring*, all set in the Birmingham area and all based on his own family experience. The characters of *The Old Order* are the workers and management of a small factory like that once run by his own father. In *Piggy-Back Rider* a young accountant has taken over just such a factory from his father, George, and is destroying the work of two generations, selling off the land in parcels and getting rid of the workforce. George and his wife, Connie, move on into *Naked in the Bull Ring* as the son and daughter-in-law of a woman of 90, strong-willed but no longer confident in mind or of her ability to control the conditions of her own life, and only able to control the lives of her own family by making those lives a nightmare.

That old woman, based on Bill's grandmother, appeared again five years later in what may be his finest play, *Curtains*. She has repeatedly asked to be helped to die, and is killed at the beginning of the second act by one of her daughters, unable to cope with her any longer. The rest of the family then attempt to behave as if the murder didn't happen. The play was commissioned by the Hampstead Theatre Club, had a considerable critical success and transferred rather inappropriately to the Whitehall Theatre, home of the Whitehall farces. It may have bemused the regular Whitehall audience and did not run for long. Shamefully, it has never been produced professionally in Britain since, although it has been performed by amateurs all over the world.

Bill's interest in communities persists throughout his work. In collaboration with David Edgar and Anne Devlin he wrote a community play, *Heartlanders*, for a cast of over a 100—again performed in Birmingham. But usually his community is a family reacting to some family disaster—euthanasia in *Curtains* or the sudden announcement by a daughter that she intends to marry in *The Bottom Drawer* (the assumption is that she must be pregnant). Or it may be the community of the workplace. Besides his use of his father's factory in the Birmingham trilogy, he used a factory making ornamental barrels in *Over a Barrel* and the management of a football club in *Over the Bar*. His characters are invariably much concerned with possessions, either the accumulation of them or the encumbrance they represent.

He has a poet's concern with imagery—in *Stitched Up*, a householder, overwhelmed with debt, simply goes into the kitchen cupboard and refuses to come out. Bill sees plays as conversations with an audience, which is why he enjoys working in regional theatres—"I know who I'm talking to." He is more interested in character than in narrative and likes to bring a group of people up against an idea or an event (or both) to see what comes of it. Consequently the plays are more conversation than action. Though its subject may be of everyday concern, the locale an ordinary house or factory, the language, the costumes, the whole approach naturalistic, a Bill play has none of the self-indulgence of a semi-improvised piece by someone like Mike Leigh. Bill is only naturalistic in the sense that Pinter is naturalistic; he has a

very sharp ear, and a delight in the extra-ordinariness of demotic speech. Of all the present crop of British dramatists, he is the playwright of the inarticulate and confused. The characters of his later plays rarely finish a sentence.

—John Bowen

BIRIMISA, George. American. Born in Santa Cruz, California, 21 February 1924. Attended school to the ninth grade; studied with Uta Hagen at the Herbert Berghof Studios, New York. Served in the United States Naval Reserve during World War II. Married Nancy Linden in 1952 (divorced 1961). Worked in a factory, as a disc jockey, health studio manager, clerk, salesman, bartender, page for National Broadcasting Company, bellhop; counterman, Howard Johnson's, New York, 1952–56; typist, Laurie Girls, New York, 1969–70. Artistic director, Theatre of All Nations, New York, 1974–76. Recipient: Rockefeller grant, 1969. Address: 627 Page Street, Apartment 6, San Francisco, California 94117, U.S.A.

PUBLICATIONS

Plays

Degrees (produced New York, 1966).
17 Loves and 17 Kisses (produced New York, 1966).
Daddy Violet (produced Ann Arbor, Michigan, and New York, 1967). Published in *Prism International* (Vancouver), 1968.
How Come You Don't Dig Chicks? (produced New York, 1967). Published in *The Alternate* (San Francisco), January 1981.
Mister Jello (produced New York, 1968; London, 1969; revised version produced New York, 1974).
Georgie Porgie (produced New York, 1968). Published in *More Plays from Off-Off-Broadway*, edited by Michael T. Smith, Indianapolis, Bobbs Merrill, 1972.
Adrian (produced New York, 1974).
Will the Real Yogonanda Please Stand Up? (produced New York, 1974).
A Dress Made of Diamonds (produced Los Angeles, 1976).
Pogey Bait! (produced Los Angeles, 1976; New York, 1977). Published in *Drummer*, 1977.
A Rainbow in the Night (produced Los Angeles, 1978).
A Rose and a Baby Ruth (produced San Francisco, 1981).

*

Manuscript Collection: Joe Cino Memorial Library, Lincoln Center Library of the Performing Arts, New York.

Theatrical Activities:
Director: **Plays**—*The Bed* by Robert Heide, New York, 1966; *The Painter* by Burt Snider, New York, 1967; *Georgie Porgie*, New York, 1971; *A Buffalo for Brooklyn* by Anne Grant, Corning, New York, 1975.

George Birimisa comments:
(1973) I write about the people I know. At this point in my life many of my friends are homosexual. I try to write

honestly about them. In writing honestly about them I believe that my plays (in particular *Georgie Porgie*) mirror the terror of a schizophrenic society that is lost in a world of fantasy. In *Daddy Violet* I believe I showed how the individual's fantasy can lead to the burning of women and children in Vietnam. The problem with my plays is that many critics label them as homosexual plays. In the United States we live at the edge of a civilization that is near the end of the line. I feel that it is important for me to throw away every fantasy and get down into the total terror of this insane society. Only then can I truly write a play that is God-affirming, that is full of light. In my new play, tentatively titled *It's Your Movie*, I'm trying to write about the only alternative left in a demonic society—the nitty-gritty love of brother for brother and sister for sister. I know I must go through the passions of the flesh before I can break through to love my brother and sister. Anything else is an illusion. I also believe that the American male is terrified of his homosexuality and this is one of the chief reasons why he is unable to love his brother. His repression creates fires of the soul and this is translated into wars and violence. If all the "closet queens" would step out into the sunshine it would be a different country. I believe the above is what I write about in my plays.

(1977) At last I have discovered that four letter word LOVE. My early plays were screams of anger and rage. I was really screaming at myself because I was a microcosm of the good and evil of the western world, and I finally realize that it is possible to walk through death and destruction, and care . . . really care.

(1992) I just re-read my comments of 1973 and 1977. *Pompous*. I gave up the theatre for the last 10 years but I'm back in it. This time it's for my personal enjoyment. Period.

* * *

George Birimisa's early play *Daddy Violet* is built on a series of cathartic acting exercises which, through a process of association and hallucinatory transformation, evoke a battle in the Vietnam war. The cruelty and destruction of the war are connected, using a technique based on improvisation, with the actor's self-loathing and sexual immaturity.

Birimisa is a fiercely moral writer; his plays are filled with compassionate rage against needless suffering, furious impatience with the human condition, desperately frustrated idealism. He links the pain of human isolation to economic and social roots.

Mister Jello starts out with a mixed bag of characters: a waspish aging transvestite, a bitchy social worker, a dreamy boy flower child, a business-like prostitute, and fat, foolish Mister Jello, who likes to pretend to be a little boy and have the prostitute as his mommy discipline him. Birimisa sets their antagonisms in perspective by reference to the social philosopher Henry George.

Georgie Porgie is a series of vignettes about homosexual relationships, almost all bitter and ugly in tone, interspersed with choral episodes quoted from Friedrich Engels. The contrast between Engels's idealistic vision of human liberty and Birimisa's variously stupid, contemptible, pitiful, self-despising characters, all imprisoned in their own compulsions, is powerful and painful.

Birimisa's writing is often crude, the language vulgar, the humor cruel, the events shocking; the author has been preoccupied with psychic pain and the consequences of neurotic patterns, and his work makes up in self-examining integrity and emotional intensity what it eschews of seductiveness and beauty. In 1976 he made what is for Americans a mythic move from East to West, from New York first to Los

Angeles, then to San Francisco. In the more affirmative pre-AIDS climate of gay liberation there, he attempted to go beyond the rage and desperation of the earlier plays to a more positive view: *Pogey Bait!* was well received in Los Angeles and ran for several months.

—Michael T. Smith

———

BLEASDALE, Alan. British. Born in Liverpool, Lancashire, 23 March 1946. Educated at St. Aloysius Infant and Junior schools, Huyton, Lancashire, 1951–57; Wade Deacon Grammar School, Widnes, Lancashire, 1957–64; Padgate Teachers Training College, teachers certificate 1967. Married Julia Moses in 1970; two sons and one daughter. Teacher, St. Columbus Secondary Modern School, Huyton, 1967–71, King George V School, Gilbert and Ellice Islands, 1971–74, and Halewood Grange Comprehensive School, Lancashire, 1974–75; resident playwright, Liverpool Playhouse, 1975–76, and Contact Theatre, Manchester, 1976–78; joint artistic director, 1981–84, and associate director, 1984–86, Liverpool Playhouse. Recipient: Broadcasting Press Guild award, 1982; Royal Television Society award, 1982; BAFTA award, 1982; *Evening Standard* award, for musical, 1985; ITV Achievement of the Decade award, 1989; Broadcasting Press Guild Television and Radio award, 1991. Lives in Liverpool. Agent: Lemon, Unna, and Durbridge, 24 Pottery Lane, Holland Park, London W11 4LZ, England.

PUBLICATIONS

Plays

Fat Harold and the Last 26 (produced Liverpool and London, 1975).
The Party's Over (produced Liverpool, 1975).
Scully, with others, adaptation of the novel by Bleasdale (produced Liverpool, 1975). London, Hutchinson, 1984.
Franny Scully's Christmas Stories, with Kenneth Alan Taylor (produced Liverpool, 1976).
Down the Dock Road (produced Liverpool, 1976).
It's a Madhouse (produced Manchester, 1976). With *Having a Ball*, London, Faber, 1986.
Should Auld Acquaintance (produced Manchester, 1976).
No More Sitting on the Old School Bench (produced Manchester, 1977). Todmorden, Yorkshire, Woodhouse, 1979.
Crackers (produced Leeds, 1978).
Pimples (produced Manchester, 1978).
Love Is a Many Splendoured Thing (for children; produced Redditch, Worcestershire, 1986). Published in *Act I*, edited by David Self and Ray Speakman, London, Hutchinson, 1979.
Having a Ball (produced Oldham, Lancashire, and London, 1981; revised version produced London, 1990). With *It's a Madhouse*, London, Faber, 1986.
Boys from the Blackstuff (televised 1982). London, Hutchinson, 1985.
Young People Today (sketch), in *The Big One* (produced London, 1983).
Are You Lonesome Tonight? (produced Liverpool and London, 1985; San Diego, 1989). London, Faber, 1985.

The Monocled Mutineer, adaptation of the book by William Allison and John Fairley (televised 1986). London, Hutchinson, 1986.
No Surrender: A Deadpan Farce (screenplay). London, Faber, 1986.

Screenplay: *No Surrender*, 1987.

Television Plays: *Early to Bed*, 1975; *Dangerous Ambition*, 1976; *Scully's New Year's Eve*, 1978; *The Black Stuff*, 1980; *The Muscle Market*, 1981; *Boys from the Blackstuff* series, 1982; *Scully* series, 1984; *The Monocled Mutineer*, 1986; *G.B.H.* series, 1991.

Novels

Scully. London, Hutchinson, 1975.
Who's Been Sleeping in My Bed? London, Hutchinson, 1977; revised edition, as *Scully and Mooey*, London, Corgi, 1984.

*

Critical Studies: *Dossier 20*, London, British Film Institute, 1984; *Boys from the Blackstuff: The Making of Television Drama* by Bob Millington and Robin Nelson, London, Comedia, 1986.

Alan Bleasdale comments:

I try *never* to look back and examine my work. I don't re-read the script or watch the video once the piece is finished. For what it's worth, I don't think a writer should know what he or she is doing! That's for the audience or critic to judge. I do know, however, that since I was a child all I have ever wanted was to be good and to do good. I should have been a social worker.

Notes such as these can sometimes become a playwright's first and last line of defence or explanation: "This is what my plays really mean!" My only explanation and defence lie between the first and last curtain.

Finally, the only three quotations I have ever managed to learn off by heart: "Any victim demands allegiance" (Graham Greene, *The Heart of the Matter*). "All my humor is based on destruction and despair. If the whole world was tranquil, without disease and violence, I'd be standing on the bread-line, right behind J. Edgar Hoover" (Lenny Bruce). "Too much talking stinks up the room" (Duke Ellington).

* * *

Although he had been writing for the theatre since the mid-1970's, it was his television series *Boys from the Blackstuff* that brought Alan Bleasdale wide recognition. In five success-ive episodes he traced, with mordant irony, the despair and madness of a group of unemployed Liverpool men and their families. The central battle is between the individual and the state. The unemployed struggle to supplement their dole money with casual earnings on building sites and in dock-yards; the Department of Employment, the social services, and the police combine to corral their clients within the government regulations. Farce turns into tragedy which re-verts to farce. While cars skid, crash, and overturn on Malloy's illegal building site at the end of the first episode, Snowy Malone, the plasterer who takes pride in his skills, falls to his death trying to escape the dole officials. Elsewhere Chrissie Todd shoots his rabbits for food, Yosser Hughes is rescued from drowning by the police he's assaulted, and the sanctimonious priest at George Malone's funeral finishes up vomiting his whiskey down a grid after the reception. Bleasdale has no more sentimental regard for his characters than they have for each other. The children are as uncom-promising as the parents. The scene where Yosser's daughter Ann Marie butts the social worker Veronica is as comic as it is shocking.

Snowy's death is echoed by that of his father in the last episode. George Malone is respected throughout the commu-nity as a socialist and a battler for citizens' rights, but the structure of Bleasdale's series questions radically whether the Malones' ideology of class solidarity is still relevant to 1980's Britain. The Malones have some analysis of why mass unem-ployment has returned. Chrissie, Yosser, Dixie, and the rest have only their native wits which, unsupported by any com-munity or educational training, can flip over into hallucina-tion. Yosser Hughes is a monomaniac, and his white face, staring red-rimmed eyes, and monotonous cry of "Gizza job" and "I can do that" immediately became the nation's most dramatic vision of unemployed misery. Chrissie's wife Angie sees clearly that jokes are not enough: "if you don't laugh, you'll cry—I've heard it for years—this stupid soddin' city's full of it," but when she screams at her husband to fight back she has no more idea than he about how it can be done.

Bleasdale's view of the professional classes is equally acer-bic. *Having a Ball*, a stage play of 1981, counterpoints the reactions of three men, Lenny, Ritchie, and Malcolm, waiting in hospital for vasectomies. They are all middle class and they are all terrified. With a woman surgeon and Malcolm's wife Doreen contemptuous of his Territorial Army "bravery," the play exposes not woman, but man, as victim. And with three simultaneous areas for stage action, the Waiting Room, the Preparation Room, and the Operating Theatre, Bleasdale exploits all the possibilities for farcial encounters and conceal-ments. But there is no harmonious resolution. The play ends with Lenny, like Yosser, screaming in despair. Through wit, mockery, and a kind of trickster role-playing, he has exposed his own and everyone else's pretensions to control and confi-dence. "Most of us are cowards most of the time," he remarks. "Until we have no choice. And all the choices seem to be going." This is Bleasdale's savage double bind which Chrissie expresses in *Boys from the Blackstuff* as "It's a way of life. The only trouble is, it's no way to live."

With *Are You Lonesome Tonight?*, Bleasdale moves away, to his cost, from his familiar territory of the North West of England. Elvis Presley, in his last hours at Graceland, has the successes and betrayals of life portrayed to him upstage. He drools over his mother, curses Colonel Parker, and comes over as a good ol' southern boy of musical genius who was led astray by unscrupulous agents. Other accounts of Elvis's last years depict a drug-ridden, gun-obsessed monster, but Bleasdale was determined that this should be a tribute to what he called the "working class hero" of his youth. It was a West End hit, but it remains unique among Bleasdale's plays for its sentimentality and uncritical adulation. The London production was memorable, not for the writing, but for the electrifyingly accurate rendition of Elvis's great early hits by Simon Bowman.

In 1986 Bleasdale returned to his strengths, anti-heroism and farce, with a 4-part television series *The Monocled Mutineer*, and a film *No Surrender*. The tricky career of Percy Toplis, a World War I conscript, is the subject of the series. He leads an uprising of conscripted men against their atro-cious conditions in the Etaples training camp in 1917. But he also impersonates officers and thoroughly enjoys their life of gambling, drinking, and whoring. Percy Toplis is neither demogogue nor ideologue. On several occasions he refuses to be called either a hero or a socialist. He is a working-class rebel who refuses all the clichés of such a figure. And he doesn't "lead" the Etaples uprising in any conventional way. Rather he finds himself in a situation where he can inflict the maximum of mayhem on a class which he both hates and simulates. "Don't get angry," he advises; "get even." Toplis is no Scarlet Pimpernel of the workers. After the war he is a poor man still hunted for his role at Etaples. He thinks he can live off a rich widow, but finds she's as big a poser as he is. Naturally he falls in love with her. When he rejoins the army it's not just to get rich by black-marketing army supplies. He admits he doesn't seem able to function outside that structure of command. Its rigidity creates his flexibility. He's not therefore the roving outsider of the romantic tradition. To be that you have to have the money and class Toplis hasn't got and never will have. The agents of the state finally eliminate this cultural hybrid on a deserted Cumbrian road, but his girlfriend's pregnancy indicates that he may be reborn. What Bleasdale has intuited is that Toplis's combination of cynicism, courage, and style is the true basis for oppositional politics in 1980's Britain. The man who invents himself from the debris all around him is the man who anticipates the new patterns of life.

No Surrender begins, continues, and ends in debris. A new manager comes to take over a decrepit nightclub in Liverpool and finds it has been double-booked by two parties of Old Age Pensioners, one Catholic and the other Protestant. Infiltrated into this gathering is a Loyalist gunman on the run. Insults escalate from the verbal to the physical, the geriatrics take strength from the fires of religious fanaticism, and the film finishes in a mayhem of fists, bottles, the police, and the Fancy Dress competition.

G.B.H. is not only about physical violence, although throughout this 10-hour, seven-episode series for Channel 4 Bleasdale certainly features back-street beatings and picket-line intimidation. The last episode culminates in the firing of the town hall of a Northern city by a mob of angry black citizens incited to revolt by a group of MI5 agents posing as Trotskyite *provocateurs*. The central incident in the life of Michael Murray, Bleasdale's rabid Labour council leader, is an unwarranted beating he received from his primary school headmaster. The narrative proposes that this has bred in him a detestation of authority which has been the driving force behind his own authoritarian assumption of power in local politics. He is unable to cope with a humane, liberal headmaster like Jim Nelson, who keeps his school open during a strike manoeuvered by Murray, and plays the good angel to Murray's devil throughout this political morality play. *G.B.H.*'s real interest, however, occurs when the personal and political collide without resolution. At these murky crossroads all is deceit and doubling. Murray's real Nemesis is one Eileen Critchley, rich when he was poor, at the same school as Murray, and a sado-masochist even as a child. She wants him to strangle her. Her refrain is "You want to please me, don't you Michael?" But he cannot do her the violence she desires. Eileen, it emerges late in the series, committed suicide at Oxford in her twenties. But in a scene with her younger sister Barbara which repeats many times she hisses "Get Michael, he's easy," and Barbara, an upper-class blonde of cool sexuality, and a member of MI5, pursues, seduces, and confuses Murray at the height of his power. *The* theme of our times, the absent father, is dramatised several times over in the criss-crossing stories of sex and politics that make up the series.

Jim Nelson also has a pathology. He is a hypochondriac with an irrational fear of bridges and a tendency to sleepwalk naked. He and his family represent the compassionate, middle-class socialism that Bleasdale clearly prefers to the conspiratorial fanaticism of Murray and his heavies. But Nelson's delusions remain farcical rather than psychological. His family is supportive, his sex-life is pure, and his morality impeccable. He is therefore dull (and woodenly acted by Michael Palin) and only interesting when he is the occasion for such scenes of hilariously black comedy as his nth interview with his doctor, or his conversation in the storm with Grosvenor, a country gentleman with a bilious contempt for the guests at his holiday retreat, particularly if they are from the North.

G.B.H. is a many-layered narrative, full of the most abrupt cutting between farce and tragedy, childhood and adulthood, the personal and the political. It does not always succeed, but its ambition far outruns any recent television scripts and its reading of the nature of obsession among public figures is very sophisticated.

—Tony Dunn

BLESSING, Lee (Knowlton). American. Born in Minneapolis, Minnesota, 4 October 1949. Educated at schools in Minnetonka, Minnesota; University of Minnesota, Minneapolis, 1967–69; Reed College, Portland, Oregon, 1969–71, B.A. in English 1971; University of Iowa, Iowa City, 1974–79, M.F.A. in English 1976, M.F.A. in speech/theater 1979. Married Jeanne Blake in 1986; two stepchildren. Teacher of playwriting, University of Iowa, 1977–79, and Playwrights' Center, Minneapolis, 1986–88. Recipient: American College Theater Festival award, 1979; Jerome Foundation grant, 1981, 1982; McKnight Foundation grant, 1983, 1989; Great American Play award, 1984; National Endowment for the Arts grant, 1985, 1988; Bush Foundation fellowship, 1987; American Theater Critics Association award, 1987; Marton award, 1988; Dramalogue award, 1988; Guggenheim fellowship, 1989. Agent: Lois Berman, Little Theatre Building, 240 West 44th Street, New York, New York 10036; or, Jeffrey Melnick, Harry Gold Agency, 3500 West Olive, Suite 1400, Burbank, California 91505. Address: 2817 West 40th Street, Minneapolis, Minnesota 55410, U.S.A.

PUBLICATIONS

Plays

The Authentic Life of Billy the Kid (produced Washington, D.C., 1979). New York, French, 1980.
Oldtimers Game (produced Louisville, Kentucky, 1982). New York, Dramatists Play Service, 1988.
Nice People Dancing to Good Country Music (produced Louisville, Kentucky, 1982; revised version produced St. Paul, Minnesota, 1984). New York, Dramatists Play Service, 1983; revised version included in *Four Plays*, 1990.
Independence (produced Louisville, Kentucky, 1984). New York, Dramatists Play Service, 1985; included in *Four Plays*, 1990.
Riches (as *War of the Roses*, produced Louisville, Kentucky, 1985). New York, Dramatists Play Service, 1986; included in *Four Plays*, 1990.
Eleemosynary (produced St. Paul, Minnesota, 1985; New York, 1989). New York, Dramatists Play Service, 1987; included in *Four Plays*, 1990.

A Walk in the Woods (produced La Jolla, California, 1987; New York and London, 1988). New York, New American Library, 1988.

Two Rooms (produced La Jolla, California, 1988). New York, Dramatists Play Service, 1990.

Cobb (produced New Haven, Connecticut, 1989). New York, Dramatists Play Service, 1991.

Down the Road (produced La Jolla, California, 1989).

Four Plays (includes *Eleemosynary*, *Riches*, *Independence*, *Nice People Dancing to Good Country Music*). Oxford, Heinemann Educational Books, 1990.

Lake Street Extension (produced New York, 1992).

Television Play: *Cooperstown*, 1993.

*   *   *

A cast of characters including a foul-mouthed nun who recites the back of cereal boxes instead of prayers, an eccentric grandmother who believes she can fly using homemade wings, an American photographer who is taken hostage in Beirut, and a Russian diplomat who prefers talking about Willie Nelson instead of nuclear arms control, reflects Lee Blessing's penchant for writing about the illogical state of the human condition. Themes embrace both public and private politics, centering around the battle to establish, nurture, and maintain human relationships. Style and subject-matter are eclectic, though Blessing's plays have certain features in common. His plays are usually short with small casts and sketchy plots.

The most interesting of his early works is *Nice People Dancing to Good Country Music*. A comedy set on a deck above a Houston Bar, it pairs together two unlikely women in order to explore the notions of discovery and acceptance. A would-be nun, Catherine, who is asked to leave the convent due to inappropriate behavior, comes to stay with her raucous aunt, who manages the bar. Catherine gets a secular education from her aunt, and from a customer of the bar, who advises her not "to remarry the world, just to date it a little." Understatement and double entendre help establish the environment necessary for the odd but realistic characters. There are a few instances in which the language is too clever and not in line with the character's personal voice. However, it is Blessing's creative use of language that distinguishes much of his work.

Eleemosynary is also a one-act play with eccentric female characters, but here Blessing uses language both as a dramatic device and as an ongoing theme. Three generations of the Westbrook women tell their stories through recollections of their shared histories, each trying to find independence but each wanting the security that dependence provides. The grandmother warns her daughter about having a child: "You'll just be something a child needs" while the daughter reveals her thoughts about her mother: "I spent my free time being delighted not to be around my mother, and wondering how she was." The granddaughter, who uses a spelling bee to bring them all together, wins the bee with the word "eleemosynary" only to realize that words neither guarantee communication nor establish relationships. In fact, the characters use words to avoid communication. Most effective is Blessing's ability to use words both to engage and to disengage the characters' emotions and their relationships with each other.

Plot is subordinate to theme in *Eleemosynary*, but structure is less traditional than Blessing's other work, with the exception of *Two Rooms*, a poignant dramatization of the imprisonment of an American hostage in Beirut and the effect it has on his wife. Blessing uses symbolism to advantage, using light and darkness to represent certain issues and maintaining a comparison of the wife's situation with that of an African hornbill bird. Hers is a desperate attempt to maintain hope while her husband's situation is exploited by the media and ignored by the government: "After they mate, the male walls the female up, in the hollow of a tree. He literally imprisons her. . . . After the eggs are hatched, he breaks down the wall again, and the whole family is united. . . . It hasn't been a prison at all. It's been . . . a fortress."

Blessing's concern about relationships is played out differently in *Independence* and *Riches*. Like *Eleemosynary*, *Independence* explores female relationships in a family void of men. The burden of maintaining familial relationships is borne by three daughters and their mentally unstable mother. However, the mother is often remarkably lucid though blatantly sardonic: "That's what family means—each generation destroying itself willingly, for what comes after." The linguistic rhythm is not as strong as it is in *Eleemosynary* and *Two Rooms*, but the plot is more cohesive. Blessing often writes about the rituals that define and reflect individuality. In *Independence* the oldest daughter forces the family to partake in a "tea time" ritual hoping that the experience will change their behavior. A funny scene, the exercise fails to effect change.

In *Riches* the husband's ritual of blowing his nose, "a big blow, then three little ones," prompts the wife's realization that she no longer wishes to be married. The play attempts to explore the notion that love is not enough to sustain a relationship. Unfortunately the first act moves slowly, in contrast with a physically violent second act. There are some interesting observations regarding human behavior: how people come to logical conclusions in rather illogical ways and some creative contrasting images. Still, the play lacks substantive dramatic action. *Riches* is similar in treatment to *Down the Road*, about a husband and wife writing team who conduct a series of interviews with a serial killer. And, like the husband and wife of *Riches*, in the end they suffer a failed marriage, theirs due to the unsuccessful results of their dealings with the murderer. The play seems truncated, but the issue of journalistic ethics serves as a unifying factor and makes the play dramatically more viable than *Riches*.

A Walk in the Woods is Blessing's most commercially successful play and has appeared on Broadway. It is based on an actual walk in the woods by Russian and American diplomats Yuli A. Kvitsinsky and Paul H. Nitze. However, the play is about personal politics and deals more with the process of how two superpowers negotiate, rather than the outcome. The plot is negligible, subordinate to the theme of American idealism versus Russian pragmatism underlying mundane conversations on topics ranging from Italian shoes to the lyrics of country music. The play's structure is cyclical, which is problematic and results in an unsatisfying ending because in the end nothing has changed; no agreement has been reached; no revelations are made. It is similar in style to an earlier and lesser play, *Oldtimers Game* in that both are vehicles for social and political issues but neither play explores these issues in any depth.

Blessing's work reflects an interest in characters whose past interferes with their future. Cyclical structures coupled with non-traditional plots create a unique style in which character and language are pivotal dramatic elements, and unique observations about relationships create impassioned moments on stage.

—Judy Lee Oliva

BOGOSIAN, Eric. American. Born in Boston, Massachusetts, 24 April 1953. Educated at Woburn High School and Woburn Drama Guild, Massachusetts, 1971–73; University of Chicago, 1973–74; Oberlin College, Ohio, 1975–76, B.A. in theater 1976. Director, The Kitchen, New York, 1977–81. Recipient: National Endowment for the Arts and New York State Arts Council grants; Drama Desk award, 1986; Obie award, 1986, 1990; Berlin Film Festival Silver Bear, 1988. Agent: George Lane, William Morris Agency, 1350 Avenue of the Americas, New York, New York 10019, U.S.A.

PUBLICATIONS

Plays

Men Inside (produced New York, 1981; revised version produced New York, 1982).
Voices of America (produced Groningen, The Netherlands, and New York, 1982).
Funhouse (produced New York, 1983).
Talk Radio (produced Portland, 1985; revised version produced New York, 1987). New York, Vintage, 1988; London, Faber, 1989.
Drinking in America (produced Boston, New York, and London, 1986). New York, Vintage, 1987; London, Faber, 1988.
Sex, Drugs, Rock & Roll (produced New York, 1988). New York, Harper, 1991.
An American Chorus (produced New York, 1989).
Dog Show (produced New York, 1992).
Notes from Underground (produced New York, 1992).

Screenplay: *Talk Radio*, 1988.

*

Theatrical Activities:
Actor: **Plays**—all his own plays.

*   *   *

Eric Bogosian's brand of performance is strongly influenced by rock concerts, Pop art, video-art, happenings, mixed media, and the blending of "high" and "low" art. Influenced by performance artists such as Cindy Sherman, Spalding Gray, Laurie Anderson, and Robert Longo, Bogosian grew impatient with traditional theater and experimented in the 1970's with alternative forms. He developed his one-man show, dazzling and offending his audience with his rogue's gallery of American males. The black stud, the spaced-out hippy, the virulently anti-semitic caller on a radio talk show, the rock star, the gang-bangers, the punks, and the homeless, all were played by this gifted theater artist in his black trousers, white oxford button-down collar shirt or T-shirt, and black ref shoes. At first his act was built around his imaginary entertainer/comedian, Ricky Paul, who ranted and gloated about the deplorable condition of the modern world. The set was generally sparse—a chair, a table, a microphone, and stand. Later, he eliminated Ricky Paul and simply played his medley of unlikely, zany, often nasty, but unforgettable characters. The monologists usually offer a warped, often angry, quasi-autobiographical account of their dispossessed selves.

Bogosian creates characters who challenge his vocal range, permitting him to play with the different accents and idioms of urban black English, a Texas drawl, burly ethnic American, or Hispanic speech. At its best, the dialogue reflects the finely observed language of the hustler, druggy weirdo, Archie Bunker racist, or rock groupie. Lacing together a stream of monologues and appropriated media images, he created his satiric or parodic assemblages, *Funhouse*, *Men Inside*, *Drinking in America*, *Talk Radio*, *Sex, Drugs, Rock & Roll*, and *An American Chorus*. A successful stand-up comic in Lower Manhattan's late-night clubs and also trained in dance, Bogosian energizes his monologues, propelling them with the power of the rock star—a characteristic of such consummate stage actors as Anthony Sher—and feeding off his audience's desire to be offended while entertained.

Bogosian began offering his monologues in New York performance art spaces such as Performance Space 122, The Kitchen, the Snafu Club, and Franklin Furnace. RoseLee Goldberg describes him as one of the founders of "artists' cabaret," a new genre spawned in New York discos. Beginning as a solo performer, Bogosian drew on Lenny Bruce, the New York deejay Alan Freed, the underground performer Brother Theodore, Bob Dylan, Jimi Hendrix, and Laurie Anderson for his inspiration. By 1982, his work crossed over from the vanguard into the mass cultural status, twice winning awards for best play, becoming the subject of films and cable specials, and appearing in book form. It is currently rumored that he is finished with monologues featuring himself and plans to write plays for others to act in.

Influenced by our media age and what is known as the hyperreal, Bogosian's works are best understood against the backdrop of the writings of Roland Barthes and Jean Baudrillard. Barthes's dissection of mass culture and its mythologies influence Bogosian's exploration of a cross-section of American cultural stereotypes. Baudrillard's analysis of the codes, structures, and practices of our consumer society are also helpful in situating Bogosian's themes. Bogosian's perspective on his material and his cultural critique address many of the same phenomena that are searchingly analyzed by Barthes and Baudrillard.

Bogosian's works are full of advertising slogans—for Kronenbrau beer, Nyquil, and Remington cigarettes—and numerous references to McDonalds, BMWs, Volvos, Peruvian cocaine, 'ludes, Jimi Hendrix, Janis Joplin, Cassius Clay, and other idols of American pop culture. His preoccupation with the media's ability to level all images and numb the mind informs his choice of the clichés and banalities uttered by his monologists.

Baudrillard defined the hyperreal as a condition in which simulations come to constitute reality itself. Drawing upon Marshall McLuhan's concept of implosion and his famous slogan that "the medium is the message," Baudrillard argues that the boundary between image or simulation and reality implodes in the postmodern world: people cannot differentiate between the real and its simulations. He finds ammunition to support this contention—one he has later modified—by citing the simulations of politics created by Reagan where the public elects the image not the man, the simulations of religions foisted on us by television evangelists, and the simulations of rape or homelessness or trials produced by television shows.

Bogosian's monologists can be read as simulations. Some of his callers on his talk show sentimentally echo the banal lyrics of Diana Ross to "reach out and touch" or Bruce Springsteen's "Arms Across America" AIDS concerts as though they form the basis of their moral beliefs. In *Sex, Drugs, Rock & Roll*, he ridicules the rock lyrics that revolutionized an era: "Freedom's just another word for nothing left to lose," or "Wanna die before I get old." Bogosian finds America's love affair with the confessional mode deeply disturbing, particularly as it is served by television, radio, and rock. With a humor that is often corrosive and with caustic wit, he offers his critique of American postmodern culture.

Barry Champlain, the radio host in *Talk Radio*, exploits the simulation. When a drugged caller pleads for help, saying that he cannot get his strung-out girlfriend to wake up, Champlain knows the call is a hoax. When he invites the caller onto the talk show, he is willing to take the risk that perhaps the caller might really do what the killer of real-life Alan Berg did, namely kill him. Alan Berg was an ex-Chicago talk show host famous for his insulting and abusive manner. In 1984 he was machine-gunned to death in the driveway of his home in Denver, Colorado by members of a Neo-Nazi hate group angered by his radio persona. Bogosian intensifies the play's taut atmosphere by staging a moment when the caller in the studio reaches into his pocket, drawing out a flash camera, not a gun, which he shoots. The moment is exactly of the kind that disturbs. Its hyperreality almost washes out the ground of reality. At one level, it is possible that the crazy caller will kill the talk show host. Such events happen in life. But are they merely imitations of what has been staged on television or marketed on talk shows? Bogosian's play raises this troubling thought at the same time as it saturates the audience in the hyperreal. The portrait of the hyper-active, egocentric, abusive talk-show host, mercurial in his mood and full of self-loathing, shows us a man just at the edge of a breakdown as every bit as disturbing as some of the pathetic or chilling life stories confessed to him by his callers. Still more frightening is the way the play mirrors its audience, making it question its own insatiable appetite for sex, violence, trouble, and confession.

In the film version of *Talk Radio* Oliver Stone changed the ending of Bogosian's stage version. The film's penultimate scene involves the shooting and death of Barry Champlain while the final images show us a postmodern mediascape in which the boundaries between information and entertainment, politics and image, implode. Callers are talking about Barry's death; they incorporate it into media patter. It has the same unreal feel about it that developed surrounding the television coverage of the Gulf War when the images that played nightly on CNN threatened to replace the reality. Bogosian's stage play is even more effective. There is no dead talk-show host; rather there is a world of sound, of talk, of narratives, most contrived, seemingly filled with beliefs for which there is no real referent. In this respect his stage play achieves some of the more nihilistic effects of Baudrillard's deeply pessimistic thinking of the 1970's.

In *Drinking in America* and *Sex, Drugs, Rock & Roll* Bogosian refines his skill at portraiture, using largely the same male types and media images and clichés, but focusing the image more sharply. Describing a schizoid America that wants to "live in piggish splendor and be ecologically responsible . . . wants to have the highest principles but win the popularity contest," Bogosian confesses to wanting both to be a big baby and a responsible citizen. In *Sex, Drugs, Rock & Roll* he says he has created 12 monologues that "take the nasty side of myself and put them out there for everyone to see." The play opens with a there-but-for-the-Grace-of-God-go-I beggar panhandling the audience. The down-and-out ex-convict shamelessly pleads with the audience to do something, give their money to him, not to the blacks in South Africa ten thousand miles away. His repeated "thank you" and "bless you" segue into the next piece, a hypocritical autobiographical promotional spiel of a British rock 'n' roll star and ex-druggie telling his imaginary talk show host how

the youth of the day should avoid his mistakes and "just say No." The other monologues include a grubby derelict cursing at the gutter; a stud bragging about the size of his penis; the host of a stag party revelling in the evening of women, porn, and drugs; Candy, talking dirty to her phone-sex caller; a wheeler-dealer; a paranoic, self-hating misogynist; and other equally obnoxious yet wholly believable types.

Bogosian is skilled both as an actor and writer. His dramatic monologues are raucous, often abrasive, rich in their specificity of character, and often capable of making their audience thoroughly uncomfortable. His characters are too recognizable. Their faults, pushed to excess and rendered without judgment, remind the audience of its own complicity in this culture of commodification and the hyperreal.

—Carol Simpson Stern

BOLAND, Bridget. British. 1913–1988.
See 4th edition, 1988.

BOLT, Carol (née Johnson). Canadian. Born in Winnipeg, Manitoba, 25 August 1941. Educated at the University of British Columbia, Vancouver, 1957–61, B.A. 1961. Married David Bolt in 1969; one son. Researcher, Dominion Board of Statistics, London School of Economics, Market Facts of Canada, and Seccombe House, 1961–72; dramaturge, 1972–73, and chair of the Management Committee, 1973–74, Playwrights Co-op, Toronto; dramaturge, Toronto Free Theatre, 1973; writer-in-residence, University of Toronto, 1977–78. Recipient: Canada Council grant, 1967, 1972; Ontario Arts Council grant, 1972, 1973, 1974, 1975. Agent: Great North Artists, 345 Adelaide Street West, Toronto, Ontario M5V 1R5. Address: 76 Herbert Avenue, Toronto, Ontario, Canada.

PUBLICATIONS

Plays

I Wish (as Carol Johnson) (produced Toronto, 1966). Published in *Upstage and Down*, edited by D.P. McGarity, Toronto, Macmillan, 1968.
Daganawida (produced Toronto, 1970).
Buffalo Jump (as *Next Year Country*, produced Regina, Saskatchewan, 1971; as *Buffalo Jump*, produced Toronto, 1972). Toronto, Playwrights, 1972.
My Best Friend Is Twelve Feet High (for children), music by Jane Vasey (produced Toronto, 1972). With *Tangleflags*, Toronto, Playwrights, 1972.
Cyclone Jack (for children; produced Toronto, 1972). Toronto, Playwrights, 1972.
Gabe (produced Alcoma, Ontario, 1972). Toronto, Playwrights, 1973.
Tangleflags (for children; produced Toronto, 1973; St. Louis,

1977). With *My Best Friend Is Twelve Feet High*, Toronto, Playwrights, 1972; published separately, 1974.
The Bluebird, adaptation of a story by Marie d'Aulnoy (produced Toronto, 1973).
Pauline (produced Toronto, 1973).
Maurice (for children; produced Toronto, 1973). Toronto, Playwrights, 1975.
Red Emma, Queen of the Anarchists (produced Toronto, 1974). Toronto, Playwrights, 1974.
Shelter (produced Toronto, 1974). Toronto, Playwrights, 1975.
Finding Bumble (for children; produced Toronto, 1975).
Norman Bethune: On Board the S.S. Empress of Asia (produced Gravenhurst, Ontario, 1976).
Okey Doke (produced Kingston, Ontario, 1976).
Buffalo Jump, Gabe, Red Emma. Toronto, Playwrights, 1976.
One Night Stand (produced Toronto, 1977). Toronto, Playwrights, 1977.
Desperadoes (produced Toronto, 1977).
TV Lounge (produced Toronto, 1977).
Star Quality (produced Louisville, 1980). Excerpt published in *Acta Victoriana* (Toronto), vol. 102, no. 2, 1978.
Deadline (produced Toronto, 1979).
Escape Entertainment (produced Toronto, 1981). Toronto, Playwrights, 1982.
Love or Money (produced Blyth, Ontario, 1981).

Radio Play: *Fast Forward*, 1976.

Television Plays: *A Nice Girl Like You* (*Collaborators* series), 1974; *Distance*, 1974; *Talk Him Down*, 1975.

*

Carol Bolt comments:

(1977) I've had a lot of opportunity to work in the theatre in the last four years, with twelve new plays commissioned. Much of this work has been inspired by the theatrical community, particularly work being done at the Toronto Free Theatre and the Théâtre Passe Muraille.

The plays often deal with "political" subjects, the characters often want to change the world, but I think my preoccupation is with the adventure, rather than the polemic, of politics. I think a play like *Red Emma* is about as political as *The Prisoner of Zenda*.

I'm interested in working in new forms of musical comedy and epic romance and in creating (or recreating) characters who are larger than life or mythic.

I'm also interested in exploring, recording, recreating, and defining Canadian concerns, characters, histories, cultures, identities. I want to create plays for this country, whether the plays are about the lost moments in Canada's past (like *Buffalo Jump*), whether they offer another view of an American mythic figure (like *Red Emma*), or whether they play at creating Canadian archetypes (*Shelter*).

I don't think this kind of cultural nationalism is parochial. I think our differences are our strengths, not our weaknesses, nationally and internationally, so I think the argument that if a Canadian play is any good the Americans or British will be happy to tell us via Broadway or the West End is specious and muddle-headed. I don't think Canadians will say anything of interest to the world until we know who Canadians are.

* * *

Through her prolific contribution to Canadian theatre Carol Bolt has shaped a unique form of social documentary using factual reference material to gain access to an imaginative Canadian mythology. Her best early plays are cohesive, rich in entertainment and dramatic values, politically inspired but romantically motivated, and imbued with a keen, sometimes riotous sense of social injustice.

Central to *Buffalo Jump*, *Gabe*, and *Red Emma* is an interest in combining theatrical styles and methods: a fluid interchange of locations loosely defined by props and emotional intensities, quick episodic scene changes, direct audience address, and the use of song to develop action or as a divertissement. This willing exhibition of the theatrical process can also be found in Bolt's approach to children's plays.

Both her adult and children's plays have a common free-form fluctuation of time, place, and space, enhanced by a strong entertainment factor which smooths abrupt or unlikely transitions with song, special lighting changes, or the emphasis of a significant prop—the train in *Buffalo Jump* or the banner of anarchy in *Red Emma*. This montage format partly results from rewriting plays in a creative collaboration with the directors and actors during the rehearsal period. *Buffalo Jump* (which originated as a revue called *Next Year Country*) and the young people's plays *Cyclone Jack* and *My Best Friend Is Twelve Feet High* were formed completely in rehearsal.

These ongoing transformations of original material also sift fiction, or rather an imaginative interpretation, into factual details aiming at a conscious redefinition of the time-blurred outlines of historical figures. Bolt has stated she would rather be interesting than accurate and rather be one-sided than give a well-rounded viewpoint honed to dullness.

The central character in *Buffalo Jump*, for example, a play about the disastrous on-to-Ottawa trek of unemployed Vancouver men during the Great Depression, combines two Canadian heroes, "Red" Walsh and "Slim" Evans, united for dramatic purposes into the single character Red Evans. A character develops not necessarily from what *is* true but from what *might* be true as the playwright understands it. The creation of myth and the reshaping of myth is more important to Bolt than the documentation of history. As she has said, "Myth is more appealing than fact. It postulates that heroism is possible, that people can be noble and effective and change things . . . what we were doing in *Buffalo Jump* was making those characters tragic heroes. It was the same with the great Native Indian runner Tom Longboat, the central character of *Cyclone Jack* and others."

Buffalo Jump, a political and social indictment of Canadian society of the 1930's, manages to be a less serious work than either *Gabe* or *Red Emma*. The play borrows from the mythology of the old west for its central metaphor, equating the workers protest march to Ottawa with a herd of buffalo about to be stampeded off a cliff. With its explicit breakdown between villains and heroes, the play might have become a modern melodrama were it not for its cut-up, cartoon style.

Gabe, based on the story of Louis Riel, the doomed Métis Indian leader of the Riel Rebellion, and his comrade in arms, Gabriel Dumont, is a constant interplay between memory images and the reality of the lives of the two modern namesakes who are the main characters of the play. The original Riel and Dumont have been refined by time into spiritual heroes who provide a constant source of romantic inspiration. Says the modern-day Louis of his historic counterpart: "Louis Riel! Was the maddest, smartest, bravest Métis bastard ever wrote his own treaty. Ever fought for the rights of his people. For their land. Fought for representation. For his people and their children." In spite of courageous poses, the figures from the past did not achieve their political ideals or their romantic

London, 1987; *Macbeth*, London, 1987; *El Sid*, London, 1988; *Poppy* by Peter Nichols, London, 1988; *Nativity* by Nigel Williams, London, 1989.

* * *

Chris Bond is one of several British dramatists who grew up under the spell of Joan Littlewood's Theatre Workshop in Stratford, East London. In his case, however, a primary attraction to the theatre began almost from his cradle. His parents had run a touring company after World War II, and Bond himself was a child actor, playing at the Shakespeare Memorial Theatre, Stratford-on-Avon, from the age of 11. He grew to love the rough-and-tumble of acting life, the performing skills and the ability to contact audiences at all levels of appreciation; and in his plays he loves to throw in effects which grab the attention—songs, dances, pieces of mime, and simple stage tricks, such as the enlarged washing machine in *Under New Management* which "Harold MacMillan" mistakes for a Mini car and thus gets spun around with the rest of the laundry.

But the direction of his work, its more serious side, derives from Littlewood. Bond has written social and historical documentaries, such as *Under New Management* and *Judge Jeffreys*, and he seeks his audiences primarily from the young, working-class, left-wing public. Although not an overtly political writer, there is a strong vein of socialist thought within his work, which sometimes emerges into didactic messages but more usually is reflected in the handling of his themes—the caricatures of establishment authority, the sympathies with the underprivileged and downtrodden.

The clearest and most striking example of this tendency is *Downright Hooligan*, first produced at the Victoria Theatre, Stoke-on-Trent, where Bond was resident dramatist. The central character, Ian Rigby, is a sort of contemporary Wozzeck, whose eyes, deep-set beneath a granite forehead, suggest a Neanderthal mentality. Permanently out of work, a fixture in the betting shop, Ian is surrounded by a society whose logical illogicalities he cannot comprehend. His mother bawls at him for masturbating in his bedroom, while her lover winks at him and tells him dirty jokes. He accidentally kills the school hamster and sticks drawing pins in its eyes to decorate the body. His headmaster is appalled by the atrocity—but he doesn't know that Ian has just paid his last respects to his grandmother, whose dead drawn face has been padded out with clutches of her own hair. One form of decorating the dead is socially acceptable—Ian's treatment of the hamster is not. Confronted by the unpredictability of society, Ian asserts himself by hitting out savagely at an elderly man and is brought before the courts as a downright hooligan.

Thus, Bond, without glamorising his hero-victim, places the blame for his behaviour upon society at large; and some critics have claimed that his impression of the repressive social forces is simplistic, belonging too much to a "them" and "us" mentality. While his portrait of Ian Rigby's background is telling and convincing, and was presented with marvellous detail by the Stoke company, *Under New Management* is almost a cartoon, agit-prop documentary, showing 12 cretinous general managers—one dressed as a schoolboy clutching a teddy bear—messing up the Fisher-Bendix factory on the outskirts of Liverpool, until the heroic workers, faced by mass redundancy, take over. It was a thoroughly lively, enjoyable production, but inevitably one-sided, partly because Bond had deliberately not interviewed anyone from the management while conducting his research.

By trying to make his plays immediately entertaining, Bond

also falls into the trap which snared some of Littlewood's productions. There is too much outer fun, too little inner content. The scenes are short and sketch-like, sometimes extended by horseplay, separated by songs and little dances, and the connecting themes are either lost or so heavily stressed that they seem merely repetitive. In the hands of a highly disciplined company, such as that of Stoke or of the old Liverpool Everyman, where Bond became artistic director, this music-hall mixture could be pulled into a tight shape. His plays usually require the concentration supplied by a firm director and an experienced team.

While striving for a casual, easy-going and lighthearted approach to the theatre, Bond in fact usually demands great restraint and professionalism from his performers—an apparent contradiction which not all directors have realised. There was a luckless production of *Judge Jeffreys* at Stratford East, where the script seemed as banal as the performances; and *Tarzan's Last Stand*, about Enoch Powell the "ape man," seemed to miss its very broad, satirical target by not taking Powell's arguments sufficiently seriously. Bond (like a somewhat similar writer of social documentaries, Alan Plater) has yet to find perhaps that dramatic structure within which his talents and social insights can be best expressed.

—John Elsom

BOND, Edward. British. Born in London, 18 July 1934. Educated at Crouch End Secondary Modern School, 1944–49. Served in the British Army, 1953–55. Married Elisabeth Pablé in 1971. Member of the English Stage Company Writers Group, Royal Court Theatre, London, from 1958. Founding member, Theatre Writers' Group (now Theatre Writers' Union), 1975; Northern Arts literary fellow, universities of Newcastle upon Tyne and Durham, 1977–79; resident writer, University of Essex, Colchester, 1982; visiting professor, University of Palermo, Italy, 1983. Recipient: George Devine award, 1968; John Whiting award, 1968; Obie award, 1976. D. Litt.: Yale University, New Haven, Connecticut, 1977. Agent: Casarotto Ramsay Ltd., National House, 60–66 Wardour Street, London W1V 3HP, England.

PUBLICATIONS

Plays

The Pope's Wedding (produced London, 1962). Included in *The Pope's Wedding* (collection), 1971.
Saved (produced London, 1965; New Haven, Connecticut, 1968; New York, 1970). London, Methuen, and New York, Hill and Wang, 1966.
A Chaste Maid in Cheapside, adaptation of the play by Middleton (produced London, 1966).
Three Sisters, adaptation of a play by Chekhov (produced London, 1967).
Narrow Road to the Deep North (produced Coventry, 1968; London and Boston, 1969; New York, 1972). London, Methuen, and New York, Hill and Wang, 1968.
Early Morning (produced London, 1968; New York, 1970). London, Calder and Boyars, 1968; New York, Hill and Wang, 1969; revised version in *Plays 1*, 1977.

Sketch in *The Enoch Show* (produced London, 1969).

Black Mass, part of *Sharpeville Sequence: A Scene, A Story, and Three Poems* (produced London, 1970). Included in *The Pope's Wedding* (collection), 1971; in *The Best Short Plays 1972*, edited by Stanley Richards, Philadelphia, Chilton, 1972.

Passion (produced London, 1971; New Haven, Connecticut, 1972). Published in *New York Times*, 15 August 1971; with *Bingo*, London, Eyre Methuen, 1974.

Lear (produced London, 1971; New Haven, Connecticut, 1973). London, Methuen, and New York, Hill and Wang, 1972.

The Pope's Wedding (collection; includes *Sharpeville Sequence* and the stories "Mr. Dog" and "The King with Golden Eyes"). London, Methuen, 1971.

The Sea (produced London, 1973; Chicago, 1974; New York, 1975). London, Eyre Methuen, 1973; with *Bingo*, New York, Hill and Wang, 1975.

Bingo: Scenes of Money and Death (and Passion) (produced Exeter, Devon, 1973; London, 1974; Cleveland, 1975; New York, 1976). London, Eyre Methuen, 1974; with *The Sea*, New York, Hill and Wang, 1975.

Spring Awakening, adaptation of a play by Wedekind (produced London, 1974; New York, 1978). Chicago, Dramatic Publishing Company, 1979; London, Eyre Methuen, 1980.

The Fool: Scenes of Bread and Love (produced London, 1975; Washington, D.C., 1976). With *We Come to the River*, London, Eyre Methuen, 1976; published separately, Chicago, Dramatic Publishing Company, 1978.

We Come to the River: Actions for Music, music by Hans Werner Henze (produced London, 1976). With *The Fool*, London, Eyre Methuen, 1976.

The White Devil, adaptation of the play by Webster (produced London, 1976).

A-A-America: Grandma Faust, and The Swing (produced London, 1976). Included in *A-A-America, and Stone*, 1976.

Stone (produced London, 1976; New York, 1981). Included in *A-A-America, and Stone*, 1976; in *Performing Arts Journal* (New York), Fall 1977.

A-A-America, and Stone. London, Eyre Methuen, 1976; revised edition, 1981.

Plays (revised versions):
1. *Saved, Early Morning, The Pope's Wedding*. London, Eyre Methuen, 1977.
2. *Lear, The Sea, Narrow Road to the Deep North, Black Mass, Passion*. London, Eyre Methuen, 1978.
3. *Bingo, The Fool, The Woman*. London, Methuen, 1987.
4. *The Worlds, The Activists Papers, Restoration, Summer*. London, Methuen, 1992.

The Woman: Scenes of War and Freedom (also co-director: produced London, 1978; Baltimore, 1983). London, Eyre Methuen, 1979 (includes stories); New York, Hill and Wang, 1979.

The Bundle: Scenes of Right and Evil; or, New Narrow Road to the Deep North (produced London, 1978; New Haven, Connecticut, 1979). London, Eyre Methuen, 1978; Chicago, Dramatic Publishing Company, 1981.

The Worlds (also director: produced Newcastle upon Tyne and London, 1979). With *The Activists Papers*, London, Eyre Methuen, 1980.

Restoration: A Pastoral, music by Nick Bicât (also director: produced London, 1981). London, Eyre Methuen, 1981; Woodstock, Illinois, Dramatic Publishing Company, 1982; revised version, with *The Cat*, London, Methuen, 1982; revised version, published separately, 1988.

Summer: A European Play (also director: produced London, 1982; New York, 1983). London, Methuen, and Chicago, Dramatic Publishing Company, 1982.

Summer, with Fables, and Service: A Story. London, Methuen, 1982.

Derek (produced Stratford-on-Avon, 1982; London, 1984). With *Choruses from After the Assassinations*, London, Methuen, 1983.

The Cat (opera libretto), music by Hans Werner Henze, adaptation of a work by Balzac (as *Die englische Katze*, produced Schwetzingen, West Germany, 1983; as *The English Cat*, produced Santa Fe, 1985; New York, 1986; Edinburgh, 1987). With *Restoration*, London, Methuen, 1982; as *The English Cat: A Story for Singers and Instrumentalists*, Mainz and London, Schott, 1983.

Choruses from after the Assassinations (produced Colchester, Essex, 1983). With *Derek*, London, Methuen, 1983.

The War Plays: A Trilogy (includes *Red, Black and Ignorant*; *The Tin Can People*; *Great Peace*) (*Red, Black and Ignorant* produced London, 1984; *The Tin Can People* produced Birmingham, 1984; also director: trilogy produced London, 1985). London, Methuen, 2 vols., 1985; revised edition, 1991.

Human Cannon (produced Edinburgh, 1986), London, Methuen, 1985.

Burns (for children; produced Birmingham, 1986).

September (produced Canterbury, Kent, 1989). Included in *Two Post-Modern Plays*, 1989.

Jackets II (produced Leicester, 1989; London 1990). Included in *Two Post-Modern Plays*, 1989.

In the Company of Men (produced Avignon, 1992). Included in *Two Post-Modern Plays*, 1989.

Two Post-Modern Plays (includes Jackets *I* and *II*, *In the Company of Men*, *September*: "Notes on Post Modernism"). London, Methuen, 1989.

Screenplays: *Blow-up*, with Michelangelo Antonioni and Tonino Guerra, 1967; *Laughter in the Dark*, 1969; *Michael Kohlhaas*, with others, 1969; *The Lady of Monza* (English dialogue), 1970; *Walkabout*, 1971; *Nicholas and Alexandra*, with James Goldman, 1971; *Fury*, with Antonio Calenda and Ugo Pirro, 1973.

Ballet Scenario: *Orpheus*, music by Hans Werner Henze, Stuttgart and New York, 1979.

Verse

The Swing Poems. London, Inter-Action, 1976.
Theatre Poems and Songs, edited by Malcolm Hay and Philip Roberts. London, Eyre Methuen, 1978.
Poems 1978–1985. London, Methuen, 1987.

*

Critical Studies: *Edward Bond* by Simon Trussler, London, Longman, 1976; *The Plays of Edward Bond* by Richard Scharine, Lewisburg, Pennsylvania, Bucknell University Press, 1976; *The Plays of Edward Bond: A Study* by Tony Coult, London, Eyre Methuen, 1977, revised edition, 1979; *Edward Bond: A Companion to the Plays*, London, TQ Publications, 1978, and *Bond: A Study of His Plays*, London, Eyre Methuen, 1980, both by Malcolm Hay and Philip Roberts, and *Bond on File* edited by Roberts, London, Methuen, 1985; *Edward Bond: A Study of His Plays* by Delia Donahue, Rome, Bulzoni, 1979; *Edward Bond* by David L. Hirst, London, Macmillan, 1985, New York, Grove Press,

1986; *The Art and Politics of Edward Bond* by Lou Lappin, New York, Peter Lang, 1987.

Theatrical Activities:
Director: **Plays**—*Lear*, Vienna, 1973; *The Woman* (co-director, with Sebastian Graham-Jones), London, 1978; *The Worlds*, Newcastle upon Tyne and London, 1979; *Restoration*, London, 1981; *Summer*, London, 1982; *The War Plays*, London, 1985.
Actor: **Plays**—Aighard in *One Leg over the Wrong Wall* by Albert Bernel, London, 1960; Christ in *Black Mass*, London, 1970.

*   *   *

Edward Bond writes the most lapidary language of today's English theatre, absorbing dialects, pastiches, metaphors, and questions into a rich mineral vein. Pithy phrases, swift scenes, and vivid characters are his building-blocks for what he calls Rational Theatre, dedicated to the creation of a rational society. Far from agit-prop, however, his plays range through history and legend, as well as the contemporary scene.

The early plays of surface realism shock by their pointless murders: young Scopey throttles an old hermit at the end of *The Pope's Wedding*; a group of youths stone a baby to death in the middle of *Saved*; at the beginning of *The Sea* Colin drowns while Hatch watches idly from the shore. However, confrontation with these deaths involves radical action on the part of Bond's protagonists. Behind its provocative title *The Pope's Wedding* dramatizes a young man's vain effort fully to understand another human being. Step by step, Scopey abandons companions, wife, job, in order to spend his time with an old hermit to learn "What yoo 'ere for?" Even in the old man's coat, communing with his corpse, he never learns.

As the title *Saved* suggests, Len is more successful. A loner, Len does not share in the bored activities of London youths who gamble, steal, fornicate. They rub a baby's face in its diaper, then pitch stones into its carriage while Len, perhaps the baby's father, watches. The baby dies, and only later does Len admit: "Well, I should a stopped yer." Rejected by the baby's mother, flirting briefly with the grandmother, Len the loner is finally "saved" by the grandfather's barely articulate plea for him to remain in their household.

The Sea opens with Colin's drowning while his friend Willie pleads vainly for help from Evens, a drunken recluse, and Hatch, a paranoid coast-guard watchman. Later Willie barely escapes a murderous attack by Hatch, who believes him to be an enemy from outer space. Despite his grief at Colin's death, contrasted with the satirized indifference of the townspeople, Willie comes to see that "The dead don't matter." Cumulatively, through these apparently realistic plays "Life laughs at death."

For the most part, Bond resembles Brecht in analyzing contemporary social injustice through parables based on legend or history. Since both playwrights see war as the cruellest social injustice, Bond explores that violence in violent plays. *Narrow Road to the Deep North* takes place in 19th-century Japan. Basho, the protagonist, follows the narrow road to the deep north in order to study, but he learns that "enlightenment is where you are." And where he is necessitates a choice between two evils, an English invader or a homegrown warlord. As the play ends, Basho is Prime Minister, his disciple falls disembowelled, and a stranger emerges from the river. Each man must make his own decisions in a time of war, and life goes on.

Of all Bond's protagonists, his Lear experiences the har-

dest enlightenment. From Shakespeare Bond borrows the large tragic conception intensified by grotesque humor. By way of Shakespeare, Bond re-enforces his own dramatic concern with moral responsibility. As in Shakespeare, Lear is an absolute autocrat. Instead of dividing his kingdom, Bond's Lear encloses it within a wall built by forced labor. Lear's two daughters foment war, and both meet violent deaths. A composite of Kent and the Fool, Bond's Gravedigger's Boy has a wife named Cordelia. After the Boy is shot and his wife raped by the daughter's soldiers, his Ghost accompanies Lear on an infernal descent through madness and blindness. The Gravedigger's Boy's Ghost is slain, Lear attains wisdom, and Cordelia attains power as head of a new autocracy. In spite of Lear's age, he tries physically to dismantle Cordelia's wall, but he is shot. Like Shakespeare's Lear, he has learned compassion, but he has also learned the necessity for socially responsible action.

In a later war parable Bond looks back to the cultural roots of the Western tradition—the Trojan War. *The Woman* (or "Scenes of War and Freedom") is a panoramic drama with Trojan Hecuba as its protagonist. Part 1, set at the walls of Troy, condenses and revises Homer's *Iliad* to show a capitalist Greece attacking a feudal Troy ruled by Hecuba. Ismene, wife of the Greek commander Hero, speaks out so passionately for peace and mercy that she is buried alive in the Trojan wall. Part 2, set on an unnamed island 12 years later, finds blind Hecuba caring for her adopted daughter, the mentally crippled Ismene. War encroaches upon freedom when the Greeks invade the island. After wise old Hecuba perpetrates a ruse for freedom, she is killed in a storm. Ismene, crippled in mind, and a miner, crippled in body, face the new day together, strangers on an island.

Bond's non-war plays deriving from history and legend zigzag sharply from comic to tragic tone. *Early Morning* puns on mourning, but the play is grotesquely hilarious in its exposé of Victorian social injustice. Proper Queen Victoria has Siamese twin sons, Crown Prince George and the protagonist Arthur. The Queen matches the former to Florence Nightingale whom she then rapes. Prince Albert, Disraeli, and Gladstone all plot against the Queen. By mid-play the whole cast is dead in Heaven, where the main activity is cannibalism, but all flesh regenerates. Arthur alone refuses to accept heavenly habit, starving himself to a second death.

Suicide also closes the grimmer *Bingo*, whose protagonist is William Shakespeare in retirement at Stratford. Aware that the land enclosure spreads starvation for its victims, Shakespeare nevertheless fails to oppose enclosure so long as his own investments are guaranteed. After a visit from drunken Ben Jonson, Shakespeare's disgust at cruelties of his fellow men shifts to self-disgust at his own failure to act: "How long have I been dead?" He answers the question by taking poison.

Like *Bingo*, *The Fool* indicts the cruelties of an acquisitive society. But unlike *Bingo*'s Shakespeare, The Fool, poet John Clare, is exploited by his social "betters." Not only does he lose his money, his poems, and his evanescent mistress, but also his sanity. Though Bond only sketches his two protagonist poets, Shakespeare and Clare, he dramatizes their society with deft economy.

Restoration dramatizes the life and death of another kind of fool, the honest servant Bob in the world of Restoration fops. Elegant, witty Lord Are deigns to marry a businessman's daughter for her dowry. She in turn has married him for entrance into the social whirl—an entrance he refuses her. In a preposterous scene she haunts him as a sourly unblithe spirit; he stabs her dead and persuades faithful Bob to take the blame. In spite of the courage and protests of Bob's black wife, he is hanged for the crime he did not commit. *Summer* stages a private story and the trilogy *The War Plays* a post-atomic epic, in impassioned pleas for social responsibility.

Bond's violent scenes and cruel humor at first attracted attention rather than appreciation, but he has gradually gathered admirers of his moral commitment theatricalized with verve and economy. Speaking against the Theatre of the Absurd—"Life becomes meaningless when you stop *acting* on the things that concern you most"—Bond has called his work the Rational Theatre. Instead of preaching a rational gospel, however, he fills an almost bare stage with whole societies from which and against which heroes arise, who learn through their suffering to act responsibly. This resembles the *pathos-mathos* of classical tragedy, but it is translated into a modern godless world.

—Ruby Cohn

BOVASSO, Julie (Julia Anne Bovasso). American. 1930–1991.
See 4th edition, 1988.

BOWEN, John (Griffith). British. Born in Calcutta, India, 5 November 1924. Educated at Queen Elizabeth's Grammar School, Crediton, Devon; Pembroke College, Oxford (editor, *Isis*), 1948–51; St. Antony's College, Oxford (Frere Exhibitioner in Indian Studies), 1951–53, M.A. 1953; Ohio State University, Columbus, 1952–53. Served in the Mahratha Light Infantry, 1943–47: captain. Assistant editor, *Sketch* magazine, London, 1953–56; copywriter, J. Walter Thompson Company, London, 1956–58; head of the copy department, S.T. Garland Advertising, London, 1958–60; script consultant, Associated Television, London, 1960–67; drama producer, Thames Television, London, 1978–79, London Weekend Television, 1981–83, and BBC, 1984. Recipient: Society of Authors travelling scholarship, 1986. Agent: (fiction) Elaine Greene Ltd., 31 Newington Green, London N16 9PU; (theatre) Casarotto Ramsay Ltd., National House, 60–66 Wardour Street, London W1V 3HP. Address: Old Lodge Farm, Sugarswell Lane, Edgehill, Banbury, Oxfordshire OX15 6HP, England.

PUBLICATIONS

Plays

The Essay Prize, with A Holiday Abroad and The Candidate: Plays for Television. London, Faber, 1962.
I Love You, Mrs. Patterson (produced Cambridge and London, 1964). London, Evans, 1964.
The Corsican Brothers, based on the play by Dion Boucicault (televised 1965; revised version produced London, 1970). London, Methuen, 1970.
After the Rain, adaptation of his own novel (produced London, 1966; New York, 1967). London, Faber, 1967; New York, Random House, 1968; revised version, Faber, 1972.
The Fall and Redemption of Man (as *Fall and Redemption,* produced London, 1967; as *The Fall and Redemption of Man,* produced New York, 1974). London, Faber, 1968.
Silver Wedding (televised 1967; revised version, produced in *We Who Are about to . . .,* later called *Mixed Doubles,* London, 1969). London, Methuen, 1970.
Little Boxes (includes *The Coffee Lace* and *Trevor*) (produced London, 1968; New York, 1969). London, Methuen, 1968; New York, French, 1970.
The Disorderly Women, adaptation of a play by Euripides (produced Manchester, 1969; London, 1970). London, Methuen, 1969.
The Waiting Room (produced London, 1970). London, French, 1970; New York, French, 1971.
Robin Redbreast (televised 1970; produced Guildford, Surrey, 1974). Published in *The Television Dramatist,* edited by Robert Muller, London, Elek, 1973.
Diversions (produced London, 1973). Excerpts published in *Play Nine,* edited by Robin Rook, London, Arnold, 1981.
Young Guy Seeks Part-Time Work (televised 1973; produced London, 1978).
Roger, in *Mixed Blessings* (produced Horsham, Sussex, 1973). Published in *London Magazine,* October-November 1976.
Florence Nightingale (as *Miss Nightingale,* televised 1974; revised version, as *Florence Nightingale,* produced Canterbury, 1975). London, French, 1976.
Heil Caesar!, adaptation of *Julius Caesar* by Shakespeare (televised 1974). London, BBC Publications, 1974; revised version (produced Birmingham, 1974), London, French, 1975.
Which Way Are You Facing? (produced Bristol, 1976). Excerpts published in *Play Nine,* edited by Robin Rook, London, Arnold, 1981.
Singles (produced London, 1977).
Bondage (produced London, 1978).
The Inconstant Couple, adaptation of a play by Marivaux (produced Chichester, 1978).
Spot the Lady (produced Newcastle upon Tyne, 1981).
The Geordie Gentleman, adaptation of a play by Molière (produced Newcastle upon Tyne, 1987).
The Oak Tree Tea Room Siege (produced Leicester, 1990).

Radio Plays: *Digby* (as Justin Blake, with Jeremy Bullmore), 1959; *Varieties of Love* (revised version of television play *The First Thing You Think Of*), 1968; *The False Diaghilev,* 1988.

Television Plays: created the *Garry Halliday* series; episodes in *Front Page Story,* *The Power Game,* *Wylde Alliance,* and *The Villains* series; *A Holiday Abroad,* 1960; *The Essay Prize,* 1960; *The Jackpot Question,* 1961; *The Candidate,* 1961; *Nuncle,* from the story by John Wain, 1962; *The Truth about Alan,* 1963; *A Case of Character,* 1964; *Mr. Fowlds,* 1965; *The Corsican Brothers,* 1965; *Finders Keepers,* 1967; *The Whole Truth,* 1967; *Silver Wedding,* 1967; *A Most Unfortunate Accident,* 1968; *Flotsam and Jetsam,* 1970; *Robin Redbreast,* 1970; *The Guardians* series (7 episodes), 1971; *A Woman Sobbing,* 1972; *The Emergency Channel,* 1973; *Young Guy Seeks Part-Time Work,* 1973; *Miss Nightingale,* 1974; *Heil Caesar!,* 1974; *The Treasure of Abbott Thomas,* 1974; *The Snow Queen,* 1974; *A Juicy Case,* 1975; *Brief Encounter,* from the film by Noël Coward, 1976; *A Photograph,* 1977; *Rachel in Danger,* 1978; *A Dog's Ransom,* from the novel by Patricia Highsmith, 1978; *Games,* 1978;

The Ice House, 1978; *The Letter of the Law*, 1979; *Dying Day*, 1980; *The Specialist*, 1980; *A Game for Two Players*, 1980; *Dark Secret*, 1981; *Honeymoon*, 1985.

Novels

The Truth Will Not Help Us: Embroidery on an Historical Theme. London, Chatto and Windus, 1956.
After the Rain. London, Faber, 1958; New York, Ballantine, 1959.
The Centre of the Green. London, Faber, 1959; New York, McDowell Obolensky, 1960.
Storyboard. London, Faber, 1960.
The Birdcage. London, Faber, and New York, Harper, 1962.
A World Elsewhere. London, Faber, 1965; New York, Coward McCann, 1967.
Squeak: A Biography of NPA 1978A 203. London, Faber, 1983; New York, Viking, 1984.
The McGuffin. London, Hamish, Hamilton, 1984; Boston, Atlantic Monthly Press, 1985.
The Girls: A Story of Village Life. London, Hamish Hamilton, 1986; New York, Atlantic Monthly Press, 1987.
Fighting Back. London, Hamish Hamilton, 1989.
The Precious Gift. London, Sinclair Stevenson, 1992.

Other (for children)

Pegasus. London, Faber, 1957; New York, A.S. Barnes, 1960.
The Mermaid and the Boy. London, Faber, 1958; New York, A.S. Barnes, 1960.
Garry Halliday and the Disappearing Diamonds [*Ray of Death; Kidnapped Five; Sands of Time; Flying Foxes*] (as Justin Blake, with Jeremy Bullmore). London, Faber, 5 vols., 1960–64.

*

Manuscript Collections: Mugar Memorial Library, Boston University; (television works) Temple University Library, Philadelphia.

Critical Studies: *Writers on Themselves*, London, BBC Publications, 1964; "The Man Behind *The Disorderly Woman*" by Robin Thornber, in *Guardian* (London), 19 February 1969; "Like a Woman They Keep Coming Back To" by Ronald Hayman, in *Drama* (London), Autumn 1970; "Bowen on the Little Box" by Hugh Hebert, in *Guardian* (London), 6 August 1971; "Author/Director," in *London Magazine*, December 1971, and "*The Guardians*: A Post Mortem," in *Plays and Players* (London), January 1972, both by Bowen.

Theatrical Activities:
Director: **Plays**—at the London Academy of Music and Dramatic Art since 1967; *The Disorderly Women*, Manchester, 1969, London, 1970; *Fall and Redemption*, Pitlochry, Scotland, 1969; *The Waiting Room*, London, 1970.
Actor: **Plays**—in repertory in North Wales, summers 1950–51; Palace Theatre, Watford, Hertfordshire, 1965.

John Bowen comments:
My plays, like my novels, are distinguished by a general preoccupation with myth (*The Truth Will Not Help Us*, *After the Rain*, *A World Elsewhere*, *Fall and Redemption*, *The Disorderly Women*, *Robin Redbreast*), and mainly with one particular myth, that of the Bacchae, which in my reading

represents the conflict between Apollonian and Dionysiac ways of living more than the mere tearing to pieces of a Sacred King. This theme, the fight in every human being and between beings themselves, rationality against instinct, is to be found somewhere in almost everything I have written.

Another common theme is of manipulation, one person using another or others, not always consciously, and sometimes "for their good." This theme has been most clearly expressed politically in the episodes I wrote for the television series *The Guardians*, and in my novel *A World Elsewhere*. A third common theme, allied to the other two, is that of self-deceit.

I think of plays as constructions (as all literary forms are, but plays and poems perhaps most), and enjoy theatricality. I like movement; plays are not talk, but action, though the talk may *be* action. I think that the cinema and television have helped the theatre in the 20th century to rediscover some of the mobility it had in the 16th. Though I like above all naturalistic acting, I hate naturalistic settings, and try to avoid waits for scene changes: in most of my plays, the scenes flow into each other by a shift of light.

I have been influenced by Ibsen and Chekhov, probably by Coward, Anouilh, Pirandello and Shaw. Of 20th-century directors, I have most admired Sir Tyrone Guthrie.

*   *   *

Before his first major stage success, with *After the Rain* in 1966, John Bowen was already well known as a novelist and theatre critic for the then prestigious *London Magazine*. His theatre columns of that period reveal a sympathetic understanding of a large variety of dramatic modes, and so it is unsurprising that his own plays have been criticised for stylistic eclecticism. Though *After the Rain* was based on one of Bowen's novels, its theatricality was immediately seen to reflect Weiss's *Marat/Sade*, particularly in the way that each member of the cast is presented as being a criminal deviant hypnotised into the therapeutic re-enactment of events related to the great deluge of the late 20th century. The meta-theatrical dimension is not developed at all, however, and Bowen's deeper interest emerges as lying in the use of archetype, particularly through sometimes startling diachronic collations. *After the Rain* displays the emblems of epic theatre from the start: a bare stage with a lectern, minimal props, placards identifying locations, and the first character (a Lecturer) delivering his opening lines to the lighting technician. All the barriers of the conventional theatre seem to have dissolved. But within a few seconds the Lecturer is referring to "life in 1968" as something prehistoric; elastic time has suddenly soared beyond the audience's experience. Early in the second act there appears a character whom audience members (but not the characters) recognise as Noah, and time bounces back violently in the other direction. The nine prisoner/characters, ostensibly drifting on a raft in the 1970's, find themselves in an arena in which the mythological merges with the futuristic, and a primitive theocracy is generated by necessity—although the Lecturer's scepticism is continually apparent. Satire of varying strengths has been directed at the figures on the raft—stock types from the 1960's—and Noah, on his first appearance, seems also a target for iconoclastic ridicule. However, it quickly becomes apparent that the Noah myth is not one of regeneration but of fossilisation; the ark is full of rotting animals, and Noah survives alone as a demented Ancient Mariner, persecuted by the anonymous gods, crazed by drinking the blood of the Shetland pony. For the protection of humanity, the ark is incinerated with Noah aboard. A new totalitarian myth is, of course, emerging, but for the audience there remains the question of whether Arthur, the autocrat of the raft society, has annihilated the Noah myth or assimilated it. The ending differs in the 1972 revised version, but essentially in both versions Arthur's divinity is challenged when he demands the sacrifice of the first baby born, and the result is a duel, with the death of the god and the birth of the new society which presents the play; at the same time, however, roles are also broken and the play ends with the insistence that the theatre has been invaded by reality.

Bowen's fascination with what he calls "myth" seems to derive from its defiance of chronology and conventional concepts of causation. His adaptation of Boucicault's *The Corsican Brothers* for television and then for the stage seems to have been stimulated by the telepathic link between the twins, and thus between Corsican and Parisian society; but the play also drops the morality of melodrama into a Brechtian limbo, heralded by the hobby-horses of the first episode and developed by numerous flippantly sardonic songs, culminating in a "Moral Finale." *Fall and Redemption* seems to consist of an iconoclastic pilfering of quaint details from the Mystery Cycles to create an acting exercise for LAMDA students, and its termination with the crucifixion (rather than Doomsday, where all the English cycles end) was interpreted as insensitivity to form; yet its Brechtian rationale is evident at least when Cain and Abel are joined by a talking horse, and inescapable in the ending, where the actors help Jesus off the cross and then come forward for applause. In another myth play for LAMDA, *The Disorderly Women*, Bowen knew that he was joining numerous playwrights of the 1960's in attempting a contemporary adaptation of *The Bacchae*; yet he was also trying to give a relatively sympathetic portrayal of Pentheus, as a ruler committed to moderation, a principle neither understood by his father nor respected by Dionysus, whose cynicism, Bowen's introduction suggests, is substantiated by Auschwitz, Hiroshima, and Vietnam.

In the 1970's Bowen's interests and techniques developed variously, with *Singles*, a comedy about sexual mercenaries, achieving a modest London critical success. The dilemma of Pentheus was expanded and domesticated in a play which did not reach London, *Which Way Are You Facing?*, a cerebral but aggressively theatrical contribution to the history of the problem play, from the sympathetic perspective of the control room of the Samaritans, monitoring the unloveliest of humanity in every corner of the auditorium. By contrast, in the much-praised *Robin Redbreast* Bowen exploits the savagery of myth which leaps from prehistory into the life of a television script editor; the dialogue of the final scene even includes a reference to *The Golden Bough*, but the structure of this play depends on psychological realism and its main impact is that of a thriller. In fact, although Bowen is best known for plays based on myth which use techniques of epic theatre, he learned his dramatic craft writing for television, and his early plays (notably *A Holiday Abroad*) show a mastery of the subtleties of realism. One of his mature plays, *The Coffee Lace*, has even been interpreted as naturalistic in its portrayal of six veteran actors who have hermetically sealed themselves off from the world after a major theatrical failure ten years previously; however, they are also fossilised grotesques, very similar in their situation to the figures of *After the Rain*. Ambivalent it may be, but the play, with its companion piece *Trevor*, must dispel the common complaint that Bowen is a humourless writer; the gentle comedy in the portrayal of the social cripples in *The Coffee Lace* is rich but compassionate.

In the 1980's, Bowen increasingly returned to his preferred early genre, fiction.

—Howard McNaughton

BRENTON, Howard. British. Born in Portsmouth, Hampshire, 13 December 1942. Educated at Chichester High School; St. Catharine's College, Cambridge, B.A. (honours) in English 1965. Married Jane Fry in 1970; two sons. Stage manager in several repertory companies; resident dramatist, Royal Court Theatre, London, 1972–73. Recipient: Arts Council bursary, 1969, 1970; John Whiting award, 1970; *Evening Standard* award, 1977, 1985. Agent: Casarotto Ramsay Ltd., National House, 60–66 Wardour Street, London W1V 3HP, England.

PUBLICATIONS

Plays

Ladder of Fools (produced Cambridge, 1965).
Winter, Daddykins (produced Dublin, 1965).
It's My Criminal (produced London, 1966).
A Sky-Blue Life, adaptation of stories by Gorky (produced London, 1967; revised version produced London, 1971). Included in *Three Plays*, 1989.
Gargantua, adaptation of the novel by Rabelais (produced Brighton, 1969).
Gum and Goo (produced Brighton, 1969; London, 1971). Included in *Plays for Public Places*, 1972.
Revenge (produced London, 1969). London, Methuen, 1970.
Heads, and The Education of Skinny Spew (produced Bradford, 1969; London, 1970). Included in *Christie in Love and Other Plays*, 1970.
Christie in Love (produced Brighton and London, 1969; Chicago, 1981). Included in *Christie in Love and Other Plays*, 1970.
Christie in Love and Other Plays. London, Methuen, 1970.
Fruit (produced London, 1970).
Wesley (produced Bradford, 1970). Included in *Plays for Public Places*, 1972.
Scott of the Antarctic; or, What God Didn't See (produced Bradford, 1971). Included in *Plays for Public Places*, 1972.
Lay By, with others (produced Edinburgh and London, 1971). London, Calder and Boyars, 1972.
Hitler Dances (produced Edinburgh and London, 1972). London, Methuen, 1982.
Plays for Public Places. London, Eyre Methuen, 1972.
How Beautiful with Badges (produced London, 1972). Included in *Three Plays*, 1989.
England's Ireland, with others (produced Amsterdam and London, 1972).
Measure for Measure, adaptation of the play by Shakespeare (produced Exeter, Devon, 1972). Included in *Three Plays*, 1989.
A Fart for Europe, with David Edgar (produced London, 1973).
The Screens, adaptation of a play by Jean Genet (produced Bristol, 1973).

Lear, adaptation of *King Lear* by Shakespeare (produced New York, 1990).

*

Theatrical Activities:
Director: **Plays**—all his own plays; *The House of Bernarda Alba* by García Lorca, San Francisco, 1963; *Mother Courage* by Brecht, Paris, 1967; *The Messingkauf Dialogues* by Brecht, Edinburgh, 1968; *Play* by Samuel Beckett, Paris, 1969, New York, 1970; *Come and Go* by Samuel Beckett, New York, 1975; *Mr. Frivolous* by Wallace Shawn, New York, 1976; *Earth Spirit* by Wedekind, New Haven, Connecticut, 1976(?); *Sunday Childhood Journeys to Nobody at Home* by Arthur Sainer, New York, 1980; *Lulu* by Wedekind, Cambridge, Massachusetts, 1980; *The Tempest*, New York, 1981; *From the Point of View of the Salt* by Liza Lorwin, New York, 1986.
Actor: **Play**—in *Wrong Guys* by Ruth Maleczech, New York, 1981.
Choreographer: **Play**—*Measure for Measure*, New York, 1976.

* * *

Lee Breuer is a dramatist as well as auteur-director, and was a founding member of the Mabou Mines experimental theatre collective in New York, a company in which he remains vitally active. His "performance poems," as he calls his playtexts, merge the American tradition of the self-conscious, extended lyric poem (Whitman, Ginsberg) with the main tendencies of European modern drama. After beginning his directorial work with the San Francisco Actors' Workshop, Breuer studied with the Berliner Ensemble and with actors who worked with Grotowski, so he knows both "presence" and the complexities of self-conscious presentational form.

The greater part of Breuer's dramatic writing is structured in the form of a labyrinthine monologue that he then "animates" in a richly physicalized stage setting and performance. The monologues telescope many identities into a single voice that in turn splices together fragments of many linguistic worlds: street language, colloquialisms, phrases from sports, science, Latin, spiritualism, etc., and above all pop imagery from the movies and the media. Through juxtaposition he develops a complex mode of irony, dominated by a sophisticated use of punning. This artistic strategy allows the poem and its speakers to subvert the efficacy of the expressive language of emotion without denying the reality of the emotion itself. Breuer's approach to dramatic language plays with the illusions of performance, emphasized by the *bunraku* puppets he so admires and often uses in his stagings of the poems.

His early poems are brief modernist beast fables in which the animal figure tells a human story. A single voice is taken up by several performers to project a fragmented self. *The Red Horse Animation* is an interior monologue about a lone voice seeking a shape for its life, as performers gyrate in evocation of a message-carrying horse. In its struggle the horse's life is stifled by the father's ethos of drudge-work and money. Just as the voice starts to feel mind and imagination coming together, the image of the horse—and potential poet—tears itself apart and dissolves into silence. *The B-Beaver Animation* tells of a stutterer—the artist who can't get his words out. He seeks to build a dam to protect his Missus and The Brood, who function as a chorus for his thoughts, which are dammed up with the detritus of his everyday experience, his learning, and his fantasies.

While working on these Animations, Breuer experimented with performance art, and both lines of work converged during the late 1970's, culminating in the hours-long *The Shaggy Dog Animation*. Here two distinct voices speak for a pair of *bunraku*-style puppets in American contemporary dress, supported by live performers who animate the puppets' bodies and their words. The story is that of the exploitative John Greed who falls in love with a faithful dog-woman who calls herself Your Dog Rose. She submits to him as one of the "bitches of the city" who are "prisoners of love." Her shaggy-dog life includes a trip to Venice, California, for movie-making, and a return to New York where she enters the art world. At her opening she shows a painted fireplug, and the art establishment comes down on her for seeing only the surface of things. She goes on to have puppies, and in a last bitter street fight with John, she ends it with him. Still, their voices merge to become one voice, as powerful in memory as they were in life.

With *A Prelude to Death in Venice* Breuer's stagings shift to solo performance, here with a triple persona: of a puppeteer (Bill); the puppet John Greed; and the movie agent Bill Morris. Expanded from a brief section of *Shaggy Dog*, life is presented as a succession of late-night calls into a pair of city street payphones which frame the figure like the two thieves framed Christ on Golgotha. He suffers the indignities of family and the movie world, with tirades to Mother, his Agent (who's "into producing reality" and is in fact himself), and finally his father. Throughout, Thomas Mann's *Death in Venice* provides an overlay of imagery and ironic contrast. Exasperated by his failed plan to shoot a movie in Venice, California, Bill the puppeteer kills John his puppet-self and thus is able to call down his father and deliver himself to momentary freedom.

A monologue of even greater complexity emerges with *Haji*, in which an American actress seated at her make-up table summons the memory of her East European father who committed suicide. They sleep together, suffer together, and he shoots himself before she can repay the money she borrowed from him, which stands for an emotional debt, too. In this fateful recollection that is her version of the traditional Moslem's trip to ancient Mecca, her father's image is superimposed upon her own, and even upon that of her son—all through a sophisticated interaction of live performer, mask, film, and video imagery. No unmasking will separate their identities, for they vibrate within one another.

Beginning in 1980, Breuer initiated a series of experiments in music-theatre with the composer Bob Telson, aiming for a synthesis of popular and high art on the order of the Brecht-Weill collaborations. Their first piece was *Sister Suzie Cinema*, a brief "Doo-Wop Opera" in which young black singers dream of a union with images on a movie-house screen. Imagination becomes reality as the ground gives way and they ride to their paradise on a huge airplane wing.

In a major experiment with Telson, *The Gospel at Colonus*, Breuer rips the Oedipus story from its Greek context and thrusts it into the world of exultation that is American black gospel singing. While this radical adaptation maintains the central events and figures of Sophocles's final masterpiece, it augments the Greek conventions with the black preacher's dramaturgy of chanting and shouting together with an onstage congregation. By the end, the audience too joins this great chorus, standing, clapping, and joyously singing along.

The transposition of the Sophoclean drama spins forward yet another strand of Breuer's auteur-directorial vision, which is, in his words, "to recreate [classic] texts through American lenses." Most recently, in his *Lear*, as a company statement tells us: "Shakespeare's *King Lear* takes on a whole new aspect in a radical, matriarchal version transported to America's Deep South, circa 1957, updating with its inter-racial casting and gender-switching, to question the family unit, old age, and the traditional structure of power."

Breuer's most ambitious effort to date is another collaboration with Telson, *The Warrior Ant*. It remains a work-in-progress, some parts already performed, which is projected as a 12-part mock epic poem to be played in four evening-long performances. In this mythological biography modeled upon those of the Japanese *samurai*, the hero Ant is mis-conceived in rape and chooses the path of individuality over that of the society of the Hill. There is a Virgilian dream-journey to hell where he discovers his true father who is termite and not ant. Renouncing the world in order to transcend this essential war within, of newly discovered parental rape-identity, he moves toward the sky by climbing a Redwood tree. Years later, reaching the top, he copulates with the Death Moth and discovers that he loves death best. Drawing upon multiple and seemingly contradictory theatrical resources and cultures —Japanese, Latino, African and more—Breuer is orchestrating in fabulous abandonment, a polyphonic cultural symphony in dramatic form.

Most jubilantly in his collaborations with Telson, music and song have led Breuer to worlds of dramatic reconciliation. But even here, as in all his work, Breuer's poetry of the theatre is predicated upon a radical synthesis of performance genres—illusory play that also is a feat of illumination.

—Bill Coco

BROPHY, Brigid. British. Born in 1929.
See 2nd edition, 1977.

BROUGHTON, John. New Zealander. Born in Hastings, 19 March 1947. Educated at Hastings Boys' High School; Massey University, Palmerston North, B.Sc. 1971; University of Otago, Dunedin, B.D.S. 1977. Served in the New Zealand Territorial Army, 1971–92: captain. Dental house surgeon, University of Otago Dental School, 1978; chair, Araiteuru Marae Council, Dunedin, 1984–90; dentist in general practice, Dunedin, 1979–89; since 1989 Maori health lecturer, Department of Preventive and Social Medicine, University of Otago Medical School, Dunedin. Recipient: *Dominion Sunday Times* Bruce Mason award, 1990. Agent: Playmarket, P.O. Box 9767, Wellington. Address: Te Maraenui, 176 Queen Street, Dunedin, New Zealand.

PUBLICATIONS

Plays

Te Hokinga Mai (*The Return Home*) (also director: produced Dunedin, 1988). Dunedin, Aoraki Productions, 1990.

Te Hara (*The Sin*) (also director: produced Dunedin, 1988). Published in *He Reo Hou: 5 plays by Maori Playwrights*, edited by Simon Garrett. Wellington, Playmarket, 1991.
Peter's Pantomime (sketch; produced Dunedin, 1989).
Nga Puke (*The Hills*) (produced Wellington, 1990). Wellington, Aoraki Press, 1992.
Hokonui Jones and the Sword of Destiny (sketch; produced Dunedin, 1990).
The Private War of Corporal Cooper (produced Dunedin, 1991).
Michael James Manaia (produced Wellington and Edinburgh, 1991). Wellington, Aoraki Press, 1991.
Marae (produced Wellington, 1992).
Anzac (produced Dunedin, 1992).

Screenplay: *Tears of Stone*, 1992.

Video: *Nga Mahi Ora* (Careers in the Health Workforce), 1990.

Other

A Time Journal for Halley's Comet (for children), with G.T. Brown. Dunedin, Double B Productions, 1985.

*

Manuscript Collection: University of Otago, Dunedin.

Critical Study: "Einblicke in die Maori-Kultur" by A.R. Glaap, in *Der Fremdsprachliche Unterricht*, (Seelze-Velber, Germany) July 1991.

John Broughton comments:
Theatre Marae has been part of Te Ao Maori (the Maori World) ever since the Maori has been in Aotearoa (New Zealand). The marae has always been an arena where real life drama is played out. However, by fusing the customs and practices of the marae with Western/European theatre a truly bicultural art form, unique to New Zealand, has evolved. This has been particularly active over the last 20 years and is still evolving and developing.

I have found that drama/theatre is a very powerful medium for the sharing of two cultures: Maori and Pakeha. It can embrace both without feeling threatening to one half. I like to think that the plays I have written, and their productions, cross both cultures in a way that is meaningful and relevant to both, resulting in enlightenment and hope for us all.

* * *

Since 1989 there has been an explosion of Maori theatre in New Zealand. Building on western traditions and writing in English, writers use the Maori language mainly for traditional forms of songs, greetings, and chants. Together with the universal themes of family life and love, Maori concerns are always tied to searching for and reclaiming the past, together with their feeling of a special relationship with the land.

In a group of about a dozen Maori playwrights newcomer John Broughton (Kahungunu on his father's side, Kai Tahu on his mother's) holds a respected position, because of his treatment of sensitive issues as well as the wide-spread acceptance of his major work *Michael James Manaia*.

Te Hara (*The Sin*), a short play for three women, tells how the building of a chicken house on sacred burial ground has terrible consequences. While a slight piece, it proved very moving in performance, and the theme of death is handled with great sensitivity. Broughton does not try to explain the beliefs held by his characters, merely displaying them in dramatic context, showing ordinary lives lived in what remains of a holistic cultural tradition overlaid with so-called European belief systems.

Te Hokinga Mai (*The Return Home*) explores Maori and European differences using Vietnam as a backdrop, a theatre of war he was to return to later on. Two soldiers, one Maori, the other European, become friends during the war. Afterwards the European visits the tribal home (*marae*) of the Maori to present the family with a greenstone pendant, all that remains of their son. In flashbacks their friendship is shown to have had a rocky start but to have strengthened and become a bridge between their cultures. Broughton uses this situation to explore differences in values, and, unashamedly didactic, to teach the European about Maori ways.

In *Nga Puke* (*The Hills*) two lonely people, a man and a woman, find love and friendship during World War II. Old-fashioned and attractively sentimental, the play reflects his continuing interest in war and its effects on people.

Broughton's first full-length play, *Michael James Manaia*, appeared in 1991. In this play for one actor we return to the Vietnam encounter, which looms large in Broughton's mind because of his first-hand experience of the New Zealand Army during the years following that conflict. The hero is a returned veteran, suffering unexplained distress since his repatriation. He remembers and re-enacts his life's experiences from childhood to the dreadful present during the course of this powerful and at times terrifying play, which shows how Broughton's command of the medium has advanced in the four years since he began to write seriously.

The first half takes us through a youth spent in the country where often harsh, often hilarious events are related. Broughton excels in giving a voice to the inarticulate, and a picture emerges of a brutal, even deprived life whose high points are lit by booze and brawling. But slowly a picture emerges of the harsh father who fought at Monte Cassino in World War II, but who never speaks of it. This looming presence is felt throughout until the horrifying climax. The second half leads us through the hell of close combat in Vietnam, and the ultimate fight with Death in the form of Hine-Nui-te-Po (Goddess of Death). The shattering climax, which combines the influences of clinging Maori myth and creeping modern chemical warfare, shocks the audience.

This performance travelled well, to the Edinburgh Festival of 1991 in fact, where it was nominated for the *Independent* Fringe Award. Demanding and receiving an outstanding performance from the actor in the solo role (Jim Moriarty), *Michael James Manaia* is a gripping play about the brutalising effects of war in a society where brutality in men was once considered normal and manly. Although there are many moments of humour, the play is horrifying rather than moving, and, as with his other plays, Broughton still tends to overwrite. Cut by 15 minutes it would be greatly improved, as several critics remarked.

To continue his engagement with the wars of this century, Broughton has written a companion piece to *Nga Puke* entitled *The Private War of Corporal Cooper*, set during World War I. While on the surface it is a naïve affirmation of the spiritual union between a nun knitting socks at home and a soldier who wears them in the trenches, the script has an unsophisticated but evocative power, while in his television script *Tears of Stone*, breaking of a *tapu* again leads to disasters for a family.

Marae, a play written for the 1992 International Festival of the Arts in Wellington, was good on the page but failed to live up to its promise in performance. Dealing with the everyday life on a *marae*, the meeting house which forms the traditional centre of village life in a Maori community, *Marae* tries to be too many things. Part myth, part love story, and part ecological treatise, the plot concerns the local council's plan to drive a new road through tribal land, and the *marae* committee's efforts to stop them. Fund raising is an issue, and a concert is planned and performed which seems to take over from the play. The audience was left with no sense of dramatic construction or focus, although the concert itself was enjoyable.

At present working on a commissioned play for Fortune Theatre, Dunedin, titled *10.45*, Broughton continues to be the quiet leader of one line of Maori playwriting in New Zealand.

—Patricia Cooke

BROWN, Kenneth H. American. Born in Brooklyn, New York, 9 March 1936. Educated at a preparatory school in Brooklyn. Served in the United States Marine Corps, 1954–57. Mail clerk, 1951–54; bartender and waiter, New York and Miami, 1958–63; bank clerk, New York, 1960; cigarette salesman, New York, 1961; resident playwright, Living Theatre, New York, 1963–67; private tutor, 1966–69, and resident playwright, 1968–69, Yale University School of Drama, New Haven, Connecticut; visiting lecturer (improvisational acting), Hollins College, Virginia, 1969; visiting lecturer (history of theatre), Hunter College, New York, 1969–70; associate professor in performance (theatrical production), University of Iowa, Iowa City, 1971. Recipient: Venice Film Festival gold medal, 1964; Rockefeller fellowship, 1965, and grant, 1967; ABC-Yale University fellowship, 1966, 1967; Guggenheim fellowship, 1966; Creative Artists Public Service grant, 1974. Agent: Mary Yost, 59 East 54th Street, New York, New York 10022. Address: 150 74th Street, Brooklyn, New York 11209, U.S.A.

PUBLICATIONS

Plays

The Brig (produced New York, 1963; London, 1964). New York, Hill and Wang, and London, Methuen, 1965.
Devices (produced New York, 1965).
The Happy Bar (produced New York, 1967).
Blake's Design (produced New Haven, Connecticut, 1968; New York, 1974). Published in *The Best Short Plays 1969*, edited by Stanley Richards, Philadelphia, Chilton, 1969.
The Green Room (produced Iowa City, 1971).
The Cretan Bull (produced Waterford, Connecticut, 1972; New York, 1974).
Nightlight (produced Hartford, Connecticut, 1973; London, 1974). New York, French, 1973.

Screenplays: *The Brig*, 1965; *Devices*, 1967.

Novel

The Narrows. New York, Dial Press, 1970.

Other

You'd Never Know It from the Way I Talk (lectures and readings). Ashland, Ohio, Ashland Poetry Press, 1990.

*

Manuscript Collection: New York Public Library.

Kenneth H. Brown comments:

I began as a playwright quite by accident. It was the best means to convey my experiences as a confined prisoner in a Marine Brig. All my plays since have been either direct or symbolic representations of my life experiences. As such, I have been classified by one theatre historian as an accidental playwright, a title I gladly accept since I adhere to the belief that all things of personal import in my life have come about as a result of pure chance. I do not take to writing as a daily chore that must be done. It is, for me, a labor of love and, as such, I engage in it only when moved to do so. As I get older, I am constantly amazed by the body of works accumulated through this philosophy.

* * *

Although Kenneth H. Brown has published poetry, a novel, *The Narrows*, and a collection of lectures and readings, *You'd Never Know It from the Way I Talk*, his most significant achievements to date have been in drama. *The Brig*, a stark and appalling indictment of militarism, stamped Brown as one of the more gifted and experimental of American dramatists of the 1960's. It placed him in a tradition with Artaud and proved him able to create what neither Artaud nor Ionesco accomplished, "theatre of cruelty" complete with a metaphysics of language. His next published play, *Blake's Design*, gave further support to the belief that Brown was a dramatist who defied labels. Moving away from the stark, purposefully flat prose of *The Brig*, Brown played with the catchy rhythms of vaudeville, embellished his prose giving it a lyrical quality, and turned away from naturalism to expressionism. Of *The Cretan Bull*, Brown says he produced a "very funny play about complete strangers who meet in Central Park at dawn and confront a very odd set of circumstances." Again Brown went in new directions, experimenting with another style, and exploring different themes. In *Nightlight*, a play produced at the Hartford Stage Company to strong critical acclaim, Brown says he wrote about "the elements of violence that are now threatening the safety of decent citizens in our big cities."

Though *The Brig* and *Blake's Design* are very different, they share many common elements. In both, an egalitarianism makes Brown select characters for his drama who reflect the ethnic and racial mix that makes up American society. In both Brown draws on music and popular songs: in *Blake's Design* the songs and dances are handled in a manner reminiscent of a vaudeville skit; in *The Brig* music is subverted and becomes an instrument of torture. The sarcastic, strident, sneering tone of a guard's voice is played contrapuntally against a clear, impersonal, unaffected voice. The breaking of a command is answered by its own often inaudible flat echo. The hideous dissonant martial music that is the tool of the fascist or authoritarian state, the kind of music that breaks a man's mind and makes him crawl like a maggot at any command, is produced by clashing garbage can lids together as if they were cymbals. Yet more hellish music derives from the sound of a voice resonating against a toilet bowl as one of the prisoners, using the cubicle as his confessional, cries out his

litany of wrongs in obedience to the guard's orders. Dance, too, figures in the plays. In *Blake's Design* Muvva and Zack sing of Zack's necrophilia with his dead, black wife while they do a soft shoe dance. In *The Brig* dance is a ritual in which the prisoners suffer repeatedly at the hands of the guards. The dance is one where men shrink, recoil, and double-over in response to the quick, sharp blows delivered by the truncheons of the Warden or the guards. This violent dance pattern is varied with a pattern of running across the stage and halting at every white line in conformity with the procedure outlined in the *Marine Corps Manual*. Finally, both plays employ a point of view that is reminiscent of naturalism. A dispassionate exact observer records precisely the world in all its minutiae as if the reality being depicted were a hard surface that can only be penetrated once it has been fully sounded. But for all these seeming similarities, the plays are, in fact, very different, both in style and in theme.

The Brig is a blatantly political play, or rather, "concept of theater," as Brown would have it called. A penal institute in Camp Fuji, the brig is the place where Marines are sent to be punished for any infraction of military orders. The set of the play duplicates as nearly as possible the specifications of the brig and its actions reenact the rules that govern its workings as set down in the *Marine Corps Manual*. The play opens with the waking of the prisoners at dawn and it closes with the putting out of the light at night. Between dawn and night, we see the prisoners repeat again and again the same gestures and motions as they are forced to dress and undress, eat and march, clean and stand at attention, for no other reason than to fulfill an order and submit to power. Nameless (they are called by number—only the guards have names), the prisoners grovel, crawl, abuse themselves, whimper silently, and try desperately to carry out any order to the letter while the military guards sadistically delight in finding new indignities for them to suffer and new punishments for their supposed failures. The discipline is without restraint or reason. Senselessly the prisoners are humiliated, beaten, and abused. The only logic that governs events is the relentless logic of power and physical force. In the course of the day, one prisoner is released, a new one enters, and a third is released to an even worse form of institutional imprisonment, the asylum. Number 26, after two weeks in the brig which follows upon 16 years of honorable military service, finds himself, against all orders and common sense, crying out his name, James Turner, and in so doing demonstrating that in the brig seemingly sane behavior is in fact insane. For two hours, the senses of the audience are assaulted as the prisoners are hollered at and harassed by the guards. Plot and character development in the ordinary sense are absent from the play. Language, stripped of all warmth, finally negates itself. The members of the audience are left responding to sounds, intonations, incantations, and not denotative meanings. They experience an agony of feeling which derives from the immediacy of the violence unleashed both on the stage and in themselves and which has little reference to the world of reason that has systematically been destroyed by the extremes to which it has been pushed on the stage.

Blake's Design depicts Zack's struggle to free himself from both his past—the black woman whose dead body he has slept with for ten years—and his illusions—Blake, or call him God, is one of them—in order to tell his son the truth, live in the present, and move out of his dark basement apartment upstairs and into the light. Zack's mulatto son, Sweek, and his two women, Muvva, with whom he has shared his bed, dead wife, and son for ten years, and Modrigal, his half-oriental mistress, all talk rather self-consciously throughout the play about man's weakness, his lies, and that part of himself which he does not know or understand and so calls God, or Blake, in an effort at understanding. The play ends when Zack unburdens himself, tells the truth, closes the door on his past, and mounts the stairs. The symbolism is rather obvious and the long talks about Blake tend to be tiresome, but the characters themselves are well imagined and the quick staccato exchanges between Sweek and Zack and the shuffling dances and songs save the play.

Brown's talents are considerable; he was one of the few genuinely original American dramatists to emerge in the early 1960's. It is the public's loss that Brown now finds the social and political environment in the United States inhospitable to writers of genuine creative talent. In his collection of lectures, he laments the breakdown in the relationship between theatre and community in the United States and starkly outlines the difficulties of trying to pursue the vocation of a writer in our era. He no longer finds his own art relevant to this crass, materialistic society. He finds this admission deeply sobering, not only because it speaks of his own failure, but because it speaks of a larger societal loss, A society that does not nurture its own art also fails itself.

—Carol Simpson Stern

———————

BULLINS, Ed. American. Born in Philadelphia, Pennsylvania, 2 July 1935. Educated in Philadelphia public schools; at William Penn Business Institute, Philadelphia; Los Angeles City College, 1958–61; San Francisco State College, 1964–65, and M.F.A. candidate since 1990; Antioch University, San Francisco, B.A. 1989. Served in the United States Navy, 1952–55. Married Trixie Warner (marriage ended). Playwright-in-residence and associate director, New Lafayette Theatre, New York, 1967–73; editor, *Black Theatre* magazine, New York, 1969–74; producing director, Surviving Theatre, New York, from 1974; writers unit co-ordinator, New York Shakespeare Festival, 1975–82; Mellon lecturer, Amherst College, Massachusetts, from 1977; public relations director, Berkeley Black Repertory, Berkeley, 1982; promotions director, Magic Theater, 1982–83; group sales coordinator, Julian Theater, 1983; playwriting teacher, Bay Area Playwrights Festival, and People's School of Dramatic Arts, 1983; instructor, City College of San Francisco, 1984–88; lecturer, Sonoma State University, California, 1987–89, and University of California, Berkeley, 1989. Recipient: Rockefeller grant, 1968, 1970, 1973; Vernon Rice award, 1968; American Place grant, 1968; Obie award, 1971, 1975; Guggenheim grant, 1971, and fellowship, 1976; Creative Artists Public Service grant, 1973; National Endowment for the Arts grant, 1974, 1989; New York Drama Critics Circle award, 1975, 1977. D.L.: Columbia College, Chicago, 1976. Address: 3617 San Pablo Avenue, #118, Emeryville, California 94608, U.S.A.

Publications

Plays

Clara's Ole Man (produced San Francisco, 1965; New York, 1968; London, 1971).   Included in *Five Plays*, 1969.
How Do You Do? (produced San Francisco, 1965; London,

1969; New York, 1980).   Mill Valley, California, Illuminations Press, 1965.
Dialect Determinism, or, The Rally (produced San Francisco, 1965).   Included in *The Theme Is Blackness*, 1973.
The Theme Is Blackness (produced San Francisco, 1966). Included in *The Theme Is Blackness*, 1973.
It Has No Choice (produced San Francisco, 1966; London, 1968).   Included in *The Theme Is Blackness*, 1973.
A Minor Scene (produced San Francisco, 1966; London, 1968).   Included in *The Theme Is Blackness*, 1973.
The Game of Adam and Eve, with Shirley Tarbell (produced Los Angeles, 1966).
In New England Winter (produced New York, 1967). Published in *New Plays from the Black Theatre*, edited by Bullins, New York, Bantam, 1969.
In the Wine Time (produced New York, 1968).   Included in *Five Plays*, 1969.
A Son, Come Home (produced New York, 1968).   Included in *Five Plays*, 1969.
The Electronic Nigger (produced New York and London, 1968).   Included in *Five Plays*, 1969.
Goin' a Buffalo: A Tragifantasy (produced New York, 1968). Included in *Five Plays*, 1969.
The Corner (produced Boston, 1968; New York, 1972). Included in *The Theme Is Blackness*, 1973.
The Gentleman Caller (produced New York and London, 1969).   Published in *A Black Quartet*, edited by Clayton Riley, New York, New American Library, 1970.
Five Plays. Indianapolis, Bobbs Merrill, 1969; as *The Electronic Nigger and Other Plays*, London, Faber, 1970.
We Righteous Bombers (as Kingsley B. Bass, Jr.), adaptation of a work by Camus (produced New York, 1969).
The Man Who Dug Fish (produced Boston, 1969; New York, 1970).   Included in *The Theme Is Blackness*, 1973.
Street Sounds (produced New York, 1970).   Included in *The Theme Is Blackness*, 1973.
The Helper (produced New York, 1970).   Included in *The Theme Is Blackness*, 1973.
A Ritual to Raise the Dead and Foretell the Future (produced New York, 1970).   Included in *The Theme Is Blackness*, 1973.
The Fabulous Miss Marie (produced New York, 1970). Published in *The New Lafayette Theatre Presents*, edited by Bullins, New York, Doubleday, 1974.
Four Dynamite Plays: It Bees Dat Way, Death List, The Pig Pen, Night of the Beast (produced New York, 1970; *It Bees Dat Way* produced London, 1970).   New York, Morrow, 1971.
The Duplex: A Black Love Fable in Four Movements (produced New York, 1970).   New York, Morrow, 1971.
The Devil Catchers (produced New York, 1970).
The Psychic Pretenders (produced New York, 1972).
You Gonna Let Me Take You Out Tonight, Baby (produced New York, 1972).
Next Time, in *City Stops* (produced New York, 1972).
House Party, music by Pat Patrick, lyrics by Bullins (produced New York, 1973).
The Theme Is Blackness: The Corner and Other Plays (includes *Dialect Determinism, or, The Rally*; *It Has No Choice*; *The Helper*; *A Minor Scene*; *The Theme Is Blackness*; *The Man Who Dug Fish*; *Street Sounds*; and the scenarios and short plays *Black Commercial No. 2, The American Flag Ritual, State Office Bldg. Curse, One-Minute Commercial, A Street Play, A Short Play for a Small Theatre*, and *The Play of the Play*). New York, Morrow, 1973.
The Taking of Miss Janie (produced New York, 1975).

Published in *Famous Plays of the '70's*, New York, Dell, 1980.

The Mystery of Phyllis Wheatley (produced New York, 1976).

I Am Lucy Terry (for children; produced New York, 1976).

Jo Anne!!! (produced New York, 1976).

Home Boy, music by Aaron Bell, lyrics by Bullins (produced New York, 1976).

Daddy (produced New York, 1977).

Sepia Star, or Chocolate Comes to the Cotton Club, music and lyrics by Mildred Kayden (produced New York, 1977).

Storyville, music and lyrics by Mildred Kayden (produced La Jolla, California, 1977; revised version produced Washington, D.C., 1979).

Michael (also director: produced New York, 1978).

C'mon Back to Heavenly House (produced Amherst, Massachusetts, 1978).

Leavings (produced New York, 1980).

Steve and Velma (produced Boston, 1980).

Bullins Does Bullins (also director: produced Oakland, California, 1988).

I Think It's Gonna Work Out Fine, with Idris Ackamoor and Rhodessa Jones (produced New York, 1990).

American Griot (produced New York, 1990).

Salaam, Huey Newton, Salaam (produced New York, 1991).Published in *Best Short Plays of 1990*, edited by Howard Stein and Glenn Young, New York, Applause, 1991.

Raining Down Stars: Sepia Stories of the Dark Diaspora, with Idris Ackamoor and Rhodessa Jones (produced San Francisco, 1992).

Screenplays: *Night of the Beast*, 1971; *The Ritual Masters*, 1972.

Novel

The Reluctant Rapist. New York, Harper, 1973.

Short Stories

The Hungered One: Early Writings. New York, Morrow, 1971.

Verse

To Raise the Dead and Foretell the Future. New York, New Lafayette Publications, 1971.

Other

Editor, *New Plays from the Black Theatre*. New York, Bantam, 1969.

Editor, *The New Lafayette Theatre Presents: Plays with Aesthetic Comments by 6 Black Playwrights*. New York, Doubleday, 1974.

*

Bibliography: *Ten Modern American Playwrights* by Kimball King, New York, Garland, 1982.

Critical Study: *Drumbeats, Masks, and Metaphor: Contemporary Afro-American Theatre* by Geneviève Fabre, translated by Melvin Dixon, Cambridge, Massachusetts, Harvard University Press, 1983; *Toward Creation of a Collective Form: The Plays of Ed Bullins* by Nicholas

Canaday, in *Studies in American Drama* (Erie, Pennsylvania), 1986.

Theatrical Activities:
Director: **Play**—*Michael*, New York, 1978; *Bullins Does Bullins*, Oakland, California, 1988; *Savage Wilds*, Berkeley, California, 1988; *Tripnology* by J. Woodward, San Francisco, 1992.

Actor: **Play**—role in *The Hotel Play* by Wallace Shawn, New York, 1981; role in *The Real Deal* by J. Woodward, San Francisco, 1988; role in *The Burial of Prejudice* by J. Woodward, San Francisco, 1991.

Ed Bullins comments:

I write plays for a number of reasons but the most simple and direct truth of the matter is that it is my work.

* * *

Though he is the most prolific, and one of the most active, figures in black American theater, Ed Bullins resists close identification with the prominent contemporary styles. With Black House and Black Arts/West in San Francisco he participated in projects to create a revolutionary theater; yet, at the same time he was capable of satirizing revolutionary ideologues in *Dialect Determinism*. He can adapt the mode of realism for his Twentieth-Century Cycle, but deflect a critic's attempt to discern its autobiographical theme with the remark that specific reference is not apt for symbolic writing like his own. Bullins's statements are often, in fact, less a commentary than an enactment of the theatrical devices of black language. There is the pretended innocence of "shuckin" that allows him to deny association with militants, the inflated language of the put-on self-description ("Ed Bullins, at this moment in time, is almost without peer in America—black, white or imported"), and the ironic humor producing elaborate games about racial stereotypes in and around his plays. Like the originators of those linguistic techniques Bullins stays loose so that he can survive the pressures of the moment and continue to evolve through performance after performance.

The best known of his works are set in the 1950's, a period that matches historically the personal deracination of the characters. They are urban people completely divorced from the southern past, the soil, and traditional culture. Shown without the coloration of myth in either their own or their creator's consciousness, they are neither idealized folk primitives so dearly beloved in the past to friendly white writers on the Negro, nor the agents of imminent revolution ardently desired by some black spokespersons. Their ghetto is both physical and moral. Excluded from accomplishments beyond those of subsisting they cannot transcend private passion or see any possibility of redemption in community. In *Clara's Ole Man*, for instance, a young student hoping to make out with a woman stumbles into a cast of grotesques who fulfill a projected sense of menace by calling in a street gang to beat him senseless.

The Twentieth-Century Cycle—about which Bullins says, in his put-on voice "there is already talk of this collective project surpassing greatness in its scope, though the work is not that astonishing, relative to Bullins' abilities"—develops its first installment, *In the Wine Time*, from a prologue in which a male narrator lyrically describes the beautiful woman who represents the goals he innocently hopes to achieve. As counterpoint the body of the play reveals through its slowly moving dialogue of a summer evening the disappointments of the youth's exhausted aunt, the frustrated hopes of her husband, and the diversion of their ambitions into a contest over

Sleeping Beauty or Coma (produced New York, 1984). Included in *Four Plays*, 1990.

Theodora, She-Bitch of Byzantium (produced New York, 1984). Included in *Three Plays*, 1992.

Times Square Angel: A Hard-Boiled Christmas Fantasy (produced New York, 1984; revised version produced New York, 1985). Included in *Three Plays*, 1992.

Gidget Goes Psychotic (produced New York, 1986). New York, French, 1986.

Pardon My Inquisition; or, Kiss The Blood Off My Castanets (produced New York, 1986). Included in *Three Plays*, 1992.

Psycho Beach Party (produced New York, 1987). Included in *Four Plays*, 1990.

Ankles Aweigh, music and lyrics by Sammy Fain and Dan Shapiro (also co-director: produced East Haddam, Connecticut, 1987). New York, French, 1987.

The Lady in Question (produced New York, 1989). Included in *Four Plays*, 1990.

Four Plays. Garden City, New York, Fireside Theatre, 1990.

House of Flowers, adaptation of the libretto by Truman Capote (produced New York, 1991). New York, French, 1991.

Red Scare on Sunset (produced New York, 1991). Garden City, New York, Fireside Theatre, 1991.

Three Plays. Garden City, New York, Fireside Theatre, 1992.

*

Manuscript Collection: Lincoln Center Library of Performing Arts, New York.

Critical Study: *Downtown* by Michael Musto, New York, Vintage, 1986.

Theatrical Activities:
Director (with Dan Siretta): **Plays**—*Ankles Aweigh*, East Haddam, Connecticut, 1987.
Actor: **Plays**—all his own plays including: Virgin Sacrifice and Madeleine Astarte in *Vampire Lesbians of Sodom*; Irish O'Flanagan in *Times Square Angel*; Chicklet in *Psycho Beach Party*; title role in *Theodora, She-Bitch of Byzantium*; Maria Garbonza and the Marquesa Del Drago in *Pardon My Inquisition*; Gertrude Garnet in *The Lady in Question*; Fauna Alexander in *Sleeping Beauty*; Mary Dale in *Red Scare on Sunset*.

Charles Busch comments:

I identify strongly with the actor-managers of the 19th century. All of my plays have been written to give my company, Theatre-in-Limbo, and myself opportunities to act. Like the theatrical monsters I emulate, I believe passionately in the eternal power of melodrama, old-fashioned comedy rhythms, and the glamorous star vehicle. I've tried to celebrate these forms and conventions as well as parody them. An audience can be thrilled by the chase but also laugh at their own easy manipulation. However, I've also tried to employ old movie and theatrical genres as starting-off points to then reflect issues of importance to me, both personal and political. Ultimately, I remain hopelessly stagestruck and I write in order to act. It's not enough for an audience to read my stories, I am compelled to get up there and tell it to them myself.

* * *

Actor-playwright Charles Busch and his cohorts at Theatre-in-Limbo are proving themselves worthy successors to Charles Ludlam, whose death in 1987 was an irretrievable loss to the comic vein of American theatre. In eight years, Busch's work has moved from burlesque sketch comedies performed for late-night coterie audiences to two-act, Off-Broadway productions with open runs. Less aesthetically dangerous and more intellectually accessible than Ludlam's sublime scavenges of Western art, Busch's deft fruit salads of B-movie conventions, femme attitudes, and subversive politics, are enormously popular with audiences and critics of all persuasions.

Although Busch insists in preface after preface that his heroines needn't be performed by men in drag, much of the power in his work is derived from a cross-dressing, decidedly gay perspective. Without Busch himself expertly glossing—indeed, outdoing—Norma Shearer or Betty Hutton or Greer Garson on the stage, making us question the construction of gender and genre, his plays might seem of little more consequence than television spoofs of best-forgotten moments in American cinema. Yet no matter how outsized the role in Busch's menagerie, from a silent screen vamp to a 12-year-old Nazi, they are meant to be performed with a sincerity and a realism that forestalls any unwelcome complicity from the audience.

The double bill of *Sleeping Beauty or Coma* and *Vampire Lesbians of Sodom* started as a weekend party for friends and became one of the longest-running plays in Off-Broadway history. In *Sleeping Beauty*, a send-up of Carnaby Street in the swinging sixties, a fashion designer, a supermodel, and a photographer hit the heights of mod London and crash semi-permanently on shoddy tabs of acid. *Vampire Lesbians* time-travels from ancient Sodom to Hollywood in the 1920's to contemporary Las Vegas to tell the tale of rival succubi who wind up as competing entertainment divas. At the conclusion, each discovers she needs the other (if only to revile her)—the rewards of feminine friendship, treated embryonically in this fairytale, is a theme that runs through all of Busch's work.

Times Square Angel is Busch's first attempt at a cinematic saga, and he continues to tailor roles for his troupe of regulars much as Molière or Preston Sturges did. Irish O'Flanagan goes from the slums of Hell's Kitchen to the top of the post-war entertainment industry, trading in her heart along the way. One Christmas Eve, with the help of a wayward angel, Irish learns the true meaning of life. Although this fantasia on *It's a Wonderful Life* overreaches itself narratively, *Times Square Angel* is full of Busch's deliriously hard-boiled dialogue.

Funnier still is *Psycho Beach Party*, an amalgam of 1960's beach movies, *Sybil*, and *Mommie Dearest*. In addition to all the surfboards, dance numbers, and petting sessions compulsory to the sandflick genre, Busch's characters are unconscious heralds of non-conformism. Chicklet must free herself by integrating her multiple personalities, and, rather than suppress their attraction for each other, beach rats Yo Yo and Provoloney openly declare their forbidden homosexual love. Liberation is again the theme when Busch returns to the 1940's with *The Lady in Question*, an anti-Nazi war melodrama. Like Irish O'Flanagan, internationally acclaimed concert pianist Gertrude Garnet is an impossibly selfish woman who only discovers her humanity through sacrifice. After her sidekick Kitty is strangled by the evil Lotte Von Elsner, Gertrude rescues a political prisoner and escapes into Switzerland on skis with the man she loves. Busch's growth as a writer is impressive; familiarity with the intertexts, among them, in this case, Hitchcock's *Notorious* and the dreadful 1950's *Bad Seed*, enhances one's appreciation of *The Lady in Question* but isn't necessary if one is to laugh at its comedy or be held in real suspense by its plot.

No less artful than his other screen "adaptations," *Red Scare on Sunset*, Busch's latest offering, was greeted with less enthusiasm. When Mary Dale, played by Busch, names names on the air in order to free Hollywood of Communist menace, audiences were confused by the author's intentions. In a culture that in a very short while has become increasingly hostile to homosexuals and to art, one can no longer afford to satirize the left with impunity. Busch is not a political writer *per se*, but his choice of material and his production style are an inherent critique of the American myths of family, assimilation, career, love, showbiz, power, and luxury. They celebrate personal freedom against the forces of evil implicity gathering just beyond the footlights. In addition to his gay audience, Busch is popular with the aging Baby Boomers given over to refabricating the hoary artifacts and attitudes of their past; yet, beneath the cartoon contours of his Hollywood tropes, Busch challenges an easy, ravenous predilection for camp by creating moments of genuine feeling. His insistence that his work be performed "straight," lends to his best plays an undeniable charm and a salutary tension.

—James Magruder

BUZO, Alexander (John). Australian. Born in Sydney, New South Wales, 23 July 1944. Educated at the Armidale School, New South Wales, 1956–60; International School of Geneva, 1962; University of New South Wales, Sydney, 1963–65, B.A. 1965. Married Merelyn Johnson in 1968; three daughters. Salesman, David Jones Ltd., Sydney, 1960; messenger, E.L. Davis and Company, Sydney, 1961; storeman-packer, McGraw-Hill Book Company, Sydney, 1967; clerk, New South Wales Public Service, Sydney, 1967–68; resident playwright, Melbourne Theatre Company, 1972–73; writer-in-residence, Sydney Teachers College, 1978, James Cook University, Townsville, 1985, University of Wollongong, 1989, and University of Central Queensland, 1991. Recipient: Australian Literature Society gold medal, 1972; Commonwealth Literary Fund fellowship, 1973; Australia Council Literature Board grant, 1974, 1978. Agent: Curtis Brown Group, 27 Union Street, Paddington, Sydney, New South Wales 2021, Australia.

PUBLICATIONS

Plays

The Revolt (produced Sydney, 1967).
Norm and Ahmed (produced Sydney, 1968; London, 1974).Included in *Norm and Ahmed, Rooted, and The Roy Murphy Show*, 1973.
Rooted (produced Canberra, 1969; Hartford, Connecticut, 1972; London, 1973). Included in *Norm and Ahmed, Rooted, and The Roy Murphy Show*, 1973.
The Front Room Boys (produced Perth, 1970; London, 1971). Published in *Plays*, Melbourne, Penguin, 1970.
The Roy Murphy Show (produced Sydney, 1971; London, 1983). Included in *Norm and Ahmed, Rooted, and The Roy Murphy Show*, 1973.
Macquarie (produced Melbourne, 1972). Sydney, Currency Press, 1971.

Tom (produced Melbourne, 1972; Washington, D.C., 1973). Sydney and London, Angus and Robertson, 1975.
Batman's Beach-head, adaption of a play by Ibsen (produced Melbourne, 1973).
Norm and Ahmed, Rooted, and The Roy Murphy Show: Three Plays. Sydney, Currency Press, and London, Eyre Methuen, 1973.
Coralie Lansdowne Says No (produced Adelaide, 1974). Sydney, Currency Press, and London, Eyre Methuen, 1974.
Martello Towers (produced Sydney, 1976). Sydney, Currency Press, and London, Eyre Methuen, 1976.
Vicki Madison Clocks Out (produced Adelaide, 1976; Louisville, 1980).
Makassar Reef (produced Melbourne and Seattle, 1978). Sydney, Currency Press, 1978.
Big River (produced Adelaide, 1980). With *The Marginal Farm*, Sydney, Currency Press, 1985.
The Marginal Farm (produced Melbourne, 1983). With *Big River*, Sydney, Currency Press, 1985.
Stingray (produced Sydney, 1987).
Shellcove Road (produced Sydney, 1989).

Screenplays: *Rod*, 1972; *Norm and Ahmed*, 1988.

Radio Plays: *File on Rod*, 1972; *Duff*, 1980; *In Search of the New Class*, 1982; *East of Singapore*, 1986.

Television Writing (animated films): *A Christmas Carol*, 1982, *Great Expectations*, 1983, *David Copperfield*, 1984, and *The Old Curiosity Shop*, 1985, all from works by Dickens.

Novels

The Search for Harry Allway. Sydney, Angus and Robertson, 1985.
Prue Flies North. Melbourne, Mandarin, 1991.

Other

Tautology: I Don't Want to Sound Incredulous But I Can't Believe It. Melbourne, Penguin, 1981; revised edition, as *Tautology Too*, 1982.
Meet the New Class. Sydney, Angus and Robertson, 1981.
Glancing Blows. Melbourne, Penguin, 1987.
The Young Person's Guide to the Theatre and Almost Everything Else. Melbourne, Penguin, 1988.

Editor (Australian edition), *Real Men Don't Eat Quiche*, by Bruce Feirstein. Sydney, Angus and Robertson, 1982.
Editor with Jamie Grant, *The Longest Game*. Melbourne, Heinemann, 1990.

*

Manuscript Collections: Mitchell Library, Sydney; National Library, Canberra; University of New South Wales Library.

Critical Studies: introduction by Katharine Brisbane to *Norm and Ahmed, Rooted, and The Roy Murphy Show*, 1973; *After "The Doll": Australian Drama since 1955* by Peter Fitzpatrick, Melbourne, Arnold, 1979; *Alexander Buzo's Rooted and Norm and Ahmed: A Critical Introduction* by T.L. Sturm, Sydney, Currency Press, 1980, and "Alexander Buzo: An Imagist with a Personal Style of Surrealism" by Sturm and "Aggressive Vernacular" by Roslyn Arnold, both in *Contemporary Australian Drama* edited by Peter

Holloway, Currency Press, 1981, revised edition, 1987; interview in *Southerly* (Sydney), March 1986; *Buzo* by John McCallum, Sydney, Methuen, 1987.

Theatrical Activities:
Director: **Play**—*Care* by Daniel Hughes, Sydney, 1969.
Actor: **Plays**—*The Alchemist* by Jonson, Sydney, 1966; *Macbird* by Barbara Garson, Sydney, 1967.

Alexander Buzo comments:

My plays are, I hope, realistic poetic comedies set in contemporary times. They are not naturalistic. The mentality behind them could be described as humanist. Magritte is my favourite painter. When I started writing, the Theatre of the Absurd was a big influence. I place emphasis on verbal precision and visual clarity, and am not terribly interested in group anarchy. I believe in literacy, professionalism, and niceness. Nearly all my plays concentrate on one central character having problems with what's around and about.

* * *

Alexander Buzo's first short play, *Norm and Ahmed*, was something of a landmark on the route to the contemporary form of the Australian play. It was only a decade from Ray Lawler's *Summer of the Seventeenth Doll* and seven years from Alan Seymour's *The One Day of the Year*, each of them regarded as quintessential Australian plays. But *Norm and Ahmed*, though not apparently revolutionary in form, gathered up a number of new popular influences which began to take the new writers in a different direction.

Norm, a middle-aged, lonely, and unimaginative storeman, stops Ahmed, a Pakistani student, on a street corner one night and engages him in reluctant conversation. Norm's character has drawn on caricatures of the conservative returned serviceman and portraits like Barry Humphries's Sandy Stone and Seymour's Alf Cook from *The One Day of the Year*. Buzo gives their xenophobia and their rigid daily rituals a new aspect by placing them in confrontation with an Asian hinterland. Norm's strikingly aggressive-defensive attitude, quite unprovoked by Ahmed, is crystallised in the final moment. Norm proffers his hand in farewell and when Ahmed takes it, Norm smashes his head.

This is the only real moment of violence in all of Buzo's writing. After that he moves into the middle class for his context; the violence turns inward into verbal persecution.

In common with other playwrights, in the late 1960's Buzo was attracted by the variety of vernacular language and the loose rhythms of Australian life. Play by play he developed towards a comedy of manners which makes one listen afresh to familiar phrases and to his satirical embroidery of the colourful cliché. It has been said with justice that if his characters stopped talking they would scream: Buzo uses language both as a weapon against and as a shield between his people and an unpleasant or mundane reality.

For Buzo is more than a satirist. Behind the writing there are loneliness and a belief that in an older society with a stronger base of religious or social dogma things might be different. The absence of religious influence in Buzo's work is almost unique among contemporary Australian playwrights. In its place is a strong poetic response to nature which the characters express in unguarded moments. Without exception Buzo's figures are alienated. Both Norm and Ahmed are aliens in the same land, trying fruitlessly to understand it. Bentley, the timid but ambitious public servant in *Rooted*, is singled out for persecution in the schoolboy gang games of the young executives for no better reason than that he is a bore. Beneath the parody of adolescent manners, the comic-strip structure of the scenes, and the jargon of the beach, the art gallery, and the public service, *Rooted* is an allegory of every young man's sense of inadequacy in a society that has no roots but other people's acceptance. In *The Front Room Boys*, which satirically records in 12 scenes the tribal rituals of a city office, all the front room boys are hunted by the unexplained power of the back room boys and in turn hunt each other. In *Tom* Buzo gives us a manufactured hero, an oil exploration trouble-shooter who speaks in monosyllables and is surrounded by the camp followers of big business while his wife suffers suburban neurosis and toothache.

In *Macquarie* Buzo abandons satire to deal with an early governor of New South Wales whose idealistic liberalism led to his downfall at the hands of the conservative power group. And in *Coralie Lansdowne Says No*, his most serious comedy of manners, a high flying young rebel facing on the other side of thirty settles for a tiresome public servant who offers durability. All of these characters are misfits, aliens like Norm in their own world, and they are swallowed up by the unquestioning values of their too-modern society.

Buzo continues to pursue this problem of rootlessness in *Martello Towers* and *Makassar Reef*, the first about the immigrant consciousness in urban Australia, the second about the migrant habits of those who touch down in the resorts of Indonesia. The setting of *Martello Towers* is an island holiday house on the Hawkesbury River, near Sydney, where Edward Martello and his estranged wife and their parents gather by accident. The family is aristocratic, two generations Australian, but still with roots in Trieste; old Martello has come to beg for a grandchild who will continue the family name. Edward says no, there are plenty of Martellos in the phone book. None of the family is happy, though they have their comforts and their brief contact with the earth and the water. They are as alienated as Norm.

This is the last of the fierce, bitter Buzo wit in the theatre, and the last of the rebelliousness. With his most recent works, *Big River* and *The Marginal Farm*, Buzo has entered a new phase, abandoning the brittleness for an overt romanticism in his examination of his characters' allegiance to their environment; and emerges with the realisation that, when men and women put down their roots in the land, they find themselves not owners but servants of it.

Big River is a portrait of Australia at Federation, moving imperceptibly from the dramatic action of a frontier community to the gentler preoccupations of suburbia. The central image is the River Murray which divides Victoria from New South Wales; and the protagonist a young widow returning to her father's vineyard for his funeral. As members of the family go their separate ways we see Adele remain, her high-flying life force captured and domesticated into a quiet contentment. A similar prey of circumstances is Toby, the heroine of *The Marginal Farm*, who takes a job as governess in Fiji in a moment of romantic restlessness. Overwhelmed at first by the beauty of the sugar cane island, she soon finds her new community a band of itinerants who one by one fly away, leaving her stranded, clinging half-heartedly to the Indian lover she has taken on an impulse of defiant individualism.

His most recent play, *Shellcove Road*, completes the cycle away from assault on current manners into overt nostalgia. Set in the Sydney house in which he grew up, the play explores a family's decision to sell the long-vacant family home. The father, a wealthy post-war immigrant, has learnt how to live solely in the present, for the mother the house is an inherited burden; but for the son, a financier, the house is haunted by the friendly ghosts of the past, and gives a sudden reminder of different values from a more secure, less worldly way of life. The surface action revolves around the choice between development and conservation; and the elegiac tone is punctuated with a subdued but characteristic Buzo wit.

Recently Buzo has moved away from the theatre to journalism, political and social satire and novel writing.

—Katharine Brisbane

BYRNE, John. British. Born in Paisley, Renfrewshire, Scotland, 6 January 1940. Educated at St. Mirin's Academy and Glasgow School of Art, 1958–63. Married Alice Simpson in 1964; one son and one daughter. Graphic designer, Scottish Television, Glasgow, 1964–66; designer, A.F. Stoddard, carpet manufacturers, Elderslie, 1966–68. Writer-in-residence, Borderline Theatre, Irvine, Ayrshire, 1978–79, and Duncan of Jordanstone College, Dundee, 1981; associate director, Haymarket Theatre, Leicester, 1984–85. Theatrical set and costume designer. Recipient: *Evening Standard* award, 1978. Agent: Casarotto Ramsay Ltd., National House, 60–66 Wardour Street, London W1V 3HP, England. Address: 3 Castle Brae, Newport-on-Tay, Fife, Scotland.

PUBLICATIONS

Plays

Writer's Cramp (produced Edinburgh and London, 1977; revised version, produced London, 1980; New York, 1986).   Published in *Plays and Players* (London), December 1977.
The Slab Boys Trilogy (originally called *Paisley Patterns*). London, Penguin, 1987.
  1. *The Slab Boys* (produced Edinburgh and London, 1978; Louisville, 1979; New York, 1980). Glasgow, Scottish Society of Playwrights, 1981; New York, French, 1982; revised version, Edinburgh, Salamander Press, 1982.
  2. *Cuttin' a Rug* (as *The Loveliest Night of the Year*, produced Edinburgh, 1979; revised version, as *Threads*, produced London, 1980; as *Cuttin' a Rug*, produced London, 1982; Washington, D.C., 1986).   *Threads* published in *A Decade's Drama: Six Scottish Plays*, edited by Richard and Susan Mellis, Todmorden, Lancashire, Woodhouse, 1981; *Cuttin' A Rug* published Edinburgh, Salamander Press, 1982.
  3. *Still Life* (produced Edinburgh, 1982; Washington, D.C., 1986).   Edinburgh, Salamander Press, 1982.
Normal Service (produced London, 1979).   Published in *Plays and Players* (London), May–June 1979.
Hooray for Hollywood (produced Louisville, 1980).
Babes in the Wood, music by John Gould, lyrics by David Dearlove (produced Glasgow, 1980).
Cara Coco (produced Irvine, Ayrshire, 1981).
Candy Kisses (produced London, 1984).
The London Cuckolds, adaptation of the play by Edward Ravenscroft (produced Leicester and London, 1985). London, French, 1986.

Radio Plays: *The Staffie* (version of *Cuttin' a Rug*); *A Night at the Alex*, 1981; *The Nitshill Writing Circle*, 1984.

Television Plays: *The Butterfly's Hoof*, 1978; *Big Deal* (*Crown Court* series), 1984; *Tutti Frutti* series, 1987; *Your Cheatin' Heart* series, 1990.

Novels

Tutti Frutti (novelization of television series).   London, BBC Publications, 1987.
Your Cheatin' Heart (novelization of television series). London, BBC Publications, 1990.

*

Theatrical Activities:
Designer (sets, costumes, and/or posters): **Plays**—*The Cheviot, The Stag, and the Black Black Oil* by John McGrath, Edinburgh and tour, 1973; *The Fantastical Feats of Finn MacCool* by Sean McCarthy, Edinburgh, 1974; *Writer's Cramp*, London, 1980; *Heaven and Hell* by Dusty Hughes, Edinburgh, 1981; *The Number of the Beast* by Snoo Wilson, London, 1982; *The Slab Boys Trilogy*, Edinburgh and London, 1982; *Other Worlds* by Robert Holman, 1982; *La Colombe* by Gounod, Buxton, Derbyshire, 1983; *McQuin's Metamorphosis* by Martyn Hobbs, Edinburgh, 1984; *The Cherry Orchard* by Chekhov, Leicester, 1984; *A Midsummer Night's Dream*, Leicester, 1984; *Candy Kisses*, London, 1984; *Dead Men* by Mike Stott, Edinburgh, 1985; *The London Cuckolds*, Leicester, 1985; *The Marriage of Figaro* by Mozart, Glasgow, 1986.

John Byrne comments:
    (1982) I think I was 11 or 12 when I wrote my first piece . . . not for the theatre, although it was highly-dramatic . . . about a cat that gets squashed under a bus. Accompanied by a linocut showing the young master in tears alongside the open coffin, it appeared in the pages of the school magazine. A slow fuse had been lit. 25 years later (in 1976) I wrote my first stage play, *Writer's Cramp*, a scherzo in J Minor for trio. This was followed by *The Slab Boys* (part 1 of a trilogy) based (but heavily embroidered) upon my own experience of working as a retarded teenager in the design studio of a carpet factory. Next came *Normal Service*, in the original draft densely packed with all sorts of motley stuffs like the haggis, but subsequently "opened up" for the stage, again based (however loosely) on a working experience, this time in television. I was trying in *Normal Service* to write a comedy without jokes, a comedy of manners, of character, the relationships within and without the office, the characters' attitudes towards one another, towards their own and each others' spouses, to their work. I can't be certain I've got the skill to cram all of that into two hours or so, which is part of the reason for my writing the aforementioned trilogy (in which the protagonists in Parts 1 and 2 are moved on 20-odd years in Part 3). In effect *The Slab Boys* trilogy will be one long play in three acts. In *Hooray for Hollywood* I transplanted the hero (F.S. McDade) of *Writer's Cramp* from Paisley to Los Angeles and looked on with mounting alarm as he proceeded to behave quite predictably. This was a ten-minute piece (part of an anthology) commissioned by the Actors' Theatre of Louisville. The distaff side of *Writer's Cramp*, *Cara Coco* (at present being rewritten), was presented by Borderline Theatre Co. in Scotland. Just now I am working on a play set in another country (other than Scotland, that is) and on one set in another time (not based on personal experience).

* * *

John Byrne was born in Paisley, a suburb of Glasgow, in 1940 and draws heavily on his past experiences and his

Scottish upbringing and adolescence for his stage writing. Unlike many of his contemporaries Byrne didn't have any success as a writer until early middle age. This success came in 1977 with his first play, *Writer's Cramp*, which transferred to London from the Edinburgh Festival and was subsequently revived. Until then Byrne had earned his living as a designer and painter, having studied art before spells in carpet manufacture and in television, periods on which he was to draw in subsequent plays. Byrne had dealings with the trendy world of art and pop music, particularly in the swinging 1960's when he had an exhibition in London and was even accorded a profile in one of the Sunday supplements. Byrne also designed LP covers and dust jackets for contemporaries such as comedian Billy Connolly and singer Gerry Rafferty and worked as a scene painter with the celebrated Scottish touring group 7:84. His contempt for the art world has led him to quit it for good and embrace the theatrical world not only as an alternative source of inspiration but, in his view, as a superior way of life. Nevertheless his painter's preoccupation with detail and his gifts of observation are stamped boldly on his work for the stage.

Writer's Cramp is an often very funny and accurate extended literary joke which parodies the styles and pretensions of arty Scotland, through the life and times of one Francis Seneca McDade. McDade, a writer, painter, and belle lettrist as well as a loveable but irredeemable mediocrity, is shown progressing from disaster to disaster: prep school, prison, literary Oxford, and swinging London, before his final demise clutching a hard-won but rather irrelevant wad of bank notes. Included among the send-ups and satires which intersperse the scenes in question are an article on Work-shy Pensioners and a disastrous musical on Dr. Spock, the latter like much of McDade's canon not advanced much further than the planning stage. However, McDade does acquire brief fame in the 1960's as an artist following a typical review from the art critic of the *Scottish Field*, one Dermot Pantalone: "When I quizzed the artist as to why so many of his pictures were painted on Formica using household brushes, his answer was to pick up a pot of Banana Yellow Deep Gloss Enamel and proceed to draw the outline of a giraffe on my overcoat. . . ." McDade and his world of poseurs and eccentrics were a rather easy target for Byrne's obvious comic and linguistic gifts. His second play, first seen at the Traverse Theatre in Edinburgh, and later in London and on television, was a very different affair. *The Slab Boys* is a lively piece of social realism cum situation comedy set in the paint-mixing room of a Glasgow carpet factory in 1957, and it draws heavily on Byrne's own past as an apprentice. The play, fiercely idiomatic and full of pungent one-liners and shop-floor banter, details a working day, in particular that of three very different apprentices: Phil, the small young rebel with a secret urge to be a painter; Spanky, the heavy and slow pal of Phil's; and Hector, shy and domiciled with an over-protective mother. It is Hector's attempt to make himself ready and presentable for the forthcoming staff dance which provides the piece with most of its narrative drive, although it is Byrne's gift for recreating the trends and preoccupations of the period (from

hit parade to comic book heroes and hairstyles) and his raucous sense of character and speech which made the play such a success.

Certainly Byrne's subsequent plays have also revealed an interest in character over narrative. *Threads* (originally *The Loveliest Night of the Year*) takes the action of *The Slab Boys* on to the evening of the "staffie" or firm dance. The dialogue is similarly colloquial, strident, and often witheringly amusing, but the action runs out of steam and relies on a series of farcical encounters in the dark which are poor compensation for the loss of the setting of the marvelously evocative slab room in the first play. Nevertheless Byrne still manages to provide the occasional telling visual effect (such as the glaring imprint of a flat iron on the back of Phil's otherwise immaculate white tuxedo).

Normal Service, which equally obviously draws on Byrne's experiences (this time as a designer for Scottish Television in the early 1960's), is set in the design room of such an organisation during a weekend in 1963 when the station's special tenth anniversary programme is due to be recorded. It depicts the internecine strife of the assembled workers who range from a cowardly, trendy media man with a kilt, to a decrepit and hilariously unsuccessful repair man, a weedy expectant father to a demonic trade-union official of Italian descent who declares war every time he answers a ringing phone. Indeed in the resulting chaos the characters and their interplay hold more sway over the audience than any development of storyline or message about technology and the chaotically minded people who service it daily.

Byrne's last substantial stage work, *Candy Kisses*, shows that his comic terrain can extend beyond Glasgow or London. It is set in 1963 in Italy where the visit of Pope Paul VI to Perugia is greeted with murderous intent by a demented fascist professor and two youthful locals with differing degrees of commitment to a Trotskyist terror group. There are varying supports: an East Coast American art student meets a draft-dodging West Coast twerp; a German fraulein attempts restoration of a Perugino fresco. Cleverly the local Italians speak with either Scots, Welsh, or Irish accents, a device which further isolates the cultural imperialists and foreigners. The plot unravels like a plate of spaghetti, although the play is hardly as substantial.

Byrne may not have kept up his steady output for the stage (though there is an amusing but insubstantial radio satire, *The Nitshill Writing Circle* which takes us back to *Writer's Cramp* territory) but he was acclaimed in 1987 for his television series *Tutti Frutti*, a whacky saga of an ageing Scottish rock-soul band on the road which starred among others one of the original Slab Boys, Robbie Coltrane. Perhaps this is the future direction for one of Britain's more engaging and unpretentious comic talents.

—Steve Grant

C

CAMPTON, David. British. Born in Leicester, 5 June 1924. Educated at Wyggeston Grammar School, 1935–41, matriculation 1940. Served in the Royal Air Force, 1942–45; in the Fleet Air Arm, 1945–46. Clerk, City of Leicester Education Department, 1941–49, and East Midlands Gas Board, Leicester, 1949–56. Recipient: Arts Council bursary, 1958; British Theatre Association Whitworth prize, 1975, 1978, 1985; Japan prize, for radio play, 1977. Agent: ACTAC (Theatrical and Cinematic) Ltd., 15 High Street, Ramsbury, Wiltshire SN8 2PA. Address: 35 Liberty Road, Glenfield, Leicester LE3 8JF, England.

PUBLICATIONS

Plays

Going Home (produced Leicester, 1950). Manchester, Abel Heywood, 1951.
Honeymoon Express (produced Leicester, 1951). Manchester, Abel Heywood, 1951.
Change Partners (produced Leicester, 1952). Manchester, Abel Heywood, 1951.
Sunshine on the Righteous (produced Leicester, 1953). London, Rylee, 1952.
The Laboratory (produced Leicester and London, 1954). London, J. Garnet Miller, 1955.
Want a Bet? (produced Leicester, 1954).
Ripple in the Pool (produced Leicester, 1955).
The Cactus Garden (produced Reading, Berkshire, 1955). London, J. Garnet Miller, 1955.
Dragons Are Dangerous (produced Scarborough, 1955).
Idol in the Sky, with Stephen Joseph (produced Scarborough, 1956).
Doctor Alexander. Leicester, Campton, 1956.
Cuckoo Song. Leicester, Campton, 1956.
The Lunatic View: A Comedy of Menace (includes *A Smell of Burning, Then . . ., Memento Mori, Getting and Spending*) (produced Scarborough, *1957; New York, 1962; Then . . .* produced London, 1980). Scarborough, Studio Theatre, 1960; *A Smell of Burning*, and *Then . . .* published New York, Dramatists Play Service, 1971.
Roses round the Door (as *Ring of Roses*, produced Scarborough, 1958). London, J. Garnet Miller, 1967.
Frankenstein: The Gift of Fire, adaptation of the novel by Mary Shelley (produced Scarborough, 1959). London, J. Garnet Miller, 1973.
Little Brother, Little Sister (produced Newcastle-under-Lyme, Staffordshire, 1961; London, 1966). Leicester, Campton, 1960.
A View from the Brink (playlets: produced Scarborough, 1960). Section entitled *Out of the Flying Pan* included in *Little Brother, Little Sister; and Out of the Flying Pan*, 1970.
Four Minute Warning (includes *Little Brother, Little Sister; Mutatis Mutandis; Soldier from the Wars Returning; At Sea*) (produced Newcastle-under-Lyme, Staffordshire, 1960;

Soldier from the Wars Returning produced London, 1961; *Mutatis Mutandis* produced London, 1967). Leicester, Campton, 4 vols., 1960.
Funeral Dance (produced Dovercourt, Essex, 1960). London, J. Garnet Miller, 1962.
Sketches in *You, Me and the Gatepost* (produced Nottingham, 1960).
Sketches in *Second Post* (produced Nottingham, 1961).
Passport to Florence (as *Stranger in the Family*, produced Scarborough, 1961). London, J. Garnet Miller, 1967.
The Girls and the Boys (revue; produced Scarborough, 1961).
Silence on the Battlefield (produced Dovercourt, Essex, 1961). London, J. Garnet Miller, 1967.
Sketches in *Yer What?* (produced Nottingham, 1962).
Usher, adaptation of the story "The Fall of the House of Usher" by Poe (also director: produced Scarborough, 1962; London, 1974). London, J. Garnet Miller, 1973.
Incident (produced 1962). London, J. Garnet Miller, 1967.
A Tinkle of Tiny Bells (broadcast 1963; produced Cumbernauld, Dumbartonshire, 1971).
Comeback (produced Scarborough, 1963; revised version, as *Honey, I'm Home*, produced Leatherhead, Surrey, 1964).
Don't Wait for Me (broadcast 1963; produced London, 1963). Published in *Worth a Hearing: A Collection of Radio Plays*, edited by Alfred Bradley, London, Blackie, 1967.
Dead and Alive (produced Scarborough, 1964). London, J. Garnet Miller, 1983.
On Stage: Containing Seventeen Sketches and One Monologue. London, J. Garnet Miller, 1964.
Resting Place (broadcast 1964; in *We Who Are about to . . .*, later called *Mixed Doubles*, produced London, 1969). London, Methuen, 1970.
The End of the Picnic (broadcast 1964; produced Vancouver, British Columbia, 1973). Included in *Laughter and Fear*, 1969.
The Manipulator (broadcast 1964; shortened version, as *A Point of View*, produced 1964; as *The Manipulator*, produced 1968). London, J. Garnet Miller, 1967.
Cock and Bull Story (produced Scarborough, 1965).
Where Have All the Ghosts Gone? (broadcast 1965). Included in *Laughter and Fear*, 1969.
Split Down the Middle (broadcast 1965; produced Scarborough, 1966). London, J. Garnet Miller, 1973.
Two Leaves and a Stalk (produced 1967). London, J. Garnet Miller, 1967.
Angel Unwilling (broadcast 1967; produced 1972). Leicester, Campton, 1972.
More Sketches. Leicester, Campton, 1967.
Ladies' Night: Four Plays for Women (includes *Two Leaves and a Stalk, Silence on the Battlefield, Incident, The Manipulator*). London, J. Garnet Miller, 1967.
Parcel (broadcast 1968). London, French, 1979.
The Right Place (produced 1970). Leicester, Campton, 1969.
Laughter and Fear: 9 One-Act Plays (includes *Incident, Then . . ., Memento Mori, The End of the Picnic, The*

Laboratory, A Point of View, Soldier from the Wars Returning, Mutatis Mutandis, Where Have All the Ghosts Gone?). London, Blackie, 1969.

On Stage Again: Containing Fourteen Sketches and Two Monologues. London, J. Garnet Miller, 1969.

The Life and Death of Almost Everybody (produced London, 1970), Leicester, Campton, 1971; New York, Dramatists Play Service, 1972.

Now and Then (produced 1970). Leicester, Campton, 1973.

Little Brother, Little Sister; and Out of the Flying Pan. London, Methuen, and New York, Dramatists Play Service, 1970.

Timesneeze (produced London, 1970). London, Eyre Methuen, 1974.

Wonderchick (produced Bristol, 1970).

Jonah (produced Chelmsford, Essex, 1971). London, J. Garnet Miller, 1972.

The Cagebirds (produced Tunbridge Wells, Kent, 1971; London, 1977). Leicester, Campton, 1972.

Provisioning (produced London, 1971).

Us and Them (produced 1972). Leicester, Campton, 1972; Chicago, Dramatic Publishing Company, 1982.

Carmilla, adaptation of a story by Le Fanu (produced Sheffield, 1972). London, J. Garnet Miller, 1973.

Come Back Tomorrow. Leicester, Campton, 1972.

In Committee. Leicester, Campton, 1972.

Three Gothic Plays (includes *Frankenstein, Usher, Carmilla*). London, J. Garnet Miller, 1973.

Eskimos, in *Mixed Blessings* (produced Horsham, Sussex, 1973). Included in *Pieces of Campton*, 1979.

Relics (produced Leicester, 1973). London, Evans, 1974.

An Outline of History (produced Bishop Auckland, County Durham, 1974). Leicester, Campton, 1981.

Everybody's Friend (broadcast 1974; produced Edinburgh, 1975). London, French, 1979.

Ragerbo! (produced Peckleton, Leicestershire, 1975). Leicester, Campton, 1977.

The Do-It-Yourself Frankenstein Outfit (produced Birmingham, 1975). London, French, 1978.

George Davenport, The Wigston Highwayman (produced Countesthorpe, Leicestershire, 1975).

What Are You Doing Here? Leicester, Campton, 1976.

No Go Area. Leicester, Campton, 1976.

One Possessed (broadcast 1977). Leicester, Campton, 1977.

Oh, Yes It Is! (produced Braunston, Northamptonshire, 1977).

Zodiac, music by John Whitworth (produced Melton Mowbray, Leicestershire, 1977). London, French, 1978.

The Great Little Tilley (produced Nottingham, 1978).

After Midnight, Before Dawn (produced Leicester, 1978). London, French, 1978.

Dark Wings (produced Leicester, 1978). Leicester, Campton, 1980.

Pieces of Campton (dialogues; includes *According to the Book, At the Door, Drip, Eskimos, Expectation, Strong Man Act, Sunday Breakfast, Under the Bush, Where Were You Last Winter?*). Leicester, Campton, 1979.

Who Calls? (produced Dublin, 1979). London, French, and Chicago, Dramatic Publishing Company, 1980.

Under the Bush (produced London, 1980). Included in *Pieces of Campton*, 1979.

Attitudes (produced Stoke-on-Trent, 1981). Leicester, Campton, 1980.

Freedom Log. Leicester, Campton, 1980.

Star-station Freedom (produced Leicester, 1981).

Look—Sea, and Great Whales. Leicester, Campton, 1981.

Who's a Hero, Then? Leicester, Campton, 1981.

Apocalypse Now and Then (includes *Mutatis Mutandis* and *The View from Here*) (produced Leicester, 1982).

Olympus (produced Leicester, 1983).

But Not Here (produced Leicester, 1983). Leicester, Campton, 1984.

Two in the Corner (includes *Reserved, En attendant François, Overhearings*). Leicester, Campton, 1983.

En attendant François (produced Chelmsford, Essex, 1984). Included in *Two in the Corner*, 1983.

Who's Been Sitting in My Chair? (produced Chelmsford, Essex, 1984).

So Why? Leicester, Campton, 1984.

Mrs. Meadowsweet (as *Mrs. M.*, broadcast 1984; revised version, as *Mrs. Meadowsweet*, produced Ulverston, Lancashire, 1985). London, French, 1986.

Cards, Cups, and Crystal Ball (produced Broadway, Worcestershire, 1985). Leicester, Campton, and Chicago, Dramatic Publishing Company, 1986.

Singing in the Wilderness (produced Leicester, 1985). London, French, 1986.

Our Branch in Brussels. London, French, 1986.

The Spectre Bridegroom, adaptation of the play by W.T. Moncrieff (also director: produced Leicester, 1987). Leicester, Campton, 1987.

Can You Hear the Music? (produced Leicester, 1988). London, French, 1988.

The Winter of 1917 (produced Bognor Regis, West Sussex, 1989). London, French, and Chicago, Dramatic Publishing Company, 1989.

Smile (produced Colefore, 1990). London, French, and Chicago, Dramatic Publishing Company, 1990.

Radio Plays: *A Tinkle of Tiny Bells*, 1963; *Don't Wait for Me*, 1963; *The Manipulator*, 1964; *Alison*, 1964; *Resting Place*, 1964; *The End of the Picnic*, 1964; *Split Down the Middle*, 1965; *Where Have All the Ghosts Gone?*, 1965; *Angel Unwilling*, 1967; *The Missing Jewel*, 1967; *Parcel*, 1968; *Boo!*, 1971; *Now You Know*, 1971 (Italy); *Ask Me No Questions* (Germany); *Holiday, As Others See Us, So You Think You're a Hero, We Did It for Laughs, Deep Blue Sea?, Isle of the Free, You Started It, Good Money, You're on Your Own, Mental Health, We Know What's Right, When the Wells Run Dry, Our Crowd, Nice Old Stick Really, On the Rampage, Victor, Little Boy Lost*, and *Tramps* (all in *Inquiry* series), from 1971; *Everybody's Friend*, 1974; *One Possessed*, 1977; *I'm Sorry, Mrs. Baxter*, 1977; *Our Friend Bimbo*, 1978, *Three Fairy Tales*, 1979, and *Bang! Wham!*, 1979 (all Denmark); *Community* series (5 episodes for schools), 1979; *Peacock Feathers*, 1982; *Kahani Apni Apni* series, 1983; *Mrs. M.*, 1984; *Cards, Cups, and Crystal Ball*, 1987.

Television Plays: *One Fight More*, with Stephen Joseph, 1956; *See What You Think* series, 1957; *Starr and Company* (serialization), 1958; *Tunnel under the World*, 1966; *Someone in the Lift*, 1967; *The Triumph of Death*, 1968; *A Private Place*, 1968; *Liar*, 1969; *Time for a Change*, 1969; *Slim John*, with others, 1971; *The Bellcrest Story*, 1972; *People You Meet*, 1972.

Other (for children)

Gulliver in Lilliput. London, University of London Press, 1970.

Gulliver in the Land of the Giants. London, University of London Press, 1970.

The Wooden Horse of Troy. London, University of London Press, 1970.

Modern Aesop Stories. Kuala Lumpur, Oxford University Press, 1976.
Vampyre, from a story by John Polidori. London, Hutchinson, 1986; New York, Barron's, 1988.
Frankenstein. London, Hutchinson, 1987.
Becoming a Playwright. London, Robert Hale, 1992.

*

Critical Studies: *Anger and After* by John Russell Taylor, London, Methuen, 1962, revised edition, 1969, as *The Angry Theatre*, New York, Hill and Wang, 1962, revised edition, 1969; *The Disarmers* by Christopher Driver, London, Hodder and Stoughton, 1964; "Comedy of Menace" by Irving Wardle, in *The Encore Reader*, London, Methuen, 1965; *Laughter and Fear* edited by Michael Marland, Glasgow, Blackie, 1969; *Investigating Drama* by Kenneth Pickering, Bill Horrocks, and David Male, London, Allen and Unwin, 1974.

Theatrical Activities:
Director: **Play**—*Usher*, Scarborough, 1962; *The Spectre Bridegroom*, 1987.
Actor: **Plays**—roles with Stephen Joseph's Theatre in the Round, Scarborough and on tour, 1957–63, including Petey in *The Birthday Party* by Harold Pinter, Birmingham, 1959, Old Man in *Memento Mori*, London, 1960, Polonius in *Hamlet*, Newcastle-under-Lyme, Staffordshire, 1962, Noah in *The Ark* by James Saunders, Scarborough, 1962, and Harry Perkins in *Comeback*, Scarborough, 1963; Cinquemani in *The Shameless Professor* by Pirandello, London, 1959; Bread in *The Blue Bird* by Maeterlinck, London, 1963.

David Campton comments:
Realizing that a play in a drawer is of no use to anyone, and that, being an ephemeral thing, it will not wait for posterity to catch up with it, I have always written with production in mind.
The circumstances of production have varied from the village hall, through radio and television, to the West End stage. (Though representation on that last has been confined to one-act plays and sketches.) This has also meant that my plays have varied in kind from domestic comedy, through costume melodrama to—as Irving Wardle coined the phrase —"comedy of menace."
My profession is playwriting, and I hope I approach it with a professional mixture of art and business. The art of playwriting is of prime importance; I hope I have never relegated it to second place. I have never written a play "because it might sell." Everything I have written has been clamouring to be written and as long as I have been able to make marks on paper, there has always been a queue of a dozen or more ideas waiting their turn to achieve solid form. But an idea can always be developed towards a particular medium, be it experimental theatre in the round or an all-female group performing in a converted schoolroom.
I dislike pigeonholes and object to being popped into one. However, one label that might fit is the title of an anthology of my plays: *Laughter and Fear*. This is not quite the same as comedy of menace, which has acquired a connotation of theatre of the absurd. It is in fact present in my lightest domestic comedy. It seems to me that the chaos affecting everyone today—political, technical, sociological, religious, etc., etc.—is so all-pervading that it cannot be ignored, yet so shattering that it can only be approached through comedy. Tragedy demands firm foundations; today we are dancing among the ruins.

* * *

David Campton is a prolific writer of short plays. The nine plays in *Laughter and Fear* include some of the best of them. *On Stage* and *On Stage Again* are collections of revue-length sketches, and many of his short plays are slight, akin to those traditional short stories that present two or three characters, reveal some significant event in their past to explain their present eccentricities, and end with an unexpected twist. In *Where Have All the Ghosts Gone?*, for example, a sensible young man intrudes on a drunken widow looking for his girlfriend, who has been too ashamed of her mother to bring him home. The mother does her best to break their attachment with a suicide attempt. She is dependent on her daughter, but also blames her for the death of her husband in a car crash, though the daughter was only five years old at the time, and now plays upon her sense of guilt. The young man, however, proposes to the daughter, and in an epilogue the mother tells the audience that the house and garden are restored and she is grandmother to twins. But the twist is still to come: "Just one big happy family. In fact to see me now, you'd never imagine . . . No, you'd never imagine that I was once a real person."
This is typical Campton territory: the crumbling house, or dowdy flat; the middle-aged or elderly middle-class woman in reduced circumstances as central character; and for theme the fight to maintain independence and defend one's individuality, sometimes successfully, as in *The Manipulator*, in which a Volpone-like bedridden woman uses gossip to blackmail, manipulate, and ensure that her daughters do not move her out of her flat. Since Campton's plays exploit the aching articulacies of the middle classes rather than the working-class inarticulacies explored by Pinter, Bond, and Stephen Lowe, they have lent themselves to radio productions.
Yet from his earliest work with Stephen Joseph's Theatre-in-the-Round in Scarborough, Campton has played with the inherent theatricality of the stage experience. This is particularly true of some of his more recent plays. In *The Life and Death of Almost Everybody*, a stage sweeper conjures characters from his imagination whom he then has trouble controlling. The committee of *In Committee*, meeting onstage, becomes aware, but refuses to acknowledge, that there is an audience present—even when "audience members" one by one replace committee members. And in *Who's a Hero, Then?* the stage is divided into an area representing a club and an "imagination area." At the club Norm is criticized for apparently letting his friend drown; each of his critics enters the imagination area in turn—through which the drowning man's cries ring each time—and does no better. The artificiality of the theatre experience is also implicit in *Timesneeze*, a play for youth performed by the National Theatre in 1970, in which a time-machine moves the hero to different places and periods.
Another kind of theatricality that Campton exploits, more successfully, is linguistic. Like Pinter, he plays with proverbs, catch-phrases, and clichés. *On Stage* includes four sketches about teenagers in which such phrases as "See you around" are by their repetition filled with all that is not being expressed. The committee members in *In Committee* are so tangled in procedural jargon that we never learn what the committee is considering. And in the high-level diplomatic encounter of *Out of the Flying Pan* the words themselves become garbled.
Campton acknowledges the influence of the Theatre of the Absurd. Ionesco's Jack, who demands a bride who is well-endowed, is first cousin to the new father who in *Mutatis Mutandis* has to break the news to his wife of their baby's

precocious development of a full head of hair (green), teeth (pointed), and tail. The baby has inherited his eyes—fine brown eyes, all three of them. Similarly reminiscent of Ionesco is *Getting and Spending*, which follows a couple's progress from marriage to old age, pursuing mutual dreams that lead to the offstage proliferation of cots and prams in the nursery, while their dreams distract them from ever actually producing offspring.

It is when the absurd serves Campton's social conscience that he produces his best plays. *Incident* is a parable on racial prejudice, in which an inn refuses admission to a weary traveller because no one named Smith is to be admitted. The most interesting aspect of the play is the way in which Campton shows how Miss Smith's companion is drawn into negotiating a compromise, only to be (rightly) abandoned by Miss Smith. In *Soldier from the Wars Returning* a soldier boasts to a barmaid of his exploits and she hands him an eye-patch, a crutch, and so on, until he leaves the bar a cripple: a parable about war and perhaps an externalizing of the hidden psychological wounds that war inflicts on all participants. *Then . . .* is a nuclear-holocaust play. A physics teacher and the reigning Miss Europe are the sole survivors; despite the social conventions that they strive to follow, feelings that neither has ever had time for flow between them, but they dare not remove the brown paper bags they wear over their heads. These absurdly slight means of protection, like children's masquerades, and their unperturbedly conventional responses to meeting, convey the frailty and limited vision of human beings, commenting more effectively in ten minutes on the threat of nuclear war than any large-scale television dramatization of the future.

Of Campton's full-length plays, the swift-moving *Jonah*, commissioned for performance at Chelmsford Cathedral in 1971, is the most interesting. Jonah is called on to warn everyone, from businessmen to the cathedral's cleaners, of the imminent destruction of their sinful city. He resists the call, knowing he will be laughed at, and the destruction occurs—though, he and the audience learn, only in a private vision for him. He calls upon people to reform, and they do. But they begin to demand when the destruction will occur and goad Jonah into declaring a date and time. No destruction occurs. No one blames Jonah for false prophecy but at the end of the play he feels humiliated: he has devoted his life to justice and punishment, not to the mercy God has shown.

Campton is a workman-like—and sometimes workaday—playwright. *Jonah*, for example, could easily be performed with one professional as Jonah and amateurs in the numerous other roles. In his hands, *Frankenstein* becomes an easily staged, almost domestic drama about Victor Frankenstein's complicated relationships with his fiancée and his best friend. He has also written a number of short plays for all-female casts. But these, unfortunately, range from the mechanical to the contrived. For example, in *Singing in the Wilderness* an ecologist and a folklorist come across Cobweb, Moth, Mustardseed, and their relatively new friend Tinkerbell, who are suffering from old age, pesticicide spraying, and the destruction of hedgerows.

Campton is an unfashionable playwright. In an age that finds critically interesting the tough-minded and difficult, the crabbed or elliptical, his inventions seem facile, especially in his full-length plays, and sometimes whimsical. His characters are usually articulate, understand each other fairly well, and his humane messages are clear. Some of his short plays deserve repeated production.

—Anthony Graham-White

CANNAN, Denis. British. Born Dennis Pullein-Thompson in Oxford, 14 May 1919; son of the late writer Joanna Cannan; brother of the writers Christine, Diana, and Josephine Pullein-Thompson. Educated at Eton College. Served in the Queen's Royal Regiment, 1939–45: mentioned in despatches. Married 1) Joan Ross in 1946 (marriage dissolved), two sons and one daughter; 2) Rose Evansky in 1965. Worked in repertory companies, 1937–39; actor at Citizens' Theatre, Glasgow, 1946–48, Bristol Old Vic, and in the West End, London. Address: 43 Osmond Road, Hove, East Sussex BN3 1TF, England.

PUBLICATIONS

Plays

Max (produced Malvern, Worcestershire, and London, 1949).

Captain Carvallo (produced Bristol and London, 1950). London, Hart Davis, 1952.

Colombe, adaptation of the play by Jean Anouilh (produced London, 1951). London, Methuen, 1952.

Misery Me! A Comedy of Woe (produced London, 1955). London, French, 1956.

You and Your Wife (produced Bristol, 1955). London, French, 1956.

The Power and the Glory, with Pierre Bost, adaptation of the novel by Graham Greene (produced London, 1956; New York, 1958). New York, French, 1959; revised version (produced Edinburgh, 1980).

Who's Your Father? (produced London, 1958). London, French, 1959.

US, with others (produced London, 1966). Published as *US: The Book of the Royal Shakespeare Production US/Vietnam/US/Experiment/Politics . . .*, London, Calder and Boyars, 1968; as *Tell Me Lies . . .*, Indianapolis, Bobbs Merrill, 1968.

Ghosts, adaptation of the play by Ibsen (produced London, 1967).

One at Night (produced London, 1971).

Les Iks, with Colin Higgins, based on *The Mountain People* by Colin Turnbull (produced Paris, 1975; as *The Ik*, produced London and Minneapolis, 1976). Chicago, Dramatic Publishing Company, 1984.

Dear Daddy (produced Oxford and London, 1976; Philadelphia, 1982). London, French, 1978.

Screenplays: *The Beggar's Opera*, with Christopher Fry, 1953; *Alive and Kicking*, 1959; *Don't Bother to Knock (Why Bother to Knock)*, with Frederic Raphael and Frederic Gotfurt, 1961; *Tamahine*, 1963; *Sammy Going South (A Boy Ten Feet Tall)*, 1963; *The Amorous Adventures of Moll Flanders*, with Roland Kibbee, 1965; *A High Wind in Jamaica*, with Stanley Mann and Ronald Harwood, 1965; *Mayerling*, with Terence Young, 1968.

Radio Plays: *Headlong Hall*, from the novel by Peacock, 1950; *The Moth and the Star*, from *Liber Amoris* by Hazlitt, 1950; *The Greeting*, from the work by Osbert Sitwell, 1964.

Television Plays: *Heaven and Earth*, with Peter Brook, 1956; *One Day at a Time*, 1977; *Home-Movies*, 1979; *Fat Chance*, from a story by Robert Bloch, 1980; *Picture of a Place*, from a work by Doug Morgan, 1980; *The Best of Everything*, from the novel by Stanley Ellin, 1981; *Way to Do It*, from a work by Jack Ritchie, 1981; *By George!*, 1982; *The Absence of*

Emily, from a work by Jack Ritchie, 1982; *The Memory Man*, from a story by Henry Slesar, 1983; *The Last Bottle in the World*, from a story by Stanley Ellin, 1986.

*

Theatrical Activities:
Actor: **Plays**—Richard Hare in *East Lynne*, based on Mrs. Henry Wood's novel, Henley-on-Thames, 1936; roles in repertory theatres, 1937–39; Citizens' Theatre, Glasgow: Hjalmar in *The Wild Duck* by Ibsen, Valentine in *You Never Can Tell* by Shaw, Hsieh Ping Quei in *Lady Precious Stream* by S.I. Hsiung, and other roles, 1946–48; Ajax and Reporter in *These Mortals* by H.M. Harwood, London, 1949; Sempronius in *The Apple Cart* by Shaw, Malvern, 1949; Kneller in *In Good King Charles's Golden Days* by Shaw, 1949; The Widower in *Buoyant Billions* by Shaw, Malvern and London, 1949, Oliver in *As You Like It*, Bristol, 1950; title role and Octavius in *Julius Caesar*, Bristol, 1950; Samuel Breeze in *A Penny for a Song* by John Whiting, London, 1951; Harold Trewitt in *All the Year Round* by Neville Croft, London, 1951. **Film**—*The Beggar's Opera*, 1953. **Television**—*The Rose Without a Thorn*, 1948; *Buoyant Billions*, 1949.

* * *

Denis Cannan is the kind of dramatist who always has a tough time of it in the English theatre: one who attempts to mix the genres. His forte, particularly in the early 1950's, was intelligent, satirical farce, much closer to the world of Giraudoux and Anouilh than that of Rattigan and Coward. After a period of prolonged silence, he dropped the comic mask and launched a couple of direct, frontal assaults on the values of our society; but he still seems a dramatist of manifest talent who has been critically undervalued and unfairly neglected by the public.

Like so many postwar English dramatists, he started out as an actor working his way round the quality repertory companies (Glasgow, Malvern, Bristol); and his first play, *Max*, was in fact staged at the 1949 Malvern Festival when he was also playing three key Shavian roles. The work is of interest now chiefly because it established the theme that was to preoccupy him for several years to come, the barren, life-destroying conflict between opposing ideologies. But it was an uncharacteristic work in that it explored the theme in slightly melodramatic terms.

Cannan really came into his own with *Captain Carvallo*, presented the following year at the St. James's under Laurence Olivier's management. This is an absolutely delightful play, a witty, bubbling farcical comedy about the absurdities of military conflict. Set behind the lines of an unspecified occupied territory, it confronts a pair of ineffectual, peace-loving partisans with a philandering enemy officer in a remote farmhouse. The enemy Captain is interested only in seducing the farm-owner's wife: the partisans, though ordered to kill the Captain, are concerned only with keeping him alive. But, although the tone of the play is light, it makes the perfectly serious point that the only sane attitude to life is to preserve it at all costs.

Misery Me!, which had a short run at the Duchess in 1955, is likewise the work of a man who, in Kenneth Tynan's words, "despises politics and is in no humour for war." And again Cannan puts to the test the English love of categorisation by encasing his theme within a light, semi-farcical framework. The setting is a moth-eaten Arcadian tavern: and the basic conflict is between a Communist and a Capitalist each determined to slay the other. Both hit on the idea of employing a suicidal young intellectual as a hired assassin and so we see two great powers forcing weapons on a man bent only on self-destruction: a resonant and neatly satirical idea in the cold-war atmosphere of mid-1950's Europe. The weakness of the play is that the characters are abstractions invented to illustrate a theme and that the play's affirmation of life boils down in the end to an endorsement of romantic love: but again Cannan shows himself capable of satirising the contemporary condition and of expressing ideas within a popular format.

His other plays of the 1950's were rather less ambitious. *You and Your Wife* was about two fractious married couples trying to sort out their problems while held captive by a couple of gangsters; *The Power and the Glory* was a proficient adaptation (done in conjunction with Pierre Bost) of the Graham Greene novel about a whiskey-priest; and *Who's Your Father?* was an ingenious farce about a snobbish nouveau-riche couple and their daughter's irresponsible fiancé.

But, after a long absence from the theatre, Cannan only surfaced again as joint writer of the Royal Shakespeare Company's corporately devised Vietnam show, *US*. His precise contribution is difficult to disentangle. But we do know that he was author of Glenda Jackson's scorching and passionate indictment of the non-involvement of the English in anything happening outside their shores and that he wrote a very specific attack on the fact that Vietnam is a "reasonable" war. "It is," he said, "the first intellectuals' war. It is run by statisticians, physicists, economists, historians, psychiatrists, mathematicians, experts on everything, theorists from everywhere. Even the atrocities can be justified by logic." In the 1950's Cannan's attack on war had been comic and oblique: now it was impassioned and direct.

One at Night attacks certain aspects of our society with punitive vigour and sharp intelligence, if not with the greatest technical skill. Its hero is a middle-aged ex-journalist and advertising man seeking discharge from a mental institution to which he has been committed after having sexual relations with a girl under 16. He argues to the middle-class hospital tribunal that, far from corrupting an innocent, he has enlarged the girl's emotional experience: but he is steadfastly refused a discharge after shattering the tribunal's complacency by uncovering the hidden fears and frailties of its individual members. What gives the play its urgency is the feeling that Cannan isn't simply exploring a fashionable intellectual thesis (only the mad are sane) but that he is sharing with us a lived-through experience. And he makes, with some power, the point that in our society it is the scramble for wealth and material possessions that increases the incidence of insanity, but that it's the self-same scramble that produces the instant cure-alls and panaceas. It's precisely the point made, in fact, by Ken Loach's film, *Family Life*.

As a dramatist, Cannan has obviously changed course radically. Where once he wrapped his message up in farce and fantasy, he now lays it right on the line. Where once he adopted a deliberately apolitical stance, he now writes with a definite sense of commitment. But, whatever the profound changes in his style and attitude, he still writes with a bristling intelligence and pungent wit. For that reason one hopes the theatre will hear more from him.

—Michael Billington

———

CARLINO, Lewis John. American. Born in New York City, 1 January 1932. Educated at El Camino College, California;

University of Southern California, Los Angeles, 1956–60, B.A. (magna cum laude) in film 1959 (Phi Beta Kappa), M.A. in drama 1960. Served in the United States Air Force, 1951–55. Married Denise Jill Chadwick; three children from previous marriage. Recipient: British Drama League prize, 1960; Huntington Hartford fellowship; Yaddo fellowship; Rockefeller grant. Lives in California. Agent: Gilbert Parker, William Morris Agency, 1350 Avenue of the Americas, New York, New York 10019, U.S.A.

PUBLICATIONS

Plays

The Brick and the Rose: A Collage for Voices (produced Los Angeles, 1957; New York, 1974; London, 1985). New York, Dramatists Play Service, 1959.
Junk Yard. New York, Dramatists Play Service, 1959.
Used Car for Sale. New York, Dramatists Play Service, 1959.
Objective Case (produced Westport, Connecticut, and New York, 1962). With *Mr. Flannery's Ocean*, New York, Dramatists Play Service, 1961.
Mr. Flannery's Ocean (includes *Piece and Precise*) (produced Westport, Connecticut, 1962). With *Objective Case*, New York, Dramatists Play Service, 1961.
Two Short Plays: Sarah and the Sax, and High Sign. New York, Dramatists Play Service, 1962.
The Beach People (produced Madison, Ohio, 1962).
Postlude, and Snowangel (produced New York, 1962).
Cages: Snowangel and Epiphany (produced New York, 1963; Leicester, 1964; *Epiphany* produced London, 1974). New York, Random House, 1963.
Telemachus Clay: A Collage for Voices (produced New York, 1963). New York, Random House, 1964.
Doubletalk: Sarah and the Sax, and The Dirty Old Man (produced New York, 1964; *Sarah and the Sax* produced London, 1971). New York, Random House, 1964.
The Exercise (produced Stockbridge, Massachusetts, 1967; New York, 1968). New York, Dramatists Play Service, 1968.

Screenplays: *Seconds*, 1966; *The Fox*, with Howard Koch, 1967; *The Brotherhood*, 1968; *Reflection of Fear*, with Edward Hume, 1971; *The Mechanic*, 1972; *Crazy Joe*, 1973; *The Sailor Who Fell from Grace with the Sea*, 1976; *I Never Promised You a Rose Garden*, with Gavin Lambert, 1977; *The Great Santini*, 1980; *Resurrection*, 1981.

Television Plays: *And Make Thunder His Tribute* (*Route 66* series), 1963; *In Search of America*, 1971; *Doc Elliot* (pilot), 1972; *Honor Thy Father*, from the novel by Gay Talese, 1973; *Where Have All the People Gone?*, with Sandor Stern, 1974.

Novels

The Brotherhood. New York, New American Library, 1968.
The Mechanic. New York, New American Library, 1972.

*

Theatrical Activities:
Director: **Films**—*The Sailor Who Fell from Grace with the Sea*, 1976; *The Great Santini*, 1980; *Class*, 1983.

* * *

Between June, 1963 and May, 1964—less than a year's time—four one-act plays and one full-length work by Lewis John Carlino were produced Off-Broadway in New York. They ranged from the vast talent and imagination of *Telemachus Clay* to the burgeoning maturity of *Cages* to the unfulfilled *Doubletalk*. With these plays, Carlino established himself as an American playwright of exceptional quality and promise. The theatre did not hear from him again for four years, as he turned to screenwriting (*Seconds*, *The Brotherhood*). In 1968 he made his Broadway debut with the sloppy and self-indulgent *The Exercise*, and the catastrophe seems to have driven him permanently from the theatre.

If critics, financial uncertainty, and the unpredictable duration of a play's run are the theatre's risks, however, film writing has its own dangers. Like too many artistic writers caught up in the American commercial maelstrom, Lewis John Carlino was lost in the hurly-burly of a marketplace too busy to notice or care. Nevertheless, the originality and craftsmanship of his stage work endure. He is a playwright who should not forget or be forgotten.

His first notable New York production was a bill of one-act plays—*Cages*. The curtain raiser, *Snowangel*, is a minor look at a constricted intellectual and an earthy prostitute, spelling out the predictable point. The main work of the program, however, is devastating.

Called *Epiphany*, it is about an ornithologist who is discovered by his wife in a homosexual act. In reaction he turns into a rooster. The Kafkaesque metaphor is theatrically powerful, visually striking, and provocative in context. But as he becomes that rooster, clucking and strutting, it turns out that he is laying eggs. Having really wanted to be a hen, he has suffered a breakdown only to find his wife all too willing to strip the coxcomb from the mask he has donned. He need no longer pretend to virility. She turns him into a female and stays to keep him that way.

Although the play came at a time when every other drama seemed to condemn women as man's arch-enemy, Carlino's imaginative story and powerful structure transcended the cliché. The dramatic scheme is faultless and the writing is for actors—something too few playwrights seem capable of doing.

As is often the case, a well received play generates production of a writer's earlier work and, within six months, Carlino's *Telemachus Clay* was presented Off-Broadway. One could only again ponder the judgment of producers for here was a drama of tremendous poetry, artistry and stage life—a drama that would never have been presented had it not been for the notices *Cages* received.

Like so many first plays, *Telemachus Clay* is a story of the artist as a young man, in this case drawn parallel to Odysseus's son. It is subtitled *A Collage for Voices*, as indeed it is, the actors perched on stools, facing the audience. The 11 of them play a host of characters, changing time and location with the magic of poetry weaving the fabric of story, thought, event, and emotion in overlapping dialogue and sound.

This is a device that risks pretension and artiness, but in *Telemachus Clay* it succeeds on the sheer beauty of language and the structural control. There are thoughts and dreams, flashbacks, memories, overheard conversation—a score of effects beyond conventional structure and justifying the form. Like *Cages* the play suffers from immature message making, but like it, too, there is a marvellous sense of theatre, of dialogue, of fantasy, and of humor.

Doubletalk underlined the flaws rather than the strengths of these earlier plays—instead of picking up on his technical finesse, strong dialogue, and sense of stage excitement, Carlino stumbled on his inclination toward point-making and his trouble with plots. These two one-act plays used coy notions instead of stories—an old Jewish lady having a chance meeting with a black musician; a virgin having a chance meeting with an aged poet. This coyness came to a head with *The Exercise*—a play about actors, improvisations, reality, and theatricality that threatened to bring Pirandello from his grave if only to blow up New York's Actors Studio, to which this play was virtually a bouquet.

The work output is slim, certainly inconsistent, and no peak of development was ever achieved. Yet, Carlino's playwriting is unmistakably artistic. Its uncertain flowering is tragically representative of too many American writers for the stage.

—Martin Gottfried

CARTER, Lonnie. American. Born in Chicago, Illinois, 25 October 1942. Educated at Loyola University, Chicago, 1960–61; Marquette University, Milwaukee, B.A. 1964, M.A. 1966; Yale University School of Drama, New Haven, Connecticut (Molly Kazan award, 1967; Shubert Fellow, 1968–69), M.F.A. 1969. Married Marilyn Smutko in 1966 (divorced 1972). Taught writing at Marquette University, 1964–65, Yale University School of Drama, 1974–75, Rockland Community College, Suffern, New York, University of Connecticut, Storrs, and New York University, 1979–86; Jenny McKean Moore Fellow, George Washington University, Washington, D.C., 1986–87. Recipient: Peg Santvoord Foundation fellowship, 1969, 1970; Guggenheim fellowship, 1971; National Endowment for the Arts grant, 1974, 1983; CBS Foundation grant, 1974; Connecticut Commission on the Arts grant, 1976, 1988; Open Circle award, 1978; PEN grant, 1978. Address: Cream Hill Road, West Cornwall, Connecticut 06796, U.S.A.

PUBLICATIONS

Plays

Adam (produced Milwaukee, 1966).
Another Quiet Evening at Home (produced New Haven, Connecticut, 1967).
If Beauty's in the Eye of the Beholder, Truth Is in the Pupil Somewhere Too (produced New Haven, Connecticut, 1969).
Workday (produced New Haven, Connecticut, 1970).
Iz She Izzy or Iz He Ain'tzy or Iz They Both, music by Robert Montgomery (produced New Haven, Connecticut, 1970; New York, 1972). Included in *The Sovereign State of Boogedy Boogedy and Other Plays*, 1986.
More War in Store, and Time Space (produced New York, 1970).
Plumb Loco (produced Stockbridge, Massachusetts, 1970).
The Big House (produced New Haven, Connecticut, 1971).
Smoky Links (produced New York, 1972).
Watergate Classics, with others (produced New Haven, Connecticut, 1973). Published in *Yale/Theatre* (New Haven, Connecticut), 1974.
Cream Cheese (produced New York, 1974).
Trade-Offs (produced New Haven, Connecticut, 1976; New York, 1977).

Bleach (produced Chicago, 1977).
Bicicletta (produced New York, 1978). Included in *The Sovereign State of Boogedy Boogedy and Other Plays*, 1986.
Victoria Fellows (produced Baltimore, 1978).
Sirens (produced New York, 1979).
The Sovereign State of Boogedy Boogedy (produced Chicago, 1985; New York, 1986). Included in *The Sovereign State of Boogedy Boogedy and Other Plays*, 1986.
The Sovereign State of Boogedy Boogedy and Other Plays (includes *Iz She Izzy or Iz He Ain'tzy or Iz They Both*, *Waiting for G*, *Bicicletta*, *Necktie Party*). West Cornwall, Connecticut, Locust Press, 1986.
Mothers and Sons (produced Chicago, 1987).
Necktie Party (produced Chicago, 1987). Included in *The Sovereign State of Boogedy Boogedy and Other Plays*, 1986.
Gulliver (produced Pittsfield, Massachusetts, 1990).
Waiting for Lefty Rose (produced New York, 1991).
I.B. Randy Jr. (produced New York, 1992).

Radio Plays: *Certain Things about the Trombone*, 1982; *Lulu*, 1983.

Television Play: *From the Top*, 1976.

*   *   *

While Lonnie Carter was studying playwriting at Yale University School of Drama he spent most of his time not writing plays, but rather attending movie retrospectives of Buster Keaton, Charlie Chaplin, the Marx Brothers, and W.C. Fields. Spending hours watching these classic comedies, he saw something in the basic physiognomy of the characters that he was trying to do verbally in his own plays. He then decided to write his own slapstick farce, *The Big House*, using a Marx Brothers film as a springboard.

Employing the original plot of the film, in which three con-men take over a prison and lock up the warden, he used the film's basic characters of Groucho, a cockney Chico, Harpo, and a minister made up to look like Chaplin. Carter's only additions were a few songs and dances. Basically what Carter ended up with was a hodge-podge of 1920's and 1930's movie comedies. The play is filled with low comedy hijinks, pratfalls galore, and very broad burlesque humor. The action proceeds at such a furious pace that by the middle of the second act the audience is out of breath and the playwright out of plot. The main trouble with Carter's *The Big House* lies in the plot and structure. It would have been fine as a one-act play or mini-musical, but it didn't work as a full-length play.

The most popular play Carter has written is called *Iz She Izzy or Iz He Ain'tzy or Iz They Both*. It had its premiere at Yale in 1970, and has since been performed regularly by university and high school drama groups. *Izzy* is set in a chaotic contemporary courtroom where a schizoid judge (Justice "Choo-Choo" Justice; half-male and half-female) is on trial for having committed the premeditated murder of his female self. In *Izzy* Carter once again uses many familiar movie gags, and supplements the action by songs with lovely lyrics that show off his audacious wit. A good example is the song sung by the frustrated Justice (Choo-Choo) Justice near the end of the play: "I'd like to have a baby/A lass or little laddie/But when it saw its mommy/Would it say 'Daddy'?"

Smoky Links is about a revolution on a mythical Scottish golf course. The main revolutionary is a symbolic Oriental golf pro who threatens the whole club while turning the Scottish accent around with his Oriental pronunciation.

In *Smoky Links*, as in most of his plays, Carter wrestles with the subject of justice. All of his main characters, Wolfgang Amadeus Gutbucket in *The Big House*, Justice (Choo-Choo) Justice in *Izzy*, and the Oriental Golf Pro in *Smoky Links*, are in some way frustrated by the law. But the characters' attitude towards justice and the law remains mostly ambiguous, except in the case of the Marx Brothers in *The Big House*. The Marx Brothers are dyed in the wool anarchists and never offer any alternative except total disruption.

Except for the highly derivative *The Big House*, Carter's sharp humor and verbal somersaults remind one more of Restoration comedy or the satires of Rabelais than the old-time Hollywood comedies. The influence of films is strong, but Carter has also a special, quite obvious talent that has yet to be developed to its fullest extent.

—Bernard Carragher

CARTWRIGHT, Jim. British. Born in Farnsworth, near Manchester, Lancashire, 27 June 1958. Educated at local schools; Royal Academy of Dramatic Art, London. Married Angela Jones in 1984. Writer-in-residence, Octagon Theatre, Bolton, Lancashire, 1989–91. Recipient: George Devine award, 1986; Beckett award, 1987; *Drama* award, 1986; *Plays and Players* award, 1986; Monte Carlo Golden Nymph award for film, 1987; Manchester *Evening News* award, 1990; *Evening Standard* award, 1992. Agent: Judy Daish Associates, 83 Eastbourne Mews, London W2 6LQ, England.

PUBLICATIONS

Plays

Road (produced London, 1986; New York, 1988).   London and New York, Methuen, 1986; revised version, 1990.
Baths (broadcast 1987; produced Bolton, Lancashire, 1990).
Bed (produced London, 1989; revised version produced Bolton, Lancashire, 1990).   London, Methuen, 1991.
To (produced Bolton, Lancashire 1989; London, 1990).   London. Methuen, 1991; as *Two*, Methuen, 1992.
Eight Miles High (produced Bolton, Lancashire 1991).
The Rise and Fall of Little Voice (produced London, 1992).   London, Methuen, 1992.

Radio Play: *Baths*, 1987.

Television Plays: *Wedded*, 1990; *Vroom*, 1990.

* * *

Jim Cartwright was the British theatre's most exciting discovery of the 1980's: a genuinely original new voice. Comparisons have been made with Osborne, Bond, and, more fruitfully, Shelagh Delaney, but Cartwright is very much his own man: a shrewd observer of North Country working-class life, a poet of the under-classes, a re-activator of demotic speech. In the course of four plays he has moved, geographically, from the Royal Court's Theatre Upstairs to the West End and from a fragmented, episodic structure (*Road*) to something closely resembling a traditional, well-made comedy (*The Rise and Fall of Little Voice*). But, although the work has progressed, the voice remains distinctive: that of a largely self-taught writer who loves the quirks and oddities of everyday speech and who has an enormous fund of sympathy for the discarded, the dispossessed, and the victims of our abrasive society.

Cartwright emerged, virtually out of the blue, in 1986 with *Road* which was given a stunning promenade production (later televised) by the Royal Court. Under the guidance of a rum-soaked narrator, Scullery, it took us on a kaleidoscopic tour of a grotty Lancastrian street: last stop before the slag-heap. One by one, it introduced us to the characters in the road: an old woman locked into sexual reverie; a fanatical, keep-fit skinhead now converted to Buddhism; an unemployed ex-Royal Air Force conscript wondering, while doing the ironing, what happened to the days of jobs, courting, and the pictures three times a week; and, most tragically of all, a young boy and girl who get into bed and jointly commit anorexic suicide.

Road was variously compared to early Osborne, *Coronation Street*, *Under Milk Wood*, and *Our Town*. But what made the play unusual was partly Cartwright's ability to mix the realism of the streets with a heightened poetic language: an out-of-work office-girl conveyed her desperation by crying "Every day's like swimming in ache." Even more remarkable was Cartwright's ability to cut through the spectator's intellectual defences and flood the stage with feeling: in the remarkable final scene an unfulfilled double tryst, fuelled by liquor and Otis Redding's recording of "Try a Little Tenderness," exploded into a song of desperate aspiration. Loose-knit the play may have been. What finally bound the episodes together was Cartwright's compassion both for the confused, bewildered young and for the old, nursing a collective memory of lost dignity and pleasure.

Cartwright's intuitive sympathy for the old was at the very heart of his next, slightly overwritten and whimsically surreal piece, *Bed*. This was a strange, dream-driven Dylanesque poem of a play showing us seven old people lying side-by-side in a vast bed and drifting through their memories: from a shelf above the bed a sleepless, red-eyed, disembodied head vituperatively abused, in a Beckettesque manner, the snoozing elders. As in *Road*, there were elegiac memories of a lost and better England and signs of Cartwright's gift for language. But although the play was full of weird, wild images— including the sight of an old married couple descending through a hole in the bed to fetch a glass of water—it lacked any sense of imaginative rigour: as Paul Taylor wrote, "if *anything* can happen in the world of a play, then what actually does is robbed of dramatic necessity."

Cartwright was back on much surer ground in the cryptically entitled *To*: a sharp, salty, quickfire evocation of the surface gaiety and underlying melancholia of English pub life, with two actors playing both the publicans and their clientèle. Once again, the structure was episodic. But Cartwright turned that to great advantage by catching, as in a series of lightning sketches, the oddity and pain behind the camaraderie of the saloon-bar. He provided some wonderfully eccentric portraits including that of a solitary widower summoning up his wife's departed spirit by touching a brown teapot and a vision of two Memphis-hooked fatties haunted by memories of the King ("Elvis died of a choked bum," one of them confidently asserts). But the Boltonian comic realism was counterpointed by a sense of the English pub as a place of gregarious solitude where, under the cheerful sluicing, you can hear the sound of breaking glass and relationships.

With *The Rise and Fall of Little Voice*, Cartwright finally harnessed all his familiar characteristics—rich language, sympathy for the underdog, streetwise wit—to a consecutive narrative. The "Little Voice" of the title is a painfully shy, waif-like agoraphobe with a hidden talent for doing impressions of Garland, Bassey, Fields, and Piaf in the privacy of her bedroom. Under pressure from her coarse, boozy, widowed mum and the mother's sleazy, spivvy agent-boyfriend, the heroine is forced to expose her peculiar talent in a tatty Northern night-club. But the irony is that, through imitating others, she finally finds her own voice.

There are obvious echoes of other plays in which a female protagonist discovers her true identity: *A Taste of Honey*, *Roots*, *Educating Rita*. But the particular appeal of this play lies in the contrast between the story's mythic, fairytale quality and the lewd, loud, lively language. Cartwright goes out of his way to emphasise the story's fable-like aspect, even showing Little Voice being rescued by a young engineer rising outside her window on a British Telecom crane. The mother is a richly-drawn vulgarian who curls her tongue round some choice Boltonian phrases: she remembers her late husband as "a length of dry stick that bored me bra-less." With *The Rise and Fall of Little Voice* Cartwright has come up with an affirmative and wholly theatrical play: one that depends on the audience's spine-tingling realization that the actress playing Little Voice is really doing her own singing. It is easily the most optimistic Cartwright has written; but, like its predecessors, it hinges on his rare ability to exploit the communal conspiracy of live theatre.

—Michael Billington

CAUTE, (John) David. British. Born in Alexandria, Egypt, 16 December 1936. Educated at Edinburgh Academy; Wellington College, Crowthorne, Berkshire; Wadham College, Oxford, M.A. in modern history, D.Phil. 1962; Harvard University, Cambridge, Massachusetts (Henry Fellow), 1960–61. Served in the British Army, in Africa, 1955–56. Married 1) Catherine Shuckburgh in 1961 (divorced 1970), two sons; 2) Martha Bates in 1973, two daughters. Fellow, All Souls College, Oxford, 1959–65; visiting professor, New York University and Columbia University, New York, 1966–67; reader in social and political theory, Brunel University, Uxbridge, Middlesex, 1967–70; Regents' lecturer, University of California, 1974; Benjamin Meaker visiting professor, University of Bristol, 1985. Literary and arts editor, *New Statesman*, London, 1979–80. Deputy chair, 1979–80, and co-chair, 1981–82, Writers Guild of Great Britain. Recipient: London Authors' Club award, 1960; Rhys memorial prize, 1960. Address: 41 Westcroft Square, London W6 0TA, England.

PUBLICATIONS

Plays

Songs for an Autumn Rifle (produced Edinburgh, 1961).
The Demonstration (produced Nottingham, 1969; London, 1970). London, Deutsch, 1970.
The Fourth World (produced London, 1973).

Radio Plays: *Fallout*, 1972; *The Zimbabwe Tapes*, 1983; *Henry and the Dogs*, 1986; *Sanctions*, 1988.

Television Documentary: *Brecht & Co.*, 1979.

Novels

At Fever Pitch. London, Deutsch, 1959; New York, Pantheon, 1961.
Comrade Jacob. London, Deutsch, 1961; New York, Pantheon, 1962.
The Decline of the West. London, Deutsch, and New York, Macmillan, 1966.
The Occupation. London, Deutsch, 1971; New York, McGraw Hill, 1972.
The Baby Sitters (as John Salisbury). London, Secker and Warburg, and New York, Atheneum, 1978.
Moscow Gold (as John Salisbury). London, Futura, 1980.
The K-Factor. London, Joseph, 1983.
News from Nowhere. London, Hamish Hamilton, 1986.
Veronica; or, The Two Nations. London, Hamish Hamilton, 1989; New York, Arcade, 1990.

Other

Communism and the French Intellectuals 1914–1960. London, Deutsch, and New York, Macmillan, 1964.
The Left in Europe since 1789. London, Weidenfeld and Nicolson, and New York, McGraw Hill, 1966.
Fanon. London, Fontana, and New York, Viking Press, 1970.
The Illusion. London, Deutsch, 1971; New York, Harper, 1972.
The Fellow-Travellers. London, Weidenfeld and Nicolson, and New York, Macmillan, 1973; revised edition, New Haven, Connecticut and London, Yale University Press, 1988.
Collisions: Essays and Reviews. London, Quartet, 1974.
Cuba, Yes? London, Secker and Warburg, and New York, McGraw Hill, 1974.
The Great Fear: The Anti-Communist Purge under Truman and Eisenhower. New York, Simon and Schuster, and London, Secker and Warburg, 1978.
Under the Skin: The Death of White Rhodesia. London, Allen Lane, and Evanston, Illinois, Northwestern University Press, 1983.
The Espionage of the Saints: Two Essays on Silence and the State. London, Hamish Hamilton, 1986.
Left Behind: Journeys into British Politics. London, Cape, 1987.
Sixty-Eight: The Year of the Barricades. London, Hamish Hamilton, and New York, Harper, 1988.

Editor, *Essential Writings*, by Karl Marx. London, MacGibbon and Kee, 1967; New York, Macmillan, 1968.

*

Critical Studies: *Anger and After* by John Russell Taylor, London, Methuen, 1962, revised edition, 1969, as *The Angry Theatre*, New York, Hill and Wang, 1962, revised edition, 1969; "Rebels and Their Causes" by Harold Hobson, in *Sunday Times* (London), 23 November 1969; "Keeping Our Distance" by Benedict Nightingale, in *New Statesman* (London), 28 November 1969; in *Plays and Players* (London), February 1970; in *Times* (London), 22 July 1971.

David Caute comments:

With one exception, my plays have all been public plays. A "public" play, like a "private" play, is of course populated by individual characters with distinctive personalities, but the real subject lies elsewhere, in some wider social or political issue. Obviously the most elementary problem for the public playwright is to present characters who are not merely ciphers or puppets—words much cherished by critics hostile to didactic theatre.

Songs for an Autumn Rifle, written in 1960, is shaped in the spirit of banal realism. By the time I wrote my next play, *The Demonstration*, seven years later, my attitude towards both fiction and drama had changed. While the necessity of commitment still imposed itself, the old forms of naturalism, realism, and illusionist mimesis seemed incompatible with our present-day knowledge about language and communication. (These ideas are developed more fully in *The Illusion*, 1971.) One is therefore working to achieve a form of self-aware or dialectical theatre which is not only about a subject, but also about the play itself as a presentation—an inevitably distorting one—of that subject. The intention is to stimulate in the audience a greater critical awareness, rather than to seduce it into empathy and catharsis. In my view, for example, the lasting impact of Brecht's *Arturo Ui* consists less in what the play tells us about Hitler than what it tells us about *knowing about Hitler*.

The kind of writing I have in mind must pay far more attention to the physical possibilities of the theatre than did the old realism or well-made play. But whereas the author was once dictator, the modern playwright finds his supremacy challenged by directors or groups of actors. Up to a point this is healthy. But only up to a point! (See my "Author's Theatre," the *Listener*, 3 June 1971.)

One of my plays, *The Fourth World*, is different: a very private play, and, I hope a funny one. It was conceived and delivered all within a week.

*   *   *

While concern with social and political issues is no longer as rare among English dramatists as it was in the 1940's and early 1950's, there are still very few who are as deeply committed as David Caute, or as deeply interested either in European politics or in committed European playwrights like Sartre. Caute's first play, *Songs for an Autumn Rifle*, was a direct response to the dilemma that the Russian treatment of the 1956 Hungarian uprising created for members of the Party. The central character is the editor of a British Communist newspaper torn between his duty to the Party and his duty to the truth as relayed to him by an honest correspondent. On a personal level he is being pressured by his wife, who is not a Party member, by the doctrinaire daughter of a Party leader who works on his paper and is in love with him, and—indirectly—by his son, a National Serviceman who brings the Cyprus question into the play, first going to military prison for refusing to serve there, then submitting to an Intelligence Officer's persuasions and later being killed.

The play plunges right into its subject matter, with several scenes set in Hungary, showing the disillusioned correspondent of the English paper in argument not only with the Hungarian rebels but with Russian soldiers, whose attitudes are not altogether at one with the orders they have to carry out.

The Demonstration is a much more sophisticated piece of playmaking dramatising the problems of student revolution in terms of drama students at a university who rebel against the play their Professor gives them to perform, insisting on substituting a play about their own experience of repressive author-itarianism at the university. Their play has the same title as the play we are watching, and we are often jerked from one level of theatrical reality to another, when, for instance, a scene between the Women's Dean and a student turns out to be a scene between two students, one of whom is playing the Woman's Dean but can come out of character to make comments on her.

There is a very funny scene of rehearsing a sequence of the Professor's play ironically representing a confrontation between a bearded guerrilla and a single peasant, with interruptions from the students playing the parts, objecting that a bourgeois audience could take comfort from the satire. There is also an effective climax to the whole play when the police constables fail to respond to the Professor's orders to remove the handcuffs from the students they have arrested and the Superintendent's moustache fails to come off when he pulls at it. Reality has taken over.

But there is more theatrical exploitation than dramatic exploration of the no-man's-land between reality and illusion, and the play is not fuelled to fulfil the Pirandellian promise of its first few scenes. There are three main flaws. One is that the basic statement it is making seems to have been too rigidly predetermined instead of being evolved during the course of the writing. The second is that while there is an admirable sympathy in general for the victims of our society—black women not admitted to hairdressing shops, students whose liberty is curtailed by rules that stem from pre-Victorian puritanism—there is not enough sympathy for the private predicaments of the characters, who remain too much like stereotypes. This applies even to the central character, Professor Bright. Caute (who himself resigned from All Souls the year after he helped to organise the Oxford Teach-In on Vietnam) has no difficulty in understanding the dilemma of a son who deplores the rule-worshipping bigotry of the university authorities but still cannot side with the rebellious students against them. So it may be a kind of personal modesty that makes him keep pulling Steven Bright away from the centre of the action. Or it may be the technical failure to provide a character Steven can confide in. Or it may be a determination to focus on social and political rather than personal problems. But his failure to project Steven's ambivalence results in the third flaw—the lack of a firm moral and structural centre. In Act 2 Steven keeps disappearing to leave the stage free for the student actors. He makes two reappearances as an actor himself, in disguise. In the first he is not recognized until after he has made a long speech—an effective *coup de théâtre*. But this does not reveal enough of what he is feeling. Instead he is crowded out by a host of peripheral characters. The stage direction at the beginning of Act 2 Scene 2 tells us that his "maliciously creative hand" can be detected in the presence on the stage of the hippies and drop-outs who reject the political aims of the student revolutionaries, and that he is seen prowling about taking occasional notes and photographs. This is not enough. He should be holding the play together and carrying it forward, even when he is left by the students who take the initiative away from him.

—Ronald Hayman

_____

CHASE, Mary (Coyle). American. 1907–1981. See 2nd edition, 1977.

_____

CHAYEFSKY, Paddy. American. 1923–1981.
See 2nd edition, 1977.

CHILDRESS, Alice. American. Born in Charleston, South Carolina, 12 October 1920. Educated at schools in Harlem, New York; Radcliffe Institute for Independent Study (scholar), Cambridge, Massachusetts, 1966–68, graduated 1968. Married to the musician Nathan Woodard; one daughter. Actor and director, American Negro Theatre, New York, 1941–52; columnist ("Here's Mildred"), Baltimore *Afro-American*, 1956–58. Artist-in-residence, University of Massachusetts, Amherst, 1984. Recipient: Obie award, 1956; Woodward School Book award, 1975; Paul Robeson award, for screenplay, 1977; Virgin Islands Film Festival award, 1977; Radcliffe Graduate Society medal, 1984; African Poets Theatre award, 1985; Audelco award, 1986; Harlem School of the Arts Humanitarian award, 1987. Agent: Flora Roberts Inc., 157 West 57th Street, New York, New York 10019, U.S.A.

PUBLICATIONS

Plays

Florence (also director: produced New York, 1949). Published in *Masses and Mainstream* (New York), October 1950.
Just a Little Simple, adaptation of stories by Langston Hughes (produced New York, 1950).
Gold Through the Trees (produced New York, 1952).
Trouble in Mind (produced New York, 1955). Published in *Black Theatre: A Twentieth-Century Collection of the Work of Its Best Playwrights*, edited by Lindsay Patterson, New York, Dodd Mead, 1971.
Wedding Band (produced Ann Arbor, Michigan, 1966; New York, 1972). New York, French, 1974.
The World on a Hill, in *Plays to Remember*. New York, Macmillan, 1968.
Young Martin Luther King (produced on tour, 1969).
String, adaptation of a story by Maupassant (produced New York, 1969). With *Mojo*, New York, Dramatists Play Service, 1971.
Wine in the Wilderness (televised 1969; produced New York, 1976). New York, Dramatists Play Service, 1970.
Mojo (produced New York, 1970). With *String*, New York, Dramatists Play Service, 1971.
When the Rattlesnake Sounds (for children). New York, Coward McCann, 1975.
Let's Hear It for the Queen (for children). New York, Coward McCann, 1976.
Sea Island Song (produced Charleston, South Carolina, 1977).
Gullah (produced Amherst, Massachusetts, 1984).
Moms: A Praise Play for a Black Comedienne, music and lyrics by Childress and Nathan Woodard (produced New York, 1987).

Screenplay: *A Hero Ain't Nothin' But a Sandwich*, 1977.

Television Plays: *Wine in the Wilderness*, 1969; *Wedding Band*, 1973; *String*, 1979.

Novel

A Short Walk. New York, Coward McCann, 1979.

Other

Like One of the Family: Conversations from a Domestic's Life. New York, Independence, 1956.
A Hero Ain't Nothin' But a Sandwich (for children). New York, Coward McCann, 1973.
Rainbow Jordan (for children). New York, Coward McCann, 1981.
Those Other People (for children). New York, Putnam, 1989.

Editor, *Black Scenes: Collections of Scenes from Plays Written by Black People about Black Experience*. New York, Zenith, 1971.

*

Critical Studies: articles by Gayle Austin and Polly Holliday, in *Southern Quarterly* (Hattiesburg, Mississippi), Spring 1987.

Theatrical Activities:
Director: **Play**—*Florence*, New York, 1949.
Actress: **Plays**—Dolly in *On Strivers Row* by Abram Hill, New York, 1940; Polly Ann in *Natural Man* by Theodore Browne, 1941; Blanche in *Anna Lucasta* by Philip Yordan, New York, 1944.

*   *   *

Most of the plays of Alice Childress are about common people. Avoiding racial stereotypes found in much of contemporary literature and drama, her works present deftly drawn and realistic portraits of human beings attempting to find a sense of dignity in a world which seems rather to appreciate less noble values. Through her dramas, Ms. Childress exposes racism in the United States and challenges each of us to redress our racial problems. Her dynamic, poignant plays prepared the commercial stage for the works of other African-American playwrights, including Lorraine Hansberry, Amiri Baraka, and Ed Bullins.

Set during the rehearsal of a melodrama about lynching in the South, *Trouble in Mind* concerns black and white cast members who become involved in a real-life drama of racial tensions arising from the portrayal of black stereotypes. The drama skillfully mirrors a world where racist and sexist problems are initially hidden under "masks," but are forced to surface. The play centers on Wiletta Mayer, a veteran actor. She is an attractive middle-aged black woman, with an outgoing personality. She has made a career out of playing stereotypical black roles, but aspires to be cast in parts more deserving of her rich talents. Initially, she readily gives advice to a novice black actor on how to ingratiate oneself; to stay on good terms with the management no matter how loathsome the production may be. When rehearsals begin, however, she cannot adhere to such a strategy when the white director uses tactics that humiliate her and the script calls for the black characters to make statements and perform actions that offend her racial pride. Consequently, by the play's end, Wiletta removes her "mask" and becomes an outspoken critic of the production even though this action puts this job and, possibly, her career in jeopardy. It is a courageous choice, but a lonely one. None of the other cast members are willing to support her.

Wine in the Wilderness, set in Harlem in 1964, examines the arrogance of the black middle class in their relations with lower income African-Americans. Bill Jameson, an artist with a privileged background, seeks a model for his painting characterizing the average African-American woman as coarse, poorly educated, and culturally illiterate. The artist's married friends, Sonny-man and Cynthia, bring to Bill the person they believe best represents this ideal—Tommy, a thirty-year-old factory worker. Despite their dubious intent, by the play's end it is Tommy who teaches the others how they are merely dilettantes masquerading as blacks. Tommy's speech and behavior communicates that being black demands a sense of unity and respect for all members of the race, no matter how different their backgrounds and lifestyles might be. Tommy's actions exemplify her philosophy as, unlike the others, she shows respect to the character Oldtimer, by asking about and calling him by his birth name. Tommy recognizes the role of black organizations in the socio-political progress of African-Americans. Like her birth name, Tomorrow, she is forward-looking, while the others are mired in the past. She identifies with current black leaders, whereas Bill talks only of dead heroes. Through Tommy, the once pretentious characters are humbled as they learn being black lies not in the way one looks, but in the way one thinks and relates to the world.

Wedding Band deals with the subject of interracial romance in an insightful, unsentimental manner unlike the usual depiction of this subject on the stage and in popular media. The drama is set in 1918 in South Carolina when it was illegal for blacks and whites to marry or cohabit. For ten years Julia, a black woman, and Herman, a white man, have nurtured a clandestine relationship held together with the promise that they will one day move to the North to marry as soon as Herman has fulfilled his financial obligations to his mother. However, Julia comes to the painful realization that marriage to Herman is nothing more than a pipe dream. She learns that Herman harbors many of the same prejudices as other whites; and he is unwilling to endure the racial taunts of others who would object to their relationship once out in the open. The recognition of the futility of their relationship also awakens a sense of racial pride within Julia. Once a passive woman, by the play's end Julia asserts her right to live the way she chooses in a country cultivated and sustained by the labors and lives of her African ancestors.

A more recent work—*Moms*—is based on the life of the famed comedienne Jackie "Moms" Mabley. A series of scenes with music and dance depict her public and private life from her performances on a early-20th century black theatre touring circuit to her death in 1975. The play pays tribute to the comedienne's impeccable comic timing and strong rapport with the audience. However, the author does not gloss over the comedienne's more ignoble traits. The play mentions her overbearing personality, miserly disposition, portrayal of degrading stereotypes, ambivalence concerning her sexual preference, and lack of personal attention to the care of her children. Still, "Moms" is a fitting, even-handed tribute and a fine tour-de-force for the appropriate black actress.

—Addell Austin Anderson

CHIN, Frank (Chew, Jr.). American. Born in Berkeley, California, 25 February 1940. Educated at the University of California, Berkeley, 1958–61; University of Iowa, Iowa City, 1961–63; University of California, Santa Barbara, A.B. in English 1966. Clerk, Western Pacific Railroad Company, Oakland, California, 1962–65; brakeman, Southern Pacific Railroad, Oakland, 1966; production writer and story editor, King-T.V. and King Screen Productions, Seattle, Washington, 1966–69; lecturer in Asian American Studies, University of California, Davis, San Francisco State College, 1969–70, and University of California, Santa Barbara, 1980; lecturer in creative writing, University of California, Berkeley, 1972, and lecturer in English, University of Oklahoma, Norman, 1988; film consultant, Western Washington State College, Bellingham, 1969–70; founder and artistic director, Asian American Theater Workshop, San Francisco, 1973–77. Recipient: Joseph Henry Jackson award, 1965; James T. Phelan award, 1966; East-West Players award, 1971; Jack J. Flaks Memorial grant, 1972; San Francisco Foundation fellowship, 1974; Rockefeller grant, 1975; National Endowment for the Arts grant, 1975, 1980; Before Columbus-American Book award, 1981, 1989; Rockefeller American Generations grant, 1991. Address: 2106 Lemoyne Street, #5, Los Angeles, California 90026, U.S.A.

PUBLICATIONS

Plays

The Chickencoop Chinaman (produced New York, 1972). With *The Year of the Dragon*, Seattle, University of Washington Press, 1981.
The Year of the Dragon (produced New York, 1974). With *The Chickencoop Chinaman*, Seattle, University of Washington Press, 1981.
Gee, Pop! (produced San Francisco, 1974).
America More or Less, with Amiri Baraka and Leslie Marmon Silko, music by Tony Greco, lyrics by Arnold Weinstein (produced San Francisco, 1976).
Lullaby, with Leslie Marmon Silko, from a story by Silko (produced San Francisco, 1976).
American Peek-a-Boo Kabuki, World War II and Me (produced Los Angeles, 1985).
Flood of Blood: A Fairy Tale (for children). Published in the *Seattle Review*, vol. 11 no. 1, 1988.

Television Plays: *Seattle Repertory Theatre: Act Two* (documentary), 1966; *The Bel Canto Carols* (documentary), 1966; *A Man and His Music* (documentary), 1967; *Ed Sierer's New Zealand* (documentary), 1967; *Seafair Preview* (documentary), 1967; *The Year of the Ram* (documentary), 1967; *And Still Champion . . .! The Story of Archie Moore* (documentary), 1967; *Mary*, 1969; *Rainlight Rainvision* (for *Sesame Street* series), 1969; *Chinaman's Chance* (documentary), 1971.

Novel

Donald Duk. Minneapolis, Coffee House Press, 1991.

Short Stories

The Chinaman Pacific and Frisco R.R. Co. Minneapolis, Coffee House Press, 1988.

Other

Rescue at Wild Boar Forest (comic book). Calgary, Water Margin Press, 1988.

The Water Margin, or Shui Hu (comic book). Honolulu, Water Margin Press, 1989.
Lin Chong's Revenge (comic book). Vancouver, Water Margin Press, 1989.

Editor, with others, *Aiiieeeee! An Anthology of Asian American Writers*. Washington, D.C., Howard University Press, 1974.
Editor, with Shawn Wong, *Yardbird Reader, volume 3*. Berkeley, California, Yardbird Publishing Cooperative, 1974.
Editor, with others, *The Big Aiiieeeee!* Seattle, Washington University Press, 1991.

*

Frank Chin comments:

Asian American theatre is dead without ever having been born, and American theatre, like American writing has found and nurtured willing Gunga Dins, happy white racist tokens, with which to pay their lip service to yellows and call it dues. No thanks.

My theatrical sense combined with my ruthless scholarly nature and need to make things right to produce ceremonial events that restored history and civility inside Japanese America, and between the Japanese Americans and Seattle and Portland. The events, called "Day of Remembrance," dramatically publicized the campaign to redress the constitutional grievances suffered by all persons of Japanese ancestry during World War II. I put together groups of Japanese-American leaders and activists to lead a return to the county fairgrounds outside of Seattle and Portland that had been converted into concentration camps for the Nikkei in 1942. The Day of Remembrance included participation by the National Guard, local politicians, a display of art and artifacts from the concentration camps, a huge pot luck dinner, and a couple thousand Japanese Americans in both cities.

Otherwise, I am out of theatre. I will not work with any theatre, producer, writer, director, or actor who has played and lives the stereotype. So, I write fiction, essays, and articles.

I have written extensively on Chinese- and Japanese-American history, culture, literature, and presence in popular local newsmagazines, television documentaries, and scholarly journals.

I have taught Asian-American history and ideas using storytelling, theatre, and writing games, in four- to five-week-long workshops for the Asian-American Studies Program at Washington State University, in Pullman, Washington; the American Thought and Literature Department at Michigan State University, in East Lansing, Michigan; in five Portland high schools for the Bilingual/ESL program of Portland Public Schools.

In response to American west-coast public schools teaching the white racist characterisation of Chinese fairytales and childhood literature as teaching misogynistic ethics and despicable morals as fact, I have, like the Cantonese and Chinese before me, wherever Chinese literature and language are banned, taken to the comic book as a tactic for making the real accessible in a hostile literary and learning atmosphere.

I am the principal editor and author of the introductory essays of *Aiiieeeee!: An Anthology of Asian American Writers*, the most influential critical work in Asian-American literature, and *The Big Aiiieeeee! The Big Aiiieeeee!* explores Chinese- and Japanese-American history and stereotyping through the history of western Christian thought and writing, Chinese- and Japanese-American writing, and the Asian fairytales and childhood literature that informed the immigrants and the structures of their political and artistic institutions from *tongs* and *tanemoshi* to railroad building and music.

*   *   *

Frank Chin's two full-length plays, *The Chickencoop Chinaman* and *The Year of the Dragon*, were presented at the American Place Theatre, New York, in 1972 and 1974, and the latter was presented to a national television audience by the Public Broadcasting Service. The historical priority of his achievement might tempt one to call Chin the doyen of Asian-American playwrights, but that would be misleading because he attacks his fellow writers—as he and his fellow-editors put it in *The Big Aiiieeeee!*—for "ventriloquising the same old white Christian fantasy of little Chinese victims," victims of their own sadomasochistic culture and of their denial of their own identity in a quest for honorary whiteness. He also claims Maxine Hong Kingston, Amy Tan, and David Henry Hwang "fake all of Asian American history and literature." He attributes the success of Hwang's *M. Butterfly* to the portrayal of the central Chinese character as "the fulfillment of white male homosexual fantasy, literally kissing ass." He remains, then, something of the Angry Young Man who is the central character in both his full-length plays.

Indeed, *The Chickencoop Chinaman* can be compared to *Look Back in Anger*. In both, we are meant to recognize the truth of the central character's highly rhetorical attacks upon society, while in the course of the play he himself is presented in such a way as to lose our sympathy. As Tam's friend Kenji says almost at the end of the play,

> I used to think it was funny, brave, man, the way you ripped everybody up with your tongue, showing 'em up for clowns and bullshit. Your tongue was fast and flashy with the sounds, man, savin your ass from this and that trouble, making people laugh, man, shooin in the girls, I used to know why you were mean and talkin all the time. I don't anymore, and you're still talkin the same crazy talk.

Tam acknowledges that he is a loner and a loser. Chin seems to try to save Tam from total alienation by having him end the play preparing Chinese food—perhaps because "food's our only common language" (*Year of the Dragon*)—while he reminisces about his grandparents. *Look Back in Anger* ends with a similarly sentimental turn-around.

The image of "The Chickencoop Chinaman making whooppee in a birdcage" recurs in both plays. The subject of Chin's plays is the difficulty Asian-American men have in establishing an independent and personal identity when doubly isolated: from a culture whose experiences the American-born Chinese has not directly known and of whose language he knows only a smattering, and from a dominant white society whose members see only stereotypes and seek to push one back—psychologically, if not physically—into the cage of Chinatown. Thus, Tam's speech "jumps between black and white rhythms and accents" for he has "no real language of my own to make sense with, so out comes everybody else's language that don't conceive." This metaphor links the sterility of the protagonist's language, however hyper-active, with a lack of manhood that all three Asian-American men in *The Chickencoop Chinaman* feel. Similarly, the corresponding slick-speaking central character in *Year of the Dragon*, Fred, swings between a phony Chinatown accent that he employs as a tourist guide and casual American English. Tam visits his friend Blackjap Kenji, who has adopted a black lifestyle, and who is sheltering Lee, who has had husbands of "all colors and decorator combinations." She passes for white but is in fact part-Chinese. Her Chinese ex-husband Tom turns up to claim her. Tam has told us that his name has been miscorrected to Tom, and Tom is an obvious alter ego. (They are even given the same line about their visits: "I didn't mean to come/walk into no situation.") Tom represents the choice Tam has not made, to become a buttoned-down, assimilated, published writer. Symbolically, he has married white, but both Tom and Tam are separated from their wives—as though neither staying in the culture nor leaving it is a satisfactory solution.

That dilemma is the subject of *The Year of the Dragon*. Again, there is a character—Fred's sister—who has "married out" and become a published author, of a successful cook-book incorporating some of Fred's tourist patter. The ironic cultural contrasts pile up. Fred's "China-crazy" white brother-in-law speaks Mandarin and admires traditional Chinese culture, while Fred speaks a little Cantonese and is contemptuous of the Chinatown culture around him. Fred's father, feeling the approach of death, has brought his first wife and Fred's real mother from China (to the dismay of his Chinese-American wife); since she speaks no English, she is a mostly silent reminder of the ties to the old country. In the younger generation, Fred's younger brother is a juvenile delinquent, responsive to his peers rather than to the authority of the family.

Fred has always spoken of wanting to get out of Chinatown and write. He helped his sister get out, and now her success and his father's death at the end of the play give him that opportunity. But Chinatown is his subject and he fears that his inspiration will dry up away from it. Deeper than that, his decision is determined by his relationship to his father, the *paterfamilias* whom Chin names simply Pa. Pa disparages the one little-magazine publication Fred has achieved, and does not introduce Fred to his fellow seniors in Chinatown (this is based on an anecdote from Chin's own life). Pa is about to give a speech at the New Year's parade in which he will acknowledge Fred's achievement in the community, but he collapses and dies in a confrontation with Fred:

Fred. You gotta do somethin for me. Not for your son, but for me.

Pa. Who you? You my son. Da's all. What else you ting you are.

The final irony is that he will continue as his father's son rather than pursue his individual dreams.

If *Chickencoop Chinaman* is akin to Osborne, *Year of the Dragon* is more like Odets in its tightly plotted family conflicts and in tone. The ideal seems to be, as Fred expresses it, that "[we] get together and we're talkin a universe, and sing." But in the hierarchical Chinese family, that does not happen.

Flood of Blood: A Fairy Tale is a lively children's play performed by a travelling Chinese troupe in which Chin mixes the Ark story, the princess to be rescued from a dragon, and shades of Turandot.

—Anthony Graham-White

————

CHRISTIE, Agatha (Mary Clarissa). British. 1890–1976. See 2nd edition, 1977.

————

CHURCHILL, Caryl. British. Born in London, 3 September 1938. Educated at Trafalgar School, Montreal, 1948–55; Lady Margaret Hall, Oxford, 1957–60, B.A. in English 1960. Married David Harter in 1961; three sons. Resident dramatist, Royal Court Theatre, London, 1974–75. Recipient: Richard Hillary memorial prize, 1961; Obie award, 1982, 1983, 1988; Susan Smith Blackburn prize, 1983, 1988; *Time Out* award, 1987; Olivier award, 1987; *Plays and Players* award, 1987; *Evening Standard* award, 1987. Agent: Casarotto Ramsay Ltd., National House, 60–66 Wardour Street, London W1V 3HP. Address: 12 Thornhill Square, London N.1., England.

PUBLICATIONS

Plays

Downstairs (produced Oxford, 1958; London, 1959).
Having a Wonderful Time (produced Oxford and London, 1960).
Easy Death (produced Oxford, 1962).
The Ants (broadcast 1962). Published in *New English Dramatists 12*, London, Penguin, 1968.
Lovesick (broadcast 1967). Included in *Shorts*, 1990.
Abortive (broadcast 1971). Included in *Shorts*, 1990.
Not, Not, Not, Not, Not Enough Oxygen (broadcast 1971). Included in *Shorts*, 1990.
The Judge's Wife (televised 1972). Included in *Shorts*, 1990.
Schreber's Nervous Illness (broadcast 1972; produced London, 1972). Included in *Shorts*, 1990.
Owners (produced London, 1972; New York, 1973). London, Eyre Methuen, 1973.
Perfect Happiness (broadcast 1973; produced London, 1974).
Moving Clocks Go Slow (produced London, 1975).
Objections to Sex and Violence (produced London, 1975). Published in *Plays by Women 4*, edited by Michelene Wandor, London, Methuen, 1985.
Light Shining in Buckinghamshire (produced Edinburgh and London, 1976). London, Pluto Press, 1978.
Vinegar Tom (produced Hull and London, 1976). London, TQ Publications, 1978; New York, French, 1982.
Traps (produced London, 1977; Chicago, 1982; New York, 1988). London, Pluto Press, 1978.
The After Dinner Joke (televised 1978). Included in *Shorts*, 1990.
Floorshow, with others (produced London, 1978).
Cloud Nine (produced Cardiff and London, 1979; New York, 1981). London, Pluto Press, and New York, French, 1979.
Three More Sleepless Nights (produced London, 1980; San Francisco, 1984). Included in *Shorts*, 1990.
Top Girls (produced London and New York, 1982). London, Methuen, 1982; revised version, Methuen, and New York, French, 1984.
Fen (produced Wivenhoe, Essex, London, and New York, 1983). London, Methuen, 1983.
Softcops (produced London, 1984). London, Methuen, 1984.
Midday Sun, with Geraldine Pilgrim, Pete Brooks and John Ashford (produced London, 1984).
Plays 1 (includes *Owners*, *Vinegar Tom*, *Traps*, *Light Shining in Buckinghamshire*, *Cloud Nine*). London, Methuen, 1985.
A Mouthful of Birds, with David Lan (produced Birmingham and London, 1986). London, Methuen, 1987.
Softcops, and Fen. London, Methuen, 1986.

Serious Money (produced London and New York, 1987).
London, Methuen, 1987; revised edition, 1990.
Icecream (produced London, 1989; New York, 1990).
London, Hern, 1989.
Hot Fudge (produced London, 1989; New York, 1990).
Included in *Shorts*, 1990.
Mad Forest (produced London, 1990). London, Hern,
1990.
Shorts (includes *Lovesick*; *Abortive*; *Not, Not, Not, Not, Not
Enough Oxygen*; *Schreber's Nervous Illness*; *The Hospital
at the Time of the Revolution*; *The Judge's Wife*; *The After-
Dinner Joke, Seagulls*; *Three More Sleepless Nights*; *Hot
Fudge*). London, Hern, 1990.
Plays 2 (includes *Softcops, Top Girls, Fen, Serious Money*).
London, Methuen, 1990.
Lives of the Great Poisoners (produced London, 1991).

Radio Plays: *The Ants*, 1962; *Lovesick*, 1967; *Identical Twins*,
1968; *Abortive*, 1971; *Not, Not, Not, Not, Not Enough
Oxygen*, 1971; *Schreber's Nervous Illness*, 1972; *Henry's Past*,
1972; *Perfect Happiness*, 1973.

Television Plays: *The Judge's Wife*, 1972; *Turkish Delight*,
1974; *The After Dinner Joke*, 1978; *The Legion Hall
Bombing*, 1978; *Crimes*, 1982.

*

Critical Studies: *File on Churchill* edited by Linda
Fitzsimmons, London, Methuen, 1989; *Caryl Churchill: A
Casebook* edited by Phyllis R. Randall, New York, Garland,
1989; *Churchill the Playwright* by Geraldine Cousin, London,
Methuen, 1989; *The Plays of Churchill* by Amelia Howe
Kritzer, London, Macmillan, 1991.

* * *

London-born and Oxford-educated, Caryl Churchill is a
highly successful playwright whose plays are designed to star-
tle and instruct. In *The Plays of the Seventies*, Roger Cornish
and Violet Ketels note that she is in the unique and enviable
position as a contemporary British playwright of having had
three plays, *Fen, Cloud Nine*, and *Top Girls*, running simultaneously in New York in the same year, 1983. Her plays are
often gutsy, outspoken, and sharp in their critique of societal
institutions. They are influenced by experimental movements
in British theatre growing up in the late 1960s. She writes an
alternative theatre, but one that is highly commercial while
also controversial.

She has been writing plays for the radio, stage, and television for more than thirty years. *Shorts* offers a representative sample of ten of her short plays written between 1965 and
1989. Two of them have never been performed; several, such
as *Lovesick* and *Abortive*, were written for radio; *The Judge's
Wife* and *The After Dinner Joke* were written for television;
and the recent *Hot Fudge* was originally intended to be a
companion to *Icecream*. One of her most successful early
plays is *The Ants*, a profoundly disturbing work about identity
and perspective, broadcast on the BBC Third Program in
1962. Her early stage play, *Owners*, produced by the Royal
Court Theatre Upstairs in 1972 offered an indictment of the
concept of property and ownership. In 1974 she became a
writer-in-residence at the Royal Court and in 1975 *Objections
to Sex and Violence* was performed on their main stage. In
1976 she became the first woman dramatist invited to join the
Joint Stock Theatre Group where she began working closely
with two directors, Max Stafford-Clark and Les Waters, who

have played an important part in her career ever since. The
majority of her subsequent plays have been produced either
on the Royal Court's main stage or in the Theatre Upstairs.
Joseph Papp's matching grant to the Joint Stock made it
possible for Churchill's plays to be brought to his Public
Theatre in New York. She also worked with the feminist
theatre group, Monstrous Regiment, where she produced
Vinegar Tom. Some of her best and most commercially profit-
able plays, *Light Shining in Buckinghamshire, Cloud Nine*,
and *Fen*, as well as some less successful albeit very interesting
experiments, *A Mouthful of Birds* and *Icecream*, have been
developed for Joint Stock. *Fen*, a play about low-paid women
potato pickers, won the distinguished Susan Smith Blackburn
prize which is awarded to outstanding women writers in the
English language. Her plays have been performed at the
National Theatre, the Barbican Pit, and the Royal Court
Theatre, as well as in repertory companies across England
and Scotland and on stages across the United States.

Her plays usually take the British people, often working-
class, for their subjects, but they travel well, in part because
of her feminist interests, topical themes, and socialist politics.
Recently, in *Icecream*, she charted the travels of an American
couple to Britain in search of their ancestors followed by the
travels of the British distant cousins to America. The clash of
the two cultures forms the backdrop to a chilling tale of
murders and deaths that connect the families. The socio-
political concerns expressed in her plays draw upon the thinking of such diverse minds as R.D. Laing, Frantz Fanon, and
Michel Foucault. Her plays offer trenchant social commentaries upon the greedy decade of mergers and acquisitions,
the appalling practices of colonialism and apartheid, and the
theme of women's oppression, whether worked out in the
17th century practice of witch-burning or the twentieth-
century phenomenon of the battered wife or child. Others
explore women's liberation, showing both its gains and its
losses. She often treats her themes with antic humour, or
ludicrous parody, while making her audience consider how
race, women-hating, and homophobia express themselves in
our culture.

Churchill is well-schooled in the craft of theatre, employing
Brechtian devices, experimenting with the formal com-
ponents of the play—the way it inhabits time and space—and
most recently experimenting with dance and movement combined with music to enhance the theatricality of her stage
images. Her experiences working in the medium of broadcast
and with Joint Stock's method of writing have both contributed importantly to the unusual texture, the overlapping of
voices, and the often episodic structure of many of her plays.
In *Traps* she keeps rerunning the action while altering it,
violating linear chronology, building a scene only to undercut
its key elements, leaving the audience perplexed about the
exact relationships between characters and the nature of the
action while absorbed by the psychological reality of the play.
Cloud Nine takes similar liberties with time and the conventions of realistic theatre.

Writing radio plays taught her much about narrative: how
characters can speak themselves, evoking the visual landscape while using words almost as musical notes, amplifying
or diminishing the hearer's sense of space and time, and
heightening the sense of anticipation. Her work in broadcast
paved the way for her technique of overlapping characters'
speeches on stage, a device she relies upon heavily since the
writing of *Top Girls*. It also schooled her in the writing of
dialogue. She often relies upon the exchange of short, staccato lines and a sparse, minimalist use of language in stage
dialogue. Occasionally she uses language lavishly, giving
characters long monologues. She opens *Serious Money* with a

scene from Thomas Shadwell's *The Volunteers, or The Stock-jobbers*, written in 1692. She then dazzles her audience with her own Shadwellian rhymed couplets throughout her play. She can also write tough, often sexually explicit dialogue. *Cloud Nine* shocked its audience with its talk of females masturbating and its use of cross-dressing and racial cross-casting to heighten the sense of the constructedness of race and gender. One of its more outlandish stage pictures occurs when a young man crawls under the late-Victorian long gown of a woman in colonial Africa, grabbing at her parts while she tries to preserve genteel appearances, belied not only by the man under her dress but also by the whip she holds, a symbol of her none-too-latent desire to see men flogged.

Her writing owes much to the protracted workshop experiences involving playwrights, actors, directors, and designers provided by the Royal Court Theatre Upstairs and Joint Stock. This format allows Churchill to work with the actors and directors in exploratory research to learn about the play's subject over a four week period, followed by an interval of up to ten weeks in which she is left to script, and concluding with a six-week period of rehearsal prior to the play's opening. At other times she has scripted during the improvisational workshop stage, bringing in new text almost daily. In one instance, she scripted collaboratively with David Lan, a playwright and anthropologist interested in rites of possession amongst Zimbabwe tribes. He scripted *A Mouthful of Birds* alongside her, both producing texts simultaneously. She seems to flourish in this setting. The workshop provides her rich thematic material and also immerses her in an environment, as it did in *Fen*. It gives her access to a wide range of characters and enables her to examine public and personal narratives, presenting private experiences set against a backdrop of historical time, institutional forces, and public events.

Churchill is a playwright of ideas. Although socialist in her political leanings, her stance is not predictable. Her work is lauded by feminists. She does not shy away from depicting powerful women corrupted by greed and ambition and deriving pleasure from the infliction of violence. She embarked on *A Mouthful of Birds*, with David Lan, providing a modern-day *Bacchae* in order to show women in the thrall of violence. Responding to feminist environmentalists and women in the peace movement, Churchill explores images that show violence and pleasure as often integral to each other. Her play concludes with women who have known the power and pleasure of violence choosing not to use it. In *Owners* and *Serious Money*, her respective protagonists, Marion, Scilla Todd, and Mary Lou Barnes are property owners, London traders, and arbitrageurs. They thrill at the power of money; they like it to come fast, and their pursuit of it knows no limits.

Churchill's plays are often satiric. They explicitly condemn their characters and the capitalist social order, but they do it with gusto. Her women are brassy. While *Serious Money* questions traditional ideas about gender and mocks the crassly sexual way in which capitalists equate money with women, considering both something that ought to be exploited, it also shows women who have been thoroughly appropriated. The fast money "Futures Song," bawdily shouting about cunts and money, which concludes the first act of the play caused a sensation when the play opened. Vulgar it is; perhaps even, finally, not necessary to Churchill's romp through the corrupt world of insider-trading, but its theatrical effect is visceral. The image conflates a chorus line with a drag ball played out in the traders' pits. Vamping in an orgy of excess, thrusting fists like pricks at the audience, and screaming out dirty words, the floor-traders, the insider dealers, the corporate raiders, and the arbitrageurs catch the audience up in a frenzy. *Softcops* is another play that revels in a 19th

century carnivalesque atmosphere where freakish side-shows are manipulated for their so-called instructional potential.

Often a topical matter of political importance is the impetus for Churchill's plays. *Serious Money* was her response to the financial scandals involving the takeover of Guinness and the arbitrageur Boesky, whose testimony finally led to the end of the era of insider-trading. Feminist concerns finding voice in the 1970's and 1980's inspired *Vinegar Tom* and *Light Shining in Buckinghamshire*. Cults of possession, demonic rites, the rise of alcoholism, particularly among women, and a growing concern with the abuse of the body—whether as the result of eating disorders or violence—led to plays like the two cited above as well as *A Mouthful of Birds*. In the case of *Vinegar Tom*, Churchill was working with a feminist group, created in 1975, which was committed to exploring socialist themes. This play not only examines witchcraft and the scapegoating of women in the 17th century, with its obvious implications for the present day, but it examined the forces behind collectivities. In *Top Girls* Churchill looks at the liberated woman, the woman freed from housework, domesticity, and child-bearing. Marlene, the managing director of the Top Girls Employment Agency, celebrates her recent promotion by throwing a party to which she invites the most unlikely cast of guests—all women overachievers, some real, some invented. Pope Joan, Chaucer's Patient Griselda, Lady Nijo, a medieval courtesan-turned-nun, and Dull Gret, a figure from a Brueghel painting, all participate in Marlene's party. Their talk is trivial; they pay little attention to each other, speaking over each others' lines, and all seemingly talking about their achievements. The play richly exploits all the trademarks of gender-bending for which Churchill is famous. She also plays fast and loose with time. In the second act, in ways reminiscent of *Cloud Nine*, the guests of the first act reappear, transformed into job applicants and interviewers in the personnel office. The play actually reveals the failure of the dream of liberation. These women are unhappy and miscast; their stories are ones of suffering, not success. The play is finally not as bleak as *Fen*. The women's suffering and sacrifices leave them incomplete and largely alone. The play's social context heightens the awareness of how gender constructs roles. Marlene is more than a victim of contemporary times—her victimage is rooted in historical institutions.

Softcops was produced by the Royal Shakespeare Company at the Pit in 1984. As in many of her plays, it probes the mainsprings of theatre—spectacle, act, and audience—taking as its subject Foucault's examination of the spectacle of the scaffold and the modern institutions of discipline and punishment worked out so brilliantly in *Discipline and Punish: The Birth of the Prison*. The play contrasts different mechanisms of control: those brought about through the witnessing of terrible punishments inflicted upon the body of the transgressor and thereby teaching the public not to commit bad acts for fear that they will suffer the agonies of the body they have watched, and those produced by eliminating the audience of the spectacle and replacing it with a single central figure well positioned to conduct surveillance of guilty parties and exert control. This latter kind of control depends on men's terror of disobedience, a fear that they will be found out, which can be produced merely by curtaining off the surveillor, so that he cannot be seen but can always see. Jeremy Bentham's architecture of the Panopticon, with its high, central watch tower, provided the ideal form of punishment, one in which very few in fact have to be imprisoned and the multitudes do not have to witness the spectacle of punishment. The consequence of the latter mechanisms of control are demonstrated in the modern-day institutions of reformatories, prisons, hospitals, and school rooms. In a play that is often funny and sometimes rather preachy, Churchill explores the close interrelationships between criminals and law-enforcers, subverting the power of authority, and finally posing the possibility that the entire institution of repressive authority might be toppled. This is a theme that she has advanced in a number of other plays from as early as *Objections to Sex and Violence*.

After more than thirty years of successful writing for the stage, there are now two book-length collections of Churchill's plays and she is the subject of a spate of critical articles and a book by Geraldine Cousin. The latter examines her use of the workshop format to develop her writing and offers an overview of her writing, considering in particular her handling of the theme of time and the possibility for revolutionary change in her plays. Churchill continues to be a fine playwright, not only because of the combination of daring and craft that is characteristic of her writing, but also because of the keen intelligence behind her plays, coupled with a high degree of wit.

—Carol Simpson Stern

CLARK, Brian (Robert). British. Born in Bournemouth, Hampshire, 3 June 1932. Educated at Merrywood Grammar School, Bristol; Redland College of Education, Bristol, teaching certificate 1954; Central School of Speech and Drama, London, 1954–55; Nottingham University, B.A. (honours) in English 1964. Served in the Royal Corps of Signals, 1950–52. Married 1) Margaret Paling in 1961, two sons; 2) Anita Modak in 1983, one stepson and one stepdaughter; 3) Cherry Potter in 1990. Schoolteacher, 1955–61 and 1964–66; staff tutor in drama, University of Hull, 1966–70. Founder, Amber Lane Press, Ashover, Derbyshire, 1978–79, Ambergate, Derbyshire, 1980–81, and Oxford since 1982. Recipient: Society of West End Theatres award, 1978; *Evening Standard* award, 1978; *Plays and Players* award, 1978; BAFTA Shell International Television award, 1979. Fellow, Royal Society of Literature, 1985. Agent: Judy Daish Associates, 83 Eastbourne Mews, London W2 6LQ, England.

PUBLICATIONS

Plays

Lay By, with others (produced Edinburgh and London, 1971). London, Calder and Boyars, 1972.
England's Ireland, with others (produced Amsterdam and London, 1972).
Truth or Dare? (produced Hull, 1972).
Whose Life Is It Anyway? (televised 1972; revised version produced London and Washington, D.C., 1978; New York, 1979). Ashover, Derbyshire, Amber Lane Press, 1978; New York, Dodd Mead, 1979.
Post Mortem (produced London, 1975). Published in *Three One-Act Plays*, Ashover, Derbyshire, Amber Lane Press, 1979.
Campion's Interview (produced London, 1976; New York, 1978–79).

Can You Hear Me at the Back? (produced London, 1979). Ashover, Derbyshire, Amber Lane Press, 1979.
Switching in the Afternoon or, As the Screw Turns (produced Louisville, 1980).
Kipling (produced London and New York, 1984).
All Change at the Wells, with Stephen Clark, music by Andrew Peggie (produced London, 1985).
The Petition (produced New York and London, 1986). Oxford, Amber Lane Press, 1986.
Hopping to Byzantium, with Kathy Levin (produced Osnabrück, Germany, 1990).

Screenplay: *Whose Life Is It Anyway?*, with Reginald Rose, 1981.

Television Plays: *Ten Torrey Canyons*, 1972; *Play in a Manger*, 1972; *Whose Life Is It Anyway?*, 1972; *Achilles Heel*, 1973; *Operation Magic Carpet*, 1973; *A Follower for Emily*, 1974; *Easy Go*, 1974; *An Evil Influence*, 1975; *The Saturday Party*, 1975; *The Eleventh Hour*, with Clive Exton and Hugh Whitemore, 1975; *Parole*, 1976; *A Working Girl*, 1976; *Or Was He Pushed*, 1976; *The Country Party*, 1977; *There's No Place . . .*, 1977; *Happy Returns*, 1977; *Cat and Mouse*, 1977; *A Swinging Couple* (*Crown Court* series), 1977; *Out of Bounds* series, with Jim Hawkins, 1977; *Mirage*, with Jim Hawkins, 1978; *Houston, We Have a Problem*, with Jim Hawkins, 1978; *Telford's Change* series, 1979; *Horse Sense* (*All Creatures Great and Small* series), 1979; *Late Starter*, 1985; *Lord Elgin and Some Stones of No Value*, with others, 1985; *House Games*, with Cherry Potter.

Other

Group Theatre. London, Pitman, 1971; New York, Theatre Arts, 1972.
Out of Bounds (for children; novelization of television series), with Jim Hawkins. London, BBC Publications, 1979.

*   *   *

Having taught drama in a university and written on group theatre, Brian Clark began his career as a playwright by collaborating with a number of younger radical dramatists on the anti-establishment political shockers *Lay By* and *England's Ireland* for Portable Theatre. There is no little irony in the fact that at about the same time he was writing the original television version of *Whose Life Is It Anyway?*, a play which six years later was to become the great "serious" West End hit of the late 1970's. Such was the critical and popular success of this play that it may be considered to have representative status. Here, it seemed, was a serious writer whose handling of an issue of contemporary relevance was, however entertaining, uncompromised by commercial success.

Whose Life Is It Anyway? concerns the claim by a man who lies in a hospital bed after a road accident, paralyzed from the neck down, to his right to die—that is, to commit suicide by choosing to be taken off the life-support machine. As its title suggests, the play's interest is in the moral argument, which culminates in the good-humored legal confrontation between the specialist, for whom life is an absolute, and the patient, who claims the right to choose suicide (eventually winning his case). The personal relationships between the patient, Ken, and the hospital staff are economically handled and often touching, and the play provides the opportunity for a virtuoso performance of an unusual kind in the central role (Tom

Conti's performance was a major factor in its success in London). The dialogue, alert, witty, and highly polished, is one of the play's most attractive features, yet its particular quality points to a major dramatic limitation. Clark is interested only in those elements of his chosen dramatic situation which can readily be verbalized. His dialectical resource is impressive, but the most interesting things about the paralyzed Ken's situation are those matters—most of them to do with psychological states—that are on the edges of the moral and legal dialectics. Ken has chosen to have his life ended and seeks to enforce his wishes with wit and pertinacity, but what of the frustration, anger, depression, and eventual self-resignation that he must be presumed to have experienced? The legal case turns on his mental state, yet psychology is unimportant to the play itself. The arguments are there, but what of the *experience* of being paralyzed?

The problem of verbalization is even more acute in Clark's second full-length stage play, *Can You Hear Me at the Back?*, though here, in a very different situation, the dramatist shows himself to be continually aware of that problem. The play deals with the attempts of the middle-aged chief architect of a New Town to break out of a professional and personal (marital) impasse. The professional planner feels that his life is "planned," devoid of spontaneity (his ideal is a "planned spontaneity"). Although he finally leaves his wife, he had previously refused to take the easy way out by going away with his best friend's wife, who has confessed her love for him. The character himself is aware that he fits only too well the self-pitying cliché of the discontented middle-class white-collar menopausal male, just as he acknowledges that the slickness and facility of his way of speaking is the verbal equivalent of what he abhors about his profession: in both cases a disorderly reality is made to submit to neat abstractions. Yet the necessary critique of the middle-class ethos represented—of which luxuriant self-scorn and guilt are an essential part—is entirely absent. Clark's own failure to reveal in the play a valid alternative way of speaking to that of his main character means that the only perspective on middle-class disillusionment offered by the work is that of the middle-class represented within it.

Implicit in Clark's attempts to combine moral argument with popular theatrical appeal is a keen awareness of an essentially middle-class liberal audience. This emerges explicitly in the quasi-biographical one-man show written for Alec McCowen, *Kipling*. Confronted by an audience composed largely of what he would term "wishy-washy liberals," and resisting crustily any demand for self-revelation, Kipling launches out on "a non-stop elegy of self-justification." The show invites the projected (liberal) audience to re-examine inherited assumptions about Kipling and to question its own beliefs and convictions; yet at least one reviewer saw it as an "accomplished exercise in audience ingratiation," carefully neutralizing a potentially disturbing subject.

Much the same could be said (and was) of Clark's two-hander *The Petition*. Here Clark returns to the issue-play mode of *Whose Life Is It Anyway?*, except that in this instance the connection between the public issue ("in a way, the Bomb is the only thing worth writing about") and the private context is not ready-made. Clark's way of making it is thoroughly conventional. The discovery by a retired General that his wife has signed an anti-nuclear petition published in the *Times* prompts disclosure of her terminal illness and of an old sexual infidelity. Arguments about nuclear confrontation and the threat of universal annihilation are thus seen within the context of a purgative conflict within marriage. The characteristic facility of the dialogue tends only to confirm the cosy domestication of a disturbing issue (though the perform-

ances of Rosemary Harris and John Mills in London were remarkable). Reviewers mentioned William Douglas-Home and Terence Rattigan.

—Paul Lawley

CLARK, John Pepper. Now writes as J.P. Clark Bekederemo. Nigerian. Born in Kiagbodo, 6 April 1935. Educated at Warri Government College, Ughelli, 1948–54; University of Ibadan, 1955–60, B.A. (honours) in English 1960, and graduate study (Institute of African Studies fellowship), 1963–64; Princeton University, New Jersey (Parvin fellowship). Married to Ebun Odutola Clark; three daughters and one son. Information officer, Government of Nigeria, 1960–61; head of features and editorial writer, Lagos *Daily Express*, 1961–62; research fellow, 1964–66, and professor of African literature, 1966–85, University of Lagos. Founding editor, *Horn* magazine, Ibadan; co-editor, *Black Orpheus*, Lagos, from 1968. Founding member, Society of Nigerian Authors. Agent: Andrew Best, Curtis Brown, 162–168 Regent Street, London W1R 5TB, England.

PUBLICATIONS

Plays

Song of a Goat (produced Ibadan, 1961; London, 1965). Ibadan, Mbari, 1961; in *Three Plays*, 1964; in *Plays from Black Africa*, edited by Fredric M. Litto, New York, Hill and Wang, 1968.
Three Plays. London, Oxford University Press, 1964.
The Masquerade (produced London, 1965). Included in *Three Plays*, 1964; in *Collected Plays, 1964–1988*, 1991.
The Raft (broadcast 1966; produced New York, 1978). Included in *Three Plays*, 1964; in *Collected Plays, 1964–1988*, 1991.
Ozidi. Ibadan, London, and New York, Oxford University Press, 1966.
The Bikoroa Plays (as J.P. Clark Bekederemo) (includes *The Boat, The Return Home, Full Circle*) (produced Lagos, 1981). Oxford, Oxford University Press, 1985; in *Collected Plays, 1964–1988*, 1991.
Collected Plays, 1964–1988 (includes *Song of a Goat, The Masquerade, The Raft, Ozidi, The Boat, The Return Home, Full Circle*). Washington, D.C., Howard University Press, 1991.

Screenplay: *The Ozidi of Atazi*.

Radio Play: *The Raft*, 1966.

Verse

Poems. Ibadan, Mbari, 1962.
A Reed in the Tide: A Selection of Poems. London, Longman, 1965; New York, Humanities Press, 1970.
Casualties: Poems 1966–68. London, Longman, and New York, Africana, 1970.
Urhobo Poetry. Ibadan, Ibadan University Press, 1980.
A Decade of Tongues: Selected Poems 1958–1968. London, Longman, 1981.

State of the Union (as J.P. Clark Bekederemo). London, Longman, 1985.
Mandela and Other Poems. Ikeja, Longman, 1988.
Collected Poems, 1958–1988. Washington, D.C., Howard University Press, 1991.

Other

America, Their America. London, Deutsch-Heinemann, 1964; New York, Africana, 1969.
The Example of Shakespeare: Critical Essays on African Literature. London, Longman, and Evanston, Illinois, North-western University Press, 1970.
The Hero as a Villain. Lagos, University of Lagos Press, 1978.

Editor and Translator, *The Ozidi Saga*, by Okabou Ojobolo. Ibadan, University of Ibadan Press, 1977.

*

Critical Studies: *John Pepper Clark* by Robert M. Wren, Lagos, Lagos University Press, 1984; *A Critical View of John Pepper Clark's "Three Plays"* by Martin Banham, London, Collins, 1985.

* * *

John Pepper Clark was awarded his B.A. at the University of Ibadan in the year Nigeria gained independence and his first play was produced and published two years later, in 1962. In his many-sided career, he has written plays less consistently than he has written poems. His *Three Plays* was followed closely by *Ozidi*, but almost twenty years passed before the trilogy *The Bikoroa Plays* appeared in 1985.

His first play, *Song of a Goat*, has been produced in various countries, and is probably the most artistically successful. Its first lines state the theme:

Masseur: Your womb
    Is open and warm as a room:
    It ought to accommodate many.
Ebiere: Well, it seems like staying empty.
Masseur: An empty house, my daughter, is a thing
    Of danger.

Ebiere's husband, Zifa, refuses to think of his sterility as permanent or of following the Masseur's suggestion that the claims of fertility be honored by his brother Tonye. When Ebiere in her frustration seduces Tonye, Zifa perverts the ritual which would legitimize that surreptitious union: he makes Tonye force the head of the sacrificed goat into a pot, which shatters. This is by analogy, as they all realize, an assault upon Ebiere's womb. Tonye hangs himself, Zifa drowns himself, and Ebiere is left pregnant. The intensity of this conflict, in which each member of the trio is both victim and aggressor, sustains this short play and sweeps us through the trappings of Greek tragedy—chorus of neighbours, a Cassandra-like aunt, a messenger speech telling of the final disaster—in which Clark dresses the story. Despite some self-conscious writing (evident also in the etymological reference of the title), overall there is an extraordinary assurance in this play.

Clark seems to have designed *The Masquerade* to offer relief from the intensity of *Song of a Goat*. He offers us "a real dance of the dragon-flies," the high-spirited wooing of Titi by a stranger, Ebiere's son Tufa. Since Clark makes Tufa innocent of any knowledge of the tragedy surrounding his conception, the wooing can be lyrically joyful, a little in the spirit of Romeo and Juliet. Only as Tufa's father investigates rumor and the past is revealed, do we return to tragedy. Unfortunately, one senses that the play's style and its denouement were willed into being. The language is full of echoes of Shakespeare and conceits in the manner of Christopher Fry. Tufa has done nothing culpable, and even with Titi's father's intransigent hostility to the marriage it takes a combination of misprision and accident to bring about the lovers' deaths.

The third of the *Three Plays*, *The Raft*, presents four men drifting down a river on a raft of logs. Differences between the characters are subordinated to atmosphere as they drift through the fog, and to the intent to convey, in Clark's phrase, the "human condition." Civil war overtook Nigeria not long after the play appeared and some read it as a prescient allegorical vision. It is true that the raft splits and carries off one of the four men, but if the work bears such meaning it is only as one metaphor among others and it cannot be pushed into the precision of an allegory.

Clark's recent trilogy, *The Bikoroa Plays*, again traces the fate of a family through successive generations. This time the focus is not on sexual relationships but on the differing ambitions of two brothers of contrasting character. They alternate in the use of the family boat, month by month, and irritations mount to the point where there is a fatal quarrel. One is shot, the other condemned to death and, ironically, the boat is split to carry each to his grave. The other two plays present the fatal quarrels of their two sons and two grandsons. This is so precise a repetition that the action becomes predictable. Yet there is less sense of the author's self-conscious control of the action. As one character says, "Fate is what we say after the event, not what we see before it." The treatment is more relaxed and less relentlessly tragic than in his first plays, in part because these are Clark's first plays in prose, but more because the brother's behavior is seen—as the action in the earlier plays is not—from the viewpoint of the community, within whose life they seek their fulfilment. Climatic scenes are trials and ceremonies. The prose easily incorporates praise-names and metaphors seem the language of the community—as when the hasty exit of an angry man evokes the comment "There goes a whirlwind with a lot of dust in its eye"—rather than a poet's invention. Beyond the community are the pressures of a changing colonial society that offers new opportunities but has destroyed the traditional ideal of "the man, the fish, the vessel, all brought together in the one act of quest by man for fish over waters spilling into the sun."

Based on an Ijaw epic that is narrated and performed over seven days, *Ozidi* is unlike Clark's other plays in length, scope, and staging demands. It too deals with blood honour and the curse on a family, worked out in this case by a son avenging his father through his own strength abetted by his grandmother's magic. But the traditional society is refracted through Clark's ironic consciousness. Ozidi is presented as a figure trapped in his destined role of warrior-avenger but at a loss to find himself and, like Goethe's Götz von Berlichingen, increasingly an outsider exemplifying anachronistic values. It has been suggested that Clark created a "parable of the talented individual in Africa today" and, indeed, Clark the modern storyteller changes Ijaw tradition in his play to have the storyteller take on the role of Ozidi.

—Anthony Graham-White

CLIFFORD, John. British. Born in Derby, 22 March 1950. Educated at Clifton College, Bristol, 1963–71; University of

Granada, Spain, 1971; University of St. Andrews, Fife, Scotland, 1968–76, M.A. (honours) in Spanish and Arabic 1971, Ph.D. 1976. Student nurse, Kirkcaldy, Fife, 1977–78; yoga instructor, Leven, Fife, 1978; lecturer in Spanish, University of St. Andrews, 1980; drama critic and dance critic, the *Scotsman*, Edinburgh, 1981–87; regular contributor and occasional presenter, Tuesday Review, BBC Radio Scotland, and Kaleidoscope, Radio 4, 1981–87; contributor to the Glasgow *Herald*, *Scotland on Sunday*, *Plays and Players*, *Nursing Times*, and the *Observer*, 1981–87; Thames Television writer-in-residence, 1986–87, and member of the play reading panel, since 1986, Traverse Theatre, Edinburgh; guest lecturer in textual studies, Queen Margaret College, Edinburgh, 1992. Recipient: Scottish Arts Council fellowship, 1983, grant, 1990; Edinburgh Festival fringe first, 1985; Spirit of Mayfest award, 1988; Gulbenkian grant, 1988; British Council grant, 1989, 1992. Agent: Alan Brodie Representation, 91 Regent Street, London W1R 7TB, England.

PUBLICATIONS

Plays

The House with Two Doors, adaptation of a play by Calderón (produced Edinburgh, 1980).
The Doctor of Honour, adaptation of a play by Calderón (produced St. Andrews, 1983).
Romeo and Juliet, adaptation of the play by Shakespeare (produced Glasgow, 1984).
Losing Venice (produced Edinburgh, 1985; London, 1987). Published in *Scot-Free*, edited by Alasdair Cameron, London, Hern, 1990.
Lucy's Play (produced Edinburgh, 1986).
Heaven Bent, Hell Bound, adaptation of a play by Tirso de Molina (produced London, 1987).
Playing with Fire (produced Edinburgh, 1987).
How Like an Angel (produced Edinburgh, 1987).
Great Expectations, adaptation of the novel by Dickens (produced Glasgow, 1988).
Schism in England, adaptation of the play by Calderón (produced London, 1989).
Inés de Castro (produced Edinburgh, 1989; London, 1991). Published in *First Run 2*, edited by Kate Harwood, London, Hern, 1990.
The House of Bernarda Alba, adaptation of the play by Lorca (produced Edinburgh, 1989).
The Magic Theatre, adaptation of the play by Cervantes (produced Edinburgh, 1989).
Ten Minute Play (produced London 1991).
Light in the Village (produced Edinburgh, 1991). London, Hern, 1991.
The Girl who Fell to Earth (produced Grantham, Lincolnshire, 1991).
Macbeth, adaptation of the play by Shakespeare (produced Perth, 1991).

Screenplay: *Santiago*, 1992.

Radio Plays: *Desert Places*, 1983; *Ending Time*, 1984; *Losing Venice*, 1986; *The Price of Everything*, 1992; *Inés de Castro*, 1992; *Celestina*, adaptation of the novel by Fernando de Rojas, 1992.

Television Plays: *Inés de Castro*, 1991; *Quevedo*, 1992.

*

John Clifford comments:
When they succeed, I like to think my plays operate like good science fiction: they take the audience somewhere else, in space or in time. They engage the imagination; also, hopefully, the senses, the emotions and the intellect.

When I write, I follow my instincts and my sense of stagecraft. I don't plan things out much, or have any particular theme in mind. What happens shouldn't come from me, but from the characters. So in a way, I don't write my plays. I try to listen out for them. I don't think much about what they mean. If they're a rich source of pleasure that is enough of an achievement.

In the end, writing's just a job. There's nothing that special about it: nothing that should single us out for special praise or exonerate us from blame. Our work does affect the world, even if only in ways we cannot measure; and we bear the responsibility for the things we write.

Certainly in these times to express just pain, disgust, and misery is something of a crime. But in any case, I don't think my plays have much to do with self-expression. I'd rather see them as small acts of resistance.

*   *   *

John Clifford's reputation rests on a highly successful series of original plays written for the Traverse Theatre in Edinburgh, and on a number of elegant translations and adaptations that have established him as one of Britain's leading interpreters of Spanish drama.

Losing Venice, the first of his plays to be produced at the Traverse, begins in the milieu of 17th century Spain and takes its principal characters on a journey across the Mediterranean to Crete and Venice before they finally return home. The free-wheeling and picaresque action of the play recounts the story of the Duke, who goes in search of winning fame by the sword. Clifford pokes fun at the vainglory of warfare and at the posturing of this military adventurer. The most beguiling qualities of all his later work are already in evidence in this piece. The handling of historical period is delicately controlled, investing the play with an air of universality that is never ponderously sought after, but which has enabled the script to travel to other parts of the world with notable success. It is characteristic of this writer's work that the drama is animated at heart by a challenging idealism, a strong sense of the light and dark in human affairs, and the need to invoke the former to combat the latter. Yet the linguistic wit is abundant, the narrative energy insatiable, and a self-deprecating comic spirit plays across the proceedings with unpredictable effect.

Lucy's Play, produced the following year, is set in Syracuse in 386 A.D. The roving, Cervantes-style dynamic of *Losing Venice* is exchanged for what is in some ways a more classical comic structure, observing a certain unity of location. The basic premises of the situation are deliberately kept simple and the comedy is woven with great purity from the interplay of relationships. The plot follows the fortunes of Lucy, whose lover Lucius departs to seek his fortune, leaving her prey to the attentions of Max, the Mayor, who is trying to raise funds that will allow him to start a war. Lucy is unable to prevent the war, but miracles ensure that after the carnage some hope survives. Clifford's improvisations and *coups de théâtre* sometimes run the risk of trading on a certain naïveté, yet they tend to work in performance by providing unique opportunities to actors and because they pursue the concerns of the play with breathtaking clarity. The wry jokes that pepper the dialogue and the sudden reversals and transformations experienced by the characters suggest a certain casualness in the composition, but this is undercut throughout: the writer pinpoints unsettling truths about economics and spirituality, about consumption and generosity.

Playing with Fire in 1987 was followed in 1989 by *Inés de Castro*. This play is inspired by a medieval story of love thwarted by politics. A Spanish princess is prevented from marrying the Portuguese heir to the throne. When he becomes King, he has her corpse dressed to preside over his court. Once again a dazzling felicity allows modern dilemmas of moral priority to leap forth from the historical source. A new maturity in the writing is signalled by the capacity to sustain a wider range of idiom: the colloquial speech of a tradesman, the wistful lyricism of the lovers, the cat-and-mouse discourse of the corridors of power—these idioms give way finally to an extraordinary speech of brutal objectivity that describes a public torture of agonizing complexity.

Inés de Castro is an original play in its own right, but of all the titles to Clifford's name as playwright, it is the one that is closest to his work as a translator. Since his version of *The House with Two Doors*, Clifford has done much to rehabilitate the Spanish Golden Age in the British theatre, and in particular to advance the reputation of Calderón as one of the great world dramatists. He has also translated Calderón's *The Doctor of Honour* and *Schism in England*, as well as providing the Actor's Touring Company with *Heaven Bent, Hell Bound*, his version of Tirso de Molina's *El condenado por desconfiado*. His translation of *The House of Bernarda Alba* was produced at the Royal Lyceum Theatre in Edinburgh. This body of work is characterized by its vigorous and always highly playable language and also by its refusal to falsify the distinct Hispanic sensibility of the originals.

His most recent Traverse play, *Light in the Village*, sees Clifford taking a brave but quite typical step into the unknown. The play is set in the Third World and confronts us with the plight of a woman seeking justice and equity in a life skewed by poverty. The impulse in the developing world towards the technology of the West is riddled with as many complications as the appeal to traditional dispensations. Indeed, by the time you get down to the local and individual level, the large global perspective has refracted into such a bewildering array of ironies that it is little more than a source of sick jokes. The play, in the end, may have fallen short of full dramatic integration, but the very scope that it aimed to take on board was impressive. It confirmed Clifford's status as one of our most important trailblazing playwrights, whose work may be leavened with humour and playfulness but is also charged with the urgency of addressing large questions. Not all of his gambles come off, but they are all unmistakably inspired by his conviction that the theatre must be a place in which we engage with fundamental issues and are made to invoke the biggest values we can lay our hands on.

—Matthew Lloyd

CLOUD, Darrah. American. Born in Illinois, 11 February 1955. Educated at Goddard College, Plainfield, Vermont, B.A. 1978; University of Iowa, Iowa City, M.F.A. in creative writing 1980, M.F.A. in theater 1981. Married David Emery Owens in 1992. Recipient: University of Iowa fellowship, 1978; National Endowment for the Arts grant, 1984; Drama League award, 1991. Lives in Catskill, New York. Agent:

Peregrine Whittlesey Agency, 345 East 80th Street, New York, New York 10021, U.S.A.

PUBLICATIONS

Plays

The House Across the Street (produced New York, 1982).
The Stick Wife (produced Los Angeles, 1987; New York and London, 1991). New York, Theatre Communications Group, 1987.
O, Pioneers! adaptation of the novel by Willa Cather, music by Kim D. Sherman (produced Seattle and New York, 1989).
Obscene Bird of Night (produced Juneau, Alaska, 1989).
The Mud Angel (produced New York, 1990).
Genesis (produced Juneau, Alaska, 1992).

Screenplay: *The Haunted*, 1991.

*

Manuscript Collection: New Dramatists, New York.

Darrah Cloud comments:

I am haughty enough to think that I might be able to speak for people who can't speak for themselves, so I write plays. Since I began meeting tremendous and brilliant actresses with no good parts to play, I have been obsessed with writing parts for women. And as a woman, I have found a language within my gender that is secret and which I want to reveal, so that it becomes a part of the norm. For in language is perspective, and in perspective is a whole new way of looking at things. I want women's ways of looking at things to be more prevalent in the world.

I think that I always write for my mother. I imagine her in the audience and I know what makes her laugh, what affects her, what she'll believe and what she won't. In that sense, I am always writing my mother as well. I guess I am constantly showing my mother to my mother, in order to let her see herself as not alone, as understood and appreciated, if only by me. My male characters are my mother. And so, obviously, are my female characters. If there is a dog in the play, it's always the dog my mother picked out for us when we were little. I am currently writing a musical about the life of Crazy Horse. Crazy Horse, in his struggle against an encroaching white world, and toward his own fulfillment as a human being, Crazy Horse is my mother.

Sometimes I put my grandmother in because she's short and funny. I have yet to write my sister. This is a goal.

I grew up in the Midwest, and there too, is a unique language based not on what is said, but on what is not said. To be midwestern is to have to intuit the subtext of conversations. If one is talking about the weather, one might actually mean something quite different; something like, "I love you," or "my wife just died and I'm lost." The weather is a very important conversational tool in the Midwest. What is not said, but felt, implied in the moment, is what I love best to write. The congress of emotions that prevent the manifestation of explanations. That creates gestures that say more than words. Open mouths with nothing coming forth from them. This strikes me as always more honest than words. I am always trying to get at the truth of a moment. And so my characters rarely say what they feel, unless they're lying, which is more honest, to me.

I believe in ghosts. I believe that animals are so much more

The Bug, written with R.S. Bailey, a San Quentin colleague, is a work in progress. A woman is harassed by obscene phone calls. Two policemen hide in an adjoining apartment, with electronic equipment that will ostensibly identify the source of the calls. But the play merges invasion of privacy into alleged obscenity.

Circumstances have walled Cluchey's life, but he has exchanged the enclosed space of prison for the enclosed space of theatre—an exchange that has liberated him and deepened public perception of prison-fostered brutalities.

—Ruby Cohn

COLLINS, Barry. British. Born in Halifax, Yorkshire, 21 September 1941. Educated at Heath School, Halifax, 1953–61; Queen's College, Oxford. Married Anne Collins in 1963; two sons and one daughter. Teacher, Halifax Education Committee, 1962–63; journalist, Halifax *Evening Courier*, 1963–71. Recipient: Arts Council bursary, 1974; Edinburgh Festival award, 1980. Agent: Lemon, Unna, and Durbridge, 24 Pottery Lane, Holland Park, London W11 4LZ, England.

PUBLICATIONS

Plays

And Was Jerusalem Builded Here? (produced Leeds, 1972).
Beauty and the Beast (for children; produced Leeds, 1973).
Judgement (produced Bristol, 1974; London, 1975; Chicago
    and New York, 1980).   London, Faber, 1974; revised ver-
    sion, Ambergate, Derbyshire, Amber Lane Press, 1980;
    New York, Urizen, 1981.
The Strongest Man in the World (produced Nottingham, 1978;
    London, 1980).   London, Faber, 1980.
Toads (produced Nottingham, 1979).
The Ice Chimney (produced Edinburgh and London, 1980).
King Canute (broadcast 1985).   Published in *Best Radio
    Plays of 1985*, London, Methuen, 1986.
Atonement (produced London, 1987).

Radio Play: *King Canute*, 1985.

Television Plays: *The Lonely Man's Lover*, 1974; *The Witches
of Pendle*, 1975; *The Hills of Heaven* series, 1978; *Dirty
Washing*, 1985; *Nada*, 1986; *Land*, 1987; *Lovebirds*, 1988.

*   *   *

Any script for solo theatre makes extraordinary demands on the creative resources of the performer, especially when, as is common with the genre, there is a virtual absence of stage directions. So Barry Collins's major work, *Judgement*, is deservedly also associated with the actors who have turned the 150-minute monologue into an engrossing theatrical debate: Peter O'Toole, Colin Blakely, and Richard Monette, to name the most successful of those who have done it in a dozen countries. Collins explains that the genesis of *Judgement* lay in an anecdote in George Steiner's epilogue to *The Death of Tragedy* concerning a war atrocity that suggests that God has grown weary of the savagery of man, and, in with-

drawing His presence, has precluded tragedy. In the anecdote, a group of imprisoned Russian officers during World War II, abandoned by the Germans, resort to cannibalism; two survivors found by the advancing Russian forces are given a good ("decent") meal and then shot, which, with the incineration of their monastery prison, obliterates the evidence of man's potential for bestiality. Collins infers (though Steiner does not say this) that the survivors were insane, and projects his play from the hypothesis that one of them preserved his sanity, to be able, "dressed in white hospital tunic and regulation slippers," to deliver his Socratic apology to his judges (the theatre audience). His implicit crime is not cannibalism (his fellow survivor would be equally culpable), but sanity: he will "defend obscenities that should strike reason dumb." At the end of the argument, the speaker insists on his right to return to active service, and speaks of himself as someone who has suffered greatly for his country.

That the play is polemical few would doubt; in fact, one way of responding to the speaker's sophistry is interpreting it as the manufacture of the warrior-hero. Theatrically, the play is also something of a milestone, in that it may be seen as an extreme form of naturalism, in which the laboratory animal finds a voice and articulates its experiences before its extermination. This reading is supported by the context that Steiner gives the story: before the Germans left, they released some of their starving police dogs on the prisoners, so that the behaviour is seen as conditioned on various animals. Read in this light, the play poses the question which obsessed writers from Cicero to Zola: what is there about man that places him above the brute beasts? That a taboo has been violated is taken for granted by the judges, whose tribal mentality insists that a scapegoat must be found so that the existence of the taboo may be reinforced, and the dignity of man reasserted; thus in the theatre there is the uncanny atmosphere of a voice coming from "the other side," voicing extraterrestrial mysteries, rather as was presented in the medieval Harrowing of Hell or *Danse Macabre* dramas.

Collins's second attempt at a full-length monologue, *The Ice Chimney*, deals with an attempt by Maurice Wilson at a solo assault on Everest in 1936, and is thus another case of human fortitude braced against superhuman afflictions. Wilson's stature as a man of principle allows a sustained expositional analysis of the circumstances that led to his heroics, but the play never generates the urgency of *Judgement*, and its development seems an awkward amalgam of Milton, Auden, and Golding. In this play, Collins's socialism is not organic to the action, and commitment appears to be to the self rather than to the society.

Though best known for monologues, Collins has also written several large-cast works of epic theatre which articulate dilemmas of socialism with a Brechtian flamboyance and a sometimes Hegelian complexity. His loose documentary about the Luddites, *And Was Jerusalem Builded Here?*, required two choruses, actors with circus skills and singing ability, projections, and costumes based on Tarot cards. Nevertheless, the play does focus on one key character, a pamphleteer, on whom is centred a perplexing array of social and domestic responsibilities. Collins's most successful large-cast play has been *The Strongest Man in the World*, a parable for the theatre about Ivan Shukhov, a Russian miner who wins an Olympic weight-lifting title as a consequence of being made to take steroids. The echoes of *Samson Agonistes* in *The Ice Chimney* become rather more explicit here, as the dissident protagonist is initially discovered back in the mines, considering the aetiology of his present condition of muscle-bound impotence, both physical and ideological. The argument of the play does have a close affinity with that of

Judgement, because Shukhov is acutely conscious of his own state as a (former) Soviet hero descended from a line of such heroes; the retribution visited on him is, again, extreme, and critics have been, predictably, divided in interpreting this as either a portrait of normal Soviet practice or a black cartoon inflating a commonplace to an enormity. Collins's stagecraft would support the latter view.

—Howard McNaughton

———————

COLLINSON, Laurence (Henry). British. Born in 1925. See 2nd edition, 1977.

———————

CONGDON, Constance S. American. Born in Rock Rapids, Iowa, 26 November 1944. Educated at Garden City High School, Kansas, 1963; University of Colorado, Colorado Springs, B.A. 1969; University of Massachusetts, Amherst, M.A., M.F.A. 1981. Married Glenn H. Johnson, Jr. in 1971; one son. Car hop, Bob's A & W Root Beer, 1960–63, columnist, Garden City *Telegram*, 1962–3, and grocery checker, Wall's IGA, 1963–65, all in Garden City; library clerk, Pikes Peak Regional District Library, 1965–66; library clerk, University of Colorado, 1966–69, and leather worker, What Rough Beast, 1969–70, all Colorado Springs; instructor in remedial writing, St. Mary's College of Maryland, St. Mary's City, 1974–76; instructor in rhetorical writing, University of Massachusetts, Amherst, 1977–81; instructor in English composition and theatre, Western New England College, Springfield, Massachusetts, 1981–83; literary manager, 1981–88, and playwright-in-residence, 1984–88, Hartford Stage Company, Connecticut, 1984–88. Recipient: American College Theatre Festival National Playwriting award, 1981; Great American Play Contest prize, 1985; National Endowment for the Arts fellowship, 1986–87; Rockefeller award, 1988; Arnold Weissberger award, 1988; Dramalogue award, 1990; Oppenheimer award, 1990; Guggenheim fellowship, 1991. Agent: Peter Franklin, William Morris Agency, 1350 Avenue of the Americas, New York, New York 10019, U.S.A.

PUBLICATIONS

Plays

Gilgamesh (produced St. Mary's City, Maryland, 1977).
Fourteen Brilliant Colors (produced Amherst, Massachusetts, 1977).
The Bride (produced Amherst, Massachusetts, 1980).
Native American (produced Portland, Maine, 1984; London, 1988).
No Mercy (produced Louisville, Kentucky, 1986). New York, Theatre Communications Group, 1985; published in *Seven Different Plays*; edited by Mac Wellman, New York, Broadway Play Publishing, 1988.

The Gilded Age, adaptation of the novel by Mark Twain (produced Hartford, Connecticut, 1986).
Raggedy Ann and Andy (for children), adaptation of the books by Johnny Gruelle, music by Hiram Titus (produced Minneapolis, 1987).
A Conversation with Georgia O'Keeffe (produced Hartford, Connecticut, 1987).
Tales of the Lost Formicans (produced Woodstock, New York, 1988; New York City, 1990). New York, Broadway Play Publishing, 1990.
Rembrandt Takes a Walk (for children), adaptation of the book by Mark Strand and Red Grooms (produced Minneapolis, 1989). Published in *Plays in Process 4: Plays for Young Audiences* (New York), vol.10 no.12, 1989.
Casanova (produced New York, 1989).
Time Out of Time (produced New York, 1990).
Mother Goose (for children), music by Hiram Titus (produced Minneapolis, 1990).
The Miser, adaptation of the play by Molière (produced Hartford, Connecticut, 1990).
Madeline's Rescue (for children), adaptation of the book by Ludwig Bemelmans, music by Mel Marvin (produced Minneapolis, 1990).
Beauty and the Beast (for children; produced Minneapolis, 1992).

*

Critical Studies: "An Interview with Constance Congdon" by Nancy Klementowski and Sonja Kuftinec, in *Studies in American Drama* (Columbus, Ohio), vol.4, 1989; "Constance Congdon: A Playwright Whose Time Has Come" by Susan Hussey, in *Organica* (Tampa, Florida), Winter 1990; "Trying to Find a Culture: An Interview with Connie Congdon" by Lisa Wilde, in *Yale/Theatre* (New Haven, Connecticut), vol.22 no.1, Winter 1990; article by Craig Gholson, in *Bomb* (New York), Fall 1991; "Connie's *Casanova*" by M. Elizabeth Osborn, in *Theatre Week* (New York), June 3–9, 1991.

Constance Congdon comments:
I have an eclectic taste in theatre, although I usually hate everything I see on Broadway. My main influences are Thornton Wilder, The Wooster Group, Caryl Churchill, also rhythm and blues and country western music, Richard Wilbur, Joni Mitchell. The American critical scene is still culturally embarrassed and defensive and trying to be something it's not—cold, cynical, politically strident, trying to out-European the changing Europeans. The American art scene is still dominated by too many people from "good" schools who have intellectual agendas that have nothing to do with what I go to theatre for. I go to have an experience that taps the mystery of living, one that comes from great passion on the part of the artist, one that has something to do with awakening or calling up the spirit that is in every theatre.
I come from about as far away from the Ivy League as is possible and am proud of it. I see myself more as an "outside artist"—one of those people who makes sculpture out of car parts in their backyard. I don't live in New York although I enjoy going in to see the work of my friends which is very good and usually found in small theatres painted flat black with bad seats and great risk or big fun (or both) going on onstage.
When I start to write a play, I imagine an empty theatre space and see who or what turns up—this is my opening image and, if I mess with it, I always pay for it and lose my

way in the play. I feel that the first things I create in a new play are like coded messages for the rest of the play, and I just return to them for clues about the rest of the play. The code is in metaphor, image, and given circumstances and I just need to see it. In *Native American*—the only naturalistic play I ever wrote—I saw, very clearly, the image of a cowboy lying face down on a couch with a sheet covering him. I also saw that the couch was outside on a porch. Then I saw an old Hudson automobile up on blocks. Some of these images were memories, I realize now, but at the time, they seemed all new and rich. Why the cowboy was on the couch, face down, gave me, bit by bit, the story and then the theme. I also knew that the play had to take place in consecutive real time. I trust these early strong impulses.

I need to entertain myself and surprise myself, so my plays are usually different from each other in style—I don't like to repeat myself. I make my living doing adaptations, and I don't recommend it to young playwrights, but it's better, for me, than teaching or trying to get media work.

*   *   *

Constance Congdon was a published poet before she was a playwright. Her plays come to her as a series of images; they are made up of many small scenes, sometimes comic, often emotionally direct, with dialogue that goes straight to the heart of the matter. When these scenes are linked together, the result reflects the world's true complexity.

Though the lives of ordinary decent people, the pleasure and pain of sexuality, the damaging effects of gender stereotypes are primary Congdon concerns, her central subject is loss. Her very first play was a dramatization of *The Epic of Gilgamesh*, at its heart the inconsolable grief of the hero at the death of his beloved friend Enkidu. The award-winning drama *No Mercy* deals with the testing of the first atomic bomb and its after-effects, but it is fundamentally about faith, and the loss of faith—in science, in religion, in life itself. Watching the scientist J. Robert Oppenheimer cross and recross the stage—the play takes place in 1945 and 1985 simultaneously, and he is lost in time—we wonder if he is dreaming this world, whose other inhabitants are the kind of undistinguished Americans this writer lovingly brings to life. Our uncertainty about who rules the play's universe is part of the point: we are watching characters lose *their* certainty, then pick themselves up and go on.

By far the most successful of Congdon's plays to date is *Tales of the Lost Formicans*, which looks at the life of contemporary suburbia through the eyes of aliens, a perspective which shows this taken-for-granted world to be complicated, mysterious, and absurd. Behind this tragicomedy lies the death of Congdon's father, many years ago, from what we now call Alzheimer's disease, but the play is really about *America's* Alzheimer's. The father in *Formicans* is far from the only character who's confused. His recently divorced daughter has moved back home with her teenaged son, who expresses in pure form the anger and distress everyone in the play feels. By donning sunglasses the play's actors become the aliens who are trying to make sense of this disoriented civilization; *Formicans* suggests that we ourselves are the aliens, attempting to distance ourselves from our own feeling. Finally we're not sure whether "real" aliens are "really" telling the story; as in *No Mercy*, this not knowing reflects our actual position in the actual world.

The opening words of Congdon's *Casanova* are the scream of a young woman in labor: "What—is—LOVE!" The playwright's answer to this most fundamental of questions is characteristically complex. An epic play not quite under control at its first showing, *Casanova* is Congdon's richest text, and may one day be seen as a revelation of the way of our own world.

Casanova's focus on sexuality and gender was presaged by an early play, *The Bride*, which brings to mind both *Our Town* and *Spring Awakening* in its depiction of the sexual awakening of four teenagers during the 1950's. In *Casanova* Congdon uses more than 60 years of her central character's life to present the full range of sexuality in men, women, and children. The famous lover is played by two actors: during the first act the old man who is writing his memoirs watches the irresistible boy he once was; after intermission Young Casanova is horrified to witness what he has become.

Congdon's *Casanova* is a feminist corrective to those one-sided memoirs; the author's deepest sympathy goes to the very young girls this man loves and leaves. Yet Young Casanova is almost wholly appealing; Congdon sees that his society gives him permission to behave as he does, that he is not so different from other men. She shows us the complicity of women: having no other power, mothers pimp their daughters, using their beauty and virginity for their own ends. The older Casanova commits monstrous acts, including rape and child seduction, but at the same time we see that he is aging, frightened, as trapped in his sexual role as any female.

In *Casanova* bedrock biological difference makes women inevitably vulnerable. Yet there is hope in the play, and it lies in those characters who transcend the usual limits of gender. The two women who come through their encounters with Casanova unscathed are bisexual, and the play's exemplar of lasting devotion is Bobo, an aging transvestite. Once tutor to Casanova's daughter, Bobo is still taking care of her 30 years later. He is Casanova's equal and opposite force, and the most memorable incarnation yet of Congdon's special feeling for gay men.

Congdon's talent flows in many directions. Her poetic gift lends itself to opera librettos; her comic sense has enlivened a series of delightful plays for the Children's Theatre of Minneapolis. Her one-woman piece about painter Georgia O'Keeffe lets her speak of her own love of the West and her complicated feeling about the position of women artists. What knowledgeable theatre people across the country have said for years is becoming more widely known: Constance Congdon is one of the most original and revelatory writers in the American theatre today.

—M. Elizabeth Osborn

CONN, Stewart. British. Born in Glasgow, Scotland, 5 November 1936. Educated at Kilmarnock Academy and Glasgow University. National Service: Royal Air Force. Married Judith Clarke in 1963; two sons. Since 1962 radio drama producer, currently Head of Drama (Radio), BBC, Edinburgh. Literary adviser, Edinburgh Royal Lyceum Theatre, 1973–75. Recipient: Eric Gregory award, 1963; Scottish Arts Council poetry prize and publication award, 1968, award, 1978; Edinburgh Festival Fringe award, for drama, 1981, 1988; New York International Radio Festival drama award, 1991. Lives in Edinburgh. Agent: Lemon,

Unna, and Durbridge, 24 Pottery Lane, Holland Park, London W11 4LZ, England.

PUBLICATIONS

Plays

Break-Down (produced Glasgow, 1961).
Birds in a Wilderness (produced Edinburgh, 1964).
I Didn't Always Live Here (produced Glasgow, 1967). Included in *The Aquarium, The Man in the Green Muffler, I Didn't Always Live Here*, 1976.
The King (produced Edinburgh, 1967; London, 1972). Published in *New English Dramatists 14*, London, Penguin, 1970.
Broche (produced Exeter, 1968).
Fancy Seeing You, Then (produced London, 1974). Published in *Playbill Two*, edited by Alan Durband, London, Hutchinson, 1969.
Victims (includes *The Sword, In Transit*, and *The Man in the Green Muffler*) (produced Edinburgh, 1970). *In Transit*, published New York, Breakthrough Press, 1972; *The Man in the Green Muffler*, included in *The Aquarium, The Man in the Green Muffler, I Didn't Always Live Here*, 1976.
The Burning (produced Edinburgh, 1971). London, Calder and Boyars, 1973.
A Slight Touch of the Sun (produced Edinburgh, 1972).
The Aquarium (produced Edinburgh, 1973). Included in *The Aquarium, The Man in the Green Muffler, I Didn't Always Live Here*, 1976.
Thistlewood (produced Edinburgh, 1975). Todmorden, Lancashire, Woodhouse, 1979.
Count Your Blessings (produced Pitlochry, Perthshire, 1975).
The Aquarium, The Man in the Green Muffler, I Didn't Always Live Here. London, Calder, 1976.
Play Donkey (produced Edinburgh, 1977). Todmorden, Lancashire, Woodhouse, 1980.
Billy Budd, with Stephen Macdonald, adaptation of the novel by Melville (produced Edinburgh, 1978).
Hecuba (produced Edinburgh, 1979; revised version produced Glasgow, 1989).
Herman (produced Edinburgh, 1981; London, 1986).
Hugh Miller (produced Edinburgh, 1988).
By the Pool (produced Edinburgh, 1988; London 1989; Cleveland, Ohio, 1991).
The Dominion of Fancy (produced Pitlochry, Tayside, 1992).

Radio Plays: *Any Following Spring*, 1962; *Cadenza for Real*, 1963; *Song of the Clyde*, 1964; *The Canary Cage*, 1967; *Too Late the Phalarope*, from the novel by Alan Paton, 1984.

Television Plays: *Wally Dugs Go in Pairs*, 1973; *The Kite*, 1979; *Blood Hunt*, 1986.

Verse

Thunder in the Air. Preston, Lancashire, Akros, 1967.
The Chinese Tower. Edinburgh, M. Macdonald, 1967.
Stoats in the Sunlight. London, Hutchinson, 1968; as *Ambush and Other Poems*, New York, Macmillan, 1970.
Corgi Modern Poets in Focus 3, with others, edited by Dannie Abse. London, Corgi, 1971.
An Ear to the Ground. London, Hutchinson, 1972.
Under the Ice. London, Hutchinson, 1978.
In the Kibble Palace: New and Selected Poems. Newcastle upon Tyne, Bloodaxe, 1987.

The Luncheon of the Boating Party. Newcastle upon Tyne, Bloodaxe, 1992.

Other

The Living Poet (radio broadcast). 1989.

Editor, *New Poems 1973–74*. London, Hutchinson, 1974.

*

Manuscript Collection: Scottish National Library, Edinburgh.

Critical Studies: interviews with James Aitchison in *Scottish Theatre* (Edinburgh), March 1969, Allen Wright in *The Scotsman* (Edinburgh), 30 October 1971, and Joyce McMillan in *Scottish Theatre News* (Glasgow), August 1981; *Towards the Human* by Iain Crichton Smith, Edinburgh, M. Macdonald, 1987.

Theatrical Activities:
Director: **Radio**—many plays, including *Armstrong's Last Goodnight* by John Arden, 1964; *The Anatomist* by James Bridie, 1965; *My Friend Mr. Leakey* by J.B.S. Haldane, 1967; *Mr. Gillie* by James Bridie, 1967; *Happy Days Are Here Again*, 1967, and *Good*, 1989, both by Cecil P. Taylor; *Wedderburn's Slave*, 1980, *The Telescope Garden*, 1986, and *Andromache*, 1989, all by Douglas Dunn; *Losing Venice* by John Clifford, 1987; *Dirt under the Carpet* by Rona Munro, 1987; *Not About Heroes*, and *In the Summer of 1918*, both by Stephen MacDonald; *Potestad* by Eduardo Pavlovsky; *Carver* by John Purser, 1991.

Stewart Conn comments:
   (1973) My plays are about human beings, and about the dilemma of human choice. I interpret this dilemma in moral terms, and visualize the characters in the plays, and their relationships, as revolving around it. As Camus wrote (in *The Plague*), "On this earth there are pestilences and there are victims, and it's up to us, so far as possible, not to join forces with the pestilences." If there is a through line in what I have written so far, it might be a reminder that we do not live our lives in isolation—but that how we behave involves, and may cause hurt to, other people. At the same time the plays are explorations: they pose questions, rather than pretending to provide any easy answers. I do not wish to impose a set of values on an audience; but like to think what I write might induce them to reassess their own. At the same time I am concerned with theatricality and with the use of words in the theatre, as also with the attempt to provide an instructive metaphor for the violence and betrayal, large and small, with which we must come to terms, within ourselves and in our society.
   (1982) I find the above all rather pretentious—and rather than "comment" again I would prefer simply to get on with the plays: that is hard enough. "We must remember who we are . . ." (Lopakhin in *The Cherry Orchard*). Perhaps my main aim now is to send the audience out into the night, ideally both transformed and entertained, in time for the last bus!

*   *   *

Stewart Conn is a poet as well as a dramatist, and his best plays, like *The King, The Sword* and *The Burning*, reveal this lyrical side. Of his full-length plays, *Broche* and *I Didn't Always Live Here* are little more than solid, competent pieces of dramatic craftsmanship; but *The Aquarium* and *The Burning* are both of considerable merit.

The Aquarium is set in a lower-middle-class Scottish home and depicts a classical father-son confrontation. The father is imbued with the puritanical work ethic and has clearly defined attitudes and beliefs, based on an old-fashioned morality, that he attempts to impose on his teenage son. The son is restless, unsure of himself and tentative in his approach to life, an attitude which is reflected in his flitting from job to job. Not unnaturally, he resists his father's attempts to make him conform, and they needle and taunt each other, with the mother ineffectually intervening, until matters come to a head when the father attempts to give his son a beating. This action triggers the son into a final break-away from his family environment. The oppressive family atmosphere is particularly well and truthfully observed in this play, and the characters have a depth and power to them that belie their slightly clichéd conception. More than any other play of his, *The Aquarium* reveals the influence of Arthur Miller, a playwright he greatly admires.

The Burning is perhaps his most impressive work to date. It deals with the 16th-century power struggle between James VI of Scotland and his cousin, the Earl of Bothwell, and its theme can be deduced from Bothwell's line to James near the end of the play: "We are the upper and nether millstones, you and I. One way or another, it is those trappt in the middle must pay the price." The play is essentially about the brutality exercised toward those caught in the middle of any struggle for religious or political power, James standing for the divine right of kings, Bothwell for self-expression and individual freedom. But both treat the people under them as expendable and use them as pawns to advance their own positions. A subsidiary theme is that of witchcraft and superstition, but it is firmly placed within the context of the battle between authority and anarchy. The characters are vibrant with life, and reflect the underlying moral and ethical problems posed by a commitment to one side or the other, in a powerful and an exact way. Another remarkable feature of the play is the hard, sinewy Scottish language, which cleverly contrives to give an impression of late 16th-century speech.

Count Your Blessings revolves around Stanley, a man on the brink of death looking back over his past life and regretting the lost opportunities for fulfilling his potentialities. A particularly powerful scene shows him as a boy berating his schoolmaster father for caving in to pressure from his headmaster employer and reneging on his commitment to address a Communist Party rally in the 1930's on the effect of government cuts in education. *Thistlewood* is an impressionistic study of the 1820 Cato Street conspiracy of a group of radicals to assassinate the British Cabinet. The play draws modern parallels in the continuing struggle between conservatism and radicalism in our society.

Of Conn's short plays *The King* is a beautifully observed picture of two men fighting each other for the same girl, with a seduction scene between Attie and Lena that is replete with an unsentimental lyricism in the language. His trio of short plays, *Victims* (*The Man in the Green Muffler*, *In Transit*, and *The Sword*), are sharply and concisely drawn pictures of situations whose implications reverberate in the mind. The first play deals with an encounter between two pavement artists, one of whom has replaced someone who has died; the second is a macabre, Pinteresque exercise in violence, between two men and an intruder whom they slowly dominate; and *The Sword*, the best of the three, is a spooky psychological study of a man and a boy, both obsessed, for different reasons, with the idea of military glory. The characterisation in all of the plays is minutely and precisely accurate, qualities reflected in the taut dialogue, with strong lyrical undertones (particularly in *The Sword*), and the craftsmanlike attention to form.

The metaphorical connotations of Conn's best plays are strengthened by his feeling for dramatic construction, his understanding of individual psychology, and his basic interest in violence and its causes, both individual and in society at large. Allied with his quality of lyricism, these give his plays a peculiar power and depth.

—Jonathan Hammond

CONNELLY, Marc(us Cook). American. 1890–1980. See 2nd edition, 1977.

COOK, Michael. Canadian. Born in London, England, 14 February 1933; emigrated to Canada, 1966; became citizen, 1971. Educated at boarding schools near London to age 15; Nottingham University College of Education, 1962–66, T.T.C. (honours) in English 1966. Served in the Royal Electrical and Mechanical Engineers, and later in the Intelligence Corps, 1949–61: staff sergeant. Married 1) Muriel Horner in 1951 (marriage dissolved 1966), eight children; 2) Janis Jones in 1967 (divorced 1973), two children; 3) Madonna Decker in 1973, four children. Farm worker and waiter, 1948–49; steel-worker and farm worker, 1961–62; schoolteacher, 1966. Specialist in drama, 1967–70, lecturer, 1970–74, assistant professor, 1974–79, and since 1979 associate professor of English, Memorial University, St. John's, Newfoundland. Drama critic, St. John's *Evening Telegram*, 1967–77; artistic director, St. John's Summer Festival, 1969–76; host of the weekly television review *Our Man Friday*, St. John's, 1973; playwright-in-residence, Banff Festival, Alberta, 1978, and Stratford Festival, 1987. Member of the Editorial Board, *Canadian Theatre Review*, Downsview, Ontario, from 1973; governor, Canadian Conference of the Arts, Ottawa, 1975–79; vice-president, Guild of Canadian Playwrights, 1978–80; member of the Newfoundland and Labrador Arts Council, 1979–82. Also actor on stage, radio, and television, mainly in character roles. Recipient: Canada Council Senior Arts grant, 1973, 1979; Labatt award, 1974, 1975, 1978, 1979; Queen's Silver Jubilee Medal, 1979; Newfoundland and Labrador Government award, 1985. Agent: Playwrights Union of Canada, 8 York Street, 6th Floor, Toronto, Ontario M5J 1R2. Address: Department of English, Memorial University, P.O. Box 4200, St. John's, Newfoundland A1C 5S7, Canada.

PUBLICATIONS

Plays

The J. Arthur Prufrock Hour (revue; also director: produced St. John's, Newfoundland, 1968).

Tiln (broadcast 1971; produced Toronto, 1972). With *Quiller*, Toronto, Playwrights, 1975.

Colour the Flesh the Colour of Dust (also director: produced St. John's, Newfoundland, 1971). Toronto, Simon and Pierre, 1972.

The Head, Guts, and Soundbone Dance (produced St. John's, Newfoundland, 1973). St. John's, Breakwater, 1974.

Jacob's Wake (produced St. John's, Newfoundland, 1974; Fox Island, Washington, 1980). Vancouver, Talonbooks, 1975.

Quiller (produced St. John's, Newfoundland, 1975). With *Tiln*, Toronto, Playwrights, 1975.

Therese's Creed (produced Montreal, 1977; London, 1982). Toronto, Playwrights, 1976.

The Fisherman's Revenge (for children; produced Trinity Bay, Newfoundland, 1976). Toronto, Playwrights, 1985.

Not as a Dream (produced Halifax, Nova Scotia, 1976). Toronto, Playwrights, 1976; New York, Doubleday, 1979.

Tiln and Other Plays (includes *Quiller* and *Therese's Creed*). Vancouver, Talonbooks, 1976.

On the Rim of the Curve (produced Gander, Newfoundland, 1977). Included in *Three Plays*, 1977.

Three Plays (includes *On the Rim of the Curve*; *The Head, Guts, and Soundbone Dance*; *Therese's Creed*). Portugal Cove, Newfoundland, Breakwater, 1977.

The Gayden Chronicles (produced Lennoxville, Quebec, 1977; Waterford, Connecticut, 1978). Toronto, Playwrights, 1979.

The Apocalypse Sonata (produced Regina, Saskatchewan, 1980).

The Deserts of Bohemia (produced San Francisco, 1980).

The Terrible Journey of Frederick Douglas (broadcast 1982). Published in *Canadian Theatre Review* (Downsview, Ontario), Fall 1986.

The Great Harvest Festival (produced Stratford, Ontario, 1986).

Radio Plays: *How to Catch a Pirate*, 1966; *A Walk in the Rain*, 1967; *No Man Can Serve Two Masters*, 1967; *The Concubine*, 1968; *Or the Wheel Broken*, 1968; *The Truck*, 1969; *A Time for Doors*, 1969; *The Iliad* (for children), from the poem by Homer, 1969; *A Midsummer Night's Dream*, from the play by Shakespeare, 1970; *To Inhabit the Earth Is Not Enough*, 1970; *Journey into the Unknown*, 1970; *Ballad of Patrick Docker*, 1971; *Tiln*, 1971; *Apostles for the Burning*, 1972; *There's a Seal at the Bottom of the Garden*, 1973; *An Enemy of the People*, from a play by Ibsen, 1974; *Love Is a Walnut*, 1975; *Travels with Aunt Jane* series (1 episode), 1975; *The Producer, The Director*, 1976; *Knight of Shadow, Lady of Silence*, 1976; *Ireland's Eye* (*The Best Seat in the House* series), 1977; *The Gentleman Amateur*, 1978; *All a Pack o' Lies*, 1979; *The Hunter*, 1980; *The Preacher*, 1981; *The Terrible Journey of Frederick Douglas*, 1982; *The Sweet Second Summer of Kitty Malone*, from the novel by Matt Cohen, 1983; *This Damned Inheritance*, 1984; *The Bailiff and the Women*, 1984; *The Ocean Ranger*, 1985; *The Saddest Barn Dance Ever Held*, 1985; *The Hanging Judge*, 1985; *The Moribundian Memorandum*, 1986:

Television Plays: *In Search of Confederation*, 1971; *Daniel My Brother*, *The C.F.A.*, and *The Course of True Love* (all in *Up at Ours* series), 1979–80.

Novel

The Island of Fire. Toronto, Doubleday, 1980.

*

Bibliography: by Don Rubin, in *Canadian Theatre Review* (Downsview, Ontario), Fall 1977.

Manuscript Collection: University of Calgary Library, Alberta.

Critical Studies: "On the Edge: Michael Cook's Newfoundland Trilogy" by Brian Parker, in *Canadian Literature* (Vancouver), Summer 1980; *The Work: Conversations with English-Canadian Playwrights* by Robert Wallace and Cynthia Zimmerman, Toronto, Coach House Press, 1982; *Major Plays of the Canadian Theatre 1934–1984* edited by Richard Perkyns, Toronto, Irwin, 1984 (includes bibliography).

Theatrical Activities:
Director: **Plays**—in St. John's, Newfoundland: *Antigone* by Jean Anouih, 1967; *The Queen and the Rebels* by Ugo Betti, 1967; *Mother Courage* by Brecht, 1968; *The J. Arthur Prufrock Hour*, 1968; *Bousille et les justes* by Gratien Gélinas, 1968; *Play* by Samuel Beckett, Labrador City, 1969; *Our Town* by Thornton Wilder, Labrador City, 1969; *Endgame* by Samuel Beckett, 1970; *The Geisha*, 1970; *Colour the Flesh the Colour of Dust*, 1971; *Hamlet*, 1972; *1 Henry IV*, 1973; *Macbeth*, 1974; *The Merchant of Venice*, 1975; *The Head, Guts, and Soundbone Dance*, Regina, Saskatchewan, 1977; *A Funny Thing Happened on the Way to the Forum* by Burt Shevelove, Larry Gelbart, and Stephen Sondheim, 1978; *Juno and the Paycock* by Sean O'Casey, 1980 and 1982; *Therese's Creed*, 1980.

Michael Cook comments:
(1977) The basic source of inspiration for my stage plays has been, and I suspect will continue to be, the people and the environment of Newfoundland. The environment is startingly dramatic; the people the inheritors of moral, social, and economic conflicts that have existed (in many instances, destructively) for three centuries. Specifically, the head-on conflict with technology has, in years of Confederation with Canada, lifted the material prosperity and hopes of the nation but has undermined the fabric of community and social life which made survival possible and gave the island its unique identity. The people, mainly of Irish and West of England origins, maintained for centuries the rich dialects, the fatalistic humour, the careless command of a savage environment that historians might associate with their forebears, the sailors of Nelson's navy, the fodder of Wellington's army. Escaping the brutal caste system of Europe they developed, despite crippling economic circumstances, a heroic individualism. Add to this a language colourful, rich, musical, scatological, varying in accent from Bay to Bay, full of the power of ancient metaphors, and I think it becomes obvious why, at times, I feel like a celebrant at a peculiarly rich, but obviously threatened, ceremony of a way of life in which individuals struggle with the timeless questions of worth and identity against an environment which would kill them if it could.

As in all such environments—the wild Coast of Clare, the weeping Hebrides, the granite coast of Cornwall—there is much in man that responds to the land in all its moods. There are, balancing energy and joy and spoken communion, madness and superstition and violence and repression and anger. There is an overwhelming sense of frustration as bureaucrats and technocrats condone the rape of the oceans.

It seems that what has occurred in Newfoundland has, or will, occur everywhere in North America. Newfoundland is the continent in microcosm. And yet, because of this vastly reduced scale, it is still possible to conceive and portray men and women in the grip of great forces, changes, emotions that are in direct conflict with everything they know and understand. There is no diffusion here through the silt of great cities. No. The changes occur where the sea still runs, where the land provides evidence of ancient struggles, and the aged provide eloquent testimony of traditional patterns of survival. I pay attention, therefore, to the realistic, the specific, the concern with the known identity and the agonised recognition of a different kind of survival. I like to think that my work speaks to the condition of all men who have only recently come to realise that somewhere in the transition between rural and industrial man they left behind a portion of their souls.

(1988) My rather gloomy forecast (above) has come true. The ocean is dying, overfishing and greed have seen to that; the quest and lust for oil have turned the traditional lifestyle about-face; and the media revolution has delivered the *coup de grâce*: metaphor and richness of dialect are all but extinct, and parking lots and four-lane highways are all the rage. Without realising it I was called upon to chronicle the death throes of a dying culture. Of all my plays, *Jacob's Wake* chronicles that most explicitly.

* * *

Although Michael Cook continues to be best known for the so-called Newfoundland Trilogy (*Colour the Flesh the Colour of Dust*, *The Head, Guts, and Soundbone Dance*, and *Jacob's Wake*), he has written some fifty radio plays of which *Tiln* (originally written for the stage), and *The Terrible Journey of Frederick Douglas* are published. He wrote for radio before the stage and continues to write for both media. It is not incidental that radio suits Cook: he is, in his own words, a "literary playwright" interested in language, and particularly in the rich, local dialect of Newfoundland. He is fascinated with sound patterns, "unable," he says, "to disassociate the sounds of words from the action that goes with them." He is also concerned with large concepts elaborately described in stage directions which can emerge imaginatively within the dialogue, but are hard to replicate on stage. Cook's protagonists are often trapped in an existential dilemma, caught between a desire for order and the apparent chaos of the external world. Three of the seven major stage plays are quasi-historical and in these Cook explores the plight of the rebel and the outsider.

In *The Gayden Chronicles*, he presents William Gayden (executed for mutiny, murder, and desertion in 1812, and upon whose diary the action is based) as such a figure. Gayden's ideas of rebellion and his own psychological make-up allow Cook to introduce the ideology of the French Revolution, Tom Paine, and William Blake as well as a critical assessment of the 19th century British Navy. In his struggle to comprehend meaning within his society and to come to terms with authority, Gayden is a hero typical of Cook.

Similar questions are raised in *Colour the Flesh the Colour of Dust* where the brief rule of a captured St. John's by the French in 1762 prompts Cook to contrast corrupt and cynical officials with the common people who survive the occupation largely unchanged though they continue to endure a cheerless society in a barren environment. Central images of birth and death frame the play but in reverse order, suggesting hope as the images move from a corpse to a baby. It is, however, hope of a universal, mythical kind; there is no individual salvation for the citizens of this time and place. Such a classical vision is typical of Cook, especially in the plays of contemporary Newfoundland where characters struggle and fail in personal

tragedies while the great forces of the sea and the land persist. In this regard, Cook shares as much with Synge as with Beckett whom he claims as a major influence on his writing.

Often Cook narrows this view of the human predicament to explore family relationships and family politics within the larger landscape of Newfoundland. In *The Head, Guts, and Soundbone Dance*, he introduces the figure of the tyrannical skipper, an Old Testament allusion who appropriately inhabits "the rock" of Newfoundland's hard, shaping terrain and who, here and in *Jacob's Wake* rails against modern society, the decline of traditional industry and values, and the loss of a patriarchal society while he symbolizes a stoic human fight against the power of Nature and mutability. In the contest between a young man and his powerful father-in-law, Skipper Pete, Cook presents the loss of an old way of life. Like the detritus of the fish they clean (the head, backbone, and guts of the title) three drunken old men dance to a folk song that sums up their decline. A version of the figure appears even in Cook's children's play, *The Fisherman's Revenge*, though the skipper has been replaced by a town merchant against whom the fisherfolk fight for economic survival.

In *Jacob's Wake*, the figure is most completely drawn and yet at its most abstract. The play was developed through a number of preliminary versions by Newfoundland's Open Group with Cook's collaboration; the published script arises from these early productions and from the first professional performance at the 1975 Festival Lennoxville. In his stage directions Cook admits to the practical difficulties of portraying a convincing apotheosis of Newfoundland culture on a naturalistic set; as the National Arts Centre production in 1986 attempted to convey, the play is essentially expressionistic. The old master lies dying upstairs in the two-level set while his presence dominates the household: his failed son (the existential victim locked between his sense of failure and his rebellion against his father's values), his repressed daughter and exploited daughter-in-law, and his three amoral grandsons. As the Biblical allusion to Jacob, the favoured son, proceeds, the story of a modern Newfoundland of unemployment, alcoholism, welfare, empty religious values, and destructive gender roles unfolds. Over a symbolic Easter weekend, the family fights out its rivalries as the wind mounts over an archetypal sea. Skipper mourns the loss of his first-born and, with him, any hope for a continuation of the sealing industry, of his old way of life. As stress within the family reaches crisis point, the storm bursts onto the stage, the soul (or force) of the Skipper appears at the door blown open by a "cosmic disaster," and the outport house transforms itself into a ship at sea. As the women are sent below, the ruined son attempts too late to steer a new course for his generation while "a ripping and rending and smashing" destroys the human world. An excellently crafted literary piece with interrelated images and allusions, significant naming, some well drawn characterizations (especially of the protagonist son), and a compelling vision of catastrophe, the play brings together themes and characters common in Cook's work and illustrates the rich sonorities of his language. The vision it presents, like that in all Cook's plays, is fundamentally tragic: Newfoundland is seen as a classic testing ground for the struggle of a trapped humankind against its own authoritarian traditions and the awesome power of a dispassionate Nature.

Since 1986, a number of new radio plays have been presented in Canada and internationally; as *End of the Road* testifies, Cook also continues to write for the stage. This as yet unproduced play examines two couples, one aged, one younger, whose antagonisms express themselves in a set of theatrical games. In the end, like the Skippers of his earlier work, the elderly couple recognize the new world will no longer admit them and commit suicide. *The Painful Education of Patrick Brown* (as yet unproduced) presents a character not unlike Cook himself, who comes as outsider to Newfoundland's unique culture and, through a "painful" process, finds a place within it. Michael Cook has had an important influence on the Newfoundland dramatic scene as newspaper reviewer, playwright and director; he now teaches at Memorial University.

—Reid Gilbert

———

COONEY, Ray(mond George Alfred). British. Born in London, 30 May 1932. Educated at Alleyn's School, Dulwich, London. Served in the Royal Army Service Corps, 1950–52. Married Linda Ann Dixon in 1962; two sons. Actor from 1946; theatrical director and producer from 1965; since 1966, director, Ray Cooney Presentations Ltd., London; director and artistic director, Theatre of Comedy Company, London, 1983–91; since 1991 owner, with George Borwick, The Playhouse Theatre, London. Address: 1/3 Spring Gardens, London SW1A 2BD, England.

PUBLICATIONS

Plays

Dickory Dock, with Tony Hilton (produced Richmond, Surrey, 1959).
One for the Pot, with Tony Hilton (produced Wolverhampton, 1960; London, 1961). London, English Theatre Guild, 1963.
Who Were You with Last Night?, with Tony Hilton (produced Windsor, 1962).
How's Your Father? (produced Richmond, Surrey, 1963).
Chase Me, Comrade! (produced London, 1964). London, English Theatre Guild, and New York, Dramatists Play Service, 1966.
Charlie Girl, with Hugh and Margaret Williams, music and lyrics by David Heneker and John Taylor (produced London, 1965). London, Chappell, 1972.
Bang Bang Beirut; or, Stand by Your Bedouin, with Tony Hilton (produced Guildford, Surrey, 1966; as *Stand by Your Bedouin*, produced London, 1967). London, English Theatre Guild, 1971.
Not Now, Darling, with John Chapman (produced Richmond, Surrey, 1967; London, 1968; also director: produced New York, 1970). London, English Theatre Guild, 1970; New York, Dramatists Play Service, 1971.
My Giddy Aunt, with John Chapman (produced Wolverhampton, 1967; London, 1968). London, English Theatre Guild, 1970; revised edition, London, Chappell, 1987.
Move Over, Mrs. Markham, with John Chapman (produced Richmond, Surrey, 1969; also director: produced London, 1971). London, English Theatre Guild, and New York, French, 1972.
Why Not Stay for Breakfast?, with Gene Stone (produced Westcliff-on-Sea, Essex, 1970; also director: produced London, 1973). London, French, 1974.

Come Back to My Place, with John Chapman (produced Westcliff-on-Sea, Essex, 1973).
There Goes the Bride, with John Chapman (produced Birmingham and London, 1974). London, English Theatre Guild, 1975.
Her Royal Highness . . .?, with Royce Ryton (also director: produced London, 1981).
Two into One (produced Leicester, 1981; also director: produced London, 1984). London, French, 1985.
Run for Your Wife (also director: produced London, 1983; New York, 1989). London, French, 1984.
Wife Begins at Forty, with Arne Sultan and Earl Barret (also director: produced Guildford, Surrey, and London, 1985). London, French, 1986.
An Italian Straw Hat, adaptation of a play by Eugène Labiche (also director: produced London, 1986).
It Runs in the Family (also director: produced Guildford, Surrey, 1987; London, 1992). London, French, 1990.
Out of Order (also director: produced Leatherhead, Surrey, and London, 1990).

Screenplays: *Not Now Comrade*, 1977; *There Goes the Bride*, with Terence Marcel, 1980; *Why Not Stay for Breakfast?*, with Terence Marcel, 1985.

Radio Plays: *Tale of the Repertory Actor*, 1971; *Mr. Willow's Wife*, with John Chapman, 1972; *Starring Leslie Willey*, 1987.

Television Plays (with Tony Hilton): *Boobs in the Wood*, 1960; *Round the Bend* (*Dial Rix* series), 1962.

*

Theatrical Activities:
Director: **Plays**—many of his own plays, and *Thark* by Ben Travers, London, 1965; *In at the Death* by Duncan Greenwood and Robert King, London, 1967; *Press Cuttings* by Shaw, 1970; *The Mating Game* by Robin Hawdon, London, 1972; *Birds of Paradise* by Gaby Bruyère, London, 1974; *See How They Run* by Philip King, London, 1984; *Pygmalion* by Shaw, London, 1984; *Three Piece Suite* by Richard Harris, Hornchurch, Essex, 1986; *Holiday Snap* by Michael Pertwee, Guildford, Surrey, 1986. **Films**—*Not Now Darling*, with David Croft, 1973; *Not Now Comrade*, with Harold Snoad, 1977; *There Goes the Bride*, 1980.
Actor: **Plays**—role in *Song of Norway* by Milton Lazarus, Robert Wright, and George Forrest, London, 1946; *Calcutta in the Morning* by Geoffrey Thomas, London, 1947; Larkin in *The Hidden Years* by Travers Otway, London, 1948; roles in repertory companies, 1952–56; *Dry Rot* by John Chapman, London, 1956; Corporal Flight in *Simple Spymen* by John Chapman, London, 1958; *One for the Pot*, London, 1961; Detective-Sergeant Trotter in *The Mousetrap* by Agatha Christie, London, 1964; Simon Sparrow in *Doctor at Sea* by Ted Willis, London, 1966; David Prosser in *Uproar in the House* by Anthony Marriott and Alistair Foot, London, 1967; Nicholas Wainwright in *Charlie Girl*, London, 1968; Timothy Westerby in *There Goes the Bride*, London, 1975; Willoughby Pink in *Banana Ridge* by Ben Travers, London, 1976; *Two into One*, Leicester, 1981, and Guildford, Surrey, 1985; *Run for Your Wife*, Guildford, Surrey, and London, both 1983, and New York, 1989; *Out of Order*, London, 1990; *It Runs in the Family*, London, 1992. **Films**—*Not Now Darling*, 1973; *Not Now Comrade*, 1977.

* * *

From the time of his first success with *One for the Pot* in 1960, Ray Cooney has sought to perfect his "talent to amuse." As one who has mastered the techniques of farce in the role of actor and producer, as well as writer, he is perhaps more qualified than most; certainly his varied abilities enable him to assess the likely response from the market-place, as well as the ivory tower, and the past 20 years have seen an increasingly imaginative use of his craft.

Farce is Cooney's chosen medium, and one in which he excels. Traditionally, its success depends less on characterisation or psychological insight than on swift and continuous action. Cooney's plays invaribly fulfil these technical demands. Starting with a humdrum situation—a forthcoming society wedding, the collection of a mink coat, the decorating of an upmarket flat—the plays rapidly develop into a maze of misunderstandings, with the impending threat of potentially disastrous confrontations. Cooney shows great skill with his plots, neatly gauging the accelerating pace and eventual climax, matching the action with a brittle, fragmented dialogue. He is also adept at exploiting such stock devices as the aside to the audience, Gilbert's comments on his partner Arnold in *Not Now, Darling* being a typical—and effective—example. A similar device is used in the same play, when Arnold, confronted by a succession of irate spouses and girlfriends about to discover "proof" of infidelity, is repeatedly reduced to hurling the "evidence"—usually underwear—out of the window. Read cold from a script, the effect appears tedious and mechanical. Onstage it works, lending added emphasis to the humour of the situation.

Repetition is a key element in Cooney's farces, the threat of discovery or catastrophic encounter continually recurring as the comic tension heightens and the possibilities grow more disastrous. *Run for Your Wife* has its bigamous taxi-driver hero striving desperately to prevent the meeting of his two wives, his position rendered more comic by the use of a split stage which reveals both women and their thoughts at the same time. *Run for Your Wife* is one of Cooney's most striking works, the action ably measured, the wit of the matching dialogue astute and keen. The same is true of *Not Now, Darling* and *Move Over, Mrs. Markham*, which show Cooney at his best. Like most of his plays, they are aimed at an upper-middle-class audience—"the tired businessman," as one reviewer puts it—and this is reflected in the locations, the former set in a high-class furrier's, the latter in "a very elegant top floor London flat." In *Not Now, Darling* Cooney contrasts the lecherous Gilbert and the prim Arnold in an escalating series of encounters as the former's amorous intrigues come home to roost. (Arnold's "I refuse to put all my bags in one exit!" must be one of Cooney's funniest lines.) *Move Over, Mrs. Markham* involves a publisher's family and friends and their liaisons, its climax a hilarious scene where a prudish best-selling author is persuaded to sign for the firm by the publisher's wife, while the publisher himself (as the butler) makes constant interruptions. All three plays are deftly executed, the interplay of character and situation sure and precise, the climaxes carefully weighted for maximum comic impact. *There Goes the Bride* is not quite equal to them. Polly Perkins, the 1920's flapper invisible to everyone but the dazed Timothy, is an overworked device, and the play lacks the "ordinariness" of Cooney's best settings. More effective is the Australian father-in-law, Babcock, in his role as that stock figure, the "funny foreigner."

Farce, like the "tired businessman," is not noted for its taste, and Cooney's plays are no exception. On the face of it, there would appear to be nothing very funny about Lebanon, but *Bang Bang Beirut* (produced in 1966) manages to wring comedy from the subject, much as Croft and Perry's *'Allo, 'Allo* has done with wartime France. Just as farce admits no

un-funny locations, Cooney also regards minorities as fair game. The "funny foreigner" is repeatedly met with in his plays, either in person or by proxy, as with Linda's awful Austrian imitation in *Move Over, Mrs. Markham*. Cooney seems to find homosexuality unbelievably amusing, and makes repeated use of its possibilities. The apparent "relationship" of Philip Markham and his partner is milked for laughs, the irony being their "discovery" by the effetely dressed Alistair, of whom Cooney seems unduly anxious to reassure us that "underneath his slightly arty exterior lurks a virile male." The bigamous husband of *Run for Your Wife* pretends to be gay himself at one point, and another camp character also makes an appearance. Many would contend that this kind of humour is on a par with racist jokes, and that the author is playing for easy laughs. No doubt Cooney, as a performer, would contend that there is no such thing. Recent plays such as *It Runs in the Family*, *Wife Begins at Forty*, and *Out of Order* display all his familiar skills, and serve to confirm his reputation, *Out of Order* especially ranking with his finest work so far. A sequel to the earlier *Two into One*, its story centres on the thwarted attempt by a junior government minister to secure a night of passion with an opposition secretary. The discovery in their hotel room of what appears to be the body of an intruder, trapped by a faulty sash window, is only the start of their troubles. Their unavailing efforts at hiding the "corpse" with the help of a bumbling PPS are further complicated by the unexpected arrival of both their spouses, the intrusive manager, a bribe-seeking waiter, and a private nurse. Cooney's script leads them—and us—adroitly through a frantic succession of hilarious scenes in which a cupboard and the faulty window figure prominently, the characters confronting each other repeatedly in varying stages of undress and potentially outrageous situations, the action matched throughout by the barbed wit of the author's dialogue. *Out of Order* provides an excellent example of Cooney's mastery of his chosen form. Nor is his work confined to the stage. In past years he has written for radio, television, and film, and his recent radio play *Starring Leslie Willey* shows a rekindling of his interest, utilising his flair for words effectively in the medium of sound.

Cooney, one feels, is not a particularly innovative writer. Rather, he is a master technician, a skilled manipulator of the conventions of his medium, where he operates to best effect. Attempts to move outside, as in *Why Not Stay for Breakfast?*, have been less satisfying. Within the limitations of his form, Cooney is altogether more impressive. Whether one laughs quite as loudly as the average businessman, or winces on occasion, the fact remains that Cooney is one of the most capable, and consistently successful, writers in the medium of farce.

—Geoff Sadler

COWARD, Noël (Pierce). British. 1899–1973. See 1st edition, 1973.

COWEN, Ron(ald). American. Born in Cincinnati, Ohio, 15 September 1944. Educated at the University of California,

Los Angeles, B.A. in English 1966; Annenberg School of Communications, University of Pennsylvania, Philadelphia, 1967–68. Taught classes in theatre at New York University, Fall 1969. Associate trustee, University of Pennsylvania. Recipient: Wesleyan University fellowship, 1968; Vernon Rice award, 1968; Emmy award, 1986, and Peabody award, 1986, for television play. Lives in Pacific Palisades, California. Agent: William Morris Agency, 151 El Camino, Beverly Hills, California 90212, U.S.A.

PUBLICATIONS

Plays

Summertree (produced Waterford, Connecticut, 1967; New York, 1968). New York, Random House, 1968.
Valentine's Day (produced Waterford, Connecticut, 1968; revised version, music by Saul Naishtat, produced New York, 1975).
Saturday Adoption (televised 1968; produced New York, 1978). New York, Dramatists Play Service, 1969.
Porcelain Time (produced Waterford, Connecticut, 1972).
The Book of Murder (televised 1974). New York, Dramatists Play Service, 1974.
Lulu, adaptation of plays by Wedekind (produced New York, 1974; as *Inside Lulu*, produced New York, 1975).

Television Plays: *Saturday Adoption*, 1968; *The Book of Murder*, 1974; *Paul's Case*, from the story by Willa Cather, 1977; *I'm a Fool*, from the story by Sherwood Anderson, 1979; *An Early Frost*, with Daniel Lipman, 1985.

* * *

The ethical crisis arising from America's involvement in the Vietnam war was a major concern for American writers in the 1960's. *Summertree*, the most successful American play of the decade to deal with this subject, was written by Ron Cowen at the age of twenty. (David Rabe's *The Basic Training of Pavlo Hummel* and *Sticks and Bones* may prove to be more significant works, but they appeared after the initial national tension over the war had peaked.) *Summertree*, which was widely produced and made into a Hollywood film, was perhaps successful more because of its timeliness than its intrinsic worth.

The play is an excessively sentimental telling of an inconsequential young man's death and life in Vietnam. As the protagonist (Young Man) lies fatally wounded under a jungle tree, he hallucinates flashback episodes from his civilian and military experience: sometimes he is twenty, sometimes he is ten. The jungle tree becomes the backyard tree in which he once built a treehouse. His recollections are of his Mother and Father, his Girl and his Buddy (Soldier). These characters are drawn by Cowen in broad strokes that critics of the production were prone to see as American archetypes: the essential constellation of personae. A critic of a less emotionally charged era is prone to see them as uninspired caricatures.

The play's most successful attribute is its three-act, cinematic structure which provides a degree of dramatic irony and gives the play substance. Its least successful is its banal dialogue. When the Young Man says to his father, late in the final act, "I want to tell the back yard goodbye," there is a cloying sentimentality which renders the moment bathetic. Yet for an audience tired of both the brutality of the war and the hysteria of the anti-war protests which shook the land in 1967, the play (and even its dialogue) struck sympathetic chords.

The play is a product of its cultural climate in yet another sense. It was written by Cowen while he was a student at the University of Pennsylvania. When the play was first presented, in the summer of 1967 at the Eugene O'Neill Memorial Theatre Foundation in Waterford, Connecticut, it underwent major re-writings at the request of its director. As it was prepared for New York production by the Repertory Theater of Lincoln Center, additional changes were introduced. The play—far more than the average commercial project—became the reflection of many concerned person's attitudes towards the war. Small wonder it found a receptive ear and was awarded the Vernon Rice award for that turbulent year. (When the movie script was being prepared this procedure got out of control. Cowen wrote a first screenplay, Rod McKuen was hired to do a second, and the shooting script was finally the work of Hollywood pros Edward Hume and Stephen Yafa. The final script owes shockingly little to Cowen's initial intentions, images, or characters.)

Cowen's subsequent career has been somewhat erratic. In 1968 *Saturday Adoption* was telecast on CBS Playhouse and in 1974 ABC aired *The Book of Murder*. Both were critical failures. The first dealt with a socially conscious young man's failures to change the world through his father's money or his pupil's achievements; the second is a coy murder mystery. Cowen's trademarks are easily seen in both: the cinematic structure, the sentimental and nostalgic tone, the domestic circumstance, the conflict over money. His weaknesses are in evidence as well: the badly motivated actions, the clichéd characters, and the clumsy dialogue which the critic for *Variety* called "goody two-shoes language." *I'm a Fool*, a television adaptation of Sherwood Anderson's story, was more successful, and *An Early Frost* won an Emmy award.

Cowen has completed subsequent stage scripts, but none has been given major production. He assisted on the book for *Billy* which flopped on Broadway in 1968. His musical *Valentine's Day* was show-cased at the Manhattan Theatre Club in 1975 but reviewed as an "unsatisfying experience." It included the Cowensque line, "I want to tell the apartment goodbye." *Inside Lulu* was a banal work, loosely based on the Wedekind plays, and created by Section Ten, the off-off-Broadway improvisational group. Cowen was their literary collaborator.

In retrospect, *Summertree* appears very much to be in the tradition of television soap opera and it is appropriate that Cowen should continue to write for the television medium. As long as his language, characters and situations remain banal, autobiographical, and domestic it is unlikely he will produce a major work. *Summertree* appears to have been less the work of a *wunderkind* than a timely reflection of a culture's anxieties.

—Thomas B. Markus

———————

CRANE, Richard (Arthur). British. Born in York, 4 December 1944. Educated at St. John's School, Leatherhead, Surrey, 1958–63; Jesus College, Cambridge, 1963–66, B.A. (honours) in classics and English 1966, M.A. 1971. Married Faynia Jeffery Williams in 1975; two sons and two stepdaughters. Actor and director: founder member, Brighton

Combination and Pool, Edinburgh. Fellow in theatre, University of Bradford, Yorkshire, 1972–74; resident dramatist, National Theatre, London, 1974–75; fellow in creative writing, University of Leicester, 1976, and University of East Anglia, Norwich, 1988; literary manager, Royal Court Theatre, London, 1978–79; dramaturg, Tron Theatre, Glasgow, 1983–84; associate director, Brighton Theatre, 1980–85; lecturer in English, University of Maryland, 1990; writer-in-residence, Birmingham Polytechnic, and tutor in playwriting, University of Birmingham, 1990–91. Member of the Board of Directors, Edinburgh Festival Fringe Society, 1973–89. Recipient: Edinburgh Festival Fringe award, 1973, 1974, 1975, 1977, 1980, 1986, 1987, 1988, 1989; Thames Television bursary, 1974; Arts Council bursary, 1974. Agent: Casarotto Ramsay Ltd., National House, 60–66 Wardour Street, London W1V 3HP, England.

PUBLICATIONS

Plays

Footlights Revue, with others (produced Cambridge, 1966).
Three Ugly Women (produced Cork and London, 1967).
The Tenant (produced Edinburgh, 1971; London, 1972).
Crippen (produced Edinburgh, 1971).
Tom Brown (produced Bradford, 1971).
Decent Things (produced Edinburgh, 1972; London, 1973).
The Blood Stream (produced Edinburgh, 1972).
Mutiny on the Bounty, music by Chris Mitchell (produced Bradford, 1972; revised version produced Brighton, 1980).
Bleak Midwinter (produced Edinburgh, 1972).
David, King of the Jews, music by Chris Mitchell (produced Bradford, 1973).
Thunder: A Play of the Brontës (produced Ilkley, Yorkshire, 1973; London, 1978). London, Heinemann, 1976.
Examination in Progress (produced Edinburgh, 1973).
Secrets (produced Belfast, 1973; London, 1974).
The Pied Piper, music by Chris Mitchell (produced Bradford, 1973).
The Quest, music by Chris Mitchell (produced Edinburgh, 1974).
The Route of All Evil (produced Edinburgh, 1974).
Humbug; or, Christmas Carol Backwards, music by Milton Reame-James (produced Bracknell, Berkshire, 1974).
Mystery Plays (produced Bracknell, Berkshire, 1974).
The King (produced Bradford, 1974).
The Bradford Revue (produced Edinburgh, 1974).
Mean Time (produced London, 1975).
Venus and Superkid (for children), music by Milton Reame-James (produced London, 1975).
Clownmaker (produced Edinburgh, 1975; London and Westport, Connecticut, 1976; New York, 1982).
Bloody Neighbours (produced London, 1975).
Manchester Tales (produced Manchester, 1975).
Gunslinger: A Wild West Show, music by Joss Buckley (produced Leicester, 1976; London, 1977). London, Heinemann, 1979.
Nero and the Golden House (produced Edinburgh, 1976).
The Perils of Bardfrod, with David Edgar (produced Bradford, 1976).
Satan's Ball, adaptation of a novel by Mikhail Bulgakov (produced Edinburgh, 1977; Berkeley, California, 1984).
Gogol (produced Brighton, 1978; London, 1979; New York, 1983).
Vanity, adaptation of *Eugene Onegin* by Pushkin (produced Edinburgh, 1980; London, 1983).

Sand (produced Brighton, 1981).
The Brothers Karamazov, adaptation of a novel by Dostoevsky (produced Edinburgh and London, 1981).
Burke and Hare (produced Glasgow, 1983).
The Possessed, with Yuri Lyubimov, adaptation of a novel by Dostoevsky (produced Paris and London, 1985).
Mutiny!, with David Essex, music by Essex (produced London, 1985).
Envy, adaptation of a novel by Yuri Olesha (produced Edinburgh, 1986).
Soldier Soldier, adaptation of a work by Tony Parker (produced Edinburgh, 1986).
Pushkin (produced Edinburgh and London, 1987).
Red Magic (produced Edinburgh and London, 1988).
Rolling the Stone (produced Edinburgh, 1989).
Phaedra, with Michael Glenny, adaptation of the play by Marina Tsvetayeva (produced London, 1990).
Baggage and Bombshells (produced Edinburgh 1991; London, 1992).

Screenplay: *Sebastian and the Seawitch* (for children), 1976.

Radio Plays: *Optimistic Tragedy*, with Faynia Williams, adaptation of the play by Vsevolod Vishnevsky, 1986; *Anna and Marina*, 1991; *Plutopia*, music by Donald Swann, 1992; *Understudies*, 1992.

Television Plays: *Nice Time* series, 1968–69; *The Billy West Show*, 1970; *Rottingdean*, 1980; *The Possessed*, with Yuri Lyubimov, 1986.

Recordings: *Mutiny!*, Phonogram, 1983, and Telstar, 1985 (and singles *Tahiti*, 1983, and *Welcome*, 1984, both Phonogram).

*

Critical Studies: in *Vogue* (London), October 1977; *Yorkshire Arts Association Magazine*, February–March 1979.

Theatrical Activities:
Director of plays in Bradford, Edinburgh, and London, and actor from 1966 in London and in repertory, on television, and in films.

*   *   *

For three weeks each year, Edinburgh is a world theatrical capital with hundreds of performances taking place both in the International Festival and on the Fringe. Many a premiere sinks into instant obscurity, but the plays of Richard Crane have left an indelible mark, taking nine coveted Edinburgh Festival Fringe awards by 1992. Over 20 years of dedication to the Edinburgh Fringe is an unusual route to dramatic success, but there is a logic to it: by collaborating with his wife, the director Faynia Williams, and working with dedicated students from universities in Bradford, Essex, and East Anglia, Crane was able to produce epic drama on a scale normally considered only by the National and Royal Shakespeare Companies. Vast themes and a large theatrical canvas became economically feasible, and his work ranged from a retelling of the Arthurian legend to the full breadth of Mikhail Bulgakov's great novel, *The Master and Margarita*.

It is interesting, then, that it was an intimate and intense play for four actors that finally elevated his reputation nationally and internationally, and many of his later plays are highly refined miniatures for perhaps no more than a single actor. Although he had already had important posts as a playwright-in-residence at the National Theatre and with the Royal Court, it was his dramatization of *The Brothers Karamazov* in 1981 that consolidated Crane's London reputation, and, indeed, a reputation in what was then the Soviet Union. It was no accident, however, that the play was quarried from Russian literature for he and Faynia Williams had begun their exploration of the Russian greats well before it was fashionable.

Before turning to *The Brothers Karamazov* and Dostoevsky, Crane had presented a string of confrontations with Russian writers, including Bulgakov, Gogol, and Pushkin. They had followed investigations into British legends, English literature and religion. At one point, he had even written a children's play called *Venus and Superkid* which was described as a "trans-galactic rock supershow based on Greek legend."

His dramatic interests have ranged from a music-hall impression of the murderer Crippen, to *Thunder*, a retelling of the Brontë family story, and *David, King of the Jews*, performed at Bradford Cathedral in 1973. His 1974 script for Bradford University, *The Quest*, offered the first serious rumblings of significant talent—in part because it was technically overambitious—and it was the Edinburgh Fringe success of that year. In the play he retold the legend of Arthurian England, with opposing factions divided into prose and poetry speakers while the audience witnessed the rise and destruction of Camelot as if watching a jousting tournament.

The following year, which also saw the production of *Bloody Neighbours* in the National Theatre's studio season at the ICA Theatre, produced *Clownmaker*. It tells the story of the relationship between Diaghilev and Nijinsky, and it was marked by shattering stage effects in Faynia Williams's production. The Ballets Russes forms the backdrop for the portrait of Diaghilev as puppet-master, and the struggles of Nijinsky to establish a separate existence create the dramatic moments. Diaghilev produces Nijinsky's first sign of animation, by providing the impetus to dance, and Nijinsky's rebellion against his homosexual relationship with Diaghilev provokes a virtual earthquake. Memorable scenes and moments of evocative dialogue did not quite jell into a total success, but the sheer theatricality was refreshing and unusual.

His adaptation of Bulgakov's novel *The Master and Margarita* appeared two years later, after a series of somewhat less ambitious works. Called *Satan's Ball*, the play marked his first serious use of Russian material and formed a vast satirical and erotic canvas for Williams's staging, again on the Edinburgh Fringe. The next collaboration was on a markedly reduced scale: a monologue, originally performed by Crane himself in a production by Williams for their own small company, the Brighton Actors' Workshop. Again, the subject was Russian, the title the name of the author, *Gogol*, with material taken from Gogol's writing, particularly "The Overcoat," and from Gogol's life. His intention was to contrast the inner life with the outer appearance, to present the spiritual substance simultaneously with the surface indications and contradictions of the body, the clothes, and the published writing.

Before *The Brothers Karamazov* promoted him to the official Edinburgh Festival, Crane and Williams produced *Vanity* on the Fringe in 1980. It was a further investigation of Russian writing, described as a "response to *Eugene Onegin*," and it cleared the way for the official invitation in 1981, which resulted in the London season and a tour of the Soviet Union.

The distinction of *The Brothers Karamazov* as an adaptation for the stage lies largely in the lucid retention of the moral and metaphysical ambiguities of Dostoevsky's novel. The originality of the work is largely in the ingenious structural emphases which significantly alter the tone of the original. Crane transforms introspective guilt into heady confessions, with each son eagerly displaying the reasons for which he might possibly have murdered his father. A familiarity with the novel helps clarify the multiple actions, but the multiple role-playing of each character is theatrically engaging on its own. There is a playfulness in giving each of the four actors a principal characterization, then diverting them to play old Fyodor (always in a fur coat) or lounging women, which provides moment to moment entertainment. Crane thrives on challenges, and more often than not meets them with original theatrical solutions.

The main developments of Crane's work remain his collaborations with Faynia Williams, both with students and latterly in radio. However, his most visible production was his collaboration with the pop star and actor David Essex on a West End musical based on *Mutiny on the Bounty*. *Mutiny!* had the merit of dispensing with the standard image of the leading mutineer, Fletcher Christian, as a recognizable hero. He was approached rather as a confused Romantic, longing for equality between officers and enlisted men. Unfortunately, the starry contributions by Essex were all too visible, keeping him moodily in view as sailors were flogged and involving him in erotic caresses with his island lover at every available chance.

Crane's most important collaboration was perhaps his work with the exiled Soviet director Yuri Lyubimov on a European co-production of a dramatization of Dostoevsky's *The Possessed* in 1985. The version reflected the director's highly personal vision of the book, but Crane's use of language was equally personal and the heightened imagery was as evident in his concentrated English as in the director's vivid staging.

Other projects, from a lively dramatization of the Soviet classic *Envy*, for the 1986 Edinburgh Festival, to a radio version of the classic communist drama by Vsevolod Vishnevsky, *Optimistic Tragedy*, continued to explore the riches of Russian writing, finally establishing a more personal tone with his impressionistic and intense study of the filmmaker Sergei Eisenstein called *Red Magic*, written as the Soviet Union lumbered towards dissolution.

Many of Crane's plays have been designed for his own performances as an actor, from his Gogol in an overcoat to a pun-rich retelling of the Sysyphus legend in *Rolling the Stone*, proving his value as an entertainer as well as a serious actor. The backstage knowledge he has accumulated as a theatrical all-rounder has been reflected in plays such as his script for radio, *Understudies*, a play about the jealousies and ambitions of those actors waiting for terrible things to happen to the star. Naturally, the roles are tailor-made for those who are already stars.

Yet serious themes with political connotations have also made repeated appearances in his work, from his dramatization of Tony Parker's book about British soldiers and their wives, *Soldier Soldier* to his 1991 play, *Baggage and Bombshells* a typically dense and imagistic shocker about women and war drawn from the rhetoric and propaganda of the Gulf War. For all his vast and varied output over the first 25 years of his writing career, Crane shows little sign of flagging creativity even if a single undisputed masterpiece has so far eluded him.

—Ned Chaillet

CREGAN, David (Appleton Quartus). British. Born in Buxton, Derbyshire, 30 September 1931. Educated at the Leys School, Cambridge, 1945–50; Clare College, Cambridge, 1952–55, B.A. in English 1955. Served as an acting corporal in the Royal Air Force, 1950–52. Married Ailsa Mary Wynne Willson in 1960; three sons and one adopted daughter. Head of English, Palm Beach Private School, Florida, 1955–57; assistant English master, Burnage Boys' Grammar School, Manchester, 1957; assistant English master and head of drama, 1958–62, and part-time drama teacher, 1962–67, Hatfield School, Hertfordshire; salesman, and clerk at the Automobile Association, 1958. Worked with Royal Court Theatre Studio, London, 1964, 1968, and Midlands Arts Centre, Birmingham, 1971; conducted three-week studio at the Royal Shakespeare Company Memorial Theatre, Stratford-on-Avon, 1971. Member of the Drama Panel, West Midlands Arts Association, 1972, and Eastern Arts, 1980. Recipient: Arts Council bursary, 1966, 1975, 1978, and grant, 1971; Foyle award, 1966; Sony award for radio, 1987. Agent: Casarotto Ramsay Ltd., National House, 60–66 Wardour Street, London W1V 3HP. Address: 76 Wood Close, Hatfield, Hertfordshire, England.

PUBLICATIONS

Plays

Miniatures (produced London, 1965). London, Methuen, 1970.
Transcending, and The Dancers (produced London, 1966). London, Methuen, 1967.
Three Men for Colverton (produced London, 1966). London, Methuen, 1967.
The Houses by the Green (produced London, 1968). London, Methuen, 1969.
A Comedy of the Changing Years (produced London, 1969).
Arthur, in *Playbill One*, edited by Alan Durband. London, Hutchinson, 1969.
Tipper (produced Oxford, 1969).
Liebestraum and Other Pieces (produced Birmingham, 1970). Included in *The Land of Palms and Other Plays*, 1973.
Jack in the Box; and If You Don't Laugh, You Cry (produced Birmingham, 1971). Included in *The Land of Palms and Other Plays*, 1973.
The Daffodil, and Sentimental Value (produced Birmingham, 1971).
How We Held the Square: A Play for Children (produced Birmingham, 1971; London, 1974). London, Eyre Methuen, 1973.
The Land of Palms (produced Dartington, Devon, 1972). Included in *The Land of Palms and Other Plays*, 1973.
George Reborn (televised 1973; produced Richmond, Surrey, 1973; London, 1977). Included in *The Land of Palms and Other Plays*, 1973.
Cast Off (produced Sheffield, 1973).
Pater Noster (in *Mixed Blessings*, produced Horsham, Sussex, 1973). Published in *Play Nine*, edited by Robin Rook, London, Arnold, 1981.
The Land of Palms and Other Plays (includes *Liebestraum*; *George Reborn*; *The Problem*; *Jack in the Box*; *If You Don't Laugh, You Cry*). London, Eyre Methuen, 1973.
The King (produced London, 1974).
Tina (produced Richmond, Surrey, 1975). With *Poor Tom*, London, Eyre Metheun, 1976.
Poor Tom (produced Manchester, 1976). With *Tina*, London, Eyre Methuen, 1976.

Tigers (produced Richmond, Surrey, 1978).
Young Sir (produced Richmond, Surrey, 1979).
Red Riding Hood (produced Stoke-on-Trent, 1979).
Getting It Right (produced Hatfield, Hertfordshire, 1980).
A Name Is More Than a Name, in *Play Nine*, edited by Robin Rook. London, Arnold, 1981.
Jack and the Beanstalk (pantomime), music by Brian Protheroe (produced London, 1982). London, French, 1987.
The Sleeping Beauty (pantomime), music by Brian Protheroe (produced London, 1983). London, French, 1984.
Red Ridinghood (pantomime), music by Brian Protheroe (produced London, 1984). London, French, 1986.
Crackling Angels (produced Beaminster, Dorset, 1987).
Beauty and the Beast (pantomime), music by Brian Protheroe (produced London, 1987).
Cinderella (pantomime), music by Brian Protheroe (produced London, 1989).

Radio Plays: *The Latter Days of Lucy Trenchard*, 1974; *The Monument*, 1978; *Hope*, 1979; *Inventor's Corner*, 1979; *The Joking Habit*, 1980; *The True Story of the Public School Strike 1990*, 1981; *Diana's Uncle and Other Relatives*, 1982; *The Spectre*, 1983; *The Awful Insulation of Rage*, 1986; *A Butler Did It*, 1990; *From a Second Home in Picardy*, 1990; *What Happened with St. George*, 1991; *Eavesdropping*, 1992.

Television Plays: *That Time of Life*, 1972; *George Reborn*, 1973; *I Want to Marry Your Son*, 1973; *Pipkins*, with Susan Pleat, 1974; *Reluctant Chickens*, 1982; *Events in a Museum*, 1983; *Goodbye Days*, 1984; *A Still Small Shout*, 1985; *Goodbye, And I Hope We Meet Again*, 1989.

Novel

Ronald Rossiter. London, Hutchinson, 1959.

*

Critical Studies: *The Second Wave* by John Russell Taylor, London, Methuen, and New York, Hill and Wang, 1971; article by Timothy J. Kidd, in *British Dramatists since World War II* edited by Stanley Weintraub, Detroit, Gale, 1982.

David Cregan comments:

1. I am a socialist because there is no other reasonable thing to be. However, all problems, as well as all interesting thoughts, seem to stem from that one position. How much does the individual matter and how much the community? Can a contemporary community ever avoid becoming systematized, and anyway how much less traumatic is it living unsystematically than systematically? How simplistic can a government be before it must be opposed totally? If material poverty produces spiritual poverty, which, with special exceptions, it does, can material wealth produce spiritual wealth? How important *is* spiritual wealth, and on what does its value depend? Can the elevation of one working class be justified if it is achieved at the expense of another working class? If freedom is no longer a meaningful conception (and it only achieves any meaning by being opposed to some form of tyranny), which qualified freedom is the most important? Of thought or from hunger? If leaders are bad, are institutions worse? What is the basic nature of man as opposed to the animals, and can it be improved?

I doubt if any of this appears overtly in any of my writing, though the head of steam is always provided by acute anxieties felt on one score or another among these and similar peculiarly 20th-century questions.

2. Since for me the best plays seem to *be* rather than to be *about*, I personally prefer the episodic forms in which characters may be presented quickly and variously, so that the architecture provides the major insights.

3. Since I have this delight in form, I find no pleasure or virtue in personal rhetoric, self-indulgent self-revelation, or absolute naturalism.

4. Delight in construction also biases me against any form of expressionism or abstract symbolism, and increasingly I use songs, jazz, and a rough poetry spoken to music for various constructional purposes.

5. Since construction of the kind so far indicated is frequently a question of rhythm, there is a "playful" quality about my work. It has a musical quality, each scene sounding forward to another. This means the plays should be acted with a care for their surface, and anyone who acts them for any individual significance, the same shall surely lose it. There are frequently large alterations in emotional stance needed between the giving and receiving of the words, and there is much pleasure in watching this.

6. I have been much influenced by farce, Ibsen, Brecht, Beckett, and the directors I have been associated with at the Royal Court. Also by the intensely magical understanding of comedy shown by Keith Johnstone.

7. I am the fourth and youngest son of an Irish shirt manufacturer. My father fought and was gassed in World War I, and sought peace and prosperity in a small Derbyshire town, where he pursued a quiet Protestant way of life. My brothers fought, and one died, in World War II. I was largely brought up by a young working-class nursemaid.

8. Writer's notes about himself are alas more revealing when they fail to confirm the impression of his work than when they succeed. This happens to more of us than is generally supposed.

* * *

In David Cregan's earliest play, *Miniatures*, the deputy headmaster says "If only one knew what every mind was thinking. If one had their habits of thought one could put in train the running of the school that way it ought to go. That's the way of achieving what is democratically best for everyone. One must have their minds, or else it is coercion." The common theme of Cregan's plays is the struggle for power and the manipulation of social conventions to achieve it. A more or less closed society that has developed its own conventions is often the setting: a school in *Miniatures* and again in *Tina*, a small town in *Three Men for Colverton*, an oasis in *The Land of Palms*, a boarding house in *Poor Tom*. In other plays the characters act as if in a closed society: in *The Dancers*, in which a middle-aged quintet dance and pair off in various combinations, and the "cozy circle" of two mutually adulterous couples of *Liesbestraum*—but where, when Jane does not find herself attracted to her husband's lover's husband, the others fear that she will seek a lover elsewhere, in which case "we'll find ourselves part of a larger community before we know where we are, with all the loss of sovereignty that will entail."

Often in Cregan's plays one set of conventions is brought into conflict with another. In his most complex play, *Three Men for Colverton*, the leader of a trio of evangelists seeks to take control of the town from the domineering Mrs. Carnock. She believes Colverton "was meant to be a stagnant pool . . . and stagnant it will remain." The uncompromising vision of the evangelists, who "hate every lubricant of living" and decry "the stern virility of man [etiolated] in the black night of consumer goods," threatens the indulgence and manipulation

of human relationships by which she maintains her dominance. Other power-seekers are the liberal vicar and an Anglican monk who uses the confessional to his own advantage.

Where existing conventions are strained or broken, new conventions are invented. In *Liebestraum* the adulterous relationships are regularized. A strict alternation of days for sleeping with one's marriage partner and with one's lover is threatened by Jane's uncertain feelings; when she does fulfil everyone's expectations by completing the sexual cross-partnering she does so on the wrong day and is denounced for the carnality. In *The Land of Palms* some British have set up a community of peace and harmony at an oasis. Three British ex-Foreign Legionnaires arrive with their military values. In *Transcending*, a short play of wonderful verve, a teenage girl escapes from the world of her parents and two of her neighbours, a young man and an older widower, all of whom have a role to offer her, by appearing at the end of the play dressed as a nun—escaping by invoking a different set of conventions.

It would be interesting to produce *Transcending* alongside the very funny *Pater Noster*, in which husband and wife are saying their bedtime prayers when the husband decides he is God, for he has created the child in her womb, and begins praying to himself despite his wife's arguments that there are other influences on conception, such as the availability of family allowances. The voice of the foetus is heard, apprehensive about the world it is to enter. We see the mother use the child to manipulate her husband and then, at the end of the play, threatening the foetus, "I'll tell him when he comes upstairs, and then you'll catch it." Even an infant is doomed in our world of manipulative conventions.

There are in Cregan's plays instinctive nonconformists. In *Miniatures* the climactic scene reveals the music teacher sitting in his store closet surrounded by all the items that have been stolen around the school. He later tries to hang himself. In *The Land of Palms* the soldier who cannot adapt to the oasis community kills himself. In *Three Men for Colverton* one of the evangelists is homosexual. He declares, "One is one and all alone and ever more shall be so. Two bodies don't make one, two minds don't make one, and I'm one." In the last scene he throws himself from a clocktower and dies. Not borne up by angels, this individualist has unwittingly destroyed the leading evangelist's power. Meanwhile, Mrs. Carnock has died, and perhaps the play's other nonconformist, a teacher who fornicates with his pupils, will establish "that dreary venture, the Arts Centre," which Mrs. Carnock had opposed, as "an act of existential heroism." In much the same spirit he will marry his latest, pregnant teenage mistress.

In Cregan's more recent short plays the nonconformists are the central characters. Tina, a teacher, dresses in jeans and leather jacket to try to reach an abused ten-year-old, whom Cregan has ironically named Dawn. In *Poor Tom* Tom murders the owner of the boarding-house to prevent him selling it. In each play much of the interest is in how the other characters react to his tearing of the social fabric.

Cregan writes dry, wry comedies. Introducing *Three Men for Colverton* he writes that "the situations of most of the characters are too painful to make me laugh. However, most of the people are themselves aware of the silliness of their positions, and this frequently leads them to act in a sillier way than ever." So it is in all his plays. The characters' self-consciousness effects a certain distancing from the audience. They often introduce themselves to the audience and sing choruses together. In *Three Men for Colverton* they move the revolving platforms Cregan envisions as setting. In *The Dancers* different records are put on and taken off, accompanied by lighting changes, while in the brief comedy *George*

Reborn the characters conduct an orchestra in snatches from well-known classical works.

The Houses by the Green is more farcical than his other full-length plays. It is a Plautine or *commedia* farce, offering the battle of two elderly men, the Commander and Mervyn Molyneux, who live in adjacent houses, for the hand of Molyneux's adopted daughter Susan, and their besting by her young lover, the servingman Oliver whom they share. Molyneux woos Susan disguised as his own friend; the Commander does likewise. Neither is aware of the other's deception. Disguised as a land developer, Oliver threatens both with their community's destruction. Even Susan disguises herself, as the developer's trollop; Oliver, puzzled, tells the audience "I must be impersonating a real person." Traditional forgiveness and marriage promises end the play when Susan, untraditionally pregnant, "is suddenly sick at the side of the stage."

—Anthony Graham-White

CRIMP, Martin (Andrew). British. Born in the United Kingdom, in February 1956. Educated at Cambridge University, graduated 1978. Married; three daughters. Thames Television writer-in-residence, Orange Tree Theatre, Richmond, Surrey, 1988–89. Recipient: *Radio Times* award, 1986. Agent: Judy Daish Associates, 83 Eastbourne Mews, London W2 6LQ, England.

PUBLICATIONS

Plays

Living Remains (produced London, 1982).
Love Games, with Howard Curtis, adaptation of the work by Jerzy Przezdziecki, from the translation by Boguslav Lawendowski (produced London, 1982).
Four Attempted Acts (produced London, 1984).
A Variety of Death-Defying Acts (produced London, 1985).
Three Attempted Acts (broadcast 1985). Published in *Best Radio Plays of 1985*, edited by Richard Imison, London, Methuen, 1986.
Definitely the Bahamas (produced London, 1987).
A Kind of Arden (produced London, 1987).
Spanish Girls (produced London, 1987).
Dealing with Clair (produced London, 1988). London, Hern, 1988.
Play with Repeats (produced London, 1989). London, Hern, 1990.
No One Sees the Video (produced London, 1990). With *Getting Attention*, London, Hern, 1991.
Getting Attention (produced Leeds and London, 1991). With *No One Sees the Video*, London, Hern, 1991.

Radio Plays: *Three Attempted Acts*, 1985; *Six Figures at the Base of the Crucifixion*, 1986.

* * *

In the short story *Stage Kiss*, Martin Crimp's narrator, a well-known actor in middle age, visits the wife from whom he is "notoriously" divorced:

The last thing my wife says to me is "Are you happy?" to which I reply "Are you?". In the theatre, these lines could prove unplayable, and I'd suggest a cut.

And yet it is in the discomforting area uncovered by this fundamental question and evasive answer that the action of Crimp's plays is developed. The appurtenances of comfort are all in place—television sets, cassette recorders, microwaves—but they are at best a distraction from, at worst a substitute for, self-recognition. The emotional hollowness of the Thatcherite society of the 1980's is exposed catastrophically to the audience, whilst the characters in the play (those who survive the violation) struggle to keep their eyes closed to it.

Crimp characteristically sprinkles the closely observed dialogue of his plays with "faint laughs" and disconcerting pauses, enforcing a recognition of the unsaid beneath the generally civilized discourse of which the plays are composed. In *Dealing with Clair*, the ostensible subject is usually the house which Mike and Liz, a monumentally unpleasant pair of libidinous yuppies, are trying to sell. Clair is their young estate agent, already inured to avarice and deception but not yet corrupted by it. Patronized by both the vendors, she is an object of casual desire for Mike and of casual jealousy for Liz, but for the enigmatic cash-buyer James, desire is not enough. *Dealing with Clair* relates unavoidably to the disappearance (presumed dead) in 1986 of a young estate agent, Suzy Lamplugh. More significant theatrically is the brilliantly sinister scene in which the solitary James conducts a soupy telephone conversation with Clair's mother while sitting on Clair's bed, emptying her handbag. With Clair and the cash-buyer both gone, the vendors are pleased to learn from a colleague of Clair's that the house has been undervalued.

The craftsmanship of *Dealing with Clair*, its use of repetition and the aural *leitmotif* of train-sounds, is unobtrusive. In *Play with Repeats*, the playwright's craft is placed in the foreground. As he might have been in one of J.B. Priestley's time-plays, Tony Steadman is given a chance to replay two crucial incidents in his unimpressive life. Unsurprisingly, he makes a worse show of it second time round. The play is more interesting for its creation and study of a casualty of competitive values than for its theatrical trickery. Tony pines for affection but earns none. He begins the play as a buttonholing pub bore, a role in which, on the reprise of his life, he is stabbed to death. His disappearance, like that of Clair in the earlier play, makes little difference to his workmates.

The self-conscious theatricality of *Play with Repeats* suggests some striving after effect. In *No One Sees the Video*, message and medium are finely synchronised. Crimp himself thinks of it as a "post-consumer play . . . it describes a world in which the equation of consumption with happiness is no longer debated, but is simply as axiomatic to everyday life as Newtonian mechanics."

Intelligent and independent though she is, Liz is drawn into the confidence trickery of market research. The question of whether she can survive without self-hatred remains open at the end of the play. Crimp's ear for the quirks and blandnesses of contemporary speech is fully displayed. Under the barrage of consumerist interrogation and the intimidating technology of video-recording, a sense of personal identity proves fragile. *No One Sees the Video* is a powerful documenting of our times.

Liz's troublesome teenage daughter Joanna is more resistant to the blandishments of consumerism than anyone else. A concern, tinged with anger, for the new generation is a feature of Crimp's work. The off-stage crying of the daughter of Liz and Mike in *Dealing with Clair* signals the self-absorption of her repulsive parents. The future of even a daughter of privilege is bleak. For Sharon in *Getting Attention*, the story is one of abuse culminating, we have to assume, in death. This is a fine and deeply disturbing play. The setting is a block of South London flats, from any one of which the sounds that emanate eerily implicate the others. The configuration of the stage contributes crucially to the action. The main area is the interior of the flat in which Carol lives with her four-year-old daughter Sharon and her common-law husband, Nick. They have a patch of garden, in which Carol sunbathes and Nick does body-building exercises. At the bottom of the garden, where it stretches out into the audience, the invisible Sharon is sometimes allowed to play. From the balcony running alongside the flats above, the lonely Bob will look at the scantily dressed Carol and the lonely Milly will try to warn her that Sharon is eating mud. Most of the time, though, Sharon is locked in her room. The concrete evidence of her existence is the light that shows above her door when she is trying to attract her mother's attention. But the play is full of noises. Bob, drinking alone, falls over in his flat (or is it Nick dealing with Sharon?). Nick and Carol make love; Bob listens to them and to the birds scratching in his chimney (though this scratching, we will eventually learn, is Sharon's sad attempt to attract attention). Every Friday, Nick brings for Carol some new gadget for home comfort and when the scratching stops, Sharon is probably dead.

—Peter Thomson

CRISTOFER, Michael. Pseudonym for Michael Procaccino. American. Born in White Horse, New Jersey, 22 January 1945. Educated at Catholic University, Washington, D.C., 1962–65; American University, Beirut, 1968–69. Recipient: Los Angeles Drama Critics Circle award, for acting, 1973, for playwriting, 1975; Pulitzer prize, 1977; Tony award, 1977; Obie award, for acting, 1980. Agent: Joyce Ketay Agency, 334 West 39th Street, New York, New York 10024, U.S.A.

PUBLICATIONS

Plays

The Mandala (produced Philadelphia, 1968).
Plot Counter Plot (produced New York, 1971).
Americomedia (produced New York, 1973).
The Shadow Box (produced Los Angeles, 1975; New York, 1977; London, 1979). New York, French, 1977.
Ice (produced Los Angeles, 1976; New York, 1979).
Black Angel (produced Los Angeles, 1978; New York, 1982; London, 1990). New York, Dramatists Play Service, 1984.
C.C. Pyle and the Bunyon Derby (produced Gambier, Ohio, 1978).
The Lady and the Clarinet (produced Los Angeles, 1980; New York, 1983; London, 1989). New York, Dramatists Play Service, 1985.
Love Me Or Leave Me, adaptation of the screenplay by Isobel Lennart and Daniel Fuchs (produced Woodstock, New York, 1989).

Screenplays: *Falling in Love*, 1985; *The Witches of Eastwick*, 1987.

*

Theatrical Activities:
Director: **Plays**—*Candida* by Shaw, New York, 1981; *Forty-Deuce* by Alan Bowne, New York, 1981.
Actor: **Plays**—roles at the Arena Stage, Washington, D.C., 1967–68, Theatre of Living Arts, Philadelphia, 1968, and Beirut Repertory Company, Lebanon, 1968–69; in *Yegor Bulichov* by Gorky, New Haven, Connecticut, 1970–71; Jules in *The Justice Box* by Michael Robert Davis, New York, 1971; *The Tooth of Crime* by Sam Shepard, Los Angeles, 1973; *Ajax* by Sophocles, Los Angeles, 1974; Colin in *Ashes* by David Rudkin, Los Angeles, 1976; *The Three Sisters* by Chekhov, Los Angeles, 1976; *Savages* by Christopher Hampton, Los Angeles; Trofimov in *The Cherry Orchard* by Chekhov, New York, 1976; Charlie in *Conjuring an Event* by Richard Nelson, New York, 1978; title role in *Chinchilla* by Robert David MacDonald, New York, 1979. **Films**—*An Enemy of the People*, 1976; *The Little Drummer Girl*, 1984. **Television**—*Sandburg's Lincoln*, 1975; *Crime Club*, 1975; *The Last of Mrs. Lincoln*, 1975; *The Entertainer*, 1976; *Knuckle*, 1976.

*   *   *

Michael Cristofer's development as a playwright, a development that includes *Plot Counter Plot*, *The Mandala*, and *Americomedia* and climaxed with *The Shadow Box* (Pulitzer Prize and Tony Award), is as instructive a lesson in how to become a playwright as *The Shadow Box* is an exciting addition to recent American drama. Like Harold Pinter and certain other contemporary dramatists, Cristofer is a gifted actor—and, with the Circle in the Square production of Shaw's *Candida*, director—and his own practical experience with theater is everywhere apparent in the play's skillful theatricality. In addition his association with the Mark Taper Forum and its director Gordon Davidson has provided a unifying center. The coalescence of three one-act plays through a series of workshops into a single contrapuntal drama, *The Shadow Box* is a process seldom possible without a secure producing environment.

The play, apparently based upon the terminal illness of two friends and Kubler-Ross's research into the state of mind of dying patients, demonstrates how the shadow of death intensifies life, merges individuality into community, and reduces times and places into a single here and now. Perhaps reflecting its origin as three draft one-act plays, *The Shadow Box* is built upon threes. Cristofer presents a trinity of characters, each surrounded by two other characters important in his personal life: Joe, a blue-collar worker, his wife, and adolescent son; Brian, an extravagant writer-intellectual, his lover, and his former wife; and Felicity, a lady of uncertain age, and both her spinster daughter and her dead daughter whose imaginary letters keep her alive. The play's set seems also to be in triplicate: three vacation cottages in the woods in a medically and psychologically controlled estate for the dying, each cottage with "*A front porch, a living room area, and a large kitchen area.*" But it is through the set's omnipresent visual image, and the constant cross-cutting this makes possible, that death's power to reduce diversity to communality and a common ground is constantly reiterated: the three cottages are in effect presented as one, and the trio of characters, who never actually meet, alternately inhabit, as the lights go down and come up, the various playing areas. The pastoral setting and the domesticity made possible by the cottage also unobtrusively place death in the context of external nature and the echoes of everyday life.

If Cristofer has a sure theatrical sense and a feeling for essential dimensions of the human experience, he also has a sense for the other indispensable ingredient of drama: language. Like a number of recent dramatists he has deliberately attempted to reverse the trend toward non-verbal theater—really the concern of dance—that characterized so much drama in the 1960's and early 1970's. The movement made important contributions but forgot the necessity to be memorably articulate. Cristofer's concern for verbal complexity is apparent immediately in the title *The Shadow Box*. In modern drama especially, titles index a play's concerns, and this one works on several complementary levels of reference. It refers to a late 19th-century device in which figures were superimposed against a chosen landscape or setting. The stationary quality of such scenes and their arbitrary arrangement express the predetermined situation of the terminally ill who are placed in a deliberately arranged environment. The term, which refers as well to a method of covering a motion picture screen so that film can be shown in daylight, expresses the play's analysis of the usually unseen, and the verb "to shadow box" connotes a fight, like the fight with death, which is ultimately an illusion. If the play begins with an emphasis upon words, it ends with an extraordinary "coda" in which life is celebrated in the face of death. The characters speak in choral fashion exchanging brief words and phrases and conclude with repetitions of the affirmative "Yes" and the final "This moment."

Ice is set in a cabin in Alaska and shows a trio of characters caught in a situation that symbolizes death in life. The subsequent *Black Angel* and *The Lady and the Clarinet* have now been seen in New York, but these somewhat counterpart plays do not sustain the promise of *The Shadow Box*. The former studies a man, Martin Engel, an apparent Nazi war criminal, and analyzes "hate," and the latter is a portrait of a woman, Luba, and her experiences with "love." Both plays interestingly suppress facts and narrative clarity and make use of simultaneous time, but in neither case are the central characters themselves created in enough depth or uniqueness to occasion or to support the playwright's relentless analyses of them. But these plays do continue Cristofer's important interest in the collaborative arts of theater.

—Gaynor F. Bradish

CROSS, (Alan) Beverley. British. Born in London, 13 April 1931; son of the theatrical manager George Cross and the actor Eileen Williams. Educated at the Nautical College, Pangbourne, Berkshire, 1944–47; Balliol College, Oxford, 1952–53. Served in the Royal Naval Reserve, 1944–48; British Army, 1948–50. Married 1) Elizabeth Clunies-Ross in 1955 (marriage dissolved), two daughters; 2) Gayden Collins in 1965 (marriage dissolved), one son; 3) the actress Maggie Smith in 1975. Seaman, Norwegian Merchant Service, 1950–52; actor, Shakespeare Memorial Theatre Company, 1954–56; production assistant for children's drama, BBC

Television, 1956. Drama consultant, Stratford Festival Theatre, Ontario, 1975–80. Recipient: Arts Council grant, 1957, and award, 1960. Agent: Curtis Brown Group, 162–168 Regent Street, London W1R 5TB, England.

PUBLICATIONS

Plays

One More River (produced Liverpool, 1958; London, 1959; New York, 1960).   London, Hart Davis, 1959.
The Singing Dolphin (for children), based on an idea by Kitty Black (produced Oxford, 1959; London, 1963).   With *The Three Cavaliers*, London, Hart Davis, 1960.
Strip the Willow (produced Nottingham and London, 1960). London, Evans, 1961.
The Three Cavaliers (for children; produced Birmingham, 1960).   With *The Singing Dolphin*, London, Hart Davis, 1960.
Belle; or, The Ballad of Dr. Crippen, with Wolf Mankowitz, music by Monty Norman (produced London, 1961).
Boeing-Boeing, adaptation of a play by Marc Camoletti (produced Oxford, 1961; London, 1962; New York, 1965). London, Evans, and New York, French, 1967.
Wanted on Voyage, adaptation of a play by Jacques Deval (produced Canterbury, 1962).
Half a Sixpence, music by David Heneker, adaptation of the novel *Kipps* by H.G. Wells (produced London, 1963; New York,   1965).   London,   Chappell,   1967;   Chicago, Dramatic Publishing Company, n.d.
The Mines of Sulphur, music by Richard Rodney Bennett (produced London, 1965; New York, 1968).   Published in *Plays of the Year 30*, London, Elek, 1965.
The Pirates and the Inca Gold (produced Sydney, 1966).
Jorrocks, music by David Heneker, adaptation of novels by R.S. Surtees (produced London, 1966).   London, Chappell, 1968.
All the King's Men (for children), music by Richard Rodney Bennett   (produced   Coventry   and   London,   1969). London, Universal Editions, 1969.
Phil the Fluter, with Donal Giltinan, music and lyrics by David Heneker and Percy French (produced London, 1969).
Victory, music by Richard Rodney Bennett, adaptation of the novel by Joseph Conrad (produced London, 1970). London, Universal Editions, 1970.
The Rising of the Moon, music by Nicholas Maw (produced Glyndebourne, Sussex, 1970).   London, Boosey and Hawkes, 1971.
Catherine Howard (televised 1970).   Published in *The Six Wives of Henry VIII*, edited by J.C. Trewin, London, Elek, 1972; revised version (produced York, 1972), London, French, 1973.
The Crickets Sing (produced Devizes, Wiltshire, 1971). London, Hutchinson, 1970.
The Owl on the Battlements (for children; produced Nottingham, 1971).
Where's Winkle? (for children; produced Liverpool, 1972).
The Great Society (produced London, 1974).
Hans Christian Andersen, with John Fearnley and Tommy Steele, music and lyrics by Frank Loesser (produced London, 1974; revised version produced London, 1976). New York, Music Theatre International, 1978.
The Mask of Orpheus, music by Nicholas Maw. London, Boosey and Hawkes, 1976.
Happy Birthday, adaptation of a play by Marc Camoletti

(produced Brighton, 1978; London, 1979). London, French, 1980.

Haworth: A Portrait of the Brontës (produced Stratford, Ontario, 1978; Birmingham, 1981). Toronto, Theatrebooks, 1978.

The Scarlet Pimpernel, adaptation of the novel by Baroness Orczy (produced Chichester, Sussex, and London, 1985). London, French, 1988.

Miranda, adaptation of a play by Goldoni (produced Chichester, 1987).

Screenplays: *Jason and the Argonauts*, with Jan Read, 1963; *The Long Ships*, with Berkely Mather, 1964; *Genghis Khan*, with Clarke Reynolds and Berkely Mather, 1965; *Half a Sixpence*, 1967; *The Donkey Rustlers*, 1969; *Mussolini: Ultimo Atto (Mussolini: The Last Act)*, with Carlo Lizzani, 1972; *Sinbad and the Eye of the Tiger*, 1977; *The Clash of the Titans*, 1981.

Television Plays: *The Nightwalkers*, from his own novel, 1960; *The Dark Pits of War*, 1960; *Catherine Howard*, 1970; *March On, Boys!*, 1975; *A Bill of Mortality*, 1975; *Miss Sugar Plum*, 1976 (Canada); *The World Turned Upside Down*, 1976 (USA).

Novels

Mars in Capricorn. London, Hart Davis, and Boston, Little Brown, 1955.

The Nightwalkers. London, Hart Davis, 1956; Boston, Little Brown, 1957.

*

Critical Studies: *Anger and After* by John Russell Taylor, London, Methuen, 1962, revised edition, 1969, as *The Angry Theatre*, New York, Hill and Wang, 1962, revised edition, 1969; introduction by J.C. Trewin to *The Mines of Sulphur*, in *Plays of the Year 30*, London, Elek, 1965.

Theatrical Activities:
Director: **Plays**—*Boeing-Boeing*, Sydney, 1964; *The Platinum Cat* by Roger Longrigg, London, 1965.
Actor: **Plays**—Agamemnon in *Troilus and Cressida*, Oxford, 1953; Soldier in *Othello*, Stratford-on-Avon, 1954; Mr. Fox in *Toad of Toad Hall* by A.A. Milne, London, 1954; Balthazar in *Much Ado about Nothing*, London, 1955; Herald in *King Lear*, London, 1955.

Beverley Cross comments:
Four main divisions of work: 1) for the commercial theatre, viz., books for musicals, boulevard comedies (i.e., *Boeing-Boeing, Half a Sixpence*); 2) librettos for modern opera (i.e., *The Mines of Sulphur, The Rising of the Moon*); 3) comedies and librettos for children (i.e., *The Three Cavaliers, All the King's Men, The Owl on the Battlements*); 4) fantasy movies (i.e., *Jason and the Argonauts, The Clash of the Titans*, etc).
Since 1969 has lived mostly abroad—in Greece, France, the US, and Canada—working on 4).

* * *

Beverley Cross has become best known as a writer of books for popular musicals (*Half a Sixpence, Jorrocks*) and of librettos for operas (*Victory, The Rising of the Moon*). He has also translated a highly successful boulevard farce (*Boeing-Boeing*), contributed one of the better episodes to a highly successful television series, *The Six Wives of Henry VIII* (*Catherine Howard*), written several lively, if less obviously

successful, plays for children, and a small number of commercially unsuccessful plays for adults. What generalisations can be made on the basis of such a spread of work?

First, that at his best he is capable of writing a vigorous, muscular, masculine dialogue which many more pretentious writers might envy. Second, that he is particularly interested in a spirit of adventure that (he feels) no longer exists in the contemporary world, and, consequently, in the character of the adventurer himself. It is significant that many of his works are set in other periods: the light children's play, *The Singing Dolphin*, among pirates in the 18th century, the serious opera, *The Mines of Sulphur*, in a remote country house at about the same time. This latter work, with its forceful language and vivid portrayal of a murderer who traps a troupe of wandering actors and is then trapped by them, shows Cross at his strongest. Another work is set in the future:

No planes to spoil the view. No trippers to litter the grass. No stinking petrol fumes to poison the air. No silly women to bitch away your time with their gossip and intrigue. Nothing to read, nothing to see. Complete freedom for the first time in my life. It's wonderful!

That is spoken by a character in *Strip the Willow*, a rather inconclusive quasi-Shavian comedy of ideas involving a tiny group of survivors of nuclear desolation, deep in the English countryside, living on their wits while the Russians and Americans divide the world between them; but the sentiment could be Cross's own.

He has written only one artistically successful play for adults; and that is his first, *One More River*, which occurs (characteristically) in a ship moored in a backwater on another continent and involves (characteristically) a mutiny. The seamen, among whom egalitarian notions have been circulating, turn on an unpopular officer and hang him, on false suspicion of having caused the death of one of their number. But they haven't the ability to exercise power, and are ignominiously forced to get an apprentice officer to navigate them upriver. The story is excitingly told, and some of the characterisation, notably of a self-satisfied, popularity-seeking bosun, is as good as some of it is melodramatic; but what makes the play interesting is its unfashionable viewpoint. Carefully, logically, it suggests that absolute democracy is mob-rule: some men are superior to others, and the others must submit to their authority. It is, of course, possible to pick holes in the argument as it emerges, for instance by pointing out that Cross does not face the possibility that the seaman's apparent inferiority may be less innate than the result of an unjust environment; but the achievement stands. *One More River* is one of the very few intelligent right-wing plays that the modern theatre has produced.

—Benedict Nightingale

_____

CROWLEY, Mart. American. 1935–1991.
See 4th edition, 1988.

_____

CURNOW, Allen. New Zealander. Born in 1911.
See 3rd edition, 1982.

_____

CURTIS, Jackie. American. 1947–1985.
See 3rd edition, 1982.

_____

D

DANIELS, Sarah. British. Born in London in 1957. Writer-in-residence, Royal Court Theatre, London, 1984. Recipient: George Devine award, 1983. Agent: Judy Daish Associates, 83 Eastbourne Mews, London W2 6LQ, England.

PUBLICATIONS

Plays

Penumbra (produced Sheffield, 1981).
Ripen Our Darkness (produced London, 1981). With *The Devil's Gateway*, London, Methuen, 1986.
Ma's Flesh Is Grass (produced Sheffield, 1981).
The Devil's Gateway (produced London, 1983). With *Ripen Our Darkness*, London, Methuen, 1986.
Masterpieces (produced Manchester and London, 1983). London, Methuen, 1984; revised version (produced London, 1984), 1984, revised version, 1986.
Neaptide (produced London, 1986). London, Methuen, 1986.
Byrthrite (produced London, 1986). London, Methuen, 1987.
The Gut Girls (produced London, 1988). London, Methuen, 1989.
Beside Herself (produced London, 1990). London, Methuen, 1990.
Head-Rot Holiday (produced London, 1992).

* * *

Sarah Daniels has been accused of many things, but never of writing boring plays. There are some critics who find her work alarming in its representations of strong, confused, complicated, or angry women. Daniels's plays rarely portray strong men, unless we count men who abuse their positions of power. In this, she has been accused of misconstruing reality, of allowing her "feminist anger" to stand in the way of writing "good theatre." But Daniels's work is not purposefully angry or intentionally controversial in critical terms.

One suspects that a good deal of the critical alarm with which some of Daniels's work has been received is a reaction to the centrality of women in the plays and to Daniels's style, which tends to be informed by street-smart rather than academic ideas about aesthetic standards. Yet Daniels's plays need no apology, for her work is highly innovative in its self-consciously radical approach to the representation of social issues of relevance to her audiences. Daniels's work is powerful: sometimes raw, sometimes unpleasantly close to reality. Her writing is fuelled by her awareness of the complexity of life in the modern world, of different forms of sexual and racial discrimination, and of class difference. But most importantly, her writing is fuelled by two qualities rare in contemporary playwriting: a penchant for black humour, and a strength and depth of vision—unacademic, straightforward,

biased, and determined—which allows Daniels to touch on subjects which others tend to gloss over or avoid altogether.

Daniels's work is often controversial, centering on themes such as pornography and violence (*Masterpieces*), rewriting of myth and reviewing of archetypal images of women (*Ripen Our Darkness*), male appropriation of women's bodies in the birthing process (*Byrthrite*), and the rights of lesbian mothers (*Neaptide*).

The best known and most controversial of her plays is *Masterpieces*, a play which deals with the issue of pornography. The central character is Rowena, a woman who watches a snuff film and who is so upset by it that she cannot separate the brutal sexual murder she has witnessed on the screen and the threat of real violence outside the cinema. When a stranger accosts her in the station, she reacts in automatic defense and shoves him; he dies on the subway line. The play shifts back and forth between exchanges with Rowena, her partner, and friends. All have different experiences of pornography, and all have difficulty seeing the issue objectively. Finally, Rowena is taken to trial for the murder of the stranger. She does not deny shoving him, but cites legal precedents of men found guilty of murder being let off with excuses such as "nagging wives." At the end of the play, Rowena describes the snuff film in graphic detail to the policewoman who waits with her for the verdict. Her final words are chilling:

> Rowena: I don't want anything to do with men who have knives or whips or men who look at photos of women tied and bound, or men who say relax and enjoy it. Or men who tell misogynist jokes.
> *Blackout.*

Masterpieces is unsettling, not only because it deals with the issue of pornography but because it challenges the distinction between soft and hard porn, and—in Rowena's final words—it suggests that the continuum from sexist jokes to real sexual violence against women is a real and dangerous one. In this way, the play depicts and challenges aspects of contemporary controversy over the pornography issue. Years after its first production *Masterpieces* is frequently produced, particularly by student and community theatre groups using it as an impetus to academic debate and social action.

Neaptide is, after *Masterpieces*, Daniels's best known and most important play, not least because it is the only play dealing with the subject of lesbianism to be produced at Britain's National Theatre. But more important is the play itself. In *Neaptide*, Daniels tells the story of Claire, a woman who finds it necessary to hide her sexual identity in order to protect her job and thereby support her young daughter. Claire is a teacher in a small secondary school, torn between defending the rights of a few lesbian pupils and remaining silent, thereby keeping the secret of her own sexuality from her peers. While she is involved in a potential child custody case, the pressure to "appear normal" is great. Meanwhile, she reads the myth of Persephone. The ending of the play is optimistic, but not overly so. Only individual women transcend such limitations: the lesbian pupils are saved when the principal of the school is embarrassed into a confession of her own homosexuality, the mother comes out of the proverbial closet and decides to fight for her child. The myth functions as a convenient analogue to contemporary problems, but not as an over-simplified model of a social corrective, nor as an all-encompassing statement about the function of roles.

Sarah Daniels often conducts research for her plays: for *Masterpieces*, she read feminist literature on the subject of pornography; for *Byrthrite* she investigated the role of mid-wives in the 17th century; for *The Gut Girls* she did local research into the history of women's work in the Deptford slaughterhouses. Before writing *Beside Herself*, Daniels contacted survivors of child sexual abuse, which is the play's underlying theme. *Beside Herself* is Daniels's latest full-length stage play, and her least realistic. It extends the earlier experimentation with myth and history into a complicated weaving of time frames, fiction, and "reality" in the world of one play. Her writing has taken another turn, however, in her most recent project, *Head-Rot Holiday*, a play for Clean Break Theatre Company involving the stories of women ex-prisoners and their children.

In all her plays, as in *Masterpieces*, Sarah Daniels takes issues of real importance to women's lives and puts them centre stage. Her plays are not easily pigeonholed: they don't quite fit the canon of great drama, and are difficult to argue for as replacements for any of the so-called classics on university reading lists. But they teach more about the power of the theatre and of the written word than do many of the texts found in the average classroom. Her work is difficult and controversial in the most positive, change-oriented sense. She is a playwright of courage and considerable talent.

—Lizbeth Goodman

DARKE, Nick. British. Born in Wadebridge, Cornwall, 29 August 1948. Educated at Newquay Grammar School, Cornwall; Rose Bruford College, Sidcup, Kent, 1967–70, diploma 1970. Has two sons. Actor in repertory, Belfast, 1970; actor and director, Victoria Theatre, Stoke-on-Trent, Staffordshire, 1971–79. Recipient: George Devine award, 1979. Agent: Casarotto Ramsay Ltd., National House, 60–66 Wardour Street, London W1V 3HP. Address: St. Julians, Sevenoaks, Kent TN15 0RX, England.

PUBLICATIONS

Plays

Mother Goose (pantomime; also director: produced Stoke-on-Trent, 1977).
Never Say Rabbit in a Boat (produced Stoke-on-Trent, 1978).
Landmarks (produced Chester and London, 1979).
A Tickle on the River's Back (produced London, 1979).
Summer Trade (produced Ilfracombe, Devon, 1979).
High Water (produced Newcastle upon Tyne and London, 1980). Published in *Plays Introduction*, London, Faber, 1984.
Say Your Prayers, music by Andrew Dickson (produced Plymouth and London, 1981).

The Catch (produced London, 1981).
The Lowestoft Man (produced on tour, 1982).
The Body, music by Guy Woolfenden (produced London, 1983). London, Methuen, 1983.
Cider with Rosie, adaptation of the work by Laurie Lee (produced Manchester, 1983).
The Earth Turned Inside Out (produced St. Austell, Cornwall, 1984).
Bud (produced Newcastle upon Tyne and London, 1985). Included in *Ting Tang Mine and Other Plays*, 1987.
The Oven Glove Murders (produced London, 1986).
The Dead Monkey (produced London, 1986). Included in *Ting Tang Mine and Other Plays*, 1987.
Ting Tang Mine (produced St. Austell, Cornwall, 1987; revised version produced London, 1987). Included in *Ting Tang Mine and Other Plays*, 1987.
Ting Tang Mine and Other Plays (includes *The Dead Monkey*, *Bud*). London, Methuen, 1987.
Campesinos (produced Stratford-on-Avon, 1989).
Kissing the Pope (produced London, 1989). Included in *Kissing the Pope: A Play and a Diary for Nicaragua*, London, Hern, 1990.

Radio Plays: *Foggy Anniversary*, 1979; *Lifeboat*, 1981.

Television Play: *Farmers Arms*, 1983.

*

Theatrical Activities:
Director: **Plays**—Victoria Theatre, Stoke-on-Trent: *Mother Goose*, *Man Is Man* by Brecht, *The Miser* by Molière, *Absurd Person Singular* by Alan Ayckbourn, *The Scarlet Pimpernel*, and *A Cuckoo in the Nest* by Ben Travers, 1977–79.
Actor: roles in more than 50 plays, Victoria Theatre, Stoke-on-Trent.

Nick Darke comments:
I consider my seven years as an actor to have been an apprenticeship for writing plays. By appearing in over 50 productions of new plays, classics, documentaries, children's plays, and community road-shows I learned firsthand the difference between good and bad dialogue, how to create characters and construct a world for the play to exist in. Most of my plays make people laugh, but I try to make an audience question its laughter. I have a low boredom threshold, and my interest in my plays lasts for exactly as long as it takes me to write them. I have strong ideas about how they should be cast and directed, and I watch them in performance to see how the audience reacts. After that my interest wanes and the next one has to be different in every respect to the last. I write quickly: the quicker it's written, the better the play. I think about a play for far longer than it takes me to write it. I type as fast as my brain works, so I dispense with the longhand stage and work straight onto the keyboard. I read my work out loud as I write it. For this reason I have to work entirely alone and out of earshot. I don't just mouth what I've written, if a scene demands decibels I supply them. If it's funny, I laugh. To see an audience laugh at something as much as I did when I first thought of it is a pleasure only another playwright could understand. I judge the success of my plays from the audience's response. My agent reads and sees my work, and I disregard her advice at my peril; she is my most valuable critic. I don't know what is a good play and what isn't. I don't know what makes some people like a play and others not. Some nights a whole audience will dislike a play, the next night they'll love it, with no perceptible change in the per-

formance. My plays tend to be ambiguous, and because the style alters with each one, nobody knows what to expect. This makes for hair-raising volatility which I don't like, but can't help. My advice to a budding playwright: Cultivate your sense of rhythm, and never go into rehearsal without a good ending.

* * *

Nick Darke, who started his theatrical career as an actor at the Victoria Theatre, Stoke-on-Trent, seems to launch himself into writing plays rather as if he were working on new roles. Energetic, versatile, imaginative, inventive, eclectic, insatiably hungry for identifications which let him disappear into a disguise, he slips unrecognisably from one style, one period, one setting to another. *The Dead Monkey* is set in contemporary California, *Ting Tang Mine* goes back to an early 19th-century Cornish copper-mining community, *A Tickle on the River's Back* takes place on a Thames barge, while the setting for *The Oven Glove Murders* is a Soho film production company. Darke lodges himself in contrasting idioms like an actor who is good at accents.

His plays, almost without exception, contain sequences which are extremely suspenseful, and others which are extremely funny, but even in his best plays, such as *The Body* and *The Dead Monkey*, the writing sometimes sinks too far below the level he is capable of achieving. The funniest sequences in *The Body* occur in the first half, which climaxes in a hilarious scene involving a muddy, half-naked corpse, a farmer who is also muddy and half-naked because he is impersonating the corpse, a cat which has just been strangled, a rat-trap, an old man wearing a gas-mask, an old woman who believes she may have been touched by divinity, three farmers who speak verse in unison and a policeman who is trying to arrest all the villagers simultaneously. Less amusing and more suspenseful, the second half of the play, set in an American airbase, works towards a climax that centres on the probability of a nuclear explosion as a young Cornish farmer, brainwashed into believing he is an American soldier, brandishes a loaded machine gun and hesitates about whether to obey the orders of a sane sergeant or a demented lieutenant who has been tied up and blindfolded but not—this was the sergeant's mistake—gagged.

The plot also introduces a rector who dresses as a Mandarin, realising that his parishioners pay no more attention to him than they would to a Chinaman. They do listen if he harangues them in Chinese, but all this is not entirely irrelevant to the plot because it convinces the psychopathic lieutenant (who suspects reds under the unlikeliest of beds) that Chinese infiltration is converting the villagers to Maoism. The solution is to ask them whether they're Communist and shoot them if they deny it.

Darke's hostility to nuclear weapons, Americans, policemen, soldiers, and capitalism is rather generalised, and his writing sags under its heavy burden of literary influences and bizarre jokes. The most obvious debt is to Brecht, who was himself indebted to Kipling for the three soldiers in *Mann ist Mann* who brainwash a civilian into taking on the identity of a missing comrade. The play also seems to have been influenced by the Auden and Isherwood of *The Dog Beneath the Skin*, by the Stoppard of *After Magritte*, and by the T.S. Eliot of the verse plays.

The Dead Monkey is a funnier, more consistent play, more accomplished, less patchy, less eclectic, though the rhythms of Tennessee Williams and Edward Albee are sometimes audible. We also feel that, as in some of the morbid *coups de théâtre* of *The Body*, Darke is trying to make us shudder. The

play opens with the monkey dead on the table. Later on in the act we learn that Dolores, the wife of an unsuccessful commercial traveller, has been supplementing her income by performing sexual tricks with the monkey. Towards the end of the act the monkey, which may have died from the physical strain, is cooked and eaten by husband and wife.

It must be conceded though, that even if Darke is trying too hard to shock, he is succeeding better than any young playwright since Stephen Poliakoff and that the play is still richer in surprising dramatic twists than in shock effects. The plot pulls the couple through a taxing series of changing situations so that, as in a play by Strindberg, they each become almost like a new person as they react to changes in their partner. Lingering love gradually gives way to implacable hatred, but the savagery of Hank's physical attack on Dolores takes us by surprise. Eventually we see her lying dead on the table in the same position as the monkey, but the aggressive husband then starts talking to his dead wife, apologising, pleading with her to come back, reminding her of what she said after the animal's death—perhaps it was looking down on them. Perhaps she is now, while he pulls the dead body off the table and clings to it as if dancing.

Like the imaginary child in Albee's *Who's Afraid of Virginia Woolf?* the monkey and the Macedonian curly pig they adopt to replace it are emblems of what is missing from their relationship, but the borrowing is unimportant in comparison with the success achieved in the sharply written sequences of marital bickering and in the chemical changes that occur in Dolores's personality and in the relationship when a well-paid job lifts her into a position financially superior to Hank's. An acute observer of the effects that money and social prestige have on sexual relationships, Darke is already starting to take his eclecticism into his stride.

—Ronald Hayman

———

DAVIES, (William) Robertson. Canadian. Born in Thamesville, Ontario, 28 August 1913. Educated at Upper Canada College; Queen's University, Kingston, Ontario; Balliol College, Oxford, 1936–38, B.Litt. 1938. Married Brenda Mathews in 1940; three daughters. Teacher and actor, Old Vic Theatre School and Repertory Company, London, 1938–40; literary editor, *Saturday Night*, Toronto, 1940–42; editor and publisher, *Examiner*, Peterborough, Ontario, 1942–63. Since 1960 professor of English, since 1962 master of Massey College, and since 1981 founding master, University of Toronto. Governor, Stratford Shakespeare Festival, Ontario, 1953–71; member, Board of Trustees, National Arts Centre. Recipient: Ottawa Drama League prize, 1946, 1947; Dominion Drama Festival prize, for play, 1948, 1949, for directing, 1949; Leacock medal, 1955; Lorne Pierce medal, 1961; Governor-General's award, for fiction, 1973; World Fantasy Convention award, for fiction, 1984; City of Toronto Book award, 1986; Canadian Authors' Association award, for fiction, 1986; Banff Centre award, 1986; Toronto Arts Lifetime Achievement award, 1986; U.S. National Arts Club Medal of Honor, 1987 (first Canadian recipient); Scottish Arts Council Neil Gunn International fellowship, 1988; Canadian Conference of the Arts diplome d'honneur, 1988; Canada Council Molson prize, 1988. LL.D.: University of Alberta, Edmonton, 1957; Queen's

University, 1962; University of Manitoba, Winnipeg, 1972; University of Toronto, 1981. D.Litt.: McMaster University, Hamilton, Ontario, 1959; University of Windsor, Ontario, 1971; York University, Toronto, 1973; Mount Allison University, Sackville, New Brunswick, 1973; Memorial University of Newfoundland, St. John's, 1974; University of Western Ontario, London, 1974; McGill University, Montreal, 1974; Trent University, Peterborough, Ontario, 1974; University of Lethbridge, Alberta, 1981; University of Waterloo, Ontario, 1981; University of British Columbia, Vancouver, 1983; University of Santa Clara, California, 1985; Trinity College, Dublin, 1990; University of Oxford, 1991. D.C.L.: Bishop's University, Lennoxville, Quebec, 1967. LL.D.: University of Calgary, Alberta, 1975; University of Prince Edward Island, Charlottetown, 1989. D.H.L.: Rochester University, Rochester, New York, 1983; Dowling College, New York, 1992. D.S.L.: Thornloe College, University of Sudbury, Ontario, 1988. Fellow, Balliol College, Oxford, 1986, and Trinity College, Toronto, 1987. Fellow, Royal Society of Canada, 1967, and Royal Society of Literature, 1984; honorary member, American Academy, 1981 (first Canadian elected). Companion, Order of Canada, 1972; Order of Ontario, 1988. Agent: Curtis Brown, 10 Astor Place, New York, New York 10003, U.S.A. Address: Massey College, 4 Devonshire Place, Toronto, Ontario M5S 2E1, Canada.

PUBLICATIONS

Plays

A Play of Our Lord's Nativity (produced Peterborough, Ontario, 1946).
Overlaid (produced Peterborough, Ontario, 1947). Included in *Eros at Breakfast and Other Plays*, 1949.
The Voice of the People (produced Montreal, 1948). Included in *Eros at Breakfast and Other Plays*, 1949.
At the Gates of the Righteous (produced Peterborough, Ontario, 1948). Included in *Eros at Breakfast and Other Plays*, 1949.
Hope Deferred (produced Montreal, 1948). Included in *Eros at Breakfast and Other Plays*, 1949.
Fortune, My Foe (produced Kingston, Ontario, 1948). Toronto, Clarke Irwin, 1949.
Eros at Breakfast (produced Ottawa, 1948). Included in *Eros at Breakfast and Other Plays*, 1949.
Eros at Breakfast and Other Plays. Toronto, Clarke Irwin, 1949.
At My Heart's Core (produced Peterborough, Ontario, 1950). Toronto, Clarke Irwin, 1950.
King Phoenix (produced Peterborough, Ontario, 1950). Included in *Hunting Stuart and Other Plays*, 1972.
A Masque of Aesop (for children; produced Toronto, 1952). Toronto, Clarke Irwin, 1952; in *Five New One-Act Plays*, edited by James A. Stone, London, Harrap, 1954.
A Jig for the Gypsy (produced Toronto and London, 1954). Toronto, Clarke Irwin, 1954.
Hunting Stuart (produced Toronto, 1955). Included in *Hunting Stuart and Other Plays*, 1972.
Leaven of Malice, adaptation of his own novel (as *Love and Libel*, produced Toronto and New York, 1960; revised version, as *Leaven of Malice*, produced Toronto, 1973). Published in *Canadian Drama* (Waterloo, Ontario), vol. 7, no. 2, 1981.
A Masque of Mr. Punch (for children; produced Toronto, 1962). Toronto, Oxford University Press, 1963.

Centennial Play, with others (produced Lindsay, Ontario, 1967). Ottawa, Centennial Commission, 1967.
Hunting Stuart and Other Plays (includes *King Phoenix and General Confession*), edited by Brian Parker. Toronto, New Press, 1972.
Brothers in the Black Art (televised 1974). Vancouver, Alcuin Society, 1981.
Question Time (produced Toronto, 1975). Toronto, Macmillan, 1975.
Pontiac and the Green Man (produced Toronto, 1977).
Dr. Danon's Cure (opera for children), music by Derek Holman (produced Toronto, 1982).

Television Play: *Brothers in the Black Art*, 1974.

Novels

The Salterton Trilogy. Toronto and London, Penguin, 1986.
  Tempest-Tost. Toronto, Clarke Irwin, 1951; London, Chatto and Windus, and New York, Rinehart, 1952.
  Leaven of Malice. Toronto, Clarke Irwin, 1954; London, Chatto and Windus, and New York, Scribner, 1955.
  A Mixture of Frailties. Toronto, Macmillan, London, Weidenfeld and Nicolson, and New York, Scribner, 1958.
The Deptford Trilogy. Toronto and London, Penguin, 1983.
  Fifth Business. Toronto, Macmillan, and New York, Viking Press, 1970; London, Macmillan, 1971.
  The Manticore. Toronto, Macmillan, and New York, Viking Press, 1972; London, Macmillan, 1973.
  World of Wonders. Toronto, Macmillan, 1975; New York, Viking Press, 1976; London, W.H. Allen, 1977.
The Cornish Trilogy. Toronto, London, and New York, Penguin, 1991.
  The Rebel Angels. Toronto, Macmillan, 1981; New York, Viking Press, and London, Allen Lane, 1982.
  What's Bred in the Bone. Toronto, Macmillan, and New York, Viking, 1985; London, Viking, 1986.
  The Lyre of Orpheus. London, Viking, 1988; New York, Viking, 1989.
Murther and Walking Spirits. Toronto, McClelland and Stewart, New York, Viking, and London, Sinclair Stevenson, 1991.

Short Stories

High Spirits: A Collection of Ghost Stories. Toronto and London, Penguin, 1982; New York, Viking Press, 1983.

Other

Shakespeare's Boy Actors. London, Dent, 1939; New York, Salloch, 1941.
Shakespeare for Young Players: A Junior Course. Toronto, Clarke Irwin, 1942.
The Papers of Samuel Marchbanks (revised editions). Toronto, Irwin, 1985; New York, Viking, 1986; London, Viking, 1987.
  The Diary of Samuel Marchbanks. Toronto, Clarke Irwin, 1947.
  The Table Talk of Samuel Marchbanks. Toronto, Clarke Irwin, 1949; London, Chatto and Windus, 1951.
  Marchbanks' Almanack. Toronto, McClelland and Stewart, 1967.
Renown at Stratford: A Record of the Shakespearean Festival in Canada 1953, with Tyrone Guthrie. Toronto, Clarke Irwin, 1953.

Twice Have the Trumpets Sounded: A Record of the Stratford Shakespearean Festival in Canada 1954, with Tyrone Guthrie. Toronto, Clarke Irwin, 1954; London, Blackie, 1955.

Thrice the Brinded Cat Hath Mew'd: A Record of the Stratford Shakespearean Festival in Canada 1955, with Tyrone Guthrie. Toronto, Clarke Irwin, 1955.

A Voice from the Attic. New York, Knopf, 1960; revised edition, New York and London, Penguin, 1990.

The Personal Art: Reading to Good Purpose. London, Secker and Warburg, 1961.

Stephen Leacock. Toronto, McClelland and Stewart, 1970.

What Do You See in the Mirror? Agincourt, Ontario, Book Society of Canada, 1970.

The Revels History of Drama in English VI: 1750–1880, with others. London, Methuen, 1975.

One Half of Robertson Davies: Provocative Pronouncements on a Wide Range of Topics. Toronto, Macmillan, 1977; New York, Viking Press, 1978.

The Enthusiasms of Robertson Davies, edited by Judith Skelton Grant. Toronto, McClelland and Stewart, 1979; New York and London, Penguin, 1991.

Robertson Davies, The Well-Tempered Critic: One Man's View of Theatre and Letters in Canada, edited by Judith Skelton Grant. Toronto, McClelland and Stewart, 1981.

The Mirror of Nature (lectures). Toronto, University of Toronto Press, 1983.

Conversations with Robertson Davies, edited by J. Madison Davis. Jackson, University Press of Mississippi, 1989.

Editor, *Feast of Stephen: An Anthology of Some of the Less Familiar Writings of Stephen Leacock*. Toronto, McClelland and Stewart, 1970; as *The Penguin Stephen Leacock*, London, Penguin, 1981.

*

Bibliography: by John Ryrie, in *The Annotated Bibliography of Canada's Major Authors 3* edited by Robert Lecker and Jack David, Downsview, Ontario, ECW Press, 1981.

Manuscript Collection: National Archives, Ottawa.

Critical Studies: *Robertson Davies* by Elspeth Buitenhuis, Toronto, Forum House, 1972; *4 Canadian Playwrights* by Mavor Moore, Toronto, Holt Rinehart, 1973; *Robertson Davies* by Patricia A. Morley, Agincourt, Ontario, Gage, 1977; "Robertson Davies Issue" of *Journal of Canadian Studies* (Peterborough, Ontario), February 1977, and of *Canadian Drama* (Waterloo, Ontario), vol. 7, no. 2, 1981; *Stage Voices* edited by Geraldine C. Anthony, Toronto, Doubleday, 1978; *Robertson Davies* by Judith Skelton Grant, Toronto, McClelland and Stewart, 1978; *Here and Now 1* edited by John Moss, Toronto, NC Press, 1979; "The Master of the Unseen World" by Judith Finlayson, in *Quest* (Toronto), vol. 8, no. 4, 1979; *Canadian Writers and Their Work* edited by Robert Lecker, Jack David, and Ellen Quigley, Downsview, Ontario, ECW Press, 1985; *Robertson Davies, Playwright: A Search for the Self on the Canadian Stage* by Susan Stone-Blackburn, Vancouver, University of British Columbia Press, 1985.

Theatrical Activities:
Actor: **Plays**—Lord Norfolk in *Traitor's Gate* by Morna Stuart, London, 1938; Stingo in *She Stoops to Conquer* by Oliver Goldsmith, London, 1939; Archbishop of Rheims in *Saint Joan* by Shaw, London, 1939; roles in *The Taming of the Shrew*, London, 1939.

Robertson Davies comments:

My plays are cast in the form of comedy because they are intended in general to be criticisms of society, even when they are set in an age other than our own; and, as I believe our age to be one of comedy and melodrama rather than one of tragedy, I have chosen to write plays that are comedies with a substantial melodramatic strain.

*   *   *

Although better known and certainly more widely acclaimed as a novelist and man of letters, Robertson Davies is one of Canada's foremost contemporary dramatists.

His earliest plays set the tone and style and introduced the themes that Davies has explored for almost 40 years. *Overlaid* and *The Voice of the People*, set in contemporary post-war Canada, *At the Gates of the Righteous*, set in upper Canada in 1860, and *Hope Deferred*, set in 17th-century Quebec, are gentle social satires attacking Canadian materialism, penchant for the utilitarian, and philistinism towards art, imagination, intellectualism—culture in general. All of these plays are short—one act in length—straightforward and essentially realistic in character portrayal, language, and structure.

Retaining the same satirical tone and realistic style, Davies elaborates on these themes in his first full-length play, *Fortune, My Foe*. The emigré puppeteer Szabo persists in pursuing his art despite rejection by and even ridicule from the Kingston establishment, but in so doing he encourages young Nicholas Hayward to remain in Canada rather than accepting a more lucrative offer from an American university. For Davies, Canadians may be narrow-minded and culturally malnourished, but there is promise in the younger generation. *At My Heart's Core*, set in upper Canada during the Rebellion of 1938, is a more complex and ambiguous play, but the conflict between practicality and imagination, science and art, cultural philistinism and cultural aspiration is a central theme. As the drunken Irish bard, Phelim, says, "We're the song birds that aren't wanted in this bitter land, where the industrious robins and the political crows get fat, and they not with a tuneful chirp among the lot of 'em."

With the founding of the Stratford Shakespearean Festival in 1953 and a general expansion of arts activities in the 1950's, Davies's attacks on Canadian cultural philistinism and provincialism became less creditable and relevant. In *A Jig for the Gypsy* he turned his attention to politics, the pretensions of the middle class, and the relationship between romantic love and marriage. Although set in Wales in 1885 and including among its cast of characters a gypsy fortune-teller and a Welsh conjuror, the dramatic situation, characters, and even particular lines are clearly intended to reflect contemporary Canadian attitudes and personalities.

As he notes in his preface to the play, romance and politics are not strange bedfellows:

The ambitions and actions of politicians, if one does not stand too near to them, are power-fully romantic, especially if they belong to a reform party with strong convictions about the perfectibility of mankind through political action. To me there is nothing odd about linking politics with fortune-telling in a play; they have been too often linked in reality, even in Canada.

The last sentence is a direct reference to Prime Minister Mackenzie King (1874–1950) who reportedly consulted fortune-tellers regularly.

Davies also has long been interested in mankind's inner life and especially in Jung's psychological theories about spiritual heredity or the "collective unconscious." He introduced these ideas in his early allegorical play *Eros at Breakfast*, subtitled "A Psychosomatic Interlude." Moreover, this play also revealed Davies's interest in dramatic techniques and forms that are more theatrical and less realistic, such as the morality play, the masque, and the extravaganza.

King Phoenix, for example, is an allegorical fantasy centering on the mythical Old King Cole; *Hunting Stuart* is a "romance of heredity" in which a contemporary Canadian civil servant, Henry Benedict Stuart, is transformed—transmigrated actually—into his illustrious ancestor, Bonnie Prince Charlie, with delightfully witty results; and *General Confession* is a historical comedy of ideas in which the main characters—Casanova, Voltaire, Cagliostro, and Amalie or the Ideal Beloved—served as Jung's archetypical *self*, *persona*, *shadow*, and *anima*. All three plays, furthermore, exploit the energy of the actor and the magic and spectacle inherent in theatrical presentation. *King Phoenix* features lavish, Druidical costumes, properties, settings, and ceremonies; *General Confession* includes magical transformations and appearances and an elaborate 18th-century mise-en-scène; while *Hunting Stuart*, to be effective, demands a certain histrionic virtuosity from the actor playing Stuart/Prince Charlie.

Davies's *A Masque of Aesop* and *A Masque of Mr. Punch*, modeled after Jonson's masques, and written for performance by the boys of Upper Canada College Preparatory School, employ a wide range of dramatic techniques and comic devices, including parody, satire, slapstick, song, farcical verse dialogue, and Punch and Judy shows. Though intended for amateur performance, they nevertheless maintain Davies's serious purpose in exposing pretensions both in art and life, while creating a vision of a better society achieved through inner peace and self-knowledge.

Leaven of Malice, adapted from his novel and subtitled "A Theatrical Extravaganza," while utilizing no formal scenery and few props, does include a number of masked figures (as in the Japanese *bunraku*) who manipulate elements of costuming and large printed signs. It also includes an elaborate five-part dream sequence and a spectacular wedding procession at the finale.

In *Question Time*, Davies attempted to combine or synthesize his social and political concerns with his interests in spiritual development. The central character, Peter MacAdam, is Canada's prime minister. He is the lone survivor of a plane crash in the Arctic Les Montagnes de Glace, and the action of the play takes place in his delirious mind as he is ministered to by an unorthodox, Edinburgh-trained Eskimo shaman. The central confrontation takes place in a fantastical mock parliament. This ironic, allegorical drama represents the self-examination of an individual and, in that the prime minister also represents Canada, of a nation. Davies, in a program note, wrote that the play was about "what power may do to a man and what that man in his turn does to the people around him and to the country he leads. . . . Canada is gravely misshaped by its reluctance to come to terms with its inmost self and to find that inmost self in its land. . . ."

Question Time also calls for fairly elaborate scenic spectacle, including a large television screen, various Arctic sound effects, the appearance of a gigantic bear, and the transformation of Les Montagnes de Glace into the Canadian House of Commons.

Davies's *Pontiac and the Green Man*, based loosely on the 1768 court martial of Major Robert Rogers (the Green Man of the title because he and his ranger regiment wore green jackets instead of the traditional British scarlet), also calls for an examination of Canadian individual and collective identity. It also is structured as a play-within-a-play, since excerpts from Rogers's own *Ponteach; or, The Savage of America* are staged during the trial.

Critical response to Davies's plays has been decidedly mixed. For example, Herbert Whittaker in the Toronto *Globe and Mail* called *Question Time* "a glittering polemic of a play," while Urjo Kareda in the Toronto *Star* labeled it "a disappointment" and "a disaster," but conceded that it was "a very grand, ambitious, and idiosyncratic disaster of the order that only Robertson Davies could have created . . . a failure with a master's signature on it." Similarly *Pontiac and the Green Man* was described by McKenzie Porter in the Toronto *Sun* as "a play full of Shavian paradox, with wit, profundity and grief, a play evoking sudden gusts of laughter, sudden chills of pity, a play rich in cutting satire on soldiers, lawyers, academics, actors, writers, women in general and even critics who, figuratively and literally, are seen to ride in the clouds." Bryan Johnson of the *Globe and Mail* labeled it "a hopeless muddle," while Gina Mallet of the *Star* walked out after two hours failing to find any "redeeming artistic importance."

These reactions to Davies's recent efforts are undoubtedly extreme, but his earlier plays also provoked varying critical responses. While many have admired his witty dialogue, original plots, strong characterizations, and thought-provoking themes, others have found his plays overwritten, over-literary, obscure, old-fashioned, sexist, and conservative.

The term most often applied to Davies's style is "Shavian" (or sometimes "Neo-Shavian"). Indeed, with his Celtic love of language, his interest in social and political ideas, his exploration of the life of the spirit, his ironic point of view, and his experimentations with various dramatic techniques and forms, there is much that Davies shares with Shaw. Davies concedes Shaw's influence (as well as Pinero's, Jonson's, and Goldsmith's), but he denies that he has ever consciously imitated a Shaw play. Davies has not written for the theatre since 1977—apart from his libretto for the children's opera *Dr. Danon's Cure*—preferring the novel to the play, and recognizing perhaps that his style of drama is unfashionable in present-day Canada.

In 1992, however, playwright and Stratford Festival literary manager Elliot Hayes adapted for the stage Davies's *Deptford Trilogy* of novels (*Fifth Business*, *The Manticore*, and *World of Wonders*). As *World of Wonders* this dramatic adaptation opened at the Stratford Festival and played in repertory as part of the 40th anniversary season—33 performances in all. The adaptation effectively adhered to the spirit of Davies's celebrated trilogy and to his penchant for theatricality. Davies publicly praised the adaptation as "admirably done," although in a sold-out lecture in Stratford he pointed out the differences between the novel and the play and advised spectators to enjoy both on their own merits.

Davies himself was lionized at the opening performance and *World of Wonders* drew large and appreciative audiences. But no matter how successful this production, it is not likely to draw Davies back to the theatre. It might, however, spark a re-examination of his plays of considerable theatricality, wit, power, and insight.

—Daniel J. Watermeier

————

DAVIS, Jack (Leonard). Australian; member of Bibbulmun tribe. Born in Perth, Western Australia, 11 March 1917.

Educated at Yarloop State School; Perth Technical College. Worked as a stockman in North West Australia; director, Aboriginal Centre, Perth, 1967–71; managing editor, Aboriginal Publications Foundation, 1972–77; joint editor, *Identity* magazine, Perth, 1973–79; teacher of creative writing, Murdoch University, Western Australia. Director and president, Aboriginal Advancement Council, 1967 and 1972; first chair, Aboriginal Lands Trust, 1971; president, Aboriginal Writers and Dramatists Association, 1980–84; member, Australia Council Aboriginal Arts Board, 1983–1988. Recipient: British Empire medal, 1977; Weickhardt award, 1980; Sidney Myer award, 1985; Australian Writers Guild award, 1986; BHP Bicentennial award, 1988; Federal creative fellowship, 1989; Ruth Adeney Koori award, 1992. D. Litt.: Murdoch University, 1985. A.M. (Member, Order of Australia), 1985. Address: 3 Little Howard Street, Fremantle, Western Australia 6160, Australia.

PUBLICATIONS

Plays

The Dreamers (produced 1973; revised version produced Perth, 1982; Portsmouth, Hampshire, 1987). With *Kullark (Home)*, Sydney, Currency Press, 1982.
Kullark (Home) (produced 1978). With *The Dreamers*, Sydney, Currency Press, 1982.
No Sugar (produced Perth, 1985). Sydney, Currency Press, 1986.
Honey Spot (for children; produced Adelaide, 1985).
Moorli and the Leprechaun (for children; produced 1986).
Barungin (Smell the Wind) (produced Perth, 1988). Sydney, Currency Press, 1989.
In Our Town (produced Perth, 1990). Sydney, Currency Perth, 1992.

Verse

The First-Born and Other Poems. Sydney and London, Angus and Robertson, 1970.
Jagardoo: Poems from Aboriginal Australia. Sydney, Methuen, 1977.
Black Life. St. Lucia, University of Queensland Press, 1992.

Other

Editor, with Bob Hodge, *Aboriginal Writing Today: Papers from the First National Conference of Aboriginal Writers*. Canberra, Australian Institute of Aboriginal Studies, 1985.
Editor, with others, *Paperbark: A Collection of Black Australian Writings*. St. Lucia, University of Queensland Press, 1990.

*

Critical Studies: "Aboriginal Australian Dramatists" by Cliff Watego, in *Community Theatre in Australia*, edited by Richard Fotheringham, Sydney, Methuen, 1987; *Jack Davis: A Life Story* by Keith Chesson, Melbourne, Dent, 1988.

*   *   *

Jack Davis was 56 years old before he tried his hand at playwriting and over 60 before he gained a professional production. He had published short stories and two books of poetry; but as a black activist in Australia he discovered late in life that the theatre was the right forum for his work.

His early childhood was spent in the forest country of south-west Western Australia and his young adult life on sheep stations in the northern Gascoigne region. But part of his early life was also spent at the Moore River Native Settlement under the notorious Western Australian Aboriginal Protection Act, which once forced blacks on to government reserves, banned fraternisation with whites, and separated families for the purpose of educating the children in the white way of life. These experiences are the material of his poetry and plays.

Since he first came to national attention with his play *Kullark* in 1978 his work has focused on bridging the gap of understanding between black and white values. For this he has received many awards from the white community, including an Hon. D. Litt and the Order of Australia. He is not the first Aboriginal to have worked in the theatre but he is the first to produce a body of work at the forefront of Australian drama; and his plays have been the occasion for creating in Western Australia a training ground for black actors and a growing demand for their performances.

Davis's first playwriting was *The Dreamers*, a short piece performed by an amateur group in 1973; it was later revised into a full-length work. A meeting with the director Andrew Ross, then working in Perth, led to the production of *Kullark* in 1979, and to a long professional association which has had an important influence upon Davis's new direction as a writer. *Kullark* is a polemical work which gathers together a variety of Aboriginal experiences at the hands of whites: fatal misunderstandings in the early settlement period; evacuation of blacks from country towns during the Depression; life under the protection laws; the granting of citizenship rights to returned soldiers; and the round of grog, poverty, and prison which has customarily made up Aboriginal family life on the fringes of white society. What stands out from the basic narrative form of this early work is the revelations it makes about the life he knows: the indigenous humour, the forbearance, the brawling acts of frustration, instinctively expressed in comic/dramatic dialogue.

These qualities show a marked advance in Davis's next play, *The Dreamers*, a domestic drama of the Wallitch family: two school-age children coping with a white education system; two layabouts on the dole and one ambitious young public servant; a dispirited father and a mother who, like all the women in Davis's plays, bears the heat and burden of the day. Uncle Worru, patriarch and storyteller, is the family's link with their Aboriginal identity and heritage, and his death brings the play to a close. As he fades from his surroundings, his spirit retreats into his tribal past. This atavistic theme mingles with the modern in the form of a tribal dancer who haunts old Worru's thoughts and ritually signals his passing, demonstrating to his white audience that the familial and telepathic links of the old society are still an important element in black consciousness today.

No Sugar returns to the theme of black oppression on the Moore River Native Settlement in a fuller and more refined form. The Millimurras are a happy-go-lucky family who live in a tent on the Northam reserve, about 60 miles east of Perth. Their peace is disrupted when they are ordered to Moore River, where they are subjected to many indignities in the name of hygiene and Christianity. Jimmy, the uncle, is a rebel and humorist who keeps the family's spirits up until he dies at an Australia Day ceremony; Gran is a reprobate who plays the system; and in the centre is the love story of Joe and Mary, who run away back to the old free life.

Concurrent with *No Sugar* came *Honey Spot*, a children's

play about a white ranger's daughter and a black family who rendezvous in the bush to invent a dance for the girl's ballet examination. Each side is at sea with the other's form of dance, and together they learn a mutual accommodation.

Barungin deals with the death while in detention of a young man arrested on suspicion of receiving stolen goods. With *The Dreamers* and *No Sugar* it completes a trilogy on the status of Aborigines called *The First-Born*. *Barungin* is the most directly political of Davis's plays: the theme is the high incidence of black deaths in police custody, the subject of a long-running judicial inquiry. It was first performed in the Australian bicentennial year of 1988 which Aborigines declared a year of mourning; and the play begins and ends with a funeral ritual. The name Wallitch means night hawk, the symbol of death, and the young man's life takes on the whole race memory of deaths at the hands of whites. The word *Barungin*, or "smell the wind", refers literally to Aboriginal sensibilities and survival skills, and metaphorically to the stench of black corpses which have littered Australian history.

In Our Town again examines life in a country town and contrasts sterile white conformity with the humorous, generous, feckless nature of Aboriginal family life. The time is 1946. David Millimurra and his white mate Larry have just been discharged from the army. David is planning to start farm contract work and to buy a house for his extended family still living in the Aboriginal reserve. Larry's sister Sue is attracted to David, but his status as a citizen and returned serviceman is soon undermined by the white community who conspire against the friendships and David's plans. Sue takes up his cause and together they resolve to face the town prejudice and work for better understanding.

—Katharine Brisbane

DAVIS, Ossie. American. Born in Cogdell, Georgia, 18 December 1917. Educated at Waycross High School, Georgia; Howard University, Washington, D.C., 1935–39; Columbia University, New York, 1948; studied acting with Paul Mann and Lloyd Richards. Served in the United States Army, 1942–45: surgical technician. Married Ruby Ann Wallace (i.e., the actress Ruby Dee) in 1948; two daughters and one son. Janitor and clerk, New York, 1938–41; member of the Rose McClendon Players, Harlem, New York, 1940–42; then writer, actor, and director; off-Broadway stage manager, 1954–55; co-host, *Ossie Davis and Ruby Dee Story Hour* and *With Ossie and Ruby* television programs. Recipient: Frederick Douglass award, 1970; Emmy award, for acting, 1970; American Library Association Coretta Scott King award, for children's book, 1979. Agent: The Artists Agency, 10000 Santa Monica Boulevard, Suite 305, Los Angeles, California 90067. Address: P.O. Box 1318, New Rochelle, New York 10802, U.S.A.

PUBLICATIONS

Plays

Goldbrickers of 1944 (produced in Liberia, 1944).
Alice in Wonder (produced New York, 1952; revised version, as *The Big Deal*, produced New York, 1953).

Purlie Victorious (produced New York, 1961). New York, French, 1961; revised version, with Philip Rose and Peter Udell, music by Gary Geld, as *Purlie* (produced New York, 1970), New York, French, 1970.
Curtain Call, Mr. Aldridge, Sir (produced New York, 1963). Published in *The Black Teacher and the Dramatic Arts*, edited by William R. Reardon and Thomas D. Pawley, Westport, Connecticut, Negro Universities Press, 1970.
Escape to Freedom: A Play about Young Frederick Douglass (for children; produced New York, 1976). New York, Viking Press, 1978.
Langston (for children). New York, Delacorte Press, 1982.
Bingo!, with Hy Gilbert, music by George Fischoff, lyrics by Gilbert, adaptation of a play by William Brashler (also director: produced New York, 1985).

Screenplays: *Gone Are the Days!*, 1963; *Cotton Comes to Harlem*, with others, 1970; *Black Girl*, with J.E. Franklin, 1973; *Countdown at Kusini*, with others, 1976.

Television Writing: *Schoolteacher*, 1963; *Just Say the Word*, 1969; *Today Is Ours*, 1974; *For Us the Living*, 1983; scripts for *Bonanza*; *NYPD*; *East Side, West Side*; and *The Eleventh Hour* series.

*

Theatrical Activities:
Director: **Plays**—*Take It from the Top* by Ruby Dee, New York, 1979; *Bingo!*, New York, 1985. **Films**—*Cotton Comes to Harlem*, 1970; *Kongi's Harvest*, 1970; *Black Girl*, 1973; *Gordon's War*, 1973; *Countdown at Kusini*, 1976. **Television**—*The Perpetual People Puzzle* (co-director), 1972; *Today Is Ours*, 1974.
Actor: **Plays**—in *Joy Exceeding Glory*, New York, 1941; title role in *Jeb* by Robert Ardrey, New York, 1946; Rudolf in *Anna Lucasta* by Philip Yordan, toured, 1947; Trem in *The Leading Lady* by Ruth Gordon, New York, 1948; Lonnie Thompson in *Stevedore* by George Sklar and Paul Peters, New York, 1948; Stewart in *The Smile of the World* by Garson Kanin, New York, 1949; Jacques in *The Wisteria Trees* by Joshua Logan, New York, 1950, 1955; Jo in *The Royal Family* by George S. Kaufman and Edna Ferber, New York, 1951; Gabriel in *The Green Pastures* by Marc Connelly, New York, 1951; Al in *Remains to be Seen* by Howard Lindsay and Russel Crouse, New York, 1951; Dr. Joseph Clay in *Touchstone* by William Stucky, New York, 1953; The Lieutenant in *No Time for Sergeants* by Ira Levin, New York, 1955; Cicero in *Jamaica* by E.Y. Harburg and Fred Saidy, New York, 1957; Walter Lee Younger in *A Raisin in the Sun* by Lorraine Hansberry, New York, 1959; Purlie in *Purlie Victorious*, New York, 1961; Sir Radio in *Ballad for Bimshire* by Loften Mitchell, New York, 1963; in *A Treasury of Negro World Literature*, toured, 1964; Johannes in *The Zulu and the Zayda* by Howard DaSilva and Felix Leon, New York, 1965; *Take It from the Top* by Ruby Dee, New York, 1979; Midge in *I'm Not Rappaport* by Herb Gardner, New York, 1987. **Films**—*No Way Out*, 1950; *Fourteen Hours*, 1951; *The Joe Louis Story*, 1953; *The Cardinal*, 1963; *Gone Are the Days!*, 1963; *Shock Treatment*, 1964; *The Hill*, 1965; *A Man Called Adam*, 1966; *The Scalphunters*, 1968; *Slaves*, 1969; *Sam Whiskey*, 1969; *Let's Do It Again*, 1975; *Countdown at Kusini*, 1976; *Hot Stuff*, 1980; *Harry and Son*, 1984; *Avenging Angel*, 1985; *I'm Not Rappaport* by Herb Gardner, 1986; *School Daze*, 1988; *Do the Right Thing*, 1989; *Jungle Fever*, 1991. **Television**—*The Green Pastures* (*Showtime* series), 1951; *The Emperor Jones* (*Kraft Theater* series), 1955; *The*

Defenders series, 1961–65; *Death Is the Door Price* (*The Fugitive* series), 1966; *The Outsider*, 1967; *The Third Choice* (*The Name of the Game* series), 1969; *Night Gallery* series, 1969; *Teacher, Teacher*, 1969; *The Sheriff*, 1971; *Billy: Portrait of a Street Kid*, 1980; *Roots: The Next Generation*, 1981; *King*, 1981; *The Tenth Level*, 1984; and *Seven Times Monday, The Doctors, The Nurses, Twelve O'Clock High, Bonanza, Hawaii Five-O*, and *All God's Children* series.

* * *

Ossie Davis is extraordinary on two counts. Loften Mitchell says in *Black Drama*, "For this tall, intelligent, graying, proud man came into the theater, interested in writing. Fortunately and unfortunately, it was learned that he is a good actor—a phenomenon rare for a writer, and detrimental as well. Mr. Davis went on to job after job working regularly as a Negro actor, never quite getting as much writing done as he wanted to do." But, despite his greater acclaim as director and actor, two of his plays are lasting contributions to dramatic literature.

The early 1950's were difficult years for black playwrights to try to get their works produced. One of the plays that did happen to make the boards—directed and produced in September 1952, in Harlem by the playwright and his friends, Maxwell Glanville, Julian Mayfield, and Loften Mitchell among others—was Davis's *Alice in Wonder*. The production, impoverished as it was, also included two of Mayfield's one-acters, *A World Full of Men* and *The Other Foot*. At the Elks Community Theater the talented group of spirited black artists "ushered in a hit show with few people in the audience" (Loften Mitchell in the *Crisis*, March 1972). Eventually Davis's charming play was optioned off to Stanley Greene and was produced successfully in downtown New York. Davis later expanded it into a full piece, *The Big Deal*.

Alice in Wonder—a reputable beginning for a gifted man—is a delightful piece. It is set in upper Harlem ("cadillac country," as Davis calls it). Alice (Ruby Dee in the original production) sees her husband Jay (Maxwell Glanville) given a sizeable contract by one of the leading television networks. In the meantime, Alice's brother (Ed Cambridge) has involved himself in a number of political affairs—one of which is an effort to restore the passport of a militant black singer. The network director asks Jay to go to Washington to testify before a government committee and to denounce the singer. Complications arise and Alice—who refuses to compromise her principles—sees that Jay is about to "sell out." She packs up and leaves. The ethos of this play is racial tension and all that it means, and it showed what Davis could do as a writer.

Purlie Victorious—warmly received by the alert New York critics at the Cort Theater, 29 September 1961—moved beyond an embryonic idea of laughter as a cure to racial bigotry, and became a dramatic experiment, and an artistic dream. The play is farcical, mocking, sparkling, resounding in ethnic wit, rapid, and unyielding as satire. Purlie Judson, a man of impatience, with a flowery evangelical style, moved by messianic mission for his race ("Who else is they got?") goes South determined to turn Big Bethel (an old barn) back into a church as an integrated symbol of freedom. Every racial cliché of southern life—and northern life for that matter—the white pro-Confederate Colonel, the Jim Crow system, the "colored" mammy and all that that image brings to mind, the Uncle Tom figures, the plantation store, the parochial cops, the stalking country sheriff, the NAACP, the Supreme Court, the church—and all that it symbolizes in both the white man's and the black man's psychology—integration, constitutional rights—are given a Swiftian examination. *Purlie Victorious* is

a series of irresistible mirrors in which men are forced to see the folly of hatred, the insanity of bigotry, and the fruitlessness of racial supremacy theories. As Davis himself says (in *Contemporary Drama*, edited by Clinton T. Oliver and Stephanie Sills, 1971), "What else can I do but laugh? . . . The play is an attempt, a final attempt to hold that which is ridiculous up to ridicule—to round up all the indignities I have experienced in my own country and to laugh them out of existence."

The dialogue is scintillating, poetic, and realistic. There are many puns, ironic uses of idiomatic expressions, and an acute awareness of the black American's sense of melody and rhythm. The satire is sharply focused with the clever use of malapropisms and misnomers: "This is outrageous—This is a catastrophe! You're a disgrace to the Negro profession! . . . That's just what she said all right—her exactly words . . . When I think of his grandpaw, God rest his Confederate soul, hero of the Battle of Chickamauga—. . . My ol' Confederate father told me on his deathbed: Feed the Negroes first—after the horses and cattle—and I've done it evah time! . . . You know something, I've been after these Negroes down here for years: Go to school, I'd say, first chance you get—take a coupla courses in advanced cotton picking. But you'd think they'd listen to me: No sireebob. By swickety!" Like many other comic works *Purlie Victorious* is an angry play. Davis allows his anger to smolder through a gem-lit comedy, and he permits his work to romp and bound through southern settings and bromidic racial situations of the most impoverished and demeaning variety. But Davis is ever in control. Like Molière he knows that people laugh at beatings, mistaken identities, disguises, clever repartee, buffoonery, indecency, and themselves when taken off guard. Thus the satire—ever corrective in the hands of an artist—is both crude and polished in aiming its fire at personal and general prejudices.

The struggle to keep the mask in place in comedy becomes a conflict between intelligence and character, craft and habit, art and nature. In Davis's principles of writing and performing there is a beautiful balance between poetry and realism.

—Louis D. Mitchell

———————

DEAN, Phillip Hayes. American. Born in Chicago, Illinois. Educated at schools in Pontiac, Michigan. Taught acting at the University of Michigan, Ann Arbor. Recipient: Dramatists Guild Hull-Warriner award, 1972; Drama Desk award, 1972. Address: c/o Dramatists Play Service, 440 Park Avenue South, New York, New York 10016, U.S.A.

PUBLICATIONS

Plays

This Bird of Dawning Singeth All Night Long (produced New York, 1968).   New York, Dramatists Play Service, 1971.
The Sty of the Blind Pig (produced New York, 1971).   New York, Dramatists Play Service, 1972.
American Night Cry (includes *Thunder in the Index, This Bird of Dawning Singeth All Night Long, The Minstrel Boy*) (produced New York, 1974).   *Thunder in the Index* and *The Minstrel Boy* published New York, Dramatists Play Service, 1972.

Freeman (produced New York, 1973). New York, Dramatists Play Service, 1973.

The Owl Killer. New York, Dramatists Play Service, 1973.

Every Night When the Sun Goes Down (produced Waterford, Connecticut, 1974; New York, 1976). New York, Dramatists Play Service, 1976.

If You Can't Sing, They'll Make You Dance (also director: produced New York, 1978).

Paul Robeson (produced New York and London, 1978). New York, Doubleday, 1978.

*

Theatrical Activities:
Director: **Play**—*If You Can't Sing, They'll Make You Dance,* New York, 1978.

*   *   *

Phillip Hayes Dean, who had been working intermittently as a playwright since the 1950's, emerged as a dramatist to watch when the Negro Ensemble Company produced *The Sty of the Blind Pig* late in 1971. The title is the name of the red-light house in which Blind Jordan, one of the last of the blind street singers, was born and which he describes in a graphic passage as a place of blood and violence and the "smell of butchered pig." (Pork would figure more directly as an image of black self-corruption in *Every Night When the Sun Goes Down.*) Blind Jordan's presence emphasizes the condition of the other three characters, whose worlds are collapsing: Weedy, the acid-tongued churchwoman, sure of her own righteousness despite a years-long affair with her minister, who goes on the annual convocation to Montgomery just in time for the 1955 bus boycott and finds the new church unrecognizable; her brother Doc, who imagines that if he can get a little money together he can become Sportin' Jimmy Sweet again in a Memphis that has disappeared; and Alberta, Weedy's daughter. She is the central figure in the play, a woman caught between a past she never really had and a future she cannot embrace; at the end, she assumes the voice and manner of her mother. The off-stage event, the burgeoning civil rights movement, is putting an end to whatever community Weedy and Doc know although the characters never see anything other than a bunch of "young folks" with "nappy hair" heading South for some reason. The most effective scene in *The Sty of the Blind Pig* is the one in which Alberta re-enacts a funeral service in which her fervor is clearly sexual, a mark of the personal and social repression in which she lives, but the strength of the piece lies in the characters as a group, the querulous sense of family even in a state of disintegration, and in the mysterious and disquieting presence of Blind Jordan.

The three plays that make up *American Night Cry,* some of which predate *The Sty of the Blind Pig,* are fables of white fear and black oppression, images of mutuality which end in madness, murder, and suicide. *Thunder in the Index, This Bird of Dawning Singeth All Night Long,* and *The Minstrel Boy* are all long on accusation, but the confrontations, despite Dean's talent for grotesque gamesplaying, are too obviously in the service of the ideational thrust of the plays. The programmatic quality of the work and the assumption of inevitable violence prepare the way for the Moloch plays. Both *Freeman* and *Every Night When the Sun Goes Down* are set in Moloch, a small industrial city in Michigan obviously suggested by Pontiac, where Dean lived for a time, but appropriately named Moloch because that god was worshipped through the sacrificial burning of children; both plays

end in fire. *Freeman* is a family play in which the titular protagonist is an ambitious and bright man constantly defeated by his inability to work in the practical world of compromise, thwarted by his working-class family, his frightened wife, and his foster brother, who has become a successful doctor. In the end, he torches the community center that he sees as a symbol of accommodation to white power and is saved from arrest at the cost of incarceration in a mental hospital. A more fully developed version of the main character in *Thunder in the Index,* Freeman is interesting dramatically as a man whose best impulses are self-destructive and harmful to those around him. Such a description may be an act of white liberal co-option, softening Dean for the mainstream of American theater, for the play is more ambiguous about Freeman. It suggests, primarily through the belated understanding of his father, that Freeman is not an instance of black hubris but of a man driven mad by an uncongenial society whose final act of violence is the inevitable end of his frustrated quest. Certainly, such a reading is suggested by *Every Night When the Sun Goes Down.* Set in a decrepit bar-hotel, peopled by whores, pimps, drunks, and crazies, it brings Blood back from prison, inspirited by a new sense of self, as a prophet who enlists this motley crew in a firebomb attack on their own environment. "And God gave Noah the Rainbow sign. No more water, the fire next time."

Paul Robeson is an unusual play in the Dean canon unless one sees the destruction of the political activist in the second act as the inevitable end of the black hero who outwitted the forces of oppression in Act 1 to become a football star, a lawyer, a famous singer and actor. Yet the celebratory frame of the play belies so Dean-like a movement. Neither convincingly Paul Robeson nor effectively Phillip Hayes Dean, it remains an anomaly in the playwright's work perhaps because Dean had his dramatic image forced on him by Robeson's biography. One of Dean's theatrical virtues is that he has a knack for non-realistic fables in which his best characters have room to develop realistically. At his weakest, the expected development never takes place; such is the case with *If You Can't Sing, They'll Make You Dance,* in which an unlikely triangle allows the protagonist's ineffectuality to expose his macho self-image. At the other extreme is *The Sty of the Blind Pig,* in which the fable, implicit in Alberta's wondering if Blind Jordan was "ever really here," gains power from those who act it out. It is not that "every character comes from some man or woman," as Dean has said, but that every character becomes a man or woman. The other plays lie between these two, at their strongest when invention and idea are less visible than the people who embody them.

—Gerald Weales

———

DEAR, Nick. British. Born in Portsmouth, Hampshire, 11 June 1955. Educated at various schools in Southampton; University of Essex, Colchester, B.A. (honours) 1977. Lives with Penny Downie; two children. Has worked as messenger boy, laundry van driver, bakery worker, garage attendant, town sergeant at Southampton Guildhall, film company administrator, and tutor in film and photography; playwright-in-residence, University of Essex, 1985; Arts Council playwright-in-residence, Royal Exchange Theatre, Manchester, 1987–88. Recipient: Pye Radio award, 1980; John Whiting award, 1987. Agent: Rosica Colin Ltd., 1 Clareville Grove Mews, London SW7 5AH, England.

PUBLICATIONS

Plays

The Perfect Alibi (produced Colchester, Essex, 1980).
Pure Science (broadcast 1983; revised version produced Stratford-on-Avon, 1986).
Temptation (produced London, 1984; New York, 1985).
In the Ruins (broadcast 1984; revised version produced Bristol, 1989; London, 1990). With *The Art of Success*, London, Methuen, 1989.
The Bed (produced Colchester, Essex, 1985; New York, 1986).
The Art of Success (produced Stratford-on-Avon, 1986; London, 1987; New York, 1989). With *In the Ruins*, London, Methuen, 1989.
Food of Love (produced London, 1988).
A Family Affair, adaptation of a play by Ostrovsky (produced London, 1988). Bath, Absolute Press, 1989.
The Last Days of Don Juan, adaptation of a play by Tirso de Molina (produced Stratford-on-Avon, 1990; London, 1991). Bath, Absolute Press, 1990.
Le Bourgeois Gentilhomme, adaptation of the play by Molière (produced London, 1992). Bath, Absolute Press, 1992.

Screenplays: *Memo*, with Ann Foreman, 1980; *The Monkey Parade*, with Ann Foreman, 1982; *The Ranter*, 1988.

Radio Plays: *Matter Permitted*, 1980; *Pure Science*, 1983; *In the Ruins*, 1984; *Jonathan Wild*, adaptation of the novel by Fielding, 1985; *Free*, 1986; *Swansong*, with David Sawer, 1989.

*

Nick Dear comments:

I mistrust writers' statements about their own work. I think there are two types of plays and of playwriting. One is concerned with money, glory, and a lot of invitations to dinner. The other is concerned with finding out something about oneself and one's place in the world—that old story—and attempting to communicate it honestly. Success is easily measured on the first count; less so on the second.

* * *

Sex, greed, disgust, and greatly heightened language are four of the basic elements which Nick Dear regularly mixes in his theatrical alchemy. His voice is a powerfully original one, at its most intense in his most famous play, *The Art of Success*, a savage portrait of the great painter, engraver, and caricaturist William Hogarth. But even in his minor plays, when he playfully borrows form and style from the likes of Steven Berkoff, Joe Orton, and Harold Pinter, as in *Pure Science*, there is no mistaking the fierceness of Dear's own vision.

Pure Science is particularly revealing of Dear's influences because it flirts with form. The elderly couple whose private life is invaded by a young Mr. Perkins could be the couple in Pinter's *A Slight Ache*, thrown off-balance by the presence of the Matchseller at their gate; or the flirtatious Mr. Perkins could be said to resemble Orton's Mr. Sloane, importing sexual and criminal danger into the house. When he speaks, Mr. Perkins uses the rough rhyme of a Berkoff Eastender, grandly elevating his larcenous inclinations through doggerel.

The moral arguments, however, are pure Dear. The chemical smells which have wafted up the stairs from the basement for the past 50 years are the evidence of unceasing experiments in alchemy—the time-honoured art of transmutating base elements into higher elements, such as lead into gold. It is that prospect which attracts the attention of Mr. Perkins, who fails to find interest in what has been achieved by his host—eternal life.

Although the latter was the grand aim of alchemy, Dear himself is clearly not convinced that scientific advancement will improve the lot of mankind; he calls on J. Robert Oppenheimer, the father of the atomic bomb, as a witness to the dangers of science and drives the four horsemen of the Apocalypse through the play. But it remains a comedy, with a workshop full of entrails for predicting the future, and it offers a cheerful reversal when the greedy, villainous, and seductive Mr. Perkins is drowned by the elderly wife—"There should be more comeuppance." The couple decide to take their secret knowledge into hiding, like many unknown others, rather than share it with a wicked world.

In Dear's play *Temptation*—where a schoolteacher hopelessly trots out examples of zoological variety to his pupils while reminding them that man destroys a species every month where evolution takes a thousand years—the bitter view of humanity is even more specific. On his way towards suicide, the teacher blurs his unspoken thoughts with his lessons, telling his children that the headmistress "has little knowledge of the world, she's not even frightened of it." His own state of mind is best summed up with the thought that he is "aware that there are 3,000 million starving and he has not gone mad." But perhaps he has, for his own grip on life has slipped through the ordinary muddle of an unwise affair and a damaged marriage.

Perhaps as evidence for the prosecution of humanity, Dear has turned to history more than once, providing a harrowing portrait of the declining George III in *In the Ruins*, but making his greatest impact with *The Art of Success*. Hogarth's chosen form of expression, the harsh morality pictures which made up such series as *The Rake's Progress*, *The Harlot's Progress*, and *Marriage à la Mode*, obviously found a sympathizer in Dear, but Hogarth's own morality was to face a rigorous test in the play.

Dear's great achievement in the play is to enter into Hogarth's world; by trawling with Hogarth through the whoring and hypocrisy of his era he etches his own series of images: Hogarth debasing a condemned murderer by sketching her in her cell against her will; Hogarth seeking degradation with prostitutes; Hogarth's wife uncovering a sheaf of drawings depicting her in sexual acts with other men. The murky desires of Hogarth's deepest imagining are shown dramatically as the force behind his own condemnations of corruption.

For all its power to shock and darkness of tone, for all the violent vigour of the language, *The Art of Success* is also comic and knowing. With its portrayal of the powers and movers of the time, of Hogarth's coup in achieving copyright for his work, it also comments on the 1980's and the commerce of art. For the duration of the play, author and subject seem to share a common vision.

Adaptation has also provided Dear with rich modes of expression, unleashing the extravagant theatrical gestures of Russian and Spanish drama through his extremely vivid English versions of classic plays. Although skilled in writing miniatures such as *Temptation*, he seems most at home when given the scope of classical drama. Perhaps the stunted theatricality of late 1980's English theatre, reduced in size commensurate with the reductions in subsidy, limited his original contributions to the theatre, but the beginning of the 1990's saw him immersed in a potentially rich collaboration, writing for the theatre of Peter Brook.

—Ned Chaillet

DEGRAFT, Joe (Joseph Coleman DeGraft). Ghanaian. 1932–1978.
See 2nd edition, 1977.

DE GROEN, Alma (née Mathers). New Zealander. Born in Foxton, 5 September 1941. Educated at Mangakino District High School, Waikato, 1954–57. Married Geoffrey De Groen in 1965; one daughter. Library assistant, New Zealand National Library Service, Wellington and Hamilton, 1958–64, and Sydney University library, Australia, 1964–65; librarian, New Zealand Trade Commission, Sydney, 1965; writer-in-residence, West Australian Institute of Technology, Perth, 1986; dramaturg, Griffin Theatre Company, Sydney, 1987; writer-in-residence, University of Queensland, St. Lucia, 1989, and Rollins College, Florida, 1989. Recipient: Canada Council grant, 1970; Australian Writers Guild award, 1985; New South Wales Premier's award, 1988; Victorian Premier's award, 1988. Agent: Hilary Linstead & Associates, Suite 302, Easts Tower, 9–13 Bronte Road, Bondi Junction, New South Wales 2022, Australia.

PUBLICATIONS

Plays

The Joss Adams Show (produced Toronto, 1970; London, 1974). Included in *Going Home and Other Plays*, 1977.
The Sweatproof Boy (produced Sydney, 1972).
Perfectly All Right (produced Adelaide, 1973). Included in *Going Home and Other Plays*, 1977.
The After-Life of Arthur Cravan (produced Sydney, 1973).
Going Home (produced Melbourne, 1976). Included in *Going Home and Other Plays*, 1977.
Chidley (produced Melbourne, 1977). Published in *Theatre Australia* (Sydney), January/February, 1977.
Going Home and Other Plays. Sydney, Currency Press, 1977.
Vocations (produced Melbourne, 1981). Sydney, Currency Press, 1983.
The Rivers of China (produced Sydney, 1987). Sydney, Currency Press, 1988.
The Girl Who Saw Everything (produced Melbourne, 1991).

Radio Play: *Available Light* (two monologues for women), 1991.

Television Plays: *Man of Letters*, adaptation of the novel by Glen Tomasatti, 1985; *Chris* (episode) in *Singles* series, 1986; *After Marcuse*, 1986; *The Women* (episode) in *Rafferty's Rules* series, 1987.

* * *

Swathed in bandages, the figure of a hospital patient, featuring in Alma De Groen's most acclaimed play, *The Rivers of China*, provides an appropriate icon for much of her work which focuses on the more painful moments of human existence while generally rejecting nihilism or despair. Always interested in relationships between the sexes, De Groen frequently foregrounds art as the contested ideological space on and through which male/female conflicts are enacted. She is deeply concerned with the role of the female artist in patriarchal society, exploring this issue not only through dialogue but also in structure which she aims to make exactly parallel to the audience's experience of a particular play. Although she has experimented with naturalism and episodic realism, De Groen's best works achieve a fluidity of form that characterises the feminist aesthetic in its ability to break down boundaries and challenge conventional expectations.

The Joss Adams Show, an early but very accomplished one-act play, exhibits precisely this fluid movement between time and place, reality and the surreal, as it presents the biting story of a young woman who beats her baby to death while those around her fail to notice how unhappy, trapped, and desperate she feels. Framed by its introduction as a television show, Joss's story positions her husband and relatives, as well as the audience, as voyeuristic accomplices to the baby's beatings. Understated, and at times even funny, the narrative clearly lays much of the blame for Joss's actions on the shoulders of an uncaring patriarchal society which provides women with few real economic and social options to cope with neglect and violence.

Going Home and *Vocations* also explore contemporary woman's search for a meaningful "home," a position or reference point from which to act without being overwhelmed by the demands of a male-dominated society. *Going Home*, which focuses on the relationships between a group of Australians living in Canada, uses the physical exile of its antagonists to stress their alienation from each other and their lack of a sense of identity rooted in place. While the men are caught up in bombast and petty rivalries over their successes and failures as expatriate artists, the women show their dislocation more elliptically through compulsive spending and eating. These symptoms point not only to general unhappiness but also to deeply felt pain that can be linked to emotional trauma, and, in Molly's case, even rape. Although most of the characters idealise the environments they left behind, the play suggests that "going home" is clearly a problematic process which involves not just physical relocation but some kind of resolution to the enacted gender conflicts. *Vocations* extends some of these themes in its representation of two couples struggling to maintain meaningful relationships with each other while they develop their individual careers. Though the four find some kind of "home" in artistic expression, the struggle for recognition and independence is clearly much harder for the women. For them, "home" remains an elusive place best posited as a feeling of connectedness with the universe and the self, a space fiercely defended but always vulnerable. In particular, Vicki's profession as an actor is not only compromised by her pregnancy but also by her partner Ross who is bent on managing the pregnancy, the baby, and everything else. Her friend Joy, a writer, faces similar usurpation when her husband uses her as the subject of his feminist novel, "packag[ing] all her pain" without first feeling it. Much of the dramatic energy of the play results from the women's efforts to resist this appropriation of their space, their vocations, and indeed their bodies. Though richly comic in its depictions of the battle of the sexes, *Vocations* nonetheless poses some complex questions about what men, as well as women, should be allowed to be.

The Rivers of China marks an important point in De Groen's development as a dramatist. It brings together many of her earlier themes, dealing even more incisively with contemporary sexual politics while merging content with form to create a visually exciting and intellectually provocative play. Indulging her interest in "walking around in other times," here De Groen follows two earlier pieces on historical figures, *Chidley* and *The After-Life of Arthur Cravan*, with an account of the last few months in the life of Katherine Mansfield. Although its major thrust is undoubtedly feminist, *The Rivers of China* also offers powerful moments for post-colonial readings through Mansfield's efforts to delineate a position for the nascent colonial woman artist immured in the territorialised spaces of the imperial patriarchal canon. To recuperate Mansfield as an historical figure is only one aim of the play. Her story is interwoven with, and indeed transformed by, a contemporary narrative set in a feminist dystopia in present-day Sydney. In this "brave new world," women have physical, economic and cultural power, while the men continually struggle for recognition and freedom of expression. But the play never suggests that this dystopia is preferable to patriachal society; rather it problematises simple inversions of the current power structures by recreating Mansfield's mind and spirit in the body of a young man who wakes up in hospital after trying to commit suicide. Structurally, the narrative disrupts chronology, taking the audience on a difficult journey that emphasises slippages between past and present, between masculine and feminine, and between sickness and health. Above all, this play is about ways of seeing.

De Groen's most recent play, *The Girl Who Saw Everything*, similarly focuses on ways of interpreting the world but its characters are more questioning of the aesthetic refractions of reality that art provides, especially when they are faced with marital breakdown and mid-life crises. Witty as always but less complex and challenging than *The Rivers of China*, this latest critique of patriarchy also avoids polemic and demonstrates a great deal of sympathy for the position of men as well as women in our society.

—Helen Gilbert

DELANEY, Shelagh. British. Born in Salford, Lancashire, 25 November 1939. Educated at Broughton Secondary School. Has one daughter. Worked as salesgirl, usherette, and photographer's laboratory assistant. Recipient: Foyle New Play award, 1959; Arts Council bursary, 1959; New York Drama Critics Circle award, 1961; BAFTA award, 1962; Robert Flaherty award, for screenplay, 1962; Encyclopaedia Britannica award, 1963; Writers Guild award, for screenplay, 1969; Cannes Film Festival award, 1985. Fellow, Royal Society of Literature, 1985. Agent: Tessa Sayle, 11 Jubilee Place, London SW3 3TE, England.

PUBLICATIONS

Plays

A Taste of Honey (produced London, 1958; New York, 1960). London, Methuen, and New York, Grove Press, 1959.

The Lion in Love (produced Coventry and London, 1960; New York, 1963). London, Methuen, and New York, Grove Press, 1961.
The House That Jack Built (televised 1977; produced New York, 1979). London, Duckworth, 1977.
Don't Worry about Matilda (broadcast 1983; produced London, 1987).

Screenplays: *A Taste of Honey*, with Tony Richardson, 1961; *The White Bus*, 1966; *Charlie Bubbles*, 1968; *Dance with a Stranger*, 1985.

Radio Plays: *So Does the Nightingale*, 1981; *Don't Worry about Matilda*, 1983.

Television Plays: *Did Your Nanny Come from Bergen?*, 1970; *St. Martin's Summer*, 1974; *The House That Jack Built* series, 1977; *Find Me First*, 1981.

Other

Sweetly Sings the Donkey. New York, Putnam, 1963; London, Methuen, 1964.

*

Critical Studies: *Anger and After* by John Russell Taylor, London, Methuen, 1969; *Feminist Theatre* by Helene Keyssar, London, Macmillan, 1984; *Look Back in Gender* by Michelene Wandor, London, Methuen, 1987.

* * *

Shelagh Delaney's *A Taste of Honey* is usually considered as part of the "angry" upsurge of the late 1950's which shook the British theatre out of its complacency and boredom. But it equally belongs with a contemporaneous spate of novels and plays from the industrial north of England whose rootedness in raw working-class experience, faithfulness to actual speech, and concern for young people are not captured by the label "angry." Delaney's hometown of Salford had already produced Walter Greenwood, who wrote the celebrated unemployment novel *Love on the Dole* (1933), and it was in the Manchester-Salford region too that Joan Littlewood was first active in the Workers' Theatre Movement before she moved her Theatre Workshop to London's East End (where Delaney's career was launched).

A Taste of Honey is set in a squalid single-room flat in a run-down area of Manchester, surrounded by "tenements, cemetery, slaughter-house," as one character caustically remarks. But the two new lodgers, a not exactly respectable or harmonious mother and daughter, are not warped by this environment. Their zest for life and plebeian *savoir vivre* never deserts them. Helen, the mother, has had many lovers in her time and soon darts off with her latest flame, a heavy-drinking car salesman with pockets full of money, to a more comfortable set-up in suburbia. Jo, an astute and quick-witted teenager, also has an affair, partly to compensate for her loneliness, partly to enjoy, much like her mother, the here and now. But hers ends in pregnancy, with her black sailor-boyfriend at large.

Despite these blows Jo manages to hold on. In Act 2 we find her mothered by Geof, a homosexual art student, whose advances she refuses. Shortly before the confinement Helen returns and drives Geof out. The play succeeds in presenting the "immoral" behaviour and unsentimental attitudes of these two struggling independent women as perfectly valid, and with the same frankness introduces Jo's racially and sexually different friends. Present-day audiences, familiar with the claims of feminism, are perhaps better equipped to appreciate the domestic centering and implicit sexual politics of the play. There is no spectacular action, intensity of dramatic conflict, or discussion of ideas, only the absorbing interest and vitality of the two strong female characters.

Naturalist elements abound in the play but it is a matter of choice for directors whether to bring the naturalism to the fore or balance it, as Littlewood did, with music-hall elements and the addressing of the audience.

The Lion in Love continues the questioning of gender roles and conventional family structures as well as reiterating the point that "young people mature quicker these days." There is the same pervasive restlessness and disorder. Yet we get a much larger picture of the rough end of a northern working-class community: three generations instead of two, the public space of a street-market instead of merely the interior of a house, a large cast with a constantly shifting focus of attention. Though the action is again slight—the younger people quit the milieu and seek their fortunes elsewhere, whereas those who have reached "the chaos of middle age" remain ineluctably stuck in it—it is difficult to say why this clearly more ambitious play is so rarely produced. It has a comparable zestful female protagonist in the figure of boozing and riotous Kit, the male characterisation is undoubtedly an advance over the earlier play, it offers a larger vista of the pressures and frustrations to which the socially marginal are exposed, and it again has its dreamlike poetic moments which temper the general picture of social disorganisation.

Given this history, Delaney's celebration of marriage in the television serial *The House That Jack Built*, written after a lapse of 15 years, came as a surprise. But it is easily overlooked that beneath the interminable rows between mother and daughter in *A Taste of Honey*, or the ill-matched couple in *The Lion in Love*, there remained a common wavelength, a possibility of understanding and a capacity for caring, which helps to explain why the break was in neither case final and *The House That Jack Built* not such a departure.

A situation with a grim end is, by contrast, to be found in the script for the prize-winning film *Dance with a Stranger*, if only in its recreation of the real-life tragedy of barmaid Ruth Ellis, who murdered her upper-class lover, and was the last woman to be hanged in Britain. Delaney wrote this scenario in close collaboration with director Mike Newell, who had chosen to dwell on the destructive internal dynamics of the relationship rather than the class issues involved. Ellis, the woman living the fast life, bears some resemblance to Delaney's earlier hedonistic protagonists. She is reluctantly drawn to the man who wants to possess her but then rejects her for a fiancée more befitting his social station. The film does not evade the class attitudes that impregnate the relationship from the start; nor does it ignore the repressive social mores of Britain in the mid-1950's. But the film's thrust is not social or documentary. The unfolding horror story of lust and obsession, jealousy and despair, ugly behaviour and deadly revenge has a more timeless dimension.

—H. Gustav Klaus

DENNIS, Nigel (Forbes). British. 1912–1989.
See 4th edition, 1988.

DEWHURST, Keith. British. Born in Oldham, Lancashire, 24 December 1931. Educated at Rydal School, 1945–50; Peterhouse, Cambridge, 1950–53, B.A. (honours) in English 1953. Married 1) Eve Pearce in 1958 (divorced 1980), one son and two daughters; 2) Alexandra Cann in 1980. Yarn tester, Lancashire Cotton Corporation, Romiley, Cheshire, 1953–55; sports writer, Manchester *Evening Chronicle*, 1955–59; presenter, Granada Television, 1968–69, and *Review* arts programme, BBC, 1972; arts columnist, the *Guardian*, London, 1969–72. Writer-in-residence, West Australian Academy of Performing Arts, Perth, 1984. Recipient: Japan prize, for television play, 1968. Agent: Alexandra Cann Representation, 68E Redcliffe Gardens, London SW10 9HE, England.

PUBLICATIONS

Plays

Running Milligan (televised 1965). Published in *Z Cars: Four Scripts from the Television Series*, edited by Michael Marland, London, Longman, 1968.
Rafferty's Chant (produced London, 1967). Published in *Plays of the Year 33*, London, Elek, 1967.
The Last Bus (televised 1968). Published in *Scene Scripts*, edited by Michael Marland, London, Longman, 1972.
Pirates (produced London, 1970).
Brecht in '26 (produced London, 1971).
Corunna! (produced London, 1971).
Kidnapped, adaptation of the novel by Robert Louis Stevenson (produced Edinburgh, 1972).
The Miser, adaptation of a play by Molière (produced Edinburgh, 1973).
The Magic Island (produced Birmingham, 1974).
The Bomb in Brewery Street (produced Sheffield, 1975).
One Short (produced Sheffield, 1976).
Luggage (produced London, 1977).
Lark Rise, adaptation of works by Flora Thompson (produced London, 1978). Included in *Lark Rise to Candleford*, 1980.
The World Turned Upside Down, adaptation of the work by Christopher Hill (produced London, 1978).
Candleford, adaptation of works by Flora Thompson (produced London, 1979). Included in *Lark Rise to Candleford*, 1980.
Lark Rise to Candleford (includes *Lark Rise* and *Candleford*). London, Hutchinson, 1980.
San Salvador (produced Louisville, 1980).
Don Quixote, adaptation of the novel by Cervantes (produced London, 1982). Oxford, Amber Lane Press, 1982.
Batavia (produced Perth, Western Australia, 1984).
Black Snow, adaptation of a novel by Mikhail Bulgakov (produced London, 1991). Bath, Absolute Press, 1991.

Screenplay: *The Empty Beach*, 1985.

Radio Plays: *Drummer Delaney's Sixpence*, 1971; *That's Charlie George Over There*, 1972; *Dick Turpin*, 1976; *Mother's Hot Milk*, 1979.

Television Plays: *Think of the Day*, 1960; *A Local Incident*, 1961; scripts for *Z Cars* series, 1962–67; *Albert Hope*, 1962; *The Chimney Boy*, 1964; *The Life and Death of Lovely Karen Gilhooley*, 1964; *The Siege of Manchester*, 1965; *The Towers of Manhattan*, 1966; *Softly Softly* series, 1967, 1975–76; *The Last Bus*, 1968; *Men of Iron*, 1969; *Why Danny Misses*

School, 1969; *It Calls for a Great Deal of Love*, 1969; *Helen*, from the play by Euripides, 1970; *The Sit-In*, 1972; *Lloyd-George*, 1973; *End Game*, 1974; *The Great Alfred* (*Churchill's People* series), 1975; *Our Terry*, 1975; *Just William* series, from books by Richmal Crompton, 1977; *Two Girls and a Millionaire*, 1978; *The Battle of Waterloo*, 1983; *What We Did in the Past*, 1986; *Joe Wilson* series, from short stories by Henry Lawson 1987 (Australia); and for *Knight Errant*, *Skyport*, *Love Story*, *Front Page Story*, *The Villains*, *The Emigrants*, *Dominic*, *Juliet Bravo*, *Van der Valk*, *Casualty*, and *Making News* series.

Novels

Captain of the Sands. New York, Viking Press, 1981; London, Cape, 1982.
McSullivan's Beach. London, Angus and Robertson, 1985.

*

Keith Dewhurst comments:

One day in June 1986 I walked into a discount bookshop in Sydney and flicked through an encyclopaedic television guide compiled by Leslie Halliwell, whom I remember with gratitude from my Cambridge days (when he managed the Rex Cinema), and the critic Phillip Purser. Two of my own television plays were accorded entries: *Men of Iron* and *The Siege of Manchester*, which had an asterisk admitting it to "Halliwell's Hall of Fame." This stunned me, in an amiable sort of way, and seems to me to be a classic example of the random fates that await the plays people write.

The Siege of Manchester was a broken-backed epic, for which I have a very soft spot, as I suppose one does for anything half-regretted, and I am delighted that Phillip Purser remembers it, but it does not seem to me to be in the same class as some other television plays I have written, such as *Albert Hope*, *It Calls for a Great Deal of Love*, *Our Terry*, *Lloyd-George*, *Men of Iron* itself, and an episode of *Juliet Bravo* called *Oscar*.

Similarly, *Lark Rise*, which was performed at the National Theatre and subsequently in various countries around the world has, I hazard, been recognised as an interesting piece, and the one in which the director Bill Bryden and myself best expressed a modern genre—the promenade play with music, that tries to make the theatre an event again. Yet the plays by which one arrived at that destination, especially *Corunna!*, aren't even in a vestibule of fame. They're out in the car park, where it's pissing with rain.

This damp obscurity I attribute mainly to the plays in question never having been published. Nor was *The Bomb in Brewery Street*, which additionally suffered from radical chic reviewers who thought that, being set in the Belfast troubles, it should provide solutions that eluded Elizabeth I, Oliver Cromwell, Henry Grattan, Gladstone, Parnell, Lloyd-George, and de Valera. In fact it is a funny and carefully researched work whose sub-text clearly favours colonial disengagement, and I wish I could hustle it into *somebody's* "Hall of Fame," but I don't suppose I will.

I can, however, close with an appropriate "Hall of Fame" reminiscence. There was an extra in *The Siege of Manchester* who was supposed to be dead in a battle scene but kept getting up. Four years later, when the director Herbert Wise and I were working on *Men of Iron*, we met this same extra in the studio corridor, clearly wearing a costume for our new play.

Herbert gripped my wrist and said: "It's George!"
George said: "Hello, Mr. Wise. I never thought I'd work for you again!"

"You wouldn't have," said Herbert, "if I'd remembered your other name."

Maybe the car park does have consolations, after all.

* * *

Keith Dewhurst is a highly skilled and conscientious dramatic craftsman. He has been prepared to write in a number of different dramatic styles, readily accepting the challenges of working for the technically demanding medium of television and of preparing for the stage adaptations of works of fiction which a large proportion of his audience already know well and love in their original form. For television he has adopted the realistic manner which is the current norm for popular entertainment, and his *Van der Valk* detective series has been well received. For the stage, however, he has often preferred to experiment with ideas taken up from Bertolt Brecht's "epic theatre," with the illusion of reality broken in order to facilitate a more direct address to the audience and to accommodate subjects which might prove unduly resistant to conventional treatment. As well as scaling down his work so that it fits comfortably on to the small screen, Dewhurst has used a number of different forms of staging, including arena style, the thrust stage with the audience seated to either side of a long ramp, and what he calls "promenade production" which goes a long way towards abolishing the traditional—or to be more accurate, the 19th-century—distinction between the public and the actors in order to create (if need be at the cost of some spoiling of the sight lines that used to be thought so important) a greater degree of intimacy and involvement. Music is not treated as a mere incidental or just to emphasise atmosphere; it serves as an essential part of the dramatic presentation in many instances. Dewhurst never loses sight of the need for the theatre to entertain, but when he comments on this he is not just repeating a commonplace and far less is he making the facile distinction of some old-fashioned critics between a theatre of entertainment and a theatre of ideas. Instead, he insists that drama can and ought to be an artistic medium which appeals to a wide range of people in a number of different ways. In this, as in his choice of dramatic mentor, Dewhurst proclaims a wide sympathy with the great mass of humanity.

His talents and his sympathy are clearly revealed in *Running Milligan*, an outstanding contribution to the BBC's epoch-making series *Z Cars*. Milligan is shown leaving prison, let out on parole to attend his wife's funeral. The policemen on patrol see him, and their immediate suspicions set the perspectives of a tragedy that is inevitable. At home Milligan predictably finds no support and cannot resist the crazy temptation of trying to run away. It is to no avail, and Barlow, who has presided over the usual police station subplot, arrives to arrest him. To some extent this is conventional enough, but Dewhurst contrives to bring out all the pathetic helplessness of Milligan, suggesting that the blame lies not with him but with his impossible situation and that society's response to his problems is no less bungling and ineffectual than his own efforts at escape. The dialogue is pared down to essentials, but in a scene near the end when Milligan tries to comfort a drink-sodden tramp whose memory is fuddled by memories of fighting in the war by telling him a fairy story, there is a sudden and disturbingly apt touch of poetry.

Rafferty's Chant, which was produced at the Mermaid Theatre, London, has a great deal more humour in its portrayal of the life and downfall of a wonderfully plausible con man in the used car trade. The dialogue is crisp and laconic, but there is a wonderful touch of romance in Rafferty's patter as he sells old bangers as if they were dream machines. The skimpy plot of this play that has more than a touch of farce to it is no more than a thread to hold together closely observed characters in a number of sketches that explore their motivations as they try to cope with one of those vitally important little matters in present-day life, the buying of a car. As we laugh with Rafferty at mankind's foibles there is no more danger of our taking any more seriously than he does the stern words he imagines a judge speaking to him before pronouncing a stiff sentence for preying on gullibility.

Following a line of development that probably owes its origins to the experiments of the French director Jean-Louis Barrault and which was certainly influenced to some extent by the work of Ariane Mnouchkine whose production of *1789* with the Théâtre du Soleil he witnessed at the Cartoucherie de Vincennes, Paris, Dewhurst has done some of his most original work in adaptations. *Corunna!*, for instance, dramatises episodes from the Napoleonic War as a ballad opera with no more than five actors reinforced by a five-piece rock band. *Kidnapped*, after Robert Louis Stevenson, was also notable for its freedom of dramatic treatment. If the problem with *Don Quixote* was an excess of text, that with *Lark Rise*, after Flora Thompson's celebrated portrait of village life in Victorian Oxfordshire, was a lack of narrative and a consequent lack of a clear central focus of attention. Dewhurst does not try to remedy this. His approach is rather to let the images of the village and its people develop before the eyes of the audience so that the succession of glimpses may add together almost as they do when we look in on real life. In this way *Lark Rise* serves as a prelude to the rather more obviously shaped *Candleford*. The texts do not read particularly well, but that criticism is no more just here than when it is levelled at television scripts. Flora Thompson's book, like the novels of Cervantes or Stevenson, remains intact for those who wish to read it. Dewhurst's aim is to find a dramatic representation of these works which functions in performance with all the different means of communication that are available in the theatre when, without the trammels and clutter of old-fashioned realism, the imagination is engaged and provoked into providing whatever may be sensed as needed to colour the pictures that are sketched before our eyes. The success of the productions of *Lark Rise* and *Candleford* is ample justification for the enterprise that Dewhurst has embarked upon.

—Christopher Smith

DICKINS, Barry. Australian. Born in Regent, Victoria, in 1949. Educated at the Preston Institute of Technology, diplomas in fine arts and education 1974. Worked at various factory jobs and as a scenic artist for television; writer-in-residence, La Mama, 1980, Victoria College of the Arts, and Playbox Theatre, 1982, all Melbourne. Recipient: Radio Broadcasting grant, 1976; APG Playwriting prize, 1978; Australia Council fellowship, 1984. Address: 63 Illawara Road, Flemington, Victoria 3031, Australia.

PUBLICATIONS

Plays

Ghosts (produced Melbourne, 1975).
The Interview (produced Melbourne, 1976).

Only an Old Kitbag (produced Melbourne, 1977).
The Great Oscar Wilde Trial (produced Melbourne, 1977).
Mag and Bag (as *The Horror of Suburban Nature Strips*, produced Melbourne, 1978). With *The Bridal Suite*, Montmorency, Victoria, Yackandandah, 1985.
The Rotten Teeth Show (produced Melbourne, 1978).
The Fool's Shoe Hotel (produced Melbourne, 1978). Montmorency, Victoria, Yackandandah, 1985.
The Bridal Suite (produced Melbourne, 1979). With *Mag and Bag*, Montmorency, Victoria, Yackandandah, 1985.
Banana Bender (produced Melbourne, 1980). With *The Death of Minnie*, Sydney, Currency Press, 1981.
The Ken Wright Show (produced Melbourne, 1980).
The Death of Minnie (produced Melbourne, 1980). With *Banana Bender*, Sydney, Currency Press, 1981.
The Golden Goldenbergs (produced Melbourne, 1980). Montmorency, Victoria, Yackandandah, 1986.
Lennie Lower (produced Melbourne, 1981). Montmorency, Victoria, Yackandandah, 1982.
One Woman Shoe (produced Melbourne, 1981). Montmorency, Victoria, Yackandandah, 1984.
A Couple of Broken Hearts (produced Melbourne, 1982).
Graeme King Lear (produced Melbourne, 1983).
Greenroom (produced Melbourne, 1985).
Beautland (produced Adelaide, 1985). Sydney, Currency Press, 1985.
More Greenroom (produced Melbourne, 1986).
Reservoir by Night (produced Melbourne, 1986).
Royboys (produced Melbourne, 1987). Sydney, Currency Press, 1987.
Eat Your Greens (produced Melbourne, 1987).
Between Engagements (produced Melbourne, 1988).
Bedlam Autos (produced Melbourne, 1989).
Perfect English (produced Melbourne, 1990).
Hymie (produced Melbourne, 1991).

Novels

Crookes of Epping. Fairfield, Victoria, Pascoe, 1984.
Ron Truffle: His Life and Bump Out. Alphington, Pascoe, 1987.
My Grandmother: Years of Wit, Warmth and Laughter. Melbourne, Penguin, 1989.

Other

What the Dickins 1–2 (humour). Melbourne, Penguin, 2 vols., 1987–89.
Gift of the Gab (humour). Melbourne, McPhee Gribble, 1988.

Illustrator, *The Barracker's Bible: A Dictionary of Sporting Slang* by Jack Hibberd and Garrie Hutchinson. Melbourne, McPhee Gribble, 1983

* * *

While not all of his plays are set specifically in his home town, Barry Dickins is very much a Melbourne writer and much of his contribution to popular culture chronicles the passing parade of everyday life in that city—mostly in a warmly humorous vein, if often tinged with poignancy. Even in Melbourne, however, his plays have been criticised sometimes for their waywardness, lack of discipline, and unorthodox dramatic structure.

Most of his work is certainly anti-naturalistic; much of it resembles the so-called "larrikin" style of La Mama and the

Pram Factory in the late 1960's and early 1970's, while some of it recalls the surrealism and absurdism of even earlier periods. The best of Dickins's work is in a broad cartoon style that is very much his own. In particular, he has developed the form of dramatic monologue—and also, at times, of true monodrama—to a high level of achievement.

The majority of Dickins's plays deal with down-and-outs, or "Aussie battlers" of one kind or another. In *Royboys*, the fluctuating fortunes of the battling, working-class, and ambiguously named Noble family are chronicled in parallel with those of their beloved and equally battling Fitzroy Football Club, a team of working-class origins but one now languishing at the bottom of a competition dominated by wealthy, sophisticated clubs which have changed the style of the game and the nature of the football league itself. Dickins uses the changing (and, in his bitingly satirical view, deteriorating) face of football as a metaphor for the gradual passing of a more leisurely and dignified lifestyle that is rapidly being supplanted by a fast-paced, impersonal world. In the end, it is the courage and determination of the Nobles that is appreciated rather than their poverty.

Similarly, the exploits of a pair of unashamedly shady but struggling used-car salesmen are celebrated (albeit with less satirical confidence) in *Bedlam Autos*, while *Mag and Bag* portrays a pair of elderly suburban sisters whose life together is reduced (like that of Beckett's tramps in *Waiting for Godot*) to insulting each other as a way of passing the time. Images of a birdcage and a trapeze serve to emphasise the two women's up-and-down relationship.

In *The Death of Minnie* and *The Bridal Suite*, the sad and broken solo female characters, Minnie and Vera, rail with considerable vigour against the bad hand life has dealt them (with alternating humour and bitterness) but still succumb to their unhappy fate. Minnie's failure in life is poignantly underlined (in a use of stage properties that is typical of Dickins) by the failure of a pop-up toaster, which finally functions (triumphantly!) only at the moment of her death. Indeed, in the later monodrama *Hymie* (the central character of which is based to some extent on an actual left-wing Melbourne Jewish artist), Hymie Slade is already dead; he regales us with anecdotes about his life and death from an elaborate and well-appointed coffin. Significantly, the Hymie of the play was not a great artist; furthermore, he and his ideals outlived even the Australian Communist Party itself, but what Dickins again values is the indomitable spirit—"the bullshit artistry"—of the melancholy solitary character.

Theatrical artists are portrayed in other plays. In *The Golden Goldenbergs*, a family of down-on-their-luck Melbourne Jewish comedians gather for a grand night of mad reminiscences, theatrical feats, and feasting; in *The Fool's Shoe Hotel*, the hotel of the title is really a sort of asylum for a troupe of battling actors and other show-business has-beens who display—in a bizarre and highly surrealist soirée—skills and tricks that were better recognised and regarded in days gone by. As in *Royboys*, Dickins laments the passing of better days, and the metaphor of popular but outmoded performance styles works well enough.

More effective, however, in their exploration of comic performers are two further monodramas: the early *Lennie Lower* and the later *Between Engagements*. In Lennie Lower, the real-life, eccentric journalist of 1930's Sydney, Dickins found a genuine soulmate for what is arguably one of his finest plays. In a very strongly developed monodrama, the physically and emotionally crippled Lower spends what turns out to be the last night of his life in a working-class pub in 1947, putting together tomorrow's funny column for his daily paper, reminiscing about his past (with the usual Dickins

alternation of nostalgia, bitterness, and surreal, ribald humour), suffering from a terminal case of writer's block and drinking himself to life . . . and death. Along the way, Lower portrays for us his long-time colleague, the cartoonist WEP, as well as his boss, Sir Frank Packer. Again, it is the vibrant if idiosyncratically perverse life of the character we remember, rather than his pitiful death. *Lennie Lower* has been often revived in Australian theatres.

Equally poignant is the excellent *Between Engagements*, portraying a perennially unemployed actor who is stuck in his flat alone—apart from a telephone, which serves as his sole lifeline to a hostile outside world and which he hopes will bring him work. Needless to say, it is reluctant to ring, despite the encouragements, threats, and wonderful "audition pieces" (speeches from his possibly remembered, possibly imagined past career at the illustrious MTC and Pram Factory) which he lavishes upon the recalcitrant instrument— not unlike Minnie and her uncooperative toaster.

A huge number of other monologues (like the various evenings at La Mama written for the actor Peter Green and bearing punning references to his name—such as *Greenroom*) are examples of Dickins's contribution to Melbourne's burgeoning comedy and cabaret circuit. However, the intentionally connected series of monologues for a female performer—*One Woman Shoe*—is a further example of his frequently insightful and sympathetic writing for women actors.

Dramaturgically unorthodox though some of them might be, Dickins's plays nevertheless teem with life (as much as with death) and, at their best, they are vigorously entertaining.

—Geoffrey Milne

DIETZ, Steven. American. Born in Denver, Colorado, 23 June 1958. Educated at the University of Northern Colorado, Greeley, 1976–80, B.A. 1980. Member, Playwrights' Center, 1980–91, co-founder, Quicksilver Stage, 1983–86, and artistic director, Midwest PlayLabs, 1987–89, all Minneapolis; resident director, Sundance Institute, Utah, 1990; associate artist, A Contemporary Theatre, Seattle, 1990–91. Recipient: Jerome Foundation fellowship, 1982, 1984; McKnight fellowship in directing, 1985, in playwriting 1989; Theatre Communications Group fellowship in directing, 1987; Society of Midland Authors award, 1988; National Endowment for the Arts fellowship, 1989. Agent: Wiley Hausam, International Creative Management, 40 West 57th Street, New York, New York 10019. Address: 4416 Thackeray North East, Seattle, Washington 98105, U.S.A.

PUBLICATIONS

Plays

Brothers and Sisters, music by Roberta Carlson (produced Minneapolis, 1982).
Railroad Tales (produced Minneapolis, 1983).
Random Acts (produced Minneapolis, 1983).
Carry On (produced Minneapolis, 1984).
Wanderlust (also director: produced Minneapolis, 1984).

Catch Me a Z, music by Greg Theisen (produced Minneapolis, 1985).

More Fun Than Bowling (produced St. Paul, Minnesota, 1986; New York, 1992). New York, French, 1990.

Painting It Red, music by Gary Rue, lyrics by Leslie Ball (produced St. Paul, Minnesota, 1986). New York, French, 1990.

Burning Desire (produced St. Paul, Minnesota, 1987).

Foolin' Around with Infinity (produced Los Angeles, 1987). New York, French, 1990.

Ten November, music and lyrics by Eric Bain Peltoniemi (produced Chicago, 1987). Published in *Plays in Process* (New York), vol. 9 no. 4, 1987; New York, French, 1990.

God's Country (produced Seattle, 1988; New York, 1992). New York, French, 1990.

Happenstance, music by Eric Bain Peltoniemi (produced Seattle, 1989).

After You (produced Louisville, 1990; New York, 1991). Published in *More Ten-Minute Plays from Actor's Theatre of Louisville*, edited by Michael Dixon, New York, French, 1992.

To the Nines (produced Seattle, 1991). Published in *The Twentieth Century*, edited by Dan Fields, Seattle, Rain City Press, 1991.

Halcyon Days (produced Seattle, 1991). Seattle, Rain City Press, 1991.

Trust (produced Seattle, 1992). Seattle, Rain City Press, 1992.

Lonely Planet (produced Seattle, 1992).

Screenplay: *The Blueprint*, 1992.

*

Theatrical Activities:

Director: **Plays**—many of his own plays; *Standing on My Knees* by John Olive, St. Paul, Minnesota, 1982; *21-A* by Kevin Kling, Minneapolis, 1984, New York, 1986; *The Voice of the Prairie* by John Olive, Minneapolis, 1985; *Harry and Claire* by Jaime Meyer, Minneapolis, 1985; *A Country Doctor* by Len Jenkin, Minneapolis, 1986; *Auguste Moderne* by Kevin Kling, Minneapolis, 1986; *T Bone N Weasel* by Jon Klein, Minneapolis, 1986, Louisville, Kentucky, 1987; *Lloyd's Prayer* by Kevin Kling, Minneapolis, 1987; *The Einstein Project* by Paul D'Andrea and Jon Klein, Minneapolis, 1987, Washington, D.C., 1992; *The Wild Goose Circus* by Russell Davis, Sundance, Utah, 1990; *Tears of Rage* by Doris Baizley, Seattle, 1991; *New Business* by Tom William, Denver, Colorado, 1991; *Home and Away* by Kevin Kling, Chicago and Minneapolis, 1992; and many readings and workshops at the Playwrights' Center, Minneapolis, 1980–91. **Opera**— *Saint Erik's Crown* by Eskil Hemberg, St. Peter, Minnesota, 1989.

Steven Dietz comments:

At the core of my interest in the theatre is a quote from Bertolt Brecht: "The modern theatre musn't be judged by whether it manages to interest the spectator in the theatre itself—but whether it manages to interest him in the world."

To that end, I have devoted many of my plays to investigations of factual events. I believe the theatre is a rehearsal of the concerns of the present moment. I believe that, as workers in this marvelous grand accident of an art form, we have a mandate to be the explorers, not the curators, of our society. Our daunting challenge, one we seldom rise to meet, is to run through the minefields before our culture does. To make the mistakes, confront the idiocy and revel in the excesses (social, sexual, religious, political) of our culture in the metaphorical safety of the theatre (where we can watch, learn, and judge)—before these same things hit us head-on in the bloody maelstrom of the world.

I believe that, at its best, the theatre can serve as a social forum, a place where members of a community can gather to confront those things which affect them. A place for reasoning and rage, laughter and loss, recognition and discussion.

I believe that, at its best, the theatre is a combustible mix of fun, fury, and eloquence.

*   *   *

Of the generation of young dramatists coming of age in the 1990's, Steven Dietz is unique in a number of ways. Although he works largely out of Seattle, his plays are frequently seen in theatres around the country, including in New York City. He is prolific, diverse, and has a "voice" which is always changing and yet recognizable as his own. Dietz pays careful attention to an issue that most playwrights of his generation and background tend to ignore or glide over: politics.

A few years ago, with *More Fun Than Bowling*, Dietz's dramaturgy came to public attention in a theatre in St. Paul, Minnesota. The theatre company is now defunct but the "voice" of Steven Dietz was unmistakable: macabre, funny, lunatic, hard-hitting, and finally disturbing in a way that many other plays of his contemporaries failed to be. Dietz showed, almost proudly, that he cared, that he had compassion, that he was not just another cool observer. The promise of *More Fun Than Bowling* has been realized recently in even more compelling work.

God's Country captured a good deal of attention because it dared to take on the headlines. The murder of radio talk show host, Alan Berg by Neo-Nazis is the mainspring of this play, where Dietz tackles thorny questions and comes up with lucid explanations. A fairly small cast is called on to play a wide range of characters in this docu-drama which dramatizes Voltaire's statement that "Anyone who has the power to make you believe absurdities has the power to make you commit injustices," which Dietz quotes in the published text of the drama. Alan Berg, "a bleeding heart with an acid tongue," had outraged the far right with his Denver talk show, his challenges to make-believe "facts." He was murdered for attempting to be reasonable and sane. As with much modern docu-drama, Dietz unfortunately resorts too often to having his characters tell us the play rather than show it to us. There is a plethora of speeches directly to the audience in this court-room drama. But montages of voices and images work well to create the atmosphere and the sense of irrationality which the madmen-murderers palm off as "salvation." The Jew-haters are themselves pathetic and dangerous, believing the "absurdities" which their leaders manufacture out of whole cloth.

In later plays, Dietz resorts to direct audience-address even more frequently, and while the speeches themselves are interesting and even fascinating, they replace dramatic conflict between characters on the stage which might have been more effectively achieved through dialogue and action.

In *Halcyon Days*, Dietz turns his attention to the American invasion of Grenada. Here again he relies on long speeches which are essentially narrative rather than theatrical. And again, we have a montage of short, snappy scenes and representative characters ranging from senators to goofy, laid-back medical students, from gift shop clerks to presidential speech writers. While the central issue of the invasion of this tiny island became moot almost instantly, what saves the play as theatre and should guarantee it a future life is its wit. As

Senator Eddie notes, "There are no comics in D.C. Comics would be redundant." Sadly, the senator's own life is engulfed by the tragedy, and comedy itself becomes redundant. Dietz proves over and over again that he can write very funny material, as when he has a character attack the murder of language: he calls it "linguicide". Euphemisms hide reality: "The old are chronologically gifted. The hungry are nourishment-free. And the homeless are architecturally-inconvenienced. . . . Murdered civilians become collateral damage, and the starving thousands . . . become disenfranchised indigenous people of color." Strong stuff emerges from hilarious spoofery, but Dietz, like many Americans, is outraged at the way his country's leaders behave and speak and lie. Such political stands are rare in American drama, but Dietz makes them work, by and large.

Trust once again uses the open stage to represent a variety of essentially cinematic settings. When Dietz lets his dialogue rip along, he is absolutely first rate, but he frequently slips back into monologue, relating the action to the audience. The fault, if it is a fault at all, is common enough in his generation of playwrights, but in *Trust* it seems intrusive. And yet Dietz has the 1990's generational jargon, attitude, value system, casual yet twitchy behavior, down pat.

Dietz's most recent play is *Lonely Planet*. It seems very different from the preceding works, except that the language is absolutely on the mark and the point that is being made is sadly only too recognizable. Two men, Jody and Carl, play games of truth and lies with each other in a map store, with the world as seen by the astronauts hanging behind them. Dietz pays direct homage to Ionesco's *The Chairs*, and in time his stage is filled with chairs, with memories which may or may not be "true." Carl complains that he is bored, but eventually we learn that his boredom is with death, which the chairs symbolize. The two characters duel with maps, play with the world, but their inner struggle emerges as we see their fear and share their anxiety. AIDS is out there, waiting, and the chairs are the chairs of their dead friends. This play is heavy in symbolism, but despite its grim center there is wit and irony which is ". . . the penicillin of modern thought." Dietz is at his best when he has Jody ponder, "We remember the wrong things. We remember the combination to our high school gym locker, we forget the name of the woman who taught us to swim. We remember the capitals of states and forget our parents' birthdays." In the end, on our lonely planet, we have only memory, however faulty, and each other.

In *Lonely Planet*, Dietz treats the audience as a character to be addressed, to have things directed at. But here the device is relevant and important because it integrates the audience as a part of the action; we should not remain passive.

—Arthur H. Ballet

DIZENZO, Charles (John). American. Born in Hackensack, New Jersey, 21 May 1938. Educated at New York University, B.A. 1962. Married Patricia Hines in 1964. Instructor in playwriting, New York University 1970–71, and Yale University, New Haven, Connecticut, 1975–76. Recipient: Yale University-ABC fellowship, 1966, and CBS fellowship, 1975; Guggenheim fellowship, 1967; National Endowment for the Arts grant, 1972. Agent: Helen Harvey Associates, 410 West 24th Street, New York, New York 10011. Address: 106 Perry Street, New York, New York 10014, U.S.A.

PUBLICATIONS

Plays

The Drapes Come (televised 1965; produced New York, 1965; Liverpool, 1973; London, 1982). New York, Dramatists Play Service, 1966; in *Off-Broadway Plays 1*, London, Penguin, 1970.
An Evening for Merlin Finch (produced New York, 1968; Coventry, 1969). New York, Dramatists Play Service, 1968; in *Off-Broadway Plays 1*, London, Penguin, 1970.
A Great Career (produced New York, 1968). New York, Dramatists Play Service, 1968.
Why I Went Crazy (produced Westport, Connecticut, 1969; New York, 1970; as *Disaster Strikes the Home*, produced Edinburgh, 1970; London, 1971).
The Last Straw, and Sociability (produced New York, 1970). New York, Dramatists Play Service, 1970.
Big Mother and Other Plays (includes *An Evening for Merlin Finch* and *The Last Straw*). New York, Grove Press, 1970.
Big Mother, music by John Braden (produced New York, 1974). Included in *Big Mother and Other Plays*, 1970.
Metamorphosis, adaptation of works by Kafka (produced New York, 1972).
The Shaft of Love (produced New York, 1975).

Television Play: *The Drapes Come*, 1965.

Other

Phoebe (for children), with Patricia Dizenzo. New York, Bantam, 1970.

*   *   *

Charles Dizenzo's plays were first produced in the off-off-Broadway workshop movement of the 1960's. Since then they have been presented by the Repertory Company of Lincoln Center, the David Merrick Arts Foundation, and the American Place Theater in New York, and in theatres in Europe.

A good example of Dizenzo's work is a pair of one-act comedies first presented at Lincoln Center's experimental Forum Theater. The first play, *A Great Career*, is an office play built on the assumption that office life is impossible, but that for all the meaningless work and the petty quarrels among employees, the office is as much "womb as tomb," or, as the heroine snarlingly calls it as the play opens, "a home away from home." It is about a harried clerical worker named Linda who has a report to prepare. During the course of the action she explodes, gets herself fired, and then realizing that there is no place else to go that is not the same she literally begs to be taken back. This description makes the play sound more painful than funny, and Dizenzo obviously wants his audience to hang on to that side of the story. The ending certainly encourages them to. We see Linda crawling around the stage picking up the papers that she scattered during her defiant scene, as a fellow employee tells her about the new bookkeeper who tried to commit suicide unsuccessfully in the men's room. In *A Great Career* Dizenzo shows the emasculating nature of office life by having men play women and women turning out to be men.

In *An Evening for Merlin Finch* the sterility of the office gives way to the silent violence of the home. Darlene Finch, an insensitive middle-class middle-American housewife, is plagued by a vengeful mother who materializes in the shape of her son Merlin. This becomes her vision of hatred and guilt. As he demonstrates in all of his plays Dizenzo is fascinated with the normality within a sick society. His plays point up the compromises which sink the soul of modern man into a dismal acceptance of everyday predicaments. Merlin, the focus of concern, is forced to play his bassoon for company. Each observation his parents make is a body blow and each gesture of contact a refusal. Merlin's life turns out to be an eternal adolescence and as he blows away on his bassoon his slim identity evaporates before our eyes. His mother's ignorance and hostility continuously undercut the comic image of Merlin's silly instrument. Here Dizenzo's dry black humor together with a carefully constructed situation exposes and explodes the Finches' severely distorted family life.

Another Dizenzo play which in its own bizarre and comic way explodes the quiet violence of family life is *Disaster Strikes the Home* (also presented under the title *Why I Went Crazy*). In this play Dizenzo submerges his audience into a complete and outrageous comic world. Once again the sexes are changed: wives are played by men, husbands by women. The reversal is not a gimmick, but a surrealistic view of the sexual strangulation that exists in the American household. Dizenzo counterpoints these outlandish images with careful, and empty, colloquial speech. The violent role reversals that take place in weak marriages epitomize Dizenzo's nightmare view of American family life.

Dizenzo's playwriting is always startlingly inventive and for the most part consistently amusing. By distorting the real world he illuminates the dark emotional silences between people which is something many contemporary playwrights attempt but seldom achieve. Although his writing has none of the manicured edge of Albee's or Ionesco's, and in places is in serious need of tightening, Dizenzo has a keen ear for the truthful phrase and a fine farceur's instint for pace. His theatrical vision is controlled and iconoclastic; he imitates no one, relying totally on his own creative talents, thereby fostering a theatrical voice which is both unique and thoroughly American.

—Bernard Carragher

DONLEAVY, J(ames) P(atrick). Irish. Born in Brooklyn, New York, United States, 23 April 1926; became Irish citizen, 1967. Educated at a preparatory school, New York; Trinity College, Dublin. Served in the United States Naval Reserve during World War II. Married 1) Valerie Heron (divorced), one son and one daughter; 2) Mary Wilson Price in 1970 (divorced), one daughter and one son. Recipient: London *Evening Standard* award, 1961; Brandeis University Creative Arts award, 1961; American Academy award, 1975. Address: Levington Park, Mullingar, County Westmeath, Ireland.

PUBLICATIONS

Plays

The Ginger Man, adaptation of his own novel (produced London and Dublin, 1959; New York, 1963). New York, Random House, 1961; as *What They Did in Dublin, with The Ginger Man: A Play*, London, MacGibbon and Kee, 1962.
Fairy Tales of New York (produced Croydon, Surrey, 1960; London, 1961; New York, 1980). London, Penguin, and New York, Random House, 1961.
A Singular Man, adaptation of his own novel (produced Cambridge and London, 1964; Westport, Connecticut, 1967). London, Bodley Head, 1965.
The Plays of J.P. Donleavy (includes *The Ginger Man*, *Fairy Tales of New York*, *A Singular Man*, *The Saddest Summer of Samuel S*). New York, Delacorte Press, 1972; London, Penguin, 1974.
The Beastly Beatitudes of Balthazar B, adaptation of his own novel (produced London, 1981; Norfolk, Virginia, 1985).

Radio Play: *Helen*, 1956.

Novels

The Ginger Man. Paris, Olympia Press, and London, Spearman, 1955; New York, McDowell Obolensky, 1958; complete edition, London, Corgi, 1963; New York, Delacorte Press, 1965.
A Singular Man. Boston, Little Brown, 1963; London, Bodley Head, 1964.
The Saddest Summer of Samuel S. New York, Delacorte Press, 1966; London, Eyre and Spottiswoode, 1967.
The Beastly Beatitudes of Balthazar B. New York, Delacorte Press, 1968; London, Eyre and Spottiswoode, 1969.
The Onion Eaters. New York, Delacorte Press, and London, Eyre and Spottiswoode, 1971.
A Fairy Tale of New York. New York, Delacorte Press, and London, Eyre Methuen, 1973.
The Destinies of Darcy Dancer, Gentleman. New York, Delacorte Press, 1977; London, Allen Lane, 1978.
Schultz. New York, Delacorte Press, 1979; London, Allen Lane, 1980.
Leila. New York, Delacorte Press, and London, Allen Lane, 1983.
DeAlfonce Tennis: The Superlative Game of Eccentric Champions: Its History, Accoutrements, Conduct, Rules and Regimen. London, Weidenfeld and Nicolson, 1984; New York, Dutton, 1985.
Are You Listening Rabbi Löw. London, Viking, 1987.
That Darcy, That Dancer, That Gentleman. London, Viking, 1990; New York, Atlantic Monthly Press, 1991.

Short Stories

Meet My Maker the Mad Molecule. Boston, Little Brown, 1964; London, Bodley Head, 1965.

Other

The Unexpurgated Code: A Complete Manual of Survival and Manners, drawings by the author. New York, Delacorte Press, and London, Wildwood House, 1975.
Ireland: In All Her Sins and in Some of Her Graces. London, Joseph, and New York, Viking, 1986.

A Singular Country, illustrated by Patrick Prendergast. Peterborough, Ryan, 1989; New York, Norton, 1990.

*

Bibliography: by David W. Madden, in *Bulletin of Bibliography* (Westport, Connecticut), September 1982.

Critical Studies: *J.P. Donleavy: The Style of His Sadness and Humor* by Charles G. Masinton, Bowling Green, Ohio, Popular Press, 1975; *Isolation and Protest: A Case Study of J.P. Donleavy's Fiction* by R.K. Sharma, New Delhi, Ajanta, 1983.

* * *

Although J.P. Donleavy is better known as a novelist, he has adapted his own novels, *The Ginger Man* and *A Singular Man*, into plays which have received fairly successful productions, and his original stage play, *Fairy Tales of New York*, won the *Evening Standard* Most Promising Playwright Award for 1961. In adjusting to the medium of the theatre, Donleavy faced two particular problems. His prose style is rich, idiosyncratic, and of a quality to encourage cult enthusiasms: but to what extent could this verbal power be incorporated into stage dialogue without leaving the impression of over-writing? His novels too are usually written from the standpoint of one man, an anti-hero such as Sebastian Dangerfield or George Smith: but in a play the audience is necessarily aware of other characters, simply because they're on the stage. If the central character talks too much, the audience's sympathy may be drawn towards the reactions of other people to him. A single angle of vision, easy to maintain in a novel, is often hard to achieve in the theatre, which is a multi-dimensional medium.

Donleavy's first play, *The Ginger Man*, revealed an uncertain control of these difficulties. The story concerns Sebastian Dangerfield, an impoverished American living with his English wife, Marion, in Dublin. He is supposedly studying law at Trinity College: but his main efforts are directed towards staving off creditors, avoiding the responsibilities of fatherhood, and raking together enough money to get drunk. In the novel Sebastian's sheer wildness, his refusal to settle down, is exciting: it is an archetypal rebellion against dreary conformity. But in the play, we are unavoidably aware of the pain Sebastian causes others—particularly Marion who leaves him, and the genteel spinster, Miss Frost, whom he seduces. And the fine uninhibited imagination of Sebastian, which provides so much fun in the book, is in the play relentlessly controlled by the physical surroundings of the set: the squalid flat at One Mohammed Road, the prim suburban house at 11 Golden Vale Park. "*The Ginger Man*," concluded Richard Gilman, "desperately requires: song, dance, lyrical fragments, voices from nowhere, shapes, apparitions, unexplainable gestures." In the format of a naturalistic play, it lost many of the qualities which made the book so remarkable. Even the theme seemed less original: the relationship between O'Keefe and Sebastian recalled the boozing friendship between Joxer and "Captain" Boyle in O'Casey's *Juno and the Paycock*.

Fairy Tales of New York is much more successful: a sequence of four related anecdotes, which almost seems to continue the ginger man's career. An American returns to his native city, with his English wife who dies on the voyage. Cornelius Christian is in the same state of desolation, harassed by poverty, guilty and grief-stricken, which faced Sebastian at the close of the earlier play. The four scenes illustrate Cornelius's gradual rehabilitation: the burial of his wife and his job at the funeral parlour, his entry into the American business world, his work-outs at a gymnasium and finally his successful (though imaginary) conquest of a snobbish head-waiter and an embarrassed girlfriend. Unlike Sebastian, however, Cornelius is a reserved quiet man—observing others and sometimes poking gentle fun at them: and this changed role for the central character, together with the much greater flexibility of form, allows Donleavy's great gifts for caricature, witty dialogue, and buoyant fun to be more evident. Nor are the episodes as unrelated and superficial as they may appear. Donleavy stresses the contrast between the democratic ideals of American society with the rigidly class-structured and snobbish habits: Christian is employed because he's been to Europe and acquired "breeding"—he dazzles the head-waiter, who refused to serve him because he wore peach shoes, by dressing as a visiting Eastern potentate wearing no shoes at all. The spurious emotionalism of the funeral parlour is related to Christian's moving grief: and the sheer falseness of an over-commercialized society is exposed with a delicate skill that only Evelyn Waugh and Edward Albee have matched.

Although *A Singular Man* lacks some of the moral seriousness (and fun) of *Fairy Tales of New York*, it too is a rewarding play: centered around the life of a fairly successful New York businessman, George Smith, his friendships and affairs with three women, Ann Martin, Sally Tomson, and Shirl. Smith is a fall guy, always missing out on the opportunities he dreams about. "The only time the traffic will stop for me," he confesses to Shirl, "is when I'm dead." His sexual fantasies focus on Sally Tomson, a gorgeous secretary, protected by her tough-guy brother and many other lovers. Her death at the end of the play, just before her marriage to a rich tycoon, crystallizes Smith's sense of cosmic defeat. But Smith never quite gives up hope: and his resilience through successive embarrassments and failures provides the mainspring for the play. *A Singular Man* is similar in construction to *Fairy Tales of New York*: a sequence of 12 anecdotal scenes, which work both on the level of isolated and very amusing revue sketches, and together as a group, the insights of one episode being carried forward to the next, until the full picture emerges both of the society and the central man. In the first scene, Smith opts out of conversation with a boring friend by answering just "Beep beep"; in the seventh, he tries the same tactics with Shirl, only to discover that his relationship with her is too charged and complex to admit such an evasion.

Donleavy's style of humour is reminiscent both of *New Yorker* cartoons and of the American dramatist Murray Schisgal, whose plays are also popular in Britain. But his jokes are never flippant—although they sometimes seem whimsical. They succeed because they're based on detailed observation and a rich command of language. Although as a dramatist, he may not yet have lived up to the promise of *Fairy Tales of New York*, he remains one of the most potentially exciting dramatists now at work.

—John Elsom

DREXLER, Rosalyn. American. Born in New York City, 25 November 1926. Self-educated. Married Sherman Drexler in 1946; one daughter and one son. Painter, sculptor, singer, and wrestler; taught at the University of Iowa, Iowa City, 1976–77. Recipient: Obie award, 1965, 1979, 1985;

Rockefeller grant, 1965 (2 grants), 1968, 1974; *Paris Review* fiction prize, 1966; Guggenheim fellowship, 1970; Emmy award, 1974. Agent: (drama) Helen Harvey Associates, 410 West 24th Street, New York, New York 10011; (literary) Georges Borchardt Inc., 136 East 57th Street, New York, New York 10022, U.S.A.

PUBLICATIONS

Plays

Home Movies; and Softly, and Consider the Nearness, music by Al Carmines (produced New York, 1964). Included in *The Line of Least Existence and Other Plays*, 1967.
Hot Buttered Roll (produced New York, 1966; London, 1970). Included in *The Line of Least Existence and Other Plays*, 1967; with *The Investigation*, London, Methuen, 1969.
The Investigation (produced Boston and New York, 1966; London, 1970). Included in *The Line of Least Existence and Other Plays*, 1967; with *Hot Buttered Roll*, London, Methuen, 1969.
The Line of Least Existence (produced New York, 1967; Edinburgh, 1968). Included in *The Line of Least Existence and Other Plays*, 1967.
The Line of Least Existence and Other Plays. New York, Random House, 1967.
The Bed Was Full (produced New York, 1972). Included in *The Line of Least Existence and Other Plays*, 1967.
Skywriting, in *Collision Course* (produced New York, 1968). New York, Random House, 1968.
Was I Good? (produced New York, 1972).
She Who Was He (produced New York, 1973).
The Ice Queen (produced Boston, 1973).
Travesty Parade (produced Los Angeles, 1974).
Vulgar Lives (produced New York, 1979).
The Writers' Opera, music by John Braden (produced New York, 1979).
Graven Image (produced New York, 1980).
Starburn, music by Michael Meadows (produced New York, 1983).
Room 17-C (produced Omaha, 1983).
Delicate Feelings (produced New York, 1984).
Transients Welcome (includes *Room 17-C*, *Lobby*, *Utopia Parkway*) (produced New York, 1984). New York, Broadway Play Publishing, 1984.
A Matter of Life and Death (produced New York, 1986).
What Do You Call It? (produced New York, 1986).
The Heart That Eats Itself (produced New York, 1987).

Novels

I Am the Beautiful Stranger. New York, Grossman, 1965; London, Weidenfeld and Nicolson, 1967.
One or Another. New York, Dutton, 1970; London, Blond, 1971.
To Smithereens. New York, New American Library, 1972; London, Weidenfeld and Nicolson, 1973; as *Submissions of a Lady Wrestler*, London, Mayflower, 1976.
The Cosmopolitan Girl. New York, Evans, 1975.
Dawn: Portrait of a Teenage Runaway (as Julia Sorel). New York, Ballantine, 1976.
Alex: Portrait of a Teenage Prostitute (as Julia Sorel). New York, Ballantine, 1977.
Rocky (novelization of screenplay; as Julia Sorel). New York, Ballantine, 1977.
See How She Runs (novelization of screenplay; as Julia Sorel). New York, Ballantine, 1978.
Starburn: The Story of Jenni Love. New York, Simon and Schuster, 1979.
Forever Is Sometimes Temporary When Tomorrow Rolls Around. New York, Simon and Schuster, 1979.
Bad Guy. New York, Dutton, 1982.

Other

Rosalyn Drexler: Intimate Emotions. New York, Grey Art Gallery, 1986.

*

Rosalyn Drexler comments:
I try to write with vitality, joy, and honesty. My plays may be called absurd. I write to amuse myself. I often amuse others.
Almost all my reviews have been excellent, but I am not produced much. It seems that every theatre wants to premiere a play. (That's how they get grants.) Therefore, if a play is done once, good or bad, that's it for the playwright—unless she is Ibsen, Shaw . . . etc.
Playwriting is my first love, I'm considered established, but I have just begun.

* * *

Rosalyn Drexler came to prominence as a novelist and playwright at a time when the absurdist symbolism of Albee was very much in vogue. Her own work of the 1960's has sometimes been called "pop art," and it has also been billed as "An Evening of Bad Taste"; whichever, it seems very much a reaction against the intellectualism and pretentiousness which surrounded the theatre of the absurd. She has remained true to her early style in the 1980's, and has found sympathetic—and still emphatically "alternative"—production milieus with groups like the Omaha Magic Theater.

Bad taste is often both the subject and the style of Drexler's plays, manipulating the audience into compromising corners. *The Investigation* presents itself as a simple if not naïve parable about a police interrogation of an adolescent murder suspect, a timid, puritanical boy who is eventually bullied by the police into suicide. Some critics found it a fashionable tract against police brutality, and hence a very slight work. The characters are, as usual in Drexler, two-dimensional, but the boy is so colourless that he is unengaging as an object of sympathy. The detective, on the other hand, is so resourceful that his techniques of sadistic attrition become the main theatrical dynamic. Much of the detective's imaginative energy is invested in verbal reconstruction of the grotesque rape and murder, putting the boy in the central role. As the audience receives no evidence from any external source, there remains the possibility that the facts which the detective narrates may be correct, and that what appears to be his sadism is in fact nausea at an outrageous crime. In the second scene there is a surprising technical twist when the murder victim's twin sister introduces herself to the audience and volunteers to re-enact the crime, using a boyfriend of hers as the accused boy. That this is parodic is obvious—they congratulate each other on their performances and show no sadness that a girl has been killed—but the mechanics of the parody are obscure. Does the scene represent the detective's hypothesis? or the boy's nightmare? or public assumptions about what happens when repression meets precociousness? The only possibility to be eliminated is that the scene shows what really happened. When questions like these are left open at the end of a play, the author can hardly be accused of triteness.

If questions are generated prodigally, Drexler also seems to have many techniques for ensuring that her plays do not become too meaningful; the title-piece for her collection, *The Line of Least Existence*, may consist of profundity or malapropism. Verbal vandalism certainly does exist in that play, but so also does an utterly unpretentious playfulness, in which words are discovered and traded just for their phatic values. Because Drexler's dramatic world is never remotely naturalistic, the reference of words is often totally unclear; one wonders whether "least existence" actually defines the dramatic cosmos as a sort of limbo, especially when at the end the central character, with a heroic irresponsibility, commits his wife and himself to a mental asylum. In *Hot Buttered Roll*, Mr Corrupt Savage, a senile bedridden billionaire, exercises his waning appetites with the assistance of a call girl and an amazonian bodyguard who from time to time throws him back into bed. The cast also includes two pimps, a "purveyor of girly girls" and a "purveyor of burly girls," but the essential action seems to be in a bunker, where all connections and relationships have been severed and the use of appetite is tentative and vicarious. As with the detective in *The Investigation*, the more scabrous parts of the dialogue sometimes have a vatic quality, so that the impact is often in its vagueness or suggestiveness. Thus the play's central image is never clearly stated, but seems to be that of (gendered) man as a sort of transplant patient, his facilities being monitored externally, his needs being canvassed through a huge mail-order system, and his responses being tested by the bizarre performances by the call girl at the foot of the bed. Very similar in rationale is *Softly, and Consider the Nearness*, in which a woman uses a television set as a surrogate world of experience.

In a later play, *Skywriting*, there are only two characters, and their referential functions are trimmed back even further: the unnamed Man and Woman seem to be archetypes, and as such make this an important work, a transition from the pop plays of the 1960's towards the mythical work of the 1970's. Beyond the fact that the diction seems closer to Drexler's Bronx than to Eden, the play is not located in any time or place. The two characters, segregated on either side of the stage, argue about the possession of a huge (projected) picture postcard of clouds. As in Shepard, the sky is perceived as a fantasy arena, and the characters instinctively take a territorial attitude to it, invading each other's minds as they defend their sexuality. This is a very clever and economical play, in which the primordial merges with the futuristic before dissolving in a throw-away ending. *She Who Was He* investigates the world of myth and ritual in an exotic, distant past; the style is lavish and operatic, but the attempt at transcendence has been problematic for audiences. In her Obie-winning *The Writers' Opera*, Drexler returns to her more familiar mode, the perversely illogical associative collage of stereotypical items. The pretentiousness and fickleness of the art world is the satirical target in this play, and this world is reflected in the domestic behaviour of the central characters, where a transsexual finds himself in an Oedipal relationship with his son. Such events differ only in degree from the ingredients of her first stage success, *Home Movies*, where outrageous farcical grotesquerie revolves round the prodigal and inventive sexuality of the characters. There, as throughout Drexler's large output of plays, novels, and novelizations, her most characteristic trait, the ridiculous pun, typifies an author who defies critical assessment while at the same time —in her own inimitable phrasing—she "shoots the vapids."

—Howard McNaughton

DUBERMAN, Martin (Bauml). American. Born in New York City, 6 August 1930. Educated at Yale University, New Haven, Connecticut, 1948–52, B.A. 1952 (Phi Beta Kappa); Harvard University, Cambridge, Massachusetts, 1952–57, M.A. 1953, Ph.D. 1957. Tutor, Harvard University, 1955–57; instructor and assistant professor (Morse Fellow, 1961–62), Yale University, 1957–62; assistant professor, 1962–65, associate professor, 1965–67, and professor of history, 1967–71, Princeton University, New Jersey. Since 1971 distinguished professor, Lehman College Graduate Center, and founder, 1986, Center for Lesbian and Gay Studies, City University of New York. Recipient: Bancroft prize, for history, 1962; Vernon Rice award, 1964; American Academy award, 1971; Manhattan Borough Presidents gold medal, 1988; George Freedley prize, 1990; Lambda Book award, 1990 (twice); Myer award, 1990. Address: 475 West 22nd Street, New York, New York 10011, U.S.A.

PUBLICATIONS

Plays

In White America (produced New York, 1963; London, 1964).   Boston, Houghton Mifflin, 1964; London, Faber, 1965.
Metaphors, in *Collision Course* (produced New York, 1968). New York, Random House, 1968).
Groups (produced New York, 1968).
The Colonial Dudes (produced New York, 1969).   Included in *Male Armor*, 1975.
The Memory Bank: The Recorder, and The Electric Map (produced New York, 1970; *The Recorder* produced London, 1974).   New York, Dial Press, 1970.
Payments (produced New York, 1971).   Included in *Male Armor*, 1975.
Soon, music by Joseph Martinez Kookoolis and Scott Fagan, adaptation of a story by Kookoolis, Fagan, and Robert Greenwald (produced New York, 1971).
Dudes (produced New York, 1972).
Elagabalus (produced New York, 1973).   Included in *Male Armor*, 1975.
Male Armor: Selected Plays 1968–1974 (includes *Metaphors*, *The Colonial Dudes*, *The Recorder*, *The Guttman Ordinary Scale*, *Payments*, *The Electric Map*, *Elagabalus*).   New York, Dutton, 1975.
Visions of Kerouac (produced New York, 1976).   Boston, Little Brown, 1977.
Mother Earth: An Epic Drama of Emma Goldman's Life. New York, St. Martin's Press, 1991.

Screenplays: *The Deed*, 1969; *Mother Earth*, 1971.

Other

Charles Francis Adams 1807–1886.   Boston, Houghton Mifflin, 1961.
James Russell Lowell.   Boston, Houghton Mifflin, 1966.
The Uncompleted Past (essays).   New York, Random House, 1969.
Black Mountain: An Exploration in Community.   New York, Dutton, 1972; London, Wildwood House, 1974; revised edition, New York, Norton, 1992.
About Time: Exploring the Gay Past.   New York, Seahorse, 1986; revised edition, New York, Dutton, 1992.
Paul Robeson.   London, Bodley Head, and New York, Knopf, 1989.

Cures: A Gay Man's Odyssey. New York, Dutton, 1991.

Editor, *The Antislavery Vanguard: New Essays on the Abolitionists.* Princeton, New Jersey, Princeton University Press, 1965.

Editor with Martha Vicinus and George Chauncey, Jr., *Hidden from History: Reclaiming the Gay and Lesbian Past.* New York, New American Library, 1989; London, Penguin, 1991.

* * *

In White America was first produced in October 1963, at a time of great optimism in American social consciousness. It was the era of the New Frontier. The play was an immediate, sustained, and internationally acclaimed success. Its author, however, was a playwright by avocation only, and his subsequent theatrical productivity has proven to reflect his true profession in subject matter, theory of communication, and evolution. Martin Duberman is a professor of history at Lehman College, a professional historian of recognized accomplishment, and author of several works in that field: *James Russell Lowell, Charles Francis Adams, The Uncompleted Past, Black Mountain: An Exploration in Community,* and *About Time.*

In White America is less a "play" in any traditional literary sense than an "evening of theatre"—it is an assemblage of documents from the history of the black American's experience of 200 years' suffering. As an historical event reflecting the social fabric of its time, the piece is significant, and at the time of its presentation it was a moving experience for all audiences. It weaves together dialogues, documents, songs, and narration with impressive sensitivity for theatrical construction and it suggests a possible form for playwrights to explore. In a 1963 essay, "Presenting the Past," Duberman argued that "the past has something to say to us . . . a knowledge of past experience can provide valuable guidelines, though not blueprints, for acting in the present." Clearly his professional concern for history provided him with his subject matter (he did not create material; he selected, edited, and shaped it). His teaching duties, moreover, led him to a belief in the theatrical and dramatic potential of oral communication: a lecturer can be more than informative. "The benefits of a union between history and drama," Duberman wrote, "would not by any means be all on one side. If theater, with its ample skill in communication, could increase the immediacy of past experience, history, with its ample material on human behavior, could broaden the range of theatrical testimony." In his preface to the printed play he added, "I chose to tell this story on the stage, and through historical documents, because I wanted to combine the evocative power of the spoken word with the confirming power of historical fact." It was the assessment of critics of the time that Duberman had succeeded in all respects. The play stimulated an awakening social consciousness, was vital in the enactment, and communicated its thesis most effectively.

In the late 1960's Duberman's attitudes towards the uses of the past and the efficacy of wedding history to theatre began to change. Perhaps the disenchantment of the New Left that followed the Kennedy and King assassinations influenced his thinking. His work for the theatre abandoned the path suggested by *In White America,* and he began to write fiction-invented drama.

Male Armor collects seven plays written between 1968 and 1974. Two are full-length. Four of the one-acts had been published previously. None had received successful production in the commercial theatre. In his introduction to the collection, Duberman professes that the plays explore a common theme, "What does it mean to be a 'man'?" The collection's title, he explains, is meant to recall Wilhelm Reich's concept of "character armor"—the devices we employ to protect ourselves from our own energy, particularly our sexual energy. Each of the plays investigates the way we build protective roles which then dominate us. For Duberman, the way to destroy these confining roles is, apparently, androgyny, either practiced or metaphorical.

Metaphors, The Electric Map, and *The Recorder* are all highly literate sparrings between consenting adults which explore the themes of power struggle and homosexuality. In *Metaphors* a young applicant to Yale University nearly seduces his admissions interviewer. *The Electric Map* and *The Recorder,* which had an unsuccessful off-Broadway production under the title *The Memory Bank,* are also duologues. The former is set before an elaborate, electrified map of the Battle of Gettysburg, and self-consciously uses this visual analogue to puff up a foolish domestic quarrel between two brothers into what the author hopes will be something akin to universality. There is a predictable undertone of latent homosexuality to the trite and poorly motivated action. *The Recorder* is an interview of the friend of a great man by an academician-historian. In it, Duberman is intrigued by the ineffectiveness and inaccuracy of historical inquiry, and the play unquestionably reflects his growing disenchantment with the study of history, as well as his growing use of sexuality as a dramatic subject. By the time of these plays, Duberman was referring to himself as "more a writer than a historian."

The newest play in *Male Armor* is *Elagabalus,* a six-scene realistic play about Adrian, a self-indulgent and affluent androgynist. Duberman writes, "Adrian is playful and daring. His gaiety may be contaminated by petulance and willfulness, but he *is* moving toward an *un*-armored territory, moving out so far that finally he's left with no protection against the traditional weaponry brought to bear against him . . . other than the ultimate defense of self-destruction." In his quest for self, Adrian stabs himself fatally in the groin, and the final image the writer offers is a gratuitous freeze-frame from the porno film "Big Stick" in which a teenage girl sucks sensuously on a popsicle. This reader was reminded of the adage that many people (Adrian? Duberman?) who are looking for themselves may not like what they find. Adrian is a boring character whose self-destruction does not seem significant.

The Uncompleted Past is a collection of Duberman's critical and historical essays which concludes with an expression of his disenchantment with the study of history and reveals why his theatrical development had moved towards fiction (in which area he appears undistinguished) and away from the documentary (in which his initial acclaim was achieved). He writes,

> For those among the young, historians and otherwise, who are chiefly interested in changing the present, I can only say . . . they doom themselves to bitter disappointment if they seek their guides to action in a study of the past. Though I have tried to make it otherwise, I have found that a "life in history" has given me very limited information or perspective with which to understand the central concerns of my own life and my own times.

It seems probable that *In White America* will stand as Duberman's major writing for the theatre, and that it will prove more significant as an event of cultural history than as either an innovation in theatrical form or the first work in the career of a significant playwright—thus belying the very attitudes towards history and theatre which Duberman has recently held.

—Thomas B. Markus

———

DUFFY, Maureen (Patricia). British. Born in Worthing, Sussex, 21 October 1933. Educated at Trowbridge High School for Girls, Wiltshire; Sarah Bonnell High School for Girls; King's College, London, 1953–56, B.A. (honours) in English 1956. Schoolteacher for five years. Co-founder, Writers Action Group, 1972; joint chair, 1977–78, and president, 1985–89, Writers Guild of Great Britain; chair, Greater London Arts Literature Panel, 1979–81; vice-chair, 1981–86, and since 1989 chair, British Copyright Council; since 1982 chair, Authors Lending and Copyright Society; vice-president, Beauty Without Cruelty; fiction editor *Critical Quarterly*, Manchester, 1987. Recipient: City of London Festival Playwright's prize, 1962; Arts Council bursary, 1963, 1966, 1975; Society of Authors travelling scholarship, 1976. Fellow, Royal Society of Literature, 1985. Agent: Jonathan Clowes Ltd., Ironbridge House, Bridge Approach, London NW1 8BD. Address: 18 Fabian Road, London SW6 7TZ, England.

PUBLICATIONS

Plays

The Lay-Off (produced London, 1962).
The Silk Room (produced Watford, Hertfordshire, 1966).
Rites (produced London, 1969). Published in *New Short Plays 2*, London, Methuen, 1969.
Solo, Old Thyme (produced Cambridge, 1970).
A Nightingale in Bloomsbury Square (produced London, 1973). Published in *Factions*, edited by Giles Gordon and Alex Hamilton, London, Joseph, 1974.

Radio Play: *Only Goodnight*, 1981.

Television Play: *Josie*, 1961.

Novels

That's How It Was. London, Hutchinson, 1962; New York, Dial Press, 1984.
The Single Eye. London, Hutchinson, 1964.
The Microcosm. London, Hutchinson, and New York, Simon and Schuster, 1966.
The Paradox Players. London, Hutchinson, 1967; New York, Simon and Schuster, 1968.
Wounds. London, Hutchinson, and New York, Knopf, 1969.
Love Child. London, Weidenfeld and Nicolson, and New York, Knopf, 1971.
I Want to Go to Moscow: A Lay. London, Hodder and Stoughton, 1973; as *All Heaven in a Rage*, New York, Knopf, 1973.
Capital. London, Cape, 1975; New York, Braziller, 1976.
Housespy. London, Hamish Hamilton, 1978.
Gor Saga. London, Eyre Methuen, 1981; New York, Viking Press, 1982.

Scarborough Fear (as D.M. Cayer). London, Macdonald, 1982.
Londoners: An Elegy. London, Methuen, 1983.
Change. London, Methuen, 1987.
Illuminations. London, Sinclair Stevenson, 1991.

Verse

Lyrics for the Dog Hour. London, Hutchinson, 1968.
The Venus Touch. London, Weidenfeld and Nicolson, 1971.
Actaeon. Rushden, Northamptonshire, Sceptre Press, 1973.
Evesong. London, Sappho, 1975.
Memorials of the Quick and the Dead. London, Hamish Hamilton, 1979.
Collected Poems. London, Hamish Hamilton, 1985.

Other

The Erotic World of Faery. London, Hodder and Stoughton, 1972.
The Passionate Shepherdess: Aphra Behn 1640–1689. London, Cape, 1977; New York, Avon, 1979.
Inherit the Earth: A Social History. London, Hamish Hamilton, 1980.
Men and Beasts: An Animal Rights Handbook. London, Paladin, 1984.
A Thousand Capricious Chances: A History of the Methuen List 1889–1989. London, Methuen, 1989.

Editor, with Alan Brownjohn, *New Poetry 3*. London, Arts Council, 1977.
Editor, *Oroonoko and Other Stories*, by Aphra Behn. London, Methuen, 1986.
Editor, *Love Letters Between a Nobleman and His Sister*, by Aphra Behn. London, Virago Press, 1987.
Editor, *Five Plays*, by Aphra Behn. London, Methuen, 1990.

Translator, *A Blush of Shame*, by Domenico Rea. London, Barrie and Rockliff, 1968.

*

Manuscript Collection: King's College, University of London.

Critical Studies: by Dulan Barber, in *Transatlantic Review 45* (London), Spring 1973; *Guide to Modern World Literature* by Martin Seymour-Smith, London, Wolfe, 1973, as *Funk and Wagnalls Guide to Modern World Literature*, New York, Funk and Wagnalls, 1973; *A Female Vision of the City* by Christine Sizemore, Knoxville, University of Tennessee Press, 1989.

Maureen Duffy comments:

(1973) I began my first play in my third year at university, finishing it the next year and submitting it for the *Observer* playwriting competition of 1957–58. I had done a great deal of acting and producing at school and at this stage my aim was to be a playwright as I was already a poet. I wrote several more plays and became one of the Royal Court Writers Group which met in the late 1950's to do improvisations and discuss problems. I have continued to write plays alternately with novels and every time I am involved in a production I swear I will never write anything else. From early attempts to write a kind of poetic social realism I have become increasingly expressionist. *Solo, Olde Tyme* and *Rites* are all on themes from Greek mythology. *Megrim*, the play I am working on at present, is a futurist study of racialism and the making of a society. I believe in theatrical theatre including all the pantomime elements of song, dance, mask and fantasy and in the power of imagery.

* * *

Maureen Duffy is firmly established as one of the foremost novelists of her generation. During the past 30 years she has also written plays; the fact that these, with the possible exception of *Rites*, have not yet received the recognition they deserve is due quite as much to an absence of a fortuitous conjunction of circumstance typical of the theatre and necessary for the achievement of success, as to the demands made on the audience by the author.

Duffy's plays are not "easy." They are densely written, pitched between fantasy and realism, and have allegorical undertones. At the centre of her work lie three short plays derived from Greek myths: The Bacchae (*Rites*), Narcissus (*Solo*), and Uranus (*Olde Tyme*).

Rites, which first appeared in an experimental programme of plays presented by the National Theatre, is set in a ladies' public lavatory, presided over by the monstrous Ada (*Agave*). Duffy describes it as a black farce. She use a chorus of modern prototypes—three office girls, a cleaner, an old tramp—and involves them in situations both modern (a girl's attempted suicide in a cubicle) and parallel to the myth. Her Dionysus is a boy doll, brought in by two women and examined with gloating curiosity; her Pentheus a transvestite lesbian, dressed like a man. She is brutally murdered as a consequence of entering this exclusive women's domain, and disposed of in the incinerator for sanitary towels. It helps to know *The Bacchae*, but it is by no means essential. The strength of the play resides in the power of the writing, the violence of its situations, and the deliberate "Peeping Tom" element.

In *Solo* her Narcissus is a man, reflecting on his image in a bathroom mirror: again a deft blending of the modern and the ancient mythical.

Olde Tyme, which deals with the castration of Uranus, is in many ways her most interesting and original play, but dramatically the least convincingly realized. It is studded with brilliant, Pirandellian ideas. Her hero is a television tycoon, keeping his employees in slavish dependence. He sustains his confidence with the help of cherished memories of his mother, a queen of the Music Halls. The slaves get their chance to revolt when he hires a derelict theatre and forces them to recreate an old Music Hall evening, with his mother as the star. This he plans to film and preserve for posterity.

Sexual fantasies are enacted, and at last his "mother" appears and punctures with her revelations the whole basis of the tycoon's life. He is destroyed ("castrated") and his minions take over. There are echoes here of Jean Genet's *The Balcony*, but the play's effectiveness is undermined by the lack of credibility of the characters. To dehumanize a three-dimensional character and make him two-dimensional will engage an audience's emotions, but you cannot flatten caricatures.

Among Duffy's other works for the stage are *The Silk Room*, which chronicles the gradual disintegration of a pop group, and a play about François Villon. The unproduced *Megrim* is an expressionist, futuristic fantasy about a secluded society. It combines the nightmarish quality of Fritz Lang's film *Metropolis* with the intellectual daring of the discussions contained in Shaw's late extravaganzas. To these Duffy has added a human, mainly sexual dimension of her own. It makes a rich but probably undigestible concoction.

More modestly, and entirely successfully, *A Nightingale in Bloomsbury Square* shows us Virginia Woolf going though a lengthy creative stocktaking prior to suicide before a spectral audience consisting of Sigmund Freud and Vita Sackville-West. It is an interrupted monologue, written with great sympathy and power.

Duffy is a writer of fierce originality and imaginative depth; hopefully, she will take the opportunity at some point to prove herself to a wider public as a dramatist, too.

—Frank Marcus

DUNBAR, Andrea. British. 1961–1991. See 4th edition, 1988.

DUNCAN, Ronald (Fredrick Henry). British. 1914–1982. See 3rd edition, 1982.

DUNN, Nell (Mary). British. Born in London in 1936. Educated at a convent school. Married the writer Jeremy Sandford in 1956 (marriage dissolved); three sons. Recipient: Rhys Memorial prize, 1964; Susan Smith Blackburn prize, for play, 1981; *Evening Standard* award, for play, 1982; Society of West End Theatre award, 1982. Agent: Curtis Brown, 162–168 Regent Street, London W1R 5TB. Address: 10 Bell Lane, Twickenham, Middlesex, England.

PUBLICATIONS

Plays

Steaming (produced London, 1981; Stamford, Connecticut, and New York, 1982). Ambergate, Derbyshire, Amber Lane Press, 1981; New York, Limelight, 1984.
Sketches in *Variety Night* (produced London, 1982).
I Want, with Adrian Henri, adaptation of their own novel (produced Liverpool, 1983; London, 1986).
The Little Heroine (produced Southampton, 1988).

Screenplay: *Poor Cow*, with Ken Loach, 1967.

Television Plays: *Up the Junction*, from her own stories, 1965; *Every Breath You Take*, 1988.

Novels

Poor Cow. London, MacGibbon and Kee, and New York, Doubleday, 1967.

The Incurable. London, Cape, and New York, Doubleday, 1971.
I Want, with Adrian Henri. London, Cape, 1972.
Tear His Head Off His Shoulders. London, Cape, 1974; New York, Doubleday, 1975.
The Only Child: A Simple Story of Heaven and Hell. London, Cape, 1978.

Short Stories

Up the Junction. London, MacGibbon and Kee, 1963; Philadelphia, Lippincott, 1966.

Other

Talking to Women. London, MacGibbon and Kee, 1965.
Freddy Gets Married (for children). London, MacGibbon and Kee, 1969.
Grandmothers. London, Chatto and Windus, 1991.

Editor, *Living Like I Do*. London, Futura, 1977; as *Different Drummers*, New York, Harcourt Brace, 1977.

*   *   *

Nell Dunn was best known in the 1960's and 1970's as a chronicler of the lives of working-class women. The child of a securely middle-class background, with a convent school education, she became fascinated by the haphazard lives of women who existed without the safety net of money or education to sustain them. In 1963 she published a collection of short stories, *Up the Junction*, which consisted of vignettes of life as she had observed it among the young in Clapham. The book, which she later adapted for television, emphasised the vitality and sharpness of perception of the women, together with their acceptance of the fate life had mapped out for them—a few short butterfly days, followed by a hopeless and unrewarding existence.

In her first novel, *Poor Cow*, Dunn centred on one woman, Joy, whose life from early on is set on a downward spiral. At 22 she has gone through one broken marriage and has a young son, Jonny. As her own life deteriorates, she transfers her hopes onto her son, trusting that his life, at least, will be better. Her epitaph on her own is: "To think when I was a kid I planned to conquer the world and if anyone saw me now they'd say, 'She's had a rough night, poor cow.'" A film was made of the book by director Ken Loach.

Dunn's stage play, *Steaming*, continues her fascination with working-class women and with the character on whom Joy was based in particular: the woman who lives for freedom and fun, but in reality remains a prisoner of her lack of self-confidence and the hard brutalities of life. Josie, the "Joy" figure, is lively, earthy, enjoys leading her men a dance, but invariably ends up the worse for it. "How come I always get hit on the left side?" she asks, after yet another beating up.

Steaming is set in a London Turkish bath, which provides Dunn with the background for what she is best at—women talking among themselves, without the constraints of a male presence. The only male, the caretaker of the Baths, is dimly glimpsed through a glass door, unable to enter the female domain. The six characters are a mixture of age and class. Apart from Josie, there is Mrs. Meadow, a repressive mother, who will not let her retarded, overweight daughter take her "plastics" off, even in the shower. There are two middle-class women—Jane, a mature student with a bohemian past, and Nancy, who shops at Peter Jones and whose husband has just left her after 22 years of marriage. The Baths are presided over by Violet, in her forties, who has worked there as attendant for 18 years and who is threatened with early retirement if the Council goes ahead with its intention to close the building.

Not a great deal happens in the play, but the humour and conversation sustain the evening. Without their clothes, and in the steamy companionship of the Baths, the women develop a sisterhood that transcends class barriers. The new entrant, Nancy, at first nervous of the milieu, is drawn in and at one point breaks down and talks about her broken marriage and the pressures that have kept her dependent on a man. Josie reveals that her seeming sexual freedom is also tied to dependence on a man's finances. Their campaign against the closure of the Baths gives them a new lease of life, and by the end Josie, after making a brilliant, if disregarded, speech at a public meeting, says she is going to get an education; Nancy, the rejected wife, announces she is "going to get fucked"; and Dawn asserts herself against her over-protective mother.

Whether this ending is anything more than a way of giving an upbeat finale to the play is a matter for debate, and Dunn's characters will probably find they are not able to change their lives greatly after their temporary euphoria. The dialogue of the working-class women has far more of a ring of truth about it than the dialogue of the middle-class women, but the author has always found a richness and rhythm in working-class speech that she fails to find in the more educated voice. *Steaming* can be regarded as a gentle piece of female consciousness-raising. It must also be one of the few feminist plays to have brought large numbers of male chauvinists in, attracted by the fact that the cast members are nude for much of the time.

I Want, written in 1972 in collaboration with Adrian Henri, is about a love affair between a well-bred, convent-educated girl but "with the devil in her" and a scholarship boy from a Liverpool terrace home. They meet in the 1920's and the play charts the course of their relationship over the next 60 years. It has moments of humour, but lacks the strength of *Steaming*. Dunn also wrote a book of interviews, *Talking to Women*, published in 1965. It is of interest for its recording of the stirrings of "female consciousness" among divergent women. In 1991 she published a sequel in *Grandmothers*. Dunn, herself a grandmother, drew on her own experiences as well as those of her friends to investigate the pleasures and pains of being a grandmother. Based on conversations with 14 of her female friends, it is particularly interesting because of the variety of backgrounds from which her subjects come, and because of the contrast between the traditional image of a grandmother and present-day reality.

Dunn's play *The Little Heroine*, which deals with a young woman's addiction to heroin, was produced during the same year as Granada Television produced her *Every Breath You Take*. This play deals with the effect on a newly divorced woman, Imogen, of finding her 13-year-old son diagnosed as diabetic. Obsessed with Tom's diet and insulin injection, she is unable to concentrate on anything else. In the end it is Tom, mature and sensible for his age, who restores her sense of proportion and helps her rebuild the life and career which she had seemed ready to abandon.

—Clare Colvin

———

DURANG, Christopher (Ferdinand). American. Born in Montclair, New Jersey, 2 January 1949. Educated at Harvard

University, Cambridge, Massachusetts, 1967–71, A.B. in English 1971; Yale University School of Drama, New Haven, Connecticut, 1971–74, M.F.A. in playwriting 1974. Drama teacher, Southern Connecticut College, New Haven, 1975, and Yale University, 1975–76. Recipient: CBS fellowship, 1975; Rockefeller grant, 1976; Guggenheim grant, 1979; Obie award, 1980, 1985; Lecomte de Nouy Foundation grant, 1981; Dramatists Guild Hull-Warriner award, 1985. Agent: Helen Merrill Ltd., 361 West 17th Street, New York, New York 10011, U.S.A.

PUBLICATIONS

Plays

The Nature and Purpose of the Universe (produced Northampton, Massachusetts, 1971; New York, 1975). Included in *The Nature and Purpose of the Universe; Death Comes to Us All, Mary Agnes; 'dentity Crisis*, 1979.

'dentity Crisis (as *Robert*, produced Cambridge, Massachusetts, 1971; as *'dentity Crisis*, also director: produced New Haven, Connecticut, 1975; London, 1986). Included in *The Nature and Purpose of the Universe; Death Comes to Us All, Mary Agnes; 'dentity Crisis*, 1979.

Better Dead Than Sorry, music by Jack Feldman, lyrics by Durang (produced New Haven, Connecticut, 1972; New York, 1973).

I Don't Generally Like Poetry But Have You Read "Trees"?, with Albert Innaurato (produced New Haven, Connecticut, 1972; New York, 1973).

The Life Story of Mitzi Gaynor; or, Gyp, with Albert Innaurato (produced New Haven, Connecticut, 1973).

The Marriage of Bette and Boo (produced New Haven, Connecticut, 1973; revised version produced New York, 1979). New Haven, Connecticut, *Yale/Theatre*, 1973; revised version (produced New York, 1985; London, 1987), New York, Dramatists Play Service, 1985.

The Idiots Karamazov, with Albert Innaurato, music by Jack Feldman, lyrics by Durang (produced New Haven, Connecticut, 1974). New Haven, Connecticut, *Yale/Theatre*, 1974; augmented edition, New York, Dramatists Play Service, 1981.

Titanic (produced New Haven, Connecticut, 1974; New York, 1976). New York, Dramatists Play Service, 1983.

Death Comes to Us All, Mary Agnes (produced New Haven, Connecticut, 1975). Included in *The Nature and Purpose of the Universe; Death Comes to Us All, Mary Agnes; 'dentity Crisis*, 1979.

When Dinah Shore Ruled the Earth, with Wendy Wasserstein (produced New Haven, Connecticut, 1975).

Das Lusitania Songspiel, with Sigourney Weaver, music by Mel Marvin and Jack Gaughan (produced New York, 1976; revised version produced New York, 1976; revised version produced New York, 1980).

A History of the American Film, music by Mel Marvin (produced Hartford, Connecticut, 1976; New York, 1978). New York, Avon, 1978.

The Vietnamization of New Jersey (produced New Haven, Connecticut, 1977). New York, Dramatists Play Service, 1978.

Sister Mary Ignatius Explains It All for You (produced New York, 1979; London, 1983). New York, Dramatists Play Service, 1980.

The Nature and Purpose of the Universe; Death Comes to Us All, Mary Agnes; 'dentity Crisis: Three Short Plays. New York, Dramatists Play Service, 1979.

Beyond Therapy (produced New York, 1981; revised version produced New York and London, 1982). New York, French, 1983.

The Actor's Nightmare (produced New York, 1981; London, 1983). With *Sister Mary Ignatius Explains It All for You*, New York, Dramatists Play Service, 1982.

Christopher Durang Explains It All for You (includes *The Nature and Purpose of the Universe, 'dentity Crisis, Titanic, The Actor's Nightmare, Sister Mary Ignatius Explains It All for You, Beyond Therapy*). New York, Avon, 1982.

Baby with the Bathwater (produced Cambridge, Massachusetts, and New York, 1983; Colchester, Essex, 1984; London, 1991). New York, Dramatists Play Service, 1984; with *Laughing Wild*, New York, Grove, 1989.

Sloth, in *Faustus in Hell* (produced Princeton, New Jersey, 1985).

Laughing Wild (produced New York, 1987; London, 1988) With *Baby with the Bathwater*, New York, Grove, 1989.

Cardinal O'Connor and *Woman Stand-up*, in *Urban Blight* (musical revue), based on an idea by John Tillinger, music by David Shire, lyrics by Richard Maltby Jr. (produced New York, 1988).

Christopher Durang at Dawn (cabaret) (produced New York, 1990).

Naomi in the Living Room (produced New York, 1991).

Screenplay: *Beyond Therapy*, with Robert Altman, 1987.

Television Writing: *Comedy Zone* series; *Carol Burnett Special*.

*

Theatrical Activities:
Director: **Play**—*'dentity Crisis*, New Haven, Connecticut, 1975; *And the Air Didn't Answer* by Robert Kerr, New York, 1989.

Actor: **Plays**—at Yale University School of Drama, New Haven, Connecticut: Gustaf in *Urlicht* by Albert Innaurato, 1971, Darryl in *Better Dead Than Sorry*, 1972, Performer in *The Life Story of Mitzi Gaynor; or, Gyp*, 1973, Bruce in *Happy Birthday, Montpelier Pizz-zazz* by Wendy Wasserstein, 1974, and Emcee in *When Dinah Shore Ruled the Earth*, 1975; at Yale Repertory Theatre: Chorus in *The Frogs* by Burt Shevelove and Stephen Sondheim, 1974, Student in *The Possessed* by Camus, 1974, and Alyosha in *The Idiots Karamazov*, 1974; Performer in *I Don't Generally Like Poetry But Have You Read "Trees"?*, New York, 1973; Performer in *Das Lusitania Songspiel*, New York, 1976, 1980; Young Cashier in *The Hotel Play* by Wallace Shawn, New York, 1981; Matt in *The Marriage of Bette and Boo*, New York, 1985; role in *Laughing Wild*, New York, 1987; Ubu's Conscience in *Ubu Roi*, adaptation of Alfred Jarry's play by Larry Sloan and Doug Wright, New York, 1989; *Christopher Durang at Dawn*, New York, 1990. **Film**—*The Secret of My Success*, 1987; *Housesitter*, 1992.

* * *

Handsomely surviving a Catholic boyhood in New Jersey and Ivy League education at Harvard and Yale (M.F.A. in playwriting), Christopher Durang has been critically ranked in the top echelon of American playwrights. Most of his plays have been popular with regional and off-the-mainline theatres, and reflect their author's penchant for parody with favorite targets being drama and film, literature, American social history and popular culture, parochial religion, and the middle-class family. National recognition arrived with the 1978 Broadway production on *A History of the American Film*. Most critics applauded Durang's satiric skills that coalesced in this inventive multi-leveled profile of the films and social history of the last 50 years.

Using a revue-type format and song lyrics by Durang, *American Film* trots out the clichés, stereotypes, and superficial attitudes toward events that bombarded American culture from *Orphans of the Storm* to *Earthquake*. The characters interchange as screen spectators and actors, as we follow the thorny path of the naively innocent heroine from poverty with a callous Cagney-like lover through speakeasies, prison, high society, wartime, to heavenly ascension. The play spoofs specific films of the 1930's and 1940's, film genres, and screen stars representing our personified ideals of toughness or innocence. And the audience watches itself identifying with the black and white morality of the western, the jingoism of World War II, and the neurotic narcissism of the postwar period. More than a revue with some skits wearing thin by the second act, this satiric farce is impudently effective.

Literature and drama, respectively, fall under attack in *The Idiots Karamazov*, written with Albert Innaurato, and *The Vietnamization of New Jersey*. The first is an irreverent send-up of Dostoevsky's novel and western literature's great books; its action combines chaotic slapstick with a profusion of literary allusions comprehensible largely to the cognoscenti. Displaying sharper comedic ability, the second play is an absurdist parody of David Rabe's anti-Vietnam play *Sticks and Bones* and of American anti-war dramas thrusting collective guilt upon docile audiences. Comic recognition, however, rests too heavily on knowledge of Rabe's drama.

The theatre and drama as satirical subjects again surface in *The Actor's Nightmare*, a hilarious curtain-raiser in which a befuddled accountant clad as Hamlet, without benefit of lines or rehearsal, finds himself on stage in a phantasmagoric play whose actors veer from Coward's *Private Lives* and Beckett plays to *Hamlet* and Robert Bolt's *A Man for All Seasons*. Ultimately thrust into a scene from the last play, the baffled hero becomes Sir Thomas More facing a suddenly realistic execution, and despite his last minute, out-of-character recanting, is not seen on stage for the curtain call—an end resembling that of Tom Stoppard's *Rosencrantz and Guildenstern*.

Setting his sights on personal relationships and the deficiencies of psychiatrists, Durang in *Beyond Therapy* chronicles the tale of two Manhattan singles in their thirties, a bisexual male lawyer and a female journalist concerned about getting herself married, who meet through a personals ad. The curious couple are ineptly coached through a courtship of insults, rejections, and threats by their respective psychiatrists: the woman's shrink, a male chauvinist who seduces his female patients, and the man's, a daffy lady who constantly carries a Snoopy doll and confuses words. In a more optimistic ending than Durang normally gives, the couple jointly reject their therapists and consider having a continued relationship perhaps even leading to marriage. There is a dazzling display of funny lines and jokes on contemporary mores, gender identity, and psychiatry. Credibility is stretched with two such divergent lovers even considering a relationship, a problem not mitigated by the lack of a final resolution scene or a well-developed farcical plot to connect the many short two-character scenes. Yet these shortcomings have not prevented the play from becoming a favorite with community and regional theatres.

Dogmatic parochial education receives barbs in Durang's Obie-winning *Sister Mary Ignatius Explains It All for You*.

The title character is a sin-smelling teaching nun who tyrannizes her students. During a lecture she is interrupted by the return of four former students who loathe her. The group ranges from a happy homosexual and unwed mother to a rape victim and a suicidal alcoholic; their recriminations rouse the nun to shoot them, and class servility is restored. The satire is sharp and wildly funny in this gem of black humor.

Absurdist portraits of the American family particularly abound in five Durang plays. *The Nature and Purpose of the Universe, Death Comes to Us All, Mary Agnes*, and *'dentity Crisis* are three short black comedies treating victimized females losing life, sanity, or identity at the hands of callous families and the traditional Catholic view of women. Although losing their bite in farcical chaos, the plays project subjects more maturely developed in two later works. The first is *Baby with the Bathwater*, a satirical farce on parenting in which two self-absorbed parents idiotically raise a male child (confusing his true gender for 15 years) who survives to young adulthood desperate to avoid his own upbringing's mistakes when becoming a father himself. The play's string of cartoon-like scenes progressively pall, despite the satirical feast they offer, and would profit from sharper variety and a greater buttressing of reality. More effective is the revised (1985) Obie-winning *The Marriage of Bette and Boo*, a trenchantly amusing dissection of the contemporary Catholic family. In 33 inventive scenes related by the family's only son and treated with farcical brilliance, a marriage moves through three decades of alcoholism, divorce, surrounding relatives representing failures of the married and single state, and a priest who dodges counsel-session questions by imitating frying bacon. At the center stand the dipsomaniac Boo and the dimwit Bette, who persists after a first surviving child producing stillborn babies against medical advice. Admitting an autobiographical connection, the playwright gives us the outrageously satiric view of society that characterizes his best work.

Durang's satiric concern with the perils of modern urban life continues in two works written since 1987. *Laughing Wild* consists of two monologues individually delivered by a man and a woman who expose their dreams and frustrations resulting from separate daily lives in which they encounter and expound upon rude taxi drivers, waiting in line, inane talk shows, attitudes of the Catholic Church towards sexual matters, and each other as they clash over a purchase of canned tuna fish in a supermarket aisle. In the play's final section the two strangers meet to re-enact the supermarket incident with varying interpretations, talk more of their overlapping dreams, and reach a hesitant truce. This funny and inventive comedy has proved popular with regional and fringe theatres. Less successful, *Naomi in the Living Room* is a dark absurdist comedy treating a self-absorbed, psychotic middle-class mother (Naomi) who rudely receives her son and his wife for a brief visit during which her son cross-dresses and behaves like his wife. The couple departs at the wife's insistence, leaving the mother in her loveless, sterile urban home.

Durang's work rises above collegiate-like preciosity to reveal a gifted satirist and farceur whose American absurdist view of the world is most delightfully successful when he furnishes a floor of reality under the dance of his characters. As a satirist writing for the stage, he is a member of an endangered species who deserves the theatre's nurturing if he is to continue to flourish. He is a needed talent in the American theatre.

—Christian H. Moe

DURRELL, Lawrence (George). British. 1912–1991. See 4th edition, 1988.

DYER, Charles (Raymond). British, Born in Shrewsbury, Shropshire, 7 July 1928. Educated at the Highlands Boys' School, Ilford, Essex; Queen Elizabeth's School, Barnet, Hertfordshire. Served in the Royal Air Force, 1944–47: flying officer. Married Fiona Thomson in 1959; three sons. Actor and director; chair and artistic director, Stage Seventy Productions Ltd. Address: Old Wob, Gerrards Cross, Buckinghamshire, England.

PUBLICATIONS

Plays

Clubs Are Sometimes Trumps (as C. Raymond Dyer) (produced Wednesbury, Staffordshire, 1948).
Who on Earth! (as C. Raymond Dyer) (produced London, 1951).
Turtle in the Soup (as C. Raymond Dyer) (produced London, 1953).
The Jovial Parasite (as C. Raymond Dyer) (produced London, 1954).
Single Ticket Mars (as C. Raymond Dyer) (produced Bromley, Kent, 1955).
Time, Murderer, Please (as C. Raymond Dyer) (produced Portsmouth, Hampshire, and London, 1956). London, English Theatre Guild, 1962.
Wanted—One Body! (as C. Raymond Dyer) (produced on tour, 1956). London, English Theatre Guild, 1961.
Poison in Jest (as C. Raymond Dyer) (produced Oxford, 1957).
Prelude to Fury (as C. Raymond Dyer) (produced London, 1959).
Red Cabbage and Kings (as R. Kraselchik) (produced Southsea, Hampshire, 1960).
Rattle of a Simple Man (produced London, 1962; New York, 1963). London and New York, French, 1963.
Gorillas Drink Milk, adaptation of a play by John Murphy (produced Coventry, 1964).
Staircase (produced London, 1966; New York, 1968). London, Penguin, 1966; New York, French, 1967.
Mother Adam (produced York, 1971; also director: produced London, 1971). London, Davis Poynter, 1972.
A Hot Godly Wind (produced Manchester, 1975). Published in *Second Playbill 3*, edited by Alan Durband, London, Hutchinson, 1973.
Futility Rites (produced in Germany, 1980).
Lovers Dancing (produced London, 1983). Oxford, Amber Lane Press, and New York, French, 1984.

Screenplays: *Rattle of a Simple Man*, 1964; *Staircase*, 1969; *Brother Sun and Sister Moon*, 1970.

Novels

Rattle of a Simple Man. London, Elek, 1964.
Charlie Always Told Harry Almost Everything. London, W.H. Allen, 1969; as *Staircase; or, Charlie Always Told Harry Almost Everything*, New York, Doubleday, 1969.

Under the Stairs. Berlin, Langen Müller, 1991.

*

Manuscript Collection: Manchester Central Library.

Critical Studies: in *Sunday Times* (London), 14 April 1966, 5 December 1971, and 29 April 1973; *Drama* (London), Winter 1967; *L'Avant Scène* (Paris), 15 January 1968; *New Yorker*, 20 January 1968; *Sipario* (Rome), August 1969; *Irish Tatler* (Dublin), December 1969.

Theatrical Activities:
Director: **Plays**—in London, Amsterdam, Rotterdam, Paris, Berlin; recently, *Mother Adam*, London, 1972, Stratford-on-Avon and London, 1973, Paris, 1981 and 1986.
Actor: **Plays**—roles in 250 plays; debut as Lord Harpenden in *While the Sun Shines* by Terence Rattigan, Crewe, Cheshire, 1947; Duke in *Worm's Eye View* by R.F. Delderfield, London and tour, 1948–50; Digger in *The Hasty Heart* by John Patrick, toured, 1950; Wilkie in *No Trees in the Street* by Ted Willis, toured, 1951; Turtle in *Turtle in the Soup*, London, 1953; Launcelot Gobbo in *The Merchant of Venice*, London, 1954; Freddie Windle in *The Jovial Parasite*, London, 1954; Maitre d'Hotel in *Room for Two* by Gilbert Wakefield, London, 1955; Keith Draycott in *Pitfall* by Falkland L. Cary, London, 1955; Dr. John Graham in *Suspended Sentence* by Sutherland Scott, London, 1955; Horace Grimshaw in *The Imperfect Gentleman* by Harry Jackson, London, 1956; Wishee Washee in *Aladdin*, London, 1956; Syd Fish in *Painted Sparrow* by Guy Paxton and E.V. Hoile, Cork, Ireland, 1956; Flash Harry in *Dry Rot* by John Chapman, London and tour, 1958; Shylock in *The Merchant of Venice*, Bromley, Kent, 1959; Viktor in *Red Cabbage and Kings*, Southsea, Hampshire, and tour, 1960; Percy in *Rattle of a Simple Man*, London, 1963; Mickleby in *Wanted—One Body!*, Guildford, Surrey, 1966. **Films**—include *Cuptie Honeymoon*, 1947; *Naval Patrol*, 1959; *The Loneliness of the Long Distance Runner*, 1962; *Rattle of a Simple Man*, 1964; *The Knack*, 1965; *How I Won the War*, 1967. **Television**—*Hugh and I* series, 1964; Charlie in *Staircase*, 1986.

Charles Dyer comments:
Outside bedtime, no one truly exists until he is reflected through the mind of another. We exist only as we think others think of us. We are not real except in our own tiny minds according to our own insignificant measurement of thought.
Animals adapt to their inadequacies without shame or discernible consciousness. Eventually, they wither to nothing, wagging their minds behind them, and die unsurprised—like frogs. Man is different, and is measured according to breadth of chest, amount of hair, inside leg, bosom and backside. He is insulted by death. He cares. And he cares more about what is seen than is hidden; yet unseen differences have greatest emotional effect.
Such as loneliness.
And I write about loneliness.
Obviously, Man is progressing towards a life, a world of Mind. Soon. Soon, in terms of creation. But with physicalities dismissed, the mind is lonelier than ever. Mind was God's accident. An unfortunate bonus. We should be more content as sparrows, spring-fluttering by the clock; a sudden day, tail-up; then the cock-bird, and satisfaction matter-of-factually; a search for straw; eggs and tomorrow automatic as the swelling of string in water. It happens for sparrows, that is all! Anything deeper is Mind. And Mind is an excess over needs. Therefore Mind is loneliness.
Rattle of a Simple Man and *Staircase* and *Mother Adam*

form a trilogy of loneliness, three plays enacted on Sundays, Bells are so damned lonely. Duologues, they are, because two seems the most sincere symbolic number, especially as man plus woman may be considered physically One. My plays have no plots, as such. Action cannot heal loneliness: it is cured only by *sharing* an action, and is emphasised by reduction of plot. And reduction of stage setting—which should, I feel, be expendable once the play is written. I detail a setting for the preparation of each duologue, that its dialogue may relate to a particular room; then, as a casting reflects its mould, the setting becomes irrevocably welded into and between the lines. The potency of these duologues is greater in drapes.

They reprimand me, occasionally, for handicapping my characters either physically or mentally: Cyrenne the prostitute and Percy, male virgin, in *Rattle of a Simple Man*; schizophrenic Adam and arthritical Mammles in *Mother Adam*; homosexual Charlie and nakedly-bald Harry in *Staircase*. And as the Trilogy grew, I locked them into barber shops and attics, depriving them even of a telephone to outside realities. This was a private challenge; yet what interest in an even face? what fault in a crooked smile? I love the courage of my imperfect characters, I despair with them—so small in a world of mindless faces, and faceless minds driving science to God's borders. In *Staircase*, man plus man situation, Charlie and Harry are lost without one another. But Charlie is too proud to admit such a fatal interdependence. He patronises Harry, taunts him, and drops "exciting" names which are anagrams of his own; he refuses to reflect anything of Harry; thus, Harry becomes an anagram, too; and even me, as their author. Charlie, Harry and me, become one; because there is no reality until we are reflected through someone else's eyes.

My characters have hope with their imperfections. They are dismayed by today's fading simplicity; today's lack of humility—no one ever wrong, always an excuse; kissing footballers without respect for the losers; and people who, from the safety of secret conscience, dismiss others as "them."

Man's disease is loneliness; God's is progress.

* * *

The opening performance of Charles Dyer's *Rattle of a Simple Man* was given at the Garrick Theatre on 19 September 1962. I had heard that it consisted of a dialogue between a mug and a tart, and, knowing nothing of Dyer's delicacy and integrity, assumed it would be full of equivocal situations. Before the end of the first act I realized I was in the presence of a new and valid talent, possessed to an astonishing degree of the capacity to find pearls among swine. In drunken football fans, in middle-aged, failing homosexual hairdressers, and the half-paralysed relics of tambourine-banging religiosity, Dyer finds not the débris of humanity, but unforgettable gleams of tenderness and self-sacrifice:

Cyrenne —Been on holiday?
Percy —I went to Morecambe. There were lots of married couples at the digs.
They took a fancy to me. I was always making them laugh. It was marvellous. I think I'll go somewhere else next year, though.

Dyer shows his skill in changing, by the simplest words, the whole mood of a scene. One can tell the very moment the light went out for Percy.

For many years Dyer travelled the country as an actor in provincial productions of London successes; and in Percy's unhappy seaside memories there may well be recollections of drab theatrical lodgings. The two homosexual barbers in *Staircase* are exceptionally bitter on this subject:

Charlie —Even me honeymoon was a—a—a holocaust: one night of passion and food-poisoning for thirteen. Maggots in the haddock, she claimed.
(Harry giggles)
Oh, I was laughing, dear. Yes. What! Lovely—your blushing bride all shivering and turgid in the promenade shelter; hurricanes whipping the shingle. Couldn't even paddle for a plague of jelly-fish.

Dyer considers and reconsiders very aspect of his work, and does not let it go until he has got out of it everything that it contains. Unlike most other eminent contemporary dramatists he is ready, even delighted, to discuss his work, its meaning, and its origin. It is clear that what he puts into his plays is but a small part of his knowledge of the people he writes about. He has written two novels, which have had considerable success, and both are treatments of themes dealt with in his plays, *Rattle of a Simple Man* and *Staircase*. Most people suppose that the novels are rewritings of the plays, but this is not true. The novels are the original work, and the plays follow after.

Thus, though *Rattle of a Simple Man* has an effect similar to that of the *nouveau roman* in that it leaves the audience with a question unanswered, Dyer is really at the opposite pole from writers like Alain Robbe-Grillet and Marguerite Duras. They leave questions open because their philosophy tells them that human knowledge is limited, whereas Dyer ends with an uncertainly only because the wealth of information with which he could resolve it would blur the clear outline of what he wishes to say.

Long before the end of *Rattle* we understand and love Cyrenne and Percy. They are characters, bruised, resilient, and in their ridiculous way curiously dignified, who make for righteousness, because they manifest sympathy and consideration for others. They are in fact people of honour.

That they are so is the basis of Dyer's outlook on the drama. He writes his plays, which are spare and austere in form, according to a classic formula of abiding power. The question with Dyer is not what his characters appear to be, but what they will do in the circumstances in which he places them. It is in my opinion a mistake to consider *Staircase* as primarily a study of homosexuality. Essentially it is a study of how under great stress a man's character may crumble, and then rebound to a level it never attained before.

Dyer is in fact the complement to Anouilh, whom in many ways he rivals in theatrical expertise. Whereas with bitter distress Anouilh discovers the sordidness of purity, Dyer—in this resembling Maupassant—comes upon purity in sordidness. Against dispiriting odds, people are capable of behaving unexpectedly well. This is one reason why Dyer's work is so much more exhilarating than that of even his most distinguished contemporaries. He is a dramatist who indulges neither in self-pity nor in recrimination.

In *Staircase*, presented by the Royal Shakespeare Company 1966–67, Dyer did a very curious thing. He gave his own name to the character played by Paul Scofield. This was the introduction of his theory that everybody is alone. He carries his theme into *Mother Adam*, but in *Staircase* all characters, on and offstage, are woven into patterns of the name Charles Dyer. It is a dramatic device to pinpoint the lack of substance in a man-man relationship where Charlie could not exist without Harry, nor Harry without Charlie. All is loneliness. And each without the other, says Dyer, would be like "a golfer holing-in-one by himself. Nobody to believe him. Nobody to prove his moment ever truly existed." Dyer is at his best when dealing with commonplace aspects of life, and discerning in them the emotional depths of their apparent shallowness. There is something both ludicrous and touching in the way Harry broods over the distresses he suffered as a scout master. Patrick Magee brought real humanity to his task of making tea for Scofield's Dyer, prissy, pampered, pomaded, a ruined god, awaiting a summons for indecent behaviour. To his lurking terror, Mr. Scofield gave a fine touch of injured vanity.

The actor who plays this splendid part—one of the best in modern drama—can be riveting, revolting, and masterly all at the same time: in his sudden bursts of panic, in his vain boastings of a largely imaginary past as a pantomime dame, in his irritability, and in his readiness, in his own terror, to wound his pitiably vulnerable companion.

Mother Adam is Dyer's most ambitious play. Adam's paralysed mother is a tyrant of extreme power, and she brings it to bear on her son, who longs—he thinks—to escape and marry. Despite its consciousness that, in one of Dyer's shining phrases, "There aren't so many silk-loined years," the play is as full of laughter as it is of heartbreak. Its dialogue is rich in curious eloquence and stirring images.

Fine as these things are, it is not in them that Dyer's mastery is to be found, but in his capacity to hold in his mind two conflicting rights, and to see, with a true compassion, that their confrontation cannot be resolved. It is because of this capacity that he has written in *Mother Adam* one of the few tragedies of our time. Adam cannot be free unless his mother is deserted; his mother cannot be cared for unless her son's life is ruined. It is this situation that Charles Dyer observes with a dancing eye and a riven heart.

I say, with the same absolute confidence with which I wrote of Pinter's *The Birthday Party* in 1958, that in the history of the contemporary theatre *Mother Adam* will rank as a masterpiece.

Dyer had previously written two fine and successful plays: *Rattle of a Simple Man* and *Staircase*. *Mother Adam* is better than either. It is more disturbing; it has deeper resonances; it is more beautifully written, with an imagination at once exotic and desperately familiar; it has a profounder pity, and a more exquisite falling close.

Loneliness haunts Dyer's imagination. Is there any solution to this terrible problem? Dyer says there is. Loneliness is the product of selfishness, and where no selfishness is, there is no loneliness. The condition of unselfishness is not easy to attain. It is within reach only of the saints. But sanctity is not an unattainable goal. We should all aim for it.

In *Mother Adam* Dyer seeks the continuing theme of Oneness. Man and mother, almost to the edges of Oedipus. The moment when Adam falls to his knees at the bedside, hugging his mother, dragging her crippled knuckles to his face, begging "Hug me! hug me! I dream of love. I need love," should represent the climax, not only of *Mother Adam*, but of the whole Loneliness Trilogy.

In two of his plays Dyer deals with subjects which, when the plays were first produced, were considered daring. The Lord Chamberlain made 26 cuts in *Staircase*, including the scene in which Harry explains his hatred of the physical side of life. The *Report on Censorship 1967* mentioned *Staircase* throughout 25 of its two hundred pages. Dyer likes to feel he is ahead of trends, but not excessively so: "In terms of eternity, the interval between Adam and Eve's nakedness and the Moment when God cast them forth in animal skins is but a finger click. The serious, most important period is what happens *after* they put on clothes."

We clothe our inadequacies. This is what Dyer's plays are all about.

—Harold Hobson

E

EASMON, R(aymond) Sarif. Sierra Leonean. Received M.B. and B.S. degrees. Practising doctor. Address: 31 Bathurst Street, Freetown, Sierra Leone.

PUBLICATIONS

Plays

Dear Parent and Ogre (produced Ibadan, Nigeria, 1961). London and New York, Oxford University Press, 1964.
The New Patriots. London, Longman, 1966.

Novel

The Burnt-Out Marriage. London, Nelson, and New York, Humanities Press, 1967.

Short Stories

The Feud and Other Stories. London, Longman, 1981.

* * *

With his unfailing sense of the comic potential in any situation, it seems likely that R. Sarif Easmon is, as Bernth Lindfors puts it, "the first African offspring of Oscar Wilde and Noël Coward." His witty, urbane plays deal with the romance of politics and the politics of romance—two areas dear to the heart of an African audience—and they move with the grace of a dancer from one finely choreographed scene to the next.

There has been some criticism of the language used by Easmon's "upper class" characters, a pure Oxford English of the type which has proven so satisfying to a generation of word-conscious and Western-educated Africans. Yet when one sees one of Easmon's plays in production there is no doubt that the language is perfectly suited to both the personalities and the social positions of the characters. After all, not all Africans speak continually in proverbs. Moreover, when Easmon introduces characters from different social backgrounds he fits their speech to their class. One need only compare the words Dauda Touray, the "parent and ogre" of Easmon's first play—"Our gratitude shall transcend champagne, Saidu!"—with those of the hired ruffian Charles Randall—"Lord 'ave mercy—Oh! For de name way me daddy and mammy gave me!"—to see the difference.

There is nothing stock about the characters in Easmon's delightful comedies. The two roguish politicians of his second play, *The New Patriots*, who are struggling for the hand of the same woman are as alive as Dauda Touray, the main character of *Dear Parent and Ogre*, yet they are not in any way a copy of the earlier character. Easmon's figures have unorthodox turns to their nature. Sekou, the young hero of *Dear Parent and Ogre*, is a son of a Yalie, a class given over to

singing (quite literally) the praises of the noble Touray family, yet he has found success in Europe as a recording star and has returned, replete with impeccable French and Rolls-Royce, to claim the hand of Dauda's daughter.

Because they deal with the themes of a new Africa, an Africa where the two suitors can be a descendant from former slaves on the one hand and from a lowly class of minstrels on the other, an Africa where champagne, moonlight, Joloff rice, and hired thugs can be blended into a scene of high comedy, Easmon's plays have attracted large audiences whenever they have been performed in West Africa. Because Easmon manages, while developing these themes, to present us with vital human characters and situations which have larger universal implications, it seems safe to say that his appeal need not be limited to African audiences.

—Joseph Bruchac

EBEJER, Francis. Maltese. Born in Dingli, 28 August 1925. Educated at Lyceum Grammar School, Valletta, 1934–39; University of Malta, Msida, 1942–43; St. Mary's College, Twickenham, Middlesex, 1948–50. Served as an English-Italian interpreter with the British 8th Army, Tripolitania, 1943–44. Married Jane Cauchi Gera in 1947; two sons (one deceased) and one daughter. Teacher, 1944–48, and school principal, 1950–77; Malta Education Department. Since 1976 guest lecturer, University of Malta. Recipient: Malta Amateur Film Circle award, for acting, 1959; International PEN (English Centre) fellowship, 1961; Fulbright travel grant (USA), 1961; Cheyney award, for producing, 1964; Dublin Television Festival award, for documentary, 1969; Malta Literary award, 1971, 1976, 1983, 1985; Phoenicia Trophy (Malta), 1982; Medal of Honor (Avignon), 1986. Agent: Eulama, via Torino 135, 1–00184 Rome, Italy; or, Peter Miller Agency, 1021 Avenue of the Americas, New York, New York 10018, U.S.A. Address: 3 Nivea Court, Swieqi Valley, St. Andrews, Malta.

PUBLICATIONS

Plays

Is-Sejha ta' Sarid (Sarid's Summons) (broadcast 1950; produced Valletta 1966). Included in *Id-Drammi 1*, 1965.

160

Cpar fix-Xemx (Fog in the Sun) (broadcast 1950). Published in *Lehen il-Malti* (Msida), April-December 1952.

Bwani (broadcast 1951; revised version produced Valletta, 1974). Included in *Id-Drammi 1*, 1965.

Iz-Zjara (The Visit) (broadcast 1952). Included in *Id-Drammi 1*, 1965.

Ix-Xorti ta' Mamzell (Mamzell's Luck) (broadcast 1953; produced Floriana, 1982). Included in *Id-Drammi 1*, 1965.

Sefora (broadcast 1954; produced Valletta, 1984). Included in *Id-Drammi 6*, 1984.

Loghba (The Game) (broadcast 1954). Included in *Id-Drammi 6*, 1984.

Rewwixta tas-Swaba' (Revolt of the Fingers) (broadcast 1955). Included in *Id-Drammi 6*, 1984.

Vaganzi tas-Sajf (produced Valletta, 1962). Included in *Id-Drammi 2*, 1970; translated by Ebejer as *Summer Holidays*, in *Collected English Plays 3*, 1980.

Boulevard (produced Valletta, 1964). Included in *Id-Drammi 2*, 1970; translated by Ebejer as *Boulevard*, in *Collected English Plays 2*, 1980.

Id-Drammi ta Francis Ebejer (The Plays of Francis Ebejer):
1. *Iz-Zjara, Is-Sejha ta' Sarid, Bwani, Ix-Xorti ta' Mamzell*. Privately printed, 1965.
2. *Menz, Boulevard, Vaganzi tas-Saif*. Privately printed, 1970.
3. *Il-Hadd Fuq Il-Bejt, L-Imnarja Zmien il-Qtil, L-Imwarrbin*. Valletta, KKM, 1973.
4. *Hitan*. Valletta, KKM, 1974.
5. *Meta Morna tal-Mellieha, Vum-Barala-Zungarè, Karnival*. Valletta, KKM, 1977.
6. *Sefora, Filfla Minn Wara Hajt* (Filfla from Behind a Wall), *Morru Sejhu lill-Werrieta, Rewwixta tas-Swaba', Loghba, X'Ma Kixifx il-Hajt*. Valletta, Mid-Med, 1984.
7. *Il-Gahan ta' Bingemma, Il-Mutur, It-Telefonata, L-Ghajta, F'Hagar Qim, In-Nasba*. Valletta, Ministry of Education, 1985.

Menz (produced Valletta, 1967). Included in *Id-Drammi 2*, 1970; translated by Ebejer as *Menz*, in *Collected English Plays 2*, 1980.

The Cliffhangers (produced Valletta, 1968). Included in *Collected English Plays 3*, 1980; translated by the author into Maltese as *L-Imwarrbin* (produced Valletta, 1974), in *Id-Drammi 3*, 1973.

Hefen Plus Zero (broadcast 1970; produced Coventry, 1981). Included in *Collected English Plays 3*, 1980.

Hitan (Walls) (televised 1970; produced Valletta, 1983). Included in *Id-Drammi 4*, 1974.

Il-Hadd Fuq Il-Bejt (Sunday on the Roof) (produced Valletta, 1971). Included in *Id-Drammi 3*, 1973.

L-Imnarja Zmien il-Qtil (Imnarja Is a Time for Killing) (produced Valletta, 1973). Included in *Id-Drammi 3*, 1973.

Vum-Barala-Zungarè (produced Valletta, 1973). Included in *Id-Drammi 5*, 1977.

X'Ma Kixifx il-Hajt (What the Wall Didn't Reveal) (televised 1973). Included in *Id-Drammi 6*, 1984.

Bloody in Bolivia (produced Floriana, 1975). Included in *Collected English Plays 1*, 1980.

Meta Morna tal-Mellieha (When We Went to Mellieha) (produced Valletta, 1976). Included in *Id-Drammi 5*, 1977.

Karnival (Carnival) (produced Valletta, 1977). Included in *Id-Drammi 5*, 1977.

Id-Dar tas-Soru (The Nun's House) (televised 1977–78). Valletta, KKM, 1977.

Golden Tut (produced Valletta, 1979; London, 1981). Included in *Collected English Plays 2*, 1980.

Morru Sejhu lill-Werrieta (Go and Call the Inheritors) (televised 1979). Included in *Id-Drammi 6*, 1984.

Collected English Plays:
1. *Mark of the Zebra, Cleopatra Slept (Badly) Here, Bloody in Bolivia*. Valletta, Aquilina, 1980.
2. *Boulevard, Golden Tut, Hour of the Sun, Menz*. Valletta, Aquilina, 1980.
3. *Saluting Battery, The Cliffhangers, Hefen Plus Zero, Summer Holidays*. Valletta, Aquilina, 1980.

Il-Gahan ta' Bingemma (The Jester of Bingemma) (produced Valletta, 1985). Included in *Id-Drammi 7*, 1985.

Il-Mutur (The Motorbike) (produced Hal Far, 1985). Included in *Id-Drammi 7*, 1985.

It-Telefonata (The Telephone Call) (produced Hal Far, 1985). Included in *Id-Drammi 7*, 1985.

L-Ghajta (The Shout) (produced Hal Far, 1985). Included in *Id-Drammi 7*, 1985.

F'Hagar Qim (At Hagar Qim) (produced Hal Far, 1985). Included in *Id-Drammi 7*, 1985.

In-Nasba (The Trap) (produced Valletta, 1985). Included in *Id-Drammi 7*, 1985.

Radio Plays: *Is-Sejha ta' Sarid*, 1950; *Cpar fix-Xemx*, 1950; *Bwani*, 1951; *Il-Karba ta' l-Art* (The Cry of the Earth), 1951; *L-Ghassiesa ta' l-Alpi* (The Guardian of the Alps), 1951; *Iz-Zjara*, 1952; *Tieqa Bla Qamar* (Window Without Moon), 1952; *Ix-Xorti ta' Mamzell*, 1953; *Majjistral* (Mistral), 1953; *Sefora*, 1954; *Loghba*, 1954; *Dawra-Durella* (Ring-a-Ring-a-Rosy), 1954; *Rewwixta tas-Swaba'*, 1955; *Hemm Barra* (Out There), 1955; *Il-Bidu Jintemm* (End of the Beginning), 1955; *'Il Hinn mill-Biza'* (Beyond Fear), 1956; *Izfen, Ors, Izfen* (Dance, Bear, Dance), 1956; *Elsie*, 1956; *It-Triq ghal Tyburn* (The Road to Tyburn), 1957; *L-Imjassra ta' Fotheringay* (The Prisoner of Fotheringay), 1957; *Mixtieq il-Kenn* (Shelter Wanted), 1957; *Hefen Plus Zero*, 1970 (Italy).

Television Plays: *Hitan*, 1970; *X'Ma Kixifx il-Hajt*, 1973; *Persuna Qieghda Tigi Investigata Dwar . . .* (A Person Is Being Interrogated Regarding . . .), 1974; *Id-Dar tas-Soru* series, 1977–78; *Morru Sejhu lill-Werrieta*, 1979.

Novels

A Wreath for the Innocents. London, MacGibbon and Kee, 1958; as *A Wreath of Maltese Innocents*, Malta, Bugelli, 1981.

Evil of the King Cockroach. London, MacGibbon and Kee, 1960; as *Wild Spell of Summer*, Malta, Union Press, 1968.

In the Eye of the Sun. London, Macdonald, 1969.

Come Again in Spring. Malta, Union Press, 1973; New York, Vantage Press, 1979.

Requiem for a Malta Fascist. Valletta, Aquilina, 1980.

Leap of Malta Dolphins. New York, Vantage Press, 1982.

Il-Harsa ta' Ruzann (Ruzann's Glance). Valletta, KKM, 1985.

Other

Translator, *The Lamplighter*, by Anton Buttigieg. Portree, Isle of Skye, Aquila, 1977.

*

Bibliography: in *Id-Drammi 7*, 1985.

Manuscript Collections: National Library of Malta, Valletta; University of Malta Library, Msida.

Critical Studies: article by Hella Jean Bartolo, in *Canadian Theatre Review* (Downsview, Ontario), Summer 1975; "The

Bicultural Situation in Malta" by Ebejer, in *Individual and Community in Commonwealth Literature* edited by Daniel Massa, Msida, University of Malta, 1979; article by Arthur Pollard, in *ACLALS Bulletin 2* (St. Lucia, Queensland), January 1979; "The Malta Theatre Connection" by Adrian Rendle, in *Contemporary Review* (London), 1980.

Theatrical Activities:
Director: **Plays**—most of his own plays; *Marching Song* by John Whiting, 1963, *The Boy Friend* by Sandy Wilson, 1965, and *The Rope Dancers* by Morton Wishengrad, 1975, all Valletta.

Francis Ebejer comments:

While I have written all my novels, except one, in English, the majority of my plays are in my native language, Maltese. Most of my plays deal with universal themes and universal humankind; in the others, universal themes are applied to a specific society, the Mediterranean-Maltese, within a cosmopolitan context. In other words, I have tried to explain life on an island steeped in antiquity yet a member of the modern world, and eying the future through the geopolitical, military, industrial, and cross-cultural concerns in the central Mediterranean.

A recurrent theme is the function and influence of the past upon the present of, as the case may be, the private individual or the colonized country striving for and trying to understand independence; in either case, the interaction of past and present might provide glimpses of alternative futures.

If it may appear that I have treated certain themes from a philosophical and/or sociological angle, all that is secondary to the attention I try to give to actual lives by three-dimensional people with their psychological, moral, and ethical strengths and weakness, integralities and contradictions.

For instance, if a character is isolated in certain psychological and moral patterns of alienation, the exercise takes on the workings of analogy, or allegory, in so far as the character comes to represent the self-flawed image of a country—in our case, Malta itself, which became a sovereign state only recently after a long history of colonization, beginning with the Phoenicians and ending with the British.

In those plays that most specifically deal with Mediterranean-Maltese society I have on several occasions gone in search of a sense of identity and continuity right to the bed-rock of Mediterranean cultures, to "the sacred groves of the goat-god and the mother-goddess"—an ethos which is still a palpable omnipresence in Catholic Malta: one wonders, in fact, whether this is as paradoxical as it may seem, since religions and pagan cults in the Mediterranean have always interlocked.

In my English plays, on the other hand, such Mediterranean aspects are touched upon only here and there, or for the most part intermittently felt, leaving me freer to explore and concentrate more upon actual relationships among disparate people caught in (semi-)existentialist conditions of life.

Thus: guilt and expiation in both the pagan sense and the Christian (*The Cliffhangers*); the various levels of freedom, starting from the snug serflike desire for non-freedom—let others do the caring!—and working upwards to freedom in responsibility (*Bloody in Bolivia*); individual and societal consciences in a conformist society (*Menz*); impotence in the face of oppression (*Saluting Battery*); the way humans at large seem destined, because of some inherent blind perversity, to miss one chance after another of a reasonably lasting fulfilment (*Boulevard*); loneliness caused by self-delusion (*Golden Tut*); the individual of vision, however weak to start with, in

an entropic society (*Hefen Plus Zero*); completely ignoring, or missing, the truth about oneself to one's own and others' detriment (*Summer Holidays*); genuine and fake identities, with particular reference to those induced by the theatre itself (*Cleopatra Slept (Badly) Here*); role-reversal under the influence of strange new places and diverted desires (*Hour of the Sun*); the black-white tension in an artist trying to make some sense of his own contradictions while not really wishing them resolved: he discerns in such an eventual symbiosis, or synthesis, a threat to his art, to his essential self (*Mark of the Zebra*).

* * *

Francis Ebejer began as a Maltese language dramatist, later writing novels and plays in English, and has continued to create in both languages. Four of his eleven *Collected English Plays* are translated from Maltese. His plays fluctuate, often during scenes within a single work, between naturalism, expressionism, symbolism, and the absurd. The four modes correspond to the various kinds of significance in the plays: the deterministic, the psychological, the social-political, and the philosophical. His early radio plays in Maltese are represented by *Hefen Plus Zero* with its science-fiction futuristic setting and philosophical themes. Moving to the theatre with *Summer Holidays*, he already had assembled many of the ingredients of his later drama, including settings so indistinct as to universalize the events while being applicable to Malta. Probably influenced by Strindberg's later plays, the dominant naturalism unexpectedly changes into expressionism and symbolism. The characters, as in *The Cliffhangers* and *Hour of the Sun* live in an apparent paradise, but bring their own hell with them. Obsessed with their past, guilt, private relations, and delusions of free choice, they are blind to the external dangers which will destroy them, the enemy soldiers literally at the door. Throughout the plays ideas of freedom are tested. While society threatens personal liberty, such freedom is often an illusion, mere adolescent rebellion, unaware of the limitations imposed by reality; isolation and role playing must be overcome through social commitment, especially to the freedom of others.

Mark of the Zebra concerns a writer whose work is unsuccessful because of an inability to reconcile sexual desires with ideals of purity; such confusion leaves him unable to write convincingly of human passions. The symbolist-absurd *Boulevard*, regarded as the start of modern Maltese theatre, reveals people continually repeating the same patterns in their life. The lack of contact between the characters reflected in incongruous, stylized dialogue, and their failure to take advantage of second chances, result in a pessimistic vision of humankind, condemned eternally to the same cycles of experience.

Set in unspecified or unlikely locations, using highly repetitive dialogue filled with such abstract moral and psychological terms as "fear" and "conscience," the plays are populated by stereotypes and caricatures who at first have no more depth than the cardboard figures used in *Menz* to suggest crowds and the "people." Such plays begin as witty exercises in the manipulation of role and power relationships, but they suddenly deepen into powerful revelations of the way emotions developed in childhood continue to influence behaviour. Comic farce erupts into a psychodrama of frantic searches for mothers, violent rebellions against fathers, murderous hatreds and stunning collapses of will. There are also Sartre-influenced existentialist implications as the surreal goonery uncovers relationships between the personal and the socio-political. *Menz* combines the comic theatre of the absurd with symbolism to show why the desire for freedom is betrayed as much by the emotional damage of the past as by social and political pressures to conform. The seemingly totally alienated Menz, symbol of freedom, is easily overcome by Ludilla B., the Governor, seductress and Mediterranean matriarch who, wearing a female lion tamer's outfit of silver tights and high black, green-sequined boots, entices him into betraying his sympathizers and letting her take care of all his decisions. As Menz's individuality leaves him he rapidly becomes senile; he says, "I'm indeed in my mother's house." The only freedom left for him is death.

In *Bloody in Bolivia* three Englishmen and an Englishwoman, absurdly attempting to sell insurance in Bolivia during a civil war, try to remain neutral, but cannot help becoming involved. While the government treats the four as possible spies, two of them are held hostage by the guerrillas, the leader of whom is the rebellious son of the dictator. Although the son's rebellion is motivated by personal obsessions, Captain Berger, who secretly works against the government for communal liberty, is a hero, as is the guerrilla leader's sister, who lives fully by risking her life for her brother. In these political plays where characters appear two-dimensional and behaviour rapidly changes, symbols give the events significance. Berger collects butterflies (symbols of beautiful freedom), while in *Saluting Battery* the ancient cannon, which the old man takes care of and which is fired as part of the rebellion, signifies sexual impotence as well as an attempted last stand for freedom. The symbolism structures what might otherwise seem mere absurdity and translates apparently arbitrary, inconsequential events into a criticism of confused, misdirected, empty lives. Not having sincerity of purpose, the characters betray themselves and others, falsely proclaim their liberty, and collapse into dependence. In *Saluting Battery* Charles, who after his dismissal from the state council leads the revolutionaries, becomes the spokesman for conformity once he is restored to his former position.

The way people are influenced by the roles they play is seen in *Hour of the Sun*, where Diana passes her discontent with marriage to Marion by having the latter imitate her. The farcical comedy of *Cleopatra Slept (Badly) Here* also concerns role-playing which, as in most of Ebejer's work, is shown as dishonest and self-defeating. The insults, advice, comments traded between the characters in the plays are similar to the nonsense game which bonds the two lonely young women in *Golden Tut*, who drive away a young man who might have redeemed them from isolation.

The use of visual symbols, sudden dramatic displays of emotion, character parts built on role-playing, and other kinds of theatricality reflects Ebejer's experience as an actor and director. His scripts suggest the kind of lighting to be used, point to significant moments of timing for entrances, and are built around such effective theatrical techniques as contrasting characters, unexpected reversals of roles, and clear parallels or contrasts between opening and concluding scenes. They are highly self-conscious plays which allude to acting and theatre while offering a surprisingly complete analysis of the human condition.

—Bruce King

EDGAR, David. British. Born in Birmingham, Warwickshire, 26 February 1948. Educated at Oundle School, Northamptonshire, 1961–65; Manchester University, 1966–69, B.A. (honours) in drama 1969. Reporter, Bradford *Telegraph and Argus*, Yorkshire, 1969–72; Yorkshire Arts Association fellow, Leeds Polytechnic, 1972–73; resident playwright, Birmingham Repertory Theatre, 1974–75; lecturer in playwriting, Birmingham University, 1974–78; literary adviser, Royal Shakespeare Company, 1984–88. Since 1988 honorary senior research fellow, Birmingham University. Recipient: John Whiting award, 1976; Bicentennial Exchange fellowship, 1978; Society of West End Theatre award, 1980; New York Drama Critics Circle award, 1982; Tony award, 1982. Lives in Birmingham. Agent: Michael Imison Playwrights, 28 Almeida Street, London N1 1TD, England.

PUBLICATIONS

Plays

Two Kinds of Angel (produced Bradford, 1970; London, 1971). Published in *The London Fringe Theatre*, edited by V.E. Mitchell, London, Burnham House, 1975.
A Truer Shade of Blue (produced Bradford, 1970).
Still Life: Man in Bed (produced Edinburgh, 1971; London, 1972).
The National Interest (produced on tour, 1971).
Tedderella (produced Edinburgh, 1971; London, 1973).
Bloody Rosa (produced Edinburgh, 1971).
Acid (produced Bradford, 1971).
Conversation in Paradise (produced Edinburgh, 1971).
The Rupert Show (produced on tour, 1972).
The End (produced Bradford, 1972).
Excuses, Excuses (produced Coventry, 1972; London, 1973; as *Fired*, produced Birmingham, 1975).
Rent; or, Caught in the Act (produced on tour and London, 1972).
State of Emergency (also director: produced on tour and London, 1972).
Not with a Bang But a Whimper (produced Leeds, 1972).
Death Story (produced Birmingham, 1972; New York and London, 1975).
The Road to Hanoi, in *Point 101* (produced London, 1972).
England's Ireland, with others (produced Amsterdam and London, 1972).
A Fart for Europe, with Howard Brenton (produced London, 1973).
Gangsters (produced London, 1973).
Up Spaghetti Junction, with others (produced Birmingham, 1973).
Baby Love (produced Leeds and London, 1973). Included in *Shorts*, 1989.
The Case of the Workers' Plane (produced Bristol, 1973; shorter version, as *Concorde Cabaret*, produced on tour, 1975).
Operation Iskra (produced on tour and London, 1973).
Liberated Zone (produced Bingley, Yorkshire, 1973; London, 1974).
The Eagle Has Landed (televised 1973; produced Liverpool, 1973).
Man Only Dines (produced Leeds, 1974).
The Dunkirk Spirit (produced on tour, 1974).
Dick Deterred (produced London, 1974; New York, 1983). New York, Monthly Review Press, 1974.
The . . . Show (produced Bingley, Yorkshire, 1974).

The Midas Connection (televised 1975). Included in *Shorts*, 1989.

O Fair Jerusalem (produced Birmingham, 1975). Included in *Plays 1*, 1987.

The National Theatre (produced London, 1975). Included in *Shorts*, 1989.

Summer Sports: Beaters, Cricket, Shotputters, Cross Country, Ball Boys (produced Birmingham, 1975; as *Blood Sports*, produced London, 1976; New York, 1987; revised version of *Ball Boys* produced London, 1977). *Ball Boys* published London, Pluto Press, 1978; in *The Best Short Plays 1982*, edited by Ramon Delgado, Radnor, Pennsylvania, Chilton, 1982; as *Blood Sports with Ball Boys*, included in *Shorts*, 1989.

Events Following the Closure of a Motorcycle Factory (produced Birmingham, 1976).

Destiny (produced Stratford-on-Avon, 1976; London, 1977). London, Eyre Methuen, 1976; revised version (produced London, 1985), Methuen, 1986.

Welcome to Dallas, J.C., adaptation of a play by Alfred Jarry (produced London, 1976).

The Perils of Bardfrod, with Richard Crane (produced Bradford, 1976).

Saigon Rose (produced Edinburgh, 1976; New York, 1982). Included in *Plays 1*, 1987.

Wreckers (produced Exeter and London, 1977). London, Eyre Methuen, 1977.

Ecclesiastes (broadcast 1977). Included in *Plays 2*, 1990.

Our Own People (produced London, 1977). With *Teendreams*, London, Methuen, 1987.

Mary Barnes (produced Birmingham, 1978; London, 1979; New Haven, Connecticut, 1980). London, Eyre Methuen, 1979; revised version, Methuen, 1984.

The Jail Diary of Albie Sachs, adaptation of the work by Sachs (produced London, 1978; New York, 1979). London, Collings, 1978.

Teendreams, with Susan Todd (produced Bristol and London, 1979). London, Eyre Methuen, 1979; revised edition, with *Our Own People*, London, Methuen, 1987.

The Life and Adventures of Nicholas Nickleby, adaptation of the novel by Dickens (produced London, 1980; New York, 1981). New York, Dramatists Play Service, 2 vols., 1982; included in *Plays 2*, 1990.

Maydays (produced London, 1983). London, Methuen, 1983; revised version, 1984.

Entertaining Strangers: A Play for Dorchester (produced Dorchester, Dorset, 1985; revised version produced London, 1987). London, Methuen, 1986.

That Summer (produced London, 1987). London, Methuen, 1987.

Plays 1 (includes *The Jail Diary of Albie Sachs*, *Mary Barnes*, *Saigon Rose*, *O Fair Jerusalem*, *Destiny*). London, Methuen, 1987.

Vote for Them, with Neil Grant (televised 1989). London, BBC Publications, 1989.

Shorts: Short Plays (includes *Blood Sports with Ball Boys*, *Baby Love*, *The National Theatre*, *The Midas Connection*). London, Hern, 1989.

Heartlanders, with Stephen Bill and Anne Devlin (produced Birmingham, 1989). London, Hern, 1989.

The Shape of the Table (produced London, 1990). London, Hern, 1990.

Plays 2 (includes *Ecclesiastes*, *The Life and Adventures of Nicholas Nickleby*, *Entertaining Strangers: A Play for Dorchester*). London, Methuen, 1990.

Plays 3 (includes *Our Own People*, *Teendreams*, *Maydays*, *That Summer*). London, Methuen, 1991.

The Strange Case of Dr. Jekyll and Mr. Hyde, adaptation of the story by Robert Louis Stevenson. London, Hern, 1991.

Screenplay: *Lady Jane*, 1986.

Radio Plays: *Ecclesiastes*, 1977; *Saigon Rose*, 1979; *A Movie Starring Me*, 1991.

Television Plays: *The Eagle Has Landed*, 1973; *Sanctuary*, from his play *Gangsters*, 1973; *I Know What I Meant*, 1974; *The Midas Connection*, 1975; *Censors*, with Hugh Whitemore and Robert Muller, 1975; *Vote for Them*, with Neil Grant, 1989.

Other

The Second Time as Farce: Reflections on the Drama of Mean Times. London, Lawrence and Wishart, 1988.

*

Critical Studies: *David Edgar, Playwright and Politician* by Elizabeth Swain, New York, Peter Lang, 1986; *File on Edgar* edited by Simon Trussler, London, Methuen, 1991.

Theatrical Activities:
Director: **Plays**—*State of Emergency*, tour and London, 1972; *The Party* by Trevor Griffiths (co-director, with Howard Davies), London, 1985.

* * *

A glance at the titles of David Edgar's many plays of the early 1970's will suggest readily enough to anyone who was aware of the chief social and political issues of the time in Britain (and not only there) the nature of his early work. Edgar himself has described his work with General Will between 1971 and 1974 as "pure unadulterated agit-prop," designed to convey information in an entertaining way and from a socialist standpoint by using satirically the forms of popular culture—pantomine, comic strip, and the like. The aim was to elucidate political and economic conditions in general by reference to particular incidents. In 1973–74 Edgar turned from agit-prop to "become a social realist," feeling the necessity to "inculcate consciousness" more forcefully and in so doing to create a truly radical "theatre of public life." Several documentary plays preceded *Destiny* which, through television and radio adaptations, brought his work before the widest possible audience (though he is well aware of the problematic nature of the "mass" audience).

Edgar describes *Destiny* as having an "agit-prop structure" —the dramatic unit is, as in Brechtian epic theatre, the presentational scene rather than the traditional long act—but it is the creation of convincing characters (without the "psychologism" which is anathema to the socialist playwright) rather than demonstration-room puppets which enables it to communicate so powerfully a sense of crisis. Though the play spans in epic fashion the period from 1947 (the year of Indian Independence and the consequent return home of the colonial army) to the mid-1970's, its main action takes place against the background of a West Midland by-election campaign and the concurrent unofficial strike of Asian workers at a local foundry. The growth of the fascist Nation Forward party, through the power of its racist rhetoric to manipulate widely differing groups and individuals into a shallow yet dangerous unit of purpose, is coolly examined, and its relation to Conservatism in its many varieties precisely analyzed. Nation Forward gains increasing popular support and the new, tough Toryism, bitter at the loss of empire, shakes off old-style sentimental-paternalist Conservatism, secretly joining forces with the fascists in order to break the Asian strike and to ensure a formidable economic basis for the hard right. The cruel irony of its final plot-twist crystallizes the play's message in terms of the individual: the pathetic local antique dealer (and before that, soldier in India) whose misdirected bitterness had driven him to join Nation Forward and who—as their adopted candidate in the by-election—has been exploited by the party to such good effect, finds out by accident that his shop was taken away from him not by Jewish property speculators (as his mentors had insinuated) but by the same businessmen who are now concluding a secret agreement with his own party leaders.

Wreckers (written for and with 7:84) and *Teendreams* (written with Susan Todd for the feminist group Monstrous Regiment) confirm Edgar's continuing belief in the validity and usefulness of collectively devised agit-prop-type work in the late 1970's. His best work of this period, however, shows a growing interest in the relation between politics and psychology—especially the psychology of suffering. This interest emerges first in *The Jail Diary of Albie Sachs*, an adaptation yet very much Edgar's own play. For the Jewish lawyer Albie, detained under the "90-day" law in his native South Africa, the suffering inflicted upon him by the state is merely destructive, depriving him of moral strength and crushing his will to political action; yet for the eponymous heroine of *Mary Barnes* the suffering caused by mental illness is something to be gone *through* (in her case in a Christ-like way). Alternative therapy, unlike conventional psychiatry, helps her to "go through" her schizophrenia towards the attainment of a stable self. In this way she becomes capable, as many "normal" people are not, of real human relationships. The play avoids the simplistic rubric of the anti-psychiatry fashion of the 1960's—that only the mad are truly sane—while at the same time allowing an implicit socio-political critique to emerge from Mary's schizophrenia and the treatment of it. Yet it is also honest about the dilemmas and conflicts within the alternative community and the causes of its eventual dissolution. *Mary Barnes* is technically an adaptation, but one which—like the immensely popular and widely seen version of *Nicholas Nickleby*, and the more recent post-Freudian *The Strange Case of Dr. Jekyll and Mr. Hyde*—brings into question the value of conventional distinctions between adaptation and original play.

Since his adaptation of *Nicholas Nickleby* (for the Royal Shakespeare Company), Edgar has continued to work on plays with and for particular groups, most recently with *Entertaining Strangers*. Written as a community play for Dorchester (by a "stranger" and on the subject of the rightness of "entertaining strangers" of different kinds), this is nonetheless a rich dramatic text in its own right, sharing significant formal characteristics with a slightly earlier play, Edgar's most important one of the 1980's, *Maydays*.

By way of an epic structure resembling that of *Destiny* (though without the feel of agit-prop), *Maydays* deals with the course of socialism since World War II. With special concentration on the impact of the crucial dates 1956 and 1968, and ending in the election year of 1979, the play attempts to articulate the shifting relations between history, ideology, and personal belief and commitment by charting the ironically interconnected progress of three men: the radical son of a vicar who becomes a Trotskyist but who, in the aftermath of 1968, grows disillusioned, is ejected from the party, and ends up in the 1980's Tory think-tank; a working-class communist who, feeling himself to have been born too late and into the wrong class, comes in the 1970's to embrace unquestioningly the authoritarian nationalism of the hard right; and a Russian army officer who, having been jolted by his experience in Hungary in 1956, is imprisoned as a dissident in the 1970's, then exiled to the West—where he finds his views being co-opted and himself used by the same right-wing authoritarian grouping. The play ends with two very different acts of protest: the subtle disruption by the Russian exile, Lermontov, of a public function organized by the right to honour him; and the stand of the women on Greenham Common. The many ironies built into the plot(s) are characteristic of Edgar's drama as a whole. Their pointedness and inevitability are intensified by the rich pattern of echo and counterpoint—in both phrase and idea—that is created by the continuous juxtaposition of the three narrative strands. The intensity is both dialectical and emotional: in a play which (among other things) examines the opposition in political discourse between thought and feeling, Edgar succeeds in provoking both.

Despite his advocacy of urban "festivals of the oppressed" as the necessary future for theatre, Edgar's own creative practice seems to have become, in the late 1980's and early 1990's, ever more social-realist. His play about the 1984 miners' strike, *That Summer*, is not the wide-ranging public drama that might have been expected, but an intimate, even domestic piece. Indeed, the miners' strike—although the desperate reality of it is registered forcefully in an indirect way—is less the subject of the play than the occasion for a witty and even poignant revaluation of late 1960's radicalism and its relevance in the Thatcher era. When a generation-of-'68 Oxford history don and his family play host in a North Wales holiday house to two teenage girls from the Welsh coalfields, the class- and culture-clashes which inevitably ensue resolve themselves, through a shift of emphasis away from class towards a shared culture of dissent, in a modest affirmation of the continuity of a tradition of radical non-compliance. ("That Summer" is both 1984 and 1968). Gay, feminist and anti-nuclear protesters are not the closest political cousins of the striking miner.

Edgar's response to revolution in eastern Europe was, dramatically speaking, a direct one. Although *The Shape of the Table* is "based on events in a number of countries, it draws most from Czechoslovakia, and is thus about a negotiated, essentially pacific and ultimately decisive overthrow of communist rule." The focus is on "high politics" rather than popular dissent or events on the street; the excitement of the play is in the manoeuvrings of the incumbent party leaders in their negotiations for survival with a radical "Public Platform" opposition led by a Havel-like dissident writer. It is a play of argument and debate, which clarifies the differing experiences of oppression on all sides and quietly qualifies the future delights of Western-style democracy. Yet it is also Edgar's most "playful" piece. The very inevitability of the outcome promotes in us the awareness of a pattern and irony which are even more pervasive than in *Destiny* or *Maydays*. The action is shadowed by the characteristic structures and motifs of fairy tale which are consistently invoked by the opposition leader Prus, and the progress of negotiations is imaged wittily by the (literal) change of shape of the table which dominates the set. The ironic reversals of plot and situation are acknowledged by the characters themselves. In the final debate, between dissident-become-president Prus and hard-line ex-first secretary, the bluntly sarcastic ex-Titoite Lutz, Prus offers a deal for Lutz's pardon which echoes the one he himself was offered in the very first scene. (Lutz refuses, thereby accepting individual responsibility and imprisonment.) And when the discrediting of an ambitious younger minister of the old regime reveals a Soviet "master-script" for large-scale liberalisation without loss of party domination, the wryly conciliatory ex-prime minister points out to the Dubček figure—an elderly "ghost" at this table from the projected "New Morning" of 1968—that "this revolution was set in train by the very people who put paid to yours. As Marx perceptively reminds us, the events of history occurring twice. First time as tragedy, the second time as farce."

—Paul Lawley

————

EGBUNA, Obi B(enedict). Nigerian. Born in 1938. Educated at a university in England; University of Iowa, Iowa City, M.A. in English 1978; Howard University, Washington, D.C., Ph.D. in English 1986. High school teacher, Bishop Shanahan College, Orlu, 1955–56, and Beaver College, Glenside, Pennsylvania, 1967; writer-in-residence and director, East Central State Writers Workshop and ECBS television, Enugu, 1973–76; honorary fellow, University of Iowa, 1976; teacher, department of African studies, 1979–81, department of German-Russian studies, 1981–86, and writer-in-residence, 1987, Howard University. Address: Apartment #B705, 3636 16th Street, NW, Washington, D.C. 20010, U.S.A.

PUBLICATIONS

Plays

Divinity (broadcast 1965). Published in *New Africa* (London), August and September 1965; Stuttgart, Ernst Klett, 1985.
The Anthill. London and New York, Oxford University Press, 1965.
Wind Versus Polygamy (televized 1966; produced Dakar, 1966).
Theatre of Power (produced Copenhagen, 1967).
The Agony (produced London, 1970).

Radio Plays: *Divinity*, 1965; *Daughters of the Sun*, 1970.

Television Play: *Wind Versus Polygamy*, 1966.

Novels

Wind Versus Polygamy: Where "Wind" Is the "Wind of Change" and "Polygamy" Is the "Change of Eves." London, Faber, 1964; as *Elina*, London, Fontana, 1978.
The Madness of Didi. London, Fontana, 1980.
The Rape of Lysistrata. Enugu, Fourth Dimension, 1980.

Short Stories

Daughters of the Sun and Other Stories. London, Oxford University Press, 1970.
Emperor of the Sea and Other Stories. London, Fontana, 1974.
The Minister's Daughter. London, Fontana, and New York, Watts, 1975.

Diary of a Homeless Prodigal. Enugu, Fourth Dimension, 1976.
Black Candle for Christmas. Enugu, Fourth Dimension, 1980.

Other

The Murder of Nigeria: An Indictment. London, Panaf, 1968.
Destroy This Temple: The Voice of Black Power in Britain. London, MacGibbon and Kee, and New York, Morrow, 1971.
The ABC of Black Power Thought. Apapa, Nigeria, di Nigro Press, 1973.

*

Theatrical Activities:
Actor: Play—Sizwe Bansi in *Sizwi Bansi Is Dead* by Athol Fugard, Iowa City, 1977.

* * *

Although Obi B. Egbuna's efforts as a dramatist include a number of radio dramas and a play entitled *Wind Versus Polygamy*, his light and frothy comedy *The Anthill* remains the only drama which he has published as such, his earlier works having been rewritten into short stories and a novel. It seems that Egbuna has chosen well, for of all his dramatic works *The Anthill* seems to be the most entertaining and the best constructed, displaying the sort of witty comedy which has made Wilde's *The Importance of Being Earnest* a perennial favorite.

In his tale of a young African painter, Bobo, who for some reason paints only anthills, Egbuna draws a number of characters (all of whom, except for Bobo, are British and white) who are just substantial enough to interest us and just stock enough to be taken less than seriously—which is necessary in any comedy which centers around a series of deaths, two real and one pretended. Even the landlady mother of the young British soldier, Tommy, who dies from a heart attack when confronted by Bobo, does not seem to be overly disturbed by her own son's death. She is more concerned that people admire her appendix, which she keeps in a jar on her mantel.

Egbuna presents us with a full house of coincidences—that the policeman who visits their room just happens to be the father of the girl who has matrimonial intentions on Bobo's friend Nigel, that Tommy dies because Bobo resembles a young African whose death Tommy caused while stationed in Tongo (Bobo's home country), that Bobo is the deceased African's twin brother, and so on. But such coincidences are as in keeping with this kind of frolic as are the puns, which flow fast and freely. The verdict of the judge that Tommy's death was his own fault—"All young British soldiers must behave like English gentlemen at home and abroad. Under no circumstances must you kill a man to whom you are not properly introduced"—is the perfect sort of climax to a story which another writer might have turned into a heavy-handed tragedy.

Underneath it all, of course, there is a deep undercurrent of seriousness. Comedy is the other side of the mask of tragedy. Egbuna himself is a serious writer—as *Destroy This Temple*, essays written while he was locked in an English prison, indicates. His other plays have dealt with the conflict between tribal ways and Christianity and the resultant agonies in the hearts of young men who are the sons of Christian Africans but advocates of Black Power. When Egbuna has

Bobo describe himself as "a typical Tongolese gentleman . . . a dedicated vindicator of African personality and I've got my Anglo-Saxon political and academic titles to prove it," the laughter is as bitter as it is sweet.

—Joseph Bruchac

————————

ELDER, Lonne, III. American. Born in Americus, Georgia, 26 December 1931. Educated at New Jersey State Teachers College (now Trenton State College); Yale University School of Drama, New Haven, Connecticut (John Hay Whitney fellow and American Broadcasting Company Television writing fellow, 1965–66; John Golden fellow and Joseph E. Levine fellow in film-making, 1967). Served in the United States Army, 1952. Married Judith Ann Johnson in 1969; two sons. Worked as a docker, waiter, and professional gambler; coordinator of the Playwrights-Directors Unit, Negro Ensemble Company, New York, 1967–69; writer, Talent Associates, New York, 1968; writer/producer, Cinema Center Films, Hollywood, 1969–70; writer, Universal Pictures, Hollywood, 1970–71, and Radnitz/Mattel Productions, Hollywood, 1971; writer/producer, Talent Associates, Hollywood, 1971; writer, MGM Pictures and Columbia Pictures, Hollywood, 1972. Recipient: Stanley Drama award, 1965; American National Theatre Academy award, 1967; Outer Circle award, 1970; Vernon Rice award, 1970; Stella Holt Memorial Playwrights award, 1970. Address: c/o Farrar Straus and Giroux, 19 Union Square West, New York, New York 10003, U.S.A.

PUBLICATIONS

Plays

Ceremonies in Dark Old Men (produced New York, 1965; revised version produced New York, 1969). New York, Farrar Straus, 1969.
Charades on East 4th Street (produced Montreal, 1967). Published in *Black Drama Anthology*, edited by Woodie King and Ron Milner, New York, New American Library, 1971.
Seven Comes Up—Seven Comes Down (produced New York, 1977–78).
Splendid Mummer (produced New York, 1988; London, 1991).
King, music by Richard Blackford, lyrics by Maya Angelou and Alistair Beaton (produced London, 1990).

Screenplays: *Sounder*, 1972; *Melinda*, 1972; *Sounder Part 2*, 1976; *Bustin' Loose*, with Roger L. Simon and Richard Pryor, 1981.

Television Plays: *Camera 3* series, 1963; *The Terrible Veil*, 1964; *NYPD* series, 1967–68; *McCloud* series, 1970–71; *A Woman Called Moses*, from a book by Marcy Heidish, 1978.

*

Manuscript Collection: Boston University.

Theatrical Activities:
Actor: **Plays**—Bobo in *A Raisin in the Sun* by Lorraine Hansberry, New York, 1959; Clem in *Days of Absence* by Douglas Turner Ward, New York, 1965.

*   *   *

A screenwriter, television scriptwriter, and dramatist, Lonne Elder III is best known in the theatre for his acclaimed work, *Ceremonies in Dark Old Men*. In the tradition of Lorraine Hansberry's *A Raisin in the Sun*, *Ceremonies* examines the struggles of an African-American family in Harlem trying to find a way to break out of the cycle of poverty and despair. In the play, the Parker family recognize few options to improve their bleak condition. An ex-vaudevillian and family patriarch, Russell Parker, depended on his now deceased wife to be the primary breadwinner for much of their 30 years of marriage. Though he earns little money as a barber, Russell finds it difficult to submit himself to the humiliation of working in the subservient jobs to which his lack of education and experience restrict him. His adult sons, Theo and Bobby, also would rather be unemployed than accept menial work. In contrast, Russell's daughter—Adele —personifies the work ethic and takes over the role of her mother by supporting and caring for the men of the family. Theo sees only one way to break this cycle through an illegal, quick money scheme.

Theo teams with Blue Haven, who ostensibly poses as a community leader, to make and sell whisky and run a numbers racket. Theo wins the support of his brother and convinces his father to join the scheme by using his barbershop as a front for the operation. Theo believes the plan will end their money problems and their dependence on his sister. In effect, he thinks it will help to heal familial wounds and bring them all closer together. Ironically, despite Theo's intent, the scheme creates more strife within the already troubled family. Bobby shuns the whisky business to join Blue Haven's thievery ring instead. Russell steals money from the till and spends more than his share of the profits on women and other pursuits. Adele becomes involved with dubious elements of the community which leads to her abuse by a male acquaintance. Theo feels used by other family members as he works day and night for the business, yet enjoys few of its rewards. At the play's end, Theo decides to give up the business and join Adele in seeking other ways to overcome their predicament. However, a price must be paid for the games the family chose to play. Bobby loses his life in a robbery attempt; and Russell is revealed as a self-centered man who places his own well-being above that of his family. With this work, Elder joins the few playwrights able to dramatize the realities of the impoverished of Black America and, specifically, the desperate, seemingly futile search of African-American males to attain a sense of dignity and financial independence.

Elder's other dramatic works lack the craft and intense emotional impact of *Ceremonies*. Commissioned by Mobilization for Youth, Inc. of New York City, *Charades on East 4th Street* was written as a vehicle to encourage young people to use legal means to protest against police brutality, however, the play seems little more than a vicarious means whereby an audience can experience the terrorization of a policeman. On the city's Lower East Side in the basement of a movie theatre, six youths hold a police officer hostage, threatening to execute him with a guillotine. Accused of raping the sister of one of the youths and brutally beating the brother of another, the officer is given little opportunity to defend himself against the charges. Adam, the group leader, initially appears to be the officer's only protector as he seems to find ways to stop the others from carrying out their death sentence. However, by the play's end, Adam is revealed as the only one willing to injure the accused. With the officer's neck on the guillotine, Adam admits it was actually his own sister who was the rape victim and forces his prisoner to admit to the crimes. He frees the man from the guillotine, but breaks both of his arms in vengeance even as the officer pleads his innocence once again. Incredibly—given their seemingly enthusiastic participation in the officer's terrorization—the other youths ultimately disapprove of Adam's actions and vow that they will now work in non-violent ways to combat police brutality.

A better written and more recent work is *Splendid Mummer*, based on the life of the famous 19th-century tragedian Ira Aldridge. Although born in the United States, Aldridge found fame on European stages, since discriminatory practices barred him from acting in the dramatic theatre of his native land. This demanding one-man show depicts various aspects of Aldridge's life from his teenage years as a valet and protégé of actor Henry Wallack to his triumphant, mature performances as Othello and Lear. While the play is laudatory towards its subject, it does not shy away from revealing less attractive aspects of Aldridge: his imperious manner or his demeanor toward his marriages and romantic conquests. By the play's end, this challenging monodrama arouses one's interest in learning more about this complex, talented man known as the "celebrated African Roscius."

—Addell Austin Anderson

ELISHA, Ron. Australian. Born in Jerusalem, Israel, 19 December 1951; brought to Australia, 1953. Educated at Melbourne High School, 1966–69; Melbourne University, 1970–75, B.Med., B.Surgery 1975. Married Bertha Rita Rubin in 1981; one son and one daughter. Since 1977 general practitioner, Melbourne. Recipient: Australian Writers Guild award, 1982, 1984, Major award, 1982, award for television, 1992; Houston International Film Festival Gold award, 1990. Agent: Judith Alexander, Cameron's Management, 163 Brougham Street, Woolloomooloo, New South Wales 2011. Address: 4 Bruce Court, Elsternwick, Victoria 3185, Australia.

PUBLICATIONS

Plays

In Duty Bound (produced Melbourne, 1979). Montmorency, Victoria, Yackandandah, 1983.
Einstein (produced Melbourne, 1981; New York, 1982; London, 1986). Melbourne, Penguin, 1986.
Two (produced Perth, 1983; London, 1987). Sydney, Currency Press, 1985; Chicago, Dramatic Publishing Company, 1990.
Pax Americana (produced Perth, 1984). Montmorency, Victoria, Yackandandah, 1990.
The Levine Comedy (produced Melbourne, 1986). Montmorency, Victoria, Yackandandah, 1987.
Safe House (produced Melbourne, 1989). Sydney, Currency Press, 1989.
Esterhaz (produced Melbourne, 1990). Sydney, Currency Press, 1990.

Television Play: *Death Duties*, 1992.

Other

Pigtales (for children). Sydney, Random Century, 1992.

*

Manuscript Collections: University College, University of New South Wales; Australian Defence Forces Academy Library, Canberra.

Critical Study: article by Helen Thompson, in *Australian Drama Studies* (St. Lucia), April 1987.

Ron Elisha comments:

Life is crammed with merciless irony. Generally speaking, we humans prefer to remain blind to this most glaring aspect of our existence choosing, instead, to imbue the workings of the universe with some profound and basic meaning. As a playwright, I'll take irony over meaning every time.

My writing is motivated by anger—anger at the poverty of human imagination that allows us to ascribe the random viciousness of existence to the perverse, backhanded machinations of some Grand Architect. We value human life far too little if we believe that it depends, for its meaning, upon the existence of a Divine Referee.

The purpose of all my writing is to restore the value of human life to its rightful place. This value is self-referential. Life is its own meaning. There is only one field of human endeavour which drives home this message with any real power: drama. And there is only one tool which is sharp enough to enable drama to rise to the occasion: irony. Taking as its foundation the twin pillars of the precepts "Live and let live" and "Do unto others. . .", the foregoing underpins all that I have written.

*   *   *

As a Jewish intellectual in the most multi-cultural city in Australia, Elisha has been able to write for an extensive university-educated audience in daily contact with the pressures and barriers of cross-cultural hybridisation. Melbourne also presents itself as the "comedy capital of Australia," but because Elisha's work exploits comedy with unusual strategies he has been called the victim of his own cleverness.

The problematic responses of a defensive migrant population have been apparent even from *In Duty Bound*, where Elisha was called an anti-Semite essentially because he wrote about racism. Australia's first major Jewish playwright, it was felt, should deal in terms of the "normal" and the "positive"—and not expose the embittered reactionary attitudes of an older generation towards mixed marriage. Persisting with what he called "rational" drama, treating the serious in a fundamentally serious way, Elisha wrote *Two* and *Pax Americana*, which left him bracketed with Louis Nowra as one of Australia's new "internationalists." The nature of *Pax* has been blurred by debate over production approaches, but the play may be seen as a satirical excursion into postmodernism, a kaleidoscopic vision of post-war, media-constructed America. *Two* takes its title from its number of characters, but also from the problems of the Manichean world view of recurrent Elisha characters; set in Germany in 1948, a woman learning Hebrew so that she can go to Israel turns out to be a former SS member, and the binaries of Jew and Arab, good and evil, self and other, are exposed to erosion.

His refusal to deal in terms of trite polarisation meant that, for Elisha, audience prejudices were simply confirmed by these early plays. In *The Levine Comedy*, he decided on a technique of audience "seduction" by packaging his serious thrust in "irrational" forms and styles. Most blatantly, the title character can acknowledge here his dialogic style by invoking the name of Woody Allen at the point of domestic tragedy, but the irrational also obtrudes in the form of abrupt changes of tone, sudden death of story elements (a device from *In Duty Bound*), and a sequence of secondary but pivotal characters who are all called Hope. If this last is in part a device from the Morality tradition, it is also reflective of Elisha's interest in psychoanalytical dissection, and the representation of universal, macrocosmic elements through single characters on stage; this interest is integral to the three plays which may be seen as his central achievements to date.

Central to both *Einstein* and *Safe House* is a male displaced character who is represented in a schizoid manner so that an older self can collide with a younger self within the character's mind, bringing "recollections from the future." Three actors play Einstein: one in 1955 at the point of death, one prospectively from 1919 until Hiroshima, and one retrogressively from 1919 to the formulation of Relativity in 1905. Throughout, Einstein speaks to Moses (another law-giver, not represented by an actor), and the finale fuses the epiphanic motif of the burning bush with a projection of the Hiroshima explosion. Einstein's interrogation of Moses recalls that of the aging Freud, and here too is the ambivalence of the man who kills his brother while in search of revelation. Other less specific facets of Hebrew history permeate the play, which opens with women's lamentation, echoing the Exilic Rachel, generic mother of Israel, "weeping for her children, refusing to be comforted, because they were not."

Safe House proceeds by a series of brilliant swivels, starting with Marx in dialogue with Tolstoy—who turns out to be one of the lesser-known Tolstoys, thinking of defecting to Australia (as a "safe house") in 1956. The first act ends with Marx administering a game of "20 questions" and concluding that Tolstoy is schizoid, something that is realised in the second act where he is represented as both Tolstoy and the Professor. Now, 30 years later, he is institutionalised, apparently in Melbourne, and the rich texture of comedy offers a back-handed gloss on Australia from a migrant perspective. A final game of "20 questions" reverses all the answers given earlier, and is preceded by a long, vatic speech in which Tolstoy cries out to Australia in the manner of a Hebrew prophet, with the inference that Australia does not hear him.

Several of Elisha's plays use music as a structuring or symbolic device; three violins, for example, reflect the conflict of the Einsteins. Only in *Esterhaz*, however, does a whole play hinge on the semiotics of music in the way that *Two* does on the Hebrew language. Here Haydn, in the employment of Esterhazy in 1772, is surrounded by musical espionage which accentuates the political dimension to composition, authorship, and authority, rather as Stalin does in Pownall's *Master Class*. For Elisha, however, the parallel is not starkly allegorical but metonymic, so that the "irrational" absurdities of antics around the palace "seduce" the audience from larger applications of music, as happened, for example, in 20th-century Fascism. When the death of a starving peasant is choreographed to the second movement of the Emperor Quartet, Gothic politics invade an art world that is trying to stay innocently Rococo.

—Howard McNaughton

ENGLAND, Barry. British. Born in London, 16 March 1934. Educated at Downside School, Bath. Served in the British Army, 1950–52. Married Diane Dirsztay in 1967; one son and one daughter. Actor in provincial repertory companies, films, and television. Recipient: Arts Council grant; Author's Club award, 1968. Agent: Patricia Macnaughton, Macnaughton Lowe Representation, 200 Fulham Road, London SW10 9PN, England.

PUBLICATIONS

Plays

End of Conflict (produced Coventry, 1961). London, Evans, 1964.
The Big Contract (produced Coventry, 1963).
The Damn Givers (produced Coventry, 1964).
Conduct Unbecoming (produced Bristol and London, 1969; New York, 1970). London, Heinemann, and New York, French, 1971.

Television Plays: *The Sweet War Man*, 1966; *The Move after Checkmate*, 1966; *An Experience of Evil*, 1966; *You'll Know Me by the Stars in My Eyes*, 1966; *The Man Who Understood Women*, 1967.

Novel

Figures in a Landscape. London, Cape, and New York, Random House, 1968.

*

Barry England comments:
I am a storyteller. I revere economy and precision.

* * *

Barry England is known for one play, *Conduct Unbecoming*. The play's well-deserved success was no doubt partly due to its unfashionably gripping story, with some help perhaps from its fashionable period setting—British India in the 1880's—and its dashing red uniforms. But, although England's approach to his subject matter is a little reminiscent of the equally unfashionable Rattigan's in *The Winslow Boy*, in that he treats a moral conflict in which there is little doubt from the outset who is right and who is wrong, *Conduct Unbecoming* is more than a simple moral tract as it is more than a thriller.

England's dramatic method is that of "putting the screws on." The dramatist chooses a completely enclosed situation, fills it with mutually conflicting characters and then deftly tightens the situation until the pips squeak. In the form of plotting, this method is inevitably an ingredient in almost every sort of play. But it is a question of where the weight of the play finally rests. Do the characters, the stage images, the philosophical, political, or social themes spill over the framework and more or less conceal it? Are they subservient to it, as in farces, thrillers, and court-room dramas? Or almost miraculously created from it, as in Racine or middle-period Ibsen?

It is quite difficult to decide where the weight falls in *Conduct Unbecoming*. An image such as the pig-sticking episode in the second scene makes a most powerful impression in its own right, but loses force for being meticulously absorbed into the final twists of the plot: there is not enough left over to expand in the mind of the audience. For all the subtlety and unexpectedness of the characters, the plot never ceases to contain them, and its neat finish seems to put them away in a box and shut the lid on them. As for England's theme, it is so organic to his method that one must ask whether he has chosen the method to explore the theme or the theme to suit the method.

His earlier plays *End of Conflict* and *The Damn Givers* argue for the primacy of the theme. *End of Conflict* is another army play, set in the New Territories of China at the time of the Korean War. Like *Conduct Unbecoming* its situation arises from the introduction of a new officer into the Mess. Its plotting is looser than that of the later play, but its theme is almost identical—the clash of an individual, still experimental code of behaviour with a traditional, collective code. For all its apparent rigidity, the army's code is shown to be flexible enough to allow good men to behave well. Indeed in *End of Conflict* the real hero is not the liberal-minded rebel who causes disaster by his inexperienced good intentions, but the liberal-minded and experienced conformist. In *Conduct Unbecoming* this clash and its outcome are more complex, but again it is the officer with "bourgeois principles" of honour who triumphs, saving the rebel from himself at the same time as restoring a true sense of honour to the regiment, whose collective pride and inflexibility had corrupted it.

The Damn Givers is a much less convincing piece, perhaps because a group of pleasure-loving socialites makes a less coherent collective than a regiment. The misfit here is a young sex-starved academic and the clash is between his awakened idea of lasting love—after he has slept with the voracious Lady Jane Moore-Fuller-Bracke—and the collective's idea of sex as one pleasure among others to be taken on the trot. England's own lack of conviction in this variation on his basic theme seems to be reflected both in the shadowy characters and the too predictable plot.

Nevertheless, it does seem clear that England's theme comes first. Because it is well defined—there is no suggestion of the infinite perplexities of life beyond the enclosed societies England studies—it is almost perfectly served by a tightly geared plot. The characters too are emanations of the theme, in the sense that their passions stop at discovering the honourable mode of conduct within a given set of rules. But since, at least in the setting of an officers' Mess in the heyday of the British Raj, such people are entirely credible, they can develop an individuality well beyond the limitations of the morality or the cliffhanger. The real strength of *Conduct Unbecoming* is in its delicately orchestrated character studies.

—John Spurling

ENRIGHT, Nick (Nicholas Paul). Australian. Born in Newcastle, New South Wales, 22 December 1950. Educated at St. Ignatius College, Riverview, New South Wales, 1962–67; Sydney University, 1968–71, B.A. 1971; New York University School of the Arts, 1975–77, M.F.A. 1977. Associate director, State Theatre Company of South Australia, Adelaide, 1978–81; teacher of acting, 1978, 1989–92, and head of acting, 1982–84, National Institute of Dramatic Art, Sydney; member, Australia Council literature board, Sydney, 1986–89; host, *Play into Opera* series, ABC-FM, 1987; cabaret performer, Tilbery Hotel, Sydney, 1989. Regular host/narrator for Sydney Symphony Orchestra, 1988–92; regular contributor of verse and features to the Sydney *Morning Herald*, the *Australian*, the *National Times*, *Theatre Australia*, and *Vogue Australia*; regular reviewer for ABC Radio, *Books and Writing* and *First Edition*. Recipient: New South Wales Premier's award, 1983; Australia Council grant, 1975–76, 1984, 1991; Australia Writers' Guild award, for radio, for television, and for best script in any medium, 1990. Agent: Hilary Linstead & Associates, Suite 302, Easts Tower, 9–13 Bronte Road, Bondi Junction, New South Wales 2022, Australia; or Intertalent, Suite 300, 131 South Rodeo Drive, Beverly Hills, California 90212, U.S.A. Address: 20 Chalder Street, Newtown, New South Wales 2042, Australia.

PUBLICATIONS

Plays

Electra, with Frank Hauser, adaptation of the play by Sophocles (produced Melbourne, 1978).
The Servant of Two Masters, with Ron Blair, adaptation of the play by Carlo Goldoni (produced Adelaide, 1978).
Oh, What a Lovely War, Mate!, adaptation of Australian scenes in the play created by Joan Littlewood and her Theatre Workshop Company (produced Adelaide, 1979).
The Venetian Twins, adaptation of the play by Carlo Goldoni, music by Terence Clarke (produced Sydney, 1979; revised version, Brisbane, 1990).
King Stag, adaptation of the play by Carlo Gozzi (produced Adelaide, 1980).
On the Wallaby (produced Adelaide, 1980). Sydney, Currency Press, 1982.
Music Is (for children; produced Adelaide, 1981).
Fatal Johnny (for children; produced Adelaide, 1982).
First Class Women (produced Sydney, 1982).
Variations, music by Terence Clarke (produced Sydney, 1982).
The Marriage of Figaro, adaptation of the play by Beaumarchais (produced Adelaide, 1983).
Summer Rain, music by Terence Clarke (produced Sydney, 1983; revised version, Sydney, 1989).
Don Juan, adaptation of the play by Molière (produced Adelaide, 1984). Sydney, Currency Press, 1984.
The Snow Queen, adaptation of the story by H.C. Andersen, music by Graham Dudley (produced Adelaide, 1985).
Daylight Saving (produced Sydney, 1989). Sydney, Currency Press, 1990.
Carnival of the Animals, music by Saint-Saens (produced Sydney, 1989). Sydney, ABC Publications, 1991.
Mongrels (produced Sydney, 1991).
St. James Infirmary (produced Penrith, New South Wales, 1992). Sydney, Currency Press, 1992.
A Property of the Clan (produced Newcastle, New South Wales, 1992).

Screenplay: *Lorenzo's Oil*, with George Miller, 1992.

Television Plays: *Come In Spinner* series, with Lissa Benyon, adaptation of the novel by F. James and D. Cusack, 1989; *Breaking Through*, adaptation of *No Longer a Victim* by Cathy-Ann Matthews, 1990.

Radio Plays: A *Ship Without a Sail* (documentary), 1985; *The Trojan Women*, adaptation of the play by Euripides, 1989; *Watching over Israel*, 1990.

Verse

The Maitland and Morpeth String Quartet (for children). Sydney, David Ell Press, 1980.

Recordings: *The Venetian Twins*, Sydney, Larrikin Records, 1981; *Carnival of the Animals* with *Peter and the Wolf*, music by Saint-Saens, Polygram Records, 1989.

*

Manuscript Collection: Australian Defence Forces Academy Library, Canberra.

Theatrical Activities:
Director: **Plays**—*American Buffalo* by David Mamet, *Twelfth Night* by Shakespeare, *Arms and the Man* by Shaw, all Adelaide, 1979; *Traitors* by Stephen Sewell, *On the Wallaby*, *A Month in the Country* by Turgenev, all Adelaide, 1980; *A Hard God* by Peter Kenna, *As You Like It* by Shakespeare, both Adelaide, 1981; *The Real Thing* by Tom Stoppard, Sydney, 1985; *Measure for Measure* by Shakespeare, Sydney, 1986.
Actor: **Plays**—with State Theatre Company of South Australia, Adelaide, 1978–81; Elyot in *Private Lives* by Noël Coward, Newcastle, 1985; Tocky in *A Happy and Holy Occasion* by John O'Donoghue, Newcastle, 1986; Saul in *As Is* by William Hoffman, Sydney, 1987; Godfrey in *Vocations* by Alma De Groen, Sydney, 1987; Max de Winter in *Rebecca* by Daphne du Maurier, Sydney, 1991. **Radio**—regular drama and feature performances since 1972; narrator, *Australia* series, 1988. **Television**—roles in *Breaking Up*, 1985; *Princess Kate*, 1987; *Willessee's Australians*, 1988; *Brotherhood of the Rose*, 1988; *Come in Spinner*, 1989; *The Paper Man*, 1990.

Nick Enright comments:
    I came to playwriting through my work as performer and director, devising, editing, adapting, or translating works for schools, community groups, and regional theatre companies. The strongest influence on the work was the circumstances of its performance. Music was usually part of the pieces which were often in a "popular theatre" vein. I was and am a pragmatist and a natural collaborator.
    Recently I have moved towards more personal work, though I have never been much interested in autobiographical revelation. Much of my work has dealt with the Australian past; that concern now seems to be coalescing with some aspects of personal history.
    I have no commitment to particular form or tone, preferring to allow the material to dictate both. My writing for stage and screen is always conceived rhythmically; and I like to think about form in musical terms.

*   *   *

Nick Enright understands the way theatre works from experience in every facet of the medium, including that of performing and directing. Because his grounding is in theatre, rather than in literature, film, or television, Enright's plays have a technical craftsmanship and assuredness which are satisfying for both the audience and the players. Much of his generation's writing, in the United States, in Australia, and in Britain, reveals ignorance of the basic elements of a theatrical event: action, characters who *show* us that action, a place in which the action takes place, and an audience which shares in the event. In short, Enright's plays may seem slightly "old-fashioned" in as much as they invariably have a strong story to show us, characters who are three-dimensional, and even a beginning, a middle, and an end, where the pieces are tied together, more or less. There is about Enright's work, over and above almost everything else, an unmistakable theatricality.
    In *On The Wallaby*, for example, Enright combines a poor Irish-Australian family struggling during the Great Depression, docudrama and Brechtian agit-prop shenanigans, and traditional British (and Australian) music-hall nonsense. It reveals a masterly command of the theatre as an instrument to entertain, inform, and move us. If the politics seem black and white today, and if the promises of the labor movements and of Communism itself have failed, never mind. The play as a play grips us with its action and its relevance, it holds the stage. This is true of almost all of Enright's work.
    Enright apparently writes for specific actors much of the time, and in *Daylight Saving* he has concocted a completely different series of theatrical conventions. Very modern, even trendy, and certainly very jokey, the play is a farce of manners, of characters, and of today. Slyly, Enright has slipped in hilarious comments on America in the 1970's (when he himself was studying there) and Australia in the 1990's. Aging yuppies, their parents, neighbors, clients, and schedules all collide in a swiftly paced, magnificently plotted series of events that boisterously amuse and reflect giddily a world that is far different from that of *On The Wallaby*. Enright is not Noël Coward, but he comes close.
    With *Mongrels*, the playwright enters quite different territory, yet he always keeps a tight hold on what the theatre is and can do best. In fact, a play is being enacted within a play, and the characters are intertwined. The witty dialogue (largely centered in "gay" chatter and allusions) is overshadowed here by a kind of darkness: theatre is a business and a dirty business at that. Who is doing what to whom at any given moment is up for grabs, it would seem, as we watch an evolution of characters from prison cells to high-rise Sydney apartments; it rings true because it is rooted in action and situation which we know is true, whether we are of the theatre or not. The mirror Enright holds up to the world in *Mongrels* reflects a less pleasant scene than the play pretends: a shadow hangs over the gags and the jabs.
    St. James Infirmary is in a way furthest away from the jamboree of *On The Wallaby*, for in this play Enright attempts to show us both morality and art (which may be closer together than we think, but which are very hard to portray on stage). We are asked to believe that a snotty young man at a Catholic boys' school is "brilliant" as an artist, that the forces which pull at him (a priest, a nurse, some adoring adolescent boys) could destroy him. But as in all melodrama, the hero is stronger than these forces and in time goes out on his own, gloriously and flamingly. The issues are less interesting than the characters or the mastery of technique which the playwright displays. (Sometimes it seems that the technique shows through, but it is always admirable craftsmanship.)
    Although he is called an Australian playwright, Nick Enright's plays "work" on the stage anywhere. Some of the lingo may seem foreign but the drift, the ideas, and the people come across without strain.
    Enright's youth, skill, and devotion to theatre promise a

handsome career, which is already well launched in the English-speaking world.

— Arthur H. Ballet

EVARISTI, Marcella. British. Born in Glasgow, 19 July 1953. Educated at Notre Dame High School for Girls, Glasgow, to 1970; University of Glasgow, 1970–74, B.A. (honours) in English and drama. Married Michael Boyd in 1982; one son and one daughter. Playwright-in-residence, University of St. Andrews, Fife, 1979–80; creative writing fellow, University of Sheffield, Yorkshire, 1979–80; writer-in-residence, universities of Glasgow and Strathclyde, 1984–85. Recipient: BBC Student Verse Competition prize, 1971; Arts Council bursary, 1975–76; Pye award, 1982. Agent: Andrew Hewson, John Johnson Authors' Agent, 45/47 Clerkenwell House, Clerkenwell Green, London EC1R 0HT, England.

PUBLICATIONS

Plays

Dorothy and the Bitch (produced Edinburgh, 1976).
Scotia's Darlings (produced Edinburgh, 1978).
Sugar and Spite (revue), with Liz Lochhead (produced Edinburgh, 1978).
Mouthpieces (revue; produced St. Andrews, 1980).
Hard to Get (produced Edinburgh, 1980).
Commedia (produced Sheffield, 1982; London, 1983). Edinburgh, Salamander Press, 1983.
Thank You For Not in *Breach of the Peace* (revue; produced London, 1982).
Checking Out (produced London, 1984).
The Works (produced Edinburgh, 1984). Published in *Plays Without Wires*, Sheffield, Sheffield Academic Press, 1989.
Terrestrial Extras (produced Glasgow, 1985).
Trio for Strings in 3 (sketch; produced, Glasgow, 1987).
Visiting Company (produced Glasgow, 1988).
The Offski Variations (produced Glasgow, 1990).

Radio Plays: *Hard to Get*, 1981; *Wedding Belles and Green Grasses*, 1983; *The Hat*, 1988; *The Theory and Practice of Rings*, 1992; *Troilus and Cressida and La-di-da-di-da*, 1992.

Television Plays: *Eva Set the Balls of Corruption Rolling*, 1982; *Hard to Get*, 1983.

*

Theatrical Activities:
Actor: **Plays**—roles in *Dorothy and the Bitch*, Edinburgh, 1976; *Twelfth Night*, Glasgow, 1979; *Sugar and Spite*, Edinburgh, 1981; *Mystery Bouffe*, Sheffield, 1982; *The Works*, Glasgow, 1985; *Terrestrial Extras*, Glasgow, 1985; Rhona Andrews in *Visiting Company*, Glasgow, 1988; *The Offski Variations*, Glasgow, 1990. **Radio**—roles in *The Works*, 1985; *The Hat*, 1988.

* * *

A rare but consistently recognizable sensibility marks the work of Marcella Evaristi. To explain it, she has frequently

remarked on her heritage; part Italian Catholic, part Jewish, altogether Glaswegian. It is a blend that has kept her a significant part of the Scottish theatre scene since her first play, *Dorothy and the Bitch*, in 1976, although her most important plays have had life south of the border in England as well.

Her qualities are seen at their most harmonious in her emotionally powerful play, *Commedia*. Set partly in Evaristi's native Glasgow and partly in Bologna, the drama marries the passionate domesticity of an Italian home in Scotland to the volatile politics of Italy in 1980. As in all her work, she reveals the most intimate details of her characters' private lives with a coroner's attention to opening up wounds, but her concerns in *Commedia* are also the ways in which the broader world determines the fate of the individual.

The play begins with edgy comedy as the adult sons of the widowed Elena bring their wives to Elena's house for their usual Chianti Hogmanay, a Scottish New Year's Eve full of "pasta, pollo alla cacciatore and wine" and seemingly lacking in the traditional whisky and tall, dark stranger "first-footing it" through the door at midnight. But there is a handsome stranger, Davide, a young teacher from Bologna working in Glasgow schools, and working on Elena's heart.

An affair between Davide and Elena, for all its uncertainties caused by a 20-year age gap, brings up less generational conflict than might be expected: the lovers are prepared to work at their differences. Typically for Evaristi, conflict erupts from within the family, from the jealousy of one of Elena's own sons. The men in Evaristi's plays regularly cling to boyhood, while the women accept whatever responsibility is required.

There are fairy-tale elements that promise a happy ending: Elena is entertainingly eccentric from the first and engages the audience's sympathy. She receives the support of an "outsider": Lucy, the American wife of the jealous son, Stefano. Davide's radical left politics provide a philosophy and a circle of friends that accommodate his relationship with Elena. But there is a bitterness in the writing; when Elena and Davide take a holiday in Bologna, it provokes a family showdown which inadvertently leads to the death of her gentler son, Cesare, one of the innocent people killed in the fascist bombing of Bologna's railway station.

The relationship subsequently fails, Lucy leaves Stefano, Elena's late-life freedom is curtailed when Cesare's widow and her daughter move in and, in effect, all the women return to a world without men. A happy ending will remain a fairy-tale until male and female relationships can survive without illusion.

There is a poetic grace and imagination in the best of Evaristi's writing that elevates the most domestic of themes. In *Commedia* Elena's conflicts are encapsulated in a song, "Tin Mags the Kitchen Witch," which divides her character into disciplinarian mother and libertarian witch, a kind of lady of misrule. In a play such as *Wedding Belles and Green Grasses* she follows two sisters and their half-sister through childhood to puberty and first boyfriends; to jobs, marriage, and divorce, lyrically raising the familiar material into ironic understanding through musical repetition of themes with subtle variations for each character.

In her major radio play, *The Hat*, her poetic imagination makes even greater leaps. The world is full of objects which are given voice; an elegant olde worlde mirror observes the troubled relationship of Marianne and her artist lover, Crispin, and comments on it to Marianne's dismay. Other inanimate characters develop conversational relationships with her, including her compact mirror and most importantly her cloche hat. The hat, despised by Crispin, can be seen symbolically as Marianne's sexuality, but the imagery of the play transcends Freud. Crispin's great achievement as an artist is a collage representing Marianne's free spirit. As Marianne establishes her own independence, the collage in its gallery deteriorates and Crispin's only hope of retaining his artistic reputation is to sexually subjugate her once again.

Women remain at the mercy of men in another of her radio plays, a potent reworking of the Troilus and Cressida story, *Troilus and Cressida and La-di-da-di-da*. Fine elevated sentiments from the two lovers begin the play, beautifully stating a bodily and spiritual commitment from each partner. When war intervenes, Troilus reluctantly becomes a soldier and continually restates his love, but Cressida is deprived of his words by other men who prostitute her. Corruption of ideals is again the natural product of male society.

Evaristi also writes well for herself as a performer, appearing in one-woman shows such as *The Offski Variations* where she further investigates the seemingly endless separations of people, from abandoned child to divorcing parents and departing partners, but her best work transcends the strong persona of her own character. She is a lyric dramatist of intense subjectivity, constantly observing the impact of society on the individual.

—Ned Chaillet

EVELING, (Harry) Stanley. British. Born in Newcastle upon Tyne, Northumberland, 4 August 1925. Educated at Rutherford College; Samuel King's School; King's College, Durham University (William Black Noble Student, 1950–51), B.A. (honours) in English 1950, B.A. (honours) in philosophy 1953; Lincoln College, Oxford, D. Phil. 1955. Served in the Durham Light Infantry, 1944–47. Married to Kate Eveling. Assistant lecturer, Department of Logic and Metaphysics, King's College, University of Aberdeen, 1955–57; lecturer, Department of Philosophy, University College of Wales, Aberystwyth, 1957–60. Senior lecturer, 1960–83, and since 1984 teaching fellow in philosophy, University of Edinburgh. Since 1970 television critic, the *Scotsman*, Edinburgh. Recipient: Earl Grey fellowship, 1955. Agent: Lemon, Unna and Durbridge, 24 Pottery Lane, Holland Park, London W11 4LZ, England. Address: c/o Fettes College, Carrington Road, Edinburgh EH4 1QX, Scotland.

PUBLICATIONS

Plays

The Balachites (produced Edinburgh, 1963). With *The Strange Case of Martin Richter*, London, Calder and Boyars, 1970.
An Unspeakable Crime (produced London, 1963).
Come and Be Killed (produced Edinburgh, 1967; London, 1968). With *Dear Janet Rosenberg, Dear Mr. Kooning*, London, Calder and Boyars, 1971.
The Strange Case of Martin Richter (produced Glasgow, 1967; London, 1968). With *The Balachites*, London, Calder and Boyars, 1970.

The Lunatic, The Secret Sportsman, and the Woman Next Door (produced Edinburgh, 1968; London, 1969). With *Vibrations*, London, Calder and Boyars, 1970.
Dear Janet Rosenberg, Dear Mr. Kooning (produced Edinburgh and London, 1969; New York, 1970). With *Come and Be Killed*, London, Calder and Boyars, 1971.
Vibrations (produced Edinburgh, 1969; London, 1972). With *The Lunatic, The Secret Sportsman, and the Woman Next Door*, London, Calder and Boyars, 1970.
Dracula, with others (produced Edinburgh, 1969; London, 1973).
Mister (produced Edinburgh, 1970; London, 1971). Published in *A Decade's Drama*, Huddersfield, Woodhouse Books, 1980.
Sweet Alice (as *Jakey Fat Boy*, produced New York 1970; as *Sweet Alice*, produced Edinburgh and London, 1971). Published in *Plays and Players* (London), March 1971.
Better Days, Better Knights (produced Edinburgh, 1971; London, 1972).
Our Sunday Times (produced Edinburgh and London, 1971).
Oh Starlings (produced Edinburgh, 1971). Published in *Plays and Players* (London), March 1971.
The Laughing Cavalier (produced London, 1971).
He Used to Play for Hearts, in *Christmas Present* (produced Edinburgh, 1971).
Caravaggio, Buddy (produced Edinburgh, 1972; London, 1977).
Union Jack (and Bonzo) (produced Edinburgh and London, 1973).
Shivvers (produced London, 1974).
The Dead of Night (produced Edinburgh, 1975).
The Buglar (sic) *Boy and His Swish Friend* (produced Edinburgh, 1983). Edinburgh, Salamander Press, 1983.

Radio Plays: *Dance ti Thy Daddy*, 1964; *The Timepiece*, 1965; *A Man Like That*, 1966; *The Devil in Summer*, with Kate Eveling, from a play by Michel Faure, 1971; *The Queen's Own*, 1976.

Television Play: *Ishmael*, 1973.

Verse

(*Poems*). Oxford, Fantasy Press, 1956.

Other

The Total Theatre. Edinburgh, Heriot Watt University, 1972.

*

Manuscript Collections: Brandeis University, Waltham, Massachusetts; National Library of Scotland, Edinburgh.

Stanley Eveling comments:
My plays seem, very roughly speaking, to oscillate between reality and unreality, between moral dramas and plays in the absurdist, or, better, Dickensian, tradition. I hanker after the former and still think that *Mister*, a sort of dramatic interface between the fantastic and the real, is the play that says most, though it doesn't have the inventive duplicity and cunning of *Dear Janet* and some others.

If I had to say what theme hovers around in all, it would be that they all seem to have something to do with beleaguered human beings, most often male ones, in circumstances that precisely don't call for his (or her) particular virtues. In

Mister's case these are heroic virtues, Nelsonian virtues; in the case of the Oblomovian Jim in *Come and Be Killed*, it is as if he were called upon to exercise the "wrong" virtues, mundane virtues that go with domesticity and responsibility, like asking Shelley to wash the nappies or the Ford Cortina, or so Jim construes it. Alec, in *Dear Janet*, is asked to play a romantic role in a young girl's dream as she is required to fulfil a dreamed-up bit of him. In *The Buglar Boy and His Swish Friend* (the most complicated play, perhaps), the characters themselves, called down from the eternal library of the imagination, attempt and fail to fulfil the tragic requirements of the play's theme, attempt and fail to take on a tragic role at a time, in an age, and with qualities that belong to comedy. This is as close as I want to get. In an as yet unproduced play, *Impossible People*, I see that the theme is that of a man called upon to perform the last male role, that of being subservient to his wife's genius. Naturally he does not succeed.

What is "ridiculous" or "absurd" is that the wrong qualities are also the right qualities, that tragic predicaments happen in comic circumstances, that is, outside the environment which would give them tragic significance. As Janet says of her own work, at the end of the play, it is carried along on "the last ripple left by the receding impulse of tragedy."

*   *   *

Stanley Eveling is a prolific and at first sight a somewhat baffling playwright: he writes in a variety of styles and almost always adopts a veiled, even blurred approach to his subject matter. But although he is a professional moral philosopher as well as a playwright and although his characters often involve themselves in philosophical argument and speculation, his plays are by no means intellectual, in the sense of being elaborately constructed to act as working models of some abstract thesis. Eveling's approach is veiled not because he is hiding the machinery, but on the contrary because he himself seems to write in the act of watching the machinery at work; he sits almost painfully close to the characters, feels them rather than thinks them, and uses one style or another, as he might use one stage or another, as at most a temporary accommodation for his stubborn and chaotic material.

This material is presented in its simplest versions in the two plays *Come and Be Killed* and *Dear Janet Rosenberg, Dear Mr. Kooning*. The first concerns an abortion, the second an abortive relationship between an ageing novelist and his female fan. The muddled, narrowly confined, squalid situations in which the characters find themselves in both plays are compounded by their own muddled, limited, and selfish reactions. "You're not wicked, you're just ignorant," says one character to another in *Come and Be Killed*: this might be a motto for all Eveling's work. Creation in general is messy, cruel, blind, and the lords of creation are no more and no less: in *The Balachites*, Eveling shows a pair of innocents, a modern Adam and Eve, corrupted not by Satan but by the ghosts of dead men; in his nearest thing to an "absurdist" play, *The Lunatic, The Secret Sportsman, and the Woman Next Door*, he shows the pathetic innocence of mental and sexual aberration.

Naturally the idea of there being such creatures as "heroes" in such a world is a fruitful source of still further pain and confusion. The story of Donald Crowhurst, who made it appear that he was winning the *Sunday Times* single-handed yacht race round the world, but turned out to have disappeared, almost certainly overboard, without ever having sailed beyond the Atlantic, forms the basis of Eveling's play *Our Sunday Times*. But he extends the story, as the title

implies, to cover a much more widespread form of bogus heroism, of cheaply bought superiority over trivial circumstances, the vicarious act of reading newspapers or watching television. The play's effect is weakened by this attempt at generalization; Eveling steps back too far from his characters. But *Mister*, in which he again treats a would-be sailor-hero, the owner of an antique shop who acts out his fantasy of being Lord Nelson, with the unfortunate complication of having a Lady Hamilton on the premises who is not content with a sexual relationship confined to fantasy, is perhaps Eveling's best play. It is certainly his saddest and funniest, his finest example of what Janet Rosenberg calls "the curious mixture of farce and misery which is the slight ripple left by the receding impulse of tragedy."

Nevertheless, although Eveling's dramatic outlook is on the whole more sad than angry, reminiscent of those world-weary but intermittently kindly doctors in Chekhov's plays, he has written at least one play in which the mixture of farce and misery is replaced by that of savage humour and despair. In *The Strange Case of Martin Richter* a German industrialist employs three ex-Nazis as household servants, not realizing or not caring what this means for his butler, who is of "Swebish" origin and whose father was murdered during the Third Reich for being "Swebish." The butler's solution is to pretend that he himself was a prominent Nazi, claim acquaintance with Hitler, constitute himself "Leader" of a neo-Nazi party and pretend to eliminate the industrialist for being "Swebish." The play ends, after several twists of fortune and a marvellously composed drunken party, with everything as it was, the industrialist once more on top of the evil heap. *Martin Richter* is the nearest thing in Eveling's work to a straight political and moral fable. It is compact and clear, a powerful and bitterly comic outcry against the nastiness, brutishness, and shortness of human life.

Shivvers, *Caravaggio*, *Buddy*, and *The Dead of Night* all deal with suicide in one form or another. The central character of *Shivvers*, having for a time assuaged his own sense of guilt by imposing vicious behaviour on a vicar and a whore, commits suicide when they shake off his domination. *Caravaggio, Buddy* is an ambitious comic fantasy—an episodic quest play somewhat reminiscent of *Peer Gynt*—whose hero fails in many attempts to commit suicide and ends up reconciled with society. The play's complex and carefully controlled shifts of style establish in dramatic rather than intellectual terms the reality and humanity of the misfit as against the unreality and inhumanity of the "organized." It is full of delightful comic inventions, such as the colloquy between Buddy and a Yeti on the slopes of Mount Everest, while just off-stage innumerable international expeditions make more or less disastrous assaults on the summit. *The Dead of Night* is a sombre piece—enlivened by a German general trying to disguise himself as a woman—set beside Hitler's bunker in Berlin and featuring the arch-suicide himself.

All three plays show Eveling sharpening his lines and clarifying his construction without losing his closeness to the characters. His themes remain the same, but his methods of exploring them become more precise and versatile.

—John Spurling

EXTON, Clive (Jack Montague). British. Born in 1930. See 1st edition, 1973.

———

EYEN, Tom. American. 1941–1991. See 4th edition, 1988.

———

F

FEIFFER, Jules (Ralph). American. Born in the Bronx, New York, 26 January 1929. Educated at James Monroe High School, New York; Art Students' League, New York, 1946; Pratt Institute, Brooklyn, 1947–48, 1949–51. Served as a cartoon animator and graphic artist in the United States Army Signal Corps, 1951–53: private. Married 1) Judith Sheftel in 1961 (separated 1971, divorced 1983), one daughter; 2) Jennifer Allen in 1983, one daughter. Assistant to the cartoonist Will Eisner, 1946–51 (ghostwriter, *The Spirit* comic, 1949–51); drew cartoon *Clifford*, 1949–51; freelance cartoonist and artist, 1951–56. Since 1956 cartoonist (*Feiffer*), *Village Voice*, New York, and since 1959 syndicated in other newspapers and magazines. Faculty member, Yale University School of Drama, New Haven, Connecticut, 1973–74. President, Dramatists Guild Foundation, 1982–83. Since 1976 director, Corporation of Yaddo, Saratoga Springs, New York. Recipient: Oscar, for cartoon, 1961; George Polk Memorial award, 1962; London Theatre Critics award, 1968; Obie award, 1968; Outer Circle award, 1968, 1969; Pulitzer prize, for cartoon, 1986; Los Angeles Critics Circle award, 1988; Venice Film Festival award, for screenplay, 1989. Address: 325 West End Avenue, New York, New York 10023, U.S.A.

Publications

Plays

The Explainers (produced Chicago, 1961; New York, 1964).
Crawling Arnold (produced Spoleto, London, and Cambridge, Massachusetts, 1961; New York, 1979). Published in *Best Short Plays of the World 1958–1967*, edited by Stanley Richards, New York, Crown, 1968.
The World of Jules Feiffer (produced Hunterdon Hills, New Jersey, 1962).
Interview, published in *Harper's* (New York), June 1962.
You Should Have Caught Me at the White House, published in *Holiday* (Indianapolis), June 1963.
Little Murders (produced New Haven, Connecticut, 1966; London and New York, 1967). New York, Random House, 1968; London, Cape, 1970.
The Unexpurgated Memoirs of Bernard Mergendeiler (produced Los Angeles, 1967; New York, 1968; Glasgow, 1969; London, 1972). Published in *Collision Course*, New York, Random House, 1968.
God Bless (produced New Haven, Connecticut, and London, 1968). Published in *Plays and Players* (London), January 1969.
Feiffer's People (produced Edinburgh and London, 1968; Los Angeles, 1971).
Dick and Jane, in *Oh! Calcutta!* (produced New York, 1969; London, 1970). New York, Grove Press, 1970.
The White House Murder Case (produced New York, 1970). New York, Grove Press, 1970.
Munro (produced New York, 1971).

Carnal Knowledge: A Screenplay (revised version produced, Houston, 1988). New York, Farrar Straus, and London, Cape, 1971.
Silverlips, in *VD Blues* (televised 1972). New York, Avon, 1973.
Watergate Classics, with others (produced New Haven, Connecticut, 1973).
Cohn of Arc, published in *Partisan Review* (New Brunswick, New Jersey), vol. 40, no. 2, 1973.
Knock, Knock (produced New York, 1976). New York, Hill and Wang, 1976.
Hold Me! (produced New York, 1977). New York, Dramatists Play Service, 1977.
Grown Ups (produced Cambridge, Massachusetts, and New York, 1981). New York, French, 1982.
A Think Piece (produced New York, 1982).
Rope-a-Dope, in *Urban Blight* (musical revue), based on an idea by John Tillinger, music by David Shire, lyrics by Richard Maltby, Jr. (produced New York, 1988).
Elliot Loves (produced New York, 1989). New York, Grove Press, 1989.
Anthony Rose (produced Philadelphia, 1989).

Screenplays: *Munro* (animated cartoon), 1960; *Carnal Knowledge*, 1971; *Little Murders*, 1971; *Popeye*, 1980; *I Want to Go Home*, 1989.

Television Plays: *Silverlips* in *VD Blues*, with others, 1972; *Kidnapped* (*Happy Endings* series), 1975.

Novels

Harry, The Rat with Women. New York, McGraw Hill, and London, Collins, 1963.
Ackroyd. New York, Simon and Schuster, 1977; London, Hutchinson, 1978.
Tantrum: A Novel-in-Cartoons. New York, Knopf, 1979; London, Sidgwick and Jackson, 1980.

Other

Sick, Sick, Sick. New York, McGraw Hill, 1958; London, Collins, 1959.
Passionella and Other Stories. New York, McGraw Hill, 1959; London, Collins, 1960.
The Explainers. New York, McGraw Hill, 1960; London, Collins, 1961.
Boy, Girl. Boy, Girl. New York, Random House, 1961; London, Collins, 1962.
Hold Me! New York, Random House, 1963.
Feiffer's Album. New York, Random House, 1963.
The Unexpurgated Memoirs of Bernard Mergendeiler. New York, Random House, 1965; London, Collins, 1966.
The Penguin Feiffer. London, Penguin.
Feiffer on Civil Rights. New York, Anti-Defamation League of B'nai B'rith, 1966.

Feiffer's Marriage Manual. New York, Random House, 1967.

Pictures at a Prosecution: Drawings and Text from the Chicago Conspiracy Trial. New York, Grove Press, 1971.

Feiffer on Nixon: The Cartoon Presidency. New York, Random House, 1974.

Jules Feiffer's America from Eisenhower to Reagan, edited by Steven Heller. New York, Knopf, and London, Penguin, 1982.

Outer Space Spirit 1952, with Will Eisner and Wallace Wood, edited by Denis Kitchen. Princeton, Wisconsin, Kitchen Sink Press, 1983.

Marriage Is an Invasion of Privacy and Other Dangerous Views. Fairway, Kansas, Andrews McMeel and Parker, 1984.

Feiffer's Children. Fairway, Kansas, Andrews McMeel and Parker, 1986.

Ronald Reagan in Movie America: A Jules Feiffer Production. Fairway, Kansas, Andrews McMeel and Parker, 1988.

Editor, *The Great Comic Book Heroes*. New York, Dial Press, 1965; London, Allen Lane, 1967.

* * *

Jules Feiffer is, first of all, a cartoonist. Long before he began to write plays, he had made a reputation as a satirist with an uncanny knack for catching the psychological, social, and political clichés which are the refuge and the cross of the college-educated middle class that provides him with an audience as well as a subject matter. His talent has always been as much verbal as visual; his ear as good as his hand. His cartoons are ordinarily strips in which two characters pursue a conversation, panel by panel, until the congenial platitudes dissolve into open aggression, naked greed, impotence, ineffectuality, pain; a variation is the strip in which a single figure—I almost said performer—speaks directly to the reader. The line between this kind of cartoon and the revue sketch is a narrow one, and a great many of Feiffer's early cartoons have crossed that line. Most of the material in *Feiffer's People* and *Hold Me!* presumably began as cartoon dialogue. Even those short works written for the theatre—*Dick and Jane*, the Feiffer sketch from *Oh! Calcutta!*, or the early one-acter *Crawling Arnold*—seem little more than extended cartoons with the stage directions standing in for the drawing.

Inevitably, Feiffer's full-length plays have been viewed—and condemned in some cases—as the work of a cartoonist. There is justice in the viewing, if not in the condemnation, for—as so often with satirists—Feiffer works in terms of stereotypes, of those figures identified by a single idiosyncrasy or a pattern of related compulsions. Even the two young men in *Carnal Knowledge* are societal types rather than psychological studies, although the labels by which we identify them may be written in the kind of psychological language that one expects to find in the balloons of Feiffer's cartoons. Feiffer tends to see his figures as more realistic than my description suggests. Just before the off-Broadway revival of *Little Murders*, Feiffer told an interviewer (*New York Times*, 26 January 1969) that his characters "are very, very real to me. I care about them as people." Yet, elsewhere in the same interview, he identified the family in the play as "a nice, Andy Hardy type family," and the Hardy family films were straight stereotype. If we read *real* in the Feiffer quotation as *true*—that is, identifiable—then the characters are real, as Andy Hardy is, as the figures in his cartoons are; we look at them and say, *oh yes, I know him*, meaning, *oh, yes, I know the type*.

The important thing about Feiffer as a playwright is that he produces unified dramatic structures—related, in some of their elements, to his cartoons and to revue sketches—in which apparently disparate material is held together by a controlling idea. In *Little Murders* the random violence that is the ostensible subject is simply the most obviously theatrical evidence of a general collapse that is reflected in technological malfunction (the failed electricity) and the impotence of traditional power-and-virtue figures (the comic turns of the judge, the detective, the priest). When Feiffer's nice American family begins to shoot people on the street, the event is not so much a culmination of the action as an open statement of what has been implicit all through the play. That last scene; the disintegration, physical and political, in *The White House Murder Case*; the sexual ignorance, and failure, that calls itself "Carnal Knowledge"—all these suggest that Feiffer has about as black a view of American society and of human possibility as one can find in the contemporary theatre.

After *Knock, Knock*, an uncharacteristic fantasy of commitment, *Grown Ups* comes home to familiar Feiffer territory with a self-pitying protagonist, faced with personal and professional collapse and a parental support system which is the presumed cause of his misery; on stage, his daughter, used as a weapon by all the adults, is something of a trial for the audience, but the television version of the play, ending with the camera on the little girl, successfully emphasizes the child as victim and the continuity of loving destructiveness within the family. *A Think Piece* concentrates on the trivia of daily existence to show, as the author says, "the nothingness that constitutes so much of our lives."

Elliot Loves and *Anthony Rose* explore familiar Feiffer themes, once again in darkly comic contexts. The titular hero of *Elliot Loves*, a nonrealistic gathering of four sketch-like scenes, is a man so unable to stop questioning, teasing, and testing his love that he ends with only a telephone cord holding him, tentatively, to his beloved. Anthony Rose is a successful playwright who turns up at a rehearsal of *The Parent Lesson*, a 25-year-old hit of his, and proceeds to rewrite it to conform to his new view of the world; the villainous father and the wronged sons exchange guilt and innocence. In the process, he takes over the production, undermining the company even as he calls them his family—a scary label since he has destroyed his own family and every theater group with which he has worked. *Elliot Loves* is the more polished script, but *Anthony Rose* is more interesting—particularly in its assumption that an author, at whatever age, uses his art to get back at the real world.

—Gerald Weales

———————

FENNARIO, David. Canadian. Born David William Wiper in Montreal in 1947. Educated at Dawson College, Montreal, 1969–71. Married Elizabeth Fennario in 1976; one child. Playwright-in-residence, Centaur Theatre, Montreal, from 1973. Co-founder, Cultural Workers Association. Recipient: Canada Council grant, 1973; Chalmers award, 1979. Address: c/o Centaur Theatre Company, 453 St. François Xavier Street, Montreal, Quebec H2Y 2TI, Canada.

PUBLICATIONS

Plays

On the Job (produced Montreal, 1975). Vancouver,
    Talonbooks, 1976.
Nothing to Lose (produced Montreal, 1976). Vancouver,
    Talonbooks, 1977.
Toronto (produced Montreal, 1978).
Without a Parachute, adaptation of his own book (produced
    Toronto, 1978).
Balconville (produced Montreal, 1979; Bath and London,
    1981). Vancouver, Talonbooks, 1980.
Changes, adaptation of his journal *Without a Parachute* (pro-
    duced Ottawa, 1980).
Moving (produced Montreal, 1983).
Blue Mondays, poems by Daniel Adams. Verdun, Quebec,
    Black Rock Creations, 1984.
Joe Beef (produced Montreal, 1985). Vancouver,
    Talonbooks, 1991.
Doctor Neil Cream (produced Toronto, 1988).
The Murder of Susan Parr (produced Montreal, 1989).
The Death of René Lévesque (produced Montreal, 1991).

Other

Without a Parachute (journal). Privately printed, 1972;
    Toronto, McClelland and Stewart, 1974.

* * *

It is difficult to consider David Fennario's work without
reference to the man himself. The connections between the
issues and attitudes of his plays and the author, his social
background, and his politics are so clear and so central that
any discussion of his *oeuvre* necessarily must take into
account his biography. This is no less true of the later work,
or of his continuing discomfort in working for established
theatres such as Montreal's Centaur Theatre where he was
first staged and where his most successful plays have been
mounted.

Fennario comes from an immigrant, working-class area of
Montreal. In this subculture, he learned to be streetwise in a
city divided between French and English factions and further
stressed by an increasingly obvious and vocal ethnic mosaic.
His personal story, which was dramatized in a one-man show,
Changes, has become a literary artifact itself, since it was the
initial and unexpected publication of his diary memoir,
Without a Parachute, which led Fennario to an unprecedented
residency with Centaur, the production of his first play, and
an immediate popular success (which has declined in the past
10 years). An extended sense of self has become characteristic of Fennario's plays: *On the Job* and *Balconville* move
further from it than, say, *Nothing to Lose*—where a protagonist exactly like the author returns to a slum exactly like his
home and talks to friends exactly like his own about how it
has been to become a famous playwright and media
personality—but even these plays exhibit the familiar setting,
figures, and tone of the author's actual background. When he
distances himself from his constructing milieu in the play
Toronto (where he not only sets aside his own territory but
moves across the border into English Canada), he writes his
least convincing play.

On the Job established the themes central to Fennario's
writing. Set in the packing room of a clothing factory on
Christmas Eve, the play's action is initiated by a special rush
order from the Eaton department store, a megabusiness

which becomes a symbol of the Canadian Establishment (in
this, as in other Canadian writing). The order requires the
shipping crew to remain through the usual half-day holiday
and brings to the surface the workers' feelings of exploitation
and powerlessness. It also allows their representative personalities to emerge: the old worker, aware of his political
weakness; the foreman, a Québécois who has risen to a
position of impotent power in the English management; the
young punk who wishes only to drink and avoid working; the
young radical who tries to incite revolution, organizing an
illegal strike which ends with the the firing of the employees.

The notion of revolution is pivotal, as it introduces
Fennario's Marxist, anarchist politics, a consistent ideology
which continues into his recent *Joe Beef*, and explains his
decision not to alter the text of *Balconville* for a 1992
remounting because, as he says in an interview in the Toronto
Globe and Mail, "times haven't really changed."

In *On the Job*, the political discussion among the men is
reproduced in extremely effective dialogue: Fennario's ear
for the dialects of Montreal is authentic and the powerful
vernacular accounts, in large part, for his early local success.
The play is full of vulgar songs, fights, props, and business
and, is lively and engaging in production. In print, it suffers
from a political vision which seems shallow and a situation
which has been explored before.

Balconville is Fennario's most successful play; the first
production broke attendance records and received ecstatic
newspaper reviews. More recently, literary critics have recon-
sidered this popularity and have attributed it more to the
relation of the play to the social milieu of its city in 1979 and
to its bold experiment in bilingualism than to an intrinsic
excellence in the drama itself.

The play is set in Pointe St. Charles, the working-class
district so familiar in Fennario's work. In this setting,
represented on stage by two double-storied apartment buildings with balconies which face each other, family groups of
English and Québécois workers display iconic traits,
establishing the linguistic and social differences between the
French and English within an otherwise similar society. These
people cannot afford to travel south to the sun in the freezing
winter or away from the inner city heat in the humid summer,
and so "vacation" in "Balconville," the crowded verandahs of
their tenements. Here, each observes the other, and petty
jealousies and language barriers explode under pressure into
family and social hatreds. The symbolism for Canadian
society is obvious and is amplified by the use of untranslated
passages in each language. The theatrical effect of this
bilingual dialogue is significant—while the characters cannot
understand one another, neither can portions of the audience
and the viewer is trapped by the text into participating in a
dramatic distillation of the frustrations of the nation. (Since
the play's first production, this device has been used in other
Canadian plays.)

Once again, characters fulfil political stereotypes of little
depth: the slum landlord and politician are monsters; the
unemployed are self-destructive victims of capitalist exploitation. The ending, in which the *quartier* burns down while
the inhabitants struggle to find some common support, offers
a facile solution to the dilemma but does offer hope for social
cooperation. The figures, however, are more rounded than
those of *On the Job*: in Thibault, Fennario creates a true
clown, and the rhythms of the dialogue, punctuated by lonely
guitar music, are well crafted and disciplined. The play also
presents female characters for the first time, figures much
more deeply drawn than the male characters who are his
normal subjects.

Disillusioned with mainstream theatre, Fennario began to

work with an amateur community group. *Joe Beef* and *Doctor Neil Cream*, written for this group, have been poorly received. *The Murder of Susan Parr*, which concerns the splintering of the Pointe St. Charles community, returns Fennario to an established playhouse but does not alter his subject.

In *Joe Beef (A History of Pointe St. Charles)*, a tavern keeper who fed a thousand workers and their families for six weeks during an organized strike in 1887 acts as Master of Ceremonies to a revisionist history of Montreal. The revue is lively, sometimes funny, and often moving, but, once again, it is single-minded in its protest and presents no solutions to the history of oppression it documents except a vague call to "stand together" and the possibility of revolution "Because. . . . Like this, we are nothing. But this . . . (*closes his hand into a fist*) we are Everything." The 19th-century capitalization of the quality the workers might achieve seems to fit the 19th-century history of the district, but seems not to offer much to audiences in the late 20th century.

In *The Death of René Lévesque*, Fennario examines the changes to the Separatist movement in Québec in an anniversary celebration of the death of its most charismatic leader. Using francophone actors to speak English lines, Fennario again plays with the accented tensions of language in the society. Characters representing a union leader, a terrorist turned bourgeois, a folk singer, and a politician depict the slide to the right of the Parti Québécois and question the ideology which might form a new nation. The play received a very mixed response, partly because it insulted some francophone viewers and partly because it mixes analysis of the struggle for independence with the Marxist polemic which is Fennario's repetitive focus.

—Reid Gilbert

FERLINGHETTI, Lawrence (Mendes-Monsanto). American. Born in Yonkers, New York, 24 March 1919; lived in France, 1920–24. Educated at Riverdale Country School, 1927–28, and Bronxville Public School, 1929–33, both New York; Mount Hermon School, Greenfield, Massachusetts, 1933–37; University of North Carolina, Chapel Hill, B.A. in journalism 1941; Columbia University, New York, 1947–48, M.A. 1948; Sorbonne, Paris, 1948–50, Doctorat de l'Université 1950. Served in the United States Naval Reserve, 1941–45: lieutenant commander. Married Selden Kirby-Smith in 1951 (divorced 1976); one daughter and one son. Worked for *Time* magazine, New York, 1945–46; French teacher, San Francisco, 1951–53. Co-founder, 1952, with Peter D. Martin, and since 1955 owner, City Lights Bookstore, and editor-in-chief, City Lights Books, San Francisco, delegate, Pan American Cultural Conference, Concepción, Chile, 1960. Also a painter: individual show—Ethel Guttmann Gallery, San Francisco, 1985. Recipient: Etna-Taormina prize (Italy), 1968. Address: City Lights Books, 261 Columbus Avenue, San Francisco, California 94133, U.S.A.

PUBLICATIONS

Plays

The Alligation (produced San Francisco, 1962; New York, 1970; London, 1989). Included in *Unfair Arguments with Existence*, 1963.

Unfair Arguments with Existence: Seven Plays for a New Theatre (includes *The Soldiers of No Country*, *Three Thousand Red Ants*, *The Alligation*, *The Victims of Amnesia*, *Motherlode*, *The Customs Collector in Baggy Pants*, *The Nose of Sisyphus*). New York, New Directions, 1963.
The Victims of Amnesia (produced London, 1989). Included in *Unfair Arguments with Existence*, 1963.
The Customs Collector in Baggy Pants (produced New York, 1964). Included in *Unfair Arguments with Existence*, 1963.
The Soldiers of No Country (produced London, 1969). Included in *Unfair Arguments with Existence*, 1963.
3 by Ferlinghetti: Three Thousand Red Ants, The Alligation, The Victims of Amnesia (produced New York, 1970). Included in *Unfair Arguments with Existence*, 1963.
Routines (includes 13 short pieces). New York, New Directions, 1964.

Novels

Her. New York, New Directions, 1960; London, MacGibbon and Kee, 1967.
Love in the Days of Rage. New York, Dutton, and London, Bodley Head, 1988.
When I Look at Pictures. Layton, Utah, Gibbs Smith, 1990.

Verse

Pictures of the Gone World. San Francisco, City Lights, 1955.
A Coney Island of the Mind. New York, New Directions, 1958.
Tentative Description of a Dinner Given to Promote the Impeachment of President Eisenhower. San Francisco, Golden Mountain Press, 1958.
One Thousand Fearful Words for Fidel Castro. San Francisco, City Lights, 1961.
Berlin. San Francisco, Golden Mountain Press, 1961.
Starting from San Francisco. New York, New Directions, 1961; revised edition, 1967.
Penguin Modern Poets 5, with Allen Ginsberg and Gregory Corso. London, Penguin, 1963.
Where Is Vietnam? San Francisco, City Lights, 1965.
To Fuck Is to Love Again; Kyrie Eleison Kerista; or, The Situation in the West; Followed by a Holy Proposal. New York, Fuck You Press, 1965.
Christ Climbed Down. Syracuse, New York, Syracuse University, 1965.
An Eye on the World: Selected Poems. London, MacGibbon and Kee, 1967.
After the Cries of the Birds. San Francisco, Dave Haselwood, 1967.
Moscow in the Wilderness, Segovia in the Snow. San Francisco, Beach, 1967.
Repeat After Me. Boston, Impressions Workshop, 1967(?).
Reverie Smoking Grass. Milan, East 128, 1968.
The Secret Meaning of Things. New York, New Directions, 1968.
Fuclock. London, Fire, 1968.
Tyrannus Nix? New York, New Directions, 1969; revised edition, 1973.
Back Roads to Far Towns after Basho. Privately printed, 1970.
Sometime During Eternity. Conshohocken, Pennsylvania, Poster Prints, 1970(?).
The World Is a Beautiful Place. Conshohocken, Pennsylvania, Poster Prints, 1970(?).

The Illustrated Wilfred Funk. San Francisco, City Lights, 1971.

A World Awash with Fascism and Fear. San Francisco, Cranium Press, 1971.

Back Roads to Far Places. New York, New Directions, 1971.

Love Is No Stone on the Moon: Automatic Poem. Berkeley, California, Arif Press, 1971.

Open Eye, with *Open Head*, by Allen Ginsberg. Melbourne, Sun, 1972; published separately, Cambridge, Massachusetts, Pomegranate Press, 1973.

Constantly Risking Absurdity. Brockport, New York, State University College, 1973.

Open Eye, Open Heart. New York, New Directions, 1973.

Populist Manifesto. San Francisco, Cranium Press, 1975; revised edition, San Francisco, City Lights, n.d.

Soon It Will Be Night. Privately printed, 1975(?).

The Jack of Hearts. San Francisco, City Lights, 1975(?).

Director of Alienation. San Francisco, City Lights, 1975(?).

The Old Italians Dying. San Francisco, City Lights, 1976.

Who Are We Now? New York, New Directions, 1976.

White on White. San Francisco, City Lights, 1977.

Adieu à Charlot. San Francisco, City Lights, 1978.

Northwest Ecolog. San Francisco, City Lights, 1978.

The Sea and Ourselves at Cape Ann. Madison, Wisconsin, Red Ozier Press, 1979.

Landscapes of Living and Dying. New York, New Directions, 1979.

The Love Nut. Lincoln, Massachusetts, Penmaen Press, 1979.

Mule Mountain Dreams. Bisbee, Arizona, Bisbee Press Collective, 1980.

A Trip to Italy and France. New York, New Directions, 1981.

The Populist Manisfestos, Plus an Interview with Jean-Jacques Lebel. San Francisco, Grey Fox Press, 1981.

Endless Life: The Selected Poems. New York, New Directions, 1981.

Over All the Obscene Boundaries: European Poems and Transitions. New York, New Directions, 1984.

Since Man Began to Eat Himself. Mt. Horeb, Wisconsin, 1986.

Wild Dreams of a New Beginning. New York, New Directions, 1988.

Recordings: *Poetry Readings in "The Cellar,"* with Kenneth Rexroth, Fantasy, 1958; *Tentative Description of a Dinner to Impeach President Eisenhower and Other Poems,* Fantasy, 1959; *Tyrannus Nix? and Assassination Raga,* Fantasy, 1971; *The World's Greatest Poets 1,* with Allen Ginsberg and Gregory Corso, CMS, 1971; *Lawrence Ferlinghetti,* Everett-Edwards, 1972; *Into the Deeper Pools . . . ,* Watershed, 1984.

Other

Dear Ferlinghetti/Dear Jack: The Spicer-Ferlinghetti Correspondence. San Francisco, White Rabbit Press, 1962(?).

The Mexican Night: Travel Journal. New York, New Directions, 1970.

A Political Pamphlet. San Francisco, Anarchist Resistance Press, 1975.

Literary San Francisco: A Pictorial History from Its Beginnings to the Present Day, with Nancy J. Peters. San Francisco, City Lights, 1980.

An Artist's Diatribe. San Diego, Atticus Press, 1983.

Leaves of Life: Fifty Drawings from the Model. San Francisco, City Lights, 1983.

Seven Days in Nicaragua Libre, photographs by Chris Felver. San Francisco, City Lights, 1984.

Editor, *Beatitude Anthology.* San Francisco, City Lights, 1960.

Editor, with Michael McClure and David Meltzer, *Journal for the Protection of All Beings 1* and *3.* San Francisco, City Lights, 2 vols., 1961–69.

Editor, *City Lights Journal.* San Francisco, City Lights, 4 vols., 1963–78.

Editor, *Panic Grass,* by Charles Upton. San Francisco, City Lights, 1969.

Editor, *The First Third,* by Neal Cassady. San Francisco, City Lights, 1971.

Editor, *City Lights Anthology.* San Francisco, City Lights, 1974.

Editor, with Nancy J. Peters, *City Lights Review 1 [3].* San Francisco, City Lights, 2 vols., 1987–89.

Translator, *Selections from Paroles by Jacques Prévert.* San Francisco, City Lights, 1958; London, Penguin, 1963.

Translator, with Anthony Kahn, *Flowers and Bullets, and Freedom to Kill,* by Yevgeny Yevtushenko. San Francisco, City Lights, 1970.

Translator, with Richard Lettau, *Love Poems,* by Karl Marx. San Francisco, City Lights, 1977.

Translator, with Francesca Valente, *Roman Poems,* by Pier Paolo Pasolini. San Francisco, City Lights, 1986.

*

Bibliography: *Lawrence Ferlinghetti: A Comprehensive Bibliography to 1980* by Bill Morgan, New York, Garland, 1982.

Manuscript Collection: Bancroft Library, University of California, Berkeley.

Critical Studies: *Ferlinghetti: A Biography* by Neeli Cherkovsky, New York, Doubleday, 1979; *Lawrence Ferlinghetti: Poet-at-Large* by Larry Smith, Carbondale, Southern Illinois University Press, 1983; *Constantly Risking Absurdity: The Writings of Lawrence Ferlinghetti* by Michael Skau, Troy, New York, Whitston, 1989; *Ferlinghetti: The Artist in His Time* by Barry Silesky, New York, Warner, 1990.

* * *

Poet of the Beat Generation, Lawrence Ferlinghetti has published two volumes of short plays in prose. Ferlinghetti's plays, like his poems, are influenced by French Existentialist attitudes to love and death, but, like his fellow Beats, he replaces French Existentialist commitment by disaffiliation. Even before he turned to plays, Ferlinghetti "performed" his poems, sometimes with jazz accompaniment. His first volume of plays, *Unfair Arguments with Existence,* uses a casual American idiom for depicting existence as we know it in modern industrial society. The progression of the seven plays in this volume is from the roughly realistic to the distinctly symbolic. The next to last play is a monologue, and the last play spurns all dialogue, striving for a more improvisational effect.

In the longest Argument with Existence, *The Soldiers of No Country,* a 60-year-old priest and a 20-year-old deserter compete for the love of 35-year-old Erma. Watching this grotesque triangle in a womblike cave are many silent people who fall, one by one, to the ground. After the priest's victory, Erma stumbles out of the cave, and the deserter threatens the priest. Though the play seems to end in ubiquitous death, a baby cries within the cave, implying the possibility of rebirth.

Hope is fainter in the next two Arguments. *Three*

Thousand Red Ants is an associational conversation between Fat and Moth, a married couple in bed. At the end Fat turns binoculars on the audience and exclaims that he sees a breakthrough, to which his wife replies under the bedclothes: "Your own! Humpty Dumpty!" In *The Alligation* Ladybird is fixated on her pet alligator, Shooky, though a Blind Indian warns her that this is dangerous. When Ladybird stretches full length on Shooky, he rolls over on top of her, and the Blind Indian calls to the audience for help. Both plays pose audience help as an implicit question.

Influenced by the Theatre of the Absurd, the next three Arguments are extended metaphors for the human condition. In *The Victims of Amnesia* a Night Clerk converses with a woman shown at four stages of diminishing age—Marie, Young Woman, Girl, Baby—all embraced in the name Mazda. At the play's end the Night Clerk *cum* Fate inveighs against all life, as the play explodes into smashing light bulbs of many sizes. But finally a single small bulb flickers in the dark before the theatre lights come up. Similarly, *Motherlode* theatricalizes the undimmed faith of a dying miner, even after the crass commercial Schmucks have despoiled the land. After the miner's death, with Schmuck triumphant, the birds still call "Love! Love!" *The Customs Collector in Baggy Pants* is set on a life-boat "full of flush-toilets which we call civilization." Assailed by a storm outside and the storm of flushing toilets on the boat, the Customs Collector shouts his determination not to die or capitulate. Ferlinghetti punctuates the Absurd with hope.

In *The Nose of Sisyphus*, however, hope is all but extinguished. In a playground that is a metaphor for the world, Sisyphus uses his false nose to try to push a globe up a slide, while assorted human beings try to scale a jungle gym. Though Sisyphus cannot persuade the people to help him, he does succeed in leading their chants. But a whistle-blowing Big Baboon slides down the slide, toppling Sisyphus, frightening the people, and robbing Sisyphus of globe and nose. Alone on stage, the Big Baboon tosses the false nose into the audience. At best, one can hope for another Sisyphus to arise from the audience.

The Nose of Sisyphus is the last play in *Unfair Arguments with Existence*, and Ferlinghetti incorporates it as the last of the 13 pieces in his second volume of plays, *Routines*. He defines a routine as

> a song and dance, a little rout, a routing-out, a runaround, a "round of business or amusement": myriads of people, herds, flowerbeds, ships and cities, all going through their routines, life itself a blackout routine, an experimental madness somewhere between dotage and megalomania, lost in the vibration of a wreckage (of some other cosmos we fell out of).

All 13 Routines focus on visual metaphors, but they read rhythmically, with the free flexible rhythms of Ferlinghetti's poems. Their subjects are love, death, and the totalitarian establishment. Just before *The Nose of Sisyphus* appears *Bore*, a call to action: "Routines never end; they have to be broken. This little routine to end all routines requires the formation of a worldwide society dedicated to the non-violent disruption of institutionalized events." Play tries to infiltrate life in Ferlinghetti's final play.

—Ruby Cohn

FIERSTEIN, Harvey (Forbes). American. Born in Brooklyn, New York, 6 June 1954. Educated at Pratt Institute, Brooklyn, B.F.A. 1973. Drag performer and actor from 1970: professional debut at Club 82 and La Mama Experimental Theatre Club, New York, 1971; roles in more than 60 plays and in several films. Recipient: Rockefeller grant; Ford grant; Creative Artists Public Services grant; Obie award, 1982; Tony award, 1983 (for writing and acting), 1984; Oppenheimer award, 1983; Drama Desk award, 1983 (for writing and acting); Dramatists Guild Hull-Warriner award, 1983; Los Angeles Drama Critics Circle award, 1984; Ace award, 1988. Agent: George Lane, William Morris Agency, 1350 Avenue of the Americas, New York, New York 10019, U.S.A.

PUBLICATIONS

Plays

In Search of the Cobra Jewels (produced New York, 1972). New York, Author, 1972.
Freaky Pussy (produced New York, 1973).
Flatbush Tosca (produced New York, 1975). New York, Author, 1975.
Torch Song Trilogy (produced New York, 1981; London, 1985). New York, Gay Presses of New York, 1981; London, Methuen, 1984.
 The International Stud (produced New York, 1978).
 Fugue in a Nursery (produced New York, 1979).
 Widows and Children First! (produced New York, 1979).
Spookhouse (produced New York, 1982; London, 1987). Published in *Plays International* (London), July 1987.
La Cage aux Folles, music and lyrics by Jerry Herman, adaptation of the play by Jean Poiret (produced Boston and New York, 1983; London, 1986).
Manny and Jake (produced New York, 1987).
Safe Sex (includes *Manny and Jake*, *Safe Sex*, *On Tidy Endings*) (produced New York, 1987; London, 1991). New York, Atheneum, 1987.
Forget Him (produced New York, 1988).
Legs Diamond, with Charles Suppon, music and lyrics by Peter Allen (produced New York, 1988).

Screenplay: *Torch Song Trilogy*, 1989.

* * *

Actor/drag queen Harvey Fierstein began writing plays at age 20 so as to create roles for himself. His first attempt concerned his efforts to clean Harry Koutoukas's apartment, a horrifying task which he undertook so that playwright would write a script for him. Instead, Fierstein wrote about the housecleaning experience in a musical—*In Search of the Cobra Jewels*, complete with a chorus of cockroaches—in which both writers appeared as themselves. Because Fierstein wanted to play a whore, he wrote *Freaky Pussy*, whose seven cross-dressing hookers live in a subway men's room. Then, longing to sing Tosca, he wrote *Flatbush Tosca*. His next, though still unproduced, play, *Cannibals*, anticipates a plot element in *La Cage aux Folles*, as two kids run off and bring shame on their tribe because they want to be straight.

The next year Fierstein began writing his Tony award-winning role, Arnold Beckoff (i.e. "beckon" versus "back off"), in the first of the *Torch Song Trilogy* plays, *The International Stud*, and the plump pixie, wit, political activist, and outspoken critic of a heterosexist society finally began attracting the attention of audiences beyond the confines of the experimental off-off-Broadway La Mama. In dialogue at once droll, direct, and distressing ("A thing of beauty is a joy till sunrise"), Arnold compulsively carries the torch for bisexual Ed; his winning that stud degrades him nearly as much as does the initial pursuit and the eventual loss. Yet he accompanies each act of dependence, each self-destructive kvetch with which he pushes Ed away from him, with a laconic quip which lets us know that Arnold understands what he's doing. Like the torch singer who capitalizes on her pain with "music to be miserable by," Arnold often allows his vulnerability to career crazily into masochistic self-pity.

Fierstein suits his form to his content by employing presentational styles in the first two plays. Thus Arnold's egocentricity finds expression when he gazes into a mirror during the opening of *The International Stud*, which also isolates Arnold and Ed in a series of self-absorbed monologues; although this is a two-character play (plus torch singer), they appear together only in the last scene, after Fierstein creates the effect of a backroom orgy by employing Arnold alone. *Fugue in a Nursery* picks up Arnold and ex-lover Ed a year after the end of their affair, as Arnold and his new flame Alan visit Ed and the "other woman" Laurel at Ed's summer home. Only slightly matured out of pure narcissism, the four, in contrapuntal scenes played upon a giant bed, engage in frequently rearranged pairings with occasionally intersecting dialogue. They're sophisticated enough to suit the fugal accompaniment (by string quartet) and plot construction, but sufficiently infantile for Arnold's bedroom to be termed "the nursery."

If *Fugue*'s duologues seem an experimental version of Noël Coward or William Wycherley, the representational domestic drama *Widows and Children First!* begins with more conventional sit-com plotting and balances deflation of sentiment with effective sentimentality. Five years after *Fugue*, we find Arnold in a period of widowhood following Alan's death—bludgeoned with baseball bats by homophobes. Ed has left Laurel, Arnold mothers his "hopelessly homo" foster son, 15-year-old David, while visiting Mrs. Beckoff rebukes her own homosexual son Arnold, giving us therefore two mothers, two widows, two sons, two referees for fights—yet only four characters. Although Arnold and Ed have matured to some degree, Ed still doesn't know what he wants and Arnold still displays a penchant for acting in ways not in his own best interest. In a moving microcosm of human paradox, Mrs. Beckoff disapproves of David when she, hilariously, mistakes him for Arnold's lover, but grows still more shocked when she learns the tie is filial. Arnold demands respect of his mother without necessarily giving it in return. David waxes wise about how to help Arnold, yet doesn't apply much insight to himself. Arnold objects to his mother's distress at homosexuality, yet loves an equally fearful man.

Fierstein's rich thematic panoply—including loneliness, loss, self-esteem, homophobia, and honesty ("What's the matter? Catch your tongue in the closet door?")—numbers among its concerns frequent allegiance to the sort of family values to which right-wing zealots love to claim sole proprietorship. Arnold can't be impersonal about sex, longing instead for romance, commitment, monogamy, and children to mother. Such conventional values imbue most of Fierstein's work ever since his groundbreaking trilogy and contribute to his popularity among heterosexual as well as gay audiences.

Spookhouse embodies contradictory attitudes towards the possibility of raising decent kids. The conscientious but destructively naïve gay social worker believes in the social system and the future. As in Tennessee Williams's *The Glass Menagerie*, the obnoxious mother's grit provides the only glue

holding together her neurotic—and in this case lower-class—family, but she knows the system has failed her kids and wants her sociopathic son imprisoned. Set in a disintegrating Coney Island amusement park ride and the home above it, *Spookhouse* serves as metaphor for the horrors in our lives we can't control. ("Life's scary enough without paying for added attractions.") These haunt us even in our safe places, such as our homes, and pop out at us when we're unable to cope with them. This black-comic melodrama, replete with rape, incest, murder, and arson, taps into our anxieties, particularly our pessimism pertaining to parenting and the urban bureaucracy, which victimizes both its clients and its employees.

The dysfunctional but straight Janiks in *Spookhouse* contrast with the stable gay family in *La Cage aux Folles*, a musical which provides a refreshing perspective refuting homophobic stereotypes. Married in all but law, Albin and Georges exceed their devotion to each other only in their love for son Jean-Michele, who poorly repays Albin's mothering by banishing him from the family flat when the boy's fiancée and her right-wing parents visit to inspect their future in-laws. Unlike the French farce original by Jean Poiret, Fierstein poignantly focuses on Jean-Michele's insensitivity and ingratitude and celebrates the commitment between the two middle-aged men, a night club owner and his androgynous drag-queen star. In addition to dramatizing loving domestic relationships, Fierstein again stresses the importance of being oneself ("I Am What I Am") and respecting oneself and others, particularly (c.f. the biblical injunction to honor them) parents.

Although this tender comedy ran on Broadway for four and a half years, Fierstein's second foray onto the musical stage proved less successful, probably because he merely attempted to salvage the work of an inexperienced librettist. When Fierstein inherited clothing designer Charles Suppon's book for the 1940's gangster musical *Legs Diamond*, scored by Australian Peter Allen, he revised characters and dialogue but retained the structure. The less said about this disastrous vanity production for the composer/star the better. The one-act, pre-AIDS comedy *Forget Him*, on the other hand, deserves an audience. The Fierstein stand-in, Michael, has paid a finder's fee for the perfect lover—handsome, rich, smart, athletic, and attentive. Yet he demands his money back because Eugene's blindness and deafness—or Michael's own insecurities—leave him troubled that someone even better, the title's "him," will come along.

With the *Safe Sex* trilogy Fierstein finally turns to the effect of AIDS on gay men's lives, representing this impact in part by means of presentational set metaphors (like *Fugue*'s bed and the spooks in *Spookhouse*). For *Manny and Jake*, he dramatizes disease-carrier Manny's ex-lovers—many now corpses—with dummies. In the title play, he visualizes for us how the men's relationship has been thrown off-balance by placing them on a seesaw, although a more recent New York revival puts them in bed, which makes the seductiveness and terrors more real.

Fear, indeed, informs all three plays. Manny, who used to live for sex, paralyzes himself with worry over infecting more men, even while praying for the renewal of romantic possibilities he regards as now blighted by his HIV status; implicitly he rejects the option of safer sex and simply laments his loss. His parallel in the title play, Ghee (played by Fierstein), also permits fears to inhibit him. HIV-negative, Ghee's terrified avoidance of sex by means of verbal attacks, retreats, and reprises really masks a greater problem: fear of intimacy. The teeter-totter metaphor expresses a relationship imbalanced by scares from AIDS, letting a lover get close, and potential loss of both lover and life. Despite the pain at their core,

Manny and Jake offers a lyrical elegy to sexual joy, while *Safe Sex* satirically mocks both Ghee's anxieties and his macho lover's unwashed ardor.

In the final treatment of fear, loss, and—dare we?—trust, *On Tidy Endings*, Fierstein employs a fully representational style and setting (repeating in this trilogy the same progression from presentational to realistic which he first used in *Torch Song*). The Fierstein character, Arthur, mourns his lover's death from AIDS, while he confronts Colin's ex-wife, there with legal papers pertaining to their shares of the inheritance. Part of that legacy turns out to be the disease, which ironically has spared Arthur but stricken the woman, probably working hard to win Arthur's trust not only for her sake but for that of her son, who needs to overcome his own grief, rage, and homophobia so as to continue to benefit from Arthur's maternal care. Like *Torch Song Trilogy*, *On Tidy Endings* prompts our laughter and tears at a son and alternately bickering and affectionate widows.

—Tish Dace

FLANNERY, Peter. British. Born in Jarrow, Tyne and Wear, 12 October 1951. Educated at the University of Manchester, B.A. (honours) in drama 1973. Director, actor, and stage manager, Manchester, 1974–76; playwright-in-residence, Royal Shakespeare Company, London, 1979–80. Member, North West Arts Association drama panel, 1980–85. Recipient: London *Sunday Times* Student Play award, 1978; Thames Television award, 1979; Arts Council bursary, 1980, 1984; John Whiting award, 1982; Beckett award, 1989. Agent: Stephen Durbridge, Lemon, Unna and Durbridge, 24 Pottery Lane, Holland Park, London W11 4LZ, England.

PUBLICATIONS

Plays

Heartbreak Hotel (produced Manchester, 1975). Todmorden, Woodhouse, 1979.
Last Resort (produced London, 1976).
Are You with Me? (produced Nottingham, 1977).
Savage Amusement (produced London, 1978; New York, 1981). London, Rex Collings, 1978.
The Boy's Own Story (produced Manchester, 1978; London, 1980; New York, 1983).
The Adventures of Awful Knawful, with Mick Ford (for children; produced London, 1978). London, Eyre Methuen, 1979.
Jungle Music (produced Manchester, 1979).
Our Friends in the North (produced Stratford-on-Avon and London, 1982). London, Methuen, 1982.
Heavy Days (produced Stratford-on-Avon, 1982).
Silence on My Radio (produced Newcastle-upon-Tyne, 1983).
Blind Justice: Five Screenplays (includes *Crime and Punishment*; *White Man, Listen*; *The One About the Irishmen*; *A Death in the Family*; *Permanent Blue*) (televised, 1988). London, Hern, 1990.
Singer (produced Stratford-on-Avon, 1989; London, 1990). London, Hern, 1989.

Radio Plays: *Small Talk*, with Elizabeth Gamlin, 1986; *Singer*, 1992.

Television Plays: *Our Friends in the North: Seven Screenplays* (includes *One Man, One Vote*; *Public Relations*; *Honour*; *Conspiracies*; *Pictures*; *Power*; *Mysteries*), 1984; *Warhill*, 1985; *Blind Justice: Five Screenplays*, 1988; *Shoot the Revolution*, 1990.

* * *

Peter Flannery, son of two generations of Jarrow shipyard workers, studied drama at Manchester University, planning to be a director. He was soon writing, however: *Heartbreak Hotel*, a rock musical; the 75-minute *Last Resort*, in which a peculiar group of people meet beside the Punch and Judy show on Blackpool beach; the one-character *The Boy's Own Story*, in which a goalkeeper explains himself between saves; and *Jungle Music*, Brecht's *In the Jungle of the Cities* as musical, updated and moved to Manchester.

Flannery first drew attention with *Savage Amusement*, staged by the Royal Shakespeare Company at the Warehouse in 1978. Set in 1982, after a Tory election victory (then in the future), four young drop-outs squatting in Hulme in south Manchester realise their dependence on a strange, detached working-class youth, and, more important, reveal a crumbling, frightening environment. Flannery explained his subject in *The Warehouse Papers*: "I was concerned about what young people in Hulme might grow up thinking and hoping. . . . Whose fault is Hulme? Can or should people from outside get involved with the place? What happens if Hulme continues to deteriorate? . . . If I am living in a society founded on civilised values, then what went wrong? . . . Though I am aware that poverty *is* a political issue, the play attempts no political solutions." Michael Billington noted that, though Flannery sympathized with his characters, he also showed "their powerlessness in the face of disintegration." More than this, Flannery created a unique and disturbing world of fear and threat, of wilderness and concentration camp, of a collapsing social fabric.

Small Talk, a sensitive study of childlessness, for radio in 1986, was followed in 1988 by the five-part *Blind Justice*, among the very few television scripts to be published. Two "alternative" lawyers, a man and a woman, dealt with various cases raising awkward questions about the legal system. Flannery visited Romania in 1990 before writing, again for television, *Shoot the Revolution*, about the fall of Ceausescu in December 1989. Using news film and a narrator, the situation in Romania was illustrated by a secret policeman, his ineffectual liberal teacher brother, a peasant girl, and an actress representing the intellectuals.

In his introduction to the text of *Blind Justice* Flannery says that he belongs "among that small band of writers which still wants to write about the big picture." This is what he has done in his two epic condition-of-England plays, *Our Friends in the North* and *Singer*.

Our Friends, episodic and ambitious, spans 1964 to 1979, with scenes in Newcastle, Soho, Scotland Yard, Parliament, and Rhodesia. Flannery expects his audience to know its British history for this period, and to pick up on his allusions to the scandals around Poulson and Dan Smith in the northeast in the 1960's. The three main plot threads are the ties between an unprincipled architect and a complacent local Labour party; corrupt police failing to act against vice in London; and the pretence that genuine sanctions were imposed on Rhodesia after the unilateral declaration of independence in 1965. The threads are linked by the parallel biographies of two Newcastle boys, one disillusioned after experience of Labour politics, the other somehow educated to understand power through crime and a spell as a mercenary in Rhodesia. The play ends with the latter and a prostitute apparently about to machine-gun a P.R. man as he leaves a restaurant, perhaps also to shoot an M.P., an oil executive, a civil servant, and three top policemen, heard but not seen in the closing minutes. *Our Friends* is about the decline and disappearance of principles and how even innocents become involved in corruption. Parliamentary democracy appears ineffective. *Our Friends* was re-written as an 11-part TV serial for the BBC, but appears to have been blocked because of the possible legal implications of its characters' being based on real people.

Flannery was prompted to write *Singer* by reading Shirley Green's biography of Peter Rachman, who became notorious nationally at the end of the 1950's as an unscrupulous and wealthy slum landlord. From the biography Flannery learned that Rachman was a survivor of the concentration camps. This led him into a year's research, a strong response to the books of Primo Levi, and so to a play about "a man's rapaciousness and the reasons behind it." The scale was Jacobean, five acts with prologue and epilogue, so *Singer* was well suited to be the first modern play staged in the Royal Shakespeare Company's Swan theatre at Stratford-on-Avon.

Chorus speeches give us briefly the dates, from wartime ("a time, and what a time, when war was not a crime but a crusade"), through Harold Wilson's 1960's ("Now the white heat of technological revolution dazzles the eyes and all the youth of England are on fire") to the Thatcherite 1980's, the years of "the Great Housekeeper, with fox-like cunning, lion's strength, and matching crocodile accessories."

Singer, a Polish Jew, is first seen as a prisoner in Auschwitz, already a wheeler-dealer, with his nephew Stefan and the German Communist, Manik, both of whom accompany him to Britain after the war. Soon he is dealing in nylons and frying pans from a public telephone box in Bayswater, charming young women (he resembles Krank in John Arden's *Waters of Babylon*), then rising to riches in property deals, evicting elderly sitting tenants. He obtains British citizenship, entertains the upper classes at a party, and at the end of Act 3 drowns in a Hampstead pond. Reappearing, he woos a girl whose crippled father proves to have been a guard at Auschwitz. He delivers soup to the homeless on the South Bank but then is led into a scheme to provide "camps" for the homeless. He has, meanwhile, found Stefan, now a photographer, who also paints scenes from the camps so that the Holocaust will be remembered: finally Stefan kills himself.

The drama is memorable for the huge title role originally played by Antony Sher. *Singer* explores the immigrant experience, the legacy of Nazism, the need to remember— Auschwitz, the Rachman era, the 1980's failing to learn from Rachman's exploitation. For Neil Taylor *Singer* was "a parable to explain the nature of modern Britain and, at the same time, the moral significance of such universals as memory and guilt."

Flannery's major stage plays require enormous casts, while all his work is controversial and anti-Establishment. One hopes that both the Royal Shakespeare Company and television companies will continue to find a place for his necessary and challenging work.

—Malcolm Page

FOOTE, (Albert) Horton (Jr.). American. Born in Wharton, Texas, 14 March 1916. Educated at the Pasadena

Playhouse Theatre, California, 1933–35; Tamara Daykarhanova Theatre School, New York, 1937–39. Married Lillian Vallish in 1945; two daughters and two sons. Actor with American Actors Theatre, New York, 1939–42; theatre workshop director and producer, King-Smith School of Creative Arts, 1944–45, and manager, Productions Inc., 1945–48, both Washington, D.C. Recipient: Oscar, for screenplay, 1963, 1983; William Inge award, for lifetime achievement in theater, 1989. D.Litt.: Austin College, Sherman, Texas, 1987; Drew University, Madison, New Jersey, 1987; American Film Institute, Los Angeles, California. Lives in New York City and Wharton, Texas. Agent: Lucy Kroll Agency, 390 West End Avenue, New York, New York 10024, U.S.A.

PUBLICATIONS

Plays

Wharton Dance (produced New York, 1940).

Texas Town (produced New York, 1941).

Out of My House (also co-director: produced New York, 1942).

Only the Heart (produced New York, 1942). New York, Dramatists Play Service, 1944.

Two Southern Idylls: Miss Lou, and The Girls (produced New York, 1943).

The Lonely (produced New York, 1943).

Goodbye to Richmond (produced New York, 1943).

Daisy Lee, music by Bernardo Segall (produced New York, 1944).

Homecoming, In My Beginning, People in the Show, The Return (produced Washington, D.C., 1944).

Themes and Variations (produced Washington, D.C., 1945?).

Celebration (produced New York, 1948).

The Chase (produced New York, 1952). New York, Dramatists Play Service, 1952.

The Trip to Bountiful (televised 1953; produced New York, 1953; London, 1956). New York, Dramatists Play Service, 1954.

The Oil Well (televised 1953; produced New York, 1991).

The Midnight Caller (televised 1953; produced New York, 1958). New York, Dramatists Play Service, 1959.

John Turner Davis (televised 1953; produced New York, 1958). Included in *A Young Lady of Property*, 1955.

The Dancers (televised 1954; produced Los Angeles, 1963). Included in *A Young Lady of Property*, 1955.

The Travelling Lady (produced New York, 1954). New York, Dramatists Play Service, 1955.

A Young Lady of Property: Six Short Plays (includes *A Young Lady of Property, The Dancers, The Old Beginning, John Turner Davis, The Death of the Old Man, The Oil Well*). New York, Dramatists Play Service, 1955.

Harrison, Texas: Eight Television Plays (includes *The Dancers, The Death of the Old Man, Expectant Relations, John Turner Davis, The Midnight Caller, The Tears of My Sister, The Trip to Bountiful, A Young Lady of Property*). New York, Harcourt Brace, 1956.

Flight (televised 1957). Published in *Television Plays for Writers*, edited by A.S. Burack. Boston, The Writer, 1957.

Old Man, adaptation of a story by Faulkner (televised 1958). Included in *Three Plays*, 1962.

Roots in a Parched Ground (as *The Night of the Storm*, televised 1960). Included in *Three Plays*, 1962.

Tomorrow, adaptation of the story by Faulkner (televised 1960). Included in *Three Plays*, 1962.

Three Plays. New York, Harcourt Brace, 1962.

The Screenplay of To Kill a Mockingbird. New York, Harcourt Brace, 1964.

Gone with the Wind, music and lyrics by Harold Rome, adaptation of the novel by Margaret Mitchell (produced London, 1972; Los Angeles, 1973).

The Roads to Home (includes *The Dearest of Friends, A Nightingale, Spring Dance*) (also director: produced New York, 1982). New York, Dramatists Play Service, 1982.

Courtship (produced Louisville, 1984). Included in *Courtship, On Valentine's Day, 1918,* 1987.

1918 (televised 1984). Included in *Courtship, On Valentine's Day, 1918,* 1987.

On Valentine's Day (televised 1985). Included in *Courtship, On Valentine's Day, 1918,* 1987.

Tomorrow (television play) and *Tomorrow* (screenplay), in *Tomorrow and Tomorrow and Tomorrow* (also includes Faulkner's story "Tomorrow"), edited by David G. Yellin and Marie Conners. Jackson, University Press of Mississippi, 1985.

The Road to the Graveyard (produced New York, 1985). New York, Dramatists Play Service, 1988.

Blind Date (produced New York, 1986). New York, Dramatists Play Service, 1986.

Lily Dale (produced New York, 1986). Included in *Roots in a Parched Ground, Convicts, Lily Dale, The Widow Claire,* 1988.

The Widow Claire (produced New York, 1986). Included in *Roots in a Parched Ground, Convicts, Lily Dale, The Widow Claire,* 1988.

Courtship, On Valentine's Day, 1918. New York, Grove Press, 1987.

Roots in a Parched Ground, Convicts, Lily Dale, The Widow Claire. New York, Grove Press, 1988.

The Man Who Climbed the Pecan Trees (produced New York, 1988). New York, Dramatists Play Service, 1989.

Selected One-Act Plays, edited by Gerald C. Wood. Dallas, Texas, Southern Methodist University Press, 1988.

Habitation of Dragons (also director: produced Pittsburgh, 1988).

Cousins, and The Death of Papa. New York, Grove Press, 1989.

To Kill a Mockingbird, Tender Mercies, The Trip to Bountiful: Three Screenplays. New York, Grove Press, 1989.

Dividing the Estate (produced Princeton, New Jersey, 1989).

Talking Pictures (produced Florida, 1990).

Screenplays: *Storm Fear,* 1955; *To Kill a Mockingbird,* 1962; *Baby, The Rain Must Fall,* 1964; *Hurry Sundown,* with Thomas Ryan, 1966; *Tomorrow,* 1972; *Tender Mercies,* 1983; *1918,* 1984; *The Trip to Bountiful,* 1985; *On Valentine's Day,* 1985; *Courtship,* 1986; *Convicts,* 1989; *Of Mice and Men,* 1991.

Television Plays: *Ludie Brooks,* 1951; *The Travelers,* 1952; *The Old Beginning,* 1952; *The Trip to Bountiful,* 1953; *A Young Lady of Property,* 1953; *The Oil Well,* 1953; *Rocking Chair,* 1953; *Expectant Relations,* 1953; *The Death of the Old Man,* 1953; *The Tears of My Sister,* 1953; *John Turner Davis,* 1953; *The Midnight Caller,* 1953; *The Dancers,* 1954; *The Shadow of Willie Greer,* 1954; *The Roads to Home,* 1955; *Drugstore: Sunday Noon,* 1956; *Flight,* 1957 (UK title: *Summer's Pride,* 1961); *Member of the Family,* 1957; *Old Man,* 1958; *Tomorrow,* 1960; *The Shape of the River,* 1960; *The Night of the Storm,* 1960; *The Gambling Heart,* 1964; *The Displaced Person,* from a story by Flannery O'Connor, 1977;

Barn Burning, from the story by Faulkner, 1980; scripts for *Gabby Hayes Show,* 1950–51; *Habitation of Dragons,* 1991.

Novel

The Chase. New York, Rinehart, 1956.

*

Critical Studies: "On Valentine's Day" by Samuel G. Freedman, in the New York *Times* Magazine, February 9, 1986; "Roots in a Parched Ground: An Interview with Horton Foote" by Ronald L. Davis, in *Southwest Review* (Dallas, Texas), Summer 1988.

Theatrical Activities:
Director: **Plays**—*Out of My House* (co-director, with Mary Hunter and Jane Rose), New York, 1942; *Goodbye to Richmond,* New York, 1946.
Actor: **Plays**—role in *The Eternal Road* by Franz Werfel, New York, 1937; with One-Act Repertory Company: Robert Emmet in *The Coggerers,* Lorenzo in *The Red Velvet Goat,* and Chief Outourou's Brother in *Mr. Banks of Birmingham,* New York, 1939; *Railroads on Parade,* New York, 1939; *Yankee Doodle Comes to Town,* toured, 1940; *The Fifth Column* by Ernest Hemingway, New York, 1940; Pharmacist in *Texas Town,* New York, 1941.

* * *

In *1918,* Horace Robedaux, the principal character of Horton Foote's Orphans' Home cycle, asks Foote's rich and perennial question: "How can human beings stand all that comes to them?". A little later, his mother-in-law indirectly answers him: "You just stand it. You keep going." Between the question and the answer lies Foote's deeply realized Texan world, where the fundamentals and the universals of many kinds of relationships are played out. We see and hear in the accents of everyday talk how sons and daughters, mothers and fathers, lovers, drunks, and crazies "stand it" and "keep going." We are not preached at, nor are the scenes or characters calculated to point morals. Instead, the plays—each of which can stand on its own dramatically—present simply and inexorably, the stuff of life. And since the cycle is set in the earlier parts of this century, our sense acts unconsciously to join that past to our own. And so the past becomes actual, both in its differences and in its similarities. There are few large-scale events; World War I, for instance, seems very far from, yet very much part of, *1918.* The central characters engage in getting and losing jobs, missing trains, flunking out of school, as well as fathering and losing children and marrying the one they love. Although life can be very bleak, Foote somehow justifies the bleakness; despite ourselves, we do not feel desperate or depressed. Through the cycle Texas becomes our world, and Horton Foote's people become our people.

The rhetoric of Foote's work suggests that the language we regularly use be taken as fully adequate to our condition, and that our condition consists precisely of the people we know, the work we do, the era in which we live. Things like a new dress (*Roots in a Parched Ground*) are significantly related to 'flu epidemics (*1918*) and Foote's methodical vision delineates the relationship and discovers the particulars of its reality. Nothing and no one is unrelated, even by choice. The Texas of 1912 and the New York City of 1992 work in the same categories of truth and falsehood, love and death, happiness and unhappiness, rejection and acceptance. The cycle lives through the coming-of-age of Horace Robedaux. From the days just before his father's early death we become part of his family because we know him at the beginning of self-definition and experience with him the sorrows and the joys. He never assumes the role of representative, however, because Foote has made his character a living one which now and again makes surprising decisions. The familiarity we have established does not breed contempt but rather respect. Horace endures partly on our behalf and our response to that endurance is to understand ourselves better—a classical purpose of theatre.

Much of Foote's drama treats the common man and woman realistically in disturbing but strangely comforting stories. The pathos which ordinary people undergo, the nobility of the neglected and the forgotten, the profound humor in unsuspected houses and families, the suffering around every corner, the substantiality of the taken-for-granted, the high stakes wagered in backstairs games—these constitute his subject. Foote's realism pertains to times and places he has both lived in and imagined; his ear for speech is true, his characters recognizable and individualized. The Orphans' Home cycle offers us aspects of life itself and it deserves to be staged as a cycle so that its full subtlety and strength can be realized.

Foote is a writer schooled in the television screenplay; a regional writer; a folk writer; a miniaturist. But, thanks to all that, he is a writer of considerable power. His one-act The Man Who Climbed the Pecan Trees treats only part of the subject of the cycle, namely, the spiritual barrenness of the arid southeast-Texas landscape. Much like Horace, Stanley has grown up in a family devoid of judgment and passion. But, unlike him, his family still "functions" because his mother keeps it alive despite its break-up. (By contrast, Horace's mother moves to Houston and leaves him to fend for himself.) The husband and father is dead before the play begins but the mother (Mrs. Campbell) keeps him alive too, in a series of inane sentimentalities which function to deaden him further and to stultify memory itself; so much so in Stanley's case that finally he can't say where in the world he is or where he's been—a fate that might well have been Horace's.

As it turns out, the same source of energy by which Mr. Campbell has gone on living since his death will now sustain his son, Mr. Stanley Campbell—Mrs. Campbell's platitudes which deny even the truth of sentiment in Stanley's obsessive lyric: "In the gloamin', Oh, my darlin'." Her manner of speaking will pen him (is penning him) in a dead-end. At play's end, he sits beside his mother, firmly on the ground but no longer of this earth. Ironically, until he "falls" back into infantile dependency, Stanley, among the evaders and euphemists, has been the truth-teller, one who sees things for what they are, even if the facts are partial. Foote's "facts" may be partial, too, but the impartiality of the theatre allows him to give us an almost complete version of American society.

—Thomas Apple

FOREMAN, Richard. American. Born in New York City, 10 June 1937. Educated at Scarsdale High School, Scarsdale, New York; Brown University, Providence, Rhode Island, 1955–59, B.A. 1959; Yale University School of Drama, New Haven, Connecticut, 1959–62, M.F.A. 1962. Married 1) Amy Taubin in 1962 (divorced 1971); 2) Kate Manheim in 1992. Writer with New Dramatists and Actors Studio, both New York, 1962–65; associate director, Film-Maker's Cinematheque, New York, 1967–68. Since 1968 founding director, Ontological-Hysteric Theatre, New York. Recipient: Obie award, 1970, 1973, 1983, 1986 (for directing), 1987, sustained achievement award, 1988; National Opera Institute grant, 1971; National Endowment for the Arts grant, 1972, 1974, and distinguished artists fellowship, 1989; Creative Artists Public Service award, 1972, 1974; Rockefeller grant, 1975; Guggenheim fellowship, 1975; Ford Foundation grant, 1980; American Academy and Institute of Arts and Letters award, 1992. Agent: Gregor F. Hall, Bookport International, 429 Third Street, Suite 2B, Brooklyn, New York 11215. Address: 152 Wooster Street, New York, New York 10012, U.S.A.

PUBLICATIONS

Plays

Angelface (also director: produced New York, 1968).
Elephant-Steps, music by Stanley Silverman (also director: produced Lenox, Massachusetts, 1968; New York, 1970).
Ida-Eyed (also director: produced New York, 1969).
Real Magic in New York, music by Stephen Dickman (produced New York, 1969).
Total Recall: Sophia = (Wisdom) Part 2 (also director: produced New York, 1970).
Dream Tantras for Western Massachusetts, music by Stanley Silverman (also director: produced Lenox, Massachusetts, 1971).
HcOhTiEnLa; or, Hotel China (also director: produced New York, 1971). Excerpts published in *Performance 2* (New York), April 1972.
Evidence (also director: produced New York, 1972; selection, as *15 Minutes of Evidence*, produced New York, 1975).
Dr. Selavy's Magic Theatre, music by Stanley Silverman, lyrics by Tom Hendry (also director: produced Lenox, Massachusetts, and New York, 1972; Oxford, 1978).
Sophia = (Wisdom) Part 3: The Cliffs (also director: produced New York, 1972). Published in *Performance 6* (New York), May–June 1973.
Particle Theory (also director: produced New York, 1973).
Honor (also director: produced New York, 1973).
Classical Therapy; or, A Week under the Influence . . . (also director: produced Paris, 1973).
Pain(t) (also director: produced New York, 1974).
Vertical Mobility: Sophia = (Wisdom) Part 4 (also director: produced New York, 1974). Published in *Drama Review 63* (New York), June 1974.
RA-D-IO (Wisdom); or, Sophia = (Wisdom) Part 1, music by David Tice (produced New York, 1974).
Pandering to the Masses: A Misrepresentation (also director: produced New York, 1975). Published in *The Theatre of Images*, edited by Bonnie Marranca, New York, Drama Book Specialists, 1977.
Hotel for Criminals, music by Stanley Silverman (also director: produced New York, 1975).
Rhoda in Potatoland (Her Fall-starts) (also director: produced New York, 1975).
Thinking (One Kind) (produced San Diego, 1975).
Le Théâtre de Richard Foreman, edited by Simone Benmussa and Erika Kralik. Paris, Gallimard, 1975.
Plays and Manifestos, edited by Kate Davy. New York, New York University Press, 1976.

Livre de Splendeurs (Part I) (produced Paris, 1976).
Lines of Vision, music by George Quincy, lyrics by María Irene Fornés (produced New York, 1976).
Slight (produced New York, 1977).
Book of Splendors (Part II): Book of Levers: Action at a Distance (also director: produced New York, 1977). Published in *Theater* (New Haven, Connecticut), Spring 1978.
Blvd. de Paris (I've Got the Shakes) (produced New York, 1978).
The American Imagination, music by Stanley Silverman (produced New York, 1978).
Luogo + Bersaglio (Place + Target) (produced Rome, 1979).
Madame Adare, music by Stanley Silverman (produced New York, 1980).
Penguin Touquet (also director: produced New York, 1981).
Café Amérique (produced Paris, 1982).
Egyptology: My Head Was a Sledgehammer (produced New York, 1983).
George Bataille's Bathrobe (produced Paris, 1984).
Miss Universal Happiness (also director: produced New York, 1985).
Reverberation Machines: The Later Plays and Essays. Barrytown, New York, Station Hill Press, 1985.
Africanis Instructus, music by Stanley Silverman (also director: produced New York, 1986).
The Cure, music by Foreman (produced New York, 1986). Included in *Unbalancing Acts*, 1992.
Film Is Evil, Radio Is Good (also director: produced New York, 1987). Included in *Unbalancing Acts*, 1992.
Love and Science (also director: produced Stockholm, 1987; Stockbridge, Massachusetts, 1990). New York, Theatre Communications Group, and London, Hern, 1991.
Symphony of Rats (also director: produced New York, 1988). Included in *Unbalancing Acts*, 1992.
What Did He See? (also director: produced New York, 1988). Included in *Unbalancing Acts*, 1992.
Lava (also director: produced New York, 1989). Included in *Unbalancing Acts*, 1992.
Eddie Goes to Poetry City: Part 1 (also director: produced Seattle, Washington, 1990).
Eddie Goes to Poetry City: Part 2 (also director: produced New York, 1991).
The Mind King (also director: produced New York, 1992).
Unbalancing Acts: Foundations for a Theater. New York, Pantheon, 1992.

Screenplays: *Out of the Body Travel*, 1975; *City Archives*, 1977; *Strong Medicine*, 1978.

*

Manuscript Collections: Lincoln Center Library of the Performing Arts, New York; Anthology Film Archives, New York.

Critical Studies: "Richard Foreman's Ontological-Hysteric Theatre" by Michael Kirby, in *Drama Review* (New York), June 1973; *Richard Foreman and the Ontological-Hysteric Theatre* by Kate Davy, Ann Arbor, Michigan, UMI Research Press, 1981.

Theatrical Activities:
Director: **Plays**—most of his own plays (also designer); *The Threepenny Opera* by Brecht, New York, 1976; *Stages* by Stuart Ostrow, New York, 1978; *Don Juan* by Molière, Minneapolis, 1981; *Three Acts of Recognition* by Botho

Strauss, New York, 1982; *Die Fledermaus* by Johann Strauss, Paris, 1984; *Dr. Faustus Lights the Lights* by Gertrude Stein, Paris, 1984; *Golem* by H. Levick, New York, 1984; *My Life My Death* by Kathy Acker, Paris, 1985; *The Birth of the Poet* by Kathy Acker, New York, 1985; *Largo Desolato* by Václav Havel, New York, 1986; *End of the World* by Arthur Kopit, Cambridge, Massachusetts, 1987; *The Fall of the House of Usher* by Arthur Yorinks and Philip Glass, Louisville, Kentucky, 1988, New York, 1989, and revised version, Florence, 1992; *Where's Dick?* by Michael Korie and Stewart Wallace, Houston, Texas, 1989; *Woyzeck* by Georg Büchner, Hartford, Connecticut, 1990; *Don Giovanni* by Mozart, Lille, France, 1991.

Richard Foreman comments:

In 1968 I began to write for the theatre which I wanted to see, which was radically different from any style of theatre that I had seen. In brief, I imagined a theatre which broke down all elements into a kind of atomic structure—and showed those elements of story, action, sound, light, composition, gesture, in terms of the smallest building-block units, the basic cells of the perceived experience of both living and art-making.

The scripts themselves read like notations of my own process of imagining a theatre piece. They are the evidence of a kind of effort in which the mind's leaps and inventions may be rendered as part of a process not unique to the artist in question (myself) but typical of the building-up which goes on through all modes of coming-into-being (human and non-human). I want to refocus the attention of the spectator on the intervals, gaps, relations and rhythms which saturate the objects (acts and physical props) which are the "givens" of any particular play. In doing this, I believe the spectator is made available (as I am, hopefully, when writing) to those most desirable energies which secretly connect him (through a kind of resonance) with the foundations of his being.

*   *   *

Richard Foreman's statement "I have developed a style that shows how it is with us, in consciousness. I don't speak in generalities. I show the mind at work, moment-by-moment" is perhaps the best starting point from which to approach his theatre. His plays eschew plot, characters, development, and even emotions in the attempt to dramatize the process of thinking itself. Each moment in the theatre corresponds to a moment in consciousness, and the relationships between them, or between the moments in the theatre, may not be immediately obvious. In *Rhoda in Potatoland* actors discuss writing, but digress to a dinner of potatoes. As in any train of thought ("Do you think using the associative method," says Foreman's Voice in *Pandering to the Masses*. "Everybody does you know."), potatoes become part of the freight, and the play begins to compare everything to a potato. After a digression for an all-girl band and a shoe store, a sign announces "THE RETURN OF THE POTATOES" and with the entrance of four human-sized potatoes, the Voice says

Now this is where the interesting part of the
evening begins. Everything up to now was
Recognizable.

Now, however
The real potatoes are amongst us
And a different kind of understanding is possible
for anybody who wants a different kind of
understanding.

Thereafter "potato" becomes a kind of counter, a word that

can replace another word or form comparisons and links with other objects. Even when the word is replaced by other words, Foreman follows the linguistic philosophy of Ludwig Wittgenstein, as he interprets it: "Use anything, to mean anything, but the system must have a rigor."

To perform consciousness rigorously, Foreman developed techniques which allow tight control over the presentation. He directs his plays using a core of performers, who have little or no classical theater training. Foreman's actors speak their lines flatly, without inflection. In some of the performances, the actors only murmur key words of their pre-recorded dialogue. Their words are frequently repeated, their sentences broken into fragments, and their phrases echoed by another actor. Foreman further ends the identity of actor and character through movement. Actors' gestures are also repeated in a hieratic style until they lose their original significance and acquire a new one from the course of the play.

The visual side of Foreman's theatre is crucial. Backdrops are used to present a fleeting image, to introduce a stray thought. Small stages reproduce the larger scene, and the actors themselves freeze into tableaux. Strings, ropes, and pieces of wood or paper stretch across the stage, link props or actors, or divide the stage into smaller frames. Buzzers, lights, and noises create other aural and visual "frames," to isolate words and actions.

No description of this odd theatre can suggest the power that these slow, measured plays can build. As the performances progress, the incomprehensible actions and incidents take their place in an overall design, not with a logical inevitability, but with a psychological appropriateness. As in Gertrude Stein's landscape plays, dialogue and incident are meant to be seen all together and simultaneously, not as a sequential development. A part of the power of the plays arises from the effort of the spectator in deciphering each individual moment like the facet in a Cubist painting, and then assembling them into a whole.

Foreman has described his plays as being what happens in his mind as he is writing a play. Recently, however, he has been increasingly directing other playwright's works, and it is possible that this expansion of his artistic universe is infecting his playwriting. *Egyptology* hints at a real setting (Egypt), and includes Louis XIV, who may have come from Foreman's having directed Molière's *Don Juan. Miss Universal Happiness* topically includes Central American guerrillas even as it asserts that "the self you seek is inside you." *The Cure* not only provides a moment of emotional contact, but even a hesitant attempt at synthesis and statement: "The pain is the cure," says one of the characters. All of this is undoubtedly happening in Foreman's mind, and while we may debate whether such a detailed presentation of one man's mind is appropriate to the theatre, that is precisely the kind of debate Foreman would enjoy: "The play's over. You're left with your own thoughts. Can you really get interested in them or are they just occurring."

—Walter Bode

_____

FORNÉS, María Irene. American. Born in Havana, Cuba, 14 May 1930; emigrated to the United States, 1945; became citizen, 1951. Educated in Havana public schools. Lived in Europe, 1954–57; painter and textile designer; costume designer, Judson Poets Theatre and New Dramatists Committee productions, 1965–70; teacher at the Teachers and Writers Collaborative, New York, privately, and at numerous drama festivals and workshops, from 1965. President, New York Theatre Strategy, 1973–80. Recipient: Whitney fellowship, 1961; Centro Mexicano de Escritores fellowship, 1962; Office for Advanced Drama Research grant, 1965; Obie award, 1965, 1977, 1979, 1982, 1984, 1985, 1988; Cintas Foundation fellowship, 1967; Yale University fellowship, 1967, 1968; Rockefeller fellowship, 1971, 1985; Guggenheim fellowship, 1972; Creative Artists Public Service grant, 1972, 1975; National Endowment for the Arts grant, 1974; American Academy award, 1985; Home Box Office award, 1986. Agent: Helen Merrill Ltd., 435 West 23rd Street, #1A, New York, New York 10011. Address: 1 Sheridan Square, New York, New York 10014, U.S.A.

PUBLICATIONS

Plays

The Widow (produced New York, 1961). Published, as *La Viuda*, in *Teatro Cubano*, Havana, Casa de las Américas, 1961.

Tango Palace (as *There! You Died*, produced San Francisco, 1963; as *Tango Palace*, produced New York, 1964; revised version produced Minneapolis, 1965). Included in *Promenade and Other Plays*, 1971.

The Successful Life of Three: A Skit for Vaudeville (produced Minneapolis and New York, 1965). Included in *Promenade and Other Plays*, 1971.

Promenade, music by Al Carmines (produced New York, 1965; revised version produced New York, 1969). Included in *Promenade and Other Plays*, 1971.

The Office (produced New York, 1966).

A Vietnamese Wedding (produced New York, 1967). Included in *Promenade and Other Plays*, 1971.

The Annunciation (also director: produced New York, 1967).

Dr. Kheal (produced New York, 1968; London, 1969). Included in *Promenade and Other Plays*, 1971.

The Red Burning Light; or, Mission XQ3 (produced Zurich, 1968; New York, 1969). Included in *Promenade and Other Plays*, 1971.

Molly's Dream, music by Cosmos Savage (produced Lenox, Massachusetts, 1968; also director: produced New York, 1968). Included in *Promenade and Other Plays*, 1971.

Promenade and Other Plays. New York, Winter House, 1971; revised edition, New York, Performing Arts Journal Publications, 1987.

The Curse of the Langston House, in *Baboon!!!* (produced Cincinnati, 1972).

Dance, with Remy Charlip (also co-director: produced London, 1972).

Aurora, music by John FitzGibbon (also director: produced New York, 1974).

Cap-a-Pie, music by José Raúl Bernardo (also director: produced New York, 1975).

Lines of Vision (lyrics only), book by Richard Foreman, music by George Quincy (produced New York, 1976).

Washing (produced New York, 1976).

Fefu and Her Friends (also director: produced New York, 1977). Published in *Wordplays 1*, New York, Performing Arts Journal Publications, 1980.

Lolita in the Garden, music by Richard Weinstock (also director: produced New York, 1977).

In Service (also director: produced Padua Hills, California, 1978).

Eyes on the Harem (also director: produced New York, 1979).

Blood Wedding, adaptation of a play by García Lorca (produced New York, 1980).

Evelyn Brown: A Diary (also director: produced New York, 1980).

Life Is Dream, adaptation of a play by Calderón, music by George Quincy (also director: produced New York, 1981).

A Visit, music by George Quincy (also director: produced Padua Hills, California, and New York, 1981).

The Danube (also director: produced Padua Hills, California, 1982; New York, 1983). Included in *Plays*, 1986.

Mud (also director: produced Padua Hills, California, and New York, 1983; revised version, also director: produced Omaha, 1985; London, 1988). Included in *Plays*, 1986.

Sarita, music by Leon Odenz (also director: produced New York, 1984; London, 1988). Included in *Plays*, 1986.

Abingdon Square (produced Seattle, 1984; New York, 1987; London, 1989).

The Conduct of Life (also director: produced New York, 1985; London, 1988). Included in *Plays*, 1986.

Cold Air, adaptation of a play by Virgilio Piñera (also director: produced New York, 1985). New York, Theater Communications Group, 1985.

Drowning, adaptation of a story by Chekhov, in *Orchards* (produced Urbana, Illinois, 1985; New York, 1986). New York, Knopf, 1986.

The Trial of Joan of Arc on a Matter of Faith (also director: produced New York, 1986).

Lovers and Keepers, music by Tito Puente and Ferrando Rivas, lyrics by Fornés (also director: produced New York, 1986). New York, Theatre Communications Group, 1987.

Art, in *Box Plays* (produced New York, 1986).

The Mothers (also director: produced Padua Hills, California, 1986).

Plays. New York, Performing Arts Journal Publications, 1986.

A Matter of Faith (produced New York, 1986).

Uncle Vanya, adaptation of the play by Anton Chekhov (also director: produced New York, 1987).

Hunger (also director: produced New York, 1988).

And What of the Night? (also director: produced Milwaukee, Wisconsin, 1989).

Oscar and Bertha (produced San Francisco, 1991).

*

Manuscript Collection: Lincoln Center Library of the Performing Arts, New York.

Critical Studies: interviews with Rob Creese in *Drama Review* (New York), December 1977, with Gayle Austin in *Theatre Times* (New York), March 1984, with Allen Frame in *Bomb* (New York), Fall 1984, and with Scott Cummings in *Theater* (New Haven, Connecticut), Winter 1985; "The Real Life of María Irene Fornés," in *Theatre Writings* by Bonnie Marranca, New York, Performing Arts Journal Publications, 1984; "Creative Danger" by Fornés, in *American Theatre* (New York), September 1985; preface by Susan Sontag to *Plays*, 1986.

Theatrical Activities:
Director: **Plays**—several of her own plays; *Exiles* by Ana Maria Simo, New York, 1982; *Uncle Vanya* by Anton Chekhov, New York, 1987; *Going to New England* by Ana Maria Simo, New York, 1990.

* * *

María Irene Fornés's scripts and dialog can seem cryptic because they pivot on an objectifying abstraction, a realistic detail, free-floating pronouns, or unstated constructs. Always current in forms and themes, her plays refuse (Susan Sontag says) to settle for "reductively psychological" or "sociological" explanations as the underlying truth. By 1982 her plays, designs, lyrics, and directing had earned Fornés a special Obie for "Sustained Achievement." She has long walked the stylistic edges of the avant-garde and experimental theater off-Broadway—especially since *Tango Palace*, *The Successful Life of Three*, and *Promenade*. If recently a few have blamed her directing for handicapping her own plays, M. E. Osborn finds her influence as a master teacher of playwriting increasingly acclaimed. This Cuban-American, by her plays, translations, projects, and workshops, has developed powerful, new Hispanic-American playwrights and repertory.

Fornés's playful attention to verbal and visual imagery from the first challenged audiences with freakishly or theatrically exalted characters, both innocent and experienced. In later, seriously passionate plays, comic provocations of a laugh or grimace reveal her fresh point of view. Even the fairly consistent, selective realism of many of her more recent and substantial works moves with the odd undulations of an idiosyncratic heart and mind. These and her considered theatricality give rise to a startling magic. Fornés is a sometimes poignant, often humorous, and always intense playwright.

An antic symbiosis of sadism and masochism in life and art locks the naïve Leopold and the strenuous Isidore into *Tango Palace*. The arrogant harangue of *Dr. Kheal*, the raucous road-show of *The Red Burning Light*, and the Jarry-Beckett scatology of *Oscar and Bertha* now seem too familiar as comic-didactic theater pieces. Their modes and themes work better in the songs and the Crosby-Hope *Road*-show format of *Promenade*. In their journey from cell to cell, Prisoners 105 and 106 must constantly trick or elude the pursuing Jailer—a dumb, sexually overactive beast. Tunnelling out of prison into a snooty banquet, 105 and 106 meet Miss Cake, ally themselves with the Servant (she seeks the meaning of life) and escape after robbing the rich Guests who nod off from stupid self-indulgence. Seeking her lost babes, Mother too joins the lengthening line of their pursuers. She and the fugitives play a tender double Pietà with two soldiers on the battlefield, before the tyrannical Mayor sends them back to jail, to escape again. The cruelty and criminality are casual. After Mother's tucking-in and the Servant's fond farewell, the prisoners remain alone, like everyone else, neither informed nor changed by their adventures.

Molly's Dream uses the Dietrich poses and bar setting of Hollywood westerns to ridicule the machismo and romance of male myths like *Bus Stop* and *The Misfits*. Movie timing and allusion activate a young couple and an older man through 10 semi-burlesque scenes in *The Successful Life of Three*. Their looks at each other (he "disdainful", she "stupid") become part of the dialog, as such a "look" becomes a whole scene in the later *Abingdon Square*. The figures and patterns of these plays of the 1960's recur with permutations throughout Fornés's works: a lover and/or beloved as jailer, spunky companions and victims, a wiser servant, a tyrannical teacher, an older man, a casual stranger, a self-loathing woman, or a mysteriously ill person. Bright "outrageousness" steps toward liberation, but *Abingdon Square* ends with a tableau of the angelically illuminated Michael appearing behind the Pietà of Marion cradling dead old Juster.

The Danube creates a bloated horror of America's naïve international meddling and policies from a European perspective. In Budapest, 1938 to whenever, nice American Paul meets sweet Eve over "Basic Sentences," chronicled in units (scenes) of Hungarian-English lessons: they marry, fall ill with a mysterious sickness, and blame each other. The last two, most difficult lessons are repeated as puppet shows and human scenes until Paul and Eve, contorted and red-spotted, both exit in a white flash explosion of pistol shot or nuclear blast. Such violence seems the inevitable doom of human agonies in Fornés's vision.

An understanding of the Hispanic family and religious heritage informs her musical chronicle *Sarita* (set in the South Bronx, 1939–47) and her viciously spare *The Conduct of Life* (set in a Latin American country). Trapped in poverty between Cuban and Yankee values and Catholic-pagan gods, Sarita from age 13 tries to follow her mind away from her incinerating passion for Julio but can't, despite his ruthless betrayals and the understanding of her "nice" new American husband Mark. Momentary vignettes and songs lead her through deepening self-hatred to stab her lover-destroyer to death. Is Mark's holding her hand in the hospital a hope of healing? *The Conduct of Life* distributes the male-dominated woman's role among three characters in relation to Orlando, who is rising on the mutilated minds and bodies of his victims to become state torturer. He ridicules the intellectual, spiritual aspirations of his wife Leticia who tolerates his humiliations and betrayals. While he ignores the older servant Olimpia who seethes with anger but will survive, he rapes, enslaves, and installs in his cellar (as servant) 12-year-old Nena. Nena "receives" those who hurt her "since maybe they are in worse pain than me." Adaptive and resisting her knowledge of his evil, Leticia grovels toward her husband and remains petulantly childish with Olimpia—until she must finally accept her responsibility and her identity with both Orlando and his victims. She shoots him and gives the child Nena the gun to shoot her. The play is a fascinating exploration of the consequences of moral distancing in human actions.

In *Fefu and Her Friends*, seven accomplished women arrive to plan a panel on education. Fefu, who considers herself alternately bright and "loathsome," proves herself "outrageous" by fixing toilets and shooting (only blanks?) her offstage husband through the window with a rifle. After falling, he dusts himself off; men are lucky. Only ballerinas lack the heavy female insides, observes friend Julia, crippled, dying of a malady, and suffering hallucinations. After the first living-room scene, Fornés divides the audience into four groups and leads them backstage to stand in the kitchen, backyard, study, and Julia's bedroom respectively, in intimate proximity to actors performing their brief scene four times; then all return to auditorium and stage. Even the ferocious Fefu who must save Julia, to maintain her own self-respect and survival, cannot do so. Fefu shoots again outside and Julia dies behind her with a red cross of blood on her forehead.

"Springtime," the most tender and the only published act of four in Fornés's powerful drama of human reachings, incest, and degradation, *And What of the Night?*, consists of 14 short scenes. The overextension of this short-scene construction device tends to fragment *Abingdon Square* (in two acts, 32 scenes), a frequently moving chronicle of the love and marriage between poor 15-year-old Marion and wealthy Juster (aged 50) from 1908 to 1917.

In *Mud*, another of her best, Fornés compassionately represents the intricacies of relationships among three characters: Mae and Lloyd (both 25) and the older Henry. Behind their ignorant and repetitiously brutal language, both Mae and Lloyd yearn to receive and provide nourishment in the

form of food, health, sex, and learning. The actors reflect their attempts to recreate themselves out of the red mud into a next phase by exiting one scene to pivot visibly in the doorway and re-enter for the next. Mae brings semi-literate Henry in to read a pamphlet on Lloyd's sickness and to teach her to read. Not wanting to live like an animal, Mae mistakes the meaner-spirited Henry for "heaven." Lloyd weeps but learns to read, cure himself, and nurse Henry who becomes more greedy, mocking and crippled. "Lloyd is good, Henry. And this is his home," Mae says before fleeing it and the men's destructive combat. Lloyd chases her, shoots and brings her back—to die like a starfish.

Perhaps, Fornés's plays imply that depriving others is a necessary way of life, as in the eternal game of euchre which occupies the four characters at the end of the grotesque little *Oscar and Bertha*, or the bleak heap that may finally absorb all in *And What of the Night?*

—John G. Kuhn

FORSYTH, James (Law). British. Born in Glasgow, Lanark, 5 March 1913. Educated at Glasgow High School, graduated 1930; Glasgow School of Art, diploma in drawing and painting 1934. Married 1) Helen Steward in 1938 (divorced 1953), two sons; 2) Louise Tibble in 1955. Served in the Scots Guards, 2nd Monmouthshire Regiment, 1940–46: captain, battalion adjutant; Bronze Cross of the Netherlands. Worked with the General Post Office Film Unit, 1937–40; dramatist-in-residence, Old Vic Company: worked with the Old Vic School and the Young Vic, 1946–48; dramatist-in-residence, Howard University, Washington, D.C., 1962; guest director and lecturer, Tufts University, Medford, Massachusetts, 1963; distinguished professor-in-residence, Florida State University, Tallahassee, 1965; director, Tufts University Program in London, 1967–71. Since 1972 artistic director, The Forsyths' Barn Theatre, Ansty, Sussex. Member of the Executive Council, League of Dramatists and Radio Writers Association, 1954–64; founding member, Theatres Advisory Council, Recipient: Arts Council bursary, 1980. Agent: Cecily Ware, 19-C John Spencer Square, London N1 2LZ; or, Harold Freedman, Brandt and Brandt, 1501 Broadway, New York, New York 10036, U.S.A. Address: Grainloft, Ansty, Haywards Heath, Sussex RH17 5AG, England.

PUBLICATIONS

Plays

Trog (broadcast 1949; produced Coventry, 1959; Tallahassee, Florida, 1964).
Brand, adaptation of the play by Ibsen (broadcast 1949; produced London, 1964). London, Heinemann, and New York, Theatre Arts, 1960.
The Medicine Man (produced London, 1950).
Emmanuel: A Nativity Play (broadcast 1950; produced London and New York, 1960). London, Heinemann, 1952; New York, Theatre Arts, 1963.
Héloïse (broadcast 1951; produced Southsea, Hampshire, and London, 1951; New York, 1958). Included in *Three Plays*, 1957; New York, Theatre Arts, 1958.

The Other Heart (broadcast 1951; produced London, 1952; also director: produced Medford, Massachusetts, 1963). Included in *Three Plays*, 1957; New York, Theatre Arts, 1964; revised version, as *Villon*, music by Gardner Read (produced New Orleans, 1981).

Adelaise (broadcast 1951; produced Ashburton, Devon, 1953). Included in *Three Plays*, 1957.

Three Plays. London, Heinemann, 1957.

The Pier (televised 1957; produced Bristol, 1958).

The Road to Emmaus: A Play for Eastertide. London, Heinemann, 1958; New York, Theatre Arts, 1972.

Joshua, music by Franz Waxman (produced Dallas, 1960). New York, Ricordi, 1959.

Dear Wormwood, adaptation of *The Screwtape Letters* by C.S. Lewis (produced Brighton, 1965). Chicago, Dramatic Publishing Company, 1961; as *Screwtape*, 1973.

Fifteen Strings of Money, adaptation of a play by Guenther Weisenhorn based on a story by Chu Su-chen (produced Pitlochry, Perthshire, 1961).

Everyman (produced Coventry, 1962).

Defiant Island (produced Washington, D.C., 1962). Chicago, Dramatic Publishing Company, 1975.

Seven Scenes for Yeni (produced Boston, 1963).

Cyrano de Bergerac, adaptation of the play by Edmond Rostand (produced Sarasota, Florida, 1963; London, 1967; New York, 1968). Chicago, Dramatic Publishing Company, 1968.

If My Wings Heal (produced Stroud, Gloucestershire, 1966).

Four Triumphant (televised 1966; as *Festival of Four*, produced Ansty, Sussex, 1976).

What the Dickens, adaptation of the novel *The Pickwick Papers* by Dickens (produced Ansty, Sussex, 1974).

Lobsterback (produced Boston and Ansty, Sussex, 1975).

No Crown for Herod (as *Christmas at Greccio*, produced Ansty, Sussex, 1976). Chicago, Dramatic Publishing Company, 1977.

The Play of Alban (produced St. Albans, 1977).

"N" for Napoleone (produced Ansty, Sussex, 1978).

When the Snow Lay Round About (broadcast 1978; as *Wenceslas*, produced Ansty, Sussex, 1980).

A Time of Harvest (produced Ansty, Sussex, 1981; as *The Threshing Floor*, broadcast 1982).

Screenplays: *The End of the Road*, with Geoffrey Orme, 1954; *Francis of Assisi*, with Eugene Vale and Jack Thomas, 1961.

Radio Plays: *The Bronze Horse*, 1948; *Trog*, 1949; *Brand*, 1949; *Emmanuel*, 1950; *Seelkie*, music by Brian Easdale, 1950; *The Other Heart*, 1951; *Adelaise*, 1951; *Héloïse*, 1951; *The Nameless One of Europe*, 1951; *For He's a Jolly Good Fellow*, 1952; *Pig*, 1953; *The Festive Spirit*, 1955; *Lisel*, 1955; *Christophe*, 1958; *Every Pebble on the Beach*, 1963; *When the Snow Lay Round About*, 1978; *The Threshing Floor*, 1982.

Television Plays: *Old Mickmack*, 1955; *The Pier*, 1957; *Underground*, from a novel by Harold Rein, 1958; *Four Triumphant*, 1966; *The English Boy*, 1969; *The Last Journey*, 1972; *The Old Man's Mountain*, 1972.

Other

Tyrone Guthrie: A Biography. London, Hamish Hamilton, 1976.

Back to the Barn. Ansty, Sussex, Grainloft, 1986.

*

Manuscript Collection: Lincoln Center Library of the Performing Arts, New York.

Theatrical Activities:
Director: **Play**—*The Other Heart*, Medford, Massachusetts, 1963.

James Forsyth comments:

(1982) The plays themselves being the playwright's *more than* personal statement to the public, I am reluctant to make other statements. I say "more than personal" and I say "play*wright*" (not playwrite) for these reasons: That Theatre, where it is more than a show for Entertainment or Propaganda purposes, is an Art—an all-arts Art—and in Art the thing wrought out of the raw material is a thing in itself and speaks for itself. I *wright* for the Theatre as a performing place for the Art of Theatre, a tough and practical and popular art. The *writing* of the playwright is only the recording art which ends up with a script. The script ends up with "the thing itself" which is the event, the production. And it is all *wrought* out of the many arts of the playwright in the fields of sight, sound, touch, etc., realized in any playhouse by all the contributory arts of those who were once, and accurately, referred to as "artistes."

I had started life as an artist painter and sculptor, and my apprenticeship to the art of the theatre, with the Old Vic Company of Guthrie and Olivier, gave me a taste for the all-arts theatre and also for epic theatre. I am a playwright because I have found that the live event of the play is the best occasion in the world for the communion with—the sharing of artistic experience with—an audience; and the art of Theatre is the best medium for creation of the concepts worth sharing.

But the all-arts theatre is a hard road in a world of theatre brutally constricted by cash considerations, a constriction relieved only a bit by subsidy of certain playhouses and the heroism of "fringe" and "off-off" companies. That is why I have directed, for the last ten years, my own plays in my own barn which is a natural playhouse with an enthusiastic audience and a company of so-called "amateurs" who have become professed to the Art of Theatre to a professional degree. But in turning away in some despair from the world of the professional theatre and showbiz in its present state to this limited but real local success in the art, I have not of course "made a living" from it, which begins to make this statement more "personal" than necessary. But by the subsidy of an Arts Council bursary I have been able to complete what could be my most important play, *The Spanish Captain*.

*   *   *

Craft is fundamental to all art, although not all craftsmen are artists, any more than every artist is a craftsman. Indeed today, as artists are promoted by PRs, craft has become somewhat unfashionable. Hence the well-made play has, of recent years, come to be regarded as something slightly old-fashioned. Yet the virtue of a well-made play is that it knows how to tell a story, how to hold an audience, and this is an essential part of the dramatist's craft.

James Forsyth is such a playwright and this term is perhaps the most pat of all for an author who has himself said (January 1972): "I have yet to wright my best play. And 'wright' is right, I am not a 'dramatist,' I am a 'playwright.' Drama is the stuff, plays are the works, and I am professed to works."

His works are prolific, a steady output over the years, from the Old Vic production of *The Other Heart* to a television series on the patron saints of England, Scotland, Ireland and

Wales, to *The Last Journey*, a 90-minute television play on Tolstoy.

The Other Heart is one of Forsyth's strongest and most powerfully constructed plays and full of excellent small character studies such as that of Marthe, the servant, who when asked why she risks her life in coming to Paris during the plague replies, "I need to help." In the character of the romantic poet, François Villon, Forsyth catches marvellously the impetuosity of young love, and the radiant recklessness of the visionary and poet. They are qualities that seem to attract him again and again. While he is drawn to "wrighting" plays about historical characters, it is noticeable how many of them are variations upon the theme of "a pair of starcrossed lovers." In this play we have Villon and Catherine de Vausselles; we have also Francis and Clare in *If My Wings Heal*, Héloïse and Abelard in *Héloïse*; in *The Last Journey*, a study of the last days of Tolstoy, Forsyth has written brilliantly of the tragic gap between a husband and wife.

The clash of the idealist with reality is perhaps, however, the profoundest recurring theme in all Forsyth's work. It has attracted him to a powerful adaptation of Ibsen's *Brand*, and in *If My Wings Heal* he sets out to explore the conflict between St. Francis of Assisi, the creative artist, poet, visionary, and Brother Elias, the ambitious administrative genius of the Franciscan Order. It was Brother Elias who wanted to turn the Friars Minor into the most powerful order within the Church, "for the sake of possession, for the possession of power." As one of the Friars remarks, "It was never Brother Francis's idea that we should be other than small bands, always on the move. We were to be the salt which is scattered."

This is a tougher and less sentimental rendering of the story of Francis of Assisi than the *Little Plays of St. Francis* by Laurence Housman, or the five-act devotional drama by Henri Ghéon, *The Marriage of St. Francis*. Only the scene of the stigmata fails. Perhaps it is an impossibility—to put on the stage a mystical experience. Perhaps only a major poet, such as T. S. Eliot, whose insight into the transcendental was close to that of the great mystics themselves, could really tackle such a scene. If Forsyth is a playwright proven he is, I think, a poet *manqué*. His weakest writing stems almost always from a tendency to poeticize, to lapse into obvious rhyming blank verse. Yet in theatre terms one can see what he is about for the steady beat and rhythm of these passages serve to carry the story forward.

David, *Andrew*, *Patrick*, and *George* (*Four Triumphant*) are four full-length plays, envisaged as a cycle, to be performed over two days. They embody not merely the history of the four patron saints but are a study of the pioneers of Christianity. Each play is self-sufficient, and yet each gains from its relation to the others.

Perhaps Forsyth's most memorable play is *Defiant Island*, the true story of Henri Christophe, the first black king of Haiti. It is a deeply moving tragedy of an idealist who is led astray by his fanatical devotion to his own ideals, so that the man is destroyed at the expense of the image of himself as the first black monarch. Finally, when Napoleon insists on "nothing less than the total extinction of every adult black, male and female," Henri Christophe, who had naively believed that all men could meet in equal justice, has to admit to himself, "I asked too much. It is a fault in me."

Henri Christophe, Brand, Abelard, Villon, Francis of Assisi are all portraits of men of thought suffused with passion; they are the solitary visionaries, the reckless romantics, the uncomfortable reformers; in the true sense of the word they are heroes. Forsyth belongs to that great tradition of bardic poets, who sang the exploits and epics of heroes. It is a

tradition that is at present a little out of fashion, but fashions change and the wheel comes full circle. When that happens Forsyth will find he has wrought his best play.

—James Roose-Evans

FOSTER, Paul. American. Born in Penns Grove, New Jersey, 15 October 1931. Educated at schools in Salem, New Jersey; Rutgers University, New Brunswick, New Jersey, 1950–54, B.A. 1954; St. John's University Law School, New York, 1954, 1957, LL.B. 1958. Served in the United States Naval Reserve, 1955–57. Since 1962 co-founder and president, La Mama Experimental Theater Club, New York. U.S. Department of State lecturer, 1975, 1976, 1977; Fulbright lecturer, Brazil, 1980; taught at University of California, San Diego, 1981, and New York University, 1983. Recipient: Rockefeller fellowship, 1967; Irish Universities award, 1967, 1971; New York Drama Critics Circle award, 1968; Creative Artists Public Service grant, 1972, 1974; National Endowment for the Arts grant, 1973; Arts Council of Great Britain award, 1973; Guggenheim fellowship, 1974; Theatre Heute award, 1977; Bulandra Foreign Play award, 1983. Address: 242 East 5th Street, New York, New York 10003, U.S.A.

PUBLICATIONS

Plays

Hurrah for the Bridge (produced New York, 1962; Edinburgh, 1967). Bogotá, Colombia, Canal Ramirez, 1965; in *Balls and Other Plays*, 1967.
The Recluse (produced New York, 1964; Edinburgh, 1967). Included in *Balls and Other Plays*, 1967.
Balls (produced New York, 1964; Edinburgh, 1967). Included in *Balls and Other Plays*, 1967.
The Madonna in the Orchard (produced New York, 1965). Published as *Die Madonna im Apfelhag*, Frankfurt, Fischer, 1968; as *The Madonna in the Orchard*, New York, Breakthrough Press, 1971; in *Elizabeth I and Other Plays*, 1973.
The Hessian Corporal (produced New York, 1966; Edinburgh, 1967). Included in *Balls and Other Plays*, 1967.
Balls and Other Plays. London, Calder and Boyars, 1967; New York, French, 1968.
Tom Paine (produced New York, 1967; expanded version produced Edinburgh and London, 1967; New York, 1968). London, Calder and Boyars, 1967; New York, Grove Press, 1968.
Heimskringla; or, The Stoned Angels (televised 1969; produced New York, 1970). London, Calder and Boyars, and New York, French, 1970.
Satyricon (produced New York, 1972). Published in *The Off-Off-Broadway Book*, edited by Bruce Mailman and Albert Poland, Indianapolis, Bobbs Merrill, 1972; in *Elizabeth I and Other Plays*, 1973.
Elizabeth I (produced New York, 1972; London, 1973). New York, French, 1972; in *Elizabeth I and Other Plays*, 1973.

Elizabeth I and Other Plays. London, Calder and Boyars, 1973.
Silver Queen Saloon (as *Silver Queen*, music by John Braden, lyrics by Foster and Braden, produced New York, 1973; revised version, as *Silver Queen Saloon*, produced New York, 1978; London, 1982). New York, French, 1976; with *Marcus Brutus*, London, Calder, 1977.
Rags to Riches to Rags (produced New York, 1974).
Marcus Brutus (produced Springfield, Massachusetts, 1975). New York, French, 1976; with *Silver Queen Saloon*, London, Calder, 1977.
A Kiss Is Just a Kiss (televised 1980; produced New York, 1983).
The Dark and Mr. Stone 1–3 (produced New York, 1985–86).

Screenplay: *Cinderella Story*, 1985.

Television Plays: *Heimskringla, or, The Stoned Angels*, 1969; *A Kiss Is Just a Kiss*, 1980 (Denmark); *Mellon*, 1980; *Smile*, 1981; *The Cop and the Anthem*, from the story by O. Henry, 1984.

Short Stories

Minnie the Whore, The Birthday Party, and Other Stories. Caracas, Venezuela, Zodiaco, 1962.

Other

Translator, with others, *Kasimir and Karoline*; *Faith, Hope, and Charity*; *Figaro Gets a Divorce*; *Judgement Day*, by Ödön Von Horváth. New York, PAJ Publications, 1986.

*

Manuscript Collection: Lincoln Center Library of the Performing Arts, New York.

Critical Studies: *The New Bohemia* by John Gruen, New York, Shorecrest, 1966; "The Theatre of Involvement" by Richard Atcheson, in *Holiday* (New York), October 1968; "The World's a Stage," in *MD Publications* (New York), October 1968; *Foster, Robbe-Grillet, Bergson: Teatro, Novela, Tiempo* by Gustavo Majia, unpublished doctoral dissertation, University of the Andes, Bogotá, 1969; *Up Against the Fourth Wall* by John Lahr, New York, Grove Press, 1970; *Le Nouveau Théâtre Américain* by Franck Jotterand, Paris, Seuil, 1970; *Selvsyn-Aktuel Litteratur og Kulturdebat* by Elsa Gress, Copenhagen, Gyldendal, 1970; *Now: Theater der Erfahrung* by Jens Heilmeyer and Pia Frolich, Cologne, Schauberg, 1971; *The Off-Off-Broadway Book* edited by Bruce Mailman and Albert Poland, Indianapolis, Bobbs Merrill, 1972.

*   *   *

The theatrical reputation of Paul Foster essentially belongs to the 1960's, when, as a highly innovative contributor to the off-off-Broadway movement, he showed greater audacity than Albee and at one stage appeared to be the mentor to the emergent Sam Shepard. The diversity of Foster's early work is much greater than his often-argued debt to Beckett would suggest. As well as abstraction, symbolism, and existentialism —for which European models may be suggested—his plays up to *Tom Paine* all have a highly idiosyncratic lyrical vein which was peculiarly suited to the ensemble techniques of the La Mama Experimental Theater Club, where all his best

work was premiered. In *Hurrah for the Bridge* an old waif, pulling a cart piled high with junk, appears to be victimised by an expressionistic group of leather-jacketed urban predators, though their autonomy is demonstrated by his eventual death at their hands, at which point he is visited by the down-and-out angel he idolises. *The Recluse* is more distinctively American in style, in its presentation of an old basement grotesque accompanied by her semi-animate mannequins and her pet cat, stuffed, which she hides in a drawer and keeps the best milk for. Foster's sympathies with the Happening and kinetic art, hinted at in these earliest plays, become rather more explicit in *Balls*, strictly a puppet play in which two pendant table tennis balls swing in and out of light; human representation comes only through recorded voices over, a nostalgic dialogue between the only two cadavers remaining in a coastal cemetery which is being eroded by the sea.

Foster's first approach to an ostensibly non-fictional subject was in *The Hessian Corporal*, subtitled "a one-act documentary play," but more like a parable for the theatre on the theme of the immorality of war, historicised to the Hessian recruitment of 1776. Though this was an important new development for Foster, it differs from his later "historical" works in that its focus is not a famous individual; his concern here is with the exploited nonentity, and the play has a social resonance which approaches the sentimental, although its relevance to Vietnam disguised this in the premiere. However, even Foster's most famous play, *Tom Paine*, is only superficially a historical portrait in any sense; in the face of surging ensemble playing and an insistent line of lyrical narrative, individuality crystallises only briefly before dissolving back into a faceless, collective context. The play poses questions about individuality; it presents conflicting elements in the traditional portrait of Paine, the visionary and the alcoholic, but by theatricality (such as fragmenting Paine and sharing him among several actors) there arises the implicit question whether such elements can coexist in the world of history or whether such a Paine is just a monster from myth. Several prominent critics felt that the play was not about a person but about a way of looking at a society, about collective impulses towards revolution. Paine himself is, theatrically and metatheatrically, a trigger device for common-sense reappraisal of the world that matters, a world which comes into focus haphazardly through the blurring devices of Paine's alcoholism and the ensemble performance.

Nor is *Elizabeth I* any more a history play or documentary. Again, two actors play the title role, but not this time to achieve schizoid characterisation; one actress does Queen Elizabeth, while the other does Elizabeth the Player Queen, a member of an itinerant company presenting a fairy-tale, cartoon-style play about the queen in the late 16th century. A few episodes, such as those concerning the death of Mary of Scotland, have some urgency, but the sterner tone and historical momentum of *Tom Paine* are all but absent; the play is generally much more frolicsome, and there is no sense of continuity between the events depicted and the world of the modern audience. A similar tone of historical vandalism permeates an earlier television play, *Heimskringla*, in which Leif Eriksson's discovery of Newfoundland is presented initially with the aura of a dramatised saga, with a massed choric incantation generating the action; however, an anachronistic flippancy soon permeates the action, with a diagram showing how to fill the stage with bubbles, and by the second-act "love-in" all intellectual pretensions have been abandoned. From this perspective, *Satyricon* would seem an almost logical development for Foster: a stage embellishment of Petronius's work in which the decadence of the *Cena* is supplemented by appearances from various Bacchantes,

Petronius himself, and Nero and Agrippina (who together enact the Foundation of Rome, the emperor playing Romulus while she plays the she-wolf). The comic grotesquerie of this play moves beyond cartoon caricature into theatrical pop art, an appropriate contribution to the Theatre of the Ridiculous. A later play with a Roman setting, *Marcus Brutus*, attempts to return to an individual focus, but again fails to target the play on contemporary issues.

Foster's subsequent plays have been diverse, and have included film scripts, but the stylistic assurance that marked his work up to *Tom Paine* has not been seen again. His sole work to attract substantial critical interest has been *A Kiss Is Just a Kiss* in which Humphrey Bogart sits centre stage and splices together personal memory and public film clips. Bogey seems intended—like Tom Paine—to offer a lens to our world, but in performance the play has lacked cohesion. Foster has never been a playwright in any conventional sense; he has been a literary collaborator in group-developed work, and his idiosyncratic habit of writing stage directions as imperatives defies any acceptance of his scripts as literature.

—Howard McNaughton

FRATTI, Mario. American. Born in L'Aquila, Italy, 5 July 1927; emigrated to the United States, 1963; became citizen, 1974. Educated at Ca'Foscari University, Venice, 1947–51, Ph.D. in language and literature 1951. Served in the Italian Army, 1951–52: lieutenant. Married 1) Lina Fedrigo in 1953 (marriage dissolved); 2) Laura Dubman in 1964; three children. Translator, Rubelli publishers, Venice, 1953–63; drama critic, *Sipario*, Milan, 1963–66, *Paese Sera*, Rome, 1963–73, *L'Ora*, Palermo, 1963–73, and since 1963 *Ridotto*, Venice. Taught at Adelphi University, Garden City, New York, and New School for Social Research, New York, 1964–65, Columbia University, New York, 1965–66, and Hofstra University, Hempstead, New York, 1973–74. Since 1968 member of the Department of Romance Languages, Hunter College, New York. Recipient: RAI-Television prize, 1959; Ruggeri prize, 1960, 1967, 1969; Lentini prize, 1964; Vallecorsi prize, 1965; Unasp-Enars prize, 1968; Arta-Terme award, 1973; Eugene O'Neill award, 1979; Richard Rodgers award, 1980. Agent: Samuel French Inc., 45 West 25th Street, New York, New York 10010. Address: 145 West 55th Street, Apartment 15-D, New York, New York 10019, U.S.A.

PUBLICATIONS

Plays

Il Campanello (produced Milan, 1958). Published in *Ridotto* (Venice), 1958; as *The Doorbell* (produced New York, 1970; London, 1972), in *Ohio University Review* (Athens), 1971.
La Menzogna (The Lie) (produced Milan, 1959). Published in *Cynthia* (Florence), 1963.
A (produced Rome, 1965). Published in *Ora Zero* (Rome), 1959; translation in *Fusta* (New Jersey), 1976.
La Partita (The Game) (produced Pesaro, 1960). Published in *Ridotto* (Venice), 1960.

Il Rifiuto (produced Mantua, 1960). Published in *Il Dramma* (Turin), October 1965; as *The Refusal* (produced New York, 1972; London, 1973), in *Races*, 1972.
In Attesa (produced La Spezia, 1960). Rome, EIST, 1964; as *Waiting* (produced New York, 1970), in *Poet Lore* (Boston), Autumn 1968.
Il Ritorno (produced Bologna, 1961). Published in *Ridotto* (Venice), 1961; as *The Return* (produced New York, 1963; London, 1972), New York, French, n.d.; in *Four by Fratti*, 1986.
La Domanda (The Questionnaire) (produced La Spezia, 1961). Published in *La Prora* (Rome), 1962.
Flowers from Lidice, published in *L'Impegno* (Bari), 1961; in *Dramatics* (Cincinnati), October 1972.
L'Assegno. Cosenza, Pellegrini, 1961; translated by Adrienne S. Mandel as *The Third Daughter* (produced New York, 1978), New York, French, n.d.
Confidenze (produced Rome, 1962). Rome, EIST, 1964; as *The Coffin* (produced New York, 1967), in *Four Plays*, 1972.
Gatta Bianca al Greenwich (produced Rome, 1962). Published in *Il Dramma* (Turin), March 1962, as *White Cat*, in *Races*, 1972.
Il Suicidio (produced Spoleto, 1962). Published in *Cynthia* (Florence), 1962; as *The Suicide* (produced New York, 1965; London, 1973), in *Four by Fratti*, 1986.
La Gabbia (produced Milan, 1963). Published in *Cynthia* (Florence), 1962; as *The Cage* (produced New York, 1966), in *The Cage, The Academy, The Refrigerators*, 1977.
The Academy (produced New York, 1963). As *L'Accademia*, Rome, EIST, 1964; as *The Academy*, in *The Cage, The Academy, The Refrigerators*, 1977.
La Vedova Bianca (produced Milan, 1963). Published in *Ridotto* (Rome), 1972; as *Mafia* (produced Tallahassee, Florida, 1966), Newark, Delaware, Proscenium Press, 1971.
La Telefonata (produced Rome, 1965). Rome, EIST, 1964; as *The Gift* (produced New York, 1966; London, 1972), in *Four Plays*, 1972.
I Seduttori (produced Venice, 1972). Published in *Il Dramma* (Turin), 1964; as *The Seducers*, music and lyrics by Ed Scott (produced New York, 1974), with *The Roman Guest*, Rome, Ora Zero, 1972.
I Frigoriferi (produced Pistoia, 1965). Published in *Ora Zero* (Udine), 1964; as *The Refrigerators* (produced New York, 1971), in *The Cage, The Academy, The Refrigerators*, 1977.
Le Spie (produced Pescara, 1967). Published as *The Spies*, in *Fusta* (New Jersey), 1978.
Eleonora Duse (produced Sarasota, Florida, 1967; New York, 1980). New York, Breakthrough Press, 1972.
Il Ponte (produced Pesaro, 1967). Published in *Ridotto* (Rome), 1967; as *The Bridge* (produced New York, 1972; London, 1980), New York, McGraw Hill, 1970.
The Victim (produced Sacramento, California, 1968; New York, 1973). As *La Vittima*, Rome, Lo Faro, 1972; as *The Victim*, in *Eleonora Duse, The Victim, Originality*, 1980.
Che Guevara (produced Toronto, 1968; New York, 1971). Published in *Enact* (New Delhi), April 1970; New York, French, 1980.
Unique (produced Baltimore, 1968). Published in *Ann Arbor Review* (Ann Arbor, Michigan), 1971.
L'Amico Cinese (produced Fano, 1969). Published in *Ridotto* (Rome), 1969; as *The Chinese Friend* (produced New York, 1972), in *Enact* (New Delhi), October 1972.
L'Ospite Romano (produced Pesaro, 1971). Rome,

ENARS, 1969; as *The Roman Guest*, with *The Seducers*, Rome, Ora Zero, 1972.

La Panchina del Venerdì (produced Milan, 1970); as *The Friday Bench* (produced New York, 1971), in *Four Plays*, 1972.

Betrayals. Cosenza, Pellegrini, 1970; in *Drama and Theatre* (Fredonia, New York), 1970.

The Wish (produced Denton, Texas, 1971; London, 1972). Included in *Four Plays*, 1972.

The Other One (produced New York, 1971). Included in *Races*, 1972.

The Girl with a Ring on Her Nose (produced New York, 1971). Published in *Janus* (Seaside Park, New Jersey), 1972.

Too Much (produced New York, 1971). Published in *Janus* (Seaside Park, New Jersey), 1972.

Cybele (produced New York, 1971).

The Brothel (produced New York, 1972). Published in *Mediterranean Review* (Orient, New York), 1971.

The 75th (produced Florence, 1974; New York, 1980). Published in *Arcoscenico* (Rome), January 1972; in *Dramatika* (New York), 1976.

Notti d'amore, published in *Tempo Sensibile* (Novara), July 1972.

The Letter (produced New York, 1978). Published in *Tempo Sensibile* (Novara), September 1972; in *Wind* (Kentucky), 1974.

The Family (produced New York, 1972). Published in *Enact* (New Delhi), October 1972.

Four Plays. Houston, Edgemoor, 1972.

Three Minidramas, published in *Janus* (Seaside Park, New Jersey), 1972.

Rapes (produced New York, 1972). Included in *Races*, 1972.

Races: Six Short Plays (includes *Rapes, Fire, Dialogue with a Negro, White Cat, The Refusal, The Other One*). Newark, Delaware, Proscenium Press, 1972.

Dialogue with a Negro (produced New York, 1975). Included in *Races*, 1972.

Teatro Americano (includes *Fuoco, Sorelle, Violenze, Famiglia*). Casale Monferrato, Tersite, 1972.

L'Ungherese (produced Florence, 1974). Published in *Tempo Sensibile* (Novara), 1972.

Dolls No More (produced London and Lafayette, Indiana, 1975). Published in *Drama and Theatre* (Fredonia, New York), Winter 1972–73.

Chile 1973 (produced Parma and New York, 1974). Published in *Enact* (New Delhi), October, November, and December 1973; in *Parola del Popolo* (Chicago), 1974.

New York: A Triptych (produced New York, 1974).

Patty Hearst, published in *Enact* (New Delhi), 1975; in *Parola del Popolo* (Chicago), 1975.

Madam Senator, music and lyrics by Ed Scott (produced New York, 1975).

Originality (produced New York, 1975). Included in *Eleonora Duse, The Victim, Originality*, 1980.

The Only Good Indian . . ., with Henry Salerno (produced New York, 1975). Published in *Drama and Theatre* (Fredonia, New York), 1975.

Tania, music by Paul Dick (produced New York, 1975).

Two Centuries, with Penelope Bradford (produced New York, 1976).

Kissinger (produced California, 1976). Published in *Enact* (New Delhi), 1976.

Messages, published in *Dramatika* (New York), 1976.

The Cage, The Academy, The Refrigerators. New York, French, 1977.

Lunch with Fratti: The Letter, Her Voice, The Piggy Bank (produced New York, 1978). *The Piggy Bank* published in *Scholia Satyrica* (Tampa, Florida), 1977.

La Croce di Padre Marcello. Turin, Elle Di Ci, 1977.

The Biggest Thief in Town (produced New York, 1978).

Birthday. New York, French, n.d.

David, Son of Sam, published in *Ars-Uomo* (Rome), 1978.

Six Passionate Women, published in *Enact* (New Delhi), 1978.

Two Women (produced New York, 1981). Published in *Zone Press* (New York), 1978.

Sette Commedie. Frascati, Tusculum, 1979.

The Fourth One (produced New York, 1980).

Caccia al Morto, Mafia. Frascati, Tusculum, 1980.

The Pill (produced New York, 1980). Published in *Scholia Satyrica* (Tampa, Florida), 1980.

Eleonora Duse, The Victim, Originality. New York, French, 1980.

Nine, book by Arthur Kopit, music and lyrics by Maury Yeston, adaptation of the screenplay 8½ by Federico Fellini (produced Waterford, Connecticut, 1981; New York, 1982). New York, French, 1983.

Half, published in *Other Stages* (New York), 1981.

Elbow to Elbow, adaptation of a play by Glauco Disalle (produced New York, 1982).

Il Pugnale Marocchino (produced L'Aquila, 1982). L'Aquila, Teatrama, 1982.

Viols, Feu (two plays) (produced Paris, 1983).

Four by Fratti (includes *The Suicide, The Return, The Victim, Eleonora Duse*). New York, French, 1986.

Our Family, Toys (two plays). New York, Griffin House Publications, 1986.

A.I.D.S. (produced London, 1987).

V.C.R. (produced Rome, 1988).

Encounter (musical) (produced Schenectady, New York, 1989).

Two Centuries, with Penelope Bradford (produced New York, 1990).

Lovers (produced New York, 1992).

Sex Commedie di Fratti. Rome, Serarcangeli, 1992.

Translations for Italian television: plays by David Shaw, Reginald Rose, Thomas W. Phipps, R.O. Hirson, J.P. Miller.

Verse

Volti: Cento Poesie (Faces: 100 Poems). Bari, Mariano, 1960.

*

Bibliography: in *Ora Zero* (Udine), 1972; in *Four Plays*, 1972.

Manuscript Collection: Lincoln Center Library of the Performing Arts, New York.

Critical Studies: by Robert W. Corrigan, in *New Theatre of Europe II*, New York, Dell, 1964, and in *Masterpieces of the Modern Italian Theatre*, New York, Collier Macmillan, 1967; by Paul T. Nolan, in *Ora Zero* (Udine), 1972, and in *La Vittima*, 1972; *Mario Fratti* by Jane Bonin, Boston, Twayne, 1982; "Italian-American Playwrights on the Rise" by G.C. Di Scipio, in *Journal of Popular Culture* (Bowling Green, Ohio), Winter 1985.

Mario Fratti comments:
I keep writing plays, at least one a year, because I have something to say. It is my way of being involved with the

world that surrounds me. It is my way to comment on the jungle we are living in. Greed and hatred prevail today. I am trying to create characters who are the victims of greed and hatred. I indicate ways to unmask them.

* * *

Mario Fratti arrived in New York in 1963 as foreign correspondent for the Italian press. He had already achieved some distinction in Italy as a playwright, and made his American debut that same year with a production of *The Academy* and *The Return* at the Theatre De Lys, starring Ron Liebman. Although a critical success, this first production failed to establish Fratti as an important New York playwright. Undaunted, Fratti continued writing prolifically. Translations of his plays appeared in prominent American literary journals and anthologies; his words were produced throughout the United States and abroad, and were evaluated in several academic studies. Fratti was a phenomenon: a European playwright based in New York achieving national and international recognition without being produced in New York. While most playwrights struggled to "crack" the New York theatrical scene, Fratti imposed himself upon the city by the weight of his international success (more than 300 productions).

Fratti is fascinated with the idea of life as theatre. Existing in an unknowable universe, caught in social systems beyond his control, man becomes an actor wearing an endless array of public and private masks as a means of survival. In such a world, deceit, treachery, and violence are commonplace. While this theme is explored by other modern writers, Fratti is unique for embracing clarity rather than obscurity in the theatre, convinced that the playwright must be the "quintessence of clarity" both for the actor and the audience. Otherwise, he is only "an hysterical poet talking to himself in front of a mirror." Fratti's rich theatrical imagination and impeccable craftsmanship assure clarity.

Comparable to the plots of the commedia dell'arte, many of his plays hinge on a deception, but the results are frequently pathetic or tragic rather than comic. While the characters are passionate, and the situation tense, the structure is coldly logical and tight, progressing like a mystery thriller: the audience's sympathies shift from one character to another; each seems to be on the side of right and the truth is elusive. However, the conclusion is not the revelation of a murderer but a provocative idea regarding the human condition. "I want to open a door in the minds of the audience," states Fratti.

In *The Cage*, Cristiano's pessimism is convincing and his isolation seems justified. Ultimately, however, his moralizing proves destructive; his murder of Pietro, the presumably cruel husband, is the megalomaniacal act of a man who would play God with other peoples' lives. Sanguemarcio, the invalid degenerate of *The Coffin*, pays to hear lurid tales of violence and perversion, aided by his trusted friend, Paoletto, who provides him with storytellers. But the tales are lies; Paoletto is a thief and parasite using the old degenerate for profit. Sanguemarcio dies when he discovers that his one trusted friend was just another of life's frauds. Fratti, however, never moralizes: deceived and deceiver are caught in a hopeless struggle for survival.

The dominant metaphor in Fratti's plays is the trap: characters trapped in situations which they attempt to escape from by violence or deception. Most of the plays are set indoors: oppressive rooms, a cage: concretized images of entrapment. Even the short, percussive titles of his plays suggest traps that have been sprung. But Fratti is not another modern pessimist. While dramatizing life's *Inferno*, he believes in man's basic goodness: "I believe in man, man notwithstanding." In *The Bridge*, a courageous policeman risks his life to save potential suicide victims, recalling a biblical parable that it is better to save one lost sheep than keep a flock. The Priest of *The Roman Guest* learns a new liberalism in America, confronts a prejudiced mob, and returns to Italy with a more profound sense of Christianity. *Che Guevara* is a heroic yet realistic depiction of the Argentinean revolutionary, a man who views his actions as expedient rather than superhuman, necessary steps toward the positive evolution of society.

Fratti also has a subtle sense of comedy. Works such as *The Academy* and *Waiting* are humorous explorations of deceit and self deception. In *The Academy*, set in postwar Italy, a fascist attempts to revenge himself upon America by maintaining an academy for gigolos in pursuit of wealthy American women. The heroine of *Waiting* feigns docility in order to lure her seducer into marriage and then punish him by making his future life a hell. *The Refrigerators*, a dark comedy, is a bizarre parable of contemporary American life and technology, a unique departure from the essential realism of Fratti's drama. Transvestism and perversion are rampant, and the madcap events have a Marx Brothers quality.

America has had a significant influence on Fratti: "This society with all its problems and conflicts is fascinating. It's the ideal society for a modern dramatist." He now writes in English as well as Italian, and evidences a remarkable ear for American dialogue: a terseness and directness that suit the compactness of his dramatic structure. Living in the heart of Manhattan's theatre district, Fratti is continually stimulated by the city, inspired by the most seemingly insignificant event or occurrence around him. "I am a great observer. Faces are incredibly revealing. Just an expression can give me an idea for a play." He describes the scene that provided him with the idea for *The Chinese Friend*, a one-act masterpiece of racial prejudice, filled with nuances regarding America's foreign policy in the Far East: "A very handsome, and elegantly attired American family passed me on the street. They seemed to be overly solicitous to a Chinese gentleman, who was, apparently, their guest."

Thematically, cynicism has tended to override Fratti's humanism in recent years. The world is too much with him of late, embittered by the cruelty, violence, and obsessive war mentality in the post-Vietnam period. But he remains deeply concerned about the poor, the underdog, the perennially helpless victims of life's more skilful and deceptive players. A recurring metaphor is exposure: men and women enmeshed in a futile battle of the sexes, exposing their penchant for foolishness, deceit, and treachery. In his darker plays, the exposure concerns buried guilts, jealousies, hatreds that end in senseless tragedy.

In the comedy *Six Passionate Women* voyeurism and self exposure dominate the lives of the film industry characters of the play. A man hater, appropriately named Mrs. Gunmore, sets out to avenge herself upon the film director, Nino, for what she regards as the male chauvinism and contempt for women evident in his work. *Nine* also centers on the travails of a film director, Guido Contini, but he is treated more sympathetically than Nino. "Sometimes I neglect you," Guido tells his suffering wife; but asks her to forgive him for his waywardness and exposure of their private life on film; it is his way of "creating and recreating." Adapted from Fellini's 8½, *Nine* dramatizes the central character's attempts toward self-understanding by exploring his guilts, desires, fantasies through his characters. The work also satirizes the film industry's incongruous marriage of crass materialism and art through the character of the German financier, Weissnicht, who backs Guido's latest film.

The Third Daughter and *Birthday* are two dark plays concerned with the theme of a father's incestuous desire for his daughter. In *The Third Daughter* Ilario decides to avenge himself upon his adulterous wife by having the offspring of her infidelity, their third daughter Alda, have an affair with a young man, thus destroying her purity, and so torment his wife. The sordid tale is complex in its implications regarding family ties, hatreds, jealousies, desires. Ilario's actual daughters are acting out their own love-hate relationship with their father: hating him for his cruel treatment of their mother, and for his preferring his stepsister to them. He has not only denied them paternal love, but aroused their jealousy, based upon their own repressed incestuous desires. *Birthday* is a fascinating dramatization of incest that becomes madness. A father annually enacts the imagined return of his runaway daughter on her birthday. Women are brought in to assume the role coached by the servant, who encourages them to please the man, and satisfy his incestuous desires.

In *The Piggy Bank* deception and exposure again prevail. A clever prostitute frightens off clients, who have paid in advance, by pretending to have venereal disease; she uses her victims, and is in turn used by her husband; a vicious game of survival with no real winners. *The Letter* is one of Fratti's short chamber plays; excellent acting vehicles—brief, intense, ambivalent.

Fratti is one of off-off Broadway's most frequently performed playwrights, a tribute to his originality and willingness to explore uncomfortable truths about contemporary life. He finds fertile ground for his drama in the most apparently insignificant moments in the passing scene of everyday life, and has a notebook filled with ideas for plays. "Look, I'll never be able to use them all in my lifetime." Let's hope he's wrong.

—A. Richard Sogliuzzo

FRAYN, Michael. British. Born in Mill Hill, London, 8 September 1933. Educated at Sutton High School for Boys; Kingston Grammar School, Surrey; Emmanuel College, Cambridge, B.A. 1957. Served in the Royal Artillery and Intelligence Corps, 1952–54. Married Gillian Palmer in 1960 (marriage dissolved 1990); three daughters. Reporter, 1957–59, and columnist, 1959–62, the *Guardian*, Manchester and London; columnist, the *Observer*, London, 1962–68. Recipient: Maugham award, 1966; Hawthornden prize, 1967; National Press award, 1970; *Evening Standard* award, for play, 1976, 1981, 1983, 1985; Society of West End Theatre award, 1977, 1982; British Theatre Association award, 1981, 1983; Olivier award, 1985; New York Drama Critics Circle award, 1986; Emmy award, 1990; *Sunday Express* Book of the Year award, 1991. Honorary fellow, Emmanuel College, 1985. Lives in London. Agent: Elaine Greene Ltd., 37 Goldhawk Road, London W12 8QQ, England.

PUBLICATIONS

Plays

Zounds!, with John Edwards, music by Keith Statham (produced Cambridge, 1957).
Jamie, On A Flying Visit (televised 1968). With *Birthday*, London, Methuen, 1990.

Birthday (televised 1969). With *Jamie, On a Flying Visit*, London, Methuen, 1990.
The Two of Us (includes *Black and Silver*, *The New Quixote*, *Mr. Foot*, *Chinamen*) (produced London, 1970; Ogunquit, Maine, 1975; *Chinamen* produced New York, 1979). London, Fontana, 1970; *Chinamen* published in *The Best Short Plays 1973*, edited by Stanley Richards, Radnor, Pennsylvania, Chilton, 1973; revised version of *The New Quixote* (produced Chichester, Sussex, and London, 1980).
The Sandboy (produced London, 1971).
Alphabetical Order (produced London, 1975; New Haven, Connecticut, 1976). With *Donkeys' Years*, London, Eyre Methuen, 1977.
Donkeys' Years (produced London, 1976; New York, 1987). With *Alphabetical Order*, London, Eyre Methuen, 1977.
Clouds (produced London, 1976). London, Eyre Methuen, 1977.
The Cherry Orchard, adaptation of a play by Chekhov (produced London, 1978). London, Eyre Methuen, 1978.
Balmoral (produced Guildford, Surrey, 1978; revised version, as *Liberty Hall*, produced London, 1980; revised version, as *Balmoral*, produced Bristol, 1987). London, Methuen, 1987.
The Fruits of Enlightenment, adaptation of a play by Tolstoy (produced London, 1979). London, Eyre Methuen, 1979.
Make and Break (produced London, 1980; Washington, D.C., 1983). London, Eyre Methuen, 1980.
Noises Off (produced London, 1981; New York, 1983). London, Methuen, 1982; New York, French, 1985.
Three Sisters, adaptation of a play by Chekhov (produced Manchester and Los Angeles, 1985; London, 1987). London, Methuen, 1983.
Benefactors (produced London, 1984; New York, 1985). London, Methuen, 1984.
Wild Honey, adaptation of a play by Chekhov (produced London, 1984; New York, 1986). London, Methuen, 1984.
Number One, adaptation of a play by Jean Anouilh (produced London, 1984). London, French, 1985.
Plays I (includes *Alphabetical Order*, *Donkey's Years*, *Clouds*, *Make and Break*, *Noises Off*). London, Methuen, 1986.
The Seagull, adaptation of a play by Chekhov (produced Watford, Hertfordshire, 1986; London, 1990). London, Methuen, 1986.
Clockwise (screenplay). London, Methuen, 1986.
Exchange, adaptation of a play by Yuri Trifonov (broadcast 1986; produced Southampton, Hampshire, 1989; London, 1990). London, Methuen, 1990.
Uncle Vanya, adaptation of a play by Chekhov (produced London, 1988). London, Methuen, 1987.
Chekhov: Plays (includes *The Seagull*, *Uncle Vanya*, *Three Sisters*, *The Cherry Orchard*, four vaudevilles). London, Methuen, 1988.
The Sneeze, adaptation of works by Chekhov (produced Newcastle-upon-Tyne and London, 1988). London, Methuen, and New York, French, 1989.
First and Last (televised 1989). London, Methuen, 1989.
Look Look (as *Spettattori*, produced Rome, 1989; as *Look Look*, produced London, 1990). London, Methuen, 1990.
Listen to This: 21 Short Plays and Sketches. London, Methuen, 1991.
Plays 2 (includes *Benefactors*, *Balmoral*, *Wild Honey*). London, Methuen, 1992.

Screenplay: *Clockwise*, 1986.

Radio Play: *Exchange*, adaptation of a play by Yuri Trifonov, 1986.

Television Plays and Documentaries: *Second City Reports*, with John Bird, 1964; *Jamie, On a Flying Visit*, 1968; *One Pair of Eyes*, 1968; *Birthday*, 1969; *Beyond a Joke* series, with John Bird and Eleanor Bron, 1972; *Laurence Sterne Lived Here* (*Writers' Houses* series), 1973; *Imagine a City Called Berlin*, 1975; *Making Faces*, 1975; *Vienna: The Mask of Gold*, 1977; *Three Streets in the Country*, 1979; *The Long Straight* (*Great Railway Journeys of the World* series), 1980; *Jerusalem*, 1984; *First and Last*, 1989.

Novels

The Tin Men.   London, Collins, 1965; Boston, Little Brown, 1966.
The Russian Interpreter.   London, Collins, and New York, Viking Press, 1966.
Towards the End of the Morning.   London, Collins, 1967; as *Against Entropy*, New York, Viking Press, 1967.
A Very Private Life.   London, Collins, and New York, Viking Press, 1968.
Sweet Dreams.   London, Collins, 1973; New York, Viking Press, 1974.
The Trick of It.   London, Viking, 1989; New York, Viking, 1990.
A Landing on the Sun.   London, Viking, 1991.

Other

The Day of the Dog (*Guardian* columns).   London, Collins, 1962; New York, Doubleday, 1963.
The Book of Fub (*Guardian* columns).   London, Collins, 1963; as *Never Put Off to Gomorrah*, New York, Pantheon, 1964.
On the Outskirts (*Observer* columns).   London, Fontana, 1967.
At Bay in Gear Street (*Observer* columns).   New York, Fontana, 1967.
Constructions (philosophy).   London, Wildwood House, 1974.
Great Railway Journeys of the World, with others.   London, BBC Publications, 1981; New York, Dutton, 1982.
The Original Michael Frayn: Satirical Essays, edited by James Fenton.   Edinburgh, Salamander Press, 1983.

Editor, *The Best of Beachcomber*, by J.B. Morton.   London, Heinemann, 1963.

*

Critical Study: introduction by Frayn to *Plays 1*, 1986.

* * *

Michael Frayn deplored the "didactic drive" of the 1970's because it replaced drama by ideology. Like his contemporary Alan Ayckbourn, Frayn consciously distinguished his work from the political drama that was sweeping the English stage at the beginning of the 1970's, asserting a return to traditional comic values. In contrast to Joe Orton, who treated tragic material as farce for shock effect, Frayn makes farce a way of exposing the insensitivity of stock responses through showing potential tragedy beneath the comic surface.

Laughter in Frayn is therefore frequently ambiguous, as in *Alphabetical Order*:

> Lucy: (. . . *starts to laugh again*) . . . I'm sorry. It's not funny!
> Nora: It's not at all funny.
> John: It's what one might call tragic irony. (*He starts to laugh*)

Frayn deals with society in terms of organizations—the news media, a manufacturing industry, the commercial theatre—which intrinsically threaten the survival of humanity. Deadening order is always subverted, however unintentionally; and the life force triumphs, though at the expense of what the individuals concerned are striving for. Thus the newspaper library of *Alphabetical Order* is overwhelmed by the accretion of trivia in the piles of yellowing newsprint. While the instant redundancy of all the facts recorded in these clippings satirizes the illusory nature of what our news-fixated culture considers important, the confusion of the library files is presented as organic: a sign of individualism surviving even in what is (taking newspaper-slang literally) a "morgue."

According to Frayn, what his plays "are all about . . . is the way in which we impose our ideas upon the world around us. In *Alphabetical Order* it is by classification, in *Make and Break* by consumption." This approach takes the form of challenging the way audiences perceive what they see on stage, and is closely related to the subjects of his plays: the way news-reportage categorizes events (in *Alphabetical Order*), or the difference between socialist and capitalist views of the world, as in *Clouds* (which reflects Frayn's disorienting experiences as a journalist in Cuba).

His most successful play, *Noises Off*, applies this to the theatre itself, taking as its title the technical term for behind-the-scenes activity that breaks the theatrical illusion. It juxtaposes backstage action with the rehearsal and performance of a mirror text: *Nothing On*, a highly artificial farce that echoes Ben Travers's *Rookery Nook*. The characters are stock figures on two overlapping levels. As actors they are the drunken old-stager, the short-sighted sex symbol, and the fading television star investing in her own show to finance retirement. And they are cast as Shavian Burglar (à la *Heartbreak House*), dumb blonde, and comic servant (duplicating the television soap role in which the aging actress made her name).

The catalyst on both back- and on-stage levels is the director. His casual affairs with both the sex symbol and the assistant stage manager (hired because her father's firm is sponsoring the production), are a real-life version of the on-stage characters' sexual activities. This behind-the-scenes promiscuity progressively disrupts the performance that he has so carefully organized in the rehearsal.

The Act I dress-rehearsal of *Nothing On* demonstrates the fragility of the ordered precision on which the performance of farce depends. Lines are forgotten, entries missed, doors jam at crucial moments or won't close; and the comedy misfires completely. It is the incompetence of the actors, not the antics of the characters, that is funny.

In the second Act—when the perspective is reversed, showing us the set from behind—the humour comes from mistaken motives and a series of emotional crises (typical of farce) that afflict the actors in the wings. The complete silence imposed on them by the ongoing performance just the other side of the thin scenery, magnifies their misunderstandings and frustrations into hysterical comedy. In fact, *Noises Off* outdoes *Nothing On* in every way. The activity behind the scenes results in double the number of men with trousers round their ankles (including the director), and two semi-nude girls instead of the one in *Nothing On*. The chaos distorts the unseen performance, finally eclipsing it, when the assistant stage manager's announcement of her pregnancy rings out through the theatre just after the curtain-lines (which are greeted with a deadly silence from the imaginary audience of *Nothing On*).

As Frayn comments: "The fear that haunts [the cast] is that the unlearned and unrehearsed—the great dark chaos behind the set, inside the heart and brain—will seep back on to the stage. . . . Their performance will break down, and they will be left in front of us naked and ashamed." And this fear is realized in the final Act, some months later in the tour, when the mayhem behind the scenes has indeed spread onto the stage. As the performers hit each other over the head, or are tripped down the backstage stairs from the "bedroom" as they exit, the stage manager is forced to enter as a stand-in for one after another, only to have the injured actor stagger into view while he is still on the set. This culminates in no fewer than three comic burglars appearing when the old soak misses his entry. Believing him to be drunk, the stage manager dashes on stage to say his crucial lines—as does the director, believing the stage manager is already on in another role—followed by the drunken actor himself. Under the pressure of such physical chaos the dialogue, uncertain at the best of times, disintegrates. In desperation the cast drag down the curtain between them and the audience.

This open theatrically—where people are presented as performers, and their social context is a stage set, so that everything relates to drama—is characteristic of the most inventive contemporary comedy, being shared by Trevor Griffiths, Peter Barnes, and Tom Stoppard.

—Christopher Innes

FREEMAN, David. Canadian. Born in Toronto, Ontario, 7 January 1945; palsied from birth. Educated at Sunnyview School for the Handicapped, Toronto, 1951–61; McMaster University, Hamilton, Ontario (news features editor, university newspaper), 1966–71, B.A. in political science 1971. Public relations officer, IBM, Don Mills, Ontario, 1970. Recipient: Ontario Council for the Arts grant, 1971; Canada Council grant, 1972, 1974; Chalmers award, 1972; Drama Desk award, 1973; Edinburgh Fringe Festival first, 1979; Los Angeles Critics Circle award (three), 1983. Agent: Agence Goodwin, 839 Shrebrooke East, Suite 2, Montreal, Quebec H2L 1K6, Canada.

PUBLICATIONS

Plays

Creeps (produced Toronto, 1971; Washington, D.C., and New York, 1973; Edinburgh, 1979; London, 1981). Toronto, University of Toronto Press, 1972; New York and London, French, 1975.
Battering Ram (produced Toronto, 1973; New York, 1975; revised version as *Le Bélier*, produced Montreal, 1984). Toronto, Playwrights, 1972.
You're Gonna Be Alright, Jamie-Boy (produced Toronto, 1974; New York, 1977; London, 1990). Vancouver, Talonbooks, 1974.

Flytrap (produced Montreal, 1976). Toronto, Playwrights, 1980.

Radio Plays: *Year of the Soul*, in *Quebec Heroes and Anti-Heroes* series, 1982.

*

Critical Study: article by G. Anthony, in *Stage Voices*, edited by Anthony, Toronto, Doubleday Canada, 1978.

David Freeman comments:

(1973) *Creeps* is an autobiographical play which takes place one afternoon in the men's washroom of a sheltered workshop for the cerebral palsied. It has four main characters: Tom, Jim, Pete, and Sam. The four congregate in the washroom in order to get away from such menial and boring tasks as sanding blocks, separating nuts and bolts, folding boxes, and weaving rugs. The main conflict is between Tom, who considers himself an abstract artist and wants to leave the workshop to devote more time to his painting, and Jim, who has recently been promoted to office work and would prefer that Tom stay in the workshop where life is less complicated. Pete is lazy and is content to let the world wait on him, while Sam is bitter, cruel, foul-mouthed, and lecherous. This afternoon they talk about sexual frustration, broken dreams, and rage at a society which has condemned them to the mercy of false charity and at themselves for accepting it. The play came out of my own experiences in such a place ten years ago, for I myself am afflicted with cerebral palsy.

(1993) *Battering Ram*, a play which explores emotional and sexual taboos, followed *Creeps*. My third work, *You're Gonna Be Alright, Jamie-Boy*, allowed me to look at the taboos and emotional trauma of the nuclear family. In *Flytrap*, I threw my audience a curve when I created a family where there should never have existed one; a middle-aged childless couple tries to play parent to a young man in his twenties.

Presently, I continue to work on a number of scripts and novels. The plays are periodically workshopped and receive readings. The novel which I am now revising tells the story of young people caught up in the changes of the late 1960's. The setting is a rural university campus. The action is a concoction of truth and the exaggerations of youth.

* * *

David Freeman's world is one of cripples, both physical and psychological, and one which mirrors the equally crippled morality, aspirations, and institutions of the "real" world which surrounds his fictional one and which causes or assists in the deforming of his various victims. It follows, therefore, that his characters and plots are naturalistic, although dramatic hyperbole often breaks into the otherwise naturalistic conception in the form of stereotype leading to caricature, as in *You're Gonna Be Alright, Jamie-Boy*, or of intensely theatrical and fantastic vignettes superimposed on the plot, as in the circus interludes of *Creeps*. The result in *Creeps* is the creation of a shockingly powerful dramatic vehicle for Freeman's bitter but balanced attack on his audience, its physical normality, its ignorance of the humiliation experienced by an adult trapped in the crippled body of a hideous child, and, finally and most unrelentingly, on its pity. It is in the dramatic rather than thematic elements that Freeman most devastatingly exposes the shallow and self-gratifying attempts of the charitable institutions to invade this "sheltered" world. In its virtually terroristic design, the play hurls its washroom set, sexual frustration, unremittingly obscene language, and grotesque mime at the audience in a *coup de théâtre* which the more controlled and mature later plays cannot approach. This design is so compelling and dramatically so powerful that in production, the audience, stunned by Freeman's ferocity, accepts elements—the exaggeration of the foul language, for example—which it would not credit in print. In the later plays, where his personal anger becomes less acute, Freeman cannot assume the same overwhelmed acceptance by his audience; regrettably, he sometimes does.

Battering Ram reworks the theme of sexual frustration, and in its removal of the physically repulsive, loses much of the dramatic strength of *Creeps*. Still, the play makes an arresting statement and, more importantly, builds it around a full characterization of the protagonist. In this focus and its largely successful execution, Freeman evidences his growth as a playwright, moving as he does into more literary and less personal devices. The play is also a movement into the more commercial theatre, employing themes which become more popular as they become less personal.

In *You're Gonna Be Alright, Jamie-Boy* Freeman creates a play in the neo-naturalistic school which became popular in Canadian drama in the 1970's. Unfortunately, in moving completely from his physically crippled familiars, Freeman created rather clichéd North American types working out a predictable pattern based on the emptiness of television-oriented lives. After the strength of the earlier plays, this reworking of a commonplace situation seems facile; in many respects it seems more like a first play than the third in a series. In its investigation of the psychology of the characters, however, it holds together well given the shallow range of personality each exhibits. Freeman looks at stereotypical characters but he looks at them reasonably well, especially through his dialogue which often picks up the verve of *Creeps* and sometimes leaps into moments of real comedy and pathos.

His fourth play, *Flytrap*, moves further into the realm of the commercial and it does so with considerable success. In its first production in Montreal, the play was called "straightforward, well crafted, entertaining and unpretentious" (Myron Galloway in the *Montreal Star*, 3 May 1976) and it has been seen as a significant example of a movement in contemporary Canadian theatre away from self-consciously social themes and into middle-class issues with a broad base of appeal. This is particularly interesting in the case of Freeman because of the very specialized concerns of *Creeps* which had previously obsessed him. The dramatic tone and staging of the play also differs: it moves at a leisurely pace through the struggle of a married but childless couple to come to terms with the new presence in their troubled marriage of a surrogate son of mature years. This strange triangle is explored without the bombast of the early work (until the end, at least, when the principals finally fight out their frustration) and the treatment is much lighter and more ironic than in the previous plays. The critical dilemma is to determine whether a more controlled discussion of average material is more or less laudable than an uncontrolled scream through the highly unusual and astonishing world of *Creeps*.

Freeman has proved himself a professional man of the theatre; he has not, however, yet matched the brilliance of his first play and that has exposed him to negative comment from those who will never be satisfied until he matches its energy but in a fully mature framework. The development of the plays to date suggests that Freeman is capable of doing just

that and when he does, he will create a play of great significance.

—Reid Gilbert

FRENCH, David. Canadian. Born in Coley's Point, Newfoundland, 18 January 1939. Educated at Harbord Collegiate High School; Oakwood Collegiate High School, Toronto, graduated 1958; studied acting at Al Saxe Studio, Toronto, 1958, Pasadena Playhouse, California, 1959, and Lawlor School of Acting, Toronto, 1960. Married Leslie Gray in 1979. Actor in Toronto, 1960–65; post office worker, 1967–68. Recipient: Chalmers award, 1973; Lieutenant-Governor's award, 1974; Canada Council grant, 1974, 1975; Dora award, 1985; Canadian Authors Association award, 1986. Agent: Shain Jaffe, Great North Artists, 350 DuPont Street, Toronto, Ontario M5R 1V9, Canada.

PUBLICATIONS

Plays

Leaving Home (produced Toronto, 1972; New York, 1974). Toronto, New Press, 1972; New York and London, French, 1976.
Of the Fields, Lately (produced Toronto, 1973; New York, 1980). Toronto, Playwrights, 1973; New York, French, 1975.
One Crack Out (produced Toronto, 1975; New York, 1978). Toronto, Playwrights, 1975.
The Seagull, adaptation of a play by Chekhov (produced Toronto, 1977). Toronto, Playwrights, 1977.
Jitters (produced Toronto and New Haven, Connecticut, 1979). Toronto, Playwrights, 1980.
The Riddle of the World (produced Toronto, 1981).
Salt-Water Moon (produced Toronto, 1984; Costa Mesa, California, 1985; Edinburgh, 1986). Toronto, Playwrights, 1985; New York, Dramatists Play Service, 1988.
1949 (produced Toronto, 1989). Vancouver, Talonbooks, 1989.
Silver Dagger (produced Toronto, 1992).

Radio Plays: *Angeline*, 1967; *Invitation to a Zoo*, 1967; *Winter of Timothy*, 1968.

Television Plays: *Beckons the Dark River*, 1963; *The Willow Harp*, 1964; *A Ring for Florrie*, 1964; *After Hours*, 1964; *Sparrow on a Monday Morning*, 1966 (USA); *A Token Gesture*, 1970; *The Tender Branch*, 1972; *The Happiest Man in the World*, from a short story by Hugh Garner, 1972; scripts for *Razzle Dazzle* children's series.

* * *

The first of David French's stage plays, *Leaving Home*, concerns the sense of displacement and frustration of a family of Irish immigrants who have been torn, not once, but twice from their roots, first from Ireland to Newfoundland and then from Newfoundland to Toronto. They carry with them the luggage of their past—Catholic-Protestant antagonisms, family loyalties and bitter dissension, a salty vituperation, and a habit of convivial overdrinking. Because of the double displacement, the past has become meaningless, yet the older generation retain it and struggle to relate it to the future. The play's theme is the ancient one of a son's need to free himself from his father, paralleled and reinforced by the theme of the alienation of the immigrant from his children in the new land.

The Mercer family organization is not unlike that in Arthur Miller's *Death of a Salesman*, with Mary Mercer loving but ineffectual in her efforts to keep the family peace and protect her husband, Jacob, and eldest son, Ben, from hurting each other. Jacob's life has been damaged by a brutal, uncaring father, the early death of his mother, and an interrupted education. In Ben, Jacob dreams of living again, successful in some socially esteemed profession and with a warm father-son relationship, yet he sneers at the university education, which is his son's path to a better life.

The action of the play takes place in the Mercer kitchen and parlour, rendered with an effect of cramped and unlovely realism, on the wedding day of the younger son, Billy, who has gotten his high school girlfriend pregnant. Significantly she is Catholic, and the daughter of Minnie Jackson, a sweetheart of Jacob's youth, a woman he did not marry because of her religion and because of her randy and slip-shod behaviour, which still both attracts and repels him. Instead he married Protestant Mary, pretty, austere, and middle-class. The wedding triggers off a series of painful reminiscences and violent reactions in Jake, not against Billy, who is marrying a Catholic, abandoning school and the traditional prejudices of the Irish in general, but against Ben, whose leaving home Jacob regards with anguish as the death of all his hopes.

The sequel to this play, *Of the Fields, Lately*, deals with Ben's return home after two futile years in the prairies, summoned ostensibly for the funeral of his aunt, but actually because of the growing frailty of his father. The play is permeated with the sense of death, but the funeral device does not create as tight a dramatic unity as the wedding in *Leaving Home*. The same temperamental antagonisms arise between Jacob and Ben, completing their alienation, shown by the use of soliloquies of reminiscence by both characters at the beginning of the play and by Ben alone after his father's death in the end. This single departure from realism frames the play declaring symbolically at the opening and reaffirming at the closing the sense of isolation felt by each character.

Yet rejection and alienation are not the whole story. Jake has a vitality lacking in his sons, although it has been warped into boasting, empty heroics at his job, and heavy drinking. Ben instinctively recognizes his father's superiority to him and feels a dogged sense of duty and even respect for Jacob, but cannot bear to be enslaved by Jacob's disappointments and dead values.

The realism of the first two plays is pushed to greater extremes in French's third, *One Crack Out*, which deals with the tawdry life of petty criminals and pool hall gamblers. The set is divided between the squalid pool hall and adjoining lavatory, and the equally squalid bedsitting room of Charlie, a pool shark, and his wife, Helen, a stripper. These claustrophobic interiors, plus eleven short scenes tumbling upon one another, build up tension as the deadline approaches when Charlie must pay the Collector the $3,000 he owes or get his hands broken.

As all his efforts to raise the money by borrowing and hustling fail, Charlie emerges as not only devious and frantic, but also as one who is capable of loyalty and unselfish feeling. With his losing streak ended through an act of pure devotion by Helen, he is able to resolve his problem in his own terms by a duel of skill. In creating Charlie's dilemma and prevent-

ing any avenue of escape, French has over-plotted the play and its emotional power is diffused by melodramatic effects such as the breathlessly approaching deadline, the complication of Charlie's sexual impotence with his wife, and the unprepared-for conversion of the Collector to accepting Charlie's challenge debt. Despite the fact that this play is less strong than French's first two, it marks a forward step in his development by moving away from the autobiographical into an invented, objective world.

French's first comedy was *Jitters*, the title of which reflects the feelings of a group of Canadian actors as they rehearse a play which they expect to be seen by an important New York director who they hope will pave their way to Broadway, the necessary seal of success in Canada. During the action they reveal the uncertainty and inferiority felt by Canadian artists in the shadow of the U.S.A.

The play begins with a trompe d'oeil effect of a play-within-a-play which the audience thinks is the real thing for the first several minutes until the director leaps up from a theatre seat calling "cut, cut!" This sudden break from "theatrical" harmony to "real life" rivalry in the past points up the personal antagonism between Jessica, who has star billing, and Patrick, the leading actor, who is outraged that his long successful career in Canada counts for less than Jessica's two flops on Broadway. It is her former director in New York who operates as a kind of nemesis, increasing both the hopes and jitters of everyone including the playwright. The director's ultimate non-attendance of the performance is the final irony of Canadian-American relations, in theatre as in everything, underscoring the Canadian sense of American imperviousness and indifference.

In *Salt-Water Moon*, his most recent work, French returns to Newfoundland and autobiographical themes with a play which precedes *Leaving Home* in time by depicting the courtship of Jacob Mercer and Mary Snow. Set on the front porch and in the yard of the summer home of the local MP, where Mary is in service, confined to the 90-minute running time of the action (there is no intermission), the play focuses narrowly on Jacob and Mary, their frustrated love, their poverty, their poignant struggle in different ways to help their families: Mary to save her sister from the brutality of an orphan asylum, and Jacob to spare his father the humiliation of being "in collar," a pernicious employment system devised by the local fishing bosses.

The play's tension arises not from suspense about whether the lovers will finally resolve their differences, but how they will do it. Their meeting after a year's absence begins in recrimination—hers for his sudden departure, and his for her becoming engaged to his arch-enemy's son. The evening proceeds with a series of explanations which reveal their experience of suffering, death, and poverty, along with their strength and tenacity. It ends with harmony being reestablished under the "salt-water moon." As always French's dialogue is affecting and funny, nostalgic and poetic with the resonance of Newfoundland Irish idiom.

—Dorothy Parker

FRIEDMAN, Bruce Jay. American. Born in New York City, 26 April 1930. Educated at De Witt Clinton High School, Bronx, New York; University of Missouri, Columbia, 1947–

51, Bachelor of Journalism 1951. Served in the United States Air Force, 1951–53: lieutenant. Married 1) Ginger Howard in 1954 (divorced 1977), three children; 2) Patricia J. O'Donohue in 1983, one daughter. Editorial director, Magazine Management Company, publishers, New York, 1953–56. Visiting professor of literature, York College, City University, New York, 1974–76. Address: P.O. Box 746, Water Mill, New York 11976, U.S.A.

PUBLICATIONS

Plays

23 Pat O'Brien Movies, adaptation of his own short story (produced New York, 1966).
Scuba Duba: A Tense Comedy (produced New York, 1967). New York, Simon and Schuster, 1968.
A Mother's Kisses, music by Richard Adler, adaptation of the novel by Friedman (produced New Haven, Connecticut, 1968).
Steambath (produced New York, 1970). New York, Knopf, 1971.
First Offenders, with Jacques Levy (also co-director: produced New York, 1973).
A Foot in the Door (produced New York, 1979).

Screenplays: *The Owl and the Pussycat*, 1971; *Stir Crazy*, 1980; *Doctor Detroit*, with others, 1983; *Splash*, with others, 1984.

Novels

Stern. New York, Simon and Schuster, 1962; London, Deutsch, 1963.
A Mother's Kisses. New York, Simon and Schuster, 1964; London, Cape, 1965.
The Dick. New York, Knopf, 1970; London, Cape, 1971.
About Harry Towns. New York, Knopf, 1974; London, Cape, 1975.
Tokyo Woes. New York, Fine, 1985; London, Abacus, 1986.
Violencia. New York, Atlantic Monthly Press, 1988.
The Current Climate. New York, Atlantic Monthly Press, 1989.

Short Stories

Far from the City of Class and Other Stories. New York, Frommer-Pasmantier, 1963.
Black Angels. New York, Simon and Schuster, 1966; London, Cape, 1967.
Let's Hear It for a Beautiful Guy and Other Works of Short Fiction. New York, Fine, 1984.

Other

The Lonely Guy's Book of Life. New York, McGraw Hill, 1978.

Editor, *Black Humor*. New York, Bantam, and London, Corgi, 1965.

*

Critical Study: *Bruce Jay Friedman* by Max F. Schulz, New York, Twayne, 1974.

Theatrical Activities:
Director: **Play**—*First Offenders* (co-director, with Jacques Levy), New York, 1973.

*   *   *

It has always been the temptation of fiction writers to turn to the theatre. From Balzac through Henry James 19th-century novelists tried their hand at playwriting, with quite mixed results. Most of us are now interested in only one of Balzac's plays, *Mercadet*, and that probably because of its influence on *Waiting for Godot*. James's plays are readily available in Leon Edel's fine edition but only specialists seem to bother to read them. The same is true for most of the plays of the other 19th-century novelists-turned-dramatist. This rule-of-thumb applies also to certain of our contemporaries: Saul Bellow and John Hawkes, for example, have turned from first-rate fiction to the theatre; the results have been somewhat frustrating and disappointing.

The case of Hawkes is instructive because his plays seem largely extensions of his novels and elaborate on certain of their themes. Hawkes had already published four superb novels by the time he brought out his collection of plays, *The Innocent Party*, in 1966. It would seem that he turned to the theatre only after he felt his position as a novelist was fairly assured. Bruce Jay Friedman appeared to follow the same pattern although he turned to playwriting earlier in his career than Hawkes. The change from fiction to drama was also managed, from all indications, with fewer problems. *Scuba Duba* and *Steambath* are clearly more stageable, if less literary, than Hawkes's plays.

But like the plays in *The Innocent Party* Friedman's work for the theatre is thematically very much tied to his fiction. *Scuba Duba* and *Steambath* use the ambience, character types, and other literary props familiar to readers of Friedman's novels and collections of stories. Guilt, failure, and frustration are words which come to mind when we look at any part of his *oeuvre*.

Scuba Duba bears the subtitle "a tense comedy"; so might almost anything else Friedman has written because laughs come always at the expense of overbearing psychic pain in all of his work. Harold Wonder, the 35-year-old worrier who uses a scythe as a more aggressive kind of security blanket, has rented a chateau in the south of France. As the play opens he laments the fact that his wife has just run off with a black man. Harold's urban Jewish intonation is evident even in his first speech: "I really needed this. This is exactly what I came here for." He feels the need to communicate his *tsuris* to anyone who will listen. An attractive young lady, Miss Janus, is all too willing to help out, but Harold—like most of Friedman's other heroes—seems especially drawn to his psychiatrist and his Jewish mother. The former, aptly named Dr. Schoenfeld, who appears in the first act as a "cut-out" and returns in the flesh in Act 2, warns him in accustomed psychiatric fashion: ". . . you've never once looked at life sideways . . ." Harold's mother seems cut from the same cloth as the mothers in Friedman's novels *Stern*, *A Mother's Kisses*, and *The Dick*. Harold speaks to her long-distance and the telephone conversation which follows should be familiar to readers of the fiction of Philip Roth, Wallace Markfield, Herbert Gold, and other American Jewish writers. Harold's mother's voice is perfectly tuned: "That's all right, Harold. I'll just consider that my payment after thirty-six years of being your mother."

As the play develops the stage gets more and more

crowded. A namedropping French landlady, an American tourist who demands proximity to a Chinese restaurant, a thief with an aphoristic turn ("All men are thieves"), an anti-American gendarme, a "wild-looking blonde" named Cheyenne who prefers "Bernie" Malamud and "those urban Jews" to C.P. Snow—all appear at one time or other. The main confrontation occurs in the second act when Harold's wife appears, followed shortly by two black men, one of whom is her lover. Harold's reaction involves much of the ambivalence experienced by Friedman Jews when in the company of blacks. The hero of Friedman's first novel, for example, went out of his way to express an affection he was never certain was compelling enough: ". . . Stern, who had a special feeling for all Negroes, hugged him [Crib] in a show of brotherhood."

Harold, schlemiel that he is, ends up by losing his wife and vows to "get started in my new life." Stern and Kenneth LePeters (the hero of The Dick) make similar resolutions and LePeters even goes to the point of leaving his wife and planning an extended trip with his daughter.

Friedman has been grouped with the so-called black humorists on several occasions. In a foreword he wrote for a collection of stories, Black Humor (which included his own story "Blank Angels"), he remarked: "There is a fading line between fantasy and reality . . ." This is evident in Scuba Duba but perhaps even more in Steambath. Almost half way through the first act, the protagonist Tandy makes the shocked discovery: ". . . We're dead? Is that what you were going to say? That's what I was going to say. That's what we are. The second I said it, I knew it. Bam! Dead! Just like that! Christ!" Until this point in the play all indications are of a real steambath; then everything suddenly dilates into symbol and "fantasy," with no noticeable change in the dramatic movement. (John Hawkes used the steambath in the fifth chapter of his novel The Lime Twig with somewhat the same symbolical intent.)

Tandy is clearly not quite ready for death and protests the Attendant's (read God) decision through the remainder of the play. He seems very like Kenneth LePeters at the end of The Dick. He is on the verge of doing things he likes—writing a novel about Charlemagne, working for a charity to help brain-damaged welders, courting a Bryn Mawr girl who makes shish kebab—after divorcing his wife and giving up his job "teaching art appreciation over at the Police Academy." Tandy shares his frustration with a blonde girl named Meredith in somewhat the way Harold Wonder shared his plight, conversationally, with Miss Janus in Scuba Duba.

Max Schulz, in a very good book on the American Jewish novel, Radical Sophistication, speaks of Friedman's manner as having something "of the stand-up comic." This is especially noticeable in Steambath. Its humor favors the incongruous and unlikely. One can almost hear Woody Allen pronouncing some of the lines with considerable relish, like Tandy's incredulous response when he realizes that God is a Puerto Rican steambath attendant or when he discovers what he stands to lose by being dead: "No more airline stewardesses . . . Newsweek . . . Jesus, no more Newsweek."

Much of the humor has to do with popular culture. Bieberman, who makes intermittent appearances, is very much taken with the actors and baseball players of the 1940's. Other characters refer to the impact made by such essentials of television as the David Frost Show and pro football (American style). Names of every variety, including those of defeated political candidates (Mario Procaccino) and editors of magazines (Norman Podhoretz), are introduced incongruously and irreverently in the conversations. Theodore Solotaroff believes that

nostalgia has a particular attraction for many Jewish writers: some of them, like Gold or Bruce Jay Friedman or Wallace Markfield or Irwin Faust, seem to possess virtually total recall of their adolescent years, as though there were still some secret meaning that resides in the image of Buster Brown shoes, or Edward G. Robinson's snarl, or Ralston's checkerboard package.

How much to the point of this remark is Steambath!

There is a good deal of the spirit of the second-generation American Jew in Friedman's plays as well as in his novels. He has caught this verbal rhythm and pulse beat in much the way that Philip Roth and Woody Allen have.

—Melvin J. Friedman

FRIEL, Brian (Bernard Patrick Friel). Irish. Born in Killyclogher, County Tyrone, 9 January 1929. Educated at St. Columb's College, Derry, 1941–46; St. Patrick's College, Maynooth, 1946–49, B.A. 1949; St. Mary's Training College (now St. Joseph's College of Education), Belfast, 1949–50. Married Anne Morrison in 1954; four daughters and one son. Schoolteacher in primary and intermediate schools in Derry, 1950–60. Since 1960 full-time writer: founder, with Stephen Rea, Field Day Theatre Company, Northern Ireland, 1980. Observer, for five months in 1963, Tyrone Guthrie Theatre, Minneapolis. Recipient: Irish Arts Council Macauley fellowship, 1963; Christopher Ewart-Biggs Memorial award, 1982; New York Drama Critics Circle award, 1989, 1991; Olivier award, 1991; Evening Standard award, 1991; Plays and Players award, 1991; Writers Guild of Great Britain award, 1991; Tony award, 1992. D.Litt.: Rosary College, Chicago, 1979; National University of Ireland, Dublin, 1983; University of Ulster, Coleraine, 1986; Queen's University, Belfast, 1992; Trinity College, Dublin, 1992. Member, Irish Academy of Letters, 1972, Aosdana, 1983, and Irish Senate, 1987. Agent: Curtis Brown, 162–168 Regent Street, London W1R 5TB, England. Address: Drumaweir House, Greencastle, County Donegal, Ireland.

PUBLICATIONS

Plays

The Francophile (produced Belfast, 1960; as The Doubtful Paradise, produced Belfast, 1960).
The Enemy Within (produced Dublin, 1962). Dublin, Gallery Press, and Newark, Delaware, Proscenium Press, 1979.
The Blind Mice (produced Dublin, 1963; Belfast, 1964).
Philadelphia, Here I Come! (produced Dublin, 1964; New York, 1966; London, 1967). London, Faber, 1965; New York, Farrar Straus, 1966.
The Loves of Cass McGuire (broadcast 1966; produced New York, 1966; Belfast, 1968; London, 1970). London, Faber, and New York, Farrar Straus, 1967.
Lovers: Part One: Winners; Part Two: Losers (produced Dublin, 1967; New York, 1968; London, 1969). New York, Farrar Straus, 1968; London, Faber, 1969.
Crystal and Fox (produced Dublin, 1968; Los Angeles, 1970; New York, 1973). London, Faber, 1970; with The Mundy Scheme, New York, Farrar Straus, 1970.

The Mundy Scheme (produced Dublin and New York, 1969). With *Crystal and Fox*, New York, Farrar Straus, 1970.

The Gentle Island (produced Dublin, 1971). London, Davis Poynter, 1974.

The Freedom of the City (produced Dublin, London, and Chicago, 1973; New York, 1974). London, Faber, 1974; New York, French, 1979.

Volunteers (produced Dublin, 1975). London, Faber, 1979.

Living Quarters (produced Dublin, 1977; New York, 1983). London, Faber, 1978; in *Selected Plays*, 1984.

Faith Healer (produced New York, 1979; London, 1981). London, Faber, 1980; in *Selected Plays*, 1984.

Aristocrats (produced Dublin, 1979; London, 1988; New York 1989). Dublin, Gallery Press, 1980; in *Selected Plays*, 1984.

Translations (produced Derry, 1980; New York and London, 1981). London, Faber, 1981; in *Selected Plays*, 1984.

American Welcome (produced Louisville and New York, 1980). Published in *The Best Short Plays 1981*, edited by Stanley Richards, Radnor, Pennsylvania, Chilton, 1981.

Three Sisters, adaptation of a play by Chekhov (produced Derry, 1981). Dublin, Gallery Press, 1981.

The Communication Cord (produced Derry, 1982; London, 1983; Seattle, 1984). London, Faber, 1983.

Selected Plays (includes *Philadelphia, Here I Come!*; *The Freedom of the City*; *Living Quarters*; *Aristocrats*; *Faith Healer*; *Translations*). London, Faber, 1984; Washington, D.C., Catholic University of America Press, 1986.

Fathers and Sons, adaptation of a novel by Turgenev (produced London, 1987). London, Faber, 1987.

Making History (produced Derry and London, 1988; New York, 1991). London, Faber, 1989.

Dancing at Lughnasa (produced Dublin and London, 1990; New York, 1991). London, Faber, 1990.

The London Vertigo, adaptation of a play by Charles MacKlin (produced Dublin, 1992).

A Month in the Country, adaptation of the play by Turgenev (produced Dublin, 1992).

Screenplay: *Philadelphia, Here I Come!*, 1970.

Radio Plays: *A Sort of Freedom*, 1958; *To This Hard House*, 1958; *The Founder Members*, 1964; *The Loves of Cass McGuire*, 1966.

Short Stories

The Saucer of Larks. New York, Doubleday, 1962; London, Gollancz, 1963.

The Gold in the Sea. London, Gollancz, and New York, Doubleday, 1966.

A Saucer of Larks: Stories of Ireland (selection). London, Arrow, 1969.

Selected Stories. Dublin, Gallery Press, 1979.

The Diviner. Dublin, O'Brien Press, and London, Allison and Busby, 1983.

Other

Editor, *The Last of the Name*, by Charles McGlinchey. Belfast, Blackstaff Press, 1986.

*

Bibliography: *Ten Modern Irish Playwrights* by Kimball King, New York, Garland, 1979.

Critical Studies: *Brian Friel* by D.E.S. Maxwell, Lewisburg, Pennsylvania, Bucknell University Press, 1973; *Brian Friel: The Growth of an Irish Dramatist* by Ulf Dantanus, Gothenburg, Sweden, Gothenburg Studies in English, 1985, London, Faber, 1987; *Brian Friel* by George O'Brien, Dublin, Gill and Macmillan, and Boston, Twayne, 1990; *Brian Friel and Ireland's Drama* by Richard Pine, London, Routledge, 1990.

* * *

Brian Friel began as a writer of short stories, and the art of the short story permeates all of his dramatic work. His drama is lyrical, intimate, and understated in ways perhaps more common to the short-story form than to the stage. Yet Friel has proved, during a career spanning 30 years, his theatrical skills in arousing and maintaining audience interest; therefore, his narrative power cannot be described satisfactorily in terms of the short-story writer. One should recall that Chekhov, the writer with whom Friel is most often compared, also had two strings to his bow.

After a few radio plays written for BBC Northern Ireland, Friel's first significant stage play (*The Enemy Within*) was written for the Abbey Theatre. The significance lies less in the play itself, a history play set in the seventh century, than in its introduction of Friel as an Abbey playwright. This tradition (founded by Yeats and Synge and carried on by O'Casey) was by 1962 much attenuated, yet the role it provided for Irish playwrights was still nominally if problematically available, to mediate between individual vision and social or socio-political reality. Friel's originality lay in his perception of the critical state of this relationship in modern Irish life. For Friel, there was an unacknowledged gap between the individual mind (and experience) and a social reality which was crumbling at an alarming rate, so that old beliefs, old values, and settled lifestyles (heretofore rendered coherent by the patriarchal nature of Irish authority) no longer retained a satisfying viability. A major statement on this alienated condition appeared in *Philadelphia, Here I Come!*, one of Friel's best and most enduring plays. Once more significantly, this play was *not* staged at the Abbey Theatre, to which Friel did not return until 1973; in the meantime he worked out his experimental and revolutionary ideas in alternative theatres in Dublin and elsewhere, under the influence of directors not tied to conventional notions of production, such as Tyrone Guthrie.

Philadelphia, Here I Come! might at first sight appear to be just one more Irish peasant play, addressing topics familiar from the canon of Irish drama. But in effect Friel subverts the tradition. His play is not mainly concerned with a conventional theme, such as emigration, the land, or a love-match. Its primary concentration is on the alienated consciousness of a young man, Gareth O'Donnell, whose relationship with his widowed father is an image of a new, privatized awareness of human isolation. Friel divides this character in two, Private and Public, to be played by two actors, "two views of the one man." Private Gar, the "alter ego," is invisible to all on stage but serves to articulate for the audience the inner thoughts and feelings of the young hero. These thoughts and feelings give a Hamlet-like dimension to the characterization, and this is where the real power of the play lies, though it is also supremely well balanced in its use of comedy and pathos.

Friel himself has said that the two plays which followed, *The Loves of Cass McGuire* and *Lovers*, share with *Philadelphia* the common theme of love. It is perhaps truer to observe that they are about loneliness and the futility of communication. Each is also theatrically experimental. After

1972, however, a very different emphasis makes its appearance in Friel's work. In January 1972 the political situation in Northern Ireland took a turn for the worse, as British paratroopers shot 13 civilians on a civil rights march in Derry. Like many another Irish writer Friel was outraged, particularly as Derry was his adopted city. He wrote *The Freedom of the City* to express his anger at the whitewashing Widgery Report, which exonerated the British army. Its premiere at the new Abbey Theatre marked Friel's return to nationalist concerns. The play, while not among Friel's best, is remarkably skilful in its adaptation of Brechtian techniques of storytelling to a current political situation, even though critics in London and New York faulted it on political grounds. On these grounds it is a play to be linked with *Translations* and *Making History*, as Friel became increasingly preoccupied with the crisis in Northern Ireland. *Translations* was staged by the Field Day Theatre Company, established by Friel and actor Stephen Rea to intervene culturally in this crisis by touring with plays which addressed specific issues. To some degree, Friel became a political dramatist.

Translations, a history play set in the year 1833, is one of Friel's best and most internationally performed plays. The action takes place in a hedgeschool and uses two distinct but here interrelated issues to explore skilfully a community in crisis, and a native culture at the point of dissolution. The issues are education and cartography, which in a colonial situation relate specifically to language and identity. Though the implications of the play are far-ranging, there is, as always in Friel, a simple human situation at its core: here, a love story between the English soldier Yolland and the Irish woman Máire (deemed to be speaking only Gaelic throughout). The tragic failure of this affair recounts a whole national disaster.

Dancing at Lughnasa, Friel's most successful play to date, shows how inadequate and even now falsifying it is to categorise him as a political playwright. The fact that it was premiered by the Abbey Theatre rather than by Field Day suggests that Friel himself felt the need to escape the confines of the Field Day ideology. *Dancing at Lughnasa* is a reminder that Friel is first and foremost an artist, a storyteller, a playwright for whom nuances of emotional experience take priority over ideas. Even in the 1970's, when his work seemed to point inevitably to the writing of *Translations*, he could confound the critics with such essentially non-political plays as *The Gentle Island*, *Living Quarters*, *Aristocrats*, and—above all—*Faith Healer*. The latter stands out as one of Friel's most original and poetic plays, occupied with the ambivalent powers of the eponymous artist figure. If *Dancing at Lughnasa* filters the doomed perfection of the past through the imagination of a boy about to develop into a writer, *Faith Healer* goes to the root of the mature artist's guilt for his failure to intervene in that doom.

Faith Healer comprises only four monologues, two from Frank and one each from his wife Grace and his impresario Teddy. In Pirandellian fashion the audience must sift the truth of what these characters contradictorily narrate. The stories they tell not only reinforce Friel's skill, but their climax also returns us to Ballybeg, the village invented for *Philadelphia, Here I Come!*. In a sense the exile of that play returns to his place of birth and is destroyed in *Faith Healer*. Thus Friel's plays inter-relate in patterns which tell not only the story of Ireland and her wounds but also the timeless story of human longing for completion, forgiveness, and love.

—Christopher Murray

————————

FRISBY, Terence. British. Born in New Cross, London, 28 November 1932. Educated at Dobwalls Village School; Dartford Grammar School; Central School of Speech Training and Dramatic Art, London, 1955–57. Married Christine Vecchione in 1963 (divorced); one son. Worked as a salesman, capstan lathe operator, factory hand, waiter, chauffeur, chucker-out at the Hammersmith Palais, etc.; since 1957 professional actor; also a producer. Resident director, New Theatre, Bromley, Kent, 1963–64. Recipient: Writers Guild of Great Britain award, for screenplay, 1970; Houston International Film Festival gold award, for comedy, 1991. Agent: Lemon, Unna, and Durbridge, 24 Pottery Lane, Holland Park, London W11 4LZ. Address: 72 Bishops Mansions, Bishops Park Road, London SW6 6DZ, England.

PUBLICATIONS

Plays

The Subtopians (also director: produced London, 1964). London, French, 1964.
There's a Girl in My Soup (produced London, 1966; New York, 1967). London and New York, French, 1968.
The Bandwagon (produced London, 1969). London, French, 1973.
It's All Right If I Do It (produced Leicester and London, 1977). London, French, 1977.
Seaside Postcard (also director: produced London, 1977). London, French, 1978.
First Night (produced London, 1987).
Just Remember Two Things: It's Not Fair and Don't Be Late (broadcast 1988). Published in *Best Radio Plays of 1988*, London, Methuen, 1988.

Screenplay: *There's a Girl in My Soup*, 1970.

Radio Play: *Just Remember Two Things: It's Not Fair and Don't Be Late*, 1988.

Television Plays: *Guilty*, 1964; *Public Eye* series, 1964; *Take Care of Madam*, 1965; *Adam Adamant* series, 1966; *More Deadly Than the Sword*, 1966; *Don't Forget the Basics*, 1967; *Lucky Feller* series, 1976; *That's Love* series, 1988–92.

*

Critical Studies: *Anger and After* by John Russell Taylor, London, Methuen, 1962, revised edition, 1969, as *The Angry Theatre*, New York, Hill and Wang, 1962, revised edition, 1969; *The Season* by William Goldman, New York, Harcourt Brace, 1969, revised edition, New York, Limelight, 1984.

Theatrical Activities:
Director: **Plays**—in various repertory companies, including plays at Bromley, Kent, 1963–64; *The Subtopians*, London, 1964; *Seaside Postcard*, London, 1977.
Actor (as Terence Holland, 1957–66): **Plays**—over 200 roles in repertory theatres in Bromley, Guildford, Lincoln, Richmond, York; London debut as Charlie Pepper in *Gentleman's Pastime* by Marion Hunt, 1958; in *A Sense of Detachment* by John Osborne, London, 1973; *X* by Barry Reckord, London, 1974; Clive Popkiss in *Rookery Nook* by Ben Travers, London, 1979; Father Mullarkey in *Once a Catholic* by Mary O'Malley, toured, 1980–81 and 1986; Birdboot in *The Real Inspector Hound* by Tom Stoppard, and Leslie in *Seaside Postcard*, toured, 1983–84; Archie Rice in

The Entertainer by John Osborne, Sonning, Berkshire, 1984; David Bliss in *Hay Fever* by Noel Coward, Manchester, 1985; other roles in London and on tour. **Radio**—Narrator in *Just Remember Two Things: It's Not Fair and Don't Be Late*, 1988. **Television**—*Play School*, 1964–66; *It Must Be Something in the Water* by Alan Plater, 1973; *Two Townsmen*, adaptation of Thomas Hardy's work by Douglas Livingstone, 1974; *Leeds—United!* by Colin Welland, 1974; *When the Boys Come out to Play* by Richard Harris, 1975; *The Brothers*, 1976; *The Madness Museum* by Ken Campbell, 1986; *Signals*, 1990; *A Strike Out of Time*, 1991; *That's Love*, 1992.

*   *   *

Terence Frisby's first play, *The Subtopians*, was greeted with eulogies when, in 1964, it was seen for the first time. It was, critics decided, funny but complex, accurately worked out, deeply felt in spite of its genuine comedy, serious in intention but almost painfully hilarious, and it had an unbreakable grip on the realities of social life in the 1960's.

Frisby was 32 when *The Subtopians* arrived to signal a newcomer whose gifts were, to say the least, so interesting that his future activities were sure to demand close attention. Part at least of the technical neatness of his first play was due to his training at the Central School of Speech Training and Dramatic Art and to his work as an actor in repertory, musicals, and films, as an entertainer in night clubs and cabaret, and as a director. There is a solid foundation of technique beneath the sometimes unkind observation and harsh comedy.

In 1966 *There's a Girl in My Soup* brought Frisby one of the greatest commercial successes in the modern theatre, running for six years in the West End and, at the same time, pleasing most of the critics. Like *The Subtopians*, it has beautifully efficient machinery and precision of observation. Its hero has the sort of position in life—he is an expert on food, writing for intellectual periodicals—which once would have pointed him out as a figure of fun but, in 1966, assured an audience that he was a leader of thought and fashion whose familiarity with the best restaurants is intrinsically romantic and enviable. Thus he is in a position to follow an exhausting, eventful career as an amorist whose endless successes are with the young who find his expertise, and the attitude towards him of those whose efforts he criticises, altogether glamorous. It is less the dialogue or anything explicit in the play than the form it takes and the succession of events which indicate that behind the parade of insatiable appetite for change and his pride in his sexual prowess he is at the same time both lonely and uncertain of his attractiveness to those whom he regards as victims. Frisby naturally chooses to study the girl whose victim he becomes, in whose life he is only a pleasant interlude. The "trendiness" and "contemporaneity" of *There's a Girl in My Soup* carried the play round a triumphal tour of the world's theatres, with productions not only throughout the English-speaking theatre but in most European countries as well as in Turkey, Israel, and Mexico.

The course of events which led to the production of Frisby's third play, *The Bandwagon*, rose out of his success as a script writer. *Guilty*, a one-off piece for the BBC in 1964, was followed by a comedy, *Don't Forget the Basics*, for Independent Television and contributions to various series, notably to *Public Eye*, which at its best gave an almost continental seediness to the activities of a provincial private detective, and *Adam Adamant*, in which adventure stories which might almost have come to birth in a boys' comic were treated with unusual and preposterous elegancies and elaborations. *The*

Bandwagon, originally *Some Have Greatness Thrust upon Them*, was to be one of BBC television's socially conscious Wednesday Plays. It chose to imagine the situation of a stupid, ugly, graceless teenage girl, a member of a family of almost appalling fecundity—her mother and her sister are both pregnant when the play begins—who discovers that, though unmarried, she is to become the mother of quintuplets. Her fecundity, before drugs inducing multiple births had won any special attention, reaches the ears of popular newspapers, who make her a heroine, and television, which interviews her. The interview comes to an end when Aurora (the most unfortunately named heroine) explains the physiological misinformation and ignorance that are responsible for her plight. Frisby's refusal to alter a line which, the BBC believed, would give unnecessary offence, led to the Corporation's refusal to produce the play.

The BBC was, perhaps, entirely wrong. The line—"My friend Syl told me it was safe standing up"—is all of a piece—with a matter-of-fact simplicity which makes Aurora almost unexploitable. Aurora is manoeuvred into marriage, and has to be hurried from the church into childbed; and so have her mother and sister. The play belongs to the tradition of broad farce, and its final scene, as the women-folk depart from the altar in agonized haste, sacrifices the precarious dignity and simplicity which have won the sympathy of the audience. *The Bandwagon*, in the good old days of curtain-raisers, could have stopped at its natural end, the silent, almost unnerving confrontation of two essentially pathetic victims of exploitation, Aurora and her husband-to-be, and have retained its integrity.

Although *The Bandwagon* seemed, when it was new, likely to follow Frisby's earlier plays and become an outstanding success, it did not do so. Possibly its depressing social milieu and its unfriendly view of what we have been taught to call the "media," as well as its combination of farce with serious moral concern, simply bothered audiences who found Aurora to be no more than a heroine of farce. In the same way, neither *It's All Right If I Do It*, and *Seaside Postcard* won any startling success. Frisby's gift for comic incident and comic dialogue, obviously rooted in a serious view of society, has not, perhaps, found its audience when it applies to areas outside the provinces and the glossy West End world of *There's a Girl in My Soup*.

—Henry Raynor

————

FRY, Christopher. British. Born Christopher Fry Harris in Bristol, 18 December 1907. Educated at Bedford Modern School, 1918–26. Served in the Non-Combatant Corps, 1940–44. Married Phyllis Marjorie Hart in 1936 (died 1987); one son. Teacher, Bedford Froebel Kindergarten, 1926–27; actor and office worker, Citizen House, Bath, 1927; schoolmaster, Hazelwood School, Limpsfield, Surrey, 1928–31; secretary to H. Rodney Bennett, 1931–32; founding director, Tunbridge Wells Repertory Players, 1932–35; lecturer and editor of schools magazine, Dr. Barnardo's Homes, 1934–39; director, 1939–40, and visiting director, 1945–46, Oxford Playhouse; visiting director, 1946, and staff dramatist, 1947, Arts Theatre Club, London. Also composer. Recipient: Shaw Prize Fund award, 1948; Foyle poetry prize, 1951; New York Drama Critics Circle award, 1951, 1952, 1956; Queen's gold medal,

1962; Royal Society of Literature Heinemann award, 1962. D.A.: Manchester Polytechnic, 1966; D.Litt.: Oxford University, 1988. Honorary Fellow, Manchester Polytechnic, 1988. Fellow, Royal Society of Literature. Agent: ACTAC Ltd, 15 High Street, Ramsbury, Wiltshire SN8 2PA. Address: The Toft, East Dean, near Chichester, West Sussex PO18 0JA, England.

PUBLICATIONS

Plays

Youth and the Peregrines (produced Tunbridge Wells, Kent, 1934).

She Shall Have Music (lyrics only, with Ronald Frankau), book by Frank Eyton, music by Fry and Monte Crick (produced London, 1934).

To Sea in a Sieve (as Christopher Harris) (revue; produced Reading, 1935).

Open Door (produced London, 1936). Goldings, Hertfordshire, Printed by the Boys at the Press of Dr. Barnardo's Homes, n.d.

The Boy with a Cart: Cuthman, Saint of Sussex (produced Coleman's Hatch, Sussex, 1938; London, 1950; New York, 1953). London, Oxford University Press, 1939; New York, Oxford University Press, 1951.

The Tower (produced Tewkesbury, Gloucestershire, 1939).

Thursday's Child: A Pageant, music by Martin Shaw (produced London, 1939). London, Girls' Friendly Society, 1939.

A Phoenix Too Frequent (produced London, 1946; Cambridge, Massachusetts, 1948; New York, 1950). London, Hollis and Carter, 1946; New York, Oxford University Press, 1949.

The Firstborn (broadcast 1947; produced Edinburgh, 1948). Cambridge, University Press, 1946; New York, Oxford University Press, 1950; revised version (produced London, 1952; New York, 1958), London and New York, Oxford University Press, 1952, 1958.

The Lady's Not for Burning (produced London, 1948; New York, 1950). London and New York, Oxford University Press, 1949; revised version, 1950, 1958.

Thor, With Angels (produced Canterbury, 1948; Washington, D.C., 1950; London, 1951). Canterbury, Goulden, 1948; New York, Oxford University Press, 1949.

Venus Observed (produced London, 1950; New York, 1952). London and New York, Oxford University Press, 1950.

Ring round the Moon: A Charade with Music, adaptation of a play by Jean Anouilh (produced London and New York, 1950). London and New York, Oxford University Press, 1950.

A Sleep of Prisoners (produced Oxford, London, and New York, 1951). London and New York, Oxford University Press, 1951.

The Dark Is Light Enough: A Winter Comedy (produced Edinburgh and London, 1954; New York, 1955). London and New York, Oxford University Press, 1954.

The Lark, adaptation of a play by Jean Anouilh (produced London, 1955). London, Methuen, 1955; New York, Oxford University Press, 1956.

Tiger at the Gates, adaptation of a play by Jean Giraudoux (produced London and New York, 1955). London, Methuen, 1955; New York, Oxford University Press, 1956; as *The Trojan War Will Not Take Place* (produced London, 1983), Methuen, 1983.

Duel of Angels, adaptation of a play by Jean Giraudoux (produced London, 1958; New York, 1960). London, Methuen, 1958; New York, Oxford University Press, 1959.

Curtmantle (produced in Dutch, Tilburg, Netherlands, 1961; Edinburgh and London, 1962). London and New York, Oxford University Press, 1961.

Judith, adaptation of a play by Jean Giraudoux (produced London, 1962). London, Methuen, 1962.

The Bible: Original Screenplay, assisted by Jonathan Griffin. New York, Pocket Books, 1966.

Peer Gynt, adaptation of the play by Ibsen (produced Chichester, 1970). London and New York, Oxford University Press, 1970.

A Yard of Sun: A Summer Comedy (produced Nottingham and London, 1970; Cleveland, 1972). London and New York, Oxford University Press, 1970.

The Brontës of Haworth (televised 1973). London, Davis Poynter, 2 vols., 1974.

Cyrano de Bergerac, adaptation of the play by Edmond Rostand (produced Chichester, 1975). London and New York, Oxford University Press, 1975.

Paradise Lost, music by Penderecki, adaptation of the poem by Milton (produced Chicago, 1978). London, Schott, 1978.

Selected Plays (includes *The Boy with a Cart, A Phoenix Too Frequent, The Lady's Not for Burning, A Sleep of Prisoners, Curtmantle*). Oxford and New York, Oxford University Press, 1985.

One Thing More; or, Caedmon Construed (produced Chelmsford, Essex, 1986; London, 1988). New York, London, King's College, and New York, Dramatists Play Service, 1987.

The Seasons, poems to accompany Julie Cooper's adaptation of Vivaldi's *The Four Seasons* (produced London, 1990).

A Journey into Light, music by Robert Walker (produced Chichester, 1992).

Screenplays: *The Beggar's Opera*, with Denis Cannan, 1953; *A Queen Is Crowned* (documentary), 1953; *Ben Hur*, 1959; *Barabbas*, 1962; *The Bible: In the Beginning*, 1966.

Radio Plays: for *Children's Hour* series, 1939–40; *The Firstborn*, 1947; *Rhineland Journey*, 1948.

Television Plays: *The Canary*, 1950; *The Tenant of Wildfell Hall*, 1968; *The Brontës of Haworth* (four plays), 1973; *The Best of Enemies*, 1976; *Sister Dora*, from the book by Jo Manton, 1977.

Verse

Root and Sky: Poetry from the Plays of Christopher Fry, edited by Charles E. and Jean G. Wadsworth. Cambridge, Rampant Lions Press, and Boston, Godine, 1975.

Other

An Experience of Critics, with *The Approach to Dramatic Criticism* by W.A. Darlington and others, edited by Kaye Webb. London, Perpetua Press, 1952; New York, Oxford University Press, 1953.

The Boat That Mooed (for children). New York, Macmillan, 1966.

Can You Find Me: A Family History. London, Oxford University Press, 1978; New York, Oxford University Press, 1979.

Death Is a Kind of Love (lecture). Cranberry Isles, Maine, Tidal Press, 1979.

Genius, Talent and Failure: The Brontës (lecture). London, King's College, 1987.

Looking for a Language (lecture). London, King's College, 1992.

Editor, *Charlie Hammond's Sketchbook*. Oxford, Oxford University Press, 1980.

Translator, *The Boy and the Magic*, by Colette. London, Dobson, 1964.

Translator, with Timberlake Wertenbaker, *Jean Anouilh: Five Plays*. London, Heinemann, 1986.

Incidental Music: *A Winter's Tale*, London, 1951; recorded by Caedmon.

*

Bibliography: by B.L. Schear and E.G. Prater, in *Tulane Drama Review 4* (New Orleans), March 1960.

Manuscript Collection: Harvard University Theatre Collection, Cambridge, Massachusetts.

Critical Studies: *Christopher Fry: An Appreciation*, London, Nevill, 1950, and *Christopher Fry*, London, Longman, 1954, revised edition, 1962, both by Derek Stanford; *The Drama of Comedy: Victim and Victor* by Nelson Vos, Richmond, Virginia, John Knox Press, 1965; *Creed and Drama* by W.M. Merchant, London, SPCK, 1965; *The Christian Tradition in Modern British Verse Drama* by William V. Spanos, New Brunswick, New Jersey, Rutgers University Press, 1967; *Christopher Fry* by Emil Roy, Carbondale, Southern Illinois University Press, 1968; *Christopher Fry: A Critical Essay*, Grand Rapids, Michigan, Eerdmans, 1970, and *More Than the Ear Discovers: God in the Plays of Christopher Fry*, Chicago, Loyola University Press, 1983, both by Stanley M. Wiersma; *Poetic Drama* by Glenda Leeming, London, Macmillan, 1989.

Theatrical Activities:
Director: **Plays**—*How-Do, Princess?* by Ivor Novello, toured, 1936; *The Circle of Chalk* by James Laver, London, 1945; *The School for Scandal* by Sheridan, London, 1946; *A Phoenix Too Frequent*, Brighton, 1950; *The Lady's Not for Burning*, toured, 1971; and others.
Actor: **Plays**—in repertory, Bath, 1937.

Christopher Fry comments:

The way a man writes for the theatre depends on the way he looks at life. If, in his experience, direction and purpose seem to be all-pervading factors, pattern and shape are necessary to his writing. The verse form is an effort to be true to what Eleanor, in *Curtmantle*, calls "the silent order whose speech is all visible things." No event is understandable in a prose sense alone. Its ultimate meaning (that is to say, the complete life of the event, seen in its eternal context) is a poetic meaning. The comedies try to explore a reality behind appearances. "Something condones the world incorrigibly" says Thomas Mendip in *The Lady's Not for Burning*—in spite of the "tragic" nature of life. The problem, a long way from being solved, is how to contain the complexities and paradoxes within two hours of entertainment: how to define the creative pattern of life without the danger of dogmatic statement. Dogma is static; life is movement. "La vérité est dans une nuance."

*   *   *

Christopher Fry's work was doubtless overrated in the fruitful years of *The Lady's Not for Burning* and *A Sleep of Prisoners*; it is most certainly underrated today. This is in part due to an integrity and consistency in the work of a playwright who has pursued his own style of the serio-comic and chosen to ignore fashion. It is as if Beckett and the theatre of the absurd had not existed, nor Brecht and the practice of epic theatre with its oblique devices of structure and technique, nor the socially and politically committed drama following Osborne's *Look Back in Anger*; and Fry's reputation has paid the price. It remains to be seen whether his neglect of contemporary trends matters in the final verdict.

In *A Yard of Sun*, Fry is still writing in that highly idiosyncratic, all-but-verse idiom of loose pentameters which drew attention to his earliest plays. Characteristically mixing the colloquial and the allusive, a minor character can say, "I pick words gingerly like a rose out of thorns," and at a stroke equalizes his role with that of a major, thus by prosaic kitchen-sink standards making all the parts equally literate and classless. Or Angelino Bruno, one of the two central characters whose families are unexpectedly united after World War II, can come out with a startling turn of expression which fixes and underscores the general statement of the stage:

What a settling-up God's having this week!
Both of us within two days. Well, once
The bit's between His teeth things start to move.

Although it may not bear close analysis as poetry on the page, verbal panache of this kind keeps Fry's stage alive when a situation is static. It is often spendthrift with the necessary economy of the action, and the idiom which refreshed the grim postwar years and dazzled the critics can now seem irrelevant, even facile.

But Fry was seeking a spiritual idiom for a contemporary and unobtrusively Christian verse drama after T.S. Eliot had prepared the ground with *Murder in the Cathedral* (1935) and *The Family Reunion* (1939). Where Eliot was concerned to find a spare and unobtrusive verse form designed to control the speech and movement on a stage of modern martyrs, Fry, in a less certain style but with more sense of the stage, aimed with abandon at a general mood to match his themes. There are moments in *A Sleep of Prisoners*, possibly the best antiwar play of its period, when the verse achieves the richness of both tonal and physical embodiment of the stage moment while exploring a verbal idea:

How ceaseless the earth is. How it goes on.
Nothing has happened except silence where sound was,
Stillness where movement was . . .

These lines are spoken by the figure of Adam just after he has witnessed the murder of Abel his son, and they enact both the father's horror and the scene's meaning.

Where, however, Eliot's profundity of vision carried him through his own inadequacies as a dramatist—notably his inability to create character which did not suffer the atrophy of symbolism—Fry came to lean on an explosive central situation fruitful in itself. This situation might lack the qualities of conflict, tension, and development, yet still be capable of holding attention. Thus *A Sleep of Prisoners* consists of a pattern of re-enacted Old Testament stories chosen to illustrate facets of the idea of violence. Each story is not only informed by the audience's own memories of the Bible, but also, because it is dreamed by a modern soldier held prisoner in a church, is automatically granted a contemporary relevance: within the structure of the play the spectator himself works to supply the missing factor in the dramatic equation, and the teaching element of a morality play is actively deduced by our application of the fiction to the fact. Nevertheless, this play suffers, as only morality plays can, from the static preconception by which morality characters tend to be fixed in their symbolic attitudes.

This play in its time startled and delighted audiences by the free use of its church setting, where at a glance the chancel could be Adam's jungle or the pulpit Abraham's mountain: as they were for *Murder in the Cathedral*, audiences were both theatregoers and congregation, and were unusually exercised by the multiplicity of association felt within the performance. There are no such props for a dramatic experience in Fry's other plays, although in *The Boy with a Cart*, a simple mystery play of spontaneous charm, *The Firstborn*, exploring the tragic dilemma of Moses and the Plagues, and *Curtmantle* he draws upon legend and history in parallel attempts to bring the remote closer to home. *Curtmantle*, too neglected a play, was his most sustained attempt at a serious character study: this chronicle play of Henry II in conflict with his Archbishop Becket is set out in a sequence of vivid episodes more in the simple manner of Bolt's episodic *A Man for All Seasons* than with the prismatic counterpoint of Brecht's epic theatre, the scenes designed to illustrate the wit, the wisdom, and the complex passions of the title part as Henry searches for a rational unity of divine and secular law.

Fry creates a drama of colour and flair, choosing a situation for its imaginative potential, often one of implicit crisis involving a clash of strong, bright personalities. His situation enables him to demonstrate a compassionate affirmation of life—an optimism which inevitably seemed escapist beside the bleak absurdist landscape of the postwar years, in spite of the tragic mode of *The Firstborn*, *Thor, With Angels* (the 1948 Canterbury Festival play) and *The Dark Is Light Enough*, plays which exemplify Fry's philosophy of maturing through crisis:

> We reach an obstacle, and learn to overcome it;
> our thoughts or emotions become knotted, and we
> increase ourselves in order to unknot them; a
> state of being becomes intolerable, and, drawing
> upon a hidden reserve of spirit, we transform it.

But he is nevertheless remembered for those early comedies of mood touched with the wit and fantasy by which he could express his most gentle and humane thinking. The prototype for this kind of comedy, and still the most regularly revived, was the one-act, *A Phoenix Too Frequent*. This was taken from the ancient tale of the young Roman widow romantically committed to a fast to the death in her husband's tomb, until she and an equally romantic young soldier agree to substitute the husband's body for the corpse the soldier was guarding with his life. With the lightest of touches, the widow decides for life, and youth and love supplant social convention and death: a joyful illustration of the life-force at work.

The spring-time comedy that made Fry's name and competed for London's attention with Eliot's *The Cocktail Party* in 1949 was his best-known play *The Lady's Not for Burning*, an extension of the style and spirit of *A Phoenix Too Frequent*. His verbal pyrotechnics were at their most assured, and the medieval colour on his stage lifted the play into a rarefied atmosphere that forced comparison with Giraudoux and the lighter Anouilh of *L'Invitation au château* (which Fry was later to translate beautifully as *Ring round the Moon*). A simple crisis again sets the play in motion, when one Thomas Mendip, desiring but denied death, is confronted with Jennet Jourdemayne, who wants to live but must die as a witch. She

envies his deathwish, he her "damnable mystery," until, to test his sincerity and her courage, Fry impudently arranges for them one last "joyous" evening together before Jennet's execution. The result is to dramatize with graceful irony Fry's sense of cosmic purpose.

His other plays designed to celebrate the seasons followed irregularly in an unpredictable range of moods, some unexpectedly sombre: *Venus Observed* (autumn), *The Dark Is Light Enough* (winter) and *A Yard of Sun* (summer). *Venus Observed* was a comedy of middle-aged disillusionment, but pleasingly balanced and without fashionable cynicism. However, *The Dark Is Light Enough* selects the year of revolutions, 1848, for its darker setting, and secures its unity in the compassionate and gracious presence of an Austrian countess, a part created by Edith Evans. With the Countess's "divine non-interference" it is demonstrated

> how apparently undemandingly
> She moves among us; and yet
> Lives make and unmake themselves in her
>   neighbourhood
> As nowhere else.

Thus the theme is one of providence, and, through the wisdom of the Countess as she recognizes the imminence of death, embodies the necessity of our respect for every human personality in its touch of grace.

To set side by side plays as contrasting as *The Lady's Not for Burning* and *The Dark Is Light Enough* is inescapably to be impressed by Fry's versatility, and by the integrity of a writer who uses his chosen medium as a way of searching out his personal philosophy whether in the vein of farce or tragedy, spring or winter. Eliot notwithstanding, Fry's is the most sustained attempt in English to write an undogmatic Christian drama in modern times.

—J.L. Styan

FUGARD, (Harold) Athol (Lannigan). South African. Born near Middleburg, Cape Province, 11 June 1932. Educated at Marist Brothers College, Port Elizabeth, 1938–45; Port Elizabeth Technical College, 1946–50; University of Cape Town, 1950–53. Married Sheila Meiring in 1956; one daughter. Seaman, *S.S. Graigaur*, 1953–54; journalist, Port Elizabeth *Evening Post*, 1954; reporter, South African Broadcasting Corporation, Port Elizabeth and Cape Town, 1955–57; clerk, Fordsburg Native Commissioner's Court, Johannesburg, 1958; stage manager and publicity agent, National Theatre Organization, 1958; worked as cleaner in London, 1960. Co-founder, Circle Players theatre workshop, Cape Town, 1957, African Theatre Workshop, Sophiatown, 1958–59, New Africa Group, Brussels, 1960, Ijinle Company, London, 1966, and The Space experimental theatre, Cape Town, 1972; director, Serpent Players, Port Elizabeth, from 1963; director of and actor in many of his own plays. Recipient: *New York Times* award, 1965; Obie award, 1971; London Theatre Critics award, 1974; Locarno Film Festival Ernest Artaria award, 1977; Berlin Film Festival Golden Bear, 1980; Yale University fellowship, 1980; New York Drama Critics Circle award, 1981, 1988; London *Evening Standard* award, 1984; Common Wealth award, 1984; Drama League award, 1986; Helen Hayes award, for direction, 1990.

D.Litt.: University of Natal, Durban, 1981; Rhodes University, Grahamstown, 1983; University of Cape Town, 1984. D.F.A.: Yale University, New Haven, Connecticut, 1983. D.H.L.: Georgetown University, Washington, D.C., 1984. Lives in Port Elizabeth. Agent: Esther Sherman, William Morris Agency, 1350 Avenue of the Americas, New York, New York 10019, U.S.A.

PUBLICATIONS

Plays

No-Good Friday (also director: produced Johannesburg, 1958; Sheffield, 1974). Included in *Dimetos and Two Early Plays*, 1977.

Nongogo (also director: produced Cape Town, 1959; Sheffield, 1974; New York, 1978). Included in *Dimetos and Two Early Plays*, 1977.

The Blood Knot (also director: produced Johannesburg, 1961; London, 1963; New York, 1964). Cape Town, Simondium, 1963; New York, Odyssey Press, 1964; in *Three Port Elizabeth Plays*, 1974.

Hello and Goodbye (also director: produced Johannesburg, 1965; New York, 1968; Leicester, 1971; London, 1973). Cape Town, Balkema, 1966; in *Three Port Elizabeth Plays*, 1974.

The Coat (produced Port Elizabeth, 1966). With *The Third Degree*, by Don MacLennan, Cape Town, Balkema, 1971.

People Are Living There (produced Glasgow, 1968; also director: produced Cape Town, 1969; New York, 1971; London, 1972). Cape Town, Buren, 1969; London, Oxford University Press, 1970.

The Occupation: A Script for Camera, in *Ten One Act Plays* edited by Cosmos Pieterse. London, Heinemann, 1968.

Boesman and Lena (also director: produced Grahamstown, 1969; revised version produced New York, 1970; London, 1971). Cape Town, Buren, 1969; New York, French, 1972; London, Oxford University Press, 1973.

Orestes (produced Cape Town, 1971). Published in *Theatre One: New South African Drama*, edited by Stephen Gray, Johannesburg, Donker, 1978.

Statements after an Arrest under the Immorality Act (also director: produced Cape Town, 1972; London, 1974; New York, 1978). Included in *Statements*, 1974.

Sizwe Bansi Is Dead, with John Kani and Winston Ntshona (also director: as *Sizwe Banzi Is Dead*, produced Cape Town, 1972; as *Sizwe Bansi Is Dead*, produced London, 1973; New Haven, Connecticut, and New York, 1974). Included in *Statements*, 1974; in *Two Plays*, 1976.

The Island, with John Kani and Winston Ntshona (also director: as *Die Hodoshe Span* produced Cape Town, 1973; as *The Island* produced London, and New York, 1974). Included in *Statements*, 1974; in *Two Plays*, 1976.

Three Port Elizabeth Plays: The Blood Knot, Hello and Goodbye, Boesman and Lena. New York, Viking Press, and London, Oxford University Press, 1974.

Statements: Three Plays. London, Oxford University Press, 1974.

Dimetos (also director: produced Edinburgh, 1975; revised version produced Nottingham, London, and New York, 1976). Included in *Dimetos and Two Early Plays*, 1977.

Two Plays: Sizwe Bansi Is Dead, and The Island, with John Kani and Winston Ntshona. New York, Viking Press, 1976.

Dimetos and Two Early Plays. London, Oxford University Press, 1977.

The Guest: An Episode in the Life of Eugène Marais, with

Ross Devenish (as *The Guest at Steenkampskraal*, televised 1977). Johannesburg, Donker, 1977.

A Lesson from Aloes (also director: produced Johannesburg, 1978; New Haven, Connecticut, New York, and London, 1980). New York, Random House, and Oxford, Oxford University Press, 1981.

Boesman and Lena, and Other Plays (includes *The Blood Knot, People Are Living There, Hello and Goodbye*). London, Oxford University Press, 1978.

The Drummer (produced Louisville, 1980).

"Master Harold" and the Boys (also director: produced New Haven, Connecticut, and New York, 1982; London, 1983). New York, Knopf, 1982; Oxford, Oxford University Press, 1983.

Marigolds in August (screenplay), with Ross Devenish. Johannesburg, Donker, 1982.

The Road to Mecca (produced New Haven, Connecticut, 1984; London, 1985; also director: produced New York, 1988). London, Faber, 1985.

A Place with the Pigs (also director: produced New Haven, Connecticut, 1987, London, 1988). London, Faber, 1988.

Selected Plays (includes *"Master Harold" and the Boys, The Blood Knot, Hello and Goodbye, Boesman and Lena*). Oxford, Oxford University Press, 1987.

My Children! My Africa! (also director: produced Johannesburg and New York, 1989; London, 1990). London, Faber, 1990.

Playland (produced Cape Town, 1992).

Screenplays: *Boesman and Lena*, 1973; *Marigolds in August*, with Ross Devenish, 1980.

Television Plays: *Mille Miglia*, 1968 (UK); *The Guest at Steenkampskraal*, with Ross Devenish, 1977.

Novel

Tsotsi. Johannesburg, Donker, and London, Collings, 1980; New York, Random House, 1981.

Other

Notebooks 1960–1977, edited by Mary Benson. Johannesburg, Donker, and London, Faber, 1983; New York, Knopf, 1984.

Writer and Region: Athol Fugard (essay). New York, Anson Phelps Stokes Institute, 1987.

*

Bibliography: *Athol Fugard: A Bibliography, Biography, Playography* by Russell Vandenbroucke, London, TQ Publications, 1977; *Athol Fugard: A Source Guide* by Temple Hauptfleisch, Johannesburg, Donker, 1982.

Manuscript Collection: National English Literary Museum, Rhodes University, Grahamstown.

Critical Studies: *Athol Fugard* by Stephen Gray, Johannesburg, McGraw Hill, 1982; *Athol Fugard* by Dennis Walder, London, Macmillan, 1984, New York, Grove Press, 1985; *Truths the Hand Can Touch: The Theatre of Athol Fugard* by Russell Vandenbroucke, New York, Theatre Communications Group, 1985.

Theatrical Activities:
Director: **Plays**—many of his own plays; *The Cure*, adaptation of *Mandragola* by Machiavelli, Grahamstown, 1963;

Woyzeck by Georg Büchner, South Africa, 1964; *Antigone* by Sophocles, Cape Town, 1965; *The Trials of Brother Jero* by Wole Soyinka, London, 1966.

Actor: **Plays**—roles in most of his own plays in South Africa; Okkie the Greek in *A Kakamas Greek* by David Herbert, Brussels, 1960; Morrie in *The Blood Knot*, New York, 1962 and 1985, London, 1966; *A Place with the Pigs*, New Haven, Connecticut, 1987; role in *The Road to Mecca*, New York, 1988. **Films**—*Boesman and Lena*, 1973; *Meetings with Remarkable Men*, 1979; *Marigolds in August*, 1980; *Gandhi*, 1982; *The Killing Fields*, 1984. **Television**—*The Blood Knot*, 1967 (UK); *The Guest at Steenkampskraal*, 1977.

* * *

Athol Fugard is a playwright in the fullest sense of the word: he is a builder of plays in the way that a shipwright is a builder of ships. Although the solitude of writing has produced a number of his finest dramas, plays at once highly personal and particular about his native South Africa and internationally accessible and meaningful, he has also used his skills as actor and director to forge collaborations which have had a profound effect on the development of South African culture. By continuing to direct his plays himself, in South Africa, the United States, and Britain, he has also continued to control the shape and expression of his ideas far more than most dramatists.

What has given particular force to his plays, individual or collaborative, is the consistent demonstration that private lives are political. His belief that this is so was formed under apartheid, an imposed division of people that made apolitical existence impossible, but dramatizing that belief means that his plays show the real dimensions of human society, to a degree seldom achieved by his contemporaries in British and American theatre.

His collaborative plays appeared in the early 1970's when the very act of collaborating with black African actors was political. Some of the plays during that period were every bit as *written* as his earliest successes such as *The Blood Knot*. Thus, *Statements After an Arrest Under the Immorality Act*, a key drama examining the carnal relations between a man and a woman whose contact was forbidden under the racial laws of South Africa, was fully scripted by him. But his most significant plays at that time for their impact on the development of black South African theatre were the two he wrote in collaboration with Winston Ntshona and John Kani, *Sizwe Bansi Is Dead* and *The Island*.

Those plays opened a dialogue with the world presenting, as *The Blood Knot* had done earlier, such theatrically exact metaphors for South Africa's racial strife that the human situation transcended the politics while at the same time illuminating the nature of the conflict. In addition the final shape of the plays, with many roles performed by two actors, was to provide an economical model for further explorations of the South African situation, such as those by Barney Simon and Percy Mtwa. *Sizwe Bansi* remains a particularly powerful statement about the effect of repression on individuals subjected to South Africa's laws. Its examination of the problem of individual identity gives a haunting, nearly mythological power.

The South African division of humanity into three groups —whites, coloured, and blacks—always had its absurdities as well as its tragedies. *Sizwe Bansi* seizes on both aspects, beginning with an actual death and ending with a symbolic transfer of identities with a dead man; in a society where access was determined by bureaucratic interpretations of race and by the possession of the right identity card, a new card could mean a new life.

Fugard's expansion of the idea into a full-length play was given additional reality through the improvisational work of Kani and Ntshona under his direction. They contributed in a similar way to *The Island*, which is set in a prison, and they undoubtedly endowed both plays with elements of speech and observed details that deepened the impact. There is none the less a dominant sense of form that evokes the two brothers of *The Blood Knot*, one light-skinned and one black, who share an identity while appearing different to the world. It is Fugard's clear theatrical structuring, combined with an exceptional literacy, that gives each of his plays a recognizable voice.

While most of his plays operate within the context determined by the politics and racial situation in South Africa, and most of his characters, regardless of race, are victims of those policies, he has extended his work equally bravely into mythic dimensions. *Dimetos*, which was commissioned by the Edinburgh Festival and subsequently performed in London, followed some of his most political pieces and attempted to explore a mythic fragment which had lodged itself in his memory. He explored it in contemporary dress, with lengthy literal discussions, around the subject of a guilty love, but while the touch of a major playwright was always evident it was a considerably more literary touch than in his more specifically South African works.

However, unlike any other playwright of comparable stature, Fugard has identified the work of the Polish director Jerzy Grotowski as a major influence on his own work. Grotowski was notable for extending the physical and vocal range of actors, and for productions which obscured the language and texts at their centres. In a similar manner, one of the major experiments made by Fugard in Cape Town was almost completely physical. He describes this experiment, *Orestes*, as "an experience which lasted about eighty minutes and which had a 'text' of about four hundred words. The rest was space, silence, and action."

Neither *Orestes* nor *Dimetos* could be described as typical; rather they are extremes of Fugard's approach to theatre and might have been explored further had he not obviously found the problems and contradictions of his country so pressing. The work beginning with *A Lesson from Aloes* is far more representative of his usual concerns, and prepared the way for the differently autobiographical dramas, *"Master Harold" and the Boys* and *The Road to Mecca* which appeared in the 1980's, and his latest work, *Playland*, the first of his plays to be premiered in South Africa for some years.

Reflecting back to notes he had made in 1961, *A Lesson from Aloes* was based on actual people caught in the closing trap of apartheid. It graphically and poignantly examined the decision of an Afrikaner of conscience who decides to cling to South Africa, drawing what sustenance he can from his native earth, while he bids farewell to a Cape Coloured friend who has been forced out. The play clearly suggested Fugard's private debate on the importance and effectiveness of remaining bound to South Africa, but *"Master Harold" and the Boys* was to bring an even more personal expression of conflict, being the self-confessedly true story of his own temptation into the assertion of racial superiority when he was a boy. The irony in the title, with the "master" being a foolish youth and the "boys" being African men of wit, generosity, and sympathy, is a statement of Fugard's guilt, and the play painfully accepts responsibility for an unforgiveable act of contempt to a black man who had been like a father to him.

The Road to Mecca, like *A Lesson from Aloes*, was more of a biographical portrait than autobiography, but the subtext was always the intolerant society of South Africa. His eccentric heroine, modelled on his mother who had sacrificed to give him an education and a woman who had reached her 70s while building her own extremely private version of Mecca, confronts the repressive community in her village of New Bethlehem, in the Great Karoo (where Fugard maintains a home). When they wish to confine her to an old people's home, she turns for support to a young woman friend who is finding it hard to come to grips with a recent abortion and her encounter with an African woman and child she encountered on the road to New Bethlehem.

In *A Place with the Pigs*, Fugard finally seemed to be moving away from his South African setting and themes. Based on the true story of a Soviet deserter from World War II who lived in secret for 40 years among the pigs on his family farm, the play was about the man's struggle to preserve his humanity while denied all human contact except that of the wife who hid him. Considered by some to form a metaphor for political repression, Fugard himself found it an expression of his own struggle with alcoholism.

His next play, *My Children! My Africa!*, was a powerful return to South Africa. A three-hander, it reflected the struggle between forces for knowledge and argument confronted by the option of revolutionary violence. The central character is a black teacher who tries to persuade his brightest black student that reason can win the struggle, offering him the choice of all the knowledge, all the words, in a dictionary, which he contrasts to one single word, a stone, which he holds in his other hand. His reward for his position is death by "necklacing," having a burning tire placed round his neck.

Reconciliation makes a more hopeful appearance in his next play. *Playland* takes place at a funfair on New Year's Eve in 1989, a month before President F.W. de Klerk announced the death of apartheid. The two characters are a black watchman, Martinus, and a white visitor to the funfair, Gideon. It is Gideon's alcohol-fuelled rantings, including a boast of killing dozens of blacks in a South African border war, that bring forth Martinus's story of killing a white man who demanded sex from his servant, Martinus's fiancée. Their sharing of shadowy histories is finally positive, offering hope of future peaceful settlement, and, as usual, the story transcends its locality. Fugard has described the play as being about "the karma of violence."

Nothing Fugard has written declines to the didactic, and though he remains a political author of the first rank, he is even more consistently a humanist. The body of his work is a glowing testament to the human spirit.

—Ned Chaillet

FULLER, Charles (H., Jr.). American. Born in Philadelphia, Pennsylvania, 5 March 1939. Educated at Villanova University, 1956–58, and La Salle College, 1965–67, both Philadelphia. Served as a petroleum lab technician in the United States Army in Japan and Korea, 1959–62. Married Miriam A. Nesbitt in 1962; two sons. Bank loan collector, counselor at Temple University, and city housing inspector, all Philadelphia, 1960's; co-founder and co-director, Afro-American Arts Theatre, Philadelphia, 1967–71; writer and director, *The Black Experience* program, WIP Radio, Philadelphia, 1970–71. Recipient: Creative Artists Public Service grant, 1975; Rockefeller grant, 1976; National Endowment for the Arts grant, 1976; Guggenheim fellow-

ship, 1977; Obie award, 1981; Audelco award, 1981, 1982; Pulitzer prize, 1982; New York Drama Critics Circle award, 1982; Outer Circle award, 1982; Hazelitt award, 1983; Mystery Writers of America Edgar Allan Poe award, for screenplay, 1985. D.F.A.: La Salle College, 1982; Villanova University, 1983. Lives in Philadelphia. Agent: Esther Sherman, William Morris Agency, 1350 Avenue of the Americas, New York, New York 10019, U.S.A.

PUBLICATIONS

Plays

The Village: A Party (produced Princeton, New Jersey, 1968; as *The Perfect Party*, produced New York, 1969).
The Rise, in *New Plays from the Black Theatre*, edited by Ed Bullins. New York, Bantam, 1969.
In My Many Names and Days (produced New York, 1972).
Candidate (produced New York, 1974).
In the Deepest Part of Sleep (produced New York, 1974).
First Love (produced New York, 1974).
The Lay Out Letter (produced Philadelphia, 1975).
The Brownsville Raid (produced Waterford, Connecticut, 1975; New York, 1976).
Sparrow in Flight, music by Larry Garner, based on a concept by Rosetta LeNoire (produced New York, 1978).
Zooman and the Sign (produced New York, 1980). New York, French, 1982.
A Soldier's Play (produced New York, 1981; Edinburgh, 1984). New York, Hill and Wang, 1982.
We (includes *Sally*, *Prince*) (produced New York, 1988).
Eliot's Coming, in *Urban Blight* (musical revue), based on an idea by John Tillinger, music by David Shire, lyrics by Richard Maltby, Jr. (produced New York, 1988).
Jonquil (produced New York, 1990).

Screenplay: *A Soldier's Story*, 1984.

Television Plays: *Roots, Resistance, and Renaissance* series, 1967; *Mitchell*, 1968; *Black America* series, 1970–71; *The Sky Is Gray*, from the story by Ernest J. Gaines (*American Short Story* series), 1980; *A Gathering of Old Men*, 1987.

*   *   *

An angry, consuming energy which propels the protagonist towards violence, an irony which humanizes him while depriving the viewer of easy categorizations: these elements characterize Charles Fuller's style. Within an American theatre tradition Fuller's work both acknowledges the seminal position of Amiri Baraka and extends the vision of the tumultuous 1960's beyond a rigid, racial schematization which in conferring upon blacks the status of victims of oppression, seemingly robbed them of any responsibility for or power over the circumstances in which they found themselves.

A former bank loan collector, college counsellor, and city housing inspector, Fuller initially gained a measure of national recognition in 1976 with *The Brownsville Raid*. Though presently out of circulation, the play is of interest because it prefigures the approach adopted in the later *A Soldier's Play*. *The Brownsville Raid* is a dramatization of the investigation into a 1906 shooting spree which culminated in President Teddy Roosevelt's unwarranted, dishonorable discharge of an entire black infantry brigade. With historical accounts as his starting point, Fuller skilfully interweaves a "whodunnit" plot with a compelling portrait of a black corporal who has his faith in the Army shattered when he refuses to comply with his officers' demand for a scapegoat. Both black and white men are presented with strengths and faults; what emerges is a composite picture of men and a society whose vision is distorted by racism.

In both *Zooman and the Sign* and *A Soldier's Play* racism appears not as a specific, external event to which the black protagonists must react; rather, its negative values have been so internalized that, propelled by their own frantic despair, the characters move relentlessly towards self-destruction. In the first play, about a father's search for his daughter's killer, a knife-toting, drug-running, 15-year-old casually admits to the audience at the outset that he is the killer. Although Zooman attempts to mask a mounting sense of entrapment with calculated bravado, his direct conversations with the audience about familial disintegration, unwanted homosexual encounters, and detention for uncommitted crimes characterize him as an alienated youth whose experiences have taught him that "niggahs can't be heroes," that blacks seemingly have no control over the atrophy engulfing their families and communities. These monologues, delivered in a street-wise, frenetic style which is nonetheless reminiscent of black toast traditions and Muhammad Ali's alliterative poetry, have the effect of humanizing Zooman, of placing him in a context where his asocial behavior becomes more understandable, and his affinity to the larger society more apparent.

Just as Zooman believes that blacks are helpless, so too do the neighbors of the slain girl, for no one will come forth as witnesses to the crime. The father's erecting a sign accusing them of moral complicity triggers only hostile recriminations from the neighbors and argument within the family itself. Symbolic of a community's failure to foster a more active, ennobling sense of its own possibilities, the sign occasions the final violence wherein Zooman is accidentally killed in his attempt to tear it down. Another black child lies dead in the street, another family grieves, and another sign goes up as momentary monument to incredible waste.

An ultimately pervasive irony, which empties the landscape of possible victors and reveals instead a society maimed by racism, is equally evident in *A Soldier's Play*. Unlike Zooman, Sergeant Waters espouses the black middle-class values of hard work, education, and racial pride as the means of self-advancement. Like Zooman, Waters, in seeking a sphere in which to exercise a masculine sense of control and dignity, has had only limited success, for he operates within the segregated Army of World War II. The search for his killer triggers a series of flashbacks which reveal him as a vicious, petty tyrant bent upon literally ridding the race of all those blues-singing, hoodoo-oriented men who he says prevent advancement; yet, they also create a measure of sympathy for this ambitious man, consumed by misplaced faith, self-hatred, and guilt.

The eventual identification of two black recruits as Waters's murderers defies the expectation, carefully nurtured by the playwright, that overt white hostility is the motivating factor. Additionally, it raises questions concerning the definition of justice, for the infantrymen have just received their long-awaited orders to ship out, in effect being granted license to kill in Europe a tyranny similar to what Waters represents at home. Compounding the irony further, Fuller provides a postscript which subverts the dramatic experience: the investigating officer reveals that the entire incident is recorded in military documents as meaningless black-on-black crime; Waters is inadvertently listed as an heroic war casualty; and the entire company is destroyed in combat. Thus, the Army learns nothing from this sorry episode.

To date, Fuller's dramatic world is dominated by driven, destructive men trying to carve out a viable place within a hostile environment. Though his characters inhabit a bleak landscape, his audiences need not: through the dramatic experience they can appreciate how racism distorts an entire society and choose to stop the human destruction.

—Sandra L. Richards

FURTH, George. American. Born George Schweinfurth in Chicago, Illinois, 14 December 1932. Educated at Northwestern University, Evanston, Illinois, B.S. in speech 1954; Columbia University, New York, 1955–56, M.F.A. 1956. Served in the United States Navy, 1958–62. Stage, film, and television actor from 1956; member of the Drama Department, University of Southern California, Los Angeles, 1979. Recipient: New York Drama Critics Circle award, 1970; Outer Circle award, 1970; Drama Desk award, 1970; Tony award, 1971. Agent: The Lantz Office, 888 Seventh Avenue, New York, New York 10106. Address: 3030 Durand Drive, Hollywood, California 90068, U.S.A.

PUBLICATIONS

Plays

Company, music and lyrics by Stephen Sondheim (produced New York, 1970; London, 1972). New York, Random House, 1970.
Twigs (includes *Emily, Celia, Dorothy, Ma*) (produced New York, 1971; Coventry, 1973). New York, French, 1972.
The Act, music by John Kander, lyrics by Fred Ebb (produced New York, 1977). New York, French, 1987.
Merrily We Roll Along, music and lyrics by Stephen Sondheim, adaptation of the play by George S. Kaufman and Moss Hart (produced New York, 1981; London, 1983).
The Supporting Cast (produced New York, 1981). New York, French, 1982.
Precious Sons (produced New York, 1986). New York, French, 1988.

*

Manuscript Collection: Northwestern University School of Speech, Evanston, Illinois.

Theatrical Activities:
Director: **Plays**—*The Supporting Cast*, Chicago, 1986; *Precious Sons*, Chicago, 1988.
Actor: **Plays**—Jordan in *A Cook for Mr. General* by Steve Gethers, New York, 1961; Junior Tubbs in *Hot Spot*, 1963; Skip in *Tadpole* by Jules Tasca, Los Angeles, 1973; Butler in *Tiny Alice* by Edward Albee; Arnold in *The Supporting Cast*, Los Angeles, 1982. **Films**—*The Best Man*, 1964; *The New Interns*, 1964; *A Rage to Live*, 1965; *A Very Special Favor*, 1965; *The Cool Ones*, 1967; *Games*, 1967; *Tammy and the Millionaire*, 1967; *The Boston Strangler*, 1968; *How to Save a Marriage—And Ruin Your Life*, 1968; *Nobody's Perfect*, 1968; *P.J.*, 1968; *What's So Bad about Feeling Good?*, 1968; *Butch Cassidy and the Sundance Kid*, 1969; *Myra Breckinridge*, 1970; *Blazing Saddles*, 1974; *Shampoo*, 1975;

Airport '77, 1977; *Cannonball Run*, 1981; *MegaForce*, 1982; *The Man with Two Brains*, 1983; *Doctor Detroit*, 1983. **Television**—*Tammy*, *Broadside*, *Mary Hartman*, *Mary Hartman* and *The Dumplings* series.

* * *

George Furth's career to date, his book for Stephen Sondheim's *Company* excepted, has been a tantalising series of near misses. Adroit as his work is, especially when he has risked innovations with the actual form of mainstream play-writing, he has rarely strayed from the narrow range of concerns that can occupy the successful Broadway play.

Twigs is essentially four one-act plays with a linking thread, providing a versatile actress with the chance to play three different sisters and their mother in the course of the evening. Taking its title from Alexander Pope ("Just as the twig is bent, the tree's inclined"), the plays are set in four different kitchens all on the same prior-to-Thanksgiving Day. All the sisters have their problems, seen mainly through a comedic lens, although the slick lines and sight-gags of the first playlet in which the garrulous recently-widowed Emily finds a possible new romance are in sharp contrast to the second, in which Celia, married to a crudely unfeeling slob whose ex-army buddy joins them for Thanksgiving, trembles on the verge of another nervous breakdown. This play begins in a vein of rumbustious comedy but gradually reveals an undertow of bleak pain. Furth does not always have time to paint in the sublest of brush strokes, one of the hazards of the one-act format; perhaps unsurprisingly, the most successful episode is the final one in which the sisters' terminally ill Mother, a formidable old lady, decides that before she dies the "Pa" with whom she has lived for so long will do right by her and marry her. The ensuing wedding scene with an understandably flustered priest may be fairly broad comedy but it has a gleeful relish, skirting the boundaries of taste, which fuels it with zest.

Furth, with an actor's background, gives all his cast good opportunities, as well as providing a virtuoso showcase for the central performer. The play had a moderate Broadway success, which was more than he achieved with *The Supporting Cast*. Set in a luxurious Malibu beachhouse, with a bushfire and a minor earthquake among the traumas of the day, the play is happiest in the realms of a wisecracking or visual comedy; it milks a recurring sight-gag of characters walking into glass patio doors, and the dialogue is crammed with sardonic one-liners, the most pungent coming from the sharp-tongued Mae. Like all the characters, all friends of first-time novelist Ellen whose novel's publication requires waivers from the real-life prototypes of her characters, Mae represents East Coast unease with Californian living ("Someone must have tipped this country on its end and everything that wasn't screwed down fell into California," as Florrie from Brooklyn puts it). The play's slight plot rests on the mixed reactions to the book before outrage turns to ego-preening; aiming for a high-octane zany comedy the play becomes progressively more desperate in its contrivances simply to keep events moving.

All of which made Furth's most recent play perhaps somewhat surprising. *Precious Sons* managed only a short run, even in a Broadway season starved of good new plays. It has many of the hallmarks of an autobiographical play: set in Furth's native Chicago in the summer of 1949, it is a solidly naturalistic play centered on the lower-middle-class household of Fred Small, hard-working and tough father in poor health, Bea his slapdash, indomitably optimistic wife, and their two very different sons (the younger with dreams of becoming an actor, the elder sneaking off to wed his Prom sweetheart), for both of whom Fred is desperate for better lives. It is a long, and sometimes flawed play (somewhat confused over Bea's motives at crucial points, especially her attitude to a projected promotion of Fred's) but offering magnificent acting opportunities, particularly in the loving, brawling volatile relationship between Fred and Bea. The play, set as it is in 1949, inevitably recalls the playwrights of that period—Inge, Miller, Williams (indeed Williams figures strongly in the story, with Freddy the younger son auditioning for the touring company of *A Streetcar Named Desire*, producing a wonderful scene in which Bea has to read Blanche to Freddy's Newspaper Boy)—but deserved a more considered critical reaction than the faint praise it received on Broadway.

Furth has had considerable success with his streamlined books for various musicals including *Company* (although *The Act* required little more than linking dialogue between Liza Minnelli's numbers) but there are signs in his work to date that there is possibly a major play yet to come from him.

—Alan Strachan

G

GAGLIANO, Frank (Joseph). American. Born in Brooklyn, New York, 18 November 1931. Educated at Queens College, New York, 1949–53; University of Iowa, Iowa City, B.A. 1954; Columbia University, New York, M.F.A. 1957. Served in the United States Army, 1954–56. Married Sandra Gordon in 1958; one son. Freelance copywriter, New York, 1958–61; promotion copywriter, McGraw-Hill Text-Film Division, New York, 1962–65. Associate professor of drama, Florida State University, Tallahassee, 1969–72; lecturer in playwriting and director of the E.P. Conkle Workshop, University of Texas, Austin, 1972–75. Since 1975 Benedum professor of playwriting, University of West Virginia, Morgantown. Visiting professor, University of Rhode Island, Providence, 1975. Recipient: Rockefeller grant, 1965, 1966; Wesleyan University-O'Neill Foundation fellowship, 1967; National Endowment for the Arts grant, 1973; Guggenheim fellowship, 1974. Lives in Pittsburgh. Agent: Gilbert Parker, William Morris Agency, 1350 Avenue of the Americas, New York, New York 10019. Address: Theatre Arts Center, University of West Virginia, Morgantown, West Virginia 26506, U.S.A.

PUBLICATIONS

Plays

Night of the Dunce (as *The Library Raid*, produced Houston, 1961; revised version, as *Night of the Dunce*, produced New York, 1966).   New York, Dramatists Play Service, 1967.
Conerico Was Here to Stay (produced New York, 1965). Included in *The City Scene*, 1966.
The City Scene (includes *Paradise Gardens East* and *Conerico Was Here to Stay*) (produced New York, 1969).   New York, French, 1966.
Father Uxbridge Wants to Marry (produced Waterford, Connecticut, and New York, 1967).   New York, Dramatists Play Service, 1968.
The Hide-and-Seek Odyssey of Madeleine Gimple (produced Waterford, Connecticut, 1967).   New York, Dramatists Play Service, 1970.
The Prince of Peasantmania (Inny), music by James Reichert (produced Waterford, Connecticut, 1968; revised version produced Milwaukee, 1970).   New York, Agency for the Performing Arts, 1968.
Big Sur (televised 1969; revised version produced Tallahassee, Florida, 1970).   New York, Dramatists Play Service, 1971.
In the Voodoo Parlour of Marie Laveau: Gris-Gris, and The Comedia World of Byron B (produced Waterford, Connecticut, 1973; as *Gris-Gris, and The Comedia World of Lafcadio Beau*, produced New York, 1974; revised version, as *Voodoo Trilogy*, produced New York, 1977; revised version, as *In the Voodoo Parlour of Marie Laveau*, produced New York, 1983).
Congo Square, music by Claibe Richardson (produced Providence, Rhode Island, 1975).

The Resurrection of Jackie Cramer, music by Raymond Benson (produced Providence, Rhode Island, and New York, 1976).
The Private Eye of Hiram Bodoni (produced New York, 1978).
The Total Immersion of Madeleine Favorini (produced Las Vegas, Nevada, 1981).
San Ysidro (cantata), music by James Reichert (produced Milwaukee, 1985).
From the Bodoni County Songbook Anthology, Book 1 (produced Morgantown, West Virginia, 1986).

Television Play: *Big Sur*, 1969.

*

Manuscript Collections: Lincoln Center Library of the Performing Arts, New York; O'Neill Theatre Center Library, Waterford, Connecticut.

Critical Studies: *Stages: The Fifty-Year Childhood of the American Theatre* by Emory Lewis, Englewood Cliffs, New Jersey, Prentice Hall, 1969; *The Nature of Theatre* by Vera M. Roberts, New York, Harper, 1971.

Frank Gagliano comments:
My whole effort in dramatic writing has been to keep a center while allowing myself the freedom of following any *seemingly* absurd path that seems to make sense. Form and impulse; the artist's great tightrope act. My favorite playwrights are Shakespeare, Georg Büchner, Chekhov, Verdi, and Bach.

* * *

Frank Gagliano is an experimental artist, uncompromising in his quest for a dramatic form that synthesizes his passion for music, language, and metaphysical themes of Christian idealism in an age of terror, disorder, perversion, and violence. "Mindlessness scares me and I'm in a mindless age," cries the heroine of *The Total Immersion of Madeleine Favorini*. Her words express the playwright's own torment. But Gagliano resembles a medieval dramatist, theatricalizing the terrors of hell to effect salvation, yet fascinated by the evils he deplores. In his plays, images of decay, violence, and death prevail over those of transcendence and salvation.

Gagliano is at war with himself. His drama is often an unresolved battleground of contradictory themes, language, and structure; winged allegories soar toward some unperceived light, burdened by the very demons they hope to evade. It is a brilliant, painful quest for truth, a journey for playwright and spectator in which the ridiculous and sublime combine in uneasy balance. Gagliano never plays it safe, and that is his great virtue as an artist.

His two-act opera, *Inny*, exemplifies the allegories of his earlier work. The dominant metaphor is that of the odyssey

215

toward some form of self-realization, though the play's structure is far more logical and compact than that of his later plays. Innocent, "Inny," rightful heir to the throne of Peasantmania, is prevented from ruling by forces of political, social, and religious corruption that dominate the country. In his struggle to obtain power, Inny journeys from innocence to wisdom. Despite the evils endured, Inny remains spiritually pure, a Christ on the throne ready to suffer for man's transgressions and leading him to salvation: "I must stay . . . I'll never understand this—the ones who chased me, beat me, betrayed me . . . I love them all."

Inny is a grand operatic spectacle of pageants, processions, dances, choruses, battles; an entourage of jaded, cruel aristocrats, hags, heroines, fools, and a wise jester, symbol of art, who ultimately dies a horrid death with Inny's beloved, Glorabella. The dominant image of the play is a huge, foreboding eye that hangs overhead: "God's surrealistic yo-yo?" cries the jester, "but where's the string?" Is the horror heaven sent, the cruel plaything of a less than benign God, or the devil's toy? The ultimate answers are beyond us; all we know for certain is that man pursues senseless evil. The innocent and wicked suffer alike. All we can hope for is that wise, beneficent, courageous leaders like Inny may ultimately triumph.

The Private Eye of Hiram Bodoni is a flawed, sprawling work intended for television, part comedy, part surrealistic nightmare. Bodoni, a private eye, is hired to discover the cause of the unexplained death of the star of a television soap opera. However, the plot is merely a device to explore the lives of the characters through their personal recollections, flashbacks, and fantasies. Although it offers some imaginative visual images and poetic dialogue, the play is confused and unresolved.

In the Voodoo Parlour of Marie Laveau, "an unsung chamber opera," is a three-character play in which a man and woman seek help and revenge from a voodoo sorceress. Under Marie Laveau's spell, the two characters give vent to nightmare and sexual fantasy:

> I wish that was me
> being humped by a donkey
> while the chic of New Orleans
> marveled at me.

The woman's gross allusion revolts the man, who dreams of pure, idealized love. Verbal images of lurid sexuality dominate the play's language, but never gratuitously, only as essential to theme and action. Marie Laveau's parlor is a microcosm of New Orleans at the turn of the century, a city of Mardi Gras, witchcraft, perversion, racial hatred, and violence. The play gains its intensity by the very limitations of its theme. Rather than Gagliano's usual depiction of the characters' torments as symptomatic of a vaster social malaise, *Marie Laveau* is concentrated on the characters as ends in themselves. The parallel to 19th-century melodramatic plots of love and revenge is deliberate—a self-contained world of passion, violence, and death. The settings and costumes are simple yet theatrically effective: a bare space, masks, skulls, bizarre headgear, the horrid implements of the voodoo ritual. The hypnotic spell of the ritual is perfectly suited to Gagliano's odyssey metaphor, the evocation of nightmare and fantasy. Through an imaginative use of scenery, costumes, and operatic dialogue, Gagliano creates a Genet-like transcendence through evil. *Marie Laveau* is powerful drama that lends itself naturally to music.

In *The Total Immersion of Madeleine Favorini* Gagliano again uses the metaphor of the journey into self through a protagonist's total immersion in fantasy, nightmare, and dreams. Madeleine, a timid librarian locked in a gynecologist's stirrups for two weeks, wanders back in fantasy to Sicily, land of her ancestors. On her journey she encounters various forms and characters: a Stalactite, the Wax Prometheus, the Goddess Materna. The actress playing Madeleine transforms herself into each of them (the other actor and actress also assume a variety of identities). Madeleine becomes imbued with the Dionysian and Christian spirit of this ancient land, an earth mother absorbing all humanity into her giant womb. In a brilliant sequence of dialogue, Madeleine and her deceased grandfather, Pazzotesto (Crazy Head), rhapsodize over the wonders of basil that covers the landscape of Sicily, creeping "up from the bottom of the green Mediterranean . . . on the beach . . . the roads, rooftops. The toilets have basil seats. The bells of the great cathedrals are covered with basil and cushion their clang." At the conclusion of the play, Madeleine is freed from the restrictions of the harsh, decadent society that nurtured her. She ascends to freedom on a crescendo of pure language. "Yes! Yes! I know what I want. I know what I mean! I want to become—language! Language!"

These final moments of the play seem to represent Gagliano's desire to free himself from the limits of drama. This work is a form of theatricalized literature or poetry rather than drama. Action becomes the exploration of character and theme instead of the resolution of some essential dramatic conflict. Gagliano's emphasis upon language as the dominant structural element of his drama can become excessive and unfocused. He has a tendency to use dialogue for the sheer richness of sound and imagery. Yet, his dialogue can also be stirring or even frightening, revealing a character's desperate need for freedom and salvation. Gagliano's drama is in transition, and its direction is unclear, but he remains one of the most daring, imaginative, and poetic playwrights of the American theatre.

—A. Richard Sogliuzzo

GALLACHER, Tom. British. Born in Alexandria, Dunbartonshire, Scotland, 16 February 1934. Writer-in-residence, Pitlochry Festival Theatre, Perthshire, 1975–78, and Royal Lyceum Theatre, Edinburgh, 1978–80. Recipient: Scottish Arts Council award, 1986. Agent: Michael Imison Playwrights, 28 Almeida Street, London N1 1TD, England.

PUBLICATIONS

Plays

Our Kindness to Five Persons (produced Glasgow, 1969). Glasgow, Scottish Society of Playwrights, 1980.
Mr. Joyce Is Leaving Paris (produced London, 1970; revised version produced Dublin, 1971; London, 1972; New York, 1978). London, Calder and Boyars, 1972.
Revival! (produced Dublin, 1972; London, 1973). With *Schellenbrack*, Glasgow, Molendinar Press, 1978.
Three to Play: Janus, Pastiche, Recital (produced Montrose, Angus, 1972; *Recital* produced London, 1973).
Schellenbrack (produced London, 1973). With *Revival!*, Glasgow, Molendinar Press, 1978.

Bright Scene Fading (produced London, 1973).

The Only Street (produced Dublin and London, 1973). Glasgow, Scottish Society of Playwrights, 1980.

Personal Effects (produced Pitlochry, 1974).

A Laughing Matter (produced St. Andrews, 1975).

Hallowe'en (produced Dundee, 1975). Glasgow, Scottish Society of Playwrights, 1980.

The Sea Change (produced Edinburgh, 1976). Glasgow, Scottish Society of Playwrights, 1980.

A Presbyterian Wooing, adaptation of the play *The Assembly* by Archibald Pitcairne (produced Pitlochry, 1976).

The Evidence of Tiny Tim, with Joan Knight (produced Perth, 1977).

Wha's Like Us—Fortunately (produced Dundee, 1978).

Stage Door Canteen, with John Scrimger (produced Perth, 1978).

Deacon Brodie, adaptation of the play by Robert Louis Stevenson and W.E. Henley (produced Edinburgh, 1978).

An Enemy of the People, adaptation of a play by Ibsen (produced Edinburgh, 1979).

Jenny (produced Pitlochry, 1979). London, French, 1980.

Natural Causes (produced Perth, 1980).

The Father, adaptation of a play by Strindberg (produced Dundee, 1980).

A Doll's House, adaptation of a play by Ibsen (produced Edinburgh, 1980).

The Parole of Don Juan (produced Perth, 1981).

The Treasure Ship, adaptation of the play by John Brandane (produced Pitlochry, 1981).

The Wild Duck, adaptation of a play by Ibsen (produced Perth, 1987).

Radio Plays: *Progress to an Exile*, 1970; *The Scar*, 1973; *Hunting Shadows*, 1975; *The Man with a Hatchet*, 1976; *Portrait of Isa Mulvenny*, 1978; *Perfect Pitch*, 1979; *Store Quarter*, 1983; *The Previous Tenant*, 1986.

Television Plays: *The Trial of Thomas Muir*, 1977; *If the Face Fits*, 1978.

Novels

Apprentice. London, Hamish Hamilton, 1983.
Journeyman. London, Hamish Hamilton, 1984.
Survivor. London, Hamish Hamilton, 1985.
The Wind on the Heath. London, Hamish Hamilton, 1987.

Short Stories

Hunting Shadows. Helensburgh, Jeffrey, 1981.
The Jewel Maker. London, Hamish Hamilton, 1986.

Other

The Way to Write for the Stage. London, Elm Tree, 1987.

*

Tom Gallacher comments:

(1977) Mainly, the plays deal with exceptions. Sometimes the exceptions are artists; sometimes it is another kind of outsider, a genius, a catalyst, or a singular man. All of them are in some way seeking to extend the meaning of their lives or the boundaries of reality.

An illustration of this can be gained from my book *The Jewel Maker* which is a fictional account of a playwright at work. There it is made clear how the work is influenced by people and events, and how the conflict of illusion and reality

extends the boundaries of the human spirit. That is the testing ground where human evolution continues to progress.

All the plays celebrate the individual. The protagonists are unmoved by Class, Party, or Movement but they are acutely conscious of the interior actions of emotion, spirit, and reason. The crises—whether sad or funny—are person to person. The conflict in comedy and drama arises from an effort to make a workable connection—between the accepted and the potential, between what we are and what we may be, between what is degrading and what is exalting.

"Only connect" was the motto which E.M. Forster placed as guardian over his novel *Howards End*. I can't think of a better motto for a writer because the motto leads to a concept of great courage and enterprise. The characters in my plays do not always master the concept or gain its acceptance by others. But if they go down they go down knowing which way is forward.

* * *

At the end of Tom Gallacher's first play, *Our Kindness to Five Persons*, an alcoholic Glaswegian author pours himself another drink and proposes a solitary toast: "Should auld acquaintance be forgot and *never* brought to mind? Yes. Please God. Yes." The play has just demonstrated a denial of the prayer; but the question, and the artist's special rights of adjudication over it, are the constant threads through the plays Gallacher has written since.

Gallacher's preoccupation with art and artist is immediately obvious on the surfaces of his plays. Writers are the central characters of at least half of them, and Gallacher often points a passage of dialogue towards the epigrammatic use of a quotation, or builds a scene around the recitation of poetry or the singing of ballads. Literary sources and models are of even greater substantive and structural importance for some of Gallacher's work. *The Sea Change* and the short radio play *The Scar* are both dream-plays-within-plays in which the stuff of the central character's imagination comes from Shakespeare. *A Presbyterian Wooing* descends from literary obscurity: *The Assembly*, a Jacobite's dramatic satire on the ecclesiastical politics and personal morals of the Edinburgh Kirk. Trimmed and embroidered into a neo-Restoration comedy of sexual hypocrisy, *A Presbyterian Wooing* demonstrates Gallacher's sensitivity to earlier dramatic modes and his ability to tune his invention and idiom to the same key. The same knack belabours Ibsen's dramaturgy and Kierkegaard's ontology in *Revival!*, the aim of which seems to be to tease the audience into reading the complete works of both Scandinavians. In *Hallowe'en*, on the other hand, Fraser's account of that ritual in pagan times is compactly reincarnated in contemporary Glasgow, and the literary *drame à clé* is cleanly unlocked in the dialogue.

The thematic purposes to which Gallacher puts these and other of his "auld acquaintance" in literature are remarkably repetitive, though the dramatic techniques he uses vary considerably. He is occupied unto the edge of obsession with the dual nature of the remembered past—omnipresent in influence and irretrievable in fact. Every one of his original plays is in large measure focused upon the relationship between dramatic past and present. In some cases, a radical time change is built into the play, its point of departure being the out-of-time introduction of the central character. *The Sea Change*, *Bright Scene Fading*, and the unproduced *A Lady Possessed* are all constructed as flashbacks in time and space through the consciousness of that character, while *Mr. Joyce Is Leaving Paris* brings the personages of Joyce's past to the front of his present consciousness. The other plays, while preserving naturalistic time schemes and the convention of the fourth wall, investigate events and relationships anterior to the action of the play, reenact them or exorcise them.

For Gallacher the memory that matters is the artistic statement of a perception about personal experience. Such a statement stands for him as evidence of the essentials of observed and observer, and as an imposition of order and connexion among these essentials. "Witness" and "pattern" are the terms which often turn up in the dialogue; another is "signpost," an indication of where someone has been and a directive to those who follow. When the plays incorporate such overt expositions of their author's understanding of art, it is not surprising that several draw attention to their own artificiality, nor that so many celebrate the triumph of artistic insight—over technology, biographical data, time, and the perceptions of the pedestrian majority of mankind.

Though the penultimate victory supplies him with some fairly strong stuff, Gallacher finds his best dramatic material in the last. Only here does he create any real competition, and only here are his aesthetic concerns communicated by more than interpretative glosses and plot gimmickry. The axis along which Gallacher most characteristically depicts these conflicts is that of an intense relationship between a gifted figure and a sympathetic sibling or comrade left behind: James and Stanislaus Joyce in *Mr. Joyce Is Leaving Paris*, Martin and Richard in *The Only Street*, and Otto and Steve in *Bright Scene Fading*. The high price of giftedness also hovers over the presentation of parent-child, husband-wife, and mentor-pupil relationships in these and other plays, but Gallacher plays a better game for higher stakes when he is dealing with doubles and shadows.

Gallacher's own practice of art as witness and as pattern is apparent in his plays and illuminates some of their more idiosyncratic aspects. His writing of dialogue is distinguished on the one hand by an accurate reproduction of spoken rhythms, with particularly precise variations for local, professional, social, and even situational idiom, and on the other hand by a wit which specializes in paradoxes, perfect squelches, and the literalisation of abstractions and figures of speech. Gallacher rarely loses this balance of an attentive ear and orderly invention.

Gallacher's patterning of his materials betrays a taste for symmetry, a mastery of plot mechanics, and an ability to exploit exposition, complication, reversal, and resolution in traditional well-made ways or to invert them for the sake of emphasis. (The exceptions to this rule of flexibility are found in his act-endings; he seems incapable of placing an interval anywhere but on the edge of a cliff in the plot). His fascination with pattern is perhaps most easily perceived in miniature in the tidy and playful plots of his three one-acts for three players (*Janus*, *Recital*, and *Pastiche*). The patterning is, however, so apparent in the full-length plays as well that it is impressively ironic that Gallacher's best and best-known play should be, superficially, his most untidy: *Mr. Joyce Is Leaving Paris*. The second half of this play saw production first. Its order is not dictated by traditional dramaturgy but, as is pointed out by one of the figures which haunt the ageing Joyce, by the order of events at an Irish wake. That the "corpse" is the sole survivor of the wake is a good instance of how Gallacher can plot a joke to great thematic purpose. The order of the first half, set much earlier in Joyce's career but written slightly later in Gallacher's, is one of the playwright's confrontations of gifted and ungifted, moving from mutual challenge, though routines long familiar to both, towards acceptance. Though Stanislaus turns up, much muted, in the second half, the two patterns converge only through the consciousness of Joyce—formal confirmation of his (and, be-

hind him, Gallacher's) claim to sole mastery of the remembered situations.

Mr. Joyce Is Leaving Paris in fact typifies Gallacher's dramatic writing as a whole as well as at its best. The qualitative difference between its parts is the difference between commendably accomplished craftsmanship and irresistibly imaginative insight. An analogous difference may be discerned in the use of theatrical resources. To these Gallacher is always attentive, using them to supplement the scripted action and dialogue in his fourth-wall dramas and pulling off some stunning isolated effects in the process. At best, however, Gallacher makes the technical parts of theatrical production indispensable to his dramatic statement. The lighting in the second half of *Mr. Joyce Is Leaving Paris*, for example, and the set for *The Sea Change* serve as visual indices to the central character's control of his memories and thus as evidence of the truth of his vision. In *The Sea Change* that vision, despite its ingenious presentation, remains derivative and diffuse. But when, as in the second half of *Mr. Joyce Is Leaving Paris*, Gallacher aligns tradition and his individual talent in perfect focus, he creates a resonant work.

—Marion O'Connor

GARDNER, Herb(ert). American. Born in Brooklyn, New York, 28 December 1934. Educated at the High School of Performing Arts, New York, graduated 1952; Carnegie Institute of Technology, Pittsburgh; Antioch College, Yellow Springs, Ohio. Married the actress Rita Gardner in 1957. Cartoonist: created *The Nebbishes* syndicated cartoon strip. Recipient: Screenwriters Guild award, 1966; Tony award, 1986; Outer Circle award, 1986; John Gassner award, 1986. Lives in New York City. Address: c/o Samuel French Inc., 45 West 25th Street, New York, New York 10010, U.S.A.

PUBLICATIONS

Plays

The Elevator (produced New York, 1952). New York, French, 1952.
A Thousand Clowns (produced New York, 1962; London, 1964). New York, Random House, 1962.
The Goodbye People (produced New York, 1968). New York, Farrar Straus, 1974; revised version (produced Los Angeles and New York, 1979), included in *A Thousand Clowns, Thieves, The Goodbye People*, 1979.
Who Is Harry Kellerman and Why Is He Saying Those Terrible Things about Me? (screenplay). New York, New American Library, 1971.
Thieves (produced New York, 1974). Included in *A Thousand Clowns, Thieves, The Goodbye People*, 1979.
Love and/or Death (produced New York, 1979).
A Thousand Clowns, Thieves, The Goodbye People. New York, Doubleday, 1979.
I'm Not Rappaport (produced Seattle and New York, 1985; Birmingham and London, 1986). New York, Doubleday, 1986.
Conversations with My Father (produced New York, 1992).

Screenplays: *A Thousand Clowns*, 1965; *Who Is Harry Kellerman and Why Is He Saying Those Terrible Things about Me?*, 1971; *Thieves*, 1976.

Television Play: *Happy Endings*, with others, 1975.

Novel

A Piece of the Action. New York, Simon and Schuster, 1958; London, W.H. Allen, 1959.

* * *

Critics keep trying to point out serious ideas in Herb Gardner's plays, but the playwright consistently wards off their attempts with a comic florish. Clearly a thoughtful man, obviously stimulated by certain prevailing attitudes of mankind, he insists that he is a writer of comedy and that his objective is to entertain audiences. Surely this is a noble and inspiring trait in a modern dramatist, particularly during a period in history when social issues are forcibly intruded into theatres at every opportunity. Unlike Robert Sherwood who, though concerned with the human condition, hid his serious thoughts behind a facade of light comedy, the like-minded Gardner looks carefully around and, like Chekhov, is genuinely amused by what he sees—the fancied and the futile attempts of man to escape the real world, the indefatigable quality of old age. Gardner, then, proceeds to use the comic techniques that bring his plays to Broadway—*A Thousand Clowns*, *The Goodbye People*, *Thieves*, and *I'm Not Rappaport*.

The world that seems funny to Gardner, however, sometimes arrests the attention of others as extremely sad. There is Max Silverman in *The Goodbye People*. This exuberant but completely unrealistic old gentleman wants to erase 20 years from passing time, rebuild his hot-dog stand on Coney Island, and bring his "Hawaiian Ecstasies" to an eager public. Moreover, he wants to do this in February, so convinced is he that his dreams can awaken "ecstasy" in a dull world. There is old Nat in *I'm Not Rappaport*, a defiant, irascible Jewish radical who refuses to be intimidated by either the establishment or the underworld and rejects any movement that intrudes upon his independence. There are all the pathetic people around the apartment building in *Thieves*, each with a problem to which no one listens, each a thief and each being robbed by passing time. And from *A Thousand Clowns* there are Murray who is tortured by the world he sees, Leo who wants to believe in himself but cannot, and Arthur who purposefully surrenders to the establishment but survives. He catches the wind and goes with it. Mainly, Gardner's characters appear to catch the cold wind straight in their faces, defiantly, stubbornly, and disastrously—and die, in one sense or another, romantically and in the glow of stage sentiment.

The comic appeal of Gardner's plays comes from his mastery of comic technique and his philosophy as a writer. Although not a storyteller and, as his plays show, somewhat contemptuous of traditional plotting in a play, he likes to hear people talk. He is also a dreamer who, like Nat, can make up little scenes which may appear as a line, a speech, or an incident—a joke, a monologue, or an episode. Like Max Silverman, Gardner does not believe in standing around and watching. One must act, wage battle even while knowing that victory is impossible. Like Murray he is afraid of "dying alive." Although called a "laureate of losers," Gardner has a sense of comic balance that contradicts this description. He sees humor, not sadness. Losers stand around; fighters keep the soul alive, and Gardner's characters, synthetic and

romanticized or caricatured as they may be, are ever hopeful, even in their fantastic, ridiculous, or childishly recalcitrant attempts to escape whatever worlds surround them. Gardner sees his people as survivors, and in juxtaposing their acts with those of others in the world he experiences he creates dramatic tension in silly-serious, comic-tragic, and pathetic-horrible situations while revealing a real comic irony.

Structurally, Gardner's plays include a lavishly encumbered stage and a love story. As visual metaphors there are the incredibly messy room in *A Thousand Clowns*, the beach that sprouts fireworks in *The Goodbye People*, the terrace in *Thieves*, and the bench in *I'm Not Rappaport*. Gardner truly loves the long monologue, the quick repartee of stand-up comedians, and the one-line gag. Jewish humor, local New York humor, visual jokes, absurd comparisons, and the unexpected retort vie for attention in a selected accumulation of odd people. In *Thieves* a character complains that "all I ever got from this neighborhood was four knife scars, two broken noses and a fruitcake wife! And they all hurt when it rains." Gardner's comedies are assuredly enhanced by good actors: his monologues are a comedian's food and wine; his dialogue can be as sprightly and as touching as the actor can create. Music also is significant in his plays to please or assault the ear as the clutter on stage may accost the eye. Within this grand expression of comic theatre where dreams cannot be answered but believing in dreams is deemed necessary, Gardner presents his characters, mainly in episodes involving the rituals of lovemaking in the modern world. Then, he stops; conclusions are not his métier.

The comic possibilities that have brought Gardner success, however, may also serve to limit his acceptance with future audiences. During the 1960's, for example, audiences applauded the rebellious youth's single-minded escape into fantasy from a real world where they found people living as "fakes." Today's audiences are more interested in contending with this real world. Carlton, the young thief in *Thieves*, is not funny to them, nor is Sally, who contends seriously and unsuccessfully with a stubbornly inhuman father. It is scarcely funny to a generation concerned with people starving in the streets that the doorman is not sleeping but dead. Gardner presents father-daughter relationships in *The Goodbye People*, *Thieves*, and *I'm Not Rappaport*, each one funny to him, each one geared to the comic sense of a different audience. In *I'm Not Rappaport* he catches the pathos as well as the comedy and with this development in his dramaturgy may advance beyond the comic banter of temporal pleasure.

—Walter J. Meserve

———————

GEE, Shirley (née Thieman). British. Born in London, 25 April 1932. Educated at Frensham Heights, Farnham, Surrey; Webber-Douglas Academy of Dramatic Art, London. Married Donald Gee in 1965; two sons. Stage and television actress, 1952–66. Member of the Radio Committee, Society of Authors, 1980–82. Since 1986 member of the Women's Committee, Writers Guild. Recipient: *Radio Times* award, 1974; Pye award, for radio play, 1979; Sony award, for radio play, 1983; Susan Smith Blackburn prize, 1984; Samuel Beckett award, 1984. Agent: John Rush, David Higham Associates, 5–8 Lower John Street, London W1R 4HA. Address: 28 Fernshaw Road, London SW10 0TF, England.

PUBLICATIONS

Plays

Typhoid Mary (broadcast 1979; produced London, 1983).
    Published in Best Radio Plays of 1979, London, Eyre
    Methuen, 1980.
Never in My Lifetime (broadcast 1983; produced London,
    1984; Stamford, Connecticut, 1987). Published in Best
    Radio Plays of 1983, London, Methuen, 1984.
Ask for the Moon (produced London, 1986). London,
    Faber, 1987.
Warrior (produced Chichester, 1989). London, French,
    1991.

Radio Plays: Stones, 1974; The Vet's Daughter, from the
novel by Barbara Comyns, 1976; Moonshine, 1977; Typhoid
Mary, 1979; Bedrock, 1979; Men on White Horses, from the
novel by Pamela Haines, 1981; Our Regiment (documentary),
1982; Never in My Lifetime, 1983; Against the Wind, 1988;
The Forsyte Chronicles, co-adaptation of The Forsyte Saga by
John Galsworthy, 1990.

Television Plays: Long Live the Babe, 1984; Flights, 1985.

*

Critical Studies: British Radio Drama edited by John
Drakakis, London, Cambridge University Press, 1981; The
Way to Write Radio Drama by William Ash, London, Elm
Tree, 1985; The Feminist Companion to Literature in English,
edited by Virginia Blain, Patricia Clements, and Isobel
Grundy, London, Batsford, 1990.

Theatrical Activities:
Actress: roles with Worthing, Hull, Malvern, and other
repertory companies, and in more than 100 television plays
and series episodes, 1952–66.

Shirley Gee comments:

I really don't like to make statements about my work; I
hope those who see or hear the plays will have the freedom to
draw their own conclusions. However, I'll try. I suppose I
write to try to understand. To make sense out of chaos. To
confront some terrors. I wonder what particular individuals
might do trapped in a particular public event or social context. I watch them grapple, try to come to terms, fight to find
the meaning of their lives. Often they are in a besieged
landscape: the dead in Stones; Mary the typhoid carrier,
imprisoned, in Typhoid Mary; British soldiers and Irish
nationals in Belfast in Never in My Lifetime; the Victorian
laceworkers and present-day sweatshop workers in Ask for
the Moon. They are tyrannised by fear or poverty or loneliness or war. Their individual needs and desires run counter to
the needs and desires of society, and must be sacrificed to that
society. Still, they behave with love and courage. They save
one another despite themselves. They beam a little light into
a dark world. I wonder what I would have done, had I been in
their place.

* * *

The list of women playwrights who have won major awards
is, although increasing daily, not long, and one might expect
Shirley Gee's name to be better known. Sadly, it is easy to
account for her comparative lack of fame: most of her work
has been written for radio, the most critically neglected medium of the past few decades. In Gee's case this is doubly
unfortunate, for her radio experience is what gives her work
for the stage its special vitality.

The radio playwright enjoys virtually unlimited freedom of
approach; as long as he or she can unlock the listener's
imagination anything is possible. Radio allows all kinds of
spatial and temporal jumps; it is possible to create and instantly change the scenery, flash backwards or forwards in
time, simply by the use of a few words or a snatch of song.
Gee has always been one of the most technically authoritative
of radio writers, and it was perhaps the triple accolade given
to her radio play Typhoid Mary—a Giles Cooper award, a
Pye award, a Special Commendation in the Italia prize—that
prompted the Royal Shakespeare Company to stage the play
and discover that its darting, fragmented structure worked
onstage with verve and power.

Typhoid Mary is Mary Mallon, the tragic Irish immigrant
who unwittingly spread the disease around New York at the
beginning of the century. Instead of narrating her story
straightforwardly, Gee creates a kaleidoscope of fragments:
in one brief scene, for example, disembodied voices chant
sensationalist newspaper headlines ("Calamity Cook Kills
Wholesale"), a lawyer pronounces on her status in dry legal
prose, a chorus sings "Molly Malone" to the accompaniment
of spoons, and Mary in the midst speaks of her pain and grief
as if she was in her own living room.

This lively variety of styles (from naturalism to the surreal)
provides an analysis of her plight from several simultaneous
angles. The spoon music stresses her background as struggling immigrant desperate to make good in a new world, and
the humming of "Molly Malone" counterpoints this; Mary is
already enshrined in popular song and in the popular imagination as a killer. The crude unthinking bias against her is fed
by the press and allowed by the law. In fact Gee allows us in a
few seconds to see Mary with the whole of American society
ranged against her, with a vividness and compression naturalistic techniques would never permit.

For all its liveliness Typhoid Mary remained a study of a
tragic individual without wider resonance. Gee's next ambitious work, also originating in radio, showed her wrestling
with political drama. Never in My Lifetime opens shatteringly
with the shooting of two British soldiers in a Belfast disco,
then flashes backwards and forwards in time to explain the
motives behind the shooting and its consequences. We follow
the lives of the soldiers—Charlie, badly wounded, with a
pregnant wife, and Tom, who dies—and the girls who lured
them into ambush—the terrorist Maire, and Tess who is
sleeping with Tom and joins Maire to save her own life when
this becomes known to the IRA. By juxtaposing past and
present, snatches of song, and snippets of Belfast life, Gee
creates their lives and evokes unforgettably the grief of their
loved ones. On a less personal level, however, the play is not
so satisfying. The breadth and daring of the structure give the
misleading impression that the play is presenting the fullest
possible spectrum of Belfast politics. In fact, the cards are
stacked. The only voice to speak for the Republican cause,
for instance, is the voice of terrorism. Through the violent
and twisted Maire, not just this killing but the whole concept
of Irish nationhood is associated with a chain of ugly and
sexually perverse imagery, contrasting with the wholesome
lyricism of the naive Tess. The soldiers are described taking
part in a brutal attack, but it is not shown, whereas the disco
incident is terrifyingly realised. Essentially the play takes a
pro-British stance while presenting itself as a slice of life; it
seems that Gee is not fully in control of her material.

Ask for the Moon, however, shows a clearer political direction, and also translates the techniques of radio into striking

visual terms. It shows simultaneously two generations of workers, Victorian lacemakers and women in a modern sweat shop. Gee's talent for conveying the texture of working life does more than lament their exploitation; she also shows how working conditions are structured to prevent unionisation. A lacemaker is forced to provide her child with opium so that the group will not slow up production; an old sweatshop hand steals another's piece-work to escape the sack. Gee makes it clear that this is forced on them despite real comradeship and caring and pride in their work. There is a touching moment when time barriers are broken and both groups join in wonder to admire a wedding veil that has cost one woman her eyesight. The women have no illusions about why they betray one another, and in the final anger of one of them, at first blind rage and then quiet planning for her own future, there is a hint that they are learning at last how to change.

—Frances Gray

GELBART, Larry. American. Born in Chicago, Illinois, 25 February 1928. Educated at John Marshall High School, Chicago; Fairfax High School, Los Angeles. Served in the United States Army, 1945–46. Married Pat Marshall in 1956; two daughters and three sons. Radio and television writer from 1947; producer or co-producer of television series including *The Marty Feldman Comedy Machine*, 1971, *M*A*S*H*, 1972–76, *Karen*, 1975, *United States*, 1980, and the *Academy Awards Show*, 1985. Artist-in-residence, Northwestern University, Evanston, Illinois, 1984–85. Recipient: Sylvania award, 1958; Emmy award, 1958, 1973; Tony award, 1963, 1990 (twice); Peabody award, 1964, 1975; Montreux Television Festival Golden Rose award, 1971; Humanitas award, 1976; Edgar Allan Poe award, 1977, 1990; Writers Guild of America award, 1977, 1978, 1982; Christopher award, 1978; Laurel award, 1981; Los Angeles Film Critics award, 1982; New York Film Critics award, 1982; National Society of Film Critics award, 1982; Pacific Broadcasting Pioneers award, 1987; Lee Strasberg award, 1990; Outer Critics Circle award, 1990 (twice); Drama Desk award, 1990; New York Drama Critics Circle award, 1990; Beverly Hills Theater Guild Spotlight award, 1991. Member, Motion Picture Academy of Arts and Sciences. D. Litt: Union College, Schenectady, New York, 1986. Address: 807 North Alpine Drive, Beverly Hills, California 90210, U.S.A.

PUBLICATIONS

Plays

My L.A. (revue; produced Los Angeles, 1948).
The Conquering Hero, with Burt Shevelove, adaptation of the work by Preston Sturges, music by Moose Charlap, lyrics by Norman Gimbel (produced New York, 1960).
A Funny Thing Happened on the Way to the Forum, with Burt Shevelove, music and lyrics by Stephen Sondheim, adaptation of plays by Plautus (produced New York, 1962; London, 1963; revised version produced Los Angeles, 1971, New York, 1972). New York, Dutton, 1963.
Jump (produced London, 1971).
Sly Fox, adaptation of *Volpone* by Ben Jonson (produced New York, 1976). New York, French, 1978.

Mastergate (produced Cambridge, Massachusetts, and New York, 1989). New York, French, 1990.
City of Angels, music by Cy Coleman, lyrics by David Zippel (produced New York, 1989; London, 1993). New York, Applause, 1990.
Power Failure (produced Cambridge, Massachusetts, 1991).
Peter and the Wolf (narration for ballet) (produced New York, 1991).

Screenplays: *The Notorious Landlady*, 1962; *The Thrill of It All*, with Carl Reiner, 1963; *The Wrong Box*, with Burt Shevelove, 1966; *Not with My Wife, You Don't*, with Norman Panama and Peter Barnes, 1966; *Oh, God*, 1977; *Movie Movie*, 1978; *Neighbors*, 1981; *Tootsie*, 1982; *Blame It on Rio*, 1984; *Barbarians at the Gate*, 1992.

Radio Writing: *Danny Thomas* ("Maxwell House Coffee Time"), 1945; *The Jack Paar Show*, 1945; *Duffy's Tavern*, 1945–47; *The Eddie Cantor Show*, 1947; *Command Performance* (Armed Forces Radio Service), 1947; *The Jack Carson Show*, 1948; *The Joan Davis Show*, 1948; *The Bob Hope Show*, 1948.

Television Writing: *The Bob Hope Show*, 1948–52; *The Red Buttons Show*, 1952; "*Honestly, Celeste!*" (*The Celeste Holm Show*), 1953; *The Patrice Munsel Show*, 1954–62; *The Pat Boone Show*, 1954; *Caesar's Hour*, 1955–57; *The Art Carney Specials*, 1958–59; *The Danny Kaye Show* (consultant), 1963; *The Marty Feldman Comedy Machine*, 1971; *M*A*S*H* series, 1972–76; *Karen*, 1975; *United States*, 1980; *Academy Award Show*, 1985, 1986; *Mastergate*, 1992.

Recordings: *Peter and the Wolf*, Philips Records, 1971; *Gulliver*, adaptation of the novel by Swift, Soundwings Records, 1989.

*

Theatrical Activities:
Director: **Plays**—*A Funny Thing Happened on the Way to the Forum*, Chichester and London, 1986. **Television**—several episodes of *M*A*S*H* series.

Larry Gelbart comments:
If anything I've ever written in any way reflects this dreamlike existence that passes for life, I can only hope that the mirror I've held up to it is sufficiently cracked.

* * *

In an age of often homogenised comedy, Larry Gelbart has helped to keep the tradition of American satirical writing alive. He has more than a trace of George S. Kaufman's lean, sharp style and, like Kaufman, he has also written for the musical theatre, undoubtedly helping the economic style and satiric thrust of his plays.

He is, in fact, one of the few book-writers of musicals whose scripts could survive without the music. *A Funny Thing Happened on the Way to the Forum*, co-authored with Burt Shevelove, was a glorious reminder back in 1962, at a time when the musical tended towards refinement, that the American musical stage had one foot in its indigenous past of vaudeville and burlesque as well as one in European operetta. *Funny Thing* exploited with gleeful zest the happy marriage between the staples of Plautine farce and those of the Orpheum Circuit's world of top bananas and bump-and-grind. Its fusion of low comedy and high-precision plotting makes it one of the endearingly funny musical comedies.

Gelbart, working solo, also later restored faith in the comedy element of musical comedy in his book for *City of Angels*, opening in 1989 at the close of a decade dominated by the sung-through spectacles of the Lloyd–Webber dominated British ascendancy.

The show came out of Gelbart's collaboration on a flop revue, *My L.A.*, which showed him "just how theatrically marvellous that marvellously theatrical city was," and his wry evocation of L.A.'s contrasted mean streets and Bel Air poolsides, filtered through pastiche of classic detective fiction and *films noirs*, helped give his script its acrid wit. It is an extremely layered script, building up complex levels of irony, but always moving the story forward, essential for a musical. It tells the story of a novelist (Stine), gradually selling out to Hollywood crassness, while simultaneously presenting scenes from his work which mirror those in his life. His work is an adaptation of one of his movies into a screenplay built around a fictional ex-cop turned private eye (Stone), the Stone scenes creating an on-stage classic private-eye movie. The Hollywood of the 1940's is created in technicolour while the movie is staged in monochrome, the two worlds coalescing as the levels of reality and fantasy combine into a hall of mirrors. Again, Gelbart's script was genuinely funny—not least in its portrait of a wonderfully monstrous movie mogul, Buddy Fidler—as it joyfully skewered Tinseltown pretensions.

Gelbart's other big theatrical success was also a study of human duplicity, greed, and gullibility—his nimble 1976 re-working of *Volpone* set in the rumbustious Barbary coast world of San Francisco at the turn of the century. *Sly Fox* has a satirical energy that gives Jonson's original some key twists. Purists might carp that he diminishes a masterpiece, but Gelbart really uses Jonson's play as a trampoline for some fast and furious fun. His language—a sinewy, muscular prose—finds a bold American equivalent for Jonson's verse, not least in his re-working of Volpone's great speeches to his gold as Foxwell S. Sly hymns his treasure-chest. And his trial scene, with his no-nonsense Judge (played by the same actor as plays Sly) presiding over a courtroom filled with cheats and chisellers, is side-splitting, especially in the evidence of the venal good-time girl Merrilee Fancy, giving her occupation to the court as "a pleasure engineer."

Gelbart's other theatrical efforts have been less successful. *Jump*, a frenetic farce centered round a zany New York family, sank under a dismal London production and *Mastergate* flopped on a Broadway no more hospitable than usual to political satire. Both were uneven pieces, but hopefully these failures will not keep Gelbart away from the theatre for long.

—Alan Strachan

GELBER, Jack. American. Born in Chicago, Illinois, 12 April 1932. Educated at the University of Illinois, Urbana, B.S. in journalism 1953. Married Carol Westenberg in 1957; one son and one daughter. Writer-in-residence, City College, New York, 1965–66; adjunct professor of drama, Columbia University, New York, 1967–72. Since 1972 professor of drama, Brooklyn College, City University of New York. Recipient: Obie award, 1960, for directing, 1972; Vernon Rice award, 1960; Guggenheim fellowship, 1963, 1966; Rockefeller grant, 1972; National Endowment for the Arts

grant, 1974; CBS-Yale fellowship, 1974. Address: Department of English, Brooklyn College, Bedford Avenue and Avenue H, Brooklyn, New York 11210, U.S.A.

PUBLICATIONS

Plays

The Connection (produced New York, 1959; London, 1961). New York, Grove Press, 1960; London, Faber, 1961.
The Apple (produced New York, 1961). New York, Grove Press, 1961.
Square in the Eye (produced New York, 1965). New York, Grove Press, 1966.
The Cuban Thing (also director: produced New York, 1968). New York, Grove Press, 1969.
Sleep (produced New York and Edinburgh, 1972). New York, Hill and Wang, 1972.
Barbary Shore, adaptation of the novel by Norman Mailer (also director: produced New York, 1973).
Farmyard, adaptation of a play by Franz Xaver Kroetz (also director: produced New Haven, Connecticut, 1975). Published in *Farmyard and Four Other Plays*, by Kroetz, New York, Urizen, 1976.
Rehearsal (also director: produced New York, 1976).
Starters (produced New Haven, Connecticut, 1980).
Big Shot (also director: produced New Rochelle, New York, 1988).
Magic Valley (produced New York, 1990).

Screenplay: *The Connection*, 1962.

Novel

On Ice. New York, Macmillan, 1964; London, Deutsch, 1965.

                              *

Bibliography: *Ten Modern American Playwrights* by Kimball King, New York, Garland, 1982.

Critical Studies: *Seasons of Discontent* by Robert Brustein, New York, Simon and Schuster, 1965, London, Cape, 1966; *Les U.S.A.: A la Recherche de Leur Identité* by Pierre Dommergues, Paris, Grasset, 1967; *Tynan: Right and Left* by Kenneth Tynan, London, Longman, 1967, New York, Atheneum, 1968; *Now: Theater der Erfahrung* edited by Jens Heilmeyer and Pia Frolich, Cologne, Schauberg, 1971; *The Living Theatre* by Pierre Biner, New York, Avon, 1972; *Theatricality* by Elizabeth Burns, New York, Harper, 1972; *Off Broadway* by Stuart Little, New York, Coward McCann, 1972; *People's Theatre in Amerika* by Karen Taylor, New York, Drama Book Specialists, 1973; introduction by Richard Gilman to *The Apple, and Square in the Eye*, New York, Viking Press, 1974.

Theatrical Activities:
Director: **Plays**—several of his own plays, and works at Lincoln Center, New Theatre Workshop, and the American Place Theatre, including *The Kitchen* by Arnold Wesker, 1966, *Kool Aid* by Merle Molofsky, 1971, *The Kid* by Robert Coover, 1972, *The Chickencoop Chinaman* by Frank Chin, 1972, *Eulogy for a Small-Time Thief* by Miguel Piñero, 1977, and *Seduced* by Sam Shepard, 1979; *Indians* by Arthur Kopit, London, 1968; *The Man and the Fly* by José Ruibal,

New York, 1982; *The House of Ramon Iglesia* by José Rivera, New York, 1983; *The Dolphin Position* by Percy Granger, New York, 1983; *Mink on a Gold Hook* by James Ryan, New York, 1986; *The Independence of Eddie Rose* by William Yellow Robe Jr., New York, 1989.
Actor: **Film**—*Another Woman*, 1988.

* * *

Jack Gelber, playwright, award-winning director, and teacher, has had one of the most important and innovative careers in contemporary American drama, and in discussing this career there are two aspects of it that must be taken into account: the kind of influence his plays had upon the improvisational and group drama of the 1960's and early 1970's, and the particular vision the plays themselves present.

The most influential of his plays is *The Connection*, produced by the Living Theatre in 1959, and its theatrical characteristics introduce the Gelber technique: the play and production represent, or seem to represent, an attack upon the "written" play. The usual authority figures of playwright and producer are parodied, plot is suppressed, and improvisation takes their place as the actors, supposedly junkies and musicians drawn from everyday life, improvise a play from their personal lives to the complementary accompaniment of Charlie Parker-type jazz. Dramatic time is ambiguous and also improvised, with the specifically allocated length of the musical passages its clearest measure. Gelber deliberately avoids detailed psychological characterization and concentrates upon communal, representative figures although three of the characters, with specific functional roles, are especially vivid: Cowboy, the "connection" who incites the events: Sister Salvation, the unexpected guest who places the play in perspective; and Leach, the everyman of the play's world who overdoses on heroin. This "spontaneous" making of a play, the seemingly improvised action with its jazz accompaniment, the use of photographers to validate another version of the happenings, the interaction with the spectators, all combine to break down the usual relationship between actors and audience, reality and illusion, play and life. The subsequent group theater movement with its distrust of authority, its emphasis upon spontaneity and community, and its attack upon the text was clearly foreshadowed, even partly suggested, by the success of Gelber's play. But it is important to note that *The Connection* is itself a carefully written text.

Gelber's subsequent plays explore and expand these characteristics of *The Connection*. *The Apple* is communal and without central characters; its action is deliberately ambiguous and chaotic; and the actors shift in and out of character and participation. *Square in the Eye* is a family play about Ed Stone, a teacher, his wife, the children, and grandparents. Here various theatrical styles, including stand-up comedy and movies, undermine realism, and the chronology of events is purposefully disrupted. In *Sleep* two sleep scientists replace the playwright; the world of the play is a sleep laboratory; time is measured in sleep cycles; and the hero Gil, whose dreams coalesce into a kind of psychological action, proves on examination to be an average everyman. His sleeping and dreams, which correspond to the waking sleep of the addicts in *The Connection*, question the nature of reality, and in the play's most important speech one of the scientists expands the ambiguity into social statement: "The fact is that we have wired up a scientifically selected sample of the entire population and we have found, I know you won't believe this, we have found that they are technically asleep." In *Rehearsal*, publicly admired by several of his fellow dramatists, a play is in rehearsal; the nervous director cannot control the perform-

ance; and the producer is an incompetent alcoholic. The theater itself becomes the setting as the play emerges from the "interpolated" digressions initiated by the actors.

These formal characteristics suggest, of course, a view of life, and it is his second play, *The Apple*, that most clearly provides its symbol. The play invites the audience to make what it will of the apple and its connotations are many, but the biblical reference to what Milton calls "the fruit of that forbidden tree" is inescapable. The Gelber dramatic world describes a society that seems to have begun with a mythic expulsion, a communal and pragmatic place without heroes where man has become his ordinary self and disappointment and death are inevitable. It is a world where a secure reality is generally illusory and a world where drugs and call it sleep become the refuge of the human imagination which cannot recall it to order.

Gelber's writing, like the title of his best known play, has many connections, connections with the contemporary theater and the world it reflects, and he is paradoxically both the American playwrights' playwright and the chronicler of the American everyman.

—Gaynor F. Bradish

GEMS, Jonathan (Malcolm Frederick). British. Born in London, 7 January 1952; son of Pam Gems, *q.v.* Educated at Stowe School, Buckinghamshire, 1965–67; Holland Park Comprehensive, London, 1967–68; Sandown Grammar, Isle of Wight, 1968–69; Royal Academy of Dramatic Art, London, 1970–71; Exeter College of Art, 1971–72. Married Catherine Hall in 1981. Founder, with Richard Branson, *Student* magazine, 1969–70; managing director, Capricorn Graphics, founder, Jonny and the Gemstones music group, and editor, *It's All Lies* (adult comic), 1970–73; deputy manager, Portobello Hotel, and managing director, Holland Mirrors, both London, 1973–75; stage manager, Open Space Theatre, London, and managing director, Jean Collette Seel fashion company, 1975–76; stage manager, Half Moon Theatre, London, 1976–77. Recipient: George Devine award, 1980; Critics Circle award, 1986; Aspen Film Festival award, 1992. Lives in Los Angeles. Agent: Sebastian Born, Curtis Brown, 161–168 Regent Street, London W1R 5TB, England.

PUBLICATIONS

Plays

Jesus Rides Out (produced London, 1978).
The Shithouse of the August Moon (produced London, 1978).
Rinni Bootsie Tutti Frutti (produced London, 1978).
The Dentist (produced London, 1979).
The Tax Exile (produced London, 1979). London, Playwrights Press, 1986.
The Secret of the Universe (produced London, 1980).
Naked Robots (produced London, 1980). With *Susan's Breasts* and *The Paranormalist*, 1989.
The Paranormalist (produced London, 1982). With *Naked Robots* and *Susan's Breasts*, 1989.
Doom Doom Doom Doom (produced London, 1984).

Susan's Breasts (produced London, 1985). With *Naked Robots* and *The Paranormalist*, 1989.
Naked Robots, Susan's Breasts, The Paranormalist. Birmingham, Oberon, 1989.

Screenplays: *White Mischief*, with Michael Radford, 1985; *The Dress*, 1990.

*

Theatrical Activities:
Director: **Plays**—some of his own plays; *The Treat* by Pam Gems, London, 1982 (co-director); *These Foolish Things* by Philip Davis, London, 1983. **Film**—*The Dress*, 1990.

Jonathan Gems comments:
I wanted to be a great playwright but instead I've ended up writing movie scripts in Los Angeles.

* * *

It would seem that Jonathan Gems has become one more in a line of younger British dramatists (Antony Minghella is another instance) wooed away from the theatre by movies. However skilled Gems's screen-writing may be, it would be sad to lose his special talent from the theatre.

Perhaps he became disillusioned by the fact that none of his plays of the 1980's made the break through into the mainstream. However successful he may have been in filling small theatres on the London fringe, he clearly wanted to reach a wider audience, not to mention make a decent living, hardly possible on fringe royalties, even with packed houses. But the fact remains that few dramatists managed to pin down with such lethal accuracy and comedic flair the subcultures of the 1980's.

Gems made a big stir with *The Tax Exile*, a rarity of modern high comedy, tracing the destruction of a decent, middle-aged man by the venality of his family. High comic spirits and a strongly moral core made an unusual combination from a young writer in 1979, and all his plays of the 1980's were fuelled by this fusion. In *Naked Robots*, as he admitted, "I wrote about me and my friends," to subsequent lack of enthusiasm when he started showing the script around, everyone rejecting it on the grounds that the characters were disgusting and the situations unbelievable ("I was baffled. This was my life!"). The RSC rescued the play and its 1980 Warehouse production remains one of the company's key achievements in new writing. Set in a warehouse dominated by a bed comprised of 10 stacked mattresses, its characters are predominantly young, either drifting like the middle-class punk Gemma or trying to carve out careers in fashion or the music industry like the central couple Desna and Nudy, and the play, tracing the shifting relationships that develop, covers a world of squats, casual sex, abortion, pop music, and drugs (Gems's dealer, Ray, is often an hilariously inept figure). He neither judges nor sentimentalises his characters; the play remains one of the most clear-eyed of its period.

The family seems less than a cosy unit in most of Gems's plays; characters like Desna and Gemma seem totally detached from their parents. And initially in *The Paranormalist* we seem again to be in the midst of the post-nuclear family with the paranormalist grandfather Sonny resented by his mixed-up psychiatrist daughter Barbara, at odds in turn with her drop-out daughter Mopsa, who is recovering from an abortion as the play begins. *The Paranormalist* is hardly short on action—it involves several paranormal experiments, Sonny's levitation, and an exorcism. Partly this was Gems's

attempt to move beyond the technical restrictions of studio theatres, but it also reflected his sense of the inexplicable and the unknown that underlines most lives. Sonny's serenity casts an increasing spell over the action which ends, after the violence of the exorcism which casts out Barbara's demons, with a beguiling scene of unity as the characters sing a harmonised version of "The Melody Lingers On" as the lights fade.

Gems's most recently produced play is *Susan's Breasts*. He wanted to tackle the theme of love but the play "became predominantly a play about people *not* falling in love," except for the mysterious character of Lemon, a disturbed but passionate young man who gives the play its emotional resonance. The play focuses on another group of young Londoners, some more affluent and distinctly less appealing than those in *Naked Robots*, the men mostly a brutish, sexist lot interested solely in financial and social success. The women—aspiring actress Susan, American model Pookie, and the drug-addict Carol—all seem to connive at the males' sexism in a mid-1980's world where love is sex and relationships are business deals. Opening with a superbly written scene at a picnic in a London park, the play moves into a new gear as Lemon's love for (and obsession with) Susan increases. Susan has been diagnosed as sterile; she casually sleeps once with Lemon and becomes pregnant (the breasts of the title now increase in size), and although Lemon escapes from the asylum in which he has been committed to plead with her, the closing implication is that Susan, faced with the loss of a movie role, will abort the child. The play's final image of Susan being comforted by the increasingly addicted Carol is another instance of Gems's ability to fuse strong theatrical images with his gift for the dialogue of his splendidly varied casts of characters.

—Alan Strachan

GEMS, (Iris) Pam(ela, née Price). British. Born in Bransgore, Dorset, 1 August 1925. Educated at Brockenhurst County High School, 1936–41; Manchester University, 1946–49, B.A. (honours) in psychology 1949. Served in the Women's Royal Naval Service, 1944–46. Married Keith Gems in 1949; two sons, including Jonathan Gems, *q.v.*, and two daughters. Research assistant, BBC, London, 1950–53. Agent: ACTAC, 16 Cadogan Lane, London S.W.1, England.

PUBLICATIONS

Plays

Betty's Wonderful Christmas (for children; produced London, 1972).
My Warren, and After Birthday (produced London, 1973).
The Amiable Courtship of Miz Venus and Wild Bill (produced London, 1973).
Sarah B. Divine! (additional material), by Tom Eyen, music by Jonathan Kramer (produced London, 1973).
Go West Young Woman (produced London, 1974).
Up in Sweden (produced Leicester, 1975; London, 1980).
Dusa, Fish, Stas, and Vi (as *Dead Fish*, produced Edinburgh, 1976; as *Dusa, Fish, Stas, and Vi*, produced London, 1976;

Los Angeles, 1978; New York, 1980). London, French, and New York, Dramatists Play Service, 1977.

The Project (produced London, 1976).

Guinevere (produced Edinburgh and London, 1976).

The Rivers and Forests, adaptation of a play by Marguerite Duras (produced London, 1976).

My Name Is Rosa Luxemburg, adaptation of a play by Marianne Auricoste (produced London, 1976).

Franz into April (produced London, 1977).

Queen Christina (produced Stratford-on-Avon, 1977; London, 1979; revised version produced London, 1982). London, St. Luke's Press, 1982.

Piaf (produced Stratford-on-Avon and London, 1978; New York, 1981). Ashover, Derbyshire, Amber Lane Press, 1979; New York, French, 1983.

Ladybird, Ladybird (produced London, 1979).

Sandra (produced London, 1979).

Uncle Vanya, adaptation of a play by Chekhov (produced London, 1979; San Francisco, 1983). London, Eyre Methuen, 1979.

A Doll's House, adaptation of a play by Ibsen (produced Newcastle upon Tyne, 1980).

Sketches in *Variety Night* (produced London, 1982).

The Treat (produced London, 1982).

Aunt Mary (produced London, 1982). Published in *Plays by Women 3,* edited by Michelene Wandor, London, Methuen, 1984.

The Cherry Orchard, adaptation of a play by Chekhov (produced Leicester, 1984).

Loving Women (produced London, 1984). Included in *Three Plays*, 1985.

Camille, adaptation of a play by Dumas fils (produced Stratford-on-Avon, 1984; London, 1985; New Haven, Connecticut, 1986). Included in *Three Plays*, 1985.

Pasionaria, music by Paul Sand, lyrics by Gems and Sand (produced Newcastle upon Tyne, 1985).

Three Plays (includes *Piaf, Camille, Loving Women*). London, Penguin, 1985.

The Danton Affair, adaptation of a work by Stanislawa Przybyszewska (produced London, 1986).

The Blue Angel, adaptation of a novel by Heinrich Mann (produced Stratford-on-Avon, 1991; London, 1992).

Television Plays: *A Builder by Trade*, 1961; *We Never Do What They Want*, 1979.

Novels

Mrs. Frampton. London, Bloomsbury, 1989.
Bon Voyage, Mrs. Frampton. London, Bloomsbury, 1990.

*

Theatrical Activities:
Actress: **Film**—*Nineteen Eighty-Four*, 1984.

* * *

Contemporary women playwrights explore areas of experience that the stage has traditionally ignored, and are developing styles designed as a radical contrast to the standard dramatic forms. Indeed, from a feminist viewpoint the category of "woman-writer" defines "a species of creativity that challenges the dominant image," since "the very concept of the 'writer' implies *maleness*." However, like Caryl Churchill, Pam Gems rejected this extreme position, declaring that "the phrase 'feminist writer' is absolutely meaningless because it

implies polemic, and polemic is about changing things in a direct political way. Drama is subversive."

Like Churchill too, Gems developed her vision and theatrical techniques through dealing with historical subjects; and their example has been influential, making the history play characteristic of women's drama over the last decade. The tension between received ideas of the past—reinforcing the subservient status of women by relegating them to invisibility—and the very different feminist perspective, contributes to the thematic complexity of such plays.

Like many women dramatists, Pam Gems came to the theatre late, after 20 years of marriage and child-raising. Starting on the fringe, her early work for feminist theatre groups included an autobiographical piece, together with two monologues about female isolation and abortion, and a satiric pantomime. *Queen Christina*, her first major play, struck a new note and established all her central themes.

As in this play, Gems's most characteristic work dramatizes the human reality of women who have been transformed into cultural symbols. These range from the 17th-century Swedish Queen who renounced her crown, and a 19th-century courtesan, to a modern nightclub singer, or most recently *The Blue Angel* image of Marlene Dietrich as vampire sexuality. In each case the character is set against a familiar and highly romanticized picture. The counter-source for the earliest of Gems's historical dramas was the classic Garbo film of an ethereal and intellectual beauty, who abdicates for love, then finds consolation in religion when the man for whom she has sacrificed everything is killed in a duel. *Piaf* turns from Hollywood myth to the sanitized commercial image of a vulnerable street-sparrow, a purely emotional being whose songs are the direct expression "of unhappiness . . . of being made helpless by love . . . of being alone." *Camille* is a reversal of both Dumas's sentimentally tragic *La Dame aux camélias* and Verdi's operatic idealization in *La Traviata*.

The deforming pressures of society are most fully explored in *Queen Christina*, who provides a test-case for issues of sexual definition, biological determinism and social programming. As the sole heir to a kingdom at war, this historical figure has been "reared as a man . . . And then, on her accession, told to marry and breed, that is to be a woman. By which time, of course, like males of her era, she despised women as weak, hysterical, silly creatures." For Gems "It is a confusion which seems as apposite as ever." Forced to abdicate, she searches Europe for a way of life in which she can be herself. She is hailed as "an inspiration" to man-hating feminists (in the shape of 18th-century French "blue-stockings") in their campaign for control over their bodies through abortion. However, she finds herself repulsed by their life-denying warfare against the opposite sex, which she recognizes as the mirror image of male domination. She seeks spiritual emancipation in the Catholic Church, but finding that the Pope is interested only in exploiting her celibacy as religious propaganda, she asserts that "We won't deny the body." Offered the kingdom of Naples, she attempts to return to her masculine role. But when it forces her to kill her lover for betraying her invading armies, she rejects the whole male ethos, setting herself against domination in all its forms, master/servant as well as man/woman. Finally—when too old to bear children—she discovers the value of maternal instincts and affirms her biological nature.

For Gems, "Whichever way we look at it, the old norms won't do any more." The play asks what it means to be "female"; and Christina's example implies that a valid definition can only be reached through "the creation of a society more suited to both sexes"—which Gems has described as her aim in writing. Her concept of drama as subversive, rather than confrontational, means working on public consciousness indirectly. In line with this, her protagonist comes to realize that positive change can only be achieved through the specifically female, undervalued qualities of "weakness," non-violent resilience, and maternal nurture: "Half the world rapes and destroys—must women, the other half, join in?"

Typically, Gems creates an opposition between what is depicted on the stage and the audience's expectations. This is most obvious in *Piaf*, where incidents from the Parisian singer's life are interpolated with renditions of her popular lyrics. The gutter milieu, her prostitution and involvement in murder, drunkenness, and drugs contrast with the glittering public persona. Piaf disintegrates under the contradiction; and when the gap between idol and real woman can no longer be disguised, society preserves the false image by divorcing musical soul from female body.

At the same time, the way the songs rise out of the scenes emphasizes that Piaf's unconventional art and her physical crudity are inseparable. Her rise to stardom is a process of continual exploitation by the men who manage or marry her, and by her public (by extension the audience for Gems's play) who project their desires onto her. Yet it is also her status as a star that enables her to assert a personal autonomy, however provisional. This is expressed through her sexual freedom, which overturns all the moral codes. And the same reversal of conventional values is reflected in the play itself, which shows Piaf not only copulating but ostentatiously pissing on stage. Physicality at its most basic (a stock way of representing reality) demolishes the socially acceptable female stereotype, promoted and imposed by men, and thus provides an example of alternative values.

—Christopher Innes

GIBSON, William. American. Born in New York City, 13 November 1914. Educated at the City College of New York, 1930–32. Married Margaret Brenman in 1940; two sons. Since 1966 co-founding president, Berkshire Theatre Festival, Stockbridge, Massachusetts. Recipient: Harriet Monroe Memorial prize (*Poetry*, Chicago), 1945; Sylvania award, for television play, 1957. Agent: Flora Roberts Inc., 157 West 57th Street, New York, New York 10019. Address: Stockbridge, Massachusetts 01262, U.S.A.

PUBLICATIONS

Plays

I Lay in Zion (produced Topeka, Kansas, 1943). New York, French, 1947.
Dinny and the Witches: A Frolic on Grave Matters (produced Topeka, Kansas, 1945; revised version produced New York, 1959). With *The Miracle Worker*, New York, Atheneum, 1960.
A Cry of Players (produced Topeka, Kansas, 1948; New York, 1968). New York, Atheneum, 1969.
The Ruby (as William Mass), libretto based on the play *A Night at an Inn* by Lord Dunsany, music by Norman Dello Joio. New York, Ricordi, 1955.
The Miracle Worker: A Play for Television (televised 1957).

New York, Knopf, 1957; stage version (produced New York, 1959; London, 1961), with *Dinny and the Witches*, New York, Atheneum, 1960; published separately London, French, 1960.
Two for the Seesaw (produced New York and London, 1958). Published in *The Seesaw Log: A Chronicle of the Stage Production*, New York, Knopf, 1959; London, Corgi, 1962.
Golden Boy, with Clifford Odets, adaptation of the play by Odets, music by Charles Strouse, lyrics by Lee Adams (produced New York, 1964). New York, Atheneum, 1965.
American Primitive (as *John and Abigail*, produced Stockbridge, Massachusetts, 1969; as *American Primitive*, produced Washington, D.C., 1971). New York, Atheneum, 1972.
The Body and the Wheel: A Play Made from the Gospels (produced Lenox, Massachusetts, 1974). New York, Atheneum, 1975.
The Butterfingers Angel, Mary and Joseph, Herod the Nut, and the Slaughter of 12 Hit Carols in a Pear Tree: A Christmas Entertainment (produced Lenox, Massachusetts, 1974; London, 1979; New York, 1980). New York, Dramatists Play Service, 1975.
Golda (produced New York, 1977). Published as *How to Turn a Phoenix into Ashes: The Story of the Stage Production, with the Text, of Golda*, New York, Atheneum, 1978; *Golda* published London, French, 1978.
Goodly Creatures (produced Washington, D.C., 1980). New York, Dramatists Play Service, 1986.
Monday after the Miracle (produced Pretoria, South Africa, Charleston, South Carolina, and New York, 1982; Northampton, 1986; London, 1990). New York, Atheneum, 1983.
Handy Dandy (produced New York, 1984). New York, Dramatists Play Service, 1986.
Raggedy Ann and Andy, music and lyrics by Joe Raposo (produced Albany, New York, 1984; as *Rag Dolly*, produced Albany, 1985; as *Raggedy Ann*, produced New York City, 1986).

Screenplays: *The Cobweb*, 1954; *The Miracle Worker*, 1962.

Television Play: *The Miracle Worker*, 1957.

Novels

The Cobweb. New York, Knopf, and London, Secker and Warburg, 1954.
Necromancer. New York, Ace Science Fiction Books, 1984.

Verse

Winter Crook. New York, Oxford University Press, 1948.

Other

A Mass for the Dead. New York, Atheneum, 1968.
A Season in Heaven, Being a Log of an Expedition after That Legendary Beast, Cosmic Consciousness. New York, Atheneum, 1974.
Shakespeare's Game. New York, Atheneum, 1978.

* * *

William Gibson began as a novelist and poet, earning a reputation with a bestselling novel (*The Cobweb*) and a collection of verse (*Winter Crook*). An early playwriting interest resulted in a short verse drama about the Apostle Peter (*I Lay in Zion*), well-tailored for church groups, which predicted larger dramas to come.

Gibson's first success on the Broadway stage came in 1958 with *Two for the Seesaw*, a two-character drama about an embittered and lonely Nebraska lawyer in New York, separated from his wife, and his affair with a generous-hearted Bronx gamine down on her luck as a dancer. Although mutual love and dependency develop between these two disparate people, the lawyer's home ties are strong enough ultimately to draw him back to his wife. The drama's chief appeal lies in its engaging portrait of the dancer, whose colorful individuality and guileless love in the face of what she realizes is a doomed relationship grasps one's attention and sympathy. The role marked the author's uncommon ability to create strong parts for women and brought recognition to the actress Ann Bancroft who continued to portray other Gibson heroines. The play won praise from the critics and a substantial Broadway run resulting in a film contract for Gibson. Later it was adapted by others as the basis of the successful musical *Seesaw*. In *The Seesaw Log* Gibson chronicles with liveliness the page-to-stage odyssey of *Two for the Seesaw* in which he reveals his disenchantment with the professional production process without minimizing the significant contribution of his collaborators.

In 1959 Gibson's short-lived off-Broadway production of *Dinny and the Witches*, a satirical fantasy with song whose good intentions exceeded its effectiveness, was followed by his greatest success: *The Miracle Worker*. Originally written as a teleplay, the biography-drama portrays the teacher Anne Sullivan's turbulent but triumphant struggle to free her savagely recalcitrant pupil, Helen Keller, from the prison of a sightless and soundless body. Encompassing the time it takes the young teacher to gain mastery over the seemingly ungovernable child in order to teach her language, the play is brought to a poignant resolution when Helen, having had her hand repeatedly doused under the water pump, excitedly discovers the connection between words and things as she writes the word "water" in her teacher's palm. Somewhat uneven and clumsy structure results from an insufficient transformation of the drama from its television form. Although critics faulted the play for its sentimentality and deficiencies in craft, they and the public agreed on its theatrical impact in presenting a compassionate portrait of the heroic teacher who made possible the greatness of Helen Keller. The play's success led to a 1962 film scripted by Gibson. Less critically successful was the 1982 sequel *Monday after the Miracle*, which focuses on the lively courtship and marriage of Anne Sullivan, still Helen Keller's companion and protector 17 years later, to the journalist John Macy, who comes to live in the Boston-area household of the two women and unavoidably disturbs their dependent relationship. Macy, unable to subordinate his private and professional needs to the now famous and articulate Helen, who is first in his wife's priorities and also sexually awakened by his presence, must leave. Critically indicted for being less emotionally powerful in material and effect than its predecessor, this thoughtful play about the difficult choices between duty and happiness offers compelling characterizations of its three leading figures and deserved better than its brief Broadway run.

Extending his experience in 1965 by collaborating on the book for a musical version of Clifford Odets's *Golden Boy*, Gibson transforms the white violinist-turned-boxer hero into a non-musical black pugilist. Aided by Sammy Davis, Jr. in the title role and a well-adapted book, the musical's New York production won moderate success.

A return to biography in the late 1960's was marked both by *American Primitive*, a lively documentary portraying John and Abigail Adams through their letters over three stormy years, and *A Cry of Players*, Gibson's dramatization of young Will Shakespeare's scantily recorded Stratford years and those of his wife Anne, who emerges as a full-bodied character enlisting our compassion. Young Will is characterized as a restless, free-living profligate, frustrated by the limitations of his village and the constricting ties of his family, who survives public punishment for poaching to join Will Kempe's troupe of players for the destiny that awaits him in London. That critics validly observed that the writer's penchant for poetic speech was marred by his lapses into either pretentious or prosaic dialogue and did not offer sufficient approval to let the play endure on Broadway, did not diminish the drama's popularity with community and college theatres.

Less successful than his other ventures into biography, Gibson's *Golda* offers the decisive days of the Arab-Israeli Yom Kippur War of 1973 as a dramatic frame to surround an episodic portrait of Israel's Golda Meir. As the Prime Minister deals with strategy crises and conflicting generals, she recalls in a series of flashbacks key public and private moments in her life stretching from her childhood to her ultimately troubled marriage and strong commitment to Zionism. Despite several strong scenes and a periodically enlivening profile of the protagonist's humor and humanity, the play failed to compress sufficiently the abundant scope of the material and to disclose the private person behind the public one. Yet Gibson merits credit for attempting to dramatize so worthy and so difficult a subject who was then still living.

In the 1980's Gibson wrote two works considerably slighter than *Monday after the Miracle*: *Handy Dandy*, a thematically pointed comedy about a conservative judge and a radical anti-armaments nun constantly brought into his court; and the book for the musical *Raggedy Ann*, concerning a doll springing to life to solve a sick young girl's parental problems, whose 1986 New York production lasted only briefly.

Gibson's work in several media demonstrates both his literary and dramatic gifts, which have resulted in some important plays of sensitivity and substance. Largely successful in dramatizing actual figures, Gibson has secured his place in American letters as an effectual writer of biography-drama.

—Christian H. Moe

GILL, Peter. British. Born in Cardiff, Glamorgan, 7 September 1939. Educated at St. Illtyd's College, Cardiff. Actor, 1957–65; associate director, Royal Court Theatre, London, 1970–72; director, Riverside Studios, Hammersmith, London, 1976–80. Since 1980 associate director, National Theatre, London, and since 1984 director, National Theatre Studio. Recipient: Belgrade International Theatre Festival prize, for directing, 1968; George Devine award, 1968; British Theatre Association award, for directing, 1985. O.B.E. (Officer, Order of the British Empire), 1980. Agent: Casarotto Ramsay Ltd., National House, 60–66 Wardour Street, London W1V 3HP, England.

PUBLICATIONS

Plays

The Sleepers Den (produced London, 1965; revised version produced London, 1969). With *Over Gardens Out*, London, Calder and Boyars, 1970.

A Provincial Life, adaptation of a story by Chekhov (produced London, 1966).

Over Gardens Out (produced London, 1969). With *The Sleepers Den*, London, Calder and Boyars, 1970.

The Merry-Go-Round, adaptation of the play by D.H. Lawrence (produced London, 1973). London, Theatreprint, 1973.

Small Change (produced London, 1976). With *Kick for Touch*, London, Boyars, 1985.

The Cherry Orchard, adaptation of a play by Chekhov (produced London, 1978).

Kick for Touch (produced London, 1983). With *Small Change*, London, Boyars, 1985.

In the Blue (produced London, 1985). With *Mean Tears*, Birmingham, Oberon, 1987.

As I Lay Dying, adaptation of the novel by Faulkner (produced London, 1985).

Mean Tears (produced London, 1987). Published in *Plays International* (London), August 1987; with *In the Blue*, Birmingham, Oberon, 1987.

*

Theatrical Activities:
Director: **Plays**—all his own plays, and *A Collier's Saturday Night* by D. H. Lawrence, London, 1965, 1968; *The Dwarfs* by Harold Pinter, Glasgow, 1966; *The Ruffian on the Stair* by Joe Orton, London, 1966; *O'Flaherty, V. C.* by Shaw, London, 1966; *The Local Stigmatic* by Heathcote Williams, London, 1966; *The Soldier's Fortune* by Thomas Otway, London, 1967; *The Daughter-in-Law* by D. H. Lawrence, London, 1967, 1968, and Bochum, 1972; *Crimes of Passion* by Joe Orton, London, 1967, 1972; *June Evening* by Bill Naughton, toured, 1967; *The Widowing of Mrs. Holroyd* by D. H. Lawrence, London, 1968; *Life Price* by Michael O'Neill and Jeremy Seabrook, London, 1969; *Much Ado about Nothing*, Stratford, Ontario, 1969, London, 1981; *Hedda Gabler* by Ibsen, Stratford, Ontario, 1970; *Landscape and Silence* by Harold Pinter, New York, 1970; *The Duchess of Malfi* by Webster, London, 1971; *Macbeth*, Stratford, Ontario, 1971; *Cato Street* by Robert Shaw, London, 1971; *A Midsummer Night's Dream*, Zurich, 1972; *Crete and Sergeant Pepper* by John Antrobus, London, 1972; *Twelfth Night*, Stratford-on-Avon, 1974; *Fishing* by Michael Weller, New York, 1975; *The Fool* by Edward Bond, London, 1975; *As You Like It*, Nottingham and Edinburgh, 1975, London, 1976; *The Changeling* by Middleton and Rowley, London, 1978; *Measure for Measure*, London, 1979; *Julius Caesar*, London, 1980; *Scrape Off the Black* by Tunde Ikoli, London, 1980; *A Month in the Country* by Turgenev, London, 1981; *Don Juan* by Molière, London, 1981; *Major Barbara* by Shaw, London, 1982; *Danton's Death* by Georg Büchner, London, 1982; *Tales from Hollywood* by Christopher Hampton, 1983; *Venice Preserv'd* by Thomas Otway, London, 1984; *Antigone*, London, 1984; *Fool for Love* by Sam Shepard, London, 1984; *A Twist of Lemon* by Alex Renton, London, 1985; *The Garden of England* by Peter Cox, 1985; *Bouncing* by Rosemary Wilton, London, 1985; *Up for None* by Mick Mahoney, London, 1985; *Mrs. Klein* by Nicholas Wright, London, 1988; *Juno and the Paycock* by

Sean O'Casey, London, 1989. **Opera**—*The Marriage of Figaro* by Mozart, Leeds, 1987. **Television**—*Girl* by James Robson, 1973; *Grace* by David Storey, 1974; *A Matter of Taste* by Alex La Guma, 1974; *Fugitive* by Sean Walsh, 1974; *Hitting Town* by Stephen Poliakoff, 1976.
Actor: **Plays**—Customer in *Last Day in Dreamland* by Willis Hall, London, 1959; Plato in *The Trial of Cob and Leach* by Christopher Logue, London, 1959; Mangolis in *The Kitchen* by Arnold Wesker, London, 1959; Marcus and A Postcard Seller in *This Way to the Tomb* by Ronald Duncan, London, 1960; Silvius in *As You Like It*, 1962; in *The Caucasian Chalk Circle* by Brecht, London, 1962. **Films**—*H.M.S. Defiant* (*Damn the Defiant!*), 1962; *Zulu*, 1964.

*   *   *

For Peter Gill, playwriting has always been incidental to his profession as director. Indeed, he is still better known as the director who first realised the theatrical potential of D. H. Lawrence's plays than as the author of any of his own works, all of which he has also directed. His special skill, both as director and as dramatist, derives from the naturalistic exploitation of subtext, usually in association with relatively inarticulate proletarian characters, so that the simplest domestic situations are weighted and economically developed for their dramatic potential. *The Sleepers Den* illustrates this method well. The Shannon family, immured in an apparently condemned Cardiff slum flat, suffers variously from claustrophobia and agoraphobia; cornered, defensive, and scared to come to grips with their real dangers, they gradually expose themselves to emotional decomposition until their whole pattern of life collapses. The subtext becomes of paramount importance because of the characters' severely limited capacity even to begin to understand their problems. The Shannons are a fragmented family: an adult brother and sister, their bedridden mother, and a daughter. There is no explanation of how this situation has evolved, and there is no evidence that anyone understands it; across the three generations, power and defense are manipulated by trivial—but effective—gestures of bribery, blackmail, and threatening. Two outsiders—a debt collector and a Catholic social worker—function as catalysts to the situation, but the revelations which are offered seem ridiculous irrelevancies; the brother confesses to the social worker that he has been doing overtime and not telling his sister, and no one seems to understand the seriousness of court action for debt. It is clear that the characters' mental state is a reflection of their environment, that their lethargy and low self-esteem have a century of conditioning behind them. The dramatic crisis comes at the end of the second act, when the sister barricades herself inside the flat as a response to a situation which is too complicated for her to understand, let alone solve; the very short last act consists in her ignoring the pleadings of her brother and the daughter, who are now forced to sleep with friends. In Gill's 1969 production it was clear that old Mrs. Shannon is dead in the last act, so that the sister has shut herself in with the corpse. The interpretation is available that, far from presenting a grotesque family incident, the play suggests a recurrent pattern, with the now insane sister usurping her dead mother's role at the end, where a hereditary family state of introverted lethargy is on the verge of re-enactment. The ambiguous omission of an apostrophe from the play's title, which has been observed in all editions, may be calculated to hint at this.

The single sealed-in set of *The Sleepers Den* is an ideal laboratory for naturalism, but in *Over Gardens Out* Gill developed similar assumptions about character evolution, but set the action in two domestic and several exterior locations. Again, several generations are represented, and surprise and vagueness about the processes of physical decay and growth are intermittently felt; but the structures of authority and rebellion between the generations are relatively unambiguous here, and mindless behaviour, though plentiful, seems attributable to individual characters rather than collective. This means that particular anti-social gestures can be isolated as particular problems, so that even through some of the severities of the action a rich vein of wry comedy persists. The central characters are two adolescent Cardiff boys of widely differing propensities (though both are intellectually limited) whose leisure hours are filled with acts of vandalism which range from the trivial to the alarming. The picaresque tone of this play is more typical of the 1960's than is *The Sleepers Den*, but the play does show an advance in terms of its warmly sympathetic characterisation. A very similar technique is deployed more adventurously in *Small Change*, where two Cardiff boys are again followed through boyhood and adolescence into manhood; for the premiere, Gill even used one of the lead actors from *Over Gardens Out* (and would use him again in *Kick for Touch*). Such an expansive chronology means that the play's naturalistic cogency is not comparable with the earlier plays, and Gill allows himself rather more intelligent and perceptive characters, who deliver nostalgic, poetical monologues, the quality of which has been questioned by critics. However, by 1976 Gill could include a climactic scene of adult anagnorisis and recrimination, in which the boyhood relationship is explicitly perceived as homosexual.

Gill's later plays use very similar material, dissected with increasingly audacious techniques. *Kick for Touch* has two Cardiff brothers, war babies, reminiscing haphazardly across a kitchen table; a woman who is married to one of them and has been the lover of both, is the linking device for a series of interior monologues and duologues, with uninvolved characters simply moving a yard or two away and freezing. Again, there is a bond of something approaching love between the men, but the finale does not pivot on this but on the mystery of a domestic tragedy. *In the Blue* has only two male characters, homosexuals, one of whom is articulate and educated. The technical novelty of this play consists in the hypothetical reinterpretation of scenes, alternative performances introduced just by the word "OR", so that there is some uncertainty as to which version represents actuality and which fantasy. Gill's naturalism has here been obscured completely; the play is almost purely expressionistic. In *Mean Tears*, chronological structuring is denied in a collation of short segments of time in which three men and two women intersect, collide, and form fragile relationships.

Gill has also written and directed numerous successful adaptations, but mention should be made of one heroic failure because its technical effrontery resembles that of his original plays. *As I Lay Dying* theatricalises the innovative narrative method of Faulkner's novel, resulting in a pattern of monologues, with varying perspectives being traded across the body of the characters' mother. The jigsaw of monologues epitomises a tendency in Gill's plays, and the maternal catalyst is also recurrent, especially in *Small Change*.

—Howard McNaughton

GILROY, Frank D(aniel). American. Born in New York City, 13 October 1925. Educated at De Witt Clinton High School, Bronx, New York; Dartmouth College, Hanover, New Hampshire, B.A. (magna cum laude) 1950; Yale University School of Drama, New Haven, Connecticut, 1950–51. Served in the United States Army, 1943–46. Married Ruth Dorothy Gaydos in 1954; three sons. Since 1964 member of the Council, and president, 1969–71, Dramatists Guild, New York. Recipient: Obie award, 1962; Outer Circle award, 1964; Pulitzer prize, 1965; New York Drama Critics Circle award, 1965; Berlin Film Festival Silver Bear, 1971. D. Litt.: Dartmouth College, 1966. Lives in Monroe, New York. Address: c/o Dramatists Guild, 234 West 44th Street, New York, New York 10036, U.S.A.

PUBLICATIONS

Plays

The Middle World (produced Hanover, New Hampshire, 1949).
A Matter of Pride, adaptation of the story "The Blue Serge Suit" by John Langdon (televised 1957). New York, French, 1970.
Who'll Save the Plowboy? (produced New York, 1962; London, 1963). New York, Random House, 1962.
The Subject Was Roses (produced New York, 1964). New York, French, 1962; included in *About Those Roses; or, How Not to Do a Play and Succeed, and the Text of "The Subject Was Roses,"* New York, Random House, 1965.
Far Rockaway (televised 1965). With *That Summer—That Fall*, New York, Random House, 1967.
That Summer—That Fall (produced New York, 1967). With *Far Rockaway*, New York, Random House, 1967.
The Only Game in Town (produced New York, 1968). New York, Random House, 1968.
Present Tense (includes *Come Next Tuesday, Twas Brillig, So Please Be Kind, Present Tense*) (produced New York, 1972). New York, French, 1973.
The Next Contestant (produced New York, 1978). New York, French, 1979.
Dreams of Glory (produced New York, 1979). New York, French, 1980.
Last Licks (produced New York, 1979; as *The Housekeeper*, produced Brighton and London, 1982).
Real to Reel (produced New York, 1987).
Match Point (produced New York, 1990).
A Way with Words (produced New York, 1991).

Screenplays: *The Fastest Gun Alive*, with Russel Rouse, 1956; *Texas John Slaughter*, 1958; *Gunfight at Sandoval*, 1959; *The Gallant Hours*, with Beirne Lay, Jr., 1960; *The Subject Was Roses*, 1968; *The Only Game in Town*, 1969; *Desperate Characters*, 1971; *From Noon till Three*, 1976; *Once in Paris*, 1978; *The Gig*, 1985.

Television Plays: *A Matter of Pride*, 1957; *Who Killed Julie Greer?* and *Up Jumped the Devil* (Dick Powell Show), 1960–61; *Far Rockaway*, 1965; *The Turning Point of Jim Malloy*, 1975; *Gibbsville* series, from stories by John O'Hara, 1976; *Nero Wolfe*, from the novel *The Doorbell Rang* by Rex Stout, 1979; *Burke's Law* series; and since 1952 plays for *U.S. Steel Hour, Omnibus, Kraft Theater, Studio One, Lux Video Theatre*, and *Playhouse 90*.

Novels

Private. New York, Harcourt Brace, 1970.
From Noon till Three: The Possibly True and Certainly Tragic

Story of an Outlaw and a Lady Whose Love Knew No Bounds. New York, Doubleday, 1973; as *For Want of a Horse*, London, Coronet, 1975.

Other

Little Ego (for children), with Ruth G. Gilroy. New York, Simon and Schuster, 1970.

*

Theatrical Activities:
Director: **Films**—*Desperate Characters*, 1971; *From Noon till Three*, 1976; *Once in Paris*, 1978; *The Gig*, 1985. **Television**—*The Turning Point of Jim Malloy* (pilot film), 1975; *Gibbsville* series, 1976; *Nero Wolfe*, 1979.

* * *

Frank D. Gilroy's bittersweet comedies consider men and male rituals: their alienation and loneliness, their difficulty communicating with and understanding women, and their insecurities in dealing with one another.

In Gilroy's first commercial success, *Who'll Save the Plowboy?*, the characters set the pattern of relationships found in his later work. Gilroy introduces us to three lives characterized by frustration, failure, and an inability to communicate honestly. Albert, the Plowboy of the title, and Helen, his wife, confront Larry, the now-dying man who saved the Plowboy's life during the war. Albert builds a castle of lies to impress his war buddy with non-existent postwar success and accomplishment, with fantasies of a happy marriage, and an imaginary strong and healthy son. Albert struts through the script like a rooster who doesn't notice that the hen house is empty. In *Plowboy* Gilroy begins to delineate the little humiliations, the deceits, and the burdensome pretenses of being a man. He also introduces us to the sexually unresponsive, adulterous woman who talks incessantly about insignificant and inappropriate things. These are the characters who populate all of Gilroy's work. In spite of *Plowboy*'s exposition and plot development, the shorthand that will become a trademark of a Gilroy script is apparent: the short, snappy repartee; the one-liner insights; the quick expressions of anger and bitterness.

The Subject Was Roses won the Pulitzer prize and is still the epitome of his style and thematic concerns. Elegant in its spareness, this play all but eliminates plot and concentrates on a moment of precisely outlined dramatic time. The World War II experiences of Timmy, another veteran, are a backdrop for the parental battlefield in his home, where his warring parents alternately use him as the cannon with which to shoot one another down. Gilroy hones his ability to communicate a complex set of emotions by focusing in exquisite detail on ordinary objects. When Nettie's waffles stick in the waffle iron, spoiling the first breakfast she's made her son in three years, her tears have less to do with a hungry son than they do with her fear of ruining an already tenuous mother-son relationship, her sense of inadequacy as a woman, and her inability to cope with losing her baby to an adult world.

Because of their terror of exposing their inner selves, Gilroy's characters are divided rather than united by emotions. They smash into one another and spin away without pausing to examine the damage. Toward the end of *The Subject Was Roses*, Timmy says: "I suspect that no one's to blame. . . . Not even me." This disavowal of any responsibility for the mess they've made of their lives is a common factor among all of Gilroy's characters.

Impressed with his Pulitzer prize and subsequent personal publicity, Gilroy admits to having felt a pressure to write something worthy of all his new-found fame. The result was the disastrous *That Summer—That Fall*, in which he tried to wed the Phaedra and Hippolytus legend to modern characters living in Manhattan's Little Italy. The play had 12 performances, and as Gilroy now says: "It proved that a boy from the Bronx shouldn't mess with the Greeks." That experience released him from what he perceived as the burden of being a Pulitzer prize-winning playwright, and enabled him to return to his own ideas and terse dramaturgy.

It is in his one-act plays that Gilroy is best able to concentrate the power of his simple descriptive style. He takes an incident and rapidly sets time, mood, and place by zeroing in on the minutest detail. In *The Next Contestant*, for example, a man who is about to be married becomes a guest on a television game show, and is challenged to call up an ex-girlfriend, who knows he's engaged, and get a date with her. If he achieves his goal, he will win a washer and dryer, a bedroom suite, a radio, television, stereo, wall-to-wall carpeting, luggage, an all-expenses-paid vacation in Miami Beach, and more. The heart of this very short play is the quick and emotionally painful telephone conversation between the contestant and the jilted ex-girlfriend. Gilroy shows the manipulation, the deceit, and the subsequent devastating disillusionment.

Gilroy is an idea man more than a plot man, and this can and does hinder him in his full-length work. *Last Licks* presents a variation on his stock characters who are involved with a one-act's worth of idea. A father, a son, and, in this case, the father's mistress, present a typical Gilroy triangular relationship filled with deception, emotional and physical sadism, drinking bouts, and tales of extramarital affairs.

Gilroy builds entire lives around rebuke and repentance. *Last Licks* is resplendent with repressed emotions and bitter speeches. Like so many of his plays, it is an often comic, but more often quite painful skirmish between the sexes, in which the primary sympathy is with the men's involvement with the world and with each other.

—Leah D. Frank

———

GODBER, John (Harry). British. Born in Upton, Yorkshire, 15 May 1956. Educated at Minsthorpe High School, South Elmsall, Yorkshire; Bretton Hall College, West Bretton, Yorkshire, 1974–78, Cert. Ed. 1977, B. Ed. (honours) 1978; Leeds University, 1978–79, M.A. in theatre 1979, graduate study, 1979–83. Teacher, Minsthorpe High School, 1981–83. Since 1984 artistic director, Hull Truck theatre company. Recipient: Edinburgh Festival award, 1981, 1982, 1984; Olivier award, 1984; Los Angeles Drama Critics Circle award, 1986. Address: Hull Truck, Spring Street Theatre, Spring Street, Hull, Yorkshire HU2 8RW, England.

PUBLICATIONS

Plays

A Clockwork Orange, adaptation of the novel by Anthony Burgess (produced Edinburgh, 1980; London, 1984).

Cry Wolf (produced Rotherham, Yorkshire, 1981).

Cramp (produced Hull, 1981; revised version, music by Tom Robinson and Hereward K, produced Edinburgh and London, 1986).

E.P.A. (produced Hull, 1982).

Happy Jack (produced Hull, 1982; London, 1985). Included in *Five Plays*, 1989.

Young Hearts Run Free: Ideas Towards a Play (produced West Bretton, Yorkshire, 1983).

September in the Rain (produced Edinburgh, 1983; London, 1984; New York, 1985). Included in *Five Plays*, 1989.

Bouncers (produced Edinburgh and London, 1984; Los Angeles, 1986; New York, 1987). With *Shakers*, London, Chappell, 1987.

Up 'n' Under (produced Edinburgh and London, 1984; New York, 1989). Oxford, Amber Lane Press, 1985.

Shakers, with Jane Thornton (produced Hull and London, 1985). With *Bouncers*, London, Chappell, 1987.

Up 'n' Under II (produced Edinburgh, 1985; New York, 1989).

Blood, Sweat and Tears (produced Hull and London, 1986).

The Ritz (televised 1987; as *Putting on the Ritz*, produced Leicester, 1987).

Teechers (produced Edinburgh and London, 1987). London, French, 1989.

Oliver Twist (for children), adaptation of the novel by Charles Dickens (produced Hull, 1987).

Salt of the Earth (produced Hull and London, 1988). London, French, 1989.

Five Plays (includes *Up 'n' Under*, *Bouncers*, *Teechers*, *September in the Rain*, *Happy Jack*). London, Penguin, 1989.

On the Piste (produced Leeds, 1990).

Happy Families (produced at 49 theatres around the United Kingdom, including London, 1991).

The Office Party (produced Hull and London, 1992).

April in Paris (produced Hull, 1992).

Television Plays: series scripts for *Grange Hill*, 1981–83, *Brookside*, 1983–84, and *Crown Court*, 1983; *The Rainbow Coloured Disco Dancer*, from work by C.P. Taylor, 1984; *The Ritz* series, 1987; *The Continental*, 1987; *My Kingdom for a Horse*, 1991.

*

Theatrical Activities:

Director: **Plays**—all of his own plays; *Imagine* by Stephen Jeffreys, *Hedda Gabler* by Ibsen, and *The Dock* by Phil Woods, Hull, 1987; *Twelfth Night* by Shakespeare, London, 1989; *Sweet Sorrow* by Alan Plater, London, 1990.

* * *

John Godber is very clear about his particular theatrical style: "the dancer and not the poet is the father of the theatre." Reading his plays gives little sense of the energy and pace of the pieces in performance, an energy and pace deriving from his resolute refusal to separate the role of writer from that of director. His involvement with the Hull Truck Company has been a happy one; their commitment to a theatre based on contemporary and community-related issues and a long pedigree of theatre derived from improvisation and intense collaboration between writer and actors has allowed him the room to experiment with an exhilarating mixture of theatrical techniques. The result has been some of the funniest and most enjoyable evenings spent in a theatre in recent years.

Plot in Godber's work is kept to a minimum, and frequently the plays have a strong if deliberately jokey documentary feel to them. In *Bouncers*, the action takes place at a provincial disco—where the events of a typical night are interspersed with flash-back scenes of anxious preparation for the great night-out by the lads and girls. Nothing particularly unusual occurs. The bouncers rehearse various degrees of aggression towards the punters, copious amounts of tears, beer, and vomit are spilt, and the characters are united in a macabre attempt to shut off the grim realities of their lives— an attempt that will be, as always, doomed. All the many characters (both male and female) are played by the same four male bouncer actors, and the effect is to enlarge the comic potential of the events but also to stress its nonparticularity. Godber is not interested in creating unique psychologically-realised characters. They are representative, standing in for an audience who may very well proceed from the theatre to such a disco—the more particularly since he is intent on attracting audiences that would not normally regard theatre as a part of their cultural experience. The club acts then as a gently symbolic location of the contemporary world at play, looking for a dream-world of alcoholic oblivion and easy sex, and finding instead a continuation of the daytime regime, ruled over by arbitrary bouncers free to admit or refuse entrance to a fun palace in which there are strict rules about dress, an expensive bar, and complete limitations on the celebration of any conceivable excess. There are tentative plans to turn the play into a movie, though it is difficult to see how the particular style of the play would mesh with the conventionally naturalistic demands of the film medium.

Shakers, written in collaboration with Jane Thornton, changes the sexual perspective. Set in a provincial wine bar run by four waitresses who again play all the other (male and female) characters, it offers an even bleaker account of the urge to escape. We see four young girls at work in the supermarket, fantasising about the birthday party to come, agonising over the choice of clothes, and seeing as the limit of their dreams the joy of actually working in a cocktail bar. But the life at Shakers presented by the four waitresses is no different from any other work situation. The hours are long, the pay is bad, and sexual harassment is not only rife, but is effectively encouraged by the unseen management. That they are the better able to analyse their situation than their male counterparts in *Bouncers* is typical of Godber's work. His strong feminist line demands this distinction. His plays are all about politically marginalised people, failures and victims of the system; for the women the victimisation is made worse by their sense of being underdogs in a world of underdogs, and they are given a stronger oppositional voice.

The pace of the productions and the constant roleswitching does little to disguise, however, a certain literalness of political analysis. Everything fits too neatly into place. His concentration on marginalised characters in an urban wasteland brings with it an inability to look beyond the boundaries of marginalisation—although it must be admitted that in performance it is a weakness that is less apparent than on more sober reflection. For these reasons his most successful play to date is *Up 'n' Under*, for here Godber has been able to use the build-up to and the actual enactment on stage of a Rugby League Sevens match as a far less prosaic metaphor of a modern world of male competition and machismo. Down-at-heel Arthur is conned into a large bet with a bent but successful businessman that he cannot train the worst amateur pub team in Yorkshire to beat the top dogs, the Cobblers Arms from Castleford. Arthur's team are dragged, understrength and unwillingly, into a training programme supervised by (horror of horrors!) a woman, and the scene is set for a *Rocky*-style conclusion—Arthur's favourite movies are the *Rocky* films—in which the underdog gets up off his backside at the last possible moment and wins. The presentation of the game, with seven actors (including their female trainer) acting out play, is the most exciting piece of total theatre I have ever seen, and tension as to the outcome is kept up throughout. This is not Hollywood, however, and our heroes lose by the odd point. But Godber's characters, though inveterate losers, always retain an optimistic strain and the play ends with the team planning a double-or-nothing bet on the result of a further match—a match which duly takes place in *Up 'n' Under II*.

The sporting theme was re-explored in *On the Piste*—the very title proclaiming its seaside postcard antecedence—which played at the Leeds Grand in the summer of 1990, and this was followed by one of the most unusual events in theatrical history. In 1991 the Little Theatre Guild of Great Britain commissioned a play for the first time. Suitably enough they turned to John Godber, and on October 12 his *Happy Families* received 49 simultaneous first performances by different U.K. companies. The story, which follows the rise of John Taylor—small-town bright lad on the make—was a typical Godber mix of sex and class warfare, and it is hard to think of a writer, at the same time both populist and popular, more suited for the Guild's ambitious commission.

—John Bull

GOLDMAN, James. American. Born in Chicago, Illinois, 30 June 1927; brother of the writer William Goldman. Educated at the University of Chicago, Ph.B. 1947, M.A. 1950; Columbia University, New York, 1950–52. Served in the United States Army, 1952–54. Married 1) Marie McKeon in 1962 (divorced 1972), one daughter and one son; 2) Barbara Deren in 1975. Since 1966 member of the Council, Dramatists Guild, and since 1967 member of the Council, Authors League of America. Recipient: Oscar, 1969; Writers Guild of America West award, 1969; Writers Guild of Great Britain award, 1969; New York Film Critics award, 1969; New York Drama Critics Circle award, 1972; Olivier award, 1987; *Evening Standard* award, 1987; Society of West End Theatres award, 1987. Agent: Owen Laster, William Morris Agency, 1350 Agency of the Americas, New York, New York 10019, U.S.A.

PUBLICATIONS

Plays

They Might Be Giants (produced London, 1961). New York, Bantam, 1970.
Blood, Sweat and Stanley Poole, with William Goldman (produced New York, 1961). New York, Dramatists Play Service, 1962.
A Family Affair, with William Goldman, music by John Kander (produced New York, 1962).
The Lion in Winter (produced New York, 1966; London, 1969). New York, Random House, and London, French, 1966).
Follies, music and lyrics by Stephen Sondheim (produced

New York, 1971; revised version produced Manchester, 1985; London, 1987). New York, Random House, 1971.
Robin and Marian (screenplay). New York, Bantam, 1976.

Screenplays: *The Lion in Winter*, 1968; *They Might Be Giants*, 1970; *Nicholas and Alexandra*, with Edward Bond, 1971; *Robin and Marian*, 1976; *White Nights*, with Eric Hughes, 1985.

Television Plays: *Evening Primrose*, music and lyrics by Stephen Sondheim, 1966; *Oliver Twist*, 1983; *Anna Karenina*, with Simon Langton, from the novel by Tolstoy, 1985; *Anastasia: The Mystery of Anna Anderson* series, 1986.

Novels

Waldorf. New York, Random House, 1965; London, Joseph, 1966.
The Man from Greek and Roman. New York, Random House, 1974; London, Hutchinson, 1975.
Myself as Witness. New York, Random House, 1979; London, Hamish Hamilton, 1980.
Fulton County. New York, Morrow, and London, Bantam, 1989.

*   *   *

James Goldman at his best is a second-rate Neil Simon: both are dramatists who entertain rather than engage their audiences. Whether he is writing situation comedies (in collaboration with his brother), *A Family Affair* and *Blood, Sweat and Stanley Poole*, historical dramas, *The Lion in Winter* and *Nicholas and Alexandra*, or a musical, *Follies*, his work is always predictable, never ranging outside of the already-tested limits of the form. Only his skillful handling of dialogue occasionally redeems his plays, but even this cannot compensate for his deficiency in imagination, nor can it conceal that his characters are stock, plots mechanical, and themes imperfectly realized.

A Family Affair and *Blood, Sweat and Stanley Poole* play like the pseudo-comedies that could be seen between 6 and 10 p.m. any weeknight on American television throughout the late 1950's and early-to-middle 1960's. One concerns itself with the bustle and bickering that typically occurs when two families attempt to plan a wedding and the guardian of the bride wants a simple, elegant "family affair" while the mother of the groom longs for something a bit fancier. The other involves an army officer, 1st Lieutenant Stanley Poole, who has been bribing the education officer, Malcolm, with goods from the supply room to pass him on the army proficiency tests. The hero-of-the-day is Private Robert Oglethorpe who runs a "cram" course for the army officers, making it possible for Poole to replace the pilfered supplies, free himself from his bondage to Malcolm, and retain his military rank by passing the proficiency exams. The plot is mechanical, the jokes are stale, the characters too familiar, and the situation—Oglethorpe's classroom for the army's dunderheads—plays like a classroom scene from *Our Miss Brooks* or *Sergeant Bilko*, replete with all the cute gimmicks and mnemonics that teach the adult student to learn the names of the five Great Lakes or to recognize "the Symphony that Schubert wrote and never finished." Even the two Goldmans' sense of theatricality falters in this play. The slapstick accident where the good guys mangle and mutilate the villainous Captain Malcolm's coveted Jag takes place off-stage and can only be recounted, supposedly hilariously, by the conspirators on the stage. The climax of the play comes when the clumsy Private

Oglethorpe, who previously got headaches whenever even the word "bayonet" was mentioned, catches the rifle Malcolm throws at him and brilliantly executes the manual of arms. The first action better fits a movie or television program than a play; the second simply lacks enough intrinsic importance to carry even the climax of a silly piece of canned comedy.

Goldman finds better success in another genre, the history or chronicle play, which had its revival in the 1960's with *Luther, Lawrence of Arabia*, and most successfully, *A Man for All Seasons*. Well done, the chronicle play examines and revitalizes characters from the past whose significance is unchallenged. It brings the past to life and, more importantly, it shows how the present has worked upon the past making it relevant. Goldman, however, seems to have overlooked this most important aspect of historical drama. It is not surprising that the dramatist of *They Might Be Giants* left the contemporary world and looked to the past to supply him with the heroes he sought, but it is regrettable that he only went to the past to acquire material and not to relate it to modern concerns. In *The Lion in Winter* Henry II of England and Eleanor of Aquitaine engage in a battle of wits as each attempts to outdo the other and settle the questions of succession, which son will marry the king's mistress, and which son will inherit the Vexin and Aquitaine. Henry, the aging monarch, still the roaring, regal lion, seeks to possess both his mistress and his wife and both their lands in order to pass England and that portion of France which is England's to John, his youngest and weakest son. Eleanor fights fiercely to hold Henry, and, failing that, to guarantee that England and her precious Aquitaine are willed to Richard Coeur de Lion. Geoffrey, the middle and cleverest son, plays brother against brother and son against father as he, too, struggles to protect what he believes should be his own. Alais, the lovely mistress, is pawn to Henry and his aged and imprisoned wife throughout the play. The dialogue in the play is witty, intelligent, pithy, and often mercurial. Henry and Eleanor alternately rage at each other and ask each other for pity in a manner reminiscent of George and Martha's quarrels in *Who's Afraid of Virginia Woolf?* But finally, the play is too contrived, the games of oneupmanship grow stale, and the audience begins to doubt that anything so real as the fate of the kingdom is at stake. The Christmas Court ends in a stalemate; the question of succession is postponed to another year; Eleanor and Henry conclude acknowledging to each other that their real enemy is time and that it will win. Goldman, meanwhile, seems to have forgotten that there was ever a real historical question raised in the play. History, and not the play, is left to tell us how the question of succession was resolved. The natures of the regal pair and not succession seem to have been the stuff of the play, but Goldman never demonstrates why these natures matter or who this King and Queen are.

More recently Goldman tried his hand at musical comedy; but he seems no more likely to be successful with this form than with the others. The book for *Follies* suffers from the same flaws that plagued his earlier works. The occasion is a reunion called by an impresario of the Weismann Follies' girls. Back to the crumbling music hall that had its heyday thirty years earlier come the showgirls who had danced for the era between the two wars. Among the guests are two girls, Sally and Phyllis, and their husbands, Buddy and Ben. As the evening progresses, we watch these pairs when they were young and in love, thirty years ago, and now, when they are old and discontented and flirting with the possibility that they can undo time and their marriages and return to the men who had jilted them before they married so long ago. The soap opera tale can be guessed. After an evening in which the couples dance and sing down memory lane and exorcize their regrets in a Follies Loveland, the couples leave their fancied past and return to drab realities and each other. The lyrics and music do much to redeem the play, and the gauzy interplay of past and present, shadows and substance, is visually well-handled and extremely well-suited to a musical that has taken sentimentality and nostalgia for its theme. A revised version of *Follies*, which Goldman and Stephen Sondheim worked on together, was a 1987 hit in London.

Goldman's difficulty in creating fully realized characters of his own fresh imagining and his lack of a significant theme continue to plague his work.

—Carol Simpson Stern

———

GOOCH, Steve. British. Born in Surrey, 22 July 1945. Educated at the Emanuel School, London, 1956–63; Trinity College, Cambridge, 1964–67, B.A. (honours) in modern languages 1967; St. John's College, Cambridge (Harper-Wood Scholar), 1967; Birmingham University, 1968–69. Assistant editor, *Plays and Players* magazine, London, 1972–73; resident dramatist, Half Moon Theatre, London, 1973–74, Greenwich Theatre, London, 1974–75, Solent People's Theatre, Southampton, 1981–82, Theatre Venture, London, 1983–84, and Croydon Warehouse Theatre, Surrey, 1986. Recipient: Arts Council bursary, 1973; Thames Television award, 1974. Agent: Casarotto Ramsay Ltd., National House, 60–66 Wardour Street, London W1V 3HP, England.

PUBLICATIONS

Plays

The NAB Show (produced Brighton, 1970).
Great Expectations, adaptation of the novel by Dickens (produced Liverpool, 1970).
Man Is Man, adaptation of the play by Brecht (produced London, 1971; New Haven, Connecticut, 1978).
It's All for the Best, adaptation of the novel *Candide* by Voltaire (produced Stoke-on-Trent, 1972; London, 1979).
Big Wolf, adaptation of a play by Harald Mueller (produced London, 1972). London, Davis Poynter, 1972.
Will Wat; If Not, What Will? (produced London, 1972). London, Pluto Press, 1975.
Nicked (produced Exeter, 1972).
The Mother, adaptation of a play by Brecht (produced London, 1973). London, Eyre Methuen, 1978.
Female Transport (produced London, 1973; Louisville, 1975; New York, 1976). London, Pluto Press, 1974.
Dick (produced London, 1973).
The Motor Show, with Paul Thompson (produced Dagenham, Essex, and London, 1974). London, Pluto Press, 1975.
Cock-Artist, adaptation of a play by Rainer Werner Fassbinder (produced London, 1974). Published in *Gambit 39–40* (London), 1982.
Strike '26, with Frank McDermott (produced London, 1975).
Made in Britain, with Paul Thompson (produced Oxford, 1976).
Landmark (as *Our Land Our Lives*, produced London, 1976; revised version, as *Landmark*, produced Wivenhoe, Essex, 1980). Colchester, Theatre Action Press, 1982.

Back-Street Romeo (produced London, 1977).
Rosie, adaptation of a play by Harald Mueller (also director: produced London, 1977).
The Women Pirates: Ann Bonney and Mary Read (produced London, 1978). London, Pluto Press, 1978.
In the Club (produced London, 1979).
Future Perfect, with Michelene Wandor and Paul Thompson (produced on tour, 1980).
Fast One (produced Southampton, 1982). Southampton, Solent People's Theatre, 1982.
Fuente Ovejuna, adaptation of the play by Lope de Vega (produced London, 1982).
Flotsam, adaptation of a play by Harald Mueller (produced Croydon, Surrey, 1985). Published in *Gambit 39–40* (London), 1982.
Home Work, adaptation of a play by Franz Xaver Kroetz (produced London, 1990). Published in *Gambit 39–40* (London), 1982.
Taking Liberties (produced London, 1984).
Good for You (produced Leicester, 1985).
Mister Fun (produced Sheffield and London, 1986).
Star Turns (produced London, 1987).
Massa (produced London, 1989). London, New Cross, 1990.
Our Say (produced Wednesbury, West Midlands, 1989).
Lulu, adaptation of *Earth Spirit* and *Pandora's Box* by Frank Wedekind (produced Edinburgh and London, 1990).
The Marquis of Keith, adaptation of the play by Frank Wedekind (produced London, 1990).

Radio Plays: *The Kiosk*, from a play by Ludvík Aškenazy, 1970; *Delinquent*, from a play by Harald Mueller, 1978; *Santis*, from a play by Martin Walser, 1980; *What Brothers Are For*, 1983; *Bill of Health*, 1987.

Other

All Together Now: An Alternative View of Theatre and the Community. London, Methuen, 1984.
Writing a Play. London, A & C Black, 1988.

Translator, *Poems and Ballads*, by Wolf Biermann. London, Pluto Press, 1977.
Translator, with Paul Knight, *Wallraff, The Undesirable Journalist*, by Günter Wallraff. London, Pluto Press, 1978; New York, Overlook Press, 1979.

*

Critical Studies: interviews in *Renaissance and Modern Studies* (Nottingham), 1977, and *Hard Times 12* (Berlin), 1980; *Alternativen im britischen Drama der Gegenwart* by Günther Klotz, Berlin, Akademie, 1978; *Stages in the Revolution* by Catherine Itzin, London, Eyre Methuen, 1980; "The Surveyor and the Construction Engineer" by Gooch, in *Theatre Quarterly 36* (London), 1980.

Theatrical Activities:
Director: **Plays**—*Work Kills!* by Bruce Birchall, London, 1975; *Consensus* by Michael Gill, London, 1976; *Rosie*, London, 1977; *Night Shift* by John Derbyshire, London, 1983.

Steve Gooch comments:
My work has developed over the years from an attempt to articulate the voice of working-class and other dispossessed sections of British society towards a general aesthetic in which the personal struggle to take control of one's life is given full emotional value within an open-eyed depiction of the social nexus surrounding it.

This has often been expressed through historical analogy and the portrayal of "hidden history," and frequently by means of multiple protagonists or groups engaged in a common, though variegated, purpose. In these plays I have attempted to reflect the increasingly collective nature of modern life, confronting the dilemma of pluralism within an ordered democratic progress.

Crucial to this "group" aesthetic is the gap between experience and thought, specifically in the way individual characters in groups "think" each other. This has also been important in my smaller-cast plays during the 1980's, where wider social conflict has tended to be treated through the microcosm of man-woman relationships. In each of these contexts language becomes the fine-tuning of communication between conflicting social aspirations and judgements. In exploring this, my translation and adaptation of European works has been invaluable in sensitising my understanding of language as the barometer of social will.

*   *   *

In contrast to other playwrights of the British 1968 generation, Steve Gooch has not, in spite of being a very prolific and versatile writer, found a firm foothold in either the major subsidised theatre companies or the mass media. This is not due to a lack of talent or of successful productions of his plays or even to a decline of the British alternative theatre scene, but rather to Gooch's adherence to a theatre for the community. A great deal of artistic energy, from the beginning of Gooch's career as a writer for the stage, has gone into the mediation, by translations or adaptations, of plays and theatrical ideas from the Romance and German languages. Gooch shows particular skill in his translations of German dramatists of the classical modernist period like the early Brecht and, more recently, Frank Wedekind, and of those contemporary playwrights (Kroetz, Harald Mueller, Martin Walser) whose preoccupation with political aspects of subjectivity mirrors his own, but he has also adapted classics like Dickens, Voltaire, Lope de Vega, and Terence.

In his original work for the stage Gooch early on found a congenial venue in the Half Moon Theatre in London's East End. One of the first results of their workshop projects was Gooch's dramatization, as *Will Wat; If Not, What Will?*, of Wat Tyler's 1381 peasants' uprising, the first proto-socialist movement in English history. In this attempt "to show what the history books usually leave out" Gooch draws on contemporary documents and alternative versions of medieval history to present the peasants' point of view in their opposition to royal militarism and exploitation by old feudal and emerging merchant interests. The play acutely balances the eventual defeat of the peasants led by John Ball and Wat Tyler against the positive growth of self-awareness of an oppressed class. History is brought on stage as a collective process whose dramaturgy has to preempt individual identification by anti-illusionist techniques such as double casting, songs, and quotes from historical documents. Similar Brechtian techniques are employed in Gooch's next historical play, also produced by the Half Moon Theatre, *Female Transport*. Again, it is history from below, this time in the more familiar scenery of early 19th-century Britain. The play gives a realistic account of the voyage to Australia of six female convicts who gradually win through to an insight into the necessity of resistance against a patriarchal class society. This socialist-feminist line in Gooch's work is elaborated in an early text that ended up as a Royal Shakespeare Company production of *The Women Pirates: Ann Bonney and Mary Read*. In this epic portrait of two historical women at the turn of the 18th century, Gooch charts, in a loose configuration of scenes interspersed with many songs, a successful if seemingly peripheral liberation from hegemonic law and morality.

While developing his Brechtian style of historical plays with a socialist, humanist, and feminist slant, Gooch collaborated on some theatrical projects that concerned sections of the contemporary working class in a more direct way. It was here that Gooch came nearest to his declared aim of writing "about working-class experience and history, and for a working-class audience and readership." In *The Motor Show* (written with Paul Thompson) Gooch tried to create a working-class community theatre from within. After local research at the Dagenham Ford plant by the group called Community Theatre, the play turned into a 24-scene documentation, in a deft cartoon-like style mixing documentary, realistic, and music hall elements, of 60 years of struggle between the Ford Company and their workers. The Community Theatre failed to set itself up in Dagenham, but the unashamedly agit-prop techniques—rescued from preachiness by witty dialogue—of *The Motor Show*, largely retained in *Strike '26* and in *Made in Britain* (a documentary about British Leyland, again written with Paul Thompson), became a model for many similar attempts by other writers. In *Our Land, Our Lives* Gooch's concern with issues involving specifically contemporary communities was placed on a more general level by being given a fictional focus in a reunion of young married people in a village barn that had served them as a meeting-place in their schooldays. The play shows the encroachment of agribusiness on traditional village life, but in the reworking of it with Essex University Theatre (under the title *Landmark*) it came to include the theme of nuclear threat. In the revised version the fields against whose sale the young people have been rallying opposition are bought up by the Ministry of Defence to be converted into a site for nuclear missiles.

In the new austerity of the 1980's Gooch has apparently redefined the range of his dramatic themes, even though he has remained faithful to the small companies and theatre groups of the dwindling alternative circuit. The move away from agit-prop didacticism is obvious even in his recent *Taking Liberties*, written in the genre of the historical play which lends itself most readily to political discourse with clear-cut messages. In this play we get an unusually broad social panorama, from patricians to plebeians, bound up in the radical agitation of the late 18th century. The carnivalesque action here focuses on the mock election of a Mayor of Garratt and reflects John Wilkes's creation of a new type of populist politics involving the London masses. The play also indicates a change in the post-1979 political atmosphere in that it does not so much rescue the utopian perspectives from the historical setting but ends in the temporary defeat of plebeian aspirations for political participation. The widening of thematic range and intended appeal finds expression in a reappropriation of realist and even naturalist theatrical approaches. This development accompanies the synthesis in Gooch's conception of his own work between John McGrath's purist reliance on popular traditions and David Edgar's more eclectic attitude towards mainstream theatrical codes. The new approach characterizes even a play with a seemingly exotic setting like *Fast One*, in which a merchant seaman is caught up in an international intrigue about the sale of arms in an unspecified South American country.

Mister Fun, written for a Sheffield-based touring group, goes even further in the direction of a naturalist tradition that the author had never completely excluded from his theatre language. The play concentrates on the lives of a young couple working on a traditional fairground. The action shows the inevitable take-over of the fair by the electronics branch of the leisure industry after a local council's abortive attempts to give it a permanent site. This process is traced in its divisive effects on the young couple's lives. In their drifting apart the girl achieves some degree of independence, whereas the eponymous hero becomes a kind of walking ad for what was once popular entertainment but which now usurps people's work and minds.

—Bernd-Peter Lange

GOODMAN, Paul. American. 1911–1972.
See 1st edition, 1973.

GORDONE, Charles (Edward). American. Born in Cleveland, Ohio, 12 October 1925. Educated at Elkhart High School, Indiana; University of California, Los Angeles; Los Angeles State College (now University), B.A. in drama 1952; New York University Television Workshop. Served in the United States Air Force. Married Jeanne Warner in 1959; two sons and three daughters. Instructor, Cell Block Theatre, Yardville and Bordontown prisons, New Jersey, 1977–78; taught playmaking, New School for Social Research, New York, 1978–79. Founder, with Godfrey Cambridge, Committee for the Employment of Negro Performers, 1962. Recipient: Obie award, for acting, 1964; Pulitzer prize, 1970; New York Drama Critics Circle award, 1970; Vernon Rice award, 1970; American Academy award, 1971. Address: 17 West 100th Street, New York, New York 10025, U.S.A.

PUBLICATIONS

Plays

A Little More Light Around the Place, adaptation of the novel by Sidney Easton (produced New York, 1964).
No Place to Be Somebody: A Black-Black Comedy (also director: produced New York, 1967). Indianapolis, Bobbs Merrill, 1969.
Gordone Is a Muthah (miscellany; produced New York, 1970). Published in *The Best Short Plays 1973*, edited by Stanley Richards, Radnor, Pennsylvania, Chilton, 1973.
Baba-Chops (produced Los Angeles, 1974; New York, 1975).
The Last Chord (produced New York, 1976).
A Qualification for Anabiosis (produced New York, 1978; revised version, as *Anabiosis*, produced St. Louis, 1979).

*

Manuscript Collection: Schomburg Collection, New York.

Critical Study: "Yes, I Am a Black Playwright, But . . ." by Gordone, in *New York Times*, 25 January 1970.

Theatrical Activities:

Director: **Plays**—about 25 plays, including *Rebels and Bugs*, 1958, *Faust* by Goethe and *Peer Gynt* by Ibsen, 1959, and *Tobacco Road* by Erskine Caldwell, *Three Men on a Horse* by George Abbott and John Cecil Holm, *Detective Story* by Sidney Kingsley, *Hell Bent fer Heaven* by Hatcher Hughes, and Eugene O'Neill's "Sea Plays," 1960; *No Place to Be Somebody*, 1967 (and later productions); *Leaving Home* by Marcia Haufrecht, 1978; *After Hours* by Virgil Richardson (co-director, with Lucien Fiiyer), 1981.

Actor: **Plays**—in *Fortunato*; Logan in *The Climate of Eden* by Moss Hart, 1952; in *Mrs. Patterson* by Greer Johnson and Charles Sebree, 1957; The Valet in *The Blacks* by Jean Genet, 1961; George of *Of Mice and Men* by Steinbeck, 1964; Jero in *The Trials of Brother Jero* by Wole Soyinka, 1967; in *Gordone Is a Muthah*, 1970. **Television**—*The Climate of Eden*, 1961.

Charles Gordone comments:
Always the search for IDENTITY.

* * *

Charles Gordone first came to public attention as an actor in the tumultuous 1961 New York production of Genet's *The Blacks*. In addition to Gordone, the cast for that production included James Earl Jones, Cicely Tyson, Godfrey Cambridge, and Cynthia Belgrave. Like the first production of *A Raisin in the Sun*, *The Blacks* inspired most of its cast members to continue and extend the 1960's renaissance of black theater. As a member of the cast of *The Blacks*, Gordone was deeply involved in discussions of the politics of the play and of the relationship of theater to the black movement.

Although Gordone continued to work in and around theater throughout the 1960's, it was not until 1969, with the first production of his major play, *No Place to Be Somebody*, that his voice was clearly heard. Gordone had difficulty finding a producer for the play until Joseph Papp agreed to do it. The productions quickly won public and critical applause. Gordone received a Drama Desk award as one of the three most promising playwrights of the year, and the play received the Pulitzer prize.

No Place to Be Somebody aptly fits a category or genre of drama defined by W. E. B. Du Bois early in this century: it is a "play of the contact of black and white." More than most plays by black American dramatists, and certainly more than most plays of the late 1960's, *No Place to Be Somebody* quickly establishes a world in which black characters and white characters not only inhabit the same space but come into direct conflict with each other. Johnny Williams, the owner of Johnny's bar where the play is set, is a young, angry black man who is obsessed with "Charlie fever," the play's organizing metaphor for black rage against white power. Johnny's rage does not take a strictly separatist form; some of his most important and ambiguous relationships are with vulnerable whites. He serves as the abusive pimp for two prostitutes—one black, the other white. He has an affair with the white, liberal college daughter of a lawyer who holds information useful to Johnny. He employs as bartender a white man whose dreams of being a "black" musician are undermined both by his ethnicity and his drug addiction. Since all of these white characters are weak and dependent on Johnny, we can read his contact with whites as a mode of reverse cultural exploitation; that is true of the structure of the relationships, but, within each one, there is at least a moment when Johnny reveals enough human concern to

suggest that something in addition to power is at stake. The complexities of Johnny's motivations are only hinted, however, and could be taken in a number of directions in performance.

Johnny's foil and eventually his foe is Gabe, a "fair-skinned" black man who plays a role and a half as unemployable actor and the author of the play-in-progress. Gabe haunts Johnny's bar from its internal and external fringes. As a Brechtian narrator, Gabe initiates each scene with a commentary on the play's intentions and limitations; he informs us, for example, that *No Place to Be Somebody* is not a social protest play. Gabe is not satisfied in his external role; he enters the world of the play, in disguise one might say, as an actor-poet who distracts and provokes the company at the bar but can not get cast in any other show in town because he is neither white nor black enough in appearance. Gabe's voice opposes Johnny's "Charlie fever" throughout the play, but his voice does not suffice. In the end, Gabe kills Johnny, and in so doing destroys both his black brother and the character created by the playwright-at-work.

No Place to Be Somebody is an unabashedly derivative play whose sources make odd and only sometimes harmonious bedfellows. The constrained barroom setting of the play is reminiscent of *The Lower Depths*, *The Iceman Cometh*, and *The Time of Your Life*; expressionistic conventions such as Gabe's lyrics and rhapsodies and Machine Dog, a materialized hallucination, interrupt the interactions on stage much as they do in the plays of Tennessee Williams and Ed Bullins; Gabe's final speeches and his appearance costumed as a black woman in mourning recall Baraka's *Dutchman* and Hawthorne's sin-laden Puritans. As many reviewers commented, the play also manages to accelerate its activity so that we find ourselves suddenly confronted with melodrama replete with an over-abundance of on-stage corpses.

In *No Place to Be Somebody* Gordone took on the difficult task of writing a drama that would at once illuminate the complex and discordant responses of black Americans to white American culture and would embrace what he himself called the "broader human context." In the 1970's he moved to the midwest and continued his struggle to "tell the story of the human comedy" through directing for the theater. His later writing includes an attempt to extend the form of the American musical with a musical version of *No Place to Be Somebody*. *Anabiosis* explores his tendency to "get sidetracked," and has been revised several times.

—Helene Keyssar

GORMAN, Clem (Brian Gorman). Australian. Born in Perth, Western Australia, 18 October 1942. Educated at St. Louis School, 1955–56, and Aquinas College, 1957–60, both Perth; University of Sydney, 1963–67, B.A., Dip. Ed.; Polytechnic of Central London, diploma in arts administration 1975. Married Sandra Dent in 1967 (divorced 1986). Freelance stage manager and theatre administrator, Sydney, 1967–68: founder, Australian Free Theatre Group; co-founder, *Masque* theatre magazine, 1968; lived in London, 1970–79; deputy administrator, Round House Trust, London, 1975–76; administrator, Moving Being dance company, Cardiff, 1976–77; administrator, Australian National Playwrights Conference, Sydney, 1982; lecturer in playwriting,

Victorian College of the Arts, Melbourne, 1984, and Adelaide University, 1985; training officer, Australian Book Publishers Association, Sydney, 1986. Since 1966 freelance journalist. Recipient: Australia Council Literature Board grant, 1980, and fellowship, 1981. Agent: Anthony Williams, 55 Victoria Street, Potts Point, New South Wales 2011, Australia.

PUBLICATIONS

Plays

I Love Your Sailor (produced London, 1976).
Let Me In, I'm a Friend of the Band (produced London, 1978).
A Manual of Trench Warfare (produced Adelaide, 1978). Sydney, Currency Press, 1979.
The Harding Women (produced Adelaide, 1980). With *A Night in the Arms of Raeleen*, Sydney, Currency Press, 1983.
The Motivators (produced Sydney, 1981). Montmorency, Victoria, Yackandandah, 1983.
A Night in the Arms of Raeleen (produced Melbourne, 1982). With *The Harding Women*, Sydney, Currency Press, 1983.
A Fortunate Life, adaptation of the autobiography by A.B. Facey (produced Melbourne, 1984).
The Journey Home (for children; produced Adelaide, 1985).
A Face from the Street (produced Canberra, 1985).
The Last Night-Club. Montmorency, Victoria, Yackandandah, 1985.

Screenplay: *The Swans Away* (documentary), 1986.

Other

The Book of Ceremonies. Bottisham, Cambridgeshire, Whole Earth Tools, 1969; revised edition, as *Making Ceremonies*, 1972; revised edition, as *The Book of Ceremony*, 1972.
Making Communes: Survey/Manual. Bottisham, Cambridgeshire, Whole Earth Tools, 1971.
People Together. St. Albans, Hertfordshire, Paladin, 1975.
Backstage Rock: Behind the Scenes with the Bands. London, Pan, 1978.

Editor, *The Larrikin Streak: Australian Writers Look at the Legend*. Sydney, Pan Macmillan, 1990.

*

Manuscript Collection: University of Queensland Press, St. Lucia.

Clem Gorman comments:
It may be—and a writer is not necessarily the best person to know—that my work is about the struggle between the female and male sides of my own nature.

* * *

Though it was only in 1978 with *A Manual of Trench Warfare* that he achieved recognition as an Australian playwright, Clem Gorman had been working in the Australian and English theatre since the mid-1960's and had written books on several aspects of the counter-culture as well as organising an experimental Sydney group theatre. In view of this background, his original published plays are surprising in that they are stylistically muted, mostly using a naturalistic structure of human relationships broken only by intermittent songs and direct audience address. Moreover, in his plays with male subjects the ostensible central theme is the traditional Australian one of mateship, questioned, tested, and analysed but not absolutely rejected. *A Manual of Trench Warfare* actually begins with a male chorus of Australian voices singing a hymn to mateship, an assertion of both working-class and nationalistic solidarity, and the first scene opens with a young soldier alone in a trench at Gallipoli writing a letter to his mother about how he killed the Turk who had killed his mate. A new trenchmate, a more garrulous Irish larrikin soldier, brings a new bond in terms of whisky, anti-authoritarianism, and comradeship in battle, but gradually Gorman's focus shifts from this traditional model of mateship to an examination of the support system which evolves between the two men and which is ultimately expressed in physical love. In the poignant final scene the Australian's patriotism has been completely displaced by his loyalty to his dying Irish mate, to the extent that he offers to shoot the corporal who has interrupted their love-making.

In *A Night in the Arms of Raeleen* the solitary female character is a catalyst for the delusory concept of mateship which twenty years previously had bound together the four males who are now having a reunion, trying to regress to their Bodgie identities in talk and dress. Raeleen, however, has recently told herself that she has got to make her "own support system now," and she defiantly asserts the sober values of middle age, forcing the men away from mutual congratulation and myth-mongering, towards a rudimentary awareness of themselves and their needs. A series of monologues from various characters, done direct to the audience under a single spotlight, shows how with a brutal cauterising of emotions Raeleen was used as the pivotal commodity in their adolescent camaraderie. But the naturalistic context of these addresses shows her emergent self-knowledge dissolving all relationships and the whole support structure, forcing them all to find independence, as a precondition for new, honest relationships. In *The Harding Women* all three characters are female, held together by their various relationships to the dead paterfamilias, dramaturgically a male equivalent of Raeleen, whom they have known as wife, as housekeeper/mistress, and as daughter. Each character has at least three monologues and songs which deal with personal crises and explain how the present situation of distrust and exploitation evolved; for these, the widow dresses in clothes of the early 1960's and speaks accusingly to her dead husband, while the other two women speak direct to the audience in a more reflective manner. A Strindbergian web of entrapment is sketched, with the acerbic hypochondriac mother venting her histrionic bitterness on the housekeeper, who had been paradoxically snared by the dead man's intended generosity, and on the daughter, who feels an irrational piety towards her mother even though she can state, "I don't need a man to look after me. I don't need a support system except my friends and colleagues at work. I don't need a system of beliefs to buttress me." But both mother and daughter have a chemical dependence, on alcohol and dope, and the ending is intensely pessimistic because, whereas the reunion at Raeleen's occurred once in twenty years, never to be repeated, for the Harding women it is an annual ritual with no prospect of relief or resolution, at least until another death occurs. The poignancy of dependence recurs in Gorman's less-known works, particularly *The Motivators*, which presents itself as two revue-style monologues which unexpectedly intersect at the end. The woman, a middle-aged "training officer," and the man, a drunken "motivator," both assert their independence, but emerge as pathetically inadequate.

The playwright Jack Hibberd has astutely observed that the Harding mother "embodies the awful oppressiveness of the 1950's in Australia," and she has a strong affinity to a recurrent type in the plays and novels of Patrick White of that period of "the great Australian emptiness." Gorman's pessimism is reinforced because that oppressiveness has invaded and infected the 1970's, and this implication underlies the ironies of his other major work, a stage adaptation of A. B. Facey's autobiography, *A Fortunate Life*. Here, Old Bert narrates from the stage the story of his life which is episodically acted out by a large cast; the narrator's persistence in refusing to see that the extraordinary saga of abandonment and deprivation is anything other than fortunate, coupled with a simplistic delivery style and a magnification of the most meagre happiness, brings an extreme pathos. Even at Gallipoli, where Bert sees the deaths of not only his mate but also his brother, there is expression of neither anger nor grief, and when his son is killed in World War II Bert's response does not go beyond losing faith in God. The terrible stoicism which accepts oppressiveness ironically belies Gorman's assertion that Australians "are a very direct and often publicly emotional people." The impregnable satisfaction of the old Facey, the obdurate larrikin, would have few answers to the emotional directness of the middle-aged Raeleen.

—Howard McNaughton

GOTANDA, Philip Kan. American. Born in Stockton, California, 17 December 1949. Educated at the University of California, Santa Barbara, B.A. in Asian studies; Hastings College, Nebraska, J.D. Co-founder, Asian American Musicians Organization; artist-in-residence, Okada House, Stanford University, California. Recipient: Rockefeller grant, 1980–81. Address: 7, 229 Willard North, California 94118, U.S.A.

PUBLICATIONS

Plays

Bullet Headed Birds (produced New York, 1981).
A Song for a Nisei Fisherman (produced Los Angeles, 1982; New York, 1983).
The Dream of Kitamura (produced New York, 1985). Published in *West Coast Plays* (San Francisco), 15/16, 1983.
The Wash (produced Los Angeles, 1985). Published in *Between Worlds: Contemporary Asian-American Plays*, edited by Misha Berson, New York, Theatre Communications Group, 1990.
Yankee Dawg, You Die (produced San Francisco, 1987; New York, 1989). New York, Dramatists Play Service, 1989.
Fish Head Soup (produced San Francisco, 1987).

*   *   *

One sees in the work of a number of Asian-American playwrights the attraction of Asian theatre styles. Thus, Philip Kan Gotanda's earliest published play, *The Dream of*

Kitamura, includes the use of masks and the crucial act from the past which haunts the characters is re-enacted with puppets. By contrast, his next two plays are realistic in their action, though *The Wash* has three locations simultaneously present throughout and *Yankee Dawg, You Die*—like *The Dream of Kitamura*—uses an abstract set of *shoji* screens.

The nonrealism of *The Dream of Kitamura* is to be seen not only in the mode of presentation but in the plotting. At the beginning of the play we hear a voice, over the chanting of a Buddhist sutra, that tells us "A crime has been committed. A robbery. A double murder. There was a witness." What we find is Rosanjin enthroned like Beckett's Hamm and so fearful of the vengeance of the demon mask Kitamura that he has hired two guards to protect him. In different pools of light we see the various interchanges between the characters, especially between Rosanjin's daughter and the young guard. At the play's end we learn that the murderer was not Rosanjin but his wife Zuma, the young guard is the victims' baby they could not find, and the older guard was witness to the crime and rescuer of the baby. Gotanda's refracted and often ritualized presentation suggests Rosanjin's state of mind even though the action does not take place within his consciousness.

The Wash takes us deep into the psyches of a married but now separated couple, perceived with deep sympathy and totally involving us in their parallel situations. After decades of marriage, in which she played a traditional supportive role, Masi has walked out on her husband Nobu. Every week she comes by to collect his dirty washing and return his clean clothes. He hardly acknowledges her visits, but his hurt is expressed by his retreating into building an elaborate kite such as he flew in his childhood. The play follows her into an affair and a new marriage with a widower, he into a very tentative relationship with a widow who runs a neighborhood restaurant at which he has come to eat regularly. He, however, cannot adjust to his wife's leaving and when she announces her remarriage isolates himself in his apartment, refusing to answer the door or the telephone. Yet Gotanda provides a subplot which allows him to suggest some hope for change in Nobu. One of two daughters has married a black man and Nobu has refused to consider this as anything but a disgrace, but when in this crisis she visits with her young son he slowly accepts the child and gives him the kite.

On the one hand, this is the story of anybody, although it is unusual in presenting such struggles for self-fulfilment among retired people in their sixties. On the other, it has particular significance for Asian-Americans. First, the central problem has been and is Nobu's internalized prohibition on the expression of emotion, perhaps even stronger in the Nisei (second-generation Japanese-Americans) because of the difficult lives they faced, notably the wartime internment to which Nobu's mind keeps returning. Even in the one scene where he asks Masi to stay the night he does so by asking her to make him breakfast (it is evening when he says this). It is this too that makes him embarrassed by the restaurant owner's small advances. Second, the length of time that it has taken Masi to face up to recognizing her own needs reflects a sense of obligation and of the importance of the family; it is perhaps only when her daughters are in their thirties that she feels free to consider herself. Third, as Michael Toshiyuki Uno, the director of the 1988 film of *The Wash*, has suggested, "if you're talking about Asian-American images in the past, there is no sexuality," and *The Wash* deals openly with sexual as well as psychological needs.

Yankee Dawg, You Die is a smaller play, in cast and in subject. It is a series of encounters between two Japanese-American film actors, the elder of whom took a Chinese name in the 1940's to improve his acceptability. This is one of the series of professional compromises that the play addresses. The young actor is at the point of moving from an Asian-American theatre company to "the industry," film and television. He expresses a mixture of admiration for the older actor's success and contempt for the compromises he has made to achieve it. At the play's end, the two friends, as they have become, try out for the same movie; the young actor takes the part of Yang, the Evil One—exactly the kind of stereotyped role he has attacked the older man for accepting —while the older actor turns down a role to appear in an independent no-budget Asian-American film.

The message is clearly put in the play's opening speech, which is repeated midway and again at the end. We see the older actor delivering a speech that he had in some long-ago war movie in which he played a Japanese soldier guarding American prisoners:

> You stupid American G.I. I know you try and escape. You think you can pull my leg. I speakee your language. I graduate UCLA, Class of '34. I drive big American car with big-chested American blond sitting next to . . . Heh? No, no, no, not "dirty floor." Floor clean. Class of '34. No, no, not "dirtyfloor." [. . .] What is wrong with you? You sickee in the head? What the hell is wrong with you? Why can't you hear what I'm saying? Why can't you see me as I really am?

Most of the rest of the play depicts the stereotyped media images of Asian-Americans and the frustrations the performers feel.

Gotanda's plays are diverse. His future work may be unpredictable, but also eagerly awaited.

—Anthony Graham-White

GOW, Michael. Australian. Born in Sydney in 1955. Educated at Sydney University, B.A. 1980. Founder-member, Thalia Theatre Company, Sydney; chair of the board, Griffin Theatre Company, Sydney, from 1986; currently associate director, Sydney Theatre Company. Recipient: New Writers fellowship, 1986; New South Wales Premier's award, 1986; Sydney Theatre Critics Circle award, 1986; Australian Writers Guild award, 1987. Address: c/o Sydney Theatre Company Ltd., Pier 4, Hickson Road, Miller's Point, Sydney, Australia.

PUBLICATIONS

Plays

The Kid (produced Sydney, 1983). Sydney, Currency Press, 1983.
The Astronaut's Wife (produced Sydney, 1984).
Away (produced Sydney, 1986; Sacramento, California, 1989). Sydney, Currency Press, 1986.
On Top of the World (produced Sydney, 1986; London, 1992).
Europe (produced Sydney, 1987; Leatherhead, Surrey, 1989). Sydney, Currency Press, 1988.
1841 (produced Adelaide, 1988). Sydney, Currency Press, 1988.

Furious (produced Sydney, 1991).
All Stops Out (for children) (produced Sydney, 1991).

Television Play: *Eden's Lost*, 1988.

* * *

With the success of his play *Away* and its numerous productions in Australia and abroad, Michael Gow was immediately considered the most exciting new writing talent in 1980's Australian theatre. The clear, sparse dialogue and sure theatrical sense of his plays owe something to his other functions as actor and director. His intertextual references to, and citation of, European models, particularly Greek and French classical tragedy and Shakespeare, led many critics to hail his plays as exemplars of a new "internationalism" in Australian theatre. Yet behind the resonant Greek allusions Gow's main subject remains the inter-generational and sexual tensions of the nuclear family, more specifically the lower-middle-class 1960's generation, alienated by international media culture and the very suburban affluence which their Depression-era parents worked so hard to bequeath them. But in the Bicentennial year of 1988 Gow wrote for the Adelaide Festival a historical play *1841*, a damning indictment of Australia's penal past which tacitly presents a dystopic and uncelebratory version of contemporary society. This was savagely condemned by the very critics who had earlier hailed the writer as an apostle of harmony and reconciliation, his subsequent silence was broken in 1991 by *Furious*, a fractured and powerful version of the *Eumenides* wherein a playwright must deal with the furies both of his family and his own vision.

Gow's first play *The Kid* is an extraordinarily assured debut, and introduces the themes of the precariousness of the family and the death of the young. The "Kid" is Aspro, whose tough sister Snake and brother Dean take him to Sydney in search of compensation for a head injury. On the road Dean initially picks up the gentle Donald, but becomes fascinated by the conviction of the abused waif Desiree's deluded allegiance to "Gard's word," this being apocalyptic nuclear visions from fundamentalist America. The quest fails, Aspro dies, and the precarious "family" of kids is shattered by the pressures of an uncomprehending official world. The tersely witty scenes are framed by operatic allusions to Valhalla and other inappropriately grandiose European cultural expressions, lending context and comment to the kids' constricted lives and their alienation amidst a plethora of post-modernist packaged "culture," whether religious slide-and-tape kits, opera albums, or fatuous coffee-table Australiana books.

Although written before *Away*, *On Top of the World* was produced after it and shows a precarious re-establishment of the family in the face of disease, emotional pain, and death. Gow's most daring and funny play, *On Top* deals with the tormented children of Clive, the widowed patriarch, who is dying of cancer in his new home on top of a Gold Coast apartment building. The estranged son Marcus brings to the family reunion the elderly Baby, a motherly working-class woman who eventually overcomes the hostility of his sister Stephanie and finds a home and function as Clive's wife. The play ends with a scene of hilarious savagery where Marcus phones to berate Baby's own ungrateful and selfish relatives, and induces the family to join in the ritual of cathartic abuse. Echoes of the Atreidae story combine with Gow's typical use of tirade and stichomythia to endow the play with classical structure and mythic resonance. For *Away* Shakespeare is used to frame the story of the dying boy Tom and the effect of his life on three 1960's families, each with some loss or grief in need of healing. The suburban rituals of the Christmas seaside family holiday provide a framework rudely shattered by the storms of nature and by various tensions caused by generational conflict and, in the case of the fragile Coral, the loss of her son in the Vietnam War. Gow's keen satire of the human and environmental costs of creeping affluence and lower-middle-class gentility is typified in the "Greek Chorus" of campers demanding "improvements" to the camp site: "a cyclone wire fence", "draining the lagoon," "banning pets," and cutting down all those "unsightly trees."

Australia's ambivalent relationship to European high culture is cleverly dramatised in the romantic comedy *Europe*. Douglas has become infatuated with Barbara, a European actor with whom he had a fling while she was acting in an international festival in Sydney; to her horror, Douglas follows her to Europe and demands the continuation of the relationship. Barbara's own ambivalence surfaces as she rebels against her entrapped role as purveyor of the classic repertoire, doomed to enact each drama to its unvarying tragic conclusion. Douglas and Barbara project onto each other their various culturally constructed longings and frustrations: his fascination with and resentment of "European" glamour and prestige; her irritation with and longing for "Australian" innocence and possibility. As these stereotypes are stripped away (Douglas proves both complicated and tenacious), the couple move towards a less illusioned and more hopeful phase of their relationship.

The historical tragedy *1841* explores the penal state of early Australia through the character of Aurora, the spirit of European revolution who fails to inspire a society already infected with European violence, acquisitiveness, and public corruption. Deadening apathy and cynicism prevent most of its inhabitants from responding to Aurora's call to resistance; so the abused innocent Lynch dies, as does Aspro (*The Kid*), without denouncing his oppressors, and the pious charade of "civilisation" continues. Gow's next play develops his interest in writing for and about the problems of young people. *All Stops Out* examines the pressures caused to kids and families by the HSC, the all-important matriculation examination. But his *Furious* utilises anew the appropriation of classic models in a play of concentrated power and confrontational force. As the writer Roland inherits from a dying woman a quest for his lost family he is possessed by them as his creative furies, beings who invade his consciousness and demand his energy and allegiance. Meanwhile his love affair with Chris develops only to be terminated by vengeful society. The overt gay theme of *Furious* has been implicit in his writing since *The Kid*, and here suggests a fragile alternative to the endemic fracturing of the nuclear family.

Gow's popularity in performance and his literary reputation remain high, as he continues to be one of the most assured and adventurous writers working today. His theatre has established a uniquely theatricalised view of Australian life wherein bold *mise en scène* and thematic intertextuality transcend a merely naturalistic or psychologising account of human interaction, in order to both contextualise historical forces and interrogate post-colonial and post-modern suburban culture.

—Veronica Kelly

GOW, Ronald. British. Born in Heaton Moor, near Manchester, Lancashire, 1 November 1897. Educated at Altrincham Grammar School, Cheshire; Manchester University, B.Sc. 1922. Served in the British Army, 1918–19. Married the actor Wendy Hiller in 1937; one daughter and one son. Worked as a chemist and schoolmaster; educational film producer. Agent: Laurence Fitch Ltd., 483 Southbank House, Black Prince Road, Albert Embankment, London SE1 7SJ England. *Died 27 April 1993.*

PUBLICATIONS

Plays

Breakfast at Eight (produced Altrincham, 1920). London, French, 1921.

The Sausage (produced Altrincham). London and New York, French, 1924.

Under the Skull and Bones: A Piratical Play with Songs (produced Altrincham). London, Gowans and Gray, and Boston, Baker, 1929.

Higgins: The Highwayman of Cranford (produced Altrincham). London, Gowans and Gray, and Boston, Baker, 1930.

Henry; or, The House on the Moor (produced Altrincham). London, Gowans and Gray, and Boston, Baker, 1931.

Five Robin Hood Plays (includes *The King's Warrant, The Sheriff's Kitchen, All on a Summer's Day, Robin Goes to Sea, The Affair at Kirklees*). London, Nelson, 1932.

The Golden West (produced Altrincham). London, Gowans and Gray, and Boston, Baker, 1932.

The Vengeance of the Gang (produced Altrincham). London, Gowans and Gray, and Boston, Baker, 1933.

O.H.M.S. (produced Altrincham, 1933). London, Deane, 1933.

Gallows Glorious (produced Altrincham and London, 1933; as *John Brown*, produced New York, 1934). London, Gollancz, 1933.

My Lady Wears a White Cockade (produced London, 1934). London, Garamond Press, 1935.

Love on the Dole, adaptation of the novel by Walter Greenwood (produced Manchester, 1934; London, 1935; New York, 1936). London, Cape, 1935; New York, French, 1936.

Compromise. London, Deane, and Boston, Baker, 1935.

The Marrying Sort. London, Garamond Press, and Boston, Baker, 1935.

The Miracle on Watling Street: A Play for the Open Air. London, Dickson and Thompson, 1935.

Men Are Unwise, adaptation of the novel by Ethel Mannin (produced London, 1937).

Ma's Bit o' Brass, based on the screenplay *Lancashire Luck* (produced Colwyn Bay and London, 1938; as *Lovejoy's Millions*, produced London, 1938). London, Deane, and Boston, Baker, 1938.

Scuttleboom's Treasure. London and New York, French, 1938.

Grannie's a Hundred. London, Deane, and Boston, Baker, 1939.

The Lawyer of Springfield (broadcast 1940). London, Deane, and Boston, Baker, 1949.

Jenny Jones, music by Harry Parr Davies, adaptation of stories by Rhys Davies (produced London, 1944).

Tess of the D'Urbervilles, adaptation of the novel by Thomas Hardy (produced London, 1946).

Jassy, adaptation of the novel by Norah Lofts (produced Wimbledon, 1947).

Ann Veronica, adaptation of the novel by H.G. Wells (produced London, 1949). London, French, 1951; revised version, with Frank Wells, music by Cyril Ornadel, lyrics by David Croft (produced London, 1969).
The Full Treatment, with Robert Morley (produced London, 1953).
The Edwardians, adaptation of the novel by V. Sackville-West (as *Weekend in May*, produced Windsor, 1959; as *The Edwardians*, produced London, 1959). London, French, 1960.
Mr. Rhodes (produced Windsor, 1961).
A Boston Story, adaptation of the novel *Watch and Ward* by Henry James (as *Watch and Ward*, produced Windsor, 1964; revised version, as *A Boston Story*, produced London, 1968). London, Theatre Guild, 1969.
This Stratford Business, adaptation of stories by Henry James (produced Cheltenham, 1971).
The Friendship of Mrs. Eckley (produced Cheltenham, 1975).
The Old Jest, adaptation of the novel by Jennifer Johnston (produced Brighton, 1980).

Screenplays: *The Man Who Changed His Mind*, 1928; *The Glittering Sword*, 1929; *Southern Roses*, 1936; *Lancashire Luck*, with A.R. Rawlinson, 1937; *Mr. Smith Carries On*, 1937; *Jig Saw*, 1942.

Radio Plays: *The Lawyer of Springfield*, 1940; *Enter, Fanny Kemble*, 1940; *Front Line Family* series, during World War II; *Mr. Darwin Comes Ashore*, 1941; *Patience on a Monument*, 1944; *Westward Ho!* (serialization), from the novel by Charles Kingsley, 1953; *Lorna Doone* (serialization), from the novel by R.D. Blackmore, 1954.

Television Play: *Trumpet in the Clouds*, 1955.

Other

Editor, *Plays for the Classroom*. London, Murray, 1933.

*

Ronald Gow comments:

The question I am being asked is "what makes me tick as a playwright?" I was brought up near Manchester with the strong belief that the Gaiety Theatre was the greatest thing that ever happened there—even greater than the Hallé—and that Brighouse, Monkhouse, and Houghton were not only household words but shining examples. We knew them all and I had even acted with the author of *Hindle Wakes*. I was definitely stage-struck and when we built a theatre in my home town I cared little whether I shifted scenery or acted or took tickets at the door. After many one-act plays and a desperate wish to be a shining example myself I began to look around for something to be angry about. Most of my plays had some compelling obsession in them. When I wrote about Bonnie Prince Charlie it became anti-war and anti-romantic. Result, a mere six weeks at the Embassy. Next play about John Brown, whose soul went marching on, brought the audience cheering to their feet at the old Shaftesbury. But a bitter anti-slavery bias and an austere title (*Gallows Glorious*) were no good in that temple of musical comedy. Two weeks. (Two nights in New York.) I was trying to write an anti-unemployment play (three million of them) but fortunately read Walter Greenwood's *Love on the Dole* and decided to dramatize that instead. Marriage necessitated making money, with no axes to grind, resulting in comedies like *Ma's Bit o' Brass* and various film scripts and a great deal of propaganda radio and film work during the war (*Front Line Family*).

Success with adapting novels led to London productions of *Tess of the D'Urbervilles*, *Ann Veronica*, *The Edwardians*, and *A Boston Story* from a Henry James novel.

* * *

Ronald Gow is a very modest man. Questioned about his work, he will say that any claim to distinction as a playwright that he may have achieved is due rather to his ability as an adaptor of borrowed plots to stage production than as an inventor of original stories. He will say this with a deprecating air, as of one ready to admit that he is operating on an artistic level rather below the highest.

How he can take this view, seeing that he is following the lead given by the most inveterate plot-borrower of them all, William Shakespeare, is not clear. One suspects Gow of being over-modest; and suspicion becomes certainty when a close critical look at his whole range of dramatic writings reveals that his early original plays were no less distinguished than his subsequent adaptations. Simply, they were less popular.

A reason for this can easily be found. Gow was educated at the grammar school at Altrincham in Cheshire, a town with easy access to Manchester. His subject was science, and his objective a B.Sc. degree at Manchester University; but during his schooldays the institution in that city which chiefly excited his interest was the Gaiety Theatre, where Miss Horniman had installed her famous regime and a whole group of angry young men were writing for her a whole series of realistic plays about social injustices of the time.

Gow, violently stage-struck, worshipped at the feet of these dramatists, came to know some of them (Harold Brighouse, Stanley Houghton, and the older Alan Monkhouse), and made up his mind that when the time came he would follow their example; meanwhile he became an enthusiastic amateur actor.

Fortunately for him, there lay at his very door the means to make the theatre an absorbing hobby without too much encroachment on the more serious business of earning a living. An amateur dramatic society at Altrincham, the Garrick, was fast becoming (and, incidentally, is still) one of the leaders in its own field. In the period after World War I when the professional stage was given over almost wholly to glittering frivolity and the general playgoing public asked for nothing better, the task of keeping a more serious theatre alive fell to amateurs who, organized and led by the newly formed British Drama League, rose nobly to the call.

As the movement gathered force and a large public responded, men like Gow found their hobby growing into something very like a profession. He himself, now a young man with his science degree behind him, working first as research chemist and then as schoolmaster, was in his spare time wholly at the Garrick Theatre's service. He acted for it, wrote for it, shifted scenery, took money at the doors. For several years he was its secretary; and when it decided to build itself its own playhouse, he even laid bricks for it. By the time when, at 33 or so, he decided to try his luck as a professional dramatist, he had had a fuller training for the craft than most.

True to the principles he had learnt as a boy, he now looked for social injustices to write about. This was easy enough so far as themes went, for he had as sharp a sense of the follies and injustices of human life as any of the Horniman dramatists whose disciple he was. Unlike them, however, he had a natural sense of period, and was apt to look to the past for his plots.

From the first, there was no question of the excellence of Gow's writing, and he soon had a play accepted for West End production. This was *Gallows Glorious*, which told the story of that John Brown whose soul, in the song, goes marching on. It was produced at the old Shaftesbury Theatre in 1933, and the first-night audience received it with rapturous applause and a standing ovation. But the Shaftesbury (destroyed by German bombs in World War II) was a big house to fill, and the general public, which was not in the mood for period pieces anyhow, showed no interest in John Brown whatever. The play limped along for two weeks and then had to be taken off.

A rather similar experience in the following year with an anti-romantic and anti-war play about Bonnie Prince Charlie must have taught him the lesson that a man writing a play-with-a-purpose should choose to set his action in the immediate present, for he next sat down to write about unemployment, the chief problem of the moment. While engaged on this he happened to read Walter Greenwood's novel *Love on the Dole*, and decided to dramatize Greenwood's story instead of going on with his own.

The great success of this play changed Gow's whole life. It made a name not only for him but for Wendy Hiller, the aspiring young actress who played his heroine and whom, in 1937, he married. It also brought him sharply to the notice of Pinewood film studios and the BBC, with the ironic result that he was, practically speaking, lost to the stage for nine years or so. Indeed, his next two stage plays, *Ma's Bit o' Brass* and *Tess of the D'Urbervilles* were both adapted to the stage from filmscripts of his own.

Ma's Bit o' Brass, a light-hearted exercise in the Lancashire idiom, ranks rather uneasily among Gow's original pieces. It never quite reached the West End, but it toured successfully and became a favourite among "Reps" and amateurs. Its author now regards it with a kind of rueful gratitude.

He wrote the film version of *Tess* for his wife, who during the war was invited to play this part in Hollywood. He himself did not quite "see" her in the part, and advised her against taking it—and, indeed, it was not one of her greatest successes. But she did well enough for John Burrell to want her to do it on the London stage, and to invite Gow to write the play. His next three West End productions—*Ann Veronica*, *The Edwardians* and the very delightful *A Boston Story*—were adaptations (as was his latest play, *The Old Jest*) but *The Friendship of Mrs. Eckley* is an original story about the Brownings.

—W.A. Darlington

GRAY, Jack. Canadian. Born in Detroit, Michigan, United States, 7 December 1927. Educated at primary and secondary schools in Ontario; Queen's University, Kingston, Ontario; University of Toronto, B.A., M.A. Married Araby Lockhart in 1952; three sons and two daughters. Assistant editor, *Maclean's Magazine*, Toronto, 1953–57; executive director and resident playwright, Neptune Theatre, Halifax, Nova Scotia, 1963; professor of integrated studies, University of Waterloo, Ontario, 1969–71; secretary general, Canadian Theatre Centre, Toronto, 1971–73; president, Association of Canadian Television and Radio Artists (ACTRA), 1978–82; special consultant on cultural policy, Department of Communications, Ottawa, 1982–83; president, League for Canadian Communications, 1984. President, International

Writers Guild, and John Gray Productions Ltd.; editor, Canadian Play Series, University of Toronto Press. Agent: Elspeth Cochrane Agency, 11–13 Orlando Road, London SW4 0LE, England. Address: 65 Pine Street, Brockville, Ontario K6V 1G6, Canada.

PUBLICATIONS

Plays

Bright Sun at Midnight (produced Toronto, 1957).
Ride a Pink Horse, music by Louis Applebaum (produced Toronto, 1958).
The Teacher (produced Stratford, Ontario, 1960).
Chevalier Johnstone (as *Louisbourg*, produced Halifax, 1964; revised version, as *Chevalier Johnstone*, produced Halifax, 1966). Toronto, Playwrights, 1972.
Emmanuel Xoc (produced Toronto, 1965).
Godiva! (produced Coventry, 1967).
Susannah, Agnes, and Ruth (broadcast 1969). Toronto, Playwrights, 1972.
Striker Schneiderman (produced Toronto, 1970). Toronto, University of Toronto Press, 1973.

Radio Plays: *To Whom It May Concern*, 1958; *The Lost Boy*, 1959; *Susannah, Agnes, and Ruth*, 1969; *The Cracker Man*, 1970; *And I Mayakovsky*, 1976.

Television Plays: *The Ledge*, 1959 (UK); *The Glove*, 1961 (UK); *Man in Town*, 1962; *The Enemy*, 1962 (UK); *The Guard*, 1963; *Miss Hanago*, 1964 (UK).

Other

The Third Strategy: A Canadian Primer of Sensible Proposals for the Solution of Insoluble Problems, with André Fortier. Ottawa, Canadian Conference of the Arts, 1984.

*

Manuscript Collection: Metropolitan Toronto Library.

Theatrical Activities:
Director: **Play**—*Clap Hands* (revue), London, 1962.

* * *

Jack Gray is a Shavian with a taste for the baroque. Most of his plays inhabit the world of witty altercation—to the detriment, occasionally, of their dramatic form. But they are on the whole well made, and the aphoristic quality of many of the speeches indicates more than superficial wit. In *Susannah, Agnes, and Ruth* the repartee is brittle:

Ian   —He'll never get over it.
Susannah —He never got over being born.

But it is more than brittle. Gray has listened to the ghastly maxims of middle-class Methodism with an attentive ear. "Don't be smart" or "A responsible parent can never be said to be interfering." Both speak for the world of O'Neill's *Ah, Wilderness!* with all the exuberance removed—a world in which we expect to hear that "the Attorney-General says that dancing on Sunday must stop in Ontario." This is only just the day before yesterday, and it does Gray credit not only that he can capture it so exactly without cause or rancour but that he can give to Susannah (the grandmother figure who is its spokesman) a toughness and a life that even the men in the play have missed. In a passage reminiscent of Strether's impassioned speech to Little Bilham in Henry James's *The Ambassadors*, Bob, one of the uncles, says to Ruth: "We've evaded life—sidestepped it—it's like a dance—one-two-side-step—one-two-step aside. . . . Don't be like we are, Ruth—take hold of life." But it is Susannah more than the rest who realizes the importance of seizing upon life and denying death. She rebukes the simpering vicar who speaks of her son and others as having died heroic deaths in France in World War I:

> They did not. They died dirty, lonely blasphemous deaths. Each year on that anniversary, Mr. Smith, I take off my mourning, I wear my gayest clothes. It's all I can do to protest the shallow sham you men make of life. It's how I would meet God—singing! We must never celebrate such deaths.

It is this festivity in the face of bleakness and heroism in spite of itself that characterize the lead in Gray's later play *Striker Schneiderman*—probably his best-known work. But there is a set-piece quality about the play, a sense of its being written for an occasion or to a prescription that does not allow it to be much more than an entertaining piece of theatre. Its elements are too predictable, even down to the tailor joke from *Endgame*.

This criticism is valid to some degree for *Chevalier Johnstone* as well, but although it too seems very much written for an occasion (not to say for television) it has a greater toughness about it, and the ending seems somehow less forced. Part of this is due to the hard-headedness of the dialogue—the absence of sentimentality and Jewish melodrama—and part to a sense that the world described, though it is two centuries away from our own, is closer to our preoccupations than are those of Schneiderman. The play has a curiously Brechtian quality—partly the result no doubt of the rapid shifting of scenes and the extravagant stage directions: "We lose the woods and stream and follow them as they walk back to, and then through, the fortress." But this Brechtian character is most obvious in the restraint of sentiment by a wit that keeps us off. This wit is directed against our prejudices—of flabby democracy and literary superstition, for instance. "I'm an Indian, not a gentleman," says Samuel, the scout who attaches himself to Johnstone while repulsing any foolish notion of mere equality. And in response to Johnstone's explanation that he reads for his recreation, "Pascal . . . Molière. And, of course, Voltaire," Drucour, his superior, asks "What do you do for healthy recreation?"

Emmanuel Xoc and *The Teacher* both suffer from flaws not so evident in the other plays. In fact, in spite of some turns of phrase in *Emmanuel Xoc*—"fifty years' caution in a man is a kink"—the play is not a good omen. It is like a combination of Puccini's *Gianni Schicchi* and Tennessee Williams's *The Milk Train Doesn't Stop Here Anymore*. But its host of characters—Tweedie, Xoc, Baptist, Fink, Fingers, Arnold, and Morgan—is too much like something out of an old Bowery Boys film for us to take the play as more than a sort of baroque exercise.

There is a similar element of fantasy in *The Teacher* (like *Emmanuel Xoc*, it has a ghost), though the fantasy is not grotesque but lyrical in a way that easily becomes sentimental. Indeed there is a studied quality about the play that, coupled with the absence of the sort of wit so evident in the later plays, gives it an unfortunate flatness. Its gestures are both towards Dylan Thomas's *Under Milk Wood* and Joyce's *The Dead*, but it fails to get beyond the sort of artificial

melodrama—complete with folksongs—that used to be the favorite of the CBC.

Fortunately Gray has come a great way since then. His later plays show both an eye for detail and an ear for wit that are badly needed. None of his plays so far is great, but some of them are very good indeed.

—D.D.C. Chambers

GRAY, John. Canadian. Born in Ottawa, Ontario, 26 September 1946. Educated at Mount Allison University, Sackville, New Brunswick, B.A. 1968; University of British Columbia, Vancouver, M.A. in theatre 1972. Has two sons. Founding director, Tamahnous Theatre, Vancouver, 1971–74; freelance director, 1972–76: directed 40 productions throughout Canada. Recipient: Los Angeles Drama Critics Circle award, 1981; Governor-General's award, 1983; Vancouver award, 1988. Address: 3392 West 37th Avenue, Vancouver, British Columbia V6N 2V6, Canada.

PUBLICATIONS

Plays

Salty Tears on a Hangnail Face (lyrics only, with Jeremy Long), book by Long, music by Gray (produced Vancouver, 1974).
18 Wheels, music and lyrics by Gray (also director: produced Toronto, 1977). Included in *Local Boy Makes Good*, 1987.
Billy Bishop Goes to War, music and lyrics by Gray (also director: as *Billy Bishop*, produced Vancouver, 1978; as *Billy Bishop Goes to War*, produced Washington, D.C., New York, and Edinburgh, 1980; London, 1981). Vancouver, Talonbooks, 1981.
Rock and Roll (also director: produced Ottawa, 1981). Published in *Canadian Theatre Review* (Downsview, Ontario), Summer 1982; included in *Local Boy Makes Good*, 1987.
Bongo from the Congo (for children; produced Vancouver, 1982).
Balthazaar and the Mojo Star (produced Vancouver, 1982).
Better Watch Out, You Better Not Die (produced Halifax, Nova Scotia, 1983).
Don Messer's Jubilee (produced Halifax, Nova Scotia, 1985). Included in *Local Boy Makes Good*, 1987.
The B.C. Review (produced Vancouver, 1986).
Local Boy Makes Good: Three Musicals (includes *18 Wheels*, *Rock and Roll*, *Don Messer's Jubilee*). Vancouver, Talonbooks, 1987.
Health, the Musical (produced Vancouver, 1989).

Screenplays: *Billy Bishop Goes to War*, 1982; *The King of Friday Night*, 1984.

Novel

Dazzled. Toronto, Irwin, 1984.

Recording: *Billy Bishop Goes to War*, Tapestry, 1979.

*

Critical Studies: "John Gray's Progress" by Judy Steed, in *Toronto Life*, May 1981; *The Work: Interviews with English-Canadian Playwrights* by Robert Wallace and Cynthia Zimmerman, Toronto, Coach House Press, 1982; *Second Stage: The Alternative Theatre Movement in Canada* by Renate Usmiani, Vancouver, University of British Columbia Press, 1983; article by David Cruise, in *Atlantic Insight* (Halifax, Nova Scotia), August 1983.

Theatrical Activities:
Director: **Plays** (selection)—most of his own plays; *The Bacchae* by Euripides, Vancouver, 1972; *Dracula Two*, Vancouver, 1974; *The Tempest*, Vancouver, 1974; *Bull Durham* by Jeremy Newson, Toronto, 1974; *Canadian Heroes Series 1* (co-director with Paul Thompson), Toronto, 1975; *Preparing* by Beverley Simons (co-director with Buzz Bense), Vancouver, 1975; *The Imaginary Invalid* by Molière, Vancouver, 1975; *Herringbone* by Thomas Cone, Vancouver, 1975 and 1976, and Lennoxville, Quebec, 1978.
Composer: music for all his own plays, and: *Bull Durham* by Jeremy Newson, Toronto, 1974; *The Imaginary Invalid* by Molière, Vancouver, 1975; *The False Messiah* by Rick Salutin, Toronto, 1975; *The Horsburgh Scandal* by Betty Jane Wylie, Toronto, 1976; *1837: The Farmer's Revolt* by Rick Salutin, Toronto, 1976; *The Farm Show* by Theatre Passe Muraille (music with Jimmy Adams), Toronto, 1976; *The Olympics Show* by Theatre Passe Muraille, Toronto, 1976; *The Great Wave of Civilization* by Herschel Hardin, Lennoxville, Quebec, 1976; *Money* by Rick Salutin, Toronto, 1976; *Le Temps d'une vie* by Roland Lepage, Toronto, 1978.

John Gray comments:

I write populist musicals in which regional and Canadian themes are placed in the broader context of the world and the human spirit. In *18 Wheels* the Canadian truck driver is the central focus for the Canadian preoccupation with physical distance and the enormous space between things and people. *Billy Bishop Goes to War* is about the World War I flying ace, and explores the various ironies that result from colonial success in an imperial war. *Rock and Roll* is about youth culture in a small Canadian town in the 1960's, from the point of view of the local rock and roll band. *Better Watch Out, You Better Not Die* is a satire on left-right attitudes in the face of old age and violent death. *Bongo from the Congo* is an afro musical about a man's search for a mystical African animal and for the grace that that animal both embodies and bestows. *Balthazaar and the Mojo Star* is a nativity jazz musical about the odyssey of a Parthian magus. *Don Messer's Jubilee* is a musical about traditional rural culture: its purpose, how it develops, and how it is destroyed in favour of international stereotypes. *Dazzled*, the novel, is a comic Bildungsroman, a cultural satire in which a Vancouver ex-hippie makes the adjustment from the romanticism of the 1960's to the neoconservatism of the 1970's. As he makes the adjustment he attempts to see beyond the media hallucinations of both eras and to understand what is really going on around him.

*　*　*

Although he can be said to belong to the large school of playwrights who chronicle Canadian social and political history, John Gray strikingly differs from other such playwrights in style and often in subject matter. He searches for signifiers of the Canadian psyche and finds them not only in conventional heroes like the World War I aviator Billy Bishop, but in an array of small-town heroes—band leaders, high school rock stars—who speak directly to the audience's local identifi-

cation with the social and musical rhythms of its country. The fact that Gray writes pop musical theatre is not coincidental to the success his work has found with audiences: the national sense he presents is young, unsure, energetic, and discordant; his theatrical design itself forms a major part of the social myths he creates. His is a satirical vision, but it is a satire full of affection. He presents documentary history, but as Jamie Portman says, "this kind of history is part cartoon, part musical hall." While his early work, in plays such as *18 Wheels* (a musical about truckers), presents issues and sounds to be heard throughout North America, there is a consistent Canadian texture to his images and attitudes. In *Don Messer's Jubilee*, which was generally well-received, Gray attempts to make an icon of a homely CBC variety show which ran on radio and television for 40 years and which, Gray suggests, is part of the Canadian personality, even if viewers of Gray's own age deplored it in their teens as old-fashioned and corny. Yet Gray ignores the generation younger than himself for whom Don Messer holds no meaning; Gray's work (which to some extent mirrors his own maturation) tends to speak directly and powerfully to the predominant, now middle-aged audience, but he has not yet explored issues unrelated to specific periods of time in Canadian social history, nor is his style in the avant-garde.

Gray first came to major international attention with his second musical, *Billy Bishop Goes to War*, a one-man show about the most celebrated Canadian war-time aviator. Accompanied by a pianist who doubles as occasional foil (Gray himself in the early productions), the narrator/actor impersonates 18 characters, including Bishop. The debt is obvious to the improvisational technique of Paul Thompson's Theatre Passe Muraille, in whose ensemble Gray worked as a young musician and from which influence *18 Wheels* first grew. In *Billy Bishop*, however, Gray finds his own voice both in the score and in his reading of history, an interpretation of Bishop which is endearing while iconoclastic. It is ironic that while showing Bishop to be "a sort of small town juvenile delinquent who, though just scraping to survive and hang on, became the toast of London," Gray makes him a hero of tremendous power and appeal. In Gray's version, Bishop becomes the peculiar hero most suited to the Canadian self-image, a hero who is swept into fame almost against his will, but who is not, in the end, unaware of his new status, nor above using it to his own advantage. Bishop realizes "I really was Number One now," but his enjoyment of the adulation does not change him or endow him with any new sense of personal purpose; in this sense he is a hero without guile, perhaps even the "hero as anti-hero," as Allan Massie called him in the *Scotsman*. He is also still the small-town boy, able to call himself "a dignitary," but ever aware that he is "A colonial dignitary, Bishop. There is a difference." He remains, as his sophisticated London benefactress, Lady St. Helier sings, "a typical Canadian/You're modesty itself." Indeed, as Bishop himself comments, "Nobody starts no wars on Canada/Where folks tend to wish each other well." It is only "once . . . in the air, [that Bishop feels] a lot better. In fact, [he feels] like a King." In this complex characterization Gray has captured a personality who seeks for security in the knowledge that he is second-best and yet who alone in an environment he can control, can scream "at the top of my lungs, I win, I WIN, I WIN!" Such a hero appeals— as the astounding commercial success of this play attests—to the Canadian sense of self. Its similar success in other Commonwealth countries and its commercial failure in New York, despite marked critical support, underlines the point: in his subtle portrait Gray has captured a hero for the colonial mind. And if that character is also likeable and embodies fears and hopes with which the audience can emphathize—and if he sings and makes airplane noises—the resulting relationship is certain to be intense and positive. As contemporary Canadian literature develops a post-modern and post-colonial discourse, however, Gray's hero begins to appear dated. His vision remains a popular one rather than one which challenges or initiates.

The play exploits its economical design: the sparse set and multiple characterizations force an audience to imagine most of the action and, in doing so, compel its involvement. The pace, the comic and often cruel caricatures, the sentiment, bravado, and charm of the protagonist, the adventure of a World War I setting, and the acting *tour de force* required of the principal actor all work together to engage an audience.

In *Rock and Roll*, Gray presents personal memoir in a play about the members of a small-town rock and roll band meeting again in middle age to restage their youth while preparing for a reunion concert. The script exists largely to allow the music to tell the story, as it does in *18 Wheels*, but the songs are Gray's best work to date, and the predictable plot is happily lost in the highly theatrical staging and hard-driving rock music. The show is pure nostalgia for those who were teenagers in the 1950s. It displays a spectrum of easy emotion —love, jealousy, a manic sense of humour, the pathos of ruined dreams, and the triumph of maturity over adolescent insecurities—and if the play can be criticized for its failure to develop any emotion (or, in fact, any plot event) past the surface, it survives in performance because the mood swings are naturalistic to the teenage characters and appropriate to the highly wrought emotions of those caught up in memory, and because the design of the play is episodic, built around the musical numbers. The play is great fun to watch, and like *Billy Bishop* presents involved patterns of music and action, establishing Gray as firmly in control of score and staging.

In *Don Messer's Jubilee*, Gray is more self-conscious about memory, more intent upon exploring the reasons for the cancellation of the popular television show than in truly recreating one of Messer's old programmes. But in his version of the old show, he presents an entertainment which Martin Knelman in *Saturday Night* calls "a lot livelier than an evening of true Messer music would be"; Gray is guilty of polishing the hero to give him more "big time" glitz, but in doing so, he is clearly myth-making: he seeks to secure the older folklore in a more contemporary aesthetic.

Recently, Gray has written and performed a series of parodic and satiric television vignettes for the CBC, capitalizing on his own popularity and a 1980's cynicism with social and political issues. He has also explored the aging process in his newest musical, *Health*, which like the TV spots, recognizes that his audience has reached middle age. The play presents an urban Everyman who is recently divorced, stressed at work, and suddenly ill. He is accompanied by a chorus of personified body parts—his brain, bowels, and phallus—who urge him in various directions, seeking mastery. Faced with the reality of his mortality, the man attempts to redefine himself and his sense of family and politics. The play is vaudevillian in design; the chorus present songs and dances against sketches of the man's life, all against a grotesque proscenium of mechanized human organs. It is a highly visual show and often amusing, but the discussion is trite and relies on the allegorical device more than on internal tension.

John Gray is an important spokesperson for Canadian culture, a role in which his widespread popularity gives him considerable influence. He also continues to enjoy a major success with audiences (although his television spots have not received uniform praise); he has uniquely been able to capture the temperament of his nation. The challenge now is for him to retain this bardic role while moving toward deeper material and in plays designed for the audience of the next century.

—Reid Gilbert

———

GRAY, Simon (James Holliday). British. Born on Hayling Island, Hampshire, 21 October 1936. Educated at a school in Montreal; Westminster School, London; Dalhousie University, Halifax, Nova Scotia, 1954–57, B.A. (honours) in English 1957; Trinity College, Cambridge, 1958–61, B.A. (honours) in English 1961, M.A. Married Beryl Mary Kevern in 1965; one son and one daughter. Harper-Wood student, 1961–62, and research student, 1962–63, Trinity College; lecturer in English, University of British Columbia, Vancouver, 1963–64; supervisor in English, Trinity College, 1964–66; lecturer in English, Queen Mary College, London, 1965–85. Since 1964 editor, *Delta* magazine, Cambridge. Recipient; *Evening Standard* award, 1972, 1976; New York Drama Critics Circle award, 1977; Cheltenham prize for literature, 1982. Honorary fellow, Queen Mary College, 1985. Lives in London. Agent: Judy Daish Associates, 83 Eastbourne Mews, London W2 6LQ, England.

PUBLICATIONS

Plays

Wise Child (produced London, 1967; New York, 1972). London, Faber, 1972.
Molly (as *Death of a Teddy Bear*, televised 1967; revised version, as *Molly*, produced Watford, Hertfordshire, and London, 1977; New York, 1978). Included in *The Rear Column and Other Plays*, 1978; in *The Rear Column, Dog Days, and Other Plays*, 1979.
Sleeping Dog (televised 1967). London, Faber, 1968.
Spoiled (televised 1968; produced Glasgow, 1970; London, 1971; New York, 1972). London, Methuen, 1971.
Dutch Uncle (produced Brighton and London, 1969). London, Faber, 1969.
Pig in a Poke (televised 1969). With *Close of Play*, London, Eyre Methuen, 1980.
The Idiot, adaptation of a novel by Dostoevsky (produced London, 1970). London, Methuen, 1971.
Butley (produced Oxford and London, 1971; New York, 1972). London, Methuen, 1971; New York, Viking Press, 1972.
Man in a Side-Car (televised 1971). Included in *The Rear Column and Other Plays*, 1978; in *The Rear Column, Dog Days, and Other Plays*, 1979.
Otherwise Engaged (produced Oxford and London, 1975; New York, 1977). Included in *Otherwise Engaged and Other Plays*, 1975.
Plaintiffs and Defendants (televised 1975). Included in *Otherwise Engaged and Other Plays*, 1975.
Two Sundays (televised 1975). Included in *Otherwise Engaged and Other Plays*, 1975.
Otherwise Engaged and Other Plays. London, Eyre Methuen, 1975; New York, Viking Press, 1976.
Dog Days (produced Oxford, 1976). London, Eyre Metheun, 1976; in *The Rear Column, Dog Days, and Other Plays*, 1979.

The Rear Column (produced London and New York, 1978). Included in *The Rear Column and Other Plays*, 1978; in *The Rear Column, Dog Days, and Other Plays*, 1979.

The Rear Column and Other Plays. London, Eyre Methuen, 1978.

The Rear Column, Dog Days, and Other Plays. New York, Viking Press, 1979.

Close of Play (produced London, 1979; New York, 1981). With *Pig in a Poke*, London, Eyre Methuen, 1980; published separately, New York, Dramatists Play Service, 1982.

Stage Struck (produced London, 1979; Chicago, 1984). London, Eyre Methuen, 1979; New York, Seaver, 1981.

Quartermaine's Terms (produced London, 1981; New Haven, Connecticut, 1982; New York, 1983). London, Eyre Methuen, 1981; revised version, Methuen, and New York, French, 1983.

Chapter 17 (produced Guildford, Surrey, 1982).

Tartuffe, adaptation of the play by Molière (produced Washington, D.C., 1982). With *The Holy Terror*, London, Faber, 1990.

The Common Pursuit: Scenes from Literary Life (produced London, 1984; New Haven, Connecticut, 1985; also co-director: produced New York, 1986; revised version, produced New York, 1987; also director: produced London, 1988). London, Methuen, 1984; New York, Dramatists Play Service, 1987.

Play 1 (includes *Butley, Otherwise Engaged, The Rear Column, Quartermaine's Terms, The Common Pursuit*). London, Methuen, 1986.

Melon (produced London, 1987; revised version, as *The Holy Terror*, broadcast 1989; also director: produced New York, 1992). London, Methuen, 1987; as *The Holy Terror*, with *Tartuffe*, London, Faber, 1990.

After Pilkington (televised 1987). London, Methuen, 1987.

Hidden Laughter (also director: produced Brighton and London, 1990). London, Faber, 1990.

Old Flames and A Month in the Country. London, Faber, 1990.

Screenplays: *Butley*, 1976; *A Month in the Country*, 1987.

Radio Plays: *Up in Pigeon Lake*, from his novel *Colmain*, 1963 (Canada); *The Holy Terror* (revised version of *Melon*), 1989.

Television Plays: *The Caramel Crisis*, 1966; *Death of a Teddy Bear*, 1967; *A Way with the Ladies*, 1967; *Sleeping Dog*, 1967; *Spoiled*, 1968; *Pig in a Poke*, 1969; *The Dirt on Lucy Lane*, 1969; *Style of the Countess*, 1970; *The Princess*, 1970; *Man in a Side-Car*, 1971; *Plaintiffs and Defendants*, 1975; *Two Sundays*, 1975; *After Pilkington*, 1987; *Old Flames*, 1990; *They Never Slept*, 1991; *Running Late*, 1992.

Novels

Colmain. London, Faber, 1963.
Simple People. London, Faber, 1965.
Little Portia. London, Faber, 1967.
A Comeback for Stark (as Hamish Reade). London, Faber, 1968.

Other

An Unnatural Pursuit and Other Pieces: A Playwright's Journal. London, Faber, 1985; New York, St. Martin's Press, 1986.

How's That for Telling 'Em, Fat Lady? A Short Life in the American Theatre. London, Faber, 1988.

Editor, with Keith Walker, *Selected English Prose*. London, Faber, 1967.

*

Theatrical Activities:
Director: **Plays**—*Dog Days*, Vienna, 1980; *The Common Pursuit* (co-director, with Michael McGuire), New York, 1986; *Hidden Laughter*, Brighton and London, 1990.

* * *

Cruel notices have dogged Simon Gray's career, but his plays have fared well with audiences, and his best are important by any standard. He is a witty, intelligent, literary playwright with a flair for the topical and gift for creating memorable characters. His genre is the comedy of manners. Frequently he combines elements from the bedroom farce with features of the whodunit. Butley's savage wit, Simon Hench's arch reserve, Quartermaine's kindly vacancy, Melon's mental sufferings, and Ronnie's words about the divine and human spirit and hidden laughter live in the landscape of the mind long after the details of the play have been forgotten. Gray's skillful control of dialogue—witty, derisive, colloquial, syntactically lively, and often irreverent—rarely fails him. His portraits of academics and the life of the literarily inclined belong beside Kingsley Amis's *Lucky Jim*. Some critics fault Gray for his lack of "magnanimity of spirit and largeness of vision." No doubt his often corrosive humor contributes to this judgement, but his poignant depiction of Quartermaine in his Chekhovian play *Quartermaine's Terms* ought to go a long way towards silencing those who argue that he lacks heart. If anything, he feels too keenly and requires humor to make life more tolerable.

Gray's plays have appeared regularly in the West End since *Wise Child* opened in 1967, shocking its London audience. In 1972, *Butley* won the *Evening Standard* Best Play award. Nonetheless, his detractors gave most of the credit to the superior actors and directors—including Alec Guinness, Simon Ward, Alan Bates, and Harold Pinter—who lent their talents to his plays. In 1979, in a particularly nasty review, James Fenton of the *Sunday Times* announced that Gray had committed "public suicide" in his thriller *Stage Struck*, and gloated that *Close of Play*, an "overblown domestic tragedy," had itself closed at the Lyttelton in less than 10 days. *Quartermaine's Terms*, an international success and the only play to win the Cheltenham prize for literature, was similarly savaged by a San Francisco radio reviewer.

Not one quick to forget or forgive slights, Gray opens his playwright's journal, *An Unnatural Pursuit and Other Pieces*, quoting Fenton's words: "Ladies and Gentlemen, the play's the thing, as Shakespeare put it. But Ladies and Gentlemen, there isn't a play here! No play at all, ladies and gentlemen." Later Gray defiantly boasts that his new play, *The Common Pursuit*, like *Quartermaine's Terms*, "has no plot." Ambiguously named after F.R. Leavis's book, the play takes revenge upon Gray's unkindly reviewers and includes a rude joke at the expense of the *Sunday Times*. Gray feared that the joke would cost him dearly and, if his account of the play's reviews and fate is accurate, his fears were warranted. Ultimately, his producers backed out of the plans to move the play from the Lyric in Hammersmith to the West End. Later, the play traveled to the United States where it was performed in New Haven; a revised version was also staged in Los Angeles.

Gray has had more than his share of flops. His adaptation of Dostoevsky's *The Idiot* entertained his audience but left the critics immodestly displaying their expertise on the Russian master while ignoring Gray's talents. *Dutch Uncle* was depressing; the critics deplored its lack of taste. *Spoiled*, with its touching exploration of a homosexual encounter between pupil and teacher—an encounter which is reworked in a number of his plays and films for television—simply failed to stir any interest. *Close of Play* did not work.

Butley was a stunning success, capturing the bitchiness, vanity, and all-too-fragile ego of a thoroughly jaundiced university lecturer. The protagonists of *Otherwise Engaged* and *Stage Struck* possess many of the traits that made Ben Butley unforgettable. Both plays had long runs in the West End. Gray's thrillers do not take advantage of a period setting. Instead they capitalize upon kinky sexuality and psychologically perverse behavior. His BBC screenplay *After Pilkington* shows him at his best. He calls it a Jamesian ghost-thriller and exploits games from childhood to chilling ends. But his stage plays in this genre lack the marvelous visual effects which made Paul Giovanni's Sherlock Holmes play *The Crucifer of Blood* such a favorite. Instead, they depend on the ingenuity of their plots and the psychological intricacies of their characters for their success. Gray's domestic comedies compare favorably with Alan Ayckbourn's, but with the important exception of *Quartermaine's Terms*, they have the same limitations. They pander to popular taste, make too much of sexual peccadilloes, be they between members of the same or of the opposite sex, and often lack love. None equals Peter Shaffer's *Black Comedy*.

In *Otherwise Engaged* and *Dog Days*, as well as in the television plays *Two Sundays* and *Plaintiffs and Defendants*, the characters of one play slip into the others while the situation remains fairly constant. In *Otherwise Engaged* a snobbish, Oxford-educated editor, Simon Hench, lives with his schoolteacher wife, Beth, and their annoying tenant David. On a day when Simon hopes to listen quietly to Wagner while his wife is away on an outing with her foreign students and a colleague, Ned, he is repeatedly interrupted. His tenant stops in, followed by his brother on an unexpected visit. Next his boisterous friend Jeff, and his current mistress Davina, barge in. Finally, Simon is confronted by an old schoolmate who accuses him, rightly, of having an affair with Joanna, a young lady in Simon's office who happens to be betrothed to the schoolmate. In the course of the day the old rivalries between the brothers are explored; Simon is propositioned by the bare-breasted Davina after she quarrels with Jeff; and Simon learns that his wife has been having an affair with Ned and now, pregnant, wants to marry him. At the play's close, Jeff and Simon turn on *Parsifal*.

Dog Days offers a variant of the same situation with different names. Peter is the junior editor whose wife, Hilary, is having an affair that threatens to destroy the marriage. His brother, Charles, is married to a vegetarian earth-mother, Alison, who has produced four children and is expecting more. After accusing Hilary of "replacing mechanical sex with spontaneous frigidity," Peter walks out to join Joanna. When pre-coital depression mars his affair, he returns contrite to Hilary who will no longer have him. Peter and Charles live a dog's life, both grovelling to people they loathe, both dependent on others in ways they had not predicted. Hilary, like Beth, cannot contemplate spending any more years in a marriage with a man who likes neither himself nor her. In the two television plays about Peter and Charles, the marriages withstand Peter's infidelities and Alison's endless cooing.

The Rear Column, a fascinating play, is based on Stanley's march to the relief of Emin Pasha in 1887 and the fate of the rear column and the five white men left behind in the encampment in the Congo with three hundred "niggers" inside and hoards of cannibals without. The play is about Major Barttelot. Left to guard the rear column, he ends up flogging, shooting, and eating the natives while Jameson, the British naturalist left behind with him, also loses all moral purpose. In his final decadence, he watches a "nigger girl" killed, cooked, and eaten so that he can sketch the rite of cannibalism with the same care he devotes to sketching the African birdlife.

Gray's plays are peopled with men discontented with themselves and ill-suited to their roles. Often these men are homosexuals. Transvestitism (*Wise Child*), bondage (*Sleeping Dog*), and sado-masochistic games (*Sleeping Dog*, *Dutch Uncle*, and *Stage Struck*) are the acts they resort to in their self-loathing. Butley has married to escape his homosexuality only to leave his wife six months later and return to his male student/lover turned colleague. Butley constantly belittles his wife, colleagues, and lover. Ultimately his corrosive humor drives them all away, leaving him too worn out and full of self-dislike to initiate yet another affair with one of his students. Butley uses words to kill. Although he cuts to the quick those who need or love him, ultimately it is he who is the victim. The nasty cut on his chin that he dabs at throughout the play physicalizes the depth of his self-dislike. Mr. Godboy, the protagonist of *Dutch Uncle*, courts punishment at the hands of a police constable noted for his strict ways. Mr. Godboy is unsuccessful in his attempt to gas his wife and upstairs tenant, but he does experience vicariously the humiliations practiced by the constable. In *Molly*, Molly and her lover kill her rich old husband—a man whose habit of spanking his "naughty" wife finally infuriates the lover. In *Sleeping Dog* a retired colonial officer torments a West Indian for being too familiar with his wife. He chains the Jamaican in the cellar of his English house, makes him confess to crimes against his wife and to homosexuality, and finally forces the man to service his wife. *Stage Struck* develops the cat-and-mouse game of *Dutch Uncle* into an extravagant panoply of stage tricks masterminded by the stage-director husband who uses suicide and murder to revenge himself upon his domineering actress wife.

Quartermaine's Terms, Gray's finest play to date, and *The Common Pursuit* depart in significant ways from the mode of *Butley* although both take school teachers and literary types for their characters. Butley and Simon Hench use language and wit trenchantly—Butley to lash out, deflecting his self-hatred against others, Hench more sparingly as an armor to prevent others from touching him. In contrast, Sir John Quartermaine, teacher in a Cambridge public school training foreign boys in English, is a man of halting phrases, few words, and nearly vacant silences. While the play traces the fortunes of the school and its small staff, we witness Sir John's retreat from his world into a drowsy sleep where he can no longer remember when or what he is teaching or even the swans on the pond near his aunt's home. He drifts in and out of reminiscences, weaving the words of Yeats's "The Wild Swans at Coole" with his own vague memories, reproducing in his own diminished way the sense of radical dislocation and displacement of Yeats's poem.

Gray's treatment of Quartermaine and the staff is richly comic. The plotting and character delineation are Chekhovian. Mr. Meadle is the play's Two-and-Twenty-Misfortunes; Quartermaine's yearnings for another era echo Anya's and Gaef's nostalgia in *The Cherry Orchard*; the characters in the play cannot remember each others' names; they murmur reassuring pleasantries while underneath they are confused and hurting. Melanie is a frustrated spinster driven to kill her sickly, hatred-ridden mother and do penance through her Christian conversion. Mr. Meadle, the accident-prone new instructor from the North Country, struggles desperately to secure both a permanent position in the school and a wife. There is a liberal sprinkling of marital infidelities and complications in the play, and it contains the suicide which often figures in Gray's plays. But its texture is different. When Quartermaine is finally dismissed by the new principal on the eve of the Christmas break, it is wrenching. All of Windscape's reasons for the firing are legitimate: Quartermaine has not been teaching for years; the other staff simply carried him on, not having the heart to do anything else. On one level it is unconscionable to pretend that Quartermaine has a role to play in an instructional institution; on another, we want to ask, "why not let him linger in the staff lounge, teaching almost not at all, rather than displace him utterly?" Gray crafts the final scene so skillfully that we are forced to balance the conflicting needs of the situation. The gentle goodnight exchanged between the two men followed by Quartermaine's lapse into silence ends the play. Echoes of Yeats's poem hover in the air. It is Gray's best ending.

The Common Pursuit departs from *Butley* in its treatment of time and its reliance on cinematic techniques for its staging and its plot development. Gray calls it a play about friendship, "English, middle-class, Cambridge-educated friendship." He has remarked that its control of time grew out of the television play *Two Sundays*. It covers 20 years and closes with a scene set 15 minutes later than its opening scene, 20 years before. Critics have anachronistically compared the play to Pinter's *Betrayal*, written a number of years after *Two Sundays*. *The Common Pursuit* is episodic, tracing the fortunes of the Cambridge friends and their literary enterprise. Many of its characters are the typical academic misfits and literary opportunists that figure in almost all of his plays. Unlike the protagonists of a number of Gray's other plays, Stuart is not the hub around which the action revolves. Stuart is what Gray calls "the spine of the play," but the play's sweeping movement over the lives of the six Cambridge friends is more akin to the structure of Virginia Woolf's novel *The Waves* than it is to the structure of Gray's other plays. Gray rightly sensed that the play might be too precious, too literary, and too elitist to please the public, but it is an effective evening of theatre, and the depiction of the group of writers, editors, scholars, and publishers is adept. Its control of time is superb and its startling epilogue a stunning piece of theatre.

Melon is a memory play presented from the perspective of its protagonist, a successful literary publisher who discovers one day that the ground has opened up under his feet: the entire routine of success around which his life has been fashioned collapses and he finds himself in the midst of a mental breakdown, recounting to his psychiatrist how it all came to be. The themes in the play are familiar: marital infidelity and breakdown, thwarted ambition, and confused sexual identity. Melon's overbearing presence, his infidelities, and his contempt for others finally undo him, but the agony of this all too familiar character-type is intensified as we see the play through his perspective. He has the unbearable task of trying to rebuild himself and trying to speak the moment when his world came apart. Gray is good at this kind of play. He employs a musical metaphor with its capacity to embrace both harmony and discord to unite his protagonist's memories. The play is fluid, evocative, and disturbing. In *Melon*, Gray affords Alan Bates another of the roles he plays so well.

Hidden Laughter is a very funny and yet deeply sad play which teases out T.S. Eliot's treatment of childish laughter and the garden in "The Four Quartets." The play's action covers 13 years, tracing the happenings in the life of a successful literary agent, his novelist wife, and two children as they seek a retreat in the life of the country. The years are full of strange happenings, near-accidents, and near-deaths. The tone moves from that of pastoral idyll to a very tentative, troubled present, full of strained relationships. The most memorable character in the play is the tolerant and yet good vicar whose life touches all the other characters in the play.

Gray is among Britain's most talented playwrights working in the traditional genre of the comedy of manners. He is well schooled in his craft, original, and able to create unforgettable characters.

—Carol Simpson Stern

GRAY, Spalding. American. Born in Providence, Rhode Island, 5 June 1941. Educated at Fryeburg Academy, Maine; Emerson College, Boston, B.A. 1965. Actor in summer stock, Cape Cod, Massachusetts, and in Saratoga, New York, 1965–67; with Performance Group, New York, 1969–75; founder, with Elizabeth LeCompte, the Wooster Group, New York, 1975. Recipient: National Endowment for the Arts fellowship, 1977; Rockefeller grant, 1980; Guggenheim fellowship, 1985; Obie award, 1985. Agent: Suzanne Gluck, International Creative Management, 40 West 57th Street, New York, New York 10019. Address: c/o The Wooster Group, Box 654, Canal Street Station, New York, New York 10013, U.S.A.

PUBLICATIONS

Plays and Monologues

Scales (also director: produced Northampton, Massachusetts, 1966; New York, 1975).
Sakonnet Point, with Elizabeth LeCompte (produced New York, 1975).
Rumstick Road, with Elizabeth LeCompte (also co-director: produced New York, 1977).
Nayatt School, with Elizabeth LeCompte (produced New York, 1978).
Three Places in Rhode Island (includes *Sakonnet Point*, *Rumstick Road*, *Nayatt School*), with Elizabeth LeCompte (produced New York, 1978).
Point Judith: An Epilog, with Elizabeth LeCompte (produced New York, 1979).
Sex and Death to the Age 14 (produced New York, 1979). Included in *Sex and Death to the Age 14* (collection), 1986.
Booze, Cars, and College Girls (produced New York, 1979). Included in *Sex and Death to the Age 14*, 1986.
India and After (America) (produced New York, 1979).
Nobody Wanted to Sit Behind a Desk (produced New York, 1980). Included in *Sex and Death to the Age 14*, 1986.
A Personal History of the American Theater (produced New York, 1980).
Interviewing the Audience (produced New York, 1981).
47 Beds (produced New York, 1981). Included in *Sex and Death to the Age 14*, 1986.

In Search of the Monkey Girl, with Randal Levenson (produced New York, 1982). New York, Aperture, 1982.

8 × Gray (produced New York, 1982).

Swimming to Cambodia, parts 1 and 2 (produced New York, 1984; London, 1985). New York, Theatre Communications Group, 1985; in *Swimming to Cambodia: The Collected Works*, 1987.

Travels Through New England (produced Cambridge, Massachusetts, 1984).

Rivkala's Ring, adaptation of a story by Chekhov, in *Orchards* (produced Urbana, Illinois, 1985; New York, 1986). New York, Knopf, 1986.

Terrors of Pleasure: The House (produced Cambridge, Massachusetts, 1985; New York, 1986; London, 1987; as *Terrors of Pleasure: The Uncut Version*, produced New York, 1989). Included in *Sex and Death to the Age 14*, 1986.

Sex and Death to the Age 14. New York, Random House, 1986; augmented edition, including *Swimming to Cambodia*, parts 1 and 2, as *Swimming to Cambodia: The Collected Works*, London, Pan, 1987.

Screenplay: *Swimming to Cambodia*, 1987.

Television Play: *Bedtime Story*, with Renée Shafransky, 1987.

*

Theatrical Activities:

Director: **Plays**—*Scales*, Northampton and Amherst, Massachusetts, 1966; *Rumstick Road* (co-director, with Elizabeth LeCompte), New York, 1977.

Actor: **Plays**—roles in all of his own plays and in numerous other plays; Hoss in *The Tooth of Crime* by Sam Shepard, New York, 1973; role in *North Atlantic* by Jim Strahs, New York, 1984; Stage Manager in *Our Town* by Thornton Wilder, New York, 1988. **Films**—*The Killing Fields*, 1984; *True Stories*, 1986; *Swimming to Cambodia*, 1987; *Clara's Heart*, 1989. **Television**—*Bedtime Story*, 1987.

*   *   *

Like Eugene O'Neill—also a New England playwright—Spalding Gray creates histrionic exorcisms of private demons. Such an autobiographical dramatist that he cheerfully admits to narcissism, Gray—again like O'Neill—in his early work is obsessed with his family and with doctors. Although Gray's subjects have evolved into his more recent experiences, his work always, unabashedly, concerns himself. An actor before he began writing roles, Gray appears in his pieces as well.

Gray initially created personal plays in collaboration with the director Elizabeth LeCompte, with whom he constructed four works named after places from his boyhood. *Sakonnet Point* recalls discontinuous images of his preschool summer beach vacations; it's as non-verbal as the infant Gray. This quiet piece built around objects and simple activities contrasts to the often frenetic and noisy *Rumstick Road*, which includes tape recordings of actual family members and of the psychiatrist who treated his mother prior to her suicide. So important are the recordings that the operator of the tape machine sits above the set in full view. Below is a doctor's examination table, on either side of which there is a room. One, containing a window through which we see a tent, is associated primarily with Gray's re-enacted past, while the other, containing a screen and slide projector, is associated more often with Gray's probing the past by stimulating his memories with mementos and tapes. The most interesting is a recording of the insensitive doctor, who tells Gray his mother's insanity is hereditary, "but don't be frightened."

Although still more fragmented and surreal, the third of Gray's *Three Places in Rhode Island*, called, after a childhood school, *Nayatt School*, begins with a seemingly straightforward lecture on T. S. Eliot's *The Cocktail Party*, from which Gray and LeCompte's script derives at least half its dialogue. While it deconstructs the Eliot play, *Nayatt School*'s imagery remains that of *Rumstick Road*: a red tent, insanity, death, Christian Science's suspicion of doctors, and preservation of past experience on tapes, film, and records—though the latter eventually are destroyed. Gray's earnest academician, a pedant intoning without passion his passion for the Eliot play, sits at a long table midway between the audience above and playing space below, where one of the rooms in *Rumstick Road* has been turned around, so we peer into it through the window. From quiet beginnings, *Nayatt School* increases its speed, ferocity, iconoclasm, and discontinuity. Farce chases punctuate scenes with a mad doctor and a parody of a horror film in which a scientist lets a giant blob of protoplasm run amok ("Get me a rewrite man quick—it's still growing"). Mindless antisocial amenities of alcohol, cigarettes, and disco music are partaken by children dressed as sophisticated adults, until characters strip and—literally—climb the walls.

Even more apocalyptic is the Gray and LeCompte part of the Rhode Island trilogy's epilogue, *Point Judith* (which also incorporates a send-up of machismo by Jim Strahs called *Rig*). Once more recur the red tent and the room frame, preservation of the past on records and film, windows which invite us in yet cut us off, and madness—this time in part by deconstruction of O'Neill's *Long Day's Journey into Night*, drowned out by a buzzer, wind, and Berlioz and accompanied by frantic farce in which objects (particularly a reversed vacuum cleaner billowing exhaust), writhing ribbons of light, and whirling bodies create cataclysmic discord. As a quieter coda, a film of men dressed as nuns and the trademark room frames concludes the piece.

After *Point Judith* Gray tired of fragmentation and deconstruction. In search of a controlled narrative form, he returned to the monologue format he'd employed in the opening of *Nayatt School* and constructed three intensely personal solo pieces. In these and his subsequent experiments in unilateral repartee, Gray reflects upon such intimate, often embarrassing details of his private life as what sort of things he did with his penis at the age of twelve. (A variation is *Interviewing the Audience*, in which, after speaking candidly of his own life, he grills spectators upon *their* experiences.) Although he condenses time and occasionally embellishes details, Gray does not fabricate. "A poetic journalist," as he terms himself, he may rearrange events to increase the humor or drama, but candor compels him to confess in *Swimming to Cambodia* (about corruption, both national and personal) that he vomited on the beach, made half as much money as others in *The Killing Fields*, was obsessed about losing his money, and patronized prostitutes. *Terrors of Pleasure* examines memories of being outfoxed by a con artist and of humiliation in Hollywood.

Whereas in those monologues Gray is largely victimized, in others he reveals his ineptitude at getting laid. Among his Woody Allen-style anxiety tales about bumbling towards the sack and fumbling in it is his ineffectual attempt to escape his confirmed heterosexuality in sex with another man. "I figured no one will know about it," Gray muses—and 200 spectators laugh.

This self-deprecatory raconteur who carries a dozen "public memories" around in his head—a nearly Homeric achievement—writes of shame—"pretty hard to maintain in New York City"—and pain, of fear, freaks, and failure, of embarrassment, banality, discomfort, and death, of greed and exploitation. With minimalist means, he confronts his paranoia and, employing a Buddhist idea, he recycles negative energy, a healing process for us as well as for him.

—Tish Dace

GREEN, Paul (Eliot). American. 1894–1981.
See 3rd edition, 1982.

GREENBERG, Richard. American. Born in East Meadow, New York, 22 February 1958. Educated at local schools; Princeton University, Princeton, New Jersey, 1976–80, A.B. in English 1980; Harvard University, Cambridge, Massachusetts, 1980–81; Yale University School of Drama, New Haven, Connecticut, 1982–85, M.F.A. in drama 1985. Member, Ensemble Studio Theater, New York. Recipient: Oppenheimer award, 1985; Dramalogue award, 1991. Lives in New York City. Agent: George Lane, William Morris Agency, 1350 Avenue of the Americas, New York, New York 10019, U.S.A.

PUBLICATIONS

Plays

The Bloodletters (produced New York, 1984).
Life Under Water (produced New York, 1985). New York, Dramatists Play Service, 1985.
Vanishing Act (produced New York, 1986). New York, Dramatists Play Service, 1987.
The Author's Voice (produced New York, 1987). New York, Dramatists Play Service, 1987.
The Maderati (produced New York, 1987). New York, Dramatists Play Service, 1987.
The Hunger Artist, with Martha Clarke and company, adaptation of a work by Franz Kafka (produced New York, 1987).
Eastern Standard (produced Seattle, 1988; New York, 1988). New York, Grove, 1989.
Neptune's Hips (produced New York, 1988).
The American Plan (produced New York, 1990). New York, Dramatists Play Service, 1990.
The Extra Man (produced Costa Mesa, California, 1991; New York, 1992).
Jenny Keeps Talking (produced New York, 1992).
Pal Joey, adaptation of the musical by Rodgers and Hart (produced Boston, Massachusetts, 1992).

Screenplays: *Ask Me Again*, 1989; *Life Under Water*, 1989.

Television Play: *The Sad Professor*, in the *Trying Times* series, 1989.

*

Richard Greenberg comments:
Self-indulgently, I consider all my work to date to constitute a public apprenticeship. My last several plays have had

quite classically constructed stories. This is a deliberate process of self-teaching, an effort to master the fundamentals of story-telling as a kind of jumping-off place for whatever the future brings. I'm non-ideological but I prefer plays that *become* ideas to those that provide forums for ideas.

* * *

Richard Greenberg's comedies explore what it is to be young, semi-gifted, white, and wealthy in Reagan-era America, with all the attendant education, anxiety, and ennui that such status confers. Exclusively set in New York City or some fashionable nearby resort, Greenberg's plays are populated by females with names better suited to pets—Minna, Rena, Dewy, and Jinx—and WASPy, dithering men saddled with names that are the inheritance of their "hegemony"—Keene, Kip, Spence, and Sky. Greenberg treats his characters with a mixture of fascination, cynicism, and envy. Often an uneasy tension exists: are they adorable but misguided eccentrics or despicably vacuous victims of their wealth and breeding?

Greenberg's characters are articulate to a fault. Where exceptions occur, the inability to express oneself properly becomes a running joke—in *The Maderati* the "Method Actor" Danton mumbles inaudibly while mediocre poet Keene never finishes his similes. In *The Author's Voice*, a hilarious and brilliant little one-act play updating the Cyrano de Bergerac story by way of the "Twilight Zone," a handsome but untalented writer is punished for relying on a misshapen gnome-like creature to provide the book he must deliver to his publisher.

Greenberg's fixation with the power of language, syntax, and literacy is evident throughout his work. Responding to the formal elocution of Eva, a German emigrée nicknamed "Czarina" in *The American Plan*, Gil exclaims, "What a sentence—wonderful!—Americans never take grammar to that kind of extreme." In *Life Under Water*, Kip tries to seduce Amy-Beth by describing a fictitious green light at the end of her dock. She responds: "That's the goddamn 'Great Gatsby.' I can read! Oh, you sensitive boys with your quotations." This is an example not only of Greenberg's propensity for making literary references, but for having other characters—and therefore the audience—recognize them.

Greenberg's one-act comedies are in many ways his most original and intriguing work; his full-length plays lack their appealing fairytale tone and surreal quality. Written in five scenes, *Vanishing Act* is a Pirandellian experiment that unfolds in a dreamy landscape peopled by wealthy but largely useless characters searching for ways to prevent physical or emotional dissipation. In the play, Minna brushes her younger sister Anya's hair while telling her a bedtime story about a woman named Carla whose husband is murdered and dismembered. The last scene jumps ahead several years to find Carla, the character in Minna's story, onstage telling *her* daughter a bedtime tale about Minna's family. As one narrative "vanishes" into another, Greenberg's structural sleight-of-hand jostles the audience's sense of reality, making manifest the infuriatingly ephemeral nature of life and art. No other Greenberg play takes such structural risks.

Life Under Water uses 17 short scenes to evoke incisively the emotionally submerged existence of pampered young people at a fashionable Hamptons beach house. Kip, a hapless teenager, runs away from home and meets Amy-Joy and her friend Amy-Beth, recently released from a mental institution. Although a short romance flares up between Kip and Beth, Kip can't sustain any sense of commitment—emblematic of many Greenberg characters (Kip and Beth could be an early sketch for Nick and Lili in *The American Plan*).

The Maderati is a broad farce satirizing a crowd of self-involved New York artists and pseudo-intellectuals. Greenberg fully embraces the traditional farce form, concluding with a *faux* murder and the couples neatly arrayed in a final tableaux. The genre and the subject allow Greenberg to give full rein to his verbal games. After the depressed poet Charlotte has been committed to an insane asylum, Dewy erroneously believes she's died, while Keene thinks she's hospitalized for an abortion. Both believe Danton should not be out of town:

Keene: He should be by her bedside.
Dewy: You mean by her *bier*.
Keene: Buying her beer, buying her flowers, buying her anything she wants.

Both *The American Plan* and *The Extra Man* feature strong, slightly demonic figures—the Miss Haversham-like Eva and the blocked writer Keith, respectively—who destructively manipulate the love affairs of those they care for most, ostensibly out of some subliminal jealousy (although sheer boredom and lack of amusement is offered as a more frightening, though unconvincing, motivation). Both plays describe the difficulty of loving another person because of the need for honesty, strength, determination, commitment, and openness—qualities invariably lacking in these cynical times. Unfortunately, the characters are so spineless and emotionally inept that they fail to generate much sympathy.

Eastern Standard most successfully details its characters' struggles to make commitments. The first act's three scenes occur at the same lunch hour and at the same restaurant, but with three different couples center-stage. In this way the action that was peripheral in one scene becomes central in another. The main character Stephen, an architect specializing in monstrous postmodern office towers ("I *am* urban blight") meets his gay friend Drew, a painter of some renown, while the girl he's loved only from a distance, Phoebe, waits to meet her brother Peter, a TV writer recently diagnosed as having AIDS. When May, a mentally unstable homeless woman, hits Peter with her Perrier bottle, Stephen has his excuse to meet his love object as he and Drew come to Peter's rescue. Act Two takes place at Stephen's Hamptons beach house, to which he's invited everyone present at the restaurant that day—eventually including May, the baglady, and Ellen, the waitress. Here all the characters struggle, not always convincingly, with commitment—Ellen to her acting career, May to sanity, Peter to the solitude imposed by the discovery he has AIDS, Drew to his artwork and his cynicism, and Stephen and Phoebe to their love for each other. Unusually for a Greenberg play, they also struggle actively with their liberal guilt, trying to gauge their personal responsibility for homelessness, an assessment occasioned by May's presence. But once it is clear no one is willing to prevent her return to the streets, May steals their valuables and disappears. The play ends rather glibly, with Drew breaking through Peter's emotional defenses, and Stephen and Phoebe engaged to each other and committed to designing and financing buildings for the homeless. As they toast their happiness, it's clear May couldn't steal what is most valuable to them—their newfound love for each other and their heightened social consciousness—highly unusual qualities for characters in the rarified world of Richard Greenberg's plays.

—John Istel

GREENE, Graham. British. 1904–1991. See 4th edition, 1988.

GREENSPAN, David. American. Born in Los Angeles, California, 17 March 1956. Educated at Beverly Hills High School, graduated 1974; University of California, Irvine, B.A. in drama 1978. Lives with William Kennon. Busboy and waiter, New York, 1978–88; playwright-in-residence, HOME for Contemporary Theatre and Art, New York, 1987–90; director and playwright-in-residence, New York Shakespeare Festival, 1990–92. Recipient: Brooklyn Arts and Cultural Association award, 1984; Art Matters grant, 1987, 1988, 1989; Revson fellowship, 1989; Rockefeller fellowship, 1989; Albee Foundation residency, 1989; Yaddo residency, 1991. Agent: Wiley Hausam, International Creative Management, 40 West 57th Street, New York, New York 10019, U.S.A.

PUBLICATIONS

Plays

Vertices, Man in a/the Chair, Pieces in the Dark, Recent Hemispheres (monologues and short pieces; produced New York, 1981–86).
The Horizontal and the Vertical (produced New York, 1986).
Dig a Hole and Bury Your Father (produced New York, 1987).
Jack (produced New York, 1987). Published in *The Way We Live Now*, edited by M. Elizabeth Osborn, New York, Theatre Communications Group, 1990.
Principia (produced New York, 1987).
The Home Show Pieces (includes *Doing the Beast, Too Much in the Sun, Portrait of the Artist, The Big Tent*) (produced New York, 1988; Glasgow, 1992). Published in *Plays in Process* (New York), 1993.
The Closet Piece (produced New York, 1989).
2 Samuel 11, Etc. (also director: produced New York, 1989; London, 1991). Published in *Plays in Process* (New York), 1990.
Dead Mother, or Shirley Not All in Vain (produced New York, 1991). Published in *Grove New American Theatre Anthology*, New York, Grove Weidenfeld, 1992.

*

Theatrical Activities:
Director: **Plays**—*Sexual Perversity in Chicago* by David Mamet, New York, 1984; *Danny and the Deep Blue Sea* by John Patrick Shanley, New York, 1986; *Kate's Diary* by Kathleen Tolan, 1989; *Wanking 'Tards* by Nicky Silver, New York, 1990; *Gonza the Lancer* by Chikamatsu Monzaemon, New York, 1990; *The Way of the World* by William Congreve, New York, 1991.

David Greenspan comments:
I think of my writing as an act of self-exploration and a form of entertainment. Sometimes I engage in research and spend long hours studying history or biography. I also work from observation and memory. Always the external instigators are filtered through the fabric of my inner life and associations.

For several years I wrote a series of autobiographical plays that dramatized private details of my personal life, attempting to capture the pedestrian obsessions and conflicts that occupy much of my experience. More recently, I have been attempting to move beyond the strictly autobiographical, and explore myself in terms of a wider social context.

* * *

David Greenspan is the most nakedly personal of playwrights. He became a writer for the theatre when he started performing excerpts from his journals, and he still often takes the central role in his pieces, which he also invariably directs. Greenspan's mother died of lupus when he was a boy; her specter shadows his entire body of work, and the tensions of a troubled family are dramatized again and again. Homoerotic fantasy is another key component of Greenspan's writing, but here, as elsewhere, his real focus is the mind, not the body. His true subject is not sex, but obsession and longing. He seeks to capture the process of thinking—especially, thinking about feeling.

Yet Greenspan's highly emotional art has always been formally experimental. Samuel Beckett, Gertrude Stein, and Robert Wilson are his acknowledged masters. Greenspan has described his early pieces as "very abstract—word-associated, fragmented, stream-of-consciousness, nonsensical in the strictest sense of the word." To include performers other than himself, he used numbers to indicate who was to speak which lines of these texts. There is little sense of character; what's dramatized is a single consciousness.

Greenspan's recent texts resemble plays more closely; they contain vivid characters who often have their own convincing voices. Yet the playwright still identifies them as Character 1 or Speaker 2, emphasizing the distance between actors and characters on the one hand, and between characters and the actual people who inspired them on the other. Any sort of actor might play any sort of character. Various actors can play the same character at different points in the play. Actors can stop playing their characters and start discussing them. Identity is fluid. Transformation, role-playing, and pretending are paramount.

The one-act *Jack* is a good introduction to Greenspan's work. It's an AIDS play, a lovely and elegiac piece for three women Speakers who stand upstage at music stands—"ideally, the image is one of floating busts," writes Greenspan—and a male Character 8 who sits surrounded by seven empty chairs. On the page the Speakers' words are printed in three columns; in the theatre they are overlapping waves of sound. In this verbal music, repetition and variation gradually build a portrait of the dead Jack. At other moments one voice breaks clear to deliver a monologue, long or short, as often about Jack's difficult mother as about Jack himself. At the center of the piece is a depiction of a primal Greenspan location: a dark park where men come for sex. It is a locus of longing, a fallen Eden, a trap. Late in the play Character 8—Jack—finally speaks, telling about getting lost as a small boy on a crowded beach, about finally seeing his father and embracing him, crying.

The Home Show Pieces and *Dead Mother, or Shirley Not All in Vain* are much bigger works, uneven, ungainly, and fascinating. *Home* contains some of this writer's wittiest scenes: in its opening section Character 1 is in bed, trying to read, then trying to hump the mattress between the interruptions of a series of phone calls which reveal his loneliness. Some years later, Character 1 sits on the toilet indulging in fantasies of fame, a playwright claiming not to read his reviews while revealing extensive knowledge of them.

The central character in *Dead Mother* is a young man, Harold, who impersonates his mother to help his brother win the woman he wants to marry. There is comedy in this *Charley's Aunt* situation, of course, but also intense drama. In one remarkable scene Harold looks into a mirror, at once accusing the mother whose identity he has put on and, as the mother, striking back. The unexpected appearance of Harold's father, who thinks he's seeing his dead wife's ghost, gives Harold the opportunity to attack his father, expressing his mother's grievances along with his own. The masquerade enables Harold not only to speak long-hidden truths to his family, but to know himself; in the end he leaves his marriage and the family business to disappear into a homosexual life.

Greenspan's most impressive and successful piece to date is *2 Samuel 11, Etc.*, which retells the David and Bathsheba story from the woman's point of view, setting it against a complex contemporary narrative that works its way to a story of a young man's encounter with a sexually predatory old man. Both narratives are evolving in the mind of Character 1, a writer, who spends the second half of the play standing in his shower recounting the second story, telling it through the dialogue of 11 characters.

Character 1 is also onstage during the first half, but all the speaking is done by Character 2: Bathsheba as she is re-imagined by the writer. As the expression of the male writer's mind, the female character speaks not only Bathsheba's story—which is wonderfully told, and filled with a complex mixture of revulsion and sympathy for the old king who seduces her, has her husband killed, and takes her into his harem—but also the homoerotic fantasies that overwhelm the writer, and the telephone conversations that represent the intrusion of everyday realities.

It's all you can do to keep up with the complicated post-intermission narrative, but the first half of *2 Samuel* is utterly clear, and so there's space for rich comedy. "I've got to find a way to get this down on paper," says Character 2, speaking for her author, who is masturbating with one hand and writing with the other. Bathsheba's jaundiced view of Old Testament patriarchy also brings wicked laughter, and there's shocking power in the juxtaposition of the Bible and what Greenspan himself calls the "pornographic ruminations" coming out of her mouth. This time the author has embodied his ideas and obsessions in a context so potent that the result is unforgettable theatre.

—M. Elizabeth Osborn

GREENWOOD, Walter. British. 1903–1974.
See 1st edition, 1973.

GRIFFITHS, Trevor. British. Born in Manchester, Lancashire, 4 April 1935. Educated at St. Bede's College, Manchester, 1945–52; Manchester University, 1952–55, B.A. in English 1955; studied for external M.A. from 1961. Served in the British Army, Manchester Regiment, 1955–57: infantryman. Married Janice Elaine Stansfield in 1960 (died 1977); one son and two daughters. Teacher of English and games in a private school, Oldham, Lancashire, 1957–61; lecturer in liberal studies, Stockport Technical College, Cheshire, 1962–65; further education officer, BBC, Leeds, 1965–72. Co-editor, *Labour's Northern Voice*, 1962–65, and series editor for Workers Northern Publishing Society. Recipient: BAFTA Writer's award, 1982. Lives in Yorkshire. Agent: Peters, Fraser, and Dunlop Group, 503/4 The Chambers, Chelsea Harbour, Lots Road, London SW10 0XF, England.

PUBLICATIONS

Plays

The Wages of Thin (produced Manchester, 1969; London, 1970).
The Big House (broadcast 1969; produced Newcastle upon Tyne, 1975). With *Occupations*, London, Calder and Boyars, 1972.
Occupations (produced Manchester, 1970; London, 1971; New York, 1982). With *The Big House*, London, Calder and Boyars, 1972; revised version, published separately, London, Faber, 1980.
Apricots (produced London, 1971). With *Thermidor*, London, Pluto Press, 1978.
Thermidor (produced Edinburgh, 1971). With *Apricots*, London, Pluto Press, 1978.
Lay By, with others (produced Edinburgh and London, 1971). London, Calder and Boyars, 1972.
Sam, Sam (produced London, 1972; revised version produced London, 1978). Published in *Plays and Players* (London), April 1972.
Gun (also director: produced Edinburgh, 1973).
The Party (produced London, 1973; revised version produced Coventry, 1974). London, Faber, 1974.
All Good Men (televised 1974; produced London, 1975). Included in *All Good Men, and Absolute Beginners*, 1977.
Comedians (produced Nottingham and London, 1975; New York, 1976; revised [women's] version produced Liverpool, 1987). London, Faber, and New York, Grove Press, 1976; revised version, Faber, 1979.
The Cherry Orchard, adaptation of a play by Chekhov, translated by Helen Rappaport (produced Nottingham, 1977). London, Pluto Press, 1978; revised edition, London, Faber, 1989.
All Good Men, and Absolute Beginners: Two Plays for Television. London, Faber, 1977.
Through the Night, and Such Impossibilities: Two Plays for Television. London, Faber, 1977.
Deeds, with others (produced Nottingham, 1978). Published in *Plays and Players* (London) May and June 1978.
Country: A Tory Story (televised 1981). London, Faber, 1981.
Sons and Lovers, adaptation of the novel by D.H. Lawrence (televised 1981). Nottingham, Spokesman, 1982.
Oi for England (televised 1982; produced London, 1982). London, Faber, 1982.
Real Dreams, adaptation of the story "Revolution in Cleveland" by Jeremy Pikser (also director: produced Williamstown, Massachusetts, 1984; London, 1986). London, Faber, 1987 (includes "Revolution in Cleveland" by Pikser).
Judgement over the Dead: The Screenplays of The Last Place on Earth, adaptation of a book by Roland Huntford (as *The Last Place on Earth*, televised 1985). London, Verso, 1986.
Fatherland (screenplay). London, Faber, 1987.
Collected Plays for Television (includes *All Good Men, Absolute Beginners, Through the Night, Such Impossibilities, Country, Oi for England*). London, Faber, 1988.
Piano (produced London, 1990). London, Faber, 1990.
The Gulf Between Us: The Truth and Other Fictions (also director: produced Leeds, 1992). London, Faber, 1992.

Screenplays: *Reds*, with Warren Beatty, 1981; *Fatherland*, 1987.

Radio Plays: *The Big House*, 1969; *Jake's Brigade*, 1971.

Television Plays: *Adam Smith* series (as Ben Rae), 1972; *The Silver Mask*, from a story by Horace Walpole (*Between the Wars* series), 1973; *All Good Men*, 1974; *Absolute Beginners* (*Fall of Eagles* series), 1974; *Don't Make Waves* (*Eleventh Hour* series), with Snoo Wilson, 1975; *Through the Night*, 1975; *Bill Brand* series, 1976; *Sons and Lovers*, 1981; *Country: A Tory Story*, 1981; *Oi for England*, 1982; *The Last Place on Earth*, 1985.

Other

Tip's Lot (for children). London, Macmillan, 1972.

*

Manuscript Collection: British Film Institute, London.

Critical Studies: *Stages in the Revolution: Political Theatre in Britain Since 1968* by Catherine Itzin, London, Eyre Methuen, 1980; *An Introduction to Fifty Modern British Plays* by Benedict Nightingale, London, Pan, 1982; *Powerplays: Trevor Griffiths in Television* by Mike Poole and John Wyver, London, British Film Institute, 1984.

Theatrical Activities:
Director: **Plays**—*Gun*, Edinburgh, 1973; *Real Dreams*, Williamstown, Massachusetts, 1984; *Saint Oscar* by Terry Eagleton, Derry, 1989, London, 1990; *The Gulf Between Us*, Leeds, 1992.

*   *   *

Trevor Griffiths is unique for the remarkable consistency with which he has probed into critical phases and issues of the international labour movement. Earlier social and political dramatists portrayed individual labour struggles or dealt with the brutal consequences of fascism, but never before have the crucial questions of socialist strategy and morality been so forcefully examined on the stage. While assuming the desirability of socialism, Griffiths is anxious to distinguish and analyse the different positions hammered out by various brands of socialism and communism, and the personal dilemmas arising out of absorbing engagement in one of these movements.

Significantly, Griffiths started with a number of plays about Continental rather than British points of crisis. *Occupations* is set in Turin at the height of the revolutionary upsurge after World War I when factories were taken over and soviets formed in many Italian cities. The play shows the workers of Turin addressed in two moving speeches by Gramsci, but its focus is less on the confrontation between capital and labour than on the controversy between Gramsci and Kabak, a secret envoy of the Comintern, over the correct estimate and handling of the situation. Kabak, who has the experience and prestige of a successful revolution behind him, stands for a communist *realpolitik*; Gramsci, by contrast, embodies a hesitant, if fervent revolutionary idealism, which is always guided by a consideration, even love, for the people he leads.

The strategic differences between these two exponents of communism are also reflected in their personal outlooks. At the end Kabak leaves behind his mistress, who is dying of cancer; Gramsci goes to Sardinia to attend to his sister on her deathbed. The political and the personal, it is suggested, should not be seen as separate concerns. This dual perspective is also expressed by the play's title (Griffiths has a predilection for succinct, ambiguous titles), which refers not only to the action taken by the Fiat workers, but also to the private undertakings of the protagonists.

One of several future historical developments hinted at towards the end of *Occupations* is Stalinism. It can be seen germinating in Kabak's ruthless pragmatism and is summed up in Gramsci's ominous words: "Treat masses as expendable, as fodder, during the revolution, you will always treat them thus." *Thermidor* gives us a glimpse of Soviet Russia in the throes of Stalinism, during the purges of 1937. This one-act play is named after the summer month of the French revolutionary calendar, in which Robespierre himself fell victim to the Terror he had unleashed in the defence of the Revolution. Here it is Anya, formerly a loyal member of the Communist Party, who will disappear in the cellars of the NKVD. The play shows her at the mercy of her interrogator, Yukhov, who twists her sentences and fabricates absurd charges. Here there is even less doubt than in the altercations between Gramsci and Kabak as to where the author's sympathies lie. Yukhov's phrase "Enemies . . . are no longer people" disqualifies him and a whole system from speaking in the name of a humanist socialism. But when Anya finally pleads innocent and Yukhov asks the rhetorical question "Are you?," this is as much the voice of the author, who cannot absolve a once diligent and influential party member like Anya of historical guilt.

In contrast to these two analytical and descriptive plays *The Party* introduces an ironical note. An assortment of non-communist and almost exclusively non-working-class leftists meet at the instigation of a progressive television producer, Joe Shawcross, to discuss the possibilities of joint revolutionary action in Britain, all against the backdrop of Parisian students mounting the barricades in May 1968. The ironic nature of the whole radical-chic congregation, and the impotence of the British (intellectual) left, are suggested from the beginning through the appearance, in the Prologue, of Groucho Marx musing at a picture of his political namesake, and Joe's masturbation prior to the arrival of the leftist partygoers. Neither of the two conflicting analyses of the situation offered by a sociology lecturer and a veteran Trotskyist respectively (the latter pointing to the necessity of building *the* Party) is entirely wrong, but equally neither is free of empty revolutionary phrase-making and worn-out slogans, as the debunking comments of an accidentally present drunken writer point out.

Occupations, *Thermidor*, and *The Party* were all conceived and written for the stage. So was *Comedians*, which is often regarded as Griffiths's best work. It is certainly his funniest, even though one finds oneself often painfully aware of the impropriety of one's laughs. For this is a comedy about the social uses of stand-up comedy, and of working-class entertainment, a comedy about the proper function of the performer and, by implication, of the dramatist. Humour for

Griffiths is too serious a business to be left in the hands of mindless word-jugglers who insult people's intelligence or pander to ethnic and sexual stereotypes.

Since the mid-1970's Griffiths's career has, however, been primarily and deliberately that of a television playwright. Few critics and scholars have appreciated this decision, and some on the left have even accused him of opportunism. The author has sought this medium out of a deep conviction that a socialist dramatist today cannot afford only to address the theatre-goer, whether in the West End or the fringe. While the one kind of theatre reaches only a middle-class audience, the other too often ends by preaching to the converted. For the vast majority of the population "drama in a dramatised society" (Raymond Williams) like ours means television drama, and as one character in *Through the Night* puts it: "whoever does not reach the capacity of the common people and fails to make them listen to him, misses his mark."

Yet what Griffiths has called the "strategic penetration" of the central channel of communication proved initially difficult. *Such Impossibilities*, commissioned by the BBC as part of a series entitled *The Edwardians*, was rejected, ostensibly on grounds of cost, but more probably because its hero, the militant labour leader Tom Mann, and its theme, the 1911 transport strike in Liverpool, a social conflict of almost civil-war like dimensions, fitted awkwardly into an ancestral gallery composed of such establishment figures as Baden-Powell, Horatio Bottomley, and Charles Stewart Rolls.

Not surprisingly, therefore, *All Good Men*, Griffiths's first major produced television play, shows the author fully alert to the power of the medium to forge consensus and to mystify. The television producer who wants to conduct an interview with the elderly Labour politician Edward Waite, a former Cabinet Minister now to be made a peer, is attacked by William, the politician's son, precisely for his seemingly disinterested, value-free pose. William, a left-wing research student, is equally critical of the historical record of the Labour Party, and the dispute between father and son over its successes, as the former sees it, or purely minor reforms ultimately solidifying capitalism, as the latter argues, forms the climax of the play. But true to his now familiar oppositional set-up, Griffiths, though sharing many of William's reservations about "Labourism," distributes the arguments fairly evenly. Moreover, Waite—like so many of Griffiths's totally committed figures—has paid a heavy price for his lifelong dedication to working-class politics. He has been deserted by his wife and is now betrayed by his son, who supplies the interviewer with compromising material about his father's past, not out of personal vindictiveness but in order to bring the internal political machinations of the Labour Party into the open.

All Good Men, like its 11-part successor *Bill Brand*, questions the parliamentary road to socialism, and scrutinises the role of the Labour Party, without writing off either completely. But as the revolutionary optimism of much of the British socialist drama of the 1970's subsided and experienced a definite check under the realities of Thatcher's Britain, Griffiths found other themes more pertinent, among them the situation of unemployed urban youths (*Oi for England*) and the construction of national myths (*The Last Place on Earth*).

Country, Griffiths's strongest play of the 1980's, is about a significant "moment" in the history of British socialism, namely Labour's landslide victory in 1945. But it looks at it from an unexpected angle, an upper-class estate in Kent, where the members of the Carlion dynasty have assembled for the annual family gathering, at which a successor to the ageing Sir Frederic, baronet and Chairman of the Board of the Carlion brewery empire, will have to be found. As the devastating election results come in, and the common people themselves symbolically lay claim to the property by trespassing and occupying a barn, incredulity and consternation alternate with wrath. But Philip, one Carlion not affected by the general stupefaction, an outsider among the pretenders for the succession not least because of his bohemian lifestyle, now energetically assumes responsibility. Philip's victory over the "old gang," his efficient and smooth dealing with the squatters, indicates the capacity of the ruling class to renew itself and adapt to unforeseen circumstances—a point already made in *Occupations*, where the Fiat manager envisages a whole paternalistic welfare programme as a palliative against future social unrest.

Griffiths's work also includes screenplays. Chief among these are *Reds* (directed by Warren Beatty) about the American journalist John Reed's involvement in the October Revolution, and *Fatherland* (directed by Ken Loach), an intriguing story of German partition and a songmaker's search for his father, who left the GDR for the West 30 years before his son.

With *Real Dreams* Griffiths has lately returned to the stage— and to an earlier preoccupation. Like *The Party*, this play about the American student movement in the late 1960's highlights the feelings of isolation and frustration behind the leftward move of many intellectuals. The attempt of a commune of white middle-class students to move out of the protected world of the campus and form a fighting alliance with Puerto Rican working people fails dismally, hampered as it is by all kinds of ethnic, cultural, sexist, and psychic blocks. But the play ends on an optimistic note: the real historical contradictions are dissolved into an anticipatory dream of perfect unity, grace, and victory— all symbolised by a trance-like Tai-Chi exercise. The limitations and self-indulgence as well as the potential power and promise of this phase of radicalism are thus brought alive. If the conclusion appears somewhat forced, the play demonstrates once again Griffiths's masterly building up of tension, and testifies to his continuing concern for the global struggle for liberation.

Perhaps the most important single theatrical influence on the later Griffiths is Chekhov, whose *The Cherry Orchard* he adapted to shrill screams of protest from critics who took issue with the downgrading of the central figure Ranevsky, and the consequent shift of emphasis from plangent sorrow over the loss of property to the acute anticipation of a revolutionary situation. Chekhov also looms large in *Piano*, which is based on the Russian's early unfinished play *Platonov* and equally set in turn-of-the-century rural society, A kindred atmosphere of imminent historical change hangs over the characters, most of them finely graded blasé upper-class, who are enmeshed in a web of failure and frustration, confusion and apathy, stalemate and deadlock —a mental and psychological state not at a great remove from that of radical intellectuals of the present day after the collapse of socialist hopes.

—H. Gustav Klaus

GRILLO, John. British. Born in Watford, Hertfordshire, 29 November 1942. Educated at Watford Boys Grammar School 1954–61; Trinity Hall, Cambridge, 1962–65, B.A. in history 1965. Professional actor: in Lincoln, Glasgow, Farnham, Brighton, London. Resident dramatist, Castle Theatre, Farnham, Surrey, 1969–70; literary associate, Soho Theatre Club, London, 1971. Recipient: Arts Council bursary, 1965.

Agent (for acting): Howes and Prior Ltd., 66 Berkeley House, Hay Hill, London W.1, England.

PUBLICATIONS

Plays

Gentlemen I . . . (produced Cambridge, 1963; London, 1968).
It Will Come or It Won't (produced Dublin, 1965).
Hello Goodbye Sebastian (produced Cambridge, 1965; London, 1968). Published in *Gambit 16* (London), 1970.
The Downfall of Jack Throb (produced London, 1967).
The Fall of Samson Morocco (produced London, 1969).
Oh Everyman Oh Colonel Fawcett (produced Farnham, Surrey, 1969).
Mr. Bickerstaff's Establishment (produced Glasgow, 1969; expanded version produced London, 1972).
History of a Poor Old Man (produced London, 1970).
Number Three (produced Bradford and London, 1970). Published in *New Short Plays*, London, Methuen, 1972.
Blubber (produced London, 1971).
Zonk (produced London, 1971).
Food (produced London, 1971).
Will the King Leave His Tea Pot (produced Edinburgh and London, 1971).
George and Moira Entertain a Member of the Opposite Sex to Dinner (produced Edinburgh and London, 1971).
The Hammer and the Hacksaw, in *Christmas Present* (produced Edinburgh, 1971).
Christmas Box, and Civitas Dei (produced London, 1972).
Snaps (*Civitas Dei, Days by the River, MacEnery's Vision of Pipkin*) (produced London, 1973).
Crackers (produced London, 1973).
Mr. Ives' Magic Punch and Judy Show (produced London, 1973).

Television Play: *Nineteen Thirty Nine*, 1973.

*

Critical Study: by Germaine Greer, in *Cambridge Review*, 29 May 1965.

Theatrical Activities:
Actor: **Plays**—Theatre Royal, Lincoln: Dabble in *Lock Up Your Daughters* by Bernard Miles, Billy Bones in *Treasure Island* by Jules Eckert Goodman, Poet in *Five to a Flat* by Valentine Kataev, Ingham in *Little Malcolm and His Struggle Against the Eunuchs* by David Halliwell, roles in *Beyond the Fringe*, Andrei in *The Three Sisters* by Chekhov, Clarence in *2 Henry IV*, Max in *The Homecoming* by Harold Pinter, Jopplin in *A Shouting in the Streets* by Elizabeth Dawson, and Rusty Charley in *Guys and Dolls* by Abe Burrows and Jo Swerling, 1966–67; Brighton Combination: Old Man in *Hello Goodbye Sebastian* and Rasputin in *The Rasputin Show* by Michael Almaz, 1968; Royal Court Theatre, London: Verlaine in *Total Eclipse* by Christopher Hampton, 1968, roles in *Erogenous Zones* by Mike Stott, 1969, Perowne in *AC/DC* by Heathcote Williams, 1970, Reporter and Deaf and Dumb Man in *Lulu* by Peter Barnes, 1971, and Marx in *Anarchist* by Michael Almaz, 1971; Glendower in *1 Henry IV*, Glasgow, 1969; Castle Theatre, Farnham: Eddy in *Tango* by Mrozek, Millionaire in *Cliffwalk* by Sebastian Shaw, Fawcett in *Oh Everyman Oh Colonel Fawcett*, and Don Pedro in *Much Ado About Nothing*, 1969–70; Soho Theatre Club, London: Nurse in *Number Three*, 1970, Thug in *Dynamo* by Christopher Wilkinson, 1971,

and Recorder in *Inquisition* by Michael Almaz, 1971; Mr. Bickerstaff in *Mr. Bickerstaff's Establishment*, London, 1972; Doc in *The Tooth of Crime* by Sam Shepard, London, 1972; Sergeant Kite in *The Recruiting Officer* by Farquhar, Hornchurch, Essex, 1972; Dr. Rank in *A Doll's House* by Ibsen, London, 1972; Poltrone in *The Director of the Opera* by Anouilh, Chichester, 1973; Gremio in *The Taming of the Shrew*, London, 1974; Ashley Withers in *The End of Me Old Cigar* by John Osborne, London, 1975; role in *Bussy d'Ambois* by George Chapman, London, 1988. **Films**—*The F and H Film*; *Dynamo*; *Firefox*, 1982; *Brazil*, 1985. **Television**—*Brideshead Revisited*, 1981; *Chessgame*, 1983; *Dog Ends*, 1984; *Blott on the Landscape*, 1985; *Mother Love*, 1989.

John Grillo comments:

(1973) Aspects of my work include 1) A writing out of private obsessive fantasies and an attempt to excite the audience by parading on the stage that which is forbidden. 2) The plays are firmly based in the lower-middle-class morality and culture of my childhood. 3) Influence of theatrical innovators and fantasists such as Ionesco and Jarry. 4) Influence of television and film. Before the age of twenty I had visited the theatre perhaps half a dozen times. 5) I do not know how my work will develop but I hope it will become more public, less private, more realistic, less fantastic.

*   *   *

John Grillo is the Alfred Jarry of modern British theatre: a clown dramatist whose plays mingle outrageous solemnity with knockabout comedy and a Rabelaisian relish for dirty jokes. His stories have the simplicity of Punch and Judy shows. Bickerstaff (in *Mr. Bickerstaff's Establishment*) murders his sleep-walking wife as an alternative to committing suicide. Emboldened by this desperate deed, he tries to take over the underworld of pimps, thugs, and prostitutes: but finally the Forces of the Law—and his wife's ghost—catch up with him and condemn him to death. Bickerstaff (like Punch) escapes and decides to "emigrate—to Beirut": where his yearning for the fleshpots of the East can be satisfied. The Nurse (in *Number Three*) is a male fascist orderly in a mental hospital, preserving a solemn repressive dignity before a torrent of sexual insults from his worst patient, Three. The King (in *Will the King Leave His Tea Pot*) retires from the Affairs of State—and his frustrated thinning wife—into a huge womb-like tea-pot: thus causing the utmost consternation among his subjects, who lose all sense of protocol. These anecdotes are told in the style of children's stories. The characters are dressed like cartoons: Bickerstaff is a "fat man with a drooping bedraggled moustache"—like Crippen. The Queen (in *Will the King Leave His Tea Pot*) "wears a long silver dress, which is frayed at the edges, a necklace of pearls, several of which are missing and two or three of which are molars." The dialogue mainly consists of torrential speeches, where wild puns, extreme thought-associations, and an almost innocent scatology provide buoyant, idiosyncratic fun. The characters talk at each other—rather than to or with—and any change in mood is underlined by asides to the audience. When the Nurse, who is trying to persuade Three to go to bed, changes his tactics, he tells the audience that he is doing so. "Poor Nurse is worried because Number Three is such a bad boy. Nurse is a very sensitive man and he cries when Number Three plays him up . . . (aside) This is called 'Making the patient feel guilty.'"

This overtness in handling the story, the dialogue, the bawdiness, and the characters gives Grillo's plays an ingenuous charm. Grillo is an actor—as well as a dramatist—and he has a performer's instinct for bizarre, shock tactics. As an actor, he

has worked extensively with fringe theatre in Britain: in the rudimentary pub theatres of London and the student theatre clubs. His plays are designed to require little in the way of staging, but to rely on actor-audience contact, in the style of music hall. He is one of the rare dramatists to exploit the essential roughness, the slapdash circumstances of fringe theatre: and therefore his plays work particularly well in pubs. Nor is the humour as unsophisticated as may appear. Grillo delights in choosing apparently "serious" themes and placing them in comic-strip settings. In his longest and perhaps most ambitious play, *Hello Goodbye Sebastian*, Grillo tells the story of an apprentice gravedigger, Sebastian, who longs for a better life and refuses to fill in a grave, because the old man whose wife occupies it believes in the resurrection of the dead. Sebastian's home life however is an unhappy one. His mother, Mary, and the lodger, Charlie, are living off his earnings: and their sex life dominates the household arrangements. Sebastian can't leave his job—to become a barber—because his mother doesn't want him to: it would destroy the precarious balance of her affair. And so Sebastian finally resigns himself to being a gravedigger: and in the final scene, he fills in the grave of the old man's wife. The allegorical overtones of Grillo's story relate it to the Theatre of the Absurd and to Ionesco's plays in particular. The suppression of innocence and adolescent hope leads to a death-centredness. Sebastian at the end of the play fills up the grave with unnecessary relish: "Half a pound of worms, landlord, down the hatch. Pound of filth, landlord. Coming, sir, down the hatch!" But this "serious" theme is handled with a flippant lightness, which does not, however, prevent the allegory from being both noticeable and important to the success of the play.

Grillo's cheerful irreverence has a habit of misfiring in the wrong surroundings. He was once the resident dramatist/actor with a repertory theatre in Farnham, a quiet country town in the South of England. His comic-strip version of the Everyman story caused the greatest possible local outrage. "They called the play," remembers Grillo, "lavatorial, smutty, schoolboyish, nihilistic, unnecessarily cruel, and what's more my acting stank." Nor was he at ease in the portentous atmosphere of avant-garde theatre clubs, which may be one reason why his plays have been under-rated by British critics. His best productions have perhaps come with the talented fringe group, Portable Theatre, who included *Zonk* and *Food* in their 1971 repertoire. Zonk is an extraordinary family comedy, involving a mother, Dora (a man in drag), a domineering father, Bone, a son, and a substitute Dora (an attractive woman in her early forties). The son's antagonism towards his father and his yearnings for sex with his mother provide a comic interpretation of Oedipalism. The son eventually disgusts the father by sucking milk from his mother's artificial penis. Not all of Grillo's plays are, however, equally extreme. His *History of a Poor Old Man* is a mock-melancholic monologue of an old man arrested for soliciting in a lavatory.

Grillo's great quality as a dramatist is that his sense of fun is infectious. The jokes tumble over each other and the uninhibitedness of the bawdry creates an easy relaxation in the theatre. He breaks down the over-solemn atmosphere of playgoing and brings back a childlike delight in trying anything once. His plays are unique, and have stayed fresh and exuberant. His technical range is severely limited, but within these limits his imagination is exhilarating.

—John Elsom

GUARE, John (Edward). American. Born in New York City, 5 February 1938. Educated at Joan of Arc Elementary School, and St. John's Preparatory School, New York; Georgetown University, Washington, D.C., 1956–60, A.B. 1960; Yale University School of Drama, 1960–63, M.F.A. 1963. Served in the United States Air Force Reserve, 1963. Married Adele Chatfield-Taylor in 1981. Assistant to the manager, National Theatre, Washington, D.C., 1960; member, Barr/Wilder/Albee Playwrights Unit, New York, 1964; founding member, Eugene O'Neill Playwrights Conference, Waterford, Connecticut, 1965; playwright-in-residence, New York Shakespeare Festival, 1976–77; adjunct professor of playwriting, Yale University, 1978. Council member, Dramatists Guild, 1971; vice-president, Theatre Communications Group, 1986. Recipient: ABC-Yale University fellowship, 1966; Obie award, 1968, 1971; *Variety* award, 1969; Cannes Film Festival award, for screenplay, 1971; New York Drama Critics Circle award, 1971, 1972; Tony award, 1972, 1986; Joseph Jefferson award, 1977; Venice Film Festival Golden Lion, National Society of Film Critics award, New York Film Critics Circle award, and Los Angeles Film Critics award, all for screenplay, 1980; American Academy Award of Merit Medal, 1981; New York Institute for the Humanities fellowship, 1987. Lives in New York City. Address: c/o R. Andrew Boose, Collyer and Boose, 1 Dag Hammarskjold Plaza, New York, New York 10017–2299, U.S.A.

PUBLICATIONS

Plays

Theatre Girl (produced Washington, D.C., 1959).
The Toadstool Boy (produced Washington, D.C., 1960).
The Golden Cherub (produced New Haven, Connecticut, 1962?).
Did You Write My Name in the Snow? (produced New Haven, Connecticut, 1963).
To Wally Pantoni, We Leave a Credenza (produced New York, 1965).
The Loveliest Afternoon of the Year, and Something I'll Tell You Tuesday (produced New York, 1966; *The Loveliest Afternoon of the Year* produced London, 1972). New York, Dramatists Play Service, 1968.
Muzeeka (produced Waterford, Connecticut, 1967; New York and Edinburgh, 1968; London, 1969). Included in *Off-Broadway Plays*, London, Penguin, 1970; in *Cop-Out, Muzeeka, Home Fires*, 1971.
Cop-Out (produced Waterford, Connecticut, 1968; New York, 1969). Included in *Off-Broadway Plays*, London, Penguin, 1970; in *Cop-Out, Muzeeka, Home Fires*, 1971.
Home Fires (produced New York, 1969). Included in *Cop-Out, Muzeeka, Home Fires*, 1971.
Kissing Sweet (televised 1969). With *A Day for Surprises*, New York, Dramatists Play Service, 1971.
A Day for Surprises (produced New York, 1970; London, 1971). With *Kissing Sweet*, New York, Dramatists Play Service, 1971.
The House of Blue Leaves (produced New York, 1971; London, 1988). New York, Viking Press, 1972.
Two Gentlemen of Verona, with Mel Shapiro, music by Galt MacDermot, lyrics by Guare, adaptation of the play by Shakespeare (produced New York, 1971; London, 1973). New York, Holt Rinehart, 1973.
Cop-Out, Muzeeka, Home Fires. New York, Grove Press, 1971.
Taking Off (screenplay), with others. New York, New American Library, 1971.

Optimism; or, The Misadventures of Candide, with Harold Stone, based on a novel by Voltaire (produced Waterford, Connecticut, 1973).
Rich and Famous (produced Lake Forest, Illinois, 1974; New York, 1976). New York, Dramatists Play Service, 1977.
Marco Polo Sings a Solo (produced Nantucket, Massachusetts, 1976; revised version produced New York, 1977). New York, Dramatists Play Service, 1977.
Landscape of the Body (produced Lake Forest, Illinois, and New York, 1977). New York, Dramatists Play Service, 1978.
Take a Dream (produced New York, 1978).
Bosoms and Neglect (produced Chicago and New York, 1979). New York, Dramatists Play Service, 1980.
In Fireworks Lie Secret Codes (produced in *Holidays*, Louisville, 1979; also director: produced separately, New York, 1981). New York, Dramatists Play Service, 1981.
Nantucket series:
 Lydie Breeze (produced New York, 1982). New York, Dramatists Play Service, 1982.
 Gardenia (produced New York, 1982; London, 1983). New York, Dramatists Play Service, 1982.
 Women and Water (produced Los Angeles, 1984; revised version produced Washington, D.C., 1985). New York, Dramatists Play Service, 1990.
Three Exposures (includes *The House of Blue Leaves*, *Landscape of the Body*, *Bosoms and Neglect*). New York, Harcourt Brace, 1982.
Hey, Stay a While, music by Galt MacDermot, lyrics by Guare (produced Chicago, 1984).
Gluttony, in *Faustus in Hell* (produced Princeton, New Jersey, 1985).
The Talking Dog, adaptation of a story by Chekhov, in *Orchards* (produced Urbana, Illinois, 1985; New York, 1986). New York, Knopf, 1986.
The House of Blue Leaves and Two Other Plays (includes *Landscape of the Body* and *Bosoms and Neglect*). New York, New American Library, 1987.
Moon over Miami (produced New Haven, Connecticut, 1989).
Six Degrees of Separation (produced New York, 1990; London, 1992). New York, Vintage, 1990; London, Methuen, 1992.
Four Baboons Adoring the Sun (produced New York, 1992). Published in *Antaeus* (New York), 1992.

Screenplays: *Taking Off*, with others, 1971; *Atlantic City*, 1980.

Television Play: *Kissing Sweet* (*Foul!* series), 1969.

*

Manuscript Collection: Beinecke Library, Yale University, New Haven, Connecticut.
Critical Study: article and checklist by John Harrop, in *New Theatre Quarterly 10* (Cambridge), May 1987.

Theatrical Activities:
Director: **Play**—*In Fireworks Lie Secret Codes*, New York, 1981.

* * *

In dramatizing philos/aphilos, the love/hate relationships in the American family, John Guare locates sources of humor in suffering, penning stinging satires, corrosive black comedies, and screwball farces about such subjects as bereavement, humiliation, betrayal, and guilt. An ironist who frequently eschews pathos, fantasist Guare speaks to our brutal realities; his comedies can move us to tears. His freewheeling imagination unfettered by the constraints of realism as he employs such presentational devices as narration, soliloquies and asides to the audience, and poetic speech, Guare nevertheless grounds his plays in contemporary American life, especially the sudden end of a family unit.

This paradoxical playwright has described one of his plays as a union of Feydeau and Strindberg. Not surprisingly, Guare depicts marriage as bondage between self-absorbed people who can't care for others, since narcissism precludes nurturing. When egocentric misfits nevertheless marry and breed, they create nightmares frequently culminating in death. Women (often more sympathetic than this dramatist's men) especially suffer from romantic or domestic ties, but sons also are victimized by family life.

His early one-acts provide the characters with bizarre backgrounds which distance us. The wayward husband in *The Loveliest Afternoon of the Year*, "a seeing eye person for blind dogs," recounts his sister's dismemberment by a polar bear and his father's death by scalding from a calliope's steam. "You're from Ohio," he explains to his mistress. "You come from a nice family. You don't understand the weirdness, the grief that people can spring from." Perhaps she gains that understanding when she dies; the man's wife shoots and kills them both.

Guare's early neo-absurdist plays also include the dreadful marital squabbles of *Something I'll Tell You Tuesday*; the characters so removed from humanity in *A Day for Surprises* that Pringle is pregnant, not with a baby, but with *The Complete Works of Dr. Spock*; and the eradication of reproductive capacity in the S&M *Cop-Out*. In *Home Fires* Guare mocks the lengths to which the Schmidts go to avoid acknowledging their family name and ties. *Muzeeka*'s Brechtian short episodes and scene titles indict marriage, which causes Argue (an anagram for Guare) to sell out his creativity, flee to kinky sex, and then ultimately escape via suicide. Marriage proves one of the rotten institutions comprising the American dream.

The House of Blue Leaves keeps the pain at a distance with increasingly antic farce, as nuns in Artie Shaughnessy's Queens apartment pursue a soldier disguised as an altar boy, prompting him to toss a bomb into the arms of the deaf movie star. In order to dramatize familial resentments of the humiliations relatives inflict on one another, Guare creates Artie, a zookeeper/composer whose singing voice is as cracked as his wife's mind. Artie's son Ronnie hates Uncle Billy for having made a fool of him, and he loathes his father for never ceasing to remind him of it. Instead of murdering his real father, Ronnie resorts to symbolic patricide by trying to kill the Pope. Because Artie can't stand his wife Bananas witnessing his failures and her knowledge that he has plagiarized his songs, he kills her. Among a group of hopeless narcissists, only Bananas can love others; therefore she is "mad." Guare dramatizes this family as unreal, phony, illusory, impermanent—like the bare tree in which blue birds momentarily perch. The family home, not the mental institution, constitutes the real "house of blue leaves."

In the cartoon *Rich and Famous*, one of the plays replete with arctic imagery, Bing turns to his parents for comfort but encounters, not warmth, but ice. They shoot him—and he shoots back—because he has failed to fulfill their own dreams. They would prefer a mentally retarded son to one who wants his own life.

In the even more baroque *Marco Polo Sings a Solo*, set in the Arctic Circle, icy images dominate, though mixed with metaphors of fire. The characters, narcissists who live only for themselves, engage in solos or quests alone. Stony McBride even owes his birth to a transexual impregnated by her own sperm—the ultimate image of self-absorption. Guare describes the play as a "comedy coming out of each character's complete obsession with self." In a house carved out of ice, all

three marriages disintegrate, but it's as though Ibsen's Nora (one wife has attended 41 productions of *A Doll's House*) has been walled in by a gigantic igloo without doors—or egress.

Landscape of the Body dramatizes relatives as helpless victims, or, as Guare puts it, "people drifting with their heads cut off." Here family members long for love, but their insecurities destroy them. After his father abandons them, Bert and his mother Betty try to begin a new life in New York, but he fears his mother won't return from a search for a husband, grabs a friend in his terror, and dies because his pal, misinterpreting this as a homosexual pass, in his own turn panics, killing and decapitating Bert. Betty's own anxieties had sent her away on a trip with an (unsuitable) admirer; those fears cost her the only person with whom she could share love (a parallel to Artie murdering his loving wife, Bananas).

Bosoms and Neglect likewise concerns loss, anxiety, egomania, and aching loneliness. Despite the farce with which Guare maneuvers Scooper, his aging mother and new girl friend, *Bosoms* forces us to experience the excruciating pain of family life. Scooper worries more about neglected authors than about his neglect of his mother or her neglect of her breast and uterine cancer—the areas of her body where he was gestated and nurtured. After Scooper tries to murder his mother, she lays bare her own regrets, anguish, and humiliation in an effort to offer him salvation, but his selfishness already has prompted him to leave the room. Horrifyingly, as she provides him with the key to understanding his recurrent nightmare, his blind mother cannot know he's not there to hear her.

Such images of loneliness, frequent throughout his career, achieve especial poignancy in *Landscape of the Body*, *Bosoms and Neglect*, and most of Guare's subsequent work. Even as he hones his ability to dramatize people cut off from other's affections, however, Guare shifts direction in another respect. While he tends to focus in the first couple of decades on families with sons, thereafter, with one exception, he writes also about daughters and sisters in his full-length plays.

That exception, *Moon over Miami* resembles the playwright's work of 20 years earlier in its blistering, Ortonesque satire targeting corruption among FBI agents, politicians, and religious con artists (a salesman of bibles which "leave out the sad parts," such as Jesus dying). The characters comprise such grotesques as agent Otis Flimbsby (weird because honest), con-man Shelley Slutsky, his mother (who sings only lewd and scatological songs in her nightclub act), and a chorus of mermaids. Beginning in Alaska, then shifting to Miami, *Moon* features more images of ice and heat, as well as extravagant efforts to connect with others. Agent Wilcox even recognizes that disillusioning people or leaving them can kill them. Suggested by the ABSCAM federal sting operation, *Moon* indicts fraud and deception. Flimsby encounters only unscrupulous charlatans except for his girlfriend, who hopes "to find a better world where Bambi runs free and Dumbo flies high and Pinocchio tells the truth and Sleeping Beauty is wide awake."

Guare originally undertook *Moon over Miami* as a film for John Belushi, who died inopportunely, as though he were a character in one of the dramatist's black-comic farces. Guare encountered better luck with another violent but amusing film script, the award-winning *Atlantic City*. Initially it depicts a bleak view of families: Sally's husband has run away with and impregnated her sister Chrissy. Yet Lou becomes a surrogate father for Sally, and Chrissy finds a surrogate mom in Grace. Perhaps substitute or chosen families nurture more tenderly and effectively than biological relatives.

In two 1980's one-acts Guare examines alienation between lovers without offspring. *In Fireworks Lie Secret Codes* concerns belonging or not belonging on the part of a gay male couple and their friends, whereas *The Talking Dog* dramatizes the unsuitable mating of a woman and her boyfriend: she agrees to both physical and emotional risk taking, while he hang glides—but hangs back from commitment.

Sabotaging or betraying relationships likewise figures prominently in Guare's full-length plays of the 1980's and early 1990's. The ambitious Nantucket trilogy evokes comparison to Eugene O'Neill's New England plays. Beginning during the Civil War, then continuing through the subsequent three decades, these melodramas offer an American fable illuminating the country's origins, nature, and future direction—just as Guare's William Dean Howells urges aspiring writer Joshua to do. The presentational and episodic *Women and Water* moves fluidly back and forth across time and permits Lydie Breeze to confide her thoughts to us directly. Guare dramatizes murder, rape, arson, and suicide in a melodrama which veers off into both satire and Senecan tragedy of blood guilt and a ghost's vengeance. Moving between hope and disillusion, Guare touches upon both betrayal, patricide, greed, lies, and the punishment of sins, and the healing of wounds and the ideals of a golden age. He balances water as a life-sustaining force against the image of the watery grave. Out of the Battle of Cold Harbor (when 17,000 men died) and other misery grows Lydie's resolution to take three men—Joshua, Dan, and Amos—and found the commune of Aipotu—Utopia spelled backwards.

The more realistic and linear *Gardenia*, though it also features murder, takes as its central image blossoms: their birth and nurturance with water, their flowering, deflowering, and withering. Other emblematic details include Lydie's conviction that her patient's baby died in punishment of the parents (innocence and guilt, sin and redemption figure prominently) and Joshua's prison assurance to the Brighton Mauler that going home constitutes a happy ending (an ironic view considering what lies ahead of Joshua). As Guare further examines ideals and disillusionment, hope and its loss, healing of old wounds and inflicting new ones, and the loneliness which engulfs Lydie, he maintains suspense by withholding from us the killing's cause.

To learn that we need *Lydie Breeze*, replete with more murder, rape, and suicide, as well as madness and syphilis. Yet this summer on Nantucket provides a sunny ending, permitting peace with the past and hope for Lydie's daughter, even while clearly suggesting a future fraught with further narcissism and corruption. This coming-of-age play of Lydie Hickman ends on the significant word "alone."

Six Degrees of Separation depicts a man singularly alone, an outsider in several senses. Black, gay, self-educated, poor, and homeless, Paul's separation from the pampered and privileged residents of condos bordering Central Park seems massive, yet, in scenes both searing and amusing, he cons them into accepting him as one of them. In this touching and hilarious commentary on human interconnections—or, often, disconnections, which separate us from ourselves as well as each other—society matron Ouisa Kittredge figures "Everybody on this planet is separated by only six people." Ouisa fears failure to forge links but also appears anxious about letting people get close, past those distancing devices at which the Kittredges and their friends excel.

As he did with *Landscape of the Body*, Guare lifted found materials from newspaper headlines: an African-American, claiming he's both Sidney Poitier's son and a friend of the Kittredge's college-student offspring, arrives in their posh apartment claiming he's been mugged in the park. When the Kittredges and several friends learn they've all, after hearing the same tale, given overnight lodging and small sums to the young man, they figure they've been victimized by a con artist. Yet he's spent their money on them (plus a male hustler) and

he's stolen nothing. His goal: becoming one of them, part of the family, and receiving parental love from Ouisa and her husband. With dramaturgy sporting monologues, dreams, jumps in time and place, and chats with the audience, Guare shows Paul's impressive bid for a foster family and the Kittredge's eventual failure to provide the affection and approval he craves.

As double-sided as the Kittredges' Kandinsky, *Six Degrees'* multiple ironies and dual tone have won it many admirers. Less popular but rich in its own right, *Four Baboons Adoring the Sun* flashes both forward (three years later, for narrative, though Guare clarifies the chronology only on the page, not the stage) and back to the courtship of Penny and Philip. The present portrays their married life in Sicily, where they dig up artifacts of the past, ostensibly archeological finds, but actually the damage to their lives which may render their union too fragile to endure.

Within 24 hours, in a classical Italian setting, events evolve which we know will end tragically, because a god, Eros, predicts disaster in the first lines: "The start of another perfect day./Something will go wrong." The newly-weds are joined by their total of nine children from their former marriages. Eros targets their first born, Wayne and Halcy, at 13 craving the romantic and sexual bliss secured by their parents, who try to thwart their youngsters' wishes. The title, which refers to a statue in which the eyes have been burned out from worshipping the sun, suggests both the ecstatic joy of love and the danger of worshipping Eros. Of each pair of lovers, the men depart, and the women remain to survive tragedy and respond affirmatively to Eros's injunction "From out of the part of your soul that's not broken, adore the Sun." If Guare in this and other plays offers hope of battered spirits reviving and flourishing, clearly those will spring from among his resilient women.

—Tish Dace

———————

GURNEY, A(lbert) R(amsdell), Jr. American. Born in Buffalo, New York, 1 November 1930. Educated at St. Paul's School, Concord, New Hampshire, 1944–48; Williams College, Williamstown, Massachusetts, 1948–52, B.A. 1952; Yale University School of Drama, New Haven, Connecticut, 1955–58, M.F.A. 1958. Served in the United States Naval Reserve, 1952–55. Married Mary Goodyear in 1957; two sons and two daughters. Since 1960 member of the faculty, and since 1970 professor of literature, Massachusetts Institute of Technology, Cambridge. Recipient: Drama Desk award, 1971; Rockefeller grant, 1977; National Endowment for the Arts award, 1982; American Academy and Institute of Arts and Letters award of merit, 1987; San Diego Theater Critics Circle award, 1988. D.D.L.: Williams College, 1984. Agent: Gilbert Parker, William Morris Agency, 1350 Avenue of the Americas, New York, New York, 10019. Address: 74 Wellers Bridge Road, Roxbury, Connecticut 06783, U.S.A.

Publications

Plays

Three People, in *The Best Short Plays 1955–56*, edited by Margaret Mayorga. Boston, Beacon Press, 1956.

Turn of the Century, in *The Best Short Plays 1957–58*, edited by Margaret Mayorga. Boston, Beacon Press, 1958.
Love in Buffalo (produced New Haven, Connecticut, 1958).
The Bridal Dinner (produced Cambridge, Massachusetts, 1962).
The Comeback (produced Cambridge, Massachusetts, 1965). New York, Dramatists Play Service, 1967.
The Rape of Bunny Stuntz (produced Cambridge, Massachusetts, 1966; New York, 1967; Richmond, Surrey, 1976). London, French, 1976.
The David Show (produced Tanglewood, Massachusetts, 1966; New York, 1968). New York, French, 1968.
The Golden Fleece (produced New York, 1968; London, 1982). Published in *The Best Short Plays 1969*, edited by Stanley Richards, Philadelphia, Chilton, 1970.
The Problem (produced Boston, 1969; London, 1973; New York, 1978). New York, French, 1968; London, French, 1973.
The Open Meeting (produced Boston, 1969). New York, French, 1969.
The Love Course (produced Boston, 1970; New York, 1973; London, 1974). Published in *The Best Short Plays 1970*, edited by Stanley Richards, Philadelphia, Chilton, 1971; published separately, London, French, 1976.
Scenes from American Life (produced Tanglewood, Massachusetts, 1970; New York, 1971; revised version produced New Haven, Connecticut and Edinburgh, 1988). Included in *Four Plays*, 1985.
The Old One-Two (produced Waltham, Massachusetts, 1973; London, 1974). New York, French, 1971; London, French, 1976.
Children, suggested by the story "Goodbye, My Brother" by John Cheever (produced London, 1974; Richmond, Virginia, and New York, 1976). London, French, 1975; included in *Four Plays*, 1985.
Who Killed Richard Cory? (produced New York, 1976; Edinburgh, 1988). New York, Dramatists Play Service, 1976; revised version, as *Richard Cory* (produced Williamstown, Massachusetts, 1984), 1985.
The Middle Ages (produced Los Angeles, 1977; New York, 1982). Included in *Four Plays*, 1985.
The Wayside Motor Inn (produced New York, 1977). New York, Dramatists Play Service, 1978.
The Golden Age, suggested by the story "The Aspern Papers" by Henry James (produced London, 1981; New York, 1984). New York, Dramatists Play Service, 1985; included in *Love Letters and Two Other Plays*, 1990.
What I Did Last Summer (produced New York, 1981). New York, Dramatists Play Service, 1983; included in *Love Letters and Two Other Plays*, 1990.
The Dining Room (produced New York, 1982; London, 1983). London, French, 1982; included in *Four Plays*, 1985.
Four Plays. New York, Avon, 1985.
The Perfect Party (produced New York, 1986; London, 1987). New York, Dramatists Play Service, 1986; included in *The Cocktail Hour and Two Other Plays*, 1989.
Another Antigone (produced San Diego, 1986; New York, 1988). New York, Dramatists Play Service, 1988; included in *The Cocktail Hour and Two Other Plays*, 1989.
Sweet Sue (produced Williamstown, Massachusetts, 1986; New York, 1987). New York, Dramatists Play Service, 1987.
Don't Fall for the Lights (dialogue only) with Terence McNally and Richard Maltby, Jr., and *White Walls*, in *Urban Blight* (musical revue), based on an idea by John Tillinger, music by David Shire, lyrics by Richard Maltby, Jr. (produced New York, 1988).

The Cocktail Hour (produced San Diego and New York, 1988; London, 1990).   Included in *The Cocktail Hour and Two Other Plays*, 1989.
Love Letters (produced New Haven, Connecticut, 1988; New York, 1989; London, 1990).   Included in *Love Letters and Two Other Plays*, 1990.
The Cocktail Hour and Two Other Plays (includes *The Perfect Party*, *Another Antigone*). New York, Plume, 1989.
Love Letters and Two Other Plays (includes *The Golden Age*, *What I Did Last Summer*).   New York, Plume, 1990.
The Snow Ball, adaptation of his own novel (produced New York, 1991).
The Old Boy (produced New York, 1991).

Screenplays: *The House of Mirth*, 1972; *The Hit List*, 1988.

Television Play: *O Youth and Beauty*, from a story by John Cheever, 1979.

Novels

The Gospel According to Joe. New York, Harper, 1974.
Entertaining Strangers. New York, Doubleday, 1977; London, Allen Lane, 1979.
The Snow Ball. New York, Arbor House, 1985.

*

Manuscript Collection: Sterling Library, Yale University, New Haven, Connecticut.

A. R. Gurney, Jr., comments:

What attracts me about the theatre are its limitations as well as its possibilities. Indeed, its best possibilities may lie in its limitations. I am as much concerned about what to leave out as about what to put in. Offstage characters and events give a kind of pressure and resonance to what is shown onstage. In fact, offstage comprises the infinite possibilities and resources of film and television. Anyone who writes plays these days is forced to explore the very restrictions of this enduring old medium. I am particularly drawn to it because I like to write about people who themselves are beginning to stretch out and push against the walls.

* * *

In recent years A. R. Gurney, Jr.'s reputation in his native America has risen sharply and his work also continues to be performed in Britain. This has been partly due to changes in the organisation of the American theatre. After Gurney's first full-length play, *Scenes from American Life*, was produced at the Forum Theatre at Lincoln Center in 1971, he had virtually nowhere else to go with his work after the Center regime changed, especially at a time when his main concern—WASP manners and mores—was out of fashion. But with a changing society that produced the Yuppie generation, Gurney's plays (especially *The Dining Room* which marked his breakthrough in the U.S.) finally found their audiences. He also formed a continuing and productive link with the Playwrights' Horizon group in New York. His work continues to expand the technical skill and that fascination with theatrical flexibility that has marked it from the outset.

Scenes from American Life is, as the title implies, a kind of montage of Americana. With a small cast including an onstage-pianist linking scenes, it uses an almost cinematic technique of dissolving and overlapping scenes to build up a series of WASP life from the 1930's to the immediate future —a christening, a debutante dance, a modern Encounter

Therapy session, and so on. Its ingenious structure at points recalls Thornton Wilder, but in its concern with archetypal American rituals and family ties, not to mention the device of an offstage character (the omnipresent Snoozer), the play indicated that Gurney had his own voice.

Offstage characters dominate his one-act plays to a great extent: *The Golden Fleece* is about a suburban couple, friends of Jason and Medea, whom the audience never sees, and in the very funny *The Open Meeting* a discussion group discovers startling new relationships while awaiting the arrival of a vanished founder member. Much of their edge derives from characters who never appear; as in Greek drama, the Gods remain offstage but people are influenced by them (or, as Gurney has said "people find their gods in other people"), and Gurney often uses or adapts classical motifs. *The Love Course* and *The Old One-Two* are both sharp satires on liberal-academic attitudes, but *The Old One-Two* develops a strain of Plautine farce as a hip young college Dean discovers an unexpected relationship with his adversary, an old-fashioned professor.

Children, first produced in London during the fallow years at home for Gurney, was "suggested by" John Cheever's 1940's story "Goodbye, My Brother"; the story, like the play, takes place in a New England summer home and has a violent confrontation between two brothers, a crucial offstage event in the play. In structure the play is much tighter than *Scenes from American Life*, covering one Saturday on a July 4th weekend in the lives of a well-to-do WASP family vacationing at their Massachusetts summer home. It is a deceptively simple study of the tensions in the family caused by the eldest son, Pokey, who rules his family as an offstage presence (only one of the offstage "Gods" in the piece—the dead father is a kind of God to all the characters). In a long final speech the Mother reverses her decision to re-marry and talks to Pokey (finally visible as a shadow on the terrace on which the play passes) casting him out to preserve the family. The scene is a fitting summation to the play which subtly exposes (not least in its aptly sparse dialogue, devoid of metaphor) a culture in erosion.

Who Killed Richard Cory?, an exploration around a WASP lawyer who in middle age finds "liberation," is a more confident handling of the techniques of *Scenes from American Life*, confirming Gurney's special ability to suggest the unease under the surface of average American life. Even more confident was *The Dining Room*, a long-running New York success later produced widely in regional theatres and abroad, a sign that Gurney's world was less recondite than it had seemed when he began his career. The dining room in which the play is set represents many such rooms in different places and times from the Depression to the present; the play is both a dissection of and an elegy to a civilisation in flux, a world centred round rituals and family occasions. Using a small cast to represent a large canvas of characters—children, patriarchs, servants, and adulterous adults alike—its stagecraft is breathtakingly assured. It can move from sharply observed social comedy as a Thanksgiving lunch collapses into disarray when the grandmother slides into happy senility to a poignant late scene in which an upright dying father instructs his son in the arrangements for his funeral.

Gurney continues to be encouragingly prolific. *What I Did Last Summer* is a touching and often very funny play centred round an adolescent boy spending a wartime summer with his mother and family on the Canadian borders, befriending a dynamic eccentric woman while the family's father—another

of Gurney's potent offstage presences—is away in the Pacific. Less successful was *The Golden Age*, an updated version of "The Aspern Papers," faintly reminiscent of the kind of star-vehicle play of Gurney's childhood. Despite an intriguing central situation—Henry James's Juliana transformed into Isobel Hastings Hoyt, fabled New York legend, possibly the original of Daisy in *The Great Gatsby* and possessor of Fitzgerald manuscripts—the play never quite worked either in London or New York (despite Constance Cummings and Irene Worth, respectively), mainly because of Gurney's inability to create a satisfactory character for his variation on James's investigative scholar. But he was quickly back to form with both *Another Antigone*, a full-length return to the culture-clash world of his academic background one-act plays, and *The Perfect Party*, a successful example of that rarity, an American artificial comedy of manners. Set in the house of a college professor hosting what he plans as "the perfect party" reflecting late 20th-century American life, the event to be reviewed by a critic from "a leading New York newspaper," the play spirals into Wildean comedy as the professor, to keep the beautiful critic's interest, finds himself embroiled in a plot with distinct echoes of *The Importance of Being Earnest*.

Gurney also adapted his novel *The Snow Ball* for the stage, an ambitiously large-cast play incorporating several scenes involving ballroom dancing, centred round the final revival of the tradition of the Snow Ball, a winter dance in Buffalo, New York. Through the various characters the play traces across several decades—its central pair comprise the socially different Jack and the rich girl Kitty, champion dancers whose lives go separate ways—Gurney again subtly conveys the changes in a city and a culture.

His autobiographical *The Cocktail Hour* was a social comedy in the Philip Barry tradition based on a playwright's return to his Buffalo family to tell them about his new play, based—to some resulting consternation—on that family, a visit which opens up some old resentments and secrets. And Gurney had an extraordinary runaway success with *Love Letters*—a simple two-handed piece in which two actors seated at a desk read letters over a 40-year period between a WASP couple, a buttoned-up man with political leanings and a more Bohemian, mixed-up woman. Once again, in this understated play, Gurney managed to cover a lot of ground as he traced the pair's relationship, beginning with formal notes after childhood parties and following them through marriages, her divorce and love affairs and their own brief affair to her death. The play was also very successful overseas, except in England where misconceived casting made the piece seem sentimentally trite. Gurney charted new ground in *The Old Boy*, his latest play, an unsettling piece, handling its time-shifts with considerable skill, in which a WASP politician revisits his old private school and has to face the truth, which might compromise his career ambitions, that his old roommate died of AIDS. His handling of WASP traditions and mores was as subtle as ever, but there was a new astringency in this play which Gurney reworked extensively following its first production in New York at Playwrights Horizons, a continually welcoming home for Gurney's work.

—Alan Strachan

H

HAILEY, Oliver. American. Born in Pampa, Texas, 7 July 1932. Educated at the University of Texas, Austin, B.F.A. 1954; Yale University School of Drama, New Haven, Connecticut (Phyllis S. Anderson fellow, 1960, 1961), M.F.A. 1962. Served in the United States Air Force, 1954–57; captain in the Reserve. Married Elizabeth Ann Forsythe in 1960; two daughters. Feature writer, Dallas *Morning News*, 1957–59; story editor, *McMillan and Wife* television series, 1972–74; creative consultant, *Mary Hartman, Mary Hartman* television series, 1976–77; co-producer, *Another Day* television series. Recipient: Vernon Rice award, 1963; Writers Guild award, for television writing, 1982. Agent: Shirley Bernstein, Paramuse Artists Associates, 1414 Avenue of the Americas, New York, New York 10019. Address: 11747 Canton Place, Studio City, California 91604, U.S.A.

PUBLICATIONS

Plays

Hey You, Light Man! (produced New Haven, Connecticut, 1962; New York, 1963; Bromley, Kent, 1971). Published in *The Yale School of Drama Presents*, edited by John Gassner, New York, Dutton, 1964.
Child's Play: A Comedy for Orphans (produced New Haven, Connecticut, 1962).
Home by Hollywood (produced New London, Connecticut, 1964).
Animal (produced New York, 1965). Included in *Picture, Animal, Crisscross*, 1970.
Picture (produced New York, 1965). Included in *Picture, Animal, Crisscross*, 1970.
First One Asleep, Whistle (produced New York, 1966). Frankfurt, Fischer, 1967.
Who's Happy Now? (produced Los Angeles, 1967; New York, 1969). New York, Random House, 1969.
Crisscross (produced Los Angeles, 1969). Included in *Picture, Animal, Crisscross*, 1970.
Picture, Animal, Crisscross: Three Short Plays. New York, Dramatists Play Service, 1970.
Orphan (produced Los Angeles, 1970).
Continental Divide (produced Washington, D.C., 1970). New York, Dramatists Play Service, 1973.
Father's Day (produced Los Angeles, 1970; New York, 1971). New York, Dramatists Play Service, 1971; revised version (produced New York, 1979; London, 1987), 1981.
For the Use of the Hall (produced Providence, Rhode Island, 1974; New York, 1977). New York, Dramatists Play Service, 1975.
And Where She Stops Nobody Knows (produced Los Angeles, 1976).
Red Rover, Red Rover (produced Minneapolis, 1977; New York, 1983). New York, Dramatists Play Service, 1979.
And Furthermore (produced Pittsburgh, 1977).
Triptych (produced Los Angeles, 1978).

I Can't Find It Anywhere, in *Holidays* (produced Louisville, 1979).
I Won't Dance (produced Buffalo, 1980; New York, 1981). New York, French, 1982.
And Baby Makes Two (produced Los Angeles, 1981).
About Time (produced Los Angeles, 1982). Published in *A.M./P.M.*, New York, Dramatists Play Service, 1983.
24 Hours. Published in *A.M./P.M.*, New York, Dramatists Play Service, 1983.
Round Trip (produced Kalamazoo, Michigan, 1984).
The Father, adaptation of a play by Strindberg (produced Philadelphia, 1984). New York, Dramatists Play Service, 1984.
Kith and Kin (produced Dallas, 1986).

Screenplay: *Just You and Me, Kid*, with Leonard Stern, 1979.

Television Plays: *McMillan and Wife* series (9 episodes), 1971–74; *Sidney Shorr: A Girl's Best Friend*, 1981; *Isabel's Choice*, 1981.

*

Critical Study: *Showcase One* by John Lahr, New York, Grove Press, 1969.

Oliver Hailey comments:

(1973) My plays are primarily the attempt to take a serious theme and deal with it comedically. Though the idea for a particular play often begins as something quite serious, I try not to start writing until I have found a comic point of view for the material.

In the case of my play that is most autobiographical, *Who's Happy Now?*, it took ten years to find that comic attitude. There had been nothing particularly funny about my childhood—and yet I felt that to tell the story without a comic perspective was to put upon the stage a story too similar to many that had been seen before. With the comic perspective came the opportunity for a much fresher approach to the material—and also, strangely, it allowed me to deal with the subject on a much more serious level than I would have risked otherwise.

Because, finally, my plays are an attempt to entertain—and when they cease to entertain—no matter how "important" what I am trying to say—they fail as plays.

* * *

Despite considerable early promise Oliver Hailey has yet to achieve either critical or commercial success in the theatre. While some of his plays have been well received in university and regional playhouses, the full-length works presented in New York City all had brief runs.

Hey You, Light Man!, written and first produced at Yale University, contrasts the reality-stained world of banal domesticity with the more glamorous role-playing offered by

262

the stage. Hailey's hero, an unhappily married actor named Ashley Knight, flees from his dreadful family to live on a stage set. There he meets a lonely young widow who has fallen asleep during a performance and is locked in the theatre. Lula Roca's husband, a stagehand, was accidentally killed by some falling equipment and her three children were all lost at a national park. One fell into a waterfall at the same time that another fell off a mountain. A third was taken by a bear. Ashley and Lula, an unlikely pair, change the direction of each other's life. Lula's experience with the illusory world of the stage permits her to develop her imaginative powers so as to face the future with new hope. Ashley, on the other hand, for whom reality could only be dreary, sees in Lula new possibilities in life off the stage and is able to make a final escape from his domestic prison. Much of the play's humor and charm stems from Lula's endearing innocence, but Hailey's somewhat redundant elaboration of his illusion vs. reality theme weakens the play. A number of oddball characters appear, but the playwright's straining for an eccentric originality is apparent. At times, however, his dialogue achieves the intended poetic effect, and his tender concern for his odd couple results in some touching moments.

First One Asleep, Whistle, which had only one performance on Broadway, reflects some of the same concerns as *Hey You, Light Man!* but lacks its offbeat charm. The milieu is again theatrical, the heroine an actress in television commercials. She has a daughter by a man not her husband and during the course of the play has an affair with a married man. This time her lover is an emotionally immature actor who is separated from his wife. As in *Light Man* the lovers eventually part, the actor returning to his wife, unaware that his mistress is pregnant. Elaine, the actress, has somehow been strengthened by this latest affair and remains confident that she will survive without a man. The ill-fated romance is complicated by the presence of Elaine's seven-year-old daughter whose innocent responses to her mother's unconventional life are the principal sources of the play's occasional humor. While Hailey avoids a sentimental "happy" ending, his characters are never very interesting and the play remains at the level of semi-sophisticated soap opera.

Who's Happy Now? also deals with domestic difficulties, but the setting is far removed from the urbane New York scene. The play takes place in Texas during the years 1941–55 and focuses on the confused reactions of a young man to the bizarre relationship between his parents. His father, a strong-willed and crude butcher, has managed to keep both his wife and mistress happy, despite the efforts of his son to alter the situation. The mistress, a waitress named Faye Precious, has lost her husband as a result of a freak accident and respects her butcher/lover (aptly named Horse) despite his continuing affection for his wife. The hero is an aspiring songwriter, his ambition inspiring disgust in Horse, and the play is a kind of comic variation of the Oedipal struggle. *Who's Happy Now?* contains some diverting musical numbers, but the mixture of irony and sentiment results in a confused tone. The frame of the play involves the hero attempting to explain to his mother, through the medium of drama, what he really felt about his parents. Such a device seems intended to point out the disparity between actual experience and its painful, often inaccurate, re-creation on stage, a theme Hailey deals with elsewhere. There are other theatrical techniques that serve to distance the audience from potentially mawkish material, but the effects, while at times inventive, ultimately manage to make a play too diffuse in impact. Despite Hailey's genuine ironic gifts, his play suffers from the lack of a firm larger design.

Continental Divide is closer to pure farce as it contrasts a wealthy couple from Long Island with the down-at-heel parents of their future son-in-law. The latter couple are visitors from their native Arkansas and the juxtaposition of rich and poor is mined of its limited potential for original insight and humor. Mr. John, the father of the groom, had killed his first wife and during the course of the play manages to wound his host twice. There are other farcical events, and whatever satiric thrusts intended by the playwright are subordinated to the broad comic effects.

Hailey's best play, *Father's Day*, despite some highly favorable reviews, ran for only one performance on Broadway. It marked a return to the urbane New York scene, and the dialogue has a pungency and bite. The characters are three divorced couples briefly reunited on Father's Day. The play focuses primarily on the complex feelings of the women, as it uncovers their ambivalent desires for both independence and security. The comic tone on the surface barely conceals the pathos of their situation, and the play has a toughminded quality normally absent in a conventional sex comedy. The characters, especially the women, are sharply drawn and while *Father's Day* at times suffers from an overly eager attempt to be topical, the playwright's verbal energy is sufficient to sustain the work. Hailey demonstrates his usual compassion and refusal to impose standard moral judgments. Here he has avoided his tendency to employ striking, if redundant or irrelevant, theatrical effects. At the close of the play, there is a reference to Chekhov's *The Three Sisters* suggesting that Hailey saw a parallel to his unhappy trio in the Russian classic. While *Father's Day* lacks the depth and resonance of Chekhov's work, its tenderness and its willingness to understand the bitterness and frustration of unfulfilled lives make the parallel not altogether inapt.

In addition to his full-length plays, Hailey has written several shorter works. *Picture*, a labored one-act play or "demonstration" is similar to *Who's Happy Now?* in its concern with the problems in recreating the past through the medium of drama. *Crisscross* is a strained sketch in which Santa Claus is crucified by his father, a carpenter resentful of his son's desire for independence. *Animal* is a brief, but effective, monologue by a mother desperately struggling to impose her will on her rebellious daughter.

It is perhaps too early to make any definitive judgment on Hailey's playwriting career. What does seem evident at this point is that he has failed in his efforts at employing conventional commercial formulas to sustain an often original point of view. Despite his refusal to provide emotionally satisfying conclusions to his plays, his dramas seem too designed to please, too eager to be charming and clever. His major themes appear rooted in the dislocations of family life and while he is often adept in revealing the sadness beneath the laugh, the shifting tone of his plays results in uncertain dramatic effects. The characters are ultimately "liberated," although their freedom contains no guarantee of happiness or security. Hailey's fondness for obvious comic devices prevents the emergence of the genuine artist he at times reveals himself to be.

—Leonard Fleischer

HAIRE, Wilson John. British. Born in Belfast, Northern Ireland, 6 April 1932. Educated at Clontonacally Elementary

School, Carryduff, County Down, 1939–46. Married 1) Rita Lenson in 1955 (marriage dissolved) five children; 2) Sheila Fitz-Jones in 1974 (marriage dissolved);3) Karen Mendelsohn in 1979 (marriage dissolved). Actor, Unity Theatre, London, 1962–67; co-director, Camden Group Theatre, London, 1967–71; resident dramatist, Royal Court Theatre, London, 1974, and Lyric Theatre, Belfast, 1976. Recipient: George Devine award, 1972; *Evening Standard* award, 1973; Thames Television award, 1974; Leverhulme fellowship, 1976. Address: 61 Lulot Gardens, London N19 5TS, England.

PUBLICATIONS

Plays

The Clockin' Hen (produced London, 1968).
The Diamond, Bone and Hammer; and Along the Sloughs of Ulster (produced London, 1969).
Within Two Shadows (produced London, 1972; New York, 1974). Published in *Scripts 9* (New York), September 1972; published separately, London, Davis Poynter, 1973.
Bloom of the Diamond Stone (produced Dublin, 1973). London, Pluto Press, 1979.
Echoes from a Concrete Canyon (produced London, 1975).
Lost Worlds: Newsflash, Wedding Breakfast, Roost (produced London, 1978). London, Heinemann, 1978.
Worlds Apart, with J.P. Dylan (produced Glasgow, 1981).

Television Plays: *Letter from a Soldier*, 1975; *The Dandelion Clock*, 1975.

*

Wilson John Haire comments:

(1988) I first began writing about Northern Ireland back in 1960. I wrote three short stories for a monthly paper called the *Irish Democrat*. My first story was called "Refuge from the Tick-Man" and I went under the pen name of "Fenian." "Fenian" is a derogatory name for Catholic in Northern Ireland. When I began writing the story of how my family fled the city of Belfast for the countryside to escape the debt collectors I became proud of that name. To me it meant someone who resists corruption and sectarian bullying. The editor of the paper persuaded me to use my real name for my second story "The Screening"—a teenage boy, pretending to be a Protestant, survives interrogation and taunts about Catholicism and gets the job for which he is applying. The third story was "The Beg." "Beg" is bag or sack in Ulster dialect. The local shipyard sheds a quarter of its workers, and the story is told through the eyes of an apprentice carpenter.

I took to writing drama in 1968 with a one-act play *The Clockin' Hen*. A broody hen hatches out her eggs under a darkening sky—in 1968 the Reverend Paisley attempts to lead a demonstration, with protection, through a Catholic ghetto and is resisted. A Catholic and Protestant are put on trial. The Catholic sees no hope of justice in a court that openly loathes him.

After that I wrote *The Diamond, Bone and Hammer, and Along the Sloughs of Ulster*. It is a sort of "Fear and Misery in the Third Reich." This play sequence was produced at the Hampstead Theatre, and later transfered to the Unity Theatre. This was not a professional production, and no reviewer appeared except for D.A.N. Jones of the *Listener*, who gave it an intelligent review. It was this one and only review that made me want to go on writing.

On opening night, Friday, 8 August 1969, the Bogside riots began, and Ulster became a topic of conversation in London.

On 12 April 1972 *Within Two Shadows* opened at the Royal Court Theatre. The media said it was the first play on the Ulster crisis to open in London. I come from a parentage of both Catholic and Protestant. I saw this as the "two shadows" in my life, and I told the tale from within the family.

Though I have not had a London production of my work recently it still continues to be alive and well within the colleges and universities in the English-speaking world. At the moment I am hoping to write some drama for radio. I have a love for language and I am hoping that radio will give me the facilities that the old Royal Court Theatre once gave.

* * *

Wilson John Haire, born in the Shankill Road, Belfast, the son of a Catholic mother and a Protestant father, has drawn much of the background material for his plays from that stark area of the tortured city. Even when the actual turmoil of Northern Ireland is not part of a play, as in *Echoes from a Concrete Canyon*, we can still feel the claustrophobic atmosphere of an unfriendly town beyond the walls of a lonely flat. Four of Haire's plays, however, are set against the background of sectarian violence, bigotry, and loneliness. He conveys the tragedy of Ulster more directly and vividly than any other contemporary playwright, drawing upon memories which reach far back into his childhood.

Haire is not a polemical writer. Political ideas interest him, particularly as part of the environments from which they come, but he is concerned more with the nature and extent of Ulster's suffering than with easy moralising. His best known play, *Within Two Shadows*, is also the most autobiographical. It deals with a working-class Belfast family, dog-eared with poverty, and torn apart by prejudices which they try to exclude but which gradually eat into their lives. In the play the mother is a Protestant, the father a Catholic, and we feel that both, at some time in their lives, have made conscientious efforts to leap over the religious barriers which divide them. But the pressure of events, the opinions of their neighbours, and the growing violence are too much for them. They try to stay away from conflict, if only to protect their children; but the children are growing up, now teenagers, and quick to enter into the rivalries, as part of their puppy-play but with fangs bared.

In *Bloom of the Diamond Stone* Haire shows what could almost have been the beginnings of that marriage, a Romeo and Juliet love affair, where the young couple from opposite sides fall in love and then have to battle against their families, the restrictions set at work, and the rigid outlooks of their former friends. In both plays Haire conveys a sense of inner honesty and goodness corrupted by circumstance. In that way, he can be an optimistic writer. His characters are not vicious in themselves, only made so by a historical backlog of revenge, fear, and defensiveness. To that extent, Ulster's torment seems the result of a curable mixture of follies, rather than the dark nightmare of the soul as other dramatists, including David Rudkin, have sometimes presented it. The British soldier searching for a "terrorist" in *Bloom of the Diamond Stone* is shown to be a likeable human being, until his fears and his job prompt him to be otherwise.

But the follies extend in all directions. They are sometimes rooted in sheer lack of understanding of the awfulness of the situation. In his first television play, *Letter from a Soldier*, Haire merely describes a soldier's effort to make his family in England understand what a tour of duty in Ulster is like. His second, *The Dandelion Clock*, concerns the particular problems facing a young girl growing up in Belfast. What sort of future can she plan for herself? The problems, however, are not just ones of comprehension. They also stem from the social organisation which is out of touch with the lives people lead.

The Clockin' Hen, Haire's first stage play, concerns a court case in which two shipyard workers of different religions are put on trial, following a Paisleyite demonstration in 1966. How do they react to the presence of the Law? Do they regard Law in any meaningful sense? And if they do not, where does an Ulsterman go? "Emotionally," Haire has said, "I am a Catholic, but intellectually I am a Protestant." This conflict is reflected in his plays. Haire perceives the need for a formal social order, but is sympathetic to the resentments caused by the existing one. To be out of touch with society, to defy, ignore, or simply have an engrained distrust of the ordering forces which are there, is equivalent to "dropping out." Haire's sympathy with Irish drop-outs, tramps, and drunkards is shown in *The Latchicoes of Fort Camden*, an unperformed play set in a London dosshouse.

Haire's skill as a dramatist reveals the strength and weaknesses of someone who chooses subjects so close to his personal experience. He can write vigorously and directly, usually naturalistically, but without the detachment needed to ensure that his plays have a clear form and that each point is made dramatically and concisely. He has indicated an intention to break away from his concentration on Northern Ireland; but in *Echoes from a Concrete Canyon*, which concerns the mental breakdown of a woman living with her daughter in a block of flats and estranged from her husband, the clotted verbosity which often accompanies autobiography is still present. Lightening touches of humour are rare; and the frequent poeticisms add heaviness rather than variety to the language. Haire in time may gain maturity as a dramatist by becoming less dependent on his background, but he may lose the force of reality which adds power to his Ulster plays. He speaks as a witness and a survivor of a continuing drama of stupidity, cruelty, and resentment. That, so far, has been his main role, and not an insignificant one, in contemporary British theatre.

—John Elsom

———

HALE, John. British. Born in Woolwich, Kent, 5 February 1926. Educated at army schools in Egypt, Ceylon, and Malta; Borden Grammar School, Sittingbourne, Kent; Royal Naval College, Greenwich. Served in the Fleet Air Arm, 1941–51: boy apprentice to petty officer, later commissioned. Married Valerie June Bryan in 1950; one son and one daughter. Stage hand, stage manager, and electrician, in variety, touring, and repertory companies, 1952–55; founder, and artistic director, Lincoln Theatre, 1955–58; artistic director, Arts Theatre, Ipswich, 1958–59 and Bristol Old Vic, 1959–61; freelance director, 1961–64; member of the Board of Governors, 1963–71, associate artistic director, 1968–71, and resident playwright, 1975–76, Greenwich Theatre, London. Since 1964 freelance writer and director. Recipient: Golden Globe award, 1970. Agent: (for plays and screenplays), Lemon, Unna and Durbridge, 24–32 Pottery Lane, Holland Park, London W11 4LZ; (for novels), Aitken and Stone Ltd., 29 Fernshaw Road, London SW10 0TG, England.

PUBLICATIONS

Plays

The Black Swan Winter (as *Smile Boys, That's the Style*, produced Glasgow, 1968; as *The Black Swan Winter*, also director: produced London, 1969). Published in *Plays of the Year 37*, London, Elek, 1970.
It's All in the Mind (also director: produced London, 1968).
Spithead (also director: produced London, 1969). Published in *Plays of the Year 38*, London, Elek, 1971.
Here Is the News (produced Beaford, Devon, 1970).
Lorna and Ted (also director: produced London, 1970).
Decibels (produced Liverpool, 1971). Published in *Prompt Three*, edited by Alan Durband, London, Hutchinson, 1976.
The Lion's Cub (televised 1971). Published in *Elizabeth R*, edited by J.C. Trewin, London, Elek, 1971.
In Memory of . . . Carmen Miranda (also director: produced London, 1975).
Love's Old Sweet Song (also director: produced London, 1976).
The Case of David Anderson, Q.C. (produced Manchester and Edinburgh, 1980; London, 1981).

Screenplays: *The Mind of Mr. Soames*, with Edward Simpson, 1969; *Anne of the Thousand Days*, with Bridget Boland, 1970; *Mary Queen of Scots*, 1972.

Radio Writing: *Micah Clarke* series, 1966.

Television Plays: *The Rules That Jack Made*, 1965; *The Noise Stopped*, 1966; *Light the Blue Touch Paper*, 1966; *Thirteen Against Fate* series, 1966; *Samson and Delilah*, *Strike Pay*, and *Her Turn*, all from short stories by D.H. Lawrence, 1966–67; *The Queen's Traitor* (5 parts), 1967; *Retreat*, 1968; *The Picnic*, 1969; *The Distracted Preacher*, 1969; *The Lion's Cub*, in *Elizabeth R* series, 1971; *The Bristol Entertainment*, 1971; *Anywhere But England*, 1972; *Ego Hugo: A Romantic Entertainment*, 1973; *Lorna and Ted*, 1973; *The Brotherhood*, 1975; *An Impeccable Elopement*, 1975; *Goodbye America*, 1976; *The Grudge Fight*, from his own novel, 1981; *Children of the North*, 1991.

Novels

Kissed the Girls and Made Them Cry. London, Collins, 1963; Englewood Cliffs, New Jersey, Prentice Hall, 1966.
The Grudge Fight. London, Collins, 1964; Englewood Cliffs, New Jersey, Prentice Hall, 1967.
A Fool at the Feast. London, Collins, 1966.
The Paradise Man. London, Rapp and Whiting, and Indianapolis, Bobbs Merrill, 1969.
Mary, Queen of Scots (novelization of screenplay). London, Pan, 1972.
The Fort. London, Quartet, 1973.
The Love School. London, Pan, 1974; New York, St. Martin's Press, 1975.
Lovers and Heretics. London, Gollancz, 1976.
The Whistle Blower. London, Cape, 1984; New York, Atheneum, 1985.

*

Theatrical Activities:
Director: **Plays**—about 150 plays in Lincoln, Ipswich, Bristol and elsewhere, including several of his own plays, and *An*

Enemy of the People by Arthur Miller, Lincoln, 1958; *Cyrano de Bergerac* by Edmond Rostand, Bristol, 1959; *The Merry Wives of Windsor*, London, 1959; *The Tinker* by Laurence Dobie and Robert Sloman, Bristol and London, 1960; *The Rehearsal* by Anouilh, Bristol and London, 1961; *The Killer* by Ionesco, Bristol, 1961; *Sappho* by Lawrence Durrell, Edinburgh, 1961; *Mother Courage* by Brecht, Hiram, Ohio, 1966. **Television**—about 16 plays, 1961–64, including *The Fruit at the Bottom of the Bowl* by Ray Bradbury, and *Drill Pig* by Charles Wood; *The Rules That Jack Made*, 1965. **Recordings**—13 Shakespeare plays, including *The Taming of the Shrew*, *Richard II*, and *Henry V*, FCM Productions.

John Hale comments:

I am both a playwright and a novelist. The plays and novels are written alternately; I buy the time with screenplays for television and films. If I have anything to say only part of it is in the plays: all of it, whatever it is, is in the plays and the novels taken together.

* * *

As a playwright, John Hale seems to share what is a common quality of actors, the ability to take up a theme, immerse himself in it, work it out, and leave it: recognizably the same actor is performing, if your concern is to look for him, yet the characters are different creations. Where other writers may work through and within an obsession, in some cases (Strindberg and Tennessee Williams) becoming trapped by it, so that their plays are like a series of studies of some vast central object too large to be contained in any one play, Hale seems to make a fresh start in each case, as if he were to say, "Here is my subject. I give myself to it. I use *this* particular piece of my own experience for it. I build it from inside, and shape it from the outside. I have made a play. I move on."

The Black Swan Winter, Hale's first stage play, was written after his own father's death, and uses memories of his father and himself. In a later play, *Love's Old Sweet Song*, Hale and his father appear again, and his grandfather also, but as supporting characters in what seems to be primarily an appalled examination of two castrating women, mother and daughter jointly devoted to the destruction of all the men around them. His novel *The Grudge Fight* used his experience of the navy, and when he wanted to return to the subject in *Spithead* he used instead the secondary experience of history. *It's All in the Mind* is his only excursion into politics, *Lorna and Ted* the only one into Suffolk, and his one-act monologue *In Memory of . . . Carmen Miranda* the only one into Samuel Beckett country, which is just as well since he seems not to be happy there.

Yet there is a moral being, Hale himself, who made all this work, even though he is modest as well as moral, and requires one to search for him. *Kissed the Girls and Made Them Cry*, *The Black Swan Winter*, and *Love's Old Sweet Song* all share a theme, the attempt to get back into one's past and find out what went wrong. The shadow of his father, a warrant officer in the Regular Army, lies upon his work and is shown in Hale's concern for fairness and his admiration of discipline, most of all self-discipline: if Forster can be boiled down to "Only connect," then Hale's two words are "Soldier on." Fairness for him means most of all fairness to other people, a decent recognition of the right to difference, but it can also mean (*Lorna and Ted*) fairness to oneself, an assertion of one's own rights, and an acceptance of responsibility.

Hale's plays are well-made in the manner, nowadays common, of a television play (or a play by Shakespeare), with a number of scenes running into each other, and a fragmented set. They are thoughtful, observed, humane, and only rarely self-indulgent. Their fault (commonly found in company with these virtues) is an occasional over-explicitness: Hale's characters, like Priestley's, too often say what they should only mean, though this is not a fault of *Lorna and Ted*, which is his most interesting play so far. He seems always to have been happiest when writing duologues (too many characters at once appear to worry him), and in this two-hander, with only a non-speaking voluptuous lady in support, his construction has been most at ease, most relaxed, least stiff.

—John Bowen

———

HALL, Roger (Leighton). New Zealander. Born in England, 17 January 1939. Educated at University College School, London, 1952–55; Victoria University, Wellington, 1963–68, M.A. (honours). Married Mavis Dianne Sturm in 1968; one daughter and one son. Worked in insurance, as a wine waiter, in factories, and as a teacher before becoming a freelance writer and editor. Teaching fellow, University of Otago, Dunedin, 1979–91; guest artist, New Mexico State University, Las Cruces, 1983. Recipient: Arts Council of New Zealand travel grant, 1975; Robert Burns fellowship, University of Otago, 1977, 1978; Turnovsky Arts award, 1987; Queen's Service Order (Q.S.O.), 1987; Commemoration medal, 1990. Agent: Casarotto Ramsay Ltd., National House, 60–66 Wardour Street, London W1V 3HP, England; or, Playmarket, P.O. Box 9767, Wellington, New Zealand.

PUBLICATIONS

Plays

Glide Time (produced Wellington, 1976; as *Roll On, Friday*, produced Southampton, 1985). Wellington, Victoria University Press, 1978.
Middle-Age Spread (produced Wellington, 1977; London, 1979). Wellington, Victoria University Press, 1978; London, French, 1980.
State of the Play (produced Wellington, 1978). Wellington, Victoria University Press, 1979.
Cinderella (produced Auckland, 1978).
Robin Hood (produced Auckland, 1979).
Prisoners of Mother England (produced Dunedin, 1979). Wellington, Playmarket, 1980.
Fifty-Fifty (produced Auckland, 1981). Wellington, Victoria University Press, 1982.
The Rose (produced Auckland, 1981).
The Quiz (broadcast 1982; produced Dunedin, 1983). Published in *On Stage 1*, edited by David Dowling, Auckland, Longman Paul, 1983.
Hot Water (produced Auckland, 1982). Wellington, Victoria University Press, 1983.
Footrot Flats, music by Philip Norman, lyrics by A.K. Grant, based on works by Murray Ball (produced Christchurch, 1983). Wellington, Playmarket, 1984.
Multiple Choice (produced Las Cruces, New Mexico, 1983; Guildford, Surrey, 1984).
Dream of Sussex Downs (produced Auckland, 1986).

Love Off the Shelf, music by Philip Norman, lyrics by Hall and A.K. Grant (produced Dunedin, 1986; Southampton, 1988).
The Hansard Show, songs by Nigel Eastgate and John Drummond (produced Wellington, 1986).
The Share Club (produced Dunedin, 1987).
After the Crash (produced Dunedin, 1988).
Mr. Punch (produced Dunedin, 1989).
You Must Be Crazy (produced Wellington, 1989).
Conjugal Rites (produced Palmerston North and Watford, Hertfordshire, 1990).
Making It Big, music by Philip Norman (produced Dunedin, 1991).

Radio Plays: *Gliding On* series, 1977–80; *Hark, Hark, The Harp!*, 1981; *Last Summer*, 1981; *The Quiz*, 1982; *Conjugal Rites* series, 1991; *The Dream Factory*, 1992; *By Degrees* series, 1992.

Television Plays: *Clean Up*, 1972; *The Bach*, 1974; *Some People Get All the Luck*, 1974; *The Reward*, 1974; *Gliding On* series, 1982–86; and series episodes for *In View of the Circumstances*, 1970–71, *Pukemanu*, 1972, *Buck House*, 1974, and *Neighbourhood Watch*, 1991; *Conjugal Rites*, 1993.

Other (for children)

Captain Scrimshaw in Space. Adelaide, Rigby, 1979; London, Arnold, 1981.
How the Crab Got a Hard Back, adaptation of a West Indian folktale. Adelaide, Rigby, 1979; London, Arnold, 1981.
Sam, Max, and Harold Meet Dracula. Wellington, Nelson, Price, 1990.
Penguin Trouble. Wellington, Nelson Price, 1991.
My Aunt Mary Went Shopping. Auckland, Ashton Scholastic, 1991.

*

Manuscript Collections: Alexander Turnbull Library, Wellington; Hocken Library, University of Otago, Dunedin.

*   *   *

Within the network of "community theatres," intimate professional theatres situated near the centre of each of New Zealand's major cities, the writing of Roger Hall has been of organic importance, reflecting their growth, their economic constraints, and especially their audience composition. His earliest theatre writing, satirical revues, dates back to the foundation period of the first of these groups, and his first major success, *Glide Time*, marked the point at which most of them had gathered sufficient momentum to regard locally written scripts as a possible commercial venture; that play's extended seasons throughout the country had a major unifying effect on the community theatres, as well as creating a sense of a national drama audience. Hall's farces of the late 1980's, *The Share Club*, *After the Crash*, and the television spin-off *Neighbourhood Watch*, used the same cluster of characters from the world of spare-time stock-market punters, which seemed precisely to correlate with the world of the audiences that the theatres were now drawing— substantially different from the students who queued for the early satirical revues.

Hall's ability to read his dominant audience has always been astute, as has been his careful development of his craft without betraying that audience's expectations and toler-ances. The satirical vein has never completely left his work, but nor has he ever overstepped his audience's inclination to laugh at itself. With *Glide Time*, the satirical target was easy: setting a satire on the public service in the capital—and premiering it there—meant easy recognition of the absurdi-ties of the daily battle against the institutional system. In *Middle-Age Spread*, the institution is marriage, but the main character's gesture of anarchy—a solitary case of marital infidelity—foreshadowed elements of the domestic farce which would be the mode of works such as *Hot Water* and *Conjugal Rites*. Even in the wording of the titles—"glide" and "spread"—was embedded the idea of escapism, or beating the system, and the audience's vicarious complicity.

An inclination to move towards the more serious dramatic statement has been apparent intermittently in Hall's work, from an attempt at psychoanalytical complexity in *State of the Play* (about a play-writing class), to *The Rose* (inspired by the 1981 Springbok rugby tour), and to *Multiple Choice*, a play about education, Hall's own early career. But even in *Glide Time* there is a filament of seriousness and poignancy, in the case of a migrant for whom the office is a partial refuge from a domestic world which is getting progressively bleaker in the face of cultural displacement. This motif he developed into a full-length work, *Prisoners of Mother England*, using mainly the revue techniques of his apprenticeship. The title charac-ters are eight of the 1,100 assisted migrants on the Captain Cook, sailing to New Zealand with visions of walking the Milford Track, big game fishing, and a land of opportunity and cheap living with people who are "more English than the English." The play shows the collapse of these delusions within the varyingly successful process of assimilation, but the scrapbook effect of the 59 short scenes, and the blatantly stereotypical presentation of many New Zealand characters through only five actors, emphasises that this is how the migrants saw—and were partially encouraged to see—them. This play, broadly autobiographical, frankly acknowledged the migrant perspective that informs much of Hall's best satire. One further treatment of the migration theme was a critical success but had a limited stage history: *Dream of Sussex Downs* returned to a more conventional form, fuller characterisation, and a sombre Chekhovian toning derived from *Three Sisters*.

Throughout this period, radio and television series devel-oped from *Glide Time* continued, and with *Footrot Flats* (from a popular New Zealand cartoon strip) Hall emerged as a writer of musicals, and continued with *Love off the Shelf*, a musical parody of Mills and Boon, and *The Hansard Show*, ingeniously derived from New Zealand's parliamentary archives, and ranging from the grotesque to the com-passionate in its glimpses of the country's emergent national identity through the lenses of politics. Since he became com-mercially successful, Hall has continued to be actively suppor-tive of innovative work by younger playwrights, especially through Playmarket workshops and his play-writing course at the University of Otago.

Internationally, Hall is best-known for the long London run of *Middle-Age Spread*, which encouraged him to script another play for the West End, *Fifty-Fifty*. Though for once there is relatively little satire in the latter play, its strength lies in two areas in which some critics have found Hall defective: female characterisation and inter-generational dynamics. The central character is an unorganised, unassertive middle-aged failure dividing up matrimonial property in the face of divorce, who encounters his adult children (including a son whose Ph.D. stands as a barrier to employment) and an assertively independent woman who is moving into his flat. The play's engagingly equivocal mood derives from the fragmentation of precisely the values that were a source of complacency to the characters of *Middle-Age Spread*.

—Howard McNaughton

———————

HALL, Willis. British. Born in Leeds, Yorkshire, 6 April 1929. Educated at Cockburn High School, Leeds. National Service 1947–52: radio playwright for the Chinese Schools Department of Radio Malaya. Married 1) the actress Jill Bennett in 1962 (marriage dissolved 1965); 2) Dorothy Kingsmill-Lunn (marriage dissolved); 3) Valerie Shute in 1973; four sons. Lives in Ilkley, West Yorkshire. Recipient: *Evening Standard* award, 1959; BAFTA award, 1988. Agent: London Management, 235 Regent Street, London W1A 2JT, England.

PUBLICATIONS

Plays

Final at Furnell (broadcast 1954).   London, Evans, 1956.
Poet and Pheasant, with Lewis Jones (broadcast 1955; produced Watford, Hertfordshire, 1958).   London, Deane, and Boston, Baker, 1959.
The Gentle Knight (broadcast 1957; produced London, 1964).   London, Blackie, 1966.
The Play of the Royal Astrologers (produced Birmingham, 1958; London, 1968).   London, Heinemann, 1960.
Air Mail from Cyprus (televised 1958).   Published in *The Television Playwright: Ten Plays for BBC Television*, edited by Michael Barry, London, Joseph, and New York, Hill and Wang, 1960.
The Long and the Short and the Tall (produced Edinburgh, 1958; London, 1959; New York, 1962).   London, Heinemann, 1959; New York, Theatre Arts, 1961.
A Glimpse of the Sea, and Last Day in Dreamland (produced London, 1959).   Included in *A Glimpse of the Sea: Three Short Plays*, 1961.
Return to the Sea (televised 1960; produced London, 1980).   Included in *A Glimpse of the Sea: Three Short Plays*, 1961.
Billy Liar, with Keith Waterhouse, adaptation of the novel by Waterhouse (produced London, 1960; Los Angeles and New York, 1963).   London, Joseph, 1960; New York, Norton, 1961.
Chin-Chin, adaptation of the play by François Billetdoux (produced London, 1960).
A Glimpse of the Sea: Three Short Plays.   London, Evans, 1961.
Celebration: The Wedding and The Funeral, with Keith Waterhouse (produced Nottingham and London, 1961).   London, Joseph, 1961.
Azouk, with Robin Maugham, adaptation of a play by Alexandre Rivemale (produced Newcastle upon Tyne, 1962).
England, Our England, with Keith Waterhouse, music by Dudley Moore (produced London, 1962).   London, Evans, 1964.
Squat Betty, with Keith Waterhouse (produced London, 1962; New York, 1964).   With *The Sponge Room*, London, Evans, 1963.
The Sponge Room, with Keith Waterhouse (produced Nottingham and London, 1962; New York, 1964).   With

Squat Betty, London, Evans, 1963; in *Modern Short Plays from Broadway and London*, edited by Stanley Richards, New York, Random House, 1969.
All Things Bright and Beautiful, with Keith Waterhouse (produced Bristol and London, 1962).   London, Joseph, 1963.
Yer What? (revue), with others, music by Lance Mulcahy (produced Nottingham, 1962).
The Days Beginning: An Easter Play.   London, Heinemann, 1964.
The Love Game, adaptation of a play by Marcel Achard, translated by Tamara Lo (produced London, 1964).
Come Laughing Home, with Keith Waterhouse (as *They Called the Bastard Stephen*, produced Bristol, 1964; as *Come Laughing Home*, produced Wimbledon, 1965).   London, Evans, 1965.
Say Who You Are, with Keith Waterhouse (produced Guildford, Surrey, and London, 1965).   London, Evans, 1966; as *Help Stamp Out Marriage* (produced New York, 1966), New York, French, 1966.
Joey, Joey, with Keith Waterhouse, music by Ron Moody (produced Manchester and London, 1966).
Whoops-a-Daisy, with Keith Waterhouse (produced Nottingham, 1968).   London, French, 1978.
Children's Day, with Keith Waterhouse (produced Edinburgh and London, 1969).   London, French, 1975.
Who's Who, with Keith Waterhouse (produced Coventry, 1971; London, 1973).   London, French, 1974.
The Railwayman's New Clothes (televised 1971).   London, French, 1974.
They Don't All Open Men's Boutiques (televised 1972).   Published in *Prompt Three*, edited by Alan Durband, London, Hutchinson, 1976.
Saturday, Sunday, Monday, with Keith Waterhouse, adaptation of a play by Eduardo De Filippo (produced London, 1973; New York, 1974).   London, Heinemann, 1974.
The Card, with Keith Waterhouse, music and lyrics by Tony Hatch and Jackie Trent, adaptation of the novel by Arnold Bennett (produced Bristol and London, 1973).
Walk On, Walk On (produced Liverpool, 1975).   London, French, 1976.
Kidnapped at Christmas (for children; produced London, 1975).   London, French–Heinemann, 1975.
Stag-Night (produced London, 1976).
Christmas Crackers (for children; produced London, 1976).   London, French–Heinemann, 1976.
Filumena, with Keith Waterhouse, adaptation of a play by Eduardo De Filippo (produced London, 1977; New York, 1980).   London, Heinemann, 1978.
A Right Christmas Caper (for children; produced London, 1977).   London, French–Heinemann, 1978.
Worzel Gummidge (for children), with Keith Waterhouse, music by Denis King, adaptation of stories by Barbara Euphan Todd (produced Birmingham, 1980; London, 1981).   London, French, 1984.
The Wind in the Willows, music by Denis King, adaptation of the story by Kenneth Grahame (produced Plymouth, 1984; London, 1985).
Treasure Island, music by Denis King, adaptation of the novel by Robert Louis Stevenson (produced Birmingham, 1984).
Lost Empires, with Keith Waterhouse, music by Denis King, adaptation of the novel by J.B. Priestley (produced Darlington, County Durham, 1985).
The Water Babies, adaptation of the novel by Charles Kingsley (produced Oxford, 1987).

Screenplays: *The Long and the Short and the Tall* (*Jungle Fighters*), with Wolf Mankowitz, 1961; with Keith Waterhouse—*Whistle Down the Wind*, 1961; *The Valiant*, 1962; *A Kind of Loving*, 1963; *Billy Liar*, 1963; *West Eleven*, 1963; *Man in the Middle*, 1963; *Pretty Polly* (*A Matter of Innocence*), 1967; *Lock Up Your Daughters*, 1969.

Radio Plays: *Final at Furnell*, 1954; *The Nightingale*, 1954; *Furore at Furnell*, 1955; *Frenzy at Furnell*, 1955; *Friendly at Furnell*, 1955; *Fluster at Furnell*, 1955; *Poet and Pheasant*, with Lewis Jones, 1955; *One Man Absent*, 1955; *A Run for the Money*, 1956; *Afternoon for Antigone*, 1956; *The Long Years*, 1956; *Any Dark Morning*, 1956; *Feodor's Bride*, 1956; *One Man Returns*, 1956; *A Ride on the Donkeys*, 1957; *The Calverdon Road Job*, 1957; *The Gentle Knight*, 1957; *Harvest the Sea*, 1957; *Monday at Seven*, 1957; *Annual Outing*, 1958; *The Larford Lad*, 1958; *The Case of Walter Grimshaw*, with Leslie Halward, 1958.

Television Plays: *Air Mail from Cyprus*, 1958; *Return to the Sea*, 1960; *On the Night of the Murder*, 1962; *The Ticket*, 1969; *The Railwayman's New Clothes*, 1971; *The Villa Maroc*, 1972; *They Don't All Open Men's Boutiques*, 1972; *Song at Twilight*, 1973; *Friendly Encounter*, 1974; *The Piano-Smashers of the Golden Sun*, 1974; *Illegal Approach*, 1974; *Midgley*, 1975; *Match-Fit*, from a story by Brian Glanville, 1976; *A Flash of Inspiration*, 1976; *Secret Army* series, 1977; *The Fuzz* series, 1977; *Hazell Gets the Boot* (*Hazell* series), 1979; *Danedyke Mystery*, from a work by Stephen Chance, 1979; *National Pelmet*, 1980; *Minder* series, 1980–86; *Christmas Spirits*, 1981; *Stan's Last Game*, 1983; *The Road to 1984*, 1984; *The Bright Side* series, 1985; *The Return of the Antelope*, and *The Antelope Christmas Special*, from his own stories, 1986; with Keith Waterhouse—*Happy Moorings*, 1963; *How Many Angels*, 1964; *Inside George Webley* series, 1968; *Queenie's Castle* series, 1970; *Budgie* series, 1971–72; *The Upper Crusts* series, 1973; *Three's Company* series, 1973; *By Endeavour Alone*, 1973; *Briefer Encounter*, 1977; *Public Lives*, 1977; *Worzel Gummidge* series, from stories by Barbara Euphan Todd, 1979; *The Reluctant Dragon* (animated), 1988.

Novel

The Fuzz (novelization of TV series). London, Coronet, 1977.

Other

They Found the World (for children), with I.O. Evans. London and New York, Warne, 1960.
The Royal Astrologer: Adventures of Father Mole-Cricket or the Malayan Legends (for children). London, Heinemann, 1960; New York, Coward McCann, 1962.
The A to Z of Soccer, with Michael Parkinson. London, Pelham, 1970.
The A to Z of Television, with Bob Monkhouse. London, Pelham, 1971.
My Sporting Life. London, Luscombe, 1975.
The Incredible Kidnapping (for children). London, Heinemann, 1975.
The Summer of the Dinosaur (for children). London, Bodley Head, 1977.
The Television Adventures [and *More Television Adventures*] *of Worzel Gummidge* (for children), with Keith Waterhouse. London, Penguin, 2 vols., 1979; complete edition, as *Worzel Gummidge's Television Adventures*, London, Kestrel, 1981.

Worzel Gummidge at the Fair (for children), with Keith Waterhouse. London, Penguin, 1980.
Worzel Gummidge Goes to the Seaside (for children), with Keith Waterhouse. London, Penguin, 1980.
The Trials of Worzel Gummidge (for children), with Keith Waterhouse. London, Penguin, 1980.
Worzel's Birthday (for children), with Keith Waterhouse. London, Penguin, 1981.
New Television Adventures of Worzel Gummidge and Aunt Sally (for children), with Keith Waterhouse. London, Sparrow, 1981.
The Last Vampire (for children). London, Bodley Head, 1982.
The Irish Adventures of Worzel Gummidge (for children), with Keith Waterhouse. London, Severn House, 1984.
The Inflatable Shop (for children). London, Bodley Head, 1984.
Dragon Days (for children). London, Bodley Head, 1985.
The Return of the Antelope (for children). London, Bodley Head, 1985.
The Antelope Company Ashore [*At Large*] (for children). London, Bodley Head, 2 vols. 1986–87.
Worzel Gummidge Down Under (for children), with Keith Waterhouse. London, Collins, 1987.
Spooky Rhymes (for children). London, Hamlyn, 1987.
Henry Hollins and the Dinosaur (for children). London, Bodley Head, 1988.
Doctor Jekyll and Mr. Hollins (for children). London, Bodley Head, 1988.
The Vampire's Holiday (for children). London, Bodley Head, 1992.
The Vampire's Revenge (for children). London, Bodley Head, 1993.

Editor, with Keith Waterhouse, *Writer's Theatre*. London, Heinemann, 1967.
Editor, with Michael Parkinson, *Football Report: An Anthology of Soccer*. London, Pelham, 1973.
Editor, with Michael Parkinson, *Football Classified: An Anthology of Soccer*. London, Luscombe, 1975.
Editor, with Michael Parkinson, *Football Final*. London, Pelham, 1975.

* * *

Willis Hall and Keith Waterhouse have written so many stage plays and television and film scripts over nearly 30 years that critics are wont to regard them as the stand-by professionals of British theatre. Their technical skill has never been doubted—but their artistry and originality often have. They were both born in Leeds in 1929 and have therefore shared a similar Yorkshire background. Both were successful individually before their long-standing collaboration began. Hall's *The Long and the Short and the Tall* was premiered by the Oxford Theatre Group in 1958: and was described by Kenneth Tynan as "the most moving production of the [Edinburgh] festival." Waterhouse's novel, *Billy Liar*, was well received in 1957. The stage version of *Billy Liar* was their first joint effort, and its success in London (where it helped to establish the names of the two actors who played the title role, Albert Finney and Tom Courtenay) encouraged them to continue in the vein of "purely naturalistic provincial working-class comedy," to quote T. C. Worsley's description. *Celebration*, *All Things Bright and Beautiful*, and *Come Laughing Home*, together with the one-act plays *The Sponge Room* and *Squat Betty*, allowed critics to regard them as the true successors of Stanley Houghton and Harold Brighouse:

and this convenient label stuck to their work, until 1965, when their farce, *Say Who You Are*, set in Kensington and concerning a middle-class *ménage à quatre*, proved an unexpected success of the season. This lively and (in some respects) ambitious sexual comedy demonstrated that their talents were not confined to one style of humour nor their sense of place to the North of England. When this barrier of mild prejudice was broken, it was remembered that Hall was responsible for perhaps the best British adaptation of a contemporary French comedy, Billetdoux's *Chin-Chin* (1960), that both had contributed widely to revues and satirical programmes (such as the BBC's *That Was the Week That Was*) and had written modern versions of Greek tragedies (such as Hall's *Afternoon for Antigone*). Their range as writers and their sophistication obviously extended beyond the narrow limits which brought them their reputations.

Nor is technical skill so common a quality among contemporary dramatists that it can be dismissed as unimportant. Hall and Waterhouse have the merits of good professionals. When they write satirically, their polemic is sharp, witty, and to the point. When they write naturalistically—whether about a provincial town in Yorkshire, a seaside amusement arcade, the war in Malaya, or Kensington—they take the trouble to know the surroundings in detail: and this groundwork enables them to discover possibilities which other writers overlook. *Celebration*, for example, presents two contrasting family events—a marriage and a funeral set in a working-class suburb of a Yorkshire town. There is no main story to hold the episodes together, nor a theme, nor even a clearly identifiable climax. But the play triumphs because the distinctive flavour of each "celebration" is captured and because the 15 main characters are each so well drawn. The slender threads of continuity which bind the episodes together reveal a sensitive insight into the nature of the society. The first act is about the wedding preparations in the backroom of a pub: Rhoda and Edgar Lucas are determined to do well by their daughter, Christine, who is marrying Bernard Fuller. But Rhoda has decided to economize by not employing Whittaker's, the firm in the town who specialize in weddings. Her efforts to ensure that the wedding breakfast doesn't let her daughter down are helped and hindered by the other members of the family: but despite the tattiness of the scene, the collapsible tables, the grease-proof paper and the dirty cups, the audience eventually is drawn to see the glowing pride and family self-importance which surround the event. Christine and Bernard survey the transformed room at the end of the act: and their contented happiness justifies the efforts. The second act is about the funeral of Arthur Broadbent, Rhoda's great-uncle and the best known eccentric of the family, who has been living in sin for years with May Beckett. The funeral is over and the pieties continue in the living room of the Lucas's house. But the family doesn't wish to acknowledge May Beckett, until she invades the house both physically (since they try to prevent her from coming) and emotionally, by expressing a grief which the conventional sentiments of the family cannot match. May's nostalgic tribute to her lost lover —so carefully prepared for in the script and emerging with an easy naturalness—is one of the truly outstanding moments of postwar British naturalistic drama: to rank with Beatie's speech at the end of Wesker's *Roots*.

This assured handling of naturalistic details is a feature of all their best plays. What other writers would have used the pub and the telephone box as so important a part of a sex comedy, replacing the more familiar stage props of a settee and a verandah? Or caught the significance of a back yard for a lonely introvert like Billy Liar? Or surrounded the pregnant unmarried girl, Vera Fawcett, in *Come Laughing Home*, with

a family whose stultifying complacency offered a convincing example of the waste land from which she is trying unsuccessfully to escape? With this unusual skill in capturing an exact milieu, Hall and Waterhouse are also adept at writing those single outstanding roles which actors love to play. The part of Private Bamforth in *The Long and the Short and the Tall* gave Peter O'Toole his first opportunity—which he seized with relish: Hayley Mills was "discovered" in their film, *Whistle Down the Wind*, with the then underrated actor, Alan Bates. Hall and Waterhouse were once criticized for writing "angry young man" parts without providing the psychological insight or rhetoric of Osborne's Jimmy Porter. John Russell Taylor wrote that

> the central characters, Bamforth and Fentrill [in *Last Day in Dreamland*], are almost identical: the hectoring angry young man who knows it all and stands for most of the time in the centre of the stage, aquiver as a rule (whether the situation warrants it or not) with almost hysterical intensity, berating the other characters, who in each case, rather mysteriously, accept him as a natural leader and the life and soul of the party. The indebtedness to *Look Back in Anger* is unmistakable. . . .

This description may apply to Fentrill, whose anger at the rundown amusement arcade seems somewhat strained since he's not forced to stay there: less so to Bamforth, whose bitterness derives from claustrophobic jungle war: and scarcely at all to the other main characters of their plays. The distinctive strength of their protagonists lies not in their volubility nor their character complexities, but in their reactions to unsympathetic surroundings. Vera Fawcett is not a stock rebel: Billy Liar doesn't rebel at all—he's too satisfied with fantasies about escape. Unlike John Osborne, Hall and Waterhouse rarely offer "mouthpiece" characters, people whose insight and rhetoric about their own problems justify their presence on the stage. Their central characters emerge from their surroundings: the environment shapes the nature of their rebellion. Their dilemmas are a typical part of their societies: and are not superimposed upon their families as a consequence of too much intelligence or education.

A fairer criticism of their work might run along these lines: while their dialogue is always lively and accurate, it rarely contains flashes of intuition. Much of the humour of *Celebration*, *Billy Liar*, and *Say Who You Are* depends upon carefully calculated repetition. The characters are sometimes given verbal catch-phrases—Eric Fawcett teases his son Brian endlessly for ordering "whisky and Scotch" in a pub—but more frequently are given habits which become irritating after a time. Eric Fawcett's life centres around making model boats (in *Come Laughing Home*); Edgar continually chides Rhoda for not arranging the wedding through Whittaker's, while his son Jack greets every newcomer with the same question, "Lend us a quid?" Often the reiteration makes a valid dramatic point—if only to illustrate the poverty of the relationships: but sometimes it seems just an easy way of establishing a person, by constantly reminding the audience of an obsession. Hall and Waterhouse often fail to reveal any deeper cause behind the nagging habit: and this lack of depth prevents the characters from seeming sympathetic. In *Say Who You Are* the two men, David and Stuart, are both self-opinionated male chauvinists: credible enough but rather uninteresting because they have so little self-knowledge. Valerie, who invents a marriage so that she can have an affair without getting too involved, is a more engaging creation— but she too seems superficial when we learn that her objections to marriage rest on a dislike of "togetherness"— "toothbrushes nestling side by side"—and on little else.

Sometimes when Hall and Waterhouse try to give an added dimension to their characters, the effect seems strained: when Vera Fawcett resigns herself to an arid future with her family from whom she cannot escape, she says "I wanted to reach out for something, but I couldn't reach far enough. It's something you need—for living—that I haven't got. I haven't really looked, but I wanted to, I was going to." This statement of her defeat doesn't dramatically match or rise to the opportunity which the play provides for her.

This superficiality has often been explained as the reverse side of the authors' facility; writers who produce so many scripts can't be expected to be profound as well. But there may be another reason. Hall and Waterhouse share a remarkable sense of form and timing, which partly accounts for the success of *Say Who You Are* and *Celebration*. David and Sarah go to two different telephones at the same time, intending to ring each other up—with the result that the numbers are always engaged and they jump to the wrong conclusion. The scenes are based on a clever use of parallels and counterpoint: but this also depends on the characters behaving with a mechanical predictability. We know what they're really going to do, and the fun comes from seeing their stock reactions fail to achieve the expected results. The formalism of the scripts, in short, sometimes prevents the characters from having an independent life: and this is the result, not so much of technical facility, as of an over-zealous care in the construction which shortsightedly ignores other possibilities. Despite these limitations, however, Hall and Waterhouse have an expertise which few other writers of the new wave of British drama can match and which accounts for the continuing popularity of their best plays.

—John Elsom

HALLIWELL, David (William). British. Born in Brighouse, Yorkshire, 31 July 1936. Educated at Bailiff Bridge Elementary School; Victoria Central Secondary Modern School, Rastrick; Hipperholme Grammar School; Huddersfield College of Art, Yorkshire, 1953–59; Royal Academy of Dramatic Art, London, diploma 1961. Founder, with Mike Leigh, Dramagraph production company, London, 1965; director and committee member, Quipu group, London, 1966–76; visiting fellow, Reading University, 1969–70; resident dramatist, Royal Court Theatre, London 1976–77, and Hampstead Theatre, London, 1978–79. Co-director, Vardo Productions Ltd. Since 1991 director, playwriting workshops, The Actor's Centre, London. Recipient: *Evening Standard* award, 1967; John Whiting award, 1978. Fellow, Royal Society of Literature. Address: 8 Crawborough Villas, Charlbury, Oxford OX7 3TS, England.

PUBLICATIONS

Plays

Little Malcolm and His Struggle Against the Eunuchs (produced London, 1965). London, French, 1966; as *Hail Scrawdyke!* (produced New York, 1966), New York, Grove Press, 1967.
A Who's Who of Flapland (broadcast 1967; produced London, 1969). Included in *A Who's Who of Flapland and Other Plays*, 1971.
The Experiment, with David Calderisi (also co-director: produced London and New York, 1967).
A Discussion (produced Falmouth, 1969). Included in *A Who's Who of Flapland and Other Plays*, 1971.
K. D. Dufford Hears K. D. Dufford Ask K. D. Dufford How K. D. Dufford'll Make K. D. Dufford (produced London, 1969). London, Faber, 1970.
Muck from Three Angles (produced Edinburgh and London, 1970). Included in *A Who's Who of Flapland and Other Plays*, 1971.
The Girl Who Didn't Like Answers (produced London, 1971).
A Last Belch for the Great Auk (produced London, 1971).
A Who's Who of Flapland and Other Plays. London, Faber, 1971.
An Amour, and A Feast (produced London, 1971).
Bleats from a Brighouse Pleasureground (broadcast 1972; produced London, 1972).
Janitress Thrilled by Prehensile Penis (also director: produced London, 1972).
An Altercation (also director: produced London, 1973).
The Freckled Bum (also director: produced London, 1974).
Minyip (also director: produced London, 1974).
Progs (also director: produced London, 1975).
A Process of Elimination (also director: produced London, 1975).
Meriel the Ghost Girl (televised 1976; also director: produced London, 1982). Published in *The Mind Beyond*, London, Penguin, 1976.
Prejudice (also director: produced Sheffield, 1978; as *Creatures of Another Kind*, produced London, 1981).
The House (produced London, 1979). London, Eyre Methuen, 1979.
A Rite Kwik Metal Tata (produced Sheffield and London, 1979).
Was It Her? (broadcast 1980; also director: produced London, 1982).
A Tomato Who Grew into a Mushroom (produced on Oxfordshire tour, 1987).

Radio Plays: *A Who's Who of Flapland*, 1967; *Bleats from a Brighouse Pleasureground*, 1972; *Was It Her?*, 1980; *Spongehenge*, 1982; *Grandad's Place*, 1984; *Shares of the Pudding*, 1985; *Do It Yourself*, 1986; *Bedsprings*, 1989; *Parts*, 1989; *There's a Car Park in Witherton*, 1992; *Crossed Lines*, 1992.

Television Plays: *A Plastic Mac in Winter*, 1963; *Cock, Hen and Courting Pit*, 1966; *Triptych of Bathroom Users*, 1972; *Blur and Blank via Checkheaton*, 1972; *Steps Back*, 1973; *Daft Mam Blues*, 1975; *Pigmented Patter*, 1976, and *Tree Women of Jagden Crag*, 1978 (*Crown Court* series); *Meriel the Ghost Girl* (*The Mind Beyond* series), 1976; *There's a Car Park in Witherton*, 1982; *Speculating about Orwell*, 1983; *Arrangements*, 1985; *Doctor Who* series (2 episodes), 1985; *The Bill* (1 episode), 1989; *Bonds*, 1990.

*

Critical Study: article in *The Gothic Impulse In Contemporary Drama* by Mary Beth Inverso, Ann Arbor, Michigan, UMI Research Press, 1990.

Theatrical Activities:
Director: **Plays**—Quipu group: many of his own plays, and *The Dumb Waiter* by Harold Pinter, *Keep Out, Love in*

Progress by Walter Hall, *The Stronger* by Strindberg, and *A Village Wooing* by Shaw, 1966; *The Experiment* (co-director, with David Calderisi), London and New York, 1967; *A Day with My Sister* by Stephen Poliakoff, Edinburgh, 1971; *The Hundred Watt Bulb* by George Thatcher, *I Am Real and So Are You*, *A Visit from the Family*, and *Crewe Station at 2 A.M.* by Tony Connor, 1972; *The Only Way Out* by George Thatcher, 1973; *We Are What We Eat* by Frank Dux, *The Knowall* by Alan C. Taylor, and *The Quipu Anywhere Show* (co-director, with Gavin Eley), London, 1973; *The Last of the Feinsteins* by Tony Connor, London, 1975; *Paint* by Peter Godfrey, London, 1977; *Lovers* by Brian Friel, Kingston, Surrey, 1978; *Jelly Babies* by Glenn Young, London, 1978.

Actor: **Plays**—Vincentio in *The Taming of the Shrew* and Seyton in *Macbeth*, Nottingham, 1962; Hortensio in *The Taming of the Shrew*, Leicester, 1962; Sydney Spooner in *Worm's Eye View* by R.F. Delderfield, Colchester, 1962; General Madigan in *O'Flaherty, V.C.* by Shaw, and Jim Curry in *The Rainmaker* by N. Richard Nash, Stoke-on-Trent, 1962; Hero in *The Rehearsal* by Anouilh, Pozzo in *Waiting for Godot* by Beckett, and The Common Man in *A Man for All Seasons* by Robert Bolt, Stoke-on-Trent, 1963; Scrawdyke in *Little Malcolm and His Struggle Against the Eunuchs*, London, 1965; Jackson McIver in *The Experiment*, London, 1967; Policeman in *An Altercation*, London, 1973; Botard in *Rhinoceros* by Ionesco, London, 1974; Frankie in *Birdbath* by Leonard Melfi, Bristol, 1975. **Films**—*Defence of the Realm*, 1986; *Mona Lisa*, 1986. **Radio**—Landlord in *Spongehenge*, 1982; Interrogator in *Bedsprings*, 1989; Hitler in *The Eagle Has Landed*, 1989, and *The Eagle Has Flown*, 1992, by Jack Higgins; Prison Officer in *Crossed Lines*, 1992.

David Halliwell comments:

Since the last edition of this book I have arrived at the essence of what I want to do as a dramatist. I have developed the means of expressing the conflicts and harmonies between the inner and outer parts of characters that I have been selecting and moving towards from the beginning of my dramatic career. Means organically centred on actors and performances which, although they can be adapted to any medium, require, in essence, no mechanical or electronic equipment.

*   *   *

David Halliwell's dramatic territory is Flapland; his perennial subject, the Hitler syndrome; the motive force of his central characters, that childish outburst of King Lear's: "I will do such things,/What they are, yet I know not, but they shall be/The terrors of the earth." Malcolm Scrawdyke, the hero of *Little Malcolm and His Struggle Against the Eunuchs*, models himself explicitly on the early Hitler, except that he wears a Russian anarchist's greatcoat in place of Hitler's raincoat. Expelled from art school, Scrawdyke enlists three variously inadequate siblings into his Party of Dynamic Erection, plans a ludicrous revenge (which never gets beyond the fantasy stage) on the man who expelled him, and succeeds only in two petty, but nonetheless unpleasant, acts of terror: the "trial" of his most articulate and independent sibling, and the beating-up of a girl who has taunted him with sexual cowardice. Scrawdyke is only a phantom Hitler, his rabble-rousing speeches are confined to the inside of his Huddersfield garret and his grasp of reality so tenuous as to constitute little danger even to his specific enemies, let alone the community at large. But the hero of Halliwell's other full-length play, *K. D. Dufford Hears K. D. Dufford Ask K. D. Dufford How K. D. Dufford'll Make K. D. Dufford*, who

actually wears a raincoat, sets his sights lower than Scrawdyke: his recipe for instant notoriety is to murder a child and he is entirely successful. Halliwell makes an ambitious attempt in this play not simply to suggest the interplay between fantasy and reality, but actually to display it, chapter and verse, on the stage, with several different versions of each scene—the real event compared with the event as imagined to his own advantage by K. D. Dufford and by each of the other main characters.

Halliwell explores the possibilities and limitations of this device in a series of short plays—*Muck from Three Angles*, *A Last Belch for the Great Auk*, *Bleats from a Brighouse Pleasureground*, and *Janitress Thrilled by Prehensile Penis*. The effect is often clumsy and ultimately superfluous since the shades of fantasy and reality pursue one another with such unerring clarity through his virtuoso monologues, that an audience must grow restive at being told by means of explicit technical devices what it has already grasped implicitly through intense dramatic sympathy.

For, however faceless, talentless, witless, loveless, lacking in courage and moral compunction these characters may be, Halliwell's comic view of them makes them irresistibly sympathetic. Something similar happens in the plays of Halliwell's contemporary Joe Orton, as well as in those of the master from whom they both learnt, Samuel Beckett. The fact that these characters would be, if met in real life, virtually sub-human, certainly pitiable or despicable to an extreme degree, is beside the point. In Halliwell's, as in Orton's and Beckett's plays, they are exaggerated dramatic representations of universal human weaknesses; and Halliwell has found and shown that, in this age of overpopulation and social disorientation, we are peculiarly vulnerable to paranoia. In *The Experiment*, partly devised by himself, partly improvised by the actors, Halliwell acted an avant-garde theatrical director "of international repute" rehearsing his company in "a modern epic translated from the Icelandic entitled *The Assassination of President Garfield*." The efforts of this director to drive his cast towards the nadir of art, to discover in the purposeless murder of a forgotten American politician deeper and deeper levels of insignificance, satirized the gullibility of audiences as much as the inflated self-admiration of certain members of the theatrical profession, but there were above all a direct demonstration of Halliwell's own special subject: the banal striving to be the unique, the insignificant the significant, the squalid reality the dream of power.

In his lightest and most charming play, *A Who's Who of Flapland*, originally written for radio but successfully translated to lunch-time theatre, Halliwell closes the circle by confronting one paranoiac with another, his equal if not his master at the gambits and routines of Flapland. Here, as in *Little Malcolm*, Halliwell relies entirely on his mastery of dramatic speech, using his native industrial Yorkshire idiom as a precision instrument to trace complex patterns of aggression, alarm, subterfuge, humiliation, triumph, surrender. The more recent plays *A Rite Kwik Metal Tata*, *The House*, and *Prejudice*, are all what one might call "polyphonic" developments of this technique, adding, for example, a cockney girl and an upper-class MP to the Yorkshire characters in *Metal Tata* and a Bradford Pakistani and an exiled Zulu to those in *Prejudice*. *The House*, set in a country mansion requisitioned as a hospital during World War I, is the least successful, since Halliwell's command of regional idioms is not matched by any sense of period, and the action is too desultory. But in *Prejudice* and *Metal Tata* the plots are strong enough to allow him to turn his characters all round and inside out in relation to each other without losing the momentum of the play. Of course this is only what the best playwrights have always done, but good methods decay into tired conventions and it is clear that Halliwell's struggle has been to remove the dead wood and reconstitute traditional polyphonic drama in the fresh terms of his own ideas and idiosyncrasies.

—John Spurling

———

HAMPTON, Christopher (James). British. Born in Fayal, the Azores, 26 January 1946. Educated at schools in Aden and Alexandria, Egypt; Lancing College, Sussex, 1959–63; New College, Oxford, 1964–68, B.A. in modern languages (French and German) 1968, M.A. Married Laura Margaret de Holesch in 1971; two daughters. Resident dramatist, Royal Court Theatre, London, 1968–70. Recipient: *Plays and Players* award, 1970, 1973, 1985; *Evening Standard* award, 1970, 1984, 1986; Los Angeles Drama Critics Circle award, 1974, 1989; Olivier award, 1986; New York Drama Critics Circle award, 1987; BAFTA award for television, 1987, for screenplay, 1990; Writers Guild of America award, 1989; Prix Italia, 1989; Academy award, 1989. Fellow, 1976, and since 1984 council member, Royal Society of Literature. Agent: Casarotto Ramsay Ltd., National House, 60–66 Wardour Street, London W1V 3HP. Address: 2 Kensington Park Gardens, London W.11, England.

PUBLICATIONS

Plays

When Did You Last See My Mother? (produced Oxford and London, 1966; New York, 1967). London, Faber, and New York, Grove Press, 1967.
Marya, adaptation of a play by Isaak Babel, translated by Michael Glenny and Harold Shukman (produced London, 1967). Published in *Plays of the Year 35*, London, Elek, 1969.
Total Eclipse (produced London, 1968; Washington, D.C., 1972; New York, 1974). London, Faber, 1969; New York, French, 1972; revised version (produced London, 1981), Faber, 1981.
Uncle Vanya, adaptation of a play by Chekhov, translated by Nina Froud (produced London, 1970). Published in *Plays of the Year 39*, London, Elek, 1971.
The Philanthropist: A Bourgeois Comedy (produced London, 1970; New York, 1971). London, Faber, 1970; New York, French, 1971; revised version, Faber, 1985.
Hedda Gabler, adaptation of a play by Ibsen (produced Stratford, Ontario, 1970; New York, 1971; London, 1984). New York, French, 1971; with *A Doll's House*, London, Faber, 1989.
A Doll's House, adaptation of a play by Ibsen (produced New York, 1971; London, 1973). New York, French, 1972; with *Hedda Gabler*, London, Faber, 1989.
Don Juan, adaptation of a play by Molière (broadcast 1972; produced Bristol, 1972; Chicago, 1977). London, Faber, 1974.
Savages (produced London, 1973; Los Angeles, 1974; New York, 1977). London, Faber, 1974; revised version, London, French, 1976.

Treats (produced London, 1976; New York, 1977; revised version produced London, 1988). London, Faber, 1976.
Signed and Sealed, adaptation of a play by Georges Feydeau and Maurice Desvallières (produced London, 1976).
Able's Will (televised 1977). London, Faber, 1979.
Tales from the Vienna Woods, adaptation of a play by Ödön von Horváth (produced London, 1977; New Haven, Connecticut, 1978). London, Faber, 1977.
Ghosts, adaptation of a play by Ibsen (produced on tour, 1978). London, French, 1983.
Don Juan Comes Back from the War, adaptation of a play by Ödön von Horváth (produced London, 1978; New York, 1979). London, Faber, 1978.
The Wild Duck, adaptation of a play by Ibsen (produced London, 1979). London, Faber, 1980; New York, French, 1981.
Geschichten aus dem Wiener Wald (screenplay), with Maximilian Schell. Frankfurt, Suhrkamp, 1979.
After Mercer, based on works by David Mercer (produced London, 1980).
The Prague Trial, adaptation of a work by Patrice Chéreau and Ariane Mnouchkine (produced Paris, 1980).
A Night of the Day of the Imprisoned Writer, with Ronald Harwood (produced London, 1981).
The Portage to San Cristobal of A.H., adaptation of the novel by George Steiner (produced London and Hartford, Connecticut, 1982). London, Faber, 1983.
Tales from Hollywood (produced Los Angeles, 1982; London, 1983). London, Faber, 1983.
Tartuffe; or, The Impostor, adaptation of the play by Molière (produced London, 1983). London, Faber, 1984.
Les Liaisons Dangereuses, adaptation of the novel by Choderlos de Laclos (produced Stratford-on-Avon, 1985; London, 1986; New York, 1987). London, Faber, 1985.
The Ginger Tree, adaptation of the novel by Oswald Wynd (televized 1989). London, Faber, 1989.
Faith, Hope, and Charity, adaptation of a play by Ödön von Horváth (produced London, 1989). London, Faber, 1989.
Dangerous Liaisons: The Film. London, Faber, 1989.
White Chameleon (produced London, 1991). London, Faber, 1991.
The Philanthropist and Other Plays (includes *Treats*, *Total Eclipse*). London, Faber, 1991.

Screenplays: *A Doll's House*, 1973; *Geschichten aus dem Wiener Wald* (*Tales from the Vienna Woods*), with Maximilian Schell, 1981; *Beyond the Limit* (*The Honorary Consul*), 1983; *The Good Father*, 1986; *Dangerous Liaisons*, 1989.

Radio Plays: *2 Children Free to Wander* (documentary), 1969; *Don Juan*, 1972; *The Prague Trial 79*, from a work by Patrice Chéreau and Ariane Mnouchkine, 1980.

Television Plays: *Able's Will*, 1977; *The History Man*, from the novel by Malcolm Bradbury, 1981; *Hotel du Lac*, from the novel by Anita Brookner, 1986; *The Ginger Tree*, adaptation of the novel by Oswald Wynd, 1989.

*

Critical Studies: *Theatre Quarterly 12* (London), October–December 1973; *Christopher Hampton: A Casebook*, edited by Robert Gross, New York, Garland, 1990.

Theatrical Activities:
Actor: **Play**—role in *When Did You Last See My Mother?*, Oxford, 1966.

* * *

Les Liaisons Dangereuses coyly preserves the original French title of an epistolary novel adroitly dramatized by Christopher Hampton—to applause on Broadway, in the West End, and on the screen. The title—French or English—aptly summarizes Hampton's own theatrical focus. Although Hampton is not an overtly political playwright, he suggests that one of the dangers to the self-absorbed partners of their liaison is their very indifference to politics.

At age 18, while still an Oxford undergraduate (reading French and German) Hampton composed his first play, *When Did You Last See My Mother?* It received a bare-boards Sunday night production at the Royal Court Theatre and was immediately snapped up for the West End. Hampton's cruel and articulate protagonist adheres to the Angry tradition established by John Osborne, but all three of Hampton's characters are involved in dangerous liaisons—a love-hate ménage of teenage boys, a brief affair between one of the boys and the mother of the other. Unlike Broadway's *Tea and Sympathy*, the latter emotion is absent from Hampton's stage. In six swift, pitiless scenes, the teenage lovers circle back to their ménage—after the automobile accident in which the self-reproachful mother is killed.

In *Total Eclipse* the cruelly brilliant teenager is the French poet Arthur Rimbaud, who formed a dangerous liaison with Paul Verlaine, a married poet nearly twice his age. Hampton steeped himself in scholarly sources about their two-year relationship, in order to dramatize its tempestuous quality, again in six scenes. This time it is Verlaine who pivots from wife to lover, again and again, until Mme. Verlaine divorces him. Lies, drink, and drugs exacerbate the homosexual liaison, which erupts twice into violence: Rimbaud coolly stabs Verlaine's hands, and on another occasion Verlaine accidentally shoots Rimbaud in the hand—and is imprisoned for two years. Hampton's final scene bears witness to his title, since both poetic talents suffer total eclipse; a derelict Verlaine is visited by the sister of the dead Rimbaud, and he fantasizes an idyllic liaison.

In spite of Hampton's two productions by the age of 21, he toyed with the idea of graduate study after taking his degree in 1968, whereupon Bill Gaskill created for him the position of resident dramatist at the Royal Court, with a slender income and no duties. Hampton proceeded to work simultaneously on translations, adaptations, and his own *The Philanthropist*, conceived as a rebuttal to Molière's *Le Misanthrope*. As the latter is an aristocratic comedy in rhyme, Hampton's play is a bourgeois comedy in prose. Since the protagonist Philip is a philologist as well as philanthropist, Hampton has marked him thrice as a lover (the translation of philo). True to Hampton's focus, Philip involves himself in dangerous liaisons—with the woman he wants to marry and with a woman who does not attract him. Spurned by both, he starts a wooing letter to still a third woman. By the end of the play, all love rejected, Philip reaches into a drawer for a gun, but when he pulls the trigger, a flame shoots out to light his cigarette. His will be a slower death, with sophisticated London as an analogue of the desert island to which Molière's misanthrope resolved to flee.

Incisive and obliquely moral about the worlds of his experience, Hampton reaches out globally in *Savages*. Triggered by the genocide of Brazilian Indians, *Savages* indicts cultured Europeans and radical South Americans for their complicity in the systematic decimation of the natives in order to acquire their land. Painting on a large canvas, Hampton parallels the public tragedy with a private one. A British Embassy official and minor poet, significantly named West, is taken hostage by Brazilian radicals who hope to trade him for their imprisoned colleagues. As the confinement of West stretches on, Hampton shows us the past in flashback—Embassy dinners, an anthropologist's distress, a pious and callous American mission, mercenaries who kill wholesale, preparations for the ceremonial gathering of Indian tribes, West's poems based on Indian legends. Then abruptly, the two plots coalesce in disaster. A bourgeois radical proves his revolutionary fervor by shooting West. A light plane bombs the Indians at their ceremony, and the pilot descends to shoot survivors. But the pilot burns all trace of the massacre, whereas West, dead, becomes a hero of the media.

Hampton retreated to another lover's triangle in *Treats*. A private term for sexual favors, the title points to the desires of two different men for Ann, married to the psychologically sadistic Dave, and intermittently living with the flaccid Patrick. When the play ends, Ann has replaced Patrick with Dave, and the sado-masochistic merry-go-round will presumably continue.

While producing these plays, Hampton worked on an unusually wide range of translations—Ibsen, Chekhov, Molière, and the lesser-known Austrian playwright Ödön von Horváth, who fired his imagination. Fleeing to Paris after the *Anschluss*, Horváth was killed at the age of 37 when a freak storm felled a tree under which he had taken shelter. In *Tales from Hollywood* Hampton invents a life for Horváth among the anti-Nazi Central European refugees in Hollywood. Mixing both easily and uneasily with the Mann family, Brecht, and others, Horváth is unable to toe any party line, as he is unable to fulfill any woman's needs. Unlike earlier Hampton heroes, Horváth is too humane and compassionate for dangerous liaisons. He withdraws from his putative afterlife, and is killed instantly by the falling tree, as recorded in history.

White Chameleon is a new departure for Hampton, since it is rooted in his own life. Set in Alexandria, Egypt, from 1952 to 1956, the play traces the effect on an English family of Egyptian social conflict. The protagonist Christopher is split in two—a boy of Hampton's own age at that time, and an adult looking back in memory. In *White Chameleon* a liaison of sympathy between young Christopher and the family servant Ibrahim proves ultimately dangerous to the latter. Little people are devoured by cataclysmic events.

Hampton is a playwright in the old English sense of the word "wright"—a craftsman who hones his tools even as he moulds increasingly large structures. As witty as his contemporaries, Hampton is more serious than most of them in his incisive dramas of cruelties of our private and public lives.

—Ruby Cohn

HANLEY, James. British. 1901–1985.
See 3rd edition, 1982.

HANLEY, William. American. Born in Lorain, Ohio, 22 October 1931. Educated at Cornell University, Ithaca, New York, 1950–51; American Academy of Dramatic Arts, New York, 1954–55. Served in the United States Army, 1952–54. Married 1) Shelley Post in 1956 (divorced 1961); 2) Patricia Stanley in 1962 (divorced 1978); two daughters. Recipient: Vernon Rice award, 1963; Outer Circle award, 1964. Agent: Georges Borchardt Inc., 136 East 57th Street, New York, New York 10022. Address: 179 Ivy Hill Road, Ridgefield, Connecticut 06877, U.S.A.

PUBLICATIONS

Plays

Whisper into My Good Ear (produced New York, 1962; London, 1966). Included in *Mrs. Dally Has a Lover and Other Plays*, 1963.
Mrs. Dally Has a Lover (produced New York, 1962; revised version, produced New York, 1988). Included in *Mrs. Dally Has a Lover and Other Plays*, 1963.
Conversations in the Dark (produced Philadelphia, 1963).
Mrs. Dally Has a Lover and Other Plays. New York, Dial Press, 1963.
Today Is Independence Day (produced Berlin, 1963; New York, 1965). Included in *Mrs. Dally Has a Lover and Other Plays*, 1963.
Slow Dance on the Killing Ground (produced New York, 1964; London, 1991). New York, Random House, 1964.
Flesh and Blood (televised 1968). New York, Random House, 1968.
No Answer, in *Collision Course* (produced New York, 1968). New York, Random House, 1968.

Screenplay: *The Gypsy Moths*, 1969.

Radio Play: *A Country Without Rain*, 1970.

Television Plays: *Flesh and Blood*, 1968; *Testimony of Two Men*, with James and Jennifer Miller, from the novel by Taylor Caldwell, 1977; *Who'll Save Our Children*, from a book by Rachel Maddox, 1978; *The Family Man*, 1979; *Too Far to Go*, from stories by John Updike, 1979; *Father Figure*, 1980; *Moviola: The Scarlett O'Hara War* and *The Silent Lovers*, from the novel by Garson Kanin, 1980; *Little Gloria . . . Happy at Last*, from the book by Barbara Goldsmith, 1982; *Something about Amelia*, 1984; *Celebrity*, 1984.

Novels

Blue Dreams; or, The End of Romance and the Continued Pursuit of Happiness. New York, Delacorte Press, and London, W.H. Allen, 1971.
Mixed Feelings. New York, Doubleday, 1972.
Leaving Mt. Venus. New York, Ballantine, 1977.

*   *   *

With a trio of one-act plays and one full-length drama William Hanley achieved a reputation in American drama which seems to have satisfied him. During a three-year period he made his appearance, created a play—*Slow Dance on the Killing Ground*—which not only reflected relevant contemporary issues but provided three acting vehicles, and disappeared from the New York theatre scene.

In spite of some serious dramaturgical weaknesses in his work Hanley was one of the few American playwrights who infused a certain amount of vitality into American drama of the early 1960's. His one-act plays are somewhat unstructured, talky, two-character plays. They are essentially conversations, but they involve perceptive thought, poetic tenderness, and the problems and feelings of generally believable people. Hanley's major concern is communication, that sometimes impossible connection between two people. Language, therefore, is important to him and his plays occasionally show a too luxuriant use of it, just as these same plays become overly concerned with discussion. Understandably, then, his sense of humanity, which is allied to his feelings for communication, frequently erupts in a distasteful sentimentality. He believes in the optimism which such sentiment suggests, however; and although his characters would seem to stumble around in an unhappy world, they do see something better. It is this vague idea of something better which he once explained as the major thought he wished his audiences for *Slow Dance on the Killing Ground* would take with them. It was a shrewd comment, however, for throughout man's history such points of view have not only been acceptable but ardently desired, especially in the theatre.

Whisper into My Good Ear presented the conversation of two old men who are contemplating suicide but change their minds. One can find a good ear for his problems: friends have value. Hanley's most popular one-act play, *Mrs. Dally Has a Lover*, is a conversation between a middle-aged Mrs. Dally and her 18-year-old lover. Before they part as the curtain falls and their affair ends the difficulty of conversation is dramatized as they are drawn in and out of their respective psychological shells. The sympathy created in this play for Mrs. Dally is further explored in *Today Is Independence Day* where she talks with her husband Sam who almost leaves her but decides to stay. Mrs. Dally also makes decisions about her own attitudes, and, although the ending of the play is sad and essentially unhappy, it is an affirmation of living.

The same comment can be made for *Slow Dance on the Killing Ground*, his only full-length Broadway success. (*Conversations in the Dark*, a discussion of the problems of husband-wife infidelity, closed in Philadelphia.) Act 1 of *Slow Dance* introduces us to three characters. None of the three—a young black genius, a middle-class white girl, a Jew who has denied his heritage and his family—can escape the violence of the world, that killing ground. In Act 2 each is unmasked, and in Act 3 a mock trial shows each one guilty. Although the play suggests that nothing can be done, there is a cohesiveness among the characters, a joint decision toward commitment and responsibility on this "killing ground," which tends to remove the play from sentimental and simply clever melodrama. Instead Hanley's insight into his characters and his obvious theme of contemporary significance have challenged critics to see *Slow Dance* as a quite substantial theatre piece.

—Walter J. Meserve

HANNAN, Chris(topher John). British. Born in Glasgow, 25 January 1958. Educated at St. Aloysius' College, Glasgow, 1969–75; University College, Oxford, 1975–78. Voluntary worker, Simon Community, Glasgow, 1978–80. Recipient: *Time Out* award, 1991; *Plays and Players* award, 1991; Charrington London Fringe award, 1991. Lives in Edinburgh.

Agent: Alan Brodie Representation, 91 Regent Street, London W1R 7TB, England.

PUBLICATIONS

Plays

Purity (produced Edinburgh, 1984).
Klimkov: Life of a Tsarist Agent (produced Edinburgh, 1984).
Elizabeth Gordon Quinn (produced Edinburgh, 1985). London, Hern, 1990.
The Orphans' Comedy (produced Edinburgh, 1986).
Gamblers, with Christopher Rathbone, adaptation of a play by Nikolai Gogol (produced Glasgow, 1987; London, 1992).
The Baby (produced Glasgow, 1990). London, Hern, 1991.
The Evil Doers (produced London, 1990). London, Hern, 1991.
The Pretenders, adaptation of the play by Henrik Ibsen (produced London, 1991).

*

Chris Hannan comments:

I'm attracted to mess; chaos. I read a couple of books about chaos theory, which I enjoyed. I can get quite into the philosophy of science. I suppose it gives me a way to think about form, patterns, order and disorder.

I like characters who believe in things however ridiculous the belief. Elizabeth Gordon Quinn, for example, is a woman who refuses to believe she's poor. To prove to herself that she's someone grand—an individual—she has a piano. Unfortunately this means she can't eat or pay the rent. She's a ridiculous and destructive woman in conflict with her family and community but also sort of heroic.

Elizabeth Gordon Quinn is quite melodramatic. Whatever I write I like the thing to have a heightened quality, a language. I admire language which is mesmeric even when it's nonsense, like in Gogol or Ben Jonson where words dance in front of the characters' eyes like the fires of hell.

I suppose I write about people who are trying to save themselves, in deformed or exotic ways. Like Macu in *The Baby* who confronts Pompey and the entire Roman State singlehandedly in a misplaced attempt to exorcise her private hurts. Or like Sammy and Tracky in *The Evil Doers* who try to save themselves from the chaos in their lives by creating more chaos.

* * *

Chris Hannan's career thus far is already notable for a number of bold and successful variations in genre. His early plays, *Klimkov*, *Elizabeth Gordon Quinn*, and *The Orphans' Comedy*, were all produced at the Traverse Theatre in Edinburgh. Of these it was *Elizabeth Gordon Quinn* that really brought his talent into the limelight. A rich and powerful piece set in a tenement in 1920's Glasgow, it is in some ways reminiscent of other Scottish work of the 1970's and 1980's, much of which has been rooted in passionate socialist convictions. Hannan's play recovers from the past an eloquent voice against historical injustice and oppression. Vivid characterization—especially of the indomitable protagonist—a robust sense of humour, and the precise evocation of period earned Hannan comparisons with Sean O'Casey, and the language of the play continually revealed a daring drive towards high style and burlesque.

The Evil Doers, which was produced at the Bush Theatre in London in 1990, presents itself as a City Comedy, a scathing satire on the pretensions of Glasgow to be European City of Culture. It is also a stunning account of a family desperately trying to stave off fragmentation in the face of alcoholism, debt, and congenital self-delusion. The writing bristles with mordant social observation—comic in the case of the teenage Heavy Metal patter, brutal in the portrayal of a young loan-shark—and contains one of the decade's finest mockeries of the Thatcherite ethic of individual enterprise. Hannan's ear for dialogue, heavily flavoured by Glaswegian slang, pinpoints evasions, blind spots, and emotional tremors with a high-definition precision sometimes equal to David Mamet's. The play deservedly earned Hannan the Most Promising Playwright award from *Plays and Players* and the Charrington Fringe Best Playwright award.

Hannan has come to a wider audience through his version of Ibsen's *The Pretenders*, produced by the RSC, but perhaps his finest, certainly his most ambitious work so far, is *The Baby*, produced at the Tron Theatre in 1990. This comparatively large-scale play adopts an Imperial Roman setting to pursue a complex meditation on the themes of innocence, violence, love, and political expediency. The structure adheres to no single dramatic model and may never have made the narrative easy to grasp—particularly in the theatre, with parts being doubled by the cast. But the play gives further proof of Hannan's versatility with language and indicates an ability also to write with the visceral effects of spectacle and physical action in mind. Passages of gory and sensational melodrama give way to moments of sudden tenderness or unexpected parallels with contemporary politics—so that one has to adjust one's mode of response continuously and at short notice. At one moment, the play seems almost to wallow in its period, like *Titus Andronicus* exploiting it for a vein of violent extremism. At another, it lurches into pressing and topical allusion, as political in its applications as *Coriolanus* or a piece by Brecht. As a playwright with a natural instinct to make demands both of his audiences and of those who produce his work, Hannan is undoubtedly one of British theatre's brightest prospects for the 1990's.

—Matthew Lloyd

HARDING, John. British. Born in Ruislip, Middlesex, 20 June 1948. Educated at Pinner Grammar School; Manchester University, 1966–69, B.A. (honours) in drama 1969. Married Gillian Heaps in 1968; one son. Agent: Michael Imison Playwrights, 28 Almeida Street, London N1 1TD, England.

PUBLICATIONS

Plays

For Sylvia, with John Burrows (produced London, 1972). Published in *The Best Short Plays 1978*, edited by Stanley Richards, Radnor, Pennsylvania, Chilton, 1978.
The Golden Pathway Annual, with John Burrows (produced Sheffield, 1973; London, 1974). London, Heinemann, 1975.
Loud Reports, with John Burrows and Peter Skellern (produced London, 1975).

Dirty Giant, with John Burrows, music by Peter Skellern (produced Coventry, 1975).
The Manly Bit, with John Burrows (produced London, 1976).

Radio Play: *Listen to My Voice*, 1987.

Television Play: *Do You Dig It?*, with John Burrows, 1976.

*

Theatrical Activities:
Actor: **Plays**—all his own plays, and *Jack and Beanstalk*, Bromley, Kent, 1969; Whitaker in *The Long and the Short and the Tall* by Willis Hall, London, 1970; Pantalone in *Pinocchio* by Brian Way, London, 1971; James in *My Fat Friend* by Charles Laurence, London, 1972; Antipholus in *The Comedy of Errors*, Hornchurch, Essex, 1973; Sir Andrew Aguecheek in *Twelfth Night*, Sheffield, 1974; *Donkeys' Years* by Michael Frayn, London, 1976; Actors Company, London: *The Importance of Being Earnest* by Wilde and *Do You Love Me?* by R.D. Laing, 1977–78; *The Circle* by W. Somerset Maugham, Chichester and tour, 1978; National Theatre, London: *The Double Dealer* by Congreve, *Strife* by Galsworthy, *The Fruits of Enlightenment* by Tolstoy, *Undiscovered Country* by Tom Stoppard, *Richard III*, and *Amadeus* by Peter Shaffer, 1978–81; *Miranda* by Beverley Cross, Chichester, 1987. **Film**—*Little Dorrit*, 1987. **Television**—*Man of Mode* by Etherege, 1980; *Baby Talk* by Nigel Williams, 1981.

* * *

See the essay on John Burrows and John Harding.

HARE, David. British. Born in Bexhill, Sussex, 5 June 1947. Educated at Lancing College, Sussex; Jesus College, Cambridge, M.A. 1968. Married Margaret Matheson in 1970 (divorced 1980); two sons and one daughter. Founding director, Portable Theatre, Brighton and London, 1968–71; literary manager, 1969–70, and resident dramatist, 1970–71, Royal Court Theatre, London; resident dramatist, Nottingham Playhouse, 1973; co-founder, 1973, and director, 1975–80, Joint Stock Theatre Company; founder, Greenpoint Films, 1982. Since 1984 associate director, National Theatre, London. Since 1981 member of the Council, Royal Court Theatre. Recipient: *Evening Standard* award, 1971, 1985; Rhys Memorial prize, 1975; USA/UK Bicentennial fellowship, 1977; BAFTA award, 1979; New York Drama Critics Circle award, 1983; Berlin Film Festival Golden Bear, 1985; *City Limits* award, 1985; *Drama* magazine award, 1988; Olivier award, 1990; *Time Out* award, 1990; *Plays and Players* award, 1990; London Theatre Critics award, 1990. Fellow, Royal Society of Literature, 1985. Lives in London. Agent: Casarotto Ramsay Ltd., National House, 60–66 Wardour Street, London W1V 3HP, England.

PUBLICATIONS

Plays

Inside Out, with Tony Bicât, adaptation of the diaries of Kafka (also director: produced London, 1968).
How Brophy Made Good (produced London, 1969). Published in *Gambit 17* (London), 1971.

What Happened to Blake? (produced London, 1970).
Slag (produced London, 1970; New York, 1971). London, Faber, 1971.
The Rules of the Game, adaptation of a play by Pirandello (produced London, 1971).
Deathsheads (sketch), in *Christmas Present* (produced Edinburgh, 1971).
Lay By, with others (produced Edinburgh and London, 1971). London, Calder and Boyars, 1972.
The Great Exhibition (produced London, 1972). London, Faber, 1972.
England's Ireland, with others (also director: produced Amsterdam and London, 1972).
Brassneck, with Howard Brenton (also director: produced Nottingham, 1973). London, Eyre Methuen, 1974.
Knuckle (produced Oxford and London, 1974; New York, 1975). London, Faber, 1974; revised version, 1978.
Fanshen, adaptation of the book by William Hinton (produced London, 1975; Milwaukee, 1976; New York, 1977). London, Faber, 1976.
Teeth 'n' Smiles, music by Nick Bicât, lyrics by Tony Bicât (also director: produced London, 1975; Washington, D.C., 1977). London, Faber, 1976.
Plenty (also director: produced London, 1978; Washington, D.C., 1980; New York, 1982). London, Faber, 1978; New York, New American Library, 1985.
Deeds, with others (produced Nottingham, 1978). Published in *Plays and Players* (London), May and June 1978.
Licking Hitler (televised 1978). London, Faber, 1978.
Dreams of Leaving (televised 1980). London, Faber, 1980.
A Map of the World (also director: produced Adelaide, Australia, 1982; London, 1983; New York, 1985). London, Faber, 1982; revised version, 1983.
Saigon: Year of the Cat (televised 1983). London, Faber, 1983.
The Madman Theory of Deterrence (sketch), in *The Big One* (produced London, 1983).
The History Plays (includes *Knuckle, Licking Hitler, Plenty*). London, Faber, 1984.
Pravda: A Fleet Street Comedy, with Howard Brenton (also director: produced London, 1985; Minneapolis, 1989). London, Methuen, 1985.
Wetherby (screenplay). London, Faber, 1985.
The Asian Plays (includes *Fanshen, Saigon: Year of the Cat, A Map of the World*). London, Faber, 1986.
The Bay at Nice, and Wrecked Eggs (also director: produced London, 1986; New York, 1987). London, Faber, 1986.
The Knife (opera), music by Nick Bicât, lyrics by Tim Rose Price (also director: produced New York, 1987).
Paris by Night (screenplay). London, Faber, 1988.
The Secret Rapture (produced London, 1988; New York, 1989). London, Faber, 1988; New York, Grove Weidenfeld, 1989.
Strapless (screenplay). London, Faber, 1990.
Racing Demon (produced London, 1990). London, Faber, 1990.
Murmuring Judges (produced London, 1991). London, Faber, 1991.
Heading Home (televized 1991). With *Wetherby* and *Dreams of Leaving*, London, Faber, 1991.
Heading Home, Wetherby, Dreams of Leaving. London, Faber, 1991.
The Early Plays (includes *Slag, Teeth 'n' Smiles, Dreams of Leaving*). London, Faber, 1992.

Screenplays: *Wetherby*, 1985; *Plenty*, 1985; *Paris by Night*, 1989; *Strapless*, 1990; *Damage*, 1992.

Television Plays: *Man above Men*, 1973; *Licking Hitler*, 1978; *Dreams of Leaving*, 1980; *Saigon: Year of the Cat*, 1983; *Heading Home*, 1991.

Other

Writing Left-Handed. London, Faber, 1991.

*

Critical Studies: by John Simon, in *Hudson Review* (New York), 1971; *The New British Drama* by Oleg Kerensky, London, Hamish Hamilton, 1977, New York, Taplinger, 1979; *Dreams and Deconstructions* edited by Sandy Craig, Ambergate, Derbyshire, Amber Lane Press, 1980; *Stages in the Revolution* by Catherine Itzin, London, Eyre Methuen, 1980; *File on Hare* edited by Malcolm Page, London, Methuen, 1990.

Theatrical Activities:
Director: **Plays**—*Inside Out*, London, 1968; *Christie in Love* by Howard Brenton, Brighton and London, 1969; *Purity* by David Mowat, Canterbury, 1969; *Fruit* by Howard Brenton, London, 1970; *Blowjob* by Snoo Wilson, Edinburgh and London, 1971; *England's Ireland*, Amsterdam and London, 1972; *The Provoked Wife* by Vanbrugh, Watford, Hertfordshire, 1973; *Brassneck*, Nottingham, 1973; *The Pleasure Principle* by Snoo Wilson, London, 1973; *The Party* by Trevor Griffiths, tour, 1974; *Teeth 'n' Smiles*, London, 1975; *Weapons of Happiness* by Howard Brenton, London, 1976; *Devil's Island* by Tony Bicât, Cardiff and London, 1977; *Plenty*, London, 1978, New York, 1982; *Total Eclipse* by Christopher Hampton, London, 1981; *A Map of the World*, Adelaide, 1982, London, 1983, New York, 1985; *Pravda*, London, 1985; *The Bay at Nice, and Wrecked Eggs*, London, 1986; *King Lear*, London, 1986; *The Knife*, New York, 1987. **Film**—*Wetherby*, 1985; *Paris by Night*, 1989; *Strapless*, 1990. **Television**—*Licking Hitler*, 1978; *Dreams of Leaving*, 1980; *Saigon: Year of the Cat*, 1983; *Heading Home*, 1991.

* * *

David Hare's early plays show a bright young man drawing on his education, writing of Kafka and Blake, and his experience: *Teeth 'n' Smiles*, about a Cambridge May Ball, audaciously linked rock band and serious play, while giving Helen Mirren a memorable part; *Slag*, superficially about women teachers, in fact reflects Hare's view of how institutions shape people. Hare also gained practical theatre experience with Portable in his twenties and accepted invitations to write, collaborating on *Lay By* and *England's Ireland*. Leftwing political convictions (always scrutinized, flexible, and rarely dogmatic) begin to show in *The Great Exhibition*, the study of a Labour M.P. burned out and sold out. His political self-education continues in his adaptation of *Fanshen*, clearly showing the condition of Chinese peasants improved after the Revolution and implying a roughly comparable need for change in Britain (though *Fanshen* was as much a Joint Stock collective effort as a distinct Hare work).

From *Brassneck* on, nearly all Hare's writing engages with the Condition-of-England, and—unusually—his scripts for film and television are also a part of his unfolding, expanding, and increasingly complex view. In a sense, the most recent play at the time of writing, *Murmuring Judges*, becomes about Part 16 of Hare on the State of the World. (With two

pieces especially, *A Map of the World* and *Saigon*, Hare's subject broadens from Britain to the whole world.) Co-written with Howard Brenton, *Brassneck* is an epic, the rise of a new style of capitalism in the Midlands from 1945 on, including operating strip-clubs and importing heroin, to a final toast to "the last days of capitalism."

Plenty, probably his best play (and surviving reasonably faithfully in the film version) also starts with World War II. Young Susan operates in occupied France full of a sense of mission and optimistically looks ahead on a sunny hillside in August: "There will be days and days and days like this." In flashback, this is the last line of the drama, and earlier we have seen Susan's disillusion, counterpointing her private life with such public events as the Festival of Britain in 1951 (changed to the 1953 Coronation in the film) and the British attack on Suez in 1956. Her friend Alice appears to be more successful at discovering a purpose in her life in peacetime. (Hare's preoccupation with how the war shaped post-war Britain is reflected also in his *Licking Hitler*, for television.)

His writing in the 1980's is sometimes tilted towards the personal, notably in the films *Wetherby* (reflecting Hare as Londoner puzzled by middle-class life in the small Yorkshire market-town), *Strapless*, and *Paris by Night*. In the Introduction to the latter, Hare writes: "Although there has been a considerable body of films and plays about the economic results of Thatcherism, there has been almost nothing of consequence about the characteristics and personalities of those who have ruled over us during these last eight years." He remedies this in *The Secret Rapture*, which contrasts a Conservative woman M.P. (a full-scale attempt to understand Margaret Thatcher) and her good sister ("a portrait of absolute goodness," wrote Michael Ratcliffe).

The Secret Rapture is one of his four plays staged at the National Theatre between 1985 and 1991 which engages urgently with the state of British society. (His fifth appearance at the National Theatre in this period was with the modest, more domestic double-bill of *Wrecked Eggs* and *The Bay at Nice*. The first of the four, *Pravda*, again co-authored with Brenton, is a ferocious, brilliant, energetic exposé of newspapers, distinguished on the stage by the powerful playing of Anthony Hopkins as an unprincipled magnate. *Racing Demon* is *about* the Church of England and to some extent about the place of religion in society now, and *Murmuring Judges* is *about* the British legal system, with emphasis on its shortcomings. Yet these are not narrowly documentary; both are theatrical and entertaining as well as thought-provoking.

Each of Hare's mature works has greater resonance when placed in sequence and in context. In his latest plays, more than any other British dramatist, he is scrutinizing the present state of the nation.

—Malcolm Page

———

HARRIS, Richard. British. Born in London, 26 March 1934. Recipient: London *Evening Standard* award, 1979, for best comedy, 1984; Molière award, Paris, 1990; New York Film and Television Festival gold medal, 1990. Agent: Lemon,

Unna, and Durbridge, 24 Pottery Lane, Holland Park, London W11 4LZ, England.

PUBLICATIONS

Plays

Partners: A Comedy (produced Edinburgh, 1969). London, Evans, 1973.
Albert: A One-Act Comedy (produced London, 1971). London, Evans, 1972.
You Must Be Virginia (produced London, 1971).
No, No, Not Yet, with Leslie Darbon (produced Windsor, 1972).
Two and Two Make Sex, with Leslie Darbon (produced Windsor and London, 1973). London, French, 1973.
Who Goes Bare?, with Leslie Darbon (produced Windsor, 1974).
Conscience Be Damned (produced London, 1975).
Correspondents' Course, with Leslie Darbon (produced Westcliff, Essex, 1976). London, French, 1976.
The Pressures of Life: Four Television Plays. London, Longman, 1977.
Outside Edge (produced London, 1979). London, French, 1980.
The Dog It Was (produced Richmond, Surrey, 1980).
The Business of Murder (produced Windsor and London, 1981). Oxford, Amber Lane, 1985.
Is It Something I Said? (produced London, 1982). London, French, 1982.
Local Affairs (produced Leicester, 1982). London, French, 1982.
Stepping Out (produced Leatherhead, Surrey and London, 1984). Oxford, Amber Lane, 1985.
The Maintenance Man (produced Leatherhead, Surrey, 1986; London, 1986). London, French, 1987.
Three Piece Suite (produced Hornchurch, Essex, 1986).
Visiting Hour (includes *Plaster, Keeping Mum, Show Business, Going Home, Waiting, Magic*) (produced London, 1987; revised version produced Richmond, Surrey, 1990). London, French, 1991.
Party Piece (produced Basingstoke, 1990). London, French, 1990.
Mixed Blessing (musical), with Keith Strachan (produced Westcliff, Essex, 1991).

Screenplays: *Strongroom*, with Max Marquis, 1965; *I Start Counting*, adaptation of the novel by Audrey Erskine Lindop, 1969; *The Lady in the Car with Glasses and a Gun*, adaptation of the novel by Sebastian Japrisot, 1970; *Orion's Belt*, adaptation of the novel by Jan Michelet, 1988; *Stepping Out*, 1991.

Radio Play: *Was It Something I Said?*, 1978.

Television Plays: *Who's a Good Boy Then? I Am*; *You Must Be Virginia*; *Saving It for Albie*; *When the Boys Come Out to Play*; *Sunday in Perspective*; *Occupier's Risk*; *Time and Mr. Madingley*; *I Can See Your Lips Move*; *A Slight Formality*; *Jack's Trade*; *Dog Ends*; *Searching for Senor Duende* and *This for the Half, Darling*, in *About Face* series, 1989; *Murder Most English*, adaptation of *The Flaxborough Chronicles* by Colin Watson; *The Prince and the Pauper*, adaptation of the novel by Mark Twain; *Plain Murder*, adaptation of the novel by C. S. Forester; *Sherlock Holmes*, adaptation of the novel by Arthur Conan Doyle; *The Darling Buds of May*, adap-

tation of the novel by H. E. Bates, 1991; *A Touch of Frost*, adaptation of the novels by R. D. Wingfield; *Shoestring* series; *Man in a Suitcase* series; *The Gamblers* series.

* * *

Few playwrights can boast one of the longest-running comedies in London as well as one of the longest-running thrillers. Richard Harris has had both, with *The Business of Murder* and *Stepping Out*. But then Harris has always been a skilled professional. His work delivers exactly what it promises for the most part; but with two plays—*Outside Edge* and *Stepping Out*—he staked a claim to be regarded as an original comic talent, more than the second-league Ayckbourn which he has sometimes been dubbed.

He seems at home in most theatrical genres. He has also written (in collaboration with Leslie Darbon) a clever farce with the misleadingly sniggering title *Two and Two Make Sex*. A typical piece of British farcical comedy—menopausal man pursing younger girl, her boyfriend attracting the older man's wife, both pairs ignorant of the complications until a late scene of near-confrontations—it naturally (being a British farce) featured sex deferred rather than sex consummated, but within the limitations of the genre, some characteristic Harris insights into women's points of view could be glimpsed underneath all the mechanics of telephone calls and close encounters on a split-level set. And *The Maintenance Man*, a fairly formula comedy centred round an eternal triangle, again provided two rounded roles for women.

Women dominated *Outside Edge* and *Stepping Out*. Set in a local cricket club, *Outside Edge* is a deceptively small-scale play; underneath the cricket jokes and sight gags gradually emerges a sense of real pain in the midst of this suburban haven, and cracks in supposedly happy marriages and relationships begin to appear like weeds on the club's lawn. Harris has again written especially good female roles—and he has created an original and endearing double-act in the shape of a role-reversal couple, she tall and lusty (memorably played by Maureen Lipman in London), coping with all the heavy building work at home, he tiny and domestic, taking over cooking and polishing. They are the happiest couple in the play.

Stepping Out has only one male role—the shy widower who is the only man in attendance at the weekly tap dance class in a North London church hall. Mavis, the ex-chorus girl instructor, the redoubtable and temperamental pianist, together with seven very contrasting pupils, comprise the rest of the cast. In the course of the play, following the class through until their appearance at the finale stepping out at a charity performance to Irving Berlin, Harris traces the patterns behind these separate lives, It is obliquely handled—much is revealed in throwaway clues rather than in confessional speeches—especially so in the case of Vera, another Harris original, an apparently brightly confident wife of an older and much-absent businessman husband, given to cheery aphorisms ("It may be February outside but it's always August under the armpits"), whose marriage, we gradually sense, is driving her into increasing isolation. Harris doesn't have room to develop all his characters to the same extent, but the play has an authenticity and sureness of rhythm that make it more than a formula hit; when this core to the play was readjusted, as for the glitzy Broadway version or for the movie, it was much less successful.

More recent Harris work has included the revue-style book for *Mixed Blessings*, a musical on marriage involving several contrasted couples which was poorly staged in its regional premiere, and several reworkings, under various titles, of a comedy now titled *Party Piece*, set in the adjoining back gardens of two socially contrasted couples and with a memorable portrait of a possessive mother. All of this suggests that Harris's drive not to repeat himself is unimpaired.

—Alan Strachan

HARRISON, Tony. British. Born in Leeds, Yorkshire, 30 April 1937. Educated at Cross Flatts County Primary, Leeds, 1942–48; Leeds Grammar School, 1948–55; University of Leeds, 1955–60, B.A. in classics 1958, postgraduate diploma in linguistics. Married 1) Rosemarie Crossfield in 1962, one daughter and one son; 2) Teresa Stratas in 1984. Schoolmaster, Dewsbury, Yorkshire, 1960–62; lecturer in English, Ahmadu Bello University, Zaria, Northern Nigeria, 1962–66, and Charles University, Prague, 1966–67; editor, with Jon Silkin and Ken Smith, *Stand* magazine, Newcastle-upon-Tyne, 1968–69; resident dramatist, National Theatre, London, 1977–79. U.K.-U.S. Bicentennial fellow, New York, 1979–80. President, Classical Association of Great Britain, 1987–88. Recipient: Northern Arts fellowship, 1967, 1976; Cholmondeley award, 1969; UNESCO fellowship, 1969; Faber memorial award, 1972; Gregynog fellowship, 1973; U.S. Bicentennial fellowship, 1979; European Poetry translation prize, 1983; Whitbread Poetry prize, 1992. Fellow, Royal Society of Literature, 1984. Agent: Peters, Fraser, and Dunlop, 503/4 The Chambers, Chelsea Harbour, Lots Road, London SW10 0XF, England.

PUBLICATIONS

Plays

Aikin Mata, with James Simmons, adaptation of *Lysistrata* by Aristophanes (produced Zaria, Nigeria, 1965). Ibadan, Oxford University Press, 1966.
The Misanthrope, adaptation of a play by Molière (produced London, 1973; Washington, D.C. and New York, 1975). London, Rex Collings, 1973; New York, Third Press, 1975.
Phaedra Britannica, adaptation of a play by Racine (produced London, 1975; New York, 1988). London, Rex Collings, 1975.
Bow Down, music by Harrison Birtwistle (produced London, 1977). London, Rex Collings, 1977.
The Passion, from the York Mystery Plays (produced London, 1977; with *The Nativity* and *Doomsday*, as *The Mysteries*, London, 1985). London, Rex Collings, 1977; in *The Mysteries*, 1985.
The Bartered Bride, adaptation of an opera by Sabina, music by Smetana (produced New York, 1978). New York, Schirmer, 1978; in *Dramatic Verse*, 1985.
The Nativity, from the York Mystery Plays (produced London, 1980; with *The Passion* and *Doomsday*, as *The Mysteries*, 1985). In *The Mysteries*, 1985.
The Oresteia, music by Harrison Birtwistle, adaptation of the plays by Aeschylus (includes *Agamemnon*, *Choephori*, *Eumenides*) (produced London, 1981). London, Rex Collings, 1981.
Yan Tan Tethera, music by Harrison Birtwistle (produced London, 1983). In *Dramatic Verse*, 1985.

The Big H, music by Dominic Muldowney (televised, 1984). Included in *Dramatic Verse*, 1985.
Dramatic Verse 1973–1985 (includes *The Misanthrope*, *Phaedra Britannica*, *Bow Down*, *The Bartered Bride*, *The Oresteia*, *Yan Tan Tethera*, *The Big H*, *Medea: Sex War*). Newcastle-upon-Tyne, Bloodaxe, 1985; as *Theatre Works 1973–1985*, London, Penguin, 1986.
Doomsday, from the York Mystery Plays (with *The Nativity* and *The Passion*, as *The Mysteries*, produced London, 1985). In *The Mysteries*, 1985.
The Mysteries, adaptation of the York Mystery Plays (includes *The Passion*, *The Nativity*, *Doomsday*) (produced London, 1985). London, Faber, 1985.
Medea: Sex War (produced London, 1991). Included in *Dramatic Verse*, 1985.
The Trackers of Oxyrhynchus (produced Delphi, 1988; London, 1990). London, Faber, 1990.
The Common Chorus. London, Faber, 1992.
Square Rounds (also director: produced London, 1992). London, Faber, 1992.

Television Plays: *Arctic Paradise*, 1981; *The Big H*, music by Dominic Muldowney, 1984; *Loving Memory* series, 1987; *V.*, 1987; *The Blasphemers' Banquet*, 1989; *The Gaze of the Gorgon*, adaptation of *The Oresteia* and *The Mysteries*, 1992.

Verse

Earthworks. Leeds, Northern House, 1964.
Newcastle Is Peru. Newcastle-upon-Tyne, Eagle Press, 1969.
The Loiners. London, London Magazine Editions, 1970.
Corgi Modern Poets in Focus 4, with others, edited by Jeremy Robson. London, Corgi, 1971.
Ten Poems from the School of Eloquence. London, Rex Collings, 1976.
From the School of Eloquence and Other Poems. London, Rex Collings, 1978.
Looking Up, with Philip Sharpe. West Malvern, Worcestershire, Migrant Press, 1979.
Continuous: 50 Sonnets from the School of Eloquence. London, Rex Collings, 1981.
A Kumquat for John Keats. Newcastle-upon-Tyne, Bloodaxe, 1981.
U.S. Martial. Newcastle-upon-Tyne, Bloodaxe, 1981.
Selected Poems. London, Viking Press, 1984; revised edition, London, Penguin and New York, Random House, 1987.
The Fire-Gap: A Poem with Two Tails. Newcastle-upon-Tyne, Bloodaxe, 1985.
V. (single poem). Newcastle-upon-Tyne, Bloodaxe, 1985; with press articles, 1989.
Anno 42. N.p., Michael C. Caine, 1987.
Ten Sonnets from the School of Eloquence. London, Anvil Press Poetry, 1987.
V. and Other Poems. New York, Farrar Straus, 1989.
A Cold Coming: Gulf War Poems. Newcastle-upon-Tyne, Bloodaxe, 1991.
The Gaze of the Gorgon. Newcastle-upon-Tyne, Bloodaxe, 1992.

Other

Translator, *Poems*, by Palladas. London, Anvil Press Poetry, 1975.

*

Bibliography: *Tony Harrison: A Bibliography 1957–1987* by John R. Kaiser, London, Mansell, 1989.

Manuscript Collections: University of Newcastle-upon-Tyne; Newcastle Literary and Philosophical Society.

Critical Studies: *Essays on Tony Harrison* edited by Neil Astley, Newcastle-upon-Tyne, Bloodaxe, 1990; *Ancient Sun, Modern Light* by Marianne McDonald, New York, Columbia University Press, 1992; "Postmodern Classics: The Verse Drama of Tony Harrison" by Romana Huk, in *British and Irish Drama Since 1960*, edited by James Acheson, London, Macmillan and New York, St. Martin's Press, 1993.

Tony Harrison comments:

It seems to me no accident that some of the world's best poetry is to be found in some of the world's best drama, and comes from those periods when poets, and I emphasise poets, worked directly with actors and wrote their pieces for specific players and spaces. This is to be found in the ancient Greek drama, for which I have had a lifelong passion, when the poet was regarded as the "didaskalos" the "teacher" of his work, and the term would involve everything now taken over by the function of director. The relationship is to be found also in the theatre of Shakespeare, the Jacobeans, Molière, Racine, Goethe, Yeats, Brecht, or in the anonymous poets who worked and reworked their texts with their illiterate players in the medieval Mysteries. My at least 25-year quest for a space for myself as a poet in the theatre, involved me in seeking the help of some of these ancients and using their stylistic resources to discover new ones for myself. And I have always thought in terms of "theatre" rather than in the compartmentalised genres of drama, music theatre, opera, remembering that opera originated when artists thought they were rediscovering Greek drama. I have always found working with composers very congenial.

I have never for a moment been interested in antique reproduction only in finding styles and conventions to confront modern issues and conflicts that the predominantly naturalistic styles seemed unable to encompass. When I first started out on my quest I found only what has been called "poetry in the theatre rather than of it" that is in works like Eliot and Fry. And indeed even the great verse classics were often played in pedestrian prose translations so far had the theatre left behind that tradition. What kept verse alive for me as a theatrical medium was not only my immersion in great theatrical poets of the past, whose styles and language I studied and often translated, but also an early appetite and relish for the verse of the music-hall recitation and the pantomime which were still vigorous enough when I was a child for me to have been influenced by them. Indeed they were my earliest experiences of theatre. I have sometimes used the resources I found in these popular forms to "unlock" or "reoriginate" the classics of the past and bring the energy of the so-called "low" art forms into the so-called "high" art forms. Sometimes I believe that there is not that great a difference between the two, and that our culture has falsely made them seem too irreconcilably distinct.

My close work with actors from the beginning of my theatrical career has led me, project by project, deeper into the everyday practicalities of theatrical production until I have reached the position of preferring to direct my own theatre pieces and to collaborate with known actors in known spaces, whether conventional theatres or not. *The Trackers of Oxyrhynchus* was devised in the National Theatre Studio with actors I had worked with on other projects, and was premiered in the unique space of the ancient stadium of Delphi in Greece. When it played subsequently in the Olivier Theatre at the National, it was radically rewritten for the new space. When the production toured to Salts Mill, Saltaire, Art

Carnuntum, Vienna, the Gasworks Theatre, Copenhagen, and the Brighton Festival I was with the company for every performance and went on making local variations in the text.

* * *

If his status as England's best-known contemporary theatre poet will probably always be controversial, Tony Harrison's achievement as a brilliant and innovative translator can scarcely be contested. Audacity sometimes hovering on the edge of verbal vandalism has characterised some of his verse, both in his collections of poetry and in his plays, but works like his *Misanthrope* and *Oresteia* have satisfied even those with a conservative concept of the translator's role. However, he is also thoroughly conversant with current translation theory, and in other works he extends the logic of transposition and refraction to move far beyond any suggestion of the play as a statement of faith to an original.

From the first, Harrison has been acutely aware of the need to read both the original and the target audience. He always regarded *Aikin Mata*, his Nigerian *Lysistrata*, as unplayable except in West Africa. Though it has been successfully staged even by the Sydney Theatre Company, *The Trackers of Oxyrhynchus* was written for a single performance at Delphi. And even the apparently conventional *The Misanthrope* was written to an audience for whom 1968 was a recent memory. However, it was *Phaedra Britannica* that confronted London with the principle of cultural transposition as an integral function in contemporary translation.

The politicisation of Racine by grounding the play in India just before the Mutiny was a brilliant piece of audience manipulation. Denied the consolation of reading the play as an object "back there" in French literature, or even as an archaeological exhibit from Greek prehistory, London theatre-goers found it folded into their own imperial history, the more fragile because its cultural sequel was already written. Reading Racine by taking a detour through India thus became an ingeniously contrived exercise in Orientalism in the theatre, a point illustrated by the response of unwitting critics who complained of the absence of (consolingly meaningless) Greek gods. In their place, Harrison offered some specifically Indian deities, but also a collective "They," a dark, menacing colonial sense of otherness. Thomas (Hippolytus), a half-caste, is rejected by his father as an "animal," his Indian blood a "lower self" that sooner or later will emerge from its "lair."

Harrison has always been conscious of himself as a Yorkshire poet, and his interest in regional material is combined with his training in comparative linguistics in *Bow Down*, a savage theatricalisation of several treatments of the "Two Sisters" ballad. Here, his technique may be compared with what Walter Benjamin (whom he admires) saw as an ideal in translation, the interlinear: Harrison collates the versions, leaving the Danish, for example, in its original. This inclination to leave "ready-mades" embedded throughout a work is more pronounced in the "sex-war" opera *Medea*, and would itself become the subject of a play in *Oxyrhynchus*.

Defiantly regionalist is *The Mysteries*, where a darts mat represents the palm-strewn road into Jerusalem, and Herod's son reads the York telephone directory before his father tears it to bits, a gesture of macho physicality that has no precedent in the Herod of the Cycle plays. The initial entrance of God on a fork-lift seems appropriate in what Harrison sees as the "post-Christian" era, but the structural awkwardness of the play (an amalgam of all four cycles) reflects the fact that it was written first just as an Easter Passion and eight years later bulked out with a Nativity (which includes a lot of Wakefield material like Cain and Noah) and a Doomsday. Between the two versions, Harrison wrote the television play *The Big H*, a highly stylised treatment of Herod in contemporary Leeds, which incorporates some of the precise stylistic features of the "Slaughter of the Innocents" play from the Cycles; formal boasting speeches from Herod and lamentation sequences from the mothers co-exist with startling liberties, like the fact that all three Herods are local schoolteachers with secret selves (called Jekyll and Hyde) with a propensity for fascism and "kiddicide." Though clearly written as a Christmas play, it was premiered by BBC2 on a Boxing Day.

The Trackers of Oxyrhynchus is a work of virtuosity which fittingly combines the proclivities of all of Harrison's best work. Grenfell and Hunt, the pioneer British papyrologists, are digging through Egyptian compost heaps and find the fragments of a satyr play, which is then realised, with themselves in the central roles of Apollo and Silenus. Harrison's keen sense of prosody is wittily indulged here, as his characteristic rhyming couplets are filled out with blanks around the papyrus word fragments, and a Caryatid maiden, a power-lifter carrying a pediment, enters and launches into a pastiche of Victorian translationese. The performance is contextualised within the frame of the Pythian Games which are then synchronised with the world of the audience with the intrusion of "new generation" satyrs as football hooligans. The play thus recreates the co-existence of the high and the low, the sacred and the profane, which Harrison's brilliant introduction argues was integral to classical Greek drama. His detractors, who have called his work kitsch, are given some substance here, in so far as compost is kitsch. But—as Silenus shrewdly observes—the full subtleties of that kitsch are accessible only to readers with a very good reading knowledge of Greek.

—Howard McNaughton

HARRON, Don(ald Hugh). Canadian. Born in 1924.
See 1st edition, 1973.

HARWOOD, Ronald. British. Born Ronald Horwitz in Cape Town, South Africa, 9 November 1934. Educated at Sea Point Boys' High School, Cape Town; Royal Academy of Dramatic Art, London. Married Natasha Riehle in 1959; one son and two daughters. Joined Donald Wolfit's Shakespeare Company in London, 1953; actor, 1953–59; presenter, *Kaleidoscope* radio programme, 1973, and television series *Read All About It*, 1978–79, and *All the World's a Stage*, 1984; artistic director, Cheltenham Festival, 1975; visitor in theatre, Balliol College, Oxford, 1986. Chairman, Writers' Guild of Great Britain, 1969; member of the Literature Panel, Arts Council of Great Britain, 1973–78. Recipient: Royal Society of Literature Winifred Holtby prize, for fiction, 1974; *Evening Standard* award, 1980; Drama Critics Circle award, 1980. Fellow, Royal Society of Literature, 1974. Agent: Judy Daish Associates, 83 Eastbourne Mews, London W2 6LQ, England.

PUBLICATIONS

Plays

Country Matters (produced Manchester, 1969).
One Day in the Life of Ivan Denisovich (screenplay). London, Sphere, 1970; New York, Ballantine, 1971.
The Good Companions, music by André Previn, lyrics by Johnny Mercer, adaptation of the novel by J.B. Priestley (produced Manchester and London, 1974). London, Chappell, 1974.
The Ordeal of Gilbert Pinfold, adaptation of the novel by Evelyn Waugh (produced Manchester, 1977; London, 1979). Oxford, Amber Lane Press, 1983.
A Family (produced Manchester and London, 1978). London, Heinemann, 1978.
The Dresser (produced Manchester and London, 1980; New York, 1981). Ambergate, Derbyshire, Amber Lane Press, 1980; New York, Grove Press, 1981.
A Night of the Day of the Imprisoned Writer, with Christopher Hampton (produced London, 1981).
After the Lions (produced Manchester, 1982). Oxford, Amber Lane Press, 1983).
Tramway Road (produced London, 1984). Oxford, Amber Lane Press, 1984.
The Deliberate Death of a Polish Priest (produced London 1985). Oxford, Amber Lane Press, and New York, Applause, 1985.
Interpreters: A Fantasia on English and Russian Themes (produced London, 1985). Oxford, Amber Lane Press, 1985.
J.J. Farr (produced Bath and London, 1987). Oxford, Amber Lane Press, 1988.
Another Time (produced Bath and London, 1989; also director: Chicago, 1991). Oxford, Amber Lane Press, 1989.
Reflected Glory (produced Darlington, Durham and London, 1992). London, Faber, 1991.

Screenplays: *The Barber of Stamford Hill*, 1962; *Private Potter*, with Casper Wrede, 1962; *A High Wind in Jamaica*, with Denis Cannan and Stanley Mann, 1965; *Drop Dead Darling* (*Arriverderci, Baby!*), with Ken Hughes, 1966; *Diamonds for Breakfast*, with N.F. Simpson and Pierre Rouve, 1968; *Eyewitness*, 1970; *Cromwell*, with Ken Hughes, 1970; *One Day in the Life of Ivan Denisovich*, 1972; *Operation Daybreak*, 1975; *The Dresser*, 1984; *The Doctor and the Devils*, 1986.

Radio Play: *All the Same Shadows*, from his own novel, 1971.

Television Plays: *The Barber of Stamford Hill*, 1960; *Private Potter*, with Casper Wrede, 1961; *Take a Fellow Like Me*, 1961; *The Lads*, 1963; *Convalescence*, 1964; *Guests of Honour*, 1965; *The Paris Trip*, 1966; *The New Assistant*, 1967; *Long Lease of Summer*, 1972; *The Guests*, 1972; *A Sense of Loss* (documentary on Evelyn Waugh), with John Selwyn, 1978; *The Way Up to Heaven*, 1979, *Parson's Pleasure*, 1986, and *The Umbrella Man*, 1986 (all in *Tales of the Unexpected* series); *Evita Péron*, 1981; *Mandela*, 1987; *Breakthrough at Reykjavik*, 1987; *Countdown to War*, 1989.

Novels

All the Same Shadows. London, Cape, 1961; as *George Washington September, Sir!*, New York, Farrar Straus, 1961.
The Guilt Merchants. London, Cape, 1963; New York, Holt Rinehart, 1969.

The Girl in Melanie Klein. London, Secker and Warburg, 1969; New York, Holt Rinehart, 1973.
Articles of Faith. London, Secker and Warburg, 1973; New York, Holt Rinehart, 1974.
The Genoa Ferry. London, Secker and Warburg, 1976; New York, Mason Charter, 1977.
César and Augusta. London, Secker and Warburg, 1978; Boston, Little Brown, 1979.

Short Stories

One. Interior. Day. Adventures in the Film Trade. London, Secker and Warburg, 1978.

Other

Sir Donald Wolfit, C.B.E.: His Life and Work in the Unfashionable Theatre. London, Secker and Warburg, and New York, St. Martin's Press, 1971.
All the World's a Stage. London, Secker and Warburg, 1984; Boston, Little Brown, 1985.
Mandela. London, Boxtree, and New York, New American Library, 1987.

Editor, with Francis King, *New Stories 3.* London, Hutchinson, 1978.
Editor, *A Night at the Theatre.* London, Methuen, 1982.
Editor, *The Ages of Gielgud: An Actor at Eighty.* London, Hodder and Stoughton, and New York, Limelight, 1984.
Editor, *Dear Alec: Guinness at Seventy-Five.* London, Hodder and Stoughton, and New York, Limelight, 1989.

*

Theatrical Activities:
Director: **Plays**—*The Odd Couple,* Manchester, 1989; *Another Time,* Chicago, 1991.
Actor: **Plays**—with Donald Wolfit's Shakespeare Company in London: roles in *Macbeth, The Wandering Jew* by E. Temple Thurston, *The Taming of the Shrew, 1 Henry IV, Hamlet, Volpone* by Jonson, *Twelfth Night, A New Way to Pay Old Debts* by Massinger, and *The Clandestine Marriage* by Garrick and Colman, 1953; Third Jew in *Salome* by Oscar Wilde, London, 1954; Captain Arago in *The Strong Are Lonely* by Fritz Hochwalder, London, 1955; repertory seasons in Salisbury and Chesterfield.

* * *

Ronald Harwood is both a popular and populist writer with a most diverse list of works—novels, television plays, screenplays, and stage plays. If there is any theme or common denominator in his work it must focus on his own deep love of the theatre (*The Dresser, After the Lions,* and *Reflected Glory* all have theatrical settings) and his concern to show how people feel rather than how they think. Most of the plays turn on a central anguished relationship, based on conflict, and have an acute sense of character, only to be expected in a novelist and dramatist brought up as an actor.

Harwood came to Britain from South Africa in 1953 and joined Donald Wolfit's Shakespeare Company as an actor and as a dresser to the great man himself. His early work included theatrical adaptations of Alexander Solzhenitsyn (*One Day in the Life of Ivan Denisovich*) and Evelyn Waugh (*The Ordeal of Gilbert Pinfold*) as well as the book for an André Previn-Johnny Mercer musical adaptation of J. B. Priestley's *The Good Companions. The Ordeal of Gilbert Pinfold* is probably

the best of his early works. It is an excellent adaptation of Waugh's late novel about an invalid on a cruise bedevilled by figments of his own imagination and is based on Evelyn Waugh's actual experiences. *Gilbert Pinfold* was produced at the Royal Exchange Theatre in Manchester in 1977 and reached London in 1979. This Manchester-London progression was repeated in 1978 with *A Family,* which played at the Haymarket Theatre. The play is designed to show that a family, however possessive, has the inner resources to remain true to itself in spite of adversity. Good though the writing is, especially the delineation of character, there is an odd sense that this is another adaptation from a novel—a "hang-over" perhaps from earlier work.

The play that established Harwood as an international success was *The Dresser,* which transferred from Manchester to the Queen's Theatre, London in 1980. The play recreates with wonderful detail and fidelity the kind of classical touring theatre which must have all but disappeared when Harwood first joined Donald Wolfit's company in 1953. The play has a wonderful and poignant quality of the end of an era about it. An aging actor/manager, simply called "Sir," struggles to play up to eight major Shakespearean roles a week as his company tours Britain in the middle of World War II. Emotionally and creatively spent, "Sir" performs each night only with the help of his dresser, Norman, who cajoles, bullies, protects, and cossets his highly strung employer. The central relationship between "Sir" and Norman is superbly realized and does much to make *The Dresser* one of the most significant and best-loved plays of the 1980's, in spite of the fact that the play has no overiding social message—an attribute considered essential at the time. It should be stressed that "Sir" is not a portrait of Sir Donald Wolfit, but rather an amalgam of several actor/managers known and read about by the author. The central role of "Sir" is a mosaic, a symbol of the age of actor/managers who were often remarkable men, dedicated not only to the classical repertoire but also to a surprisingly high degree of performance. As "Sir" acts King Lear on what proves to be the last night of his life, other stories of ambition, loyalty, loneliness, and betrayal are played out off-stage, acting as a counterpoint and making this the most moving and empathetic of all Harwood's work. *The Dresser* proved to be a hard act to follow and indeed, although *After the Lions* shares the same backstage setting, it did not transfer to London after its Manchester premiere. This play deals with a grim period in the life of the great Sarah Bernhardt, the point in her career when her leg was amputated. The main focus of the play is the attempt of Pitou, Bernhardt's secretary, to get the great actress to retire and not face a humiliating American tour. Skilful though the writing is, the play does not have the atmospheric immediacy of *The Dresser,* although the major roles must be coveted by the acting establishment.

Tramway Road, seen briefly in London in 1984, is a fine play. Two of its major characters are a married expatriate English couple trapped in a bitter relationship. The man teaches elocution to a South African youth who dreams of a theatre in London. But the boy is "reclassified" as a half-caste and his future is destroyed. Faced with the boy's dilemma, the husband acts with a weakness it is difficult to forgive. The play is essentially a clash between the wistfulness of what might have been and the reality of the cruelty of bigotry. Written with deep conviction and truth, this play reminds one of the works of Athol Fugard, so it is interesting to note what Ronald Harwood himself has to say about the piece in an interview in the April 1992 edition of *Plays and Players:* "My stand (the condemnation of South Africa) was honourable, and it was certainly fashionable at the time. But it is easy to pontificate when one is 6000 miles away. I think Athol Fugard is a wonderful writer and a proper witness to what happened there. I'm not a proper witness, I wasn't there." In spite of Harwood's protests, *Tramway Road* remains the most under-valued of all his plays.

The year 1985 was a prolific one. *The Deliberate Death of a Polish Priest* was presented at the Almeida Theatre in London. This documentary play was based on the transcripts of a trial and other material arising out of the murder of Father Jerzy Popieluszko in 1984. The priest was a political activist and all the words of Father Popieluszko and the witnesses are their own. Disarmingly simple, the tragic story —and its attempted cover-up—has a deep emotional impact. On a totally different emotional level, *Interpreters*, which enjoyed a long London run, also looks at the last days of the Cold War. The play's focus is the visit to England by the Soviet president. As the itinerary is carefully examined, the English translator Nadia (who is of Russian descent) and the Russian, Victor, face each other at the conference table. But Nadia and Victor were embroiled in a passionate affair a decade earlier and we eagerly watch the renewal of this romance even though we suspect the rejuvenated liaison cannot last.

In *Another Time*, presented in London in 1989, Harwood returned both to a South African setting and to a re-exploration of the themes of the family. Initially set in Cape Town in the 1950's, the play examines the life of Leonard Lands, 17 years old, the only child of immigrant parents and a gifted pianist. In order to achieve success commensurate with his talent, Leonard must study in Europe. Act Two takes place 35 years later, in London, and Leonard has reached another turning point in his life. Harwood skilfully examines the price Leonard has paid for his single-minded devotion to his music and the effect this has had on his relationship to his family.

Ronald Harwood's latest play, *Reflected Glory*, opened in London in 1992. Like much of his work, the play turns on a central, troubled relationship. Here, the struggle is between two brothers: Michael is a playwright whose latest script exposes the deepest personal secrets of his family: the other brother, restauranteur Alfred, has tried and failed to injunct the play, causing a long and acrimonious rift with his sibling. *Reflected Glory* concerns the attempt by Michael to effect a "so-called" reconciliation—in fact, he is trying to clear the ground for his latest play which will examine his relationship with Alfred. Funny, heartfelt, and with autobiographical overtones, *Reflected Glory* is in many ways Harwood's best play since *The Dresser*.

—David E. Kemp

HASTINGS, Michael (Gerald). British. Born in Lambeth, London, 2 September 1938. Educated at Alleyn's School, 1949–53; apprentice, Kilgour French and Stanbury, bespoke tailors, London, 1953–56. Married Victoria Hardie in 1975; two sons and one daughter from previous marriage. Recipient: Arts Council award, 1956; Encyclopaedia Britannica award, 1965; Maugham award, 1972; Writers Guild award, 1972; Emmy award, 1973; British Screenwriters Guild award, 1975; *Evening Standard* award, 1979. Fellow, Royal Geographical Society. Agent: Andrew Hewson, John

Johnson Ltd., Clerkenwell House, 45–47 Clerkenwell Green, London EC1R 0HT. Address: 2 Helix Gardens, London S.W.2, England.

PUBLICATIONS

Plays

Don't Destroy Me (produced London, 1956; New York, 1957). London, Nimbus, 1956.
Yes, and After (produced London and New York, 1957). Included in *Three Plays*, 1966.
The World's Baby (produced London, 1965). Included in *Three Plays*, 1966.
Lee Harvey Oswald: A Far Mean Streak of Indepence Brought on by Negleck (as *The Silence of Lee Harvey Oswald*, produced London, 1966). London, Penguin, 1966.
Three Plays (includes *Don't Destroy Me*; *Yes, and After*; *The World's Baby*). London, W.H. Allen, 1966.
The Silence of Saint-Just (produced Brighton, 1971). London, Weidenfeld and Nicolson, 1970.
The Cutting of the Cloth (produced London, 1973).
For the West (Uganda) (produced London, 1977). Included in *Three Plays*, 1980.
Gloo Joo (produced London, 1978). Included in *Three Plays*, 1980.
Full Frontal (produced London, 1979). Included in *Three Plays*, 1980.
Carnival War (as *Carnival War a Go Hot*, produced London, 1979). With *Midnite at the Starlite*, London, Penguin, 1981.
Midnite at the Starlite (as *Midnight at the Starlight*, televised 1980; as *Midnite at the Starlite*, produced Birmingham, 1981). With *Carnival War*, London, Penguin, 1981.
Three Plays. London, Penguin, 1980.
Two Fish in the Sky (produced New York, 1982).
The Miser, adaptation of a play by Molière (produced Cambridge, 1982).
Tom and Viv (produced London, 1984; New York, 1985). London, Penguin, 1985.
Going to a Party (for children; produced London, 1984).
The Emperor, with Jonathan Miller, adaptation of a novel by Ryszard Kapuscinski (also co-director: produced London, 1987). London, Penguin, 1988.
A Dream of People (produced London, 1990).
Three Political Plays (includes *The Emperor*, *For the West (Uganda)*, *Lee Harvey Oswald*). London, Penguin, 1990.
Death and the Maiden, adaptation of the play by Ariel Dorfman (produced London, 1991; New York, 1992). London, Hern, 1991.

Screenplays: *Bedtime*, 1968; *The Nightcomers*, 1972.

Television Plays: *The Game*, from his novel, 1961, revised version, 1973; *For the West (Congo)*, 1965; *Blue as His Eyes the Tin Helmet He Wore*, 1967; *Camille '68*, 1968; *Ride, Ride*, 1970; *The Search for the Nile* (documentary), with Derek Marlowe, 1971; *Auntie Kathleen's Old Clothes*, 1977; *Murder Rap*, 1980; *Midnight at the Starlight*, 1980; *Michael Hastings in Brixton* (documentary), 1980; *Stars of the Roller State Disco*, 1984.

Novels

The Game. London, W.H. Allen, 1957; New York, McGraw Hill, 1958.

The Frauds. London, W.H. Allen, 1960; New York, Orion Press, 1961.

Tussy Is Me: A Romance. London, Weidenfeld and Nicolson, 1970; New York, Delacorte Press, 1971.

The Nightcomers. New York, Delacorte Press, 1972; London, Pan, 1973.

And in the Forest the Indians. London, Hodder and Stoughton, 1975.

Short Stories

Bart's Mornings and Other Tales of Modern Brazil. London, Hodder and Stoughton, 1975.

Verse

Love Me, Lambeth, and Other Poems. London, W.H. Allen, 1961.

Other

The Handsomest Young Man in England: Rupert Brooke: A Biographical Essay. London, Joseph, 1967.

Sir Richard Burton: A Biography. London, Hodder and Stoughton, 1978.

*

Manuscript Collections: Princeton University, New Jersey; University of Texas, Austin.

Theatrical Activities:
Director: **Play**—*The Emperor* (co-director, with Jonathan Miller), London, 1987.

*   *   *

Michael Hastings's first play was produced at the now defunct New Lindsey Theatre in Notting Hill when he was only 18, winning him instant fame as one of the youngest dramatists ever to have had his work performed. *Don't Destroy Me* showed an ear for the casual but revealing remark, though the dialogue was never fully controlled. Hastings's second play, *Yes, and After*, was three times as long (i.e., four and a half hours), indicating an increasing ease with the medium. It was also a mature work in many respects. He exploited his ability at dialogue, his minor characters were well observed, and, significantly, the female characters came at least as fully to life as the male ones: the daughter in this play is one of his finest creations. Both these plays were considered significant additions to the new drama of the angry young men.

Hastings returned to the stage only after nine years. For five years he had not written at all, having spent time educating himself while living frugally in France, Germany, and Spain. The education was less digested, in dramatic terms, than was desirable: *The World's Baby* is a sceptical chronicle of British life from the 1920's to the 1950's. The central character, Anna, begins as a Dionysian dispenser of sex. While her Cambridge boyfriends change as a result of wartime experiences, Anna's anti-bourgeois convictions remain intact. Hastings's Jewish and working-class background might lead one to expect sympathy with Anna's views, but their

effect is pitilessly to transform her from charming (if childish) impetuousness to menopausal crankiness. Is Anna to be seen as a victim of circumstances, as a symbol of her times, or simply as an individual? She is a little of each but not enough of any to be quite convincing. If Hastings's technique had not grown any more coherent, he certainly had come better to understand how people behave under emotional stress.

Hastings discovered the vein which he was to mine most successfully with his first popular success, *The Silence of Lee Harvey Oswald*. The playwright's background had given him an undeniable instinct for character, his self-education gave him a sense of what is topical, and he rightly focused on the person rather than on history. He had read through the 26-volume Warren Commission Report, but the purpose of his play was to understand what was enigmatic in the alleged assassin. Structured on Oswald's declining marriage, the play's emotional power is generated by the explosive brutality of Oswald's treatment of his wife. When she attempts to desert him, their sense of loneliness and exhaustion, which prompts Oswald to plead with her for her return, is equally tellingly handled. The play moves from verbatim transcripts of evidence by Oswald's wife and mother, to dramatisations of episodes described by them. The two women hold different views of the man, his mother believing him to be a framed CIA agent, his wife thinking that he killed Kennedy to gain notoriety. (The play's popularity may have also come from the perpetually appealing techniques and suspense of cross-examination, which has a key place in the technique of the play.) The two views are, however, presented flatly. Oswald remains impenetrable, and Hastings's concern for truth is precisely what prevents the play from achieving the insight of art.

In his play on Saint-Just, Hastings violently couples the documentary material with invented dialogue about twisted revolutionary heroes. Saint-Just's powerful and mysterious silence for the 30 hours preceding his execution is made into the play's crucial anti-climax, showing Hastings at his technically adventurous best. *For the West*, on Idi Amin, is a better blend of documentary and imaginative material, and it is assisted by a large part of it taking place in Amin's dreams.

In the third stage of his playwriting career, Hastings was preoccupied with racial themes. *Gloo Joo* and *Carnival War* are perhaps the best known of the plays on these themes, but Hastings's undoubtedly serious concern is undercut by the farcical mode in which he chooses to treat strongly divisive issues. *Carnival War* combines larking about the Notting Hill Carnival with buffoonery aimed against the police, reminiscent of some of Hastings's earlier plays, especially the television play *Blue as His Eyes the Tin Helmet He Wore*. Notwithstanding this, Hastings's plays about black people have enjoyed considerable success in Africa and the Caribbean.

Tom and Viv is based on the allegation that T. S. Eliot's first wife Vivien Haigh-Wood was committed to an asylum not because she was a lunatic but because, emotionally troubled as she was, she indulged in behaviour that Eliot and his Bloomsbury friends found embarrassing. The controversial nature of this thesis was compounded by the uncertainty regarding its factual basis. History will reveal the truth of the matter. This satirical and sometimes sickening play succeeds as a startling recreation of the period and of period characters, eloquently portraying the savagery of the two societies that destroyed Viv: the landed merchant class of her origin and her husband's glittering literary set who considered her a boor.

Hastings is a dramatist of ever-widening range (extended even further in his recent *The Emperor*), but he still seems in search of a completely congenial dramatic form; there remains a gulf between the inner and outer worlds of his plays.

—Prabhu S. Guptara

HAUPTMAN, William (Thornton). American. Born in Wichita Falls, Texas, 26 November 1942. Educated at Wichita Falls Senior High School, graduated 1961; University of Texas, Austin, B.F.A. in drama 1966; Yale University School of Drama, New Haven, Connecticut, M.F.A. in playwriting 1973. Married 1) Barbara Barbat in 1968 (divorced 1977), one daughter; 2) Marjorie Erdreich in 1985, one son. Instructor in playwriting, Adelphi College, Garden City, New York, 1973–75, and Yale University School of Drama, 1976; performer with Cadillac Cowboys rockabilly band, La Jolla, California, Summer 1985. Recipient: CBS grant, 1976; National Endowment for the Arts grant, 1977; Obie award, 1977; Guggenheim grant, 1978; Boston Theatre Critics Circle award, 1984; Tony award, 1985; San Diego Drama Critics Circle award, 1985; Dramalogue award, 1986; Jesse Jones award, for fiction, 1986. Agent: Rick Leed, Agency for the Performing Arts, 888 Seventh Avenue, New York, New York 10106. Address: 240 Warren Street, Apartment E, Brooklyn, New York 11201, U.S.A.

PUBLICATIONS

Plays

Heat (produced New Haven, Connecticut, 1972; revised version produced New York, 1974). New York, French, 1977.
Shearwater (produced New Haven, Connecticut, 1973; New York, 1974). Published in *Performance* (New York), vol. 1, no. 5, March–April 1973.
Domino Courts (produced New York, 1975). With *Comanche Cafe*, New York, French, 1977.
Comanche Cafe (produced New York, 1976). With *Domino Courts*, New York, French, 1977.
The Durango Flash (produced New Haven, Connecticut, 1977).
Big River, music and lyrics by Roger Miller, adaptation of the novel *Adventures of Huckleberry Finn* by Mark Twain (produced Cambridge, Massachusetts, 1984; New York, 1985). New York, Grove Press, 1986.
Gillette (produced Cambridge, Massachusetts, 1985; revised version produced La Jolla, California, 1986). New York, Theatre Communications Group, 1985.

Television Play: *A House Divided* series (3 episodes), 1981.

Novel

The Storm Season. New York, Bantam, 1992.

Short Stories

Good Rockin' Tonight. New York, Bantam, 1988.

*

William Hauptman comments:

I find as I get older I'm more interested in writing what I know about, and what I really know about is working class, because that's where I'm from. . . . When you get older you realize that there's a reason why the forms exist; they've been created by a process that's hundreds of years long. Story and character are still the most important things. The style comes and goes, but stories about people remain.

* * *

There is a remarkable wholeness about William Hauptman's dramatic writing that transcends the working-class milieu in which his plays are set. His characteristic preoccupations surface even in *Big River*, his Tony award-winning book for the 1985 Broadway musical based upon Mark Twain's *Adventures of Huckleberry Finn*. An awareness of the outdoors, the land, and forces of nature permeates this writing and generates some striking scenic images. That visual sensibility is supplemented by his strongly imagistic use of sound: the distant dog bark that ends *Domino Courts*, the low rumble that seems to comment upon Carroll's line "Now we can have some peace and quiet, right, honey?" in *Heat*, a passing train, the howl of a coyote, droning cicadas, and specific musical selections that often mock a character's pipe dreams.

All of his plays are episodically constructed; like the early Tennessee Williams, William Hauptman might be better described as a "scenewright" than a playwright. That loose construction, however, is metaphorically appropriate for these studies of characters infected by wanderlust. The car on the road or the raft on the river offer them an aimless mobility that might bring "the answer" to drifters like Huck and Jim in *Big River*, Mickey and Bobby in *Gillette*, and Roy in *Domino Courts*, or to those who merely dream of travel, like Ronnie in *Comanche Cafe* and Joe Billy in *Heat*. Above all, Hauptman's characters seem to be in search of their own identities. Huck Finn declares in song his determination "to be nobody but himself." "Hell—let's be ourselves," Floyd pleads with Roy, whom he accuses of flaunting a "phony personality." In *Heat* Carroll says, "I've got a club. When you belong you can be anyone you want." Mickey, the fortyish drifter in *Gillette*, says "You look at that town and you see all the towns that ever were, and every person you've ever been. . . . There's somebody inside me who's bigger and better than I've ever been yet." But his young friend Bobby, a novice on the road, seeks to define himself in terms of an occupation.

Friendship between two men is the basis for all of Hauptman's full-length plays as well as for the one-act *Domino Courts*. Huck and Jim, Mickey and Bobby, Carroll and Harley, and Floyd and Roy all experience a pattern of alternating closeness and estrangement in their relationships. Each craves self-sufficiency but fears loneliness. The pattern is reiterated structurally by an alternation of scenes set in town with scenes set on the river or prairie or desert. When they are in town, the men feel trapped and have to get away from "civilization"; but out in the country, with the town's lights twinkling in the distance, they feel as if they are missing out on some action. Similarly, they are often torn between their need for freedom and their desire for the comfort of a woman's love. Mickey sums up the conflict most of them have faced: "Long time ago, I decided not to go for the house and kids. I was going for the other dream—freedom and a big score at the end of the road."

Women cause the greatest stress on the men's friendships. *Gillette* deals most directly with this problem, for both Mickey and Bobby must choose between binding themselves to the women who seem to be so right for them or remaining buddies as before. In *Domino Courts* Floyd and Roy get at each other through their women. In both of these plays and in *Heat*, the men often behave like little boys showing off for the women or for each other. They speak of "staying up all night" as if it were a special affirmation of manhood. Between women this sort of bonding is rare in Hauptman's plays; they are usually too afraid of losing their man. Occasionally that wariness will be dissolved in a spontaneous appreciation of "something in common," as in *Heat* when Susan and Billie find that they have both shoplifted. They devote much effort to learning, as Ronnie says in *Domino Courts*, "how to deal with men," even as they tell each other: "Don't cry, honey, no man's worth it." It is a major breakthrough when a woman like Jody in *Gillette* learns that she need not be dependent upon a man.

Hauptman's best writing to date is probably *Gillette*, about a couple of oil rig roughnecks who dream of making "big coin" in a northeastern Wyoming boom town. Originally published in Theatre Communications Group's "Plays in Process" series in 1985, it was extensively revised by Hauptman for its 1986 production at La Jolla Playhouse. *Variety's* review sums up the appeal of this compelling portrait of blue-collar America: "It is earthy, rousing, contemporary and tough-minded—a very funny, well-written, well-staged, well-played serious comedy with a Saroyanesque strain in oddly touching moments. And like Saroyan, Hauptman's long suit is dialog and the creating of strong, highly individual, often eccentric characters."

—Felicia Hardison Londré

HAVIS, Allan. American. Born in New York City, 26 September 1951. Educated at City College, New York, B.A. 1973; Hunter College, New York, M.A. 1976; Yale University, New Haven, Connecticut, M.F.A. 1980. Married Cheryl Riggins in 1982. Film instructor in children's program, Guggenheim Museum, New York, 1974–76; writer-in-residence, Case Western Reserve University, Cleveland, Ohio, 1976; theatre critic, *Our Town*, New York, 1977; playwriting instructor, Foundation of the Dramatists Guild, New York, 1985–87, Ulster County Community College, Stone Ridge, New York, 1986–88, Old Dominion University, Norfolk, Virginia, 1987, Sullivan County Community College, Loch Sheldrake, New York, 1987, and since 1988, University of California at San Diego, La Jolla. Recipient: John Golden award, 1974, 1975; Case Western Reserve University Klein award, 1976; Dramatists Guild/CBS award, 1985; Playwrights USA award, 1986; National Endowment for the Arts fellowship, 1986; Rockefeller fellowship, 1987; Guggenheim fellowship, 1987; New York State Foundation for the Arts fellowship, 1987; Albee Foundation for the Arts fellowship, 1987; Kennedy Center/American Express grant, 1987; MacDowell fellowship, 1988; McKnight fellowship, 1989; Hawthornden fellowship, 1989; University of California Faculty Summer fellowship, 1989; California Arts Council fellowship, 1991; Rockefeller residency, Bellagio Centre, Italy, 1991. Agent: Helen Merrill, 435 West 23rd Street, New York, New York 10011, U.S.A.; or Peters, Fraser, and Dunlop Group, 503/4 The Chambers, Chelsea Harbour, Lots Road, London SW10 0XF, England. Address: 531 Palomar Avenue, La Jolla, California 92037, U.S.A.

PUBLICATIONS

Plays

The Boarder and Mrs. Rifkin (produced New York, 1974).
Oedipus Again (produced Cleveland, 1976).
Watchmaker (produced New York, 1977).
Heinz (produced New Haven, Connecticut, 1978).
Interludes (produced New Haven, Connecticut, 1978).
Family Rites (produced New Haven, Connecticut, 1979).
The Road from Jerusalem (produced New York, 1984).
Holy Wars (produced Cambridge, Massachusetts, 1984).
Morocco (produced New York, 1984). Included in *Plays in Process* (New York), 1985; in *Morocco, Mink Sonata, Hospitality*, 1989.
Mink Sonata (also director: produced New York, 1986). In *Morocco, Mink Sonata, Hospitality*, 1989.
Duet for Three (produced New York, 1986).
Mother's Aria (also director: produced New York, 1986).
Einstein for Breakfast (produced New York, 1986).
Haut Goût (produced Norfolk, Virginia, 1987). Published in *Plays in Process* (New York), vol.8 no.5, 1987.
Hospitality (produced Philadelphia, 1988; London, 1989). In *Morocco, Mink Sonata, Hospitality*, 1989.
Morocco, Mink Sonata, Hospitality. New York, Broadway Play Publishing, 1989.
A Daring Bride (produced New Haven, Connecticut, 1990).
Lilith (produced New York, 1990). New York, Broadway Play Publishing, 1991.

Other

Albert the Astronomer (for children). New York, Harper, 1979.

*

Theatrical Activities:
Director: **Plays**—some of his own plays.

* * *

"We had a passion for strange dark risks," says Claire, the modern-day demon lover in Allan Havis's *Lilith*, getting at the essence of the mysterious and disturbing work of this American playwright. Havis's plays tend toward the Kafkaesque. Their worlds are nightmares of unreason in which a well-off white American male, often Jewish, is lured by the siren song of the Other—a woman, or a man of dark skin: an Arab, a Haitian. Whether or not a formal investigation is taking place, dialogue is filled with the threat of attack, the tension of defense. The white man is victimized, betrayed. He may be goaded to murder; nonetheless his antagonist always wins.

Havis is a cryptic storyteller. Critic James Leverett wrote of one play that characters "encounter one another in circumstances that are fraught but far from clear." This is generally true, and the playwright's elegant and elliptical language resists reduction to straightforward meaning or moral. Still, the sexual and racial tensions at the heart of Havis's plays are uncomfortably familiar, and this dramatist's most important achievement may prove to be the revelation of what it feels like to be a white male, an American, in an age in which he senses his long ascendancy coming to an end.

Morocco, Havis's best and most successful play to date, was described by Mel Gussow in the New York *Times* as "an absorbing cat-and-mouse game in which one cannot always distinguish the cat from the mouse." The first act consists of 10 brief scenes representing 10 days during which Kempler, a Jewish-American architect, attempts to secure his wife's release from a Moroccan jail. Kempler's antagonist, the nameless Arab Colonel who runs the prison, is given to remarks like "Is this secrecy Jewish?" Havis knows his audience will think the worst of the Moroccan and the best of the architect and his banker wife, and therefore assume that a charge of prostitution and a diagnosis of syphilis have been trumped up—at least until they witness the tension-filled second-act conversation between husband and wife, which takes place at an expensive restaurant in Spain "some days later." Increasingly it seems possible that Mrs. Kempler, who is part Arab and part Spanish gypsy, is in fact promiscuous; it is also apparent that her husband is inclined to jealousy, paranoia, and masochism. The third act finds him back in the Colonel's office, confessing to the murder of his wife—who promptly appears to collect her husband. She takes him away only after her exchanges in Arabic with the Colonel show that Kempler is the odd man out. This play takes place—the phrase is Gussow's—in "a Morocco of the mind."

Haut Goût mines similar terrain. A rich Jewish doctor insists on taking leave from his New York suburban life to spend several months in Haiti testing a milk formula he has developed to combat infant mortality. This innocent abroad promptly finds himself entangled with the ruler of the island, who incarnates Americans' most prejudicial notions about such figures: Le Croix is an army general, a communist, a torturer, a heroin addict, a homosexual—and, as Dr. Gold discovers, a person with AIDS (though that term is not used). Gold resists Le Croix's persistent sexual advances, but is nonetheless under his spell; the doctor is less successful in standing up to Latch, the U.S. State Department official who pressures him to murder the general. (Latch, we are given to understand, arranged the deaths of seven babies in Gold's study—deaths the doctor naïvely blames himself for.) Gold gives Le Croix a lethal injection and returns home a broken man, but in the last scene the general turns up in Scarsdale with his perpetual attendant, a woman said to be able to raise the dead. They poison Dr. Gold, and Le Croix ends the play with talk of togetherness in death. Filled with the guilt of the privileged, the American has sought his own destruction.

A sinister view of United States government is central to the ironically titled *Hospitality*, in which two Immigration agents—one white, one black—work to break two detainees, one a female Colombian journalist, the other a rightwing Israeli politician. They induce diarrhea in the woman; she gives names; in the end she is released, though it is now impossibly dangerous for her to return home. The Jew is beaten, and his insulin is withheld; he dies of a stroke. Happy Logan, the agent who administered the beating, is in a neat reversal the designated victim of the subsequent investigation. His presumed buddy, the black agent Fuller, will not help him, and may have set him up. His personal as well as professional life a shambles, Logan kills himself. He is a particularly clear example of a white American destroyed through his dealings with the Other.

Mink Sonata, at least initially, attempts a lighter tone. The most absurdist of these plays, its focus is the relationship between an affluent father and his troubled daughter, Roberta. She has an alter ego, Blake, "stylish, self-confident and very attractive"; played by the same actress, Blake enables sexual fantasies to surface. Nearly every relationship in a Havis play is notable for talk about what would ordinarily be subliminal sexual tension.

There is considerable comedy, too, in the first act of *Lilith*, in which Adam and his pre-Eve wife wrangle before a Voice,

that of an archangel conducting the hearing that will result in the couple's separation and the creation of Adam's new mate. "Strindberg as directed by Mike Nichols" is Havis's description of his post-intermission depiction of present-day Claire's power to disrupt family life by seducing Arnold (the act's Adam), sexually initiating his 10-year-old son, and, at moments, casting her spell over Eppy, the wife and mother who is the act's Eve. Throughout the play Adam is inept and helpless in the face of Lilith's determination to have children; once again male power is shown to be illusory.

—M. Elizabeth Osborn

HAWKES, John (Clendennin Burne Jr.). American. Born in 1925.
See 3rd edition, 1982.

HELLER, Joseph. American. Born in 1923.
See 3rd edition, 1982.

HELLMAN, Lillian (Florence). American. 1905–1984.
See 3rd edition, 1982.

HENDRY, Tom (Thomas Best Hendry). Canadian. Born in Winnipeg, Manitoba, 7 June 1929. Educated at Bishop Taché School and Norwood Collegiate Institute, St. Boniface, Manitoba; Kelvin Technical High School, Winnipeg, graduated 1947; University of Manitoba, Winnipeg, 1947; Manitoba Institute of Chartered Accountants, admitted to membership 1955. Married 1) Irene Chick in 1958 (divorced 1963); 2) Judith Carr in 1963; two sons and one daughter. Owner, Thomas Hendry, C.A., 1956–58, and partner, Hendry and Evans, 1958–61, Winnipeg; founder and partner, Theatre 77, Winnipeg, 1957–58; manager and producer, Rainbow Stage, Winnipeg, 1958–60; founder and general manager, Manitoba Theatre Centre, Winnipeg, 1958–63; secretary-general, Canadian Theatre Centre, Toronto, 1964–69; editor, *Stage in Canada*, Toronto, 1965–69; literary manager, Stratford Festival, Ontario, 1969, 1970; founding director, Playwrights Co-op, 1971–79 and Playwrights Canada, 1979–82, Toronto; co-founder and producer, Toronto Free Theatre, 1971–82; co-founder, Banff Playwrights Colony, and head of the Playwriting Department,

Banff Centre, Alberta, 1974–76; audit officer, Department of National Revenue, Toronto, 1982–84; chair, Task Force on National Arts Centre, Ottawa, 1986. Consultant, 1984–85, and since 1985 policy director, Toronto Arts Council; since 1986 Barker Fairley distinguished visitor in Canadian culture, University College, Toronto. Recipient: Canada Council travel grant, 1963, Senior Arts grant, 1973, and grant, 1977; Centennial medal, 1967; Lieutenant-Governor's medal, 1970; Queen's Silver Jubilee medal, 1977; Toronto Drama Bench award, 1982. Fellow, Bethune College, York University, Downsview, Ontario, 1978. Address: 34 Elgin Avenue, Toronto, Ontario M5R 1G6, Canada.

PUBLICATIONS

Plays

Do You Remember? (televised 1954; revised version, music by Neil Harris, produced Winnipeg, 1957).
Trapped! (for children; produced Winnipeg, 1961).
Do Not Pick the Flowers (mime play; produced Winnipeg, 1962).
All about Us (revue), with Len Peterson, music by Allan Laing (produced Winnipeg, 1964).
Fifteen Miles of Broken Glass (televised 1966). Published in *A Theatre Happening*, Toronto, Nelson, 1968; revised version (produced Toronto, 1970), Toronto, Playwrights, 1972.
Satyricon, music by Stanley Silverman, adaptation of the work by Petronius (produced Stratford, Ontario, 1969).
How Are Things with the Walking Wounded? (as *The Walking Wounded*, produced Lansing, Michigan, 1970; as *How Are Things with the Walking Wounded?*, produced Toronto, 1972). Toronto, Playwrights, 1972.
That Boy—Call Him Back (produced Lansing, Michigan, 1970; Toronto, 1971). Published in *Performing Arts in Canada* (Toronto), Winter 1972.
You Smell Good to Me, and Séance (produced Toronto, 1972). Toronto, Playwrights, 1972.
The Missionary Position (produced Vancouver, 1972). Toronto, Playwrights, 1972.
Dr. Selavy's Magic Theatre (lyrics only), with Richard Foreman, music by Stanley Silverman (produced Lenox, Massachusetts, and New York, 1972; Oxford, 1978).
Aces Wild, music by Hendry and Stephen Jack, lyrics by Hendry (also director: produced Hamilton, Ontario, 1972).
Friends and Lovers (includes *You Smell Good To Me* and *The Missionary Position*). Toronto, Playwrights, 1972.
Gravediggers of 1942, music by Stephen Jack, lyrics by Hendry (produced Toronto, 1973; London, 1984). Toronto, Playwrights, 1973.
The Dybbuk (lyrics only), book by John Hirsch, music by Allan Laing, adaptation of the play by S. Ansky (produced Winnipeg, 1974; Los Angeles, 1975). Winnipeg, Peguis, 1975.
Naked at the Opera (produced Banff, Alberta, 1975). Toronto, Co-opera, 1976.
A Memory of Eden (produced Banff, Alberta, 1975).
Apart from Everything, Is Anything the Matter? (produced Banff, Alberta, 1975).
Byron, music by Stephen Jack (produced Toronto, 1976).
Confidence (produced Banff, Alberta, 1976).
Séance II, published in *Quarry* (Kingston, Ontario), Winter 1978–79.
Hogtown: Toronto the Good, music by Paul Hoffert (produced Toronto, 1981).
East of the Sun, West of the Moon (produced Toronto, 1986).

Screenplays: *Box Car Ballet* (documentary), 1955; *A City in White* (documentary), 1956; *A House Divided* (documentary), 1957; *The Day the Freaks Took Over*, 1972; *Aces Wild*, 1974; *Private Places*, with Ron Kelly, 1976.

Radio Plays: *Wolf, Adolph, and Benito*; *The Steps Behind Her*; *Sea and Sky*, 1951–59.

Television Plays: *Do You Remember?*, 1954; *The Anniversary*, from a short story by Chekhov, 1965; *Fifteen Miles of Broken Glass*, 1966; *Last Man on Horseback*, 1969; *I Was Never in Kharkov*, 1972; *Pickles*, 1976; *Royal Suite* series (3 episodes), 1976; *Santa Claus from Florida*, 1976; *King of Kensington* series (6 episodes), 1977–78, 1981; *Welcome to Canada*, 1977; *The Central Tech Tiger*, 1977; *Volcano*, 1978; *Please Say You're Real*, 1978.

Other

The Canadians (on English-Canadian theatre). Toronto, Macmillan, 1967.
Theatre in Canada: A Reluctant Citizen. Toronto, Committee for an Independent Canada, 1972.
Cultural Capital: The Care and Feeding of Toronto's Artistic Assets. Toronto, Toronto Arts Council, 1985.
L'École/The School with Michel Garneau. Montréal, Stanke, 1985.
Task Force on the National Arts Centre: Accent on Access/ Favoriser l'accessibilité (English and French texts). Ottawa, Government of Canada, 1986.

*

Manuscript Collections: Public Archives of Canada, Ottawa; Toronto Public Library.

Critical Study: *The Work: Conversations with English-Canadian Playwrights* by Robert Wallace and Cynthia Zimmerman, Toronto, Coach House Press, 1982.

Theatrical Activities:
Director: **Play**—*Aces Wild*, Hamilton, Ontario, 1972.
Actor: roles in *The Jacksons and Their Neighbours* and other radio and television series, early 1950's.

Tom Hendry comments:
   I cannot explain why I write plays, or why I choose the subjects that I do. The people in the plays reflect the people in my life—mostly they are outsiders. Paradoxically, I believe that if you examine anyone closely you will find that in some important area of his life he is an outsider, a non-participant. I believe that civilized society is a system of institutionalized violence directed at the individuals who make it up, and that to some extent each of us is aware of and opposes this violence. I believe that how people behave is as important as why they behave as they do. I believe that the damage we do to each other will only abate and finally cease when more perfect forms of communication—akin to ESP—are discovered and taught to everyone. Therefore I believe that dreams and nightmares and fairy tales are the only things worth writing or writing about. My plays say what I have to say.

* * *

   Tom Hendry fills the plays from his most prolific period of writing for the stage with articulate and sophisticated characters, with artists, models, *literati*, and successful businessmen. His is a world of chic parties, brittle dialogue, liquor, drugs, and sexual freedom of a marked homosexual ambiance—a world of falsity. In expressing a set of attitudes typical of young urbanites of the 1970's, these plays also present central themes and figures which can be found in Hendry's earliest plays and which recur in the more recent work. In this world of stereotypes, the very shallowness of the fictional personalities is true to the real world they represent, and Hendry draws them accurately: his world is less erudite than is Waugh's, but it is also less guilty and self-indulgent than is Crowley's and, therefore, more credible. At times, Hendry draws elements out of even these predictable characters that bring them to life, but the strains of the mannered drawing-room comedy are more than reminiscent and when Hendry is imitative he is as shallow as his characters and as boring. In a play like *How Are Things with the Walking Wounded?* an unevenness arises between those sections which work out an original pattern and those which seem superimposed snatches of Noël Coward, a difficulty in integrating material (especially lyrics) which persists through the later musical collaborations. This is unfortunate, since a maturation of craft can be seen through this period and, apart from the sense of *déjà vu* which besets it, *Walking Wounded* is a fine play. Unfortunately also, Simone is correct in remarking of herself and her fellow characters, "we do tend to talk a lot, darling."

The plays produced at the Toronto Free Theatre rework the related themes of the outsider, the "non-participant" as Hendry has called him, and the prostitute he becomes in a world based on selling out as a solution to loneliness or failure. The figure first appears in the television play *Fifteen Miles of Broken Glass* in the person of an under-aged air force cadet who is left out when the war ends three years before he can join it. The bombing of Hiroshima ends the protagonist's heroic dreams, forcing him to connect with reality. The outsider becomes representative of Canada in this war play and, more strongly, in the later *Gravediggers of 1942*, which overlays a campy musical comedy subplot on the shocking events of the Dieppe raid. Here the thesis is a more intellectual statement of the Hendry theme, with the prostitution symbolically extended to a cynical self-destruction of the Canadian psyche in the person of the ingenue Judy who finally capitulates to Hitler's offers of wealth and power. Kept outside the principal action and sacrificed by stronger powers, made as ineffectual as the naive Canadian kids in the subplot trying to become part of the war effort by putting on a show to sell war bonds, "Our Lady of the Peace Tower" accepts one solution to being outside: she learns to prostitute herself. By doing so, she completes the series of characters in *You Smell Good to Me*, *The Missionary Position*, and *Walking Wounded*; seen from various vantages, Albert-Steven-Willy is the same character and Regan–Rene–Barbara–Judy, although they display different external characteristics and even genders are simply facets of the hustler figure.

Gravediggers suffers from often clumsy lyrics and an uneven relationship of song to plot, a problem which caused the later musical collaboration *Hogtown: Toronto the Good* to fail in production though its concept is sound and its scale ambitious. *Hogtown* presents a dialectic on the legislation of public morality, and, once again, it presents the struggle as a battle between the establishment and the outsider. Once again, that outsider is a prostitute—a famous brothel keeper from Toronto's past. Like *Gravediggers* and a series of musical collaborations since *Satyricon*, this play attempts to join a debate on heroism through often hopeless action (a theme explored most completely in *Byron*) to the apparatus of the Broadway musical. Each of these entertainments is an excit-

ing cooperative project, but each remains in need of further revision and completion; Hendry has not yet achieved the complex mix of cynicism and froth he seeks, has not yet brought his highly interrelated plays together to produce the one play to which all the others point.

Hendry now works as an arts administrator and has recently prepared a pivotal report on cultural funding. He has turned away from writing for the stage, but has recently adapted *Fifteen Miles of Broken Glass* to film.

—Reid Gilbert

HENLEY, Beth (Elizabeth Becker Henley). American. Born in Jackson, Mississippi, 8 May 1952. Educated at Southern Methodist University, Dallas, B.F.A. 1974; University of Illinois, Urbana, 1975–76. Actress, Theatre Three, Dallas, 1972–73, with Southern Methodist University Directors Colloquium, 1973, and with the Great American People Show, New Salem, 1976; teacher, Dallas Minority Repertory Theatre, 1974–75. Recipient: Pulitzer prize, 1981; New York Drama Critics Circle award, 1981; Oppenheimer award, 1981. Lives in Los Angeles. Agent: Gilbert Parker, William Morris Agency, 1350 Avenue of the Americas, New York, New York 10019, U.S.A.

PUBLICATIONS

Plays

Am I Blue? (produced Dallas, 1973; revised version produced Hartford, Connecticut, 1981; New York, 1982). New York, Dramatists Play Service, 1982.
Crimes of the Heart (produced Louisville, 1979; New York, 1980; London, 1983). New York, Viking Press, 1982.
The Miss Firecracker Contest (produced Los Angeles, 1980; London, 1982; New York, 1984). New York, Dramatists Play Service, 1985.
The Wake of Jamey Foster (produced Hartford, Connecticut, and New York, 1982). New York, Dramatists Play Service, 1983.
The Debutante Ball (produced Costa Mesa, California, 1985; New York, 1988; London, 1989). Jackson, University of Mississippi Press, 1991.
The Lucky Spot (produced New York, 1987; London, 1991). New York, Dramatists Play Service, 1987.
Abundance (produced Costa Mesa, California, 1989; New York, 1990).
Control Freaks (also director: produced Chicago, 1992).

Screenplays: *The Moon Watcher*, 1983; *True Stories*, with Stephen Tobolowsky, 1986; *Crimes of the Heart*, 1987; *Nobody's Fool*, 1987; *Miss Firecracker*, 1990.

* * *

Portraying women who seek to define themselves outside of their relationships with men and beyond their family environment is a unifying factor in all of Beth Henley's plays.

Surprisingly, her first play to be produced in New York, *Crimes of the Heart*, won the Pulitzer prize and most of her work continues to be compared to it. There are strong similarities between her plays, not only in theme but also in plot; but it is Henley's characters who provide unique contributions to the dramaturgy. The McGrath sisters in *Crimes of the Heart* are probably the most traditionally well-developed characters in that each has a strong connection to the plot; each grows from her experience; and each comes to understand others better. However, in *The Debutante Ball*, *The Wake of Jamey Foster*, and the more recent *Abundance*, Henley masterfully creates characters who explore their identities within a complex plot and who transcend their experience with uncertain and unexpected results.

The Debutante Ball is a quirky play filled with Henley's typical southern humor and Chekhovian characters. The play includes action that is not often dramatized, such as women cutting themselves shaving, and an unsympathetic treatment of a deaf girl. The ball serves as a structural device for all the characters to come together in hopes of re-establishing their place in society. However Teddy the debutante cannot go through with the façade and in the end she is left bleeding all over her ball gown, having aborted a child. Pregnant by a one-armed man with a scarred face, whom Teddy had called ugly, she explains that: "I kinda just did it to be polite. I couldn't take on any more, ah, bad feelings, guilt."

In *The Wake of Jamey Foster* the occasion is the burial of Marshael's husband, Jamey. The unhappy and bitter widow eventually resolves her feelings and, like the debutante, is actually empowered by the difficulties and troubled feelings that the death has brought to light. In *Abundance* two pioneer women, Macon Hill and Bess Johnson, are also empowered by the unexpected twists of fate which in the end leave them both looking like freaks, a powerful physical representation of disfigured dreams.

Death, disaster, and freakish accidents play a major role in all of Henley's plays. However, Henley's treatment of this recurring motif is often humorous. Most of her southern characters accept such events matter-of-factly, so that when Babe shoots her husband in *Crimes of the Heart*, or when Bess is kidnapped by the Indians in *Abundance*, or when orphan Carnelle in *The Miss Firecracker Contest* speaks nonchalantly about people dying—"It seems like people've been dying practically all my life, in one way or another"—it is never maudlin.

Structurally Henley relies on storytelling, especially those stories in which female characters can turn to other female characters for help. She often employs one or two female characters to center her story around, usually an occasion of some sort and then adds dimension to the plot with minor characters who are bleakly comic or mildly eccentric. Leon, the slow-witted brother in *The Wake of Jamey Foster*, Cassidy, the pathetic tom-boy teenager in Henley's least successfuly play *The Lucky Spot*, or Delmount, the mentally unstable cousin in *The Miss Firecracker Contest*, are all good examples. These secondary characters reinforce a comic pathos established by the central characters. The cruelties of life befall all Henley's characters and the playwright is adept in dramatizing their sadness with a rare duality of expression that creates laughter and tears. One of the most memorable examples is that of Cassidy who clings to a dream in which a "furry animal" pledged his love for her.

Male characters often serve as plot devices and are rarely fully developed, especially problematic in *Abundance* with the character of Elmore, an opportunist who shows up late in the play to help Bess write about her ordeal of being kidnapped and living with the Indians for five years. Brighton in *The Debutante Ball* and Doc in *Crimes of the Heart* are

necessary to advance the plot but remain one-dimensional. Male characters rarely take any definite positive action, but rather serve as the impetus for action by the female characters. Will in *Abundance* and, to a lesser degree, Brocker in *The Wake of Jamey Foster*, are exceptions.

Linguistically, Henley's style couples witty dialogue with poetic colloquial speech that at its best produces a powerful personal voice for her characters, especially when the playwright trusts the simplicity and honesty of her southern characters. Language becomes forced when Henley moves beyond descriptions of experience. When characters reveal how they feel, Henley makes good use of her own strong feelings and observations. However, she is less successful in descriptive metaphors, which are especially clumsy in the opening scenes of *Abundance*, an epic play that spans 25 years beginning in the late 1860's. The dialogue creates a forced rhythm unnatural and uncharacteristic of Henley. For example, in the early moments of the play Bess says: "Thanks kindly. I'm near pined t'death with famine." Later in the play Henley overuses metaphor as when Bess says: "I try not to show my hurt. I hide it in different parts of the house. I bury jars of it in the cellar; throw buckets of it down the well; iron streaks of it into the starched clothes and hang them in the closet."

Crimes of the Heart is Henley's most fully integrated play in terms of dramatic elements, but *Abundance* is her most ambitious. The latter contains many elements of earlier plays including freak accidents, female bonding, and the exploration of identity. It also shares one of the less successful dramaturgical strategies seen in other plays where too much happens between scenes; character transformations happen in mental space so that it is difficult to believe the changes that occur, especially in the character of Bess. The problem is more pervasive in *Abundance* because of the epic nature of the play. Still, the play is Henley's most sober and explicit work, fillcd with a strong sense of irony and uncompromising in its depiction of the evils that befall women who sell out their identities to men.

—Judy Lee Oliva

———————

HENSHAW, James Ene. Nigerian. Born in Calabar, 29 August 1924. Educated at Christ the King College, Onitsha; National University of Ireland, Dublin, M.B. 1949; University of Wales, T.D.D. 1954. Married Caroline Nchelem Amadi in 1958; five sons and three daughters. Physician: medical consultant to Government of Eastern Nigeria, 1955–78: controller of medical services in Southern Eastern State (now Cross River State), 1968–72, and senior consultant on tuberculosis control, Rivers State, 1973–78. Member, National Council on Health, 1968–72, and Nigerian Medical Council, 1970–72. Recipient: Henry Carr Memorial Cup, 1953. Knight, Order of St. Gregory the Great, 1965; Officer, Order of the Niger, 1977. Address: Itiaba House, 4 Calabar Road, P.O. Box 1249, Calabar, Nigeria.

PUBLICATIONS

Plays

This Is Our Chance (produced Dublin, 1947). Published in *This Is Our Chance*, 1957.

This Is Our Chance: Plays from West Africa (includes *The Jewels of the Shrine, A Man of Character, This Is Our Chance*).   London, University of London Press, 1957; *The Jewels of the Shrine* published in *Plays from Black Africa*, edited by Fredric M. Litto, New York, Hill and Wang, 1968.

A Man of Character (produced Ilorin, 1970).   Published in *This Is Our Chance*, 1957.

Children of the Goddess and Other Plays (includes *Companion for a Chief* and *Magic in the Blood*).   London, University of London Press, 1964.

Magic in the Blood (produced Newcastle-upon-Tyne, 1987). Published in *Children of the Goddess and Other Plays*, 1964.

Medicine for Love. London, University of London Press, 1964.

Dinner for Promotion. London, University of London Press, 1967.

Enough Is Enough: A Play of the Nigerian Civil War (produced Benin City, Nigeria, 1975).   Benin City, Ethiope, 1976.

A Song to Mary Charles, Irish Sister of Charity (produced Owerri, 1981).   Calabar, Etewa, 1984.

*

Critical Studies: "Modern Drama in West Africa" by O. Ogunba, in *Perspectives in African Literature*, edited by Christopher Haywood, London, Heinemann, 1971; "Drama and Theatre in Nigeria" by Y. Ogunbiyi, in *Nigeria Magazine* (Lagos), 1982; "The Politics of Literary Syllabus: The Marginalization of James Ene Henshaw's Plays" and "Ene Henshaw and the Beginnings of Popular Plays in Nigeria" by A. Bamikunie, in *Nigeria Magazine* (Lagos), Vol.53 No.1, 1985.

James Henshaw comments:

(1988) I usually try (as much as I can) to make sure that those people who watch my plays do not return to their homes sadder than they have been. That is why the plays are mostly described as "comedies," even though there are more tragic situations in some of them than in some "tragic" plays. The comedy medium has, however, worked well for the type of audiences I have always had in mind, namely the youths, especially Nigerian youths.

Through many of my plays and the introductory essays that accompany them I have tried to make it clear that I was writing about Africans and for Africans. To me the preoccupation of making the "white man" understand the "black man" through African writing has never been as important as the need to make one Nigerian understand the other, or one African understand the other better. The plays are therefore always relevant to the culture and environment of the play goers. In addition to introductory essays, I usually give simple instructions to help players who might not have someone to direct them. Occasionally I am invited to see the plays and I think I enjoy them like anyone else in the audience. I have been particularly impressed by the variety of productions.

* * *

James Ene Henshaw occupies a unique position in African/ Nigerian literary drama, coming as he does between the "coarse plays" of the Onitsha Market literature tradition of the 1950's and early 1960's and the more sophisticated and better constructed plays of Wole Soyinka and the other university-trained dramatists. One thing for which Henshaw

should be remembered is the fact that his was the first attempt to write what could be regarded as authentic African drama to be performed by African people. He set out, as he says in the preface to *This Is Our Chance*, to write plays "whose scenes take place in surroundings" not "far removed from the African's own" and in which things spoken about have a "relationship with the problems of the African audience."

As a playwright, Henshaw captures the pulse and moods of his West African society. It is quite possible to see his plays as chronologically reflecting the moral concerns and social development of his region since they usually deal with the prevailing political and ethical preoccupations of certain moments in West African history. In *This Is Our Chance* Henshaw looks at a West Africa before colonialism and before Christianity. Koloro is almost virgin Africa with all its traditions intact, even if there are already cracks and friction represented by the indomitable Bambulu, the rebellious Princess Kudaro, and the moderately radical Enusi. Here Henshaw begins his exploration of the theme of tradition in conflict with modernity, a theme which dominates his consciousness in later plays like *Children of the Goddess* and *Companion for a Chief*. One key statement which Henshaw seems to be making in these plays is that societies are capable of generating change from within and that where there are external influences, compromise and accommodation should become the watchword. This, coming as it did in the 1950's and 1960's when the norm was a wholesale sweeping-away of traditional African value systems for foreign Euro-Christian ones, was a new kind of thinking. And this may well explain Henshaw's popularity across a wide spectrum of West African society, for his audiences could relate to his concerns which, in a sense, were their concerns.

Essentially, Henshaw's plays can broadly be divided into two categories, the traditional plays and the contemporary plays. In the first group, Henshaw seems concerned with exploring the tensions that arise when his African traditions are faced with new "modernising" influences from outside and to this extent these plays depict an Africa caught in the throes of transition. Henshaw's voice strikes a middle ground because for him, much as we do not have to remain static by clinging to outmoded traditional practices like the killing of twins in *Children of the Goddess*, the silly superstitions of *This Is Our Chance*, and sacrificing human beings to accompany great chiefs when they die as in *Companion for a Chief*, neither should we abandon all traditional codes of behaviour so as to make way for a strange and undigested modernity.

It is obvious that while Henshaw accepts that the missionaries, the Mcphails and Wilberforce, are agents of good, he cautions that these "good Christians" could become destabilising if they showed no respect for the culture and opinions of the people they had come to Christianize. For Henshaw, the traditional African culture and the Euro-Christian culture can learn a lot from each other and thus avoid the unnecessary tensions which a stubborn rejection and a callous denigration could give rise to. And does this make Henshaw a traditionalist or a modernist? I think he is neither, for he is both, and this I believe is why his plays escape the tag of being moral tracts or a preaching theatre. While his ambivalence tends to deprive his plays of a deeper significance, it allows him a measure of distance from his subjects and characters and this in the end ensures that delightful comic spirit which is never absent from a Henshaw play. It is this and the fact of his being a pioneer of African literary drama that ensured his popularity in the 1950's, 1960's, and 1970's.

In the contemporary plays the themes range from Kobina's stubborn honesty and integrity in the face of domestic and social pressure in *A Man of Character*, the confrontation between the filial irresponsibility of youth and the crafty doggedness of the old of *The Jewels of the Shrine*, to the mild feminism, blind hero-worship, and judicial corruption of *Magic in the Blood*. It also includes the corrupt politics and social excesses of *Medicine for Love*, the cool and devious manipulations in *Dinner for Promotion*, and the more serious and sombre reflections of the post-civil war play *Enough Is Enough*. What one notices in the progress of Henshaw's drama is that as he moved away from traditional concerns, his plays began also to lose that pervading sense of community which characterised *This Is Our Chance* and *Children of the Goddess*. The feeling of the possible communal catastrophe and chaos of these two is replaced by a detached vision of individuals struggling through personal dilemmas and mishaps as Ewia and Kobina are in *Medicine for Love* and *A Man of Character* respectively.

Through the two phases, however, Henshaw still manages to show us his highly developed sense for the comic through deft twists in situations, delightful turns of phrase, and character manipulations for effect. Some of his characters are so memorable that they become household names. Who can forget Bambulu, that artist and master of the big phrase and pose! His comic antics and exuberant pedantry provided ample elocutionary meat for many budding actors and actresses. His famous salvo to Princess Kudaro—"This is the child of my brain, the product of my endeavour, and the materialisation of my inventive genius"—is a speech that became popular and synonymous with African drama and acting in the 1960's. Most of us growing up then knew Bambulu and his famous speech by heart before we chanced on *This Is Our Chance*.

Henshaw is thus important for giving us the first really stageable African plays, and, simple as these plays were, they were filled with memorable African characters and situations.

—Osita Okagbue

HERBERT, John. Pseudonym for John Herbert Brundage, Canadian. Born in Toronto, Ontario, 13 October 1926. Educated in public schools, 1932–43; Art College of Ontario, Toronto, 1947–49; New Play Society School of Drama, Toronto, 1955–58; Volkoff Ballet School, Toronto, 1956; National Ballet School of Canada, 1957. Commercial artist, Toronto, 1943–46; served 6-month sentence in reformatory, Guelph, Ontario, 1946; worked at various jobs in the U.S.A., 1947, 1950–54; artistic director, Adventure Theatre, 1960–62, and New Venture Players, 1962–65, both Toronto; artistic director and producer, Garret Theatre Company, Toronto, 1965–71; artistic director, Medusa Theatre, 1972–74; associate editor, Arteditorial Company, Toronto, 1975–82; resident dramatist and associate director, Smile Company, Toronto, 1984–85. Lecturer in drama, Ryerson Polytechnical School, Toronto, summers 1969–70, York University, Downsview, Ontario, Summer 1972, New College, University of Toronto, summers 1973–76, Three Schools of Art, Toronto, 1975–81, and Tappa School of Art, 1982–83. Dancer, Garbut Roberts's Dance Drama Company; actor, dancer, and set and costume designer with other companies. Recipient: Dominion Drama Festival Massey award, 1968 (refused); Chalmers award, 1975. Agent: Ellen Neuwald Inc., 905 West End Avenue, New York, New York 10025, U.S.A. Address: Suite B-1, 1050 Yonge Street, Toronto, Ontario M4W 2L1, Canada.

PUBLICATIONS

Plays

They Died with Their Boots On: *A Marsh-Melodrama* (produced Canoe Lake, Ontario, 1942).
Private Club (also director: produced Toronto, 1962).
A Household God (also director: produced Toronto, 1962).
A Lady of Camellias, adaptation of a play by Dumas fils (also director: produced Toronto, 1964).
Closer to Cleveland (also director: produced Toronto, 1967).
Fortune and Men's Eyes (produced New York, 1967; London, 1968). New York, Grove Press, 1967; in *Open Space Plays*, edited by Charles Marowitz, London, Penguin, 1974.
World of Woyzeck, adaptation of a play by Georg Büchner (also director: produced Toronto, 1969).
Beer Room (produced Toronto, 1970). Included in *Some Angry Summer Songs*, 1976.
Close Friends (produced Toronto, 1970). Included in *Some Angry Summer Songs*, 1976.
Born of Medusa's Blood (also director: produced Toronto, 1972).
Omphale and the Hero (produced Toronto, 1974). Published in *Canadian Theatre Review 3*, (Toronto), Summer 1974.
Some Angry Summer Songs (includes *Pearl Divers*, *Beer Room*, *Close Friends*, *The Dinosaurs*) (also director: produced Toronto, 1974). Vancouver, Talonbooks, 1976.

Screenplay: *Fortune and Men's Eyes*, 1971.

Other

Belinda Wright and Jelko Yuresha (biography). London, Kaye Bellman, 1972.

*

Manuscript Collection: University of Waterloo, Ontario.

Critical Studies: by Nathan Cohen, in *Canadian Writing Today* edited by Mordecai Richler, London, Penguin, 1970; "Damnation at Christmas" by Ann P. Messenger, in *Dramatists in Canada* edited by W.H. New, Vancouver, University of British Columbia Press, 1972; "Sexuality and Identity in *Fortune and Men's Eyes*" by Neil Carson, in *Twentieth Century Literature* (Los Angeles), July 1972.

Theatrical Activities:
Director: **Plays**—*Mourning Becomes Electra* by O'Neill, Toronto, 1957; Adventure Theatre, Toronto: *The Chalk Garden* by Enid Bagnold, 1961, and *Dear Brutus* by J.M. Barrie, 1962; New Venture Players, Toronto: *Private Club* and *A Household God*, 1962, and *A Lady of Camellias*, 1964; Garret Theatre, Toronto: *The Maids* by Jean Genet and *Escurial* by Michel de Ghelderode, 1965, *The Sea Gull* by Chekhov, 1966, *Closer to Cleveland*, 1967, *Doberman* by David Windsor and *Gin Rummy* by S. Bordenvik, 1968, and *World of Woyzeck*, 1969; *Born of Medusa's Blood*, Toronto, 1972; *Some Angry Summer Songs*, Toronto, 1974; *The Gnädiges Fräulein* by Tennessee Williams, Toronto, 1976; *Close Friends*, Toronto, 1976.
Actor: **Plays**—Shylock in *The Merchant of Venice*, Toronto, 1939; Thisbe in *A Midsummer Night's Dream*, Toronto, 1939; Juliet in *Romeo and Juliet*, Toronto, 1949; Father in *The Monkey's Paw* by W.W. Jacobs and L.N. Parker, Toronto,

1941; Farmer in *The Arkansas Traveller*, Toronto, 1942; Singer in *The Rising of the Moon* by Lady Gregory, Canoe Lake, Ontario, 1942; Carmen in *They Died with Their Boots On*, Canoe Lake, Ontario, 1942; Dancer in *Paris after Midnight* by Betty Rohm, Canadian tour, 1953; Tom in *The Glass Menagerie* by Tennessee Williams, Toronto, 1956: Octavius and Doctor in *The Barretts of Wimpole Street* by Rudolf Besier, Toronto, 1957; Orin in *Mourning Becomes Electra* by O'Neill, Toronto, 1957; Trigorin in *The Sea Gull* by Chekhov, Toronto, 1958; Dr. Sloper in *The Heiress* by Ruth and Augustus Goetz, Toronto, 1958; Professor Tobin in *The Druid Circle* by John van Druten, Toronto, 1959; Mental Patient in *The Wall* by Vyvyan Frost, Toronto, 1960; Rhangda in *A Balinese Legend* by Garbut Roberts, Toronto, 1967; title role in *The Gnädiges Fräulein* by Tennessee Williams, Toronto, 1976.

John Herbert comments:

(1973) My life in theatre goes back as far as I can remember, for I fell in love with the art as a small child. I saw Leonide Massine dance the Cuban Sailor in a production of *Gaîté Parisienne* with a touring company. I saw and heard some of the greatest artists of the theatre at Toronto's Royal Alexandra, in the days when all artists of magnitude travelled the world for us, and I have never lost my passion as a member of the audience. I visit the theatre constantly to see and hear what others are thinking, feeling, and doing. Occasionally, the original thrilling convulsion of surprise returns, as when the Bolshoi Ballet dances, or when Laurence Olivier plays the father in O'Neill's *Long Day's Journey into Night*, or whenever I encounter a new young voice in the theatre, whether it belong to playwright, director, or player. I cannot say that I care more about writing a play than for directing, acting, designing, or dancing. I try to live in the theatre as one would revel as a swimmer in the ocean. The tides must always be felt, powerful, endless, timeless, and terrible as life itself.

* * *

John Herbert's reputation as the *enfant terrible* of Canadian drama arose almost entirely from the acclaim with which his *Fortune and Men's Eyes* was first greeted. That it was well written and without the worst aspects of nationalistic theatre recommended it highly to audiences weary of the sentimental quest for the great Canadian play.

Having said that, though, it is necessary to say that *Fortune and Men's Eyes* is not a great play. Its attractions are that it can easily be performed by a small cast with a modest competence and few resources for sets. Its weakness is that, for all its Sartrean setting, it is sentimental in another way—in its depictions of good and evil in "Western" terms. Smitty, the first-time criminal, who is at the center of the play, is essentially a Victorian character. He is corrupted not by defects present in his own character but by the circumstances of his confinement. In fact, we have very little sense of what sort of person he is, and in that sense his transformation from bewildered innocence to black awareness is artificial. His last speech—"I'll pay you all back"—reminds us of Malvolio's "I'll be revenged on the whole pack of you." But the comparison reveals the thinness of the conflict.

Something of this artifice is manifested in Smitty's diction. To Mona, the Blanche DuBois of this underworld whose brutalization is the moment of Smitty's awakening, he says, "You keep your secrets, like Greta Garbo—under a hat." And his revulsion from Mona is too articulate for the character that he is meant to be: "Let me out of here! I'll go to the bloody concert—anywhere—where there is life."

It is the tendency toward caricature that weakens the play and exposes it as trading both in a fashionable subject and on the need for social reform. Neither of these things would in itself have prevented the play from retaining some permanent stature—Ibsen's *Ghosts* is an example of similar defects—were it not for the fact that the characters seem manufactured. Mona is too weak, and "her" penchant for great books too exaggerated. (It is from "her" attempt to make analogies between the banal life of Kingston Pen and Shakespeare's relation to Southampton that the somewhat precious title comes.) Queenie is credible enough as a caricature queen but not as a person. "Her" vocabulary is just not credible. "Does Macy's bother Gimbel's?" is not a phrase that we believe he, as a Canadian, in a Canadian prison, would use. The author is coming through. It is, in fact, in precisely this absence of particular places and definable voices that the play is weakest. To be everywhere is to be nowhere.

This is not to say that the play is without dramatic force. In its first production and again in its London premiere, it was shocking in the forthrightness of its language and action. But more than shock and a passable narrative are required in a play of stature. And not even these are present in *Omphale and the Hero*, where an archetypal whore-meets-hustler situation is the venue for a great deal of bathetic language and a plot that creaks at every joint. It is sad to see Herbert's talent wasted on bad Tennessee Williams.

—D.D.C. Chambers

———

HERLIHY, James Leo. American. Born in Detroit, Michigan, 27 February 1927. Educated at Black Mountain College, North Carolina, 1947–48; Pasadena Playhouse, California, 1948–50; Yale University School of Drama, New Haven, Connecticut (RCA Fellow), 1956–57. Served in the United States Naval Reserve, 1945–46; petty officer. Taught playwriting at City College, New York 1967–68; distinguished visiting professor, University of Arkansas, Fayetteville, 1983. Lives in Los Angeles. Agent: Jay Garon-Brooke Associates, 415 Central Park West, New York, New York 10025, U.S.A.

Publications

Plays

Streetlight Sonata (produced Pasadena, California, 1950).
Moon in Capricorn (produced New York, 1953).
Blue Denim, with William Noble (produced New York, 1958; Swansea, Wales, 1970). New York, Random House, 1958.
Crazy October, adaptation of his story "The Sleep of Baby Filbertson" (also director: produced New Haven, Connecticut, 1958).
Terrible Jim Fitch (produced Chicago, 1965; London, 1973).
Stop, You're Killing Me (includes *Terrible Jim Fitch*; *Bad Bad Jo-Jo*; *Laughs, Etc.*) (produced Boston, 1968; New York, 1969; *Bad Bad Jo-Jo* produced London, 1970; *Laughs, Etc.* produced London, 1973). New York, Simon and Schuster, 1970.

Novels

All Fall Down. New York, Dutton, 1960; London, Faber, 1961.

Midnight Cowboy. New York, Simon and Schuster, 1965; London, Cape, 1966.
The Season of the Witch. New York, Simon and Schuster, and London, W.H. Allen, 1971.

Short Stories

The Sleep of Baby Filbertson and Other Stories. New York, Dutton, and London, Faber, 1959.
A Story That Ends with a Scream and Eight Others. New York, Simon and Schuster, 1967; London, Cape, 1968.

Other

The Sleep of Reason, photographs by Lyle Bongé. Highlands, North Carolina, Jargon, 1974.

*

Manuscript Collection: Boston University.

Theatrical Activities:
Director: **Play**—*Crazy October*, New Haven, Connecticut, 1958.
Actor: **Plays**—roles at the Pasadena Playhouse, California; in *The Zoo Story* by Edward Albee, Boston and Paris, 1961; title role in *Terrible Jim Fitch*, Chicago, 1965. **Films**—*In the French Style*, 1963; *Four Friends* (*Georgia's Friends*), 1981.

* * *

So I'll get on a bus to Hell.
Which will probably be
another San Pedro—or Times Square or Tia Juana or
Dallas—and I'll make out all right. I can make out in
places
like Hell. I've had practice.

                                                    —*Terrible Jim Fitch*

Embattled innocence and vulnerable corruption, often shading into each other, define the limits of James Leo Herlihy's drama. The innocent, struggling in a hostile society they inadvertently threaten, sometimes perish, sometimes triumph, and occasionally become embodiments of the corruption they once challenged. In Herlihy's unpublished fantasy *Moon in Capricorn*, Jeanne Wilkes has an actual star in her heart, a condition producing untrammelled happiness, often objectified in her tendency toward impromptu dancing. Such behavior causes incomprehension, pain, and hostility in those around her (including a typical Herlihy psychotic cripple), and ultimately Jeanne's own death. Another unpublished play, *Crazy October*, derived from Herlihy's story "The Sleep of Baby Filbertson," focuses on a mother who tyrannizes her simple-minded son until he unearths a literal family skeleton that could destroy her, a reversal suggesting both the victory of innocence and its transmutation into corrupt power. Despite the presence of Tallulah Bankhead in a showy role, the play failed to reach New York, perhaps because the conventional plotline, which punishes the wicked Mrs. Filbertson, lacked an irony consistent with the black-comic atmosphere and characterizations.

Herlihy's least representative play, *Blue Denim*, written in collaboration with William Noble, was both a critical and financial success and became a popular film. In some ways the archetypal version of the misunderstood adolescent theme of the 1950's, *Blue Denim* partially transcends the genre through clever scenic symbolism and a sympathetic portrait of the adults. The setting, the Detroit home of Major Bartley, his wife, their 23-year-old daughter Lillian, and 15-year-old son Arthur, provides simultaneous views of both the main-floor existence of the family and the basement refuge of Arthur and his friends, Janet and Ernie, a combination hideaway and copy of the adult world upstairs (the boys' beer parodies the Major's serious brandy drinking). Though the play fails to explore the full possibilities of the semi-underground life of the adolescents, the setting suggests that their rebellion (the sexual union of Janet and Arthur, Janet's abortion, the boys' forgery to help pay for the abortion) will be short-lived. The young are already aping their elders.

The bluejeans of the title, a familiar image in Herlihy, stress Arthur's sexual vulnerability (in Herlihy's novels like *Midnight Cowboy* and *All Fall Down* the garment displays sexual aggressiveness or commercial availability). The innocence of Arthur and Janet causes her pregnancy and encounter with a shady abortionist. However, the painful experience does not destroy the youngsters, nor turn them into variants of the abortionist or Lillian's gangster suitor. Ultimately, Arthur and Janet will become part of the world of the Major, a muted version of Herlihy's familiar grotesque, whose "game leg" results not from 18 years army service but from a ludicrous fall on a department store escalator. Though Arthur seems the logical protagonist and achieves an insight into his relationship with his parents, Janet's plight generates more interest; unfortunately, most of her anguish occurs offstage, and Arthur's once-removed reactions seem too inarticulate to reveal either his own feelings or to echo Janet's. Thus, in a sense, Major Bartley, the faintly ridiculous, faintly grotesque personification of the American Legion outlook, emerges as the focal figure and the catalyst in Arthur's maturation. Though the Major's sudden prominence unbalances the play, his changing role seems designed less to please a predominantly middle-aged Broadway audience than to convey the decency latent in such a man: his belief that feeding Arthur huge quantities of food will effect the desired reconciliation may be simplistic, but works convincingly in the play and amusingly underscores Arthur's youthfulness.

Herlihy's next dramatic work, *Stop, You're Killing Me*, is a collection of three one-act plays that experiment in varying ways with the monologue and attempt to create a nightmare vision of a violent America. In *Laughs, Etc.*, a single-character play in the Ruth Draper tradition, Gloria, the middle-aged wife of a lawyer, reminisces to unseen friends and husband about her recent party at which she fed vicariously off the lives of some East Village neighbors and the young female addict they had befriended. Gloria's nastiness inadequately disguises a vulnerability stemming from her childlessness, the source of her quasi-sexual, quasi-maternal obsession with her "safe" homosexual neighbors. Gloria's stress on her essential purity, as she describes the effect of a popular song heard across the courtyard, is predictably ludicrous: "It was as if we were all seven again, and taking our first Holy Communion together. There was this feeling of the oneness of humanity, the sort of thing Dostoevski raved about." However, the irony becomes obtrusive when Gloria, having spent generously for the party, refuses to provide $35 in drug money for the girl, who dies the next day from the forced withdrawal. Not only is it difficult to understand why none of the men living in an expensive building could find the necessary money, but it is also difficult to accept the play's assessment of the girl as a violated innocent whom only Gloria sees as grotesque: "Then Michael said, Gloria, I hope you'll try to bring her out, will ya? Try to get to know her a little? She's very worthwhile, she has all kinds of original thoughts, insights, ideas, she has her own little window on the world." This view seems as falsely sentimentalized as Gloria's reaction to the song. Despite Gloria's shallowness and bitchery, it is easy to share her indignation at the charge that ". . . this same dreadful Gloria is responsible for shelling out thirty-five smackeroos to save the life of every drug fiend in Manhattan." The play fails to make a $35 drug purchase an index either to the girl's purity or Gloria's compassion, and seems a rigged attempt to flay the would-be hip bourgeois. Since Gloria's auditors apparently respond to her lines, the monologue does not intensify her sense of isolation and remains merely a technical exercise.

Bad Bad Jo-Jo begins with what is essentially a telephone monologue by Kayo Hathaway, creator of the pop novel and movie figures, Bad Bad Jo-Jo and Mama, allegorical right-wing dispensers of violent law and order in a mother-dominated society. A poster depicts them as "a little old lady with tiny eyeglasses and sensible shoes leading an enormous apelike young man by a chain. The young man wears an Uncle Sam hat that is too small for him." The play parodies the Frankenstein myth when two young men invade Kayo's home and don the garb of Jo-Jo and Mama in order to murder their creator ritualistically. Though Kayo protests, "Is it really and truly necessary to point out to you that I do not kill people? I am in show business," he is responsible for the violence he commercializes. The play, least effective of the three because of its predictable conclusion and use of camp humor to satirize a camp culture hero like Kayo, merely dwells on varieties of corruption and creates neither a sense of justice at Kayo's death, nor sufficient irony to define the climax as more than an exercise in sadism.

Terrible Jim Fitch, Herlihy's best play, focuses on a man who robs churches, a character with rich folklore resonance and the allegorical dimensions of Spenser's Kirkrapine. In a variation of Strindberg's method in *The Stronger*, Jim addresses his monologue to the silent, but responsive Sally Wilkins, a former singer whose face he once scarred in a fit of rage. The motel room setting helps build a powerful sense of Jim's loneliness and frustration, as he half-threatens, half-begs a reaction from Sally:

> What am I talking about, Sal, something about sleeping in cars? Help me! Answer me, goddam you. . . . Some day, some day, lady, you are not gonna answer me, and God help—I got it! Sleeping in cars! One night in a saloon in Key West, I got in a fist fight and when it was daylight I went to sleep in a car and had this dream about philosophy. There! I remembered—without anybody helping me.

Jim eventually loses his battle for control in the face of loneliness heightened by Sally's unspoken hostility (her behavior underlines the effectiveness of the monologue); but Jim is sometimes capable of raw tenderness: "If I was God, I'd hear you." However, his final plea apparently goes unanswered and leads to Sally's death: "Come on Sally, let me quit now. I'm beggin you. What's my name? Just say what my name is. You don't have to call me darling with it, but just say that one thing. Say my name. Once." The play illuminates Jim's blend of "criminal mentality" and vulnerability, and implies their genesis without sociological jargon or condescension. The inevitability of the conclusion heightens the tension and helps create that fusion of corruption and innocence toward which all Herlihy's plays aspire.

—Burton S. Kendle

HEWETT, Dorothy (Coade). Australian. Born in Perth, Western Australia, 21 May 1923. Educated at Perth College; University of Western Australia, Perth, 1941–42, 1959–63, B.A. 1961, M.A. 1963. Married Lloyd Davies in 1944 (marriage dissolved 1949), one son (deceased); lived with Les Flood, 1950–59, three sons; married Merv Lilley in 1960, two daughters. Millworker, 1950–52; advertising copywriter, Sydney, 1956–58; senior tutor in English, University of Western Australia, 1964–73. Writer-in-residence, Monash University, Melbourne, 1975, University of Newcastle, New South Wales, 1977, Griffith University, Nathan, Queensland, 1980, La Trobe University, Bundoora, Victoria, 1981, and Magpie Theatre Company, Adelaide, 1982. Poetry editor, *Westerly* magazine, Nedlands, Western Australia, 1972–73. Member of the editorial board, *Overland* magazine, Melbourne, since 1970, and *Sisters* magazine, Melbourne, since 1979; since 1979 editor and director, Big Smoke Books, and review editor, *New Poetry*, both Sydney. Member of the Communist Party, 1943–68. Recipient: Australian Broadcasting Corporation prize, for poetry, 1945, 1965; Australia Council grant, 1973, 1976, 1979, 1981, 1984, lifetime emeritus fellowship, 1988; Australian Writers Guild award, 1974, 1982, 1986; International Women's Year grant, 1976, Australian prize, for poetry, 1986; Grace Levin prize, for poetry, 1988; Mattara Butterfly Books prize, for poetry, 1991; Nettie Palmer prize, for non-fiction, 1991; Victorian Premier's award, 1991. A.O. (Member, Order of Australia), 1986. Agent: Hilary Linstead and Associates, 302 Easts Towers, 9–13 Bronte Road, Bondi Junction, New South Wales 2022. Address: 496 Great Western Highway, Faulconbridge, New South Wales 2776, Australia.

PUBLICATIONS

Plays

Time Flits Away, Lady (produced 1941).
This Old Man Comes Rolling Home (produced Perth, 1966; revised version produced Perth, 1968). Sydney, Currency Press, 1976.
Mrs. Porter and the Angel (produced Sydney, 1969). Included in *Collected Plays 1*, 1992.
The Chapel Perilous; or, The Perilous Adventures of Sally Banner, music by Frank Arndt and Michael Leyden (produced Perth, 1971). Sydney, Currency Press, 1972; London, Eyre Methuen, 1974.
Bon-Bons and Roses for Dolly (produced Perth, 1972). ith *The Tatty Hollow Story*, Sydney, Currency Press, 1976.
Catspaw (produced Perth, 1974).
Miss Hewett's Shenanigans (produced Canberra, 1975).
Joan, music by Patrick Flynn (produced Canberra, 1975). Montmorency, Victoria, Yackandandah, 1984.
The Tatty Hollow Story (produced Sydney, 1976). With *Bon-Bons and Roses for Dolly*, Sydney, Currency Press, 1976; included in *Collected Plays 1*, 1992.
The Beautiful Miss Portland. Published in *Theatre Australia* (Sydney), November-December and Christmas 1976.
The Golden Oldies (produced Melbourne, 1976; London, 1978). With *Susannah's Dreaming*, Sydney, Currency Press, 1981.
Pandora's Cross (produced Sydney, 1978). Published in *Theatre Australia* (Sydney), September-October 1978.
The Man from Mukinupin (produced Perth, 1979). Sydney, Currency Press, 1980.
Susannah's Dreaming (broadcast 1980). With *The Golden Oldies*, Sydney, Currency Press, 1981.

Golden Valley (for children; produced Adelaide, 1981). With *Song of the Seals*, Sydney, Currency Press, 1985.
The Fields of Heaven (produced Perth, 1982).
Song of the Seals (for children), music by Jim Cotter (produced Adelaide, 1983). With *Golden Valley*, Sydney, Currency Press, 1985.
Christina's World (opera libretto; produced Sydney, 1983).
The Rising of Peter Marsh (produced Perth, 1988).
Zoo with Robert Adamson (produced Wagga Wagga, New South Wales, 1991).
Collected Plays 1 (includes *This Old Man Comes Rolling Home, Mrs. Porter and the Angel, The Chapel Perilous, The Tatty Hollow Story*). Sydney, Currency Press, 1992.

Screenplays: *For the First Time*, with others, 1976; *Journey among Women*, with others, 1977; *The Planter of Malata*, with Cecil Holmes, 1983.

Radio Plays: *Frost at Midnight*, 1973; *He Used to Notice Such Things*, 1974; *Susannah's Dreaming*, 1980.

Novel

Bobbin Up. Sydney, Australasian Book Society, 1959; revised edition, London, Virago Press, 1985.

Short Stories

The Australians Have a Word for It. Berlin, Seven Seas, 1964.

Verse

What about the People, with Merv Lilley. Sydney, Realist Writers, 1962.
Windmill Country. Sydney, Edwards and Shaw, 1968.
The Hidden Journey. Newnham, Tasmania, Wattle Grove Press, 1969.
Late Night Bulletin. Newnham, Tasmania, Wattle Grove Press, 1970.
Rapunzel in Suburbia. Sydney, New Poetry, 1975.
Greenhouse. Sydney, Big Smoke, 1979.
Journeys, with others, edited by Fay Zwicky. Melbourne, Sisters, 1982.
Alice in Wormland. Newcastle-upon-Tyne, Bloodaxe, 1987.
A Tremendous World in Her Head. Sydney, Dangaroo Press, 1989.
The Upside Down Sonnets. Springwood, New South Wales, Butterfly Books, 1991.

Other

Wild Card (autobiography). Melbourne, McPhee Gribble, and London, Virago, 1990.

Editor, *Sandgropers: A Western Australian Anthology*. Nedlands, University of Western Australia Press, 1973.

*

Manuscript Collections: Australian National Library, Canberra; Fisher Library, University of Sydney; Flinders University, Adelaide, South Australia.

Critical Studies: "Quest or Question? Perilous Journey to the Chapel" by Reba Gostand, in *Bards, Bohemians, and Bookmen* edited by Leon Cantrell, St. Lucia, University of Queensland Press, 1976; "Confession and Beyond" by Bruce

Williams, in *Overland* (Sydney), 1977; *After "The Doll"* by Peter Fitzpatrick, Melbourne, Arnold, 1979; *Contemporary Australian Playwrights* edited by Jennifer Palmer, Adelaide, University Union Press, 1979; interview with Jim Davidson, in *Meanjin* (Melbourne), 1979; articles by Brian Kiernan and Carole Ferrier, in *Contemporary Australian Drama* edited by Peter Holloway, Sydney, Currency Press, 1981, revised edition, 1986; *Dorothy Hewett: The Feminine as Subversion* by Margaret Williams, Sydney, Currency Press, 1992.

* * *

It is hard to be indifferent to the work of Dorothy Hewett. Everything she has goes into it, provoking in the observer anger, distaste, admiration, extravagant praise and partisanship, and, on two occasions, threat of court action. First a poet, author of one important novel and much left-wing journalism, she turned to playwriting in 1965. Her materials are the female psyche and the burden that men and society lay on the romantic imagination and the artistic soul. She disclaims any autobiographical intention, bending her mind as she does to the universal experience of the artist as woman through her own painful experience of the role; but it is nevertheless true that most of her characters can be identified by a style of language and imagery that refers noticeably to her own life and literary experience.

The progress of her work shows a steady motion from dramatic narrative to ritual poetry; and much of the discomfort she causes stems from her defiant intrusion of the private nature of the poetic experience into the naked public arena of the theatre.

Her first play, *This Old Man Comes Rolling Home*, remains her most immediately accessible and contains some of her best dramatic writing. It is the story of a household of communist activists in Redfern, an inner Sydney suburb, in the early 1950's, the fierce time of the unsuccessful attempt by Sir Robert Menzies to ban the Communist Party. The play was a response to her own time in Redfern and is an acknowledgement of what she calls her "love affair with the working class."

Two early dramatic influences were Patrick White and Tennessee Williams, both of them moving out of realism towards a poetic interpretation of the ordinary man and woman. Like them but in her own way she has since progressed into a landscape not "real" in the accepted sense but born of and reflecting the mind and sensibilities of Hewett and her characters. She made a leap into this landscape with *Mrs. Porter and the Angel*, a play in which a deranged woman teacher wanders through the gathering dark to the houses of her colleagues in search of an imaginary dog. The play is replete with black dog images of impotence and closet sexuality, of men and women destroying each other out of their own fantasies. And yet the play adds up to a kind of celebration of the good and evil in them all: it shares the optimism of *This Old Man*, a comedy of poverty which pays tribute to the force of life and laughter.

Journeys are endemic to Hewett's writing. The major journey to date is that taken by Sally Banner in *The Chapel Perilous*, her most widely performed play. In it she audaciously compares to the questing of Malory's heroes a woman's search for spiritual truth through literary striving, sexual adventures, marriage, communism, and public recognition. In *Bon-Bons and Roses for Dolly* her heroine is a teenager of the 1940's, indulged by her emotionally starved parents and grandparents and fed on the fairy floss of the Hollywood movie. In Act 2 Dolly returns, middle-aged, to the now crumbling Crystal Palace—a meeting of two empty and neglected monuments to second-hand dreams.

Hewett's rock opera *Catspaw* in different style offers a drop-out guitar player in search of the real Australia. In a ribald grand parade of legendary characters the author postulates that most of these enlightened minds were stick-in-the-mud conservatives.

The Tatty Hollow Story and *Joan* return to the theme of the female predicament and demonstrate how women rise to the roles men create for them. The former ritually brings together the five lovers of the mysterious Tatty Hollow, whom each remembers in a different fantasy. At last, in retaliation for what she sums up as a wasted life, Tatty takes revenge on them and dissolves—and the play with her—into a poetic madness. *Joan* is the Joan of Arc story as a rock opera with four eponymous heroines—Joan the peasant, Joan the soldier, Joan the witch, and Joan the saint.

The Golden Oldies, a savage mood piece on the round of domestic duty and mutual exploitation which is the lot of many women, emerges in retrospect as a turning point for Hewett's imagination, an exorcism of the past. Leaving us with the image of an old woman's death and her daughter sifting through the flotsam of a lifetime, Hewett moves away from her exploration of isolation towards unifying the elements of life. In the work which follows she begins to live down the old defiance and absorb the destructive forces, which had hitherto preoccupied her, into a total creative vision.

Pandora's Cross is a nostalgic attempt to rally the old creative forces of the once bohemian Kings Cross, today a haunt of drug addicts and racketeers. The play contains some of her best poetry but suffers, like other work from this middle period, from unresolved dramatic action. In 1979, however, the challenge of writing a festive work for the Western Australian sequicentennial celebrations, drew from her a play which changed her fortunes and reconciled her with the State of her birth. *The Man from Mukinupin* mingles childhood memories of the wheat-farming district in which she grew up with a dense education in Shakespeare and the English and Australian Romantics. The play is set during World War I, and she brings to the story of a grocer's daughter and her sweetheart, and of their darker siblings, a half-Aboriginal whore and her outcast lover, a world view of the good and evil forces over which the mad water diviner Zeek Perkins presides, Prospero-like, in a parched but magical land.

This was the beginning of what has come to be known as Hewett's pastoral period, which produced in close succession *Susannah's Dreaming*, a radio play about the tragic intrusion of adult brutality into the magical sea-world of a retarded innocent; *The Fields of Heaven*, about the takeover of a farming community by an ambitious escapee from Mussolini's Italy; and two children's plays, *Golden Valley*, set in the wheatfields, and *Song of the Seals*, set in a mystical sub-Antarctic bay, which use the forces of nature, in the form of people transmuted into birds and fish, to fight the intrusion of acquisitive outsiders into their rural harmony.

Hewett's work is informed by a strongly literary background and an incorrigible romanticism which contrasts oddly with her critical armoury. Part of the romanticism is an attention-getting daring and a determination to prove that life can be beautiful—a desire so strong in some plays that the energy consumes an often shaky structure. The source of her romanticism can be traced to the artistic isolation of her girlhood in Western Australia and her private schooling which together encouraged poetry and idealism. Her long allegiance to the Communist Party was an emotional, even a religious commitment, which, after her expulsion in 1968, left her isolated, bereft of beliefs, and newly aware of her

mortality—a sense confirmed by the senility and death of her mother. These factors are strongly represented in the work of her middle period and come to an end with the sudden force of *The Man from Mukinupin*. Hewett's subsequent works still take the same journey through idealism to understanding but they carry a new optimism and a new acceptance of the follies of life; a new recognition of the splendour and the resilience of the human spirit.

—Katharine Brisbane

HIBBERD, Jack (John Charles Hibberd). Australian. Born in Warracknabeal, Victoria, 12 April 1940. Educated at Marist Brothers College, Bendigo, Victoria; University of Melbourne, M.D. 1964. Married 1) Jocelyn Hibberd in 1969 (divorced 1977), one daughter and one son; 2) Evelyn Krape in 1978, one son. Practising physician, 1965–66, 1970–73, and since 1986. Member, Australia Council Theatre Board, 1977–79; first president, Melbourne Writers' Theatre; editor, "Performing Arts in Australia" issue of *Meanjin*, Melbourne, 1984. Currently wine columnist, Melbourne *Age*. Recipient: Australia Council fellowship, 1973, 1977, 1981. Address: 125 Wooralla Drive, Mount Eliza, Victoria 3930, Australia.

PUBLICATIONS

Plays

Brain Rot (produced Carlton, Victoria, 1967; augmented version produced Melbourne, 1968). Section *Who?* published in *Plays*, Melbourne, Penguin, 1970; *Just Before the Honeymoon* in *Kosmos II* (Clayton, Victoria), 1972; *One of Nature's Gentlemen* in *Three Popular Plays*, 1976; selections in *Squibs*, 1984.
White with Wire Wheels (produced Melbourne, 1967). Published in *Plays*, Melbourne, Penguin, 1970.
Dimboola: A Wedding Reception Play (produced Carlton, Victoria, 1969). Melbourne and London, Penguin, 1974.
Marvellous Melbourne, with John Romeril (produced Melbourne, 1970). Published in *Theatre Australia* (Potts Point, New South Wales), July-September 1977.
Customs and Excise (also director: produced Carlton, Victoria, 1970; augmented version, as *Proud Flesh*, produced Carlton, Victoria, 1972).
Klag (produced Melbourne, 1970).
Aorta (produced Melbourne, 1971).
A Stretch of the Imagination (also director: produced Carlton, Victoria, 1972; London, 1982; Richmond, Virginia, 1983). Sydney, Currency Press, 1973; London, Eyre Methuen, 1974.
Women!, adaptation of a play by Aristophanes (produced Carlton, Victoria, 1972).
Captain Midnight V.C., music by Lorraine Milne (produced Carlton, Victoria, 1973). Montmorency, Victoria, Yackandandah, 1984.
The Architect and the Emperor of Assyria, adaptation of a play by Fernando Arrabal (produced Carlton, Victoria, 1974).
The Les Darcy Show (produced Adelaide, 1974). Included in *Three Popular Plays*, 1976.

Peggy Sue; or, The Power of Romance (produced Carlton, Victoria, 1974; revised version produced Melbourne, 1983). Montmorency, Victoria, Yackandandah, 1982.
Goodbye Ted, with John Timlin (produced 1975). Montmorency, Victoria, Yackandandah, 1983.
A Toast to Melba (also director: produced Adelaide, 1976). Included in *Three Popular Plays*, 1976.
The Overcoat, music by Martin Friedel, adaptation of a story by Gogol (produced Carlton, Victoria, 1976; London, 1978). With *Sin*, Sydney, Currency Press, 1981.
Three Popular Plays. Melbourne, Outback Press, 1976.
Memoirs of a Carlton Bohemian, published in *Meanjin* (Melbourne), no. 3, 1977.
Sin (opera libretto), music by Martin Friedel (produced Melbourne, 1978). With *The Overcoat*, Sydney, Currency Press, 1981.
A Man of Many Parts (produced Perth, 1980).
Mothballs (produced Melbourne, 1981). Published in *Meanjin* (Melbourne), no. 4, 1980.
Liquid Amber (produced Wodonga, Victoria, 1982). Included in *A Country Quinella*, 1984.
Lavender Bags, published in *Aspect*, no. 25, 1982.
Glycerine Tears (produced Melbourne, 1983; London, 1985). Published in *Meanjin* (Melbourne), no. 4, 1982; with *The Old School Tie*, as *Duets*, 1989.
Squibs: A Collection of Short Plays (includes selections from *Brain Rot* and *Asian Oranges*, *A League of Nations*, *The Three Sisters*, *Death of a Traveller*). Brisbane, Phoenix, 1984.
A Country Quinella: Two Celebration Plays (includes *Dimboola* and *Liquid Amber*). Melbourne, Penguin, 1984.
Death Warmed Up, published in *Scripsi* (Melbourne), vol. 2, no. 4, 1984.
Odyssey of a Prostitute, published in *Outrider* (Indooroopilly, Queensland), 1985.
Duets (includes *The Old School Tie*, *Glycerine Tears*) (produced Melbourne, 1989). Montmorency, Victoria, Yackandandah, 1989.

Novels

Memoirs of an Old Bastard. Melbourne, McPhee Gribble, 1989.
The Life of Riley. Melbourne, Mandarin, 1991.

Other

The Barracker's Bible: A Dictionary of Sporting Slang, with Garrie Hutchinson. Melbourne, McPhee Gribble, 1983.

Translator, *Le vin des amants: Poems from Baudelaire*. Toorak, Victoria, Gryphon, 1977.

*

Manuscript Collections: Australian National Library, Canberra; Melbourne University Archives; La Trobe University Library, Bundoora, Victoria; Eunice Hanger Collection, University of Queensland, St. Lucia.

Critical Studies: "Snakes and Ladders" by Margaret Williams, in *Meanjin* (Melbourne), no. 2, 1972; "Assaying the New Drama" by A. A. Phillips, in *Meanjin* (Melbourne), no. 2, 1973; *After "The Doll"* by Peter Fitzpatrick, Melbourne, Arnold, 1979; interviews in *Contemporary Australian Playwrights* edited by Jennifer Palmer, Adelaide, University Press, 1979, *Sideways from the Page* by Jim Davidson, Sydney, Fontana, 1983, and with Elizabeth Perkins in *Linq* (Townsville, Queensland), vol. 11, no. 1, 1983; articles by Peter Pierce, Charles Kemp, and Paul McGillick, in *Contemporary Australian Drama* edited by Peter Holloway, Sydney, Currency Press, 1981; *Hibberd* by John Hainsworth, Melbourne, Methuen Australia, 1987; *Jack Hibberd* by Paul McGillick, Amsterdam, Rodopi, 1988.

Theatrical Activities:
Director: **Plays**—several of his own plays, and *Bedfellows* by Barry Oakley, Carlton, Victoria, 1975.

Jack Hibberd comments:

(1977) I have striven over the last ten years to write specifically of an Australian experience on matters of social aberration and folly, history, politics, popular myth, and individual torment. As a playwright, I believe implacably in the necessity for practical involvement in theatre. Though my plays do not evolve out of laboratory and workshop situations, I believe theatre is the best context in which to attempt dramaturgical diversity and innovation.

(1988) Over the last ten years I have been less concerned to write specifically of Australian experience but more sweepingly of human conduct in a context of comico-tragic formal experiment, especially in my monodramas and other theatrical sorties into the actor-audience farce.

*   *   *

Jack Hibberd's work consistently explores the formal possibilities of the theatre, and does so within a rigorously articulated philosophy of the nature and function of the theatre. Moreover, his use of language, within a carefully thought-out position on its role in the theatre, is equally informed and imaginative. Hibberd's plays successfully marry form and content in the context of a notion of the theatre not only as a place for communal celebration, but also as a metaphor for life itself. Consequently, his plays speak directly in a theatrical language rather than a verbal language which then needs to be translated. A Hibberd play is always primarily a theatrical experience in which the audience is never allowed to forget that it is in a theatre and participating in a social event. Hibberd remains a significant figure in the Australian theatre, not in spite of, but actually *because* of his refusal to write for the theatre since 1984 as a protest against invidious values which he feels have come to predominate.

The first period of Hibberd's work (1967 to 1976), was one in which he found his own voice and experimented with themes and forms. Early short plays like *Who?* worked through the influences of Pinter and Beckett applied to an Australian setting and using Australian English. The menace of Pinter surfaced in Hibberd in the form of a simmering violence endemic to mateship—violence to someone who opts out of the tribe, towards women, and towards any of the refinements which contradict the exaltation of crudity characteristic of "ocker" mateship. These themes inform Hibberd's first full-length play, *White with Wire Wheels*, which is also his first explicitly anti-naturalistic play, using nightmare sequences and with one actress playing all the female roles.

Hibberd's major play in this first period, *A Stretch of the Imagination*, is what Hibberd terms a monodrama—a play for one person who enacts and re-enacts his own life for his own entertainment rather than an audience as in a monologue—a form he has returned to and refined several times since. Monk O'Neill is a recluse, living in a hut in the Australian outback. Through Monk, Hibberd goes beyond describing the "ocker" to an exploration of the existential alienation which is equally responsible for producing "ockers," soccer hooligans, or Hitlers. Through the particularly of this very Australian character who re-lives, often fictionalising, the events which have led to his present miserable predicament (though this is a misery never acknowledged by Monk, who insists he is happy in his rejection of other people), Hibberd achieves a universality of appeal which has resulted in this play being performed all over the world, despite many difficulties in the cultural and linguistic translation of its marked Australian language and humour.

Hibberd's other major success from this period is *Dimboola*, which has also been performed all over the world and is, indeed, the most-produced Australian play ever. *Dimboola* had a two-fold origin, namely Hibberd's interest in achieving a viable form of audience participation and in creating a truly "popular" form of theatre which embodied his concept of theatre as social celebration. The play depicts a wedding reception in a country town where the audience are guests sitting at tables and are served food and drink. It exploits and explores the rituals inherent in wedding receptions, like the testing of strengths of "the two recently conjugated tribes," as Hibberd describes them—one Catholic, the other Presbyterian. The setting is not a conventional theatre, but an actual reception hall and the audience's participation is natural rather than coerced. The play also allows for improvisation and character development based on basically stereotypic characters. *Dimboola* probably signals Hibberd's discovery of himself as a comic writer who, like Gogol (whom he admires), uses a comic vision to accommodate what he sees as a hostile universe.

Hibberd's exploration of "popular" theatre produced three other plays in 1976, two of which, *A Toast to Melba* and *The Les Darcy Show*, used famous and archetypal Australians to explore the nature of the myths Australians use to explain themselves.

With his free adaptation of Gogol's short story, *The Overcoat*—which he calls "a theatrical double somersault and half-pike from the springboard of Gogol's insane prose"—Hibberd moved into another phase of writing which saw a broadening of his formal explorations, a universalising of his themes and settings which were no longer necessarily Australian. Likewise, his use of the Australian vernacular is no longer *de rigeur*, but often functions as a defamiliarising device, drawing attention to the insane and contradictory world which Hibberd's characters increasingly come to inhabit.

Music is always important in Hibberd's work, often taking the form of a Brechtian commentary on the action and sometimes a more explicit role as in *Melba* or in *Sin*, his opera parody based on the seven deadly sins (inspired by Kurt Weill's oratorio) with music by Martin Friedl, which is as much a spoof on orchestral players as a rumination on the role of the artist in contemporary society.

In his seven monodramas, Hibberd develops the notion of the theatre as a metaphor—a notion which finds its most sophisticated form in what is probably his best play after *Stretch*, *Odyssey of a Prostitute*. Based on a story by Maupassant of a country girl forced into prostitution, Hibberd's play is essentially a farce with a dark underbelly, celebrating the theatre as entertainment but seeing it also as a metaphor for a menacingly unpredictable universe. In the words of the Actor who introduces Act 2: "It is life . . . that is a dream. Theatre's the real thing. One long scream." The play is highly theatrical, with a square in Paris serving as a performance area in which characters act out their stories. The play simultaneously draws attention to its own theatrical-

ity and satirises the theatre, using Shakespearean conceits and songs to comment on the action.

While Hibberd's mature work explores the idea that the theatre and life are metaphors for one another, it reveals a preoccupation with what Hibberd clearly feels is the untenable role of the artist in late 20th-century society.

—Paul McGillick

HILL, Errol (Gaston). American. Born in Trinidad, 5 August 1921; naturalized U.S. citizen. Educated at the Royal Academy of Dramatic Art (British Council scholar), London, diploma 1951; University of London, diploma in dramatic art 1951; Yale University, New Haven, Connecticut, B.A., M.F.A. 1962, D.F.A. 1966. Married Grace L.E. Hope in 1956; four children. Drama tutor, University of the West Indies, Kingston, Jamaica, 1952–58; creative arts tutor, University of the West Indies, Trinidad, 1958–65; teaching fellow in drama, University of Ibadan, Nigeria, 1965–67; associate professor of drama, Richmond College, City University, New York, 1967–68. Associate professor of drama, 1968–69, professor of drama, 1969–76, Willard professor of drama and oratory, 1976–89, and since 1989 emeritus professor, drama department, Dartmouth College, Hanover, New Hampshire. Chancellor's distinguished professor, University of California, Berkeley, 1983. Founder, Whitehall Players, Trinidad; editor, Caribbean Plays series, University of the West Indies, 1954–65. Editor, *ATA Bulletin of Black Theatre*, Washington, D.C., 1971–76. Recipient: Rockefeller fellowship, 1958, 1959 and teaching fellowship, 1965–67; Theatre Guild of America fellowship, 1961; Bertram Joseph award for Shakespeare Studies, 1985; Barnard Hewitt award, for theatre history, 1985; Guggenheim fellowship, 1985; Fulbright fellowship, 1988. Address: 3 Haskins Road, Hanover, New Hampshire 03755, U.S.A.

PUBLICATIONS

Plays

Oily Portraits (as *Brittle and the City Fathers*, produced Trinidad, 1948). Port-of-Spain, Trinidad, University of the West Indies, 1966.
Square Peg (produced Trinidad, 1949). Port-of-Spain, Trinidad, University of the West Indies, 1966.
The Ping Pong: A Backyard Comedy-Drama (broadcast 1950; produced Trinidad, 1953). Port-of-Spain, Trinidad, University of the West Indies, 1955.
Dilemma (produced Jamaica, 1953). Port-of-Spain, Trinidad, University of the West Indies, 1966.
Broken Melody (produced Jamaica, 1954). Port-of-Spain, Trinidad, University of the West Indies, 1966.
Wey-Wey (produced Trinidad, 1957). Port-of-Spain, Trinidad, University of the West Indies, 1958.
Strictly Matrimony (produced New Haven, Connecticut, 1959; London, 1977). Port-of-Spain, Trinidad, University of the West Indies, 1966; in *Black Drama Anthology*, edited by Woodie King and Ron Milner, New York, New American Library, 1971.
Man Better Man (produced New Haven, Connecticut, 1960;

London, 1965; New York, 1969).   Published in *The Yale School of Drama Presents*, edited by John Gassner, New York, Dutton, 1964; in *Plays for Today*, edited by Hill, London, Longman, 1986.
Dimanche Gras Carnival Show (produced Trinidad, 1963).
Whistling Charlie and the Monster (carnival show; produced Trinidad, 1964).
Dance Bongo (produced New York, 1965).   Port-of-Spain, Trinidad, University of the West Indies, 1966; in *Caribbean Literature: An Anthology*, edited by G.R. Coulthard, London, University of London Press, 1966.

Radio Play: *The Ping Pong*, 1950 (UK).

Other

The Trinidad Carnival: Mandate for a National Theatre. Austin, University of Texas Press, 1972.
Why Pretend? A Conversation about the Performing Arts, with Peter Greer.   San Francisco, Chandler and Sharp, 1973.
Shakespeare in Sable: A History of Black Shakespearean Actors.   Amherst, University of Massachusetts Press, 1984.
The Jamaican Stage 1655–1900.   Amherst, University of Massachusetts Press, 1992.

Editor and Contributor, *The Artist in West Indian Society: A Symposium.*   Port-of-Spain, Trinidad, University of the West Indies, 1964.
Editor, *A Time and a Season: 8 Caribbean Plays.*   Port-of-Spain, Trinidad, University of the West Indies, 1976.
Editor, *Three Caribbean Plays for Secondary Schools.*   Port-of-Spain, Trinidad, Longman, 1979.
Editor, *The Theater of Black Americans: A Collection of Critical Essays.*   Englewood Cliffs, New Jersey, Prentice Hall, 2 vol., 1980.
Editor, *Plays for Today.*   London, Longman, 1986.
Editor, *Black Heroes: Seven Plays.*   New York, Applause, 1989.

*

Bibliography: *Black Theatre and Performances: A Pan-African Bibliography* by John Gray, New York, Greenwood Press, 1990.

Manuscript Collection: Baker Library, Dartmouth College, Hanover, New Hampshire.

Theatrical Activities:
Director: **Plays**—more than 120 plays and pageants in the West Indies, England, the United States, and Nigeria.
Actor: **Plays**—more than 40 roles in amateur and professional productions in the West Indies, England, the United States, and Nigeria.

Errol Hill comments:

I was trained first as an actor and play director. I began writing plays when it became clear to me, as founder of a Trinidad theatre company (the Whitehall Players, later merged with the New Company to become the Company of Players), that an indigenous West Indian theatre could not exist without a repertoire of West Indian plays. The thrust of my work as playwright has been to treat aspects of Caribbean folk life, drawing on speech idioms and rhythms, music and

dance, and to evolve a form of drama and theatre most nearly representative of Caribbean life and art. As drama tutor for the University of the West Indies I carried this message to every part of the Caribbean and have written plays by way of demonstrating what could be done to provide a drama repertoire for Caribbean theatre companies.

*   *   *

Errol Hill demonstrates a remarkable talent in two separate but closely associated artistic fields—namely, playwriting and literary criticism. Presently Chairman of the Department of Drama at Dartmouth College, he is the author of one-act plays and full-length dramas; he has edited the Caribbean Plays series and is the author of many articles and reports. *The Trinidad Carnival: Mandate for a National Theatre* is a definitive contribution to the study of a rich folklore.

Man Better Man, Hill's most outstanding theatrical success, tells of a young suitor for the hand of Petite Belle Lily. The suitor's method is to challenge the village stick-fighting champion to a decisive duel. The young lover resorts to the supernatural means of his vibrant culture. He goes to the village obeahman, Diable Papa, and is subsequently cheated by the quack magician. He receives a herb, "Man Better Man"—a known cure which guarantees invincibility. With characteristic humility, Hill once wrote to me the following explanation:

It [*Man Better Man*] was for me little more than an experiment in integrating music, song, and dance into dramatic action, and using the calypso form with its rhymed couplets to carry the rhythm and make the transitions occur more smoothly. . . . I never had an orchestral score of the music for the play. Since most of it is traditional-based, with a few numbers "composed by me," . . . I simply provided a melodic line and left it to each production to create their own orchestration. Much of the music should appear to be improvised anyway with, ideally, the musicians carrying their instruments as part of the chorus on stage.

Hill's play celebrates, in a ritualized form, the triumphal pleasure of comedy. Richard F. Shepard said in the *New York Times* (3 July 1969): "Mr. Hill has encapsuled an authentic folk tale flavor, letting us know something about a people, his people, whose history antedates steel drum bands. It is quaint, yet not condescending; ingenuous, yet not silly." On the surface the musical play gleams with a tropical panache; beneath are the threatened subtleties and hidden meanings. Thus that magic, that mystery which the festive Greeks knew very well, is engaged—no, released—by Hill on a richly set Caribbean stage. The connection between the author's skill in portraying effects obtained by the juxtaposition of the real with the assumed—one of the several functions of comedy— and his symbolic comic vision is the dynamic element of this work.

C. L. R. James was deeply moved when Hill produced and directed a lengthy skit in Trinidad of dramatic, musical, festive, and political impact. He observed that the audience enjoyed it while "the authorities" did not approve. Hill's venture to me is completely West Indian, and completely Greek. Sir William Ridgeway in *The Origin of Tragedy* (1910) and *The Dramas and Dramatic Dances of Non-European Races* (1915) could have been speaking of West Indian drama as well as Greek tragedy when he states that the heavy emphasis on ghosts, burial rites, and ancestor worship could not be derived from such a deity as Dionysus alone. The art must be related to hero and ancestor worship and the cult of the dead. For example, in *Man Better Man* Hannibal, Calypsonian, enjoys a position roughly analogous to the Anglo-Saxon court *scop*. He immortalizes the island's heroes in song, and his repertoire constitutes a veritable oral chronicle. Pogo's homeric cataloguing of famous stick-fighters displays the continuity of the heroic tradition. Villagers manifest an awareness that they see tradition-in-the-making. "Excitement for so/More trouble and woe/A day to recall/When you grow old."

Medieval courtly conventions are carried off to the Caribbean setting in the most graceful and lyrical moods. Courtly love comes forward and all action stems from Tim Briscoe's desire to win a woman's affection through a demonstration of physical prowess. He expresses his longing in courtly love terms for Petite Belle Lily. Tim displays those familiar symptoms of "heroes"—the conventional lover's malady—when he says "I cannot eat by day, come the night/Cannot sleep, what a plight." Petite Belle Lily shows her indifference—perhaps medieval, perhaps Petrarchan—to her lover's sorry state which is so fitting and proper to her courtly heroine-like state. The stick-fight itself—traditionally accompanied by a calinda—between Tim and Tiny Sata is reminiscent of a medieval tournament whose proceedings are governed by ritualized and rigid customs. Aspects of trial-by-combat are ever-present, along with strong emphasis on personal honor and its defence. Indeed, stick-fighting is envisioned among these island dwellers as a folk institution. The fighter is a true folk hero, like Beowulf or Achilles, who embodies not only the primitive drive of the islanders, but also the qualities which they esteem most highly—physical courage, prowess in battle, personal honor. The reigning champion becomes a personification of the communal ideal.

The tension between Diable Papa—a fake and a counterfeit who, by means of voodoo, makes money from the primitive fears of the people—and Portagee Joe supplies the intellectual focus of the drama. The obeahman—the holder of all the local rituals, spells, and incantations—represents the power of illusion and mass deception. Portagee Joe, who successfully challenges Diable Papa's authority, is the typical "village atheist"—whose cynicism or rationalism keeps him outside the circle of communal belief. "The social significance of the play lies in the relationship between Portagee Joe and his customers: They were not 'niggers' to him and he is not 'white' to them," writes Mrs. Stanley Jackson, in a letter to the *New York Times*. "A man could be judged as a man seventy years ago in Trinidad. . . . The author of *Man Better Man* knew his material extremely well."

Lastly, Diable Papa, who is a fraud, nevertheless reflects some picaresque influences. He is reminiscent of the medieval and Tudor horrific-comic depiction of stock diabolic figures. But the obeahman is balanced against the broader irony of the play's resolution. Tim Briscoe qua anti-hero, although defeated, emerges as a hero in spite of himself. Diable Papa, confounded by supposedly "supernatural" happenings and spectral visitations, is actually victimized by the very beliefs he has fostered in the villagers.

The drama is a picture of thoughtful delight. The audience —even the reader—becomes an extension of the stage. One cannot help recalling throughout the work Michael Rutenberg's advice to directors: "Break through the proscenium!" The ceremonial interaction of chorus, dancers, actors, and calypsonian sequences—responsorial in nature (countermelodies are used by Diable Papa and Minee)—and the lively verse—incantatorial in quality and reflecting the natural rhythmic delivery of the West Indian speech pattern—all go to picture and re-emphasize the profundity of life, dying,

and existence when tragic and comic values meet in confrontation.

—Louis D. Mitchell

HIVNOR, Robert (Hanks). American. Born in Zanesville, Ohio, in 1916. Educated at the University of Akron, Ohio, A.B. 1936; Yale University, New Haven, Connecticut, M.F.A. 1946; Columbia University, New York, 1952–54. Served in the United States Army, 1942–45. Married Mary Otis in 1947; two sons and one daughter. Political cartoonist and commercial artist, 1934–38; instructor, University of Minnesota, Minneapolis, 1946–48, and Reed College, Portland, Oregon, 1954–55; assistant professor, Bard College, Annandale-on-Hudson, New York, 1956–59. Recipient: University of Iowa fellowship, 1951; Rockefeller grant, 1968. Address: 420 East 84th Street, New York, New York 10028, U.S.A.

PUBLICATIONS

Plays

Martha Goodwin, adaptation of the story "A Goat for Azazel" by Katherine Anne Porter (produced New Haven, Connecticut, 1942; revised version broadcast, 1959).
Too Many Thumbs (produced Minneapolis, 1948; New York, 1949; London, 1951). Minneapolis, University of Minnesota Press, 1949.
The Ticklish Acrobat (produced New York, 1954). Published in *Playbook: Five Plays for a New Theatre*, New York, New Directions, 1956.
The Assault upon Charles Sumner (produced New York, 1964). Published in *Plays for a New Theatre: Playbook 2*, New York, New Directions, 1966.
Love Reconciled to War (produced Baltimore, 1968). Published in *Break Out! In Search of New Theatrical Environments*, edited by James Schevill, Chicago, Swallow Press, 1973.
"I" "Love" "You" (produced New York, 1968). Published in *Anon* (Austin, Texas), 1971.
DMZ (includes the sketches *Uptight Arms, How Much?, "I" "Love" "You"*) (as Osbert Pismire and Jack Askew; produced New York, 1969).
A Son Is Always Leaving Home. Published in *Anon* (Austin, Texas), 1971.
Apostle/Genius/God. Published in *Bostonia* (Boston), January/February, 1990.

*

Critical Studies: "The Pleasure and Pains of Playgoing" by Saul Bellow, in *Partisan Review* (New York), May 1954; *The Theatre of the Absurd* by Martin Esslin, New York, Doubleday, 1961, London, Eyre and Spottiswoode, 1962, revised edition, London, Penguin, 1968, Doubleday, 1969; *American Drama since World War II* by Gerald Weales, New York, Harcourt Brace, 1962; *The New American Arts* edited by Richard Kostelanetz, New York, Horizon Press, 1965; by Albert Bermel, in *New Leader* (New York), 1966; by A. W.

Staub, in *Southern Review* (Baton Rouge, Louisiana), Summer 1970.

* * *

The economics of theatre are all too cruel to art: because a play costs so much more to produce than, say, a novel, many important texts are rarely, if ever, presented. Those particularly victimized by such economic discrimination include older playwrights who have neither the time nor energy necessary to launch non-commercial productions on their own. There is no doubt, in my judgment, that Robert Hivnor has written two of the best and most original American postwar dramas, but it is lamentable that our knowledge of them, as well as his reputation, must be based more upon print than performance and that lack of incentive keeps yet other plays half-finished. The first, called *Too Many Thumbs*, is more feasible, requiring only some inventive costuming and masks to overcome certain difficulties in artifice. It tells of an exceptionally bright chimpanzee, possessed of a large body and a small head, who in the course of the play moves up the evolutionary ladder to become, first, an intermediate stage between man and beast, and then a normal man and ultimately a god-like creature with an immense head and a shrivelled body. The university professors who keep him also attempt to cast him as the avatar of a new religion, but unending evolution defeats their designs. Just as Hivnor's writing is often very funny, so is the play's ironically linear structure also extremely original (preceding Ionesco's use of it in *The New Tenant*), for by pursuing the bias implicit in evolutionary development to its inevitable reversal, the play coherently questions mankind's claim to a higher state of existence. *The Ticklish Acrobat* is a lesser work, nonetheless exhibiting some true originality and typically Hivnorian intellectual comedy; but here the practical difficulty lies in constructing a set whose period recedes several hundred years in time with each act.

Hivnor is fundamentally a dark satirist who debunks myths and permits no heroes; but unlike other protagonist-less playwrights, he is less interested in absurdity than comprehensive ridicule. *The Assault upon Charles Sumner* is an immensely sophisticated history play, regrettably requiring more actors and scenes than an unsubsidized theatre can afford, and an audience more literate than Broadway offers. Its subject is the supreme example of liberal intellectuality in American politics—the 19th-century Senator from Massachusetts, Charles Sumner, who had been a distinguished proponent of abolition and the Civil War. Like Sumner's biographer David Donald, Hivnor finds that Sumner, for all his saintliness, was politically ineffectual and personally insufferable. The opening prologue, which contains some of Hivnor's most savage writing, establishes the play's tone and thrust, as it deals with the funeral and possible afterlife of the last living Negro slave. "Sir, no American has ever been let into heaven." "Not old Abe Lincoln?" the slave asks. "Mr. Lincoln," Sumner replies, "sits over there revising his speech at the Gettysburg. . . ."

Extending such negative satire, Hivnor feasts upon episodes and symbols of both personal and national failure, attempting to define a large historical experience in a single evening. While much of the imagery is particularly theatrical, such as repeating the scene where Preston Brooks assaults Sumner with a cane, perhaps the play's subject and scope are finally closer, both intrinsically and extrinsically, to extended prose fiction.

—Richard Kostelanetz

HOAR, Stuart (Murray). New Zealander. Born in New Plymouth, 17 June 1957. Educated at James Cook High School, Auckland, 1970–74. Clerk, Department of Education, Auckland, 1975; film sound recordist, Television New Zealand, Auckland, 1976–81; part-time cleaner, Auckland, 1982–87; literary fellow, Auckland University, 1990. Recipient: Bruce Mason award, 1988. Agent: Playmarket, Box 9767, Wellington, New Zealand.

PUBLICATIONS

Plays

Squatter (produced Auckland, 1987). Wellington, Victoria University Press, 1988.
American Girl (broadcast 1988; produced Dunedin, 1992). Published in *Three Radio Plays*, edited by Michael Peck, Wellington, Victoria University Press, 1989.
Scott of the Antarctic (broadcast 1989; produced Wellington, 1990).
Exile (produced Auckland, 1990).
A Long Walk Off a Tall Rock (produced Wellington, 1991).
Cool Gangs (produced Auckland, 1992).
The Pulp Explosion (produced Christchurch, 1992).
The Boat (produced Auckland, 1992).

Screenplay: *Lovelock*, 1992.

Radio Plays: *The Birdwatchers*, 1983; *Sea Pictures*, 1984; *Emmet City*, 1984; *The Tigers, the Man on the Vine, and the Wild Strawberry*, 1985; *Crystal of Life*, 1985; *The Man Who Would Be Perfect*, 1986; *Contact*, 1986; *The Second Crusade*, 1986; *Horses*, 1986; *American Girl*, 1988; *Rios Negroes*, 1988; *Hank Williams Laid Down in the Back of My Car and Died*, 1988; *Scott of the Antarctic*, 1989; *Terror and Virtue*, 1989; *Past Lives, Present Mind*, 1990; *The Boat*, 1990; *The Chinese Figure*, 1990; *The Voyage*, 1991; *Ohura*, 1991; *Appointment with Samarra*, 1992; *Travels of the Ship's Surgeon Zuynprit in and about Neu Zeelandt*, 1992.

*

Stuart Hoar comments:
I believe in plays which contain outsights rather than insights, which are aligned outwards into society rather than inwards into the individual, which will make an attempt to apprehend the rational and irrational behaviour contained within any situational frame. Such analysis need not be mechanical, indeed its particular strength, in dramatic form, will be the way imagination, emotion, and thought are used to build each unique situation that a play is, or should be. I believe in plays which actually liberate the imagination from its fetters of an anticipated and expected response. Instead of a closed (and ultimately comfortable) system in which a play generates empathetic reaction to the sum of its representations, there are the potential and the precedent for an open theatre of poetry, paradox, and parable in which the sum of the play's disrepresentations add up to a whole greater than its parts.

* * *

After a short stay at university, Stuart Hoar worked as a film sound recordist, which may be where he developed his ear for the rhythms of dialogue. Apart from that, there is little that is autobiographical in his work; his settings range all over the known world and across time. He began his playwriting with radio plays at the age of 24, and between 1983 and 1992 26 of his plays were broadcast by Radio New Zealand.

His first full-length stage play, *Squatter*, was produced in Auckland in 1987 and the following year in Wellington. Apart from being set in recognisably historic times, Canterbury in the 1890s when the Liberal government was forcibly breaking up the bigger sheep stations, *Squatter* is deliberately non-naturalistic. Hoar insists that complete identification with his characters is not required from his actors, and he seeks critical detachment rather than suspension of disbelief from his audience. His occasional didacticism almost demands an exchange of ideas.

Squatter investigates generational political struggles between greedy capitalists—the Bilstrode family who are landowners (or squatters)—and rather disorganised revolutionaries consisting of Elisabeth the cook, Tuckler the socialist idealist, Wade the ineffectual manager, and Snape, a farcical grotesque of a butler. These four plan to oust Bilstrode, his wily son William and daughter Florence, but as well as being unable to organise themselves they are diverted by the activities of a couple of roving characters, Bracken, a photographer, and Olive, a murderer. Florence is also accompanied by Amy, who is looking for some security of her own.

The plot is violent; even the props include dead sheep and rabbits. There is an early murder of a roustabout by Olive, Elisabeth is bloodily killed offstage, a hasty hanging is rigged on stage for Tuckler, wrongly thought to have killed Elisabeth, and finally a fatal shooting and devastating fire brings all their plans to nothing more than "floating telegrams of ash."

Sons' memories of their fathers is a theme running through the soliloquies in which several characters address the audience. Bilstrode and his son demonstrate their own relationship, and the feeling between Olive and Bracken is very much like that between father and son. These generational exchanges underline the political theme of old systems having to give way to the new.

The final scene emphasises Hoar's Brechtian allegiance, with the four dead characters carrying placards displaying slogans, as the remaining actors scavenge in the ruins and find pieces of human bone. The last sound is of hunting dogs closing in on the murderer, as the placards give their message: This Space For Hire. The image that remains is of the eternal land, scraped and burnt down to the bone by exploiters of several kinds.

A fascinating play which was welcomed critically but was too demanding to become popular, *Squatter* contains elements of farce, parable, social satire, comedy of manners, and melodrama. Hoar uses modern colloquial language whose incongruity in the mouths of period figures is acceptable because he is more interested in exploring ideas—in this case "how people face moral ideas, whether to make a stand or just talk about it, whether to act on principle or look after oneself. Most do the latter."

Stuart Hoar is perhaps not a typical New Zealand playwright in that he does not write about local concerns, nor in contemporary settings. His next work was a version of Alexander Dumas's *The Three Musketeers*, which combined the high romance of the original with a fast-moving action-packed plot—indeed one critic described it as 17th-century *Star Wars*.

Exile, first called *Exile in Stonehurst*, emerged in 1990. Set in 1939, it is a satire on literary attitudes and their inability to bring about change in society. Three German exiles arrive in Auckland to escape Hitler and are at first welcomed enthusiastically by the tiny literary community. Consisting of recognisable caricatures it is dryly amusing, as the local community dances from bed to bed with and around the newcomers. By

contrasting the indigenous writers with the exotic arrivals and a staunch local Everyman who is cheerfully going off to war, Hoar shows New Zealand's isolation, narrow-mindedness, and the futility of some literary pretensions. Lines such as "Brush away the shallow fripperies of mateship and behold the ice-people of the South Pacific" mark *Exile* as a play which has moved on from celebrating the specialness of being a New Zealander to critically assessing just what that means.

Branching into opera libretto and turning one of these—*A Long Walk Off a Tall Rock*—into a full-length play have given Hoar experience in dealing with the grand emotions. This latest play tells a story of the fate of pure and unrequited love in a society which is driven purely by profit. The idea comes from an actual event in Auckland in 1984 when a stripper, trapped in a violent marriage, had an affair with a dwarf. The lovers hire a member of the Mongrel Mob to kill the husband. On this story Hoar based his play (written entirely in verse), which became both operatic and surreal in a dynamic student production.

Hoar deliberately prevents the audience from getting excited and involved with characters and therefore suffers the risk of audience indifference. Recently however, *American Girl*, first broadcast in 1988, has been staged at Otago University and perhaps shows a change to a more sympathetic style. This versatile and prolific playwright is on the move.

—Patricia Cooke

HOFFMAN, William M. American. Born in New York City, 12 April 1939. Educated at the City University, New York, 1955–60, B.A. (cum laude) in Latin 1960 (Phi Beta Kappa). Editorial assistant, Barnes and Noble, publishers, New York, 1960–61; assistant editor, 1961–67, and associate editor and drama editor, 1967–68, Hill and Wang, publishers, New York; literary adviser, *Scripts* magazine, New York, 1971–72; visiting lecturer, University of Massachusetts, Boston, Spring, 1973; playwright-in-residence, American Conservatory Theatre, San Francisco, 1978, and La Mama, New York, 1978–79. Since 1980 Star professor, Hofstra University, Hempstead, New York. Recipient: MacDowell Colony fellowship, 1971; Colorado Council on the Arts and Humanities grant, 1972; Carnegie Fund grant, 1972; PEN grant, 1972; Guggenheim fellowship, 1974; National Endowment for the Arts grant, 1975, 1976; Drama Desk award, 1985; Obie award, 1985; New York Foundation for the Arts grant, 1985. Lives in New York City. Agent: International Creative Management, 40 West 57th Street, New York, New York 10019, U.S.A.

PUBLICATIONS

Plays

Thank You, Miss Victoria (produced New York, 1965; London, 1970). Published in *New American Plays 3*, edited by Hoffman, New York, Hill and Wang, 1970.
Saturday Night at the Movies (produced New York, 1966). Published in *The Off-Off-Broadway Book*, edited by Albert Poland and Bruce Mailman, Indianapolis, Bobbs Merrill, 1972.

Good Night, I Love You (produced New York, 1966).
Spring Play (produced New York, 1967).
Three Masked Dances (produced New York, 1967).
Incantation (produced New York, 1967).
Uptight! (produced New York, 1968).
XXX (produced New York, 1969; as *Nativity Play*, produced London, 1970). Published in *More Plays from Off-Off-Broadway*, edited by Michael T. Smith, Indianapolis, Bobbs Merrill, 1972.
Luna (also director: produced New York, 1970). As *An Excerpt from Buddha*, published in *Now: Theater der Erfahrung*, edited by Jens Heilmeyer and Pia Frolich, Cologne, Schauberg, 1971.
A Quick Nut Bread to Make Your Mouth Water (also director: produced New York, 1970). Published in *Spontaneous Combustion: Eight New American Plays*, edited by Rochelle Owens, New York, Winter House, 1972.
From Fool to Hanged Man (produced New York, 1972). Published in *Scenarios* (New York), 1982.
The Children's Crusade (produced New York, 1972).
Gilles de Rais (also director: produced New York, 1975).
Cornbury, with Anthony Holland (produced New Haven, Connecticut, 1977). Published in *Gay Plays*, edited by Hoffman, New York, Avon, 1979.
The Last Days of Stephen Foster (televised 1977). Published in *Dramatics* (Cincinnati), 1978.
A Book of Etiquette, music by John Braden (produced New York, 1978; as *Etiquette*, produced New York, 1983).
Gulliver's Travels, music by John Braden, adaptation of the novel by Swift (produced New York, 1978).
Shoe Palace Murray, with Anthony Holland (produced San Francisco, 1978). Published in *Gay Plays*, edited by Hoffman, New York, Avon, 1979.
The Cherry Orchard, Part II, with Anthony Holland (produced New York, 1983).
As Is (produced New York, 1985; London, 1987). New York, Random Housc, 1985.

Television Writing: *Notes from the New World: Louis Moreau Gottschalk*, with Roger Englander, 1976; *The Last Days of Stephen Foster*, 1977; *Whistler: 5 Portraits*, 1978.

Verse

The Cloisters: A Song Cycle, music by John Corigliano. New York, Schirmer, 1968.
Wedding Song. New York, Schirmer, 1984.

Other

Editor, *New American Plays 2, 3 and 4*. New York, Hill and Wang, 3 vols., 1968–71.
Editor, *Gay Plays: The First Collection*. New York, Avon, 1979.

*

Manuscript Collections: University of Wisconsin, Madison; Lincoln Center Library of the Performing Arts, New York.

Theatrical Activities:
Director: **Plays**—*Thank You, Miss Victoria*, New Brunswick, New Jersey, 1970; *Luna*, New York, 1970; *A Quick Nut Bread to Make Your Mouth Water*, New York, 1970, Denver, 1972; *XXX*, New York, 1970; *First Death* by Walter Leyden Brown, New York, 1972; *Gilles de Rais*, New York, 1975.
Actor: **Plays**—Frank in *The Haunted IIost* by Robert Patrick,

New York, 1964; Cupid in *Joyce Dynel* by Robert Patrick, New York, 1969; Twin in *Huckleberry Finn*, New York, 1969.
Film—*Guru the Mad Monk*, 1970.

William M. Hoffman comments:

(1982) In 1980 the Metropolitan Opera commissioned me to write a libretto for their 1983–84 season. The composer chosen was John Corigliano. We decided to complete the trilogy of operas on Figaro, using Beaumarchais's last play, *La Mère coupable* (*The Guilty Mother*), as our port of embarkation.

This libretto capped a decade of work with historical materials. My subjects included Gilles de Rais, the actual Bluebeard of 15th-century France; *Gulliver's Travels* and Emily Post's *Book of Etiquette* (1934 edition), in musical adaptation; James McNeill Whistler, Stephen Foster, and Louis Moreau Gottschalk, in plays for television; and Jesus.

My three collaborations with Anthony Holland were also historically founded. *Cornbury* is based on the life of the transvestite English governor of New York in the early 18th century. *Shoe Palace Murray* is located in New York in the 1920's. And *The Cherry Orchard, Part II* is set in Russia of the 1905–17 era.

But now after finishing the libretto, I have returned to the more personal material of my earliest plays, which all took place in contemporary times. I am currently working on a semiautobiographical play and a novel set in my neighborhood, SoHo.

*   *   *

William M. Hoffman's early work *Spring Play* is about a young man leaving home, girlfriend, and innocence and coming to New York City, where he meets a variety of exciting, corrupting people and experiences, and comes to some grief in his growing up. The style of the play is romantic and poetic, a kind of hallucinatory naturalism. Since then Hoffman has edited several anthologies of new American plays, and his awareness of contemporary styles and modes of consciousness is reflected in his own work. *Thank You, Miss Victoria* is a brilliant monologue in which a mother-fixated young business executive gets into a bizarre sado-masochistic relationship on the telephone. *Saturday Night at the Movies* is a bright, brash comedy, and *Uptight!* a musical revue. The eccentrically titled play *XXX* has as characters Jesus, Mary, Joseph, the Holy Ghost, and God. It retells the story of Jesus's life in a personal, free-form, associative, hip, provocatively beautiful fashion. The play is conceived as an ensemble performance for five actors. *Luna* is a light show. *A Quick Nut Bread to Make Your Mouth Water* is an ostensibly improvisatory play for three actors constructed in the form of a recipe, and the nut bread is served to the audience at the finish of the performance. In one production the author himself directed, he incorporated a group of gospel singers into the play.

Hoffman has explored forms other than drama, seeking a renewal of dramatic energies, attempting to expand theatrical possibilities and the audience's awareness. *From Fool to Hanged Man* is a scenario for pantomime, based on imagery from the Tarot. By contrast with much of Hoffman's earlier work, which made a point of the possibility of enlightenment, in which innocence was rewarded at least with edifying experience, here the innocent hero moves blindly, almost passively, through a bleak succession of destructive encounters and is finally hanged. The beauty of the work only emphasizes its despair. Characteristically, the forces at work are not worldly or political but seem to exist in the individual state of mind. *The Children's Crusade* is another dance-pantomime of naive and sentimental innocence brought down by the mockery and hostility of the corrupt, historically worn-out world. The theme parallels a widespread shift of attitude in the United States; to follow Hoffman's work is to observe a representative contemporary consciousness.

Although *Gilles de Rais* embraces depravity, most of Hoffman's subsequent work treats lighter subjects. In this vein are *The Cherry Orchard, Part II, Shoe Palace Murray,* and *Cornbury,* all collaborations with Anthony Holland. *The Cherry Orchard, Part II* is a political satire, incorporating lyrical and melodramatic elements, which opens and closes with the final moments of Chekhov's play and co-opts the character of Irina from *The Three Sisters.* It traces the evolution between 1903 and 1918 of a group of Moscow intellectuals from Tolstoyan pacifists to Bolsheviks. Comedies both, *Shoe Palace Murray* takes place in a New York footwear store in 1926, while *Cornbury* dramatizes the life of an early governor of New York, a transvestite who ruled in Queen Anne's leftover clothing. With the songwriter John Braden, Hoffman has also written two musicals, *Gulliver's Travels* and *A Book of Etiquette.* Another musical project—suggested by the third play in Beaumarchais's trilogy *The Guilty Mother*—is the libretto to *A Figaro for Antonia* for the composer John Corigliano, commissioned by the Metropolitan Opera.

As Is returns to serious matters: the mysterious and, so far, incurable illness AIDS, which in America has struck male homosexuals particularly hard. Blending humor with rage and sorrow, playing freely with time and place, *As Is* makes its larger social commentary within the context of an old-fashioned love story—only here the lovers are gay men, one of whom has a fatal, infectious disease. Hoffman's most popular play to date, *As Is* transferred from the Circle Repertory Company to Broadway.

—Michael T. Smith and C. Lee Jenner

HOLDEN, Joan. American. Born in Berkeley, California, 18 January 1939. Educated at Reed College, Portland, Oregon, B.A. 1960; University of California, Berkeley, M.A. 1964. Married 1) Arthur Holden in 1958 (divorced); 2) Daniel Chumley in 1968, three daughters. Waitress, Claremont Hotel, Berkeley, 1960–62; copywriter, Librairie Larousse, Paris, 1964–66; research assistant, University of California, Berkeley, 1966–67. Since 1967 playwright, publicist, 1967–69, and business manager, 1978–79, San Francisco Mime Troupe. Editor, Pacific News Service, 1973–75; instructor in playwriting, University of California, Davis, 1975, 1977, 1979, 1983, 1985, 1987. Recipient: Obie award, 1973; Rockefeller grant, 1985. Address: San Francisco Mime Troupe, 855 Treat Street, San Francisco, California 94110, U.S.A.

PUBLICATIONS

Plays

L'Amant Militaire, adaptation of a play by Carlo Goldoni, translated by Betty Schwimmer (produced San Francisco and New York, 1967). Published in *The San Francisco Mime Troupe: The First Ten Years,* by R. G. Davis, Palo Alto, California, Ramparts Press, 1975.

Ruzzante; or, The Veteran, adaptation of a play by Angelo Beolco, translated by Suzanne Pollard (produced Hayward, California, 1968).

The Independent Female; or, A Man Has His Pride (produced Los Angeles, 1970). Included in *By Popular Demand,* 1980.

Seize the Time, with Steve Friedman (produced San Francisco, 1970).

The Dragon Lady's Revenge, with others (produced San Francisco, 1971; New York, 1972). Included in *By Popular Demand,* 1980.

Frozen Wages, with Richard Benetar and Daniel Chumley (produced San Francisco, 1972). Included in *By Popular Demand,* 1980.

San Fran Scandals, with others (produced San Francisco, 1973). Included in *By Popular Demand,* 1980.

The Great Air Robbery (produced San Francisco, 1974).

Frijoles; or, Beans to You, with others (produced San Francisco, 1975). Included in *By Popular Demand,* 1980.

Power Play (produced San Francisco, 1975).

False Promises/Nos Engañaron (produced San Francisco, 1976; New York, 1978). Included in *By Popular Demand,* 1980.

The Loon's Rage, with Steve Most and Jael Weisman (produced on tour, 1977). Published in *West Coast Plays 10* (Berkeley, California), Fall 1981.

The Hotel Universe, music by Bruce Barthol (produced La Rochelle, France, 1977). Published in *West Coast Plays 10* (Berkeley, California), Fall 1981.

By Popular Demand: Plays and Other Works by The San Francisco Mime Troupe (includes *False Promises/Nos Engañaron; San Fran Scandals; The Dragon Lady's Revenge; The Independent Female; Frijoles; Frozen Wages* by Holden, and *Los Siete* and *Evo-Man*). San Francisco, San Francisco Mime Troupe, 1980.

Factperson, with others (produced San Francisco, 1980). Published in *West Coast Plays 15–16* (Berkeley, California), Spring 1983.

Americans; or, Last Tango in Huahuatenango, with Daniel Chumley (produced Dayton, Ohio, and London, 1981; New York, 1982).

Factwino Meets the Moral Majority, with others (produced San Francisco, 1981; New York, 1982). Published in *West Coast Plays 15–16* (Berkeley, California), Spring 1983.

Factwino vs. Armaggedonman (produced San Francisco, 1982). Published in *West Coast Plays 15–16* (Berkeley, California), Spring 1983.

Steeltown, music by Bruce Barthol (produced San Francisco, 1984; New York, 1985).

1985, with others (produced San Francisco, 1985).

Spain/36, music by Bruce Barthol (produced Los Angeles, 1986).

The Mozamgola Caper, with others (produced San Francisco, 1986). Published in *Theater* (New Haven, Connecticut), Winter 1986.

Ripped van Winkle, with Ellen Callas (produced San Francisco, 1988).

Seeing Double, with others (produced San Francisco and New York, 1989).

Back to Normal, with others (produced San Francisco, 1990).

The Marriage of Figaro, adaptation of a play by Beaumarchais (produced San Francisco, 1990).

*

Manuscript Collection: University of California, Davis.

Critical Studies: "*Hotel Universe*: Playwriting and the San Francisco Mime Troupe" by William Kleb, in *Theater* (New Haven, Connecticut), Spring 1978; "Joan Holden and the San Francisco Mime Troupe," in *Drama Review* (New York), Spring 1980, and *New American Dramatists 1960–1980*, London, Macmillan, and New York, Grove Press, 1982, both by Ruby Cohn.

Joan Holden comments:

I write political cartoons. For years, I was ashamed of this. I agreed meekly with those critics who said, "*mere* political cartoons." To please them, and led astray by well-wishers who'd say, "You can do more—you could write *serious* plays," I've tried my hand, from time to time, at realism. Each time I've been extremely impressed, at first, with the solemnity of what I've written. Rereading those passages, I always find I've written melodrama. The fact is, I'm only inspired when I'm being funny. Writing comedy is not really a choice: it's a quirk. On a certain level, making things funny is a coward's way of keeping pain at arm's length. But that same distance allows you to show certain things clearly: notably, characters' social roles, their functions in history. These generalities, not the specifics which soften them, interest caricaturists—who have serious reasons for being funny, and in whose ranks I now aspire to be counted.

For 20 years, I've written for a permanent company, for particular actors, directors, and composers, and in collaboration with them. This has put conditions on my writing; it has also supplied a nearly constant source of ideas, and a wonderful opportunity to learn from mistakes.

*   *   *

Joan Holden has been the principal playwright of the San Francisco Mime Troupe, which has always performed with words as well as gesture. Although chance led to this association, a 30-year career was launched.

The Holden/Goldoni *Military Lover/L'Amant Militaire* drew large audiences to nearly 50 park performances, and Holden wrote: "Comedy, which in its basic action always measures an unsatisfactory reality against its corresponding ideal, may be the revolutionary art form *par excellence*." It became Holden's art form *par excellence*, pitting satirized Establishment figures of unsatisfactory reality against the satisfactory dream of working-class harmony and celebration.

After the Mime Troupe went collective in 1970, *The Independent Female* expressed the new spirit. *Commedia* characters gave way to those of soap opera with satiric telltale names—Pennybank for a business tycoon, Heartright for a junior executive, Bullitt for a militant feminist. A pair of lovers is faced with an obstacle to their marriage, as in soap opera. But subverting the genre, Holden identifies the obstacle as the young ingénue's growing independence. Instead of dissolving the obstacle for a happy curtain clinch, Holden sees a happy ending in sustained feminist revolt which the audience is asked to link to working class revolt.

The Dragon Lady's Revenge is grounded in another popular form, the comic strip, with assists from Grade B movies, and its intricate plot involves the corrupt American ambassador in Long Penh, his soldier son, a CIA agent Drooley, and the titular Dragon Lady, as well as the honest native revolutionary Blossom. Holden shifted from global to local politics with *San Fran Scandals* blending housing problems into vaudeville. Science fiction and detective story were then exploited for *The Great Air Robbery*.

In the mid-1970's the San Francisco Mime Troupe reached out beyond the white middle class, actively recruiting Third World members, and Holden's scripts reflect their new constituency. *Frijoles* (Spanish for beans) zigzags from a Latin American couple to a North American couple, joining them at a food conference in Europe, and joining them in identical class interests. As *Frijoles* travels through space, *Power Play* travels through time in order to indict the anti-ecological monopoly of the Pacific Gas and Electric Company.

By 1976, America's bicentennial year, Holden was in firm command of her style: a specific issue attacked through a popular art form; simple language and clean story line; swift scenes often culminating in a song. The group wished to present a play on the uncelebrated aspects of American history—the role of workers, minorities, women. Based on collective research, Holden scripted *False Promises*, which deviated from her usual satiric formula in presenting heightened realism of working-class characters. They continue to appear in such subsequent plays as *Steeltown* and the final play of the Factwino trilogy. In *Factperson* the person of the title is an old black baglady with the power to cite facts that contradict the lies of the media. In *Factwino vs. Armaggedonman* "the double-headed dealer of doom" or the military-industrial powers subjugate an old black wino with alcohol, but in the most recent Factwino play he emerges triumphant through his own research beneath lies: "Everybody has to find their own power." *Ripped van Winkle* is a hilarious reversion to satire, when a 1960's hippy awakens from a 20-year acid trip, adrift in Reaganomics. Local or global, probing character, or tickling caricature, Holden theatricalizes current events with theatrical verve.

—Ruby Cohn

———

HOLLINGSWORTH, Margaret. Canadian. Born in Sheffield, England, in 1940; emigrated to Canada, 1968; became citizen, 1974. Educated at Hornsey High School, London; Loughborough School of Librarianship, Leicestershire, A.L.A.; Lakehead University, Thunder Bay, Ontario (gold medal), B.A. 1972; University of British Columbia, Vancouver, M.F.A. in theatre and creative writing 1974. Journalist, editor, librarian, and teacher in England, 1960–68; chief librarian, Fort William Public Library, Ontario, 1968–72. Since 1972 freelance writer. Assistant professor, David Thompson Centre, University of Victoria, Nelson, British Columbia, 1981–83; writer-in-residence, Concordia University, Montreal, 1985–86, Stratford Festival Theatre, Ontario, 1987, and University of Western Ontario, London, Ontario, 1989–90; since 1992 assistant professor of creative writing, University of Victoria, British Columbia. Recipient: Association of Canadian Television and Radio Artists award, 1979; Chalmers award, 1985; Dora Mavor Moore award, 1986, 1987. Lives in Victoria. Address: c/o Playwrights Union of Canada, 8 York Street, 6th Floor, Toronto, Ontario M5J 1R2, Canada.

PUBLICATIONS

Plays

Bushed (produced Vancouver, 1974). With *Operators*, Toronto, Playwrights, 1981.

Operators (produced Vancouver, 1975; revised version produced 1981). With *Bushed*, Toronto, Playwrights, 1981.

Dance for My Father. Vancouver, New Play Centre, 1976.

Alli Alli Oh (produced Vancouver, 1977). Toronto, Playwrights, 1979.

The Apple in the Eye (broadcast 1977; produced Vancouver, 1983). Included in *Willful Acts*, 1985.

The Writers Show (revue), with others (produced Vancouver, 1978).

Mother Country (produced Toronto, 1980). Toronto, Playwrights, 1980.

Ever Loving (produced Victoria, British Columbia, 1980). Toronto, Playwrights, 1981.

Islands (produced Vancouver, 1983). Toronto, Playwrights, 1983.

Diving (produced Vancouver, 1983). Included in *Willful Acts*, 1985.

War Babies (produced Victoria, British Columbia, 1984). Included in *Willful Acts*, 1985.

It's Only Hot for Two Months in Kapuskasing (produced Toronto, 1985). Included in *Endangered Species*, 1989.

Willful Acts (includes *The Apple in the Eye*, *Ever Loving*, *Diving*, *Islands*, *War Babies*). Toronto, Coach House Press, 1985.

The Green Line (produced Stratford, Ontario, 1986).

Endangered Species (includes *The House That Jack Built*, *It's Only Hot for Two Months in Kapuskasing*, *Prim and Duck, Mama and Frank*). Toronto, One Act Press, 1989.

Prim and Duck, Mama and Frank (produced Toronto, 1991). Included in *Endangered Species*, 1989.

Alma Victoria (produced Nanaimo, British Columbia, 1990).

There's a Few Things I Want to Tell You (produced Vancouver, 1992).

Making Greenpeace (produced Vancouver, 1992).

Radio Plays: *Join Me in Mandalay*, *Prairie Drive*, *As I Was Saying to Mr. Dideron*, *Wayley's Children*, and *War Games*, from 1973; *The Apple in the Eye*, 1977; *Webster's Revenge*, 1977; *Operators*, 1986; *Alli Alli Oh*, 1986; *Responsible Party*, 1986; *Woman on the Wire*, 1986; *Surreal Landscape*, *The Cloud Sculptors of Coral D*, *Sailing Under Water*, *A Mother in India*, from 1986; *Mussomeli-Dusseldorf*, adaptation of the radio play by Dacia Maraini, 1991.

Television Plays: *Ole and All That*, 1968 (UK); *Sleepwalking* (*AirWaves* series), 1986; *Scene from a Balcony*, 1987; *The Last Demise of Julian Whittaker*, 1989.

Short Stories

Sailing Under Water. Vancouver, Lazara Press, 1989.

*

Critical Studies: "Margaret Hollingsworth," in *The Work: Conversations with English Canadian Playwrights*, edited by Cynthia Zimmerman, Toronto, Coach House Press, 1982; introduction by Ann Saddlemyer to *Willful Acts*, 1985; "Readings in Review: *Willful Acts*," by Rina Fraticelli, in *Canadian Theatre Review* (Downsview, Ontario), Summer 1986; "Alienation and Identity: The Plays of Margaret Hollingsworth," in *Canadian Literature* (Vancouver), no. 118, Autumn 1988; "Margaret Hollingsworth," in *Fair Play: 12 Women Speak/ Conversations with Canadian Playwrights*, edited by Judith Rudakoff and Rita Much, Toronto, Simon and Pierre, 1990.

Margaret Hollingsworth comments:

(1988) My work is very wide-ranging in style and subject. Constantly recurring themes are the search for a home, sex roles and sexual stereotypes, and war. My latest plays are *The Green Line* which is set on the green line in Beirut, and *Marked for Marriage*, a 3-act farce set against the background of the survival games which are an extremely popular pseudo-military outdoor activity among Canadian men.

Some of my more experimental work, such as *Prim and Duck, Mama and Frank*, has yet to get beyond the workshop production stage, since there are very few outlets for experimental work in Canada at this time.

*   *   *

Margaret Hollingsworth, born in England, emigrated to Canada at the age of 28. Now she insists: "Canada is what I write about. Canada is where I come from; it's what feeds me. My plays always, in some way, come out of Canada." She believes, as she said in a 1982 interview, that her distinctive style accounts for the infrequent staging of her work: "It tends to read flat but it isn't flat in production. Often directors are very tentative about how to handle it because it doesn't fall into any category. It isn't like what anyone else is doing. My work has got a surreal level to it. That's the way I see life. I see it in a very surreal way but rooted in practical realism." The broad trend of Hollingsworth's work ranges from relatively conventional drama (perhaps shaped by the assumptions of the New Play Centre in Vancouver) to more obscure styles and technique, linked with her gradual evolution of her own female aesthetic.

Bushed and *Operators*, early one-acts, are set in northern Ontario. *Bushed* depicts tired immigrant men in a laundromat and *Operators* features two women nightshift workers whose long-term friendship is disrupted by a newcomer. These are pieces of mood, of place, and of displacement.

Ever Loving (an ironic title) is her most accessible drama. In 38 scenes, starting in 1970 and going back as far as 1938, we see three war marriages between near-strangers: a Dundee fishergirl with an Ontario millworker of Irish descent; a posh Englishwoman with a Ukrainian Prairie farmer; and an Italian aristocrat with a would-be musician in Nova Scotia. Hollingsworth includes pre-war life, first meetings, courtship, crossing the Atlantic, and the ups and downs of 25 years. "Canada's roots," writes Helen Thomson, are shown as in "other and older cultures," while "Canadian nationalism excludes its women, and is only a spurious emotion in men." *Ever Loving* explores an important aspect of recent Canadian experience; it is about romance though it avoids all the clichés; and it is unobtrusively adventurous structurally (with two or three separate actions onstage at the same time; inter-weaving date and comment with 29 popular songs; and juxtaposing different accents and speech rhythms).

The murder of Francis Rattenbury by his wife's toy boy, perhaps aided by the wife, was a sensation in England in 1935. Rattenbury, an architect, worked mostly in British Columbia. The story prompted two plays, *Cause Célèbre*, by Terence Rattigan, and—distantly—*Molly*, by Simon Gray. Hollingsworth's treatment, *Alma Victoria*, commissioned for the 1990 Nanaimo Festival, occurs largely before the murder, with the first half in the 1920's, promisingly sketching the English-style middle-class way of life in Victoria, British

Columbia. Rattenbury, at 58, abandons his wife for young Alma, a successful New York pianist and already twice married. The more routine conclusion in Bournemouth has Rattenbury drinking and in decline while his wife composes songs. The focus becomes a troubled woman circumscribed by her times.

Though Hollingsworth was active in the Campaign for Nuclear Disarmament in Britain, her political principles become overt only in *Woman on the Wire*. She explained that she lacked the confidence to write politically explicitly for a long time as "part of being a woman. You don't feel that your voice is important enough to matter. It takes a lot of writing to be able to get to the point where I feel confident enough to do that." In *Woman on the Wire*, Kate, a Canadian wife and mother, is drawn to the peace camp at the missile base at Greenham Common. The tension of night beside the barbed-wire is created, with a lonely male sentry on one side and a female look-out on the other. Both are tired, jumpy, afraid. In snippets, we learn how Kate had to accompany her manager husband to London and how an English friend first takes her to the Common, then how the commitment becomes more vital than the marriage. Another camper is a teacher who found she could teach war because it was history, but not peace, because it was politics. Kate proclaims polemically: "Just being here can make a difference to life on this planet." *Woman on the Wire* shows the usual enterprise in structure, as when song, the husband's "I love you," and the trial judge's "How do you plead?" are intercut and overlapped.

Mother Country shows Hollingsworth attempting to create on both a literal and a super-realist level. The characters are an English emigré family, three daughters returning to celebrate their dominating mother's 65th birthday, on an island off the British Columbia coast. The themes were stated succinctly by Cynthia Zimmerman: it is a play "about country and culture, about belonging and home."

Hollingsworth believes, as she told the Vancouver *Sun* in 1984, that womens' drama is "unlinear, concerned with getting inside people's heads, into the thought process. There's an earthy rhythmic sense to a lot of female writing, an effort to be more universal, to find a wholeness, a diffusing quality." Later she explains that she seeks "a poetic drama that isn't self-conscious." In a 1985 article she probed further into the problems of the woman dramatist: the domination of men as decision-makers in the theatre; the tendency for women to write for ensembles, "always a stumbling block to smooth production"; but also the way that a true woman's way defies the rules of playwriting; "The concept of a hero is perhaps a male invention, a male need." Women prefer to write of "inner states and tensions," which often do not "fit neatly into an accepted dramatic form."

An early piece such as *The Apple in the Eye* shows concern with the differences between a woman's public and private voice, together with puzzles about precisely what the apple represents. The four self-published short scripts collected as *Endangered Species* reveal Hollingsworth clearly pushing in new directions, ignoring the expectations of mainstream theatre. To select two of these, *Poppycock* develops from work with masks and clowning. Here time is "scrambled" and three well-researched relationships are brought together; H.D. and Ezra Pound, Dora Maar and Picasso, and Winifred Wagner and Hitler, with the same actor playing the three men. The semi-absurdist *Prim and Duck, Mama and Frank* has its four characters in four different rooms, with the movements of the play entitled Feet, Hands, Body, and Head.

While commentators have examined Hollingsworth's work in the light of her degree in psychology and through the influence of Pinter, neither provides the key; nor is she precisely "absurd" or "surrealist." Using short forms and evolving her own kind of non-realism, her work is increasingly individualistic, even idiosyncratic. Her writing is characterized by care for language, by focus on women in a man's world, and by a continuing restless search for something new, the perfect form of self-expression. But will these plays be produced—preferably without the restrictions of low budgets and short rehearsal periods—before she is discouraged?

—Malcolm Page

HOLMAN, Robert. British. Born in Guisborough, Cleveland, 25 August 1952. Educated at Lawrence Jackson School, Guisborough, 1963–69; Prior Pursglove Sixth Form College, Guisborough, 1969–71. Bookstall assistant, Paddington Station, London, 1972–74; resident dramatist, National Theatre, London, 1978–80, and Royal Shakespeare Company, Stratford-on-Avon, 1984. Recipient: Arts Council bursary, 1974; George Devine award, 1978; Fulbright fellowship, 1988. Agent: Casarotto Ramsay Ltd., National House, 60–66 Wardour Street, London W1V 3HP, England.

PUBLICATIONS

Plays

The Grave Lovers (produced Edinburgh, 1972).
Progress in Unity (produced Teesside, 1972).
Coal (produced London, 1973).
The Natural Cause (produced London, 1974).
Mud (produced London, 1974). With *German Skerries*, London, Heinemann, 1977.
Outside the Whale (produced Edinburgh, 1976; London, 1978). With *Rafts and Dreams*, London, Methuen, 1991.
German Skerries (produced London, 1977). With *Mud*, London, Heinemann, 1977.
Emigres, adaptation of the play by Sławomir Mrozek (produced London, 1978; New York, 1979). Published in *New Review* (London), 1979.
Rooting (produced Edinburgh, 1980).
Other Worlds (produced London, 1983). London, Methuen, 1983.
Today (produced Stratford-on-Avon, 1984; London, 1985). London, Methuen, 1985.
The Overgrown Path (produced London, 1985). London, Methuen, 1985.
Making Noise Quietly: A Trilogy (includes *Being Friends*, *Lost*, *Making Noise Quietly*) (produced London, 1986; Los Angeles, 1989). London, Methuen, 1987.
Across Oka (produced Stratford-on-Avon, 1988; London, 1989). London, Methuen, 1988.
Rafts and Dreams (produced London, 1990). With *Outside the Whale*, London, Methuen, 1991.

Television Plays: *Chance of a Lifetime*, 1979; *This Is History, Gran*, 1984.

Novel

The Amish Landscape. London, Hern, 1992.

* * *

Allusive and carefully crafted, Robert Holman's plays explore the interpenetration of ordinary lives and large historical events. The Great Depression, the Spanish Civil War, World War II, the Holocaust, the destruction of Nagasaki, and the continuation of research on the hydrogen bomb—such realities darken the worlds shaping and shaped by his characters, worlds which in turn illuminate the contradictions and complexities of these realities. History is not a backcloth—nor even a stage—for these characters, but a sense of pattern which reveals, and is revealed by, their actions or inactions. Time and again his protagonists articulate this simple truth: "It's important. History. Our lives."

Perhaps his strongest and most ambitious play to date is *The Overgrown Path*. This opens with a playlet performed by primary-school children in modern-day Nagasaki. It recounts the experience of a girl called Etsuko on the day the atomic bomb was dropped. When the playlet ends, Etsuko is identified as the children's schoolteacher. The rest of the drama takes place on the Greek island of Tinos where Daniel Howarth, a 73-year-old British academic, has retired from the world with Beth, his second wife. Four years his junior, she is American and a doctor. As a member of a medical relief team in Nagasaki in 1945, she had witnessed the effects of the bomb and, during her time there, had befriended a 10-year-old orphan of the blast called Etsuko. Daniel's career had been in atomic physics and he had led the research programme on the hydrogen bomb throughout the 1950's. They met and married in the 1960's. To their escape on Tinos comes Daniel's daughter by his first marriage, and a bright questioning disciple—in his late thirties—who is hesitating before embarking on what clearly could be a brilliant academic career. From the lives of these four people come stories and processes of learning which reveal patterns of design and accident that help to bring both characters and historical "facts" into a felt relationship. As Daniel says to his inquisitive disciple: "I'm not a historian, but it seems to me we look at history in the wrong way. We have to look at ourselves first. At our own stories. When we stop repeating our own failings, and take responsibility for our actions, maybe we have a chance."

This need to "take responsibility" is a recurring motif. It is something Joe Waterman, in an earlier play *Other Worlds*, is running away from. It is something his betrothed, at their last tragic meeting, insists upon:

Joe: It's other people messed it up, not us.
Emma: It's us.

It is something that, by the end of the play, Joe learns to do. *Other Worlds* takes place during the final decades of the 18th century when enclosure by private Acts of Parliament was dividing communities and challenging custom. The barriers of enmity and suspicion raised by one such Act, separating the world of the fishers and the world of the farmers on an isolated stretch of the north Yorkshire coast, are reinforced by the threat of an invasion from France. Fear of the unknown and of the reciprocal violence engendered by enclosure is portrayed through such vivid stage imagery as the unexpected irruption of a shipwrecked gorilla dressed in a blue woollen sailor's jumper, his capture in a fishing net, and his imprisonment and eventual execution as a Frenchman alongside a vagrant girl who, dressed in boy's clothes, is

thought to be a French spy and whose protestations of gender are not believed. The absurdity of such images highlights how, in a collision of closed worlds, any sense of identity, shared humanity, or responsibility to otherness becomes constrained. Against these implosive forces are posited a belief in education and learning, hope—"when you've lost hope, you've lost everything"—and the need not to drift or run away but to take on the responsibility for one's actions.

In all of Holman's work, a care for detail is balanced by an impressionistic style designed to engage an audience in a continual process of inference, surprise, reassessment, and understanding concerning both events and people. In many of his plays events move backwards and forwards in time, as—for example—in *Today*, where they move from 1936 to 1920 to 1922 to 1937 to 1946. In this drama, we are drawn into the experiences of the relatives, friends, and casual acquaintances of Victor Ellison, a Yorkshire music teacher who, struggling to compose something out of his life, goes to fight in Spain. Their experiences articulate differences in opportunities, aspirations, economics, class, and region before and during the Great Depression. The shifts in time sharpen our sense of the choices and restrictions facing these figures as well as highlighting how chance and accident can affect the direction of events. These shifts in perspective involve the audience in seeing and revising why and how these things happened. Holman's approach to characterisation deepens this involvement. New, often contradictory, facets of character are continually juxtaposed, making us modify, even change outright, our sense of what motivates each person.

We get to know Holman's characters through partial and accidental revelations and encounters. This allusive approach is best exemplified in *Lost*, the shortest of the one-act plays comprising the trilogy *Making Noise Quietly*. A young naval lieutenant visits his sister's mother-in-law to commiserate on her son's death in the Falklands. They have not met before. She does not know who he is. The mother has not heard that her son is dead. She does not even know that he was married. These facts—along with details of family relationships, their social backgrounds, and respective pasts—are disclosed in a seemingly haphazard way which exposes an emotional muddle of "little lies" in the front room of a small terraced house in Redcar, a muddle that parallels and illuminates the moral murk of the Falklands War.

—Leslie du S. Read

————

HOME, William Douglas. British. 1912–1992.
See 4th edition, 1988.

————

HOPKINS, John (Richard). British. Born in London, 27 January 1931. Educated at Raynes Park County Grammar School; St. Catharine's College, Cambridge, B.A. in English. Served in the British Army (national service), 1950–51. Married 1) Prudence Balchin in 1954; 2) the actress Shirley Knight in 1970; two daughters. Worked as television studio

manager; writer, BBC Television, 1962–64. Since 1964 free-
lance writer. Recipient: two Screenwriters Guild awards.
Agent: William Morris Agency, 31–32 Soho Square, London
W1V 6AP, England. Address: Hazelnut Farm, R.F.D. 1,
Fairfield, Connecticut 06430, U.S.A.

PUBLICATIONS

Plays

A Place of Safety (televised 1963). Published in *Z Cars:*
Four Scripts From the Television Series, edited by Michael
Marland, London, Longman, 1968.
Talking to a Stranger: Four Television Plays (includes
Anytime You're Ready I'll Sparkle, *No Skill or Special*
Knowledge Is Required, *Gladly My Cross-Eyed Bear*, *The*
Innocent Must Suffer) (televised 1966). London, Penguin,
1967.
A Game—Like—Only a Game (televised 1966). Published in
Conflicting Generations: Five Television Plays, edited by
Michael Marland, London, Longman, 1968.
This Story of Yours (produced London, 1968; New Haven,
Connecticut, 1981). London, Penguin, 1969.
Find Your Way Home (produced London, 1970; New York,
1974). London, Penguin, 1971; New York, Doubleday,
1975.
Economic Necessity (produced Leicester, 1973; New York,
1976).
Next of Kin (produced London, 1974).
Losing Time (produced New York, 1979). New York,
Broadway Play Publishing, 1983.
Absent Forever (produced Cleveland, Ohio, 1987).

Screenplays: *Two Left Feet*, with Roy Baker, 1963;
Thunderball, with Richard Maibaum, 1965; *The Virgin*
Soldiers, with John McGrath and Ian La Fresnais, 1969;
Divorce—His, Divorce—Hers, 1972; *The Offence*, 1973;
Murder by Decree, 1980; *The Holcroft Covenant*, with
George Axelrod and Edward Anhalt, 1982; *The Power*, with
John Carpenter and Gerald Brach, 1983.

Television Plays: *Break Up*, 1958; *After the Party*, 1958; *The*
Small Back Room, 1959; *Dancers in Mourning*, 1959; *A*
Woman Comes Home, 1961; *A Chance of Thunder* (6 parts),
1961; *By Invitation Only*, 1961; *The Second Curtain*, 1962;
Look Who's Talking, 1962; *Z Cars* series (53 episodes),
1962–65; *The Pretty English Girls*, 1964; *I Took My Little*
World Away, 1964; *Parade's End* (serialization), from the
novel by Ford Madox Ford, 1964; *Time Out of Mind*, 1964;
Houseparty (ballet scenario), 1964; *The Make Believe Man*,
1965; *Fable*, 1965; *Horror of Darkness*, 1965; *A Man Like*
Orpheus, 1965; *Talking to a Stranger* (4 parts), 1966; *Some*
Place of Darkness, music by Christopher Whelen, 1966; *A*
Game—Like—Only a Game, 1966; *The Gambler* (serializa-
tion), from a novel by Dostoevsky, 1968; *Beyond the Sunrise*,
1969; *The Dolly Scene*, 1970; *Some Distant Shadow*, 1971;
That Quiet Earth, 1972; *Walk into the Dark*, 1972; *The Greeks*
and Their Gifts, 1972; *A Story to Frighten the Children*, 1976;
Double Dare, 1976; *Fathers and Families* (6 plays), 1977;
Smiley's People, with John le Carré, from the novel by le
Carré, 1982.

* * *

With well over 50 scripts for the television series *Z Cars*,
and several short television plays behind him, John Hopkins

is not primarily a writer for the stage. It was on the newer
medium that his reputation was made, and continues to stand
at its highest. Indeed, one important critic called his tetralogy, *Talking to a Stranger*, "the first authentic masterpiece
written directly for television," and there must be many
others who, though perhaps charier of the word "masterpiece," would agree that no finer dramatic work has yet been
seen on it. It is undeniably impressive in itself: it also makes a
helpful introduction to the first plays Hopkins was subsequently to write for the theatre, *This Story of Yours* and
Find Your Way Home.

Each of the four plays involves approximately the same
day, and each is written from the stance of a different member of the same family, the father, the mother, and their two
grown-up children, Alan and Teresa. All are characterized in
striking depth; all, with the possible exception of the son, are
thoroughly self-absorbed, more inclined to talk in monologue
than dialogue; all, again except for him, stand in danger of
being overwhelmed by their own self-destructive feelings; all,
including him, are lonely and dissatisfied. The tetralogy opens
with Teresa, bustling with frantic neurosis, and ends with the
mother, dead by her own hand, and, between the two,
Hopkins avoids none of the emotional collisions and unplea-
santness that his plot generates. Where most contemporary
writers would hedge, or tread warily, or retreat into irony, he
strides in wholeheartedly and sometimes repetitively, using
straightforward, unpretentious, naturalistic language. Not
surprisingly, he has been accused of dramatic overstatement,
even melodrama.

But "melodrama" occurs when a writer presents extremes
of feeling which are neither justified by his material nor
empathetically understood by himself. In *Talking to a*
Stranger the emotions on display are no more than the "objective correlative" of the dramatic situation, so painstakingly
assembled; and, equally, Hopkins has a thorough grasp of the
people he has created. He gives the impression of knowing,
instinctively, how they would react to any new event. The
question is: can we say as much for his stage plays? And the
proper answer would seem to be: not quite.

This Story of Yours seems almost to be accusing Hopkins's
scripts for *Z Cars* of romanticizing their subject, the police
(though in fact they were widely admired for their wry realism). It is a study of the mind of Detective-Sergeant Johnson,
trapped in an unfulfilling marriage and at once disgusted and
fascinated by work that, characteristically, Hopkins describes
in lurid detail. He breaks, and, in a scene of considerable
dramatic intensity, beats to death an alleged child rapist: an
act that is doubly self-destructive, since it wrecks his career
and since it is clearly a way of sublimating his loathing for his
own hideous thoughts and corrupt desires. *Find Your Way*
Home mainly concerns two homosexuals, one young, unhappy, and apparently a part-time prostitute, the other a
married man, and ends with them settling down seriously to
live together, having confessed their mutual love. By bringing
on a distraught wife, and by accentuating the crudity and
sadness of the homosexual subculture, Hopkins is at pains to
make this decision as difficult as possible. But his view evidently is that it is the right one. The older man has "found his
way home," to a more honest and fulfilling way of life.

From this, it will be seen that Hopkins's view of the world is
bleak: and what seems "melodramatic" in his work is often
only his way of emphasizing his belief that people are lonely
and perverse, full of black thoughts and longings. If a relationship is capable of any success at all, which is doubtful, it
can be only after each partner has accepted his own and the
other's emotional inadequacies, as the protagonists of *Find*
Your Way Home are beginning to do. It is an outspoken,

unfashionable moral stance which, to be persuasive, may need the more thorough characterization we find in *Talking to a Stranger*. There are psychological gaps left open in the stage plays, and notably in *Find Your Way Home*, whose scheme forces Hopkins to the dubious assumption that a young man who has gone very far in self-destructive promiscuity may be capable of sustained affection in a mature relationship. Hopkins achieves his effects by accumulating the emotional evidence as thickly as he can, and may therefore need more space, more time, than other contemporary writers in order to do so.

—Benedict Nightingale

HOROVITZ, Israel (Arthur). American. Born in Wakefield, Massachusetts, 31 March 1939. Educated at the Royal Academy of Dramatic Art, London, 1961–63; City College, New York, M.A. in English 1972. Married 1) Elaine Abber in 1959 (marriage annulled 1960); 2) Doris Keefe in 1961 (divorced 1972), one daughter and two sons. 3) Gillian Adams in 1981, twin daughter and son. Stage manager, Boston and New York, 1961–65; playwright-in-residence, Royal Shakespeare Company, London, 1965; instructor in playwriting, New York University, 1967–69; professor of English, City College, 1968–73; Fanny Hurst professor of theatre, Brandeis University, Waltham, Massachusetts, 1973–75. Founder, New York Playwrights Lab, 1977; founder, 1980, and producer and artistic director, Gloucester Stage Company, Massachusetts. Columnist, *Magazine Littéraire*, Paris, 1971–77. Recipient: Obie award, 1968, 1969; Rockefeller fellowship, 1969; Vernon Rice award, 1969; Drama Desk award, 1969; *Jersey Journal* award, 1969; Cannes Film Festival Jury prize, 1971; New York State Council of Arts fellowship, 1971, 1975; National Endowment for the Arts fellowship, 1974, 1977; American Academy award, 1975; Fulbright fellowship, 1975; Emmy award, 1975; Christopher award, 1976; Guggenheim fellowship, 1977; French Critics prize, 1977; Los Angeles Drama Critics Circle award, 1980; Goldie award, 1985; Eliot Norton Prize, 1986; Boston Best Play award, 1987. Agents: William Morris Agency, 1350 Avenue of the Americas, New York, New York 10019, U.S.A., and 31–32 Soho Square, London W1V 6AP, England.

PUBLICATIONS

Plays

The Comeback (produced Boston, 1958).
The Death of Bernard the Believer (produced South Orange, New Jersey, 1960).
This Play Is about Me (produced South Orange, New Jersey, 1961).
The Hanging of Emanuel (produced South Orange, New Jersey, 1962).
Hop, Skip, and Jump (produced South Orange, New Jersey, 1963).

The Killer Dove (produced West Orange, New Jersey, 1963).
The Simon Street Harvest (produced South Orange, New Jersey, 1964).
The Indian Wants the Bronx (produced Waterford, Connecticut, 1966; New York and Watford, Hertfordshire, 1968; London, 1969). Included in *First Season*, 1968; in *Off-Broadway Plays*, London, Penguin, 1970.
Line (produced New York, 1967; London, 1970; revised version produced New York, 1971). Included in *First Season*, 1968.
It's Called the Sugar Plum (produced Waterford, Connecticut, 1967; New York and Watford, Hertfordshire, 1968; London, 1971). Included in *First Season*, 1968; in *Off-Broadway Plays*, London, Penguin, 1970.
Acrobats (produced New York, 1968; London, 1980). New York, Dramatists Play Service, 1971.
Rats (produced New York, 1968; London, 1969). Included in *First Season*, 1968.
Morning (in *Chiaroscuro* produced Spoleto, Italy, 1968; in *Morning, Noon, and Night* produced New York, 1968). Published in *Morning, Noon, and Night*, New York, Random House, 1969.
First Season: Line, The Indian Wants the Bronx, It's Called the Sugar Plum, Rats. New York, Random House, 1968.
The Honest to God Schnozzola (produced Provincetown, Massachusetts, 1968; New York, 1969). New York, Breakthrough Press, 1971.
Leader (produced New York, 1969). With *Play for Trees*, New York, Dramatists Play Service, 1970.
Play for Trees (televised 1969). With *Leader*, New York, Dramatists Play Service, 1970.
Shooting Gallery (produced New York, 1971). With *Play for Germs*, New York, Dramatists Play Service, 1973.
Dr. Hero (as *Hero*, produced New York, 1971; revised version, as *Dr. Hero*, produced Great Neck, New York, 1972; New York City, 1973). New York, Dramatists Play Service, 1973.
The Wakefield Plays (produced New York, 1978). Included in *The Wakefield Plays* (collection), 1979.
  1. *Alfred the Great* (also director: produced Paris and Great Neck, New York, 1972; New York City, 1973). New York, Harper, 1974.
  2. *Our Father's Failing* (produced Waterford, Connecticut, 1973; New York, 1974).
  3. *Alfred Dies* (produced New York, 1976).
Play for Germs (in *VD Blues*, televised 1972). With *Shooting Gallery*, New York, Dramatists Play Service, 1973.
The First, The Last, and The Middle: A Comedy Triptych (produced New York, 1974).
The Quannapowitt Quartet (produced New Haven, Connecticut, 1976). 3 plays in *The Wakefield Plays* (collection), 1979.
  1. *Hopscotch* (also director: produced Paris and New York, 1974; London, 1980). With *The 75th*, New York, Dramatists Play Service, 1977.
  2. *The 75th* (produced New York, 1977). With *Hopscotch*, New York, Dramatists Play Service, 1977.
  3. *Stage Directions* (produced New York, 1976; Richmond, Surrey, 1978). With *Spared*, New York, Dramatists Play Service, 1977.
  4. *Spared* (also director: produced Paris and New York, 1974). With *Stage Directions*, New York, Dramatists Play Service, 1977.
Turnstile (produced Hanover, New Hampshire, 1974).
The Primary English Class (produced Waterford, Connecticut, 1975; also director: produced New York,

1975; Richmond, Surrey, 1979; London, 1980). New York, Dramatists Play Service, 1976.

Uncle Snake: An Independence Day Pageant (produced New York, 1975). New York, Dramatists Play Service, 1976.

The Reason We Eat (produced Stamford, Connecticut, and New York, 1976).

The Lounge Player (produced New York, 1977).

Man with Bags, adaptation of a play by Eugène Ionesco, translated by Marie-France Ionesco (produced Baltimore, 1977). New York, Grove Press, 1977.

The Former One-on-One Basketball Champion (produced New York, 1977). With *The Great Labor Day Classic*, New York, Dramatists Play Service, 1982.

Cappella, with David Boorstin, adaptation of the novel by Horovitz (produced New York, 1978).

The Widow's Blind Date (produced New York, 1978). New York, Theatre Communications Group, 1981.

Mackerel (produced Hartford, Connecticut, 1978; revised version produced Washington, D.C., 1978). Vancouver, Talonbooks, 1979.

A Christmas Carol: Scrooge and Marley, adaptation of the story by Dickens (produced Baltimore, 1978). New York, Dramatists Play Service, 1979.

The Good Parts (produced New York, 1979). New York, Dramatists Play Service, 1983.

The Great Labor Day Classic (in *Holidays*, produced Louisville, 1979; produced separately New York, 1984). With *The Former One-on-One Basketball Champion*, New Dramatists Play Service, 1982.

The Wakefield Plays (collection; also includes *The Quanna-powitt Quartet* except for *The 75th*). New York, Avon, 1979.

Sunday Runners in the Rain (produced New York, 1980).

Park Your Car in Harvard Yard (produced New York, 1980).

Henry Lumper (produced Gloucester, Massachusetts, 1985; New York, 1989). New York, Dramatists Play Service, 1990.

Today, I Am a Fountain Pen, adaptation of stories by Morley Torgov (produced New York, 1986). New York, Dramatists Play Service, 1987.

A Rosen by Any Other Name, adaptation of a novel by Morley Torgov (produced New York, 1986). New York, Dramatists Play Service, 1987.

The Chopin Playoffs, adaptation of stories by Morley Torgov (produced New York, 1986). Included in *An Israel Horovitz Trilogy*, 1987.

North Shore Fish (produced Gloucester, Massachusetts, and New York, 1986). New York, Dramatists Play Service, 1989.

Year of the Duck (produced Portland, Maine, 1986; New York, 1987). New York, Dramatists Play Service, 1988.

An Israel Horovitz Trilogy (includes *Today, I Am a Fountain Pen*; *A Rosen by Any Other Name*; *The Chopin Playoffs*). New York, Nelson Doubleday, 1987.

Faith, Hope, and Charity (three one-acts) with Terrence McNally and Leonard Melfi (produced New York, 1988). New York, Dramatists Play Service, 1989.

Strong-Man's Weak Child (also director: produced Los Angeles, 1990).

Fighting over Beverly (produced Gloucester, Massachusetts, 1993).

Screenplays: *Machine Gun McCain* (English adaptation), 1970; *The Strawberry Statement*, 1970; *Believe in Me* (*Speed Is of the Essence*), 1970; *Alfredo*, 1970; *The Sad-Eyed Girls in the Park*, 1971; *Camerian Climbing*, 1971; *Acrobats*, 1972; *Fast Eddie*, 1980; *Fell*, 1982; *Berta*, 1982; *Author! Author!*,

1982–83; *Light Years*, 1985; *A Man in Love*, with Diane Kurys, 1988.

Television Plays: *Play for Trees*, 1969; *VD Blues*, with others, 1972; *Start to Finish*, 1975; *The Making and Breaking of Splinters Braun*, 1976; *Bartleby the Scrivener*, from the story by Melville, 1978; *A Day with Conrad Green*, from a story by Ring Lardner, 1978; *The Deer Park*, from the novel by Norman Mailer, 1979.

Novels

Cappella. New York, Harper, 1973.

Nobody Loves Me. Paris, Minuit, 1975; New York, Braziller, 1976.

*

Manuscript Collections: Lincoln Center Library of the Performing Arts, New York; Sawyer Free Library, Gloucester, Massachusetts.

Critical Studies: *Thirty Plays Hath November* by Walter Kerr, New York, Simon and Schuster, 1969; *Opening Nights* by Martin Gottfried, New York, Putnam, 1970; *The Playmakers* by Stuart W. Little and Arthur Cantor, New York, Dutton, 1970, London, Reinhardt, 1971; in *Études Anglaises* (Paris), Summer 1975.

Theatrical Activities:
Director: **Plays**—several of his own plays in English and French, and *Chiaroscuro: Morning, Noon and Night*, by Horovitz, Leonard Melfi, and Terrence McNally, Spoleto, Italy, 1968. **Film**—*Acrobats*, 1972. **Television**—*VD Blues*, 1972.
Actor: **Film**—*The Strawberry Statement*, 1970.

Israel Horovitz comments:
(1988) Much of life has changed for me.

I used to aspire to run 10 kilometers under 30 minutes. Breaking 40 minutes for the same distance is now quite satisfactory.

My family and my work remain as they were to me before: holy.

(1993) Not much has changed. Happy to break 45 minutes for 10 kilometers.

* * *

Israel Horovitz has produced a large volume of work since the 1970's, leaving audiences with the impression of a writer with broad concerns, varying aesthetic impulses, and an impish overview of the human condition. The Horovitz work wants to reach out to a community we call America; often it addresses that community in rudimentary terms, in buoyant cadences, in colloquial jargon (and the colloquialisms will change with the times) about the perverse innocence of the New World, and about the blatant, if also diluted, examples of good and evil within it. And all this is revealed in good-humoured fashion by an older brother who can speak to that afternoon headache known to us as the Land of the Free and the Home of the Brave. Morning in America is not to be recycled, but Afternoon in America is having its extended, slightly sickening nap. Israel is somewhat inducing it to sleep on and somewhat inducing it to get on its feet, and Horovitz is positioned as a kind of Puckish moralist-voyeur over an uneasy, fitfully napping, sometimes racist Gulliver.

First performed in 1968 at the Astor Place Theatre in New York City, *The Indian Wants the Bronx* presents a luminous title, suggesting what in fact it isn't. This Indian isn't a Native American demanding the return of ancestral lands which have been renamed the Grand Concourse and Tremont Avenue; instead he is a Hindu momentarily trapped in Manhattan by two juvenile hoods while waiting for a bus to take him to his English-speaking son somewhere in the bombed-out vista still known as the Bronx. The Indian, named Gupta, has just landed in the U.S., has neither a working knowledge of what passes for English nor of the habits of white slum kids idling between self-induced bouts of trouble. Gupta, unfortunately dependent on the kindness of strangers to help him relocate the son he is visiting and from whom he has momentarily been separated, is caught in a luckless encounter. We gather from the moment Horovitz's two louts, Joey and Murph, come careening into view, disturbing the silence of a September night on upper Fifth Avenue with their aggressive rendition of a rock-and-roll number (the import of which is that "Baby, you don't care"), that Gupta is in for an ugly encounter, at least a touch of misery before he is ever reunited with his son. The louts, before they turn their attention to Gupta, have been trying to make the September night unbearable for a lady they call Pussyface, a social worker whose caseload has included Joey and Murph. Pussyface's apartment apparently faces the aforementioned bus stop and the lady is being serenaded with snippets and variations from the "Baby, you don't care" cycle. We deduce that "baby" is either out of town, fast asleep, indifferent to, or highly annoyed at the public attention presently being showered on her. The impromptu concert goes on intermittently, the boys curse, sulk, and play ugly physical games, but in due time they begin to terrorize the Indian. Why do they terrorize him? He's an innocent, an alien, and the play needs tension.

The work's major problem is that it is essentially an anecdote which Horovitz has to loosen into movement. An anecdote is a self-enclosed organism which is perfectly satisfied with itself; it moves nowhere on its own, one has to "make something" of it. The anecdote may have threads but having been unravelled, even threads need to be transformed. In *Indian* there is no plausible reason for the bus never arriving except that it's necessary for Horovitz's story; also necessary is that Gupta speak not a word of English and that he be on his own in a strange city, unable to make contact with his son except through a phone number that he can't read. Horovitz sets up the conditions whereby Gupta has to be terrorized. But the terrorizing is an arbitrary development, and one has to ask, what do we learn from it other than that human actions are sometimes arbitrary?

Albee's *Zoo Story* can be viewed as a similarly arbitrary work. That is, the writing of the narrative takes on an arbitrariness, and it pushes the story into another arbitrariness. In the Horovitz play, there is even less necessity than in the Albee. People in the world do sometimes terrorize one another but not always. One would think that something in Joey and Murph, which might only be understood viscerally, has to give way and take over in order to manifest the terror. In André Gide's *Lafcadio's Adventures* there is an arbitrary murder, but it is a willed arbitrariness; Gide's hero wants not to resist the impulse to arbitrariness. Perhaps Horovitz needed to employ arbitrariness for the sake of theatricality.

Henry Lumper, some two decades later, begins with necessity. Horovitz creates, sets, and produces the play in Gloucester. It deals with serious concerns of the Gloucester townspeople that are familiar to many: drugs, mass unemployment, deception, alcoholism, violence, community dis-

location and, as in *Indian*, our relationship to those we see as aliens. In the 1970's, disciples of Reverend Moon, more popularly known as "Moonies," moved into the fishing village of Gloucester, creating much tension and bitterness among townspeople who envisioned the cult movement destabilizing the village. As Horovitz tells it, the area was also invaded by condo developers buying up precious waterfront property and drug runners moving in on the fishing industry. Overlaid on this contemporary drama is Shakespeare's *Henry IV*, with the Bolingbrokes and the Percys as principal players, and Prince Hal, or alcoholic loser Hal Boley, as the principal among principals. Hal Boley can't find himself, it's post-Vietnam, Hal can't commit, he's into drugs, booze, and erotic pleasures. He will eventually redeem himself, tackle the issues, become a responsible Boley, put the town back on its feet, and provide moral clarification for a community under siege.

Horovitz has given us a contemporary morality play, a work that has to do both with economics and with saving the soul of a people. In its best moments, and there are many of them, *Henry Lumper* is a moving, heartfelt work, with clarity and believable people. Horovitz uses an open stage and cinematic devices, quick dissolves between characters, so that a whole layer of subjectivity is beautifully present. One might argue that Shakespeare simply gets in the way of the story and one wastes time hunting for parallels. But the work has fine strengths and here Horovitz has moved far beyond the arbitrariness and unconvincing staginess of *Indian*. It's a play, perhaps too heavily coated with morality, that nevertheless moves as if under its own steam and that's a significant movement.

—Arthur Sainer

HORSFIELD, Debbie. British. Born in Manchester, 14 February 1955. Educated at Eccles Grammar School, Manchester, 1966–73; Newcastle University, B.A. (honours) in English literature 1977. Assistant administrator, Gulbenkian Studio Theatre, Newcastle-upon-Tyne, 1978–80; assistant to the artistic director, Royal Shakespeare Company, London, 1980–83; writer-in-residence, Liverpool Playhouse, Liverpool, 1983–84. Recipient: Thames Television award, 1983. Agent: Sheila Lemon, Lemon, Unna, and Durbridge, 24 Pottery Lane, Holland Park, London W11 4LZ, England.

PUBLICATIONS

Plays

Out on the Floor (produced London, 1981).
Away from It All (produced London, 1982).
The Next Four Years, Parts 1–2 (produced Liverpool, 1983).
All You Deserve (produced London, 1983).
Red Devils (produced Liverpool, 1983; London, 1984; New York, 1989). Included in *Red Devils Trilogy*, 1986.
True Dare Kiss (produced Liverpool, 1983; London, 1985). Included in *Red Devils Trilogy*, 1986.
Command or Promise (produced Liverpool, 1983; London, 1985). Included in *Red Devils Trilogy*, 1986.
Touch and Go (produced London, 1984).

Revelations (produced Chichester, Sussex, 1985).
Red Devils Trilogy.   London, Methuen, 1986.
Royal Borough (produced London, 1987).
In Touch (produced Coventry, 1988).
Making Out (televised 1989).   London, Transworld, 1989.

Radio Play: *Arrangements*, 1981.

Television Plays: *Face Value*, in *Crown Court* series, 1982;
Out on the Floor, 1983; *Making Out* series, 1989–91.

* * *

Debbie Horsfield is among the most successful of Britain's young women playwrights, primarily due to the popularity of her television drama writing. Her original idea for *Making Out* was to focus on working-class women's issues. Horsfield sets the series in a factory; thus, rather than putting one woman at the centre of a largely male world, she has created a community of women who live and work with men, yet who are not primarily identified through their relationships (social or sexual) with those men. *Making Out* reached a wide audience eager to see reflections of real women on the screen. Significantly, the series is not only written by a woman (Horsfield) but has tended to be directed and produced by women as well.

The same focus on strong, realistic women is what fuels Horsfield's writing for the theatre. Her best-known theatre work is the *Red Devils Trilogy*. All three plays in the trilogy focus on the same four characters: Alice, Nita, Phil, and Beth. These four young women grow up together and their relationships, careers, hopes, and fears develop as they share their experiences and their love of football (Manchester United, to be precise). Of course, Manchester United is not only the name of a football team, but is also an accurate phrase to describe the relationship between the four central female characters, all from Manchester, all united as friends whose lives develop in different ways but stem from common roots and shared experiences.

In this trilogy of comic plays, the same idea which gives energy to *Making Out* likewise fuels the power of the theatre performance: women working and playing together, women who share interests (non-stereotypically "feminine" interests at that), women who like each other and enjoy each other's company, women who know how to make each other laugh, just as Horsfield clearly knows how to make her audiences laugh. The power of Horsfield's writing is her combination of unusual scenarios and settings for women with a frank, unsentimental, yet playful style. The working-class settings invite men as well as women into the worlds of the plays. Working-class situations are rarely portrayed as well in the theatre. Thus, the *Red Devils Trilogy* has a certain interest, even for those with no interest in football.

In the first play, *Red Devils*, the four central characters are Manchester schoolgirls on their way to the 1979 Cup Final at Wembley Stadium. The action takes place in Manchester before the game, in London during the game, and at a motorway service station between the two cities after the game. The cast of characters is laid out on the page of the published version in the shape of a football formation, with Horsfield's name (as author) in the goal box. This playful presentation of the "facts" of the performance is in keeping with the mood of the play: like much of Horsfield's work (including several of her earlier plays), it emphasizes female friendship and the enjoyment which women, like men, find in each other's company. Petty differences are presented in a humorous rather than a "catty" way.

The same positive spirit enlivens the remaining two plays in the trilogy: *True Dare Kiss* and *Command or Promise*, both staged in London's Cottesloe Theatre (The Royal National Theatre) in 1985. In both of these plays, the same four characters have grown up and remain friends, sharing different aspects of their adult lives, as well as their continued love of football. The plays have been criticized for being "too much like soap opera," a criticism which says as much about our cultural expectations as it does about the plays. It is true that the depiction of the young women's lives in these later plays is channeled through multiple storylines, familiar from televised soap operas and serials (and very effectively utilized in Horsfield's own television success, *Making Out*). But to identify the form of the plays as a fault is misleading: they are episodic and weighted with the conflicting and overlapping stories of four different women's lives. Relationships are represented between women and men, women and work, women and higher education, women and cultural trends (punk culture and football). Yet the uniting thread of the four stories, as they develop and grow in the three plays of the *Red Devil's Trilogy*, is the relationship between the four women. That focus on women's friendship is still uncommon on the stage. Debbie Horsfield has begun to make it more acceptable, and has thereby opened the way for other playwrights to experiment with a wide range of common but little-represented experiences in contemporary theatre.

—Lizbeth Goodman

————

HOWARD, Roger. British. Born in Warwickshire, 19 June 1938. Educated at Dulwich College, London; Royal Academy of Dramatic Art, London, 1956–57; Bristol University, 1958; University of Essex, Colchester, M.A. 1976. National Service in Royal Armoured Service Corps, 1958: sentenced to imprisonment for refusal to wear uniform: dishonourable discharge. Married Anne Mary Zemaitis in 1960; one son. Teacher, Nankai University, Tientsin, China, 1965–67; manager, Collets Bookshop, Peterborough, 1967–68, and Bookshop 85, London, 1968–72; teacher, Peking University, 1972–74; playwright-in-residence, Mercury Theatre, Colchester, 1976; Arts Council fellow in creative writing, University of York, 1976–78; Henfield writing fellow, University of East Anglia, Norwich, 1979. Since 1979 lecturer, and founding director, Theatre Underground, and since 1980 editor, New Plays series, University of Essex. Member, Council of Management, Society for Anglo-Chinese Understanding, and editorial committee, *China Now* magazine, London, 1970–72; member of the editorial committee, *Platform* magazine, London, 1978–82; since 1980 founder, Theatre Action Press, Colchester; guest professor, Janus Pannonius University, and visiting director, Pécs Little Theatre, Pécs, Hungary, 1991. Recipient: Arts Council bursary, 1975. Address: Department of Literature, University of Essex, Wivenhoe Park, Colchester, Essex CO4 3SQ, England.

PUBLICATIONS

Plays

Bewitched Foxes Rehearsing Their Roles (produced London, 1968).

New Short Plays 1, with Leonard Melfi and Carey Harrison (includes *The Carrying of X from A to Z, Dis, The Love Suicides at Havering, Seven Stages on the Road to Exile*). London, Methuen, 1968.

Fin's Doubts (produced London, 1969). Privately printed, 1968.

The Love Suicides at Havering (produced London, 1969). Included in *New Short Plays 1*, 1968.

The Carrying of X from A to Z (produced Papua New Guinea, 1971). Included in *New Short Plays 1*, 1968.

Dis (produced York, 1971). Included in *New Short Plays 1*, 1968.

Seven Stages on the Road to Exile (produced Carlisle, 1970). Included in *New Short Plays 1*, 1968.

Season (produced London, 1969).

Simon Murdering His Deformed Wife with a Hammer (produced London, 1969).

The Meaning of the Statue (produced London, 1971). Included in *Slaughter Night and Other Plays*, 1971.

Writing on Stone (produced London, 1971). Included in *Slaughter Night and Other Plays*, 1971.

Slaughter Night and Other Plays: The Meaning of the Statue, The Travels of Yi Yuk-sa to the Caves at Yenan, Returning to the Capital, Writing on Stone, Korotov's Ego-Theatre, Report from the City of Reds in the Year 1970, The Drum of the Strict Master, The Play of Iron, Episodes from the Fighting in the East, A New Bestiary. London, Calder and Boyars, 1971.

The Travels of Yi Yuk-sa to the Caves at Yenan (produced Colchester, 1976). Included in *Slaughter Night and Other Plays*, 1971; in *Scripts 4* (New York), February 1972.

The Drum of the Strict Master (produced Colchester, 1976). Included in *Slaughter Night and Other Plays*, 1971.

Korotov's Ego-Theatre (produced Edinburgh, 1978). Included in *Slaughter Night and Other Plays*, 1971.

Episodes from the Fighting in the East (produced Edinburgh, 1978). Included in *Slaughter Night and Other Plays*, 1971; in *Scripts 4* (New York), February 1972.

Report from the City of Reds in the Year 1970 (produced Cambridge, 1978). Included in *Slaughter Night and Other Plays*, 1971.

The Auction of Virtues, in *Point 101* (produced London, 1972). Published in *Y* (York), 1977.

Sunrise. Peking, Peking University, 1973.

Klöng 1, Klöng 2, and the Partisan (produced Colchester, 1976).

Notes for a New History (produced Colchester, 1976).

The Tragedy of Mao in the Lin Piao Period (produced London, 1976). Included in *The Tragedy of Mao in the Lin Piao Period and Other Plays*, 1989.

The Great Tide (produced Colchester, 1976).

A Feast During Famine (produced London, 1977).

Travelling Players of the Dawn (produced York, 1977).

The Play of Margery Kempe (produced York and London, 1978). Included in *The Tragedy of Mao in the Lin Piao Period and Other Plays*, 1989.

Women's Army (produced Nottingham and London, 1978).

Joseph Arch (produced London, 1978).

Queen (produced Alsager, Cheshire, 1979). Included in *The Tragedy of Mao in the Lin Piao Period and Other Plays*, 1989.

Memorial of the Future: A Rag (produced Norwich, 1979). With *The Society of Poets*, Colchester, Theatre Action Press, 1979.

The Society of Poets: A Grotesquery (produced Norwich, 1979). With *Memorial of the Future*, Colchester, Theatre Action Press, 1979.

A Break in Berlin (produced Colchester, 1979). Colchester, Theatre Action Press, 1981.

The Siege (produced Colchester, 1981). Published as *The Violent Irruption and Terrible Convulsions of the Siege During the Late Lamentable Civil War at Colchester in the Year 1648*, Colchester, Theatre Action Press, 1981.

White Sea (produced Colchester, 1982). Included in *The Tragedy of Mao in the Lin Piao Period and Other Plays*, 1989.

Partisans (produced Colchester, 1983). London, Actual Size, 1983.

The Speechifier, published in *Double Space*, no. 2, 1984–85.

Contact (produced Nottingham, 1985). Included in *Britannia and Other Plays*, 1990.

The Tragedy of Mao in the Lin Piao Period and Other Plays (includes *The Play of Margery Kempe, White Sea, Queen*). Colchester, Theatre Action Press, 1989.

Britannia and Other Plays (includes *A Break in Berlin, The Siege, Partisans, The Speechifier, Contact*). Colchester, Theatre Action Press, 1990.

The Christ-Bringer's Comedy (produced Colchester, 1992).

Novels

A Phantastic Satire. Bala, Merioneth, Chapple, 1960.
From the Life of a Patient. Bala, Merioneth, Chapple, 1961.

Short Stories

Four Stories, with *Twelve Sketches*, by Tony Astbury. London, Mouthpiece, 1964.
Ancient Rivers. Warwick, Greville Press, 1984.

Verse

To the People. . . . London, Mouthpiece, 1966.
Praise Songs. Tientsin, Tianjin Ribao, and London, Mouthpiece, 1966.
Senile Poems. London, Actual Size, 1988.

Other

The Technique of the Struggle Meeting. London, Clandestine, 1968.
The Use of Wall Newspapers. London, Clandestine, 1968.
The Hooligan's Handbook: Methods of Thinking and Action. London, Action, 1971.
Method for Revolutionary Writing. London, Action, 1972.
Mao Tse-tung and the Chinese People. London, Allen and Unwin, and New York, Monthly Review Press, 1977.
Le théâtre chinois contemporain. Brussels, La Renaissance du Livre, 1978; as *Contemporary Chinese Theatre*, London, Heinemann, 1978.

Editor, *Culture and Agitation: Theatre Documents.* London, Action, 1972.

*

Critical Studies: "*The Drum of the Strict Master* at the Essex University Theatre" by Howard, in *Theatre Quarterly* (Cambridge), no. 24, 1976; *Contradictory Theatres* edited by Leslie Bell, Colchester, Theatre Action Press, 1985; "The Dramatic Sense of Life: Theatre and Historical Simulation" by Howard, in *New Theatre Quarterly* (Cambridge), no. 3, 1985.

Roger Howard comments:

(1973) In revolutionary war, plays are performed to show scenes of the struggle in which fighters who actually took part replay their "parts" as examples to other fighters. Their short, instructional plays go back over the battle just ended in order to point out the lesson to be learnt for the next round. They educate by showing the audience—other fighters—the significance of their actions.

Such drama is deeply rooted in the day-to-day work experience of the people. It captures their imagination because it closely expresses themselves. At the same time it is a higher form of artistic expression than mere realism, because it shows the people's actions in their relationship to the new, evolving, and advancing socialist morality. Their plays are agitation in the service of the people's advance and an aid in the overthrow of the old society.

My short plays are part of the same process. Preparing for the situation where there will be open military warfare, they are agitational plays in the wider war which engulfs us all, the war between classes which takes many forms and which will not cease until classes cease. Each play is located at a point where a certain stage of development in struggle has been reached, and where the choices are open as to what the following stage should be.

The point reached at the opening of each play may be either a victory or a defeat for revolutionary advance. The body of the play then develops the initial point by showing the contending sides and conflicting interests, giving visual and verbal guidelines from the particular instance to the wider significance in the form of interpolated screen captions, extended sound words, lyrical or didactic verses, or actual physical combat.

The characters are shown in their class as well as in their individual roles; they are individuals who express class positions in the way they think, speak, act, and interact. Their conflicts therefore elicit humour, grotesquery, poetry, reason, tragedy, and decision.

The resolution of the conflicts between the characters, as of those within one character, is resolution not of a "personality" to his "destiny" or of the "mind" to the "universe," still less of the "underdog" to his "station in life." It is a resolution that will give the revolutionary protagonist, the positive character, his due as the man who has history on his side in an era when capitalism is in decline and the many forces of socialism are in the ascendant. It is therefore a resolution of *ideas*, by which the conscious, active man triumphs over the slave in man, whether it be in himself or in others. For some, the resolution comes as a condemnation: they are the negative characters, the reactionaries, backward rejects of history. For others, the resolution comes too late; for them they have their message to pass on to a new generation. For all our mistakes, man is learning to advance. The point of resolution in each play is therefore an ideological point, to be perceived as such by the audience.

So the characters of the plays are representations of contradictory class position as they appear in individual human beings. This gives the positive characters greater dimensions than those of mere self-contained, alienated individuals at odds with society for their own sake, just as in life itself the activists of revolution are so much greater figures than those who merely talk about it or those who use socialism for their personal advantage.

Our oppression will last for as long as we remain afraid; if only we act, we lose our fear. Oppressors tremble when they lose their grip on our terror. The revolutionary characters in my plays are heroic because they are no longer afraid. And they are no longer afraid because they have become con-

scious. They know that as active workers, conscious of class, they hold the future in their hands. I warm to those men and women in our century who, raising the people to raise themselves, and growing thus in stature, have reminded mankind of its dignity. My heart is stung when I hear of their deeds; they are few of them famous and most suffered great privation and even death. My plays can hardly emulate their lives but they are some sort of small monuments, not for us to gaze at and pity, but to stir us to action. They rescue from the great killings some memorials of actions that teach us to kill more precisely in future: our killers.

(1977) The idea of people as doers, as much as sufferers, has been pushed into the background in much of recent drama that has become academically respectable, from Ibsen to Beckett. The idea that people are capable of directing their future more completely has been neglected.

In my short plays I have introduced prototypes of such representative men and women. The transition I am now making from short to full-length plays will give the idea of renewal more scope. The first long play, *The Tragedy of Mao in the Lin Piao Period*, is a 19-scene construction of the shifts in the relationship between two men striving to remake men and themselves. Then follows a trilogy on turning points in English history, from tribalism to feudalism, to capitalism, and to socialism.

(1982) The trilogy—*The Earth-Founding*, *The Force in the Land* and *The Great Tide*—has expanded into a series of full-length historical plays which now includes *Bread, Meat and Higher Learning* about the Marian suppression of the protestants, *The Siege* about clashes of inner self and outer self-interest in the radical debates of the English Civil War at the time of the Siege of Colchester (a play commissioned by the Mercury Theatre), and *Joseph Arch* about the founding of the agricultural workers' union. In these plays and in *A Break in Berlin* I have attempted to develop a method of characterisation that dialectically relates the inner person to his or her outer status in historical change, relying increasingly heavily on a dynamic use of dialogue as "spoken action" to present multi-dimensional and many-layered representations of characters caught in their personal "moments" inside the "movement" of changing societies. I still use a variety of dramatic forms—comic extravaganza in *Queen*, a study of the psychological effects of rule on the personality of Elizabeth II; epic in *Joseph Arch*, now expanded into a 37-scene play retitled *The Weight of Many Masters*; comic grotesquery in *The Society of Poets*; naturalism in *A Break in Berlin*; dynamic verbal-action theatre in *The Siege*. I have developed a notion of socialist tragedy which attempts to use a method of writing plays to show the processes of a person's life in terms of the extent to which he or she must submit to necessity and the extent to which he or she remains free (and willing) to act. *The Force in the Land*, *The Tragedy of Mao*, *A Break in Berlin* and *The Siege* are examples of such attempts. Increasingly I have felt the need to bring my critical, scholarly, and theoretical work on theatre, which has appeared largely in journals, together with the practice of production and the teaching of ideas of theatre. My work at Essex University is to do with the idea content of new English theatre writing and I have initiated a New Plays Scheme whereby each year M.A. drama students are given the opportunity of working on the production of a play with a specially commissioned theatre writer. I have founded the Theatre Underground in this connection in order to explore the possibility of a materialist and dialectical method of theatre writing and production practice. Theatre Underground's productions are of new English and overseas plays which have to do with representing, in a variety of theatre forms and by dialectical characterisation, a dramatic appraisal of men and women in their personal and their social lives in the connections of their personae to the wider forces of their time. The Theatre Underground scripts published in Essex University New Plays series—*A Break in Berlin* was the first—are accompanied by production notes and introductory material which provide a discourse about the play both as a piece of dramatic literature and as a theatre piece for performance. In Theatre Underground work my own ideas develop alongside the work of others whose research and practice is in overlapping areas and who have become involved in the concepts embodied by Theatre Underground. My plans for the future include plays about George Stephenson, Hitler, Ernst Toller and early English socialists; and a play about the rise and tribulations of the "alternative" theatre of the 1970's.

(1988) My exploration of socialist tragedy has extended to five new plays. *White Sea*, an ironic drama with music, traces the effects of their labour on the consciousness of a group of theatre workers helping to dig the White Sea Canal in the Soviet Union in the early 1930's. The "tragedy of expediency" occurs where Stalinist social and political euphoria, associated with the Five-Year Plan, meets the necessities of material reality—and plain human inadequacies. *Partisans* is a series of grotesque and savage scenes in the comic and disturbing life of a freedom-seeking actress in the English "alternative" theatre of the 1960's and 1970's. She turns from drugs to terrorism and goes from prison to a peace camp before gaining a sense of her own identity as that of a victim's mental and emotional dissolution in a surrounding pre-nuclear chaos. The published edition contains a short essay by Charles Lamb on aspects of the play's dramaturgy. This "tragedy of liberation," whose main character, Cindy, bears some resemblance to Gerda in *A Break in Berlin* and Margery in *The Play of Margery Kempe* in her tortured questing, was followed by a tragedy of confinement, *The Speechifier*. Based on *The Orator*, a play by the Lithuanian writer Kazys Saja, the play is set in the family apartment of the ghost-writer of a Leader of a tyrannical state. The writer loses himself in obedience to his master, achieving a most perfect acquiescence rewarded when his family is gassed, trapped in their flat. *Britannia* (unproduced) is a dream play about the state of England. Christian Wager embarks on a journey of self-exposure from early-mediaeval hermetic spirituality, through Tudor state-forming and Victorian empire-building to Thatcherite monetarist opportunism, before learning how an intellectual has to conform to the powers-that-be. This latter-day Faust is chided by his female double, Wager 2, for not learning from a regicide who at least had the nobleness to crown with his own suicide his repeated failure through the ages to remove the monarch, while Wager signs a deal with the King ensuring merely his own degenerate survival. *Contact* is a four-hander in 17 scenes, a contemporary tragedy of romantic love in a Europe divided by ideologies and united in opportunism. A young Polish woman and an English poet have a brief affair across the borders, an idealistic contact which collapses in a bitter war of self-interest.

All these plays reflect a new idea of tragedy in which human drives reach the limits imposed on them by necessity in one form or another. They reflect a notion of a tragic moment as resulting from a collision that is socially produced as well as personally motivated. Much of the theory attached to these ideas is published in *Contradictory Theatres*, a collection of essays and documentation about the work of the Theatre Underground at Essex University, which also contains essays by other hands on *A Break in Berlin* and *White Sea*.

(1993) After directing *The Play of Margery Kempe* at Pécs

Little Theatre in Hungary, I was commissioned to write *The Christ-Bringer's Comedy*, produced by Theatre Underground at Essex University for the centenary conference on 1492 and for the Essex Festival. The central figure of Columbus commits the *hubris* of taking the name of God in vain in his pursuit of possessions, a lonely questing figure who has features of both Don Juan and Faust. The central act is concerned with Columbus's discoveries, but the first and third acts find him, Faust-like, travelling through time before and after the life-span of the historical figure, when he meets not only Venus but the Spanish Arabian mystic poet Ibn Al-'Arabi, Saint Catherine of Genoa, the poet Lesya Ukrainka, a rabbi of Chernobyl called Menahem Nahum, and the neo-Confucian philosopher Wang Yang-ming. Despite his consultations with such figures, from whom he asks guidance in his longings, he never really understands the nature of either the new world he discovered or of the Europeans and Indians he affected to offer to save. Living by fire, he dies by fire, as Venus prophesises, when he is sucked into the flames of a nuclear power plant at melt-down.

* * *

Roger Howard is a genuine original, whose plays combine an essentially Maoist political stance with a range of diverse and eclectic styles, including Brechtian epic theatre, slapstick, music hall, and cartoon theatre. In his introductory essay to his collection *Slaughter Night* he makes the point that, in the present political situation, it is the playwright's task to divide and agitate, not to help in the creation of culture, which is part of the "deep sleep" our rulers want to impose on us. His plays are sharp, clear, and carry out this task of division with an admirable precision, though their form is very far from being conventional agitational socialist realism. This essay, which of necessity considers the plays more as cultural objects than as means of heightening political consciousness, is an exercise in contradictions, an example of the dialectical relationship between politics and art; but it is true to say that the best of the plays do work on an artistic and aesthetic level over and above their directly political one.

Howard's plays fall into three distinct phases. First, there are the lyrical pre-China pieces, like *Season* and *Simon Murdering His Deformed Wife with a Hammer*, which propagate a William Morris-type socialism through semi-abstract poetic characters and language. *Season* shows the struggle between urban and rural values; while *Simon* shows a young man trying to educate his wife to his own level of political consciousness, failing and murdering her as a result. Then come more complex plays, like *The Love Suicides at Havering*, which shows a group of people attempting to overcome their psychological inhibitions as a necessary precondition to achieving a revolutionary situation, and *Fin's Doubts*, which shows in symbolist form the full cycle of a revolution. A group of revolutionaries overthrow an era of reactionary repression, achieve the first stages of a revolution, and impose temporary authoritarian measures to consolidate its achievements; by a process of bureaucratic ossification this authoritarianism becomes permanent, and the whole cycle starts off again.

Howard went to China as a teacher for two years and the result can be seen in the artistically and politically more mature plays in *Slaughter Night*. The title play juxtaposes Sauer, the Dog King, and the Writer, a nice, cosy arrangement with the Writer reflecting Sauer's interests through his works until two Wolves and an Outlaw show him the error of his ways. *The Meaning of the Statue* shows a young man in conversation with the statue of a general. Essentially, it is about the loss of spontaneity and fluidity in a revolutionary situation occasioned by its bureaucratic organisation, symbolised by the youth being shot by the statue and being put, in the same fixed position, in the statue's place. *Returning to the Capital* uses the characters of Seami Motokiyo and his son, the fashioners of the first Noh plays, to point the differences between and consequences of being a reformist, like Seami, and a revolutionary. *Writing on Stone* is about a couple romanticising the past in lyrical images and being afraid to face up to the implications of the present. *Korotov's Ego-Theatre* shows the irrelevance and sterility of individualist concepts of art in a revolutionary situation; *Episodes from the Fighting in the East*, the erratic progress of a revolution and the shifts of power that take place within it; while *A New Bestiary* hilariously satirises, through animal imagery, types of people pretending to be revolutionaries who are in fact, without realizing it, on the revolutionaries' side. They all use language and sound in a most original way.

The *Tragedy of Mao in the Lin Piao Period* examines the ideological differences between Mao and the PLA commander-in-chief Lin (who was killed in an air crash in 1971 while fleeing to Moscow) and their origins in the civil war struggles of the 1930's. It is a subtle stylistic mixture of realism and a kind of heightened poetry, which in its totality gives some idea of how China's peasant-based socialism has evolved.

Howard has been little performed as yet; his plays are, however, eminently actable and stageable. They condense more into their brief spans, both in thought and style, than most full-length plays.

—Jonathan Hammond

———————

HOWARTH, Donald. British. Born in London, 5 November 1931. Educated at the Grange High School for Boys, Bradford; Esme Church Northern Children's Theatre School, 1948–51. Stage manager and actor in various repertory companies, 1951–56. Literary manager, Royal Court Theatre, London, 1975–76. Recipient: Encyclopaedia Britannica award, 1961; George Devine award, 1971. Agent: Casarotto Ramsay Ltd., National House, 60–66 Wardour Street, London W1V 3HP, England.

PUBLICATIONS

Plays

Lady on the Barometer (also co-director: produced London, 1958; as *Sugar in the Morning*, produced London, 1959).
All Good Children (produced Bromley, Kent, 1960; also director: produced London, 1964). London, French, 1965.
Secret of Skiz, adaptation of a play by Zapolska (produced Bromley, Kent, 1962).
A Lily in Little India (televised 1962; also director: produced London, 1965). London, French, 1966.
Ogodiveleftthegason (also director: produced London, 1967).
School Play, in *Playbill One*, edited by Alan Durband. London, Hutchinson, 1969.
Three Months Gone (produced London, 1970). London, French, 1970.

Othello Sleges Blankes, adaptation of the play by Shakespeare (also director: produced Cape Town, 1972).
Scarborough (also director: produced Cape Town, 1972).
The Greatest Fairy Story Ever Told, adaptation of a play by Kathleen Housell-Roberts (also director: produced New York, 1973).
Meanwhile, Backstage in the Old Front Room (produced Leeds, 1975).
Ibchek (also director: produced Grahamstown, South Africa, 1979).
Adventures of a Black Girl, adaptation of the novel *Adventures of a Black Girl in Her Search for God* by Shaw (also director: produced Cape Town, 1980).

Screenplay: *Gates to Paradise*, 1968.

Radio Play: *Reece*, 1989.

Television Plays: *A Lily in Little India*, 1962; *Stanley*, 1972.

*

Critical Study: introduction by Michael Billington to *New English Dramatists 9*, London, Penguin, 1966.

Theatrical Activities:
Director: **Plays**—several of his own plays, and *This Property Is Condemned* by Tennessee Williams, London, 1960; *Miniatures* by David Cregan, London, 1965; *Play Mas* by Mustapha Matura, London, 1974; *Mama, Is Terry Home for Good?* by James Edward Shannon, Johannesburg, 1974; *Parcel Post* by Yemi Ajibade, London, 1976; *Rum an' Coca Cola* by Mustapha Matura, London, 1976, New York, 1977; *Waiting for Godot* by Beckett, London, Cape Town, and New York, 1981.
Actor: **Plays**—roles in repertory, 1951–56; Salvation Army Captain in *Progress to the Park* by Alun Owen, London, 1959.

Donald Howarth comments:
Art is what you don't do. Less is more.

* * *

One of the pleasures of reading through Donald Howarth's earlier plays in sequence—*Sugar in the Morning, All Good Children, A Lily in Little India, Ogodiveleftthegason*, and *Three Months Gone*—is the pleasure of seeing a playwright finding his way to an individual and successful compromise between naturalism and freewheeling expressionism by dint of returning again and again to the same themes and the same characters but never to the same style. He has worked hard, and at its worst his writing is laborious, but he has been capable from the beginning of sustaining passages of comedy which deftly combine truthfulness with elegant and compelling theatrical rhetoric. Finally, in *Three Months Gone*, he achieved a sureness of touch that enables him to tie fantasy material down to solid surfaces and to draw dividends from all his earlier stylistic experiments. *Ogodiveleftthegason* is the play in which he takes the most expressionistic short cuts and spans over the greatest amount of human experience. It is his least successful play, though, not because it is the least comic or the least realistic, but because it is the most shapeless and the least able to gain an audience's sympathy for the characters or sustain its interest in them—partly because their identity keeps changing. *Three Months Gone*, while no less remote from the slow development of the conventional naturalistic three-act play, has a storyline strong enough to keep the colourful balloons of fantasy that both main characters fly tethered securely to a solid matter-of-factness.

Mrs. Broadbent, the sexually frustrated landlady in *Sugar in the Morning*, and Grannie Silk, her obstinately vulgar, cheerful, warm-hearted, interfering mother, are both rough prototypes of Mrs. Hanker in *A Lily in Little India* and *Three Months Gone*, who combines the main characteristics of both of them without having Mrs. Broadbent's pretensions to gentility or her ineptness at finding food for her sexual appetites. A clear picture of suburban life emerges in *Sugar in the Morning* but much of the basic energy is spent on drawing it. Decisions about which lodgers to take, clipping the privet hedge, arguments about noisy radios and washing hung up outside windows, rent collecting, drinking cups of tea in the landlady's room, hurrying for the twenty-to-eight bus, finding a shilling for the gas meter, discussing whether to have a baby—in using episodes like these as its currency, the play makes them all seem equally important. None of the characters in *Sugar in the Morning* reappears in *All Good Children* but Rev. Jacob Bowers and his daughter and son, Anna and Maurice, are in both *All Good Children* and *A Lily in Little India*, which introduces Mrs. Hanker and her son Alvin, who are to reappear in *Three Months Gone*, together with Anna and Maurice. The whole of the action of *All Good Children* is set in a converted farmhouse in South Yorkshire, but the 60-year-old minister is about to retire and to move his family to the suburb where we find them in the two subsequent plays. The new theme introduced in *All Good Children*, which will recur persistently in the later work, is the relationship between Protestant morality and sexual deprivation. Jacob Bowers, now a devout anti-sensualist, has been very different when younger, and became a minister only because of guilt feelings after his affair with a minister's daughter had caused the old man's death. Unlike his younger brother, Clifford, who has been more of a conformist, Maurice has reacted violently against his Puritanic upbringing and becomes a sailor. His letters, with their juicy descriptions of local brothels, have been Anna's main life-line, and the love she feels for Maurice verges on the incestuous, but after her mother's death, caused by an on-stage fall down a staircase, she rejects her chance of breaking out of the family cage and condemns herself, after 20 years of imprisonment, to staying with her father.

The plot of *All Good Children* is developed mostly through speeches that rake over the past. *A Lily in Little India* is a less Ibsenite play, and physical action bulks larger in it. The action, like the stage, is divided between the Bowers' house and the Hankers'. We see Anna waiting on the old father who has spoiled her life by his narrowness, and writing letters to the brother through whom she is still vicariously living; in the other house a selfishly sensual landlady is trapping a reluctant postman into an affair regardless of the harm done to her sensitive son, who finds happiness only in growing a lily and in his encounters with Anna. When the mother, poised on a ladder outside his bedroom window, threatens to destroy his beloved lily, he throws water in her face causing her to fall backwards, and moves into Anna's house when his mother goes to hospital. The characters win considerable sympathy and interest, and there are some very funny and some very touching moments, but the comedy and the seriousness do not quite balance or reinforce each other as one comes to feel they should and, though the dialogue has been praised by Michael Billington (in his Introduction to the Penguin *New English Dramatists 9*) as "a just sufficiently heightened version of ordinary speech," it sinks sometimes into self-consciousness and just occasionally into sentimentality.

But the dialogue of *Three Months Gone* is virtually unflawed. The rapid shifts in and out of Anna's fantasies, and later Alvin's, give Howarth the opportunity to penetrate funnily but compassionately their private views of themselves, each other, and the two other main characters, Maurice and Mrs. Hanker, who are sexually so much more robust. There is a hilarious scene in which Mrs. Hanker, bullying Alvin to find the pluck to make Anna marry him, makes him propose to her while she pretends to be Anna, and this is followed by a sequence in which Maurice makes a pass at him under guise of teaching him how to make a woman submit. The audience's uncertainty about which sequence represents fantasy, which reality, is often an advantage.

The later plays are different and less successful. *The Greatest Fairy Story Ever Told* is a skittish pantomime full of arch chinoiserie. There are characters called Much Too Yin and Too Much Yang and jokes about Pon-Ting's fabric hall and the Royal Courtyard. *Meanwhile, Backstage in the Old Front Room* is highly serious, ambitiously moving further away from naturalism than any of Howarth's earlier works. It leans on both Beckett and Genet: *Endgame* is feminised in the relationship between the dominating old woman who never leaves her wheelchair and the blind younger women, possibly her daughter, who lives with her. The power games and the extremism in making the characters speak out their thoughts are reminiscent of Genet's *The Maids*. The influence is domesticated into a family setting, but not altogether digested.

—Ronald Hayman

———

HOWE, Tina. American. Born in New York City, 21 November 1937. Educated at Sarah Lawrence College, Bronxville, New York, B.A. 1959; Chicago Teachers College, 1963–64. Married Norman Levy in 1961; one son and one daughter. Since 1983 adjunct professor, New York University; since 1990 visiting professor, Hunter College, City University of New York. Recipient: Rosamond Gilder award, 1983; Rockefeller grant, 1983; Obie award, 1983; Outer Critics Circle award, 1983, 1984; John Gassner award, 1984; National Endowment for the Arts grant, 1984; Guggenheim fellowship, 1990. Honorary degree: Bowdoin College, Brunswick, Maine, 1988. Agent: Flora Roberts Inc., 157 West 57th Street, New York, New York 10019, U.S.A.

PUBLICATIONS

Plays

Closing Time (produced Bronxville, New York, 1959).
The Nest (produced Provincetown, Massachusetts, 1969; New York, 1970).
Museum (produced Los Angeles, 1976; New York, 1977). New York, French, 1979.
Birth and After Birth, in *The New Women's Theatre*, edited by Honor Moore. New York, Random House, 1977.
The Art of Dining (produced Washington, D.C., and New York, 1979). New York, French, 1980.
Appearances (produced New York, 1982).
Painting Churches (produced New York, 1983; Southampton, 1991; London, 1992). New York, French, 1984.

Three Plays (includes *Museum, The Art of Dining, Painting Churches*). New York, Avon, 1984.
Coastal Disturbances (produced New York, 1986). New York, French, 1987.
Approaching Zanzibar (produced New York, 1989). New York, Theatre Communications Group, and London, French, 1989.
Coastal Disturbances: Four Plays (includes *Painting Churches, The Art of Dining, Museum*). New York, Theatre Communications Group, 1989.
Teeth. Published in *Antaeus* (New York), no.66, Spring 1991.
Swimming (produced New York, 1991).

*

Critical Studies: *Creating Theater: The Professionals' Approach to New Plays* by Lee Alan Morrow and Frank Pike, New York, Vintage, 1986; *Interviews with Contemporary Women Playwrights* edited by Kathleen Betsko and Rachel Koenig, New York, Beech Tree Books, 1987; *A Search for Postmodern Theater: Interviews with Contemporary Playwrights* by John L. DiGaetani, New York, Greenwood Press, 1991.

* * *

Tina Howe is a marvelously perceptive observer of contemporary mores, and much of the pleasure one receives from her plays comes from her comic skewering of pretentious amateur art critics, couples moaning orgasmically over the yuppie menu of their dreams, and thoroughly enlightened parents thoroughly unable to cope with their monstrous four-year-old. At their best, however, her comedies probe beneath the surface to reveal the inextricable mixture of the humorous and horrific to which modern culture—including art, ritual, and table manners—is a barely adequate response.

Although it already hints of better things to come, *The Nest* is the least satisfying of Howe's full-length plays. The influence of Ionesco and Beckett, whose work Howe admires, is evident here in the use of repeated scenes as well as in the heavy reliance on verbal and physical farce. Still, this play about a trio of female roommates lacks the satirical and emotional bite of her subsequent creations even as it offers glimpses of her prodigious imagination.

"Family life has been over-romanticized; the savagery has not been seen enough in the theatre and in movies," Howe once complained. She attempts to fill this gap with *Birth and After Birth*, a sometimes hilarious, often frightening portrait of the Apples. As their name implies, the Apples (including a four-year-old son played by an adult actor) are a parody of the TV-fare all-American family, continually declaring how happy they are and continually belying this claim. What keeps *Birth and After Birth* from being simply another satire on Ozzie and Harriet is not only Howe's accurate portrait of the physical and emotional brutality inherent in family life but her disturbingly negative exploration of why women choose to have—or not to have—children. Despite the often broad slapstick, *Birth and After Birth* is one of Howe's darkest comedies.

Museum is less a plotted play than a wonderful series of comic turns as visitors—singly and in groups—wander through an exhibit entitled "The Broken Silence." As Howe has acknowledged in interviews, all of her plays are about art, and *Museum* examines the complex interrelationships among creator, creation, and viewers. On one level, *Museum* reveals what fools art makes of us (witness the young woman pain-

stakingly copying an all-white canvas); on another level, however, it shows that artworks cannot fully exist except in the presence of an audience, foolish or not. Finally, in one of the comically horrific monologues that seem an essential part of the Howe landscape, a museum-goer recounts a foraging expedition she took with Agnes Vaag, a young artist represented in the show but never seen on stage. The story reveals the frightening, non-rational roots of art. Vaag, at once a mysterious being who makes "menacing constructions" out of animal carcasses and a ludicrous figure who lugs suitcases through state parks, may well be Howe's archetypal artist.

Another loosely knit comedy, *The Art of Dining* combines Howe's obsession with food (first manifest in *The Nest*) and her concern with art and its consumption. Because the fragility of art is a repeated motif throughout Howe's canon, in a sense food is for her the ultimate artistic medium: it must be destroyed to be appreciated. Set in a restaurant, *The Art of Dining* contains one of Howe's most brilliant creations, Elizabeth Barrow Colt, a wonderfully comic and pathetic figure who embodies every cliché about writers; comfortable only in the world of the imagination, she's a genius with a pen but a total failure with a soup spoon. In *The Art of Dining*'s spectacular conclusion—all the restaurant guests gathered around a flaming platter of crepes tended by the female chef—Howe uses Elizabeth to point out the connection between art and ritual as well as the redemptive power of artistic creation, a theme that runs through several of Howe's works.

Howe's biggest critical success to date is *Painting Churches*, in some ways her most conventional play as well as one of her most lyrical. Returning to the favorite subject of the American playwright—the nuclear family—Howe gives us a comedy about the necessity of acceptance: a daughter accepting the inevitable decline of her aging parents, parents accepting their daughter as a capable adult (and artist). Howe's quirky sense of humor and her distinctive verbal and visual idiom mark the work as uniquely her own, however familiar her starting point. Although Howe denies that she is an autobiographical writer, there is obviously a kinship between the playwright and Mags Church, the young artist who learns that the portrait she is painting of her parents reveals her as well as them. In a moving final tour-de-force that erases the line between Mags' painting and Howe's play, the stripped-bare stage becomes the portrait, the aging characters rescued from decline for the space of a magical moment.

Howe favors unusual settings—a museum, a restaurant kitchen—and the beach locale of *Coastal Disturbances* is as much metaphor as place: like human beings and their relationships, the sand and ocean remain essentially the same over millennia yet change from moment to moment. The main character is a young woman photographer; appropriately, the play is divided into numerous short scenes that rely heavily on visual effects—resembling, in other words, a sequence of snapshots. Although the central situation, a love triangle, is not Howe's most original, her verbal and especially her visual wit are amply in evidence.

Swimming shares the beach location and largely affirmative vision of *Coastal Disturbances*, while *Teeth* is a serio-comic meditation on fear set, appropriately, in a dentist's office. These two add to the small but growing canon of Howe's one-act plays, which also includes *Appearances*, an encounter between a dressing room attendant and a painfully awkward customer. *Approaching Zanzibar*, Howe's latest major work, is a "road play" that follows a family of four on a cross-country trip to visit a dying relative (an elderly artist reminiscent of Georgia O'Keeffe). The Blossoms' journey is both physical and metaphysical as they engage in hilarious—and sometimes nasty—travel games while wrestling with anxieties about change, loss, and death. Not only is this the first of Howe's plays to exploit multiple settings, but its relatively large cast also represents a deliberate attempt on the playwright's part to include a wider range of characters in terms of ethnicity as well as age. Despite being one of Howe's most complex and ambitious works, however, *Zanzibar* received mixed reviews and enjoyed only a brief New York run.

Howe has acknowledged her debt to Absurdist writers, a debt more apparent in her earlier work than in her most recent plays. Like many other American playwrights, Howe doesn't quite share the nihilistic vision of her European counterparts; although salvation is transitory and more likely to be aesthetic than religious or social, there are moments of redemption in most of her plays. Her work has grown in emotional depth over the years and her focus on art and the artist has become stronger. Women artists are her favored protagonists: she writes from a clearly female perspective even if not from a consistently feminist one. Howe's comedies reveal a playwright with a fine sensitivity to the terrors of existence, a splendidly anarchic sense of humor, and a willingness to take risks on the stage.

—Judith E. Barlow

HUGHES, Dusty. British. Born in Boston, Lincolnshire, 16 September 1947. Educated at Queen Elizabeth Grammar School, Wakefield, Yorkshire, 1957–65; Trinity Hall, Cambridge, 1965–68, M.A. (honours) in English. Has one daughter. Assistant director, Birmingham Repertory Theatre, 1970–72; theatre editor, *Time Out*, London, 1973–76; artistic director, Bush Theatre, London, 1976–79; script editor, *Play for Today* series, BBC Television, 1982–84. Member, Arts Council Drama panel, 1975–80. Recipient: London Theatre Critics award, 1980; Edinburgh Festival award, 1981. Agent: Sebastian Born, Curtis Brown Group, 162–168 Regent Street, London W1R 5TB, England.

PUBLICATIONS

Plays

Grrr (produced Edinburgh, 1968).
Commitments (produced London, 1980). With *Futurists*, London, Faber, 1986.
Heaven and Hell (produced Edinburgh and London, 1981).
Molière; or, The Union of Hypocrites, adaptation of a play by Mikhail Bulgakov (produced Stratford-on-Avon, 1982; London, 1983). London, Methuen, 1983.
From Cobbett's Urban Rides, in *Breach of the Peace* (produced London, 1982).
Bad Language (produced London, 1983).
Philistines, adaptation of a play by Maxim Gorky (produced Stratford-on-Avon, 1985; London, 1986). Oxford, Amber Lane Press, 1985; New York, Applause, 1986.
Futurists (produced London, 1986). With *Commitments*, London, Faber, 1986.
Jenkin's Ear (produced London, 1987). London, Faber, 1987.
Metropolis, music by Joe Brooks, adaptation of the Fritz Lang film (produced London, 1989).
A Slip of the Tongue (produced Chicago and London, 1992).

Screenplays: *Cries from the South*, 1986; *In Hiding*, 1987; *Tom*, 1991; *Crimes of Passion*, 1992.

Television Play: *The Secret Agent*, adaptation of the novel by Joseph Conrad, 1992.

*

Theatrical Activities:
Director: **Plays**—Bush Theatre, London: *The Soul of the White Ant* by Snoo Wilson, 1976; *Blood Sports* by David Edgar, 1976; *Vampire* by Snoo Wilson, 1977; *Happy Birthday, Wanda June* by Kurt Vonnegut, Jr., 1977; *In at the Death* by Snoo Wilson and others, 1978; *A Greenish Man* by Snoo Wilson, 1978; *Wednesday* by Julia Kearsley, 1978.

* * *

Dusty Hughes emerged in the 1980's with several dramatic works to his credit and more to come. An early experience with the left-wing's not having transformed him into a "good Bolshevik" has shaped the subject and concerns of his produced plays. The plays pursue a theme of disenchantment with the Marxist-Socialist ideal turned sour or repressive, as well as with middle-class aspirations which disclose emptiness and produce social and personal inertia.

Standing as immediate examples are Hughes's three best works: *Commitments*, *Futurists*, and an adaptation, *Molière; or, The Union of Hypocrites*.

Commitments introduces a small group of left-wing activists in 1973 using as live-in headquarters the London flat of a tolerant bourgeois dilettant reluctant to join their cause. Forming a focal and substantially dimensionalized triumvirate are the charming but undirected benefactor, an actress strongly committed to "the Party," and her working-class actor-lover. Fellow workers drop in as the group discusses politics and strategies and performs menial Party tasks, while outside the 1974 Labour government comes to power owing little to the Party's efforts or workers. Malaise affects the group's interrelationships: the flat-owner, motivated to become politically active, now ends up returning to his wastrel ways persuaded that the Party is "authoritarian and not a little unrealistic"; and the politically committed actress loses her lover, who returns to his wife. The drama offers a trenchant picture of disillusioned leftists whose cause and commitments have seemed wasted effort.

In *Futurists* Hughes takes us to 1921 post-revolution Petrograd, where great and mediocre artists, journalists, political hacks, striking sailors, and Bolshevik informers mingle in a sweaty nightclub. The drama centers on the Futurist poets—the famous figures of Mandelstam, Mayakovsky, Anna Akhmatova, and others are vividly recreated—who are drawn together by a fervent revolutionary belief that they have something to say but are initially unaware that their individualistic, unconventional thought and expression will eventually doom them. They proclaim their art and reveal their loss of equilibrium in the excitement of revolutionary confusion, while beyond the nightclub the revolution has gone wrong. The poets have relied for protection on their hero Gorky, friend of Lenin, who presides over them like a one-man arts council, but finds he cannot save them from the firing squads or being otherwise silenced. In the new society the artist is an endangered species: the mediocre survive, the talented grow silent or die. Central to the action, the tubercular Gorky becomes a tragic figure losing his self-assured belief that "people don't kill poets" as he becomes increasingly powerless to help his friends and is even warned by Lenin to leave the country. Hughes fills his characters and their world with vibrant life and a dire meaning, tellingly visualized in the 1986 London production as the colorfully grotesque Futurist trappings of the artists' cabaret are progressively stripped away to reveal the ominous black and red banners of Stalin. Yet with Anna Akhmatova's final recitation of a forbidden poem, Hughes reminds us that poetry outlasts revolutions.

That the playwright was drawn to adapt Mikhail Bulgakov's *Molière* is understandable. The play focuses on Molière's relationship to Louis XIV, as a sardonic paradigm of the Russian Bulgakov's position as a writer under Stalin, who in 1936 banned the play after seven performances. Hughes, in portraying a freethinking Molière incurring the wrath of Mother Church in mounting *Tartuffe* and suffering its banishment and his own fall from grace, demonstrates how the artist must demean himself before tyrannical and faction-influenced authority. Rejecting his long-time mistress Madeleine for a disastrous marriage with her supposed younger sister, Molière is informed upon by a dismissed actor in his company. This allows the religious cabal unscrupulously to engineer Molière's fall from favor by extracting Madeleine's confession that his wife is actually their mutual daughter, thus forcing the King's disapproval and his capitulation to their condemnation of the artist. The lively portrait of Molière, who switches from the impetuous actor-manager-writer backstage to a grovelling sycophant when in the presence of his sovereign, is both dramatically powerful, if perhaps historically exaggerated (as is the use of the unproven incest rumor), and thematically lucid. Molière underestimates the power of church and state with its near-omnipotent king and informer-ridden society resembling Stalinist Russia. The play is effective as theatre and as political statement.

Several further works also are underscored by socio-political themes. A critically unsuccessful (yet in its 1989 London production, visually spectacular) musical adaptation of Fritz Lang's 1927 film *Metropolis*, with an uninspired libretto by Hughes, presents a futuristic vision of a city where workers toil in subterranean factories under the dictatorship of an above-ground capitalist élite. A workers' revolt blows up the city, paving the path for a less harsh future whose power structure may or may not be significantly changed for the better. In *A Slip of the Tongue*, the question of whether freedom obligates a sense of responsibility to the political world or gives license to indulge hedonistic impulses is embodied in the actions of a noted dissident and womanizing writer who leaves the long harassment of a unspecified Eastern European country after the Berlin Wall crumbles to become a globe-trotting lecturer rather than a needed helper in framing a new government. This imperfect play drew popular attention in a 1992 Chicago world premiere with John Malkovitch as the anti-hero protagonist. *Jenkin's Ear*, in its focus on a disillusioned ex-foreign correspondent pursuing a missing female friend in a Central American country like Honduras, concerns the moral issue of whether getting a story is worth people's lives. The rapid inertness of middle-class values infecting the generations underlines *Bad Language*, a wryly comic survey of Cambridge undergraduates touched by the malady of sameness, and *Philistines*, an adaptation of Gorky's flawed yet compelling first play in which Hughes incisively presents a blackly comic portrait of a turn-of-the-century *petit bourgeois* Russian provincial family unable to change their ineffectual lives, and foreshadowing the national upheaval.

Productively engaged in turning out new work, Hughes continues to earn recognition as a playwright committed to creating dramas of substance that thoughtfully examine or offer parallels to the socio-political tapestry of this time.

—Christian H. Moe

HUTCHINSON, Ron. British. Born near Lisburn, County Antrim, Northern Ireland; brought up in Coventry, Warwickshire. Educated at schools in Coventry. Worked at various jobs, including fish gutter, carpet salesman, scene shifter, and bookseller, all Coventry; clerk, Ministry of Defence and Ministry of Labour, Coventry; social worker and claims investigator, Department of Health and Social Security, Coventry, 5 years. Resident writer, Royal Shakespeare Company, London, 1978–79. Moved to Los Angeles in 1988. Recipient: George Devine award, 1978; John Whiting award, 1984; Emmy award, 1989; Ace award, 1989. Agents: Judy Daish Associates, 83 Eastbourne Mews, London W2 6LQ, England; and Merrily Kane, The Artists Agency, 10000 Santa Monica Boulevard, #305, Los Angeles, California 90067, U.S.A.

PUBLICATIONS

Plays

Says I, Says He (produced Sheffield, 1977; London, 1978; New York, 1979). Part 1 published in *Plays and Players* (London), March and April 1978; complete play published Newark, Delaware, Proscenium Press, 1980.
Eejits (produced London, 1978).
Jews/Arabs (produced London, 1978).
Anchorman (produced London, 1979).
Christmas of a Nobody (produced 1979).
The Irish Play (produced London, 1980).
Into Europe (produced London, 1981).
Risky City (broadcast 1981; produced Coventry, 1981).
The Dillen, adaptation of a work by Angela Hewins (produced Stratford-on-Avon, 1983).
Rat in the Skull (produced London, 1984; New York, 1985). London, Methuen, 1984.
Mary, After the Queen, with Angela Hewins (produced Stratford-on-Avon, 1985).
Curse of the Baskervilles, from a story by Arthur Conan Doyle (produced Plymouth, 1987).
Babbit: A Marriage, adaptation of a novel by Sinclair Lewis (produced Los Angeles, 1987).
Pygmies in the Ruins (produced Belfast, 1991; London, 1992).

Radio Plays: *Roaring Boys*, 1977; *Murphy Unchained*, 1978; *There Must Be a Door*, 1979; *Motorcade*, 1980; *Risky City*, 1981; *Troupers*, 1988; *Larkin*, 1988.

Television Plays: *Twelve Off the Belt*, 1977; *Deasy Desperate*, 1979; *The Last Window Cleaner*, 1979; *The Out of Town Boys*, 1979; *Deasy*, 1979; *The Winkler*, 1979; *Bull Week*, 1980; *Bird of Prey* series, 1982 and 1984; *Connie* series, 1985; *The Marksman*, from the novel by Hugh C. Rae (*Unnatural Causes* series), 1987; *The Murderers Among Us: The Simon Wiesenthal Story*, 1988; *Dead Man Walking*, 1988; *Red King,*

White Knight, 1990; *The Josephine Baker Story*, 1990; *Prisoners of Honor*, 1991; *Blue Ice*, 1992.

Novel

Connie (novelization of television series). London, Severn House, 1985.

*   *   *

The value of Ron Hutchinson's drama derives largely from its consistent concentration on the Irish experience *outside* Ireland—an experience which serves in his plays to crystallize native Irish problems. The focus is only incidentally social in character. *Risky City* offers a forceful account, in the form of deathbed flashbacks, of the wasting of a Coventry–Irish youth by his inner-city environment, but his experience is not presented as a specifically Irish one. More characteristic is Hutchison's first stage play, *Says I, Says He*, in which the "Old Firm" of two picaresque Ulster navvies, the "roaring boy" Hannafin and the "clean-shave" Phelan, leave their terrorist siblings, and the beautiful dancer for whose hand they are rivals, to conquer London. Financial success for Phelan (gained, ironically, not without obscure threats of Ulster-style violence) attracts the attention of the terrorists, but turns out to be illusory, a matter of the "gab." Reunited, the two plan to leave for England again but are gunned down.

With its musical numbers (some of them uproariously obscene, all of them broadly ironic), *Says I, Says He* resembles a navvies' version of Stewart Parker's *Catchpenny Twist*—another Irish play in which the aspiring heroes ultimately fail to escape political violence. Where Parker has musicians, Hutchinson, as his title suggests, has talkers—but they are no less *performers*: the play consists of a series of comic sketch-episodes (in which the humour is not often a matter of inflection) crowned by Phelan's final fibbing performance ("You took *me* in. With *your* act"). However, in this play Hutchinson is content to revel in his characters' gift of the gab rather than to reflect upon it. The comedy is not of the serious kind.

Eejits also focuses on performers. But here the four violently argumentative members of a London-based Ceilidh band are not under threat from terrorists; rather they carry their national(ist) factionalism around with them. The same predicament receives thorough and hilarious treatment, again in connection with a performance, in *The Irish Play*. In a broken-down Midlands Irish club, the embattled President O'Higgins, striving to retain his control and dignity in the face of the machinations of the opposing Roche faction, endorses the presentation of a nationalistic historical play (agit-prop Ferguson) as part of his plan to endow the bibulous membership with a "historical perspective." As to history, he discovers that "it's all around us, that's the trouble," when, in debate, committee, and finally rehearsal, the ancient alignments of civil war emerge: "Constitutionals versus Hill-men"; Collins versus De Valera; Kerry versus Wexford. In a comic metaphor of internecine self-destruction, the building is jointly wrecked by the warring factions, leaving only the bewildered step-dancer who "plays recorder and dances in the rubble."

The playwriter Ruari in *The Irish Play* declares that he is "trying to understand my country . . . my countrymen . . . myself." Hutchinson himself has said of his most successful and best play, *Rat in the Skull*: "I wanted to write this play to sort out my personal reactions to what is going on in Ireland. . . . You find out who you are in the process." Certainly this feels like a work energized by a personal imperative. For the first time, Hutchinson's abrasively comic dialogue and his preoccupation with performance are concentrated into a sustained scrutiny of the self-awareness and self-understanding catalyzed within an Irishman by his presence in England.

Rather than a plot, *Rat in the Skull* presents a situation and poses a question. The framework is not naturalistic. Under a screen, showing clinical photographs of Michael Patrick De Valera Demon Bomber Roche after his clinical beating-up by Detective-Inspector Nelson of the Royal Ulster Constabulary in Paddington Green police station, are played out the interrogation of Roche by Nelson which led up to the beating, and the consequent interviews, by the Irish "specialist" Superintendent Harris, of Nelson and of the young policeman detailed to be present at the interrogation. The case had been "stitched up," and Nelson had come to London only because of the possibility of the prisoner's turning informer; so why the very deliberative act of violence? The weary Harris reaches for extenuating personal circumstances (an unfaithful wife and a recently dead father), persuading Nelson to accept an "unfit discharge," but neither he nor the baffled, indifferent Constable Naylor can conceive of the complex relation between history and personal identity which renders these Irishmen intimate in conflict—to the exclusion of the Englishman—and which alone points to the explanation. Nelson's fierce parodies of sectarian rhetoric and his sudden changes of tone and address turn the interrogation into a terrible comic performance—one calculated not only to "get inside" and break Roche but also to discomfit an English public which, he senses, stereotypes him in the role of "unclean" Paddy. As Naylor, the "audience" to the interrogation, says: "Roche hasn't said a word the sod, but he's straight man to Nelson . . . it's him and Roche on me." But Nelson is also inflicted with the performer's self-scrutinizing distance. The eponymous rat-in-the-skull images the doubt and self-awareness that persuade him to "break step" for the first time with his Protestant forebears by acknowledging, through this calculated gesture of violence, that he is not a state-sanctioned fighter in a "Holy War" but rather one of "two fellas in a ditch, clubbing each other, till the one dropped dead." *Rat in the Skull* capitalizes thematically on the talent for punchy, stylized dialogue that has always been apparent in Hutchinson's work for both stage and television (*Bird of Prey* and *Connie*), and in so doing enriches that most vital tradition within Irish drama—its concern with the nature and power of rhetoric.

Since the late 1980's, Hutchinson has lived and worked in America, writing scripts for film and television. His most recent stage play could be seen as an apologia, a treatment of the playwright's "quarrel with himself" over his leaving Ireland. For D.I. Nelson there is no way out: his decisive act of violent (self-) confrontation condemns him to inevitable violent death. But for Harry Washburn, in *Pygmies in the Ruins*, an even more intricate acknowledgement of the guilty historical roots of his own personal identity sanctions self-justification and release, so that emigration—a "going *to*" America—can be distinguished from exile—a "running *from*" Ireland. Act I of *Pygmies* "takes place simultaneously in Belfast 1991 and Belfast 1871." Again, a mystery informs the action. When Washburn, a police photographer with artistic pretensions, cracks up after working on yet another (apparently) sectarian murder, he becomes obsessed with the unsolved murder in 1871 of a pathetic domestic servant-girl. In 1871 we see Dr. Mulcahy's investigation of that earlier case; though thwarted, it nonetheless reveals the dark underside of that "Progress" which has earned Belfast prosperity and civic pride. The police-photographer and the physician from Dublin are both examples of the artist as witness, intimate with, yet professionally detached from their surroundings. The double whodunit changes radically when, in Act II, the two "meet" in Washburn's hallucinatory consciousness to play out a nightmare trial-scene. Mulcahy joins with the play's other characters to embody the sick man's feelings of guilt at not only his own life and calling (with its "aesthetic of extinction") but also the "bloody knot of rope" which binds the identity of a whole culture: "the idea of the North," "the mystery of us." They are pygmies in the ruins of a city. Suicide is arrested and recovery begins only when Washburn comes to realize that the very strenuousness of his self-confrontation is a mark of the "voluntary man," the free individual. Reality returns, and Washburn, defying the charge of "quitting," prepares to leave for America with his lover and "a kind of peace."

—Paul Lawley

HWANG, David Henry. American. Born in Los Angeles, California, 11 August 1957. Educated at Stanford University, California, 1975–79, A.B. in English 1979; Yale University School of Drama, New Haven, Connecticut 1980–81. Married Ophelia Y.M. Chong in 1985. Recipient: Dramalogue award, 1980, 1986; Obie award, 1981; Golden Eagle award, for television writing, 1983; Rockefeller fellowship, 1983; Guggenheim fellowship, 1984; National Endowment for the Arts fellowship, 1985; Tony award, 1988; Outer Critics Circle award, 1988; Drama Desk award, 1988. Lives in Los Angeles. Agent: Paul Yamamoto and William Craver. Writers and Artists Agency, 70 West 36th Street, #501, New York, New York 10018, U.S.A.

PUBLICATIONS

Plays

FOB (produced Stanford, California, 1978; New York, 1980). Included in *Broken Promises: Four Plays*, 1983.
The Dance and the Railroad (produced New York, 1981; in *Broken Promises*, produced London, 1987). Included in *Broken Promises: Four Plays*, 1983.
Family Devotions (produced New York, 1981). Included in *Broken Promises: Four Plays*, 1983.
Sound and Beauty (includes *The House of Sleeping Beauties* and *The Sound of a Voice*) (produced New York, 1983; *The House of Sleeping Beauties* in *Broken Promises*, produced London, 1987). *The House of Sleeping Beauties* included in *Broken Promises: Four Plays*, 1983; *The Sound of a Voice* published New York, Dramatists Play Service, 1984.
Broken Promises: Four Plays. New York, Avon, 1983.
Rich Relations (produced New York, 1986).
As the Crow Flies (produced Los Angeles, 1986).
Broken Promises (includes *The Dance and the Railroad* and *The House of Sleeping Beauties*) (produced London, 1987).
1000 Airplanes on the Roof, music by Philip Glass (produced Vienna, Philadelphia, and New York, 1988; Glasgow, 1989). Layton, Utah, Gibbs Smith, 1989.
M. Butterfly (produced New York, 1988; Leicester and London, 1989). New York, New American Library, 1989; London, Penguin, 1989.

FOB and Other Plays (includes *The Dance and the Railroad*, *The House of Sleeping Beauties*, *1000 Airplanes on the Roof*, *Family Devotions*, *The Sound of a Voice*). New York, New American Library, 1990.
The Voyage, music by Philip Glass (produced New York, 1992).

Television Play: *Blind Alleys*, 1985.

*

Theatrical Activities:
Director: **Plays**—*A Song for a Nisei Fisherman*, 1980, and *The Dream of Kitamura*, 1982, both by Philip Kan Gotanda, San Francisco; *FOB*, New York, 1990.

David Henry Hwang comments:
I'm interested in the dust that settles when worlds collide. Sometimes these worlds are cultural, as in my explorations of a Chinese past meeting an American present. Sometimes they are spiritual, as in *Rich Relations*, where the gung-ho materialism of a California family struggles with its Christian mysticism. Most of the time I also try to walk the fine line between tragedy and comedy. I'm fascinated by America as a land of dreams—people pursue them and hope some day to own one.

* * *

"The element it shares with my previous work has to do with a concern for identity," says David Henry Hwang in the introduction to *1000 Airplanes on the Roof*. "To me, all the really interesting human dilemmas are basically internal searches." His comment is as misleading as it is true, for the internal searches in his plays are hedged by external pressures and prejudices. This fact is obvious in the title (*Broken Promises*) which Hwang gave to the collection of his first four plays. Historically, the promise that was broken for so many Chinese immigrants was the dream of the Gold Mountain, an America where fortunes could be picked up off the street. Hwang, the son of immigrants, conventionally educated at choice American universities, is not only interested in the broken promises of the past, but is also concerned about the loss implicit in an embracing of the emblems of American success and the confusions embodied in being a hyphenated person, a Chinese-American.

Essentially a non-realistic dramatist, Hwang does not develop his characters in the conventional way by the accumulation of psychological details. They emerge through formal presentational modes as varied as Chinese opera (*The Dance and the Railroad*) and the television sitcom (*Family Devotions*). Neither the opera nor the sitcom is allowed to retain its classic form, however, for artistically as well as ideationally Hwang is preoccupied in the early plays with the ground on which the hyphenated American struggles to define himself. The tension of inclusion/exclusion which marks these plays operates in a less narrowly ethnic context in the later work, and the early use of non-realistic techniques (the role-playing in *FOB*, for instance) prepares the way for the extreme theatricality of *M. Butterfly* and *1000 Airplanes*, in which Jerome Sirlin's projections come close to upstaging both Philip Glass's music and Hwang's text.

FOB is a three-way struggle between Dale, who is accepted —almost—as something other than "a Chinese, a yellow, a slant, a gook"; Grace, his first-generation cousin who has been in the States since she was a child; and Steve, the bumptious newcomer, the FOB (Fresh Off the Boat). The final pairing of Steve and Grace, who sometimes become the hero Gwan Gung and Fa Mu Lan, the Woman Warrior, suggests that the Chinese in America must hold onto some sense of being Chinese, but it is instructive that at the end they are heading for a fashionable disco in a rented limousine. There is a similar but more moving cross-over in *The Dance and the Railroad*, in which Lone tries to separate himself from his fellow immigrant workers by going to the mountain-top to practice the movements of Chinese opera. Ma, who wants both to dance with Lone and to be one of "the guys" down below, improvises—with Lone's blessing—an opera, at once comic and touching, which uses the vocabulary of traditional art in a new American context and which frees Lone of his need to stand apart. In *Family Devotions*, it is the visiting uncle from the mainland, more Chinese than Communist, who teaches his great nephew that, before he can escape the twin traps of materialism and Christianity which his family represents, he must recognize his face—reflected in the back of the violin that will open his path to the future—and carry his Chinese self into his American world.

Between *Family Devotions* and *M. Butterfly*, seven years later, there were several plays—including the elegantly suggestive, Japanese-based *Sound and Beauty*—but it was with *M. Butterfly* that Hwang scored his greatest success. Much of that success came from the surface slickness of the work, in part the contributions of the director and the designer, and the somewhat lurid content of the story around which the play is built. Yet, *M. Butterfly* is Hwang's most complex treatment of the crises of identity, one that allows for political, sexual, and social considerations more convoluted than those in the early work. The scandalous story, borrowed from a real event, is the account of a French diplomat and his mistress, a Chinese actress on whom he thought he had fathered a child, charged with spying; the trial reveals, to the apparent surprise of the diplomat, that the mistress is a man. In the end, the diplomat dons the robes discarded by his lover and, like Madame Butterfly, kills himself to prove that there is a love deep enough to die for. The suicide is simply an audience-pleasing charade unless playgoers recognize the act as an illustration of the arbitrariness and elusiveness of sexual and ethnic stereotypes. The assumptions underlying the affair—Western male assumptions—are that both women and Asians are submissive, accepting the invasion of the male, the Westerner. It is an admonitory tale for a time in which such assumptions are under attack.

With *1000 Airplanes on the Roof*, Hwang's protagonist is stripped of ethnic identification. He or she (the role was designed to be played by either a man or a woman) is ill-at-ease in the ordinary world in which he presumably lives, constantly on the run from both the here-and-now, and a half-remembered encounter with extraterrestrials, a painful but transcendent event. An interview with a doctor allows him to disown all extraordinary elements in his life, frees him from the threat implied in recurrent lines ("It is better to forget. It is pointless to remember. No one will believe you. You will have spoken heresy. You will be outcast."), lets him see "only the glow of neon" in the sky but robs him of the sound like a thousand airplanes on the roof. Although the "science fiction music-drama" gives Hwang his most experimental vehicle to date, his text is largely a platitude about the contemporary sense of alienation. Neither his words nor Glass's music have the force or the imagination of Sirlin's design. Perhaps it is time for Hwang to jump (space)ship and get back to the land of broken promises and broken butterflies.

—Gerald Weales

I

INGE, William (Motter). American. 1913–1973.
See 1st edition, 1973.

INNAURATO, Albert. American. Born in Philadelphia, Pennsylvania, 2 June 1947. Educated at Temple University, Philadelphia, B.A.; California Institute of the Arts, Valencia, B.F.A. 1972; Yale University School of Drama, New Haven, Connecticut, M.F.A. 1975. Playwright-in-residence, Playwrights Horizons, New York, 1983; adjunct professor, Columbia University, New York, and Princeton University, New Jersey, 1987. Recipient: Guggenheim grant, 1975; Rockefeller grant, 1977; Obie award, 1977; National Endowment for the Arts grant, 1986, 1989; Drama League award, 1987. Agent: George Lane, William Morris Agency, 1350 Avenue of the Americas, New York, New York 10019. Address: 325 West 22nd Street, New York, New York 10011, U.S.A.

PUBLICATIONS

Plays

Urlicht (produced New Haven, Connecticut, 1971; New York, 1974). Included in *Bizarre Behavior*, 1980.
I Don't Generally Like Poetry But Have You Read "Trees"?, with Christopher Durang (produced New Haven, Connecticut, 1972; New York, 1973).
The Life Story of Mitzi Gaynor; or, Gyp, with Christopher Durang (produced New Haven, Connecticut, 1973).
The Transfiguration of Benno Blimpie (produced New Haven, Connecticut, 1973; New York, 1975; London, 1978). New Haven, Connecticut, Yale/Theatre, 1976; London, TQ Publications, 1977.
The Idiots Karamazov, with Christopher Durang, music by Jack Feldman, lyrics by Durang (also director: produced New Haven, Connecticut, 1974). New Haven, Connecticut, Yale/Theatre, 1974; augmented edition, New York, Dramatists Play Service, 1981.
Earth Worms (produced Waterford, Connecticut, 1974; New York, 1977). Included in *Bizarre Behavior*, 1980.
Gemini (produced New York, 1976). New York, Dramatists Play Service, 1977.
Ulysses in Traction (produced New York, 1977). New York, Dramatists Play Service, 1978.
Passione (also director: produced New York, 1980). New York, Dramatists Play Service, 1981.
Bizarre Behavior: Six Plays (includes *Gemini, The Transfiguration of Benno Blimpie, Ulysses in Traction, Earth Worms, Urlicht, Wisdom Amok*). New York, Avon, 1980.

Coming of Age in SoHo (also director: produced Seattle and New York, 1984; revised version produced New York, 1985). New York, Dramatists Play Service, 1985.
Best Plays (includes *Coming of Age in SoHo, The Transfiguration of Benno Blimpie, Gemini*). New York, Gay Presses of New York, 1987.
Gus and Al (produced Denver, Colorado, 1987; New York, 1988). New York, Dramatists Play Service, 1989.
Magda and Callas (produced Philadelphia, 1988). New York, Theatre Communications Group, 1989.

*

Theatrical Activities:
Director: **Plays**—*The Idiots Karamazov*, New Haven, Connecticut, 1974; *Passione*, New York, 1980; *The Transfiguration of Benno Blimpie*, New York, 1983; *Herself as Lust*, New York, 1983; *Coming of Age in SoHo*, Seattle 1984, New York, 1984 and 1985.
Actor: **Play**—*I Don't Generally Like Poetry But Have You Read "Trees"?*, New York, 1973.

* * *

In his Introduction to his collection of plays *Bizarre Behavior* the extraordinarily talented Albert Innaurato expresses understandable annoyance at the frequency with which critics misunderstand his plays or insist upon discussing connections between them. But to misread is always the critic's risk and to search out the connections, when they do indeed exist, one of his obligations. When considered together, Innaurato's individual plays delineate, as the work of such an important and promising dramatist must, a unique, powerfully held vision of the human condition. This vision is characterized by the skillful manipulation of vividly contrasting dramatic elements that ignite the plays' tensions and yield to their reconciliations. Most prominent among these are satiric farce, comedy, and pathos; the beauty-and-the-beast combination of the grotesque and the beautiful; and the religious and the blasphemous. Among a rather extensive list of more specific dualities are his characters' outward appearances and contrasting inner realities; their often "bizarre behavior" and their rather different inner impulses; and a frequent doubling of times and places that parallel these dichotomies of character and action. Innaurato also explores the psychological terrain of sexual ambiguity, seems to exploit aspects of the disease of overeating, bulimia, with the necessary purgation, here Aristotelian rather than Roman-orgy in nature, and from music borrows the concepts of aria and counterpoint.

The multiple dualities of *Gemini*, his most commercially successful play, with a run of over four years at a small Broadway house, are indicated by the title from which the hero Francis Geminiani, "plump" and "a little clumsy," derives his name. At the time of his 21st birthday, his fellow Harvard students, the attractive and very WASP Judith

Hastings and her freshman younger brother, arrive for an unexpected visit to his Italian and Catholic South Philadelphia home. At his symbolic coming of age, climaxed by a disastrous birthday feast, Francis is forced to investigate openly his inner life and to admit that he is attracted emotionally not only to the sister but to her brother as well. But despite the potential pathos of the central situation, as Harvard and South Philadelphia, his college friends and his overfed, rough-talking, but good-hearted neighbors collide, the results are a raucous comic festival, as lively as an Italian street *festa* and funnier than anything Neil Simon could devise. In *Passione* Innaurato returns to South Philadelphia to explore the emotional problems of a middle-aged couple and to contrast the parents with their happy son, a clown, who is incongruously married to the fat lady of the circus.

Innaurato's most recent, more interesting, and less successful play *Coming of Age in SoHo* is a kind of counterpart or sequel to *Gemini* and brings to the foreground some of its preoccupations. The hero Bartholomew Dante has left his wife to write in a loft in SoHo and like his predecessor also comes of age, this time at 36. There is again much wild humor, triggered here by his wife's South Philadelphia family headed by her father, the Mafia don Cumbar' Antonio, and the unexpected entrance of three boys, the brothers Odysseus ("WASP culture") and Trajan from St. Paul's and Harvard, and his own forgotten son Puer, the result of a long-ago affair with a German terrorist. But the play's intent is serious. The brothers with their classical names, poor Puer ("boy" and the *puer* complex) who seeks a brother and finds his father, and the Dante-Beatrice allusions index the play's assemblage of elements of what might be called the *gemini* concept: the linkage of narcissism, dual or ambivalent identity, and creativity. Aspects of this concept underlie Albee's much earlier *The American Dream* and are present in the plays of Peter Shaffer, particularly *Equus*.

But the brilliant, darkly beautiful *The Transfiguration of Benno Blimpie*, Innaurato's finest work thus far, belongs to a differently imagined South Philadelphia than *Gemini* and is more characteristic of his other plays. The fat, unattractive Benno, with his delicate inner life, is eating himself to death. As he controls the play's dramatic time, he comments upon and verbally participates in scenes of his past emotional yearnings and rejections. The play ends with a startling cannibalistic image as Benno, before the quick black-out, "*lowers the meat cleaver as though to cut off some part of himself.*"

The same dark intensity is present in *Earth Worms*, one of the most widly imaginative plays by any recent dramatist. Arnold Longese, the sexually ambiguous hero, manages to beget a child with a country girl from the south. He brings her back to South Philadelphia, and there they are surrounded by his blind grandmother who lives on the floor, two transvestites, and a group of hustlers. At the end of the play the grandmother dies, the family home is becoming a whorehouse, and the hero is mutilated by three vindictive nuns. Ingredients for an unintended comedy? Perhaps. But here they combine into Magritte-like fragments of a vivid tragicomic nightmare. The short play *Urlicht* belongs to a similar dramatic world, features outrageously comic religious situations, and is peopled in part by incongruous nuns.

Innaurato's plays clearly make allusions to his awareness of the grandeur and comedy of the classical past. *Gemini* and *Ulysses in Traction*, with its implications of inhibited enterprise, make the suggestions in their titles; the mad nuns who become like giant cockroaches as they swarm over the hero of *Earth Worms* recall the Furies. But in their effects the plays bring to mind that modern gothic playwright Michel de Ghelderode, and they seem more properly gothic and medie-

val. Francis in *Gemini* and Arnold in *Earth Worms* wander like modern everymen through their distorted worlds, and Innaurato's most memorable characters resemble frightening or wildly comic gargoyles. But in familiar phrases from Shakespeare and Yeats, most of his characters have "that within which passeth show": they have Dionysus's "beating heart" rather than stone "in the midst of all."

—Gaynor F. Bradish

ISHERWOOD,   Christopher   (William   Bradshaw). American. 1904–1986. See 3rd edition, 1982.

ISITT, Debbie. British. Born in Birmingham, 7 February 1966. Educated at Lordswood Girls' School, Birmingham, 1977–82; Coventry Centre for the Performing Arts, 1983–85. Dancer, Unique, Birmingham, 1978–82; receptionist, Hendon Business Association, Birmingham, 1982–83; actor, Cambridge Experimental Theatre Company, European tour, 1985–86; co-founder and since 1986, artistic director, Snarling Beasties Theatre Company, Longford, Coventry; guest director, Coventry Centre for Performing Arts, 1991, Other Theatre of Comedy Trust, London, 1992, and Repertory Theatre, Heilbronn, Germany, 1992. Recipient: *Scottish Daily Express* award, 1988; Independent Theatre award, 1989; Perrier Pick of the Fringe award, 1989, 1990; *Time Out* Theatre award, 1990/91; Edinburgh Fringe Festival first, 1992. Agent: Nick Marston, A. P. Watt Ltd., 20 John Street, London WC1N 2DR. Address: c/o Snarling Beasties Coventry Touring Theatre Co-op Ltd., 36 Sydnall Road, Longford, Coventry CV6 6BW, England.

PUBLICATIONS

Plays

Gangsters (produced Edinburgh, 1988).
Punch and Judy: The Real Story (also director: produced Edinburgh and London, 1989).
Valentino (also director: produced Birmingham and London, 1990).
Femme Fatale (also director: produced Edinburgh and London, 1990).
The Woman Who Cooked Her Husband (produced Warwick and London, 1991).
You Never Know Who's Out There (produced London, 1992).

Television Play: *The Lodger*, 1992.

*

Theatrical Activities:
Director: **Plays**—all her own plays; *East* by Steven Berkoff, Edinburgh, 1986.

Actor: **Plays**—all her own plays; *A Midsummer Night's Dream*, European tour, 1985–86.

Debbie Isitt comments:

Writing for me has to have a purpose and that purpose is usually to reach people and hopefully make them feel something, see something, hear something, think something, and maybe even do something. In my experience writing for the theatre is vitally important; I am not reliant very often on producers, publicists, marketing machines, sponsors, donors, editors, censors, men in suits and women in shoulder pads to be able to create and get my work seen. Part of this freedom comes from directing and appearing in my own work; I only have to find a willing person to let me have a space, find others willing to push themselves and take a few risks and put it on. This is the most important bit—to put it on and say—this is what I wanted to say and it's how I wanted to say it—it is a truthful interpretation of what I intended and let people take from it what they wish. I could not stand to be part of a system that compromised my plays, that shaped them and bent them and formed them into someone else's. If a writer is not herself behind the words then she is not a writer. She should put herself on the line and create dramas that draw people into her world just for the duration of the play; even if the world is one from her imagination it is HER imagination and no one else's that we should be sharing. So much emphasis is put on criteria for funding, fitting in, opting out. I would like to think I can maintain control of my writing, although as I move some way into film I begin to see that things are very difficult, there seems to be little room for guts, imagination, and risk.

I tend to choose themes that are at once personal and close to home while smacking of larger social issues. Heterosexual relationships and the dark forces seething behind contemporary marriage is a theme that I am drawn to time and again. Social myths and secrets that we hide and disguise and twist to fit in and conform. Domestic violence, tranvestism, betrayal, phobias, lies are the stuff my plays are made of. They are real and surreal fusing together. Music is a massive influence, especially the great works of contemporary heros like Frank Sinatra, Ella Fitzgerald, Patsy Cline. The woman's psyche being put centre stage is another of my interests; I like to put women into certain situations to see how they react and then make them do things and think things and say things that we're not supposed to and see how the men react. It's really a very interesting process. I also like to leave room for movement and mime and visual techniques often influenced by films and incorporate it on the stage. Above all I think I like to be truthful to the characters, the situation, and myself. The plays are usually funny even though they are often dark. I cannot stand to get depressed—we need to recognize the funny side of pain and guilt and grief. We also need fight and spirit and punch and my plays must be performed with pace and vitality. I am not the sentimental type—just the mental type.

* * *

Debbie Isitt's plays are inextricably linked to her productions in which she usually also acts. The company was formed in 1986 and called Snarling Beasties (Steven Berkoff's creative slang for testicles) because Isitt fancied the idea of strait-laced bureaucrats unwittingly referring to male genitalia in the course of deciding whether or not to give the company money. After their inaugural production of Berkoff's *East* at Edinburgh, it fell upon Isitt to come up with some follow-up material. Not for her the luxury of dwelling on every syllable; her best work has been produced under the pressure of the deadline of the Edinburgh Festival. *Punch and Judy*, *Femme Fatale*, and *The Woman Who Cooked Her Husband* are a trio of plays exploring the underbelly of heterosexual relationships on the themes of wife-battering, transvestism, and adultery respectively. In production her words are supported by an expressionistic, mimetic presentation of character, loud popular music, and a set that hits you between the eyes. The effect is intensely theatrical and reminiscent of Berkoff in the aggressive use of rhyming couplets. Such an upfront presentation is exhilarating to watch, although sometimes one wonders whether it is the raucous music that is providing the uplift rather than Isitt's words.

Judging from Isitt's work, she is not a woman in need of courses in assertiveness. Her approach is unashamedly partisan: men appear as boorish, unimaginative wimps with little or nothing to recommend them. *The Woman Who Cooked Her Husband* was inspired by the real-life case of Nicholas Boyce in 1985 in which Boyce chopped his wife up and distributed the pieces because he could no longer stand her nagging. The Judge, summing up, said that Boyce was sorely provoked and he only served six years for manslaughter. In contrast, Sara Thornton is serving life for killing her husband after being abused for years. Such an imbalance of justice fuels Isitt's anger. *The Woman Who Cooked Her Husband* depicts a triangular relationship between Kenneth, his wife Hilary, and Laura, his mistress. Kenneth is torn between Laura's skills in bed and Hilary's in the kitchen. Hilary has devoted her life to serving up tempting delicacies in the belief that a well-fed man will never leave her. Through flashback, we see Kenneth's first encounters with the sulky Laura who can hardly summon up enough energy to open a packet of fish fingers. Cringing, shifty, and a poor liar, Kenneth continues to meander between the two until Laura takes matters into her own hands and spills the beans to Hilary, forcing Kenneth to leave her. At a strange reunion, Kenneth salivates as he anticipates his first good meal for a long time, but Hilary, finally supported by Laura, has other ideas for the menu.

There is no doubt that Kenneth is the most unpleasant character on stage and there can be few audiences who wouldn't cheer Hilary on in her grisly deed. But Isitt also criticises the wife's tendency to blame "the other woman" instead of her spouse. The woman, it seems, is seen as inadequate if she is left and criticised as a homewrecker if she does the leaving. Isitt doesn't see that marriage has much to offer a woman. So one-sided and dogmatic is the approach that it can inspire resistance in an audience. It is the black humour that transforms the bile into something more memorable.

Femme Fatale, the second play in the trilogy, is more complex because for once Isitt doesn't have all the answers. Georgia and Jimmy could be a model couple, with lots of disposable income and a good sex life, only Jimmy is drawn irresistibly towards a black cubicle at the back of the stage where he is transformed into Jessica. Apart from the shock and distaste, what enrages Georgia is that Jessica should be such a paragon of femininity, lying on the sofa painting her nails and eager to do all she can to make their domestic life run smoothly. Her perfection challenges Georgia's refusal to be a slave to the sink or her husband. Jimmy likes to dress up because he says it makes him feel "free from pressure." But being a woman is far from being free of pressure. Isitt tentatively explores why transvestites are drawn to such stereotypical images of femininity, tottering around on high heels and crowned with their beehive hairdos—everything that feminists are trying to escape. As Georgia gets more aggressive, so Jimmy becomes more passive. Beneath the feminist rhetoric, there is some sympathy for the man who feels he has to adopt the clothes of a woman in order to explore the more feminine side of his nature. But Isitt never loses sight of the fact that discovering one's husband dressed in a pair of one's knickers does have a funny side.

Since the trilogy the Other Theatre of Comedy Trust commissioned *You Never Know Who's Out There*, which explores the seedy, racist and misogynist world of the Northern club and is reminiscent of Trevor Griffiths's *Comedians*. A power struggle amongst the performers results in much spilling of blood but little illumination. Snarling is Isitt's hallmark. Now that we know that she is not afraid to show her teeth, it would make a change if she occasionally concealed them.

—Jane Edwardes

J

JEFFREYS, Stephen. British. Born in London, 22 April
1950. Educated at Stationers' Company's School, London,
1961–68; Southampton University, B.A. (honours) in English
language and literature, 1972, and research student for
M.Phil, 1972–74. Driver for Silexeine Paints, London, 1969,
and Jeffreys Brothers (Billiards) Ltd., London, 1972–74;
teacher, Upton House Comprehensive School, London,
1974–75; lecturer in drama and English, Cumbria College of
Art and Design, 1975–78; writer-in-residence, Brewery Arts
Centre, and founder, Pocket Theatre, Cumbria, 1978–80;
writer-in-residence, Paines Plough, London, 1987–89; since
1991 part-time literary associate, Royal Court Theatre,
London. Recipient: *Sunday Times* National Student Drama
award, 1977; Edinburgh Fringe first, 1978, 1984; *Evening
Standard* award, 1989; Critics Circle award, 1989; *Plays and
Players* award, 1989. Agent: Tom Erhardt, Casarotto
Ramsay Ltd., National House, 60–66 Wardour Street,
London W1V 3HP, England.

Publications

Plays

Where the Tide Has Rolled You (produced Southampton,
1973).
Counterpoint (produced Southampton, 1975).
Like Dolls or Angels (produced Carlisle, Cumbria and
London, 1977).
Mobile 4 (produced Carlisle, Cumbria and London, 1978).
London, French, 1979.
Darling Buds of Kendal (produced Kendal, Cumbria, 1978).
Year of the Open Fist (for children; produced Kendal,
Cumbria, 1978).
The Vigilante Trail (produced Kendal, Cumbria, 1979).
Jubilee Too (produced Warwick and London, 1980).
Watches of the Night (broadcast, 1981; produced Kendal,
Cumbria, 1981).
Imagine (produced Edinburgh, 1981).
Peer Gynt with Gerry Mulgrew, adaptation of the play by
Henrik Ibsen (produced Kendal, Cumbria, 1981).
Hard Times, adaptation of the novel by Dickens (produced
Kendal, Cumbria, 1982; London and New York, 1987).
London, French, 1987.
Futures (produced Kendal, Cumbria, 1984).
Carmen 1936, adaptation of the novel by Prosper Mérimée
(produced Edinburgh, 1984; Baltimore and London, 1985).
Clearing House (produced Kendal, Cumbria, 1984).
Returning Fire (produced London, 1985).
Desire (produced Edinburgh, 1986).
The Garden of Eden (produced Carlisle, Cumbria, 1986).
Valued Friends (produced London, 1989; New Haven,
Connecticut, 1990). Published in *First Run 2*, edited by
Kate Harwood, London, Hern, 1990.
The Clink (produced Plymouth and London, 1990).
London, Hern, 1990.

A Jovial Crew, adaptation of the play by Richard Brome
(produced Stratford-on-Avon and London, 1992).

Radio Plays: *Like Dolls or Angels*, 1979; *Watches of the
Night*, 1981; *Absolute Decline*, 1984; *Carmen 1936*, 1992.

*

Theatrical Activities:
Director: **Plays**—for the Pocket Theatre, Cumbria, 1979:
Stone by Edward Bond; *Games* by James Saunders; *The
Vigilante Trail*.

Stephen Jeffreys comments:
I think of myself in the widest sense as an entertainer, and I
write plays partly out of a desire to create exciting events. I
like audiences to laugh, to be moved, and to be confronted
—to have a big experience. I am interested in telling stories
and use different techniques—naturalism, epic theatre—in
the service of narrative. As a playwright working in live
theatre I want to give audiences an evening they cannot have
in front of the television or in the cinema, an experience
which depends on their sharing a space with live actors.

* * *

Stephen Jeffreys is one of the most strikingly versatile
British playwrights to have come to the fore during the
1980's. His output spans a number of ingenious translations
and dramatic adaptations as well as original plays in an impressive variety of genres. The most characteristic features of
his work are an unerring comic instinct, a shrewd eye for
topical relevance, and a brilliant theatrical nous for turning
limited resources to rich account.

After the success of *Like Dolls or Angels*, his "study of a
stuntman on the skids," Jeffreys was involved with the
setting-up of Pocket Theatre Cumbria, which was to become
one of the most successful of the small-scale touring companies. His association with the company continued through the
premieres of several of his plays including *Watches of the
Night* and *Futures*, and allowed Jeffreys to develop a natural
talent for writing with specific requirements in mind. He also
began to explore subject matter to which he would return one
way or another: his early play about John Lennon, *Imagine*,
evinced a fascination with the world of popular music that
crops up to telling effect in his later work (it's suggestively
used to mark the passage of time in *Valued Friends* and to
give one of the characters a secret life in *Going Concern*, a
new play based on the Jeffreys family business of making
billiard tables, which is as yet unproduced).

Pocket Theatre also first produced Jeffreys's version of
Dickens's *Hard Times*. This model of how to preserve the
quintessential flavours of a prose writer in a purely theatrical
format has deservedly become a staple for touring companies
both in Britain and abroad. Other adaptations to his name are
Peer Gynt and most recently *A Jovial Crew*, from the original

by Richard Brome, for a production by Max Stafford–Clark with the Royal Shakespeare Company that has been applauded for its deft underscoring of modern resonances in pre-Civil War drama.

The same gift for dynamic interpretation of historical material is evident in *Carmen 1936*, his play about the Spanish Civil War produced by the Scottish company Communicado, which won a Fringe First in 1984. In the late 1980s, Jeffreys wrote two fine plays on occasional pretexts: *Returning Fire*, which celebrated the return of Halley's Comet, and *The Garden of Eden*, a large-scale piece for the community of Carlisle that used a cast of 150. The first of these plays was produced by Paines Plough, the new writing company for whom he also wrote *The Clink*. This Jacobean revenge comedy may have felt over-long in the theatre, but it nonetheless displays a vivid control of pastiche and cunningly pitched anachronism.

This body of work displays Jeffreys's impressive knack of finding the right dramatic idiom for each project, his ability to write to the strengths of a particular company or to tease theatrical magic out of the narrowest of briefs. By the mid-1980's Jeffreys had confirmed his potential as a collaborative writer *par excellence*, a strikingly ingenious dramatic craftsman, but not one, perhaps, with a distinctive personal voice. *Valued Friends*, produced at Hampstead Theatre in 1989 and revived there a year later, marked a new leap forward in that it more conspicuously exploited the writer's own experience of the here and now. This superbly written response to the property boom is palpably founded on an insider's observations of the dramatic situation at hand, and manipulates the sympathies of the audience with ironical aplomb. The play tells the story of a group of friends who have shared a flat since they were students. When a property developer tries to buy them out, their attitudes and relationships become subject to a process of erosion. The major decisions of their lives are eventually governed by the housing market and the greed it inexorably instils. Jeffreys's handling of the characters is wry and clear-sighted, but also notably tolerant. Many of his contemporaries, having seized on the same scenario, would have turned in a more two-dimensional issue-drama. It's not that Jeffreys's humour and wit shirk any political responsibility: they're simply deployed with a sure sense of how the audience's desire to identify with the characters will entangle them in the same quagmire of values and commitments. The play deservedly won awards for its author, and interestingly took on new shades and tonalities in its second production, after the boom had turned to bust—a measure of its subtlety and stature, which many a more conventional critique of Thatcherism would never have been able to emulate.

—Matthew Lloyd

JELLICOE, (Patricia) Ann. British. Born in Middlesbrough, Yorkshire, 15 July 1927. Educated at Polam Hall, Darlington, County Durham; Queen Margaret's, Castle Howard, Yorkshire; Central School of Speech and Drama, London (Elsie Fogarty prize, 1947), 1944–47. Married 1) C. E. Knight-Clarke in 1950 (marriage dissolved 1961); 2) Roger Mayne in 1962, one son and one daughter. Actress, stage manager, and director, in London and the provinces, 1947–51; founding director, Cockpit Theatre Club, London, 1952–54; lecturer and director, Central School of Speech and

Drama, 1954–56; literary manager, Royal Court Theatre, London, 1973–75; founding director, 1979–85, and president, 1986, Colway Theatre Trust. O.B.E. (Officer, Order of the British Empire), 1984. Agent: Casarotto Ramsay Ltd., National House, 60–66 Wardour Street, London W1V 3HP, England.

PUBLICATIONS

Plays

Rosmersholm, adaptation of the play by Ibsen (also director: produced London, 1952; revised version produced London, 1959). San Francisco, Chandler, 1960.
The Sport of My Mad Mother (also co-director: produced London, 1958). Published in *The Observer Plays*, London, Faber, 1958; revised version, London, Faber, 1964; with *The Knack*, New York, Dell, 1964.
The Lady from the Sea, adaptation of a play by Ibsen (produced London, 1961).
The Knack (produced Cambridge, 1961; also co-director: London, 1962; Boston, 1963; New York, 1964). London, Encore, and New York, French, 1962.
The Seagull, with Adriadne Nicolaeff, adaptation of a play by Chekhov (produced London, 1964).
Der Freischütz, translation of the libretto by Friedrich Kind, music by Weber (produced London, 1964).
Shelley; or, The Idealist (also director: produced London, 1965). London, Faber, and New York, Grove Press, 1966.
The Rising Generation (produced London, 1967). Published in *Playbill 2*, edited by Alan Durband, London, Hutchinson, 1969.
The Giveaway (produced Edinburgh, 1968; London, 1969). London, Faber, 1970.
You'll Never Guess (also director: produced London, 1973). Included in *3 Jelliplays*, 1975.
Two Jelliplays: Clever Elsie, Smiling John, Silent Peter, and A Good Thing or a Bad Thing (also director: produced London, 1974). Included in *3 Jelliplays*, 1975.
3 Jelliplays (for children; includes *You'll Never Guess*; *Clever Elsie, Smiling John, Silent Peter*; *A Good Thing or a Bad Thing*). London, Faber, 1975.
Flora and the Bandits (also director: produced Dartington, Devon, 1976).
The Reckoning (also director: produced Lyme Regis, Dorset, 1978).
The Bargain (also director: produced Exeter, 1979).
The Tide (also director: produced Axminster, Devon, 1980).
The Western Women, music by Nick Brace, adaptation of a story by Fay Weldon (also co-director: produced Lyme Regis, Dorset, 1984).
Changing Places (produced Woking, Surrey, 1992).

Other

Some Unconscious Influences in the Theatre. London and New York, Cambridge University Press, 1967.
Devon: A Shell Guide, with Roger Mayne. London, Faber, 1975.
Community Plays: How to Put Them On. London, Methuen, 1987.

*

Theatrical Activities:
Director: **Plays**—*The Confederacy* by Vanbrugh, London, 1952; *The Frogs* by Aristophanes, London, 1952; *Miss Julie*

by Strindberg, London, 1952; *Rosmersholm* by Ibsen, London, 1952; *Saint's Day* by John Whiting, London, 1953; *The Comedy of Errors*, London, 1953; *Olympia* by Ferenč Molnár, London, 1953; *The Sport of My Mad Mother* (co-director, with George Devine), London, 1958; *For Children* by Keith Johnstone, London, 1958; *The Knack* (co-director, with Keith Johnstone), London, 1962; *Skyvers* by Barry Reckord, London, 1963; *Shelley*, London, 1965; *You'll Never Guess*, London, 1973; *Two Jelliplays*, London, 1974; *A Worthy Guest* by Paul Bailey, London, 1974; *Six of the Best*, London, 1974; *Flora and the Bandits*, Dartington, Devon, 1976; *The Reckoning*, Lyme Regis, Dorset, 1978; *The Bargain*, Exeter, 1979; *The Tide*, Axminster, Devon, 1980; *The Poor Man's Friend* by Howard Barker, Bridport, Dorset, 1981; *The Garden* by Charles Wood, Sherborne, Dorset, 1982; *The Western Women* (co-director, with Chris Fog and Sally-Ann Lomax), Lyme Regis, Dorset, 1984; *Entertaining Strangers* by David Edgar, Dorchester, Dorset, 1985.

* * *

The major plays by new young writers in London between 1956 and 1959 included *Look Back in Anger, The Birthday Party, Roots, Serjeant Musgrave's Dance, A Resounding Tinkle, The Long and the Short and the Tall, Flowering Cherry, Five Finger Exercise, The Hostage, A Taste of Honey* —and Ann Jellicoe's *The Sport of My Mad Mother* at the Royal Court, the heart of this activity.

Since this impressive debut, Jellicoe has written only three other full-length stage plays, two of them slight. The 16 brief scenes of *Shelley* take the poet from his Oxford years, through two marriages, to Harriet Westbrook and Mary Godwin, to his drowning in Italy. *Shelley*, subtitled "the Idealist," is written as though for a 19th-century touring company of twelve: heavy, walking gentleman, juvenile, and so on. Jellicoe remarks that as a writer she is tackling a new set of problems here, working "within a set narrative framework—partly for the sheer technical discipline involved." Shelley interests her because he is very young, and trying to be good: "the problems of goodness which are so much more interesting than those of evil." He is tragic because of "his blindness to the frailty of human nature." *Shelley* is a flat work, with conspicuous explanatory sections in which the poet talks like a letter or tract.

The Giveaway turns on a suburban housewife who wins a competition prize of ten years' supply of cornflakes (which are conspicuously on stage); she has had to pretend to be under 14. While the only production may not have done it justice, *The Giveaway* seems to be a clumsy attempt to write a farce, with a hint of satire on consumerism and a touch of the kind of non-verbal comedy Jellicoe had written earlier.

Jellicoe's best play, *The Knack*, is an exuberant, liberating, youthful comedy. Three young men share a flat: Tolen (he has only this one curious name), who has "the knack" of success with women; likeable Colin, who lacks it and envies Tolen; and the garrulous Tom, half outside the sex war. Enter Nancy, a lost, gawky, 17-year-old Northerner, looking for the YWCA, who will give Tolen a chance to demonstrate his knack. The staccato, repetitive dialogue skims along like jazz, and is sometimes hard to follow on the page. A bed provides comic business (they pretend it is a piano), as do entries through the window. An undercurrent is Tolen's Nazi characteristics, and whether negotiation is possible with such people. (The film, scripted by Charles Wood and directed by Richard Lester, is substantially changed, and also great fun.)

Jellicoe's *succès d'estime*, *The Sport of My Mad Mother*, is much more unusual and demanding. This is about four London teenagers and three people they come across, a liberal American, a retarded girl of 13, and Greta, an Australian who comes to represent also the Hindu goddess of destruction and creation, Kali. Yet character, plot, dialogue hardly matter. This is a piece to be brought to life by a director, and, to make reading really difficult, stage-directions are few. The form is non-linear; Jellicoe writes in the Preface to the revised text of 1964 that the play "was not written intellectually according to a prearranged plan. It was shaped bit by bit until the bits felt right in relation to each other and to the whole. It is an anti-intellect play not only because it is about irrational forces and urges but because one hopes it will reach the audience directly through rhythm, noise and music. . . . Very often the words counterpoint the action or intensify the action by conflicting with it." *The Sport of My Mad Mother* is highly original (especially for Britain and for the 1950's) in its Artaudian use of ritual, in its stress on physical expressiveness, in its use of speech and drums for rhythms, in its audacious non-literary form and apparent shapelessness, and in its search for the roots of arbitrary violence. Proper recognition and appreciation will require a readily available film version, as yet unmade.

In 1972 Jellicoe told Carol Dix in the *Guardian*: "Directing, as I see it, is an interpretative art, and writing is a creative art, and it's a bloody relief not to have to be creative any longer. The impulse to create is linked with the aggressive instinct."

A ten-year silence ended when in 1978 Jellicoe moved to Lyme Regis, Dorset; she has since staged numerous community plays in the southwest. These ambitious works involve many local people (up to 180 onstage), use the town as the setting and have a promenade production. Jellicoe wrote the first, *The Reckoning*, about the Monmouth Rebellion of 1685. Allen Saddler described it in *Plays and Players*: "It is all action. The mayor and his cronies scramble about in a frenzy, people rush by in terror, beg for mercy or confide strange secrets in your ear. A girl who is pregnant by a Catholic finds herself in a strange dilemma, proclamations are read from various parts of the hall. Soldiers burst in. Bands play. Prisoners are dragged off screaming. Brawls break out just where you are standing. Events proceed so quickly that there is no time to examine the Catholic or the Protestant case." *The Western Women*, about the part played by women in the siege of Lyme in the Civil War, was re-written by Jellicoe from a script by Fay Weldon. Another local history piece, *The Bargain*, concerned Judge Jeffreys and was commissioned by the Southwest Music Theatre. Jellicoe in her essay in *Women and Theatre* writes of the satisfaction of this community activity: "It was extraordinary, the people of Lyme, in rehearsal and in performance, watching a play about themselves. There is a unique atmosphere. It's partly the promenade style of performance, partly that the play is specially written for the town, but it has never failed, that excitement, they just go wild. . . . What I love about it is slowly building something in the community."

In May 1992 Jellicoe took up the challenge of devising a community play for Woking, Surrey, a place lacking much history or sense of identity. Her *Changing Places* focused on women, on Ethel Smythe, composer and militant suffragette, contrasting her with a working-class woman—outside the middle-class movement for votes-for-women—who achieves self-realisation as a nurse in World War I. Jellicoe appears unlikely to return to the Royal Court, or to the West End, as her fulfilment now comes from her community work in the West Country.

—Malcolm Page

JENKIN, Len (Leonard Jenkin).American. Born in New York City, 2 April 1941. Educated at Columbia University, New York, 1958–63, 1969–71, B.A. in English 1962, M.A. 1963, Ph.D. in English 1972. Has one daughter. Lecturer in English, Brooklyn College, New York, 1965–66; associate professor of English, Manhattan Community College, 1967–79. Since 1980 associate professor, Tisch School of the Arts, New York University. Since 1983 associate artistic director, River Arts Repertory Company, Woodstock, New York. Recipient: Yaddo fellowship, 1975; National Endowment for the Arts fellowship, 1979, 1982; Rockefeller fellowship, 1980; Christopher award, 1981; American Film Festival award, 1981; Creative Artists Public Service grant, 1981; Obie award, 1981 (for writing and directing), 1984; MacDowell fellowship, 1984; Guggenheim fellowship, 1987. Agent: Scott Hudson, Writers and Artists Agency, 19 West 44th Street, Suite 1000, New York, New York 10036, U.S.A.

PUBLICATIONS

Plays

Kitty Hawk (produced Stratford, Connecticut, 1972; New York, 1974; London, 1975).
Grand American Exhibition (produced New York, 1973).
The Death and Life of Jesse James (produced Los Angeles, 1974; New York, 1978).
Mission (produced New York, 1975).
Gogol: A Mystery Play (also director: produced New York, 1976). Published in *Theatre of Wonders: Six Contemporary American Plays*, edited by Mac Wellman, Los Angeles, Sun and Moon Press, 1986.
Kid Twist (produced San Francisco, 1977; New York, 1983).
New Jerusalem (produced New York, 1979).
Limbo Tales (includes *Highway*, *Hotel*, *Intermezzo*) (also director: produced New York, 1980; London, 1982). New York, Dramatists Play Service, 1982.
Five of Us (produced Seattle, 1981; New York, 1984). New York, Dramatists Play Service, 1986.
Dark Ride (also director: produced New York, 1981). New York, Dramatists Play Service, 1982.
Candide; or, Optimism, adaptation of the novel by Voltaire (produced Minneapolis, 1982). New York, Theatre Communications Group, 1983.
A Country Doctor, adaptation of a story by Kafka (also director: produced San Francisco, 1983; New York, 1986).
My Uncle Sam (also director: produced New York, 1984). New York, Dramatists Play Service, 1984.
Madrigal Opera, music by Philip Glass (produced Los Angeles, 1985).
American Notes (also director: produced Los Angeles, 1986; New York, 1988). New York, Dramatists Play Service, 1988.
A Soldier's Tale, adaptation of a libretto by Ramuz, music by Stravinsky (produced New York, 1986).
Poor Folks Pleasure (also director: produced Seattle, 1987).
Pilgrims of the Night (also director: produced Seattle, 1991).

Screenplays: *Merlin and Melinda*, 1977; *Blame It on the Night*, 1985; *Welcome to Oblivion*, 1989; *Nickel Dreams*, 1992.

Television Plays: *More Things in Heaven and Earth*, 1976, and *See-Saw*, 1977 (*Family* series); *Road Show* (*Visions* series), 1976; *Eye of the Needle* (*Quincy* series), 1977; *Games of Chance* (*Incredible Hulk* series), 1979; *Family of Strangers*, 1980; *Days and Nights of Molly Dodd*, 1989.

Novel

New Jerusalem. Los Angeles, Sun and Moon Press, 1986; London, Harper Collins, 1990.

Other

Editor, with Leonard Allison and Robert Perrault, *Survival Printout*. New York, Random House, 1973.

*

Theatrical Activities:
Director: some of his own plays.

Len Jenkin comments:
I always like the opening: the houselights fade, the room goes black, the voices around me quiet, the first lights come up in the toybox, and the figures start to move.

Once that's over, for something to hold me, as author or audience, there needs to be a continuing sense of *wonder*, as powerful as that in fairy tales, moonlight, or dreams. This can be present in any sort of work for the stage—realistic to sublimely outrageous—and it's a quality that can't be fused into or onto something with clever staging or sideways performances. It's gotta be there, in the text and through and through.

The other thing that needs to be there for what I'd consider to be "Theatre" to exist is what I call *heart*. This doesn't mean I want to look at people struggling bravely through their emotional problems. It means that the author is not primarily an entertainer; that he/she is instead a preacher, and a singer, and a human being. And that the deep twined nature of what binds us and what makes us free is going to be out there on the stage.

I want to see theatre energetically stomping around the U.S.A. and the rest of the world. Put on plays by the highway side. I want to see tractor-trailers full of men in hats and beautiful women, pulling into town and setting up on the high school football field. I'll be glad to be in the cab of the first truck in line—the one that says "ALIVE" in a bullet on its side.

*   *   *

In *American Notes* one character might be speaking of almost any of Len Jenkin's characters when he says, "You have fallen through an American crack, and them is deep." Another says, "You know, there's a lot of people who think their life is what happens to them. Get a job, get married, eat an ice cream cone. It's a great life. There's another kind of people who don't connect what happens to them with their lives at all. Their life is something else . . . hopefully."

It is about the latter that Jenkin writes. Yearning for something outside their lives, his characters are interested in the sleazy dreams offered by supermarket tabloids and carnival pitchmen, and in extraterrestrial beings. *American Notes* is more than an *Our Town* of the current rural depression for, as in most of Jenkin's plays, the characters are isolated beings, who are as likely to address the audience in monologues as engage with other characters.

The central characters of *Gogol*, *Five of Us*, and *Dark Ride* are all artists of a kind: a playwright, a writer who is more successful at writing pornographic romances pseudonymously than the artistic novel in his desk drawer, the translator of a meaningless and maybe fake Chinese mystical work. Journalists, would-be writers, and an ex-director of slasher films haunt the margins of his plays. Other purveyors of dreams are the salesmen, offering encyclopedias, love potions, views of the crocodile Bonecrusher, or novelties to trick and surprise people. This last salesman, the eponymous Uncle Sam, might speak for Jenkin when he says "These gags break the rules in people's heads. If there weren't any rules, I'd be outta business." Jenkin plays with theatrical conventions and seems to disclaim any deeper intentions. As 10 characters repeat, one after another, at the end of *Dark Ride*, "I'm not interested in philosophy. Just tell me how it ends." But, as Jenkin's epigraph to *American Notes*, from Blake's "America: A Prophecy," suggests, "Tho' obscur'd, this is the form/Of the Angelic land," his plays are driven by deeper concerns, spelled out most clearly in *American Notes*:

> Last few weeks, I've seen a lot of dreams with my eyes open, just riding down the road. I drive through these towns, one after the other, and they all got a main street, and on it is a place to buy groceries, Food Town—a place to eat, Marv's Broiler—and a place to get fucked-up, Hi-Hat tavern. And when you go through these places in America, the question is always "Anybody home?" The answer is obvious. No. Basically, there is nobody home in America, Pauline. Except you.

> There are people out there, after all. They go way back, and they came outta the sky and the dirt, just like us. And they got secrets, just like us.

His plays commonly center upon quests, presented wryly— even mockingly—as what might be called *drames noirs*.

Gogol, *Dark Ride*, and *My Uncle Sam* all portray rather absurd quests in which gangsters or the police dog the footsteps of the central character as he stumbles toward an unclear goal. And most of the decidedly unreligious pilgrims of *Pilgrims of the Night* who wait through the night at a ferry terminal in the middle of nowhere, are hoping to contact extraterrestrials who are reported to have crashed in the forest across the river. All these plays have narrator figures and an episodic structure full of seedy eccentrics who typically offer the audience an introductory account of themselves. *My Uncle Sam*, one of the most fascinating of Jenkin's plays, has various levels of commentary upon the action: from the Author; from his Uncle Sam in old age; from Sam when young and on his quest; from an audio cassette from the Universal Detective Agency that instructs him step by step; and from a series of Narrators dressed appropriately for the successive settings. His version of *Candide*, which might be described as an un-quest play, has an equally elaborate set of narrative devices and characters. In both *Candide* and *Gogol* a play within the play is presented; in *Pilgrims of the Night* the characters arrange to while away the night by telling stories, which we see enacted.

This overt, sometimes flamboyant, theatricality brings a joyousness or aesthetic pleasure that gives the audience something of that transfiguring experience whose want his characters unconsciously or consciously feel. For example, in "Hotel," one of his *Limbo Tales*, a "starved, stalled, and stranded" salesman talks to the audience in his hotel room. On either side of him are the other two rooms with only a large audio speaker in each: from one we hear a writer painfully composing "Kubla Khan," interrupted not by a person from Porlock but by a lightning-rod salesman, and from the other a teenage drug-addict who is visited by acquaintances who leave with her last 20 dollars. And yet the salesman gets a phone call from his dead father; before he leaves to avoid eviction he quotes the Bible, "For ye shall go out with joy, and be led forth with peace: the mountains and the hills shall break forth before you into singing, and all the trees of the field shall clap their hands"; and finally, with his room and the stage empty, we see the shadow of a dove briefly on the windowshade and hear the writer begin to type again. Like *Waiting for Godot*, Jenkin's plays are about the inability of man not to hope.

—Anthony Graham-White

JOHN, Errol. Citizen of Trinidad and Tobago. 1924–1988. See 4th edition, 1988.

JOHNSON, Terry. British. Born 20 December 1955. Educated at Queens School, Bushey, Hertfordshire; University of Birmingham, 1973–76, B.A. in drama 1976. Actor in late 1970's, and director. Recipient: *Plays and Players* award, 1982; *Evening Standard* award, 1983; John Whiting award, 1991. Lives in London. Agent: Phil Kelvin, Goodwin Associates, 12 Rabbit Row, London W8 4DX, England.

PUBLICATIONS

Plays

Amabel (produced London, 1979).
Days Here So Dark (produced Edinburgh and London, 1981).
Insignificance (produced London, 1982; New York, 1986). London, Methuen, 1982; New York, Methuen, 1986.
Bellevue (produced on tour, 1983).
Unsuitable for Adults (produced London, 1984; Costa Mesa, California, 1986). London, Faber, 1985.
Cries from the Mammal House (produced Leicester and London, 1984).
Tuesday's Child, with Kate Lock (televised 1985; produced London, 1986). With *Time Trouble*, London, Methuen, 1987.
Time Trouble (televised 1985). With *Tuesday's Child*, London, Methuen, 1987.
Imagine Drowning (produced London, 1991). London, Methuen, 1991.

Screenplays: *Insignificance*, 1985; *Killing Time*, 1985.

Television Plays: *Time Trouble*, 1985; *Tuesday's Child*, with Kate Lock, 1985; *Way Upstream*, adaptation of the play by Alan Ayckbourn, 1988.

*

Theatrical Activities:
Director: **Plays**—*The Woolgatherer* by William Mastrosimone, London, 1985; *I've Been Running* by Clare McIntyre, London, 1986; *Candy and Shelley Go to the Desert* by Paula Cizmar, London, 1986; *Bedroom Farce* by Alan Ayckbourn,

Bolton, 1987; *Children of the Dust* by Anne Aylor, London, 1988; *Rag Doll* by Catherine Johnson, Bristol, 1988; *Sleeping Nightie* by Victoria Hardie, London, 1989; *Death of a Salesman* by Arthur Miller, York, 1989; *Just Between Ourselves* by Alan Ayckbourn, 1991. **Television**—*Time Trouble*, 1985; *Way Upstream* by Alan Ayckbourn, 1988; *Rag Doll* by Catherine Johnson, 1988; *The Lorelei* by Nick Dunning, 1989; *Man in Heaven* (episode 3: *Falling in Love*), 1990; *Ball on the Slates* by Bryan Elsley, 1990.

*   *   *

Boldness of conception and a subtle control in execution are richly combined in Terry Johnson's drama. Thus *Insignificance*, despite all the potential for lurid sensation in a scenario which brings together an Einstein-figure, a Marilyn Monroe-figure, a Joe DiMaggio-figure, and a Senator McCarthy-figure in a New York hotel room in 1953, impresses as a sustained dramatic scrutiny, within a basically naturalistic framework, of the nature of celebrity and of the human need for celebrities. It is a play about wants. The far-from-dumb-blond Actress arrives at the Professor's hotel room wanting to talk to him, to prove her knowledge (of his theories especially), and finally to sleep with him; the Ballplayer wants the Actress to come home and *make* a home; the Senator, meanwhile, wants the Professor to co-operate with him and his committee, and to back an anti-Soviet nuclear programme. The Professor himself wants only to be left alone to retreat with his calculations about the shape of the universe. He it is who articulates a Theory of *existential* Relativity, concerning the need of each individual to feel a centre of identity which in modern Western culture results in the erection of "false gods" as guarantors and measures of personal wholeness—the neon-lit image of the Actress's famous skirt-blown-up pose; the Ballplayer immortalized on a million bubble-gum cards; the omniscient Professor dubbed "True Child of the Universe." Yet the Actress, whose desperate desire for a child is thwarted even within the play itself (she miscarries when the Senator strikes her), ultimately recognizes the despair implicit in the Professor's refusal to confront his own fear—of an impending nuclear devastation for which he feels responsible. The repulsive Senator, self-proclaimed "gentleman and . . . solipsist," is the extreme embodiment of the "madman's scheme of things" that the Professor and the Actress, in their different ways, both diagnose as general: so convinced is he of a self-centred universe that he can claim to have *invented* them all to fulfil his purposes.

The ability of Johnson fully and powerfully to *dramatize* complex ideas and arguments is also evident in *Unsuitable for Adults*. The setting—an upstairs pub-theatre in Soho—is very different from that of *Insignificance*, but the concentration is again upon a vital lack of personal identity in modern culture. The resolution is gender-based. The feminist alternative comedian Kate attempts to convince the asthmatic lunchtime stripper Tish of her unthinking collusion with a culture which turns women into images and potential objects of violence; but Kate's real *experience* of feminism and her extrication from her own hopeless involvement with Nick, a brilliant impressionist whose pretence and avoidance of moral responsibility in his private life are an extension of his act, can take place only with self-acknowledgement and self-understanding. While the other acts—Tish's schoolgirl strip, Nick's impressions, the magician Keith's feeble escapism—provide images of fantasy or compensation for an audience which as a result of that remains "captive," Kate attempts aggressively to confront both them and herself with her sca-

brous Lenny Bruce-style act (a considerable opportunity for the performer). But her routine gradually falls apart, and verbal violence comes to a cathartic physical climax when she deliberately mutilates a finger: "the body turns against the mind and says, 'Enough. I want to stop this now.'" In the play's Epilogue Kate withdraws to a Dartmoor cottage with Tish (who is recovering from a serious asthma attack). The performances are over, and the stripping is now a discovery of truth, both moral and physical: it reveals an essentially *natural* identity in which both women partake.

The very considerable philosophical ambition of *Insignificance* and *Unsuitable for Adults* is fully disclosed only as the carefully worked dramatic pattern of each play becomes apparent. Each is notable for a stylistic texture which is varied and flexible, natural and uninsistent; climaxes are violent, but there are no shocks of structure or style. In *Cries from the Mammal House*, however, there is a clear relation between philosophical ambition and theatrical experiment. Hitherto in Johnson's work, metaphor has provided a crucial means of dialectical organization within a broadly naturalistic structure; but now a single, diagnostic dramatic metaphor is proposed at the outset and subsequently explored in a theatrical mode replete with bizarre detail, blackly comic juxtaposition, and stylistic variation. The point of reference is expressionism—in plot as in style. When a half-Celtic bastard bird-conservationist arrives at the zoo kept by his brother for the funeral of their father, the zoo's founder, he finds it in a state of terminal decay. Despite the efforts of his wife, Anne (who falls in love with the visitor), the despairing brother Alan is impotent to reverse the trend of death and morbid preservation begun by the morally corrupt founding father himself, and the zoo is sold. Renewal comes only after the "Birdman" David has undertaken a "dreamlike" journey to Mauritius in search of the pink pigeon and returns to England, having experienced the company of strange colonial survivors and kidnap by a Creole tribe, with a real live Dodo. The zoo animals have by now been killed, prior to his suicide, by Alan; but as the play ends, David and Anne, together with her daughter Sally (formerly traumatized but now released) and his three Mauritian companions, plan a "new lease of life" for the zoo—under the sign not of the decadent Western father but of an Eastern enlightenment (and with the "absurd cry" of the Dodo).

Johnson's most recent play, *Imagine Drowning*, also has a richly symbolic setting with much characteristically grotesque detail: a chaotic guest-house on the Cumbrian coast in the shadow (or "glow") of Sellafield Nuclear Power station. Into this modern "haunted house," with its bizarre menagerie, comes a young woman called Jane, who is in search of her radical journalist husband David. An intricately worked double time-scheme enables the intertwined presentation of the crises of self undergone by both David (a few weeks earlier) and Jane. David gives way to a reactionary individualist pessimism and confronts the "cold, black nugget" of the homicidal impulse within himself; Jane experiences the depressive "schism" of mind and body. However, the play's resolution is unconvincing because the full dramatic realization of the "journey of the soul" is limited by the presence of two figures of ethical authority through whom the playwright offers explicit diagnosis and commentary. Both figures are, inevitably, marginal to society, if not actually outside it: the severely disabled Tom, whose political activism is presented with affectionate (self-) irony, attempts to stir the couple to political action, and catalyses Jane's confrontation of her relation to David; Buddy, "grounded" American ex-astronaut and now mystical beach-bum, forces each to be "baptized into the new age" by immersion in the sea, thus effecting a death-and-rebirth consonant with his holistic philosophy. The dominance of these figures inhibits exploration of the play's most interesting character, the mysterious, eccentric survivor, Brenda, "a very slow woman" who keeps the guest house. Buddy's philosophy recognizes "connection," but the causal link made by the playwright between the deathly effects, moral and physical, of Sellafield, and the homicidal activities of Brenda's imprisoned mass-murderer husband, seems rather a matter of ideological correctness than of the fresh perception of the relation between self and society of which we know Johnson to be capable. The large symbolic ambitions of this "dream play about the pain we're all immersed in" are frustrated by the very urgency of the need to deliver a message about the "moral, political and sexual confusion" of the 1980's and the possibility of renewal in the future.

—Paul Lawley

———————

JOHNSTON, (William) Denis. British. 1901–1984.
See 3rd edition, 1982.

———————

JOHNSTONE, Keith. British. Born in Brixham, Devon. Married to Ingrid Johnston. Director of the Theatre Studio, 1965–66, and associate director, 1966, Royal Court Theatre, London; director, Theatre Machine Improvisational Group; taught at Royal Academy of Dramatic Art, London, and Statens Teaterskole, Copenhagen. Currently associate professor of drama, University of Calgary. Co-director, Loose Moose Theatre Company, Calgary. Address: Department of Drama, University of Calgary, Calgary, Alberta T2N 1N4, Canada.

PUBLICATIONS

Plays

Brixham Regatta, and For Children (produced London, 1958).
The Nigger Hunt (produced London, 1959).
Gloomy Go Round (produced London, 1959).
Philoctetes, adaptation of the play by Sophocles (produced London, 1964).
Clowning (produced London, 1965).
The Performing Giant, music by Marc Wilkinson (also co-director: produced London, 1966).
The Defeat of Giant Big Nose (for children; also director: produced on Welsh tour, 1966).
Instant Theatre (produced London, 1966).
Caught in the Act (produced London, 1966).
The Time Machine (produced London, 1967).
The Martians (produced London, 1967).
Moby Dick: A Sir and Perkins Story (produced London, 1967).

Wakefield Mystery Cycle (also director: produced Victoria, British Columbia, 1968).
Der Fisch (also director: produced Tübingen, 1971).
The Last Bird (produced Aarhus, Denmark, 1973). Toronto, Playwrights, 1981.
Shot by an Elk (produced Kingston, Ontario, 1974).
Robinson Crusoe (produced Calgary, Alberta, 1976).

Other

Impro: Improvisation and the Theatre. London, Faber, and New York, Theatre Arts, 1979; revised edition, London, Eyre Methuen, 1981.

*

Theatrical Activities:
Director: **Plays**—*Eleven Plus* by Kon Fraser, London, 1960; *The Maimed* by Bartho Smit, London, 1960; *The Triple Alliance* by J.A. Cuddon, London, 1961; *Sacred Cow* by Kon Fraser, London, 1962; *Day of the Prince* by Frank Hilton, London, 1962, 1963; *The Pope's Wedding* by Edward Bond, London, 1962; *The Knack* by Ann Jellicoe (co-director, with Jellicoe), London, 1962; *Edgware Road Blues* by Leonard Kingston, London, 1963; *The Cresta Run* by N.F. Simpson, London, 1965; *The Performing Giant* (co-director, with William Gaskill), London, 1966; *The Defeat of Giant Big Nose*, Welsh tour, 1966; *Wakefield Mystery Cycle*, Victoria, British Columbia, 1968; *Der Fisch*, Tübingen, 1971; *Waiting for Godot* by Beckett, Alberta, 1972.

Keith Johnstone comments:
(1973) I began writing plays when the Royal Court commissioned me in 1957. They were about physical sensations, often sensations experienced in infancy, expressed in visual images.

When I began writing again in 1966 it was only to provide suitable scripts for improvisors and short "entertainment" pieces. Most of my work from 1965 to 1970 was with my group Theatre Machine. We toured in many parts of England, gave demonstrations to teachers and trainee teachers, and hammered out an effective formula. *Instant Theatre* was the Theatre Machine in an early show. We were the only British group to be invited to Expo 67 in Montreal, and toured in Denmark, Germany, Belgium, Yugoslavia, and Austria.

I am at present writing an account of my improvisational methods, and am returning to writing "real" plays. *Brixham Regatta* was given a Sunday night production at the Mermaid in about 1969 and it looked O.K. to me. This has made me feel that there might be some point in trying a serious work again.

I dislike "sets." I think theatre should be popular. I think theatre should "freak-out" the audience rather than offer conversation pieces. Favourite play—*Do It!* performed by the Pip Simmons Group.

*   *   *

Keith Johnstone's work has been relatively little exposed and it can hardly be claimed that he has had much direct influence on the British theatre; but in a more subtle and pervasive manner, his work played an important role in the British theatre of the 1960's. To a large extent this was initially confined to his work at the Royal Court for the English Stage Company during one of its most creative periods. Associated with the Court from 1957, he was a co-director of the 1965–66 season and director of the Theatre Studio, from which emerged Johnstone's Theatre Machine Group, whose work, based on improvisations, has influenced a large number of younger English actors and writers.

The first efforts of the Court Studio to gain widespread attention consisted of a 1965 Christmas show, *Clowning*. Designed for both children and adults, each performance was unpredictable and different, basing itself on mime and improvisation exercises originated in the Court's acting classes. Its theme, broadly, was the making of clowns, examining whether and how they can be trained. Taking a few basic situations from which the actors could take off into improvisation, the show intriguingly experimented with that sense of the unexpected and dangerous which Johnstone evidently sees as a major clowning skill, in its concentration on the immediacy of the theatrical moment. Some aspects of this work were elaborated in Johnstone's most interesting play to date, *The Performing Giant*, produced in a double-bill with Cregan's *Transcending* at the Court in 1966. The play received a poor reception at the time; critics seemed to lack a critical vocabulary with which to cope with a kind of theatre which later many other experimental groups were to make easier for them. Basically the play is an allegory of the adolescent's attempt to understand the mysteries and puzzles of the outside world as well as the processes of the developing body; a group of pot-holers encounter a giant and explore the terrain of his inside as a potential tourist Disneyland only to have the giant rebel and defeat them with the aid of the female pot-holer with whom he falls in love. To most critics the play seemed merely strange and extravagant; charging it with whimsical obscurity in its initial premise, they missed the

denseness of the developing fantasy and the way in which Johnstone's allegory worked, not as a planned series of concepts but as an immediate theatrical experience, using a loose basic structure as a starting-point in a manner parallel to the work of another Court dramatist, Ann Jellicoe, in *The Sport of My Mad Mother*. It would be interesting to see *The Performing Giant* revived, for it is a more important play than was noticed at the time.

Johnstone's other work in England has been mainly in the shape of further Theatre Machine shows, each one progressively more adventurous, or of adaptations (such as his excellent version of Sophocles's *Philoctetes*). His sense of the possibilities of theatre, coupled with his ability to work within the terms of fantasy without sentimentality or whimsy, marks him as an original voice too rarely heard.

—Alan Strachan

JONES, LeRoi. See BARAKA, Amiri.

K

KALCHEIM, Lee. American. Born in Philadelphia, Pennsylvania, 27 June 1938. Educated at Trinity College, Hartford, Connecticut, B.A.; Yale University School of Drama, New Haven, Connecticut, one year. Recipient: Rockefeller grant, 1965; Emmy award, 1973. Agent: Susan Schulman, 454 West 44th Street, New York, New York 10036. Address: RD #2, West Center Road, West Stockbridge, Massachusetts 01266, U.S.A.

PUBLICATIONS

Plays

A Party for Divorce (produced New York, 1963).

Match Play (produced New York, 1964). Published in *New Theatre in America*, edited by Edward Parone, New York, Dell, 1965.

. . . And the Boy Who Came to Leave (produced Minneapolis, 1965; New York, 1973). Published in *Playwrights for Tomorrow 2*, edited by Arthur H. Ballet, Minneapolis, University of Minnesota Press, 1966.

An Audible Sigh (produced Waterford, Connecticut, 1968).

The Surprise Party (produced New York, 1970).

Who Wants to Be the Lone Ranger (produced Los Angeles, 1971).

Hurry, Harry, with Jeremiah Morris and Susan Perkis, music by Bill Weeden, lyrics by David Finkle (produced New York, 1972).

Prague Spring (produced Providence, Rhode Island, 1975; New York, 1976).

Win with Wheeler (produced Waterford, Connecticut, 1975). New York, French, 1984.

Winning Isn't Everything (produced New York, 1978).

Breakfast with Les and Bess (produced New York, 1983). New York, French, 1984.

Friends (produced New York, 1984; also director: revised version, produced New York, 1989).

Moving (produced Lenox, Massachusetts, 1991). New York, French, 1991.

The Tuesday Side of the Street (produced Lenox, Massachusetts, 1991).

Television Plays: *Reunion*, 1967; *Let's Get a Closeup of the Messiah*, 1969; *Trick or Treat*, 1970; *All in the Family* series, 1971–72; *Is (This) Marriage Really Necessary*, 1972; *The Class of '63*, 1973; *The Bridge of Adam Rush*, 1974; *The Comedy Company*, 1978; *Marriage Is Alive and Well*, 1980.

*

Lee Kalcheim comments:

I am a realist. So, my plays are realistic. Comic. Dramatic. Strongly based on characters. I grew up with the realistic writers of the 1950's. Found myself sitting in the middle of the avant garde movement with an inherited style. And then as the theatre began to be less faddish (in New York) it became apparent that I could indeed maintain my love of character—of reality—and survive as a playwright. My work in improvisational theatre and film began to broaden my work. My later work became more fragmented or film like. Less . . . living-roomish. But I realized that for all the excitement of theatrical effects (I have tried various experiments with mixed media), the thing that still moved me most, standing in rehearsal watching my plays, were those one to one scenes. Those scenes where two people faced each other, wanting something from each other. Those scenes where something happened between people. They washed out all the media effects, or unusual transitions, or whatever. They were theatre at its strongest. And I suppose I keep coming back to those in my plays. I do write film. But I keep coming back to the theatre for the excitement of those live, vibrant scenes —that put flesh and blood out there in front of you.

* * *

"It makes me very sad and very happy to be a playwright," was Lee Kalcheim's answer to a request for a statement which could introduce this piece about him. It serves well. Kalcheim is indeed a melancholy and a joyful chronicler. But what made him almost unique among the American dramatists of his generation was his ability to bustle, hustle, and earn his own way *as a writer*. While most "young playwrights" are weaving their tortured ways through the mazes of foundations and endowments and theatre boards seeking grants, honoraria, subsistences, and other encouraging hand-outs, Kalcheim energetically and quite successfully went into the *business* of writing.

He has a good mind and that intelligence which reflects both cool observations and warm insights into the characters he creates. More than storytelling, Kalcheim is people-telling. His plays, he says, are about "human ideas": as a playwright he is less concerned with the usual ideas *per se* than he is with the humanness of those ideas, with the humanity which generates those ideas.

Moreover, as even a quick reading or viewing of his work for the stage reveals, Kalcheim is fascinated by human loneliness. What for other, more abstract writers is a concern with the condition of loneliness, for Kalcheim becomes both a compassionate and an uninvolved concern for the human being as an alone creature: yes, both passionate and uninvolved, both sad and happy. People trying—desperately, lazily, sadly, hopefully, hilariously, pathetically, ridiculously —to make contact with other people is what his plays not only are but are about.

At the end of *An Audible Sigh*, one of the characters, Gale, says, "You see . . . I want to be loved, but I don't want to have strings attached." And there, indeed, is the rub. Kalcheim's people are lonely, loving but afraid of being loved and even of being un-lonely. They sometimes seem to enjoy their loneliness and find sanctuary in their states of not being loved. Driven in part by fear of being possessed and by desire to possess, the characters are intensely vulnerable. Their bulwarks seem all terribly sturdy and well-planned but facing in the wrong direction.

In play after play, Kalcheim examines these qualities. Even more personally, he exhibits a unique ability to watch and be part of the action, *and* to double the effect, to watch the watchers (himself included) and the actors. Again and again, Kalcheim seems to be writing much the same play—each time in a different guise but each time about the same qualities, sensibilities. If these feelings and events are indeed his own experiences (love, divorce, joining, separation, regret, hope, need, fear, tenacity, escape), he is quite excellent at turning that experience into theatrical action, because Kalcheim the writer is a very astute observer of Kalcheim the man.

Moreover, his technique works unusually well: he juxtaposes comedy and drama with almost metronomic regularity, but at the critical heart of the matter is a much more important and profound juxtaposition: The Fear of Death poised against An Immortality Assured, if one may capitalize such sentiments any more.

Kalcheim has been writing since he was eleven years old, and he says that when his first playlet was produced, he wept at the recognition of his own voice "up there." If he has turned now more and more to film and television to earn a living, his first and enduring love is perhaps not a person (ironically) but the theatre. As with many media writers, Kalcheim plays the game of running down his own television writing, but nonetheless he speaks with justified pride about the way his voice is now heard "up there."

—Arthur H. Ballet

———

KANIN, Garson. American. Born in Rochester, New York, 24 November 1912. Educated at local schools to age 15; attended American Academy of Dramatic Arts, New York, 1932–33. Served in the United States Army Signal Corps, 1941–42; private; Air Force, 1942–43, and the Office of Strategic Services, 1943–45; captain, on Staff on SHAEF (European Theatre Operations). Married the actress and playwright Ruth Gordon in 1942 (died 1985). Jazz musician, Western Union messenger, stock boy and advertising proofreader at Macy's, New York, burlesque comedian, and summer camp social director, 1929–32; assistant to the playwright and director George Abbott, *q.v.*, 1935–37; radio interviewer and actor; on production staff, Samuel Goldwyn Productions, Hollywood, 1937–38. Since 1938 freelance director and producer: formed Kanin Productions, 1967. Recipient: New York Film Critics Circle award, 1945; Oscar, for documentary, 1946; Sidney Howard Memorial award, 1946; Donaldson award, for play and direction, 1946; American Academy of Dramatic Arts award of achievement, 1958; New York Public Library Literary Lion award, 1985; elected to the Theater Hall of Fame, 1985. Agent: William Morris Agency, 1350 Avenue of the Americas, New York, New York 10019. Address: 200 West 57th Street, New York, New York 10019, U.S.A.

PUBLICATIONS

Plays

Born Yesterday (also director: produced New York, 1946; London, 1947).   New York, Viking Press, 1946.

The Smile of the World (also director: produced New York, 1949).   New York, Dramatists Play Service, 1949.
The Rat Race (also director: produced New York, 1949). New York, Dramatists Play Service, 1950.
The Live Wire (also director: produced New York, 1950). New York, Dramatists Play Service, 1951.
The Amazing Adèle, adaptation of a play by Pierre Barillet and Jean-Pierre Grédy (also director: produced Westport, Connecticut, 1950).
Fledermaus, adaptation of the libretto by Haffner and Genée, music by Johann Strauss, lyrics by Howard Dietz (also director: produced New York, 1950).   New York, Boosey and Hawkes, 1950.
The Good Soup, adaptation of a play by Félicien Marceau (also director: produced New York, 1960).
Do Re Mi, music by Jule Styne, lyrics by Betty Comden and Adolph Green, adaptation of his own novel (also director: produced New York, 1960; London, 1961).
A Gift of Time, adaptation of *Death of a Man* by Lael Tucker Wertenbaker (also director: produced New York, 1962). New York, Random House, 1962.
Come on Strong, based on his own stories (also director: produced New York, 1962).   New York, Dramatists Play Service, 1964.
Remembering Mr. Maugham, adaptation of his own book (produced New York, 1966).
Adam's Rib, with Ruth Gordon (screenplay).   New York, Viking Press, 1972.
Dreyfus in Rehearsal, adaptation of a play by Jean-Claude Grumberg (also director: produced New York, 1974). New York, Dramatists Play Service, 1983.
Peccadillo (also director: produced St. Petersburg, Florida, 1985).
Happy   Ending (also   director: produced   Bristol, Pennsylvania, 1989).

Screenplays: *Woman of the Year* (uncredited), 1942; *The More the Merrier* (uncredited), 1943; *From This Day Forward*, with Hugo Butler, 1946; *Born Yesterday* (uncredited), 1950; *It Should Happen to You*, 1953; *The Girl Can't Help It*, with Frank Tashlin and Herbert Baker, 1957; *The Rat Race*, 1960; *High Time*, 1960; *Where It's At*, 1969; *Some Kind of a Nut*, 1969; with Ruth Gordon—*A Double Life*, 1947; *Adam's Rib*, 1949; *The Marrying Kind*, 1952; *Pat and Mike*, 1952.

Television Plays: *An Eye on Emily, Something to Sing About*, and *The He-She Chemistry* (*Mr. Broadway* series), 1963–64; *Josie and Joe; Hardhat and Legs*, with Ruth Gordon, 1980; *Scandal*, 1980.

Novels

Do Re Mi.   Boston, Little Brown, 1955.
Blow Up a Storm.   New York, Random House, 1959; London, Heinemann, 1960.
The Rat Race.   New York, Pocket Books, and London, Ace, 1960.
Where It's At.   New York, New American Library, 1969.
A Thousand Summers.   New York, Doubleday, 1973; London, Hart Davis MacGibbon, 1974.
One Hell of an Actor.   New York, Harper, 1976; London, Barrie and Jenkins, 1979.
Moviola: A Hollywood Saga.   New York, Simon and Schuster, 1979; London, Macmillan, 1980.
Smash.   New   York,   Viking   Press,   1980;   London, Macmillan, 1981.

Cordelia? New York, Arbor House, and London, Severn House, 1982.

Short Stories

Cast of Characters: Stories of Broadway and Hollywood. New York, Atheneum, 1969.

Other

Remembering Mr. Maugham. New York, Atheneum, and London, Hamish Hamilton, 1966.
Tracy and Hepburn: An Intimate Memoir. New York, Viking Press, 1971; London, Angus and Robertson, 1972.
Hollywood: Stars and Starlets, Tycoons and Flesh-Peddlers, Movie-Makers and Moneymakers, Frauds and Geniuses, Hopefuls and Has-Beens, Great Lovers and Sex Symbols. New York, Viking Press, 1974; London, Hart Davis MacGibbon, 1975.
It Takes a Long Time to Become Young. New York, Doubleday, and London, Prior, 1978.
Together Again! The Stories of the Great Hollywood Teams. New York, Doubleday, 1981; as *Great Hollywood Teams*, London, Angus and Robertson, 1982.

*

Theatrical Activities:
Director: **Plays**—assistant director, to George Abbott, of *Three Men on a Horse* by Abbott and John Cecil Holm, New York, 1935, *Boy Meets Girl* by Bella and Sam Spewack, New York, 1935, *Brother Rat* by John Monks, Jr., and Fred F. Finklehoffe, New York, 1936, and *Room Service* by John Murray and Allen Boretz, New York, 1937; director of *Hitch Your Wagon* by Sidney Holloway, New York, 1937; *Too Many Heroes* by Dore Schary, New York, 1937; *The Ragged Path* by Robert E. Sherwood, New York, 1945; *Years Ago* by Ruth Gordon, New York, 1946; *Born Yesterday*, New York, 1946; *How I Wonder* by Donald Ogden Stewart, New York, 1947; *The Leading Lady* by Ruth Gordon, New York, 1948; *The Smile of the World*, New York, 1949; *The Rat Race*, New York, 1949; *The Amazing Adèle*, Westport, Connecticut, 1950; *The Live Wire*, New York, 1950; *Fledermaus*, New York, 1950, 1966; *Into Thin Air* by Chester Erskine, London, 1955; *The Diary of Anne Frank* by Frances Goodrich and Albert Hackett, New York, 1955; *Small War on Murray Hill* by Robert E. Sherwood, New York, 1957; *A Hole in the Head* by Arnold Schulman, New York, 1957; *The Good Soup*, New York, 1960; *Do Re Mi*, New York, 1960, London, 1961; *Sunday in New York* by Norman Krasna, New York, 1961; *A Gift of Time*, New York, 1962; *Come On Strong*, New York, 1962; *Funny Girl* by Isobel Lennart, New York, 1964; *I Was Dancing* by Edwin O'Connor, New York, 1964; *A Very Rich Woman* by Ruth Gordon, New York, 1964; *We Have Always Lived in the Castle* by Hugh Wheeler, New York, 1966; *Remembering Mr. Maugham*, Los Angeles, 1969; *Idiot's Delight* by Robert E. Sherwood, Los Angeles, 1970; *Dreyfus in Rehearsal*, New York, 1974; *Ho! Ho! Ho!* by Ruth Gordon, Stockbridge, Massachusetts, 1976; *Peccadillo*, St. Petersburg, Florida, 1985. **Films**—*A Man to Remember*, 1938; *Next Time I Marry*, 1938; *The Great Man Votes*, 1939; *Bachelor Mother*, 1939; *My Favorite Wife*, 1940; *They Knew What They Wanted*, 1940; *Tom, Dick and Harry*, 1941; *Night Shift*, *Fellow Americans*, and *Ring of Steel* (documentaries), 1942; *Woman of the Year*, 1942; *German Manpower* (documentary), 1943; *Night Stripes* (documentary), 1944; *Battle Stations* (documentary), 1944; *A Salute to France* (*Salut à France*) (documentary), with Jean Renoir, 1944; *The True Glory* (documentary), with Carol Reed, 1945; *Where It's At*, 1969; *Some Kind of Nut*, 1969. **Television**—*Born Yesterday*, 1956.
Actor: **Plays**—Tommy Deal in *Little Ol' Boy* by Albert Bein, New York, 1933; Young Man in *Spring Song* by Bella and Sam Spewack, New York, 1934; Red in *Ladies' Money* by George Abbott, New York, 1934; Al in *Three Men on a Horse* by George Abbott and John Cecil Holm, New York, 1935; Izzy Cohen in *The Body Beautiful* by Robert Rossen, New York, 1935; Green in *Boy Meets Girl* by Bella and Sam Spewack, New York, 1935; Vincent Chenevski in *Star Spangled* by Robert Ardrey, New York, 1936; Garson Kanin in *Remembering Mr. Maugham*, Los Angeles, 1969. **Film**—*Bachelor Mother*, 1939. **Radio**—*March of Times* news re-enactments, *The Goldbergs*, *Aunt Jenny's Real Life Stories*, *The Theatre Guild on the Air*, *Five-Star Final*, *The NBC Theatre*, *The Honeymooners*—*Grace and Eddie*, 1935–37.

*   *   *

Born Yesterday is conventionally cited as Garson Kanin's only commercial and critical success, his only twin birth. The other plays are either dismissed utterly or damned with faint praise. But such a division into the worthwhile and the worthless assumes both that the number of times a writer can earn money and praise matters definitively, and that an accomplishment must be repeatable to be substantial. That *Born Yesterday* is great drama cannot be argued conclusively. But to argue that its quality seems anomalous and, therefore, negligible begs the question rather than answering it. (In this respect, the anomalies are the Arthur Millers and the Neil Simons.) When Harry Brock, king junk dealer and influence-strongman, and his floozie, Billie Dawn, meet Paul Verrall, *New Republic* reporter, in the nation's capital, a dose of culture makes a "dumb blonde" wise and a powerful "low-life" weak. The combined force of the embattled ideals of the American Revolution and the reality of love defeat post-war domestic corruption in the same way that the force of democracy had just defeated Nazi Germany, Fascist Italy, and Imperial Japan. Kanin brings the higher, eminently practical yet optimistic lessons of the war home.

Played today, his play reveals, among other things, that 50 years of *The New Republic* and other "popular" voices have not managed to restrain plutocracy in Washington. *Born Yesterday* can be seen as the post-war theatrical analog of *Mr. Smith Goes to Washington*; we feel a similar vindication of the small people, especially since the United States and the Allies had won a famous victory. But when Ed Devery (a former Assistant U.S. Attorney General gone to seed) toasts the "dumb chumps and all the crazy broads, past, present, and future—who thirst for knowledge—and search for truth. . . . and civilize each other—and make it so tough for sons-of-bitches like you [the bribed Senator Hedges]—and you [Brock]—and me," we are embarrassed at the extreme ironies we hear in the word "broads," and in the phrases "civilize each other," and "make it so tough." That world isn't this world, and the difference obtains as much in the national life and character as in the dramatic literature. Paul and Billie did—and would continue to—"make it tough" for the Brocks and their cronies, and audiences and readers could be assured that the balance of power had shifted *representatively* in *Born Yesterday*. Hitler and Mussolini had been joined by Brock, Devery, and Hedges on the junkpile of history. We know different—and differently. Kanin catches the innocence of a people victorious and generous, a condition of mind almost wholly lacking and a state of the nation almost wholly nostalgic now. *Born Yesterday* is a period piece which reconstitutes American's original brash promise and it does so with real humor and point. After all, Judy Holliday became a *bona fide* star in *Born Yesterday* and her brief, brilliant career can be said to form a counterpart to the brief and brilliant career of the Billie Dawns and Paul Verralls; in retrospect, Kanin's *brilliant* career lasted about as long. The first flush of peace seems to have conferred a hard-won yet easy freedom which the 1950's and 1960's continually wore away. Kanin's highest achievement took place while peace was becoming the Cold War and once that time settled in, his special command of a time of innocence lost its relevance.

As a man of the working theatre, Kanin (actor, director, playwright) knew its special requirements; that he succeeded in Hollywood as well as in New York testifies to *working* knowledge. The popular theatre lives by such versatile, common, and regular talents. Yet acting, directing, and writing for the stage should not be so described, except relatively since almost no one manages to sustain over 40 years a career, let alone careers, in show business. To manage it argues something uncommon and extraordinary. And Kanin managed it. Practical lessons are best learned not from works of genius but from works of the accomplished; the commercial theatre needs productive perseverance of the kind Kanin lived by, not simply in terms of continuity but energy and creativity, too. *Born Yesterday* belongs to the grand tradition of Broadway comedy, just as Kanin belongs four-square to the grand tradition of Broadway.

His later plays such as *The Rat Race* and *A Gift of Time* fall short of *Born Yesterday*'s standard, offering little but schematic plots and clichéd dialogue. By this time, however, Kanin had basically left writing for a stage he had been apparently in process of leaving for some years. He spent much of his effort in directing plays by others and in writing essays and fiction. Judging a dramatist involves assessing the ongoing exigencies of the theatre to which the play is offered. Demands which emphasize commercial viability impose curious restrictions on playwrights. Producing texts of high aesthetic or social merit often seems irreconcilable with producing scripts of high earning potential.

—Thomas Apple

KARNAD, Girish (Raghunath). Indian. Born in Matheran, Maharashtra, 19 May 1938. Educated at Karnataka University, Dharwad, 1954–58, B.A. in mathematics and statistics 1958; Bombay University (Dakshina fellow), 1958–59; Magdalen College, Oxford University (Rhodes scholar), 1960–63, M.A. in philosophy, politics, and economics 1963. Married Saraswathy Ganapathy in 1980; one daughter and one son. Assistant manager, 1963–69, and manager, 1969–70, Oxford University Press, Madras; director, Film and Television Institute of India, Pune, 1974–76; president, Karnataka State Nataka Academy, 1976–78; visiting professor and Fulbright scholar-in-residence, University of Chicago, 1987–88. Member, Ministry of Information and Broadcasting Special Commission on Film, 1976, Indo–U.S. Sub-Commission on Education and Culture, Joint Committee for Films and Broadcasting, 1979, and Ministry of Human Resource Development, Department of Culture Committee on Cultural Dissemination Through Mass Media, 1987; mem-

ber of the governing councils of the National School of Drama, Film, and T.V. Institute of India, Shri Ram Centre for Arts and Culture, and Indian Institute of Mass Communications; Indian co-chair, Indo–U.S. Sub-Commission on Education and Culture, Joint Media Committee, 1984–93, and chair, Sangeet Natak Akademi (National Academy of the Performing Arts), 1988–93. Recipient: Mysore Rajyotsava award, 1970; Homi Bhabha fellowship, for folk theatre, 1970–72; President's gold medal, for film, 1970; National award, for film direction, 1972, for screenplay, 1978; Sangeet Natak Akademi award, 1972; Kamaladevi award, 1972; President's silver medal, for feature film, 1974; Karnataka State award, for acting, 1991; Golden Lotus award, for documentary, 1989. Padma Shri, 1974; Padma Bhushan, 1992. Address: 301 Silver Cascade, Mount Mary Road, Bombay 400 050, India.

PUBLICATIONS

Plays

Yayati (produced in Hindi, Bombay, 1967). Published in Kannada, Dharwad, Manohara Grantha Mala, 1961.
Ma Nishada (broadcast in Kannada, 1963). Published in Kannada, New Delhi, Sahitya Akademi, 1986.
Tughlaq (produced in Urdu, Delhi, 1966; in English, Bombay, 1970; in Kannada, Bangalore, 1971). Published in Kannada, Dharwad, Manohara Grantha Mala, 1964; in English, New Delhi, Oxford University Press, 1972.
Hayavadana (produced in Kannada, Bangalore, 1972; in Hindi, Bombay, 1972; in English, Madras, 1972; London, 1988). Published in Kannada, Dharwad, Manohara Grantha Mala, 1971; in English, Calcutta, Oxford University Press, 1975.
Evam Indrajit, translation of the play by Badal Sircar (produced Bombay, 1985). New Delhi, Oxford University Press, 1974.
Anjumallige (produced in Kannada, Bangalore, 1978). Published in Kannada, Dharwad, Manohara Grantha Mala, 1977.
Hittina Hunja (produced in Hindi as *Bali*, Bombay, 1987). Published in Kannada, Dharwad, Manohara Grantha Mala, 1980.
Nagamandala (produced in Kannada, Bangalore, 1988). Published in Kannada, Dharwad, Manohara Grantha Mala, 1989; in English, New Delhi, Oxford University Press, 1990.
Taledanda (produced in Kannada, Gadag, 1991). Published in Kannada, Dharwad, Manohara Grantha Mala, 1990.

Screenplays: in Kannada: *Samskara*, 1969; *Vamsha Vriksha* with B.V. Karanth, 1971; *D.R. Bendre* (documentary), 1973; *Kaadu*, 1973; *Tabbaliyu Neenade Magane*, with B.V. Karanth, 1977; *Bhumika*, 1977; *Kondura*, 1977; *Ondanondu Kaladalli*, 1978; in Hindi: *Utsav*, 1984; in English: *Kanaka-Purandara* (documentary), 1973; *Kalyug*, 1980; *The Lamp in the Niche 1–2* (documentary), 1989.

Radio Play: *Ma Nishada* (in Kannada), 1963.

*

Theatrical Activities:
Director: **Plays**—with the Madras Players, 1964–69. **Films**—*Vamsha Vriksha*, 1971; *Kaadu*, 1973; *Tabbaliyu Neenade Magane*, with B.V. Karanth, 1977; *Ondanondu Kaladalli*,

1978; *Utsav*, 1984; *Cheluvi* (in Hindi), 1992. **Television**—*Woh Gar* (in Hindi) by Kirtinath Kurtkoti, 1984.
Actor: **Plays**—with the Madras Players, 1964–69; lead roles in *Oedipus Rex* and *Jokumaraswamy*, Bangalore, 1972. **Film**—*Samskara*, 1969; *Vamsha Vriksha*, 1971; also several Hindi feature films. **Television**—several Hindi television films and serials.

Girish Karnad comments:

My generation was the first to come of age after India gained independence. It therefore had to face tensions that had been suppressed but now had come to the surface and demanded resolution: tensions between the country's cultural past and its colonial experience, between the attractions of the Western mode of thought and our own traditions.

In my first play I automatically turned to the *Mahabharata* for source material and have since then continued to borrow from mythology, history, legends, and oral tales. These narrative traditions are still alive in India and widely shared, even in the cities. The problem was to find a theatrical form which could do justice to this inheritance.

Such theatre as existed in our cities in the 1960's, derived from Victorian models and later from naturalistic drama, was clearly inadequate. I turned to the traditional theatre of my childhood, still surviving in small towns and villages, from which the urban playwright felt divorced. The aim was to identify the structure of expectations and conventions about entertainment underlying these forms on which one could base a fresh rapport with the audience.

To my delight, I have found that these various devices—half-curtains, masks, music, mime, the mixing of human and non-human elements—allow for greater technical complexity and hence a more sensitive exploration of contemporary issues. They permit a simultaneous viewing of alternative points of view without which one could not handle the immense contradictions of life in India today.

* * *

Girish Karnad is one of a handful of Indian playwrights who have completely reshaped the form and content of theatre in India since its independence. In doing this they have rejected the British theatrical structures which existed until 1947, and the agit-prop styles which developed with the Independence struggle. This group, writing in their various Indian languages, have drawn from the epics, the religious stories, and the folk tales of India to use them as modern metaphors. Moreover, they have reinterpreted this material by using conventions and structures of Indian classical and folk drama to forge a dynamic new national style.

Of this group, Karnad is the only one to translate his work into English, and the three translated plays give a wonderful insight into his abilities and his vision. He writes in Kannada, the language of his culturally-rich native state, Karnataka, and his plays are translated into many other Indian languages, often before appearing in English. In all his work he treats traditional material as a metaphor, but he teasingly avoids giving a moral message, preferring to open up a challenge for the audience where it must make its own decisions. The seriousness of his dilemmas is without doubt; he is an intellectual observer of his society, but his abilities as a man of the theatre to draw from the clownesque and the traditional relationship of storyteller to audience which is found in Indian folk drama gives a wonderful lightness of touch to his subject matter. Masks, music, dance, and song enrich his verbal structures to create very accessible theatre.

His earliest play in English, *Tughlaq*, was an immediate success in 1970. The play takes place in Delhi in 1327 and follows the reign of the Muslim ruler of Northern India, Sultan Muhammad Tughlaq. But it is not an historical chronicle; it is an allegory of power and idealism as it charts the labyrinthine efforts of Tughlaq to achieve, and be seen to achieve, his ideal liberal society. It follows the trickery, deceit, force, and violence in which he indulges to attain this. The contradiction between his methods and his ideal destroys him.

The opening scene shows a Muslim dhobi paid to pose as a Hindu Brahmin to demonstrate that it is possible for a Hindu to bring a successful case against a Muslim ruler. This character, Aziz, and his friend, Aazam, are like the clowns of the traditional Nataka drama. Aziz, using blatant deceit to achieve success, mirrors Tughlaq's less honest attempts. As similar events occur, we uncover the layers of the play from historical myth to modern allegory, which was conceived in the days after Nehru's era of idealism led to political disillusionment.

Hayavadana, his next play to be translated into English, has a curious genesis. Karnad took the theme from Thomas Mann's *The Transposed Heads*, but Mann had taken the story from the Sanskrit Kathasaritsagara. The central story is that of two close friends, Devadatta and Kapila, the former a refined philosopher and poet, the latter a "man of the body." When Devadatta falls in love with and marries Padmini, Kapila is soon also drawn towards her. They try to solve these complications in an hilarious scene where both men behead themselves and Padmini obtains a boon from a very bored goddess Kali to restore their heads and their lives. In the dark she mistakes the heads and places them on the wrong bodies! The resulting confusion leads to essential questions as to who is her husband and the father of her expected child. Karnad does explore the question of head versus body but goes further to question the tangled identities within a relationship. Finally the two composite men again die, in a duel. None of this is shown as tragic, and to underline this the play is set in the framework of a storyteller who at the beginning meets a sad creature, half-man, half-horse (Hayavadana of the title) who longs to be whole. The storyteller sends him off to a temple. At the end of the play the creature returns and has been made whole, a whole horse!

In *Nagamandala* (subtitled *Play with a Cobra*), Karnad's most recent success in several languages, he mixes two folk tales and presents his material using all the energy of Indian folk theatre. The first story, which again provides the framework for the whole piece, concerns a man in a temple telling us he will die if he cannot stay awake the whole night. A chorus of flames, from the lights which are put out at night, introduce a character called Story, who can only exist if someone will listen to her and pass on the story. The man agrees. Her story is the central portion of the play. It concerns a young woman, Rani, who marries Apanna, a husband who locks her in their new home and returns only to eat at midday. Unhappy, she resorts to a magic potion to make her husband love and stay with her. She cannot go through with it and tips the mixture on an anthill. It is drunk by a king cobra (Naga) who falls in love with her and visits her each night in her husband's shape. She thus sees her husband as a cruel tyrant by day and a caring lover by night and cannot understand. When she is pregnant her husband accuses her of infidelity before the village court, but she chooses trial by plunging her hand into the snake's lair, whilst proclaiming she has touched none of the male sex except her husband and the snake. It is the truth; the cobra does not bite her but spreads its hood over her in view of everyone. It is proclaimed a miracle, and she a goddess incarnate. Her husband is obliged to spend the rest of his life in her service. The cobra dies of sorrow, the story has been told, the man has listened all night and has been saved by hearing the story. And of course it has been passed on to us. It is perhaps the least demanding of the three plays but celebrates the folk idiom and shows how it allows for many ways of seeing. It is this complex seeing which is the effective core of Karnad's work. And he clothes the core with the entertainment implicit in traditional Indian theatre. In this way he challenges us, with entertainment.

—John Martin

————————

KEANE, John B(rendan). Irish. Born in Listowel, County Kerry, 21 July 1928. Educated at Saint Michael's College, Listowel, graduated 1947. Married Mary O'Connor in 1955; three sons and one daughter. Chemist's assistant, 1946–51; street sweeper and furnace operator, Northampton, England, 1952–54. Since 1955 pub owner-operator, Listowel. Weekly columnist Limerick *Leader* and Dublin *Evening Herald*. Since 1973 president, Irish PEN. D. Litt: Trinity College, Dublin, 1977; D.F.A.: Marymount Manhattan College, New York, 1984. Address: 37 William Street, Listowel, County Kerry, Ireland.

PUBLICATIONS

Plays

Sive (produced Listowel, County Kerry, 1959; London, 1960). Dublin, Progress House, 1959; Elgin, Illinois, Performance, n.d.
Sharon's Grave (produced Cork, 1960; New York, 1961; London, 1988). Dublin, Progress House, 1960; Elgin, Illinois, Performance, n.d.
The Highest House on the Mountain (produced Dublin, 1961). Dublin, Progress House, 1961.
Many Young Men of Twenty (produced Cork, 1961; London, 1987). Dublin, Progress House, 1961; in *Seven Irish Plays 1946–1964*, edited by Robert Hogan, Minneapolis, University of Minnesota Press, 1967.
No More in Dust (produced Dublin, 1962).
Hut 42 (produced Dublin, 1963). Dixon, California, Proscenium Press, 1963.
The Man from Clare (produced Cork, 1963). Cork, Mercier Press, 1963.
The Year of the Hiker (produced Cork and Chicago, 1964). Cork, Mercier Press, 1964.
The Field (produced Dublin, 1965; New York, 1976). Cork, Mercier Press, 1967.
The Roses of Tralee (produced Cork, 1966).
The Rain at the End of the Summer (produced Cork, 1967). Cork, Mercier Press, 1967.
Big Maggie (produced Cork, 1969; New York, 1973). Cork, Mercier Press, and New York and London, French, 1969.
Faoiseamh (produced Dublin, 1970). Dublin, Avel Linn, n.d.
The Change in Mame Fadden (produced Cork and Chicago, 1971). Cork, Mercier Press, 1973.
Moll (produced Killarney, County Kerry, 1971; New York, 1977). Cork, Mercier Press, 1971, revised edition, 1991.

The One-Way Ticket (produced Listowel, County Kerry, 1972). Elgin, Illinois, Performance, 1972.
Values: The Spraying of John O'Dovey, Backwater, and The Pure of Heart (produced Cork, 1973; *The Pure of Heart* produced London, 1985). Cork, Mercier Press, 1973.
The Crazy Wall (produced Waterford, 1973). Cork, Mercier Press, 1974.
Matchmaker (produced Dublin, 1975).
The Good Thing (produced Limerick, 1976). Cork, Mercier Press, 1976; Newark, Delaware, Proscenium Press, 1978.
The Buds of Ballybunion (produced Cork, 1979). Cork, Mercier Press, 1979.
The Chastitute (produced Dublin, 1980). Cork, Mercier Press, 1981.
Three Plays (includes *Sive, The Field, Big Maggie*). Cork, Mercier Press, 1990.

Radio Plays: *Barbara Shearing*, 1959; *A Clutch of Duckeggs*, 1970; *The War Crime*, 1976 (UK); *The Talk Specific*, 1979; *The Battle of Ballybooley*, 1980.

Novel

The Bodhrán Makers. Dingle, County Kerry, Brandon, 1986; New York, Vanguard Press, 1988.

Short Stories

Death Be Not Proud and Other Stories. Cork, Mercier Press, 1976.
More Irish Short Stories. Cork, Mercier Press, 1981.
Love Bites and Other Stories. Cork, Mercier Press, 1991.

Verse

The Street and Other Poems. Dublin, Progress House, 1961.

Other

Strong Tea. Cork, Mercier Press, 1963.
Self-Portrait. Cork, Mercier Press, 1964.
Letters of a Successful T.D. [*an Irish Parish Priest, an Irish Publican, a Love-Hungry Farmer, a Matchmaker, an Irish Civic Guard, a Country Postman, an Irish Minister of State*]. Cork, Mercier Press, 8 vols., 1967–78.
The Gentle Art of Matchmaking. Cork, Mercier Press, 1973.
Is the Holy Ghost Really a Kerryman? Cork, Mercier Press, 1976.
Unlawful Sex and Other Testy Matters. Cork, Mercier Press, 1978.
Stories from a Kerry Fireside. Cork, Mercier Press, 1980.
Unusual Irish Careers. Cork, Mercier Press, 1982.
Man of the Triple Name. Dingle, County Kerry, Brandon, 1984.
Owl Sandwiches. Dingle, County Kerry, Brandon, 1985.

*

Bibliography: *Ten Modern Irish Playwrights* by Kimball King, New York, Garland, 1979.

Critical Studies: in *Seven Irish Plays 1946–1964* edited by Robert Hogan, Minneapolis, University of Minnesota Press, 1967, and *After the Irish Renaissance* by Hogan, University of Minnesota Press, 1967, London, Macmillan, 1968; *Fifty Years Young: A Tribute to John B. Keane* edited by John M. Feehan, Cork, Mercier Press, 1979; *Festival Glory in Athlone* by Gus Smith, Dublin, Aherloe, 1979; *The Irish Theatre* by Christopher Fitz-Simon, London, Thames and Hudson, 1983; *Modern Irish Drama 1891–1980* by D. E. S. Maxwell, Cambridge, Cambridge University Press, 1984.

John B. Keane comments:

I regard the playwright of today as a man who must speak for his people, to speak up and to speak out, to say what vested interests, politicians, and big business are afraid to say. I believe that men should be tried for not speaking out when doing so would benefit their fellows and ultimately save lives. Those guilty of not doing so are criminals in every sense of the word. Most men have moral courage, but moral courage without skill to impose one's views is like a steed without a rider. I feel strongly about exploring the ills of modern Ireland and the world, for the anguish of our times is the Frankenstein monster that has been created by our convenient and long silences. We reap this anguish because we have encouraged its growth by pulling the bedclothes over our heads, hoping that the ogres might go away and that dawn might purify all. That is why we are fast approaching a post-Christian era. This is why speaking out early and often is so essential if there is to be a decent quality of life. I look to life as it is lived around me and listen to a language that is living. It would be against my nature to ignore a living speech and a living people. I sometimes feel I would die without these to sustain me. Playwriting is my life. Just as a tree spreads its roots into the earth, I spread my recording impulses around the breasts of my people and often into their very cores. People need to be recorded, to be witnessed; they expect and deserve it. I feel a responsibility to my people, a duty to portray them accurately and with dignity lest they are falsely delineated. There is a lot of love and humour in my plays, for without love and humour there is nothing. Where there is love there is every virtue you care to think of: love begets all that is great and constant. Think of that word "constant." That's what love is. That is the rock to which I have anchored myself, and I think my best is to come.

* * *

In the programme notes to the 1991 Field Day Theatre Company's production of Thomas Kilroy's *The Madame MacAdam Travelling Theatre*, Christopher Murray recalls a story about Anew McMaster, the director of an Irish Shakespearean company which toured Ireland after World War II:

> When the first All-Ireland amateur drama festival took place in Athlone in 1953 McMaster played that same week in Galway (some fifty miles away) to empty houses. On the last night he came forward dressed as King Lear at the end of the play, took out a pair of spectacles and read to the sparse audience a few lines of bitter protest at his desertion. Taking off his spectacles and putting away the text of his address he delivered his parting shot. "I will leave you to the amateurs."

The most detailed record of John B. Keane's early success as a dramatist is recorded in *Festival Glory in Athlone* (1979), Gus Smith's account of 25 years of amateur drama in Ireland. The real value of the book lies in its documentation of the relationships and tensions between a resurgent amateur theatre in Ireland and a moribund professional one during this period. The All-Ireland Drama Festival culminating in Athlone was, and remains in essence, a circuit of competitive festivals. Unlike McMaster, many "professionals" were happy to hire their services as adjudicators for the amateur stage, the broad aim being to provide some kind of basic training in the form of qualified advice from the adjudicators and to make awards for merit, which not infrequently provided the only means for an individual to find confirmation in his or her aspirations to make a career in the theatre. However, the festivals are, by their nature, social occasions. Audiences, spurred on by the spirit of festivity, frequently exceeded those the professional stage could attract, hard pressed as it was by outmoded stages, inadequate facilities, increasingly large wage bills, and a largely unimaginative repertoire. Accordingly, the festivals not infrequently occasioned invidious and unnecessary comparisons.

John B. Keane's first stage success, *Sive*, a tragic story of a young illegitimate girl unwillingly matched to marry an old man and who as a consequence takes her own life, started out as an amateur production of a script originally submitted to, and rejected by, both the Abbey Theatre and RTE (the Irish Radio and Television Service). However, Micheal O hAodha, an executive with RTE, suggested that Keane try it out on an amateur company. Subsequently O hAodha was to adjudicate this production in positive terms as "a carbon copy of an Abbey production." Tomas McAnna, an employee of the Abbey and subsequently its artistic director, was less kind. In his adjudication he intimated that the obvious success of the play was due to the fact that it had been "rewritten in the way suggested by the Abbey Theatre," a point which Keane himself has always vigorously rebutted.

Keane's success with the amateurs was quickly followed by interest from professional companies keen to premiere his work (initially the Southern Theatre Group based in Cork; later, Gemini Productions under the direction of Barry Cassin in Dublin). Nevertheless, his initial outstanding success on the amateur stage has over the years consistently been used by critics to undervalue his achievement. The tendency has been to compare him negatively to other writers: "Geographically, but not imaginatively, the locale [of Keane's plays] is George Fitzmaurice's countryside, no longer so evocative of demonic dolls . . . Keane's Kerry is an indecisive countryside which falls short of wider identifications," as D. E. S. Maxwell wrote in *Modern Irish Drama 1891–1980* (1984). "The language of the early plays shares the North Kerry quirkiness of [Fitzmaurice]" according to Christopher Fitz-Simon's *The Irish Theatre* (1983). Neither of these writers is concerned with Keane's continuing ability, certainly with his major plays, to attract and hold his audiences' attention; and recent interest in his work (mainstage productions at the Abbey Theatre and a film of *The Field*, starring Richard Harris) suggest that the significance of his impact on the Irish stage is due for reappraisal.

Most of Keane's published plays were written between 1959 and 1979; since then, the bulk of his output has been poetry or prose, complemented by a substantial contribution to the developing success of the annual Listowel Writers' Festival. His dialogue is characteristically robust and colourful; his sense of the visual is atypically acute in a dramatic tradition that is so wordbound. His images shift easily along the continuum that links the intimate with the primeval, enabling him to move unselfconsciously from moments of domestic tedium to eruptions of mythic energy and ritual power. Hence his characters, while appearing to be larger than life, are at once familiarly real and strangely archetypal. It is this flexibility of definition in his characterisation that keeps the tendency to burlesque and melodrama in check. In *Sharon's Grave* he creates a grotesque double-headed monster which he dismembers in the last scene. At the point where Dinzie Conlee, the malignant cripple and his hulking brother Jack, on whose back he is forcibly borne, are about to mutilate the girl Trassie, Jack sets Dinzie down to settle a score with Peadar, Trassie's fiancé. The apotheosis of the cripple's impotence is an illustration of Keane's ability to exercise remarkable control over the tone of his plays. Again, Maxwell, writing about *The Field*, rationalises a text rather than the performance on which it is predicated when he observes that while Bull McCabe "emanates a brooding menace . . . the play never brings him, its story, and the telling of its story into 'The Present' . . . aircraft, electricity, television . . . remain trappings." Behind this criticism, typical of most, lies an assumption that Keane, unlike the better known Brian Friel (who frequently deals with the same kind of conjunctions, notably in *Translations*) is unequal to the task of writing for the stage.

James N. Healy, who was to create many of Keane's major roles, suggests that the rural background of the plays is something that is part of the "living present" rather than the recent past. This is more perceptive. Keane is at his most Irish when he is dealing with practical metaphysics; the central theme in *The Field* is the foregrounding of an immutable and atavistic relationship between man and the space he inhabits: "When you'll be gone, Father, to be a Canon . . . and the Sergeant to be a superintendent, Tadgh's children will be milking cows and keeping donkeys out of the ditches . . . and if there's no grass there's the end of me and mine."

Paradoxically, the progress of Keane's drama, while it is nearly always set in the present, records a loss of intensity as it withdraws from the elemental conflicts at the outer reaches of civilisation (*The Highest House on the Mountain*) to the contemporary and sentimental perspective of Ireland from a North of England building site (*Hut 42*, Keane's first Abbey premiere). It is a compliment to his genius to say that in the whole of the canon of his dramatic output he strongly resists the temptation to work to a formula while writing around issues about which he feels best qualified to write. His dialogue is assured; he is strongly attracted to local themes. His declared conventional interests (walking, reading, occasional beer-drinking) are, to a degree, at variance with his observations that little in life can be conventional and realistic at the same time. But with John B. Keane there is, as there was with Brecht, a nagging feeling that he owes his considerable success to being comprehensively misunderstood.

—Paul J.A. Hadfield

KEATLEY, Charlotte. British. Born in London in 1960. Educated at Manchester University, B.A. in drama 1982; University of Leeds, M.A. in theatre arts 1983. Theatre critic for the Yorkshire *Post*, *Times Educational Supplement*, *Plays and Players*, Glasgow *Herald*, 1980–86, and for the *Financial Times*; writer, actor, and director in performance art and community theatre in Leeds and Manchester, 1982–84; teacher in drama in primary and secondary schools around Britain, 1985–86; Judith E. Wilson visiting fellow in English, Cambridge University, 1988–89; lecturer in playwriting and theatre skills, University of London, Royal Court Young People's Theatre and Women's National Touring Theatre, London, University of Birmingham, and Vassar College, Poughkeepsie, New York, 1988–92. Recipient: *Sunday Times* award, for acting, 1980; Manchester *Evening News* award, 1987; George Devine award, 1987; *Plays and Players* award,

1989; Edinburgh Fringe first, for direction, 1991. Agents: Peregrine Whittlesey Agency, 345 East 80th Street, New York, New York 10021, U.S.A.; and Rod Hall, A.P. Watt, 20 John Street, London WC1N 2DL, England.

PUBLICATIONS

Plays

Underneath the Arndale (produced Manchester, 1982).
Dressing for Dinner (produced Leeds, West Yorkshire, 1982).
An Armenian Childhood, with Pete Brooks and Steve Schill (produced Leeds, 1983).
The Legend of Padgate, music by Mark Vibrans (also director: produced Warrington, Cheshire, 1986).
Waiting for Martin (produced Manchester and London, 1987).
My Mother Said I Never Should (produced Manchester, 1987; London, 1989; New York, 1990). London, Methuen, 1988; revised version, London, Methuen, 1989.
You're a Nuisance Aren't You, in *Fears and Miseries of the Third Term*, with others (produced Liverpool and London, 1989).
The Singing Ringing Tree (for children), music by Errollyn Wallen (produced Manchester, 1991).

Radio Plays: *My Mother Said I Never Should*, 1989; *Citizens* series, with others, 1989–90.

Television Play: *Badger* (for children), 1989.

*

Theatrical Activities:
Director: **Plays**—*The Legend of Padgate*, Warrington, Cheshire, 1986; *Autogeddon* by Heathcote Williams, Edinburgh, 1991.

* * *

Charlotte Keatley is one of the youngest playwrights to have a main stage performance at the Royal Court. Her play *My Mother Said I Never Should* received wide-spread acclaim after its run at that theatre. It was compared by reviewers to the work of Sharman MacDonald in its depiction of generations of women learning about themselves and each other. This play is Keatley's primary claim to fame in the theatre, though she has also written *Underneath the Arndale* and *Dressing for Dinner*. In addition, she is known as one of the writers of the television serial *Citizens*. She is currently at work on another full-length play.

In interview in 1989, Charlotte Keatley compared her work to that of the early feminist and alternative theatres. She said: "When you start making plays about your own experiences and in your own language, there is so much to say that the temptation is to say it all quickly and crudely, and so you throw up big signs. After that, you can become more sophisticated and more subtle in the way you say things, which I would say started happening in the late seventies." Keatley's work has developed in a similar way, from the dark humour of *Dressing for Dinner* to the more sophisticated balance of humour and drama which is explored in *My Mother Said I Never Should*.

Keatley performed in her play *Dressing for Dinner*, a visual theatre piece devised and produced by Keatley's own company, The Royale Ballé. The (unpublished) play centred on the image of the feminine woman and her essential item of apparel: the obligatory "little black number." It experimented with images and ideas, movement and gesture, in a form which borrowed both from 1980's feminist thought and the theatrical styles of visual and performance theatre artists such as Clare MacDonald. Visual tricks such as comparing— through innuendo and layered symbolism—the dressing of a woman and the dressing of a fish in aspic were utilized as "shock techniques" which first made the audience laugh, and then made them question the source of their laughter.

Keatley continued to experiment with "shock techniques" in her later work, and most notably in *My Mother Said I Never Should*. But in the latter, the "shock" is primarily directed at audience empathy rather than such radical questioning of audience values and motives. Both *Dressing for Dinner* and *My Mother Said* explore the relations between generations of women and their shared experiences and memories. Yet *My Mother Said I Never Should* is a much more sophisticated piece of writing, and of theatre. It can be studied as a script or literary text, chronicling the lives of four generations of women in war-torn and post-war Britain. It can also be studied in larger terms as a performance of self in society, that is, it can be analyzed as a play informed by feminist politics and theories, played out in the differences between generations of woman.

Keatley, of course, belongs to one of those generations. But her skill as a playwright has transcended the limitations of the author's own perspective, offering instead a play which can be—and often is—seen to be filtered through the perspective of different generations. In fact, as Keatley herself has observed when sitting in the audience of her own play, members of the audience tend to identify with a particular character, and with her generation. The critical conception of "the gaze" is manipulated in terms of generational difference rather than gender difference.

Gender is, though, also a crucial consideration in the play. No male characters appear on stage. Yet unlike many women's plays which are criticized for the lack of men or for "cardboard depictions of men," Keatley seems somehow to have sidestepped that kind of red-herring criticism, partly through humour and partly through a skillful manipulation of audience expectation in regard to the invisible male characters. While no men appear on stage in *My Mother Said I Never Should*, Keatley has incorporated references to male characters in the script: husbands and partners are referred to and seem at times to be present in the wings as the women on stage shout questions and comments to them. This manipulation of audience expectation is used to comic effect, but also has a more serious purpose. In Keatley's words: "I finally decided to do the play without men at all because I wanted to present whole ways of being for women which only happen when the men have gone out of the room."

That introduction to female characters as they appear when no men are present is one of Keatley's greatest contributions. That men seemed to enjoy the plays as well is a tribute to the quality of the writing. With or without male characters, the creation of plays which deal intelligently and evocatively with the performance of gender roles on stage makes Keatley a playwright whose work should be read and seen.

—Lizbeth Goodman

KEEFFE, Barrie (Colin). British. Born in London, 31 October 1945. Educated at East Ham Grammar School, London. Married 1) Dee Truman in 1969 (divorced 1979); 2) the writer Verity Bargate in 1981 (died 1981), two stepsons; 3) Julia Lindsay in 1983. Actor, at Theatre Royal Stratford East, London, 1964, and National Youth Theatre, 3 years; reporter, *Stratford and Newham Express*, London, to 1969, and for news agency to 1975; dramatist-in-residence, Shaw Theatre, London (Thames TV Playwright scheme), 1977, and Royal Shakespeare Company, 1978; associate writer, Theatre Royal Stratford East, 1986–1991. Since 1977 member of the Council, National Youth Theatre; since 1978 member of the Board of Directors, Soho Poly Theatre, London. Recipient: French Critics prize, 1978; Mystery Writers of America Edgar Allan Poe award, for screenplay, 1982. Agent: Lemon, Unna, and Durbridge, 24 Pottery Lane, Holland Park, London W11 4LZ; and, Gilbert Parker, William Morris Agency, 1350 Avenue of the Americas, New York, New York 10019, U.S.A. Address: 110 Annandale Road, London SE10 0JZ, England.

PUBLICATIONS

Plays

Only a Game (produced London, 1973).
A Sight of Glory (produced London, 1975).
Gimme Shelter: Gem, Gotcha, Getaway (*Gem* produced London, 1975; *Gotcha* produced London, 1976; trilogy produced London, 1977; New York, 1978). London, Eyre Methuen, 1977; New York, Grove Press, 1979.
My Girl (produced London, 1975; revised version produced London, 1989). With *Frozen Assets*, London, Methuen, 1989.
A Certain Vincent, with Jules Croiset, adaptation of letters of Vincent Van Gogh (also director: produced Amsterdam and London, 1975).
Scribes (produced Newcastle upon Tyne, 1975; London, 1976; New York, 1977).
Here Comes the Sun (produced London, 1976). Published in *Act 3*, edited by David Self and Ray Speakman, London, Hutchinson, 1979.
Barbarians: A Trilogy: Killing Time, Abide with Me, In the City (*Abide with Me* produced London, 1976; trilogy produced London, 1977). London, Eyre Methuen, 1978.
Up the Truncheon (produced London, 1977).
A Mad World, My Masters (produced London, 1977; San Francisco, 1978; revised version produced London, 1984). London, Eyre Methuen, 1977.
Frozen Assets (produced London and San Francisco, 1978; revised version produced London, 1987). London, Eyre Methuen, 1978.
Sus (produced London, 1979; New York, 1983). London, Eyre Methuen, 1979.
Heaven Scent (broadcast 1979). Published in *Best Radio Plays of 1979*, London, Eyre Methuen, 1980.
Bastard Angel (produced London, 1980). London, Eyre Methuen, 1980.
Black Lear (produced Sheffield, 1980).
She's So Modern (produced Hornchurch, Essex, 1980).
Chorus Girls, music by Ray Davies (produced London, 1981).
A Gentle Spirit, with Jules Croiset, adaptation of a story by Dostoevsky (also director: produced Amsterdam, 1981; London, 1982).
The Long Good Friday (screenplay). London, Methuen, 1984.

Better Times (produced London, 1985).   London, Methuen, 1985.

King of England (produced London, 1988).   With *Bastard Angel*, London, Methuen, 1989.

Not Fade Away (produced London, 1990).   In *Wild Justice, Not Fade Away, Gimme Shelter*, 1990.

Wild Justice (produced London, 1990).   In *Wild Justice, Not Fade Away, Gimme Shelter*, 1990.

Wild Justice, Not Fade Away, Gimme Shelter: Three Plays. London, Methuen, 1990.

Screenplay: *The Long Good Friday*, 1981.

Radio Plays: *Good Old Uncle Jack*, 1975; *Pigeon Skyline*, 1975; *Self Portrait*, 1977; *Heaven Scent*, 1979; *Paradise*, 1989.

Television Plays: *The Substitute*, 1972; *Nipper*, 1977; *Not Quite Cricket*, 1977; *Champions*, 1978; *Hanging Around*, 1978; *Waterloo Sunset*, 1979; *No Excuses* series, 1983; *King*, 1984; *Betty*, 1990.

Recording: *A Certain Vincent*, RCA; *No Excuses*, CBS.

Novels

Gadabout.   London, Longman, 1969.
No Excuses (novelization of his television series).   London, Methuen, 1983.

Other

Editor, *The 1984 Verity Bargate Award Short Plays.* London, Methuen, 1985.
Editor, *The Verity Bargate Award New Plays 1986.*   London, Methuen, 1987.
Editor, *The Verity Bargate Award New Plays 1988.*   London, Methuen, 1987.

*

Theatrical Activities:
Director: **Plays**—*A Certain Vincent*, Amsterdam and London, 1975; *A Gentle Spirit*, Amsterdam, 1981, London, 1982.

*   *   *

In the days when Barrie Keeffe worked for a local newspaper in East London, one of his assignments was the astrology column which, even more than most astrology columns, was a piece of total imagination written under the byline of "Kay Sera." The random assignment of different fates to his readers must have given his employers some indication of his developing dramatic gifts, but it was another assignment which profoundly coloured his future work. At the end of an interview with the pro-censorship campaigner Mary Whitehouse, later to be the recognizable target of his satire, *She's So Modern*, he asked her whom the people were that she professed to speak for. With a metaphorical pat on the head, she replied: "Ordinary, decent people; like you and me." The plays which followed that interview, whether comedies or dramas, frequently troubled Mrs. Whitehouse, particularly when broadcast on television, but Keeffe's explorations of British racism and alienated youth certainly followed his own concerns with decency. What is remarkable, for a writer so very much of his time and place, is how

successful the plays have been in other countries and how they have endured.

Revivals began in the mid 1980's, when Keeffe found that *Frozen Assets*, his play written for the Royal Shakespeare Company in 1978, was being performed and revalued. His radio version of the play, somewhat less profane but no less powerful than the stage version, was being broadcast by the BBC in his own updated adaptation and stage revivals were being scheduled in acknowledgement that the basic story of a Borstal boy on the run in London had survived with its comical cynicism intact. Indeed, the picture the play paints of East London as a community destroyed by property speculation was provided with additional poignancy in the wake of the yuppie invasion of dockland.

Similarly, 1986 had seen revivals of his 1977 trilogy of one-act plays, *Gimme Shelter*, which included the play *Gotcha* about a schoolboy who held his teachers hostage with matches held over the open petrol tank of a motorcycle. The arguments in that play had not dated, nor had the level of resentment he had first measured in schools where pupils were being dumped, unprepared, into a society which could not provide them with jobs. Another apparently topical play, *Sus*, about a black man arrested under the now abolished "sus" law where people could be held by the police on grounds of suspicion alone, has also survived the progress of time and continues to appear in various productions, both in Britain and abroad, though it was very specifically set on the night of Margaret Thatcher's first electoral victory. At the heart of its survival is the recognizable human pain of the man falsely accused of his wife's death.

Despite the continued interest in his early plays, and the undoubted influence of his plays about disaffected British youth, the flood of his stage plays from the 1970's had subsided to a trickle in the mid-1980's. The plays that appeared in the 1980's were notably different from the scripts of the 1970's, as with the short-lived musical he wrote with Ray Davies of The Kinks, *Chorus Girls*, a political entertainment taken from an obscure comedy by Aristophanes, *Thesmophoriazusae*. Similar in some ways to the satirical comedy he wrote in 1977 for the Joint Stock Company, *A Mad World, My Masters* (with the title and the spirit of the free-flowing plot borrowed from the Jacobean writer Thomas Middleton), the play tapped a classical source for a very current inspiration and concerned the kidnapping of Prince Charles by dedicated feminists. Ill-directed, the play had only a local success in London's Theatre Royal, Stratford East, the theatre for which it was designed. None the less it was witty, often uproariously so, with several excellent songs from Davies, and its presentational format marked a breakthrough in Keeffe's technique.

The play which followed four years later, *Better Times*, was another departure, part documentary about East London's historical Poplar Rent Strike and again part East End comedy in the mood of *A Mad World*. Meticulous in its recreation of the courtroom scenes and backroom dramas surrounding an important moment in British socialist history, and admirable for it, the most telling demonstration of Keeffe's talent was in the imaginary scenes with his patented version of an East End Keystone Cop. Though cheered by his East London audiences, the play was received with bemusement by several of his critics. It has often been the wayward force of his comedy which has bewildered reviewers, but the touch of absurdism in his work remains another of the qualities which keeps the apparently topical subject-matter of the plays alive.

Keeffe's work has long benefited from associations with specific companies, beginning with the National Youth Theatre and achieving a major impetus from the late Verity

Bargate's support at London's Soho Poly Theatre. It was in that small venue that both his youth trilogies, *Gimme Shelter* and *Barbarians*, were developed, and something of the claustrophobic power of those pictures of aimless young Londoners can probably be ascribed to their original performance space which he exploited to its full. The trilogies boldly gave his inarticulate and angry young men a rich imagistic language, both abusive and tender, which has been much imitated by younger writers. Keeffe, however, has varied his dramatic offerings much more than his followers and his own influences range visibly from Plautus—the twins in *She's So Modern*—to Chekhov.

Bastard Angel was written for the Royal Shakespeare Company. Belying its own gutsy story of a female rock singer rattling painfully through despair in the mansion which she bought in order to humiliate servants who had humiliated her when she was a young singer, the play took its inspiration from Chekhov's *Platonov* and key images from each of the four acts of the Russian play have been retained. More cataclysmic by far than the Chekhov original, with the rock star entering into a sexual relationship with her own son, the play manages to retain autumnal beauty in the midst of violent events and blasting music. The later television version, *No Excuses*, carried the story further but lacked the focus of the stage version which is a major work.

Throughout the 1980's, he developed a successful continuing relationship with London's Theatre Royal, Stratford East, once the home of Joan Littlewood. A split with the theatre came in 1991, but his work with Philip Hedley there produced two of his best later plays, *My Girl* and *Wild Justice*, both written for the actor Karl Howman.

My Girl is a claustrophobic comedy, highly impassioned and often painful, about the relationship between a social worker and his wife. The constant caring for strangers which is his job seems to deprive him of the devotion appropriate to his heavily pregnant wife and their child, but a crisis is reached when his attraction to a client threatens their marriage. Never simply about the relationship, since the fundamental anxiety concerns Sam's inability to reconcile his own ideals with the stress of his underpaid job, it is none the less a powerful love story. *Wild Justice* is a modern revenge play, triggered by the death of a child and as blackly insistent as any Jacobean revenge tragedy. It contains some of the very best of Keeffe's writing.

With the success of his screenplay *The Long Good Friday*, a film which seized the initiative from American crime movies to mingle East End villainy, the IRA, international crime, and a unique political perspective, Keeffe moved into the rank of writers constantly courted by Hollywood, a not altogether happy arrangement given the tendency of moviemakers to demand their Hollywood version of his vision. Prior to that he had contributed notably to British television, particularly with his audacious comedy, *Waterloo Sunset*, with its portrait of an elderly white woman who walks out on an old folks' home and moves in with a black family in South London. (It later became the stage play *Not Fade Away*.)

His short prize-winning radio play *Heaven Scent*, about crime and perfume, is a model of radio technique and beautifully demonstrates his own gift for characterization and storytelling. Radio also saw the premiere of his epic drama about Robespierre, *Paradise*, a play of great power and historical clarity which recognizes, as few other sources do, the extreme youth of the makers of the French Revolution. Vast in its intention and achievement, the play has yet to find a stage performance.

Adept in all areas of drama, he has also written the novel of *No Excuses*, providing interesting commentary on the intentions of the story; losing, however, the touch of Chekhov which made the original play so effective. With his exuberant language and uninhibited vision of the potential of the stage, his greatest gifts are theatrical—few writers have his ability to create searing images through the speech of their characters.

—Ned Chaillet

KELLY, George (Edward). American. 1887–1974. See 1st edition, 1973.

KEMPINSKI, Tom. British. Born in London, 24 March 1938. Educated at Hall School; Abingdon Grammar School; Cambridge University (open scholar). Married. Actor, 1960–71. Recipient: London Drama Critics award, 1980. Agent: Alan Brodie Representation, 91 Regent Street, London W1R 7TB, England.

PUBLICATIONS

Plays

The Peasants Revolt (produced Essex, 1971).
The English Civil War (produced London, 1972).
Moscow Trials (produced London, 1972).
Pageant of Labour History (4 plays; produced London, 1973).
The Ballad of Robin Hood, with Roger Smith (produced London, 1973).
October, with Roger Smith (produced 1973).
Sell-Out (1931), with Roger Smith, music by Kempinski and Smith (produced London, 1974).
Flashpoint (as Gerrard Thomas) (produced London, 1978).
What about Borneo? (produced London, 1978).
The Workshop, adaptation of a play by Jean-Claude Grumberg (produced London, 1979; as *The Workroom*, produced New Haven, Connecticut, 1982).
Japanese Noh Plays (for children; produced Leicester, 1979).
Mayakovsky, adaptation of a work by Stefan Schütz (produced London, 1979).
Duet for One (produced London, 1980; New York, 1981). London, French, 1981.
Dreyfus, adaptation of the play by Jean-Claude Grumberg (produced London, 1982).
The Beautiful Part of Myself (produced Watford, Hertfordshire, 1983).
Life of Karl Marx, with Roger Smith (produced London, 1984).
Self-Inflicted Wounds (produced Mold, Clwyd, 1985).
Separation (produced London, 1987). London, French, 1989.
Sex Please, We're Italian (produced London, 1991).
A Free Country, adaptation of a play by Jean-Claude Grumberg (produced London, 1991).
When the Past Is Still to Come (produced London, 1992).

Screenplay: *Duet for One*, with Jeremy Lipp and Andrei Konchalovsky, 1987.

*

Tom Kempinski comments:

There are two kinds of oppression in the world: the oppression of one group in society by another, and the oppression of one part of a person by another part of the same person. I write about both kinds, because I have experienced both—and also studied and struggled to change both.

My historical plays are influenced by English radio comedy of the 1950's, and include songs and music which I compose.

My "personal" plays are characterised by attempts to penetrate beneath the surface of people's deeds to their inner, and often concealed motives. These plays are written in a "naturalistic" "style," and—in a country that keeps a stiff upper lip (since 1800?) in order not to show weakness to wogs, niggers, wops, and other human beings which Britain has conquered—are found to be just a touch emotional.

Top people—whether parents or dictators—prefer lies of all kinds, because they invent these lies to maintain their superior status in the world.

* * *

Tom Kempinski writes about strong people under unbearable pressure, charting the process of their bravely resisted but inevitable collapse. Stephanie Abrahams in *Duet for One* is a classical musician struck down by multiple sclerosis and compelled to face a life without the music that has been the centre of it; Isaac Cohen in *Self-Inflicted Wounds* is a dedicated Nazi-hunter who finds his courage faltering when it comes time to publish his research; Carter in *Flashpoint* is a wise-cracking soldier whose method of coping with army routine is tested in a crisis.

Given these outlines, it is not surprising that Kempinski's plays sometimes skirt the edge of soap opera and melodrama. *Duet for One*, which consists entirely of Stephanie's sessions with an overly wise psychologist, follows a predictable emotional outline, at least in part: one knows from the minute she enters bravely denying a psychological problem that she will eventually break down and cry, "I-can-never-never-play-the-the-the-violin again" (it happens at the end of Act 1), just as one can predict that the laconic psychologist will eventually make an eloquent pull-yourself-together speech (Act 2). *Self-Inflicted Wounds* is also a bit schematic in the way that Cohen's affair with a young girl and his own family secrets are twisted back on the main plot to be used against him by his enemies. And the action of *Flashpoint*, which involves an armed soldier going berserk and taking his platoon hostage in an attempt to stop the execution of a deserter, threatens to lose sight of its ideas in the melodramatic action.

But these dangers, not always avoided, are almost inevitable, given Kempinski's determination to find the sources and limits of his protagonists' strength. Notably, the process is not simple or direct, and the discoveries made are complex and sometimes surprising. Stephanie Abrahams does not go from bold defiance to simple despair—that predictable breakdown is only the end of the first act. Kempinski sees that despair is a step, not a conclusion; it is followed by self-denial and self-abasement, as Stephanie tries to convince herself that she doesn't care about her loss of dignity and self-control; by self-deceit, as the fear of losing her husband is raised to deflect the psychologist from deeper probing; and only then by the loss of all defenses and the admission of the very elementary fears that everything else was covering, an

admission that Kempinski sees as the bravest step of all and the basis for hope.

Similarly, Cohen's perplexing hesitancy to publish the damning results of his research is not explained or exposed simply. Each revelation is a little more true than the one before it, but not itself the entire truth. Even at the end, when Cohen admits that he might have deliberately sabotaged himself by giving his enemies the means to discredit him, his reasons are a subtle mixture of weakness and strength, betrayals of his own morality and higher affirmations of it. And Carter is also shown to be more complex than one might first expect: his wise-guy attitude does not keep him from being the strongest participant in the hostage crisis or bar him from sympathy for his weaker comrades. It is only after the crisis is over and he learns how those outside had manipulated both gunman and hostages that Carter momentarily breaks, showing in his sense of betrayal a core of faith in the military that his sneers had hidden.

Kempinski's one attempt at comedy, *Sex Please, We're Italian*, merely proves that his talents do not lie in that area. This would-be romp about townsfolk trying to hide their many sexual peccadillos from a visiting clergyman is leadenly unfunny, without the manic energy or insane internal logic that successful farce demands.

Duet for One remains the strongest of Kempinski's plays, largely because it is such a successful theatrical piece: its effectiveness as a vehicle for a sensitive actress disguises or counterbalances its weaknesses. It is also the most tightly focused of his plays: making the "enemy" a disease frees Kempinski from having to create melodramatic events and also eliminates any potentially distracting political overtones. Like many well-meaning political writers, Kempinski tends to become less controlled and more simplistic the closer he comes to his own passionate convictions. To the extent that *Self-Inflicted Wounds* is about Nazism, *Flashpoint* about the British military presence in Northern Ireland, or *Dreyfus* about anti-semitism, they are at their weakest and most diffuse; Kempinski's strengths are always in the personal dramas.

—Gerald M. Berkowitz

———

KENNA, Peter (Joseph). Australian. 1930–1987. See 4th edition, 1988.

———

KENNEDY, Adrienne (Lita, née Hawkins). American. Born in Pittsburgh, Pennsylvania, 13 September 1931; grew up in Cleveland, Ohio. Educated in Cleveland public schools; Ohio State University, Columbus, B.A. in education 1953; Columbia University, New York, 1954–56. Married Joseph C. Kennedy in 1953 (divorced 1966); two sons. Joined Edward Albee's workshop in 1962. Lecturer in playwriting, Yale University, New Haven, Connecticut, 1972–74, Princeton University, New Jersey, 1977, and Brown University, Providence, Rhode Island, 1979–80; chancellor's distinguished lecturer, University of California, Berkeley, 1986. Member of the Board of Directors, PEN, 1976–77. Recipient: Obie award, 1965; Guggenheim fellowship, 1967; Rockefeller grant, 1967, 1969, 1973; New England Theatre Conference grant; National Endowment for the Arts grant, 1972; CBS-Yale University fellowship, 1973; Creative Artists Public Service grant, 1974. Agent: Bridget Aschenberg, 40 West 57th Street, New York, New York 10019. Address: 325 West 89th Street, New York, New York 10024, U.S.A.

PUBLICATIONS

Plays

Funnyhouse of a Negro (produced New York, 1964; London, 1968).   New York, French, 1969.
The Owl Answers (produced Westport, Connecticut, and New York, 1965).   Included in *Cities in Bezique*, 1969.
A Beast's Story (produced New York, 1965).   Included in *Cities in Bezique*, 1969.
A Rat's Mass (produced Rome, 1966; New York and London, 1970).   Published in *New Black Playwrights*, edited by William Couch, Jr., Baton Rouge, Louisiana State University Press, 1968.
The Lennon Play: In His Own Write, with John Lennon and Victor Spinetti, adaptation of works by Lennon (produced London, 1967; revised version produced London, 1968; Albany, New York, 1969).   London, Cape, 1968; New York, Simon and Schuster, 1969.
A Lesson in Dead Language (produced New York and London, 1968).   Published in *Collision Course*, New York, Random House, 1968.
Boats (produced Los Angeles, 1969).
Sun: A Poem for Malcolm X Inspired by His Murder (produced London, 1969).   Published in *Scripts 1* (New York), November 1971.
Cities in Bezique: 2 One-Act Plays: The Owl Answers and A Beast's Story.   New York, French, 1969.
An Evening with Dead Essex (produced New York, 1973).
A Movie Star Has to Star in Black and White (produced New York, 1976).   Published in *Wordplays 3*, New York, Performing Arts Journal Publications, 1984.
Orestes and Electra (produced New York, 1980).   Included in *In One Act*, 1988.
Black Children's Day (produced Providence, Rhode Island, 1980).
A Lancashire Lad (for children; produced Albany, New York, 1980).
In One Act (includes *Funnyhouse of a Negro*, *The Owl Answers*, *A Lesson in Dead Language*, *A Rat's Mass*, *Sun*, *A Movie Star Has to Star in Black and White*, *Electra*, *Orestes*).   Minneapolis, University of Minnesota Press, 1988.
She Talks and Beethoven: 2 One-Act Plays.   Published in *Antaeus* (New York), no.66, Spring 1991.

Other

People Who Led to My Plays (memoirs). New York, Knopf, 1987.
Deadly Triplets: A Theatre Mystery and Journal. Minneapolis, University of Minnesota Press, 1990.

*

Adrienne Kennedy comments:
    My plays are meant to be states of mind.

* * *

As black power gathered strength in America in the 1960's, the dramatist Adrienne Kennedy, who is black, was discovering more uses for the word Negro. She marks the beginnings of celebratory blackness with *Funnyhouse of a Negro* in which a woman's personal history of miscegenation, rape, and madness inscribes the larger history of black experience in white America, a history that Americans now sanitize and democratize under the rubric "race relations." Kennedy makes no totalizing claims to represent anyone, but the play's motifs resonate sharply in collective history.

In her New York apartment, Kennedy's "Negro-Sarah" enshrines an enormous statue of Queen Victoria and, in the course of the play, splits into a hunchbacked Jesus, the Duchess of Hapsburg, the African liberation leader Patrice Lumumba, and even Queen Victoria—each denoted as "One of Herselves." This is history and identity in a funnyhouse of distorted mirrors whose reflections are as unthinkable in racist America emerging from the 1950's as Sarah herself, child of a light-skinned black woman supposedly raped by her missionary black husband in Africa. Slowly Sarah's incarnations emerge from darkness to narrate bits of the original trauma: the missionary zeal of the father who "wanted the black man to rise from colonialism," the mother who "didn't want him to save the black race and spent her days combing her hair . . . and would not let him touch her in their wedding bed and called him black," the daughter conceived in violence, who rejects the father but resembles him and watches her mother lapse into madness, then death, the remembered sign for which is hair falling out.

Throughout the play, shining hairless skulls appear in dialogue and enacted fantasy until Sarah tries to stifle her father's (and her race's) claim on her by bludgeoning him with an ebony mask. Yet he returns: "He keeps returning forever, coming back ever and keeps coming back forever." Sarah's white friends whose (Victorian) culture "keep [her] from reflecting too much upon the fact that [she is] a Negro" cannot protect her from this returning and recurring repressed racial memory, signified by the repeated sound of knocking and the obsessively repeated images of fallen hair, kinky and straight, on a white pillow; of yellowness, the sickly white color of Sarah's skin; of swarming ravens and of death's-heads. The expressionistic funnyhouse of Sarah's memory defies linear logic. Her father hangs himself—or does not—in two versions of the story, but the last play image shows Sarah herself hanged, reclaimed by the jungle that engulfs the stage. Sarah's split subjectivity bears the scars of Afro-American history; her identification with her mother and murderous repression of her father's culture engage the discourses of feminism and psychoanalysis, and reveal the desire and exclusion embodied in Kennedy's "Negro."

The Owl Answers brilliantly extends these issues through the laminated identities of Kennedy's protagonist, She who is Clara Passmore who is the Virgin Mary who is the Bastard who is the Owl, whose history generates another violently skewed family romance, this time with a poor black mother and the "Richest White Man in the Town." Gradually a story emerges of a bastard daughter of miscegenous union, adopted by the Reverend Passmore, renamed Clara, but who carries her black mother's color and a passion for her white father's culture, "the England of dear Chaucer, Dickens and dearest Shakespeare," whose works she reads as a child in the Passmore library, and later disseminates as a "plain, pallid" schoolteacher in Savannah, Georgia. The glorious fathers of literary history merge with those of Christian myth as God's white dove (associated with Reverend Passmore's preaching) replaces the jungle father's black ravens in *Funnyhouse*. Her black mother called a whore, the adopted Clara identifies with the Virgin Mary, but in a fantasy visit to England the white fathers who have colonized her desire refuse Clara access to St. Paul's where she imagines burying her own white father, and lock her in the Tower of London. Rejected by her father, but unable to bury or repress him, Clara is imprisoned in her own history. In the play's associative logic the Tower is also a New York subway car in which the adult Clara, lost in guilt and rage, picks up a Negro man, introduces herself as Mary, addresses him as God, and tries to stab him.

The surrealistic Tower (dominant white culture) and the High Altar (sacrificial Christianity) are the phallic edifices against which Clara Passmore measures her being. Ultimately she transforms into the screeching Owl, symbol of her black mother and her criminal origins: "The Owl was [my] beginning." Although her adopted status allows her to "pass more," Clara belongs to the owls as she cannot belong to the world of "Buckingham Palace, . . . the Thames at dusk, and Big Ben" or the "Holy Baptist Church . . . on the top of the Holy Hill." Near the end of the Play, Clara kneels to pray: "I call God and the Owl answers."

This summary conveys nothing of Kennedy's surrealistic spectacle: "There is the noise of the train, the sound of moving steel on the track." "The WHITE BIRD's wings should flutter loudly"—a cacophony that should evoke, says Kennedy, "a sense of exploding imprisonment."

Two shorter works, *A Lesson in Dead Language* and *A Rat's Mass*, add new elements of Kennedy's bestiary. In the first Western culture in the form of a Latin lesson and a schoolteacher, costumed from waist up as a White Dog, and Christian doctrine in the form of enormous statues of Jesus, Joseph, Mary, two Wise Men, and a shepherd, instruct and overwhelm seven little girls, whose initiation into menstruation marks them (and their white dresses) as guilty. In *A Rat's Mass* redemptive authority resides in a schoolmate, Rosemary, who refuses to expiate the incestuous crime of Brother and Sister Rat; and the sister goes mad. In this as in all of Kennedy's beautifully crafted plays, cultural exclusion translates into sexual terror and guilt, the signs of "Negro" womanhood.

Funnyhouse of a Negro won an Obie, but Kennedy's work is rarely discussed or performed in the United States.

—Elin Diamond

KESSELMAN, Wendy (Ann). American. Teaching fellow, Bryn Mawr College, Pennsylvania, 1987. Also a composer and songwriter. Recipient: Meet the Composer grant, 1978, 1982; National Endowment for the Arts fellowship, 1979; Sharfman award, 1980; Susan Smith Blackburn prize, 1980; Playbill award, 1980; Guggenheim fellowship, 1982; Ford Foundation grant, 1982; McKnight fellowship, 1985; ASCAP Popular award, for musical theatre, 1992. Agent: George Lane, William Morris Agency, 1350 Avenue of the Americas, New York, New York 10019; and, Jane Annakin, William Morris Agency Ltd., 31–32 Soho Square, London W1V 6AP, England. Address: P.O. Box 680, Wellfleet, Massachusetts 02667, U.S.A.

PUBLICATIONS

Plays

Becca (for children), music and lyrics by Kesselman (produced New York, 1977).   New Orleans, Anchorage Press, 1988.
Maggie Magalita (produced Washington, D.C., 1980; New York, 1986).   New York, French, 1987.
My Sister in This House, music by Kesselman (produced Louisville and New York, 1981; revised version produced Leicester and London, 1987).   New York, French, 1982.
Merry-Go-Round (produced Louisville, 1981; New York, 1983).
I Love You, I Love You Not (one-act version produced Louisville, 1982; New York, 1983; full-length version produced St. Paul, 1986; New York, 1987).   New York, French, 1988.
The Juniper Tree: A Tragic Household Tale, music and lyrics by Kesselman (produced Lenox, Massachusetts, 1982; New York, 1983).   New York, French, 1985.
Cinderella in a Mirror (produced Lenox, Massachusetts, 1987).
The Griffin and the Minor Cannon, music by Mary Rodgers, lyrics by Ellen Fitzhugh (produced Lenox, Massachusetts, 1988).
A Tale of Two Cities, adaptation of the novel by Dickens (produced Louisville, 1992).
The Butcher's Daughter (produced Cleveland, Ohio, 1993).

Fiction (for children)

Franz Tovey and the Rare Animals. New York, Quist, 1968.
Angelita. New York, Hill and Wang, 1970.
Slash: An Alligator's Story. New York, Quist, 1971.
Joey. New York, Lawrence Hill, 1972.
Little Salt. New York, Scholastic Press, 1975.
Time for Jody. New York, Harper, 1975.
Maine Is a Million Miles Away. New York, Scholastic Press, 1976.
Emma. New York, Doubleday, 1980.
There's a Train Going by My Window. New York, Doubleday, 1982; London, Hodder and Stoughton, 1983.
Flick. New York, Harper, 1983.
Sand in My Shoes. Westport, Connecticut, Hyperion, 1993.

*

Critical Study: "Wendy Kesselman: Transcendence and Transformation" by Jay Dickson, in *Harvard Advocate* (Cambridge, Massachusetts), 1986.

Theatrical Activities:
Actor: **Play**—role in *The Juniper Tree*, New York, 1983.

* * *

Already an author of children's books, Wendy Kesselman began her playwriting career with *Becca*, a play ostensibly for a young audience, though older spectators responded to the implicit subtext of parental neglect and a brother's abuse of his sister. Kesselman charms tiny tots with her book, lyrics, and music, particularly the songs for caged animals (parrot, salamander, grasshopper, and bullfrog) and the creatures (rats, Ida the Spider, escaped snake, and witches) who terrify Becca when her bullying brother Jonathan, as a means of controlling her, locks her in the closet. Yet Kesselman teaches as well as entertains: relegated to his room by parents who never appear but by implication both ignore him and dictate his every move, Jonathan mirrors that behavior by neglecting to provide his pets with food and water and tyrannizing his sister, treating her like a toy doll, not a person. He eventually learns to respect others, relinquishes his pets (after Becca tells them they can free themselves), and stops hitting and threatening his sister. Jonathan changes because Becca changes first, finding the courage to put a stop to his dehumanizing treatment, to take control of her own life, and to toss onto the closet floor the long white dress which reduced her to a mere object. The most amazing moment in this startling feminist parable occurs when Becca rebels against her tormentor and it finally dawns on us that she is not a doll.

Becca prefigures Kesselman's later dramas in its use of her own music, its parallels (Becca and the pets) and contrasts (the pets versus the creatures, Becca versus Jonathan), and its themes of loneliness, maturation, violence to soul and body, fear, family relations, control, and courage. Kesselman continues to write about children and adolescents and about gender inequities, while expanding this exploration to include conflicts fueled by disparities of class, age, and culture. Further, she imbues her plays with a feminist sensibility to the ways patriarchal, social, and economic structures stunt women's minds and stifle their souls.

Kesselman's early masterpiece *My Sister in This House* exemplifies the way in which she keeps her viewpoint implicit, never preaching, always dramatizing. She constructs the play in a dazzling series of parallels and contrasts, satirizing life in the drawing room and dining room, while portraying with compassion life in the kitchen and garret. Conversations between the maids and between the mother and daughter for whom they slave frequently intersect, the concerns of each economic class reflecting those of the other. But so great is the social stratification separating them that not until the play's bloody climax do the two sets of women converse across class lines. Instead the Danzards beckon or point or nod or, when the white glove detects dust, scowl. Yet the sisters and the two women who employ them share a common obstacle to their humanity and self-actualization: female existence in a time and place (France in the early 1930's) which permit their sex only a domestic function. Conservative arbiters of conduct require women without men to repress their sexuality as well as their needs for personal and professional fulfillment. While the women in both social strata lead empty lives, at least the sisters provide each other with the tender love and sex missing from their vacuous employers' existence. Yet the young women's inability to control their own economic destinies dooms both them and their bourgeois nemeses, as the impulse towards aggression, though stifled, on both sides builds and builds.

When Jean Genet based *The Maids* on the same horrendous Le Mans double murder committed by incestuous sisters, he wasn't attempting to create sympathetic portraits of the killers, but Kesselman accepts that challenge. She succeeds by depicting impoverished innocents trapped in a claustrophobic world devoid of stimulation, affection, or purpose except for each other's solace. After the mutual enthusiasm of the Danzards and the sisters gives way to suspicion and fear, Madame explodes with a venomous denunciation which guarantees that the sisters will be thrown on the street without references, food, or shelter; this tragedy can end only in the destruction of all four bleak lives.

A prize-winning composer as well as a dramatist, Kesselman has supplied music for most of her texts. By the end of *My Sister*, we're already deeply affected by the play's action, but Kesselman enhances its impact by the recurrence of the musical refrain "Sleep my little sister, sleep." In *The Juniper Tree: A Tragic Household Tale* Kesselman renders the drama's macabre murder, dismemberment, cannibalism, revenge, and resurrection both funnier and more horrifying by describing and enacting events with lovely solos and eerie duets. As usual, Kesselman takes a child's perspective in dramatizing this Grimm's fairy-tale about parental abuse. Both narrating and acting out the plot in the style of story theatre, *The Juniper Tree* portrays the irrational but compulsive murder of a child by (as in her *Cinderella in a Mirror*) a wicked stepmother, who compounds the crime by blaming her own daughter for the boy's death, then cooking him and serving him as soup for supper. Among Kesselman's funny, folksy touches are the men's descriptions of their personal activities, the father's ravenous appetite—gruesomely comic—and the daughter's disgust at her father's gross table manners while he unknowingly devours his son.

Merry-Go-Round, using as music only a title song, considers childhood largely by depicting its outcome in young adults: we see a similar child within each quite different grown-up. The play's structure jumps from present to past, not with flashbacks, but with the adults re-enacting the earlier scenes. After they reconnect with their past selves, their roots, their early powerful bond broken by their parents, and their loneliness after Michael moved away, Daisy and Michael consummate sexually their earlier relationship, coming full circle—as the title suggests. Kesselman keeps all this understated, implicit, subtle, but authentically evokes the feelings engendered by a reunion of former soul mates.

In *Maggie Magalita* Kesselman depicts an immigrant adolescent struggling to win acceptance from her classmates in New York City while responding with embarrassment to her Spanish-speaking grandmother. Eventually their culture clash educates them both, after screaming arguments, sullen rejection, and cruelties to the aging Abuela which correspond to what her tormentors inflicted upon little Magalita before she became Americanized into Maggie. In addition to her characteristic theme of loneliness—Magalita's as well as Abuela's—Kesselman dramatizes such values as respect for those who are different, self-acceptance, and courage when confronting pressures to conform. Although set largely in the family apartment, the episodes shift freely from present to past and among such other locales as the zoo, the seashore, and Maggie's high-school. The playwright visually expresses her protagonist's transformation from Latin American to North American when the teenager dons flashy sunglasses and earrings and a baggy T-shirt bearing a photo of a rock group.

In *I Love You, I Love You Not* the dramatist narrows this confrontation of cultures and generations to its essentials: wilful adolescent Daisy (a favorite name?) and Nana, her grandmother from the Old World. Jewish rather than Hispanic, Daisy (the flower used in playing the ambivalent petal-plucking game of the play's title) actually wants to learn the language of her heritage (in this case German) so as to deprive her parents of the capacity to speak privately in her presence, whereas Nana, a Holocaust survivor, hates the tongue of her persecutors, who killed Nana's sisters and parents. As in *Becca*, Kesselman keeps Daisy's parents offstage, but employs them as a formidable hostile presence. Like this playwright's other domestic dramas, this one also compels our attention to the love/hate relations within a family. While the high-strung teenager spends this weekend in her rites of passage to maturity skirmishing with her grandmother, her parents intrude by telephone as they attempt to remove her from her grandmother's nurturing care. "Care" proves the operative word. Never maudlin—indeed, Daisy proves spoiled, narcissistic, self-indulgent, childish—*I Love You, I Love You Not* dramatizes the volatile but nurturing relationship between an emotionally needy, insecure youngster and the woman who can develop her fragile "Daisy" into hardier stock with survival skills, capable of overcoming her intolerance, guilt, and especially fears.

In the late 1980's Kesselman began work on two more musical plays, each set in France during the Revolution. Both again in some part concern young people, contrast classes, and dramatize events in brief episodes, and each ends with execution by guillotine. In *A Tale of Two Cities* she adapts Dickens' novel, whereas *The Butcher's Daughter* breaks audacious new ground. *A Tale of Two Cities* employs the parallels of Charles and Sydney, young Thérèse and young Lucie, the burning of shoemaking tools and burning the Bastille, Lucie's imprisoned father and then little Lucie's imprisoned father. Kesselman also utilizes flashbacks, building suspense about events we can't fully comprehend when we first observe them, until we grasp how Thérèse Defarge's sister was raped on her wedding day by the Évremondes, who killed her husband, father, and brother. The latter's moving song "Quieting the Frogs" proves one of the best among Kesselman's extraordinary compositions for musical theatre.

The Butcher's Daughter's parallels constitute the play's whole structure, as we follow the destinies of two young women, one adopted by a butcher, the other the daughter of the executioner who decapitates the butcher's daughter at the end, when the executioner's daughter hangs herself. A grandmother lives in each household; images of blood permeate the play, which indicts such male-driven acts as capital punishment and incest. Once more, the world proves pernicious to women of any talent or spirit, so utterly denying them autonomy and equity they cannot survive. Kesselman selects as one of her central figures the pioneer playwright and feminist Olympe de Gouges, and both women's spirits soar. The women interact only twice, for a few wordless but indelible moments. Linking the two protagonists, the street singer Pierrot knows, loves, and celebrates them both—just as Kesselman sings of women young and old, timid and bold, some of the most memorable female characters in contemporary drama.

—Tish Dace

KILROY, Thomas. Irish. Born in Callan, County Kilkenny, 23 September 1934. Educated at Christian Brothers School, Callan; St. Kieran's College, Kilkenny; University College, Dublin, 1953–59, B.A. 1956, higher diploma in education 1957, M.A. in English 1959. Married 1) Patricia Cobey in 1963 (divorced 1980), three sons; 2) Julia Lowell Carlson in 1981. Headmaster, Stratford College, Dublin, 1959–64; visiting lecturer in English, University of Notre Dame, Indiana, 1962–63; visiting professor of English, Vanderbilt University, Nashville, 1964–65; assistant lecturer, Department of Modern English and American Literature, University College, Dublin, 1965–73; lecturer, School of Irish Studies, Dublin, 1972–73. Visiting professor, Sir George Williams University and McGill University, both Montreal, 1973, University College, Galway, 1975–76 and 1979, Dartmouth College, Hanover, New Hampshire, 1976, University College, Dublin,

1977–78, and Bamberg University, West Germany, 1984; Examiner in Modern English, Trinity College, Dublin, and Thomond College, Limerick, 1983. Recipient: *Guardian* prize, for fiction, 1971; Royal Society of Literature Heinemann award, for fiction, 1972; Irish Academy prize, 1972; American-Irish Foundation award, 1974; Arts Council of Ireland bursary, 1976; Bellagio Study Centre grant, 1986; Rockefeller grant, 1986. Fellow, Royal Society of Literature, 1972; member, 1973, and member of the Council, 1979, Irish Academy of Letters; member, Aosdana, 1986. Lives in Kilmaine, Mayo, Ireland. Agent: Casarotto Ramsay Ltd., National House, 60–66 Wardour Street, London W1V 3HP, England.

PUBLICATIONS

Plays

The Death and Resurrection of Mr. Roche (produced Dublin, 1968; London, 1969; New York, 1978). London, Faber, and New York, Grove Press, 1969.
The O'Neill (produced Dublin, 1969).
Tea and Sex and Shakespeare (produced Dublin, 1976).
Talbot's Box (produced Dublin and London, 1977). Dublin, Gallery Press, and Newark, Delaware, Proscenium Press, 1979.
The Seagull, adaptation of a play by Chekhov (produced London, 1981). London, Eyre Methuen, 1981.
Double Cross (produced Derry and London, 1986). London, Faber, 1986.
Ghosts, adaptation of the play by Henrik Ibsen (produced Dublin, 1988).
The Madame MacAdam Travelling Theatre (produced Derry, 1991; New York, 1992). London, Methuen, 1991.

Radio Plays: *The Door*, 1967; *That Man, Bracken*, 1986.

Television Plays: *Farmers*, 1978; *The Black Joker*, 1981.

Novel

The Big Chapel. London, Faber, 1971.

Other

Editor, *Sean O'Casey: A Collection of Critical Essays*. Englewood Cliffs, New Jersey, Prentice Hall, 1975.

*

Bibliography: *Ten Modern Irish Playwrights* by Kimball King, New York, Garland, 1979.

Critical Studies: articles by Christopher Murray, in *Ireland Today* (Dublin), 1982, and by Gerald Dawe, in *Theatre Ireland 3* (Belfast), 1982; "The Fortunate Fall: Two Plays by Thomas Kilroy" by Anthony Roche, in *The Writer and the City* edited by Maurice Harmon, Gerrard's Cross, Buckinghamshire, Smythe, 1984; "A Haunted House: The Theatre of Thomas Kilroy" by Frank McGuinness, in *Irish Theatre Today* edited by Barbara Hayley and Walter Rix, Würzburg, Königshausen & Neumann, 1985; "Thomas Kilroy" by Anthony Roche, in *Post-War Literatures in English: A Lexicon*, Groningen, Netherlands, Noordhoff, 1989.

* * *

Thomas Kilroy is probably best known on both sides of the Atlantic for *The Death and Resurrection of Mr. Roche*, a tragicomedy which demonstrates his flair for funny yet trenchant dialogue in a style reminiscent of O'Casey. In this play, as well as in his historical portraits of Matt Talbot in *Talbot's Box* and William Joyce and Brendan Bracken in *Double Cross*, his characters are strongly defined, and his sense of dramatic structure is adroit. He is quite eclectic in his dramaturgy; his plays have little in common except an apparent rejection of the strong naturalistic tradition of many Abbey playwrights. His first play, *Mr. Roche*, is basically realistic in style, while his second, *The O'Neill*, is a historical work about Owen Roe O'Neill, the Irish opponent of Queen Elizabeth I. *Talbot's Box* is a penetrating psychological study notable for its use of expressionistic devices. *Tea and Sex and Shakespeare* is a thin comedy which teeters on the edge of absurdist theater. *Double Cross* is a curious dramatic diptych, a study of two political opposites who figured prominently in the propaganda battles of England and Germany in World War II. A decade separated a fine adaptation of Chekhov's *The Seagull* from a brilliant updating of Ibsen's *Ghosts*. Kilroy's most recent work, *The Madame MacAdam Travelling Theatre*, is a meditation on acting and the theatre imposed on a humorous account of a down-at-heel company of actors touring rural Eire in the early 1940s. Some of Kilroy's themes are traditionally Irish; others are universal (e.g., the "aloneness" of spiritual isolation, the theatre as a "doubling" of reality).

In *The Death and Resurrection of Mr. Roche* an all-male drinking party seemingly turns tragic when one of the group dies suddenly, or so it appears. Kelley, a mid-thirties civil servant of peasant background, has extended a casual invitation to assorted patrons of Murray's Bar to return to his small, desolate Dublin flat for further drinking. Last to arrive is Mr. Roche, the oldest of the lot and a known homosexual to whom Kelley is openly hostile. After they are even further into their cups, they begin to torment him, and he "dies" suddenly after they have forced him into a cubbyhole of a cellar. While two of the drinkers, Doc and Kevin, are out attempting to dispose of the body, Kelley and Seamus have what is thematically the most significant scene of the play. In an account of a sexual encounter with Roche, Kelley reveals his homosexual tendencies, and Seamus confesses he is trapped in marriage to a girl whose "sameness is beginning to drive me mad." At a carefully chosen moment, Doc and Kevin reappear with a very live Mr. Roche and an explanation that never quite includes how Doc could have pronounced him dead in the first place.

The central theme is the stultifying effect—the spiritual and cultural sterility—that contemporary urban life has had on young Irish men who were able to leave small family farms and villages and make careers in Dublin. They are descendants of the early "peasant play" characters who, unconsciously at least, longed to leave behind the hard life on the land, the narrow provinciality of the village, and the stifling influence of parents and clergy for the headier life of Dublin, England, or America. Kilroy's Irish are cousins to Brian Friel's Gar who leaves the small family business for the United States in *Philadelphia, Here I Come!* The father-son conflict, the Irish generational gap, is well behind Kilroy's characters; they have made their escape and feel lucky. However, they have, as they sadly admit, lost contact with their families. Kelley thinks he has a very good job, and Seamus, with whom he grew up, is proud of being a teacher and, until he thinks about it, is happily married. Their reu-

nion over several pints becomes a melancholy soul-baring in which Seamus admits that he is not just attempting to recapture the pleasure of their last reunion two years ago. "Twas more like I was trying to get back to ten years ago. What was healthy then is sick now. . . . Why haven't you changed even a little? . . . You're in the same situation as you were when you came to Dublin—" Kelley angrily insists that he's "the success of my family," while Seamus concludes sadly that he's "as happy as ever I'll be." Their conversation concludes with Kelley's unwelcome revelation that he had, in fact, invited Roche to the apartment before and that once they had had sexual relations.

Homosexuality is Kilroy's second theme, along with Irish hypocrisy. Kelley's hostile attitude toward Roche is made clear quite early to underline his hypocrisy: "I won't let the likes of him over that step. . . ." After Roche's "death," Kelley is terrified that their acquaintance will come out: "Prison I can take. It's the bad name that leaves me wake at the knees." However, Roche is, in Kevin's words, "not a bad auld skin." In fact, Roche speaks for Kilroy in a plea for sympathy and understanding for all his characters, for homosexuality is here the playwright's metaphor for "aloneness." Through Roche, Kilroy strongly condemns their lifestyle, their drinking bouts to assuage loneliness and uncertainty, the waste of their lives. When Kelley condescendingly rejects Roche's sympathy, the homosexual makes a plea for all of them: "We all need sympathy now and again. . . . There's little comfort as it is, in this world. . . . Who am I or you to deny someone the single object which makes each day bearable?" Writing in 1968, Irving Wardle praised *Mr. Roche* as "the most important new work ever presented by the Dublin Theatre Festival."

Tea and Sex and Shakespeare was Kilroy's contribution to the 1976 Dublin Festival and has not been published. It involves the fantasies of a blocked writer named Brien. In one fruitless day spent in his Dublin attic workroom, he plays out his dreams involving his wife, Elmina, who is, in fact, at work; his neighbor, Sylvester, who finds him a nuisance but fancies his wife; his comic landlady and her nubile daughter, Deirdre, to whom he is tutor; and finally Mummy and Daddy, his in-laws, who might have escaped from a short play by Edward Albee. Brien's dream world centers around dramatic suicides and seductions, with dialogue quoted or paraphrased from Shakespeare, the subject of his tutorials with the buxom Deirdre. The plot and characters are exceedingly thin. The play ends on a poignantly serious note as the long-suffering wife remonstrates with Brien: "You build your absurd jokes around you like a high wall so that no one can reach you," she charges. Brien responds that he is only trying to say "I'm alone." Her reply—"And who in this world isn't alone?"—reiterates the theme of spiritual isolation that Kilroy mined far more effectively and dramatically in *Talbot's Box*. This comedy of the frustrated, haunted creative person is only moderately successful.

Talbot's Box rarely matches the humor of *Mr. Roche*, but in its central character there is a highly effective study of religious zealotry, a subject the dramatist had dealt with in his novel *The Big Chapel* a few years earlier. Matt Talbot was a Dublin workman and mystic who died in 1925, and as early as 1931 a movement was underway for his canonization. On his death, it was discovered that for many years he had been wearing heavy chains and cords around his body, arms, and legs and that some of the rusty chains had sunk into the flesh. The play is an inquiry into the psyche of Talbot. The action comes through four actors who portray a variety of different roles, with costume changes made on stage. The playwright touches a number of social bases: for example, Talbot's role in the Transport Strike of 1913 sets his unique vision against the background of labor troubles, just as his encounters with the Church demonstrate that in his zealous humiliation of the flesh he is as unmanageable as Shaw's St. Joan. In the key scene of the play, Talbot tells the priest, "I knows the darkness! . . . 'Tis in every man, woman 'n child born inta the world." For him, "the darkness is Gawd," and "there's no peace till ya walk through it inta some kinda light." The humiliation of the flesh is "only the way for me to know the darkness of me own body." In Kilroy's own words *Talbot's Box* is a play "about aloneness, its cost to the person and the kind of courage required to sustain it."

Kilroy's next work for the stage was a highly effective adaptation of Chekhov's *The Seagull*. Now set on an estate in the West of Ireland, this transplanted Russian classic shows no signs of a sea-change in its passage from one predominantly rural, 19th-century culture to another.

Double Cross is concerned with the problem of "doubleness or doubling, . . . the way things repeat themselves in life or attract their opposites." This is the "basis of acting or role-playing," Kilroy writes in an introduction, as well as the impetus behind "the universal desire . . . to make up and tell stories, thereby inventing a reality which may reflect everyday life but is still distinct from it." *Double Cross* attempts "to move along the lines from role-playing and fiction-making to the act of political treason." William Joyce, born in Brooklyn in 1906, arrived in England (via Ireland and Northern Ireland) in 1921. By 1933 he had become a member of Sir Oswald Mosley's British Union of Fascists. In 1939 he went to Germany where he joined German Radio. Before the year was out, he had become the infamous Lord Haw-Haw, probably Goebbels's best known radio commentator and apologist for the Nazi regime. Kilroy finds Joyce's "opposite" in Brendan Bracken, born 1901 in Tipperary, who by dint of systematic cultivation of the rich, famous, aristocratic, and politically powerful, rose, by 1939, to be Churchill's Parliamentary Private Secretary at the Admiralty and, by 1941, to be Minister of Information, whose responsibility it was to counteract the effect of Lord Haw-Haw's broadcasts.

Double Cross is divided into two halves: "The Bracken Play: London" and "The Joyce Play: Berlin." The first scene of "the Bracken Play" introduces both Joyce and Bracken (played by the same actor) as well as an actor and actress who both narrate and play a variety of characters, most notably Churchill and Lord Beaverbrook and the two women in the lives of Joyce and Bracken. Structurally, each play is made up of a series of free-flowing scenes which chronicle, in the case of Bracken, his political maneuverings and his affair with a woman called Popsie, while still allowing him to look back at his modest beginnings in Ireland and ahead to his own death (by cancer) in 1958. Joyce's "Berlin Play" focuses on his relations with his second wife, Margaret, and an interview (after his capture by the Allies) with Lord Beaverbrook. He was hanged as a war criminal in 1946.

For Kilroy this is a play about "two men who invented themselves," Bracken as an actor on the English political scene of the late 1930's and the war years, and Joyce as "a creator of fictions" driven to an invented self by a "deep, angry impatience," with life. Both came of unremarkable Irish backgrounds; both invented lives for themselves in English society; both tried to imitate his oppressor, Joyce by his anti-British propaganda, and Bracken by his very "English" attitude toward Ireland. Each of the plays is a tour de force for both the dramatist and the actor, with the first being the better of the two. Yet, as Irving Wardle wrote in the London *Times*, Kilroy's idea that "social play-acting in some way leads to fascism and treason" is not effectively projected.

However, the play remains a fascinating study of "doubles/opposites." Kilroy followed *Double Cross* with a radio play on the same subject—or the Bracken half of it—called *That Man, Bracken*, which is an effective distillation of material used in the earlier work.

Kilroy's adaptation of Ibsen's *Ghosts* is a highly effective updating, justifiably received with enthusiasm in its first production at the 1988 Dublin Theatre Festival. The scene is now a provincial Irish town, but most importantly, the time is moved up to the late 1980's. Certain changes, which are both natural and effective, make the play very contemporary. First, Oliver Aylward (like Ibsen's Oswald Alving) has come home to die; he is in the final stages of AIDS. Second, there is a hint that his father introduced him to drugs (probably marijuana) in his childhood (Kilroy's variation on Oswald's story of how, when a small boy, he became ill by smoking his father's pipe). Third, Oliver's rejection of the "ghosts" theme —that the fathers' sins are visited on the children—is more forceful, coupled as it is with his assertion of personal responsibility. Fourth, the euthanasia theme is far more acceptable now than it would have been for much of the life of Ibsen's play, and since Helen Aylward (Ibsen's Helene Alving) seems a more "liberated" woman than her original, there is reason to suppose that Oliver won't be allowed to suffer very long. All four characters—even Father Manning (Pastor Manders)—are drawn with greater precision than in most translations of Ibsen. Kilroy's excoriation of the social hypocrisies surrounding marriage and the family are more trenchant in this adaptation: "There is more evil propagated inside family life than in any other human organisation that I know of," says Oliver. Finally, even the image/symbol of the sun is employed with more resonance in the final moment of the play. This adaptation is so timely and effective that a modern classic becomes a brand-new play.

Kilroy's most recent work for the stage, *The Madame MacAdam Travelling Theatre*, is a highly original play which generated a negative critical response at the 1991 Dublin Theatre Festival. This is not a play that is strong in either plot (quite complex) or characterization (certainly adequate). Set in a very small town in rural Ireland during the Emergency (the World War II years when the country was neutral), *Madame MacAdam* concerns a small, third-rate British travelling theatre company which, by the merest chance, winds up in the Free State. They are depleted in number (only five), and they have run out of petrol. Unable to move on, they become involved in: a crooked greyhound race (through which they hope to obtain petrol); the search for a missing child; the seduction of a local teenager by a young actor in the company; and somewhat incidentally, a performance of an Irish melodrama dealing with the 18th-century patriot Robert Emmet and his love, Sarah Curran.

Interweaving these various strands of plot, Kilroy sometimes satirizes, sometimes parodies, as he employs the most hackneyed materials of melodrama in a setting that only occasionally hints at realism (e.g., the drone of war planes overhead which may be either German or English). As Madame MacAdam says in her first speech: "Tonight we offer the usual fare. A love story. A lost child. Villainy at large. While in the background the drums of war. And at the end, that frail salvation of the final curtain. What else is there?"

Kilroy employs projected scene headings of a melodramatic nature which evoke silent film subtitles but which also recall the scene captions employed (to quite a different end) in Brechtian theater. Their function is, of course, not only to acknowledge and so mitigate the episodic nature of the plot but also to gently tease the banal ingredients. Madame herself begins the play with a speech (above) that finally seems directed more to the audience in the real theater than to the rural Irish who watch Robert Emmet court Sarah.

The various plot strands form a context for a running commentary (by several characters) on the acting profession and the nature and function of the theater. This is really what the play is about: the actor's artistic urge for expression; his triumph in making an audience "believe"; the ephemeral nature of his achievement; the healing and transforming power of theater; "the greatest mystery of all"—becoming another person; "human error and human frailty . . . and the second-rate" as the foundation for "the miracle of theatre." Madame (thought to be based on the famous actor-manager of that period, Anew McMaster) is comically pompous, but she can also be wisely succinct: "To keep at bay the principle of chaos. That is what is urgent." Although not necessarily his best, *Madame MacAdam* is Kilroy's most complex and demanding play.

—Gene A. Barnett

KINGSLEY, Sidney. American. Born in 1906.
See 2nd edition, 1977.

KOCH, Kenneth. American. Born in Cincinnati, Ohio, 27 February 1925. Educated at Harvard University, Cambridge, Massachusetts, A.B. 1948; Columbia University, New York, M.A. 1953, Ph.D. 1959. Served in the United States Army, 1943–46. Married Mary Janice Elwood in 1955; one daughter. Lecturer in English, Rutgers University, New Brunswick, New Jersey, 1953–54, 1955–56, 1957–58, and Brooklyn College, 1957–59; director of the Poetry Workshop, New School for Social Research, New York, 1958–66. Lecturer, 1959–61, assistant professor, 1962–66, associate professor, 1966–71, and since 1971 professor of English, Columbia University. Associated with *Locus Solus* magazine, Lans-en-Vercors, France, 1960–62. Recipient: Fulbright fellowship, 1950, 1978; Guggenheim fellowship, 1961; National Endowment for the Arts grant, 1966; Ingram Merrill Foundation fellowship, 1969; Harbison award, for teaching, 1970; Frank O'Hara prize (*Poetry*, Chicago), 1973; American Academy award, 1976; American Academy of Arts and Letters award of merit, 1987. Address: Department of English, 414 Hamilton Hall, Columbia University, New York, New York 10027, U.S.A.

PUBLICATIONS

Plays

Bertha, music by Ned Rorem (produced New York, 1959). Included in *Bertha and Other Plays*, 1966.
The Election (also director: produced New York, 1960). Included in *A Change of Hearts*, 1973.
Pericles (produced New York, 1960). Included in *Bertha and Other Plays*, 1966.
George Washington Crossing the Delaware (in *3 x 3*, produced New York, 1962; produced separately, London, 1983). Included in *Bertha and Other Plays*, 1966.
The Construction of Boston (produced New York, 1962). Included in *Bertha and Other Plays*, 1966.
Guinevere; or, The Death of the Kangaroo (produced New York, 1964). Included in *Bertha and Other Plays*, 1966.
The Tinguely Machine Mystery; or, The Love Suicides at Kaluka (also co-director: produced New York, 1965). Included in *A Change of Hearts*, 1973.
Bertha and Other Plays (includes *Pericles, George Washington Crossing the Delaware, The Construction of Boston, Guinevere; or, The Death of the Kangaroo, The Gold Standard, The Return of Yellowmay, The Revolt of the Giant Animals, The Building of Florence, Angelica, The Merry Stones, The Academic Murders, Easter, The Lost Feed, Mexico, Coil Supreme*). New York, Grove Press, 1966.
The Gold Standard (produced New York, 1969). Included in *Bertha and Other Plays*, 1966.
The Moon Balloon (produced New York, 1969). Included in *A Change of Hearts*, 1973.
The Artist, music by Paul Reif, adaptation of the poem "The Artist" by Koch (produced New York, 1972). Poem included in *Thank You and Other Poems*, 1962.
A Little Light (produced Amagansett, New York, 1972).
A Change of Hearts: Plays, Films, and Other Dramatic Works 1951–1971 (includes the contents of *Bertha and Other Plays*, and *A Change of Hearts*; *E. Kology*; *The Election*; *The Tinguely Machine Mystery*; *The Moon Balloon*; *Without Kinship*; *Ten Films: Because, The Color Game, Mountains and Electricity, Sheep Harbor, Oval Gold, Moby Dick, L'Ecole Normale, The Cemetery, The Scotty Dog*, and *The Apple*; *Youth*; and *The Enchantment*). New York, Random House, 1973.
A Change of Hearts, music by David Hollister (produced New York, 1985). Included in *A Change of Hearts* (collection), 1973.
Rooster Redivivus (produced Garnerville, New York, 1975).
The Art of Love, adaptation of a poem by Mike Nussbaum (produced Chicago, 1976).
The Red Robins, adaptation of his own novel (produced New York, 1978). New York, Performing Arts Journal Publications, 1979.
The New Diana (produced New York, 1984).
Popeye among the Polar Bears (produced New York, 1986).
One Thousand Avant-Garde Plays (produced New York, 1987). New York, Knopf, 1988.
The Construction of Boston, music by Scott Wheeler (produced Boston, 1989).
Some Avant-Garde Plays (produced Portland, Maine, 1990).

Screenplays: *The Scotty Dog*, 1967; *The Apple*, 1968.

Novel

The Red Robins. New York, Random House, 1975.

Short Stories

Interlocking Lives, with Alex Katz. New York, Kulchur Press, 1970.
Hotel Lambosa and Other Stories. Minneapolis, Coffee House Press, 1993.

Verse

Poems. New York, Tibor de Nagy, 1953.
Ko; or, A Season on Earth. New York, Grove Press, 1960.

Permanently. New York, Tiber Press, 1960.

Thank You and Other Poems. New York, Grove Press, 1962.

Poems from 1952 and 1953. Los Angeles, Black Sparrow Press, 1968.

When the Sun Tries to Go On. Los Angeles, Black Sparrow Press, 1969.

Sleeping with Women. Los Angeles, Black Sparrow Press, 1969.

The Pleasures of Peace and Other Poems. New York, Grove Press, 1969.

Penguin Modern Poets 24, with Kenward Elmslie and James Schuyler. London, Penguin, 1973.

The Art of Love. New York, Random House, 1975.

The Duplications. New York, Random House, 1977.

The Burning Mystery of Anna in 1951. New York, Random House, 1979.

From the Air. London, Taranman, 1979.

Days and Nights. New York, Random House, 1982.

Selected Poems 1950–1982. New York, Random House, 1985.

On the Edge. New York, Viking, 1986.

Seasons on Earth. New York, Viking, 1987.

Selected Poems. Manchester, Carcanet, 1991.

Other

John Ashbery and Kenneth Koch (A Conversation). Tucson, Interview Press, 1965(?).

Wishes, Lies, and Dreams: Teaching Children to Write Poetry. New York, Random House, 1970.

Rose, Where Did You Get That Red? Teaching Great Poetry to Children. New York, Random House, 1973.

I Never Told Anybody: Teaching Poetry Writing in a Nursing Home. New York, Random House, 1977.

Editor, with Kate Farrell, *Sleeping on the Wing: An Anthology of Modern Poetry, with Essays on Reading and Writing*. New York, Random House, 1981.

Editor, with Kate Farrell, *Talking to the Sun: An Illustrated Anthology of Poems for Young People*. New York, Holt Rinehart, 1985; London, Viking Kestrel, 1986.

*

Theatrical Activities:
Director: **Plays**—*The Election*, New York, 1960; *The Tinguely Machine Mystery* (co-director, with Remy Charlip), New York, 1965.

* * *

Kenneth Koch is a genuine man of letters, though that epithet seems inappropriate for a writer whose natural instincts are comic and parodic. In addition to writing much first-rate poetry and some striking fiction, he has been one of America's best teachers of writing—not only inspiring several promising younger poets, but also popularizing the idea of poetry writing in elementary education. His book *Wishes, Lies, and Dreams* details his own experience in the New York City public schools, and thus establishes a pedagogical example that is currently imitated all over the United States. Koch has also written short plays over the past three decades, most of which originated as responses to his personal experience as a graduate student of literature, a college professor, a serious poet, and a participant in the New York art scene. Perhaps because of their occasional inspiration, many of

these shorter works remained too attached to their original circumstances to be presented again. His second collection, *A Change of Hearts*, includes several new pieces, all of which are typically Kochian, none particularly better than his past work.

On one hand, Koch is a bemused absurdist and a giggler, incapable of taking anything too seriously, whose plays exploit situations and/or subjects for their available humor. On the other, he is a "New York School" poet capable of extraordinary acoherent (as distinct from incoherent) writing, such as the marvelous nonsense of these concluding lines from his early play, *Pericles*:

> And we stood there with pure roots
> In silence in violence one two one two
> Will you please go through that again
> The organ's orgasm and the aspirin tablet's speechless
>   spasm.

In structure, his plays tend to be collections of related sketches, strung together in sequences of varying duration, allowing imaginative leaps between the scenes. The best also reveal his debt, both as playwright and as poet, to the French surrealists and dadaists.

Bertha and Other Plays collects most of Koch's early works in chronological order. The very best, *George Washington Crossing the Delaware*, originated as a response to Larry Rivers's painting of the same title (and the play is appropriately dedicated to the artist). Koch's compressed historical play ridicules several kinds of clichés: the myths of American history, the language of politicians, war films, military strategies, patriotism, and much else. The theme of Koch's multiple burlesques, here and elsewhere, is that the accepted familiar versions are no more credible than his comic rewritings. The play also reveals Koch's love of Apollinaire's great poem *Zone* (1918) by scrambling space and time. The British general refers at one point to "the stately bison," which did not enter popular mythology until the 19th-century and certainly could not be seen on the East Coast; and the play takes place in "Alpine, New Jersey," which is nowhere near the Delaware River.

In the ten short-short scenes of his earlier mini-epic, *Bertha*, whose text runs less than ten pages, Queen Bertha of Norway uses power to assuage her evident madness, attacks Scotland only to halt at the frontier, shoots lovers for their sins, only to win the confidence, nonetheless, of both her armies and their captives. (The historical source of this burlesque is less obvious than for *George Washington*, but several possibilities come to mind.) Koch's book also includes *Guinevere*, an early work with some marvelous nonsense writing; and "Six Improvisational Plays," four of which are prose texts that suggest a performance (much like a script for a "happening"); and the book closes with scenes from *Angelica*, an opera about 19th-century French poetry that was written for the American composer Virgil Thomson but never performed.

Koch's more recent plays are likewise filled with marvelous moments. In *The New Diana*, essentially a satire of the myth of poets and their muses, he has live turkeys appear, speaking indigenous language: CAGED TURKEY: Mishiki wai now-uga gan! Ish tang. TURKEY ON TABLE: Nai shi mai ghee itan, korega. *Popeye among the Polar Bears*, likewise a series of vignettes, has the wit and representational freedom we've come to associate with Koch's verse plays. *The Red Robins* is, by contrast, an adaptation of Koch's sole novel, published a few years before; it differs from other Koch theater in having considerably longer speeches.

In the mid-1980's he developed a working relationship with

Barbara Vann and her colleagues at the Medicine Show, a New York Off-Broadway theater, which produced an operatic version of *A Change of Hearts* (from his second collection).

Whereas Koch is clearly a major American poet, is he yet a major playwright? His dramatic texts are unique in the ways that all major work is unique. They are radical enough for Ruby Cohn to write (in *New American Dramatists 1960–1980*, 1982), "I find the plays of poet Kenneth Koch, which I have never seen performed, too childish to examine in a book intended for adults." Such dismissal would not occur unless Koch's texts took risks with theatrical language and yet, to my senses, they don't take enough risks within their premises and don't sustain their innovations to sufficient length. There is nothing in Koch's theater equal to his two book-length poems, *When the Sun Tries to Go On* (written in 1953, but not published until 1969) and *Ko; or, A Season on Earth*—but symptoms of such ambition abound in his work. It should also be noted that Koch, like his poetic colleagues John Ashbery and Frank O'Hara (both of whom also wrote plays), belongs to the counter-tradition of American playwriting—a theater of poets and novelists that emphasizes not naturalism but fantasy; not character but circumstance; not events but essence.

—Richard Kostelanetz

KONDOLEON, Harry. American. Born in New York City, 26 February 1955. Educated at Hamilton College, Clinton, New York (Bradley Playwriting prize, 4 times), 1974–77, B.A. 1977; Yale University, New Haven, Connecticut (Kazan award, 1979, 1980), M.F.A. 1981. Member, playwrights and directors unit, Actors Studio, New York, 1978–80, and Manhattan Theatre Club, 1982–84. Instructor in playwriting, New School for Social Research, 1983–84, and Columbia University, 1985–87, both New York. Recipient: International Institute of Education fellowship, 1977; Oppenheimer award, 1983; Obie award, 1983; New York Foundation for the Arts grant, 1984; National Endowment for the Arts grant, 1985. Agent: George Lane, William Morris Agency, 1350 Avenue of the Americas, New York, New York 10019, U.S.A.

PUBLICATIONS

Plays

The Cote d'Azur Triangle (produced New York, 1980). New York, Vincent FitzGerald, 1985.
The Brides, music by Gary S. Fagin (also director: produced Stockbridge, Massachusetts, 1980; as *Disrobing the Bride*, also director: produced New York, 1981). Published in *Wordplays 2*, New York, Performing Arts Journal Publications, 1982.
Rococo (produced New Haven, Connecticut, 1981).
Andrea Rescued (produced New York, 1982). Montclair, New Jersey, Caliban Press, 1987.
Self Torture and Strenuous Exercise (produced New York, 1982). Published in *The Best Short Plays 1984*, edited by Ramon Delgado, Radnor, Pennsylvania, Chilton, 1984.

Slacks and Tops (produced New York, 1983). New York, Dramatists Play Service, 1983.
Christmas on Mars (produced New York, 1983). New York, Dramatists Play Service, 1983.
The Vampires (produced Seattle, 1984; also director: produced New York, 1984). New York, Dramatists Play Service, 1984.
Linda Her, and The Fairy Garden (produced New York, 1984). New York, Dramatists Play Service, 1985.
Anteroom (produced New York, 1985). New York, Dramatists Play Service, 1985.
Play Yourself (produced Norfolk, Virginia, 1988).
The Poet's Corner (produced New York, 1988).
Zero Positive (produced New York, 1988). New York, Dramatists Play Service, 1989.
Love Diatribe (produced Seattle, 1990).

Television Play: *Clara Toil*, 1982.

Novel

The Whore of Tjampuan. New York, Performing Arts Journal Publications, 1987.

Verse

The Death of Understanding. Montclair, New Jersey, Caliban Press, 1986.

*

Theatrical Activities:
Director: **Plays**—*The Brides*, Stockbridge, Massachusetts, 1980; *Disrobing the Bride*, New York, 1981; *The Vampires*, New York, 1984; *Rich Relations* by David Henry Hwang, New York, 1986.

* * *

With just a handful of plays, Harry Kondoleon has mapped out a territory where the brittle wit of high comedy of manners and the breakneck plot-twists of farce fuse with the primal fears, monstrous egotism, and logic of dreams. There, the bedrock of social existence—loving partnerships, family life, the company of friends—are depicted as barely preferable to purgatory. There is no suggestion that these are bourgeois constraints. The elemental world—as represented by children (dead and alive) and fairies—is viewed as damaged and damaging. No one is innocent in this world. Salvation is not a possibility. It is a measure of Kondoleon's unique—one is tempted to say warped—perspective that all this is presented as hilarious.

A voice out of bedlam wailing of love and loss, to the formal rhythm of the tango: this is Screamin' Jay Hawkins's rendition of "I Put a Spell on You." This song is integral to *The Vampires* (but could serve as anthem to any Kondoleon play). Zivia, a zombie 13-year-old, plays it as she wanders around her aunt and uncle's chic home, mainlining heroin and wondering what happened to her brother. Dispatching her to an ashram only creates new problems. Meanwhile, her elders are establishing aberrant and obnoxious behaviour as normative. Particularly notable is Uncle Ian, who has taken to sleeping during the day and biting his wife in the neck at night.

Linda Her is set in a sparse bedroom on a humid night in a summer cottage upstate somewhere. Carol walks out on her sleeping husband, his daughter, her best friend. She does this because Linda Her, the most popular girl in her husband's nursery class, died. Some years ago. ". . . I picture her so clearly. This very beautiful, bright girl, who everyone likes, with her whole life ahead of her and then one day many years later boom you find out she doesn't exist anymore—isn't that scary?" asks Carol. And goes.

Linda Her is the curtain raiser and complement to *The Fairy Garden*. The stark bedroom is replaced with a lush garden and the ornate lives of its inhabitants. Mimi and Roman are men and lovers and best friends with Dagny who is married to Boris, but he is old and ugly and she wants to live with her boyfriend The Mechanic. So Dagny cuts off Boris's head. Luckily a fairy appears who restores Boris's head to his shoulders and elopes with him. (The Fairy, it should be noted, is more fond of diamonds than Zsa Zsa Gabor and charges for wishes granted.) Mimi leaves Roman for Dagny which leaves The Mechanic to seduce Roman except that Roman prefers the agony of being alone to the pain of being dependent and vulnerable.

This is soap opera taken to demented and dislocating extremes. Everyone acts out of boredom, malice, and self-interest, communicating only to feed and confirm their obsessive urges. "I thought Boris was kind of cute in a boyish innocent kind of way, and he'd be fun to kiss and hold for a few minutes," the Fairy tells Roman while predicting that Mimi and Dagny—who have torn Roman's world apart—will be together, "A week, two weeks, maybe even a month." Kondoleon takes groups at crisis point, but though the group fragments and realigns, no change occurs. The pace merely accelerates.

When asked his wish, Roman (Kondoleon's most fully realized character) replies, "I want the world to disappear," and—in a remarkable visual coup—the Fairy (kind of) obliges. Like Carol's flight into the unknown or Ian's vampirism, Roman is yearning for a state of otherness, in a world where death—or at least oblivion—is preferable to life suffused with loss.

This does not sound like the stuff of comedy. Yet there has been no playwright this side of Joe Orton who relishes the awfulness of people in the way Kondoleon does. This mordant delight is contagious. There is also the vicarious thrill of observing characters totally unfettered by propriety. Best of all there is the dialogue, where the barbed wisecrack and the hysterical outburst attain new heights of elegance and wit. With all this to delight in, it is a shame that there is a tinge of misogyny. For no apparent reason, the female characters are even more horrendous than the male.

Kondoleon's outlandish vision is usually taken as satirical but could equally be his perception of reality. This ambiguity only serves to make the plays more complex and interesting. Like the creature in *Alien*, Kondoleon has burst forth, spewing the entrails of American domestic comedy in his wake. He is the most arresting playwright at work in America today.

—Joss Bennathan

KOPIT, Arthur (Lee). American. Born in New York City, 10 May 1937. Educated at Lawrence High School, New York, graduated 1955; Harvard University, Cambridge, Massachusetts, A.B. (cum laude) 1959 (Phi Beta Kappa). Married to Leslie Ann Garis; two sons and one daughter.

Playwright-in-residence, Wesleyan University, Middletown, Connecticut, 1975–76; CBS fellow, 1976–77, adjunct professor of playwriting, 1977–80, Yale University, New Haven, Connecticut. Since 1981 adjunct professor of playwriting, City College, New York. Since 1982 Council member, Dramatists Guild. Recipient: Shaw Travelling fellowship, 1959; Vernon Rice award, 1962; Outer Circle award, 1962; Guggenheim fellowship, 1967; Rockefeller grant, 1968, 1977; American Academy award, 1971; National Endowment for the Arts grant, 1974; Wesleyan University Center for the Humanities fellowship, 1974; Italia prize, for radio play, 1979; Tony award, 1982. Lives in Connecticut. Agent: Audrey Wood, International Creative Management, 40 West 57th Street, New York, New York 10019, U.S.A.

PUBLICATIONS

Plays

The Questioning of Nick (produced Cambridge, Massachusetts, 1957; New York, 1974; London, 1981). Included in *The Day the Whores Came Out to Play Tennis and Other Plays*, 1965.

Gemini (produced Cambridge, Massachusetts, 1957).

Don Juan in Texas, with Wally Lawrence (produced Cambridge, Massachusetts, 1957).

On the Runway of Life, You Never Know What's Coming Off Next (produced Cambridge, Massachusetts, 1957).

Across the River and into the Jungle (produced Cambridge, Massachusetts, 1958).

To Dwell in a Place of Strangers, Act 1 published in *Harvard Advocate* (Cambridge, Massachusetts), May 1958.

Aubade (produced Cambridge, Massachusetts, 1958).

Sing to Me Through Open Windows (produced Cambridge, Massachusetts, 1959; revised version produced New York, 1965; London, 1976). Included in *The Day the Whores Came Out to Play Tennis and Other Plays*, 1965.

Oh Dad, Poor Dad, Mamma's Hung You in the Closet and I'm Feelin' So Sad: A Pseudoclassical Tragifarce in a Bastard French Tradition (produced Cambridge, Massachusetts, 1960; London, 1961; New York, 1962). New York, Hill and Wang, 1960; London, Methuen, 1962.

Mhil'daim (produced New York, 1963).

Asylum; or, What the Gentlemen Are Up To, And As for the Ladies (produced New York, 1963; *And As for the Ladies* produced, as *Chamber Music*, London, 1971). *Chamber Music* published in *The Day the Whores Came Out to Play Tennis and Other Plays*, 1965.

The Conquest of Everest (produced New York, 1964; London, 1980). Included in *The Day the Whores Came Out to Play Tennis and Other Plays*, 1965.

The Hero (produced New York, 1964; London, 1972). Included in *The Day the Whores Came Out to Play Tennis and Other Plays*, 1965.

The Day the Whores Came Out to Play Tennis (produced Cambridge, Massachusetts, 1964; New York, 1965). Included in *The Day the Whores Came Out to Play Tennis and Other Plays*, 1965.

The Day the Whores Came Out to Play Tennis and Other Plays. New York, Hill and Wang, 1965; as *Chamber Music and Other Plays*, London, Methuen, 1969.

Indians (produced London, 1968; Washington, D.C., and New York, 1969). New York, Hill and Wang, 1969; London, Methuen, 1970.

An Incident in the Park, in *Pardon Me, Sir, But Is My Eye Hurting Your Elbow?*, edited by Bob Booker and George Foster. New York, Geis, 1968.

What's Happened to the Thorne's House (produced Peru, Vermont, 1972).

Louisiana Territory; or, Lewis and Clark—Lost and Found (also director: produced Middletown, Connecticut, 1975).

Secrets of the Rich (produced Waterford, Connecticut, 1976). New York, Hill and Wang, 1978.

Wings (broadcast 1977; produced New Haven, Connecticut, and New York, 1978; London, 1979). New York, Hill and Wang, 1978; London, Eyre Methuen, 1979.

Nine (book), music and lyrics by Maury Yeston, from an adaptation by Mario Fratti of the screenplay *8½* by Federico Fellini (produced Waterford, Connecticut, 1981; New York, 1982). New York, French, 1983.

Good Help Is Hard to Find (produced New York, 1981). New York, French, 1982.

Ghosts, adaptation of a play by Ibsen (produced New York, 1982; Southampton, 1986). New York, French, 1984.

End of the World (produced New York, 1984; as *The Assignment*, produced Southampton, 1985). New York, Hill and Wang, and London, French, 1984.

Bone-the-Fish (produced Louisville, Kentucky, 1989; revised version as *The Road to Nirvana*, produced New York, 1991). New York, Hill and Wang, 1991.

Phantom, music and lyrics by Maury Yeston (produced Houston, 1991).

Radio Play: *Wings*, 1977.

Television Plays: *The Conquest of Television*, 1966; *Promontory Point Revisited*, 1969; *Starstruck*, 1979; *Hands*, 1987; *Hands of a Stranger* series; *Phantom of the Opera* series; *In a Child's Name*.

*

Bibliography: *Ten Modern American Playwrights* by Kimball King, New York, Garland, 1982.

Critical Study: *Sam Shepard, Arthur Kopit, and the Off Broadway Theater* by Doris Auerbach, Boston, Twayne, 1982.

Theatrical Activities:
Director: **Plays**—*Oh Dad, Poor Dad, Mamma's Hung You in the Closet and I'm Feelin' So Sad*, Paris, 1963; *Louisiana Territory*, Middletown, Connecticut, 1975. **Television**—*The Questioning of Nick*, 1959.

*   *   *

"Do I exaggerate?" asks Michael Trent in his first speech in *End of the World*. "Of course. That is my method. I am a playwright." The line is a comic one which becomes ironic in the face of a theme—the prospect of global annihilation—which turns even the grandest theatrical exaggeration into austere understatement. Out of context, the words provide a suitable description of the way Arthur Kopit works.

At 23, fresh out of Harvard, Kopit escaped—or appeared to escape—the cocoon of university production when *Oh Dad, Poor Dad, Mamma's Hung You in the Closet and I'm Feelin' So Sad* was published by a house that specializes in serious drama and went on to production in London and New York. A fashionable success, it established Kopit as a dramatist, but it also saddled him with the label "undergraduate playwright" which stayed with him long after the playfulness of *Oh Dad* had given way to the mixed-genre method that marks his best and most complex plays. One reason the

epithet stuck is that the work that immediately followed *Oh Dad* lacked the flash of that play and offered little substance in consolation. *The Day the Whores Came Out to Play Tennis and Other Plays*, which contained some of his student work along with his post-*Oh Dad* efforts, seemed to confirm the critics who saw him simply as a clever young man noodling around.

Such a judgment is far too dismissive. Although some of *Oh Dad*'s games—the parody references to Tennessee Williams, for instance—seem too cute in retrospect, it is an early indication of the dramatic virtues that have become increasingly apparent in Kopit's work: a facility with language, an ear for the clichés of art and life, an eye for the effective stage image (the waltz scene in which Madame Rosepettle breaks Commodore Roseabove, for instance), a strategic use of caricature, the talent for being funny about a subject that is not at all comic. All of these are in evidence in *Oh Dad* and all of them are in the service of a serious theme (or one that seemed serious in 1960)—the emasculation of the American male by the too protective mother, the iron-maiden temptress and the little girl as seducer.

In an interview in *Mademoiselle* (August 1962), Kopit said, "Comedy is a very powerful tool . . . You take the most serious thing you can think of and treat it as comically as you can." Although he invoked Shaw, *Oh Dad* is the immediate reference. Since then, he has thought of more serious things —war, death, nuclear destruction—and has treated them seriously. And comically, as *Indians* and *End of the World* indicate. The Bantam edition of *Indians* (1971) prints a long interview with John Lahr in which Kopit identifies his play as a response to "the madness of our involvement in Vietnam," but he chose to approach the subject obliquely, going back to the eviction of the American Indian from his land. The play shows the distance between official words and deeds, the power of platitude and the way in which myths are made and used. The central figure is Buffalo Bill, who begins as a friend of the Indians and ends—a star of his own show—as an apologist for slaughter. The play moves back and forth between comic and serious scenes, from the broad farce of the play within the play and the cartoon Ol' Time President to the powerful accusatory ending in which the Wild West Show is invaded by the dead Indians. For some, the funny scenes fit uncomfortably with the solemn subject matter, but they are not simply entertaining decoration. The comedy is thematic. The disastrous production of the Ned Buntline melodrama at the White House is both an instance of the creation of myth and a critique of it.

End of the World is a similar fusion of genres. It concerns a playwright who is commissioned to write a play about the dangers of nuclear proliferation—as Kopit was, in fact—and finds that he can only do so by writing a play about a playwright who . . . The parody private-eye frame of the play (the playwright as detective), the agents' lunch at the Russian Tea Room and the three interviews in which the rationale of nuclear stockpiling and scenarios of destruction are presented as comic turns are all central to the play's assumption that there are personal, artistic, and official ways of not facing up to the impending horror. What Michael Trent learns in the play is that all the nuclear strategists know the situation is hopeless but do not believe what they know, and that he was chosen to write the play because, like the men he interviews, he has an attraction to evil and destruction. A painful and funny play, it provides no solution, only an insistence on the probability of catastrophe and, unlike the conventional post-bomb melodrama, no promise of rebirth.

If *Indians* and *End of the World* share dramatic method, *Wings* is an indication of Kopit's unpredictability. There are funny lines in the play, but it is primarily a lyric exploration of death. It is about a woman who suffers a stroke, struggles to make her fragmented speech fit her still coherent thoughts and, after a second stroke, becomes eloquent as she sees herself flying into the unknown. A wing-walker in her youth, her profession/art provides the main metaphor for her final sense of exhilarating discovery. The play evokes both the concerned narrowness of medicine's perception of the woman and the imagination that continues to carry her above her stammering exasperation with herself and those around her. It is an indication—along with *Indians* and *End of the World* —that Kopit is wing-walking far above the bravura flight of *Oh Dad.*

—Gerald Weales

———

KOPS, Bernard. British. Born in London, 28 November 1926. Educated in London elementary schools to age 13. Married Erica Gordon in 1956; four children. Has worked as a docker, chef, salesman, waiter, lift man, and barrow boy. Writer-in-residence, London Borough of Hounslow, 1980–82; lecturer in drama, Spiro Institute, 1985–86, and various educational authorities, 1989–90. Writer-in-residence, Polka Theatre, London, 1991–92. Recipient: Arts Council bursary 1957, 1979, 1985, 1990, 1991; C. Day Lewis fellowship, 1981–83. Agent: David Higham Associates, 5–8 Lower John Street, London W1R 4HA. Address: 35 Canfield Gardens, Flat 1, London N.W.6, England.

PUBLICATIONS

Plays

The Hamlet of Stepney Green (produced Oxford, London, and New York, 1958). London, Evans, 1959.
Goodbye World (produced Guildford, Surrey, 1959).
Change for the Angel (produced London, 1960).
The Dream of Peter Mann (produced Edinburgh, 1960). London, Penguin, 1960.
Stray Cats and Empty Bottles (produced Cambridge, 1961; London, 1967).
Enter Solly Gold, music by Stanley Myers (produced Wellingborough, Northamptonshire, and Los Angeles, 1962; London, 1970). Published in *Satan, Socialites, and Solly Gold: Three New Plays from England*, New York, Coward McCann, 1961; in *Four Plays*, 1964.
Home Sweet Honeycomb (broadcast 1962). Included in *Four Plays*, 1964.
The Lemmings (broadcast 1963). Included in *Four Plays*, 1964.
Four Plays (includes *The Hamlet of Stepney Green, Enter Solly Gold, Home Sweet Honeycomb, The Lemmings*). London, MacGibbon and Kee, 1964.
The Boy Who Wouldn't Play Jesus (for children; produced London, 1965). Published in *Eight Plays: Book 1*, edited by Malcolm Stuart Fellows, London, Cassell, 1965.
David, It Is Getting Dark (produced Rennes, France, 1970). Paris, Gallimard, 1970.
Moss (televised 1975; produced London, 1991).
It's a Lovely Day Tomorrow, with John Goldschmidt (televised 1975; produced London, 1976).

More Out Than In (produced on tour and London, 1980).
Ezra (produced London, 1981).
Simon at Midnight (broadcast 1982; produced London, 1985).
Some of These Days (produced London, 1990; as *Sophie! Last of the Red Hot Mamas*, produced London, 1990).
Playing Sinatra (produced Croydon, Surrey, 1991; London, 1992).
Androcles and the Lion (for children; produced London, 1992).
Dreams of Anne Frank (for children; produced London, 1992).
Who Shall I Be Tomorrow? (for children; produced London, 1992).

Radio Plays: *Home Sweet Honeycomb*, 1962; *The Lemmings*, 1963; *Born in Israel*, 1963; *The Dark Ages*, 1964; *Israel: The Immigrant*, 1964; *Bournemouth Nights*, 1979; *I Grow Old, I Grow Old*, 1979; *Over the Rainbow*, 1980; *Simon at Midnight*, 1982; *Trotsky Was My Father*, 1984; *More Out Than In*, 1985; *Kafe Kropotkin*, 1988; *Colour Blind*, 1989; *Congress in Manchester*, 1990; *The Ghost Child*, 1991; *Soho Nights*, 1992; *Sailing with Homer*, 1992.

Television Plays: *I Want to Go Home*, 1963; *The Lost Years of Brian Hooper*, 1967; *Alexander the Greatest*, 1971; *Just One Kid*, 1974; *Why the Geese Shrieked*, and *The Boy Philosopher*, from stories by Isaac Bashevis Singer, 1974; *It's a Lovely Day Tomorrow*, with John Goldschmidt, 1975; *Moss*, 1975; *Rocky Marciano Is Dead*, 1976; *Night Kids*, 1983; *The Survivor* series, 1991–92.

Novels

Awake for Mourning. London, MacGibbon and Kee, 1958.
Motorbike. London, New English Library, 1962.
Yes from No-Man's Land. London, MacGibbon and Kee, 1965; New York, Coward McCann, 1966.
The Dissent of Dominick Shapiro. London, MacGibbon and Kee, 1966; New York, Coward McCann, 1967.
By the Waters of Whitechapel. London, Bodley Head, 1969; New York, Norton, 1970.
The Passionate Past of Gloria Gaye. London, Secker and Warburg, 1971; New York, Norton, 1972.
Settle Down Simon Katz. London, Secker and Warburg, 1973.
Partners. London, Secker and Warburg, 1975.
On Margate Sands. London, Secker and Warburg, 1978.

Verse

Poems. London, Bell and Baker Press, 1955.
Poems and Songs. Northwood, Middlesex, Scorpion Press, 1958.
An Anemone for Antigone. Lowestoft, Suffolk, Scorpion Press, 1959.
Erica, I Want to Read You Something. Lowestoft, Suffolk, Scorpion Press, and New York, Walker, 1967.
For the Record. London, Secker and Warburg, 1971.
Barricades in West Hampstead. London, Hearing Eye, 1988.

Other

The World Is a Wedding (autobiography). London, MacGibbon and Kee, 1963; New York, Coward McCann, 1964.

Neither Your Honey nor Your Sting: An Offbeat History of the Jews. London, Robson, 1985.

Editor, *Poetry Hounslow.* London, Hounslow Civic Centre, 1981.

*

Manuscript Collections: University of Texas, Austin; Indiana University, Bloomington.

* * *

Bernard Kops's work is informed by tension between the despair—not for himself, but for humanity—from which suicide beckons, and a redeeming joy of life. Contradictions inform such poems as "Shalom Bomb," "Sorry for the Noise—We're Dancing," and "First Poem," which injoins "let's dance upon the desolation." Despite his clarity of vision about the mess we're making of the world and the death which awaits us—necessarily as individuals, with increasing probability collectively as well—Kops's celebratory rejoinder sets to dancing the feet of those high-spirited people who populate his novels and poems and plays.

Although occasionally mislabeled a kitchen-sink realist, Kops writes neither gritty nor cozy domestic drama. More often presentational than representational, offering parables upon human nature, his plays are theatrical poetry employing language—in its rhythms, rhymes, word play, and word choice—and conflicts not so much contemporary as timeless.

Unlike other "poetic" playwrights, however, Kops creates not a rarefied atmosphere but robust crackpots, energetic con-artists and their gullible targets, and colorful characters whose values he satirizes even as he nudges them towards reform and affirmation of life. A writer poised between tears and laughter, Kops has increasingly emphasized palpable passion; of late he leaves spectators more often touched than chuckling.

Kops frequently depicts old people made anxious by mortality, yet he emphasizes the imperative to live. Although such plays as *Just One Kid, Change for the Angel, Goodbye World,* and *It's a Lovely Day Tomorrow* don't flinch from death snatching people prematurely or tempting them to end their own lives, Kops holds up those characters who harbor a death wish as negative examples not to be emulated. Thus Danny Todd's initial respect for independent lives in *Home Sweet Honeycomb* is commendable, and his ultimate embrace of the firing squad which killed his brother signifies his dehumanization. Sam Levy and Peter Mann both learn through their skirmishes with death to embrace life. Appreciating only on his death bed that he's let life slip by, Sam in *The Hamlet of Stepney Green* returns as a ghost to inspire love of life in his son. Peter Mann grows from a lad convinced nothing's worth living for to exuberance about life. An anti-nuclear and anti-war play, *The Dream of Peter Mann* makes a compelling argument against mass destruction; life is worth living. The remarkable black comedy *The Lemmings* likewise carries in its criticism of suicide implicit affirmation. After Norman and Iris follow their parents into the water, the sound of seagulls and sea devastates us because they should have lived.

Frequently Kops dramatizes means of surviving bereavement or failure. Moss chooses life in the face of grief for his beloved grandson. Moss survives by taking up painting and giving away his money, while Harry of *Rocky Marciano Is Dead* maintains his independence by nurturing the potential of a black boxer. *The Lost Years of Brian Hooper* and *Simon at Midnight* likewise demonstrate the efficacy of hopes and dreams in combating futility and fear of death; without them, life is meaningless.

Repeatedly interfering with these characters' happiness are their wealth and/or greed. The miser Moss has agonized over the loss of his sweet-shop profits to thieving kids; his salvation lies in divesting himself of his fortune. Sam Levy and Peter Mann have been distracted from life's beauty by pursuit of riches from pickled-herring or shrouds. The successful right-wing writer in *David, It Is Getting Dark* is driven so far as to plagiarize the work of a Jewish writer living in penury. The title character of *Enter Solly Gold*, as he fleeces a family of vulgar snobs, releases them from materialism to enjoyment of life. *The Boy Who Wouldn't Play Jesus* dramatizes a Christmas lesson about giving which turns the boy into a social activist. Distressed that Christianity "hasn't really happened yet," he appeals to the cast members' consciences and cancels the nativity play. As long as children are starving, Jesus cannot be born.

For many years Kops's work displayed ambivalence towards women. Although occasionally rapturous about romantic love, Kops gives David Levy and Peter Mann traditional women who want nothing in life but to sacrifice themselves for their mates. His men most often are hen-pecked or neglected or part of a bickering couple in a marriage not exactly made in heaven. His sons fall victim to overbearing mothers who smother them or even—in *Home Sweet Honeycomb* and *The Lemmings*—send them to their deaths. Such stereotypes of domineering mothers and controlling wives have, however, given way in several recent Kops plays to more fully developed women. The runaway in *Night Kids* who resorts to prostitution to survive inspires compassion both when she's on the streets and as she returns to her indifferent parents. Leading female characters in *Sophie! Last of the Red Hot Mamas* (about Sophie Tucker) and *Kafe Kropotkin* (about an anarchist collective) even show signs of autonomy and competence. Sandra of *Playing Sinatra* survives and escapes, leaving the two men, her friend and her symbiotic sibling, trapped in the creepy South London house obsessing over Sinatra recordings instead of living. The female character in *Who Shall I Be Tomorrow?*, on the other hand, mines herself more deeply in pathetic poverty.

Kops's masterpiece *Ezra* attempts to reconcile Ezra Pound's poetic genius with the fascism and anti-semitism he espoused. Playful in tone and fluid in structure, *Ezra* dramatizes Pound's postwar imprisonment. Mocking his situation and those who accuse him of treason with snatches of pop songs, Pound chats with Mussolini and Vivaldi. Not a one-dimensional villain, Pound argues in his defense: "A poet listens to his own voice." Implicitly, Kops condemns the confiscation of Pound's literary manuscripts as evidence and defends his right to free expression. After his release, troubled by his former views, Pound goes to the Ghetto Vecchio in Venice, where he appeals to the Jews there to vouch for him. As he is answered only by the wind, Pound cannot understand why the houses are empty. Kops appears to forgive the poet's complicity in genocide out of a humanity which the poet cannot discover in himself until too late, when Pound reaches a chilling anagnorisis, a recognition that those Jews he loved have perished because of policies he championed.

—Tish Dace

KOUTOUKAS, H. M. American. Born in Endicott, New York, 4 June 1947. Educated at Harpur College, Binghamton, New York; Maria Ley-Piscator Dramatic Workshop, New School for Social Research, New York, 1962–65; Universalist Life Church, Modesto, California, Ph.D. Associated with the Electric Circus and other theatre groups in New York; founder Chamber Theatre Group, New York; member, the Ridiculous Theatrical Company, New York. Recipient: Obie award, 1966; National Arts Club award; Professional Theatre Wing award. Agent: Nino Karlweis, 250 East 65th Street, New York, New York 10021. Address: c/o Judson Church, Washington Square, New York, New York 10012, U.S.A.

PUBLICATIONS

Plays

The Last Triangle (produced New York, 1965).
Tidy Passions; or, Kill, Kaleidoscope, Kill (produced New York, 1965). Published in *More Plays from Off-Off-Broadway*, edited by Michael T. Smith, Indianapolis, Bobbs Merrill, 1972.
All Day for a Dollar (produced New York, 1966).
Medea (produced New York, 1966).
Only a Countess (produced New York, 1966).
A Letter from Colette (also director: produced New York, 1966).
Pomegranada, music by Al Carmines (produced New York, 1966).
With Creatures Make My Way (produced New York, 1967).
When Clowns Play Hamlet (also director: produced New York, 1967).
View from Sorrento (produced New York, 1967).
Howard Kline Trilogy (produced New York, 1968).
Christopher at Sheridan Squared (produced New York, 1971).
French Dressing (revue), with others (produced New York, 1974).
Grandmother Is in the Strawberry Patch (produced New York, 1974).
The Pinotti Papers (produced New York, 1975).
One Man's Religion (produced New York, 1975).
Star Followers in an Ancient Land, music by Tom O'Horgan and Gale Garnett (also director: produced New York, 1975).
The Legend of Sheridan Square (produced New York, 1976).
Turtles Don't Dream (also director: produced New York, 1977).
Too Late for Yogurt (also director: produced New York, 1978).
The Butterfly Encounter, music by David Forman (produced New York, 1978).
A Hand Job for Apollo (produced New York, 1988).
When Lightning Strikes Twice (includes *Awful People Are Coming Over So We Must Be Pretending to Be Hard at Work and Hope They Will Go Away, Only a Countess May Dance When She's Crazy*) (produced New York, 1991).

*

Theatrical Activities:
Director: **Plays**—several of his own plays.

* * *

H. M. Koutoukas wrote a very large number of plays—

several dozen—in the decade beginning about 1963. Most of them he produced himself in a wide variety of situations. He is the quintessential off-off-Broadway dramatist: in addition to showing his work in the usual coffee houses, churches, and lofts, he put on plays in art galleries, concert halls, movie theatres, and, on commission, at parties as private entertainment for the rich. He gained a considerable though largely underground following, but this did not bring him readier access to stages. The theatre scene has changed, there is less personal rapport between producers and artists, more commercial pressure, and since the mid-1970's Koutoukas's output has declined.

His plays have a special tone and flavor that are all his own and immediately recognizable. He often writes in verse, and the characters and situations are the product of a highly fanciful imagination and an elaborately refined sensibility. Most of his plays are designated "camps" rather than drama or comedies, and the style is flamboyantly romantic, idiosyncratic, sometimes self-satirizing, full of private references and inside jokes, precious, boldly aphoristic, and disdainful of restrictions of sense, taste, or fashion. Koutoukas is perhaps the last of the aesthetes. Underlying the decoration, his characteristic themes concern people or creatures who have become so strange that they have lost touch with ordinary life, yet their feelings are all the more tender and vulnerable —the deformed, the demented, the rejected, the perverse.

Medea is an adaptation of the Greek play in which the action is set in a laundromat, and in the author's production Medea was played by a man. On the surface a ridiculous notion, the play vividly articulates the situation of a woman from a more primitive, natural, expressive culture trapped among the over-civilized, calculating Greeks and conveys a sympathetic insight into her desperation. The characters in *Tidy Passions; or, Kill, Kaleidoscope, Kill* include a high priestess and several witches of a broken-down cobra cult, a dying dove, Narcissus, and Jean Harlow, who proclaims, "Glamour is dead." *With Creatures Make My Way* is set in a sewer where the single character, neither man nor woman, finally consummates an eternal love with a passing lobster. *A Letter from Colette*, in the naturalistic mode, sweetly tells of romance between an aging woman and a handsome young delivery boy. *Pomegranada* opens in the Garden of Eden and is about tarnish. *Christopher at Sheridan Squared* is an hallucinatory documentary about the Greenwich Village street where Koutoukas has lived for years.

In the mid-1980's Koutoukas re-emerged as an actor and theatrical personality. He presented his students, the School for Gargoyles, in his play *A Hand Job for Apollo*, and appeared at La Mama in *The Birds*. Joining the Ridiculous Theatrical Company, he won acclaim for his performances in revivals of several plays by the late Charles Ludlam, appearing in London as well as New York. His plays *Awful People Are Coming Over So We Must Be Pretending to Be Hard at Work and Hope They Will Go Away* and *Only a Countess May Dance When She's Crazy*, under the collective title *When Lightning Strikes Twice*, were presented by the Ridiculous, starring Everett Quinton, in 1991.

—Michael T. Smith

—————

KRAUSS, Ruth (Ida). American. Born in Baltimore, Maryland, 25 July 1911. Educated in public elementary schools; at Peabody Institute of Music, Baltimore; New School for Social Research, New York; Maryland Institute of Art, Baltimore; Parsons School of Art, New York, graduate. Married David Johnson Leisk (i.e., the writer Crockett Johnson) in 1940 (died 1975). Address: c/o Scholastic Books, 730 Broadway, New York, New York 10003, U.S.A.

PUBLICATIONS

Poem-Plays

The Cantilever Rainbow.   New York, Pantheon, 1965.
There's a Little Ambiguity Over There among the Bluebells and Other Theatre Poems.   New York, Something Else Press, 1968.
If Only.   Eugene, Oregon, Toad Press, 1969.
Under Twenty.   Eugene, Oregon, Toad Press, 1970.
Love and the Invention of Punctuation.   Lenox, Massachusetts, Bookstore Press, 1973.
This Breast Gothic.   Lenox, Massachusetts, Bookstore Press, 1973.
If I Were Freedom (produced Annandale-on-Hudson, New York, 1976).
Re-examination of Freedom (produced Boston, 1976).   West Branch, Iowa, Toothpaste Press, 1981.
Under 13.   Lenox, Massachusetts, Bookstore Press, 1976.
When I Walk I Change the Earth.   Providence, Rhode Island, Burning Deck, 1978.
Small Black Lambs Wandering in the Red Poppies (produced New York, 1982).
Ambiguity 2nd (produced Boston, 1985).

Productions include: *A Beautiful Day, There's a Little Ambiguity Over There among the Bluebells, Re-Examination of Freedom, Newsletter, The Cantilever Rainbow, In a Bull's Eye, Pineapple Play, Quartet, A Show, A Play—It's a Girl!, Onward, Duet* (or *Yellow Umbrella*), *Drunk Boat, If Only, This Breast,* many with music by Al Carmines, Bill Dixon, and Don Heckman, produced in New York, New Haven, Boston, and other places, since 1964.

Fiction (for children)

A Good Man and His Good Wife.   New York, Harper, 1944; revised edition, 1962.
The Carrot Seed.   New York, Harper, 1945.
The Great Duffy.   New York, Harper, 1946.
The Growing Story.   New York, Harper, 1947.
Bears.   New York, Harper, 1948.
The Happy Day.   New York, Harper, 1949.
The Big World and the Little House.   New York, Schuman, 1949.
The Backward Day.   New York, Harper, and London, Hamish Hamilton, 1950.
The Bundle Book.   New York, Harper, 1951.
A Hole Is to Dig: A First Book of First Definitions.   New York, Harper, 1952; London, Hamish Hamilton, 1963.
A Very Special House.   New York, Harper, 1953.
I'll Be You and You Be Me.   New York, Harper, 1954.
How to Make an Earthquake.   New York, Harper, 1954.
Charlotte and the White Horse.   New York, Harper, 1955; London, Bodley Head, 1977.
Is This You? New York, Scott, 1955.
I Want to Paint My Bathroom Blue.   New York, Harper, 1956.
The Birthday Party.   New York, Harper, 1957.

Monkey Day.   New York, Harper, 1957.
Somebody Else's Nut Tree and Other Tales from Children.   New York, Harper, 1958.
A Moon or a Button.   New York, Harper, 1959.
Open House for Butterflies.   New York, Harper, and London, Hamish Hamilton, 1960.
"Mama, I Wish I Was Snow" "Child, You'd Be Very Cold."   New York, Atheneum, 1962.
Eye Nose Fingers Toes.   New York, Harper, 1964.
The Little King, The Little Queen, The Little Monster, and Other Stories You Can Make Up Yourself, illustrated by the author.   New York, Scholastic, 1966.
This Thumbprint: Words and Thumbprints, illustrated by the author.   New York, Harper, 1967.
Little Boat Lighter Than a Cork.   Westport, Connecticut, and New York, Magic Circle Press-Walker, 1976.
Minestrone: A Ruth Krauss Selection, illustrated by the author.   New York, Greenwillow, 1981.
Big and Little.   New York, Scholastic, 1987.

Verse (for children)

I Can Fly.   New York, Simon and Schuster, 1950.
A Bouquet of Littles.   New York, Harper, 1963.
What a Fine Day for . . . , music by Al Carmines.   New York, Parents' Magazine Press, 1967.
I Write It.   New York, Harper, 1970.
Everything under a Mushroom.   New York, Four Winds Press, 1974.
Somebody Spilled the Sky.   New York, Greenwillow, 1979.

*

Manuscript Collection: Dupont School, Wilmington, Delaware.

Ruth Krauss comments:
    All the "works"—or "plays"—are essentially poems—with an approach from the words themselves, rather than ideas, plot, etc. (This division cannot be made in so cut-and-dried a fashion.) The interpretation is *mostly* left completely to the director—i.e., one line can be made to take dozens of forms in actual presentation.
    Part of the philosophy behind this is: say *anything*—and leave it to the director to see what happens. This does not always work out for the best—depending on the director.

* * *

The nature of Ruth Krauss's work is that it is bursting with health, bursting with greenery, with fresh promise. This nutritional assault, this vitality asserts itself beyond all the emotions of the day, all of which, sadness, wistfulness, and hilarity, appear ephemeral beside the steady residue of glowing good health.
    But health seems to issue from a steadying optimism and a kind of bravery, an ability to look the universe in the eye. Nothing cannot be looked at, nothing is so awful that it cannot be faced, perhaps mended, always accepted.
    But the world that she sees appears to be without serious menace, without horror; it appears to be essentially benign, so that in effect what Krauss faces is what she perhaps near-sightedly envisions. The bursting sense to her work is matched by a quieter sense, one of comic wistfulness. And one of whimsy. The world viewed in comic tranquility.
    I recall a series of Krauss whimsies. A number of years ago the Hardware Poets, long since gone not only from

Manhattan but from the planet, presented an evening of her works which, if memory doesn't betray me, had the generic term of seven-second plays. I may be inventing this name but they certainly *felt* like seven-second plays. They were little, exploding, comic pellets which appeared, exploded and disappeared in dazzling succession for many long minutes. Or what appeared to be many long minutes. They were delightful charmers, about nothing that I can now possibly recall, except the essential sense of them—comic energy organisms, dramatic meteorites which lasted long enough to be retained forever in the spirit.

My sense of Krauss's work is that it consists of fragmented interruptions in the more sombre concourse of human events, healthy winks from over the fence. The fragments give off the sense also of interrupting shards of sunlight in a universe grown perceptibly greyer as the years go on. Here are excerpts from a Krauss fragment, a monologue called *If Only* which Florence Tarlow, a performer with an especially dry wit, delivered with comic gravity at the Judson Poets Theatre in New York:

If only I was a nightingale singing
If only I was on my second don't-live-like-a-pig week
If only the sun wasn't always rising behind the next hill
If only I was the flavor of tarragon
If only I was phosphorescence and a night phenomena
    at sea
If only Old Drainpipe Rensaleer as we used to call him
    hadn't hit bottom in Detroit the time he made a
    fancy dive and got absentminded and forget to turn
    and all his shortribs got stove in he got sucked
    down the drain-pipe because the grate wasn't on
If only I didn't have to get up and let our dog out now
If only the glorious day in April because it has no
    beginning or end that all Flatbush had awaited
    impatiently between creation and construction had
    come
If only I was Joyce and had written Finnegans Wake
    only then I'd be gone

If only somebody would kiss me on the back of the
    neck right now

If only those degraded bastards hadn't monkeyed
    around with the Oreo Sandwich pattern

Krauss is a playwright to turn to when both the flesh and spirit grow weak.

—Arthur Sainer

KUREISHI, Hanif. British. Born in London, 5 December 1954. Educated at King's College, University of London, B.A. in philosophy. Writer-in-residence, Royal Court Theatre, London, 1981 and 1985–86. Recipient: George Devine award, 1981; *Evening Standard* award, for screenplay, 1985. Agent: Lemon, Unna, and Durbridge, 24 Pottery Lane, Holland Park, London W11 4LZ, England.

PUBLICATIONS

Plays

Soaking the Heat (produced London, 1976).
The Mother Country (produced London, 1980).

The King and Me (produced London, 1980). Included in *Outskirts, The King and Me, Tomorrow—Today!*, 1983.
Outskirts (produced London, 1981). Included in *Outskirts, The King and Me, Tomorrow—Today!*, 1983.
Tomorrow—Today! (produced London, 1981). Included in *Outskirts, The King and Me, Tomorrow—Today!*, 1983.
Cinders, from a play by Janusz Glowacki (produced London, 1981).
Borderline (produced London, 1981). London, Methuen, 1981.
Artists and Admirers, with David Leveaux, from a play by Alexander Ostrovsky (produced London, 1982).
Birds of Passage (produced London, 1983). Oxford, Amber Lane Press, 1983.
Outskirts, The King and Me, Tomorrow—Today! London, Calder, and New York, Riverrun Press, 1983.
Mother Courage, adaptation of a play by Brecht (produced London, 1984).
My Beautiful Laundrette (screenplay; includes essay "The Rainbow Sign"). London, Faber, 1986.
Sammy and Rosie Get Laid (screenplay). London, Faber, 1988.
London Kills Me (screenplay). London, Faber, 1991.

Screenplays: *My Beautiful Laundrette*, 1985; *Sammy and Rosie Get Laid*, 1988; *London Kills Me*, 1991.

Radio Plays: *You Can't Go Home*, 1980; *The Trial*, from a novel by Kafka, 1982.

Novel

The Buddha of Suburbia. London, Faber, 1990; New York, Penguin, 1991.

*   *   *

Hanif Kureishi is often assumed to be a purely Asian writer, but for the most part his earlier plays look at events through the eyes of characters who are white. Kureishi himself was born in London of mixed parentage, with an English mother and Pakistani father. He grew up without feeling that he was different from his classmates and has always thought of himself as an Englishman. However, the need for an Asian voice in contemporary theatre and the current concern with problems that affect Asians have caused him to examine that other aspect of his heritage.

After two early plays produced in 1980, *The Mother Country* at Riverside Studios and *The King and Me* (about a couple's obsession with Elvis Presley) at the Soho Poly, Kureishi's more ambitious play *Outskirts* received a production at the Royal Shakespeare Company Warehouse in 1981. It centres on two men who grew up together in the straggling suburbs around Orpington and on the eventual divergence of their lives. Del, who has always tagged along with the more dominant Bob, makes the break from their dead-end working-class background and trains as a teacher. Bob, who leaves school early for a well-paid job, finds himself on the unemployment scrapheap. In his bitterness, he turns to the National Front where he says, "We're strong men, together. Men worn down by waiting. Abused men. Men with no work. Our parents made redundant. Now us.. . ." But the racialism he expresses now is a reminder of an evening ten years ago when he and Del had beaten up a Pakistani. On that occasion, Del had taken the initiative in violence, and the shadow of that incident haunts him now that he is a respectable teacher.

Outskirts has an awkwardness of construction in the way it moves from past to present and back again, and the appearance at intervals of Bob's mother is not always successfully dealt with. But nonetheless, Kureishi gets inside the skin of young men who thought, with the end of school and a wage packet each week, that the world was theirs: "I tell you," says Bob, "it's all waiting for a boy like me. Cars, clothes, crumpet." Kureishi also illuminates the lot of the women. Bob's wife, Maureen, returns from having had an abortion rather than bring up a child in a home with no money, to be told by Bob's mother, who is prematurely old, "You did the right thing. Sometimes I wish I'd done the same. I know it's wicked to say that. But I think it. I do."

In *Borderline*, written after a workshop collaboration with Joint Stock and produced at the Royal Court in 1981, Kureishi turns to the problems of Asian immigrants. The idea of writing about Asians in Britain came from the Court's artistic director, Max Stafford-Clark, and Kureishi was at first nervous of writing from outside his own experience. His misgivings proved unnecessary, and with the combination of several weeks of meeting and talking with Asians in Southall, and the inspiration of his imagination and his own past, he was able to write a play about the Asian dilemma in England. For him, writing about Pakistanis in England is also a way of writing about the English and the way England has changed.

Borderline is concerned with the lives of several Asians who are trying to survive in an indifferent or hostile community. An English observer, Susan, a journalist writing an article on Asians in England, takes the role at times of commentator on what Kureishi himself heard during his research: "All the people I've spoken to have been beaten or burnt or abused at some time. You speak to them, they say they like England, it is democratic, or just or good. And then say what's been done to them here. Such viciousness in England." The play also deals with conflict among the Asians—those who try to maintain an Asian way of life, and those who adopt English morals and attitudes. The parents of Amina decide to send her back to an arranged marriage in Pakistan, but she realises that she has become English and, whether she likes it or not, England is her home.

Birds of Passage deals with a lower middle-class family in Sydenham who have fallen on hard times. There are resonances of *The Cherry Orchard* as the family are forced to sell their house to an Asian former lodger. The father of the family, a self-educated Labour councillor, does not realise times have changed until he loses his job. His daughter, despite her education, has taken to prostitution on the side, and his wife's sister and her husband, at one time affluent on the proceeds of selling central heating, suddenly find that the bottom has dropped out of the market. Kureishi writes about his ineffectual characters with affection, and there is what amounts to a hymn of praise to suburbia from the father. "Out here we live in peace, indifferent to the rest of the world. We have no sense of communal existence but we are tolerant, not cruel." The least sympathetic character is the Asian, Asif, the spoilt, indolent son of rich parents. Asif despises poor Pakistani immigrants and is smugly upwardly mobile. The play is not primarily about racial attitudes, but about the effect of the recession on people in Britain who believed in the optimism of the 1960's and then had to face unemployment in the early 1980's.

Kureishi's script for the film *My Beautiful Laundrette* brought him to the attention of a wider public. A small-budget movie, directed by Stephen Frears, it caught the imagination of critics and audiences. Several of the characters and situations of his stage plays are enlarged on here. The outwardly modest but sexually experienced Amina of *Border-line* has her counterpart in the film, as does the amoral young entrepreneur Asif of *Birds of Passage*, while the intense and, in the film's case, homosexual, relationship of the two boys who grew up together echoes the relationship of Del and Bob in *Outskirts*.

Kureishi's second film, *Sammy and Rosie Get Laid*, was larger, more diffuse, and in the end less satisfactory. It featured polemical discussions on drugs, and the gay incidents seemed to be extraneous rather than a development of the story. Sammy, an Asian, and Rosie, English, living in Brixton, have an uneasy relationship. Sammy's Pakistani politician father arrives in London, to find that the pleasant and gentlemanly England he remembers has vanished. He is haunted by the ghost of a man with a battered face, a reminder of his responsibility for torture in Pakistan. The film has raw, strong images, but suffers from Kureishi's ambition to give a dissertation on everything that is wrong in Britain in the Thatcherite 1980's.

Kureishi's next film, which he directed, *London Kills Me*, narrows the theme to the London drug scene. Clint, a young member of a drug-dealing posse, is half in love with a heroin addict Sylvie, but she is stolen from him by the posse leader, Muffdiver. The smalltime posse tries to get in with the big-time dealers but only end by alienating them. Clint, having been unlucky in love and crime, decides to go straight and takes a job as a waiter in a diner. His first ingratiating smile at a customer implies he will be a success in his new occupation. Although the film is set against the drug scene, it concentrates on the triangular relationship and the symbolic search by Clint for the "true shoe" after his have been stolen when he is beaten up by a couple of dealers to whom he owes money. The ending is ambiguous. The spontaneous street hustler has turned into a paid performer in waiter's costume, yet there is an air of futility about his friends who decide to continue the life of flight and disguise.

Kureishi's novel, *The Buddha of Suburbia*, has an autobiographical element. It is the story of Karim Amir, "an Englishman born and bred—almost," who lives with his English mother and Indian father in a dull South London suburb. It is his dream to escape to London proper and to the world of sex and drugs. Finally his father, "the Buddha of Suburbia," leads the way with his glamorous mistress, Eva, and introduces him to the exciting life of the city. Karim becomes an actor and falls under the influence of the charismatic theatre director Matthew Pike, star of the flourishing alternative theatre. The play Karim is in transfers to New York, where he re-encounters his old schoolfriend Charlie, now a rock star and into sado-masochism. The book is strong on dialogue and characters—some of which are clearly borrowed from real life. It is episodic in construction and reads at times like a source book for the recurring themes in his plays.

—Clare Colvin

KUSHNER, Tony. American. Born in New York City, 16 July 1956. Grew up in Lake Charles, Louisiana. Educated at Columbia University, New York, B.A. 1978; New York University, M.F.A. in directing 1984. Since 1989 guest artist, New York University Graduate Theatre Program, Yale University, New Haven, Connecticut, and Princeton University, New Jersey. Director, Literary Services, Theatre Communications Group, New York, 1990–91; playwright-in-residence, Juilliard School of Drama, New York, 1990–92. Recipient: National Endowment for the Arts directing fellowship, 1985; Princess Grace award, 1986; New York State Council on the Arts playwriting fellowship, 1986; New York Foundation for the Arts playwriting fellowship, 1987; John Whiting award, 1990; Kennedy Center/American Express Fund for New American Plays award, 1990, 1992; National Arts Club Kesselring award, 1991; Will Glickman playwriting prize, 1992; *Evening Standard* award, 1992. Lives in Brooklyn. Agent: Joyce Ketay, 334 West 89th Street, New York, New York 10024, U.S.A.

PUBLICATIONS

Plays

Yes, Yes, No, No (for children; produced St. Louis, Missouri, 1985). Published in *Plays in Process* (New York), vol. 7, no. 11, 1987.
Stella, adaptation of the play by Goethe (produced New York, 1987).
A Bright Room Called Day (produced San Francisco, 1987; London, 1988; New York, 1991). New York, Broadway Play Publishing, 1991.
Hydriotaphia (produced New York, 1987).
The Illusion, adaptation of a play by Pierre Corneille (produced New York, 1988; revised version produced Hartford, Connecticut, 1990). New York, Broadway Play Publishing, 1991.
Widows, with Ariel Dorfman, adaptation of the novel by Dorfman (produced Los Angeles, 1991).
Angels in America, Part One: Millennium Approaches (produced San Francisco, 1991; London, 1992; New York, 1993). London, Hern, 1992; with *Angels in America, Part Two: Perestroika*, New York, Theatre Communications Group, 1993.
Angels in America, Part Two: Perestroika (produced Los Angeles, 1992; London and New York, 1993). With *Angels in America, Part One: Millennium Approaches*, New York, Theatre Communications Group, 1993.

*   *   *

Tony Kushner dreams on a grand scale. He creates manifestations of Satan, Death, and the soul as readily as other dramatists invent ordinary humans. A passionate political thinker and devoted student of Bertolt Brecht, Kushner writes plays suffused with historical consciousness and often filled with political argument. Behind the torrents of his language lie models of extravagant prose—his play *Hydriotaphia* was inspired by the 17th-century essayist Sir Thomas Browne—and the poetry of centuries. Though Kushner has an acute ear for the ways all sorts of people speak, his dialogue frequently breaks into poetry, which can rhyme or be very free. A Romantic with a capital R, he is also a gay activist; his work is death-haunted, yet full of hope.

Kushner has shot to prominence with his two-part, roughly seven-hour *Angels in America*. *Angels* is the first significant Kushner play to be rooted wholly in contemporary life; it depicts the catastrophe of AIDS in New York City. This emotionally powerful subject works to bring the recondite stuff of Kushner's earlier plays to a much larger audience.

The Illusion, freely adapted from Corneille's *L'illusion comique*, shows Kushner reveling in romance. The play is full of poetic hyperbole at once indulged in and mocked, but

above all enjoyed. Kushner's braggart soldier Matamore is a Don Quixote, the embodiment of the play's absurd and melancholy beauty. The love of theatre, of its magic and its transformations, at this play's heart is a key element in *Angels* as well.

Kushner wrote his first important play, *A Bright Room Called Day*, in "deepest-midnight Reagan America"; since then it has been extensively revised. In the Weimar Germany of 1932–33 a circle of friends disintegrates under the pressures of Hitler's rise to power, one after another forced into hiding or exile until just one woman, Agnes, is left cowering in her apartment. This story is periodically interrupted by Zillah Katz, a contemporary American "with Anarcho-Punk tendencies," who in the version staged at New York's Public Theater in 1991 comes to Berlin and lands in the same apartment; finally she and Agnes inhabit each other's dreams. Kushner keeps rewriting Zillah's lines because she is there to draw parallels with the current political situation in the United States. "Overstatement is your friend: use it," advises Zillah, comparing Reagan and Bush to Hitler. For subsequent productions, Kushner writes, he "will cheerfully supply new material, drawing appropriate parallels between contemporary and historical monsters and their monstrous acts, regardless of how superficially outrageous such comparisons may seem. To refuse to compare is to rob history of its power to inform present action."

One of the bravest of *Bright Room*'s characters, a woman artist named Gotchling, says that "the dreams of the Left are always beautiful." Her words catch at the essence of Kushner's art: "As an artist I am struck to the heart by these dreams. These visions. We progress. But at great cost." Words very like these recur at the end of *Angels in America*.

Subtitled "A Gay Fantasia on National Themes," *Angels* is an epic play for eight actors, its theatricality heightened by casting them in a number of roles—often characters of the opposite sex—in addition to their primary one. Twin plots center on two troubled couples. Prior has AIDS and his lover Louis, unable to cope, leaves him. Joe and Harper are Mormons; their marriage is falling apart because Joe is losing his lifelong battle to repress his homosexuality and Harper's way of dealing is to retreat into Valium-assisted visions. As in a 19th-century novel, the two stories interweave: Louis and Joe become lovers; Harper and Prior meet in a mutual hallucination. Joe and Louis both work at a Federal Court building in Brooklyn, giving scope for plenty of political argument between the conservative Mormon and the liberal Jew.

Even more important to the play's political nexus is Roy M. Cohn, Joe's father-figure and the embodiment of the naked desire for power that underlies politics and corrupts it. Kushner has made of this historical figure a monster, a profane, bigoted, brazen criminal. He is also the life-force incarnate. Cohn fights the whole world, and revels in the struggle. A gay man dying of AIDS (however closeted, however much he insists he has liver cancer), he is furious and unafraid. He brings to *Angels in America* acid comedy and demonic energy; he summons complicated feeling; and after he dies he comes back to dominate yet more scenes.

Millennium Approaches is not only the first part's title; it is the feeling that underlies the entire work. Prior's illness seems to open him to a sense of apocalypse; at the end of Part One an angel crashes through his bedroom ceiling. In the second part, *Perestroika*, Prior journeys to heaven to reject the role of prophet, to reject the angel's message of stasis, to ask for more life. By the January 1990 epilogue, set at the Bethesda angel's fountain in Central Park, where no water flows in winter, he has been living with AIDS for five years. Prior and his friends tell us the story of the original fountain of Bethesda: when the Millennium comes—"not the year two thousand, but the capital M Millennium"—the waters that heal all pain will flow again.

Angels in America is a work of such size and scope, so filled with poetry and felt thought, that it brings to mind *Faust* and *Peer Gynt*. Whether its resolution will meet with the acclaim that greeted *Millennium Approaches* in San Francisco and London has yet to be seen. What's already clear is that *Angels* is one of the most ambitious, exciting, and talented plays ever written in America. In it one encounters an enormously gifted young writer coming into his full power.

—M. Elizabeth Osborn

L

LAFFAN, Kevin (Barry). British. Born in Reading, Berkshire, 24 May 1922. Married Jeanne Lilian Thompson in 1952; three sons. Repertory actor and director until 1950; director of productions, Pendragon Company, 1950–52, and Everyman Theatre Company, 1953–58, both Reading. Recipient: ATV Television award, 1959; Irish Life award, 1969; National Union of Students award, 1969; *Sunday Times* award, 1970. Agent: ACTAC (Theatrical and Cinematic) Ltd., 16 Cadogan Lane, London S.W.1, England.

PUBLICATIONS

Plays

Ginger Bred (as Kevin Barry) (produced Reading, 1951).
The Strip-Tease Murder (as Kevin Barry), with Neville Brian (produced Reading, 1955).
Winner Takes All (as Kevin Barry) (produced Reading, 1956).
First Innocent (as Kevin Barry) (produced Reading, 1957).
Angie and Ernie, with Peter Jones (produced Guildford, Surrey, 1966).
Zoo Zoo Widdershins Zoo (produced Leicester, 1969). London, Faber, 1969.
It's a Two-Foot-Six-Inches-above-the-Ground World (produced Bristol, 1969; London, 1970). London, Faber, 1970.
The Superannuated Man (produced Watford, Hertfordshire, 1971).
There Are Humans at the Bottom of My Garden (produced London, 1972).
Adam and Eve and Pinch Me (produced London, 1974).
Never So Good (produced London, 1976).
The Wandering Jew (produced London, 1978).
The Dream of Trevor Staines (produced Chichester, 1983).
Adam Redundant (also director: produced London, 1989).

Screenplays: *It's a Two-Foot-Six-Inches-above-the-Ground World* (*The Love Ban*), 1973; *The Best Pair of Legs in the Business*, 1973.

Radio Play: *Portrait of an Old Man*, 1961.

Television Plays: *Lucky for Some*, 1969; *The Best Pair of Legs in the Business*, 1969; *You Can Only Buy Once*, 1969; *Castlehaven* series, 1970; *Kate* series, 1970; *A Little Learning*, 1970; *The Designer*, 1971; *Decision to Burn*, 1971; *Fly on the Wall* (trilogy), 1971; *The General*, 1971; *Emmerdale Farm*, 1972, 1977; *Justice* series, 1973; *The Reformer*, 1973; *Getting Up*, 1973; *Beryl's Lot* series, with Bill McIlwraith, 1973, 1977; *After the Wedding Was Over*, 1975; *It's a Wise Child*, 1975; for Bud Flanagan programme.

Novel

Amos Goes to War with M. Mitchell. Molesey, Surrey, Venus Publications, 1987.

*   *   *

Anybody leaving the theatre after the first performance of Kevin Laffan's *Zoo Zoo Widdershins Zoo* would probably have been amazed to discover that the writer was a man in his forties. Laffan's study of a group of young people—the eldest are in their early twenties—sharing a house and everything in it while refusing to work and turning to petty crime—shop-lifting, robbing telephone booths, and cheating gas meters—when money is scarce, seems to have come exactly out of the way of life it re-creates.

Laffan, however, was born in 1922 and *Zoo Zoo Widdershins Zoo* was his first real success. It won an award from the National Union of Students, which wanted a play for production in universities. If the occasion of the play suggested its theme, only Laffan's complete understanding of his characters, their idioms, attitudes and rejection of social responsibility, can account for the play's authenticity and for its cool, morally neutral tone. It captures and makes comprehensible a gaiety which seems to grow out of the apparently depressing life-style these people have adopted. Cleverly, it is a play entirely about a minute community, and there is a feeling that the audience, as well as the squatters, is betrayed when the couple whose house has become a home for the group manoeuvre the others out and, suddenly, revert to conventional bourgeois habits.

Zoo Zoo Widdershins Zoo is almost plotless, carefully designed to seem as aimless as the way of life it observes, and its alternations of intensity and relaxation are all conveyed in the limited, inexplicit dialogue which exploits its young people's idiom.

This was by no means Laffan's first play. He began his career in the theatre as an actor; with others, he helped to found the Everyman Theatre Company in Reading and in 1959 won an award from ATV for a television play *Cut in Ebony* which was never produced because it deals, in terms of comedy, with problems of race and colour. Laffan, abandoning acting and direction, earned the time to write plays by undertaking any other writing that would pay, including a not very successful series of television programmes for the comedian Bud Flanagan. His television plays, *Lucky for Some*, *You Can Only Buy Once*, and *The Best Pair of Legs in the Business*, however, established him as a playwright in this medium, and *Castlehaven*, a television serial doing for a Yorkshire community what *Coronation Street* did for Lancashire, became a fixed part of commercial television schedules outside London.

Laffan's stage play *Angie and Ernie* was produced outside London. *The Superannuated Man* won an Irish Life award in 1969 but was produced only in 1971. But *Zoo Zoo Widdershins Zoo*, after its university production, was given a successful commercial production in London and impressed the critics, with the result that *It's a Two-Foot-Six-Inches-above-the-Ground World*, first seen at the Theatre Royal, Bristol, was able to travel to London and make a distinct impression there; it considers, in a very individual tone of toughly angry, affectionate hilarity, the effects on a young Catholic husband and wife of their Church's refusal to permit any means of birth control. Catholics complained that Laffan's play misrepresents the Church's attitude, but in its own terms, as a work for the theatre, it is entirely successful.

The marriage of a young Liverpool Catholic is falling into ruins; his wife, a Protestant girl who was converted to Catholicism only in order to marry him, has provided him with three sons; another child would probably kill her, while sexual abstinence, which suits the wife even less than it suits the husband, is destroying the marriage. The voice of the Church is transmitted by a young priest who expresses the Catholic prohibition at its most extreme and unyielding. A totally permissive view is offered by an outsider—a van driver making a delivery at the middle son's Catholic primary school. The father's prudery had prevented him from teaching his children anything about their physical functions, so that the van driver's use of the school lavatory, arousing the child's interest in an adult masculine body, costs the unfortunate driver—an energetic and undeviating lecher—his job.

These people argue their cases with great energy, and the play dresses the situation in continual high spirits. When all else fails, the wife's surreptitiously acquired and so far unused collection of contraceptive pills comes in useful; they can, for example, be mistaken for aspirins. It would not be fair to accuse Laffan of pulling his punches in the interests of good taste or of scrupulous intellectual fairness in his presentation of opposed points of view. He is, however, far more deeply involved through his emotions than through any desire to solve intellectual arguments, and under the hard-edged hilarity of its presentation, there is a touching awareness of the painful situation of two simple, good, likeable people trapped by the husband's earnest conviction.

Laffan's progress has been slow. *There Are Humans at the Bottom of My Garden* did not rival the success of its predecessor, and his later work for television, notably the skilfully written *Emmerdale Farm* and the more predictable *Justice* series, won a loyal television following without suggesting any of the tougher moral and social implications of his work for the theatre. A handful of television plays and two unusual comedies, differing so widely in tone and aim as *Zoo Zoo Widdershins Zoo* and *It's a Two-Foot-Six-Inches-above-the-Ground World*, suggest that his other plays deserve careful study by some enterprising theatre manager.

—Henry Raynor

LAN, David. South African. Born in Cape Town, 1 June 1952. Educated at the University of Cape Town, 1970–72, B.A. in English 1972; London School of Economics, 1973–76, B.Sc. in social anthropology 1976, Ph.D. 1983; research associate, University of Zimbabwe, Harare, 1980–82. Moved to England, 1972; lived in Zimbabwe, 1980–82. Member of the Editorial Board, *Journal of Southern African Studies*, Oxford. Recipient: John Whiting award, 1977; George Orwell Memorial award, 1983. Agent: Judy Daish

Associates, 83 Eastbourne Mews, London W2 6LQ, England.

PUBLICATIONS

Plays

Painting a Wall (produced London, 1974; New York, 1980). London, Pluto Press, 1979.
Bird Child (produced London, 1974).
Homage to Been Soup (produced London, 1975).
Paradise (produced London, 1975).
The Winter Dancers (produced London, 1977; Los Angeles, 1978; New York, 1979). Included in *Desire and Other Plays*, 1990.
Not in Norwich (produced London, 1977).
Red Earth (produced London, 1978).
Sergeant Ola and His Followers (produced London, 1979; New York, 1986). London, Methuen, 1980; revised version in *Desire and Other Plays*, 1990.
Flight (produced Stratford-on-Avon, 1986; London, 1987; New York, 1992). London, Methuen, 1987.
A Mouthful of Birds, with Caryl Churchill (produced Birmingham and London, 1986). London, Methuen, 1986.
Ghetto, with Jeremy Sams, adaptation of the play by Joshua Sobol (produced London and New York, 1989). London, Hern, 1989.
Desire (produced London, 1990). Included in *Desire and Other Plays*, 1990.
Desire and Other Plays (includes *The Winter Dancers*, *Sergeant Ola and His Followers*). London, Faber, 1990.
Hippolytos, adaptation of the play by Euripides (produced London, 1991). London, Almeida Theatre Scripts, 1991.

Television Plays: *The Sunday Judge*, 1985; *The Crossing*, 1988; *Streets of Yesterday*, 1989; *Welcome Home Comrades*, 1989; *Dark City*, 1990.

Other

Guns and Rain: Guerrillas and Spirit Mediums in Zimbabwe. London, Currey, and Berkeley, University of California Press, 1985.

*

Theatrical Activities:
Director: **Plays**—*A New Way to Pay Old Debts* by Massinger, Cape Town, 1971; *The Sport of My Mad Mother* by Ann Jellicoe, Cape Town, 1972.

* * *

David Lan is a South African, so he begins with a subject. His one-act *Painting a Wall* and his full-length play *Bird Child* both deal with aspects of apartheid. The first is slight, impressionistic, a short story. Two coloured men and an Indian paint a wall, helped by a coloured boy. The Indian has lost his child, and makes an unsuccessful attempt at suicide by drinking paint. The boy runs away. The men paint pictures on the wall, but must paint over them. They talk and paint. The wall is finished. They leave.

In *Bird Child* the characters are white, mostly students in collision with the police. In protesting against the denial of freedom to her mother's maid, the heroine discovers the nature of freedom for herself. The other protagonists are locked by the system into predetermined attitudes. This is Lan's most immediately accessible play, owing particularly to his handling of Krou, the Colonel of Police, an intelligent, logical, and resourceful man, by no means a target for the scoring of easy liberal points.

Lan's next play, the one-act *Homage to Been Soup*, is only 12 pages long, no more than a technical exercise. *Paradise*, which followed, was more ambitious and interesting. Lan appears to have been inspired by Goya's *Horrors of War*, and set his play in Northern Spain in 1808, the year of Bonaparte's invasion. His characters—deserters from the French army, Spanish peasants and their landlord, his wife and school-teacher daughter—have no particularity of time and place, and the play might more suitably have been set in a non-particular Whiting-Land, into which his two most successful images, a simpleton who teaches the others his private unintelligible non-language, and the birds which move their nests from trees about to be chopped down, might fit more successfully. Lan's concern with the nature of freedom is noble, his images striking, and his own search for a language and ideas more complex than those of his earlier plays is admirable.

A new direction came with *The Winter Dancers* and *Sergeant Ola and His Followers*, the first two of a trilogy of anthropological plays. (Lan had taken a doctorate in social anthropology at the London School of Economics.) In *The Winter Dancers*, he used the work of Boas on the Kwakiutl of Vancouver Island, for *Sergeant Ola* Peter Worsley's research into cargo cults in Papua New Guinea. Both plays use ritual and magic, both are concerned with the statement (explicit in *The Winter Dancers*), "White men are eating up the world."

In *The Winter Dancers* the shaman, Carver, knows that he cures the sick by trickery and sleight of hand. Others believe in his power; he knows he has none. Yet the cures are genuine. When finally he comes to believe in his own power he has already lost it, because the white men have destroyed the people's belief, and he is killed by the chief of the tribe in order to preserve the legend. In *Sergeant Ola* there is no longer any power in the people but only in the "wetmen" who have taken away the people's ancestors, and offered them Adam and Eve instead. The wetmen have all the cargo (riches) and the people are merely offered pay (which is not cargo) for doing the wetmen's work, while the wetmen manifestly do no work at all. The attempts of the people to make cargo come again by ignorant imitation, amounting to parody, of what they have observed of the wetmen's ways is both comic and piteous.

Lan's next play *Flight* is more complex. The narrative is neither strong nor straightforward, the action moving between 1930, when a Jewish family flees from persecution in Lithuania, to 1980 when the next generation is leaving Zimbabwe. The title and a prologue to the play suggest that its theme is the perpetual uprooting, settlement elsewhere, and subsequent uprooting of the Jews under persecution, but my own view is that the title may be ironic, and the real flight may be from political reality, that centuries of persecution have made the Jews politically aware and active, but have also contributed to the development of a family loyalty which occludes political vision and vitiates action. Because of its complexity, the play demands to be seen more than once.

In 1980 Lan went to live in Zimbabwe and work with the Shona. From this time comes the third play of the anthropological trilogy, *Desire*. The play is set in the Zambezi Valley. The war is over, freedom won. The spirit of a dead girl, a guerrilla shot during the war by soldiers, possesses her friend, Rosemary, who becomes ill every time she tries to live with her husband. The possession is ended—ritually as one would

expect from Lan, with ancestors participating—when it is discovered that the dead girl's own father, Rosemary's father, and Rosemary's husband were all involved in causing the girl's death. *Desire*, like the other two plays of the set, is lively and energetic. Lan has a talent for expressing in language and action the behaviour and beliefs of people whom the West would call primitive. He has said that he does not wish his plays to be "lectures with feet," but to some extent they have become so. They are illustrative, and the illustrations of primitive behaviour are formed into parables which are themselves illustrations.

For the time being, Lan seems to have reached the end of a period of development. He has worked in television and film over the past few years, but his work for the theatre has not been prolific, and consists, apart from *Desire*, of two "versions," the first (with Jeremy Sams) of *Ghetto*, a play with dancing and music by the Israeli playwright, Joshua Sobol, about the last two years of the ghetto at Vilna before the last occupants were murdered by the Germans, the second a version of the *Hippolytos* of Euripides. *Ghetto* is a play about a society in destruction, full of passion and bitter laughter, using ritual and music as Lan's own work does, and admirably suited to his methods. This cannot be said of *Hippolytos*.

—John Bowen

LAURENTS, Arthur. American. Born in Brooklyn, New York, 14 July 1917. Educated at Cornell University, Ithaca, New York, B.A. 1937. Served in the United States Army, 1940–45: sergeant; radio playwright, 1943–45 (Citation, Secretary of War, and *Variety* radio award, 1945). Stage director. Director, Dramatists Play Service, New York, 1961–66. Council member, Dramatists Guild, from 1955. Recipient: American Academy award, 1946; Sidney Howard Memorial award, 1946; Tony award, for play, 1967, for directing, 1984; Vernon Rice award, 1974; Golden Globe award, 1977; Screenwriters Guild award, 1978; elected to the Theatre Hall of Fame, 1983; Sydney Drama Critics award, for directing, 1985. Agent: Shirley Bernstein, Paramuse Artists, 1414 Avenue of the Americas, New York, New York 10019. Address: Dune Road, Quogue, New York 11959, U.S.A.

PUBLICATIONS

Plays

Now Playing Tomorrow (broadcast 1939). Published in *Short Plays for Stage and Radio*, edited by Carless Jones, Albuquerque, University of New Mexico Press, 1939.
Western Electric Communicade (broadcast 1944). Published in *The Best One-Act Plays of 1944*, edited by Margaret Mayorga, New York, Dodd Mead, 1944.
The Last Day of the War (broadcast 1945). Published in *Radio Drama in Action*, edited by Erik Barnouw, New York, Farrar and Rinehart, 1945.
The Face (broadcast 1945). Published in *The Best One-Act Plays of 1945*, edited by Margaret Mayorga, New York, Dodd Mead, 1945.
Home of the Brave (produced New York, 1945; London, 1948; as *The Way Back*, produced London, 1949). New York, Random House, 1946.

Heartsong (produced New Haven, Connecticut, 1947).

The Bird Cage (produced New York, 1950). New York, Dramatists Play Service, 1950.

The Time of the Cuckoo (produced New York, 1952). New York, Random House, 1953.

A Clearing in the Woods (produced New York, 1957). New York, Random House, 1957; revised version, New York, Dramatists Play Service, 1960.

West Side Story, music by Leonard Bernstein, lyrics by Stephen Sondheim (produced New York, 1957; London, 1958). New York, Random House, 1958; London, Heinemann, 1959.

Gypsy, music by Jule Styne, lyrics by Stephen Sondheim, adaptation of a book by Gypsy Rose Lee (produced New York, 1959; also director: produced London, 1973). New York, Random House, 1960.

Invitation to a March (also director: produced New York, 1960; Hereford, 1965). New York, Random House, 1961.

Anyone Can Whistle, music by Stephen Sondheim (also director: produced New York, 1964; Cheltenham, Gloucestershire, 1986). New York, Random House, 1965.

Do I Hear a Waltz?, music by Richard Rodgers, lyrics by Stephen Sondheim (produced New York, 1965). New York, Random House, 1966.

Hallelujah, Baby!, music by Jule Styne, lyrics by Betty Comden and Adolph Green (produced New York, 1967). New York, Random House, 1967.

The Enclave (also director: produced Washington, D.C., and New York, 1973). New York, Dramatists Play Service, 1974.

Scream (also director: produced Houston, 1978).

The Madwoman of Central Park West, with Phyllis Newman, music by Peter Allen and others, adaptation of the play *My Mother Was a Fortune Teller* by Newman (also director: produced Buffalo and New York, 1979).

A Loss of Memory (produced Southampton, New York, 1981). Published in *The Best Short Plays 1983*, edited by Ramon Delgado, Radnor, Pennsylvania, Chilton, 1983.

Nick and Nora, music by Charles Strowse, lyrics by Richard Maltby, Jr. (also director: produced New York, 1991).

Screenplays: *The Snake Pit*, with Frank Partos and Millen Brand, 1948; *Rope*, with Hume Cronyn, 1948; *Anna Lucasta*, with Philip Yordan, 1949; *Caught*, 1949; *Anastasia*, 1956; *Bonjour Tristesse*, 1958; *The Way We Were*, 1973; *The Turning Point*, 1977.

Radio Plays: *Now Playing Tomorrow*, 1939; *Hollywood Playhouse*, *Dr. Christian*, *The Thin Man*, *Manhattan at Midnight*, and other series, 1939–40; *The Last Day of the War*, *The Face*, *Western Electric Communicade*, and other plays for *The Man Behind the Gun*, *Army Service Force Presents* and *Assignment: Home* series, 1943–45; *This Is Your FBI* series, 1945.

Television: *The Light Fantastic*, 1967.

Novels

The Way We Were. New York, Harper, 1972; London, W.H. Allen, 1973.

The Turning Point. New York, New American Library, 1977; London, Corgi, 1978.

*

Manuscript Collection: Brandeis University, Waltham, Massachusetts.

Theatrical Activities:
Director: **Plays**—*Invitation to a March*, New York, 1960; *I Can Get It for You Wholesale* by Jerome Weidman, New York, 1962; *Anyone Can Whistle*, New York, 1964; *The Enclave*, Washington, D.C., and New York, 1973; *Gypsy*, London, 1973, New York, 1974 and 1989; *My Mother Was a Fortune Teller* by Phyllis Newman, New York, 1978; *Scream*, Houston, 1978; *The Madwoman of Central Park West*, Buffalo and New York, 1979; *So What Are We Gonna Do Now?* by Juliet Garson, New York, 1982; *La Cage aux Folles* by Jean Poiret, adapted by Harvey Fierstein, Boston and New York, 1983, Sydney, 1985, London, 1986; *Birds of Paradise* by Winnie Haltzman and David Evans, New York, 1987; *Nick and Nora*, New York, 1991.

Arthur Laurents comments:

Too much of today's theatre brings "The Emperor's New Clothes" to my mind. Style is considered content; formlessness is considered new technique; character is reduced to symbol and/or type; and story has been banished—not necessarily a loss—in favor of incident which is usually too thin and too undramatic to fuse an entire play. Moreover, the dominant tone is modish pessimism or militancy, both of which can be as sentimentally romantic as effulgent optimism.

All a matter of taste, of course. My own is for a heightened theatricality and for new forms—but I still believe that form is determined by content and requires control. I want characters in a play, I want to be emotionally involved; I want social content; I want language and I want a *level* of accessibility. (I suspect obscurantism of being the refuge of the vague, the uncommitted, and the chic.) Although I do not demand it, I prefer optimism—even if only implied. For I think man, naturally evil or not, is optimistic. Even the bleakest has hope: why else does he bother to write?

For the United States, for New York, I want subsidized theatres with permanent companies playing repertory. I think that is the most important need of the American playwright and would be of the greatest aid in his development.

* * *

One of the most promising dramatists appearing immediately after World War II was Arthur Laurents. His first success in New York, *Home of the Brave*, showed both his skill as a dramatist and his insight into human nature as he dramatized the ethnic and individual problems of a Jewish soldier in a battle situation. During the following 15 years Laurents wrote four plays—*The Bird Cage*, *The Time of the Cuckoo*, *A Clearing in the Woods*, and *Invitation to a March* —which continued to demonstrate his theatrical powers and his inclination to write serious drama. Unfortunately, in neither area—theatricality or intellectual penetration—was he able to sustain or develop a first-rate drama for the American commercial theatre. Perhaps he recognized either the personal or public impasse. At any rate, toward the end of this period Laurents had begun to devote more of his talents to musical comedy with considerable success. His creation of the books for *West Side Story* and *Gypsy* gave these musicals the careful integration and character development which distinguish them among modern musicals. During the next decade he collaborated on musicals but without significant success, and seemed to abandon his career in legitimate drama—a disappointment for critics who had felt his earlier promise.

Laurent's seriousness as a dramatist was most evident in the themes that he chose to develop. The fearful uncertainties of the lonely person trying to find a meaningful identity in a world full of frustrations and strangers—this is a dominant theme in his works. Generally, his major character was trying to discover the essentials of love which Laurents seemed to believe would lead to a revelation of self. Although his psychological penetration into his major characters suggests a generally acute perception of humanity, his dramatized solutions tend more consistently toward theatricality than a probing concern for mankind. In other words, the problems that he considers—a person's fears, frustrations, feeling of alienation—place Laurents among these seriously concerned with modernity, but his insistence that sex is fundamental to all such problems limits both his psychology and his insight.

In three of his four plays since his initial success his major characters have been women whose psychological problems have driven them toward disaster. (The other play, *The Bird Cage*, tells the story of Wally, a vicious egomaniac and owner of a night club, whose abuse of everyone stems from his own sexual frustrations.) In *The Time of the Cuckoo* Leona Samish is that warm but lonely woman whose pathos rests in her inability to know and have faith in herself or accept the love of others. Sorry for herself and bitter towards life and thus unable to get what she most desires, she is that dangerous person who destroys. Virginia, the heroine of *A Clearing in the Woods*, sees herself as the destroyer although she wants desperately to be loved. Discovering that someone does truly care, she can work toward a position where she accepts both herself and the real world around her. *Invitation to a March* tells of a girl who, at first, wants to "march" along with the ordinary world and its seemingly inherent problems of love, sex, and divorce. But she changes, rejects the "march" and finds love with one who said "come dance with me." Uncharacteristically for a Laurents play, a strongly made decision becomes the climax of this one, and perhaps both the author and his characters abandon the ordinary world as idealism seems a possible alternative to drudgery. Unfortunately, no further step has been dramatized.

Although Laurents has not been an innovator in technical theatre, he has courageously employed distinctive techniques in his plays. While *The Bird Cage* employs a rather obvious use of theatrical symbol, the "clearing in the woods" with its "magic circle" is well integrated into the structure of the play where three characters—Ginna, Nora, Jigee—act out particular ages in the heroine's life and tease her for her inability to accept what "they" contribute to her present problems. The frequent "front" delivery to the audience in an attempt to indicate unspoken and personal feelings was unsuccessful even in a semi-fantasy such as *Invitation to a March*. Music becomes a dominant part of several of his plays, as might be expected of a dramatist interested in musical comedy. In all of Laurents's theatre works his care in the creation of his characters is a major asset. Whether in musical comedy or straight drama, through an integration of theme and theatrical technique Laurents has tried to express his views on psychological and social life in the modern world.

—Walter J. Meserve

LAVERY, Bryony. British. Born in Wakefield, Yorkshire, 21 December 1947. Educated at the University of London,

1966–69, B.A. (honours) in English 1969. Artistic director, Les Oeufs Malades, 1976–78, Extraordinary Productions, 1979–80, and Female Trouble, 1981–83, all London. Resident dramatist, Unicorn Theatre for Young People, London, 1986–88; artistic director, Gay Sweatshop, London, 1989–91. Agent: Andrew Hewson, John Johnson Ltd., Clerkenwell House, 45–47 Clerkenwell Green, London EC1R 0HT. Address: 17 Maitland Road, London E15 4EL, England.

PUBLICATIONS

Plays

Of All Living (produced London, 1967).
Days at Court (produced London, 1968).
Warbeck (produced London, 1969).
I Was Too Young at the Time to Understand Why My Mother Was Crying (also director: produced London, 1976).
Sharing (also director: produced London, 1976).
Germany Calling, with Peter Leabourne (produced London, 1976).
Grandmother's Footsteps (also director: produced London, 1977).
Snakes (produced London, 1977).
The Catering Service (also director: produced London, 1977).
Floorshow, with others (produced London, 1978).
Helen and Her Friends (also director: produced London, 1978).
Bag (also director, produced London, 1979).
Time Gentlemen Please (cabaret; produced London, 1979).
The Wild Bunch (for children; produced London, 1979). Published in *Responses*, edited by Don Shiach, London, Thomas Nelson, 1990.
Sugar and Spice (for children; produced Ipswich, Suffolk, 1979).
Unemployment: An Occupational Hazard? (for children; also director: produced London, 1979).
Gentlemen Prefer Blondes, adaptation of the novel by Anita Loos (produced London, 1980).
The Joker (for children; also director: produced London, 1980).
The Family Album (also director: produced London, 1980).
Pamela Stephenson One Woman Show (cabaret; produced London, 1981).
Missing (also director: produced Colchester, Essex, and London, 1981).
Zulu, with Patrick Barlow (produced London, 1981).
Female Trouble (cabaret; produced London, 1981).
The Black Hole of Calcutta, with Patrick Barlow (produced London, 1982).
Götterdämmerung; or, Twilight of the Gods, with Patrick Barlow and Susan Todd (produced London, 1982).
For Maggie, Betty and Ida, music by Paul Sand (produced London, 1982).
More Female Trouble (cabaret), music by Caroline Noh (produced London, 1982).
Uniform and Uniformed, and Numerical Man (broadcast 1983). Published in *Masks and Faces*, edited by Dan Garrett, London, Macmillan, 1984.
Hot Time (produced London, 1984).
Calamity (produced London, 1984).
Origin of the Species (produced Birmingham, 1984; London, 1985). Published in *Plays by Women: Six*, edited by Mary Remnant, London, Methuen, 1987.
The Wandsworth Warmers (cabaret; also director: produced London, 1984).

The Zulu Hut Club (for children; produced London, 1984).
The Wandsworth Warmers Christmas Carol Concert (cabaret; also director: produced London, 1985).
Over and Out (also director: produced on tour, 1985).
Witchcraze (produced London, 1985). Published in *Herstory*, edited by Gabrial Griffin and Elaine Aston, Sheffield, Sheffield Academic Press, 1991.
Getting Through (additional lyrics only), by Nona Shepphard, music by Helen Glavin (produced on tour, 1985; London, 1987).
The Wandsworth Warmers in Unbridled Passions (cabaret; also director: produced London, 1986).
Sore Points (for children; produced London, 1986).
Mummy, with Sally Owen and L. Ortolja (produced London, 1987).
Madagascar (for children; also director: produced London, 1987).
The Headless Body, music by Stephanie Nunn (produced London, 1987).
The Dragon Wakes (for children; produced London, 1988).
Puppet States (produced London, 1988).
The Drury Lane Ghost, with Nona Shepphard (produced London, 1989).
Two Marias (produced London, 1989). Included in *Her Aching Heart, Two Marias, Wicked*, 1991.
Wicked (produced London, 1990). Included in *Her Aching Heart, Two Marias, Wicked*, 1991.
Her Aching Heart (produced London, 1990). Included in *Her Aching Heart, Two Marias, Wicked*, 1991.
Kitchen Matters (produced London, 1990).
Her Aching Heart, Two Marias, Wicked. London, Methuen, 1991.
Flight (produced London, 1991).
Peter Pan, with Nona Shepphard (produced London, 1991).
The Sleeping Beauty, with Nona Shepphard (produced London, 1992).

Radio Plays: *Fire the Life-Giver*, 1979; *Changes at Work* series, 1980; *Let's Get Dressed*, 1982; *Uniform and Uniformed*, 1983; *Numerical Man*, 1983; *Magical Beasts*, 1987; *Cliffhanger* series, 1990; *Laying Ghosts*, 1992.

Television Plays: *Revolting Women* series, with others, 1981; *Rita of the Rovers*, 1989; *The Cab Wars*, 1989.

Video: *The Lift*, 1988; *Twelve Dancing Princesses*, 1989.

*

Critical Study: "But Will Men Like It; or, Living as a Feminist Writer Without Committing Murder" by Lavery, in *Women and Theatre* edited by Susan Todd, London, Faber, 1984.

Theatrical Activities:
Director: **Plays**—most of her own plays; *More Female Trouble* (revival), London, 1983; *Homelands: Under Exposure* by Lisa Evans, and *The Mrs. Docherties* by Nona Shepphard (co-director, with Shepphard), London, 1985; *Hotel Destiny* by Tasha Fairbanks, London, 1987.

* * *

Bryony Lavery's plays are comic in the best sense of the term, funny, and engaging at a popular level. As Lavery's work tends to deal with controversial issues, including the representation of lesbian and gay sexuality and the funding of

the theatre itself, its popularity is all the more significant. Lavery has worked in British alternative theatre for many years; she was, for instance, one of the early contributors to the work of both Gay Sweatshop and Monstrous Regiment. In the 1970's, Lavery collaborated with Caryl Churchill and Michelene Wandor on *Floorshow*, the Monstrous Regiment's cabaret. She also worked on the Regiment's cabaret *Gentlemen Prefer Blondes* and on comic shows such as *Female Trouble* and *More Female Trouble*, as well as in writing full-length plays. More recently, she has worked in children's theatre, theatre in education, and in teaching playwriting.

By drawing on this wide range of experience, Lavery has developed a voice which is quite unique in British theatre. Her style is intelligent and comic without being too sarcastic or snide; her writing reveals a certain jolly approach to important topical issues. In this way, Lavery has succeeded in developing a style which reaches beyond the typical middle-class forms of farce and drawing-room humour. Her work is self-consciously aware of those forms, but has found a balance between parody and celebration which is politically effective because it makes the plays so engaging, so enjoyable to read and watch.

Origin of the Species and *Her Aching Heart* are probably Lavery's best-known plays. Both illustrate Lavery's skill for combining humour with serious social commentary.

Origin of the Species was first produced by Monstrous Regiment in 1984, with Gillian Hanna as Molly, the anthropologist looking for said origins, who finds them in Victoria, the living creature-woman she unearths, played by Mary McCusker. Directed by Nona Shepphard, this play was ambitious in its scope (all of history) but remarkably unambitious in its use of resources: two actors, minimal sets and props, a small playing space. The power of the play is in its language and its use of humour. Similarly, *Her Aching Heart* is a sophisticated piece of writing, another two-hander which combines wit and parodies of courtly and poetic language with the representation of social issues in entertaining form.

Her Aching Heart was first produced in 1990 at the Oval House, London, directed by Claire Grove and performed by Nicola Kathrens and Sarah Kevney. The play is a "lesbian historical romance" which casts two modern-day women as the readers of bodice-ripping fiction, and concurrently as the heroines and heroes of that fiction. Modern-day characters Molly and Harriet engage in a budding romance in "real life" which parallels the stories of Molly, the servant girl, and Lady Harriet of Helstone Hall, the fiery aristocrat of the novel. Molly and Harriet read the novel and engage in the fictional romance, while they begin to know each other through telephone conversations. The audience gets to know the story, the highs and lows and misunderstandings of their romance, through the narratives and songs of these two central characters. They sing of love and of longing, and the songs are enriched by their references to stereotyped images of romance lifted from fiction and fairytales. That the two lovers are both women is important, but is not the key to the play's politics. Rather, the interweaving of the modern and the "historical," the real and the fictional, the serious and the silly, results in a complicated play which is a delight to read and to watch.

Her Aching Heart toured twice with the Women's Theatre Group in 1990 and 1991, both times with great success. That the play is so accessible and so amusing, as well as so beautifully constructed, makes the choice of a lesbian story-line all the more significant. Similarly, the play engages with gender, class, and power as issues intrinsic to an informed examination of bodice-ripper as a popular form, and to the expectations involved in reading romantic fiction. Yet all these important considerations are represented as parts of the larger fabric of the play rather than as "politically correct" issues to be evaluated in and of themselves.

Of course, not all Lavery's work is written for two actors. Some of the work has been much larger in scale, and some has been immediately linked to contemporary social issues. In 1990, for instance, Lavery wrote *Kitchen Matters*, a play for Gay Sweatshop. As a mixed group with feminist politics, Sweatshop has promoted women's work since its founding in 1974. Sweatshop's struggle with viability in the current economic climate of the arts inspired Bryony Lavery to write the play as an "epic comedy." In a humorously self-referential scene, *Kitchen Matters* opens with a narrator (a woman at a typewriter) discussing her decision to write a (the) play:

> . . . There were some kids in a touring theatre
>   company.
> They were Gay they were Poor they were Minority
> but they wanted a show.
> I had to help them out.
> I'm a writer with a Large Soul and Big Bills.
> My brain met up with my heart and they took a walk
> down into my guts to see what was there.
> The place was full of undigested matter.
> I chewed it over.
> A heavenly light shone on my blank A4 paper.
> I lit my two hundred and thirty-fourth cigarette.
> I started to write.

Lavery's enjoyment of and facility with language is evident even in this short extract. So is her dedication to the theatre. The narrator of this scene, like Lavery, wrote for the benefit of the theatre company. The play was highly successful, and reached many people from different communities, of different classes and sexual orientations. It was a political play with a point to make. But the comedy made the point, and the self-conscious nature of the humour made it all the more powerful as a play.

Lavery's current work is even larger in scale. In early 1992, she was at work on another "epic", but one which involves "a cast of 17" and which is "set in the tomb of an 11th-century Chinese Emperor." Whether or not such an ambitious play will find sufficient financial backing in Britain is a large question, and no doubt one which Lavery will weave into the humour of the play itself.

One thing is certain: if there is a contemporary playwright whose work deserves more attention—on theatrical and social grounds—it is Bryony Lavery.

—Lizbeth Goodman

LAWLER, Ray(mond Evenor). Australian. Born in Footscray, Melbourne, Victoria, in 1921. Left school at age 13. Married Jacklyn Kelleher; three children. Worked in a foundry, 1934–45; actor, Sid Turnbull's Melbourne Repertory Company, 1946–49; actor and producer, National Theatre Company, Melbourne, 1950–54; director, Union Theatre Repertory Company, Melbourne University, 1954–55; lived in Denmark, England, and mainly in Ireland, early 1960's–1975; director and literary adviser, Melbourne Theatre Company, 1976–86. Recipient: Playwrights Advisory Board prize, 1955; London *Evening Standard* award, 1958.

O.B.E. (Officer, Order of the British Empire), 1981. Agent: Curtis Brown, 27 Union Street, Paddington, New South Wales 2021, Australia.

PUBLICATIONS

Plays

Cradle of Thunder (produced Melbourne, 1949).
Summer of the Seventeenth Doll (produced Melbourne, 1955; London, 1957; New York, 1958). London, Angus and Robertson, and New York, Random House, 1957.
The Piccadilly Bushman (produced Melbourne, 1959; Liverpool, 1965). London, Angus and Robertson, 1961.
The Unshaven Cheek (produced Edinburgh, 1963).
A Breach in the Wall (televised 1967; produced Canterbury, Kent, 1970).
The Man Who Shot the Albatross (produced Melbourne, 1972).
Kid Stakes (produced Melbourne, 1975). Included in *The Doll Trilogy*, 1978.
Other Times (produced Melbourne, 1976). Included in *The Doll Trilogy*, 1978.
The Doll Trilogy (includes *Kid Stakes*, *Other Times*, *Summer of the Seventeenth Doll*). Sydney, Currency Press, 1978.
Godsend (produced Melbourne, 1982).

Television Plays: *A Breach in the Wall*, 1967; *Sinister Street* serial, from the novel by Compton Mackenzie, 1968; *Cousin Bette* serial, from the novel by Balzac, 1971; *The Visitors* serial, from the novel by Mary McMinnies, 1972; *Two Women* serial, from a novel by Alberto Moravia, 1972; *Mrs. Palfrey at the Claremont*, from the novel by Elizabeth Taylor, 1973; *After the Party*, from the story by W. Somerset Maugham, 1974; *Seeking the Bubbles* (*The Love School* series), 1975; *True Patriots All*, 1975; *Husband to Mrs. Fitzherbert*, 1975.

*

Theatrical Activities:
Actor: **Play**—Barney Ibbot in *Summer of the Seventeenth Doll*, Melbourne, 1955, London, 1957.

* * *

Ray Lawler's reputation as one of Australia's most distinguished playwrights is still based largely on one extremely successful play, *Summer of the Seventeenth Doll*. The play came at a crucial time, not only for the narrow world of the Australian theatre but for Australian culture generally. The 1950's were a time of national self-consciousness, when former ideas of "Australianness" were being, to a certain extent, reassessed. The *Doll* took the traditional legend of the laconic, hard-bitten Australian bushman, which had been an important part of the national self-image since the 1890's, and dragged it, almost literally, kicking and screaming into the cities to face the realities of postwar urban Australia.

The play had a sudden popular impact when it first appeared. Its warm portrayal of distinctive bush and city character-types was greeted with delighted recognition by middle-class audiences for whom the original legend had in fact only ever been an exotic dream. The two tough cane-cutters, Roo and Barney, who come down from the Queensland cane-fields each year to spend the "lay-off" season whooping it up in Melbourne, represented a vanishing national type with whom the city audiences liked to identify.

The *Doll* shows these two legendary characters failing to deal with the new urban Australia. The romantic dream of the lay-offs—times of innocent loving fun for the men and their barmaid girlfriends—is already beginning to fail as the play opens. Olive, Roo's woman, tries to sustain her vision of a nobler life than that which the "soft city blokes" have to offer, and she clings to it even when it brings personal tragedy for her, but the world of the soft city blokes wins, practically if not emotionally. For contemporary audiences, perhaps, the portrayal of Olive as a foolish woman who refuses to grow up (confirmed in the expanded *The Doll Trilogy*) has dated. There is some justice in her claim to have found a serious alternative to marriage, but after a series of reversals at the end we are left with a final ironic triumph of the legend, as Roo and Barney stagger out to head back north, leaving Olive alone in her grief.

The *Doll's* appeal, even for foreign audiences who know nothing of the bush legend, is based in the solid, old-fashioned virtues of well-made realism: detailed and consistent characterisation, a wonderfully rich use of vernacular, and a complex and carefully plotted action. These were virtues which Lawler showed he was still a master of when he came, 20 years after the original appearance of the *Doll*, to write the two additional plays which make up the trilogy, *Kid Stakes* and *Other Times*.

The extraordinary success of the *Doll* meant that Lawler's next plays, before the completion of the trilogy, were bound to be received with disappointment. *The Piccadilly Bushman* is a technically competent play which explores the self-image of an Australian expatriate actor who has achieved success as an actor in England and returns to confront what he now sees as his embarrassing "colonial" past. *The Man Who Shot the Albatross* is an historical play about a much-treated subject in Australian drama: the colonial Governor Bligh, struggling to deal with mutinous local bigwigs, and haunted by the memory of the other more famous mutineers on the *Bounty*. The play presents its subject largely in terms of personal conflict between Bligh and the politically astute landowner, John Macarthur—avoiding any wider historical or political exploration. For this reason, perhaps, it seemed rather old-fashioned in 1972. Neither of these two plays has had much impact in the Australian theatre.

Lawler lived abroad during the great upsurge in Australian drama of the early 1970's, but he returned in the mid-1970's to produce two plays which revived his reputation: *Kid Stakes* and *Other Times*. These plays are set prior to the *Doll*. They go back to the first and the ninth "lay-offs," introducing the appealing character of Nancy, whose memory so dominates the *Doll*, and generally filling in the background to what had by the mid-1970's become a well-known and well-loved part of the national heritage. *Kid Stakes* is a play of great charm. Its delightful portrait of an innocent young Australian society before World War II showed Lawler at his full strength, lamenting the loss of a simpler world. *Other Times*, set during the war, in winter, is written in a minor key, introducing a note of bitterness which anticipates the tragedy of the *Doll*.

The effect of the trilogy, ironically, was to lessen the impact of the original play. The new plays take so much trouble to plant hints anticipating the action of the *Doll* that the brilliant Ibsenite exposition in the original becomes rather pointless and the story and characters move into a new world of sophisticated soap opera. Again, however, the warmth and richness with which these familiar characters are developed make this one of the most charming works in the New Wave of Australian drama.

In 1982 Lawler produced his first major work since the trilogy, *Godsend*. The "godsend" is the discovery in a small rural church in Kent of the lost tomb of St. Thomas à Becket. Each of the four central characters—a traditionalist Catholic bishop, the Anglican Archbishop, an idealistic parson, and his agnostic wife—has a different interest in the holy remains, and through their conflict the play explores the nature of religious faith and the difficulties of sustaining it. Stylistically the play is a departure from the well-made realism of *The Doll Trilogy*, especially in its complex use of direct audience address. It is the work of a mature dramatist, with accomplished skills, which has not yet had the impact it deserves.

Lawler's place in the development of Australian drama is still assured by the *Doll*. If he has never repeated that success, it is perhaps partly because his dramatic interests have become less relevant to the issues which now involve Australian audiences, but he remains one of the most technically capable of all Australian dramatists, and one who has contributed some of the best-loved characters in the culture.

—John McCallum

LAWRENCE, Jerome. American. Born in Cleveland, Ohio, 14 July 1915. Educated at Ohio State University, Columbus, B.A. 1937; University of California, Los Angeles, 1939–40. Director of summer stock, Connellsville, Pennsylvania, then Pittsfield, Massachusetts, summers 1934-37; reporter and telegraph editor, Wilmington *News-Journal*, Ohio, 1937; editor, New Lexington *Daily News*, Ohio, 1937–38; continuity editor, KMPC Radio, Beverly Hills, California, 1938, 1939; senior staff writer, Columbia Broadcasting System, Hollywood and New York, 1939–41; scenario writer, Paramount Pictures, Hollywood, 1941. Expert consultant to the Secretary of War during World War II: co-founder of Armed Forces Radio Service, and radio correspondent in North Africa and Italy (wrote and directed the official Army-Navy programs for D-Day, VE Day and VJ Day). Since 1942 partner, Lawrence and Lee, and since 1955 president, Lawrence and Lee Inc., New York and Los Angeles. Founder and national president, Radio Writers Guild; co-founder and president, American Playwrights Theatre, 1970–85; co-founder and judge, Margo Jones award; founder and board member, Writers Guild of America; council member, Dramatists Guild and Authors League of America; member of the advisory board, Eugene O'Neill Foundation, American Conservatory Theatre, 1970–80, Board of Standards of the Living Theatre, Plumstead Playhouse, Stella Adler Theater, and Ohio State University School of Journalism. Professor, Banff School of Fine Arts, Alberta, Canada, 1950–53; member, U.S. State Department Cultural Exchange Panel, 1962–70. Master playwright, New York University, 1967, 1968; visiting professor of playwriting, Ohio State University, 1969; lecturer, Salzburg Seminar in American Studies, 1972; visiting professor, Baylor University, Waco, Texas, 1976; William Inge lecturer, Independence Community College, Kansas, 1983, 1986–91; professor of playwriting, University of Southern California, Los Angeles, 1984–92. Contributing editor, *Dramatics* magazine, Cincinnati. Recipient: New York Press Club award, 1942; *Radio-TV Life* award, 1948, 1952; Peabody award, 1949, 1952; *Radio-TV Mirror* award, 1952, 1953; *Variety* award, 1954, 1955; Donaldson award, 1955; Outer Circle award, 1955; British Drama Critics award, 1960; Moss Hart Memorial award, 1967; Ohio State University

Centennial award, 1970, and Alumni medal, 1985; American Theatre Association award, 1979; International Thespian Society Directors award, 1980; William Inge award, 1983; Valentine Davies award, 1984; Emmy award, 1988 (twice); Southeastern Theater Conference award, 1990; elected to Theater Hall of Fame and College of Fellows of the American Theatre, 1990. D.H.L.: Ohio State University, 1963; D.Litt.: Fairleigh Dickinson University, Rutherford, New Jersey, 1968; College of Wooster, Ohio, 1983; D.F.A.: Villanova University, Pennsylvania, 1969. Agent: Robert Freedman Dramatic Agency, 1501 Broadway, New York 10036; and, Mitch Douglas, International Creative Management, 40 West 57th Street, New York, New York 10019. Address: 21056 Las Flores Mesa Drive, Malibu, California 90265, U.S.A.

PUBLICATIONS

Plays

Laugh, God!, in *Six Anti-Nazi One-Act Plays*. New York, Contemporary Play Publications, 1939.

Tomorrow, with Budd Schulberg, in *Free World Theatre*, edited by Arch Oboler and Stephen Longstreet. New York, Random House, 1944.

Inside a Kid's Head, with Robert E. Lee, in *Radio Drama in Action*, edited by Erik Barnouw. New York, Farrar and Rinehart, 1945.

Look, Ma, I'm Dancin', with Robert E. Lee, music by Hugh Martin, conceived by Jerome Robbins (produced New York, 1948).

The Crocodile Smile, with Robert E. Lee (as *The Laugh Maker*, produced Hollywood, 1952; revised version, as *Turn on the Night*, produced Philadelphia, 1961; revised version, as *The Crocodile Smile*, also director: produced Flatrock, North Carolina, 1970). New York, Dramatists Play Service, 1972.

Inherit the Wind, with Robert E. Lee (produced Dallas and New York, 1955; London, 1960). New York, Random House, 1955; London, Four Square, 1960.

Shangri-La, with Robert E. Lee and James Hilton, music by Harry Warren, adaptation of the novel *Lost Horizon* by Hilton (produced New York, 1956). New York, Morris Music, 1956.

Auntie Mame, with Robert E. Lee, adaptation of the work by Patrick Dennis (produced New York, 1956; London, 1958). New York, Vanguard Press, 1957; revised version, music by Jerry Herman, as *Mame* (produced New York, 1966; London, 1969), New York, Random House, 1967.

The Gang's All Here, with Robert E. Lee (produced New York, 1959). Cleveland, World, 1960.

Only in America, with Robert E. Lee, adaptation of the work by Harry Golden (produced New York, 1959). New York, French, 1960.

A Call on Kuprin, with Robert E. Lee, adaptation of the novel by Maurice Edelman (produced New York, 1961). New York, French, 1962.

Sparks Fly Upward, with Robert E. Lee (as *Diamond Orchid*, produced New York, 1965; revised version, as *Sparks Fly Upward*, produced Dallas, 1967). New York, Dramatists Play Service, 1969.

Live Spelled Backwards (produced Beverly Hills, California, 1966). New York, Dramatists Play Service, 1970.

Dear World, with Robert E. Lee, music by Jerry Herman, based on *The Madwoman of Chaillot* by Giraudoux (produced New York, 1969).

The Incomparable Max, with Robert E. Lee (also director: produced Abingdon, Virginia, 1969; New York, 1971). New York, Hill and Wang, 1972.

The Night Thoreau Spent in Jail, with Robert E. Lee (produced Columbus, Ohio, and 154 other theatres, 1970). New York, Hill and Wang, 1970.

Jabberwock: Improbabilities Lived and Imagined by James Thurber in the Fictional City of Columbus, Ohio, with Robert E. Lee (produced Columbus, Ohio, 1972). New York, French, 1974.

First Monday in October, with Robert E. Lee (also director: produced Cleveland, 1975; New York, 1978). New York, French, 1979.

Whisper in the Mind, with Norman Cousins and Robert E. Lee (produced Tempe, Arizona, 1990).

The Plays of Lawrence and Lee, edited by Alan Woods (includes: *Inherit the Wind*, *Auntie Mame*, *The Gang's All Here*, *Only in America*, *A Call on Kuprin*, *Diamond Orchid*, *The Night Thoreau Spent in Jail*, *First Monday in October*). Columbus, Ohio, Ohio State University Press, 1992.

The Angels Weep. Published in *Studies in American Drama: 1945 to the Present*. (Columbus, Ohio), 1992.

Screenplays, with Robert E. Lee: *My Love Affair with the Human Race*, 1962; The *New Yorkers*, 1963; *Joyous Season*, 1964; The *Night Thoreau Spent in Jail*, 1972; *First Monday in October*, 1982.

Radio Plays: *Junior Theatre of the Air* series, 1938; *Under Western Skies* series, 1939; *Nightcap Yarns* series, 1939, 1940; *Stories from Life* series, 1939, 1940; *Man about Hollywood* series, 1940; *Hollywood Showcase* series, 1940, 1941; *A Date with Judy* series, 1941, 1942; *They Live Forever* series, 1942; *Everything for the Boys* series, 1944; *I Was There* series; with Robert E. Lee—*Columbia Workshop* series, 1941–42; *Armed Forces Radio Service Programs*, 1942–45; The *World We're Fighting For* series, 1943; *Request Performance* series, 1945–46; *Screen Guild Theatre* series, 1946; *Favorite Story* series, 1946–49; *Frank Sinatra Show*, 1947; *Dinah Shore Program*, 1948; The *Railroad Hour*, 1948–54; *Young Love* series, 1949–50; *United Nations Broadcasts*, 1949–50; *Halls of Ivy* series, 1950–51; *Hallmark Playhouse* series, 1950–51; *Charles Boyer Show*, 1951; other freelance and special programs, 1941–50.

Television Plays: *Lincoln, The Unwilling Warrior*, 1975; with Robert E. Lee—*The Unexpected* series, 1951; *Favorite Story* series, 1952–53; *Song of Norway*, 1957; *West Point*, 1958; *Actor*, music by Billy Goldenburg, 1978.

Other

Oscar the Ostrich (for children; as Jerome Schwartz). New York, Random House, 1940.

Actor: The Life and Times of Paul Muni. New York, Putnam, 1974; London, W.H. Allen, 1975.

Editor, *Off Mike: Radio Writing by the Nation's Top Radio Writers*. New York, Essential, 1944.

*

Bibliography: in *Studies in American Drama: 1945 to the Present* (Columbus, Ohio). 1992.

Manuscript Collections: Lawrence and Lee Theatre Research Institute, Ohio State University, Columbus; Lincoln Center Library of the Performing Arts, New York; Kent State

University, Ohio; Widener Library, Harvard University, Cambridge, Massachusetts; Ziv-United Artists film and transcription library.

Critical Study: "The Greatest Sport in the World" (interview with Christopher Meeks), in *Writer's Digest* (Cincinnati), March 1986.

Theatrical Activities:
Director: **Plays**—*You Can't Take It with You* by George S. Kaufman and Moss Hart, *The Imaginary Invalid* by Molière, *Anything Goes* by Howard Lindsay and Russel Crouse, *The Green Pastures* by Marc Connelly, *Boy Meets Girl* by Bella and Sam Spewack, *H.M.S. Pinafore* and *The Pirates of Penzance* by Gilbert and Sullivan, and *Androcles and the Lion* by Shaw, in summer stock, 1934–37; *Mame*, Sacramento, California, 1969; *The Incomparable Max*, Abingdon, Virginia, 1969; *The Crocodile Smile*, Flatrock, North Carolina, 1970; *The Night Thoreau Spent in Jail*, Dublin, 1972; *Jabberwock*, Dallas, 1974; *Inherit the Wind*, Dallas, 1975; *First Monday in October*, Cleveland, 1975.

Jerome Lawrence comments:
Robert E. Lee and I have been called by various critics: "the thinking man's playwrights." In our plays and in our teaching we have attempted to be part of our times. We have done all we can to encourage truly national and international theatre, not confined to a few blocks of real estate in Manhattan or London's West End. Thus, we have sought to promote the growth of regional and university theatres through the formation of American Playwrights Theatre, to bring new and vital and pertinent works to all of America and all of the world.

It has been my privilege to travel to more than a hundred countries, often on cultural-exchange missions. At home, through the years, we have tried to encourage new and untried playwrights, stimulating their work through teaching and through the annual Margo Jones Award.

In our plays we have hoped to mirror and illuminate the problems of the moment—but we have attempted to grapple with universal themes, even in our comedies. We have tried for a blend between the dramatic and the entertaining: our most serious works are always leavened with laughter (*Inherit the Wind* is an example) and our seemingly frivolous comedies (*Auntie Mame*, *Mame*, *Jabberwock*) have sub-texts which we hope say something important for the contemporary world. We are pleased and gratified that our plays have been translated and produced in 34 languages.

We are lovers of the living theatre and intend to continue working and living in it.

*   *   *

"Eatable things to eat and drinkable things to drink," comments a shocked character in Dickens's short story "Mugby Junction," describing a visit to France. The British railway station buffet is the object of Dickens's scorn, and the news that French railways provide edible and easily assimilated food causes the staff of Mugby Junction's restaurant to come close to catatonic fits.

Many a critic, professional *or* amateur, might, in snobbish chorus, make similar comments about the works of collaborators Jerome Lawrence and Robert E. Lee. "Playable plays to play—or readable plays to read!" might be their disbelieving cry. The expressions of disapproval and disdain might be almost as extreme as those of the 19th-century railway grotesques, for both playability and readability are cardinal points

of the works of Lawrence and Lee. Their plots are tight, their characters cleanly developed, their dialogue smooth. Actors like them for they present strong speeches and well developed scenes, and although this might be considered old-fashioned playwriting it is clear that audiences like it too. Their most successful work, *Inherit the Wind* (first presented at the National Theatre in New York, April 1955, after a run in Dallas under a great encourager of new talent, Margo Jones) was the third longest-running serious play in the history of Broadway. It is based on the famous Scopes Trial in Tennessee (the "Monkey Trial") when Darwinism and traditional religion had a head-on crash in a rural American setting. It featured Paul Muni and Ed Begley, who made the dialogue of this solid courtroom drama flow back and forth like a mounting tide. The script is very readable; although not deep it is most engaging in a theatrical, if not an intellectually involving way. The effect of putting two great contemporary orators, pitted one against the other, as the core of the play makes for compelling speeches, and the device of the trial itself provides a rounded dramatic vehicle, still open-ended enough to allow one of the protagonists to stand at the end weighing copies of the Bible and Darwin while planning the appeal. Today's audience (even though we would like to think ourselves beyond quaint beliefs) can still become emotionally involved over God versus gorilla. Good and forceful fare, it has been produced around the world.

Many of the works of Lawrence and Lee are lighter, mirroring their ability to zero in on the essentially sentimental underbelly of the average Broadway audience. Their evident enjoyment of the sentimental is one of their secrets. By far the largest part of the Broadway audience is out for fun, a pleasurable look at the land of never-never, which is why the musical when successful is always such a huge money-spinner. Lawrence and Lee pull off a clever trick with *Inherit the Wind* for it has many elements of the musical, yet gives patrons the self-importance of feeling they have seen something serious. They are also at home in creating an impossible character like *Auntie Mame*, first produced in New York in 1956. This giddy American dame was adored onstage, although she probably would not have been tolerated for more than a moment beyond Manhattan or Wilshire Boulevard. Many of the members of the audience would have come from suburban patios like the satirized Upsons (whose house in Connecticut is called "Upson Downs"—Lawrence has a weakness for rather ponderous puns in conversation and his own California house is called "Writers to the Sea") but the social comment is kept gentle and the medicine is never too strong. An amusing evening and intended to be nothing more no doubt, yet for this writer the play only sparked into life when Beatrice Lillie played the part in the London production.

Auntie Mame became the very successful musical *Mame* (May 1966) which Lawrence and Lee also wrote, featuring the then relatively unknown Angela Lansbury. Their collaboration on a monolithic musical called *Dear World* based on the Giraudoux play *The Madwoman of Chaillot* was less successful. However, it's hard to find fault with writers when faced with the complexities of producing musicals in New York City where music, lyrics, choreography, special songs, production numbers, direction, elaborate costumes, and staggering scenery—along with equally staggering costs— seem often to overwhelm the basic book.

Nevertheless Lawrence and Lee seem happier when they are away from the big-time musical stage, as witness their commitment to a play entitled *The Night Thoreau Spent in Jail*. This play, first presented at Ohio State University in 1970, is an interesting experiment. Some years ago, intent on trying to circumvent the sterile Broadway scene where serious plays are concerned, the partners set up American Playwrights Theatre in Columbus, Ohio. It was a deliberate move away from New York in a laudable attempt to develop new audiences for serious drama, with the plays of dramatists, known and unknown, presented in a new "circuit"—the network of resident and university theatres across America. Each writer was guaranteed a number of *different* productions in various spots on this new circuit and many were produced before Lawrence and Lee launched one of their own—*Thoreau*, a subject of particular interest to young audiences, for it deals with one of the first cases of civil disobedience in America. Later collaborations include *Jabberwock* and *First Monday in October*.

Their hand with humour can, unfortunately, be a little heavy, and when tackling such a delicate exponent of the art as Max Beerbohm in *The Incomparable Max* they became caught in a morass that was anything but Maxian. There are times when the pair cleaves dangerously close to the jungle of clichés.

Lawrence and Lee collaborate easily—each has a veto, "but it's a positive one" says Lawrence. They both feel they can, and do, learn from criticism. Their contribution to American drama is perhaps most significant when one looks at the number of nations that know them from the many translations of their principle works. *Inherit the Wind* has been translated into 28 different languages while the citizens of Ireland, Israel, Holland, Germany, Bangladesh, and Russia, among others, have been given an eye-opening view of a Yankee philosopher's protest in *Thoreau*.

—Michael T. Leech

LAWSON, John Howard. American. 1894–1977.
See 2nd edition, 1977.

LEE, Robert E(dwin). American. Born in Elyria, Ohio, 15 October 1918. Educated at Northwestern University, Evanston, Illinois; Drake University, Des Moines, Iowa; Ohio Wesleyan University, Delaware, 1935–37. Served in the United States Army, 1942–45: Expert Consultant to the Secretary of War, 1942; co-founder, Armed Forces Radio Service; writer-director, Armed Forces Radio Service, Los Angeles, 1942–45: Special Citation, Secretary of War, 1945. Married Janet Waldo in 1948; one son and one daughter. Astronomical observer, Perkins Observatory, Delaware, Ohio, 1936–37; director, WHK-WCLE Radio, Cleveland, 1937–38; director, Young and Rubicam, New York and Hollywood, 1938–42; professor of playwriting, College of Theatre Arts, Pasadena Playhouse, California, 1962–63. Since 1942 partner, Lawrence and Lee, and since 1955 vice-president, Lawrence and Lee Inc., New York and Los Angeles; since 1966, lecturer, University of California, Los Angeles. Co-founder and judge, Margo Jones award; co-founder, American Playwrights Theatre. Recipient: New York Press Club award, 1942; City College of New York

award, 1948; *Radio-TV Life* award, 1948, 1952; Peabody award, 1949, 1952; *Radio-TV Mirror* award, 1952, 1953; *Variety* award, 1954, 1955; Donaldson award, 1955; Outer Circle award, 1955; British Drama Critics award, 1960; Moss Hart Memorial award, 1967; William Inge award, 1988; elected to Theater Hall of Fame and College of Fellows of the American Theatre, 1990. Lit.D.: Ohio Wesleyan University, 1962; M.A.: Pasadena Playhouse College of Theatre Arts, 1963; H.H.D.: Ohio State University, Columbus, 1979; Litt.D.: College of Wooster, Ohio, 1983. Agent (Attorney): Martin Gang, 6400 Sunset Boulevard, Hollywood, California 90028. Address: 15725 Royal Oak Road, Encino, California 91436, U.S.A.

PUBLICATIONS

Plays

Inside a Kid's Head, with Jerome Lawrence, in *Radio Drama in Action*, edited by Erik Barnouw. New York, Farrar and Rinehart, 1945.

Look, Ma, I'm Dancin', with Jerome Lawrence, music by Hugh Martin, conceived by Jerome Robbins (produced New York, 1948).

The Crocodile Smile, with Jerome Lawrence (as *The Laugh Maker*, produced Hollywood, 1952; revised version, as *Turn on the Night*, produced Philadelphia, 1961; revised version, as *The Crocodile Smile*, produced Flatrock, North Carolina, 1970). New York, Dramatists Play Service, 1972.

Inherit the Wind, with Jerome Lawrence (produced Dallas and New York, 1955; London, 1960). New York, Random House, 1955; London, Four Square, 1960.

Shangri-La, with Jerome Lawrence and James Hilton, music by Harry Warren, adaptation of the novel *Lost Horizon* by Hilton (produced New York, 1956). New York, Morris Music, 1956.

Auntie Mame, with Jerome Lawrence, adaptation of the work by Patrick Dennis (produced New York, 1956; London, 1958). New York, Vanguard Press, 1957; revised version, music by Jerry Herman, as *Mame* (produced New York, 1966; London, 1969), New York, Random House, 1967.

The Gang's All Here, with Jerome Lawrence (produced New York, 1959). Cleveland, World, 1960.

Only in America, with Jerome Lawrence, adaptation of the work by Harry Golden (produced New York, 1959). New York, French, 1960.

A Call on Kuprin, with Jerome Lawrence, adaptation of the novel by Maurice Edelman (produced New York, 1961). New York, French, 1962.

Sparks Fly Upward, with Jerome Lawrence (as *Diamond Orchid*, produced New York, 1965; revised version, as *Sparks Fly Upward*, produced Dallas, 1967). New York, Dramatists Play Service, 1969.

Dear World, with Jerome Lawrence, music by Jerry Herman, based on *The Madwoman of Chaillot* by Giraudoux (produced New York, 1969).

The Incomparable Max, with Jerome Lawrence (produced Abingdon, Virginia, 1969; New York, 1971). New York, Hill and Wang, 1972.

The Night Thoreau Spent in Jail, with Jerome Lawrence (produced Columbus, Ohio, and 154 other theatres, 1970). New York, Hill and Wang, 1970.

Jabberwock: Improbabilities Lived and Imagined by James Thurber in the Fictional City of Columbus, Ohio, with Jerome Lawrence (produced Columbus, Ohio, 1972). New York, French, 1974.

Ten Days That Shook the World, based on reports from Russia by John Reed (also director: produced Los Angeles, 1973).

First Monday in October, with Jerome Lawrence (produced Cleveland, 1975; New York, 1978). New York, French, 1979.

Sounding Brass (produced New York, 1975). New York, French, 1976.

Whisper in the Mind, with Norman Cousins and Jerome Lawrence (produced Tempe, Arizona, 1990).

The Plays of Lawrence and Lee, edited by Alan Woods (includes *Inherit the Wind, Auntie Mame, The Gang's All Here, Only in America, A Call on Kuprin, Diamond Orchid, The Night Thoreau Spent in Jail, First Monday in October*). Columbus, Ohio, Ohio State University Press, 1992.

Screenplays, with Jerome Lawrence—*My Love Affair with the Human Race*, 1962; *The New Yorkers*, 1963; *Joyous Season*, 1964; *The Night Thoreau Spent in Jail*, 1972; *First Monday in October*, 1982; with John Sinn—*Quintus*, 1971.

Radio Plays: *Empire Builders* series, 1938; *Opened by Mistake*, 1940; *Flashbacks* series, 1940–41; *Three Sheets to the Wind*, 1942; *Task Force*, 1942; *Ceiling Unlimited*, 1942; *Meet Corliss Archer*, 1942; *Suspense*, 1943; *The Saint* 1945; with Jerome Lawrence—*Columbia Workshop* series, 1941–42; *Armed Forces Radio Service Programs*, 1942–45; *The World We're Fighting For* series, 1943; *Request Performance* series, 1945–46; *Screen Guild Theatre* series, 1946; *Favorite Story* series, 1946–49; *Frank Sinatra Show*, 1947; *Dinah Shore Program*, 1948; *The Railroad Hour*, 1948–54; *Young Love* series, 1949–50; *United Nations Broadcasts*, 1949–50; *Halls of Ivy* series, 1950–51; *Hallmark Playhouse* series, 1950–51; *Charles Boyer Show*, 1951; other freelance and special programs, 1941–50.

Television Plays: *A Colloquy with Paul*, 1961; with Jerome Lawrence—*The Unexpected* series, 1951; *Favorite Story* series, 1952–53; *Song of Norway*, 1957; *West Point*, 1958; *Actor*, music by Billy Goldenburg, 1978.

Other

Television: The Revolution. New York, Essential, 1944.

*

Bibliography: in *Studies in American Drama: 1945 to the Present* (Columbus, Ohio) 1992.

Manuscript Collections: Lawrence and Lee Theatre Research Institute, Ohio State University, Columbus; Lincoln Center Library of the Performing Arts, New York; Kent State University, Ohio.

Critical Study: "The Greatest Sport in the World" (interview with Christopher Meeks), in *Writer's Digest* (Cincinnati), March 1986.

Theatrical Activities:
Director: **Plays**—*Only in America*, Los Angeles, 1960; *The Night Thoreau Spent in Jail*, Los Angeles, 1970; *The Gang's All Here*, Los Angeles, 1972; *Ten Days That Shook the World*, Los Angeles, 1973.

Robert E. Lee comments:
The devil's name is Dullness. An eraser is sometimes more essential than a pencil. But merely to entertain is fatuous. Writing for today is really writing for yesterday; I try to write for tomorrow.

* * *

See the essay on Jerome Lawrence and Robert E. Lee.

———

LEIGH, Mike. British. Born in Salford, Lancashire, 20 February 1943. Educated at North Grecian Street County Primary School; Salford Grammar School; Royal Academy of Dramatic Art, London, 1960–62; Camberwell School of Arts and Crafts, London, 1963–64; Central School of Art and Design, London, 1964–65; London Film School, 1965. Married the actress Alison Steadman in 1973; two sons. Founder, with David Halliwell, Dramagraph production company, London, 1965; associate director, Midlands Arts Centre for Young People, Birmingham, 1965–66; actor, Victoria Theatre, Stoke-on-Trent, Staffordshire, 1966; assistant director, Royal Shakespeare Company, 1967–68; lecturer, Sedgley Park and De La Salle colleges, Manchester, 1968–69, and London Film School, 1970–73. Recipient: Chicago Film Festival and Locarno Film Festival awards, 1972; George Devine award, 1974; *Evening Standard* award, 1982, 1989; Venice Film Festival Critics award, 1988; Stars de Demain Coup de Coeur, 1989; Peter Sellers Comedy award, 1989; National Society of Film Critics Best Film award, 1991. Agent: Peters, Fraser, and Dunlop Group, 503/4 The Chambers, Chelsea Harbour, Lots Road, London SW10 0XF, England.

PUBLICATIONS

Plays

The Box Play (produced Birmingham, 1965).

My Parents Have Gone to Carlisle (produced Birmingham, 1966).

The Last Crusade of the Five Little Nuns (produced Birmingham, 1966).

Waste Paper Guards, (produced Birmingham, 1966).

NENAA (produced Stratford-on-Avon, 1967).

Individual Fruit Pies (produced Loughton, Essex, 1968).

Down Here and Up There (produced London, 1968).

Big Basil (produced Manchester, 1969).

Epilogue (produced Manchester, 1969).

Glum Victoria and the Lad with Specs (produced Manchester, 1969).

Bleak Moments (produced London, 1970).

A Rancid Pong (produced London, 1971).

Wholesome Glory (produced London, 1973).

The Jaws of Death (produced Edinburgh, 1973; London, 1978).

Dick Whittington and His Cat (produced London, 1973).

Babies Grow Old (produced Stratford-on-Avon, 1974; London, 1975).

The Silent Majority (produced London, 1974).

Abigail's Party (produced London, 1977). With *Goose-Pimples*, London, Penguin, 1983.

Ecstasy (produced London, 1979). With *Smelling a Rat*, London, Hern, 1989.

Goose-Pimples, (produced London, 1981). With *Abigail's Party*, London, Penguin, 1983.

Smelling a Rat (produced London, 1988). With *Ecstasy*, London, Hern, 1989.

Greek Tragedy (produced Sydney, 1989; Edinburgh and London, 1990).

Screenplays: *Bleak Moments*, 1972; *The Short and Curlies*, 1987; *High Hopes*, 1988; *Life Is Sweet*, 1991.

Radio Play: *Too Much of a Good Thing*, 1979 (banned).

Television Plays: *A Mug's Game*, 1973; *Hard Labour*, 1973; "Five Minute Films": *The Birth of the 2001 FA Cup Final Goalie, Old Chums, Probation, A Light Snack*, and *Afternoon*, all 1975; *The Permissive Society*, 1975; *Nuts in May*, 1976; *Knock for Knock*, 1976; *The Kiss of Death*, 1977; *Who's Who*, 1979; *Grown-Ups*, 1980; *Home Sweet Home*, 1982; *Meantime*, 1983; *Four Days in July*, 1985.

*

Critical Study: *The Improvised Play: The Work of Mike Leigh* by Paul Clements, London, Methuen, 1983.

Theatrical Activities:
Director of all his own plays and films.

* * *

"My work" said Mike Leigh in a recent interview, "is always very strictly scripted with serious literary considerations."

Such words should be taken into account when assessing Leigh's plays, for a misconception has grown up—caused perhaps by his famous improvisational method—that his work is simply a "slice of life." Nothing could be further from the truth—though, as anyone who has seen his plays will attest, this method does give his pieces a very recognizable form and flavour.

Leigh produces his work through a process that is, broadly speaking, collaborational. A group of actors is selected and each is presented with the germ of a character. They are then asked to go away and develop these characters, using their own experience and imagination. At the end of several weeks, or months, they are reassembled and, under Leigh's direction, a play is put together. The accent here is on "under Leigh's direction": although he welcomes, indeed expects, creative input from his actors, Leigh remains very much in control. "I function as author and director," he has said. "There's no committee involved."

Such a process produces a very particular kind of play. Plots are simple, almost non-existent; language is idiomatic, even vulgar. There are no great dramatic moments, no soaring lyrical flights—little, indeed, that is "theatre" in the usual sense. What there *is* is a close and exact study of suburban angst which uses the smallest words and actions to highlight undercurrents of malice and frustration. It's Artaud moved to Pinner, one might say, or Beckett in Brooklyn. What it's not is simply a "slice of life."

Leigh's first major success, and still his most popular play, was *Abigail's Party*. Eponymous Abigail is having a thrash; intimidated, her mother Sue retreats to the lurid drawing room of neighbour Beverley, a former beautician, and of her estate agent husband Laurence. Two other guests arrive;

what should be a "lovely evening" then degenerates into a hilariously grotesque nightmare of jealousy, cruelty, and indifference. We laugh at Leigh's characters, but we laugh uneasily: in their material wealth and spiritual poverty they are, perhaps, a little too close for comfort.

Ecstasy, Leigh's next play, stands a little apart from his other pieces. Here the characters are working-class rather than lower middle-class; and, though desperate, Jean and Dawn, and Mike and Len, manifest a clumsy warmth and sympathy quite absent from, say, *Abigail's Party*. Particularly moving are the songs that end the play—songs whose sweetness (and occasional indecency) accentuate the characters' human pathos to an almost unbearable degree.

Two years later came *Goose-Pimples*, a return, at least in tone, to the world of *Abigail's Party*. Jackie, trainee croupier and lodger, brings home Muhammed, a small-time Arab businessman, for a drink. He thinks she's a prostitute; she thinks he's an oil-sheik. Into this misunderstanding barges her landlord, a car dealer, a colleague of his from work, and the colleague's wife. What follows is a parody of West End farce, with exits and entrances and muddles galore. At the end of the piece the two Englishmen, in a fit of drunken and entirely spurious gallantry, assault and humiliate Muhammed—a graphic depiction of the violence and xenophobia undercutting British society. It's a brutal moment; the shadow of Pinter, one feels, is hovering nearby.

After several years of film and television work Leigh returned to the stage with *Smelling a Rat*. More a playlet than a play, it is, perhaps, the slightest of Leigh's pieces. Of greater substance is *Greek Tragedy*, which Leigh directed in Australia in 1989. This project was something of a risk, for by his own admission Leigh knew nothing of Greek-Australian society. Using, however, a cast drawn entirely from this ethnic group he overcame this difficulty, producing by his collaborational method a play every bit as accurate and discomforting as his British pieces. A tragedy in more than one sense (it observes, for example, the classical unities), *Greek Tragedy* portrays the sterile, loveless marriage of Kalliope and Alex, two workers in the rag trade for whom the Australian dream has scarcely come true. Into their stifled lives burst Larry and Vicki, emigrant success stories and monsters *par excellence*; the stage is then set for another of Leigh's studies in suburban cruelty and frustration. If it all sounds a little familiar—*Goose-Pimples*, as it were, translated Down Under—it's still horribly unerring; one waits with interest to see what Leigh will do next.

—John O'Leary

———

LEONARD, Hugh. Pseudonym for John Keyes Byrne. Irish. Born in Dublin, 9 November 1926. Educated at Presentation College, Dun Laoghaire, 1941–45. Married Paule Jacquet in 1955; one daughter. Civil servant, Dublin, 1945–59; script editor, Granada Television, Manchester, 1961–63; literary editor, Abbey Theatre, Dublin, 1976–77; programme director, Dublin Theatre Festival, 1978–80. Recipient: Italia prize, for television play, 1967; Writers Guild of Great Britain award, 1967; Tony award, 1978; New York Drama Critics Circle award, 1978; Outer Circle award, 1978; Vernon Rice award, 1978; Sagittarius prize. D.H.L.: Rhode Island College, Providence, 1980; D. Litt.: Trinity College, Dublin,

1989. Agent: Lemon, Unna, and Durbridge, 24 Pottery Lane, Holland Park, London W11 4LZ, England. Address: 6 Rossaun, Pilot View, Dalkey, County Dublin, Ireland.

PUBLICATIONS

Plays

The Italian Road (produced Dublin, 1954).

The Big Birthday (produced Dublin, 1956).

A Leap in the Dark (produced Dublin, 1957).

Madigan's Lock (produced Dublin, 1958; London, 1963; Olney, Maryland, 1970). With *Pizzazz*, Dublin, Brophy, 1987.

A Walk on the Water (produced Dublin, 1960).

The Passion of Peter Ginty, adaptation of the play *Peer Gynt* by Ibsen (produced Dublin, 1961).

Stephen D, adaptation of the works *A Portrait of the Artist as a Young Man* and *Stephen Hero* by James Joyce (produced Dublin, 1962; London, 1963; New York, 1967). London, Evans, 1965.

Dublin One, adaptation of the stories *Dubliners* by James Joyce (produced Dublin, 1963).

The Poker Session (produced Dublin, 1963; London, 1964; New York, 1967). London, Evans, 1963.

The Family Way, adaptation of a play by Eugène Labiche (produced Dublin, 1964; London, 1966).

The Late Arrival of the Incoming Aircraft (televised 1964). London, Evans, 1968.

A View from the Obelisk (televised 1964; in *Scorpions*, produced Dublin, 1983).

The Saints Go Cycling In, adaptation of the novel *The Dalkey Archives* by Flann O'Brien (produced Dublin, 1965).

Mick and Mick (produced Dublin, 1966; as *All the Nice People*, produced Olney, Maryland, 1976; New York, 1984). London, French, 1966.

A Time of Wolves and Tigers (televised 1967; produced in *Irishmen*, Olney, Maryland, and Dublin, 1975). Included in *Suburb of Babylon*, 1983.

The Quick, and The Dead (produced Dublin, 1967).

The Au Pair Man (produced Dublin, 1968; London, 1969; New York, 1973). Published in *Plays and Players* (London), December 1968; New York, French, 1974.

The Barracks, adaptation of the novel by John McGahern (produced Dublin, 1969).

The Patrick Pearse Motel (produced Dublin and London, 1971; Olney, Maryland, 1972; New York, 1984). London, French, 1972.

Da (produced Olney, Maryland, and Dublin, 1973; London, 1977; New York, 1978). Newark, Delaware, Proscenium Press, 1976; revised version, London, French and New York, Atheneum, 1978.

Summer (produced Olney, Maryland, and Dublin, 1974; London, 1979; New York, 1980). London, French, 1979.

Suburb of Babylon (includes *A Time of Wolves and Tigers*, *Nothing Personal*, *The Last of the Last of the Mohicans*) (as *Irishmen*, produced Olney, Maryland, and Dublin, 1975). London, French, 1983.

Some of My Best Friends Are Husbands, adaptation of a play by Eugène Labiche (produced London, 1976).

Liam Liar, adaptation of the play *Billy Liar* by Keith Waterhouse and Willis Hall (produced Dublin, 1976).

Time Was (produced Dublin, 1976). Included in *Da, A Life, Time Was*, 1981.

A Life (produced Dublin, 1979; London and New York, 1980). London, French, 1980; New York, Atheneum, 1981.

Da, A Life, Time Was. London, Penguin, 1981.

Kill (produced Dublin, 1982; New York, 1986.)

Pizzazz (produced Dublin, 1983). London, French, 1986.

Scorpions (includes *A View from the Obelisk*, *Roman Fever*, *Pizzazz*) (produced Dublin, 1983).

The Mask of Moriarty, based on characters by Arthur Conan Doyle (produced Dublin, 1985; Leicester, 1987).

Moving (produced Dublin, 1992).

Screenplays: *Great Catherine*, 1967; *Interlude*, with Lee Langley, 1967; *Whirligig*, 1970; *Percy*, with Terence Feely, 1970; *Our Miss Fred*, 1972; *Widows' Peak*, 1986; *Da*, 1989.

Radio Plays: *The Kennedys of Castleross* series.

Television Plays: *The Irish Boys* (trilogy), 1962; *Saki* series, 1962; *A Kind of Kingdom*, 1963; *Jezebel Ex-UK* series, 1963; *The Second Wall*, 1964; *A Triple Irish*, 1964; *Realm of Error*, 1964; *My One True Love*, 1964; *The Late Arrival of the Incoming Aircraft*, 1964; *Do You Play Requests?*, 1964; *A View from the Obelisk*, 1964; *The Hidden Truth* series, 1964; *Undermind* series, 1964; *I Loved You Last Summer*, 1965; *Great Big Blond*, 1965; *Blackmail* series, 1965; *Public Eye* series, 1965; *Simenon* series: *The Lodger* and *The Judge*, 1966; *Insurrection* (8 parts), 1966; *Second Childhood*, 1966; *The Retreat*, 1966; *Silent Song*, from a story by Frank O'Connor, 1966; *The Liars* series, 1966; *The Informer* series, 1966; *Out of the Unknown* series, 1966–67; *A Time of Wolves and Tigers*, 1967; *Love Life*, 1967; *Great Expectations* (serialization), from the novel by Dickens, 1967; *Wuthering Heights* (serialization), from the novel by Emily Brontë, 1967; *No Such Things as a Vampire*, 1968; *The Corpse Can't Play*, 1968; *A Man and His Mother-in-Law*, 1968; *Assassin*, 1968; *Nicholas Nickleby* (serialization), from the novel by Dickens, 1968; *Conan Doyle* series: *A Study in Scarlet* and *The Hound of the Baskervilles*, 1968; *Hunt the Peacock*, from a novel by H.R.F. Keating, 1969; *Talk of Angels*, 1969; *The Possessed* (serialization), from a novel by Dostoevsky, 1969; *Dombey and Son* (serialization), from the novel by Dickens, 1969; *Somerset Maugham* series: *P & O*, 1969, and *Jane*, 1970; *A Sentimental Education* (serialization), from a novel by Flaubert, 1970; *The Sinners* series, 1970–71; *Me Mammy* series, 1970–71; *White Walls and Olive Green Carpets*, 1971; *The Removal Person*, 1971; *Pandora*, 1971; *The Virgins*, 1972; *The Ghost of Christmas Present*, 1972; *The Truth Game*, 1972; *Tales from the Lazy Acres* series, 1972; *The Moonstone* (serialization), from the novel by Wilkie Collins, 1972; *The Sullen Sisters*, 1972; *The Watercress Girl*, from the story by H.E. Bates, 1972; *The Higgler*, 1973; *High Kampf*, 1973; *Milo O'Shea*, 1973; *Stone Cold Sober*, 1973; *The Bitter Pill*, 1973; *Another Fine Mess*, 1973; *Judgement Day*, 1973; *The Travelling Woman*, 1973; *The Hammer of God*, *The Actor and the Alibi*, *The Eye of Apollo*, *The Forbidden Garden*, *The Three Tools of Death*, and *The Quick One* (*Father Brown* series), 1974; *London Belongs to Me*, from the novel by Norman Collins, 1977; *Bitter Suite*, 1977; *Teresa*, *The Fur Coat*, and *Two of a Kind*, from stories by Sean O'Faolain, 1977; *The Last Campaign*, from the novel *The Captains and the Kings* by Jennifer Johnston, 1978; *The Ring and the Rose*, 1978; *Strumpet City*, from the novel by James Plunkett, 1980; *The Little World of Don Camillo*, from a novel by Giovanni Guareschi, 1981; *Good Behaviour*, from a work by Molly Keane, 1983; *O'Neill* series, 1983; *The Irish R.M.* series, 1985; *Hunted Down*, from a story by Dickens, 1985; *Troubles*, 1987; *Parnell and the Englishwoman* (serialization), from his own novel, 1991.

Novel

Parnell and the Englishwoman. New York, Atheneum, 1990.

Other

Leonard's Last Book (essays). Enniskerry, County
Wicklow, Egoist Press, 1978.
A Peculiar People and Other Foibles (essays). Enniskerry,
County Wicklow, Tansy, 1979.
Home Before Night: Memoirs of an Irish Time and Place.
London, Deutsch, 1979; New York, Atheneum, 1980.
Leonard's Year (journalism). Dublin, Canavaun, 1985.
Out After Dark (memoirs). London, Deutsch, 1989.
Rover and Other Cats (memoirs). London, Deutsch, 1992.

*

Bibliography: *Ten Modern Irish Playwrights* by Kimball
King, New York, Garland, 1979.

Theatrical Activities:
Actor: **Play**—in *A Walk on the Water*, Dublin, 1960.

Hugh Leonard comments:
(1973) Being an Irish writer both hampers and helps me:
hampers, because one is fighting the preconceptions of
audiences who have been conditioned to expect feyness and
parochial subject matter; helps, because the writer can utilise
a vigorous and poetic idiom which enables him to combine
subtlety with richness. Ireland is my subject matter, but only
to the degree in which I can use it as a microcosm; this
involves choosing themes which are free of Catholicism and
politics, both of which I detest, and which deprive one's work
of applicability outside Ireland.

For many years I was obsessed with the theme of betrayal
(*A Walk on the Water* and *The Poker Session*)—its effects and
its inevitability. My work then began to reflect a preoccupation with defining and isolating the essence of the new prosperity, which I used as the subject for satire (*The Patrick
Pearse Motel* and *Thieves*, as yet unproduced). By and large
—and after the event—my work reflects Ibsen's observation
that to be a writer is to sit in judgment on oneself; and
perhaps for this reason I now want to write a play which, like
A Walk on the Water and *Pandora*, is autobiographical. Like
most writers I am involved in seeking a form. A play takes me
a long time to write, and my methods involve—partly deliberately, partly because of how I work—various subterranean
levels. At times this leads to an excess of cleverness, stemming perhaps from a lack of faith in one's own powers. Now
that I have learned both the requirements and the uses of the
dramatic form I would like to use a simplicity of style combined with visual situations—the image in my mind is the
scene in which Lavinia confronts her mother across her
father's corpse in *Mourning Becomes Electra*.

Like all writers who achieve middle-age, I am conscious of
having wasted time, and also of having at last arrived at a
sense of identity. Ideally, I would now like to write my
"failures"; i.e., plays written as pure acts of self-expression,
without any hope of their being staged. I am conscious that
my main faults are the cleverness (in the structural sense)
which I have mentioned and at times an irresponsible sense of
comedy, which is not so much out of place as inclined to give
my work an unintended lightness. These faults at least I know
and can guard against. I regard myself as an optimist, and the
theme that emerges from my plays is that life is good if it is
not misused. But this is only an impression which—again

after the event—I have gleaned from revisiting my work. As
Moss Hart has said, one begins with two people on a stage,
and one of them had better say something pretty damn quick!
One starts to write, and one's own character and beliefs—not
consciously defined—shapes, limits, enriches, pauperises,
and defines one's work. Choice of subject and form are the
cartridge case which contains the bullet. A play is an accident:
often one writes the right play at the wrong time in one's life,
and vice-versa; often one begins to write it that vital fraction
in time before it has ripened in one's skull—or a moment too
late, when it has gone cold. One goes on trying.

*   *   *

In the masterful autobiography of his early years, *Home
Before Night*, Hugh Leonard tells of his gradual progress into
the stifling prize of a job in the Irish civil service. The book is
an eloquent statement of reconciliation, exploring his illegiti-
macy and family relationships, and is a rich lode of characters, full of personalities that are developed further in his
plays. There is a passage toward the end where he records his
first serious experience of theatre-going, when he visited the
Abbey's production of Sean O'Casey's *The Plough and the
Stars*. His prose crystallizes that experience, communicating
the personal epiphany that made him a playwright. Rushing
from the theatre to a train, he found himself in a compartment with a courting couple, sulking at his presence: "The
pair of them could strip to their skins for all he cared. He
looked away from them through the window and saw his
reflection in the dark glass. It was amazing how calm he
looked. His breath in the unheated compartment threw a mist
upon the glass, but even then he could see, as if it was out
there by the tracks, the door he would escape through."

Since O'Casey Irish playwrights have made Ireland their
major subject. Leonard has claimed his place in that tradition,
but there are essential differences, and he has always looked
for broader applicability. He works mainly through the
emergent middle classes of Ireland, with conflicts more suburban than urban and politics and religion as mere ghosts in the
background. They are, of course, inescapable ghosts.

His best plays explore the characters of his own life, and
stretch from *A Walk on the Water* to *A Life*, with 20 years of
experience between the plays and a rare, deepening texture
that demonstrates his own increased understanding of the
past. Memory is also the form of many of his adaptations,
including his first international success, *Stephen D*, a dramatization of James Joyce's autobiographical books. Using both
A Portrait of the Artist as a Young Man and Joyce's earlier,
more straightforward version of the book, *Stephen Hero*,
Leonard showed his sympathy for the metaphysical flight of
Dedalus—Joyce's own exile from church, family, and Ireland
—as directly as if telling his own story.

His earliest plays found him more within the Irish dramatic
tradition, even showing a concern with politics, but the form
of *A Leap in the Dark* suggested his alienation from the
violent course Irish politics often took. On a New Year's Eve
in Dublin, a father and son fall out over the new troubles in
Northern Ireland, with the son opposing the violence so
completely that his best friend tries to show the reasoning
behind the border raids by confessing his own part in them.
The son, Charles, then discovers that another raid is in the
making and sets out to inform the police. On his return to the
house, he is shot.

It is rare that such scenes are depicted in Leonard's work,
but his private path has wandered in many directions. After
his start in theatre, writing plays for the Dublin Theatre
Festival, he learned the disciplines of prolificacy by writing a

serial called *The Kennedys of Castlerosse* for commercial radio. He went from Irish radio to British television, editing scripts, writing dramas and churning out numerous series. In the midst of that work, and while providing a steady stream of original plays for the stage, he continued adapting the work of other writers. Before *Stephen D*, there was the Irish *Peer Gynt*, which he called *The Passion of Peter Ginty*. Flann O'Brien's surreal humour in *The Dalkey Archives* went to the stage as *The Saints Go Cycling In* and *Billy Liar* was transformed into an Irish play for the Abbey as *Liam Liar*.

Leonard, who is known to most of Ireland as Jack Byrne, or plain Jack, since they reject the pseudonym of Hugh Leonard, is quick to point out that an Irish literary movement is when two playwrights are on speaking terms. Nonetheless he has found himself at the centre of Irish letters on several occasions, including the stormy year he spent as literary manager of the Abbey and during his spell of literary management as one of the directors of the important Dublin Theatre Festival. Those positions were dignified by his presence, for there is no doubt that he is a major playwright of international importance.

For a long time he had a rewarding relationship with a theatre in Olney, Maryland, just outside Washington, D.C. Plays such as *The Patrick Pearse Motel* and *Da* were mounted in Olney well before New York took notice. New York, however, finally did with *Da* what London regularly refused to do with Leonard's critically well-regarded work; it gave him a major popular success.

The play is a joyous one, undisguisedly about the death of Leonard's own stepfather, the Da of the title. At the father's death the son flies from London to Dublin for the funeral, only to find that the old man wanders in to discuss the funeral and claim his place in his stepson's heart and mind. Leonard links past and present with the son's younger self, who is also on hand, reliving the traumas of adolescence, fighting it out with his mother, and getting furiously annoyed with his Da. The memories of the past and the details of the present, which include putting the meagre effects of the father into order, are so ingeniously layered that farce, understanding, and frustrated fury all manage to coexist, and, from Leonard's precise evocation of individuals at different points in time, the love that comes from understanding is conveyed.

A minor figure from *Da* is the character of Drumm, a man who figures in the autobiography as the civil servant who brings Leonard into the civil service. In *Da* he complains of "tummy trouble" which is revealed as cancer in the next memory play, *A Life*. Again, past and present coexist, with Drumm irascibly trying to make his peace with the girl he failed to marry in his youth while witnessing his younger self making all the original mistakes that foretold his old age as a bundle of attitudes and principles. The delicacy of Leonard's imagery and the richness of his comedy deflects the maudlin potential of the story, and the affirmation of life is reflected even in the final sentence when Drumm confronts the imminence of death and says to his wife, "Let's make a start." In those plays, Leonard is a writer at the height of his powers and he confirms his ability to extend the specific to a large audience: it is as if he were a master of the spectator's memories as well as his own.

A spectacular Dublin story about money siphoned out of Leonard's accounts saw to it that Leonard spent the greater part of his time for a few years after *A Life* concentrating on the more lucrative expression of films, but he never abandoned the theatre. His most notable advance was *Kill*, a dinner-party metaphor about Irish politics with some acidly presented characters all too recognizable to the Irish audience. His presentation of the Irish government as covert

collaborators with terror alienated some of his audience, but not permanently. His Sherlock Holmes adventure, *The Mask of Moriarty*, was the hit of the 1985 Dublin Theatre Festival despite a notorious interview with the play's leading actor which gave away the twist in the play before it opened.

Although a number of friendly notices greeted an English production of *The Mask of Moriarty* at Leicester's Haymarket Theatre the following year, with the twist that Holmes's enemy Moriarty had had surgery to become Holmes's double being widely publicized again, it failed to find a West End home. Leonard's subsequent successes included a movie version of *Da* and a major television series, *Parnell and the Englishwoman*, a story about the Irish leader Charles Stewart Parnell and an adulterous affair which destroyed his career. Perhaps the lurking point, that without that affair Parnell's leadership might have kept Ireland from later years of bloodshed, was not finely enough expressed, but Leonard's novel of the same story won him the Sagittarius prize for first novel by an author over 60.

His 1992 play, *Moving*, saw him in the familiar geographical territory of the Dublin seaside town of Dalkey, but his attempt to chart an ordinary suburban family's rise over the 30 years from 1957 to 1987 showed its scheme rather too clearly. From childish skipping of mass to gay rights years later, from household pride to high pretension, the family called Noone represent an Ireland which cannot find its way. Overall, however, Leonard's art represents a potent expression of Ireland as he sees it, from where it moulds the individual.

—Ned Chaillet

LESSING, Doris (May, née Tayler). British. Born in Kermansha, Persia, 22 October 1919; moved with her family to England, then to Banket, Southern Rhodesia, 1924. Educated at Dominican Convent School, Salisbury, Southern Rhodesia, 1926–34. Married 1) Frank Charles Wisdom in 1939 (divorced 1943), one son and one daughter; 2) Gottfried Lessing in 1945 (divorced 1949), one son. Au pair, Salisbury, 1934–35; telephone operator and clerk, Salisbury, 1937–39; typist, 1946–48; journalist, Cape Town *Guardian*, 1949; moved to London, 1950; secretary, 1950; member of the Editorial Board, *New Reasoner* (later *New Left Review*), 1956. Recipient: Maugham award, for fiction, 1954; Médicis prize (France), 1976; Austrian State prize, 1981; Shakespeare prize (Hamburg), 1982; W.H. Smith Literary award, 1986; Palermo prize (Italy), 1987; Mondello prize (Italy), 1987; Cavour award (Italy), 1989. Honorary doctorate: Princeton University, New Jersey, 1989, University of Durham, 1990. Associate member, American Academy, 1974; honorary fellow, Modern Language Association (U.S.A.), 1974; distinguished fellow in literature, University of East Anglia, Norwich, 1991. Agent: Jonathan Clowes Ltd., Iron Bridge House, Bridge Approach, London, NW1 8BD, England.

PUBLICATIONS

Plays

Before the Deluge (produced London, 1953).
Mr. Dollinger (produced Oxford, 1958).

Each His Own Wilderness (produced London, 1958). Published in *New English Dramatists*, London, Penguin, 1959.

The Truth about Billy Newton (produced Salisbury, Wiltshire, 1960).

Play with a Tiger (produced Brighton and London, 1962; New York, 1964). London, Joseph, 1962; in *Plays by and about Women*, edited by Victoria Sullivan and James V. Hatch, New York, Random House, 1973.

The Storm, adaptation of a play by Alexander Ostrovsky (produced London, 1966).

The Singing Door (for children), in *Second Playbill 2*, edited by Alan Durband. London, Hutchinson, 1973.

The Making of the Representative for Planet 8 (opera libretto), music by Philip Glass, adaptation of the novel by Lessing (produced London, 1988).

Television Plays: *The Grass Is Singing*, from her own novel, 1962; *Care and Protection* and *Do Not Disturb* (both in *Blackmail* series), 1966; *Between Men*, 1967.

Novels

The Grass Is Singing. London, Joseph, and New York, Crowell, 1950.

Children of Violence:
  Martha Quest. London, Joseph, 1952; with *A Proper Marriage*, New York, Simon and Schuster, 1964.
  A Proper Marriage. London, Joseph, 1954; with *Martha Quest*, New York, Simon and Schuster, 1964.
  A Ripple from the Storm, London, Joseph, 1958; with *Landlocked*, New York, Simon and Schuster, 1966.
  Landlocked. London, MacGibbon and Kee, 1965; with *A Ripple from the Storm*. New York, Simon and Schuster, 1966.
  The Four-Gated City. London, MacGibbon and Kee, and New York, Knopf, 1969.

Retreat to Innocence. London, Joseph, 1956; New York, Prometheus, 1959.

The Golden Notebook. London, Joseph, and New York, Simon and Schuster, 1962.

Briefing for a Descent into Hell. London, Cape, and New York, Knopf, 1971.

The Summer Before the Dark. London, Cape, and New York, Knopf, 1973.

The Memoirs of a Survivor. London, Octagon Press, 1974; New York, Knopf, 1975.

Canopus in Argos: Archives:
  Shikasta. London, Cape, and New York, Knopf, 1979.
  The Marriages Between Zones Three, Four, and Five. London, Cape, and New York, Knopf, 1980.
  The Sirian Experiments. London, Cape, and New York, Knopf, 1981.
  The Making of the Representative for Planet 8. London, Cape, and New York, Knopf, 1982.
  The Sentimental Agents. London, Cape, and New York, Knopf, 1983.

The Diaries of Jane Somers. New York, Vintage, and London, Joseph, 1984.
  The Diary of a Good Neighbour (as Jane Somers). London, Joseph, and New York, Knopf, 1983.
  If the Old Could—(as Jane Somers). London, Joseph, and New York, Knopf, 1984.

The Good Terrorist. London, Cape, and New York, Knopf, 1985.

The Fifth Child. London, Cape, and New York, Knopf, 1988.

Short Stories

This Was the Old Chief's Country. London, Joseph, 1951; New York, Crowell, 1952.

Five: Short Novels. London, Joseph, 1953.

No Witchcraft for Sale: Stories and Short Novels. Moscow, Foreign Language Publishing House, 1956.

The Habit of Loving. London, MacGibbon and Kee, and New York, Crowell, 1957.

A Man and Two Women. London, MacGibbon and Kee, and New York, Simon and Schuster, 1963.

African Stories. London, Joseph, 1964; New York, Simon and Schuster, 1965.

Winter in July. London, Panther, 1966.

The Black Madonna. London, Panther, 1966.

Nine African Stories, edited by Michael Marland. London, Longman, 1968.

The Story of a Non-Marrying Man and Other Stories. London, Cape, 1972; as *The Temptation of Jack Orkney and Other Stories*, New York, Knopf, 1972.

Collected African Stories. New York, Simon and Schuster, 1981.
  1. *This Was the Old Chief's Country*. London, Joseph, 1973.
  2. *The Sun Between Their Feet*. London, Joseph, 1973.

(Stories), edited by Alan Cattell. London, Harrap, 1976.

Collected Stories: To Room Nineteen and *The Temptation of Jack Orkney*. London, Cape, 2 vols., 1978; as *Stories*, New York, Knopf, 1 vol., 1978.

London Observed. London, Cape, 1991.

The Real Thing. New York, HarperCollins, 1991.

Verse

Fourteen Poems. Northwood, Middlesex, Scorpion Press, 1959.

Other

Going Home. London, Joseph, 1957; revised edition, London, Panther, and New York, Ballantine, 1968.

In Pursuit of the English: A Documentary. London, MacGibbon and Kee, 1960; New York, Simon and Schuster, 1961.

Particularly Cats. London, Joseph, and New York, Simon and Schuster, 1967.

A Small Personal Voice: Essays, Reviews, Interviews, edited by Paul Schlueter. New York, Knopf, 1974.

Prisons We Choose to Live Inside. Montreal, CBC, 1986; London, Cape, and New York, Harper, 1987.

The Wind Blows Away Our Words, and Other Documents Relating to Afghanistan. London, Pan, and New York, Vintage, 1987.

The Doris Lessing Reader. London, Cape, and New York, Knopf, 1989.

*

Bibliography: *Doris Lessing: A Bibliography* by Catharina Ipp, Johannesburg, University of the Witwatersrand Department of Bibliography, 1967; *Doris Lessing: A Checklist of Primary and Secondary Sources* by Selma R. Burkom and Margaret Williams, Troy, New York, Whitston, 1973; *Doris Lessing: An Annotated Bibliography of Criticism* by Dee Seligman, Westport, Connecticut, Greenwood Press, 1981; *Doris Lessing: A Descriptive Bibliography of Her First Editions* by Eric T. Brueck, London, Metropolis, 1984.

Critical Studies (selection): *Doris Lessing* by Dorothy Brewster, New York, Twayne, 1965; *Doris Lessing*, London, Longman, 1973, and *Doris Lessing's Africa*, London, Evans, 1978, New York, Holmes and Meier, 1979, both by Michael Thorpe; *Doris Lessing: Critical Studies* edited by Annis Pratt and L.S. Dembo, Madison, University of Wisconsin Press, 1974; *Notebooks/Memoirs/Archives: Reading and Re-reading Doris Lessing* edited by Jenny Taylor, London and Boston, Routledge, 1982; *Doris Lessing* by Lorna Sage, London, Methuen, 1983; *Doris Lessing* by Mona Knapp, New York, Ungar, 1984; *Doris Lessing* edited by Eve Bertelsen, Johannesburg, McGraw Hill, 1985; *Critical Essays on Doris Lessing* edited by Claire Sprague and Virginia Tiger, Boston, Hall, 1986; *Doris Lessing: The Alchemy of Survival* edited by Carey Kaplan and Ellen Cronan Rose, Athens, Ohio University Press, 1988; *Doris Lessing* by Ruth Whittaker, London, Macmillan, 1988; *Doris Lessing* by Jeannette King, London, Arnold, 1989; *Understanding Doris Lessing* by Jean Pickering, Columbia, University of South Carolina Press, 1990.

* * *

In any theatre, a deal of talent must go to waste, especially among playwrights, but it is a great pity that Doris Lessing's career as a playwright should have been abortive. One of the failures of George Devine's successful regime at the Royal Court was its failure to help her to go on from *Each His Own Wilderness*, which was given a Sunday night production in 1958. Though it was dismissed by many of the critics as a novelist's play can so readily be dismissed, simply by describing it as "a novelist's play," in fact it was remarkably free from the flaws that might have been expected—flat characters, over-leisurely development, verbal analysis written out as dialogue, lack of dramatic drive. Lessing had, on the contrary, a very keen instinct for how to ignite a situation theatrically.

By building the play around a mother–son conflict and empathizing successfully with the son, she steered clear of the pitfall of subordinating all the other characters to the woman she could most easily identify with. Myra Bolton is an attractive, middle-aged campaigner for left-wing causes, warm, well-meaning, but gauche in human relationships, liable to inflict unintended pain not only on her son but on the three men in the play she has had relationships with—two of her own generation, one of her son's. The muddles and misunderstandings of these involvements are all developed in a way that contributes richly to the play's dramatic texture, and the untidiness we see on the set—the hall of her London house—contributes visually to the impression of an inability to keep things under control.

The men are all well characterized—the sad, ageing, lonely politician, the architect trying to embark on a new marriage with a young girl, the opportunistic 22-year-old son of a woman friend, and above all Tony, the son, who returns from National Service to find Myra did not know which day to expect him. His pained anger at his own inability to commit himself to any outside reality and at the lack of understanding between them mounts effectively through the play, reaching a climax when he discovers that Myra has sold the house he loves more than anything, intending to help him by raising money to set him up on his own in a flat. It may be a well-made play but it is made remarkably well, with an unusual talent for keeping a number of relationships simultaneously on the boil, and it catches the flavour of the life of left-wing intellectuals in the 1950's. Showing private people devoting their lives to protesting about public issues, Lessing success-

fully merges personal and political themes. Like the characters in John McGrath's play, these people are all "plugged-in to history."

Lessing had started writing for the theatre five years earlier, in 1953, and of the three plays she turned out *Mr. Dollinger* was also produced in 1958, earlier in the year, at the Oxford Playhouse, and *The Truth about Billy Newton* was produced in 1960 at Salisbury. But the only play of hers to receive a full-scale London production was *Play with a Tiger* which was written in 1958 and had a seven-and-a-half week run at the Comedy in 1962 with Siobhan McKenna as the central character, who is, unfortunately, very much more central than any of the characters in *Each His Own Wilderness*.

Lessing was determined to turn her back on both naturalism and realism. "It is my intention," she wrote in a 1963 note on the play,

> that when the curtain comes down at the end, the audience will think: Of course! In this play no one lit cigarettes, drank tea or coffee, read newspapers, squirted soda into Scotch, or indulged in little bits of "business" which indicated "character." They will realize, I hope, that they have been seeing a play which relies upon its style and its language for its effect.

But it starts off naturalistically in an underfurnished room with a litter of books and cushions, paraffin heaters, a record player, and a telephone. There are also sound effects of traffic noises. Anna Freeman is a woman of "35 or so" who lives as a literary freelance, has a son by a broken marriage and has recently decided not to marry an Englishman who is about to settle for a safe job on a woman's magazine. She is in love with an American Jew who would never settle and if she had been entertaining ideas of marrying him, these would be killed off in Act 1 by the visit of a nice young American girl who announces that she is going to have Dave's baby.

The play's starting points, in other words, are all naturalistic and there is even a naturalistic cliché neighbour who fusses about an invisible cat. But towards the end of Act 1 the walls disappear, and though the neighbour is going to reappear and the play is still going to make gestures towards satisfying the audience expectations that its first half-hour has aroused, its centre has been shifted. With only a few interruptions from other characters, about 62 pages of the 92-page script are taken up with a dialogue between Anna and Dave. But the language and the style cannot depart completely from those of the naturalistic beginning. Some of the writing in it is very good, some of it bad and embarrassing, especially when they play games reminiscent of the psychoanalytical situation.

Even the best sections of the dialogue, which make a defiant and articulate declaration of rights on behalf of the woman against the male predator, tend to generalize the play away from its roots in the specific predicament of a specific woman. In reacting against naturalism, Lessing is renouncing all its disciplines, some of which were very useful to her in *Each His Own Wilderness*. *Play with a Tiger* may look more like a public statement and it was seized on by feminist groups, whose performances unbalanced the central relationship by failing to give Dave equal weight with Anna. Lessing complained about this in a 1972 postscript, but the fault is basically in the play, which is really more private than *Each His Own Wilderness*, and more self-indulgent, in that the dialogue is spun too directly out of personal preoccupations.

—Ronald Hayman

LEVY, Benn W(olfe). British. 1900–1973.
See 1st edition, 1973.

————

LEVY, Deborah. British. Born in South Africa in 1959. Educated at Dartington College of Arts, Devon, 1978–81, B.A. (hons.) in theatre language 1981; fellow in creative arts, Trinity College, Cambridge, 1989–91. Since 1992 writer and director for MANACT Theatre Company, Cardiff and London. Agent: Leah Schmidt, Curtis Brown, 162–168 Regent Street, London W1R 5TB, England.

PUBLICATIONS

Plays

Pax (produced Edinburgh and London 1984: Baltimore, 1985). London, Methuen, 1985.
Clam (produced London, 1985). London, Methuen, 1985.
Our Lady (produced Edinburgh and London, 1986).
Heresies (produced London, 1987). With *Eva and Moses*, London, Methuen, 1987.
Eva and Moses. With *Heresies*, London, Methuen, 1987.
Blood Wedding, (libretto) adaptation of the play by Federico García Lorca (produced London, 1992). London, Novello, 1992.
The B File (also director: produced Cardiff, 1992). London, Methuen, 1992.
Call Blue Jane (produced London, 1992).

Television Plays: *Celebrating Quietly*, 1988; *Lickin' Bones*, 1990; *The Open Mouth*, 1991.

Novel

Beautiful Mutants. London, Cape, 1987; New York, Viking, 1989.

Short Stories

Ophelia and the Great Idea. London, Cape, and New York, Viking, 1986.

Verse

An Amorous Discourse in the Suburbs of Hell. London, Cape, 1990.

Other

Editor, *Walks on Water: Five Performance Texts.* London, Methuen, 1992.

*

Deborah Levy comments:

I now mostly direct my own texts for the theatre, working with ensemble companies who come from diverse arts backgrounds and cultures. I hope to create with them as writer and director, work that is visual, visceral, kinetic, and physical.

* * *

A female world without patriarchy can be deduced from Deborah Levy's dramatic work. Its primary substances are bread, fruit, and eggs, its primary symbols are fish, the sea, and the moon, and its religion is a combination of Goddess-worship and the ritual aspects of Catholicism and Judaism. Children (female) are parented by the whole community, which is itself inter-generational and the collective guardian of a herstory of revolutionary élan as well as domestic drudgery. The wisest women are witches and eccentrics like The Keeper in *Pax* and Leah in *Heresies*. Money-making is the most abhorred activity, art-making the best. Even the betrayers can be redeemed, such as Mayonnaise (*Heresies*) who is the beautiful wife and mistress respectively of a securities-dealer (Edward) and a commercial architect (Pimm), and who forces her lover's ex-wife and child to return to Budapest. Her hair falls out and, it is implied, she loses Pimm, but she is welcomed into the circle of women at the end who gather to hear Leah's final composition. The Domesticated Woman's presence in *Pax* is intensely resented by the fiercely independent and autocratic Keeper, but she is accepted by the other younger women, The Mourner (a geologist), and H.D., the hidden daughter of The Keeper, but also a reference, presumably, to the great American Modernist writer Hilda Doolittle. When The Mourner leaves at the end she gives an egg to the Domesticated Woman, a symbol not just of fertility but also of professional expertise. The Mourner specialises in the egg fossils of dinosaurs. The two older women come to look on the younger generation with a wry affection. "We have," observes The Keeper, "two young women between us. Mad as nettles in a storm." In an end-note to the play Levy admits she began by detesting what the Domesticated Woman represented and finished with respect and even liking for her. Perhaps Mary, the devout Catholic servant of Pimm, best sums up the ideal existence: "I'd like a house with a garden and a tree." Active, mobile women are respected in the plays but the settings are all interiors and rapid movements of flight or travel are either in retrospect or prospect.

These, along with emotionally numb men and distracted hunts for fathers and mothers, are the commonplaces of second-wave feminist Utopias; indeed, there are distinct echoes of the first, Edwardian wave. The posed eccentricity of Leah playing the piano in a hat rimmed with lighted candles, and of her companion, Violet, trampling a tub of grapes, recalls the desperate bohemianism of Gudrun and Ursula in *Women in Love*. Mayonnaise's staccato statements of inconsequent desires ("I want to be a Catholic") echo the disjointed utterances of Evelyn Waugh's Agatha Runcible, and H.D., with her fishing-rod and her cigars, can trace her ancestry back to Una Troubridge and Vita Sackville-West. But Levy defamiliarises these themes by a persistent preoccupation with Eastern Europe, as site both of terrible history and of a more humane community. In *Clam* Alice and Harry, a domestic couple, who double as Lenin and Krupskaya, another domestic couple, play out a history of the defeat of revolution. A fishtank, as in *Heresies*, is a key prop. It is a cornucopia of objects to provoke fantasies. Alice imagines the sea bringing in Poland and Latvia and other Eastern bloc countries like fish so that "a little boy kissed the Ukraine . . . a woman in a bikini put Poland on her belly." For Cholla, domestic cleaner and mother of Pimm's child, Hungary is her lost homeland of song and fecundity, a culture she rejected for that of the frozen English and to which she now wishes to return. Leah remembers the Russians as beautiful in their revolution and The Keeper counterpoints a refrain of "I want to go back to Vienna/Prague etc." with horrific recollections of the Holocaust. Cholla fled from Hungary at the age of 17 because of the claustrophobia of family life, but now she dreams of her mother standing on Liberty Bridge "in her red shoes . . . calling me." Cholla sums up East/West relations in a prescient line: "The West only likes Eastern Europe when she cries."

Levy is both of and not of the performance art movement of the 1980's. She has an interest in visual theatre and her symbol for the imagined funeral of H.D.'s father, one bright light on a polished marble column, effectively condenses a multiplicity of signs. Music strains to become a language in its own right under Leah's promptings and the abrupt emotional shifts of Mayonnaise and Krupskaya are typical of the distrust of continuous narrative in much performance art. But Levy also has a traditional interest in plot and character-conflict. The many histories that are recounted indicate a concern for verbal language that many performance artists would consider quite outmoded. One suspects that Levy is still struggling to reconcile her commitment to a distinctive female voice in theatre with her determination to find her own voice. Too often her characters, particularly male, mouth attitudes rather than dramatise situations. With the decline of feminism and the collapse of communism she will be forced back onto her own linguistic resources, although, in true postmodernist fashion, she may find her way to them through the words of others, as her libretto-version of Lorca's *Blood Wedding* for The Women's Theatre Trust would seem to indicate.

—Tony Dunn

LINNEY, Romulus. American. Born in Philadelphia, Pennsylvania, in 1930. Educated at Oberlin College, Ohio, A.B. 1953; Yale University School of Drama, New Haven, Connecticut, M.F.A. 1958. Served in the United States Army, 1954–56. Actor and director in stock for 6 years; stage manager, Actors Studio, New York, 1960; has taught at the Manhattan School of Music, University of North Carolina, Chapel Hill, University of Pennsylvania, Philadelphia, Brooklyn College, Princeton University, New Jersey, Columbia University, New York, Hunter College, New York, and Connecticut College, New London. Recipient: National Endowment for the Arts grant, 1974; Obie award, 1980, for sustained achievement, 1992; Guggenheim fellowship, 1980; Mishima prize, for fiction, 1981; American Academy award, 1984; Rockefeller fellowship, 1986; American Theater Critics Association award, 1988, 1990; Helen Hayes award, 1990. Lives in New York City. Agent: Gilbert Parker, William Morris Agency, 1350 Avenue of the Americas, New York, New York 10019, U.S.A.

PUBLICATIONS

Plays

The Sorrows of Frederick (produced Los Angeles, 1967; Birmingham, 1970; New York, 1976). New York, Harcourt Brace, 1966.
The Love Suicide at Schofield Barracks (produced New York, 1972). With *Democracy and Esther*, New York, Harcourt Brace, 1973; one-act version (produced Louisville, 1984),

in *The Best Short Plays 1986*, edited by Ramon Delgado, New York, Applause, 1986.
Democracy and Esther, adaptation of the novels by Henry Adams (as *Democracy*, produced Richmond, Virginia, 1974; revised version produced Milwaukee, 1975). With *The Love Suicide at Schofield Barracks*, New York, Harcourt Brace, 1973; as *Democracy*, New York, Dramatists Play Service, 1976.
Holy Ghosts (produced New York, 1974). With *The Sorrows of Frederick*, New York, Harcourt Brace, 1977.
The Seasons, Man's Estate (produced New York, 1974).
Appalachia Sounding (produced on tour, 1975).
Old Man Joseph and His Family (produced New York, 1977). New York, Dramatists Play Service, 1978.
Childe Byron (produced Richmond, Virginia, 1977; revised version produced Louisville, New York, and London, 1981). New York, Dramatists Play Service, 1981.
Just Folks (produced New York, 1978).
The Death of King Philip, music by Paul Earls (produced Boston, 1979). New York, Dramatists Play Service, 1984.
Tennessee (produced New York, 1979). New York, Dramatists Play Service, 1980.
El Hermano (produced New York, 1981). New York, Dramatists Play Service, 1981.
The Captivity of Pixie Shedman (produced New York, 1981). New York, Dramatists Play Service, 1981.
Goodbye, Howard (produced New York, 1982). Included in *Laughing Stock*, 1984.
Gardens of Eden (produced New York, 1982).
F.M. (also director: produced Philadelphia, 1982; New York, 1984). Included in *Laughing Stock*, 1984.
April Snow (produced Costa Mesa, California, 1983; New York, 1987). Included in *Three Plays*, 1989.
Laughing Stock (includes *Goodbye, Howard*; *F.M.*; *Tennessee*) (produced New York, 1984). New York, Dramatists Play Service, 1984.
Wrath, in *Faustus in Hell* (produced Princeton, New Jersey, 1985).
Sand Mountain (includes *Sand Mountain Matchmaking* and *Why the Lord Come to Sand Mountain*) (produced New York, 1986). New York, Dramatists Play Service, 1985.
A Woman Without a Name (produced Denver, 1986). New York, Dramatists Play Service, 1986.
Pops (includes *Can Can*, *Claire de Lune*, *Ave Maria*, *Gold and Silver Waltz*, *Battle Hymn of the Republic*, *Songs of Love*) (produced New York, 1986). New York, Dramatists Play Service, 1987; *Ave Maria* produced as *Hrosvitha* in *Three Poets*, 1989.
Heathen Valley, adaptation of his own novel (produced Denver, 1986). New York, Dramatists Play Service, 1988.
Yancey (produced New York, 1988). Included in *Three Plays*, 1989.
Juliet (produced New York, 1988). Included in *Three Plays*, 1989.
Pageant, with others, music and lyrics by Michael Rice (produced Little Rock, Arkansas, 1988).
Precious Memories, adaptation of a story by Chekhov (also director: produced New York, 1988); as *Unchanging Love* (produced New York, 1991), New York, Dramatists Play Service, 1991.
Three Plays (includes *Juliet*, *Yancey*, *April Snow*). New York, Dramatists Play Service, 1989.
Three Poets (includes *Komachi*, *Hrosvitha*, *Akhmatova*; also director: produced New York, 1989). New York, Dramatists Play Service, 1990.
2 (produced Louisville, 1990). Included in *Six Plays*, 1993.

Ambrosio (produced New York, 1992).   Included in *Seventeen Short Plays*, 1992.
Seventeen Short Plays (includes *Ambrosio, The Love Suicide at Schofield Barracks, Sand Mountain Matchmaking, Why the Lord Come to Sand Mountain, Komachi, Hrosvitha, Akhmatova, Can Can, Claire de Lune, Gold and Silver Waltz, Songs of Love, Juliet, Yancey, The Death of King Philip, El Hermano, The Captivity of Pixie Shedman, Goodbye, Howard*).   Newbury, Vermont, Smith and Kraus, 1992.
Six Plays (includes *F.M., Childe Byron, Tennessee, 2, April Snow, Heathen Valley*).   New York, Theatre Communications Group, 1993.

Television Plays: *The 34th Star*, 1976; episodes for *Feelin' Good* series, 1976–77.

Novels

Heathen Valley.   New York, Atheneum, 1962; London, Cassell, 1963.
Slowly, By Thy Hand Unfurled.   New York, Harcourt Brace, 1965; London, Cassell, 1966.
Jesus Tales.   San Francisco, North Point Press, 1980.

Other

Editor, with Norman A. Bailey and Domenick Cascio, *Ten Plays for Radio*.   Minneapolis, Burgess, 1954.
Editor, with Norman A. Bailey and Domenick Cascio, *Radio Classics*.   Minneapolis, Burgess, 1956.

*

Manuscript Collection: Lincoln Center Library for the Performing Arts, New York.

Theatrical Activities:
Director: **Plays—** *F.M.*, Philadelphia, 1982; *Sand Mountain Matchmakers*, New York, 1989.

Romulus Linney comments:
   My plays and novels are drawn from either historical subjects or memories of my childhood in Tennessee and North Carolina, or direct personal experiences.

*   *   *

   Romulus Linney has worked at the writer's trade as playwright, novelist, and television scriptwriter. His dramatic writing thus far has garnered awards and resulted in more than 15 plays produced on and off Broadway, in American regional theatres, and abroad. Widely ranging in subject and structure, Linney's plays show him to be a distinctive writer of uncommon literacy.
   Linney often develops in his dramas a pattern of action in which his protagonists enter or mature in environments where they confront values repressive of their own worth as individuals. Usually tempted or victimized by such values, these characters experience them while testing or evaluating them against their own needs and beliefs and ultimately reaching a decision to accept or reject them. This pattern is evident in at least six plays: *The Love Suicide at Schofield Barracks, Democracy, Holy Ghosts, A Woman Without a Name, Tennessee,* and *The Sorrows of Frederick.*
   Within the framework of a military inquiry, *The Love Suicide at Schofield Barracks* reveals the events behind the

bizarre double suicide in 1970 of an army general and his wife in Hawaii at a Schofield Barracks Officers' Club party. As witnesses testify, a compassionate portrait emerges of a patriotic professional soldier whose beliefs become so shattered by Vietnam that with his wife he perpetrates—in the guise of a classic Japanese drama—a ritualistic suicide expressing disapproval of the war and America's conduct. The play generates considerable tension as the event is finally pieced together, and makes a strong statement about war and individual responsibility for national morality. The author also has written an equally powerful one-act version preserving the original's skillfully orchestrated characters.
   Democracy, a combined dramatization of two Henry Adams 19th-century novels, introduces a wealthy widow and an agnostic photographer, two attractive and intelligent women who enter Washington's 1875 presidential society during the corruption-ridden Grant administration, to be individually charmed, courted, and proposed to by two attractive men of high station whose beliefs they abhor. They courageously reject the men and leave Washington. Major characters are richly drawn; the values of 19th-century American democracy are examined in a manner both provocative and dramatic.
   In *Holy Ghosts* a runaway wife flees a boorish husband to find sanctuary with a Pentecostal sect whose members seek redemption from self-loathing by surviving the handling of poisonous snakes. When the husband angrily comes to reclaim his newly converted wife and lets his low self-esteem turn him into a convert during the cult's ritual, the wife abandons the sect, resolving to achieve independence and self-realization. This theatrically intriguing drama of redemption colorfully recreates the rural Southern milieu and its dispossessed. Also rising above domestic strife and despair by achieving self-recognition is the title character in *A Woman Without a Name*, a drama adapted from Linney's novel *Slowly, By Thy Hand Unfurled*. She is an uneducated, small-town Southern wife and mother tormented both by her turn-of-the-century family's afflictions and by its unfair calumny of her regarding its travails. With despairing self-doubt she records memories of family experiences in a journal as characters come forward re-enacting events and interacting with her as participant, and becomes progressively literate and liberated as she absolves herself of guilt and discovers her self-worth in a starkly yet imaginatively conceived portrait of feminine endurance and self-discovery. Similarly effective, the Obie-winning *Tennessee* portrays an elderly 1870 Appalachian woman, her family's sole survivor, who recalls her youth and realizes that her late husband cheated her of independence by tricking her into a frontier marriage's stern service. The richly rounded protagonist and vividly detailed exposition create a definitive world of the past with present parallels. (Appearing in a short-play trilogy collectively entitled *Laughing Stock, Tennessee* accompanies two efficacious comedies: *Goodbye, Howard*, about three sisters' confused death-watch over a brother; and *F.M.*, focusing on a talented rough-diamond student writer who shocks dilettante classmates in a creative writing course.)
   The Sorrows of Frederick offers a psychological portrait of Prussia's philosopher-king Frederick the Great. In a series of sharply-etched scenes, Linney unravels the chronicle of a father-dominated prince who as a king forsakes great artistic and intellectual gifts to pursue power and finds himself a victim of his life at its end. Enriched by elevated dramatic language and fully rounded characterizations, the drama revivifies Frederick and, like the aforementioned five dramas, exemplifies Linney's concern with characters resolving their destinies by their choice of values. Treating a less regal

tyrant, *2* thoughtfully examines the character of Hermann Goering during the 1945–46 Nuremberg trials as he reveals the self-deception and unrepentant Nazi prejudices existing within all nations and all would-be world conquerors.

Apparent in Linney's work is a penchant for comedy, romance, and the one-act form which is demonstrated by two collective works of short plays, *Sand Mountain* and *Pops*. Strong in homespun humor, *Sand Mountain* encompasses two Appalachian folklore yarns about, respectively, a discriminating young widow who rejects a bragging band of eligible men for a truth-telling widower, and the visit of Jesus and St. Peter, in human disguise, to a mountaineer family. *Pops*, consisting of six comically rich one-acts, treats forms of love, young and old, from the romantic to the aesthetic. Among the collection's funniest works are those of a progeny-opposed oldsters' romance (*Songs of Love*) and a 10th-century abbess's defense of Hrosvitha's, and her own, right to create art (*Ave Maria*). The latter, retitled *Hrosvitha*, accompanies *Komachi*, an adapted Japanese Nō drama, and *Akhmatova*, demonstrating the Russian poetess's calm ethical courage in confronting a Stalinist inquisition in an admirable short-play collection entitled *Three Poets*.

In a darker mode, two more recent works trenchantly depict the tight rural world of Appalachia: *Unchanging Love* —based on a Chekhov story and formerly entitled *Precious Memories*—exposes the corruption and lack of social compassion within a merchant family; and Linney's adaptation of his novel *Heathen Valley*, whose narrator-protagonist disavows and opposes church hierarchy and dogmatism to advocate his community's need for social goodness.

A writer of substance and range, Romulus Linney creates plays that crackle with challenging issues and theatricality, and evince by the spectrum of their structural variety an imaginative craftsman. He is a major talent among contemporary dramatists.

—Christian H. Moe

LIVINGS, Henry. British. Born in Prestwich, Lancashire, 20 September 1929. Educated at Park View Primary School, 1935–39; Stand Grammar School, Prestwich (scholarship), 1940–45; Liverpool University, 1945–47, read Hispanic studies. Served in the Royal Air Force, 1950–52. Married Judith Francis Carter in 1957; one son and one daughter. Worked for Puritex, Leicester, then actor with Theatre Royal, Leicester, and many repertory companies; associated with the BBC programme *Northern Drift*. Recipient: *Evening Standard* award, 1961; Encyclopaedia Britannica award, 1965; Obie award, 1966. Agent: Lemon, Unna, and Durbridge, 24 Pottery Lane, Holland Park, London W11 4LZ. Address: 49 Grains Road, Delph, Oldham, Lancashire OL3 5DS, England.

PUBLICATIONS

Plays

Stop It Whoever You Are (produced London, 1961). Published in *New English Dramatists 5*, London, Penguin, 1962.
Big Soft Nellie (as *Thacred Nit*, produced Keswick, Cumberland, 1961; as *Big Soft Nellie*, produced Oxford and London, 1961). Included in *Kelly's Eye and Other Plays*, 1964.
Nil Carborundum (produced London, 1962). Published in *New English Dramatists 6*, London, Penguin, 1963.
Kelly's Eye (produced London, 1963). Included in *Kelly's Eye and Other Plays*, 1964.
There's No Room for You Here for a Start (televised 1963). Included in *Kelly's Eye and Other Plays*, 1964.
The Day Dumbfounded Got His Pylon (broadcast 1963; produced Stoke-on-Trent, 1965). Published in *Worth a Hearing: A Collection of Radio Plays*, edited by Alfred Bradley, London, Blackie, 1967.
Kelly's Eye and Other Plays. London, Methuen, and New York, Hill and Wang, 1964.
Eh? (produced London, 1964; Cincinnati and New York 1966). London, Methuen, 1965; New York, Hill and Wang, 1967.
The Little Mrs. Foster Show (produced Liverpool, 1966; revised version, also director: produced Nottingham, 1968). London, Methuen, 1969.
Brainscrew (televised 1966; produced Birmingham, 1971). Published in *Second Playbill 3*, edited by Alan Durban, London, Hutchinson, 1973.
Good Grief! (includes *After the Last Lamp, You're Free, Variable Lengths, Pie-Eating Contest, Does It Make Your Cheeks Ache?, The Reasons for Flying*) (produced Manchester, 1967). London, Methuen, 1968.
Honour and Offer (produced Cincinnati, 1968; London, 1969). London, Methuen, 1969.
The Gamecock (produced Manchester, 1969). Included in *Pongo Plays 1–6*, 1971.
Rattel (produced Manchester, 1969; London, 1974). Included in *Pongo Plays 1–6*, 1971.
Variable Lengths and Longer: An Hour of Embarrassment (includes *The Reasons for Flying, Does It Make Your Cheeks Ache?*) (produced London, 1969).
The Boggart (produced Birmingham, 1970). Included in *Pongo Plays 1–6*, 1971.
Conciliation (produced Lincoln, 1970; London, 1971). Included in *Pongo Plays 1–6*, 1971.
The Rifle Volunteer (produced Birmingham, 1970; London, 1971). Included in *Pongo Plays 1–6*, 1971.
Beewine (produced Birmingham, 1970; London, 1971). Included in *Pongo Plays 1–6*, 1971.
The ffinest ffamily in the Land (produced Lincoln, 1970; London, 1972). London, Methuen, 1973.
You're Free (produced London, 1970).
GRUP (televised 1970; produced York, 1971).
Mushrooms and Toadstools (produced London, 1970). Included in *Six More Pongo Plays*, 1974.
Tiddles (produced Birmingham, 1970). Included in *Six More Pongo Plays*, 1974.
Pongo Plays 1–6. London, Methuen, 1971; revised versions, music by Alex Glasgow, 1976.
This Jockey Drives Late Nights, adaptation of a play by Tolstoy (produced Birmingham, 1972; London, 1980). London, Eyre Methuen, 1972; revised version, 1976.
Daft Sam (televised 1972; produced London, 1976). Included in *Six More Pongo Plays*, 1974.
The Rent Man (produced Stoke-on-Trent, 1972). Included in *Six More Pongo Plays*, 1974.
Cinderella: A Likely Tale, adaptation of the story by Perrault (produced Stoke-on-Trent, 1972; London, 1973). London, Dobson, 1976.
The Tailor's Britches (produced Stoke-on-Trent, 1973). Included in *Six More Pongo Plays*, 1974.

Glorious Miles (televised 1973; produced Sheffield, 1975).
Jonah (produced Manchester, 1974).   London, Pulpit Press, 1975.
Six More Pongo Plays Including Two for Children (includes *Tiddles, The Rent Man, The Ink-Smeared Lady, The Tailor's Britches, Daft Sam, Mushrooms and Toadstools*). London, Eyre Methuen, 1974.
Jack and the Beanstalk, music by Alex Glasgow (produced London, 1974).
Jug, adaptation of a play by Heinrich von Kleist (produced Nottingham, 1975; revised version produced London, 1986).
The Astounding Adventures of Tom Thumb (for children; produced London, 1979).
Don't Touch Him, He Might Resent It, adaptation of a play by Gogol (produced Chipping Norton, Oxfordshire, 1984).
This Is My Dream: The Life and Times of Josephine Baker (produced London, 1987).
The Great Camel Rumbles and Groans and Spits (produced Waterloo, Ontario, 1988). Published in *New Plays 1*, edited by Peter Terson, Oxford, Oxford University Press, 1988.
The Public, adaptation of a play by Federico García Lorca (produced London, 1988). Published in *Lorca, Plays: Three*, edited by Gwynne Edwards, London, Methuen, 1991.
The Barber of Seville, adaptation of the play by Beaumarchais (produced Stoke-on-Trent, 1989).
Stop the Children's Laughter (produced Bolton, Greater Manchester, 1990).

Radio Plays: *After the Last Lamp*, 1961; *The Weavers*, from a play by Hauptmann, 1962; *The Day Dumbfounded Got His Pylon*, 1963; *A Public Menace*, from the play by Ibsen, 1964; *Nelson Cape Requests the Pleasure*, 1967; *The Government Inspector*, from a play by Gogol, 1969; *The Dobcross Silver Band* (documentary), 1971; *The Red Cockerel Crows*, from a play by Hauptmann, 1974; *A Most Wonderful Thing*, 1976; *Crab Training*, 1979; *Urn*, 1981; *The Moorcock*, 1981.

Television Plays: *The Arson Squad*, 1961; *Jack's Horrible Luck*, 1961; *There's No Room for You Here for a Start*, 1963; *A Right Crusader*, 1963; *Brainscrew*, 1966; *GRUP*, 1970; *Daft Sam*, 1972; *Glorious Miles*, 1973; *Shuttlecock*, 1976; *The Game*, from the play by Harold Brighouse, 1977; *The Mayor's Charity*, 1977; *Two Days That Shook the Branch*, 1978; *We Had Some Happy Hours*, 1981; *Another Part of the Jungle* and *I Met a Man Who Wasn't There* (*Bulman* series), 1985.

Short Stories

Pennine Tales.   London, Methuen, 1983.
Flying Eggs and Things: More Pennine Tales. London, Methuen, 1986.

Other

That the Medals and the Baton Be Put on View: The Story of a Village Band 1875–1975. Newton Abbot, Devon, David and Charles, 1975.

*

Critical Study: *Anger and After* by John Russell Taylor, London, Methuen, 1962, revised edition, 1969, as *The Angry Theatre*, New York, Hill and Wang, 1962, revised edition, 1969.

Theatrical Activities:
Director: **Plays**—*Stop It Whoever You Are*, Nottingham; *The Little Mrs. Foster Show*, Nottingham, 1968; *Trinity Tales* by Alan Plater, Sheffield.
Actor: **Plays**—with the Century Theatre, the Midland Theatre Company, Coventry, Theatre Workshop, Stratford East, and other repertory and London theatres. **Radio**—*Northern Drift* (miscellany). **Television**—*Cribbins, Livings and Co.*, 1976; *Get the Drift*, 1976; *Night People* by Alan Plater, 1978.

Henry Livings comments:
To me, a show is an opportunity for communal imaginings, actors and audience together, for which I provide the material. When I first wrote plays, I felt there weren't enough plays which were fun, and that plot and naturalism were overwhelming the other aspects (fun, magic, social observation, the sculptural kinetics, the social connection that can be set up in a theatre); I now feel that I neglected story too much: I still feel it's better to know the story beforehand —if we're wondering what happens next, how can we pay attention to what's happening now?—but I try to steal a good story as well. I would like to make plays that are neither a simple narrative nor a flat picture, but a complete experience to carry out of the building, so that we could look around us with new eyes and say "Oh yes, that's right." For this I go mostly for laughter, because for me laughter is the shock reaction to a new way of looking at something: even a pun questions our security in the solidity of words. I also believe that we are what we do, rather than having some kind of permanent identifiable reality: the materials of art, observation, ritual, symbol, gesture, community give us a chance to focus for a moment, and then go forward with fresh hope that we matter and that what we do signifies. For this reason again I try to choose as a principal character or characters someone who isn't normally a big deal in our thinking—not that I'm not interested in power, as we all are, but that I want to see how it works and on whom. I have only once had the worm turning (in *Stop It*), and then only on Mrs. Warbeck, the scold, which is a good gag; but have frequently shown the humble to be indestructible—which I consider to be a fair observation of what goes on: we do survive, in our millions, in spite of famine, war, and pestilence.

*   *   *

Henry Livings's success in presenting "a new way of looking at something" is arguably at the core of the "controversies" over his work. Some critics suggest a lack of compassion, an absence of distinction between victims and oppressors, and a neglect in providing "positive action and solution." They suggest that a playwright who focuses on the underdog is required, at the least, to invest his underdog with momentary glory, preferably illustrating a victory for the individual over authority.

Livings lets them down by rejecting the conventional approaches. As he says, his characters are people not "normally a big deal," or, as he describes Perkin Warbeck, "very insignificant." None exhibits particularly redeeming personal characteristics or grows in our affections. Those who attempt revenge do so in inept and insignificant ways. Perkin Warbeck in *Stop It Whoever You Are* is an old, cantankerous lavatory cleaner brow-beaten by his wife for never having attained the social heights of schoolmate Alderman

Oglethorpe. His seduction by precocious 14-year-old Marilyn inspires Warbeck with enough energy to express his resentment by attempting to soak Oglethorpe when the official entourage, on discovering that the new library they are opening has no public convenience, is forced to use the factory lavatory. Perkin back-handedly soaks his boss, and is sacked. He collapses and is taken home to die, only to return through a medium to haunt his wife.

Warbeck's revenge is something of an own-goal. Stanley, in *Big Soft Nellie*, a stuttering milksop electrician, unable to elicit the acknowledgement that the business depends on his ability to repair electrical goods, temporarily steals his employers' television and cannot even get himself arrested. Livings avoids the usual manner of dealing with the humble and ignored. He neither heroicises them nor elaborates personal detail to elicit sympathy. For Livings, the fact of their existence is justification enough and merits attention. What his characters all have in common, besides their indisputable insignificance, is their inability or unwillingness to play that game that doles out significance, to acknowledge the importance of the construct that those around them take for granted as the source of relevance and social cohesion. Their lack of participation, rather than elevating them to "heroic" heights, exposes the essential arbitrariness of the construct itself. Thus, it is not "authority" but the system justifying it that is in the dock.

Livings has often been linked with the Irish playwright Brendan Behan. Some of the common aspects of their work may well be the effect of their experiences with Joan Littlewood at Theatre Workshop (Livings acted in Behan's *The Quare Fellow*). Livings's plays are constructed of a series of short music-hall skits, each relatively complete in itself. Both his frequent use of a compere-type narrator and his broad seaside-postcard-like characters retain an aura of the music hall. However, he also shares with Behan a fundamental respect and fondness for the natural anarchy of human life, the inherent, chaotic unreasonableness of human emotion and day-to-day ingenuity, and a moral resistance to attempts to control and categorise through the imposition of organised hierarchical structures. Like Behan, he sees the systems of institutional ordering as destructive to the anarchic, unpredictable spirit and innate dignity which express the irreducible value of human life.

In his straight-talking northern manner, Livings does not attempt to elevate the humble or to invest the insignificant with glory. Rather, he insists dignity is inviolable and concentrates on exposing the constructs that attempt to make it negotiable by denying the many and augmenting the few, exposing their arbitrariness through highlighting their ludicrousness. Once seen as arbitrary, they might lose their power and become changeable if not dispensable.

We find Livings's characters in ludicrous situations. Viewed from an unquestioning everyday perspective, however, these situations, on the face of it, are fairly ordinary and mundane. It is the perspective created through the dogged unchangeability of his characters' worm's-eye view that renders the circumstances ridiculous. In *Eh?*, for example, a young man obsessed with growing mushrooms acquires a job in a factory which requires only that he turn the central machine on and off. From the point of view of the employer or the factory staff one can safely assume that there would be little remarkable about the situation. The machine is the heart of their purpose; the lad, the smallest cog in their impressive wheel. Onstage, however, even the visual image of the individual dwarfed by the immense machine necessitates an assessment of fundamental values. The obsessive technology that surrounds him (including a musical door) compounds the

appalling waste of human energy and renders the situation ludicrous. The "unresolved" ending in which the young man, his girlfriend, and the mushrooms rise in a cloud of smoke as the machine explodes offers no practical solutions, but sustains the question of where our values should lie and compounds the instigating assumption of the original image: that the constructs we embrace to organise and assess our lives are arbitrary, ludicrous, and demeaning.

The central characters of the plays are ordinary, unremarkable people who can't, won't, or don't know how to play the game that seems to occupy and give importance to those around them. Their denial is not the expression of heroic integrity, nor is it a moral stand, but arguably the source of their insignificance: they simply don't seem able to see the Emperor's New Clothes. Unacknowledged, the structures themselves lose their inevitability and the behaviour sustaining them appears ludicrous—at worst, destructive to human nature, at best, arbitrary and bemusing.

Nil Carborundum, whose title sums up the main thrust of Livings's work ("Don't let them grind you down"), provides perhaps the clearest example of his argument. Neville is serving out his National Service as a cook. He arrives in camp as a war game is about to commence. ("It is assumed for the purpose of the Surprise Enterprise that the Home Counties have been dislocated by ground-to-ground nuclear missiles. . . . Umpires will wear yellow armbands.") Because Neville doggedly refuses to acknowledge any role except that of cook, every possible attitude towards the war game is played out, from total engagement to the embittered irony of the Commander, to Neville's refusal to recognise its existence. Neville's denial exposes the game as a ludicrous construction and a waste of human energy and ingenuity. In contrast with Arnold Wesker, whose *Chips with Everything* poses National Service and the army as a metaphor for human life, Livings presents it as exemplary of the arbitrariness of social constructs and their denial of human value. Neville's resistence is never heroic, but his behaviour suggests that, faced with such ludicrous, demeaning demands, the best one can do—even the most positive act possible—is to deny one's participation, not on self-aggrandised principle, but in fact, thus exposing the construct itself to evaluation.

In *There's No Room for You Here for a Start* (a television play), the tentative relationship between Lily, a lonely aging landlady and her lodger, Len, a one-armed semi-tramp, is sharply contrasted with the obsessive, officious demands of the council that she cut her hedge to the regulation height. It is not difficult to assess the relative importance of the emotional needs of two lonely, isolated people (the play is possibly the first to deal with the effects of child abuse) and regulation-size hedges. Nor is it difficult to understand how Len's desperate desire to protect Lily leads him to meet the council's authoritarian aggression with a gun. The excessiveness of his response highlights the ludicrousness of theirs. The hedge is, unsurprisingly, cut to council regulation height. However, Len and Lily are condemned to lonely futures.

Livings's most serious piece is the disturbing, poetic *Kelly's Eye*. Set in 1939, it is a Conradian story of a man, self-isolated as a result of a guilty, painful past, drawn back into social interaction and inevitable destruction through emotional engagement. Livings makes no attempt to exonerate Kelly for the murder of his friend; at best, it is indicative of a growing violence and chaos, as well as Kelly's lack of self-knowledge. Kelly's constant memories of soldiering in World War I give us more insight into the deed than Kelly can.

Kelly meets young Anna on an isolated beach when he rescues her from her callous boyfriend. Love grows between them. Reluctantly, Kelly moves into town with her where, as he feared, Anna's wealthy father and the law soon track him down. Kelly commits suicide. Kelly's story, however, is never permitted the vestiges of special significance; the murder, his and Anna's love for each other, his capture, and his suicide are overshadowed by news that war has been declared, another man-made construct that overlooks the value and dignity of the "insignificant" man.

Livings's writing has been described as "comic strip," but the broad, colourful, and splendidly bizarre style presents a difficult vision suggesting that the systems by which we order and evaluate are not "natural" formations but arbitrary constructs that might be reassembled, changed, or dispensed with in favour of simple compassion and respect, or even a whole-hearted embracing of the fundamental anarchy of human nature.

—Elaine Turner

LOCHHEAD, Liz. Scottish. Born in Motherwell, Lanarkshire, 26 December 1947. Educated at Dalziel High School, Motherwell, 1960–65; Glasgow School of Art, 1965–70, diploma in art. Art teacher at Bishopbriggs High School, Glasgow, and other schools in Glasgow and Bristol. Recipient: BBC Scotland prize, 1971; Scottish Arts Council award, 1973, and fellowship, 1978. Address: 11 Kersland Street, Glasgow G12 8BW, Scotland.

PUBLICATIONS

Plays

Blood and Ice (produced Edinburgh, 1982; revised version, produced London, 1984). Edinburgh, Salamander Press, 1982; New York, Methuen, 1983.
Tickly Mince (revue), with Tom Leonard and Alisdair Gray (produced Glasgow, 1982).
The Pie of Damocles (revue), with others (produced Glasgow, 1983).
A Bunch of Fives, with Tom Leonard and Sean Hardie (produced Glasgow, 1983).
Silver Service. Edinburgh, Salamander Press, 1984.
Dracula, adaptation of the novel by Bram Stoker (produced Edinburgh, 1985). With *Mary Queen of Scots Got Her Head Chopped Off*, London, Penguin, 1989.
Tartuffe, adaptation of the play by Molière (produced Edinburgh, 1985). Edinburgh, Polygon, 1985.
Mary Queen of Scots Got Her Head Chopped Off (produced Edinburgh and London, 1987). With *Dracula*, London, Penguin, 1989.
The Big Picture (produced Glasgow, 1988).
Patter Merchant (produced Edinburgh, 1989).
Jock Tamson's Bairns, with Gerry Mulgrew (produced Glasgow, 1990).
Quelques Fleurs (produced Edinburgh and London, 1991).

Screenplay: *Now and Then*, 1972.

Radio Play: *Blood and Ice*, 1990.

Television Play: *Sweet Nothings* in *End of the Line* series, 1984.

Verse

Memo for Spring. Edinburgh, Reprographia, 1972.
The Grimm Sisters. London, Next Editions, 1981.
Dreaming Frankenstein, and Collected Poems. Edinburgh, Polygon, 1984.
True Confessions and New Clichés. Edinburgh, Polygon, 1985.

*

Critical Study: "Feminist Nationalism in Scotland: *Mary Queen of Scots Got Her Head Chopped Off*" by Ilona S. Koren-Deutsch, in *Modern Drama* (Toronto), September 1992.

Theatrical Activities:
Actor: **Play**—*The Complete Alternative History of the World, Part 1*, Edinburgh, 1986.

*   *   *

Once upon a time there were *twa queens* on the wan green island, and the wan green island was split inty two kingdoms. But no equal kingdoms, naebody in their richt mind would insist on that.
—La Corbie, *Mary Queen of Scots
Got Her Head Chopped Off*

Liz Lochhead is a teller of tales, the author of strongly narrative plays, dramatic monologues, and poetry. The stories she recounts are often drawn from popular memory and folk culture but are retold with a distinctively female voice. History, myth, and memory interconnect and are analysed and deconstructed in a body of work that finds reference in both literary and popular culture. In common with other contemporary women writers Lochhead has been attracted to the images and the conventions of the Gothic and has discovered in fairytales and in childhood rhymes a new set of metaphors for the role of women in society. Like Angela Carter, Lochhead twists the familiar to find a dark and bloody unconscious with new perspectives on the assumed truths of our society.

Lochhead's plays retell the stories of Mary Shelley and Frankenstein, Mary Queen of Scots and Elizabeth I, Tartuffe, and Dracula with a compelling mix of traditional Scots, contemporary vernacular dialogue, and a subtle lyricism that contemporary theatre writing often effaces in favour of bald realism. Lochhead is not afraid to mix the prosaic and the poetic in one play, one scene, one speech. This combination brings to her already credible and recognisable characters new heights of tragedy or pathos. In *Quelques Fleurs* the extended monologues of Verena and her oilrig-worker husband, Derek (characters as recognisable in a Scottish context as Mike Leigh's characters are within English culture), are written in a mordantly idiomatic and scathingly witty prose to blackly comic effect.

Across a range of genres and subjects Lochhead writes about women and about monsters. Rarely, however, does she write about monstrous women. Focusing on the experiences of women in history, in literature, and in our contemporary world, Lochhead's writing uncovers society's fears of the *unheimlich* aspects of the feminine. Her plays foreground the social and domestic, sexual and creative roles of women within societies which politically and culturally marginalise and devalue their work and their lives. Lochhead takes the common view of these women—Mary as *femme fatale* and Elizabeth as scheming politician in *Mary Queen of Scots Got Her Head Chopped Off*, Mary Shelley as daughter of Mary

Wollstonecraft and William Godwin and lover and wife of Percy Bysshe Shelley, with Elise as mere downtrodden maid, in *Blood and Ice*—and peels back the mythology, drawing out the essential humanity of the person. She strives to find in each of her creations a more empowering identity than has traditionally been projected.

Lochhead's plays reset the role of women within both historical and contemporary society with a ubiquity of language that draws on her skills as poet and performer. The subjects of her plays may be historically diverse but they are united by an energetic, vibrant, and precise use of language.

Blood and Ice, her first full-length play, achieved after several revisions, is essentially a memory play with characters and spirits emerging from the life and imagination of Mary Shelley. Time, place, and degree of "reality" are all signalled in the prose and the verse of the text. In a play dealing with Mary Shelley's creativity and the writing process, with commentary on the lives of both Shelley and Byron, there is a deliberate overemphasis on the importance of words. Language is used to mark shifts in time and space, memory and imagination. Variations in tone suggest in turn the lyricism of the idyll of Lake Geneva, the artificiality of the conversation and society of Mary's Romantic companions, the prosaic language of domestic duties and responsibilities, and the obsessive and violent nature of her imagination and her creativity.

The nature and value of creativity is also examined by presenting alternative visions of Mary Shelley as mother and author. The process of writing the novel is mirrored in her role as mother (to her children and in her increasingly maternal relationships with Shelley and her half-sister Claire) and as creator of the fiction of *Frankenstein*. This is further compared to the character of Frankenstein bringing life to his monster. Society's restricting expectations of roles of wife/lover and mother are described as problematic—particularly to the creative and powerful woman. *Blood and Ice* shows that society demands a heavy price from the woman who steps outside the framework of family and wants to be more than muse to another's imagination. At the end of the play Mary Shelley may be left isolated and alone but Lochhead has recovered her and her life from a distraction of myths and received ideas to posit an impression of her heroine as a person, as a mother, and as a writer in her own right.

As with *Blood and Ice*, the demands of society upon woman to be wife and mother is a central theme of *Mary Queen of Scots Got Her Head Chopped Off*. In this play, however, the dramatic conflict is not played out in private places or in the psyche of one woman but in the public sphere and the political conflicts of two nations. The play's narrator, chorus, and sometime conscience La Corbie poses the central riddle of the play: ". . .I ask you, when's a queen a queen/ And when's a queen juist a wummin?"

Plays like *Blood and Ice*, *Mary Queen of Scots Got Her Head Chopped Off*, and *Dracula*, although written with a strongly narrative spine, are structurally dense—with complex layerings of temporal, geographic, and psychological spaces. Lochhead uses doubling with psychological intent, actors being required to play two, three, or even four different but fundamentally linked characters. Mary and Elizabeth are matched at each step by parallel and complimentary characters, each time played by the same actors. The pairings of the maids Marian and Bessie, the beggars Mairn and Leezie, and the children Marie and Wee Betty each reveal another facet of Lochhead's project to show the similarities in the problems faced by Mary and Elizabeth in particular, but also by other women both in the time-frame of the drama and in our own age.

Scottish theatre writing is often criticised for its essential nostalgia and preoccupation with the nation's history, and certainly *Mary Queen of Scots Got Her Head Chopped Off* is a play about a privileged moment in Scotland's political development. Typically of Lochhead, however, the play energises the discourse of nostalgia through the use of rhymes and games. Using *Doppelgänger* for all the main players in the drama and an omnipresent narrator who speaks in an eclectic version of 16th-century Scots, and introducing parallel scenes within contemporary culture, her use of the past is very much more precise and focused than is the case with plays that offer a more straightforward version of historical drama. Lochhead sets out to reinterpret the past and to draw out a new and political agenda for the contemporary audience. She mixes the introspection of much of Scottish culture with a desire to develop a new set of images and a new system of metaphors for the depiction of domestic and psychological drama. The activation of memory as well as history is again reflected in her use of language. The play ends with the characters of the drama transformed into children playing a demonic game in which Mary/Marie is again the victim of prejudice and group hysteria.

Just as the received images society holds of Mary Shelley are dissected in *Blood and Ice*, so in *Mary Queen of Scots Got Her Head Chopped Off* Lochhead re-examines the mythology associated with both Mary and Elizabeth and again finds disturbing parallels between the demands made of the women in the play and the prejudices that still limit their expectations and ambitions. The play functions as an explicit metaphor for contemporary society.

Lochhead's plays re-examine the deeply rooted prejudices and assumptions held by our culture. Using the conventions of historical drama in *Mary Queen of Scots Got Her Head Chopped Off*, restoring the real horror and tragedy of *Dracula*, and revealing the isolation of women as different as Mary Shelley and Verena, Lochhead rewrites the myths of our culture to reinstate the experiences and the voices of women.

—Adrienne Scullion

LORD, Robert. New Zealander. 1945–1992.
See 4th edition, 1988.

LOWE, Stephen. British. Born in Nottingham, 1 December 1947. Educated at the University of Birmingham, 1966–70, B.A. (honours) in English 1969. Actor and director, Stephen Joseph Theatre-in-the-Round, Scarborough, Yorkshire, 1975–78; senior lecturer, Dartington College of Arts, Devon, 1978–82; resident playwright, Riverside Studios, London, 1984. Since 1984 artistic director, Meeting Ground Theatre Company, Nottingham. Recipient: George Devine award, 1977. Agent: Judy Daish Associates, 83 Eastbourne Mews, London W2 6LQ, England.

PUBLICATIONS

Plays

Comic Pictures (includes *Stars* and *Cards*) (produced London, 1972; revised version produced Scarborough, 1976; London, 1982). *Cards* published London, French, 1983; *Stars* included in *Moving Pictures: Four Plays*, 1985.
Touched (produced Nottingham, 1977). Todmorden, Yorkshire, Woodhouse, 1977; revised version (produced London, 1981; New York, 1982), London, Eyre Methuen, 1981.
Shooting, Fishing and Riding (produced Scarborough, 1977).
Sally Ann Hallelujah Band (produced Nottingham, 1977).
The Ragged Trousered Philanthropists, adaptation of the novel by Robert Tressell (produced Plymouth and London, 1978; New York, 1987). London, Joint Stock, 1978; revised version (produced London, 1983), London, Methuen, 1983.
Fred Karno's Bloody Circus (produced London, 1980).
Moving Pictures (as *Glasshouses*, produced London, 1981; as *Moving Pictures*, produced Leeds, 1985). Included in *Moving Pictures: Four Plays*, 1985.
Tibetan Inroads (produced London, 1981). London, Eyre Methuen, 1981.
Strive (produced Exeter, 1983; London, 1987). Included in *Moving Pictures: Four Plays*, 1985.
The Trial of Frankenstein (produced Plymouth, 1983).
Seachange (produced London, 1984). Included in *Moving Pictures: Four Plays*, 1985.
Keeping Body and Soul Together (produced London, 1984) Published in *Peace Plays 1*, edited by Lowe, London, Methuen, 1985.
Moving Pictures: Four Plays. London, Methuen, 1985.
Desire (produced Nottingham, 1986).
Demon Lovers (produced Loughborough, Leicestershire and London, 1987).
The Storm, adaptation of a play by Alexander Ostrovsky (produced London, 1987).
Divine Gossip (produced London, 1988). With *Tibetan Inroads*, London, Methuen, 1988.
William Tell, adaptation of the play by Schiller (produced Sheffield, 1989).
Paradise (musical; produced Nottingham, 1990).

Television Plays: *Cries from a Watchtower*, 1979; *Shades*, 1982; *Kisses on the Bottom*, 1985; *Albion Market* series, 1986; *Coronation Street* series, 1989; *Families* series, 1990; *Ice Dance*, 1990; *Flea Bites*, 1992; *In Suspicious Circumstances*, 1992; *Tell-Tale Hearts*, 1992.

Other

Editor, *Peace Plays 1*. London, Methuen, 1985.
Editor, *Peace Plays 2*. London, Methuen, 1989.

*

Critical Studies: "Letters from a Workshop: *The Ragged Trousered Philanthropists*," in *Dartington Papers 2* (Totnes, Devon), 1978, and "Peace Plays: Peace as a Theatrical Concern," in *Englische Amerikanische Studien* (Munich), nos. 3–4, 1986, both by Lowe.

Stephen Lowe comments:
The best introductions to my work are, of course, the plays. But some central concerns, or obsessions, are clear even to me, and have taken me into plays set in the past, and into plays set on the other side of the world—in Tibet. One concern is to explore moments of real change in society, to discover perhaps an optimistic vision that might inspire us through the present moment of change. A large number of them *I* would call political love stories; these have often led me into an exploration of "inner language" through dreams and fairy and folk tale elements.

As Joyce pointed out, there are probably only three subjects worth writing about—politics, religion, and sex. I have discovered in my work that the clear divisions between these create a false perspective, and the interrelation of all these elements is, to me, a crucial theatrical concern, in both form and content.

*   *   *

Stephen Lowe's career as a professional playwright started with a production of two short plays, *Cards* and *Stars* at the Library Theatre in Scarborough while Lowe was employed there as an actor. Since then, his plays have been regularly premiered and performed on all the major British stages, on radio, and on television.

His work as a playwright is characterised by a sustained interest in exploration and experiment, both in dramatic technique and in the process of production. Largely because of this, his work is hard to classify. Much of his work deals with material derived from being born in, and spending most of his life around, Nottingham. His plays not uncommonly cover issues that broadly characterise the texture of D.H. Lawrence's work: local dialect, intense interest in sexuality, the preoccupations of working-class people, and, most distinctively, a powerfully subjective view of the artistic imagination as the means to free the individual from the social and personal myths that circumscribe the actions in their daily lives. In Lowe, as in Lawrence, it is this distinctive voice that gives, to the broadly provincial tone of his work, a resonance and allusiveness that make him undoubtedly one of the most significant British writers of the last decade. As a complement to this, his theatrical interests and activities challenge his own residual prejudices about "the spirit of place," sustained by a concern to balance the subjective elements of his writing against a wider, universal perspective.

Nowhere are these tensions more explicit than in his first major successful play, *Touched*, first directed at the Nottingham Playhouse by Richard Eyre, taken on tour and then revived by Bill Gaskill for the Royal Court in 1981. The play is set in the 100-day period between May and August 1945, between the end of the war in Europe and the dropping of the atomic bomb on Hiroshima. Against a collage of sounds and images which document the processes of a world adjusting with difficulty to peace, Lowe reveals the quiet, relentless tragedy of an extended family, through a structured defoliation of the private hopes and fears of the women left at home to sustain the life of a community unmanned by the war.

The burden of the play rests on Sandra, a married woman in her mid-thirties who sees the chance to confront the old hierarchies with her decision to carry a child begotten in an opportunistic relationship with an Italian prisoner of war. The plot is complicated by an 18-year-old epileptic boy's unsolicited declaration to Sandra's family that he is the father of her child. It transpires that his admission of paternity arises from a wish to offer her a measure of protection from the stigma of straying outside the tribe, and to expiate his sin of spying on Sandra's illicit lovemaking with the prisoner of war. In gratitude, Sandra presents herself to Johnny, but he cannot "touch" her. Like all the men in the play, he cannot function as a man where the traditional myths based on a male-orientated world are challenged. This desolate vision of the impending return of the men at the end of the war is un-relieved throughout the play. The nature of the ambiguous peace is reflected in our final realisations that Sandra's preg-nancy is an illusion, and ratified in the final ironies in General MacArthur's voice-over: "Men everywhere walk upright in the sun . . . The entire world is at peace . . . The Holy Mission is completed."

Touched is an important play in that it prefigures most of Lowe's thematic concerns, not the least of which is a belief that, in order to deal with the myths it embodies, history cannot be treated like a "theme park," detached from the present. For Lowe, the historic "moment" is often the main-spring of dramatic action; it is inevitable that while the "moments" he employs to test out his hypotheses are gener-ally accessible ones, they invariably have personal resonances for him. In *Touched*, the interest in 1945 grew out of ex-tended discussion with his aunt and his mother and his father's trials in the 8th Army. In *Moving Pictures*, perhaps the most autobiographical of his plays, the "moment" is 1963–64, the age of mobility and the growth of the nuclear family: the shift from street community to high-rise flat. *Strive* is a short play based on the Falklands War, a "moment" he develops with more complexity in *Seachange*, also based on the Falklands War, but again linked to a personal odyssey Lowe made some years earlier across the Aegean Sea. His grandfather, who had fought in the Gallipoli campaign during World War I, was killed when the ship he was on went down after aerial bombardment. In the introduction to the play, Lowe recalls how on his odyssey he imagined how he might have "passed over the clear waters of his grandfather's grave," re-enacting "the uncertain intimacy of those who love each other through blood, but [who] are only too aware of the sea of time that divides them."

The link between history and the imagination is under-stated in *Touched*. It is given more detailed examination in *Tibetan Inroads*, *Moving Pictures*, *Demon Lovers*, and *Divine Gossip*. *Demon Lovers* is, in effect, an imaginative construc-tion of the love story between the Moors Murderers Ian Brady and Myra Hindley, and the gothic horror of an art (in this case, a video) worked out of the suffering they inflicted on their victims, Lowe is powerfully interested in the relation-ship between imagination, creativity, and art. In *Demon Lovers*, and earlier in *The Trial of Frankenstein*, he alludes to the negative power of an imagination denied expression. *Divine Gossip* reveals the more positive, though no less potent, manifestation of creativity in action. The play has an historical setting: 1929, the year in which three of Lowe's heroes (George Orwell, Harry Crosby, and D.H. Lawrence) were all in Paris. It juxtaposes aspects of maleness—in art, sexuality, and the desire for death—upon a story of Louise Brooks's *Pandora's Box* and a French prostitute aspiring to be Louise Brooks.

Through *Touched*, Lowe earned an early reputation for being a writer of women's plays. *The Ragged Trousered Philanthropists* and *Divine Gossip* clearly prove this is not the case. Between these poles lies *Shooting, Fishing and Riding*, a play about rape, inspired by the feminist writer Susan Brownmiller's book, *Against Our Will*. While he considers this piece to have been unsuccessful, his most recent work for television, *Tell-Tale Hearts*, a psychological thriller set in Edinburgh and Glasgow, returns to this early theme of sexual abuse within relationships.

Lowe is at his most articulate and assured in writing about inter-personal relationships. *Tibetan Inroads* is an exemplary work from a number of perspectives. The play is based around the vicissitudes of natural love and the penalties and consequences of disrupting social convention. If *Tibetan Inroads* makes any single statement about people it is that they are endlessly unknowable, possessing in equal measure the mystical, intangible capacities for compassion and abuse. But above all, his characterisations reveal a care for, and love of, the extraordinary richness, diversity, and complexity across the spectrum of human behaviour. Characteristic of this is the uproariously comic, plangent scene from *Moving Pictures* in which adolescent brothers and sisters try to con-struct a Lawrentian sex-movie in a studio improvised out of the parent's front parlour.

Lowe's evocations of mood and period are wrought with great skill and economy. It is germane to note how his progress as a dramatist has been paralled by his continuing workshop and community projects. Those workshops aimed to politicise the imagination of the participants—on the one hand to give responsibility denied them in their ordinary lives, on the other, to discover new ways of understanding history and art.

—Paul Hadfield

———

LOWELL, Robert (Traill Spence, Jr.). American. 1917–1977.
See 2nd edition, 1977.

———

LUCAS, Craig. American. Born in Atlanta, Georgia, 30 April 1951. Educated at Boston University, Massachusetts, B.F.A. (cum laude) 1973. Since 1987 associate artist, South Coast Repertory, Costa Mesa, California, and since 1989 member, Circle Repertory, New York. Recipient: Drama-logue award 1986; Los Angeles Drama Critics award, 1986; George and Elizabeth Marton award, 1986; Guggenheim fellowship, 1987; Rockefeller grant, 1989; Tony award, 1989; Outer Critics Circle award, 1989; Obie award, 1990; Sun-dance Film Festival Audience award, 1990. Lives in New York City. Agent: Peter Franklin, William Morris Agency, 1350 Avenue of the Americas, New York, New York 10019, U.S.A.

PUBLICATIONS

Plays

Marry Me a Little, with Norman Rene, music and lyrics by Stephen Sondheim (produced New York, 1980; London, 1982).
Blue Window, music by Craig Carnelia (produced New York, 1984; London, 1989). With *Reckless*, New York, Theatre Communications Group, 1989.
Three Complaints, music by Stewart Wallace (produced New York, 1985).
Missing Persons (produced New York, 1985).

Three Postcards, music and lyrics by Craig Carnelia
(produced Costa Mesa, California and New York, 1987;
Edinburgh, 1992).
Prelude to a Kiss (produced Costa Mesa, California, 1988;
New York, 1990). New York, Dutton, 1990.
Reckless, music by Craig Carnelia (produced New York,
1988). With *Blue Window*, New York, Theatre
Communications Group, 1989.
Orpheus in Love (libretto), music by Gerald Busby (pro-
duced New York, 1992).
Throwing Your Voice (produced New York, 1992).

Screenplays: *Longtime Companion*, with Norman Rene,
1990; *Prelude to a Kiss*, with Norman Rene, 1991.

Television Play: *Blue Window*, with Norman Rene, 1987.

*

Manuscript Collection: Boston University, Special Collections, Boston, Massachusetts.

Theatrical Activities:
Actor: **Plays**—role as Confederate Sniper in *Shenandoah* by
James Lee Barrett, New York, 1975, and Nathan, 1976–77;
Gentleman of the Court in *Rex*, book by Sherman Yellen,
music by Richard Rodgers, lyrics by Sheldon Harnick, New
York, 1976; male singer and standby Max Jacobs in *On the
Twentieth Century*, book and lyrics by Betty Comden and
Adolph Green, music by Cy Coleman, New York, 1978;
member of the company, *Sweeney Todd, the Demon Barber
of Fleet Street*, book by Hugh Wheeler, music and lyrics by
Stephen Sondheim, New York, 1979; *Marry Me A Little* by
Lucas and Norman Rene, music and lyrics by Stephen
Sondheim, New York, 1980.

* * *

Several of Craig Lucas's plays are prefaced by epigraphs
from other authors, which give pointers to the journeys taken
in his work. W. H. Auden's aptly-titled "Leap Before you
Look" provides the motto to *Reckless*, at the startling opening in which the heroine Rachel, a happy suburban housewife, anticipating a happy Christmas with her husband and
kids, is suddenly told by her husband that he has taken out a
contract on her life. As an intruder breaks in downstairs,
Rachel climbs out of the bedroom window. Windows in
Lucas's world have something of the mystery of the nursery
window in *Peter Pan*, and in *Reckless* Rachel's defenestration
begins one of the roller-coaster journeys on which Lucas
takes his audiences.
Reckless is an unusual Christmas fable—fleeing into the
snowy night, Rachel is given a lift by Lloyd, who takes her to
the Springfield, Massachusetts home which he shares with the
crippled Pooty, who is also deaf and dumb. But as Pooty
reveals to Rachel later, she so adored Lloyd when she first
saw him at the centre for the physically handicapped where he
works that she has only pretended to be deaf and dumb
because she felt that only if she were somehow needier than
others would she get special attention from Lloyd. This is
only one of several revelations in the play—that Lloyd walked
out on a wife with multiple sclerosis is another ("The past is
the nightmare you wake up to every day," he says)—as it
traces Rachel's journey through a wacky parody of television
game-shows ("Your Money or your Wife?") and her encounters with different doctors, all played by the same actor
(Lucas has some sharp fun at psychiatry's expense in these

sections), to eventual self-discovery and maturity. It ends
with Rachel as a doctor herself, interviewing her now-
adolescent son (who, of course, does not recognise her) who
has had problems sleeping, troubled by his family's past, in a
scene which climaxes in a curiously affecting sense of reconciliation at another Christmas time.
The audience goes on another journey in *Blue Window*, a
play of dazzling technical achievement, which takes place in
five separate New York apartments simultaneously. It's
Sunday night and Libby is preparing to give a party (relying
on her friend Griever for telephonic advice); other guests
include a lesbian couple and a composer and his girl. Before,
during, and after the party, Lucas weaves their conversations
into a complex mesh of overlapping dialogue, scoring verbal
music against an abstract blue setting and building up against
this slightly sterile background the patterns of young(ish)
professional mid-1980's Manhattan, anxious and self-
defensively wry (especially in Griever's often outrageous
cadenzas) with some splendid running sight-gags (Libby's
encounter with a caviare jar breaks off a cap on a tooth,
forcing her to mask her mouth for much of the evening). On
the page, it might seem over-wistful and fatally arch, but in
performance *Blue Window* combines social comedy with a
melancholy substrain to potent effect.
Lucas's association with the Circle Repertory Company in
New York continued with a recent play, *Prelude to a Kiss*,
which then moved to Broadway for a long run. E. M.
Forster's *aperçu* from *Howard's End* that "Death destroys a
man, but the idea of death is what saves him" suggests the
dark urban fairytale at the centre of the play.
Prelude to a Kiss represents the boldest of Lucas's journeys
to date. In Manhattan, a young man (Peter) falls in love with
a young girl (Rita) he meets at a party. There are just a few
clues (Rita's insomnia, for example) that suggest perils lurking behind the idyll of their courtship. At their wedding at
Rita's parents' New Jersey home, an unsettling incident
occurs, with an uninvited old man kissing Rita and then going
on his way. Rita seems oddly affected by the encounter, and
her oddness increases on the couple's Jamaican honeymoon.
By the disturbing close of Act One, we have begun to realise
that a transmigration of souls has taken place, and the second
act traces Peter's dilemma; with Rita's soul residing in the
body of an old man dying of cancer, can he still love her?
Love makes Peter resourceful enough to engineer a way by
which to regain Rita's soul, and the play ends with their
reunion after a typical Lucas tragi-comic journey. The play
occasionally falls into the trap of becoming overslick, even
fey, but obliquely—as he does in much of his work—Lucas
reaffirms the power of love in an age of fears which compromise it. And the hairpin bends Lucas has to negotiate in
the rides he creates give his best work a sense of exhilarating
adventure.

—Alan Strachan

———

LUCIE, Doug. British. Born in Chessington, Surrey, 15
December 1953. Educated at Tiffin Boys' School, 1965–72:
Worcester College, Oxford, 1973–76, B.A. (honours) in
English 1976. Resident playwright, Oxford Playhouse
Company, 1979–80; visiting playwright, University of Iowa,
Iowa City, 1980. Recipient: *Time Out* award, 1988. Agent:

Michael Imison Playwrights, 28 Almeida Street, London N1 1TD, England.

PUBLICATIONS

Plays

John Clare's Mad, Nuncle (produced Edinburgh, 1975).
Rough Trade (also director: produced Oxford, 1977).
The New Garbo (produced Hull and London, 1978).
We Love You (also director: produced London, 1978).
Oh Well (also director: produced Oxford, 1978).
Heroes (also director: produced Edinburgh and London, 1979).
Fear of the Dark (produced London, 1980).
Poison (also director: produced Edinburgh, 1980).
Strangers in the Night (produced London, 1981).
Hard Feelings (produced Oxford, 1982; London, 1983). With *Progress*, London, Methuen, 1985.
Progress (produced London, 1984; New Haven, Connecticut, 1986; New York, 1989). With *Hard Feelings*, London, Methuen, 1985.
The Key to the World (produced Leicester and London, 1984).
Force and Hypocrisy (produced London, 1986).
Fashion (produced Stratford-on-Avon, 1987; London, 1988; Chicago, 1992). London, Methuen, 1987.
Doing the Business (produced London, 1990).
Grace (produced London, 1993).

Television Plays: A *Class of His Own*, 1984; *Funseekers*, with Nigel Planer, 1987.

*

Theatrical Activities:
Director: **Plays**—some of his own plays; student productions of *The Duchess of Malfi* by Webster, *The Comedy of Errors*, and *Hitting Town* by Stephen Poliakoff.
Actor: **Plays**—*We Love You*, London, 1978; *Oh Well*, Oxford, 1978.

* * *

Wherever people congregate there will be rich pickings for those with an ear for the nuances of speech and a nose for the ridiculous. Since comedy of manners was invented, the drawing room has provided the playwright with a suitable microcosm for bourgeois society. Where once there were drawing rooms there are now communal living spaces. At some point in the 1970's Doug Lucie moved into yours or mine. He has captured the social mores and hypocrisies of a particular social strata—at university and beyond—and pilloried us on stage for our general amusement and embarrassed recognition.

Lucie has not dealt exclusively with the cynicism, power games, and capacity for self-delusion of his contemporaries. *The New Garbo* anticipated the interest in the actress Frances Farmer. *Strangers in the Night* flirted with a lurid expressionism redolent of mid-period Sam Shepard. But it is as the persistent chronicler of his peers that Lucie has gained his reputation. *We Love You* dealt with adolescent rebel posturing. *Heroes* showed six undergraduates in a shared house in Oxford and contrasted them with a different group living there ten years before. *Hard Feelings* is set in Brixton in 1981. Inside another shared house they bicker and pose. Outside,

they riot. *Progress* is marriage and careers and sexual politics. Will is a Channel 4 researcher; Ronee is a social worker. What with the lodger, the battered wife they adopt, the phone calls from Ronee's lesbian lover, and Will's men's group ("We're trying to change our attitudes by being open and supportive without resorting to traditional, hierarchical structures"), their living room achieves honorary communal status.

Lucie's plays unfold with an ease and grace which belie a precise construction and rigorous comic technique. Lucie has an insidious way with his exposition; scenes end at precisely the right moment—the structure never sags; the comic effect derives from incongruous juxtaposition and savage undercutting. With a good designer to capture the latest nuances of interior decor and personal accessories, an evening at a Lucie play can provide an irresistible but excruciating portrait of the way we carry on, as our foibles are exposed in a relentlessly funny and viciously acute way.

Is it replication or exaggeration? There are those who say Lucie lacks subtlety. True, he assembles predictable characters in unsurprising combinations. *Progress* is a title with heavy-handed irony. In *Hard Feelings* the living room blinds are always down, which is perhaps an overemphatic metaphor. But unless Lucie aspires to subtlety, lack of it is neither here nor there. One cannot scourge discreetly. Yet who is being scourged and why? It may be that Lucie feels himself an interloper in the world he describes, but his sympathies are always with the outsider, regardless of their actions and attitudes. When Tone, the outsider in *Hard Feelings*, bellows, "people aren't kind of things, they're people," he articulates the author's—and the audience's—outrage. But in *Progress* the outsiders are Mark and Lenny. Mark is a gutter-press journalist with a spectacular line in sexist banter. Lenny uses his wife "as a sparring partner and she doesn't box." He also rapes her. Being bereft of privilege or pretense does not accord integrity by default, and it seems untypically naïve of Lucie even to hint that this is the case.

I do not think, as some do, that Lucie is trivial, but he often trivialises. Comedy of manners is, almost by definition, concerned with surfaces. Too often the dictates of this comic form constrain Lucie. When human beings are reduced to plot functionaries, however brilliantly, it is difficult to care much about what happens to them. Points are half-raised then abandoned, lest the pace slacken. Despite his huge talent, Lucie often seems wilfully insubstantial.

It is possible that Lucie will transcend the civilising parameters he has set himself and attain the corroscating heights of great satire. Interestingly, his 1984 play *The Key to the World* moved out of the drawing room and towards a more humane and less comic vision. Whatever direction Lucie takes, he is a dramatist of rare wit and exceptional powers of observation.

—Joss Bennathan

LUDLAM, Charles. American. 1943–1987.
See 3rd edition, 1982.

LUDWIG, Ken. American. Born in York, Pennsylvania, 15 March 1950. Educated at York Suburban High School, 1968; Haverford College, Pennsylvania, B.A. (magna cum laude) 1972; Trinity College, University of Cambridge, England, LL.M. 1975; Harvard Law School, Cambridge, Massachusetts, J.D. 1976. Married Adrienne George in 1976; one daughter. Attorney (Of Counsel), Steptoe and Johnson, law firm, Washington, D.C., 1976–89. Lives in Washington, D.C. Agent: Gilbert Parker and Peter Franklin, William Morris Agency, 1350 Avenue of the Americas, New York, New York 10019, U.S.A.

PUBLICATIONS

Plays

Class Night (sketches) (produced Haverford and Bryn Mawr, Pennsylvania, 1970 and 1972).
Divine Fire (produced Washington D.C., 1979; New York, 1980).
Sullivan and Gilbert (produced Milford, New Hampshire, 1983; New York, 1984). New York, French, 1989.
Postmortem (produced Milford, New Hampshire, 1984). New York, French, 1989.
Dramatic License (produced Cleveland, Ohio, 1985).
Lend Me a Tenor (as *Opera Buffa*, produced Milford, New Hampshire, 1985; as *Lend Me a Tenor*, produced London, 1986; New York, 1989). London, French, 1986; New York, French, 1989.
Crazy for You, adaptation of *Girl Crazy* by George and Ira Gershwin (produced Washington, D.C., 1991; New York, 1992; London, 1993).

*

Theatrical Activities:
Director: **Play**—*Who's Afraid of Virginia Woolf* by Edward Albee, Haverford and Bryn Mawr, Pennsylvania, 1972.

Ken Ludwig comments:
The tradition of stage comedy that I admire most is what scholars call "high comedy" and I like to call "muscular comedy." It's the kind of comedy which, while firmly rooted in reality and the emotions of the characters, bursts off the stage, has a story filled with unexpected twists and turns, contains a broad range of characters from different levels of society, and abounds in word play—all in all, a reflection of our real lives, but somehow "bigger." The most distinguishing hallmark of this kind of comedy is some form of confusion, deception, or mistake, either in the workings of the plot or at the core of the structure.
The tradition began about 2,000 years ago with that irreverent Roman, Plautus. It re-emerged in the comedies of Shakespeare where mistaken identities and deception abound (*viz.*, in my opinion, the greatest comedies ever written, *Twelfth Night*, *As You Like It*, *Much Ado About Nothing*, and *A Midsummer Night's Dream*). Then came Goldsmith and Sheridan (*She Stoops to Conquer* and *The Rivals*) in the 18th century. In the 19th century the tradition is best seen in the comic operas of Rossini and Donizetti. And in our own century the tradition re-emerges in the stage comedies of Kaufman and Hart, Hecht and MacArthur, the screen comedies of Lubitsch and Sturges, and in the uniquely American musical comedies that were written in the 1920's and 1930's.

This is the form of drama, which, when it has greatness about it, touches me most deeply. My goal as a writer is to reinvent this tradition for our own times.

*   *   *

It is hardly surprising that Ken Ludwig should have achieved his biggest success to date with *Crazy for You*, his 1990's reworking of the 1930's book to the old Gershwin musical *Girl Crazy*. Music runs like a seam through Ludwig's plays and it was surely that musical sense and his sharp ear for the rhythm and shaping of a scene that made him the ideal choice to reconstruct the show's libretto affectionately.
Sullivan and Gilbert, Ludwig's play about the volatile relationship between Gilbert and Sullivan, may not tread any noticeably new ground, but it integrates the accompanying Savoy Opera songs with adroit smoothness, and the play has some astute scenes revealing the pitfalls of artistic collaboration.
Lend Me a Tenor is that rarity, a completely successful modern farce. Leading comedy writers have either failed signally in this tricky field (Neil Simon with *Rumours*) or skirted with homage to the form (such as Alan Ayckbourn paying tribute to Ben Travers in *Taking Steps*), with—in Britain at least—only Ray Cooney left to fly the flag for farce. So *Lend Me a Tenor* was doubly welcome—a farce which had all the classic Swiss-watch precision of plotting as it handled the spiralling complexities of its initially simple central situation, while retaining wit and heart. In a hotel suite in 1930's Cleveland, an imperious Opera House manager faces disaster when the Italian tenor ("Il Stupendo") booked to sing Otello at an important charity gala falls into a drunken stupor and is presumed dead (the scene of this assumption, involving the misunderstanding of the goodbye note from the tenor's jealous wife, may be a familiar farce staple—Ayckbourn uses it too in *Taking Steps*—but here it's superbly funny, because so credibly plotted and planted). To save the day, the impresario's dogsbody, Max, besotted by his employer's daughter, gets the chance to realise his operatic ambitions when he puts on blackface to win acclaim as Otello. Of course Il Stupendo awakes and dresses in costume, leading to a post-performance second act of hair's-breadth near-misses as real and substitute Otellos enter and exit through the suite's multiple doors, while the aphrodisiacs of fame and seductive music figure more strongly as various swooning females crowd the suite.
The play works well (it achieved an especially buoyant success in Jerry Zaks's high-octane New York production) not just because of its meticulous timing and passages of climactic lunacy (reaching the heights of some vintage Marx Brothers sequences), but also because of the spine of the plot, the old standby of understudy blossoming into star, given extra mileage here by a genuinely appealing central character; the audience moves progressively towards Max throughout the play as he looks like winning both his girl and musical fame.
Theatrical ambitions are also at the heart of Ludwig's expert book for *Crazy for You*—his hero, Bobby Childs, dreams of a dancing career in the Zangler Follies in 1930's New York, but is forced to act for his affluent family law firm to repossess a bankrupt Western township. Out in Deadrock, Nevada, there just happens to be a disused theatre and Bobby falls for the owner's daughter. Ludwig then cheekily re-works his central *Tenor* device with Bobby impersonating the flamboyant Zangler, only for the real Zangler to turn up. The script has a blithe, spring-heeled invention that will no doubt

have producers besieging Ludwig for more of the same, but it is to be hoped that he will also come up with another play as funny as *Lend Me a Tenor*.

—Alan Strachan

———

LUKE, Peter (Ambrose Cyprian). British. Born in St. Albans, Hertfordshire, 12 August 1919. Educated at Eton College; Byam Shaw School of Art, London; Atelier André Lhote, Paris. Served in the Rifle Brigade, in the Western Desert, Italy, and Northwest Europe, 1940–46: Military Cross, 1944. Married 1) Carola Peyton-Jones (died); 2) Lettice Crawshaw (marriage dissolved), one son (deceased) and one daughter; 3) the actress June Tobin in 1963, two sons and three daughters. Sub-editor, Reuters, 1946–47; worked in the wine trade, 1947–57; book critic, *Queen* magazine, London, 1957–58; story editor, *Armchair Theatre* programme, 1958–60, and editor, *Bookman* programme, 1960–61, and *Tempo* arts programme, 1961–62, all for ABC Television, London; drama producer, BBC Television, London, 1963–67. Since 1967 freelance writer, producer, and director: director, Gate Theatre, Dublin, 1977–80. Recipient: Italia prize, for television production, 1967; Tony award, 1969. Agent: Lemon, Unna, and Durbridge, 24 Pottery Lane, Holland Park, London W11 4LZ, England.

PUBLICATIONS

Plays

Hadrian VII, based on *Hadrian the Seventh* and other works by Frederick Rolfe, "Baron Corvo" (produced Birmingham, 1967; London, 1968; New York, 1969). Published as *The Play of Hadrian VII*, London, Deutsch, 1968; New York, Knopf, 1969.
Bloomsbury (produced London, 1974). New York and London, French, 1976.
Rings for a Spanish Lady, adaptation of a play by Antonio Gala (also director: produced Dublin, 1977).
Proxopera, adaptation of the novel by Benedict Kiely (produced Dublin, 1978).
Married Love: The Apotheosis of Marie Stopes (produced Leatherhead, Surrey, 1985; London, 1988).
Yerma, adaptation of the play by Federico García Lorca (produced London, 1987). Published in *Lorca, Plays: One*, edited by Gwynne Edwards, London, Methuen, 1987.

Radio Plays: *Nymphs and Satyrs Come Away*, 1985; *The Last of Baron Corvo*, 1989; *The Other Side of the Hill* (includes *The Road to Waterloo* and *It's a Long Way to Talavera*), 1991.

Television: *Small Fish Are Sweet*, 1959; *Pig's Ear with Flowers*, 1960; *Roll On, Bloomin' Death*, 1961; *A Man on Her Back*, from a story by William Sansom, 1966; *The Devil a Monk Wou'd Be*, from a story by Daudet, 1967; *Anach Cuan: The Music of Sean O Riada*, 1967; *Black Sound—Deep Song: The Andalusian Poetry of Federico García Lorca*, 1968; *Honour, Profit, and Pleasure*, with Anna Ambrose, 1985.

Novel

The Other Side of the Hill. London, Gollancz, 1984.

Short Stories

Telling Tales: The Short Stories of Peter Luke. The Curragh, County Kildare, Goldsmith Press, 1981.

Other

Sisyphus and Reilly: An Autobiography. London, Deutsch, 1972.
Paquito and the Wolf (for children). The Curragh, County Kildare, Goldsmith Press, 1981.
The Mad Pomegranate and the Praying Mantis: An Andalusian Adventure, London, Mantis Press, 1984.

Editor, *Enter Certain Players: Edwards-MacLiammóir and the Gate 1928–1978*. Dublin, Dolmen Press, 1978.

*

Critical Studies: by Ronald Bryden in *Observer* (London), 21 April 1968; by Harold Hobson in *Sunday Times* (London), 21 April 1968; "Peter Luke Used to Be a Television Producer. Then He Escaped" by Luke, in *Listener* (London), 12 September 1968; by Clive Barnes in *New York Times*, 9 January 1969; "*Hadrian VII* Is Alive and a Hit" by John Chapman, in *San Francisco Examiner*, 5 October 1969.

Theatrical Activities:
Director: **Plays**—*Hadrian VII*, Dublin, 1970; *Rings for a Spanish Lady*, Dublin, 1977. **Television**—*Hamlet at Elsinore*, 1963; *A Passage to India*, 1966; *Silent Song*, 1967; *Anach Cuan: The Music of Sean O Riada*, 1967; *Black Sound—Deep Song: The Andalusian Poetry of Federico García Lorca*, 1968.

Peter Luke comments:
(1977) To write an introduction to my work as a playwright is difficult because to date there is relatively little of it. I did not write my first play until I was nearly forty. The oeuvre, such as it is to date, consists of four original plays for television and one dramatization of a novel by William Sansom for the same medium. In addition there are two films d'auteur commissioned by the BBC. They are respectively, and perhaps significantly, about a musician and a poet. Then there is the stage play, *Hadrian VII*, which was first written in 1961 but was not produced until 1967. *Bloomsbury*, produced by Richard Cottrell in 1974, ran for only five weeks due to the American recession as it affected Throgmorton Street and the tourist trade and a petulant notice from Harold Hobson (anagram: Dora Snobhol). (1988: Since then *Married Love* has had an airing, but has not yet reached the West End.)

I would like to be able to give some indication of the direction in which I think I am going, but this is difficult. Certainly I am more than ever interested in poetry, which is not to say that I am immediately contemplating a play in verse. But if I can see a development in my work, it is towards the articulate. Language is my preoccupation and I feel that the theatre, now as in the past, and quite irrespective of present day vogues and trends, should be the place to use it in.

The choice of medium was made for me. My father, Harry Luke, was a writer but early on I decided that I wanted to paint and I had already spent two years studying when the war broke out in 1939. Nineteen—nearly twenty—years later, in 1959, my first television play, *Small Fish Are Sweet*, starring Donald Pleasence and Katherine Blake, was produced. Several others followed hard upon. What happened in between is told in an essay in autobiography, *Sisyphus and Reilly*.

I did not intend to become a playwright. It happened by accident. I do not even now consider myself to be solely a writer of plays, though I suppose few writers can have been so fortunate as to have had an international success on the scale of *Hadrian VII*. Indeed, how many playwrights have had a major success which began as a flop? Thanks to Hadrian, however, I am now free to write what I want to and my intention for the foreseeable future is to alternate plays with books. This I find very therapeutic and my one concern now is that the results will justify the therapy, and that the therapy will give me a long life in which to write a great deal more.

* * *

Peter Luke was almost 40 when, in 1958, he became a story editor for ABC Television, and began writing television plays. In 1963, he joined the BBC, with whom he stayed until 1967. Since then he has worked as a freelance writer, producer, director, and translator, as well as writing a historical novel, short stories, and two autobiographical reminiscences.

In 1967 Luke adapted Frederick Rolfe's novel, *Hadrian the Seventh*, for the stage. In an otherwise faithful rendering, he made one major change. In the novel, the protagonist is a young man called George Arthur Rose. Luke has described his play as "a biography of Rolfe himself in terms of his 'Hadrian' fantasy."

Hadrian VII begins with Rolfe being visited by two bailiffs. They present him with a writ, resulting from a series of petty debts, which he refuses to sign. Left alone to his "imagining," he fantasizes that the two bailiffs are a Bishop and a Cardinal come to persuade him to accept ordination. They invite him to Rome, where he learns that he has been elected Pope. He calls himself Hadrian VII, and immediately announces his intention of dissolving the "temporal" Church and selling the Vatican's treasure and real estate. The cardinals are outraged. Meanwhile, Jeremiah Sant, who knew Rolfe before his election, tries to wheedle money out of him. Hadrian refuses to give him any, but offers to help save his soul instead. Sant thereupon draws a revolver and shoots Hadrian, who dies requesting that Sant be forgiven his crime. The final scene shows the bailiffs confiscating Rolfe's belongings, among them the manuscript of his masterpiece. The play's enormous success in the late 1960's can be attributed to two factors. The contrast between the "real" Rolfe in his seedy garret and Rolfe as he imagines himself is dramatically very effective; and the theme—individuality vs. authority—is perennial.

Luke's next play, *Bloomsbury*, portrays the group of friends which surrounded Lytton Strachey, as seen through the eyes of Virginia Woolf. Towards the end of the play, she says: "Yes, I have created an art form out of them all. . . . I have orchestrated their movements like the waves." Although the concept is clever, the various relationships and attitudes explored lack the dramatic interest of his previous work.

Proxopera—a coinage for "operation proxy"—is adapted from a novel by Benedict Kiely, who described his story as "a condemnation of the interference by violent men in the lives of the innocent." A group of IRA gunmen are holding a family at gunpoint. They threaten to kill the women and child if Binchey, a retired schoolmaster, does not drive a bomb into town for them. He agrees, and sets off to do so, but when he sees his town in the early morning light, he can't bring himself to aid in the murder of any of its citizens. He tells two soldiers what he is carrying. They rescue his family, but Binchey dies of a heart attack after safely exploding the bomb.

Married Love: The Apotheosis of Marie Stopes opens light-heartedly, contrasting Stopes's academic brilliance and her emotional immaturity. After chasing a Japanese professor to no avail, she marries a man who is impotent. As a result, she comes to think that contraception could be used to produce a better species. George Bernard Shaw persuades her that it would be better employed to help women to avoid unwanted pregnancies. Her subsequent achievement in promoting contraception is set against her sense of personal emptiness. Early in the play, she tells Shaw: "I only know that I haven't got something that I feel I ought to have." She never acquires it. She never settles; is never satisfied. The play maintains a fine balance between comedy and domestic tragedy. It is certainly Luke's best work since *Hadrian VII*.

Ez, commissioned by the Hampstead Theatre Company (and not yet produced), is about the non-trial for treason of Ezra Pound. The first act is set in a cage in a Pisan prison; the second, in St. Elizabeths hospital in Washington where Pound spent more than a decade. Some of Pound's best work belongs to this period, but Luke is more concerned with the contradictions inherent in his character: an egotist, he would share his scraps of food with a cat; a racist, he made friends easily with blacks. He emerges as a victim of a genius inseparable from irresponsibility. But when he is eventually released, he is no longer so sure that what he believed in was right. His confession that he was at fault brings the play to a close. It is a plea for tolerance.

Luke has also written many successful television plays and documentaries, from *Small Fish Are Sweet* in 1959, to *Honour, Profit, and Pleasure*, about Handel, co-written with Anna Ambrose, in 1985. And he has made two excellent translations from the Spanish. *Rings for a Spanish Lady*, from a prize-winning play by Antonio Gala, is the story of how El Cid's widow, who represents Spain, is compelled by the king to forego her love for Don Minaya and accept her widowhood. Luke describes his translation of Lorca's *Yerma* as "the first unbowdlerized version."

Although Luke's subjects vary widely, their themes are closely related. In all his plays, the main character's dreams or plans are threatened by a society which has no place for his or her kind of individuality. His work is a call for greater understanding between individuals.

—Terence Dawson

LYNNE, James Broom. British. Born in 1920. See 1st edition, 1973.

LYSSIOTIS, Tes. Australian. Educated at Rusden State College, Melbourne, degree in teaching. Married in 1974; two children. Secondary school teacher, from 1975–81, and 1983; drama consultant for the Knox Region, 1980; playwright-in-residence, La Mama, 1984, and LaTrobe University, 1991, both Melbourne. Address: 33 Lorraine Drive, East Melbourne, Victoria 3151, Australia.

PUBLICATIONS

Plays

I'll Go to Australia and Wear a Hat (produced Melbourne, 1982).
Come to Australia They Said (produced Melbourne, 1982).
Hotel Bonegilla (produced Melbourne, 1983).
On the Line (produced Melbourne, 1984).
The Journey (produced Melbourne, 1985).
Café Misto (produced Melbourne, 1986).
A White Sports Coat (produced Melbourne, 1988).
The Forty Lounge Café (produced Melbourne, 1990). Sydney, Currency, 1990.
The Past Is Here (produced Melbourne, 1991).
Zac's Place (for children; produced Melbourne, 1991).

Radio Play: *A Small Piece of Earth*, 1990.

* * *

Biculturalism is at the heart of the multilingual plays of Greek-Australian writer-director Tes Lyssiotis: "I grew up aware that I wasn't just Greek and I wasn't just Australian—I'm both." The daughter of a proxy bride who came to Australia in 1949 from the island of Cythera, she draws on her own background in exploring the historical experiences of southern European migrant women. *I'll Go to Australia and Wear a Hat* contrasts the bleak and barren reality of low-paid menial work which awaited migrant women in the 1950's with their expectations of Australia as "a paradise, a place where men made money and women got to be ladies with fine jewellery and sophisticated hats." Workshopped with an all-woman cast, this semi-documentary play incorporated extracts from parliamentary debates, editorials, and letters from newspapers of the period expressing prevalent, often openly racist, Anglo-Australian attitudes towards migrants of non-English-speaking background (NESB). It also showed the value of migrant oral history as dramatic material: "It dawned on me that my mother had so many stories to tell. I believe the most ordinary people have the most extraordinary stories to tell if you talk to them."

Come to Australia They Said examined the experiences of Italian migrants in Australia during World War II, and their internment as enemy aliens, as well as the widening generation gap within Italo-Australian families. Lyssiotis drew on the experiences of the Italian actors in her cast, and although she does not speak Italian herself, she stresses the importance of workshopping material with NESB actors in their native languages. *Hotel Bonegilla* was developed with actors of Greek, Italian, and German backgrounds, and dealt with the infamous eponymous migrant camp formed from temporary army huts in 1947. As many as 10,000 migrants of 32 different nationalities lived at Bonegilla until more permanent housing and employment could be found for them elsewhere. The play opens with a slow-motion imagistic sequence inspired by Theodoros Angelopoulos's film *The Travelling Players*—a strong influence on Lyssiotis's work—in which a group of migrants carrying suitcases enter through the audience and form a tableau. The alienation of the different language groups becomes a vehicle for comedy: Italian, Greek, and German families forced to share cramped adjacent cubicles attempt with disastrous results to discuss the misfortunes of communal living, while a Greek girl looking for the place where her brother sleeps is misunderstood as wanting to sleep with her brother, and a camp official asks if anyone can speak "European" to interpret for her. *Hotel Bonegilla* also re-enacts the riots which occurred in the camp when poor food, lack of work and money, the remote and alienating environment, and racist attitudes became too much to bear, and tanks were sent in to quell the violence.

In 1984 Lyssiotis formed the Filiki Players with actors Nikos Zarkadas and Lu Beranek, and as writer-in-residence at La Mama Theatre in Melbourne she was commissioned to write *On the Line* about migrant factory workers. She had spent a year working with a group of women suffering from repetitive strain injuries from working on production lines, and built their experiences at home and at work into the play. The following year she devised *The Journey*, a "collage of events" selected from her four previous plays, which transferred to the larger Universal Theatre in Melbourne and later toured other states of Australia, bringing national attention to her work for the first time, although critical response to the play's inevitable discontinuities was not always positive. It was not until the German periodical *Theater Heute* described the play as "a synthesis, by minimal means, of history and individual fates, of stage play and reality, as it is seldom seen in Germany" that the importance of her work began to be fully recognised. Playbox Theatre in Melbourne commissioned her to write *The Forty Lounge Café*, her only published play to date. Using songs and sections of dialogue in Greek, it draws on Lyssiotis's mother's sometimes comic experiences working in her brother-in-law's family fish and chip shop in rural Australia as a basis for flashbacks to the protagonist Elefteria's childhood and adolescence in Greece. As she states to her sister when she returns to Greece for her mother's funeral in the play's final scene, Elefteria's whole life has been a sacrifice:

> "I was working in the orphanage, so Irini could have some kind of dowry. I worked so my younger sister could marry . . . She sent me away, I didn't ask to be married to a stranger. Did anyone ever ask me what I wanted? Why did she send me away? I curse the day I set foot on that plane. For years I was a servant to this family."

Elefteria's forced subjugation to the welfare of others makes her determined to provide an upbringing for her daughter Toula which makes the most of her cultural heritage. She counters Toula's dismissal of Greece as "just a bunch of old rocks" and her adoption of Anglo-Australian attitudes by insisting on passing on to her Greek skills and traditions. In a play dominated by mourning, sadness, and deprivation the briskness of the café scenes provide welcome moments of levity. In the monologue *A White Sports Coat* a pregnant playwright reminisces about her mother, her Greek family home, and her Australian childhood while desperately trying to finish her play before she gives birth to her child. *Zac's Place* focuses on the dilemmas of a young Greek-Australian torn between the romanticised notions of Greece, of his father, who wants to close down the family milk bar and go back to their homeland, and the peer pressure of his Australian friends. Lyssiotis presents Greek-Australian migrant experience "from the inside out," but avoids the "ghetto" of much non-Anglophonic Australian community theatre, and rejects the tokenism of multiculturalism: "I don't want to be labelled as 'multicultural'. I want to be regarded as an artist, and the fact that I am working on things to do with migrants is irrelevant. It could just as well be elephants or disabled people."

—Tony Mitchell

M

MacDONALD, Sharman. British. Born in Glasgow, Scotland in 1951. Educated at Edinburgh University. Married to Will Knightley; two children. Thames Television writer-in-residence, The Bush Theatre, London, 1984–85. Recipient: *Evening Standard* award, 1984. Agent: Patricia MacNaughton, MacNaughton Lowe Representation, 200 Fulham Road, London SW10 9PN, England.

PUBLICATIONS

Plays

When I Was a Girl, I Used to Scream and Shout. . . (produced London, 1984; Costa Mesa, California, 1989). London, Faber, 1985.
The Brave (produced London, 1988). Included in *When I Was a Girl, I Used to Scream and Shout. . ., When We Were Women*, 1990.
When We Were Women (produced London, 1988). Included in *The Brave, When I Was a Girl, I Used to Scream and Shout. . .*, 1990.
When I Was a Girl, I Used to Scream and Shout. . ., The Brave, When We Were Women: Three Plays. London, Faber, 1990.
All Things Nice (produced London, 1991). London, Faber, 1991.
Shades (produced London, 1992).
Winter Guest (produced London, 1993).

Television Play: *Wild Flowers*, 1990.

Novels

The Beast. London, Collins, 1986.
Night, Night. London, Collins, 1988.

*   *   *

Familial bonds, the confusions of adolescence, a Celtic heritage—all are powerfully recurrent themes in Sharman MacDonald's work, which deals with mother/child relationships with an emotional charge and engaging comedy that mark her as a distinctive voice in the British theatre. Celtic writers seem especially strong on this territory—many of the scenes between MacDonald's adolescent girls Fiona and Vari in *When I Was A Girl, I Used To Scream and Shout. . .* recall the Edna O'Brien of *A Pagan Place*. But MacDonald's landscape of small Scottish towns where the climate seems to be predominantly grey and rainy is very much her own.

She made an electrifying debut with *When I Was A Girl, I Used To Scream and Shout. . .*, which transferred from the tiny Bush Theatre to enjoy a long West End run with Julie Walters initially starring. MacDonald was an actress for some years before becoming a full-time writer, and this play—like the work of many actor-dramatists—had refreshingly lively dialogue which at once stamped her as an original. The play may have relatively little plot, but as it swings across time (it moves between 1983, when it was written, 1955, and 1960), a complex web of family tensions and bonds is built up.

It opens on a rocky beach on the east coast of Scotland in 1983, with the 32-year-old Fiona, unmarried and childless, revisiting a childhood haunt with her mother Morag, one of MacDonald's outstanding creations—a garrulous, warm, but often sharp-tongued woman, much given to commenting on the lack of a grandchild ("A woman's body is a clock that runs down very rapidly," she is prone to remark). Later in the play it transpires that Fiona was pregnant at 15—the scenes in flashback involving the 17-year-old Ewan who fathers the child are superbly written—a deliberate move on Fiona's part, in the complicated emotional relationship between Fiona and Morag, to prevent her mother going abroad with a new man, ending in an abortion with Morag remaining at home. All the 1983 scenes between Morag and Fiona beautifully convey the loving but acerbic relationship between them, and equally assured are the time-shifts to 1955, with Fiona and her friend Vari giggling through their first sexual fumblings and comparing notes on boys, and to 1960 with Fiona's decision, made with the devastating candour of adolescence, to use Ewan to father her child. Tough and tender as well as funny, it was a remarkable first play.

There was a cooler reaction to MacDonald's subsequent work; it is not an uncommon pattern for British critics to moderate their enthusiasm for dramatists to whose early work they awarded high praise. But it must be admitted that *The Brave* and *When We Were Women*, both produced in 1988, were somewhat disappointing. *The Brave* was an admirable effort to break away from a Scottish setting; set in Morocco, it had a startling opening sequence by an hotel poolside with Ferlie, a Scottish woman in her mid-thirties, lumbered with what transpires to be the dead body of a Moroccan whom she has killed in self-defence. She and her sister Susan, a political terrorist who has jumped bail and fled to Morocco where Ferlie has been visiting her, spend most of the play trying to get rid of the body, finally burying it in the desert on the site of the crumbling movie-set for *Samson and Delilah*, with the help of two engineers working in Morocco and taking a brief vacation at the hotel. This pair—the spaced-out Robert, endlessly strumming his guitar, and his friend Jamie, a Scottish exile with false teeth and an abrasive wit—provide much of the vitality in a play which only fitfully sparks into life. There are some splendid scenes, specially Susan's efforts to steal a spade from the poolside with which to bury the body while her sister distracts the barman, and Jamie gives the play energy whenever he is on stage, his raw Scottish vigour reminding both the sisters and the audience that geography cannot fundamentally alter cultural heritage, but too often the play remains obstinately arid.

When We Were Women, which came out of work at the National Theatre Studio, may bear some of the hallmarks of laboratory conditions, but it was a significant technical experiment for MacDonald too. Again, the background is Scotland

—this time during World War II—and centres round another of MacDonald's young heroines. Isla lives with her mother, the indomitable Maggie, and her common-law husband Alec. Written in a series of short scenes, alternating between Isla's life at home and her encounters with a serviceman, Mackenzie, the play subtly evokes the sense of time suspended during war. Isla becomes pregnant by Mackenzie, who marries her only for the marriage to be revealed as bigamous. At the close the family is left turned in on itself.

All Things Nice also covered familiar MacDonald terrain while she continued to experiment technically. The play inhabits two worlds. Scotland again provides one, with another adolescent heroine in 15-year-old Moira, staying with her Gran and her "paying guest," the Captain, and becoming aware of life in the company of her best friend Linda. Parallel with these scenes, earthy and funny, we also focus on the isolated figure of Rose, Moira's mother, absent with Moira's father who is working for a Middle-Eastern oil company. Rose's increasingly revealing letters disclose a woman trapped in an unhappy marriage and beginning to seek refuge in drink and affairs. MacDonald traces the tension between the two worlds with delicate precision, and the scenes between Moira and Linda have all the insight into the closed world of adolescence that distinguished *When I was a Girl. . .*, whilst the figure of the bedridden Captain, cajoling and frightening, reveals again her ability to create rich male roles as well as female ones.

MacDonald returned to the embrace of the commercial theatre with *Shades*, with Pauline Collins starring in what is perhaps the richest role MacDonald has yet written. Once again, a mother/child relationship is at the heart of the play, which begins with a widowed mother in her forties dressing to go out to a dance with a new man friend and which, for virtually the entire first act, consists of a dialogue between the woman, Pearl, and her 10-year-old son. This act delicately probes the unusual relationship—flirtatious as well as possessive—between a single parent and a sensitive child, while the second act contains a beautifully-handled scene with Pearl's new man backing off from further commitment once he realises how strong her love remains for her husband, who died young. The play is fundamentally a chamber piece and suffered to a degree from the commercial pressures of playing in a large West End theatre. The experience of the production seems to have been tricky for MacDonald, who announced shortly before the play's opening that she would not be writing for the theatre again. It is to be hoped she will change her mind.

—Alan Strachan

MacDOUGALL, Roger. British. Born in 1910.
See 3rd edition, 1982.

MACHADO, Eduardo. American. Born in Havana, Cuba in 1953. Moved to the United States in 1956. Lives in New York. Agent: William Craver, The Writers and Artists Agency, 19 West 44th Street, Suite 1000, New York, New York 10036, U.S.A.

PUBLICATIONS

Plays

Rosario and the Gypsies, music by Rick Vartorella (produced New York, 1982).
The Modern Ladies of Guanabacoa (produced New York, 1983). Included in *The Floating Island Plays*, 1991.
Broken Eggs (produced New York, 1984). Published in *On New Ground* (an anthology of Hispanic plays), edited by Betty Osborne, New York, Theatre Communications Group, 1986.
Fabiola (produced New York, 1985). Included in *The Floating Island Plays*, 1991.
When It's Over, with Geraldine Sher (produced New Haven, Connecticut, 1986).
Wishing You Well (produced New York, 1987).
Why to Refuse (produced New York, 1987).
A Burning Beach (produced New York, 1988).
Don Juan in New York City (produced New York, 1988).
Garded (opera libretto) (produced Philadelphia, 1988).
Once Removed (produced New Haven, Connecticut, 1992). Published in *Plays in Process* (New York) vol. 9, no. 3, 1988.
The Day You'll Love Me, adaptation of the play by José Ignacio Cabrujas (produced Los Angeles, 1989; London, 1990).
Cabaret Bambu (produced New York, 1989).
Related Retreats (also director: produced New York, 1990).
Pericones (produced New York, 1990).
Stevie Wants to Play the Blues, music by Fredric Myrow, lyrics by Machado and Myrow (produced Los Angeles, 1990).
In the Eye of the Hurricane (produced Louisville, 1991). Included in *The Floating Island Plays*, 1991.
The Floating Island Plays (includes *The Modern Ladies of Guanabacoa*, *Fabiola*, *Broken Eggs*, *In the Eye of the Hurricane*). New York, Theatre Communications Group, 1991.

Television Plays: *Death Squad*, 1989: *China Rios, HBO*, 1989; *In the Heat of Saturday Night*, 1990.

*

Theatrical Activities:
Actor: **Play**—role in *A Visit* by Maria Irene Fornés, New York, 1981.

* * *

With his teacher and mentor Irene Fornés, Eduardo Machado stands at the forefront of Hispanic-American drama, which is an increasingly important component of theatre in the United States. His plays, unlike those of Fornés, are not innovative in form. The best of them—Machado is prolific, and his work uneven—bring Chekhov to mind: in the tempestuous and yet ordinary life of a household may be seen the end of an era, the remaking of a society. The highly individual characters are viewed with a critical yet compassionate eye. The plays are tragicomic, filled with absurdity, pettiness, energy, and grief.

Sent from his homeland as a child, the Havana-born

Machado knows at first hand the loss of privilege, the experience of exile. In all his major work this dramatist seeks the meaning of his people's history. *A Burning Beach* symbolically represents Cuban society in the late 19th century, at the time of the short-lived uprising led by the poet José Martí; this decadent world of Yankee imperialists, landowners of Spanish descent, and Afro-Cuban servants is clearly doomed. The Bay of Pigs débâcle is the background event in *Once Removed*, which chronicles the misadventures of an emigrant family in Florida and then in Texas; Machado's most satiric play, it is also full of affectionate admiration for the bumbling perseverance of its displaced persons. But the richest of Machado's works is the quartet published as *The Floating Island Plays*. Autobiographically based, they make up an epic 20th-century drama, encompassing the stories of several Cuban families linked by marriage and then by exile in the United States. This is poetic history, in which details of characters' lives shift to meet the needs of an individual play, and it is high comedy, laying bare personal and societal shortcomings at every turn.

Each of the *Floating Island* plays shows an extended family struggling with fundamental change. Set in the Cuba of 1928–31, *The Modern Ladies of Guanabacoa* depicts the domestic rituals of a society that is conservative, Catholic, and patriarchal. As the title suggests, these values are under siege, and in the end the head of the household, a proud Basque who excels at womanizing rather than moneymaking, is shot dead, possibly by an enraged husband, possibly by a government displeased by the expansion of the family's bus routes, possibly at the instigation of his son-in-law, a taxi driver who is using the family money and his own ability to make their fortune. Remarkably fair to all his characters, the playwright nonetheless exhibits throughout his work a special sympathy for those out of power: women, homosexual men, all those from a lower class and with darker skin. Not that such Machado creations are weak people. Women, here and in other plays, are the survivors; they frequently get what they want. In these home-centered plays they are often dominant figures.

Fabiola covers the period 1955–67, and introduces *Floating Island*'s central catalytic (though offstage) event—the rise of Fidel Castro. Portraying a wealthy family related by marriage to that of the previous play, this work is the quartet's least comic and most daring. Its terrain is Gothic, at its heart the desperate love of one brother for another. The less committed partner in this incestuous relationship must flee the country; his needier brother finally slits his wrists as yet more family members leave for the United States. Years of luxury end in anguish and guilt.

In the Eye of the Hurricane dramatizes the nationalization of the bus company established in the first play. It is 1960, and the taxi driver, in his climb to wealth, has apparently forgotten where he came from. He and his wife, attempting to keep their buses through public protest, are shocked when their efforts are made ludicrous by a lack of support: the populace cheers the takeover. Family members who lent romantic support to Castro's revolution come to see what it really means.

The resolution—if that is the right word—of this epic story takes place in 1979 at a country club in suburban Los Angeles, where three generations of displaced Cubans gather for a wedding. *Broken Eggs* is the blackest of comedies. Though these Cuban-Americans are once again reasonably well off, their tight family structure has come apart. The bride's parents have divorced and her father is remarried to an Argentinian. Nearly everyone is drug-dependent: the older generation downs valium and alcohol, the younger

snorts cocaine. Though family lives throughout the *Floating Island Plays* are filled with squabbles, tensions, and power struggles, nastiness has reached a new level. Yet for all this we see that both the family and Cuba are inescapable. More than one character in more than one play quotes Christopher Columbus: "This is the most beautiful land that human eyes have seen." The loss of Eden is the quintessential American theme. Machado knows that you can't go home again.

—M. Elizabeth Osborn

———————

MacLEISH, Archibald. American. 1892–1982. See 3rd edition, 1982.

———————

MAC LOW, Jackson. American. Born in Chicago, Illinois, 12 September 1922. Educated at the University of Chicago, 1939–43, A.A. 1941; Brooklyn College, New York, 1955–58, A.B. (cum laude) in Greek 1958. Formerly married to the painter Iris Lezak; two children. Freelance music teacher, English teacher, translator, and editor, 1950–66; reference book editor, Funk and Wagnalls, 1957–58, 1961–62, and Unicorn Books, 1958–59; copy editor, Alfred A. Knopf, 1965–66, all in New York. Member of the editorial staff, and poetry editor, 1950–54, *Now, Why?* (later *Resistance*), a pacifist-anarchist magazine; instructor, American Language Institute, New York University, 1966–73; poetry editor, *WIN* magazine, New York, 1966–75. Recipient: Creative Artists Public Service grant, 1973, 1976; PEN grant, 1974; National Endowment for the Arts fellowship, 1979. Address: 42 North Moore Street, New York, New York 10013, U.S.A.

PUBLICATIONS

Plays

The Marrying Maiden: A Play of Changes, music by John Cage (produced New York, 1960).
Verdurous Sanguinaria (produced New York, 1961).   Baton Rouge, Louisiana, Southern University, 1967.
Thanks: A Simultaneity for People (produced Wiesbaden, 1962).
Letters for Iris, Numbers for Silence (produced Wiesbaden, 1962).
A Piece for Sari Dienes (produced Wiesbaden, 1962).
Thanks II (produced Paris, 1962).
The Twin Plays: Port-au-Prince, and Adams County, Illinois (produced New York, 1963).   New York, Mac Low and Bloedow, 1963.
Questions and Answers. . . . : A Topical Play (produced New York, 1963). New York, Mac Low and Bloedow, 1963.
Asymmetries No. 408, 410, 485 (produced New York, 1965).
Asymmetries, Gathas and Sounds from Everywhere (produced New York, 1966).
A Vocabulary for Carl Fernbach-Flarsheim (produced New York, 1977).   New York, Mac Low, 1968.

Performance Scores and Broadsides (published New York, Mac Low): *A Vocabulary for Sharon Belle Mattlin* [*Vera Regina Lachman, Peter Innisfree Moore*], 1974–75; *Guru-Guru Gatha*, 1975; *1st Milarepa Gatha*, 1976; *1st Sharon Belle Mattlin Vocabulary Crossword Gatha*, 1976; *Homage to Leona Bleiweiss*, 1976; *The WBAI Vocabulary Gatha*, 1977, revised edition, 1979; *A Vocabulary Gatha for Pete Rose*, 1978; *A Notated Vocabulary for Eve Rosenthal*, 1978; *Musicwords (for Phill Niblock)*, 1978; *A Vocabulary Gatha for Anne Tardos*, 1980; *Dream Meditation*, 1980; *A Vocabulary Gatha for Malcolm Goldstein*, 1981; *1st* [*2nd*] *Happy Birthday, Anne, Vocabulary Gatha*, 1982; *Unstructured Meditative Improvisation for Vocalists and Instrumentalists on the Word "Nucleus,"* 1982; *Pauline Meditation*, 1982; *Milarepa Quartet for Four Like Instruments*, 1982; *The Summer Solstice Vocabulary Gatha*, 1983; *Two Heterophonics from Hereford Bosons 1 and 2*, 1984; *Phonemicon from Hereford Bosons 1*, 1984.

Radio Writing: *Dialog unter Dichtern/Dialog among Poets*, 1982; *Thanks/Danke*, 1983; *Reisen/Traveling*, 1984 (all Germany); *Locks*, 1984.

Composer: incidental music for *The Age of Anxiety* by W.H. Auden, produced New York, 1954; for *The Heroes* by John Ashbery, produced New York, 1955.

Verse

The Pronouns: A Collection of 40 Dances—for the Dancers—6 February-22 March 1964. New York, Mac Low, 1964; London, Tetrad Press, 1970.
August Light Poems. New York, Caterpillar, 1967.
22 Light Poems. Los Angeles, Black Sparrow Press, 1968.
23rd Light Poem: For Larry Eigner. London, Tetrad Press, 1969.
Stanzas for Iris Lezak. Barton, Vermont, Something Else Press, 1972.
4 Trains, 4–5 December 1964. Providence, Rhode Island, Burning Deck, 1974.
36th Light Poem: In Memoriam Buster Keaton. London, Permanent Press, 1975.
21 Matched Asymmetries. London, Aloes, 1978.
54th Light Poem: For Ian Tyson. Milwaukee, Membrane Press, 1978.
A Dozen Douzains for Eve Rosenthal. Toronto, Gronk, 1978.
Phone. New York, Printed Editions, 1978.
Asymmetries 1–260: The First Section of a Series of 501 Performance Poems. New York, Printed Editions, 1980.
Antic Quatrains. Minneapolis, Bookslinger, 1980.
From Pearl Harbor Day to FDR's Birthday. College Park, Maryland, Sun and Moon, 1982.
"Is That Wool Hat My Hat?" Milwaukee, Membrane Press, 1983.
Bloomsday. Barrytown, New York, Station Hill Press, 1984.
French Sonnets, Composed Between January 1955 and April 1983. Tucson, Black Mesa Press, 1984.
The Virginia Woolf Poems. Providence, Rhode Island, Burning Deck, 1985.
Representative Works 1938–1985. New York, Roof, 1986.

Recordings: *A Reading of Primitive and Archaic Poems*, with others, Broadside; *From a Shaman's Notebook*, with others, Broadside.

*

Critical Studies: "Jackson Mac Low Issue" of *Vort 8* (Silver Spring, Maryland), 1975, and *Paper Air* (Blue Bell, Pennsylvania), vol. 2, no. 3, 1980.

Theatrical Activities:
Actor: **Plays**—in *Tonight We Improvise* by Pirandello, New York, 1959, and other plays.

*   *   *

Jackson Mac Low is recognized as America's leading dramatist of the aleatoric school, which uses chance-structured materials and is best known by its principal musical exponent, John Cage. Mac Low's works for the theatre have been performed in the U.S.A., Canada, Germany, Brazil and England, although few have ever been commercially published in a complete form.

Mac Low's original interest was musical composition, though after 1939 he became increasingly involved in poetry. During the 1940's Mac Low contributed to such anarchist publications as *Now, Why?* (later called *Resistance*) and was poetry editor for *WIN*, for the Workshop In Nonviolence. Most of his poems are, however, designed for live performance and Mac Low has described himself as a "Writer and Composer of Poetry, Music, Simultaneities, and Plays."

The most active phase of his theatre activity begins with Prester John's Company in New York in 1949 (one of the most interesting early off-off-Broadway groups), as co-director and actor in various Paul Goodman plays, and continues in a long association with the Living Theatre beginning in 1952, originally as composer for productions of John Ashbery's *The Heroes*, W.H. Auden's *The Age of Anxiety*, etc., but also as an actor, and eventually as dramatist.

The major phase of his dramatic corpus begins also with his association with the Living Theatre and, at about the same time, with John Cage. There are two sets of "Biblical Poems" and a "Biblical Play," performed in 1955, and a major play called *Lawrence*, based on writings by D.H. Lawrence. These pieces are extremely static and resemble Gagaku oratorios of words. The climax of this group of works is *The Marrying Maiden* performed in repertoire by the Living Theatre in 1960–61 with a sound score by John Cage. This play is totally lyrical and abstract, and it includes actions to be determined by the performers using a randomizing process. The Living Theatre's production was extremely conventional and inappropriate; it failed to bring out the uniqueness of the piece which was, as a result, unpublished except as an acting script and has not been performed since. About the works of this time, Mac Low has written:

> All during the 1940's and 1950's, many poems of mine in all modes express a pacifistic and libertarian political viewpoint strongly related to religious attitudes derived from Taoism, Buddhism, and mystical Judaism (Chassidism and Cabala). . . . These religious and political views, along with the more libertarian schools of psychotherapy [e.g. Paul Goodman], helped make me receptive to the use of chance operations and to the interpenetration of art works and the environment. . . .

Mac Low's performance works are structured as social models in which each participant participates as a co-equal and direction is self-guidance and by working-out, rather than being along doctrinaire, authoritarian, or imposed-visionary lines. The sound of the lines is as important as the sense (the sound often *is* the sense), resulting in a uniquely musical theatre experience.

After *The Marrying Maiden* the plays become more choric

—there is action, usually in unison and repetitive—though the texts remain more musical than semantic. As with *Lawrence*, the pieces take their names from some aspect of their source material. For instance, one major work of this period is *Verdurous Sanguinaria*, which is derived from a botanical text on wild flowers. Another is *The Twin Plays*, mentioned before, two plays with identical action in all respects, but one of which uses combinations of the letters in the name "Port-au-Prince" and the other proverbs collected from "Adams County Illinois" which become the names for their respective plays. Another of these works is *Questions and Answers Incredible Statements the Litany of Lies Action in Freedom Statements and Questions All Round Truth and Freedom in Action; or, Why Is an Atom Bomb Like a Toothbrush? A Topical Play* which takes political texts reflecting Mac Low's views, treats it as a litany, then randomizes the actions.

Simultaneous with Mac Low's theatre work (and not necessarily completely separate from it) Mac Low's poems were developing in parallel blocks. There are early works such as *Peaks and Lamas* (1957, included in the magazine *Abyss*, Spring 1971). There is *Stanzas* for *Iris Lezak*, a massive cycle of over 400 pages, written more or less immediately after *The Marrying Maiden* and in some ways paralleling it. And at the end of *Stanzas*, the work develops into the *Asymmetries*, another large cycle (unpublished in any complete form but, like the Iris Lezak stanzas, often performed). These poems are overwhelmingly ear-oriented. They include long silences, difficult to approximate on a printed page apart from performance. They may be "poetry" but they partake of theatre, especially of the heard elements. Many are "simultaneities," by Mac Low's term, but theatre in fact.

Starting in the late 1950's the theatre of Happenings began to develop, with its emphasis on the simple image. The acme of Happenings was the Fluxus group, which performed in Europe, Japan, and the U.S.A. many works by George Brecht, Ben Vautier, Ay-o, Dick Higgins, Bob Watts, Wolf Vostell, Yoko Ono, Chieko Shiomi, and others. In 1962 and the years immediately following, the Fluxus group published and performed a number of Mac Low pieces. Mac Low's third major body of performance works relates to the Fluxus kind of piece. Many of these pieces, such as *Thanks* or *Questioning*, have sets of directions and intentions as scripts, and these are filled in improvisatorially by the performer. Others, such as the *Gathas* (a series begun in 1961), are purely choric "simultaneities," in which the readers read the sounds in any direction. Still other performance pieces are "buried" in other cycles, such as the *8th Light Poem* which is a scenario, written in a fairly typical Happenings vein. There also exist film scenarios from this period and in this style, the best known of which is *Tree* in which the cameraman is asked to photograph a tree, unmoving and static, through a day.

Mac Low's cycle of odes, highly personal poems in classical form, do not use chance in any direct way and suggest a more direct and semantic phase in his work.

—Dick Higgins

MADDY, Yulisa Amadu. Sierra Leonean. Born in Freetown, 27 December 1936. Educated at schools in Sierra Leone; Rose Bruford College, Sidcup, Kent, diploma 1965;

City of London University, postgraduate diploma in arts administration; research fellow, Leeds University, from 1986. Married Abibatu Kamara in 1986; six children. Worked for Sierra Leone Railways; radio producer, Denmark and Britain, early 1960's; director and dancer, Comedia Hus, Copenhagen, 1966; director and actor, British Council Theatre, Freetown, 1968–69; tutor in drama and African literature, Evelyn Hone College, University of Zambia, Lusaka, 1969–70; artistic director, Keskidee Arts Centre, London, 1971–73; acting director, Sierra Leone Ministry of Tourism and Culture, Freetown, 1974–77; instructor in dance and drama, Morley College, London, 1979–80; fellow in theatre arts, Ibadan University, Nigeria, 1980–81; senior lecturer in performing arts, Ilorin University, Nigeria, 1981–83; visiting professor of performing arts, Special Education Resource Center, Bridgeport, Connecticut, 1983–85; Fulbright senior scholar, University of Maryland, College Park, and Morgan State College, Baltimore, 1985–86. Since 1986 artistic director, Gbakanda Afrikan Tiata, Leeds. Recipient: Sierra Leone National Arts Festival prize, for fiction, 1973; Gulbenkian grant, 1978; Edinburgh Festival award, 1979. Address: 19 Francis Street, Leeds, Yorkshire LS7 4BY, England.

PUBLICATIONS (early works as Pat Amadu Maddy)

Plays

Alla Gbah (produced London, 1967). Included in *Obasai and Other Plays*, 1971.
Obasai and Other Plays. London, Heinemann, 1971.
Gbana-Bendu (produced London, 1973; Baltimore, 1986). Included in *Obasai and Other Plays*, 1971.
Yon-Kon (televised 1982; produced Bridgeport, Connecticut, 1984). Included in *Obasai and Other Plays*, 1971.
Life Everlasting (produced London, 1972). Published in *Short African Plays*, edited by Cosmo Pieterse, London, Heinemann, 1972.
Big Breeze Blow (produced Freetown, 1974). Privately printed, 1984.
Take Tem Draw di Rope (produced Freetown, 1975).
Put for Me (produced Freetown, 1975).
Nah We Yone Dehn See (produced Freetown, 1975).
Big Berrin (in Krio: Big Death) (produced Freetown, 1976; Washington, D.C., 1984). Privately printed, 1984.
A Journey into Christmas (produced Ibadan, 1980).
Drums, Voices and Words (produced London, 1985).

Radio Plays: *If Wishes Were Horses*, 1963 (UK); and plays for Cross River Broadcasting, Sierra Leone Broadcasting, and Zambia Broadcasting.

Television Writing: *Saturday Night Out* series, 1980 (Nigeria); *Yon-Kon*, 1982 (Nigeria); and plays for Sierra Leone Broadcasting.

Novel

No Past, No Present, No Future. London, Heinemann, 1973.

Short Stories

Ny Afrikansk Prose, edited by Ulla Ryum. Copenhagen, Vendelkaer, 1967.

*

Critical Study: *The Development of African Drama* by Michael Etherton, London, Hutchinson, 1982.

Theatrical Activities:
Director: **Plays**—all of his own plays; *The Trials of Brother Jero* by Wole Soyinka, Copenhagen, 1966, Freetown, 1969; *Theatre of Power* by Obi B. Egbuna, Copenhagen, 1967; *The Road* by Wole Soyinka, Freetown, 1968, Lusaka, 1970; *Dalabani* by Mukhtarr Mustapha, London, 1972; *Anansi and Bra Englishman* by Manley Young, London, 1972; *Onitsha Market Play*, London, 1973; *Cherry and Wine* by Jimi Rand, London, 1973; *Sighs of a Slave's Dream* by Lindsey Barrett, London, 1973; *Alla Gbah*, Freetown, 1974; *Gbakfest* (National Theatre Festival), Freetown, 1976; *Pulse* by Alem Mezgebe, London, 1979, Ibadan, 1980; *The Refund*, Ilorin, Nigeria, 1982; *The Chattering and the Song* by Femi Osofisan, Ilorin, Nigeria, 1983; *Gbana-Bendu*, Ilorin, Nigeria, 1983; *12 Days at the Round House*, London, 1986. **Television**—*Saturday Night Out* series, 1980; *Yon-Kon*, 1982.
Actor: **Plays**—Chume in *The Trials of Brother Jero* by Wole Soyinka, Copenhagen, 1966; Student in *Theatre of Power* by Obi B. Egbuna, Copenhagen, 1967; Professor in *The Road* by Wole Soyinka, Freetown, 1968, Lusaka, 1970; Brother Jero in *The Trials of Brother Jero*, Freetown, 1969; *Dalabani* by Mukhtarr Mustapha, London, 1972; *Life Everlasting*, London, 1972; *Onitsha Market Play*, London, 1973; *Sighs of a Slave's Dream* by Lindsey Barrett, London, 1973; *Alla Gbah*, Freetown, 1974; *Big Breeze Blow*, Freetown, 1974; *Take Tem Draw di Rope*, Freetown, 1975; *Put for Me*, Freetown, 1975; *Nah We Yone Dehn See*, Freetown, 1975; Awoko in *Big Berrin*, Freetown, 1976, Washington, D.C., 1984; Dictator in *Pulse* by Alem Mezgebe, London, 1979, Ibadan, 1980; *A Journey into Christmas*, Ibadan, 1980; Bobby in *Big Breeze Blow*, Ibadan, 1981; Student in *The Refund*, Ilorin, Nigeria, 1982; *Drums, Voices and Words*, London, 1985; *12 Days at the Round House*, London, 1986; Shadow in *Gbana-Bendu*, Baltimore, 1986. **Television**—Pagu in *Yon-Kon*, 1982.

Yulisa Amadu Maddy comments:

To make a statement introducing my work as a playwright is not easy for I am still asking questions which have yet to be answered; questions which demand honest, direct, and altruistic answers from publishers, critics, distributors, and a great many institutions and individuals. These people have yet to come to terms with the history, traditions, social, political, and economic background of this playwright; who and what he is; what he represents—this African from the so-called Third World.

I have always held Dylan Thomas in great esteem, not only because he was a great poet but because without him, the world would never have known, experienced, and enjoyed the wealth of knowledge and greatness in Amos Tutuola's Yoruba folktale, *The Palm-Wine Drinkard*. Tutuola's work, written in his own cryptic pidgin English, was looked upon with disdain and rejected as non-literary by his own country-men and other African men of letters ("Euro-Afros"). Things haven't changed much—or have they? I am very happy that I am recognised as an "Afrikan Writer"; but first as a Sierra Leonean. I do not strive to satisfy American or European academics, researchers or Africanists. My direction is Africa —the people; whatever I write identifies with the people I know, from whom I came.

It will never be easy for most critics to be enthusiastic about my plays because they cannot discuss my characters without destroying them. My critics expose their own limitations with regard to their ignorance of the grassroots, the vital human

relationships that I share very closely with those characters in their own world.

I took to creative writing, especially playwriting, because it gives me the freedom to experiment with the senses and emotions, the foibles and frailties of people, but mostly because I enjoy probing the fears, jealousies, greed, and power that influence their lives. Fools I detest; nonetheless, I prefer them to the religious hypocrite, the bigoted politician, the insincere academic poser. My fascination and sympathy have always been with and for the rejects, the down-trodden, and the over-zealous who fail only because they believe and follow blindly. Even the truth must be proved. When I wrote my first play, *If Wishes Were Horses*, while a student at Rose Bruford College, I was mocked, ridiculed, and laughed at. When the play was accepted and broadcast by the BBC African Service it dawned on me that the mockery and laughter were the incentive, inspiration, and encouragement I needed which I never got from my tutors and those elites of my own kind. So I have continued to write.

It is true that my plays speak out on behalf of the masses. My protagonists are drawn mostly from among the under-dogs, the underprivileged. I caution against despair, apathy, and inertia. I urge them to come to terms with the realities of the world they live in, to use their common sense, plan their own strategies, and take individual and collective decisions as men and women in control of their own principles, not those dictated to them. They should be people who respect themselves—who understand their indigenous traditions, love their country, are ready to make sacrifices, even to die for it; are willing to make mistakes and ready to correct those mistakes: all of which leads to individual freedom and self-determination. From this basis they are prepared to face the world as men and women in control of their own destinies.

If posterity judges my work adversely, as some critics have done, the youth will always be there to prove it wrong. I believe in the young and unafraid Africans. For them, I will continue to write as I feel and like and want.

* * *

Mixing absurdist comedy, ritualistic theatre, and Brechtian alienation effects with dialect, African proverbs, satire, political and social allusions, a rich, highly poetic stage language, parodies (especially of Christian missionary songs), and his own songs, Yulisa Amadu Maddy has tried to move beyond elite art to a popular yet political theatre for the African urban population. From European fringe theatre of the 1960's he returned to Africa, where he has increasingly worked in pidgin English and local languages. His published plays are similar to his partly autobiographical novel, *No Past, No Present, No Future*, in being critical of the characters and their actions and in not choosing sides between them. The plays present highly stylized versions of representative African social problems but offer no solutions. Maddy aims to demystify and raise consciousness.

The early one-act play *Yon-Kon* contains many of the ingredients developed at more length in his other works, including the relationship of personal freedom to communal activity. Although the setting is an African prison (details suggest Maddy has Sierra Leone in mind), it is symbolic of the prison of the world in which the convicts are forced to keep up an absurd, endless march "Right, left, left, right." A store clerk who has been sentenced to two weeks imprisonment objects to the march and is hurt by the others who demand that he respect Yon-Kon, their leader, who makes them chant "We must not steal, we must not fight, we must obey the laws." When the new convict continues to assert his rights, he is attacked and after a struggle is accused of killing another prisoner who probably died from a weak heart. When Yon-Kon asks for £200 to have the prison doctor testify that the dead man died of a stroke, the clerk foolishly says he will trust justice. He is unjustly sentenced to a further seven years imprisonment for manslaughter and loses his life savings as a consequence.

Yon-Kon illustrates both the insecurity of a life of routine, and the ways in which law responds to money, prestige, and the views of the community. The new convict believes in bourgeois ideals of truth, justice, and personal rights, but he cannot survive the cruelty and absurdity of the world as represented by the prison, where power and leadership are more important than truth. Bully, leader, cynic, hypocrite, middleman between the prisoners and prison officials, leader of a criminal gang, enforcer of prison discipline, Yon-Kon appears adjusted to the reality of his environment: "I don't feel free outside. I will never feel free or enjoy anything outside prison. Prison was built for people like me. I will always make new friends there. I will have people to command." At the play's end he is once more making the others march "Right, left, left, right," while the convicts chant "We must behave—as good citizens should."

Alla Gbah, possibly influenced by Camus's *L'Étranger*, portrays the last hours of Joko Campbell, a 27-year-old student condemned to death for killing his mistress. Maddy is here particularly concerned with the relationship of love to freedom. Joko ran away from home as his mother made him feel helpless, "like a child." Claiming not to have time for the "ethics of decadent puritan society" he falls in love with a Mrs. Manly, a woman of his mother's age who is notorious for seducing students. He idealizes her, and finds in his love a way of transforming his dull, purposeless existence into a new life; but when he catches her making love to another man Joko kills her in defence of his manhood. Although Joko is a Dostoevskian hero who defines himself by "creating and killing," his notions are tested by a moral realism. Rejecting "money, education, morals, society," Joko wants to find "Love, selfless love. Freedom" and "Above all, happiness" among the underprivileged. But despite his proud defiance, as the play ends he is alone in his cell with one hour to live, frightened, crying "I need you mother." Independence means learning the hard facts of life through trial and error.

Obasai, another short play, is a farcical yet hard-boiled portrait of modern African society. It concerns the decision of a tough village schoolboy to leave his mother, brother, and "good society" to join some swindlers in creating a new life for himself as a fisherman. Women, as in all Maddy's plays, seem seductively threatening, hypocritical, agents of conformity, whom the protagonist must reject. As society is corrupt there is little to choose between the good and the swindlers. The dialogue often takes on the power of Jacobean satire: "Easy, Dad. He's a real punk. Look how he's running to meet the bitch. She wears his trousers and he wears her frock." Maddy's dramas are Jonsonian comedies where crooked characters play upon and bring out the hypocrisy of society, while the attractiveness of the swindlers puts the audience's own values into question.

A common Maddy target is the African ruling class, especially the Europeanized Creole elite of Sierra Leone, which is contrasted to the downtrodden labourers and peasants through whose eyes the dramatist attempts to see reality. The long play *Gbana-Bendu*, with its wry, arch, exaggerated, melodramatic style, is concerned with the robbery of Africa by the governing elite and the improbability of the people in a democracy willingly ridding themselves of their oppressors. The attempt by two drunken tramps to save a virgin from

being sacrificed becomes symbolic of the condition of Africa. The traditional masqueraders are revealed to be thieves who rob the people's houses during ceremonies, and keep the sacrificial maidens for their own sexual use. The rhetoric of tradition and convention sanctifies their misdeeds. When she refuses to be saved from the sacrifice and claims that she must fulfil her duty, the virgin at first appears a symbol for the self-repression of traditional Africa. In a surprising twist, however, we learn that she is in cahoots with the chief masquerader, whom she loves; she uses her supposed loyalty to convention as a means to trick others. Although Maddy demystifies both traditionalist and nationalist rhetoric, the ending of the play becomes confusing, as the tramps are unreliable and might be making up the explanations they offer. In a final irony, as the tramps discuss whether they are becoming corrupted by others, they are themselves trapped by the crowd.

Many of Maddy's later plays in Krio and pidgin have not been published. *Big Berrin*, for which he was imprisoned, concerns corruption in Sierra Leone and the hopeless condition of the urban poor. According to Michael Etherton in *The Development of African Drama* (1982), the central character is a schoolteacher who, not having been paid for months, creates his own church through which he can exploit others. The play shows that the local politicians, businessmen, religious leaders, and other members of the establishment have continued the ways of the colonial powers in robbing the people.

—Bruce King

MALTZ, Albert. American. 1908–1985.
See 3rd edition, 1982.

MAMET, David (Alan). American. Born in Flossmoor, Illinois, 30 November 1947. Educated at Rich Central High School; Francis W. Parker School; Goddard College, Plainfield, Vermont, B.A. in English 1969; Neighborhood Playhouse School, New York, 1968–69. Married 1) Lindsay Crouse in 1977 (divorced), one daughter; 2) Rebecca Pidgeon in 1991. Actor in summer stock, 1969; stage manager, *The Fantasticks*, New York, 1969–70; lecturer in drama, Marlboro College, Vermont, 1970; artist-in-residence, Goddard College, 1971–73; founder and artistic director, St. Nicholas Company, Plainfield, Vermont, 1972, and St. Nicholas Players, Chicago, 1974–76; faculty member, Illinois Arts Council, 1974; visiting lecturer, University of Chicago, 1975–76 and 1979, and New York University, 1981; teaching fellow, Yale University School of Drama, New Haven, Connecticut, 1976–77; associate artistic director, Goodman Theatre, Chicago, 1978–84; associate director, New Theater Company, Chicago, 1985. Since 1988 associate professor of film, Columbia University, New York. Contributing editor, *Oui* magazine, 1975–76. Recipient: Joseph Jefferson award, 1974; Obie award, 1976, 1983; New York State Council on the Arts grant, 1976; Rockefeller grant, 1976; CBS-Yale University fellowship, 1977; New York Drama Critics Circle award, 1977, 1984; Outer Circle award, 1978; Society of West End Theatre award, 1983; Pulitzer prize, 1984; Dramatists Guild Hull-Warriner award, 1984; American Academy award, 1986; Tony award, 1987. Agent: Howard Rosenstone, Rosenstone/Wender, 3 East 48th Street, 4th Floor, New York, New York 10017, U.S.A.

PUBLICATIONS

Plays

Lakeboat (produced Marlboro, Vermont, 1970; revised version produced Milwaukee, 1980). New York, Grove Press, 1981.
Duck Variations (produced Plainfield, Vermont, 1972; New York, 1975; London, 1977). With *Sexual Perversity in Chicago*, New York, Grove Press, 1978; in *American Buffalo, Sexual Perversity in Chicago, Duck Variations*, 1978.
Mackinac (for children; produced Chicago, 1972?).
Marranos (produced Chicago, 1972–73?).
The Poet and the Rent: A Play for Kids from Seven to 8:15 (produced Chicago, 1974). Included in *Three Children's Plays*, 1986.
Squirrels (produced Chicago, 1974). New York, French, 1982.
Sexual Perversity in Chicago (produced Chicago, 1974; New York, 1975; London, 1977). With *Duck Variations*, New York, Grove Press, 1978; in *American Buffalo, Sexual Perversity in Chicago, Duck Variations, 1978*.
American Buffalo (produced Chicago, 1975; New York, 1976; London, 1978). New York, Grove Press, 1977; in *American Buffalo, Sexual Perversity in Chicago, Duck Variations*, 1978.
Reunion (produced Louisville, 1976; New York, 1979; London, 1981). With *Dark Pony*, New York, Grove Press, 1979.
The Woods (also director: produced Chicago, 1977; New York, 1979; London, 1984). New York, Grove Press, 1979.
All Men Are Whores (produced New Haven, Connecticut, 1977; London, 1990). Included in *Short Plays and Monologues*, 1981.
A Life in the Theatre (produced Chicago and New York, 1977; London, 1979). New York, Grove Press, 1978; London, Methuen, 1989.
The Revenge of the Space Pandas; or, Binky Rudich and the Two-Speed Clock (produced Chicago, 1977). Included in *Three Children's Plays*, 1986.
Dark Pony (produced New Haven, Connecticut, 1977; New York, 1979; London, 1981). With *Reunion*, New York, Grove Press, 1979.
The Water Engine: An American Fable (produced Chicago and New York, 1977; London, 1989). With *Mr. Happiness*, New York, Grove Press, 1978.
Prairie du Chien (broadcast 1978; produced New York, 1985; London, 1986). Included in *Short Plays and Monologues*, 1981; with *The Shawl*, London, Methuen, 1989.
American Buffalo, Sexual Perversity in Chicago, Duck Variations: Three Plays. London, Eyre Methuen, 1978.
Mr. Happiness (produced New York, 1978; London, 1984). With *The Water Engine*, New York, Grove Press, 1978.
Lone Canoe; or, The Explorer, music and lyrics by Alaric Jans (produced Chicago, 1979).

The Sanctity of Marriage (produced New York, 1979). With *Reunion* and *Dark Pony*, New York, French, 1982.
Shoeshine (produced New York, 1979). Included in *Short Plays and Monologues*, 1981.
A Sermon (also director: produced New York, 1981; London, 1987). Included in *Short Plays and Monologues*, 1981.
Short Plays and Monologues (includes *All Men Are Whores, The Blue Hour: City Sketches, In Old Vermont, Litko, Prairie du Chien, A Sermon, Shoeshine*). New York, Dramatists Play Service, 1981.
Edmond (produced Chicago and New York, 1982; London, 1985). New York, Grove Press, 1983; London, Methuen, 1986.
The Disappearance of the Jews (produced Chicago, 1983).
Glengarry Glen Ross (produced London, 1983; Chicago and New York, 1984). New York, Grove Press, and London, Methuen, 1984.
Red River, adaptation of a play by Pierre Laville (produced Chicago, 1983).
Five Unrelated Pieces (includes *Two Conversations; Two Scenes; Yes, But So What*) (produced New York, 1983). Included in *Dramatic Sketches and Monologues*, 1985.
The Dog (produced 1983). Included in *Dramatic Sketches and Monologues*, 1985.
Film Crew (produced 1983). Included in *Dramatic Sketches and Monologues*, 1985.
4 A.M. (produced 1983). Included in *Dramatic Sketches and Monologues*, 1985.
Vermont Sketches (includes *Pint's a Pound the World Around, Deer Dogs, Conversations with the Spirit World, Dowsing*) (produced New York, 1984). Included in *Dramatic Sketches and Monologues*, 1985).
The Frog Prince (produced Louisville, 1984; New York, 1985). Included in *Three Children's Plays*, 1986.
The Spanish Prisoner (produced Chicago, 1985).
The Shawl (produced Chicago and New York, 1985; London, 1986). With *Prairie du Chien*, New York, Grove Press, 1985; London, Methuen, 1989.
The Cherry Orchard, adaptation of a play by Chekhov (produced Chicago, 1985). New York, Grove Press, 1987.
Cross Patch (broadcast 1985; produced New York, 1990). Included in *Dramatic Sketches and Monologues*, 1985.
Goldberg Street (broadcast 1985; produced New York, 1990). Included in *Dramatic Sketches and Monologues*, 1985.
Vint, adaptation of a story by Chekhov, in *Orchards* (produced Urbana, Illinois, 1985; New York, 1986). New York, Knopf, 1986.
Dramatic Sketches and Monologues (includes *Five Unrelated Pieces, The Power Outrage, The Dog, Film Crew, 4 A.M., Food, Pint's a Pound the World Around, Deer Dogs, Columbus Avenue, Conversations with the Spirit World, Maple Sugaring, Morris and Joe, Steve McQueen, Yes, Dowsing, In the Mall, Cross Patch, Goldberg Street*). New York, French, 1985.
Goldberg Street: Short Plays and Monologues. New York, Grove Press, 1985.
Three Children's Plays. New York, Grove Press, 1986.
Speed-the-Plow (produced New York, 1987; London, 1988). New York, Grove Press, 1988; London, Methuen, 1989.
House of Games (screenplay). New York, Grove Press, 1987; London, Methuen, 1988.
Things Change, with Shel Silverstein (screenplay). New York, Grove Press, 1988; London, Methuen, 1989.
Where Were You When It Went Down? in *Urban Blight* (musical revue), based on an idea by John Tillinger, music by David Shire, lyrics by Richard Maltby, Jr. (produced New York, 1988).

Bobby Gould in Hell (produced New York, 1989; London, 1991).

Uncle Vanya, adaptation of the play by Chekhov (produced Harrogate, 1990). New York, Grove Press, 1989.

Five Television Plays (includes *A Waitress in Yellowstone, The Museum of Science and Industry Story, A Wasted Weekend, We Will Take You There, Bradford*). New York, Grove Weidenfeld, 1990.

We're No Angels (screenplay). New York, Grove Weidenfeld, 1990.

Three Sisters, adaptation of the play by Chekhov. New York, Grove Weidenfeld, 1991.

Homicide (screenplay). New York, Grove Weidenfeld, 1992.

Oleanna (produced New York, 1992; London, 1993).

Screenplays: *The Postman Always Rings Twice*, 1981; *The Verdict*, 1982; *The Untouchables*, 1987; *House of Games*, 1987; *Things Change*, with Shel Silverstein, 1988; *We're No Angels*, 1990; *Homicide*, 1991; *Glengarry Glen Ross*, 1992.

Radio Plays: *Prairie du Chien*, 1978; *Cross Patch*, 1985; *Goldberg Street*, 1985; *Dintenfass*, 1989.

Verse

The Hero Pony. New York, Grove Weidenfeld, 1990.

Other

Writing in Restaurants (essays). New York, Viking, 1986; London, Faber, 1988.

The Owl (for children), with Lindsay Crouse. New York, Kipling Press, 1987.

Warm and Cold (for children), with Donald Sultan. New York, Grove Weidenfeld, 1988.

Some Freaks (essays). New York, Viking, 1989; London, Faber, 1990.

On Directing (essays). New York, Viking, 1991.

*

Bibliography: *Ten Modern American Playwrights* by Kimball King, New York, Garland, 1982.

Critical Studies: *David Mamet* by C.W.E. Bigsby, London, Methuen, 1985; *David Mamet* by Dennis Carroll, London, Macmillan, and New York, St. Martin's Press, 1987.

Theatrical Activities:
Director: **Plays**—*Beyond the Horizon* by O'Neill, Chicago, 1974; *The Woods*, Chicago, 1977; *Twelfth Night*, New York, 1980; *A Sermon*, New York, 1981. **Films**—*House of Games*, 1987; *Things Change*, 1988; *Homicide*, 1991.

* * *

David Mamet's rise to the forefront of American drama has been seen as the triumph of the minimalist, of the theatre poet indulging in language for its own sake, of the apologist for the big-mouthed home-baked philosopher. His plays have been attacked for their lack of clarity, for their plotlessness, for their obscenity, for their articulation of a poetics of loss without any compensatory dimensions. Critics have said his work is without subtext; others have implied that it consists of nothing but subtext. All of this is true in one sense or other, but the stridency of response is itself an indicator that the

Mamet phenomenon has implicated the audience as a vital constituent of what happens in the play: clarity is a commodity which is as much in the audience's hands as in the characters'.

Most of Mamet's plays seem in some way fragmentary. Though he did not begin screen-writing until the 1980's, with *The Postman Always Rings Twice*, his plays almost from the start looked like something made on the editing table, with sometimes brutal cross-cutting. The 30 brief scenes which make up *Sexual Perversity in Chicago* do have a chronological linearity that is absent from the 14 episodes of *Duck Variations*, but it is left to the audience—placed by the title as voyeur of perversity—to read through the displacement activity that passes as dialogue and write its own construction of the homosocial sexuality behind the talk. Mamet's use of the fragment cogently illustrates the response theorists' view of the audience function as "creatively filling in gaps."

Like the presentation of behaviour, the philosophies that spill out of Mamet's early characters are fractured slogans chipped out of a broader cultural context. These contexts are always so well-known as to have their own mythology. The gangster, the real estate salesman, the Jewish patriarch, the sexual hijacker—each has an ethic that has been articulated and endorsed by decades of film and popular culture. That the characters are losers in the face of the myth does nothing to invalidate the myth, but it does open up the dimension of loss. The failure of the three would-be crooks in *American Buffalo* to achieve any part of their scheme does not undermine the notion of the big burglary as a faith to live by, any more than the males in *Sexual Perversity* will cease to live in hope of the big sexual coup. But the reading of this as loss, meaninglessness, or sterility is ambivalent because the texture of language brings a lyricism that is both bonding and possibly healing, if not regenerative. *American Buffalo* ends with compassion. *The Disappearance of the Jews* may be about the disappearance of something, but that does not mean that nothing is left. Whether they reach for fiction or for rhetoric, the characters seldom stop reaching.

Bonding may be loveless or even adversarial in Mamet. *Glengarry Glen Ross* has its four salesmen wedged within the real estate system, a system that says that two of them must be debased, to become waste products, the condition of so many Mamet characters. But the predatory cycle takes in not only the salesmen themselves, but also clients, who are trapped by the wonderful spirals of sales blather into buying junk land. Again, language is the bond: the first act ends with Roma's virtuoso cadenza on the general theme of the human condition, and the sudden—brilliantly comic—revelation that he is talking to a complete stranger. But the laughter is also reflexive, in that the audience has been absorbed in the barroom philosophy almost as much as the client.

Mamet has not been averse to describing some of his plays as "classical tragedies," apparently because of their tone and themes of rejection and betrayal. But it is also noticeable that in these plays he moves beyond episodic structure to give a precisely defined diachronic placing which observes unities of both place and time. The whole claustrophobic action of *American Buffalo* occurs in a junkshop within a single day, while *The Woods* dramatises the recurrent Mamet question—why don't men and women get on?—by putting the two characters in a cabin in the woods for a single night. Though in both plays the characters are firmly positioned within a social fantasy system, their more sustained action has gratified critics who want to give Mamet characters an individual psychology.

That Mamet's plays look at gender delineations as well as sexuality is clear from the content of the male fantasies that pervade his work. But the gendering of characters through fantasy as well as through social constructions means that female characters in particular can be ambivalent in stature. This is especially clear when, as in *The Shawl* and *Speed-the-Plow*, two male characters confront a woman who intrudes on their relationship. In the latter play, some Hollywood tycoons run up against a temporary secretary who, given a script to read, comes up with a verdict that divides them. The secretary can be played dumb or shrewd, as a product of the male gaze or as a generator of it, like the non-appearing woman in *A Life in the Theatre*.

A similar complexity of female characterisation is in his first filmscript for his own direction, *House of Games*, and in the sequel to *Speed-the-Plow*, *Bobby Gould in Hell*. Structurally, both of these may be seen as modern morality plays, a genre Mamet had experimented with in *Edmond*, a descent into the hell of New York. Here, the American Everyman figure of the title is precipitated through the grotesqueries of the city's lower depths and brought to the brink of his own judgement, sketched with an extravagance that contrasts sharply with the economy of the earlier plays. But *Edmond* is also important for its reminder that Mamet is primarily a regional playwright, who writes plays not *for* New York but *at* it.

—Howard McNaughton

MANAKA, Matsemela. South African. Born in Alexandra, South Africa in 1956. Artist, musician, poet, and playwright. Since 1976 founder-member, Soyikwa Theatre Group, Soweto. Lives in Diepkloof, Soweto. Address: c/o The Market Theatre, P.O. Box 8656, Johannesburg 2000, South Africa.

PUBLICATIONS

Plays

The Horn (produced Soweto, 1978).
Egoli, City of Gold (produced Soweto, 1979; Erlangen, West Germany, 1980). Johannesburg, Soyinkwa-Ravan, 1979.
Pula (*Rain!*) (produced Soweto, 1982; Edinburgh, 1983; London, 1984). Published in *Market Plays*, edited by Stephen Gray, Johannesburg, Ad. Donker, 1986; Braamfontein, Skotaville, 1990.
Imbumba (*Unity*) (produced Soweto, n.d.; Edinburgh, 1983; London, 1984).
Children of Asazi (produced Soweto, 1985; New York, 1986).
Goree, music by Motsumi Makhene (produced Soweto, 1985; New York, 1989).

Other

Editor, *Echoes of African Art*. Braamfontein, Skotaville, 1987.

*

Critical Studies: *"In Township Tonight!": South Africa's Black City Music and Theatre* by David Coplan, Johannesburg, Soyinkwa-Ravan, 1985; *Black Theater, Dance, and Ritual in South Africa* by Peter Larlham, Ann Arbor, Michigan, UMI Research Press, 1985; *Theatre and Cultural Struggle in South Africa* by Robert Mshengu Kavanagh, London, Verso, 1985; *"Repainting the Damaged Canvas: The Theatre of Matsemela Manaka,"* in *Commonwealth: Essays and Studies* (Dijon), no.14, 1, 1991.

Theatrical Activities:
Director: **Plays**—all his own plays.

* * *

Matsemela Manaka's most anthologized play, *Children of Asazi*, deals with homelessness, toys with incest, and exposes the systematic destruction of the black family unit by the racist South African government. What is remarkable about the work, apart from its plot which makes ingenious use of the structure of indigenous African folk-tales, is that its very advocacy of resistance is rooted in love and attachment to place. Diliza, the hero, is a young politically conscious firebrand who has sworn to defy the government bulldozers coming to mow down Alexandra, the city where he lives with his father in a shack. Against his father's instructions, he attends a meeting aimed at mobilizing the people against enforced evacuation. On his return, he discovers that one of the most vocal men at the meeting, Ntate Majika, is actually a rich, sneaky, two-faced character who has evicted a poorer black neighbour, Ntate Mabu, from his house and sent him into the streets by offering bribes (whisky) to the administration officer responsible for allocating houses. Diliza unmasks Majika and forces him to confess several other acts of sabotage against the inhabitants of Alexandra which include confiscating the money collected by the residents to get a lawyer to defend them against forceful removal. Majika had actually invested the money for the benefit of his own stomach, wife, and children. His argument is that when the period of investment elapses, the money will be used to defend all the residents who would have been arrested while protesting against removals. He claims it is the devil that made him do it. Diliza summons the spirits of the land who assist him in exorcising the thieving devil in Majika. The spirits actually appear on stage in a mock ritual, thereby enhancing the work's visual effect.

Central to the play, however, is Diliza's love affair with Charmaine who, at the beginning of the play, is pregnant with Diliza's child. In a complicated plot which unfolds through conflicting stories told by Nduna, Diliza's father, and his grandmother, Gogo, we learn at first that Charmaine is Diliza's sister, only to be told that Charmaine's mother is another woman who is dead. Before this revelation, Charmaine had suggested to Diliza that they run away and resettle somewhere else or abort the child. The story comes to a happy ending because Diliza insists on finding out who his real mother is. This stubborn quest is a subtle metaphor for the average South African's yearning to be earthed where his umbilical cord is buried, namely, his native land. So, even though the play ends happily for the couple, a greater threat to their future and unborn child looms: a palpable and audible menace in the play, the sound of bulldozers in the distance. This existential anguish is articulated by Gogo:

As we were going up the hill from the bridge, I saw my best Sunday hat, rollerskating down the donga . . . One of my little friends, a girl, noticed the hat and screamed: "There goes your hat!" . . . When she came back with the hat, she found us in tears. My home was no more. I looked at the little children and saw citizens whose citizenship was like an ice cream under the heat of the sun.

This thematic preoccupation is further pointed up when Diliza, out of compassion, takes in the homeless and disguised Gogo, not knowing that she is his grandmother. She is accepted into an already crowded shack.

> Nduna: There you are! It fits like a garage and two rooms in the backyards of Soweto. Look at that! It's a three room house already. Innovation! . . . we grew up sleeping in the kitchen, maGogo. Thirteen of us . . . in a room divided into two rooms by means of a curtain . . . We may not be able to stretch our feet, but one day we will.

Thus, naïve and simple as it may appear on the surface, a careful reading of *Children of Asazi* reveals that beneath the love story and trite plot of mistaken identities lies a terrifyingly mapped geography of dispossession and its devastating impact on three generations of black South Africans who have never had a decent roof over their heads. Manaka's forte in this play is the traditional folk-tale technique into which he weaves songs, proverbs, ironies, idiomatic expressions, reversals, flashbacks, mime, and a measure of contemporaneity through jazz music. These elements reduce the tedium of words and the racy, crisp, one-line dialogue suggests that the play will move swiftly in performance.

Manaka's other well-known play, *Egoli, City of Gold* was devised in a workshop and performed to overwhelmingly high audience turnouts at the Space Theatre in 1979. It has also travelled abroad and was so provocative that the South African government had to ban it. The play chronicles the experiences of two miners, migrant labourers, living in men's compounds and separated from their families. Surrounded by walls day and night, they see their lives as prison sentences. Working in the mines for paltry pay, to them, is one long process of asphyxiation by inhaling gold dust. To make things worse, they realize that the huge profits from exported gold are used by the South African government to consolidate white rule, infrastructure, health, and general welfare while the black population is left to starve in ghettos, slums, and black townships. Manaka uses mime, songs, poetry, and symbolism to paint this canvas of exploitation in which human and economic energies are mined from the land without thought for its rightful owners. Characteristically, the playwright empowers the characters with an insurrectionary consciousness and in one of the scenes they dream and re-enact through mime the process of freeing themselves from their bondage. Their desperation is embedded in the words "Egoli. City of misery. City of hate."

Though both plays demonstrate a successful experimentation with form and message, Manaka leans quite often towards the sentimental and melodramatic instead of the deeper characterization which, in future, could give his plays a greater tragic force.

—Esiaba Irobi

MANKOWITZ, (Cyril) Wolf. British. Born in London, 7 November 1924. Educated at East Ham Grammar School, London; Downing College, Cambridge, M.A. in English 1946. Served as a volunteer coal miner and in the British Army during World War II. Married Ann Margaret

Seligmann in 1944; four sons. Play and film producer: with Oscar Lewenstein, 1955–60; independently, 1960–70; with Laurence Harvey, 1970–72. Owner, Pickwick Club restaurant, London, 1963–70; also antique and art dealer. Moved to Ireland in 1971. Since 1982 adjunct professor of English, and adjunct professor of theatre arts, 1987–88, University of New Mexico, Albuquerque. Honorary consul to the Republic of Panama in Dublin, 1971. Exhibition of Collages, Davis Gallery, Dublin, 1990. Recipient: Society of Authors award, for poetry, 1946; Venice Film Festival prize, 1955; BAFTA award, 1955, 1961; Oscar, for screenplay, 1957; Film Council of America golden reel, 1957; *Evening Standard* award, 1959; Cork Film Festival International Critics prize, 1972; Cannes Film Festival grand prize, 1973. Address: The Bridge House, Ahakista, Durrus, near Bantry, County Cork, Ireland; or, 2322 Calle Halcon, Sante Fe, New Mexico 87505, U.S.A.

PUBLICATIONS

Plays

Make Me an Offer, adaptation of his own novel (televised 1952; revised version, music and lyrics by Monty Norman and David Heneker, produced London, 1959).
The Bespoke Overcoat (produced London, 1953). London, Evans, 1954; New York, French, n.d.
The Baby, adaptation of a work by Chekhov (televised 1954; produced London, 1981). Included in *Five One-Act Plays*, 1955.
The Boychik (produced London, 1954).
It Should Happen to a Dog (televised 1955; produced Princeton, New Jersey, 1967; London, 1977). Included in *Five One-Act Plays*, 1955.
Five One-Act Plays. London, Evans, 1955; New York, French, n.d.
The Mighty Hunter (produced London, 1956). Included in *Five One-Act Plays*, 1955.
The Last of the Cheesecake (produced London, 1956). Included in *Five One-Act Plays*, 1955.
Expresso Bongo, with Julian More, music and lyrics by David Heneker and Monty Norman (produced London, 1958). London, Evans, 1960.
Belle; or, The Ballad of Dr. Crippen, with Beverley Cross, music by Monty Norman (produced London, 1961).
Pickwick, music and lyrics by Cyril Ornadel and Leslie Bricusse, adaptation of the novel by Dickens (produced London, 1963).
Passion Flower Hotel, music and lyrics by Trevor Peacock and John Barry, adaptation of the novel by Rosalind Erskine (produced London, 1965).
The Samson Riddle (produced Dublin, 1972; as *Samson and Delilah*, produced London, 1978). London, Vallentine Mitchell, 1972.
Jack Shepherd, music by Monty Norman (produced Edinburgh, 1972; as *Stand and Deliver*, produced London, 1972).
Dickens of London (televised 1976). London, Weidenfeld and Nicolson, 1976; New York, Macmillan, 1977.
The Hebrew Lesson (screenplay). London, Evans, 1976.
The Irish Hebrew Lesson (produced London, 1978; New York, 1980).
Iron Butterflies (produced Albuquerque, 1985). Two acts published in *Adam International Review* (London), 1984.

Screenplays: *Make Me an Offer*, with W.P. Lipscomb, 1954; *A Kid for Two Farthings*, 1955; *The Bespoke Overcoat*, 1955;

Trapeze, 1955; *Expresso Bongo*, 1959; *The Two Faces of Dr. Jekyll* (*House of Fright*), 1960; *The Millionairess*, with Ricardo Aragno, 1960; *The Long and the Short and the Tall* (*Jungle Fighters*), with Willis Hall, 1961; *The Day the Earth Caught Fire*, with Val Guest, 1961; *Waltz of the Toreadors*, 1962; *Where the Spies Are*, with James Leasor and Val Guest, 1965; *Casino Royale*, with others, 1967; *La Vingt-cinquième Heure* (*The Twenty-fifty Hour*), 1967; *The Assassination Bureau*, with Michael Relph, 1969; *Bloomfield* (*The Hero*), with Richard Harris, 1970; *Black Beauty*, with James Hill, 1971; *The Hebrew Lesson*, 1972; *Treasure Island*, with Orson Welles, 1973; *The Hireling*, 1973; *Almonds and Raisins* (documentary), 1983.

Television Plays: *Make Me an Offer*, 1952; *The Baby*, 1954; *The Girl*, 1955; *It Should Happen to a Dog*, 1955; *The Killing Stones*, 1958; *Love Is Hell*, 1966; *Dickens of London* series, 1976; *Have a Nice Death*, from the story by Antonia Fraser (*Tales of the Unexpected* series), 1984.

Novels

Make Me an Offer. London, Deutsch, 1952; New York, Dutton, 1953.
A Kid for Two Farthings. London, Deutsch, 1953; New York, Dutton, 1954.
Laugh Till You Cry: An Advertisement. New York, Dutton, 1955; included in *The Penguin Wolf Mankowitz*, 1967.
My Old Man's a Dustman. London, Deutsch, 1956; as *Old Soldiers Never Die*, Boston, Little Brown, 1956.
Cockatrice. London, Longman, and New York, Putnam, 1963.
The Biggest Pig in Barbados: A Fable. London, Longman, 1965.
Raspberry Reich. London, Macmillan, 1979.
Abracadabra! London, Macmillan, 1980.
The Devil in Texas. London, Royce, 1984.
Gioconda. London, W.H. Allen, and New York, Freundlich, 1987.
The Magic Cabinet of Professor Smucker. London, W.H. Allen, 1988.
Exquisite Cadaver. London, Deutsch, 1990.
A Night with Casanova. London, Sinclair Stevenson, 1991.

Short Stories

The Mendelman Fire and Other Stories. London, Deutsch, and Boston, Little Brown, 1957.
Expresso Bongo: A Wolf Mankowitz Reader. New York, Yoseloff, 1961.
The Blue Arabian Nights: Tales of a London Decade. London, Vallentine Mitchell, 1973.
The Days of the Women and the Nights of the Men: Fables. London, Robson, 1977.

Verse

XII Poems. London, Workshop Press, 1971.

Other

The Portland Vase and the Wedgwood Copies. London, Deutsch, 1952.
Wedgwood. London, Batsford, and New York, Dutton, 1953; revised edition, London, Barrie and Jenkins, 1980.
Majollika and Company (for children). London, Deutsch, 1955.

ABC of Show Business. London, Oldbourne Press, 1956.
A Concise Encyclopedia of English Pottery and Porcelain, with R.G. Haggar. London, Deutsch, and New York, Hawthorn, 1957.
The Penguin Wolf Mankowitz. London, Penguin, 1967.
The Extraordinary Mr. Poe: A Biography of Edgar Allan Poe. London, Weidenfeld and Nicolson, and New York, Summit, 1978.
Mazeppa: The Lives, Loves, and Legends of Adah Isaacs Menken: A Biographical Quest. London, Blond and Briggs, and New York, Stein and Day, 1982.

*

Manuscript Collection: Mugar Memorial Library, Boston University.

Theatrical Activities:
Director: **Film**—*The Hebrew Lesson*, 1972.

Wolf Mankowitz comments:
  There have been some quite good notes and notices on odd works of mine from time to time, but I really could not give details. Let's just say that they all agreed that I was somewhat over-diversified and altogether too varied, and generally speaking, pragmatic, which means, I suppose, opportunistic in the way one tends to be if one is a professional writer. Lately my writing has been described as erudite, sophisticated, always funny, sometimes bizarre—so whether I'm getting better or worse, I am certainly continuing. I have never considered myself to be a playwright. I think of myself as a storyteller, and I tend to use whatever form the story seems to me to require.

*   *   *

  In his early novels and short stories Wolf Mankowitz displayed a sure grasp of the dramatic, that sense of character and situation which makes for good theatre. *Make Me an Offer* and *A Kid for Two Farthings* are both simple, direct narratives, sensitive and funny; it was natural enough to see them transcribed for the stage and the screen. Since then, Mankowitz has joyfully embraced show biz at all levels; he has become an impresario, he is a screenwriter who adapts his own scripts and those of others, and he has put every form of popular entertainment on celluloid. The films to which he has contributed range in their appeal from the glamorous (*The Millionairess*) to the horrific (*The Two Faces of Dr. Jekyll*), from adventure (*The Day the Earth Caught Fire*) to schmaltz (*Black Beauty*).
  Mankowitz has certainly found his spiritual home in Shaftesbury Avenue but that hasn't shaken his allegiance to the basic principles of storytelling first learnt in the East End; he still employs a powerful mixture of cynicism and sentiment, still reveres the past, still delights in patterns of speech and idiosyncrasies of behaviour. At a guess, his central character in *Make Me an Offer* is something of a self-portrait. "Who knew better than he that nothing is given, that everything passes, the woods decay. He was the ultimate human being. He resigned himself to make a profit." *Expresso Bongo* is a further comment on commercialisation, a musical set in Soho, where the promoters of pop live in the continued hope of overnight successes, sudden fortune.
  Of Mankowitz's one-act plays, *The Bespoke Overcoat* has always attracted praise for its technical skill and depth of feeling. It is published together with four smaller pieces, one entitled *It Should Happen to a Dog*, another, *The Last of the*

Cheesecake. As one might expect, these are anecdotes of Jewish life, poignant, comic, and shrewd. *The Bespoke Overcoat* is something more, a celebration of that stubborn reverence for life which the good adhere to, however desperate their circumstances. Morry the tailor ("a needle like Paganini") can never give his friend the longed-for overcoat, since Fender has died in poverty. But human values are not negated by death: this truth is triumphantly stated in Morry's speeches and, at the close of the play, in his chanting of the Kaddish. Pathos is the dominant mood in another early play, *The Boychik*; this is a study of hopeless ambition, that of an elderly actor who, with his son, dreams of reopening the decaying theatre where he was once a star.

Mankowitz has made an important contribution to postwar drama, which is not always acknowledged by those who distrust box office success. His picture of Jewish life is convincing for its realism and memorable for its use of symbolism, as in *A Kid for Two Farthings*. He has eschewed the avant garde but is nevertheless a highly sophisticated playwright who understands the traditions of the European theatre and has worked against the parochialism of the English stage.

—Judy Cooke

MANN, Emily. American. Born in Boston, Massachusetts, 12 April 1952. Educated at Radcliffe College, Cambridge, Massachusetts, B.A. in English 1974 (Phi Beta Kappa); University of Minnesota, Minneapolis (Bush Fellow), 1974–76, M.F.A. in theater arts 1976. Married Gerry Bamman in 1981 (divorced), one son. Associate director, Guthrie Theatre, Minneapolis, 1978–79; resident director, BAM Theater Company, Brooklyn, New York, 1981–82; member of the board, 1983–87, and vice-president of the board, 1984–86, Theatre Communications Group, and director, New Dramatists workshop for play development, 1984–91, both New York. Since 1989 artistic director, McCarter Theatre Center for the Performing Arts, Princeton, New Jersey; artistic associate, Crossroads Theatre, New Brunswick, New Jersey, 1990; lecturer, Council of the Humanities and Theatre and Dance program, Princeton University, New Jersey, 1990. Recipient: Obie award, 1981 (for writing and directing); Guggenheim fellowship, 1983; Rosamond Gilder award, 1983; National Endowment for the Arts grant, 1984, 1986; Creative Artists Public Service grant, 1985; Edinburgh Festival Fringe first award, 1985; McKnight fellowship, 1985; Dramatists Guild award, 1986; Playwrights USA award, 1986; Helen Hayes award, 1986; Home Box Office U.S.A. award, 1986. Lives in Princeton, New Jersey. Agent: George Lane, William Morris Agency, 1350 Avenue of the Americas, New York, New York 10019, U.S.A.

PUBLICATIONS

Plays

Annulla, An Autobiography (as *Annulla Allen: The Autobiography of a Survivor*, also director: produced Minneapolis, 1977; revised version, as *Annulla, An Autobiography*, produced St. Louis, 1985; New York,

1988). New York, Theatre Communications Group, 1985.

Still Life (also director: produced Chicago, 1980; New York, 1981; Edinburgh and London, 1984). New York, Dramatists Play Service, 1982; published in *Coming to Terms: American Plays and the Vietnam War*, edited by James Reston, Jr., New York, Theatre Communications Group, 1985.

Execution of Justice (produced Louisville, 1984; also director: produced New York, 1986). Published in *New Playwrights 3*, edited by James Leverett and Elizabeth Osborn, New York, Theatre Communications Group, 1986.

Nights and Days, adaptation of a play by Pierre Laville, published in *Avant-Scène* (Paris), July 1984.

Betsey Brown, adaptation of the novel by Ntozake Shange, book by Shange and Mann, music by Baikida Carroll, lyrics by Shange, Mann, and Carroll (also director: produced Philadelphia, 1989).

*

Theatrical Activities:
Director: **Plays**—*Cold* by Michael Casale, Minneapolis, 1976; *Ashes* by David Rudkin, Minneapolis, 1977, and Cincinnati, 1980; *Annulla Allen*, Minneapolis, 1977; *Surprise, Surprise* by Michel Tremblay, Minneapolis, 1978; *On Mount Chimborazo* by Tankred Dorst, Minneapolis, 1978; *Reunion* and *Dark Pony*, by David Mamet, Minneapolis, 1978; *The Glass Menagerie* by Tennessee Williams, Minneapolis, 1979, Princeton, New Jersey, 1990; *He and She* by Rachel Crothers, New York, 1980; *Still Life*, Chicago, 1980, New York, 1986; *Oedipus the King* by Sophocles, New York, 1981; *A Tantalizing* by William Mastrosimone, Louisville, 1982; *The Value of Names* by Jeffrey Sweet, Louisville, 1982, and Hartford, Connecticut, 1984; *A Weekend near Madison* by Kathleen Tolan, Louisville and New York, 1983; *Execution of Justice*, Minneapolis, 1985, New York, 1986; *A Doll's House* by Ibsen, Hartford, Connecticut, 1986; *Hedda Gabler* by Ibsen, La Jolla, California, 1987; *Betsey Brown*, Philadelphia, 1989, Princeton, New Jersey, 1990; *The Three Sisters* by Chekhov, Princeton, New Jersey, 1991.

* * *

Emily Mann has referred to her work as "theatre of testimony." Documentary drama is her métier, and recent history has provided her subjects ranging from the horrors of war, to peacetime violence, to the revolution in gender roles and sexual politics. Her first three stage plays are based wholly or in part on interviews with the people whose stories she tells.

Annulla, An Autobiography is the prototype. Mann visited the protagonist, a survivor of Nazism, in 1974, and the work hews so closely to what the playwright heard in Annulla Allen's London kitchen that she credits her as co-author. The short play turns Annulla's own words into an uninterrupted monologue. Annulla's privileged girlhood in Galicia is a distant memory, eclipsed by the Nazi terror. Her self-assurance and unsemitic good looks helped her escape the camps and rescue her Jewish husband from Dachau. Now widowed, she cares for a demanding invalid sister. However compelling her harrowing story, Annulla insists, "It is not me who is interesting, it is my play." An enormous manuscript covers her kitchen table, stage center. Annulla's play argues for global matriarchy as the solution to evil and barbarism. "If women would only start thinking, we could change the world," she observes, declaring women incapable of the monstrous acts of Hitler or Stalin.

Still, Annulla is unable to read out representative passages from her work in progress. The manuscript is so disorganized and the need to get dinner for her ailing sister so pressing that she loses patience sifting through the jumbled pages. Therein lies Mann's point. However reasoned Annulla's thesis or promising her creativity, she is chronically distracted by more traditional female roles and by the anxieties and guilt which stem from her terrible past. Annulla can no more impose order on her play than she can on her life. Mann does not try to do that for her. In setting down the unmediated monologue of this scarred but plucky woman, Mann makes a statement about her own role. *Annulla* testifies to the freedom for creativity exercised by the playwright who recognizes that, by sheer accident of time and place, she was spared the life of her co-author and subject.

In *Still Life* Mann again draws on interviews with real people who become the *dramatis personae*. She calls this work a documentary, specifying that it be produced with that genre's characteristic objectivity. That tone is the first of the ironies that mark this work about the virulent psychic and emotional conditioning suffered by a Vietnam veteran and about the troubled society to which he returns. As a Marine, Mark learned that he could kill civilians as easily as enemy soldiers. After the war, he cannot get rid of the memory of having wielded power over life and death. His obsession is alternately the source of rage, guilt, and physical pleasure. Incapable of talking either to those who were not in Vietnam, or to those who were, Mark turns to drugs, crime, and domestic violence. He is not too self-centered to appreciate that his wife, Cheryl, whom he abuses, is as much of a casualty of the war years as he. Cheryl wants to return to the securities of a traditionalism more alive in her memories than in post-1960's America. She longs to play the roles her mother did, noting that, except in wartime, it is women who protect men—a point of view strikingly antithetical to that of Annulla Allen. Mark's mistress Nadine has done battle with all manner of "naughtiness." "A woman with many jobs and many lives," in Mann's words, Nadine describes herself as being so busy that she sleeps with her shoes on. The observation is metaphoric. Nadine steps over troubled waters, never feeling the cold or agitation, and never plunging beneath the surface. Mark can tell Nadine his ugly truths, for absolutely nothing offends, disturbs, or even touches her.

Still Life is staged so as to make palpable the lack of genuine communication between Mark, who lives in the past, Cheryl, who yearns for an unrealizable future, and Nadine, who hovers above an unexamined present. The three characters sit side by side behind a table, like members of a panel discussion—or witnesses at a trial. They talk about, but rarely to, one another, their intersecting speeches often juxtaposed ironically. So, for example, Nadine's innocence about her near fatal pregnancies overlaps the ingenuous Cheryl's shock in coming upon Mark's pictures of war casualties. Projections on a screen behind the actors underscore the hopelessness of anyone's enjoying the full understanding of others. Gruesome pictures of horribly mutilated war injured, for instance, illustrate Mark's inability to talk to his parents who supported the war. Indeed, this seething play whose self-possessed characters never touch one another on stage ironically reflects a society where people, however uncommunicating, are continually in violent and destructive collision.

The notion of the audience as jury, implicit in *Still Life*, is central to *Execution of Justice*. Significantly, the work was commissioned by the Eureka Theatre of San Francisco. Its subject is the 1978 murder of George Moscone, Mayor of San Francisco, and Harvey Milk, a City Supervisor and the first avowed homosexual voted into high public office. The play brings to the stage the case of the People against Dan White, the assassin. It demonstrates the instability of White, who had been elected a City Supervisor, resigned, changed his mind and, when Moscone refused to reappoint him to his former post, vented his rage by shooting him and Milk. Mann bases her script on the transcript of the trial, reportage, extensive interviews with some of the principals, as well as what she calls in a prefatory note "the street." The play neatly synthesizes background pertinent to the case, such as the evolution in the social and political spheres caused by the migration to San Francisco of a large homosexual population. It recreates the climate of fear provoked by the mass deaths in Jonestown, Guyana, and the reputed connections between James Jones and liberal elements in San Francisco. The play captures effectively the unprecedented violence that stalked American political life in the 1970's.

As the testimony piles up, one appreciates the implausible defense arguments (e.g., the famous "Twinkies defense," which attributed criminal behavior to the accused's junk food diet) and its unlikely claim that the murders were purely politically and not homophobically motivated. *Execution of Justice* shows that what was really on trial was conservative values, outraged and threatened by the growing power of the gay community. The use of video projections and film clips from documentaries intensify the passions of the trial; the inclusion of reporters and photographers heightens its immediacy. Though Mann treats this explosive material with an even hand, there is no question that she wants the audience as jury to find that Dan White's conviction and light jail sentence for the lesser charges of voluntary manslaughter amount to the miscarriage of justice referred to in the play's title.

Mann's penchant for transforming life to the stage takes a new turn with *Betsey Brown*, a rhythm and blues musical. She came to the project at the invitation of Ntozake Shange who began it as a short story, turned it into a performance piece produced in 1979 at the Kennedy Center as *Boogie Woogie Landscapes*, and finally rewrote it as a novel. Shange and jazz trumpeter-composer Baikida Carroll approached Mann for help in reworking the piece for the stage. The result was a full-fledged collaboration, a musical whose 28 songs color and interweave the various strands of a distinctly contemporary story.

The eponymous Betsey Brown is a young African-American woman who comes of age in St. Louis of 1959. The first stirrings of the civil rights movement form the background for a number of issues the play explores. The most obvious is, of course, racism, both within the black community and from white society threatened by integration. At least as consequential is the question of a role model for teenage Betsey. On one side is her mother, a "modern" woman who briefly abandons her family to pursue her own intellectual needs. Notwithstanding, she is genuinely concerned about educating her daughters to become cultivated members of a society which hardly encourages the self-actualization of black women. On the other side is the comforting figure of the Browns' housekeeper, a traditional woman who sings gospel songs with exquisite conviction. Her other accomplishments include commonsensical strategies for pleasing a man and consoling a crying child. Reviews of *Betsey Brown*'s premiere prove the success of the work in moving beyond its delineation of the tensions and beauties of black life to dramatize universal problems of parental responsibilities to children in a radically changing world.

In addition to her work for the stage, Mann has written three screenplays (none yet produced). *Naked* (1985), based on the book by Jo Giese Brown, is subtitled *One Couple's Intimate Journey Through Infertility*. *Fanny Kelly* (1985) dramatizes the true story of an intrepid pioneer woman captured by the Sioux. *You Strike a Woman, You Strike a Rock* (1990) is a script on the Greensboro Massacre, commissioned by NBC Theatre. These scripts are distinguished by tight, suspenseful plots as well as the credible characterizations that Mann has made her signature.

—Ellen Schiff

MAPONYA, Maishe. South African. Born in Johannesburg, 4 September 1951. Educated at Diepkloof Secondary School, Soweto, 1969–71; Orlando High School, 1972–73; University of Leeds, 1986–87. Supervisor, Liberty Life Assurance, Johannesburg, 1974–83; coordinator, Bahumuts (drama group), Diepkloof, 1976–88; vice chair, P.A.W.E., Johannesburg, 1991–93. Recipient: Standard Bank Young Artists award, 1985; Wesley Guild's Best Diepkloof Poet prize, 1986. Address: Dramatic Art Department, University of Witwatersrand, PO Wits 2050, Johannesburg, South Africa.

PUBLICATIONS

Plays

The Hungry Earth (produced London, 1981). Johannesburg, Polyptoton, 1981.
Umongikazi (*The Nurse*) (produced Edinburgh and London, 1983). Johannesburg, Polyptoton, 1983.
Dirty Work (produced London, 1985). Johannesburg, Polyptoton, 1985.
Gangsters (produced London, 1985; New York, 1986). Johannesburg, Polyptoton, 1985; New York, Braziller, 1986.
The Valley of the Blind, with V. Amani Waphtali (also co-director; produced London, 1987).
Jika (produced New York, 1988).
Busang Meropa (*Bring Back the Drums*) (produced Birmingham, 1989).

Radio Play: *Gangsters*, 1987.

Recordings: *Busang Meropa* (*Bring Back the Drums*), Johannesburg, S.F.B., 1988; *Azikho*, Johannesburg, Tusk Records, 1991.

*

Theatrical Activities:
Director: **Plays**—most of his own plays; *Changing the Silence* by Don Kinch, London, 1985; *The Coat* by Athol Fugard, Johannesburg, 1990; *Two Can Play* by Trevor Rhone, Johannesburg, 1992; *A Raisin in the Sun* by Lorraine Hansberry, 1992.
Actor: **Plays**—roles in most of his own plays, and in *The Hungry Earth*, London, 1981.

* * *

Maishe Maponya's plays can be described as theatrical hand-grenades to be detonated for maximum impact on the sensibilities of the audience. The themes are unabashedly political and each work offers us an excruciating insight into the impact of apartheid on different segments of the black South African population. The playwright tries to assault the reader with knife-blade images of the experiences of several classes of workers and other artistic professions straining against the strictures and structures of white-controlled establishments which are draconically manipulated to deny black South Africans maximum participation, career advancement, and self-fulfilment. Persecution and prejudice can be said to be Maponya's creative obsessions.

In *The Hungry Earth*, his earliest published play, we are dragged on a tour of five symbolic settings which epitomise the degradation of black South African migrant labourers. In the first setting, The Hostel, four men—Mathloko (Suffering), Usiviko (Shield), Beshwana (Loin-cloth), and Sethotho (Imbecile)—are asleep in a labourers' hostel when Usiviko wakes up from a nightmare in which he claims he has seen Umlungu (the Whiteman) leaving the land with goods plundered from the sweat and toil of the original owners of the land. The scene recaptures the history of their dispossession and the consequent hardship wrought upon them by European settlers. Sethotho, the imbecile, plays the devil's advocate, pointing out the material and economic benefits of the white man's control of South Africa. In a symbolic dance, the four men mime their determination to reclaim their land and its bounties just as their ancestors resisted colonialism. Their act of defiance is traced to "Isandlwana," meaning "Little Hill," where the Zulus fought a battle against the British in 1879 and inflicted heavy casualities on them. Also evoked through the dance is the memory of "Umgungudlovu," "Surrounding of the Elephant," another battlefield where the Zulus routed the Boers in 1838. Subsequent scenes expose the exploitation of children in sugar plantations where they labour for 10 hours every day, after trekking six miles each morning, only to be paid 50 cents by the white owners. The beauty of this scene lies in the manner in which the four men transform themselves into children with one of them doubling as a father, a visitor, searching for his child in several plantation barracoons. The final scene displays the four men in a mine as the roof of the pit caves in on them, killing 41 black miners, hence the title of the play.

Maponya's other plays employ this episodic structure, which makes for fluidity of scene changes and easy transformation of characters, as is characteristic of many South African protest plays. His major contribution to the corpus of plays created by other black and white liberal playwrights is the presentation of the experience and effects of segregation in an uncompromising and urgent manner, calling for a pragmatic black blacklash instead of the survivalist tendency found, for example, in *Sizwe Bansi Is Dead*.

Umongikazi (*The Nurse*) portrays the dilemma of black nurses working in a white-administered hospital. Through the maltreatment of three characters, Felize, Nyamezo, and Maria, the play highlights the bureaucratic double standards employed by the South African Nursing Association in the promotion of the workers, a strategy which leaves black nurses perennially at the foot of the career ladder. Generous with statistics, Maponya informs us that there are 4,000 black doctors for 23 million black people, whereas 12,000 abound for a mere 5 million whites. In one striking scene a white paediatrician refuses to treat a new-born black baby because "tomorrow it'll be the one that will snatch my bag."

Gangsters, however, is this playwright's masterpiece. Its edge over the other works is the dextrous use of flashbacks with which the playwright chronicles the hounding, arrest, torture, and death of Rasecheba, a poet accused of writing inflammatory verses. It starts at the end, and a carefully disarranged sequence of past meetings and incidents leads to the theatrical finale where the policemen who tortured the hero to death are at a loss as to the explanation they will give to the inquisition and the court as plausible accounts for the poet's death. Rejected suggestions include "hanged himself from the cell window . . . fell to his death from a seventh storey floor trying to escape interrogation [the interrogation room is actually on the first floor] . . . slipped on a tablet of wet soap [this is rejected because it has been used too often to explain away the death of black people held in detention]." By shifting the emphasis from the poet's death to the process of his death, the playwright succeeds in presenting Rasecheba's tormentors as professional homicides who, for once, are embattled with guilt, thus giving the work a near-tragic impetus. Another revealing insight in *Gangsters* is the nature of the circumstances, mainly economic, that force black policemen to become informers or to persecute their own people. Jonathan, a black policeman in the play, becomes Whitebeard's hatchet-man simply because Whitebeard, his boss, is paying for the education of Jonathan's children in Swaziland.

Dirty Work, portrays a paranoid white security officer, Peter Hannekon, giving a lecture on the state-of-the-art security equipment devised and imported by the South African government to forestall any invasion by black people. However, and hilariously enough, any little sound off-stage sends Hannekon trembling. He finally dies of a heart attack towards the end of the lecture, trying to exorcise the terror conjured up in him by "invade," a word which he cannot pronounce.

Maponya's weaknesses as a playwright include poor character development, speechifying, and an irritating tendentiousness which sometimes becomes overtly propagandist. His strengths include the "poverty" of his theatre, its Brechtian dynamic, and the infusion of local colour into his work through indigenous songs, dances, languages, and mime. The racy dialogue in the interrogation scenes of *Gangsters* and the macabre humour towards the end are commendable. However, more than his present monochromatic imagination Maponya needs a deeper insight into human nature.

—Esiaba Irobi

MARCHANT, Tony. British. Born in London, 11 July 1959. Educated at St. Joseph Academy School. Recipient: Edinburgh Festival award, 1982; *Drama* award, 1982. Agent: Lemon, Unna, and Durbridge, 24 Pottery Lane, Holland Park, London W11 4LZ, England.

PUBLICATIONS

Plays

Remember Me? (produced London, 1980).
Thick as Thieves (includes *London Calling* and *Dealt With*) (produced London, 1981). London, Methuen, 1982.
Stiff (produced London, 1982).

Raspberry (produced Edinburgh and London, 1982). Included in *Welcome Home, Raspberry, The Lucky Ones*, 1983.
The Lucky Ones (produced London, 1982). Included in *Welcome Home, Raspberry, The Lucky Ones*, 1983.
Welcome Home (produced Hemel Hempstead, Hertfordshire, and London, 1983). Included in *Welcome Home, Raspberry, The Lucky Ones*, 1983.
Welcome Home, Raspberry, The Lucky Ones. London, Methuen, 1983.
Lazydays Ltd. (produced London, 1984).
The Attractions (produced London, 1987). Oxford, Amber Lane, 1988.
Speculators (produced London, 1987). Oxford, Amber Lane, 1988.

Television Plays: *Raspberry*, 1984; *Reservations*, 1985; *This Year's Model*, 1988; *The Money Men*, 1988; *Death of a Son*, 1989; *The Attractions*, 1989; *Take Me Home*, 1989; *Goodbye Cruel World*, 1992.

*

Tony Marchant comments:
I started writing at 20, and for the past seven or eight years I have written about my generation in various situations—unemployed, trapped in office conformity, at war, in a state of sexual confusion. The experiences of my characters differ vastly: from having fought in the Falklands (*Welcome Home*) to confronting the "stigma" of infertility (*Raspberry*). Generally the plays are about people attempting to confound the expectations of their environment. They are mostly excluded from the mainstream of society, but suffer from its judgement. They all question these judgements and ultimately defy them. Theirs is a plea for dignity.

* * *

Tony Marchant's work so far marks him as the spokesman for people not normally given a voice. His earliest plays toured schools and youth clubs and he has tended to work in theatres which have a strong sense of community, such as the Theatre Royal at Stratford East, a regular clientele, such as the now closed Soho Poly, or for touring companies like Paines Plough—in short in intimate locations which allow his greatest strengths free play. He has a sharp eye for the minutiae of characterisation, allied to the ability to endow his characters with a high level of articulacy that still seems to keep within the bounds of naturalism. *Thick as Thieves*, for example, shows a group of unemployed London teenagers; the first part, *London Calling*, depicts them merely wandering about flirting with the notion of casual violence; but there is also a clear sense that at least some of them are thinking out their situation in a remarkably organised way. They take on the unthinking prejudices of Pimple, a mate who is toying with the ideas of the National Front; but while they are clear about who not to blame for their situation, they cannot conceive of a way out and their very real linguistic energy is dissipated in destructive self-parody. They are only too aware that they are prime subjects for well-meaning, ineffectual documentary: when Pimple remembers bonfires on the tatty dump that is now their social space, Paul responds sardonically "Our heritage—building things with rubbish and setting light to 'em." The idea of waste is made overt in the second play, *Dealt With*, in which Paul and the others confront a personnel officer who has rejected him; they harass him without much effect and the play ends with the boys on the run from the security guard, except for Paul, now on the verge of suicide. Here the focus is split: on the one hand there is a simple clash between the deprived and the prosperous, on the other a contrast between the dreams with which Paul invests this confrontation and the inadequacy of the personnel officer as a target for his rage. Marchant sometimes seems lost between the two and the somewhat melodramatic ending looks like a way of dodging the issue.

In his play about the Falklands aftermath, *Welcome Home*, we are shown a group of young men who have found at least a temporary alternative—the Army. Marchant gives a scrupulous account of both the benefits and the cost of that alternative on a personal level. In the discipline of the "cherry berets" the boys have found both self-image and self-respect. They have developed a comradeship which can show itself in uproarious horseplay but also in their care that a comrade's funeral shall turn out well. In return the Army demands not just their lives but also the right to control their self-expression. As the Corporal points out, the funeral is part of their public duty to be heroes "as advertised on TV"; when one of them messes up the discipline of the procession he isn't simply punished by the Army for violating its image—he assists the process, breaking down from pure shame. The Corporal treats him with savage violence, but his motivation is not the reflex action of a man addicted to "bull"; it is rather a clumsy attempt at shock therapy, an attempt to help while staying within the permitted boundaries of the Para image; this, Marchant implies, is the real cost of the Army as an outlet for youthful energy and courage—the damage it does to the best human instincts.

Raspberry is perhaps the clearest celebration of the human ability to transcend immediate oppression. Two women share a gynaecological ward—one for an abortion, the other for yet another operation for her infertility. Despite the insensitivity of the system that has flung them together, symbolised by the hostility of the nurse towards the young abortion patient, they achieve a close and mutually comforting relationship. Lacking any common ground, they unite against their surroundings in an almost surreal spirit. What starts as a near-quarrel turns, in the face of an angry nurse, to a mischievous assertion that they have been playing games; this then becomes something like fact as they improvise a "party" to transform the grimness of the pre-operation evening; this leads in turn to a genuine relationship; the moment when they hold each other in the face of their shared pain is a touching moment of theatre. This ability to show the play instinct at work in the unlikeliest settings, and the comradeship arising out of it, is perhaps Marchant's major strength. At present the naturalism of his sets and plots precludes a close analysis of the underlying politics. One simply accepts that, unjust as it is, this is the present situation. However, he shows clearly the resources that are there to fight it; the linguistic energy of his characters is a lively symbol of human energy in the face of oppression. For change to occur, Marchant implies, that energy needs only to be harnessed.

—Frances Gray

MARCUS, Frank (Ulrich). British. Born in Breslau, Germany, 30 June 1928; emigrated to England in 1939. Educated at Bunce Court School, Kent (evacuated to Shropshire), 1939–43; St. Martin's School of Art, London,

1943–44. Married Jacqueline Sylvester in 1951; one son and two daughters. Secretary, salesman, and manager, T.M.V. Ltd., London, 1944–54; manager, Marshal's Antiques (Silver), London, 1954–65. Actor, director, and scenic designer, Unity Theatre, Kensington, London; founder, International Theatre Group. Theatre critic, the *Sunday Telegraph*, London, 1968–78; regular contributor to *Plays and Players*, London, *London Magazine*, and *Dramatists Guild Quarterly*, New York. Since 1984 television critic, *Plays International*, London. Recipient: *Evening Standard* award, 1965; *Plays and Players* award, 1965; *Variety* award, 1966. Agent: Casarotto Ramsay Ltd., National House, 60–66 Wardour Street, London W1V 3HP. Address: 8 Kirlegate, Meare, near Glastonbury, Somerset BA6 9TA, England.

PUBLICATIONS

Plays

Minuet for Stuffed Birds (also director: produced London, 1950).
Merry-Go-Round, adaptation of a play by Schnitzler (as *Reigen—La Ronde*, produced London, 1952). London, Weidenfeld and Nicolson, 1953.
The Man Who Bought a Battlefield (produced London, 1963).
The Formation Dancers (produced London, 1964; revised version, produced London, 1971). Published in *Plays of the Year 28*, London, Elek, 1965.
The Killing of Sister George (produced Bristol and London, 1965; New York, 1966). London, Hamish Hamilton, 1965; New York, Random House, 1967.
Cleo (produced Bristol, 1965). Excerpt, as *Cleo and Max*, published in *London Magazine*, February 1966.
The Window (televised 1966; produced London, 1969; New York, 1973). London, French, 1968; New York, French, 1970.
Studies of the Nude (produced London, 1967).
Mrs. Mouse, Are You Within? (produced Bristol and London, 1968). Published in *Plays of the Year 35*, London, Elek, 1969.
The Guardsman, adaptation of a play by Ferenc Molnár (produced Watford, Hertfordshire, 1969; London, 1976; New York, 1980). London, Eyre Methuen, 1978.
Blank Pages: A Monologue (televised 1969; also director: produced London, 1972; New York, 1973). London, French, 1973; in *The Best Short Plays 1974*, edited by Stanley Richards, Radnor, Pennsylvania, Chilton, 1974.
Notes on a Love Affair (produced London, 1972). Published in *Plays of the Year 42*, London, Elek, 1973.
Christmas Carol (produced London, 1972; New York, 1973; as *Carol's Christmas*, produced London, 1975).
Keyholes (produced New York, 1973).
Beauty and the Beast (produced Oxford, 1975). Published in *Plays of the Year 46*, London, Elek, 1978.
Anatol, adaptation of the play by Schnitzler (produced London, 1976). London, Methuen, 1982.
Portrait of the Artist (mime; produced London, 1976).
Blind Date: An Anecdote (produced London, 1977). London, French, 1977; in *The Best Short Plays 1979*, edited by Stanley Richards, Radnor, Pennsylvania, Chilton, 1979.
The Ballad of Wilfred II (produced London, 1978).
The Merman of Orford (mime; produced Niagara-on-the-Lake, Ontario, 1978).
The Weavers, adaptation of a play by Gerhart Hauptmann (produced London, 1980). London, Eyre Methuen, 1980.
La Ronde, with Jacqueline Marcus, adaptation of a play by

Schnitzler (televised 1982; produced London, 1991). London, Methuen, 1982.
From Morning to Midnight, adaptation of a play by Georg Kaiser (produced London, 1987).

Screenplays: *The Snow Tiger*, 1966; *The Formation Dancers*, 1972.

Radio Plays: *The Hospital Visitor*, 1979; *The Beverley Brooch*, 1981; *The Row over La Ronde*, 1982.

Television Plays: *Liebelei*, 1954; *The Window*, 1966; A *Temporary Typist*, 1966; *The Glove Puppet*, 1968; *Blank Pages*, 1969; *Carol's Story*, 1974; *La Ronde*, with Jacqueline Marcus, 1982.

*

Manuscript Collection: Boston University Libraries.

Critical Studies: "The Plays of Frank Marcus" by Irving Wardle, in *London Magazine*, March 1966; "The Comedy is Finished" by Marcus, in *London Magazine*, June–July 1971.

Theatrical Activities:
Director: **Plays**—*House of Regrets* by Peter Ustinov, London, 1948; *The Servant of Two Masters* by Carlo Goldoni, London, 1949; *Minuet for Stuffed Birds*, London, 1950; *The Broken Jug* by Heinrich von Kleist, London, 1950; *Husbands and Lovers* by Ferenc Molnár, London, 1950; *The Man of Destiny* by Shaw, London, 1950; *Reigen* (*La Ronde*) by Arthur Schnitzler, London, 1952; *Georges Dandin* by Molière, London, 1953; *This Property Is Condemned* by Tennessee Williams, London, 1953; *The Killing of Sister George*, toured, 1967; *Blank Pages*, London, 1972.
Actor: **Play**—The General in *House of Regrets* by Peter Ustinov, London, 1948; Silvio in *The Servant of Two Masters* by Carlo Goldoni, London, 1949; title role in *The Man with the Flower in His Mouth* by Pirandello, London, 1950; Priest in *The Broken Jug* by Heinrich von Kleist, London, 1950; Napoleon in *The Man of Destiny* by Shaw, London, 1950; Orlando in *Angelica* by Leo Ferrero, London, 1951; The Son in *My Friend, The Enemy* by Sheila Hodgson, London, 1952.

*   *   *

A quality that has distinguished all Frank Marcus's mature plays is his sympathetic, though not sentimental, understanding of the behaviour of women in love, using the word "love" in its widest possible sense. The examination of feminine amatory practice in its various forms has been his theme in play after play. In two of them, *Cleo* and *Notes on a Love Affair*, it furnishes virtually the whole material of the plot.
Marcus's first play to achieve any kind of commercial success was *The Formation Dancers*, a light-hearted foursome in which one man borrows another man's mistress for a brief episode. His wife, to reclaim his fidelity, feigns an affair with this other man. The plot, in fact, is triviality itself; but two points are worth observing. One is the insistence that it is the two women who are always in command. The other is the drawing of the mistress, a Chelsea demi-beatnik of a type more common in 1964 (the date of the play) than now, who recurs several times in later work.

A much more detailed portrait of what is pretty well the same character appears in *Cleo*. This play is a theme and variations; the protagonist, that same demi-beatnik, as intelligent as she is footloose, is observed in a series of encounters with assorted men. (It may be significant that in 1953 Marcus published a translation of Schnitzler's *Reigen*, best known as the film *La Ronde*.) In this play it is clear that woman is unarguably the dominant sex, even if her dominance cannot always insure her against disaster. A later play, *Studies of the Nude*, was a developed version of one of the episodes from *Cleo*. Schnitzler's *Anatol*, adapted by Marcus ten years after *Cleo*, gives an idea of where he got the story from, only here the sexes are reversed.
Between *The Formation Dancers* and *Cleo* came what is certainly Marcus's most imaginative play so far, *The Killing of Sister George*. This is a penetrating study of a lesbian love affair. The "masculine" woman of the association is a once-successful actress whose career has dwindled to a steady part in a radio soap opera from which the producers now intend to drop her. She shares her life with a girl who appears to be merely young and silly, but who is later revealed as not so young and mentally retarded, the object not only of love but of a genuinely charitable beneficence. It is the younger girl, however, who at the end of the play has moved into a greater happiness and left the older woman on the brink of despair: the dominance is once again attributed to the weaker vessel. This play, in which the events mark an almost uninterrupted sequence of sadness, is nevertheless hilariously funny throughout: an imaginative masterpiece. Its sensitivity was somewhat obscured in a subsequent film version, in which Marcus did not have a hand.
After *Sister George*, Marcus's next piece dealt with characters almost defiantly ordinary. This was *Mrs. Mouse, Are You Within?*, once more a comedy of which the storyline is unrelieved tragedy. It is set among mildly trendy middle-class people in London, and once again there is a strong female part at the core, though on this occasion, for once, she is a character to whom things happen rather than a character who makes things happen. What happens is that she becomes pregnant by a passing association with a black neighbour. The lover decamps; the boring man to whom she has been engaged for eight years is so stuffy that she sends him away; and her Marxist landlord, in whom she has never felt much interest, makes a proposal of marriage to which she agrees from the depths of her despair.
The ordinariness of the characters is an asset to the play, in that vast misfortunes seem vaster when they light on little people. But *Mrs. Mouse* has not quite the imaginative spark of *Sister George* nor the wit of *The Formation Dancers*, though there is plenty of good comedy and real pathos in it. The *Cleo* character is once more recognisable in the heroine's younger sister.
Notes on a Love Affair is more romantic and less comic than any of Marcus's previous work. In this, a woman novelist stuck on a play sets up a love affair between a former lover of hers and a colourless girl who works for her dentist, so that she may observe their mutual reactions. As so often, the experiment progresses through realms of comedy to final heartbreak. The play does not mark any advance on Marcus's part, unless in his willingness to adopt the Pirandellian shift of having his heroine explain directly to the audience what she is doing. But it is a moving play, and contains two fine parts for actresses.
Marcus has also made several adaptations, including a stylish translation of Molnár's *The Guardsman*, and written several plays for television, one of which, a short two-hander called *The Window*, has also been seen in the theatre. There

is some significance in the Molnár translation. If there is any detectable influence in Marcus's work, it is in Molnár and Schnitzler that you will find it.

—B.A. Young

MASON, Bruce (Edward George). New Zealander. 1921–1982. See 3rd edition, 1982.

MASTROSIMONE, William. American. Born in Trenton, New Jersey, 19 August 1947. Educated at Pennington Preparatory School, New Jersey, 1963–66; Tulane University, New Orleans, 1966–70; Rider College, Trenton, New Jersey, 1973–74, B.A. in English 1974; Rutgers University, New Brunswick, New Jersey, 1974–76, M.F.A. 1976. Recipient: Los Angeles Drama Critics Circle award, 1982; Outer Circle award, 1983; John Gassner award, 1983. Agent: George Lane, William Morris Agency, 1350 Avenue of the Americas, New York, New York 10019. Address: 715 First Avenue West, Apartment 202, Seattle, Washington 98119, U.S.A.

PUBLICATIONS

Plays

The Woolgatherer (produced New Brunswick, New Jersey, 1979; New York, 1980; London, 1985). New York, French, 1981.
Extremities (produced New Brunswick, New Jersey, 1980; New York, 1982; London, 1984). New York, French, 1984.
A Tantalizing (produced Louisville, 1982). New York, French, 1985.
Shivaree (produced Seattle, 1983). New York, French, 1984.
The Undoing (produced Louisville, 1984).
Nanawatai (produced in Norwegian, Bergen, Norway, 1984; produced in English, Los Angeles, 1985). New York, French, 1986.
Tamer of Horses (produced New Brunswick, New Jersey, 1985; revised version produced Los Angeles, 1986; revised version produced Seattle, 1987).
Cat's-Paw (produced Seattle, 1986). New York, French, 1987.
The Understanding (produced Seattle, 1987; New York, 1989).
Sunshine (produced New York, 1989).

Screenplays: *Extremities*, 1986; *The Beast*, 1988.

Television Play: *Sinatra* series, 1992.

*

Manuscript Collection: Boston University.

* * *

When *Extremities* opened off-Broadway in 1982, it proved to be one of the most controversial plays of the season, on or off Broadway. Some critics suggested that William Mastrosimone's tense drama about a would-be rapist and his implacable woman captor attracted audiences because there wasn't more powerful fare available. Some dismissed the play as an exercise in old-fashioned melodrama, with onstage violence to whet the visual appetites of jaded television viewers. Actually, Mastrosimone, inspired by a 55-year-old woman rape victim—as he explained in "The Making of Extremities," had touched a raw nerve among theatre-goers in general and women in particular. The fear of and revulsion against, violent, vicious, and unprovoked sexual attacks were very real. That angry or unbalanced male members of some minority groups were perceived as the usual rapists found resonance in the play, whose very disturbed potential ravisher is named Raul. This, some suggested, was invoking racial stereotypes, and confronting a seemingly helpless young woman, Marjorie, with this cunning, shifty criminal seemed a deliberate attempt to exploit current fears.

This is unfair to Mastrosimone, although he clearly cares more for victims' rights and safety than he does for those of wrong-doers. In *Extremities* the naked threat of violence and violation is presented almost immediately, but fortunately Marjorie is able to turn the tables and take Raul captive. His deviousness and threats, as the play progresses, make her decide—driven by rage—to kill him and bury the body in her garden. Her roommates return and react variously, suggesting standard social reactions to such a situation when it is merely hypothetical. At the close, there is a catharsis—somewhat schematic—for both Raul and Marjorie, but it offers no magic solutions to the problem. In addition to the exercise of physical violence on stage, Mastrosimone offers audiences a tightly constructed cat-and-mouse plot, whose outcome is not easily guessed. What is especially appealing, however, as in other Mastrosimone plays, is his ability not only to capture the rhythms and idioms of conversation of various social groups, but also to make them the proper expression of his characters. David Mamet is often praised for his ear for common or raffish speech; Mastrosimone is also adept, but in a different way. Where Mamet's characters may seem involved in an aimless stream-of-consciousness, Mastrosimone's are generally trying to achieve some end, to move the plot forward at the very least.

In *The Woolgatherer*, there is almost no major plot action. Rose, a fragile, disturbed girl, who displaces her terrors and misadventures on a mythical friend, Brenda, brings home Cliff, a trucker looking for a sexual encounter. Their banter —his jocular, angry, or uncomprehending; hers tense, poetic, pained—are the substance of the play, as they come to know and trust each other. The title refers to her collection of men's sweaters, begged from previous visitors. *A Tantalizing*, a one act play, is also a two-character exercise, but this time it's the man, Ambrose, who is unbalanced. Dafne, a young woman who has watched this once well-dressed, confident lawyer spend his days in a parking lot, doing imaginary business on a disconnected telephone he carries with him, has brought him to her apartment, though it's not clear why. No matter what comforts or refreshments she offers, he is peremptory, corrective, fussy, revealing reasons for his failure in life. At the close, she succeeds in getting him to lay aside his ragged clothing for some of her late father's fine garb.

Mastrosimone can manipulate three or more characters on stage at the same time, with effective exchanges of dialogue, but he seems to prefer confrontations between two people, with others brought on—if at all—only when required by the plot. *Shivaree* has echoes of *Butterflies Are Free*, with the difference that Chandler, its protagonist, is hemophiliac, not blind. His overprotective mother drives a cab to pay the bills, while he saves ice-cream money to pay for a session with a prostitute. He finds himself and romance, however, with a neighboring exotic dancer named Shivaree.

Nanawatai deals with the fates of a Soviet tank-team, trapped in a mountain cul-de-sac by Afghan rebels. The title is supposedly the tribal word for sanctuary: once uttered, enemies must protect the one who begs it. A Russian soldier claims it and is spared. Later, his former comrades do so as well, but implacable Afghan women, impatient with the seeming softness of their men, slaughter the helpless Soviets. Interestingly, this was premiered in Norway rather than the United States.

Cat's-Paw goes beyond *Extremities* in dealing with topical terrors and in subtly satirizing American manners and mores. Jessica Lyons, a weekend television anchor-woman, who wants a major news scoop to improve her position, is brought blindfolded to make a television interview with Victor, who has just blown up a car loaded with explosives outside the Environmental Protection Agency in Washington, D.C. He and his small group are using terror tactics to protest government failures to protect the public from toxic wastes. To that end, he's kidnapped a culpable minor EPA official, David Darling, whom he threatens to kill. Lyons's past television coups have shown her unblinking in the face of horrors; Victor hopes to use her talents to get his message to the world and, perhaps, blow up the White House as she reports the event on television. The willingness of the media to exploit— or to trivialize—horrors to win audiences, the very real threat of toxic wastes and official coverups, and the various aspects of terrorism are all effectively used dramatically. It's especially provocative that the maniacal killer seems to espouse all the pieties of the Sierra Club and be willing to destroy unknown innocents for the greater good of mankind. The verbal sparring between Victor and Lyons is notable; the situation, cinematic.

In *The Undoing* there are overtones of Tennessee Williams: Lorraine Tempesta, who runs a chicken-slaughtering and dressing shop, drinks too much, longs for a man, and harasses her dating daughter. A year before, her husband Leo had been killed in a terrible traffic accident; at the site, she laughed. Now she's overcome with guilt. Into the shop comes a one-eyed man who wants to help out. He proves to be the driver of the other wrecked car, come to make amends. There's also a kind of Greek-Italian chorus, two old women, Mrs. Corvo and Mrs. Mosca.

Tamer of Horses combines elements familiar in other Mastrosimone plays. Childless Ty and Georgiane have taken a youthful black offender, Hector, as a foster child. Ty, orphaned and separated from his brother Sam, who died young as a criminal, wants to give another youth in trouble a chance for a new life. Ty, who is a classics teacher, reaches Hector through a retelling of *The Iliad*, but he cannot break him of old thieving, lying ways. Especially chilling is Hector's recreation of a subway mugging. Touched by the two and their caring, Hector nonetheless departs. With his talent for authentic ethnic dialogue and his apparent belief that one cannot even teach a *young* dog new tricks, Mastrosimone has found a voice and themes for the audiences of his time.

As so many other talented younger playwrights, Mastrosimone has found cinema and television more lucrative markets than the theatre. Nonetheless he has told an interviewer he prefers the "instant gratification," which a writer can get in the theatre from both audience and critics. He can also discover rapidly what audiences and critics think, reactions which are delayed or muted with film and television.

A novice in film-making, he was so disgusted with what was done to *Extremities* that he walked out in mid-production. *The Beast* is based on his drama of the Soviet-Afghan confrontation, *Nanawatai*.

The Understanding is autobiographical in tone, dealing with a sternly independent immigrant Italian father—a stone-carver—in Tenafly, New Jersey, and his alienated son. The father threatens to shoot officials who want to evict him from the stone house he built himself in order to build a freeway ramp. His son, Raff, arrives, ostensibly to introduce his fiancée, Janice, but actually to persuade the old man to leave his home peacefully. Old wounds are probed and new threats explored. Father and son arrive at an understanding on two levels.

Also with a small cast, *Sunshine*—which the writer is adapting for the screen—also probes emotional wounds. Sunshine is a "porn queen" stripper who performs for ogling males in a glass-booth under seductive pink lights. At home she has a pet lobster in a glass-tank, an obvious symbol. Repulsed by her life, she flees to take shelter from a murderous husband with Nelson, a burned-out paramedic. He protects himself from the world with indifference, but she manages to get under his skin. They are both in glass-booths, but finally they also have an understanding. The idea came from a nine-hour talk with an actual stripper who took shelter with Mastrosimone from her porn-king spouse. The play, he says is "about the effect pornography has on the people who perform it."

—Glenn Loney

MATHEW, Ray(mond Frank). Australian. Born in Sydney, New South Wales, 14 April 1929. Educated at Sydney Boys' School; Sydney Teacher's College, 1947–49. Schoolteacher in New South Wales, 1949–51; freelance journalist, 1951–52; staff member, Commonwealth Scientific and Independent Research Organisation, Sydney, 1952–54; tutor and lecturer, Workers Education Association, University of Sydney, 1955–60; left Australia in 1961, and has lived in London, Italy, and New York. Recipient: Commonwealth Literary Fund grant, 1951, 1956; Arts Council of Great Britain bursary, 1960. Address: c/o Currency Press, P.O. Box 452, Paddington, New South Wales 2021, Australia.

PUBLICATIONS

Plays

Church Sunday (produced Ballarat, Victoria, 1950).
We Find the Bunyip (produced Sydney, 1955). Published in *Khaki, Bush and Bigotry*, edited by Eunice Hanger, St. Lucia, University of Queensland Press, 1968; as *Three Australian Plays*, Minneapolis, University of Minnesota Press, 1969.
Lonely Without You (produced Hobart, 1957).
The Bones of My Toe (produced Brisbane, 1957). Published in *Australian One-Act Plays 1*, edited by Eunice Hanger, Adelaide, Rigby, 1962.
A Spring Song (produced Brisbane, 1958; Edinburgh and London, 1964). St. Lucia, University of Queensland Press, 1961.

Sing for St. Ned (produced Brisbane, 1960).
The Life of the Party (produced London, 1961).

Radio Plays: *The Love of Gotama*, 1952; *The Medea of Euripides*, 1954.

Novel

The Joys of Possession. London, Chapman and Hall, 1967.

Short Stories

A Bohemian Affair.   Sydney, Angus and Robertson, 1961.
The Time of the Peacock, with Mena Abdullah. Sydney, Angus and Robertson, 1965; New York, Roy, 1968.

Verse

With Cypress Pine.   Sydney, Lyre-Bird Writers, 1951.
Song and Dance.   Sydney, Lyre-Bird Writers, 1956.
South of the Equator.   Sydney, Angus and Robertson, 1961.

Other

Miles Franklin. Melbourne, Landsdowne Press, 1963.
Charles Blackman. Melbourne, Georgian House, 1965.

* * *

By the time Ray Mathew's first important play, *We Find the Bunyip*, was produced he had been a schoolteacher, radio scriptwriter, university tutor, and poet. Before leaving Australia to live in Italy five years later he had published his second and third volumes of poetry, one minor and three full-length plays, as well as having written most of the short stories later collected in *A Bohemian Affair*. The fourth major play was written a year later, the novel in 1965–66.

One of the dimensions used in surveying a playwright's work is the breadth of his technical resource, another the innovations which arose from his experimental structures. On both Mathew scores unusually well.

Technically he is the most sophisticated playwright Australia has produced. His range of dramatic devices, particularly in the area of dialogue, is remarkable and it is difficult to find any instance where a structure obtrudes or is used merely as dramatic ornamentation. Even in *Sing for St. Ned*, which uses some expressionistic devices to achieve alienation, the technical means to Mathew's end remain in control, always revealing rather than distracting from his sub-text.

Mathew's work as a poet had material influence on his drama, many of his more interesting sequences using modes common to both. His dialogue is based on idiomatic syntax, built into rhythmical blocks with caesurae and stresses placed as they are by the sub-group to which each character belongs. This leaves the impression of real speech but creates a denser texture and much broader emotional range.

Repetition is a favourite device, sometimes used to reinforce the texture of ostensibly colloquial chatter, sometimes to establish key phrases without obvious emphasis, frequently to restore significance to devalued words. In *We Find the Bunyip* the key word "happy" occurs thirty times, in as many emotional colours, in one short stretch of dialogue—its original coinage is re-established and it takes a final, ironic, value with considerable impact. In performance the point of the sub-text is clearly established but both the use of the device and the rather formal structure of the sequence go unnoticed.

Mathew's ability to create freshly observed characters, his avoidance of stereotype and his lack of condescension give him much in common with those older playwrights, Lawler, Seymour, Beynon, and Sumner Locke Elliott who, using more conventional moulds, were working in Australia during the same period.

Both *A Spring Song* and *We Find the Bunyip* are closely related to biographical sources, a point which perhaps gives each its authoritative, unforced grasp of the value systems in Australian provincial life. In each play the young middle-class schoolmaster is plummeted among those with whom he appears to have little in common: instead of using them to look on in anger or play the quasi-narrator, Mathew has both characters interact with their new setting, sometimes in wry puzzlement, always with compassion and delight. The myth of Australian egalitarianism is not invoked, neither is there a single extraneous gag for the benefit of the middle-class audience at the expense of the humble.

The very rapid modification of emotional colour necessary in Mathew dialogue is typical of a later period of playwriting than that in which it was conceived. What might now be dismissed as "pinteresque" was written before Pinter was published. Equally innovatory in the middle 1950's, when it was written, was *Sing for St. Ned*, one of the earliest plays to use extensive sequences in which the cast was encouraged to use the techniques of improvisation. Originally intended for college and university use, this play developed a number of devices now taken for granted in educational theatre. Simultaneous discovery is as common in the arts as in science, logical innovation often arising from experiments in several test-tubes.

Mathew's plays do not "read" well, largely because they depend more on the Chekhovian interaction of characters than upon a strong plot line and resolution. On the printed page his deliberately unsensational vocabulary (much closer to Australian reality than to stereotype stage-Australian vernacular) and the subtle flexibility of his emotional colours both contribute to the same difficulty. The doyenne of Australian drama critics, Eunice Hanger, was the first to perceive Mathew's substantial technical resource, other commentators having often missed the carefully concealed technique. Some find the plays unattractive because Mathew does not attempt to capitalise, as a later crop of playwrights have, on the popular Australian sociological and psychological myths.

Mathew's work was not maximised, either quantitatively or qualitatively, at its point of origin. His characteristic qualities needed to be confirmed and consolidated by major Australian directors and actors. When staged in England, with that form of Cockney-cum-Loamshire which passes there for an Australian dialect, the plays—perhaps predictably—failed.

—Reid Douglas

———

MATURA, Mustapha. Citizen of Trinidad and Tobago. Born in Trinidad, 17 December 1939. Educated at Belmont Boys Roman Catholic Intermediate School, 1944–53. Married Mary Margaret Walsh in 1964; three children. Worked as an office boy and in a solicitor's firm, 1954–57, stocktaker in hotel, 1958–59, insurance salesman, 1959–60, and tally clerk on the docks, 1960–61, all in Trinidad; moved to England,

1961; hospital porter, 1961–62, display assistant in a cosmetic factory, 1962–65; stockroom assistant in a garment factory, 1966–70. Founding chair, Black Theatre Co-operative, London, 1978. Recipient: Arts Council bursary, 1971; John Whiting award, 1972; George Devine award, 1973; *Evening Standard* award, 1975; *Caribbean Times* award, for directing, 1982. Agent: Judy Daish Associates, 83 Eastbourne Mews, London W2 6LQ, England.

PUBLICATIONS

Plays

Black Pieces (includes *Party*, *Indian*, *Dialogue*, *My Enemy*) (produced London, 1970). With *As Time Goes By*, London, Calder and Boyars, 1972.
As Time Goes By (produced Edinburgh and London, 1971). With *Black Pieces*, London, Calder and Boyars, 1972.
Bakerloo Line (produced London, 1972).
Nice (produced London, 1973). Included in *Nice, Rum an' Coca Cola, and Welcome Home Jacko*, 1980.
Play Mas (produced London, 1974; New York, 1976). London, Marion Boyars, 1976.
Black Slaves, White Chains (produced London, 1975).
Bread (produced London, 1976).
Rum an' Coca Cola (produced London, 1976; New York, 1977). Included in *Nice, Rum, an' Coca Cola, and Welcome Home Jacko*, 1980.
More, More (produced London, 1978).
Another Tuesday (produced London, 1978).
Independence (produced London, 1979). Included in *Play Mas, Independence, and Meetings*, 1982.
Welcome Home Jacko (produced London, 1979; New York, 1983). Included in *Nice, Rum, an' Coca Cola, and Welcome Home Jacko*, 1980.
A Dying Business (produced London, 1980).
Nice, Rum an' Coca Cola, and Welcome Home Jacko. London, Eyre Methuen, 1980.
One Rule, music by Victor Romero and John Laddis (produced London, 1981).
Meetings (produced New York, 1981; also director: produced London, 1982). New York, French, 1982; included in *Play Mas, Independence, and Meetings*, 1982.
Play Mas, Independence, and Meetings. London, Methuen, 1982.
The Playboy of the West Indies (produced Oxford and London, 1984; Chicago, 1988).
The Trinidad Sisters, adaptation of *The Three Sisters* by Chekhov (produced London, 1988).
The Coup (produced London, 1991).

Screenplay: *Murders of Boysie Singh*, 1972.

Television Plays: *No Problem* series, with Farrukh Dhondy, 1983; *There's Something Wrong in Paradise*, 1984; *Black Silk* series, with others, 1985.

Other

Moon Jump (for children). London, Heinemann, and New York, Knopf, 1988.

*

Theatrical Activities:
Director: **Plays**—*Meetings*, London, 1982; *Fingers Only* by Yemi Ajibade, London, 1982.

Mustapha Matura comments:
In my writing I have tried to examine the effects of colonialism, political and psychological, on the colonisers and the colonised, hoping that in the magic process of theatre these experiences will lead to eventual liberation.

* * *

The prolific Mustapha Matura was hailed as "the most perceptive and humane black dramatist presently writing in Britain" by Benedict Nightingale as early as 1979. Matura's earlier plays were taken up by the Royal Court and Theatre Upstairs and by the different sections of the London fringe represented by the ICA, the Almost Free, and the Bush. His *Play Mas* was the only work by a Caribbean writer to transfer to the West End. With *The Coup* in 1991 he became the first Caribbean writer to be staged by the National Theatre. In 1978 Matura co-founded the Black Theatre Co-operative with Charlie Hanson; the Co-op has produced his *Welcome Home Jacko* and *One Rule*. Matura gained wider exposure in the 1980's through television scripts: a musical examining black politics through Kid Creole's shipwreck in the Caribbean, *There's Something Wrong in Paradise*; a series about a black barrister in London, devised with Rudy Narayan, *Black Silk*; and a Channel 4 comedy series about five young blacks, *No Problem*, written with Farrukh Dhondy. The 40-minute *Black Slaves, White Chains* is a curiosity in his work, an allegory in which three manacled slaves are discouraged from escape by tempters who offer sex, religion, and books. Two finally accept an offer of work, leaving the third still defiant.

Matura's other plays are best divided into those set among West Indians living in England and plays set in the Caribbean.

As Time Goes By is the most entertaining of the former group. It concerns a plausible Trinidadian East Indian mystic and con-man, a Jonsonian rogue, living in Notting Hill, who solves everyone's problems, for a fee. Other characters include the West Indian father worried that his son has turned into a cockney skinhead and the white hippie couple who steal the con-man's best "pot." His wife longs to return to Trinidad: "Trinidad en much but is we own is a heaven compared to dis. . . . Look, child, is five years I here and every night a go ter bed a pray dat when a open my eyes in de morning a go see de sun shining, home." Matura wants his comedy taken seriously: "*As Time Goes By* is about a black man living in this country and how he's escaping from the realities of being a black man and not looking at the world, this country, in any political context. A lot of it is about his escapism and how he's pretending and not being himself, not being black, not being his own true identity." The jokes and high spirits cover a desperation and near-despair about the struggle to make a bare living in a hostile environment. *Welcome Home Jacko* looks at unemployed boys in a rundown London youth club, who profess faith in rastafarianism but are eventually forced, by the return of Jacko from prison, into a more accurate perception of their blackness.

Play Mas is one of Matura's more ambitious dramas of change in Trinidad. The first half presents Samuel working as a dogsbody in a tailor's shop, being pushed around by his East Indian bosses, mother and son. The time is the early 1950's with the Peoples' National Movement emerging. Samuel goes to a political meeting instead of sweeping the floor, and is sacked. Play Mas, the Carnival, arrives and people revel in the streets in striking costumes. The second half is set several years later, after independence. Samuel has become the local police chief, seeking the source of arms coming to guerrillas on the island. A State of Emergency could prevent Carnival, but Samuel is persuaded to lift the ban, and the Carnival provides an apparent happy ending.

Rum an' Coca Cola has only two characters, composers of calypsos, on a Trinidad beach. The very form of calypso is shown to be degraded by the need to perform "Rum an' Coca Cola," with its refrain, "working for the Yankee dollar." As usual with Matura, the surface lightness is deceptive: he feels passionately about the state of his own part of the Third World.

"In *Independence*," writes Matura in his Author's Note, "I wanted to show that colonialism is a state of mind as well as a political reality and to examine the conflicts created by the leftovers of such attitudes." In this drama two barmen in an old, little-used hotel offer contrasting views. The older clings to memories of the good old days when the hotel was full of tourists while the younger wants to be a farmer and completely discard the colonialism which lingers with the hotel—which the older finally burns down.

Meetings focuses on another facet of independent Trinidad: the successful, though they have riches as well as self-government, are, in Matura's words, "people living outside their landscape, with problems that neither inheritance can solve." *Meetings* is about an affluent Americanised couple, seen in their sterile labour-saving kitchen, enjoying a Mercedes, air-conditioning, and a swimming-pool. Both lead a hectic life of business meetings. The man, however, influenced by a new young cook in the household, discovers a preference for traditional foods, breadfruit and coconut leaves. This leads to growing commitment to his roots, talking to old people with tales of slave revolts, and to taking part in a shango, an ecstatic African-based ritual—to the horror of his wife, who says that she did not marry a monkey-man. She, meanwhile, sinks into the corruption that follows selling illegally imported cigarettes, and satire turns to tragedy.

The Coup, subtitled "a play of revolutionary dreams," is based on the attempted coup against Eric Williams in 1970. Here Matura uses farce to allude lightly to serious issues of power and the Third World.

The Playboy of the West Indies is an audacious rewriting of J.M. Synge's classic. Matura moves the location from County Mayo to the remote Trinidadian fishing village of Mayaro, so one outpost of the English-speaking world becomes another. Widow Quin becomes Mama Benin, the shebeen becomes a rum-shop, and the local girls bring gifts of molasses and freshwater oysters. The time is 1950; many men are emigrating and the girls fear they will not find husbands. Synge's eloquent Irish poetry becomes a racy, idiomatic, earthily comic Caribbean speech.

The Trinidad Sisters transfers *The Three Sisters* to Port-of-Spain at the start of World War II, with the women dreaming of going to Cambridge. Vershinin is the only white. The colonial world will soon crumble, as Chekhov's Russia did. Matura justified his work: "It's a wonderful vehicle for familiarising the European who knows the play with West Indian parallels, but also for black Europeans who are soon not going to know anything about the West Indies."

Matura has remarked: "I respond differently to each new play I write. . . . So it would be less than accurate, and misleading, to find one common perception throughout my work." Matura's subjects are the state of former black colonies and of blacks in Britain, usually treated with apparent lightness, and with a mastery of all the possibilities of Trinidadian speech.

—Malcolm Page

MAY, Elaine. American. Born in 1932.
See 2nd edition, 1977.

McCABE, Eugene. Irish. Born in Glasgow, Scotland, 7 July 1930. Educated at Castleknock College, Dublin; University College, Cork, B.A. 1953. Married Margôt Bowen in 1955; one daughter and three sons. Since 1955 farmer in County Monaghan. Chair Patrick Kavanagh Society, 1970–73. Recipient: *Irish Life* award, 1964; Prague Festival award, for television play, 1974; Irish Critics award, for television play, 1976; Royal Society of Literature Winifred Holtby prize, for fiction, 1977; Reading Association of Ireland award, for children's book, 1987. Agent: Macnaughton Lowe Representation, 200 Fulham Road, London SW10 9PN, England. Address: Drumard, Clones, County Monaghan, Ireland.

PUBLICATIONS

Plays

The King of the Castle (produced Dublin, 1964; New York, 1978). Dublin, Gallery Press, and Newark, Delaware, Proscenium Press, 1978.
Breakdown (produced Dublin, 1966).
Pull Down a Horseman (produced Dublin, 1966). With *Gale Day*, Dublin, Gallery Press, 1979.
Swift (produced Dublin, 1969).
Victims (trilogy; includes *Cancer, Heritage, Victims*), adaptation of his own fiction (televised 1976; produced Belfast, 1981). Cork, Mercier Press, 1976; *Cancer* published Newark, Delaware, Proscenium Press, 1980.
Roma, adaptation of his own story (televised 1979). Dublin, Turoe Press, 1979.
Gale Day (televised 1979; produced Dublin, 1979). With *Pull Down a Horseman*, Dublin, Gallery Press, 1979.

Television Plays: *A Matter of Conscience*, 1962; *Some Women on the Island*, 1966; *The Funeral*, 1969; *Victims* (trilogy), 1976; *Roma*, 1979; *Gale Day*, 1979; *Music at Annahullion*, from his own short story, 1982; *The Year of the French*, with Pierre Lary, from the novel by Thomas Flanagan, 1983.

Novel

Victims: A Tale from Fermanagh. London, Gollancz, 1976.

Short Stories

Heritage and Other Stories. London, Gollancz, 1978.

Other

Cyril: The Quest of an Orphaned Squirrel (for children). Dublin, O'Brien Press, 1986.

*   *   *

Eugene McCabe's output is small: one could wish for more plays from such a talent. In the 1980's he turned more to fiction and television as his media, winning much acclaim for his adaptation of Thomas Flanagan's best-selling historical novel *The Year of the French*. As playwright, McCabe belongs to the 1960's, when he was instrumental, together with such dramatists as Brian Friel, Thomas Murphy, and John B. Keane, in revitalizing the moribund Irish theatre (symptomatic of which was the Abbey Theatre's ultra-conservatism at this period).

McCabe's plays have a forthrightness that must be seen in the context of theatrical and cultural conditions in an Ireland emergent from isolationism and about to come to terms with changes and challenges brought by television, the EEC, air travel, and an affluence deriving from unprecedented industrial development. *The King of the Castle* challenged certain taboos in Irish society by presenting for contemplation the spectacle of a childless couple goaded by social attitudes towards sex and fertility into hiring a surrogate father. The setting is a farm in County Monaghan, where Scober Mac Adam is harvesting and has many hired hands and petty farmers in assistance. A proud and powerful figure, Scober is all too sensitive to the mocks and jeers of those who look on his pretty wife Tressa and fault Scober for her childlessness. The imagery and atmosphere of the harvest reinforce Scober's bitter sense of sterility, and unknown to Tressa he encourages a young labourer, Matt Lynch, to think of her as in need of him. When she discovers the monstrous notion that Scober has planned, Tressa, a sympathetic character, is shattered. Ironically, Scober has succeeded only in driving her further away from him than ever, while the mockery of the "chorus" of Hardy-esque locals is not silenced but increased. Written with sensitivity as well as appropriate frankness, this play is McCabe's greatest claim to attention as a dramatist. It is, one might say, an Irish *Desire under the Elms*. It won for McCabe the prestigious *Irish Life* award.

Two unpublished plays followed: *Breakdown* and *Swift*. Neither was a success. *Breakdown*, a play about the new Ireland of big business deals and shady ethical standards, could nevertheless be regarded as rather old-fashioned in its moral approach, "pure Ibsen through the idiom," as the *Irish Times* reviewer put it. *Swift* was a major production at the Abbey with Tyrone Guthrie directing, Tanya Moisiewitch designing, and Micheál MacLiammóir from the Gate Theatre starring as Swift. The *Irish Times* reviewer described the play as "an episodic, impressionistic chronicle" and found it somewhat tedious, in spite of (or can it have been because of?) the stars descending amid the homely Abbey company. The subsequent television adaptation of *Swift* indicated that the proper medium for McCabe's main theme, Swift's madness, was film rather than theatre. But in tackling the theme for the stage he was joining a long and distinguished line of Irish dramatists fascinated by the mysteries of Swift's biography: Yeats, Lord Longford, and Denis Johnston, for example.

The greater success on television of *Swift* may have inclined McCabe towards that medium and away from the stage. Yet he did, in fact, write once more for the stage with *Gale Day*, a short play about Patrick Pearse. This was written at a time when revisionist historians were depicting Pearse as less than heroic, and, indeed, seriously flawed. *Gale Day* puts Pearse on trial and presents him as sympathetic and courageous in spite of the charges laid against him. This play makes a pendant to an earlier short piece in which Pearse and James Connolly hold a debate over the true nature of Irish republicanism, *Pull Down a Horseman*. McCabe does not take sides between the romantic idealist and the socialist.

With his three-part television drama on the Northern Ireland situation, *Cancer*, *Heritage*, and *Victims*, McCabe reached a wider audience with enormous success. Using fiction that McCabe had either already published or was about to publish, these plays carried a documentary quality that was both new and powerful on Irish television. From his native vantage point in the border county of Monaghan adjoining the rural population of Fermanagh that is sharply divided on sectarian lines, McCabe can communicate through codes of language and skilful subtext startling and even shocking insights into the ways violence blasts through coexistence and undermines human feeling. As one character puts it in *Heritage*: "men who don't want to hate are pushed to it" and must take sides. McCabe probably said all he wanted to say about the Northern Ireland tragedy in these three plays. Subsequently, he wrote a simple study of a tramp figure, an Irish Mad Tom, in *Roma*, based on a story with the same title already published in *Heritage and Other Stories*. The confused mind of the old man could be seen as an image of Irish consciousness strained by the twin forces of loyalty to traditional pieties and the necessity to see and accept changes in moral standards when doors are opened to foreign influences. The concern with "breakdown" under one kind of strain or another has been McCabe's enduring theme as a playwright, and it is found again even in so minor a piece as *Roma*.

—Christopher Murray

McCARTEN, Anthony (Peter Chanel Thomas Aquinas). New Zealander. Born in New Plymouth, 28 April 1961. Educated at Francis Douglas Memorial College, New Plymouth, graduated 1979; Victoria University, Wellington, B.A. 1987. Married Fiona Mathieson in 1988 (divorced 1992); one son. Journalist, Taranaki *Herald*, New Plymouth, 1979–82; musician, Anthony Takes A Bath, Wellington, 1989. Recipient: Queen Elizabeth II Arts Council grant, 1989, 1990, 1991; New Zealand *Listener* award, 1991: Wellington Theatre Critics award, 1991. Agent: Playmarket, P.O. Box 9767, Wellington, New Zealand; and, Casarotto Ramsay, National House, 60–66 Wardour Street, London W1V 3HP, England.

PUBLICATIONS

Plays

Cyril Ellis, Where Are You? (produced Wellington, 1984).
Yellow Canary Mazurka (produced Wellington, 1987).
Ladies Night, with Stephen Sinclair (produced Auckland, 1988; Oldham, Greater Manchester, 1989; London, 1990).
Pigeon English (produced Wellington, 1989).
Weed (produced Wellington, 1990).
Via Satellite (produced Wellington, 1991).
Hang On a Minute Mate! (produced Wellington, 1992).

Short Stories

A Modest Apocalypse. Auckland, Godwit Press, 1991.

*

Anthony McCarten comments:

I come from out of a rural farming tradition, small towns and ordinary people are my characters. My plays, by and large, try to place these ordinary people in extraordinary situations, thereby forcing them to reveal their true character. Often as not, they are funny.

*   *   *

To write nine plays in nine years and have most of them staged at least once is not a bad start for a New Zealand playwright who has only just passed his 30th birthday. When one of these plays also becomes a runaway success, tours extensively in Australasia, and goes on to three tours of Britain produced by Michael Codron, then to Europe in translation, and even makes money, then that playwright can be said to have arrived.

And yet there is the feeling that Anthony McCarten is still searching for a winning formula rather than trying to express his own, deeply felt ideas. In his first play, *Cyril Ellis, Where Are You?*, McCarten experimented with form and came up with a mixture of the bizarre and the comic. A group of widely disparate people travel by train on Christmas Eve 1951, a date all New Zealanders remember as the Tangiwai Disaster, when a train ploughed into a swollen river causing many deaths. He was partly successful in showing the alienated condition of New Zealanders, and he was welcomed as a promising new talent.

Yellow Canary Mazurka addressed the plight of those lonely and rejected people who live in high-rise apartments and only just manage to communicate. Comedy was his mode, because that is what audiences in Wellington resolutely seemed to want, and the play was again well-received, and the tragicomedy of the situation recognised. A second production in Auckland was considered "as tight a piece of writing as one could wish for . . . a crazy love story, part black comedy, part Pinteresque farce, which functions as a perfect paradigm of urban angst."

In 1987 he collaborated with Stephen Sinclair to produce the phenomenally successful *Ladies Night*, which encouraged him to claim to be "the first New Zealander of his generation to emerge as an international force in the writing of plays". While this is too grandiose a claim at present, it may well soon prove to be true.

Ladies Night tells of five young men despairingly on the dole, who decide to try anything to earn some money, including stripping at a night club. Arrogantly confident at first that they have nothing to learn, they are forced to change their ideas about what women want and to sharpen their performance skills while improving their physiques. They learn some of life's lessons and emerge sharper, nastier, but certainly more confident—and much, much richer. Their highly charged strip-acts end the play, each performer having developed his own specialty act to fit his personality. Audiences for *Ladies Night* came from the wider non-theatre-going crowd and many young women made multiple visits to watch what became a dramatised version of a sex show, but with laughs.

Ladies Night has had numerous productions and resists critical disapproval, quickly becoming the most widely-seen New Zealand play ever. Translated, it has gone to Germany, Austria, Spain, and Italy, proving that some pleasures are common to women the world over.

By the time his fourth play, *Pigeon English*, made it to the stage in 1989, it had been three or four years in preparation. A whimsical satire on local government bureaucrats faced with the dilemma of removing pigeons from the town hall clock, it failed to live up to expectations.

Weed took up the plight of New Zealand's farmers faced with financial ruin after oil shocks, stock market crashes, and European Community exclusions, with the happy suggestion of a really lucrative cash crop—marijuana—to help them

trade their way out of difficulties in true monetarist manner. Originally titled *A Secret Economy*, this genuinely Kiwi play has proved popular and has had revivals all over the country.

Consistent only in that he writes comedy in various shades of black, McCarten next explored the rich vein of domestic comedy with *Via Satellite*. A family (consisting of mother, four remaining daughters, and the husband of one of them) wait for the appearance on television of a fifth daughter about to go for gold at the Olympics. They also await the even more disruptive arrival of a television crew to film the family watching the event for satellite relay to the waiting world. Civil war has been raging in this family for a long time, and each knows and dreads the moves the other will make. Each responds in her own way to the success of the famous sister and the play gives fine opportunities for dynamic and comic performances from five women. When the crew arrives the complications intensify and all is only just resolved by curtain time. Farce is hovering, but is kept at bay. McCarten lays claim in programme notes and interviews to a more serious intent, saying that he is examining the way a family brings up its members, and that there may be some connection between the success of one and the failure of another. The play does not justify these claims, but it has brilliant dialogue, funny situations, and skilful construction. McCarten is becoming a master of comedy.

Barry Crump is a New Zealand writer of yarns about blokes in the bush, and McCarten's next enterprise, *Hang On a Minute Mate!* was to adapt some of these into a full-length play. Overburdened by a complicated revolving set and a Model-A Ford trundling on and off, the play was too long and cumbersome in performance, although the theatre proved that careful marketing could find a new audience for this genre.

A solo piece for a modern young man who expresses his dislocation from and dysfunction in today's society, called *Let's Spend the Night Together*, is emerging from workshop and rehearsed reading. Together with Stephen Sinclair again, he has *Legless* or *The Curse of the Wedgecombes* ready to go into production. This comedy-spoof murder mystery with allegorical overtones of the split between Britain and her erstwhile Dominions may well prove another hit for this team. Meanwhile McCarten's path continues upwards and his ambition drives him towards international markets for his plays.

—Patricia Cooke

————————

McCLURE, Michael (Thomas). American. Born in Marysville, Kansas, 20 October 1932. Educated at the University of Wichita, Kansas, 1951–53; University of Arizona, Tucson, 1953–54; San Francisco State University, B.A. 1955. Married Joanna Kinnison in 1954 (divorced), one daughter. Assistant professor, 1962–77, associate professor, 1977, and since 1978 professor, California College of Arts and Crafts, Oakland. Playwright-in-residence, American Conservatory Theatre, San Francisco, 1975; associate fellow, Pierson College, Yale University, New Haven, Connecticut, 1982. Editor, with James Harmon, *Ark II/Moby I*, San Francisco, 1957. Recipient: National Endowment for the Arts grant, 1967, 1974; Guggenheim fellowship, 1971; Magic Theatre Alfred Jarry award, 1974; Rockefeller fellowship,

1975; Obie award, 1978. Agent: Helen Merrill Ltd., 361 West 17th Street, New York, New York 10011. Address: 5862 Balboa Drive, Oakland, California 94611, U.S.A.

PUBLICATIONS

Plays

!The Feast! (produced San Francisco, 1960). Included in *The Mammals*, 1972.

Pillow (produced New York, 1961). Included in *The Mammals*, 1972.

The Growl, in *Four in Hand* (produced Berkeley, California, 1970; produced separately New York, 1976). Published in *Evergreen Review* (New York), April–May 1964.

The Blossom; or, Billy the Kid (produced New York, 1964). Milwaukee, Great Lakes Books, 1967.

The Beard (produced San Francisco, 1965; New York, 1967; London, 1968). Privately printed, 1965; revised version, New York, Grove Press, 1967.

The Shell (produced San Francisco, 1970; London, 1975). London, Cape Goliard Press, 1968; in *Gargoyle Cartoons*, 1971.

The Cherub (produced Berkeley, California, 1969). Los Angeles, Black Sparrow Press, 1970.

The Charbroiled Chinchilla: The Pansy, The Meatball, Spider Rabbit (produced Berkeley, California, 1969). Included in *Gargoyle Cartoons*, 1971.

Little Odes, Poems, and a Play, The Raptors. Los Angeles, Black Sparrow Press, 1969.

The Brutal Brontosaurus: Spider Rabbit, The Meatball, The Shell, Apple Glove, The Authentic Radio Life of Bruce Conner and Snoutburbler (produced San Francisco, 1970; *The Meatball* and *Spider Rabbit* produced London, 1971; New York, 1976; *The Authentic Radio Life of Bruce Conner and Snoutburbler* produced London, 1975). Included in *Gargoyle Cartoons*, 1971.

Gargoyle Cartoons (includes *The Shell, The Pansy, The Meatball, The Bow, Spider Rabbit, Apple Glove, The Sail, The Dear, The Authentic Radio Life of Bruce Conner and Snoutburbler, The Feather, The Cherub*). New York, Delacorte Press, 1971.

The Pansy (produced London, 1972). Included in *Gargoyle Cartoons*, 1971.

Polymorphous Pirates: The Pussy, The Button, The Feather (produced Berkeley, California, 1972). *The Feather* included in *Gargoyle Cartoons*, 1971.

The Mammals (includes *The Blossom, !The Feast!, Pillow*). San Francisco, Cranium Press, 1972.

The Grabbing of the Fairy (produced Los Angeles, 1973). St. Paul, Truck Press, 1978.

The Pussy, The Button, and Chekhov's Grandmother; or, The Sugar Wolves (produced New York, 1973).

McClure on Toast (produced Los Angeles, 1973).

Gorf (produced San Francisco, 1974). New York, New Directions, 1976.

Music Peace (produced San Francisco, 1974).

The Derby (produced Los Angeles, 1974; revised version produced New York, 1981).

General Gorgeous (produced San Francisco, 1975; Edinburgh, 1976). New York, Dramatists Play Service, 1982.

Two Plays. Privately printed, 1975.

Sunny-Side Up (includes *The Pink Helmet* and *The Masked Choir*) (produced Los Angeles, 1976). *The Pink Helmet* included in *Two Plays*, 1975; *The Masked Choir* published in *Performing Arts Journal* (New York), August 1976.

Minnie Mouse and the Tap-Dancing Buddha (produced San Francisco, 1978). Included in *Two Plays*, 1975.

Two for the Tricentennial (includes *The Pink Helmet* and *The Grabbing of the Fairy*) (produced San Francisco, 1976).

Range War (produced Tucson, 1976).

Goethe: Ein Fragment (produced San Francisco, 1977). Published in *West Coast Plays 2* (Berkeley, California), Spring 1978.

Josephine the Mouse Singer, adaptation of a story by Kafka (produced New York, 1978). New York, New Directions, 1980.

The Red Snake (produced San Francisco, 1979).

The Mirror (produced Los Angeles, 1979).

Coyote in Chains (produced San Francisco, 1980).

The Velvet Edge. Privately printed, 1982(?).

The Beard, and VKTMS: Two Plays, (*VKTMS* produced New York, 1988). New York, Grove Press, 1985.

Television Play: *The Maze* (documentary), 1967.

Video: *Love Lion*, 1991.

Novels

The Mad Cub. New York, Bantam, 1970.

The Adept. New York, Delacorte Press, 1971.

Verse

Passage. Big Sur, California, Jonathan Williams, 1956.

Peyote Poem. San Francisco, Wallace Berman, 1958.

For Artaud. New York, Totem Press, 1959.

Hymns to St. Geryon and Other Poems. San Francisco, Auerhahn Press, 1959.

The New Book: A Book of Torture. New York, Grove Press, 1961.

Dark Brown. San Francisco, Auerhahn Press, 1961.

Two for Bruce Conner. San Francisco, Oyez, 1964.

Ghost Tantras. Privately printed, 1964.

Double Murder! Vahrooooooohr! Los Angeles, Wallace Berman, 1964.

Love Lion, Lioness. Privately printed, 1964.

13 Mad Sonnets. Milan, East 128, 1964.

Poisoned Wheat. Privately printed, 1965.

Unto Caesar. San Francisco, Dave Haselwood, 1965.

Mandalas. San Francisco, Dave Haselwood, 1966.

Dream Table. San Francisco, Dave Haselwood, 1966.

Love Lion Book. San Francisco, Four Seasons, 1966.

Hail Thee Who Play. Los Angeles, Black Sparrow Press, 1968; revised edition, Berkeley, California, Sand Dollar, 1974.

Muscled Apple Swift. Topanga, California, Love Press, 1968.

Plane Pomes. New York, Phoenix Book Shop, 1969.

Oh Christ God Love Cry of Love Stifled Furred Wall Smoking Burning. San Francisco, Auerhahn Press, 1969(?).

The Sermons of Jean Harlow and the Curses of Billy the Kid. San Francisco, Four Seasons, 1969.

The Surge. Columbus, Ohio, Frontier Press, 1969.

Hymns to St. Geryon, and Dark Brown. London, Cape Goliard Press, 1969; San Francisco, Grey Fox Press, 1980.

Lion Fight. New York, Pierrepont Press, 1969.

Star. New York, Grove Press, 1971.

99 Theses. Lawrence, Kansas, Tansy Press, 1972.

The Book of Joanna. Berkeley, California, Sand Dollar, 1973.

Transfiguration. Cambridge, Massachusetts, Pomegranate Press, 1973.

Rare Angel (writ with raven's blood). Los Angeles, Black Sparrow Press, 1974.

September Blackberries. New York, New Directions, 1974.

Solstice Blossom. Berkeley, California, Arif Press, 1974.

Fleas 189–195. New York, Aloes, 1974.

A Fist Full (1956–1957). Los Angeles, Black Sparrow Press, 1974.

On Organism. Canton, New York, Institute of Further Studies, 1974.

Jaguar Skies. New York, New Directions, 1975.

Man of Moderation. New York, Hallman, 1975.

Flea 100. New York, Hallman, 1975.

Ah Yes. Berkeley, California, Poythress Press, 1976.

Antechamber. Berkeley, California, Poythress Press, 1977.

Antechamber and Other Poems. New York, New Directions, 1978.

Fragments of Perseus. New York, Jordan Davies, 1978.

Letters. New York, Jordan Davies, 1978.

Seasons, with Joanna McClure, Berkeley, California, Arif, 1981.

The Book of Benjamin, with Wesley B. Tanner. Berkeley, California, Arif, 1982.

Fragments of Perseus (collection). New York, New Directions, 1983.

Fleas 180–186. Berkeley, California, Les Ferriss, 1985.

Selected Poems. New York, New Directions, 1986.

Rebel Lions. New York, New Directions, 1991.

Other

Meat Science Essays. San Francisco, City Lights, 1963; revised edition, San Francisco, Dave Haselwood, 1967.

Freewheelin' Frank, Secretary of the Angels, as Told to Michael McClure by Frank Reynolds. New York, Grove Press, 1967; London, New English Library, 1974.

Scratching the Beat Surface. Berkeley, California, North Point Press, 1982.

Specks (essays). Vancouver, Talonbooks, 1985.

Testa Coda. New York, Rizzoli, 1991.

Editor, with David Meltzer and Lawrence Ferlinghetti, *Journal for the Protection of All Beings 1 and 3*. San Francisco, City Lights, 2 vols., 1961–69.

*

Bibliography: A *Catalogue of Works by Michael McClure 1956–1965* by Marshall Clements, New York, Phoenix Book Shop, 1965.

Manuscript Collections: Simon Fraser University, Burnaby, British Columbia; University of California, Berkeley.

Critical Studies: "This Is Geryon," in *Times Literary Supplement* (London), 25 March 1965; interview in *San Francisco Poets* edited by David Meltzer, New York, Ballantine, 1971, revised edition, as *Golden Gate*, San Francisco, Wingbow Press, 1976; "Michael McClure Symposium" in *Margins 18* (Milwaukee), March 1975.

Theatrical Activities:
Actor: **Films**—*Beyond the Law*, 1968; *Maidstone*, 1971.

Michael McClure comments:
    Theatre is an organism of poetry—weeping, and laughing, and crying, and smiling, and performing superhuman acts—on a shelf in space and lit with lights.

*   *   *

Michael McClure's curious and highly personal amalgams of Artaud, pop art playfulness, surrealism, and Eastern mysticism seek to bridge the Romantic gap, to join the mind and body in what he calls *spiritmeat*. His first attempt in this ambitious project was a succès de scandale, *The Beard*, in which two archetypes of American dreams, Jean Harlow and Billy the Kid, confront each other outside time and place. Harlow's challenge, "Before you can pry any secrets from me, you must first find the real me! Which one will you choose?" counterpoints Billy's "You're divine," and "You're a bag of meat," two McClurean identities. *The Beard* avoids the implied metaphysics of meaty divinity, since rational argument could only intensify the split between the senses and the spirit. Instead, Billy and Harlow's verbal duel becomes increasingly sexual and violent, pulsating to an ecstatic climax rather than a resolution.

McClure has tried to extend our concept of what humanity is, first by emphasizing man's animality. *!The Feast!* was written in grahr language, sound-poetry based on animal grunts growls, howls and groans, which gradually evolved into mystical imagery:

> There's no light in the closed rose but a tiny black cherub sleeps there and sings to the creatures that walk in the cliffs of the Lily's pollen, moving from shadow to light in the drips of rain. The seen is as black as the eye seeing it.

At its best, such language is difficult to sustain in the theatre and for *Gargoyle Cartoons* and subsequent plays up to *Minnie Mouse and the Tap-Dancing Buddha* McClure returned to the more direct statement of *The Beard*. These plays present his metaphysics in what is almost a parody of Beat slang: "from the moment of birth till the hour we're zapped and boogie to the grave, we're thoroughly enwrapped in the realms of being. How can we know nothing, and know especially that even nothing isn't something, if there's always *Being* there?" Although these bald statements have little dramatic value, the best of the plays are oddly unsettling glimpses of human nature, and humans and nature. The combination spider and rabbit of *Spider Rabbit* wanders absent-mindedly onstage, and decides to show and tell. Producing a head from his bag he saws it open: "BOY AM I HUNGRY! This is the brain of a soldier. BOY, do I hate war. (The head quivers as Spider Rabbit proceeds to eat it with the spoon.) I'M OUT OF CARROTS. BOY, DO I HATE WAR." Few of the plays blend social satire and sight gag so sharply, but they all have a reckless playfulness, a freedom to explore the theatre's sensuous possibilities and the audience's expectations about the theatre.

Despite their frequent childishness, McClure felt these plays illustrated the universe's basic nature, which embraces the silly and shallow as well as the profound. More recently, however he decided "I'd carried that stream of comedies where the universe created the plays to an extreme that completed my expectations and satisfactions in that mode. So at this time, I've nothing further to say in that vein." Since then (about 1978), his work has focused largely on the relation of art to society. In *Goethe: Ein Fragment*, Mephistopheles offers a callow, arrogant young Goethe a deal: if Goethe will write a play that immortalizes the devil, the playwright will receive a second life. This alternate life is the play called *Faust*, and with this arrangement, McClure plays with the relative importance of the artist and his creation. Not only is the devil a more sympathetic character than Goethe, both of them frequently become subordinate to the play *Faust*. As Mephistopheles says, "Everything real or imagined exists everywhere at once," and McClure suggests that what is imagined is less mortal than ordinary reality, a state that is performed behind a scrim in *Goethe: Ein Fragment*.

Like *Goethe* and the clumsy *The Red Snake* (based on James Shirley's 1641 *The Cardinal*), McClure's *Josephine the Mouse Singer* is drawn from existing literature, Kafka's delicate and eloquent short story. The play won an Obie award for its script before it was produced in New York, and its best dialogue is the narration taken directly from Kafka. However, McClure effectively dramatizes the central problem: Is Josephine's art, brilliant as it is, more important than the dull grey mouse society? Josephine, proud and demanding, is willing to break all the rules of society in order to give it better art, but at the same time she threatens to destroy it. Neither, Kafka nor McClure is foolhardy enough to try to resolve this dilemma, but in dramatizing it, McClure produced some of the best writing of his career.

—Walter Bode

—————

McGEE, Greg(ory William). New Zealander. Born in Oamaru, 22 October 1950. Educated at Waitaki Boys High School; University of Otago, Dunedin, LL.B. 1973. Married Mary Davy; one daughter. Literary fellow, University of Auckland, 1982. Agent: Playmarket, P.O. Box 9767, Wellington. Address: 8 John Street, Ponsonby, Auckland 2, New Zealand.

PUBLICATIONS

Plays

Foreskin's Lament (produced Auckland, 1980). Wellington, Victoria University Press, 1981.
Tooth and Claw (produced Wellington, 1983). Wellington, Victoria University Press, 1984.
Out in the Cold (produced Auckland, 1983). Wellington, Victoria University Press, 1984.
Whitemen (produced Auckland, 1986).

Television Plays: *Free Enterprise*, 1982; *Mortimer's Patch* series, 1984; *Roche* series, 1985.

*

Greg McGee comments:

The colour, vitality, humour, and general excess I have tried to bring to my work, particularly *Foreskin's Lament*, *Out in the Cold*, and *Whitemen*, are reactions against the traditional literary perception of New Zealand as a dull, grey, colourless place which forced most of our writers and artists into cultural exile. Even those who stayed, like Frank Sargeson, seem in their work to share this "colonial" view of New Zealand as culturally bankrupt. It has been a view that has been too easily accepted by our novelists and short story writers, many of whom felt unable to work here.

I have no such difficulties and I glory in the idiosyncrasies of a very inventive New Zealand colloquial English. The burgeoning Maori writing presence does not seem to be having any difficulties, either, in throwing off the yoke of

what, after all, was a very pakeha (white) perception of this land.

*   *   *

From its first production in 1980, Greg McGee's *Foreskin's Lament* was immediately recognised as the most strident piece of confrontational realism in New Zealand drama. For some theatre-goers, the play was simply about rugby: the first act set in a changing room on practice night, the second act at a party after the Saturday match. Most people, however, also followed the argument of the character nicknamed Foreskin, that the rugby player is "the heart and bowels" of New Zealand society, the greatest influence on New Zealand law and ethics; rugby, with its associations of brutality and insensitivity, thus becomes a metaphor for New Zealand life, the "larger game." The team is a herd, which represents a society, and the action essentially consists of an individual detaching himself from the herd, articulating his independence, and then being absorbed back into the herd. Foreskin's mission is not to undermine rugby or destroy the team, of which he is the (valued) fullback; he simply wants to encourage them to play better rugby, to teach them a primitive altruism on the field. The coach, whose ethic is to "kick shit out of everything above grass height," protests that he "does not understand the meaning of the word" altruism, and in the second half of the play Foreskin's defeat is reflected in his retreat into the coach's language. As Foreskin realises that his stance is hopeless, he moves into his "lament," which begins as a parody of a formal speech at the party (echoing the speech which the acting captain made at the start of the act), although the subject now is the death of a team-mate; gradually, the speech turns into a more general threnody for the lost heroes of New Zealand rugby, and the style becomes increasingly poetical, with invented verbs of loss and fragmentation. The stance of the individual against the collective has obvious parallels in Ibsen and Bond, and the central action (a villainous scheme against the captain, resulting in his death) is the stuff of sporting melodrama. However, McGee's depiction of the bonds which give cohesion to the team, and the nuances of language in which the slogans are asserted, questioned, and reasserted, constitute the finest piece of social realism in New Zealand drama to that point. (The published script of *Foreskin's Lament* is based on the version used in the premiere productions; McGee has subsequently modified the play considerably, and the performance script held by his agents does not even contain the final poetical "lament.")

McGee's second play, *Free Enterprise*, was a disappointment, a television situation comedy about the thwarting of a cafe owner. His next two stage plays, however, were much more substantial. *Tooth and Claw* is set in a law office (McGee's own profession), with a large central screen serving sometimes as a window (suggesting that events in the city are being monitored from the executive tower) and sometimes a depiction of the lawyer's mental state, illustrating his anxieties, for his own reflective scrutiny. Before the first lines of dialogue, a black-and-white screen image of civic anarchy, being viewed in dismay by the lawyer, suggests that there is again to be a metaphorical expansion of the action; however, it also becomes clear that there is really disorder in the streets, and that the lawyer's nightmare is derived from a recent incident in which he was actually assaulted and robbed by a Maori activist (who expressionistically appears on stage as a mime). The immediate action consists of politely veiled blackmail from a former student flatmate who is now a speculator and entrepreneur, manipulations which are reflected in two senior law partners as well. The guilty past is analysed and confessed in clinical detail, a method which contrasts strongly with the remarkable vagueness with which the wider present and imminent future are depicted.

In the same year as *Tooth and Claw*, *Out in the Cold* was premiered as a stage play, although its outline was already familiar from McGee's short story of the same title. Summarised, it sounds like a situation comedy: Judy, a former student and now a solo mother, tries to pass herself off as a man to get a well-paid heavy labouring job in the chamber at the local freezing works. The imminent general peripeteia which will occur when her real identity is discovered—as it is transparently obvious it will be—means that there is a good deal of comic suspense pivoting on the inevitable rethinking of attitudes. However, like rugby in the earlier play, the meat works is here a metaphor for Kiwi masculinity—or the packaging of masculinity—and the facility with which it can be penetrated and possibly punctured means that the overt comedy is supported by rich implicit ironies. A 1985 television version began with a brief introduction without dialogue in which Judy, sunbathing naked, got up, cut her hair and dressed as a man before going to the employment room at the freezing works; this clarified some of the possible early ambiguities in the stage version, and generated strong sympathy with Judy from the start. The screen also allowed meticulous coverage of the butchery process, and the camera dwelt on the labyrinthine concrete expanses of the works, which became even more clearly a physical correlative to a bizarre social system.

McGee's fourth stage play, *Whitemen*, was a resounding critical and commercial failure, and has not been published. However, such has been the continuing impact of his earlier works that several companies have successfully mounted second productions, exploring different approaches.

—Howard McNaughton

———

McGRATH, John (Peter). British. Born in Birkenhead, Cheshire, 1 June 1935. Educated at Alun Grammar School, Mold, Wales; St. John's College, Oxford (Open Exhibitioner), 1955–59, Dip.Ed. Served in the British Army (national service), 1953–55. Married Elizabeth MacLennan in 1962; two sons and one daughter. Farm worker, Neston, Cheshire, 1951; play reader, Royal Court Theatre, London, and television writer and director, 1959–65. Founder and artistic director, 7:84 Theatre Company, 1971–88 (divided into Scottish and English companies, 1973); since 1983 founding director, Freeway Films. Since 1989 director, Channel Four Television, London. Judith E. Wilson fellow, Cambridge University, 1979. Agent: Casarotto Ramsay Ltd., National House, 60–66 Wardour Street, London W1V 3HP, England. Address: c/o Freeway Films, 67 George Street, Edinburgh EH2 2JG, Scotland.

PUBLICATIONS

Plays

A Man Has Two Fathers (produced Oxford, 1958).
The Invasion, with Barbara Cannings, adaptation of a play by Arthur Adamov (produced Oxford and Edinburgh, 1958).

The Tent (produced Edinburgh and London, 1958).
Why the Chicken (produced Edinburgh, 1959; revised version produced on tour, 1960).
Tell Me Tell Me (produced London, 1960). Published in *New Departures* (London), 1960.
Take It (produced London, 1960).
The Seagull, adaptation of a play by Chekhov (produced Dundee, 1961).
Basement in Bangkok, music and songs by Dudley Moore (produced Bristol, 1963).
Events While Guarding the Bofors Gun (produced London, 1966). London, Methuen, 1966.
Bakke's Night of Fame, adaptation of the novel *A Danish Gambit* by William Butler (produced London, 1968). London, Davis Poynter, 1973.
Comrade Jacob, adaptation of the novel by David Caute (produced Falmer, Sussex, 1969).
Random Happenings in the Hebrides; or, The Social Democrat and the Stormy Sea (produced Edinburgh, 1970). London, Davis Poynter, 1972.
Sharpeville Crackers (produced London, 1970).
Unruly Elements (includes *Angel of the Morning*, *Plugged-in to History*, *They're Knocking Down the Pie-Shop*, *Hover Through the Fog*, *Out of Sight*) (produced Liverpool, 1971; *Plugged-in to History*, produced London, 1971; *Out of Sight*, *Angel of the Morning*, *They're Knocking Down the Pie-Shop*, and *Hover Through the Fog*, produced London, 1972). *Angel of the Morning*, *Plugged-in to History* and *They're Knocking Down the Pie-Shop*, published as *Plugged-in*, in *Plays and Players* (London), November 1972.
Trees in the Wind (also director: produced Edinburgh and London, 1971, New York, 1974).
Soft or a Girl (produced Liverpool, 1971; revised version, as *My Pal and Me*, also director: produced Edinburgh, 1975).
The Caucasian Chalk Circle, adaptation of a play by Brecht (produced Liverpool, 1972).
Prisoners of the War, adaptation of the play by Peter Terson (produced Liverpool, 1972).
Underneath (also director: produced Liverpool, 1972; London, 1978).
Serjeant Musgrave Dances On, adaptation of the play *Serjeant Musgrave's Dance* by John Arden (produced Stirling, 1972).
Fish in the Sea, music by Mark Brown (produced Liverpool, 1972; revised version produced London, 1975). London, Pluto Press 1977.
The Cheviot, the Stag, and the Black, Black Oil (also director: produced Edinburgh, 1973). Kyleakin, Isle of Skye, West Highland Publishing, 1973; revised version, 1975; revised version, London, Eyre Methuen, 1981.
The Game's a Bogey (also director: produced Aberdeen, 1974). Edinburgh, Edinburgh University Student Publications, 1975.
Boom (also director: produced Golspie, Sutherland, 1974; revised version produced Aberdeen, 1974). Published in *New Edinburgh Review*, August 1975.
Lay Off (also director: produced Lancaster and London, 1975).
Little Red Hen (also director: produced Edinburgh, 1975; London, 1976). London, Pluto Press, 1977.
Oranges and Lemons (also director: produced Amsterdam, 1975; Birmingham, 1977).
Yobbo Nowt, music by Mark Brown (also director: produced York and London, 1975; as *Mum's the Word*, produced Liverpool, 1977; as *Left Out Lady*, produced New York, 1981). London, Pluto Press, 1978.

The Rat Trap, music by Mark Brown (also director: produced Amsterdam and London, 1976).

Out of Our Heads, music by Mark Brown (also director: produced Aberdeen, 1976; London, 1977).

Trembling Giant (English version) (produced Lancaster, 1977).

Trembling Giant (Scottish version) (also director: produced Dundee and London, 1977).

The Life and Times of Joe of England (also director: produced Basildon, Essex, and London, 1977).

Big Square Fields, music by Mark Brown (produced Bradford and London, 1979).

Joe's Drum (also director: produced Aberdeen, 1979). Aberdeen, People's Press, 1979.

Bitter Apples, music by Mark Brown (produced Liverpool, 1979).

If You Want to Know the Time (produced London, 1979).

Swings and Roundabouts (also director: produced Aberdeen, 1980). Included in *Two Plays for the Eighties*, 1981.

Blood Red Roses (also director: produced Edinburgh, 1980; London, 1981; revised version produced Liverpool, 1982). Included in *Two Plays for the Eighties*, 1981.

Two Plays for the Eighties. Aberdeen, People's Press, 1981.

Nightclass, music by Rick Lloyd (also director: produced Corby, Northamptonshire, and London, 1981).

The Catch, music by Mark Brown (produced Edinburgh, 1981).

Rejoice!, music by Mark Brown (produced Edinburgh and London, 1982).

On the Pig's Back, with David MacLennan (produced Kilmarnock, Ayrshire, 1983).

The Women of the Dunes (produced in Dutch, Ijmuiden, Netherlands, 1983).

Women in Power; or, Up the Acropolis, music by Thanos Mikroutsikos, adaptation of plays by Aristophanes (also director: produced Edinburgh, 1983).

Six Men of Dorset, music by John Tams, adaptation of a play by Miles Malleson and Harry Brooks (produced Sheffield and London, 1984).

The Baby and the Bathwater: The Imperial Policeman (produced Cumbernauld, Dunbartonshire, 1984; revised version produced Edinburgh, 1985; London, 1987).

The Albannach, music by Eddie McGuire, adaptation of the novel by Fionn MacColla (produced Edinburgh, 1985).

Behold the Sun (opera libretto), with Alexander Goehr, music by Goehr (produced Duisburg, West Germany, 1985).

All the Fun of the Fair, with others (produced London, 1986).

Border Warfare (also director: produced Glasgow, 1989).

John Brown's Body (also director: produced Glasgow, 1990).

Watching for Dolphins (produced London, 1991).

Screenplays: *Billion Dollar Brain*, 1967; *The Bofors Gun*, 1968; *The Virgin Soldiers*, with John Hopkins and Ian La Fresnais, 1969; *The Reckoning*, 1970; *The Dressmaker*, 1989.

Television Plays: scripts for *Bookstand* series, 1961; *People's Property* (*Z Cars* series), 1962; scripts for *Tempo* series, 1963; *Diary of a Young Man* series, with Troy Kennedy Martin, 1964; *The Entertainers* (documentary), 1964; *The Day of Ragnarok*, 1965; *Mo* (documentary), 1965; *Shotgun*, with Christopher Williams, 1966; *Diary of a Nobody*, with Ken Russell, from the novel by George and Weedon Grossmith, 1966; *Orkney*, from stories by George Mackay Brown, 1971; *Bouncing Boy*, 1972; *Once upon a Union*, 1977; *The Adventures of Frank*, from his play *The Life and Times of Joe*

of England, 1979; *Sweetwater Memories* (documentary), 1984; *Blood Red Roses*, 1986; *There Is a Happy Land*, 1987.

Other

A Good Night Out: Popular Theatre: Audience, Class and Form. London, Eyre Methuen, 1981.

The Bone Won't Break: On Theatre and Hope in Hard Times. London, Methuen, 1990.

Translator, with Maureen Teitelbaum, *The Rules of the Game* (screenplay), by Jean Renoir. London, Lorrimer, 1970.

*

Bibliography: by Malcolm Page, in *New Theatre Quarterly* (Cambridge), November 1985.

Manuscript Collection: University of Cambridge.

Critical Studies: *Disrupting the Spectacle* by Peter Ansorge, London, Pitman, 1975; *British Theatre since 1955* by Ronald Hayman, London and New York, Oxford University Press, 1979; *Stages in the Revolution* by Catherine Itzin, London, Eyre Methuen, 1980; *Dreams and Deconstructions* edited by Sandy Craig, Ambergate, Derbyshire, Amber Lane Press, 1980; "Three Socialist Playwrights" by Christian W. Thomsen, in *Contemporary English Drama* edited by C.W.E. Bigsby, London, Arnold, and New York, Holmes and Meier, 1981, and "The Politics of Anxiety" by Bigsby, in *Modern Drama* (Toronto), December 1981; *Modern Scottish Literature* by Alan Bold, London, Longman, 1983; interview with Oscar Moore, in *Plays and Players* (London), April 1983.

Theatrical Activities:
Director: **Plays**—many of his own plays, and *Bloomsday* by Allan McClelland, Oxford, 1958; *The Birds* by Aristophanes, Oxford, 1959; Live New Departures series of plays, 1961–64; *The Eccentric* by Dannie Abse, London, 1961. **Television**— *Bookstand* series, 1961; *The Compartment* by Johnny Speight, 1961; *Z Cars* series (8 episodes), 1962; *The Fly Sham* by Thomas Murphy, 1963; *The Wedding Dress* by Edna O'Brien, 1963; *The Entertainers* (documentary), 1964; *The Day of Ragnarok*, 1965; *Mo* (documentary), 1965; *Shotgun* by McGrath and Christopher Williams, 1966; *Double Bill* by Johnny Speight, 1972; *Z Cars: The Final Episode*, 1978; *The Adventures of Frank*, 1979; *Come to Mecca* by Farrukh Dhondy, 1983; *Blood Red Roses*, 1986.

John McGrath comments:
(1973) My plays, I now realize, have been from the beginning about the relationship of the individual to other individuals and thence to history. They have pursued this theme in many ways, poetic, comic, tragic, realistic, and latterly more and more freely. Music is now coming to play a more important part in my plays, to help break through the barriers of naturalism which I can no longer tolerate. My work has never suited London (West End) audiences or ways of thinking: it is now being seen by working-class audiences from Orkney to Plymouth, and by young audiences all over the country in the new university theatres and art labs and studio theatres, via the 7:84 Theatre Company. I have also benefited from a thriving relation with the Everyman Theatre, Liverpool, under the direction of Alan Dosser, as previously from working with directors as perceptive and helpful as Ronald Eyre, Anthony Page, and Richard Eyre in Edinburgh.

My plays are not difficult to approach, although they tend to have many levels of meaning embedded fairly deeply under them as well as on the surface. The key, if key is needed, is a growing political consciousness allied to a growing feeling for individual human beings, with all the contradictions that alliance involves.

* * *

The enormity of John McGrath's contribution to the field of contemporary drama will probably never be fully realised, largely because of the way in which he has latterly chosen to direct his energies. Active in the theatre as an undergraduate writer, he immediately went on to earn a place in history as one of the key developers of the dominant mode of modern television naturalism—during his time with the BBC he was jointly responsible for the hugely influential *Z Cars* series. Rejecting a full-time career in television, he turned first to the conventional professional theatre. After *Events While Guarding the Bofors Gun*, a play deriving from his own experience in Army National Service in the 1950's, linkable thematically and in stature with Arnold Wesker's *Chips with Everything*, he produced *Bakke's Night of Fame*, an adaptation of a novel, as well as working on a number of screenplays, including that for his own *The Bofors Gun*.

Interest in the political consciousness of his characters was apparent from the outset but the demands of television and the conventional professional theatre for a well-crafted play with a resolved narrative proved inhibiting. The sense of class confrontation and ideological moulding in *The Bofors Gun*, for instance, is never matched by any strand in the play which suggests a way out of the fatalistically conceived framework of plot and society. What McGrath sought was a way of presenting individuals in conflict with their social context, but in ways which suggested the possibility of change through self-education and experience. This was to involve him in a conscious turning-away from the conventional theatre with what he saw as, at best, its minimally questioning analysis of capitalist society. The problem for him was as much that of audience as theatrical style: "the audience has changed very little in the theatre, the social requirements remain constant, the values remain firmly those of acceptability to a metropolitan middle-class audience, with an eye to similar acceptability on the international cultural market."

The real break with his past—and a consistent turning away from the politically restricting naturalistic mode—came in 1968. McGrath had started work on the first of a long series of plays about Scotland's history and its struggles, *Random Happenings in the Hebrides*. The play was to deal with the attempts of a young Scottish Labour MP to work for change for his island community within the confines of the parliamentary system. In the middle of writing the play, the barricades went up in Paris. McGrath went over and rethought the play, placing a greater emphasis on a non-parliamentary oppositional strategy, but seeing all the time the conflict between the need for political organisation and the immediacy of action that he had witnessed in France. It was a theme that was to dominate much of his later work, taking him progressively further away from naturalism and into various models of agit prop theatre in pursuit of an audience that could be defined in terms of its political potential rather than its interest in the theatre as such.

By 1970, when *Random Happenings* was first produced, McGrath had started a formative period of work with the Liverpool Everyman—including a series of playlets about contemporary Britain, *Unruly Elements* (later retitled *Plugged-in to History*). In 1971 McGrath founded 7:84, a

socialist theatre group intent on taking plays into the kind of non-theatrical venues shunned by the conventional theatrical establishment. Since then he has worked largely in Scotland, producing a string of plays dealing with Scottish socialist strategy in a variety of historical and contemporary contexts —with the occasional production for the English offshoot of 7:84. Productions have varied from the didactic intensity of the first 7:84 piece, *Trees in the Wind*, to offerings, such as the political pantomime *Trembling Giant*, that make use of the loosest of narrative structures to put across a deliberately crude analysis. McGrath's clear awareness of the dangers of arguing for an impossibly simple solution to a highly complex problem—the dilemma of all revolutionaries living in a non-revolutionary age—is brilliantly articulated in the humour and wit of the plays, frequently inviting the audience into the never self-contained discourse. The general method is summed up well by Joe's tongue-in-cheek invitation to the audience to take its seats again after the interval in *Joe's Drum*, a play written in response to the election of a Conservative administration and the failure of the Scottish Assembly vote. They are assured that they should not be frightened off by the fear of weighty material. "It's yer ain true story told in biased argument, highly selective history and emotional folksong. Are ye all back that's comin' back? Right—lock the doors."

McGrath's—and 7:84's—insistence on a theatre that should not only offer enlightenment but entertainment is a key part of the play's acceptance. McGrath has moved progressively away from the kind of consumer society cultural parody that has proved a staple of so much agit prop theatre—as in the "Beat the System" TV show in *The Game's a Bogey*—in search of popular cultural roots that oppose those offered by the consumerist system. The use of the Highland ceilidh form for the first Scottish 7:84 tour in 1973, of *The Cheviot, the Stag, and the Black, Black Oil*, gave McGrath the structure of a traditional evening entertainment through which to tell the story of Scottish exploitation through history to the, then, oil boom. In subsequent plays he was to make the link between the music as part of an oppositional cultural history and the need to question contemporary representations a major part of the shows' dynamics.

McGrath's is a questioning development of agit prop, and his conclusions are usually open-ended, witnessing a small personal achievement perhaps but not proclaiming the imminence of revolutionary change. And in this context, his depiction of the particular dilemma of women caught in the dual webs of capitalism and a male-oriented ideology has emerged as a major theme in his work. In *Joe's Drum* his wife is a continual presence, chipping away at masculine vanities, and in a play such as *Yobbo Nowt* all the emphasis is placed on the struggles of a wife after she has ejected an unfeeling husband. Her discovery of the way in which the system operates against the "have-nots" parallels her own discovery of individual potential, and the play ends with a small personal leap forward.

McGrath has continued to produce work at a prolific rate— always with a central interest in the way in which the individual can operate against the increasingly sophisticated and endlessly elastic models of late capitalist society. The overall effect is to suggest the way in which the various manifestations of authority and oppression are a part of a single system and thus linkable, as they are from one play to another—each then becoming just one in a series of views through the different windows of a part of the same enormous construction. In *Blood Red Roses*, he traced the political struggles of Bessie from the 1950's to the present day; she is just one of what is by now a very large political family assured of an audience away from the subsidised and commercial theatres of London where reputations are made. However, his insistence on the continual tracing of that struggle has itself been a great struggle and, as McGrath recounts in *The Bone Won't Break*, the establishment, and in particular that part of the establishment holding the purse-strings of the Arts Council, has continually opposed the efforts of McGrath and 7:84—to the extent that the company has at last ceased to operate. As a result, stage productions from McGrath have become less frequent of late—although the 1990 *John Brown's Body* at Glasgow's Tramway, in which the dominant stage feature was a huge platform along three walls from which the ruling-class characters controlled and directed the workers and audience on stage level, saw him continue unabashed. More energy has inevitably gone into work for film and television, but no let-up in activity is to be anticipated. A popular writer in a genuine sense, McGrath will continue to be active long after the reputations of many participants in what he sees as an integral part of the capitalist system have been forgotten.

—John Bull

_____

McGRATH, Tom. British. Born in Rutherglen, Lanarkshire, 23 October 1940. Educated at Glasgow University, degree in drama and English. Married; four daughters. Director, Third Eye Centre, Glasgow; founding editor, *International Times* underground newspaper, London, 1960's; writer-in-residence. Traverse Theatre, Edinburgh, and University of Iowa, Iowa City. Since 1990 associate literary director, Scottish Arts Council, Edinburgh. Also a jazz pianist. Agent: Michael Imison Playwrights, 28 Almeida Street, London N1 1TD, England.

PUBLICATIONS

Plays

Laurel and Hardy (produced Edinburgh, 1976; as *Mr. Laurel and Mr. Hardy*, produced London, 1976).
The Hard Man, with Jimmy Boyle (produced Edinburgh and London, 1977). Edinburgh, Canongate, 1977.
The Android Circuit (produced Edinburgh, 1978).
Sisters (produced London, 1978; revised version produced Southampton, 1985).
Animal (produced Edinburgh, 1979).
The Innocent (produced London, 1979).
1–2–3: Who Are You Anyway?, *Very Important Business*, *Moondog* (produced Edinburgh and London, 1981).
The Phone Box (for children; produced on tour, 1983).
Pals (produced Cumbernauld, Dunbartonshire, 1984).
Kora (produced Edinburgh, 1986).
Thanksgiving (produced Glasgow, 1986).
Private View, with Mhairi Grealis (produced Edinburgh, 1987).
Trivial Pursuits (produced Edinburgh, 1988).

Radio Play: *The Silver Darling*, from the novel by Neil Gunn, 1982.

Televisions Plays: *The Nuclear Family*, 1982; *Blowout*, 1984; *The Gambler*, 1984; *End of the Line*, 1984.

Composer: music for *The Great Northern Welly Boot Show*, book by Tom Buchan, lyrics by Billy Connolly, Edinburgh and London, 1972.

* * *

For a long time, the original success of Tom McGrath's most completely achieved play, *Animal*, kept it out of circulation in England. Although the hit of the 1979 Edinburgh Festival, when it was presented as an official offering by the Traverse Theatre, it was snapped up by American entrepreneurs and the English rights were blocked. The absurdity of such absolute control was reflected by its middling success when it was finally produced south of the Scottish border long after its ecstatic notices. None the less, it remains his most dazzling theatrical conceit.

Originally mounted in an ascending structure of scaffolds and platforms, the play observed the drama of life in a colony of apes, with the intrusive presence of zoologists observing them. The real spectacle and abiding image of the play was the movement and inter-relationships of the apes themselves. With the animals portrayed by loose-limbed actors and actresses, the effect was of life observed through a series of mirrors. The animals were watched by the humans, while the apes aped the humans they were watching. Insights and comedy came through the parallel dramas, and, ironically, dramatic communication was hindered most by the necessity of speech among the humans.

Before becoming a dramatist, McGrath was himself an outside observer of sorts. He edited Britain's most influential counter-cultural periodical, *International Times*, part of the exploding drug culture of the 1960's. That experience was brought to his play for the Royal Shakespeare Company, *The Innocent*, which followed a progression from the use of drugs for pleasure to addiction and withdrawal in an attempt to consider the implications of a selfish pursuit of pleasure on the dreams of the lost "alternative society." It was the first of his plays even to suggest personal experience and observation, and most of his work through the 1970's was notable for his wide-ranging interests. Science fiction and dramatized biography were perhaps the strongest elements.

His first play, which appeared at the Edinburgh Festival in 1976 and later transferred to London, was *Mr. Laurel and Mr. Hardy*, a private view of the off-screen life of the best comic team of the first Hollywood era. McGrath takes the ambitious route of showing both lives independently as well as matching his two actors for some of the on-screen routines. For McGrath, the attraction of Stan Laurel is obviously his Glasgow beginnings, but Oliver Hardy is given equal biographical substance. The play is notable for its contemplation of the team's pathetic final years, with Laurel alone, still writing routines for himself and his old partner, but speaking both parts.

McGrath's second play, a violent dramatization of the life of a reformed Glasgow gangster, appeared the following year. *The Hard Man* was written with Jimmy Boyle, who told the story under his own name in the book *A Sense of Freedom*, which McGrath had a hand in. The story is essentially an odyssey through childhood and gang warfare in the Glasgow slums, culminating in a criminal career which included brutal murder. There is a further dimension to the story, which could tell of Boyle's rehabilitation in prison and his emergence as a sculptor. The play does not go that far; rather it provides a form of ritual re-enactment of the street violence which accentuates key moments in the life of Johny Byrne, the fictional Boyle. Inside prison, jailed for murder, Byrne remains the fiercely proud street-fighter, resisting the regimentation and sadism of the prison and finally reaching a peculiar transcendence in a cramped cage where he squats and smears excrement over himself.

That power was missing from McGrath's fantasy *The Android Circuit*, and from his portrait of three girls growing up in London's East End, *Sisters*. Moments of that force are again visible in a trilogy which he wrote for the Traverse and BBC radio, *1–2–3*, which McGrath described as "plays about male identity written from a feminist viewpoint by a man." The plays are chiefly connected by a cast of three (two men and a woman), and the first play, *Who Are You Anyway?*, blazes a trail of gender confusion as male love and bonding are transferred to love of a woman. The final play appears to pick up the thread of *The Innocent* and shows the two men and woman reinventing a myth about woman as witch, or specifically as priestess of the moon. *Moondog* begins with a drop-out Scot pictured in his chosen solitude in the Highlands, greeting the morning with a chant before being interrupted by an old friend who comes bearing unwanted business propositions. A further interruption is in the form of the woman who arrives with a different purpose, in the nature of human sacrifice.

The trilogy failed in London, but found an audience for the same production at the Toronto Theatre Festival of 1981 and McGrath himself spent a year at the University of Iowa directing the Playwrights' Workshop there. Returning to Scotland, he returned to Scottish themes, notably with *Kora*, a documentary drama about the struggle of tenants in a Dundee housing estate to improve conditions, but filled with flashes of McGrath's theatrical invention and optimism. The American experience was satirically reflected through his short play, *Thanksgiving*, written for Glasgow's Tron Theatre. As part of a trilogy including plays by other Glasgow-based writers, it was designed to accommodate original music by Edward McGuire, but rather more theatrically made use of the spectral presence of the musicians as he dissected the consumerism of America's Thanksgiving Day, with a bossy television set and a woman reasonably declaring her love for two men during "the year of the Ayatollah." It passes more as amused observation than enlightening comment, and if his work in the 1980's is less visible than his work of the 1970's, it is similarly diverse and sympathetic.

While he continued to supply original plays and adaptations to the Scottish theatre, from the Edinburgh Lyceum to Cumbernauld Theatre Company, by the 1990's McGrath had moved into a new role with perhaps even more influence on the future of Scottish drama. As associate literary director of the Scottish Arts Council he masterminded training and astute subsidy to become regarded as a "guru" of Scottish playwrights. His own work still represented a major part of his time, but perhaps reverting to his early days, when as a founder member of the *International Times* he was concerned with enfranchising the disaffected into an alternative society, his inspiration to others is proving to be a major achievement.

—Ned Chaillet

McGUINNESS, Frank. Irish. Born in Buncrana, Donegal, 29 July 1953. Educated at Carndonagh College, Donegal, 1966–

71; University College of Dublin, 1971–76, B.A., and M.Phil in medieval studies. Lecturer, University of Ulster, Coleraine, Londonderry, 1977–79, University College of Dublin, 1979–80, and since 1984 St. Patrick's College, Maynooth, County Kildare. Since 1992 director, The Abbey Theatre, Dublin. Member of Aosdanna, from 1991. Recipient: Rooney prize, 1985; Harvey's award, 1985; *Evening Standard* award, 1986; *Plays and Players* award, 1986; Cheltenham prize, 1986; Charrington award, 1987; Ewart-Biggs Peace prize, 1987; Edinburgh Fringe first, 1988; Prague prix des journalists, 1989. Agent: Sheila Lemon, Lemon, Unna, and Durbridge, 24 Pottery Lane, Holland Park, London W11 4LZ, England.

PUBLICATIONS

Plays

The Factory Girls (produced Dublin, 1982; London, 1988). Dublin, Monarch Line, 1983; revised edition, Dublin, Wolfhound, 1988.
Borderlands (produced Dublin, 1984). Published in *Three Team Plays*, edited by Martin Drury, Dublin, Wolfhound, 1988.
Observe the Sons of Ulster Marching Towards the Somme (produced Dublin, 1985; London, 1986; Boston, 1988). London, Faber, 1986.
Baglady (produced Dublin, 1985; London and Springfield, Connecticut, 1988). With *Carthaginians*, London, Faber, 1988.
Gatherers (produced Dublin, 1985).
Innocence: The Life and Death of Michelangelo Merisi Caravaggio (produced Dublin, 1986). London, Faber, 1987.
Yerma, adaptation of the play by Federico García Lorca (produced Dublin, 1987).
Rosmersholm, adaptation of the play by Henrik Ibsen (produced London, 1987).
Carthaginians (produced Dublin, 1988; London, 1989; Williamstown, New York, 1991). With *Baglady*, London, Faber, 1988.
Times in It (produced Dublin, 1988).
Peer Gynt, adaptation of the play by Henrik Ibsen (produced Dublin, 1988). London, Faber, 1990.
Mary and Lizzie (produced London, 1989). London, Faber, 1989.
Beautiful British Justice (sketch) in *Fears and Miseries of the Third Term* (produced Liverpool and London, 1989).
The Bread Man (produced Dublin, 1990).
Three Sisters, adaptation of the play by Anton Chekhov (produced Dublin and London, 1990). London, Faber, 1990.
Threepenny Opera, adaptation of the play by Bertolt Brecht (produced Dublin, 1991).
Someone Who'll Watch over Me (produced London and New York, 1992).

Television Plays: *Scout*, 1987; *The Hen House*, 1990.

*

Manuscript Collection: National Library of Ireland.

Frank McGuinness comments:
    After 20 years or more of civil war, Ireland still stumbles forward, keeping its head just above water. I want my plays to

trace the steps of that stumbling, to be steeped in that unholy water. Having lost the certainness of faith and fatherland, this country is in the business of finding new languages, new laws. Theatre is likewise radically shaken. *Someone Who'll Watch over Me*, *Mutabilitie*, and another project will, I hope, form a contingently linked trilogy, giving what are new lives to those lies, the conflict of Ireland and England, the edging of Ireland to Europe.

* * *

"It is possible that there is no other memory than the memory of wounds." The epigraph to *Carthaginians*, taken from Czestaw Milosz, could stand as epigraph to the whole of Frank McGuinness's work. The characteristic Irish preoccupation with (in his own words) "the effect that the past has on our present" finds distinctive form in his plays through an exploration of the relationship between culture (whether local or national) and personal identity in which the past is experienced as both a burden and a source of energy. McGuinness has described his plays as "attempts to give what was lost a voice," and the constant formal and stylistic experimentation of his work evidences his continuing effort to articulate the relationship between the personal and the cultural spheres as part of a project of recuperation and regeneration. The necessity to *give voice* also guarantees the essentially theatrical nature of the work. McGuinness's plays find their resolutions in acts of *utterance*, of a ritual or quasi-ritual nature: song, recitation, oratory, incantation, or naming. Above all, these plays are shaped by the imperative of *confession*, which, though sacramental in feeling, is valued as an act of *human* reciprocity. By giving voice we keep our words to the voiceless.

McGuinness's first play, *The Factory Girls*, prefigures the dramatic movement of his later ones. The confrontational response of a group of five women to the threat of redundancy leaves them in an apparently hopeless situation, but it also catalyses a realisation in each of an independence gained through bonding. In this terminal situation, individuality and collectivity are found to be mutually sustaining. This realisation, in a much more richly contextualised form, assumes a pivotal position in McGuinness's best-known (and best) play, the award-winning *Observe the Sons of Ulster Marching Towards the Somme*. As a piece in which a writer from a Catholic background addresses empathetically the experience of Protestant Ulstermen at one of the vital symbolic moments of Loyalist historical memory, the play was, quite properly, regarded as a significant act of fellowship. Yet it is the perception of "something rotten" at the heart of a "dying" Unionist culture that prompts the characters to question, in their different ways, both the idea of inevitable death as "sacrifice" and the familiar rhetoric of blood which embodies that idea. The play is in four named parts, each evoking a ritual of a secular character. Part 1, "Remembrance," is a monologue set in the present, in which the elderly, blind Kenneth Pyper affirms his fidelity to the sacrifice of "the irreplaceable ones," his immediate comrades on the Somme in 1916, then calls up their ghosts to help him answer the question of "why we let ourselves be led to extermination." The "ghosts," including Pyper's own very different younger self, play out the events leading up to 1 July 1916. In "Initiation," the eight young Ulstermen gather in a makeshift barracks where the homosexual Pyper, failed sculptor and "black sheep" of an ascendancy family, with a disastrous French marriage behind him and a death-wish driving him on, mocks Unionist culture—by fierce parody—as only an insider could, and vows "I'll take away your peace." In "Pairing" the stage is divided to evoke

four numinous locations: Boa Island, a church, a rope-bridge, and the Twelfth Field. The men are home on leave, but "the guns are home" too, and the realisation that "we *are* the sacrifice" brings about within each of the four pairings a dissolution of identity, personal and cultural. Yet the same moment also yields a visionary clarity of understanding. The fellowship and even (homosexual) love that enables each man to refashion himself as an independent being is finally tested and proven in Part 4, "Bonding." As they wait in the trenches to go over the top in this "last battle," their ritual preparations affirm the potency of Protestant rhetoric not as triumphalist threat and self-justification but as common inheritance and shared medium of identity. It is Pyper, remade in the bond, who delivers the final prayer; the battle-cry of "Ulster" reaches paroxysm and his younger and elder selves join hands to "Dance in this deserted temple of the Lord."

The symbolic mode developed through *Sons of Ulster*, *Innocence* (a play about Caravaggio, another homosexual artist-figure), and the densely powerful monologue *Baglady*, finds its most daring embodiment—both visual and verbal—in McGuinness's play about Northern Catholic culture, *Carthaginians*. Once again the focus is on an isolated group of individuals in crisis, but here the isolation is self-imposed and the situation even more openly symbolic. This is a play of waiting. Although the setting is a real place in real time, and the dialogue-style predominantly naturalistic, the action is largely internalised, articulated not through conventional narrative but through image, symbol, and quasi-ritual utterance. Six people—three women and three men—are camped out in Derry city graveyard awaiting the fulfilment of a vision of the dead rising in the burial ground. The world they create for themselves, in this place of ancient resonances, is one which effects strange inversions and suspensions of normal experience by the attempt to mediate between the living and the dead. The group is anchored to everyday fact and reality only through the kind offices of Dido Martin, "patriot and poof," the queen of this particular Carthage and the representative of quite another kind of camp. As with Pyper and Caravaggio, homosexuality here constitutes not a social "issue" but a perspective offering clarification and insight. By virtue of his gender position and through his theatricality (he even writes a parodic play for them) Dido delivers a criticism of the culture of the living even as he is mediating it to the group. Each of the graveyard dwellers nurses the "wound" of a deep personal loss or torment of political conscience, but these are subsumed in the overshadowing memory of a great communal wound: Bloody Sunday, a day in 1971 when British troops shot dead several civilians during a protest march in Derry. The confessional rites of personal release are finally sealed by the communal invocation, as Sunday dawns, of the names of the victims of the atrocity. The dead are present as silent "Listeners," and the living are enjoined to include themselves in a general forgiveness. As "they sleep in the graveyard," the vigilant Dido affirms the survival of the city ("Carthage has not been destroyed"), discards the accumulated detritus of Northern Catholic culture, and leaves Derry to "walk the earth."

Where the symbolic intensities of *Carthaginians* seem indebted to Lorca, the fantastic narrative of *Mary and Lizzie*, with its constant reference to "popular forms of English art" (pantomime and television comedy) and Irish folk tradition (ballad and myth), announces its affiliation to *Peer Gynt* (which McGuinness has translated). This is the playwright's most direct treatment of voicelessness. "Frederick Engels lived with two Irishwomen, Mary and Lizzie Burns"; they showed him the "Condition of the Victorian Working Class" in Manchester. For this reason they are, for McGuinness, "probably the most important Irish people of the 19th century, in terms of world history." Yet they are remembered only by the single line in Engels's *Life*: they *are* their name(s). Neither fully "historical" nor fully "mythical," Mary and Lizzie, like Pyper, Caravaggio, and Dido, move between two distinct realms. In the world of Myth, a nameless shadowy territory projected by Irish song, folklore, and ritual, and defined by darkness and the earth, they are first sent out from the arboreal City of Women to "kiss and tell," then shown the future, in the forms of a Magical Priest (son of Mother Ireland), representing both Protestantism and Catholicism in a "killing combination," and a ritual Feast of Famine—complete with balladeering Pig. They escape to England and the realm of History, where, after "passing the time" with the young Queen Victoria (a pantomime dame), they descend to the "open sewer" of Manchester. There they agree to guide a fearful Engels through the nameless "dark" of the "dangerous poor," and so become silent collaborators in his project to "change the world." The sisters' insistence on sexuality and the body disrupts the philosophical double-act of Engels and Karl Marx, and at "Dinner with Karl and Jenny" (Marx's wife—herself tormented by the suppression of her contribution) the reason and abstraction of "scientific" socialism is posed against the instinctive physicality and lyrical utterance of Mary and Lizzie. As Jenny reads Engels's terrible account of the Manchester Irish, the illiterate sisters counter his betrayal by singing the folk-song "She Moved Through the Fair." Finally, the regenerative power of song and the earth is decisively affirmed in the face of a vision of the "night to come," brought about in the name of political ideologies and attested to by nameless "Women of the Camps" in choric song. Even after Mary's "death," song can unite the sisters with their mother to wander the earth (like McGuinness's other mediator-figures) and "sing the songs of those who were never sung about." The linkage of myth, song, and the earth bears witness to the endurance of the voiceless.

The Bread Man returns to the (historical) present to address the problematic relationship between southern and Northern Ireland. The experience of guilt, distrust, dispossession, and despair surrounding a fraternal bereavement is given wider symbolic resonance through a dramaturgy of the interior recalling that of *Innocence*. This play met with general critical disappointment, but the consistency of thematic focus and the variety of formal treatment to be found in McGuinness's drama as a whole combine to inspire confidence in the quality of his future work.

—Paul Lawley

McINTYRE, Clare. British. Member, Nottingham Playhouse TIE Company, 1977–78, The Women's Theatre Group, London, 1979–81, and Common Stock, London, 1981. Recipient: Beckett award, 1989; *Evening Standard* award, 1990; London Drama Critics award, 1990. Agent: Leah Schmidt, Curtis Brown Group, 162–168 Regent Street, London W1R 5TB, England.

PUBLICATIONS

Plays

Better a Live Pompey than a Dead Cyril, with Stephanie Nunn, adaptation of the poems and writings of Stevie Smith (produced London, 1980).

I've Been Running (produced London, 1986).
Low Level Panic (produced London, 1988). Published in *First Run*, edited by Kate Harwood, London, Hern, 1989.
My Heart's a Suitcase (produced London, 1990). London, Hern, 1990.

Radio Play: *I've Been Running*, 1990.

*

Theatrical Activities:
Actor: **Plays**—role in *Better a Live Pompey than a Dead Cyril*, by McIntyre with Stephanie Nunn, London, 1980; Mrs. Kendal in *The Elephant Man* by Bernard Pomerance, Plymouth, 1982; Dawn in *Steaming* by Nell Dunn, Chester, 1985; Gwendolen in *The Importance of Being Earnest* by Oscar Wilde, Chester, 1985; Jane in *Crystal Clear*, Nottingham, 1986; Jan in *Bedroom Farce* by Alan Ayckbourn, Bolton, 1987; Linda in *Kafka's Dick* by Alan Bennett, Leeds, 1988. **Films**—*The Pirates of Penzance*, 1981; *Krull*, 1982; *Plenty*, 1984; *Empire State*, 1986; *Security*, 1987; *A Fish Called Wanda*, 1988. **Television**—*Hotel du Lac*, 1985; *Splitting Up*, 1990.

*   *   *

Clare McIntyre was an actress working in theatre and film for several years before she turned full-time to writing. As a member of the Women's Theatre Group she produced a delightful compilation of the work of Stevie Smith. Her first original play was *I've Been Running*, directed by Terry Johnson and performed at the Old Red Lion in London. It focuses on a female health freak whose fears are kept at bay by feverish activity. McIntyre is one of a long line of female playwrights whose work has been encouraged and nurtured by a combination of the Women's Playhouse Trust and Max Stafford-Clark at the Royal Court. Both *Low Level Panic* and *My Heart's a Suitcase* reveal an uncanny ability to reflect the obsessions and anxieties of contemporary women. Like Caryl Churchill, her plays attract a huge female following, but there is no reason why men shouldn't also enjoy her wit and shrewd observation.

The panic in *Low Level Panic* is engendered in a couple of female flat-sharers when confronted with the images of women peddled by advertising and pornography. The territory is similar to Sarah Daniels's but without her aggression. Mary, Jo, and Celia are preparing for a party. McIntyre cleverly sets all but two of the play's scenes in the bathroom, the very place where women minutely examine their bodies and almost invariably find them wanting. Lying in the bath, Jo imagines herself as the heroine of a sexual fantasy, a leggy model gliding through the cocktail bars of London's hotels, clinking glasses of Martini and meeting the admiring eyes of a rich handsome stranger across a crowded room. Such glacial perfection and anonymity is in complete contrast with Jo's vision of herself as overweight and over-talkative, especially when confronted with a roomful of people at a party. Far from being an expression of her own sensuality, her fantasy makes her feel both humiliated and undesirable. It is also in sharp contrast with the reality experienced by Mary when, in one of just two scenes set outside the bathroom, she is stopped on her way home and raped. As a result she can no longer dress up for a party without feeling she is asking to be attacked again. The pornographic magazine she discovers in their dustbin appears to her to be a legal incitement to men to attack women. In contrast, Celia, the third member of the flat and the least developed as a character, dishes out advice on the right colour of eyeshadow as though life simply consists of trapping the right man. The intimate dialogue about spots, herpes, and even unattractive clitorises is sharply observed and very amusing. But above all it is the confusion and naïvety of her characters that McIntyre captures so accurately.

Anxiety is also a theme in *My Heart's a Suitcase*. Chris is 30 years old, a waitress and distinctly unhappy about it: "What's wrong with being a waitress is that it's a shit job with shit money, no shitting pension and zero fucking prospects." She has a capacity to complain that rivals Jimmy Porter's in Osborne's *Look Back in Anger*. *My Heart's a Suitcase* is a play of the 1980's, a time when everybody was supposed to be getting richer but Chris, who is middle-class, articulate, has a degree, and could presumably earn money if she set her mind to it, is paralysed. Her life is drifting by while she is obsessed with the horrors of the world, an obsession intensified after being attacked by a man with a gun on the tube. Her more placid friend Hannah faces the possibility of real paralysis in the form of multiple sclerosis. The two of them travel down to the seaside together, invited to spend the weekend in an empty flat belonging to a rich ex-boyfriend of Chris's. Thus Chris is given plenty of opportunity to rail against the injustice of some people having money while she has a pittance. She is confronted with real riches when Colin's wife, Tunis, arrives at the flat trailing her consumer goods behind her and throws a tantrum when she discovers her specially made curtains don't fit. Tunis doesn't even have to work for her money but fritters her time away in endless shopping sprees. McIntyre, however, avoids drawing too neat a moral; Tunis is indolent but not a villain and is discontented without being wildly unhappy. It is not that Chris is particularly greedy; it is more that she imagines that wealth would make her happy, although a strange religious phantom called Luggage suggests that it is a woman's role in life to make do with her lot. This phantom, together with that of the man who attacked her, are the least engaging aspects of the play. Most enjoyable is Chris's ability to articulate her discontent with such ferocious gusto. She may be maddening but it is hard to dislike her, and McIntyre makes a rare attempt to present the rich complexities of female friendship onstage. She is a humorous, observant playwright with a deep understanding of the female psyche, and, if she is not diverted into television, could well produce a major play in the future.

—Jane Edwardes

McLURE, James. American. Born in Louisiana. Address: c/o Dramatists Play Service, 440 Park Avenue South, New York, New York, 10016, U.S.A.; and, Chappell Plays Ltd., 129 Park Street, London W1Y 3FA, England.

Publications

Plays

Lone Star (produced Louisville and New York, 1979; London 1980). New York, Dramatists Play Service, 1980.
Pvt. Wars (produced New York, 1979; London, 1980). New York, Dramatists Play Service, 1980.
1959 Pink Thunderbird (includes *Lone Star* and *Laundry and Bourbon*) (produced Princeton, New Jersey, 1980; London, 1989).
Laundry and Bourbon (produced Ashland, Oregon, 1980; London, 1986). New York, Dramatists Play Service, 1981.
The Day They Shot John Lennon (produced Princeton, New Jersey, 1983; London, 1990). New York, Dramatists Play Service, 1984.
Thanksgiving (produced Louisville, 1983).
Wild Oats: A Romance of the Old West, adaptation of the play by John O'Keeffe (produced Los Angeles, 1983). New York, Dramatists Play Service, 1985.
Lahr and Mercedes (produced Denver, 1984).
The Very Last Lover of the River Cane (produced Louisville, 1985).
Max and Maxie (produced New York, 1989). New York, Dramatists Play Service, 1989.

*

Theatrical Activities:
Actor: **Plays**—in *The Death and Life of Jesse James* by Len Jenkin, New York, 1978; *Music Hall Sidelights* by Jack Heifner, New York, 1978.

*   *   *

James McLure is a playwright and actor who became recognized for two one-acts, *Lone Star* and *Pvt. Wars*, that were produced on Broadway in 1979. It is *Lone Star* that best characterizes the nature and dilemma of McLure's favorite protagonist: a southwestern country bumpkin, good ole boy veteran who returns as an adult to a tamer and duller world which both baffles and bores him. This character or his counterpart, appearing in several McLure plays, is a displaced romantic unable to function well in an adult world that no longer operates by his values.

Set in the littered backyard of a small-town Texas bar, *Lone Star* focuses on the swaggering figure of Roy, a former high school hero now back in town after a hitch in Vietnam and not adjusting well. He drinks Lone Star beer and gasses with his hero-worshipping but slower younger brother about his military and amorous exploits and his three loves: his wife, his country, and his 1959 pink Thunderbird convertible. At the evening's end only one love is left intact, for Roy learns that his brother has slept with his young wife and that his cherished Thunderbird has been borrowed and demolished by a fatuous hardware store clerk ever jealous of Roy. Though the symbols of Roy's youth are destroyed or tarnished, he bounces back at the conclusion dimly realizing he can no longer merely muse on the past. Validly praised by critics for its earthy humor and the salty regional idiom of its roistering language, the short play represents McLure at his most effective.

Less successful than its companion piece, *Pvt. Wars* is a black comedy set in an Army hospital where three recuperating Vietnam veterans tease, torment, and even solace each other to disguise their anxiety about returning to the uncertainties of civilian life. Like *Lone Star*'s Roy, they will have to confront a different world. The trio includes a Georgia hillbilly (Gately) given to fiddling with a dead radio, a street-wise hipster (Silvio) addicted to "flashing" nurses even though he is now possibly impotent, and a prissy rich kid (Natwick) who misses his mother. The men's encounters, depicted in 12 sketch-like scenes, project an off-beat humor; but the play's episodic structure forces too fragmentary a quality on the action and characters.

Conceived as a companion piece to *Lone Star* and set in the latter's same mythical Texas town at the home of Roy and his wife Elizabeth, *Laundry and Bourbon* is a short comedy introducing three women on a hot summer afternoon. Elizabeth, the intelligent young lady of the house, folds laundry and sips bourbon while chatting with a gabby neighbor, Hattie. Their talk is interrupted by the self-righteous and unwelcome Amy Lee, the gossipy wife of the hardware clerk met in *Lone Star*. Amidst self-generated bits of gossip, Amy Lee purposefully blurts out that Roy has been seen with another woman. Displaying an inner strength and an understanding of her husband's turmoil since returning from Vietnam, Elizabeth realizes Roy's need for her and her love for him and resolves to be waiting for him when he returns home whatever the opinion of others. In this comedy McLure's humor, characters, and dialogue are richly successful. It stands alongside *Lone Star* as the playwright's strongest work.

Wild Oats is a loose adaptation of John O'Keeffe's 18th-century comedy of the same name keeping the plot structure of the original while transferring the action's locale and characters to the legendary American Old West. The plot and characters are a send-up of old-fashioned melodrama's clichés and stereotypes involving long-lost sons found and forgiven, long-estranged parents reunited, and mistaken identities ultimately revealed. While *Wild Oats* suffers from a surfeit of complications and characters, it yet emerges as an amusing theatrical romp disclosing its author's promising hand for theatricality and parody.

The Day They Shot John Lennon is comprised of a series of encounters between a group of strangers gathered at the New York City site of John Lennon's assassination. The disparate group, whose motives vary from curiosity and shock to theft, includes the veterans Silvio and Gately (of *Pvt. Wars*) now out of Army hospital and practicing pickpockets. Caught in a theft, Gately reveals his serious mental disturbance and Silvio his protective overseeing of his friend. The total group's interaction throughout point up the assassination's larger significance: that violence and ugliness continue to exist in the communal soul and are too soon forgotten even when witnessed. McLure credibly portrays contemporary urbanites with point and poignancy, demonstrating that his territory goes beyond the southwest.

That he is an actor as well as a writer contributes to McLure's strengths, which include a sharp eye for character, a gifted ear for regional idiomatic speech, and an uncommon comic flair extending to the examination of American myths and mores. If he can stretch effectively beyond the one-act form in which he is most comfortable, McLure should have a productive future.

—Christian H. Moe

McNALLY, Terrence. American. Born in St. Petersburg, Florida, 3 November 1939. Educated at schools in Corpus Christi, Texas; Columbia University, New York (Evans Traveling Fellow, 1960), 1956–60, B.A. in English 1960 (Phi Beta Kappa). Stage manager, Actors Studio, New York, 1961; tutor to John Steinbeck's children, 1961–62; film critic, *Seventh Art*, New York, 1963–65; assistant editor, *Columbia College Today*, New York, 1965–66. Since 1981 vice-

president, Dramatists Guild. Recipient: Stanley award, 1962; Guggenheim fellowship, 1966, 1969; Hull Warriner award, 1973, 1987, 1989; Obie award, 1974; American Academy award, 1975. Agent: Gilbert Parker, William Morris Agency, 1350 Avenue of the Americas, New York, New York 10019. Address: 218 West 10th Street, New York, New York 10014, U.S.A.

PUBLICATIONS

Plays

The Roller Coaster published in *Columbia Review* (New York), Spring 1960.

And Things That Go Bump in the Night (as *There Is Something Out There*, produced New York, 1962; revised version, as *And Things That Go Bump in the Night*, produced Minneapolis, 1964; New York, 1965; London, 1977). Included in *The Ritz and Other Plays*, 1976.

The Lady of the Camellias, adaptation of a play by Giles Cooper based on the play by Dumas fils (produced New York, 1963).

Next (produced Westport, Connecticut, 1967; New York, 1969; London, 1971). Included in *Sweet Eros, Next, and Other Plays*, 1969.

Tour (produced Los Angeles, 1967; New York, 1968; London, 1971). Included in *Apple Pie*, 1969.

Botticelli (televised 1968; produced Los Angeles, 1971; London, 1972). Included in *Sweet Eros, Next, and Other Plays*, 1969; in *Off-Broadway Plays 2*, London, Penguin, 1972.

Sweet Eros (produced Stockbridge, Massachusetts, and New York, 1968; London, 1971). Included in *Sweet Eros, Next, and Other Plays*, 1969; in *Off-Broadway Plays 2*, London, Penguin, 1972.

¡ Cuba Si! (produced Provincetown, Massachusetts, and New York, 1968). Included in *Sweet Eros, Next, and Other Plays*, 1969.

Witness (produced New York, 1968; London, 1972). Included in *Sweet Eros, Next, and Other Plays*, 1969.

Noon (in *Chiaroscuro* produced Spoleto, Italy, 1968; in *Morning, Noon, and Night*, produced New York, 1968). Published in *Morning, Noon, and Night*, New York, Random House, 1968.

Apple Pie (includes *Next, Tour, Botticelli*). New York, Dramatists Play Service, 1969.

Last Gasps (televised 1969). Included in *Three Plays*, 1970.

Bringing It All Back Home (produced New Haven, Connecticut, 1969; New York, 1972). Included in *Three Plays*, 1970.

Sweet Eros, Next, and Other Plays. New York, Random House, 1969.

Three Plays: ¡ Cuba Si!, Bringing It All Back Home, Last Gasps. New York, Dramatists Play Service, 1970.

Where Has Tommy Flowers Gone? (produced New Haven, Connecticut, and New York, 1971). New York, Dramatists Play Service, 1972.

Bad Habits: Ravenswood and Dunelawn (produced East Hampton, New York, 1971; New York City, 1974). New York, Dramatists Play Service, 1974.

Let It Bleed, in *City Stops* (produced New York, 1972).

Whiskey (produced New York, 1973). New York, Dramatists Play Service, 1973.

The Ritz (as *The Tubs*, produced New Haven, Connecticut, 1973; revised version, as *The Ritz*, produced New York, 1975). Included in *The Ritz and Other Plays*, 1976.

The Ritz and Other Plays (includes *Bad Habits*, *Where Has Tommy Flowers Gone?*, *And Things That Go Bump in the Night*, *Whiskey*, *Bringing It All Back Home*). New York, Dodd Mead, 1976.

Broadway, Broadway (produced New York, 1978).

It's Only a Play (produced New York, 1982). New York, Nelson Doubleday, 1986.

The Rink, music by John Kander, lyrics by Fred Ebb (produced New York, 1984; Manchester, 1987; London, 1988). New York, French, 1985.

The Lisbon Traviata (produced New York, 1985). Included in *Three Plays*, 1990.

Frankie and Johnny in the Claire de Lune (produced New York, 1987; London, 1989). Included in *Three Plays*, 1990.

Don't Fall for the Lights (dialogue only), with A.R.Gurney and Richard Maltby, Jr., *Street Talk*, and *Andre's Mother* in *Urban Blight*, (musical revue), based on an idea by John Tillinger, music by David Shire, lyrics by Richard Maltby, Jr. (produced New York, 1988).

Faith, Hope, and Charity, with Israel Horovitz and Leonard Melfi (produced New York, 1988). New York, Dramatists Play Service, 1989.

Prelude and Liebstod (produced New York, 1989).

Up in Saratoga (produced San Diego, 1989).

Three Plays (includes *The Lisbon Traviata*, *Frankie and Johnny in the Claire de Lune*, *It's Only a Play*). New York, New American Library, 1990.

Kiss of the Spider Woman, adaptation of the novel by Manuel Puig, music by John Kander, lyrics by Fred Ebb (produced Purchase, New York, 1990; London, 1992).

Lips Together, Teeth Apart (produced New York, 1991).

Screenplays: The *Ritz*, 1976; *Frankie and Johnny*, 1991.

Television Plays: *Botticelli*, 1968; *Last Gasps*, 1969; *The Five Forty-Eight*, from the story by John Cheever, 1979, *Mama Malone series*, 1983.

* * *

It's a long way from Terrence McNally's one-act plays to the rather woozy *And Things That Go Bump in the Night* to the manic antics of *The Ritz* to the hilarious bitchiness of *The Lisbon Traviata* to the wistful sadness of *Lips Together, Teeth Apart* to the upbeat quirkiness of the characters in *Frankie and Johnny in the Claire de Lune* and back to the sharp and incredibly funny goings-on in *It's Only a Play*.

There are a number of unifying elements which are evident in all of McNally's plays: a love of music and theatre; a clever, often biting, wit; a sense of where middle-America thinks it is; and an aura of the confessional with the characters as penitents and the audience as priest. This latter characteristic in lazy writers simply takes the form of narrative monologue but in McNally's work it can be genuinely revealing and often hilarious.

One-act plays seem slightly out of fashion these days, but they are wonderful entrances to production for new writers, and well over 20 years ago McNally was pumping out some biting and successful playlets. One favorite is *Whiskey*, which is as funny at times as any one-act play since *Box and Cox*. It begins with the disastrous appearance of a drunken television cast at the Houston Astrodome and eventually exposes an endearing bunch of fakers. What is clear in this play, as in so many of McNally's pieces, is his infatuation with and amusement by theatre and show people.

Other one-act plays which should continue to find pro-

ductions include *Tour*, which is a funny and very accurate portrait of an American couple abroad; they are an easy target, however, and McNally later finds more amusing Americans to tease. For those of us who saw James Coco as the reluctant and shy draftee in *Next*, this short play will always be a highlight of off-Broadway. *Botticelli* is different in almost every way as we see two soldiers in Vietnam playing the word-game Botticelli as they "kill a gook"; what is truly frightening (and provokes anger) in this one-act play is the fact that these Americans are intelligent, clever, and educated, yet they have become murderers.

McNally wrote *Hope*, the middle play in *Faith, Hope, and Charity*, which is located in Central Park. As with a good many of McNally's plays, many brand products are named; the device seems to locate the time and the characters but can at times be overdone. In *Hope* several characters wait on Easter Sunday for the sun to rise, which it almost fails to do. The sadness in the play is reflected in an exchange in which a nun says, "Sometimes I think that Christ died in vain. Isn't that terrible?" and another character replies, "Sometimes I think everyone dies in vain. Isn't that worse?" Heavy stuff, indeed, and a portent of heavier stuff to come with the age of AIDS.

With *Sweet Eros*, in which a young lady is tied to a chair and tormented, McNally achieved a good deal of notoriety, but the play flounders in a monologue, which seems to be the purpose of the work itself. Likewise, *Witness* is basically one very long funny speech by a window cleaner, given a memorable performance by the late James Coco again.

Given the nature of one-act plays, however, McNally's considerable reputation as one of America's leading playwrights will rest instead on his full-length plays. *And Things That Go Bump in the Night* received a lot of attention, in part because of its homosexual hero and its experimental format, but also because at heart the play is honest and fascinating. It takes itself very seriously indeed. A later work, *Where Has Tommy Flowers Gone?*, brings to the foreground some of McNally's favorite leitmotifs: the theatre, the outsider, the long monologue with the hero addressing the audience as a character in the play. Theatre and cinema references abound in Tommy's monologues, and the dramatic conventions which are routed in Tommy's various drag outfits are explored skillfully and with good humor. Again, products and product names are almost the "scenery" of this play, but beneath it all is a boy so alienated from the world that he is making a bomb to blow the whole thing up. Thus again, beneath the humor of *Where Has Tommy Flowers Gone?*, there is a deep and disturbing anger which lifts the play from mere frippery to something more profound.

Recently, McNally has written at least four major theatre pieces, all of which have had major success with audiences, just as did the earlier, commercial *The Ritz*, which takes place in a gay bathhouse.

Lips Together, Teeth Apart brings together two men and two women at a house on Fire Island. The brother of one of the women has died of AIDS, and she is deciding what to do with the place. McNally juggles his onstage and offstage characters with enormous skill, combining the running gags and an abiding sense of tragedy, death, fear, and loneliness. Chloe says, quite wisely, as she babbles incessantly, "I talk too much probably because it's too horrible to think about what's really going on." The contrast between this sense of horror and death is sharp as the gays next door noisily celebrate the Fourth of July—if we cannot laugh and at least pretend, we all wallow in sadness and self-pity. There is much in McNally's *Lips Together, Teeth Apart* which echoes the best of Chekhov. This is a play which is much more than merely topical and clever, giving us four distinct and touching characters; it is a play that confronts a deep ache in most of us.

Frankie and Johnny in the Claire de Lune, on the other hand, is a realistic bringing-together of two unheroic figures: a brassy, frightened waitress and her suitor, Johnny, who is hardly the hunk of the week. Together, in Frankie's walk-up, one-room apartment, they find and lose each other, and find themselves finally. Another of McNally's devices is used here very successfully: the integration of appropriate music which comes from "real" sources and is not merely background or mood-inducing pabulum. Frankie and Johnny talk and love and talk some more, but not for a moment are we, the audience, bored or alienated, because we find our own real or hoped-for love in these characters. The film version seemed less intimate but was equally moving, and once the film has had its run, it is likely that the play will continue to have a life of its own in theatres all over the world. It deserves a returning audience.

The Lisbon Traviata is both an achingly funny play and a sad commentary on a love affair that is not just breaking up, but is already broken to pieces. The "opera queens" who dote on, and live for, opera divas are hoist on their own petards. Mendy, the "queen" who has to, simply absolutely must, have a copy of Maria Callas (who else?) singing the "Lost One" in Lisbon, is one of the funniest (and most pathetic) characters of modern drama. A lonely man, he wants so much to be loved but his caustic wit and his obsessions would frighten off a saint. Stephen knows that his relationship with Mike is over, that Paul has come between them, but he cannot quite accept his loss. McNally has created a poignant and very funny play. It may (even now) shock some audiences, but it will survive and thrive in theatre wherever humor, self-exploration, and honesty are permitted.

The funniest play in recent years is *It's Only a Play*. Not since Michael Frayn's *Noises Off* has there been a farce about theatre and theatre people to equal the sheer joy and madness of this play. *It's Only a Play* is an almost perfect reflection of what it was to produce a play on Broadway. (Is it McNally's own *The Ritz* that he is remembering?) The maniacal characters "celebrating" the opening night at the producer's smart apartment are so brilliantly drawn that one need never have seen a theatre person to know that that these are the real thing, properly exaggerated for farce. In the fabled tradition of *The Torchbearers* (those inept amateurs) and *Light up the Sky* (those greedy professionals), McNally has skewered his beloved showbusiness, and I honestly cannot remember a play at which the audience screams with laughter in just this way. It is all outrageous, improbable, and absolutely on the mark.

It is safe to assume that Terrence McNally is not only a leading American playwright but a caring, skillful, and successful man who has only just begun to explore his theatrical territory with these diverse and wonderful plays. He's well beyond "promised"; he has delivered.

—Arthur H. Ballet

MEDNICK, Murray. American. Born in Brooklyn, New York, 24 August 1939. Educated at Fallsburg Central School, New York; Brooklyn College, 1957–60. Artistic co-director,

Theatre Genesis, New York, 1970–74. Founder with others and since 1978 artistic director, Padua Hills Playwrights Workshop and Festival, Los Angeles, California. Playwright-in-residence, Florida State University, Tallahassee, 1972, State University of New York, Buffalo, 1973, California State University, Long Beach, 1973, La Verne College, California, 1978–82, and Pomona College, Claremont, California, 1983, 1984. Recipient: National Endowment for the Arts grant, for poetry, 1967; Rockefeller grant, 1968, 1972; Obie award, 1970; Guggenheim grant, 1973; Creative Artists Public Service grant, 1973; Los Angeles Theatre League Ovation Lifetime Achievement award, 1992. Address: 10923 Ayres Avenue, Los Angeles, California 90064, U.S.A.

PUBLICATIONS

Plays

The *Box* (produced New York, 1965).
The Mark of Zorro (produced New York, 1966).
Guideline (produced New York, 1966).
Sand (produced New York, 1967; London, 1970). Published in *The New Underground Theatre*, New York, Bantam, 1968.
The Hawk: An Improvisational Play, with Tony Barsha (produced New York, 1967). Indianapolis, Bobbs Merrill, 1968.
Willie the Germ (produced New York, 1968). Published in *More Plays from Off-Off-Broadway*, edited by Michael T. Smith, Indianapolis, Bobbs Merrill, 1972.
The Hunter (produced New York, 1968). Indianapolis, Bobbs Merrill, 1969.
The Shadow Ripens (also director: produced San Diego and New York, 1969).
The Deer Kill (produced New York, 1970). Indianapolis, Bobbs Merrill, 1971.
Cartoon (produced New York, 1971).
Are You Lookin'? (also director: produced New York, 1973).
Black Hole in Space (produced New York, 1975).
Taxes (also director: produced New York, 1976). Published in *Wordplays 3*, New York, Performing Arts Journal Publications, 1984.
The Coyote Cycle (7 plays) (also director: produced Los Angeles, 1978–80; complete cycle produced Santa Fe, 1984). Published in *West Coast Plays* (Berkeley, California), 1981; *Coyote V: Listening to Old Nana*, in *Plays from Padua Hills*, edited by Mednick, Claremont, California, Pomona College, 1983.
Solomon's Fish (produced New York, 1979).
The Actors' Delicatessen, with Priscilla Cohen (produced New York, 1984).
Scar (also director: produced San Francisco, 1985).
Zohar (also director: produced Los Angeles, 1985).
The Pitch (produced San Francisco, 1985). Published in *Articles*, 1986.
Face (produced Los Angeles, 1986).
Heads (produced Los Angeles, 1987).
Shatter 'n Wade (produced Los Angeles, 1990). Published in *Best of the West*, edited by Mednick, Los Angeles, Padua Hills Press, 1991.

Television Plays: *Iowa*, 1977; *Blessings*, 1978.

Other

Editor, *Plays from Padua Hills*. Claremont, California, Pomona College, 1983.

Editor, *Best of the West.* Los Angeles, California, Padua
Hills Press, 1991.

*

Theatrical Activities:
Director: **Plays**—several of his own plays, and *Blue Bitch* by
Sam Shepard, New York, 1973.
Actor: **Plays**—*The Actors' Delicatessen*, San Francisco, 1984;
Zohar, Los Angeles, 1985.

* * *

Murray Mednick is one of the important American dramatists who came of age in the 1960's. In the decade beginning in
1965 he produced some dozen plays, developing increasing
technical strength, clarity, and complexity and extending his
vision with passionate conviction. His plays and the worlds
they evoke are often dominated by ugly, crushing economic
and personal pressures that lie behind the American pretense
of equality and social justice. The humor is often bitter.
Another recurring feature has been the attempt to place
contemporary experience in the context of native American
myth.

Mednick did most of his early work at Theatre Genesis, a
church-sponsored theater on the lower East Side in New
York. A poet before he turned to drama, he wrote several
one-act plays in the mid-1960's, then moved onto larger
forms. *Sand* shows an ageing, used-up American couple who
are visited by a formal ambassador, their horrible regressive
stupor unbroken by the news that their son is dead in the
(Vietnam) war. The dead soldier's body is brought in at the
end on a meat hook. *Willie the Germ* is about a down-and-out
man working as a dishwasher for a grotesque family of Coney
Island freaks who endlessly seduce him into incomprehensible machinations that always get him into trouble. He
yearns to escape but is kept in his place by put-downs and an
invisible electric force field operated by an anonymous
Button-Pusher in the audience. At the end he is destroyed
and castrated by the monstrous representatives of "society."

Mednick has also created plays with groups of actors, using
improvisation to draw material from their lives and imaginations into a form devised by the dramatist. *The Hawk* is a
play about a drug pusher and his victims. The victims' self-
revealing monologues were developed by the actors and
framed in a formal, ritualistic structure. The play employed a
novel and experimental set of technical acting devices and
was remarkably successful in shaping very loose, idiosyncratic
material within an elegantly disciplined and cohesive form.
The Shadow Ripens was based on an Eskimo legend and
embodied the idea of descending to dangerous non-rational
depths of being in quest of wisdom and authenticity.

Mednick continued to produce plays that emphasized language and carefully crafted writing. *Are You Lookin'?* is a
fragmented, highly subjective study of the effect of heroin use
on personal emotional life. *The Hunter* depicts a hip, tight
friendship between two men. They are united by a common
enemy, a middle-aged hunter obsessed with the Civil War,
whom they nail to a tree; and they are driven to mutual
mistrust by a woman. The play's pared-down, ambiguous
style shows Mednick moving toward the visionary.

The young hero of *The Deer Kill* has moved to an old farm
seeking a simple, virtuous life. His good nature and well-
being are sorely tried—by crazed friends from the city, one of
whom kills himself, by his unfaithful wife, and by the local
authorities, because his dog has killed a deer. The play is
more realistic than Mednick's early work, a clear, rich, and
affecting study of the struggle to live morally in contemporary
America.

In the middle 1970's Mednick, Brooklyn-born, moved
from New York to Los Angeles, where he has continued to
broaden and deepen his achievement. The cartoon-like
Taxes, his take on the vaunted California lifestyle, ironically
recapitulates the devices of the freshly historic New York
avant-garde. The playwright's biting clarity of vision communicates a new compassion for his characters.

With Maria Irene Fornés, John Steppling, and Sam
Shepard, Mednick founded the Padua Hills Playwrights
Workshop and Festival in Los Angeles in 1978, and he con-
tinues as artistic director.

Padua Hills took the form of theater without a theater—
natural settings were the only stage available. This led to
Mednick's extraordinary *The Coyote Cycle*, seven plays
developed between 1978 and 1984. Drawing on Native
American imagery, including the Coyote/Trickster tradition
and the Hopi creation myths, as well as contemporary culture
and experimental theatre, *The Coyote Cycle* is an environmental warning and prayer for planetary salvation. All-night
performances of the cycle have taken audiences into rugged
landscapes for a unique theatrical and conceptual experience.

By the early 1990's Mednick had also written *Scar*, *Shatter
'n Wade*, and *Heads*. In *Scar*, set in the New Mexico mountains, a successful rock musician encounters a "loser" from his
past who forces him to confront deep responsibilities to earth
and being. The teeming, finely honed talk in *Shatter 'n Wade*
implies sharp contemporary anxieties and aggressions, its
mounting menace and fear mirroring society at the raw interface with individual consciousness. The direct, apocalyptic
Heads is clean, mean, and powerful, unflinchingly mythic,
and beautifully spare in its language.

Mednick uses theater as a free poetic medium, and the dark
intensity of his vision, as well as the intelligence of his forms,
fuses many levels of meaning. His latest works have won
fervent admiration, and he continues to enlarge the meaning,
artistry, and emotional effect of his plays.

—Michael T. Smith

———

MEDOFF, Mark (Howard). American. Born in Mount
Carmel, Illinois, 18 March 1940. Educated at the University
of Miami, 1958–62, B.A. 1962; Stanford University,
California, 1964–66, M.A. 1966. Married Stephanie Thorne
in 1972 (second marriage); three daughters. Supervisor of
publications, Capitol Radio Engineering Institute,
Washington, D.C., 1962–64. Instructor, 1966–71, assistant
professor, 1971–74, associate professor, 1974–79, since 1979
professor of drama (currently head of the department of
theatre arts), since 1975 dramatist-in-residence, and artistic
director, 1982–87, American Southwest Theatre Company,
all at New Mexico State University, Las Cruces. Chair of the
Awards Committee, American College Theatre Festival,
1985–86. Recipient: Drama Desk award, 1974, 1980; New
Mexico State University Westhafer award, 1974; John
Gassner award, 1974; Joseph Jefferson award, for acting,
1974; Guggenheim fellowship, 1974; Tony award, 1980;
Outer Circle award, 1980; New Mexico Governor's award,
1980; Society of West End Theatre award, 1982; Obie award,
1984. D.H.L.: Gallaudet College, Washington, D.C., 1981.

Agent: Gilbert Parker, William Morris Agency, 1350 Avenue of the Americas, New York, New York 10019. Address: Department of Theatre Arts, New Mexico State University, Las Cruces, New Mexico 88003, U.S.A.

PUBLICATIONS

Plays

The Wager (produced Las Cruces, New Mexico, 1967; New York, 1974).   New York, Dramatists Play Service, 1975.
Doing a Good One for the Red Man (produced Las Cruces, New Mexico, 1969).   Included in *Four Short Plays*, 1974.
The Froegle Dictum (produced Albuquerque, New Mexico, 1971).   Included in *Four Short Plays*, 1974.
The War on Tatem (produced Las Cruces, New Mexico, 1972).   Included in *Four Short Plays*, 1974.
The Kramer (produced San Francisco, 1972).   New York, Dramatists Play Service, 1976.
When You Comin Back, Red Ryder? (produced New York, 1973).   New York, Dramatists Play Service, 1974; included in *The Hero Trilogy*, 1989.
The Odyssey of Jeremy Jack (for children), with Carleene Johnson (produced Las Cruces, New Mexico, 1975).   New York, Dramatists Play Service, 1974.
Four Short Plays (includes *The Froegle Dictum, Doing a Good One for the Red Man, The War on Tatem, The Ultimate Grammar of Life*).   New York, Dramatists Play Service, 1974.
The Wager: A Play, and Doing a Good One for the Red Man, and The War on Tatem: Two Short Plays.   Clifton, New Jersey, James T. White, 1975.
The Halloween Bandit (produced Huntington, New York, 1976; New York City, 1978).
The Conversion of Aaron Weiss (produced Minneapolis, 1977).
Firekeeper (produced Dallas, 1978).
The Last Chance Saloon (also director: produced Las Cruces, New Mexico, 1979).
Children of a Lesser God (produced Los Angeles, 1979; New York, 1980; London, 1981).   New York, Dramatists Play Service, 1980; Ambergate, Derbyshire, Amber Lane Press, 1982.
The Hands of Its Enemy (produced Los Angeles, 1984; New York, 1986).   New York, Dramatists Play Service, 1987.
The Majestic Kid, music by Jan Scarborough, lyrics by Medoff and Scarborough (produced San Francisco, 1985; New York, 1988).   Included in *The Hero Trilogy*, 1989.
Kringle's Window (produced Las Cruces, New Mexico, 1985).
The Heart Outright (produced Santa Fe, 1986; New York, 1989).   Included in *The Hero Trilogy*, 1989.
The Hero Trilogy (includes *When You Comin' Back, Red Ryder?, The Majestic Kid, The Heart Outright*).   Salt Lake City, Peregrine Smith, 1989.
Big Mary.   New York, Dramatists Play Service, 1989.

Screenplays: *Good Guys Wear Black*, with Bruce Cohn and Joseph Fraley, 1978; *When You Comin' Back, Red Ryder?*, 1979; *Off Beat*, 1986; *Apology*, 1986; *Children of a Lesser God*, with Hesper Anderson, 1987; *Clara's Heart*, 1988.

Radio Plays: *The Disintegration of Aaron Weiss*, 1979.

*

Theatrical Activities:
Director: **Plays**—some of his own plays; *Waiting for Godot* by Samuel Beckett; *The Effect of Gamma Rays on Man-in-the-Moon Marigolds* by Paul Zindel; *Jacques Brel Is Alive and Well and Living in Paris*; *The Birthday Party* by Harold Pinter; *One Flew over the Cuckoo's Nest* by Dale Wasserman; *Equus* by Peter Shaffer; *The Hotel Baltimore* by Lanford Wilson; *Head Act* by Mark Frost; *The Hold Out* by Tony Stafford; *Xmor* by Jan Scarborough and Barbara Kerr; *Vanities* by Jack Heifner; *A Flea in Her Ear* by John Mortimer; *Deadline for Murder*.
Actor: **Plays**—Andrei Bolkonski in *War and Peace*; Marat in *Marat/Sade* by Peter Weiss; Pozzo in *Waiting for Godot* by Samuel Beckett; Teddy in *When You Comin Back, Red Ryder?*; Harold Gorringe in *Black Comedy* by Peter Shaffer; Bro Paradock in *A Resounding Tinkle* by N.F. Simpson; Lenny Bruce in *The Soul of Lenny Bruce*; Dysart in *Equus* by Peter Shaffer; Deeley in *Old Times* by Harold Pinter; Scrooge in *A Christmas Carol*; Bellman in *The Hands of Its Enemy*, Los Angeles, 1984.

Mark Medoff comments:
  My work is simply a reflection of my own spirit, my fears, sorrows, and fires.

*   *   *

Mark Medoff's characters are nostalgic, hoping for redemption in the face of a disappearing way of life. This life exists in various forms: in some of Medoff's plays we mourn the lost idealism of the 1960's, in some the disappearing myth of the west. In all of them characters are defending against a changing world, whether through violence, verbal wit, or the hope of love.

The Kramer is a dream play depicting a power-hungry young man's seemingly gratuitous attempt to take over a secretarial school and simultaneously transform the lives of everyone in it. In a touch of rather heavy-handed symbolism Kramer's profile is marred by a cancerous mole. The men in his way—the obligatory conservative supervisor, the unambitious secretary Artie Malin—are no match for Kramer's cynicism, his verbal game-playing, or his eventual transition from verbal to physical violence. Or the women either. Kramer's persuasiveness is based on his apparent ability to know, verbatim, the past lives of his antagonists. He easily persuades Judy Uichi to leave her Japanese amputee husband on the grounds that: "the idealism of your youth having dissipated, he's a lodestone around your neck." Equally as easily he persuades Artie Malin to leave his unattractive wife, Carol May. Ironically, it is Carol May, who seems to be Kramer's weakest opponent, who is actually his only true adversary. Carol May is the only character who seems capable of genuine feeling, and it is her voice that we remember: "You understand you're trying to drown me. . . . Why are you doing this? . . . Is it me—or is it that you just want to destroy things? . . . Haven't you ever loved another person very, very much?"

Teddy in *When You Comin Back, Red Ryder?* is, like Kramer, a figure of violence who far exceeds everyone around him in both intelligence and physical strength. But Teddy is a more complex character. Though initially his disruption of the New Mexico diner appears as gratuitous as Kramer's takeover, it becomes evident that Teddy's real threat is not only his violence but also his ability to destroy the illusions around which lives are constructed. Teddy shares Kramer's uncanny insight into others' pasts, and his readings of people are both cruel and accurate. If Teddy is evil he is also a catalyst for change, forcing decisions and realizations that have long been avoided. In addition, Medoff allows an insight that we don't get into Kramer: we see what Teddy is mourning. Calling himself one of the "disaffected" youth, he asks of the old western heroes, "What in the hell happened to those people?" and announces at the end of the play, "This is the last dance then, gang. Time's gone and I'm gonna ride off into the sunrise." Teddy's tragedy is both his misused brilliance and his ability to accept life's divergence from myth.

The Wager is in many ways a transition between Medoff's earlier works and *Children of a Lesser God*. Leeds shares with Kramer and Teddy the qualities of violence, verbal wit, and cruel if brilliant insight. But the violence here is transformed to suggest emotional vulnerability. As in *The Kramer* the protagonist's only real match is a woman. The verbal pyrotechnics between Leeds and Honor are clearly a defense against their attraction to one another. Leeds's ability to overcome this defensiveness, even if with great resistance, and Honor's recognition that words are often destructive to understanding suggest greater depth of character than that possessed by any of Medoff's earlier protagonists, and, in addition, for Medoff, a change of key.

The singular quality of *Children of a Lesser God* is its lyricism, relying on the same fluid and dream-like staging employed in *The Kramer*. The play begins and ends in James's memory. James, like his predecessors, is bright and somewhat disaffected, a former Peace Corps volunteer who tells us, "I saved Ecuador." Unlike his predecessors, he retains in the face of the cynicism of his somewhat stereotypical supervisor and students at a school for the non-hearing both some measure of idealism and an openness to feeling, although his tendency to what Robert Brustein has called "pop psychoanalysis" can become annoying. Also unlike his predecessors, James shares the stage. He has a co-protagonist.

Sarah Norman, one of James's non-hearing students, who signs because she will not speak, provides the play with much of its lyrical eloquence. The relationship between James and Sarah, initially a power struggle between teacher and student, becomes a love affair and then reverts to a power struggle. The issues Medoff explored in earlier works are now complicated by the conflict between power and feeling. James acknowledges the inherent ambiguity of his motives: do they stem from a desire to help or a desire to control? Sarah, for her part, is "determined to preserve her wholeness inside a deaf world . . . deafness . . . is a condition of being 'other,' and this otherness has its sufficient rewards." She signs to James: "I live in a place you can't enter. It's out of reach. . . . Deafness isn't the opposite of hearing, as you think. It's a silence full of sound. . . ." Their final confrontation is a recognition of simultaneous love and difference—a difference that is, despite love, irresolvable, James acknowledging: "Yes, I'm a terrific teacher: Grow, Sarah, but not too much. Understand yourself, but not more than I understand you. Be brave, but not so brave you don't need me anymore," and Sarah: "I'm afraid I would just go on trying to change you. We would have to meet in another place; not in silence or in sound but somewhere else. I don't know where that is now."

The play's eloquence is, paradoxically, inherent in its characters' inability to make themselves understood. The fact is that the two protagonists speak separate languages. Although this linguistic difference is muted by James's simultaneous translation of Sarah's signing, the play does give an indication, at least, of the imperative to understand those who are "inarticulate" in our language. Those who are non-vocal, Medoff suggests, do not necessarily have nothing to say. The struggle to be heard is a common theme, and

Brustein, in his review, expresses his irritation, calling the play "a chic compendium of every extant cliché about women and minority groups. . . ." But the frequency with which a theme is explored does not necessarily relate to its importance; if anything the repetition of an idea may indicate the necessity of coming to terms with it. Gerald Weales has written of this play that: "Since no marriage—however close, however loving—can make two people one . . . the special cases of James, as teacher, and Sarah, as unwilling pupil, can become metaphors for any marriage." James's final nostalgia for a love that is real and yet not realizable is at the heart of the play's poignance, a poignance the later screenplay, by resorting to a happy ending, fails to retain.

Two later plays by Medoff are less successful in their reiteration of earlier themes. Aaron, in the musical *The Majestic Kid*, is like Leeds, concerned with issues of love and distance, with lost idealism. But the characters are unrealized. Aaron's love affair with Lisa is abrupt and therefore unimportant. It is difficult to know how to take the Laredo Kid, a movie character brought to life who knows all the old western plots by heart—movie as karma?—but cannot decipher the present script. And the ideological and political concerns of Aaron's long-time lover and co-worker, A.J., jar with her flip one-liners. *The Hands of Its Enemy* also concerns a woman who cannot hear. But *Enemy* is more conceptional than *Children*, a play within a play which juxtaposes a psychological exploration of the characters of a playwright and her director with the rehearsal process for their play. The central theme again centers around issues of distance and the need to trust, but here the struggle is at times cloying and overdone.

At his weakest Medoff may occasionally go too far in one direction or the other, becoming either gratuitous or overly sentimental. But in his best plays he is able to combine a frighteningly realistic depiction of the cruelties we wittingly or unwittingly commit with a simultaneous acknowledgement of our tremendous vulnerability.

—Elizabeth Adams

MELFI, Leonard (Anthony). American. Born in Binghamton, New York, 21 February 1935. Educated at Binghamton Central High School; St. Bonaventure University, New York, 1956–57; American Academy of Dramatic Arts. Worked as a waiter and carpenter, lecturer, New York University, 1969–70. Columnist ("Notes of a New York Playwright"), *Dramatists Guild Quarterly*, New York. Recipient: Eugene O'Neill Memorial Theatre Foundation award, 1966; Rockefeller grant, 1966, 1967; Guggenheim fellowship, 1978. Lives in New York City. Agent: Helen Harvey Associates, 410 West 24th Street, New York, New York 10011, U.S.A.

PUBLICATIONS

Plays

Lazy Baby Susan (produced New York, 1965).
Sunglasses (produced New York, 1965).
Pussies and Rookies (produced New York, 1965).
Ferryboat (produced New York, 1965). Included in *Encounters*, 1967.
Birdbath (produced New York, 1965; Edinburgh, 1967; London, 1969). Included in *Encounters*, 1967; in *New Short Plays 1*, London, Methuen, 1968.

Times Square (produced New York, 1966; Edinburgh and London, 1967). Included in *Encounters*, 1967.

Niagara Falls (produced New York, 1966; revised version produced Los Angeles, 1968; London, 1976). Published in *New Theatre for Now* (*New Theatre in America 2*), edited by Edward Parone, New York, Dell, 1971.

Lunchtime (produced New York, 1966; London, 1969). Included in *Encounters*, 1967.

Halloween (produced New York, 1967; London, 1969). Included in *Encounters*, 1967.

The Shirt (produced New York, 1967). Included in *Encounters*, 1967.

Encounters: 6 One-Act Plays. New York, Random House, 1967.

Disfiguration (produced Los Angeles, 1967).

Night (in *Chiaroscuro* produced Spoleto, Italy, 1968; in *Morning, Noon, and Night,* produced New York, 1968). Published in *Morning, Noon, and Night*, New York, Random House, 1969.

Stars and Stripes, in *Collision Course* (produced New York, 1968). New York, Random House, 1968.

Stimulation (produced New York, 1968; London, 1969).

Jack and Jill (produced New York, 1968; revised version, produced as part of *Oh! Calcutta!*, New York, 1969, 1976–89; London, 1970). New York, Grove Press, 1969.

The Breech Baby (produced New York, 1968).

Having Fun in the Bathroom (produced New York, 1969).

The Raven Rock (produced New York, 1969).

Wet and Dry, and Alive (produced New York, 1969).

The Jones Man (produced Provincetown, Massachusetts, 1969).

Cinque (produced London, 1970; New York, 1971). Published in *Spontaneous Combustion: Eight New American Plays*, edited by Rochelle Owens, New York, Winter House, 1972.

Ah! Wine! (produced New York, 1974).

Beautiful! (produced New York, 1974).

Horse Opera, music by John Braden (produced New York, 1974).

Sweet Suite (produced New York, 1975).

Porno Stars at Home (produced New York, 1976). New York, French, 1980.

Eddie and Susanna in Love (produced New York, 1976).

Fantasies at the Frick; or, (The Guard and the Guardess) (produced New York, 1976). New York, French, 1980.

Butterfaces (produced New York, 1977).

Taxi Tales (five plays; produced New York, 1978). Included in *Later Encounters*, 1980.

Rusty and Rico, and Lena and Louie (produced New York, 1978). Included in *Later Encounters*, 1980.

Later Encounters: Seven One-Act Plays (includes *Taxi Tales—Taffy's Taxi, Tripper's Taxi, Toddy's Taxi, The Teaser's Taxi, Mr. Tucker's Taxi—Rusty and Rico, Lena and Louie*). New York, French, 1980.

Amorous Accidents (produced Los Angeles, 1981).

The Dispossessed (produced New York, 1982).

Eve Is Innocent (produced New York, 1983).

Rosetti's Apologetics, music by Mark Hardwick (produced New York, 1983).

The Little Venice Makes a Good Drink (produced Binghamton, New York, 1985).

Lily Lake (produced Binghamton, New York, 1986).

Faith, Hope, and Charity, with Terrence McNally and Israel Horovitz (produced New York, 1988). New York, Dramatists Play Service, 1989.

Screenplay: *La mortadella* (*Lady Liberty*), 1971.

Television Plays: *The Rainbow Rest*, 1967; *Puck! Puck! Puck!*, 1968; *What a Life!*, 1976.

*

Critical Study: *American Playwrights: A Critical Survey* by Bonnie Marranca and Gautam Dasgupta, New York, Drama Book Specialists, 1981.

Theatrical Activities:
Actor: **Plays**—Knute Gary in *Beautiful!*, New York, 1974; Room Service in *Sweet Suite*, New York, 1975; Richard DeRichard in *The Dispossessed*, New York, 1982; Rosetti in *Rosetti's Apologetics*, New York, 1983. **Films**—*La mortadella* (*Lady Liberty*), 1971; *Rent Control*, 1983.

Leonard Melfi comments:
A personal statement introducing my plays?
Well . . . "I borrow from life and pay back my debt by giving my imagination."
Or, maybe . . . "Plays about my fellow human beings in and out of trouble, like all of us at various times. In other words: celebrating the human condition, the miracle and mystery of life, no matter what."
Or, maybe . . . "I take people who wake up in the morning and ask themselves: 'Are you happy?', and then they answer immediately to themselves: 'Yes, I am!' . . . and I throw them together with the other group, who, when they ask themselves the very same question, always answer immediately: 'No, I'm not!' (There's always a play in that situation!)."
Why I feel so great about writing plays (among other certain reasons)? Well, once in my father's roadhouse restaurant and bar in Upstate New York where I grew up, a bunch of hunters walked in to drink and eat and my father was behind the bar. One of the men asked: "By the way: what does your son down in New York City do anyway?" And my father smiled and proudly replied (he had gone as far as the sixth grade): "My son does the same thing that Shakespeare did!"

*   *   *

It's just like a sort of Utopia . . . all those windows with all those people behind all of those windows: living and breathing and trying to love too. Well, I just love it all, my dear Louie Pussycat! All of them trying like holy hell and holy heaven to be wholly holy happy as much as it's humanly possible in all of our rather only half-happy lives instead of our wholly happy lives. . .!

Lena of *Lena and Louie* shows the best and the worst of Leonard Melfi's playwriting. The exuberance and visionary optimism are as typical of his work as the shallow sentiment and flabby prose. Although Melfi has never fulfilled the promise of his early plays, and may have reneged on it, he has consolidated his dramatic territory and remained constant to it.

Melfi gained his first foothold in theatre when he began writing one-act plays for Ellen Stewart's Cafe La Mama, one of the birthplaces of off-off-Broadway. To fit the one-act form, Melfi stripped his characters of all but one or two qualities, usually the need for love or the need for sex, or both. Similarly, the plays of *Encounters* revolved around those brief moments when human contact becomes possible. Such moments are particularly rare in large cities, and Melfi's plays are as New York as pavement, filled with specific references to the city and its people. Presented at La Mama, they were always on intimate terms with their audiences.

The plays range in style from a necessarily narrowed realism to a highly stylized fantasy occasionally reminiscent of Michael McClure's cartoon plays. *Birdbath*, one of Melfi's best known plays, brings together a superficially composed young man and an excessively nervous young woman who can speak of little but her mother. Their encounter brings out the man's obsessive need to write and the woman's murder of her mother that morning, and the bond between them that results from these revelations brings them together, and the play ends with Frankie's valentine to Velma. In contrast, *Times Square* is a masquelike fantasy about the people who inhabit New York's most offensive block of sex-shows and other adult temptations. The characters, however, are childlike, hopeful dreamers whose innocence is only confirmed by the fluid, anything-can-happen life of Times Square. When the angelic Melissa Sobbing is hit by a car, she is revivified with a kiss, and for a moment Times Square really is a street of dreams.

Melfi's world has its nightmares too, which come with a sudden violence that counterpoints oddly its romance. In *Encounters* the violence exploded into the romance with a sharpness and suddenness that enriched the plays. In *Later Encounters* and Melfi's longer plays the dark side of New York has been increasingly absorbed and softened by the light. Although Lena and Louie freeze to death in Central Park, their deaths are an apotheosis. They die "in each other's arms, with the two most beautiful smiles on their faces: smiling like one has never seen smiling ever before in one's life; smiling smiles that told of things like, well, things like . . . forever!"

Melfi's longer plays are essentially enlarged one-acts, with small casts and limited aims. In *Porno Stars at Home* the characters begin an evening with their facades intact, smoothly congratulating themselves on their style and dash. Before the evening is out, they've reduced their styles to shreds, and are trying desperately to put them back together. Unfortunately, their psychological strip uncovers little of interest, little more than "Baby, all I do all of the time is to try and not be scared anymore, that's all," or "I just want something to hang on to before it's too late." Although an able craftsman of the theatre, Melfi has so far failed to pursue his well-worn themes and situations into new territory.

—Walter Bode

————

MERCER, David. British. 1928–1980.
See 2nd edition, 1977.

————

MILLAR, (Sir) Ronald (Graeme). British. Born in Reading, Berkshire, 12 November 1919. Educated at Charterhouse School, Surrey; King's College, Cambridge. Served in the Royal Naval Volunteer Reserve, 1940–43: sub-lieutenant. Since 1977 deputy chair, Theatre Royal, Haymarket, London. Knighted, 1980. Agent: Ian Bevan, 37 Hill Street, London W1X 8JY. Address: 7 Sheffield Terrace, London W.8, England.

PUBLICATIONS

Plays

Murder from Memory (produced London, 1942).
Zero Hour (produced London, 1944).
The Other Side, adaptation of the novel by Storm Jameson (produced London, 1946).
Frieda (produced London, 1946). London, English Theatre Guild, 1947.
Champagne for Delilah (produced London, 1949).
Waiting for Gillian, adaptation of the novel *A Way Through the Wood* by Nigel Balchin (produced London, 1954). London, French, 1955.
The Bride and the Bachelor (produced London, 1956). London, French, 1958.
A Ticklish Business (produced Brighton, 1958; as *The Big Tickle*, produced London, 1958). London, French, 1959.
The More the Merrier (produced London, 1960). London, French, 1960.
The Bride Comes Back (produced London, 1960). London, French, 1961.
The Affair, adaptation of the novel by C.P. Snow (produced London, 1961; Washington, D.C., 1964). New York, Scribner, 1962; London, French, 1963.
The New Men, adaptation of the novel by C.P. Snow (produced London, 1962). Included in *The Affair, The New Men, The Masters*, 1964.
The Masters, adaptation of the novel by C.P. Snow (produced London, 1963). Included in *The Affair, The New Men, The Masters*, 1964.
The Affair, The New Men, The Masters: Three Plays Based on the Novels and with a Preface by C.P. Snow. London, Macmillan, 1964.
Robert and Elizabeth, music by Ron Grainer, lyrics by Millar, adaptation of the play *The Barretts of Wimpole Street* by Rudolf Besier (produced London, 1964). London, French, 1967.
On the Level, music by Ron Grainer (produced London, 1966).
Number 10, adaptation of the novel by William Clark (produced Glasgow and London, 1967). London, Heinemann, 1967.
They Don't Grow on Trees (produced London, 1968). London, French, 1969.
Abelard and Heloise, based on *Peter Abelard* by Helen Waddell (produced Exeter and London, 1970; New York, 1971). London and New York, French, 1970.
Parents' Day, adaptation of the novel by Edward Candy (produced London, 1972).
Odd Girl Out, adaptation of the novel by Elizabeth Jane Howard (produced Harlow, Essex, 1973).
The Case in Question, adaptation of the novel *In Their Wisdom* by C.P. Snow (produced London, 1975). London, French, 1975.
Once More with Music (produced Guildford, Surrey, 1976).
A Coat of Varnish, adaptation of the novel by C.P. Snow (produced London, 1982). London, French, 1983.

Screenplays: *Frieda*, with Angus Macphail, 1947; *So Evil My Love*, with Leonard Spiegelgass, 1948; *The Miniver Story*, with George Froeschel, 1950; *Train of Events*, with others, 1950; *The Unknown Man*, with George Froeschel, 1951; *Scaramouche*, with George Froeschel, 1951; *Never Let Me Go*, with George Froeschel, 1953; *Rose Marie*, 1954; *Betrayed*, with George Froeschel, 1954.

*

Theatrical Activities:
Actor: **Plays**—in *Swinging the Gate* (revue), London, 1940; Prince Anatole Kuragin in *War and Peace* by David Lucas, London, 1943; Cully in *Mr. Bolfry* by James Bridie, London, 1943; David Marsden in *Murder for a Valentine* by Vernon Sylvaine, London, 1944; Flight Lieutenant Chris Keppel in *Zero Hour*, London, 1944; Penry Bowen in *Jenny Jones* by Ronald Gow, London, 1944; Roy Fernie in *We Are Seven* by Ian Hay, London, 1945; Colin Tabret in *The Sacred Flame* by W. Somerset Maugham, London, 1945; Smith in *Murder on the Nile* by Agatha Christie, London, 1946. **Films**—*The Life and Death of Colonel Blimp*, 1943; *Beware of Pity*, 1945.

* * *

Ronald Millar was born in Reading in 1919. When he was a small boy his mother, an actress, wishing him to be protected from the glamorous uncertainties of stage life, sent him to a good preparatory school to receive a classical education. At the end of his time there he sat for scholarships at several of the great public schools. He was offered one at Harrow, but refused it on the advice of his headmaster, who had his eye on Winchester. At the Winchester examination, however, he happened to be out of sorts and narrowly missed an award; but he did gain one at Charterhouse.

From his mother's point of view this was an unhappy accident; for at that time Charterhouse, of all the great public schools, had the closest connection with the theatre and the largest number of old boys who were actors. And from there young Ronald went on to King's, which of all the colleges in Cambridge had the strongest theatrical tradition.

The outcome was fairly predictable. Millar joined various University acting clubs, showed talent, gained experience—incidentally, he was given the leading part in the triennial Greek play which is traditionally a great dramatic event at Cambridge—and was inevitably attracted to the professional stage. Then service in the Royal Navy delayed his final decision; but by the time he was invalided out he had made up his mind. He did not return to Cambridge to take his degree, but turned actor at once.

However, the years spent with the classics were not wasted. There are many worse forms of training for a writer, and Millar's ambition to be a dramatist was at least as strong as his desire to act, and was to prove much more lasting. His second play, *Zero Hour*, was produced at the Lyric in June 1944, with himself in the cast, and his third, *Frieda* (about a girl escaped from Nazi Germany), at the Westminster in 1946. This had a fair success on the stage and a bigger one as a film.

In 1949 Millar suffered a deep disappointment. Returning to England after an interlude spent writing filmscripts in Hollywood, he brought with him a light comedy, *Champagne for Delilah*, which was instantly accepted for West End production. To all the experts who handled it, it seemed certain to have a huge success, and it was received with acclaim on its prior-to-London tour. But on arrival at the New Theatre it proved a dead failure, and nobody has ever been able to suggest why. Seven years later, however, Millar must have felt compensated by an ironic twist of fate when another play, *The Bride and the Bachelor*, ran for more than 500 performances after having been given a hostile reception by nearly all the critics. Later still, in 1960, a sequel to this piece, *The Bride Comes Back*, also ran very well.

By this time Millar had enough successful work to his credit to prove that one of his outstanding qualities was his versatility. From the seriousness of *Frieda* to the frivolity of the two "Bride" plays was a big step and a vivid contrast in styles; and he now proceeded to demonstrate further uses to which his versatility might be put.

The year 1961 saw the beginning of a whole series of plays adapted by Millar from novels or other literary sources, the first of them being a stage version of C.P. Snow's story of college life at Cambridge, *The Affair*. As a Cambridge man himself, Millar was familiar with the atmosphere so truthfully rendered by the book, and, given a free hand, matched that atmosphere quite perfectly. Then came a setback. Manager after manager refused to believe that a play so local in its application could interest the general public. At last Henry Sherek, who had been Millar's backer for *Frieda* and *Champagne for Delilah*, accepted the risk, and was rewarded with critical favour and a year's run.

A second play from a Snow novel, *The New Men*, followed in 1962 and had no success; but a second Cambridge piece, *The Masters*, was staged in 1963 and ran even longer than *The Affair* had, and in 1975 yet another, *The Case in Question*, ran very well.

The particular talent which carried Millar to his notable successes in this field is an ability to turn a novelist's narrative prose into dialogue without losing his personal flavour, added to which is an ability where necessary to write in scenes of his own invention in a style to fit in with the rest.

This was perhaps not an especially difficult task in the case of the two Cambridge plays, where novelist and adapter had in common a detailed knowledge of and feeling for the atmosphere they wished to convey; but it became a problem of much delicacy in the case of Millar's next, and much more serious play, *Abelard and Heloise*. The main materials for this play were Helen Waddell's book about Peter Abelard and the famous letters, and the task was to find an idiom which would convey both these elements. This was done with such skill that the play drew not only the more serious playgoers but also the general public. Produced in May 1970, it ran into 1972.

One other proof of Millar's versatility should be noted. In 1964 he wrote both the book and lyrics for *Robert and Elizabeth*, the musical version of *The Barretts of Wimpole Street*, which ran for two and a half years.

—W.A. Darlington

MILLER, Arthur. American. Born in New York City, 17 October 1915. Educated at Abraham Lincoln High School, New York, graduated 1932; University of Michigan, Ann Arbor (Hopwood Award, 1936, 1937), 1934–38, A.B. 1938. Married 1) Mary Slattery in 1940 (divorced 1956), one son and one daughter; 2) the actress Marilyn Monroe in 1956 (divorced 1961); 3) the photographer Ingeborg Morath in 1962, one daughter. Worked in automobile supply warehouse, 1932–34; member of the Federal Theatre Project, 1938; writer for CBS and NBC Radio Workshops. Associate professor of drama, University of Michigan, 1973–74. International president, PEN, London and New York, 1965–69. Recipient: Theatre Guild award, 1938; New York Drama Critics Circle award, 1947, 1949; Tony award, 1947, 1949, 1953; Pulitzer prize, 1949; National Association of Independent Schools award, 1954; American Academy Gold medal, 1959; Brandeis University Creative Arts award, 1969; Peabody award, for television play, 1981; Bobst award, 1983; National Arts Club medal of honor, 1992; City University of New York Edwin Booth award, 1992; Commonwealth award, 1992. D.H.L.: University of Michigan, 1956; Honorary degree: Hebrew University, Jerusalem, 1959; Litt.D.: University of East Anglia, Norwich, 1984. Member, American Academy, 1981. Lives in Connecticut. Agent: Kay Brown, International Creative Management, 40 West 57th Street, New York, New York 10019, U.S.A.

PUBLICATIONS

Plays

Honors at Dawn (produced Ann Arbor, Michigan, 1936).
No Villain (*They Too Arise*) (produced Ann Arbor, Michigan, 1937).
The Pussycat and the Expert Plumber Who Was a Man, and *William Ireland's Confession*, in *100 Non-Royalty Radio Plays*, edited by William Kozlenko. New York, Greenberg, 1941.
The Man Who Had All the Luck (produced New York, 1944; London, 1960). Published in *Cross-Section 1944*, edited by Edwin Seaver, New York, Fischer, 1944.
That They May Win (produced New York, 1944). Published in *Best One-Act Plays of 1944*, edited by Margaret Mayorga, New York, Dodd Mead, 1945.
Grandpa and the Statue, in *Radio Drama in Action*, edited by Erik Barnouw. New York, Farrar and Rinehart, 1945.
The Story of Gus, in *Radio's Best Plays*, edited by Joseph Liss. New York, Greenberg, 1947.
The Guardsman, radio adaptation of a play by Ferenc Molnár, and *Three Men on a Horse*, radio adaptation of the play by George Abbott and John Cecil Holm, in *Theatre Guild on the Air*, edited by William Fitelson. New York, Rinehart, 1947.
All My Sons (produced New York, 1947; London, 1948). New York, Reynal, 1947; in *Collected Plays*, 1957.
Death of a Salesman: Certain Private Conversations in Two Acts and a Requiem (produced New York and London, 1949). New York, Viking Press, and London, Cresset Press, 1949.
An Enemy of the People, adaptation of a play by Ibsen (produced New York, 1950; Lincoln, 1958; London, 1988). New York, Viking Press, 1951; London, Walker, 1989.
The Crucible (produced New York, 1953; Bristol, 1954; London, 1956). New York, Viking Press, 1953; London, Cresset Press, 1956; augmented version (with additional scene, subsequently omitted), New York, Dramatists Play Service, 1954.
A View from the Bridge (produced New York, 1955). With *A Memory of Two Mondays*, New York, Viking Press, 1955; revised version (produced London, 1956), New York, Dramatists Play Service, 1956; London, Cresset Press, 1957.
A Memory of Two Mondays (produced New York, 1955; Nottingham, 1958). With *A View from the Bridge*, New York, Viking Press, 1955; in *Collected Plays*, 1957.
Collected Plays (includes *All My Sons, Death of a Salesman, The Crucible, A Memory of Two Mondays, A View from the Bridge*). New York, Viking Press, 1957; London, Cresset Press, 1958.
After the Fall (produced New York, 1964; Coventry, 1967; London, 1990). New York, Viking Press, 1964; London, Secker and Warburg, 1965.
Incident at Vichy (produced New York, 1964; Brighton and London, 1966). New York, Viking Press, 1965; London, Secker and Warburg, 1966.
The Price (produced New York, 1968; also director: produced London, 1969). New York, Viking Press, and London, Secker and Warburg, 1968.

Fame, and The Reason Why (produced New York, 1970). *Fame* published in *Yale Literary Magazine* (New Haven, Connecticut), March 1971.
The Creation of the World and Other Business (produced New York, 1972; Edinburgh, 1974). New York, Viking Press, 1973; in *Collected Plays 2*, 1981; revised version, as *Up from Paradise*, music by Stanley Silverman (also director: produced Ann Arbor, Michigan, 1974; New York, 1983), New York, French, 1984.
The Archbishop's Ceiling (produced Washington, D.C., 1977; revised version produced Cleveland, 1984; Bristol, 1985; London, 1986). London, Methuen, 1984; with *The American Clock*, New York, Grove Press, 1989.
The American Clock, adaptation of the work *Hard Times* by Studs Terkel (produced Seattle, 1979; New York, 1980; Birmingham, 1983; London, 1986). London, Methuen, 1983; with *The Archbishop's Ceiling*, New York, Grove Press, 1989.
Playing for Time, adaptation of a work by Fania Fenelon (televised 1980; produced Edinburgh, 1986). New York, Bantam, 1981; in *Collected Plays 2*, 1981.
Collected Plays 2 (includes *The Misfits, After the Fall, Incident at Vichy, The Price, The Creation of the World and Other Business, Playing for Time*). New York, Viking Press, and London, Secker and Warburg, 1981.
Eight Plays (includes *All My Sons, Death of a Salesman, The Crucible, A Memory of Two Mondays, A View from the Bridge, After the Fall, Incident at Vichy, The Price*). New York, Doubleday, 1981.
Two-Way Mirror (includes *Elegy for a Lady* and *Some Kind of Love Story*) (also director: produced New Haven, Connecticut, 1982; Edinburgh, 1984; London, 1989). *Elegy for a Lady* published New York, Dramatists Play Service, 1982; *Some Kind of Love Story* published Dramatists Play Service, 1983; both plays published London, Methuen, 1984.
Danger! Memory! (includes *I Can't Remember Anything* and *Clara*) (produced New York, 1987; London, 1988). London, Methuen, 1986; New York, Grove Press, 1987.
Speech to the Neighborhood Watch Committee in *Urban Blight* (musical revue), based on an idea by John Tillinger, music by David Shire, lyrics by Richard Maltby, Jr. (produced New York, 1988).
Plays 3 (includes *The American Clock, The Archbishop's Ceiling, Two-Way Mirror*). London, Methuen, 1990.
Everybody Wins (screenplay). London, Methuen, 1990; New York, Grove Weidenfeld, 1990.
The Last Yankee (produced New York, 1991; London, 1993). New York, Dramatists Play Service, 1991.
The Ride Down Mount Morgan (produced London, 1991).

Screenplays: *The Story of G.I. Joe* (uncredited), 1945; *The Witches of Salem*, 1958; *The Misfits*, 1961; *Everybody Wins*, 1990; *The Crucible*, 1992.

Radio Plays: *The Pussycat and the Expert Plumber Who Was a Man, William Ireland's Confession, Grandpa and the Statue, The Story of Gus, The Guardsman, Three Men on a Horse*, early 1940's; *The Golden Years*, 1987 (UK).

Television Play: *Playing for Time*, 1980.

Novels

Focus. New York, Reynal, 1945; London, Gollancz, 1949.
The Misfits (novelization of screenplay). New York, Viking Press, and London, Secker and Warburg, 1961.

Short Stories

I Don't Need You Any More.   New York, Viking Press, and
London, Secker and Warburg, 1967.

Other

Situation Normal.   New York, Reynal, 1944.
Jane's Blanket (for children).   New York, Crowell Collier,
and London, Collier Macmillan, 1963.
In Russia, photographs by Inge Morath.   New York, Studio,
and London, Secker and Warburg, 1969.
The Portable Arthur Miller, edited by Harold Clurman.
New York, Viking Press, 1971; London, Penguin, 1977.
In the Country, photographs by Inge Morath.   New York,
Studio, and London, Secker and Warburg, 1977.
The Theater Essays of Arthur Miller, edited by Robert A.
Martin.   New York, Viking Press, and London, Penguin,
1978.
Chinese Encounters, photographs by Inge Morath.   New
York, Farrar Straus, and London, Secker and Warburg,
1979.
"Salesman" in Beijing.   New York, Viking, and London,
Methuen, 1984.
Timebends (autobiography).   New York, Grove Press, and
London, Methuen, 1987.

*

Bibliography: "Arthur Miller: The Dimension of His Art: A
Checklist of His Published Works," in *Serif* (Kent, Ohio),
June 1967, and *Arthur Miller Criticism (1930–1967)*,
Metuchen, New Jersey, Scarecrow Press, 1969, revised edi-
tion as *An Index to Arthur Miller Criticism*, 1976, both by
Tetsumaro Hayashi; *Arthur Miller: A Reference Guide* by
John H. Ferres, Boston, Hall, 1979.

Manuscript Collections: University of Texas, Austin;
University of Michigan, Ann Arbor; New York Public
Library; Library of Congress, Washington, D.C.

Critical Studies (selection): *Arthur Miller*, Edinburgh, Oliver
and Boyd, and New York, Grove Press, 1961, and *Miller: A
Study of His Plays*, London, Eyre Methuen, 1979, revised
edition as *Miller the Playwright*, Methuen, 1983, both by
Dennis Welland; *Arthur Miller* by Robert Hogan,
Minneapolis, University of Minnesota Press, 1964; *Arthur
Miller: The Burning Glass* by Sheila Huftel, New York,
Citadel Press, and London, W.H. Allen, 1965; *Arthur Miller:
Death of a Salesman: Text and Criticism* edited by Gerald
Weales, New York, Viking Press, 1967; *Arthur Miller* by
Leonard Moss, New York, Twayne, 1967, revised edition,
1980; *Arthur Miller, Dramatist* by Edward Murray, New
York, Ungar, 1967; *Arthur Miller: A Collection of Critical
Essays* edited by Robert W. Corrigan, Englewood Cliffs,
New Jersey, Prentice Hall, 1969; *Psychology and Arthur
Miller* by Richard I. Evans, New York, Dutton, 1969; *The
Merrill Guide to Arthur Miller* by Sidney H. White,
Columbus, Ohio, Merrill, 1970; *Arthur Miller: Portrait of a
Playwright* by Benjamin Nelson, New York, McKay, and
London, Owen, 1970; *Arthur Miller* by Ronald Hayman,
London, Heinemann, 1970, New York, Ungar, 1972;
Twentieth-Century Interpretations of The Crucible edited by
John H. Ferres, Englewood Cliffs, New Jersey, Prentice Hall,
1972; *Studies in Death of a Salesman* edited by Walter J.
Meserve, Columbus, Ohio, Merrill, 1972; *Critical Essays on
Arthur Miller* edited by James J. Martine, Boston, Hall, 1979;

Arthur Miller: New Perspectives edited by Robert A. Martin,
Englewood Cliffs, New Jersey, Prentice Hall, 1982; *Arthur
Miller* by Neil Carson, London, Macmillan, and New York,
Grove Press, 1982; *Twentieth-Century Interpretations of
Death of a Salesman* edited by Helene Wickham Koon,
Englewood Cliffs, New Jersey, Prentice Hall, 1983; *Conver-
sations with Arthur Miller* edited by Matthew C. Roudané,
Jackson, University Press of Mississippi, 1987; *File on Miller*
edited by C.W.E. Bigsby, London, Methuen, 1988.

Theatrical Activities:
Director: **Plays**—*The Price*, London, 1969; *Up from
Paradise*, Ann Arbor, Michigan, 1974; *Two-Way Mirror*,
New Haven, Connecticut, 1982; *Death of a Salesman*,
Beijing, 1983, Stockholm, 1992.
Actor: **Play**—Narrator in *Up from Paradise*, Ann Arbor,
Michigan, 1974. **Television**—*The Civil War*.

Arthur Miller comments:
   I have, I think, provided actors with some good things to do
and say. Beyond that I cannot speak with any certainty. My
plays seem to exist and that's enough for me. What people
may find in them or fail to find is not in my control anymore; I
can only hope that life has not been made less for what I've
done, and possibly a bit more.

*   *   *

How may a man make of the outside world a home?

   I am constantly awed by what an individual is, by the
endless possibilities in him for good and evil, by his
unpredictability, by the possibilities he has for any
betrayal, any cruelty, as well as any altruism, any
sacrifice.

—Arthur Miller

   Arthur Miller writes primarily about man's relationship to
society and the issues of personal identity and human dignity.
Throughout, he has used the realistic form. His statement of
purpose—to write "a drama of the whole-man"—conveys his
interest in psychology as well as morality. Miller frequently
uses what T.S. Eliot called the "objective correlative" ("a set
of objects, a situation, a chain of events which shall be the
formula of that *particular* emotion") in order to combine an
extraordinarily forceful theater with uncanny psychological
insights and lyrical and poetic vision. His aim is a theater that
"teaches, not by proposing solutions but by defining
problems."
   The *Collected Plays* of 1957 portray the individual struggling against the laws of society, family, and even selfhood—
torn between either the dreams the dog-eat-dog world has
imposed upon him and his essential goodness, or torn between his deepest wishes for the simple life and the needs he
feels obliged to meet. Set against a ruthless capitalist system
that ignores or uses the common man, his identity frequently
consists of merely accommodating himself to an essentially
alien universe (society) and the act of painstakingly supporting his family. Sometimes, however, he learns that he never
was in fact connected with family or job, let alone society, or
that the values of each were equally spurious.
   Miller's first successful play, *All My Sons*, portrays the
conflict between the idealistic son (Chris) and his materialisti-
cally corrupted father (Joe Keller). To retain his business,
Keller has shipped out defective plane parts which have
ultimately caused the deaths of many fliers. The seeds of the
great *Death of a Salesman* are here—from the stage setting
(with the Keller's house and the impinging presence of the

more successful neighbors) to the use of poetic images (wind, the car), to even specific rhetorical cadences ("Nobody in this house dast take her faith away"). Here is the eternally forgiving, self-deluding wife-mother; her idealistic sons (one has committed suicide for his principles); the poignant and misguided bond between father and son; and the father's suicide to expiate a lifetime of wrong commitment. Here is Miller's vision of the terrible rat-race of ordinary, business reality, and one's better knowledge of the need to love other men. One bears a responsibility to the other, and "can be better! Once and for all you can know there's a universe of people outside and you're responsible to it." This, however, becomes increasingly difficult to enact, as one's love for his family may also tear him apart: "There's nothin' he could do that I wouldn't forgive. Because he's my son. Because I'm his father and he's my son."

Miller's masterpiece, *Death of a Salesman*, measures the enormous gap between America's promise of inevitable success and the devastating reality of one's concrete failure. Commitment to false social values blinds one to the true values of human experience—the comforts of personal relationships, of family and friendship, of love. Identity and commitment are again the subject. Willie Loman, who might well exemplify Miller's definition of the tragic hero (in his important essay "Tragedy and the Common Man"), has completely sold himself to what is at best an anachronistic dream —that anyone can get ahead. This is what he has been brought up to believe, the promise of his mythic (salesmen) heroes. While Willie has pursued this for 40 years and has sold it to his two sons, he is blind to its contemporary meaninglessness and to his own (and their) failure. But Willie *is* a great salesman—of the old American dream—and even his wife, the loyal Linda, lives in a world of self-generating lies and illusions. What Willie comes to realize on this single day of the play—his "recognition scene"—is that he has totally overlooked his true wealth, that he is a deeply loved father. Ironically, armed with this knowledge, he defies the system that has until now defeated him. He commits suicide to give his sons the only thing his society respects—cash. In defiance, irony, and profound bitterness, Miller sends Willie to his death with the same illusion he has lived by—though Willie is now fully aware of and in control of it. This is Miller's most bitter picture of the system that uses the little man—that eats the orange and throws away the peel. As tattered and self-pitying as Willie sometimes appears, he is one of the theater's most poignant and moving figures.

Miller has connected the origins of *The Crucible* with McCarthyism, with the "political, objective knowledgable campaign from the far Right [which] was capable of creating not only a terror, but a new subjective reality, a veritable mystique which was gradually assuming even a holy resonance." Specifically about the Salem witch trials of 1692, the play also treats the national paranoia, hysteria, and general immorality that characterized the McCarthy witch-hunts. Miller bitterly attacks the society that rewards the suppression of freedom in the name of "right" and conformity. Two lines summarize his focus: the rhetorical "Is the accusor always holy?" and "You must understand . . . that a person is either with this court or he must be counted against it, there be no road between." Although this has been called a modern morality play, Miller goes beyond black/white characterizations to portray his figures' petty rivalries and moral ambiguities. He probes the political, social, and psychological needs of both those who capitulate and those who resist. Mr. Proctor, after defying the court's demands, finally regains his name (also important to Willie and Keller) and dies in another act of defiance. Once again, Miller illustrates his

conviction that one can assert his "personal dignity" and "act against the scheme of things that degrades." As he puts it in *All My Sons*, one can be "better."

A Memory of Two Mondays, which Miller has expressed an especial fondness for, brings back the depression years. It was produced initially with *A View from the Bridge*, which treats the hardworking and likeable Eddie Carbone who, out of blind love toward his niece-ward, informs on the illegal immigrants he is presumably safeguarding; one is his niece's boyfriend. Blind to what really drives him ("You can never have her"), and defiant of community, family, and natural law, he endures public humiliation for his act of treason. His grief is overwhelming as he cries the familiar: "I want my name"; he draws a knife and once again Miller's protagonist precipitates his own death. Although the play is, as Miller intended, simpler than *Salesman*, it recalls it in many ways: two men in conflict with a third, an authority figure; the (surrogate) father's blind worship of his charge ("She's the best"); the ever-supportive and loving wife; it also retains certain expressionistic elements (the narrator functions like a Greek chorus and frames each section in mythic terms).

For the next nine years, Miller wrote short stories, prose essays (the important "The Shadow of Gods"), and the screen-play *The Misfits*. With *After the Fall* he turns from the family and one's obligation to connect with the social world to a more existential statement: the recuperative and regenerative powers of love, the question of personal or universal guilt, and the necessity of man to justify himself to himself (rather than the system)—the need for human community and love, and the fact that one *is* his brother's keeper. Despite the many critical attempts to pigeonhole *After the Fall* autobiographically (with Maggie as Miller's wife, Marilyn Monroe), Miller has said that the play is no more autobiographical than his other work. It treats, he continues, the self-destructiveness of a character who views herself as "pure victim." In this stream-of-consciousness drama, Quentin, the protagonist, subjects all of his values to scrutiny. His statement—"the bench was empty. No judge in sight. And all that remained was the endless argument with oneself, this pointless litigation of existence before any empty bench"— and the tone of the entire piece redefines Miller's conviction that one must come to terms with his own acts and values. As Quentin confronts his parents, wives, and the various situations of his recent and past life, Miller suggests that we all bear the mark of Cain; we are all born after the fall and are responsible for all our acts. After such knowledge *is* forgiveness: the play ends with the affirmative "Hello."

Themes of commitment, responsibility, and integrity continue in *Incident at Vichy*, where the aristocrat Von Berg (the mirror image of Quentin) transfers his own freedom to the Jewish Leduc and accepts his own death. Miller raises questions about sacrifice and guilt ("the soul's remorse for his own hostility"). The play investigates the need we all have for scapegoats and the suffering "other." "You must face your own complicity," he writes, "with . . . your own humanity." One must accept not only his own evil (and goodness) but also the sacrifices and kindness of others.

The Price returns to two brothers, the poles of love and money, the sacrifices and selfishness of each, and the terrible lack of relationship that always existed between the two—the terrible "price" that rivalry and lovelessness exact. Unlike Von Berg in *Incident*, the brothers have given nothing, and they therefore have nothing. Gregory Solomon, the antiques dealer, teaches that one must give without expecting repayment; he understands the gratuitousness of love. One must embrace community while realizing the utter isolation that is finally the human condition.

Although in 1972 Miller said that his plays were becoming more mythical, *The Creation of the World and Other Business* (about God's conflict with Lucifer over the behavior of Adam and Eve, and Cain and Abel) is an existential query into the nature of individual responsibility. Miller's most recent works have been less than successful. *The American Clock* is a series of vignettes in which the fate of a Depression family—the not particularly heroic Baums—is intertwined with that of a remarkably heroic nation during the 1930's. An overly ambitious effort, Miller describes it "as though the whole country were really the setting"; it was intended, he explains, to be "a mural for the theater inspired by Studs Terkel's *Hard Times.*" The two minidramas of *Two-Way Mirror*, on the other hand, are extremely modest, although they are intended as "passionate voyages through the masks of [agonizing] illusion." *Elegy for a Lady* focuses on a middle-aged man who, while selecting a gift for his dying mistress, indulges in a conversation on the pain of love with the boutique proprietress. In *Some Kind of Love Story* a detective visits an old girlfriend, now a call girl, who may be the key figure in clearing a murder suspect. The 20-minute *The Last Yankee* treats two men—one, an affluent businessman with seven children; the other, a carpenter with no children—who meet in a mental hospital. They are waiting to visit their wives, both of whom suffer from severe depression. The men discuss the possible reasons for their wives' illness, in the course of which they realize that the women's symptoms, and obviously their causes—specifically, their marriages—are totally different. At the end of the play, as the social and economic rivalries between the men become dominant, Miller evokes a subtle perspective on the ubiquitousness of human need and self-absorption, both of which inevitably destroy personal relationships.

The Ride Down Mount Morgan is presumably a "comedy" about bigamy, although Miller himself describes his sombre subject as "what it takes out of a man to get everything he wants in marriage and life." While there are some comic moments, the play really focuses on marital deception and responsibility. Miller portrays a 50ish husband named Lyman Felt—a Willy Loman gone astray, a one-time poet, now salesman (insurance) magnate, who has gone the limits of marital infidelity. Lyman is a nine-year bigamist, who has negotiated "two sublimely happy marriages . . . without being humbled." Throughout the play, Lyman (and Miller) rationalizes his clearly immoral life. That is to say, as he "loves each wife equally," he prides himself on his efforts to understand true selfhood. "You can either be true to yourself or to other people," he says, and, "A loser lives someone else's life. I've lived my own life." The play is constructed as a series of flashbacks in Lyman's hospital room following his car accident on icy Mount Morgan. It is here that the two wives, Leah and Theodora (one a young Jewish businesswoman; the other, a WASPY older woman) first meet and learn the truth. Ultimately, each rejects him as a deceptive liar. Miller said of the play: "We have no solution to this problem. We have an instinctual life, and we have a social life," a variation of Lyman's remark to his lawyer: "Look, we're all the same." Perhaps more pertinent to Miller's audience, however, is Lyman's revelation: "I know what's wrong with me—I could never stand still for death! Which you've got to do, by a certain age, or be ridiculous—you've got to stand there nobly and serene and let death run his tape out your arms and around your belly and up your crotch until he's got you fitted for that last black suit. And I can't. I won't! So I'm left wrestling with this anachronistic energy which God has charged

me with and I will use it till the dirt is shoveled into my mouth."

—Lois Gordon

<hr>

MILLER, Jason. American. Born John Miller in Long Island City, New York, 22 April 1939. Educated at St. Patrick's High School, Scranton, Pennsylvania; Scranton University, B.A. 1961; Catholic University, Washington D.C., 1962–63. Married Linda Gleason in 1963 (divorced 1973); one daughter and two sons. Stage and film actor. Recipient: New York Drama Critics Circle award, 1972; Tony award, 1973; Pulitzer prize, 1973. Address: c/o Screen Actors Guild, 7750 Sunset Boulevard, Los Angeles, California 90046, U.S.A.

PUBLICATIONS

Plays

Three One-Act Plays: Lou Gehrig Did Not Die of Cancer, It's a Sin to Tell a Lie, The Circus Lady (produced New York, 1970).   New York, Dramatists Play Service, 1972.
Nobody Hears a Broken Drum (produced New York, 1970). New York, Dramatists Play Service, 1971.
That Championship Season (produced New York, 1972; London, 1974).   New York, Atheneum, and London, Davis Poynter, 1972.

Screenplay: *That Championship Season*, 1982.

Television Play: *Reward*, 1980.

Verse

Stone Step. New York, Jadis Yumi, 1968.

*

Theatrical Activities:
Director: **Film**—*That Championship Season*, 1982.
Actor: **Plays**—Champlain Shakespeare Festival, Vermont; Cincinnati Shakespeare Festival; New York Shakespeare Festival; Edmund in *Long Day's Journey into Night* by O'Neill; Tom in *The Glass Menagerie* by Tennessee Williams; Pip in *Pequod* by Roy S. Richardson, New York, 1969; Poker Player in *The Odd Couple* by Neil Simon, Fort Worth, Texas, 1970; Assistant in *The Happiness Cage* by Dennis J. Reardon, New York, 1970; Rogoshin in *Subject to Fits* by Robert Montgomery, New York, 1971; in *Juno and the Paycock* by O'Casey, Washington, D.C., 1971. **Films**—*The Exorcist*, 1972; *The Nickel Ride*, 1975; *The Devil's Advocate*, 1977; *Marilyn—The Untold Story*, 1980; *Twinkle, Twinkle Killer Kane (The Ninth Configuration)*, 1980; *Monsignor*, 1982; *Toy Soldiers*, 1984. **Television**—*A Home of Our Own*, 1975; *F. Scott Fitzgerald in Hollywood*, 1976; *The Dain Curse*, 1978; *Vampire*, 1979; *The Henderson Monster*, 1980; *The Best Little Girl in the World*, 1981; *A Touch of Scandal*, 1984.

* * *

Jason Miller's *That Championship Season* is a solid, vibrant play. The solidity comes in part from the familiar structure of the play—too familiar, at points—but Miller's freshness of detail saves the evening.

The event that occasions the drama has been used a lot: it is a reunion, in this case of four members of a champion high-school basketball team of twenty years ago. The fifth man on stage is the now-retired coach who has taught them that winning is all that counts—in basketball and in life. As Walter Kerr pointed out, the set itself is familiar—limp lace curtains and a steep staircase that recalls the conventional naturalism of William Inge's *The Dark at the Top of the Stairs*.

In fact, the experienced play-goer knows within two minutes what the arc of things will be: the men have come together to celebrate and live again their triumph, but before the night is out it will be revealed how everything has gone rotten somehow. And so it turns out. One of the players is now mayor of the small Pennsylvania town, and he is proud of it. But underneath he is a loser—and indeed it is obvious he will be thrown out of the forthcoming election.

Another team-mate has been his chief financial backer—a man made rich through the strip-mining that ecologists condemn. But now he sees the mayor will lose, so he wants to shift his backing to another candidate.

A third player is now a school principal who wants to be superintendent. When the mayor tells him that he can't back him because it will hurt his own candidacy, the superintendent angrily blurts out that the strip-miner is sleeping with the mayor's wife, and he says he'll tell the whole town if they don't support him. But he is a mediocrity; he knows it, his own young son knows it, and everyone on stage knows it. The coach calls his bluff, knowing he is even too much of a mediocrity to do something so substantial as tell the town about the mayor's wife.

The fourth player is now an alcoholic but he nevertheless sees things more clearly than the rest. It is he who brings up Martin. In basketball there are five players: Martin was the fifth, and at first he is mourned as if dead. Ultimately it is revealed that he has simply gone away, turning his back on the coach and his dogmas. It was Martin who, at the coach's direction, broke the ribs of the "nigger" who was the star of the other team, and it's clear that's the only reason our boys won.

The play uncovers the dark underside of that old triumph and the abject failure beneath any gloss of current success. The coach is shown to be a bigot, a right-wing supporter of Joe McCarthy, a champion of the ugly ethic that to win is to be good.

So the route of the play is familiar and so are the figures. But the figures are not cardboard—Miller fills in their dimension with the rich detail of an orthodox novelist. And the play is not without surprises. In particular it is verbally surprising. Lines are fresh and newly honed. And the humor is painfully superb. Cautioning the mayor not to exploit the fact of his handicapped child, the alcoholic says, "You lose the mongoloid vote right there." And he denies he has a liquor problem: "I can get all I want."

Miller's limitation, at least in this play, is his conventionality, his predictability. But many regard the theatrical experimentation on the American scene as unrewarding, and other traditionalists have lost the vitality that Miller found in this play. It's a somber comment on American theatre that one of the most promising plays of the early 1970's could have been written in the early 1950's.

—Thomas J. McCormack

MILLER, Susan. American. Born in Philadelphia, Pennsylvania, 6 April 1944. Educated at Pennsylvania State University, University Park, B.A. 1965; Bucknell University, Lewisburg, Pennsylvania, M.A. 1970. Instructor in English, Pennsylvania State University, 1969–73; lecturer in playwriting, University of California, Los Angeles, 1975–76; playwright-in-residence, Mark Taper Forum Theatre, Los Angeles, 1975. Recipient: Rockefeller grant, 1975; National Endowment for the Arts grant, 1976; Obie award, 1979. Agent: Joyce Ketay Agency, 334 West 89th Street, New York, New York 10024, U.S.A.

PUBLICATIONS

Plays

No One Is Exactly 23 (produced University Park, Pennsylvania). Published in *Pyramid 1* (Belmont, Massachusetts), 1968.
Daddy, and A Commotion of Zebras (produced New York, 1970).
Silverstein & Co. (produced New York, 1972).
Confessions of a Female Disorder (produced Hartford, Connecticut, 1973). Published in *Gay Plays*, edited by William M. Hoffman, New York, Avon, 1979.
Denim Lecture (produced Los Angeles, 1974).
Flux (produced New York 1975; London, 1976; revised version produced New York, 1977, 1982).
Cross Country (produced Los Angeles, 1976; New York, 1977). Published in *West Coast Plays* (Berkeley, California), 1978.
Nasty Rumors and Final Remarks (produced New York, 1979).
Arts and Leisure (produced Los Angeles, 1985).
For Dear Life (produced New York, 1989).
It's Our Town, Too (produced Los Angeles, 1992).

Television Plays: *Home Movie* (*Family* series); *One for the Money, Two for the Show*, with Nedra Deen; *A Whale for the Killing*; *Visions* series.

* * *

In Susan Miller's *Arts and Leisure*, the character J.D. Salinger inquires of the Professor—about a student's films—"Does her work astonish you?" Miller's startling explorations of women's minds and hearts do just that, especially creating the shock of recognition in spectators who, like her characters, write, teach, or experience turbulent relationships. Miller's plays most frequently explore issues of intimacy and of evolving sexual identity. In contrast to her self-protective Dina in *Flux*, who pleads "I'm not eager to expose private agonies," Miller persists in such probing, in plays characterized by their whimsy yet potential violence, passion yet playfulness.

Most of Miller's full-length plays include a tap dance, and nearly all her funny dramas or poignant comedies end on an upbeat note—with Jake's optimism, with Ronnie's self-discovery, with Jess regaining her confidence, with Salinger gladly relinquishing his manuscripts, with Perry beginning a new life; in fact, the last line of *Cross Country* finds Perry greeting new companions. Although the title of *Nasty Rumors and Final Remarks* suggests that Raleigh's demise concerns Miller, actually the dramatist focuses on the life of this quicksilver woman, who can't be confined by her hospital bed or defined by her friends, lovers, or offspring; hence, even Raleigh after her stroke seems affirmative. So does Miller's reply to the Republican's 1992 convention; although *It's Our Town, Too*, because it follows the structure of her model by Thornton Wilder, ends at the graveyard, it affirms respect for those who are different, for values other than those of fundamentalist Christians, and for families other than the old-fashioned model of homemaker mother, wage-earning father, two children, and a dog.

Miller's language provides part of her plays' fascination. She builds her rhythms into her lines so their catchy cadences prove actor-proof. In natural dialogue, fragmented but also filled with expressive turns of phrase, her characters fumble to express their panic or pleasure, occasionally achieving eloquent accuracy. *Cross Country*, for instance, says of Perry's wrenching herself out of her marriage to take off in search of professional and personal fulfilment: "There is a moment, like the black holes in space, of complete and irrevocable loss. To allow that moment is to let go of the sides of time, to fall into another place where it is not likely any of your old friends will recognize you again." Often Miller's lines provide witty insights into women's lives, as when a character remarks that, because we are so often interrupted while looking after others, "Women live longer just to finish their conversations."

Miller chooses as her characters writers and others in the arts, usually women in crisis or transition, experiencing problems living with others or in their own skin. One of several protagonists bearing names unusual for women, Ronnie in *Confessions of a Female Disorder* makes the transition from puberty to marriage and career while struggling to avoid confronting her attraction to women. The title expresses both Ronnie's love of women and a female penchant for abnegation. Perry leaves her marriage to find herself. *Flux*'s iconoclast Jess, on the edge and unable to contain her emotions or control those she inspires in others, turns on her students to her considerable charms instead of to English, making a mess in the classroom and in her personal life as well. *Nasty Rumors and Final Remarks* takes dying Raleigh on an adventure of self-discovery; nobody else could tame her enough to know her. Catherine and Jake in *For Dear Life* differ too profoundly to sustain their relationship: she always expects the worst, while her husband flees her pessimism, which begins to infect him. Yet, ironically, she proves correct in her fears that their marriage will crumble.

Such early Miller works as the Jewish-American rites-of-passage black comedy *Silverstein & Co.* and her one-act *No One is Exactly 23* employ absurdist styles. As her craft developed, however, Miller suited her form to her objective, often combining presentational and representational conventions in the same play and varying her structure to fit her purpose. Although frequently employing surface verisimilitude, Miller sticks to that style throughout only in *Arts and Leisure*, in which the Professor and Ginny break into the New Hampshire farmhouse of J.D. Salinger—"the Greta Garbo of American letters"—threatening to blow up his home unless the reclusive but compulsive writer turns over all his unpublished manuscripts. Establishing immediate suspense and then sustaining it throughout, Miller confines the action to less than 24 hours on a single set.

At the other extreme, Miller's most surprising play structurally, *Cross Country*, employs huge chunks of narration (distributed among the cast, rather than assigned to a single narrator) as well as stage directions which the actors speak aloud, as in chamber theatre. This highly episodic play dramatizes some scenes in a single sentence, or gives one line to two characters who interact on stage simultaneously, but in fact separately, with protagonist Perry. Miller begins by des-

cribing what happens after the play's middle, and the narrative occurs mostly in the past tense. After repeatedly jumping around in its chronology, however, *Cross Country* eventually moves forward to Perry's new life on the West Coast.

Miller experiments with chronology in another fashion with *For Dear Life*, which disrupts linear progression through time by moving from a "present" in Act I, to 18 years later in Act II, to 16 years before that in Act III. In other words, Act III occurs about two years after Act I, but the intervening act flashes far forward. The style, meanwhile, moves from mostly representational to often presentational. Miller unifies the unusual construction with a speech which we watch Jake prepare during the first act and which his son quotes at the end of the play, when he's supposed to be one year old—but we see him then as the teenager he was in the previous act. The disrupted chronology of the play's construction permits Miller to show us in Act III the problems which cause the divorce which Act II has already shown us does occur. The couple in the third act wait for their happiness to end—as we know it must. Not only Act II but the title also tells us that they are hanging on for dear life, clinging to a relationship as though to a lifeline, even though logic dictates letting go.

Confessions of a Female Disorder, perhaps the most fluid of all Miller's unconventionally constructed plays, takes Ronnie from her first menstrual period and the start of her search for a man through her gathering with other women in her kitchen to begin exploring facets of themselves. So presentational and episodic is this play that Miller hops Ronnie out of a shower straight into her shrink's office in mid-lather and pops husband David in "out of sequence," a line which acknowledges to spectators that we all know this is a play, not a slice of life. "Cheerleaders" and "Lettermen" jump in and out of the action both to comment and to take minor roles (such as the guys who offer her a sexual experience superior to her first time); when coercing her into marriage, Ronnie's shrink turns into a minister.

Although Miller has revised *Flux* several times, each version employs presentational, episodic scenes conveying the quality of dreams and nightmares which do for the collapse of female self-esteem what Arthur Miller (no relation) did for male disintegration in *Death of a Salesman*. Moving freely from the classroom, Saul's bedroom, Jess's house, Jess's office, and her mentor's office or classroom, Miller dramatizes Jess's disorienting mismatch of expectations with those of her students and partner. Such construction and style convey what Jess and her students experience emotionally rather than factually; thus, the mentor performs a con artist's shell game, the students don pyjamas and brush their teeth in the classroom, and a voice-over about student evaluations accompanies an orgy. Clearly Jess and her students populate each other's dreams.

Miller's most unusual temporal distortions occur in *Nasty Rumors and Final Remarks*; while Raleigh experiences a cerebral haemorrhage on one side of the stage, others elsewhere deal with its aftermath. Only one preliminary scene has established Raleigh's personality before the stroke. As time passes, Raleigh begins narrating and describing herself in the third person, past tense (somewhat like *Cross Country*); while she's supposed to be in a coma and dying, we see her talking to us and eavesdropping on her male lover, her female lover, her friend. Raleigh's ramblings round the hospital are intersected by flashbacks which dramatize her relationships to these people who have gathered to wait for her death. These presentational episodes connect so seamlessly in a montage of past events and present passions that we scarcely notice the technique, till everyone gathers to bid goodbye to the dead woman.

Raleigh has proven unreliable, unpredictable, unfaithful, and unnerving to all who care about her. Yet when the play ends, we miss her, as we do all Miller's protagonists—usually brilliant, beautiful, bisexual women who fascinate and bewilder their admirers, who cannot tame their whirlwind natures. In dramatizing them Miller explores such themes as how to couple successfully, how to balance professional and personal fulfillment, how to know and be oneself, and how to behave responsibly towards others without betraying oneself. Miller balances her evocation of anxiety and loneliness with a sense of elation at rising to the challenges of intimacy and career. Repeatedly she achieves the trademark Miller effect of locating our hidden lacerations, then tickling those wounds till we're convulsed.

—Tish Dace

MILNER, Ron(ald). American. Born in Detroit, Michigan, 29 May 1938. Educated at Northeastern High School, Detroit; Highland Park Junior College, Detroit; Detroit Institute of Technology; Columbia University, New York. Writer-in-residence, Lincoln University, Pennsylvania, 1966–67; taught at Michigan State University, East Lansing, 1971–72. Founding director, Spirit of Shango theatre company, and Langston Hughes Theatre, Detroit. Recipient: John Hay Whitney fellowship, 1962; Rockefeller grant, 1965. Address: c/o Crossroads Theatre Company, 320 Memorial Parkway, New Brunswick, New Jersey 08901, U.S.A.

PUBLICATIONS

Plays

Who's Got His Own (produced New York, 1966).   Published in *Black Drama Anthology*, edited by Milner and Woodie King, New York, New American Library, 1971.
The Monster (produced Chicago, 1969). Published in *Drama Review* (New York), Summer 1968.
The Warning: A Theme for Linda (produced New York, 1969).   Published in *A Black Quartet: Four New Black Plays*, New York, New American Library, 1970.
(M)Ego and the Green Ball of Freedom (produced Detroit, 1971).   Published in *Black World* (Chicago), April 1971.
What the Wine-Sellers Buy (produced Los Angeles, 1973; New York, 1974).   New York, French, 1974.
These Three (produced Detroit, 1974).
Season's Reasons (produced Detroit, 1976; New York, 1977).
Jazz Set, music by Max Roach (produced Los Angeles, 1979; New York, 1982).
Crack Steppin' (produced Detroit, 1981).
Roads of the Mountaintop (produced New Brunswick, New Jersey, 1986).
Don't Get God Started, music and lyrics by Marvin Winans (also director: produced New York, 1987).
Checkmates (produced Los Angeles, 1987; New York, 1988).

Other

Editor, with Woodie King, *Black Drama Anthology*.   New York, New American Library, 1971.

*   *   *

Playwright Ron Milner is considered one of the more exciting writers who came to national prominence during the explosive Black Theatre movement of the 1960's. Much like his contemporaries, Ed Bullins and Amiri Baraka, he was influenced by both the social and political conditions of those times. A native Detroiter, Milner, who has often been called "the people's playwright," has had his works described as being rich in the authentic texture of life in the urban black setting. He has repeatedly been praised for his powerful use of language and observation of character. His characters often examine their self-perceptions and identity while questioning their place in a complex and oppressive world. This introspection enables them to come to a new understanding of themselves, thereby changing how they relate to that world.

Reminiscent of Lorraine Hansberry's *A Raisin in the Sun*, Milner's first full-length play, *Who's Got His Own*, portrays the damaged relationships of a recently widowed mother with her alienated son and embittered daughter. The drama explores the impact that living in a racist society has on black manhood. Opening with the funeral of the domineering patriarch, the son—Tim, Jr.—is forced to address the conflicting feelings of disgust and love he has for his father. After Mrs. Bronson reveals several unspoken truths about her husband, Tim, Jr. and his sister, Clara are better able to understand their father in a new way, thereby coming to terms with those feelings.

Milner's next play, a one-act drama called *The Warning: A Theme for Linda*, again examines the theme of black manhood. However, unlike *Who's Got His Own*, the issue is dealt with entirely through the unpleasant and whimsical experiences of women. Linda, a 17-year-old girl living in an impoverished section of Detroit, daydreams about men and what it means to be a woman. In contrast to her fantasies, Linda's alcoholic mother and resentful grandmother tell her of their disastrous encounters with men, warning her to stay clear of them. Finally, after deciding to discard both the imaginary men of her dreams and those of the stories told by her mother and grandmother, Linda instead decides to begin a serious, sexual relationship with her boyfriend, Donald. She confronts him with the challenge of sharing their futures together as equals in mind, body, and soul.

In 1973, Milner combined his concern for the temptations besetting urban black youth with an examination of the destructive black role models of pimps and drug-dealers created by Hollywood. Set in Detroit, *What the Wine-Sellers Buy* deals with a young high-school boy choosing between good and evil. The boy, Steve Carlton, is forced to decide whether to follow the advice of a pimp named Rico who suggests that he turns his girlfriend into a prostitute to raise money for Steve's sick mother. By following Rico's advice, Steve would simultaneously satisfy his mother's medical needs while condemning his girlfriend Mae to a life of depravity. Steve's struggle with his conscience allowed Milner again to address the theme of black male responsibility. Finally, Steve comes to the correct moral decision by understanding that the cost would be too high for himself and his girlfriend.

Set in Detroit in the late 1980's, *Checkmates* depicts the vast differences in the value systems of two generations of African-American couples: a young upwardly mobile professional pair, and their older, middle-class, traditionally-minded landlords. Milner shows the world in which we live as one devoid of the strong moral and social values it once had. Initially the younger couple—Sylvester and Laura—appear to have it all: successful careers, good looks, love, and financial security. As the play progresses, their commitment to one another is tested as they confront growing individual needs. For Laura, it is her desire for a career that justifies having an abortion without Sylvester's knowledge. Sylvester displays self-centeredness when he becomes physically abusive after increased feelings of paranoia regarding his job and the discovery of Laura's abortion. Eventually the distrust created between Laura and Sylvester pushes them both into the arms of other lovers. Their "anything goes" code of behavior actually helps to create a division in their relationship during times of strife. Rather than bringing them closer, Sylvester and Laura's troubles enlarge the division between them which eventually makes their love for one another seem futile, and finally leads to divorce.

In contrast, through reminiscent flashbacks we see that the older couple of Frank and Mattie have also dealt with infidelity, physical abuse, and the frustrations of racism on the job. However, in each of these experiences Frank and Mattie chose personal sacrifice over self-centered behavior; children were not seen as being in conflict with individual desires, and adultery and physical abuse was simply not tolerated. It is through their lives that we see how these sacrifices for the marriage have strengthened their relationship. Because of their more traditional value system, Frank and Mattie's world is more stable. Theirs is a code of behavior which helps them live through troubled times.

—Gary Anderson

MINGHELLA, Anthony. British. Born in Ryde, Isle of Wight, 6 January 1954. Educated at the University of Hull, Yorkshire (Reckitt Travel Award), B.A. (honours) 1975. Lecturer in drama, University of Hull, 1976–81. Recipient: London Theatre Critics award, 1984, 1986. Lives in London. Agent: Judy Daish Associates, 83 Eastbourne Mews, London W2 6LQ, England.

Publications

Plays

Mobius the Stripper, adaptation of the story by Gabriel Josipovici (also director: produced Hull, 1975).
Child's Play (also director: produced Hull, 1978).
Whale Music (also director: produced Hull, 1980; London, 1981). Included in Whale Music and Other Plays, 1987.
A Little Like Drowning (produced Hemel Hempstead, Hertfordshire, 1982; London, 1984). Included in Whale Music and Other Plays, 1987.
Two Planks and a Passion (produced Exeter, 1983; London, 1984). Included in Whale Music and Other Plays, 1987.
Love Bites (produced Derby, 1984).
What If It's Raining? (televized 1986). Included in Interior: Room, Exterior: City, 1989.
Made in Bangkok (produced London, 1986). London, Methuen, 1986.
Whale Music and Other Plays. London, Methuen, 1987.
Hang Up (broadcast 1987). Included in Interior: Room, Exterior: City, 1989.
Cigarettes and Chocolate (broadcast 1988). Included in Interior: Room, Exterior: City, 1989.

Interior: Room, Exterior: City (includes Cigarettes and Chocolate, Hang Up, What If It's Raining?). London, Methuen, 1989.
Living with Dinosaurs and One-Act Plays and Sketches. London, Methuen, 1991.
Plays 1 (includes Made in Bangkok, Whale Music, A Little Like Drowning, Two Planks and a Passion). London, Methuen, 1992.
Truly, Madly, Deeply (screenplay). London, Methuen, 1992.

Screenplay: Truly, Madly, Deeply, 1991.

Radio Plays: Hang Up, 1987; Cigarettes and Chocolate, 1988.

Television Plays: Studio series, 1983; What If It's Raining? 1986; Inspector Morse, from a novel by Colin Dexter, 1987; Storyteller series, 1987 (USA); Signals (opera), music by John Lunn and Orlando Gough, 1989; Driven to Distraction, episode in Inspector Morse series, 1990.

Novels

On the Line (novelization of television series). London, Severn House, 1982.
The Storyteller (novelization of television series). London, Boxtree, 1988.

*

Theatrical Activities:
Director: **Plays**—some of his own plays. **Film**—Truly, Madly, Deeply, 1991.

* * *

Anthony Minghella emerged as one of the most consistently adventurous younger British dramatists of the 1980's. He is a writer refreshingly prepared to tackle a wide variety of subjects, and his plays have been marked by an unsentimental humanism and steadily growing technical confidence as he moved from relatively small-scale work in studio and fringe theatres to wider exposure in the commercial sector.

Whale Music was an early indication of Minghella's original voice; with an all-female cast (Minghella has continued to write superb roles for actresses), it is structured round a diverse group of women waiting in a seaside town for a student friend to have her baby. While the play at times seems over-schematic and, in its succession of short scenes, at points jerkily constructed (the dissolving scenes worked much more surely in a later television version), it still creates a recognisable milieu with understated precision. Tender, ironic, and funny, it contains some memorable writing, particularly a long speech from the drifting Stella, giving room to the pregnant Caroline, savagely corrosive in its picture of the men she encounters in her one-night stands.

A Little Like Drowning is also written in a succession of short scenes, but here ambitiously spanning the years with its fulcrum in the break-up of an Anglo-Italian couple's marriage. Moving between the present on an English beach where the old Leonora recalls her life to her granddaughter, to her 1920's marriage to Alfredo in Italy and Alfredo's affair and later life in Dublin with Julia, the play seamlessly links time and space—a scene in 1939 with Alfredo packing to leave Leonora has both Leonora and Julia on stage, unaware of each other, the scene playing as if their dialogue is totally independent. Minghella continued to explore and celebrate his own Anglo-Italian inheritance, this time on a more epic scale, in *Love Bites*. The first act is set in wartime England, concentrating on two Italian-immigrant brothers, Angelo and Bruno, establishing themselves in the ice-cream business. Particularly impressive in this act is Minghella's handling of Angelo's affair with Elizabeth, a schoolteacher who becomes pregnant by him and to whose love he cannot finally respond; his suggestion of the curiously suspended quality of time during wartime is especially evocative. The second act leaps into the present, set in a convention hotel with Angelo about to be inaugurated as President of the Ice Cream Group of Great Britain. Minghella handles his large cast and canvas here with a sharp sense of focus, painting a vivid picture of the family's tribal relationships among the different generations. Bruno, in disappointed middle age, realises that he has let himself be trapped by the past but comes to realise in a powerfully written late scene that he and Angelo are essentially alike after all; in such scenes, Minghella's control of the play's changes of mood is continuously sure.

He moved completely away from such material in *Two Planks and a Passion*, set in late 14th-century York, where a troubled Richard II, his wife, and his friend the Earl of Oxford have escaped the court's pressures while the workmen's guilds prepare the Mystery Plays for the Feast of Corpus Christi. The play weaves several strands—the royals' mischievous exploitation of local bourgeois snobbery, rivalry among the artisans for patronage, and the workers rehearsing the Crucifixion—including some scenes of high comedy (especially that involving the King mercilessly teasing the fawning mayor during an innovative golf game), gradually drawing them together as the rehearsal becomes a moving performance witnessed by the royal party. The play may occasionally suffer from the lack of one truly dynamic central character but it remains an engaging, grave, and totally individual play.

Two Planks and a Passion gradually brought Minghella into the critical spotlight and a "Most Promising Playwright" award rightly came his way in 1984. That promise was amply confirmed by his first major West End play, *Made in Bangkok*. The play covers a group of English tourists and businessmen in Bangkok; often sharply and satirically funny, its moods keep boldly changing, emerging as a very dark comedy indeed about personal as well as cultural exploitation. He again created a challengingly complex leading female role in Frances, wife of a devious and finally frightening businessman, the only character not tainted by some form of exploitation, and he again demonstrates his ability to handle a multi-scene and intricately interlocking play with accomplished control. He also reaffirmed the theatre's ability to shock, to jolt an audience's moral attitude, as in the scene in which Edward, a repressed homosexual dentist, finally makes a sickeningly pathetic bid for the favours of the hotel-worker guide who has helped him. Minghella's dispassionate (and compassionate) handling of all his characters gave the play a depth of texture that made one intrigued to see in what direction he will travel next.

—Alan Strachan

MITCHELL, Adrian. British. Born in London, 24 October 1932. Educated at Greenways School, Wiltshire; Dauntsey's School, West Lavington, Wiltshire; Christ Church, Oxford (editor, *Isis* magazine, 1954–55), 1952–55. Served in the Royal Air Force, 1951–52. Reporter, Oxford *Mail*, 1955–57, and *Evening Standard*, London, 1957–59; columnist and reviewer, *Daily Mail*, *Woman's Mirror*, the *Sun*, the *Sunday Times*, *Peace News*, *Black Dwarf*, *New Statesman*, and the *Guardian*, all London. Instructor, University of Iowa, Iowa City, 1963–64; Granada fellow in the arts, University of Lancaster, 1967–69; fellow, Wesleyan University Center for the Humanities, Middletown, Connecticut, 1971–72; resident writer, Sherman Theatre, Cardiff, 1974–75; visiting writer, Billericay Comprehensive School, Essex, 1978–80; Judith E. Wilson fellow, Cambridge University, 1980–81; resident writer, Unicorn Theatre for Young People, London, 1982–83. Recipient: Eric Gregory award, 1961; P.E.N. prize for translation, 1966; Tokyo Festival award, for television, 1971. Fellow, Royal Society of Literature, 1988. Agent: Peters, Fraser, and Dunlop Group, 503–504 The Chambers, Chelsea Harbour, Lots Road, London SW10 0XF, England.

PUBLICATIONS

Plays

The Ledge (libretto), music by Richard Rodney Bennett (produced London, 1961).
The Persecution and Assassination of Jean-Paul Marat as Performed by the Inmates of the Asylum of Charenton under the Direction of the Marquis de Sade [*Marat/Sade*], adaptation of a play by Peter Weiss (produced London, 1964; New York, 1965). London, Calder, 1965; New York, Atheneum, 1966.
The Magic Flute, adaptation of the libretto by Schikaneder and Giesecke, music by Mozart (produced London, 1966).
US, with others (produced London, 1966). Published as *US: The Book of the Royal Shakespeare Production US/Vietnam/US/Experiment/Politics . . .*, London, Calder and Boyars, 1968; as *Tell Me Lies*, Indianapolis, Bobbs Merrill, 1968.
The Criminals, adaptation of a play by José Triana (produced London, 1967; New York, 1970).
Tyger: A Celebration of the Life and Work of William Blake, music by Mike Westbrook (produced London, 1971). London, Cape, 1971.
Tamburlane the Mad Hen (for children; produced Devon, 1971).
Man Friday, music by Mike Westbrook (televised 1972; produced London, 1973). With *Mind Your Head*, London, Eyre Methuen, 1974.
Mind Your Head, music by Andy Roberts (produced Liverpool, 1973; London, 1974). With *Man Friday*, London, Eyre Methuen, 1974.
The Government Inspector (as *The Inspector General*, produced Nottingham, 1974; revised version, as *The Government Inspector*, produced London, 1985). London, Methuen, 1985.
A Seventh Man, music by Dave Brown, adaptation of the book by John Berger and Jean Mohr (produced London, 1976).
White Suit Blues, music by Mike Westbrook, adaptation of works by Mark Twain (produced Nottingham and London, 1977).
Houdini: A Circus-Opera, music by Peter Schat (produced Amsterdam, 1977; Aspen, Colorado, 1980). Amsterdam, Clowns, 1977(?).
Uppendown Mooney (produced Welwyn Garden City, Hertfordshire, 1978).

The White Deer (for children), adaptation of the story by James Thurber (produced London, 1978).

Hoagy, Bix, and Wolfgang Beethoven Bunkhaus (produced London, 1979; Indianapolis, 1980).

In the Unlikely Event of an Emergency, music by Stephen McNeff (produced Bath, 1979; London, 1988).

Peer Gynt, adaptation of the play by Ibsen (produced Oxford, 1980).

The Mayor of Zalamea; or, The Best Garrotting Ever Done, adaptation of a play by Calderón (produced London, 1981). Edinburgh, Salamander Press, 1981.

Mowgli's Jungle, adaptation of *The Jungle Book* by Kipling (pantomime; produced Manchester, 1981).

You Must Believe All This (for children), adaptation of "Holiday Romance" by Dickens, music by Nick Bicât and Andrew Dickson (televised 1981). London, Thames Television-Methuen, 1981.

The Wild Animal Song Contest (for children; produced London, 1982).

Life's a Dream, with John Barton, adaptation of a play by Calderón (produced Stratford-on-Avon, 1983; London, 1984).

A Child's Christmas in Wales, with Jeremy Brooks, adaptation of the work by Dylan Thomas (produced Cleveland, 1983).

The Great Theatre of the World, adaptation of a play by Calderón (produced Oxford, 1984).

C'mon Everybody (produced London, 1984).

Animal Farm (lyrics only), book by Peter Hall, music by Richard Peaslee, adaptation of the novel by George Orwell (for children; produced London, 1984; Baltimore, 1986). London, Methuen, 1985; Chicago, Dramatic Publishing Company, 1986.

The Tragedy of King Real (screenplay), in *Peace Plays 1*, edited by Stephen Lowe. London, Methuen, 1985.

Satie Day/Night (produced London, 1986).

The Pied Piper (for children), music by Dominic Muldowney (produced London, 1986). Birmingham, Oberon, 1988.

Mirandolina, adaptation of a play by Goldoni (produced Bristol, 1987).

The Last Wild Wood in Sector 88 (produced Rugby, 1987).

Love Songs of World War Three (produced London, 1988).

Fuente Ovejuna, adaptation of the play by Lope de Vega (produced London, 1988).

Woman Overboard, adaptation of a play by Lope de Vega, music by Monty Norman (produced Watford, 1988).

The Patchwork Girl of Oz, adaptation of the story by L. Frank Baum (for children; produced Watford, 1988).

Anna on Anna (produced Edinburgh and London, 1988; Baltimore, 1990).

The Tragedy of King Real (produced Ongar, Essex, 1989).

Triple Threat (produced London, 1989).

Greatest Hits (produced London, 1992).

Screenplays: *Marat/Sade*, 1966; *Tell Me Lies* (lyrics only), 1968; *The Body* (commentary), 1969; *Man Friday*, 1976; *The Tragedy of King Real*, 1983.

Radio Play: *The Island* (libretto), music by William Russo, 1963.

Television Plays: *Animals Can't Laugh*, 1961; *Alive and Kicking*, 1971; *William Blake* (documentary), 1971; *Man Friday*, 1972; *Somebody Down There Is Crying*, 1974; *Daft As a Brush*, 1975; *The Fine Art of Bubble Blowing*, 1975; *Silver Giant, Wooden Dwarf*, 1975; *Glad Day*, music by Mike Westbrook, 1979; *You Must Believe All This*, 1981; *Juno and*

Avos, from a libretto by Andrei Voznesensky, music by Alexei Rybnikov, 1983.

Initiated and helped write student shows: *Bradford Walk*, Bradford College of Art; *The Hotpot Saga, The Neurovision Song Contest*, and *Lash Me to the Mast*, University of Lancaster; *Move Over Jehovah*, National Association of Mental Health; *Poetry Circus*, Wesleyan University; *Mass Media Mash* and *Mud Fair*, Dartington College of the Arts, 1976 and 1977.

Novels

If You See Me Comin'. London, Cape, and New York, Macmillan, 1962.

The Bodyguard. London, Cape, 1970; New York, Doubleday, 1971.

Wartime. London, Cape, 1973.

Man Friday. London, Futura, 1975.

Verse

(Poems). Oxford, Fantasy Press, 1955.

Poems. London, Cape, 1964.

Peace Is Milk. London, Peace News, 1966.

Out Loud. London, Cape Goliard Press, and New York, Grossman, 1968; revised edition, as *The Annotated Out Loud*, London, Writers and Readers, 1976.

Ride the Nightmare: Verse and Prose. London, Cape, 1971.

Cease-Fire. London, Medical Aid Committee for Vietnam, 1973.

Penguin Modern Poets 22, with John Fuller and Peter Levi. London, Penguin, 1973.

The Apeman Cometh. London, Cape, 1975.

For Beauty Douglas: Collected Poems 1953–1979. London, Allison and Busby, 1982.

Nothingmas Day (for children). London, Allison and Busby, 1984.

On the Beach at Cambridge: New Poems. London, Allison and Busby, 1984.

Love Songs of World War Three (collected song lyrics). London, Allison and Busby, 1989.

Greatest Hits (collected song and lyrics). Newcastle upon Tyne, Bloodaxe, 1992.

Recording: *Poems*, with Stevie Smith, Argo, 1974.

Other (for children)

The Adventures of Baron Munchausen. London, Walker, 1985.

The Baron Rides Out [*on the Island of Cheese, All at Sea*]. London, Walker, and New York, Philomel, 3 vols., 1985–87.

Leonardo, The Lion from Nowhere. London, Deutsch, 1986.

Our Mammoth [*Goes to School, in the Snow*]. London, Walker, 3 vols., 1987–88; San Diego, Harcourt Brace, first 2 vols., 1987–88.

Rhinestone Rhino. London, Methuen, 1989.

Editor, *Strawberry Drums*. London, Macdonald, 1989.

Other

Naked In Cheltenham (miscellany). Cheltenham, Gastoday, 1978.

Tourist Snapshots of Chile. London, Chile Solidarity Campaign, 1985.

Editor, with Richard Selig, *Oxford Poetry 1955.* Oxford, Fantasy Press, 1955.
Editor, *Jump, My Brothers, Jump: Poems from Prison,* by Tim Daly. London, Freedom Press, 1970.

*

Theatrical Activities:
Actor: **Plays**—*C'mon Everybody*, London, 1984; *Love Songs of World War Three*, London, 1988; *Triple Threat*, London, 1989; *Greatest Hits*, London, 1992.

* * *

"A truthful colour supplement. As you turn the pages, conflicting images hit you." Adrian Mitchell's description of his stage show *Mind Your Head* may to some extent be applied to all his dramatic creations. Impossible to pigeon-hole into any one form, they mingle genres indiscriminately, juxtaposing pathos with horror and ribald humour. Instead of adhering to the norms of dramatic artifice, Mitchell appears to seize the chaos and disturbance of modern life and transfer it whole to the stage. Constants of his work are its anarchic individualism and the opposition of its author to establishment mores.

Irony lies at the root of Mitchell's dilemma. A notable "performance" poet, adept in a structured, concentrated medium, he nevertheless strives continually to dispense with the formal restraints of language. Equally, as a playwright, he attempts to eschew established theatrical conventions. Overall, Mitchell's work recalls the 1960's and its legacy of protest, which had a profound influence on his thinking. Together with his contemporary Christopher Logue, he featured prominently in anti-Vietnam War demonstrations, taking part in the famous public poetry readings and contributing to the radical stage show *US*.

All the same, this aspect of Mitchell's writing may be over-stressed. His plays are perhaps more traditional and less unorthodox than they appear at first glance. Centuries ago, Aristophanes combined fantasy, social comment, satire, and personal invective against establishment figures, the action interspersed with song and dance routines. In much the same way, Mitchell's dramas blend the 1960's "happening" with elements of pantomime and old-time music hall, their seemingly random progress broken by songs and comic patter from various members of the cast. *Mind Your Head* typifies this approach, a surreal revamping of the Hamlet legend, built around the passengers and crew of a London bus. Mitchell allows his humour a free rein, using parodies of comic and pop song styles for some of the key passages—Hamlet's Soliloquy, for example, is performed as a Frankie Howerd monologue—and bestowing the names of jazz musicians on his characters. The pantomime atmosphere of the show, with its songs and jokes, provides for audience participation, which accords with Mitchell's "performance" style. A similar work is *Tyger*, where scenes from the daily life of the poet William Blake are expanded to include a fantasy moon-voyage, and several establishment "names" are mercilessly caricatured in song-and-dance form. Mitchell's affinity with Blake is spiritual rather than stylistic, and he is able to evoke the nature of the man by judicious quotation, while retaining his own mixed-genre method of presentation.

Mitchell's television plays tend to show more formal organ-ization than his stage dramas. *Glad Day* is an exception, another Blake tribute where Mitchell manages to transfer some of the spontaneous energy of *Tyger* to the small screen. Like several of Mitchell's dramas, *Glad Day* involved the close co-operation of Mike Westbrook, whose musical accompaniments gave an added power to Blake's poetry, not least in the memorable "Song of the Slave" whose lyrics are intensified by the jazz arrangement. More typical of the television plays is *Man Friday*, a significant work which Mitchell later adapted for the stage and as a novel. It embodies many of Mitchell's most profound beliefs on the theory of white supremacy, which he contrasts with the foundations of so-called "primitive" societies. In a series of dialogues between Crusoe and the "savage" Friday, Mitchell adroitly ridicules not only the white man's "civilizing" mission, but also popular concepts of nationalism, crime and punishment, and property ownership. The stage version, which allows for more audience interaction, is a strong work, but the original television play is the more enduring. Ironically, as with other Mitchell creations, its organized structure ensures its success.

The throwaway "instant" quality of some of Mitchell's writing, his ability to create for specific occasions, may perhaps explain his skill in adapting the work of other writers. His earliest success in this field came in the 1960's, with his verse translation of Weiss's *Marat/Sade*, whose blend of social comment and gallows humour evidently appealed to him. Since then, he has produced versions of works by Dickens, Gogol, Calderón, Goldoni, and—more recently—Baum and Lope de Vega. *You Must Believe All This*, taken from a Dickens original, shows Mitchell to be an adept writer for children, to whom audience participation is a natural response, a skill which is further confirmed by his rearrangement of L. Frank Baum's fables in *The Patchwork Girl of Oz*, and outside the field of drama by his growing number of illustrated books for younger readers. Mitchell fractures the original texts to obtain the desired result, altering language and adding or deleting scenes, usually to good effect. His adaptation of Gogol's *The Government Inspector* inserts the famous "troika" scene and speech from *Dead Souls*, and provides Khlestakov with a startling airborne departure, both of which work dramatically and are in keeping with the lurking unease that underlies this particular "comedy." Similarly, his versions of Calderón's *Life's a Dream* and *The Mayor of Zalamea* break with the fluency of their Spanish originals in favour of a popular, slangy English verse-form which conveys greater impact than a strict translation. Calderón's exploration of the major human themes, his matching of sentiment with grim humour, is clearly to Mitchell's taste, and thus far the results have been interesting. The same may be said of *Woman Overboard*, his highly individual reworking of Lope de Vega's play *The Dog in the Manger*. This gift for adaptation is far from being the least of Mitchell's talents, and his efforts in this field deserve comparison with the best of his original plays, which continue unabated. Recent examples of the latter include his one-act musical satire on the world's worst airline, *In the Unlikely Event of an Emergency*, and three longer productions which Mitchell describes as "compilation shows of songs and poems," namely *Triple Threat*, *Love Songs of World War Three*, and *Greatest Hits*. These last have Mitchell appearing as a leading performer onstage as well as in his customary role of author, and are proof that he has lost none of his power and drive. If anything his creative energy seems to have increased, with fresh concepts and approaches being constantly sought in his latest dramas. *Anna on Anna*, his one-woman show portraying the life of poetess Anna Wickham, and specially written for the actress Illona Linthwaite, is a perfect example in this respect. While it remains to be seen where these explorations will lead Mitchell in future, one suspects that the answers will be well worth waiting for.

—Geoff Sadler

———————

MITCHELL, (Charles) Julian (Humphrey). British. Born in Epping, Essex, 1 May 1935. Educated at Winchester College, Hampshire, 1948–53; Wadham College, Oxford, B.A. 1958; St. Antony's College, Oxford, M.A. 1962. Served in the Royal Naval Volunteer Reserve, 1953–55: midshipman. Member, Arts Council Literature Panel, 1966–69; formerly, Governor, Chelsea School of Art, London. Chair, Welsh Arts Council Drama Committee, 1988–92. Recipient: Harkness fellowship, 1959; Rhys Memorial prize, 1965; Maugham award, 1966; International Critics prize, for television play, 1977; Christopher award, for television play, 1977 (U.S.A.); Florio prize, for translation, 1980; Society of West End Theatre award, 1982. Lives in Newport, Gwent, Wales. Agent: Peters, Fraser, and Dunlop Group, 503–504 The Chambers, Chelsea Harbour, Lots Road, London SW10 0XF, England.

PUBLICATIONS

Plays

A Heritage and Its History, adaptation of the novel by Ivy Compton-Burnett (produced London, 1965). London, Evans, 1966.
A Family and a Fortune, adaptation of the novel by Ivy Compton-Burnett (produced Guildford, Surrey, 1966; Seattle, 1974; London, 1975). London, French, 1976.
Shadow in the Sun (televised 1971). Published in *Elizabeth R*, edited by J.C. Trewin, London, Elek, 1972.
Half-Life (produced London, 1977; New York, 1981). London, Heinemann, 1977.
Henry IV, adaptation of the play by Pirandello. London, Eyre Methuen, 1979.
The Enemy Within (produced Leatherhead, Surrey, 1980).
Another Country (produced London, 1981; New Haven, Connecticut, 1983). Ambergate, Derbyshire, Amber Lane Press, 1982; New York, Limelight, 1984.
Francis (produced London, 1983). Oxford, Amber Lane Press, 1984.
After Aida; or, Verdi's Messiah (produced London, 1986). Oxford, Amber Lane Press, 1986.
The Evils of Tobacco, adaptation of a work by Chekhov, translated by Ronald Hingley (produced London, 1987).

Screenplays: *Arabesque*, with Stanley Price and Pierre Marton, 1966; *Another Country*, 1984; *Vincent and Theo*, 1990.

Radio Documentary: *Life and Deaths of Dr. John Donne*, 1972.

Television Plays: *Persuasion*, from the novel by Jane Austen, 1971; *Shadow in the Sun*, 1971; *The Man Who Never Was*, 1972; *A Perfect Day*, 1972; *Fly in the Ointment*, 1972; *A*

Question of Degree, 1972; *The Alien Corn*, from a story by W. Somerset Maugham, 1972; *Rust*, 1973; *Jennie*, 1974; *Abide with Me*, from the book *A Child in the Forest*, by Winifred Foley, 1976; *Staying On*, from the novel by Paul Scott, 1980; *The Good Soldier*, from the novel by Ford Madox Ford, 1981; *The Weather in the Streets*, from the novel by Rosamond Lehmann, 1984; episodes for *Inspector Morse* series, 1987–92; *All the Waters of Wye* (documentary), 1990; *Survival of the Fittest*, 1990.

Novels

Imaginary Toys. London, Hutchinson, 1961.
A Disturbing Influence. London, Hutchinson, 1962.
As Far as You Can Go. London, Constable, 1963.
The White Father. London, Constable, 1964; New York, Farrar Straus, 1965.
A Circle of Friends. London, Constable, 1966; New York, McGraw Hill, 1967.
The Undiscovered Country. London, Constable, 1968; New York, Grove Press, 1970.

Short Stories

Introduction, with others. London, Faber, 1960.

Other

Truth and Fiction (lecture). London, Covent Garden Press, 1972.
Jennie, Lady Randolph Churchill: A Portrait with Letters, with Peregrine Churchill. London, Collins, 1974; New York, St. Martin's Press, 1975.

Editor, with others, *Light Blue, Dark Blue: An Anthology of Recent Writing from Oxford and Cambridge Universities*. London, Macdonald, 1960.

*   *   *

Julian Mitchell's success as a playwright makes nonsense of claims that the well-made play is dead. He is a skilful craftsman whose work fits well into a British theatrical tradition as defined by, say, Terence Rattigan. Dialogue is all in his work, and the plays offer audiences an invitation into a world of polite discourse in which, if voices are occasionally raised, there is always someone present to push the argument forward into its next phase. He is not an innovative writer but he is always a polished one, as might be expected from someone who came late to the stage after an extensive literary apprenticeship. The 1990's have seen him embarked in yet another direction with his screenplay for *Vincent and Theo*, but his reputation as a writer in the 1960's rested solely on his activities as a novelist. The 1970's saw him established as a regular writer and adapter for television—his work included dramatisations of Austen's *Persuasion*, Paul Scott's *Staying On*, and Ford Madox Ford's *The Good Soldier*, as well as a contribution to the *Elizabeth R* series—and it was only in the 1980's that he really began to receive serious attention as a stage dramatist. Indeed, two of his earliest stage plays, *A Heritage and Its History* and *A Family and a Fortune*, were both adapted from novels by Ivy Compton-Burnett, and it is always apparent that he writes as a novelist converted to the stage.

His first novel was compared by one critic with the work of

Aldous Huxley, and his plays all have a dedicated commitment to a series of theatrical debates that makes the comparison only too inviting. At worst, the characters serve as convenient mouth-pieces for opposing views—in *Half-Life*, for instance, that most predictable of all West End formats, a country-house weekend, is the venue for a political discussion with an assorted bunch of over-articulate people, and there is scarcely any sense of theatre about the events depicted. All is wit and verbal sword-play. But at best the debate is more open, and nowhere more so than in his most successful play to date, *Another Country*.

In *Another Country* Mitchell offers one of many recent analyses of the "betrayal" of their class by the Cambridge Communist school of the 1930's. What makes his account interesting is that he transfers the action back to the penultimate year of their public-school days, placing the thoughts of the pro-Stalinist Judd and the flamboyantly gay Bennett (Guy Burgess in thin disguise, as is made explicit in the film version) in the context of that institution which is intended to mould them for their future roles as statesmen and administrators. The familiar use of the school as metaphor of the state, not of the country at large but of its ruling-class, allows Mitchell to show how an essentially apolitical Bennett might be led into the world of espionage both as a reaction to the brutal punishing of his sexual appetites by an institution which serves only to heighten their appeal, and as an extension of the need to be continually in disguise, leading a double life, which he sees as his fate.

The economic need to restrict the size of the cast (although the play eventually transferred to the West End, it started its life at the Greenwich Theatre) does much to increase the sense of enclosure, of claustrophobia, that confronts any boy who cannot, or will not, fit into the system ready created for him. Bennett actually spends a great deal of time in the play acknowledging the attention of his off-stage and never-seen young lover and peering through binoculars at what is happening outside the particular room he is in—including the early sighting of the removal of the body of a boy who has hanged himself in the bell tower, a victim of the sexual double-standards of the school.

After Aida presents a similarly enclosed stage, in this instance to consider the events leading up to Verdi's agreement to compose *Otello*. It is difficult not to compare the play with Shaffer's *Amadeus*, but it stands up very well to the exercise, being a much less pretentious re-animation of musical history. A preoccupation with the past is also evident in Mitchell's earlier play, *Francis*, which takes a long sweep through the life of St. Francis and his attempts to hang on to his ideal of poverty in the face of pressure from both the established church and his increasingly wealthy new order. As a character Francis is Mitchell's most successful creation, with a stronger sense of internal conflict apparent than in most of his protagonists who are allowed to dominate the action simply by the superiority of their wit and rhetoric. Francis's attempt to relive the Spartan life of his Christ unites the rebellious instincts of Bennett with the puritan discipline of Judd in *Another Country*, and here the corrupt oppression of church and papacy take the place of the school. As in all his plays, the voice of the rebel is allowed a place—as it is with the young Prue Hoggart in *Half-Life*—but the resolution of the plays, having suggested a plausible reason for the rebellion, is always to suggest the impossibility of real change.

History, for Mitchell, teaches a lesson of conflict in which the terms of reference remain essentially unchanged. In all his plays there is little sense of new ground being broken, either theatrically or intellectually, but if the mainstream is to continue to demand a steady diet of well-made plays then at least there is always evidence of an articulate intelligence behind Mitchell's work; and that is certainly to be welcomed in the increasingly dull world of contemporary West End theatre.

—John Bull

———

MITCHELL, Loften. American. Born in Columbus, North Carolina, 15 April 1919. Educated at De Witt Clinton High School, Bronx, New York, graduated 1937; City College, New York, 1937–38; Talladega College, Alabama, B.A. in sociology 1943; Columbia University, New York, 1947–51, M.A. Served in the United States Naval Reserve, 1944–45: seaman second class. Married Helen Marsh in 1948; two sons. Actor, stage manager, and press agent, 115th Street People's Theatre and Harlem Showcase, New York, 1946–52; social worker, with Gypsy families, 1947–58, and in Day Center Program for Older Persons, 1959–66. Department of Welfare, New York; professor of African-American Studies and Theatre, State University of New York, Binghamton, 1971–85, now professor emeritus. Editor, NAACP *Freedom Journal*, 1964. Recipient: Guggenheim fellowship, 1958; Rockefeller grant, 1961; Harlem Cultural Council award, 1969; State University of New York Research Foundation award, 1974; Audelco award, 1979. Address: 88–45 163rd Street, Jamaica, New York 11432, U.S.A.

Publications

Plays

Shattered Dreams (produced New York, 1938).

Blood in the Night (produced New York, 1946).

The Bancroft Dynasty (produced New York, 1948).

The Cellar (produced New York, 1952).

A Land Beyond the River (produced New York, 1957). Cody, Wyoming, Pioneer Drama Service, 1963.

The Phonograph (produced New York, 1961).

Tell Pharaoh (televised 1963; produced New York, 1967). Published in *The Black Teacher and the Dramatic Arts*, edited by William R. Reardon and Thomas D. Pawley, Westport, Connecticut, Negro Universities Press, 1970.

Ballad for Bimshire, with Irving Burgie (produced New York, 1963; revised version produced Cleveland, 1964).

Ballad of the Winter Soldiers, with John Oliver Killens (produced New York, 1964).

Star of the Morning: Scenes in the Life of Bert Williams (produced Cleveland, 1965; revised version produced New York, 1985). Published in *Black Drama Anthology*, edited by Woodie King and Ron Milner, New York, New American Library, 1971.

The Final Solution to the Black Problem in the United States; or, The Fall of the American Empire (produced New York, 1970).

Sojourn to the South of the Wall (produced 1973; revised version produced 1983).

The Walls Came Tumbling Down, music by Willard Roosevelt (produced New York, 1976).

Bubbling Brown Sugar, concept by Rosetta LeNoire, music by Danny Holgate, Emme Kemp, and Lilian Lopez (produced New York, 1976; London, 1977). New York, Broadway Play Publishing, 1985.

Cartoons for a Lunch Hour, music by Rudy Stevenson (produced New York, 1978).
A Gypsy Girl (produced Pine Bluff, Arkansas, 1982).
Miss Waters, To You, concept by Rosetta LeNoire (produced New York, 1983).

Screenplays: *Young Man of Williamsburg*, 1954; *Integration: Report One*, 1960; *I'm Sorry*, 1965.

Radio Writing: *Tribute to C.C. Spaulding*, 1952; *Friendly Advisor* program, 1955; *The Later Years* program, 1959–62.

Television Plays: *Welfare Services*, 1960's; *Tell Pharaoh*, 1970.

Novel

The Stubborn Old Lady Who Resisted Change.   New York, Emerson Hall, 1973.

Other

Black Drama: The Story of the American Negro in the Theatre.   New York, Hawthorn, 1967.

Editor, *Voices of the Black Theatre*.   Clifton, New Jersey, James T. White, 1975.

*

Manuscript Collections: State University of New York, Binghamton; Boston University; Talladega College, Alabama; Schomburg Collection, New York.

Critical Studies: *Negro Playwrights in the American Theatre 1925–1959* by Doris E. Abramson, New York, Columbia University Press, 1969; article by Ja A. Jahannes, in *Afro–American Writers after 1955* edited by Thadious M. Davis and Trudier Harris, Detroit, Gale, 1985.

Theatrical Activities:
Actor: **Plays**—with the Progressive Dramatizers and the Rose McClendon Players, both New York; Victor in *Cocktails*, and Aaron in *Having Wonderful Time* by Arthur Kober, 1938; Angel in *The Black Messiah* by Dennis Donoghue and James H. Dunmore, 1939.

*   *   *

For his work as a black theatre historian, the American theatre owes a great debt to Loften Mitchell. His books— *Black Drama* and *Voices of the Black Theatre*—and numerous essays contain invaluable information and insights on Afro-American contributions to the theatre. Mitchell's plays reflect his passionate interest in the black theatre and black American history in general. With few exceptions, his plays and librettos inform the audience of the tribulations and achievements of well known black entertainers and historical figures.

Black pride, unity, and perseverance during times of adversity form recurrent themes in Mitchell's plays. These concepts are often voiced in rhetorical discourses by characters drawn along simplistic, ideological lines. His protagonists based on historical individuals speak and act as though already aware of the significance of their achievements to future generations. After the black characters have suffered in conflicts with external forces motivated by racial prejudice

and self-interests, the plays end on a triumphant note as the blacks learn how to endure the hardships and, in some cases, prevail over their adversaries.

Tell Pharaoh surveys the history of black Americans; the characters speak of their illustrious African heritage, bitter experiences as slaves, and ongoing struggles for the same civil rights and opportunities enjoyed by white Americans. The drama identifies black American heroes and martyrs, and celebrates the contributions of blacks to various aspects of American life. As in most of his works, Mitchell includes a tribute to his beloved Harlem and uses music to set the mood and underscore the sentiments of the play. The concluding harangue against Pharaoh—a symbolic persecutor of blacks, Latins, Asians, Indians, and other groups—dates the work and typifies the rhetoric of the revolutionary activists of the 1960's.

Based on real events, *A Land Beyond the River* depicts the story of a rural, black South Carolina community which through the judicial system sought the right to send its children to any school receiving public funds. In Mitchell's dramatization, a sickly but courageous black woman— Martha Layne—proposes the law suit and her husband— Joseph—rallies the support of other black citizens and a sympathetic white physician. "Uncle Toms" and white bigots attempt to undermine their efforts. Intimidating threats and the burning of the Layne home aggravate Martha's precarious condition and result in her death. The events create dissension among the blacks and encourage most to accept a local court decision to provide a "separate, but equal" school for blacks. However, in a stirring speech punctuated with biblical references, Joseph contends that black children would not receive parity with whites through the ruling. Instead, he convinces his peers to appeal the case to a higher court in order to achieve their original objective of obtaining equal access to services and facilities enjoyed by white students. Despite the clichés and simplistic characterizations, the drama provides a moving historical portrait of valiant individuals bound by a common cause in the civil rights movement.

A more recent work—*Miss Waters, To You*—is based on the life of Ethel Waters. A series of scenes with musical numbers depict Waters's transition from a struggling 17-year-old divorcée to an accomplished actress and singer. The play includes appearances by such noted entertainers as Bessie Smith, Lena Horne, Duke Ellington, and Cab Calloway. These blacks provide each other with moral support and teach Waters how to endure the racial prejudice and indignities of their profession. However, such scenes weaken the credibility of the play as a true portrait of Waters's life. In fact, her animosity toward some black entertainers, such as Miss Horne, is quite well known. The drama also glosses over certain of Waters's ignoble traits which would place her in a less exalted light. As in his other tributes to black entertainers —*Bubbling Brown Sugar* and *Star of the Morning: Scenes in the Life of Bert Williams*—Mitchell chose to portray black role models of high esteem with few, if any, unadmirable attributes.

—Addell Austin Anderson

MOLLOY, M(ichael) J(oseph). Irish. Born in Milltown, County Galway, 3 March 1917. Educated at St. Jarlath's

College and in a seminary for 4 years. Farmer, 1950–72. Recipient: Irish Arts Council award, 1972. Address: Milltown, Tuam, County Galway, Ireland.

PUBLICATIONS

Plays

Old Road (produced Dublin, 1943). Dublin, Progress House, 1961.
The Visiting House (produced Dublin, 1946). Published in *Seven Irish Plays 1946–1964*, edited by Robert Hogan, Minneapolis, University of Minnesota Press, 1967.
The King of Friday's Men (produced Dublin, 1948; London, 1949; New York, 1951). Dublin, Duffy, 1954; included in *Three Plays*, 1975.
The Wood of the Whispering (produced Dublin, 1953; London, 1963; New York, 1975). Dublin, Progress House, 1961; included in *Three Plays*, 1975.
The Paddy Pedlar (produced Dublin, 1953). Dublin, Duffy, 1954; included in *Three Plays*, 1975.
The Will and the Way (produced Dublin, 1955). Dublin, Bourke, 1957.
A Right Rose Tree (produced Dublin, 1958).
Daughter from over the Water (produced 1962; produced Dublin, 1964). Dublin, Progress House, 1963.
The Wooing of Duvesa (produced Dublin, 1964).
The Bitter Pill, in *Prizewinning Plays of 1964*. Dublin, Progress House, 1965.
Three Plays. Newark, Delaware, Proscenium Press, 1975.
Petticoat Loose (produced Dublin, 1979). Newark, Delaware, Proscenium Press, 1982.
The Bachelor's Daughter (produced Dublin, 1985).

* * *

M.J. Molloy may be Ireland's most genuine folk-dramatist. He is certainly the most distinguished contributor to this genre since Synge. Unlike Synge, who was a stranger to rural Ireland and had to be educated about its culture, Molloy is a native of County Galway and still lives there, in simple circumstances very like those he describes in his plays. Most of his plays have been produced either at the Abbey Theatre or by the Abbey Theatre Company. They represent a 45-year effort to provide for the Irish theater the sort of play Yeats said was needed to make Irish people conscious of their own history. Molloy has singlemindedly written plays which deal with the experience of the Irish countryman. A broadly educated man himself, he has witnessed and understood the changes which in the past 40 years have moved rural Ireland away from what Molloy regards as its feudal traditions and toward a society less certain of its values and more vulnerable to the exploitation of its land and its people.

In all of Molloy's plays there is nostalgia for a time when men had a proper regard for each other and for the land, a time when depopulation had not reduced rural Ireland to a gaggle of testy and self-righteous bachelors, a time before technology and an unscrupulous middle class purloined the land. Not surprisingly, since he is a dramatist rather than an historian, Molloy's plays do not deal with that ancient age of social order, but rather with periods of conflict, of moments when one can observe the old order passing. A self-confessed romantic, Molloy can see no good coming out of this change.

Two of Molloy's early plays, *The King of Friday's Men* and *The Visiting House*, might be regarded as paradigms of the worlds that have been lost. Set in late 18th-century Mayo and Galway, *The King of Friday's Men* reveals a large society still responsive to the old feudal structure of lord and peasant. The play concerns a lord's obsession with his right to have as his mistresses the unmarried daughters of his tenant farmers. His exploitation of a feudal right provokes disorder in the land and leads ultimately to the violent death of the lord. Molloy is not naive in his romantic attachment to Ireland's feudal past. As a Catholic, he believes that human nature has been self-seeking and violent since the Fall and can never change. Nevertheless, all the characters in *The King of Friday's Men* share the same social and moral values. Lord and tenant both know when privilege has been exploited.

The Visiting House has a contemporary setting and reveals a shrunken social order. Unlike *The King of Friday's Men* in which action ranges all over Galway and Mayo, and an heroic Bartley Dowd wipes out a contingent of the lord's men with a few swipes of his shillelagh, *The Visiting House* is confined to the single setting which Molloy has used for most of his plays. The heroics are rhetorical rather than physical as characters called The Man of Learning and The Verb-to-Be nightly take their positions by the fire and engage in a merry flyting match. Within these narrowed circumstances, however, *The Visiting House* does reveal a social order based on ownership of the land. A once flourishing institution barely more than a memory when Molloy wrote his play, the visiting house was the place where small farmers gathered and where each had respect and a social identity.

Molloy's other plays deal more directly with the breakdown of traditional Irish rural life. *Old Road* is about the depopulation caused by farmers being unable to divide their small farms any further. Only the oldest son may inherit the land. Others must leave the community for Dublin or England. *The Wood of the Whispering* also has depopulation for its theme. Molloy assembles an array of zany and impotent old bachelors who lust after the one or two girls left in the village. Their lives pass in the shadow of ancient Castle D'Arcy, a reminder to Molloy's audience of a time when society was stable. *The Will and the Way* has to do with a rural community whose visiting house is threatened by the arrival of a city-type who has no feeling for community life and nearly succeeds in destroying it.

In his more recent plays Molloy has been unable to maintain the gentle comic spirit and ironic distance which characterize his earlier work. The last traces of genuine rural Irish life are being destroyed by technology, especially by television which gives the Irish a false sense of being a national community while at the same time imposing a radical isolation of one man from another. *A Right Rose Tree* presents a rural Ireland so fraught with social problems that the play is more like documentary than drama. It deals with the period 1921–23, when the Irish countryside rises up against the English only to witness even more bloody battles of brother against brother when the Black and Tans have left. The utter lawlessness which results permits the base to inherit the earth. The lines from Yeats which give the play its title assert the purposefulness of violence—"There's nothing but our own red blood/Can make a right Rose tree." For Molloy violence has no such creative energy. The final horror of *A Right Rose Tree*, the symbolic killing of a landlord by insensitive, ignorant, and cowardly men, leaves nothing of value after it.

—Arthur E. McGuinness

MOORE, (James) Mavor. Canadian. Born in Toronto, Ontario, 8 March 1919. Educated at University of Toronto secondary schools, graduated 1936; University of Toronto, 1936–41 (Leonard Foundation Scholar), B.A. (honours) in philosophy and English 1941. Served in the Canadian Army Intelligence Corps, 1941–45: captain (psychological warfare). Married 1) Darwina Faessler in 1943 (divorced), four daughters; 2) the writer Phyllis Grosskurth in 1969; 3) Alexandra Browning in 1982, one daughter. Feature producer, Toronto, 1941–42, chief producer for the International Service, Montreal, 1944–45, and Pacific Region producer, Vancouver, 1945–46, CBC Radio; teacher, Academy of Radio Arts, Toronto, 1946–49; managing producer, New Play Society, Toronto, 1946–50, 1954–57; radio director, 1946–50, and executive television producer, 1954–60, United Nations Information Division, New York; chief producer, 1950–53, and assistant television program director, 1954, CBC Television, Toronto; drama critic, Toronto *Telegram*, 1958–60; stage director, Canadian Opera Company, Toronto, 1959–61, 1963; general director, Confederation Centre, Charlottetown, Prince Edward Island, 1963–65; founder and artistic director, Charlottetown Festival, 1964–67; general director, St. Lawrence Centre for the Arts, Toronto, 1965–70. Since 1961 president, Mavor Moore Productions Ltd., Toronto; since 1970 professor of theatre, York University, Downsview, Ontario; member, 1974, member of the Executive Committee, 1975, and since 1979 chair, Canada Council. Since 1953 member of the Board of Directors, later senator, Stratford Festival, Ontario; chair, Canadian Theatre Centre, 1957–58; since 1958 governor, National Theatre School, Montreal; founding chair, Guild of Canadian Playwrights, 1977. Recipient: Peabody award, 1947, 1949, 1957; Canadian Association of Authors and Artists award, for television writing, 1955; Centennial Medal, 1967. D.Litt.: York University, 1969; LL.D.: Mount Allison University, Sackville, New Brunswick, 1982. Officer, Order of Canada, 1973. Agent (Canada): Canadian Speakers and Writers Service, 44 Douglas Crescent, Toronto, Ontario; (U.K. and U.S.A.): ACTAC Ltd., 16 Cadogan Lane, London S.W.1, England. Address: 176 Moore Avenue, Toronto, Ontario M4T 1V8, Canada.

PUBLICATIONS

Plays

Court Martial, with Earle Birney (broadcast 1946). Published in *Words on Waves: Selected Radio Plays* by Birney, edited by Howard Fink, Kingston, Ontario, Quarry Press, 1985.
Spring Thaw (revue; produced Toronto, 1947 and later versions, 1948–57, 1961–65). Sketch *Togetherness* published in *A Treasury of Canadian Humor*, edited by Robert Thomas Allen, Toronto, McClelland and Stewart, 1967.
Who's Who (also director: produced Toronto, 1949).
The Best of All Possible Worlds, adaptation of the novel *Candide* by Voltaire (broadcast 1952; revised version, as *The Optimist*, broadcast 1954; revised version, as *The Best of All Possible Worlds*, music and lyrics by Moore, produced Toronto, 1956).
The Hero of Mariposa, music and lyrics by Moore, adaptation of *Sunshine Sketches of a Little Town* by Stephen Leacock (broadcast 1953; as *Sunshine Town*, also director: produced Toronto, 1956).
The Ottawa Man, adaptation of a play by Gogol (televised 1958; revised version, also director: produced Toronto,

1961; revised version produced Lennoxville, Quebec, 1972).
Louis Riel (opera libretto), with Jacques Languirand, music by Harry Somers (produced Toronto, 1967; Washington, D.C., 1975).
Yesterday the Children Were Dancing, adaptation of a play by Gratien Gélinas (also co-director: produced Charlottetown, Prince Edward Island, 1967). Toronto, Clarke Irwin, 1969.
Johnny Belinda, lyrics by Moore, musical version of the play by Elmer Harris (produced Charlottetown, Prince Edward Island, 1968).
Getting In (broadcast 1968; as *The Interview*, televised 1973). New York, French, 1972.
The Pile (broadcast 1969). Included in *The Pile, The Store, Inside Out*, 1973.
Man Inc., adaptation of a play by Jacques Languirand (produced Toronto, 1970).
The Argument (broadcast 1970). Published in *Performing Arts in Canada* (Toronto), Winter 1973.
The Store (broadcast 1971). Included in *The Pile, The Store, Inside Out*, 1973.
Inside Out (televised 1971). Included in *The Pile, The Store, Inside Out*, 1973.
Anne of Green Gables (additional lyrics, with Elaine Campbell), book by Donald Harron, music by Norman Campbell, lyrics by Harron and Campbell, adaptation of the novel by L.M. Montgomery (produced Charlottetown, Prince Edward Island, 1971).
Come Away, Come Away (broadcast 1972). Published in *Encounter: Canadian Drama in Four Media*, edited by Eugene Benson, Toronto, Methuen, 1973.
Customs (broadcast 1973). Published in *Cues and Entrances*, edited by Henry Beissel, Toronto, Gage, 1977.
The Pile, The Store, Inside Out. Toronto, Simon and Pierre, 1973.
The Roncarelli Affair, with F.R. Scott (televised 1974). Published in *The Play's the Thing*, edited by Tony Gifford, Toronto, Macmillan, 1976.
Abracadabra, music by Harry Freedman (produced Courtenay, British Columbia, 1979).
Love and Politics, music and lyrics by Moore, adaptation of the play *The Fair Grit* by Nicholas Flood Davin (produced St. Catherines, Ontario, 1979).
Fauntleroy, music and lyrics by Johnny Burke, adaptation of the novel *Little Lord Fauntleroy* by Frances Hodgson Burnett (produced Charlottetown, Prince Edward Island, 1980).

Radio Plays: more than 100 plays, including *Court Martial*, with Earle Birney, 1946; *The Best of All Possible Worlds*, 1952 (revised as *The Optimist*, 1954); *The Hero of Mariposa*, 1953; *Fast Forward*, 1968; *Getting In*, 1968; *The Pile*, 1969; *The Argument*, 1970; *The Store*, 1971; *A Matter of Timing*, 1971; *Come Away, Come Away*, 1972; *Customs*, 1973 (USA); *Time Frame*, 1974; *Freak*, 1975.

Television Plays: more than 50 plays, including *Catch a Falling Star*, 1957; *The Ottawa Man*, 1958; *The Well*, 1961; *The Man Born to Be King*, 1961; *The Man Who Caught Bullets*, 1962; *Mary of Scotland*, 1966; *Inside Out*, 1971; *The Interview*, 1973; *The Roncarelli Affair*, with F.R. Scott, 1974.

Verse

And What Do You Do? A Short Guide to the Trades and Professions. Toronto and London, Dent, 1960.

Other

4 Canadian Playwrights: Robertson Davies, Gratien Gélinas, James Reaney, George Ryga. Toronto, Holt Rinehart, 1973.
Slipping on the Verge: The Performing Arts in Canada with Theatre as a Case Study. Washington, D.C., Canadian Embassy, 1983.

Editor, *The Awkward Stage: The Ontario Theatre Study.* Toronto, Methuen, 1969.
Editor, *An Anthology of Canadian Plays.* Toronto, New Press, 1973.

*

Theatrical Activities:
Director: **Plays**—*King Lear*, Toronto, 1948; *Heartbreak House* by Shaw, Toronto, 1948; *The Circle* by W. Somerset Maugham, Toronto, 1948; *The Government Inspector* by Gogol, Toronto, 1948; *Who's Who*, Toronto, 1949; *Macbeth*, Toronto, 1949; *The Tempest*, Toronto, 1949; *Sunshine Town*, Toronto, 1956; *The Ottawa Man*, Toronto, 1961, Charlotte-town, Prince Edward Island, 1966; *The Fourposter* by Jan de Hartog, Halifax, Nova Scotia, 1963; *Dial M for Murder* by Frederick Knott, Halifax, 1963; *Floradora*, Vancouver, 1964; *Julius Caesar*, Vancouver, 1964; *An Evening with Wayne and Shuster*, Charlottetown, 1965; *Laugh with Leacock*, Charlottetown, 1965; *Yesterday the Children Were Dancing* (co-director), Charlottetown, 1967. **Television and Radio**—productions for CBC, United Nations (New York), CBS and NBC (USA).
Actor: **Plays**—roles with the New Play Society, Toronto, the Crest Theatre, the Charlottetown and Vancouver Festivals, and other theatre companies, including title role in *King Lear*, Toronto, 1948, 1963; title role in *Riel*, Toronto, 1948; Escalus in *Measure for Measure*, Stratford, Ontario, 1954; Caesar in *Caesar and Cleopatra* by Shaw, Toronto and Vancouver, 1962; Undershaft in *Major Barbara* by Shaw, Halifax, 1963. **Television**—starring roles in numerous Canadian drama series. **Radio**—roles in numerous CBC productions, CBS and NBC (USA), etc.

* * *

Mavor Moore is Canada's most ubiquitous man-about-theatre. In the last 40 years he has had great success as actor, producer, director, festival impresario, and theatre administrator. Now, as professor of theatre at York University in Toronto, he has a period of relative calm in which he can once more concentrate on writing. For most of his career as a playwright for the stage, he has mainly adapted the work of other writers and adapted it very often for his own direction. Or he has worked as a librettist in cooperation with composers and co-writers.

In the area of musical drama Moore created a lively version of Mariposa, that sleepy little town which Stephen Leacock wrote about in *Sunshine Sketches*. In *Sunshine Town* Moore wrote a book, music, and lyrics which had the right period feeling; it has had several revivals.

On another occasion, for his Charlottetown Festival, he wrote a musical version of *Johnny Belinda* based on the Broadway play by Elmer Harris. Again, the quality of the writing and the success of his director, Alan Lund, made even the story of a deaf-mute who is raped a good and satisfying musical.

Louis Riel is an opera rather than a musical; with a score composed by Harry Somers, it was a notable addition to the Canadian Opera Company's repertoire for the Centennial Year of 1967. Moore went to history—Riel is a key figure in the French-English debate which still is a central part of Canada's polity—and managed to create a full-blooded set of characters, even though from time to time the dialogue was more operatic than dramatic. Generally, though, Moore's greatest gift as a dramatist is his skill in dialogue, perhaps because he has written so much for radio—a purely verbal medium.

Moore's best known play is *The Ottawa Man*, an adaptation of Gogol's *The Government Inspector*. Only Moore's talent for dialogue could have made it the success it is because the central situation, which is firmly rooted in the official corruption of czarist Russia, cannot be easily transplanted to the relative honesty of 19th-century pioneer Manitoba. But the fact is that one doesn't question this while the play is being acted; nor is one too aware of the fact that the characters are all stereotypes rather than people. What one is aware of is the farcical encounter between two Irishmen, a French-Canadian Catholic, a German immigrant, and an English remittance man—all of whom speak in an uncannily accurate style and accent.

In recent years Moore has written several one-act plays, mainly for radio and television. Character is not important in them, but ideas and verbal play on those ideas are. In fact, so little character is necessary for embodying the ideas that in some of the plays none of the characters has a name: in *Come Away, Come Away*, which is about an old man facing death and a little girl fascinated by the encounter, the characters are Old Man and Little Girl; in *The Pile*, a fable about modern business and ecology, the characters are X and Y; and in *Getting In*, a play with a really strange resonance, P is the official and T is an applicant.

Perhaps the most significant of these plays is *The Argument* which, through its dialogue alone, establishes characters who are identified only as M—a man—and W—a woman. But their dialogue, their argument, creates an interaction which convinces one that Moore is capable of writing longer and more solid work.

—Arnold Edinborough

MORNIN, Daniel. British. Born in Belfast, 10 January 1956. Educated at Orangefield Primary School, 1961–67, and Orangefield Secondary, 1967–71, both Belfast. Served in the Royal Navy as ordinary seaman, 1974–77. Married Aine Beegan in 1991; one son. Agent: Judy Daish, Judy Daish Associates, 83 Eastbourne Mews, London W2 6LQ, England.

PUBLICATIONS

Plays

Mum and Son (produced London, 1981).
Kate (produced London, 1983).
Getting Out (as *Short of Mutiny*; produced London, 1983).
Comrade Ogilvy (produced London, 1984).
By the Border (produced London, 1985).

The Murderers (produced London, 1985).
Built on Sand (produced London, 1987).
Weights and Measures (produced London, 1987).
At Our Table (produced London, 1991).

Television Play: *Border Country*, 1991.

Novel

All Our Fault. London, Hutchinson, 1991.

*

Daniel Mornin comments:

I seem to be attracted to themes that are, I hope, more enduring than they are fashionable, themes that lie beneath "the passing scene" to give strength to a play between the lines. I have always hoped that this provokes thought, incites curiosity so that the play remains with the audience a good while longer than the length of time they have sat in their seats: even if they dislike the play (my plays are often not likeable) I hope they remember it. Recently I have become interested in "morality," the fragile, fictive morality of the intellect, the "the what should be" and the human morality of "what is" of experience, often the violent experience that comes when society (as in Northern Ireland for a time) breaks down, or as with my new play a man fights in a war.

*   *   *

Daniel Mornin's work to date clearly illustrates the instinct to retreat from the images that shaped the experience of his early life in Belfast. At the same time, the public acts of brutality and intolerance that have come to symbolise the divided city in which he grew up, are frequently discovered in the landscapes of his plays. This paradox is resolved in his treatment of his material. The violence that lies at the heart of the sectarian divisions in his native city is central to much of his work, though his instinct is not to deal with it as a purely local phenomenon. Rather, he presents a world view in which metaphysical degeneracy and moral corruption appear to be the inevitable concomitants of what "being human" is all about. *Mum and Son* (directed at the Riverside Studios by David Leveaux), his professional début, documents a welter of emotional screw-ups inflicted on a dutiful son by his intense, isolated, insecure, possessive, predatory, massively irritating mother. The situation is aggravated by an aura of mystery concerning the boy's father and further notched up, first by the presentation of apparently incontrovertible facts surrounding the mystery of the father, then by the subsequent contradiction of these "facts."

Mornin's obsession with the darker, hardly performable, aspects of behaviour is mediated through his intuitive flair for writing dialogue and his masterly control of tone. His working method is to return to themes and rework situations. He is rarely content to set aside a plot or a dramatic structure until he has exhausted the possibilities inherent in them. His best work exemplifies his extraordinary control over the imaginative and technical demands made by the, largely, realistic situations he depicts. Yet his work as a whole suggests that he cannot readily meet the need to devise structures of sufficient formal complexity to match the brilliance of his dialogue.

There are two aspects of Mornin's one-act play, *By the Border*, which illustrate the tensions underlying his thematic and structural preoccupations. The first is the employment of the brother-sister theme which, over the span of plays he has written, has increasingly been overlaid with the archetypal and symbolic resonances of Greek tragedy. This theme

initially appeared in *Kate* (widely regarded as one of the best of his plays), a focused, painful, thought-provoking, and accurate study of an incestuous relationship between the son and daughter of a "mixed" marriage. The second is a "delaying" device which, in *By the Border*, takes the form of a character who remains onstage for a large part of the play without saying anything, thus raising questions in the audience's mind over the character's reasons for being there.

The reference to Greek tragedy is clearly intended to heighten the universality of Mornin's dramas, though there is no wide agreement that the plays subjected to this treatment are either more focused or more accessible than those which are not. It is worth noting that Mornin's best dialogue is contained in scenes with the structural simplicity of Greek drama; specifically in the interplay between two (or three) actors. It therefore seems superfluous to emphasise structural principles at the expense of dramatic action.

Roland Barthes encapsulates the generic problems of imposing the patterns of tragedy on the close, psychological perspectives of modern drama in his essay "Putting on the Greeks" (*Critical Essays*, 1972). He reminds us: "the sentiments (of characters in the Greek drama) are not at all psychological in our modern sense of the word . . . pride is not a sin here, a marvelous and complicated disease; it is an offence against the city, it is a political excess."

Mornin's developing fondness for classical themes may to some extent be a response to the ethos of the theatre that has encouraged his writing. Yet his promise and potential as a playwright stem from his ability to evaluate his achievements with fastidious care, and to see the art of playwriting essentially as a provisional and experimental one.

His latest play, *At Our Table* (directed at the Royal National Theatre by Jenny Killick), represents an attempt to reconcile the distinctions Barthes draws between modern and classical Greek theatre. Again, Mornin's major structural device (developed out of *By the Border*) is to delay the revelation which will confirm the full horror of the apparently ordinary domestic drama played out before us. The characters grow in significance throughout the play through a conscious finessing of the distinction between the "public" and "private" sentiments of the characters.

Virtually all of Mornin's plays underline the provisionality of his dramaturgy. *Weights and Measures* (directed at the National Theatre Studio by John Burgess) is a striking example of a play that shows how complex is the relationship between the expansion of Mornin's thematic interests and his developing technical skill. Based on the life of Denis Nilssen, the serial killer, it is set in a house, stratified to reveal activities on various levels. In the upper part of the house there are scenes between a "yuppie" and two women who, in the course of the play, spiritually destroy him. In the lower level, the Nilssen figure plays out a number of brilliant scenes with an actor who appears, in various guises, as different people. The play, however, is caught between the theoretical compactness of its formal symmetry and the practical problems of reconciling an audience to the confusing demands of dividing the stage space equally between scenes of widely differentiated dramatic interest. *Weights and Measures* is an important play, however, in that Mornin is consciously working to consolidate his practical achievements as a writer of taut, psychologically threatening dialogue while shifting the emphasis of his muse away from personal experience towards imagination and research.

Built on Sand (directed at the Royal Court Theatre Upstairs by Lindsay Posner), has an imaginative setting on the island of Crete; but the additional device of refracting the topical evils of Belfast, in a reworking of *The Murderers*, through the mirror of classical mythology is neither felicitous nor efficient.

The Murderers is generally regarded as one of his best plays. It appears (though Mornin does not acknowledge this) to be based on an account of the Shankill Butchers, a group of Protestant paramilitaries who achieved notoriety in the 1970's through a series of indiscriminate and bestial murders. Its formal achievement is to extend the play's climax (the mutilation, in the back room of a public house, of a young man culled from the street) to an unbearable pitch. The play is a detailed anatomy of the clash of working-class men, not as an undifferentiated mass, but as a complex of interdependent relationships initiated in blood and tribal fealty and compacted in the thrall of unmitigated horror. In *The Murderers*, more than in any other of Mornin's plays, there is a distinctive and malodorous atmosphere. The darkness exemplifies Mornin's ability to sustain the tension between character and action in a way that is deeply shocking.

As *The Murderers* illustrates, Mornin's depiction of women is overshadowed by his brilliant observation and astute handling of situations in which men are thrown together, by design or accident. Mornin shows consummate skill in dramatising homophile relationships, not as narrowly homoerotic and homosexual, but centring rather on the dark, secretive interdependence of men as members of a group. *Short of Mutiny* is set mainly below decks of a Royal Navy destroyer, and casts a cold eye over the behaviour of predominantly young seamen, working to discharge themselves dishonourably from the service so as to avoid paying themselves "out." Set against them are the ship's officers who, realising the game and also trapped themselves, cannily avoid the predicted confrontation. As a counterpoint to the main action, there are intensely disturbing scenes involving the time-hardened older men, reduced to making ships to go in bottles.

Short of Mutiny requires over 20 people to perform it, one of the reasons for the long delay in its production. Mornin's willingness to adapt to the demands of modern theatrical production is subsequently reflected in plays of smaller casts. He has written for radio, and a first novel, *All Our Fault*, is being filmed for television. In 1992 he was working on a new play for the Royal National Theatre. His unschematic view of his function as an artist, coupled with an ability to attract actors and directors of the highest calibre to stage his work, indicates that, in the foreseeable future, his playwriting career is assured.

—Paul Hadfield

MORRISON, Bill. Irish. Born in Ballymoney, County Antrim, Northern Ireland, 22 January 1940. Educated at Dalriada Grammar School, Ballymoney, 1951–58; Queen's University, Belfast, 1958–62, LL.B. (honours) 1962. Married Valerie Lilley in 1968. Actor in Belfast, Dublin, and London, from 1963; resident writer, Victoria Theatre, Stoke-on-Trent, Staffordshire, 1969–71; radio drama producer, BBC, Belfast, 1975–76; resident writer, Everyman Theatre, 1977–78, lecturer in creative writing, C.F. Mott College, 1977–78, drama producer, Radio City, 1979–81, and associate director, 1981–83, and artistic director, 1983–85, Playhouse Theatre, all Liverpool. Since 1978 board member, Merseyside Young People's Theatre, Liverpool, since 1981 board member,

Playhouse Theatre, and since 1985 chair, Merseyside Arts Drama Panel. Recipient: Ford Foundation grant, 1972; Arts Council bursary, 1975; Pye award, for radio feature, 1981. Agent: Michael Imison Playwrights, 28 Almeida Street, London N1 1TD, England.

PUBLICATIONS

Plays

Love and a Bottle, adaptation of the play by George Farquhar (produced Dublin, 1966; Nottingham, 1969).
Laugh But Listen Well (produced Dublin, 1967).
Conn and the Conquerors of Space (for children; also director: produced Falmer, Sussex, 1969; London, 1971).
Please Don't Shoot Me When I'm Down (produced Manchester, 1969; London, 1972).
Jupiter-5 (for children; produced Stoke-on-Trent, 1970; London, 1971).
Aladdin and His Magic Lamp (for children; also director: produced Stoke-on-Trent, 1971).
Tess of the d'Urbervilles, adaptation of the novel by Hardy (produced Stoke-on-Trent, 1971). London, Macmillan, 1980.
Sam Slade Is Missing (broadcast 1971; produced Derby, 1972; London, 1974). Published in *The Best Short Plays 1973*, edited by Stanley Richards, Radnor, Pennsylvania, Chilton, 1973.
The Time Travellers (for children; produced Stoke-on-Trent, 1971).
Patrick's Day (produced New Haven, Connecticut, 1972).
The Love of Lady Margaret (broadcast 1972; produced London, 1973).
Ellen Cassidy (broadcast 1974; produced Liverpool, 1978).
The Emperor of Ice-Cream, adaptation of the novel by Brian Moore (broadcast 1975; produced Dublin, 1977).
The Irish Immigrants Tale (produced Liverpool, 1976).
Flying Blind (produced Liverpool, 1977; London, 1978; New York, 1979). London, Faber, 1978.
Time on Our Hands (produced Belfast, 1979).
Dr. Jekyll of Rodney Street (produced Liverpool, 1979).
Scrap! (produced Liverpool, 1982; London, 1985).
Cavern of Dreams, with Carol Ann Duffy (produced Liverpool, 1984).
Run, Run, Runaway (for children; produced Liverpool and London, 1986).
Be Bop a Lula (musical; produced Liverpool, 1988).

Radio Plays: *Sam Slade Is Missing*, 1971; *The Love of Lady Margaret*, 1972; *The Great Gun-Running Episode*, 1974; *Ellen Cassidy*, 1974; *Crime and Punishment*, from a novel by Dostoevsky, 1975; *Crow's Flight*, from a play by Dimitri Kehaidis, 1975; *The Emperor of Ice-Cream*, 1975; *Simpson and Son*, 1977; *The Big Sleep*, *The High Window*, *The Lady in the Lake*, *The Little Sister*, and *The Long Goodbye*, all from the novels by Raymond Chandler, 1977; *Maguire*, 1979; *The Spring of Memory* (feature), 1981; *Blues in A-Flat*, 1989.

Television Plays: *McKinley and Sarah*, 1973; *Joggers*, 1978; *Potatohead Blues*, 1982; *Shergar*, 1986; *A Safe House*, 1990.

*

Theatrical Activities:
Director: **Plays**—*On Approval* by Frederick Lonsdale, Dublin, 1967; *The Lion in Winter* by James Goldman,

London, 1969; *Two Gentlemen of Verona*, London, 1969; *Conn and the Conquerors of Space*, Falmer, Sussex, 1969; *Aladdin and His Magic Lamp*, Stoke-on-Trent, 1971; Playhouse Theatre, Liverpool: *A Doll's House* by Ibsen, *Ladies in Waiting* by Ellen Fox, *These Men* by Mayo Simon, *Skirmishes* by Catherine Hayes, *Walking on Walter* by Claire Luckham, *A Lesson from Aloes* by Athol Fugard, *I Want* by Nell Dunn and Adrian Henri, *Breezeblock Park* by Willy Russell, *Alfie* by Bill Naughton, *Cavern of Dreams*, and *The Divvies Are Coming* by Eddie Braben, 1981–85; *The Beastly Beatitudes of Balthazar B* by J.P. Donleavy, London, 1983. Actor: **Plays**—roles at Arts Theatre, Belfast, and with Ulster Theatre Company, 1963–65; Nick in *Who's Afraid of Virginia Woolf?* by Edward Albee, Dublin, 1966; Barney Muldoon in *Illuminatus!* by Robert Anton Wilson, Liverpool, 1978. **Film** —*Sinful Davey*, 1969.

Bill Morrison comments:

(1982) I was born in Ireland but I was born in the British part of it. I was born during a war and have lived in the shadow of war since. I am more an Ulster writer than an Irish one. My language has the particular rhythms of that place, my characters and subjects are violently shaped by it, my use of comedy is dictated by it. I write in order to try to make sense of what happens to me and what I see around me and I hope by that to make a record of how people felt and lived in a particular time and place, which I take to be the job of the writer in any society.

I also write for an audience. I am proud of the fact that my work has been performed in twelve countries. The excitement and persistence of theatre is that it is the form which depends on the creative participation of the audience to complete it. The audience always affects and often profoundly alters the quality of the artistic event. To me the theatre is a laboratory of human communication, a place of constant experiment. The glory of the nature of it is that it has to be on the human scale. Technology does change and improve but it barely affects the essential experience. Writing for radio, TV, or film is rewarding because of the audience it reaches but it is not the same. Theatre is the only human activity I have found which embraces and needs all levels of skill and talent in its making and where, despite all its internal conflicts, the need and advantage of co-operating always wins. The event is always greater than the individual. It is always communal.

That is how it should be. It is why I now run a theatre with other writers. However, I regret the fact that, apart from a community tour of a show *Time on Our Hands* which I devised with a company, my work remains unperformed in Northern Ireland.

(1988) The purpose of the writer in society is to record how people feel about the time they live in and the events in it. I try to make sense of what I feel and see around me, and mostly fail—which is why I write comedy and farce. The story of my time is the story of murder exposed as farce.

* * *

Following up his own proposition that since 1969 "the trouble with being an Ulster playwright has been trouble," Bill Morrison wrote in 1977: "the best of my work, or at least the most important to me, has been about my country and the people who try to survive in it. The plays have been about my struggle to understand the disease in my society which caused its intense, unbearably prolonged and homicidal breakdown. But they have also been about my struggle to find a form which would encompass it." This comment conveniently suggests the characteristics which give Morrison's drama its

force: his exploration of the problematic relation between cultural and personal spheres in the Ulster context, and the formal experimentation from play to play that such an exploration necessarily entails. Moreover, in a writer who believes, as Morrison does, that "the theatre is ultimately the only way of fully discovering oneself," the "struggle to find a form" makes itself felt as a moral as well as an artistic imperative.

The struggle was complicated for Morrison in the early 1970's by a lack of sympathy he encountered in theatre (and television) for his exploratory treatment of the Ulster situation. Finding an outlet instead in radio, he experimented with the use of stereo in adaptations (notably *Crime and Punishment*) and, in his first original radio play, *The Love of Lady Margaret*, satisfyingly exploited the potential of the medium for narrative ambiguity in the rendering of an isolated consciousness and its labyrinth of ultimately self-thwarting fictions.

The aptness of the radio medium to the playwright's concerns is powerfully (though perhaps not consistently) apparent in *Ellen Cassidy*—a later stage version of which the author considers to have been unsatisfactory. Here the troubled consciousness belongs to the 34-year-old Armagh-born Protestant Ellen. Now in London, estranged from yet still haunted by her Irish husband, and awaiting the arrival of her young lover, she engages with the constraints and outcomes of an Ulster upbringing in a fluid series of recollections, reflective monologues, and flashbacks. The writing is often richly imaged, and at the heart of the play is the symbolic opposition of blood—the issue of menstruation, of sexual and sectarian violence, the pulsing badge of cultural belonging, something *inside* the self and controlling it—and water, an element outside the self which for Ellen promises cool, free-floating identity. As a woman, Ellen has experienced in both her upbringing and her relationships the stifling cultural consequences of the evolutionary determinism expatiated upon by her older lover, the biologist Gorman. When it becomes clear that the men in her life are, in their different ways, all pathetically enslaved by their cultural conditioning and its "stories," she finally proclaims her independence of all three and of "the old old days of pain": "My name is Ellen Cassidy and I live all alone."

Because of—or perhaps despite—the lyrical power of its monologues, *Ellen Cassidy* cannot help but bring to mind Morrison's admission that at this time he was "using plays as a form of psychoanalysis." *Flying Blind* signals a breakthrough for Morrison in its achievement of a decisively *im*personal form for the articulation of his characteristic preoccupations. The brooding and often painful energies of *Ellen Cassidy* are here gathered, shaped, and endowed with a bitter comic trajectory by the crisp dialogue and coolly contrived sudden mayhem of farce. The result is, as one critic has put it, "a world where the laws of farce and tragedy are interchangeable."

The increasingly fevered comings and goings of *Flying Blind* take place in and around the "imaginatively furnished" living room of an Ulster medical rep, Dan Poots, a supplier of "happy pills" who has dedicated himself to survival in an environment he considers to be in the grip of a "perversion of the spirit." He retreats between stereo headphones, listening to the music of his hero, Charlie "Bird" Parker, who "found the terms of membership unacceptable"—as Dan now does. Even before the darkly funny (and, for him, bladder-stretching) incursions of two groups of terrorists—a Protestant murder-squad and vengeful Catholics—Dan's strategy for survival is seriously disturbed by the demands of his concerned wife Liz, and by her old flame the sociologist Michael, who has returned to his native Ulster, laden with simplistic socio-political solutions and a desperation born of childlessness, determined to "save" Liz (or, failing that, her babysitter). Meanwhile the lawyer Boyd, recently forced out of politics by terrorist death-threats, is alarmed to find his sexual impulses arising only in the revolver he brandishes—and even that fails to go off at the climactic moment. In fact sex, that generic stipulation of farce, is here ingeniously invested with a pivotal diagnostic function. The pathetic impotence of the men in the play is symptomatic of a diseased society in which, as Dan realizes, potency exists not in sexual relationships but in the self-destructive violence of history's "blind men," the terrorists. Hence the moral force behind the farce when Dan and his generous (though unfulfilled) neighbour Bertha confront imminent death by undressing to make love right in front of the panic-stricken terrorists who are threatening them. In the end a fatal mêlée (graced by a bucket of piss and a purblind terrorist called Magoo) disrupts the reconciliation of friends and neighbours, and happy ending gives way to familiar stalemate.

Following the success of *Flying Blind* and after a group of Raymond Chandler adaptations for radio, Morrison worked on radio scripts in the U.S.A. and on a number of television projects, most of them either abortive or disappointing, in Britain. His last important stage play before his spell as director at the Liverpool Playhouse (1981–85) was *Scrap!* Here again farce is the formal basis, but the action is rather less riotous than in *Flying Blind*, and there are interwoven elements of the thriller-mode—or even of whodunnit.

Scrap! is centrally concerned with betrayal—personal, cultural, and political. The high-ranking English policeman Cleaver (a.k.a. Butcher) aims "to solve the problems of a whole country" by an appeal to what he considers to be the "eternal verities"—"bribery, blackmail, and betrayal." His plan is to lure the key Protestant terrorist organizer Sidney Mulligan out of Belfast to Liverpool and to deliver him over to the Catholic terrorist leader Madigan as part of a deal involving the military-strategic co-operation with Britain of a prospective non-neutral "new" united Ireland. To this end Cleaver brings over to Liverpool Mulligan's schoolgirl daughter Kate, who has gone to the police with her father's operational notebooks in her possession. Kate, ironically, is glad to escape Belfast, and with it the childhood innocence that makes her a potential blood-sacrifice on the altar of Ulster's history, yet at the same time she is torn at the prospect of betraying her father and all that he stands for. She manages to deposit the vital documents with his cousin, the English scrap-dealer Tommy Atkins (who is unaware of the fact). When Mulligan himself arrives in Liverpool, impelled less by his concern for the notebooks than by the desperation and "black pain" he feels at the disappearance of the child in whose innocence he invests all his surviving values, he is drawn into a deadly, yet also farcical, pattern of intrigue and betrayal. The plainly allegorical design of the play is reinforced by the co-ordination of symbolic structure and setting: the mirror-lined basement bar of the second half realizes visually the darkly oppressive phantom-world of Ulster history which shuts out the "sweet daylight" of freedom and reduces the Protestants to the contorted scrap of Britain. At the climax, Cleaver's underhand plans go grotesquely wrong, and the powerful Protestant Mulligan, having wrapped himself in a waistcoat of dynamite and lit the fuse, grasps the disarmed Catholic Madigan under one arm and the crooked Englishman Cleaver under the other, as he asks: "which among us deserves to be saved?" This final stage-image crystallizes the deadlock Morrison has always sought to confront and to understand through his drama—in the belief that such understanding would also constitute a kind of self-discovery.

A further strand of Morrison's work is constituted by his imaginative realizations of "true stories" which are in some way enigmatic or remarkable. Into this category fall the television films *Shergar* (about the kidnap of the racehorse), and *A Safe House* (about the Maguire case), and the stage play *Be Bop a Lula*. Based on research by Spencer Leigh, *Be Bop a Lula* tells the story of rock 'n' rollers Gene Vincent and Eddie Cochran on their 1960 British tour, during which the latter died in a car crash. The narrative, woven around no less than 30 songs (performed live), concentrates on the relationship between the broodingly violent and self-destructive Vincent, with his crippled leg and black leathers, and the fresh but fated Cochran. Cochran is the rising star, but the final image of the play is of the already fading Vincent sitting on his friend's coffin. The play is a kind of requiem, a contribution to (pre-Beatles) rock mythology rather than an exploration of it. "Great drama it isn't," wrote one reviewer, "but it is good rock and roll."

—Paul Lawley

———

MORTIMER, John (Clifford). British. Born in Hampstead, London, 21 April 1923. Educated at Harrow School, Middlesex, 1937–40; Brasenose College, Oxford, 1940–42, B.A. 1947; called to the bar, 1948; Queen's Counsel, 1966; Master of the Bench, Inner Temple, 1975. Served with the Crown Film Units as scriptwriter during World War II. Married 1) Penelope Dimont in 1949 (divorced 1971), one son and one daughter; 2) Penny Gollop in 1972, two daughters. Drama critic, *New Statesman, Evening Standard*, and *Observer*, 1972, all London; member of the National Theatre Board, 1968–88; president, Berkshire, Buckinghamshire, and Oxford Naturalists' Trust, from 1984; chair, League of Dramatists; chair of the council, Royal Society of Literature, from 1989; chair, Royal Court Theatre, from 1990; president, Howard League for Penal Reform, from 1992. Recipient: Italia prize, for radio play, 1958; Screenwriters Guild award, for television play, 1970; BAFTA award, for television series, 1980; *Yorkshire Post* award, 1983. D. Litt.: Susquehanna University, Selinsgrove, Pennsylvania, 1985; University of St. Andrews, Fife, 1987; University of Nottingham, 1989; LL.D.: Exeter University, 1986. C.B.E. (Commander, Order of the British Empire), 1986. Lives in Henley-on-Thames, Oxfordshire. Agent: Peters, Fraser, and Dunlop Group, 503–504 The Chambers, Chelsea Harbour, Lots Road, London SW10 0XF, England.

PUBLICATIONS

Plays

The Dock Brief (broadcast 1957; produced London, 1958; New York, 1961). In *Three Plays*, 1958.
I Spy (broadcast 1957; produced Salisbury, Wiltshire, and Palm Beach, Florida, 1959). In *Three Plays*, 1958.
What Shall We Tell Caroline? (produced London, 1958; New York, 1961). In *Three Plays*, 1958.
Three Plays: The Dock Brief, What Shall We Tell Caroline?, I Spy. London, Elek, 1958; New York, Grove Press, 1962.
Call Me a Liar (televised 1958; produced London, 1968). In

Lunch Hour and Other Plays, 1960; in *The Television Playwright: Ten Plays for B.B.C. Television*, edited by Michael Barry, New York, Hill and Wang, 1960.

Sketches in *One to Another* (produced London, 1959). London, French, 1960.

The Wrong Side of the Park (produced London, 1960). London, Heinemann, 1960.

Lunch Hour (broadcast 1960; produced Salisbury, Wiltshire, 1960; London, 1961; New York, 1977). In *Lunch Hour and Other Plays*, 1960; published separately, New York, French, 1961.

David and Broccoli (televised 1960). In *Lunch Hour and Other Plays*, 1960.

Lunch Hour and Other Plays (includes *Collect Your Hand Baggage, David and Broccoli, Call Me a Liar*). London, Methuen, 1960.

Collect Your Hand Baggage (produced Wuppertal, Germany, 1963). In *Lunch Hour and Other Plays,* 1960.

Sketches in *One over the Eight* (produced London, 1961).

Two Stars for Comfort (produced London, 1962). London, Methuen, 1962.

A Voyage round My Father (broadcast 1963; produced London, 1970). London, Methuen, 1971.

Sketches in *Changing Gear* (produced Nottingham, 1965).

A Flea in Her Ear, adaptation of a play by Feydeau (produced London, 1966; Tucson, Arizona, 1979). London and New York, French, 1967.

A Choice of Kings (televised 1966). In *Playbill Three*, edited by Alan Durband, London, Hutchinson, 1969.

The Judge (produced London, 1967). London, Methuen, 1967.

Desmond (televised 1968). In *The Best Short Plays 1971*, edited by Stanley Richards, Philadelphia, Chilton, 1971.

Cat among the Pigeons, adaptation of a play by Feydeau (produced London, 1969; Milwaukee, 1971). New York, French, 1970.

Come As You Are: Four Short Plays (includes *Mill Hill, Bermondsey, Gloucester Road, Marble Arch*) (produced London, 1970). London, Methuen, 1971.

Five Plays (includes *The Dock Brief, What Shall We Tell Caroline?, I Spy, Lunch Hour, Collect Your Hand Baggage*). London, Methuen, 1970.

The Captain of Köpenick, adaptation of a play by Carl Zuckmayer (produced London, 1971). London, Methuen, 1971.

Conflicts, with others (produced London, 1971).

I, Claudius, adaptation of the novels *I, Claudius* and *Claudius the God* by Robert Graves (produced London, 1972).

Knightsbridge (televised 1972). London, French, 1973.

Collaborators (produced London, 1973). London, Eyre Methuen, 1973.

The Fear of Heaven (as *Mr. Lucy's Fear of Heaven*, broadcast 1976; as *The Fear of Heaven*, produced with *The Prince of Darkness* as *Heaven and Hell*, London, 1976). London, French, 1978.

Heaven and Hell (includes *The Fear of Heaven* and *The Prince of Darkness*) (produced London, 1976; revised version of *The Prince of Darkness*, as *The Bells of Hell* produced Richmond, Surrey, and London, 1977). *The Bells of Hell* published London, French, 1978.

The Lady from Maxim's, adaptation of a play by Feydeau (produced London, 1977). London, Heinemann, 1977.

John Mortimer's Casebook (includes *The Dock Brief, The Prince of Darkness, Interlude*) (produced London, 1982).

When That I Was (produced Ottawa, 1982).

Edwin (broadcast 1982). In *Edwin and Other Plays*, 1984.

A Little Hotel on the Side, adaptation of a play by Feydeau and Maurice Desvalliers (produced London, 1984). In *Three Boulevard Farces*, 1985.

Edwin and Other Plays (includes *Bermondsey, Marble Arch, The Fear of Heaven, The Prince of Darkness*). London, Penguin, 1984.

Three Boulevard Farces (includes *A Little Hotel on the Side, A Flea in Her Ear, The Lady from Maxim's*). London, Penguin, 1985.

Die Fledermaus, adaptation of the libretto by Henri Meilhac and Ludovic Halévy, music by Johann Strauss (produced London, 1989). London, Viking, 1989.

Screenplays: *Ferry to Hong Kong*, with Lewis Gilbert and Vernon Harris, 1959; *The Innocents*, with Truman Capote and William Archibald, 1961; *Guns of Darkness*, 1962; *I Thank a Fool*, with others, 1962; *Lunch Hour*, 1962; *The Running Man*, 1963; *Bunny Lake Is Missing*, with Penelope Mortimer, 1964; *A Flea in Her Ear*, 1967; *John and Mary*, 1969.

Radio Plays: *Like Men Betrayed*, 1955; *No Hero*, 1955; *The Dock Brief*, 1957; *I Spy*, 1957; *Three Winters*, 1958; *Lunch Hour*, 1960; *The Encyclopedist*, 1961; *A Voyage round My Father*, 1963; *Personality Split*, 1964; *Education of an Englishman*, 1964; *A Rare Device*, 1965; *Mr Luby's Fear of Heaven*, 1976; *Edwin*, 1982; *Rumpole*, from his own stories, 1988; *Glasnost*, 1988.

Television Plays: *Call Me a Liar*, 1958; *David and Broccoli*, 1960; *A Choice of Kings*, 1966; *The Exploding Azalea*, 1966; *The Head Waiter*, 1966; *Hughie*, 1967; *The Other Side*, 1967; *Desmond*, 1968; *Infidelity Took Place*, 1968; *Married Alive*, 1970; *Swiss Cottage*, 1972; *Knightsbridge*, 1972; *Rumpole of the Bailey*, 1975, and series, 1978, 1979, 1987, 1988; *A Little Place off the Edgware Road, The Blue Film, The Destructors, The Case for the Defence, Chagrin in Three Parts, The Invisible Japanese Gentlemen, Special Duties*, and *Mortmain* all from stories by Graham Greene, 1975–76; *Will Shakespeare*, 1978; *Rumpole's Return*, 1980; *Unity*, from the book by David Pryce-Jones, 1981; *Brideshead Revisited*, from the novel by Evelyn Waugh 1981; *Edwin*, 1984; *The Ebony Tower*, from the story by John Fowles, 1984; *Paradise Postponed*, from his own novel, 1986; *Summer's Lease*, from his own novel, 1989; *The Waiting Room*, 1989; *Titmuss Regained*, from his own novel, 1991.

Ballet Scenario: *Home*, 1968.

Son et Lumière scripts: *Hampton Court*, 1964; *Brighton Pavilion*, 1965.

Novels

Charade. London, Lane, 1948.

Rumming Park. London, Lane, 1948.

Answer Yes or No. London, Lane, 1950; as *The Silver Hook*, New York, Morrow, 1950.

Like Men Betrayed. London, Collins, 1953; Philadelphia, Lippincott, 1954.

The Narrowing Stream. London, Collins, 1954; New York, Viking, 1989.

Three Winters. London, Collins, 1956.

Will Shakespeare: The Untold Story. London, Hodder and Stoughton, 1977; New York, Delacorte Press, 1978.

Paradise Postponed. London and New York, Viking, 1985.

Summer's Lease. London and New York, Viking, 1988.

Titmuss Regained. London and New York, Viking, 1990.

The Rapstone Chronicles (includes *Paradise Postponed, Titmuss Regained*) London and New York, Viking, 1991.
Dunster. London and New York, Viking, 1992.

Short Stories

Rumpole. London, Allen Lane, 1980.
  Rumpole of the Bailey. London, Penguin, 1978; New York, Penguin, 1980.
  The Trials of Rumpole. London, Penguin, 1979; New York, Penguin, 1981.
Regina v. Rumpole. London, Allen Lane, 1981.
  Rumpole's Return. London, Penguin, 1980; New York, Penguin, 1982.
  Rumpole for the Defence. London, Penguin, 1982.
Rumpole and the Golden Thread. New York, Penguin, 1983.
The First Rumpole Omnibus (includes *Rumpole of the Bailey, The Trials of Rumpole, Rumpole's Return*). London, Penguin, 1983.
Rumpole's Last Case. London, Penguin, 1987; New York, Penguin, 1988.
The Second Rumpole Omnibus (includes *Rumpole for the Defence, Rumpole and the Golden Thread, Rumpole's Last Case*). London, Viking, 1987; New York, Penguin, 1988.
Rumpole and the Age of Miracles. London, Penguin, 1988; New York, Penguin, 1989.
Rumpole à la Carte. London and New York, Viking, 1990.

Other

No Moaning of the Bar (as Geoffrey Lincoln). London, Bles, 1957.
With Love and Lizards (travel), with Penelope Mortimer. London, Joseph, 1957.
Clinging to the Wreckage: A Part of Life. London, Weidenfeld and Nicolson, and New Haven, Connecticut, Ticknor and Fields, 1982.
In Character (interviews). London, Allen Lane, 1983.
The Liberty of the Citizen (lecture), with Franklin Thomas and Lord Hunt of Tanworth. London, Granada, 1983.
Character Parts (interviews). London, Viking, 1986.

Editor, *Famous Trials*, edited by Harry Hodge and James H. Hodge. London, Viking, and New York, Penguin, 1984.
Editor, *Great Law and Order Stories*. London, Bellew, 1990.

*

Manuscript Collections: Boston University; University of California, Los Angeles.

Critical Study: *Anger and After* by John Russell Taylor, London, Methuen, 1962, revised edition, 1969, as *The Angry Theatre*, New York, Hill and Wang, 1962, revised edition, 1969.

John Mortimer comments:

(1982) Comedy, I remember saying when my plays were first performed, is the only thing worth writing in this despairing age. Twenty years later the world has offered no call for a change of attitude. It may be that only in the most secure and optimistic ages can good tragedies be written. Our present situation, stumbling into a misty future filled with uncertainty and mistrust, is far too serious to be described in terms that give us no opportunity to laugh.

*   *   *

As a barrister, John Mortimer has been a doughty advocate of the freedom of the stage from censorship, and as a public figure he is respected as a staunch left-wing intellectual, albeit with an uninhibited taste for the good life and a hearty dislike of what he is wont to call the "nanny state." His own most successful plays, however, have been agreeable and witty middle-class entertainments. They are deftly crafted and beautifully scripted, with well-observed characters who are presented, sometimes, in plots of such simplicity as to be little more than a single extended situation, and his theatrical style departs from traditional realistic canons only in a certain fluidity of staging. His remarkable expertise in the difficult form of the one-act play has tempted some critics to suggest that Mortimer is less at home with longer plays, but this is not entirely fair, for he does know how to develop ideas and characters. Mortimer's skilled theatrical craftsmanship is exemplified particularly well in his translations of *A Flea in Her Ear*, *Cat among the Pigeons*, and *The Lady from Maxim's*, three French farces by Georges Feydeau. Above all, however, Mortimer is associated in the public mind with the *Rumpole* television series. Rumpole is, in Mortimer's phrase, an Old Bailey hack, and each of the many half-hour episodes presents an entertaining if undemanding intertwining of three elements: the battles of a bumbling but liberal-minded barrister to defend the flawed individuals who are his clients against the English legal system; the everyday squabbles between the oddly assorted partners in chambers in London; and Rumpole's domestic difficulties with his harridan of a wife, Hilda, or, as the British public has come to call her, "She Who Must be Obeyed."

The Dock Brief, which was Mortimer's first play to be produced, contains much that is to be found again and again in his work. Set in the cells beneath the courtroom, it is economical to produce, but imagination and the provision of acting opportunities compensate for any lack of extravagance in staging. Hilariously funny yet sad in all its implications, the play juxtaposes a very human prisoner charged with killing his wife and a totally incompetent ageing barrister who dreams that presenting the case for the defence will win him the reputation for which he has always yearned. In the cell he attempts to play out the court room drama which he foresees, but in court, we are told, he fails dismally. A happy paradox, however, results in an unexpected happy ending.

Another of Mortimer's early plays, the very popular one-act *Lunch Hour* illustrates two more characteristic aspects of his work. As a barrister specialising in divorce cases, Mortimer was well acquainted with the world of sleazy hotels and the clientele that used them for their assignations. With an attractive blend of wit and sympathy, *Lunch Hour* shows what this may well mean in personal terms. Sex, it turns out, is really only a secondary consideration here, and once again, as in *The Dock Brief*, there are beguiling episodes which raise the question of the relationship between individuals' true selves and the roles that they are called upon to assume in life. Mortimer is also interested, in what some might regard as a very English way, with life in English private schools, and this is represented for the first time in the sensitive and closely observed early play *What Shall We Tell Caroline?*, in which, of course, it transpires that putting the question in quite those terms represents a fundamental misunderstanding of the headmaster's 18-year-old daughter.

Many theatre-goers regard *A Voyage round My Father* as Mortimer's greatest achievement, and both on stage, with Alec Guinness in the lead, and on television with Laurence Olivier, it made a great impression. Mortimer's father was a noted figure in the courts, both for the style of his advocacy and for the fact that he was blind, and *A Voyage* is a marvellously rich portrayal of this impossibly difficult character in counterpoint to John Mortimer's life from childhood through adolescence to maturity. The situations can become hilarious as the blind barrister deliberately flouts every bourgeois convention; the dialogue has all the brilliance one might expect from men whose stock-in-trade is the ability to speak well; the social observation is sharp; and with all this there is also great sympathy for a wounded human being who fights to retain his dignity. Symbolic of the blind barrister's determination not to be daunted by his affliction is his passionate concern for the beauty of his garden. By the end the audience feels almost guilty for enjoying looking at the summer flowers he cannot see.

The *Judge* also explores the legal world, this time from the angle of a judge who, at the end of his career, returns not only to his home town in the provinces but to unresolved aspects of his past. The tone is more serious than in many of Mortimer's plays, and the public has generally preferred rather lighter fare, such as *Collect Your Hand Baggage*, with its whimsically deflating ending, *Two Stars for Comfort*, set in a modest hotel, and clever short plays like those collected in *Come As You Are* which reveal, in a form and with an attitude that demands little of the audience, an acute awareness of just what makes people tick.

—Christopher Smith

MOSEL, Tad. American. Born in Steubenville, Ohio, 1 May 1922. Educated at Amherst College, Massachusetts, B.A. 1947; Yale University, New Haven, Connecticut, 1947–49; Columbia University, New York, M.A. 1953. Served in the United States Army Air Force, 1943–46: sergeant. Clerk, Northwest Airlines, 1951–53. Visiting critic in television writing, Yale University School of Drama, 1957–58. Member of the Executive Board, *Television Quarterly*, Syracuse, New York; member of the Executive Council, Writers Guild of America. Recipient: Pulitzer prize, 1961; New York Drama Critics Circle award, 1961. D. Litt.: College of Wooster, Ohio, 1963; D.F.A.: College of Steubenville, 1969. Agent: William Morris Agency, 1350 Avenue of the Americas, New York, New York 10019. Address: 400 East 57th Street, New York, New York 10022, U.S.A.

PUBLICATIONS

Plays

The Happiest Years (produced Amherst, Massachusetts, 1942).
The Lion Hunter (produced New York, 1952).
Madame Aphrodite (televised 1953; revised version, music by Jerry Herman, produced New York, 1962).
My Lost Saints (televised 1955). Published in *Best Television Plays*, edited by Gore Vidal, New York, Ballantine, 1956.
Other People's Houses: Six Television Plays (includes *Ernie Barger Is Fifty, The Haven, The Lawn Party, Star in the Summer Night, The Waiting Place*). New York, Simon and Schuster, 1956.
The Out-of-Towners (televised 1956). Published in *Television Plays for Writers: Eight Television Plays*, edited by A.S. Burack, Boston, The Writer, 1957.

The Five-Dollar Bill (televised 1957). Chicago, Dramatic Publishing Company, 1958.
Presence of the Enemy (televised 1958). Published in *Best Short Plays 1957–1958*, edited by Margaret Mayorga, Boston, Beacon Press, 1958.
All the Way Home, adaptation of the novel *A Death in the Family* by James Agee (produced New York, 1960). New York, Obolensky, 1961.
Impromptu (produced New York, 1961). New York, Dramatists Play Service, 1961.
That's Where the Town's Going (televised 1962). New York, Dramatists Play Service, 1962.

Screenplays: *Dear Heart*, 1964; *Up the Down Staircase*, 1967.

Television Plays: *Jinxed*, 1949; *The Figgerin' of Aunt Wilma*, 1953; *This Little Kitty Stayed Cool*, 1953; *The Remarkable Case of Mr. Bruhl*, 1953; *Ernie Barger Is Fifty*, 1953; *Other People's Houses*, 1953; *The Haven*, 1953; *Madame Aphrodite*, 1953; *The Lawn Party*, 1955; *Star in the Summer Night*, 1955; *Guilty Is the Stranger*, 1955; *My Lost Saints*, 1955; *The Waiting Place*, 1955; *The Out-of-Towners*, 1956; *The Five-Dollar Bill*, 1957; *The Morning Place*, 1957; *Presence of the Enemy*, 1958; *The Innocent Sleep*, 1958; *A Corner of the Garden*, 1959; *Sarah's Laughter*, 1959; *The Invincible Teddy*, 1960; *Three Roads to Rome: Venus Ascendant, Roman Fever, The Rest Cure*, from stories by Martha Gellhorn, Edith Wharton, and Aldous Huxley, 1960; *That's Where the Town's Going*, 1962.

Other

Leading Lady: The World and Theatre of Katharine Cornell, with Gertrude Macy. Boston, Little Brown, 1978.

*   *   *

Tad Mosel gained attention as one of the leading American writers for live television in the 1950's. His scripts were ideally suited for the medium in their restricted scope, focus on intimate details, and Chekhovian naturalism within a thoroughly contemporary American suburban milieu. An earlier one-act play written for the stage, *Impromptu*, has become a minor classic in its treatment of illusion and reality by means of a theatrical metaphor. A group of actors find themselves on a stage to which they have been summoned in order to improvise a play. Their groping efforts point up the recognition that life itself is essentially an improvisation in which roles are assumed and identity is elusive. Mosel handles this potentially trite and sentimental concept with wit and restraint.

Mosel's most successful work, however, was *All the Way Home*, a stage adaptation of James Agee's novel, *A Death in the Family*. Mosel's play captures the essence of the subjective, introspective novel while providing it with an external, theatrical form. In its depiction of several generations of a family and its compassionate rendering of death, birth, and the process of emotional maturing, the work has echoes of Thornton Wilder, an impression that is reinforced by Mosel's fluid handling of time and space. Especially noteworthy is the economy of dialogue, which is related to Mosel's sure sense of the power of the stage to communicate in unverbalized, visual terms.

—Jarka M. Burian

MOTTON, Gregory. British. Born in London, 17 September 1961. Lives with Lotta Kjellberg; one daughter. Recipient: Arts Council bursary, 1989; Royal Literary Fund grant, 1991. Agent: Rod Hall, A.P. Watt, 20 John Street, London WC1N 2DR, England.

PUBLICATIONS

Plays

Chicken (produced London, 1987). With *Ambulance*, London, Penguin, 1987.
Ambulance (produced London, 1987). With *Chicken*, London, Penguin, 1987.
Downfall (produced London, 1988). With *Looking at You (Revived) Again*, London, Methuen, 1989.
Looking at You (Revived) Again (produced Leicester and London, 1989). With *Downfall*, London, Methuen, 1989.
The Ghost Sonata, adaptation of the play by August Strindberg (produced London, 1989).
The Pelican, adaptation of the play by August Strindberg (produced London, 1989).
Picture of Dorian Gray, adaptation of the novel by Oscar Wilde (produced Leicester, 1990).
Woyzeck, adaptation of the play by Georg Büchner (produced London, 1992). London, Hern, 1992.

Screenplay: *Kleptophilia*, 1992.

Radio Plays: *The Jug*, 1991; *Lazy Brién*, 1992.

* * *

In a 1988 *Guardian* review of *Downfall*, Gregory Motton's third drama in two years, Michael Billington detected "the birth of a new genre: Urban Impressionism." Occasioned by the congruent staging of Nick Ward's *The Strangeness of Others* (to which many reviewers unfavourably compared Motton's work), the label is no less useful than many another —"surrealism," Billington went on to suggest; "tragi-farcical nightmare," opined Paul Taylor of the *Independent*. Motton "[is] fast making a name for himself," Sheridan Morley ventured in *Punch*, as "the dramatic poet of urban disintegration." A drama wilfully (if not always clearly) focused on social damage and dissidence and at the same time fashioning an expressionist, sometimes symbolist mode of address does not lend itself easily to shorthand account: abrupt shifts of mood and register, dialogue gracelessly demotic then poetically or portentously inflected, violence and comedy charged by incipient wandering and waste make clear that dramatic naturalism is as residual a feature of Motton's stagecraft as his characters are the residues and casualties of psychosocial "development."

A break with naturalism is hardly apparent from the settings of the earlier plays, *Chicken*—"an abandoned working men's cafe" and "a street outside [a] doorway"—and *Ambulance*—"Ellis's room" and "the street, outside a launderette"; however, the interplay between road and room, as it were, shapes a series of narratives which, in both plays, elliptically explore what have become Motton's ruling concerns: commitment and communication, power and loss. Indeed, the title *Ambulance* has much to do with the impairment of characters' motor functions: the crippled Clivey, locked into a relation with Louise, is then mothered by Mary who is herself unable to carry her legs beyond a certain radius of Holloway Prison; meanwhile, the uncertainly gendered

Ellis injures herself jumping from a stifling room onto the pavement outside, thus prompting the ambulance's arrival. Ambulancemen figure as anonymous powers of capture and disablement, much as, in *Chicken*, the "party" that Pat (the patriarch) menacingly invokes and the role he assumes of Secretary of State for Sanitation and Education (to include "secrecy"), suggest individual disempowerment by bureaucracy and factional interests. Commitment, along with individual desire for personal and professional growth, is readily transmuted into involuntary committal.

Indeed, individuals (periodically but always problematically forming couples) wander through an increasingly fractured narrative line across the plays, forcing out an ever more compacted set of dramatic co-ordinates: lost, abandoned, imagined children, for example—with the sense of continuity, history, and relation they suggest—are repeatedly invoked. The killing of the chicken in the play of that title is a matricidal act (no eggs), the breaking of a food chain by a usurping father. The "pain of separation," as Johnny terms it in *Ambulance* (on occasions, from that which one never possessed) includes loss of memory, relation, and aspiration, of visible and attainable goals, even as seekers with binoculars search the skies and invoke the "cosmos." The same play's Pedro, increasingly wracked with bodily spasms, can still claim, however, that "Life goes on" even when, at the play's close, the "battering ram" (an ambulance crew) hoves into view.

Downfall, a drama divided into 56 brief scenes, is forbiddingly dense and oblique with its networks of verbal and circumstantial patterning, its snatches of biblical and occult narrative, its characters (Tower Man, Spanish Lover, Violent Man) emblematically rather than socially situated. More so than in the earlier drama, dialogue swings from the barely articulate outburst or stumbling exchange to outpourings of garrulous but vacuous energy or fitfully focused portentousness; pointed concentration slides off into offhand nonsequitur. At the same time, despite—perhaps because of—having each scene titled as an episode, Motton's dramatic—but more especially visual—imagination has developed to incorporate wildly different modes and circumstances: the Violent Man hounded by a swooping helicopter, Hetty and Rolo itinerant but grounded beneath the choric Tower Man, Secret Service man Geronimo progressively losing power and position in respect of the "sides" which the play, as carnival, insists on dislocating. Such circumstances recur and are refashioned to punctuate material which might otherwise overreach itself.

A moment of tender (if not quite literally touching) intimacy between "two strays" just before the play's close ("There are lots of people in the world," Clancy, not for the first time, remarks) serves to highlight Motton's emphasis on permissive rather than repressive commitment in a world open to surveillance, institutional power, and false prophets, all emanating from on high upon a falling world. In a shadowing of the Christian story (with "skulduggery" as Gethsemane and Dover "the nation's Calvary" at the play's end) *Downfall* enacts the struggle to remain upright (in every sense of that word) along a modern *via dolorosa* of betrayal, suffering, guilt, and despair. Along the way there are any number of false epiphanies (and a conspicuously unachieved annunciation) ending with "a long road stretching out" before three figures themselves stretched across the skyline and Motton's concluding dance (of death?).

The debt to Strindberg (several of whose plays Motton has translated for production) is most evident in his more tightly worked, economically constructed "ghost" play *Looking at You (Revived) Again*. It presents a triangle of figures—a man, Abe, "dark woman" Mrs. James (the wife whom, it seems, from reconstructed dramas of the past, Abe has abandoned and whose children he affects to be seeking) and "Peragrin's daughter" whom Abe consorts with as "the dark side . . . the invisible side of (his) soul." "p.d." (as she is known) finally overshadows not only the crippled Mrs. James, now upstanding, and transforms herself into a figure of mannikin beauty, but also overshadows Abe (who claims to have been "eclipsed" entirely) with the promise of a child which will stir him to a sense of responsibility. Inset narrated stagings of a wedding, threats from landlords and bailiffs, desolate settings, and sickness notwithstanding, the lack of social specificity and the more tightly worked psychodramas of repression, transference and working through make this, Motton's most recent play, a studied rejection of naturalism. One might indeed be forgiven for seeking the play's public concerns less with "urban disintegration" and contemporary British culture than with European Jewry and for locating its dramatic kinship within European Expressionism.

—James Hansford

———————

MOWAT, David. British. Born in Cairo, Egypt, 16 March 1943. Educated at Bryanston School, 1956–60; New College, Oxford, 1961–64, B.A. (honours) in English language and literature 1964; University of Sussex, Falmer, 1964–66. Cilcennin fellow, University of Bristol, 1973–75; director of the Playwrights Workshop, University of Iowa, Iowa City, 1978; fellow, Virginia Center for Creative Arts, 1979. Since 1984 director of the Playwriting Workshop, Actors Centre, London. Recipient: Arts Council bursary, 1970, 1971, 1976, 1977, 1983. Agent: Casarotto Ramsay Ltd., National House, 60–66 Wardour Street, London WIV 3HP. Address: 7 Mount Street, Oxford OX2 6DH, England.

PUBLICATIONS

Plays

Jens (produced Falmer, Sussex, 1965; London, 1969). Included in *Anna-Luse and Other Plays*, 1970.
Pearl (produced Brighton, 1966).
1850 (produced London, 1967).
Anna-Luse (produced Edinburgh, 1968; London, 1971; New York, 1972). Included in *Anna-Luse and Other Plays*, 1970.
Dracula, with others (produced Edinburgh, 1969; London, 1973).
Purity (produced Manchester, 1969; London, 1970; New York, 1972). Included in *Anna-Luse and Other Plays*, 1970.
Anna-Luse and Other Plays. London, Calder and Boyars, 1970.
The Normal Woman, and Tyyppi (produced London, 1970).
Adrift, with others (produced Manchester, 1970).
The Others (produced London, 1970). London, Calder and Boyars, 1973.
Most Recent Least Recent (produced Manchester, 1970).
Inuit (produced London, 1970).
Liquid (produced London, 1971).
The Diabolist (produced London, 1971).

John (produced London, 1971).
Amalfi, based on *The Duchess of Malfi* by Webster (produced Edinburgh, 1972).
Phoenix-and-Turtle (produced London, 1972; New York, 1976). Published in *The London Fringe Theatre*, edited by Victor Mitchell, London, Burnham House, 1975.
Morituri (produced London, 1972).
My Relationship with Jayne (produced London, 1973).
Come (produced London, 1973).
Main Sequence (produced Bristol, 1974).
The Collected Works (produced London, 1974; New York, 1977).
The Memory Man (produced Bristol, 1974).
The Love Maker (produced Bristol, 1974).
X to C (produced Bristol, 1975).
Kim (produced Sheffield, 1977; London, 1980).
Winter (produced Iowa City, 1978; London, 1983).
The Guise (produced Birmingham and London, 1979; New York, 1991).
Hiroshima Nights (produced Milton Keynes, Buckinghamshire, and London, 1981).
The Midnight Sun (produced London, 1983).
Carmen (produced Chichester, 1984).
The Almas (produced London, 1989).

Radio Plays: *To Die in Africa*, 1989; *Singing and Dancing in Kanpur*, 1991.

Short Stories

New Writers 11, with others. London, Calder and Boyars, 1974.

* * *

The name of David Mowat is familiar to those who frequent experimental fringe theatres. He began his career as one of the band of writers who provide much of the repertoire of short plays produced on the lunch-time circuit.

Many of these playwrights seem almost indistinguishable from each other: indeed, some half dozen of them indulge occasionally in corporate efforts. Their methods are freewheeling, their subject matter often sensational, and their intention to subvert the existing social structure by means of shock effects. They command respect on account of their talent and seriousness of purpose, although their playing out of sadistic and erotic fantasies induces doubt as often as cheers.

From these writers, Mowat stands conspicuously apart. There is present in his work an obsessive search for truth: "What information, useful information for the living of our lives, are we getting from this person?" asks the Narrator in a direct address to the audience in *Phoenix-and-Turtle*. In the same play he also observes "There's no obscenity so obscene as the horrid spectra of untruth lurking in the centre of one's home." The speaker is a Lecturer in English who has been sacked as a result of a liaison with a student; who has just burnt the manuscript of his book on the subject of the eponymous Shakespeare poem; who feels compelled to tell his wife that she has not long to live; and who—after an incestuous attack on his daughter—discovers that the girl is already pregnant. All these lies are brought into the open but, characteristically, the very act of telling the truth by means of the basic lie of theatre is also questioned. The author likens art to putting a frame around lies and, by making them scan or rhyme, pretending to give them a moral purpose.

Fat-Man (from the same period but not yet produced),

deals allegorically with the rifts in the political left. Using as a motto a dictum of Mao Tse-tung's—"When the body is healthy, the feelings are correct"—the scene is set in a gymnasium threatened with demolition. The name of three of its four characters—Fatman, Cripple, and Little-Boy—indicate the satirical nature of the problem: each one has passionate convictions regarding the desired use of the gymnasium. The play is subtitled "the exercise of power"; needless to say, Mowat offers no easy solutions. His adaptation of *The Duchess of Malfi* and his approving quotation of Webster's remark that all life is a torture chamber may point to a vein of pessimism, but this, too, could be misleading. There is a quality of nagging obsession in Mowat's plays. His zeal for uncovering the truth has an echo of Ibsen, his haunted, nightmarish fantasies remind one of Strindberg. Of living authors, only Pinter comes to mind: Mowat, too, is a master of mystery and economy and his plays, though often difficult to comprehend at first sight, share with Pinter's the power to keep an audience spellbound.

He has travelled a long way since he wrote *Jens*: a comparatively straightforward piece of symbolism in which animals and humans mingle surrealistically. His most impressive early play was *Anna-Luse*. Here, a blind young girl gets up in the morning, goes through a ritual of stock-taking of her body and her possessions, and is visited by a girlfriend (also blind), a confused young man, and a dubious P.T. instructor. The last was the victim of a gang of thugs on the way over. Drenched but undaunted, he proceeds to give the girls some strange therapy, which induces in Anna-Luse a phantom pregnancy and childbirth. It is, however, the Instructor who is revealed most surprisingly: he ends, curled up like a baby, at Anna-Luse's breast.

Mowat's plays are by no means solemn. In *The Diabolist*, for example, a worried mum is introduced to her daughter's new boyfriend. He is the epitome of the ordinary bloke, but turns out unexpectedly to be a devil-worshipper. Apart from a macabre and not altogether unsuccessful ending, this sketch is as funny as anything produced by the absurdists.

The surface of these plays is in most cases shabbily suburban and lower middle class. They gain from being staged with absolute naturalism; the tension between manner and matter becomes then increasingly menacing. The rug is slowly and unnervingly pulled from under our feet, and we leave the theatre with our heads buzzing with questions which have no easy or formal solutions but which demand to be asked, if not answered.

Mowat's full-length play *John* belongs in this category. Its hero spends the entire play in a catatonic trance. The unease engendered by his silence, and its effect on the other, superficially "ordinary" characters, provides an exciting evening. Sudden irruptions of extreme violence occur regularly in Mowat's work, but they never appear gratuitously.

The short play *Come* seems to me wilfully enigmatic. Here a distraught father attempts to persuade his estranged daughter to return to him. He lies in wait for her in a room adjoining an intellectual party which becomes an orgy. Nothing is achieved, and neither the motives nor the narrative makes any comprehensible sense.

The full-length play *The Collected Works* is Mowat's most lucid and fully realized to date. The setting is a library; the books, like the eyes of accumulated wisdom and disillusion, stare down at the turbulent emotional tangle involving a researcher, a love-sick girl, the sterile Chief Librarian, and his beautiful wife. Taking as his theme the tensions between life and art, Mowat contrasts the messiness and unexpectedness of the former with the unalterable composure of the latter. There is much sly comedy as the characters explain

themselves in lengthy monologues. Once again, he writes in a deliberate undertone, but the surface simmers with unease and bubbles with incipient volcanic explosions.

With his sensitivity, his depth, and his increasing technical assurance, there is every chance that he will emerge from his present, somewhat esoteric, milieu and give us a play of real significance, with "useful information for the living of our lives."

—Frank Marcus

———

MTWA, Percy. South African. Born in Wattville, Benoni. Dancer and musician, Daveyton; stores clerk, Dunlop Industries, Johannesburg; founder-singer, Percy and the Maestros. Recipient: Edinburgh Fringe first, 1987. Address: c/o The Market Theatre, P.O. Box 8656, Johannesburg 2000, South Africa.

PUBLICATIONS

Plays

Woza Albert!, with Mbongeni Ngema and Barney Simon (produced Johannesburg, 1981; Edinburgh, London, and Los Angeles, 1982; New York, 1984). London, Methuen, 1983; published in *Woza Afrika! An Anthology of South African Plays*, edited by Duma Ndlovu, New York, Braziller, 1986.
Bopha! (*Arrest!*) (also director: produced Johannesburg, n.d.; New York, 1986; London, 1987). Published in *Woza Afrika! An Anthology of South African Plays*, edited by Duma Ndlovu, New York, Braziller, 1986.

*

Theatrical Activities:
Director: **Play**—*Bopha!*, New York, 1986; London, 1987.
Actor: **Plays**—role in *Mama and the Load* by Gibson Kente, Johannesburg, 1979, and roles in *Woza Albert!*.

*   *   *

Though his international reputation rests on two plays, Percy Mtwa has a substantial performing career in South Africa, North America, and Britain which shows that his dramatic creativity goes far beyond verbal scripting, to explore many areas of theatre semiotics. While observing affinities with Grotowski's "poor theatre"—intense physicality with minimal props and costuming—critics have also complained that Mtwa's plays are unsophisticated, their thought is not profound, and the actors' accents make what dialogue there is hard to follow. This failure to acknowledge that Mtwa's commitment is not to a Shavian theatre of ideas but to a confrontational theatre of resistance also evades a pivotal fact of his plays' theatrical interactiveness, that their politics of language casts the audience as complicit in the situation on stage.

Woza Albert!, co-written with the actor Mbongeni Ngema and the white director Barney Simon, announces its activist function in the title: "woza" means "rise up!"—from death, sleep, or passivity. Its running motif is what would happen if Morena, a Christ-like Messiah, should visit South Africa, and most of its 26 scenes present workplace situations showing black oppression, white exploitation, and police brutality. Long before he arrives, Morena serves as a catalyst for the aspirations of the ordinary people, but with his appearance the play takes on more overtly parabolic tones, with his arrest, death, and resurrection. In the final graveyard scene Morena searches for a name on a tombstone beginning with L so that he can raise Lazarus, but finds instead that of the title figure, Albert Luthuli, the Zulu chief who was president of the ANC, and the play ends with a dancing, celebratory invocation to other dead heroes of South African freedom, black and white, to "rise up."

If the recurrent themes are of oppression, the tone of the play is of vitality, with the actors' bodies making an insistent statement of indefatigability and playfulness. The absurdities that surround the figure of Morena, arriving by jumbo jet and eventually gunned down by a military helicopter, merge with the playfulness of performance but only partly disguise the fact that basically this is a theological play, contesting the religious ideology of apartheid, and advancing a Christianity of liberation. There is no subtlety in the indictment of white religious posturing when it turns out that Morena cannot understand Afrikaans, nor is it difficult to see white supremist tactics when a black worker is paid to play Judas and another is imprisoned on Robben Island with only the Bible to read. Other religious allusions are less overt, like the longest scene in the play where the Coronation Brickyard recalls the Israelites in bondage in Egypt making bricks for Pharaoh.

Bopha! (*Arrest!*) does to the law what *Woza Albert!* does to religion, but builds up to starker images of township violence. Here, the Judas motif occupies the whole play, in the form of a black police sergeant who forces the recruitment of his reluctant brother and also confronts his politically-active son's resistance. If the brutality of the final episodes is grim, there is also a filament of rich comedy in the subversive behaviour of the brother recruited into the force, as well as an optimistic ending to the violent absurdity of the police state with the resignation of the sergeant.

Though they are resistance plays, Mtwa's works look forward to a unified, multi-cultural South African society. This vision is reinforced in the theatre by the use of only two or three actors to play many characters. The actor's sometimes half-naked body becomes a screen onto which is projected many different identities, black and white, an effect of condensation not unlike the sequence of photographs of the dead heroes at the end of the BBC television abridgement of *Woza Albert!*, and the figure of the Messiah is inscribed on the martyrs. Also, by parodying the idea of miracles, the plays do not run a risk of obsolescence with the collapse of apartheid. By the time that Peter Brook directed his French version of *Woza Albert!* at the Théâtre des Bouffes du Nord, some sections required rewriting in the light of reform, but it was clear that the supporting social, economic, and religious system will remain highly problematic long after the legal demolition of apartheid.

Within the dialogue of resistance, Mtwa casts the audience as a complicit mediator. When the actors play blacks in Johannesburg pleading with white motorists for jobs, the front of the stage becomes the car window, the auditorium the car interior, and the theatre-goer the privileged minority with the power to act or ignore. In both plays, the actors constantly work frontally, engaging the audience rather than each other even during dialogue, and their hand gestures speak a language of appeal, enquiry, and indictment.

Like much recent South African drama, both plays com-bine several languages, the meaning of which can not always be easily inferred in performance. Sometimes this works for comic irony, as when Zulu is used to abuse a white boss behind his back, or when an Afrikaans policeman is confronted with "big English". But language is also used as a blocking device to prevent the access of other characters or a white audience, staking out a precise cultural territory through language and claiming it as one's own. For this reason, the production history of Mtwa's plays is particularly interesting: their political dynamics have fluctuated radically with every audience group, from their black township origins to their showcase status at international festivals like Edinburgh and Paris. Like the black actor's skin, black language—including Black English—is a text that must be understood in a multicultural society.

—Howard McNaughton

———

MUNRO, Rona. Scottish. Born in Aberdeen, 7 September 1959. Educated at Mackie Academy, Stonehaven; Edinburgh University, 1976–80, M.A. in history (honours). Married Edward Draper in 1981; one son. Writer-in-residence, Paines Plough Theatre Company, London, 1985–86. Recipient: McClaren award for radio, 1986; Susan Smith Blackburn prize, 1991; *Evening Standard* award, 1991; London Theatre Critics Circle prize, 1992; *Plays and Players* award, 1992. Agent: Casarotto Ramsay Ltd., National House, 60–66 Wardour Street, London W1V 3HP, England.

PUBLICATIONS

Plays

The Salesman (produced Edinburgh, 1982).
The Bang and the Whimper (produced Edinburgh, 1982).
Fugue (produced Edinburgh, 1983). Edinburgh, Salaman-der, 1983.
Touchwood (for children; produced Aberdeen, 1984).
The Bus (for children; produced Edinburgh, 1984).
Ghost Story (for children; produced Glasgow, 1985).
Piper's Cave. Published in *Plays by Women: Five*, edited by Michelene Wandor and Mary Remnant, London, Meth-uen, 1985.
The Biggest Party in the World (produced Edinburgh, 1986).
Dust and Dreams (produced Fareham, Hampshire, 1986).
The Way to Go Home (produced London, 1987).
Winners (produced Leeds, 1987).
Off the Road (produced Leeds, 1988).
Saturday at the Commodore (produced Isle of Skye, 1989). Published in *Scot Free*, edited by Alasdair Cameron, London, Hern, 1990.
Bold Girls (produced Cumbernauld, Strathclyde, 1990; London, 1991). Published in *First Run 3*, edited by Matthew Lloyd, London, Hern, 1991.
Your Turn to Clean the Stair (produced Edinburgh, 1992).

Radio Plays: *Kilbreck* series, 1983–84; *Watching Waiters*, 1986; *Dirt under the Carpet*, 1987; *Citizens* series, 1988; *Elsie*, 1990; *Elvis*, 1990; *Eleven*, 1990; *Three Way Split*, 1992.

Television Plays: *Hardware*, 1984; *Biting the Hands*, 1989; 3 episodes in *Dr. Who* series, 1989; *Say It with Flowers* in *Casualty* series, 1990.

*

Rona Munro comments:

I am a Scottish playwright, a woman playwright, and an Aberdonian playwright, not necessarily in that order. All of these facts inform my writing but don't define it. Up till now a lot of my writing has concerned itself with issues around gender and sexual politics and as yet there's no sign of that preoccupation wearing off. I'm concerned to address these issues from a broad, human perspective, and as far as possible to write entertainingly and honestly, reflecting women's and men's lives as I perceive them rather than as I would choose them to be. I'm concerned to assert my place as part of a living tradition, a distinctive Scottish culture, and to explore the possibilities of writing in Scots as well as in English. I am also apparently incapable of writing anything without slipping a few gags in and will probably always choose to write drama that is liberally laced with comedy.

* * *

Rona Munro is one of Scotland's most innovative young playwrights. Her use of language and particularly of Aberdonian dialect in some of her work, and her creative weaving of Celtic myth into her contemporary scenarios, both serve to enrich her theatre writing immensely. Her own experiences as a student, cleaner, and experienced traveller have also influenced her work, lending it a voice which is at once true to her working-class origins and informed by world affairs and global issues.

An early play, *Fugue*, was commissioned in 1982 and staged at the Traverse Theatre, Edinburgh in 1983. Another early work, *Ghost Story*, was staged at the Tron Theatre, Glasgow, in 1985. She has also written for television and radio, but her theatre work is her true forte, and has been influenced by her work with (and has been influential upon the work of) both Paines Plough Theatre Company and her own women's comedy duo, the Msfits, founded with colleague Fiona Knowles. But her best-known plays—and deservedly so—are *Piper's Cave* and *Saturday at the Commodore*.

Piper's Cave is a curiously surreal play, a two-hander between a young woman (Jo) and a mysterious man who appears to be older than his 30-odd years (Alisdair). A third "character" of sorts is the unseen spirit of the landscape. Munro gives this spirit a "local habitation and a name," as well as a good number of lines in the script: the landscape is called "Helen." Helen is present from the opening of the play, but she comes into her own about half-way through, when she speaks as frequently as do the two "real" characters. Whether or not she is speaking, however, Helen's presence is crucial throughout, for this is a play about the power of the environment, and one which challenges ingrained essentialist notions about "Mother Nature." At the same time, it addresses the issues of gender and power, sex and violence.

Piper's Cave, as Rona Munro reveals in the published afterword to the play, "actually exists," though she exercised some creative licence in terms of its location. Similarly, the issues which Munro deals with in the play are quite real. Yet the play experiments with reality and myth by combining them, drawing on one to enrich the other. The play introduces young Jo as a modern woman, and Alisdair as a version of the legendary "piper who walked into the hill and never came out." Helen is the natural world, and she has a mighty wit. But Jo and Alisdair also have their "other-worldly" sides: Alisdair is, or thinks he is, the legendary piper; Jo becomes, or thinks she becomes, the Selky, the seal woman of Celtic myth. At the play's end, we hear splashing: the sound of waves which could be made by Jo, or by Helen, or which might be the sound of curtains closing on a thought-provoking play.

While in *Piper's Cave* only Alisdair spoke regularly in dialect, all of *Saturday at the Commodore* is written to be performed in a strong Aberdonian. The play is quite short (only five pages in the published version); a one-woman monologue of sorts, commissioned by 7:84 Scotland as part of a series of short pieces by "Voices of Today's Scotland." The use of dialect is crucial, due to the setting of both the play and its performances (it was first performed at the Isle of Skye in 1989).

Lena is the 30-year-old central character, or narrator, who relates the story of *Saturday at the Commodore*, a story of one woman's memories of childhood and adolescence in Scotland. The play is a story, a narrative which somehow conjures up vivid images of other places and people, most notably Nora, Lena's "best mate" and the girl she fancied as well. The development into womanhood, from being a student to being a teacher, through one heterosexual relationship to a life of independence—all this is told in a narrative which is relaxed, wry, witty, and immensely engaging. The dialect makes it Lena's story, and a uniquely Scottish story. Yet Munro's ability to create likeable characters and familiar, evocative situations makes it a larger story as well, one worth staging and re-staging to see what different communities and different audiences may make of it.

—Lizbeth Goodman

———————

MURDOCH, (Jean) Iris. British. Born in Dublin, Ireland, 15 July 1919. Educated at the Froebel Education Institute, London; Badminton School, Bristol; Somerville College, Oxford, 1938–42, B.A. (first class honours) 1942; Newnham College, Cambridge (Sarah Smithson student in philosophy), 1947–48. Married the writer John Bayley in 1956. Assistant principal in the Treasury, London, 1942–44; administrative officer with the United Nations Relief and Rehabilitation Administration (UNRRA) in London, Belgium, and Austria, 1944–46; fellow, St. Anne's College, Oxford, and university lecturer in philosophy, Oxford University, 1948–63; honorary fellow of St. Anne's College from 1963; lecturer, Royal College of Art, London, 1963–67. Recipient: James Tait Black Memorial prize, 1974; Whitbread award, 1974; Booker prize, 1978; Shakespeare prize (Hamburg), 1988; National Arts Club (U.S.A.) medal of honor, 1990. D. Litt.: Oxford University, 1987. Member, Irish Academy, 1970; honorary member, American Academy, 1975, and American Academy of Arts and Sciences, 1982; honorary fellow, Somerville College, 1977, and Newnham College, 1986. Companion of literature, Royal Society of Literature, 1987. C.B.E. (Commander, Order of the British Empire), 1976; D.B.E. (Dame Commander, Order of the British Empire), 1987. Lives in Oxford. Agent: Ed Victor Ltd., 162 Wardour Street, London W1V 4AT, England.

PUBLICATIONS

Plays

A Severed Head, with J.B. Priestley, adaptation of the novel by Murdoch (produced Bristol and London, 1963; New York, 1964). London, Chatto and Windus, 1964.

The Italian Girl, with James Saunders, adaptation of the novel by Murdoch (produced Bristol, 1967; London, 1968). London, French, 1969.

The Servants and the Snow (produced London, 1970). With *The Three Arrows*, London, Chatto and Windus, 1973; New York, Viking Press, 1974.

The Three Arrows (produced Cambridge, 1972). With *The Servants and the Snow*, London, Chatto and Windus, 1973; New York, Viking Press, 1974.

Art and Eros (produced London, 1980). Included in *Acastos*, 1986.

The Servants (opera libretto), adaptation of her play *The Servants and the Snow*, music by William Mathias (produced Cardiff, 1980).

Acastos: Two Platonic Dialogues (includes *Art and Eros* and *Above the Gods*). London, Chatto and Windus, 1986; New York, Viking, 1987.

The Black Prince, adaptation of her own novel (produced London, 1989). Included in *Three Plays*, 1989.

Three Plays (includes *The Servants and the Snow*, *The Three Arrows*, *The Black Prince*). London, Chatto and Windus, 1989.

Radio Play: *The One Alone* (in verse), music by Gary Carpenter, 1987.

Novels

Under the Net. London, Chatto and Windus, and New York, Viking Press, 1954.

The Flight from the Enchanter. London, Chatto and Windus, and New York, Viking Press, 1956.

The Sandcastle. London, Chatto and Windus, and New York, Viking Press, 1957.

The Bell. London, Chatto and Windus, and New York, Viking Press, 1958.

A Severed Head. London, Chatto and Windus, and New York, Viking Press, 1961.

An Unofficial Rose. London, Chatto and Windus, and New York, Viking Press, 1962.

The Unicorn. London, Chatto and Windus, and New York, Viking Press, 1963.

The Italian Girl. London, Chatto and Windus, and New York, Viking Press, 1964.

The Red and the Green. London, Chatto and Windus, and New York, Viking Press, 1965.

The Time of the Angels. London, Chatto and Windus, and New York, Viking Press, 1966.

The Nice and the Good. London, Chatto and Windus, and New York, Viking Press, 1968.

Bruno's Dream. London, Chatto and Windus, and New York, Viking Press, 1969.

A Fairly Honourable Defeat. London, Chatto and Windus, and New York, Viking Press, 1970.

An Accidental Man. London, Chatto and Windus, 1971; New York, Viking Press, 1972.

The Black Prince. London, Chatto and Windus, and New York, Viking Press, 1973.

The Sacred and Profane Love Machine. London, Chatto and Windus, and New York, Viking Press, 1974.

A Word Child. London, Chatto and Windus, and New York, Viking Press, 1975.

Henry and Cato. London, Chatto and Windus, 1976; New York, Viking Press, 1977.

The Sea, The Sea. London, Chatto and Windus, and New York, Viking Press, 1978.

Nuns and Soldiers. London, Chatto and Windus, 1980; New York, Viking Press, 1981.

The Philosopher's Pupil. London, Chatto and Windus, and New York, Viking Press, 1983.

The Good Apprentice. London, Chatto and Windus, 1985; New York, Viking Press, 1986.

The Book and the Brotherhood. London, Chatto and Windus, 1987; New York, Viking, 1988.

The Message to the Planet. London, Chatto and Windus, 1989; New York, Viking, 1990.

Verse

A Year of Birds. Tisbury, Wiltshire, Compton Press, 1978.

Other

Sartre, Romantic Rationalist. Cambridge, Bowes, and New Haven, Connecticut, Yale University Press, 1953; as *Sartre, Romantic Realist*, Brighton, Harvester Press, 1980.

The Sovereignty of Good over Other Concepts (lecture). Cambridge, University Press, 1967.

The Sovereignty of Good (essays). London, Routledge, 1970; New York, Schocken, 1971.

The Fire and the Sun: Why Plato Banished the Artists. London, and New York, Oxford University Press, 1977.

Reynolds Stone (address). London, Warren, 1981.

The Existential Political Myth. Birmingham, Delos Press, 1989.

*

Bibliography: *Iris Murdoch and Muriel Spark: A Bibliography* by Thomas T. Tominaga and Wilma Schneidermeyer, Metuchen, New Jersey, Scarecrow Press, 1976; *Iris Murdoch: A Reference Guide* by Kate Begnal, Boston, Hall, 1987.

Manuscript Collection: University of Iowa, Iowa City.

Critical Studies: *Iris Murdoch* by Rubin Rabinovitz, New York, Columbia University Press, 1968, *Iris Murdoch* by Frank Baldanza, New York, Twayne, 1974; *Iris Murdoch* by Donna Gerstenberger, Lewisburg, Pennsylvania, Bucknell University Press, 1974; *Iris Murdoch: The Shakespearian Interest*, New York, Barnes and Noble and London, Vision Press, 1979, and *Iris Murdoch*, London, Methuen, 1984, both by Richard Todd, and *Encounters with Iris Murdoch* edited by Todd, Amsterdam, Free University Press, 1988; *Iris Murdoch: Work for the Spirit* by Elizabeth Dipple, Chicago, University of Chicago Press, 1981, London, Methuen, 1982; *Iris Murdoch's Comic Vision* by Angela Hague, Selinsgrove, Pennsylvania, Susquehanna University Press, 1984; *Iris Murdoch: The Saint and the Artist* by Peter J. Conradi, London, Macmillan, and New York, St. Martin's Press, 1986; *Iris Murdoch* edited by Harold Bloom, New York, Chelsea House, 1986; *A Character Index and Guide to the Fiction of Iris Murdoch* by Cheryl K. Bove, New York, Garland, 1986; *Iris Murdoch* by Deborah Johnson, Bloomington, Indiana University Press, and Brighton, Sussex, Harvester Press, 1987; *Iris Murdoch: Figures of Good* by Suguna Ramanathan, London, Macmillan, 1990.

* * *

Iris Murdoch has published one volume of plays, *Three Plays*, which includes *The Servants and the Snow*, *The Three Arrows*, and her adaptation of her novel *The Black Prince*. In addition, she has published *Acastos*, a volume containing two philosophical plays in the form of Platonic dialogues, *Art and Eros* and *Above the Gods*. The drama critic Harold Hobson praised Andrew Cruickshank's performance of *Art and Eros*, saying that he conducted "a Socratic enquiry with philosophic zeal and illuminating theatrical skill." *Above the Gods* inquires into the differences between morality and religion. Murdoch wrote both her Platonic plays so that they could be performed either in modern dress or in period costume. In a period version of *Above the Gods*, she suggests casting the servant as a black man born of a Nubian mother. This choice on her part shows her willingness to unsettle a modern British audience, questioning religion, values, British ideas of empire, and slavery. Before Murdoch tried her own playwriting, she collaborated with J.B. Priestley in the stage adaptation of her novel *A Severed Head*, and with James Saunders on the adaptation of *The Italian Girl*. The experienced hands of her collaborators made these plays more actable than her own later ones—indeed, *A Severed Head* was a theatrical success. Her play *The Black Prince* is her first attempt to adapt one of her own novels into a play without the benefits of an experienced theatrical collaborator. It is a witty, fast-paced drama, about love, death and art that testifies to her sure hand as a master of the dramatic as well as the narrative mode.

The play version of *A Severed Head* diminishes the complexity and obscurity of Murdoch's novel while it preserves its zany, quick-paced, very British high comedy. Physical farce, unexpected entrances, surprise discoveries, and unanticipated twists of plot all contribute to the effect. In "Against Dryness," Murdoch described her own novel as one in which Sartre's "facile idea of sincerity" is tested against the "hard idea of truth." When Martin is confronted by his wife's affair with her analyst, he tries broadmindedly to take it in his stride. Unwilling to confess his own affair, and himself attracted to the American analyst, he suffers passively as his wife flaunts her infatuation and asks his approval of her plan to move into her lover's home. It takes Honor Klein, the half-sister of the analyst and a Cambridge anthropologist, to function as the "dark god" of this play. Manipulating all the other characters, she forces Martin to submit to irrational and primitive forces, to understand the "hard idea of truth," and to give himself over to his love for her, however temporary and however imperfectly understood. The play rivals Restoration comedy in the variety of its sexual pairings. Martin passes through the stages of the outraged husband, latently homosexual lover to his wife's lover, complacent cuckold, violent lover, and lover surrendering to a higher, more mysterious, primitive love. Variations of incest are explored in the relationship between Honor and her half-brother and Antonia and her brother-in-law. In many ways *A Severed Head* is a modern *The Cocktail Party*. T. S. Eliot's one-eyed Reilly becomes Murdoch's Honor Klein. Both plays examine religious feeling and neurotic obsessions.

Murdoch's other plays, with the exception of *The Black Prince*, confirm that her gifts are as a novelist; nevertheless, they are also interesting in their own right. In her novels, Murdoch the storyteller and Murdoch the moral philosopher, struggling with ideas of freedom and contingency and accident and pattern, live fairly comfortably together. In her plays, the two fight each other and conspire to flatten her characters in ways that the novel can accommodate or avoid. She is often unable to find the dialogue that believably captures her hybrid characters—half-mythic, half-natural. She strikes the best balance in *The Black Prince* but she does so at the expense of her intellectual inquiry into the nature of art, love, and ethics.

The Servants and the Snow is a compact play which, like Strindberg's *Miss Julie*, depends for its effect on the pressure that the environment and past exert on the characters. The snow madness imprisons the characters; it covers and holds the blood guilt of the past. Basil, a landowner who returns to the isolated country house of his father who has died six months earlier, finds himself accountable for his father's crimes. He feels unequal to the task of being master to his 200 or more servants. Too anxious to play benevolent master, and too scrupulously "sincere" in his efforts to examine his own situation and motives, he finds himself forced to atone for his father's affair with a servant girl, Marina, which led to the death of the girl's husband at the hand of her jealous master. To prevent the erosion of his own authority, Basil is persuaded to re-enact his father's crime—to deflower the servant girl on her nuptial night. Neither Marina nor Oriane can tolerate weak men. Like the girl in Sylvia Plath's poem "Daddy," they prefer the "boot in the face" administered by the brute Daddy/husband. Marina consents to the marriage because it will figuratively give her back her dead master and dead husband. Oriane loathes Basil's sentimentality and misguided sense of guilt and cannot abide the injury to her pride posed by Marina. In a jealous rage, Oriane kills her husband during Marina's wedding vows and welcomes the arrival of her brother, the General, who knows how to treat servants as swine and give commands. The play examines the nature of power and the relationship of past to present. It also examines moral character. The final action fulfills Murdoch's ideas about accident and free will, but it cannot wholly contain the ideas. The characters in the play are too reductive.

The Three Arrows depends heavily for its effect upon ritual action and theatricality. Some of its moments are brilliant. Set in medieval Japan, the play explores the choices available to Prince Yorimitsu, a political prisoner held captive by the Emperor and a pawn of the Shogun, the real ruler. Yorimitsu's avowed ambition is to be a leader of the forces of the North and seize the power of the Shogun. The play abounds with deceits and stratagems. Necessity conspires to defeat moral purpose and free will. Yorimitsu is forced to choose between the contemplative life, an honorable death, love, or his ambition for power. The choices he ultimately exercises are constrained: he acts without properly knowing the motives of those who act against him, or understanding the meaning of the choices put to him. At the end of the play he is free, the Shogun dead, the princess he loved dead, and the young Emperor the willing accomplice in his escape. Intellectually the play is fascinating, but its plot unfolds too slowly and the motives behind certain actions are incompletely conceptualized.

Murdoch's most recent play, presented at the Aldwych Theatre in 1989 to considerable critical acclaim, is adapted from one of her finest and most difficult novels, a novel more novelistic than any she has written. Offering her most protracted and penetrating examination of aesthetics and the relation of art to human behavior, *The Black Prince* is a highly self-reflexive and elaborately mediated novel. It tells the story of Bradley Pearson, a fussy, aging, recently retired taxman and blocked writer, and his ordeal with love and art. It is introduced by two forewords and concluded by five postscripts, four written by the principal dramatic characters: Christian, Pearson's ex-wife; Francis, his "unfrocked" physician brother-in-law; Rachel, the battered and vengeful wife of Pearson's literary rival, Arnold Baffin, and mother of Julian; and Julian, the Baffin's 20-year-old daughter with whom the 58-year-old Pearson (53 in the play version) falls absolutely in love. The fifth postscript is written by Pearson's mysterious editor and cell-mate, Loxias, his alter ego and muse, the god

Apollo in disguise, who finally compels Pearson to answer to Apollonian truth and goodness, replacing the dark creative god Eros with the higher god Apollo. Murdoch's play could hardly do justice to the intricacy of the novel's struggle with form and formlessness. She does, in her play version, combine the dramatic and narrative modes, allowing Pearson to step forward and address the audience directly, with veiled references to his final transformation. She also concludes the play with an epilogue where four characters offer their highly eschewed and self-serving interpretations of the play's central action, the murder of Baffin. Notably missing from the play is any reference to Loxias, the editor and Apollo figure. No doubt Murdoch's instincts were right in this regard. The novelistic techniques and the ambiguous, often tortuous structure, could not but damage the play. She does treat the theme of *The Black Prince* in her play version, developing the relationship between Julian, decked out in her Hamlet costume, and Hamlet, and also enabling the audience to understand the relationship of Bradley Pearson's struggle to write with Shakespeare's. However, without a familiarity with the novel these references in the play may not adequately convey the theme. What does succeed, and very well, is her highly comic and ironic treatment of the three interwoven crises: Pearson's struggles with his sister's failed marriage and suicide; his rivalry with Baffin, over both women and art; and his immersion in his love for Julian which leads to the play's denouement, Rachel's murder of Baffin for which Pearson is tried and convicted.

Murdoch's wit and irony and gift for character, her fondness for patterning and artifice, serve her well when she adapts her novels for the stage.

—Carol Simpson Stern

MURPHY, Arthur Lister. Canadian. 1906–1985. See 3rd edition, 1982.

MURPHY, Tom (Thomas Murphy). Irish. Born in Tuam, County Galway, 23 February 1935. Educated at Vocational School, Tuam; Vocational Teachers' Training College, Dublin. Married Mary Hippisley; three children. Apprentice fitter and welder, Tuam, 1953–55; engineering teacher, Vocational School, Mountbellow, County Galway, 1957–62. Actor and director, 1951–62. Member of the Board of Directors, 1972–83, and since 1986 writer-in-association, Irish National Theatre (Abbey Theatre), Dublin; Regents lecturer, University of California, Santa Barbara, 1981; writer-in-association, Druid Theatre, Galway, 1983–85. Founding member, Moli Productions, Dublin, 1974. Recipient: Irish Academy of Letters award, 1972; Independent Newspapers award, 1983; Harvey's award, 1983, 1986; *Sunday Tribune* award, 1985. Member, Irish Academy of Letters, 1982, and Aosdána, 1984. Agent: Alexandra Cann Representation, 68E Redcliffe Gardens, London SW10 9HE, England; and, Bridget Aschenberg, International Creative Management, 40

West 57th Street, New York, New York 10019, U.S.A. Address: 46 Terenure Road West, Dublin 6, Ireland.

PUBLICATIONS

Plays

On the Outside, with Noel O'Donoghue (produced Cork, 1961; New Haven, Connecticut, 1976). With *On the Inside*, Dublin, Gallery Press, 1976; included in *A Whistle in the Dark and Other Plays*, 1989.
A Whistle in the Dark (produced London, 1961; New Haven, Connecticut, and New York, 1969). New York, French, 1971; included in *A Whistle in the Dark and Other Plays*, 1989.
Famine (produced Dublin, 1966; London, 1969; New York, 1981). Dublin, Gallery Press, 1977; included in *Plays: One*, 1992.
The Fooleen (as *A Crucial Week in the Life of a Grocer's Assistant*, televised 1967; as *The Fooleen*, produced Dublin, 1969). Dixon, California, Proscenium Press, 1970; Dublin, Gallery Press, 1978; as *A Crucial Week in the Life of a Grocer's Assistant*, included in *A Whistle in the Dark and Other Plays*, 1989.
The Orphans (produced Dublin, 1968; Newark, Delaware, 1971). Newark, Delaware, Proscenium Press, 1974.
The Morning after Optimism (produced Dublin, 1971; New York, 1974). Cork, Mercier Press, 1973.
The White House (produced Dublin, 1972).
On the Inside (also director: produced Dublin, 1974; New Haven, Connecticut, 1976). With *On the Outside*, Dublin, Gallery Press, 1976; included in *A Whistle in the Dark and Other Plays*, 1989.
The Vicar of Wakefield, adaptation of the novel by Goldsmith (produced Dublin, 1974).
The Sanctuary Lamp (produced Dublin, 1975; New York, 1980). Dublin, Poolbeg Press, 1976; revised version, Dublin, Gallery Press, 1984.
The J. Arthur Maginnis Story (produced Dublin, 1976).
Conversations on a Homecoming (televised 1976; produced Galway, 1985; New York, 1986; London, 1987). Dublin, Gallery Press, 1986; included in *After Tragedy*, 1988.
Epitaph under Ether (also director: produced Dublin, 1979).
The Blue Macushla (produced Dublin, 1980). Included in *Plays: One*, 1992.
The Informer, adaptation of the novel by Liam O'Flaherty (also director: produced Dublin, 1981; Louisville, 1982).
She Stoops to Conquer, adaptation of the play by Goldsmith (produced Dublin, 1982).
The Gigli Concert (produced Dublin, 1983; Costa Mesa, California, 1984; London, 1992). Dublin, Gallery Press, 1984; included in *After Tragedy*, 1988.
Bailegangáire (produced Galway, 1985; London, 1986; New Haven, Connecticut, 1987). Dublin, Gallery Press, 1986; included in *After Tragedy*, 1988.
A Thief of a Christmas (produced Dublin, 1985).
After Tragedy: Three Irish Plays (includes *The Gigli Concert*, *Conversations on a Homecoming*, *Bailegangáire*). London, Methuen, 1988.
A Whistle in the Dark and Other Plays (includes *A Crucial Week in the Life of a Grocer's Assistant*, *On the Outside*, *On the Inside*). London, Methuen, 1989.
Too Late for Logic (produced Dublin, 1989). London, Methuen, 1990
The Patriot Game (produced Dublin, 1991). Included in *Plays: One*, 1992.

Plays: One (includes *Famine, The Patriot Game, The Blue Macushla*). London, Methuen, 1992.

Television Plays: *The Fly Sham*, 1963; *Veronica*, 1963; *A Crucial Week in the Life of a Grocer's Assistant*, 1967; *Snakes and Reptiles*, 1968; *Young Man in Trouble*, 1970; *The Moral Force, The Policy, Relief* (trilogy), 1973; *Conversations on a Homecoming*, 1976; *Speeches of Farewell*, 1976; *Bridgit*, 1981; *Fatalism*, 1981.

*

Bibliography: *Ten Modern Irish Playwrights* by Kimball King, New York, Garland, 1979.

Critical Studies: "Thomas Murphy Issue" of *Irish University Review* (Dublin), Spring 1987; *The Politics of Magic: The Work and Times of Tom Murphy* by Fintan O'Toole, Dublin, Raven Arts Press, 1987.

Theatrical Activities:
Director: **Plays**— *On the Outside/On the Inside*, Dublin, 1974; *Famine*, Dublin, 1978; *The Well of the Saints* by J.M. Synge, Dublin, 1979; *Epitaph under Ether*, Dublin, 1979; *The Informer*, Dublin, 1981.

Tom Murphy comments:

My plays attempt to recreate the feeling or the mood of life rather than to represent it: they attempt to create something that can be identified with, felt or recognised. The emotional and/or spiritual truth is, if anything, more important than the intellectual truth. The mood can be the theme of the play.

* * *

Apart from *A Whistle in the Dark*, which made Kenneth Tynan and other notables sit up in the early 1960's, Tom Murphy's plays have not won the international recognition they deserve. It is significant that when *Conversations on a Homecoming* was staged by the Galway Druid Theatre Company at the Pepsico International Arts Festival in New York in 1986 he was spoken of in reviews as if he were new on the scene.

The main reason for this unwarranted neglect internationally seems to lie in Murphy's exploration of themes that are particularly (though not exclusively) Irish, in a form that uncompromisingly makes strenuous demands on audiences. A typical Murphy play, while not necessarily set in Dublin and possibly as vague in setting as the dreamlike forest in *The Morning after Optimism*, is occupied with a spiritual deprivation and a social humiliation that are endemically Irish. The grounding, the "objective correlative," is invariably a situation potentially explosive, deriving from feelings powerfully responsive to defects in a particular community, society, or national institution. Unless one is familiar with the grounding, the plays may appear obscure or the level of feeling inexplicably intense, and the language (Murphy's strongest weapon) perhaps in excess of the apparent facts. This is to say that atmosphere and mood are of primary importance. For example, *The Sanctuary Lamp*, to the puzzlement of some British reviewers covering the Dublin Theatre Festival in 1975, caused disturbance among its first audiences at the Abbey Theatre, and comparison was made with the initial impact of O'Casey's *The Plough and the Stars* (1926), when riots occurred. Murphy's play was regarded by some as highly blasphemous. The satiric and iconoclastic feelings released in it arise out of a church setting, taken over by three outcast characters, Harry and Francisco, who used to have a circus act of a sleazy nature, and Maudie, a runaway orphan frightened into believing that Jesus has taken away her baby because she is bad. Francisco has pursued Harry for defecting, and to spring upon him the shattering news that Harry's wife, who formed part of their dubious circus act in rich people's houses, is dead from an overdose of drugs. Harry, for his part, is heart-sick at the death of his little daughter Teresa, and is burning with feelings of revenge against life and God. He takes the job of sacristan and custodian of the lamp that signifies the divine presence. When Francisco arrives pursuing the fugitive from himself, they argue in the locked church at night over the effects on their lives of the "metaphysical monster" the Catholic Church. With a bottle of altar wine in one hand Francisco delivers from the pulpit his bitter jeremiad against contemporary Catholicism. But when all passion's spent, the three characters settle down for the night in a confession box, forming a fellowship against the dark, and tending the lamp as a gesture of human rather than of divine presence.

Murphy's plays, besides being uncompromising as passionate indictments of hypocrisy of every kind, are also theatrically demanding. Some, such as the historical drama *Famine*, are almost unrelieved Theatre of Cruelty. One of his best and most ambitious plays, *The Gigli Concert*, ran for three and a half hours at the Abbey Theatre, and Murphy refused at that time to cut it. The director and cast of such plays face huge problems, but overcoming them has provided the Irish theatre with some of its greatest achievements in the 1970's and early 1980's. *The Gigli Concert* may be described as a fantastic reworking of the Faust story so as to explore and express in contemporary terms the nature of damnation and of magical release. The plot centres on a self-made Irish millionaire's visit during a mental breakdown to one J.P.W. King, a professed "dynatologist," actually an abandoned practitioner of an American quasi-science. The "patient" wants to sing like Beniamino Gigli. It is an obsession arising from recurring depression caused by guilt. In this regard he could be compared with Ibsen's Solness (*The Master Builder*) and Osborne's Maitland (*Inadmissible Evidence*). King gets caught up in the pursuit of this impossible ambition and Gigli's voice, on record, begins to fascinate him also. "He's the devil!" the Irish Man warns him. But when the latter backs away, preferring to return to society with all his neuroses intact, and King's Gretchen figure has told him she is dying of cancer, while Helen accuses him of making obscene telephone calls, King feels compelled to go on with the mad scheme of trying himself to sing like Gigli. He turns to conjuring and in a theatrically challenging scene he manages to bring off the impossible: the "magic" of theatre and its illusion allows the audience to believe that this hopeless case has transcended the barriers of the normal. King then plugs in the cassette player once more and pressing the repeat button lets Gigli sing on forever while he takes off elsewhere.

Bailegangáire, another extraordinary play, breaks new ground. Written when Murphy was playwright-in-association at the Druid Theatre in Galway, it has a good deal of Irish (i.e., Gaelic) words and phrases and it deals with Irish tragic material in a style that seems to marry Synge and Beckett. The play combines two levels and two situations in two time periods. On one level an old woman, Mommo, raves in a senile manner in bed, endlessly telling a story of a tragic event in her history, but never finishing the tale. On another level her granddaughters, Mary and Dolly, while caring for her try at the same time to come to terms with their own lives. Often their conversations take place while Mommo raves on at the same time. Each of the women is in fact trying to seize hold of her life, but it happens that Mommo holds the key to the happiness of all three. Mary, the nurse, realising that Mommo's obsession with the story relates to her own need to shape her life, forces her to finish the tale for the first time. It concerns a laughing contest in which Mommo's husband won over a local champion but caused his death and subsequently the death of another grandchild. The full facts have the effect of drawing Mary and Dolly closer to Mommo, and, rather like the three characters who settle down for the night at the end of *The Sanctuary Lamp*, these three women settle down in Mommo's bed and, in knowledge and understanding, find peace. The beautiful and moving ending was powerfully rendered by Siobhan McKenna as Mommo in the first production, which travelled to the Donmar Warehouse, London, in 1986. The play, while being well received, was found to be somewhat mystifying to some English reviewers, who could make sense of it only as allegory, with Mommo as Ireland obsessed with her history.

Too Late for Logic tried to consolidate the new direction Murphy began to take with *The Gigli Concert*, towards what he calls "after tragedy." These later plays tend to move beyond tragedy into a mood of acceptance. A new attitude towards women, now dramatised as holding the key to sanity and survival, is still developing in Murphy's work. *Too Late for Logic* is in one sense merely a play about the suicide of an academic too bound up in Schopenhauer; but in a wider sense the play explores how Christopher might have learned from the women in his life. Instructive as this learning process may be it lacks the dramatic fire of Murphy's earlier plays, since the form chosen is to begin with the suicide of Christopher and make him the observer of his own self-defeat. It remains to be seen if Murphy can move beyond this self-obsessive phase and integrate his new quasi-feminist sympathies with dramatic inventiveness.

Murphy's only serious rival among his Irish contemporaries is Brian Friel, who in a programme note for *The Blue Macushla* paid tribute to Murphy's unique talent, his restless and uncompromising imagination. By his refusal to write the popular play, and by his digging afresh every time into the daunting recesses of passion and folly, Murphy has shown himself to be one of the best, if the most unpredictable, of modern Irish dramatists.

—Christopher Murray

MURRELL, John. Canadian. Born in the United States, 15 October 1945. Educated at schools in Alberta; University of Calgary, Alberta, B.A. in drama. Married; one daughter. Schoolteacher for five years; playwright-in-residence, Alberta Theatre Projects, Calgary, 1975; associate director, Stratford Festival, Ontario, 1978; head of the theatre section, Canada Council, from 1988. Recipient: Clifford E. Lee award, 1975. Address: c/o Talonbooks, 201–1019 East Cordova, Vancouver, British Columbia V6A 1M8, Canada.

PUBLICATIONS

Plays

Metamorphosis.   Edmonton, Alberta Department of Culture, 1970.

Haydn's Head (produced Edmonton, 1973).
Power in the Blood (produced Edmonton, 1975).
Arena (produced Calgary, 1975).
Teaser, with Kenneth Dyba (produced Calgary, 1975).
A Great Noise, A Great Light (produced Calgary, 1976).
Waiting for the Parade: Faces of Women in War (produced Calgary, 1977; London, 1979; St. Paul, 1982). Vancouver, Talonbooks, 1980.
Memoir (produced Guelph, Ontario, 1977; London, 1978; revised version produced Calgary, 1981). New York, Avon, 1978.
Uncle Vanya: Scenes from Rural Life, adaptation of a play by Chekhov (produced Stratford, Ontario, 1978; Portsmouth, New Hampshire, 1979; London, 1982). Toronto, Theatrebooks, 1978.
Mandragola, adaptation of the play by Machiavelli (produced Calgary, 1978).
Bajazet, adaptation of the play by Racine (produced Toronto, 1979).
The Seagull, adaptation of a play by Chekhov (produced Stratford, Ontario, 1980).
Farther West (produced Calgary, 1982). With *New World*, Toronto, Coach House Press, 1985.
New World (produced Ottawa, 1984). With *Farther West*, Toronto, Coach House Press, 1985.
October (also director: produced Toronto, 1988).
Democracy (produced Douglas, Alaska, 1991).

*

Theatrical Activities:
Director: **Play**—*Mrs. Warren's Profession* by Shaw, Calgary, 1981.

*   *   *

Though John Murrell has several unpublished scripts and translations to his credit, he is known primarily for the internationally successful works *Memoir* and *Waiting for the Parade*. These were preceded by several other pieces. *Power in the Blood*, loosely about the American evangelist Amy Semple McPherson, was followed by two comedies commissioned by Pleiades Theatre, Calgary, and then by *A Great Noise, A Great Light*, about the late 1930's in Alberta.

Waiting for the Parade interweaves the stories of five women through several years of World War II in Calgary. The eldest, Margaret, is pessimistic, a widow with one son in the navy and one imprisoned for anti-war activities. Catherine, a factory-hand, is a total contrast, a promiscuous extrovert whose husband is a prisoner-of-war. Eve is an idealistic teacher with a husband too old to join the army. They are bossed by the energetic, bigoted Janet, who is compensating for her spouse, a radio announcer who is not contributing to the war effort (she is more thinly characterized than the others). Detached from the foursome is a seamstress, German-born Marta, whose father is interned for supposed Nazi sympathies. These women variously talk, plan, and argue while rolling bandages and taking fruit to troop trains at the station: the detail of wartime life, with appropriate songs, is good. *Waiting for the Parade* is gentle and poignant, sometimes comic.

Memoir is about 77-year-old Sarah Bernhardt in 1922, during the last year of her life, composing her memoirs on an island off the Brittany coast, occasionally acting a fragment of her greatest roles. The only other character is her pedantic, spinsterish, middle-aged male secretary, dubious about theatre, a bad actor, who has to play all the other parts—a manager, a doctor, Oscar Wilde. Bernhardt's biography is obliquely revealed. "Old actors do not die; they simply rehearse their dying," comments Keith Garebian. The play touches on such themes as the relationship between art and life and that between a great artist and lesser mortals. Murrell always writes eloquently, risking over-writing: an early work such as this is marked by lines like "a tall gray woman with a voice like a clay jug thrown against a stone wall." The 1981 version of the play is substantially altered, and improved. *Memoir* has been very successful, translated into more than 20 languages, and performed in 35 countries.

Two of Murrell's subsequent plays are more ambitious, with larger casts. Though directed by Robin Phillips, neither drew much national or international attention. *Farther West*, which the author labels "a romance," is loosely based on the life and death of an actual Calgary brothel-mistress, May Buchanan. Starting in Rat Portage, Ontario, in 1886, she travels west to Calgary and then has to take refuge in Nose Creek. She is pursued by Seward, an obsessive, puritanical policeman who continues the hunt for her even after leaving the force, and Shepherd, a rancher who loves her and wants to marry her. They pursue her to Vancouver, where in 1892 Shepherd kills her. In a powerful final scene, Seward pushes her corpse in a rowing-boat out into English Bay. The play is strongly charged with sex—the first half ends in what Mark Czarnecki called "the most erotic simulated lovemaking ever to see the Canadian stage"—yet May can perform the sex act while keeping her true self inviolate. She never stops seeking her West: "Thomas Shepherd of Sheep River! That's not the sort of kindling to start fires under me. I've got to travel farther, much farther, before I find anybody." In her West there are "no rules, no laws, no judges." Instead, she seeks her independence: "I prefer my own kind of pleasure, my own kind of peace and my own pennies to anybody else's dimes!" The West as myth, in fact, is partly caught in this drama, though perhaps impossible to embody on the stage.

New World takes place on one summer day on China Beach on Vancouver Island, looking out to the Pacific. The seven characters include an unhappy English woman painter (Old World) and her brother, an American maker of rock videos (New World). Between the two worlds are a third sibling, an ageing photographer (anglophone Canadian) and his assistant, a cook and bisexual (francophone Canadian). The sadness of both the failed painter and the successful photographer is exposed. There's lots of plot: the French-Canadian will go off with the rock-video man's wife, but include him too, while her daughter starts to fall in love with the photographer's young apprentice. Yet *New World* is not centrally a play of character or plot. On the contrary, what matters for Murrell are the references to *The Tempest*, the sea and the sun; the use of Puccini's music; the photographer taking endless self-portraits; a beautiful blue Japanese fishing float, found on the beach, which is admired, broken, mended, and, at the last moment of the third scene, "spontaneously explodes into a thousand bright fragments." Murrell aspires here to write what Jamie Portman called a "tone poem" beyond the banalities of character and plot (it resembles some of Michel Tremblay's later work and David Storey's *Early Days*); he has not achieved this difficult ambition.

Murrell's next two plays return to real people and to artists, whom he calls the most tormented and least successful of people. *October* is about an actress, a dancer, and a writer. Both acts take place outside an inn at Fiesole, near Florence. In the first half, in 1913, Eleanora Duse tries, in a personal and pessimistic way, to console Isadora Duncan, whose two children have just drowned. The encounter prompts Duse's return to the stage. The second half takes place 11 years earlier, with Duse having a ferocious quarrel with her lover, D'Annunzio. Murrell sees that genius and monstrosity may go together, and that the passion and commitment of these Europeans "has something to teach us in this culture."

His subject is Americans in *Democracy*, Ralph Emerson visiting Walt Whitman in 1863, during the Civil War. The rationalist and the romantic discuss the war, their country, its future; the play is static and subdued, of words and ideas. The other two characters are soldiers, one blinded, the other a deserter. Christopher Newton commented that "it is a dense set of variations on themes suggested by the writings of Emerson and Whitman. *Democracy* is a complex metaphor which addresses the problems that many of us face today when dealing with the deaths of young men, whether in war or, closer to home, from AIDS."

Murrell is a fine craftsman in his use of both language and music. After modest, very effective small-scale pieces, he gropes towards a poetic theatre in *New World* and encompasses epic and myth in the audacious *Farther West*.

—Malcolm Page

MUSAPHIA, Joseph. New Zealander. Born in London, England, 8 April 1935. Educated at a primary school in Australia, and at Christchurch Boys' High School, New Zealand. Married Marie Beder in 1966; one son and one daughter. Shop assistant, Ballintyne's, Christchurch, 1950–51; motor mechanic, David Crozier's, Christchurch, 1951–54; commercial artist, Stuart Wearn, Christchurch, 1954–55, Wood and Braddock, Wellington, 1955, John Haddon, London, England, 1956–57, and for agencies, Wellington, 1958–60; cartoonist, New Zealand *Listener*, Wellington, 1958–60; fish and chip shop owner, Wellington, 1971–73. Since 1974 columnist, the *Dominion* and *Sunday Times*, both Wellington. Writing fellow, Victoria University, Wellington, 1979. Recipient: New Zealand State Literary Fund grant, 1963; New Zealand Arts Council grant, 1974, 1976. Agent: Playmarket, P.O. Box 9767, Wellington. Address: 75 Monro Street, Wellington 3, New Zealand.

PUBLICATIONS

Plays

Free (produced Wellington, 1961). Published in *Landfall 68* (Christchurch), December 1963.
Virginia Was a Dog (broadcast 1963; produced Wellington, 1968).
The Guerilla (produced Sydney, 1971). Sydney, Currency Press, 1976.
Victims (produced Wellington, 1973). Published in *Act 20* (Wellington), August 1973.
Obstacles (produced Wellington, 1974). Published in *Act 25* (Wellington), December 1974.
Mothers and Fathers (produced Wellington, 1975). Sydney, Currency Press, 1977.
Hunting (produced Wellington, 1979).
Shotgun Wedding (produced Wellington, 1980). Wellington, Playmarket, 1981.
The Hangman (produced Wellington, 1983).
Mates (produced Wellington, 1986).

Screenplay: *Don't Let It Get You*, 1966.

Radio Plays: more than 120 plays, including *Out of the Passing Crowd*, 1962; *A Seat in the Sun*, 1963; *Bread Crumbs for the Pigeons*, 1963; *Suddenly It's Tomorrow*, 1963; *Virginia Was a Dog*, 1963; *This Business of Being Alive*, 1963; *The Cause of Something*, 1965; *This Side of Life*, 1965; *The Marriage*, 1965; *See Mr. Roberts*, 1966; *Too Many Cooks*, 1966; *The Listener with the Pop-up Toaster*, 1966; *Be Good If You Could but You Can't*, 1967; *Has Anybody Here Seen Christmas?*, 1967; *Once upon a Blind Date*, 1968; *Think!*, 1968; *A Fair Go for Charlie Wellman*, 1968; *The Spook*, 1968; *A Jolly Roger for Christmas*, 1969; *The Old Man and the Sea and Christmas Dinner*, 1973; *Going On*, 1974; *I Was a Teenage Matchmaker*, 1975; *Sound Furious*, 1976; *Never Let It Be Said*, 1977; *Flotsam and Jetsam*, 1977; *Hello Goodbye*, 1979; *Mind Jogging*, 1980; *Just Desserts*, 1982; *That'll Be the Day*, 1983.

Television Plays: episode in *Buck House* series, 1974; scripts for *Joe's World* and *In View of the Circumstances* series.

*

Joseph Musaphia comments:

While I have tried both serious and comedy writing and acting, I prefer comedy. Receiving an immediate, vocal response from the members of an audience is the one vital peculiarity comedy has that allows its creator conclusive proof that his effort was worthwhile. By the same token, I hope that what the audience initially laughed at supplies them with food for thought for some time after their amusement has died down. If I had to describe my attitude towards my writing, it would probably be best summed up by a description used by a local critic in reviewing *Mothers and Fathers*. Michael Dean referred to me in the New Zealand *Listener* as a "moral democrat." Having checked out his description in as many tomes as are available to me, I have decided that it just might be inoffensive enough to be acceptable to this playwright, who is not at all happy to be categorized or to write about his own work. I don't enjoy being asked what a play of mine "was getting at," because if the play worked on stage the question should not have to be asked. I can say that after a preposterously varied existence, I count myself very lucky indeed to be making such an enjoyable living out of a typewriter. If audiences continue to get half the pleasure out of watching my plays as I get writing them, I have no complaints.

* * *

Joseph Musaphia's plays for the theatre all in a sense develop out of the early one-act piece *Free*, which is about personal freedom. Musaphia has delighted in exploring the ways people hold down and exploit others, especially in sexual relationships, in order to satisfy purely selfish needs of their own. His plays are comedies—in fact, more than any other New Zealand playwright he uses some of the elements of 19th-century farce—but the moral implications seldom leave any doubt that it is his intention, as he would say, to hit his audience hard.

Musaphia found an apt vehicle for this in *The Guerilla*. Adam King, an ordinary man (though the name might suggest Original Egotism), frustrated by all the minor indignities imposed by petty officialdom on suburban life, barricades himself in his house with some hand grenades and his de facto wife and demands to see the Prime Minister. (It is characteristic that King's success in persuading the police to pass in to him an armalite rifle, a farcical detail which seems to remove the play from the world of possibility, actually occurred in the incident on which the play is based.) Musaphia likes to use such a character, apparently harmless, whom life drives into aberration if not madness. In *Obstacles* a bedridden woman sexually teases her father's friend into a position where she can blackmail them both into performing her slightest wish—yet still needs their assistance to reach the loo. Much of the comedy rises out of situations thus extrapolated, so to speak, from ordinary life into the world of farce.

Farce is not often connected with strong moral concern, and it is a sign of Musaphia's not-so-farcical nature that he has more difficulty with his last than with his first acts. He can catch an audience's attention effortlessly. The bickering couple of a dead marriage in *Shotgun Wedding* are interrupted by the entry of the husband's partner from a recent naughty weekend—in full bridal dress! It is a superb *coup de théâtre*. Equally fine is the opening of *Mothers and Fathers*, in which a suburban couple place by telephone the following advertisement: "Mature, liberated, rational, childless couple are willing to pay five thousand dollars to suitable woman prepared to volunteer her body for impregnation by male half of the aforementioned married couple."

Musaphia is unwilling to resolve the complications which arise from such openings with either a wedding or a pistol shot. Life is good for a laugh, but is also a serious matter, and when all passions are spent returns to its habitual grey.

The more complicated plots tend to diverge rather than converge in the last act. *Victims* (which capitalises splendidly on its 1900 setting and parallels the ignorance of strait-laced Victorian puritanism with modern societies for the preservation of community standards) opens with almost the entire cast standing around a grave, but ends with couples separated into three different bedrooms. Even when violence is used, as in the underrated *Hunting*—in which two middle-aged divorcees, feeling their way gingerly towards a relationship they both desperately want, are interrupted by the return of their grown-up children, also the victims of sexual mistakes, clamouring for their parents' undivided protection and attention—nothing is really resolved. This crisis of middle age also dominates Musaphia's latest play, *Mates*, where the same difficulty in finding a satisfying "action" or shape allows the initial power of the piece to drain away.

Mothers and Fathers, by far Musaphia's most successful play, avoids any madness or extreme nastiness, and presents four characters not one of whom is really unsympathetic. Their sexual needs and antagonisms result in a realignment of forces: the two husbands, rendered irrelevant, are left confronting their two ex-wives, who have joined against the common enemy and occupied the house—an example of aggressive feminism to be paralleled in most of the other plays. If Musaphia's men are not quite so rampantly chauvinist as some of his women, no doubt Musaphia would agree that their world is so arranged that they don't need to be so self-centred to get their way.

Musaphia has often contributed to the successful production of his plays as either director or actor. His audiences, though, have been suspicious of the taste shown in exploiting such pitiful and sometimes unpleasant characters for such uproarious farcical laughter. There is not a doubt that Musaphia can make his audiences laugh; but they have not always liked being hit so hard at the same time.

—John Thomson

N

NAUGHTON, Bill (William John Francis Naughton). British 1910–1992. See 4th edition, 1988.

———

NELSON, Richard. American. Born in Chicago, Illinois, 17 October 1950. Educated at Hamilton College, Clinton, New York, 1968–72, B.A. 1972. Married Cynthia B. Bacon in 1972; one daughter. Literary manager, BAM Theater Company, Brooklyn, New York, 1979–81; associate director, Goodman Theatre, Chicago, 1980–83; dramaturg, Guthrie Theatre, Minneapolis, 1981–82. Recipient: Watson fellowship, 1972; Rockefeller grant, 1979; Obie award, 1979, 1980; National Endowment for the Arts fellowship, 1980, 1985; Guggenheim fellowship, 1983; ABC award, 1985; Playwrights USA award, 1986; HBO award, 1986; *Time Out* award (London), 1987. Agent: Peter Franklin, William Morris Agency, 1350 Avenue of the Americas, New York, New York 10019. Address: 32 South Street, Rhinebeck, New York 12572, U.S.A.

PUBLICATIONS

Plays

The Killing of Yablonski (produced Los Angeles, 1975).
Conjuring an Event (produced Los Angeles, 1976; New York 1978). Included in *An American Comedy and Other Plays*, 1984.
Scooping (produced Washington, D.C., 1977).
Jungle Coup (produced New York, 1978). Published in *Plays from Playwrights Horizons*, New York, Broadway Play Publishing, 1987.
The Vienna Notes (produced Minneapolis, 1978; New York and Sheffield, 1979). Published in *Wordplays 1*, New York, Performing Arts Journal Publications, 1980.
Don Juan, adaptation of a play by Molière (produced Washington, D.C., 1979).
The Wedding, with Helga Ciulei, adaptation of a play by Brecht (produced New York, 1980).
The Suicide, adaptation of a play by Nikolai Erdman (produced Chicago, 1980).
Bal (produced Chicago, 1980). Included in *American Comedy and Other Plays*, 1984.
Rip Van Winkle; or, "The Works" (produced New Haven, Connecticut, 1981). New York, Broadway Play Publishing, 1986.
Il Campiello, adaptation of the play by Goldoni (produced New York, 1981). New York, Theatre Communications Group, 1981.
Jungle of Cities, adaptation of a play by Brecht (produced New York, 1981).
The Marriage of Figaro, adaptation of a play by Beaumarchais (produced Minneapolis, 1982; New York, 1985).
The Return of Pinocchio (produced Seattle, 1983; New York, 1986). Included in *An American Comedy and Other Plays*, 1984.
An American Comedy (produced Los Angeles, 1983). Included in *An American Comedy and Other Plays*, 1984.
Accidental Death of an Anarchist, adaptation of a play by Dario Fo (produced Washington, D.C., and New York, 1984). New York, French, 1987.
Three Sisters, adaptation of a play by Chekhov (produced Minneapolis, 1984).
Between East and West (also co-director: produced Seattle, 1984; London, 1987). Published in *New Plays USA 3*, edited by James Leverett and M. Elizabeth Osborn, New York, Theatre Communications Group, 1986.
An American Comedy and Other Plays. New York Performing Arts Journal Publications, 1984.
Principia Scriptoriae (produced New York and London, 1986). New York, Broadway Play Publishing, and London, English Theatre Guild, 1986.
Chess (revised version), with Tim Rice, music by Benny Andersson, lyrics by Björn Ulvaeus (produced New York, 1988).
Some Americans Abroad (produced Stratford-on-Avon, 1989; New York, 1990). London, Faber, 1989.
Eating Words (broadcast 1989). Published in *Best Radio Plays of 1989*, London, Methuen, 1990.
Sensibility and Sense (televized 1990). London, Faber, 1989.
Two Shakespearean Actors (produced Stratford-on-Avon, 1990; London, 1991). London, Faber, 1990.
Columbus and the Discovery of Japan (produced London, 1992). London, Faber, 1992.

Radio Plays: *Languages Spoken Here*, 1987; *Roots in Water*, 1989; *Eating Words*, 1989; *Advice to Eastern Europe*, 1990.

Television Play: *Sensibility and Sense*, 1990.

Other

Editor, *Strictly Dishonorable and Other Lost American Plays*. New York, Theatre Communications Group, 1986.

*

Theatrical Activities:
Director: **Play**—*Between East and West* (co-director, with Ted D'Arms), Seattle, 1984.

* * *

Richard Nelson is seriously funny: his writing is often comic, but never frivolous, and he uses laughter to deepen an audience's understanding of character and situation. Farcical misunderstanding is one of the ways he achieves that, and it is no surprise to find a Broadway adaptation of Dario Fo's

485

Accidental Death of an Anarchist among his scripts (along with versions of Goldoni and Molière), but his plays are perhaps even more notable for a rare thoughtfulness. For a few seasons that thoughtfulness caught audiences in his native United States by surprise, and he was considered suspiciously foreign and probably political.

In a nicely ironic turn of fortune, his reputation in the American theatre grew when he achieved considerable success in a foreign country. His 1986 play *Principia Scriptoriae* was tepidly received in its first production in New York but won prizes and a flurry of admiring reviews when David Jones directed it for the Royal Shakespeare Company. It proved to be only the first of several highly successful plays for the RSC, plays which were subsequently produced to great effect in the United States.

His next play for the RSC, *Some Americans Abroad*, was a comedy about a group of American tourists on a cultural tour of the literary landmarks of England. A knowing and witty piece about American pretension, subterfuge, and enthusiasm, it ingeniously forced spectators into recognition of aspects of themselves. The majority of the audience was naturally British, but they were laughing at the Americans on stage while sharing the theatre with a healthy number of culture-hungry Americans who were finding large parts of their own itinerary recreated in the play.

The later long-running New York production at Lincoln Center demonstrated just how subtly Nelson had pitched his comedy. Where London audiences had been greatly amused by the eagerness of the tourists to experience British culture, New Yorkers accepted such enthusiasm as natural, an understandable white Anglo-Saxon search for European roots. They found their laughter in the acutely observed academic rivalries in the play.

Some Americans Abroad shares with much of Nelson's work a concern with roots and rootlessness, with that endemic 20th-century condition of exile. His play *The Return of Pinocchio* imagines that the wooden puppet who became a boy had left Italy to star in a Walt Disney movie and later became a wealthy entertainer. After World War II he returns to his Italian village where he finds the misery of starvation, prostitution, and theft. But the play is about an American cloak of protective naïvety which permits the American dream of "making it big" to thrive by ignoring the reality of the world.

Between East and West is another story of the uprooted, about Gregor and Erna Hasek, Czech emigrés in their 50's who confront the American experience as Gregor attempts to rebuild his career as a stage and film director in America. The Communist Party, by lying, has made it possible for Gregor to return, but succeeds only in luring the homesick Erna back. Gregor remains alone in a country he still sees as the land of opportunity, directing a play which is finally dismissed as "too European." It contains some of his finest writing, including a scene where Gregor rehearses Erna in Chekhov's *Three Sisters*, trying to correct her English pronunciation while she defiantly reverts to Czech—it is entirely acted in English and uses his own adaptation of Chekhov.

Between East and West also represents another of Nelson's concerns, the function of the intellectual in society. The play which most thoroughly examines that in an American context is *Sensibility and Sense*. It is a fine and delicate drama about the aging of ideals and idealists, focusing particularly on two women as they were in 1937 and as they are in 1986. Their history parallels the history of the intellectual left in those years, and articulates the painful divisions as one woman writes scathingly about the other—who is dying, but certainly not going gently.

The RSC offered the premieres of the next two major plays by Nelson. *Two Shakespearean Actors* was his retelling of the rivalry of two actors, the American Edwin Forrest and the Englishman William Charles Macready. In 1849 they were presenting competing Macbeths in neighbouring theatres in New York's Astor Place and the jingoistic followers of Forrest started a riot which resulted in 34 deaths.

Nelson's play had fun recreating the contrasting styles of the two actors with simultaneous rehearsals of *Macbeth*, and there is loving comic detail in the backstage and bar room banter of the theatrical companies, but the key to the play is an artistic coming-together of Forrest and Macready on the stage of a shuttered theatre as the riot rages in the streets. Despite all the posturing that has gone before, they find their artistic intentions share a belief that could be called sacred. Like *Some Americans Abroad*, it demonstrated Nelson's understanding of audiences on each side of the Atlantic. His British audiences chose the side of Macready, and laughed at the American's perceived crudity. On Broadway, where the play proved itself as a large-scale work, it was injected with American pace yet somehow tilted decisively in Forrest's favour.

Columbus and the Discovery of Japan, his contribution to the 500th anniversary of the discovery of America, suffered a severe critical divide on the RSC's main London stage. Many reviewers felt that the three-hour piece, mistakenly performed in rather small boxes on the vast Barbican stage, was a small-scale play. But the play very effectively dramatizes the contradictions of Columbus himself. His greatness of vision and pettiness of character combine to get him his ships and get him to America and the issues of the play are exceptionally large-scale. To achieve this, Nelson called on the opposing techniques of Brecht and Chekhov to create a "Chekhovian epic," vast and intimate. Passionate admirers of the play recognized that and also recognized the way in which his recurring theme of rootlessness applied to the drifting life of Columbus.

Perhaps his play *Roots in Water* (which has yet to receive a full production on stage), a sequence of 12 short plays spanning the years 1977 to 1988, contains his most specific statement on rootlessness. A husband comforting his ex-wife as her new marriage fails recites something he has been writing: "'Roots in water. We live but there's nowhere to settle.' A poem. That I've been working on for a long time." Coming at the end of the sequence, when year by year he has demonstrated the post-Vietnam, post-Watergate malaise that affected his generation in particular, it none the less seemed to indicate that he himself was continuing to work on that poem, on that clear statement about how Americans had come to that particular disaffected point.

His skill at mastering dramatic forms has also extended to prize-winning radio plays for the BBC, where Americans abroad were directly confronted with cultural conflicts in part prompted by their disaffection with their own country. In *Languages Spoken Here*, a second-generation Polish-American in London finds himself out of his depth when he tries to help an exiled Polish novelist with a translation; in *Eating Words*, a self-exiled American novelist finds a brotherhood through his friendship with an English novelist dying of AIDS; in *Advice to Eastern Europe* a young American would-be filmmaker finds romance and utter political confusion when he gets romantically entangled with a young Czech woman, a filmmaker who idealizes the United States.

—Ned Chaillet

NEWMAN, G(ordon) F. British. Born in Kent in 1947. Married to Rebecca Hall; two children. Recipient: BAFTA award, 1992. Agent: Elaine Steel, 21 Brookfield, 5 Highgate Hill West, London N6 6AS. Address: Wessington Court, Woolhope, Hereford, HR1 4QN, England.

PUBLICATIONS

Plays

Operation Bad Apple (produced London, 1982). London, Methuen, 1982.
An Honourable Trade (produced London, 1984). London, Methuen, 1984.
The Testing Ground, from his own novel (produced London, 1989).

Screenplay: *Number One*, 1985.

Television Plays: *Law and Order* series, 1978; *Billy*, 1979; *The Nation's Health*, 1984; *1996*, 1989; *Here Is the News*, 1990; *For the Greater Good*, 1991; *Black and Blue*, 1992.

Novels

Sir, You Bastard. London, W.H. Allen, 1970; New York, Simon and Schuster, 1971; as *Rogue Cop*, New York, Lancer, 1973.
Billy: A Family Tragedy. London, New English Library, 1972.
The Player and the Guest. London, New English Library, 1972.
The Abduction. London, New English Library, 1972.
You Nice Bastard. London, New English Library, 1972.
Three Professional Ladies. London, New English Library, 1973.
The Split. London, New English Library, 1974.
The Price. London, New English Library, 1974.
You Flash Bastard. London, New English Library, 1974.
The Streetfighter. London, Star, 1975.
A Detective's Tale. London, Sphere, 1977.
The Guvnor. London, Hart Davis MacGibbon, 1977; as *Trade-Off*, New York, Dell, 1979.
A Prisoner's Tale. London, Sphere, 1977.
A Villain's Tale. London, Sphere, 1977.
The List. London, Secker and Warburg, 1979.
The Obsession. London, Granada, 1980.
Charlie and Joanna. London, Granada, 1981.
The Men with the Guns. London, Secker and Warburg, 1982.
The Nation's Health. London, Granada, 1983.
Law and Order. London, Granada, 1983.
Set a Thief. London, Joseph, 1986.
The Testing Ground. London, Joseph, 1987.
Trading the Future. London, Macdonald, 1992.

*

G. F. Newman comments:

I declare myself to be a radical vegan (pure vegetarian), one who has hitherto sought to change corrupt and oppressive institutions through political ideas. But lately I've realised that change comes only from the heart of man (and woman), rather than as a consequence of the political clothes he wears. It comes when we recognise a true ideal and are brave enough to run with it; when we see truth and are strong enough to stand and defend it. Recognising that the exploitation of one species paves the way to the exploitation of all others is such a

truth; acknowledging the interconnectedness of all living creatures on this planet is such an ideal. If we want to change society, if we want a fairer, more just, more compassionate society, first we must extend justice and compassion beyond our immediate family and our own kind to every living creature. Until we do so we will never be without racial or national or sexual strife; we will never sustain lasting beneficial change. To every action there is reaction; our troubled human condition is largely the result of what we do to the "other nations" who share this earth with us. If there were political solutions to be had we would almost certainly have them by now, and all of our problems would have been legislated away. Due process is part of the problem, not the solution; only when we gain self-recognition will we start to approach solutions. In my work I strive to create mirrors that reflect some of the problems that confront us to help me gain self-recognition.

*   *   *

G. F. Newman is known above all as the author of fiction, and though he has turned to dramatic form from time to time, it is not in the theatre that he has made his name. On television, his *The Nation's Health* and *Law and Order*, for instance, created quite a stir, but that was more on account of their highly controversial content than because of specifically dramatic qualities, and the published versions take the form of novels.

Operation Bad Apple, which was given its first performance at the Royal Court Theatre, London, on 4 February 1982, reveals both the strengths and weaknesses of Newman as a dramatist. There is a sense of commitment which has to be respected, and the action moves speedily to make its points. The play shares with several of Newman's novels the central character of Detective Chief Inspector Terry Sneed, and indeed the whole work might be well thought of as a deft dramatisation of an episode from his chronicles of the world of "bent" London coppers, which had special relevance at the time. The first scene introduces the theme of the investigation, by police drafted in from Wiltshire, of complaints about possible misconduct in the Metropolitan Police. It is not long before we come to appreciate that there is indeed genuine cause for concern. As the investigators fret about the impact on their family lives of a lengthy absence from home in the debilitating moral atmosphere of the capital, they come into contact with corruption at every level, with brutal policemen abusing their power both in their relationships with brother officers and with the criminal classes. What becomes increasingly plain, however, is the fact that the powerful and cynical Sneed is the most guilty of all the policemen, though his subordinates too are portrayed as disreputable, grasping, and cowardly. To conclude this disheartening drama Newman offers a scene in which two pillars of the establishment are seen out on a golf-course organising a totally immoral cover-up in an effort to avert any criticism of the status quo.

The effect is certainly striking, but there is no escaping the feeling that Newman is rather too keen to shock by exposing what he plainly feels are the disgraceful inadequacies of the police force. No doubt he has a point, but a little more balance and perspective might be fairer and would certainly make for better drama because the audience would not have quite the same feeling of being pushed in one direction.

The dramatic style of the play is fluid, cutting swiftly from one brief scene to the next, almost in cinematic style, and with the audience largely left to make sense of the juxtapositions without formal explanations. Characters are used functionally, rather than developed for their own sake, and there is a certain reliance on social type which is in harmony with the general thrust of a play that shows, in many ways, more interest in groups and classes than in people as such. Some quite lengthy speeches are the expression of the way certain individuals impose their will on those around them. The incessant use of bad language, which some might regard simply as realistic, also serves as an effective and constant reminder of moral degradation.

—Christopher Smith

———————

NGEMA, Mbongeni. South African. Born in Umkumbane, Durban. Recipient: Edinburgh Fringe first, 1987. Address: c/o The Market Theatre, P.O. Box 8656, Johannesburg 2000, South Africa.

PUBLICATIONS

Plays

Woza Albert!, with Percy Mtwa and Barney Simon (produced Johannesburg, 1981; Edinburgh, London, and Los Angeles, 1982; New York, 1984). London, Methuen, 1983; published in Woza Afrika! An Anthology of South African Plays, edited by Duma Ndlovu, New York, Braziller, 1986.
Asinamali! (We Have No Money!) (also director: produced New York, 1986). Published in Woza Afrika! An Anthology of South African Plays, edited by Duma Ndlovu, New York, Braziller, 1986.
Sarafina!, music by Ngema and Hugh Masekela (produced New York, 1987).
Too Harsh (produced Johannesburg, n.d.).
The Last Generation (also director: produced Johannesburg, n.d.).

Screenplay: Sarafina!, with William Nicholson, 1992.

*

Theatrical Activities:
Director: Plays—some of his own plays; Sheila's Day by Duma Dnlovu, New Brunswick, New Jersey, 1989.
Actor: Plays—role in Isigcino by Lucky Mavundla; Working Class Hero by Kessie Govender; Mama and the Load by Gibson Kente, Johannesburg, 1979; Woza Albert!. Films—role in Sarafina!, 1992.

* * *

Mbongeni Ngema's reputation as a playwright came to world attention with the production and publication of the critically acclaimed Woza Albert! which he devised and co-wrote with Percy Mtwa and Barney Simon. The play is remarkable in the sense that it uses the minimum of stage props, lighting, actors, and instead employs dramatic devices such as songs, dance, and mime, in a panoramic yet poignant examination of the quality of life in contemporary South Africa. The resilience of black people as they endure, challenge, and rebel against the machinery of apartheid is its thematic province. But what sets it apart from many other

South African plays which often, in a tendentious manner, assault the readers or audience with these disturbing issues is Mbongeni Ngema's sense of humour. This helps the work's aesthetic distancing. But the comic potential of this work is disturbing. It harbours a subterfuge. As we read the play, we can easily infer that the laughter therein is the only psychic valve for a people who can no longer cry.

Woza Albert! employs the ingenious concept of the Messiah (Morena) coming to visit present-day South Africa. An invisible interviewer tries to get the reactions and opinions of a cross-section of the black population (played by only two actors, Mtwa and Ngema). Their witty and sarcastic responses and their constant mutation into different characters fill the stage with a dynamic visual theatricality as well as an historical insight into the origins of the dispossession of the black citizens. In one of the most stunning scenes, two passengers travelling in a train are asked for their view of the visit. They answer: "He will be taken to all the nice places in the country. Like the game reserve where he can lie down with a leopard and a lamb. . . . And then on a Thursday—the gold mines to watch." At this point they mime deafening drills and perform a short, ironic dance routine which is supposed to signify the happiness of the black gold miners. They then suggest that Christ should also be taken to see Sun City, the Las Vegas of South Africa, where he will inspect a guard of honour mounted by prostitutes and gambling machines. Finally they ask: "When the television cameras turn on him, will he be smiling? Will he be joyous?" They conclude that he will be crying and go on to improvise a speech which articulates the reason for Christ's tears. "What place is this . . . where old people weep over the graves of children? . . . How was it permitted? I've passed people with burning mouths . . . and the other side I see people . . . living in glass and gold." It is this interface between black and white, wealth and poverty, comfort and misery, life and death that informs both the poetic framework and political agenda of Woza Albert! Its dramatic strength lies in the improvisational latitude the imagined situation gives the actors to comment wryly on a vast number of issues pertinent to the present apartheid state while also allowing them space to criticise the shortcomings of their own black people. The dialogue is crisp, the scenes brief, and the re-enactments precise. It ends on an affirmative note in a graveyard where Christ is asked to raise the spirits, not bodies, of the dead black African leaders who have championed the insurrection against racism. Notable among these names is Albert Luthuli, after whom the play is named.

Mbongeni Ngema's other technically competent work is Asinamali! (We Have No Money!) which, as a slogan, is the black South African equivalent of "Won't pay; can't pay!" It deals with the problems of unemployment, economic hardship, and homelessness and translates, in theatrical terms, as a bitter indictment of the white-controlled South African labour bureaucracy. Because black people spend as long as six months looking for jobs in white-reserved townships, they logically cannot pay their rents. Asinamali! recreates, through vivid vignettes, this vicious circle of orchestrated dehumanization and its aftermath, a protest which ends in a massacre as armed white police enforcement agents move in with tanks and decimate the agitating citizens.

Set in prison with five characters—Solomzi, Thami, Bongani, Bheki, and Bhoyi—the play makes a distinction between the image of the prisoners as they are stigmatized by members of the society and the reality of the political and social conditions that lead to their crimes and consequent incarceration. The play uses a series of brilliantly re-enacted flashbacks to expose the humanity of the characters who first appear on stage as common felons. Employing a cinematographic technique characteristic of the dramaturgy of Ngema, these five characters people the stage with as many as 20 other human presences. Bongani alone plays 11 characters. The other characters almost equal his feat as they mimic and impersonate other absent personages to give dramatic conviction to the stories of their lives.

One very memorable flashback in the play deals with sexual politics and unfolds in the scene where Thami recalls his seduction by a white pig-farmer's wife. This scene re-emphasizes Ngema's gift for subversive humour:

> Thami: . . . Mrs Van Niekerk always called me to come help buy her groceries on Saturdays. I would sit at the back seat of the car. . . . One day she started to ask me; "how do you feel when you see a white woman?" . . . I WANT THEM! . . . One night she called me in; "Thami, kom hier, come into the house." A child asked from another room; "mommy, who is speaking Zulu in the house?" she said: "Ag . . . it's Radio Zulu, I am trying to learn Zulu, go to sleep honey." . . . It became daily bread.

Thami continues to enjoy his daily bread until the day its ecstasy makes him forget to lock the pigsty gate. The pigs escape. Mr Van Niekerk returns and Thami is sent to prison.

These two plays are the most representative of Ngema's vision and craftsmanship as a playwright. The direction of his work in a post-apartheid society is an open question, since his inspiration seems strongly rooted in the experience of the present.

—Esiaba Irobi

NGUGI, wa Thiong'o. Formerly wrote as James T. Ngugi. Kenyan. Born in Kamiriithu, near Limuru, Kiambu District, 5 January 1938. Educated at Kamaandura School, Limuru; Karing'a School, Maanguũ; Alliance High School, Kikuyu; University College, Kampala, Uganda (editor, *Penpoint*), 1959–63, B.A. 1963; Leeds University, Yorkshire, 1964–67, B.A. 1964. Married Nyambura in 1961; five sons and three daughters. Columnist ("As I See It"), early 1960's, and reporter, 1964, Nairobi *Daily Nation*; editor, *Zuka*, Nairobi, 1965–70; lecturer in English, University College, Nairobi, 1967–69; fellow in creative writing, Makerere University, Kampala, 1969–70; visiting lecturer, Northwestern University, Evanston, Illinois, 1970–71; senior lecturer, associate professor, and chair of the Department of Literature, University of Nairobi, 1972–77; imprisoned under Public Security Act, 1977–78; left Kenya, 1982; now lives in London. Recipient: East African Literature Bureau award, 1964. Address: c/o Heinemann Educational Books, Halley Court, Jordan Hill, Oxford OX2 8EJ, England.

PUBLICATIONS

Plays

The Black Hermit (produced Kampala, Uganda, 1962; London, 1988). London, Heinemann, 1968.
This Time Tomorrow (broadcast 1967). Included in *This Time Tomorrow*, 1970.
This Time Tomorrow (includes *The Rebels* and *The Wound in the Heart*). Nairobi, East African Literature Bureau, 1970.
The Trial of Dedan Kimathi, with Micere Mugo (produced London, 1984). Nairobi, Heinemann, 1976; London, Heinemann, 1977.
Ngaahika Ndeenda (in Kikuyu), with Ngugi wa Mirii (produced Limuru, 1977). Nairobi, Heinemann, 1980; as *I Will Marry When I Want*, London, Heinemann, 1982.

Radio Play: *This Time Tomorrow*, 1967.

Novels

Weep Not, Child. London, Heinemann, 1964; New York, Collier, 1969.
The River Between. London, Heinemann, 1965.
A Grain of Wheat. London, Heinemann, 1967.
Petals of Blood. London, Heinemann, 1977; New York, Dutton, 1978.
Caitaani Mutharaba-ini (in Kikuyu). Nairobi, Heinemann, 1980; as *Devil on the Cross*, London, Heinemann, 1982.
Matigari (in Kikuyu). Nairobi, Heinemann, 1986; translated by Wangui wa Goro, London, Heinemann, 1989.

Short Stories

Secret Lives and Other Stories. London, Heinemann, and New York, Hill, 1975.

Other

Homecoming: Essays on African and Caribbean Literature, Culture, and Politics. London, Heinemann, 1972; New York, Hill, 1973.
The Independence of Africa and Cultural Decolonisation, with *The Poverty of African Historiography*, by A.E. Afigbo. Lagos, Afrografika, 1977.
Writers in Politics: Essays. London, Heinemann, 1981.
Detained: A Writer's Prison Diary. London, Heinemann, 1981.
Education for a National Culture. Harare, Zimbabwe Publishing House, 1981.
Barrel of a Pen: Resistance to Repression in Neo-Colonial Kenya. London, New Beacon, and Trenton, New Jersey, Africa World Press, 1983.
Decolonising the Mind: The Politics of Language in African Literature. London, Currey, 1986.
Njamba Nene and the Cruel Chief (for children). Nairobi, Heinemann, 1986.
Njamba Nene's Pistol (for children). Nairobi, Heinemann, 1986.
Writing Against Neocolonialism. London, Vita, 1986.
Walter Rodney's Influence on the African Continent. London, Friends of Bogle, 1987.

*

Bibliography: *Ngugi wa Thiong'o: A Bibliography of Primary and Secondary Sources 1957–1987* by Carol Sicherman, London, Zell, 1989.

Critical Studies: *Ngugi wa Thiong'o* by Clifford Robson, London, Macmillan, 1979, New York, St. Martin's Press, 1980; *Ngugi wa Thiong'o: An Exploration of His Writings* by David Cook and Michael Okenimkpe, London, Heinemann, 1983; *East African Writing in English* by Angela Smith,

London, Macmillan, 1989; *Mother, Sing for Me: People's Theatre in Kenya* by Ingrid Björkman, London, Zed Books, 1989. *Ngugi wa Thiong'o: The Making of a Rebel: A Source Book in Kenyan Literature and Resistance* by Carol Sicherman, 1990.

* * *

Ngugi wa Thiong'o's plays are the minor works of a major novelist. Indeed, one book on his work tacitly ignores the plays. Nevertheless, his first play remains important for its historical priority and in his later work he offers an aesthetic —and, indeed, moral—example of how dramatists may serve a popular audience. For several years after its production in 1962, Ngugi's *The Black Hermit* was the only full-length play in English from East Africa. Written just before Kenya achieved independence, the play is a pessimistic look at the rival claims of traditional and modern ways of life, traditional and modern religions, public service and private fulfilment. Unfortunately, the claims of nation, ideology, family, and love are only touched upon, not explored. The shuffling of the different issues—now one, now another held before us— produces melodrama. The author himself has called the play "very confused."

Remi, the first of his tribe to go to college, loved Thoni, who married his brother while he was away. On the death of his brother, Remi's father urged him to follow tradition and marry his brother's wife. This he did, though he felt that he could never love one who was another's. He fled from her, and from the expectations of the tribe that he would be their political leader, to the city and the love of a white girl. The play opens with the efforts of his mother and wife to get him to return; the pastor will visit Remi on their behalf. Meanwhile, the elders also send emissaries, bearing "medicine." Weighing the Bible in one hand, the "medicine" in the other, Remi is moved by these "pieces of superstition" and returns home. He holds a successful political rally, against tribalism, but while he discusses future plans a woman enters with a letter from

She who was kind.
She who was true.
A tender sapling growing straight.
Though surrounded by weed.

His wife had loved him, and deep down he had loved her, but she had heard him say that he had been wrong to follow custom in marrying her, and so committed suicide, leaving the letter to state that she has always loved him. The play ends with Remi kneeling beside her body and declaring "I came to break Tribe and Custom, Instead, I've broken you and me."

More interesting is a short radio play, *This Time Tomorrow*. A slum, ironically named Uhuru (Freedom) Market, is to be bulldozed because "tourists from America, Britain and West Germany are disgusted with the dirt that is slowly creeping into a city that used to be the pearl of Africa." In the slum live Njango, wife of a freedom fighter, and her dreaming daughter Wanjiro. During the play, Wanjiro's lover persuades her to move into his house, and Njango attends a protest meeting, led by the Stranger, a former freedom fighter who is arrested. A bulldozer razes the hut as Njango ends the play: "If only we had stood up against them! If only we could stand together!" Against the actualities of the situation, caught in a soliloquy of Wanjiro's—"How often have I leaned against this very post, and watched the city awake. Just now, noise is dead in the city. It is so dark outside—the crawling maggots in the drains are hidden"—are set the bland

phrases of the journalist, with which the play opens—"The filthy mushrooms—inhabited by human beings—besieging our capital city, came tumbling down yesterday."

As an epigraph to his collection of essays *Writers in Politics*, Ngugi quotes Karl Marx: "The profound hypocrisy and inherent barbarism of bourgeois civilization lies unveiled before our eyes, turning from its home, where it assumes respectable forms, to the colonies, where it goes naked. . . ." The struggle against colonialism is dramatized in *The Trial of Dedan Kimathi*, while *I Will Marry When I Want* attacks the new black bourgeois exploiters. Both dramatize his views insistently and even stridently.

Kimathi was a leader of the Mau Mau rebellion, captured and shot by the British. In Ngugi's play Kimathi's brief arraignment and trial frame four "trials" of his resolution in his cell, reminiscent of the visits of the tempters to Eliot's Becket. The last of these is followed by a flashback to a trial over which Kimathi presided, to judge traitors in the guerrilla ranks. Woven between are scenes which focus on a boy and a girl whom a female colleague of Kimathi's recruits for a rescue attempt. They allow Ngugi to describe the life of the most destitute, stress women's contribution to the liberation struggle, and show the spirit of revolt passed to the next generation. The complexity of the play's structure saves it from being too pietistic or too obviously didactic.

There are flashbacks to the independence struggle in *I Will Marry When I Want*, but they seem to serve more as excuses for the songs and dances that befit a popular piece rather than to have a dramatic purpose. The play has a narrower focus than *The Trial of Dedan Kimathi*, showing the destruction of a simple bourgeois family who are both hypocritically Christian and the black tools of foreign capitalism. The didactic message is spelled out by a neighbor raisonneur.

All Ngugi's plays contrast tradition with the exploitation of (neo-)colonialists and their agents. Disgust at official and religious cant is sharpened by a sense that Uhuru has brought nothing to the common people. A believer in the collectivization of economic resources and the "release of a people's creative spirit [through] the active work of destroying an inhibitive social structure and building a new one" (*Homecoming*), Ngugi developed *I Will Marry When I Want* in his home village as "a community product." Its performance led to his being jailed for a year amid charges that he was subverting national unity by promoting the Kikuyu language in which it was written. His last attempt to develop a drama of the people was *Maitu Njuriga* (Mother, Sing for Me), with songs in five of Kenya's languages. Its performance was not allowed, but many people saw a series of "rehearsals."

—Anthony Graham-White

———————

NICHOLS, Peter (Richard). British. Born in Bristol, 31 July 1927. Educated at Bristol Grammar School, 1936–44; Bristol Old Vic Theatre School, 1948–50; Trent Park Teachers' Training College, Hertfordshire, 1955–57. Served in the Royal Air Force, 1945–48. Married Thelma Reed in 1959; three daughters (one deceased) and one son. Actor, in repertory, television, and films, 1950–55; teacher in primary and secondary schools, 1957–59; has also worked as a park keeper, English language teacher in Italy, cinema commissionaire, and clerk. Visiting playwright, Guthrie Theatre,

Minneapolis, 1977. Governor, Greenwich Theatre, London, 1970–76; member, Arts Council Drama Panel, 1972–75. Recipient: Arts Council bursary, 1961; *Evening Standard* award, 1967, 1969, 1978, 1982, 1985; John Whiting award, 1968; Ivor Novello award, 1977; Society of West End Theatre award, 1978, 1982; Tony award, 1985; New York Drama Critics Circle award, 1989. Fellow, Royal Society of Literature, 1983. Agent: Casarotto Ramsay Ltd., National House, 60–66 Wardour Street, London W1V 3HP. Address: The Old Rectory, Hopesay, Craven Arms, Shropshire SY7 8HD, England.

PUBLICATIONS

Plays

Promenade (televised 1959). Published in *Six Granada Plays*, London, Faber, 1960.
Ben Spray (televised 1961). Published in *New Granada Plays*, London, Faber, 1961.
The Hooded Terror (televised 1963; produced Bristol, 1964).
A Day in the Death of Joe Egg (produced Glasgow and London, 1967; New York, 1968). London, Faber, 1967; as *Joe Egg*, New York, Grove Press, 1967.
The Gorge (televised 1968). Published in *The Television Dramatist*, edited by Robert Muller, London, Elek, 1973.
The National Health; or, Nurse Norton's Affair (produced London, 1969; Chicago, 1971; New York, 1974). London, Faber, 1970; New York, Grove Press, 1975.
Hearts and Flowers (televised 1970). Included in *Plays 1*, 1987.
Forget-Me-Not Lane (produced London, 1971; New Haven, Connecticut, 1973). London, Faber, 1971.
Neither Up nor Down (produced London, 1972). Included in *Plays 1*, 1987.
The Common (televised 1973). Revised version in *Plays 1*, 1987.
Chez Nous (produced London, 1974; New York, 1977). London, Faber, 1974.
The Freeway (produced London, 1974; Milwaukee, 1978). London, Faber, 1975.
Harding's Luck, adaptation of the novel by E. Nesbit (produced London, 1974).
Privates on Parade (produced London, 1977; New Haven, Connecticut, 1979; New York, 1989). London, Faber, 1977.
Born in the Gardens (also director: produced Bristol, 1979; London, 1980). London, Faber, 1980.
Passion Play (produced London, 1981). London, Eyre Methuen, 1981; as *Passion* (produced New York, 1983), New York, French, 1983.
Poppy, music by Monty Norman (produced London, 1982). London, Methuen, 1982.
Privates on Parade (screenplay). London, Star, 1983.
A Piece of My Mind (produced Southampton and London, 1987).
Plays 1 (includes *Forget-Me-Not Lane*, *Hearts and Flowers*, *Neither Up nor Down*, *Chez Nous*, The *Common* revised version, *Privates on Parade*). London, Methuen, 1987; revised edition, as *Plays: One* (includes *A Day in the Death of Joe Egg*, *The National Health*, *Forget-Me-Not Lane*, *Hearts and Flowers*, *The Freeway*), London, Methuen, 1990.
Plays: Two (includes *Chez Nous*, *Privates on Parade*, *Born in the Gardens*, *Passion Play*, *Poppy*). London, Methuen, 1990.

Screenplays: *Catch Us If You Can* (*Having a Wild Weekend*), 1965; *Georgy Girl*, with Margaret Forster, 1966; *A Day in the Death of Joe Egg*, 1972; *The National Health*, 1973; *Privates on Parade*, 1983; *Changing Places*, 1984.

Television Plays: *Walk on the Grass*, 1959; *After All*, with Bernie Cooper, 1959; *Promenade*, 1959; *Ben Spray*, 1961; *The Big Boys*, 1961; *The Reception*, 1961; *The Heart of the Country*, 1962; *Ben Again*, 1963; *The Hooded Terror*, 1963; *The Continuity Man*, 1963; *The Brick Umbrella*, 1964; *When the Wind Blows*, 1965; *The Gorge*, 1968; *Majesty*, from a story by F. Scott Fitzgerald, 1968; *Winner Takes All*, from a story by Evelyn Waugh, 1968; *Daddy Kiss It Better*, 1968; *Hearts and Flowers*, 1970; *The Common*, 1973.

Other

Feeling You're Behind: An Autobiography. London, Weidenfeld and Nicolson, 1984.

*

Critical Studies: *The Second Wave* by John Russell Taylor, London, Methuen, and New York, Hill and Wang, 1971; interview in *Playback 2* by Ronald Hayman, London, Davis Poynter, 1973; *The New British Drama* by Oleg Kerensky, London, Hamish Hamilton, 1977, New York, Taplinger, 1979; *British Television Drama* edited by George W. Brandt, London, Cambridge University Press, 1981; *Landmarks of Modern British Drama: The Seventies* edited by Roger Cornish and Violet Ketels, London, Methuen, 1986.

Theatrical Activities:
Director: **Plays**—*A Day in the Death of Joe Egg*, London, 1971; *The National Health*, Minneapolis, 1977; *Born in the Gardens*, Bristol, 1979; *Forget-Me-Not Lane*, London, 1990.

*   *   *

Few dramatists have had more success than Peter Nichols in making their characters reveal their attitudes towards a problem, towards each other, towards society; and in this media age, when everyone's opinion is solicited, known, and categorized, the writer who is an artist at encapsulating attitude is likely to achieve wide popularity.

In, for example, *A Day in the Death of Joe Egg*, Nichols demonstrates admirably his ability to deal with a forbidden subject (in 1967), that of the paraplegic, the spastic, the "vegetable" (referred to in many ways during the course of the play). There was a surge of approval as a new barrier of inhibition was swept away: this is very flattering to an audience. Nichols manages to present an uncomfortable subject in a kind of hectic, hectoring way that is contrived not to offend. He incorporated every possible range of emotional response. We come away feeling there's something in the problem for all of us.

Nichols's jokes always cut near the bone, and in the revival of *Joe Egg*, directed by the author himself, one sometimes had the feeling there was no bone left to cut near. Possibly there may be something too quiescent at the back of the parents' games. They constantly exercise their instantly dismissable feelings at the expense of their "problem." Sometimes, one feels, a sustained and heartfelt cry of pain might be more cathartic. But pain is not an attitude. The main reservation concerns the theme. One looks in vain for some guiding idea to capture the imagination. Here and there Nichols throws in a possibility, as when, for instance, he points out that we are all cripples in some way, all limited. While the peripheries of the problem never relax their hold, a central issue obstinately fails to materialize. Nichols's method is to touch upon all, moving forward with brittle and lightning force in case he loses his audience.

The National Health, produced at the National Theatre in 1969, combines many Anouilhesque qualities and shortcomings. Half of this play is a comic comment on the human race, the conclusion being that each of us is entitled to his own death—half a gallop through every known attitude to health. The result has a lively spontaneous progress, is well-organized, but, ultimately, on the thin side.

In *Forget-Me-Not Lane* the debt to Anouilh appears even greater, as a middle-aged man asks himself what went wrong in his marriages and re-examines his childhood and his life with his parents during World War II. The device of shuttling the action back and forth between past and present results in much high comedy and some sharp theatrical moments. *Chez Nous* presents the much-trodden situation of two friendly married couples, Dick and Liz, Diana and Phil, on holiday in the Dordogne, who are driven to the brink of splitting up. The marital tug of war that we have already seen in *Joe Egg* and *Forget-Me-Not Lane* is organized in greater depth and comic intensity than Nichols has used previously, and in his presentation of the boulevard twist of fate—that Dick's daughter has given birth to Phil's son—Nichols pulls off a memorable *coup de théâtre*. Some critics found it highly improbable, but the combination of artificiality and the earthy—even squalid—way the couples express themselves towards each other produces an enjoyable, if not exactly profound, sense of truth.

In *Passion Play* Nichols drives even more relentlessly down the path of adultery by a device of splitting the main characters, Eleanor and James, into double identities (a device similar to that of Brian Friel in *Philadelphia, Here I Come!*). Again it's the many-sidedness of life he attempts to pay tribute to, but what promises much by way of exploring the inner states of the pair never lives up to expectations. No larger vision appears than that of lost apes in pursuit of ultimate sexiness: this may, of course, be sound comment, or may equally point to the shortcoming that virtuosity has become an end in itself.

With minor plays such as *The Freeway* Nichols returns to the episodic comic style of *The National Health*, though with less success. A great motorway (the FI) has been built running North to South, and in a week-end jam a number of marooned motorists commingle in the form of a glorified variety entertainment. Though there is some sharply observed satire, we seem, like the cars themselves, not to arrive anywhere in particular. But by the same token, *Privates on Parade* succeeds admirably. It is a mixture of cynical squaddie comment and concert routines of an army entertainment troupe around 1950, and in it Nichols again demonstrates his skill as pure entertainer. *Harding's Luck* is a straightforward adaptation of E. Nesbit's children's novel, using the author as narrator. The central character is Dickie, the crippled urchin from Deptford. He is elevated by the hospitality of a genteel family, finds out he is well-connected, and finally is submitted to a magical transformation backwards in time—from an Edwardian childhood into a Jacobean youth.

Poppy is an ambitious attempt to do with pantomime convention what *Privates on Parade* did with the concert party, but it is much less successful. Taking as his subject the Opium Wars in mid-19th-century China, Nichols satirizes British imperial commercialism in a mixture of styles, and reveals,

ultimately, that he has little that is vitally comic or original to add to what became a hackneyed target for entertainers in the 1980's.

—Garry O'Connor

NKOSI, Lewis. British. Born in Durban, South Africa, 5 December 1936. Educated at public schools in Durban; Zulu Lutheran High School; M.L. Sultan Technical College, Durban, 1961–62; Harvard University, Cambridge, Massachusetts (Nieman Fellow), 1962–63. Married Bronwyn Ollerenshaw in 1965; twin daughters. Staff member, *Ilanga Lase Natal* (Zulu newspaper), Durban, 1955–56, *Drum* magazine and *Golden City Post*, Johannesburg, 1956–60, and *South African Information Bulletin*, Paris, 1962–68; radio producer, BBC Transcription Centre, London, 1962–64; National Education Television interviewer, New York, 1963; literary editor, *New African* magazine, London, 1965–68; Regents lecturer on African Literature, University of California, Irvine, Spring 1971. Currently professor of English, University of Zambia, Lusaka. Recipient: Dakar Festival prize, for essays, 1965; C. Day Lewis fellowship, 1977; Macmillan Silver Pen award, 1987. Agent: Deborah Rogers, Rogers, Coleridge, and White Ltd., 20 Powis Mews, London W11 1JN, England. Address: Department of English, University of Zambia, P.O. Box 31338, Lusaka, Zambia.

PUBLICATIONS

Plays

The Rhythm of Violence (produced London, 1963). London, Oxford University Press, 1964; in *Plays from Black Africa*, edited by Fredric M. Litto, New York, Hill and Wang, 1968.
Malcolm (televised 1967; produced London, 1972).
The Chameleon and the Lizard (libretto; produced London, 1971).

Screenplay: *Come Back Africa*, 1959.

Radio Plays: *The Trial*, 1969; *We Can't All Be Martin Luther King*, 1971.

Television Play: *Malcolm*, 1967 (Sweden).

Novel

Mating Birds. Nairobi, East African Publishing House, 1983; London, Constable, and New York, St. Martin's Press, 1986.

Other

Home and Exile (essays). London, Longman, 1965; revised edition, 1983.
The Transplanted Heart: Essays on South Africa. Benin City, Nigeria, Ethiope, 1975.
Tasks and Masks: Themes and Styles of African Literature. London, Longman, 1981.

*

Theatrical Activities:
Actor: **Play**—Father Higgins in *No-Good Friday* by Athol Fugard, Johannesburg, 1958.

*   *   *

When Lewis Nkosi's *The Rhythm of Violence* was published in 1964 it was hailed as the first play by a black South African to appear in print since Herbert Dhlomo's *The Girl Who Killed to Save* (1935). Because of its sensitive handling of the explosive issues of South African racism the play was widely acclaimed and Nkosi was seen by some as being in the vanguard of a new black South African theatre. Since then Nkosi has published short stories and essays (a form in which he seems to excel), but his visible dramatic output has been limited to three radio and television plays.

Since the mid-1960's the immediacy of the South African situation, the terrific tensions it creates (which Nkosi himself has noted in his speculations on the dearth of recent plays and novels from South Africa), have made it difficult for the black South African writer to do anything other than the personal forms of essay, short story, and autobiography. Drama is written for an audience, and the stricter, though more subtle, laws which developed after the Sharpeville Massacre made it difficult for a mixed audience to come together in South Africa.

Thus we are left with only one major work in theatre on which to judge Nkosi, *The Rhythm of Violence*, an outstanding first play, an important one. There are some weaknesses in the play. Certain of the scenes tend to drag and some of the characters seem static, almost unreal—especially Tula and Sarie, the Zulu boy and Boer girl who are caught in the web of destruction. Nkosi's moral, however, that violence is mindless, that it destroys both the guilty and the innocent, and that violence begets more violence, is effectively acted out. Nkosi also does an excellent job in presenting the two Boer policemen, Jan and Piet, in such a way that we see beyond the harshness of their exterior into their confused souls. They are the most fully realized characters in the play and in one masterful scene, when Jan pretends to be a black politician and is carried away in his part ("You spoke just like a native communist," says Piet in a shocked voice), Nkosi makes it clear that the possibility for understanding between men does exist—unless the rhythm of violence prevents such understanding from developing.

—Joseph Bruchac

NOONAN, John Ford. American. Born in New York City, 7 October 1943. Educated at Fairfield Preparatory School, Connecticut, graduated 1959; Brown University, Providence, Rhode Island, A.B. in philosophy 1964; Carnegie Institute of Technology, Pittsburgh, M.A. in dramatic literature 1966. Married Marcia Lunt in 1962 (divorced 1965); three children. Taught Latin, English, and history at Buckley Country Day School, North Hills, Long Island, New York, 1966–69; stagehand, Fillmore East Rock Theatre, New York, 1969–71; stockbroker, E.F. Hutton Company, New York, 1971–72; professor of drama, Villanova University, Pennsylvania, 1972–73. Recipient: Rockefeller grant, 1973. Agent: Joan Scott Inc., 162 West 56th Street, New York, New York 10019. Address: 484 West 43rd Street, New York, New York 10036, U.S.A.

PUBLICATIONS

Plays

The Year Boston Won the Pennant (produced New York, 1969). New York, Grove Press, 1970.
Lazarus Was a Lady (produced New York, 1970).
Rainbows for Sale (produced New York, 1971). Published in *The Off-Off-Broadway Book*, edited by Albert Poland and Bruce Mailman, Indianapolis, Bobbs Merrill, 1972.
Concerning the Effects of Trimethylchloride (produced New York, 1971).
Monday Night Varieties (produced New York, 1972).
Older People (also director: produced New York, 1972).
Good-By and Keep Cold (produced New York, 1973).
A Noonan Night (produced New York, 1973).
A Sneaky Bit to Raise the Blind, and Pick Pack Pock Puck (produced New York, 1974).
Where Do We Go from Here? (produced New York, 1974).
Getting Through the Night (produced New York, 1976).
A Coupla White Chicks Sitting Around Talking (produced New York, 1979; London, 1983). New York, French, 1981.
Listen to the Lions (produced New York, 1979).
Some Men Need Help (produced New York, 1982). New York, French, 1983.
Talking Things Over with Chekhov (produced Burbank, California, 1987; New York, 1990).
Nothing But Bukowski (includes *The Raunchy Dame in the Chinese Raincoat, The Heterosexual Temperature in West Hollywood*) (produced New York, 1987).
All She Cares About Is the Yankees. New York, French, 1988.
My Daddy's Serious American Gift (produced Los Angeles, 1989).
Stay Away a Little Closer (produced New York, 1990).
Recent Developments in Southern Connecticut (produced Cincinnati, 1990).

Screenplays: *Septuagenarian Substitute Ball*, 1970; *The Summer the Snows Came*, 1972.

*

Manuscript Collection: Lincoln Center Library of the Performing Arts, New York.

Critical Studies: "Theatre as Mystery," in *Evergreen Magazine* (New York), December 1969, and reviews in *Village Voice* (New York), May 1971 and May 1972, all by John Lahr; "John Ford Noonan Dons Glad Rags at Stockton" by Noreen Turner, in *The Press* (Atlantic City, New Jersey), June 1989.

Theatrical Activities:
Director: **Play**—*Older People*, New York, 1972.
Actor: Since 1967 in summer stock, regional and off-Broadway theatres, and in television and films.

John Ford Noonan comments:
In *The Year Boston Won the Pennant*, Marcus Sykowski, a once legendary baseball pitcher who has mysteriously lost his glove arm and is now in search of a chrome limb to take its place, discusses pitching as follows:

I am a pitcher. Pitching is my job. I have lost an arm, but I will earn it back. I have science on my side. I'm no college man. I never got a degree. I am no thinker, no man whose job it is to lead or be understood. I am a pitcher. I stand on the mound. I hold the ball, smile, get the feel I'm ready. I rear, I fire, and that ball goes exactly where I tell it 'cause I tell it to, 'cause it was me who threw it, the great Sykowski. What else must they know. . . . One strike, two strikes, three strikes, four, five, six, seven, eight, nine . . . the whole side, 'cause when you're pouring rhythm sweet, when you got it, really got it, they can't see it, they can't smell it, they can't touch it, they can't believe it. . . . It's yours, all yours . . . it's magic.

I believe Marcus is speaking of more than throwing a baseball.

*   *   *

John Ford Noonan's plays veer in style from conventional realism to fantasy and contain a range of American character types from baseball players and firemen to transvestites, gangsters, old people, and deserted wives. They have earned Noonan critical and popular attention since his first full-length play's production in 1969. Themes interweaving his plays encompass Saroyanesque concern for the vulnerability of the world's little people and the need to help one another. While believing in the communion of saints, Noonan largely avoids sentimentality in his work and sees the dark forces lurking in the sunlight. Characters in early plays tend toward caricatures and are often enmeshed in conflicts with mythic implications.

His more recent work discloses characters of realistic dimension while thematically supporting W.H. Auden's thought that "we must love one another or die." *A Coupla White Chicks Sitting Around Talking*, Noonan's deservedly most popular work, is a two-character comedy effectively emphasizing that good can come from unlikely relationships. In Westchester County suburbia a prim WASP housewife, Maude Mix, angry and lost at the latest desertion by her philandering husband, finds herself called upon by Hannah Mae, a prying Texan wife and new next-door neighbor, who makes uninvited daily visits and offers practical but unwelcome advice after deducing Maude's situation. Maude cannot rid herself of the loud-mouth do-gooder even when she truthfully reports that Hannah's oafish husband has forced her into bed on a surprise visit. Hannah leaves her husband and moves in with Maude; a symbiotic friendship develops. Maude learns to accept her marriage's futility and regains self-esteem and the strength to go it alone, while Hannah returns to her now-penitent husband but promises to maintain daily visits to Maude. The comedy offers a perceptive look at two delightfully defined contemporary women undergoing loss and gain. Although differing in details, a reverse-gender repetition of the above play appears in the more recent but less successful *Some Men Need Help*. A career-disillusioned young WASP advertising executive, Singleton, deserted by his wife, is drowning himself in liquor and self-loathing in his Connecticut home when he is visited by an overbearing lower-class ex-Mafioso neighbor who inexplicably insists on saving him. Singleton cannot eject the unwelcome Good Samaritan, even with racist slurs, yet eventually is persuaded to undergo detoxification and to change his self-destructive attitude. While overly reminiscent of its predecessor, this well-intentioned comedy about two men who grow to like each other relays Noonan's message that help is possible when you love your neighbor.

More characteristic of his individual voice, Noonan's earlier plays are often less realistic in style and context than these later ones. *The Year Boston Won the Pennant* employs fantasy and Brechtian techniques to chronicle the odyssey through a callous society of the maimed baseball pitcher Marcus Sykowski, who wishes to regain his former fame and the ability he enjoyed before mysteriously losing his arm. Throughout 14 mockingly titled scenes, the impractical but courageously aspiring Sykowski visits family and friends seeking solace and money to buy a prosthetic limb, only bewilderingly to encounter attempted exploitation and unprovoked betrayal or violence, while at the same time an anti-war revolution occurs in the streets unnoticed by all. Constantly pursued by a mysteriously menacing gangster, Sykowski is assassinated when pitching a dream-like comeback game. The victimized hero seems to be a metaphor for a baffled, maimed Vietnam-era America self-destructively pursuing an impossible quest for lost prestige and driven by forces of greed and unconscionable irrationality. This dark comedy, sometimes ambiguously uneven in style and characterization, does more than confirm Leo Durocher's observation that "good guys finish last."

The hysteria and inclination toward fantasy of ordinary people are often subjects in Noonan's work of the 1970's. In *Rainbows for Sale*, a youthful firehouse custodian meets his older self to find him a deceased racist fireman who has gone on a maniacal shooting spree in an ethnic neighborhood. The play effectively mixes fantasy with forcibly graphic narrative. The difficulties of ageing are well represented with empathy and irony in *Older People*, a cycle of 15 sketch-like short plays with interludes of song—a Noonan characteristic—dealing with the new fears and waning sexual powers of the elderly. While the sketches range in quality, the work's contrast between its sad and wistful subject matter and its farcical form is engaging.

Concern with fantasy and the bizarre as well as domestic alienation is sustained in several Noonan plays of the 1980's, which tend to be less successful than earlier works. In *Talking Things Over with Chekhov*, a budding playwright has hallucinatory conversations with Chekhov about literary philosophy. The playwright renews a friendship with a former actress lover, desperate for a comeback after suffering a nervous breakdown, by offering her a starring role in his explicit autobiographical play about their past relationship. Her casting has been confirmed by a willing producer. However, when the playwright secures a more advantageous producer who will cast another actress, she is desolate despite the writer's claim that the play is the truly major star. The two-character piece begins awkwardly and totters between comedy and an uneven examination of obsession. *Listen to the Lions* deals with a Boston Irish family, peopled by insufficiently drawn yet colorful characters unable to relate to each other. *My Daddy's Serious American Gift* focuses on a girl who tells of having found her father dead in her home with a killer wanting her to call it suicide. The implausible story is not sufficiently rescued by its bizarre quality.

In a 1989 interview, Noonan claimed that a playwright has to listen to the child in himself and to write about things that pop into his head. That philosophy continues to be borne out, not always with success, in his work. Yet Noonan remains a talented dramatist with a zany, acerbic, and perceptive comic vision of the world. He continues to be an individual voice worthy of attention.

—Christian H. Moe

NORMAN, (John) Frank. British. 1930–1980.
See 2nd edition, 1977.

NORMAN, Marsha (née Williams). American. Born in Louisville, Kentucky, 21 September 1947. Educated at Durrett High School, Louisville; Agnes Scott College, Decatur, Georgia, B.A. in philosophy 1969; University of Louisville, 1969–71, M.A. 1971. Married 1) Michael Norman in 1969 (divorced 1974); 2) Dann C. Byck, Jr., in 1978 (divorced 1986); 3) Tim Dykma in 1987. Worked with disturbed children at Kentucky Central State Hospital, 1969–71; teacher, Brown School, Louisville, from 1973; book reviewer and editor of children's supplement (*Jelly Bean Journal*), Louisville *Times*, mid-1970's; playwright-in-residence, Actors Theatre, Louisville, 1977–78, and Mark Taper Forum, Los Angeles, 1979; since 1988 treasurer, the Dramatists Guild. Recipient: American Theater Critics Association prize, 1978; National Endowment for the Arts grant, 1978; Rockefeller grant, 1979; John Gassner award, 1979; Oppenheimer award, 1979; Susan Smith Blackburn prize, 1983; Pulitzer prize, 1983; American Academy award, 1986; Tony award, 1991. Lives in Long Island, New York. Agent: Jack Tantleff, The Tantleff Agency, 375 Greenwich Street, New York, New York 10013, U.S.A.

PUBLICATIONS

Plays

Getting Out (produced Louisville, 1977; New York, 1978; London, 1988). New York, Avon, 1980.
Third and Oak: The Laundromat (produced Louisville, 1978; New York, 1979). New York, Dramatists Play Service, 1980.
Third and Oak: The Pool Hall (produced Louisville, 1978). New York, Dramatists Play Service, 1985.
Circus Valentine (produced Louisville, 1979).
Merry Christmas, in *Holidays* (produced Louisville, 1979).
'Night, Mother (produced Cambridge, Massachusetts, 1982; New York, 1983; London, 1985). New York, Hill and Wang, 1983; London, Faber, 1984.
The Holdup (produced San Francisco, 1983). New York, Dramatists Play Service, 1987.
Traveler in the Dark (produced Cambridge, Massachusetts, 1984; revised version produced Los Angeles, 1985; New York, 1990).
Four Plays (includes *Getting Out, Third and Oak, The Holdup, Traveler in the Dark*). New York, Theatre Communications Group, 1988.
Sarah and Abraham (produced Louisville, 1988).
The Secret Garden, music by Lucy Simon, adaptation of the novel by Frances Hodgson Burnett (produced Norfolk, Virginia, 1990; New York, 1991).
D. Boone (produced Louisville, 1992).

Television Plays: *It's the Willingness* (*Visions* series), 1978; *In Trouble at Fifteen* (*Skag* series), 1980.

Novel

The Fortune Teller. New York, Random House, 1987; London, Collins, 1988.

*

Theatrical Activities:
Director: **Play**—*Semi-Precious Things* by Terri Wagener, Louisville, 1980.

* * *

"I know now, all these years and plays later, that I always write about solitary confinement." If this realisation only came to Marsha Norman with the anthologising of *Getting Out* in 1988, it also eluded critics who generalised on her early successes and tended to find a playwright grasping at various fragments of social significance and dissecting them within a broad spectrum of dramaturgic experimentation. Yet the focalising drive towards the character locked within herself certainly is a recurrent motif, and relates suggestively to another of Norman's statements quoted in *The Feminist Companion to Literature in English*: "What you cannot escape seeing is that we are all disturbed kids."

Norman's perception derives from her early experience working with disturbed children, partly at the Kentucky Central State Hospital, and is most obviously illustrated in *Getting Out*. But most of her plays take place at the intersection of the confined and the disturbed. *Third and Oak: The Laundromat* parodies the idea of "standing by your man" in its portrait of two women accidentally meeting in the middle of the night carrying shirts which are the relics of relationships they want to think still survive; but it ends with an assertion of the strength of solitude. If *The Holdup* presents itself as a parody of the frontier myth, it is also a study of a very naïve young man's detachment from a suffocating mother to a point of self-sufficient isolation. *Traveler in the Dark* is more complex in its structuring of relationships, but the same dynamics recur in the central character of Sam, the famous surgeon trying to place himself as father, husband, and son, fleeing back to his (now absent) mother when his professional skills leave him stranded and helpless beside a dying friend. But it is Norman's two full-length plays with female protagonists that most amply illustrate her skills at feminising and contemporising the problem play.

If the material of *Getting Out* sounds in synopsis rather like a case study with obvious elements of social didacticism, its technique is reminiscent of O'Neill's *Strange Interlude* in its schizoid presentation of the main character: the whole action follows the first day of notional freedom for Arlene, just released on parole after serving a murder sentence, but unable to detach from her "criminal" self, Angie, played by another actor. Detachment, however, is just the obverse of the integration she seeks into society, into a straight career, and into her fragmented family, but the quest for some kind of bonding is thwarted by the people she meets: her former pimp and her prison guard, both with an agenda of brutal exploitation, her mother who in effect rejects her, and her new neighbour, another ex-con who still carries the ambience of the prison with her. Instead, integration comes with the self she has tried to exorcise, and the play's ending has Arlie and Arlene laughing playfully together, an interesting anticipation of Caryl Churchill's finale to *Cloud Nine*.

Jessie Cates, whose suicide is the entire action of *'Night, Mother*, is a restatement and development of this integration. As the often-quoted introductory statement emphasises, she has only just got herself together: only in the last year has she "gained control of her own mind and body," and the choice of suicide is the triumphant result of that control. But in the period before that control, there is a quest for identity as daughter, wife, and mother, a search through pockets of silence most graphically illustrated by her epileptic fits. This abnormality, read as a biological deviance parallel to Arlie's anti-social propensities, means that Jessie too has constantly been generating her own state of solitary confinement.

Because they have both in different senses been "inside," Jessie and Arlene are both highly receptive to "reports" of the personal history that they have been out of touch with. The murder for which Angie was locked up is relayed back to her by people who saw it covered on television. Jessie wants to know what she, her other self, looks like during fits, and this is directly related to the search for control that is central to all of Norman's protagonists. Arlene's hunt for normal work will bring her to meet strangers who nevertheless know the television image of Arlie, a gaze as brutal, as impersonal, and as invasive as the thought of the two-way mirrors in the prison washrooms. The reductiveness of this is severe, a total denial of adult dignity, like Jessie regressing to a condition of infantile dependence when she wets herself during fits—and only knowing it has happened because others told her that they cleaned her up.

Such a crisis of identity reflects the blur of societal positioning that both women face. An absent father confronts them with an Oedipal/Electral ambiguity. Society tells both of them that they have failed as mothers of the sons who are having their own problems of integration. And both are threatened by the blackmail of dependence from one of Jane Gallop's "phallic mothers," through whom, in Luce Irigaray's terms, there is the prospect of "femininity" being "effaced to leave room for maternity"—especially as these mothers do not hesitate to hit them with evidence of their own incompetence as mothers. But in their ultimate refusal to disavow themselves in the face of such pressures, or to annihilate the "disturbed kid" in themselves and now in society at large, there is the defiant insistence that the dismantling of structures may not just be anarchic but may bring a more integrated sense of self—if, necessarily, in confinement. Jessie's final wish for her son may serve as Norman's final gloss on the anxieties of modern mothercraft: if he spends his inheritance on dope, she hopes it is at least good dope.

—Howard McNaughton.

NOWRA, Louis. Australian. Born in Melbourne, Victoria, in 1950. Educated at La Trobe University, Bundoora, Victoria. Married Sarah de Jong in 1974. Writer-in-residence, University of Queensland, Brisbane, 1979, Lighthouse Company, Adelaide, 1982, Playbox Theatre, Melbourne, 1985, and Capricornia Institute, 1987; associate artistic director, Sydney Theatre Company, 1980, and Lighthouse Company, 1983. Recipient: Australian Literature Board fellowship, 1975, 1977–79, 1981, 1983. Agent: Hilary Linstead and Associates, Suite 302, Easts Tower, 9–13 Bronte Road, Bondi Junction, New South Wales 2022, Australia.

PUBLICATIONS

Plays

Kiss the One-Eyed Priest (produced Melbourne, 1973).
Albert Names Edward (broadcast 1975; produced Melbourne, 1976). Radio version published in *Five Plays for Radio*, edited by Alrene Sykes, Sydney, Currency Press, 1976; stage version published with *Inner Voices*, Currency Press, 1983.
Inner Voices (produced Sydney, 1977; London, 1982). Sydney, Currency Press, 1978.
Visions (produced Sydney, 1978). Sydney, Currency Press, 1979.
The Lady of the Camellias, adaptation of a play by Dumas fils (produced Sydney, 1979).
Inside the Island (produced Sydney, 1980). With *The Precious Woman*, Sydney, Currency Press, 1981.
The Precious Woman (produced Sydney, 1980). With *Inside the Island*, Sydney, Currency Press, 1981.
Cyrano de Bergerac, adaptation of the play by Rostand (produced Sydney, 1980).
The Song Room (broadcast 1980). Stage version published in *Seven One-Act Plays*, edited by Rodney Fisher, Sydney, Currency Press, 1983.
Death of Joe Orton (produced Adelaide, 1980).
Beauty and the Beast (produced Sydney, 1980).
Lulu, adaptation of a play by Frank Wedekind (produced Adelaide, 1981).
Spellbound (produced Adelaide, 1982; London, 1986).
Royal Show (produced Adelaide, 1982).
The Prince of Homburg, adaptation of a play by Heinrich von Kleist (also director: produced Adelaide, 1982).
Sunrise (produced Adelaide, 1983). Sydney, Currency Press, 1983.
The Golden Age (produced Melbourne, 1985; Bristol, 1992). Sydney, Currency Press, 1985.
Whitsunday (opera), music by Brian Howard (produced Sydney, 1988).
Capricornia, adaptation of the novel by Xavier Herbert (produced Sydney, 1988). Sydney, Currency Press, 1988.
Byzantine Flowers (produced Sydney, 1989).
Summer of the Aliens (as *The Summer of the Aliens*, broadcast 1989; as *Summer of the Aliens* produced Melbourne, 1992). Sydney, Currency Press, 1992.
Cosi (produced Sydney, 1992). Sydney, Currency Press, 1992.

Radio Plays: *Albert Names Edward*, 1975; *The Song Room*, 1980; *The Widows*, 1986; *The Summer of the Aliens*, 1989.

Television Plays: *Displaced Persons*, 1985; *Hunger*, 1986; *The Lizard King*, 1987.

Novels

The Misery of Beauty: The Loves of Frogman. Sydney and London, Angus and Robertson, 1976.
Palu. Woollahara, New South Wales, Pan, 1987; New York, St. Martin's Press, 1989.

Other

Editor, *The Cheated*. Sydney, Angus and Robertson, 1979.

*

Critical Study: *Louis Nowra* edited by Veronica Kelly, Amsterdam, Rodopi, 1987.

Theatrical Activities:
Director: **Plays**—*The Prince of Homburg*, Adelaide, 1982; *The Marriage of Figaro* by Beaumarchais, Adelaide, 1983; *Not about Heroes* by Stephen MacDonald, Melbourne, 1985; *The Lighthouse* by Peter Maxwell Davies, Sydney, 1985.

* * *

Louis Nowra was born in a raw post-war suburb of outer Melbourne. His comic and savage theatrical parables obliquely image the cultural disjunctions of contemporary Australian experience. Yet his early plays puzzled some observers by being, it seemed, set in perversely exotic locales such as 18th-century Russia (*Inner Voices*) or Paraguay during the genocidal 1870's War of the Triple Alliance (*Visions*). With its violence, farce, and formal stylisation, his theatre presents a wry view of the savageries of "history," wherein the Australian working-class idiom and perspective of the characters remain nonetheless unmistakeable. Yet Nowra rejects the naturalistic style: "I was bemused by American and English naturalism which left me with the impression of whingeing men in grubby cardigans and women shouting at their husbands." Nor does he participate in the post-1970's tradition of Australian naturalism; finding it both theatrically and ideologically constricting. Concomitantly and despite stylistic similarities in his early writing, he resists assimilation with the Brechtian project, rejecting what he sees as its programmatic closure. His theatre owes more to expressionistic, mythical, and musical modes, offering an expansive, highly visual, and tonally mixed dramaturgy, through which the contradictions and decentred consciousness of a multicultural and multiracial society are explored with a complexity unequalled in contemporary Australian writing.

Ivan, true heir to the Russian throne (*Inner Voices*), has been imprisoned all his life in a fortress, knowing no language but his name. A bloody military coup precipitously releases Ivan into language; as puppet-tsar he is forced to mouth, with hilarious lack of politesse, political proclamations and trite Englightenment philosophy. As the pathetically stunted consciousness of Ivan struggles towards expression, he becomes a tyrant, mutilating and imprisoning his former tutors in an attempt to drown out the sound of what have now become his own truly inner voices. Finally Ivan is imprisoned anew, a solitary figure screaming for silence like an image in a Francis Bacon painting. The motifs of crippled, mute or aphasic characters, of language acquisition—and, by association, the process of cultural transmission—are insistent in Nowra's theatre and suggest a political dimension. "Teaching" is a power manoeuvre, neither disinterested nor innocuous. Later plays continue to explore the marginalised state of the postcolonial subject and his or her gradual emergence into a new hybridised and empowering consciousness, signified frequently by Nowra's most arresting literary device, the invention of powerful and poetic creolised speech registers.

Visions enlarges upon the anti-imperial theme of *Inner Voices*. It introduces the first of Nowra's many powerful female roles in Madame Lynch, dubiously Parisian courtesan now married to Lopez, military dictator of Paraguay. In this fantasia on historical themes, Lynch acts as the snobbish transmitter of *haute bourgeoise* European "culture" to a "backward" nation, an imposition which ends in their own overthrow at the cost of Paraguay's catastrophic military defeat. Juana the blind girl, a brutalised victim of the invasion, speaks of her mystical visions in a private language

which Lopez tries in vain to understand. As the first of Nowra's "Aboriginal" characters—figures whose dislocation and endurance embody the discursive position of black experience within white Australia—her fate here is to eventually parrot Lynch's visions of "culture." But in later plays, particularly *The Golden Age* and *Byzantine Flowers*, the colonised character, frequently of mixed racial origin, is able to transcend the brutalities of colonisation and use the language "taught" to her to speak her own visions and procure her own autonomy.

In 1980 Nowra shocked some and delighted others by setting *Inside the Island* actually in Australia, albeit in the past. The time is 1912, three years before Gallipoli, the location a remote wheat property whose semi-feudal social relations, based on a suppressed history of black dispossession, are apocalyptically disrupted when a squad of young visiting soldiers are infected by ergotism and run wild in a destructive orgy. The poison in the flour—a common method of massacre of Aboriginals—is the unwitting gift of the matriarch Lillian Dawson, who believes that off-white flour is good enough for working-class lads for their "civilised" picnic and cricket match. Expressionistic images of white flannels streaked in blood, of raging bushfires and violent self-mutilation show the eruption both of the suppressed past and of the immediate future, since the imagery of the ergotism scene draws on accounts of the hell of the Somme offensive: the poisoned legacy is and remains imperialism. A more recent version of Australia's client-state status is central to *Sunrise* the first of Nowra's plays to utilise extensively his somewhat paradoxical appreciation of high-style comedy of manners. Bourgeois rituals are wittily exposed at the Easter gathering of a privileged Adelaide family, whose various guilts and nightmares include collaboration in the 1950's British nuclear tests at Maralinga. Again, a purgative bushfire threatens the resurgence of a violent past in a society which attempts to forget history.

Probably Nowra's most engaging and resonant play, *The Golden Age* examines Tasmanian history through the discovery in 1939 of a "lost" tribe of whites, descended from convict outcasts and speaking a richly earthy patois. Because of their inbred genetic degeneration, the clan's matriarch bravely decides to seek reintegration with the world of "rack 'n' cat" which had so savagely exiled their ancestors. Once in Hobart, however, they are confined in a lunatic asylum, in the politically expedient belief that they provide evidence for Nazi eugenicism. This incarceration obviously alludes to the last Tasmanian Aboriginals, imprisoned last century in these same grim convict remnants. The play's ending is ambiguous. Betsheb, the last survivor, is returned to her forest home, but her lover Francis, the traumatised soldier, may not be able to survive there with her. In a powerful ending, Betsheb promises "Nowt more outcastin'."

In his adaptation of Xavier Herbert's novel *Capricornia*, in *Byzantine Flowers*, and his Bicentennial opera *Whitsunday*, Nowra further empowers his part-Aboriginal or Kanak heroine. In the case of the two latter pieces, by using the powers of love, sexual charisma, or survival cunning, she comes into her own inheritance and begins to restore to her world something of what has been lost. Most recently, Nowra has mined a rich vein of overtly semi-autobiographical writing, where the Australian tradition of the yarn mixes painfully with wildly comic situations. The engaging *Summer of the Aliens*, the first of a projected trilogy, shows Lewis at the age of 14 trying to understand his own emotions plus a bizarre-seeming array of his family's and neighbour's activities. Perhaps they have been taken over by aliens from UFOs, he surmises, though he comes to realise that such perturbing behaviour is merely an attribute of humanity, himself included. Its sequel *Cosi* has the now 21-year-old drop-out directing Mozart's opera—without the music—for the inhabitants of a mental institution. An extended homage to the refined style of its model, despite the black humour, *Cosi* is a witty example of the in-joke rehearsal play genre. It presents humanity as pitifully fragile, sometimes appalling, but always spiritually resilient; an endless source of delight and dismay which dogmas cannot easily contain.

—Veronica Kelly

————

NUGENT, Elliott (John). American. 1899–1980. See 2nd edition, 1977.

————

O

O'MALLEY, Mary (Josephine). British. Born in Bushey, Hertfordshire, 19 March 1941. Resident writer, Royal Court Theatre, London, 1977. Recipient: *Evening Standard* award, 1978; Susan Smith Blackburn prize, 1978; *Plays and Players* award; Pye award, for television play. Address: c/o Salmon Publishing, The Bridge Mills, Galway, Republic of Ireland.

PUBLICATIONS

Plays

Superscum (produced London, 1972).
A 'nevolent Society (produced London, 1974).
Oh If Ever a Man Suffered (produced London, 1975).
Once a Catholic (produced London, 1977; New York, 1979). Ashover, Derbyshire, Amber Lane Press, and New York, French, 1978.
Look Out . . . Here Comes Trouble (produced London, 1978). Ashover, Derbyshire, Amber Lane Press, 1979.
Talk of the Devil (produced Watford, Hertfordshire, 1986; revised version produced Bristol, 1986).

Television Plays: *Percy and Kenneth*, 1976; *Oy Vay Maria*, 1977; *Shall I See You Now?*, 1978; *On the Shelf*, 1984.

Other

A Consideration of Silk. Galway, Salmon Publishing, 1990.

* * *

Mary O'Malley came into the public eye with her mischievous play *Once a Catholic*, which premiered at the Royal Court Theatre in 1977, and then transferred to the West End. The play won awards from the London *Evening Standard* and *Plays and Players*. The play is a warm but sharply retrospective look at a Catholic girls' convent in the 1950's, with the youth rebellion of that decade given added edge by the repressiveness of the nuns. All the girls are called "Mary," and the play is a witty and perceptive extended sit-com, which is such good fun that it would undoubtedly offend no-one. In its way it even was able to test the taboos of the commercial theatre, in a scene where one of the shocked nuns discovers a packet of Tampax hidden in the lavatory, and a final act of sacrilege when one of the girls affixes a plasticine penis to a statue of Christ in the school chapel—for which Mary the scape-goat (the only one who genuinely wants to become a nun) is blamed.

There is a satirical edge to O'Malley's writing which derives from a sensitivity to the very ordinary pains and ironies of daily life—and also to the iconography of domestic experience, which is so important to people. This latter was the main feature of her play *Look Out . . . Here Comes Trouble*, staged by the Royal Shakespeare Company at the Warehouse in London in 1978. The play was set in a psychiatric ward, but

floundered in the material detail, and although the comic pain was a feature in the lives of the characters, it never became part of the structural fabric of the play. Somehow O'Malley appears to be caught between the potentialities of a more ruthless satirical approach and a familiar, lightly comic sit-com approach.

—Michelene Wandor

————

O'NEILL, Michael. British. Educated at Northampton Grammar School; Cambridge University. Teacher. Agent: Curtis Brown, 162–168 Regent Street, London W1R 5TB, England.

PUBLICATIONS

Plays (with Jeremy Seabrook)

Life Price (produced London, 1969).
Morality (produced London, 1971).
Millennium (produced London, 1973).
Our Sort of People (produced London, 1974).
Sex and Kinship in a Savage Society (produced London, 1975).
Sharing (produced London, 1980).
Black Man's Burden (produced London, 1980).

Radio Plays: *The Bosom of the Family*, 1975; *Living Private*, 1978; *Our Children's Children*, 1980; *Life Skills*, 1985.

Television Plays: *Skin Deep*, 1971; *Soap Opera in Stockwell*, 1973; *Highway Robbery*, 1973; *A Clear Cut Case*, 1973; *A Stab in the Front*, 1973; *Children of the Sun*, 1975; *Beyond the Call of Duty* (*Crown Court series*), 1976; *A State of Welfare*.

* * *

It was Genet whose beliefs about society radically changed when he discovered that, according to the most advanced and accurate statistics available, the percentage of criminals remained the same whichever class or system held power at a particular moment. Michael O'Neill and Jeremy Seabrook's early work suffers from the widespread delusion that it is only as a result of capitalism, the "ceaseless gutting of their body and spirit in the name of enterprise, profits, efficiency," that

499

there is a social sediment at the bottom of society, providing both aggressors and victims for horrible crime. For in their first performed play, *Life Price*, the pre-destined victim, Debbie, and the typical child murderer, George Reginald Dunkley, are both observed against a landscape of "neglected mounds of detritus, crumbling terraces, derelict buildings, and the housing estate itself, all cabbage-stalks and dilapidated creosote fences, maculated concrete, rusting bed-springs and motor-bikes, dead chrysanthemums and dingy paintwork."

A State of Welfare, a television play, is a much better organized work about an American scent spray firm moving into England, and its impact on the household of an average worker. Here the theme of a working-class boy bettering himself, by taking French lessons with an executive's wife, and so coming into conflict with his father—the two sides of industry get together over dinner in a powerful scene reminiscent of Ibsen's *The League of Youth*—forms a substantial and colourful central thread.

Morality is an even more domestic story than *A State of Welfare*. A family called the Pargeters are trying to make their son Nick "get on" by passing his A-level exams and winning a place at university. When it is discovered that Nick is having a homosexual affair with his progressive and sensitive teacher, Larry, the family is up in arms at the scandal this will cause in the neighbourhood. However, when Nick's parents manage to summon up the courage to go and see Larry, Larry calms them down with a hypocritical assertion of "morality." The psychology—and morality—may be crude compared with other plays about divided loyalty, but *Morality* is a lively portrayal of family conflict. As in *Life Price* the authors would seem to be saying it is society which is to blame for the cynicism and destructiveness of young people towards their elders. This is an attitude supported by concrete, almost documentary writing, not by the continual assertion of a doctrinaire point of view.

In *Millennium*, set in a semi-detached house on a Northampton estate, there's a gap of 53 years between the first part and the second. The authors present for comparison the life-style of Florrie's family, and that of Doll her grand-daughter, in a broader and more sentimental way than in the earlier plays. In Florrie's family one of the girls is dying of scarlet fever, while about her rage the violences of poverty, the stringencies of life caused by the father's status as a hired man. The rebel son, common to both generations, in the first part merely burns his sister's boots (cost, 8/6), while in the second he has, as part of a gang, tied up a boy, cut his hair, and tried to extort money from his parents. The boot-burning satisfies the instinct for anger at the circumstances, and it is punished and purged within the family unit. The second misdemeanour is a matter for the courts, showing the impersonality of justice and how the family has broken down. The time gap achieves a neat and forceful comparison.

Dramatically striking, too, is the Pirandellian twist by which Florrie's family advance on their petty-minded materialist descendants and engage in a battle of wits. The author's sympathies clearly lie with the earlier brood, on whom a huddled statuesque dignity is conferred. Grim and monochrome as they appear, they have the virtue of discipline and look to the after-life for their reward.

Sex and Kinship in a Savage Society is a less successful treatment of the same theme of family disintegration. In *Black Man's Burden* the family is Jamaican. We hear imposing astral voices with Jamaican accents telling the heroine Melvita her child-to-be is the New Messiah. The family settles in England and the problems of assimilating such a striking notion into a society with a National Health service intent on

imposing its own solution on visionaries gives the authors opportunity, once more, for striking contrasts, this time comic, beguiling speech rhythms, and exact evocations of place.

—Garry O'Connor

O'SULLIVAN, Vincent (Gerald). New Zealander. Born in Auckland, 28 September 1937. Educated at University of Auckland, M.A. 1959; Lincoln College, Oxford, B.Litt. 1962. Married. Editor, *Comment*, 1963–66, and literary editor, New Zealand *Listener*, 1978–79, both Wellington; lecturer, Victoria University, Wellington, 1963–66; senior lecturer, 1965–75, and reader, 1977–78, Waikato University, Hamilton; visiting fellow, Yale University, New Haven, Connecticut, 1976; writer-in-residence, Victoria University, 1981, University of Tasmania, Hobart, 1982, and Deakin University, Geelong, Victoria, 1982; playwright-in-residence, Downstage Theatre, Wellington, 1983; ARGS research fellow, Flinders University of South Australia, Bedford Park, 1984–86; writer-in-residence, University of Queensland, St. Lucia, 1987. Since 1988 professor of English, Victoria University, Wellington. Recipient: Commonwealth scholarship, 1960; Macmillan Brown prize, 1961; Jessie MacKay award, 1965; Farmers poetry prize, 1967, 1971; Fulbright award, 1976; Wattie Book award, 1979; New Zealand Book award, 1981. Address: c/o John McIndoe Ltd., 51 Crawford Street, P.O. Box 694, Dunedin, New Zealand.

PUBLICATIONS

Plays

Shuriken (produced Wellington, 1983). Wellington, Victoria University Press, 1985.
Ordinary Nights in Ward Ten (produced Wellington, 1984).
Jones and Jones (produced Wellington, 1988). Wellington, Victoria University Press, 1989.
Billy (produced Wellington, 1989). Wellington, Victoria University Press, 1990.
Cobbers (as *The Lives and Loves of Harry and George*, produced Wellington, 1990).

Novel

Miracle: A Romance. Dunedin, McIndoe, 1976.

Short Stories

The Boy, the Bridge, the River. Dunedin, McIndoe, 1978.
Dandy Edison for Lunch and Other Stories. Dunedin, McIndoe, 1981.
Survivals. Wellington, Port Nicholson Press, 1985.
The Snow in Spain. Wellington, Allen and Unwin, 1990.

Verse

Our Burning Time. Wellington, Prometheus, 1965.
Revenants. Wellington, Prometheus, 1969.
Bearings. Wellington and London, Oxford University Press, 1973.

From the Indian Funeral. Dunedin, McIndoe, 1976.
Butcher & Co. Wellington, Oxford University Press, 1977; London, Oxford University Press, 1978.
Brother Jonathan, Brother Kafka. Wellington and Oxford, Oxford University Press, 1980.
The Rose Ballroom and Other Poems. Dunedin, McIndoe, 1982.
The Butcher Papers. Auckland, Oxford University Press, 1986.
The Pilate Tapes. Auckland, Oxford University Press, 1986.

Other

New Zealand Poetry in the Sixties. Wellington, Department of Education, 1973.
Katherine Mansfield's New Zealand. Melbourne, Lloyd O'Neal, 1974; London, Muller, 1975.
James K. Baxter. Wellington, Oxford University Press, 1976; London, Oxford University Press, 1977.
Finding the Pattern, Solving the Problem: Katherine Mansfield the New Zealand European (lecture). Wellington, Victoria University Press, 1989.

Editor, *An Anthology of Twentieth-Century New Zealand Poetry*. London, Oxford University Press, 1970; revised edition, Wellington and London, Oxford University Press, 1976; revised edition, 1987.
Editor, *New Zealand Short Stories 3*. Wellington, Oxford University Press, 1975; London, Oxford University Press, 1976.
Editor, *The Aloe, with Prelude*, by Katherine Mansfield. Wellington, Port Nicholson Press, 1982; Manchester, Carcanet, and Atlantic Highlands, New Jersey, Humanities Press, 1983.
Editor, with M.P. Jackson, *New Zealand Writing Since 1945*. Auckland, Oxford University Press, 1983.
Editor, with Margaret Scott, *The Collected Letters of Katherine Mansfield 1: 1903–1917*. Oxford and New York, Oxford University Press, 1984; *2: 1918–1919*, 1987.
Editor, *Collected Poems*, by Ursula Bethell. Auckland, Oxford University Press, 1985.
Editor, *The Poems of Katherine Mansfield*. Auckland, Oxford University Press, 1988.
Editor, *Selected Letters by Katherine Mansfield*. Oxford, Clarendon Press, 1989.

*   *   *

Vincent O'Sullivan's early poems—especially the *Butcher & Co.* sequences—demonstrated his gift for characterisation, and it was not surprising that he should eventually turn his attention to the stage.

In at least two respects his first play, *Shuriken*, established a pattern for most of his subsequent work. Like *Billy* and the as yet unproduced *Yellow Brides* (which treats love in much the same way as *Shuriken* treats war), it dramatises a clash between white Antipodean society and the indigenous cultures of the Pacific Rim. And, like all his plays, it exhibits some inventive mixing of theatrical modes.

Shuriken focuses on a fatal clash in a New Zealand prisoner-of-war camp for the Japanese in 1943. The prisoners and their minders inhabit different worlds, with only Tiny (the camp interpreter) and "Charlie" (the most tractable of the Japanese) capable of any movement between the two. The Camp Commandant characterises the difference as one between "thinking white and thinking yellow." Tiny sums it up less colourfully:

The point is we can see history in two ways. . . . There's the bird's eye view that gives you the grand scale. The sweep of time where none of us individually matters a damn. . . . The Japs stand for [this view]. We stand for the opposite. . . . We don't think about history. We think about us.

Not surprisingly, then, the Japanese see their captors as:

a group of men. . ., with no memory of the past, no sense of destiny for the future, a present defined by what? A certain number of sheep, a full stomach, a King on the other side of the world who regards your dead as his right. A king who is a man like yourselves.

The Japanese Emperor is, of course, a god, and the Japanese prisoners' loyalty to him, coupled with their proud military tradition and their lack of concern for the individual, precludes any acceptance of defeat, surrender, or imprisonment. This intransigence leads eventually to the fatal showdown with their reluctant and uncomprehending captors. To accentuate the prisoners' proud sense of their culture, O'Sullivan builds certain Japanese theatrical conventions into the play—notably a snatch of Nō drama, featuring the spirit of a dead prisoner in Act I.

The New Zealanders, "lost in the featureless landscape of a world without history" (as one reviewer put it), lack such distinctive cultural forms, and tend to lapse into the imported idiom of music hall for their more stylised moments. But one character among them—the Maori soldier, Tai—does have an authentic culture, to which he gives memorable expression at the end of Act I, where he delivers a moving elegy—"both a soliloquy and a traditional Maori lament"—for his brother-in-law, killed in battle by the Japanese.

Tai remains rather on the fringe of the action in *Shuriken*, but in *Billy* O'Sullivan puts an Aboriginal character (loosely modelled on the famous Bennelong) firmly at the centre of things. The play opens with a beautifully contrived image of the colonisation of Australia. The principals enter one by one, and remove dust-covers "suggesting mounds, hillocks etc." from the furniture, thus transforming an Australian landscape into a Victorian drawing-room. The ensuing colonial ensemble eventually breaks down into a series of fragmentary scenes in which the Europeans one by one encounter Billy, who, being (unlike Bennelong) a deaf-mute, serves as "the Other" by which they define themselves. As one character puts it, "I am looking at something so empty, so foreign to me, that I only see back myself."

Through Billy's mime, some startling sound effects (e.g. the "clamour of magpies"), and a few vignettes of minor (mainly Irish) characters, a picture of a more authentic Australia slowly emerges, but, apart from one highly stylised scene in which Elizabeth acts as Billy's mouthpiece, this Australia remains below the symbolic threshold of language —as the final stage-direction indicates:

With the spot narrowing to his face, [Billy] opens his mouth, straining to utter some sound. It is painful, guttural, perhaps slowly developing into a painful scream. He sinks to his knees, still making this protracted sound. It is accompanied by or taken over by the sound of a didgeridoo. The lights snap back on, into mid-party. BILLY is still kneeling on the floor, the others dance gaily about him, a jig or reel.

Billy, like *Shuriken*, grafts stylised sequences of one kind or another onto a realistic base. O'Sullivan's other plays employ this same formula, generally drawing on music hall for the stylised episodes. *Jones and Jones*, the best—and (since O'Sullivan is a noted Mansfield scholar) the most authoritative—of the plays spawned by the centenary of Katherine Mansfield's birth, makes a particularly apt use of music hall. In his Author's Note, O'Sullivan explains that his intention was "to present something that was faithful to my idea of the kind of woman she was, and yet to avoid any suggestions of 'naturalism' or stage biography. I took my lead from her own passion for music hall."

The play charts the relationship between Mansfield and Ida Baker, with cameo roles for a number of other notables, including D.H. Lawrence, who at one point "enters through a trap in the floor . . . wearing a miner's helmet." The stolid character of Baker often provides a linking device for the stylised antics of the others, but by the end Mansfield too is wanting to leave the superficial world of music hall behind; she "wouldn't mind being real . . . for a change," and, as she sets out on her fateful final voyage to Fontainebleau, her husband, John Middleton Murry, comments, "She thinks the only way to truth is through shedding our false selves." Her own last speech expresses a wish "to become so simple that the light shines through me."

This development from role-playing to sincerity is in effect reversed in *Cobbers*. The play works backwards through the lives of two men who have lived together since their 20's. Initially they appear to be harmless old codgers, whose fondness for music hall merely underlines their appealing eccentricity. But the play eventually reveals that they are—and always have been—ruthlessly exploitative and manipulative. As with Mansfield, a love of music hall becomes in effect a metaphor for heartlessness.

O'Sullivan's best plays seldom range beyond this blend of realism and music hall, but he is certainly capable of a wider range of styles. *Ordinary Nights in Ward Ten*, an obscure allegory of love and time, is bewilderingly eclectic, while *Kurtspiel* (as yet unproduced) uses Brechtian techniques effectively—especially in the first act—to depict the career of Kurt Weill.

—Richard Corballis

OGUNYEMI, Wale. Nigerian. Born in Igbajo, Oyo State in 1939. Member, Orisun Theatre, Ibadan, and University of Ibadan Theatre Arts Company; senior artist and writer, Institute of African Studies, University of Ibadan; writer-in-residence, the Workshop Theatre, University of Leeds, 1974–75; deputy project director, Unibadan Masques, Ibadan, 1976. Recipient: Nigerian Writers Guild award, 1982; University of California African Arts award. Address: c/o Institute of African Studies, University of Ibadan, Ibadan, Nigeria, West Africa.

PUBLICATIONS

Plays

Business Headache (produced Ibadan, n.d.). Oshobogo, Adeyeye Print, 1966.
The Scheme (produced Ibadan, 1967). Published in *Three Nigerian Plays*, edited by Ulli Beier, London, Longman, 1967.
Be Mighty Be Mine (produced Ibadan, 1968). Published in *Nigeria Magazine* (Lagos), no.97, 1968.

Eshu Elegbara (produced Ibadan, 1968). Ibadan, Orisun, 1970.
Aare Akogun, adaptation of *Macbeth* by Shakespeare (produced Ibadan, 1968).
Obaluaye (musical; produced Ibadan, 1968). Ibadan, Institute of African Studies, University of Ibadan, 1972.
Ijaye War (produced Ibadan, n.d.). Ibadan, Orisun, 1970.
Kiriji (produced Ibadan, 1971). Lagos, African Universities Press, 1976.
The Vow (produced Ibadan, 1972). London, Macmillan, 1985.
The Divorce (produced Ibadan, 1975). Ibadan, Onibonoje Press, 1977.
Langbodo, adaptation of a work by D.O. Fagunwa (produced Lagos, 1977; London, 1984). Lagos, Nelson, 1979.
Eniyan, adaptation of *Everyman* (produced Ibadan, 1982). Ibadan, Ibadan University Press, 1987.
The Sign of the Rainbow (produced Ibadan, n.d.).

Television Plays: *Be Mighty Be Mine*, 1968; *For Better for Worse* series; *Bello's Way* series, *Cock Crow at Dawn* series, 1978–82.

Radio Play: *We Can Always Create*.

*   *   *

Wale Ogunyemi combines live theatre practice with television and radio drama and is one of the most versatile theatre practitioners in contemporary Nigeria. Yet his dramatic texts have received very little critical attention, ironically for the very reason that they are popular with audiences—they are not exotic literary texts. Ogunyemi may be categorised as a transitional dramatist who occupies a critical watershed between the populist vernacular folk drama pioneered by Ogunde and developed by Duro Ladipo, Moses Olaiya, Kola Ogunmola, and the 200 or more Yoruba travelling theatres on the one hand, and on the other, the consciously exotic literary dramatic enterprises of English expression pioneered by James Ene Henshaw but gaining stature through Wole Soyinka, J.P. Clark, Ola Rotimi and the generation of emergent dramatists. It is for this reason that Ogunyemi's drama belongs more with total theatre (combining dance, music, spectacle, and dialogue) than with "profound" dramatic texts.

Among Ogunyemi's most popular subjects are traditions and myths, and conflict, both of values and of cultures. They also include history and social satire. Of his published texts, his major plays include *The Vow*, *The Scheme*, and *Obaluaye*, which deal with value conflict; *Ijaye War* and *Kiriji*, both historical dramas; *The Divorce*, and his television serials *For Better for Worse* and *Bello's Way*, all offering commentary on social and domestic problems in contemporary Nigerian society. His most accomplished play to date, at least at the level of craft and dramaturgy, is his play *Langbodo*, Nigeria's major dramatic entry for the 1977 Second World Black and African Festival of Arts and Culture (FESTAC). It is a dramatization of Wole Soyinka's novel *Forest of a Thousand Demons*, imaginatively translated from the Yoruba classical novelist D.O. Fagunwa's work *Ogboju Ode Ninu Igbo Irunmale*. It is a play in the heroic quest tradition, adapted into a nationalist journey towards social redemption from decadence, corruption, and malaise. Ogunyemi also adapted Shakespeare's *Macbeth* as *Aare Akogun* for the Nigerian stage.

The Vow contrasts indigenous African values with the so-called modern European values. This, of course, is an overtrodden dramatic path in Nigeria. On the level of plot, an ultra-conservative king sets out to thwart his western-educated son's plan to marry a foreign girl who already carries his child, and to force him to accept a pre-arranged partner in accordance with "our grandfathers' ways." Tension mounts as both father and son are rigidly committed to their convictions. Fearing disgrace, the father employs charm, which backfires and leads to his committing suicide. An atmosphere of tragedy surrounds the king but as a tragic figure he lacks the depth of character and complexity that could secure audience sympathy. The verse of the play is thin and the dialogue lacks the subtlety and richness of diction required of tragedy.

In *Obaluaye*, Ogunyemi utilizes the techniques of Yoruba folk drama to demonstrate how individual protagonists in a society in a state of cultural flux can avert tragedy through syncretic accommodation of indigenous African and Western Christian religions. *Obaluaye* narrates a story of a village head, Baalé, who, being a Christian convert, treats his native traditions and customs with neglect and contempt. He refuses, and urges his people to refuse, to worship the gods of the land. The gods' anger is manifested in the visitation of the Smallpox King, Soponna, and the disease plagues the whole community with widespread mortal consequences. Baalé's recommendation of increased vaccination proves abortive and Baalé himself falls victim of Obaluaye's curse. He dies, and is resurrected by an Ifa priest. Baalé performs the required rites and pledges to observe them regularly. The King and the land gain expiation and the moral is drawn: "Christianity does not say we shouldn't observe tradition." The play is realised mainly through music and dance.

The second category of Ogunyemi's drama embraces historical themes. *Ijaye War* and *Kiriji* portray fratricide among the Yorubas of Nigeria in the 18th and 19th centuries. *Ijaye War* represents the ceaseless battles among the Yoruba in the 1860's, referred to as the Ijaye-Ibadan Wars, which eventually fragmented the old Oyo Empire. Alafin Atiba defies age-old tradition by making the king-makers approve his appointment of his first son, Adelu, his successor. Even though his stated aim is to prevent the usual interminable crisis over succession, tradition holds that the crown prince die with the king, not succeed him. The next in succession protests at this breach with tradition but it is the fierce opposition of Kurunmi, the Aare Ona Kakanfo (generalissimo) of Oyo and the Lord of Ijaye, that culminates in the next round of wars. Kurunmi says tradition is inviolable and must be protected, and thus challenges Adelu's ascension to the throne. Adelu gains the support of Ibadan, while, as he gathers his forces, Kurunmi receives an ally in the Egba people. In the battle that ensues, Kurunmi loses his five highly-valued sons and deeply grieved, he commits suicide. The play maintains extreme fidelity to actual history, but to such an extent that it is ultimately a reconstruction of historical events rather than a creative work of imagination.

The same criticism can be applied to *Kiriji*, which dramatises the late 19th-century revolt of the Ekiti and Ijesha people against the tyrannical imperialism of Ibadan, represented in the play by Aare Latosa and his inexhaustible appetite for new territories. The war ends in stalemate, and the epilogue represents a peace agreement via a mutually convenient truce. There is not much, beyond spectacle and effective depiction of battles on stage, of dramatic quality requiring special mention in the play.

Langbodo is, no doubt, the most deserving of critical attention of Ogunyemi's plays. The play is artistically profound and technically rewarding. It is a play of epic proportions encompassing all the major political cultures in Nigeria, and all the ethno-linguistic sectors of Nigerian society. In terms of dramaturgy, the play combines the forms of song, dance, narration, audience participation, and mime. A journey motif is embodied in the seven leading hunters who are asked by the king to undertake a journey to Mount Langbodo in the depths of the forest of demons and bring back peace and plenty for their people. The journey symbolises a quest for the social regeneration and redemption sorely needed in a society in the throes of decadence and socio-spiritual ennui, such as Nigeria was at the time the play was produced.

Ogunyemi is a brilliant actor and director, yet his plays, with their improvisational bent, need greater depth of vision and subtlety of diction if they are to achieve an enduring value and aesthetic significance.

—Olu Obafemi

* * *

OSBORNE, John (James). English. Born in London, 12 December 1929. Educated at Belmont College, Devon. Married 1) Pamela Lane in 1951 (marriage dissolved 1957); 2) the actress Mary Ure in 1957 (marriage dissolved 1963); 3) the writer Penelope Gilliatt in 1963 (marriage dissolved 1968), one daughter; 4) the actress Jill Bennett in 1968 (marriage dissolved 1977); 5) Helen Dawson in 1978. Journalist, 1947–48; toured as an actor, 1948–49; actor-manager, Ilfracombe Repertory, 1951; also in repertory, as actor and stage manager, in Leicester, Derby, Bridgewater, and London; co-director, Woodfall Films, from 1958; director, Oscar Lewenstein Plays Ltd., London, from 1960. Member of the Council, English Stage Company, London, 1960–82. Recipient: *Evening Standard* award, 1956, 1965, 1968; New York Drama Critics Circle award, 1958, 1965, Tony award, 1963; Oscar, for screenplay, 1964; Writers Guild Macallan award, for lifetime achievement, 1992. Honorary Doctor: Royal College of Art, London, 1970. Member, Royal Society of Arts. Address: c/o Faber and Faber Ltd., 3 Queen Square, London WC1N 3AU, England.

PUBLICATIONS

Plays

The Devil Inside Him, with Stella Linden (produced Huddersfield, Yorkshire, 1950).
Personal Enemy, with Anthony Creighton (produced Harrogate, Yorkshire, 1955).
Look Back in Anger (produced London, 1956; New York, 1957). London, Faber, and New York, Criterion, 1957.
The Entertainer, music by John Addison (produced London, 1957; New York, 1958). London, Faber, 1957; New York, Criterion, 1958.
Epitaph for George Dillon, with Anthony Creighton (produced Oxford, 1957; London and New York, 1958). London, Faber, and New York, Criterion, 1958.
The World of Paul Slickey, music by Christopher Whelen (also director: produced Bournemouth and London, 1959). London, Faber, 1959; New York, Criterion, 1961.
A Subject of Scandal and Concern (as *A Matter of Scandal and Concern*, televised 1960; as *A Subject of Scandal and Concern*, produced Nottingham, 1962; New York, 1966).

London, Faber, 1961; Chicago, Dramatic Publishing Company, 1971.

Luther (produced Nottingham and London, 1961; New York, 1963). London, Faber, 1961; New York, Criterion, 1962.

Plays for England: The Blood of the Bambergs, Under Plain Cover (produced London, 1962; New York, 1964–65). London, Faber, 1963; New York, Criterion, 1964.

Tom Jones: A Film Script. London, Faber, 1964; New York, Grove Press, 1965.

Inadmissible Evidence (produced London, 1964; New York, 1965). London, Faber, and New York, Grove Press, 1965.

A Patriot for Me (produced London, 1965; New York, 1969). London, Faber, 1966; New York, Random House, 1970.

A Bond Honoured, adaptation of a play by Lope de Vega (produced London, 1966). London, Faber, 1966.

The Hotel in Amsterdam (produced London, 1968). With *Time Present*, London, Faber, 1968; in *Four Plays*, 1973.

Time Present (produced London, 1968). With *The Hotel in Amsterdam*, London, Faber, 1968; in *Four Plays*, 1973.

The Right Prospectus (televised 1970). London, Faber, 1970.

Very Like a Whale (televised 1980). London, Faber, 1971.

West of Suez (produced London, 1971). London, Faber, 1971; in *Four Plays*, 1973.

Hedda Gabler, adaptation of the play by Ibsen (produced London, 1972; Abingdon, Virginia, 1982). London, Faber, 1972; Chicago, Dramatic Publishing Company, 1974.

The Gift of Friendship (televised 1972). London, Faber, 1972.

A Sense of Detachment (produced London, 1972). London, Faber, 1973.

Four Plays: West of Suez, A Patriot for Me, Time Present, The Hotel in Amsterdam. New York, Dodd Mead, 1973.

A Place Calling Itself Rome, adaptation of *Coriolanus* by Shakespeare. London, Faber, 1973.

The Picture of Dorian Gray: A Moral Entertainment, adaptation of the novel by Oscar Wilde (produced London, 1975). London, Faber, 1973.

Jill and Jack (as *Ms.; or, Jill and Jack*, televised 1974). With *The End of Me Old Cigar*, London, Faber, 1975.

The End of Me Old Cigar (produced London, 1975). With *Jill and Jack*, London, Faber, 1975.

Watch It Come Down (produced London, 1976). London, Faber, 1975.

You're Not Watching Me, Mummy (televised 1980). With *Try a Little Tenderness*, London, Faber, 1978.

A Better Class of Person (An Extract of Autobiography for Television), and God Rot Tunbridge Wells. London, Faber, 1985.

The Father, adaptation of a play by Strindberg (produced London, 1989). With *Hedda Gabler*, London, Faber, 1989.

Déjàvu (produced London, 1992). London, Faber, 1992.

Screenplays: *Look Back in Anger*, with Nigel Kneale, 1959; *The Entertainer*, with Nigel Kneale, 1960; *Tom Jones*, 1963; *Inadmissible Evidence*, 1968; *The Charge of the Light Brigade*, with Charles Wood, 1968.

Television Plays: *Billy Bunter*, 1952, and *Robin Hood*, 1953 (*For the Children* series); *A Matter of Scandal and Concern*, 1960; *The Right Prospectus*, 1970; *The Gift of Friendship*, 1972; *Ms.; or, Jill and Jack*, 1974; *Almost a Vision*, 1976; *You're Not Watching Me, Mummy*, 1980; *Very Like a Whale*,

1980; *A Better Class of Person*, 1985; *God Rot Tunbridge Wells*, 1985.

Other

A Better Class of Person: An Autobiography 1929–1956. London, Faber, and New York, Dutton, 1981.

Too Young to Fight, Too Old to Forget. London, Faber, 1985.

Almost a Gentleman: An Autobiography 1956–1966. London, Faber, 1991.

*

Bibliography: *John Osborne: A Reference Guide* by Cameron Northouse and Thomas P. Walsh, Boston, Hall, 1974.

Critical Studies: *Anger and After* by John Russell Taylor, London, Methuen, 1962, revised edition, 1969, as *The Angry Theatre*, New York, Hill and Wang, 1962, revised edition, 1969, and *Look Back in Anger: A Casebook* edited by Taylor, London, Macmillan, 1968; *John Osborne* by Ronald Hayman, London, Heinemann, 1968, New York, Ungar, 1972; *Osborne* by Martin Banham, Edinburgh, Oliver and Boyd, 1969; *The Plays of John Osborne: An Assessment*, London, Gollancz, and New York, Humanities Press, 1969, and *John Osborne*, London, Longman, 1969, both by Simon Trussler; *John Osborne* by Alan Carter, Edinburgh, Oliver and Boyd, 1969, New York, Barnes and Noble, 1973; *Theatre Language: A Study of Arden, Osborne, Pinter, and Wesker* by John Russell Brown, London, Allen Lane, and New York, Taplinger, 1972; *John Osborne* by Harold Ferrar, New York, Columbia University Press, 1973; *Anger and Detachment: A Study of Arden, Osborne, and Pinter* by Michael Anderson, London, Pitman, 1976; *Coping with Vulnerability: The Achievement of John Osborne* by Herbert Goldstone, Washington, D.C., University Press of America, 1982; *John Osborne* by Arnold P. Hinchliffe, Boston, Twayne, 1984; *File on Osborne* edited by Malcolm Page, London, Methuen, 1988.

Theatrical Activities:
Director: **Plays**—with the Huddersfield Repertory Company, 1949; *The World of Paul Slickey*, Bournemouth and London, 1959; *Meals on Wheels* by Charles Wood, London, 1965; *The Entertainer*, London, 1974; *Inadmissible Evidence*, London, 1978.
Actor: **Plays**—Mr. Burrells in *No Room at the Inn* by Joan Temple, Sheffield, 1948; on tour and in repertory in Ilfracombe, Bridgwater, Camberwell, Kidderminster, Derby, 1948–56; with the English Stage Company, London: Antonio in *Don Juan* by Ronald Duncan, 1956, Lionel in *The Death of Satan* by Ronald Duncan, 1956, roles in *Cards of Identity* by Nigel Dennis, 1956, Lin To in *The Good Woman of Setzuan* by Brecht, 1956, The Commissionaire in *The Apollo de Bellac* by Giraudoux, 1957, and Donald Blake in *The Making of Moo* by Nigel Dennis, 1957; Claude Hicket in *A Cuckoo in the Nest* by Ben Travers, London, 1964. **Films**—*First Love*, 1970; *Get Carter*, 1971; *Tomorrow Never Comes*, 1978; *Flash Gordon*, 1980. **Television**—*The Parachute* by David Mercer, 1968; *The First Night of Pygmalion* by Richard Huggett, 1969; *Lady Charlotte*, 1977.

* * *

The staging of *Look Back in Anger* in May 1956 is frequently cited as the start of a dramatic renaissance in Britain.

While Beckett's *Waiting for Godot* had been praised the previous year and Brendan Behan's *The Quare Fellow* was to open two weeks later, the statement is broadly true. *Look Back in Anger* established the English Stage Company at the Royal Court as a writers' theatre and because of its success, many young authors turned to plays instead of fiction, or found it easier to have their work performed.

Look Back in Anger presents Jimmy Porter, an eloquent young man running a sweet stall in a provincial town. He is a graduate of a university which was not even redbrick, but white tile. His wife Alison is upper-middle-class, as he often reminds her; later her ex-Indian Army father appears. Cliff, a young Welshman, shares the flat; an actress, Helena, moves in, eventually sharing Jimmy's bed, and his wife moves out, returning—with whimsical talk of bears protecting squirrels—at the end.

I was one of the young people in the gallery at the Royal Court in the summer of 1956. For the first time ever I saw people similar to people I knew on the stage, talking in the same way—though none could sustain wit and raciness in the way Jimmy did. These characters talked about the same subjects. I scribbled memorable lines from the play all over my programme: the diplomat who was "the platitude from outer space"; "I must say it's pretty dreary living in the American Age—unless you're an American of course"; "There aren't any good, brave causes left. If the big bang does come, and we all get killed off, it won't be in aid of the old-fashioned grand design."

Jimmy Porter was angry at the apathetic mid-1950's. Five months later he could have joined protests at the British invasion of Suez and less than two years later he might have marched to Aldermaston with the newly-formed Campaign for Nuclear Disarmament. I remember too from the Royal Court gallery Mary Ure as Alison in her slip: the play had a sexiness almost unknown on the British stage at the time. Kenneth Tynan's review in the *Observer* had drawn me to the drama: Osborne had presented "post-war youth as it really is" in "the best young play of the decade."

While *Look Back in Anger* is a key document to the mood of the 1950's, it survives for its presentation of class, male versus female, and the generation gap in terms of pre- and post-war, and especially for the eloquence of Jimmy.

The Entertainer followed, a more ambitious work looking at three generations and picturing the state of England through the metaphor of the decline of the music-hall. Archie Rice, third-rate comedian, who sings "Why should I bother to care?" finally refuses to flee to Canada, publicly because "you can't get draught Bass in Toronto," in fact because being English is still so important to him. His proudest moment was when two nuns looked at him and crossed themselves. His neglected wife looks back to the heyday of the music-halls when she sings "The boy I love he's up in the gallery." Archie points to the analogy with England with "Don't clap too hard, we're all in a very old building." Archie's son is kidnapped, then killed, at Suez, and his daughter cries out, in the most subversive speech heard till then in a London theatre: "What's it all in aid of—is it really just for the sake of a gloved hand waving at you from a golden coach?"

Both *Look Back in Anger* and *The Entertainer* were quite well presented in films made at the time.

Five more substantial Osborne plays were staged in the 1960's. *Inadmissible Evidence*, about a lawyer whose public and private lives are disintegrating, was a drama of forceful, inimitable invective rivalling that of Jimmy Porter. *Luther* turned to history, to the roots of protest, for a spectacular stage piece which finally focused on psychological explanations for Luther's revolt. *A Patriot for Me*, also with a big cast, examined a homosexual scandal in Austro-Hungary before World War I, a theme which challenged the Lord Chamberlain's censorship. *The Hotel in Amsterdam*, a quiet conversation piece, has six people in the film business escaping their boss for a weekend. *Time Present*, which contrasts sisters—an actress and an earnest Labour MP—facing the approaching death of their father, has been undervalued. These last two plays are ensemble work, in contrast to the earlier ones: lesser characters are granted a right-of-reply.

Osborne's output in a long career includes other full-length plays: an ill-fated musical, *The World of Paul Slickey*; adaptations and translations; and short plays and work for television.

Osborne's work comes full cycle, and possibly concludes, with *Déjàvu* in 1992. He returns to Jimmy Porter 36 years later, living in comfort in Shropshire, still accompanied by Cliff. An Alison is still at the ironing board (his daughter by a failed second marriage) while the men read the Sunday papers. The new Helena is a friend of the daughter. The older Jimmy is even more prone to extended monologue than he was in *Look Back in Anger*, and Osborne seems to enjoy annoying his audience by non-stop attacks on progressives, gays, feminists, Australians, the lower-middle-class, and change in the Church of England. *Déjàvu* has two strengths: intriguing oblique comment on *Look Back in Anger*, as play and myth, and the pain seen in Jimmy, sinking with claret, his teddy bear, and the Book of Common Prayer.

Angered by the critical reception of *Déjàvu*, Osborne wrote in the *Spectator* (London): "No more plays, no more journalism for me" (20 June 1992). As his most polished and entertaining work in recent years has been two volumes of autobiography (*A Better Class of Person* vividly recreates a pre-1939 upbringing), this choice of words allows us to expect more non-fiction.

—Malcolm Page

OSGOOD, Lawrence. American. Born in 1929.
See 3rd edition, 1982.

OSOFISAN, Femi (Babafemi Adeyemi Osofisan). Nigerian. Born 16 June 1946. Educated at schools in Ilesha, Ife-Ife, and Erunwon; Government College, Ibadan; University of Dakar, Senegal, D.E.S. 1968; University of Ibadan, B.A. 1969, Ph.D. 1974; University of Paris III, 1971–73. Since 1973 member of the faculty, currently professor in theatre arts, University of Ibadan. Visiting professor, University of Benin, Lomé, Togo Republic, 1980, University of Pennsylvania, Philadelphia, 1983, University of Benin, Benin City, Nigeria, 1983–85, University of Ife, Ife-Ife, 1985–86, and University of Iowa, Iowa City, 1991; visiting fellow, University of Cambridge, 1986, Cornell University, Ithaca, New York, 1992, and St. Alfred College, England, 1992. Founding member of the Editorial Board, the *Guardian*, Lagos, 1984–85. Currently editor, *Opon Ifa: Ibadan Poetry Chapbooks*.

Drama consultant, FESTAC 77, Lagos; artist-in-residence, Henri Clewes Foundation, La Napoule, France, 1990; guest writer, Japan Foundation, Japan, 1991; drama consultant, MAMSER, Abuja, 1991–92. President, Association of Nigerian Authors, 1989, 1990; vice-president for West Africa, Pan-African Writers Association, from 1992. Recipient: Association of Nigerian Authors prize, 1983, 1986; Fulbright fellowship, 1986. Address: Department of Theatre Arts, University of Ibadan, Ibadan, Nigeria.

PUBLICATIONS

Plays

Odudwa, Don't Go! (produced Ibadan, 1968).
You Have Lost Your Fine Face (produced Ibadan, 1969).
A Restless Run of Locusts (produced Akure, 1970). Ibadan, Onibonoje Press, 1975.
Red Is the Freedom Road (produced Ibadan, 1974). Included in *Morountodun and Other Plays*, 1982.
The Chattering and the Song (produced Ibadan, 1974). Ibadan, Ibadan University Press, 1977.
Who's Afraid of Solarin? (produced Ibadan, 1977). Calabar, Scholars Press, 1978.
Once upon Four Robbers (produced Ibadan, 1978). Ibadan, BIO, 1982.
Farewell to a Cannibal Rage (produced Ibadan, 1978; revised version produced Benin City, 1984). Ibadan, Evans, 1986.
Morountodun (produced Ibadan, 1979; revised version produced Ife-Ife, 1980). Included in *Morountodun and Other Plays*, 1982.
Fires Burn But They Die Hard (televized 1981). Included in *Birthdays Are Not for Dying and Other Plays*, 1991.
The Inspector and the Hero (televized 1981). Included in *Birthdays Are Not for Dying and Other Plays*, 1991.
Birthdays Are Not for Dying (produced Ibadan, 1981). Ibadan, Evans, 1987.
The Oriki of a Grasshopper (produced Ibadan, 1981; revised version produced Benin City, 1985). Included in *Two Short Plays*, 1986.
No More the Wasted Breed (produced Ibadan, 1982). Included in *Morountodun and Other Plays*, 1982.
Morountodun and Other Plays. Ikeja, Longman, 1982.
Midnight Hotel (produced Ibadan, 1982). Ibadan, Evans, 1986.
Altine's Wrath (televised 1983; produced Ibadan, 1983). Included in *Two Short Plays*, 1986.
Esu and the Vagabond Minstrels (produced Benin City, 1984; revised version produced Ife-Ife, 1986). Ibadan, New Horn Press, 1987.
Two Short Plays. Ibadan, New Horn Press, 1986.
Twingle-Twangle A-Twynning Tayle (produced Ibadan, 1988). Lagos, Longman, 1992.
Aringindin and the Nightwatchmen (produced Ibadan, 1989). Ibadan, Heinemann Educational, 1992.
Another Raft (produced Ibadan, 1989). Lagos, Malthouse Press, 1990.
Yungba-Yungba and the Dance Contest (produced Ibadan, 1990). Ibadan, Heinemann Educational, 1992.
Birthdays Are Not for Dying and Other Plays. Lagos, Malthouse Press, 1991.

Television Plays: *The Inspector and the Hero*, 1981; *Fires Burn But They Die Hard*, 1981; *Altine's Wrath*, *A Debt to the Dead*, *A Date with Danger*, *The New Cathedral*, *At the Petrol Station*, *Mission Abandoned*, *A Hero Comes Home*, *Operation Rat-Trap*, *To Kill a Dream* (all in *Visitors* series), 1983.

Novels

Kolera Kolej. Ibadan, New Horn Press, 1975.
Cordelia (as Okinba Launko). Lagos, Malthouse Press, 1990.

Verse

Minted Coins (as Okinba Launko). Ibadan, Heinemann Educational, 1986.

Other

Beyond Translation: Tragic Paradigms and the Dramaturgy of Ola Rotimi and Wole Soyinka. Ife-Ife, Ife Monographs on African Literature, 1986.
The Orality of Prose: A Comparatist Look at the Works of Rabelais, Joyce, and Tutuola. Ife-Ife, Ife Monographs on African Literature, 1986.

Translator, *Theatre and Nationalism: Wole Soyinka and LeRoi Jones*, by Alain Ricard. Ife-Ife, University of Ife Press, 1978.

*

Theatrical Activities:
Director: all of his own plays.
Actor: since 1963 lead roles with many companies including The Orisun Theatre Company, the Unibadan Masques, the University of Ibadan Theatre Ensemble, and the Kakaun Sela Company.

Femi Osofisan comments:
My works belong to what is now customarily described as the second generation of modern Nigerian writing, following that of Wole Soyinka and Chinua Achebe. The distinctive features of our dramaturgy are (a) the concern to produce works that are directly relevant to the political and social struggles of our times, and particularly from a combattant, leftist perspective, without however being dogmatic or pedantic. In most cases, this had meant a violent rejection of the sometimes exotic, and sometimes anthropological works of our predecessors, and of the tragic-metaphysical emphasis of their explorations; and (b) the equal concern to produce works that are easily accessible, readable, and simple, without being simplistic. In my case, it has meant a predilection for plays which are more or less open-ended, in which the audience is called upon to involve itself, take positions, and, even, decide the resolutions for the actors. Thus we have created a novel aesthetics, based on a vigorous and lively experimentation with form and mechanics, and the resuscitation of the traditional resources of folklore and festival, masques and myth, ritual and extemporisation. The driving aim is to entertain our audience, but also, and crucially, to change our world.

* * *

University professor, theatre director, newspaper columnist, and poet, Femi Osofisan is part of a generation which has experienced Nigerian independence only as an empty slogan. Thus, he fashions a committed literature designed to reawaken a collective, imaginatively self-critical sensibility and break the enduring shackles of religion, custom, and colonialism in favor of a more humane, egalitarian society. Within Nigeria he is often viewed as a radical who would completely destroy the past, but his radicalism actually builds positively upon the best of tradition while seeking to encourage pervasive change.

For analytical convenience, Osofisan's works may be separated into the broad categories of realistic protest plays, satiric adaptations of European models, and a particularly African form of "total theatre." *A Restless Run of Locusts*, *Red Is the Freedom Road*, and *The Oriki of a Grasshopper* fit into the first category. Here, the playwright registers the widespread political corruption, brutality, intellectual failure, and rhythm of repression, coup, and counter-coup of post-independence Nigeria. His *No More the Wasted Breed* rejects an acceptance of martyrdom, articulated in Wole Soyinka's *The Strong Breed*, and illuminates in persuasive dramatic form aspects of the quarrel—albeit friendly—which many younger intellectuals have with their distinguished mentor.

European dramatic literature provides a ready source for adaptation in such plays as *Who's Afraid of Solarin?* and *Midnight Hotel*. The former play is a loose adaptation of Gogol's *The Inspector General*, and the latter, through its use of farcical complications and acerbic songs, rendered from an oversized songbook, borrows from both Feydeau and Brecht. More importantly for Nigerian audiences which may be unaware of the European originals, these plays satirize the rampant materialism of the upper classes. As such, they may be considered an ingenious contemporary development of the traditional, age-grade satires in which the unempowered expressed their dissatisfaction with the privileged.

To date, Osofisan's most conceptually and stylistically complex plays are *The Chattering and the Song*, *Farewell to a Cannibal Rage*, *Once upon Four Robbers*, *Morountodun*, and *Esu and the Vagabond Minstrels*. Illustrative of an African concept of drama, these plays incorporate non-verbal elements like dance and music into a spoken text; insist upon theatre as artifice through frequent role-changes and story-telling techniques; conjoin spatial and temporal frames into a seamless experiential present; and place high value on episodic and open-ended structures which challenge audiences to impose meaning upon the event.

The Chattering and the Song, the first Osofisan play written in this genre, contains many of the themes upon which the playwright subsequently elaborates. The play traces a path whereby university-trained supporters of a farmers' movement move from an unfocused anger about social injustice to an active understanding of the process of social change. Games, or the construction of illusory systems in which the characters invest belief, are the vehicles through which this evolution is accomplished. Thus, the characters play a number of riddling and card games, with each new round being a repetition with significant variation; riddling, which is designed to develop intellectual prowess through experimentation with trope and which epitomises the temporary resolution of apparent paradox, becomes a metaphor for an appropriate revolutionary stance which acknowledges dialectical development yet maintains commitment to an egalitarian ideal.

The initial irony of would-be revolutionaries unwittingly betraying espoused principles within the context of a game is repeated in their later re-enactment of a play-within-the-play, for the most flamboyant radical begins awkwardly in his role of ruler but grows more overbearing the longer he is called upon to defend his privileged position. The historical drama which these characters enact is itself a radical re-interpretation of recorded fact; the alteration enables

Osofisan to posit identity as multiple, contextual, and susceptible to change, qualities which in turn necessitate continuous re-evaluation of material circumstances. The confrontational climax of the historical drama is rendered in song, dance, and drumming, sensorially rich devices which satisfy his audiences' inherited expectations concerning aesthetic structures most suited for conveying deep emotion. Yet, this appeal to the senses is followed by an intellectual argument, couched in terms of myth, another popular mode of expression which Osofisan has elsewhere characterized as a "pedagogical explanation of knowledge by means of metaphor." The abrupt disruption of the play-within-the-play offers the audience a graphic image of its potential to reject and redirect a hegemonic social reality; the moment anticipates the final deconstruction of form when the actors jettison their roles entirely and encourage the audience to join in acknowledging the positive thrust of the farmers' movement.

Thus, Osofisan offers in plays like *The Chattering and the Song* what Brecht defines as a "fighting" popular theatre. With sophisticated irreverence, he re-interprets core values, thereby challenging audiences to reclaim for themselves the power to alter their world.

—Sandra L. Richards

OVERMYER, Eric. American. Born in Boulder, Colorado, 25 September 1951. Educated at Reed College, Portland, Oregon, B.A. 1976; Florida State University, Tallahassee, 1977; Brooklyn College, City University of New York, 1979–81. Married 1) Melissa Cooper in 1978; 2) Ellen McElduff in 1991. Literary manager, Playwrights Horizons, New York, 1981–84; associate artist, Center Stage, Baltimore, Maryland, 1984–91; story editor, *St. Elsewhere* television series, 1986–87; visiting associate professor of playwriting, Yale University, and associate artist, Yale Repertory Theater, New Haven, Connecticut, 1991–92. Recipient: Le Comte du Nouy, 1984; McKnight fellowship, 1986; National Endowment for the Arts fellowship, 1987; New York Foundation for the Arts fellowship, 1987; Rockefeller fellowship, 1987. Agent: George Lane, William Morris Agency, 1350 Avenue of the Americas, New York, New York 10019. Address: 366 West 11th Street, New York, New York 10014, U.S.A.

PUBLICATIONS

Plays

Native Speech (produced Los Angeles, 1983; New York, 1991). New York, Broadway Play Publishing, 1984.
On the Verge, or The Geography of Yearning (produced Baltimore, Maryland, 1985; New York, 1987; London, 1989). New York, Broadway Play Publishing, 1986.
The Double Bass, with Harry Newman, adaptation of the play by Patrick Süskind (produced New York, 1986).
In a Pig's Valise, music by August Darnell (produced Baltimore, Maryland, 1986; New York, 1989). New York, Broadway Play Publishing, 1989.
In Perpetuity Throughout the Universe (produced Baltimore, Maryland, and New York, 1988). New York, Broadway Play Publishing, 1988.

Hawker. Published in *Plays from New Dramatists*, edited by Christopher Gould, New York, Broadway Play Publishing, 1989.
Mi Vida Loca (produced New York, 1990). New York, Broadway Play Publishing, 1991.
Don Quixote de La Jolla (produced La Jolla, California, 1990).
Kafka's Radio (produced New York, 1990).
The Heliotrope Bouquet by Scott Joplin and Louis Chauvin (produced Baltimore, Maryland, 1991).
Dark Rapture (produced Seattle, 1992).

Television Plays: *St. Elsewhere* series, 1985–88; *The Days and Nights of Molly Dodd* series, 1988–90; *Sisters* series, 1990–91.

*

Eric Overmyer comments:
I am interested in the authentically theatrical. Hermann Broch stated that he wrote novels in order to discover that which can only be discovered by writing a novel. I write plays in order to discover what can only be discovered by writing plays. I am interested in discovering the limits of the theatre, its possibilities and its impossibilities. I am interested in language, first and always: a charged, mythic, poetic, theatrical language. And imagination: mythic, poetic, epic. I am interested in bravura performance style which is necessary to an authentically theatrical experience. I am not interested in naturalism, in small plays with small ideas which need small performances, in plays which are really faux cinema; in short, in the kind of plays the dramaturg James Magruder refers to as "talking about my problems in your living room." I am interested in plays which are contradictory, complex, many-layered, and many-faceted, which are unencumbered by reductive, mechanistic psychology, motive, and biography. In other words, I am interested in reversal instead of transition, in wrought language rather than humdrum speech, in leaps of the imagination not tedious exposition, in classic plays, and in contemporary plays which embody classical virtues and present classical challenges. I prefer to work with directors who direct classical plays as if they were contemporary, and contemporary plays as if they were classical. I am not an avant-gardist, I am a nouveau-classicist.

* * *

As one of only two playwrights currently toiling in the American theater for whom language is both object and muse (the other is Mac Wellman), Eric Overmyer suffers many fools. Directors, actors, and the critical establishment charge him with wilfull obscurity and arrant pedantry, and chide him for a perceived resistance to closure. He runs foul of editors and proofreaders who insisted, for example, upon changing his line "Give it me" in *In Perpetuity Throughout the Universe* to "Give it *to* me" through every stage of publication. The choice of "give it me" over "give it to me" is no trifling matter in an Overmyer play; those deaf to the difference deny the characters their territory. Smoothing over this particular imperative, or paraphrasing Overmyer into standard usage, denies the author his right to remain a non-naturalistic word jockey spinning lines outside the adamantly realist boundaries of the American theater. The standard new American play—standard play in standard prose—can be boiled down to the formula "Talking about *my* problems in *your* apartment." Apartments count for nothing in Overmyer's euphonic universe; his people more often than not turn up in dreams or on the airwaves or on terra incognita. Their language, their logorrheic pulse, is their main chance to talk their way into a

known state of being and recognize themselves. How well the audience knows them when they get there is another matter.

Overmyer's second play, *On the Verge, or The Geography of Yearning*, is one of the most important new works to emerge in American drama in the last 30 years. Mary, Alex, and Fanny, three intrepid Victorian lady explorers, set out for adventure with machetes and pith helmets in 1888. As they progress, the terrain becomes increasingly unfamiliar. Unknown objects—eggbeaters, side-view mirrors—turn up; words and phrases they've never heard or used before spring to their lips—I like Ike, Cool Whip, tractor opera. They discover that they are, in fact, bivouacking their way along the continuum of American pop. They pause in 1955; Alex and Fanny, enthralled by post-war consumer culture, remain in this most ideal of climates, leaving Mary to venture ever forward, yearning into the future. *On the Verge* traverses the twin peaks of American literature, the urge to know and the urge to go, charting with unflagging theatricality the giddy debasement of American speech on the open market. "I have seen the future and it is slang."

The theme of what control an artist, particularly the writer, can exert over his work—in a sense, the question of reception theory—recurs throughout Overmyer's work. *In Perpetuity Throughout the Universe* is a dark, vertiginous ride through the conspiracist mentality of racist America in which a doubled cast of good guys and bad guys ghost-write hate primers, creating enemies to keep the populace permanently paranoid and off-kilter. The title is a phrase from an author's contract regarding future rights to sequels and spinoffs. *Don Quixote de La Jolla*, built during five weeks of site-specific collaboration at the La Jolla Playhouse, is an insidiously faithful tweak on the tale of the mad knight and his doughty sidekick. Overmyer offers a baleful rumination on what weight, if any, that mighty and mightily unread 16th-century classic would have on a Southern Californian populace raised on "Lady of Spain" and the terminally trashy *Man of La Mancha*. Not surprisingly, the lambada leaves Cervantes in the dust in another one of Overmyer's hilarious acts of cultural anthropology.

In his 1991 play (the fifth to be presented at Baltimore's Center Stage), *The Heliotrope Bouquet by Scott Joplin and Louis Chauvin*, Overmyer creates a fluid, overlapping dreamscape that encompasses both historical and hallucinatory locations. Joplin, the foremost composer of piano ragtime, and Chauvin, an illiterate contemporary whose musical gifts were said to have surpassed Joplin's, wrote "The Heliotrope Bouquet," a slow-drag two-step, in 1906. This rhapsodic moment occasions the play. Inasmuch as the historical material is scarce and largely conjectural, *Heliotrope* is less an historical restitution of Chauvin's place in American culture and African-American history than it is a dialectical meditation on artistic collaboration. Although grounded in the sporting house context of ragtime America, the conflict between "slow and cautious Joplin," who lives with an eye on the future, and Chauvin, who burns brightly in the moment and believes that it only lasts "as long as a man stays awake," raises larger, unanswered questions "still to be heard in the ether and the House of God." What is posterity to a dead man? What is success—does it come from a rag well performed before friends or in copies of sheet music tucked inside a stranger's piano bench? What is worth recalling—bundles of heliotrope set down on a table or notes bunched on the musical stave? Is art the moment of creativity or the fact of duration?

As with all of Overmyer's work, a main source of *Heliotrope*'s drama is its poetic idiom. As richly syncopated as ragtime, the play can be said to mimic the structure of a piano rag as certain lines are repeated throughout, passed from character to character like a musical phrase set in different keys. *Heliotrope*'s language is sensational; better than merely original, it is particular. Overmyer states his own case best when he writes in his production notes for *On the Verge*: "The language of the play . . . cannot, must not, should not be naturalized or paraphrased. Rhythm and sound are sense."

—James Magruder

OWEN, Alun (Davies). British. Born in Liverpool, Lancashire, 24 November 1925. Educated at Cardigan County School, Wales; Oulton High School, Liverpool. Married Mary O'Keeffe in 1942; two sons. Stage manager, director, and actor, 1942–59. Recipient: Screenwriters and Producers Script of the Year award, 1960; Screenwriters Guild award, 1961; *Daily Mirror* award, 1961; Golden Star, 1967; Banff International Television Festival prize, 1985. Lives in London. Agent: Julian Friedmann, Blake Friedmann Agency, 37–41 Gower Street, London WC1E 6HH, England.

PUBLICATIONS

Plays

The Rough and Ready Lot (broadcast 1958; produced London, 1959). London, Encore, 1960.
Progress to the Park (broadcast 1958; produced London, 1959). Published in *New English Dramatists 5*, London, Penguin, 1962.
Three T.V. Plays (includes *No Trams to Lime Street*; *After the Funeral*; *Lena, Oh My Lena*). London, Cape, 1961; New York, Hill and Wang, 1963.
The Rose Affair (televised 1961; produced Cardiff, 1966). Published in *Anatomy of a Television Play*, London, Weidenfeld and Nicolson, 1962.
Dare to Be a Daniel (televised 1962). Published in *Eight Plays: Book 1*, edited by Malcolm Stuart Fellows, London, Cassell, 1965.
A Little Winter Love (produced Dublin, 1963; London, 1965). London, Evans, 1965.
Maggie May, music and lyrics by Lionel Bart (produced London, 1964).
The Game (includes *The Winner* and *The Loser*) (produced Dublin, 1965).
The Goose (produced Dublin, 1967).
The Wake (televised 1967). Published in *Theatre Choice: A Collection of Modern Short Plays*, edited by Michael Marland, London, Blackie, 1972.
Shelter (televised 1967; produced London, 1971). London, French, 1968.
George's Room (televised 1967). London and New York, French, 1968.
There'll Be Some Changes Made (produced London, 1969).
Norma, in *We Who Are About to . . .*, later title *Mixed Doubles* (produced London, 1969; revised version produced London, 1983). London, Methuen, 1970.
Doreen (televised 1969). Published in *The Best Short Plays 1971*, edited by Stanley Richards, Philadelphia, Chilton, 1971.
The Male of the Species (televised 1969; produced Brighton and London, 1974). Published in *On Camera 3*, edited by Ron Side and Ralph Greenfield, New York, Holt Rinehart, 1972; published separately London, French, 1975.
Lucia (produced Cardiff, 1982).

Screenplays: *The Criminal* (*The Concrete Jungle*), with Jimmy Sangster, 1960; *A Hard Day's Night*, 1964; *Caribbean Idyll*, 1970.

Radio Plays: *Two Sons*, 1957; *The Rough and Ready Lot*, 1958; *Progress to the Park*, 1958; *It Looks Like Rain*, 1959; *Café Society*, 1982; *The Lancaster Gate End*, 1982; *Colleagues*, 1982; *Kisch-Kisch*, 1983; *Soft Impeachment*, 1983; *Tiger*, 1984; *Halt*, 1984; *Earwig* series, 1984; *Widowers*, 1985.

Television Plays: *No Trams to Lime Street*, 1959; *After the Funeral*, 1960; *Lena, Oh My Lena*, 1960; *The Ruffians*, 1960; *The Ways of Love*, 1961; *The Rose Affair*, 1961; *The Hard Knock*, 1962; *Dare to Be a Daniel*, 1962; *You Can't Win 'em All*, 1962; *The Strain*, 1963; *Let's Imagine* series, 1963; *The Stag*, 1963; *A Local Boy*, 1963; *The Other Fella*, 1966; *The Making of Jericho*, 1966; *The Fantasist*, 1967; *The Wake*, 1967; *Shelter*, 1967; *George's Room*, 1967; *Stella*, 1967; *Thief*, 1967; *Charlie*, 1968; *Gareth*, 1968; *Tennyson*, 1968; *Ah, There You Are*, 1968; *Alexander*, 1968; *Minding the Shop*, 1968; *Time for the Funny Walk*, 1968; *The Ladies*, 1969; *Doreen*, 1969; *Spare Time*, 1969; *Park People*, 1969; *You'll Be the Death of Me*, 1969; *The Male of the Species* (U.S. title: *Emlyn, MacNeil, Cornelius*), 1969; *Joan*, 1970; *Hilda*, 1970; *And a Willow Tree*, 1970; *Just the Job*, 1970; *Female of the Species*, 1970; *Joy*, 1970; *Ruth*, 1971; *Funny*, 1971; *Pal*, 1971; *Giants and Ogres*, 1971; *The Piano Player*, 1971; *The Web*, 1972; *Ronny Barker Show* (3 scripts); *Buttons*, 1973; *Flight*, 1973; *Lucky*, 1974; *Left*, 1975; *The Vandy Case*, 1975; *Forget-Me-Not* (6 plays), 1976; *The Fetch*, 1977; *The Look*, 1978; *Passing Through*, 1979 (Ireland); *The Runner*, 1980; *Sealink*, 1980; *Lovers of the Lake*, from the story by Sean O'Faolain, 1984; *Unexplained Laughter*, from the novel by Alice Thomas Ellis, 1989; *Come Home Charlie and Face Them*, from the novel by R.F. Delderfield, 1990.

*

Theatrical Activities:
Actor: **Plays**—with the Birmingham Repertory Company, 1943–44; Gotti in *The Lonely Falcons* by P.N. Walker-Taylor, London, 1946; Jepson in *Humoresque* by Guy Bolton, London, 1948; Rolph in *Snow White and the Seven Dwarfs*, London, 1951; with Sir Donald Wolfit's Company at the Old Vic, London, 1951: in *Tamburlaine the Great* by Marlowe, Charles in *As You Like It*, Curan and Herald in *King Lear*, Officer in *Twelfth Night*, Salarino in *The Merchant of Venice*, Sexton in *Macbeth*, Gonzales Ferera in *The Wandering Jew* by J. Temple Thurston, a Lord and Joseph in *The Taming of the Shrew*; with the English Stage Company at the Royal Court, London, 1957; Clifford in *Man with a Guitar* by Gilbert Horobin, and Smith in *The Waiting of Lester Abbs* by Kathleen Sully, London, 1957; Reader in *The Samson Riddle* by Wolf Mankowitz, Dublin, 1972. **Films**—*Valley of Song* (*Men Are Children Twice*), 1953; *Every Day Except Christmas*, 1957; *In the Wake of a Stranger*, 1959; *I'm All Right Jack*, 1959; *Jet Storm*, 1959; *The Servant*, 1963.

* * *

The main strengths of Alun Owen's work have always been its accuracy of observation, its depth of characterization, and the power and fluency of its dialogue, sometimes reaching the level of poetry. *Progress to the Park*, set in the Liverpool of the late 1950's, is a vivid and detailed portrait of working-class life in that town at the period. The play's central theme is the vice-like grip that religious intolerance has on the city's inhabitants; and is expressed through the central relationship between Bobby Laughlin, a Protestant boy, and Mag Keegan, a Catholic girl. Their potential love is stifled and destroyed by the bigoted attitudes of their elders. There are a number of sharply defined character studies, including members of the Laughlin and Keegan families; and of Teifion Davies, the detached, ironic young Welshman who has a love-hate relationship to his home town, which is reflected in his commentary on the action. The play teems with vitality and power, each episode flowing effectively and relentlessly into and out of each other but related strongly to the central theme.

The Rough and Ready Lot is set in monastery in a Spanish colony in South America a few years after the end of the American Civil War and revolves around four "soldiers of fortune"—Kelly, O'Keefe, Morgan, and the Colonel. They are in a lull between fighting, ostensibly on the side of the Indians in their bid to free themselves from their Spanish oppressors; in the meantime, the four men talk. O'Keefe is a fanatical Catholic; Morgan an equally fanatical political revolutionary; the Colonel is a "realist," who thinks he knows the motives for people's actions but is, in fact, incredibly blinkered; while Kelly just takes life as it comes. They argue and try to impose their views on the others, sometimes in bursts of magnificent rhetoric; but in the end only Kelly survives. As Irving Wardle said in a review, "Its dialogue flows beautifully; its characters are conceived in depth and, as embodiments of conflicting principles, they are disposed in a pattern of geometric symmetry; the plot is constructed solidly and attaches itself tenaciously to the governing theme."

In the musical *Maggie May*, written with Lionel Bart, Owen returns to the Liverpool scene and gives us another teeming, vital slice of life. The early and mid-1960's was also the time of his award-winning television plays, also set on Merseyside, *No Trams to Lime Street*, *Lena, Oh My Lena*, and *After the Funeral*; and his sharp and witty script for the Beatles' first and best film, the semi-documentary *A Hard Day's Night*. By contrast, *The Rose Affair*, also a television award-winner, was a modernized version of the fairy-tale *Beauty and the Beast*, the Beast-figure an isolated, high-powered businessman, the Beauty a girl he falls in love with from afar; stylistically, it had some bold innovations for its time and also had some pithy things to say on the split between being a public and a private person.

In recent years, most of Owen's work has been for television, and includes *Shelter*, a play about the confrontation between an aggressive working-class man and an alienated young middle-class woman, and *Dare to Be a Daniel*, in which a young man with a grudge against his former schoolteacher returns to the small town where he comes from to gain his revenge.

Owen adapted his 1969 television play *The Male of the Species* for the stage in 1974. Consisting of three short plays, this work purports to show how women are exploited by men. Mary MacNeil is shown in her encounters with three crucial male figures: her father, a master carpenter; her employer, a suave, urbane barrister; and the "office cad." The trouble is, however, that the men are all depicted as attractive, while Mary is portrayed as the willing victim. The perhaps unconscious male chauvinism of the play is disappointing in a writer of Owen's talent.

—Jonathan Hammond

OWENS, Rochelle. Pseudonym for Rochelle Bass. American. Born in Brooklyn, New York, 2 April 1936. Educated at Lafayette High School, Brooklyn, graduated 1953. Married George Economou in 1962. Worked as a clerk, typist, telephone operator. Founding member, New York Theatre Strategy. Visiting lecturer, University of California, San Diego, 1982; adjunct professor, and host of radio program *The Writer's Mind*, University of Oklahoma, Norman, 1984; distinguished writer-in-residence, Brown University, Providence, Rhode Island. Recipient: Rockefeller grant, 1965, 1975; Ford grant, 1965; Creative Artists Public Service grant, 1966, 1973; Yale University School of Drama fellowship, 1968; Obie award, 1968, 1971, 1982; Guggenheim fellowship, 1971; National Endowment for the Arts grant, 1974; Villager award, 1982; New York Drama Critics Circle award, 1983. Agent: Dramatists Guild, 234 West 44th Street, New York, New York 10036. Address: 1401 Magnolia, Norman, Oklahoma 73072, U.S.A.

PUBLICATIONS

Plays

Futz (produced Minneapolis, 1965; New York, Edinburgh, and London, 1967). New York, Hawk's Well Press, 1961; revised version in *Futz and What Came After*, 1968, in *New Short Plays 2*, London, Methuen, 1969.
The String Game (produced New York, 1965). Included in *Futz and What Came After*, 1968.
Istanboul (produced New York, 1965; London, 1982). Included in *Futz and What Came After*, 1968.
Homo (produced Stockholm and New York, 1966; London, 1969). Included in *Futz and What Came After*, 1968.
Beclch (produced Philadelphia and New York, 1968). Included in *Futz and What Came After*, 1968.
Futz and What Came After. New York, Random House, 1968.
The Karl Marx Play, music by Galt MacDermot, lyrics by Owens (produced New York, 1973). Included in *The Karl Marx Play and Others*, 1974.
The Karl Marx Play and Others (includes *Kontraption, He Wants Shih!, Farmer's Almanac, Coconut Folksinger, O.K. Certaldo*). New York, Dutton, 1974.
He Wants Shih! (produced New York, 1975). Included in *The Karl Marx Play and Others*, 1974.
Coconut Folksinger (broadcast 1976). Included in *The Karl Marx Play and Others*, 1974.
Kontraption (produced New York, 1978). Included in *The Karl Marx Play and Others*, 1974.
Emma Instigated Me, published in *Performing Arts Journal 1* (New York), Spring 1976.
The Widow, and The Colonel, in *The Best Short Plays 1977*, edited by Stanley Richards. Radnor, Pennsylvania, Chilton, 1977.

Mountain Rites, in *The Best Short Plays 1978*, edited by Stanley Richards. Radnor, Pennsylvania, Chilton, 1978.
Chucky's Hunch (produced New York, 1981).   Published in *Wordplays 2*, New York, Performing Arts Journal Publications, 1982.
Who Do You Want, Peire Vidal? (produced New York, 1982).   With *Futz*, New York, Broadway Play Publishing, 1986.

Screenplay: *Futz* (additional dialogue), 1969.

Radio Plays: *Coconut Folksinger*, 1976 (Germany); *Sweet Potatoes*, 1977.

Television Play (video): *Oklahoma Too: Rabbits and Nuggets*, 1987.

Short Stories

The Girl on the Garage Wall.   Mexico City, El Corno Emplumado, 1962.
The Obscenities of Reva Cigarnik.   Mexico City. El Corno Emplumado, 1963.

Verse

Not Be Essence That Cannot Be.   New York, Trobar Press, 1961.
Four Young Lady Poets, with others, edited by LeRoi Jones. New York, Totem-Corinth, 1962.
Salt and Core.   Los Angeles, Black Sparrow Press, 1968.
I Am the Babe of Joseph Stalin's Daughter.   New York, Kulchur, 1972.
Poems from Joe's Garage.   Providence, Rhode Island, Burning Deck, 1973.
The Joe 82 Creation Poems.   Los Angeles, Black Sparrow Press, 1974.
The Joe Chronicles 2.   Santa Barbara, California, Black Sparrow Press, 1979.
Shemuel.   St. Paul, New Rivers Press, 1979.
French Light.   Norman, Oklahoma Press with the Flexible Voice, 1984.
Constructs.   Norman, Oklahoma, Poetry Around, 1985.
Anthropologists at a Dinner Party.   Tucson, Arizona, Chax Press, 1985.
W. C. Fields in French Light.   New York, Contact II, 1986.
How Much Paint Does the Painting Need? New York, Kulchur, 1988.
Paysanne: New and Selected Poems 1961–1988.   New York, Contact, 1990.

Recordings: *A Reading of Primitive and Archaic Poetry*, with others, Broadside; *From a Shaman's Notebook*, with others, Broadside; *The Karl Marx Play*, Kilmarnock, 1975; *Totally Corrupt*, Giorno, 1976; *Black Box 17*, Watershed Foundation, 1979.

Other

Editor, *Spontaneous Combustion: Eight New American Plays*.   New York, Winter House, 1972.

*

Manuscript Collections: Mugar Memorial Library, Boston University; University of California, Davis; University of Oklahoma, Norman; Lincoln Center Library of the Performing Arts, New York; Smith College, Northampton, Massachusetts.

Critical Studies: by Harold Clurman and Jerome Rothenberg in *Futz and What Came After*, 1968; review by Jane Augustine in *World 29* (New York), 1974; "Rochelle Owens Symposium" in *Margins 24–26* (Milwaukee), 1975; *American Playwrights: A Critical Survey* by Bonnie Marranca and Gautam Dasgupta, New York, Drama Book Specialists, 1981; *Women in American Theatre* edited by Helen Krich Chinoy and Linda Walsh Jenkins, New York, Crown, 1981; *American Women Writers* by Linda Mainiero, New York, Ungar, 1981; article by Owens in *Contemporary Authors Autobiography Series 2* edited by Adele Sarkissian, Detroit, Gale, 1985; Len Berkman, in *Parnassus* (New York), 1985.

Theatrical Activities:
Director and actor: **Television**—*Oklahoma Too: Rabbits and Nuggets*, 1987.

Rochelle Owens comments:
   I am interested in the flow of imagination between the actors and the director, the boundless possibilities of interpretation of a script. Different theatrical realities are created and/or destroyed depending upon the multitudinous perceptions and points of view of the actors and director who share in the creation of the design of the unique journey of playing the play. There are as many ways to approach my plays as there as combinations of people who might involve themselves.
   The inter-media video *Oklahoma Too* uses poetry and images juxtaposed. The structures both linguistic and visual offer exciting projections of my continuous investigation of making art.

*   *   *

   Rochelle Owens came to the attention of the theatre public with her first play, *Futz*, whose shocking subject and inventive language launched her theatrical career. Owens's plays are distinguished by intense poetic imagery that springs from primordial human impulses of the subconscious and by the passionate and often violent struggle of her characters to survive within their repressive societies. Although a moralist who satirizes human frailty with parody, dialect, and the comic grotesque, Owens is also a compassionate observer who imbues her characters with tragic dimensions.
   Futz is preceded by a quotation from Corinthians: "Now concerning the things whereof ye wrote to me: It is good for a man not to touch a woman." Cyrus Futz loves his pig, Amanda, and is persecuted by the community. Majorie Satz lusts for all men and wheedles an invitation to share Futz's sexual pleasure with his pig. Oscar Loop is driven to madness and murders Ann Fox when they inadvertently witness the Futz-Amanda-Majorie orgy. Majorie kills Amanda for revenge. Oscar is condemned to hang and Futz is sent to prison where he is stabbed by Majorie's brother. Puritanical society punishes innocent sensuality.
   The String Game also explores the conflict between puritanism and natural impulse. Greenland Eskimos play the string game to ward off winter boredom. They are admonished for creating erotic images by their Italian priest, Father Bontempo; yet he longs for his own string game: warm spaghetti. Half-breed Cecil tempts Bontempo with a promise of pasta in exchange for the support of Cecil's commercial schemes. While gluttonously feasting, the priest chokes to death. The saddened Eskimos refuse to comply with Cecil's business venture and stoically return to their string games.

Istanboul dramatizes a cultural clash and *Homo* a class struggle. In *Istanboul* Norman men are fascinated by hirsute Byzantine women, and their wives by the smooth-skinned Byzantine men. In a religious frenzy St. Mary of Egypt murders the barbaric Norman, Godfrigh, and sensual Leo makes love to Godfrigh's wife as they wait for the Saracens to attack. *Homo* presents the mutual greed and contempt of Nordic and Asiatic. A surrealistic exploration of racial and class conflict the dramatic energy of the play in which revolution comes and goes, and workers continue their brutality.

Human perversion and bloody primitive rites prevail in Owens's most savage play, *Beclch*. In a fantasy Africa, four white adventurers intrude upon the natural innocence of a village. Queen Beclch, a monster of excess, professes her love for young Jose, then introduces him to the cruelty of cockfighting. She promises Yago Kingship, if he will contract elephantiasis. When Yago cannot transcend the pain of his deformity, he is forced mercilessly by the villagers to strangle himself. Beclch moves further into excess, and Jose flees in disgust. Since a queen cannot rule without a male consort, Beclch prepares herself for death as voluptuously as she lived.

A promise of social progress resides in Owens's first play with music, *The Karl Marx Play*. As in *Homo*, linear time is ignored and through a montage of scenes, past and present, a human portrait of Marx emerges in this, Owens's most joyful play. Her Marx is drained by illness, poverty, and lust for his aristocratic wife. All those who surround him demand that he complete *Das Kapital*, particularly his friend Engels and a 20th-century American black, Leadbelly. Though Marx denies his Jewish heritage, he invokes Yahweh for consolation, but it is finally Leadbelly who actively ignites the man of destiny to fulfill his mission.

He Wants Shih! is an elegant poetic tragedy. Lan, son of the last Empress of the Manchu dynasty, abdicates the warlike legacy of his mother, ignores the adoring Princess Ling, loves his stepbrother Bok, and is enthralled with his stern mentor Feng. Steeped in Eastern philosophy and the supernatural, this surrealistic archetypal myth of individuation is dramatized with ritual, masks, and pseudo-Chinese dialect. The dismembered head of the Empress continues to speak on stage while Western imperialists decimate the Chinese. Acknowledging his homosexuality in the final scene, Lan-he transforms into Lanshe. Total renunciation of sex and empire ends this fantastic play.

As *He Wants Shih!* explores the quest for selfhood, *Kontraption* examines dehumanization in a technological world. On an empty terrain Abdul and Hortten share their lives and sexual fantasies. Abdul's intolerance of their repulsive laundryman, Strauss, drives him to murder, and he is in turn transformed by a magician into a mechanical contraption. When Abdul attempts to transcend his own grotesque condition he falls to his death, leaving behind a disconsolate Hortten.

Owens returns to historical biography in *Emma Instigated Me*. The life of Emma Goldman, the 19th-century anarchist, is juxtaposed against a contemporary Author, Director, and female revolutionaries. Once again linear time is dissolved. The characters change from one to another, from character into actor into bystander. The theatricality of the play becomes its most important objective.

Owens continues to experiment. *Chucky's Hunch* was acclaimed by New York critics as hilarious and impelling. In contrast to her multi-character dramas, the solitary Chucky, a middle-aged failure, narrates a series of recriminating letters to one of his three ex-wives. Similarly in *Who Do You Want, Peire Vidal?*, two characters assume multiple roles. In this play-within-a-play a Japanese-American professor is among the transformational characters in a series of episodic confrontations. Owens's fantastic imagery, charged language, and daring confrontation with subconscious impulse remains unique in American theatre.

—Elaine Shragge

OWUSU, Martin. Ghanaian. Born in Agona, Kwaman, 11 July 1943. Educated at the University of Ghana, Legon, 1963–66, diploma in drama and theatre studies 1966; University of Bristol, 1971–73, M. Litt. in drama 1975; Brandeis University, Waltham, Massachusetts, 1976–79, Ph.D. in English and American literature 1979. Married Margaret Owusu in 1966; one daughter and two sons. Tutor, St. Augustine's College, 1966–69, and Mfantsipim School, 1969–71, both Cape Coast; lecturer, University of Cape Coast, 1973–76; assistant professor, Mass Bay Community College, 1979–82, Brandeis University, 1981–82, University of Rhode Island, Kingston, 1982–83, and Emerson College, Boston, 1984, and 1986–87. Since 1987 senior lecturer, and drama coordinator, 1988–91, University of Ghana, Legon. Recipient: British Council fellowship, 1971; ECRAG award, for acting, 1988, and for television, 1989. Address: c/o School of Performing Arts, University of Ghana, P.O. Box 25, Legon, Near Accra, Ghana.

PUBLICATIONS

Plays

The Story Ananse Told (produced Legon, 1967). London, Heinemann, 1971.
The Mightier Sword (produced Cape Coast, 1967). Included in *The Sudden Return and Other Plays*, 1973.
The Adventures of Sasa and Esi, Sasa and the King of the Forest. Accra, Ghana Publishing House, 1968.
The Adventures of Sasa and Esi, Sasa and the Witch of the Forest. Accra, Ghana Publishing House, 1968.
Anane (televised 1968; produced Legon, 1989). Included in *The Sudden Return and Other Plays*, 1973.
The Sudden Return (produced Legon, 1991). Included in *The Sudden Return and Other Plays*, 1973.
The Sudden Return and Other Plays (includes *The Mightier Sword, The Pot of Okro Soup, Anane, A Bird Called "Go-Back-for-the-Answer"*). London, Heinemann, 1973.
Python: The Legend of Aku Sika (produced Legon, 1989). Accra, Asempa Publishers, 1992.

Television Play: *Anane*, 1968.

*

Martin Owusu comments:
My plays are set in historic, mythological, and modern Ghana. I draw my material and forms largely from traditional sources. I am ceaselessly seeking to move in new directions. While I have a profound awareness of playwriting fashions in Europe and America, I am attempting to create forms that are more directly related to African experience. I am particularly interested in the mysterious and the supernatural. At the same time, I explore the effect of man's social background on his manners and morality.

* * *

Martin Owusu's first published play, *The Story Ananse Told*, taps the rich theatrical fount of the *anansesem* storytelling tradition of the Akans of Ghana. Owusu does not just flirt with the traditional storytelling form; rather he explores its essence and mode which he uses as his guiding aesthetic for creating a theatre that is contemporary while being firmly rooted in tradition. It is the dialectical tension between the traditional and the modern which makes his plays so engaging. He seems chiefly concerned with experimenting with African traditional forms of song, dance, mime, and folklore in order to make these elements intrinsically part of contemporary African theatre. It is in *The Sudden Return and Other Plays* that he successfully realises this intention.

The five plays that make up this collection are *The Sudden Return*, *The Mightier Sword*, *The Pot of Okro Soup*, *Anane*, and *A Bird Called "Go-Back-for-the-Answer"*. *The Sudden Return* possesses a "sparse and lyrical economy" and is a moving and truly "pathetic story of a middle aged revenu seeking spiritual solace for a tortured conscience." Kojo's sudden return after a 15-year absence startles as well as pleases members of his extended family, but only for a while, for he is a deeply troubled man virtually on the brink of a mental collapse. Through a series of flashbacks, Owusu reveals to the audience that Kojo, in order to get rich, had killed his wife and two daughters through ritual magic and in doing so had set his soul on fire. The climax of the play is his psychic disintegration in full view of his people, for his guilt can no longer be hidden from the world. *The Sudden Return* is a play that aspires to the tense and emotional heights of tragedy but somehow falls short because the central character cannot rise above the flaccid image of a sad soul caught in a web of anguish and the trauma of a personal past. However, it is richly textured by a neat mix of the indigenous myths, legends, and superstitions of Ghana.

The second play, *The Mightier Sword*, is a historical drama with a tripartite structure that helps to control the terrain as well as the action of the drama. Although not as emotionally and theatrically powerful as *The Sudden Return*, it is successful as a recreation of a past contained within a written history. It is concerned with dramatising certain incidents in the history of the once-powerful and extensive empire of Ghana, especially the internecine wars that raged endlessly between Ashanti and Denkyira. The central conflict revolves around the rivalry between Osei Tutu of Ashanti and Ntim Gyakari of Denkyira, while the main action is the unprovoked insults and diplomatic blunders of the latter and his subsequent defeat in the war that he brought about. As documentary drama it succeeds and is at times captivating, but as effective stage drama, it is weak because its poetry limps, while the action and the lines remain static and narrative most of the time.

A Pot of Okro Soup and *A Bird Called "Go-Back-for-the-Answer"* return to the *anansesem* tradition of *The Story Ananse Told*. Here Ananse is up to his usual tricks and his victims are a gullible couple, Apraku and Akosua, whom he tricks into giving him food in exchange for a useless piece of stone which he claims is capable of making the most delicious okro soup. This is vintage Ananse. However his scams are never malicious, merely survivalist, as in *A Bird . . .* in which our indomitable hero tricks his way into the ranks of the elders of Nana Kuntu's court. It is a rich tradition of storytelling theatre that Owusu exploits in his Ananse plays; with this character, his audience can be assured of boundless comedy full of delightful characters and lively situations. The Ananse plays are full of verve as the *anansegoro* tradition provides a versatile and dynamic structure of music, mime, and dialogue that make the plays interesting to read and stage.

The last play in the collection, *Anane*, is a tragicomedy and is also influenced by the storytelling form, for it observes the formulaic opening, and has a narrator who stands outside the action telling and commenting on the story. It is about Anane, the wayfarer, who as a baby is picked up in the bush by Bofo. He is brought up to believe that Bofo and his wife are his real parents, and that their only daughter is his sister. But when it appears that the hatred and taunts of the girl are going to lead to disaster and a sad end for Anane, his real father turns up as Stranger, who in actual fact is a king. In this play Owusu explores another style of storytelling in which the narrator remains always outside the action, unlike in the Ananse tales where Ananse is usually the narrator as well as the main character.

On the whole, Owusu is to be commended for his sophisticated experiments with Ghanaian traditional theatre forms which he successfully adapts for the modern theatre. His plays blend music, song, dance, proverb, myth, and legend in a rich theatrical mix which can be more fully appreciated in performance. He has contributed immensely in the drive towards the creation of an African theatre that would exist comfortably on the African stage as well as on all stages of the world. And in general, although his universe is his African cultural environment, his characters and themes belong to all humanity.

—Osita Okagbue

————————

OyamO. American. Born Charles F. Gordon in Elyria, Ohio, 7 September 1943. Educated at Admiral King High School, Lorain, Ohio, graduated 1962; Miami University, Oxford, Ohio, 1963–65; studied journalism, U.S. Naval Reserve, 1966 (honorable discharge); New York University, 1967–68; theater lighting program, Brooklyn College, New York, 1968; Harlem Youth Speaks/First Light Video Institute, New York, 1974; College of New Rochelle, New York, B.A. 1979; Yale University School of Drama, New Haven, Connecticut, M.F.A. 1981. Assistant technical director, New Lafayette Theatre, 1967–69, assistant stage manager, American Place Theatre, 1970, founder, The Black Magicians, theatre company, 1970, and master electrician, Negro Ensemble Company, 1971, all New York; teacher in creative writing, Afro-American Cultural Center, Buffalo, New York, 1972, Street Theatre, Eastern Correctional Institute, Napanoch, New York, 1975–76, Afro-American Cultural Center, New Haven, Connecticut, 1978, and College of New Rochelle, New York, 1979–82; writer-in-residence, Emory University, Atlanta, Georgia, 1982–83, and Playwrights Center, Minneapolis, 1984; visiting lecturer, Playwrights Workshop, Princeton University, New Jersey, 1986–87. Adjunct associate professor in playwriting, 1989–90, and since 1990 associate professor, University of Michigan, Ann Arbor. Recipient: Rockefeller grant, 1972, 1983; New York State Council on the Arts fellowship, 1972, 1975, 1982, 1985; Guggenheim fellowship, 1973; Ohio Arts Council award, 1979; Yale University School of Drama Molly Kazan award, 1980; McKnight fellowship, 1984; National Endowment for the Arts fellowship, 1985, 1992. Address: 814 Stimson, Ann Arbor, Michigan 48103; or, 157 West 120th Street, No. 3, New York, New York 10027, U.S.A.

PUBLICATIONS

Plays

Chumpanzees (produced New York, 1970).

The Negroes (produced New York, 1970). Published in *Black Troupe Magazine* (New York), vol.1, no.2, 1970.

Outta Site (produced New York, 1970). Published in *Black Theatre Magazine* (New York), vol.1, no.4, 1970.

The Thieves (produced Seattle, 1970).

Willie Bignigga (produced New York, 1970). Published in *Dramatika*, (New York), vol.3, no.1, 1970.

The Last Party (produced New York, 1970).

The Lovers (also director: produced New York, 1971).

The Advantage of Dope (produced Buffalo, New York, 1971).

His First Step in *The Corner* (produced New York, 1972). Published in *The New LaFayette Theatre Presents*, edited by Ed Bullins, New York, Grove Press, 1974.

The Breakout (produced Waterford, Connecticut, 1972; New York, 1975). Published in *Black Drama: An Anthology*, edited by Woodie King and Ron Milner, New York, n.p., 1972.

The Juice Problem (produced Waterford, Connecticut, 1974).

Crazy Niggas (produced Napanoch, New York, 1975).

A Star Is Born Again (for children) (produced New York, 1978).

Mary Goldstein and the Author (produced New York, 1979). Chicago, Third World Press, 1989.

The Place of the Spirit Dance (produced New Haven, Connecticut, 1980).

The Resurrection of Lady Lester (produced New Haven, Connecticut and New York, 1981). Published in *Plays U.S.A.: 1*, edited by James Leverett, New York, Theatre Communications Group, 1981.

Distraughter and the Great Panda Scanda (musical; produced Atlanta, Georgia, 1983).

Old Black Joe (produced San Francisco, 1984).

Every Moment (produced San Francisco, 1986).

The Temple of Youth (for children) (produced New York, 1987).

Fried Chicken and Invisibility (produced New York, 1988).

Singing Joy (produced New York, 1988).

An Evening of Living Colors, music by Olu Dara (produced Trenton, New Jersey, 1988; New York, 1989).

The Stalwarts (produced New York, 1988).

Return of the Been-To (produced New York, 1988).

Let Me Live (produced New York, 1991).

One Third of a Nation, adaptation of a play by Arthur Arent (produced Fairfax, Virginia, 1991).

Famous Orpheus (produced New Brunswick, New Jersey, 1991).

Angels in the Men's Room (produced New York, 1992).

Sanctuary (sketches) (produced New York, 1992).

Other

The Star That Could Not Play (for children). New York, OyamO Ujamaa, 1974.

Hillbilly Liberation (collection of plays and prose). New York, OyamO Ujamaa, 1976.

*   *   *

The dramas of OyamO are rarely confined by a realistic style. His works often juxtapose myth and reality and require actors to play multiple roles. His gift for the use of language evokes an intense emotional impact, while creating vivid visual images.

Although inspired by the life of Lester Young, the author does not profess his play, *The Resurrection of Lady Lester*, to be a docudrama of the famed saxophonist. Termed as a "poetic mood song," the lyrical quality of the dialogue provides one with impressions of the man and his music, instead of the cold facts which usually encumber bio-dramas. Although not featured in chronological order, scenes from the musician's life seem to flow seamlessly into one another as though streaming from Young's memory. Perhaps the most poignant of these scenes are those which illustrate his intimate professional and personal relationship with legendary singer Billie Holiday. In the end, the play manages not to be a lament for Young's tragic death, but celebrates the musician who plays his instrument from the depths of his soul.

Set in the early 1970's, *Fried Chicken and Invisibility* examines a former militant who believes he has found a scheme to obtain success in a racist American society. Traveling to a writer's conference by train, William Price and Winston McRutherford share rum and fried chicken, while discussing their experiences as African-Americans. Price, a strong-willed young man in his late 20's, recalls his turbulent youth in an impoverished neighborhood and his revolutionary activities during the 1960's. Reminiscent of the hero in Ralph Ellison's novel *The Invisible Man*, Price argues for invisibility as a strategy for survival. As long as he fits the ineffectual, stereotypical image whites have created for blacks, he believes whites will not see him as a threat and therefore target him for death. Price assumes the posture of a black revolutionary; by play's end, however, his true disposition is revealed. The young man tries to proposition McRutherford's wife who he mistakenly assumes is white, and the opinion of the whites at the writer's conference seems unduly important to him even though McRutherford informs him of its ineffectuality in furthering one's career. Thus, the drama indicts Price as a hypocritical man of few convictions unless in regard to his own self-interest.

Set in Atlanta in 1932, *Let Me Live* gives a moving portrayal of men caught in an unjust and cruel penitentiary system. The drama provides glimpses into the lives of eight African-American prisoners with scenes alternating between their current predicament and episodes revealed by memory. Mirroring prevailing socio-political conditions of the outside world, the penal system encourages the men to turn on each other for their basic needs or perversions. One recently imprisoned man, Angelo Herndon, struggles not to fall prey to the base intentions of his captors. An ardent communist jailed for organizing the disenfranchised, Herndon provides the other prisoners with the hope his socialist allies will provide the legal assistance needed to free them from their hellish existence. Drawing on his strong convictions as a source of inspiration, he refuses to despair when one of his cellmates dies from lack of medical attention or when the attorney sent to advise them proves unsympathetic and ineffectual. Attempting to break his spirit, a masochistic prison informant and enforcer—Shonuff—brutally rapes Herndon after intoxicating him with liquor. However, at play's end, when given the opportunity to deal his abuser a fatal blow, he chooses against the animalistic action. Although another prisoner decides to kill Shonuff, Herndon's personal stance against barbarism represents a tribute to those who refuse to relinquish their humanity under inhumane conditions.

Famous Orpheus is based on the mythological legend of the lovers Orpheus and Eurydice, and inspired by the film adaptation of the story, *Black Orpheus*. The poetic drama uses touches of humor to explore the connection between myth and reality. In Trinidad, an acting troupe of singing and dancing performers portrays the story guided by a "Calypsonian Griot." Orpheus—a famed guitarist—appears eager to marry his fiancée, Mariella, even though she does not share his passion for music. However, when collecting his newly made guitar, Orpheus falls desperately in love with the instrument maker's niece, Eurydice. During the revelry of Carnival, a mysterious figure representing death stalks Eurydice as he has done since she left her home in Tobago. When the figure reveals his presence to Eurydice, she runs for her life with the figure in pursuit. Orpheus gives chase as far as the wharf and tries in vain to fight the figure. Eurydice becomes entangled in an electric cable and falls to her death in the ocean. Obsessed with his love for Eurydice, Orpheus attempts to retrieve her from the Underworld. There he meets such mythological beings as Charon, Pluto, and Persephone. Ironically, these legendary figures speak in the rhythms and style of the Trinidadian people, sprinkling their dialogue with specific references to modern-day popular culture. Receiving his request to retrieve the dead Eurydice, Orpheus is allowed to return with her to the land of the living provided he does not look at her until they have left the Underworld. Unfortunately, Eurydice's feelings of neglect compel her to force Orpheus into looking at her, thus breaking his agreement. A heartbroken Orpheus returns to his own world, only to be killed by his jealously insane ex-fiancée.

—Addell Austin Anderson

———

P

PAGE, Louise. British. Born in London, 7 March 1955. Educated at High Storrs Comprehensive School, Sheffield; University of Birmingham, 1973–76, B.A. in drama and theatre arts 1976; University of Wales, Cardiff, 1976–77, post-graduate diploma in theatre studies 1977. Yorkshire Television fellow in creative writing, University of Sheffield, 1979–81; resident playwright, Royal Court Theatre, London, 1982–83; associate director, Theatre Calgary, Alberta, 1987. Recipient: George Devine award, 1982; J.T. Grein award, 1985. Agent: Phil Kelvin, Goodwin Associates, 12 Rabbit Row, London W8 4DX. Address: 6-J Oxford and Cambridge Mansions, Old Marylebone Road, London NW1 5EC, England.

PUBLICATIONS

Plays

Want-Ad (produced Birmingham, 1977; revised version produced London, 1979).
Glasshouse (produced Edinburgh, 1977).
Tissue (produced Birmingham and London, 1978; Connecticut, 1985; New York, 1992). Published in *Plays by Women 1*, edited by Michelene Wandor, London, Methuen, 1982.
Lucy (produced Bristol, 1979).
Hearing (produced Birmingham, 1979).
Flaws (produced Sheffield, 1980).
House Wives (produced Derby, 1981).
Salonika (produced London, 1982; New York, 1985). London, Methuen, 1983.
Falkland Sound/Voces de Malvinas (produced London, 1983).
Real Estate (produced London, 1984; Washington, D.C., 1985; New York, 1987). London, Methuen, 1985.
Golden Girls (produced Stratford-on-Avon, 1984; London, 1985). London, Methuen, 1985.
Beauty and the Beast (produced Liverpool and London, 1985). London, Methuen, 1986.
Goat (produced Croydon, Surrey, 1986).
Diplomatic Wives (produced Watford, 1989). London, Methuen, 1989.
Plays: One (includes *Tissue, Salonika, Real Estate, Golden Girls*). London, Methuen, 1990.
Adam Was a Gardener (produced Chichester, 1991).
Like to Live (produced New York, 1992).
Hawks and Doves (produced Nuffield, 1992).

Radio Plays: *Saturday, Late September*, 1978; *Agnus Dei*, 1980; *Armistice*, 1983.

Television Play: *Peanuts* (*Crown Court* series), 1982.

* * *

Although Louise Page's work may lack the strident militancy expected of modern women writers, her contribution lies in her singling out the experiences of women as keystones to an examination of social conditioning. These women are unexceptional, lacking in unique personality traits. Their right to be the centre of the drama stems from the situations they are in, unremarkable situations in themselves, but personal crises to the characters through whom we see the contradictions between our socially conditioned expectations and our private experience of life. By isolating these ordinary women and their mundane crises, Page explores and exposes the social preconceptions by which people define and judge, analysing the ways in which these assumptions limit our lives, complicate our decisions, and contradict our experiences.

Page adopts different theatrical styles to highlight this tension between socially conditioned expectations and private experience. In plays as different in form as *Tissue, Salonika,* and *Real Estate,* the most frequent single word is "expect," and the action of the plays is played out against a background of expectations, making the audience aware of the contradictions and distortions these ingrained preconceptions place upon individual behaviour. *Tissue,* for example, is not so much a play about breast cancer as a play in which the crisis of breast cancer serves as a focus for the examination of assumptions about female sexuality and value.

A straight narrative about a woman fighting breast cancer would, by definition, imply themes of personal heroism. The structure of *Tissue* changes the emphasis from personality and the fact of cancer to the associated ideas that make facing breast cancer more difficult for both victim and associates. Scenes from Sally's life, unconnected by time or space, irrelevant in themselves, are magnetized by Sally's cancer; their juxtaposition highlights the complex socially conditioned assumptions which create the feminine mystique. Their sequence has the logic of memory, setting each other off through association of word, image, or emotional logic and building an analysis of the obsessive connections between breasts and sexuality, sex and love, and the evaluation of women by physical appearance we absorb from childhood. Sally herself is barely a character at all. She displays no individual personality traits; her thoughts and reactions are not so much personal as situational, the responses of a woman who has breast cancer.

Breasts define womanhood. They are assumed to be the measure of attractiveness, synonymous with sexuality and prerequisites for love, happy partnership, and future. The mystique created round the female body is shown through the play to prevent realistic and healthy attitudes towards oneself and others. Sally's mother, who treated Sally's growing breasts as objects of magical impurity, is afraid to touch her own to test for cancer. Sally's boss tells of his wife who "wrecked her life trying to keep her body whole. I did not ask her to be beautiful but to be there." Although we would consciously reject the evaluation of a woman solely on the size of her breasts, the progress of the play illuminates the way these assumptions infiltrate our lives and inform our behaviour.

Through stylistic choices, Page depersonalizes the characters in order to accentuate their situations and responses. All the men and women, except Sally, are meant to be played by the same actor and actress. Direct speeches to the audience and other theatrical devices like the content-related sequence of scenes and the quick-fire lists (the "possible causes" of cancer in Scene 28) serve to demystify by removing the personal elements and emphasizing the situational behaviour and its constriction through preconceptions. The construction of the play encourages audiences to go beyond their fear of cancer and recognize the social conditioning which exacerbates their fears but which, through unravelling and understanding, can be overcome. Cancer, terrifying as it is, becomes not the end of the road, but a pathway through distorted preconceptions of femininity and the examination of the taboos of both cancer and sexuality.

Sally's greatest fear when she finds she has cancer is not that she will die, but that she will cease to be attractive to men and thus be unable to love and be loved. Only at the end, when she has a new lover, and after she has confronted, with us, the moments of her life which make up the fearful, complex confusion between her appearance and her value as a woman does she take joy in the very fact of living.

Salonika, too, celebrates the indefatigable life force which defies physical limitation, while making us aware of our assumptions and their limiting effect on our lives. The play's dream-like quality not only stems from the World War I soldier's ghost rising from the sands; the situation itself flies in the face of expectation. The mother and daughter on holiday to visit the father's grave are 84 and 64 years old. The mother has a 74-year-old lover who has hitch-hiked to Greece to be with her. In a world where love is assumed to be the reserve of the young and beautiful, these very facts cause a sense of unreality and demand that we take note of our preconceptions.

Within the play, too, the characters are constantly evaluating the expectations they held in the light of experience:

Ben	—(the ghost)—I didn't think you'd be a daughter.
Enid	—Didn't you?
Ben	—No. That's why I said to call a girl Enid. Because I thought you'd be a boy.
Leonard	—You expect everything in you to shrivel. All the hate and the longing. The lust. You don't expect to have them any more. But there isn't much else so you have them all the more. I could kill now. If I had the strength. . . . That's not what you expect.

Life as we live it defies expectation. The young man on the beach suddenly dies, leaving the old to bury him.

This dichotomy between social preconceptions and personal experience is elaborated in a more realistic form in *Real Estate*. Here Gwen, a middle-aged woman, lives with Dick, her second husband, outside Didcot where she runs a small estate agency. Her daughter Jenny, a successful London buyer, returns for the first time since she ran away 20 years before. Jenny is pregnant and has come to claim the care and attention mothers are expected, automatically, to provide. Gwen, conventional as she appears, does not revert to type. Although she dreads losing contact with Jenny again, she resists her intrusion into her life.

We assume, without thinking, that the younger, modern woman would introduce a life-style free from preconceptions and conventions. But Jenny, the very image of the modern independent woman, demands conventional responses from others. The "modernness" she brings with her is calloused,

self-centred, and totally material. She carelessly lets the dog out; she refuses to marry Eric, the child's father, while demanding his attention. When she insinuates herself into the business Gwen has founded on honesty, loyalty, and personal concern, Jenny's first act is to encourage a client to gazump.

Almost by definition, we expect a middle-aged, middle-class woman's life to be circumscribed by convention and socially approved roles, but, without proselytizing, Gwen and Dick have evolved a life-style that suits them both: "I can't ask you to stay for supper because I don't know if there's enough. Are you expecting to be asked to stay? Dick's province, not mine. He's the one who knows how long the mince has been in the freezer. How many sheets there are which haven't been turned edge to edge." Dick even embroiders tapestries! Indeed, the men in the play could not be more amenable. Eric, though divorced, appears sympathetic to his wife and is actively committed to the care of his daughter. Jenny considers this a liability; when her needs conflict with the child's, she demands priority although she refuses Eric her commitment. While Gwen has no desire to be a mother, again, nor a grandmother, Dick longs for a baby on whom to lavish loving care.

Gwen cannot share her life with Jenny. Their expectations and values are mutually exclusive. Without fuss, leaving to Dick the traditional role she once imagined for herself, Gwen takes the little acorn she planted at the play's start and plants it in the forest; like Jenny, it is well able to continue its growth on its own, though probably more willing. The placing of Gwen at the centre of the play challenges our assumptions. We are led to consider the limitations these preconceptions force upon individual lives and their lack of validity as bases for judgement and the evaluation of human behaviour. While retaining our sympathy, Gwen foils our expectations, setting them in relief so we might evaluate them.

Page structures her plays to call into question our assumptions about character, behaviour, and role and to stress that the roots of these automatic expectations and responses are in social conditioning rather than personality and psychology. Her choice of unexceptional women in unexceptional circumstances places emphasis on the way these preconceptions infiltrate the very fabric of our lives, laying bases for misunderstanding and regret and corrupting moments of crisis and decision.

—Elaine Turner

* * *

PARKER, (James) Stewart. British. 1941–1988. See 4th edition, 1988.

* * *

PARKS, Suzan-Lori. American. Educated at Mount Holyoke College, South Hadley, Massachusetts, B.A. in English and German literature (Phi Beta Kappa) 1985; the Drama studio, London, 1986. Guest lecturer, Pratt Institute, New York, 1988, University of Michigan, Ann Arbor, 1990, and Yale University, New Haven, Connecticut, and New York University, both 1990 and 1991; playwriting professor, Eugene Lang College, New York, 1990; writer-in-residence,

New School for Social Research, New York, 1991–92. Recipient: Mary E. Woolley fellowship, 1989; Naomi Kitay fellowship, 1989; National Endowment for the Arts grant, 1990, and playwriting fellowship, 1990, 1991; New York Foundation for the Arts grant, 1990; Rockefeller Foundation grant, 1990; Obie award, 1990. Agent: Wiley Hausam, International Creative Management, 40 West 57th Street, New York, New York 10019, U.S.A.

PUBLICATIONS

Plays

The Sinner's Place (produced Amherst, Massachusetts, 1984).
Betting on the Dust Commander (produced New York, 1987). New York, Dramatists Play Service, 1990.
Imperceptible Mutabilities in the Third Kingdom (produced New York, 1989).
Greeks (produced New York, 1990).
The Death of the Last Black Man in the Whole World (produced New York, 1990). Published in *Theatre* (New Haven), Summer/Fall 1990.
The America Play (produced New York, 1991).
Devotees in the Garden of Love (produced Louisville, 1991).

Screenplay: *Anemone Me*, 1990.

Radio Plays: *Pickling*, 1990; *The Third Kingdom*, 1990; *Locomotive*, 1991.

Video: *Poetry Spots*, 1989; *Alive from Off Center*, 1991.

*   *   *

A playwright with the linguistic sensibilities of a Gertrude Stein or James Joyce, who recognizes that "the world is in the word" and attempts to stage that world following the example of Samuel Beckett; who eschews stage directions, citing the model of Shakespeare: "If you're writing the play—why not put the directions in the writing"; and who draws on her own experiences as an African-American woman living in a white, male culture but who denies that her works are only about being black: "I don't want to be categorized in any way." This is Suzan-Lori Parks.

Parks sees her main task as writer to "Make words from world but set them on the page—setting them loose on the world." Others may employ neologisms, lexical transformations, phonetic shifts, spelling variations, and repetitions to further the plot and point to the theme. In Parks's plays language is the theme, and the omission of even a letter can change the direction of a play or the life of a people. "Before Columbus thuh worl usta be *roun* they put uh /d/ on thuh end of roun makin roun. Thusly they set in motion thuh end. Without that /d/ we coulda gone on spinnin for ever. Thuh /d/ think ended things ended" says Queen-then-Pharaoh Hatshepsut in *The Death of the Last Black Man in the Whole Entire World*. Fixed in place by an imposed language that defines them but is not their own, Parks's people—just as Joyce's and Beckett's—seek to get out from under the weight of words. "Talk right or you're outa here," Molly is told by her boss in *Imperceptible Mutabilities in the Third Kingdom*. A phoneme, the /sk/ in ask, defeats her as she struggles against a language—and a world—in which "Everything in its place."

Parks's first produced play is a tetraptych, whose title she

carefully defines: *Imperceptible*: "That which by its nature cannot be perceived or discerned by the mind or the senses"; *Mutabilities*: "things disposed to change"; *in the Third Kingdom*: ". . . that of fungi. Small, overlooked, out of sight, of lesser consequence. All of that. And also: the space between." The four playlets—"Snails," "Third Kingdom," "Open House," "Third Kingdom (reprise)," and "Greeks"— offer a composite picture of African-American experience, starting with contemporary time, moving backward to a mythic retelling of the black forced journey from Africa and concluding with two "family plays" depicting the terrible results of such displacement and estrangement from both language and self.

The absence of traditional narrative is counteracted by formal structures: all have five characters whose names either rhyme or are the same; "Snails," is divided into six and "Open House," and "Greeks" seven sections. Each makes use of slides and photographs offering an intertextual archival history. In each the angle of vision is, to invoke Beckett, "trine: centripetal, centrifugal and . . . not": the characters seen by white society, see themselves thus reflected but still struggle to see beyond the stereotype, the "not."

"Snails" describes three roommates, each wounded by words and each carrying two names: the one she chooses and the one by which she is known in the white community, names that "whuduhnt ours." They are visited by a robber who "didn't have no answer cause he didn't have no speech" and his opposite, a loquacious Naturalist named Lutsky, spouting the latest anthropological terminology, who comes to study the habits of the women, disguised as cockroach, the contemporary version of the fly on the wall, and who also doubles as the "exterminator" called to rid the women of the pest. Of the two it is Lutsky, Parks suggests, who is the true thief: he steals their voice by fixing them with his words the better to classify and study them.

"Third Kingdom" offers a melodic, mythic retelling of the black voyage from Africa to America, chanted by characters whose names range from Kin-Seer, Us-Seer, Shark-Seer, Soul-seer, to Over-seer. A refrain opens the section and punctuates the piece and the reprise: "Last night I dreamed of where I comed from. But where I comed from diduhnt look like nowhere like I been." The speakers evoke images of a lost home, of a voyage, and of the boat that carried them. While Shark-Seer denies their collective experience, "But we are not in uh boat!" Us-Seer insists, "But we iz."

"Open House" is a composite black/white family portrait in which Aretha Saxon, a black servant/surrogate mother to a white girl and boy is being "let go because she's gone slack." But before she leaves/expires she is subjected to "an extraction" in which her teeth are tortuously yanked from her mouth by the efficient Miss Faith, who records in the process the parallel extraction/eradication of African-American history from white memory.

Parks's last play, "Greeks," is her most powerful. The modern retelling of the Odysseus legend, focuses on the Smith family—Sergeant, Mrs. Sergeant, Buffy, Muffy, and Duffy—the mother and children awaiting the return of the father who will bring with him "his Distinction" won by faithfully serving his country in the white man's army. While they make periodic visits to "see their maker" each furlough followed by the birth of a child, and Mrs. Smith takes pride in her own mark of distinction—looking as if "You ain't traveled a mile nor sweated a drop"—Sergeant Smith waits in vain, returning finally in old age, like Odysseus, to a family that barely recognizes him. Legless, broken, he helplessly explains his dream: "Always wanted to do me somethin noble. . . . Like what they did in thuh olden days." The only glory open to him, however, is to break the fall of "that boy fallin out thuh sky. . . . I saved his life. I aint seen him since." This section ends where the first play began: the character recognizing the position of blacks in America: "we'se slugs."

The Death of the Last Black Man in the Whole Entire World is even more experimental and language-centered: a series of poetic phrases or melodious riffs depicting the life and times of Parks's composite African-American couple—Black Man with Watermelon and Black Woman with Fried Drumstick—surrounded by characters with names evoking black soul food—Lots of Grease and Lots of Pork—literary figures—And Bigger and Bigger and Bigger (after Richard Wright), and ancient times—Queen-then-Pharaoh Hatshepsut.

Beginning with the line, "The Black man moves his hands," Parks takes her people on a linguistic voyage back through African-American experience, historic and literary, animating her characters as she plays with a set of phrases and transformations, concluding with "Thuh black man he move. He move. He hans," words carved on a rock to be remembered: "because if you dont write it down we will come along and tell the future that we did not exist." Unlike the earlier play, the characters laugh at the end, having thrown off and stomped on the controlling "/d/."

Again strict form undergirds the work. The title is repeated nine times through the seven sections of the play, the first six times ending in "world," the last three "worl," allowing the Black Man to go from a fixed figure in a borrowed language to a self-animated speaker. The commensurate female experience moves from provider of chicken to supporter and encourager. Her words end the play.

Parks's work is audacious, upending traditional dramaturgy and replacing action with language shifts. Building on the earlier experiments of Ntozake Shange and Adrienne Kennedy, Parks moves even further, creating a theatre of poetry, in which the very power of language is reaffirmed by showing its potential to stand as subject and theme.

—Linda Ben-Zvi

PATRICK, John. American. Born John Patrick Goggan in Louisville, Kentucky, 17 May 1905. Educated at Holy Cross School, New Orleans; St. Edward's School, Austin, Texas; St. Mary's Seminary, LaPorte, Texas. Served in the American Field Service in India and Burma, 1942–44: captain. Radio writer, NBC, San Francisco, 1933–36; freelance writer, Hollywood, 1936–38. Recipient: Pulitzer prize, 1954; New York Drama Critics Circle award, 1954; Tony award, 1954; Donaldson award, 1954; Foreign Correspondents award, 1957; Screen Writers Guild award, 1957; William Inge award for lifetime achievement in theater, 1986. D.F.A.: Baldwin Wallace College, Berea, Ohio, 1972. Address: 22801 Wilderness Way, Boca Raton, Florida 33428, U.S.A.

PUBLICATIONS

Plays

Hell Freezes Over (produced New York, 1935).
The Willow and I (produced New York, 1942). New York, Dramatists Play Service, 1943.

The Hasty Heart (produced New York and London, 1945). New York, Random House, 1945.
The Story of Mary Surratt (produced New York, 1947). New York, Dramatists Play Service, 1947.
The Curious Savage (produced New York, 1950; Derby, 1966). New York, Dramatists Play Service, 1951.
Lo and Behold! (produced New York, 1951). New York, French, 1952.
The Teahouse of the August Moon, adaptation of a novel by Vern Sneider (produced New York, 1953; London, 1954). New York, Putnam, 1954; London, Heinemann, 1955; revised version as *Lovely Ladies, Kind Gentlemen*, music and lyrics by Stan Freeman and Franklin Underwood (produced New York, 1970), New York, French, 1970.
Good as Gold, adaptation of a novel by Alfred Toombs (produced New York, 1957).
Juniper and the Pagans, with James Norman (produced Boston, 1959).
Everybody Loves Opal (produced New York, 1961; London, 1964). New York, Dramatists Play Service, 1962.
It's Been Wonderful (produced Albuquerque, 1966). New York, Dramatists Play Service, 1976.
Everybody's Girl (produced Miami, 1967). New York, Dramatists Play Service, 1968.
Scandal Point (produced Albuquerque, 1967). New York, Dramatists Play Service, 1969.
Love Is a Time of Day (produced New York, 1969). New York, Dramatists Play Service, 1970.
A Barrel Full of Pennies (produced Paramus, New Jersey, 1970). New York, Dramatists Play Service, 1971.
Opal Is a Diamond (produced Flat Rock, North Carolina, 1971). New York, Dramatists Play Service, 1972.
Macbeth Did It (produced Flat Rock, North Carolina, 1972). New York, Dramatists Play Service, 1972.
The Dancing Mice (produced Berea, Ohio, 1972). New York, Dramatists Play Service, 1972.
The Savage Dilemma (produced Long Beach, California, 1972). New York, Dramatists Play Service, 1972.
Anybody Out There? New York, Dramatists Play Service, 1972.
Roman Conquest (produced Berea, Ohio, 1973; Altrincham, Cheshire, 1980). New York, French, 1973.
The Enigma (produced Berea, Ohio, 1973). New York, Dramatists Play Service, 1974.
Opal's Baby: A New Sequel (produced Flat Rock, North Carolina, 1973). New York, Dramatists Play Service, 1974.
Sex on the Sixth Floor: Three One Act Plays (includes *Tenacity, Ambiguity, Frustration*). New York, French, 1974.
Love Nest for Three. New York, French, 1974.
A Bad Year for Tomatoes (produced North Royalston, Ohio, 1974). New York, Dramatists Play Service, 1975.
Opal's Husband (produced Flat Rock, North Carolina, 1975). New York, Dramatists Play Service, 1975.
Noah's Animals: A Musical Allegory (produced Berea, Ohio, 1975). New York, French, 1976.
Divorce, Anyone? (produced North Royalston, Ohio, 1975). New York, Dramatists Play Service, 1976.
Suicide, Anyone? (produced St. Thomas, U.S. Virgin Islands, 1976). New York, Dramatists Play Service, 1976.
People! Three One Act Plays: Boredom, Christmas Spirit, Aptitude (produced North Royalston, Ohio, 1976). New York, French, 1980.
That's Not My Father! Three One Act Plays: Raconteur, Fettucine, Masquerade (produced St. Thomas, U.S. Virgin Islands, 1979). New York, French, 1980.

That's Not My Mother: Three One Act Plays: Seniority, Redemption, Optimism (produced St. Thomas, U.S. Virgin Islands, 1979).   New York, French, 1980.

Opal's Million Dollar Duck (produced St. Thomas, U.S. Virgin Islands, 1979).   New York, Dramatists Play Service, 1980.

The Girls of the Garden Club (produced Berea, Ohio, 1979).   New York, Dramatists Play Service, 1980.

The Magenta Moth.   New York, Dramatists Play Service, 1983.

It's a Dog's Life (includes *The Gift, Co-Incidence, The Divorce*).   New York, French, 1984.

Danny and the Deep Blue Sea (produced Louisville, 1984).

The Reluctant Rogue, or, Mother's Day.   New York, Dramatists Play Service, 1984.

Cheating Cheaters.   New York, Dramatists Play Service, 1985.

The Gay Deceiver.   New York, Dramatists Play Service, 1988.

The Doctor Will See You Now.   New York, Dramatists Play Service, 1991.

Screenplays: *Educating Father*, with Katharine Kavanaugh and Edward T. Lowe, 1936; *36 Hours to Live*, with Lou Breslow, 1936; *15 Maiden Lane*, with others, 1936; *High Tension*, with others, 1936; *Midnight Taxi*, with Lou Breslow, 1937; *Dangerously Yours*, with Lou Breslow, 1937; *The Holy Terror*, with Lou Breslow, 1937; *Sing and Be Happy*, with Lou Breslow and Ben Markson, 1937; *Look Out, Mr. Moto*, with others, 1937; *Time Out for Romance*, with others, 1937; *Born Reckless*, with others, 1937; *One Mile from Heaven*, with others, 1937; *Big Town Girl*, with others, 1937; *Battle of Broadway*, with Lou Breslow and Norman Houston, 1938; *Five of a Kind*, with Lou Breslow, 1938; *Up the River*, with Lou Breslow and Maurine Watkins, 1938; *International Settlement*, with others, 1938; *Mr. Moto Takes a Chance*, with others, 1938; *Enchantment*, 1948; *The President's Lady*, 1953; *Three Coins in the Fountain*, 1954; *Love Is a Many-Splendored Thing*, 1955; *High Society*, 1956; *The Teahouse of the August Moon*, 1956; *Les Girls*, with Vera Caspary, 1957; *Some Came Running*, with Arthur Sheekman, 1958; *The World of Susie Wong*, 1960; *The Main Attraction*, 1962; *Gigot*, with Jackie Gleason, 1962; *The Shoes of the Fisherman*, with James Kennaway, 1968.

Radio Plays: *Cecil and Sally* series (1100 scripts), 1929–33.

Television Play: *The Small Miracle*, with Arthur Dales, from the novel by Paul Gallico, 1972.

Verse

Sense and Nonsense. New York, French, 1989.

*

Manuscript Collection: Boston University.

*   *   *

John Patrick began his career as an NBC script writer who became noted for radio dramatizations of novels. He first reached Broadway in 1935 with *Hell Freezes Over*, an unsuccessful and short-lived melodrama concerning polar explorers whose dirigible crash-lands in Antarctica. Patrick continued writing, primarily Hollywood film scripts. His next play, also unsuccessful, was *The Willow and I*, a forced but sensitively written psychological drama about two sisters competing for the love of the same man and destroying each other in the struggle.

During World War II Patrick served as an ambulance driver with the British Army in North Africa, Syria, India, and Burma. His experience furnished the background for *The Hasty Heart*. Set in a military hospital behind the Assam-Burma front, the action centers on a dour Scottish sergeant sent to the convalescent ward unaware that a fatal illness condemns him to early death. His wardmates, knowing the prognosis, extend their friendship. But the Scot's suspicious nature and uncompromising independence nearly wrecks their good intentions. He gradually warms to his companions until he discovers his fatal condition and concludes that their proffered fellowship is merely pity. Ultimately he comes to accept his wardmates' goodwill, poignantly demonstrating Patrick's premise: "the importance of man's acknowledgement of his interdependency." Although some critics doubted that the stubbornly misanthropic protagonist could be capable of change, the majority found the play's effect credible and warming. It enjoyed a substantial run before being made into a motion picture, and evinced its author's growth as a dramatist in dealing more incisively with plot structure, characterization, and the effect of inner states of mind on conduct and character.

Patrick's next three plays failed to win popular approval. Based on historical events, *The Story of Mary Surratt* depicts the trial and conviction of the Washington landlady sentenced to the gallows by a vindictive military tribunal for complicity in the assassination of Abraham Lincoln. Patrick's view was that Mrs. Surratt, whose misguided son had become involved in Booth's plot, was an innocent victim of 1865 postwar hysteria. Although the drama was a compassionate protest against injustice and the vengeful concept of war guilt, playgoers did not want to be reminded of a probable miscarriage of justice in their own history at a time when war crime trials were a present reality. Critical opinion was divided, and the production failed. The drama, despite some turgidity of dialogue and the minor portrait of its title character, still emerges as a substantial work which deserved a better fate.

Patrick turned to comedy in *The Curious Savage*. The story focuses on a charmingly eccentric wealthy widow, insistent on spending her millions on a foundation financing people's daydreams, whose mendacious stepchildren commit her to a sanatorium where she finds her fellow inmates more attractive than her own sane but greedy family; with the help of the former she outwits the latter. While admitting the play's affectionate humor, critics fairly faulted the author for treating his rational "villains" too stridently and his irrational characters too romantically. Although it had only a brief run on Broadway, *The Curious Savage* has been popular with regional theatres. A sequel, *The Savage Dilemma*, was published in 1972, but not presented in New York.

Other comedies followed. *Lo and Behold!* introduces a rich, solitude-loving writer who dies, having stipulated in his will that his house be kept vacant as a sanctuary for his spirit, and returns in ghostly form to find the premises occupied by three incompatible ghosts whom he ultimately persuades to leave after all join forces to resolve a stormy courtship between a lingering housemaid and the estate's executor.

In 1953 Patrick achieved a Broadway triumph with *The Teahouse of the August Moon*, based on a novel by Vern Sneider. The play is a satire on the American Army of Occupation's attempts following World War II to bring democracy to the people of Okinawa. Amidst amusing clashes of mores and traditions, a young colonel with a past record of failure abandons standard Occupation procedure, builds the teahouse the villagers have longed for rather than a school-house, and a distillery producing a local brandy which brings them prosperity. His obtuse commanding officer visits the village and hotly orders an end to such unorthodox practices but is overridden by a Congressional declaration that the colonel's methods are the most progressive in Okinawa. Critic John Mason Brown accurately commented that "no plea for tolerance between peoples, no editorial against superimposing American customs on native tradition has ever been less didactic or more persuasive." The comedy captivated audiences and critics alike to become one of America's most successful plays, winning both the Pulitzer Prize and a New York Critics Circle award. Patrick rewrote it as a screenplay and later as a short-lived musical called *Lovely Ladies, Kind Gentlemen*.

Other comedies by Patrick include *Good as Gold* and *Everybody Loves Opal*. The former, a dramatization of a novel by Alfred Toombs, concentrates on a botanist who discovers a formula for changing gold into soil that will grow enormous vegetables but who cannot persuade Congress to give him the contents of Fort Knox. This farcical satire on politics constructed on one joke failed to find support. The title character of *Everybody Loves Opal* is a kindly recluse, living in a dilapidated mansion, who reforms three intruding petty crooks with her faith in the goodness of man. The comedy's fun was intermittent and its run short. Patrick has written several sequels.

Several other Patrick plays, mostly comedies, have been published, but not produced on Broadway. Patrick is a prolific writer of radio, film, and play scripts, but his reputation as a major craftsman in the American theatre rests chiefly on *The Teahouse of the August Moon*, one of the most successful American comedies.

—Christian H. Moe

PATRICK, Robert (Robert Patrick O'Connor). American. Born in Kilgore, Texas, 27 September 1937. Educated at Eastern New Mexico University, Portales, three years. Host, La Mama, 1965, secretary to Ruth Yorck, 1965, and doorman, Caffe Cino, 1966–68, all New York; features editor and contributor, *Astrology Magazine*, New York, 1971–72; columnist, *Other Stages*, New York, 1979–81. Artist-in-residence, Jean Cocteau Repertory Theater, New York, 1984. Recipient: *Show Business* award, 1969; Rockefeller grant, 1973; Creative Artists Public Service grant, 1976; International Thespians Society award, 1980; Janus award, 1983. Address: 2848 Wathen, Atwater, California 95301, U.S.A.

PUBLICATIONS

Plays

The Haunted Host (produced New York, 1964; London, 1975). Included in *Robert Patrick's Cheep Theatricks!*, 1972; in *Homosexual Acts*, London, Inter-Action, 1976.
Mirage (produced New York, 1965). Included in *One Man, One Woman*, 1978.

Sketches (produced New York, 1966).
The Sleeping Bag (produced New York, 1966).
Halloween Hermit (produced New York, 1966).
Indecent Exposure (produced New York, 1966).
Cheesecake (produced New York, 1966). Included in *One Man, One Woman*, 1978.
Lights, Camera, Action (includes *Lights, Camera Obscura, Action*) (produced New York, 1966; in *My Dear It Doesn't Mean a Thing*, produced London, 1976). Included in *Robert Patrick's Cheep Theatricks!*, 1972.
Warhol Machine (produced New York, 1967).
Still-Love (produced New York, 1968). Included in *Robert Patrick's Cheep Theatricks!*, 1972.
Cornered (produced New York, 1968). Included in *Robert Patrick's Cheep Theatricks!*, 1972.
Un Bel Di (produced New York, 1968). Published in *Performance* (New York), 1972.
Help, I Am (produced New York, 1968). Included in *Robert Patrick's Cheep Theatricks!*, 1972.
See Other Side (produced New York, 1968). Published in *Yale/Theatre* (New Haven, Connecticut), 1969.
Absolute Power over Movie Stars (produced New York, 1968).
Preggin and Liss (produced New York, 1968). Included in *Robert Patrick's Cheep Theatricks!*, 1972.
The Overseers (produced New York, 1968).
Angels in Agony (produced New York, 1968).
Salvation Army (produced New York, 1968).
Joyce Dynel: An American Zarzuela (as *Dynel*, produced New York, 1968; revised version, as *Joyce Dynel*, produced New York, 1969). Included in *Robert Patrick's Cheep Theatricks!*, 1972.
Fog (produced New York, 1969). Published in *G.P.U. News* (Milwaukee), 1980.
The Young of Aquarius (produced New York, 1969).
I Came to New York to Write (produced New York, 1969; Edinburgh, 1975). Included in *Robert Patrick's Cheep Theatricks!*, 1972.
Oooooooops! (produced New York, 1969).
Lily of the Valley of the Dolls (produced New York, 1969; Edinburgh, 1972).
One Person: A Monologue (produced New York, 1969; London, 1975). Included in *Robert Patrick's Cheep Theatricks!*, 1972.
Silver Skies (produced New York, 1969).
Tarquin Truthbeauty (produced New York, 1969).
Presenting Arnold Bliss (produced New York, 1969; in *The Arnold Bliss Show*, produced Edinburgh, 1972).
The Actor and the Invader (in *Kinetic Karma*, produced New York, 1969; in *The Arnold Bliss Show*, Edinburgh, 1972).
Hymen and Carbuncle (produced New York, 1970). Included in *Mercy Drop and Other Plays*, 1979.
A Bad Place to Get Your Head (produced New York, 1970).
Bead-Tangle (includes *La Répétition*) (produced New York, 1970).
Sketches and Songs (produced New York, 1970).
I Am Trying to Tell You Something (produced New York, 1970).
Angel, Honey, Baby, Darling, Dear (produced New York, 1970).
The Golden Animal (produced New York, 1970).
Picture Wire (produced New York, 1970).
The Richest Girl in the World Finds Happiness (produced New York, 1970). Included in *Robert Patrick's Cheep Theatricks!*, 1972.
A Christmas Carol (produced New York, 1971).
Shelter (produced New York, 1971).

The Golden Circle (produced New York, 1972).   New York, French, 1977(?).

Ludwig and Wagner (produced New York, 1972).   Included in *Mercy Drop and Other Plays*, 1979.

Youth Rebellion (produced New York, 1972).

Songs (produced New York, 1972).

Robert Patrick's Cheep Theatricks!, edited by Michael Feingold. New York, Winter House, 1972.

The Arnold Bliss Show (includes *Presenting Arnold Bliss*, *The Actor and the Invader*, *La Répétition*, *Arnold's Big Break*) (produced Edinburgh, 1972). Included in *Robert Patrick's Cheep Theatricks!*, 1972.

Play-by-Play (also director: produced New York, 1972; revised version produced Chicago and London, 1975). New York, French, 1975.

Something Else (produced New York, 1973; in *My Dear It Doesn't Mean a Thing*, produced London, 1976). Included in *One Man, One Woman*, 1978.

Cleaning House (produced New York, 1973).   Included in *One Man, One Woman*, 1978.

The Track of the Narwhal (produced Boston, 1973).

Judas (produced New York, 1973).   Published in *West Coast Plays 5* (Berkeley, California), Fall 1979.

Mercy Drop; or, Marvin Loves Johnny (produced New York, 1973).   Included in *Mercy Drop and Other Plays*, 1980.

The Twisted Root (produced New York, 1973).

Simultaneous Transmissions (produced New York, 1973). Published in *The Scene/2 (Plays from Off-Off-Broadway)*, edited by Stanley Nelson, New York, The Smith/New Egypt, 1974.

Hippy as a Lark (produced New York, 1973).

Imp-Prisonment (produced New York, 1973).

Kennedy's Children (produced New York, 1973; London, 1974). London, French, 1975; New York, Random House, 1976.

Love Lace (produced New York, 1974).   Included in *One Man, One Woman*, 1978.

How I Came to Be Here Tonight (produced Los Angeles, 1974).

Orpheus and Amerika, music by Rob Felstein (produced Los Angeles, 1974; New York, 1980).

Fred and Harold, and One Person (produced London, 1975). Published in *Homosexual Acts*, London, Inter-Action, 1976.

My Dear It Doesn't Mean a Thing (includes *Lights, Camera Obscura*, *Action*, *Something Else*) (produced London, 1976).

Report to the Mayor (produced New York, 1977).

Dr. Paroo (produced New York, 1981). Published in *Dramatics* (Cincinnati), 1977.

My Cup Ranneth Over (produced New York and London, 1978).   New York, Dramatists Play Service, 1979.

Mutual Benefit Life (produced New York, 1978).   New York, Dramatists Play Service, 1979.

T-Shirts (produced Minneapolis, 1978; New York, 1980). Published in *Gay Plays*, edited by William M. Hoffman, New York, Avon, 1979.

One Man, One Woman (produced New York, 1979).   New York, French, 1978.

Bank Street Breakfast (produced New York, 1979). Included in *One Man, One Woman*, 1978.

Communication Gap (produced Greensboro, North Carolina, 1979; as *All in Your Mind*, produced New York, 1981).

The Family Bar (produced Hollywood, 1979).   Included in *Mercy Drop and Other Plays*, 1979.

Mercy Drop and Other Plays (includes *The Family Bar* and

The Loves of the Artists: Ludwig and Wagner, Diaghilev and Nijinsky, and *Hymen and Carbuncle*).   New York, Calamus, 1979.

Diaghilev and Nijinsky (produced San Francisco, 1981). Included in *Mercy Drop and Other Plays*, 1979.

Sane Scientist (produced New York, 1981).

Michelangelo's Models (produced New York, 1981).   New York, Calamus Press, 1983.

24 Inches, music by David Tice, lyrics by Patrick (produced New York, 1982).

The Spinning Tree (produced Ada, Ohio, 1982; New York, 1983).

They Really Love Roba (produced New York, 1982).

Sit-Com (produced Minneapolis, 1982). Published in *Blueboy* (New York), June 1982.

Willpower, published in *Curtain* (Cincinnati), May 1982.

Blue Is for Boys (produced New York, 1983).

Nice Girl (produced New York, 1983).

Beaux-Arts Ball (produced New York, 1983).

The Comeback (produced New York, 1983).

The Holy Hooker (produced Madison, Wisconsin, 1983).

50's 60's 70's 80's (produced New York, 1984).

Big Sweet, music by LeRoy Dysart (produced Richmond, Virginia, 1984). Published in *Dramatics* (Cincinnati), 1984.

That Lovable Laughable Auntie Matter in "Disgustin' Space Lizards" (produced New York, 1985).

Bread Alone (produced New York, 1985).

No Trojan Women, music by Catherine Stornetta (produced Wallingford, Connecticut, 1985).

Left Out (produced Arroyo Grande, California, 1985). Published in *Dramatics* (Cincinnati), 1985.

The Hostages (produced New York, 1985).

The Trial of Socrates (produced New York, 1986).

Bill Batchelor Road (produced Minneapolis, 1986).

On Stage (produced Ralston, Nebraska, 1986).

Why Are They Like That? (produced Spokane, Washington, 1986).

Desert Waste (produced New York, 1986).

La Balance (produced New York, 1986).

Pouf Positive (produced New York, 1986).   Published in *Out/Write* (San Francisco), 1988.

Lust (produced New York, 1986).

Drowned Out (produced New York, 1986). Published in *One-Acts for High Schools*, Montana, Merriwether Press, 1986.

The Last Stroke (produced New York, 1987).

Explanation of a Xmas Wedding (produced New York, 1987).

Let Me Not Mar That Perfect Dream (produced New York, 1988). Published in *The James White Review* (Minneapolis), 1987.

Untold Decades (produced New York, 1988).   New York, St. Martin's Press, 1988.

The Trojan Women (produced New York, 1988).

Hello, Bob (produced New York, 1990). Published in *Stages* (New York), 1991.

Evan on Earth (produced Sacramento, California, 1991).

Un-tied States (produced Denver, Colorado, 1991).

Interruptions (produced Bakersfield, California, 1992).

Screenplays: *The Haunted Host*, 1969; *The Credit Game*, 1972.

*

Manuscript Collection: Lincoln Center Library of the Performing Arts, New York.

Theatrical Activities:
Director: **Plays**—*Wonderful, Wonderful* by Douglas Kahn,
and excerpt from *The Approach* by Jean Reavey, La Mama,
New York, 1965; artistic director of *Bb Aa Nn Gg!!!*, New
York, 1965; created Comic Book Shows at the Caffe Cino,
New York, 1966; assistant director to Tom O'Horgan and
Jerome Savary, Brandeis University, Waltham, Massachu-
setts, 1968; originated *Dracula*, Edinburgh, 1968; reopened
Bowery Follies, New York, 1972; *Silver Queen* by Paul
Foster, New York, 1973; directed many of his own plays.
Actor: **Plays**—at Caffe Cino, La Mama, and Old Reliable in
his own plays and plays by Powell Shepherd, Soren Agenoux,
John Hartnett, Stuart Koch, H.M. Koutoukas, and William
M. Hoffman.

Robert Patrick comments:

(1973) My plays are dances with words. The words are
music for the actors to dance to. They also serve many other
purposes, but primarily they give the actors images and
rhythms to create visual expressions of the play's essential
relationships. The ideal production of one of my plays would
be completely understandable even without sound, like a
silent movie. Most of my plays are written to be done with a
minimum of scenery, although I have done some fairly lavish
productions of them. My plays fall into three general classes:
1) simple histories, like *I Came to New York to Write*; 2)
surrealistic metaphors, like *The Arnold Bliss Show*, *Lights,
Camera, Action*, and *Joyce Dynel*, and 3) romances, like *Fog,
Female Flower* (unproduced), and both *The Golden Animal*
and *The Golden Circle*. Basically, I believe the importance of
a play to be this: a play is an experience the audience has
together; it is stylized to aid in perception and understanding;
and, above all, it is done by live players, and it is traced in its
minutest particulars, so that it can serve as a warning (if it is a
tragedy or comedy) or as a good example. Nothing must be
left out or it becomes merely ritual. The time of the ritual is
over. The essential experience must replace it.

*   *   *

Robert Patrick's conception of theatrical form and purpose
was molded at the Caffe Cino. He had been working there at
odd jobs in the early 1960's and, influenced by Joe Cino's
creative energy along with playwrights like Lanford Wilson,
Paul Foster, David Starkweather, and the entire Cino gang,
he wrote his first play, *The Haunted Host*. In fact, he got
his name with that production in a typical Cino haphazard
manner. Marshall Mason (later artistic director of Circle
Repertory Company and chief interpreter of Lanford
Wilson's dramas) was rushing out to get *The Haunted Host*
programs printed. Patrick, who was acting in his own show,
asked that Mason break up his name and list Robert Patrick
and Bob O'Connor, one for playwright and the other for
actor, because he didn't want people concentrating on the
fact that the playwright and actor were the same person.
When Mr. Mason came back with the program, Robert
Patrick O'Connor was known as Robert Patrick, playwright.

The Cino was a place in which theatrical rules did not exist.
Experimentation with form and content was common, and
wits-only, wing-it living was the norm. Although when the
Cino closed it was shrouded in tragedy, for most of its years
the key word there was fun. Entertainment was the only
guideline anyone followed, and this free-wheeling, fun-
obsessed lifestyle turned a naive young Texan named Bob
O'Connor into the most prolific playwright of his generation.
As he says of the off-off-Broadway movement which began,
in part, at the Cino, "For the first time a theatre movement

began, of any scope or duration, in which theatre was considered the equal of the other arts in creativity and responsibility; never before had theatre existed free of academic,
commercial, critical, religious, military, and political restraints. For the first time, a playwright wrote from himself,
not attempting to tease money, reputation, or licences from
an outside authority."

To analyze the numerous plays Patrick has written and
produced since 1964 on a script by script basis would be to
miss the profound contribution of the overall body of his
work. His genius stems not from some artfully crafted style or
from deep, intellectual questioning, but rather from an
uncanny ability to record and reflect the world around him.
Kennedy's Children, his best known play, captures the mood
of an entire era, and serves as a mirror of morals for a lost
decade.

In *Kennedy's Children* the characters, all of whom we now
recognize as 1960's stereotypes, sit separately in a bar. We're
presented with their interior monologues. The alienation, the
loneliness, and the confusion that were so apparent in
America's youth throughout the tumultuous years of Vietnam
are so accurately portrayed in *Kennedy's Children* that it is
difficult to imagine a more perfect example of the crumbling
American dream post-Vietnam.

To read Patrick for clues to a specific style is to get trapped.
For most of his career, his style has been unique only in its
absence, a fact which often drives his critics to despair. It
could only be described, perhaps, as Cinoese, or off-off-
Broadway eclectic. As he continues to write, he appears to be
coalescing his vast mental resources into a genuine effort to
produce works which deal with an unchanging human condition. The classical themes of love, greed, pride, and tormented self-doubt abound in all his plays, but never as
obviously mirrored as in his most current works. In fact, he
now says he is striving to write "classical Greek drama." If his
style is elusive, his subject certainly is not. Patrick is pure
romantic and in play after play writes primarily about relationships and heterosexual marriage. In recent years he has
become known as a gay playwright and, although he is currently using gay themes again, in fact most of his "gay" plays
are early works which have been re-discovered in the current
rage for gay theatre. Although *Michelangelo's Models* is
about how a man and a boy do get together, theirs is a
basically traditional relationship, and this play, too, is about
how people do or do not form unions. It is this general appeal
to the traditional which gives his plays not only an international popularity, but which also accounts for his enormous
effect on high school audiences. Young people are drawn to
him as to a pied piper and it is to them that he is most
expressive about the great excitement the art of theater can
generate. He travels extensively to high schools across the
country encouraging students to write for and/or to become
involved with theater.

Aside from stating the obvious, that his story is the subject
of his play, like apples are the subjects of a Cézanne painting,
and that his stories are about couples getting together or not
getting together and about how society affects a relationship,
there is no generalizing about a Patrick play. From the stark
classic tragedy of *Judas* to the innovative oratorio of an age,
Kennedy's Children, to the retrograde Renaissance fantasia
of *Michelangelo's Models*, he has been a man in love with
playwriting. He has improvised full-scale musicals in four
days (*Joyce Dynel* and *A Christmas Carol*), provided
occasional entertainments (*The Richest Girl in the World
Finds Happiness*, *Play-by-Play*, *Halloween Hermit*), whipped
out formal experiments (*Lights, Camera, Action*; *Love Lace*;
Something Else), manufactured commercial successes (*My*

Cup Ranneth Over, *Mutual Benefit Life*), helped the developing gay theatre (*Mercy Drop*, *T-Shirts*, *The Haunted Host*), and piled up eccentricities (*The Golden Animal*, *Lily of the Valley of the Dolls* and the unproduced *Female Flower*). His first collection, *Robert Patrick's Cheep Theatricks!*, was only an arbitrary gleaning of the 150 works he had accumulated by 1972; his second, *One Man, One Woman*, ranged from 1964 to 1979; his third, *Mercy Drop and Other Plays*, from 1965 through 1980. Many works are still unpublished and unproduced.

Patrick believes that words are music for the actors to dance to, and that rhythms have to help the actors build up emotions. He is very conscious of vocabulary and of how words give the actors images to act out, tell an audience story facts and plot facts or jokes or bits of poetry. In *Michelangelo's Models* Ignudo, the peasant boy who wants to marry Michelangelo, talks in Okie dialect. And Michelangelo's speech varies between the formal patterns of the other characters and the slang that unites him to Ignudo. Patrick's fascination with words sometimes gets him tangled in verbiage, but it creates a type of security blanket for this off-off-Broadway baby. Playwrights who regularly work off-off-Broadway never know if they're going to have sets, lights, music, or anything, so writing for a bare floor and some actors is a form of artistic self-preservation. Then, if you can get lights and background music to set the mood it's all the better. If Patrick is sometimes overly expository it can be traced directly to the Caffe Cino where the lights sometimes went out and action had to be described to an audience in the dark.

—Leah D. Frank

PERELMAN, S(idney) J(oseph). American. 1904–1979. See 2nd edition, 1977.

PHILLIPS, Caryl. British. Born in St. Kitts, West Indies, 13 March 1958; brought to England in 1958. Educated at schools in Leeds to 1974, and in Birmingham, 1974–76; Queen's College, Oxford, 1976–79, B.A. (honours) 1979. Founding chair, 1978, and artistic director, 1979, *Observer* Festival of Theatre, Oxford; resident dramatist, The Factory, London 1981–82; writer-in-residence, Literary Criterion Centre, Mysore, India, 1987, and Stockholm University, Sweden, 1989. Since 1990 visiting writer, Amherst College, Massachusetts. Member of the Board of Directors, Bush Theatre, London, 1985–88; member, British Film Institute Production Board, London, 1985–88. Recipient: Arts Council bursary, 1983; Malcolm X prize, 1985; Martin Luther King Memorial prize, 1987; *Sunday Times* Young Writer award, 1992. Lives in London. Agent: Judy Daish Associates, 83 Eastbourne Mews, London W2 6LQ; or, Curtis Brown, 162–168 Regent Street, London W1R 5TB, England.

PUBLICATIONS

Plays

Strange Fruit (produced Sheffield, 1980; London, 1982). Ambergate, Derbyshire, Amber Lane Press, 1981.

Where There Is Darkness (produced London, 1982). Ambergate, Derbyshire, Amber Lane Press, 1982.
The Shelter (produced London, 1983). Oxford, Amber Lane Press, 1984; New York, Applause, 1986.
The Wasted Years (broadcast 1984). In *Best Radio Plays of 1984*, London, Methuen, 1985.
Playing Away (screenplay). London, Faber, 1987.

Screenplay: *Playing Away*, 1986.

Radio Plays: *The Wasted Years*, 1984; *Crossing the River*, 1986; *The Prince of Africa*, 1987; *Writing Fiction*, 1991.

Television Plays: *The Hope and the Glory*, 1984; *The Record*, 1984; *Lost in Music*, 1985.

Novels

The Final Passage. London, Faber, 1985; New York, Penguin, 1990.
A State of Independence. London, Faber, and New York, Farrar Straus, 1986.
Cambridge. London, Bloomsbury, 1991; New York, Knopf, 1992.

Short Stories

Higher Ground. London, Viking, 1986; New York, Viking, 1989.

Other

The European Tribe (travel). London, Faber, and New York, Farrar Straus, 1987.

*

Caryl Phillips comments:
My dominant theme has been cultural and social dislocation, most commonly associated with a migratory experience.

*　*　*

Few British dramatists have been equally at home in fiction and in the theatre, but Caryl Phillips is a playwright well on his way to a reputation that overlaps a variety of categories. Most of his work has been concerned with the immigrant experience of blacks in Britain, but his perspective is both historical and international and he has applied his talent with success to drama for the stage, television, radio, and cinema. In addition, with his first two books he made a mark in the demanding form of the novel. Journalism, too, has proved a fruitful form, provoking thoughtful essays on such significant predecessors as James Baldwin. Indeed, Baldwin is an unmistakeable model and inspiration and the clear, passionate view of the United States which was seen in Baldwin's early essays, when he was able to combine a knowledge of the American South with a European perspective, is reflected in Phillips's view of Britain, though Phillips goes further and applies Baldwin's measures to Europe as well. For Phillips, it is Europe that has made him a "black" writer. In the preface to his play in two parts, *The Shelter*, he says: "In Africa I was not black. In Africa I was a writer. In Europe I am black. In Europe I am a black writer. If the missionaries [for which read critics] wish to play the game along these lines then I do not wish to be an honorary white."

Although born in St. Kitts in the West Indies, and very

conscious of his Caribbean heritage, he is a child of Leeds in England where he was reared, and his accent is Yorkshire. His plays have persistently explored the conflicts of immigration, looking at the yearning for a homeland which has achieved mythological significance and at the reality of life in a society which views the immigrant as an outsider because of colour. While immigration has remained his major theme, he has maintained an ironic distance that sees slavery as the first immigration, and that it was very much an immigration imposed on the African by Europeans and North Americans.

His perspective is finally more mid-Atlantic than Caribbean, and the title of his first play, *Strange Fruit*, is drawn directly and knowingly from the Billie Holiday song about lynching. As in much of his later work, the subject is a West Indian family held together by a single parent but pulled between two hemispheres. Although Vivien has educated her sons in England, they feel drawn to the black culture of the Caribbean.

In his next and more ambitious play, *Where There Is Darkness*, the pull of the islands is felt by a West Indian man, Albert, who 25 years earlier fled his home for the promises of England, first making a girl pregnant so her father would pay their passage to the "motherland." Phillips sets the play on the eve of Albert's return to the Caribbean, during and after a farewell party for the white friends and colleagues he has gathered in his years as a social worker. In his London garden Albert confronts the guilt of his betrayals, including the sacrifice of his first wife to his ambition, and his inability to bring the son he loves into his vision of success.

While remembering that his own father had advised him that the only way out of the gutters and up to the mountains was through exile, and foreign wealth, the sacrifice he was prepared to make was the gift of his son to England. When he took his father-in-law's money for the passage it was to the admonition that: "The child belongs to England." His disappointment when his son announces that he is leaving university to marry his pregnant black girlfriend proves the final blow in his struggle for self-justification. At the beginning of the play, Albert's confrontation with his accommodations to white society has driven him into the garden with a raging headache. At the end of the play he has stripped down to his trousers to plunge into an imaginary sea. His Faustian bargain has torn his spirit apart.

Everywhere in Phillips's work he is concerned with the price paid for admission into the white man's world, "the price of the ticket" in Baldwin's phrase. In his novel, *The Final Passage*, as in his plays of immigration, it is confrontation with the bitter reality of England that is the revelation. But the final passage is not really a voyage made by choice. It is rather the completion of a journey that began with the "middle passage," the crossing of the Atlantic from Africa to the New World in English slave ships. For the black men and women of his dramas, every choice is the result of a desperate search for a homeland to replace the Africa which they lost in generations past when their ancestors were ripped from their tribes. The final passage for the black people of the Commonwealth is the attempt to complete the voyage to English society.

In *The Shelter*, a play which takes on the potent image, taboo for so long, of black men with white women, he first imagines a shipwreck which throws together a freed slave and a white widow on a desert island at the end of the 18th century. His use of the period language is too fussy to wholly express his ideas and the ex-slave is so demonstrably superior to the English woman in thought and poetic speech that his slow transformation in her mind from ape to man is devalued, but it does nicely prepare the way for the second act: an examination of a sexual relationship between a black immigrant and a white woman in the London of the 1950's. At that key moment in the history of immigration, the man and woman can only meet in a pub by pretending to be strangers. When their relationship is revealed by a kiss they sacrifice their right to sit together but a more fundamental decision is being made. The woman has chosen to bear the man's child despite his announcement that he wants to return "home," alone.

Radio is a medium which has allowed Phillips the means to explore his ideas with greater ambition, beginning with his prize-winning play, *The Wasted Years*. In that piece he was able to recreate the pressures of school and family life on two brothers, products of the wave of immigration so ironically reflected by "news reports" describing the original arrival of the previous generation, "these dashing chaps in their colourful hats and big smiles." His starkly refined short radio play, *Crossing the River*, looked at the triangle of the slave heritage, from Africa to the United States and Britain, and his most powerful radio piece, *The Prince of Africa*, was the richly imagined story of the crossing of a slave ship. Although the destination of the ship was Boston, Massachusetts, it was a play which was firm in its condemnation of England as a nation of slavers and gave little sympathy to the guilty captain who refused to take personal responsibility for his cargo.

With a finely disciplined command of language, and wide experience of a world well beyond the triangle of the slave heritage, Phillips promises to be a dramatist who will continue to broaden the understanding of his audiences, particularly when he is allowed to drop the burden of his label as a "black" writer.

—Ned Chaillet

PIELMEIER, John. American. Born in Altoona, Pennsylvania, 23 February 1949. Educated at Catholic University, Washington, D.C., 1966–70, B.A. (summa cum laude) in speech and drama 1970 (Phil Beta Kappa); Pennsylvania State University, University Park (Shubert Fellow), 1970–73, M.F.A. in playwriting 1978. Married Irene O'Brien in 1982. Actor, 1973–82: numerous roles in regional theatres, including Actors Theatre of Louisville, Guthrie Theatre, Minneapolis, Alaska Repertory Theatre, Anchorage, Center Stage, Baltimore, and Eugene O'Neill Playwrights Conference, Waterford, Connecticut. Recipient: National Endowment for the Arts grant, 1982; Christopher award, for television play, 1984; Humanitas award, for television play, 1984. D.H.L.: St. Edward's University, Austin, Texas, 1984. Agent: Jeannine Edmunds, Artists Agency, 230 West 55th Street, Suite 17-D, New York, New York 10019. Address: R.R.1, Box 108, Horton Road, Cold Spring, New York 10516, U.S.A.

PUBLICATIONS

Plays

Soledad Brother (produced University Park, Pennsylvania, 1971).
A Chosen Room (produced Minneapolis, Minnesota, 1976).

Agnes of God (produced Louisville, 1980; New York, 1982; London, 1983). New York, New American Library, 1985.

Jass (produced New York, 1980).

Chapter Twelve: The Frog (produced Louisville, 1981).

Courage (produced Louisville, 1983; New York, 1984).

Cheek to Cheek (produced Louisville, 1983).

A Gothic Tale (also director: produced Louisville, 1983). Included in *Haunted Lives*, 1984.

Haunted Lives (includes *A Witch's Brew, A Ghost Story, A Gothic Tale*) (produced Edinburgh, 1986). New York, Dramatists Play Service, 1984.

The Boys of Winter (produced New York, 1985).

Evening (produced Cincinnati, 1986).

In Mortality (produced Louisville, 1986).

Sleight of Hand (produced New York, 1987).

The Classics Professor (produced New York, 1988).

Steeple Chase (produced New York, 1989).

Impassioned Embraces. New York, Dramatists Play Service, 1989.

Willi, music by Matthew Selman (produced Big Fork, Montana, 1991).

Young Rube, music and lyrics by Matthew Selman (produced St. Louis, Missouri, 1992).

Screenplay: *Agnes of God*, 1985.

Television Play: *Choices of the Heart*, 1983.

*

Theatrical Activities:

Director: **Play**—*A Gothic Tale*, Louisville, 1983.

Actor: **Plays**—Jasmine in *Memphis Is Gone* by Dick Hobson, New York, 1975; Tommy in *Female Transport* by Steve Gooch, Lymon in *Ballad of the Sad Café* by Edward Albee, and Boy in *Welcome to Andromeda* by Ron Whyte, all Louisville, 1975; Junior in *Waterman* by Frank B. Ford, Billy in *The Collected Works of Billy the Kid* by Michael Ondaatje, Burnaby in *The Matchmaker* by Thornton Wilder, and Kid in *Cold* by Michael Casale, all Minneapolis, 1976; Dorcas in *Gazelle Boy* by Ronald Tavel, and Dennis in *Scooter Thomas Makes It to the Top of the World* by Peter Parnell, both Waterford, Connecticut, 1977; roles in *Holidays*, and Mark in *The Shadow Box* by Michael Cristofer, both Louisville, 1979, Mark Levine in *Today a Little Extra* by Michael Kassin, Louisville, 1980; role in *The Front Page* by Ben Hecht and Charles MacArthur, Baltimore, 1980; Lysander in *A Midsummer Night's Dream*, Anchorage, Alaska, 1981; and numerous other roles.

John Pielmeier comments:

I consider myself primarily a writer for actors, and then a theatrical storyteller. I am fascinated with music and the myths of history, though *Agnes of God* is an exception to the latter. Some of my best work (*Jass* and *The Boys of Winter*) illustrates this fascination clearly. I consider writing a collaborative effort with actors and audience, and a play is never finished until it is on its feet for several weeks or for several productions. J.M. Barrie and Thornton Wilder are the playwrights closest to my heart—so in the end I suppose I am something of a theatrical romantic.

* * *

The playwright and actor John Pielmeier is indebted to regional theatre, where much of his work has been developed and presented. National attention was achieved with *Agnes of God*, whose successful Broadway engagement was preceded by nine regional productions. The drama's concern with the conflict between the real and the imagined, the rational and the irrational, is one constantly catching Pielmeier's interest.

In the published play's introduction, Pielmeier confesses that *Agnes of God* sprang from his questioning concern as a lapsed Catholic with the possibility of saints and miracles today, augmented by an evocative headline about a nunnery infanticide. The drama's circumstances are that a stigmatic and emotionally disturbed young nun, who as a child was abused by a sadistic mother, gives birth in her convent to a child later found strangled in a wastepaper basket. The saintly nun Agnes (from Latin "lamb"), who hears divine voices, claims to remember nothing about the child's conception, birth, or death. A court psychiatrist, a lapsed Catholic woman harboring a grudge against nuns, is sent to discover whether Agnes is sufficiently sane to stand trial for manslaughter. Proceeding as a narrator and detective-like investigator, the anticlerical doctor becomes absorbed with Agnes, beginning to question her own pragmatic values in the face of the situation's supernatural overtones. The overt conflict arises between the doctor and the convent's Mother Superior, later revealed to be Agnes's aunt, who is protective of Agnes and believes in the possibility of a parthenogenetic miracle. At the investigation's climax, Sister Agnes re-enacts under hypnosis the child's conception, still leaving unanswered the question of divine or human fatherhood. Yet the psychiatrist's anguished self-questioning emerges as the central issue. Unavoidable is a comparison to Peter Shaffer's *Equus*, whose plot is similar and which is more successful in the depth of its protagonist physician and in the examination of the questions raised. Nonetheless, Pielmeier has written a theatrically powerful play whose well-orchestrated female characters and strong dramatic climaxes provide an exciting theatre experience. The question of faith and miracles initially posed, while understandably not answered, tends to become obscured by the psychological issues triggering the second act's revelations erupting after an exposition-laden first act. The play stimulates the emotions but leaves the intellect confused. Pielmeier also wrote the screen version of the play.

The enigmatic dichotomy of the natural and unnatural interconnects three three-character one-acts collectively titled *Haunted Lives*. In the least effective but still eerie *A Witch's Brew*, a brother engages his doubting sister and her boyfriend in a grisly childhood game (pretending objects passed around in darkness are human body parts) in a semi-dark farmhouse basement where he claims his mother murdered and buried his long-absent father. The brother has played the game in earnest. *A Ghost Story*, a more successfully developed piece, presents two hiking strangers seeking shelter from a wintry blizzard in an isolated Maine cabin where they are joined by a mysterious girl who participates in telling frightening stories, one involving the throat-cutting of hikers by an unknown murderer. One hiker, once his companions fall asleep, tells the audience of a recurring dream, realized at the play's conclusion, in which his dead sister appears and cuts the throat of a hiker whom she first seduces. In *A Gothic Tale*, the final and most chilling tale, a young woman obsessed with the need to be loved and her manservant imprison a young rake in an island mansion tower, warning him that he will die unless admitting love for the woman. At the end of six weeks, depicted in sex scenes, the gradually starved prisoner's aversion turns to terror and capitulation as he dies discovering the skeletons of men preceding him. The drama's cumulative effect of impending doom is strong. *Haunted Lives* is a well-crafted minor work again demonstrating Pielmeier's theatrical skill.

In addition to *Courage*, a monodrama about J.M. Barrie, and *Choices of the Heart*, a teleplay about a religious worker murdered in El Salvador, two other works show an extension of Pielmeier's range. The musical *Jass* (dialect for "jazz"), with story-and-mood songs by the playwright, tells an unfocused story of the demise of a New Orleans Storyville redlight district house facing legal closure in 1917. An anti-war drama short-lived on Broadway, *The Boys of Winter*, delineates seven Marines who are wiped out on a Vietnam hilltop in 1968, except for their lieutenant who on his return coldbloodedly kills seven innocent Vietnamese civilians. The atrocity is rationalized in the men's monologues, offering the controversial premise that we all are guilty of My Lais. Despite flaws, the play's dialogue projects a salty reality, and its bloody incidents gather theatrical force.

Pielmeier is a dramatist of proven theatrical expertise; the nature of his development and the durability of his plays will be discovered by the future.

—Christian H. Moe

PIÑERO, Miguel (Antonio Gomez, Jr.). American. 1946–1988.
See 4th edition, 1988.

PINNER, David. British. Born in Peterborough, Northamptonshire, 6 October 1940. Educated at Deacon's Grammar School, Peterborough; Royal Academy of Dramatic Art, London, 2 years. Married the actress Catherine Henry Griller in 1965; one daughter and one son. Has acted with repertory companies in Sheffield, Coventry, Windsor, and Farnham, and in London. Playwright-in-residence, Peterborough Repertory Theatre, 1974. Recipient: 4 Arts Council bursaries. Agent: Elspeth Cochrane Agency, 11–13 Orlando Road, London SW4 0LE. Address: 18 Leconfield Avenue, London SW13 0LD, England .

PUBLICATIONS

Plays

Dickon (produced Hornchurch, Essex, 1966). Published in *New English Dramatists 10*, London, Penguin, 1967.
Fanghorn (produced Edinburgh and London, 1967). London, Penguin, 1966.
The Drums of Snow (televised 1968). Published in *New English Dramatists 13*, London, Penguin, 1968; revised version (produced Stanford, California, 1970; Oxford, 1974), in *Plays of the Year 42*, London, Elek, 1972.
Marriages (also director: produced London, 1969).
Lightning at the Funeral (produced Stanford, California, 1971).
The Potsdam Quartet (produced Guildford, Surrey, 1973;

revised version produced London, 1980; New York, 1982). Leominster, Herefordshire, Terra Nova, 1980; New York, French, 1982.
Cartoon (produced London, 1973).
An Evening with the GLC (produced London, 1974).
Hereward the Wake (produced Peterborough, 1974).
Shakebag (produced London, 1976). Published in *Green River Review* (University Center, Michigan), 1976.
Lucifer's Fair (produced London, 1976).
The Last Englishman (broadcast 1979; also director: produced Richmond, Surrey, 1990).
Screwball (produced Plymouth, 1982).
Revelations (produced Grinnell, Iowa, 1986).
The Teddy Bears' Picnic (produced Chester, 1988).
Skin Deep (produced Chester, 1989).

Radio Plays: *Dickon*, 1966; *Lightfall*, 1967; *Cardinal Richelieu*, 1976; *The Ex-Patriot*, 1977; *Keir Hardie*, 1978; *The Square of the Hypotenuse*, 1978, *Talleyrand*, 1978; *Drink to Me Only*, 1978; *The Last Englishman*, 1979; *Fings Ain't What They Used to Be*, 1979.

Television Plays: *The Drums of Snow*, 1968; *Strange Past*, 1974; *Juliet and Romeo* (Germany), 1976; *The Potsdam Quartet*, 1979; *Leonora*, 1981, *The Sea Horse*, 1982.

Novels

Ritual. London, Hutchinson, 1967.
With My Body. London, Weidenfeld and Nicolson, 1968.
There'll Always Be an England. London, Blond and Briggs, 1985.

*

Manuscript Collection: Grinnell College, Iowa.

Theatrical Activities:
Director: **Plays**—*Marriages*, London, 1969; *All My Sons* by Arthur Miller, London, 1976; *The Three Sisters* by Chekhov, London, 1976, *The American Dream* by Edward Albee, London, 1977; *Suddenly Last Summer* by Tennessee Williams, London, 1977; *The Last Englishman*, Richmond, 1990; *Macbeth*, London, 1992; *Andromache* by Euripides, London, 1992.
Actor: **Plays**—Hornbeck ·in *Inherit the Wind* by Jerome Lawrence and Robert E. Lee, Perth, Scotland, 1960; Ross in *Macbeth* and Magpie in *Naked Island* by Russell Bladdon, Coventry, 1961, Gratiano in *The Merchant of Venice*, Newcastle upon Tyne, 1963; title role in *Billy Liar* by Keith Waterhouse and Willis Hall, Windsor, 1964; Cassius in *The Man Who Let It Rain* by Marc Brandel, London, 1964; Laertes in *Hamlet*, Bassanio in *The Merchant of Venice*, and Edmund in *King Lear*, Sunderland, 1964–65; Lopahin in *The Cherry Orchard* by Chekhov, Hornchurch, Essex, 1965; Sergeant Trotter in *The Mousetrap* by Agatha Christie, London, 1966; Joseph in *Revelations*, Grinnell, Iowa, 1986. **Film**—*Robbery*, 1967. **Television**—*The Growing Pains of P. C. Penrose* by Roy Clarke, 1975; *The Prince Regent* by Robert Muller, 1979, *Henry V*, 1979; *Fame Is the Spur*, by Howard Spring, 1982; *A Murder Is Announced* by Agatha Christie, 1985.

* * *

David Pinner's *Fanghorn* may have misfired in the 1967 production and it may fail to sustain the comic impact and inventiveness of the first two acts in the third, but the talent is unmistakable. What is remarkable about the writing is its energy. It begins with a middle-aged man beheading roses with a sword, then fencing flirtatiously with his 16-year-old daughter, before switching to making her jump by slashing at her legs. And it sustains a brisk pace in visual surprises and twists in the plot. Occasionally an uncertain note is struck with deliberately over-written lines like "Look at that gull battering his whiteness against the hooks of the wind!" But there are also some very funny lines and plenty of intriguing changes of direction in the dialogue, which builds up to the entrance of Tamara Fanghorn, a tough-talking, leather-clad sophisticate, who arrives before she is expected, and from upstairs. Subsequent developments make it look as though she is in league with the wife to humiliate the husband, who is First Secretary to the Minister of Defence. Act 2 ends with him naked except for his pants, his hands tied with his belt and his feet with the telephone wire. As the curtain falls Tamara is brandishing a cut-throat razor and threatening "Now I am going to cut off what offends me most!" When the curtain rises on Act 3, we find him denuded only of his moustache. The crucial twist comes when his disillusioned wife has walked out on him and we find that this is what he and Tamara had wanted all along.

Dickon is centred more ordinarily on family relationships. It is vitiated by perfunctoriness and superficiality in most of its characterisation, but there is a glowingly affectionate portrait of a lower-middle-class father trying to fight off the awareness of cancer, and then later fighting with pain. But the end piles on the drama too heavily, with one son powdering morphine tablets to put the dying man out of his agony, the other son giving them to him and then the two of them fighting and laughing hysterically.

There is a curious reprise of these themes in *The Potsdam Quartet*. Act 1 ends with the leader revealing to the cellist that for ten years he has been suffering from Parkinson's Disease, and the cellist, who had thought he was going mad, reacts with a joyful demonstration of relief. How the cellist could have remained ignorant of his own condition is never adequately explained and there are only cursory references to the illness in Act 2, in which the biggest climax is provided by a quarrel between the second violin and the viola player, who are lovers, John (second violin) threatens Ronald (viola) that he is going to have the boyfriend of the leader's daughter, and Ronald responds by swallowing a succession of sleeping pills.

The play is set in an ante-room at the Potsdam Conference in 1945. The string quartet (which is based on the Griller Quartet) play two quartets to Churchill, Stalin, and Truman. Act 1 takes place immediately after the first quartet and Act 2 immediately after the second. Apart from the four musicians the only character is a Russian guard who hardly ever speaks. The characters are well contrasted and there is some amusing dialogue, but it is a realistic play in which the action is limited to what can go on in one room between four men who know each other extremely well. Act 1 cannot always avoid the pitfall of making them tell each other things they all know in order to give information to the audience and Act 2 resorts to making them all drunk in order to increase the ratio of action to talk. It lacks the energy and the courage of *Fanghorn* but after writing many unproduced plays in the six intervening years, Pinner cannot be blamed for playing safe, though the theatre can be blamed for failing to nourish the talent he originally showed.

Perhaps his two best plays are two one-acters produced at the Soho Poly. *Cartoon* is about an alcoholic cartoonist drying out in a clinic just up the road from the pub where he customarily spends his lunch-hour drinking grapefruit juice and weeping as he regularly wins money out of the fruit machine. *An Evening with the GLC* is set in a television studio where a Labour Councillor and his wife are exposed to a live interview conducted by their son. They both walk a little too willingly into the traps which are set for them, but the exposure of political dishonesties is nonetheless effective. Written when Pinner was resident playwright at Peterborough, *Hereward the Wake* is another historical play with dialogue in the modern idiom.

—Ronald Hayman

PINNOCK, Winsome. British. Born in London in 1961. Educated at Goldsmiths' College, London, B.A. (honours) in English and drama 1982. Playwright-in-residence, Tricycle Theatre, London, 1989–90, and since 1991 Royal Court Theatre, London. Recipient: Unity Theatre Trust award, 1989; George Devine award, 1991; Thames Television award, 1991. Agent: Lemon, Unna, and Durbridge, 24 Pottery Lane, Holland Park, London W11 4LZ, England.

PUBLICATIONS

Plays

The Wind of Change (produced London, 1987).
Leave Taking (produced Liverpool, 1988; London, 1990). Published in *First Run*, edited by Kate Harwood, London, Hern, 1989.
Picture Palace (produced London, 1988).
A Rock in Water (produced London, 1989). Published in *Black Plays: Two*, edited by Yvonne Brewster, London, Methuen, 1989.
A Hero's Welcome (produced London, 1989).
Talking in Tongues (produced London, 1991).

Television Plays: episode in *South of the Border* series, 1988; episode in *Chalkface* series, 1991.

*   *   *

Winsome Pinnock is widely acknowledged as one of the leading young talents currently writing for the British theatre. She is also known as one of a very small circle of black women playwrights whose work is regularly produced at mainstream theatres in Britain, most notably at the Royal Court.

Though Pinnock was born and educated in London, her work is influenced by an awareness of the role of a Caribbean heritage in the lives of black communities in England. Some of her most recent work has also dealt with the theme of civil rights. These two interests combine and enrich the language, as well as the themes, of her plays.

One of Pinnock's best-known plays is *A Hero's Welcome*, first presented as a rehearsed reading at the Royal Court in 1986, and given a full production—in a revised version—at the Theatre Upstairs in 1989 (produced by the Women's Playhouse Trust). The play is set in Jamaica and tells a story of family tension and young love, framed in the traditions and expectations of West Indian culture but informed by the British context of its writing and production. It centres on three young women, Minda, Sis, and Ishbel. All three grow up in a small Caribbean community in 1947. All are looking for a way out of poverty, for better lives, and Len, the returning "hero" (charged with a strong sexual drive which is exciting and enticing to the young women) seems to symbolize that kind of possibility and hope. Only the two older women characters, Nana and Mrs. Walker, are able to offer the wisdom of age and experience which keeps the girls in line, in their community. That such a play found a wide and diverse audience is itself an achievement, but more important was the national recognition which this production brought to Pinnock.

Also in 1989—in fact, one month before *A Hero's Welcome* was given its full production—the Theatre Upstairs premiered Pinnock's *A Rock in Water*. This play broke new ground for Pinnock and for London audiences, in its powerful evocation of a recent historical figure: Claudia Jones, the founder of the Notting Hill Carnivals in the mid-1950's and a dedicated worker at one of the first black presses, the *West Indian Gazette*. In bringing Jones to public attention, Pinnock engaged in a process of "writing [black] women into history." And as Jones was not just any woman, the play also engaged audiences in a recognition of the importance of location and cultural identity in the lives of black women and men. The play chronicles the life of Claudia Jones in Trinidad and Harlem as well as in London, where she lived only after she was exiled to England after being accused of "un-American activities."

A Rock in Water was commissioned by the Royal Court's Young People's theatre and was developed through workshops with actors. But Pinnock also did her own research by interviewing people who had known Claudia Jones: she brought the woman to life through the memories of contemporaries and co-workers, including the actress Corinne Skinner-Carter (who was featured in *A Hero's Welcome*). The play was performed by 14 members of the Young People's Theatre, all of whom had been closely involved in the development of the ideas which Pinnock wove into the play.

Leave Taking was first produced at the Liverpool Playhouse Studio in 1988, the same year which saw the national tour of *Picture Palace*, produced by the Women's Theatre Group. While *Picture Palace* focused on the roles which women play and the images which are used in advertising and the media in Britain, *Leave Taking* followed on from *A Hero's Welcome* in its cross-cultural focus. *Leave Taking* was given a revival in 1990, when it was directed by Jules Wright and produced by the Women's Playhouse Trust at the Royal Court. The play's popularity is related to its scope and its intelligent yet humorous view of relationships between individuals and their cultural identities. *Leave Taking* also introduced the theme of cultural difference in the coming of awareness of individuals and groups of black women and men, a topic which is rarely dealt with in British theatre. *Leave Taking* was revived for a run at the Belgrade Theatre, Coventry in May 1992.

Pinnock's most recent play, *Talking in Tongues*, was performed at the Royal Court Theatre (directed by Hetty MacDonald), when Pinnock was writer-in-residence there in 1991. In this play, Pinnock's concern with the intermingling of cultures, identities, and voices is further developed within the story of a number of black and white friends and colleagues who come together at a New Year's Eve party. Sexuality and inter-racial relationships are represented, as are the themes of competition and identification between blacks and whites, women and men. As in her other work, the use of dialect frames the play with the sound and rhythm of another language. The film adaptation of *Talking in Tongues* is already underway.

In these plays, as in most of Pinnock's work to date, the realist drama focuses on the central dilemma of the black woman coming to terms with (predominantly) white British society. Pinnock's talent as a playwright is enriched in all of her work by her keen awareness of the nuances of language, and by her ability to reach out to and communicate with the many different "communities" and individuals who make up the audiences of her plays.

—Lizbeth Goodman

PINTER, Harold. British. Born in Hackney, London, 10 October 1930. Educated at Hackney Downs Grammar School, 1943–47; Royal Academy of Dramatic Art, London, 1948. Conscientious objector: no military service. Married 1) the actress Vivien Merchant in 1956 (divorced 1980), one son; 2) the writer Lady Antonia Fraser in 1980. Professional actor, 1949–60, and occasionally since then; also a director; associate director, National Theatre, London, 1973–83; director, United British Artists, 1983; since 1988 editor and publisher, Greville Press, Warwick, and since 1989 member of the editorial board, *Cricket World*. Recipient: *Evening Standard* award, 1960; Newspaper Guild of New York award, 1962; Italia prize, for television play, 1962; Berlin Film Festival Silver Bear, 1963; Screenwriters Guild award, for television play, 1963, for screenplay, 1963; New York Film Critics award, 1964; BAFTA award, 1965, 1971; Tony award, 1967; Whitbread award, 1967; New York Drama Critics Circle award, 1967, 1980; Shakespeare prize (Hamburg), 1970; Writers Guild award, 1971; Cannes Film Festival Golden Palm, 1971; Austrian State prize, 1973; Pirandello prize, 1980; Commonwealth award, 1981; Donatello prize, 1982; British Theatre Association award, 1983, 1985; Bobst award, 1984. D.Litt.: universities of Reading, 1970, Birmingham, 1971, Glasgow, 1974, East Anglia, Norwich, 1974, Stirling, 1979, Hull, 1986, and Sussex, 1990; Brown University, Providence, Rhode Island, 1982. Honorary fellow, Modern Language Association (USA), 1970; fellow, Royal Society of Literature; honorary member, American Academy and Institute of Arts and Letters, 1984, and American Academy of Arts and Sciences, 1985; honorary fellow, Queen Mary College, London, 1987. C.B.E. (Commander, Order of the British Empire), 1966. Lives in London. Agent: Judy Daish Associates, 83 Eastbourne Mews, London W2 6LQ, England.

PUBLICATIONS

Plays

The Room (produced Bristol, 1957; also director: produced London, 1960; New York, 1964). Included in *The Birthday Party and Other Plays*, 1960.
The Birthday Party (produced Cambridge and London, 1958; San Francisco, 1960; New York, 1967). London, Encore, 1959; included in *The Birthday Party and Other Plays*, 1960; revised version, London, Methuen, 1965.

Sketches in *One to Another* (produced London, 1959). London, French, 1960.

Sketches in *Pieces of Eight* (produced London, 1959). Included in *A Slight Ache and Other Plays*, 1961; in *The Dwarfs and Eight Revue Sketches*, 1965.

A Slight Ache (broadcast 1959; produced London, 1961; New York, 1962). Included in *A Slight Ache and Other Plays*, 1961; in *Three Plays*, 1962.

The Dumb Waiter (produced, in German, Frankfurt, 1959; London, 1960; Madison, Wisconsin, and New York, 1962). Included in *The Birthday Party and Other Plays*, 1960.

The Dwarfs (broadcast 1960; also director: produced London, 1963; revised version produced Edinburgh, 1966; Boston, 1967; New York, 1974). Included in *A Slight Ache and Other Plays*, 1961, in *Three Plays*, 1962.

The Birthday Party and Other Plays (includes *The Dumb Waiter* and *The Room*). London, Methuen, 1960; as *The Birthday Party and The Room* (includes *The Dumb Waiter*), New York, Grove Press, 1961.

The Caretaker (produced London, 1960; New York, 1961). London, Methuen, 1960; with *The Dumb Waiter*, New York, Grove Press, 1961.

Night School (televised 1960). Included in *Tea Party and Other Plays*, 1967; in *Early Plays*, 1968.

A Night Out (broadcast 1960; produced Dublin and London, 1961; New York, 1971). Included in *A Slight Ache and Other Plays*, 1961; in *Early Plays*, 1968.

A Slight Ache and Other Plays (includes *The Dwarfs, A Night Out*, and sketches). London, Methuen, 1961.

The Collection (televised 1961; also co-director; produced London, 1962; New York, 1963; revised version, televised 1978). London, French, 1962; in *Three Plays*, 1962.

Three Plays. New York, Grove Press, 1962.

The Lover (televised 1963; also director: produced London, 1963; New York, 1964). Included in *The Collection, and The Lover*, 1963; published separately, New York, Dramatists Play Service, 1965.

The Collection, and The Lover (includes the prose piece *The Examination*). London, Methuen, 1963.

The Compartment (unreleased screenplay), in *Project 1*, with Samuel Beckett and Eugène Ionesco. New York, Grove Press, 1963.

Dialogue for Three, published in *Stand* (Newcastle upon Tyne), vol. 6, no. 3, 1963.

Tea Party (televised 1965; produced New York, 1968; London, 1970). London, Methuen, 1965; New York, Grove Press, 1966; revised version, London, Karnac, 1968.

The Homecoming (produced London, 1965; New York, 1967). London, Methuen, 1965; New York, Grove Press, 1966; revised version, London, Karnac, 1968.

The Dwarfs and Eight Revue Sketches (includes *Trouble in the Works, The Black and White, Request Stop, Last to Go, Applicant, Interview, That's All, That's Your Trouble*). New York, Dramatists Play Service, 1965.

The Basement (televised 1967; produced New York, 1968; London, 1970). Included in *Tea Party and Other Plays*, 1967; in *The Lover, The Tea Party, The Basement*, 1967.

Tea Party and Other Plays. London, Methuen, 1967.

The Lover, The Tea Party, The Basement. New York, Grove Press, 1967.

Early Plays: A Night Out, Night School, Revue Sketches. New York, Grove Press, 1968.

Sketches by Pinter (produced New York, 1969). Included in *Early Plays*, 1968.

Landscape (broadcast 1968; produced London, 1969; New York, 1970). London, Pendragon Press, 1968; included in *Landscape, and Silence*, 1969.

Silence (produced London, 1969; New York, 1970). Included in *Landscape, and Silence*, 1969.

Landscape, and Silence (includes *Night*). London, Methuen, 1969; New York, Grove Press, 1970.

Night, in *Mixed Doubles* (produced London, 1969). Included in *Landscape, and Silence*, 1969.

Five Screenplays (includes *The Caretaker, The Servant, The Pumpkin Eater, Accident, The Quiller Memorandum*). London, Methuen, 1971; modified version, omitting *The Caretaker* and including *The Go-Between*, London, Karnac, 1971; New York, Grove Press, 1973.

Old Times (produced London and New York, 1971). London, Methuen, and New York, Grove Press, 1971.

Monologue (televised 1973; produced London, 1973). London, Covent Garden Press, 1973.

No Man's Land (produced London, 1975; New York, 1976). London, Eyre Methuen, and New York, Grove Press, 1975.

Plays 1–4. London, Eyre Methuen, 1975–81; as *Complete Works 1–4*, New York, Grove Press, 1977–81.

The Proust Screenplay: A la Recherche du Temps Perdu. New York, New Directions, 1977; London, Eyre Methuen-Chatto and Windus, 1978.

Betrayal (produced London, 1978; New York, 1980). London, Eyre Methuen, 1978; New York, Grove Press, 1979.

The Hothouse (also director: produced London, 1980). London, Eyre Methuen, and New York, Grove Press, 1980; revised version (produced Providence, Rhode Island, and New York, 1982), Methuen, 1982.

Family Voices (broadcast 1981; produced London and Cambridge, Massachusetts, 1981). London, Next Editions, and New York, Grove Press, 1981.

The Screenplay of The French Lieutenant's Woman. London, Cape, and Boston, Little Brown, 1981.

The French Lieutenant's Woman and Other Screenplays (includes *Langrishe, Go Down* and *The Last Tycoon*). London, Methuen, 1982.

Other Places (includes *Family Voices, Victoria Station, A Kind of Alaska*) (produced London, 1982). London, Methuen, 1982; New York, Grove Press, 1983; revised version, including *One for the Road* and omitting *Family Voices* (produced New York, 1984; London, 1985).

Precisely (sketch), in *The Big One* (produced London, 1983).

One for the Road (also director: produced London, 1984; in *Other Places*, produced New York, 1984). London, Methuen, 1984; revised version, Methuen, 1985; New York, Grove Press, 1986.

Mountain Language (also director: produced London, 1988). London, Faber, 1988; New York, Grove Press, 1989.

The Heat of the Day, adaptation of the novel by Elizabeth Bowen (televized 1989). London, Faber, 1989.

The Comfort of Strangers and Other Screenplays (includes *Reunion, Turtle Diary, Victory*). London, Faber, 1990.

Party Time (also director: produced London, 1991). With *Mountain Language*, London, Faber, 1991.

The New World Order (also director: produced London, 1991).

Screenplays: *The Servant*, 1963; *The Guest (The Caretaker)*, 1964; *The Pumpkin Eater*, 1964; *The Quiller Memorandum*, 1966; *Accident*, 1967; *The Birthday Party*, 1968; *The Go-Between*, 1971; *The Homecoming*, 1973; *The Last Tycoon*, 1976; *The French Lieutenant's Woman*, 1981; *Betrayal*, 1982; *Turtle Diary*, 1985; *The Trial*, 1989; *Reunion*, 1989; *The Handmaid's Tale*, 1990; *The Comfort of Strangers*, 1990; *The Remains of the Day*, 1991.

Radio Plays: *A Slight Ache*, 1959; *The Dwarfs*, 1960; *A Night Out*, 1960; *Landscape*, 1968; *Family Voices*, 1981; *Players*, 1985.

Television Plays: *Night School*, 1960; *The Collection*, 1961, revised version, 1978; *The Lover*, 1963; *Tea Party*, 1965; *The Basement*, 1967; *Monologue*, 1973; *Langrishe, Go Down*, from the novel by Aidan Higgins, 1978; *Mountain Language*, 1988; *The Heat of the Day*, 1989; *Party Time*, 1992.

Novel

The Dwarfs. London, Faber, and New York, Grove Weidenfeld, 1990.

Verse

Poems, edited by Alan Clodd.   London, Enitharmon Press, 1968; revised edition, 1971.
I Know the Place.   Warwick, Greville Press, 1979.

Other

Mac (on Anew McMaster).   London, Pendragon Press, 1968.
Poems and Prose 1949–1977.   London, Eyre Methuen, and New York, Grove Press, 1978; revised edition, as *Collected Poems and Prose*, Methuen, 1986.

Editor, with John Fuller and Peter Redgrove, *New Poems 1967: A PEN Anthology*.   London, Hutchinson, 1968.
Editor, with Geoffrey Godbert and Anthony Astbury, *100 Poems by 100 Poets*.   London, Methuen, 1986; New York, Grove Press, 1987.

*

Bibliography: *Pinter: A Bibliography: His Works and Occasional Writings with a Comprehensive Checklist of Criticism and Reviews of the London Productions* by Rudiger Imhof, London, TQ Publications, 1975; *Harold Pinter: An Annotated Bibliography* by Steven H. Gale, Boston, Hall, and London, Prior, 1978.

Critical Studies (selection): *Harold Pinter*, New York, Twayne, 1967, revised edition, 1981, and *Harold Pinter*, New York, St. Martin's Press, 1975, London, Macmillan, 1976, both by Arnold P. Hinchliffe; *Harold Pinter* by Ronald Hayman, London, Heinemann, 1968, New York, Ungar, 1973, revised edition, Heinemann, 1980; *Harold Pinter* by John Russell Taylor, London, Longman, 1969; *Stratagems to Uncover Nakedness: The Dramas of Harold Pinter* by Lois Gordon, Columbia, University of Missouri Press, 1969; *Harold Pinter: The Poetics of Silence* by James H. Hollis, Carbondale, Southern Illinois University Press, 1970; *Harold Pinter* by Alrene Sykes, St. Lucia, University of Queensland Press, and New York, Humanities Press, 1970; *The Peopled Wound: The Plays of Harold Pinter* by Martin Esslin, London, Methuen, and New York, Doubleday, 1970, revised edition, as *Pinter: A Study of His Plays*, Methuen, 1973, New York, Norton, 1976, revised edition, Eyre Methuen, 1977, revised edition, as *Pinter: The Playwright*, Methuen, 1982; *The Dramatic World of Harold Pinter: Its Basis in Ritual* by Katherine H. Burkman, Columbus, Ohio State University Press, 1971; *Pinter: A Collection of Critical Essays* edited by Arthur Ganz, Englewood Cliffs, New Jersey, Prentice Hall, 1972; *The Plays of Harold Pinter: An Assessment* by Simon

Trussler, London, Gollancz, 1973; *The Pinter Problem* by Austin E. Quigley, Princeton, New Jersey, Princeton University Press, 1975; *The Dream Structure of Pinter's Plays: A Psychoanalytic Approach* by Lucina Paquet Gabbard, Rutherford, New Jersey, Fairleigh Dickinson University Press, 1976; *Where the Laughter Stops: Pinter's Tragi-Comedy*, Columbia, University of Missouri Press, 1976, and *Harold Pinter*, London, Macmillan, and New York, Grove Press, 1982, both by Bernard F. Dukore; *Butter's Going Up: A Critical Analysis of Harold Pinter's Work* by Steven H. Gale, Durham, North Carolina, Duke University Press, 1977, and *Harold Pinter: Critical Approaches* edited by Gale, Madison, New Jersey, Fairleigh Dickinson University Press, 1986; *Harold Pinter: A Critical Evaluation* by Surendra Sahai, Salzburg, Austria, Salzburg Studies in English Literature, 1981; *Canters and Chronicles: The Use of Narrative in the Plays of Samuel Beckett and Harold Pinter* by Kristin Morrison, Chicago, University of Chicago Press, 1983; *Harold Pinter* by Guido Almansi and Simon Henderson, London, Methuen, 1983; *Pinter: The Player's Playwright* by David T. Thompson, London, Macmillan, and New York, Schocken, 1985; *Pinter's Comic Play* by Elin Diamond, Lewisburg, Pennsylvania, Bucknell University Press, 1985; *Harold Pinter: You Never Heard Such Silence* edited by Alan Bold, London, Vision Press, and New York, Barnes and Noble, 1985; *Making Pictures: The Pinter Screenplays* by Joanne Klein, Columbus, Ohio State University Press, 1985; *Harold Pinter: The Birthday Party, The Caretaker, and The Homecoming: A Casebook* edited by Michael Scott, London, Macmillan, 1986; *Pinter's Female Portraits: A Study of Female Characters in the Plays of Pinter* by Elizabeth Sakellaridou, London, Macmillan, 1988; *Harold Pinter: Towards a Poetics of His Plays* by Volker Strunk, Bern, Switzerland, Peter Lang, 1989; *Pinter in Play* by Susan Merritt, Durham, North Carolina, Duke University Press, 1990; *Harold Pinter: A Casebook* by Lois Gordon, New York, Garland, 1990.

Theatrical Activities:
Director: **Plays**—*The Birthday Party*, Oxford and Cambridge, 1958; *The Room*, London, 1960; *The Collection* (co-director, with Peter Hall), London, 1962; *The Lover*, London, 1963; *The Dwarfs*, London, 1963; *The Birthday Party*, London, 1964; *The Man in the Glass Booth* by Robert Shaw, London, 1967, New York, 1968; *Exiles* by James Joyce, London, 1970; *Butley* by Simon Gray, Oxford and London, 1971; *Next of Kin* by John Hopkins, London, 1974; *Otherwise Engaged* by Simon Gray, Oxford and London, 1975, New York, 1977; *Blithe Spirit* by Noël Coward, London, 1976; *The Innocents* by William Archibald, New York, 1976; *The Rear Column* by Simon Gray, London, 1978; *Close of Play* by Simon Gray, London, 1979; *The Hothouse*, London, 1980; *Quartermaine's Terms* by Simon Gray, London, 1981; *Incident at Tulse Hill* by Robert East, London, 1981; *The Trojan War Will Not Take Place* by Jean Giraudoux, London, 1983; *The Common Pursuit* by Simon Gray, London, 1984; *One for the Road, and Victoria Station*, London, 1984; *Sweet Bird of Youth* by Tennessee Williams, London, 1985; *Circe and Bravo* by Donald Freed, London, 1986; *Mountain Language*, London, 1988; *Vanilla* by Jane Stanton Hitchcock, Bath and London, 1990; *Party Time*, London, 1991; *The New World Order*, London, 1991. **Film**—*Butley*, 1976. **Television**—*The Rear Column* by Simon Gray, 1980; *The Hothouse*, 1981.
Actor (as David Baron and Harold Pinter): **Plays**—with Anew McMaster's theatre company in Ireland, 1950–52; with Donald Wolfit's theatre company, Kings Theatre,

Hammersmith, London, 1953, numerous provincial repertory companies, 1953–60; Mick in *The Caretaker*, London, 1964; Goldberg in *The Birthday Party*, Cheltenham, 1964; Lenny in *The Homecoming*, Watford, Hertfordshire, 1969; Deeley in *Old Times*, Los Angeles, 1985; Hirst in *No Man's Land*, London, 1992. **Radio**—*Monologue*, 1975; *Rough for Radio* by Samuel Beckett, 1976; *Two Plays* by Václav Havel, 1977. **Films**—*The Servant*, 1963; *Accident*, 1967; *The Rise and Rise of Michael Rimmer*, 1970. **Television**—*Rogue Male*, 1976; *Langrishe, Go Down*, 1978; *The Birthday Party*, 1986.

* * *

In a remarkably prolific period between 1957 and 1965, Harold Pinter established himself as the most gifted playwright in England and the author of a unique dramatic idiom. Popularly labelled "the Pinteresque," Pinter's theater is not "of the absurd"; nor is it a "drama of menace," both of which portray the gratuitous visitation upon innocent victims of external forces of terror or "the absurd." Actually, "the Pinteresque" consists of a much more frightening visitation: Pinter's comfortable people (at least through *Silence* and *Landscape*), unlike the innocents of Kafka's or even Beckett's worlds, are besieged by their own internal fears and longings and their own irrepressible guilts and menacing sexual drives, and it is these which invariably wage successful war against the tidy life-styles they have constructed in order to survive from day to day.

Pinter's characters, usually enclosed in a room, organize their lives with the "games people play." But in their games or role-playing—where each has agreed to a specific scenario with implicit limits and taboos—they often say one thing but really feel and often communicate another. During their exchanges, in fact, the verbal is only the most superficial level of communication. The connotations of their words and their accompanying gestures, or pauses, or *double-entendres*—and their hesitations and silences—really communicate a second level of meaning often opposed to the first. Pinter himself has said of language: "The speech we hear is an indication of that which we don't hear. It is a necessary avoidance, a violent, sly, and anguished or mocking smoke screen which keeps the other in its true place. When true silence falls we are left with echo but are nearer nakedness. One way of looking at speech is to say that it is a constant stratagem to cover nakedness." Indeed, one way of looking at Pinter's plays is to say that they are dramatic stratagems that uncover nakedness.

Into his characters' rooms, and into their ritualized and verbal relationships, a stranger invariably enters, whereupon language begins to disintegrate, and the protection promised by the room becomes threatened. The commonplace room, in fact, becomes the violent scene of mental and physical breakdown. What occurs, in effect, is that the characters *project on to* the stranger—an intruder into their precarious, psychic stability—their deepest fears. The so-called victimizers—Goldberg and McCann in *The Birthday Party*; Riley in *The Room*; the blind, mute matchseller in *A Slight Ache*; the visiting, unfamiliar sister-in-law in *The Homecoming*; the old, garrulous, and admittedly opportunistic Davies in *The Caretaker*; and even the mechanical dumb waiter in *The Dumb Waiter*—all function as screens upon which the characters externalize their own irrationality, that side of themselves which the games have ultimately been inadequate to hide. Pinter's "intruders" are, in a sense, his technique for leading his characters to expose their true identities. What is, of course, simultaneously funny and horrific is that the games constructed—and even the "intruders" or screens, which are mirror images of the characters—contain within themselves the boring lives already lived *and* the violence struggling for expression.

In Pinter's first play, *The Room*, Rose coddles, feeds, clothes, and emasculates her silent husband, Bert, fittingly portrayed as a child (he has agreed to play the passive child in their relationship), wearing a silly hat and reading comic books. Protective of her precarious stability she admits: "This is a good room. You've got a chance in a place like this. . . . It's cold out. . . . It's murder." When a young couple enters (a mirror of Rose and Bert many years before), thinking her flat free, she actually experiences them as potential "murderers." This is exacerbated by her landlord's (Kidd's) retaliatory remarks (because of her earlier putdown) and his mention that a blind, black man in the basement (an obvious image of her subterranean mind) is waiting to "see" her. For the rest of the play, Rose acts out her rage, sexual appetite, and then guilt toward the black Riley, as though re-enacting an earlier Oedipal crime. From her "You're all deaf and dumb and blind, the lot of you," she succumbs to his "Sal [a childhood name]. . . . I want you to come home" and caresses his eyes and head. With Bert's return, following this enactment of her most basic instinctual/tabooed behavior, she becomes blind.

In *The Birthday Party* a young man has similarly secluded himself in order to hide from some lingering childhood guilt. When the two strangers Goldberg and McCann enter his seaside retreat, Stanley becomes violent and projects upon them his own fantasies and guilts: "You stink of sin"; "you contaminate womankind. . . . Mother defiler. . . . You verminate the sheet of your birth." Later at a "celebration," his landlady, Meg, with whom Stanley has structured a safe though flirtatious child-lover relationship, and the neighbor, Lulu, along with Goldberg and McCann, act out both Stanley's taboo Oedipal impulses and his repulsion and guilt toward these drives. As Rose became blind, Stanley becomes mute. In *The Dumb Waiter* two hitmen lose control when some actually very funny messages descend on the building's dumb waiter and the w.c. misfunctions, whereupon their carefully measured roles are upset. In *The Caretaker* the intrusion of a harmless (though manipulative and highly verbal) old man threatens the carefully designed relationship of two brothers. In *The Homecoming* a presumably stable all-male household is exposed in all its rage, confused sexuality, and utter precariousness when an unknown woman (the visiting wife of a third son) appears. Her mere presence threatens everyone's identity. In *The Basement* and *Tea Party* Pinter returns to his earlier triangular patterns, and focuses on the breakdown of orderly and controlled behavior for displays of cuckoldry and homosexuality.

Silence and *Landscape* indicate a new direction. The same childless couples inhabit these plays, but they have long ago learned that playing games will not assure their relationship. Nothing is certain in their isolated rooms, and least of all, identity or connection. Each not only fails to understand himself (unable to distinguish fantasy from experience) but he can never know the stranger who calls himself his spouse. There is a kind of finality in these plays but also a poignancy about these people so inextricably locked within themselves.

The plays demand a more poetic reading—for the lyrical sense of the characters' rationalizations, hopes, fears, and fantasies, which are true at one and the same time. Still in the tradition of Joyce, Woolf, and Beckett, Pinter has now moved from earlier explorations of the underside of self (and what Freud called "the seething cauldron" beneath logical thought and act) to a dramatic rendering of the simultaneous levels of fantasy and real experience that equally occupy the individual. He has said of the complexities and ultimate mystery of human behavior: "The desire for verification on the part of us all, with regard to our own experience and the experience of others, is understandable, but cannot always be satisfied. I suggest there can be no hard distinctions between what is real and what is unreal, nor between what is true and what is false. A thing is not necessarily either true or false; it can be both true and false."

The details, characters, and images of *Silence* and *Landscape* are similar, as though each were two halves of a whole. Poetic images of growing old, they tell of brief and unfulfilled love affairs. Their details are of walks in the country, moments in pubs, and flights of birds; recollections are illuminated by memories of fading sunlight or grey clouds or gusts of rain. Speakers interrupt their wistful thoughts with lusty outbursts about the most mundane of matters. Every word, gesture, color, and mood reverberates, and each character's reveries define the others; although their conversations are not directed to the other, each one explains the way in which life has passed the other by, although to him that insight remains unfathomable. Just as these people fail to connect, their poetically connected insights, their common pain and joy, and their repetition of words and gestures suggest a universality about human nature. Pinter has clearly moved toward new, poetic dimensions; interestingly, he also published his first volume of poems at this time, although they were written as early as his first plays.

Old Times returns to issues of possible and real homosexual and heterosexual commitment, fidelity, and friendship. Pinter's triangle (two women and a man) suggests any number of possibilities and combinations: "There are some things one remembers even though they may never have happened. There are things I remember which may never have happened but as I recall them so they take place." *No Man's Land* recreates a male world of potential comforters and predators with each man locked in a precarious linguistic world of identity. "No man's land" is that mysterious realm of truth and self-knowledge, of one's comprehension of oneself and one's world that "never moves, which never changes, which never grows older, but which remains forever, icy and silent."

Almost as though Pinter had begun with a line from *Old Times* (where one man tells another he "proposed" that his wife "betray" him), *Betrayal* treats multiple betrayals among friends, spouses, lovers (and even within the self)—in a fascinating structural manipulation of time. Perhaps inspired by his screenplay of Proust's *A la recherche*, it begins two years after an affair ended and in nine scenes moves back in time. Humor, banality, poetry, violence, diluted passion, and pain merge in a poignant evocation of time and one's eternal separation from both innocence and responsibility.

The Hothouse, written in 1958 but not published until 1980, focuses on the sanatorium in which the mute Stanley in *The Birthday Party* might have been committed. Staff members chatter in banal, funny, and threatening conversations about sex and the variations of power and control. Playing with traditional symbolism—there has been both a birth and death; the play occurs on Christmas; the characters (in this hothouse) are named Roote, Cutts, Lush, and Lamb—Pinter raises serious and ambiguous issues about sanity and insanity, "leaders" and "followers." At the end, a gratuitous mass murder of the staff is committed, but the perpetrator remains ambiguous: is it one of the patients? Is it one of the staff?

The London production of *Other Places* included *Victoria Station*, *A Kind of Alaska*, and *Family Voices*; in New York, *One for the Road* replaced *Family Voices*, originally a radio play. There is a curious unity in the three remaining works, as they anatomize primitive responses to menace and loyalty. *Tours de force* in concreteness, they are finely chiselled por-

traits of the contingency of human experience; they simultaneously evoke the most abiding of human encounters with evil or kindness.

The very short *Victoria Station* portrays the conversation between a taxi despatcher and a driver who, after picking up a female passenger, loses all sense of place and identity. The despatcher becomes his brother's keeper. *One for the Road* conveys a series of frightening confrontations between a banal, Goldberg-like torturer (vaguely representative of God and country) and his victims—a tortured man, his brutally assaulted wife, and their eventually murdered son. In the most affecting of the group, *A Kind of Alaska*, a woman in her mid-forties "erupts to life" after nearly 30 years of sleeping sickness. Pinter depicts her rebellious, bewildered, foolish, angry, and gallant responses in a combination of hallucination, childlike language, and erotic wish fulfilment. The reality of her lost youth and lost love, along with her sister's and doctor's unshakable loyalty, create a powerful work.

Pinter's work since the late 1980's has been political in the extreme. He has announced, repeatedly, that he feels a responsibility to pursue his role as "a citizen of the world in which I live, [and] insist upon taking responsibility." This responsibility consists of both speaking out publicly and writing about the political oppression of the individual through the subversive function of language. As such, *Mountain Language* treats the oppression of an unnamed people in an unspecified totalitarian state for the crime of retaining their own (mountain) language. In the first of four brief scenes, Pinter portrays a mother and wife who wait an entire day before being permitted to visit their imprisoned husband and son—each man apparently arrested for retaining his now-outlawed language. As one officer reminds the women: "Your language is forbidden. It is dead. No one is allowed to speak your language." Already terrorized by two guards and their dogs, the women, even when permitted to see the prisoners, are subjected to additional ridicule and sexual menace. As the elderly mother visits her son—and both are forbidden to speak in their native language—a "voice over" (tape) plays out their thoughts; but the guards' double-talk destroys any possibility of communication. In the next of these stark, rapid scenes, a young woman sees the hooded figure of her badly tortured husband and is told she can save him only if she sleeps with an administrator. In the final scene, when the state arbitrarily changes the law and the mother is told she "can speak in her own language. Until futher notice," she has become too terrorized to do so, and her son collapses before her eyes. The play is a frightening image, as Pinter explained, of what happens when people are deprived of "expressing their own identity through their own language."

The New World Order, billed as "a short satiric response to the Gulf War," is a 10-minute play whose title is taken from one of George Bush's political phrases. It portrays the gratuitous torture two men inflict upon an innocent. In a small room two captors stand and discuss what to do with their victim, who sits silent and blindfolded before them. As they play word games punctuated by Pinter's meticulous pauses, they increase the prisoner's apprehension of his impending torture. In essence, the two men play ironic variations on the theme "He has no idea what we are going to do with him," and the victim, like the audience, has "some idea," "a faint idea," "a little idea" and constructs any series of possible tortures. The guards also remind each other about their power in language—for example, they tease their victim with contradictory and vulgar sexual epithets (He is "a cunt" and then "a prick"); they proceed to question whether he is a peasant or theologian. At one point, the more vocal terrorist becomes silent. "I feel pure," he says, as if through sheer power and authority he had reached a transcendent state. In Pinter's somewhat mysterious climax, we are told that not only will his partner but the prisoner as well will shake his hand "in about thirty-five minutes." It would appear that what was the peasant, theologian, or just plain Pinter innocent has either been driven entirely mad or has totally capitulated to authority. The new world order has reduced all dissent or individuality to blind conformity.

—Lois Gordon

PLATER, Alan (Frederick). British. Born in Jarrow-on-Tyne, County Durham, 15 April 1935. Educated at Pickering Road Junior and Infant School, Hull, 1940–46; Kingston High School, Hull, 1946–53; King's College, Newcastle upon Tyne (University of Durham), 1953–57; qualified as architect (Associate, Royal Institute of British Architects), 1961. Married 1) Shirley Johnson in 1958 (divorced 1985), two sons and one daughter; 2) Shirley Rubinstein, three stepsons. Worked in an architect's office, Hull, 1957–60. Since 1960 full-time writer. Co-founder, Humberside Theatre (formerly Hull Arts Centre), 1970; co-chair, Writers Guild of Great Britain, 1986–87. Recipient: Writers Guild award, for radio play, 1972; Sony award, for radio play, 1983; Royal Television Society award, 1984, 1985; New York and San Francisco film festival awards, 1986; Broadcasting Guild award, 1987; BAFTA writers and drama series award, 1988; Variety Club of Great Britain award, 1989. D. Litt.: Hull University, 1985. Honorary Fellow, Hull College of Higher Education, 1983; Fellow, Royal Society of Literature, 1985. Lives in London. Agent: Alexandra Cann Representation, 68E Redcliffe Gardens, London SW10 9HE, England.

PUBLICATIONS

Plays

The Referees (televised 1961; produced Stoke-on-Trent, 1963).
The Mating Season (broadcast 1962; produced Stoke-on-Trent, 1963). Published in *Worth a Hearing: A Collection of Radio Plays*, edited by Alfred Bradley, London, Blackie, 1967.
A Smashing Day (televised 1962; revised version, music by Ben Kingsley and Robert Powell, produced Stoke-on-Trent, 1965; London, 1966).
The Rainbow Machine (broadcast 1962; produced Stoke-on-Trent, 1963).
Ted's Cathedral (produced Stoke-on-Trent and London, 1963).
A Quiet Night (televised 1963). Published in *Z Cars: Four Scripts from the Television Series*, edited by Michael Marland, London, Longman, 1968.
See the Pretty Lights (televised 1963; produced London, 1970). Published in *Theatre Choice: A Collection of Modern Short Plays*, edited by Michael Marland, London, Blackie, 1972.
The Nutter (televised 1965; revised version, as *Charlie Came to Our Town*, music by Alex Glasgow, produced Harrogate, Yorkshire, 1966).

Excursion (broadcast 1966). Included in *You and Me*, 1973.
The What on the Landing? (broadcast 1967; produced Coventry, 1968; London, 1971).
On Christmas Day in the Morning (*Softly, Softly* series; televised 1968). Included in *You and Me*, 1973.
Hop Step and Jump (produced Scarborough, Yorkshire, 1968).
Close the Coalhouse Door, music by Alex Glasgow, adaptation of stories by Sid Chaplin (produced Newcastle upon Tyne and London, 1968). London, Methuen, 1969.
Don't Build a Bridge, Drain the River!, music by Michael Chapman and Mike Waterson (produced Hull, 1970; revised version, music by Mike O'Neil, produced Hull, 1980).
Simon Says!, music by Alex Glasgow (produced Leeds, 1970).
And a Little Love Besides (produced Hull, 1970; London, 1977). Included in *You and Me*, 1973.
King Billy Vaudeville Show, with others (produced Hull, 1971).
Seventeen Per Cent Said Push Off (televised 1972). Included in *You and Me*, 1973.
The Tigers are Coming—O.K.? (produced Hull, 1972).
You and Me: Four Plays, edited by Alfred Bradley. London, Blackie, 1973.
Swallows on the Water (produced Hull, 1973).
When the Reds Go Marching In (produced Liverpool, 1973).
Annie Kenney (televised 1974). Published in *Act 3*, edited by David Self and Ray Speakman, London, Hutchinson, 1979.
Tales of Humberside, music by Jim Bywater (produced Hull, 1975).
Trinity Tales, music by Alex Glasgow (televised 1975; produced Birmingham, 1975).
Our Albert (produced Hull, 1976).
The Fosdyke Saga, with Bill Tidy (produced London, 1977). London, French, 1978.
Drums along the Ginnel (produced London, 1977).
Fosdyke 2, with Bill Tidy (produced London, 1977).
Short Back and Sides (televised 1977). Published in *City Life*, edited by David Self, London, Hutchinson, 1980.
Well Good Night Then . . . (produced Hull, 1978).
Skyhooks (produced Oldham, Lancashire, 1982).
On Your Way, Riley!, music by Alex Glasgow (produced London, 1982).
A Foot on the Earth (produced Newcastle upon Tyne, 1984).
Prez, music by Bernie Cash (produced Hull and London, 1985).
Rent Party, from an idea by Nat Shapiro (produced London, 1989).
Sweet Sorrow (produced Edinburgh and London, 1990). London, Square One, 1990.
Going Home (produced Newcastle upon Tyne, 1990). London, Square One, 1990.
I Thought I Heard a Rustling (produced London, 1991). Oxford, Amber Lane, 1991.

Screenplays: *The Virgin and the Gypsy*, 1970; *Juggernaut*, 1974; *It Shouldn't Happen to a Vet* (*All Things Bright and Beautiful*), 1976; *Priest of Love*, 1982; *The Inside Man*, 1984.

Radio Plays: *The Smokeless Zone*, 1961; *Counting the Legs*, 1961; *The Mating Season*, 1962; *The Rainbow Machine*, 1962; *The Seventh Day of Arthur*, 1963; *Excursion*, 1966; *The What on the Landing?*, 1967; *Fred*, 1970; *The Slow Stain*, 1973; *5 Days in '55* (*The Gilberdyke Diaries*), 1976; *Tunes*, 1979; *Swallows on the Water*, 1981; *The Journal of Vasilije Bogdanovic* (*In a Strange Land* series), 1982; *Tolpuddle*, with

Vince Hill, 1982; *Who's Jimmy Dickenson?*, from his play *Well Good Night Then . . .*, 1986.

Television Plays: *The Referees*, 1961; *A Smashing Day*, 1962; *So Long Charlie*, 1963; *See the Pretty Lights*, 1963; *Z Cars* series (18 episodes), 1963–65; *Ted's Cathedral*, 1964; *Fred*, 1964; *The Incident*, 1965; *The Nutter*, 1965; *Softly, Softly* series (30 episodes), 1966–76; *To See How Far It Is* (trilogy), 1968; *The First Lady* series (4 episodes), 1968–69; *Rest in Peace, Uncle Fred*, 1970; *Seventeen Per Cent Said Push Off*, 1972; *The Reluctant Juggler* (*The Edwardians* series), 1972; *Tonight We Meet Arthur Pendlebury*, 1972; *It Must Be Something in the Water* (documentary), 1973; *Brotherly Love*, 1973; *The Land of Green Ginger*, 1974; *The Needle Match*, 1974; *Goldilocks and the Three Bears*, 1974; *Wish You Were Here* (documentary), 1974; *Annie Kenney* (*Shoulder to Shoulder* series), 1974; *The Loner* series, 1975; *The Stars Look Down*, from the novel by A.J. Cronin, 1975; *Trinity Tales* series, 1975; *Willow Cabins*, 1975; *Practical Experience*, 1976; *Oh No—It's Selwyn Froggit* series, 1976; *A Tyneside Entertainment* (documentary), 1976; *Seven Days That Shook Young Jim* (*Going to Work* series), 1976; *We Are the Masters Now*, 1976; *There Are Several Businesses Like Show Business*, 1976; *The Bike*, 1977; *Short Back and Sides*, 1977; *Middlemen* series, 1977; *By Christian Judges Condemned*, 1977; *For the Love of Albert* series, 1977; *Give Us a Kiss, Christabel*, 1977; *The Eddystone Lights* (documentary), 1978; *The Party of the First Part*, 1978; *Curriculee Curricula*, music by Dave Greenslade, 1978; *Night People*, 1978; *Flambards*, from works by K.M. Peyton, 1979; *The Blacktoft Diaries*, 1979; *Reunion*, 1979; *The Good Companions*, from the novel by J.B. Priestley, 1980; *Get Lost!* series, 1981; *Barchester Chronicles*, from novels by Trollope, 1981; *The Clarion Van*, from a work by Doris Neild Chew, 1983; *Feet Foremost*, from a story by L.P. Hartley, 1983; *Bewitched*, from the story by Edith Wharton, 1983; *The Consultant*, from the novel *Invitation to Tender* by John McNeil, 1983; *Pride of Our Alley*, 1983; *The Crystal Spirit: Orwell on Jura*, 1983; *Thank You, Mrs. Clinkscales*, 1984; *The Solitary Cyclist*, from a story by Arthur Conan Doyle, 1984; *Edward Lear: On the Edge of the Sand*, 1985; *The Beiderbecke Affair* series, 1985; *A Murder Is Announced*, from the novel by Agatha Christie, 1985; *Coming Through*, 1985; *The Man with the Twisted Lip*, from a story by Arthur Conan Doyle, 1986; *Death Is Part of the Process*, from a novel by Hilda Bernstein, 1986; *Fortunes of War*, from novels by Olivia Manning, 1987; *The Beiderbecke Tapes*, 1987; *A Very British Coup*, from the novel by Chris Mullin, 1988; *The Beiderbecke Connection*, 1988; *Campion*, from the works of Margery Allingham, 1989; *A Day in Summer*, from the novel by J.L. Carr, 1989; *Misterioso*, from his own novel, 1991; *The Patience of Maigret*, from the novel by Georges Simenon, 1992; *Maigret and the Burglar's Wife*, from the novel by Georges Simenon, 1992.

Novels

The Beiderbecke Affair. London, Methuen, 1985.
The Beiderbecke Tapes. London, Methuen, 1986.
Misterioso. London, Methuen, 1987.
The Beiderbecke Connection. London, Methuen, 1992.

Other

The Trouble with Abracadabra (for children). London, Macmillan, 1975.

*

Critical Studies: introduction to *Close the Coalhouse Door*, 1969, "What's Going On Behind the Coalhouse Door," *in Sunday Times* (London), 9 February 1969, "The Playwright and His People," in *Theatre Quarterly 2* (London), April–June 1971, "One Step Forward, Two Steps Back," in *New Statesman* (London), 3 November 1972, "Views," in *Listener* (London), 29 November 1973, and "Twenty-Five Years Hard," in *Theatre Quarterly 25* (London), 1977, all by Plater; "The London Show" by Yorick Blumenfeld, in *Atlantic* (Boston), August 1969; *The Second Wave* by John Russell Taylor, London, Methuen, and New York, Hill and Wang, 1971; "Trinity Collage" by Peter Fiddick, in *Guardian* (London), 12 December 1975; article by Albert Hunt, in *British Television Drama* edited by George W. Brandt, London, Cambridge University Press, 1981.

Alan Plater comments:

(1973) Authors introducing their work fill me with gloom, like people explaining jokes: if I didn't laugh or cry before the explanation, nothing is likely to change afterwards. Therefore all I can do is look down the laundry list of my work to date and try to work out why I bothered, apart from what Mr. Perelman calls "the lash of economic necessity."

The clue lies in the place of birth and the present address: I was born and have always lived in industrial communities. I live in a place that works for a living. I never ran barefoot other than from choice. I have always eaten well and have never been deprived of anything that mattered: but I have always been close enough to the inequalities and grotesque injustices of our society to get angry about them.

(1977) Essentially I am writing a segment of the history of a society that was forged by the Industrial Revolution. This is less earnest and painful than it sounds; if an idea is important enough it is worth laughing at and one professional associate defined my method as taking fundamentally serious concepts like Politics and Religion and Life and Death and kicking the Hell out of them with old jokes. At any rate, the evidence of the more-or-less knockabout shows we've done around the regions is that people laugh the louder if the fun is spiced with a couple of centuries of inherited prejudice.

The other thought prompted by the laundry list is that not many writers have tangled with as rich and diverse a company of people and subjects: D.H. Lawrence, Mrs. Pankhurst, Sandy Powell, and Les Dawson would look good on any music-hall poster, though there might be some dispute over billing. At any rate, it underlines my feeling that it's the job of the writer at all times to head for the nearest tightrope and, in the words of Max Miller, Archie Rice, or both: "You've got to admit, lady, I do have a go."

(1982) Very little changes. The inequalities and injustices of 1973 are still there and I'm still heading for the tightrope as in 1977. We've got a new dog called The Duke (after Ellington) and I've had a programme banned by the BBC, which is a distinction of a sort. I copied some words by Jean Rhys and pinned them on the wall behind my desk. She says: "All of writing is a huge lake. There are great rivers that feed the lake, like Tolstoy and Dostoevsky. And there are trickles, like Jean Rhys. All that matters is feeding the lake. I don't matter. The lake matters. Nothing else is important. . . ."

(1988) After all that worthy stuff about living in an industrial community, here I am writing this paragraph in downtown N.W.3. In the famous words of Mr. Vonnegut: so it goes. We grow older, we change, we pursue happiness and sometimes find it. Professionally, I still head for the tightrope and Jean Rhys is still with me. So, for that matter, is The Duke.

* * *

Alan Plater is one of several dramatists whose work has done much to further the cause of British regional theatre. Although some of his plays have been seen in London and he has written widely for national television and the cinema, for many years his energies were directed towards ensuring the success of the ambitious Hull Arts Centre, a small 150-seat theatre. This physical home was also apparently a spiritual one, for his plays are set in the northeast of England and are largely concerned with the particular problems and history of the area. "Central to the greater part of my writing," he once stated, "is man's relationship to his work": and work in this context means particularly coal-mining and deep-sea fishing, two regional industries. Plater admires the "genuine solidarity and craft-consciousness" of those whose jobs involve "hideous physical working conditions": and he has captured the sheer pride in overcoming fear and danger which distinguishes the miners in his highly successful musical documentary, *Close the Coalhouse Door*. Plater identifies wholeheartedly with the community he describes: he shares the passion for football, and once, when he was asked about his literary influences, he replied by mentioning the popular music-hall names of his youth—Norman Evans, Mooney and King. He also expresses with great fire many of the social and political attitudes (some might call them prejudices) which characterize the region: a hatred of the bosses, who are usually portrayed as effete Southerners, a respect for Trade Union tradition, a somewhat over-generalized call for revolution which is coupled with a suspicion of change, a brashly extrovert dismissal of all forms of theatre which lack working-class appeal and a socialism which refuses to accept that Labour politicians are better than stooges for capitalistic con-men.

His work falls into two main categories. Plater has written several carefully observed naturalistic plays, such as *See the Pretty Lights* and *A Smashing Day*, which were both rewritten for the stage from television scripts. In 1966 Plater met the composer and songwriter Alex Glasgow and together they have collaborated on several musical documentaries, among them *Charlie Came to Our Town* and *Close the Coalhouse Door*. The documentaries, unlike the naturalistic plays, combine many styles of writing—cross-talk sketches, songs, impassioned oratory, summaries of historical incidents, and much satire—which are all loosely brought together by a general theme, the history of Hull or the struggle of miners to gain decent living standards.

These two styles reveal different qualities. *See the Pretty Lights* is a gentle, warm, and moving account of a meeting between a middle-aged man and a teenage girl at the end of a pier. Both lead dull lives: and the bright lights of the seaside and their momentary friendship helps to relieve—but also to underline—their social frustrations. The hero of *A Smashing Day* is a young man, Lennie, who suffers from bored aimlessness: he meekly accepts his job, the odd nights at the palais with his mates who never become friends, and the routine drink. But he senses that a more exciting life awaits him somewhere if only he could find out where. He goes steady with a girl, Anne, and drifts towards marriage, which he doesn't want: and the social pressures are such that he persists in marrying her even after meeting Liz, an independent and sensitive girl with whom he falls in love. Many critics felt that the increased length of the stage play failed to achieve the concentrated power of the television script, and *A Smashing Day* was not successful in London. But it did provide an excellent part for the then unknown actor, Hywel Bennett, and revealed Plater's ability to describe an apparently uninteresting person in some depth. Lennie is never allowed to be either a pathetic person or an angry young man: and despite

his shy insecurity which leaves an impression of spinelessness, his situation is both moving, credible, and strong enough to hold the play together.

If the naturalistic plays are distinguished by restraint and accuracy, the documentaries have entirely the opposite qualities: panache, a cheerful display of class bias, and loose, anything-goes technique. The best known is *Close the Coalhouse Door*, which was remarkably successful in Newcastle but received only a limited run in London, a fact which could be interpreted in several ways. The episodes of mining history are told within the context of a golden "wedding" reception in the Millburn family, who step out of a photograph to tell stories of strikes and hardships. Some scenes were particularly powerful: the death of a miner, the rivalry between families and men, the bitterness against the blackleg miners who went back to work too soon after the General Strike. Plater stressed the complicated mixture of affection and fear for the pits, together with a scorn of modernization programmes whose effect was to send miners back on the dole. The songs by Alex Glasgow caught the friendly liveliness of music halls and pubs, and in Newcastle it became a cult show. "Workers turned up in their thousands once the word got round," recalled Plater: the large Playhouse Theatre was filled to capacity night after night—the audiences would sit in the aisles, even on the steps to the stage.

Why did the show receive such a tepid reception in London? The answer is a complex one, revealing much about Plater's work. Plater has offered two reasons—that London audiences are prejudiced against working-class plays and that in any case they could not be expected to share the associations of the North. Both may be true: but isn't it the job of a dramatist to convey the importance of his theme to those who do not belong to the background? London critics generally commented on the superficial characterization of the play, on the rather simplistic dialogue and form, and on the one-sided interpretations of history. These objections to Plater's documentaries were confirmed by two subsequent shows which didn't come to London: *Simon Says!*, a wholesale attack on the British ruling classes represented by Lord Thing, the Chairman of the MCC (the governing board of English cricket), and *And a Little Love Besides*, a scathing account of the uncharitable Church. The critical charge against both these plays was that the satire was too sweeping and naïve to hit any real targets. Plater's documentaries are seen at their best perhaps either when the subject contains real and deeply felt observations or when the general sense of fun takes over. *Charlie Came to Our Town*, Plater's first documentary with Alex Glasgow, is a delightfully light-hearted musical about an eccentric anarchist.

Plater's two styles complement each other: and it is sad perhaps that they haven't been combined in one play. The naturalistic plays are small-scale and lack the passionate energy of the documentaries: the documentaries are too vaguely polemical and lack the construction of the naturalistic plays. Plater is a prolific writer, whose talents seem hard to control. But his adaptability is shown by the skill with which he has adjusted to the various media: his contributions to the *Z Cars* detective series on television and his screenplay for D.H. Lawrence's *The Virgin and the Gypsy* have been rightly praised. This energetic eagerness to tackle any task which interests him helped revitalize the theatre in the northeast and suggests that in future his many abilities may be contained within undeniably good plays.

—John Elsom

POLIAKOFF, Stephen. British. Born in London, 1 December 1952. Educated at Westminster School, London; King's College, Cambridge, 1972–73. Married Sandy Welch in 1983; one daughter. Writer-in-residence, National Theatre, London, 1976–77. Recipient: *Evening Standard* award, 1976; BAFTA award, 1980; Venice Film Festival prize, 1989; Bergamo Film Festival prize, 1991. Agent: Casarotto Ramsay Ltd., National House, 60–66 Wardour Street, London W1V 3HP, England.

PUBLICATIONS

Plays

Granny (produced London, 1969).
Bambi Ramm (produced London, 1970).
A Day with My Sister (produced Edinburgh, 1971).
Lay-By, with others (produced Edinburgh and London, 1971). London, Calder and Boyars, 1972.
Pretty Boy (produced London, 1972).
Theatre Outside (produced London, 1973).
Berlin Days (produced London, 1973).
The Carnation Gang (produced London, 1974).
Clever Soldiers (produced London, 1974). Included in *Plays: One*, 1989.
Heroes (produced London, 1975).
Hitting Town (produced London, 1975; New York, 1979). Included in *Hitting Town, and City Sugar*, 1976.
City Sugar (produced London, 1975; New York, 1978). Included in *Hitting Town, and City Sugar*, 1976.
Hitting Town, and City Sugar. London, Eyre Methuen, 1976; revised edition 1978.
Strawberry Fields (produced London, 1977; New York, 1978). London, Eyre Methuen, 1977.
Shout Across the River (produced London, 1978; New York, 1979). London, Eyre Methuen, 1979.
American Days (produced London, 1979; New York, 1980). London, Eyre Methuen, 1979.
The Summer Party (produced Sheffield, 1980). London, Eyre Methuen, 1980.
Caught on a Train (televised 1980). With *Favourite Nights*, London, Methuen, 1982.
Favourite Nights (produced London, 1981). With *Caught on a Train*, London, Methuen, 1982.
Soft Targets (televised 1982). With *Runners*, London, Methuen, 1984.
Breaking the Silence (produced London, 1984). London, Methuen, 1984.
Runners (screenplay). With *Soft Targets*, London, Methuen, 1984.
Coming in to Land (produced London, 1987). London, Methuen, 1987.
Playing with Trains (produced London, 1989). London, Methuen, 1989.
She's Been Away, and Hidden City (screenplays). London, Methuen, 1989.
Plays: One (includes *Clever Soldiers, Hitting Town, City Sugar, Shout Across the River, American Days, Strawberry Fields*). London, Methuen, 1989.
Sienna Red (produced London, 1992). London, Methuen, 1992.

Screenplays: *Runners*, 1983; *Hidden City*, 1988; *She's Been Away*, 1989; *Close My Eyes*, 1991.

Television Plays: *Stronger Than the Sun*, 1977; *Bloody Kids*, 1980; *Caught on a Train*, 1980; *Soft Targets*, 1982.

*

Theatrical Activities:
Director: **Films**—*Hidden City*, 1988; *Close My Eyes*, 1991.

* * *

Stephen Poliakoff first achieved recognition with the two related plays *Hitting Town* and *City Sugar* in 1975. The plays attacked a series of readily identifiable targets—the tackiness and squalor of new inner-city developments, the alienating effects of fast-food shops and discos, the banality of pop radio D.J.s. But here, as so often subsequently, the rather crude political context is less the real subject of the drama than a convenient backdrop against which a series of strangely vulnerable oddball characters rehearse their particular desperation. Poliakoff's is a theatre of individual gesture rather than generalised political analysis. Although his plays appear to offer a series of thematically related attacks on contemporary society in loosely political terms. it is the emotional subtext that is most important.

In *Hitting Town*, it is the awkward movement of a lonely woman and her waywardly embittered younger brother through a desolate provincial night on the town and towards an incestuous bed that creates most of the dramatic tension, just as in the more recent screenplay for *Runners* it is the tentative efforts of the father to achieve some kind of relationship with his young runaway daughter that holds the audience's attention, rather than the more general theme of hopelessness in the face of mass youth unemployment that the film presents as its primary concern. And indeed the daughter is not presented as a passive victim of circumstances. Like so many of Poliakoff's central protagonists she is a survivor, shell-shocked but still in possession of a tentative resilience, surviving in a half-glimpsed London world of the dispossessed by distributing advertising literature.

Poliakoff returns continually to city nightlife. It is when his characters can be displayed at their loneliest—a situation which brings about the very existence of the all-night radio phone-in which provides the structural continuity of *City Sugar*. And it is this pervading sense of isolation in supposedly crowded locations that gives his plays their peculiar clarity, for Poliakoff's stage city is a curiously unpopulated one. In *Hitting Town* the sister and brother first visit a Wimpy Bar in which the only other person present is a waitress who will again be the sole witness to their dialogue in the shopping precinct. Whether other people are assumed to be present, and thus a further cause of the sister's worry at her brother's deliberately provocative behaviour, is deliberately left unclear, but no such ambiguity exists by the time the three of them arrive at a disco in which the only direct evidence of the presence of others comes from the voice of the unseen D.J.

Again, in *Favourite Nights*, Catherine, language teacher by day and escort by night, takes her German businessman student and her sister to a casino in which we otherwise see only a croupier, an American punter, and Alan, an official of the club. The absence of characters who must be understood to be present in night spots such as discos and casinos intensifies the way in which Poliakoff's characters see themselves as a part of, and yet separate from, the contemporary world. Catherine's manic attempts to beat the bank yet again in order to avoid the sexual compromise potentially involved in letting her client pay for their evening out is seen as if in a filmic close-up from which all the extras are excluded; and the attempts to communicate with her lover, Alan, in a locale in which contact between staff and punters is banned, is given a curious intensity by the presence of spy cameras unsupported by any other realised members of the casino management.

It is not surprising, given all this, that the medium of film has come to seem increasingly attractive to Poliakoff. In *Hidden City*, the first film he directed, the fascination with the city as secret world is still evident. A bored mathematical psychologist meets up with a strange young woman who reveals a literal underworld of tunnels and hidden chambers in pursuit of officially dead newsreel film footage, stumbling by accident on evidence of a long-since buried nuclear scandal. But afterwards it is the image of the "hidden city" rather than the concern with the hidden scandal that remain in the mind.

Even when Poliakoff moves out of a city environment, as in *Strawberry Fields*, he takes his characters from London and up the motorway vertebrae of England, in and out of service stations and lay-bys which are as unpopulated as his all-night bars and casinos. Kevin and Charlotte set off to meet at pre-arranged points others members of the fascist group to which they belong. In this instance, the lack of contact with any other characters—with the exception of a police constable and a hitchhiker, who are shot dead at the ends of the first and second acts respectively—stresses their lack of contact with any reality, other than Kevin's half-remembered images of the 1960's, to support their ideology. They see themselves increasingly as latter-day Bonnies and Clydes, but the paranoia of persecution and pursuit on which their stance is built is undercut by the non-appearance of the police who are supposedly chasing them.

This thematic use of the journey is another manifestation of the characters as socially and politically rootless and unconnected to the details of everyday life. In his 1980 television play, *Caught on a Train*, Poliakoff uses a railway journey across Europe in which a series of characters—from a collection of anarchically politicised football hooligans to a young American thoroughly disenchanted with Europe—meet in transit without ever properly communicating as an informing metaphor for an account of the contemporary malaise. This film marked a major development in his work and, interestingly, he was to return to the central motif of the train journey in his most impressive stage play to date—*Breaking the Silence*.

For the first time since his earliest work Poliakoff moves the action into the past, Russia in the immediate aftermath of the revolution. Nikolai, a wealthy Jewish aristocrat based loosely on the playwright's own Russian grandfather, is turned out of his spacious accommodation and is made telephone surveyor of the Northern Railway. To this end he is given a train to patrol a region where telephone poles have yet to be erected, all the time working single-mindedly towards his life's ambition of producing the first synchronised talking pictures. He is to be thwarted, and the play finishes as he prepares for exile in England, his pictures as silent as the northern region's telephone system. It is again a journey of isolation, in which all attempts at communication are literally and metaphorically denied; but it is also another story of a survivor. Poliakoff has for the first time properly united the individual concerns of the narrative with a larger thematic structure. His concern with the links between the political worlds of the east and west, and thus with his own sense of cultural duality, was continued in *Coming in to Land*, which opened at the National Theatre in 1987, and in *Playing with Trains*, and certainly, given the rapidly changing nature of the

political map of Europe, there is good reason to hope that he will continue to be preoccupied by this larger social arena.

—John Bull

POLLOCK, Sharon (née Chalmers). Canadian. Born in Fredericton, New Brunswick, 19 April 1936. Educated at the University of New Brunswick, Fredericton, 2 years. Married Ross Pollock in 1954; six children. Actress in New Brunswick, and with touring group, Prairie Players, Calgary; head of the playwriting division, Department of Drama, University of Alberta, Edmonton, 1976–77; director of the Playwrights' Colony, Banff School of Fine Arts, Alberta, 1977–81; playwright-in-residence, Alberta Theatre Projects, Calgary, 1977–79, National Arts Centre, Ottawa, 1981, 1982, and Regina Public Library, Saskatchewan, 1986–87; dramaturge, 1982–83, associate artistic director, 1983–84, and artistic director, 1984, Theatre Calgary. Member, 1979–80, and chair 1980–81, Canada Council Advisory Arts Panel; vice-chair Playwrights Canada National Executive, 1981–83. Recipient: Dominion Drama Festival award, for acting, 1966; Nellie award, for radio play, 1981; Governor-General's award, 1981, 1986; Alberta award of excellence, 1983; Chalmers award, 1984; Canada Council Senior Arts grant, 1984; Alberta Writers Guild award, 1986; Alberta Literary Foundation award, 1987. Honorary Doctorate: University of New Brunswick, 1986. Address: 319 Manora Drive N.E., Calgary, Alberta T2A 4R2, Canada.

PUBLICATIONS

Plays

A Compulsory Option.   Edmonton, Department of Culture, Youth, and Recreation, 1970; revised version (produced Vancouver, 1972; as *No! No! No!* produced Toronto, 1977), Vancouver, New Play Centre, 1972.
Walsh (produced Calgary, 1973).   Vancouver, New Play Centre, 1972; revised version (produced Stratford, Ontario, 1974), Vancouver, Talonbooks, 1974.
New Canadians (for children; produced Vancouver, 1973).
Superstition Throu' the Ages (for children; produced Vancouver, 1973).
Wudjesay? (for children; produced Vancouver, 1974).
A Lesson in Swizzlery (for children; produced New Westminster, British Columbia, 1974).
The Rose and the Nightingale (for children), adaptation of the story by Oscar Wilde (produced Vancouver, 1974).
The Star-child (for children), adaptation of the story by Oscar Wilde (produced Vancouver, 1974).
The Happy Prince (for children), adaptation of the story by Oscar Wilde (produced Vancouver, 1974).
And Out Goes You? (produced Vancouver, 1975).
The Komagata Maru Incident (produced Vancouver, 1976; London, 1985).   Toronto, Playwrights, 1978.
Blood Relations (as *My Name Is Lisbeth*, produced New Westminster, British Columbia, 1976; revised version, as *Blood Relations*, produced Edmonton, 1980; New York, 1983; Derby and London, 1985). Included in *Blood Relations and Other Plays*, 1981; in *Plays by Women 3*, edited by Michelene Wandor, London, Methuen, 1984.

Tracings: The Fraser Story (collective work), with others (produced Edmonton, 1977).

The Wreck of the National Line Car (for children; produced Calgary, 1978).

Mail vs. Female (produced Calgary, 1979).

Chautauqua Spelt E-N-E-R-G-Y (for children; produced Calgary, 1979).

One Tiger to a Hill (produced Edmonton, 1980; revised version produced Lennoxville, Quebec, and New York, 1981). Included in *Blood Relations and Other Plays*, 1981.

Generations (produced Calgary, 1980). Included in *Blood Relations and Other Plays*, 1981.

Blood Relations and Other Plays. Edmonton, NeWest Press, 1981.

Whiskey Six (produced Calgary, 1983).

Doc. Toronto, Playwrights, 1986.

Other Play: *The Great Drag Race; or, Smoked, Choked, and Croaked* (for children).

Radio Plays: *Split Seconds in the Death Of*, 1971; *31 for 2; We to the Gods; Waiting; The B Triple P Plan; In Memory Of; Generation*, 1980; *Sweet Land of Liberty*, 1980; *Intensive Care; Mary Beth Goes to Calgary; Mrs. Yale and Jennifer* (8 episodes); *In the Beginning Was*.

Television Plays: *Portrait of a Pig*; *The Larsens*; *Ransom*; *Free Our Sisters, Free Ourselves*; *The Person's Case*; *Country Joy* (6 episodes).

*

Manuscript Collection: University of Calgary, Alberta.

Theatrical Activities:

Director: **Plays**—some of her own plays, and *Betrayal* and *A Slight Ache* by Harold Pinter; *The Mousetrap* by Agatha Christie; *Scapin* by Molière; *The Gingerbread Lady* by Neil Simon; *The Bear* and *A Marriage Proposal* by Chekhov; *Period of Adjustment* by Tennessee Williams; *The Indian Wants the Bronx* by Israel Horovitz; *The Effect of Gamma Rays on Man-in-the-Moon Marigolds* by Paul Zindel; *Buried Child* by Sam Shepard; and others.

Actress: **Plays**—roles in some of her own plays, and title role in *Lysistrata* by Aristophanes; Nancy in *The Knack* by Ann Jellicoe; Amanda in *Private Lives* by Noël Coward; Miss Cooper in *Separate Tables* by Terence Rattigan; Bunny in *The House of Blue Leaves* by John Guare; Nell in *Endgame* by Samuel Beckett; Maddy in *All That Fall* by Arthur Miller; Polina in *The Seagull* by Chekhov; title role in *Miss Julie* by Strindberg; Alison in *Look Back in Anger* by John Osborne; The Psychiatrist in *Agnes of God* by John Pielmeier; and others.

* * *

Sharon Pollock's early plays are typical of the large branch of Canadian theatre which directly explores the country's history, employing documents but moving from them in a subjective response to events and an investigation of character and political process. In a note to the text of *The Komagata Maru Incident*, Pollock posits that drama "is a theatrical impression of an historical event seen through the optique of the stage and the mind of the playwright."

Her first play, *A Compulsory Option*, is a rather simple exercise in farce which does not fit this documentary model and which has been overshadowed by the later plays which do. It is, however, an amusing play with witty insights, especially into predictable academic character traits.

In her second play, *Walsh*, Pollock began to experiment with what has been considered her typical form. In the first version of the play, for example, broadcasted speeches taken from historical sources preceded each scene to provide necessary background; this rather awkward attempt at documentation was replaced in the published version by a Prologue which occurs out of time and which shows us the eventual moral decline of the protagonist while simultaneously providing fewer but more easily assimilated historical details. The play recreates the dilemma of Major John Walsh of the Northwest Mounted Police who, in 1876, is caught in the middle between the Canadian government of Sir John A. MacDonald (symbolized by Queen Victoria as Great White Mother) and the American Indian nations as symbolized by Chief Sitting Bull. Sitting Bull is cast as a shamanistic figure, and when critics have sometimes found the character overly pious to the point of unreality, they have ignored the fact that he is intended not as rounded character in a drama but as mystical *exemplum* of his dying race, caught in a modern European world it cannot resist and true to the primitive but doomed values of the "Sacred Hoop" of life. Major Walsh, a strict militarist, attempts to extend white logic to the Indian view of the world and discovers that he does not himself wish to accept the detached political logic of his white superiors. He also discovers that considerations other than reason and fair play motivate the Canadian government. In one short and highly dramatic speech, however, he capitulates in the face of these discoveries, reverting to his background and his sense of duty, and by doing so seals his own moral doom. The young recruit, Clarence, functions in the play as a mirror to Walsh's spiritual decline, learning to see the Indians as human beings even as Walsh forces himself to manage them as political pawns. The interesting discussion which these two figures embody becomes a central theme of the play: the man without responsibility can remain idealistic and humane; the bureaucrat trapped between forces he cannot control but must administer suffers and often falls victim to the events of history. The staging echoes this stark reality —a few representative figures on an almost bare stage play out a tiny portion of the larger event and do so in an unadorned and internalized landscape.

The same trapped figure reappears in *The Komagata Maru Incident* in the person of the spy, William Hopkinson. In this play, Pollock returns to a form similar to that of *Walsh* after an experiment in history seen as burlesque in *And Out Goes You? Komagata Maru* concerns the historic refusal of the turn-of-the-century provincial government to allow a boatload of East Indian refugees to enter the country. The ship remains in harbour for two months, and the play explores the racial and legal aspects of the event. Sent as a spy, Hopkinson is forced to come to terms with his own racial self-image (he is half-East Indian) and with his attempts to survive in a white world by denying his cultural background. The rendering of Hopkinson is rounder than that of Walsh; the issues are not as clear cut and the protagonist fights not only the social values which surround him but the weaker side of his own personality. The stagecraft is similarly more sophisticated than it was in *Walsh*: the action moves back and forth from the ship to other locales; the secondary characters and motives are interesting in themselves; and the thematic action is less directly stated. The theme, though it centres on a serious local problem of a particular time, is universal enough to affect other audiences and its considerations of the roles of fear, envy, and ambition speak to us all.

Although these first plays concern the reactions of men to

historical events, the later plays show a growing interest by Pollock in the reactions of women in general and herself in particular. Her most successful play, *Blood Relations*, a reworking of an idea she first wrote as *My Name Is Lisbeth*, is a study of the American murderer Lizzie Borden in the context both of her feminine struggle to resist a role carved out for her by 19th-century society and her attempt to discover her own identity as a agent with Will. The play makes its point not only in the text, but by a powerful staging in which Lizzie switches roles with her Actress friend and watches "herself" repeat the action which led to the murder. The question of her guilt is played out in this mirror world and extended through an elaborate pattern of blood imagery to include the audience. As part of the folklore which condemns her, the play suggests, Americans and even Canadians are as guilty of the murder as is Lizzie. This contention is supported not only in the double action, but in Pollock's most successful writing, a well-designed and intricate web of language which demonstrates a significant leap from the earlier dialogue.

The most recent major play, the semi-autobiographical *Doc*, continues Pollock's search into the feminine memories of family. Although the play has not attracted the critical attention of *Blood Relations*, it has reinforced the notion that Pollock has, in the later plays, found a more literary voice. The writing here is highly compelling, the speeches often beautiful in themselves, and the general tone softer and more intimate. By moving steadily away from the directly documentary and away, as well, from the heroes themselves (be they male or female) into the philosophical implications of her events and characters, Pollock is creating plays which exist beyond the confines of the history they employ; her new plays have become more important than the subjects which have inspired them.

—Reid Gilbert

POMERANCE, Bernard. American. Born in Brooklyn, New York, in 1940. Educated at the University of Chicago. Co-founder, Foco Novo theatre group, London, 1972. Recipient: New York Drama Critics Circle award, Tony award, Obie award, and Outer Circle award, all 1979. Lives in London. Address: c/o Faber and Faber Ltd., 3 Queen Square, London WC1N 3AU, England.

PUBLICATIONS

Plays

High in Vietnam, Hot Damn; Hospital; Thanksgiving Before Detroit (produced London, 1971).   Published in *Gambit 6* (London), 1972.
Foco Novo (produced London, 1972).
Someone Else Is Still Someone (produced London, 1974).
A Man's a Man, adaptation of a play by Brecht (produced London, 1975).
The Elephant Man (produced Exeter and London, 1977; New York, 1979).   New York, Grove Press, 1979; London, Faber, 1980.
Quantrill in Lawrence (produced London, 1980).   London, Faber, 1981.

Melons (produced London, 1985; New Haven, Connecticut, 1987).

Novel

We Need to Dream All This Again. New York, Viking, 1987.

* * *

An American living in England, Bernard Pomerance found productions for his early plays in London's fringe theater of the 1970's. Yet it was his play *The Elephant Man*, produced on Broadway in 1979 subsequent to an English premiere and an off-off Broadway presentation, that established Pomerance as a playwright. An immense critical and popular success, the play won several awards including an Obie and one from the New York Drama Critics Circle.

The title of the biography-drama was a sideshow term applied to John Merrick (1863–90), a noted teratoid "freak" of Victorian England, so hideously malformed by an incurable and then unknown disease (now diagnosed as neurofibromatosis) that he was cruelly exploited as a traveling show oddity. Rescued from such exhibition by the anatomist Dr. Frederick Treves, he was given safe shelter in London Hospital, Whitechapel, which raised public donations for his maintenance and became his home for six years before his death in 1890. Merrick became a curio studied by science and visited by fashionable society who found him a man of surprising intelligence and sensitivity. Treves's published account of Merrick's life sparked Pomerance's interest in the subject.

In 22 often trenchant short scenes identified by title placard, *The Elephant Man* effectively employs a presentational and Brechtian style to tell its story. In Act 1 Treves encounters Merrick in a sideshow, later offers him shelter after a mob almost kills him, and determines with condescending compassion to create for his patient the illusion of normality. To this purpose, he enlists the actress Mrs. Kendal to befriend Merrick. The second act shifts focus from physician to patient as we watch the progress of Treves's social engineering. The "Elephant Man" fits himself into the role of the correct Victorian gentleman, but not without questioning the rules he is told to obey.

As the metamorphosis continues, fashionable society lionizes him for he lets them see him not as an individual but as a mirror of qualities they like to claim. Noting to Mrs. Kendal that sexual loneliness continues to isolate him from other men and that he has never seen a naked woman, the actress kindly obliges by baring her breasts only to be interrupted by a scandalized Treves who orders her out for her impropriety: she does not return. Interpreting the experience as defining his own limitations, Merrick realizes his normality has been an illusion, and he suicidally lets his huge head drop unsupported, causing strangulation. Simultaneously with his patient's development, Treves comes to question his principles and those of his class and painfully perceives Merrick's subtle exploitation by science and society. Pomerance is concerned with the theme that compassion, society and its conventional morality, and the idea of normality are at bottom destructive illusions.

Pomerance's play is at once theatrically effective, emotionally compelling, and intellectually provoking. Yet the drama has some problems. More ideas are unleashed than are developed, and some of these are overstated in the later scenes. Moreover, the shift in focus from Treves to Merrick and then back to the former near the conclusion unbalances the center of the play: the physician's loss of self-assurance demands more preparation. But such problems are minor when considering the play's overriding strengths.

As John Merrick is an exemplary victim of 19th-century greed, intolerance, and samaritanism, the aging Apache leader Caracol alias John Lame Eagle in *Melons* is a noble-turned-vengeful-savage exploited and oppressed by white civilization. Regarded as a messiah by his southwest Pueblo settlement, Caracol confronts his old U.S. Cavalry adversary now (in 1906) representing an oil company with drilling rights on the Indian's land, recalls past humiliations at white hands, and ultimately reveals his ritual decapitation of two geologists sent by the company to find oil on the reservation. This revelation causes at the climax both his death and that of his white antagonist. Caracol's doomed attempts to hold onto the ancient ways and his white enemy's callous materialism reflect the Indian's inability to accommodate the conquering culture. Pomerance employs as a narrator an Indian activist raised by whites who encompasses the tension between both cultures and is powerless to prevent the conflict's bloody conclusion. The narrator strides back in time to tell us the Caracol story in a fractured narrative burdened with commentary, flashbacks, and a lengthy narrator-Caracol debate which hinders the forward momentum and immediate action of the play. Many critics viewing the 1985 London production by the Royal Shakespeare Company faulted the play's structural and storytelling flaws, and the consequent shortcomings in overall theatrical effectiveness, while praising its ambitions.

Quantrill in Lawrence, an earlier play, displays similar deficiencies in craft and the playwright's characteristic attraction to historical settings and situation. This play combines a plot derived from Euripides's *Bacchae* with the burning of Lawrence, Kansas, in 1863 by the Confederate outlaw Quantrill. The liberation of women and of suppressed desires are the play's thematic concerns.

Pomerance is a talented playwright committed to tackling large themes. His work is notable for its continuing interest in biographical and historical sources as means by which to examine contemporary problems.

—Christian H. Moe

PORTER, Hal. Australian. 1911–1984.
See 3rd edition, 1982.

POTTER, Dennis (Christopher George). British. Born in Joyford Hill, Coleford, Gloucestershire, 17 May 1935. Educated at Christchurch Village School; Bell's Grammar School, Coleford; St. Clement Danes Grammar School, London; New College, Oxford (editor, *Isis*, 1958), B.A. (honours) in philosophy, politics and economics 1959. Married Margaret Morgan in 1959; one son and two daughters. Member of the Current Affairs Staff, BBC Television, 1959–61; feature writer, then television critic, *Daily Herald*, London, 1961–64; leader writer, the *Sun*,

London, 1964; television critic, *New Statesman*, London, 1967, 1972, 1974–75; book reviewer, the *Times*, London, 1967–73 and the *Guardian*, London, 1973; television critic, *Sunday Times*, London, 1976–78. Labour candidate for Parliament, East Hertfordshire, 1964. Recipient: Writers Guild award, 1965, 1969; Society of Film and Television Arts award, 1966; BAFTA award, 1979, 1980; Italia prize, 1982; San Francisco Film Festival award, for television play, 1987; Broadcasting Press Guild award, for television play, 1987. Agent: Judy Daish Associates, 83 Eastbourne Mews, London W2 6LQ. Address: Morecambe Lodge, Duxmere, Ross-on-Wye, Herefordshire HR9 5BB, England.

PUBLICATIONS

Plays

Vote Vote Vote for Nigel Barton (televised 1965; revised version produced Bristol, 1968). Included in *The Nigel Barton Plays*, 1968.
The Nigel Barton Plays: Stand Up, Nigel Barton, Vote Vote Vote for Nigel Barton: Two Television Plays. London, Penguin, 1968.
Son of Man (televised 1969; produced Leicester and London, 1969). London, Deutsch, 1970.
Follow the Yellow Brick Road (televised 1972). Published in *The Television Dramatist*, edited by Robert Muller, London, Elek, 1973.
Only Make Believe (televised 1973; produced Harlow, Essex, 1974).
Brimstone and Treacle (produced Sheffield, 1978; London, 1979; New York, 1989). London, Eyre Methuen, 1978.
Blue Remembered Hills (televised 1979; produced London, 1991). Included in *Waiting for the Boat*, 1984.
Sufficient Carbohydrate (produced London, 1983). London, Faber, 1983.
Waiting for the Boat: Dennis Potter on Television (includes *Joe's Ark*, *Blue Remembered Hills*, and *Cream in My Coffee*). London, Faber, 1984.
The Singing Detective (televised 1986). London, Faber, 1986; New York, Vintage, 1988.
Christabel (televised 1988). London, Faber, 1988.

Screenplays: *Pennies from Heaven*, 1982; *Brimstone and Treacle*, 1982; *Gorky Park*, 1983; *Dreamchild*, 1985; *Track 29*, 1988; *Secret Friends*, 1991.

Television Plays: *The Confidence Course*, 1965; *Alice*, 1965; *Stand Up, Nigel Barton*, 1965; *Vote Vote Vote for Nigel Barton*, 1965; *Emergency—Ward 9*, 1966; *Where the Buffalo Roam*, 1966; *Message for Posterity*, 1967; *The Bonegrinder*, 1968; *Shaggy Dog*, 1968; *A Beast with Two Backs*, 1968; *Moonlight on the Highway*, 1969; *Son of Man*, 1969; *Lay Down Your Arms*, 1970; *Angels Are So Few*, 1970; *Paper Roses*, 1971; *Traitor*, 1971; *Casanova* (series of six plays), 1971; *Follow the Yellow Brick Road*, 1972; *Only Make Believe*, 1973; *A Tragedy of Two Ambitions*, from a story by Hardy, 1973; *Joe's Ark*, 1974; *Schmoedipus*, 1974; *Late Call*, from the novel by Angus Wilson, 1975; *Double Dare*, 1976; *Where Adam Stood*, from the book *Father and Son* by Edmund Gosse, 1976; *The Mayor of Casterbridge*, from the novel by Hardy, 1978; *Pennies from Heaven*, 1978; *Blue Remembered Hills*, 1979; *Blade on the Feather*, 1980; *Rain on the Roof*, 1980; *Cream in My Coffee*, 1980; *Tender Is the Night*, from the novel by F. Scott Fitzgerald, 1985; *The Singing Detective*, 1986; *Visitors*, from his play *Sufficient*

Carbohydrate, 1987; *Brimstone and Treacle*, 1987; *Christabel*, 1988; *Blackeyes*, from his novel, 1989; *Lipstick on Your Collar*, 1993.

Novels

Hide and Seek.   London, Deutsch, 1973.
Pennies from Heaven (novelization of television series). London, Quartet, 1981.
Ticket to Ride.   London, Faber, 1986.
Blackeyes.   London, Faber, 1987; New York, Vintage, 1988.

Other

The Glittering Coffin.   London, Gollancz, 1960.
The Changing Forest: Life in the Forest of Dean Today. London, Secker and Warburg, 1962.

*

Theatrical Activities:
Director: **Film**—*Secret Friends*, 1991. **Television**—*Blackeyes*, 1989.

* * *

Dennis Potter presents, albeit with a great deal of brittle humour and some acerbic comments on present-day life in Britain, an arrestingly grim view of mankind's eternal plight. He shows how beings are condemned to journey through lives which are often physically or psychologically painful as they more or less consciously search for a glory that has departed, for a god whose existence they vaguely intuit though he remains tantalisingly aloof and who might release them from their agonising and incurable sense of disinheritance. Only human relationships can sometimes assuage man's grief, but all too often they only make it worse. Education may well have served to increase Potter's feeling of alienation from certain traditional values that might have supported him, and his attitudes have no doubt been shaped to some degree by prolonged and distressing ill-health. But if he had been a French intellectual, critics would have had little hesitation in referring to Jansenism with its uncompromising condemnation of moral laxness and, above all, to Pascal's doctrine of fallen man's perennial and insatiable craving to know a god who remains hidden despite all the efforts of the reason to discover him. Within such a context, the combination of metaphysical despair with a heartfelt attachment to socialist values would not seem in the least unusual either.

For the most part Potter has written for television, scoring several notable successes, among them the famous *Pennies from Heaven* and *The Singing Detective*, which aroused very considerable public interest. *Christabel* is a powerful and effective reworking for the small screen of *The Past Is Myself*, an autobiographical work by Christabel Bielenberg, an intelligent and articulate woman who married a German lawyer in 1934 and witnessed at first-hand the horrors of the Nazi period in Germany in the 1930's and during World War II. Television is a medium that Potter handles with great skill, notably paring down his dialogue and leaving it to the screen image to convey much of what he has to say about the characters. Even such early works as *The Nigel Barton Plays* show many of his constant themes. *Stand Up, Nigel Barton*, presents the agonies of the bright boy at school, squirming with embarrassment when he finds he is becoming teacher's pet and realising that he is, in two senses, becoming alienated from the fellow members of his class. At home things are little

better as Nigel's father, a Nottinghamshire miner, tries to make sense of his son's education, and Oxford is presented more as Babylon than as the new Jerusalem which it had seemed when viewed as the goal of every educational ambition. *Vote Vote Vote for Nigel Barton* takes idealism down another peg, going behind the scenes of contemporary British politics as Nigel stands as Labour candidate in a by-election which he knows he cannot win. Party loyalty and the sheer impossibility of denying the recent past impel him to go forward until at last despair wins the upper hand. Only then are human values reasserted, and in his hour of deepest self-doubt his wife Anne sees that, in a world where compromise is the pre-condition of such limited success as will ever be possible, Nigel has personal qualities that matter. Another television play, *Follow the Yellow Brick Road*, takes disillusionment further. Jack is an actor, and the sense that authenticity has departed from his life is neatly conveyed by his paranoid illusion that he is being continuously photographed, while his disgust at materialist values is expressed by reference to the futile banalities of the dog-food commercials in which he has to play a ridiculous part. In *Cream in My Coffee* the familiar device of juxtaposing two time-sequences as a couple visit a seaside hotel before their marriage and return 30 years later neatly demonstrates, in a play also notable for its evocation of period, another failure in human relations. With *Joe's Ark* Potter tackles the issue of death with a directness uncommon in television drama. As Lucy lies dying of cancer she talks the matter over with her doctor; he admits he has no cure, or explanation either; then he adds that "every doctor eventually expects his patient to *collude* with him," and in the acceptance of the inevitable there is some comfort.

Brimstone and Treacle was written for television in the mid-1970's, but the BBC refused to screen it until 1987. Potter was naturally outraged, but it is not too hard to see why there were doubts about screening a play in which a girl who has long lain in a coma tended by her distraught parents recovers consciousness after being assaulted and raped by a young man with a whiff of Satanism about him. All the same, as well as revealing Potter's theatrical skills, the stage version of the play bravely tackles a taboo subject and offers some paradoxical optimism at the end.

So too does *Sufficient Carbohydrate*. On a Greek island an English couple are holidaymaking with an ill-assorted American couple who are accompanied by their callow son. The Englishman, Jack, has been forced into selling his food processing company to an American conglomerate, and now manoeuvres are going on to force him to resign the post he was fobbed off with after the merger. Junk food, summed up in vitriolic attacks on sodium monoglutamate, the additive that brings out the flavour, and on efforts to regulate the genes of mushrooms so that they breed identical in shape for easy marketing, is the focus for Jack's attacks on all that the modern world has to offer him. He drinks more than is good for him and equally often gets drunk on words, indulging himself in torrents of abuse about the sins and follies of the modern world. All the frustration of an existence that seems to have no solid purpose is brought out in the sexual tensions that are created, when Jack's wife, her patience exhausted, turns to the American while his wife casts her eyes on his son by a former marriage. Exceedingly funny in its lashing, highly articulate, and allusively literate humour, *Sufficient Carbohydrate* is deftly constructed for the stage, not betraying in any way that its author has had much of his experience in television. Played out amid the beauties of the setting on a Greek island and in a situation where, as it would in a classical drama, no outside force will come to complicate or solve the characters' problems, the human dilemmas hold our attention because the characters are so well observed. At first Jack irritates because of his self-pity, and his idealism seems close to self-indulgence and wishful thinking. Gradually his struggle becomes something grander as he sees, however dimly, a vision of values that will serve to nourish the human spirit in a materialistic age.

—Christopher Smith

———

POWNALL, David. British. Born in Liverpool, 19 May 1938. Educated at Lord Wandsworth College, Long Sutton, Hampshire, 1949–56; University of Keele, Staffordshire, 1956–60, B.A. (honours) 1960. Married 1) Glenys Elsie Jones in 1961 (divorced 1971), one son; 2) Mary Ellen Ray in 1972, one son. Personnel officer, Ford Motor Co., Dagenham, Essex, 1960–63; personnel manager, Anglo-American, Zambia, 1963–69; resident writer, Century Theatre touring group, 1970–72, and Duke's Playhouse, Lancaster, 1972–75; founder and resident writer, Paines Plough Theatre, Coventry, 1975–80. Recipient: John Whiting award, for drama, 1982, 1986. Fellow, Royal Society of Literature, 1976. Agent: Andrew Hewson, John Johnson Ltd., 45–47 Clerkenwell Green, London EC1R 0HT, England.

Publications

Plays

As We Lie (produced Cheltenham, 1973). Zambia, Nkana-Kitwe, 1969.
How Does the Cuckoo Learn to Fly? (produced on tour, 1970).
How to Grow a Guerrilla (produced Preston, Lancashire, 1971).
All the World Should Be Taxed (produced, Lancaster, 1971).
The Last of the Wizards (for children; produced Windermere, Cumbria, and London, 1972).
Gaunt (produced Lancaster, 1973).
Lions and Lambs (produced on Lancashire tour, 1973).
The Dream of Chief Crazy Horse (for children; produced Fleetwood, Lancashire, 1973). London, Faber, 1975.
Beauty and the Beast, music by Stephen Boxer (produced Lancaster, 1973).
The Human Cartoon Show (produced Lancaster, 1974).
Crates on Barrels (produced on Lancashire tour, 1974; London, 1984).
The Pro (produced London, 1975).
Lile Jimmy Williamson (produced Lancaster, 1975).
Buck Ruxton (produced Lancaster, 1975).
Ladybird, Ladybird (produced Edinburgh and London, 1976).
Music to Murder By (produced Canterbury, 1976; Miami, 1984). London, Faber, 1978.
A Tale of Two Town Halls (produced Lancaster, 1976).
Motocar, and Richard III, Part Two, music by Stephen Boxer

(produced Edinburgh and London, 1977). London, Faber, 1979.
An Audience Called Édouard (produced London, 1978). London, Faber, 1979.
Seconds at the Fight for Madrid (produced Bristol, 1978).
Livingstone and Sechele (produced Edinburgh, 1978; London, 1980; New York, 1982).
Barricade (produced on tour, 1979).
Later (produced London, 1979).
The Hot Hello (produced Edinburgh, 1981).
Beef (produced London, 1981; New York, 1986). Published in *Best Radio Plays of 1981*, London, Methuen, 1982.
Master Class (produced Leicester, 1983; London, and Washington, D.C., 1984; New York, 1986). London, Faber, 1983.
Pride and Prejudice, adaptation of the novel by Jane Austen (produced Leicester, 1983; New Haven, Connecticut, 1985; London, 1986).
Ploughboy Monday (broadcast 1985). Published in *Best Radio Plays of 1985*, London, Methuen, 1986.
The Viewing (produced London, 1987).
Black Star (produced Bolton, Lancashire, 1987).
The Edge (produced London, 1987).
King John's Jewel (produced Birmingham, 1987).
Rousseau's Tale (produced London, 1991).
My Father's House (produced Birmingham, 1991).
Nijinsky: Death of a Faun (produced Edinburgh, 1991).
Dinner Dance (produced Leicester, 1991; London, 1992).

Radio Plays: *Free Ferry*, 1972; *Free House*, 1973; *A Place in the Country*, 1974; *An Old New Year*, 1974; *Fences*, 1976; *Under the Wool*, 1976; *Back Stop*, 1977; *Butterfingers*, 1981; *The Mist People*, 1981; *Flos*, 1982; *Ploughboy Monday*, 1985; *Beloved Latitudes*, from his own novel, 1986; *The Bridge at Orbigo*, 1987; *A Matter of Style*, 1988; *Plato Not Nato*, 1990; *The Glossomaniacs*, 1990; *Bringing Up Nero*, 1991.

Television Plays: *High Tides*, 1976; *Mackerel Sky*, 1976; *Return Fare*, 1978; *Follow the River Down*, 1979; *Room for an Inward Light*, 1980; *The Sack Judies*, 1981; *Love's Labour* (*Maybury* series), 1983; *The Great White Mountain* (*Mountain Men* series), 1987; *Something to Remember You By*, 1991.

Novels

The Raining Tree War. London, Faber, 1974.
African Horse. London, Faber, 1975.
God Perkins. London, Faber, 1977.
Light on a Honeycomb. London, Faber, 1978.
Beloved Latitudes. London, Gollancz, 1981.
The White Cutter. London, Gollancz, 1988; New York, Viking, 1989.
The Gardener. London, Gollancz, 1990.
Stagg and His Mother. London, Gollancz, 1991.

Short Stories

My Organic Uncle and Other Stories. London, Faber, 1976.

Verse

An Eagle Each: Poems of the Lakes and Elsewhere, with Jack Hill. Carlisle, Cumbria, Arena, 1972.
Another Country. Liskeard, Cornwall, Harry Chambers/Peterloo Poets, 1978.

Other

Between Ribble and Lune: Scenes from the North-West, photographs by Arthur Thompson. London, Gollancz, 1980.
The Bunch from Bananas (for children). London, Gollancz, 1980; New York, Macmillan, 1981.

Editor, with Gareth Pownall, *The Fisherman's Bedside Book*. London, Windward, 1980.

*   *   *

David Pownall has written prolifically in the 1970's, 1980's, and early 1990's: eight novels, and numerous plays for the stage, radio, and television. Partly because few of the plays are published. he had little attention until the success of *Master Class* at the Old Vic in 1984. A second well-known stage work is an adaptation of Jane Austen's novel *Pride and Prejudice*.

A few of Pownall's plays are conventional pieces of story-telling, for instance, *Ladybird, Ladybird*, which shows Miriam's return to Liverpool after 50 years in the United States. A young war widow, she had escaped her environment, leaving a baby son behind. Now she comes back for a first meeting with her grandchildren, two men and a girl in a wheelchair, and the play shows the twists, turns, shifts, and complexities in these new relationships. Other stories set in the present are *Fences*, for radio, in which an upper-class girl falls in love with a stable-boy, and two for television, *Return Fare*, in which a discharged mental patient goes to live with his brother, and *Follow the River Down*, where an old man relives his life as he follows a river to its mouth.

In Pownall's most distinctive plays, something quite unexpected breaks through, identifiable reality changing to fantasy or taking on ritualistic aspects. In the early, strange *How to Grow a Guerrilla* an English garden has run wild and turned to jungle. A moronic youth plays soldiers, and a take-over by gangsters is followed by one by black police. *Motocar* is set in Rhodesia ten days before independence (indefinitely in the future when Pownall wrote it in 1976), in a mental hospital run by whites for blacks. A suspected black terrorist, named Motocar, is brought in for psychiatric examination. A poetic ritual eventually develops in which the blacks force the four whites to relive aspects of the black experience of oppression.

Most of this group of plays uses historical events and changes and adapts them. *Richard* III, *Part Two* ingeniously weaves together George Orwell in 1984 and Richard III in 1484 by way of a board game about Richard, called Betrayal. Games and men must both be properly marketed for success —Richard failed in this, while Orwell knew it. The 30-character *Seconds at the Fight for Madrid* is set in November 1936. The audience meets English, Americans, Germans, a Russian, peasants, beggars, who discuss the fate of three showgirls and a musician who have blundered into this military zone. The picture of the Spanish Civil War is completed with appearances by the king, Franco, Hitler, and, since Pownall is ever imaginative, Don Juan and Don Quixote. *Barricade*, set in the Spanish countryside in May 1937, has anarchists joined by two gypsies and a young English army officer on a cycling holiday. The gypsies, in curious stylized scenes, attempt to awaken the Englishman politically. *An Audience Called Édouard* starts with the pose of two men and two women as in *Le Déjeuner sur l'herbe*; Manet, unseen, is imagined painting this somewhere among the audience. The chatter of the foursome is disturbed by two intruders from the river, one of whom is Karl Marx, indeed a disruptor of the

harmony of La Belle Époque. In *The Bridge at Orbigo*, for radio, a referee and a footballer retracing the pilgrim route to Santiago de Compostela are guided into the past by a priest. Most difficult of all, in *Music to Murder By* a Californian woman musicologist conjures up the ghosts of Gesualdo, an Italian Renaissance composer, and Philip Heseltine, alias Peter Warlock, a scholar and composer who killed himself in 1930, as an illustration of links between creativity and violence.

A third group of plays treats historical subjects more objectively. *All the World Should Be Taxed* emphasises political elements in the Nativity story. *The Dream of Chief Crazy Horse*, written for schools with 70 parts, surveys ten thousand years of Red Indian history. In *Livingstone and Sechele* the young missionary David Livingstone makes his first convert, Sechele, chief of the Crocodile people, in South Africa, and is obliged to scrutinize his own faith. The other characters are their wives, submissive Mary and Mokoton, a fifth wife, scheming to keep her man from the outsiders. *Black Star* takes a really obscure subject, Ira Aldridge, the black American actor touring in Shakespeare in Poland in 1865. *Bringing Up Nero*, for radio, is a discussion between the young Nero and his tutor, the playwright Seneca, so the theme is whether a writer can influence a tyrant.

Two plays of 20th-century local history were written for Lancaster. *Buck Ruxton* deals with two brutal murders by a Parsee doctor in 1935. *Lile Jimmy Williamson* looks at the man who was the "uncrowned king" of Lancaster from the 1880's to the 1920's. He was a millionaire linoleum manufacturer, and Liberal MP from 1892 on. Pownall explained that Williamson "monopolised the city's industry so that he could pay subsistence wages and control the movement of employment. . . . I wasn't grinding any particular political axe. I was fascinated to find out what happened and why. Especially why it was allowed."

Birmingham Repertory Theatre commissioned *My Father's House*, about Joseph Chamberlain and his sons Neville and Austen, the most famous family in British politics. Pownall remarks that writing about real people "is a relief from creating fictional characters. It gives you a new flavour and uses a different part of your mind."

Pownall has also written three unique "danceplays." *Nijinsky: Death of a Faun*, set on the day Nijinsky hears of the death of Diaghilev, was written for Nicholas Johnson, a dancer who had never acted before. The others were for the Kosh company: *The Edge*, for one voice, about a mother estranged from her daughter, and *Dinner Dance*, which brings seven people into a kitchen. Pownall's work here is pioneering and original.

The wide-ranging historical interests and the musical aspect of *Music to Murder By* come together in *Master Class*, set in the Kremlin in 1948. Stalin, shown as a subtle manipulator, and Zhdanov, a bully, summon two famous composers to condemn their kind of music and to require them to meet Communist Party expectations in future. Shostakovich wants to be loyal, to work within the Soviet system, while Prokofiev feels himself outside it. As Stalin has all the power, the conflict is uneven, and, from outside the drama, audiences may know that the composers survived this confrontation. The second half has additional interest when the men try to compose a Georgian folk-cantata to show their conformity. Though some critics have argued that Pownall trivializes the issues, *Master Class* poses important questions about art and politics, elitism and social purpose, and the distance between modern music and the general public.

Pownall is a man overflowing with ideas, eagerly moving on to the next work rather than perfecting the previous one. His difficulty in gaining wider recognition, though, arises from the demands he makes on his audiences, whether to care about controversy in Russia in 1948 or to go more than halfway towards him in the strange world of *Richard* III, *Part Two*, *An Audience Called Édouard* and *Music to Murder By*.

—Malcolm Page

———————

PRIESTLEY, J(ohn) B(oynton). British. 1894–1983.
See 3rd edition, 1982.

———————

R

RABE, David (William). American. Born in Dubuque, Iowa, 10 March 1940. Educated at Loras College, Dubuque, B.A. in English 1962; Villanova University, Pennsylvania, 1963–64, 1967–68, M.A. 1968. Served in the United States Army, 1965–67. Married 1) Elizabeth Pan in 1969, one son; 2) the actress Jill Clayburgh in 1979. Feature writer, New Haven *Register*, Connecticut, 1969–70. Assistant professor, 1970–72, and from 1972, consultant, Villanova University. Recipient: Rockefeller grant, 1967; Associated Press award, for journalism, 1970; Obie award, 1971; Tony award, 1972; Outer Circle award, 1972; New York Drama Critics Circle citation, 1972, and award, 1976; *Variety* award, 1972; Dramatists Guild Hull-Warriner award, 1972; American Academy award, 1974; Guggenheim fellowship, 1976. Agent: Ellen Neuwald Inc., 905 West End Avenue, New York, New York 10025. Address: c/o Grove/Atlantic Monthly Press, 841 Broadway, New York, New York 10003, U.S.A.

PUBLICATIONS

Plays

Sticks and Bones (produced Villanova, Pennsylvania, 1969; New York, 1971; London, 1978). With *The Basic Training of Pavlo Hummel*, New York, Viking Press, 1973.
The Basic Training of Pavlo Hummel (produced New York, 1971). With *Sticks and Bones*, New York, Viking Press, 1973.
The Orphan (produced New York, 1973). New York, French, 1975.
In the Boom Boom Room (as *Boom Boom Room*, produced New York, 1973; revised version, as *In the Boom Boom Room*, produced New York, 1974; London, 1976). New York, Knopf, 1975; revised version (produced New York, 1986), New York, Grove Press, 1986.
Burning (produced New York, 1974).
Streamers (produced New Haven, Connecticut, and New York, 1976; London, 1978). New York, Knopf, 1977.
Goose and Tomtom (produced New York, 1982). New York, Grove Press, 1986.
Hurlyburly (produced Chicago and New York, 1984; also director: revised version produced Los Angeles, 1988). New York, Grove Press, 1985; revised edition, New York, Grove Weidenfeld, 1990.
Those the River Keeps (produced Princeton, New Jersey, 1991). New York, Grove Weidenfeld, 1991.

Screenplays: *I'm Dancing as Fast as I Can*, 1982; *Streamers*, 1983; *Casualties of War*, 1989.

*

Bibliography: *David Rabe: A Stage History and a Primary and Secondary Bibliography* by Philip C. Kolin, New York, Garland, 1988.

Manuscript Collection: Mugar Memorial Library, Boston University.

* * *

David Rabe's corrosive portrait of American life evolves within a series of metaphoric arenas—living rooms, military barracks, disco bars—where his characters collide violently against each other, but where, primarily, they struggle with their own society-fostered delusions. The revised edition of *In the Boom Boom Room*, published in 1986, is mischievously dedicated to "the wolf at the door" but the creature is already well within Rabe's theatrical house and the psyches of those who dwell inside it.

Two Rabe plays, forming with *Streamers* what has come to be known as his Vietnam trilogy, burst onto the New York stage in 1971 when both were produced by Joseph Papp at the Shakespeare Festival Public Theatre. Rabe denies that they are specifically "anti-war" plays, maintaining that he neither expected nor intended them to wield any political effect, that they merely define a condition as endemic to the "eternal human pageant" as family, marriage, or crime. ("A play in which a family looks bad is not called an 'antifamily' play. A play in which a marriage looks bad is not called an 'anti-marriage' play. A play about crime is not called an 'anticrime' play.")

But *The Basic Training of Pavlo Hummel* and *Sticks and Bones* portray the dehumanization and senseless horror of the Vietnam era with the sustained raw power now ordinarily associated only with certain films produced well after American troop withdrawal (*Apocalypse Now*, *The Killing Fields*, *Platoon*, *Full Metal Jacket*). Poor Pavlo Hummel's basic training functions as ritual throughout the play, contributing significantly to Rabe's theatrical stylization of an essentially realistic dramatic structure. Rabe's "realism" is invariably a realism heightened, stretched beyond traditional limits through (as in *Sticks and Bones* and *Hurlyburly*) dazzling language-play or (as in *Pavlo Hummel*) surreal fracturing of time and space and the ominous on-and-off-stage drifting of Ardell, a character seen only by Pavlo. Such blending of the real and surreal characterizes Rabe's style and serves both to rattle a viewer's preconceptions and to reinforce (as in *Sticks and Bones*) a given figure's alienation from those closest to him. It also prevents a play with a simple-minded hero from itself becoming simple-minded by complicating the theatrical conventions that develop Pavlo into an Army-trained killer who is ironically killed himself, not on the battlefield but in a brothel squabble. A sense of verisimilitude nevertheless underpins Rabe's stylistic virtuosity, the details of the Vietnam plays clearly emanating not only from the playwright's imagination but from his own Army experience in a hospital support unit at Long Binh as well.

While *Pavlo Hummel* focuses on pre-combat preparation for war, *Sticks and Bones* concerns its grotesque stateside aftermath. The naïve Pavlo may be blind to the reality of war but David, the embittered veteran of *Sticks and Bones*, has been literally—physically—blinded *by* it. Torn by the atrocities he has witnessed, tormented by his psychological and physical infirmity, David must be expelled from the bosom of the family whose artificial tranquility he is determined to destroy. Pavlo knows too little, David too much, and both must therefore die.

Despite its intensely serious subject, the method of *Sticks and Bones* is often wildly comic, dependent upon the clichéd conventions of situation comedy which Rabe transforms into a vehicle for macabre parody of American delusion. The play resonates, however, with overtones of American domestic tragedy, notably Miller's *Death of a Salesman* and O'Neill's *Long Day's Journey into Night*. Generically complex, articulated in language that alternates between poetic and vernacular extremes, *Sticks and Bones* remains the most important American play to come out of the Vietnam experience.

Streamers, adapted to the screen by Rabe and the director Robert Altman in 1983, expands the thematic scope of the earlier plays but most resembles *Pavlo Hummel* in its barracks setting. The violence inherent in the military system is here expanded, linked by Rabe to institutionalized racism and homophobia camouflaged in the rhetoric of patriotism.

Hurlyburly, a title that reflects the chaos of its characters' lives, veers in a different direction. The word appears in the opening lines of *Macbeth*, which Rabe considered using in their entirety to name each of his three acts, respectively: "When Shall We Three Meet Again?," "In Thunder Lightning or in Rain?," and "When the Hurlyburly's Done, When the Battle's Lost and Won." Though he rejected the idea, he writes in the Afterword to the play that he "felt for a long time that the play was in many ways a trilogy, each act an entity, a self-contained action however enhanced it might be by the contents of the other acts and the reflections that might be sent back and forth between all three." (Rabe is an astute commentator on the art of playwriting—his own and others'. See also his Introduction to *Pavlo Hummel* and the Author's Note to *Sticks and Bones*.)

Like that of *Streamers* and *Pavlo Hummel*, the world of *Hurlyburly* is male-centered, but the barracks of those plays shifts to the living room of a small house in the Hollywood Hills, inhabited by Rabe's least sympathetic outcasts. Cut off from their wives and children by divorce or separation, the men of *Hurlyburly* waver violently between macho boasting and episodes of confessional self-loathing as they seek solace in drugs, alcohol, and uncommitted affairs. Their hostility toward women, whom they regard as "broads" or "bitches," masks their inability to reconcile male behavior codes learned as children with expectations demanded by their liberated partners. These boy-men lack a moral center and represent for Rabe a characteristically American rootlessness.

Their anger is articulated in the stylized excesses and violence of the play's language, in the four-letter words that punctuate the dialogue but, more subtly, in the winding convolutions of speech: parenthetical expressions, self-interruptions, thoughts within thoughts, the repetitions and circularity that contribute to the work's considerable length and O'Neillian power. Eddie, Mickey, and Phil fear silence even more than they fear tuning into their own feelings, and thus keep talking, even if doing so runs the risk of accidental self-revelation. In this regard, an early stage direction notes that "in the characters' speeches phrases such as 'whatchamacallit,' 'thingamajig,' 'blah-blah-blah' and 'rapateta' abound. These are phrases used by the characters to keep themselves talking and should be said unhesitatingly with the authority and conviction with which one would have in fact said the missing word." The play's dialogue is extraordinary in its rich mix of funny, vulgar, savagely articulate language.

Rabe maintains that *Hurlyburly* contains no spokesman, that "no one in it knows what it is about." But the Age of Anxiety, documented by the disasters ticked off nightly on the 11 o'clock news, determines how his characters, and his audience, live. Rabe may claim that no single person in his play knows what it means, but *Hurlyburly*'s thematic core is expressed clearly in the drunken Eddie's furious lament for an absent God:

> The Ancients might have had some consolation from a view of the heavens as inhabited by this thoughtful, you know, meditative, maybe a trifle unpredictable and wrathful, but nevertheless UP THERE—this divine onlooker—we have bureaucrats devoted to the accumulation of incomprehensible data—we have connoisseurs of graft and the filibuster—virtuosos of the three-martini lunch for whom we vote on the basis of their personal appearance. The air's bad, the water's got poison in it, and into whose eyes do we find ourselves staring when we look for providence? We have emptied out the heavens and put oblivion in the hands of a bunch of aging insurance salesmen whose jobs are insecure.

Hurlyburly is Rabe's most intricate, verbally dazzling theatrical statement to date, a view even more strikingly apparent since the publication of the dramatist's definitive edition of the play in 1990. In this version Rabe restores and revises text cut or altered for the 1984 production directed by Mike Nichols in Chicago and on Broadway. This new, even more corrosive version of *Hurlyburly* emerges from a process of revision culminating in a 1988 production of the play, directed by Rabe himself, at the Westwood Playhouse in Los Angeles.

Also prominent in Rabe's most recent work are his screenplay for *Casualties of War*—a film with which Rabe expressed dissatisfaction, but one which searingly reflects Rabe's continuing obsession with the Vietnam conflict; and *Those the River Keeps*, a play which returns to the terrain of *Hurlyburly* from a fresh perspective.

—Mark W. Estrin

RANSLEY, Peter. British. Born in Leeds, Yorkshire, 10 December 1931. Educated at Pudsey Grammar School, Yorkshire, 1942–49; Queen Mary College, University of London, 1950–52. Married 1) Hazel Rew in 1955 (divorced 1970); 2) Cynthia Harris in 1974, one son. Journalist, social worker, and development manager of a publishing company, then freelance writer. Recipient: First Commonwealth Film and TV Festival Gold medal, 1980. Agent: Sheila Lemon, Lemon, Unna, and Durbridge, 24 Pottery Lane, Holland Park, London W11 4LZ, England.

PUBLICATIONS

Plays

Disabled (produced Manchester, 1969; as *Dear Mr. Welfare*, televised 1970; revised version, as *Disabled*, produced London, 1971). Published in *Plays and Players* (London), June 1971.
Ellen (produced Manchester, 1970; London, 1971). Published in *Plays and Players* (London), April 1971.

The Thomson Report (produced London, 1972).
Runaway (produced London, 1974).
Nothing Special (produced London, 1981).

Television Plays: *Dear Mr. Welfare*, 1970; *Black Olives*, 1971; *Night Duty*, 1972; *Blinkers*, 1973; *A Fair Day's Work*, 1973; *Bold Face Condensed*, 1974; *Mark Massey Is Dead*, 1974; *Big Annie*, 1974; *Jo and Ann*, 1974; *The House on the Hill*, 1975; *The Healing Hand*, 1975; *Henry and Jean*, 1975; *To Catch a Thief*, 1978; *Couples*, 1978; *Hospital Roulette*, 1979; *Minor Complications*, 1980; *Kate*, 1980; *Bread of Blood*, from the book *A Shepherd's Life* by W.H. Hudson, 1981; *Shall I Be Mother?*, 1983; *The Best Chess Player in the World* (*Tales of the Unexpected* series), from a story by Julian Symons, 1984; *The Price*, 1985; *Inside Story*, 1986; *Sitting Targets*, 1989; *Underbelly*, 1992.

Novels

The Price (novelization of television series). London, Corgi, 1984.
The Hawk. London, Hodder and Stoughton, 1988; New York, Viking, 1989.
Bright Hair About the Bone. London, Hodder and Stoughton, 1991.

* * *

Peter Ransley's first two plays, *Ellen* and *Disabled*, are based upon actual persons. For a period Ransley was a social worker, and in his first play, *Disabled*, he writes about one particular old man. In *Ellen* he depicts a playwright from the North who is writing a play about Ellen, a tramp who lives on his doorstep. When the play was staged at the Hampstead Theatre Club the real-life Ellen came to see the play about herself.

The central character in *Disabled*, Barker, is a problem case, dirty, smelly, cantankerous; further, he is in a disputed area where three welfare districts meet, so that responsibility for him is passed from department to department. He alienates all who try to help him, task force, home help, male nurse. But, as Ted, a character in *Ellen*, remarks, "Help is a cruel word." Both plays are concerned with the need to consider individuals as people, and not as "cases." Again, as Ted says in *Ellen*, "Labels. That's what makes people acute cases. The labels people stick on them."

At the end of the first act of *Disabled* a young man enters, an unidentified social worker called Mike. Barker gets him to talk about his marriage, which is on the rocks. He has not had intercourse with his wife for three years (the same length of time that Barker has been without sex since his accident), and after her last miscarriage Mike's wife took up social work. Like the wife Clare in *Ellen*, she is a frigid and sterile person. When she appears at the end of the play she says to Barker, "You are my case," to which he replies, "I am my own case."

Disabled is about the reversal of roles; it probes and poses such questions as who is the helper and who the helped. As Barker begins to tap Mike's dilemma we realize that it is Mike who, psychologically, is disabled. And when at the final curtain Barker is left alone saying "Poor bastard," it is perhaps less of himself that he is thinking than of Mike. In another sense it is also both of them, for in this play, not wholly successfully, Ransley attempts to merge two styles, naturalism and fantasy. In a central scene (finely directed at the Hampstead Theatre Club by Vivian Matalon with Leonard Rossiter as Barker and Peter McEnery as Mike), Barker gets Mike to make up his face like a woman. (Barker used to be a ventriloquist and do an act on the halls with his wife, Maisie.) Empathetically, almost mediumistically, Barker begins to take on the voice of Mike's wife (whom he has never met). By assuming the persona of Mike's wife he is able to uncover Mike's neurosis. At the climax of this curious scene he persuades Mike to lift him out of his wheel chair and to dance with him. As they dance so "Barker's limbs come to life" (author's stage directions). The moment the wife enters the room Barker collapses and falls to the floor.

What the author is trying to convey is that it is Mike whose psychological limbs have been brought to life by Barker's insight and understanding. And in the process of having to think about another human being, Barker finds a role for himself—he, too, comes to life.

Ransley described, in an audience discussion about the play, how at one point in his relationship with the particular old man who provided the play's genesis, he lost his temper and hit the old man. He was at once ashamed of himself but the old man laughed and laughed. For the first time someone had responded to him not as a "case," as a disabled person requiring a special attitude, but as a human begin. By losing his temper Ransley had revealed a true involvement with the old man, they had begun to relate to each other as people.

Ellen is a considerable advance in complexity and skill. While developing further the major theme of *Disabled*, it also touches upon the dilemma of the provincial artist. At one point Ted says to the playwright "We've both come a long way since those old Brummy days. I wasn't sure it was right for you to come to London because it is more of a challenge in the provinces, and you do lose contact with the source of your material—aren't you losing contact with your sources, cockalorum?" to which the playwright replies, "Trust you to go straight to the heart of my neuroses."

One of the arguments for "Drama-in-Education" is that it provides an additional teaching medium, and as such enables any subject from history to geography to English or science, to be taught, or handled, dramatically. Similarly, Ransley's plays are essays in sociology presented through the medium of drama. Carefully and sensitively he dissects aspects of our society. In *Runaway* he brings under his microscope a working-class family in a remote part of Yorkshire who have fallen under the shadow of cancer. The father is an old trade union man who failed to expose the risks of a dangerous chemical used in the manufacture of car tyres in the local factory. The resulting cancer which has crippled his best friend Charlie now threatens him. His 11-year-old grandson, the runaway of the title, and the best written part, is at the centre of the conflicts within this family. The writing is spare, pared to the bone, and beautifully understated.

Ransley's is a quiet and thoughtful talent but one which has a way of lingering on in the memory, of exercising one's conscience in everyday life.

—James Roose-Evans

RATTIGAN, Terence (Mervyn). British. 1911–1977.
See 2nd edition, 1977.

RAYSON, Hannie. Australian. Born in Brighton Beach, Melbourne, 31 March 1957. Educated at Brighton High School, Melbourne, 1969–72; Melbourne Church of England Girls Grammar, 1973–74; University of Melbourne, Parkville, Victoria, B.A. 1977; Victorian College of the Arts, Melbourne, Victoria, diploma of art in dramatic art 1980. Lives with James Grant; one son. Co-founder, writer and actor, Theatre Works, Melbourne, 1981–83; writer-in-residence, The Mill Theatre, Geelong, 1984, Playbox Theatre, Melbourne, 1985, LaTrobe University, Bundoora, Victoria, 1987, Monash University, Clayton, Victoria, and Victorian College of the Arts, Melbourne, 1990. Recipient: Queen Elizabeth II Silver Jubilee award, 1981; Australian Writers Guild award, 1986, 1990; Victorian Green Room award, 1990; New South Wales Premier's Literary award, 1990. Agent: Hilary Linstead and Associates, Suite 302, Easts Tower, 9–13 Bronte Road, Bondi Junction, New South Wales 2022, Australia.

PUBLICATIONS

Plays

Please Return to Sender (produced Melbourne, 1980).
Mary (produced Melbourne, 1981). Montmorency, Victoria, Yackandandah, 1985.
Leave It Till Monday (produced Geelong, 1984).
Room to Move (produced Melbourne, 1985). Montmorency, Victoria, Yackandandah, 1985.
Hotel Sorrento (produced Melbourne, 1990). Sydney, Currency Press, 1990.

Television Plays: *Sloth*, 1992; episode in *Sins* series, 1993.

*

Hannie Rayson comments:
My plays to date have been a response to particular contemporary social phenomena which at the outset I want to understand more fully. I seek subject matter which is full of contradiction and spend large tracts of time doing research. I begin with a big question, for example, in *Room to Move*, how has feminism affected Australian men or in *Hotel Sorrento*, how does the experience of expatriation alter one's perception of home?
Articulating the intellectual context occurs in tandem with the process of immersing myself in the world of the play: the characters, their lives, relationships, and so on. I am neither polemical nor didactic but I do want my work to be dense with ideas which have a critical relationship with the narrative. My ambition is to write plays which send audiences into the night with much to talk about.

* * *

Hannie Rayson's early work was in collaborative and community theatre, and the influence of that experience is evident in the problem-based plots and episodic structures which are characteristic of her writing. The first of her plays to achieve publication and some prominence, *Mary*, was directly a product of that involvement, and was developed in close consultation with relevant interest groups. Rayson acknowledges in her foreword to the published text both their contribution to the project, and the challenge which she herself faced as a fifth-generation Australian in dramatizing authentically the experience of a teenage Greek girl caught between her parents' culture and the very different expectations and rituals of Australian adolescents. *Mary* works very effectively, though, to catch sympathetically and with some humour the painfulness of the conflict.

Room to Move marked Rayson's transition into the mainstream subsidized theatre, and it has proved a very popular piece. It was hailed at the time as representing a belated recognition of feminist concerns in the Australian theatre, though that seems a partial distortion of the real achievement of the play. Rayson's subject is less the reappraisal of the role of women in relationships and the wider society than the impact which such reappraisals have had in those areas, particularly on the men who have been challenged with adjusting to them. The practical consequence of this approach is, in a sense, the reinforcement of the privileged status which men have enjoyed (or suffered from) in recent Australian plays as the principal agents of wit and momentum in the dialogue; reviewers frequently likened Rayson's presentation of the comedy of marital strife to that of David Williamson. But *Room to Move* has a further dimension, through the mediating presence of the elderly Peggy, who demonstrates that age and a warm cardigan offer no exemption from the need for challenge and intimacy in relationships. Like the more routine business of gender politics, her situation is treated with a nicely balanced sense of its pain and poignancy and its potential for farce.

Hotel Sorrento is Rayson's most ambitious play, and established her as a playwright of real substance. At its centre is the interaction, past and present, between three sisters; it has suitably Chekhovian elements of wryness and compassion, and establishes credibly a number of lines of conflict, most of them unresolvable. There are other aspects reminiscent of Chekhov: a strong sense of nostalgia for a lovelier and more innocent past, which in Rayson's depiction of the little seaside town of Sorrento is allowed to pass largely without analysis; a lively and articulate range of surrounding characters with a tendency to pontificate on the state of the nation; and, most tellingly, a subtle and powerful sense of the dignity and beauty which can co-exist with the silliness of people. The central images of the beach and the pier are handled very evocatively here, and catch for the first time in Australian theatre something of the mythological importance which looking out from the fringes of the continent to the water has in constructions of the Australian identity; it is a way of seeing which is just as fundamental as the more characteristic literary stance which looks inward to the arid centre.

Hotel Sorrento has more than its share of good conversation, and now and then the debate structure, and the much-canvassed matter of Australian identity, becomes a little stodgy; another limitation is the skeleton in the cupboard which underlies the sisters' wariness, which seems at once too prosaic and too melodramatic to account for the intricacies of their relationship. But it is a very moving and intelligent piece, impressive in its reach, and almost certainly built to last; it testifies to Rayson's growing stature in the contemporary Australian theatre.

—Peter Fitzpatrick

———

REANEY, James (Crerar). Canadian. Born in South Easthope, Ontario, 1 September 1926. Educated at Elmhurst Public School, Easthope Township, Perth County; Central

Collegiate Vocational Institute, Stratford, Ontario, 1939–44; University College, Toronto (Epstein award, 1948), B.A. 1948, M.A. 1949, graduate study, 1956–58, Ph.D. in English 1958. Married Colleen Thibaudeau in 1951; two sons (one deceased) and one daughter. Member of the English Department, University of Manitoba, Winnipeg, 1949–56. Since 1960 professor of English, Middlesex College, University of Western Ontario, London. Founding editor, *Alphabet* magazine, London, 1960–71. Active in little theatre groups in Winnipeg and London: founder, Listeners Workshop, London, 1966. Recipient: Governor-General's award, for poetry, 1950, 1959, for drama, 1963; President's medal, University of Western Ontario, 1955, 1958; Massey award, 1960; Chalmers award, 1975, 1976. D.Litt.: Carleton University, Ottawa, 1975. Officer, Order of Canada, 1975; Fellow, Royal Society of Canada, 1978. Agent: Sybil Hutchinson, 409 Ramsden Place, 50 Hillsboro Avenue, Toronto, Ontario M5R 1S8. Address: Department of English, University of Western Ontario, London, Ontario N6A 3K7, Canada.

PUBLICATIONS

Plays

Night-Blooming Cereus, music by John Beckwith (broadcast 1959; produced Toronto, 1960). Included in *The Killdeer and Other Plays*, 1962.
The Killdeer (produced Toronto, 1960; Glasgow, 1965). Included in *The Killdeer and Other Plays*, 1962; revised version (produced Vancouver, 1970), in *Masks of Childhood*, 1972.
One-Man Masque (also director: produced Toronto, 1960). Included in *The Killdeer and Other Plays*, 1962.
The Easter Egg (produced Hamilton, Ontario, 1962). Included in *Masks of Childhood*, 1972.
The Killdeer and Other Plays. Toronto, Macmillan, 1962.
The Sun and the Moon (produced London, Ontario, 1965). Included in *The Killdeer and Other Plays*, 1962.
Names and Nicknames (for children; produced Winnipeg, 1963). Rowayton, Connecticut, New Plays for Children, 1969.
Aladdin and the Magic Lamp, *Apple Butter*, *Little Red Riding Hood* (puppet plays; also director: produced London, Ontario, 1965). *Apple Butter* included in *Apple Butter and Other Plays*, 1973.
Let's Make a Carol (for children), music by Alfred Kunz. Waterloo, Ontario, Waterloo Music, 1965.
Ignoramus (for children; produced London, Ontario, 1966). Included in *Apple Butter and Other Plays*, 1973.
Listen to the Wind (also director: produced London, Ontario, 1966). Vancouver, Talonbooks, 1972.
The Canada Tree (produced Morrison Island, Ontario, 1967).
Colours in the Dark (for children; produced Stratford, Ontario, 1967). Vancouver and Toronto, Talonbooks-Macmillan, 1970.
Geography Match (for children; produced London, Ontario, 1967). Included in *Apple Butter and Other Plays*, 1973.
Three Desks (produced London, Ontario, 1967). Included in *Masks of Childhood*, 1972.
Don't Sell Mr. Aesop (produced London, Ontario, 1968).
Genesis (also director: produced London, Ontario, 1968).
Masque, with Ron Cameron (produced Toronto, 1972). Toronto, Simon and Pierre, 1974.
Masks of Childhood, edited by Brian Parker. Toronto, New Press, 1972.

All the Bees and All the Keys, music by John Beckwith (for children; produced Toronto, 1972). Erin, Ontario, Press Porcépic, 1976.
Apple Butter and Other Plays for Children. Vancouver, Talonbooks, 1973.
The Donnellys: A Trilogy. Erin, Ontario, Press Porcépic, 1983.
  1. *Sticks and Stones* (produced Toronto, 1973). Erin, Ontario, Press Porcépic, 1975.
  2. *The St. Nicholas Hotel* (produced Toronto, 1974). Erin, Ontario, Press Porcépic, 1976.
  3. *Handcuffs* (produced Toronto, 1975). Erin, Ontario, Press Porcépic, 1977.
Baldoon, with C.H. Gervais (produced Toronto, 1976). Erin, Ontario, Porcupine's Quill, 1976.
The Dismissal; or, Twisted Beards and Tangled Whiskers (produced Toronto, 1977). Erin, Ontario, Press Porcépic, 1979.
The Death and Execution of Frank Halloway; or, The First Act of John Richardson's Wacousta (produced Timmins, Ontario, 1977). Published in *Jubilee 4* (Wingham, Ontario), 1978; complete version, as *Wacousta!* (produced Toronto, 1978), Erin, Ontario, Press Porcépic, 1979.
At the Big Carwash (puppet play; produced Armstrong, British Columbia, 1979).
King Whistle! (produced Stratford, Ontario, 1979). Published in *Brick 8* (Ilderton, Ontario), Winter 1980.
Antler River (produced London, Ontario, 1980).
Gyroscope (produced Toronto, 1981). Toronto, Playwrights, 1983.
The Shivaree (opera), music by John Beckwith (produced Toronto, 1982).
I the Parade (produced Waterloo, Ontario, 1982).
The Canadian Brothers, from a novel by John Richardson (produced Calgary, 1983). Published in *Major Plays of the Canadian Theatre 1934–1984*, edited by Richard Perkyns, Toronto, Irwin, 1984.
Serinette (opera) (produced Guelph, Ontario, 1986).
Crazy to Kill (opera) (produced Guelph, Ontario, 1988).

Radio Plays: *Blooming Cereus*, 1959; *Wednesday's Child*, 1962; *Canada Dash, Canada Dot* (3 parts), music by John Beckwith, 1965–67.

Verse

The Red Heart. Toronto, McClelland and Stewart, 1949.
A Suit of Nettles. Toronto, Macmillan, 1958.
Twelve Letters to a Small Town. Toronto, Ryerson Press, 1962.
The Dance of Death at London, Ontario. London, Ontario, Alphabet, 1963.
Poems, edited by Germaine Warkentin. Toronto, New Press, 1972.
Selected Shorter [and Longer] Poems, edited by Germaine Warkentin. Erin, Ontario, Press Porcépic, 2 vols., 1975–76.
Imprecations: The Art of Swearing. Windsor, Ontario, Black Moss Press, 1984.
Performance. Goderich, Ontario, Moonstone Press, 1990.

Other

The Boy with an "R" in His Hand. Toronto, Macmillan, 1965.
14 Barrels from Sea to Sea. Erin, Ontario, Press Porcépic, 1977.

Take the Big Picture. Erin, Ontario, Porcupine's Quill, 1986.

*

Manuscript Collections: University of Toronto; Toronto Public Library.

Critical Studies: *James Reaney* by Alvin A. Lee, New York, Twayne, 1968; *James Reaney* by Ross G. Woodman, Toronto, McClelland and Stewart, 1971; *James Reaney* by J. Stewart Reaney, Agincourt, Ontario, Gage, 1977; *Approaches to the Work of James Reaney* edited by Stan Dragland, Downsview, Ontario, ECW Press, 1983.

Theatrical Activities:
Director: **Plays**—*One-Man Masque*, Toronto, 1960; *Aladdin and the Magic Lamp*, *Apple Butter*, and *Little Red Riding Hood*, London, Ontario, 1965; *Listen to the Wind*, London, Ontario, 1966; *Genesis*, London, Ontario, 1968.
Actor: **Plays**—in *One-Man Masque*, Toronto, 1960.

James Reaney comments:

These plays are interested in telling stories. I like using choral and collage techniques. The plays, particularly the children's plays, are based on watching children play on streets and in backyards. So—Plays as play.

* * *

When James Reaney turned to drama in the late 1950's, he had already won well deserved recognition as a poet with the volumes *The Red Heart* (1949) and *A Suit of Nettles* (1958), both awarded Governor General's awards. The early plays show Reaney struggling to master the elements of the dramatist's craft, a struggle that is not always successful. *The Killdeer*, first produced in 1960, reveals weaknesses typical of Reaney's work at this time—a sensational and melodramatic plot (a female prisoner, accused of murder, is made pregnant by the protagonist to save her from the gallows; Madame Fay is unmasked in a final courtroom scene); crude characterization; uncertain motivation. But if the other plays of this period—*The Easter Egg*, *The Sun and the Moon*, *Listen to the Wind*, and *Three Desks*—reveal similar weaknesses, they are also plays rich in poetry featuring a non-realistic approach to theatre which relies on non-linear plots, and the representation of mythic patterns through theatrical effects. If the reader or viewer is disconcerted by these early plays it is because there are so many unexpected and unprepared for shifts in Reaney's dramatic voice.

Some of Reaney's best work is represented by his 1960's plays for children—*Names and Nicknames*, *Geography Match*, and *Ignoramus*. *Colours in the Dark*, commissioned by the Stratford Festival and produced by John Hirsch at the Avon Theatre, Stratford, in 1967, is the best of these children's plays; it also appeals to adult audiences. It dispenses almost entirely with plot, motivation, and conventional structure replacing them with structural elements related to the play's thematic concerns—the letters of the alphabet, the books of the Bible, the seasons. The play's key structural element which gives coherence to the multiple incidents and to the rapid switches in mood is provided by poems which Reaney had already published and which are themselves given coherence by the dominant "Existence" poem. Central to these elements or motifs is the archetypal theme of a Fall and possible redemption.

Many critics regard Reaney's Donnelly trilogy (produced between 1973 and 1975 by Toronto's Tarragon Theatre) as his best work. His recreation of the events surrounding the 1880 murder of the Donnelly family of southwestern Ontario by Orangemen combines in a striking way history, folktales, myth, music, dancing, mime, and an inventive use of props. The first part, *Sticks and Stones*, is a vivid celebration of the Donnelly family and a powerful foreshadowing of their death. While rooted in naturalistic detail, the play suggests that the Donnellys are outsiders, as mythic in stature as Oedipus or the Ancient Mariner. The other two plays of the trilogy—*The St. Nicholas Hotel and Handcuffs*—are less effective because they repeat the essential story of the murder of the Donnellys. In them the mythic gives way to the naturalistic and drama is too often subsumed in literal documentary. But if the trilogy is marred by Reaney's excesses and if the published text seems confusing (nine actors must carry more than 70 roles), the true values of the work can best be seen in production where the complex nexus of symbols and the larger-than-life characters carry dramatic conviction. Reaney's plays are best understood *as process* rather than in terms of the printed text.

Following the Donnelly trilogy Reaney turned to dramatizing Canadian historical themes as in *Baldoon* (with C.H. Gervais), *The Dismissal*, *Wacousta!*, and *The Canadian Brothers*, the last two based on melodramatic novels by Major John Richardson, a deservedly neglected early nineteenth-century writer. These late plays have not been well received. In such 1980's plays as *King Whistle!* and *Antler River* Reaney has further reduced the scope of his themes by dramatizing incidents in the history of his own immediate neighbourhood—Stratford and London, Ontario; these plays have not gained provincial or national attention.

Although Reaney is generally held in high regard as a dramatist, his work is uneven, revealing a conflict between his innate academicism and the populist theatricality to which he aspires.

—Eugene Benson

———

REARDON, Dennis J. American. Born in Worcester, Massachusetts, 17 September 1944. Educated at Tulane University, New Orleans, 1962–63; University of Kansas, Lawrence (Hopkins Award, 1965, 1966), 1963–66, B.A. in English (cum laude) 1966; Indiana University, Bloomington, 1966–67. Served in the United States Army, 1968–69. Married in 1971 (separated); one daughter. Playwright-in-residence, University of Michigan, Ann Arbor (Shubert Fellow, 1970; Hopwood Award, 1971), 1970–71, and Hartwick College, Oneonta, New York. Since 1985 member of the English Department, State University of New York, Albany. Recipient: Creative Artists Public Service grant, 1984; Weissberger Foundation award, 1985; National Play award, 1986; National Endowment for the Arts fellowship, 1986. Lives in Guilderland Center, New York. Agent: Susan Schulman, 454 West 44th Street, New York, New York 10036, U.S.A.

PUBLICATIONS

Plays

The Happiness Cage (produced New York, 1970). New York, French, 1971.

Siamese Connections (produced Ann Arbor, Michigan, 1971; New York, 1972).

The Leaf People (produced New York, 1975).   Published in *Plays from the New York Shakespeare Festival*, New York, Broadway Play Publishing, 1986.

The Incredible Standing Man and His Friends (also co-director: produced Oneonta, New York, 1980).

Steeple Jack (produced Portland, Maine, 1983; New York, 1985).

Subterranean Homesick Blues Again (produced Louisville, 1983; New York, 1984).

Comment, music by Merrill Clark (produced New York, 1985).

New Cures for Sunburn (produced Albany, 1986).

*

Manuscript Collection: Lincoln Center Library of the Performing Arts, New York.

Critical Study: *Uneasy Stages* by John Simon, New York, Random House, 1975.

Theatrical Activities:
Director: **Play**—*The Incredible Standing Man and His Friends* (co-director), Oneonta, New York, 1980.

Dennis J. Reardon comments:

The central dynamic in my plays exists in the tension between what is "real" and what is "made up." I often mix carefully researched and recognizably topical material with the stuff of dreams, and I am seldom precise about where one mode leaves off and the other begins. My intent is to push beyond the suffocating ephemera of journalistic facts into a more iconic realm where the only reality is a metaphor.

* * *

Among the plays of America's contemporary dramatists, Dennis J. Reardon's work is distinguished by an energy that assaults the intellect as well as the emotions. With an audacity arising first from his youthful enthusiasm and then from a greater understanding of his craft, Reardon has experimented with theatrical effect in order to enhance his stories and to communicate his vision of man to audiences from whom he clearly demands intellectual involvement while besieging their senses with a variety of staged actions. Yet he remains basically a storyteller, albeit one with a bit of the Irish dark side showing. His subject is the plight of man immemorial, a condition he explores with all of the anxieties, frustrations, and reactions to the violent freedoms of the 1960's that marked his own maturing years. To date, his career divides into two distinct periods. *The Happiness Cage*, *Siamese Connections*, and *The Leaf People* brought him immediate recognition on Broadway as well as a sense of being both victor and victim in a world he did not fully understand. After a period of "self-willed" oblivion he began writing again in 1980 and has produced a half-dozen plays that reveal the vibrancy of his earlier work accentuated through experience and by the more balanced probing of the demons and saints, facts and fates, that persistently follow the modern Everyman.

The plays of Reardon's early period remain as daringly theatrical as anything he has written. Because he is always idea-oriented, however, his heavy emphasis upon a depressing view of humanity in these plays changes in subsequent work without bringing a complete denial to his philosophical

stance. Feeling that he has "the power to bring an untold amount of happiness into this miserable world," Dr. Freytag of *The Happiness Cage* experiments upon his patients to find a cure for schizophrenia. Then one patient questions Freytag's assessment of his condition as "lonely, confused, frightened, and thoroughly unhappy" and asserts that he is simply a man, that he is a unique human being. Moreover, he wants to know what happiness means. Apparently sharing Nathaniel Hawthorne's definition of the "unpardonable sin," Reardon mocks the stupid cruelty of the veteran's hospital where Freytag works and the flagrant hypocrisy of its management toward the lonely, confused, frightened, and thoroughly unhappy doctor. The "brooding, barren immensity" of the Kansas farm in *Siamese Connections* provides a metaphor for the story of two brothers—the favored one who was killed in Vietnam and the one who survived but did not know how to kill the ghosts that made him into a homicidal monster, resentful of his brother, unable to escape, condemned. In *The Leaf People*, a most demanding play for actors and technicians, Reardon underscored one of the ironies of life while dramatizing mankind's murderous pathway to power. The action takes place in the Amazon rain forest where a rock star searches for his father, an Irish apostle named Shaughnessey who has discovered, and wants to save the Leaf People. Internal conflict prevents the Leaf People from protecting themselves from the invisible greed of the outside world, the apostle dies, the son fails as a messenger of their danger, and disaster results. Eventually, new residents in the area say that they "never heard of any tribe called the Leaf People."

In all of Reardon's plays since 1980 there is a persistent probing of man's sensitivities and sensibilities, but his overall perspective is obviously comic as he writes about the human comedy. Laughter, however, is not his objective; understanding is. If people laugh, it is as likely the laughter of pain or startled hilarity, a dark and improbable humor. *The Incredible Standing Man and His Friends*, "a parody of dysfunction on both the societal and individual levels," may produce such confused laughter with its stereotypical characters in an absurd world. Who helps and what happens to the inarticulate man in a situation people do not understand? *Steeple Jack*, Reardon's most balanced view of life, dramatizes the trials of a young girl, tortured by fears and despairs, who is guided to hope by an illiterate busboy and a self-anointed apostle who preaches at perpetual man as he trudges on toward Armageddon. In *Subterranean Homesick Blues Again* the cavern tour guide, Charon, appropriately delivers his querulous tourists with ironic politeness to that place where "the turbulence and confusion of your days beneath the Sun are ended." Both *Security* and *Club Renaissance* in *Unauthorized Entries* (written 1984; unpublished) show the insubstantiality of modern times where a whimsical fate controls. A darker humor prevails in *New Cures for Sunburn* where the disastrous impulses of family cruelty and morbidity climax in a loss of human dignity for all. In opposition to such bleak pictures of grotesque man, *Sanctuary for Two Violins* (*Under Assault*) (written 1984; unpublished) repeats the hope of *Steeple Jack* as two old violinists heroically resist the assaults of life and survive to create the music described in the final line of the play, "How lovely!"

Having chosen the stage on which to project the conflicts and crises of modern man, Reardon finds that he has a great deal to say—about moral obligations, a mechanical society, illusions of security, destructive cynicism, fraudulence and perversity, the destructive forces of vulgarity. In order to underline his concerns, he is an explorer in contemporary theatre. Music plays an important role in his art—rock music, popular ballads, a sonata for two violins. Like many writers—such as Thornton Wilder whom he appears to admire—Reardon experiments with the concept of time and the complexity of its adequate expression on stage. In *Siamese Connections* the dead and the living exist together; in *The Incredible Standing Man* life hangs waiting for a traffic light to change; dance movements in *Sanctuary for Two Violins* project timeless assaults on life. In these experiments with time, some of Reardon's plays suggest the vertical approach of the Nō drama, unfettered by realistic representation or linear progression of thought. Space—on stage or imagined—also stabs Reardon's consciousness and moves him toward shifting scenes divided by numerous blackouts. His work is also marked by that relentless energy, now carefully orchestrated in such plays as *Steeple Jack*, *Standing Man*, and *Sanctuary for Two Violins*, to produce compelling and thoughtful drama.

—Walter J. Meserve

RECKORD, Barry. Jamaican. Born in Jamaica. Educated at Oxford University, 1952. Lived in London until 1970; now lives in Jamaica. Address: c/o Tricycle Theatre, 269 Kilburn High Road, London NW6 7JR, England.

PUBLICATIONS

Plays

Adella (produced London, 1954; revised version, as *Flesh to a Tiger*, produced London, 1958).
You in Your Small Corner (produced Cheltenham, 1960; London, 1961).
Skyvers (produced London, 1963). Published in *New English Dramatists 9*, London, Penguin, 1966.
Don't Gas the Blacks (produced London, 1969).
A Liberated Woman (also director: produced New York, 1970; London, 1971).
Give the Gaffers Time to Love You (produced London, 1973).
X (produced London, 1974).
Streetwise, music and lyrics by Reckord (produced London, 1982).
White Witch (produced London, 1985).

Radio Play: *Malcolm X*, 1973.

Television Plays: *In the Beautiful Caribbean*, 1972; *Club Havana*, 1975.

Other

Does Fidel Eat More Than Your Father: Cuban Opinion. London, Deutsch, and New York, Praeger, 1971.

*

Theatrical Activities:
Director: **Play**—*A Liberated Woman*, New York, 1970.
Actor: **Play**—Guy in *A Liberated Woman*, London, 1971.

*   *   *

Barry Reckord's studies of the effects of exploitation are thorough and broad-based. In his early play *Flesh to a Tiger* we are let in to the struggle of people in a Jamaican slum trying to emancipate themselves from superstition without falling under white domination. Della is a beautiful but poor woman, and her child is dying. She has to choose between the local "shepherd's" magic and the English doctor's medicine. Half-fearful of magic and half in love with the doctor, she encourages him to be insulted in the end—for what he regards as his "weakness." She finally smothers the baby and stabs the shepherd.

But exploitation is basically a class evil, rather than a racial one, and Reckord illustrates this impressively in his most famous play, *Skyvers*, which is an authentic picture of students in a London comprehensive school just before they drop out. The beautifully preserved "cockney patter" is another triumph of the play. As with *Flesh to a Tiger*, it deals with the incipient violence which results from frustration and limited choice. The children are surrounded by parents and teachers who are social failures; and they dream about football stars, pop singers and big-time criminals. Even if we deny that such schools are "invented" to suppress talent, the effect is the same. And the sight of "criminally ill-educated" uncertain boys suddenly acting with confidence and more than a hint of violence when they get together as a group should be a warning.

Having looked at exploitation of the group, Reckord then examined the other side of the coin—liberation of the individual. In *Don't Gas the Blacks* he introduced a black lover to test the professed liberalism of a middle-class Hampstead couple, and succeeds in exposing the racialism of the one and in destroying the sexual fantasies of the white woman about the black man. In *A Liberated Woman* the experiment is taken one stage further, where it is the husband who is black and the wife's lover white. Does the wife's liberation extend to her having a white lover?

Reckord is also interested in establishing the link between social and economic exploitation and the obsession of blacks to ape white bourgeois values. The aping can be seen in a lighter vein in *You in Your Small Corner*, where it is the black bourgeois family in Brixton who are the custodians of "culture." It is they who are educated, who "talk posh" and the English who are down-trodden and "common." The black mother (the successful owner of a club) doesn't want her son to get serious about the local girls, but to wait until he goes up to Cambridge where he will meet "people of his own class."

In the television play *In the Beautiful Caribbean*, however, the mood is darker. Nothing much seems to have changed in Jamaica since *Flesh to a Tiger* 14 years earlier, except that now the class and race battles are fought to the death. The society does really seem to be in disintegration because of the many special interests hostile to each other. There's the American exploitation of bauxite, the drugs industry, the subordination of the black working classes by the black middle classes, unemployment, the generation gap, and more.

This is not new in itself; what is new is the people's refusal to be abused indefinitely and this brings about the black power uprising. We trace this from One Son who is fired from his job as captain of a fishing boat, becomes interested in politics, and starts selling a black power newspaper. He is thrown in jail, beaten and killed because the police think he knows where the black power guns are hidden. His friend Jonathan, a barrister, and therefore middle-class, finally manages to forego white power temptations, and becomes a persuasive black power orator instead. And as so often happens, the end is bloodshed and defeat.

—E.A. Markham

REDDIN, Keith. American. Born in New Jersey, 7 July 1956. Educated at Northwestern University, Evanston, Illinois, B.S. 1978; Yale University School of Drama, New Haven, Connecticut, M.A. 1981. Married Leslie Lyles in 1986. Recipient: McArthur award, 1984; San Diego Critics Circle award, 1989, 1990. Agent: Peter Franklin, William Morris Agency, 1350 Avenue of the Americas, New York, New York 10019, U.S.A.

PUBLICATIONS

Plays

Throwing Smoke (produced Atlanta, Georgia, 1980). With *Desperadoes* and *Keyhole Lover*, New York, Dramatists Play Service, 1986.
Life and Limb (produced Costa Mesa, California, 1984; New York, 1985). New York, Dramatists Play Service, 1985.
Desperadoes (produced New York, 1985). With *Throwing Smoke* and *Keyhole Lover*, New York, Dramatists Play Service, 1986.
Rum and Coke (produced New Haven, Connecticut, 1985; New York, 1986). New York, Broadway Play Publishing, 1986.
Keyhole Lover (produced New York, 1987). With *Desperadoes* and *Throwing Smoke*, New York, Dramatists Play Service, 1986.
Desperadoes, Throwing Smoke, Keyhole Lover. New York, Dramatists Play Service, 1986.
Highest Standard of Living (produced Costa Mesa, California and New York, 1986). New York, Broadway Play Publishing, 1987.
After School Special (produced New York, 1987; as *The Big Squirrel*, produced New York, 1987).
Plain Brown Wrapper (5 sketches) (produced New York, 1987).
Big Time (produced Chicago, Illinois, 1987; New York and London, 1988). New York, Broadway Play Publishing, 1988.
Nebraska (produced La Jolla, California, 1989; New York, 1991). New York, Broadway Play Publishing, 1990.
Life During Wartime (produced La Jolla, California, 1990; New York, 1991). New York, Dramatists Play Service, 1991.
Innocents' Crusade (produced New Haven, Connecticut, 1991; New York, 1992).

Television Plays: *Big Time*, 1988; *The Heart of Justice*, 1990; *Praha*, 1991.

*

Theatrical Activities:
Actor: **Plays**—Third red soldier, art student, fifth comrade, fourth airman, and Dockerill in *No End of Blame* by Howard Barker, New York, 1981; Geoffrey in *A Taste of Honey* by Shelagh Delaney, New York, 1981; Melvin McMullen in *Cliffhanger* by James Yaffe, 1985; Leo Davis in *Room Service* by John Murray and Allen Boretz, New York, 1986; Dr. William Polidori in *Bloody Poetry* by Howard Brenton, New York, 1987; role in *Precious Memories* by Romulus Linney, New York, 1988; role in *Just Say No* by Larry Kramer, New York, 1988; Dennis Post in *The Bug* by Richard Strand, Louisville, Kentucky, 1989; role in *Buzzsaw Berkeley* by Doug Wright, New York, 1989.

*   *   *

That Keith Reddin is considered one of America's most political playwrights is less an accurate assessment of his dramaturgical preoccupations than it is an indictment of a nation of historical amnesiacs. Indeed, Reddin is part of a disenchanted generation of American writers, baby boomers who were raised on television and the homespun, fictitious ideals of American supremacy, who matured post-Watergate and wish to combat the critical forces of amnesia and nostalgia in the national psyche with their writing, an even more pressing task in the wake of 12 years of Republican rule. With varying degrees of *naïveté*, these writers display a political consciousness rather than set any agendas. While many of Reddin's plays are set around textbook "topics" and incidents like the Korean War (*Life and Limb*), the Cold War (*Highest Standard of Living*), the Bay of Pigs invasion (*Rum and Coke*), or the use of nuclear power (*Nebraska*), what Reddin does, like most filmmakers and playwrights in the American grain, is use political events and cultural patterns as a backdrop for an individual's struggle with fractious personal relationships. The political is traduced by the personal, and the result is a sharply satirical, uneasy sketch about one more episode in the ongoing saga of America's moral complacency.

A Reddin play typically centres around a well-meaning, bright, and unsuspecting gull who joins a powerful organization, only to gradually awaken to its incorporated evil. The hero is given opportunities to stand against the juggernaut (or at least get out), but is shown to be either too powerless or too passive to make a difference. When he does speak out, events have passed him by and/or he sustains a sudden and tragic personal loss. The play at hand then becomes an opportunity for the sadder-but-wiser narrator to detail his loss of innocence for the audience; as Jake, the raw CIA recruit who finds himself unable to stem the tide in Cuba, states at the outset of *Rum and Coke*, "this is how I got messed up in something called the Bay of Pigs."

Jake's admission, offhand yet personal, an invitation that deflects pain through mockery, is an example of Reddin's characteristic tone. Reddin is an actor; and, although he doesn't perform in his own work, he writes, for better and for worse, for the actor. The scenes are taut, brisk, and highly verbal, yet the characters often seem underwritten until actors flesh out the conflicts with their presence. Even the minor characters are provided with monologues or non-naturalistic outbursts to the audience that showcase the actor's talents. A Reddin play, unconcerned with subtextual moorings and structural transitions, is performed at high velocity and high pitch, the comedy arising from abrupt shifts in tone and emphasis and a predilection for the grotesque detail in everyday circumstance.

Reddin makes use of a post-modern sensibility. Having the theologian Calvin make a visit from the 16th century to deliver an ad hoc diatribe against the utter debasement of contemporary language and finish with a reference to Yul Brynner in *The King and I* is a very Reddin moment. Since one of his themes is the anaesthetizing effect of popular culture and the media on the individual, his plays bristle with references to ancient advertising slogans, household products, songs, old movies, political buzzwords, etc. In production, his comedies feature virtual "soundtracks" of popular recordings as commentary to the action. Reddin is also something of a fantasist. In two very different plays, the love interests of the heroes die unexpectedly. In *Life and Limb*, just as things are finally looking better for Franklin and Effie in 1950's suburbia, Effie is killed in a freak movie theatre accident, presumably because she has committed adultery and must pay for it. In *Life During Wartime*, Gail is the victim of a senseless murder in which her young lover

Tommy is an unwitting yet circumstantial accessory. Both of these deaths—of highly sympathetic characters—are completely shocking. The playwright himself can't seem to part with them or face up to his dramaturgical choice and so, in each instance, he has the dead woman return from the other world and console her grieving man.

Comic resurrection or patent, infantile wish-fulfilment? Reddin would seem to want it both ways, seeking theatrical resolution while showing such a gesture to be false. His heroes and heroines connect best when they are in different spaces. While they walk the earth, they are pulled irresistibly to become like everyone else—amoral, compromised, money-mad, power-driven. Time and again Reddin shows that the blows come when least expected, that people are much more evil than one expects, and that the web of complicity is always more extensive than one assumed; in a society administered by the corrupt and controlled by the media, how can one hope to keep one's hands clean? All that one can do is bear witness. If his earliest plays could be seen as fashionably cynical political cartoons, his later work demonstrates a more profound treatment of individual loss. Small wonder then that his latest play, which opened in 1991, is titled the *Innocents' Crusade*.

—James Magruder

REID, Christina. Irish. Born in Belfast, 12 March 1942. Educated at Everton Primary School, 1947–49, Girls Model School, 1949–57, and Queens University, 1982–83, all Belfast. Married in 1964 (divorced 1987); three children. Worked in various office jobs in Belfast, 1957–70; writer-in-residence, Lyric Theatre, Belfast, 1983–84, and Young Vic Theatre, London, 1988–89. Recipient: Ulster Television Drama award, 1980; Thames Television Playwriting award, 1983; George Devine award, 1986. Agent: Alan Brodie Representation, 91 Regent Street, London W1R 7TB, England.

PUBLICATIONS

Plays

Did You Hear the One About the Irishman . . .? (produced New York, 1982; London, 1987). With *The Belle of Belfast City*, London, Methuen, 1989.
Tea in a China Cup (produced Belfast, 1983; London, 1984). With *Joyriders*, London, Methuen, 1987.
Joyriders (produced London, 1986; New York, 1992). With *Tea in a China Cup*, London, Methuen, 1987.
The Last of a Dyin' Race (broadcast 1986). Published in *Best Radio Plays of 1986*, London, Methuen, 1986.
My Name, Shall I Tell You My Name (broadcast 1987; produced London, 1990).
The Belle of Belfast City (produced Belfast, 1989). With *Did You Hear the One About the Irishman . . .?*, London, Methuen, 1989.
Les Miserables, adaptation of the novel by Victor Hugo (produced Nottingham, 1992).

Radio Plays: *The Last of a Dyin' Race*, 1986; *My Name, Shall I Tell You My Name*, 1987; *The Unfortunate Fursey*, adaptation of the novel by Mervyn Wall, 1989; *Today and Yesterday in Northern Ireland*, for children, 1989.

Television Play: *The Last of a Dyin' Race*, 1987.

*

Christina Reid comments:

I come from a long line of Irish storytellers. The women of my mother's family didn't just sit still and tell tales, they dressed up and enacted a mixture of fact and fiction through song, dance, and dialogue, as much for their own enjoyment as to entertain us children. It is my earliest memory of theatre. In my plays, characters often tell their story as naturally in song and dance as they do in words, and much of my writing to date has been about the women and children of Northern Ireland. There are strong parts for men in the plays, but there are usually more women in the cast, and the main storyline tends to be mostly theirs. I don't set out to do this in any causal way; it is simply how I write, but I do think that too often Northern Ireland is portrayed on stage and screen as if "the troubles" and male violence is the whole rather than a part of life there, and that this leaves too many songs unsung.

* * *

Much as the weaver of homespun interlaces strands of yarn, Christina Reid alternates the tragedies of Belfast life with her ironic humor. Her plays are at once soft and abrasive, delicate and resilient, and they blanket us in warmth. Her portraits of working-class people are well crafted, their characters revealed quickly and neatly by series of humble incidents. Woven into the comfort of the ordinary is the horror of the extraordinary; entwined in the pain is the ache of laughter. The effect is outrageous: prejudice, deprivation, and death are reduced to commonplace events that we can understand, no matter where we live.

Outrage is a natural reaction to Reid's first play, the one-act *Did You Hear the One About the Irishman . . .?*. It is a 1980's romance à la Victor Hugo in that "the sublime and the grotesque" co-exist. Allison, a Protestant, and Brian, a Catholic, are idealists in an imperfect world. Neither can understand why it could be dangerous for them to marry, even though Brian's father was murdered and both have relatives in the Long Kesh prison where political prisoners are held. Their dialogue is witty and gentle, in contrast to the pleading of their families and the warnings of the prisoners. Periodic appearances are made by an Irishman who reads from a list of "Permitted Christmas Parcels" for the prison, thereby injecting reality, and by a comedian whose anti-Irish jokes are increasingly ominous. In counterpoint to Allison's and Brian's joke about forming their own peaceful "Apathy Party," the comedian talks of the inevitable violent deaths the Irish must suffer. The tragic conclusion is expected, yet the theatrical impact is not diminished. Reid makes effective use of black humor.

Tea in a China Cup is a lovely, quiet play. Though it takes place during the Troubles, it is concerned more with pride—making the proper impression and not airing dirty linen in public. It is the maintenance of dignity that obsesses Beth's working-class Protestant family, and fear of becoming caught in the same domestic trap that motivates Beth. In the first scene Beth must buy a grave plot for her mother, Sarah, who is dying of cancer. Reid's ironic faculty is evident immediately as Beth must decide between the Catholic and Protestant sections of the new cemetery, lest her mother stand out "like a sore thumb." Always aware of tradition, Sarah hopes only to live until 12th of July, when the Orangemen will again march past her window. She cautions Beth to remember all the family stories after she is gone, and Beth tells us about the men who went to war, the women who laid out the dead, her own friendship with a Catholic girl, and the importance of having what her grandmother called "a wee bit of fine bone china." But the china which to Sarah symbolizes the last vestige of civilization in a city of soldiers and Catholics is a bane to Beth. As Reid leads us through 30 years in the life of this family, Beth matures. In the end, still loving them all, she is able to break free of the restrictions which bound the women to home and custom. Superstition, prejudice, and tradition are cast aside in one last ironic act; hope is possible.

Less optimistic is *Joyriders*, a spirited evocation of what it means to be a poor Catholic teenager in Belfast. Sandra, Maureen, Arthur, and Tommy are four residents of the deplorable Divis Flats housing development who are given a chance to prove themselves in a youth training program. Two are young offenders, one was scarred when the army accidentally shot him, and one lives alone with her glue-sniffing brother. Reid first places these characters in a theatre, watching the end of Sean O'Casey's *Shadow of a Gunman* with their social worker Kate. By their reactions to the dialogue, their characters are instantly defined. Tommy, possibly a half-caste, is defensive; the disfigured Arthur is a joker; Sandra is practical; Maureen is a romantic. Together, they form a kind of family which Kate leads through various vicissitudes to a conclusion even she cannot control. The startling reversal is reminiscent of the well-made play. *Joyriders* is a particularly ironic title, since the activity brings this group only momentary joy and lasting misery. More ironic still is Kate's realization that the entire training course is the ultimate joyride because, when it ends, the participants have little chance of finding jobs. The course itself is constantly threatened with extinction. Sandra, Maureen, Arthur, and Tommy will all rejoin the cycle of hopelessness. In several ways, the play ends by coming full circle. Reid creates a sensitive portrait of teenagers trying to find their identities in a society that has no place for them. The issue is the fate of children from what Reid quotes as "the worst housing development in Western Europe."

The Belle of Belfast City takes its title from a music-hall song sung by Dolly, the ageing child star and matriarch of this play's family. As three generations gather, their reunion is marred by Jack, a loyalist who protests against the Anglo-Irish Agreement with the Reverend Ian Paisley. All of Dolly's women—Belle, the half-caste granddaughter; niece Janet, the victim of her brother Jack's incestuous attentions; the brave Vi and the idealistic Rose, Dolly's daughters—are subject to the males in power. Jack, the conservative Protestant zealot, and Tom, a strong-arm English "businessman," both harass the women. Each copes in her own valiant way, but is swept along on the political undercurrent which ripples through this play. Eventually Vi is persuaded to sell her shop. Rose fears the right-wing Catholic stand, so like Jack's, which limits women's rights. Reid is more straightforward about her politics than usual.

Reid's themes are women and their submissive role in Northern Ireland, their families, and the damage caused to both by the Troubles. She speaks sympathetically yet unsentimentally, and with the authority of one who knows the people and the customs about which she writes. It is a tribute to her skill that we can receive her message while being entertained. In no sense do we feel we have been subjected to a lecture, and yet we are filled with rage. In the midst of a lovely story is the inescapable presence of oppression, of a cycle of hopelessness despite courage. It is Reid's humor which gives

resilience to her characters and provides a fascinating contrast to degradation and horror. Her frequent use of music also adds texture to her plays.

—Carol Banks

RENÉE. New Zealander. Born Renée Gertrude Jones in Napier, 19 July 1929. Educated at primary schools to age 12; extra-mural study at Massey University, Palmerston North, from 1967: B.A. (University of Auckland) 1979. Married in 1949 (divorced); three sons. English and drama teacher in secondary schools, Wairoa, and at Long Bay College, Auckland, 1975–81; member, Womenspirit Collective, 1979–85, and Broadsheet Collective, Auckland, 1982–84; organised and led several writing workshops, 1983–85; playwright-in-residence, Theatre Corporate, Auckland, 1986; Robert Burns fellow, Otago University, Dunedin, 1989. Actress and director with Napier Repertory Players, Wairoa Community Theatre, and in Auckland. National vice-president, P.E.N., 1992. Recipient: Queen Elizabeth II Arts Council grant, 1982, and award, 1986. Lives in Dunedin. Agent: Playmarket, P.O. Box 9767, Wellington, New Zealand.

PUBLICATIONS

Plays

Secrets: Two One-Woman Plays (produced Auckland, 1982; revised version produced Auckland, 1987). With *Setting the Table*, Wellington, Playmarket, 1984.
Breaking Out (produced Wellington, 1982).
Setting the Table (produced Auckland, 1982). With *Secrets*, Wellington, Playmarket, 1984.
What Did You Do in the War, Mummy? (also director: produced Auckland, 1982).
Asking for It (also director: produced Kaikohe, 1983).
Dancing (produced Auckland, 1984).
Wednesday to Come (produced Wellington, 1984). Wellington, Victoria University Press, 1985.
Groundwork (produced Auckland, 1985).
Pass It On (produced Auckland, 1986). Wellington, Victoria University Press, 1986.
Born to Clean, songs by Jess Hawk Oakenstar and Hilary King (produced Auckland, 1987).
Form (for children). Dunedin, McIndoe, 1990.
Jeannie Once (produced Dunedin, 1990). Wellington, Victoria University Press, 1991.
Touch of the Sun (produced Dunedin, 1991).
Missionary Position (produced Dunedin, 1991).
Te Pouaka Karaehe (*The Glass Box*) (also director: produced Wellington, 1992).
Tiggy Tiggy Touchwood (produced Dunedin, 1992).

Television Plays: *Husbands and Wives* (*Country G.P.* series), 1985; *Beginnings and Endings*, *Strings*, and *Sheppard Street* (*Open House* series), 1986.

Novel

Willy Nilly. Auckland, Penguin, 1990.

Short Stories

Finding Ruth. Auckland, Heinemann, 1987.

*

Manuscript Collection: University of Canterbury, Christchurch; Playmarket, Wellington.

Theatrical Activities:
Director: **Plays**—*What Did You Do in the War, Mummy?*, New Zealand tour, 1982; *Asking for It*, New Zealand tour, 1983; *Te Pouaka Karaehe* (*The Glass Box*), Wellington, 1992.

* * *

In the decade since Renée began writing plays, she has remained true to the principles which first inspired her. These are to celebrate the lives of ordinary working women and to give prominence to their undervalued struggles in times of social change, whilst writing with humour and a light touch. She is widely respected as New Zealand's most prolific and versatile woman dramatist, exploring themes of gender, class, and race. Perhaps because her work coincided with the upsurge in feminist thinking, and because it certainly filled a need for more and better parts for women in plays, all the major professional theatres performed her plays during the 1980's.

Setting the Table, written in January 1981, shows women as intelligent, humorous, and strong, in a naturalistic play that also handles radical feminist questions. Set in the kitchen and revolving around four women who run a refuge for battered women, the action arises out of an angry husband who follows one of the workers home while looking for his wife. Sheila, who works at a public hospital, has become so angered by living in a culture which accepts rape that she takes the opportunity to intimidate a violent man. She injures him with a knife, ties a yellow ribbon around his penis, and hangs a sign on him saying "This man is a rapist." The central issue which follows from this action is whether it is ever necessary —or acceptable—to retaliate with violence in a violent situation.

Her best-known work is a historical trilogy which began in 1984 with *Wednesday to Come* (set in the 1930's), followed with *Pass It On* (set in 1951), and completed in 1990 by *Jeannie Once* (set in 1879). The stories of four generations of working-class women during times of upheaval are told. *Wednesday to Come* is also set in a kitchen but this time during the Depression, while a march of the unemployed to Parliament passes the house. Inside a young woman is waiting for the body of her husband (who has committed suicide in a work camp) to be returned to her. Four generations of women live together, represented by five well-drawn characters who retain their individuality while signifying class oppression and working women's invincibility.

Pass It On takes the action forward, while keeping the teenagers Jeannie and her brother from the previous play, to the 1951 waterfront confrontation when men fought each other in the streets and it was against the law to help strikers or to publish any news about them. A hand-written broadsheet is being printed and distributed (hence the title) and the technique this time is Brechtian rather than naturalistic. Several actors are used to fill many smaller roles and the effect is more didactic than in the earlier play.

Jeannie Once goes back to the first Jeannie, the old grandmother of *Wednesday to Come*, and explores her first years in New Zealand in 1879. Again Renée tries new ways of telling her story, using music-hall songs and many characters in shorter scenes. Women are the strong centre of this group of people from Britain trying to make a new life in a distant colony. Issues of racial prejudice appear in the victimisation of 19-year-old Martha, a Maori accused of stealing.

A racial theme is also obvious in *Groundwork*, set during the 1981 South African Springbok rugby tour of New Zealand, which takes the play inside prison and in flashback to a suburban home. Lesbian relationships are also thematic in this play, as they were covertly in *Setting the Table* and *Breaking Out*, and more overtly in *Belle's Place*.

Missionary Position is a full length play in which three bagladies seek refuge from life's realities at the bottom of the social heap by living in a film-star fantasy, casting themselves as Garbo, Monroe, and Dietrich. As she has often done, Renée uses music to counterpoint the action. *Touch of the Sun* is a comedy with strong roles for two women playing sisters sorting through the extensive wardrobe of their dead mother and discovering that things were not quite as they imagined in her life. The dominant presence of the dead mother looms over their lives, and always will.

Maori values set alongside success in the European world is the theme of *Te Pouaka Karaehe* (*The Glass Box*). "I think people get caught up in the glass box [of the city] and that becomes a barrier. Just living in the city and learning city ways and playing city games, you forget some of the things about home," Renee said of this play. Handicapped by three off-stage characters who do not appear but are constantly talked about, *The Glass Box* gives good opportunities for Maori women actors but the focus is diffused over several cultural and political issues, weakening the impact. *Tiggy Tiggy Touch Wood* is a tragi-comedy about a woman who, as the result of a vicious attack years before, has been braindamaged. Cared for by a friend who loves her, the time has come when a decision has to be made about putting her in a home.

Renée has added television scripts, a collection of short stories (*Finding Ruth*), a film treatment, and a novel (*Willy Nilly*) to her output, while plays continue to be her first line of creative communication with a society not by any means fully adjusted to the feminist point of view. Work in progress includes a novel, *Daisy and Lily, Lazy and Silly*, due in September 1993 for Women's Suffrage year in New Zealand.

—Patricia Cooke

———

REXROTH, Kenneth. American. 1905–1982.
See 3rd edition, 1982.

———

RHONE, Trevor D. Jamaican. Born in Kingston, 24 March 1940. Educated at a school in St. Catherine; Beckford and Smith's School (now Jago High School), Spanish Town, 1952–57; Rose Bruford College, Sidcup, Kent, 1960–63. Married Camella King in 1974; one daughter and two sons. Writer, Jamaican Broadcasting Corporation, Kingston, 1958–

60; teacher in Jamaica, 1963–64 and 1965–69; actor in England, 1964–65; founder, Theatre '77 (Barn Theatre), Kingston, 1965. Since 1969 freelance writer. Agent: Wiley Hausam, International Creative Management, 40 West 57th Street, New York, New York 10019, U.S.A. Address: c/o Drumbeat Series, Longman Group Ltd., 5 Bentinck Street, London W1M 5RN, England.

PUBLICATIONS

Plays

Smile Orange (produced Kingston, 1971; Waterford, Connecticut, and London, 1972). Included in *Old Story Time and Other Plays*, 1981.
The Web (produced Waterford, Connecticut, 1972).
School's Out (produced Kingston, 1975; London, 1986). Included in *Old Story Time and Other Plays*, 1981.
Old Story Time (also director: produced Nassau, 1979; London, 1984). Included in *Old Story Time and Other Plays*, 1981.
Old Story Time and Other Plays. London, Longman, 1981.
Two Can Play (produced London, 1983; New York, 1985). With *School's Out*, London, Longman, 1986; published separately, Lexington, Kentucky, KET, 1986.
One Stop Driver, music by Louis Marriott (produced London, 1989).

Screenplay: *Smile Orange*, 1974.

*

Theatrical Activities:
Director: **Plays**—*Old Story Time*, Nassau, 1979, and London, 1984; *Smile Orange*, London, 1992. **Film**—*Smile Orange*, 1974.
Actor: **Play**—Russ Dacres in *School's Out*, Kingston, 1975.

* * *

Filmmaker, actor, and teacher of acting, Trevor Rhone is Jamaica's best known playwright and one of the few Caribbean dramatists to be often performed outside the region. Having started the Barn Theatre in Kingston, he has a highly professional understanding of theatre economics, and the technical abilities and limitations of most drama groups. Written for small casts, using readily available stage props, requiring few set changes, his plays can be easily and inexpensively performed. They are entertaining while treating serious social problems. Rhone writes good acting parts and has a talent for suggesting dialect without clouding meaning for standard-English speakers. He has a sense of what makes people tick, how they behave towards each other. While he shows people influenced by their environment, their problems are personal and require will to resolve. The plays are Jamaican in subject matter and nationalist in perspective, but their themes are universal. Rhone is especially concerned with domination on a personal and national level, and with the ways self-interest destroys communal values.

Rhone's first success, *Smile Orange*, is built upon a contrast between the real and the tourist Jamaica, as found at a third-rate Montego Bay hotel. Language is representative of cultural and racial identification, as is shown by the hotel telephone operator's shift from the standard English she uses on her job to the dialect forms she uses in conversation with friends. "Me see one or two dry-up looking white people but

[*hiss*] is today dem say di season start proper." In an impoverished society, both personal and national relationships are established by financial considerations: "Is money I looking. Him have nutten to offer." As the workers feel dependent on the American tourists, they suffer from racial self-hatred: "di boss man have a black man out front as Assistant Manager. Di tourist don't like dat, you know, and I don't blame dem." A satire about the corrupting effect of the tourist economy on Jamaica, *Smile Orange* shows a society in which self-respect and sense of community have been lost, with the result that the characters feel trapped by circumstances, exploit each other, and look towards America for their redemption. "When it get down to di nitty-gritty is each man for himself." Driven rather by self-interest than vocation, dignity, ethics, or sense of community, the hotel employees are unreliable, even malicious. In the background a band plays cheerful music, but tableware is polished with spit and banana skins are left dangerously on the floor.

School's Out, a satirical exposé of the failure of local schools since independence, offers a disillusioned view of Jamaica and of human motives. The missionary school, representative of the nation, is perhaps best symbolized by the non-functioning toilet to which the characters often refer. Overflowing for weeks, its stink pervades the school but no one will have it fixed as it is the responsibility of the apparently absent headmaster, whose unopened door is always present on stage. The teaching staff and chaplain are late to their classes, find excuses to dismiss them early and by not doing their duty have left the school's canteen and other activities in the control of unsupervised students whose hooliganism the teachers then use to justify themselves. When a new white teacher begins to restore order, he is accused of asserting himself and of racial pride. As the play's symbolism suggests, he is a Christ-like leader whose involvement cuts through the stereotypes and who looks after the students' personal and moral welfare. Seeing their sinecures threatened, the other teachers start rumours of his sexual involvement with the students, which lead to his resignation and the return of disorder and incompetence.

In *School's Out* the staff are divided by politics. The conservatives do nothing to prevent a drop in standards while praising the past when the school had high standards and excluded the masses. Meanwhile the semi-literate products of recent mass education drive out the good, and hire others like themselves. The obvious analogy is to Jamaican society since independence. The evil of self-interest triumphs over national reform.

The relationships between the political, racial, moral, and religious aspects of Rhone's writing are clear in *Old Story Time*, where a black mother's initial hatred for and eventual acceptance of her black daughter-in-law is symbolic of Jamaica's coming to terms with itself and overcoming both black and colonial self-hatred. As in the other plays relations between characters are illustrative of the national mentality. The play covers 40 years of Jamaican social history, from a time when anything black was condemned as inferior, to a present when many of the same prejudices linger on under the surface of national independence. The villain is "a high brown man," who ruthlessly pursues his own self-interest and cheats others, especially trusting blacks.

The use of a *conteur* in *Old Story Time* is a technically effective way of moving back and forth in time. While the use of a traditional oral literary frame reinforces the play's concern with the revaluation of blackness, it allows dramatization of revelations about the past. Similarly, the use of obeah by the mother, the highly educated son's belief in its effectiveness, and the exorcism, half-obeah and half-Christian, of the mother's hatred are both psychologically probable and a statement about African survivals in the New World. The ending is sentimental, but the ceremonial exorcism is good spectacle.

Set in Kingston in the late 1970's, when politics has resulted in a near civil war, with people locking themselves into their houses while the sounds of machine guns are heard in the near distance, *Two Can Play* translates women's liberation to a Jamaican context. The national situation has contributed to the crisis of a marriage in which the husband has dominated, exploited, and humiliated his wife, leaving her sexually and emotionally unsatisfied. Unable to jump the legal and financial hurdles to emigrate to America, the husband collapses into futile incompetence, whereas the wife proves to be daring, disciplined, and quick-thinking. Having reached America on her own, she returns to Jamaica, now conscious of her abilities, to demand that her husband treat her better. To a nation where violence appears to have destroyed society, America may seem the promised land, but by the play's conclusion, when the husband and wife can emigrate to the United States, they have learned that American cities are also dangerously violent and marked by racial prejudice and conflict.

—Bruce King

RIBMAN, Ronald (Burt). American. Born in New York City, 28 May 1932. Educated at Brooklyn College, New York, 1950–51; University of Pittsburgh, B.B.A. 1954, M.Litt. 1958, Ph.D. 1962. Served in the United States Army, 1954–56. Married Alice Rosen in 1967; one son and one daughter. Assistant professor of English, Otterbein College, Westerville, Ohio, 1962–63. Recipient: Obie award, 1966; Rockefeller grant, 1966, 1968, 1975; Guggenheim fellowship, 1970; Straw Hat award, 1973; National Endowment for the Arts grant, 1974, fellowship, 1986–87; Creative Artists Public Service grant, 1976; Dramatists Guild Hull-Warriner award, 1977; Playwrights U.S.A. award, 1984; Kennedy Center New American Play grant, 1991. Lives in South Salem, New York. Agent: Samuel Gelfman, B.D.P. and Associates, 10637 Burbank Boulevard, North Hollywood, California 91601, U.S.A.

PUBLICATIONS

Plays

Harry, Noon and Night (produced New York, 1965). With *The Journey of the Fifth Horse*, Boston, Little Brown, 1967.
The Journey of the Fifth Horse, based in part on "The Diary of a Superfluous Man" by Turgenev (produced New York, 1966; London, 1967). With *Harry, Noon and Night*, Boston, Little Brown, 1967; published separately, London, Davis Poynter, 1974.
The Final War of Olly Winter (televised 1967). Published in *Great Television Plays*, New York, Dell, 1969.
The Ceremony of Innocence (produced New York, 1967). New York, Dramatists Play Service, 1968.
Passing Through from Exotic Places (includes *The Son Who Hunted Tigers in Jakarta, Sunstroke, The Burial of Esposito*) (produced New York, 1969). New York, Dramatists Play Service, 1970.
The Most Beautiful Fish (televised 1969). Published in *New York Times*, 23 November 1969.
The Son Who Hunted Tigers in Jakarta (produced New York, 1989). Included in *Passing Through from Exotic Places*, 1970.
Fingernails Blue as Flowers (produced New York, 1971). Published in *The American Place Theatre*, edited by Richard Schotter, New York, Dell, 1973.
A Break in the Skin (produced New Haven, Connecticut, 1972; New York, 1973).
The Poison Tree (produced Philadelphia, 1973; revised version produced Philadelphia, 1975; New York, 1976). New York, French, 1977.
Cold Storage (produced New York, 1977; London, 1986). Garden City, New York, Nelson Doubleday, 1976.
Five Plays (includes *Cold Storage*; *The Poison Tree*; *The Ceremony of Innocence*; *The Journey of the Fifth Horse*; *Harry, Noon and Night*). New York, Avon, 1978.
Buck (produced New York, 1983). New York, Theatre Communications Group, 1983.
Sweet Table at the Richelieu (produced Cambridge, Massachusetts, 1987). Published in *American Theatre* (New York), July/August 1987.
The Cannibal Masque (produced Cambridge, Massachusetts, 1987).
A Serpent's Egg (produced Cambridge, Massachusetts, 1987).
The Rug Merchants of Chaos (produced Pasadena, California, 1991).

Screenplay: *The Angel Levine*, with Bill Gunn, 1970.

Television Plays: *The Final War of Olly Winter*, 1967; *The Most Beautiful Fish*, 1969; *Seize the Day*, from the novella by Saul Bellow, 1985; *The Sunset Gang* series (includes *Yiddish, The Detective, Home*), from the short stories by Warren Adler, 1991.

*

Bibliography: in *The Work of Ronald Ribman: The Poet as Playwright* by Susan H. Dietz, University of Pennsylvania, unpublished dissertation, 1974.

Manuscript Collection: New York Public Library.

Critical Studies: "Journey and Arrival of a Playwright" by Robert Brustein, in *New Republic* (Washington, D.C.), 7 May 1966; *The Jumping-Off Place*, New York, Harcourt Brace, 1969, and "Ronald Ribman: The Artist of the Failure Clowns," in *Essays on Contemporary American Drama* edited by Hedwig Bock and Albert Wertheim, Munich, Hueber, 1981, both by Gerald Weales; articles by Anne Roiphe, 25 December 1977, and by Leslie Bennetts, 6 March 1983, both in *New York Times* theatre section; *Harvard Guide to Contemporary American Writing* edited by Daniel Hoffman, Cambridge, Massachusetts, Harvard University Press, 1979.

* * *

Ronald Ribman is a difficult playwright to characterize. The surface dissimilarity among his works gives each of his plays a voice of its own, but all are variations on the dramatist's own voice—on his preoccupation with recurrent themes, on his commitment to language that is at once complex and dramatic. Perhaps because he is also a poet (although not so good a poet as he is a playwright), he is essentially a verbal dramatist, fascinated by the nuances of language—the way a well-chosen adverb can alter the first meaning of a sentence, the way an extended metaphor can come to characterize its speaker through both content and style. Yet he is aware of and, often in key scenes, dependent on visual images that give particular force to the words; consider the scene in *Harry, Noon and Night* in which Immanuel cleans a fish while sparring verbally with Archer, the aggressive chop-chop-chop altering seemingly innocent statements.

The chief thematic concern of the playwright is with man caught between aspiration and possibility. "Well, all my characters are crying out against the universe they can't alter," he once told an interviewer, but the inalterable force varies from play to play. Sometimes it seems to lie primarily within the character (Harry of *Harry, Noon and Night*), sometimes to be dictated by the assumptions of society (the prisoners in *The Poison Tree*). More often it is a combination of these two. Finally, in *Cold Storage*, it lies in the fact of human mortality.

His first two plays—*Harry, Noon and Night* and *The Journey of the Fifth Horse*—deal with "failure clowns," "fifth horses," to borrow the "loser" images of the two plays. Underlying *Harry* is a conventional psychological drama about a young man perpetually in the shadow of his successful older brother. Yet, Harry can be victimizer as well as victim, and so can Immanuel, who routs the brother in Scene 2, but is himself the captive clown of Scene 3. Add the German setting with its references to the Nazis, "the Dachau circus," and the metaphor of the failure clown spreads to suggest the human condition. All this in a very funny comedy. The fifth horses of *Journey*, which grows out of Turgenev's "The Diary of a Superfluous Man," are Turgenev's hero and the publisher's reader who finally rejects the manuscript; the second character is only an ironic note in the original story, but Ribman creates him fully, his real and his fantasy lives, and lets him recognize and cry out against the identification he feels with the man whose diary he is reading.

With his television play, *The Final War of Olly Winter*, and *The Ceremony of Innocence*, Ribman seemed to be moving into overt social drama, into a direct pacifist statement brought on by the general distress with the American presence in Vietnam. Similarly *The Poison Tree* seemed to some an explicit commentary on prison conditions and racial bigotry, a reading that perhaps contributed to its commercial failure as the theater moved away from the social/political concerns of the 1960's. Although the social implications of these dramas are real enough, they are plays that deal with familiar Ribman themes and display the complexities of structure and language already familiar from the early plays. *The Ceremony of Innocence* is an historical drama which uses flashback scenes to explain why Ethelred will not come out of seclusion to defend England against the Danish invasion. He prefers to stand aside from a society which, mouthing the rhetoric of honor, chooses war over peace and special privilege over public welfare; still, the failures of his society—so forcefully expressed in a speech of the disillusioned idealist Kent—are reflections of Ethelred's inability to rule even himself, giving way, as he does at crucial moments, to an anger that belies his faith in the rational mind. In *The Poison Tree*, in which the prison is largely peopled by black convicts and white guards, Ribman develops his titular metaphor to show that all the characters are creatures of the situation. The manipulative guard who is his own victim, too easily a caricature in production, is actually the Kent of this play, finally as

helpless as the leading prisoner, the one who prefers feeling to dehumanizing theory, but is incapable of non-violent, regenerative action.

With *Cold Storage* Ribman returned to the exuberance, the inventiveness that characterized *Harry, Noon and Night*. Primarily a two-character play, *Cold Storage* is set in the terminal ward of a New York hospital. Given that setting, it is perhaps surprising to find such vitality, so much luxury of language, such wild humor, but these qualities are as important to the play's content as they are to its texture. Parmigian, a dying fruit merchant with an incredible frame of reference and a compulsive need to talk (silence is death), assaults Landau, gets him to release his secret guilt at having survived the Holocaust. As Landau learns to live, Parmigian comes to accept the fact of death. The play ends with a community of two, a conspiracy of sorts against the human condition, and leaves the audience with a marvelously replenishing sense of life.

The "crying out" is more muted in *Buck* and *Sweet Table at the Richelieu*, but they provide opposition to the inevitable—the one an image, the other a character. The titular protagonist of *Buck*, a director for a sex-and-violence television company, fails to humanize his product, to modify the cruel behavior of his colleagues, to solve his offstage personal problems, but the play ends with the new snow falling, bringing the promise of cleansing even though it will quickly turn to dirt and slush. As the patrons of the Richelieu, a metaphorical luxury spa, exit for the last sleighride, the less self-obsessed of the guests is defined as the Lady of Enduring Hope although she knows that no one can stay long enough to taste all the glories on the sweet table.

There is a quartet of failing clowns in *The Rug Merchants of Chaos*, two couples who have wandered the world, trying to succeed with one impossible business after another. When we meet them, escaping on a rattletrap ship from Cape Town, after a fire they set for the insurance got out of hand, it is only the latest installment of lives which one character describes as "hanging so delicately between farce and destruction." At the end there is exhilaration when they go over the side of the ship, ready to risk themselves and their hopes in an open boat miles from any shore.

—Gerald Weales

RICHARDSON, Jack (Carter). American. Born in New York City, 18 February 1935. Educated at Columbia University, New York, 1954–57, B.A. (summa cum laude) in philosophy 1957 (Phi Beta Kappa); University of Munich (Adenauer Fellow), 1958. Served in the United States Army, in France and Germany, 1951–54. Married Anne Grail Roth in 1957; one daughter. Recipient: Brandeis University Creative Arts award, 1963. Address: c/o Simon and Schuster, 1230 Avenue of the Americas, New York, New York 10020, U.S.A.

PUBLICATIONS

Plays

The Prodigal (produced New York, 1960). New York, Dutton, 1960.

Gallows Humor (produced New York, 1961; Edinburgh, 1964; London, 1987). New York, Dutton, 1961.
Lorenzo (produced New York, 1963).
Xmas in Las Vegas (produced New York, 1965). New York, Dramatists Play Service, 1966.
As Happy as Kings (produced New York, 1968).
Juan Feldman, in *Pardon Me, Sir, But Is My Eye Hurting Your Elbow?*, edited by Bob Booker and George Foster. New York, Geis, 1968.

Novel

The Prison Life of Harris Filmore. London, Eyre and Spottiswoode, 1961; Greenwich, Connecticut, New York Graphic Society, 1963.

Other

Memoir of a Gambler. New York, Simon and Schuster, 1979; London, Cape, 1980.

*

Theatrical Activities:
Actor: **Film**—*Beyond the Law*, 1968.

* * *

At the outset of the 1960's four young playwrights, Edward Albee, Jack Richardson, Arthur Kopit, and Jack Gelber, held the attention of the American theatre as its best prospects for the future since the postwar emergence of Tennessee Williams and Arthur Miller. The four became acquainted, and in the season of 1962–63 they were simultaneously active in the Playwrights' Unit of the Actors Studio in New York. Jack Richardson's particular position in this rather brilliant quartet was achieved by the success of two splendid plays produced off-Broadway, *The Prodigal*, his retelling in his own contemporary idiom of the Orestes story, and *Gallows Humor*, two linked tragicomic plays in a modern setting. In these plays Richardson stands apart from his three immediate contemporaries for certain defining characteristics unmistakably his own, characteristics that also mark his subsequent and somewhat parallel pair of Broadway plays, *Lorenzo* and *Xmas in Las Vegas*.

The plays, all vividly theatrical, are intentionally intellectual in the French tradition—somewhat unusual in American drama, although less so perhaps for a graduate in philosophy from Columbia University—and for their almost neo-classical emphasis upon verbal precision and formal control. At the same time, the plays share a conscious concern for previous dramatic materials and conventions, classical, medieval, Renaissance, and are unified by Richardson's persistent and strongly held view of the human predicament as man's forced participation in a destructive conflict between fundamental opposites: life, individuality, imaginative illusion, but chaos on the one hand; or death, conformity, reality, and order on the other.

The first pair of plays, *The Prodigal* and *Gallows Humor*, are written with an exhilarating wit and a Shavian exuberance hard to match in recent drama in English, and they are contrasting but complementary in method, with the classically inspired play modern by implication and the modern by medieval allusion universal or timeless in intent. In the former play Richardson personifies his characteristic and paradoxically grouped opposites in the figures of Aegisthus and Agamemnon, and in their conflicting views of man as either lesser or greater than he is Richardson also reflects Aristotle's definitions of comedy and tragedy. Orestes, the perfect tragicomic hero, succeeds for a time in avoiding either view and the destructive oppositions Aegisthus and Agamemnon represent. He seeks instead to "walk along the shore" and adopts the detachment of "laughter." But this modern stance, interestingly prophetic of the disillusion of youth in the later 1960's, proves a precarious stasis which cannot hold, and the murder of his father compels Orestes's participation in the battle of extremes he sought to avoid. The seeming inevitability of his decision is doubly reinforced in the play by the revenge theme of the myth itself and by the return motif of the biblical reference to the prodigal son, and at the play's close Orestes identifies his own decision with the general fate of man:

> The sea will always roar with Electra's cry; the waters will always rush toward Agamemnon's vengeance. It will cleanse or wash away the earth entirely, but it will never change . . . I can resist these forces no longer. I will go back, murder, and say it's for a better world.

In *Gallows Humor* the two component plays are linked by their common theme and by the fact that each play exactly reverses the central characters, condemned and executioner, and their points of view, and the effect of reversal is heightened by the appearance of the actors in the first play as their counterpart selves in the second. Walter, the condemned murderer, has a surprising passion for order and conformity, strives to keep his cell immaculate, and to go to his death with his "number patch" in place. But in the last hours, at the imminence of death, he is seduced back toward a celebration of life, illusion, and chaos by the prison prostitute Lucy. In the second play, Phillip the executioner, properly "dressed in the trousers, shirt, and tie of his official uniform," has an irresistible attraction toward revolt and wishes for the coming solemnities "to dress up like a headsman from the Middle Ages" in "a black hood." But his cold and practical wife Martha reasons him back toward conformity and order. The hood, Lucy's face, like a "carnival mask," the essential brutality of the execution itself, and the appearance of Death from the old Morality Plays to deliver the Prologue, give the play its comparative time metaphor. Although modern appearances are confusing, and Death complains that it is now difficult for him to "tell the hangman from the hanged," Richardson's essential oppositions, life or death, order or disorder, conformity or individuality, illusion or reality, and hangman or hanged, are reasserted as Walter and Phillip, modern ambiguities to the contrary, do end up playing their destined roles.

To an extent *Lorenzo* is a Renaissance variation of *The Prodigal*, but with a special emphasis upon illusion and reality, and the gambling metaphor in *Xmas in Las Vegas*, with its insistence upon the either/or of winner and loser, repeats the executioner-condemned contraries of *Gallows Humor* in a zany world and manner reminiscent of Kaufman and Hart and *You Can't Take It with You*. Lorenzo, "director of the theatrical troupe 'Theatre of the First Dove,'" is caught up in the midst of a "small war of the Renaissance" in Italy, and like Orestes he tries vainly not to become involved in the destructive conflict of opposites, polarized here in the impractical Duke, Filippo, and his general, the realist Van Miessen. In *Xmas in Las Vegas* Wellspot is the inveterate gambler condemned to lose, and Olympus, the casino owner, is the financial executioner. Olympus, with his suggestion of the gods, gambling as fate or destiny, and the sacrificial connotations of Christmas all enlarge the dimension of this modern parable.

popular County Durham folktale for his opera *The Lambton Worm*. In recent years she has also produced translations—or, as she significantly prefers to call them, "singing versions"—of the texts of Monteverdi's *The Return of Ulysses*, Cavalli's *La Calisto*, Handel's *Agrippina*, and Mozart's *Così fan Tutte*. These meticulously worked versions, which reveal a rare combination of verbal and musical sensitivity, have set high standards in this very testing art form. They have made an important contribution to the growing trend, exemplified at its best by Kent Opera, of performing, both in the theatre and on television, the masterpieces of the operatic repertory in English.

—Christopher Smith

RITTER, Erika. Canadian. Born in Regina, Saskatchewan in 1948. Educated at McGill University, Montreal, B.A. 1968; University of Toronto, M.A. in arts and drama 1970. Teacher, Loyola College, Montreal, 1971–74; playwright-in-residence, Stratford Festival, 1985; host of *Dayshift,* CBC radio program, 1985–87. Recipient: Chalmers award, 1980; ACTRA award, 1982. Agent: Shain Jaffe, Great North Artists, 350 DuPont Street, Toronto, Ontario M5R 1V9, Canada.

PUBLICATIONS

Plays

A Visitor from Charleston (produced Winnipeg, 1975). Toronto, Playwrights Co-op, 1975.
The Splits (produced Toronto, 1978). Toronto, Playwrights Co-op, 1978.
Winter 1671 (produced Toronto, 1979). Toronto, Playwrights Co-op, 1979.
The Automatic Pilot (produced Calgary, Alberta, 1980). Toronto, Playwrights Co-op, 1980.
The Passing Scene (produced Toronto, 1982).
Murder at McQueen (produced Toronto, 1986).

Radio Plays: *The Road to Hell*; *Dayshift*; *Miranda*, 1985; *Smith and Wesson*; *The Girl I Left Behind Me*.

Other

Urban Scrawl (essays and sketches). Toronto, Macmillan, 1984.
Ritter in Residence (essays and sketches). Toronto, McClelland and Stewart, 1987.

*

Critical Study: *The Work: Conversations with English-Canadian Playwrights*, edited by Robert Wallace and Cynthia Zimmerman, Toronto, Coach House Press, 1982.

* * *

Erika Ritter's first published play, *A Visitor from Charleston*, produced in 1975, concerns Eva, a youngish divorcée and frustrated would-be actress, who drowns the tedium of a routine library job and a dull ex-husband in a world of romantic fantasy created by repeated viewings of *Gone with the Wind*, viewings which continue after her separation from her husband and which number 47 as the play opens. Eva is deterred from seeing the film for the 48th time by a door-to-door cosmetic salesman pushing a line called "Instant Fantasie," promising rejuvenation and glamour, all the things Eva experiences vicariously in Rhett and Scarlett, who are eternally young, frozen in time on film. For the period of the play, Eva heckles and badgers the salesman, distracting him from his patter to reveal her life's disappointments and expose his frauds and weaknesses, all in the hope that "Instant Fantasie" products will somehow prove to be her own personal *Gone with the Wind*. Peering into the mirror as she tries out the new blushers and mascaras, recalling the face of her youth, triggers a series of three memory scenes, each one increasing her disillusionment, and confirming her sense that love and artistic fulfilment are impossible except in the movies.

The two major themes of male/female relationships and the creating of art, along with a number of motifs and technical devices introduced in *A Visitor from Charleston*, continue with variations throughout the five following plays, all (with the exception of the anachronistic historical play, *Winter 1671*) contemporary, urban, and full of corrosively witty one-liners and self-deprecating anecdotes.

The Splits, Ritter's next play, produced in 1978, is about Megan, a television script writer, trying to organize her career as well as come to terms with the three men in her life—Hal, the Tuesday-Thursday lover she met in group therapy; David, her story editor and well-meaning, though weak friend; and Joe, her boorish, abusive, cadging ex-husband. In the end they all split, Hal willingly, Joe by force, trashing Megan's apartment while declaring she's the only woman he ever loved, and David by default. Most important is Megan's departure. The play closes with her picking up her purse and typewriter from the wreckage and walking out, the upbeat ending of a courageous woman who has rejected palliatives and mediocre solutions for a creative life on her own terms.

The Automatic Pilot is Ritter's most accomplished work to date. It concerns Charlie, a writer of soap operas by day and a stand-up comedienne by night, who uses the disasters of her personal life as material for her comic routines. Again Ritter deals with male/female relationships, but this time from both perspectives: Charlie's (the female lead) in the first act and Gene's (her lover) in the second. Because Ritter refuses to oversimplify the difficulties of the current situation for unattached, self-supporting, successful professional women who also want a fulfilling and secure love relationship with a decent man who can accept equality of the sexes, her plays never take a straight feminist direction. She refuses just to blame "patriarchal" society, and insists that many women (like Charlie) are their own worst enemies. This leads to a very shrewd analysis of elements of character which are self-defeating in women. Yet while Ritter sees their unhappiness as "largely a product of their own mentality and their attitude about themselves", she does recognize that there is a link between this and society as a whole: "My characters tend to do a lot of wistful wandering; they tend to be indecisive people because they live in an indecisive age." Both men and women are affected by this modern indecisiveness, as even macho Nick, one of Charlie's pick-ups in *The Automatic Pilot*, slumps wearily and says he feels old. And the root of Charlie's difficulty (as both Gene, her lover, and Alan, her ex-husband, point out) is that, despite her independence and apparent cynical toughness, ultimately she depends on other people for respect and a sense of self. In reaction against this dependency, Charlie tries constantly to see herself as the victim of the people whose respect she feels she has lost. As Ritter explains, "[Charlie] wants to contrive circumstance so that she, in her own mind, is free from guilt or blame. . . . She manipulates situations so that the other person is responsible, because she's more comfortable with the role of the person who is acted upon."

The form that this self-contempt takes is her routine as a stand-up comedienne at the Canada Goose, a night club employing amateurs. On one level, joking is Charlie's method of coming to terms with the harshness of experience by laughing at herself, but on another level it is an appeal for the audience's approval and sympathy. The technique of comic self-deprecation that started as a defense mechanism becomes an emotional necessity for her. Gradually she starts to see her actual experience in terms of the show, instead of vice versa. As the audience watches Charlie's routine in the "show within the play," it sees creation in process at the same time as the destruction of Charlie's life. The saddest result is that when she does win the love of a totally decent man, Gene, she can't accept it; she has to spoil it because she only feels comfortable and safe in her habitual mixture of self-contemptuous misery, projected as comedy to win admiration of an audience.

In the meantime, Gene, the only male character in all the plays who represents Ritter's point of view, also turns his personal experience into a novel, comically entitled *Deathless Prose*. However, he is not hooked into the process as Charlie is, but uses his art to try to understand. Beneath the often farcical situations and constant wisecracks are extremely perceptive comments on human behaviour and art, typical of the bitter-sweet, comic-sad mixture of most of Ritter's work.

Six years later *Murder at McQueen* was produced, a play again focusing on women and their relations with men and with their own particular forms of self-expression. Three of the four women, each a decade apart in age, has an affair with a macho, amoral talk-show host, appropriately named Rex. The eldest, Mitzi, founds a successful women's club, The McQueen, as therapy following the break-up, but after five years she still yearns for him. Secretly her best friend, Norah, a beautiful young lawyer in her 20's, annoyed by the chauvinist tack Rex takes in his talk show, telephones her protest and, both intrigued, they meet and end up in bed, Rex enthralled for the first time despite numerous affairs, and Norah attracted, but feeling she has betrayed Mitzi. Ultimately she rejects Rex, to his astonishment and dismay, but also leaves the club and Mitzi.

This plot is framed by a chorus figure, Blythe, a writer and teacher of detective fiction, and non-member of the club who observes and receives confidences from members. She suffers from the same unsatisfactory love experiences as the others—separation, rejection, fulfilment through fantasy. When her fictional detective, Butler, appears in the flesh investigating a fire at the club and crank calls to Rex, she finds illusion merging wonderfully with reality at first until fantasy is overwhelmed by sordid facts. The "Murder" in the play's title refers to the betrayal of friendships, the death of hope and trust, and concomitantly, the growth of cynicism, despair, and loneliness.

Ritter's plays are all written in the style and tradition of the Comedy of Manners, where her shrewd eye for modern "yuppie" attitudes and ear for ways of talking are captured in often brilliant verbal wit. In fact, the wit is so ubiquitous and sharp that the audience sometimes forgets Ritter's technical skill. The juxtaposing of two modes of fantasy, the movie and the cosmetics, in her first play, *A Visitor from Charleston*, creating a kind of literary *trompe d'oeil*, and the mode of sliding into memory through the mirror, are effects which she varies imaginatively in later plays, creating clever transitions from one level to another so that we see the relationship between real life and performance, fantasy and human need that is central to Ritter's vision.

—Dorothy Parker

ROCHE, Billy (William Michael Roche). Irish. Born in Wexford, 11 January 1949. Educated at Mercy Convent School, Wexford, 1954–57; Christian Brothers, Primary and Secondary, 1957–66. Married Patti Egan in 1973; three daughters. Barman, Shamrock Bar, Wexford, 1967–69; upholsterer, Smiths Car Factory, Wexford, 1969–73 and 1978–80; builders' labourer, London, 1973–75; barman, Stonebridge Lounge, Wexford, 1976; factory worker, Wexford, 1976–78. Singer with The Roach Band, 1975–80; playwright-in-residence, The Bush Theatre, London, 1988. Recipient: *Plays and Players* award, 1988, 1989; John Whiting award, 1989; George Devine award, 1990; Edinburgh Fringe first, 1990; Thames Television award, 1990; London Theatre Fringe award, 1992; *Time Out* award, 1992. Lives in Wexford. Agent: Leah Schmidt, Curtis Brown Group, 162–168 Regent Street, London W1R 5TB, England.

PUBLICATIONS

Plays

Johnny Nobody (produced Wexford, 1986).
A Handful of Stars (as *The Boker Poker Club*, produced Wexford, 1987; as *A Handful of Stars*, produced London, 1988). Published in *First Run*, edited by Kate Harwood, London, Hern, 1989.
Amphibians (produced Wexford, 1987; revised version produced London, 1992).
Poor Beast in the Rain (produced London, 1989). London, Hern, 1990.
Belfry (produced London, 1991). Included in *The Wexford Trilogy*, 1992.
The Wexford Trilogy (includes *A Handful of Stars*, *Poor Beast in the Rain*, *Belfry*) (produced London, 1992). London, Hern, 1992.

Novel

Tumbling Down. Dublin, Wolfhound Press, 1986.

*

Theatrical Activities:
Actor: **Plays**—Spud Murphy in *Johnny Nobody*, Wexford, 1986; Stapler in *The Boker Poker Club*, Wexford, 1987; Eagle in *Amphibians*, Wexford, 1987; Willy Diver in *Aristocrats* by Brian Friel, London, 1988. **Films**—role in *Strapless* by David Hare, 1990. **Television**—*The Bill*, 1992.

Billy Roche comments:
It is my fascination with my hometown of Wexford in Ireland that forms the basis of all my work so far. I had hoped

that I'd be over it all by now but instead I find my fascination deepens with every play I write. It is mainly the language of the people of Wexford that I'm after—poetic, strange, sly language that can be so devastatingly economic, particularly in the affairs of the heart, and yet has the knack of going right to the core of the matter. Like many other writers before me I keep returning to the place of my birth like a salmon swimming home perhaps because I just long to see my own face in the water or at the very least I really wouldn't mind finding the little fellow I used to be once upon a time.

*   *   *

"The play is set in Wexford, a small town in Ireland." The thematic territory of Billy Roche's *The Wexford Trilogy* is as economically defined and focused as its geographical setting. What is presented in each of the plays is less a plot than a situation of stagnation in which the thwarted energies and desires of the individual continually seek expression—or even resolution in action. The paralysis of a provincial milieu in which, although "it's nobody's fault," "everyone's to blame," is familiar from Joyce's *Dubliners* and the stream of Irish writing that emerges from it, but Roche's treatment is distinctive in its particularity and resonance. Indeed, his writing is notable (especially in view of its themes) for its deep and unembarrassed relation to its artistic roots: not only Joyce and the Irish short story, but Chekhov—mediated perhaps through the 1970's plays of Brian Friel. The affection manifest in the presentation of many of the characters, and the fullness with which the Wexford context is suggested, tend to pull against the astringencies of a Joycean or Chekhovian irony, but the sense of small-town stagnation is nevertheless potent. Not the least Joycean feature of Roche's writing is the pervasive reference to popular culture—film and pop song— which functions as ironic counterpoint to the action. Also noticeable is the way that stereotypes familiar from O'Casey are displaced and rotated. In all three plays, those who ultimately constrain, command, influence, or stand as symbols are versions of the stoical, forebearing mother and the feckless, extravagant father. But these figures are always unseen, offstage: their determining presence is made all the more apparent by their physical absence.

A Handful of Stars, the first play of the *Trilogy*, is set in a "scruffy pool hall," the favourite haunt of local teenage rebel and self-styled "King of the Renegades," Jimmy Brady. For Jimmy, to "grow up" would be for him to join the "livin' dead," wrapped up in a "nice neat little parcel." Progressively isolated by the loss of his girlfriend (who leaves him because he is "not going to change") and the impending marriage of his best friend, Jimmy realises that he has not "a ghost of a chance" of avoiding the fate of his drunken ne'er-do-well father. He "wages war on everybody," and seals his alienation from local society by attempting to hold up a shop. Taking refuge in the pool hall, he wrecks the privileged preserve of its "élite" members. Before the Garda arrives, the over-the-hill local boxer, Stapler, a surrogate father for Jimmy, steadies him, but can offer only weary words: "Most of us wage war on the wrong people." Jimmy would "rather be an ejit than a creep," and there seems no other option. His parents' momentary happiness now appears like a "mirage," and his arrest will, he knows, consign his mother to further silent torment. Among other things, the play is a tribute to the "young rebels" of 1950's and 1960's Hollywood—"Brando and Dean, Newman, Clift and McQueen." Yet the rebel here represents not a "misunderstood" generation posed against a smug "adult" orthodoxy but a culture split against itself and "screamin'."

For his second play Roche originally projected a piece which was to focus on a Jimmy-like rebel who would refuse his cultural identity, "run for the hills," and join the Carnival. But the Bush Theatre prevailed on the playwright to reconsider and he turned this scenario inside out, effecting in the process a decisive shift of thematic emphasis. *Poor Beast in the Rain* centres not on departure but on that most pervasive trope of Irish literature—return. According to Roche himself, this is "a rainy day sort of a play which is held together by an ancient Irish Myth as Danger Doyle returns like Oisín to the place of his birth, 'just because he wanted to see his auld mates again.' Danger Doyle, who is a sort of grown-up Jimmy Brady, ran away with another man's wife ten years ago and the play is really about all the people the pair of them left behind." The setting is an "old fashioned betting shop"— owned by the abandoned husband, Steven, and run by him and his daughter Eileen—on the weekend of the All-Ireland Hurling Final, in which the local team is successful. For the frequenters of the betting shop, "the ranks of the left behind," the commonest strategy of consolation is the mythologisation of the past and the veneration of its "characters," be they local wild boys or hurling heroes. Danger Doyle has escaped only to a depressed and workaday existence in England. Yet when he returns, feeling "like a fugitive," it is not to "kiss the past's arse" but to persuade Eileen to go back with him to visit her dejected mother. He also tries to set his "auld mates" free from their devotion to glamorised memories of himself. This entails not a demythologisation (which is revealed as the other, disillusioned, side of the rhetorical coin) but an assurance that, as he says to an embittered old flame, "I don't have what you seem to think I took from yeh." Only when his name is "washed away" will she cease to conceive of herself as a "poor beast" left out "in the rain": to those "reachin' for the moon," the here-and-now can only ever be an "auld snare."

The third play of the *Trilogy*, *Belfry*, signals an interesting formal shift. A split stage and retrospective structure permit a fluidity of action and promote an intimacy with the consciousness of a single individual. Events are framed, punctuated, and indeed ordered, by an expansive and occasionally lyrical narrative addressed "to the audience" in which the "little sacristan'" Artie O'Leary discloses why, in his "queer auld whisperin' world," the "only life he's ever known," he now has "a story to tell." His story is of a furtive, though passionate, adulterous affair with the church helper Angela, and of how she "tapped a hidden reservoir" by releasing him from a life dominated by a tyrannical mother and bounded by his necessary involvement with the rites of birth, marriage, and death. On his mother's death, the illegitimate Artie can become his "father's son again"—a wild "Jack-the-lad" in his free time. It is a small enough victory in a "small enough life," but a not insignificant one when those around him are so thwarted. The young priest Pat laments a life "surrounded by dead and dying," and turns to drink again; Angela attempts to mend her continuing sense of exclusion from her husband's life by moving on to another affair; and the husband himself, Donal, having confronted Artie and then resumed their friendship, broods over his fading status as local handball star. Only Dominic, the backward and endearingly sparky altar boy for whom Artie is a surrogate father, stands apart. He is beaten by Artie, who believes (wrongly) that he has revealed the affair to Donal, and he is killed in an accident whilst escaping from the special school to which he has been sent. But it is his surprise birthday party that Artie's narrative poignantly revisits; it is Dominic who, ringing out "I Can't Get No Satisfaction" on the church bells, and announcing his ambition to make people happy, embodies the "capacity" for happiness in the play. In *Belfry*, as elsewhere in *The Wexford Trilogy*, Roche manages to avoid not just the sentimentality of a facile hope but the equally insidious sentimentality of a self-pitying despair.

—Paul Lawley

————

ROMERIL, John. Australian. Born in Melbourne, Victoria, 26 October 1945. Educated at Brighton Technical School and High School, South Australia; Monash University, Clayton, Victoria, 1966–71, B.A. (honours) in English 1970. Writer-in-residence, Australian Performing Group, Melbourne, 1974, Western Australian Institute of Technology, Bentley, 1977, University of Newcastle, New South Wales, 1978, Jigsaw Theatre Company, Canberra, 1980, Troupe, Adelaide, 1981, Flinders University, Bedford Park, South Australia, 1984, Magpie, Adelaide, 1985, and National University of Singapore, 1986–87; Mathew J. Cody artist-in-residence, Victorian Arts Centre, Melbourne, 1985. Also a director and actor. Recipient: Australian Council for the Arts travel grant, 1972; Canada-Australia prize, 1976; Victorian Government Drama fellowship, 1988. Agent: Almost Managing, P.O. Box 1034 Carlton, Victoria 3053, Australia.

PUBLICATIONS

Plays

A Nameless Concern (produced Melbourne, 1968).
The Kitchen Table (produced Melbourne, 1968). Included in *Two Plays*, 1971.
Scene One, with John Minter (produced Melbourne, 1969).
The Man from Chicago (produced Melbourne, 1969).
The American Independence Hour (produced Melbourne, 1969).
Mr. Big, The Big, Big Pig (produced Melbourne, 1969).
In a Place Somewhere Else (produced Melbourne, 1969).
I Don't Know Who to Feel Sorry For (produced Melbourne, 1969). Sydney, Currency Press, 1973; London, Eyre Methuen, 1975.
Chicago Chicago (produced Melbourne, 1970). Published in *Plays*, Melbourne, Penguin, 1970.
200 Years (produced Melbourne, 1970).
Marvellous Melbourne, with Jack Hibberd (produced Melbourne, 1970). Published in *Theatre Australia* (Potts Point, New South Wales), July–September 1977.
Dr. Karl's Kure (produced Melbourne, 1970).
The Magnetic Martian Potato (produced Melbourne, 1971).
Whatever Happened to Realism (produced Melbourne, 1971).
Mrs. Thally F (produced Melbourne, 1971). Published in *Seven One-Act Plays*, edited by Rodney Fisher, Sydney, Currency Press, 1983.
Two Plays (includes *The Kitchen Table* and *Brudder Humphrey*). Clayton, Victoria, Kosmos, 1971.
Rearguard Action (produced Melbourne, 1971).
Hackett Gets Ahead, with Bill and Lorna Hannan (produced Melbourne, 1972).
He Can Swagger Sitting Down (produced Melbourne, 1972).
Bastardy (produced Melbourne, 1972). Montmorency, Victoria, Yackandandah, 1982.

A Night in Rio and Other Bummerz, with Tim Robertson (produced Melbourne, 1973).
The Earth, Air, Fire, and Water Show (produced Melbourne, 1973).
Waltzing Matilda: A National Pantomime with Tomato Sauce, with Tim Robertson (produced Melbourne, 1974). Montmorency, Victoria, Yackandandah, 1984.
The Floating World (produced Melbourne, 1974). Sydney, Currency Press, 1975; London, Eyre Methuen, 1976; revised version, Currency Press, 1982.
The Golden Holden Show (produced Melbourne, 1975).
Dudders, with John Timlin (produced Melbourne, 1976).
The Radio-Active Horror Show (produced Melbourne, 1977).
The Accidental Poke (produced Melbourne, 1977). Published in *Popular Short Plays for the Australian Stage*, edited by Ron Blair, Sydney, Currency Press, 1985.
Mickey's Moomba (produced Melbourne, 1979).
Carboni (produced Melbourne, 1980).
700,000 (produced Canberra, 1980).
Samizdat (produced Adelaide, 1981).
Centenary Dance (produced Adelaide, 1984).
The Kelly Dance (produced Adelaide, 1984). Montmorency, Victoria, Yackandandah, 1986.
Definitely Not the Last (produced Adelaide, 1985).
Jonah, music by Alan John, adaptation of the novel by Louis Stone (produced Sydney, 1985; revised version, produced Adelaide, 1991).
Legends, with Jennifer Hill and Chris Anastassiades (produced Melbourne, 1985). Montmorency, Victoria, Yackandandah, 1986.
Koori Radio (produced Hobart, 1987).
The Impostor, adaptation of a play by Sha Yexin (produced Melbourne, 1987).
Top End, with Tim Robertson and Don Watson (produced Melbourne, 1988).
History of Australia, with Tim Robertson and Don Watson (produced Melbourne, 1989).
Lost Weekend (produced Adelaide, 1989).
Black Cargo, adaptation of a story by John Morrison (produced Melbourne, 1991).
The Reading Boy (produced Adelaide, 1991).
Working Out (produced Melbourne, 1991).

Television Plays: *Bonjour Balwyn*, 1969; *The Best of Mates*, 1972; *Charley the Chequer Cab Kid*, 1973; *The Great McCarthy*, from a novel by Barry Oakley, 1975; *6 of the Best* series, 1981–82; *Mr. Steam and Dry*, 1986.

Other

6 of the Best: An Introduction to the Television Drama Series. Melbourne, Transition Education Advisory Committee, 1984.

*

Critical Studies: interview in *Meanjin* (Melbourne), no. 3, 1978; article by Romeril, in *Theatre Australia* (Potts Point, New South Wales), April 1979; interview in *Australian Drama Studies* (St. Lucia), no. 17, 1990; *State of Play* by Len Radic, Ringwood, Victoria, Penguin, 1991.

John Romeril comments:
    I take my prime duty as a playwright to be the recording and representation of contemporary Australian reality on the stage. Politically I'm of a left-wing persuasion, hence interested in plays of ideas. However, I operate on the premise

that if you want people to entertain ideas you must first entertain people. Thus the kind of theatre I try to make is above all lively, full of colour, movement, wit and style, fused with content of pressing concern.

* * *

For 25 years John Romeril has been Australia's most prolific yet neglected playwright. Few of his works are in print, and those mostly in small-run desktop editions, while critical comment has been almost non-existent. Much of his output has been performed by community or educational institution-based companies, and have been for particular occasions or audiences. An example is *Koori Radio* which was devised for Hobart's Salamanca Theatre Company and dealt with the supposed genocide of Aboriginal people in that state. Other scripts as various as *The Kelly Dance*, about the 19th-century bushranger, and *Legends*, about young people groping towards self-esteem, have been worked up from improvisations with trainee actors in Adelaide and Melbourne respectively, and the latter even credits two students as co-authors.

One of only two writers to have made successful long-term professional careers in the Australian theatre since the dramatic renaissance of the late 1960's (David Williamson is the other), Romeril nevertheless consciously welcomes these collaborative and specialised projects as being consistent with his democratic political views, and they make up more than three-quarters of his dramatic opus. In nearly all such work the resulting scripts (though not necessarily the performances) lack the clarity of a final singular penning, many are unpublished, and most have had only the single originating production. *The Kelly Dance*'s popular historical subject matter has made it an exception, with minor publication and many subsequent seasons throughout Australia, but all have been produced in small venues by amateur or semi-professional companies. This play is a good introduction to Romeril's "community-style" pieces, with a bush-dance setting maximising audience participation and the consequent informal atmosphere unifying the short, episodic scenes and rambling structure; such projects might best be characterised as "entertainments with ideas."

However, as well as being a "public servant of the pen," Romeril has had occasional moderate success as a single author of mainstream professionally performed plays, and has insisted on being seen as a "hybrid" talent, working across the full spectrum of staging possibilities. Again there have been specialised commissions such as *The Reading Boy*, a children's piece on an ecological theme performed by puppets, but after some 14 years during which his work was ignored by the mainstream professional companies, the 1980's brought him large theatre and large-scale attention. Major restagings of his early success *The Floating World* in Melbourne in 1982 and in Sydney in 1986 can largely be attributed to its appearance on secondary school English syllabi at that time, but there have also been two state company productions of a musical adaptation of the Louis Stone novel *Jonah*; a community-style piece, *Top End*, set in Darwin and perhaps mistakenly given formalised staging by the Melbourne Theatre Company in 1988; and a Chekhovian, or perhaps more accurately Shavian, comedy, *Lost Weekend*, which had two major productions in 1989.

Lost Weekend pits a narrow-minded trade-unionist recovering from a stroke against an aristocratic grazier and ex-army officer; the setting is the farm homestead which, like the stately homes of England, has been reduced to offering tourist accommodation. Romeril's allegory of an Australia caught between patronising colonial and idealistic national constructions of society is finely balanced against the pragmatic response to new economic realities of the grazier's wife, and a scatty but sane serving girl who acts as disbelieving chorus to the eccentric gathering. A weak ending mars this important play, and *Jonah* has been Romeril's biggest critical and commercial success to date in a revised 1991 production in Adelaide. It is a sharp but colourful Brechtian satire charting the uncheckable rise of a seedy street thug who turns from booting fallen rivals to bootmaking.

Unfortunately, neither *Lost Weekend* nor *Jonah* have yet been published. Consequently Romeril continues to be known in schools and universities, nationally and internationally, principally through *The Floating World*, now nearly 20 years old. A formally experimental comedy-drama, it combines cartoon characters and an increasingly dream-like narration to tell the story of Les Harding, a former prisoner-of-war on the notorious Thailand-to-Burma railway, who many years later reluctantly joins his wife on a holiday cruise to Japan. As the journey progresses, Les's oafish and bigoted behaviour becomes increasingly disturbed as his memories of horror, loss, and suffering begin to consume him. Originally staged in the characteristically informal surroundings which provide the warmth and vibrancy that Romeril's hard-edged anti-romantic stories need to succeed as entertainment, *The Floating World* has adapted uneasily to proscenium production. (It is no coincidence that the acclaimed *Jonah* season, although by a state company using star actors, avoided formal theatre blocking and had the actors moving amongst the audience, clearing a space for each successive location.)

New productions of *The Floating World* have made significant script deletions and staging reinterpretations—with Romeril's consent, consistent with his belief in relating performance to contemporary social context. The play was queried for possible racism when first produced and, while this was certainly not the author's intention, its increasingly subjective engagement with Les's internal agony can be misinterpreted as endorsement of his chauvinist outbursts and can distort the play in performance. The 1986 Sydney Theatre Company production removed a number of scenes satirising cheap Japanese imported goods, replacing them with images of Japanese traditional culture; unfortunately such revisions are yet to be incorporated in the published script.

In an Australian theatre industry which has increasingly marginalised political, experimental, and non-commercial work, Romeril has shown an exceptional ability to shift styles and subjects in order to survive, and new editions and projected works of critical analysis may revive interest in a writer currently poorly served by scholarship and the written record.

—Richard Fotheringham

ROTIMI, Ola. Nigerian. Born in Sapele, 13 April 1938. Educated at Methodist Boys' High School, Lagos, 1952–56; Boston University (president, African Students Union, 1962–63), 1959–63, B.F.A. 1963; Yale University School of Drama, New Haven, Connecticut (Rockefeller scholar, 1963–66; Student Drama prize, 1966), 1963–66, M.F.A. 1966. Married Hazel Mae Gaudreau in 1965; three sons and one daughter. Executive director and artistic director, University of Ife Theatre, Ife-Ife, 1973–77. Since 1977 director of the university theatre, dean of student affairs, 1979–80, dean of the faculty of humanities, 1982–84, and since 1982 head of the department of creative arts, all University of Port Harcourt. Recipient: *African Arts* prize, 1969; Oxford University Press prize, 1970; Nigerian National Festival of the Arts prize, 1974. Address: Department of Creative Arts, University of Port Harcourt, P.M.B. 5323, Port Harcourt, Rivers State, Nigeria.

PUBLICATIONS

Plays

Our Husband Has Gone Mad Again (produced Ibadan and New Haven, Connecticut, 1966). Ibadan, Oxford University Press, 1977.
The Gods Are Not to Blame (produced Ife-Ife, 1968; London, 1978). Ibadan, Oxford University Press, 1971.
Kurunmi: An Historical Tragedy (produced Ife-Ife, 1969). Ibadan, Oxford University Press, 1971.
Holding Talks (produced Ife-Ife, 1970). Ibadan, Ibadan University Press-Oxford University Press, 1979.
Ovonramwen Nogbaisi (produced Ife-Ife, 1971). Benin City, Ethiope, and London, Oxford University Press, 1974.
Initiation into Madness, adaptation of a play by Adegoke Durojaiye (produced Ife-Ife, 1973).
Grip Am (produced Ife-Ife, 1973).
Akassa Youmi (produced Port Harcourt, 1977).
If: A Tragedy of the Ruled (produced Port Harcourt, 1979). Ibadan, Heinemann, 1983.
Hopes of the Living-Dead (produced Port Harcourt, 1985). Ibadan, Spectrum Books, 1988.

*

Bibliography: by O. Lalude, in *Bibliographic Series 1*, Port Harcourt, University of Port Harcourt Library, 1984.

Critical Studies: interview in *Dem Say* (Austin, Texas), 1974; *African Theatre Today* by Martin Banham and Clive Wake, London, Pitman, 1976; "Three Dramatists in Search of a Language" by Dapo Adelugba, in *Theatre in Africa* edited by Oyin Ogunba and Abiola Irele, Ibadan, Ibadan University Press, 1978; "Ola Rotimi's Search for Technique" by Akanju Nasiru, in *New West African Literature* edited by Kolawole Ogungbesan, London, Heinemann, 1979; "The Search for a Popular Theatre" by Biodun Jeyifo, in *Drama and Theatre in Nigeria* edited by Yemi Ogunbiyi, Lagos, Nigeria Magazine, 1981; article by Alex C. Johnson, in *African Literature Today 12* edited by Eldred Jones and Eustace Palmer, London, Heinemann, 1981; *Beyond Translation: Tragic Paradigms and the Dramaturgy of Ola Rotimi and Wole Soyinka* by Femi Osofisan, Ife-Ife, Ife Monographs on African Literature, 1986.

Theatrical Activities:
Director: **Plays**—all his own plays; *King Christophe* by Aimé Césaire, Ife-Ife, 1970; *Rere Run* by Dejo Okediji, Ife-Ife, 1973; *Wahala* by Babalola Fatunwase, Ife-Ife, 1973; *The Curse* by Kole Omotosho, Ife-Ife, 1975; *The Family* by Comish Ekiye, Ife-Ife, 1976; *Sizwe Bansi Is Dead* by Athol Fugard, John Kani, and Winston Ntshona, Port Harcourt, 1984; *The Emperor Jones* by Eugene O'Neill, Port Harcourt, 1985; *Behold My Redeemer* by Rasheed Gbadamosi, Port Harcourt, 1986.

Ola Rotimi comments:
My creative passion is for a people's theatre informed by that which also impels it, namely: the spasms of the socio-political tendons of Africa yesterday, today, and tomorrow.

* * *

Of the generation of Nigerian playwrights who began writing in the late 1960's, Ola Rotimi exhibits the surest sense of drama as a plastic, three-dimensional form incorporating the spoken word, dance, music, mime, and the massing of bodies in space for the creation of spectacle. This sense of theatrical possibility is found equally in his high or stylistically elevated dramas and in his more realistic, socio-political plays.

Characteristic of this "high" style are the tragedy *The Gods Are Not to Blame* and the historical dramas *Kurunmi* and *Ovonramwen Nogbaisi*. Each play distances its concerns by locating events in the previous century; treats the gods as an awesome, unseen presence rather than as a physical manifestation; molds music, mime, and ritual elements to create a varied social panorama; employs dance in an efficacious manner designed to enhance collective well-being; and makes extensive use of traditional poetic forms for the expression of values central to the community portrayed. The best known play of this group, *The Gods Are Not to Blame*, is also a good example of the blend of theatre traditions to which Rotimi is heir, for he obtained degrees in directing and playwriting from Boston and Yale universities in the United States and, following his return to Nigeria in 1966, began researching traditional Yoruba performance modes as part of his direction of the Ori Olokun Acting Company.

Adapted from the Oedipus story, *The Gods Are Not to Blame* strives to reject the fatalistic relationship of man to god, contained in the Greek original, by using as a central visual image the shrine of Ogun, the Yoruba god associated with iron and, by implication, with the creation of technologies designed to extend man's manipulation of the environment. In Rotimi's hands the source of the protagonist's downfall becomes the learned, social conditioning of ethnic paranoia.

But this adaptation is not fully successful, for Yoruba attitudes concerning fate only superficially approximate an interpretation of Greek tragedy as attributable to a single character flaw. Furthermore, Rotimi's subsequent explanation that the drama, first produced in 1968 during the Nigerian Civil War, was intended as a direct commentary on current events is not fully satisfactory, for such a position invalidates the centrality of the prophecy imposed by the original, and runs the risk of reducing the war's complex causes to a single issue. Rather, it seems that in this instance the choice of material identifies Rotimi with the period in modern African literatures when writers were eager to validate their cultures in terms which the former colonial masters could appreciate.

A similar borrowing from Western perspectives seems evident in *Kurunmi* and *Ovonramwen Nogbaisi*, for these historical dramas concerning internecine Yoruba wars and the British conquest of the Benin Empire hinge upon the great-man theory of history, antithetical to an African emphasis on personality as collective. While the latter play is not entirely persuasive because the king's failure of will seems insufficiently motivated, *Kurunmi* is an impressive evocation of a world under fatal pressure. Through the manipulation in English of Yoruba expressive modes governing the use of proverbs and lyrical structures or the easy movement between the spiritual/tragic realm and the secular/comic world, Rotimi creates an effective defense of tradition and culture as the sole element which distinguishes humans from other life forms. Yet, true to historical accounts and his own contemporary reality, the playwright brings his protagonist to the ironic realization that this defense visits widescale destruction and eventual decline upon the entire nation.

In contrast, later realistic plays like *If: A Tragedy of the Ruled* and *Hopes of the Living-Dead* tackle current social concerns directly and explore the dynamic interplay between leaders and followers. The first play, loosely adapted from Errol John's Caribbean drama *Moon on a Rainbow Shawl*, is an impassioned plea for the rejection of self-interest in favor of a collective vision of national health. The latter play, while conforming to sketchy historial accounts, projects the sobering image of Nigeria as a nation of lepers threatened with sure extinction unless they learn to work collectively for the benefit of all.

In these socio-political plays the playwright achieves a theatrical plasticity similar to that of the stylistically elevated plays. The simultaneous playing of several scenes and massing of actors in such a way as to convey separate foci which momentarily converge and allow for the settling on a common purpose; the successful integration of various Nigerian languages with pidgin and English to capture the dream of a truly pluralistic society; and the use of music to evoke a poignant sense of the possibility of a shared, human grandeur all distinguish Rotimi as one of the best playwrights of contemporary Nigerian drama.

—Sandra L. Richards

RUDKIN, (James) David. British. Born in London, 29 June 1936. Educated at King Edward's School, Birmingham, 1947–55; St. Catherine's College, Oxford, 1957–61, M.A. 1961. Served in the Royal Corps of Signals, 1955–57. Married Alexandra Margaret Thompson in 1967; two sons and two daughters. Assistant master of Latin, Greek and music, County High School, Bromsgrove, Worcestershire, 1961–64. Recipient: *Evening Standard* award, 1962; John Whiting award, 1974; Obie award, 1977; New York Film Festival gold medal, 1987; Society of Authors scholarship, 1988; European Film Festival Special Jury award, 1990. Agent: Casarotto Ramsay Ltd., National House, 60–66 Wardour Street, London W1V 3HP, England.

PUBLICATIONS

Plays

Afore Night Come (produced Oxford, 1960; London, 1962). Included in *New English Dramatists 7*, London, Penguin, 1963; published separately, New York, Grove Press, 1966.
Moses and Aaron, translation of the libretto, music by Schoenberg (produced London, 1965). London, Friends of Covent Garden, 1965.
The Grace of Todd, music by Gordon Crosse (produced Aldeburgh, Suffolk, and London, 1969). London, Oxford University Press, 1970.
Burglars (for children; produced London, 1970). Published in *Prompt Two*, edited by Alan Durband, London, Hutchinson, 1976.

The Filth Hunt (produced London, 1972).
Cries from Casement as His Bones Are Brought to Dublin (broadcast 1973; produced London, 1973). London, BBC Publications, 1974.
Ashes (produced Hamburg, 1973; London, 1974; Los Angeles and New York, 1976). London, Pluto Press, 1978.
Penda's Fen (televised 1974). London, Davis Poynter, 1975.
No Title (produced Birmingham, 1974).
The Sons of Light (produced Newcastle upon Tyne, 1976; London, 1978). London, Eyre Methuen, 1981.
Sovereignty under Elizabeth (produced London, 1977).
Hippolytus, adaptation of the play by Euripides (produced Stratford-on-Avon, 1978; London, 1979). London, Heinemann, 1980.
Hansel and Gretel (produced Stratford-on-Avon, 1980; London, 1981).
The Triumph of Death (produced Birmingham, 1981). London, Eyre Methuen, 1981.
Peer Gynt, adaptation of the play by Ibsen (produced Stratford-on-Avon, 1982; London. 1983). London, Methuen, 1983.
Space Invaders (produced Stratford-on-Avon and London, 1984).
Will's Way (produced Stratford-on-Avon and London, 1985).
The Saxon Shore (produced London, 1986). London, Methuen, 1986.
Deathwatch, and The Maids, adaptations of plays by Jean Genet (produced London, 1987).
When We Dead Awaken, adaptation of the play by Ibsen (produced London, 1990). Bath, Absolute Press, 1990.

Screenplays (additional dialogue, uncredited): *Fahrenheit 451*, 1966; *Mademoiselle*, 1966; *Testimony*, 1987; *December Bride*, 1989.

Radio Plays: *No Accounting for Taste*, 1960; *The Persians*, from the play by Aeschylus, 1965; *Gear Change*, 1967; *Cries from Casement as His Bones Are Brought to Dublin*, 1973; *Hecuba*, from the play by Euripides, 1975; *Rosmersholm*, from the play by Ibsen, 1990.

Television Plays: *The Stone Dance*, 1963; *Children Playing*, 1967; *House of Character*, 1968; *Blodwen, Home from Rachel's Marriage*, 1969; *Bypass*, 1972; *Atrocity*, 1973; *Penda's Fen*, 1974; *Pritan* and *The Coming of the Cross* (*Churchill's People* series), 1975; *The Ash Tree*, from the story by M.R. James, 1975; *The Living Grave* (*Leap in the Dark* series), 1981; *Artemis 81*, 1981; *Across the Water*, 1983; *White Lady*, 1987; *Gawain and the Green Knight*, from the Middle English poem, 1991.

Ballet Scenario: *Sun into Darkness*, 1966.

*

Theatrical Activities:
Director: **Television**—*White Lady*, 1987.

* * *

David Rudkin's *Afore Night Come* is one of the most mature and assured first plays of the postwar period, though in retrospect it can be seen to contain its author's chief dramatic preoccupations only (as it were) in solution, uncrystallized. Primitive chthonic forces long repressed by culture and individual psychology reassert themselves with great violence when a group of fruit-pickers on a Midlands farm single out a casual worker—a strange, "educated" Irish tramp—as scapegoat for their personal, moral, and economic failings and carry out his ritual murder in the sinister, though apparently numinous presence of a crop-spraying helicopter. Thematic elements which are to become central in Rudkin's later work—homosexuality, sexual infertility, the threat of nuclear devastation, England's Irish problem—are present but not developed. Indeed, thematic coherence seems less important to Rudkin at this stage of his career than the recognizably Pinteresque menace which can be generated by the rhythms of a judiciously charged dialogue. It is perhaps for this reason that, though the crucial sacrificial event of *Afore Night Come* is obviously two-edged, the energy of the play makes itself felt as essentially negative.

By contrast, Rudkin's work after his 12-year self-imposed apprenticeship is energized by his passionate commitment to a powerful central *idea*. The primitive impulses of *Afore Night Come* reveal their creative aspect in the concentration on the reintegration and realization of the self that occurs in the gradual, painful liberation from a complex web of repression. On the evidence of his work, Rudkin believes that the power-wielders of modern civilization, and especially the various Christian churches with their capacity for psychological conditioning, function only by burying or perverting for their own dark ends original, natural forces and beliefs. His dramatic response is to affirm the continuity of these forces, on several different levels simultaneously—psychological, sexual, cultural, historical—using those forms which many modern artists have regarded as the enduring repositories of non-rational or even anti-rational values: image, fable, and myth. The quasi-physical impact of Rudkin's dramatic language, with its intense compression and often eccentric syntax, itself reflects these values. Hence also the importance to Rudkin of dialect, the concrete, poetic language of the authentic, geographically rooted self which he repeatedly sets against abstract discourse, the rootless, "Flat Urban Academic" that "will bury our theatre." (The Norwegian acts of his *Peer Gynt* are translated into the "stylized rural Ulster speech" of his own childhood.)

Ashes is a harrowing autobiographical play which rotates the theme of sexual infertility through a series of wider perspectives, political, anthropological, and existential, in handling the problem of free will and determinism. However, the roughly contemporaneous television play *Penda's Fen* offers a more satisfying dramatic realization of his preoccupations. The growth of an adolescent boy in Worcestershire away from social, religious, educational, and sexual constraints into mature selfhood is articulated through images of a local landscape in which the natural forces of Penda's Fen are being perverted, in the modern Pinvin, to menacing scientific ends, through suggestive sequences of music (which, together with sound-effects, has always been more important to Rudkin than scenery or props), and through a series of dream-images which reveal to the boy his homosexuality. Here, as elsewhere in Rudkin's work, homosexuality is important less as a social reality than as an idea: it is the humane "mixed" state which stands as a critique of the conventional phallic "manliness" of society's power-wielders. Having realized that Christianity has "buried" the authentic Jesus—just as "Pinvin" (a real place) has buried Penda's Fen—the boy Stephen rejects power and inherits, in a vision of Penda himself (the last of the English pagan kings) "the sacred demon of ungovernableness."

The key work in Rudkin's oeuvre, at which he worked from 1965 to 1976, is *The Sons of Light*, a massive, multi-layered fable with science-fiction elements and a tripartite mythic structure: "The Division of the Kingdom," "The Pit," "Surrection." The ancient paradigm drawn on by Rudkin is perhaps most familiar from the Christian *Harrowing of Hell*, but the play's fundamental design (as well as its title) is indebted above all to the heresy of Manichaeanism, with its characteristic cosmological dualism. A new pastor and his three sons arrive on a remote Scottish Atlantic island to find it (literally) divided and in the grip of a patriarchal religion of wrath. The island's subterranean industrial complex, an obscene dystopia masterminded by an expressionist-style German scientist, dehumanises and mechanises its workers, allaying any residual stirrings with the (purely functional) promise of religious transcendence. Two of the pastor's sons are killed, but amid terrible violence and purgative suffering, the third son, the "cold" burning "angel" John, descends into this "pit," initiates a fresh consciousness of self in the workers, and destroys the complex, thus uniting the body of the island and reclaiming it for its inhabitants. Simultaneously the identity of a schizophrenic girl, hitherto an outcast, is reintegrated and she is made whole. The structural parallel is underscored by the destruction on several levels of the baneful Father, the figure who, as always in Rudkin, holds in place the structures of repression: sexual, familial, and political. This extraordinary conjunction of Reichian psychotherapy and Artaudian theatre within the arena of myth is a distinctive and powerful achievement.

Rudkin's fiercely idiosyncratic brand of psycho-history is most clearly embodied in *The Triumph of Death*, an extravagant Gothic panorama which dramatises the annihilation or demonisation of natural modes of being and worship by medieval Christianity in its perverted ("Crosstian") project of ideological self-definition and cultural domination (in the name of "Salvation"). With its insistently excremental symbolism, its appropriation of Christian imagery for the evocation of polymorphous ("natural") sexuality and its reconception of Christian mythological figures (most notably "Jehan"/Joan of Arc), this is undoubtedly Rudkin's riskiest and most challenging work. Indeed, its oddity is a strength (the epigraph insists that the past both is and is not "another country"). Its gravest limitation is a degree of schematisation which *The Sons of Light*, despite shared concerns and imagery, and the fundamental dualism of its structure, largely avoids. *The Triumph of Death*, for all its anti-rationalist primitivism and its fluid Artaudian dramaturgy, is a thesis play: "Our fracture is our fall," and civilisation is founded on repression.

The Saxon Shore attempts to combine an individual's quest for selfhood with an historical vision. The context is also implicitly political, and in Rudkin this means (as in *Ashes*, *Cries from Casement as His Bones Are Brought to Dublin*, and *Across the Water*) the Irish problem. The play is set in Britain in AD 410. The Roman empire is crumbling fast; on the North Sea coast, the displaced native British Celts and a "plantationer" Saxon community face each other across Hadrian's Wall in the presence of a disgruntled and demoralised colonial army. The allegory of the Ulster situation (a Saxon Defence Regiment aids the scornful Roman soldiers and Saxons-turned-nocturnal-werewolves compulsively perpetrate acts of terror) serves as framework for the story of Athdark, a "child growed stale" from mother-domination, who shows "the beginnings of a man" by the end of the play. The structure of the story recalls that of a fable or folktale, whilst resemblances of narrative pattern and tone, as well as verbal echoes, indicate Rudkin's continuing creative-critical engagement with *Peer Gynt*. (*The Dream of Gerontius* and *King Lear* are also, as ever in Rudkin, important intertexts.) But despite the play's variety of English (and a speculative version of Celtic), its dramatic language is disappointingly thin and lacking in resonance. Moreover, the relation between the historical conditions and the development of the individual is never as fully or coherently articulated as it is in Rudkin's best work.

—Paul Lawley

———————

RUGANDA, John. Ugandan. Born in Uganda in 1941. Educated at Makerere University, Kampala, B.A. (honours) in English literature. Member, the Makerere Free Travelling Theatre, and founder-member, the Makonde Group, editorial and sales representative, Oxford University Press's East Africa Branch, 1972, and senior fellow in creative writing, Makerere University, 1973, all Kampala. Founder-member, the Nairobi Travelling Theatre, Kenya. Address: c/o Heinemann Kenya, PO Box 45314, Nairobi, Kenya.

PUBLICATIONS

Plays

The Burdens (produced Kampala, 1972). Nairobi, Oxford University Press, 1972.
Black Mamba (produced Kampala, 1972). With *Covenant of Death*, Nairobi, East African Publishing House, 1973.
Covenant of Death. With *Black Mamba*, Nairobi, East African Publishing House, 1973.
The Floods (produced Nairobi, 1979). Nairobi, East African Publishing House, 1980.
Music Without Tears (also director: produced Nairobi, 1981). Nairobi, Bookwise, 1982.
Echoes of Silence (also director: produced Nairobi, 1985). Nairobi, Heinemann, 1986.

*

Critical Study: *Notes on John Ruganda's "The Burdens"*, Nairobi, Heinemann, 1977.

* * *

It was *The Burdens* that brought John Ruganda to prominence as a playwright in Uganda. Wamala, the major character in the play, had once been a teacher but through two masterstrokes of chicanery, wriggled himself into the post of a minister. His first political ploy was to seduce and marry Tinka, daughter of a very influential chief, thereby securing for himself a formidable political constituency. The second move was to give a demagogic speech on the eve of Uganda's independence. It won him the position he desired. As a minister, with the extraordinary fringe benefits accompanying the post, Wamala and his family cut themselves off from ordinary people and preferred only to drink with kings. But Power and Time plan their revenge on him. As the play starts, Wamala is at the bottom of the social heap. He can no longer feed his family. His wife, a more resourceful person, confronts their new humiliating reality by brewing and selling a local brand of alcohol, *enguli*. Their two children starve. Unable to face the penury, Wamala escapes into alcohol. His favourite haunt is, ironically, "The Republic," a bar where he

recalls the more pleasant days of old with his former political cronies. Very late one night, he returns and, inspired by alcohol, decides to meet an old architect, Vincent Kanagonago, a prospective politician, and sell him the ideas of (1) running Kanagonago's electioneering campaign as a master sloganeer and, (2) partnership in the establishment of a company that would manufacture matchsticks with two heads which can be lit when struck even on wet surfaces. In a brilliant play-within-a-play, he re-enacts this meeting with his wife acting the rich, condescending Kanagonago. Somewhere along the line, illusion blurs into reality and Wamala attempts to strangle his wife believing that she really is Kanagonago. Wamala's leap to murder comes after he realizes that Kanagonago, to whom he has sold his idea, is actually the owner of Associated Matches, the company with a match-manufacturing monopoly in the country. One other hilarious moment is the scene in which Wamala, in a reverie, relives his days of glory at a political rally using the audience as the electorate. It ends tragically when Tinka murders her half-crazed husband fearing that, with his progressing state of diminished responsibility, he might kill her first. *The Burdens* is a well-knit play, employing only four characters. The dialogue is precise, digital and contrapuntal. It is a competent, satirical study of post-independence disillusionment in African politics.

In *Music Without Tears*, John Ruganda explores the collective hysteria which engulfed Uganda in the post-Idi Amin period of the country's turbulent history. Odie is bitter that his brother, Wak, had fled the country 10 years earlier to escape the tortures and disappearances. With the country liberated by a new military government, he returns but is insensitive to the brutalities still going on. Odie argues that the punishment for this nonchalance should be death. His sister, Stella, insists Odie should see a psychiatrist in order to curb his bloodlust. He turns on her and accuses her of betraying the honour of the family by sleeping with Ali, the army commander, who signed the paper for the death of their father, a former minister for tourism. Ali was also in charge of a drunken platoon that raped Stella and her classmates, including some nuns, a few years ago. A study in tyranny, even within the family, *Music Without Tears* reveals the after-effects of military rule on the psyche of an abused and savaged populace.

In *The Floods*, Ruganda again probes the psychosomatic disorder that befalls a society where the craze for power and position makes meaningful human relationship impossible. Bwogo, a former chief of the State Research Bureau (the Ugandan version of the FBI and KGB), has been made redundant since the Boss, Idi Amin, was ousted from power. He lives with Nankya, a pseudo-intellectual, who is bent on getting to the top of the academic ladder by fair or foul means. Bwogo, still suffering from the cannibalistic streak which characterized his days in power, plans and announces on radio that a flood is going to sweep off all the inhabitants of a symbolic island on Lake Victoria. His scheme is to get Nankya and her mother on the government-approved Noah's Ark, a "rescue" boat whose passengers are consequently exterminated. Bwogo's negative actions stem from jealousy and guilt. In one of the phantasmagoric moments of this dark play, Bwogo sees apparitions of those he killed coming to take his life. *The Floods* is a disturbing study in physical and verbal cannibalism. It is divided into waves instead of scenes and acts, with each wave symbolizing the wash of violence rising and ebbing in Bwogo's mind. Its greatest strength, however, is Ruganda's evocative language. Here is a memorable passage by a fisherman who functions as narrator and communal memory in the play:

KYEYUNE: It was early evening when I set sail . . . I paddled on and on to the centre of the lake. Then all of a sudden the net on my right became heavy . . . I knew it was a big catch. Do you know what it was, son? A man. A military man. Dead. Three long nails in his head, his genitals sticking out in his mouth. A big stone round his neck. His belly ripped open and the intestines oozing out . . . I looked at the body and froze with fright. Here was a man . . . who probably had a wife and children . . . What had he done to come to such an unmourned-for end? Had he, perhaps, in a moment of enthusiasm, uttered an unwelcome word to his masters?

Ruganda's weaknesses as a playwright include sloganeering, poor character delineation through dialogue, excessive intellectualizing, and unrelieved cynicism. His strengths are the ferocious honesty with which he dissects his society and his experimentation with theatrical forms which, when they work, give his psychodramas, on page and in performance, a psychotherapeutic power.

—Esiaba Irobi

RUSSELL, Willy (William Martin Russell). British. Born in Whiston, Lancashire, 23 August 1947. Educated at schools in Knowsley and Rainford, Lancashire; Childwall College of Further Education, Lancashire, 1969–70; St. Katharine's College of Higher Education, Liverpool, 1970–73, Cert.Ed. Married Ann Margaret Seagroatt in 1969; one son and two daughters. Ladies' hairdresser, Liverpool and Kirkby, 1963–68; labourer, Bear Brand warehouse, 1968–69, and teacher, Shorefields Comprehensive, 1973–74, Liverpool. Since 1974 freelance writer. Associate director, 1981–83, and since 1983 honorary director, Liverpool Playhouse; since 1982 founding director, Quintet Films, London. Writer-in-residence, C.F. Mott College of Education, Liverpool, 1976; fellow in creative writing, Manchester Polytechnic, 1977–79. Also folk song composer and singer: performances (with group Kirbytown Three) in clubs and on radio and television since 1965. Recipient: Arts Council bursary, 1974; *Evening Standard* award, 1974; London Theatre Critics award, 1974; Society of West End Theatre award, 1980, 1983, 1988; Golden Globe award, 1984; Ivor Novello award, 1985. M.A.: Open University, Milton Keynes, Buckinghamshire, 1983. Agent: Casarotto Ramsay Ltd., National House, 60–66 Wardour Street, London W1V 3HP. Address: W.R. Ltd., 43 Canning Street, Liverpool L8 7NN, England.

PUBLICATIONS

Plays

Keep Your Eyes Down (produced Liverpool, 1971).
Blind Scouse (includes *Keep Your Eyes Down, Playground, Sam O'Shanker*) (produced Liverpool, 1972; revised version of *Sam O'Shanker*, music by Russell, produced Liverpool, 1973).
Tam Lin (for children), music by Russell (produced Liverpool, 1972).
When the Reds, adaptation of the play *The Tigers Are Coming—O.K.?* by Alan Plater (produced Liverpool, 1973).

Terraces, in *Second Playbill 1*, edited by Alan Durband. London, Hutchinson, 1973; collection published as *Terraces*, 1979.
John, Paul, George, Ringo and Bert (produced Liverpool and London, 1974).
The Cantril Tales, with others (produced Liverpool, 1975).
Breezeblock Park (produced Liverpool, 1975; London, 1977). London, French, 1978.
Break In (televised 1975). Published in *Scene Scripts 2*, edited by Michael Marland, London, Longman, 1978.
I Read the News Today (broadcast 1976). Published in *Home Truths*, London, Longman, 1982.
One for the Road (as *Painted Veg and Parkinson*, produced Manchester, 1976; as *Dennis the Menace*, produced Norwich, 1978; as *Happy Returns*, produced Brighton, 1978; as *One for the Road*, produced Nottingham, 1979). London, French, 1980; revised version (produced Liverpool, 1986; London, 1987), 1985.
Our Day Out (televised 1977). Published in *Act 1*, edited by David Self and Ray Speakman, London, Hutchinson, 1979; revised version, songs and music by Bob Eaton, Chris Mellors, and Russell (produced Liverpool and London, 1983), London, Methuen, 1984.
Stags and Hens (produced Liverpool, 1978; London, 1984). London, French, 1985.
Lies (televised 1978). Published in *City Life*, edited by David Self, London, Hutchinson, 1980.
Politics and Terror (televised 1978). Published in *Wordplays 1*, edited by Alan Durband, London, Hutchinson, 1982.
The Boy with the Transistor Radio (televised 1980). Published in *Working*, edited by David Self, London, Hutchinson, 1980.
Educating Rita (produced London, 1980; Chicago and New York, 1987). London, French, 1981.
Blood Brothers (produced Liverpool, 1981; revised version, music and lyrics by Russell, produced Liverpool and London, 1983). London, Hutchinson, 1986.
Educating Rita, Stags and Hens, and Blood Brothers. London, Methuen, 1986.
Shirley Valentine (produced Liverpool, 1986; London, 1988; New York, 1989). With *One for the Road*, London, Methuen, 1988.

Screenplays: *Educating Rita*, 1983; *Shirley Valentine*, 1989; *Dancin' thru the Dark*, from *Stags and Hens*, 1990.

Radio Play: *I Read the News Today*, 1976.

Television Plays: *King of the Castle*, 1973; *Break In*, 1975; *The Death of a Young, Young Man*, 1975; *Our Day Out*, 1977; *Lies*, 1978; *Politics and Terror*, 1978; *The Daughters of Albion*, 1979; *The Boy with the Transistor Radio*, 1980; *One Summer* series, 1983.

Verse

Sam O'Shanker: A Liverpool Tale. Liverpool, Mersey Yarns, 1978.

Other

Published Music: *I Will Be Your Love and OOee boppa OOee boppa*, RSO, 1974; *Dance the Night*, Paternoster, 1980; *Blood Brothers*, Paternoster-Russell Music, 1983; *The Show*, Timeact-Russell Music-Paternoster, 1985; *Mr. Love*, Russell Music-Warner Brothers, 1986.

Film Music: *Shirley Valentine*, with George Hatzinassios, 1989.

*

Critical Study: "Willy Russell: The First Ten Years" by Timothy Charles, in *Drama* (London), Summer 1983.

Theatrical Activities:
Director: **Play**—*Educating Rita*, Liverpool, 1981.
Actor: **Plays**—Narrator in *Blood Brothers*, Liverpool, 1985, and *Shirley Valentine*, Liverpool, 1986. **Film**—*Educating Rita*, 1983.

Willy Russell comments:

I am loath to make any specific statement on the nature of my work as I reserve the right to dismiss on Thursday the statement I made on Wednesday. However, in a letter of 1984, written to a BBC producer to explain why I would not be writing a play I wrote the following (I think for me it will remain as true on a Thursday as it is on a Wednesday):

To write a play one must passionately believe in something which one wants to communicate. The writer might want to tell of the ills of the world, or of his love for another, of society's folly, of mankind's goodness and baseness. He may want to argue a political cause or just show off his wit. Whatever, it is something which requires a passionate belief in telling what one has to tell. I heard David Edgar say recently that (to paraphrase) writing becomes more difficult as one gets older because as one gets older one gets less certain. Perhaps what he meant was that with age one sees the corollary to every argument, that the radical turns merely liberal. I don't want to be liberal. But *what* do I, personally, want to communicate? What is it that I am deeply concerned with at present? Am I being too heavy on myself? When going through this pre-play torture have I *ever* felt concerned with anything? Is total emptiness a necessary condition in the prelude to writing a play?

I don't want to write what I've already written. I want to learn. I want to write a play which forces me to develop the talent I have. Talent must not go back on itself and stagnate. It is a nerve-wracking process but truly it is better to write nothing than to write something which one has already written. It's only with pushing against the barriers, stretching the boundaries, staring at the abyss that the imagination soars and poetry can be achieved. I believe that no great play was ever written at any significant distance from the abyss—they are all written on the edge. Think of Moss Hart saying that one never learns to be a playwright, only how to write one particular play. The next play, no matter how "successful" the playwright, is something about which he knows nothing. He cannot know how to write it, has no guidelines because, before he has written it, it has never existed. Every play is a trip back to the beginning and a walk through hell all over again.

What do I want to say? What moves me? What story do I want to tell? I believe that every play I have ever written has, ultimately, been one which celebrates the goodness of man; certainly, the plays have included emptiness, despair, possibly even baseness. But it is the goodness that I hope the audience is left with. I really don't want to write plays which are resigned, menopausal, despairing, and whingeing. I don't want to use any medium as a platform for displaying the smallness and hopelessness of man. Man is man because madly,

possibly stupidly but certainly wonderfully, he kicks against the inevitability of life. He spends his life looking for answers. There probably are no answers but the fact that man asks the questions is the reason I write plays.

* * *

What happens when you grow beyond the class and the culture you were born into? When is freedom real and when is it a fake? What is true knowledge? These are the central questions posed by Willy Russell's major plays since the mid-1970's.

Breezeblock Park is set in the houses of two sisters, Betty and Reeny. It is Christmas and therefore a time for competitive consumption. Betty and Reeny try to outdo each other over costly furniture, bathroom fittings, and central-heating systems. Betty's husband Ted is obsessed with his new car and sees himself as an intellectual with his knowledge of *Mastermind* and his ambitions as an author. Betty's brother Tommy represents a vulgar alternative to this working-class gentility when he gives Betty a vibrator as a Christmas present and prefers to celebrate in the pub rather than in his sister's tasteful front room. Gender roles are strictly defined. The women's territory is the home, particularly the kitchen. Their talk is of clothes, food, children, and relationships. The men work away from the home and their talk is of sport, politics, and general knowledge. Everyone, however, closes ranks over the play's central issue—the pregnancy of Betty's daughter Sandra. Their code demands that she marry the father. There's no shame in "being in the club." As Tommy explains: "It's a bloody secret society they've got goin'. They have a great time." But Sandra is different. She reads, she's interested in ideas, she hangs around with students; in fact, her lover, Tim, is a student. After a strong talking-to by the men, Tim is ready to do the decent thing, but Sandra stands firm. She'll have the child, but she'll live with Tim, unmarried, in a student house. "I want a *good* life, Mother," she shouts at Betty. "I want to sit around and talk about films and—and music." And Betty replies, "You begrudge me every bit of pleasure I have ever had." The two cultures, gentility and bohemianism, are irreconcilable. In a skilful last scene Sandra breaks through the menacing circle of her relations, but only because her mother steps aside. Tim meekly follows her.

Another wedding fails and another escape takes place in *Stags and Hens*. It is stag night for Dave and hen night for Linda before they get married. But both parties have booked into the same dance-hall in Liverpool. On a single set, which consists of the Ladies' and Gents' loos side by side, the differing codes of sex, drink, and clothes are enacted in dialogue which is witty, vulgar, sentimental, and bitter. Linda, we discover, is uneducated but discontented with her girlfriends' cheerful acceptance of the conventions of their class. It isn't so much the consumer world of *Breezeblock Park* that is satirised as the competitive world of grabbing a girl or keeping a man. In a shrewd theatrical move, Dave, the groom at tomorrow's "wedding," stays dead drunk throughout the play, which puts the spotlight even more fiercely on Linda. She finally rejects her world by leaving with Peter, lead singer of the band and an old flame who's made good in London. But the last word is given to Eddy, the leader of Dave's friends. It is he, like Tommy in the earlier play, who organises local solidarity against the outsider. "Don't you come makin' people unhappy," he warns Dave. "She's our mate's tart. We look after our mates. We stick with them." Eddy, however, is younger than Tommy. He has to construct a myth of freedom for his class and culture in the dead wastes of Merseyside. Peter may be a successful artist but Eddy assures everyone, "You could do that, what he does if you wanted to. You can do anythin' he can do. We all can." All they can do is get drunk, draw their names on the toilet walls, and try to chat up women. Eddy is furious when Linda gets out, but still optimistic for the future. The play ends with his staggering out of the Gents carrying the still-oblivious Dave over his shoulder and muttering, "She's gone. Well y've got no baggage weighin' y' down. There's nothin' holdin' us back now Dave. We can go anywhere."

With *Educating Rita* all these themes are very sharply expressed and focused by Rita herself. She's already outpaced Sandra and Linda by enrolling on an Open University course, but the early encounters between her directness and the cultured evasiveness of her tutor Frank reveal real cultural gulfs. But, as she shows in a series of brilliant observations in Act 1, Scene 4, she knows very well what she's leaving behind and why she wants to change. Her class may have a certain level of affluence but it hasn't got meaning, it hasn't got culture as meaningful life. "I just see everyone pissed, or on the Valium, tryin' to get from one day to the next." Since Rita doesn't believe in a distinct working-class culture—"I've read about that. I've never seen it though"— she wants the knowledge and skills that Frank can give her. "What do you want to know?" he asks her at their first tutorial. "Everything," she replies. By the end she's certainly acquired a poise, a sophistication—"I know what clothes to wear, what plays to see"—and a contempt for Frank she didn't have at the beginning. She's escaped her origins and she knows how much everyone resents this kind of mobility. "They hate it when one of them tries to break away."

In the musical *Blood Brothers*, Russell shifts to men and their life chances. Twin brothers, separated at birth, are brought up by natural and fake mothers, in working-class and middle-class environments. Another Linda shuttles between the two. Each sees advantages in the other's situation, but it is working-class Mickey who suffers unemployment, depression, and jealousy over Linda. Edward goes to university and becomes a local politician. He helps his brother with housing and a job but, in a melodramatic ending, Mickey shoots his brother because he thinks Linda has slept with him

and gets shot down himself by the police. So, once again, the women progress as the men go under.

The pattern is repeated with *Shirley Valentine* but this is the least complex of Russell's plays. It is a monologue in two acts by a 42-year-old Liverpool housewife who moves from her downbeat kitchen to a downmarket *taverna* in Greece. With typical Scouse wit she tells her tale of taking off for a holiday in Greece with a feminist friend, leaving her boorish husband and her two layabout children. She has an affair with a Greek waiter and although she knows he seduces all his clients she gains new confidence in herself from his flattery. She gives us sharp verbal sketches of oafish English families abroad and a self-portrait in which stoicism and romanticism are equally mixed. Shirley is pre-Rita in her self-awareness but she has made a decisive break in her life-pattern by going to Greece and staying there although her linguistic and cultural resources are still so slender that we have to doubt whether she really has achieved a breakthrough. The play ends with her waitressing at the *taverna* and waiting for her husband who is desperate to get her back. It's a fantasy that she could stay on—she would be ostracised by all the local women as a whore—but the hope is that her husband will treat her with new respect at home. *Shirley Valentine* is an entertaining piece, which had a long London run, but it represents a step backward from Russell's earlier successes.

—Tony Dunn

RYGA, George. Canadian. 1932–1987.
See 3rd edition, 1982.

S

SACKLER, Howard. American. 1929–1982.
See 3rd edition, 1982.

———

SAINER, Arthur. American. Born in New York City, 12 September 1924. Educated at Washington Square College, New York University (John Golden award, 1946), 1942–46, B.A. 1946; Columbia University, New York, 1947–48, M.A. in philosophy 1948. Married 1) Stefanie Janis in 1956 (divorced 1962); 2) Maryjane Treloar in 1981, two sons and two daughters. New York editor, *TV Guide*, New York, 1956–61; film critic, *Show Business Illustrated*, Chicago, 1961; founding editor, *Ikon*, New York, 1967. Book critic since 1961, book editor, 1962, and drama critic, 1961–65 and since 1969, *Village Voice*, New York; film and theatre editor, *American Book Review*, New York, 1986–90. Member of the English or Theatre department, C.W. Post College, Brookville, New York, 1963–67, 1974–75, Bennington College, Vermont, 1967–69, Chautauqua Writers' Workshop, New York, 1969, Staten Island Community College, New York, 1974–75, Hunter College, New York, 1974, 1980–81, Adelphi University, Garden City, New York, 1975, Wesleyan University, Middletown, Connecticut, 1977–80, Middlebury College, Vermont, 1981–83, since 1985 New School for Social Research, New York, and since 1990 Sarah Lawrence College, Bronxville, New York. Member of the Academic Council and program adviser, Campus-Free College, Boston, 1971–74. Co-producer, Bridge Theatre, New York, 1965–66. Recipient: Office for Advanced Drama Research grant, 1967; Ford grant, 1979, 1980; Berman award, 1984. Agent: Anne Edelstein, 137 Fifth Avenue, New York, New York 10010. Address: 565 West End Avenue, New York, New York 10024, U.S.A.

PUBLICATIONS

Plays

The Bitch of Waverly Place (produced New York, 1964).
The Game of the Eye (produced Bronxville, New York, 1964).
The Day Speaks But Cannot Weep (produced Bronxville, New York, and New York City, 1965).
The Blind Angel (produced New York, 1965).

Untitled Chase (produced New York, 1965).
God Wants What Men Want (also director: produced New York, 1966).
The Bombflower (also director: produced New York, 1966).
The Children's Army Is Late (produced Brookville, New York, 1967; New York City, 1974).
The Thing Itself (produced Minneapolis, 1967; New York, 1972; Published in *Playwrights for Tomorrow 6*, edited by Arthur H. Ballet, Minneapolis, University of Minnesota Press, 1969.
Noses (produced New York, 1967).
OM: A Sharing Service (produced Boston, 1968).
Boat Sun Cavern, music by George Prideaux and Mark Hardwick (produced Bennington, Vermont, 1969; New York, 1978).
Van Gogh (produced New York, 1970).
I Piece Smash (produced New York, 1970). Published in *The Scene/2 (Plays from Off-Off-Broadway)*, edited by Stanley Nelson, New York, The Smith/New Egypt, 1974.
I Hear It Kissing Me, Ladies (produced New York, 1970).
Images of the Coming Dead (produced New York, 1971).
The Celebration: Jooz/Guns/Movies/The Abyss (produced New York, 1972).
Go Children Slowly (produced New York, 1973).
The Spring Offensive (produced New York, 1974).
Charley Chestnut Rides the I.R.T., music by Sainer (produced New York, 1975).
Day Old Bread: The Worst Good Time I Ever Had (produced New York, 1976).
The Rich Man, Poor Man Play, music by David Tice and Paul Dyer (produced New York, 1976).
Witnesses (also director: produced New York, 1977).
Carol in Winter Sunlight, music by George Prideaux (produced New York, 1977).
After the Baal-Shem Tov (produced New York, 1979).
Sunday Childhood Journeys to Nobody at Home (produced New York, 1980).

Television Plays: *A New Year for Margaret*, 1951; *The Dark Side of the Moon*, 1957; *A Man Loses His Dog More or Less*, 1972.

Other

The Sleepwalker and the Assassin: A Study of the Contemporary Theatre. New York, Bridgehead, 1964.
The Radical Theatre Notebook. New York, Avon, 1975.

*

Critical Studies: "The Greening of American-Jewish Drama" by Ellen Schiff, in *Handbook of American-Jewish Literature*, New York, Greenwood, 1988.

Theatrical Activities:
Director: **Plays**—several of his own plays; *Lord Tom Goldsmith* by Victor Lipton, New York, 1979; *The Desire for a City* by Norah Holmgren, New York, 1985.
Actor: **Plays**—*OM: A Sharing Service*, Boston, 1968; *The Children's Army Is Late*, Parma, Italy, 1974.

Arthur Sainer comments:

(1973) I like to believe I write plays to find out something—about self, about self in cosmos, about the cosmos, I try to make something in order to understand something. Sometimes the plays use ideological material but they aren't ideological plays. Ultimately if they work they work as felt experience.

For some time I was fascinated by the juxtaposition of live performers and visual projections, concerned with an enlarged arrested image operating on a level other than that of the "real" performer. That period ran from *The Game of the Eye* (1964) through *Boat Sun Cavern* (written in 1967, produced in 1969). But I've lost interest in projections, I want the magic to be live, immediate, home-made. And I want the mistakes to be live ones.

Language—I've gone from many words, *God Wants What Men Want* (written in 1963), to few words, *The Blind Angel* (1965), *The Bombflower* (1966), to some words, *Images of the Coming Dead* (1971). None of these approaches is superior to the others. It depends on what the play needs and what the playwright needs at that time. Bodies are no more or less useful than the utterances that emerge from them. Only truth is useful.

Words are useful, but so is everything else. I don't hold with Grotowski's belief that every conceivable element other than the performer ought to be stripped away. Everything created by God, everything designed or decimated by the hands of man, is potentially viable and important, all of it is a testament to this life. But I've come lately (in *The Spring Offensive*) to believe in an economy of means—forget the lights, forget the setting—to believe in the magic of what is obviously being put together by hand before our eyes.

Much theatre leaves me cold, and most audiences disturb me. I don't want to make audiences particularly happy or excite them anymore. I don't want them to be sitting there judging the play, to be weighing its excellences and faults. I want the audiences to be seized and ultimately to become the play. We like to say that a really fine play changed its audience, but a really fine play also creates the condition where its audience can change it. The play ultimately is the product of this mutual vulnerability.

* * *

Theatre's ability to reproduce the external, everyday details of human life is balanced by its need to incorporate the internal, imaginative reality of its characters. Arthur Sainer's plays combine the two kinds of reality by allowing the characters to retain their unique contributions to life, while linking them into a living whole. Whether describing radical politics of the 1960's, the shifting forces at work in love and marriage, the alienation of the poor and dispossessed, a subway conductor's imminent death, or other contemporary struggles with life, Sainer is sensitive to both the effect of daily routines and rituals, and the pressure of people upon one another. His real subjects are not the events that happen to people in the course of a play, but rather the way people change and are changed by life around them.

This concentration on people produces plays that are plotless in the usual sense, but obey a rigorous internal logic. Louis, the protagonist of *The Thing Itself*, says

In the theatre to which we are offering our blood, there are no characters to be created. There are no consistencies, no patterns. Instead there are irrelevancies, inconsistencies, mistakes, broken thoughts. There is an impulse toward chaos, another toward assimilation. In our theatre there is no stage and no story, there is only human life pushed into a corner, threatened with extinction. And human life threatened with human life. And always mistakes.

The statement is unusually blunt for Sainer, whose dialogue is most often more oblique and questioning, and *The Thing Itself* unusually pessimistic and bitter, but Louis does describe Sainer's primary attitude toward drama's means and goals. Louis and his friends—Harold, who eats obsessively; Althea, a sympathetic prostitute who is brutal toward her brutal customers—are coping with the thing itself, the degradation of life in an impersonal, almost savage, city environment.

As in most of Sainer's plays, *The Thing Itself* is frequently interrupted by mimed scenes, fantasies, monologues, songs, slides, and films. Sainer has used most of the techniques available to contemporary playwrights—from Brechtian alienation to improvisation and audience participation—quite skillfully, but in every case they are expressions of the contradictory, tumultuously human life of the plays. A trilogy—*Images of the Coming Dead*, *The Children's Army Is Late* and *Carol in Winter Sunlight*—follows the growth and evolution of a family: the shifting stresses on David and Carol resulting from David's immersion in filmmaking. Carol's increasing desire to escape the trap of the family, the love both bear for their children, and their concern for their aging parents combine to create a broad and penetrating portrait of the family. In addition, the logic of this portrait calls up a series of mythological and allegorical scenes: a group of figures who begin in naked innocence, gradually become a mindlessly hardworking society, and are beset by aggressive renegades; Hector and Achilles fight their epic combat; and two characters named Allan and Albert re-enact the tragedy of Cain and Abel with a modern twist. The evolution of the human race vibrates against the evolution of the family, and the depiction of the family, sharp and sensitive as it is, is extended and expanded.

Sainer's ability to mesh the intimacy of everyday life and the development of civilization combines with his inquiries into the meaning of Jewish history to focus his plays on death. In *The Children's Army Is Late*, David searches to find and film a dying man. *Charley Chestnut Rides the I.R.T.* is filled with the bewilderment and agony of an ordinary subway conductor who suddenly faces death from a terminal illness. However, the interest in death stems from its use as a reflection of life. *After the Baal-Shem Tov* tells the story of a Jew who survives a German concentration camp to start life anew in the United States. Israel is an innocent, gentle man with an irritating habit of questioning everything. As he makes his way in America, visits a kibbutz in Israel, and becomes the editor of a respected Jewish newspaper, he loses his naivety but not his questions. Recalling his liberation from the concentration camp, he sings

Here in the new world, the absent
From the dead take on new life,
The skeletons take on new flesh.

What's it like now for the absent from the dead?
What's it like now? Shoving, running,
Piling up things, looking into faces.
It's stupid life, it's joyous days.

Israel gives up everything and everyone he has gained in

order to "redeem the promises," and there is throughout Sainer's plays an intensely human attempt to redeem the gift of life, to understand the death of people, of ideas, and of relationships in order to appreciate them more fully.

—Walter Bode

SÁNCHEZ-SCOTT, Milcha. American. Born in Bali in 1955. Lived in Colombia and Mexico until 1969. Educated in London and in California. Has lived in California since 1969. Member of New Dramatists, New York. Recipient: Drama-logue award (seven times); Vesta award, 1984; Rockefeller award, 1987. Agent: George Lane, William Morris Agency, 1350 Avenue of the Americas, New York, New York 10019. Address: 2080 Mount Street, Los Angeles, California 90068, U.S.A.

PUBLICATIONS

Plays

Latina (produced Los Angeles, 1980). Published in *Necessary Theater: Six Plays About the Chicano Experience*, edited by Jorge A. Huerta, Houston, Texas, Arte Publico Press, 1989.
Dog Lady and The Cuban Swimmer (produced New York, 1984; London, 1987). Published in *Plays in Process* (New York), vol.5, no.12, 1984.
Roosters (produced New York, 1987). Published in *On New Ground: Contemporary Hispanic-American Plays*, edited by M. Elizabeth Osborn, New York, Theatre Communications Group, 1987.
Evening Star (produced New York, 1988). New York, Dramatists Play Service, 1989.
Stone Wedding (produced Los Angeles, 1989).
El Dorado (produced Costa Mesa, California, 1990).

* * *

Of pan-American and pan-Pacific ancestry, Milcha Sánchez-Scott has felt the shock of sexist prejudice as a Latina in California. Since 1980 she has dramatised the humor and resolution of the disempowered. These qualities, along with the devotion of displaced communities, hold back for a moment the relentless oppression of economics and negative assumptions. Sánchez-Scott finds holes within harsh realities through which stream magical visions, spells, miraculous cures, transformations, and an old religious faith in past and future. Dual language allows her characters an alternative to the dominant one, whether Spanish or English. Words let them escape from mundanity into unique eloquence. Such language supplies a textual correlative for the immediately visualized and physicalized images.

In *Latina*, her first play, a remarkable playwriting voice made Sánchez-Scott's bilingual and bi-level dramatic visions clear, rich, and effective—even for materialistic, English-speaking audiences. In the prologue to *Latina*, New Girl journeys from a Peruvian mountain village to cross the barbed-wire American border. The originally plaintive Peruvian flute resounds "triumphantly" with American pop music and traffic, as we see a bus stop in front of FELIX SANCHEZ DOMESTIC AGENCY on Wilshire Boulevard

in Los Angeles. Two tanned mannequins stand in the window of the comically sleazy entrepreneur's agency; the maternal dummy in white holds a pink doll, and the naughty maid in black holds a feather duster. Dressed carefully in the American style, Sarita enters briskly to say how embarrassing it is to be thought car-less, a maid-for-hire, Latina, or available at 23 in Los Angeles. Overhearing this but speaking no English, old Eugenia the yu-yu vendor and cleaning lady offers "niña Sarita" a cure for her malady. Sarita, still denying, answers in effortless Spanish, rebukes in English, and translates for the audience. Eugenia ritually sprinkles water to sweep, and Sarita, hearing a rooster, admits she sees her grandmother sweeping a dirt road in 1915 Juarez. Then, joking bawdily about using Lava soap, they reveal Sarita's frustrated television-acting career and the old woman's affectionate pride in it. New Girl, dressed in the Peruvian style, furtively seeking domestic work, panics at the word "immigration" in Sarita's reassurance, and bites the hand that places Latinas in WASP households. As Don Felix approaches to open his shop, Eugenia still prays before they make their daily bet: is he wearing his Mickey Mouse or sailboat pajama top today? What's the point of praying? Sarita blurts in Spanish, and before going in, pauses to assure her audience, "I let her win."

These first few moments of *Latina* typify Sánchez-Scott's career. Seven comically disparate Latin women (eight, including Sarita), awaiting jobs in the agency, gossip about their desperate realities and party. The mannequins appear in Sarita's mind, mock her abject servility to WASP's and failure to defend Alma, and don rebozos to go to the park as sisters. What one lets oneself be called is important. New Girl lets them reduce her five names to "Elsa Moreno," accepts Sarita's exchanging her carefully chosen disguise for her Peruvian clothes, and with the help of Eugenia's charm and prayer and everyone's generosity, gets a placement. Sarita—in learning to accept Eugenia's prayer and bet (that her own audition overcame television's prejudice against "exotics") and divest herself of her disguise in order to help others—gets beyond her "mal educada" status to find her own dignity. "Sarita Gomez" will play her television role, and she attacks the intolerable Mrs. Camden. *Latina* ends with an immigration raid arresting all the "illegal" women as another New Girl creeps toward the barbed wire.

The Cuban Swimmer shows the Suarez family from Long Beach in the Pacific Ocean halfway to Catalina Island. Daughter Margarita is swimming in the invitational race, and her father (coach), mother (a former Miss Cuba), the praying Abuela (grandmother), and the younger brother with binoculars and punk sunglasses follow on their boat. Margarita, losing concentration, is apparently drowned by exhaustion, the oil slick ("rainbows"), and the family's hopes and demands, but mostly by the condescension of being called a simple Cuban amateur and brave little loser by the sexist American television reporter in a helicopter. Sinking to the bottom, she swims to the rhythm of "Hail Mary" into blackout. Abuela, who shouted "Assholes!" after the vanishing helicopter, invokes ancestors and saints as the grieving family reports the swimmer lost: "My little fish is not lost!" The same television reporter, in a nicely ambiguous phrase, describes to the family and the world "a miracle!"—the lost, little Cuban swimmer "is now walking on the waters, through the breakers," first "onto the beach." Abuela recognizes "sangre de mi sangre"—blood of my blood.

In *Dog Lady*, pretty, 18-year-old Rosalinda Luna will successfully and literally "run like a dog" to win the big race, and run on beyond the barrio's Castro-street—with the prayerful support of her decorous mother and the yu-yu spell and incantation of old Luisa Ruiz, the mentally and physically unkempt dog-keeper and "healer" next door. But Jesse, the 15-year-old tomboy, receives the audience's attention, her mother's scolding, her sister's trust, and half the bouquet an infatuated 18-year-old intended for the star. Suddenly transformed into a beautiful señorita, Jesse asks, "You really turn into a dog?" Rosalinda puts the yu-yu around Jesse's neck, explaining, "You have to work very hard." The two actions—winning and reluctantly coming-of-age—frame soaring fantasies, functional but very funny misunderstandings, and sparkling dialogue.

Evening Star offers another two houses on Castro Street and another reluctant coming-of-age; Olivia Peña, aged 14, in parochial school uniform, and Junior Rodriguez, aged 16, search for stars from his roof. A 30-year-old male vendor is the keeper of lore and cures (like Eugenia, Abuela, the dog lady, and *Our Town*'s Stage Manager). Grandmother Tina Peña puzzles with the vendor over the significance of a white rose miraculously appearing in her garden that morning. It should signify birth, they agree—before the old man Peña, throwing rocks, drives the vendor off. Both hardworking households are impoverished and have problems with daughters. Peña drove off their lost Sarita who left behind her child Olivia, and the abandoned Mrs. Rodriguez at first does the same when her lanky 15-year-old admits her own pregnancy. However, as Lilly Rodriguez gives birth upstairs in the Peñas' house, little epiphanies, tendernesses, and strengths bloom like roses. Mama Rodriguez rushes in to help her baby, and old Peña, who can't go in and can't pray, throws a humanistic rock at heaven. The vendor is heard: "The sun is rising. Another day of life. Try not to abuse it." Despite gritty details, poetic monologues, Old Peña's comic grouchiness and his daily ritual with Olivia (painstakingly, penuriously crossing off from his mailing list Hispanic names found in the obituaries), real theatrical magic seems slight, and too much of the affirmation gratuitous.

In *Roosters*, a multi-levelled conflict is set among farm workers who are laboring to achieve some dignity and respite. Sánchez-Scott divides allegorically-named males and females into contrasting types and lets the drama bring them to fertile reconciliation. In a prologue the handsome Gallo, in his forties, explains how, at the cost of a prison term for manslaughter, he "borrowed" a high-flying ("like dark avenging angels") Filipino bolina named MacArthur to breed with his old red Cuban hen ("a queen" to whom you would never give "a second look" yet who killed every "stag") to create the prize-fighting cock Zapata. As he stalks and pricks his crossbred Hispanic-Pacific rooster (a male dancer) with a stiletto, Gallo croons "Show Daddy watcha got" and delights when "son" Zapata attacks and draws blood. Now, all anxiously await the homecoming of husband-lover, brother and father. Willed the bird by his grandfather during his father's absence, Gallo's 20-year-old son Hector plans to first-fight Zapata tonight and sell him to finance a better life for his mother (Juana), tortilla-rolling aunt (Chata), and mystical younger sister (Angelita). The women preparing food anticipate more hardship and loneliness. Angelita with her cardboard wings and tombstones, prayers to saints, disappearances, and imaginary tea-parties can see the shadows stalking her father and brother and must choose sides. The predicted cockfight between Hector and Gallo allows rightful shares of nobility to each generation, character, and way of living. Sánchez-Scott achieves this persuasively.

—John G. Kuhn

SAROYAN, William. American. 1908–1981.
See 2nd edition, 1977.

————

SAUNDERS, James A. British. Born in Islington, London, 8 January 1925. Educated at Wembley County School; University of Southampton. Married Audrey Cross in 1951; one son and two daughters. Formerly taught English in London. Since 1962 full-time writer. Recipient: Arts Council bursary, 1960, 1984; *Evening Standard* award, 1963; Writers Guild award, 1966. Lives in Twickenham, Middlesex. Agent: Casarotto Ramsay Ltd., National House, 60–66 Wardour Street, London W1V 3HP, England.

PUBLICATIONS

Plays

Cinderella Comes of Age (produced London, 1949).
Moonshine (produced London, 1955).
Dog Accident (broadcast 1958; revised version produced London, 1969). Published in *Ten of the Best*, edited by Ed Berman, London, Inter-Action Imprint, 1979.
Barnstable (broadcast 1959; produced Dublin and London, 1960). London, French, 1965.
Alas, Poor Fred: A Duologue in the Style of Ionesco (produced Scarborough, 1959; London, 1966). Scarborough, Studio Theatre, 1960.
The Ark, music by Geoffrey Wright (produced London, 1959).
Ends and Echoes: Barnstable, Committal, Return to a City (produced London, 1960). *Return to a City* included in *Neighbours and Other Plays*, 1968.
A Slight Accident (produced Nottingham, 1961; London, 1971; Chicago, 1977). Included in *Neighbours and Other Plays*, 1968.
Double, Double (produced London, 1962). London, French, 1964.
Next Time I'll Sing to You, suggested by a theme from *A Hermit Disclosed* by Raleigh Trevelyan (produced London, 1962; revised version produced London and New York, 1963). London, Deutsch, and New York, Random House, 1963.
Who Was Hilary Maconochie? (produced London, 1963). Included in *Savoury Meringue and Other Plays*, 1980.
The Pedagogue (produced London, 1963). Included in *Neighbours and Other Plays*, 1968.
Neighbours (produced London, 1964; New York, 1969). Included in *Neighbours and Other Plays*, 1968.
A Scent of Flowers (produced London, 1964; New York, 1969). London, Deutsch, and New York, Random House, 1965.
Triangle, with others (produced Glasgow, 1965; London, 1983).
Trio (produced Edinburgh, 1967). Included in *Neighbours and Other Plays*, 1968.
The Italian Girl, with Iris Murdoch, adaptation of the novel by Murdoch (produced Bristol, 1967; London, 1968). London, French, 1969.
Neighbours and Other Plays (includes *Trio*; *Alas, Poor Fred*; *Return to a City*; *A Slight Accident*; *The Pedagogue*). London, Deutsch, 1968.
Haven, later called *A Man's Best Friend*, in *We Who Are*

about to . . ., later called *Mixed Doubles* (produced London, 1969).   London, Methuen, 1970.

The Travails of Sancho Panza, based on the novel *Don Quixote* by Cervantes (produced London, 1969). London, Heinemann, 1970.

The Borage Pigeon Affair (produced London, 1969). London, Deutsch, 1970.

Savoury Meringue (produced London, 1971; New York, 1981).   Included in *Savoury Meringue and Other Plays* 1980.

After Liverpool (broadcast 1971; produced Edinburgh and London, 1971; New York, 1973).   London, French, 1973.

Games (produced Edinburgh and London, 1971; New York, 1973).   London, French, 1973.

Opus (produced Loughton, Essex, 1971).

Hans Kohlhaas, adaptation of the story by Heinrich von Kleist (produced London, 1972; as *Michael Kohlhaas*, produced London, 1987).

Bye Bye Blues (produced Richmond, Surrey, 1973; London, 1977).   Included in *Bye Bye Blues and Other Plays*, 1980.

Poor Old Simon (in *Mixed Blessings*, produced Horsham, Sussex, 1973; produced separately, New York, 1981). Included in *Savoury Meringue and Other Plays*, 1980.

Random Moments in a May Garden (broadcast 1974; produced London, 1977).   Included in *Bye Bye Blues and Other Plays*, 1980.

A Journey to London, completion of the play by Vanbrugh (produced London, 1975).

Play for Yesterday (produced Richmond, Surrey, 1975; London, 1983).   Included in *Savoury Meringue and Other Plays*, 1980.

The Island (produced London, 1975).   Included in *Bye Bye Blues and Other Plays*, 1980.

Squat (produced Richmond, Surrey, 1976).

Mrs. Scour and the Future of Western Civilisation (produced Richmond, Surrey, 1976; London, 1983).

Bodies (produced Richmond, Surrey, 1977; London, 1978; New Haven, Connecticut, 1981). Ashover, Derbyshire, Amber Lane Press, and New York, Dramatists Play Service, 1979.

Over the Wall (produced London, 1977). Published in *Play Ten*, edited by Robin Rook, London, Arnold, 1977.

What Theatre Really Is, in *Play Ten*, edited by Robin Rook. London; Arnold, 1977.

Player Piano, adaptation of the novel by Kurt Vonnegut (produced London, 1978).

The Mountain (produced Bristol, 1979).

The Caucasian Chalk Circle, adaptation of a play by Brecht (produced Richmond, Surrey, 1979).

Birdsong (produced Richmond, Surrey, 1979; New York, 1984).   Included in *Savoury Meringue and Other Plays*, 1980.

The Girl in Melanie Klein, adaptation of the novel by Ronald Harwood (produced Watford, Hertfordshire, 1980).

Savoury Meringue and Other Plays, Ambergate, Derbyshire, Amber Lane Press, 1980.

Bye Bye Blues and Other Plays (includes *The Island* and *Random Moments in a May Garden*). Ambergate, Derbyshire, Amber Lane Press, 1980.

Fall (produced Richmond, Surrey, 1981; London, 1984). London, French, 1985.

Nothing to Declare (broadcast 1982; produced Richmond, Surrey, 1983).

Menocchio (broadcast 1985).   Published in *Best Radio Plays of 1985*, London, Methuen, 1986.

Redevelopment, adaptation of a play by Václav Havel (produced Richmond, Surrey, 1990).   London, Faber, 1990.

Making It Better (broadcast 1991; produced London, 1992). London, French, 1992.

Radio Plays: *Love and a Limousine*, 1952; *The Drop Too Much*, 1952; *Nimrod's Oak*, 1953; *Women Are So Unreasonable*, 1957; *Dog Accident*, 1958; *Barnstable*, 1959; *Gimlet* (version of *Double, Double*), 1963; *It's Not the Game It Was*, 1964; *Pay As You Go*, 1965; *After Liverpool*, 1971; *Random Moments in a May Garden*, 1974; *The Last Black and White Midnight Movie*, 1979; *Nothing to Declare*, 1982; *The Flower Case*, 1982; *A Suspension of Mercy* (*Murder for Pleasure* series), from the novel by Patricia Highsmith, 1983; *Menocchio*, 1985; *The Confidential Agent*, from the novel by Graham Greene, 1987; *Headlong Hall*, from the novel by Thomas Love Peacock, 1988; *Making It Better*, 1991.

Television Plays: *Just You Wait* (version of *Double, Double*), 1963; *Watch Me I'm a Bird*, 1964; *The White Stocking, New Eve and Old Adam, Tickets Please, Monkey Nuts, Two Blue Birds, In Love*, and *The Blue Moccasins*, all from works by D.H. Lawrence, 1966–67; *The Beast in the Jungle*, from the story by Henry James, 1969; *Plastic People*, 1970; *The Unconquered*, 1970; *Craven Arms*, from a story by A.E. Coppard, 1972; *The Mill*, 1972; *The Black Dog*, 1972; *Blind Love*, from the story by V.S. Pritchett, 1977; *The Healing Nightmare*, 1977; *People Like Us*, with Susan Pieat and Ian Curteis, from the novel by R.F. Delderfield, 1978; *Bloomers* series, 1979; *The Sailor's Return*, from the novel by David Garnett, 1980; *The Captain's Doll*, from the story by D.H. Lawrence, 1983; *The Magic Bathroom*, 1987.

* * *

James Saunders's work is characterized by a diversity of style which is unusual even among the more eclectic of his contemporaries. He can be compared to a startling variety of other writers, and, should his scripts survive without attribution, future generations of scholars might assign them in something like this fashion: to Harold Pinter the revue sketch investment of the commonplace with interest found in *Double, Double* and the schematic exploration of open marriage found in *Bye Bye Blues*; to John Mortimer the charming coincidence of complementary handicaps which permits two self-pitying people to unite in *Blind Love*; to Samuel Beckett the seemingly plotless philosophizing of *Next Time I'll Sing to You*; to John Arden and Margaretta D'Arcy the episodic structure and satire of inept and hypocritical public officials in *The Borage Pigeon Affair*; to Eugène Ionesco or N.F. Simpson the absurdist farce of such one-acts as *Who Was Hilary Maconochie?*, *Alas, Poor Fred*, and *A Slight Accident*; to Simon Gray the mutual torment inflicted by sophisticates in extremis found in *Bodies*; to Peter Handke the invitation to spectators to reject the play found in the fragmented *Games*; to Henry Livings the music-hall flavor of *Savoury Meringue*; and to any one of dozens of realistic dramatists the belligerence and bewilderment of the interracial psychological study *Neighbours*.

Although Saunders's stylistic range is breathtaking our 21st-century literary detectives might discover his authorship by recognizing his distinctive situations and themes. His dramatis personae are frequently couples, and he is constantly investigating how people can relate to others, care about others, commit themselves to others, and sustain the relationship long term. The alienated Saunders character often lives close to the edge. He or she finds difficulty wrenching meaning from a life rendered pointless by death and unbearable by loneliness or, paradoxically, by the proximity of people. He probes the false values exemplified in various interpersonal relations, and illuminates the responsibility people assume or evade for the choices they make. He's a humanist sympathetic to the underdog or the rebel, and deeply suspicious of the games people play to keep their emotions at bay or to score points off others. Yet he's expert at dramatizing those often urbane games, and such is the ambiguity of his situations—particularly in his more recent work—that spectators may be forgiven for wondering whether his commiseration for the losers isn't balanced by a certain admiration for the victor's skill.

Saunders has created a constellation of wonderfully ineffectual characters. There's the driver in *Gimlet* whose bus passes through—but is really bypassed by—life. There's the befuddled actor in *Triangle* who's "not quite sure whether I'm trying to play myself or trying not to play myself." There are the musicians in *Trio* who can't perform because they're under attack by flies. There's the teacher in *The Pedagogue* who loses control of his pupils as well as his faith in mankind. There are the men and women in *After Liverpool* who often botch their desultory attempts to talk to each other. There's the wife in *A Slight Accident* who's flustered by her husband's failure to get up off the floor after she's murdered him and poor Pringle's confusion when he's reminded that he killed the title character in *Alas, Poor Fred*. There's the deceased protagonist of *A Scent of Flowers* whose inability to inspire in her family any accessible love has led her to suicide. In *Next Time I'll Sing to You* there's little Lizzie who's lost because she's replacing her twin sister in the role without benefit of either rehearsal or script. There are the ridiculous attempts of the macho men in *The Island* to bully their superiors (the women) into liking them. ("If I had been expecting anything," quips one of the gals, "they'd be a disappointment.") And there are those archetypal sufferers of indignity in *The Travails of Sancho Panza*.

Repeatedly Saunders has dramatized the tension between such poles as independence and dependence or our responsibility for choices versus our lack of control over events. In an early radio play which later became the street theatre piece *Dog Accident*, for instance, Saunders confronts passersby with a dispute between—seemingly—two of their number over a dog who's just been run over. They disagree over whether the dog's demise was its own fault and, later, over whether the dog's really dead or still suffering. Why, argues the indifferent one, should they care about a dying dog when large-scale catastrophe strikes people every day? The other momentarily opts for bothering, then either can't sustain or can't stomach the pain and prefers to go to lunch. Our mutual interdependence and the complex determinants of an event also inform *Bye Bye Blues*, in which three separate couples discuss one or more automobile accidents in which they're all somehow involved or implicated.

Saunders's best-known play, *Next Time I'll Sing to You*, picks as its subject a hermit, Jimmy Mason, who died in Essex in 1942. Another writer might have considered Mason's solitary life and death more conventionally and sentimentally. But Saunders suggests the aimlessness of life with a form which itself rambles. This presentational style and non-linear "plot" may communicate subliminally that life is disordered suffering. Ostensibly, however, the play is a comedy in which the characters are actors making disconnected attempts to put on a play about Mason. They crack jokes, discuss whether they're asleep, and confuse the actress who is supposedly a substitute for her sister. Perhaps five minutes is devoted to conveying the facts of Mason's life. Gradually such philosophical issues as the nature of man and the purpose of life are raised. *Next Time I'll Sing to You*, like *Waiting for Godot*, employs off-beat characters and structure to raise fundamental human questions. After we wonder why Mason lived alone—or, indeed, why he lived—we come to wonder whether his solitude differs only superficially from our own. If we're better off than Mason, the reason may only be "One thing about us—at least we're not dead."

Although well known, *Next Time I'll Sing to You* has been regarded by some critics as pretentious or incomprehensible. Neither charge could be levelled at Saunders's best play, *Bodies*. Though seemingly more realistic—because it's set in recognizable contemporary homes—*Bodies* is one of Saunders's many plays which combine presentational and representational styles. It also epitomizes his highly verbal work; hearing it is much more important than seeing it.

In *Bodies* Saunders portrays two couples who many years before had affairs with each others' mates. Act 1 intercuts monologues, in which each of the four recalls the affairs, with duologues on their approaching reunion with their ex-lovers. Act 2 brings them, at that reunion, into present confrontation with their pasts. The couples have handled their mid-life crises—or passages—quite differently. Anne and Merwyn—who have considered themselves unromantic pragmatists—muddle along experiencing their anxiety at reaching middle age, their panic at disillusionment in the things they once held dear, their terror at lack of self-esteem. David and Helen, on the other hand, have reached, by means of a new therapy, a state untroubled by emotions of any kind. They insist people are only bodies, and happiness and unhappiness don't exist.

We are meant to wonder whether feelings are valuable. Especially if these passions are painful, is it preferable, like tranquil and twitchless David and Helen, to be therapeutically freed from suffering, from the insistence on finding meaning in experience? Or is that insensitive, unresponsive to life, and is one therefore better off—as Peter Shaffer's *Equus* and innumerable other contemporary British plays suggest—with one's neuroses intact? But if Saunders initially sets up a dichotomy between detached David and Helen and the troubled teacher Merwyn, he subtly suggests that the latter also escapes his emotional traumas, though his means is not therapy, but mental agility liberally laced with alcohol. An off-stage student, meanwhile, has left Merwyn's English seminar and fled his feelings still more effectively by killing himself. Ultimately what Saunders has dramatized, then, is alternative routes to wasting one's personal emotional riches.

Saunders has been blessed with sufficient royalties from his German productions to earn a living and the long-term willingness of two London groups (the Questors and the Richmond Fringe at the Orange Tree) to try whatever he happens to write. Free from worry over whether each new work will prove a commercial success, Saunders has been able to write to please himself. Perhaps this has encouraged self-indulgence in scenes sometimes simultaneously cerebral and long-winded. Yet when he avoids verbosity, Saunders succeeds with versatility, ingenuity, whimsy, suspense, wit, and an emotional sensitivity which permits him to touch us without growing maudlin. Both in depth and in range, his plays continue to intrigue longer than might the work of a more uniform playwright.

—Tish Dace

SCHARY, Dore. American. 1905–1980.
See 2nd edition, 1977.

SCHENKAR, Joan M. American. Born in Seattle, Washington, 15 August 1946. Educated at St. Nicholas School, Bennington College, Bennington, Vermont, and a collection of graduate schools. Advertising copywriter, social worker, and researcher, all New York, 1960's; coffee and doughnut vendor, 1973, and church organist, Congregational Church, 1974, both Vermont; playwright-in-residence, Joseph Chaikin's Winter Project, New York, 1977 and 1978, Polish Laboratory, New York, 1977, Florida Studio Theatre, Sarasota, Florida, 1980, Changing Scene, Denver, Colorado, 1982, Centre d'essai des auteurs dramatiques, Montreal, and Composer-Librettist's Workshop, New York, both 1985, Minnesota Opera New Music Theatre Ensemble, Minneapolis, 1986–88, and Kentucky Foundation for Women, Louisville, Kentucky, 1988. Visiting fellow, Cummington Community Arts, Cummington, Massachusetts, 1978, Ragdale Foundation, Lake Forest, Illinois, 1979, and MacDowell Art Colony, Peterborough, New Hampshire, 1980; teacher, School of Visual Arts, New York, 1978–91; founder and artistic director, Force Majeure Productions, New York, from 1987. Since 1992 director, The Performance Series, North Bennington, Vermont. Recipient: National Endowment for the Arts grant, 1977, 1978, 1980, 1982, fellowship, 1981; Creative Artists Public Service fellowship, 1979–80; Lowe Foundation grant, 1983; Playwrights Forum award, 1984; Arthur Foundation grant, 1984, 1989; New York State Council on the Arts grant, 1986, 1989, 1992; Schubert Travel grant, 1988; Vermont Community grant, 1991. Agent: Casarotto Ramsay Ltd., National House, 60–66 Wardour Street, London W1V 3HP, England. Address: P.O. Box 814, North Bennington, Vermont 05257, U.S.A.

PUBLICATIONS

Plays

The Next Thing (produced Los Angeles, 1976).
Cabin Fever (produced Los Angeles, 1976; New York, 1977; London, 1986). New York, French, 1984.
Last Words (produced New York, 1977).
Signs of Life (produced New York, 1979; London, 1983). Published in *The Women's Project Anthology* edited by Julia Miles, New York, Performing Arts Journal Publishers, 1980.
The Lodger (produced New York, 1979).
Mr. Monster (produced New York, 1980).
The Last of Hitler (also director: produced New York, 1981).
Between the Acts (also director: produced New York, 1984).
Fulfilling Koch's Postulate (also director: produced New York, 1985; London, 1986).
Joan of Arc (produced Minneapolis, 1986).
Family Pride in the 50's (produced New York, 1986). Published in *The Kenyon Review* (Kenyon, Ohio), Spring 1993.
Fire in the Future (produced Minneapolis, 1987; also director: produced New York, 1988).
Hunting Down the Sexes (includes *Bucks and Does, The Lodger*) (produced New York, 1987).
Nothing Is Funnier than Death (produced New York, 1988).
The Universal Wolf (produced New York, 1991). New York, Applause Books, 1992.

*

Critical Studies (selection): "Foodtalk in the Plays of Caryl Churchill and Joan Schenkar" by Vivian M. Patraka, in *The Theatre Annual* (Akron, Ohio), 1985; "Mass Culture and Metaphors of Menace in Joan Schenkar's Plays" by Vivian M. Patraka, in *Making a Spectacle, Feminist Essays on Contemporary Women's Theatre* edited by Lynda Hart, Ann Arbor, Michigan, University of Michigan Press, 1989; "History and Hysteria, Writing the Body in *Portrait of Dora* and *Signs of Life*" by Ann Wilson, in *Modern Drama* (Toronto, Ontario), March 1989; "Crossing the Corpus Callosum" by Elin Diamond, in *The Drama Review* (New York), Summer 1991.

Theatrical Activities:
Director: Plays—*The Last of Hitler*, New York, 1981; *Between the Acts*, New York, 1984, 1989; *Fulfilling Koch's Postulate*, New York, 1985; *Fire in the Future*, New York, 1988.

Joan Schenkar comments:

My most serious intention as a writer for the stage is to enter a clear condition of nightmare thru the comedy of precise vernacular . . . Some truths are so terrible they can only be approached by laughter—which is why I write comedies of menace. In the best of all possible productions, I will have made you laugh at something horrible.

*   *   *

Dreams, history, and fantasy serve as raw material for the elliptical, determinedly non-naturalistic plays of Joan Schenkar. Her style is heavily influenced by cartoons, comic strips, feminist theory and literature, radio, television, circus, and sideshow. Schenkar's stated purpose "is to make comedies of tragic subjects," and she wields her macabre, demonic sense of humor like a scalpel, dissecting varied topics—the Victorians' destructive attitude toward women, the insidious spread of anti-Semitism, the power and precariousness of a scientific outlook, and the surreal normality of American suburbia.

Schenkar gives a number of her plays the subtitle "a comedy of menace." Her three primary works in this vein—*Cabin Fever*, *Fulfilling Koch's Postulate*, and *Family Pride in the 50's*—all share this subversive manic humor. *Cabin Fever*, the funniest and most menacing, reads like a Stephen King story as dramatized by Samuel Beckett. Three characters, called One, Two, and Three, never move from their dilapidated New England front porch as they try to stave off the dreaded disease of the title. Underneath their reserved, almost formal manner, terror lurks: they know "it comes in threes." "What does?" one character asks. "Death," assures another. With each repetition of this litany their anxiety spirals. When talk turns to the cannibalism that's been running rampant in this backwoods community, One twitches in her seat as Two and Three recall the last time they sampled human flesh. Although they jocularly threaten to eat One, she gets the last laugh, and the play ends with her brandishing knife and fork.

Influenced by the Katzenjammer Kids comic strip, Schenkar purposefully confines herself to a 300-word vocabulary for *Fulfilling Koch's Postulate*. Like *Cabin Fever*, Schenkar provides her characters with a one-line litany: "Nothing is funnier than death." Her sets are always exaggerated metaphors that serve as an extra character and this one is no exception, featuring a lip-shaped proscenium and a playing space made into an esophagus. Within this frame the stage is split between the kitchen, from which a household chef, based on the infamous historical figure known as Typhoid Mary, spreads her deadly contagion, and the laboratory in which Dr. Koch tries to track down the disease's root. As the cook cooks and the scientist probes, the culinary activities take on shades of sinister experimentation while Koch's dissections become utterly domestic. *Family Pride in the 50's* is a heavy-handed satire on an easy target: the idyllic post-war decade dominated by frosted flakes, family holiday dinners, and fights over the television set. Everyone resembles everyone else—two brothers married two sisters, each with two children. As the eldest child Joan retches violently, everyone blithely continues their family squabbles. When the children play "doctor," they use real knives and instruments, much like the dramatist did: "When I was a kid I used to collect knives. . . . I had a surgeon's puncture tool. . . . And I'd take people's blood samples." The play ends with the children sitting around the table:

> Maureen: You gonna deal those cards? Or do I have to cut 'em with my knife.
> Joan: Tch tch. Such language sis. Tch tch tch. Such *language* at the *dinner* table.

Schenkar's preoccupation with science—or what she calls "false science"—underlies two other historically based plays, *The Last of Hitler* and *Signs of Life*. The former is a dream play picturing the Führer in what Schenkar envisions as his version of Hell—a "Kozy Kabin" in Florida, a state with a large population of Jews. Once again, Schenkar works with a split stage, but this one is divided by an enormous 1940's radio that spews anti-Semitism, less visible than Typhoid Mary's infection but just as deadly. As Dr. Reich and his office skeleton perform ventriloquist routines reminiscent of Charlie McCarthy's, Hitler and Eva Braun fight off cancer and their own Jewishness. *Signs of Life*, the most successful of Schenkar's imaginative treatments of history, features Henry James and Dr. Sloper, the inventor of the "uterine guillotine," taking tea and toasting "the ladies" who Schenkar believes helped make the men famous—Henry's invalid sister Alice, and Jane Merritt, P.T. Barnum's sideshow star dubbed the "Elephant Woman," on whom Sloper performed experimental surgery. The play clearly demonstrates how both women were transformed into freaks, victims of Victorian patriarchy's malevolence toward women.

Between the Acts, an absurdist surreal fairytale set in the garden of the wealthiest man in the world, gives allegorical voice to Schenkar's feminist and political concerns. At a climactic moment, the rich capitalist Martin Barney and his daughter's lesbian lover the artist Romaine Brooks, circle each other like boxers. Instead of trading physical blows, they shout out famous names. When Barney yells "J.P. Morgan" Romaine is momentarily staggered, but she strikes back with "Emily Brontë, Emily Dickinson, Virginia Woolf!" and crumples the industrialist, who wails, "Genius! Good God! I have nothing to fight genius with." Featuring a gigantic Venus Fly Trap that serves as a trysting spot, a riding crop that spews magic dust, and a dog in a tutu performing bourrées in silhouette, this is one of Schenkar's wildest efforts.

Hunting Down the Sexes, composed of two compact and vicious one-acts, literalizes these gender wars. Part One, *Bucks and Does*, focuses on three men, Rap, Ape, and Ab, at their hunting cabin. The play opens with Rap masturbating in synchronized motion with Ab's ritualistic cleaning of the guns. Schenkar then takes Freud's theories to their harrowing extreme: Rap, who insists on calling does "pretty brown girls," tells his mates, "There's nothing like pulling a trigger and watching 'em drop. I always come when they drop." Of course, the does, portrayed by actresses, get their final revenge when Rap staggers into the cabin with his crotch bloodied by a stray bullet. In Part Two, *The Lodger*, a pair of spinsterish women debate the tortures they'll inflict on their

male prisoner, captured in the guerilla war between genders raging around their Victorian New England home.

Schenkar's works all limn the body/brain duality. Images of blood, ritualistic "bloodings," and blood samples appear in virtually every play, while the fragile intellectual systems holding reality together go haywire. Schenkar's stagecraft, using varied performance traditions—from cartoons to shadow-puppets—and structural devices—from entr'actes to epilogues—matches her imagination to provide, in the best of her work, insightful entrées to the dualities duelling for body and soul in Western society.

—John Istel

———

SCHEVILL, James (Erwin). American. Born in Berkeley, California, 10 June 1920. Educated at Harvard University, Cambridge, Massachusetts, B.S. 1942. Served in the United States Army, 1942–46. Married Margot Helmuth Blum in 1966; two daughters by an earlier marriage. Member of the faculty, California College of Arts and Crafts, Oakland, 1950–59; member of the Faculty, 1959–68, and director of the Poetry Center, 1961–68, San Francisco State College. Professor of English 1969–85, professor emeritus since 1985, and director of the creative writing program, 1972–75, Brown University, Providence, Rhode Island. Founding member, Wastepaper Theatre, Providence; since 1983 president, Rhode Island Playwrights Theatre. Recipient: National Theatre Competition prize, 1945; Dramatists Alliance Contest prize, 1948; Fund for the Advancement of Education fellowship, 1953; Phelan prize, for biography, 1954, for play, 1958; Ford grant, 1960; Rockefeller grant, 1964; William Carlos Williams award (*Contact* magazine), 1965; Roadstead Foundation award, 1966; Rhode Island Governor's award, 1975; Guggenheim fellowship, 1981; McKnight fellowship, 1984; American Academy award, 1991, literary award, 1992. M.A. (ad eundem): Brown University, 1969; D.H.L.: Rhode Island College, Providence, 1986. Agent: Helen Merrill Ltd., 435 West 23rd Street, No. 1A, New York, New York 10011. Address: 1309 Oxford Street, Berkeley, California, U.S.A.

PUBLICATIONS

Plays

High Sinners, Low Angels, music by Schevill, arranged by Robert Commanday (produced San Francisco, 1953). San Francisco, Bern Porter, 1953.
The Bloody Tenet (produced Providence, Rhode Island, 1956; Shrewsbury, Shropshire, 1962). Included in *The Black President and Other Plays*, 1965.
The Cid, adaptation of the play by Corneille (broadcast 1963). Published in *The Classic Theatre 4*, edited by Eric Bentley, New York, Doubleday, 1961.
Voices of Mass and Capital A, music by Andrew Imbrie (produced San Francisco, 1962). New York, Friendship Press, 1962.
The Master (produced San Francisco, 1963). Included in *The Black President and Other Plays*, 1965.

American Power: The Space Fan, and The Master (produced Minneapolis, 1964).   Included in *The Black President and Other Plays*, 1965.

The Black President and Other Plays. Denver, Swallow, 1965.

The Death of Anton Webern (produced Fish Creek, Wisconsin, 1966).   Included in *Violence and Glory: Poems 1962-1968*, 1969.

This Is Not True, music by Paul McIntyre (produced Minneapolis, 1967).

The Pilots (produced Providence, Rhode Island, 1970).

Oppenheimer's Chair (produced Providence, Rhode Island, 1970).

Lovecraft's Follies (produced Providence, Rhode Island, 1970).   Chicago, Swallow Press, 1971.

The Ushers (produced Providence, Rhode Island, 1971). Included in *Five Plays*, 1993.

The American Fantasies (produced New York, 1972).

Emperor Norton Lives! (produced Salt Lake City, 1972; revised version, as *Emperor Norton*, music by Jerome Rosen, produced San Francisco, 1979).

Fay Wray Meets King Kong (produced Providence, Rhode Island, 1974). Published in *Wastepaper Theatre Anthology*, edited by Schevill, 1978.

Sunset and Evening Stance; or, Mr. Krapp's New Tapes (produced Providence, Rhode Island, 1974).   Published in *Wastepaper Theatre Anthology*, edited by Schevill, 1978.

The Telephone Murderer (produced Providence, Rhode Island, 1975).   Published in *Wastepaper Theatre Anthology*, edited by Schevill, 1978.

Cathedral of Ice (produced Providence, Rhode Island, 1975). Wood Hole, Massachusetts, Pourboire Press, 1975.

Naked in the Garden (produced Providence, Rhode Island, 1975).

Year after Year (produced Providence, Rhode Island, 1976).

Questioning Woman (produced Providence, Rhode Island, 1980).

Mean Man I (also director: produced Providence, Rhode Island, 1981).

Mean Man II (also director: produced Providence, Rhode Island, 1982).

Edison's Dream (produced Providence, Rhode Island, 1982).

Galileo, with Adrian Hall, adaptation of the play by Brecht (produced Providence, Rhode Island, 1983).

Cult of Youth (produced Minneapolis, 1984).

Mean Man III (also director: produced Providence, Rhode Island, 1985).

Time of the Hand and Eye (produced Providence, Rhode Island, 1986).

The Planner (also director: produced Providence, Rhode Island, 1986).

Collected Short Plays. Athens, Swallow Press-Ohio University Press, 1986.

The Storyville Doll Lady (also director: produced Providence, Rhode Island, 1987).

Perelman Monologue (produced Providence, Rhode Island, 1987).

Mother O; or, The Last American Mother (produced Providence, Rhode Island, 1990).   Included in *Five Plays*, 1993.

Sisters in the Limelight (produced Providence, Rhode Island, 1990).

American Fantasies (produced Rostock, East Germany, 1990).

The Garden on F Street, with Mary Gail (produced Providence, Rhode Island, 1992).

Five Plays (includes *Lovecraft's Follies, The Ushers, The Last Romantics, Mother O; or, The Last American Mother,*

Shadows of Memory: A Double Bill About Dian Fossey and Djuna Barnes).   Athens, Ohio, Swallow Press, 1993.

Radio Plays: *The Sound of a Soldier*, 1945; *The Death of a President*, 1945; *The Cid*, 1963 (Canada); *The Death of Anton Webern*, 1972.

Novel

The Arena of Ants.   Providence, Rhode Island, Copper Beech Press, 1977.

Verse

Tensions.   San Francisco, Bern Porter, 1947.

The American Fantasies.   San Francisco, Bern Porter, 1951.

The Right to Greet.   San Francisco, Bern Porter, 1955.

Selected Poems 1945–1959.   San Francisco, Bern Porter, 1960.

Private Dooms and Public Destinations: Poems 1945–1962. Denver, Swallow, 1962.

The Stalingrad Elegies.   Denver, Swallow, 1964.

Release.   Providence, Rhode Island, Hellcoal Press, 1968.

Violence and Glory: Poems 1962–1968.   Chicago, Swallow Press, 1969.

The Buddhist Car and Other Characters.   Chicago, Swallow Press, 1973.

Pursuing Elegy: A Poem about Haiti.   Providence, Rhode Island, Copper Beech Press, 1974.

The Mayan Poems.   Providence, Rhode Island, Copper Beech Press, 1978.

Fire of Eyes: A Guatemalan Sequence.   Providence, Rhode Island, Copper Beech Press, 1979.

The American Fantasies: Collected Poems 1: 1945–1981. Athens, Swallow Press-Ohio University Press, 1983.

The Invisible Volcano.   Providence, Rhode Island, Copper Beech Press, 1985.

Ghost Names/Ghost Numbers.   Providence, Rhode Island, Walter Feldman, 1986.

Ambiguous Dancers of Fame: Collected Poems 2: 1945–1985. Athens, Swallow Press-Ohio University Press, 1987.

Quixote Visions.   Providence, Rhode Island, Ziggurat Press, 1991.

Recording: *Performance Poems*, Cambridge, 1984.

Other

Sherwood Anderson: His Life and Work. Denver, University of Denver Press, 1951.

The Roaring Market and the Silent Tomb (biographical study of the scientist and artist Bern Porter).   Oakland, California, Abbey Press, 1956.

Bern Porter: A Personal Biography.   Gardiner, Maine, Tilbury House, 1992.

Editor, *Six Historians*, by Ferdinand Schevill.   Chicago, University of Chicago Press, and London, Cambridge University Press, 1956.

Editor, *Break Out! In Search of New Theatrical Environments*.   Chicago, Swallow Press, 1973.

Editor, *Wastepaper Theatre Anthology*.   Providence, Rhode Island, Pourboire Press, 1978.

*

Manuscript Collection: John Hay Library, Brown University, Providence, Rhode Island.

Critical Study: unpublished thesis by Wanda Howard, University of Rhode Island, Kingston, 1981.

Theatrical Activities:
Director: **Plays**—Wastepaper Theatre, Providence: *Mean Man I–III*, 1981–85; *The Planner*, 1986; *The Storyville Doll Lady*, 1987.

James Schevill comments:
(1973) My early plays were verse plays. Recently, my plays have been written in prose. However, as a poet, I still believe in poetry as the roots of the theatre, and do my best to upend a theatre that is too literal and prosaic. I want an action that is both theatrical and poetic, that can use the disturbing images of our time to create a new vitality on stage. To achieve this vitality, I like to use dramatic, historical contrasts to give a play depth and perspective. Today the great possibilities of playwriting lie in the recognition that a play can range in time and space as widely as a film, that it can be as exciting in movement as a film, and that the great advantage it continues to have over film is the live actor who is capable of instantaneous, extraordinary transformations in character and situation.

*   *   *

A lyric poet, James Schevill has been consistently drawn to the theatre, but his plays are written largely in prose. Composed of history, current events, and fantasy, they theatricalize injustice in contemporary America.

The Bloody Tenet takes its title from the self-defense of Roger Williams when he was persecuted for religious unorthodoxy. Schevill's play sets Williams's story as a play within a play, and the outer frame is a dialogue between a middle-aged Journalist and a voluptuous Evangelist. As the inner play dramatizes Williams's condemnation by orthodox authority, the frame play dramatizes a facile orthodoxy paying lip service to liberty. Schevill's play finally confronts his moderns with Williams himself, who refuses to choose between the Journalist's critique of his inadequacies and the Evangelist's idolization of him. In verse Roger Williams reemphasizes his belief in individual paths to God.

Moving from religion to politics, Schevill paired his next two plays under the title *American Power*. The first play, *The Space Fan*, is subtitled a play of escape, and the second one, *The Master*, a play of commitment. The titular Space Fan is a zany lady who communicates with beings in outer space, and a suspicious government therefore assigns an Investigator to spy on her activities. Through the course of the play the Space Fan converts the Investigator to her free way of life, and as they join in a dance the Investigator declares: "For the first time in my life, I feel that I've become a real investigator."

In the companion play, *The Master*, investigation is more insidious. An attractive young woman, the Candidate, is guided by the Master in examinations which will culminate in a degree of General Mastery. During the examination the Master imposes upon the Candidate various roles, such as Army Officer, Indian squaw, Minute Man, Southern rebel, and finally corpse. Master and Candidate then oppose each other with their respective autobiographies, which erupt into scenes that glorify American power. The subtitles of both plays emerge as ironic: *The Space Fan* is a play of escape from American power, and *The Master*, a play of commitment, satirizes (and implicitly condemns) commitment to American power.

Schevill's next play, *The Black President*, is rooted in American oppression of blacks, but it reaches out to indict the whole white racist world. Moses Jackburn, a black American, is captain of a fascimile slaveship that is manned by the blacks of many countries. He sails the ship up the Thames to London, demanding to speak with the British Prime Minister. He is met with pious platitudes, then mercantile bargaining, and finally threats of force. Rather than surrender the ship, Jackson orders his crew to blow it up. While awaiting extradition to America, he is visited by Spanish Carla with whom he shares a fantasy life in which she helps him campaign for the presidency, to become the first "Black President." Back in the reality of his prison, Jackburn denounces his dream, but still hopes for "a little light."

In *Lovecraft's Follies* Schevill indicates his concern about man's enslavement by technology. H.P. Lovecraft, a Rhode Island recluse, was one of the first science-fiction writers to stress its gothic horrors. The protagonist of Schevill's play, Stanley Millsage, is a physicist at a space center, who has developed a Lovecraft fixation-fear of the horrors that science can perpetrate, which are theatricalized scenically to serve as a cathartic journey for the protagonist. Thus freed from his Lovecraft fixation, Millsage decares: "Well, that's the end of Lovecraft's follies. . . ." But the figure of Lovecraft, alone on stage, says mockingly to the audience: "Maybe!"

That "Maybe" leads to Schevill's next major play, *Cathedral of Ice*, in which technology again brings horror. On stage is a dream machine: "With our machine's modern computer device/We conjure up a vast Cathedral of Ice./ . . . I become Dream-Fuehrer, power to arrange." The drama fancifully traces the results of Hitler's power mania; in seven scenes he confronts historical and imaginary figures. Inspired by Napoleon and Charlemagne, Hitler summons an architect to "create for eternity our famous German ruins." Converting people's weaknesses into cruel and theatrical strengths, Hitler builds on the legends of Karl May and Richard Wagner. He refuses to tarnish his own legend by marrying Eva Braun. Above all he harnesses science to his monstrous destructive dream. But Night and Fog, actual characters, erode his structures. Even as the gas chambers destroy their multitudes, the Nazis are destroyed by their own manias, so that Hitler finally seeks glory in a *Liebestod* in the Cathedral of Ice.

In fantastic theatrical shapes Schevill's drama explores the realities of power and politics. Using music, dance, ritual, projections, Schevill the poet has reached out to embrace many possibilities of theatre.

—Ruby Cohn

———————

SCHISGAL, Murray (Joseph). American. Born in Brooklyn, New York, 25 November 1926. Educated at the Brooklyn Conservatory of Music; Long Island University, New York; Brooklyn Law School, LL.B. 1953; New School for Social Research, New York, B.A. 1959. Served as a radioman in the United States Navy, 1944–46. Married Reene Schapiro in 1958; one daughter and one son. Jazz musician in 1940's; lawyer, 1953–55; English teacher, Cooper Junior High School, East Harlem, and other private and public schools in New York, 1955–59. Since 1960 full-time writer. Recipient: Vernon Rice award, 1963; Outer Circle award, 1963; Los Angeles and New York Film Critics award, National Society of Film Critics award, and Writers Guild award, all for screenplay, 1983. Lives in New York City. Agent: Bridget

Aschenberg, International Creative Management, 40 West 57th Street, New York, New York 10019, U.S.A.

PUBLICATIONS

Plays

The Typists, and The Tiger (as *Schrecks: The Typists, The Postman, A Simple Kind of Love*, produced London, 1960; revised versions of *The Typists* and *The Postman* produced as *The Typists, and The Tiger*, New York, 1963; London, 1964). New York, Coward McCann, 1963; London, Cape, 1964.

Ducks and Lovers (produced London, 1961). New York, Dramatists Play Service, 1972.

Luv (produced London, 1963; New York, 1964). New York, Coward McCann, 1965.

Knit One, Purl Two (produced Boston, 1963).

Windows (produced Los Angeles, 1965). Included in *Fragments, Windows and Other Plays*, 1965.

Reverberations (produced Stockbridge, Massachusetts, 1965; as *The Basement*, produced New York, 1967). Included in *Fragments, Windows and Other Plays*, 1965.

Fragments, Windows and Other Plays (includes *Reverberations, Memorial Day, The Old Jew*). New York, Coward McCann, 1965.

The Old Jew, Fragments, and Reverberations (produced Stockbridge, Massachusetts, 1966). Included in *Fragments, Windows and Other Plays*, 1965.

Fragments (includes *The Basement* and *Fragments*) (produced New York, 1967). Included in *Fragments, Windows and Other Plays*, 1965.

Memorial Day (produced Baltimore, 1968). Included in *Fragments, Windows and Other Plays*, 1965.

Jimmy Shine, music by John Sebastian (produced New York, 1968; revised version, as *An Original Jimmy Shine*, produced Los Angeles, 1981). New York, Atheneum, 1969.

A Way of Life (produced New York, 1969; as *Roseland*, produced Berlin, 1975; as *The Downstairs Boys*, produced East Hampton, New York, 1980).

The Chinese, and Dr. Fish (produced New York, 1970). New York, Dramatists Play Service, 1970.

An American Millionaire (produced New York, 1974). New York, Dramatists Play Service, 1974.

All Over Town (produced New York, 1974). New York, Dramatists Play Service, 1975.

Popkins (produced Dallas, 1978). New York, Dramatists Play Service, 1984.

The Pushcart Peddlers (produced New York, 1979). Included in *The Pushcart Peddlers, The Flatulist, and Other Plays*, 1980.

Walter, and The Flatulist (produced New York, 1980). Included in *The Pushcart Peddlers, The Flatulist, and Other Plays*, 1980.

The Pushcart Peddlers, The Flatulist, and Other Plays (includes *A Simple Kind of Love Story, Little Johnny, Walter*). New York, Dramatists Play Service, 1980.

Twice Around the Park (includes *A Need for Brussels Sprouts* and *A Need for Less Expertise*) (produced New York, 1982; Edinburgh, 1984). Included in *Luv and Other Plays*, 1983.

Luv and Other Plays (includes *The Typists, The Tiger, Fragments, The Basement, The Chinese, The Pushcart Peddlers, The Flatulist, Twice Around the Park*). New York, Dodd Mead, 1983.

The New Yorkers (produced New York, 1984).

Jealousy (produced New York, 1984). With *There Are No Sacher Tortes in Our Society!*, New York, Dramatists Play Service, 1985.

Closet Madness and Other Plays (includes *The Rabbi and the Toyota Dealer* and *Summer Romance*). New York, French, 1984.

The Rabbi and the Toyota Dealer (produced Los Angeles, 1985). Included in *Closet Madness and Other Plays*, 1984.

Old Wine in a New Bottle (produced in Flemish, Antwerp, 1985). New York, Dramatists Play Service, 1987.

Schneider (produced Stockbridge, Massachusetts, 1986).

Road Show (produced New York, 1987). New York, Dramatists Play Service, 1987.

Man Dangling. New York, Dramatists Play Service, 1988.

Screenplays: *The Tiger Makes Out*, 1967; *Tootsie*, with others, 1983.

Television Plays: *The Love Song of Barney Kempinski*, 1966; *Natasha Kovolina Pipishinsky*, 1976.

Novel

Days and Nights of a French Horn Player. Boston, Little Brown, 1980.

*   *   *

In the mid-1960's Murray Schisgal's plays were hailed as a step ahead of the avant-garde and more absurd than the work of the absurdists. He was frequently grouped with the new author-stars of American theater—Edward Albee, John Guare, Arthur Kopit, Jack Gelber—whose work, like Schisgal's, was first seen in the United States off-Broadway. As Schisgal notes with irony in the preface to his plays *The Typists, and The Tiger*, this recognition by American critics came only after he had achieved significant success as a playwright in England. *The Typists* and *The Tiger*, two one-acts, and a full-length play, *Ducks and Lovers*, were in fact all first produced in London, and Schisgal's eventual Broadway hit, *Luv*, was optioned in London as early as 1961. After the popular success of *Luv*, which opened in London in 1963 and New York in 1964, Schisgal's career as a playwright seemed assured. He continued to write new plays at a remarkably steady pace through the 1960's and 1970's; most of his new works were produced and published. Critics, however, quickly lost interest in his work, and he has thus become one of the few American playwrights who has genuinely sustained a career in the theater but has no defined place in American culture or drama history.

Much of the oddity of Schisgal's reception can be discovered in the comic constancy and contemporaneity of his work. He is a satirist of daily life in America and of the clichés of that life. His plays evoke a zany world that teeters between lunacy and good sense. In each of his plays, there is at least one character whose social role is ostensibly ordinary but whose manner of inhabiting that role is eccentric and perverse. Nowhere is this disclosure of the volatile, chaotic energy of ordinary people better accomplished than in *The Tiger*. The plot is simply and potentially melodramatic: Ben, a postman, kidnaps Gloria, a suburban housewife; he intends to rape her. We encounter the two as Ben enters his dingy, cluttered basement apartment with Gloria slung over his shoulder. Any expections we might have of soap-opera melodrama are quickly thwarted by the peculiar behavior of both characters. Ben's notion of rape begins with a peck on Gloria's cheek and includes playing her a recording of

Tchaikovsky's first piano concerto; Gloria is so impressed by Ben's quasi-philosophic utterances that she repeatedly forgets that she, not he, is the victim in this situation. Ben's hyperbolic frustration turns out to be the perfect match for Gloria's fertile boredom, and, as we laugh at the two equally naïve lovers groping for each other like adolescents, we are finally able to laugh, too, at the self-indulgence of our own overly promoted ennui.

The Tiger delights both because it enables us to laugh at our inflation of contemporary causes and because almost every line is a surprise. While remaining within a recognizable world, Schisgal captures the inanity of our assertions and our memories. Like *The Tiger*, Schisgal's full-length work *Luv* is a comedy of contemporary manners and obsessions. The classic triangle—a man, his wife, and his best friend—erupts and renegotiates its connections in *Luv* with much the same irreverence for marriage and other institutions that emerged in *The Tiger*. Milt, Harry, and Ellen of *Luv* clearly deserve each other; no-one else would take any one of them as seriously as they do each other or themselves. In this play, as in *The Tiger*, Schisgal's magic is that of the true clown; he makes us laugh at every near-catastrophe including the suicide attempts of each character. In the end, however, *Luv* does not sustain its wit, and one is left with the uneasy sense that, having displayed love itself as a false totem, the play's most lasting image is of a dog peeing on someone's leg.

Relentless in his deflation of each new passion in American society, Schisgal's plays since the late 1960's have become less funny and more acute in the social issues they address. Of the plays written since *Luv*, two, *Jimmy Shine* and *All Over Town*, are particularly rich in the experience they provide for an audience. *All Over Town* assaults every facile "solution" that was embraced in the late 1960's and early 1970's: welfare, psychiatry, ecology, liberalism, racial and sexual "liberation" are all reduced to confetti in an upper-class New York apartment that becomes a carnival of errors. Although Schisgal has since written other plays in his distinctive satiric mode, *All Over Town* so expands the madness and so multiplies the cast of characters that it conveys an aura of finality—in this mode at least. In contrast, *Jimmy Shine*, while orthodox in dramaturgy, exemplifies a powerful new mode in Schisgal's writing. In *Jimmy Shine* Schisgal quietly controls the tentative, unsatisfied struggles of his artist-hero to find meaning without ornamentation. Schisgal's persistent presentation of the humorous aspects of sexuality and the painful burdens of human love are presented in *Jimmy Shine* without the usual parodic refractions. Perhaps it is the integrity so transparent in *Jimmy Shine* that continues to draw community and academic theater companies to Schisgal's plays.

—Helene Keyssar

* * *

SEABROOK, Jeremy. British. Born in Northampton in 1939. Educated at Northampton Grammar School; Gonville and Caius College, Cambridge; London School of Economics, diploma in social administration 1967. Teacher in a secondary modern school for two years; social worker, Inner London Education Authority, 1967–69, and with Elfrida Rathbone Association, 1973–76. Agent: Curtis Brown, 162–168 Regent Street, London W1R 5TB, England.

PUBLICATIONS

Plays

Life Price with Michael O'Neill (produced London, 1969).
Morality, with Michael O'Neill (produced London, 1971).
Millennium, with Michael O'Neill (produced London, 1973).
Our Sort of People, with Michael O'Neill (produced London, 1974).
Sex and Kinship in a Savage Society, with Michael O'Neill (produced London, 1975).
Yesterday's News, with Joint Stock (produced Aldershot, Hampshire, and London, 1976).
Sharing, with Michael O'Neill (produced London, 1980).
Black Man's Burden, with Michael O'Neill (produced London, 1980).
Heart-Throb, with Caroline Hutchison and Anna Mottram (produced London, 1988).

Radio Plays: *Birds in a Gilded Cage*, 1974; *A Change of Life*, 1979; *A Mature Relationship*, 1979; *Golden Opportunities*, 1982; with Michael O'Neill—*The Bosom of the Family*, 1975; *Living Private*, 1978; *Our Children's Children*, 1980; *Life Skills*, 1985.

Television Plays, with Michael O'Neill: *Skin Deep*, 1971; *Soap Opera in Stockwell*, 1973; *Highway Robbery*, 1973; *A Clear Cut Case*, 1973; *A Stab in the Front*, 1973; *Children of the Sun*, 1975; *Beyond the Call of Duty* (*Crown Court* series), 1976; *A State of Welfare*.

Other

The Unprivileged: A Hundred Years of Family Life and Tradition in a Working-Class Street. London, Longman, 1967.
City Close-Up. London, Allen Lane, and Indianapolis, Bobbs Merrill, 1971.
Loneliness. London, Temple Smith, 1971; New York, Universe, 1975.
The Everlasting Feast. London, Allen Lane, 1974.
A Lasting Relationship: Hormosexuals and Society. London, Allen Lane, 1976.
What Went Wrong? Working People and the Ideals of the Labour Movement. London, Gollancz, 1978; New York, Pantheon, 1979.
Mother and Son: An Autobiography. London, Gollancz, 1979; New York, Pantheon, 1980.
Working-Class Childhood. London, Gollancz, 1982.
Unemployment. London, Quartet, 1982.
The Idea of Neighbourhood: What Local Politics Should Be About. London, Pluto Press, 1984.
A World Still to Win: The Reconstruction of the Post-War Working Class, with Trevor Blackwell. London, Faber, 1985.
Landscapes of Poverty. Oxford, Blackwell, 1985.
Life and Labour in a Bombay Slum. London, Quartet, 1987.
The Politics of Hope: Britain at the End of the Twentieth Century, with Trevor Blackwell, London, Faber, 1988.
The Leisure Society. Oxford, Blackwell, 1988.
The Race for Riches: The Human Cost of Wealth. Basingstoke, Marshall Pickering, 1988.

The Myth of the Market. Hartland, Devon, Green Books, 1990.

*   *   *

See the essay on Michael O'Neill and Jeremy Seabrook.

———

SELBOURNE, David. British. Born in London, 4 June 1937. Educated at Manchester Grammar School; Balliol College, Oxford, B.A. (honours) 1958; Inner Temple, London, called to the Bar, 1959. Lecturer, University of Aston, Birmingham, 1963–65; Tutor in Politics, Ruskin College, Oxford, 1965–86. Recipient: Aneurin Bevan Memorial fellowship, 1975; Southern Arts Association award, 1979; Indian Council of Social Science research award, 1979; Social Science Research Council award, 1980; Periodical Publishers Association award, 1986. Address: c/o Xandra Hardie, 9 Elsworthy Terrace, London NW3 3DR, England.

PUBLICATIONS

Plays

The Play of William Cooper and Edmund Dew-Nevett (produced Exeter, 1968). London, Methuen, 1968.
The Two-Backed Beast (produced Liverpool, 1968). London, Methuen, 1969.
Dorabella (produced Edinburgh, 1969). London, Methuen, 1970.
Samson (produced London, 1970). With *Alison Mary Fagan*, London, Calder and Boyars, 1971.
Alison Mary Fagan (produced Auckland, New Zealand, 1972). With *Samson*, London, Calder and Boyars, 1971.
The Damned. London, Methuen, 1971.
Class Play (produced London, 1972). Published in *Second Playbill 3*, edited by Alan Durband, London, Hutchinson, 1973.
Three Class Plays (for children; produced London, 1973).
What's Acting? and Think of a Story, Quickly! (for children; produced London, 1977). London, Arnold, 1977.
A Woman's Trial (produced in Bengali, as *Shrimatir Bichar*, Calcutta, 1982).

Other

Brook's Dream: The Politics of Theatre. London, Action Books, 1974.
An Eye to China. London, Black Liberator Press, 1975.
An Eye to India: The Unmasking of a Tyranny. London, Penguin, 1977.
Through the Indian Looking-Glass: Selected Articles on India 1976–1980. Bombay, Popular Prakashan, and London, Zed Press, 1982.
The Making of A Midsummer Night's Dream: An Eye-Witness Account of Peter Brook's Production. London, Methuen, 1982.
Against Socialist Illusion: A Radical Argument. London, Macmillan, and New York, Schocken, 1985.
Left Behind: Journeys into British Politics. London, Cape, 1987.
Death of the Dark Hero: Eastern Europe 1987–1990. London, Cape, 1990.

Editor, *In Theory and in Practice: Essays on the Politics of Jayaprakash Narayan.* New Delhi, Oxford University Press, 1985; Oxford and New York, Oxford University Press, 1986.
Editor, *A Doctor's Life: The Diaries of Hugh Selbourne M.D., 1960–1963.* London, Cape, 1989.

*

Critical Studies: introductions by John Russell Brown to *The Play of William Cooper and Edmund Dew-Nevett*, 1968, by Stuart Hall to *An Eye to China*, 1975, and by Selbourne to *What's Acting? and Think of a Story, Quickly!*, 1977.

*   *   *

David Selbourne writes with consistent strategy. He chooses simple actions that involve basic motives with the minimum of complication through story or the representation of the process of everyday living. So he is free to move his characters into ever-changing relationships with each other, and with their own reactions. In the one-act *Samson* a boy tries to break away from his father in twelve short scenes. In *Dorabella* a spinster is attracted to the boyfriend of her hairdresser. In *The Play of William Cooper and Edmund Dew-Nevett* a simpleton and would-be artist seeks happiness and finds corruption.

These are intellectual plays in that they are based on a clear view of how time, power, imagination, thought, and passions work together. But they are realized with a sensual awareness that seeks to create brilliant juxtapositions, activity and language that can take actors and audiences directly to total, undisguised confrontations.

Almost all the dialogue is in a verse form that serves to accentuate thrust and concision. It also holds attention for the echoes from mystical poets and the Old Testament that play a large part in creating the overall impression of the plays. The echoes are purposefully easy to catch and, more than this, they live together with a lively response to ordinary talk and responses. This style with its radiant images offsets the restricted nature of the play's actions, where man is repeatedly shown caught by his own conditions of living. *The Damned* presents self-deception and domination with calculated ruthlessness, but even in this painful drama the words spoken show how the hope of free life is still the characters' true source of energy. At the end of *William Cooper* the simpleton can "fly no more," but he has only just recognized again "Light blazing into my head."

Two plays are in a separate category, for in the one-act *Alison Mary Fagan* and the short *Class Play* Selbourne has placed real people in dramatic forms: in the first an actress who faces herself, her life and her career, and in *Class Play* three pupils and a teacher facing school and life. These are difficult plays to perform, for the dialogue is still shockingly direct and the situations continually changing, but at the centre of the drama is a person who performs or children who are manipulated, and these are to be seen without artifice, recognized as if outside a theatre.

Selbourne is a writer of teeming imagination and clear determination. He has never fallen in with a fashionable mode of writing for the stage. He has worked on his own, confident in the validity of his purpose. He stakes everything he knows; to share that risk is an exhilarating and demanding enterprise that leaves a permanent mark.

—John Russell Brown

———

SEWELL, Stephen. Australian. Born in Sydney in 1953. Educated at the University of Sydney, B.S. 1975. Writer-in-residence, Nimrod Theatre, Sydney, 1981–82. Recipient: Australian Writers Guild award, 1982; New South Wales Premier's award, 1985. Agent: Hilary Linstead and Associates, Suite 302, Easts Tower, 9–13 Bronte Road, Bondi Junction, New South Wales 2022, Australia.

PUBLICATIONS

Plays

The Father We Loved on a Beach by the Sea (produced Brisbane, 1978).   Sydney, Currency Press, 1976.
Traitors (produced Melbourne, 1979; London, 1980).   Sydney, Alternative Publishing Co-operative, 1983.
Welcome the Bright World.   Sydney, Alternative Publishing Co-operative, 1983.
The Blind Giant Is Dancing (produced Adelaide, 1983).   Sydney, Currency Press, 1983; revised version, 1985.
Burn Victim, with others (produced Sydney, 1983).
Dreams in an Empty City (produced Adelaide, 1986; London, 1988).   Sydney, Currency Press, 1986.
Hate (produced Sydney, 1988).
Miranda (produced Brisbane, 1989).
Sisters (also director: produced Melbourne, 1991; London, 1992).
King Golgrutha (produced Adelaide, 1991).
In the City of Grand-Daughters (produced Melbourne, 1993).
Dust (produced Adelaide, 1993).

Screenplay: *Isabelle Eberhardt*, 1993.

* * *

The first production of *Traitors* in 1979 established Stephen Sewell as one of the most exciting and challenging of the new generation of Australian playwrights. His work is distinctive for the power and complexity of its political vision, and in this sense is perhaps more appropriately compared with recent left-wing British theatre than with the mostly comic, mostly celebratory style of satire which has dominated Australian stages over the past two decades. *The Blind Giant Is Dancing* and *Dreams in an Empty City*, share some of the central concerns of that local tradition, however, in the ways they present patterns of social (and particularly marital) interaction which offer distinctive images of contemporary Australia. But always in Sewell's work the analysis of interpersonal politics is conducted in the context of structures of power which exist beyond the individual, and beyond the immediate culture. Sewell is a Marxist of a fairly sceptical and speculative kind, and while his plays have provoked a hostile reaction from some critics who find them ponderous and propagandistic, such a view seems to be a response to his overtly ideological approach to theatre rather than to the complex political vision which the plays actually present. Sewell's description of Marxism as a "tenable hypothesis" fairly indicates his own awareness of the complexity of the issues he deals with; it gives no sense, though, of the importance in the disintegrating world which his plays depict of finding some system of value which is "tenable," or of the passion with which such a commitment can be held.

The Father We Loved on a Beach by the Sea, Sewell's first play, was to some extent a dress-rehearsal for the presentation, in the more recent plays, of aspects of the familial culture in terms which attempt as well to define the forces which create them. It also anticipated something of the structural complexity demanded by Sewell's later more elaborate explorations of political cause and effect. *The Father*'s juxtaposition of two time-frames (remembrance of things past as experienced by Joe, a quintessential Aussie "battler," and a hypothetical revolutionary future focused on Dan, his activist son) entails an ambitious mixture of playing styles which is developed still more challengingly in *The Blind Giant* and *Dreams in an Empty City*. Here these elements are less satisfyingly reconciled than in the later plays; perhaps the absence of a point of present vantage between warmly stereotypical past and coldly nightmarish future contributes to the sense that there is some uncertainty of focus behind the power of the play. Where the treatment of "little people" in Sewell's later work reflects his premise that the political and the personal are inextricable or identical, the image of the family in *The Father* appeals quite directly to the feelings of unresolved guilt, love, and resentment which most of us have for our parents.

Traitors and *Welcome the Bright World* were greeted as distinguished instances of the "new internationalism" in Australian drama which followed the very self-consciously Australian "new wave" of the late 1960's and early 1970's. The settings of the two plays—respectively, Stalinist Russia between world wars and Germany through the 1970's—certainly looked like a conspicuous refusal to be parochial. In the light of the distinctively local emphasis of the two latest plays, that choice might be seen either as having no significance at all beyond Sewell's particular interests at the time, or as a controlling response to the personal dimensions of *The Father*. The relevance of a concept like "internationalism" to Sewell's work can be sought more profitably in the nature of his political analysis and the theatrical company he (metaphorically) keeps than in matters of literal placement.

Traitors is the most concentrated of his plays. The historicity and episodic structure look Brechtian, but there is not much ground for rational reflection; the play's intensity comes from the unrelenting pressure of its depiction of the efforts of individuals to find some place for love and some sense of personal purpose in a society where betrayal and oppression appear to pre-empt such things. Here the personal is the political in a particularly overt and uncomplicated way; although the ideological commitments of all the characters make self-abnegation seem a moral imperative, *Traitors* explores the tensions which that creates.

Soviet factionalism provided a somewhat esoteric base for *Traitors*; the combination of revolutionary politics in Germany, different forms of consciousness of being Jewish, and the state of contemporary physics made a more demanding one for *Welcome the Bright World*. This play confirmed a general critical conception of Sewell as a playwright whose reach, excitingly but rather wilfully, would always exceed his grasp. As in *Traitors*, there is a great deal going on, most of it very powerful and disturbing, and all of it suggesting that this is a writer who will not make theatrical compromises in his mission to address an audience intelligently. The unwieldiness of the structure becomes in a sense an aspect of the play's power, in its seeming guarantee that there are forces here which are beyond containment.

The two most recent plays have found forms of containment which have not been at the expense of the intensity of the idea. In returning to aspects of Australian society as his subject, Sewell has in both cases drawn on a central myth to encompass the action beyond its immediate political reference—the Faust story in *The Blind Giant*, and the Christ story in *Dreams in an Empty City*. *Welcome the Bright World* foreshadowed this development, in its treatment of the effort of much modern nuclear theory to establish the principles which relate the smallest detectable (or imaginable) particle to the largest forms of matter; unification theory became a metaphor not only for the essential interrelatedness of political structures, but for the form of the play itself. But where that central metaphor requires a good deal of explanatory play on blackboards with quarks and neutrinos, *The Blind Giant* and *Dreams* appeal to analogies which are quite as rich and more broadly available.

The Blind Giant deals with political corruption at all levels of Australian society, though its focus is on the corrosiveness of compromise in the development of its central character, a crusader on the Labor left. There is nothing simplistic about this concern, though, since the exploration of power structures from the domestic to the international is complicated in the action by the elusiveness of answers to all questions about the sources of power, and by individual psychological patterns of assertion and submission. It is perhaps in the latter area that the play's major strength lies; its treatment of sexual and familial politics seems to offer more durable insights than the remarkably accurate short-term prophecies which emerge from its presentation of Australian political life.

The force which in *The Blind Giant* threatens to undermine all positions of integrity is cynicism, and no-one in the play (apart from a rather unlikely Chilean freedom-fighter) seems to find an answer to it. In *Dreams* that force is given its full spiritual dimension in the form of corrupting despair; even the most venal of the financial predators in this play appeal at some point to a perception of the world as irredeemably fallen in order to mask their opportunism with moral repugnance. The enemy of political change is not the dominant system in itself, but the sickness which breeds it. *Dreams* ends, like *The Father* and *The Blind Giant*, on a note of apocalyptic fantasy; here it is nothing less than the collapse of international capitalism. But for all the risks involved in its giant subject, and in its allegorical methods which transpose Christian virtue into a context of secular revolution, *Dreams* works, very powerfully and movingly.

Sewell is a young playwright whose achievement is already very impressive. The only thing which can be confidently predicted about the way in which his work might develop in the future is that it is sure to be exciting.

—Peter Fitzpatrick

SEYMOUR, Alan. Australian. Born in Perth, Western Australia, 6 June 1927. Educated at Fremantle State School, Western Australia; Perth Modern School. Freelance film and theatre critic and educational writer, Australian Broadcasting Commission, Perth and Sydney, 1950's; actor, Perth and Sydney, 1950's; contributor, *Overland* and *Meanjin*, both Melbourne, and Sydney *Bulletin-Observer*, from 1950's; co-founding director, Sydney Opera Group, 1953–58; theatre critic, *London Magazine*, 1962–65; lived in Izmir, Turkey, 1966–71. Recipient: Sydney Journalists' Club prize, 1960; Australian Council for the Arts grant, 1974. Address: 74 Upland Road, London SE22 0DB, England.

PUBLICATIONS

Plays

Swamp Creatures (produced Canberra, 1958).
The One Day of the Year (produced Adelaide, 1960; London, 1961). Sydney, Angus and Robertson, 1962; included in *Three Australian Plays*, London, Penguin, 1963; revised version, in *Three Australian Plays*, edited by Alrene Sykes, Melbourne, Penguin, 1985.
The Gaiety of Nations (produced Glasgow, 1965; London, 1966).
A Break in the Music (produced Perth, 1966).
The Pope and the Pill (produced London, 1968).
Oh Grave, Thy Victory (produced Canberra, 1973).
Structures (produced Perth, 1973).
The Wind from the Plain, adaptation of a novel by Yashar Kemal (produced, in Finnish, Turku, Finland, 1974–75).
The Float (produced Adelaide, 1980).

Radio Plays: *Little Moron*, 1956; *The Man Who Married a Dumb Wife*, from a work by Rabelais, 1956; *A Winter Passion*, 1960; *Donny Johnson*, 1965 (Finland).

Television Plays (UK): *Richard II*, from the play by Shakespeare, 1958 (Australia); *The Runner*, 1960 (Australia); *Lean Liberty*, 1962; *And It Wasn't Just the Feathers*, 1964; *Auto-Stop*, 1965; *The Trial and Torture of Sir John Rampayne*, 1965; *Stockbrokers Are Smashing But Bankers Are Better*, 1965; *Fixation*, from a work by Miles Tripp, 1973; *The Lotus*, *Tigers Are Better-Looking*, and *Outside the Machine*, from stories by Jean Rhys, 1973–74; *Eustace and Hilda*, from the novels by L.P. Hartley, 1977; *Sara Dane* series, from the novel by Catherine Gaskin, 1981 (Australia); *Frost in May*, from the novel by Antonia White, 1982; *The Tribute*, from a work by Jane Gardam, 1983; *The Ghostly Earl*, from a story by R. Chetwynd-Hayes, 1984; *The Box of Delights* series, from the book by John Masefield, 1984; *Tudawali* (documentary), 1987 (Australia); *Menace Unseen* series, 1988; *The Lion, The Witch, and the Wardrobe* series, 1988, *Prince Caspian* series, 1989, *The Voyage of the "Dawn Treader"* series, 1989, and *The Silver Chair* series, 1990, all based on *The Chronicles of Narnia* by C.S. Lewis; *The Care of Time*, adaptation of a novel by Eric Ambler, 1991; *The House of Eliott* series, 1991.

Novels

The One Day of the Year. London, Souvenir Press, 1967.
The Coming Self-Destruction of the United States of America. London, Souvenir Press, 1969; New York, Grove Press, 1971.

*

Manuscript Collection: Mitchell Library, Sydney.

Critical Studies: "Seymour's Anzac Play" by Max Harris, in *Nation* (Sydney), April 1961; introduction by Harry Kippax to *Three Australian Plays*, 1963; *Profile of Australia* by Craig McGregor, London, Hodder and Stoughton, 1966; essay in *On Native Grounds* edited by C.B. Christesen, Sydney, Angus and Robertson, 1967; introduction by Charles Higham to *Australian Writing Today*, London, Penguin, 1968; *The Great Australian Stupor* by Ronald Conway, Melbourne, Sun, 1971; article by Alrene Sykes, in *Australian Literary Studies* (Hobart, Tasmania), vol. 6, 1974, and by Sykes and

Keith Richardson, in *Australasian Drama Studies* (St. Lucia, Queensland), April 1984; *After "The Doll"* by Peter Fitzpatrick, Melbourne, Arnold, 1979; *Contemporary Australian Playwrights* edited by Jennifer Palmer, Adelaide, University Union Press, 1979.

Theatrical Activities:
Director: **Play**—*The One Day of the Year*, Australia tour, 1961. **Operas**—with Sydney Opera Group: *The Telephone, The Medium, Amahl and the Night Visitors*, and *Amelia Goes to the Ball*, all by Menotti; *Impresario* by Mozart; *The Secret of Susanna* by Wolf-Ferrari; *Une Education manquée* by Chabrier; and *The Jumping Frog of Calaveras County* by Lukas Foss, Sydney and Australia tours, 1953–58.

Alan Seymour comments:

(1973) As a theatre critic and student of theatre history and especially modern theatre experiments, I am concerned with the research for new forms. Paradoxically, the play of mine most widely performed in Australia and other countries, *The One Day of the Year*, is least typical of my work and intentions, its simple neo-realist form stemming from a conscious artistic choice as the best means to communicate my feelings on the subject of lingering militarism and a need of national self criticism, in the Australian theatre situation of the late 1950's.

Like many Australian playwrights I have in the last decade lived abroad, although the wisdom of this decision is obviously arguable. It is generally held that writers from theatrically under-developed countries need to live abroad because the more open possibilities in, for instance, London make their professional life easier. In my view, life abroad is more difficult. My creative life had I stayed at home would have developed more smoothly, though on more predictable lines. In London, though moderately successful as a television playwright and critic during the first half of the 1960's, I found that, as a playwright for the theatre, I had lost my national voice and not found a new "international" one to replace it.

By 1965 this and other problems drove me to live a more isolated life, to think things through, and after five years in Izmir, Turkey, I feel I have a more complex understanding of contemporary life. Certainly some creative problems have been unblocked. Now returned at least temporarily to London, I am interested in the developing Fringe theatre and the perennial problem of how to reinvigorate the traditional theatre. Radical politics and social problems are a continuing preoccupation.

In 1973 I revisited Australia as a guest of the first Australian National Playwrights' Conference.

(1982) In 1980 the problem referred to above was brought home to me most pointedly. My first new stage play for some years was produced by the State Theatre Company in Adelaide's Festival Centre to positive audience reaction and universally bad critical response. The deliberately theatrical, at times non-naturalistic and jokily satirical style affronted the critics. I'd thought the views of a passionately involved yet geographically and culturally distanced commentator would give Australian audiences an interestingly different slant on their society. The tone and content outraged the critics. The richness and complexity gained from living around the world were somehow excluded from the piece by the choice of a glib stylization, a real error of judgment. Welcome both in the U.K. and Australia as an experienced and dedicated craftsman in television writing, I have yet to develop in the theatre as I'd have wished to.

* * *

Born in Australia, now living in England, Alan Seymour is a cosmopolitan rather than a specifically "Australian" playwright. His earliest plays were for the most part set nominally in Australia, but the setting might have been anywhere. The swamp where two elderly sisters and their servant perform weird experiments in *Swamp Creatures* is supposedly "a dank and fertile part of the Australian bush," but there is no hint of gum leaves, however rank and decayed, in the grim setting. Donny Johnson, the Don Juan hero of the play *Donny Johnson*, could be a pop singer anywhere; it just happens that the play moves from a country town in New South Wales to Sydney. Since Seymour left Australia in 1961, one stage play, *A Break in the Music*, has returned to Australia to deal with family memories of life there in the 1930's and 1940's, but for the rest he has ranged widely. His short play *The Gaiety of Nations* took up the theme of Vietnam; his novel *The Coming Self-Destruction of the United States of America* deals with race conflicts in the U.S., and his television plays have covered a wide range of countries and situations.

Risking over-simplification, one might say that Seymour's plays fall into two broad categories, sometimes of course overlapping: on the one hand, compassionate but comic-satiric observation of ordinary people, plays that are convincingly "real"; and on the other hand, plays which are grotesque, macabre, occasionally bordering on the grand guignol, and with characters larger than life. Included in the first type would be the delightful television drama *And It Wasn't Just the Feathers*, about the short-lived relationship between a frightened, lonely old woman with a passion for feathers, and a tough, drifting young man, and the two specifically Australian plays *A Break in the Music* and *The One Day of the Year*.

The One Day of the Year, though an early play, is still probably Seymour's most important work, and it has become part of Australian theatrical and social history. "The one day of the year" is Anzac Day, 25 April, when Australians traditionally mourn their war dead. For Alf Cook, returned soldier, the day is sacred, fraught with implications of courage, mateship, masculinity; it is the day when, marching with old comrades, he is no longer an ordinary little man who drives a lift but someone of importance, once more part of a group, "They make a fuss of y'for once. The speeches and the march . . . and y're all mates." For his son Hughie, now a university student and ironically becoming estranged from his parents by the education they have struggled to give him, the Day is also, though he only half comprehends this, a symbol—a symbol of all that he is struggling to free himself from in his working-class background. Hughie comes into violent conflicts with his father when he and Jan, a girlfriend from a higher social level, collaborate to produce an article and pictures for the university newspaper; the subject is Anzac Day, and the message, loud and clear through Hughie's photographs of drunken "old diggers," is that the real significance of the so-called day of mourning is that it is an excuse for an almost national booze-up. The play comes to a slightly sentimental conclusion, suggesting that though Alf cannot change, he has gained greater insight into himself, and Hughie for his part has learned a little more tolerance of the father he loves and in some ways resembles. Seymour presents with great insight the strengths and weaknesses of each point of view; the dream as well as the drunkenness in Alf's concept of Anzac Day, and, in Hughie's, idealism combined with lack of understanding and compassion for what he has not experienced, and, of course, the need of youth to assert itself and its values. *The One Day of the Year* is basically not a play about Anzac Day or even conflicting ideas of nationalism, but the conflict of generations, heightened by disparity in education. On its first production the play roused considerable indignation, mostly from older Australians who felt with some justice that the sacred nature of Anzac Day had been assailed. In fact, *The One Day of the Year* is dramatically weighted in favour of the older, more colourful "lower class" characters, Alf, his taciturn wife Dot, and Wacka, the only real Anzac in the play; against these, the better-educated Hughie is pallid and almost priggish, his socially superior girlfriend Jan frankly unreal. Alf, Wacka, and Dot have the advantage of a distinctive idiom—Alf with his intolerable reiteration of "I'm a bloody Australian . . ." which, with all its implications of unthinking complacency, is turned against him when Jan tells him sweetly, "You're so right, Mr. Cook." The automatic invitation, "'ave a cuppa tea" has comedy, kindliness—and finally the horrors of strangling, inescapable banality.

The second category of Seymour plays could be represented by such dramas as *The Shattering* (unproduced), *Donny Johnson*, and *Swamp Creatures*. In *Swamp Creatures* two sisters and their servant mate different species of animals, producing obscene monsters which prowl through the swamps at night and finally turn on the human beings who made them. It is a slow, highly theatrical revelation of horrors which also carries a message, clearly embedded in the symbolism, a message a good deal less hackneyed when Seymour wrote the play than it is now; that science may in the end turn and rend its creator.

As with most writers, certain characteristic themes and forms of expression recur in Seymour's plays. There is for instance a touch of caricature about many of his best characters, a surprising number of whom are older women, very like Dot Cook in *The One Day of the Year*. Seymour's plays for the most part end in one of two ways: with the main characters trapped unwillingly in some painful situation (*The One Day of the Year*, *Donny Johnson*, *Swamp Creatures*, the unproduced *Screams from a Dark Cellar*) or else in Pinter-like isolation (*A Winter Passion*, *And It Wasn't Just the Feathers*, *The Shattering*). Seymour has himself pointed out two recurring motifs, the conflict of generations which occurs in most of his plays, and the less frequent but still observably repeated situation of someone being kidnapped.

The Float, according to Seymour, is concerned with "the interaction of public and private in people's lives," and its climax is the dismissal of a fictional head of government, Ruff Mottram—a glance back at the controversial sacking of the Australian prime minister, Gough Whitlam, in 1975. The play had a mixed reception in Australia, its bleak portrayal of Australian society being, possibly, a contributing cause.

Some of Seymour's best drama writing has been for television, and particularly noteworthy are his sensitive adaptations of the Jean Rhys stories *The Lotus*, *Tigers Are Better-Looking*, and *Outside the Machine*, and of *The Narnia Chronicles* by C.S. Lewis. He is also a novelist, a knowledgeable and perceptive drama critic, and the author of many short stories and articles.

—Alrene Sykes

SHAFFER, Anthony (Joshua). British. Born in Liverpool, Lancashire, 15 May 1926; twin brother of Peter Shaffer, *q.v.* Educated at St. Paul's School, London; Trinity College, Cambridge (co-editor, *Granta*), graduated 1950. Conscript coalminer, Kent and Yorkshire, 1944–47. Married 1) Carolyn Soley, two daughters; 2) the actress Diane Cilento in 1985. Barrister, 1951–55; journalist, 1956–58; partner in advertising film production agency, 1959–69. Recipient: Tony award, 1971; Mystery Writers of America Edgar Allan Poe award, for screenplay, 1973. Lives in Wiltshire. Agent: Peters, Fraser, and Dunlop Group, 503–504 The Chambers, Chelsea Harbour, Lots Road, London SW10 0XF, England.

PUBLICATIONS

Plays

The Savage Parade (produced London, 1963; as *This Savage Parade*, produced London, 1987).
Sleuth (produced London and New York, 1970). New York, Dodd Mead, 1970; London, Calder and Boyars, 1971.
Murderer (produced Brighton and London, 1975). London, Boyars, 1979.
Widow's Weeds (produced Brisbane, Queensland, 1977; Plymouth, 1987).
Whodunnit (as *The Case of the Oily Levantine*, produced Guildford, Surrey, 1977; London, 1979; revised version, as *Whodunnit*, produced New York, 1982; Brighton, 1987). New York, French, 1983.

Screenplays: *Mr. Forbush and the Penguins*, 1971; *Frenzy*, 1972; *Sleuth*, 1973; *The Wicker Man*, 1974; *Masada*, 1974; *The Moonstone*, 1975; *Death on the Nile*, 1978; *Absolution*, 1981; *Evil Under the Sun*, 1982; *Appointment with Death*, 1988.

Television Play: *Pig in the Middle*.

Novels

How Doth the Little Crocodile? (as Peter Antony, with Peter Shaffer). London, Evans, 1952; as Peter and Anthony Shaffer, New York, Macmillan, 1957.
Withered Murder, with Peter Shaffer. London, Gollancz, 1955; New York, Macmillan, 1956.
The Wicker Man (novelization of screenplay), with Robin Hardy. New York, Crown, 1978; London, Hamlyn, 1979.
Absolution (novelization of screenplay). London, Corgi, 1979.

*   *   *

It is not often that a writer has the opportunity to create a literary fashion and even a new genre, but theatrical thrillers and mysteries can legitimately be divided into pre-*Sleuth* and post-*Sleuth*, indicating more than their date of composition. The traditional stage or film mystery is a variant on the classic English Country House mystery novel, a whodunnit in which a crime is committed and the audience tries to guess which of several suspects is the criminal, while the author carefully directs our suspicions in the wrong directions. In *Sleuth* Anthony Shaffer created the whodunwhat, where not only the identity of the criminal but the nature of the crime—indeed, the reality and reliability of everything we've seen with our own eyes—is part of the mystery.

Sleuth begins in an orthodox way, as a man enlists the aid of his wife's lover in a complex plot to rob himself; this way lover and wife can afford to run off, husband will be free to marry his own mistress, and the insurance company will pay for everything. No sooner has the audience settled in to see whether they'll pull it off and whether one will doublecross the other than we discover that this isn't what has been going on at all; the whole project is a convoluted cover for a murder. And no sooner is that fact absorbed than we are told that the murder we thought we watched happening didn't really happen. (Oh yes it did, we're told a moment later. Oh no it didn't, we're shown a bit after that.) A policeman has come to arrest the murderer. (Oh no he hasn't. Oh yes he has.) In fact, a second murder entirely has happened offstage (Oh no . . .) and the murderer has planted clues implicating the innocent party, which he dares him to find because the police are really coming this time (Oh no . . .). Even the program and cast list can't be trusted.

Of course *Sleuth* has its antecedents, among them Patrick Hamilton's *Gas Light* and the Hitchcock film *Suspicion* (Is the man really trying to kill his wife or is she imagining it?) and the Clouzot film *Diabolique* (Who of the three main characters are the murderers and who the victims?). But Shaffer concentrates and multiplies the questions and red herrings, and dresses them in an entertaining mix of psychology (the husband is a compulsive games-player), social comment (husband is a snob, lover working class), in-jokes (husband writes mysteries of the classic whodunnit kind), and black humor (one plot twist somehow requires a character to dress as a clown). And everything moves so quickly and effortlessly that there is added delight in the author's skill and audacity in so repeatedly confusing us. *Sleuth* was an immense worldwide success that quickly bred dozens of other thrillers of the new genre, notable among them Ira Levin's *Deathtrap* and Richard Harris's *The Business of Murder*. The Agatha Christie-type whodunnit, with corpses who didn't get up again and a murderer who was Someone In This Room, seemed hopelessly old-fashioned when compared to plays in which the audience had to figure out what was really happening before moving on to the question of who was guilty.

Oddly, Shaffer's own follow-ups in the genre he created are rather limp. *Murderer* opens with a 30-minute silent sequence during which we watch a particularly gruesome murder and dismemberment, followed by the arrival of a policeman, the discovery of the grisly evidence and the confession of the criminal—only to be told then that it was all a fake, the pastime of a crime buff reenacting a famous murder. So far, so good, but when the buff then turns his hand to an actual murder, the plot twists are less inevitable and less delightful than in *Sleuth*. Two actual murders take place, one with the wrong victim and one with the wrong murderer, but everything seems forced and unlikely, and requires extensive advance set-ups or after-the-fact explanations. It is ultimately an unpleasant play, working too hard to shock and surprise, and thus removing the pleasure of shock and surprise.

The Case of the Oily Levantine (revised for America as *Whodunnit*) is openly labelled "A Comedy Thriller," and is lighter and more entertaining than *Murderer* though sometimes just as strained and self-conscious. Its first act is a high-spirited parody of the whodunnit genre, with the title character blackmailing everyone in sight—titled dowager, retired officer, debutante, even the butler—until an unidentified one of them murders him. The best touch, with some of *Sleuth*'s flair, is that we periodically hear the disguised voice of the murderer giving teasing clues; it will refer, for example, to lighting a cigarette, only to have each character onstage light up as our hope of catching the criminal fades. As one might predict by now, Act 2 begins with the discovery that nothing we saw in Act 1 was real, except the murder. This twist owes a debt to the 1973 film *The Last of Sheila*, and the working-out

of the new version of the murder is unconvincing and unengrossing, despite forced in-jokes both literary and theatrical. There is a satisfying final joke, though, as the solution is shown to be a twist on one of the traditional whodunnit's oldest clichés.

Shaffer's continuing skill as a craftsman of mystery and thrills is seen in his film work, notably for the film version of *Sleuth* and Hitchcock's *Frenzy*. In the theatre, however, his reputation must rest on *Sleuth* and on the genre it created.

—Gerald M. Berkowitz

SHAFFER, Peter (Levin). British. Born in Liverpool, Lancashire, 15 May 1926; twin brother of Anthony Shaffer, *q.v.* Educated at a preparatory school in Liverpool; Hall School, London; St. Paul's School, London; Trinity College, Cambridge (co-editor, *Granta*), 1947–50, B.A. in history 1950. Conscript coalminer, Chislet colliery, Kent, 1944–47. Worked in Doubleday bookstore, an airline terminal, at Grand Central Station, Lord and Taylors department store, and in the acquisition department, New York Public Library, all New York, 1951–54; staff member, Boosey and Hawkes, music publishers, London, 1954–55; literary critic, *Truth*, London, 1956–57; music critic, *Time and Tide*, London, 1961–62. Recipient: *Evening Standard* award, 1958, 1980, 1988; New York Drama Critics Circle award, 1960, 1975; Tony award, 1975, 1981; Outer Critics Circle award, 1981; Vernon Rice award, 1981; New York Film Critics Circle award, 1984; Los Angeles Film Critics Association award, 1984; Oscar, for screenplay, 1985; Hamburg Shakespeare prize, 1989. C.B.E. (Commander, Order of the British Empire), 1987. Lives in New York City. Agent: Macnaughton Lowe Representation, 200 Fulham Road, London SW10 9PN, England; or, Robert Lantz, The Lantz Office, 888 Seventh Avenue, New York, New York 10106, U.S.A.

PUBLICATIONS

Plays

Five Finger Exercise (produced London, 1958; New York, 1959). London, Hamish Hamilton, 1958; New York, Harcourt Brace, 1959.
The Private Ear, and The Public Eye (produced London, 1962; New York, 1963). London, Hamish Hamilton, 1962; New York, Stein and Day, 1964.
The Merry Roosters' Panto, music and lyrics by Stanley Myers and Steven Vinaver (produced London, 1963; as *It's about Cinderella*, produced London, 1969).
Sketch in *The Establishment* (produced New York, 1963).
The Royal Hunt of the Sun: A Play Concerning the Conquest of Peru (produced Chichester and London, 1964; New York, 1965). London, Hamish Hamilton, and New York, Stein and Day, 1965.
Black Comedy (produced Chichester, 1965; London, 1966; New York, 1967). Included in *Black Comedy, Including White Lies*, 1967.
White Lies (produced New York, 1967). Included in *Black Comedy, Including White Lies*, 1967; as *White Liars* (pro-

duced London, 1968), London, French, 1967; revised version (produced London and New York, 1976), French, 1976.

Black Comedy, Including White Lies: Two Plays. New York, Stein and Day, 1967; as *White Liars, Black Comedy: Two Plays*, London, Hamish Hamilton, 1968.

Shrivings (as *The Battle of Shrivings*, produced London, 1970; revised version, as *Shrivings*, produced York, 1975). London, Deutsch, 1974; with *Equus*, New York, Atheneum, 1974.

Equus (produced London, 1973; New York, 1974). London, Deutsch, 1973; with *Shrivings*, New York, Atheneum, 1974.

Amadeus (produced London, 1979). London, Deutsch, 1980; revised version (produced New York, 1980; London, 1981), New York, Harper, and London, Penguin, 1981.

The Collected Plays of Peter Shaffer (revised texts; includes *Five Finger Exercise, The Private Ear, The Public Eye, The Royal Hunt of the Sun, White Liars, Black Comedy, Equus, Shrivings, Amadeus*). New York, Harmony, 1982.

Black Mischief (produced Bristol, 1983).

Yonadab (produced London, 1985).

Lettice and Lovage (produced Bath and London, 1987; revised version, produced London, 1988; New York, 1990). London, Deutsch, 1988; New York, Harper and Row, 1990.

Whom Do I Have the Honour of Addressing? (broadcast 1989). London, Deutsch, 1990.

The Gift of the Gorgon (produced London, 1992).

Screenplays: *Lord of the Flies*, with Peter Brook, 1963; *The Public Eye (Follow Me!)*, 1972; *Equus*, 1977; *Amadeus*, 1984.

Radio Plays: *Alexander the Corrector*, 1946; *The Prodigal Father*, 1957; *Whom Do I Have the Honour of Addressing?*, 1989.

Television Plays: *The Salt Land*, 1955; *Balance of Terror*, 1957.

Novels

The Woman in the Wardrobe (as Peter Antony). London, Evans, 1951.

How Doth the Little Crocodile? (as Peter Antony, with Anthony Shaffer). London, Evans, 1952; as Peter and Anthony Shaffer, New York, Macmillan, 1957.

Withered Murder, with Anthony Shaffer. London, Gollancz, 1955; New York, Macmillan, 1956.

*

Critical Studies: *Peter Shaffer* by John Russell Taylor, London, Longman, 1974; *Peter Shaffer* by Dennis A. Klein, Boston, Twayne, 1979; *File on Shaffer* edited by Virginia Cooke and Malcolm Page, London, Methuen, 1987; *Peter Shaffer: Roles, Rites and Rituals in the Theater* by Gene A. Plunka, Teaneck, New Jersey, Fairleigh Dickinson University Press, 1988.

* * *

In 1958, when Peter Shaffer's *Five Finger Exercise* achieved critical acclaim in London, it was difficult to reconcile its middle-class tone and formal elements with the breed of theatre of Britain's Angry Young Men then flourishing. A well-made drawing-room drama set in a weekend cottage in

Suffolk, *Five Finger Exercise* probed the Harringtons' marital strife and its devastating effects upon their nervous, literary son and the secretive, young German tutor brought into the household to educate their volatile 14-year-old-daughter. The intricately wrought monologues of the five characters are played and replayed against a background of music. The family relationships are dangerously out of balance and the intrusion of the outsider threatens to destroy them. Only after numerous variations of the same theme does the play find resolution.

Five Finger Exercise placed Shaffer in the traditions of the well-made play while he was also compared briefly with John Osborne and Harold Pinter. Other plays by Shaffer show his flair for the highly theatrical spectacle and epic theatre. His use of framing and narration derive from dramatists such as Thornton Wilder, Tennessee Williams, Robert Bolt, and Bertolt Brecht. His narrators control the prism through which the work is viewed and provide a structure which offers his play of intellect a wider range.

Shaffer's use of the conventions of presentational aesthetics emerge clearly in *The Royal Hunt of the Sun, Equus, Amadeus*, and *Yonadab*. His narrators interrupt the play's action and dart backwards and forwards, violating the conventions of the fourth wall and addressing the audience directly, inviting them to participate in the experience of epic theatre as it was articulated by Brecht. The epic mode provides solutions to some of the technical problems apparent in *Five Finger Exercise* and very much evident in *Shrivings*, a play marred by too much ideological talkiness and an inadequate objective correlative for the play's ideas. His brilliantly conceived narrators—Old Martin in *The Royal Hunt of the Sun*, the analyst Dysart in *Equus*, Salieri in *Amadeus*, and Yonadab in the eponymous play—rivet the audience's attention, offering a self-conscious examination of the play's narration and story line without diminishing its nakedly dramatic elements.

His two recent works, the stage play *Lettice and Lovage* and the play for broadcast *Whom Do I Have the Honour Of Addressing?*, more nearly resemble his comedies of the 1960's. Abandoning the conventions of the frame and epic theatre, they nonetheless display his interest in narrative technique.

Lettice, a whimsical tour guide, has been hired by the Preservation Trust (a thinly disguised National Trust) to show parties around Britain's historical houses. A devotee of history and invention, Lettice's creative spirit is too restless to allow her merely to recite her official text. The play opens with her regaling a group of tourists with stories about a great staircase constructed from Tudor oak that dominates the grand hall of the all-too-dreary Fustian House. After several more recitations, she constructs ever more melodramatic accounts of the stairs and the house's inhabitants, introducing the Virgin Queen herself, Gloriana, into her tale. She thrives on her own theatrical romanticizing and role-playing, deviating wildly from historical fact in her desperate attempts to make one of the dullest Elizabethan houses in England more interesting. The first act concludes with her being fired by the severe, duty-bound Lotte. Act II finds Lotte befriending Lettice, and the two women quaff Lovage, an herbal brew, enlarging, enlivening, and enlightening their souls, spirits, and eyes as they share their pasts and rebel against the drabness of their lives. In the third act, Lettice coaxes her apparent accuser, Lotte, into allowing her to replay their enactment of Charles the First's beheading in front of Bardolph, an attorney who has come to defend Lettice from Lotte's charges of attempted murder. In both the first and third act, Shaffer breaks the fourth wall with entrances from the auditorium and with addresses to both an on-stage and off-stage audience. Throughout the play, there are readings of letters as well as constant variations upon an official, transcribed text. Both devices thicken the play's texture. In all these small ways, Shaffer manipulates techniques of narrative to interrupt the dramatic mode.

Angela Parsons, the deeply self-deluded monologist of his radio play *Whom Do I Have the Honour of Addressing?*, similarly interweaves readings of her correspondence into her stage narration as she speaks her supposed last and only words about her life and death into a tape-recorder. Shaffer sets both of these later works in the present and abandons the use of flashbacks and the presence of a narrator. In the radio play, he offers another level of mediation of the play's dramatic action through the device of the tape-recorder used in a manner reminiscent of Beckett in *Krapp's Last Tape*.

Two other elements have been staples of almost all Shaffer's plays. Music is an integral aspect of their soundscape, and elements from detective fiction figure prominently in his treatment of plot and character. He served for a number of years as music critic for *Time and Tide* in London. Before he became a successful playwright, he co-authored two detective novels with his brother, Anthony Shaffer, author of *Sleuth*. Shaffer's light and playful one-act play *The Public Eye* presents Julian Christoforou, a raisin-and-yogurt-eating private eye, who meddles in the domestic life of Charles and Belinda Sidley, prying in a detective-like way into their souls and psyches. Ultimately, this British eccentric teaches the couple how to experience love again and how to play. Shaffer uses the character of the detective and the devices of detective fiction—disguised identities, the dreary business of sleuthing, the perfunctory discovery scene, the interrogation scene, the establishing of fees—to structure his frivolous one-act play. Many of the same devices can be found in Shaffer's superbly crafted farce *Black Comedy* as well as in *Equus*, *Amadeus*, *Lettice and Lovage*, and *Whom Do I Have the Honour of Addressing?*

Black Comedy depends for its comic effect on a clever theatrical trick of the eye and mind. While the stage is lit, its fictive world is dark; when the stage is black, the characters are inhabiting a fully lit fictive world. Because of this simple reversal, the audience relishes the delight of watching a stage full of characters groping around in the darkness but actually flooded with light as a result of a blown fuse in the London flat of Brindsley Miller in early evening. Miller, a young sculptor, is trying to impress his debutante fiancée's father, Colonel Melkett, by selling one of his sculptures to an elderly, deaf millionaire art collector. To insure the evening's success, Brindsley and his fiancée have swiped numerous pieces of elegant Regency furniture from the flat of his modish neighbor, a closet homosexual and owner of an antique china shop. As the evening advances towards its complete dissolution, Brindsley is forced to drag the furniture from his apartment back to its owner's, right before the darkened eyes of the owner, his father-in-law-to-be, his mistress who has paid a surprise visit, a spinster, his alcoholic upstairs neighbor, and his silly, spoilt fiancée. The scene is hilarious. Comic timing is essential to its success. Brindsley's misstep which causes him to fall neatly down the entire flight of stairs as he attempts to return calmly from his bedroom requires that the actor display no trace of the knowledge that he is facing an uncomfortable fall. The moment when Brindsley passes under the outstretched arms of his father-in-law and fiancée as they are exchanging a glass of lemonade and he is holding a Regency chair in one hand and a Wedgwood bowl in the other is another brilliant comic moment. All the deft timing of exits and entrances, sudden falls, rapid movements of almost all

the major pieces of stage furniture, combined with the sharp white light which glaringly exposes the goings-on to the audience, testify to the importance of the genre of detective fiction and film in Shaffer's imagination. The exposed light bulb and the interrogation scenes of detective fiction probably contributed to the game of hide-and-seek executed in this delightful farce.

In *Amadeus* the debt is even more apparent. The play opens with the word "assassin" hissed and savagely whispered by the chorus of rumour on the stage, rising to a crescendo, and punctuated with the names of Mozart and Salieri. By the end of the second scene Salieri, the narrator, promises the audience one final performance, to be entitled, "The Death of Mozart; or, Did I Do It?" The audience is plunged into a world of a whodunnit in which they are the detective and Salieri is the villain. Shaffer's revised version clarified the London version's dramatic structure, implicating Salieri more directly in Mozart's death and replacing Greybig with Salieri as the Masked Figure and Messenger of Death who appears to Mozart in the penultimate scene of the play.

Yonadab continues in this tradition. Yonadab, the cousin of Amnon and Absalom, David's sons, is the treacherous confidant of both brothers. He plays the one against the other, abetting the scene of Tamar's incestuous rape by her half-brother Amnon and later assisting Absalom in the slaying of Amnon. He is also the reporter of the lurid scene to the audience. Again, the play's focus on reporters and news, on a lurid tale of intrigue, ambition, incest, and murder, on the cunning ways such plots transpire, and on the way villains are punished all reflect the sure hand of a writer familiar with detective fiction.

In both *Lettice and Lovage* and *Whom Do I Have the Honour of Addressing?* the protagonists are guilty of assault; in one case, accidentally, in the other, the justifiable albeit violent reaction to the sordid happenings resulting from Angela's infatuation with a Hollywood stage idol half her age. Both plays can be seen as the confessions of confused, romantic souls—their crimes being an over-active imagination in a colourless world.

Music is also an essential aspect of Shaffer's theatrical talent. In *White Lies*, later revised as *White Liars*, Shaffer used a tape-recording to surround the audience with the inner monologues and dialogues of Sophie, his fortune-telling protagonist. In *The Private Ear* Bob's great passion is music and the gramophone; his failed romance is with a girl he met at a concert. *Five Finger Exercise* depends on the music of Bach and Brahms and the stuck recording of a gramophone repeating over and over a portion from Mahler's Symphony No. 4 to dramatize the suicide attempt of the young German tutor whose father's participation in the Nazi party has driven him to England. Shaffer described *The Royal Hunt of the Sun*'s brilliant score written by Marc Wilkinson: "To me its most memorable items are the exquisitely doleful lament which opens Act II, and, most amazing of all, the final Chant of Resurrection, to be whined and whispered, howled and hooted, over Atahuallpa's body in the darkness, before the last sunrise of the Inca Empire." *Amadeus* soars with the music of Mozart and Salieri and a score that reflects how Salieri probably imagined Mozart's music. *Lettice and Lovage* opens with lugubrious Elizabethan music. In its final farcical act, Bardolph is marching about the stage banging upon an invisible drum and calling out his "PAM-TITITI-PAMS," joined by Lettice's soprano doubling of his cries in imitation of the martial music that accompanied King Charles I's execution in 1649.

Finally, Shaffer is a playwright of ideas. Perhaps his eloquent exposition of them failed in *Shrivings*, but the battle between Dysart and Alan Strang in *Equus*, Pizarro and Atahuallpa in *The Royal Hunt of the Sun*, Salieri and Mozart in *Amadeus*, and Yonadab and David's brothers all intelligently explore man's struggle for meaning in a world in which death dominates and religion holds no salvation. Alan Strang, the boy who blinded six horses, knows a savage god; Atahuallpa is the Son of the Sun God; Pizarro has no faith, nor, until the very end, love or passion. East and west collide; faithfulness is played against faithlessness; passion and violence against impotence; passivity and Eastern love against skepticism and violence; and passionate creativity against classical balance and duty.

Some have criticized Shaffer's recent plays for owing too much of their success to the brilliance of their leading actors and too little to their themes and plots. *Lettice and Lovage* was written for Maggie Smith who brilliantly captured Lettice's extravagance of nature. The third act is slightly forced, even in its revised version. Originally the play concluded with Lettice and Lotte setting out to bomb a select number of London's most abominable post-World War II municipal monstrosities. In the revised version, they set out to create their own "E.N.D. Tours" to London's aesthetically disgusting buildings. The radio play also exploits Dame Judi Dench's voice and relies upon the eccentricities of its protagonist and the lurid details of its close to carry it. But both are plays for women, a departure for Shaffer whose earlier plays have lacked major women's roles, and both have a whimsicality and winning poignancy.

It is to Shaffer's credit that he excels in creating plays with stunning spectacles, lavish soundscapes, dramatic action, and a powerful artillery of rhetoric as well as more theatrically modest ones in which it is the delicious play of words and invention that charms us.

—Carol Simpson Stern

SHANGE, Ntozake. American. Born Paulette Williams in Trenton, New Jersey, 18 October 1948; took name Ntozake Shange in 1971. Educated at schools in St. Louis and New Jersey; Barnard College, New York, 1966–70, B.A. (cum laude) in American studies 1970; University of Southern California, Los Angeles, 1971–73, M.A. in American studies 1973. Married David Murray in 1977 (2nd marriage; divorced); one daughter. Faculty member, Sonoma State College, Rohnert Park, California, 1973–75, Mills College, Oakland, California, 1975, City College, New York, 1975, and Douglass College, New Brunswick, New Jersey, 1978. Since 1983 associate professor of drama, University of Houston. Artist-in-residence, Equinox Theatre, Houston, from 1981, and New Jersey State Council on the Arts. Recipient: New York Drama Critics Circle award, 1977; Obie award, 1977, 1980; Columbia University medal of excellence, 1981; Los Angeles *Times* award, 1981; Guggenheim fellowship, 1981. Address: Department of Drama, University of Houston–University Park, 4800 Calhoun Road, Houston, Texas 77004, U.S.A.

PUBLICATIONS

Plays

For Colored Girls Who Have Considered Suicide When the Rainbow Is Enuf (produced New York, 1975; London, 1980). San Lorenzo, California, Shameless Hussy Press, 1976; revised version, New York, Macmillan, 1977; London, Eyre Methuen, 1978.

A Photograph: Lovers-in-Motion (as *A Photograph: A Still Life with Shadows*, *A Photograph: A Study of Cruelty*, produced New York, 1977; revised version, as *A Photograph: Lovers-in-Motion*, also director: produced Houston, 1979). New York, French, 1981.

Where the Mississippi Meets the Amazon, with Thulani Nkabinda and Jessica Hagedorn (produced New York, 1977).

Spell #7 (produced New York, 1979; London, 1985). Included in *Three Pieces*, 1981; published separately, London, Methuen, 1985.

Black and White Two-Dimensional Planes (produced New York, 1979).

Boogie Woogie Landscapes (produced on tour, 1980). Included in *Three Pieces*, 1981.

Mother Courage and Her Children, adaptation of a play by Brecht (produced New York, 1980).

From Okra to Greens: A Different Kinda Love Story (as *Mouths* produced New York, 1981; as *From Okra to Greens*, in *Three for a Full Moon*, produced Los Angeles, 1982). New York, French, 1983.

Three Pieces: Spell #7, A Photograph: Lovers-in-Motion, Boogie Woogie Landscapes. New York, St. Martin's Press, 1981.

Three for a Full Moon, and Bocas (produced Los Angeles, 1982).

Educating Rita, adaptation of the play by Willy Russell (produced Atlanta, 1983).

Three Views of Mt. Fuji (produced New York, 1987).

Betsey Brown, adaptation of her own novel, with Emily Mann, music by Baikida Carroll, lyrics by Shange, Mann, and Carroll (also director: produced Philadelphia, 1989).

The Love Space Demands: A Continuing Saga (produced London, 1992). New York, St. Martin's Press, 1991; included in *Plays: One*, 1992.

Plays: One (includes *For Colored Girls Who Have Considered Suicide When the Rainbow Is Enuf*, *Spell #7*, *I Heard Eric Dolphy in His Eyes*, *The Love Space Demands: A Continuing Saga*). London, Methuen, 1992.

Novels

Sassafrass: A Novella. San Lorenzo, California, Shameless Hussy Press, 1977.

Sassafrass, Cypress and Indigo. New York, St. Martin's Press, 1982; London, Methuen, 1983.

Betsey Brown. New York, St. Martin's Press, and London, Methuen, 1985.

Verse

Melissa and Smith. St. Paul, Bookslinger, 1976.

Natural Disasters and Other Festive Occasions. San Francisco, Heirs, 1977.

Nappy Edges. New York, St. Martin's Press, 1978; London, Methuen, 1987.

A Daughter's Geography. New York, St. Martin's Press, 1983; London, Methuen, 1985.

From Okra to Greens: Poems. St. Paul, Coffee House Press, 1984.

Ridin' the Moon West in Texas: Word Paintings. New York, St. Martin's Press, 1988.

Other

See No Evil: Prefaces, Essays, and Accounts 1976–1983. San Francisco, Momo's Press, 1984.

*

Theatrical Activities:

Director: **Plays**—*The Mighty Gents* by Richard Wesley, New York, 1979; *The Spirit of Sojourner Truth* by Bernice Reagon and June Jordan, 1979; *A Photograph: Lovers-in-Motion*, Houston, 1979; *Betsey Brown*, Philadelphia, 1989.

Actor: **Plays**—The Lady in Orange in *For Colored Girls Who Have Considered Suicide When the Rainbow Is Enuf*, New York, 1976; in *Where the Mississippi Meets the Amazon*, New York, 1977; in *Mouths*, New York, 1981.

* * *

The production of *For Colored Girls Who Have Considered Suicide When the Rainbow Is Enuf* established Ntozake Shange as a major force in American theatre. True to the Xhosa name she had received in 1971, she was indeed "one who brings her own things" and "walks with lions." Shange has now moved from the spotlight, but she remains one of the finest English-language verse dramatists, forging a poetry compelling in both its social immediacy and its broad vision.

For Colored Girls is a collage of poems mixed with song and dance celebrating the lives of black girls who previously had not been considered a fit subject for dramatic presentation. Structured around rhythmic pulses, the play charts the passage from the self-conscious bravado of "we waz grown," proclaimed at the moment of high school graduation and loss of virginity, through a variety of alternatively funny and painful experiences with men, to the hard-gained knowledge of one's self-worth found in the closing affirmation, "i found god in myself & i loved her fiercely." Belying the women's anguish and seeming predilection towards the negative is their willingness to dance—dance and music being metaphors for the courage to venture into the world with grace, to seek intimate connections with others, and to celebrate the nearly limitless potentiality of life.

The play unlocked emotional doors rarely touched in American theatre. For many women, experiencing a performance became a quasi-religious moment in which some of their deepest feelings were acknowledged and a healing of wounds achieved. For countless other audiences it energized a highly charged debate about male-female relationships and the image of black men in American literature.

Shange's subsequent plays *A Photograph: Lovers-in-Motion* and *Boogie Woogie Landscapes* continue to use a rites-of-passage theme, but the exploration is carried forth within a more clearly delineated social context and a more conventional dramatic form. Thus, in *A Photograph* the male protagonist's identification with both Alexandre Dumas père and the illegitimate Dumas fils serves as a metaphor for his confusion, and the shedding of this fantasy is an indication of the extent to which he moves towards a healthier creative vision. Similarly, Layla in *Boogie Woogie Landscapes* relives her own emotional geography in order to reconcile the possibility of personal love with social struggle. But given the ways in which society distorts personality, love is tenuous, more often a momentary grasping for, rather than solid achievement of, unity.

With *Spell #7* the playwright moves further into the public arena by tackling the iconography of the "nigger." Manipulating the power of music, minstrel performers banish a huge, all-seeing black-face mask along with their stage personae in order to create a safe space in which secret hopes, fears, and dreams may be articulated. But two confessions centering around the shattering of faith puncture the whimsical or contained quality of most of the fantasies and reveal an almost overwhelming anguish. Although the master of ceremonies intervenes to reassure the audience that it will enjoy his black magic, and although the actors conjure forth the joyous spirit of a black church with the chant, "bein colored and love it," the mask returns. In reading the play we are left to wonder whether the actors and audience have indeed enjoyed the freedom of their own definitions and/or whether Shange has performed a sleight of hand which simply allows the drama to end on a positive note. The answer lies finally in the extent to which the communion between actors and audience creates a countervailing force to the hideous minstrel mask and in the audience members' ability to find within their own lives resolutions to the play's purposeful contradictions.

The most recently published play, *From Okra to Greens: A Different Kinda Love Story*, explores further the intersection of the personal and the political. Present are the now-familiar Shange themes of nearly overwhelming brutalization balanced by the transcendence of dance-music-poetry. But significantly new is the shared articulation of many of these experiences by both a male and female protagonist and the effective merger of the personal and the political into a whole which allows them to move forward. Thus, the play closes with the couple bidding their "children" emerge from the ghettoes, bantustans, barrios, and favelas of the world to fight against the old men who would impose death, to dance in affirmation of their unbreakable bond with nature itself.

Within a black theatre tradition Shange seems to have been influenced most by Amiri Baraka and Adrienne Kennedy. Characteristic of her dramaturgy are an attack upon the English language which she as a black woman finds doubly oppressive; a self-consciousness as a writer linked to a determination to reclaim for oppressed peoples the right of self-definition; and a use of poetry, music, and dance to approximate the power of non-linear, supra-rational modes of experience. A poet, Shange brings to the theatre a commitment to it as a locus of eruptive, often contradictory, and potentially healing forces whose ultimate resolution lie beyond the performance space.

—Sandra L. Richards

———

SHANLEY, John Patrick. American. Born in New York City, 13 October 1950. Educated at New York University, B.S. 1977. Recipient: Oscar, 1987; Writers Guild of America award, 1987; Los Angeles Drama Critics Circle award, 1987. Agent: Esther Sherman, William Morris Agency, 1350 Avenue of the Americas, New York, New York 10019. Address: 630 Ninth Avenue, Suite 800, New York, New York 10036, U.S.A.

PUBLICATIONS

Plays

Saturday Night at the War (produced New York, 1978).
George and the Dragon (produced New York, 1979).
Welcome to the Moon and Other Plays (includes *The Red Coat, Down and Out, Let Us Go out into the Starry Night, Out West, A Lonely Impulse of Delight*) (produced New York, 1982). New York, Dramatists Play Service, 1985.
Danny and the Deep Blue Sea (produced Waterford, Connecticut, 1983; New York, 1984; London, 1985). New York, Dramatists Play Service, 1984.
Savage in Limbo (produced New York, 1985; London, 1987). New York, Dramatists Play Service, 1986.
the dreamer examines his pillow (produced Waterford, Connecticut, 1985; New York, 1986). New York, Dramatists Play Service, 1987.
Women of Manhattan (produced New York, 1986). New York, Dramatists Play Service, 1986.
All for Charity (produced New York, 1987).
Italian American Reconciliation (also director: produced New York, 1988). New York, Dramatists Play Service, 1989.
The Big Funk (produced New York, 1990). New York, Dramatists Play Service, 1991.
Beggars in the House of Plenty (produced New York, 1991). New York, Dramatists Play Service, 1992.
Thirteen by Shanley (includes *Danny and the Deep Blue Sea, The Red Coat, Down and Out, Let Us Go out into the Starry Night, Out West, A Lonely Impulse of Delight, Welcome to the Moon, Savage in Limbo, Women of Manhattan, the dreamer examines his pillow, Italian American Reconciliation, The Big Funk, Beggars in the House of Plenty*). New York, Applause, 1992.
What is this Everything? (produced New York, 1992).

Screenplays: *Moonstruck*, 1987; *Five Corners*, 1988; *The January Man*, 1989; *Joe Versus the Volcano*, 1990; *Alive*, 1993.

* * *

The theatre of John Patrick Shanley is primarily about the loss and pain caused by love. In Shanley's plays love leaves none of its converts with sufficient air; it robs people of options, stultifies, sends reason packing, and embraces suffering. People really suffer in Shanley's plays; they are primed for pain, they can't wait to taste its joys, and such longed-for suffering is fully orchestrated through the arrival of the protagonist, love. Love creates a state where everything diminishes other than the pain it generates. People seem to understand that they have lost something but love holds them in a delicious stupor; they seem not to know what has been lost and spend their days heaving, sighing, and breathing heavily.

Shanley has important strengths—in particular a wonderful ear for the sound of working-class Italian-Americans. He portrays the language as having too many syllables, adopting a flatfooted formality, a kind of hardhat existentialism. Probably nobody speaks like this:

Aldo: . . . a lot of people have an expression of this problem. They had something horrible for a long time, and then they get away from it, and then they miss it.

or like this:

Huey: I feel this pain that makes me weak. The pain is that place in me where I'm hurt from the divorce. . . . I

tried to go into the future and be new, but it don't work for me.

—*Italian American Reconciliation*

But, for all their verbal constructions and cadences with an authentic ring, for all their rhetorical poetry of loss and exhortation of grief and baying to the heavens, Shanley's characters inhabit a self-perpetuating prison. These protagonists have not found a way of moving past self-absorption into that place where the world transacts its mundane but necessary business.

Shanley's early collection *Welcome to the Moon and Other Plays* contains some seemingly uncertain, sometimes uncontrolled pieces, but they do display an engaging energy and a foreshadowing of both the strengths and weaknesses of his later works.

Down and Out is raw Shanley, a work consciously without subtext which comes at us from that cloudy lyricism fashioned by William Saroyan in his early plays. The allegorical figures are named Love and Poet. Love is fixing a dinner of water and beans when Poet arrives home sick and discouraged. He wanted a library book but the library was not open. A shrouded figure now comes to the house and demands his library card. Poet wants to write new poems but "I cannot write them. Because I have no pencil." Another shrouded figure holds out "Money! Money! Money!"

Love: Look how green it is! How green!
Poet: It's beautiful! Can I have it?
Figure: Give me your soul. Give me your soul.
Love: Never! Get out get out get out!

and later:

Poet: No one wants my poetry. The man in the newspaper said I am an untalented fool. The man in the newspaper was right. We are alone. Unknown. We live on beans.

But Love inspires the Poet:

Love: The darkest thing has come and led to a moment of despair. But look! See here! I am your Love who has never left you! I can turn a tiny lock and open up your soul again! (She opens the box, which is his soul. It plays music. The poet is bathed in a powerful light. He rises up.)

In *Let Us Go out into the Starry Night*, ghosts and monsters are chewing at the head of a tormented young man and clawing at his stomach. The man explains to the young woman who seeks him out that one of these monsters is the ghost of his mother.

Man: She doesn't look too bad today really. Some nights she visits me looking like a rotting side of beef and carrying a big knife.

They kiss and decide to merge their dreams:

Man: How did we get here?
Woman: We got here by being serious.

In *Welcome to the Moon* Stephen abandons his wife and returns to the Bronx, to a "lowdown Bronx bar." He confides in his old buddy, Vinnie, that he has never got over his girlfriend, Shirley, whom he hasn't seen for 14 years but whose memory has poisoned his marriage. Stephen breaks down and weeps and is shortly joined in his weeping by Ronny, another member of the old Bronx gang who has been trying to kill himself because of his own unrequited love. It is hard to establish where Shanley is positioning himself. His overlay of irony seems to be a defense against the expected charge of sentimentality. One is left suspecting that Shanley's characters are unable to deal with the world, that they need to surrender to that controlling creature Love who will mend all pencils, retrieve library cards, cook beans, and keep one from loneliness and suicide.

By 1988 Shanley had developed an almost seamless aesthetic. Huey, in *Italian American Reconciliation*, desperately wants to return to his former wife, Janice, who not only detested him but shot his dog and threatened him with the same gun. Janice is a nightmare and Huey has everything a man could want in sweet, gentle Teresa, but he is convinced that Janice took "his power to stand up and be a man and take. I want it back. I think Janice has it. I think she took that power from me, or it's sitting with her." Shanley seems to identify with Huey's belief system, his people seeing only themselves. Huey is blinded by his belief in the castrating powers of Janice; in an important sense Huey has created his Janice, a woman he can't possibly see. One has to question what kind of consuming love is taking place, how the world of the Bronx and of broken people is ever going to mend. Perhaps Shanley has to borrow Janice's gun and shoot love right out the door. But then what are we left with?

—Arthur Sainer

SHAW, Irwin. American. 1934–1984.
See 3rd edition, 1982.

SHAW, Robert (Archibald). British. 1927–1978.
See 2nd edition, 1977.

SHAWN, Wallace. American. Born in New York City, 12 November 1943; son of the editor William Shawn. Educated at the Dalton School, New York, 1948–57; Putney School, Vermont, 1958–61; Harvard University, Cambridge, Massachusetts, 1961–65, B.A. in history 1965; Magdalen College, Oxford, 1966–68, B.A. in philosophy, politics, and economics 1968, M.A.; studied acting with Katharine Sergava, New York, 1971. Lives with Deborah Eisenberg. English teacher, Indore Christian College, Madhya Pradesh, India, 1965–66; teacher of English, Latin, and drama, Church of Heavenly Rest Day School, New York, 1968–70; shipping clerk, Laurie Love Ltd., New York, 1974–75; Xerox machine operator, Hamilton Copy Center, New York, 1975–76. Recipient: Obie award, 1975, 1986, 1991; Guggenheim fellowship, 1978. Agent: Casarotto Ramsay Ltd., National House, 60–66 Wardour Street, London W1V 3HP, England.

PUBLICATIONS

Plays

Our Late Night (produced New York, 1975). New York, Targ, 1984.
In the Dark, music by Allen Shawn (also director: produced Lenox, Massachusetts, 1976).

A Thought in Three Parts (as *Three Short Plays: Summer Evening, The Youth Hostel, Mr. Frivolous*, produced New York, 1976; as *A Thought in Three Parts*, produced London, 1977). Published in *Wordplays 2*, New York, Performing Arts Journal Publications, 1982.
The Mandrake, adaptation of a play by Machiavelli (produced New York, 1977; as *Mandragola*, music and lyrics by Howard Goodall, produced London, 1984).
The Family Play (produced New York, 1978).
Marie and Bruce (produced London, 1979; New York, 1980). New York, Grove Press, 1980; with *My Dinner with André* (screenplay), London, Methuen, 1983.
My Dinner with André, with André Gregory (produced London, 1980).
My Dinner with André (screenplay), with André Gregory. New York, Grove Press, 1981; with *Marie and Bruce*, London, Methuen, 1983.
The Hotel Play (produced New York, 1981). New York, Dramatists Play Service, 1982.
Aunt Dan and Lemon (produced London and New York, 1985). London, Methuen, and New York, Grove Press, 1985.
The Fever (produced New York and London, 1991). New York, Farrar Straus, and London, Faber, 1991.

Screenplay: *My Dinner with André*, with André Gregory, 1981.

*

Theatrical Activities:
Director: **Play**—*In the Dark*, Lenox, Massachusetts, 1976.
Actor: **Plays**—in *Alice in Wonderland*, New York, 1974; Prologue and Siro in *The Mandrake*, New York, 1977; Ilya in *Chinchilla* by Robert David MacDonald, New York, 1979; in *My Dinner with André*, London, 1980; Father, Jasper, and Freddie in *Aunt Dan and Lemon*, London and New York, 1985; *The Fever*, New York and London, 1991. **Films**—*Manhattan*, 1979; *Starting Over*, 1979; *All That Jazz*, 1980; *Atlantic City*, 1980; *Simon*, 1980; *My Dinner with André*, 1981; *Lovesick*, 1983; *Strange Invaders*, 1983; *Deal of the Century*, 1983; *Micki and Maude*, 1984; *Crackers*, 1984; *The Bostonians*, 1984; *The Hotel New Hampshire*, 1984; *Heaven Help Us*, 1985; *Prick Up Your Ears*, 1987; *Radio Days*, 1987; *The Moderns*, 1989; *We're No Angels*, 1990; and other films. **Television**—*Saigon: Year of the Cat*, 1983.

* * *

Shock has always been one side-effect of Wallace Shawn's dramatic writing, a rather curious side-effect when one thinks of the man himself in his amiable and benign intelligence. Joint Stock's 1977 production of *A Thought in Three Parts* at London's ICA Theatre started the forces of oppression on a particularly merry chase. Within 24 hours of the play's opening there were calls for prosecution on the grounds of obscenity and there were detectives sitting in the audience. Within a week the Charity Commissioners had initiated an inquiry into the ICA's charitable status. Within two months, the Government had announced that it was setting up a committee to consider the law of obscenity generally, at the same time specifically declining to prosecute *A Thought in Three Parts*.

After the dust settled, the reputation of the three one-act plays that made up the evening was invisible for the outrage that had been engendered. Rarely had London's critics been so disturbed by a theatrical event, and that event showed the danger of taking sex seriously in the theatre. The clownish romping of such shows as *Oh! Calcutta!* had given way to something considerably more threatening.

A dangerous aura of violence hung over the evening despite the jokey comedy and naked sexual frolicking of the actors in the second of the plays, the one which caused the greatest outrage. Something more akin to horror than joy came through, and rather than real copulation there was real fear. The first part, *Summer Evening*, takes place in a hotel room in a foreign city where a man and a woman exchange trivial words about eating, reading, and card-playing. Underneath the conversation is the spectre of brutal sexuality, and phrases break through the trivia to reveal the real state of play: "I just had a picture. I thought of you strangling me."

Rather than viewing sex as communication, the second play analyses the essentially solitary experience of orgasm. The selfishness of much sexual gratification percolates through the distractions presented of oral foreplay, intercourse, and group masturbation in *The Youth Hostel*. Shawn compresses time and emotional responses so that the blinding number of orgasms signal changing relationships between five young people spending the night together. The comedy of the dialogue, in language suitable for *True Teenage Romances*, is a deceiving technique that sharpens the human isolation of his characters when their sexual energies are exhausted.

Mr. Frivolous, the final play, begins and remains with the isolation of an individual, an elegant man breakfasting alone in an elegant room. His monologue skates through idle sexual fantasy, from basic heterosexuality to images of gropes with a priest and the possibilities of bondage. Shawn's very public musings on sexuality are finally too dour to be erotic. He stimulates the mind, not the body.

Shawn first made an impact on the off-off-Broadway scene when André Gregory directed the play *Our Late Night* for the experimental company called the Manhattan Project. An obvious precursor to *A Thought in Three Parts*, the play dramatized the drifting unconscious thoughts of two young people quietly going to bed. Around the two there was a swirl of couples discussing sexuality, food, and other encounters.

Shawn's collaboration with Gregory on that production led to the remarkable play by Shawn and Gregory called *My Dinner with André*, which was made into a film by Louis Malle. Gregory had spent the best part of two decades exploring the expanding boundaries of the theatrical avant-garde, finally chasing the aesthetic experience into a forest in Poland, to the Findhorn community in Scotland, to India, Tibet, and the Sahara Desert. Shawn had spent those years consolidating a reputation as an actor in films with Woody Allen, and with such plays as *Marie and Bruce* which drew attention to him without intensifying the scandal.

The form of *My Dinner with André* is seductive and misleading. It pretends to be an account of an actual dinner that Shawn had with Gregory, "a man I'd been avoiding literally for years," and Shawn himself became the character who introduces and frames the play, indeed playing the part of Wally Shawn opposite Gregory's André in both the stage version and the film. The play's conflict is Shawn's New York rationality confronted with Gregory's telling of the "paratheatrical" activities he had had since quitting the theatre after directing *Our Late Night* in 1975.

No such dinner occurred, but the conversation actually took place, extended well beyond the 100 or so pages of the final script. Shawn and Gregory taped lengthy meetings where Gregory detailed his adventures and conclusions against the curious and sane encouragement of Shawn's scepticism. Gregory talked of the project he undertook in a Polish forest with 40 musicians, creating "experiences" with the encouragement of his friend the Polish director Jerzy Grotowski. He elaborated on his search by telling of a Japanese monk he befriended, and with whom he ate sand in the desert. Shawn responded that he liked electric blankets and that happiness could be a cup of cold coffee in which no cockroach had drowned during the night.

The piece is an aesthetic debate of great interest and value, and while the bulk of the ideological contribution is Gregory's, Gregory credits Shawn with the dramatic sensibility that shaped the debate and made the unfolding of the story so mesmerizing. It is Shawn's own characterization of himself as a cynic that gives a forum to Gregory's ideas, and it makes for a significant contribution to the search for artistic forms and meaning that followed the explosion of experiment in the 1960's. Shawn's own openness to thoughtful and radical inquiry into the nature of art and human experience is hearteningly matched by his disciplined skills of expression.

The amused cynicism evident in his own plays was reflected in Shawn's translation and adaptation of Machiavelli's *Mandragola*, with its jaundiced view of human relationships, but it was his original play *Aunt Dan and Lemon* which again stirred the audience into shock. In some ways a meditation on the Nazi atrocities, it was most disturbing for the cold way in which it portrayed the spiritually damaged woman called Lemon, the narrator of the piece. Beginning by welcoming the audience, including the "little children. How sweet you are, how innocent," she went on to tell the story of a friend of her parents, an American academic teaching at Oxford called Aunt Dan, who had regaled her with strange tales when she was 11. Aunt Dan's stories were sometimes about the heroism of Henry Kissinger when he ordered bombing attacks on Vietnam, or about a woman who had been Aunt Dan's lesbian lover and who had killed a man by strangling him with her stockings. The lesson that Lemon learns is that comfort is bought by assigning the killing to others, and that it is really hypocritical to condemn the Nazis who, after all, had been very successful against the Jews. Profoundly disturbing, the play is a mesmerizing blend of narration and enactment which tries, with mixed success, to comprehend the nature of human cruelty and the negotiated truce with justice that affects all non-political people.

Shawn's 1991 play for one character, *The Fever*, was an even more specific meditation on justice and injustice, virtually a call for revolution. "This piece was written," he writes, "so that it could be performed in anyone's flat or home, for an audience of 10 or 12, as well as in public places, and it was designed to fit a very wide spectrum of performers." Shawn himself has performed it in dining-rooms and at London's Royal National Theatre, and it would be very hard to measure its impact for it is basically a call for people to change, for those theatre-going civilized people who have money to switch sides and join the poor.

The performer describes waking up in a hotel room in a poor country, reviewing his or her own reconsideration of the privilege that has come with money. In a post-Marxist world, it rehearses with passion Marx's analysis of the value of things, of commodities, so that the value of labour is recognized. By graphic reference to torture and oppression which protects privilege, he indicts his audience and the comfortable notion of gradual change—but finally the character speaking cannot relinquish his or her own wealth. The dramatic and political journey is never completed.

—Ned Chaillet

SHEARER, Jill. Australian. Born in Melbourne, 14 April 1936. Secretary, Japanese Consulate-General, Brisbane, 1966–79. Recipient: Big River Festival prize, for poetry, 1973; Monash Alexander Special award, 1976; New South Wales Society of Women Writers award, 1976; Utah Cairns Centenary award, 1976; McGregor Literary award, 1987; Australia Council grant, 1989. Address: c/o Playlab Press, P.O. Box 185, Ashgrove, Brisbane 4060, Queensland, Australia.

PUBLICATIONS

Plays

The Trouble with Gillian (produced Brisbane, 1974).
The Foreman (produced Brisbane, 1976). Sydney, Currency Press, 1979.
The Boat (produced Brisbane, 1977). Published in Can't You Hear Me Talking to You, St. Lucia, University of Queensland Press, 1978.
The Kite (produced Brisbane, 1977). Included in Echoes and Other Plays, 1980.
Nocturne (produced Brisbane, 1977). Included in Echoes and Other Plays, 1980.
Catherine (produced Goulburn, New South Wales, 1978). Melbourne, Edward Arnold, 1977.
Stephen (produced Brisbane, 1980). Included in Echoes and Other Plays, 1980.
Echoes and Other Plays (includes The Kite, Nocturne, Stephen). Ashgrove, Playlab Press, 1980.
Release Lavinia Stannard (produced Brisbane, 1980).
A Woman Like That (produced Brisbane, 1986).
Shimada (produced Melbourne, 1987; New York, 1992). Sydney, Currency Press, 1989.
Comrade (produced Brisbane, 1987). Ashgrove, Playlab Press, 1987.

Radio Play: A Woman Like That, 1989.

*

Manuscript Collection: Fryer Library, University of Queensland, St. Lucia, Brisbane.

Critical Study: "Telling It in Multiple Layers: an interview with Jill Shearer" by Helen Gilbert, in Australasian Drama Studies (St. Lucia, Brisbane), 21, October 1992.

Jill Shearer comments:
Whilst I'm interested in all aspects of contemporary society, I'm drawn to writing about individuals and families often caught up in larger events. Living and working in Australia I'm increasingly interested in exploring Asian cultures (as I did in my play Shimada) increasingly linked as they are with my own.

* * *

Beginning with numerous one-act plays written in the 1970's and produced mostly by amateur companies, Jill Shearer's work exhibits a passionate concern with social issues and tackles such wide-ranging and often controversial topics as abortion, industrial work practices, conservation, race relations, and foreign economic influence in Australia. Most often, these broader issues are played out in localized settings through the representation of ordinary people and family situations. The Foreman, for example, condemns racism not through a primary focus on interactions between Aboriginal and non-Aboriginal Australians but by revealing the effects of prejudice on an Aboriginal family whose relationships become strained when the breadwinner is rejected by his white "mates" after he receives a well-deserved promotion.

Other plays such as Echoes, The Trouble with Gillian, Stephen, and The Boat also foreground family tensions, although these are often more powerfully suggested by the characters' desperate attempts to sustain some semblance of harmony or normality than by any overt confrontations. The Boat depicts a man's regression into a child-like fantasy world after he loses his job and sense of purpose. His wife and son choose not to disabuse him of his belief that the daily fishing trips played out in the living room of their conventional suburban home are mere fictions. In Echoes, the representation of a family on holiday at the beach is similarly energized by a forced but unsustainable congeniality which side-steps problems and masks hostilities. In both texts, subterranean conflict is kindled by an outsider who threatens to fracture the fragile integrity of the family unit, but despite its fissures, this structure proves resistant to the "truths" the outsider might offer. Short, sharp, and narrowly focused, both plays construct vivid impressions of the roles people play in order to cope with difficult situations. Characterized by deft touches of the bizarre combined with a vague sense of threat, they are strongly evocative of Pinter's work, as is Nocturne, a very short scenario which positions a cellist at the top of a mountain road playing with wild abandon, oblivious to all else but the music, while a walker becomes increasingly frustrated and aggressive as she tries to make conversation. Here, Shearer's use of silence and the unfinished line or trail-away phrase also owes much to Pinter's influence.

To the extent that she evokes clearly recognizable images of tropical Australia, Shearer could be called a regionalist writer. Nocturne owes something of its uncomfortable ambience to the disjunction between a highly minimalist set, an abstract tree beside a white strip of road, and the dialogue's insistent references to the panoramic view from the tangled rainforest where the antagonists sit to the nearby coastline and beyond. Echoes features the Great Barrier Reef as a deceptively calm retreat wherein nature's bounty is balanced only by its potential destructiveness. This dual aspect of nature which represents both threat and promise acts here as a metaphorical parallel for the characters themselves while in The Kite, the healing powers of the beach and the sand are harnessed to dissuade a young woman from committing suicide.

Though not pursuing an obvious feminist agenda, Shearer consistently creates strong women characters and her one historical play, Catherine, clearly argues for a reconsideration of women's roles in Australia's past and present. Constructed as a play within a play, Catherine explores the relationship between a female convict on the second fleet and a rakish upper-class gentleman who has taken her by intimidation, if not force, for his mistress. While the viewer's interest is directed toward this tale, the framing narrative questions the passivity attributed to Catherine when the actor who plays her insists on presenting a character with more verve than the director sees fit. Primarily, the play sets out to rescue Catherine and other convict women from the margins of imperial history, but it also voices a powerful indictment of the convict system even while celebrating the tenacity of the oppressed and dispossessed who were transported to Australia to found a nation.

Stylistically, Shearer's recent work strives towards heigh-

Sam Shepard comments:

(1973) I'm interested in exploring the writing of plays through attitudes derived from other forms such as music, painting, sculpture, film, all the time keeping in mind that I'm writing for the theatre. I consider theatre and writing to be a home where I bring the adventures of my life and sort them out, making sense or non-sense out of mysterious impressions. I like to start with as little information about where I'm going as possible. A nearly empty space which is the stage where a picture, a sound, a color sneaks in and tells me a certain kind of story. I feel that language is a veil hiding demons and angels which the characters are always out of touch with. Their quest in the play is the same as ours in life—to find those forces, to meet them face to face and end the mystery. I'm pulled toward images that shine in the middle of junk. Like cracked headlights shining on a deer's eyes. I've been influenced by Jackson Pollock, Little Richard, Cajun fiddles, and the Southwest.

* * *

In spite of his prolific output—some 40 plays since the mid 1960's—Sam Shepard's invention never flags, and his achievements sometimes tower high. More than any contemporary American playwright, he has woven into his own dramatic idiom the strands of a youth culture thriving on drugs, rock music, astrology, science fiction, old movies, detective stories, cowboy films, and races of cars, horses, dogs. More recently he strives for mythic dimensions in family plays.

Growing up in Southern California, Shepard fell almost accidentally into playwriting when he went to New York City: "The world I was living in was the most interesting thing to me, and I thought the best thing I could do maybe would be to write about it, so I started writing plays." Since the time was the 1960's and the place was the lower East Side, Shepard's short plays were produced off-off-Broadway. Today he finds it difficult to remember these early efforts, which tend to focus on a single event, the characters often talking past one another or breaking into long monologues. However puzzling the action, these plays already ring out with Shepard's deft rhythms.

Within three years of these first efforts, in 1966, 23-year old Shepard produced his first full-length play, *La Turista*, punning on the Spanish word for tourist and the diarrhea that attacks American tourists in Mexico. Perhaps influenced by Beckett's *Waiting for Godot*, *La Turista* is also composed of two acts in which the second virtually repeats the first. However, questionable identities and mythic roles are at once more blatant and more realistic than in Beckett. In both of Shepard's acts Kent is sick, and his wife Salem (both named for cigarette brands) sends for a doctor, who, more or less aided by his son, essays a cure. But the first act is set in a Mexican hotel room and the illness is *la turista*, whereas the second act is set in an American hotel room and the illness is sleeping sickness. Playing through film stereotypes, Kent breaks out of the theater and perhaps out of illness as well.

Other plays followed swiftly, some published in 1971 in two volumes aptly named for the first and longest play in each book. In the six plays of *The Unseen Hand* almost all the main characters are threatened by unseen hands. Two plays of *Mad Dog Blues* camp the popular arts they embrace affectionately. In the title play two friends, Kosmo, a rock star, and Yahoudi, a drug dealer, separate to seek their respective fortunes. Kosmo takes up with Mae West, and Yohoudi with Marlene Dietrich. Each pair becomes a triangle when Kosmo annexes Waco, Texas, and Yahoudi Captain Kidd, for whose treasure they all hunt. Tumbling from adventure to adventure, Yahoudi shoots Captain Kidd, Marlene goes off with Paul Bunyan, Kosmo and Mae West find the treasure, but Jesse James makes off with treasure and Mae West. Finally Mae suggests that they all go to the Missouri home of Jesse James, and the play ends in festive song and dance.

A longer play from 1970 also ends in comic celebration. The punning title *Operation Sidewinder* refers to an American army computer in the shape of a sidewinder rattlesnake. By the play's end, however, it becomes an actual snake and Hopi Indian religious symbol through whose symbiotic power a disoriented young couple is integrated into an organic society—even as in New Comedy. To attain this, the pair has to avoid a revolutionary conspiracy, military backlash, several corpses, and their own highly verbal confusion.

It is generally agreed that *The Tooth of Crime* is Shepard's most impressive play. He has commented: "It started with language—it started with hearing a certain sound which is coming from the voice of this character, Hoss." And the play's strength remains in language, a synthesis of the slangs of rock, crime, astrology, and sports. Hoss has played by the code and moved by the charts, but he senses that he is doomed. Gradually, the doom takes the shape and name of Crow, a gypsy killer. Alerted through Eyes, warned by the charts of Galactic Jack, doped by his doctor, comforted by his moll, Hoss prepares for his fate, "Stuck in my image." In Act 2, Hoss and Crow, has-been and would-be, duel with words and music—"Choose an argot"—as a Referee keeps score. In the third Round the Ref calls a TKO, and Hoss kills the Referee. Unable to bend to Crow's wild ways, Hoss prefers to die, in the manner of classical heroes but in contemporary idiom: "A true gesture that won't never cheat on itself 'cause it's the last of its kind."

Ironically, this American tragedy was written when Shepard was living in London, where his *Geography of a Horse Dreamer* sprang from English dog-racing. On home ground in California, Shepard wrote *Action* about two passive American couples, *Killer's Head* about a cowboy in the electric chair, *Angel City* about horror and horror movies in Hollywood, *Suicide in B Flat* about pressures leading to artistic suicide. These plays are at once newly inventive and stylistically consistent in their nonrealistic images, unpredictable characters, and rich language grounded in colloquialism and soaring to manic monologue. Shepard's most mercurial achievement in pure monologue is the creation of two pieces for the actor Joseph Chaikin—*Tongues* and *Savage/Love*.

While becoming more involved in his career as a film actor, Shepard has written what he himself calls a "family trilogy," although there is no carryover of characters in *Curse of the Starving Class*, *Buried Child*, and *True West*. In these plays Shepard follows O'Neill in dramatizing a tragic America, mired in sin. In *Curse* the sin is betrayal of the land to soulless speculators. In *Buried Child* it is incest, cruelty, and murder that stifle freedom and creativity in the young. *True West* is at once funnier on its surface and more focused in its opposition of two brothers with divergent lives and attitudes toward the true West.

The love/hate relation within a pair carries over from *True West* to *Fool for Love*, but the pair is now half-siblings and whole lovers. May and Eddie are alternately ecstatic and sadistic in one another's presence in a tawdry motel room, while their father observes them from an offstage vantage. When, at play's end, the motel room goes up in flames, it is not only the end of their inconclusive incest, but of Shepard's own subjection to conventional play-making, with exposition, plot, and resolution. Shepard punctuates this stage of his career by acting the part of Eddie in the movie version, where flashbacks are unfortunately shown.

A Lie of the Mind divides the stage between a rootless and a rooted family, a violent representative of the old West, and a family where the victimized women exude tenderness, Shepard implies that America must look forward with a gentleness that belies its violent past. More boldly, Shepard denounces the violence of war in *States of Shock*. Into a family restaurant a nameless American colonel wheels a wounded young veteran, Stubbs, who may prove to be his son. As conflict escalates between the bellicose colonel and the injured Stubbs, a white man and woman think only of their own appetites, but the black waitress finally heals Stubbs. Percussion and projections cause the action to resonate far beyond the confines of a family restaurant.

Shepard has absorbed American pop art, media myths, and the Southwestern scene to recycle them in many—perhaps too many—image-focused plays in which the characters speak inventive idioms in vivid rhythms. At his best—*La Turista, Mad Dog Blues, The Tooth of Crime, A Lie of the Mind*—Shepard achieves his own distinctive coherence through beautifully bridled fantasy.

—Ruby Cohn

SHERMAN, Martin. American. Born in Philadelphia, Pennsylvania, 22 December 1938. Educated at Boston University, 1956–60, B.F.A. 1960. Playwright-in-residence, Playwrights Horizons, New York, 1976–77. Recipient: Wurlitzer Foundation grant, 1973; National Endowment for the Arts fellowship, 1980; Dramatists Guild Hull-Warriner award, 1980; Rockefeller fellowship, 1985. Agent: Casarotto Ramsay Ltd., National House, 60–66 Wardour Street, London W1V 3HP; and, Johnnie Planko, William Morris Agency, 1350 Avenue of the Americas, New York, New York 10019, U.S.A. Address: 35 Leinster Square, London W.2, England.

PUBLICATIONS

Plays

A Solitary Thing, music by Stanley Silverman (produced Oakland, California, 1963).
Fat Tuesday (produced New York, 1966).
Next Year in Jerusalem (produced New York, 1968).
The Night Before Paris (produced New York, 1969; Edinburgh, 1970).
Things Went Badly in Westphalia (produced Storrs, Connecticut, 1971). Published in *The Best Short Plays 1970*, edited by Stanley Richards, Philadelphia, Chilton, 1970.
Passing By (produced New York, 1974; London, 1975). Published in *Gay Plays 1*, edited by Michael Wilcox, London, Methuen, 1984.
Soaps (produced New York, 1975).
Cracks (produced Waterford, Connecticut, 1975; New York, 1976; Oldham, Lancashire, 1981). Published in *Gay Plays 2*, edited by Michael Wilcox, London, Methuen, 1986.
Rio Grande (produced New York, 1976).
Blackout (produced New York, 1978).
Bent (produced Waterford, Connecticut, 1978; London and

New York, 1979). Ashover, Derbyshire, Amber Lane, 1979; New York, Avon, 1980.
Messiah (produced London, 1982; New York, 1984). Oxford, Amber Lane, 1982.
When She Danced (produced Guildford, Surrey, 1985; London, 1988; New York, 1990). Oxford, Amber Lane, 1988.
A Madhouse in Goa (includes *A Table for a King* and *Keeps Rainin' All the Time*) (produced London, 1989). Oxford, Amber Lane, 1989.

Television Play: *The Clothes in the Wardrobe*, adaptation of Alice Thomas Ellis's *The Summerhouse Trilogy*, 1993.

*

Theatrical Activities:
Director: **Play**—*Point Blank* by Alan Pope and Alex Harding, London, 1980.

* * *

Although Martin Sherman is an American playwright born and bred, his parentage is Russian, and he displays a European consciousness as well as an unusual sensitivity to the music of language. Small wonder he prefers historical periods (including earlier in this century) to the present-day and European settings to American. Although *Bent* and *Passing By* focus on male-identified men, in the leading roles of *Rio Grande, Messiah, When She Danced*, and *A Madhouse in Goa* Sherman has created remarkably complex and individualized portraits of women. Sherman brings a keen intellect to bear on his materials, yet crafts plays which, far from aridly cerebral, are palpably permeated with the deepest feeling. Generalizations about his work, however, are dangerous, for he does not repeat himself. Equally at home with comedy and drama, Sherman works in styles as diverse as his subjects, and his eccentric characters populate works of often audacious originality.

Sherman's volatile and varied subjects include satire of soap operas (*Soaps*); a dying woman who, when visited by an alien from another planet, is tempted to go off with him in his space ship (*Rio Grande*); a charming, light comedy about two gay men who, shortly after meeting, develop hepatitis and care for each other (*Passing By*); and a hippie whodunnit so crazed the killer's identity is never revealed (*Cracks*). That madcap comedy of death, described by a British critic as "Agatha Christie on acid," is a counterculture *Ten Little Indians*, but also a satire of narcissism which Joe Orton might have written had he spent the 1960's in California.

The characters in these and other Sherman plays are outsiders because they are gay or Jewish or foreign or female or strangers in a strange land. In *Messiah*, seeing the Cossacks torture her husband to death has rendered Rebecca mute, while in *A Madhouse in Goa* aphasiac Daniel's language is as dislocated as this gay genius—an "other"—is from his world. Seven languages are spoken in *When She Danced* because nearly everyone in the play is an expatriate from another country. The men in *Bent* represent exiles within their own country, because of their differences thrown into a concentration camp to die.

Although this literal and metaphorical alienation devastates spectators, Sherman's survival kit contains, above all, humor. In *Messiah* his Rachel—a skeptical yet compassionate figure who seems to embody the author's spirit more than any of Sherman's other creations—endures because she is blessed with an ironic sensibility which perceives God's exquisite humor and turns even her denial of God's existence into a scream directed at the Deity.

This dark, personal, and painful play set in 17th-century Poland and Turkey concerns not the title character, who never appears, but a clever yet homely woman whose life the news of the "false Messiah" Sabbatai Sevi profoundly alters. From a claustrophobic village to a barren foreign shore, Rachel and what family remains after her husband dies in a literal leap of faith journey in search of salvation. In liberation from dogma and sexual repression and in self-reliance, however, fear and doubt accompany the removal of boundaries. Such exiles must do without, equally, both restrictions and security. Rich in eroticism, brooding mysticism, and earthy humor, *Messiah* dramatizes a courageous, autonomous woman, a resilient and female Job, experiencing metaphysical conflicts often reserved for male heroes. In her soul, as well as in the play as a whole, doubt, superstition, and disillusionment war against buoyant spirits, wit, kindness, and faith—in God, in the future, and in self.

Whereas religion opposes sexuality in *Messiah*, in *Bent* the source of oppression is governmental. A play which has changed the popular perception of Holocaust victims as solely Jewish, *Bent* has been staged in 35 countries worldwide. Its initial urbane comedy quickly moves into a nightmare about men whom Nazis required to wear, not yellow stars, but pink triangles. Forced into complicity in his lover's murder, in order to survive Max also denies his homosexuality and proves he's not "bent" by having sex with a 13-year-old girl's corpse. Yet Max moves beyond betrayal and self-contempt. In the dehumanizing circumstances of Dachau, his humanity emerges as he affirms the possibility of love and self-sacrifice, embraces his gay identity, and defies those who imprison his soul. In the play's most amazing scene, Max even makes love to another prisoner without their ever making physical contact.

When She Danced finds affirmation, not through intense suffering, but in comedy of wit. This day in the life of Isadora Duncan takes its tone from Preston Sturges's 1940's films because that writer/director grew up around the Duncan household. A touching and amusing valentine to genius, this comedy finds the 46-year-old, improvident, charismatic dancer living in Paris with her young husband Sergei, with whom she shares no common tongue. Much of the humor derives from the troubles communicating experienced by characters speaking in seven languages and from the arrival of a translator. Isadora's instincts that language is highly overrated—"We never had it in America"—prove prophetic, as communication promotes discord and chaos, as well as hilarious misunderstandings.

A Madhouse in Goa moves, like *Bent*, from wit to poignance. Naturally, neither of its two parts takes place in Goa. The brittle, mannered comedy of *A Table for a King* unfolds at a Corfu resort in the 1960's, while the stormy weather of *Keeps Rainin' All the Time* occurs on Santorini "one year from now," after nuclear accidents have altered world weather patterns so drastically that rain continually drenches the Greek isles. The former's narrator is a gay, Jewish, socially awkward young American whose insecurities are assailed by a garrulous southern matron who mocks and mothers him and whose loneliness is momentarily assuaged by the clever Greek waiter who seduces him.

This fellow's wallowing in melancholy seems only minor self-indulgence when contrasted to the second assortment of self-pitying people all wrapped up in their own needs but none too adept at satisfying them. Only gradually does a spectator appreciate that among this self-absorbed crew is the same American, this time in his forties. Not exactly the same man, though, for it appears Daniel is the *author* of the first part, which dramatizes, not the real events of twenty years ago, but a fictionalization which conveniently omits the painful truths that would have reduced his novel's commercial appeal. That sell-out, however, is minor compared to plans for a musical film version of *A Table for a King* presented by a born-again Hollywood producer, who may be the most mercilessly satirized Sherman creation. The self-preoccupied Daniel's stroke-induced aphasia prevents his communicating to the others surrounding him—his male nurse, his dying friend Heather, her hacker son, the producer's girlfriend. Thus when Heather's fears of religious extremists, carcinogenic food, AIDS, and getting nuked require reassurance, Daniel intones "Apple sauce."

The despair underlying Sherman's humor, as well as the imaginative situation and plotting, recall David Mercer, particularly *Duck Song*. Underneath the jokes lurks anguish for a doomed world, a perception which prompted the comical woman of Part 1 to commit herself to the titular Indian asylum. Sherman smashes his other characters' lives, leaving Daniel no audience for his incomprehensible and bitter wit. Unlike the Sherman plays which have dramatized survival, *A Madhouse in Goa*—like Beckett's *Endgame*—distills dread for the very future of humanity.

—Tish Dace

SHERMAN, Stuart. American. Born in the United States, 9 November 1945. Has worked at the Kitchen and the Performing Garage, New York. Recipient: National Endowment for the Arts fellowship; Creative Artists Public Service grant; New York State Council on the Arts grant; Northwest Area Foundation grant; Massachusetts Council for the Arts and Humanities grant; Art Matters grant; MacDowell Colony residency; Asian Cultural Council travel grant; prix de Rome, 1991. Address: 166 West 22nd Street, 6A, New York 10011, U.S.A.

PUBLICATIONS

Plays

Spectacles (produced New York, Amsterdam, Paris, Frankfurt, Hamburg, Sydney, and Tokyo, 1975–90).
The Classical Trilogy: Hamlet, Oedipus, Faust.
    Hamlet (produced Amsterdam, 1981; New York, 1982).
    Faust (produced Frankfurt, 1982).
    Oedipus (produced Minneapolis, 1984).
The Second Trilogy: Chekhov, Strindberg, Brecht (produced New York, 1986).
    Chekhov (produced Cambridge, Massachusetts and New York, 1985).
    Brecht (produced Frankfurt, 1985; New York, 1986).
    Strindberg (produced Melbourne, Australia, 1986; New York, 1986).
The Man in Room 2538 (produced New York, 1986).
It is Against the Law to Shout "Fire!" in a Crowded Theater: or, "Fire! Fire!" (produced New York, 1986).
This House Is Mine Because I Live in It (produced New York, 1986).

Endless Meadows, and So Forth (produced New York, 1986).

Chattanooga Choo-Choo (Für Elise) (produced New York, 1987).

An Evening of One-Act Plays (produced New York, 1987).

Slant (produced Amherst, Massachusetts, 1987).

Crime and Punishment; or, The Book and the Window (produced New York, 1987).

"A" is for "Actor" (produced New York, 1987).

The Yellow Chair (produced New York, 1987).

One Acts and Two Trilogies. Imperial Beach, California, Video Research Institute Theater Library, Contemporary Scripts, Series 1, No.10, 1987.

But What Is the Word for "Bicycle"? (produced New York, 1988). As *Aber wie heisst das Wort für "Fahrrad"?*, Cologne, Kölner Ensemble Publication, 1990.

In a Handbag; or, Oscar's Wilde: or, The Importance of Being More or Less Earnest (produced New York, 1988).

Objects of Desire (produced New York, 1989).

The Play of Tea; or, Pinkies Up! (produced New York, 1989).

Knock, Knock, Knock, Knock (produced New York, 1989).

Taal Eulenspiegel (produced Ghent, Belgium, 1990).

Solaris, adaptation of the novel by Stanislaw Lem (produced Aachen, Germany, 1992). Cologne, Kölner Ensemble Publication, 1992.

*

Theatrical Activities:

Plays—acted in and directed all his own plays.

* * *

It is difficult to write about Stuart Sherman's theatre, for his work is often complex; yet at moments the complexity speaks to something quite simple.

Sherman's work is generally described as performance art, under which rubric works as diverse as Charlotte Moorman's naked cello recitals, the Spalding Gray meditative monologues about wonders and miseries recalled in tranquillity, and George Jessel's telephone calls to his mother might be grouped. One of the elements in Sherman's work that assures the categorizers that Stuart is performance-arting is its non-linear, non-sequential narrative, but sometimes his plots are sequential and sometimes his plays are non-narrative. Another element is Sherman's use of the presentational, the mode that indicates that the players, even when they do not speak directly to the audience, are always aware of them. Heightening the presentational mode is an absence of psychological depth, whereby the player often takes on an allegorical persona (e.g., good dental hygiene), or becomes a metaphor for urban anxiety. Thus we understand that the player is presenting rather than being, and even as it distances us from emotional catharsis, it permits us to collaborate in the understanding that presumably we (performer and spectator) are all thinking together. What we are all thinking about is not always clear.

In the early 1970's, Sherman would set up a small card table on West Broadway in the heart of Soho in New York City. It was always some daytime hour, a handful of pedestrians might wander by, a few would stop out of curiosity, allow themselves to be amused or not, and then move on to other amusements. No one was threatened by the Stuart Sherman who stood behind the card table. If the work was not always accessible, it was modest enough not to challenge whatever agenda you might be developing for yourself. In fact there was something almost incorrigibly domestic, therefore incorrigibly reassuring about these ostensibly sober and brief

cartoon-like romps. The very card table looked as if it had been lifted out of Sherman's mother's kitchen, and the objects used by Sherman might have come out of that same kitchen (for example, a homely set of salt and pepper shakers, some plastic cups and saucers). The whole arsenal of props suggested banal domesticity—before the street audience floated unthreatening plastic, dime-store paper, cellophane, kitchen variety glass, bits of linoleum, and the inevitable formica. The Sherman work might speak of magical or homely events that could befall any reasonable middle-class urban type, or there might be an abstract portrait of some local celebrity out of the downtown art scene. There was something particularly engaging and refreshing about the modesty of means, about the self-effaciveness of the performer who plied his art with the homeliest of weapons in full daylight, open to the scrutiny of whoever might be passing. Granted that the street chosen was fast becoming a major thoroughfare for downtown gallery-hoppers, there was still a beguiling innocence about the herky-jerky, open-faced Sherman performance and its rickety card-table technology.

Sherman had already been performing indoors, but within a year or two he shifted to more sophisticated sites like the Kitchen and the Performing Garage. His work began to embrace the more complex technology of lights, projections, and other staples from the arena of mixed media. And now it was customary to see other performers working in tandem with Sherman. What these performers very often had in common was a seeming ability to convey that not only were they not acting but they hadn't the first clue as to how one might create a character onstage. In a very real sense one was still in Stuart's mother's kitchen, and the performers had decided to dress up in "acting clothes" and do something that somebody said was "acting." It is not that one or more of them might not have had considerable training in performance, but rather that what seemed to be required for Sherman's material, which still dealt with abstract portraits and non-linear narratives, was a kind of somnambular persona which acted as cipher rather than character. So the "acting," it seemed, needed to conform to the comforting artifice of gracelessness, "graceless" material which was at the same time particularly heartfelt.

In 1986 Sherman premiered *The Man in Room 2538*, a two-character play set in a bar-restaurant atop a hotel in Tokyo. The customer, played by Sherman, is waiting at the bar; he wants to eat his dinner at a window seat but all such seats are occupied. While he waits he and the bartender carry on a low-key philosophical discourse. The customer, who dines here every night on "the usual," steak teriyaki and Kirin beer, recounts how he took the elevator to the 25th floor and stood outside room 2538:

> I don't see, inside the room, a man sitting by the window, looking out, holding a book on his lap. I don't see this. I don't see the color of the walls, which are slightly blue. I don't feel the fit of the man's shoes. . . . I don't see, feel, or hear any of these things.

Later the customer sees himself "more and more clearly, sitting by a window . . . and I order something to eat and something to drink. . . ." The customer is either recounting last night's "usual" or tonight's "usual" which will materialize when a window seat becomes vacant. What seems to connect what he doesn't see inside room 2538 with what he does see in the bar-restaurant are 2,538 dots of light, precisely 2,538 dots joined to make the seen and the unseen. The bartender, a rationalist, is slowly drawn into the customer's mathematical fixation.

The narrative here is linear, but what gives the play its

substance is not simply the apparent "content," the intellectual, discursive byplay, but also the exterior of the byplay, the hallucinatory manner within which the byplay carries on its life. The content and its exterior manner are both shaped in the spirit of the mathematical logic of Kurt Godel and the hallucinatory loop drawings of M.C. Escher in which phenomenon come together in an endless, mirror-like "reality." It seems that Sherman is coming into his own in this work. He has been trying to see into things, and many of his works, which he sometimes calls "Spectacles" or "Portraits," have to do with this attempt at seeing. Perhaps that is why representational acting is not appropriate. If one were to accept the premise that representation is the grossest of lies, then there is a particular value in devising the obvious artifice of "structures" wherein performers perform separate events side by side and over and over, sometimes with variations, sometimes with ritual-like actions, none especially "convincing" except that we are convinced that someone is "performing" them.

Sherman's *Classical Trilogy*, comprising *Hamlet*, *Faust*, and *Oedipus* and his *Second Trilogy*, comprising *Chekhov*, *Brecht*, and *Strindberg*, combine ritual abstractions with readings of fragments from various plays, and seem to be an attempt to "play" these plays in the manner children might "play" them at home. These trilogies could be regarded as analogs, abstractions of the plays, but the obviousness of the playing suggests that this is Sherman's way of making the plays his own, of finding a new reality, of seeing that he is seeing, as if once again he were making a play in the Sherman kitchen of days gone by.

—Arthur Sainer

SHERRIFF, R(obert) C(edric). British. 1896–1975.
See 1st edition, 1973.

SIMON, Barney. South African. Born in Johannesburg, 13 April 1933. Educated at Fairview Junior School, Jeppe Preparatory School, and Jeppe Boys High, all Johannesburg. Copywriter, E. Lindsay Smithers, 1958–62, copy chief, J. Walter Thompson, 1962–66, editor, *The Classic Magazine*, 1964–71, founder-director, Phoenix Players, 1965–68, and creative director, Central Advertising, 1966–68, all Johannesburg; associate editor, *New American Review*, New York, 1969–70; founder-director, Mirror 1, 1970–72; founder, with Mannie Manim, and director, The Company, 1973–76. Since 1976 founder, with Mannie Manim, and artistic director, The Market Theatre and, since 1990, The Market Theatre Laboratory, both Johannesburg. Chair of Celebration, Derry, 1992. Recipient: Ford Foundation grant, 1970; Edinburgh Festival Fringe award, 1982, 1987; Los Angeles Critics award, 1982; Bay Area award, 1983; *City Limits* award, 1984; Obie award, 1984, 1986; Vita award, 1985, 1991, 1992; Rockefeller grant, 1989, 1992. Agent: Patricia MacNaughton, MacNaughton Lowe Representation, 200 Fulham Road, London SW10 9PN, England. Address: c/o The Market Theatre, P.O. Box 8656, Johannesburg 2000, South Africa.

PUBLICATIONS

Plays

Phiri, with others (produced Johannesburg, 1972).
Hey Listen (produced Johannesburg, 1973).
Six Characters in Search of an Author, adaptation of a play by Pirandello (produced Johannesburg, 1973).
People, with others (produced Johannesburg, 1973).
People Too, with others (produced Johannesburg, 1974).
Joburg, Sis! (includes *Men Should Cry More Often*, *Miss South Africa*, *I Live in a Building*, *Cape Town Is Fantastic*, *Our War*) (also director: produced Johannesburg, 1974). Johannesburg, Bataleur Press, 1974.
Storytime, with others (includes *The Yellow Star*) (also director: produced Johannesburg, 1975). *The Yellow Star* published Johannesburg, Quarry, 1976.
Medea, adaptation of a play by Franz Grillparzer (also director: produced Cape Town, 1978; Edinburgh, 1983; London, 1983).
Cincinatti, with others (produced Johannesburg, 1979). Johannesburg, Haum Educational, 1984.
Call Me Woman, with others (produced Johannesburg, 1980).
Cold Stone Jug, adaptation of the play by Stephen Gray (also director: produced Cape Town, 1980). Cape Town, Human and Rousseau, 1982.
Marico Moonshine and Manpower, with others (produced Johannesburg, 1981).
Woza Albert!, with Mbongeni Ngema and Percy Mtwa (also director: produced Johannesburg, 1981; Edinburgh, London, and Los Angeles, 1982; New York, 1984). London, Methuen, 1983; in *Woza Afrika! An Anthology of South African Plays*, edited by Duma Ndlovu, New York, Braziller, 1986.
Black Dog–Inj Mayama, with others (also director: produced Johannesburg, Edinburgh, and London, 1984).
Born in the R.S.A., with others (also director: produced Johannesburg, 1985; New York, Edinburgh, and London, 1986). In *Woza Afrika! An Anthology of South African Plays*, edited by Duma Ndlovu, New York, Braziller, 1986.
Outers, with others (produced Johannesburg, 1985).
The Dybbuk, adaptation of the play by S. Ansky (produced Johannesburg, 1986).
Klaaglied vir Kous (produced Johannesburg, 1986).
Written by Hand, with others (produced Boston, Massachusetts, 1987).
Score Me with Ages, with others (produced Johannesburg, 1989).
Eden and Other Places, with others (produced Johannesburg, 1989).
Inyanga—About Women in Africa, with others (produced Johannesburg, 1989).
Singing the Times, with others (produced Johannesburg, 1992).

Television Plays: *Six Feet of the Country*, 1982; *Good Climate, Friendly Inhabitants*, 1982; *City Lovers*, 1982; *Born in the R.S.A.*, 1986; *Woza Albert!*, 1987.

Other

Editor, *Familiarity Is the Kingdom of the Lost*, by Dugmore Boetie. London, Cresset Press, 1969; New York, Dutton, 1970.

*

Critical Study: *The Best of Company: The Story of Johannesburg's Market Theatre* by Pat Schwartz, Johannesburg, Ad Donker, 1988.

Theatrical Activities:
Directed, adapted, and workshopped many plays.

Barney Simon comments:

Because of my opposition to the segregation of audiences and players in apartheid South Africa, I never considered a professional career in South African theatre. From 1954 to 1958 I lived in London. For a short period, around 1957, I worked backstage for Joan Littlewood's Theatre Workshop. This was a definitive influence on my understanding of the horizons and freedoms of theatre and its role in the life of a community.

When I returned to South Africa I met Athol Fugard, then struggling to make theatre in the black townships. Our communication was immediate and electric. In 1961 Fugard was employed to run a workshop theatre at the African Music and Drama Association at Dorkay House, Johannesburg. His first production was *The Blood Knot* which he had just written. He was directing and performing in the play. He invited me to participate as "third eye." This was the beginning of a long and committed association. When he moved to Port Elizabeth I continued to work at Dorkay House with a multi-racial group. I earned my living as an advertising copywriter.

In the mid-sixties, because of political pressures we were forced to leave Dorkay House and I founded Phoenix Players (in a condemned mansion) which performed to invited, free audiences which rendered multi-racial theatre legal. You could have blacks as guests as long as you didn't serve liquor.

Between 1968 and 1970, I lived and worked in America as a director, writer, and editor. Upon my return to South Africa I founded a company called Mirror 1—"a reflecting surface in which we might find an image of ourselves." We performed plays relevant to our situation on campuses, in backyards and lounges. Concurrently I began to work in mission hospitals in the Transkei and Zululand, working with black nurses in the creation of songs to traditional melodies and plays through which they communicated with traditional, largely illiterate communities. The work extended to urban communities and squatter camps. We once played in a backyard next door to a man under house arrest so that he could watch over his fence. The procedure with the nurses was to begin with awareness exercises and gossip, followed by incognito field-trips into their villages where they "spied" on their potential subjects and audiences and considered their lives. Subsequently I used the same procedure with professional actors in Johannesburg, and in this way many Market Theatre pieces were created. There is an Ehassidic saying "God created man because He loves to listen to stories." I believe that actors and audiences are made in His image. My procedure is (without knowledge of him) similar to Mike Leigh's, except that the majority of my "made" plays were made within a normal four-week period. I slept with my lights on and a pen clutched in my hand. At present I am negotiating to have a decade of this work published.

* * *

Barney Simon is known for his work as a theatre director but essentially he has been "happiest creating plays, including musicals, through workshops with actors." The genesis of Simon's interest in improvised theatre may be traced to his having worked with Joan Littlewood in the 1950's and with Athol Fugard, the well-known South African playwright and director who has done similar work, notably with Winston Ntshona and John Kani, to produce the highly successful and internationally acclaimed *Sizwe Bansi Is Dead* and *The Islands*. Simon worked with Fugard in the first production of the latter's *The Blood Knot* in 1961.

To date, Simon is credited with a number of plays, most of which have emerged from workshops and improvisations with the members of his multi-racial Market Theatre in Johannesburg. Among his written plays are *Phiri* (described as a black musical version of *Volpone*), *Cold Stone Jug*, *Joburg, Sis!*, and *Miss South Africa*. His collectively devised works with actors include *People*, *Storytime*, *Call Me Woman*, *Cincinatti* [sic], *Woza Albert!*, and *Born in the R.S.A.* The last two are the best known of his workshop creations.

Woza Albert! and *Born in the R.S.A.* represent a tradition of theatre and performance much influenced by the "poor theatre" philosophy and experiments of the Polish director Jerzy Grotowski. This style of play-making and performance has since become a hallmark of much contemporary political theatre of South Africa from Athol Fugard onwards. Usually, these plays are collectively devised and process- rather than product-oriented and often employ non-naturalistic styles of performance to inform while entertaining their readers and audiences. The characters in the plays are very often drawn from the suppressed communities of South African apartheid society. The two plays also represent the dream of crossing the racial barriers which alone can bring a much needed peace to South Africa's segregated and intensely troubled socio-cultural milieu. *Woza Albert!*, which first brought Simon and his two black actors/collaborators (Mbongeni Ngema and Percy Mtwa) into the international theatre limelight, has been described as "an act of affirmation" because it testifies to the ability of the human spirit and imagination to rise creatively above the soul-deadening repression of an inhuman social system. The characters/actors in this play of racial agony still manage to wrest hope from the pits of despair and this they offer to the audience: it is a play that offers us laughter through a torrent of tears.

In theatrical terms, the play is simple—two black actors come upon an empty stage/space and with minimal props begin to present to the audience poignant and hilarious images of South African urban life, on a stage filled with villains, heroes, and clowns, clearly understating the sheer will and defiance that makes survival possible in an inhuman environment. What amazes most in this theatre of "poor means" is the enormous amount of histrionic ability required of the actors in order to actualize for the audience the gripping reality of the drama of racial/communal anguish—over an exhilarating space of two hours, the two actors range freely and effortlessly through a wide spectrum of characters and situations that reflect the gory details of life for blacks under apartheid. The play's strength lies in its simple details which challenge and force the audience to become co-creators of the mise-en-scène with the performers.

Born in the R.S.A., while still in the mould of the former, is more of a "docudrama" since the seven actors/characters actually play themselves, and only occasionally assume other personae. It employs the traditional storytelling style of collective narration done in relay mode involving all the actors/characters who talk about themselves, but who while doing this are actually talking about each other and about their South Africa. Structurally complex, each personal story maintains a kind of linear continuity which is often broken by other stories. Yet all create a uniquely clear and unbroken narrative. You can actually pick a character/actor and follow his/her narration, but each acquires a broader perspective and a deeper significance when seen in the context of the whole which is the human anguish and tension of the South African situation.

This new direction in Simon's theatre work and the fact that the Market Theatre which he founded with Mannie Manim was for a long time South Africa's only integrated theatre, clearly shows him to be an artist who is politically committed and who believes in utilizing the resources of the theatre medium to examine the human condition and dilemma in a racially repressive and inhuman environment. In a recent interview Simon aptly stated the philosophy behind his work in the theatre, which is to "present plays that are relevant to our lives, that open hearts and minds," and he does this through helping his actors to "create personal texts" from their South African landscape. In doing so, he seems to have moved away from the mere directing and adapting of *Phiri* to genuinely creating plays of the moment that fuse the traditional elements of his South African culture while using and extending the techniques of "poor theatre" as he and his collaborators do in *Woza Albert!* and *Born in the R.S.A.*

—Osita Okagbue

————————

SIMON, (Marvin) Neil. American. Born in the Bronx, New York, 4 July 1927. Educated at De Witt Clinton High School, New York, graduated 1943; New York University, 1944–45; University of Denver, 1945–46. Served in the United States Army Air Force, 1945–46: corporal. Married 1) Joan Baim in 1953 (died 1973), two daughters; 2) the actress Marsha Mason in 1973 (divorced 1983); 3) Diane Lander in 1987. Radio and television writer, 1948–60. Recipient: Emmy award, for television writing, 1957, 1959; Tony award, 1965, 1970, 1985, 1991; London *Evening Standard* award, 1967; Shubert award, 1968; Writers Guild of America West award, for screenplay, 1969, 1971, 1976; PEN Los Angeles Center award, 1982; New York Drama Critics Circle award, 1983; Outer Circle award, 1983, 1985; New York State Governor's award, 1986; Pulitzer prize, 1991. L.H.D.: Hofstra University, Hempstead, New York, 1981; Williams College, Williamstown, Massachusetts, 1984. Address: c/o G. DaSilva, 10100 Santa Monica Boulevard, No. 400, Los Angeles, California 90067, U.S.A.

PUBLICATIONS

Plays

Sketches (produced Tamiment. Pennsylvania, 1952, 1953).
Sketches, with Danny Simon, in *Catch a Star!* (produced New York, 1955).
Sketches, with Danny Simon, in *New Faces of 1956* (produced New York, 1956).
Adventures of Marco Polo: A Musical Fantasy, with William Friedberg, music by Clay Warnick and Mel Pahl. New York, French, 1959.
Heidi, with William Friedberg, music by Clay Warnick, adaptation of the novel by Johanna Spyri. New York, French, 1959.
Come Blow Your Horn (produced New Hope, Pennsylvania, 1960; New York, 1961; London, 1962). New York and London, French, 1961.
Little Me, music by Cy Coleman, lyrics by Carolyn Leigh,

adaptation of the novel by Patrick Dennis (produced New York, 1962; London, 1964; revised version produced New York, 1982; London, 1983). Included in *Collected Plays 2*, 1979.
Barefoot in the Park (as *Nobody Loves Me*, produced New Hope, Pennsylvania, 1962; *as Barefoot in the Park*, produced New York, 1963; London, 1965). New York, Random House, 1964; London, French, 1966.
The Odd Couple (produced New York, 1965; London, 1966; revised [female] version produced New York, 1985). New York, Random House, 1966.
Sweet Charity, music by Cy Coleman, lyrics by Dorothy Fields, based on the screenplay *Nights of Cabiria* by Federico Fellini and others (produced New York, 1966; London, 1967). New York, Random House, 1966.
The Star-Spangled Girl (produced New York, 1966). New York, Random House, 1967.
Plaza Suite (includes *Visitor from Mamaroneck*, *Visitor from Hollywood*, *Visitor from Forest Hills*) (produced New York, 1968; London, 1969). New York, Random House, 1969.
Promises, Promises, music and lyrics by Burt Bacharach and Hal David, based on the screenplay *The Apartment* by Billy Wilder and I.A.L. Diamond (produced New York, 1968; London, 1969). New York, Random House, 1969.
Last of the Red Hot Lovers (produced New York, 1969; Manchester and London, 1979). New York, Random House, 1970.
The Gingerbread Lady (produced New York, 1970; Windsor and London, 1974). New York, Random House, 1971.
The Prisoner of Second Avenue (produced New York, 1971). New York, Random House, and London, French, 1972.
The Sunshine Boys (produced New York, 1972; London, 1975). New York, Random House, 1973.
The Comedy of Neil Simon (includes *Come Blow Your Horn*; *Barefoot in the Park*; *The Odd Couple*; *The Star-Spangled Girl*; *Plaza Suite*; *Promises, Promises*; *Last of the Red Hot Lovers*). New York, Random House, 1972.
The Good Doctor, music by Peter Link, lyrics by Simon, adaptation of stories by Chekhov (produced New York, 1973; Coventry, 1981; London, 1988). New York. Random House, 1974; London, French, 1975.
God's Favorite (produced New York, 1974). New York, Random House, 1975.
California Suite (includes *Visitor from New York*, *Visitor from Philadelphia*, *Visitor from London*, *Visitor from Chicago*) (produced Los Angeles. New York, and London, 1976). New York, Random House, 1977.
The Goodbye Girl (screenplay 1977) stage version, music by Marvin Hamlisch, lyrics by David Zippel (produced Chicago, 1992; New York, 1993).
Chapter Two (produced Los Angeles and New York, 1977; London, 1981). New York. Random House, and London, French, 1979.
They're Playing Our Song, music by Marvin Hamlisch, lyrics by Carol Bayer Sager (produced Los Angeles, 1978; New York, 1979; London, 1980). New York, Random House, 1980.
Collected Plays 2 (includes *The Sunshine Boys*, *Little Me*, *The Gingerbread Lady*, *The Prisoner of Second Avenue*, *The Good Doctor*, *God's Favorite*, *California Suite*, *Chapter Two*). New York, Random House, 1979.
I Ought to Be in Pictures (produced Los Angeles and New York, 1980; Perth, Scotland, 1983; London, 1986). New York, Random House, 1981.
Fools (produced New York, 1981). New York, Random House, 1982.

Brighton Beach Memoirs (produced Los Angeles, 1982; New York, 1983; London, 1986).   New York, Random House, and London, French, 1984.

Actors and Actresses (produced Stamford, Connecticut, 1983).

Biloxi Blues (produced Los Angeles, 1984; New York, 1985). New York, Random House, 1986.

Broadway Bound (produced New York, 1986; London, 1991).   New York, Random House, 1987.

Rumors (produced New York, 1988; revised version produced Chichester, West Sussex, 1990).   New York, Random House, 1990.

Jake's Women (produced San Diego, 1990; revised version produced New York, 1992).

Lost in Yonkers (produced New York, 1991; London, 1992). New York, Random House, 1991.

Collected Plays 3 (includes *Sweet Charity, They're Playing Our Song, I Ought to Be in Pictures, Fools, The Odd Couple* [female version], *Brighton Beach Memoirs, Biloxi Blues, Broadway Bound*). New York, Random House, 1992.

Screenplays: *After the Fox*, with Cesare Zavattini, 1966; *Barefoot in the Park*, 1967; *The Odd Couple*, 1968; *The Out-of-Towners*, 1970; *Plaza Suite*, 1971; *The Heartbreak Kid*, 1972; *The Last of the Red Hot Lovers*, 1972; *The Prisoner of Second Avenue*, 1975; *The Sunshine Boys*, 1975; *Murder by Death*, 1976; *The Goodbye Girl*, 1977; *The Cheap Detective*, 1978; *California Suite*, 1978; *Chapter Two*, 1979; *Seems Like Old Times*, 1980; *Only When I Laugh*, 1982; *I Ought to Be in Pictures*, 1982; *Max Dugan Returns*, 1983; *The Lonely Guy*, with Ed Weinberger and Stan Daniels, 1984; *The Slugger's Wife*, 1985; *Brighton Beach Memoirs*, 1987; *Biloxi Blues*, 1988; *The Marrying Man*, 1991.

Radio: scripts for *Robert Q. Lewis Show*.

Television: *Phil Silvers Show*, 1948; *Tallulah Bankhead Show*, 1951; *Your Show of Shows*, 1956; *Sid Caesar Show*, 1956–57; *Jerry Lewis Show*; *Jacky Gleason Show*; *Red Buttons Show*; *Sergeant Bilko* series, 1958–59; *Garry Moore Show*, 1959–60; *The Trouble with People*, 1972; *Happy Endings*, with others, 1975; *Broadway Bound*, 1992.

*

Bibliography: *Ten Modern American Playwrights* by Kimball King, New York, Garland, 1982.

Manuscript Collection: Harvard University, Cambridge, Massachusetts.

Critical Studies: *Neil Simon* by Edythe M. McGovern, New York, Ungar, 1979; *Neil Simon* by Robert K. Johnson, Boston, Twayne, 1983.

*   *   *

In a time of turmoil and despair in the commercial theatre both in Britain and in America, it is encouraging to note that neither Neil Simon nor Alan Ayckbourn has been seriously deterred by dismissive or hostile criticism. Some fifty years ago on both sides of the Atlantic, there were a number of playwrights who regularly produced new works, confidently expecting professional productions. Today, writers' grants and play-workshops proliferate, as producers, directors,

actors, critics, and even audiences wonder where the interesting new plays are to be found. At least in the commercial sector, some already renowned playwrights find it difficult to get a production. In the United States, Simon is almost alone as a successful dramatist who is expected to continue concocting comedies and musicals which please audiences.

Unlike Ayckbourn, who is able to develop and test his new works at Scarborough's Stephen Joseph Theatre before they are shown in the West End, Simon's scripts are customarily commercially mounted and "tried out" in Los Angeles and elsewhere in regional America before coming to Broadway. It has been suggested that Simon may well be the most successful playwright—in terms of royalties and other income from his varied ventures on stage, in films, and on television—who has ever lived. At various times, he has had three and four productions running simultaneously on Broadway, not to mention touring ensembles, stock and amateur productions, and foreign stagings.

His fortunes with many critics, however, have been rather different. Initially, with early domestic comedies such as *Come Blow Your Horn* and *Barefoot in the Park*, he was welcomed as a fresh new voice, with a particular comic talent for pointing up the pangs and problems of urban family life. He was also fortunate in receiving slickly professional productions with impressive performers to bring his visions of contemporary middle-class angst to life. The fact that most new Simon scripts rapidly became long-running hits, significant commercial money-spinners, helped attract even wider audiences. It's an axiom that people would rather see hits than flops. Once in the theatre, however, spectators were obviously amused by Simon's comic techniques, but they also clearly responded to characters and situations they could recognize.

It has been repeatedly pointed out, by regional and foreign critics and producers, that the farther removed from New York a Simon production is, the less easily do audiences respond and empathize. Some explain this by suggesting that Simon's concerns are largely with urban and suburban New Yorkers, which may well be of interest to audiences elsewhere, without striking any personal sparks of instant recognition. A few of Simon's detractors, however, insist that his comedy is not only one of New York insularity, but more specifically of materialistic, middle-class New York Jews, thus making it less immediately accessible to non-Jews beyond the Hudson. Whatever the merits of this argument, in the mid-1980's such nation-wide American Simon successes as his autobiographical *Brighton Beach Memoirs* and *Biloxi Blues* were produced by Britain's subsidized National Theatre rather than by a West End commercial management.

While some object to what they perceive as a regional, cultural, economic, or even ethnic bias in Simon's choice of subject matter, others—notably critics, rather than audiences—complain about what is often seen as the playwright's major fault: his obvious addiction to the "one-liner" comic comment, which seems to elicit boisterous laughter, regardless of the dramatic context in which it occurs. A cursory reading of Simon's comedies and musical comedy books will readily reveal this penchant for the quick, often sarcastic quip, which in fact is more often to be heard in New York conversations than elsewhere in America. This is a distinctive element in Simon's comic writing, and its genesis can be traced to his early collaboration with his brother, Danny Simon, when they were gag-writers for such television series as the *Phil Silvers Show* and the *Sid Caesar Show*, where the smart retort and the devastating comic put-down were major provokers of laughter. The gift of making people laugh in the theatre is to be prized, but this talent in Simon has been viewed, by critics who would like to admire him more, as rather a curse than a dramatic inspiration.

Despite his commercial success and even such official recognitions as the Tony, Shubert, and *Evening Standard* awards, Simon has been sensitive to critical objections. In conversation, he is an informed, concerned, compassionate, serious human being; a Simon interview is not a barrage of hilarious one-liners. He has repeatedly pointed out—to answer critical charges that his comedies are all artificial constructs, manipulations of stereotypes in stock situations— that the most succesful of his works, from the first, have been firmly rooted in his personal experience, or that of close friends and family. That's true of *Come Blow Your Horn* and *The Odd Couple*, in terms of the brothers Simon. As television collaborators, Simon has noted, brother Danny was rumpled and disorganized, while brother Neil was always neat and tidy: out of this experience came the comic conflicts of sloppy Oscar and fussy Felix. *Barefoot in the Park* reprised the New York apartment experiences of the newlywed Neil Simons.

Last of the Red Hot Lovers, a series of amorous miscarriages on the part of a frustrated fish merchant with variously fixated women, was inspired by the so-called Sexual Revolution of the 1960's, when many middle-aged men and women feared the new freedoms were passing them by. (Women in the Broadway audience would shout advice to James Coco, playing the forlorn would-be seducer: "Jimmy! *She's* not right for you!") Whatever demanding critics may say, popular audiences readily respond to Simon's view of man and life.

The Star-Spangled Girl is a construct, as Simon has admitted, acknowledging that it didn't work as he hoped it would. *Plaza Suite*, in which the same suite in the famed New York hotel is the scene of three quite different but amusing encounters, may be viewed as a comic tour de force, but the situations are all based on realities. (In fact, Simon's film *The Out-of-Towners* is a dramatised expansion of an opening *Plaza Suite* monologue, omitted on Broadway.)

When Simon tried to show his critics—and his public—that he was capable of dealing thoughtfully and dramatically with a serious subject, *The Gingerbread Lady* was dismissed or disparaged as having been damaged by his recourse to the familiar device of the comic quip. This play was clearly inspired by the self-destructiveness of Judy Garland. Simon explored the possible reasons for her loss of confidence and bad habits; he also was intrigued by the idea of an often hurt but still loving daughter effectually becoming a mother to her own mother, to protect her from herself. Another showbusiness situation was probed in *The Sunshine Boys*, exploring the behind-the-scenes hostilities—continuing into old age —of vaudeville teams such as Smith and Dale. *The Prisoner of Second Avenue* continues to excite interest, however, with its mordant humor all the more valid as seemingly successful, highly paid executives are suddenly fired, with no prospects of re-employment. As if to answer those who complain that Simon only writes about New Yorkers, *California Suite* did for Los Angeles what *Plaza Suite* did for Manhattan.

Chapter Two—in which Simon came to terms with the sorrow and rage at the loss of his first wife through cancer and began a new relationship—at last was a serious subject which critics and public could accept as an honest, deeply felt vision of suffering and redemption, leavened with sharp personal satire and comic quips. Curiously, the most recent Simon comedies, the saga of a young playwright's growing up, have been critically praised as a kind of break-through in comic technique. Actually, however, the semi-autobiographical *Brighton Beach Memoirs* (childhood in Brooklyn), *Biloxi*

Blues (1940's army experience), and *Broadway Bound* (young man with a typewriter) exemplify one of the oldest known dramatic structures. Simon's alter-ego, Eugene Morris Jerome (*pace* Eugene O'Neill), functions as a genial narrator, who interrupts his first-person story to step into dramatised episodes. It's efficient as a technique, but it's hardly an innovation.

Rumors was a disappointment after the trilogy, for the basic situation and characters were stereotypical constructs of no particular interest, animated merely by the confusions and misunderstandings rumors make possible. Simon himself described it as a farce, but it lacked the essential elements of farce, except for a setting with a number of doors. Unlike Feydeau, however, Simon did not know how to use the doors for suspense or comic effect. A colorful, manic Broadway production glossed over the weakness of the script.

After that slump, *Lost in Yonkers* was doubly welcomed by critics and public. It was hailed as even more honest and autobiographical than the trilogy. It focused again on two boys—Simon brothers surrogates—growing up with a tyrannical, embittered, and crippled grandmother in a shabby Yonkers flat, while their loving but feckless father tries to survive the Depression on the road. A gangster uncle and a childlike aunt provide love and occasional adventure for the boys. At last Simon was awarded a Pulitzer prize as well as the 1991 Tony for best play, his work being deemed sufficiently serious. The characters, it is true, were much more distinctive and less generic, but as in previous Simon plays, every one of them had a string of smart "one-liner" retorts which were vintage Simon, and yet not out of character.

Jake's Women, which tried out in San Diego in 1990, only to be halted on its way to Broadway by Simon himself, was rethought and rewritten to achieve a popular—if not critical —success in New York. The dramaturgy was intricate and engaging, as Jake, a Simon-like playwright, summons up his own imaginings of the women in his fantasy and real lives. His long-dead first wife turns up at will, but, like his newer estranged wife, a possible future wife, and his daughter by the first wife, seen at two different ages, she can only express the thoughts, emotions, and words which the playwright assigns her in his fantasies. This play is "*Chapter Two¹/₂*," also autobiographical as *Chapter Two* was, in that the spectre of a beloved but deceased first wife is ruining the playwright's emotional relationships with subsequent lovers. Even the writer's female therapist is made to see things his way. It's a clever conceit in performance, but it plumbs no new depths in the Simon or human psyche which weren't already explored in *Chapter Two*.

Over the years, Simon has also shown himself a skilled adaptor of other materials, as in the musicals *Little Me* (Patrick Dennis's novel), *Sweet Charity* (Federico Fellini's film), and *Promises, Promises* (Billy Wilder's film), and in the plays *The Good Doctor* (Chekhov's short stories), *God's Favorite* (*The Book of Job* on Long Island's North Shore: Simon's answer to MacLeish's *J.B.*), and *Fools* (suggested by Sholem Alecheim's stories of Chelm). For the cinema, he has drafted effective screenplays of some of his own plays, as well as some originals, such as *The Goodbye Girl* and *Murder by Death*, the first a popular romantic comedy, the second, a puzzling disaster.

Despite periodic renunciations of Broadway, carping critics, the pace of New York life, or East Coast values, Simon does seem to draw his primary inspiration and stimulation from this scene. And, although some denigrators would insist that with Simon, "Nothing succeeds like *excess*," his large, impressive, continuing body of comedies, endorsed to a greater or lesser degree by audiences at home and abroad, is an undeniable achievement by a distinctive talent with a penetrating intelligence. It is a record all the more impressive in a time when so few playwrights are regularly creating effective comedies.

—Glenn Loney

SIMONS, Beverley (née Rosen). Canadian. Born in Flin Flon, Manitoba, 31 March 1938. Educated at Banff School of Fine Arts, Alberta, 1956; McGill University, Montreal, 1956–57; University of British Columbia, Vancouver, 1958–59, B.A. (honours) in English and theatre 1959. Married to Sidney B. Simons; three sons. Lived in Europe, 1959–61. Recipient: Canada Council grant, 1967, and award, 1972. Lives in Vancouver. Address: c/o Playwrights Union of Canada, 8 York Street, 6th Floor, Toronto, Ontario M5J 1R2, Canada.

PUBLICATIONS

Plays

Twisted Roots (as Beverley Rosen), in First Flowering, edited by Anthony Frisch. Toronto, Kingswood House, 1956.
The Birth (produced Montreal, 1957).
A Play (produced Montreal, 1957).
The Elephant and the Jewish Question (produced Vancouver, 1968). Vancouver, New Play Centre, n.d.
Green Lawn Rest Home (produced Burnaby, British Columbia, 1969). Toronto, Playwrights, 1973.
Crabdance (produced Seattle, 1969). Vancouver, In Press, 1969; revised version (produced Vancouver, 1972), Vancouver, Talonbooks, 1972.
Preparing (produced Burnaby, British Columbia, 1973). Included in Preparing (collection), 1975.
Preparing (includes Prologue, Triangle, The Crusader, Green Lawn Rest Home). Vancouver, Talonbooks, 1975.
Prologue, Triangle, The Crusader (produced Toronto, 1976). Included in Preparing, 1975.
If I Turn Around Quick, published in Capilano Review (North Vancouver), Summer 1976.
Leela Means to Play (produced Waterford, Connecticut, 1978). Published in Canadian Theatre Review 9 (Downsview, Ontario), Winter 1976.

Television Play: The Canary, 1968.

*

Critical Studies: "Beverley Simons Issue" of Canadian Theatre Review 9 (Downsview, Ontario), Winter 1976.

*   *   *

Crabdance is Beverley Simons's best-known work and remains her outstanding achievement. In it the commonplace world is transformed by Sadie Golden's hyper-sensitive perceptions, salesmen becoming sons, lovers, and husband as Sadie projects onto them her feelings about sex, motherhood, and her femaleness. At the critical hour of 3 p.m. she dies out

of the lacerating existence in which "Mama's gone a-hunting/ She's taken off her own white skin. . . ." The salesmen are recognizably objective figures as well as emanations from Sadie, and the play's relation to experience is powerfully present through distorted images. The great success of Crabdance lies in the perilous balance between observation and feeling, the known world and Sadie's vision of it.

In an earlier one-act play, Green Lawn Rest Home, less ambitious than Crabdance but the most finished and unified of her plays, Simons also makes the internal perceptions of the characters modify the presentation of outward reality and brilliantly fuses lyrical and satirical perspectives. Society's prettification of senility and dying is critically observed while, at the same time, the mortifications before death, the leaking away of life in anguish, the tiny passions of the geriatrics, are seen and felt from within. A "date" which consists of a walk to the gate of the rest home becomes, for the old couple subjectively presented, the equivalent of the most violent adolescent sexuality. Simons conveys feelingly the real hardness of the green pebbles which, from a little distance away, give the illusion of lawns.

Leela Means to Play presents, sporadically, clear moral views of the operations of legal justice through a kind of trial-by-encounters of a judge. The play is a full-length aggregation of very short scenes, related in theme but not through plot or sequence—gobbets of allegory in which the representation of modern life is distorted by an intensely feeling consciousness. There is no equivalent of Sadie Golden, however, to give focus and coherence in this play. In this work Simons relies too naïvely on her audience's recognition of the personality behind it. The play seems to have been untimely snatched from the authorial womb, still trailing unsynthesized bits of Beckett, Genet, Albee, and Nō-via-Yeats, unfinished though very much alive.

The title piece of Preparing gives us (like Crabdance) a dramatization of the passionately sensitive perceptions of Simons. This monologue requires an actress skilled in mime and with a set of voices adequate to portray the several ages of woman. From adolescence to womanhood the speaker undertakes preparations for imposed sexual roles ending with ultimate resistance ("fuck 'em all") to all the impositions. Two other short pieces in this collection are too clamantly "experimental"; one, The Crusader, employs masks in a novel but clumsy way; in the other, Triangle, light and movement give us the geometry of bonding and victimage in the relationships of three characters. In both the moral view is rather heavily imposed and not offset by studious "theatricality."

In an earlier play, The Elephant and the Jewish Question (published only in mimeographed form), Simons showed herself capable of handling a conventional structure and natural speech, though the piece is rather stickily embedded in "Jewish atmosphere." The great development from this to Crabdance is an indication of Simons's strengths. Her work is marked by her exploration of various ways of presenting lyrical, internalized characters within an objective framework. But her genuine distinctiveness seems to be still overlayed and obscured by studious imitation and anxiety about form.

—Michael Sidnell

SIMPSON, N(orman) F(rederick). British. Born in London, 29 January 1919. Educated at Emanuel School, London,

1930–37; Birkbeck College, University of London, 1950–54, B.A. (honours) 1954. Served in the Royal Artillery, 1941–43, and the Intelligence Corps, 1943–46. Married Joyce Bartlett in 1944; one daughter. Staff member, Westminster Bank, London, 1937–39; teacher, College of St. Mark and St. John, London, 1939–41, and City of Westminster College, London, and extra-mural lecturer, 1946–62; literary manager, Royal Court Theatre, London, 1976–78. Address: c/o Simon Brett, 12 Blowhorn Street, Marlborough, Wiltshire SN8 1BT, England.

PUBLICATIONS

Plays

A Resounding Tinkle (produced London, 1957; Bloomington, Indiana, and New York, 1961). Published in *The Observer Plays*, London, Faber, and New York, French, 1958; shortened version included in *The Hole and Other Plays and Sketches*, 1964.
The Hole (produced London, 1958; New York, 1961). London and New York, French, 1958.
One Way Pendulum (produced London, 1959; New York, 1961). London, Faber, 1960; New York, Grove Press, 1961.
Sketches in *One to Another* (produced London, 1959). London, French, 1960.
Sketches in *You, Me and the Gatepost* (produced Nottingham, 1960).
Sketches in *On the Avenue* (produced London, 1961).
Sketches in *One over the Eight* (produced London, 1961).
The Form (produced London, 1961). New York and London, French, 1961.
Oh (produced London, 1961). Included in *The Hole and Other Plays and Sketches*, 1964.
The Hole and Other Plays and Sketches (includes shortened version of *A Resounding Tinkle*, and *The Form*, *Gladly Otherwise*, *Oh*, *One Blast and Have Done*). London, Faber, 1964.
The Cresta Run (produced London, 1965; Louisville, 1968). London, Faber, 1966; New York, Grove Press, 1967.
We're Due in Eastbourne in Ten Minutes (televised 1967; produced London, 1971). Included in *Some Tall Tinkles*, 1968; in *The Best Short Plays 1972*, edited by Stanley Richards, Philadelphia, Chilton, 1972.
Some Tall Tinkles: Television Plays (includes *We're Due in Eastbourne in Ten Minutes*, *The Best I Can Do by Way of a Gate-Leg Table Is a Hundredweight of Coal*, *At Least It's a Precaution Against Fire*). London, Faber, 1968.
Playback 625, with Leopoldo Maler (produced London, 1970).
How Are Your Handles? (includes *Gladly Otherwise*, *Oh*, *The Other Side of London*) (produced London, 1970; *Gladly Otherwise* produced New York, 1988).
Was He Anyone? (produced London, 1972; New York, 1979). London, Faber, and Chicago, Dramatic Publishing Company, 1973.
In Reasonable Shape (produced London, 1977). Published in *Play Ten*, edited by Robin Rook, London, Arnold, 1977.
Anyone's Gums Can Listen to Reason, in *Play Ten*, edited by Robin Rook. London, Arnold, 1977.
Inner Voices, adaptation of a play by Eduardo De Filippo (produced London, 1983). Oxford. Amber Lane Press, 1983.
Napoli Milionaria, adaptation of a play by Eduardo De Filippo (produced London, 1991).

Screenplays: *One Way Pendulum*, 1964; *Diamonds for Breakfast*, with Pierre Rouve and Ronald Harwood, 1968.

Radio Plays: *Something Rather Effective*, 1972; *Sketches for Radio*, 1974.

Television Plays: *Make a Man*, 1966; *Three Rousing Tinkles* series: *The Father by Adoption of One of the Former Marquis of Rangoon's Natural Granddaughters*, *If Those Are Mr. Heckmondwick's Own Personal Pipes They've Been Lagged Once Already*, and *The Best I Can Do by Way of a Gate-Leg Table Is a Hundredweight of Coal*, 1966; *Four Tall Tinkles* series: *We're Due in Eastbourne in Ten Minutes*, *In a Punt with Friends Under a Haystack on the River Mersey*, *A Row of Potted Plants*, and *At Least It's a Precaution Against Fire*, 1967; *World in Ferment* series, 1969; *Charley's Grants* series, 1970; *Thank You Very Much*, 1971; *Elementary, My Dear Watson*, 1973; *Silver Wedding*, 1974; *An Upward Fall* (*Crown Court* series), 1977; *Wainwrights' Law* series, 1980.

Novel

Harry Bleachbaker. London, Harrap, 1976; as *Man Overboard: A Testimonial to the High Art of Incompetence*, New York, Morrow, 1976.

*

Manuscript Collections: Indiana University, Bloomington; University of Texas, Austin; University of California, Berkeley.

Critical Studies: *The Theatre of the Absurd* by Martin Esslin, New York, Doubleday, 1961, London, Eyre and Spottiswoode, 1962, revised edition, London, Penguin, 1968, Doubleday, 1969; *Curtains* by Kenneth Tynan, London, Longman, and New York, Atheneum, 1961; *Dramatic Essays* by Nigel Dennis, London, Weidenfeld and Nicolson, 1962, Westport, Connecticut, Greenwood Press, 1978.

N.F. Simpson comments:
   The question that, as a writer, one is asked more frequently than any other is the question as to why of all things it should be plays that one has chosen to bring forth rather than, say, novels or books about flying saucers. The answer in my own case lies, I think, in the fact that there is one incomparable advantage which the play, as a form, has over the novel and the book about flying saucers; and this is that there are not anything like as many words in it. For a writer condemned from birth to draw upon a reservoir of energy such as would barely suffice to get a tadpole from one side of a tea-cup to the other, such a consideration cannot but be decisive. Poetry admittedly has in general fewer words still, and for this reason is on the face of it an even more attractive discipline; but alas I have even less gift for that than I have for writing plays, and if I had the gift for it, it would be only a matter of weeks before I came up against the ineluctable truth that there is just not the money in it that there is in plays. Not that, the way I write them, there is all that much money in those either.
   As for methods of work, what I do is to husband with jealous parsimony such faint tremors of psychic energy as can sometimes be coaxed out of the permanently undercharged batteries I was issued with at birth, and when I have what might be deemed a measurable amount, to send it coursing down the one tiny channel where with any luck it might do some good. Here it deposits its wee pile of silt, which I allow to accumulate, with the barely perceptible deliberation of a coral reef to the point where it may one day recognise itself

with a start of surprise as the small and unpretentious magnum opus it had all along been tremulously aspiring to.

As for why one does it there are various reasons—all of them fairly absurd. There is one's ludicrously all-embracing sense of guilt mainly. I walk the streets in perpetual fear and trepidation, like someone who expects, round the very next corner, to meet his just deserts at the hands of a lynch mob carried away by fully justified indignation. To feel *personally* responsible not only for every crime, every atrocity, every act of inhumanity that has ever been perpetrated since the world began, but for those as well that have not as yet been so much as contemplated, is something which only Jesus Christ and I can ever have experienced to anything like the same degree. And it goes a long way to account for what I write and why I write it. For not only must one do what one can by writing plays to make amends for the perfidy of getting born; one must also, in the interests of sheer self-preservation, keep permanently incapacitated by laughter as many as possible of those who would otherwise be the bearers of a just and terrible retribution. One snatches one's reprieve quite literally laugh by laugh.

My plays are about life—life as I see it. Which is to say that they are all in their various ways about a man trying to get a partially inflated rubber lilo into a suitcase slightly too small to take it even when *uninflated*. Like most Englishmen, of which I am proud to be one, I have a love of order tempered by a deep and abiding respect for anarchy, and what I would one day like to bring about is that perfect balance between the two which I believe it to be peculiarly in the nature of English genius to arrive at. I doubt very much whether I ever shall, but it is nevertheless what I would like to do.

* * *

N. F. Simpson is perhaps the most typical English exponent of the so-called Theatre of the Absurd (a term introduced by Martin Esslin to describe the drama of a world without God: "cut off from his religious metaphysical and transcendental roots, man is lost, all his actions become senseless"—his position in the universe is essentially absurd). The roots of such drama lie in the French theatre, in the work of Jarry and Artaud, and may be seen today in the plays of Ionesco and Genet. Simpson indeed has many affinities with Ionesco, not least a stage on which anything can happen and, however bizarre, be taken as normal by the actors. Describing the Paradock couple in a foreword to *Some Tall Tinkles*, Simpson commented: "Nothing is so preposterous that it may not happen here before the day is out."

Simpson's English precedents are the fantasy and nonsense worlds of Lewis Carroll and Edward Lear. Simpson's absurd world contains, however, a strong vein of social criticism; a manic sense of humour cloaks a satirical and often savage commentary on British institutions and suburban life.

Simpson first came to public notice with *A Resounding Tinkle*, which won the *Observer* play competition for 1957. It was first performed in a shortened version in December 1957. The original version takes place in the Paradocks' home. Two comedians explore Bergson's theory of laughter and an apologetic author-figure commiserates with the audience:

I agree. A pretty epileptic start. We're going to see what we can do in the next scene about pulling the thing together.

In Act Two an over-large elephant has been delivered to the Paradocks' back garden; they decide to swap it for their neighbour's snake, which is "too short" for her (it arrives in a pencil box). The Paradocks' son appears, dressed as a woman ("Why, you've changed your sex"). A parody of the BBC's

Critics' Forum ensues, with the critics (Mustard Short, Denzil Pepper, Miss Salt, and Mrs. Vinegar) discussing "The performance we have all been watching"—after which the author exits, dazed. A man in a bowler hat tells the producer the audience have "had about as much as they can take of this" and the play ends with the full cast toasting the audience.

The second version is tighter and less conscious of itself as a play, cutting the author and comics and concentrating on the Paradocks, their animal interests, and the fact that Mr. Paradock has been asked to form a government by someone "working through the street directory." This version was performed in a double bill with *The Hole*, a play in which the action centres on a hole in the road. A "visionary" sits by the hole, awaiting a spiritual happening; a crowd gathers round him and each member presents differing philosophical speculations as to the purpose of the hole, until a workman emerges from it, stating that it contains an electrical junction box. The visionary is finally left alone, still awaiting his miracle; as a crowd member comments: "it is upon this cavity that we build our faith."

One Way Pendulum, "a farce" set in another suburban household, established Simpson's popularity with audiences. Mabel Groomkirby "takes in her stride most of what happens around her," including son Kirby's ambition to teach several hundred speak-your-weight machines the Hallelujah Chorus. Since they can speak, they should be capable of singing, thinks Kirby, who has "a very logical turn of mind." He is moreover, a Pavlovian—unable to eat until a cash register "pings"—and feels compelled to wear black. Needing "a logical pretext" for this, he commits 43 murders! Kirby intends his singing weighing machines to act as sirens to lure large crowds to the North Pole, where they will all jump— and, in landing, alter the tilt of the world's axis, provoking a new ice age, guaranteed to cause sufficient regular deaths for Kirby's sartorial purposes.

Such details emerge gradually, via his father's obsession with the law, which leads him to build a replica of the Old Bailey in his living room. This becomes the focus of Act Two, when a judge appears and Kirby's trial ensues—a brilliant satire of the legal system. The judge finally discharges Kirby because, in sentencing him:

We may be putting him beyond the reach of the law in respect of those other crimes of which he might otherwise have become guilty. The law, however, is not to be cheated in this way. I shall therefore discharge you.

The Cresta Run, an equally hilarious satire of espionage, was followed in 1972 by *Was He Anyone?*, a merciless exposure of bureaucracy and the social services. It demolishes the committees and departments responsible for rescuing Albert Whitbrace, a bookie's runner, who ran off a liner and is still in the Mediterranean after two and a half years awaiting rescue. A piano is flown out to keep him occupied and he is finally proficient enough to give a concert with the Leningrad Symphony Orchestra, who join him for the purpose. His rescue becomes more urgent as his lifejacket becomes waterlogged and he begins to sink. Finally some "woolly-minded do-gooder" throws him a lifebelt, knocking him unconscious, and he drowns. "Was he anyone?" someone enquires, with the chilling response: "I don't think he was, fortunately." The play is perhaps Simpson's strongest satirical statement about society, and he reworked and enlarged these ideas into his only novel, *Harry Bleachbaker*.

—Rosemary Pountney

SINCLAIR, Stephen (Kennedy). New Zealander. Born in Auckland, 30 December 1956. Educated at Victoria University of Wellington, B.A. in Maori studies, 1980. Warehouse employee, Lands Bags, 1977, dishwasher, Plimmer House Restaurant, 1978–79, research assistant, Maori Studies Department, Victoria University of Wellington, 1979, writer, actor, director, Wellington Arts Centre, 1980–81, translator of Maori manuscripts, National Archives, 1982, writer, actor, director, Taotahi Maori and Polynesian Theatre Group, 1982–84, postman, New Zealand Post Office, 1983–85, and administration officer, New Zealand Actors Equity, Wellington Branch and New Zealand Writers Guild, Southern Branch, 1986–87, all Wellington. Agent: Playmarket, P.O. Box 9767, Wellington, New Zealand; and, Casarotto Ramsay, National House, 60–66 Wardour Street, London W1V 3HP, England. Address: 189 Marine Parade, Seatoun, Wellington, New Zealand.

PUBLICATIONS

Plays

Le Matau (*The Hook*), with Samson Samasoni (produced Wellington, 1984).
Big Bickies, with Frances Walsh (produced Dunedin, 1988).
Ladies Night, with Anthony McCarten (produced Auckland, 1988; Oldham, Manchester, 1989; London, 1990).
The Sex Fiend, with Danny Mulheron (produced Wellington, 1989).
Caramel Cream (produced Wellington, 1991).

Other Plays: *The Howzie Show*, 1981; *Scars of Welfare*, 1983; *The Alhambra's Master*, 1987.

Screenplays: *Meet the Feebles*, with Peter Jackson, Danny Mulheron, and others, 1992; *Brain Dead*, with Frances Walsh.

*

Stephen Sinclair comments:

I write plays for the excitement of presenting ideas in dramatic form and to explore the imaginative possibilities of the stage. Much of my energy has been devoted to creating theatre which depicts relations between Maori and Pakeha, trying to offer an alternative to both the conservative and liberal versions of race relations in New Zealand.

In recent years I've been having fun with popular forms: farce, murder mystery, etc. At a time when even the most ravenous culture vultures have abandoned the fly-blown carcass of the avant garde, it seems imperative to create theatre which has meaning and appeal to a wide audience. Theatre in New Zealand runs the risk of going the same way as poetry— of becoming an art form patronised only by a tiny cultural elite. However, the situation is not hopeless. Contrary to a widespread misconception, inventive, imaginative theatre and the general public are not mutually exclusive!

*   *   *

Stephen Sinclair can turn his hand to any form or genre. Film scripts with Peter Jackson, such as *Meet the Feebles* (the first splatter-puppet movie) and zombie comedy *Brain Dead*, come as easily to him as a musical or drama. His historical epic *The Alhambra's Master* is a drama with chorus about betrayal among Wellington seafarers at the turn of the cen-

tury, with great potential for staging on a bare platform with evocations of Wellington's harbour and city of that time. He can also write parody or parable with ease and has made collaborative writing almost his trade-mark.

A poet with published work in *Landfall*, Sinclair's first production *The Howzie Show*, in 1981, was a group effort about inner-city living which set the pattern for co-writing. *Scars of Welfare* pilloried the Social Welfare dole queues long before they became the scandal they are today. Perhaps the time for this production has come. Then in 1984 he wrote *Le Matau* (The Hook), with Samson Samasoni, for the Maori and Polynesian theatre group Taotahi, about the changes made by a Samoan immigrant as he adapts to New Zealand life and values. This play was the first exploration of the Pygmalion theme in Sinclair's work, together with his interest in race relations and lives lived in the modern city.

The film *Brain Dead* was conceived as a musical in collaboration with Frances Walsh in 1987 as well as the later film, and discussions are under way to stage it when the movie is released, in spite of the difficulties presented by its technical (and gory) requirements.

Collaborating with Frances Walsh again, Sinclair co-wrote the musical *Big Bickies*, a grotesque parable about an archetypical New Zealand couple who win the big prize in a lottery. Deliberately using cliché for satirical purposes, *Big Bickies* exposed the cynical way society exploits the naïve.

His next and most widely performed collaborative work, the commercial blockbuster *Ladies Night*, which Sinclair wrote with Anthony McCarten, brought him fame and some financial fortune. This has had numerous productions and tours in New Zealand, Australia, Canada, and Britain and has resisted critical disapproval to become the New Zealand play seen by the biggest audiences ever. Translated, it has gone to Germany, Austria, Spain, and Italy proving that some pleasures are common to women the world over.

Ladies Night tells of five young men despairingly on the dole, who decide to try anything to earn some money, including stripping at a night club. Arrogantly confident at first that they have nothing to learn, they are forced to change their ideas about what women want and to sharpen their performance skills while improving their physical trim. They learn some of life's lessons and emerge—sharper, nastier but certainly more confident—and much much richer. Their highly charged strip acts end the play, each having developed his own specialty-act to fit his personality. Audiences for *Ladies Night* came from the wider non-theatre-going crowd and many young women made multiple visits to watch what became a dramatized version of a sex show, but with laughs.

Collaboration with Danny Mulheron followed, resulting in the farce *The Sex Fiend*. Close working on the structure of this notoriously difficult form paid off, as the play was very well paced and proved extremely popular as well as critically acceptable. Sensitive "New Age" man, Matthew, has just been elected Sexual Harassment Officer at university. One evening his live-in girl friend Anna invites her friends, including a lesbian feminist poetry group, to use their flat for a reading. At the same time staunch lad Brent arrives armed with porno videos and hunting for booze and birds. In true farcical style, these and other disparate elements have to be kept apart by the increasingly frenetic Matthew, making full use of doors, stairs, mistaken identity, and discarded clothes, his own and others'. There is much harassment of the feminist poets and unexpected encounters enliven everybody's evening. All kinds of extreme attitudes of the modern post-feminist age get a sound thrashing in this very funny farce.

Sinclair next tried his hand alone at a straight comedy-drama about race and sexual relations called *Caramel Cream*, performed in 1991. This play is completely different in feeling from his preceding work, although touching again on the Pygmalion theme of *Le Matau*, and continues to demonstrate the surprising versatility of this writer. The plot concerns two inept burglars who, while avoiding the police, hide in a social welfare office where they are disturbed by lonely Claire, who is working late. She befriends them and an attraction begins to form between her and Mitch, a Maori, while Peter, a European, is suspicious of their friendship. The comic mood at the start doesn't last and we can see that the affair is doomed. Apparently Sinclair doesn't want us to think that anything can halt the slide back into violence and mindless crime from which Claire had tried to rescue Mitch. The title with its contrast of brown on the outside and white inside, is of course satirical. Structural weakness, in that there is no satisfactory dramatic climax, and the numerous short scenes in four separate settings make *Caramel Cream* disjointed on stage: perhaps it is better suited to film. Sinclair is still experimenting.

The current work in progress, again collaborating with Anthony McCarten, is a satire on the English country house murder mystery (with a New Zealand input) called *Legless*. Its alternative title, *The Curse of the Wedgecombes*, conveys its flavour better. On one level a simple comedy with a twist, it can be seen as an allegory of relations between xenophobic Britain and her old dominions, now that the European Community looms as the new club to belong to. This clever and always interesting writer is just getting into his stride.

—Patricia Cooke

SLADE, Bernard. Canadian. Born Bernard Slade Newbound in St. Catherines, Ontario, 2 May 1930. Educated at 13 schools in England and Wales, including John Ruskin School, Croydon, Surrey, and Caernarvon Grammar School. Married Jill Hancock in 1953; one daughter and one son. Moved to Canada in 1948: worked in a customs office, 1948; actor, 1949–57; co-founder, Garden Centre Theatre, Vineland, Ontario, 1954; television writer, 1957–74: wrote scripts for Canadian Broadcasting Corporation, CBS, ABC, and NBC; guest lecturer, Columbia University, New York, New York University, and University of California, Los Angeles. Recipient: Drama Desk award, 1975. Agent: Jack Hutto, 405 West 23rd Street, New York, New York 10011. Address: 1262 Lago Vista Place, Beverly Hills, California 90210, U.S.A.; and, Flat 3, 4 Egerton Place, London S.W.3., England.

PUBLICATIONS

Plays

Simon Says Get Married (produced Toronto, 1960).
A Very Close Family (produced Winnipeg, 1963).
Same Time, Next Year (produced Boston and New York, 1975; London, 1976). New York, Delacorte Press, 1975.
Tribute (produced Boston and New York, 1978; Northampton, 1984). New York, French, 1978.
Romantic Comedy (produced New York, 1979; Watford, Hertfordshire, and London, 1983). Garden City, New York, Doubleday, 1980.

Fling! New York, French, 1979.
Special Occasions (produced New York, 1982; revised version, also director: produced London, 1983). New York, French, 1982.
Fatal Attraction (produced Toronto, 1984; London, 1985). New York, French, 1986.
An Act of the Imagination (produced as *Sweet William*, Guildford, Surrey, 1987). New York, French, 1988.
Return Engagements (produced Westport, Connecticut and New York, 1988). New York, French, 1989.

Screenplays: *Stand Up and Be Counted*, 1972; *Same Time, Next Year*, 1978; *Tribute*, 1980; *Romantic Comedy*, 1983.

Television Plays: *The Prize Winner*, 1957 (revised version, as *The Long, Long Laugh*); *Men Don't Make Passes*, *Innocent Deception*, *The Gimmick*, *Do Jerry Parker*, *The Most Beautiful Girl in the World*, *The Big Coin Sound*, *The Oddball*, *The Reluctant Angels*, *A Very Close Family* and *Blue Is for Boys*, 1958–64; *Bewitched* series (16 episodes), 1963–64; pilot films for series: *Love on a Rooftop*, *The Flying Nun*, *The Partridge Family*, *Bridget Loves Bernie*, *The Girl with Something Extra*, *Mr. Deeds Goes to Town*, *The Bobby Sherman Show*, and *Mr. Angel*, 1964–74; 80 scripts for other series.

*

Manuscript Collection: Boston University, Massachusetts.

Critical Studies: article by Robert Berkvist, in *New York Times*, 13 April 1975; article by William A. Davis, in *Critical Survey of Drama* edited by Frank N. Magill, Englewood Cliffs, New Jersey, Salem Press, 1985.

Theatrical Activities:
Director: **Play**—*Special Occasions*, London, 1983.
Actor: **Plays**—roles in 300 plays throughout Canada, and on Canadian television, 1949–57; George in *Same Time, Next Year*, Edmonton, 1977.

* * *

Bernard Slade, while not so prolific as Neil Simon, has been Simon's only serious rival as a consistently commercially successful Broadway dramatist in recent years. His work is ultra-professional and, while occasionally unusually adventurous technically, artfully tailored to prevailing Broadway taste.

He had a phenomenal long-running early hit with *Same Time, Next Year*, a rare example of a successful two-character play, recalling Jan de Hartog's *The Fourposter* with adultery instead of marriage at its centre and similarly spanning the years. It follows the love affair of Doris and George, both happily married to their respective partners and with children, in a California hotel room (hardly changing in the play's six scenes), an affair which occupies one weekend every year between 1951 and 1975. The play is an accomplished laughter-rouser, especially in the scene in which an all-too pregnant Doris appears for the 1961 weekend; although somewhat overreliant on strings of smart one-liners and with noticeably grinding gear changes at more serious moments, as when George cracks up over the death of his son in Vietnam, it never descends into a sniggering comedy of adultery, and a genuine relationship emerges as Slade traces the changes in the couple over a quarter of a century of shifting middle-class American values.

In *Special Occasions* Slade again used only two characters in a shifting time-scale. In 14 scenes moving from 1970 to 1979 and set in various locales in California, New York, and Colorado, the play uses the "special occasions"—weddings, christenings, anniversaries, funerals—in the lives of a divorced couple, Amy and Michael. Slade often writes with both insight and economy into the different levels of the couple's dependence although, as in *Same Time, Next Year*, the play is at its happiest in the groove of broad mainstream comedy. Technically, in the handling of the time-shifts in an unnaturalistic manner, using almost filmic dissolves and links between the major scenes, the play is adventurous but the technique cannot compensate for a distinct air of predictability in its substance.

Romantic Comedy, a valentine to the kind of charmingly elegant comedy that once dominated Broadway and an unabashed star-vehicle play, cunningly updated an apparently moribund genre, complete with a glimpse of 1970's nudity. Set in the luxurious New York penthouse of Jason Carmichael, a successful Broadway dramatist looking for a new collaborator on the eve of his marriage, setting, style, and tone recall the world of Philip Barry in the developing relationship (again over a period of years—the mid-1960's to 1979 here) between Carmichael and Phoebe Craddock, a classic ugly duckling who develops into a beautiful swan. The play has one memorably funny scene involving the collaborators and Carmichael's sharp female agent after a disastrous opening night, but becomes a good deal too lachrymose instead of the bitter-sweet light comedy intended, as well as stiltedly over-written, in its final scenes. Even more manipulative a star-vehicle was *Tribute*, initially set in a Broadway theatre at a tribute evening to Scottie Templeton, a middle-aged screenwriter (described as "a mixture of Noël Coward, the Marx Brothers, and Peter Pan"), the participants including his agent, his doctor (it transpires that Scottie has terminal cancer), and his son. In the flashback scenes into which the play dissolves behind the scrim of the theatre setting, set in Scottie's townhouse, the complex relationship between father and son comes to be the emotional fulcrum of the evening as the two men, both wary of each other, finally make their peace. The play certainly delivered a juicy central role (performed by Jack Lemmon) and adroitly mixed pathos with slapstick comedy; it never risked alienating its public, however, always recovering with a cleverly timed gag from any hint of over-seriousness, especially evident in its sentimental ending.

Slade may yet come up with a play which charts territory more challenging than that of a skilled Broadway professional, one in which the content matches the interesting variations he has played to date with the actual form of the conventional commercial play. However, that play was certainly not *Fatal Attraction*, a would-be glossy thriller with a famous actress under a death-threat which was a disappointingly muddled farrago falling well beneath the standards of models such as *Deathtrap*.

—Alan Strachan

SMITH, Dodie (Dorothy Gladys Smith). British. 1896–1990. See 4th edition, 1988.

SMITH, Michael T(ownsend). American. Born in Kansas City, Missouri, 5 October 1935. Educated at the Hotchkiss School, Lakeville, Connecticut, 1951–53; Yale University, New Haven, Connecticut, 1953–55. Married Michele Marie Hawley in 1974 (divorced 1989); two sons. Theatre critic, 1959–74, and associate editor, 1962–65, *Village Voice*, New York (Obie award judge, 1962–68 and 1972–74); teacher, New School for Social Research, New York, 1964–65, Project Radius, Dalton, Georgia, 1972, and Hunter College, New York, 1972; instrument maker, Zuckermann Harpsichords, Stonington, Connecticut, 1974–77 and 1979–85; arts editor, Taos *News*, New Mexico, 1977–78; music, art, and theatre critic, New London *Day*, Connecticut, 1982–86; assistant press secretary to Edward I. Koch, Mayor of New York City, 1986–89; since 1992 music critic, Santa Barbara *News-Press*. Also director, lighting designer, and musician: manager, Sundance Festival Theatre, Upper Black Eddy, Pennsylvania, 1966–68; producer, Caffe Cino, New York, 1968; director, Theatre Genesis, New York, 1971–75, and Boston Early Music Festival and Exhibition, 1983–85; manager, 14th Street Lighting, New York, 1989–90; since 1990 lighting director, The Living Theater, New York. Recipient: Brandeis University Creative Arts award, 1965; Obie award, for directing, 1972; Rockefeller grant; 1975; MacDowell Colony fellowship, 1991. Address: 1801 Olive Avenue, Santa Barbara, California 93101, U.S.A.

PUBLICATIONS

Plays

I Like It (also director: produced New York, 1963). Published in *Kulchur* (New York), 1963.
The Next Thing (produced New York, 1966). Published in *The Best of Off-Off-Broadway*, edited by Smith, New York, Dutton, 1969.
More! More! I Want More!, with John P. Dodd and Remy Charlip (produced New York, 1966).
Vorspiel nach Marienstein, with John P. Dodd and Ondine (also director: produced New York, 1967).
Captain Jack's Revenge (also director: produced New York, 1970; London, 1971). Published in *New American Plays 4*, edited by William M. Hoffman, New York, Hill and Wang, 1971.
A Dog's Love, music by John Herbert McDowell (produced New York, 1971).
Tony (produced New York, 1971).
Peas (also director: produced Denver, 1971).
Country Music (also director: produced New York, 1971). Published in *The Off-Off-Broadway Book*, edited by Albert Poland and Bruce Mailman, Indianapolis, Bobbs Merrill, 1972.
Double Solitaire (also director: produced Denver, 1973).
Prussian Suite (also director: produced New York, 1974).
A Wedding Party (also director: produced Denver, 1974; New York, 1980).
Cowgirl Ecstasy (also director: produced Denver, 1976; New York, 1977).
Life Is Dream, adaptation of a play by Calderón (also director: produced Taos, New Mexico, 1979).
Heavy Pockets (also director: produced Westerly, Rhode Island, 1981).
Sameness, with Alfred Brooks (produced Denver, 1990).

Verse

American Baby. Westerly, Rhode Island, Fast Books, 1983.
A Sojourn in Paris. Westerly, Rhode Island, Fast Books, 1985.

Other

Theatre Journal, Winter 1967. Columbia, University of Missouri Press, 1968.
Theatre Trip (critical journal).   Indianapolis, Bobbs Merrill, 1969.

Editor, with Nick Orzel, *Eight Plays from Off-Off-Broadway.* Indianapolis, Bobbs Merrill, 1966.
Editor, *The Best of Off-Off-Broadway.*   New York, Dutton, 1969.
Editor, *More Plays from Off-Off-Broadway.* Indianapolis, Bobbs Merrill, 1972.

*

Theatrical Activities:
Director: **Plays**—many of his own plays, and *Three Sisters Who Are Not Sisters* by Gertrude Stein, New York, 1964; *Icarus's Mother* by Sam Shepard, New York, 1965; *Chas. Dickens' Christmas Carol* by Soren Agenoux, New York, 1966; *Donovan's Johnson* by Soren Agenoux, New York, 1967; *With Creatures Make My Way* by H.M. Koutoukas, New York, 1967; *The Life of Juanita Castro* by Ronald Tavel, Denver, 1968; *Dr. Kheal* by Mariá Irene Fornés, Denver, 1968; *Hurricane of the Eye* by Emmanuel Peluso, New York, 1969; *Eat Cake* by Jean-Claude van Itallie, Denver, 1971; *XXX* by William M. Hoffman, Denver, 1971; *Bigfoot* by Ronald Tavel, New York, 1972; *Tango Palace* by Mariá Irene Fornés, New York, 1973; *Krapp's Last Tape* by Beckett, *The Zoo Story* by Albee, and *West Side Story* by Arthur Laurents, Taos, New Mexico, 1977–78; *A Shot in the Dark* by Harry Kurnitz, Kingston, Rhode Island, 1985; *Curse of the Starving Class* by Sam Shepard, New London, Connecticut, 1985.

Michael T. Smith comments:

Circumstances too narrowly personal to be called historical have more to do with the extent and character of my plays than any political or career agenda I may have chosen and willed. It has seemed to me that the real (as opposed to manifest) content of anything I write produces itself from affinities and perceptions that I haven't much control over. In fact they control me, define me. The challenge is to find a form that transmits them, that enables me to share these infinitely intimate flashes of truth and beauty.

* * *

It all seems to refer to something else, but it is difficult to figure out what that something else is.
—*Country Music*

I offer the following tale as a model for the unconscious process that seems to underlie the plays of Michael T. Smith:

He has gone to a lot of trouble to arrange his materials. The plantain was picked while Venus was ascendant, the hair was surreptitiously cut from the sleeping girl, the circle was drawn in clean sand by the flowing stream, and now the words so carefully memorized are pronounced correctly. All these elements must be in order to produce the *event*.

Dutifully he summons demons to aid him. From the inner recesses of his consciousness and the stream, from his spinal column and the beech tree, from his shoulder and his dog, demons fly to him. He is protected from danger by the limits of his circle.

He perceives the demons as scraps of old arguments,

flashes of relieved emotions, a slight feeling of unease. Is he coming down with a cold? Why did he think of his mother? Will he stay with his lover?

His experience tells him to say "Get ye hence" to the demon-thoughts. He must go further. He's tired of emotion, bored with dialectic. "There must be something else," he thinks.

What does he want tonight? To be loved? To hate? Make fertile? Kill? None of these. Tonight he wants to be *wise*. He does not want information; he has plenty of facts. He knows that hens lay eggs, soldiers kill, lovers love. No, he wishes to know how and where to stand in relation to all his knowledge.

He throws a little something on the fire. It flares briefly, and suddenly a similar flare lights his mind. He thinks of nothing at all for some moments of eternity. The muscles of his neck relax.

After which he addresses the world as the wind makes his hair fly: "Who are you, Moon? Who are you, Stream? Who are you, Dog? Who are you, Man?"

I certainly do not wish to say that Smith is a practitioner of black or white arts. What I do mean to suggest is that Smith, like many other artists of this time, wants to explore lines of inquiry that in earlier times might have been called religious.

As the magician or priest juxtaposes disparate and often illogical elements toward a magical goal, Smith arranges his material without the superficially logical glue that audiences since Ibsen have come to expect.

Smith's stories often seem discontinuous in characterization and time. The actress playing the daughter in *Peas* is also asked to play her own mother, grandmother, and lover's other girlfriend. In *Country Music* costumes and make-up are changed drastically and abruptly. In *The Next Thing* the sequence of events is arranged aesthetically; reaction does not necessarily follow action, although within any small section time is "normal." In *Point Blank* (as yet unproduced) the opening stage direction reads, "This is a loop play. Begin anywhere, repeat several times, stop anywhere."

Thus in spite of fairly naturalistic dialogue the audience is somewhat disoriented by a Smith play. In fact because the dialogue is so "normal" Smith creates enormous tension by letting his characters play freely with role and time.

Smith's homely subject matter, which is most often the family, also is at variance with his treatment. Unlike most playwrights who write about the family, Smith is uninterested in commenting either unfavorably or favorably about his subject.

As the priest or witch places such ordinary elements as bread, wine, and plants in the context of the cosmos, so Smith exposes his characters to time, nature, and politics.

In *Country Music* two couples are exposed to the vagaries of time and weather. Their loves seem more affected by these elements than by psychology. Change seems to occur the same way buds grow. In *Captain Jack's Revenge* the characters are subject to art and politics. In the first act the people consciously try to order their awareness by means of television, radio, stereo, slide and movie projectors, telephone, and the doorbell. In the second act we see how the minds of these same people have been shaped by the actions of remote figures in American history.

Yet Smith does not tell us that we are doomed by weather, time, politics, psychology, or the media. He is pointing two ways at once, both at the solidity of certain facts, the bread and the wine, and at the cosmic context of these facts.

Yes, the couple in *Country Music* are subject to powerful forces outside their control, but look at the stars, look at the different kinds of light we can see—candlelight, sunshine, moonlight, twilight, dawn. The actors prepare food on stage and then eat it. All these experiences are called for by the author as his characters love, grow apart, leave.

Yes, the white people in *Captain Jack's Revenge* are doomed to the Indians' revenge for the crimes of their ancestors, but notice the beauty of the revenge, the glorious but mind-numbing media, the alluring but confusing drugs.

From Smith's magical (I might say "objective") point of view comes the curiously unemotional language. Rarely do his people lose their cool. They love passionately, they hate, they murder, but their language does not often reflect this. Does the playwright feel that emotion is such a heavy element on stage that the total stage picture would be unduly dominated by it? As the son says in *Peas*. "I want other people to be there without making a point of it."

Smith's plays are not designed to weigh ten tons of emotions. The audience must not be distracted from being aware they are seeing a model, not a slice, of life. The altar or voodoo dolls are not naturalistic representations either. Perhaps the logic of a Smith play is: If you can portray a situation objectively, with the freedom to be playful, if you can see the total picture, if you can arrange the elements of existence, you can induce a state of mind that allows us to see the magic of everyday life.

—William M. Hoffman

SNYDER, William (Hartwell, Jr.). American. Born in 1929. See 2nd edition, 1977.

SOFOLA, Zulu. Nigerian. Born in Issele-Uku, 22 June 1935. Educated at Virginia Union University, Richmond, B.A. in English (cum laude) 1959; Catholic University of America, Washington, D.C., M.A. in drama 1966; University of Ibadan, Ph.D. in tragic theory 1977. Married J.A. Sofola in 1960; four sons and one daughter. Coordinator of extra-mural programme, University of Ibadan, 1968–70; acting head of the performing arts department, 1985–87, and since 1989 head of department, University of Ilorin, Kwara State; senior visiting professor, State University of New York, Buffalo, New York, 1988–89. Recipient: African-American scholarship, 1961–62; Ford Foundation fellowship, 1969–72; University of Missouri award, 1971; African Writers Project award, 1980; Ife International Book Fair award, 1987; Fulbright fellowship, 1988. Address: c/o Department of the Performing Arts, Faculty of Arts, University of Ilorin, Ilorin, Kwara State, Nigeria.

PUBLICATIONS

Plays

The Disturbed Peace of Christmas (produced Ibadan, 1969). Ibadan, Daystar Press, 1971.
Wedlock of the Gods (also director: produced Columbia, Missouri, 1971). London, Evans Brothers, 1973.

The Operators (produced Ibadan, 1973). Included in *Lost Dreams and Other Plays*, 1992.
King Emene (produced Ibadan, 1975). Ibadan, Heinemann, 1974.
Old Wines Are Tasty (produced Ibadan, 1975). Ibadan, University Press, 1981.
The Sweet Trap (produced Ibadan, 1975; also director: produced Buffalo, New York, 1988). Ibadan, University Press, 1977.
The Wizard of Law. London, Evans Brothers, 1976.
The Deer and the Hunters Pearl (produced Ibadan, 1976).
Memories in the Moonlight (produced Ibadan, 1977). London, Evans Brothers, 1986.
Song of a Maiden (produced Ilorin, 1977). Ibadan, University Press, 1991.
Queen Omu-Ako of Oligbo (also director: produced Buffalo, New York, 1989).
Eclipso and the Fantasia (produced Ilorin, 1990).
Lost Dreams (produced Ilorin, 1991). Included in *Lost Dreams and Other Plays*, 1992.
The Showers (produced Ilorin, 1991). Included in *Lost Dreams and Other Plays*, 1992.
The Love of the Life. Included in *Lost Dreams and Other Plays*, 1992.
Lost Dreams and Other Plays (includes *Lost Dreams*, *The Operators*, *The Love of the Life*, *The Showers*). Ibadan, Heinemann, 1992.

Other plays: *The Ivory Tower*; *A Celebration of Life*.

*

Theatrical Activities:
Director: **Plays**—*Wedlock of the Gods*, Columbia, Missouri, 1971; *King Emene*, Ibadan, 1978; *The Sweet Trap*, Buffalo, New York, 1988; *Queen Omu-Ako Oligbo*, Buffalo, New York, 1989.

Zulu Sofola comments:
My main areas of research are into the African concept of tragedy, the creative process, the artist in traditional society, and African aesthetics. In my plays I explore the tragic factor in African cosmology in a search for an Afro-centric theory that may help the African scholar to better define African humanity. Consequently in my plays I have treated the aspects in traditional society where customs and moral precepts set themselves at war against individual citizens, as is the case in: *Wedlock of the Gods*; *Song of a Maiden*, where a university intelligentsia reject the philosophy of "town and gown" and become irrelevant; *Queen Omu-Ako of Oligbo*, where the traditional female arm of government confronts the warring camps of the Federal Government of Biafra in defence of the citizens in the Ani'ocha area of Delta State; and in *The Sweet Trap* where a misguided elite engage in a meaningless gender debate, a battle of the sexes.

*   *   *

Zulu Sofola is the first published and established female Nigerian dramatist and theatre practitioner of English expression. The main thematic concerns and preoccupations of her textual/dramatic output are the utilization of tradition to address various other contemporary issues and concepts such as the state and status of women in modern society, the individual in contending western and indigenous African cultures, and individual and group moralities as influenced and determined by religious persuasions, social and communal ethics, and history.

Zulu Sofola's plays employ elements of magic, legend, myth, ritual, and folklore to explore the enduring conflicts between indigenous African traditionalism and Western-induced modernism with an often undisguised preference for the former. In her exploration and examination of this conflict, the patriarchal male supremacy survives or is at best gently admonished to accommodate and recognize the importance of women in a male-dominated society. Some of her major plays also manifest her vision of individual and group tragedy, mainly derived from her indigenous African perception and cosmology. Again, this conception of tragedy arises from individual protagonists and female representatives of the women's liberation movement who attempt to break the existing harmonious culture of patriarchy. Her most produced play, *Wedlock of the Gods*, explores the repercussions of an attempt to violate traditional lores and order. Her other important plays which examine traditional issues include *King Emene*, *Old Wines Are Tasty*, and *Memories in the Moonlight*. Her more contemporary plays which deal with women's struggle for liberation and the conflict between academia (gown) and the macro-society (town) are *The Sweet Trap* and *Song of a Maiden* respectively.

Myth, legend, and magic enrich and structure her dramaturgy in traditional themes where characters who defy age-old conventions are revealed as treading tragic paths. Uloko and Ugwoma in *Wedlock of the Gods* are passionate and genuine lovers who cannot consummate their love in marriage because an older and more acceptable (to the parents) suitor exists. As it turns out, the older suitor dies shortly after marrying Ugwoma and the two lovers return to their original purpose of getting married without waiting for the prescribed traditional mourning period and rites for the late husband to pass. As expected, the enraged mother-in-law makes it her responsibility to set tradition back on course by evoking her magical powers to destroy the new couple. Here is an oversimplified mythopoesis in which tragedy equates defiance of traditional codes and mores.

This tradition of imposing an elderly man on an unwilling young girl who has already chosen her partner recurs in the play *Memories in the Moonlight*. In the end, Abiona marries her dream man and the plot is resolved via metaphysics and traditional contrivance where an arranged parent/suitor reconciliation takes place.

The Sweet Trap employs a traditional cleansing ceremony (Okebadan Festival, an exclusive male cult accomplished by licence and permitted abuse of the female sex) to celebrate a traditionally Nigerian supremacy of the man over his wife or wives. In this play, using the three-act dramatic structure, Sofola counsels—against the growing wave of feminism in the country, particularly in university circles where she teaches—that harmonious matrimony requires that a wife recognize and accept her husband's supremacy, with, of course, a gentle appeal to husbands to accord their wives due emotional regard. The plot takes off in Femi Sotubo's university residence. Femi applies brute force and chauvinism to deny his wife the right to celebrate her birthday. Encouraged by her friends and with the promise of a venue to celebrate the birthday, Clara Sotubo changes from an initial position of docility and submission to one of violent defiance and self-assertion. The party goes on. As it turns out, the birthday party ends in a fiasco and humiliation as the Okebadan celebrants intrude on the arena and generously dole out abuse to the women, who in confusion blame each other for being responsible for initiating the party. After the disruption, the resolution of the play comes from Dr. Jinadu, who advises Clara to apologise to her husband, advice she gleefully takes and complies with. She cringes on her knees for stubbornly

going against "tradition." The thesis of the play is an advocation of female submission in order to avert matrimonial disharmony.

Sofola's conceptual vision of tragedy grows out of her traditionalist vision of a particular African world view which emphasizes that iconoclasm and unorthodoxy disrupt cosmic harmony and wreak historical discontinuity on the communal psyche. An individual in this perception is independent within a communal equilibrium. Tragedy occurs when that independence is extended beyond the communal ethos and cosmos. Tragedy can be averted through conformity or atonement and expiation. In the play *King Emene*, a usurpation of the throne has taken place through intrigue and a murder contrived by Emene's mother in order to deprive the deceased of his due right of ascendancy and place his own son on the throne. Inevitably, disharmony occurs and the kingdom is troubled. King Emene aggravates the situation when he rejects the admonition of elders that he should not perform the rites which usher in the Peace Week because a heinous crime needing cleansing and propitiation has been committed. Oblivious of the facts of the situation, Emene interprets this as a plot against him and proceeds with the rites during which he is suddenly and mysteriously attacked by a boa. He is shamed and inevitably commits suicide. Thus, unexpiated crime and defiance of traditional wisdom occasion the tragedy of King Emene.

Sofola's thematic concerns with tragedy, metaphysics, gender problems, and individual and societal conflict with a growing Western modernism are all anchored structurally and perceptually in certain traditionalist aesthetics. Technically, her plays are simple and accessible, at times bordering on oversimplification. Her dialogue and characterization oscillate between the sketchy and the profound. Her language is clear and unobtrusive, ranging between standard English usage and direct translation from her vernacular African linguistic sources and background, and partly responsible for audience interest in her theatre.

—Olu Obafemi

SOWANDE, Bode. Nigerian. Born in Kaduna, Nigeria, 2 May 1948. Educated at the University of Ife (now Obafemi Awolowo University), Ife-Ife, 1967–71, B.A. in French (honours) 1971; University of Dakar, Senegal, 1969, diplôme d'études françaises 1970; University of Sheffield, England, 1973–77, M.A. in dramatic literature 1974, Ph.D. 1977. Married with children. Resident playwright, Orisun Theatre, Lagos, 1968–71; founder, 1972, and since 1972 resident playwright Odu Themes, and Odu Themes Meridian (drama studio), 1986, both Ibadan; senior lecturer, department of theatre arts, University of Ibadan, 1977–90; visiting lecturer, universities of Sheffield, Leeds, and Kent, England, 1988, and universities of Rome, L'Aquila, and Lecce, Italy, 1990–91; international theatre residence, France, 1990. Recipient: T.M. Aluko prize, for creative writing, 1966; University of Ife creative writing prize, 1968; University of Sheffield Edgar Allen award, for academic proficiency, 1975; Association of Nigerian Authors Drama award, 1987, 1989; British Council fellowship, 1988; French National award, 1991. Address: c/o Odu Themes Meridian, 33 Oyo Road, Orita, U.I., P.O. Box 14369, U.I. Post Office, Ibadan, Nigeria.

PUBLICATIONS

Plays

The Night Before (produced Ibadan, 1972). Included in
    Farewell to Babylon and Other Plays, 1979.
Lamps in the Night (produced Ibadan, 1973).
Bar Beach Prelude (televised 1974; produced London, 1976).
A Sanctus for Women (as *The Angry Bridegroom*, produced
    Sheffield, England, 1976). Included in *Farewell to
    Babylon and Other Plays*, 1979.
Afamako—the Workhorse (produced Ibadan, 1978).
    Included in *Flamingo and Other Plays*, 1986.
Farewell to Babylon (produced Ibadan, 1978). Included in
    Farewell to Babylon and Other Plays, 1979.
Kalakutu Cross Currents (produced Ibadan, 1979).
The Master and the Frauds (produced Geneva, Switzerland,
    1979). Included in *Flamingo and Other Plays*, 1986.
Farewell to Babylon and Other Plays. London, Longman,
    1979.
Barabas and the Master Jesus (produced Ibadan, 1980).
Flamingo (produced Ibadan, 1982; London, 1992). Included
    in *Flamingo and Other Plays*, 1986.
Circus of Freedom Square (produced L'Aquila, Italy, 1985).
    Included in *Flamingo and Other Plays*, 1986.
Flamingo and Other Plays. London, Longman, 1986.
Tornadoes Full of Dreams (produced Lagos, 1989). Lagos,
    Malthouse Press, 1990.
Arelu, adaptation of *The Miser* by Molière (produced Lagos,
    1990).
Ajantala-Pinocchio (produced Chieri, Italy, 1992).

Radio and Television Plays: *Bar Beach Prelude*, 1974; *Get a
Pigeon from Trafalgar Square*, 1975; *Beggar's Choice*, 1976;
Acada Campus series, 1980–82; *Flamingo* series, 1982;
Penance series, 1983; *My Brother's Keeper* (13 episodes),
1983; *Without a Home* series, 1984; *Dream for the Sun*, 1988.

Novels

Our Man the President. Ibadan, Spectrum, 1981.
Without a Home. London, Longman, 1982.
The Missing Bridesmaid. Ibadan, A.B.M, 1988.

*

Theatrical Activities:
Actor: **Plays**—Baba Fakunle in *The Gods Are Not to Blame*
by Ola Rotimi, Ibadan, 1968; chorus leader in *Chaka* by
Léopold Sedar Senghor, Ibadan, 1970; Old man in *A Sanctus
for Women*, Sheffield, 1976; Bello in *Afamako—the
Workhorse*, Ibadan, 1978; Monrian in *Farewell to Babylon*,
Ibadan, 1978; Monrian in *Flamingo*, Ibadan, 1982.

Bode Sowande comments:
    Writing came to me and from within me as a pleasure but
the creative sensibility teaches me its attendant responsibility.
Whatever the roots of my African self, I realize that in the
global continent the human spirit flows into the countless
branches of the same expression. At every turn values should
be naturally renewed, and in a crisis-torn world, a militant
hope is the needed virtue for today's heroism.
    I dread pigeon-holing, but I celebrate the variety of
nature's expression in man, and salute the original genius of
creating names for the world's objects and people.
    I consider today's man as an exile from his natural heritage.
If only to go back "home," I believe that fine creative writing

is a necessary compass for today's map in education and in
leisure.
    In the creative arts, in the living theatre, in "good" tele-
vision, story telling and documentation, I am in my element.

*   *   *

    Bode Sowande belongs to the second generation of drama-
tists in Nigeria with its conscious, materialist approach to
society. The first generation includes notable Nigerian playwrights and dramatists such as Henshaw, Soyinka, and Clark.
    Sowande's major plays draw dramatic conflicts around
clear class antagonism and attempt a dialectical interpretation
of this problem, proposing successful ethical solutions in
favour of the underprivileged working and peasant masses.
However, Sowande can be distinguished from his colleagues
of the avant garde generation of dramatists in Nigeria, which
include Femi Osofisan, Kole Omotoso, and Tunde Fatunde,
by his philosophy of Spiritual Nationalism, a vision which
circumscribes ideology within metaphysical consciousness.
His major play, which actually establishes this mediational
philosophy of materialism, is *Farewell to Babylon*, the sequel
to *The Night Before*, and in the same collection as *A Sanctus
for Women*. Sowande's other major plays, apart from
his numerous television scripts and radio dramas, include
Circus of Freedom Square, *Afamako—the Workhorse*, and
Tornadoes Full of Dreams, this last a drama commissioned by
the French Cultural Centre in Lagos commemorating the
bicentenary of the 1789 French Revolution. His recent play
Arelu is a free adaptation into Yoruba of Molière's *The
Miser*, again sponsored by the French Embassy in Lagos. All
of these plays manifest eloquently the dramatist's faithful
identification with the issues which plague contemporary society and which need urgent attention. The issues range from
oppression and exploitation by the dominant political elite of
the underprivileged, to the alienation and disillusionment of
young people, to the growing aggressive materialism with its
lethal potential for a virile social culture, and general social
incoherence.
    Most of these features of social decadence are already
amply evident in his early play, *The Night Before*. The play
narrates, in a non-lineal episodic form, the experience of six
undergraduate students on the eve of their graduation ceremony. The anticipated euphoria of this kind of moment is
submerged for these young intellectuals by sombre reflections
and reveries of an unenviable past which casts shadows on the
promise of a bright future. The night turns into a confessional
and expositional one where hidden truths of the past are laid
bare. Their individual and collective activism has been
marred by certain individual failings which disarm them from
the challenges of the outside world. Onita, the perceptive
artist, is unable to accommodate the banality of the environment. Moniran's optimism is blighted by memories of his lost
Students' Union electioneering campaigns. Dabira burns his
academic gown as a symbol of his renunciation of the convocation which has been undermined by the romance treachery
perpetrated by Onita and Ibilola. Nibidi and Moye make up
their minds to join the aggressive, acquisitive world outside.
    The central theme of the play, which is conveyed through a
combination of the play-within-the-play device, role playing,
flashbacks, and the direct address formula—all of which are
experiments within the Brechtian epic dramatic mode—is the
inevitable sense of defeat and frustration which a pervasively
and rabidly corrupt social order engenders in otherwise
idealistic young people. There is a kind of critical realism in
this play which is rather cynical in view of the revolutionary
promise of the beginning. Rather than gathering the strands

of the imperative of struggle which the idealism of the students potentially manifests, the play flounders into a cataloguing of the tales and narratives of failed progressives. A revolutionary outlook gives way to cynicism and open-ended despair.

Farewell to Babylon is a more purposeful and more emphatic political statement than *The Night Before*. There are definite programmes of action by the committed individual characters in the play. Onita and Moniran, erstwhile colleagues in the earlier play, join opposing sides of the social system. Moniran joins the military dictatorship while Onita joins the Farmers' Movement. The play's events bear a strong resemblance to the Agbekoya uprising of the late 1960's in the Western State of Nigeria where the military government invoked state apparatus to smash a massive people's revolt. Moniran becomes head of the state police called the Octopus which harasses and arrests vast numbers of revolutionary farmers, student activists, and progressive intellectuals. Moniran's fiancée Jolomitutu is also turned into a police detective and sent among the farmers where she successfully undermines the position of Dansaki, the farmers' leader, and extracts vital information in the process. Onita, a university don who resigns his lecturing job to join the farmers' movement, is arrested and faces, in the process of interrogation, his age-long friend and colleague Moniran. The encounter leads to a dialogic revelation of their positions as revolutionaries during which Onita contemptuously spits in the face of his doubted friend. The death of Onita at the hands of Cookey, his psychopathic fellow-inmate in prison, denies him the knowledge of the true and continuing identity of Moniran, who dethrones the dictatorial president in a coup under Major Kasa during which a compromise with the farmers and the promise of a civil democracy are achieved.

Using the dramaturgical devices of pantomime, visual and kinetic effects, song, and dialogue, Sowande proposes a revolution which is at once political as well as spiritual and abstract. This proposition is, however, only suggested in the play. A recognition of metaphysics and spiritualist abstractions as viable instruments for attaining an alternative social order is shown in *A Sanctus for Women*, where the Yoruba legend of Olurombi is evoked to caution against aggressive and uncritical materialism in society.

Both in his plays and in his numerous radio and television series such as *Acada Campus* and the serialized novel *Without a Home*, socio-political transformation is seminal to Sowande's creative ideology and vision.

—Olu Obafemi

SOYINKA, Wole (Akinwande Oluwole Soyinka). Nigerian. Born in Abeokuta, 13 July 1934. Educated at St. Peter's School, Ake, Abeokuta, 1938–43; Abeokuta Grammar School, 1944–45; Government College, Ibadan, 1946–50; University College, Ibadan (now University of Ibadan), 1952–54; University of Leeds, Yorkshire, 1954–57, B.A. (honours) in English. Married; has children. Play reader, Royal Court Theatre, London, 1957–59; Rockefeller research fellow in drama, University of Ibadan, 1961–62; lecturer in English, University of Ife, Ifelfe, 1963–64; senior lecturer in English, University of Lagos, 1965–67; head of the department of theatre arts, University of Ibadan, 1969–72 (appoint-

ment made in 1967); professor of comparative literature, and head of the department of dramatic arts, University of Ife, 1975–85; Goldwin Smith professor of Africana studies and theatre, Cornell University, Ithaca, New York, from 1988. Visiting fellow, Churchill College, Cambridge, 1973–74; visiting professor, University of Ghana, Legon, 1973–74, University of Sheffield, 1974, Yale University, New Haven, Connecticut, 1979–80, and Cornell University, 1986. Founding director, 1960 Masks Theatre, 1960, and Orisun Theatre, 1964, Lagos and Ibadan, and Unife Guerilla Theatre, Ifelfe, 1978; co-editor, *Black Orpheus*, 1961–64; editor, *Transition* (later *Ch'indaba*) magazine, Accra, Ghana, 1975–77. Secretary-general, Union of Writers of the African Peoples, 1975. Tried and acquitted of armed robbery, 1965; political prisoner, detained by the Federal Military Government, Lagos and Kaduna, 1967–69. Recipient: Dakar Festival award, 1966; John Whiting award, 1967; Jock Campbell award (*New Statesman*), for fiction, 1968; Nobel prize for literature, 1986; AGIP-Mattei award, 1986; Benson medal, 1990; Premio Letterario Internazionale Mondello, 1990. D.Litt: University of Leeds, 1973; Yale University, 1981; Paul Valéry University, Montpellier, France, 1984; University of Lagos; Morehouse College, Atlanta, 1988; University of Bayreuth, Germany, 1989. Fellow, Royal Society of Literature; member, American Academy, and Academy of Arts and Letters of the German Democratic Republic. Commander, Federal Republic of Nigeria, 1986, Legion of Honour (France), 1989, and Order of the Republic of Italy, 1990; Akogun of Isara, 1989; Akinlatun of Egbaland, 1990. Agent: Morton Leavy, Leavy Rosensweig and Hyman, 11 East 44th Street, New York, New York 10017; or Carl Brandt, Brandt and Brandt, 1501 Broadway, New York, New York 10036, U.S.A. Address: P.O. Box 935, Abeokuta, Nigeria.

PUBLICATIONS

Plays

The Swamp Dwellers (produced London, 1958; New York, 1968). Included in *Three Plays*, 1963; in *Five Plays*, 1964.
The Lion and the Jewel (produced Ibadan, 1959; London, 1966). Ibadan, London, and New York, Oxford University Press, 1963.
The Invention (produced London, 1959).
A Dance of the Forests (produced Lagos, 1960). Ibadan, London, and New York, Oxford University Press, 1963.
The Trials of Brother Jero (produced Ibadan, 1960; Cambridge, 1965; London, 1966; New York, 1967). Included in *Three Plays*, 1963; in *Five Plays*, 1964.
Camwood on the Leaves (broadcast 1960). London, Eyre Methuen, 1973; in *Camwood on the Leaves, and Before the Blackout*, 1974.
The Republican and *The New Republican* (satirical revues; produced Lagos, 1963).
Three Plays. Ibadan, Mbari, 1963; as *Three Short Plays*, London, Oxford University Press, 1969.
The Strong Breed (produced Ibadan, 1964; London, 1966; New York, 1967). Included in *Three Plays*, 1963; in *Five Plays*, 1964.
Childe Internationale (produced Ibadan, 1964). Ibadan, Fountain, 1987.
Kongi's Harvest (produced Ibadan, 1964; New York, 1968). Ibadan, London, and New York, Oxford University Press, 1967.
Five Plays: A Dance of the Forests, The Lion and the Jewel,

The Swamp Dwellers, The Trials of Brother Jero, The Strong Breed. Ibadan, London, and New York, Oxford University Press, 1964.
Before the Blackout (produced Ibadan, 1965; Leeds, 1981). Ibadan, Orisun, 1971; in *Camwood on the Leaves, and Before the Blackout*, 1974.
The Road (produced London, 1965; also director: produced Chicago, 1984). Ibadan, London, and New York, Oxford University Press, 1965.
Rites of the Harmattan Solstice (produced Lagos, 1966).
Madmen and Specialists (produced Waterford, Connecticut, and New York, 1970; revised version, also director: produced Ibadan, 1971). London, Methuen, 1971; New York, Hill and Wang, 1972.
The Jero Plays: The Trials of Brother Jero, and Jero's Metamorphosis. London, Eyre Methuen, 1973.
Jero's Metamorphosis (produced Lagos, 1975). Included in *The Jero Plays*, 1973.
The Bacchae: A Communion Rite, adaptation of the play by Euripides (produced London, 1973). London, Eyre Methuen, 1973; New York, Norton, 1974.
Collected Plays:
1. *A Dance of the Forests, The Swamp Dwellers, The Strong Breed, The Road, The Bacchae.* London and New York, Oxford University Press, 1973.
2. *The Lion and the Jewel, Kongi's Harvest, The Trials of Brother Jero, Jero's Metamorphosis, Madmen and Specialists.* London and New York, Oxford University Press, 1974.
Camwood on the Leaves, and Before the Blackout: Two Short Plays. New York, Third Press, 1974.
Death and the King's Horseman (also director: produced IfeIfe, 1976; Chicago, 1979; also director: produced New York, 1987; Manchester, 1990). London, Eyre Methuen, 1975; New York, Norton, 1976.
Opera Wonyosi, adaptation of *The Threepenny Opera* by Brecht (also director: produced IfeIfe, 1977).Bloomington, Indiana University Press, and London, Collings, 1981.
Golden Accord (produced Louisville, 1980).
Priority Projects (revue; produced on Nigeria tour, 1982).
Requiem for a Futurologist (also director: produced IfeIfe, 1983). London, Collings, 1985.
A Play of Giants (also director: produced New Haven, Connecticut, 1984). London, Methuen, 1984.
Six Plays (includes *The Trials of Brother Jero, Jero's Metamorphosis, Camwood on the Leaves, Death and the King's Horseman, Madmen and Specialists, Opera Wonyosi*). London, Methuen, 1984.
A Scourge of Hyacinths (broadcast 1990). Published with *From Zia with Love*, London, Methuen, 1992.

Screenplay: *Kongi's Harvest*, 1970.

Radio Plays: *Camwood on the Leaves*, 1960; *The Detainee*, 1965; *Die Still, Dr. Godspeak*, 1981; *A Scourge of Hyacinths*, 1990.

Television Plays: *Joshua: A Nigerian Portrait*, 1962 (Canada); *Culture in Transition*, 1963 (USA).

Novels

The Interpreters. London, Deutsch, 1965; New York, Macmillan, 1970.
Season of Anomy. London, Collings, 1973; New York, Third Press, 1974.

Verse

Idanre and Other Poems. London, Methuen, 1967; New York, Hill and Wang, 1968.
Poems from Prison. London, Collings, 1969.
A Shuttle in the Crypt. London, Eyre Methuen-Collings, and New York, Hill and Wang, 1972.
Ogun Abibimañ. London, Collings, 1976.
Mandela's Earth and Other Poems. New York, Random House, 1988; London, Deutsch, 1989.

Other

The Man Died: Prison Notes. London, Eyre Methuen-Collings, and New York, Harper, 1972.
In Person: Achebe, Awoonor, and Soyinka at the University of Washington. Seattle, University of Washington African Studies Program, 1975.
Myth, Literature, and the African World. London, Cambridge University Press, 1976.
Aké: The Years of Childhood (autobiography). London, Collings, 1981; New York, Vintage, 1983.
The Critic and Society (essay). IfeIfe, University of Ife Press, 1981.
The Past Must Address Its Present (lecture). N.p., Nobel Foundation, 1986; as *This Past Must Address Its Present*, New York, Anson Phelps Institute, 1988.
Art, Dialogue and Outrage: Essays on Literature and Culture. Ibadan, New Horn, 1988.
Isara: A Voyage Around "Essay." New York, Random House, 1989; London, Methuen, 1990.

Editor, *Poems of Black Africa.* London, Secker and Warburg, and New York, Hill and Wang, 1975.

Translator, *The Forest of a Thousand Daemons: A Hunter's Saga*, by D.O. Fagunwa. London, Nelson, 1968; New York, Humanities Press, 1969.

*

Bibliography: *Wole Soyinka: A Bibliography* by B. Okpu, Lagos, Libriservice, 1984.

Critical Studies: *Wole Soyinka* by Gerald Moore, London, Evans, and New York, Africana, 1971, revised edition, Evans, 1978; *The Writing of Wole Soyinka* by Eldred D. Jones, London, Heinemann, 1973, revised edition, 1983, 2nd revised edition, London, Curry, 1988; *The Movement of Transition: A Study of the Plays of Wole Soyinka* by Oyin Ogunba, Ibadan, Ibadan University Press, 1975; *Komik, Ironie, und Satire im Dramatischen Werk von Wole Soyinka* by Rita Bottcher-Wobcke, Hamburg, Buske, 1976; *A Dance of Masks: Sengher, Achebe, Soyinka* by Jonathan Peters, Washington, D.C., Three Continents, 1978; *Notes on Wole Soyinka's The Jero Plays* edited by E.M. Parsons, London, Methuen, 1979; *Critical Perspectives on Wole Soyinka* edited by James Gibbs, Washington, D.C., Three Continents, 1980, London, Heinemann, 1981, and *Wole Soyinka* by Gibbs, London, Macmillan, and New York, Grove Press, 1986; *The Lion and the Jewel: A Critical View* by Martin Banham, London, Collings, 1981; *Theatre and Nationalism: Wole Soyinka and LeRoi Jones* by Alain Ricard, Ife-Ife, University of Ife Press, 1983; *A Writer and His Gods: A Study of the Importance of Yoruba Myths and Religious Ideas in the Writing of Wole Soyinka* by Stephan Larsen, Stockholm, University of Stockholm, 1983; *Wole Soyinka and Modern*

Tragedy: A Study of Dramatic Theory and Practice edited by Ketu E. Katrak, Westport, Connecticut, Greenwood Press, 1986; *Wole Soyinka: An Introduction to His Writing* by Obi Maduakar, London, Garland, 1986; *Before Our Very Eyes: Tribute to Wole Soyinka* edited by Dapo Adelugba, Ibadan, Spectrum, 1987; *Index of Subjects, Proverbs and Themes in the Writings of Wole Soyinka* by Greta M.K. Coger, New York, Greenwood, 1988; *The Essential Soyinka: A Reader*, edited by Henry Louis Gates, Jr., New York, Pantheon, 1991.

Theatrical Activities:
Director: **Plays**—by Brecht, Chekhov, Clark, Easmon, Eseoghene, Ogunyemi, Shakespeare, Synge, and his own works; *L'Espace et la Magie*, Paris, 1972; *The Biko Inquest* by Jon Blair and Norman Fenton, IfeIfe, 1978, and New York, 1980.
Actor: **Plays**—Igwezu in *The Swamp Dwellers*, London, 1958; Obaneji and Forest Father in *A Dance of the Forests*, Lagos and Ibadan, 1960; Dauda Touray in *Dear Parent and Ogre* by R. Sarif Easmon, Ibadan, 1961; in *The Republican*, Lagos, 1963; **Film**—*Kongi's Harvest*, 1970; **Radio**—Konu in *The Detainee*, 1965.

* * *

Wole Soyinka's dramatic concerns are as varied as the settings of his plays. Key themes that run through Soyinka's plays are his preoccupation with death, his fascination with the creative-destructive principle as embodied in the contradictory essence of Ogun (his creative Muse), and a belief in the ever-recurring cycle of human stupidity and violence. Added to these are his faith in special individuals whose singular acts of courage alone can save an errant humanity always on the verge of self-destruction. These themes are found in varying degrees in most Soyinka plays, sometimes individually and sometimes in combination.

Death holds a unique place in Soyinka's dramatic consciousness as can be seen from *The Road, Death and the King's Horseman, The Strong Breed, Requiem for a Futurologist, Camwood on the Leaves, A Dance of the Forests*, and *The Bacchae: A Communion Rite*. The first two plays explore death as both a ritual process and a phenomenon of transition in Yoruba metaphysics. *The Road* deals with the Yoruba ritual of *agemo*, the neither-nor phase between the moment of death and the physical dissolution of the flesh. Professor interrupts the death process of Murano in order to study this phase in the transition from one plane of existence to another. The tragedy in the play arises from this sacrilege and act of hubris which Professor pays for with his own life. A similar interruption of a ritual process of death by Pilkings leads to tragedy for Elesin and the Yoruba world in *Death and the King's Horseman*. Soyinka's explorations are anchored on the notion that death, like birth, is merely a stage in the process of life—that life exists on three planes and that crossing from one to another requires a rite of passage and a journey through the gulf of transition. An understanding of this helps to understand Soyinka's drama, especially the complex plays like *A Dance of the Forests* where the intercrossing between the planes of the dead, the living, the unborn, and the gods provides the dynamics and tension, and *Death and the King's Horseman*, in which Elesin is expected to commit suicide so as to accompany the dead Alafin to the world of the ancestors.

In *The Strong Breed*, Eman belongs to the eponymous group whose duty it is to carry the sins of the community every year. His tragedy is that in trying to avoid this lighter fate of being "carrier" for his own community, he meets the heavier fate of becoming "scapegoat" for another community. What unites these plays is Soyinka's request that his audience understand death not as the sad end that it is in some cultures, but rather as a journey into knowledge and life. *Requiem for a Futurologist* is a satiric reaction to a 1983 prediction that a prominent Nigerian dramatist was going to die in an accident. But despite treating Godspeak's "death" as a farce, Soyinka continues to probe the deeper significance of death. The play asks very disturbing questions which are left unanswered in the end.

What Soyinka does brilliantly in his "death" plays is use them to examine the notion of tragedy. Tragedy to Soyinka does not always mean death for the major character. The tragic moments are often those when the central character courageously enters the gulf of transition, confronts the forces that guard it, and finally emerges with new knowledge to energize his community. His tragedy is therefore an individual experience undertaken on behalf of the community. Pentheus dies so that Thebes might be saved from the vengeance of Dionysus and we are therefore not surprised when at the end of *The Bacchae* the entire community celebrates with wine spurting from his impaled head. Olunde's death in *Death and the King's Horseman*, Professor's in *The Road*, Eman's in *The Strong Breed*, and Erinjobi's in *Camwood on the Leaves* all have this quality of communal beneficence. This view of tragedy is peculiarly African.

The recurring cycle of human stupidity is the theme of *Dance of the Forests*, where the human community, in celebrating its history, refuses to acknowledge the crimes of the past. The cycle of crime and violence will persist unless a courageous individual breaks it. Demoke could have, but he returns the Half-Child to its dead mother and the cycle continues. *Madmen and Specialists* is Soyinka's exploration of this cycle in a Nigeria just out of a civil war. In the nihilist philosophy of AS, he states the eternal futility of human action: "AS was the Beginning, AS is Now, AS ever shall be. . .." This philosophy of despair asserts that there is never change in human existence since life returns to its ordained path. And even when power-crazy Bero kills Old Man, his action promises no escape; instead, it is back to another cycle of human misery and cannibalism which is the reality of war.

Soyinka creates strong characters by endowing them with the creative-destructive impulse of Ogun, the god of war and of creativity. Most of his heroes—Elesin in *Death and the King's Horseman*, Professor in *The Road*, Demoke in *A Dance of the Forests*, Eman in *The Strong Breed*, Dionysus in *The Bacchae*, Daoudu and Segi in *Kongi's Harvest*—all share in the singular ability to be both creative and destructive. Also, they all in a way breach the gulf of transition like Ogun did as the first victim/hero of Yoruba tragic rites. And their vitality stems from the tension between their contradictory essences.

Although Soyinka writes about the myths, rituals, and metaphysics of the Yoruba, his plays escape parochialism. This is because he merely uses his Yoruba origins as a creative fount and anchor in his exploration of contemporary Nigerian and universal concerns. His plays are statements on prevailing political, ethical, and social issues. Even his most ritualistic plays are political and social, pointing to the fact that his is a mind sensitive to the environment. From the delightful *The Lion and the Jewel*, in which he looks at modernity versus tradition, through the hugely successful satire on religious charlatanism and susceptibility of *The Jero Plays*, *The Swamp Dwellers*, in which he pits the near-violent but deep-seated anguish of Igwezu against the corrupt priesthood of Kadiye, to the domestic comedy *Childe Internationale*, Soyinka remains the barometer of his society. His very political plays are *Kongi's Harvest*, his attack on the burgeoning dictators all over the African continent represented by Kongi, *Opera Wonyosi*, and *A Play of Giants* in which he attacks Africa's well-known quartet—Bokasa, Amin, Nguema, and Mobutu. *Opera Wonyosi* deals with madness and corruption in Bokasa's Central African Republic, while *A Play of Giants* portrays the four dictators as unfortunate aberrations that are only fit for Madame Tussaud's Chamber of Horrors. In the last, Soyinka is at his satiric best as he paints these human monstrosities as oversized and grotesque buffoons who have no place in human society and history.

However, Soyinka's major contribution to theatre is his attempt to create a theatre that is genuinely African. He has gone back to his Yoruba heritage and enriched his writing with its rituals, dances, songs, and beliefs. But above all, he has borrowed and adapted for contemporary African and non-African audiences the very rich Yoruba theatre sensibility, which he integrates with his firm knowledge of world theatre styles and traditions. The result is a vibrant theatre that is uniquely Soyinkan.

—Osita Okagbue

SPEIGHT, Johnny. British. Born in Canning Town, London, 2 June 1920. Educated at St. Helen's School. Married Constance Barrett in 1956; two sons and one daughter. Worked in a factory, as a jazz drummer and insurance salesman; then writer for BBC radio and television. Recipient: Screenwriters Guild award, 1962, 1966, 1967, 1968; *Evening Standard* award, 1977; Pye award, for television writing, 1983. Address: Fouracres, Heronsgate, Chorleywood, Hertfordshire, England.

PUBLICATIONS

Plays

Mr. Venus, with Ray Galton, music and lyrics by Trevor H. Stanford and Norman Newell (produced London, 1958).
Sketches in *The Art of Living* (produced London, 1960).
The Compartment (televised 1961; produced Pitlochry, Perthshire, 1965).
The Knacker's Yard (produced London, 1962).
The Playmates (televised 1962; as *Games*, produced London, 1971).
If There Weren't Any Blacks You'd Have to Invent Them (televised 1965; produced Loenersloot, Holland, and London, 1965). Loenersloot, Holland, Mickery, 1965; London, Methuen, 1968.
Sketches in *In the Picture* (produced London, 1967).
The Salesman (televised 1970; produced London, 1970).
Till Death Us Do Part. London, Woburn Press, 1973.
The Thoughts of Chairman Alf (produced London, 1976).
Elevenses (sketch), in *The Big One* (produced London, 1983).

Screenplays: *French Dressing*, with others, 1964; *Privilege*, with Norman Bogner and Peter Watkins, 1967; *Till Death Us Do Part*, 1968; *The Alf Garnett Saga*, 1972.

Radio Writing: for the *Edmondo Ros*, *Morecambe and Wise*, and *Frankie Howerd* shows, 1956–58; *Early to Braden* show,

1957–58; *The Deadly Game of Chess*, 1958; *The April 8th Show* (*7 Days Early*), 1958; *Eric Sykes* show, 1960–61.

Television Writing: for the *Arthur Haynes* show; *The Compartment*, 1961; *The Playmates*, 1962; *Shamrot*, 1963; *If There Weren't Any Blacks You'd Have to Invent Them*, 1965; *Till Death Us Do Part* series, 1966–75, 1981; *To Lucifer a Sun*, 1967; *Curry and Chips* series, 1969; *The Salesman*, 1970; *Them* series, 1972; *Speight of Marty* series, 1973; *For Richer . . . For Poorer*, 1975; *The Tea Ladies* series, with Ray Galton, 1979; *Spooner's Patch* series, with Ray Galton, 1980; *The Lady Is a Tramp* series, 1982; *In Sickness and in Health*, 1985.

Other

It Stands to Reason: A Kind of Autobiography. London, Joseph-Hobbs, 1973.
The Thoughts of Chairman Alf: Alf Garnett's Little Blue Book; or, Where England Went Wrong: An Open Letter to the People of Britain. London, Robson, 1973.
Pieces of Speight. London, Robson, 1974.
The Garnett Chronicles: The Life and Times of Alf Garnett, Esq. London, Robson, 1986.

*

Theatrical Activities:
Actor: **Films**—*The Plank*, 1967; *The Undertakers*, 1969; *Rhubarb*, 1970.

* * *

Johnny Speight is one of those writers whose success in television has become a trap. Unlike almost every other writer of comic series for peak-hour viewers, he has been a source of controversy, scandal, and outrage as well as having been rewarded with a popularity which has proved to be less than totally advantageous to him. He was a factory worker before World War II, and it was not until 1955 that his determination to succeed as a writer bore any fruit. His first work was writing scripts for such comedians as Frankie Howerd, Arthur Askey, Cyril Fletcher, Eric Sykes, and others. When he began to write for Arthur Haynes, he showed an ability to create unusual material rather than the power to exploit the familiar gifts of an established comedian. For Haynes, Speight created the character of a tramp whose aggressive, rebarbative personality had a striking originality.

It was through a series of programmes for BBC television, *Till Death Us Do Part*, that Speight became a household name. His work became a battleground over which "permissive" liberals fought the old-fashioned viewers who believe in verbal restraint, the importance of good taste and the banishment of certain topics, notably religion, from light entertainment. What Speight wrote was originally in essence a cartoon, a cockney version of the north country Andy Capp, in which attitudes almost everybody would condemn as antisocial were derided. Four people—husband and wife, their daughter and son-in-law—inhabit the sitting room of a slum house; they have nothing in common except their bitter dislike for each other. The father, Alf Garnett, is barely literate, full of misconceived, misunderstood, and ignorant prejudices about race, politics, and religion; his language is atrocious. His wife is reduced almost to the state of a vegetable, coming to life only when her detestation of her husband finds some opportunity of expressing itself. The son-in-law, as ignorantly and stupidly of the left as Garnett is of the right, is a

Liverpool-Irish Roman Catholic, who dresses flamboyantly, wears his hair long, and does no work whatever; his only spell of activity was an inefficient attempt to swindle social security officials. The daughter agrees in all things with her husband, but it is plain that her agreement is the result of his effectiveness as a lover rather than of any intellectual processes of argument.

Through these appalling people, Speight was able for a time to lambast senseless racial and political prejudices while making cheeky fun of the Royal Family, the church, and anything else which drifted into what passes in the Garnett household for conversation, and Garnett for a time was a very effective weapon against bigotry and stupidity. Unfortunately, his effectiveness as a vehicle for satire tended to diminish as the monstrous energy with which he was created slipped out of control and allowed him to take possession of each episode of a series which continued long after the original impetus had exhausted itself and which began to show something dangerously ambivalent in Speight's attack on racialism. The creation of two Garnett films demonstrated that Speight's monsters were at their most popular when there was nothing left to say about them, so that *Till Death Us Do Part* seemed to turn into an incubus from which the author was unable to escape.

Curry and Chips, another effort to stifle racial prejudice by allowing it to be voiced in its most extreme forms by the stupid, lacked the vitality of *Till Death Us Do Part*, and a later series, *Them*, in which two tramps dreamed of grandeur, their dreams contrasted sharply with the reality of their way of life, was notable only for the gentleness of its comedy, proving that Speight was capable of more than the stridency of life with the Garnett family.

Such work, for all the energy of Garnettry, and the strength with which the leading monster had been created, made it seem that Speight had moved a long way in the wrong direction. In 1961, his first television play proper, *The Compartment*, had nothing to do with the sort of writing which later made him notorious. In a compartment of an old-fashioned train which has no corridor, a businessman is alone with a practical joker who persecutes him for the length of the journey; it becomes the joker's amusement to convince his pompous, easily frightened companion that he is helpless in the company of an armed, murderous psychopath. There are no motives, no explanations, no rationalisations; the events simply happen with a sort of uneasy humour. A year later, the same joker, selling "jokes" and tricks from door to door, finds himself sheltered for a night by a strange, psychopathic girl who is the only inhabitant of a big house. *The Playmates*—for the girl wants to join in fun with the traveller's samples—shares the disregard for motives and explanations already shown by *The Compartment*. A third play, offering, it seems, another aspect of the experience of the joker, was equally effective. The ideas were fashionable at the time when it was avant garde and exciting to offer allegiance to The Theatre of the Absurd, but Speight produced his genuine shocks and *frissons*.

Both *The Compartment* and a later television play, *If There Weren't Any Blacks You'd Have to Invent Them*, were adapted for stage performances but, despite some success, proved to belong to the screen rather than the stage. *If There Weren't Any Blacks* exploited Speight's reputation, won from the Garnett series, as a passionate opponent of racialism, and makes its point amusingly and convincingly with none of the ambivalence which crept into *Till Death Us Do Part* when Garnett took control of the series and began to speak as a character in his own right rather than as an instrument designed by his creator to ridicule the politically idiotic.

Speight's only genuine play for the theatre, not adapted from television material, *The Knacker's Yard*, won some praise for the vigour and imaginativeness of its dialogue.

It is impossible not to think of Speight as a creator of grotesque, disturbing characters who is trapped by television into a situation which demands that he repeat, with diminishing returns, a success which rapidly lost its inventiveness. Thus, he pays the penalty of his originality.

—Henry Raynor

SPENCER, Colin. British. Born in London, 17 July 1933. Educated at Brighton Grammar School, Selhurst; Brighton College of Art. Served in the Royal Army Medical Corps, 1950–52. Married Gillian Chapman in 1959 (divorced 1969); one son. Paintings exhibited in Cambridge and London; costume designer. Chair, Writers Guild of Great Britain, 1982-83. Agent: (plays) Casarotto Ramsay Ltd., National House, 60–66 Wardour Street, London W1V 3HP; (novels) Richard Scott Simon, 43 Doughty Street, London WC1N 2LF. Address: 2 Heath Cottages, Tunstall, near Woodbridge, Suffolk IP12 2HQ, England.

PUBLICATIONS

Plays

The Ballad of the False Barman, music by Clifton Parker (produced London, 1966).
Spitting Image (produced London, 1968; New York, 1969). Published in *Plays and Players* (London), September 1968.
The Trial of St. George (produced London, 1972).
The Sphinx Mother (produced Salzburg, Austria, 1972).
Why Mrs. Neustadter Always Loses (produced London, 1972).
Keep It in the Family (also director; produced London, 1978).
Lilith (produced Vienna, 1979).

Television Plays: *Flossie*, 1975; *Vandal Rule OK?* (documentary), 1977.

Novels

An Absurd Affair. London, Longman, 1961.
Generation:
  Anarchists in Love. London, Eyre and Spottiswoode, 1963; as *The Anarchy of Love*, New York, Weybright and Talley, 1967.
  The Tyranny of Love. London, Blond, and New York, Weybright and Talley, 1967.
  Lovers in War. London, Blond, 1969.
  The Victims of Love. London, Quartet, 1978.
Asylum. London, Blond, 1966.
Poppy, Mandragora, and the New Sex. London, Blond, 1966.
Panic. London, Secker and Warburg, 1971.
How the Greeks Kidnapped Mrs. Nixon. London, Quartet, 1974.

Other

Gourmet Cooking for Vegetarians. London, Deutsch, 1978.

Good and Healthy: A Vegetarian and Wholefood Cookbook. London, Robson, 1983; as *Vegetarian Wholefood Cookbook*, London, Panther, 1985.

Reports from Behind, with Chris Barlas, illustrated by Spencer. London, Enigma, 1984.

Cordon Vert: 52 Vegetarian Gourmet Dinner Party Menus. Wellingborough, Northamptonshire, Thorsons, 1985; Chicago, Contemporary, 1987.

Mediterranean Vegetarian Cooking. Wellingborough, Northamptonshire, Thorsons, 1986.

The New Vegetarian: The Ultimate Guide to Gourmet Cooking and Healthy Living. London, Elm Tree, and New York, Viking, 1986.

The Vegetarian's Healthy Diet Book, with Tom Sanders. London, Dunitz, 1986; as *The Vegetarian's Kitchen*, Tucson, Arizona, Body Press, 1986.

One-Course Feasts. London, Conran Octopus, 1986.

Feast for Health: A Gourmet Guide to Good Food. London, Dorling Kindersley, 1987.

Al Fresco: A Feast of Outdoor Entertaining. Wellingborough, Northamptonshire, Thorsons, 1987.

The Romantic Vegetarian. Wellingborough, Northamptonshire, Thorsons, 1988.

The Adventurous Vegetarian. London, Cassell, 1989.

Which of Us Two? The Story of a Love Affair. London, Viking, 1990.

Editor, *Green Cuisine: The Guardian's Selection of the Best Vegetarian Recipes*. Wellingborough, Northamptonshire, Thorsons, 1986.

*

Critical Study: interview with Peter Burton, in *Transatlantic Review* 35 (London), 1970.

Theatrical Activities:
Director: **Play**—*Keep It in the Family*, London, 1978.

*   *   *

Harold Hobson, reviewing Colin Spencer's musical play *The Ballad of the False Barman* in the *Sunday Times*, referred to "Mr. Spencer's great and complicated skill unified by [his] overwhelming sense of evil. This is its aesthetic strength." Certainly there is something in the play that both attracts and alienates. I recall that, as artistic director of the Hampstead Theatre Club where it was premiered, I sent it to nine directors before the tenth, Robin Phillips, accepted it. Yet re-reading it now for what must be about the twelfth time I find that my first impression is unchanged. The play still seems to me like an impassioned sermon by John Donne, written with the sensuality of Genet, the cogency (especially in the lyrics) of Brecht, and the high camp of Ronald Firbank. If this sounds like mirroring too many influences it should be remembered that it is, after all, a play about disguises. The setting is a bar in Brighton to which come all the so-called "dregs of society." They are welcomed by an enigmatic barman (played by a woman) who fulfills their needs:

Give me the right to exploit you,
Tell me your private dream,
I can fix anything, just leave it to me.

The play's central theme is the opposition of corruption, in the person of the barman, and goodness, in the person of Josie. As the Barman says to Josie. "Your goodness is a thorn in our flesh."

When Josie's lover, a gigolo and burglar called Bill, is thrown into prison, Josie is shown out of the bar. No one will help her. (En route Spencer makes a scathing attack on conventional morality, on the inhumanity of the professional clergyman, the police, and the judiciary.) Josie is driven to accept the hospitality of a mysterious Duke whose advances she has long resisted. But now she says, "I am too tired to do anything else."

She enters the Duke's house with its many rooms. "Explore them," says the Duke, "I will give you thoughts like new children. I will uncover areas of feeling, of rhythm, and motion, which will astonish, amaze, excite. . ." to which Josie replies, "You have shown me things in myself that I never dreamt were there. . . . You have shown me mirrors." The Duke answers, "The more you know, the greater you will grow."

No critic at the time realized what Spencer was doing here. Brilliantly, more alarmingly than in any Mystery play of York or Wakefield, he has updated the story of the serpent in the Garden of Eden, the temptation to eat of the Tree of Knowledge of good *and* evil. The death of Josie's baby comes in this context as a brutal, dream-potent image of death of innocence, the expulsion from Eden. At the end of the play Josie says to the Duke, "You are all the terror in my soul. You are the darkness that I have always feared but when I was laid in your arms I knew such peace." Throughout Spencer is dealing with the metaphysic of evil, with what Jung calls the *shadow* side of experience. Anyone who has read Jung's *Answer to Job* will recognise that ultimate goodness cannot be separated from the question of ultimate evil. And though there is undoubtedly a force of evil, the powers of darkness, just as there is a force of good, Spencer questions whether what we call evil is necessarily always evil. And whether what we call good is necessarily always good. We have first to come to terms with our shadow side and only then is a transformation possible. It is only when Prospero ceases to call Caliban "a devil, a demi-devil," and says "This thing of darkness I acknowledge as my own," that Caliban, his shadow side, is enabled to say, "Henceforth I'll seek for grace."

Josie comes to see that her goodness was no more than "simplicity, easily destroyed and now quite worthless." She becomes a whore. "I began to do what you all do because I thought you'd understand. How does sin destroy what's good?" Yet she is not corrupted. She merely sheds the shell of naïvety which we, all too often and mistakenly, call innocence. For, as Amanda, the militant Christian in the play, remarks, "It's difficult to go naked in this world."

What Josie finally learns is that "You can't act being good. It just exists in itself. Goodness is a thing apart. It is itself." And because she believes this she will not accept the only society she knows, that of the Bar. She cries out, "Are we in this modern world trapped so vilely in our flesh? No, no, no, no!"

It is with this affirmation that the play ends. And it seems to me in retrospect that no production has yet done the play credit. It is all too easy to be carried away by the surface camp (admittedly a part of the play's fabric) and to neglect its deep moral purpose.

For, fundamentally, Spencer is a moralist. What he does, more urgently than any other contemporary writer, more wittily and with refreshing humour, is to question accepted conventions. In *The Sphinx Mother* (a modern version of the Oedipus story) there is a moving scene at the beginning of the second act between Clare (the Jocasta figure) and Owen (the Oedipus figure):

Clare—There has never been such a partnership of power and goodness.
Owen—How can that be! Goodness based on corruption?
Clare—Where was the corruption? I have experienced no cruelty or violence from you, nor given you any. We trod softly through each other's lives and gave freely.

Clare challenges Owen's terrible self-mutilation, "all that he showed was his pathetic weakness." Through her, Spencer challenges,

our abstract ideas of what life and love ought to be. It is these abstract ideas that cause violence and aggression. Can you not accept that we did love each other, totally? If a son has lain with his mother for a quarter of a lifetime is that as grotesque as we think it is?

In other plays, notably the comedies *The Fruiting Body* (not yet produced) and *Spitting Image*, Spencer continues to question and probe. *Spitting Image*, a "happy play" as Spencer had it billed, revealed, as John Russell Taylor observed in a brilliant review, that the author has learnt from a writer like Firbank that camp nonsense can sometimes cut deep. And though, on the surface, *Spitting Image* is about two homosexuals one of whom gives birth to a baby by the other, he has used this fantastic particular instance in order to illuminate a believable, disturbing reality. "If the birth is fantastic," writes Taylor,

the opposition Gary and Tom encounter, the ways and means by which the authorities seek to suppress the awkward individual, the special case which obstinately refuses to fit into the nearest convenient pigeon-hole, are too unforgettably credible. The fantastic particular is made to stand effectively for the host of less eye-catching realities, and the social comment reaches its target unerringly.

If sometimes, as in certain passages from *The Sphinx Mother*, or *The Ballad of the False Barman*, Spencer seems almost florid, baroque in his writing, it is because in these passages (such as Bill's loneliness speech in prison and the Duke's long arias) he is trying to pierce below the external observable reality to that anguish of spirit that cannot really be put into words. In these passages he employs, deliberately, a convoluted, imagistic, surreal style of writing, digging out the kind of uncomfortable and embarrassing images that perhaps occur only in dreams. He is concerned to articulate the lost areas of human experience. In the unproduced *Summer at Camber—39* (the setting is the outbreak of World War II) he has Hester say,

I feel trapped, Maud. I'm thirty-nine and I feel trapped. I don't think I'll ever get free . . . so many things there are battering begging to speak, not just from inside of me, but . . . so much . . . I don't quite understand. You don't understand. Eddy can't understand, ever . . . what am I doing? How long must I stay without . . . being able to know . . . more?

The intensity of emotion conveyed by those dots, those broken phrases, is what increasingly concerns theatre. As Stanislavsky wrote at the turn of the century, "It is necessary to picture not life itself as it takes place in reality, but as we vaguely feel it in our dreams, our visions, our moments of spiritual uplift." Virginia Woolf said that she wanted to write "books about silence; about the things people do not say,"

but because she, like Spencer, was a writer, she had to try to use words. How to reach the centre is the shared concern of many different artists. One cry rings through all these explorations, the cry of Josie in *The Ballad of the False Barman*, "Who among you cares enough? Stop all this deceit, please, oh, please. Stop all these disguises!"

—James Roose-Evans

SPURLING, John. British. Born in Kisumu, Kenya, 17 July 1936. Educated at Dragon School, Oxford, 1946–49; Marlborough College, Wiltshire, 1950–54; St. John's College, Oxford, 1957–60, B.A. 1960. Served in the Royal Artillery (national service), 1955–57. Married Hilary Forrest (i.e., the writer Hilary Spurling) in 1961; one daughter and two sons. Plebiscite officer for the United Kingdom in Southern Cameroons, 1960–61; announcer, BBC Radio, London, 1963–66; radio and book reviewer, the *Spectator*, London, 1966–70, and other publications. Henfield fellow, University of East Anglia, Norwich, 1973, art critic, *New Statesman*, London, 1976–88. Lives in London. Agent: Patricia MacNaughton, MacNaughton Lowe Representation, 200 Fulham Road, London SW10 9PN, England.

PUBLICATIONS

Plays

Char (produced Oxford, 1959).
MacRune's Guevara As Realised by Edward Hotel (produced London, 1969; Walla Walla, Washington, 1971; New York, 1975). London, Calder and Boyars, 1969.
Romance, music and lyrics by Charles Ross (produced Leeds and London, 1971).
In the Heart of the British Museum (produced Edinburgh and London, 1971). London, Calder and Boyars, 1972.
Shades of Heathcliff (produced Sheffield, 1971; London, 1972). With *Death of Captain Doughty*, London, Boyars, 1975.
Peace in Our Time (produced Sheffield, 1972).
Death of Captain Doughty (televised 1973). With *Shades of Heathcliff*, London, Boyars, 1975.
McGonagall and the Murderer (produced Edinburgh, 1974).
On a Clear Day You Can See Marlowe (produced London, 1974).
While Rome Burns (produced Canterbury, 1976).
Antigone Through the Looking Glass (produced London, 1979).
The British Empire, Part One (produced Birmingham, 1980). London, Boyars, 1982.
Coming Ashore in Guadeloupe (produced Harrogate and London, 1982).

Radio Plays: *Where Tigers Roam*, 1976; *The Stage Has Nothing to Give Us* (documentary), 1980; *The British Empire: Part One: Dominion over Palm and Pine*, 1982, *Part Two: The Christian Hero*, 1982, *Part Three: The Day of Reckoning*, 1985; *Daughters and Sons*, from the novel by Ivy Compton-Burnett, 1985; *Fancy Pictures: A Portrait After Gainsborough*, 1988; *Discobolus*, 1989.

Television Plays: *Hope*, 1970; *Faith*, 1971; *Death of Captain Doughty*, 1973; *Silver*, 1973.

Novel

The Ragged End.   London, Weidenfeld and Nicolson, 1989.

Other

Beckett: A Study of His Plays, with John Fletcher. London, Eyre Methuen, and New York, Hill and Wang, 1972; revised edition, Eyre Methuen, 1978; revised edition, as *Beckett the Playwright*, Methuen, and New York, Farrar Straus, 1985.
Graham Greene. London, Methuen, 1983.

Editor, *The Hill Station: An Unfinished Novel, and An Indian Diary*, by J.G. Farrell. London, Weidenfeld and Nicolson, 1981.

*

John Spurling comments:

(1977) *MacRune's Guevara* was written from a desire to create an event in space rather than to turn out something recognisable as a play (I imagined it being performed in an art gallery rather than a theatre): at the same time I wanted to represent to myself my own conflicting reactions to Che Guevara and to attack certain forms of artistic and political cant which were dominant in the theatre at the time—perhaps still persist.

I found the idea for the more complex structure of *In the Heart of the British Museum* in Frances Yates's book on Renaissance theories of *The Art of Memory*, but after completing five scenes I put the play away. I took it up again as a commission for the Traverse Workshop Theatre, under Max Stafford-Clark's direction. The piece, with its emphasis on song and dance, was finished with this particular company in mind, but since I had felt the need for just such a company to perform it even before I knew of the company's existence, the original structure did not have to be altered. The subject matter comprises Aztec and Chinese legend, the recent Chinese Cultural Revolution, the exile of the Roman poet Ovid, and some of the subject matter of Ovid's own poems. The central theme is also Ovid's, the idea of Metamorphosis, and this is an important element in the structure.

Shades of Heathcliff grew directly out of being commissioned for Ed Thomason's Crucible Vanguard Theatre in Sheffield. A play for Sheffield seemed to call for a version of *Wuthering Heights*; the company consisted only of three actors and one actress, and, performing in a small space, dictated that it be a chamber piece and that the characters of the four Brontë children and of the novel itself be melted together.

Peace in Our Time was commissioned by the Crucible Theatre, Sheffield. It is the first part of a larger work called *Ghosts and Monsters of the Second World War*, which I have yet to finish. This first part is set in Hell, where the characters (Hitler, Stalin, Mussolini, Chamberlain, et al.) replay some of the political games of 1935–39.

McGonagall and the Murderer is a short play commissioned by the Pool Theatre, Edinburgh. A man who has failed to assassinate Queen Victoria and is now confined in Broadmoor tries to win a second chance by entering the mind of the poet McGonagall, himself on the road to Balmoral. *On a Clear Day You Can See Marlowe* was first written in 1970 and revised in 1974 for the Major Road Company. The play is something of a companion piece to *MacRune's Guevara*—a collage of the few known facts about the playwright Marlowe, much speculation (both reasonable and ludicrous), and versions of his own work in modern rehearsal.

(1988) *While Rome Burns*, commissioned by the Marlowe Theatre, Canterbury under its then director, David Carson, is a futuristic version of Edgar Allan Poe's story "The Masque of the Red Death." A company of travelling players visits an island off the coast of Britain, the last refuge of a group of well-heeled, middle-class people who have fled from a major catastrophe on the mainland. *Antigone Through the Looking Glass*, also commissioned by David Carson for a production at the King's Head, Islington, London, is roughly the same length as Sophocles' *Antigone* which is being acted off-stage, while we watch the performers coming and going in the green-room.

The British Empire trilogy, covering the period 1820–1911, with a cast of over 200 characters, was intended for the stage. Part One was performed in the studio at Birmingham Rep as a promenade production (directed by Peter Farago with a cast of only 9) and then adapted for BBC Radio 3, which also commissioned Parts Two and Three. I am still hoping to see the whole seven-hour work on the stage, preferably performed in one day or at least on successive evenings.

Coming Ashore in Guadeloupe was started in 1973 for a Dutch company which folded, but substantially revised in 1982 for the Cherub Theatre Company and its director Andrew Visnevski. It is a panorama (in fairly concise form) of the European discovery and conquest of America, featuring Columbus, Cortes, Pizarro, Raleigh, Verrazzano, and others, but viewed much of the time through the eyes of the Indian inhabitants.

* * *

John Spurling's work has veered from the technically innovative and exciting to the commonplace, and some of it is probably best forgotten—for example, the sentimental musical drawing-room comedy *Romance*. However, he has produced three plays which will almost certainly survive: *MacRune's Guevara*, *In the Heart of the British Museum*, and *While Rome Burns*.

There is in most of Spurling's plays a profound concern with history and experience. And indeed with what happens to history. In *MacRune's Guevara* it is suggested that the real Guevara was an enigmatic figure of whom we are unlikely to know anything that finally matters. History, present in the play in the form of press reports, and problematic enough by itself, is only one of the ways in which the audience sees Guevara. Other viewpoints come from the actors in the play, as well as from the narrator, Edward Hotel, who is the supposed dramatist. Hotel has recently occupied a room in which the failed Scots-Irish artist MacRune lived just before his death. MacRune had covered the walls of this room with pencil sketches of some 17 scenes of Guevara's Bolivian campaign. These sketches, now faint and sometimes indistinguishable from other marks on the wall, are a parallel to the press reports about Guevara; and these are thrown into a discussion on the nature of history, with Hotel's own views of the subject, and MacRune's supposed views of it—which we are told, with questionable reliability, are heretical from a Marxist point of view. From all this, Guevara emerges as partly ineffectual and partly valiant, guerrilla hero but also a dupe of higher powers, on the one hand an inspirer of love who does not allow himself to be swayed by it from his cause, and on the other a merely simple-minded killer of bourgeois Belgians in an interlude located in the Congo. At the end of his life, he appears disillusioned, though as brave as ever, a man who did not amount to much in life but who has acquired mythic dimensions in death. One critic called this play "an honest magnification of the author's own confusion"; it is, in fact, the exact opposite: a sophisticated attempt to say "No clothes" about a king. Through Guevara, Spurling is also making a point about all contemporary heroes.

The multi-viewpoint technique of *MacRune's Guevara*, of which Spurling was one of the pioneers, was further elaborated in his next notable play, *In the Heart of the British Museum*. Three narratives are interwoven here: the disgrace and rehabilitation of a Chinese professor during the Cultural Revolution, the exile and death of Ovid, and the temptation and fall of the Aztec god Quetzalcoatl and his succession by the grimmer god Texcatlipoca. These themes elaborate and comment on each other. In contrasting power and war with culture and intelligence, in setting history against myth, reputation against reality, Spurling does not take sides. He makes it quite clear that he is not quarrelling with others: it is of his quarrel with his own multitudinous and contradictory responses to Guevara, myth, history, power, and intelligence, that Spurling makes his artistic work. By his omnivorous, witty plays he hopes to make us experience all of reality and thus progress to that profound understanding which is at the heart of all things.

Yet the understanding towards which he stretches his hands is nothing if not radically critical, especially of contemporary fads and blind spots—witness the concern in the title of *While Rome Burns* (loosely structured on Poe's "The Masque of the Red Death"). In this, a privileged few escape from Britain to an island fortress where they are burdened neither with incomes nor with taxes, and are cottoned from news of the world without. War games and cricket, costume balls and leisured adultery, suggestive of a luxury cruise without a destination, are what constitute their concerns. This island sanctuary is approached by an assassin. Disconnected set-pieces provide mannered comic moments which reveal the butterfly character of the protagonists, and their growing sense of dread. We identify with their fear, and yet we cannot help seeing that this beauty is terrible and deserves to be destroyed.

Spurling has written conventional plays with competence; at his best, however, he avoids the comforts of security. Melodrama and the music hall, comedy and tragedy, the neat plot and the predictable one, are alike eschewed. Sometimes Spurling pares away, peels off layer after layer; at other times he takes strange or unexpected angles, comparing like with what appears at first glance to be wholly unlike. Finally, his work functions as parable, icon, mystic text; and, at his finest, he persuades drama to aspire to the condition of poetry.

—Prabhu S. Guptara

STARKWEATHER, David. American. Born in Madison, Wisconsin, 11 September 1935. Educated at the University of Wisconsin, Madison, 1953–57, B.A. in speech 1957. Editor of a visitors newspaper in New York. Recipient: Creative Artists Public Service grant, 1975; Rockefeller grant, 1978. Address: 340 West 11th Street, New York, New York 10014, U.S.A.

PUBLICATIONS

Plays

Maggie of the Bargain Basement, music by Starkweather (ballad opera; produced Madison, Wisconsin, 1956).
Excuse Me, Pardon Me (produced Madison, Wisconsin, 1957).
You May Go Home Again (produced New York, 1963). Published in *The Off-Off-Broadway Book*, edited by Albert Poland and Bruce Mailman, Indianapolis, Bobbs Merrill, 1972.
So Who's Afraid of Edward Albee? (produced New York, 1963).
The Love Pickle (produced New York, 1963; Edinburgh, 1971).
The Family Joke (produced New York, 1965).
The Assent (produced New York, 1967).
Chamber Comedy (produced Washington, D.C., 1969).
A Practical Ritual to Exorcise Frustration after Five Days of Rain, music by Allan Landon (also co-director: produced New York, 1970).
The Poet's Papers: Notes for an Event (produced Boston, 1971). Published in *New American Plays 3*, edited by William M. Hoffman, New York, Hill and Wang, 1970.
The Straights of Messina (produced New York, 1973).
Language (also director: produced New York, 1974).
The Bones of Bacon (produced New York, 1977).

*

Manuscript Collection: Lincoln Center Library of the Performing Arts, New York.

Theatrical Activities:
Director: several of his own plays.

David Starkweather comments:
(1973) Two mirrors facing what do they reflect?

Slice the mind in fives, Consciousness stage center. One way wings of Memory, staging areas of attention seeking self-ordering re-experience, detouring terror into ritual belief: Subconscious. Opposite wings of Appetite, senses drawn to sources of actuation, pulled always into foreign homes: Superconscious. Deeper still surrounding wings as well as centers, forms in the mind's structure beneath conception, containing all potential concepts like the possibilities of a medium; Unconscious. Facing Other Consciousness awareness of other centers of awareness, the possibilities of union/conflict with/within all potential spectators. The boundaries between these modes of mindworks the symbol, always blocking one way, all ways disappearing another.

My current vision of theatre is a head, the bodies of the audience resonating chambers like the jugs beneath the stage in the classic Nō, feeling their behavioral imaginations. Sound surrounds but the eyes are in front perceiving SENSES in terms of each other. Vision is figure to sound's ground and vice versa because each word has an aural and visual component. A noun is a picture (visual/spatial) and a verb is a melody (aural/temporal) relation. The split between being and doing dissolves when nouns are just states verbs are in at a given moment. The central human art form is the spoken word.

We laugh at people who are out of control. We laugh with people who are shoulder to shoulder. And we call it tragedy when a hero who is behind us loses.

If you write a play and do it badly that play is about

incompetence. My plays in their forms hope to suggest what competence is. Moving toward an ideal. And I deal this round. Place your bets. It's a show of competence. All plays are about knowing. Being is where they're at. What I seek in a word is Order. In a feeling a release of energy.

For themes I have recognized a clear line of development in my last three plays: 1) there is nothing you can know without limiting your ability to know something equally true; 2) the only thing we need to believe is that there is nothing we need to believe; and 3) the only taboo is on taboos.

I write consistently about changing minds.

A number of works, my most ambitious, are as yet unproduced: *Owey Wishey Are You There?*, 1965, *The Wish-House*, 1967.

* * *

Ham—And where are you?
Noah—I am here and it is now. And all around is mystery.
—*A Practical Ritual to Exorcise Frustration after Five Days of Rain*.

It's not that he hates his family, his religion, or the rest of the society; it's just that he can't stand their noise. Most people he knows participate in the trivia of family life and the charades of state. They believe that somewhere there is *one* person who will solve the riddle of their emotional needs, that the state must be protected, especially from within, that there is a god who sits on a throne, somewhere.

So the young man leaves his home, not to be mean or ornery, but because he'll go crazy if he stays. He goes Downtown, where there are so many people that no one will notice him, or Downtown to the wilderness, where there are no people. And now he is in the Downtown part of his mind, where memories of his former life rise and beckon him to return and resume the old ties. He replies to their telephone calls and to his dreams that their lives are meaningless and their ways are mindless and hold no allure.

But the old ways are alluring to him in his solitude, and part of him wants to go home. However, gradually, painfully, he withdraws into the land of light, and now he's totally alone with his mind. Soon he *is* his mind and alone he's together. At this still point fears arise in their pure form and threaten his sanity. Fears: of pain, of people, of death, of body functions.

He discovers that these fears cannot be conquered in their essence but must be met in their actuality, and so, here he goes, folks, back to the "real world" to conquer his fears. But this time he's armed; around his waist he carries self-containment; his vest is armored with enlightenment; his helmet is pure reason.

There are no trumpets on his return. People have scarcely noticed he's been gone, so busy have they been with their own wars and marriages. When he approaches the natives he finds that things are as they've always been between him and them: they don't see what he sees. So he withdraws again, and returns again armed with new weapons. The cycle is endless, the man is lonely, but filled with love. His attitude is increasingly ironic.

This portrait of the saintly exile is a composite of the heroes and mock heroes that form the core of David Starkweather's work, the recalcitrant lover Colin of *So Who's Afraid of Edward Albee?*, the errant son David of *You May Go Home Again*, the would-be suicide Alan of *The Assent*, the wandering Poet of *The Poet's Papers*, and both Sonny and Pittsburgh, who together form the hero of *Language*. They are all versions of the Odysseus/Christ/dropout anti-heroes of our time.

Colin, one of Starkweather's earliest creations, is merely disgusted by the System and puzzled by his disgust. David, created later, overwhelmed by his ambiguous feelings toward his family, goes into exile. Alan, guilty in exile, longs for death. The Poet, more comfortable in his separation from society, wanders the earth watching it destroy itself. And Sonny and Pittsburgh, who have in different ways plumbed the mysteries of isolation, now seek a way back into a society they have left.

In all of his plays, but especially in *The Family Joke* and *The Wish-House* (unproduced), Starkweather provides ample reason for self-exile, and incidentally offers savage but concerned criticism of Western society. In *The Family Joke* the nuclear family is seen as the System's breeding factory. Children must be raised, no matter what the cost to the parents. *The Wish-House* presents an almost paranoid view of the methods of mind control that the System is willing to employ. For the enemy, here represented by a Dr. Brill, is in possession of the same knowledge that Starkweather's exile-heroes have struggled so hard to obtain: "All that you consider yourself to be is merely the stopper to contain what you really are. All that you do most easily, by habit and without thought, is only to avoid your most beautiful and dangerous nature."

In counterpoint to some of the most glorious abstractions in contemporary theatre, architectural visions that spring from contemplation of the basic dualities of thought, Starkweather weaves the anxieties that often accompany advanced thought: fears of death, impotence, blood, piss, and shit.

In *The Poet's Papers* the war between the two divisions of mankind, the Orals and the Anals, is conducted in lyrical language. In *The Assent* the System prefers control of urination to control of theft: "Petty theft raises the living standard of the worker . . . and stimulates cash flow. Whereas urine . . . involves the production of a non-salable commodity and is therefore a general drain on the corporate effort." In *Language* Sonny, a virgin, admits: "I think that potency has something to do with murder."

In the plays of Starkweather we have a most complete view of what in olden times would have been called a saint: the man who leaves his society, goes into physical and psychical exile, searches for his god, and brings back the golden fleece to an indifferent world. In play after play, in growing clarity, Starkweather shows us the dangerous yet exciting journey, the abandoned society, and the funny, heartbreaking return. He even allows us glimpses of the fleece:

He goes away within
miles from the common road
to bring back for this world
something lovely something pure
Thank you, man.

—William M. Hoffman

———

STAVIS, Barrie. American. Born in New York City, 16 June 1906. Educated at New Utrecht High School, Brooklyn, New York, graduated 1924; Columbia University, New York, 1924–27. Served in the Army Signal Corps, Plans and Training section, 1942–45: technical-sergeant. Married 1) Leona Heyert in 1925 (divorced 1939); 2) Bernice Coe in 1950, one son and one daughter. Foreign correspondent in

Europe, 1937–38; freelance journalist after World War II. Co-founder, and member of the board of directors, New Stages theatre group, 1947, and United States Institute for Theatre Technology, 1961–64 and 1969–72; visiting fellow, Institute for the Arts and Humanistic Studies, Pennylvania State University, University Park, 1971. Recipient: Yaddo fellowship, 1939; National Theatre Conference award, 1948, 1949. Fellow, American Theatre Association, 1982. Lives in New York City. Address: c/o Benjamin Zinkin, 635 Madison Avenue, New York, New York 10022, U.S.A.

PUBLICATIONS

Plays

In These Times (produced New York, 1932).

The Sun and I (produced New York, 1933; revised version produced New York, 1937).

Refuge: A One-Act Play of the Spanish War (produced London, 1938). New York, French, 1939.

Lamp at Midnight: A Play about Galileo (produced New York, 1947; Bristol, 1956). New York, Dramatists Play Service, 1948; revised version, South Brunswick, New Jersey, A.S Barnes, and London, Yoseloff, 1966; revised version, Chicago, Dramatic Publishing Company, 1974; one-hour school and church version (produced Chicago, 1972; New York, 1973), Dramatic Publishing Company, 1974.

The Man Who Never Died: A Play about Joe Hill (produced St. Paul, 1955; New York, 1958). New York, Haven Press, 1954; revised version, South Brunswick, New Jersey, A.S. Barnes, and London, Yoseloff, 1972.

Banners of Steel: A Play about John Brown (produced Carbondale, Illinois, 1962). South Brunswick, New Jersey, A.S. Barnes, and London, Yoseloff, 1967; revised version, as *Harpers Ferry: A Play about John Brown* (produced Minneapolis, 1967).

Coat of Many Colors: A Play about Joseph in Egypt (produced Provo, Utah, 1966). South Brunswick, New Jersey, A.S. Barnes, and London, Yoseloff, 1968.

Joe Hill (opera libretto), music by Alan Bush, adaptation of the play *The Man Who Never Died* by Stavis (produced Berlin, 1970).

Galileo Galilei (oratorio) music by Lee Hoiby, adaptation of the play *Lamp at Midnight* by Stavis (produced Huntsville, Alabama, 1975).

The Raw Edge of Victory (as *Washington*, produced Midland, Texas, 1976). Published in *Dramatics* (Cincinnati), April and May 1986.

Novels

The Chain of Command (novella). New York, Ackerman, 1945.

Home, Sweet Home! New York, Sheridan House, 1949.

Other

John Brown: The Sword and the Word. South Brunswick, New Jersey, A.S. Barnes, and London, Yoseloff, 1970.

Editor, with W. Frank Harmon, *The Songs of Joe Hill.* New York, People's Artists, 1955.

*

Manuscript Collections: Lincoln Center Library of the Performing Arts, New York; Pennsylvania State University, University Park.

Critical Studies: "Barrie Stavis: The Humanist Alternative" by Herbert Shore, in *Educational Theatre Journal* (Washington, D.C.), December 1973; interview in *Astonish Us in the Morning: Tyrone Guthrie Remembered* by Alfred Rossi, London, Hutchinson, 1977, Detroit, Wayne State University Press, 1981; "Humanism Is the Vital Subject" (interview), in *Dramatics* (Cincinnati), March-April 1978; "A History, A Portrait, A Memory" by Stavis, in *Time Remembered: Alan Bush: An Eightieth Birthday Symposium* edited by Ronald Stevenson, Kidderminster, Worcestershire, Bravura, 1981; "How Broad Should the Theatre's Concerns Be?" by Daniel Larner, in *Dramatics* (Cincinnati), May 1981; "Barrie Stavis Issue" of *Religion and Theatre* (St. Paul), August 1981; *American Theater of the 1960's* by Zoltán Szilassy, Carbondale, Southern Illinois University Press, 1986; "Barrie Stavis: Sixty Years of Craft and Commitment" by Ezra Goldstein, in *Dramatics* (Cincinnati), April 1986.

Barrie Stavis comments:

(1973) I wrote my first full-length play when I was 19 years old. I had my first production when I was 26. Fortunately there are no scripts in existence. About a dozen plays followed—all since destroyed.

The material and form of these early plays were derivative, echoing closely the dominant writing and production modes of the American stage. I refer to the Theatre of Illusion where the play is naturalistic in concept and style, generally romantic in approach. The physical envelope of such plays consists of a box set, usually a four-walled room with the fourth wall removed so that the audience can "peek in" and see what happens to those "real" people on the stage.

I was gradually becoming dissatisfied with this kind of stage and its "imitation of life." It could not contain the statements I was trying to make in the theatre. But at that time I did not know how to break away from the narrow restrictions of the romantic-naturalism and the pseudo-realism of the Theatre of Illusion. I knew (though certainly not as clearly as I know it now) that I was concerned with writing plays where the driving force of the characters was the clash of their *ideas*, not their subjective emotions.

Form is dictated by content and should grow out of function. Thus, I was also searching for a form which would be consonant with my material. I was seeking a freedom and a plastic use of the stage which the box set could not give me. I began studying Shakespeare intensively. Shakespeare was, and remains even to this day, my major theatre influence, followed by the Bible for its style, and its ruthlessly candid and objective way of telling a story. My study of the Elizabethan theatre, along with Greek theatre and the Roman amphitheatre, gradually led me to devise what I designated (1933–34) as "Time-Space Stage"—a stage where both time and space could be used with fluidity.

In 1939 I began to work on *Lamp at Midnight*. It took three years to complete. It was in this play that I first achieved a successful synthesis of content and form. The characters in the play are embattled over basic philosophic concepts; and the plastic use of time and space on the stage proved to be the perfect medium for expressing the conflict of ideas.

It was then that I realized I wanted to write further plays exploring this use of the stage. Although all the plays in the series would have the same major theme, each play would be independent unto itself with the common theme developed from a different axis of observation.

The series proved to be a tetralogy exploring the problems of men who have ushered in new and frequent drastic changes in the existing social order—men who are of their time and yet in advance of their time. And I have been concerned with examining the thrust they exercise on their society, and the counter-thrust society exerts on them.

It is the essence of nature and of man to undergo continual change. New forms evolve from old, mature, and, as the inevitable concomitant of their maturation, induce still newer forms which replace them. This is the historical process.

This process of change is gradual. It is not always perceived nor clearly apparent. Yet it is constant and inexorable. At a given moment when historical conditions are ripe, a catalyst enters and fragments the existing culture, setting into motion a new alignment of forces, a new series of relationships, which gradually become stabilized, codified.

It is this process of change that I endeavor to capture in my plays: the precise moment in history when society, ripe for change, gives birth to the catalyst who sets the dynamics of change into accelerated motion.

The four plays in their order are: *Lamp at Midnight* (Galileo Galilei), *The Man Who Never Died* (Joe Hill), *Harpers Ferry* (John Brown), *Coat of Many Colors* (Joseph in Egypt). In the first of these plays, *Lamp at Midnight*, I dramatize the story of Galileo Galilei, the first human being to turn his new, powerful telescope to the night skies, there to discover the true motion of our solar system, a discovery unleashing a host of scientific and social consequence which heralded the coming Industrial Age. In *The Man Who Never Died* I dramatize the story of Joe Hill, troubador, folk poet, and trade union organizer, who was framed on a murder charge and who, during the 22 months of his prison stay, grew to heroic proportions. In *Harpers Ferry* I dramatize the story of John Brown's raid on Harpers Ferry, a raid which was the precursor to the Civil War. In *Coat of Many Colors* I dramatize the story of Joseph in Egypt, the world's first great agronomist and social planner, and I explore the theme of power and its uses. These four plays have been so designed that they can be performed by a single basic acting company. Further, all four plays can be produced on the same basic unit set.

Galileo Galilei, Joe Hill, John Brown, Joseph—these men have certain things in common. They were put on trial for their thoughts and deeds, found guilty, and punished. Yet their very ideas and acts achieved their vindication by later generations. Thus does the heresy of one age become the accepted truth of the next.

I have chosen to write plays about men who have an awareness of social and moral responsibility, plays that have faith in man's capacity to resolve his problems despite the monumental difficulties facing him. Why? Because I believe in ethical commitment. I believe that man is capable of ultimately solving the problems of the Nuclear Age.

Today, much theatre writing is obsessed with frustration and defeat. One trend of such playwriting deals with personality maladjustments and sexual aberration. This theatre is preoccupied with such matters as who goes to bed with whom, the gap in communication between parent and adolescent, the need to show that sex is either rape or submission. There is intense concern with subjective, neurotic problems, very little concern with the objective and social conditions of the world in which the characters live and the impact of the world upon them. It is as though the characters were living in a vacuum tube. Outside is the pulsating, throbbing world, but within the tube they function only insofar as their psyches collide with one another. Of the outside world, there is barely a reflection. A second contemporary trend is the writing of plays which explore the thesis that the human condition is hopeless because man is utterly dislocated in his society, that rational thought is a snare, that human life is purposeless, that action is without point for it will accomplish no result. There is in such plays no release for the affirmative emotion of an audience.

However, I believe with Chekhov that "Every playwright is responsible not only for what man is, but for what man can be." With Aristophanes, I seek to banish the "little man and woman affair" from the stage and to replace it with plays which explore ideas with such force and clarity as to raise them to the level of passion. Today especially, it should be the responsibility of the playwright to search out those situations which, by the inherent nature of the material, will capture the emotions and the intellect of an audience and focus it on men and women striving creatively for a positive goal.

(1988) I am now engaged in another tetralogy. The overall thematic examination of these four plays is *War, Revolution, and Peace*. In them, I explore George Washington, Abraham Lincoln, Miguel Hidalgo, and Simon Bolivar. Thus, I deal with the four liberators of the Western Hemisphere. In these plays I am concerned with the movement of colony to nation, of subject to citizen.

The material I handle is historical, but like the four plays of my first tetralogy, they are highly contemporary. We have been living in a century of war. There was the Japanese-Russian war in the first years of the century. Then came the famous/infamous assassination in Sarajevo which ushered in World War I. From then on until today, the world has been embroiled in wars, large and small. At this moment, there are over 50 different wars raging throughout the world. Thus, focusing on the theme of *War, Revolution, and Peace* is very much of our time.

I have completed the first play of the tetralogy: *The Raw Edge of Victory*, which deals with George Washington and the Revolutionary War. I'm half way through the second play, which focuses on Abraham Lincoln and the Civil War. Since I spend approximately five years on each play, it is obvious that I have accounted for the next ten years of my writing life!

* * *

A mere glance at the men Barrie Stavis has chosen to write about is indicative of his own passions, goals, intentions: John Brown, Joe Hill, Galileo, the biblical Joseph, and now in various stages of completion, works about George Washington, Hidalgo, Bolivar, and Lincoln.

There is about Stavis an almost Talmudic fury when he discusses his work and when he writes. This is in strange contrast to the man himself: warm, friendly, hopeful, and eager. Stavis is intellectually always aware ("conscious" might be an even better word) of what he is doing, dramaturgically and theatrically. His experience in theatre goes back further than most, and he has worked with almost every kind of theatre—getting his plays on to stages, everywhere.

Beyond grassroots experiences, there is a playwright, Stavis, who is very like the protagonists in his own plays: a man with a vision. It is a driving, almost monomaniacal vision which he, the artist, holds in careful check.

Just as his first tetralogy dealt with, in his words, "four aspects of mankind," all of his plays are precisely predicated. *Lamp at Midnight* (seen by twenty million in one night on a Hallmark Hall of Fame telecast) is "about Truth" (no small feat to undertake in a single play); *The Man Who Never Died* is "about Human Dignity"; *Harpers Ferry* is "about Freedom"; and *Coat of Many Colors* is "about Power." Stavis writes that kind of play deliberately, and there are abundant audiences and theatres in the United States and abroad eagerly seeking these plays: they have something to say, say it clearly, and are "about" something. As with good textbooks (*good* textbooks, mind), his work is pedantic, fascinating, and satisfying.

Stavis celebrated his 80th birthday shortly after the first play in his projected second tetralogy was published in *Dramatics*. This drama is about George Washington's heroic efforts to hold together the colonial army in the face of foreign intrigues, English military superiority, congressional neglect, domestic opportunism, and defeatism, despair, and dissatisfaction in the ranks. Stavis calls this epic drama *The Raw Edge of Victory*, and it is a potent brew of all the conflicts which raged as the Revolutionary War dragged on and on. The real role of black slaves and women in the war is forcefully demonstrated, as are the grim realities of keeping the troops in line, which Washington does with unflinching severity—even though he understands the reasons for rebellion in the ranks. Unlike the earlier plays, there are touches of humor here—even gallows-humor, as well as contrasts between the roughness of camp life and the sophisticated Court of King Louis XVI. Stavis's extensive research fortunately doesn't parade itself; it is abundantly evident in the dramatic revelation of how Washington and his army won the war and at what cost.

As with any conscientious teacher, Stavis is a superb researcher, who reads and studies about and around the men he will put on stage. Eventually, out of that research comes the spine of the play, the direction dictated by the material. His own humanistic background, of course, controls the aesthetics and even the politics of the play, and his experience controls the shape of the work, but the man and the artist avoid the merely pedantic, the narrowly polemic, the purely didactic. The five years he works on any single play make it fairly inevitable as a work: big, intellectual, more than a little "preachy" but almost always theatrical.

Stavis is a grassroots playwright. Middle America listens to the voice of history, and it is history that Stavis purveys most astutely and clearly. Grandeur and pageantry are second nature to the themes and the shapes of his work. His best work, I think, is *The Man Who Never Died*. It is no small accident that the play deals with an early "liberal," an American labor leader martyred and misplaced in time and place. That this play comes most successfully to the stage finally in the form of a German opera is really no surprise to those most familiar with Stavis's work.

He denies a tendency to romanticism and insists on the classicistic nature of his work. As did Brecht, Stavis claims to be more concerned with the *how* of an action than with the *why*. And in fact, his plays (the Joseph play possibly excepted) tend to Seriousness, with a capital S. There is generally little to amuse one in a Stavis play; the solemnity of the central figure is reflected in the almost complete lack of humor in the play itself. Even love is dealt with clinically and analytically. He leaves it to the total action to *move* his audiences: the themes that last, the appeal to noble if belated stances, the hero out of time.

Stavis, quite seriously and realistically, sees his own work as primarily influenced by both Shakespeare and the Holy Bible. If there are more rabbinic research and prophetic polemicism than there are lyricism and joy, Stavis cannot be faulted: he is after all very much a writer of his time and place, with a keen eye on the lessons of the past.

It might seem overly ambitious or optimistic for a playwright at age 80 to be looking forward to completing three more epics, all linked by the theme *War, Revolution, and Peace*. But Stavis has already been doing his years of research on Bolivar, Miguel Hidalgo, and Lincoln. Indeed, the life of Bolivar—whose own officers betrayed the vision of South American democracy for which he fought the war of liberation from Spain—has obsessed him for some time. The new tetralogy, he says, will explore in depth the "processes of throwing off oppression to gain freedom." He's focusing on "the movement of colony to nation, of subject to citizen," but the processes, as in *The Raw Edge of Victory*, are to be illuminated by the central characters of the liberators. In 1986, he was already halfway through his drama about Lincoln, with 2½ epics to go. Knowing Stavis at all is to know that his plays will indeed deliver.

He is a "pro." Methodical, organized, enthusiastic, and almost pristinely professional as he is, there is a double irony in the fact that he has never really had a hit on Broadway. Yet he represents professional theatre to literally dozens of colleges and repertory companies not only in the United States but around the world. To non-Americans, particularly, as Tyrone Guthrie indicated, Stavis represents the clearest and "most American" voice of the time. As perhaps is still true with O'Neill, Stavis seems most American to those who are least American, and he seems most "universal" to his American audiences.

There is, in any event, no mistaking Stavis's intent and purpose. If heroic drama has gone out of fashion in an era of the anti-hero, Stavis persistently views history and man's passage through that history as essentially Heroic with a capital H.

Finally, Stavis is quite the opposite in one crucial aspect from the heroes of his plays. While each of them is a man *out* of joint with his own time, Stavis is *of* his time and writes for that broadest, most fundamental of audiences: people, not critics.

—Arthur H. Ballet

STEPPLING, John. American. Born in California, 18 June 1951. Founder, with Sam Shepard and others, Padua Hills Playwrights Workshop and Festival, Los Angeles, 1978; founder and co-artistic director, Heliogabalus Company, 1986–89. Recipient: Rockefeller fellowship, 1984; National Endowment for the Arts grant; PEN West award, 1989. Agent: Michael Perctzian, William Morris Agency, 151 El Camino Drive, Beverly Hills, California 90212. Address: 844 Brooks Avenue, Venice, California 90291, U.S.A.

PUBLICATIONS

Plays

The *Shaper* (produced Louisville, Kentucky, 1985).
The Dream Coast (produced Los Angeles, 1986). New York, Dramatists Play Service, 1987.
Pledging My Love (produced San Francisco, 1986).
Standard of the Breed (produced Los Angeles, 1988).
Teenage Wedding (produced Los Angeles, 1990; New York, 1991).
Deep Tropical Tan (produced Los Angeles, 1990; New York, 1992).

The Thrill (produced Los Angeles, 1991).
Storyland and Theory of Miracles.   Published in *Best of the West*, edited by Murray Mednick, Los Angeles, Padua Hills Press, 1991.
Sea of Cortez (produced Los Angeles, 1992).

Screenplay: *52 Pick-up*, with Elmore Leonard, 1986.

* * *

In John Steppling's enigmatic evocations of life on the edge of the emotional abyss, the American Dream has been neither deferred nor exploded. Instead, his characters' aspirations have leaked from their souls like corrosive toxic sludge. His four major full-length plays—*The Shaper, The Dream Coast, Standard of the Breed,* and *The Thrill*—are all set on a West Coast whose spiritual, if not physical, focus is the scuzzy underside of Los Angeles and Hollywood.

All the plays are written in short, enigmatic blackout scenes that resolutely avoid a traditional dramatic trajectory composed of rising and falling action, therefore structurally mimicking the emptiness of the characters' emotional lives, which seem measured out in small epiphanies that come across as continuous dénouements. His spare use of language and heavy emphasis on silence and pauses are reminiscent of the German playwright Franz Xaver Kroetz. The sometimes glacial pace of his action coupled with his low-life subjects help inject all his plays with a dark, unseen, but pervasive sense of danger and potential menace.

Wilson, the ageing owner of a rundown Los Angeles motel in *The Dream Coast*, perhaps best describes the world view of Steppling's characters when he remembers being with his son: "I took him out—and everything seemed fine. He'd be having fun—he was only a little boy, three, four years old, so it was a kind of fun that little kids have, like it's an easy thing—but it was drab; underneath it not very deep, right under the surface was this drabness—sordid, sad—yeah, very sad, an awful sickness, an illness of sadness. . . ." The play, a *Grapes of Wrath* for the 1980's, finds two transplanted Okies—Marliss, a pliable 23-year-old and Weldon, approaching 40—in residence at Wilson's motel. Marliss doesn't "have any dreams about California"; instead, she's content to hang out by the pool and pop whites, smoke joints, score some coke. She ends up naked and semi-conscious on a transvestite's motel room floor as Bill, a grease-stained auto mechanic, drops his pants and lowers himself onto her. Wilson, haunted throughout the play by his ex-wife's harpings injected onstage via audiotape, finally allows his financially strapped motel to be torched for the insurance money.

The Shaper also explores failed dreams through the increasing insolvency of a small business. Set in Bud and Del's rundown surfboard shop, the title literally refers to Bud's occupation as a surfboard sculptor; metaphorically it suggests the influence of Del, in jail for cocaine possession at the play's outset, who lures Bud not only into acts of infidelity and petty larceny, but also into the whole soulless environment in which their dissipation has occurred. Reesa, Del's half-sister, has recently arrived in California from Ohio and she ogles the other characters' tans and tells them how she always imagined Bud as a "shiny golden beach boy." The great distance between her ideal and the sordid reality forms the vacuous grand canyon at the heart of Steppling's plays.

The Thrill, like *The Dream Coast*, is an ironic title. Linda, another of Steppling's young impressionable women unable to generate any self-motivation, hangs out at a Southern California shopping mall. There she encounters two small-time con-artists, working their way west from Providence,

Rhode Island. Walter found Nat when he was 19 and reminds his partner that he was "the most beautiful thing I'd ever seen." But their partnership, like Bud and Del's, is doomed since Nat has managed to forcefully seduce the docile Linda (one scene consists solely of Nat forcing himself sexually on her in a telephone booth in the mall while her friend Beverly watches). However, the "thrill" of her relationship is all Linda has to fill her life; her passivity is such that when her father sends her a large check for her 21st birthday, she willingly hands it over to Nat, who then disappears with the money. The play ends with Linda sharing lunch with her aunt who runs a small fabric store in the mall—a perfect image of bland domesticity—in which she's recently started working now that the source of her "thrills" has vanished.

Standard of the Breed departs slightly from these other plays in that it takes place not in the Los Angeles area but in Jack's Nevada desert home outside Las Vegas (although the dreams crash just as resoundingly there) where he raises mastiffs, "the largest dogs in the world." A more significant difference is that the characters haven't yet completely surrendered their hopes and dreams to despair. The play unfolds at a dreamlike pace over the course of one night, beginning when twentysomething Cassie, a mixed-up young L.A. girl, arrives at Jack's doorstep after having left her unwitting boyfriend asleep in their room at a Vegas hotel. She's come to buy a mastiff puppy and escape her relationship. Jack explains that the standard for breeding dogs is "perfection," a metaphor for these humans as well (although such a project is ultimately destined for failure). The play is also about leaving, and like all Steppling's work, the characters are in transit to or from some half-idealized existence. Reese, Jack's boss at the casino, deserts his girlfriend Teela, who hoped to go to L.A. to try to make it as a singer. Jack decides to head to Sacramento and get drunk for a while, and encourages Cassie to dump her life and head out into the desert with her puppy by her side: "Leave it—That's a fine thing to do. All you need to take is the yearning." The play ends with Jack letting his prized mastiffs loose into the desert morning where they'll surely die slow painful deaths.

Some critics take exception to Steppling's plays, not only for the manner in which they continually portray young females as hapless victims of older, predatory males, but for their perceived soullessness. In an interview Steppling maintains his prerogative: "we live in patriarchy, it's very sexist. I'm writing what I see. . . . And everyone's a victim, really. Men and women are just subjugated in different kinds of ways." To Steppling's admirers, such arguments are beside the point; for, they feel, few U.S. dramatists so effectively describe the underbelly of human aspiration and futility.

—John Istel

STEWART, Douglas (Alexander). Australian. 1913–1985. See 3rd edition, 1982.

STOPPARD, Tom. British. Born Tom Straussler in Zlin, Czechoslovakia, 3 July 1937; moved to Singapore, 1939,

Darjeeling, India, 1942, and England, 1946. Educated at Dolphin School, Nottinghamshire, 1946–48; Pocklington School, Yorkshire, 1948–54. Married 1) Jose Ingle in 1965 (marriage dissolved 1971), two sons; 2) Miriam Moore-Robinson (i.e., the writer Miriam Stoppard) in 1972, two sons. Journalist, *Western Daily Press*, Bristol, 1954–58, and Bristol *Evening World*, 1958–60; then freelance journalist and writer: drama critic, *Scene*, London, 1962–63. Member of the board, Royal National Theatre, London, from 1989. Recipient: Ford grant, 1964; John Whiting award, 1967; *Evening Standard* award, 1967, 1973, 1975, 1979, 1983; Italia prize, for radio play, 1968; Tony award, 1968, 1976, 1984; New York Drama Critics Circle award, 1968, 1976, 1984; Shakespeare prize (Hamburg), 1979; Outer Circle award, 1984; Drama Desk award, 1984. M.Lit.: University of Bristol, 1976; Brunel University, Uxbridge, Middlesex, 1979; University of Sussex, Brighton, 1980; honorary degrees: Leeds University, 1980; University of London, 1982; Kenyon College, Gambier, Ohio, 1984; York University, 1984. Fellow, Royal Society of Literature. C.B.E. (Commander, Order of the British Empire), 1978. Lives in Iver, Buckinghamshire. Agent: Peters, Fraser, and Dunlop Group, 503–504 The Chambers, Chelsea Harbour, Lots Road, London SW10 0XF, England.

PUBLICATIONS

Plays

A Walk on the Water (televised 1963; produced Hamburg, 1964); revised version, as *The Preservation of George Riley* (televised 1964); as *Enter a Free Man* (produced London, 1968; New York, 1974). London, Faber, 1968; New York, Grove Press, 1972.

The Dissolution of Dominic Boot (broadcast 1964). Included in *The Dog It Was That Died and Other Plays*, 1983.

"M"Is for Moon among Other Things (broadcast 1964; produced Richmond, Surrey, 1977). Included in *The Dog It Was That Died and Other Plays*, 1983.

The Gamblers (produced Bristol, 1965).

If You're Glad I'll Be Frank (broadcast 1966; produced Edinburgh, 1969; London, 1976; New York, 1987). With *Albert's Bridge*, London, Faber, 1969; revised version, published separately, New York and London, French, 1978.

Tango, adaptation of a play by Slawomir Mrozek, translated by Nicholas Bethell (produced London, 1966). London, Cape, 1968.

A Separate Peace (televised 1966). London, French, 1977; in *Albert's Bridge and Other Plays*, 1977.

Rosencrantz and Guildenstern Are Dead (produced Edinburgh, 1966; revised version produced London and New York, 1967). London, Faber, and New York, Grove Press, 1967; screenplay published as *Rosencrantz and Guildenstern Are Dead: The Film*, London, Faber, 1991.

Albert's Bridge (broadcast 1967; produced Edinburgh, 1969; New York, 1975; London, 1976). With *If You're Glad I'll Be Frank*, London, Faber, 1969; in *Albert's Bridge and Other Plays*, 1977.

Teeth (televised 1967). Included in *The Dog It Was That Died and Other Plays*, 1983.

Another Moon Called Earth (televised 1967). Included in *The Dog It Was That Died and Other Plays*, 1983.

Neutral Ground (televised 1968). Included in *The Dog It Was That Died and Other Plays*, 1983.

The Real Inspector Hound (produced London, 1968; New York, 1972). London, Faber, 1968; New York, Grove Press, 1969.

After Magritte (produced London, 1970; New York, 1972). London, Faber, 1971; New York, Grove Press, 1972.

Where Are They Now? (broadcast 1970). With *Artist Descending a Staircase*, London, Faber, 1973; in *Albert's Bridge and Other Plays*, 1977.

Dogg's Our Pet (produced London, 1971). Published in *Ten of the Best*, edited by Ed Berman, London, Inter-Action Imprint, 1979.

Jumpers (produced London, 1972; Washington, D.C., and New York, 1974). London, Faber, and New York, Grove Press, 1972; revised version, Faber, 1986.

Artist Descending a Staircase (broadcast 1972; produced London, 1988; New York, 1989). With *Where Are They Now?*, London, Faber, 1973; in *Albert's Bridge and Other Plays*, 1977.

The House of Bernarda Alba, adaptation of the play by García Lorca (produced London, 1973).

Travesties (produced London, 1974; New York, 1975). London, Faber, and New York, Grove Press, 1975.

Dirty Linen, and New-found-land (produced London, 1976; Washington, D.C., and New York, 1977). London, Faber, and New York, Grove Press, 1976.

The Fifteen Minute Hamlet (as *The [Fifteen Minute] Dogg's Troupe Hamlet*, produced London, 1976). London, French, 1978.

Albert's Bridge and Other Plays (includes *Artist Descending a Staircase, If You're Glad I'll Be Frank, A Separate Peace, Where Are They Now?*). New York, Grove Press, 1977.

Every Good Boy Deserves Favour: A Play for Actors and Orchestra, music by André Previn (produced London, 1977; Washington, D.C., 1978; New York, 1979). With *Professional Foul*, London, Faber, and New York, Grove Press, 1978.

Professional Foul (televised 1977). With *Every Good Boy Deserves Favour*, London, Faber, and New York, Grove Press, 1978.

Night and Day (produced London, 1978; Washington, D.C., and New York, 1979). London, Faber. 1978; New York, Grove Press, 1979; revised version, Faber, 1979.

Albert's Bridge Extended (produced Edinburgh, 1978).

Undiscovered Country, adaptation of a play by Schnitzler (produced London, 1979; Hartford, Connecticut, 1981). London, Faber, 1980.

Dogg's Hamlet, Cahoot's Macbeth (produced Warwick, London, Washington, D.C., and New York, 1979). London, Faber, and New York, French, 1980.

On the Razzle, adaptation of a play by Johann Nestroy (produced Edinburgh and London, 1981; Washington, D.C., 1982). London, Faber, 1981.

The Real Thing (produced London, 1982). London, Faber, 1982; revised version (produced New York, 1984), 1984.

The Dog It Was That Died (broadcast 1982). Included in *The Dog It Was That Died and Other Plays*, 1983.

The Love for Three Oranges, adaptation of the opera by Prokofiev (produced on tour, 1983).

The Dog It Was That Died and Other Plays (includes *The Dissolution of Dominic Boot, "M" Is for Moon among Other Things, Teeth, Another Moon Called Earth, Neutral Ground, A Separate Peace*). London, Faber, 1983.

Rough Crossing, adaptation of a play by Ferenc Molnár (produced London, 1984; revised version produced New York, 1989; London, 1990). London, Faber, 1985.

Squaring the Circle: Poland 1980–81 (televised 1984). With *Every Good Boy Deserves Favour* and *Professional Foul*, London, Faber, 1984.

Four Plays for Radio (includes *Artist Descending a Staircase, Where Are They Now?, If You're Glad I'll Be Frank, Albert's Bridge*). London, Faber, 1984.

Dalliance, adaptation of a play by Schnitzler (produced London, 1986). With *Undiscovered Country*, London, Faber, 1986.

Largo Desolato, adaptation of the play by Václav Havel (produced Bristol, 1986; London, 1987). London, Faber and New York, Grove Press, 1987.

Brazil (screenplay), in *The Battle of Brazil* by Jack Mathews. New York, Crown, 1987.

Hapgood (produced London, 1988). London, Faber, 1988.

The Radio Plays 1964–1983. London, Faber, 1990.

Arcadia (produced London, 1993). London, Faber, 1993.

Screenplays: *The Romantic Englishwoman*, with Thomas Wiseman, 1975; *Despair*, 1978; *The Human Factor*, 1980; *Brazil*, with Terry Gilliam and Charles McKeown, 1985; *Empire of the Sun*, 1988; *Rosencrantz and Guildenstern Are Dead*, 1990.

Radio Plays: *Dissolution of Dominic Boot*, 1964; *"M" Is for Moon among Other Things*, 1964; *If You're Glad I'll Be Frank*, 1966; *Albert's Bridge*, 1967; *Where Are They Now?*, 1970; *Artist Descending a Staircase*, 1972; *The Dog It Was That Died*, 1982; *In the Native State*, 1991.

Television Plays: *A Walk on the Water*, 1963 (revised version, as *The Preservation of George Riley*, 1964); *A Separate Peace*, 1966; *Teeth*, 1967; *Another Moon Called Earth*, 1967; *Neutral Ground*, 1968; *The Engagement*, from his radio play *The Dissolution of Dominic Boot*, 1970 (USA); *One Pair of Eyes* (documentary), 1972; *The Boundary* (*Eleventh Hour* series), with Clive Exton, 1975; *Three Men in a Boat*, from the novel by Jerome K. Jerome, 1975; *Professional Foul*, 1977; *Squaring the Circle*, 1984.

Novel

Lord Malquist and Mr. Moon. London, Blond, 1966; New York, Knopf, 1968.

Short Stories

Introduction 2, with others. London, Faber, 1964.

*

Bibliography: *Tom Stoppard: A Reference Guide* by David Bratt, Boston, Hall, 1982.

Critical Studies: *Tom Stoppard* by C.W.E. Bigsby, London, Longman, 1976, revised edition, 1979; *Tom Stoppard* by Ronald Hayman, London, Heinemann, and Totowa, New Jersey, Rowman and Littlefield, 1977, 4th edition, Heinemann, 1982; *Beyond Absurdity: The Plays of Tom Stoppard* by Victor L. Cahn, Madison, New Jersey, Fairleigh Dickinson University Press, 1979; *Tom Stoppard* by Felicia Hardison Londré, New York, Ungar, 1981; *Tom Stoppard: Comedy as a Moral Matrix* by Joan Fitzpatrick Dean, Columbia, University of Missouri Press, 1981; *The Stoppard Plays* by Lucina Paquet Gabbard, Troy, New York, Whitston, 1982; *Shakespearean Parallels and Affinities with the Theatre of the Absurd in Stoppard's Rosencrantz and Guildenstern Are Dead* by Anja Easterling, n.p., 1982; *Tom Stoppard's Plays* by Jim Hunter, London, Faber, and New York, Grove Press, 1982; *Tom Stoppard* by Thomas R.

Whitaker, London, Macmillan, and New York, Grove Press; 1983; *Stoppard: The Mystery and the Clockwork* by Richard Corballis, New York, Methuen, 1984, Oxford, Amber Lane Press, 1985; *Tom Stoppard: An Assessment* by Tim Brassell, London, Macmillan, and New York, St. Martin's Press, 1985; *File on Stoppard* edited by Malcolm Page, London, Methuen, 1986, *Tom Stoppard* by Susan Rusinko, Boston, Twayne, 1986; *Stoppard the Playwright* by Michael Billington, London, Methuen, 1987; *The Theatre of Tom Stoppard* by Anthony Jenkins, London and New York, Cambridge University Press, 1987, revised edition, 1989; *Tom Stoppard: A Casebook* edited by John Harty, III, New York, Garland, 1987; *Tom Stoppard: The Artist as Critic* by Neil Sammells, London, Macmillan, 1988; *Tom Stoppard: Rosencrantz and Guildenstern Are Dead, Jumpers, Travesties: A Casebook* edited by T. Bareham, London, Macmillan, 1990; *Tom Stoppard: The Moral Vision of the Major Plays* by Paul Delaney, London, Macmillan, 1990.

Theatrical Activities:
Director: **Play**—*Born Yesterday* by Garson Kanin, London, 1973; *The Real Inspector Hound*, London, 1985. **Film**—*Rosencrantz and Guildenstern Are Dead*, 1990.

*   *   *

Tom Stoppard vaulted to international renown in 1967 with *Rosencrantz and Guildenstern Are Dead*. It remains undoubtedly his best-known and most often produced work, although it can now be seen as juvenilia within the context of a dramatic talent that has matured steadily in both craft and thematic scope. A characteristic—if somewhat self-conscious—verbal agility has anchored his *oeuvre* as he developed his craft by exploring a variety of dramatic modes, writing for radio, television, and motion pictures as well as for the stage, both mainstream and experimental. Exercising his stylistic virtuosity upon other writers' plot structures, he has also made a number of free adaptations of plays from other languages.

After several years as a journalist and sometime theatre reviewer, in 1960 Stoppard wrote his first play, *A Walk on the Water*, which did not reach the legitimate stage until 1968 (in a revised version, titled *Enter a Free Man*). Meanwhile, it was a series of radio and television plays that launched him as a professional dramatist. Several of those early radio plays—notably *If You're Glad I'll Be Frank, Albert's Bridge*, and *Artist Descending a Staircase*—have in recent years been brought to the stage. Their creative use of the radio medium, however, tends to gimmickry at the expense of character, as in *Artist Descending a Staircase*, an ingenious search backward and forward in time for the truth about the circumstances of the artist's death, which had been captured on a tape recording that lends itself to clever ambiguity of interpretation. In the 1991 radio play *In the Native State*, a more subtle and graceful exploitation of the medium's unique properties fuels the story's implicit eroticism and places the focus on an intriguing web of human interactions, between English and Indian people, between people in 1930 and in the present. The radio plays' trajectory from artifice to interest in characters with real emotions parallels the development of Stoppard's writing for the stage.

The title characters of *Rosencrantz and Guildenstern Are Dead* are the school chums of Shakespeare's *Hamlet*, who have been summoned to Elsinore without knowing what is expected of them. Stoppard's play shows the two characters adrift in somebody else's plot, just as the Absurdists focused upon modern man's rudderlessness in a world he cannot control. While the action of *Hamlet* proceeds in the background, the two innocents play games to pass the time in a manner clearly inspired by Beckett's *Waiting for Godot*. Their desire to overcome the fixity of the work of art in which they must function echoes the premise of Pirandello's *Six Characters in Search of an Author*. The complex interrelationships of life and art are demonstrated with particular theatrical flair in the pair's scenes with the Players who come to perform for Claudius at Elsinore.

Two recurring themes in Stoppard's short plays of the 1960's and early 1970's, as well as in his novel *Lord Malquist and Mr. Moon*, are the relativity of truth and the urge to discern some pattern in the world's chaos. In *Albert's Bridge*, a well-educated young man opts to spend his life painting a suspension bridge, because it sets him above the fray of daily existence which can now be perceived as "dots and bricks, giving out a gentle hum." *The Real Inspector Hound* amusingly toys with the boundary between art and life by having two theatre critics get caught up in the murder mystery drama they are watching. The stage picture at the beginning of *After Magritte* is like a surrealist painting, but the action of the play reveals a kind of manic logic behind the visual nonsense.

The same concerns reappear in Stoppard's two major mid-career full-length plays *Jumpers* and *Travesties*. Although the philosophical discourse may become a bit heavy-handed in *Jumpers*, it must still be counted among his best plays for the brilliance of its theatrical conceits. The intellectual argument of the play, a dialectic between moral philosophy and logical positivism, is reified in stage metaphors like the human pyramid of middle-aged philosophers in jump suits, whose shaky performance inadvertently demonstrates the false logic of a relativistic philosophical system. However, the search for absolutes by philosopher George Moore is constantly subverted by events in his own household that cannot be understood at face value.

Travesties is a dazzling foray into a crucial moment in political and cultural history—filtered through the self-serving memory of a senile minor figure, Henry Carr, who worked at the British Consulate in Zurich during World War I. He comes into contact with Lenin, who is preparing the way for a revolution in Russia; Tristan Tzara, who seeks through Dada to overthrow 25 centuries of artistic convention; and James Joyce, who is already working on the novel that will revolutionize modern literature. Fitting these characters into the borrowed structure of Wilde's *The Importance of Being Earnest* (which was produced by the English Players under Joyce's direction in Zurich in 1917), Stoppard examines the responsibility of the artist to society.

As a kind of busman's holiday from his West End fare, Stoppard wrote a few short pieces for various "alternative theatre" projects undertaken by director Ed Berman, who had premièred *After Magritte*. Berman's community service organization Inter-Action included a children's theatre company called Dogg's Troupe, for which Stoppard wrote the one-act farce *Dogg's Our Pet*. In this play, as in the later paired one-acts *Dogg's Hamlet/Cahoot's Macbeth*, Stoppard makes fun of the arbitrariness of language by having some of his characters speak Dogg's language, which is composed of English words used to mean different things. The stage action in these plays is the construction of a speaker's platform, a stage, or a wall, using slabs, planks, bricks, and cubes—just as language uses the various parts of speech to construct a meaning. *Dogg's Hamlet* incorporates an earlier playlet, *The [Fifteen-Minute] Dogg's Troupe Hamlet*, which is a very funny condensation of Shakespeare's *Hamlet*, followed by a two-minute version as an encore.

In 1976 the American-born Berman asked Stoppard to write a play that would celebrate both the American bicentennial and Berman's naturalization as a British citizen. Stoppard responded by sandwiching the brief sketch, *New-found-land*, into his longer farce, *Dirty Linen*. Set in a House of Commons meeting room, *Dirty Linen* shows the foibles of members of the Select Committee on Promiscuity in High Places; they finally come to accept the common-sense opinions of the attractive Maddie Gotobed who has been sexually involved with most of them. When the Committee adjourns for 15 minutes, two new characters enter and use the room for a discussion of Berman's citizenship application, which leads to a long and cleverly evocative panegyric monologue about America as seen through foreign eyes.

Some of Stoppard's best writing has come from his moral outrage at totalitarian violations of human rights. Invited by André Previn to write a play that would involve a collaboration of actors and a live orchestra on the stage, Stoppard realized that by making the orchestra a figment of one character's imagination, he could set the play in an insane asylum and write about the Soviet practice of confining political prisoners there along with genuine lunatics. For all its serious subject matter, *Every Good Boy Deserves Favour* contains some supremely witty dialogue. It also features a child, Sacha, whose observation of the system's injustice and of his dissident father's integrity has matured him beyond his years. A boy named Sacha also plays a crucial role in the television play *Professional Foul*, which draws its metaphors from a soccer match that is played in Czechoslovakia while British philosophers attend a conference there. In the course of the tense drama, Sacha courageously helps one of them to smuggle his dissident father's doctoral thesis to England for publication. Another television play, *Squaring the Circle*, traces the 1980–81 workers' Solidarity movement in Poland and makes of that complex history a clear and absorbing narrative for the layman. Stoppard's premise is that the concept of a free trade union like Solidarity is as irreconcilable with the Communist bloc's definition of socialism as is the mathematical impossibility of turning a circle into a square with the same area. The brilliantly theatrical short piece *Cahoot's Macbeth* must also be classed as one of Stoppard's "plays of commitment."

Night and Day is a play of transition in Stoppard's development, for it continues his concern for human rights in the face of totalitarianism while it branches into a tentative exploration of romantic emotion. It is above all a play about journalism, a lively demonstration of the pros and cons of a free press. Ruth Carson is the wife of a British mine owner in a fictitious African country where a British-educated black dictator's rule is challenged by a Soviet-backed rebel countryman. The most idealistic of the three journalists who converge upon the Carson home becomes Ruth's fantasy-lover.

In *The Real Thing*, for the first time in Stoppard's canon, the human story is allowed to take precedence over ideological concerns or stylistic conceits. Yet there is a bit of everything in this romantic comedy that does not shy away from either human pain or politics; there is perhaps even a touch of autobiography in that the protagonist Henry Boot is a playwright. His speech, using a cricket-bat metaphor to uphold standards in language and thought, is dramatic writing at its best, a stylistic high point in the work of a writer for whom style has always been the strong suit.

Hapgood, too, may be seen as a compendium of earlier Stoppardian features: a small boy, political intrigue, a glimmer of romantic interest, attempts to discern a pattern in seemingly random events, and a complicated plot illustrating the premise that the truth depends upon where you are standing. Just as Stoppard had mastered certain philosophical arguments in order to write *Jumpers*, he learned particle physics in order to write his espionage comedy-thriller *Hapgood*, in which a Russian-born physicist may be a double or triple agent. Using the behavior of subatomic particles as a metaphor ("there is *no such thing* as an electron with a definite position and a definite momentum"), Stoppard's plot employs two real sets of twins and one fake pair to give dramatic shape to the notion that there is no fixity in human affairs.

During the increasingly long periods between his plays, Stoppard has devoted himself to writing screenplays, directing, and adapting plays in translation. He regards his adaptations as a crucial component of his work, and the liberties he takes with the originals establishes his versions in a category apart from literary translation. *Rough Crossing*, for example, borrows some of the characters and the situation from Ferenc Molnár's *The Play at the Castle* (also known as *The Play's the Thing*), but moves them from a castle on the Italian Riviera to a transatlantic ocean liner. By imposing spatial and temporal boundaries on the action, Stoppard heightens the dramatic tension even as he indulges in a variety of comic distractions. Certainly, Stoppard is long past needing such projects as short refresher courses in the craft of playwriting. They might be seen as tributes to his peers from one who has attained the status of world-class dramatist.

—Felicia Hardison Londré

STOREY, David (Malcolm). English. Born in Wakefield, Yorkshire, 13 July 1933; brother of the writer Anthony Storey. Educated at Queen Elizabeth Grammar School, Wakefield, 1943–51; Wakefield College of Art, 1951–53; Slade School of Fine Art, London, 1953–56, diploma in fine arts 1956. Married Barbara Rudd Hamilton in 1956; two sons and two daughters. Played professionally for the Leeds Rugby League Club, 1952–56; associate artistic director, Royal Court Theatre, London, 1972–74. Fellow, University College, London, 1974. Recipient: Macmillan award (U.S.) for fiction, 1960; Rhys Memorial award, for fiction, 1961; Maugham award, for fiction, 1963; *Evening Standard* award, 1967, 1970; New York Drama Critics Circle award, 1971, 1973, 1974; Faber Memorial prize, 1973; Los Angeles Drama Critics Circle award, 1973; Obie award, 1974; Booker prize, for fiction, 1976. Address: c/o Jonathan Cape Ltd., 20 Vauxhall Bridge Road, London SW1V 2SA, England.

PUBLICATIONS

Plays

The Restoration of Arnold Middleton (produced Edinburgh, 1966; London, 1967). London, Cape, 1967; New York, French, 1968.
In Celebration (produced London, 1969; Los Angeles, 1973; New York, 1984). London, Cape, 1969; New York, Grove Press, 1975.
The Contractor (produced London, 1969; New Haven, Connecticut, 1970; New York, 1973). London, Cape, 1970; New York, Random House, 1971.

Home (produced London and New York, 1970). London, Cape, 1970; New York, Random House, 1971.
The Changing Room (produced London, 1971; New Haven, Connecticut, 1972; New York, 1973). London, Cape, and New York, Random House, 1972.
The Farm (produced London, 1973; Washington, D.C., 1974; New York, 1976). London, Cape, 1973; New York, French, 1974.
Cromwell (produced London, 1973; Sarasota, Florida, 1977; New York, 1978). London, Cape, 1973.
Life Class (produced London, 1974; New York, 1975). London, Cape, 1975.
Mother's Day (produced London, 1976). London, Cape, 1977.
Sisters (produced Manchester, 1978; London, 1989). Included in *Early Days, Sisters, Life Class*, 1980.
Early Days (produced Brighton and London, 1980). Included in *Early Days, Sisters, Life Class*, 1980.
Early Days, Sisters, Life Class. London, Penguin, 1980.
Phoenix (produced London, 1984).
The March on Russia (produced London, 1989; Cleveland, Ohio, 1990). London, French, 1989.
Stages (produced London, 1992). Included in *Plays 1*, 1992.
Plays 1 (includes *The Contractor*, *Home*, *Stages*, *Caring*). London, Methuen, 1992.

Screenplays: *This Sporting Life*, 1963; *In Celebration*, 1976.

Television Play: *Grace*, from the story by James Joyce, 1974.

Novels

This Sporting Life. London, Longman, and New York, Macmillan, 1960.
Flight into Camden. London, Longman, 1960; New York, Macmillan, 1961.
Radcliffe. London, Longman, 1963; New York, Coward McCann, 1964.
Pasmore. London, Longman, 1972; New York, Dutton, 1974.
A Temporary Life. London, Allen Lane, 1973; New York, Dutton, 1974.
Saville. London, Cape, 1976; New York, Harper, 1977.
A Prodigal Child. London, Cape, 1982; New York, Dutton, 1983.
Present Times. London, Cape, 1984.

Verse

Storey's Lives: Poems 1951–1991. London, Cape, 1992.

Other

Writers on Themselves, with others. London, BBC Publications, 1964.
Edward, drawings by Donald Parker. London, Allen Lane, 1973.

*

Manuscript Collection: Boston University, Massachusetts.

Critical Studies: "No Goodness or No Kings" by Susan Shrapnel in *Cambridge Quarterly*, Autumn 1970; *The Second Wave*, London, Methuen, and New York, Hill and Wang, 1971, and *David Storey*, London, Longman, 1974, both by John Russell Taylor; "David Storey: Novelist or Playwright?"

by Mike Bygrave, in *Theatre Quarterly 1* (London), April-June 1971; by Marie Peel, in *Books and Bookmen* (London), March 1972; interview in *Plays and Players* (London), September 1973; "The Ironic Anger of David Storey" by William J. Free, in *Modern Drama* (Toronto), December 1973; "Poetic Naturalism in David Storey" in *New British Drama on the London Stage 1970–1985* by Richard Allen Cave, Gerrards Cross, Smythe, 1987; *The Plays of David Storey: A Thematic Study* by William Hutchings, Edwardsville, Illinois, Southern Illinois Press, 1988.

Theatrical Activities:
Director: **Television**—*Portrait of Margaret Evans*, 1963; *Death of My Mother* (D.H. Lawrence documentary), 1963.

* * *

David Storey's achievement as a dramatist has to be measured alongside the contribution made by Lindsay Anderson, who directed several of Storey's productions at London's Royal Court Theatre. Anderson may well have inspired Storey to branch out into the theatre following his auspicious beginning as a realistic novelist in the early 1960's. Anderson was certainly largely responsible for transforming Storey's most minutely detailed scripts into viable theatrical experiences.

Storey began as a playwright with *The Restoration of Arnold Middleton*, concerning a free spirit who rebels against conventional suburban mores. Both in style and in outlook, this resembled a number of other plays at the time by Tom Stoppard, David Mercer, and John Antrobus, and, though competent, was not truly indicative of Storey's main direction in the theatre.

In Celebration and *The Contractor* were far more distinctive. Each drew from their original novels a quality that was completely Storey's own in the matter-of-fact rendering of Northern working-class life. As grim as Lawrence's earlier evocations of Nottinghamshire mining communities, these were more subdued in tone, seeking simply to render a portrait of the way industrial life had fragmented family relationships, though the undercurrents of almost tribal unity and custom remained. *In Celebration* provides pointed comparisons with Mercer's *Ride a Cock Horse* in its refusal to let migration southward develop into Mercer's celebrated Northern chip on the shoulder. Storey's family of working-class lads return home for their parents' wedding anniversary. The scars of upbringing are manifest; so are the recriminations. But the protest is muted, less by inertia than by the sheer inability to come to terms with transition, even to the point of articulating that something is wrong.

It was an impressive feat, not least because Storey had dared to present something "internal" and "reflective" on a London stage and at a time when the waves of agitprop were beginning to break. Anderson's production concentrated on ensemble playing to underscore the theme of kinship, and Alan Bates and Constance Chapman gave memorable performances in an unglamorous evening that was, for all that, compelling.

The Contractor developed these strands as far as they can go, one feels from Storey's career afterwards. Each of the untoward elements of the earlier play were now fully exploited. Storey refined narrative to the point where there were no dramatic cruces to be explored. Several itinerant labourers appear on stage in desultory fashion to assemble a marquee for a wedding. The audience watches as actors simulate the very business their characters are required to do. They remain in role, but most of the theatricality is provided by their common initiative in successfully performing a set task by the time the act concludes. After the break the actors repeat the process in reverse, and when the marquee is finally dismantled the play ends, as unceremoniously as it begins.

For ensemble playing, this could only be matched by an audience being invited to attend a workshop of actors working with a given group in some highly organized game-playing. As a piece of scripted theatre, it bypassed areas of sleight-of-hand to emerge as a genuine piece of naturalism, closer to real experience than Arnold Wesker's *The Kitchen* had been, because the suspension of disbelief was "unnecessary." Life and art mirrored each other as they had never done before.

To say Storey had set himself an impossible task by trying to move on from this point is to give a far more rounded picture of Storey's career than he does himself. He continued to write plays interspersed with as many novels. Most of them, too, reveal a ready ability to experiment. All of the subsequent plays are at least watchable, and even when he has relied too heavily on existing models, including his own, he has done so with the clear aim of creating something new.

The Changing Room and *Home*, for example, closely followed *The Contractor* in Anderson productions at the Royal Court. But if the one suggested that writer and director were working to a formula (with a still-life depiction of a Northern amateur rugby team), the other compelled audiences to look at Storey anew. *Home*'s lingering achievement—it has to be said—is likely to be as a vehicle for a Gielgud–Richardson double act late in their careers when non-specialist audiences were eager to see two lions of the London stage performing the epitome of their talents. The production duly transferred into the West End and enabled the English Stage Company, at the Royal Court, to enter a turbulent decade of fringe production at least financially solvent. As a play, *Home* now bears too many traces of Beckett's influence to be seen as a development of Storey's canon. *Mother's Day* is, similarly, Ortonesque, while *Sisters* (an early play staged at Manchester) betrays so many uncomfortable similarities to *A Streetcar Named Desire* that it is tempting to wonder why the author did not simply write a transatlantic version of the Williams play.

On more native ground, however, Storey has enjoyed both critical and popular success with further examples of working-class life. If one is perplexed by the apparent absence of a centre to Storey's work, it is worth recalling that he trained as an artist at the Slade, and that the point of a play like *Early Days*, about a politician living out his retirement in bemused and gentle autocracy, may be less to raise searching questions about the condition of England than to offer an impressionistic pastoral better suited to comparison with John Constable's landscapes than with the crazy-quilt landscape of left-wing drama. (The play, incidentally, enabled Richardson to end his career on a note of triumph.)

Painting (and art generally) was the theme of the earlier *Life Class*, which presents a group of faintly-motivated art students, tutored by Alan Bates, trying to create something out of ubiquitous drabness, and failing, as the play fails, to catch hold of anything substantial.

The Farm, *Cromwell*, *The March on Russia*, and *Stages* complete Storey's dramatic output to date. He has said that he used the Brontës as inspiration in writing the first of these, and although the information is of tangential significance, this return to the theme of Northern family life, with women at the centre, is a solid achievement. *Cromwell* with its epic structure and its distance on passion, is more circumspect, though Brian Cox held the production together and revealed the author's mordant wit. *The March on Russia* was very much a reprise. At work again with a now U.S.-domiciled Anderson, Storey seemed content to revive their earliest collaboration under a new title. It is hard, anyway, to see *The March on Russia* as very much more than that. In it, as well, Storey may have been searching, himself, for a centre to his dramatic work. More likely this is to be found, however, in the one milestone of *The Contractor*.

—James MacDonald

STOTT, Mike. British. Born in Rochdale, Lancashire, 2 January 1944. Attended Manchester University. Stage manager, Scarborough Library Theatre, Yorkshire, and playreader, Royal Shakespeare Theatre, 3 years; script editor, BBC Radio, London, 1970–72; Thames Television resident writer, Hampstead Theatre Club, London, 1975. Agent: Michael Imison Playwrights, 28 Almeida Street, London N1 1TD, England.

PUBLICATIONS

Plays

Mata Hari (produced Scarborough, 1965).
Erogenous Zones (produced London, 1969).
Funny Peculiar (produced Bochum, Germany, 1973; Liverpool, 1975; London, 1976). Ashover, Derbyshire, Amber Lane Press, 1978.
Lenz, adaptation of the story by Georg Büchner (produced London, 1974; New York, 1979). Todmorden, Lancashire, Woodhouse, 1979.
Plays for People Who Don't Move Much (produced London, 1974; section produced as *Men's Talk*, Edinburgh, 1974).
Midnight (produced London, 1974).
Other People (produced London, 1974).
Ghosts, adaptation of a play by Wolfgang Bauer (produced London, 1975).
Lorenzaccio, adaptation of the play by Alfred de Musset (produced Exeter, 1976).
Followed by Oysters (produced London, 1976; as *Comings and Goings*, produced Liverpool and London, 1978).
The Scenario, adaptation of a play by Anouilh (produced Bellingham, Northumberland, 1976).
Soldiers Talking, Cleanly (televised 1978). London, Eyre Methuen, 1978.
The Boston Strangler (produced London, 1978).
Grandad (produced Croydon, Surrey, 1978).
Strangers (produced Liverpool, 1979).
Ducking Out, adaptation of a play by Eduardo De Filippo (produced London, 1982).
Dead Men (produced Southampton, 1982).
Pennine Pleasures (produced Oldham, Lancashire, 1984).
The Fling, adaptation of a work by Asher (produced London, 1987).
The Fancy Man (broadcast 1987; produced London, 1988). Published in *Plays International* (Shrewsbury, Shropshire), November 1988.

Radio Plays: *Lucky*, 1970; *When Dreams Collide*, 1970; *Early Morning Glory*, 1972; *Lincoln*, 1973; *Richard Serge*, 1973;

The Bringer of Bad News, 1973; *The Doubting Thomases*, 1973; *The Fancy Man*, 1987.

Television Plays: *The Flaxton Boys*, 1969; *Susan*, 1973; *Thwum*, 1975; *Our Flesh and Blood*, 1977; *Pickersgill People* series, 1978; *Soldiers Talking, Cleanly*, 1978; *One in a Thousand*, 1981; *The Last Company Car*, 1983; *The Practice* series, 1985–86.

* * *

Mike Stott's 1976 West End success with his comedy *Funny Peculiar* may well represent the culmination of his search for an ideal, or at least clinching, formula for the permissive sex comedy.

His search began with *Erogenous Zones*, a collection of sketches for performance by a company of six, centred round the twin themes of love and homicide. The mixture here is one of strip cartoon wit and woman's magazine cliché, the main charm residing in the way passion is reduced to absurdity through being couched in dumb and deadpan phrases. The types are instantly recognizable—the doughy sweetheart, the sadistic cop, the clean-limbed officer doing press-ups, the big beefy success, the mad gunman, the obsessive lawyer—with the point always clear before the pay-offs. Stott shows cleverness in catching the comedy of the obvious, while managing to avoid repetition.

In *Other People* the form is sometimes laboured though the dialogue is often sharp. It begins with an arresting image of a "flasher" naked under his plastic, see-through mac, and a pretty Czech girl who frightens him away by her eagerness to participate in anything he might suggest. But an arresting image does not make a play, and the web of relationships Stott establishes—between a successful businessman, Dave, who ends by taking an overdose, an out-of-work Italian father-of-five who is given a cheque by the dying man to solve all his problems, a lonely widow of 51 who lacks love, and her daughter, married to Dave's friend Geoff—fails to form a coherent pattern of comic interest. The writing is often vivid, as in the Italian's fantasy of selling underwear to Arabs in hair-covered boxes—"We buy the hair, we comb it, shampoo, and we stick it on the boxes. And those Arabs, those Greeks, they go CRAZY in the shops, just to stroke our sexy hairy boxes. Believe me, Mr. Brock, I know those men, the foreigners, the Aristotles, the Ahmeds. They KILL each other to be stroking a hairy English box." The theme of sexual permissiveness is provocatively explored, with the sound of couples making love upstairs and one couple trying to initiate group sex. But it's hard to make out what Stott's intention is, whether he's attempting genuine social observation or merely exploiting current fashion.

Funny Peculiar has a mock moral ending. The hero, Trevor, a North Country grocer proclaiming the virtues of sexual freedom, falls down into his cellar, pursued by a sex-hungry puritan lady of advanced years, and is consequently rendered helpless in plaster and straps on a hospital bed. There he becomes the passive object of wife and mistress's oral lust. A new and up-to-date version of the "tu l'a voulu, Georges Dandin" idea, Trevor's obsession with sex is kept simmering in naked cavorting among the council-estate flower beds and in his attempts to preach to the unconverted customers of his shop (losing custom as a result).

The best writing is found in the scenes when he tries to convince his wife to leap on to the freedom bandwagon and when he upbraids her for sexual ordinariness. Her defence is so heartfelt and real it really seems that her subsequent conversion to his way of thinking is engineered for the sake of the plot. There's one piece of slapstick—a fight with confectionary between a visiting confectionary salesman and Trevor—which must rate as one of the best scenes of comic anarchy ever seen on the West End stage.

In his versions of Büchner's *Lenz* and Wolfgang Bauer's *Ghosts* Stott demonstrates more fragmented skills as an adaptor and translator from the German. *Lenz*, originally a short story about a Strasbourg intellectual who believes he can raise a girl from the dead, is written in numerous short scenes (in Büchner's own expressionistic manner) which fail to come to grips with any central issue. The original of *Ghosts* is a roughed up rewrite of Brecht's satire on a lower-middle-class wedding party, using socially more sophisticated though dramatically more crude characters.

In later plays Stott has not shown he can move beyond formula writing. *The Boston Strangler*, for all its rape and murder in intended subtle variations—ensuring constant changes of wigs and underwear in the actress playing all the victims—cumulatively diminishes interest in the crimes of a psychopath. *Comings and Goings* promises to be better. Jan, a teacher, married to a cream-cracker executive, deserts him and arrives in the household of a pair of homosexuals. But development is lost in favour of generalized encounters confirming the rule of licence and ending with vapid literary parallels. The characters have little genuineness and the comings and goings lack dramatic direction. Stott seems to have come to the position of despising the people he writes about. *Grandad*, too, displays a tawdry lack of charity, becoming unrelievedly tedious. Stott returned to formula writing in the television series *The Practice*, an examination of life in a medical centre.

—Garry O'Connor

SUNDE, Karen. American. Actor, Colorado Shakespeare Festival, Boulder, Colorado, 1967, The New Shakespeare Company, San Francisco, 1967–68, Arrow Rock Lyceum, Arrow Rock, Missouri, 1969–70, and CSC Repertory, New York, 1971–85; associate director, CSC Repertory, New York, 1975–85. Recipient: Bob Hope award, 1963; American Scandinavian Foundation travel grant, 1981; Finnish Literature Center Production grant, 1982; Villager award (three times), 1983; McKnight fellowship, 1986; Aide de la Création grant, 1987. Address: 23 Leroy Street, Number 8, New York, New York 10014, U.S.A.

PUBLICATIONS

Plays

The Running of the Deer (produced New York, 1978).
Balloon (produced New York, 1983). New York, Broadway Play Publishing, 1983.
Philoctetes, adaptation of the play by Sophocles (also director: produced New York, 1983).
Dark Lady (produced Santa Maria, California, 1986; Dublin, 1988). Wilton, Connecticut, Dramatic Publishing Company, 1985.
Kabuki Othello (produced Philadelphia, 1986).
To Moscow (produced Minneapolis, 1986; New York, 1991).

Quasimodo (musical), adaptation of Victor Hugo's *The Hunchback of Notre Dame*, with Christopher Martin (produced Woodstock, New York, 1987).
Anton, Himself (produced Louisville, Kentucky, 1988). Published in *Moscow Art Theatre*, edited by Michael Bigelow Dixon, Louisville, Kentucky, Actors' Theatre of Louisville, 1989.
Kabuki Macbeth (produced Davis, California, 1989).
Haiti: A Dream (produced Atlanta, Georgia, 1990).
Masha, Too (produced Philadelphia, 1991).
Achilles (produced Kourion, Cyprus and Philadelphia, 1991).
In a Kingdom by the Sea (produced Madison, New Jersey and New York, 1992).

Radio Plays: *The Sound of Sand*, 1963; *Balloon*, 1987; *Haiti: A Dream*, 1991.

*

Manuscript Collection: Lincoln Center Library for the Performing Arts, New York.

Theatrical Activities:
Director: **Plays**—*Exit the King* by Ionesco, New York, 1978; *Philoctetes* by Sophocles, New York, 1983.
Actor: **Plays**—some 60 roles performed off Broadway including: Ruth in *The Homecoming* by Pinter, 1972–76; Celimene in *The Misanthrope* by Molière, and Viola in *Twelfth Night*, 1973–74; Hedda in *Hedda Gabler* by Ibsen, 1974–77; Antigone in *Antigone* by Anouilh, 1975–77; Isabella in *Measure for Measure*, 1975; Hesione in *Heartbreak House* by Shaw, 1976–77; Rebekka West in *Rosmersholm* by Ibsen, 1977–78; Countess Aurelie in *The Madwoman of Chaillot* by Giraudoux, 1978; Portia in *The Merchant of Venice*, 1980; Jocasta and Antigone in *Oedipus Rex*, *Antigone*, and *Oedipus at Colonus* by Sophocles, 1980–81; Aase in *Peer Gynt* by Ibsen, 1981–82; Lotte in *Big and Little* by Botho Strauss, 1983–84; Alice in *Dance of Death* by Strindberg, 1984; Clytemnestra in *The Orestia* by Aeschylus, 1984–85. **Television**—Mary Brewster in *The Mayflower*, 1980.

Karen Sunde comments:
I follow my nose—and here's all I know: that rhythm is important to me. And economy. And passion. That the live current between audience and stage is everything.

* * *

With a voice both poetic and theatrical, Karen Sunde's plays dramatize historical epochs in epic scope, making hers a distinctive, even unique, contemporary American drama, more akin to European than to other American plays. She tackles topics of war and politics to produce usually presentational, often explosive theatre which many would swear could not have been created by a woman. Yet she imbues her mythic vision of the bellicose and patriarchal nature and direction of the United States and the world with a sense of what women can or do contribute to modifying these.

Sunde's twenty works for stage and screen fall into three related groups: the historical plays, the treatments of classics, and the glimpses of a painful present shaping a deplorable, but possibly salvageable future.

The first of her three consecutive plays set during or immediately after the American Revolution, *The Running of the Deer*, with its huge canvas and varied vistas, dramatizes the ravages of cold, starvation, and battle on George Washington's troops in order to probe the character of

American male heroes, while the second, *Balloon*, achieves the same goal by setting in a theatrical framework worthy of Jean Genet another American founding father, Ben Franklin, so he can spar with his Tory son and woo his French mistress, Helvetius, who fears losing her autonomy in marriage to a man as passionately committed to his vocations as to his lovers. An appropriate protagonist for a play about hope and progress, Franklin strives and achieves, yet his painful interpersonal relations have diluted his triumphs.

Deborah: The Adventures of a Soldier (an unproduced television play), like several of Sunde's subsequent plays, investigates female heroism, or, in this case, the male model of heroism achieved by an astonishing woman warrior, Deborah Sampson, who enlists in the Continental Army as "Robert Shurtliffe," and rises to leadership among men while battling with the British. As Sunde remarks of her version of this actual historical woman's triumphs, "When war is real, issues confused, deaths bitter, a woman has to finally decide who she is." This one can outshoot, outthink, and outrun the men, but should she continue to do so? Sunde humorously recounts Deborah's adventures both as a soldier and as a woman trying to pass for a man (with women coming on to "him") and falling in love with a sergeant who thinks she's male. Sunde's background as an actor in Shakespeare's plays certainly sensitized her to the comedic possibilities of employing a woman playing a man. But the dramatist also conveys the war's pathos, its pain, and its cost in lives lost.

Sunde continues to explore female heroism in *The Flower's Lost Child* (an unproduced play), which portrays what the playwright describes as "America's romance with violence." Instead of colonists resisting taxation without representation and throwing off an oppressor's rule, Sunde chooses hippie revolutionaries in 1970 New York. The shift in period changes our perspective, forcing us to distance ourselves from terrorists, to question the appropriateness of bombs in the pursuit of peace. Yet she dramatizes these idealists sympathetically. A resourceful and brave leader, Anne had worked with Martin Luther King and embraced non-violence. Now, disillusioned by his assassination, she has abandoned marches and rallies in favor of dynamite. This tragedy creates a powerful sense of fate because Sunde frames the entire play as flashback by beginning with firemen sifting through rubble and dismembered bodies, and then enhances the suspense by surrounding her characters with explosives.

In her as yet unproduced and untitled gothic thriller about British serial killer John George Haigh, set in 1948, Sunde builds tension by hinting at a murder and the threat to the lives of two courageous women, a spirited teenager and another more mature woman, who struggle to foil their amoral terrorizer.

Sunde again depicts a female hero in *Dark Lady*, which, set against the plague's slaughter, dramatizes the relationship between Shakespeare and Renaissance England's best-known woman poet, Emilia Bassano. Sunde creates in her a passionate woman whose humanity, courage, spirit, and generosity equal—and ultimately exceed—the Bard's.

In three further plays, Sunde dramatizes actual characters in events which plausibly might have occurred. *To Moscow* concerns Chekhov, his actress wife Olga Knipper, Konstantin Stanislavsky, and the beginnings of the Moscow Art Theatre. The title evokes Chekhov's three sisters' unrealized intention to return from their provincial backwater to Moscow. Sunde chooses as four of the six central characters women whom Chekhov exploits. But in one, Olga, he finds (like Shakespeare in Emilia) his equal. Sunde completes her Russian trilogy with two matching one-act portraits, one of the narcissist Chekhov titled *Anton, Himself*, the other,

Masha, Too, of his sister, as she struggles to summon the courage to tell him she plans to marry. We conclude from *Anton* that her brother will not let her leave him. While viewers need know nothing about Chekhov to enjoy these three, Sunde interlards the action with jokes about the plays and stories, especially intriguing to knowledgeable viewers.

While penning her history plays Sunde undertook a related approach to indicting human folly, by means of our literary myths, one from Victor Hugo, three from Shakespeare's plays, and one from Homer's *Iliad*. Sunde's musical version of *The Hunchback of Notre Dame*, which she wrote with director Christopher Martin, fashions the novel into a fluid work which contrasts with the long, carefully demarcated scenes in that other Hugo musical, *Les Misérables*. More opera than musical and boasting a score ranging from ecclesiastic to gypsy, the galvanic *Quasimodo* dramatizes the theme that people should experience, not repress, their passions: "Man is man, not stone."

Providing further evidence of her versatility, Sunde created four Kabuki plays for Japanese director Shozo Sato, who has staged them in Kabuki style but with American performers. Although *Kabuki Othello* preserves the Shakespearean outlines, Sunde makes Iago's motivation clearer and eliminates the Bard's racism and sexism. Asian ritual reinforces the tragedy's inevitability. Far from inviting any unfavorable comparisons to the original, Sunde creates her own distinctive imagery—delicate, tender, and eventually heroic for Desdemona, demonic for the Ainu Othello—and, in Emilia's lines, a healthy sarcasm about machismo and female subservience. In her *Kabuki Macbeth* and, the as yet unproduced, *Kabuki Richard* the dramatist also evokes a theatrical mixture of the original plots and their archetypes with Eastern culture—samurai, shoguns, karma, and Shiva intertwined with ghosts, witches, and severed heads.

In *Achilles* Sunde converts material from *The Iliad* into a mythic anti-war tragedy. She emphasizes the macho lust for glory which leads to the razing of Troy and massive, senseless slaughter, reminding us of the continuing cost of personal and international bravado. Sunde's searing script dramatizes pride, arrogance, and savagery—and their aftermath of grief, when Achilles joins Priam in mourning Hector's death after the bereaved father kisses the "victor's" hand. Focusing her work for us through the eyes of the enslaved Briseis, "only a woman," a prize of battle, who has learned "the purpose of life is war," Sunde employs an archetypal example to promote peace and recognition of our common humanity.

Sunde likewise dramatizes conflicts from a humanist perspective in a series of prescient plays looking towards the global future. *House of Eeyore* (an unproduced play), which takes its title from A. A. Milne's *Winnie the Pooh* stories, employs dream research, a gubernatorial campaign, and an ageless native American psychic (named after the female spirit Gaia) to awaken a prominent American family to its spiritual and social responsibilities.

Whereas the visionary middle-class woman in *House of Eeyore* works as a research physician, Gaye in *Countdown: Earth* (an unproduced screenplay), saves the western half of the planet because of her skill as a geophysicist—not to mention her bravery in carrying out a daredevil rescue while dangling above a volcano starting to erupt. Still a third woman scientist, this one discovering a cure for cancer, plays a prominent role in *Over the Rainbow* (another unproduced screenplay), but here Sunde chooses as her protagonist another healer, the scientist's little girl. Both *Countdown: Earth* and *Over the Rainbow* employ science fiction to arouse concern about our planet's survival.

In three further plays Sunde hopes for a better tomorrow

even as she explores the roots of misery today. The prophetic *Haiti: A Dream* dramatizes the flight to Florida of Haitian boat people by focusing on a man and his wife and the Old Woman empowered by voodoo who tries unsuccessfully to inspire them both to recognize their own strength to lead their people. In a similar spirit of fantasizing about a better way, *How His Bride Came to Abraham* (an unproduced play), creates an extraordinary modern pacifist myth in which a wounded male Israeli soldier and a female Palestinian terrorist experience each other's passionate hunger for their homes and rights. Sunde describes this tragedy as "today's violent news stories in fairy-tale form," but it indelibly etches itself upon viewers' souls because of the human encounter, as wary people drop their guard with an enemy.

The multi-media *In a Kingdom by the Sea*, based upon the abduction of Marine Lt. Col. William Higgins, presents simultaneously the efforts of the UN peacekeepers to free one of their own—here named Hogan—and Hogan himself, who appears in both past and present, in both monologue and dialogue, to share with us the "key to America," and to his character: football and women—in Hogan's case the woman whom, since high school, he has tried to impress with a uniform. In contrast to *How His Bride Came to Abraham*'s wartime dream of peace and love, *In a Kingdom by the Sea* dramatizes the subversion of the UN peacekeeping forces' efforts in Lebanon by those on both sides for whom macho bravado means more than would an end to hostility.

A balloon will rise, but what, Sunde inquires in *Balloon*, of humanity? Her plays consider whether we have reason to hope.

—Tish Dace

SUTHERLAND, Efua (Theodora, née Morgue). Ghanaian. Born in Cape Coast, 27 June 1924. Educated at St. Monica's School and Training College, Cape Coast; Homerton College, Cambridge, B.A.; School of Oriental and African Studies, London. Married William Sutherland in 1954; three children. Schoolteacher in Ghana, 1951–54. Since 1958 founding director, Experimental Theatre Players (now Ghana Drama Studio), Accra. Founder, Ghana Society of Writers (now the University of Ghana Writers Workshop) and Kusum Agoromba children's theatre group, Legon. Cofounder, *Okyeame* magazine, Accra. Address: Institute of African Studies, University of Ghana, P.O. Box 25, Legon, Ghana.

PUBLICATIONS

Plays

Foriwa (produced Accra, 1962).   Accra, State Publishing Corporation, 1967; New York, Panther House, 1970.
Edufa, based on *Alcestis* by Euripides (produced Accra, 1962; London, 1987).   London, Longman, 1967; in *Plays from Black Africa*, edited by Fredric M. Litto, New York, Hill and Wang, 1968.
Anansegoro: You Swore an Oath, in *Présence Africaine 22* (Paris), Summer 1964.
Vulture! Vulture! Two Rhythm Plays (for children; includes *Tahinta*), photographs by Willis E. Bell. Accra, Ghana Publishing House, 1968; New York, Panther House, 1970.
Ananse and the Dwarf Brigade (for children; produced Cleveland, 1971).
The Marriage of Anansewa: A Storytelling Drama (produced Accra, 1971).   London, Longman, 1975.

Other plays: *Odasani*, version of *Everyman*; adaptation of Chekhov's *The Proposal*; *The Pineapple Child*; *Nyamekye*; *Tweedledum and Tweedledee*, adaptation of *Alice in Wonderland* by Lewis Carroll.

Verse (for children)

Playtime in Africa, photographs by Willis E. Bell.   London, Brown Knight and Truscott, 1960; New York, Atheneum, 1962.

Other

The Roadmakers, with Willis E. Bell, photographs by Bell. Accra, Ghana Information Services, and London, Neame, 1961.
The Original Bob: The Story of Bob Johnson, Ghana's Ace Comedian, illustrated by Willis E. Bell. Accra, Anowuo, 1970.
The Voice in the Forest: A Tale from Ghana. New York, Philomel, 1983.

*   *   *

It is impossible to consider Efua Sutherland's plays apart from her work as a founder and organiser of theatres and troupes. One might infer, indeed, that she has considered this work more important than her writing since a number of her plays have never appeared in print.

In the mid-1950's Sutherland set up a society to write for children, and her concern with children has been a continuing one. For them she has written many plays, sometimes based upon traditional tales. Only the two extremely brief "rhythm plays" and *Anansegoro: You Swore an Oath* have appeared in print, the latter without her advance knowledge. The narrative framework of *Anansegoro*, with a storyteller and a chorus whose members also play minor parts, is appropriate to its retelling of a common folktale of a deer who turns into a beautiful woman, and whom Ananse eventually loses when he tells the secret of her identity. The short play is vigorous, simple, and highly theatrical. Children can take pleasure in the story, the song, and the dance, adults in the sophistication of the presentation.

Sutherland brought playwriting and theatrical production together in Ghana, for the few plays that predate Ghanaian independence in 1957 and the founding of her Experimental Theatre players in 1958 were essentially closet dramas. Moreover, from the start she aimed to bring drama to the people. She was thus concerned with bringing drama to children and encouraging their participation; with drawing upon local folk stories, lyrics, and dances; and with performing in Twi as well as in English. With funding from American foundations and with government support the first professional theatre, the Ghana Drama Studio, was built and opened in 1961. In 1962 the Drama Studio became a part of the newly established School of Music and Drama at the University of Ghana. Continuing her concern with reaching the ordinary person, Sutherland designed a courtyard theatre. This was, I believe, the first African attempt to design a theatre that drew on indigenous tradition rather than copying European proscenium stages.

She has adapted various works, from *Alice in Wonderland* to *Everyman*, which remain unpublished. Her full-length play *Edufa*, however, is less an adaptation than a counter-argument to Euripides' *Alcestis*, since the values given to many of the characters are reversed. In Euripides' play, because of his reputation for hospitality the gods allow Admetus to let someone else die for him. Even in the midst of his grief for his wife, Alcestis, he courteously plays host to the visiting Heracles, who then pursues Death, wrests Alcestis away from him, and returns her to Admetus. Euripides' play was designed to be presented not as a tragedy but in place of a satyr play. *Edufa*, however, is a tragedy, ending with the Alcestis-figure's death. Moreover, with heavy irony, the action is set against an annual ceremony in which funeral songs are sung as evil is expelled from the town. Evil is to be found in Edufa, Sutherland's Admetus-figure, a selfish member of the new class of privileged *nouveaux riches* who, behind his facade of a man emancipated from traditional beliefs by his education, secretly resorts to diviners. Similarly, the Heracles character is a seedy intellectual. In contrast, the father, a self-centred hypocrite in Euripides, becomes a representative of the dignity and wisdom of the older generation. The focus, as the shift from wife to husband in the title suggests, is on the educated modern man and the loss of moral orientation that has come with his alienation from traditional values.

Of Sutherland's other two full-length plays, *Foriwa* was first written in Twi and intended for performance in the street of any small town. Labaran, a university graduate, tells us in the play's opening soliloquy

This is my office, this street: the people who use it are my work and my education.

I am keeping vigil here, placing my faith in some daybreak after this long night, when the townsmen shall wake and shake my soul with vibrant talk. . . .

I was impatient at the beginning: in haste. Seeing the raggedness of my people's homes, I was ashamed, even angry. I heard it screamed: Progress! Development! I wanted it far and everywhere.

From this straightforward statement of the theme, we anticipate—quite correctly—that the play will end with his triumph. Yet the play is distinctively original. First, Sutherland eschews the conflict between generations, and between tradition and modernization, around which many African plays about social change are based. Labaran's allies are the retired postmaster and the Queen-Mother who, de-spite her traditional role, is a reformer. Second, the tone of the play is set not by the struggle for social change, but by the joyous youthfulness and self-discovery of Foriwa, the Queen-Mother's daughter, who has just returned from training as a teacher. She and Labaran take the length of the play to fall in love. Since he is a Hausa from the distant north, this is yet another symbol of unity for progress. The play's climax is the Queen-Mother's use of a traditional ceremony—again, Sutherland emphasizes the alliance of old and new—to win endorsement for change. The play is without villains, for the message is that all must cooperate; even the elders, Labaran says, "have come as far as they are able."

The Marriage of Anansewa is a sprightly divertissement. Ananse, a traditional figure who is a combination everyman and trickster, encourages four wealthy chiefs to woo his daughter. When each announces his imminent arrival to claim his bride, the only way out is for Anansewa to "die." This has the double advantage that it frees her father from any obligation to return their gifts and allows him to discover the character of each suitor and his motives in seeking the match. Of course, it is the last one to send his condolences who alone is worthy of her, and she miraculously revives to marry the Chief-Who-Is-Chief. Since the wooing is all by messenger, and since Anansewa is silent while she is "dead," Sutherland can keep her untainted by her father's mercenary schemes. By keeping her uninvolved, however, Sutherland also leaves her character undeveloped.

Each of Sutherland's plays experiments with the involvement of the spectators. *Edufa* keeps the Euripidean chorus and was intended for presentation in the Ghana Drama Studio's courtyard theatre, with spectators and actors entering through the same gate. *Foriwa* was written for street performance and the hero explains his intentions directly to the audience. Most ambitiously and successfully, *The Marriage of Anansewa* attempts to recapture the atmosphere of traditional story-telling sessions, not only with a storyteller and a busy onstage property man, but also by keeping the performers onstage throughout as an onstage audience with whom Sutherland hopes the real audience will "feel as one," perhaps even joining in the play's many songs.

—Anthony Graham-White

T

TABORI, George. British. Born in Budapest, Hungary, 24 May 1914. Educated at Zrinyl Gymnasium. Served in the British Army Middle East Command, 1941–43; lieutenant. Married 1) Hanna Freund (divorced 1954); 2) the actress Viveca Lindfors (divorced), one son, one daughter, and one stepson. Former artistic director, Berkshire Theatre Festival, Stockbridge, Massachusetts. Recipient: British Film Academy award, 1953. Address: 172 East 95th Street, New York, New York 10028, U.S.A.; or, c/o Suhrkamp Verlag, Lindenstrasse 29–35, Postfach 4229, 6000 Frankfurt am Main, Germany.

PUBLICATIONS

Plays

Flight into Egypt (produced New York, 1952). New York, Dramatists Play Service, 1953.

The Emperor's Clothes (produced New York, 1953). New York, French, 1953.

Miss Julie, adaptation of a play by Strindberg (also director: produced New York, 1956).

Brouhaha (produced Brighton and London, 1958; New York, 1960).

Brecht on Brecht (produced New York and London, 1962). New York, French, n.d.

The Resistible Rise of Arturo Ui: A Gangster Spectacle, adaptation of the play by Brecht (produced New York, 1963; Edinburgh, 1968; London, 1969). New York, French, 1972.

Andorra, adaptation of the play by Max Frisch (produced New York, 1963).

The Guns of Carrar, adaptation of a play by Brecht (produced Syracuse, New York, 1963; New York City, 1968). New York, French, 1970.

The Niggerlovers: The Demonstration, and Man and Dog, music by Richard Peaslee (produced New York, 1967).

The Cannibals (produced New York, 1968). Published in *The American Place Theatre*, edited by Richard Schotter, New York, Dell, 1973; published separately, London, Davis Poynter, 1974.

Mother Courage, adaptation of a play by Brecht (produced Washington, D.C., 1970).

Pinkville, music by Stanley Walden (produced Stockbridge, Massachusetts, 1970; New York, 1971).

Clowns (also director: produced Tübingen, 1972).

Talk Show (produced Bremen, 1976).

Changes (produced Munich, 1976).

Mein Kampf: A Farce (produced Edinburgh and London, 1989).

Weisman and Copperface (produced London, 1991).

Screenplays: *I Confess*, with William Archibald, 1953; *The Young Lovers*, with Robin Estridge, 1954; *The Journey*, 1959; *No Exit*, 1962; *Secret Ceremony*, 1968; *Parades*, 1972; *Insomnia*, 1975.

Novels

Beneath the Stone the Scorpion. London, Boardman, 1945; as *Beneath the Stone*, Boston, Houghton Mifflin, 1945.

Companions of the Left Hand. London, Boardman, and Boston, Houghton Mifflin, 1946.

Original Sin. London, Boardman, and Boston, Houghton Mifflin, 1947.

The Caravan Passes. London, Boardman, and New York, Appleton Century Crofts, 1951.

The Journey: A Confession. New York, Bantam, 1958; London, Corgi, 1959.

The Good One. New York, Pocket Books, 1960.

Other

Ich wollte, meine Tochter läge tot zu meinen Füssen und hätte die Juwelen in den Ohren: Improvisationen über Shakespeares Shylock: Dokumentationen einer Theaterarbeit. Munich, Hanser, 1979.

*

Theatrical Activities:
Director: **Plays**—*Miss Julie* by Strindberg, New York, 1956; *Brecht on Brecht*, toured, 1962; *Hell Is Other People*, New York, 1964; *The Cannibals* (co-director, with Marty Fried), Berlin, 1970; *Pinkville*, Berlin, 1971; *Clowns*, Tübingen, 1972; *Kohlhaas*, Bonn, 1974; *Emigrants*, Bonn, 1975; *Afore Night Come* by David Rudkin, Bremen, 1975; *The Trojan Women* by Euripides, Bremen, 1976.

* * *

George Tabori's world recalls the Sherwood Anderson title *Dark Laughter*. What a world—betrayal, repression, violence, cannibalism, and, unlike the Greeks', no redemption. And envisioned more and more as a black comedy. But not quite. The flavor is sardonic, tongue-in-cheek, but beneath this is absolutely no acceptance of the world as is. Beneath the sardonic tone we can apprehend the eyes of an anguished, lacerated soul who has seen mankind in one perversion, one degradation after another, seen Hungary in its fascistic period earlier in the century, Germany in the Nazi era, and America in its growing role as police-butcher of the world, has seen it all, and yet whose outcry marks him as one who still believes in the impossible dream of brotherhood. I have the sense that Tabori is too angry, too disgusted to *want* to believe, but that past his disgust, past his disillusionment, there is a tremendous yearning, a cavernous yearning to believe in the possibility of a decent society.

Early Tabori is represented by *The Emperor's Clothes*, the tale of a "fuzzy-headed idealist" intellectual (my quotes) in Budapest who appears to renounce all his beliefs when he falls into the hands of the secret police, but who emerges as a man with backbone. Under torture he rediscovers his manhood. In short, Tabori at his most idealistic.

But then the world grows darker and Tabori begins to shift from naturalism toward a more abstract, less lyrical, and far harsher theatre. He began adapting Brecht, e.g., *Brecht on Brecht* and *Arturo Ui*, and his own work became more detached, more sardonic, more abstract, more song-and-dance oriented. By the time of *The Cannibals* in 1968, the work was very dry, very dark, very bitter, very removed. In a Nazi concentration camp, the prisoners decide to cook and eat their friend Puffi, the fat man who has just died. Hirschler says:

> (To Uncle who is protesting the cannibalism) Listen, Uncle, let's have some perspective. The cake is too small. Whenever you eat, you take a crumb out of someone else's mouth. At this very moment, while you're making such a fuss, millions are starving to death in India; but today we may have stumbled on the most elegant solution. The graveyards are full of goodies; the chimneys are going full blast, and nice fat suicides come floating down every river and stream. All that perfectly good stuff going to waste.

Shades of Swift's *A Modest Proposal*. And the cannibalism, which Tabori treats both literally and as a metaphor, is painted as inexorable. At the end of the play, the Loud-speakers place the action in historic context:

> . . . some savages eagerly desire the body of a
>   murdered man
> So that his ghost may not trouble them,
> For which reason I recommend, dear brethren in
>   Christ,
> The Jew's heart, in aspic or with sauce vinaigrette,
> So soft it will melt in your mouth.

In The *Niggerlovers* Tabori views the racial tensions that afflict the U.S., but any sympathy is sublimated. No one comes off with any saving grace, the white liberals are stupid or saccharine or slightly perverted, the blacks are corroded with cynicism. No action seems to be of any help, there is no way out.

Pinkville studies the development of an American killer—specifically how the U.S. army takes a non-violent, righteous young man, and using his very righteousness, subverts him into the killer it needs to massacre Vietnamese. Again the action is inexorable. Everything becomes grist for the army's purpose. Again the world is so self-enclosed that there is no way out.

And yet the way out is through the action of Tabori's art. For the very work is a cry. The sardonic element has within it a taint of satisfaction, as if the worst is always somehow satisfying, but the worst is also an indictment of us, ultimately a call. For the early heroes are gone, no heroes left in the later plays, nothing for us to emulate. You and I become the only possible heroes left to Tabori and to the world.

—Arthur Sainer

TALLY, Ted. American. Born in Winston-Salem, North Carolina, 9 April 1952. Educated at Yale University, New Haven, Connecticut (John Golden fellowship 1976–77; Kazan award, 1977; Field prize, 1977), B.A. 1974, M.F.A. 1977. Married; one son. Taught at Yale University; artist-in-

residence, Atlantic Center for the Arts, 1983. Member of the Dramatists Guild, Writers Guild, Academy of Motion Picture Arts and Sciences, and the Artistic Board, Playwrights Horizons, New York. Recipient: CBS-Yale fellowship, 1977; Creative Artists Public Service grant, 1979; John Gassner award, 1981; National Endowment for the Arts fellowship, 1983; Obie award, 1984; Guggenheim fellowship, 1985; Christopher award, 1988; Oscar, 1992; Writers Guild award, 1992; Chicago Film Critics award, 1992; Saturn award, 1992. Lives in Pennsylvania. Agent: (theatre) Helen Merrill Ltd., 361 West 17th Street, New York, New York 10011; (film) Arlene Donovan, International Creative Management, 40 West 57th Street, New York, New York 10019, U.S.A.

PUBLICATIONS

Plays

Terra Nova (produced New Haven, Connecticut, 1977; Chichester, Sussex, 1980; London, 1983; New York, 1984). London, French, 1981; New York, Dramatists Play Service, 1982.
Night Mail and Other Sketches (produced New York, 1977).
Word of Mouth (revue), with others (produced New York, 1978).
Hooters (produced New York, 1978). New York, Dramatists Play Service, 1978.
Coming Attractions, music by Jack Feldman, lyrics by Feldman and Bruce Sussman (produced New York, 1980). New York, French, 1982.
Silver Linings: Revue Sketches. New York, Dramatists Play Service, 1983.
Little Footsteps (produced New York, 1986; London, 1987). New York, Dramatists Play Service, 1986.
Taxi from Hell in *Urban Blight* (musical revue), based on an idea by John Tillinger, music by David Shire, lyrics by Richard Maltby, Jr. (produced New York, 1988).
The Gettysburg Sound Bite (produced New York, 1989).

Screenplays: *White Palace*, with Alvin Sargent, 1990; *The Silence of the Lambs*, 1991.

Television: *The Comedy Zone* series, 1984; *Holy Angels*, with others, 1986; *The Father Clements Story*, with Arthur Heineman, 1987.

*

Ted Tally comments:
I have sometimes been asked whether my plays share any particular theme. Though they have been diverse both stylistically and in terms of subject matter, I think there are at least two common threads: a fascination with rites of passage, and a concern for the prices one must pay in pursuit of a dream.

*   *   *

Ted Tally writes in versatile voices. Since 1977 productions of his plays at showcase American theaters (including the Yale Repertory Theater, the O'Neill Theater Center in Waterford, Connecticut, the Mark Taper Forum in Los Angeles, and the audaciously innovative Playwrights Horizons in New York City), in Stockholm, and at the Chichester Festival Theatre have earned him recognition as an important dramatic talent.

Tally's prodigious promise is revealed stunningly in *Terra*

Nova, his most widely produced and justifiably praised work to date. His subject is specific and based in reality: Englishman Robert Scott's doomed 1911–12 race to the Antarctic against the Norwegian Roald Amundsen. But the play's method and implications are mythic and poetic; they free Tally from the confines of a history play and enable him to universalize his literal subject through stylized language, setting, and dramatic structure. Set in the mind of the dying Scott as he records final entries in his diary, *Terra Nova* portrays its hero's hallucinatory evaluation of the sources that have driven him and his unlucky band of men to the Antarctic. The procession of stage images shifts seamlessly, cinematically, within the frozen present, the past, the future —all reflected through the anguished mind of Scott, whose story co-exists as exciting theatrical adventure and as the wellspring for a series of complex moral debates.

Tally dissects the core of heroism even as he concedes the needs of nations to create heroes and the symbiotic needs of special men, sometimes tragic men like Scott, to enact the roles their societies write for them. Related to the play's central, ambivalent issue are the vanishing points between national pride and jingoism, patriotic sacrifice and familial irresponsibility, a shrinking British Empire and a future (toward which the play points) bereft of Old Style Heroes. "The world is changing," Amundsen says in Scott's imagined future. "England, Norway, Europe—The Great War changed everything, you wouldn't know it today [1932]. It's a smaller place, but not a more neighbourly one. A frightened place, a world of shopkeepers and thieves. Where is the heroic gesture in such a world? The man who can keep his bread on the table is a hero. Where on such an earth are men who walk like gods? Dead and gone, with Columbus and Magellan." In his haunted fear of failure and conflicting drive to defy man's ordinary boundaries, Scott resembles Ibsen's Master Builder Solness. Possibly, as Amundsen calls him, "the most dangerous kind of decent man," possibly a true representative of the last breed of genuine hero, possibly a complete sham. Scott is one of the few realized tragic heroes in the recent American drama.

In *Coming Attractions* the subject is still celebrity but the mode is wild satire. Amundsen's prediction in *Terra Nova* has come true: no heroes are left. But television and the tabloids, memoir publishers and movie writers, hungry for heroes to feed an insatiable American public, fabricate them out of killers, madmen, and Real People. *Coming Attractions* takes deadly aim at many targets: Miss America contests, television news, talk and variety shows, inept law enforcement, an even more inept judicial system, old time religion, advertising, and—especially—an American society that encourages fleeting fame or infamy to masquerade as authentic accomplishment. To appear on television, even for a moment, is the Promised End. Tally's shift from the poetic voices of *Terra Nova* to the parodies in *Coming Attractions* of show biz vernacular, press agentry, and media hype is dazzling. Outrageous puns (Criminal to Judge: "I demand that you give me the chair!" Judge: "Then where would I sit?"), burlesque routines, movie clichés, and mordantly hilarious situations (the play concludes with the televised musical electrocution of its killer-hero: "Live from Death Row—it's—The Execution of Lonnie Wayne Burke!") combine in a lunatic blend of the Marx Brothers, Artaudian theatre of cruelty, Paddy Chayefsky's *Network*, and Sinclair Lewis's *Elmer Gantry*.

Tally's other work reflects his discomfort with stylistic uniformity. *Hooters* is a rites-of-passage sex comedy. Three early unproduced film scripts belong to three separate genres: situation comedy (*Couples Only*); epic (*Empire*, on which Tally worked for a year with director Lindsay Anderson); New

York police thriller (*Hush-a-Bye*). In the underrated play *Little Footsteps* ("an exceptionally literate sitcom," *New York Times* critic Frank Rich called it), the teenage courtship dance of *Hooters* evolves into marriage and in-law rituals as a young couple await the arrival of their firstborn. "We've got nothing against your religion, Ben; it's you we hate," his mother-in-law casually informs the beleaguered hero in the play's pungent dialogue.

Like most serious American playwrights of the past decade, Tally deplores the exorbitant costs of Broadway theatre which result in productions appealing to "the widest possible audience" and having "more and more to do with sensation and effect, less to do with any food for thought." His plays are primarily associated with strong regional theatre companies and with Playwrights Horizons in New York City, the highly regarded company with which he has been identified periodically since the beginning of his career.

Tally's disenchantment with the theatre appears for now to have driven him entirely to screenwriting, a shift that, with his adaptation of *The Silence of the Lambs*, has brought him financial reward and critical acclaim (including an Oscar) rarely earned for his stage work. He embraces film writing for its opportunities to reach "a wider audience and to be less subject to the whims of critics." He rejects the notion that Hollywood "sucks up writers and destroys them," maintaining that his work with director Jonathan Demme on *The Silence of the Lambs* was a thoroughly enjoyable collaborative effort; he anticipates the prospect of a sequel with relish.

In recognition of what he calls the inevitable "streamlining" that must occur in screen adaptation, Tally's screenplay for the film eliminates the multiple points of view which occur in Thomas Harris's novel. "The book goes inside the minds not just of Clarice Starling, but of Lecter, of Gumb, the killer she is pursuing, and of Jack Crawford, her mentor at the F.B.I.," Tally told a New York Times interviewer. "I thought really that the entire story had to concentrate on Clarice, that every scene had to concentrate as much as possible on what she is seeing and what she is feeling and what she is thinking. The heart of the story was between Clarice and Lecter, that strange sexual power struggle, that chess game between this young woman and this man—this monster." That "this monster," performed memorably by Anthony Hopkins, becomes the film's unforgettable character, a Norman Bates for the 1990's, is a particular consequence of Tally's dialogue, which manages to externalize Lecter's dangerous complexity and dark humour without turning him into a caricature.

"Success is a bitch. Grab her, and have her—but don't stand under her window with a mandolin," says Amundsen, the cynical, pragmatic leveler of Scott's romantic imagination in *Terra Nova*. "Ain't life a bitch?" muses theatrical agent Manny Alter to the man condemned to electrocution in *Coming Attractions*. In *Terra Nova* heroism comes to an end but genuine myths are born. In *Coming Attractions* travesty is the only legitimate vehicle for a society in which violence and bad taste alone capture the public imagination. Hannibal (the Cannibal) Lecter sprang to mythical status as an icon of popular cinema culture following the release of *The Silence of the Lambs*. It is no small irony that Ted Tally's most explicit flirtation with violence and bad taste captured the public imagination as none of his plays has yet been able to do.

—Mark W. Estrin

TAVEL, Ronald. American. Born in Brooklyn, New York, 17 May 1941. Educated at Brooklyn College; University of Wyoming, Laramie, B.A., M.A. 1961. Screenwriter, Andy Warhol Films Inc., 1964–66; playwright-in-residence, Play-House of the Ridiculous, New York, 1965–67, Theatre of the Lost Continent, New York, 1971–73, Actors Studio, New York, 1972, Yale University Divinity School, New Haven, Connecticut, 1975, 1977, Williamstown Theatre Festival, Massachusetts, Summer 1977, New Playwrights Theatre, Washington, D.C., 1978–79, Cornell University, Ithaca, New York, 1980–81, Centrum Foundation, Fort Worden State Park, Washington, 1981, and Millay Colony for the Arts, New York, 1986; lecturer in foreign languages, Mahidol University, Thailand, 1981–82; visiting professor of creative writing, University of Colorado, Boulder, 1986. Since 1984 member of the Education Division, Theater for the New City, New York. Literary adviser, *Scripts* magazine, New York, 1971–72; drama critic, *Stages* magazine, Norwood, New Jersey, 1984; theatre editor, *Brooklyn Literary Review*, 1984–85. Recipient: Obie award, 1969, 1973; American Place Theatre grant, 1970; Creative Artists Public Service grant, 1971, 1973; Rockefeller grant, 1972, 1978; Guggenheim fellowship, 1973; National Endowment for the Arts grant, 1974; New York State Council on the Arts grant, 1975; ZBS Foundation grant, 1976; New York Foundation for the Arts fellowship, 1985; Yaddo fellowship, 1986. Agent: Helen Merrill Ltd., 361 West 17th Street, New York, New York 10011. Address: 780 Carroll Street, Brooklyn, New York 11215; or, 438 West Broadway, Apartment 1, New York, New York 10012, U.S.A.

PUBLICATIONS

Plays

Christina's World, published in *Chicago Review*, Winter-Spring 1963.
The Life of Juanita Castro (produced New York, 1965). Included in *Bigfoot and Other Plays*, 1973.
Shower (produced New York, 1965). Included in *Bigfoot and Other Plays*, 1973.
Tarzan of the Flicks (produced Plainfield, Vermont, 1965). Published in *Blacklist 6* (Maplewood, New Jersey), 1965.
Harlot (scenario), published in *Film Culture* (New York), Spring 1966.
The Life of Lady Godiva (produced New York, 1966). Published in *The New Underground Theatre*, edited by Robert Schroeder, New York, Bantam, 1968.
Indira Gandhi's Daring Device (produced New York, 1966). Included in *Bigfoot and Other Plays*, 1973.
Screen Test (produced New York, 1966).
Vinyl (produced New York, 1967). Published in *Clyde* (New York), vol. 2, no. 2, 1966.
Kitchenette (also director: produced New York, 1967). Included in *Bigfoot and Other Plays*, 1973.
Gorilla Queen (produced New York, 1967). Published in *The Best of Off-Off-Broadway*, edited by Michael T. Smith, New York, Dutton, 1969.
Canticle of the Nightingale (produced Stockholm, 1968).
Cleobis and Bito (oratorio; produced New York, 1968).
Arenas of Lutetia (also director: produced New York, 1968). Published in *Experiments in Prose*, edited by Eugene Wildman, Chicago, Swallow Press, 1969.
Boy on the Straight-Back Chair, music by Orville Stoeber (produced New York, 1969). Included in *Bigfoot and Other Plays*, 1973.

Vinyl Visits an FM Station (produced New York, 1970). Published in *Drama Review* (New York), September 1970.
Bigfoot, music by Jeff Labes (produced New York, 1970). Included in *Bigfoot and Other Plays*, 1973.
Words for Bryan to Sing and Dance (produced New York, 1971).
Arse Long—Life Short (produced New York, 1972).
Secrets of the Citizens Correction Committee (produced New York, 1973). Published in *Scripts 3* (New York), January 1972.
Bigfoot and Other Plays. New York, Winter House, 1973.
Queen of Greece (produced New York, 1973).
The Last Days of British Honduras (produced New York, 1974).
Playbirth (produced New York, 1976).
The Clown's Tail (produced New York, 1977).
Gazelle Boy (produced Waterford, Connecticut, 1977).
The Ovens of Anita Orangejuice: A History of Modern Florida (produced Williamstown, Massachusetts, 1977; New York, 1978).
The Ark of God (produced Washington, D.C., 1978).
The Nutcracker in the Land of Nuts, music by Simeon Westbrooke (produced New York, 1979).
My Foetus Lived on Amboy Street (broadcast 1979; also director: produced New York, 1985).
The Understudy (produced Ithaca, New York, 1981).
Success and Succession (produced New York, 1983).
Notorious Harik Will Kill the Pope (also director: produced New York, 1986).
Thick Dick (also director: produced New York, 1988).

Screenplays: *Harlot*, 1964; *Phillip's Screen Test*, 1965; *Screen Test*, 1965: *Suicide*, 1965; *The Life of Juanita Castro*, 1965; *Horse*, 1965; *Vinyl*, 1965; *Kitchen*, 1965; *Space*, 1965; *Hedy; or, The 14-Year-Old Girl*, 1966; *Withering Sights*, 1966; *The Chelsea Girls*, 1966; *More Milk Evette*, 1966.

Radio Play: *My Foetus Lived on Amboy Street*, 1979.

Novel

Street of Stairs. New York, Olympia Press, 1968.

*

Manuscript Collections: Mugar Memorial Library, Boston University: Lincoln Center Library of the Performing Arts, New York; University of Wisconsin Center for Theatre Research, Madison.

Critical Studies: "The Pop Scene," in *Tri-Quarterly 6* (Evanston, Illinois), 1966, and "Pop Goes America," in *New Republic* (Washington, D.C.), 9 September 1967, both by Peter Michelson; "Ronald Tavel: Ridiculous Playwright" by Dan Isaac, in *Drama Review* (New York), Spring 1968; "Toward Eroticizing All Thought," in *New York Times*, 5 January 1969, and "Ronald Tavel: Celebration of a Panic Vision," in *Village Voice* (New York), 6 March 1969, both by Gino Rizzo; "A Kid Named Toby" by Jack Kroll, in *Newsweek* (New York), 24 March 1969; *American Playwrights: A Critical Survey* by Bonnie Marranca and Gautam Dasgupta, New York, Drama Book Specialists, 1981.

Theatrical Activities:
Director: **Plays**—*The Life of Juanita Castro*, Chicago, 1967; *Kitchenette*, New York, 1967; *Arenas of Lutetia*, New York, 1968; *Infinity*, New York, 1972; *A Streetcar Named Desire* (in

Thai, as *Ourrat*) by Tennessee Williams, Bangkok, 1981; *The Zoo Story* (in Thai) by Edward Albee, Bangkok, 1982; *Clash of the Bra Maidens*, New York, 1984; *My Foetus Lived on Amboy Street*, New York, 1985; *The Tell-Tale Heart*, East Meadow, New York, 1985; *Talent*, East Meadow, New York, 1985; *Notorious Harik Will Kill the Pope*, New York, 1986; *Thick Dick*, New York, 1988. **Films**—*Harlot*, 1964; *Phillip's Screen Test*, 1965; *Screen Test*, 1965; *The Life of Juanita Castro*, 1965; *Horse*, 1965; *Vinyl*, 1965; *Space*, 1965; *It Happened in Connecticut*, 1965; *Hedy; or, The 14-Year-Old Girl*, 1966; *Withering Sights*, 1966; *The Chelsea Girls* (*Toby Short* and *Hanoi Hanna* episodes), 1966.

Actor: **Plays**—roles in *In Search of the Cobra Jewels* by Harvey Fierstein, New York, 1972, and in all his directed plays. **Films**—in all his directed films, and in *Fifty Fantasticks*, 1964; *Bitch*, 1965; *Jail*, 1967; *Suicide Notations: Fire Escape*, 1972; *Infinity*, 1974.

Ronald Tavel comments:

(1973) My earliest tales were delivered Homerically. At the age of six or seven I took the first step toward giving them permanent form: comic books. While these comics were shameless imitations of the pictorial styles featured in the funnies we read at that time, there was, I fancy, something more urgent in my stories and characterizations. I wrote my first (verse) play (or fragment of one) in my sophomore year in high school and ten verse plays (or fragments of ones) followed that effort. The last of these have reached print but only one (*Cleobis and Bito*) was ever produced. In 1965, after two years of writing, directing, and acting in films, I turned again to playwriting. These were the one-acters that inaugurated The Theatre of the Ridiculous movement—a term I invented to catch the attention of critics and lower them into a category in order to facilitate their work. The term "Ridiculous" should not be taken too seriously (!) unless you want to re-define that word as Professor Peter Michelson did in his essay on the new American absurdity (*New Republic*, 9 September 1967). I sought in these abstract satires to find a distinctly American language for the stage and that is a continuing preoccupation in my later and mercilessly longer "tragedies." In the early plays I also attempted to destroy plot and character, motivation, cause, event, and logic along with their supposed consequences. The word was All: what was spoken did not express the moment's preoccupation; rather, the preoccupation followed the word. In *The Life of Lady Godiva* I reached, cynically, for the Aristotelian principles of playmaking. While cynicism is the major thrust of *Godiva*, a near decade of concern with *The Poetics* was worming its way, re-evaluated, to the core of my chores. *Gorilla Queen* progresses by building and abolishing, rebuilding and reabolishing, etc., the Aristotelian constructs. The full-length plays after *Gorilla Queen* obey, I believe, without too much objection, the Greek's difficult insights. While I have no single favorite, I am particularly fond of *Shower* because it continues to mystify me, am protective of *Arenas of Lutetia* because no one else will be, and consider *Bigfoot* (if you will allow me to play critic) my most ambitious and best play to date.

(1988) Although my recent fellowships and judging and teaching appointments are apparently for my abstract work in theatre, I have continued to create as many formal pieces: partly because I feel that formal values, following the disappearance of American education, are threatened in serious contemporary theatre; and partly because I believe that our present situation is not more keenly scrutinized by the abstract than the formal. (My previous solution, in larger works, was always to combine the two.)

Because of the growing idiosyncratic nature of serious plays, it has become common in the last decade for American dramatists to direct their own work. Reluctantly, I have joined their ranks. Since directing forces a stronger confrontation with space, time, flesh, clothes, and light than words alone do, and requires no rewards or rejuvenations outside itself, it helps the playwright to that closer understanding of the unity of theatre which he irresponsibly surrendered in the past century and a half.

* * *

Ronald Tavel is one of the originators of the mode Susan Sontag identified as "camp." From the start he writes with an unmistakable voice, relentlessly punning, answering back to his own word-plays, philosophizing, art-conscious, joking, ridiculous as the Marx Brothers, and turning his formidable energy to the service of a passion for justice, with a Cassandra's terror of self-righteousness, a not-to-be-thwarted demand for meaning, self- and god-knowledge.

This thrust is evident even in a pop joke like *The Life of Juanita Castro* which takes its authenticity from *Life* magazine. *Indira Gandhi's Daring Device* drew a swift protest from the government of India, and *How Jacqueline Kennedy Became Queen of Greece* was muted (but in title only) to *Queen of Greece*. These plays are travesty, but Tavel is out for serious game, and has loaded them with real facts and arguments.

Gorilla Queen, his first play on a large scale, is a spoof on jungle movies, unique in its crazy playfulness, rococo, smart-aleck language, outlandishly scrambled sexuality, and self-consciousness about art. From the epilogue (delivered by a gibbon holding a purple rose): ". . . art ain't never 'bout life, but life *is* only 'bout art. Dis rose?—oh, it ain't no symbol like ya mighta thought, an dat's cause it ain't got nothing' to do wit life either. Dis here rose is all 'bout art. Here, take it—(He throws the rose into the audience.)"

In *Bigfoot* the work began to reveal, not just refer to, its depth and power. Here Tavel's subject is brothers, in the image of Jacob and Esau. On a profound level of derangement the one, an intellectual monastic and schoolteacher, suspects the other, a forest ranger, of being not human, confusing him with the Bigfoot, the legendary man-ape of the Pacific Northwest. Set in the majestic forest and the monastery schoolroom, *Bigfoot* is a play of immense complexity. The surface is no longer pop or campy but the post-realist strategies are in flood: a fictional lighting girl gets caught up in the *more real* fiction of the play's far-fetched story; the Playwright's Brother is a character *ex machina*, played in the production Tavel supervised by his own brother—what a thing to do in a play about mythic fratricide!

The Ovens of Anita Orangejuice is a boisterous, savage satire about Anita Bryant's 1977 campaign against gay rights. Subtitled "A History of Modern Florida," it is a wisecrack that turns into a nightmare. For all its frenzied hilarity, it makes a thought-provoking, emotionally compelling case. In *Gazelle Boy* a middle-aged missionary in the north woods loses her head over a wild boy, which leads to tragedy of profoundly unsettling dimensions. It is a beautiful play, dense with religion. Here sex is a reaching for the divine. *The Understudy* is about sex murder: the play's playwright may have done the killings he has written about, which the audience is ultimately shown in literal gore; a demented understudy tries to save him, and steal the writer's being, by recommitting them himself.

My Foetus Lived on Amboy Street takes a far more tender tone. The play appears to be, of all things, a prenatal autobiography. The writer experiments here with an expressionistically abstracted, outwardly geometrical stagecraft. The persona of the play's ego images himself as a spider, while the company of players patch in the various roles as freely as the author counterposes multiple vernaculars of lyricism and melodrama. *Notorious Harik Will Kill the Pope*, which Tavel himself staged at the Theatre for the New City in New York in 1986, crammed the stage with movie types (Turhan Bey and Lana Turner are among the characters) in a flashy complexity of scenes. The frivolity of its trashy satirical style— Tavel never resists a pun—masks a sustained demolition of the religious establishment which, like all his themes, the writer gives every sign of meaning.

—Michael T. Smith

TAYLOR, Cecil P(hilip). British. 1929–1981.
See 2nd edition, 1977.

TERRY, Megan. American. Born Marguerite Duffy in Seattle, Washington, 22 July 1932. Educated at Banff School of Fine Arts, Alberta, summers 1950–53, 1956; University of Washington, Seattle, 1950, 1953–56, B.Ed. 1956; University of Alberta, Edmonton, 1951–53. Drama teacher and director of the Cornish Players, Cornish School of Allied Arts, Seattle, 1954–56; founding member, 1963, and director of the playwrights workshop, 1963–68, Open Theatre, New York; writer-in-residence, Yale University School of Drama, New Haven, Connecticut, 1966–67; founding member, Women's Theatre Council, 1971; founding member and treasurer, New York Theatre Strategy, 1971; Bingham professor of humanities, University of Louisville, 1981; Hill professor of fine arts, University of Minnesota, Duluth, 1983; visiting artist University of Iowa, Iowa City, 1992. Since 1971 resident playwright and literary manager, Omaha Magic Theatre. Recipient: Stanley award, 1965; Office of Advanced Drama Research award, 1965; ABC-Yale University fellowship, 1966; Rockefeller grant, 1968, 1987; Obie award, 1970; National Endowment for the Arts grant, 1972, fellowship, 1989; Earplay award, 1972; Creative Artists Public Service grant, 1973; Guggenheim fellowship, 1978; Dramatists Guild award, 1983; Nebraska Artist of the Year Governors award, 1992. Agent: Elisabeth Marton, 96 Fifth Avenue, New York, New York 10011. Address: 2309 Hanscom Boulevard, Omaha, Nebraska 61805; or, c/o Omaha Magic Theatre, 1417 Farnam Street, Omaha, Nebraska 68102, U.S.A.

PUBLICATIONS

Plays

Beach Grass (also director: produced Seattle, 1955).
Seascape (also director: produced Seattle, 1955).
Go Out and Move the Car (also director: produced Seattle, 1955).

New York Comedy: Two (produced Saratoga, New York, 1961).
Ex-Miss Copper Queen on a Set of Pills (produced New York, 1963; Edinburgh, 1987). With *The People vs. Ranchman*, New York, French, 1968.
When My Girlhood Was Still All Flowers (produced New York, 1963).
Eat at Joe's (produced New York, 1964).
Calm Down Mother (produced New York, 1965; London, 1969). Indianapolis, Bobbs Merrill, 1966.
Keep Tightly Closed in a Cool Dry Place (produced New York, 1965; London, 1968). Included in *Four Plays*, 1967.
The Magic Realists (produced New York, 1966). Included in *Three One-Act Plays*, 1972.
Comings and Goings (produced New York, 1966; Edinburgh, 1968). Included in *Four Plays*, 1967.
The Gloaming, Oh My Darling (produced Minneapolis, 1966). Included in *Four Plays*, 1967.
Viet Rock: A Folk War Movie (also director: produced New York, 1966; London, 1977). Included in *Four Plays*, 1967.
Four Plays. New York, Simon and Schuster, 1967.
The Key Is on the Bottom (produced Los Angeles, 1967).
The People vs. Ranchman (produced Minneapolis, 1967; New York, 1968). With *Ex-Miss Copper Queen on a Set of Pills*, New York, French, 1968.
Home; or, Future Soap (televised 1968; revised version, as *Future Soap*, produced Omaha, 1987). New York, French, 1972.
Jack-Jack (produced Minneapolis, 1968).
Massachusetts Trust (produced Waltham, Massachusetts, 1968). Published in *The Off-Off-Broadway Book*, edited by Albert Poland and Bruce Mailman, Indianapolis, Bobbs Merrill, 1972.
Changes, with Tom O'Horgan (produced New York, 1968).
Sanibel and Captiva (broadcast 1968). Included in *Three One-Act Plays*, 1972.
One More Little Drinkie (televised 1969). Included in *Three One-Act Plays*, 1972.
Approaching Simone (produced Boston and New York, 1970). Old Westbury, New York, Feminist Press, 1973.
The Tommy Allen Show (also director: produced Los Angeles and New York, 1970). Published in *Scripts 2* (New York), December 1971.
Grooving (produced New York, 1972).
Choose a Spot on the Floor, with Jo Ann Schmidman (produced Omaha, 1972).
Three One-Act Plays. New York, French, 1972.
Couplings and Groupings (monologues and sketches). New York, Pantheon, 1973.
Susan Peretz at the Manhattan Theatre Club (produced New York, 1973).
Thoughts (lyrics only), book by Lamar Alford (produced New York, 1973).
Nightwalk, with Sam Shepard and Jean-Claude van Itallie (produced New York and London, 1973). Published in *Open Theater*, New York, Drama Book Specialists, 1975.
St. Hydro Clemency; or, A Funhouse of the Lord: An Energizing Event (produced New York, 1973).
The Pioneer, and Pro-Game (produced Omaha, 1973; New York, 1974). Holly Springs, Mississippi, Ragnarok Press, 1975.
Hothouse (produced New York, 1974). New York, French, 1975.
Babes in the Bighouse (produced Omaha, 1974; New York, 1976). Omaha, Magic Theatre, 1979.

All Them Women, with others (produced New York, 1974).

We Can Feed Everybody Here (produced New York, 1974).

Hospital Play. Omaha, Magic Theatre, 1974.

Henna for Endurance. Omaha, Magic Theatre, 1974.

The Narco Linguini Bust (produced Omaha, 1974).

100,001 Horror Stories of the Plains, with others (produced Omaha, 1976). Omaha, Magic Theatre, 1979.

Sleazing Towards Athens. Omaha, Magic Theatre, 1977; revised version (produced Omaha, 1986), 1986.

Willie-Willa-Bill's Dope Garden. Birmingham, Alabama, Ragnarok Press, 1977.

Brazil Fado (produced Omaha, 1977). Omaha, Magic Theatre, 1977; revised version (produced Santa Fe, 1978), 1979.

Lady Rose's Brazil Hide Out (produced Omaha, 1977).

American King's English for Queens (produced Omaha, 1978). Omaha, Magic Theatre, 1978.

Goona Goona (produced Omaha, 1979). Omaha, Magic Theatre, 1985; New York, Broadway Play Publishing, 1992.

Attempted Rescue on Avenue B: A Beat Fifties Comic Opera (produced Chicago, 1979). Omaha, Magic Theatre, 1979.

Fireworks, in *Holidays* (produced Louisville, 1979). Colorado Springs, Meriwether Publishing, 1992.

Running Gag (lyrics only), book by Jo Ann Schmidman (produced Omaha, 1979). Omaha, Magic Theatre, 1981.

Objective Love I (produced Omaha, 1980). Omaha, Magic Theatre, 1985.

Scenes from Maps (produced Omaha, 1980). Omaha, University of Nebraska, 1980.

Advances (produced Omaha, 1980). Omaha, Magic Theatre, 1980.

Flat in Afghanistan (produced Omaha, 1981). Omaha, Magic Theatre, 1981.

Objective Love II (produced Omaha, 1981). Omaha, Magic Theatre, 1985.

The Trees Blew Down (produced Los Angeles, 1981). Omaha, Magic Theatre, 1981.

Winners (produced Santa Barbara, California, 1981).

Kegger (produced Omaha, 1982).

Fifteen Million Fifteen-Year-Olds (produced Omaha, 1983). Omaha, Magic Theatre, 1983.

Mollie Bailey's Traveling Family Circus, Featuring Scenes from the Life of Mother Jones, music by Jo Anne Metcalf. New York, Broadway Play Publishing, 1983.

X-rayed-iate (produced Omaha, 1984).

Katmandu, published in *Open Spaces* (Columbia, Missouri), 1985.

Family Talk (produced Omaha, 1986).

Sea of Forms (collaborative work), text and lyrics with Jo Ann Schmidman (produced Omaha, 1986). Omaha, Magic Theatrc, 1987.

Walking Through Walls (collaborative work), text and lyrics with Jo Ann Schmidman (produced Omaha, 1987). Omaha, Magic Theatre, 1987.

Dinner's in the Blender (produced Omaha, 1987). Omaha, Magic Theatre, 1987.

Retro (produced Omaha, 1988).

Amtrak (produced Omaha, 1988). Hattiesburg, University of Southern Mississippi Press, 1990.

Headlights (produced Little Rock, Arkansas, 1988).

Do You See What I'm Saying? (produced Chicago, 1990). New York, French, 1991.

Body Leaks, with Sora Kimberlain and Jo Ann Schmidman (produced Omaha, 1990).

Breakfast Serial (produced Omaha, 1991).

Sound Fields: Are We Hear (produced Omaha, 1992).

Radio Plays: *Sanibel and Captiva*, 1968; *American Wedding Ritual Monitored/Transmitted by the Planet Jupiter*, 1972.

Television Plays: *The Dirt Boat*, 1955; *Home; or, Future Soap*, 1968; *One More Little Drinkie*, 1969.

Other

Editor, with Jo Ann Schmidman and Sora Kimberlain, *Right Brain Vacation Photos: New Plays and Production Photographs 1972–1992*, Omaha, Magic Theatre, 1992.

*

Manuscript Collections: Kent State University, Kent, Ohio; Hope College, Holland, Michigan; Lincoln Center Library of the Performing Arts, New York; Omaha Public Library.

Critical Studies: "Who Says Only Words Make Great Drama?" by Terry, in *New York Times*, 10 November 1968; "Megan Terry: Mother of American Feminist Theatre," in *Feminist Theatre* by Helene Keyssar, London, Macmillan, 1984, New York, Grove Press, 1985; "(Theoretically) Approaching Megan Terry" by Elin Diamond, in *Art and Cinema 3* (New York), 1987; "Making Magic Public: Megan Terry's Traveling Family Circus" in *Making a Spectacle*, edited by Lynda Hart, Ann Arbor, University of Michigan Press, 1989.

Theatrical Activities:
Director: **Plays**—with the Cornish Players, Seattle: *Beach Grass*, *Seascape*, and *Go Out and Move the Car*, 1955; with the Open Theatre's Playwrights Workshop, New York, 1962–68; *Viet Rock*, New York, 1966; *The Tommy Allen Show*, Los Angeles, 1970; and other plays. **Television**—*The Dirt Book*, 1955.
Actor (as Maggie Duffy): **Plays**—Hermia in *A Midsummer's Night Dream*, title role in *Peter Pan* by J.M. Barrie, Kate in *Taming of the Shrew*, and other roles, Banff School of Fine Arts, Alberta, 1950–53; (as Megan Terry): roles in *Body Leaks*, 1991, and *Sound Fields*, 1992, both Omaha.

Megan Terry comments:
   I design my plays to provoke laughter—thought may follow.

*   *   *

"Roughly political, generally unintelligible, devoutly gymnastic." Walter Kerr's assessment seems strikingly at odds with the playwright who has more recently been acknowledged as the "Mother of American Feminist Drama." Yet the energy, vitality, and diversity of Megan Terry's work in the 1960's was often mistaken for lack of control or purpose, especially as many of those plays seemed to merge with the cultures of pop, protest, and the hippies. She became best known for *Viet Rock: A Folk War Movie*, a pivotal theatrical rallying-point against the Vietnam War, but one which could also too easily be dismissed as politically superficial, without acknowledging the dramaturgically innovative features it shared with most of her early work.

Calm Down Mother, Terry's first major contribution to a feminist theatre, is subtitled "A Transformation for Three Women," referring to an improvisatory technique developed by Terry and Joseph Chaikin in the early period of the Open Theatre. To the audience, a transformation simply appeared as a dissolving of character, location, or any other apparently concrete reality, so that the given circumstances that might be thought to define role would be constantly protean. Many different fragments of identity crystallize briefly in *Calm Down Mother* to provide a tapestry of female experience similar to Ntozake Shange's notion of the choreopoem. Though some found the play shocking for its up-front physicality, it was also generally received as celebratory of women reclaiming their bodies in the theatre.

The transformation was, more intellectually, conceptualized within psychoanalysis to reveal fragments of personality or role that are not easily integrated into one's preferred identity, so that the "tapestry" of *Calm Down Mother* is also a condensation. This becomes clearer in two plays dealing with male criminals, *The People vs. Ranchman* and *Keep Tightly Closed in a Cool Dry Place*. The latter has three actors in a prison cell working through a murder and a trial in which they were complicit; the clustering of responses to the event, the exposure of repressed self-images, and the merging of figures from history and the screen, constitute the central action, with the notion of transformation being facilitated by the actors occasionally connecting to form a machine.

Other plays of the 1960's experiment with other styles. *Ex-Miss Copper Queen on a Set of Pills* can be read as Gothic realism in its picturing of two female scavengers encountering the title character in a New York street at night, but it also has an hallucinatory fabric as the Queen "fights through drugs and drink" to make contact with them. *The Magic Realists* is transformational in its whimsical presentation of a businessman paranoiacally in retreat from his family and other responsibilities, but it also has elements of dream, jazz, male fantasy, and the consoling retreat into an ersatz pioneering ethos, derived from stage and screen more than from history books. *Home; or, Future Soap*, written for television and rescripted for stage, is a science-fiction vision of population explosion carried to an extreme in which its nine characters are born and die in the same room; yet it too has a social concern as it scrutinizes principles such as home, family, and children.

Terry's most lasting play, as a reading script, has been *Approaching Simone*, ostensibly a stage biography of Simone Weil. The play's seriousness and appeal to authenticity certainly acted as a corrective to those who had found her earlier work trite; it was widely praised for its audacity in presenting an affirmative portrait of a genius, and also for finding theatricality in an apparently untheatrical life. Yet Terry also saw the play as the culmination of 15 years of developing her dramatic technique. In its combination of stark statements to the world, couched in a context of sometimes severe or shocking stylization, there is a boldness of dramatic strategy that matches the choice of subject.

At the height of her New York success, and having won an extensive international reputation, Terry joined the Omaha Magic Theatre in the early 1970's; with that group, she has remained highly productive, but much of her work has been local or regional in its application. Her "social action theatre" or "community problem plays" are extensively researched and workshopped within the community that they in a sense document, and on tour their performance is accompanied by a "scholar" such as a psychiatrist or historian who will facilitate discussion with the audience after the show. Subjects like juvenile alcohol abuse (in *Kegger*), domestic violence (in *Goona Goona*), and incarceration of women (in *Babes in the Bighouse*) are of obvious community concern, but her plays also deal with issues such as illiteracy (in *Headlights*), how behaviour is shaped by language imbalance (in *American King's English for Queens*), and communication within families (in *Family Talk* and *Dinner's in the Blender*). But serious-

ness of social commitment could be found in Terry from the start: there is a case study in *Copper Queen* that might almost offer a gloss to *Kegger*. And neither has sheer playfulness deserted her in the face of earnestness: she is still writing plays such as *Amtrak*, about a pick-up on a train, which combines satire, iconoclasm, and a self-reflexive structure, with a hint of the artistic anarchy of the 1960's.

—Howard McNaughton

TERSON, Peter. Pseudonym for Peter Patterson. British. Born in Newcastle upon Tyne, Northumberland, 24 February 1932. Educated at Heaton Grammar School; Newcastle upon Tyne Technical College; Redland Training College, Bristol, 1952–54. Served in the Royal Air Force, 1950–52. Married Sheila Bailey in 1955; two sons and one daughter. Draughtsman, 1948–50; games teacher, 1953–65. Resident writer, Victoria Theatre, Stoke-on-Trent, Staffordshire, 1966–67; associated with the National Youth Theatre. Recipient: Arts Council bursary, 1966; John Whiting award, 1968; Writers Guild award, 1971. Agent: Lemon, Unna, and Durbridge, 24 Pottery Lane, Holland Park, London W11 4LZ, England.

PUBLICATIONS

Plays

A Night to Make the Angels Weep (produced Stoke-on-Trent, 1964; London, 1971). Published in *New English Dramatists 11*, London, Penguin, 1967.
The Mighty Reservoy (produced Stoke-on-Trent, 1964; London, 1967). Published in *New English Dramatists 14*, London, Penguin, 1970.
The Rat Run (produced Stoke-on-Trent, 1965).
All Honour Mr. Todd (produced Stoke-on-Trent, 1966).
I'm in Charge of These Ruins (produced Stoke-on-Trent, 1966).
Sing an Arful Story, with others (produced Stoke-on-Trent, 1966).
Jock-on-the-Go, adaptation of the story "Jock-at-a-Venture" by Arnold Bennett (produced Stoke-on-Trent, 1966).
Holder Dying (extracts produced Stoke-on-Trent, 1966).
Mooney and His Caravans (televised 1966; produced London, 1968). With *Zigger Zagger*, London, Penguin 1970.
Zigger Zagger (produced London, 1967). With *Mooney and His Caravans*, London, Penguin, 1970.
Clayhanger, with Joyce Cheeseman, adaptation of the novel by Arnold Bennett (produced Stoke-on-Trent, 1967).
The Ballad of the Artificial Mash (produced Stoke-on-Trent, 1967).
The Apprentices (produced London, 1968). London, Penguin, 1970.
The Adventures of Gervase Beckett; or, The Man Who Changed Places (produced Stoke-on-Trent, 1969). Edited by Peter Cheeseman, London, Eyre Methuen, 1973.
Fuzz (produced London, 1969).
Inside-Outside (produced Nottingham, 1970).
The Affair at Bennett's Hill, (Worcs.) (produced Stoke-on-Trent, 1970).

Spring-Heeled Jack (produced London, 1970).   Published in *Plays and Players* (London), November 1970.

The 1861 Whitby Lifeboat Disaster (produced Stoke-on-Trent, 1970; London, 1971). Todmorden, Yorkshire, Woodhouse, 1979.

The Samaritan, with Mike Butler (produced Stoke-on-Trent and London, 1971).   Published in *Plays and Players* (London), July 1971.

Cadium Firty (produced London, 1971).

Good Lads at Heart (produced London, 1971; New York, 1979).

Slip Road Wedding (produced Newcastle upon Tyne and London, 1971).

Prisoners of the War (produced Newcastle upon Tyne, 1971; London, 1983).

But Fred, Freud Is Dead (produced Stoke-on-Trent, 1972). Published in *Plays and Players* (London), March 1972.

Moby Dick, adaptation of the novel by Melville (produced Stoke-on-Trent, 1972).

The Most Cheerful Man (produced Stoke-on-Trent, 1973).

Geordie's March (produced London, 1973).

The Trip to Florence (produced London, 1974).

Lost Yer Tongue? (produced Newcastle upon Tyne, 1974).

Vince Lays the Carpet, and Fred Erects the Tent (produced Stoke-on-Trent, 1975).

The Ballad of Ben Bagot (televised 1977).   Published in *Prompt 2*, edited by Alan Durband, London, Hutchinson, 1976.

Love Us and Leave Us, with Paul Joyce (produced London, 1976).

The Bread and Butter Trade (produced London, 1976; revised version produced London, 1982).

Twilight Joker (produced Brighton, 1977; London, 1978).

Pinvin Careless and His Lines of Force (produced Stoke-on-Trent, 1977).

Family Ties: Wrong First Time; *Never Right, Yet Again* (produced London, 1977).   Published in *Act 2*, edited by David Self and Ray Speakman, London, Hutchinson, 1979.

Forest Lodge (produced Salisbury, 1977).

Tolly of the Black Boy (produced Edinburgh, 1977).

Rattling the Railings (produced London, 1978). London, French, 1979.

The Banger (produced Nottingham, 1978).

Cul de Sac (produced Chichester, 1978; London, 1979).

England, My Own (produced London, 1978).

Soldier Boy (produced London, 1978).

VE Night (produced Chichester, 1979).

The Limes, and I Kid You Not (produced London, 1979).

The Pied Piper, adaptation of the poem by Robert Browning, music by Jeff Parton (produced Stoke-on-Trent, 1980). London, French, 1982.

The Ticket (produced London, 1980).

The Night John (produced London, 1980).

We Were All Heroes (produced Andover, Hampshire, 1981).

Aesop's Fables, music by Jeff Parton (produced Stoke-on-Trent, 1983).   London, French, 1986.

Strippers (produced Newcastle upon Tyne, 1984; London, 1985).   Oxford, Amber Lane Press, 1985.

Hotel Dorado (produced Newcastle upon Tyne, 1985).

The Weeping Madonna. Published in *New Plays 1: Contemporary One-Act Plays*, edited by Terson, Oxford, Oxford University Press, 1988.

Radio Plays: *The Fishing Party*, 1971; *Play Soft, Then Attack*, 1978; *The First Flame*, 1980; *The Rundle Gibbet*, 1981; *The Overnight Man*, 1982; *The Romany Trip* (documentary), 1983; *The Top Sail at Imberley*, 1983; *Madam Main Course*, 1983; *Poole Harbour*, 1984; *Letters to the Otter*, 1985; *When Youth and Pleasure Meet*, 1986; *The Mumper*, 1988; *Blind Down the Thames*, 1988; *Stones, Tops, and Tarns*, 1989; *Tales My Father Taught Me*, 1990.

Television Plays: *Mooney and His Caravans*, 1966; *The Heroism of Thomas Chadwick*, 1967; *The Last Train Through the Harecastle Tunnel*, 1969; *The Gregorian Chant*, 1972; *The Dividing Fence*, 1972; *Shakespeare—or Bust*, 1973; *Three for the Fancy*, 1973; *Dancing in the Dark*, 1974; *The Rough and the Smooth*, 1975; *The Jolly Swagman*, with Paul Joyce (*Crown Court* series), 1976; *The Ballad of Ben Bagot*, 1977; *The Reluctant Chosen*, 1979; *Put Out to Grass*, 1979; *Atlantis*, 1983; *Salvation Army* series.

Other

The Offcuts Voyage. Oxford, Oxford University Press, 1988.

Editor, *New Plays 1: Contemporary One-Act Plays*. Oxford, Oxford University Press, 1988.

Editor, *New Plays 2: Contemporary One-Act Plays*. Oxford, Oxford University Press, 1988.

Editor, *New Plays 3: Contemporary One-Act Plays*. Oxford, Oxford University Press, 1989.

* * *

Peter Terson has been called a "primitive," a term which (in its complimentary sense) is intended to mean that his technique is artless, his observation fresh and original, and his naturally prolific talent untainted by too much sophistication. This somewhat backhanded tribute, however, belittles his ability. Few dramatists have the sheer skill to write success- fully for both the small "in the round" theatre company at the Victoria, Stoke-on-Trent, and the large casts of the British National Youth Theatre, whose London productions take place in conventional proscenium arch theatres. Nor is Terson unknowledgeable about recent trends in the theatre. He insisted, for example, that Harry Philton in *Zigger Zagger*, the boy who escapes from the mindless enthusiams of a football crowd to learn a trade, should not "mature or have a *Roots*-like vision of himself"—thus pushing aside one cliché of contemporary naturalistic drama. One under-rated aspect of Terson's style is the way in which he either avoids an idea which has become too fashionable or twists it to his own ends. In *The Mighty Reservoy* he plays with the Lawrentian theme of the dark, elemental forces of nature and makes it seem both credible as a psychological obsession and (through this haunting power over the mind) a force indeed to be feared. Terson is, however, ruthless with the pretentiousness of middle-class theatre: on receiving a Promising Playwright's award from Lord Goodman, he enquired whether Green Shield stamps went with it. This latent cheekiness is also part of his plays. Although he rarely ventures into the class pole- mic of some of Alan Plater's documentaries, he usually cari- catures people in authority: magistrates and social workers (in *Zigger Zagger*), scientists and business tycoons (in *The Ballad of the Artificial Mash*) and the paternalistic firm (in *The Apprentices*). He chooses working-class rather than middle-class themes and environments, and writes with par- ticular passion about his own childhood in Newcastle upon Tyne, the poverty and unemployment of the 1930's. This refusal to accept the normal attitudes of the West End coupled with his strong regional loyalties, may help to account for his reputation as a "primitive": but for this very reason the term is misleading. He doesn't write popular West

End comedies because he doesn't choose to do so; he doesn't write about middle-class families in the grip of emotional dilemmas because the problems which he tackles seem to him more important. He is a highly skilled writer with a particular insight into Northern working-class societies and whose plays have, at best, a richness of imagination and an infectious humour.

Terson's first plays were produced at the Victoria Theatre, Stoke-on-Trent, a pioneering Midlands company directed by Peter Cheeseman whose work concentrates on "in the round" productions, plays with local associations and documentary plays. Terson caught immediately the company style and became their resident playwright in 1966. His first plays, *A Night to Make the Angels Weep* and *The Mighty Reservoy*, were naturalistic comedies, but with strong underlying themes. *The Mighty Reservoy* is set in the Cotswolds, on a large reservoir built on a hill, which is guarded by Dron. The reservoir is presented as a passionate force of water, which might at any time swamp the surrounding villages. Dron has an affectionate pride towards it: and he introduces his friend Church to its mysteries, among them that the water demands one human sacrifice before it will be satisfied. Church eventually becomes this sacrifice. But the dialogue between the two men ranges from intimate, slightly drunken chat about their dissatisfactions about life to a passionate yearning for union with nature. *Mooney and His Caravans*, another two-person play written for the Victoria Theatre, represents a different type of "drowning": a couple on a caravan site are gradually driven away from their home by the aggressive commercialism of Mooney, whom they admire and who owns the site. With these small cast, tightly knit naturalistic plays, Terson also wrote several looser, more flexible and easy-going works, such as *Jock-on-the-Go*, a picaresque tale about a lad on the make in 19th-century Yorkshire, and *The Ballad of the Artificial Mash*, a horror story about the effect of hormone poultry foods on a salesman, one of the first and most effective plays about environmental pollution. Both these plays were in the style of the Stoke documentaries: short scenes, mainly satirical, brought together by songs and dances written and performed by the company. Although Terson left the Victoria Theatre in 1967, the influence of its informal atmosphere, the economy of means and the easiness of story-telling (using a narrator and props to indicate change of locale) remained with Terson as a formative inspiration. He has since written other plays for the company, including *But Fred, Freud Is Dead*, an amusing Northern comedy.

In 1966 Michael Croft, the director of the National Youth Theatre, invited Terson to write a play for his largely amateur group of schoolchildren and young adults. Terson's first play for the company, *Zigger Zagger*, was enormously successful, although its story seems flimsy and episodic. Harry Philton leaves school without distinction, and drifts from one job to another, from his unhappy home to his well-intentioned brother-in-law, sustained at first by his love of football. Eventually, however, this craze for football leaves him and he settles down to a proper trade apprenticeship. Terson sets this story against a background of a (pre-hooligan) football terrace, with fans whose songs and attitudes comment on the main events of the story. The exuberance of the production, the nostalgia and fervour of the football crowds provide an unforgettable image of surging humanity, charged with a youthful energy which only heightened the sad frustrations of Harry's career. *The Apprentices* tackled a somewhat similar theme, but more naturalistically. Bagley, a young tearaway, works reluctantly in a local factory—playing football whenever he has the opportunity. He deliberately scorns all opportunities for promotion, determined to leave the town and his

job as soon as he can: but he is trapped into an unwise marriage and at the end of the play he is resigned to a dull frustrating future. *Spring-Heeled Jack* and *Good Lads at Heart*, two other plays written for the National Youth Theatre, explore the frustrations of the misfits in an impoverished society.

Although Terson's plays have a much greater variety and range than is often supposed, he usually limits himself to social surroundings with which he is familiar: and perhaps the least satisfactory part of this limitation is that he shares some stock reactions, say, about the awfulness of progress and the craftsmanship of the past which are expressed rather too often in his plays. He also fails to pare down his documentary plays to the dramatic essentials. But his influence in British regional theatre has been considerable, and more than any other contemporary dramatist he carries forward the ideas of social drama pioneered by Joan Littlewood.

—John Elsom

TESICH, Steve. American. Born Stoyan Tesich in Titovo Uzice, Yugoslavia, 29 September 1943; emigrated to the United States, 1957; became citizen, 1961. Educated at Indiana University, Bloomington, B.A. 1965 (Phi Beta Kappa); Columbia University, New York, M.A. in Russian 1967, and further graduate study. Married Rebecca Fletcher in 1971. Caseworker, Brooklyn Department of Welfare, late 1960's. Recipient: Rockefeller grant, 1972; New York Film Critics award, Writers Guild award, and Oscar, all for screenplay, 1979. Agent: International Creative Management, 40 West 57th Street, New York, New York 10019, U.S.A.

PUBLICATIONS

Plays

The Carpenters (produced New York, 1970). New York, Dramatists Play Service, 1971; London, Davis Poynter, 1976.

Lake of the Woods (produced New York, 1971). Included in *Division Street and Other Plays*, 1981.

Baba Goya (produced New York, 1973). Included in *Division Street and Other Plays*, 1981; as *Nourish the Beast* (produced New York, 1973), New York, French, 1974.

Gorky, music by Mel Marvin (produced New York, 1975). New York, French, 1976.

Passing Game (produced New York, 1977). New York, French, 1978.

Touching Bottom (*The Road, A Life, Baptismal*) (produced New York, 1978; London, 1990). New York, French, 1980.

Breaking Away (screenplay). New York, Warner Books, 1979.

Division Street (produced Los Angeles and New York, 1980; revised version produced New York, 1987). Included in *Division Street and Other Plays*, 1981.

Division Street and Other Plays (includes *Baba Goya, Lake of the Woods, Passing Game*). New York, Performing Arts Journal Publications, 1981.

The Speed of Darkness (produced Chicago, 1989; New York, 1991).

Square One (produced New York, 1990). New York, Applause, 1990.
On the Open Road (produced Chicago, 1992). New York, Applause, 1992.

Screenplays: *Breaking Away*, 1979; *Eyewitness (The Janitor)*, 1981; *Four Friends (Georgia's Friends)*, 1981; *The World According to Garp*, 1982; *American Flyers*, 1985; *Eleni*, 1986.

Novel

Summer Crossing. New York, Random House, 1982; London, Chatto and Windus, 1983.

* * *

Though still best known as the Oscar-winning writer of the film *Breaking Away*, Yugoslavian-born Steve Tesich launched his writing career in the theatre and continues to work primarily in that medium. Like David Mamet, Tesich loves "the rhythm of alternating between the mediums, the fact that whatever is confining in one form isn't in the other." His plays are generally quirkier and more personal than his screenplays, and have received sympathetic but mixed critical comments.

The typical Tesich play centers around family relationships. His characters are often archetypal and eccentric, his themes moral and societal. He writes in a variety of genres, from comedy and tragicomedy to musicals, farces, and even Beckett-like absurdism.

Tesich's early plays, written in the 1970's for the American Place and other Off-Broadway theatres, were mostly upbeat paeans to the progressive, economically-secure America that had welcomed the young Tesich and his family. In his more recent plays, however, Tesich's outlook has grown decidedly darker.

His first produced play, *The Carpenters*, has been called *The Master Builder* in reverse. Whereas Ibsen's Solness builds a beautiful house for a family he has helped ruin, the inept father in *The Carpenters* struggles to keep his home from collapsing around his wife and children, all of whom search desperately for happier, purer, more natural lives. The play was well received by the critics: John Simon called it "a play of witty insight and fierce foresight," and Clive Barnes sensed "an air of Greek tragedy about it."

Nourish the Beast, originally entitled *Baba Goya*, garnered Tesich his best notices. In this serious comedy, a matriarch struggles to hold together a diverse extended family, which includes her dying fifth husband, an unhappy daughter, a son in the police force, and other engaging characters. To *Newsweek*'s Jack Kroll, this play proved Tesich "one of the most promising young American playwrights," whose work echoed Archie Bunker, Ionesco, and Sam Shepard, though it lacked "the shock that comes with the real moral force of [David Rabe's] *Sticks and Bones*." Richard Watts likened it to Saroyan's work in its "warm friendliness," and other critics compared it to George Kaufman and Moss Hart's Pulitzer prize-winning *You Can't Take It with You*. Despite these strong notices, the play has not aged well: after a 1989 revival, even Tesich acknowledged that it seemed dated.

Tesich wrote several more notable off-Broadway plays, including *Passing Game* and *Touching Bottom*, before *Division Street* opened on Broadway. In this knockabout farce, a 1960's student leader seeks obscurity in 1980 Chicago as an insurance adjuster, but is immediately surrounded by the same type of people he is trying to avoid, including some old comrades. Some critics praised its colorful cast of charac-

ters, but others considered it either an anachronistic radical call to arms, or (missing Tesich's purpose entirely) a piece of shallow American chauvinism. Even after a 1987 rewrite, which changed the original rousing ending to a more somber meditation, *Newsweek*'s Mark Chalon Smith still dismissed the play as "a flag-waver" with "a cloyingly goofy side." Though the critics were cool, audience enthusiasm has since made it Tesich's most-produced play.

Tesich wrote no new plays for almost a decade, devoting himself almost exclusively to film writing until *The Speed of Darkness*. In this stark drama, a pillar of society is visited by his now-homeless old Vietnam buddy, who forces him and his family to confront the moral and physical pollution of America. The play was compared by critics to Ibsen's *An Enemy of the People* and Miller's *All My Sons*, but as Edwin Wilson noted in the *Wall Street Journal*, it has "too many issues crammed into an obvious dramatic structure." Frank Rich wrote that although it is "at times its author's most pretentious play, it is also his most ambitious and, potentially, a major breakthrough." Unhappily, the play's Broadway production coincided exactly with the Gulf War, and it closed after only 36 performances.

Square One is a love story set in a tidy, structured brave new world where all art is purified for public consumption by a huge governmental bureaucracy. Reviewers responded warmly to the work's relevance to the controversy over government sponsorship of the arts. *Time* called it a "witty and touching work . . . likely to be topical again all too soon," and Liz Nicholls of the *Edmonton Journal* was impressed by "its radical argument that artists themselves are corrupt . . . in that their ends are always suspect."

In Tesich's latest play, *On the Open Road*, two tramps meet during an unspecified "time of civil war," decide to travel to "The Land of the Free," and are crucified alongside a mute Christ. Commenting on this work, Tesich has said that he has no doubt man will survive, "but I'm not so sure he'll survive as a human being." To *Time*'s Georgia Harbison, the play blends "metaphysical ambition and gothic excess," and is filled with "echoes of Kerouac, Beckett and Reaganomics interwoven with Tesich's moral fervor." The play's "philosophical and theological vaudeville" reminds Hedy Weiss of the *Chicago Sun-Times* of Beckett, Dostoevsky, Brecht, Hannah Arendt, and "doomsday landscapes of Mad Max"; its characters, though, "too often sound like mouthpieces rather than human beings."

A talented and committed writer, Tesich's work continues to evolve, and he continues to give much of his most personal and heartfelt work to the stage rather than to the screen. "Now the only thing I will write for the theater," he said recently, "is something that involves a moral issue. Nothing else interests me."

—Paul Nadler

———

THOMAS, Gwyn. British. 1913–1981.
See 2nd edition, 1977.

———

THOMPSON, Judith. Canadian. Born in Montreal, 20 September 1954. Educated at Queen's University, Kingston,

Ontario, 1973–76, B.A. in English drama 1976; National Theatre School, Montreal, 1976–79. Married Gregor Campbell in 1983; two daughters and one son. Nurse aide, Ongwanada Hospital, 1974, and social worker, Ministry of Social Services, 1977, both Kingston, Ontario; private tutor, Toronto, 1979. Recipient: Governor-General's award, 1984, 1990; Chalmers award, 1988, 1991; Nellie award, for radio, 1989; Toronto Arts award, 1990. Lives in Toronto. Agent: Great North Artists, 350 Dupont Street, Toronto, Ontario M5R 1V9, Canada.

PUBLICATIONS

Plays

The Crackwalker (produced Toronto, 1980; also director: New York, 1987; London, 1992). Toronto, Playwrights, 1988.
White Biting Dog (produced Toronto, 1984). Toronto, Play-wrights, 1984.
Pink (produced Toronto, 1986). Included in The Other Side of the Dark, 1989.
Tornado (broadcast 1987). Included in The Other Side of the Dark, 1989.
I Am Yours (produced Toronto, 1987). Included in The Other Side of the Dark, 1989.
The Other Side of the Dark. Toronto, Coach House, 1989.
Lion in the Streets (also director: produced Toronto, 1990). Toronto, Coach House, 1991.
Hedda Gabler, adaptation of the play by Ibsen (also director: produced Niagara-on-the-Lake, Ontario, 1991).

Radio Plays: Quickening, 1984; A Kissing Way, 1986; Tornado, 1987.

Television Plays: Turning to Stone, 1986; Don't Talk, 1992.

*

Critical Study: "'Cause You're the Only One I Want: The Anatomy of Love in the Plays of Judith Thompson" by George Totes in Canadian Literature (Vancouver), 118, 1988.

Theatrical Activities:
Director: **Plays**—The Crackwalker, New York, 1987; The Crucible by Arthur Miller, Fredericton, New Brunswick, 1989; Lion in the Streets, Toronto, 1990; Hedda Gabler, Niagara-on-the-Lake, Ontario, 1991.

Judith Thompson comments:
I believe that the voice is the door to not only the soul of an individual, but the soul of a nation, and within that, the soul of a culture, a class, a community, a gender. When I write a play it is as if I am walking into dark woods—do not know what I will find, but the most interesting stories happen when I stumble on raw mythology. I have worked in radio, television, and film, but I believe that the stage has by far the most power. There is a rock, an actor and words—when the technology all collapses—the play will survive.

* * *

Judith Thompson's haunting and challenging plays evaluate love relationships and betrayals, the destructive force of cities and contemporary lifestyles, and physical and spiritual pain. Dreams and the effects of dreams expressionistically shape the plays which have had a considerable impact in Canada

in the last decade. The evil beast that exists in every subconscious—sometimes resulting in murder—confronts good, though not in a didactic manner. Thompson's plays refer to worms, snakes, and lions, and are sometimes punctuated by screams of agony which are frequently difficult to decipher. The characters try to deal with their evil, peeling back the layers of the selves they have constructed to hide the nightmares. Because of the self protection that many characters engage in, they do not listen to the seers and psychics.

Class and generational tensions exist in every play, with birth being a recurrent image of the search for love, acceptance, and belonging in this world. The characters of Thompson's plays are people for whom life means psychic hardship and pain, but they are not extraordinary people: they are merely undisguised versions of Everyman, and thus deserving of empathy. Reflecting both this tension and the ordinariness of the characters, bodily functions and fluids, epilepsy, and cancer are not modestly overlooked.

The plays are not naturalistic in style. But much of the dialogue is naturalistic and the accents and pronunciations clearly indicate the ages, education, and frames of mind peculiar to each character. Thompson talks of standing in her characters' blood to really feel who they are.

The Crackwalker centres on two couples who are friends. Sandy and Joe are working-class, while Theresa and Alan are unable to hold jobs and to react independently. They unsuccessfully imitate Joe and Sandy: a desperate Alan helplessly kills his baby in fear and in an ironic gesture of protection. As Alan slips down between the cracks to the world "below" the sidewalk, he finds the company of the Crackwalker, a "drunken Indian" who symbolizes, among other things, social and economic failure. Joe and Sandy—sickened by Alan and by the naïve Theresa's acceptance of the horrifying world around her—escape to Alberta, but they will never escape from their fear of the Crackwalker.

Pink is a brief monologue about Lucy, a white South African girl, whose black nurse, Nellie, is killed in an uprising. It explores the insidiousness of apartheid through Lucy's insistence that the pink colour of her favourite cake is real, and through her demands that nothing, insidious or not, is her fault. Pink is not real: black is.

The radio drama Tornado pursues the struggle of having babies and stealing babies that is developed in I Am Yours. Dee in I Am Yours must accept her mother's death, represented by the evil blob she paints that lives behind the wall. Encephalitis is the metaphor Dee uses to describe the nightmarish control that her subconscious has over her, and Toilane also talks of his head filling with water. Dee's one-night stand with Toilane produces a baby that Toilane abducts, with the help of his mother, because he needs to care for someone. The title, from a locket Dee's father gave to her, refers to all the characters, each of whom seeks love, understanding, and belonging.

White Biting Dog is also about possession and fear of losing one's self and others. Pony, a psychic, arrives at the Race household, feeling that she is on a mission. Her dog, recently dead, appeared to Cape Race, who was about to jump to his death. The dog convinced him that if he saved his father from death, Cape too would experience a salvation. Dogs reappear throughout the play, and Pony especially misses her white biting dog. Desperately searching for his release, Cape tries to bring his estranged parents back together. The only two surviving characters are Cape and his mother, Lomia, who hope that the deaths (one metaphoric, two literal) will at least provide the hope that they need to keep living. Pony's suicide is the blood sacrifice that will, she hopes, effect the change in Cape. The play uses music, particularly drum beats and song, to provide a rhythm. Once again the nightmares terrorize many of the characters who frequently try to create other selves to survive, covering up the "bad" implicit in everyone.

Lion in the Streets presents another devilish creature who is haunting a murdered, intellectually disadvantaged Portuguese girl who must both warn others of the lion and decipher what happened to her, before she can be released from its clutches and the hold that life still has on her. She becomes a Cassandra figure to the many other characters who attempt to cope with cancer, poverty, childcare, and weight problems. The play ends with the girl's crucifixion-cum-wedding which expiates her lion only. The other characters must fight their own lions.

Thompson's plays are also visually exciting. Favouring a staging that allows for different levels, the plays graphically demonstrate the evils that everyday life uncovers in the world and in the characters considering ways to exorcize the beasts.

—Joanne Tompkins

THOMPSON, Mervyn (Garfield). New Zealander. 1936–1992.
See 4th edition, 1988.

TOWNSEND, Sue (Susan Lilian Townsend). British. Born in Leicester, 2 April 1946. Educated at South Wigston Girls High School, Leicestershire. Married 1) in 1964 (divorced 1971), two sons and one daughter; 2) Colin Broadway in 1985, one daughter. Member of the Writer's Group, Phoenix Arts Centre, Leicester, 1978. Recipient: Thames Television bursary, 1979. Lives in Leicester. Agent: Anthony Sheil Associates, 43 Doughty Street, London WC1N 2LF, England.

PUBLICATIONS

Plays

In the Club and Up the Spout (produced on tour, 1979).
Womberang (produced London, 1980; as *The Waiting Room*, produced Leicester, 1982). Included in *Bazaar and Rummage, Groping for Words, and Womberang*, 1984.
The Ghost of Daniel Lambert, music by Rick Lloyd (produced Leicester, 1981).
Dayroom (produced Croydon, Surrey, 1981).
Bazaar and Rummage (produced London, 1982). Included in *Bazaar and Rummage, Groping for Words, and Womberang*, 1984.
Captain Christmas and the Evil Adults (produced Leicester, 1982).
Groping for Words (produced Croydon, Surrey, 1983; revised version, as *Are You Sitting Comfortably?*, produced Watford, Hertfordshire, 1986; as *Groping for Words*, produced London, 1988). Included in *Bazaar and Rummage, Groping for Words, and Womberang*, 1984.

Clients (produced Croydon, Surrey, 1983).
Bazaar and Rummage, Groping for Words, and Womberang. London, Methuen, 1984.
The Great Celestial Cow (produced Leicester and London, 1984). London, Methuen, 1984.
The Secret Diary of Adrian Mole Aged 13³/₄, songs by Ken Howard and Alan Blaikley (produced Leicester and London, 1984). London, Methuen, 1985.
Ear, Nose and Throat (produced Chichester, West Sussex, 1988). London, Methuen, 1989.
Ten Tiny Fingers, Nine Tiny Toes (produced Manchester, 1989). London, Methuen, 1990.
Disneyland It Ain't (produced London, 1990).

Radio Plays: *The Diary of Nigel Mole Aged 13³/₄*, 1982; *The Growing Pains of Adrian Mole*, 1984; *The Great Celestial Cow*, 1985; *The Ashes*, 1991.

Television Plays: *Revolting Women* series, 1981; *Bazaar and Rummage*, 1984; *The Secret Diary of Adrian Mole* series, 1985; *The Growing Pains of Adrian Mole*, 1987; *The Refuge* series, with Carole Hayman, 1987; *Think of England* series, 1991.

Novels

The Adrian Mole Diaries. London, Methuen, 1985; New York, Grove Press, 1986.
  The Secret Diary of Adrian Mole Aged 13³/₄. London, Methuen, 1982; New York, Avon, 1984.
  The Growing Pains of Adrian Mole. London, Methuen, 1984.
Rebuilding Coventry: A Tale of Two Cities. London, Methuen, 1988; New York, Grove Weidenfeld, 1990.
Adrian Mole from Minor to Major. London, Methuen, 1991.

Other

The True Confessions of Adrian Albert Mole, Margaret Hilda Roberts, and Susan Lilian Townsend. London, Methuen, 1989.
Mr. Bevan's Dream. London, Chatto and Windus, 1989.

*

Sue Townsend comments:
I suppose I write about people who do not live in the mainstream of society. My characters are not educated; they do not earn high salaries (if they work at all). I look beneath the surface of their lives. My plays are about loneliness, struggle, survival, and the possibility of change.

Strangely, they are also comedies. Comedy is the most tragic form of drama.

* * *

Sue Townsend writes compassionate comedy whose power comes from its intermittently hard edge. A comedy with serious intentions is nothing new. But what is distinctive about the sometimes gentle, sometimes tough comedy Townsend writes is her ability to balance buoyant laughter with biting social commentary. In what she has called "problem plays," Townsend presents groups whose troubles are conventionally ignored: agoraphobics, adult illiterates, Asian women immigrants. In her most recent work, she has written increasingly on politically volatile issues like national health and institutional attitudes to childbearing and children. She is optimistic that by comically encouraging awareness of such groups and issues in a diverse audience (she hopes to attract working-class people back to the theatre) her theatre can contribute to social change.

In *Bazaar and Rummage* genial comedy cushions the revealing and disturbing study of three agoraphobics and their two social workers. Here Townsend refines the tendencies already apparent in her early theatre script *Womberang*, tendencies which characterize most of her plays: a group and not an individual is at the center of the action, the play refuses conventional descriptions of its plot, and the comedy is generated by community and concern. Townsend describes plays like *Bazaar*, which offer a "group against the world," as "closet plays," "enclosed plays," to emphasize her focus on neglected social problems. In *Bazaar* she engages her predilection for dealing with "the change in [such] a group" by presenting a trio of agoraphobics venturing from home for the first time in years, flanked by the two amateur social workers attempting to aid them. Instead of focusing on one of the characters and her progress toward health, Townsend balances the advances and setbacks in the lives of all five women; progress toward self-understanding is not a function of individual awareness but of group members supporting one another through crises. The plot which such communal character development creates is more circular than linear. There is a passing of awareness from one character to another until the group's collected courage allows for a collective exit onto an Acton street. Townsend's approach to comedy in this play occasioned a notable critical debate. The marriage of very funny lines to a feminist message moved some reviewers to dismiss the effort as "glib," "quirky," or "not too seriously meant," and motivated Michael Billington to warn the playwright that laughter "can't be used simply to decorate." But Townsend herself describes the combination of comedy and women as natural. Laughter, she explains, is "how women cope and have coped for centuries." She sees comedy as the most powerful tool available to her as an aid in reaching people; and in *Bazaar*, by allowing her audience to laugh with the agoraphobics, she encourages compassion and enables reflection. While theatre critics have found comedy variously revolutionary or reactionary, Townsend uses it to approach tough social issues and sees it—perhaps for that reason—as "a basic need of the human body."

Townsend's concern turns from women's special problems to the class issue of illiteracy in *Are You Sitting Comfortably?* (an earlier version was called *Groping for Words*). The play shares its class-conscious focus with *The Secret Diary of Adrian Mole Aged 13¾*, the play version of Townsend's successful novel. Both plays portray working-class characters seeking personal and social validation, but to the very light touch of *Adrian Mole* Townsend adds, in *Are You Sitting Comfortably?*, a pointed political message—a condemnation of the British class structure which seems to require illiterates. The play's class conflict is manifest in the encounter of the well-positioned, middle-class Joyce—the novice literacy instructor—and her three working-class students, George, Thelma, and Kevin. As in *Bazaar*, Townsend again keys the play's action to the symbiotic developments within this group. By the end of the play Joyce must acknowledge that her liberalism effects little social change, but Kevin vocalizes what all the others are scared to. In the play's chilling ending, he realizes that the world doesn't "want us to read! There ain't room for all of us is there?" This painful truth gels not just in Kevin, however, but also in the group. The audience, too, must join in this difficult collective realization, for as it laughs, it is being asked, 'are *you* sitting comfortably?" This play may be the clearest example of Townsend's comic gifts,

but also evidence of her commitment to using comedy to urge re-thinking and re-considering.

In two recent works, Townsend moves further in her engagement with political issues. *Ten Tiny Fingers, Nine Tiny Toes* is set in a future where two couples are curiously joined in their attempt to maintain some control over their offspring. In a right-wing society strictly compartmentalized by class, Lucinda and Ralph, the equivalent of an upper-working-class couple, conceive a baby in a government-sanctioned laboratory procedure. In distinct contrast, Dot and Pete, unskilled labourers relegated to perish on the fringes of organized society, conceive naturally—and illegally. When the two mothers meet, awaiting childbirth in a shared hospital room, they bond through recognition of how much the institutions around them devalue both women and the life they produce. Their connection empowers them to challenge the government hegemony. When Lucinda's daughter is destroyed by the authorities because of a deformity (a missing toe), the two conspire to share the breastfeeding and rearing of Dot's baby boy. With both husbands rejected (for their failure to behave admirably to the stress of births gone wrong), the two women face an uncertain future together; yet, as in previous plays, Townsend provides an upbeat ending in which these women brave the future on their own terms. In the one-act *Disneyland It Ain't*, children again provide the focus as Maureen pleads with "Mr. Mouse" to visit her dying 10-year-old daughter. As the British mother and the American carnival worker puzzle through his reluctance to help, her rage and his fear frame a discussion which ranges from national health insurance to consumerism to religious apostasy. All the while, the grim specter of the dying child shadows the caustic and clever dialogue. In theatrical shorthand, Townsend displays her ability to combine the trials of day-to-day survival with a hope she and her most burdened characters manage to eke out.

In fiction as well as in drama, Townsend continues to fuse comedy and serious matter. In her novel *Rebuilding Coventry*, Townsend creates a slightly bizarre, often comic, but deadly serious narrative centered on a woman who discovers she has options in her life only as a result of unintentionally murdering a man strangling his wife. Townsend's feminism and class consciousness—active in both genres—are leading her on a constant quest for new forms and formats. But it is in her plays especially where she has worked, through her comedy, to bring people together both inside and outside of the play's frame.

—Susan Carlson

TRAVERS, Ben. British. 1886–1980.
See 2nd edition, 1977.

TREVOR, William. Pseudonym for William Trevor Cox. Irish. Born in Mitchelstown, County Cork, 24 May 1928. Educated at St. Columba's College, Dublin, 1942–46; Trinity College, Dublin, B.A. 1950. Married Jane Ryan in 1952; two sons. History teacher, Armagh, Northern Ireland, 1951–53; art teacher, Rugby, England, 1953–55; sculptor in Somerset, 1955–60; advertising copywriter, Notley's, London, 1960–64. Recipient: *Transatlantic Review* prize, for fiction, 1964; Hawthornden prize, for fiction, 1965; Society of Authors travelling fellowship, 1972; Allied Irish Banks prize, for fiction, 1976; Heinemann award, for fiction, 1976; Whitbread award, 1976, 1983; Irish Community prize, 1979; BAFTA award, for television play, 1983. D. Litt.: University of Exeter, 1984; Trinity College, Dublin, 1986; D. Litt.: Queen's University, Belfast, 1989; National University, Cork, 1990. Member, Irish Academy of Letters. C.B.E. (Commander, Order of the British Empire), 1977. Lives in Devon, England. Agent: Peters, Fraser, and Dunlop Group, 503–504 The Chambers, Chelsea Harbour, Lots Road, London SW10 0FX, England; and Sterling Lord Literistic Inc., 1 Madison Avenue, New York, New York 10010, U.S.A.

PUBLICATIONS

Plays

The Elephant's Foot (produced Nottingham, 1965).
The Girl (televised 1967; produced London, 1968). London, French, 1968.
A Night with Mrs. da Tanka (televised 1968; produced London, 1972). London, French, 1972.
Going Home (broadcast 1970; produced London, 1972). London, French, 1972.
The Old Boys, adaptation of his own novel (produced London, 1971). London, Davis Poynter, 1971.
A Perfect Relationship (broadcast 1973; produced London, 1973). London, Burnham House, 1976.
The 57th Saturday (produced London, 1973).
Marriages (produced London, 1973). London, French, 1973.
Scenes from an Album (broadcast 1975; produced Dublin, 1981). Dublin, Co-op, 1981.
Beyond the Pale (broadcast 1980). Published in *Best Radio Plays of 1980*, London, Eyre Methuen, 1981.
Autumn Sunshine, adaptation of his own story (televised 1981; broadcast 1982). Published in *Best Radio Plays of 1982*, London, Methuen, 1983.

Radio Plays: *The Penthouse Apartment*, 1968; *Going Home*, 1970; *The Boarding House*, from his own novel, 1971; *A Perfect Relationship*, 1973; *Scenes from an Album*, 1975; *Attracta*, 1977; *Beyond the Pale*, 1980; *The Blue Dress*, 1981; *Travellers*, 1982; *Autumn Sunshine*, 1982; *The News from Ireland*, from his own story, 1986; *Events at Drimaghleen*, 1988; *Running Away*, 1988.

Television Plays: *The Baby-Sitter*, 1965; *Walk's End*, 1966; *The Girl*, 1967; *A Night with Mrs. da Tanka*, 1968; *The Mark-2 Wife*, 1969; *The Italian Table*, 1970; *The Grass Widows*, 1971; *O Fat White Woman*, 1972; *The Schoolroom*, 1972; *Access to the Children*, 1973; *The General's Day*, 1973; *Miss Fanshawe's Story*, 1973; *An Imaginative Woman*, from a story by Thomas Hardy, 1973; *Love Affair*, 1974; *Eleanor*, 1974; *Mrs. Acland's Ghosts*, 1975; *The Statue and the Rose*, 1975; *Two Gentle People*, from a story by Graham Greene, 1975; *The Nicest Man in the World*, 1976; *Afternoon Dancing*, 1976; *The Love of a Good Woman*, from his own story, 1976; *The Girl Who Saw a Tiger*, 1976; *Last Wishes*, 1978; *Another Weekend*, 1978; *Memories*, 1978; *Matilda's England*, 1979; *The Old Curiosity Shop*, from the novel by Dickens, 1979;

Secret Orchards, from works by J.R. Ackerley and Diana Petre, 1980; *The Happy Autumn Fields*, from a story by Elizabeth Bowen, 1980; *Elizabeth Alone*, from his own novel, 1981; *Autumn Sunshine*, from his own story, 1981; *The Ballroom of Romance*, from his own story, 1982; *Mrs. Silly (All for Love* series), 1983; *One of Ourselves*, 1983; *Broken Homes*, from his own story, 1985; *The Children of Dynmouth*, from his own novel, 1987; *August Saturday*, from his own novel, 1990.

Novels

A Standard of Behaviour. London, Hutchinson, 1958.
The Old Boys. London, Bodley Head, and New York, Viking Press, 1964.
The Boarding-House. London, Bodley Head, and New York, Viking Press, 1965.
The Love Department. London, Bodley Head, 1966; New York, Viking Press, 1967.
Mrs. Eckdorf in O'Neill's Hotel. London, Bodley Head, 1969; New York, Viking Press, 1970.
Miss Gomez and the Brethren. London, Bodley Head, 1971.
Elizabeth Alone. London, Bodley Head, 1973; New York, Viking Press, 1974.
The Children of Dynmouth. London, Bodley Head, 1976; New York, Viking Press, 1977.
Other People's Worlds. London, Bodley Head, 1980; New York, Viking Press, 1981.
Fools of Fortune. London, Bodley Head, and New York, Viking Press, 1983.
The Silence in the Garden. London, Bodley Head, and New York, Viking, 1988.
Two Lives (includes *Reading Turgenev* and *My House in Umbria*). London and New York, Viking, 1991.

Short Stories

The Day We Got Drunk on Cake and Other Stories. London, Bodley Head, 1967; New York, Viking Press, 1968.
Penguin Modern Stories 8, with others. London, Penguin, 1971.
The Ballroom of Romance and Other Stories. London, Bodley Head, and New York, Viking Press, 1972.
The Last Lunch of the Season. London, Covent Garden Press, 1973.
Angels at the Ritz and Other Stories. London, Bodley Head, 1975; New York, Viking Press, 1976.
Lovers of Their Time and Other Stories. London, Bodley Head, 1978; New York, Viking Press, 1979.
The Distant Past and Other Stories. Dublin, Poolbeg Press, 1979.
Beyond the Pale and Other Stories. London, Bodley Head, 1981; New York, Viking Press, 1982.
The Stories of William Trevor. London and New York, Penguin, 1983.
The News from Ireland and Other Stories. London, Bodley Head, and New York, Viking, 1986.
Nights at the Alexandra (novella). London, Century Hutchinson, and New York, Harper, 1987.
Family Sins and Other Stories. London, Bodley Head, and New York, Viking, 1990.

Other

Old School Ties (miscellany). London, Lemon Tree Press, 1976.

A Writer's Ireland: Landscape in Literature. London, Thames and Hudson, and New York, Viking, 1984.

Editor, *The Oxford Book of Irish Short Stories.* Oxford and New York, Oxford University Press, 1989.

*

Manuscript Collection: University of Tulsa, Oklahoma.

* * *

A successful novelist and prolific television and radio dramatist before turning in any real measure towards the theatre, William Trevor has been somewhat unlucky in his career as far as his full-length plays are concerned. *The Elephant's Foot* closed during its prior-to-London tour, and *The Old Boys* had a particularly unfortunate opening in London with its star's first-night nerves hindering the flow of a play whose full effect depended on the subtleties of its verbal nuances; and although the central performance improved immeasurably during its original limited Mermaid Theatre run and throughout a subsequent provincial tour, sadly the play did not find a West End theatre.

The Elephant's Foot (along with his early one-acter *The Girl*) represents something of a false start for Trevor. Both reveal his unusual gift for dialogue, particularly that of characters enmeshed in their own sense of failure and for those verging on the sinister or seedy, but both remain somewhat inert, heavily relying as they do on a central situation, of strange intruders entering domestic scenes, itself something of a cliché-situation in the theatre of the early 1960's. In *The Girl*, set in suburban London (one of Trevor's favourite locales, both in novels and plays), a mysterious teenage girl descends on the Green household, convincingly claiming to be Mr. Green's daughter, the result of a single drunken escapade with a prostitute. Her arrival, not surprisingly, divides the family, until it is revealed, with the near-curtain arrival of the girl's violent young friends, that Green is only the latest in a long list of prostitute mother's clients, to be descended on and terrorised in turn by the loutish teenage gang. It is adroit and suspenseful enough to sustain its length, although the ghost of Pinter looms heavily over the play, even to some extent over the dialogue, particularly in the opening sections between the Green family, laden with pauses and the reiteration of the clichés of suburban small-talk. *The Elephant's Foot* is similarly burdened with a top-heavy plot and reliance on a closing "surprise." An elderly couple, Colonel and Mrs. Pocock, who live apart except for their Christmas reunion with their twin children, in the midst of preparing their Christmas meal are invaded by the bizarre stranger Freer (first-cousin to the splendid con-man Swingler in *The Old Boys*) and his mute associate Tiger. Freer gradually unsettles the Pococks, frightening them by anticipating the non-arrival of their children, but he fails to insinuate Tiger into the household in the twins' place and the play closes with the Pococks again alone preparing to resume their old domestic battle. After a promising opening, with a very funny verbal tussle between the Pococks over the unfortunate selection of the Christmas brussels sprouts, the play collapses in the second act, only sustaining itself to the final curtain by resorting to coincidence and unconvincing metaphysical overtones. Nevertheless, *The Elephant's Foot* revealed that Trevor was capable of an individual dramatic verbal style (which his early novels, largely in dialogue, had pointed towards), a stylized counterpointing of the colloquial with the rhetorical which owes a little to Ivy Compton-Burnett but essentially remains very much his own.

This was further developed in *The Old Boys*, his own adaptation of his Hawthornden prize-winning novel of the same name, which revealed too Trevor's special understanding of elderly characters, particularly in those scenes set in a London residential hotel populated entirely by old boys of the same minor public school and tyrannised over by a dragoness of a Matron-surrogate. In its study of an old schoolboy rivalry extending from out of the past to influence a struggle over the presidency of the Old Boys' Association, the play is by turns hilarious and deeply touching, although the first act never satisfactorily solves some problems of construction in the adaptation process. But the climatic scene as old Mr. Jaraby at last realises the futility of his grudges and ambitions and, now a widower preparing to join the other old men at the Rimini Hotel, launches into a speech of life-affirming anarchy at the expense of the bullying proprietrix, stands as one of Trevor's finest achievements. Since *The Old Boys* Trevor has enjoyed considerable success with one-act plays often adapted from previous television and radio plays or from short stories. Most of these are acutely observed and tightly written duologues between different kinds of victims—the lonely, deserted, or repressed characters Trevor reveals so compassionately. Some of these, such as *A Night with Mrs. da Tanka*, a hotel encounter between a sad drunken divorcée and a shy bachelor, suffer in the transition to the stage and seem curiously artificial. But the best of them—especially *Going Home*, in which a precocious schoolboy and a spinster Assistant Matron, travelling in a train compartment together for the holidays, painfully realise their mutual loneliness—capture moments of crisis in their characters' lives and give them a genuine life on stage beyond the confines of the original medium from which they were adapted. Likewise, some of the best scenes in *The Old Boys* are those not in or most freely adapted from the original novel; hopefully before long Trevor may emerge with a new full-length play original in all senses of the word.

—Alan Strachan

———

TSEGAYE GABRE-MEDHIN. Ethiopian. Born in Ambo, Shewa, 17 August 1936. Educated at Zema and Kine Ethiopian Orthodox Church Schools, 1945–48; Ambo Elementary School, 1948–52; General Wingate and Commercial Secondary schools, 1952–56; Blackstone School of Law, Chicago, LL.B. 1959. Married Laketch Bitew in 1961; three daughters. Studied British theatre at the Royal Court Theatre, London, and French theatre at the Comédie Française, Paris, 1959–60; director, 1961–71, and general manager, 1967–74, Haile Selassie I Theatre (now Ethiopian National Theatre), Addis Ababa; editor, Oxford University Press, Addis Ababa, 1971; research fellow, University of Dakar, Senegal, from 1971; permanent secretary, Ministry of Culture and Sports, Addis Ababa, 1975–76; assistant professor of theatre arts, Addis Ababa University, 1977; secretary general, Ethiopian Peace, Solidarity and Friendship House, 1979. Currently adviser, Ministry of Culture, Addis Ababa. Recipient: Unesco fellowship, 1959; International Theatre Institute fellowship, 1965; Haile Selassie I prize, 1966; Fulbright fellowship, 1966, 1971, 1975, 1985; Gold Mercury award, 1982. Commander, Senegal National Order,

1971. Address: Ministry of Culture, P.O. Box 1907, Addis Ababa, Ethiopia.

PUBLICATIONS

Plays

Belg (Autumn) (produced Addis Ababa, 1957). Addis Ababa, Berhanena Selam, 1962.

Yeshoh Aklil (Crown of Thorns) (produced Addis Ababa, 1958). Addis Ababa, Berhanena Selam, 1959.

Askeyami Lijagered (The Ugly Girl) (produced Addis Ababa, 1959).

Jorodegif (Mumps) (produced Addis Ababa, 1959).

Listro (Shoe Shine Boy) (produced Addis Ababa, 1960).

Igni Biye Metahu (Back with a Grin) (produced Addis Ababa, 1960).

Chulo (Errand Boy) (produced Addis Ababa, 1961).

Kosho Cigara (Cheap Cigarettes) (produced Addis Ababa, 1961).

Yemama Zetegn Melk (Mother's Nine Faces) (produced Addis Ababa, 1961).

Tewodros (in English; produced Addis Ababa, 1962; revised version produced Addis Ababa, 1983; London, 1987). Published in *Ethiopian Observer* (Addis Ababa), vol. 10, no. 3, 1966.

Othello, adaptation of the play by Shakespeare. Addis Ababa, Oxford University Press, 1963.

Tartuffe, adaptation of the play by Molière (produced Addis Ababa, 1963).

The Doctor in Spite of Himself, adaptation of a play by Molière (produced Addis Ababa, 1963).

Oda Oak Oracle: A Legend of Black Peoples, Told of Gods and God, Of Hope and Love, Of Fears and Sacrifices (produced Addis Ababa, 1964). London and New York, Oxford University Press, 1965.

Azmari (in English; produced Addis Ababa, 1964). Published in *Ethiopian Observer* (Addis Ababa), vol. 10, no. 10, 1966.

Yekermo Sew (The Seasoned) (produced Addis Ababa, 1966). Addis Ababa, Berhanena Selam, 1967.

Petros (produced Addis Ababa, 1968).

King Lear, adaptation of the play by Shakespeare (produced in part, Addis Ababa, 1968).

Macbeth, adaptation of the play by Shakespeare (produced in part, Addis Ababa, 1968). Addis Ababa, Oxford University Press, 1972.

Hamlet, adaptation of the play by Shakespeare (produced in part, Addis Ababa, 1968). Addis Ababa, Oxford University Press, 1972.

Kirar Siker (Kirar Tight-Tuned) (produced Addis Ababa, 1969).

Ha Hu Besidist Wer (A-B-C in Six Months) (produced Addis Ababa, 1974). Addis Ababa, Berhanena Selam, 1975.

Enat Alem Tenu (Mother Courage), adaptation of the play by Brecht (produced Addis Ababa, 1975). Addis Ababa, Berhanena Selam, 1975.

Atsim Beyegetsu (Skeleton in Pages) (produced Addis Ababa, 1975).

Abugida Transform (produced Addis Ababa, 1976).

Collision of Altars. London, Collings, 1977.

Melikte Proletarian (produced Addis Ababa, 1979).

Mekdem (Preface) (produced Addis Ababa, 1980).

Gamo (produced Addis Ababa, 1981).

Zeray (produced Asmara, Eritrea, 1981).

Zikegna Abera (produced Addis Ababa, 1986).

Verse

Issat Woy Ababa (Fire of Flower). Addis Ababa, Berhanena Selam, 1973.

Other

Ethiopia: Footprint of Time (travel), photographs by Alberto Tessore. Udine, Italy, Magnus, 1984.

*

Tsegaye Gabre-Medhin comments:

I do not think in English or French but in Ethiopian first. My cultural personality is formed out of a background which consciously resists being re-created in the image of any and all supremacist alien values. I write for a people who for many thousands of years have developed a conscious taste for their own poetic heritage, in one of their own scripts, and in one of their own indigenous languages. In the literature of one of the children of Kam: of Meroe, of Nubia, of Egypt, of Ethiopia— of the cradles of the world's earliest civilization. The people are still the judges of my plays which mirror them. They are still the critics of the poetry and culture that make them, and which in turn they themselves make.

If for instance a British poet *naturally* felt hard put to think or dream his verse in Chinese it is because (a) Chinese is not the natural expression of British culture, (b) Chinese literature forms the Chinese personality, makes and develops first a Chinese universal man and not first a Briton or a British personality, and (c) the said British poet is not yet re-created in the image of the Chinese. Can any African artist-poet or playwright (unless of course his culture is already killed in him and replaced by something else) afford to think or dream his verse in anything less than what is his indigenous African expression FIRST? Just like *no* Chinese literature can make a truly British culture, so there is *no* English, French, Dutch, or Portuguese, etc., literature which can make a truly African culture.

*   *   *

Tsegaye Gabre-Medhin has written and directed plays in Amharic, including Amharic versions of Shakespeare and Molière. In his English plays both the phrasing and the poetic conception suggest that he is experimenting with the transferral of devices alien to modern English. In *Oda Oak Oracle*, for instance:

Loneliness is
When the ripe fruit fails,
To make the bird
Aware of its existence.
Loneliness is
When the avoided heart,
Growing stale every night,
Wears a mask of bitterness,
While the tense veins
Growing frantic and mad
Scratch at the mask
Of a stricken heart.
Loneliness is
When the aged mule
Rubs its flank
Against the deserted trunk
Of a dead bush.
Loneliness is
When the moon is left cold

Among a glowing
Jungle of stars.

The rich elaboration contributes to the florid, torrid melodrama.

In *Oda Oak Oracle* the oracle has decreed marriage between Shanka and Ukutee, and the sacrifice of their first-born to the ancestors. To avoid this, Shanka refuses to consummate the marriage. In humiliation and frustration Ukutee offers herself to Shanka's friend, Goaa. He brings to the play the perspective of another society, for he had once been taken away by strangers and instructed by them in the Gospel. His criticism of the oracle and traditional beliefs feeds Shanka's doubts. By the last act Ukutee is in labour. Cloud darkens the valley and there is perturbation among the elders at the lack of sun. The oracle commands a combat between Goaa and Shanka, the victor to be flogged from the valley by Ukutee. Goaa is killed and Ukutee consents to whip out Shanka because the oracle has promised that she will then bear a fine son. In fact, she dies giving birth to a daughter and the play ends with Shanka holding the child as a mob approaches to stone both of them to death.

This doom-laden play Albert Gerard, in his *Four African Literatures* (1971), finds to be "one of the finest plays to have been written in Africa." Personally, I find the extremely short lines awkward and their divisions of little help to the speaker; moreover the climax of the play seems to pile up punishments over-ingeniously.

The resignation of a 6th-century emperor after he has lost his army to disease, the political impotence of his sons, and the disintegration of the empire from religious sectarianism is the subject of *Collision of Altars*. Gabre-Medhin's theatrical experience is evident in the ingeniously complex setting and epic scale, but character development seems precluded by the number of representatives of different religions and political interests, and by the public nature of most of the scenes. Gabre-Medhin, in any case, is interested in presenting the conflicts on a symbolic dimension. The ultimate effect is of a vast threnody.

More interesting, I believe, are two short plays which appeared in the *Ethiopia Observer*. *Tewodros* is an account of a mid-19th-century commoner who rose to be Emperor. He had a vision of uniting Ethiopia, but his rule was troubled by various revolts and ended by British invasion. Showing both concern for the welfare of the common people and bloody ruthlessness, Tewodros is an ambiguous figure, and the interest of Gabre-Medhin's play lies not in his Tamburlaine-like career, but in the doubts expressed by his first and second wives and by others around him:

Washing my hands in other's blood and watching mine flow out has occupied the best years of my life. The one exciting activity I can remember of my only son is the lashing of his paper sword and his shouting of the war-cry "zeraf" . . . until finally I heard him repeat the same thing on the battlefield once and for all . . . then he bled to death in my arms. What has the poor peasant to live for, Princess, if he can't afford to question why his children should sing war songs and not read the Book of Life?

The same note is struck in *Collison of Altars*.

The most successful of his plays is *Azmari*. *Azmaris* are professional singers, and female *azmaris* are considered little better than courtesans. Gabre-Medhin's play portrays the tensions in a family, in each generation of which a member is called to be "the expressive medium for Nature's passions"—and so Lulu considers herself. The centre of the play is her clash with her mother, who resents her being "out with that moaning harp of hers day and night, and never lifting a finger to help the family," and maintains that a minstrel's is "no decent folk's way of life." Who is betraying whom, the member of the family who rejects the call of music, or the artist who does not help support it?

Unlike Gabre-Medhin's other plays, *Azmari* has only one violent action, the smashing of Lulu's harp. As in Chekhov, the significant action takes place offstage—Lulu has played at the marriage of the man she loved, who has jilted her for a socially acceptable bride—and no resolution is offered. The use of music as an emotional punctuation of the scenes is dramatically relevant. Grandiloquence, too, is used dramatically, for it is set off against the everyday speech of those in the family who refuse music's call.

—Anthony Graham-White

TURNER, David. British. 1927–1990.
See 4th edition, 1988.

U

UHRY, Alfred. American. Born in Atlanta, Georgia, 3 December 1936. Educated at Brown University, Providence, Rhode Island, 1958. Married Joanna Kellogg in 1959; four daughters. Member, 1987, and since 1990 president, Young Playwrights Foundation, New York; since 1988 council member, Dramatists Guild, New York; since 1991 member of the faculty, New York University School of the Arts. Recipient: Pulitzer prize, 1988; Marton award, 1988; Outer Critics Circle award, 1988; Los Angeles Drama Critics Circle award, 1989; Oscar, 1990. Lives in New York. Agent: Flora Roberts, 157 West 57th Street, New York, New York 10019, U.S.A.

PUBLICATIONS

Plays

Here's Where I Belong, adaptation of *East of Eden* by John Steinbeck, book by Alex Gordon, music by Robert Waldman (produced New York, 1968).
The Robber Bridegroom, adaptation of the novella by Eudora Welty, music by Robert Waldman (produced New York, 1974). New York, Drama Book Specialists, 1978.
Swing, book by Conn Fleming, music by Robert Waldman (produced Washington, D.C., 1980).
Little Johnny Jones, adaptation of a musical by George M. Cohan (produced New York, 1982).
America's Sweetheart, adaptation of a novel by John Kobler, with John Weidman, music by Robert Waldman (produced Hartford, Connecticut, 1985).
Driving Miss Daisy (produced New York, 1987; Ipswich, Suffolk, 1990). New York, Dramatists Play Service, 1987.

Screenplays: *Mystic Pizza*, 1988; *Driving Miss Daisy*, 1989; *Rich in Love*, 1992.

* * *

Alfred Uhry was awarded the Pulitzer prize in 1988 for his first and only full-length play, *Driving Miss Daisy*, and an Oscar for the best screenplay adaptation of the play. Uhry's earlier work was primarily as a lyricist and librettist. His long-time collaboration with composer Robert Waldman resulted in Tony and Drama Desk award nominations in 1976 as lyricist and librettist for *The Robber Bridegroom*. Waldman composed the incidental music for the Playwrights Horizons première of *Driving Miss Daisy*. Uhry's work prior to the success of *Driving Miss Daisy* was primarily on lesser-known musicals including, *Here's Where I Belong*, based on Steinbeck's *East of Eden*; *Swing*; *Little Johnny Jones*, which starred Donny Osmond; and *America's Sweetheart*, about Al Capone. None of these musicals received critical acclaim. Even *The Robber Bridegroom*, a musical based on the novella by Eudora Welty, met with mixed reviews, with one reviewer noting that the score was "self-consciously rural" with "few bright moments." However, Uhry's work on such musicals

along with his long stint as a teacher of play- and lyric-writing proved to be beneficial once the playwright decided to write about his childhood in Atlanta and of his grandmother, an elderly Southern woman who had a black chauffeur who drove her for nearly 25 years.

Driving Miss Daisy is really a long one-act, that takes place in various locations in Atlanta from 1948 to 1973. There are 24 "shifts" in scene, though the play is not formally divided into scenes. The action centers around Daisy Werthan, a widow who progresses in age from 72 to 97 during the course of the play. Her son Boolie Werthan, who ages from 40 to 65, hires a black chauffeur, Hoke Coleburn. Hoke is 60 when the play begins.

The play is deceptively simple in presentation. There is no traditional plot or conflict. The structure is episodic, moving chronologically forward, but the large span of time does not resonate with meaning; nor does it punctuate any vast issues or polemics. The dramatic action is sustained through the growing relationship between Daisy and Hoke. Boolie serves more as a transitional device than as a pivotal character, though the playwright does use Boolie to demonstrate the up-and-coming Southern Jewish businessman.

What distinguishes *Driving Miss Daisy* from other plays written during the 1980's is the subtlety with which the playwright empowers his dramaturgy, enabling him to address issues of race and ethnicity and to explore conflicts of old versus young, rich versus poor, Jew versus gentile, while maintaining the emphasis on the very human relationship that develops between Daisy and Hoke. Uhry's dramaturgy is economical in every way. Exposition is provided via dialogue concerning cars and insurance and the church that people attend, so that necessary information regarding geography, economy, and time is provided by scant verbal signposts.

When the subject of hiring a driver for the ageing Miss Daisy is broached by Boolie, Daisy responds innocently with "I still have rights. And one of my rights is the right to invite who I want—not who you want—into my house. . . . What I do not want—and absolutely will not have is some—some chauffeur sitting in my kitchen. . . ." This technique of introducing ideas and issues—in this case, that of human rights—is a technique that Uhry employs subtly, but also deftly. The notion of prejudice is handled in the same way—both issues are strong undercurrents in the play; and issues that Daisy comes to understand better through her friendship with Hoke, though she never articulates anything beyond saying to Hoke "You're my best friend."

Uhry is a master of understatement. What is not said in *Driving Miss Daisy* is significant. Equally compelling is Uhry's use of metaphor which serves both to punctuate the humor and to reveal the differences in characters' lifestyles and points of view. Hoke's response to Boolie's inquiry regarding Hoke's ability to handle Miss Daisy is a good example. Hoke replies with "I use to wrastle hogs to the ground at killin' time, and ain' no hog get away from me yet."

Driving Miss Daisy is a play about dignity in which all the characters strive to hold onto their personal integrity against

an environment of prejudice, change, and economic instability. The Southern dialect in counterpoint with the colloquial expressions create a lyrical rhythm that greatly
contributes to the overall effect of the play. The simple
images called for by Uhry throughout the play are meant to
capture glimpses of these characters' lives, so that in effect
these people become representative of types as well as individuals. The play, then, becomes representative of a time in
history and tells about that time via this one story.

Perhaps the only drawback of Uhry's play is that with the
simplicity of the dramaturgy the play requires a strong cast to
sustain the subtextual notions of the play as well as to sustain
the constant leaps in time and place. In addition the juxtaposition of one "scene" to the next has no symbolic meaning so
that the shifts become predictable and tension is difficult to
sustain. Still, *Driving Miss Daisy* reflects Uhry's expertise in
cinematic dramaturgy, and it is a play that continues to be
produced successfully in regional theatres.

—Judy Lee Oliva

USTINOV, Peter (Alexander). British. Born in London, 16
April 1921. Educated at Gibbs Preparatory School, London;
Westminster School, London, 1934–37; London Theatre
Studio, 1937–39. Served in the Royal Sussex Regiment,
Royal Army Ordnance Corps, 1942–46; with Army
Kinetograph Service, 1943, and Directorate of Army
Psychiatry. Married 1) Isolde Denham in 1940 (divorced
1950), one daughter; 2) Suzanne Cloutier in 1954 (divorced
1971), two daughters and one son; 3) Hélène du Lau d'Alle-
mans in 1972. Actor, writer, and director. Co-director,
Nottingham Playhouse, 1963. Rector, University of Dundee,
1968–73. Since 1969 Goodwill Ambassador, Unicef.
Recipient: Golden Globe award, 1952; New York Drama
Critics Circle award, 1953; Donaldson award, 1953; *Evening
Standard* award, 1956; Royal Society of Arts, Benjamin
Franklin medal, 1957; Emmy award, for acting, 1957, 1966,
1970; Oscar, for acting, 1961, 1965; Peabody award, for
acting, 1972; Unicef award, 1978; Jordanian Independence
medal, 1978; Prix de la Butte, 1978; Variety Club award, for
acting, 1979; City of Athens gold medal, 1990; Greek Red
Cross medal, 1990; medal of honour, Charles University,
Prague, 1991. D.M.: Cleveland Institute of Music, 1967;
D.L.: University of Dundee, 1969, University of Ottawa,
1991; D.F.A.: La Salle University, Philadelphia, 1971; D.
Litt.: University of Lancaster, 1972; University of Toronto,
1984; D.H.L.: Georgetown University, Washington, D.C.,
1988. Fellow, Royal Society of Arts; Fellow, Royal Society of
Literature, 1978. C.B.E. (Commander, Order of the British
Empire), 1975; Commander, Order of Arts and Letters
(France), 1985; Order of Istiglal, Hashemite Kingdom of
Jordan; Order of the Yugoslav Flag; elected to the Académie
des Beaux-Arts, Paris, 1988; knighted, 1990; Chancellor,
University of Durham, 1992. Agent: William Morris Agency,
31–32 Soho Square, London W1V 5DG, England. Address:
11 rue de Silly, 92110 Boulogne, France.

PUBLICATIONS

Plays

The Bishop of Limpopoland (sketch: produced London,
1939).
Sketches in *Swinging the Gate* (produced London, 1940).

Sketches in *Diversion* and *Diversion 2* (produced London,
1940, 1941).
Fishing for Shadows, adaptation of a play by Jean Sarment
(also director: produced London, 1940).
House of Regrets (produced London, 1942). London, Cape,
1943.
Beyond (produced London, 1943). London, English
Theatre Guild, 1944; in *Five Plays*, 1965.
Blow Your Own Trumpet (produced Liverpool and London,
1943). Included in *Plays about People*, 1950.
The Banbury Nose (produced London, 1944). London,
Cape, 1945.
The Tragedy of Good Intentions (produced Liverpool, 1945).
Included in *Plays about People*, 1950.
The Indifferent Shepherd (produced London, 1948).
Included in *Plays about People*, 1950.
Frenzy, adaptation of a play by Ingmar Bergman (produced
London, 1948).
The Man in the Raincoat (also director: produced Edinburgh,
1949).
Plays about People. London, Cape, 1950.
The Love of Four Colonels (also director: produced
Birmingham and London, 1951; New York, 1953).
London, English Theatre Guild, 1951; New York,
Dramatists Play Service, 1953.
The Moment of Truth (produced Nottingham and London,
1951). London, English Theatre Guild, 1953; in *Five
Plays*, 1965.
High Balcony (produced London, 1952).
No Sign of the Dove (also director: produced Leeds and
London, 1953). Included in *Five Plays*, 1965.
Romanoff and Juliet (produced Manchester and London,
1956; New York, 1957). London, English Theatre Guild,
1957; New York, Random House, 1958; revised version, as
R Loves J, music by Alexander Faris, lyrics by Julian More
(produced Chichester, 1973).
The Empty Chair (produced Bristol, 1956).
Paris Not So Gay (produced Oxford, 1958).
Photo Finish: An Adventure in Biography (also director:
produced Dublin and London, 1962; New York. 1963).
London, Heinemann, 1962; Boston, Little Brown, 1963.
The Life in My Hands (produced Nottingham, 1964).
*Five Plays: Romanoff and Juliet, The Moment of Truth, The
Love of Four Colonels, Beyond, No Sign of the Dove*.
London, Heinemann, and Boston, Little Brown, 1965.
Halfway Up the Tree (produced on tour, Germany, 1967; also
director: produced New York and London, 1967). New
York, Random House, 1968; London, English Theatre
Guild, 1970.
*The Unknown Soldier and His Wife: Two Acts of War
Separated by a Truce for Refreshment* (produced New
York, 1967; also director: produced Chichester, 1968;
London, 1973). New York, Random House, 1967;
London, Heinemann, 1968.
Who's Who in Hell (produced New York, 1974).
Overheard (produced Billingham, County Durham, and
London, 1981).
The Marriage, adaptation of an opera libretto by Gogol,
music by Mussorgsky (also director: produced Milan, 1981;
Edinburgh, 1982).
Beethoven's Tenth (produced Paris, 1982; Birmingham,
London, and Los Angeles, 1983; New York, 1984).
An Evening with Peter Ustinov (produced London, 1990; San
Francisco, 1991).

Screenplays: *The New Lot* (documentary), 1943; *The Way
Ahead*, with Eric Ambler, 1944; *The True Glory* (documen-

tary), with others, 1944; *Carnival*, with others, 1946; *School for Secrets* (*The Secret Flight*), 1946; *Vice Versa*, 1948; *Private Angelo*, with Michael Anderson, 1949; *School for Scoundrels*, with others, 1960; *Romanoff and Juliet*, 1961; *Billy Budd*, with Robert Rossen and De Win Bodeen, 1962; *Lady L.*, 1965; *Hot Millions*, with Ira Wallach, 1968; *Memed, My Hawk*, 1984.

Television Plays: *Ustinov ad lib*, 1969; *Imaginary Friends*, 1982.

Novels

The Loser. London, Heinemann, and Boston, Little Brown, 1961.
Krumnagel. London, Heinemann, and Boston, Little Brown, 1971.
The Old Man and Mr. Smith. London, O'Mara, 1990; New York, Arcade, 1991.

Short Stories

Add a Dash of Pity. London, Heinemann, and Boston, Little Brown, 1959.
The Frontiers of the Sea. London, Heinemann, and Boston, Little Brown, 1966.
The Disinformer. London, O'Mara, and New York, Arcade, 1989.

Other

Ustinov's Diplomats: A Book of Photographs. New York, Geis, 1961.
We Were Only Human (caricatures). London, Heinemann, and Boston, Little Brown, 1961.
The Wit of Peter Ustinov, edited by Dick Richards. London, Frewin, 1969.
Rectorial Address Delivered in the University, 3rd November 1972. Dundee, University of Dundee Press, 1972.
Dear Me (autobiography). London, Heinemann, and Boston, Little Brown, 1977.
Happiness (lecture). Birmingham, University of Birmingham, 1980.
My Russia. London, Macmillan, and Boston, Little Brown, 1983.
Ustinov in Russia. London, O'Mara, 1987; New York, Summit, 1988.
Ustinov at Large (articles). London, O'Mara, 1991.

Recordings: Writer and performer—*Mock Mozart, and Phoney Folk Lore*, Parlophone; *The Grand Prix of Gibraltar*, Orpheum; narrator—*Peter and the Wolf*; *The Nutcracker Suite*; *The Soldier's Tale*; *Háry János*; *The Little Prince*; *The Old Man of Lochnagar*; *Grandpa*; *Babar and Father Christmas*.

*

Critical Studies (includes filmographies and bibliographies): *Peter Ustinov* by Geoffrey Willans, London, Owen, 1957; *Ustinov in Focus* by Tony Thomas, London, Zwemmer, and Cranbury, New Jersey, A.S. Barnes, 1971.

Theatrical Activities:
Director: **Plays**—*Fishing for Shadows*, London, 1940; *Squaring the Circle* by Valentine Katayev, London, 1941; *The Man in the Raincoat*, Edinburgh, 1949; *Love in Albania* by Eric Linklater, London, 1949; *The Love of Four Colonels*, Birmingham and London, 1951; *A Fiddle at the Wedding*, by Patricia Pakenham-Walsh, Brighton, 1952; *No Sign of the Dove*, Leeds and London, 1953; *Photo Finish*, Dublin and London, 1962; *Halfway up the Tree*, New York, 1967; *The Unkown Soldier and His Wife*, Chichester, 1968, London, 1973. **Films**—*School for Secrets* (*The Secret Flight*), 1946; *Vice Versa*, 1948; *Private Angelo*, with Michael Anderson, 1949; *Romanoff and Juliet*, 1961; *Billy Budd*, 1962; *Lady L.*, 1965; *Hammersmith Is Out*, 1972, *Memed, My Hawk*, 1984. **Operas**—*L'Heure Espagnole* by Ravel, *Gianni Schicchi* by Puccini, and *Erwartung* by Schoenberg (triple bill), London, 1962; *The Magic Flute* by Mozart, Hamburg, 1968; *Don Quichotte* by Massenet, Paris, 1973; *Don Giovanni* by Mozart, Edinburgh, 1973; *Les Brigands* by Offenbach, Berlin, 1978; *The Marriage* by Mussorgsky, Milan, 1981, Edinburgh, 1982; *Mavra* and *The Flood* by Stravinsky, Milan, 1982; *Katja Kabanowa* by Janáček, Hamburg, 1985; *The Marriage of Figaro* by Mozart, Salzburg and Hamburg, 1987.
Actor: **Plays**—Waffles in *The Wood Demon* by Chekhov, Shere, Surrey, 1938; in *The Bishop of Limpopoland*, London, 1939; Aylesbury Repertory Company: in *French Without Tears* by Terence Rattigan, *Pygmalion* by G.B. Shaw, *White Cargo* by Leon Gordon, *Rookery Nook* by Ben Travers, and *Laburnum Grove* by J.B. Priestley, 1939; Reverend Alroy Whittingstall in *First Night* by Reginald Denham, Richmond, Surrey, 1940; *Swinging the Gate* (revue), London, 1940; M. Lescure in *Fishing for Shadows*, London, 1940; *Hermione Gingold Revue*, London, 1940; *Diversion and Diversion 2* (revues), London, 1940, 1941; Petrovitch in *Crime and Punishment* by Rodney Ackland, London, 1946; Caligula in *Frenzy*, London, 1948; Sergeant Dohda in *Love in Albania* by Eric Linklater, London, 1949; Carabosse in *The Love of Four Colonels*, London, 1951; The General in *Romanoff and Juliet* London, 1956, New York, 1957; Sam Old in *Photo Finish*, London, 1962, New York, 1963; Archbishop in *The Unknown Soldier and His Wife*, Chichester, 1968, London, 1973; Boris Vassilevitch Krivelov in *Who's Who in Hell*, New York, 1974; title role in *King Lear*, Stratford, Ontario, 1979, 1980; Stage Manager in *The Marriage*, Milan, 1981, Edinburgh, 1982; Ludwig in *Beethoven's Tenth*, Paris, 1982, Birmingham, London, and Los Angeles, 1983, New York, 1984; *An Evening with Peter Ustinov*, London, 1990, San Francisco, 1991. **Films**—*Hullo Fame!*, 1941; *Mein Kampf, My Crimes*, 1941; *One of Our Aircraft Is Missing*, 1941; *The Goose Steps Out*, 1942; *Let the People Sing*, 1942; *The New Lot*, 1943; *The Way Ahead*, 1944; *The True Glory* 1945; *School for Secrets* (*The Secret Flight*), 1946; *Vice Versa*, 1947; *Private Angelo*, 1949; *Odette*, 1950; *Quo Vadis*, 1951; *Hotel Sahara*, 1951; *The Magic Box*, 1951; *Beau Brummell*, 1954; *The Egyptian*, 1954; *Le Plaisir* (*House of Pleasure*) (narrator), 1954; *We're No Angels*, 1955; *Lola Montès* (*Lola Montez, The Sins of Lola Montes*), 1955; *I girovaghi* (*The Wanderers*), 1956; *Un angel paso sobre Brooklyn* (*An Angel over Brooklyn, The Man Who Wagged His Tail*), 1957; *Les Espions* (*The Spies*), 1957; *The Adventures of Mr. Wonderful*, 1959; *Spartacus*, 1960; *The Sundowners*, 1960; *Romanoff and Juliet*, 1961; *Billy Budd*, 1962; *La donna del mondo* (*Women of the World*) (narrator), 1963, *The Peaches* (narrator), 1964; *Topkapi*, 1964; *John Goldfarb, Please Come Home*, 1964; *Lady L.*, 1965; *The Comedians*, 1967; *Blackbeard's Ghost*, 1967; *Hot Millions*, 1968; *Viva Max!*, 1969; *Hammersmith Is Out*, 1972; *Big Truck and Sister Clare*, 1973; *Treasure of*

Matecumbe, 1976; *One of Our Dinosaurs Is Missing*, 1976; *Logan's Run*, 1976; *Robin Hood* (voice in animated film), 1976; *Un Taxi mauve* (*The Purple Taxi*), 1977; *The Last Remake of Beau Geste*, 1978; *The Mouse and His Child* (narrator), 1978; *Doppio delitto* (*Double Murders*), 1978; *Death on the Nile*, 1978; *Tarka the Otter* (narrator), 1978; *Winds of Change* (narrator), 1978; *Ashanti*, 1979; *Charlie Chan and the Curse of the Dragon Queen*, 1981; *The Great Muppet Caper*, 1981; *Grendel, Grendel, Grendel* (voice in animated film), 1981; *Evil under the Sun*, 1982; *Memed, My Hawk*, 1984; *Appointment with Death*, 1988; *The French Revolution*, 1989; *Lorenzo's Oil*, 1991. **Television**—*The Life of Dr. Johnson*, 1957; *Barefoot in Athens*, 1966; *In All Directions* series; *A Storm in Summer*, 1970 (USA); *Lord North*, 1972; *The Mighty Continent* (narrator), 1974; *A Quiet War*, 1976 (USA); *The Thief of Bagdad*, 1978; *Jesus of Nazareth*, 1979; *Einstein's Universe* (narrator), 1979; *Imaginary Friends* (5 roles), 1982; *The Well-Tempered Bach*, 1984; *13 at Dinner*, 1985; *Dead Man's Folly*, 1986; *Peter Ustinov's Russia*, 1986 (Canada); *World Challenge*, 1986 (Canada); *Murder in Three Acts*, 1986; narrator for *History of Europe*, *The Hermitage* and *The Ballerinas*; *Peter Ustinov in China*, 1987; *Around the World in Eighty Days*, 1988–89; *The Secret Identity of Jack the Ripper*, 1989–90; *The Mozart Mystique*, 1990; *Ustinov on the Orient Express*, 1991–92.

Peter Ustinov comments:

I believe that theories should emerge as a logical consequence of practice, and not be formulated in a coldly intellectual climate for eventual use. I therefore regard myself as a practical writer who began to write in the period of the proscenium arch, but who survived into the epoch of the arena and platform stages. The theatre, to survive, must do what film and television cannot do, and that is to exploit the physical presence of the audience. Naturalism was the logical reaction against romanticism, but the poetry inherent in all valid works of any school emerges more easily on film and even more easily on television than on the stage, and the time of the "fourth wall" has passed. Also, with the extraordinarily graphic quality of current events diffused by the news media, and the growing public sense of irony and scepticism about the nature and possibilities of government, tragedy and comedy have been chased for ever from their ivory towers. This is the time of the tragic farce, of the comic drama, of the paradox, of the dramatized doubt. In my plays as in my non-dramatic works I have always been interested in the comic side of things tragic and in the melancholy side of things ribald. Life could not exist without its imperfections, just as the human body could not survive without germs. And to the writer, the imperfections of existence are life-blood.

* * *

Like Noël Coward, with whose versatility his own was often compared when he was establishing himself, Peter Ustinov had a dazzling early break in his career. While he was appearing in a Herbert Farjeon revue, Farjeon gave one of Ustinov's manuscripts to James Agate, then at the height of his influence on the *Sunday Times*. Following Agate's lavish praise of *House of Regrets*, it was produced in 1942. It is very much a young man's play; its story of Russian émigrés living in genteel poverty in wartime London is an often self-consciously "atmospheric" piece, but it shows already Ustinov's sympathetic identification with eccentrics and the

aged in his picture of the old Admiral and General plotting their coup to re-enter Russia. In the immediately following period Ustinov's plays appeared with impressive frequency, perhaps too frequently for their own good. Too many could be described in the terms he uses to label *Blow Your Own Trumpet*, a fantasy set in an Italian restaurant—"An idea rather than a play in the ordinary sense of the word." *The Tragedy of Good Intentions*, a chronicle play about the Crusades, is unfocused and verbose; *The Indifferent Shepherd*, his closest approach to a conventional well-made West End play, centred round a clergyman's crisis of conscience, is lacklustre despite its sincerity; and *No Sign of the Dove*, a resounding critical failure, a re-working of the Noah legend, despite a fine neo-Firbankian opening of high style, dwindles into a tepid mixture of late Shaw and bedroom-door farce. The initial impetus in these earlier plays is rarely sustained consistently.

At the same time, Ustinov's unique gift for the fantastic was developing more surely. *The Banbury Nose*, tracing a great military family through three generations in reverse order (a kind of *Milestones* backwards), is a technical tour de force, but in the scenes between the wife and the men who have loved her Ustinov also reveals a sure understanding of the threads of response between people. Although his 1950's work produced some oddly muffled efforts—such as *The Moment of Truth*, an over-inflated political drama—he also produced *The Love of Four Colonels* and *Romanoff and Juliet*, at his inventive best in both. *The Love of Four Colonels*, set in a European state disputed by the Allies, enjoyably satirizes national characteristics as the four Colonels try to awaken the Sleeping Beauty's love in pastiche scenes in which they play out their own hopes and ideals, while *Romanoff and Juliet* adapts the Romeo and Juliet story in the Cold War context of rival Russian and American embassies in "the smallest country in Europe." Underneath the fairy tales and Ruritanian trappings there is a shrewd core of humanist understanding of contemporary problems, although with Ustinov's polyglot ancestry this inevitably emerges in an international rather than a local context.

His later output continued to develop earlier themes. *Photo Finish* recalls *The Banbury Nose* in its flashback time-sequence, presenting a famous writer in confrontation with his younger selves as he contemplates the mirror of the past. *The Unknown Soldier and His Wife* is a further exploration of some material in *The Tragedy of Good Intentions* but a much surer play. It sweeps in time from ancient Rome to medieval England to modern times, linked by the same recurring characters who emerge whenever war comes and who control its course. Occasionally it threatens to become a series of admittedly amusing anti-war sketches, but it contains some of Ustinov's most pungent writing.

Certainly few of Ustinov's plays have a tight plot progression; as in his novels he is happier in a more picaresque style. His ancestry perhaps partly explains his drawing on the Russian literary tradition blending tragedy and comedy and his best plays have a strong tension between the two. He once stressed the influence of music on his work and there is indeed a Mozartian strain which informs his best plays which, despite an apparent surface plotlessness, have an internal rhythm which gives them strong theatrical movement. This could hardly be said of a string of disappointing work in more recent years. *Halfway up the Tree*, a tired comedy of the drop-out generation, was sadly jaded, but still not so distressingly feeble as *Who's Who in Hell*. This has a splendid initial idea; it is set in an anteroom of Hell where the ultimate destination of new arrivals (including the U.S. President and the Russian Premier) is decided. But the promise of a sharp political comedy is torpedoed by stale jokes and a woefully jejune level of intellectual argument. *Overheard*, a lachrymose comedy of diplomatic life, was similarly thin, while *Beethoven's Tenth* was not entirely a return to form. Again, there is a hugely promising initial premise—Beethoven materialises as the result of a trance by a psychic au pair in the house of a London music critic and is shortly cured of his deafness, also speaking perfect English. The play seems poised to take off into an exhilarating comedy of ideas but apart from a

closing scene to the first act in which the critic's wife, an ex-singer, sings "An die ferne Geliebte" to the composer's accompaniment—as good a scene as anything Ustinov has written—the rest of the play never recovers the buoyancy of the opening.

—Alan Strachan

V

VALDEZ, Luis (Miguel). American. Born 26 June 1940. Educated at San Jose State University, California. Married Guadalupe Valdez in 1969; three children. Union organizer, United Farmworkers, Delano, California, to 1967. Since 1965 founding director, El Teatro Campesino, Delano, 1965–69, Fresno, 1969–71, and since 1971 San Juan Bautista, California. Recipient: Obie award, 1968; Emmy award, for directing, 1973; Rockefeller grant, 1978. Address: 705 Fourth Street, San Juan Bautista, California 95045, U.S.A.

PUBLICATIONS

Plays

Las dos caras del patroncito (produced Delano, 1965). Included in *Actos*, 1971.
La quinta temporada (produced Delano, 1966). Included in *Actos*, 1971.
Los vendidos (produced Delano, 1967). Included in *Actos*, 1971.
The Shrunken Head of Pancho Villa (produced Delano, 1968).
La conquista de Mexico (puppet play; produced Delano, 1968). Included in *Actos*, 1971.
No saco nada de la escuela (produced Fresno, 1969). Included in *Actos*, 1971.
The Militants (produced Fresno, 1969). Included in *Actos*, 1971.
Vietnam campesino (produced Fresno, 1970). Included in *Actos*, 1971.
Soldado razo (produced Fresno, 1970; New York, 1985). Included in *Actos*, 1971.
Huelguistas (produced Fresno, 1970). Included in *Actos*, 1971.
Bernabé (produced Fresno, 1970). Published in *Contemporary Chicano Theatre*, edited by Roberto Garza, Notre Dame, Indiana, University of Notre Dame Press, 1976.
Actos. San Juan Bautista, Cucaracha, 1971.
El Virgen del Tepeyac (produced San Juan Bautista, 1971).
Dark Root of a Scream (produced Los Angeles, 1971; New York, 1985). Published in *From the Barrio: A Chicano Anthology*, edited by Lillian Faderman and Luis Omar Salinas, San Francisco, Canfield Press, 1973.
Los olivos pits (produced San Juan Bautista, 1972).
Mundo (produced San Juan Bautista, 1973).
La gran carpa de los rasquachis (produced San Juan Bautista, 1973).
El baille de los gigantes (produced San Juan Bautista, 1973).
El fin del mundo (produced San Juan Bautista, 1975).
Zoot Suit (produced Los Angeles, 1978; New York, 1979).
I Don't Have to Show You No Stinking Badgers (produced Los Angeles, 1986).

Screenplays: *Zoot Suit*, 1982; *La Bamba*, 1987.

Other

Pensamiento Serpentino: A Chicano Approach to the Theatre of Reality. San Juan Bautista, California, Cucaracha, 1973.

Editor, with Stan Steiner, *Aztlan: An Anthology of Mexican American Literature.* New York, Knopf, 1972.

*

Theatrical Activities:
Director: **Plays**—most of his own plays. **Films**—*Zoot Suit*, 1982; *La Bamba*, 1987.
Actor: **Film**—*Which Way Is Up?*, 1977. **Television**—*Visions* series, 1976.

* * *

Best known as the founder of the Teatro Campesino (Farmworkers Theatre) in 1965, Luis Valdez is a man of many talents: actor, playwright, screenwriter, essayist, stage and film director, and he is the leading practitioner of Chicano theater in the United States. From the earliest agit-prop pieces he directed and wrote, termed *actos*, to his professionally produced *Zoot Suit*, first a play and then a film, Valdez has attempted to portray the Chicano's reality.

The very term "Chicano" connotes a political attitude, cognizant of a distinctive place in the so-called "American melting-pot," and Valdez became a major proponent of this self-imposed designation when his teatro toured the country asserting a cultural and political distinction. Valdez has termed *Zoot Suit* an "American play," this in deference to his belief that Chicanos are a part of the American society and should not be excluded from what this society has to offer its citizens. Valdez's dramatic themes always reflect Chicanos in crisis, never pretending that Chicanos have been fully accepted into the American mainstream. His characters are always in conflict with some aspect of the system, and more often than not, that manifestation of the power structure is presented by non-Chicanos, or "Anglos." Although the characters in power find it easy to manipulate the subordinate Chicanos, Valdez's audiences discover that whether the heroes win or lose it is they who can win through collective action.

Las dos caras del patroncito (The Two Faces of the Boss) and *La quinta temporada* (The Fifth Season) are *actos* that reveal the plight of striking farmworkers, solved through unionization. When Valdez decided to leave the union in 1967 he sought an independent theater company, not focused solely on labor movement and farmworker themes. The next *acto*, *Los vendidos* (The Sellouts), explored various stereotypes of Chicanos and satirized the "sellout" who attempted to assimilate into a white, racist society. *No saco nada de la escuela* (I Don't Get Anything Out of School) exposed some inequities in the educational process and *La conquista de*

Mexico (The Conquest of Mexico) paralleled the fall of the Aztecs with the disunity of Chicano activists of the day. The use of masks, farcical exaggeration, stereotyped characters, improvisation, and social commentary in the *actos* reflects Valdez's work with the San Francisco Mime Troupe prior to his founding the teatro. While the *actos* are brief agit-prop statements, Valdez's plays explore other theatrical forms.

Beginning with his first play, *The Shrunken Head of Pancho Villa*, originally written and produced while he was a student, Valdez has written non-realistic statements, mingling fantasy and farce, comedy and pathos. All of Valdez's plays issue forth from a family structure. *The Shrunken Head of Pancho Villa* pits the assimilationist against the *pachuco* social bandit: two brothers whose life-styles reflect the extremes within the barrio. *Bernabé* revolves around a village idiot who gains a spiritual release when he symbolically marries *La Tierra* (The Earth) who appears to him as a symbol of the Mexican Revolution of 1910.

There is much of the Spanish religious folk theatre in Valdez's plays, combined with a new message of social justice. The playwright uses allegorical and mythological figures to present his messages, combatting the evils of the war in Vietnam in the *actos Vietnam campesino* and *Soldado razo* (Private Soldier) or the expressionist play *Dark Root of a Scream*. He exposes the need for a balance with Mother Nature in the ritualistic *El fin del mundo* (The End of the World), *La gran carpa de los rasquachis* (The Great Tent of the Underdogs), and *Mundo* (a title based on the name of the protagonist, Reimundo, or "king of the world"). Beginning with *Bernabé*, each of the plays combines indigenous mythology with contemporary problems. *La gran carpa de los rasquachis* most notably unites the Virgin of Guadalupe with Quetzalcoatl, the meso-American Christ-figure, calling for unity among all people.

In *Zoot Suit* Valdez unites all the elements of his theater to create a statement that cannot be classified without listing its parts: the *acto*, Living Newspaper, the *corrido* (dramatized Mexican ballads), selective realism, and fantasy. The play is narrated by an archetypal "pachuco," a barrio character type that has always fascinated the playwright. This enigmatic figure glides in and out of the action, a fantastical symbol of the Chicano's defiance and ability to survive between two cultures: the Mexican and the Anglo. *Zoot Suit* was the first Chicano play to reach Broadway, and though the New York critics generally disliked the play, it broke box-office records in Los Angeles. The play reminded its audiences that current Chicano struggles have their precedents in such events as the Sleepy Lagoon Murder Trial, which exposed a biased system of justice in the 1940's. Valdez's hit film *La Bamba*, the story of Chicano pop singer Ritchie Valens, reached the Anglo audience in a big way in 1987.

From *actos* to *Zoot Suit*, Valdez remains a singular example of a Chicano who has consistently recreated the struggles and successes of the Chicanos with a clarity of vision and style, however controversial the themes, that makes him a true man of the theater.

—Jorge A. Huerta

---

van ITALLIE, Jean-Claude. American. Born in Brussels, Belgium, 25 May 1936; moved to the United States, 1940; became citizen, 1952. Educated at Great Neck High School, New York; Deerfield Academy, Massachusetts; Harvard University, Cambridge, Massachusetts, A.B. 1958; New York University, 1959; studied acting at the Neighborhood Playhouse, New York. Editor, *Transatlantic Review*, New York, 1960–63; playwright-in-residence, Open Theatre, New York, 1963–68; freelance writer on public affairs for NBC and CBS television, New York, 1963–67; taught playwriting at the New School for Social Research, New York, 1967–68, 1972, Yale University School of Drama, New Haven, Connecticut, 1969, 1978, 1984–85, and Naropa Institute, Boulder, Colorado, 1976–83; lecturer, Princeton University, New Jersey, 1973–86, New York University, 1982–86, 1992, University of Colorado, Boulder, Fall 1985, 1987–91, and Columbia University, New York, Spring 1986; visiting Mellon professor, Amherst College, Massachusetts, Fall 1976, and Middlebury College, Vermont, 1990. Recipient: Rockefeller grant, 1962; Vernon Rice award, 1967; Outer Circle award, 1967; Obie award, 1968; Guggenheim fellowship, 1973, 1980; Creative Artists Public Service grant, 1973; National Endowment for the Arts fellowship, 1986. Ph.D.: Kent State University, Kent, Ohio, 1977. Address: Box 729, Charlemont, Massachusetts 01339, U.S.A.

PUBLICATIONS

Plays

War (produced New York, 1963; Edinburgh, 1968; London, 1969). Included in *War and Four Other Plays*, 1967; in *America Hurrah: Five Short Plays*, 1967.
Almost Like Being (produced New York, 1964). Included in *War and Four Other Plays*, 1967; in *America Hurrah: Five Short Plays*, 1967.
I'm Really Here (produced New York, 1964; London, 1979). Included in *War and Four Other Plays*, 1967.
The Hunter and the Bird (produced New York, 1964). Included in *War and Four Other Plays*, 1967.
Interview (as *Pavane*, produced Atlanta, 1965; revised version, as *Interview*, produced New York, 1966; London, 1967). Included in *America Hurrah: Five Short Plays*, 1967.
Where Is de Queen? (as *Dream*, produced New York, 1965; revised version, as *Where Is de Queen?*, produced Minneapolis, 1965). Included in *War and Four Other Plays*, 1967.
Motel (as *America Hurrah*, produced New York, 1965; revised version, as *Motel*, produced New York, 1966; London, 1967). Included in *America Hurrah: Five Short Plays*, 1967.
America Hurrah (includes *Interview, TV, Motel*) (produced New York, 1966; London, 1967). New York, Coward McCann, 1967; with *War* and *Almost Like Being*, as *America Hurrah: Five Short Plays*, London, Penguin, 1967.
The Girl and the Soldier (produced Los Angeles, 1967). Included in *Seven Short and Very Short Plays*, 1975.
War and Four Other Plays. New York, Dramatists Play Service, 1967.
Thoughts on the Instant of Greeting a Friend on the Street, with Sharon Thie (produced Los Angeles, 1967; in *Collision Course*, produced New York, 1968). Included in *Seven Short and Very Short Plays*, 1975.
The Serpent: A Ceremony, with the Open Theatre (produced Rome, 1968; New York, 1970). New York, Atheneum, 1969.
Take a Deep Breath (televised 1969). Included in *Seven Short and Very Short Plays*, 1975.
Photographs: Mary and Howard (produced Los Angeles, 1969). Included in *Seven Short and Very Short Plays*, 1975.

Eat Cake (produced Denver, 1971). Included in *Seven Short and Very Short Plays*, 1975.

Mystery Play (produced New York, 1973). New York, Dramatists Play Service, 1973; revised version, as *The King of the United States*, music by Richard Peaslee (also director: produced New York, 1973), New York, 1975.

Nightwalk, with Megan Terry and Sam Shepard (produced New York and London, 1973). Published in *Open Theater*, New York, Drama Book Specialists, 1975.

The Sea Gull, adaptation of a play by Chekhov (produced Princeton, New Jersey, 1973; New York, 1975). New York, Harper, 1977.

A Fable, music by Richard Peaslee (produced New York, 1975). New York, Dramatists Play Service, 1976.

Seven Short and Very Short Plays (includes *Photographs*, *Eat Cake*, *The Girl and the Soldier*, *Take a Deep Breath*, *Rosary*, *Harold*, *Thoughts on the Instant of Greeting a Friend on the Street*). New York, Dramatists Play Service, 1975.

The Cherry Orchard, adaptation of a play by Chekhov (produced New York, 1977). New York, Grove Press, 1977.

America Hurrah and Other Plays (includes *The Serpent*, *A Fable*, *The Hunter and the Bird*, *Almost Like Being*). New York, Grove Press, 1978.

Medea, adaptation of the play by Euripides (produced Kent, Ohio, 1979).

Three Sisters (produced New York, 1979). New York, Dramatists Play Service, 1979.

Bag Lady (produced New York, 1979). New York, Dramatists Play Service, 1980.

Uncle Vanya, adaptation of a play by Chekhov (produced New York, 1983). New York, Dramatists Play Service, 1980.

Naropa, music by Steve Gorn (produced New York, 1982). Published in *Wordplays 1*, New York, Performing Arts Journal Publications, 1980.

Early Warnings (includes *Bag Lady*, *Sunset Freeway*, *Final Orders*) (produced New York, 1983). New York, Dramatists Play Service, 1983.

The Tibetan Book of the Dead; or, How Not to Do It Again, music by Steve Gorn (produced New York, 1983). New York, Dramatists Play Service, 1983.

Pride, in *Faustus in Hell* (produced Princeton, New Jersey, 1985).

The Balcony, adaptation of a play by Jean Genet (produced Cambridge, Massachusetts, 1986).

The Traveler (produced Los Angeles, Leicester, and London, 1987).

Struck Dumb (produced Los Angeles, 1989; New York, 1991). Published in *Best One-Act Plays: 1990–1991*, New York, Applause, 1991.

Ancient Boys (produced Boulder, Colorado, 1990; New York, 1991).

Screenplays: *The Box Is Empty*, 1965; *Three Lives for Mississippi*, 1971.

Television Writing: scripts for *Look Up and Live* series, 1963–65; *Hobbies; or, Things Are All Right with the Forbushers*, 1967; *Take a Deep Breath*, 1969; *Picasso: A Painter's Diary*, 1980.

Other

Calcutta (journal). Kent, Ohio, Kent State University Libraries, 1987.

*

Manuscript Collections: Kent State University, Ohio; Harvard University Library, Cambridge, Massachusetts.

Critical Studies: by Walter Kerr, in *New York Times*, 11 December 1966; "Three Views of America," in *The Third Theatre* by Robert Brustein, New York, Knopf, 1969, London, Cape, 1970; *Up Against the Fourth Wall* by John Lahr, New York, Grove Press, 1970; "Jean-Claude van Itallie Issue" of *Serif* (Kent, Ohio), Winter 1972.

Theatrical Activities:
Director: **Plays**—*The King of the United States*, New York, 1973; *The Tempest* by Shakespeare, New York, 1984; *The Balcony*, New York, 1989.

Jean-Claude van Itallie comments:

I seem to have been most intent on playing with new forms that might express a clear theatre optic. I have worked as a playwright in solitude. I have adapted and translated into English from a foreign language. I have worked as a poet in collaboration with a theatre director and actors, and with actors alone. I have written for puppets. I have written screenplays and specifically for television. I question theatre but I remain married to it, more or less. I agree that language itself helps to keep us isolated but I continue to write. I want to write with greater clarity, but from the heart. I like to work with other artists in the theatre, and to imagine the audience as a community of friends.

The 1960's were an exciting time of revolt and reformation. In the vanguard, theater destroyed preconceptions and invented new disciplines to express re-found truths underlying the mendacity of the commercial and political world. The 1970's were a time of retrenchment; I worked on new versions of classics making contact with my heritage as a playwright, my lineage. What now? In form, working to synthesize the discoveries of the 1960's, and the rediscoveries of the 1970's. Political lies and corruption of power have become mundane; we are concerned now with our self-caused possible destruction of the world. What is the relationship between runaway technology and short-sighted pollution of air, food, and water, on the one hand, and spiritual poverty on the other? This is a time to clarify and acknowledge the split between body and mind in the individual and the world, and in that acknowledgement to effect a healing.

*   *   *

The early plays of Jean-Claude van Itallie, in terms of their brevity, wit, and social commentary, may be taken to resemble the early one-acts of Ionesco or, better, Chekhov—and later in his career van Itallie composed luminous American versions of the major Chekhov plays. The decisive difference between van Itallie's drama and that of the classic moderns lies in the realm of form. He is preoccupied with multiple levels of experience, with the mask behind the mask, and with states of awareness outside the province of the everyday. His crystalline perceptions give rise to complex modes of characterization, a concern with indeterminate time, and a montage approach to dramatic activity and language.

Van Itallie's essential stage vocabulary is there at the start, in his off-off-Broadway debut with *War*. He describes the play as a "formal war game, a duel" between two male actors of different generations who metamorphose into father and son. They are visited by the shimmering vision of a nameless great actress of the Edwardian era who addresses them as her children and transforms their gritty New York loft which is crammed with theatrical paraphernalia, into a sunny, cheerful park. At the end the men form an emblem of a two-headed eagle of war, each male identity locked into that of the other.

The rich theatrical implications of this meditation on appearances, on essential conflict, and on the role-nature of personality quickly matured when in the same year van Itallie began writing for the newly organized Open Theatre under the direction of Joseph Chaikin. In its shattering of received theatrical forms, its canonization of the workshop process, and its philosophical daring, the Open Theatre provided van Itallie with a subtle instrument for testing the limits of theatrical representation. For the Open Theatre he contributed numerous sketches, improvisations, and short plays, including *The Hunter and the Bird*; among his most successful are the pop-art Hollywood comedies informally known as "the Doris Day plays": *Almost Like Being* and *I'm Really Here*, with a wacky Doris D. in love with Just Rock and then the deadly Rossano.

Van Itallie's chief works for the Open Theatre came in his last years with the company. A triptych of one-acts under the title *America Hurrah* begins with *Interview*, a rhythmic weaving of ritualized daily behavior and speech that starts and concludes in the anonymous offices of an employment agency where all the applicants are named Smith. *TV* dramatizes the menace and trivializing power of the mass media, with a trio watching television in the viewing room of a television-ratings company: the television images break free of the set and engulf the viewers. *Motel: A Masque for Three Dolls* unfolds within a tacky midwestern motel room where a huge Doll Motel-Keeper spews forth an unctuous monologue about the room and its furnishings which represent the mail-order-catalogue surface of a violent America. Man Doll and Woman Doll enter the room and proceed to tear the place apart, have sex, and destroy the Motel-Keeper.

The theme of violence done to persons through the exigencies of the social contract is taken up again in *The Serpent*. Here, in an even more sophisticated interplay of layered actions, contemporary violence is linked back to its ancient sources and seen as a central aspect of the human condition. As it simultaneously presents and confronts the values in its story, this "ceremony" for actors explores the themes and the events of Genesis, and the Tree of Life is a tangle of men who embody the serpent. God's fixing of limits upon Adam and Eve is viewed as humanity's projection of its own need for limits, and the self-consciousness that results from the Fall leads to Cain and Abel and the unending human battle, in which each is "caught between the beginning and the end" and unable to remake the past.

After leaving the Open Theatre, van Itallie wrote and staged *The King of the United States*, a stark political fable about the need for an office of rule supported by agents of the status quo to give order to life. *Mystery Play* recycles the characters and themes of *The King* and inverts its tone and style in an elegantly paced farce-parody of the whodunnit, presided over by a Mystery Writer who likes to play detective.

In 1975 van Itallie collaborated again with Chaikin on *A Fable*, a folktale for adults. In picaresque episodes a Journeyor leaves her impoverished village in search of help, and in her wanderings over a wide and storied landscape she comes to celebrate the need to transcend the beast within.

With *Early Warnings* van Itallie returned to smaller forms and a second triptych, on the theme of accommodation. The warnings are directed at the audience, for the characters already have made their choices. *Bag Lady* presents a day in the street life of the witty Clara who is organizing her bags and keeping only the essential shards of her identity. The

perky actress Judy Jensen in *Sunset Freeway* breezes along in her car at dusk on the L.A. freeway, immersed in her identity of commercial actress. She speaks to her toy giraffe, imagines a nuclear holocaust, spots Warren Beatty, and, looking out upon the glories of consumer culture, she's in heaven. In *Final Orders* space program agents Angus and Mike listen to instructions from a computer and hold on to one another, poised for the holocaust that now is at hand.

Among van Itallie's most ambitious projects is a theatrical version of *The Tibetan Book of the Dead; or, How Not To Do It Again*, a ritual for the dead in which the characters are emanations of the Dead One, speaking, chanting, and dancing within a huge skull and upon a floor mandala. In its style and complexity, and in its debt to an ancient text, it resembles *The Serpent*, but its landscape lies beyond history and legend in an essentialized world of the spirit.

The whole of van Itallie's dramatic universe is dedicated to a process of vital experimentation through the counterpoint of language, mask, and gesture. His is a philosophy of theatrical play underscored with social critique. Central to his vision are the inadequacies of being and a knowledge of exile. And above all, a knowledge too of the brutalities that are visited upon the self as it seeks to make its way in a world almost willfully estranged from organic life.

—Bill Coco

VIDAL, Gore (Eugene Luther Gore Vidal, Jr.). American. Born in West Point, New York, 3 October 1925. Educated at Los Alamos School, New Mexico, 1939–40; Phillips Exeter Academy, New Hampshire, 1940–43. Served in the United States Army, 1943–46: warrant officer. Editor, E.P. Dutton, publishers, New York, 1946. Lived in Antigua, Guatemala, 1947–49, and Italy, 1967–76. Member of the advisory board, *Partisan Review*, New Brunswick, New Jersey, 1960–71; Democratic-Liberal candidate for Congress, New York, 1960; member of the President's Advisory Committee on the Arts, 1961–63; co-chair, New Party, 1968–71. Recipient: Mystery Writers of America award, for television play, 1954; Cannes Film Critics award, for screenplay, 1964; National Book Critics Circle award, for criticism, 1983. Address: La Rondinaia, Ravello, Salerno, Italy; or c/o Random House Inc., 201 East 50th Street, New York, New York 10022, U.S.A.

PUBLICATIONS

Plays

Visit to a Small Planet (televised 1955). Included in *Visit to a Small Planet and Other Television Plays*, 1956; revised version (produced New York, 1957; London, 1960), Boston, Little Brown, 1957; in *Three Plays*, 1962.
Honor (televised 1956). Published in *Television Plays for Writers: Eight Television Plays*, edited by A.S. Burack, Boston, The Writer, 1957; revised version as *On the March to the Sea: A Southron Comedy* (produced Bonn, Germany, 1961), in *Three Plays*, 1962.
Visit to a Small Planet and Other Television Plays (includes *Barn Burning, Dark Possession, The Death of Billy the Kid,*

A Sense of Justice, Smoke, Summer Pavilion, The Turn of the Screw). Boston, Little Brown, 1956.

The Best Man: A Play about Politics (produced New York, 1960). Boston, Little Brown, 1960; in *Three Plays*, 1962.

Three Plays (includes *Visit to a Small Planet, The Best Man, On the March to the Sea*). London, Heinemann, 1962.

Romulus: A New Comedy, adaptation of a play by Friedrich Dürrenmatt (produced New York, 1962). New York, Dramatists Play Service, 1962.

Weekend (produced New York, 1968). New York. Dramatists Play Service, 1968.

An Evening with Richard Nixon and . . . (produced New York, 1972). New York, Random House, 1972.

Screenplays: *The Catered Affair*, 1956; *I Accuse*, 1958; *The Scapegoat*, with Robert Hamer, 1959; *Suddenly, Last Summer*, with Tennessee Williams, 1959; *The Best Man*, 1964; *Is Paris Burning?*, with Francis Ford Coppola, 1966; *Last of the Mobile Hot-Shots*, 1970; *The Sicilian*, 1970; *Gore Vidal's Billy the Kid*, 1989.

Television Plays: *Barn Burning*, from the story by Faulkner, 1954; *Dark Possession*, 1954; *Smoke*, from the story by Faulkner, 1954; *Visit to a Small Planet*, 1955; *The Death of Billy the Kid*, 1955; *A Sense of Justice*, 1955; *Summer Pavilion*, 1955; *The Turn of the Screw*, from the story by Henry James, 1955; *Honor*, 1956; *The Indestructible Mr. Gore*, 1960; *Vidal in Venice* (documentary), 1985; *Dress Gray*, from the novel by Lucian K. Truscott IV, 1986.

Novels

Williwaw. New York, Dutton, 1946; London, Panther, 1965.

In a Yellow Wood. New York, Dutton, 1947; London, New English Library, 1967.

The City and the Pillar. New York, Dutton, 1948; London, Lehmann, 1949; revised edition, Dutton, and London, Heinemann, 1965.

The Season of Comfort. New York, Dutton, 1949.

Dark Green, Bright Red. New York, Dutton, and London, Lehmann, 1950.

A Search for the King: A Twelfth Century Legend. New York, Dutton, 1950; London, New English Library, 1967.

The Judgment of Paris. New York, Dutton, 1952; London, Heinemann, 1953; revised edition, Boston, Little Brown, 1965; Heinemann, 1966.

Messiah. New York, Dutton, 1954; London, Heinemann, 1955; revised edition, Boston, Little Brown, 1965; Heinemann, 1968.

Three: Williwaw, A Thirsty Evil, Julian the Apostate. New York, New American Library, 1962.

Julian. Boston, Little Brown, and London, Heinemann, 1964.

Washington, D.C. Boston, Little Brown, and London, Heinemann, 1967.

Myra Breckinridge. Boston, Little Brown, and London, Blond, 1968.

Two Sisters: A Memoir in the Form of a Novel. Boston, Little Brown, and London, Heinemann, 1970.

Burr. New York, Random House, 1973; London, Heinemann, 1974.

Myron. New York, Random House, 1974; London, Heinemann, 1975.

1876. New York, Random House, and London, Heinemann, 1976.

Kalki. New York, Random House, and London, Heinemann, 1978.

Creation. New York, Random House, and London, Heinemann, 1981.

Duluth. New York, Random House, and London, Heinemann, 1983.

Lincoln. New York, Random House, and London, Heinemann, 1984.

Empire. New York, Random House, and London, Deutsch, 1987.

Hollywood. New York, Random House, and London, Deutsch, 1990.

Novels as Edgar Box

Death in the Fifth Position. New York, Dutton, 1952; London, Heinemann, 1954.

Death Before Bedtime. New York, Dutton, 1953; London, Heinemann, 1954.

Death Likes It Hot. New York, Dutton, 1954; London, Heinemann, 1955.

Short Stories

A Thirsty Evil: Seven Short Stories. New York, Zero Press, 1956; London, Heinemann, 1958.

Other

Rocking the Boat (essays). Boston, Little Brown, 1962; London, Heinemann, 1963.

Sex, Death, and Money (essays). New York, Bantam, 1968.

Reflections upon a Sinking Ship (essays). Boston, Little Brown, and London, Heinemann, 1969.

Homage to Daniel Shays: Collected Essays 1952–1972. New York, Random House, 1972; as *Collected Essays 1952–1972*, London, Heinemann, 1974.

Matters of Fact and of Fiction: Essays 1973–1976. New York, Random House, and London, Heinemann, 1977.

Sex Is Politics and Vice Versa (essay). Los Angeles, Sylvester and Orphanos, 1979.

Views from a Window: Conversations with Gore Vidal, with Robert J. Stanton. Secaucus, New Jersey, Lyle Stuart, 1980.

The Second American Revolution and Other Essays 1976–1982. New York, Random House, 1982; as *Pink Triangle and Yellow Star and Other Essays*, London, Heinemann, 1982.

Vidal in Venice, edited by George Armstrong, photographs by Tore Gill. New York, Summit, and London, Weidenfeld and Nicolson, 1985.

Armegeddon? Essays 1983–1987. London, Deutsch, 1987; as *At Home*, New York, Random House, 1988.

A View From the Diner's Club: Essays 1987–1991. London, Deutsch, 1991.

Editor, *Best Television Plays*. New York, Ballantine, 1956.

*

Bibliography: *Gore Vidal: A Primary and Secondary Bibliography* by Robert J. Stanton, Boston, Hall, and London, Prior, 1978.

Manuscript Collection: University of Wisconsin, Madison.

Critical Studies: *Gore Vidal* by Ray Lewis White, New York, Twayne, 1968; *The Apostate Angel: A Critical Study of Gore Vidal* by Bernard F. Dick, New York, Random House, 1974; *Gore Vidal* by Robert F. Kiernan, New York, Ungar, 1982.

Theatrical Activities:
Actor: **Film**—*Roma* (*Fellini Roma*), 1972.

* * *

Eschewing all consideration of Gore Vidal as a novelist and short story writer the critic must associate his theatrical production with its kinship to cinema and television, i.e., Vidal's plays are quite stageable yet are intrinsically cinematographic or televisionistic. They have a modernity about them that facilitates their being restructured for each medium—because they are thematically and linguistically hinged loosely but integrally, and the characters drawn in such a manner that in displacing a character, in changing a tempo, or shifting psychology for a particular medium, Vidal does not violate the play's integrity. Critics have envied Vidal's facile success on television and stage; but his success would not be forthcoming were he not an extremely proficient stylist. True, Vidal has a grudge against a complacent "bourgeois" society and likes to jab at sensitive and vulnerable spots, and he succeeded cinematographically in *Suddenly Last Summer*. The film *Lefthanded Gun* (based on his television play on the Billy the Kid legend) succeeded; but *Myra Breckinridge* failed because the producers were not faithful to Vidal.

His themes—extreme and tabooistic in his novels—are more traditional in his plays, mainly war and politics. But the persistent leitmotiv in all his works is man bereft in the modern world. Should man relinquish certain values? Find new ones? Vidal assigns satire for the first alternative, irony for the second. Vidal the person seems to opt for relative values, and creates types (as do all playwrights) to epitomize these values; yet Vidal the writer, in creating the antagonistic types to exemplify certain absolutes, finds himself with characters possessing more dramatic qualities and effectiveness—which indicates that Vidal the writer is instinctively more sage than Vidal the person. Since the antagonist stands well in his own defence he wins dramatic or tragic sympathy; hence, the thesis comes to no social conclusion and the spectator is left with the unresolved futility of modern life. This is good dramaturgy.

Weekend is the least effective of Vidal's plays. It is an attempt to profit from the topical concern about miscegenation which the author encrusts on a political campaign (not unlike *The Best Man*); but the situation and the characters are not real enough for good satire, nor exaggerated enough to make good farce. Vidal's merit as a playwright, however, is best demonstrated in his trilogy: *Visit to a Small Planet*, *On the March to the Sea*, *The Best Man*.

Visit to a Small Planet is the story of a one-man invasion from outer space—an extraterrestrial being who is intent on creating a state of war between his world and ours. This "man" is called Kreton (may all warmongers bear this epithet!) and almost succeeds in creating a war hysteria on earth through certain well-conceived comic situations. It was because of these situations that the play became a very successful television series. However, its anti-war theme is ineffective because we cannot associate the Kreton's world with our own cretin world. After all, it was they who wanted war, not us humans. The audience can't help but feel self-righteous at the end when Kreton is led off to his celestial kindergarten. In attempting a satire on war Vidal created an excellent science-fiction farce with characterizations that are memorable—the pixie Kreton, the prototype of the war-loving general, Tom Powers, and Roger Felding, an equally ambitious television commentator.

Although the theme of *On the March to the Sea* is shopworn—the disasters wrought on Southern families, par-ticularly that of John Hinks, by the ravages of the Civil War—this play is poignant and highly dramatic. The characters are all believable, with the possible exception of Captain Taylor of the Union Army—flamboyant, too philosophic (war participants, i.e., soldiers, are never introspective not contemplative, at least about ethical or social problems, during bellicose engagements). Vidal thought a lot of this character and gave him the final words of the play; but the character really caught in the maelstrom of life and war, John Hinks, was the authentic tragic figure of the play. The play is in a war setting and the war pervades all. Yet as the title aptly indicates, the main theme is not Sherman's march to the sea, but a series of incidents that take place *on* the march to the sea. The question of what is human dignity (the answer to one's own conscience) and honor (the answer to social conscience) is put literally through a trial by fire. The characters, even though typified (intentionally so) are all quite well drawn, except for Colonel Thayer, who is the "heavy."

But Colonel Thayer is too celluloidish a character to be really cruel. The cruelty prize goes to Clayton, son of John Hinks, too young and self-centered to understand his father's anguish. Though *Visit to a Small Planet* was intended as a satire on war, *On the March to the Sea* is infinitely more effective as an anti-war drama.

The Best Man shows the struggle between two presidential aspirants, jockeying, scratching, and grubbing for the nomination of their party. The play is a well-wrought urn, perfectly structured, containing political characters that emulate Hollywoodian stereotypes (Vidal had every intention of doing this), effective dialogue, with each character keeping to his program. The suspenseful outcome of the nomination is solved by an honorable, classical, and justified theatrical technique: President ex-machina. The solution is not only theatrically perfect, but thematically perfect, in that the person eventually to be nominated is of little importance.

The main theme—does one have to be a demogogue to be successful in political life? Vidal gives us such a selection of presidential aspirants that they seem *inverosimil* and incredible. But as the old Italian quip says, "If it's not a wolf, it's a dog." This is ingeniously planted in the mind of the spectator and this is why *The Best Man* is extremely good satire.

—John V. Falconieri

VOGEL, Paula (Anne). American. Born in Washington, D.C., 16 November 1951. Educated at Bryn Mawr College, Pennsylvania, 1969–70, 1971–72; Catholic University, Washington, D.C., 1972–74, B.A.; Cornell University, Ithaca, New York, 1974–77, A.B.D. Various jobs including secretary, moving van company packer, factory packer, computor processor, electronics factory worker, 1969–71; lecturer in women's studies and theatre, Cornell University, Ithaca, New York, 1977–82; artistic director, Theater with Teeth, New York, 1982–85; production supervisor, theatre on film and tape, Lincoln Center, New York, 1983–85; associate professor and director of graduate playwriting program, Brown University, Providence, Rhode Island, from 1985. Since 1990 artistic director, Theatre Eleanor Roosevelt, Providence, Rhode Island; since 1992 board member, Circle Repertory Company, New York. Recipient: Heerbes-McCalmon award, 1975, 1976; American College Theatre

Festival award, 1976; Samuel French award, 1976; American National Theatre and Academy-West award, 1977; National Endowment for the Arts fellowship, 1980, 1991; MacDowell Colony fellowship, 1981, 1989; Bunting fellowship, 1990; Yaddo fellowship, 1992; McKnight fellowship, 1992; Bellagio fellowship, 1992; AT&T award, 1992. Agent: Peter Franklin, William Morris Agency, 1350 Avenue of the Americas, New York, New York 10019. Address: c/o Box 1852, Brown University, Department of Creative Writing, Providence, Rhode Island 02912, U.S.A.

PUBLICATIONS

Plays

Swan Song of Sir Henry (produced Ithaca, New York, 1974).
Meg (produced Ithaca, New York, 1977; New York, 1979). New York, French, 1977.
Apple-Brown Betty (produced Louisville, Kentucky, 1979).
The Last Pat Epstein Show Before the Reruns (produced Ithaca, New York, 1979).
Desdemona (produced Ithaca, New York, 1979; New York, 1985).
Bertha in Blue (produced New York, 1981).
The Oldest Profession (produced New York, 1981).
And Baby Makes Seven (produced San Francisco, 1986).
The Baltimore Waltz (produced New York, 1992). New York, Dramatists Play Service, 1992.
Hot 'n' Throbbing (produced New York, 1992).

*

Theatrical Activities:
Director: **Plays**—*The Lower Rooms* by Eliza Anderson, Providence, Rhode Island.
Actor: **Plays**—Sister George in *The Killing of Sister George* by Frank Marcus, Washington, D.C., 1972.

* * *

Paula Vogel's plays, while imaginatively dramatizing the conflict between the life force and death, prompt us to re-examine such topics as the feminization of poverty, the non-traditional family, the AIDS epidemic, and domestic violence (both in late 20th-century America and in the context of a revisit to Shakespeare's *Othello*). Despite the topicality of her comedies sporting a sting, these plays tend to salute the salutary nature of fantasy. Although clearly writing from a feminist perspective, Vogel does not portray her women uncritically or her men unsympathetically.

Nevertheless Vogel laments the unnecessarily Darwinian nature of people's odds of survival—a sort of law of the jungle by which the more muscular, wealthy, or powerful white, Protestant men enjoy the advantage. Prodigy Cecil, one of three fantasy children in *And Baby Makes Seven*, quotes Darwin to this effect: "Never forget that every single organic being around us strives to increase in numbers; that each lives by a struggle at some period in its life; that heavy destruction inevitably falls either on the young or the old. . . . Thus, from war or nature, from famine and death, all organic beings advance by one general law—namely, Multiply, Vary, Let the Strongest Live, and the Weakest Die. . . ."

The Oldest Profession depicts the effects wrought by the feminization of poverty among the elderly during the Reagan years. In a tiny New York City park at 72nd and Broadway, four still-working prostitutes in their 70's and their madame,

aged 83, quietly chat about their fees, their clients and their simple meals—which provide a precarious pleasure and sustenance, given their low incomes. These hookers preserve their self-respect and their dignity except for the occasional necessity of beating off the incursions of a rival's encroachment on their territory. Although Vogel's premise that ladies of the night keep plying their trade till they drop might seem far-fetched, *The Oldest Profession* reflects the reality that senior citizens do service their own generation in this manner—what else are they trained to do and how else, deprived of health insurance and Social Security payments, can they eke out an existence? Vogel's shrewd social criticism even locates them in the building occupied by Zabar's Delicatessen, which really did evict the elderly tenants living upstairs when it expanded into selling housewares.

Vogel evinces a keen ear for her characters' colloquial speech, an intuitive understanding of their honor, pride, and enjoyment in their work, and subtlety in dramatizing their deprivations, ambitions, conflicts, and mutual nurturing. She gives us 10 minutes or so to warm to these women before we learn that they are anything more than just widows enjoying the sun. By this time we're perfectly prepared to recognize their importance to their clients and their value as people—for this represents the most respectful play ever written on this topic. As we laugh at such quips as "Vera's not just a woman with a Past; she's a woman with an Epic," we respond to Vogel's views of their struggle to survive on income insufficient to meet expenses, their efforts to exercise some control over their destinies, their compassion, their sisterhood, their respect for others and themselves, and their loneliness as, one by one, they die.

Although a comedy (especially in its, as yet unreleased, cinematic version, which takes the women away from their park bench and includes their satisfied customers), *The Oldest Profession*, like Vogel's other plays, stresses the women's mortality. *And Baby Makes Seven* initially seems a more carefree comedy about a contented though non-traditional family composed of Ruth, her pregnant partner Anna, Peter (the gay man who has fathered Anna's child), and three imaginary children made quite real to the adults (and to us) by Ruth and Anna. The situation quickly grows sinister, however, after Peter insists the kids must go before baby arrives. Once more Vogel hooks us with her characters' charm before telling us the truth about them. When we hear the boys talking in the dark about how babies are made, we can't resist lovable Henri from Albert Lamorisse's 1955 film *The Red Balloon*, prodigy Cecil, and Orphan—a wild boy brought up by a pack of dogs, who wants to name the baby Lassie. Soon infanticide occupies the grown ups. Combining whimsy and menace, the fantasy threatens to career off into violence while still encompassing the playful interaction of the lesbian lovers and their friend. After eight-year-old Henri tries to blackmail Anna into buying him a pony by claiming to be the father of her child, all three kids are killed off. (Orphan, most amusingly, dies of rabies, while quoting dog references from Shakespeare, such as "Out, damned spot.") Yet the parents come to appreciate their need for both illusions and playfulness and, in Vogel's happiest ending, quickly recapture both.

Vogel repeats this mingling of fantasy and death in *The Baltimore Waltz*, this time replacing the earlier plays' realism with a fluid presentational approach which combines narrative, lectures, language lessons, a slide show, and quick two- and three-person scenes set in the United States and Europe. Vogel creates simultaneously a compassionate comedy about death, a bedroom farce, and a satire on American AIDS policy, which fails urgently to pursue a cure because so many of the victims have been those "different" (from our rulers) and powerless. "If just one grandchild of George Bush caught this thing during toilet training, that would be the last we'd hear about the space program," laments a character.

But Vogel conjures a disease which targets single elementary school teachers, because they haven't a mother's immunity to their pupils' viruses. Although set in a ward at Baltimore's Johns Hopkins Hospital, this fantasy waltzes protagonist Anna around Europe in a two-fold quest: to find a cure for Acquired Toilet Disease and to enjoy sex, so that she can, before her untimely demise, make up for all those years of celibacy while forcing herself to remain a good little girl. Vogel forces spectators not in a high-risk group to consider for the first time the possibility of their own impending deaths, struck down by a mysterious illness the government doesn't care to fight fiercely. An AIDS play for those unaware souls who ignore the epidemic's ravages, *The Baltimore Waltz* proves another Vogel comedy which wins our sympathies before showing its hand: only after we can't help caring about Anna does the play, by substituting slides of Baltimore for views of Europe, let us know she's merely a surrogate for her dying sibling, AIDS-victim Carl (Vogel's brother, to whose memory she dedicates the play "because I cannot sew"). This ferocious comedy, playful and poignant, written in lieu of a panel for the AIDS memorial quilt, veers quickly then from nightmarish satire of medical quackery, to bereavement, to a magical waltz.

The plays which tackle violence, however, cannot offer such an upbeat conclusion. *Hot 'n' Throbbing* tells the truth: domestic violence escalates to murder. And *Desdemona* creates no happy ending to avoid its protagonist's death. We're stuck with how Shakespeare ends his play—though Vogel stops her comedy's action prior to that tragedy's crisis. Yet the intersection of their plots at *Desdemona*'s conclusion in the hair-brushing scene renders chilling the loss of life awaiting the high-spirited woman we've been delighting in earlier.

Vogel's imaginative recreation of Desdemona provides us with everything which Shakespeare denies us: full portraits of the three women (the only characters here), high spirits which do not willingly suffer their men's foolishness, no easy acquiescence to being victimized, even a lusty, frank sexuality. This provocative, startling comedy takes from Shakespeare its setting in Cyprus, Amelia's theft of the handkerchief, and the women's names. But where Shakespeare's Desdemona today must appear foolish to endure Othello's violent and unwarranted jealousy, Vogel's gives him cause to be jealous by exulting in an earthy, exuberant sexuality as she beds every man on the island save Cassio. Weaving such irony through her short, pithy episodes Vogel depicts women as often coarse, mainly honest, and so sensual they seem on the verge of seducing each other. The women's relations are marred, however, by petty jealousies, betrayals, and rivalries.

Vogel shows us we must blame the social system, implicitly responsible for denying the women sisterhood in a common cause, forcing them instead to depend on destructive men who exercise over them the power of life and death. Denied meaningful, remunerative employment, a woman can slave in a kitchen while promoting the advancement of a husband she despises (Amelia's choice), run a bawdy house (Bianca's choice), or prostitute herself (Desdemona's choice). Separated by class, financial status, and education (like the women in Wendy Kesselman's *My Sister in This House*), the women trust each other too little, too late—and therefore Desdemona will die, ironically having just made plans to leave her husband the next morning.

Ostensibly more in control, *Hot 'n' Throbbing*'s Charlene, an empowered, professional woman and feminist, has obtained a restraining order against the husband who has beaten her for years. At her computer, she supports herself and her kids by writing women's erotica for a feminist film company; like Desdemona's hooking, this has earned her independence. Yet gender power imbalances leave her vulnerable to violence. The husband breaks down the door, manipulates both her compassion for him and their teenagers' responses, and finally kills her.

Charlene has created powerful images of a dominant woman and submissive partner, but later, just before she is murdered, a male crew reverse the roles and turn the script into a snuff film. Even the daughter has fantasized about bondage and pain. If Vogel permits us any hope for women at this funny but dark and frightening play's conclusion, it emerges when the daughter dons knee-socks, flannel shirt, overalls, and heavy boots, thereby ensuring she's no sex object, before taking her own place at the computer. There she begins to write the play we've just seen, the sort of play Paula Vogel dramatizes, with the power to transform people and thus alter the world.

—Tish Dace

VONNEGUT, Kurt, Jr. American. Born in 1922. See 3rd edition, 1982.

W

WALCOTT, Derek (Alton). British. Born in Castries, St. Lucia, West Indies, 23 January 1930. Educated at St. Mary's College, Castries, 1941–47; University College of the West Indies, Mona, Jamaica, 1950–54, B.A. 1953. Married 1) Fay Moyston in 1954 (divorced 1959), one son; 2) Margaret Ruth Maillard in 1962 (divorced), two daughters; 3) Norline Metivier in 1982. Teacher, St. Mary's College, Castries, 1947–50 and 1954, Grenada Boy's Secondary School, St. George's, Grenada, 1953–54, and Jamaica College, Kingston, 1955; feature writer, *Public Opinion*, Kingston, 1956–57; feature writer, 1960–62, and drama critic, 1963–68, *Trinidad Guardian*, Port-of-Spain. Co-founder, St. Lucia Arts Guild, 1950, and Basement Theatre, Port-of-Spain; founding director, Little Carib Theatre Workshop (later Trinidad Theatre Workshop), 1959–76. Assistant professor of creative writing, 1981, and since 1985 visiting professor, Boston University. Visiting professor, Columbia University, New York, 1981, and Harvard University, Cambridge, Massachusetts, 1982, 1987. Recipient: Rockefeller grant, 1957, 1966, and fellowship, 1958; Arts Advisory Council of Jamaica prize, 1960; Guinness award, 1961; Ingram Merrill Foundation grant, 1962; Borestone Mountain award, 1964, 1977; Royal Society of Literature Heinemann award, 1966, 1983; Cholmondeley award, 1969; Audrey Wood fellowship, 1969; Eugene O'Neill Foundation fellowship, 1969; Gold Hummingbird medal (Trinidad), 1969; Obie award, for drama, 1971; Jock Campbell award (*New Statesman*), 1974; Guggenheim award, 1977; *American Poetry Review* award, 1979; Welsh Arts Council International Writers prize, 1980; MacArthur fellowship, 1981; Los Angeles *Times* prize, 1986; Queen's gold medal for poetry, 1988; W.H. Smith award, for poetry, 1991; Nobel prize, for literature, 1992. D. Litt.: University of the West Indies, Mona, 1973. Fellow, Royal Society of Literature, 1966; Honorary Member, American Academy, 1979. O.B.E. (Officer, Order of the British Empire), 1972. Agent: Bridget Aschenberg, International Famous Agency, 1301 Avenue of the Americas, New York, New York 10019, U.S.A. Address: 165 Duke of Edinburgh Avenue, Diego Martin, Trinidad.

PUBLICATIONS

Plays

Cry for a Leader (produced St. Lucia, 1950).
Senza Alcun Sospetto (broadcast 1950; as *Paolo and Francesca*, produced St. Lucia, 1951?).
Henri Christophe: A Chronicle (also director: produced Castries, 1950; London, 1952). Bridgetown, Barbados Advocate, 1950.
Robin and Andrea, published in *Bim* (Christ Church, Barbados), December 1950.
Three Assassins (produced St. Lucia, 1951?).
The Price of Mercy (produced St. Lucia, 1951?).
Harry Dernier (as *Dernier*, broadcast 1952; as *Harry Dernier*,

also director: produced Mona, 1952). Bridgetown, Barbados Advocate, 1952.
The Sea at Dauphin (produced Trinidad, 1954; London, 1960; New York, 1978). Mona, University College of the West Indies Extra-Mural Department, 1954; in *Dream on Monkey Mountain and Other Plays*, 1970.
Crossroads (produced Jamaica, 1954).
The Charlatan (also director: produced Mona, 1954?; revised version, music by Fred Hope and Rupert Dennison, produced Port-of-Spain, 1973; revised version, music by Galt MacDermot, produced Los Angeles, 1974; revised version produced Port-of-Spain, 1977).
The Wine of the Country (also director: produced Mona, 1956).
The Golden Lions (also director: produced Mona, 1956).
Ione: A Play with Music (produced Kingston, 1957). Mona, University College of the West Indies Extra-Mural Department, 1957.
Ti-Jean and His Brothers (produced Castries, 1957; revised version, also director: produced Port-of-Spain, 1958; Hanover, New Hampshire, 1971; also director: produced New York, 1972; London, 1986). Included in *Dream on Monkey Mountain and Other Plays*, 1970.
Drums and Colours (produced Port-of-Spain, 1958). Published in *Caribbean Quarterly* (Mona), vol. 7, nos. 1 and 2, 1961.
Malcochon; or, The Six in the Rain (produced Castries, 1959; as *The Six in the Rain*, produced London, 1960; as *Malcochon*, produced New York, 1969). Included in *Dream on Monkey Mountain and Other Plays*, 1970.
Jourmard; or, A Comedy till the Last Minute (produced St. Lucia, 1959; New York, 1962).
Batai (carnival show; also director: produced Port-of-Spain, 1965).
Dream on Monkey Mountain (also director: produced Toronto, 1967; Waterford, Connecticut, 1969; New York, 1970). Included in *Dream on Monkey Mountain and Other Plays*, 1970.
Franklin: A Tale of the Islands (produced Georgetown, Guyana, 1969; revised version, also director: produced Port-of-Spain, 1973).
In a Fine Castle (also director: produced Mona, 1970; Los Angeles, 1972). Excerpt, as *Conscience of a Revolutionary*, published in *Express* (Port-of-Spain), 24 October 1971.
Dream on Monkey Mountain and Other Plays (includes *Ti-Jean and His Brothers*, *Malcochon*, *The Sea at Dauphin*, and the essay "What the Twilight Says"). New York, Farrar Straus, 1970; London, Cape, 1972.
The Joker of Seville, music by Galt MacDermot, adaptation of the play by Tirso de Molina (produced Port-of-Spain, 1974). With *O Babylon!*, New York, Farrar Straus, 1978; London, Cape, 1979.
O Babylon!, music by Galt MacDermot (also director: produced Port-of-Spain, 1976; London, 1988). With *The Joker of Seville*, New York, Farrar Straus, 1978; London, Cape, 1979.

Remembrance (also director: produced St. Croix, U.S. Virgin Islands, 1977; New York, 1979, London, 1980). With *Pantomime*, New York, Farrar Straus, 1980.

The Snow Queen (television play), excerpt published in *People* (Port-of-Spain), April 1977.

Pantomime (produced Port-of-Spain, 1978; London, 1979; Washington, D.C., 1981; New York, 1986). With *Remembrance*, New York, Farrar Straus, 1980.

Marie Laveau, music by Galt MacDermot (also director: produced St. Thomas, U.S. Virgin Islands, 1979). Excerpts published in *Trinidad and Tobago Review* (Tunapuna), Christmas 1979.

The Isle Is Full of Noises (produced Hartford, Connecticut, 1982).

Beef, No Chicken (produced New Haven, Connecticut, 1982; London, 1989). Included in *Three Plays*, 1986.

Three Plays (includes *The Last Carnival*; *Beef, No Chicken*; *A Branch of the Blue Nile*). New York, Farrar Straus, 1986.

The Last Carnival (produced Stockholm, Sweden, 1992). Included in *Three Plays*, 1986.

To Die for Granada (produced Cleveland, Ohio, 1986).

The Odyssey, adaptation of the epic by Homer (produced Stratford-on-Avon, 1992).

Radio Plays: *Senza Alcun Sospetto*, 1950; *Dernier*, 1952.

Verse

25 Poems. Port-of-Spain, Guardian Commercial Printery, 1948.

Epitaph for the Young: XII Cantos. Bridgetown, Barbados Advocate, 1949.

Poems. Kingston, Jamaica, City Printery, 1951.

In a Green Night: Poems 1948–1960. London, Cape, 1962.

Selected Poems. New York, Farrar Straus, 1964.

The Castaway and Other Poems. London, Cape, 1965.

The Gulf and Other Poems. London, Cape, 1969; as *The Gulf*, New York, Farrar Straus, 1970.

Another Life. New York, Farrar Straus, and London, Cape, 1973.

Sea Grapes. London, Cape, and New York, Farrar Straus, 1976.

The Star-Apple Kingdom. New York, Farrar Straus, 1979; London, Cape, 1980.

Selected Poetry, edited by Wayne Brown. London, Heinemann, 1981.

The Fortunate Traveller. New York, Farrar Straus, 1981; London, Faber, 1982.

The Caribbean Poetry of Derek Walcott and the Art of Romare Bearden. New York, Limited Editions Club, 1983.

Midsummer. New York, Farrar Straus, and London, Faber, 1984.

Collected Poems 1948–1984. New York, Farrar Straus, and London, Faber, 1986.

The Arkansas Testament. New York, Farrar Straus, 1987; London, Faber, 1988.

Omeros. New York, Farrar Straus, 1989; London, Faber, 1990.

*

Bibliography: *Derek Walcott: An Annotated Bibliography of His Works* by Irma E. Goldstraw, New York, Garland, 1984.

Critical Studies: *Derek Walcott: Memory as Vision* by Edward Baugh, London, Longman, 1978; *Derek Walcott: Poet of the Islands* by Ned Thomas, Cardiff, Welsh Arts Council, 1980; *Derek Walcott* by Robert D. Hamner, Boston, Twayne, 1981; *The Art of Derek Walcott* edited by Stewart Brown, Bridgend, Glamorgan, Seren, 1989.

Theatrical Activities:
Director: many of his own plays.

*   *   *

Although primarily a poet—and as such, one of the best writing in English today—Derek Walcott is also an accomplished playwright, whose interest in drama was kindled at an early age. A youthful stage designer, he has for some time supervised acting workshops in Trinidad, where he has also campaigned for the establishment of a national Caribbean theatre. His plays afford dramatic treatment to themes expressed in his poetry, exploring concepts of personal and racial identity, the brooding presence of evil, and the inevitability of exile and separation. Walcott's efforts to comprehend and utilize the nature of his own mixed ancestry in his writing explain much of the tension and conflict that underlies his work. The descendant of European masters and African slaves officially denied a history of their own, he strives in poems and dramas alike to maintain a balance between the two. Walcott's affection for European literature, demonstrated clearly in his mastery of poetic and dramatic styles, is genuine but wary, and in his recent play, *The Last Carnival*, he indicates the dangers of wholesale acceptance of European models by Caribbean artists. At the same time he strongly asserts the heritage of his black forebears, drawing on patterns of Caribbean speech, and African-derived chanting, drumming, and dance in many of his plays. His vision focuses powerfully on the quest for self-knowledge and self-realization in a world where, as the child of two conflicting cultures, he might fairly claim with his fictional character Shabine: "I had no nation now but the imagination."

Walcott's early dramas present native Caribbean figures in heroic and tragic roles, countering the accepted European pantheon of "greats." For a writer trying to recreate a history with meaning for his black compatriots, the Haitian revolution offers evident attractions. *Henri Christophe: A Chronicle* portrays the life, ambition, and eventual downfall of the rebel who became Emperor of Haiti, and Walcott has returned more recently to the events of this period with *Haitian Earth* (as yet unproduced). More typical of his work as a dramatist are those plays which have lowly, downtrodden peasants as their leading characters. In *Malcochon*, *The Sea at Dauphin*, and *Dream on Monkey Mountain* woodcutters, charcoal-burners, and fishermen take centre stage, their subsistence lifestyles presented in the bleakest possible light. Walcott strips away all heroic pretensions from them, revealing his creations as squalid, vulnerable individuals. Makak, for instance, whose nightmare vision provides the core of the play in *Dream on Monkey Mountain*, bears a name which invites comparison with the simian macaque. This allusion to mankind's prehuman ancestry is clear in the text itself: "In the beginning was the ape, and the ape had no name, so God called him man." A further, sinister dimension is also suggested, in the dehumanizing racist stereotype of all blacks as monkeys. Makak, in his dream, struggles to free himself from the power of the White Goddess, whiteness here—as in *Moby Dick*—symbolizing death and negation. With its bleak, compelling insights, its presentation of "the wretched of the earth," *Dream on Monkey Mountain* ranks among Walcott's strongest dramatic statements. Another significant work, *Ti-Jean and His Brothers*, makes effective use of drumming and chanting as background to a play whose dialogue is imbued with Creole speech patterns. Ti-Jean, the untutored peasant, holds the central role in a Caribbean morality play, encountering and overcoming the Devil in his many guises by a combination of luck and mother-wit. His victory, achieved at tragic cost, is given a native context by its "chorus" of chants and drum-rhythms. *The Joker of Seville* reveals talent of another kind, being a remarkable reworking of the Don Juan legend from Molina's Spanish original in which Walcott reshapes the classic material to a valid creation of his own. Following Juan, the amoral, heartless lecher-hero, to his final destruction, he sets the action not in Spain but Trinidad, where Latin and African cultures fuse uneasily together. The stage is devised as a symbolic bull-ring where stick-fighters and masked dancers echo the dialogue with comments and chanted choruses. *O Babylon!* has a more modern setting, its action centring on a confrontation between developers and Rastafarian squatters on the eve of Haile Selassie's visit to Jamaica. Walcott presents scenario and players in a manner at once comic and profound, the complex natures and motives of his characters displayed in speeches which make inspired use of Rastafarian, Jamaican, and English languages. Music and dance again complement the inevitable irony of the play's conclusion.

Three Plays, an impressive triptych from the 1980s, shows Walcott once more exploring major themes in a contemporary Trinidadian setting. *The Last Carnival* traces the shared relationships of a land-owning Creole family and their "adopted" English sibling as colonialism gives way to independence, and the trauma of revolution. The image of the carnival—at once a vain attempt by the thwarted artist Victor to impose the canons of European culture on his unresponsive audience, and a symbolic final gesture of the old order—is effectively contrasted with the surface radicalism of the young revolutionaries, for whom war is another kind of carnival, and one equally doomed to failure. The gradual change in Agatha, the working-class English woman who renounces her own radical politics on Victor's death to become the mainstay of the establishment, is convincingly shown, as is her tense relationship with the isolated, unbalanced Victor and his earthy Creolised brother Oswald. In the end, the one hope for salvation is the exile chosen by Clodia, the Agatha of a new generation. *Beef, No Chicken*, like *O Babylon!*, presents the conflict of developers and "little men" in terms of comic farce. Its central theme is the struggle of small-time restaurateur Otto Hogan to fight off the efforts of a corrupt council to bypass his premises with a major highway. Modern reality is represented by the shopping-mall magnate Mongroo, who regards bribery and coercion as an integral part of "civilization," and a mayor who sees pollution as evidence of progress. Otto's futile attempts to hold up the road by "haunting" workmen in the guise of a female ghost are complicated by a hilariously varied cast which includes a television crew, Cuban revolutionaries, and the members of the council. In the end, he is forced to abandon his principles and join the rat-race, running for mayor as the council and Mongroo are exposed on television. *A Branch of the Blue Nile* is set in a small theatre workshop in Port-of-Spain, and follows the lives of actors and director as they examine their relationships through rehearsals, improvisations, and performance in a modern version of *Antony and Cleopatra*. Walcott depicts players and setting superbly in a powerful, moving drama where acting is presented as a holy or profane transformation, a state of grace or possession which defines

and limits the continuing flux of life. The poetic strength of his dialogue—in blank verse speeches, taped conversations, and island dialect—lends an individual voice to all three plays, and in particular to the last, which is surely one of his most impressive achievements.

—Geoff Sadler

WALKER, George F(rederick). Canadian. Born in Toronto, Ontario, 23 August 1947. Educated at Riverdale Collegiate, Toronto, graduated 1965. Married Susan Purdy in 1980; two daughters. Playwright-in-residence, 1971–76, and artistic director, 1978–79, Factory Theatre Lab, Toronto; resident playwright, New York Shakespeare Festival, 1981. Recipient: Canada Council grant, 1971 (and 4 subsequent grants); Chalmers award, 3 times; Governor-General's award, 1986. Agent: Great North Artists, 350 Dupont Street, Toronto, Ontario M5V 1V9, Canada.

PUBLICATIONS

Plays

The Prince of Naples (produced Toronto, 1971). Toronto, Playwrights, 1972.
Ambush at Tether's End (produced Toronto, 1971). Toronto, Playwrights, 1972.
Sacktown Rag (produced Toronto, 1972). Toronto, Playwrights, 1972.
Bagdad Saloon (produced Toronto and London, 1973). Toronto, Playwrights, 1973.
Demerit (produced Toronto, 1974).
Beyond Mozambique (produced Toronto, 1974). Toronto, Playwrights, 1975.
Ramona and the White Slaves (also director: produced Toronto, 1976). Included in *Three Plays*, 1978.
Gossip (produced Toronto and Chicago, 1977). Toronto, Playwrights, 1980.
Zastrozzi, The Master of Discipline (produced Toronto, 1977; London, 1978; Seattle, 1979; New York, 1982). Toronto, Playwrights, 1977.
Three Plays (includes *Bagdad Saloon*, *Beyond Mozambique*, *Ramona and the White Slaves*). Toronto, Coach House Press, 1978.
Filthy Rich (produced Toronto, 1979; Evanston, Illinois, 1982; London, 1984; New York, 1985). Toronto, Playwrights, 1981.
Rumours of Our Death, music by John Roby, lyrics by Walker and Roby (also director: produced Toronto, 1980). Published in *Canadian Theatre Review* (Downsview, Ontario), Winter 1980.
Theatre of the Film Noir (also director: produced Toronto, 1981; London, 1983). Toronto, Playwrights, 1981.
Science and Madness (produced Toronto, 1982). Toronto, Playwrights, 1982.
The Art of War: An Adventure (also director: produced Toronto, 1983; New York 1987). Toronto, Playwrights, 1983.
Criminals in Love (produced Toronto, 1984). Toronto, Playwrights, 1985.

The Power Plays (includes *Gossip*, *Filthy Rich*, *The Art of War*).   Toronto, Coach House Press, 1984.
Better Living (produced Toronto, 1986; Poughkeepsie, New York, 1987).   Included in *East End Plays*, 1987.
Beautiful City (produced Toronto, 1987).   Included in *East End Plays*. 1987.
East End Plays (includes *Criminals in Love*, *Better Living*, *Beautiful City*).   Toronto, Playwrights, 1987.
Nothing Sacred, adaptation of Turgenev's *Fathers and Sons* (produced Los Angeles, 1988; New York, 1992).   Toronto, Coach House Press, 1988.
Love and Anger.   Toronto, Coach House Press, 1990.

Radio Plays: *The Private Man*, 1973.

Television plays: *Sam, Grace, Doug, and the Dog*, 1976; *Microdrama*, 1976; *Strike*, 1976; *Overlap*, 1977; *Capital Punishment*, 1977.

*

Critical Studies: *Factory Lab Anthology* edited by Connie Brissenden, Vancouver, Talonbooks, 1974; "Playnotes" by Richard Horenblas, in *Scene Changes* (Toronto) October 1975; in *University of Toronto Quarterly*, Spring 1980.

Theatrical Activities:
Director: **Plays**—some of his own plays; *The Extremist* by Ilya Denykin, Toronto, 1976.

*   *   *

George F. Walker's origins are in the theatre of the absurd. The earliest plays have situations and humour similar to those of *Waiting for Godot* and Stoppard's plays. In *Ambush at Tether's End* a corpse hangs upstage while Galt and Bush engage in dialogue like that of Vladimir and Estragon or Rosencrantz and Guildenstern as they wait for someone to take responsibility. Notes found on the corpse humorously introduce themes of free will and determinism, liberty and responsibility. Trapped in a situation they did not create, unable to act, the two repeatedly attempt suicide but lack the courage. The play is characterised by verbal wit, idiomatic absurdities ("you're here to put your foot down if it gets out of hand"), and economical development of character.

Written during a time when American legends were becoming the subject matter of literature, *Bagdad Saloon* shows the inappropriateness of American myths to other nations. Such American characters in the play as Henry Miller, Gertrude Stein, and Doc Halliday assume they are famous and act as they wish, whereas the non-Americans seek a formula to imitate. Significantly, the heir to the legendary heroes of the Old West and the American writers of the Left Bank is a soldier who returns from the war in Vietnam, thus ending illusions about America. This period of chaotic, highly fragmented, cartoon-like dramas, with their exaggerated actions and simplified characters, continues with *Beyond Mozambique*, a take-off on art about exotic places. While the natives beat drums and collect arms to rebel, the mad Europeans, like many of Walker's characters, no longer can distinguish reality from fantasy. There are parodies of *The Three Sisters*, *Frankenstein*, Graham Greene's "whisky priest," and Hollywood films. Evil appears to rule; society is in a state of collapse and no one knows what to do or much cares. The starkly bleak vision of *Ramona and the White Slaves* probes the depths of the psyche, its perversions, the nature of power, and the wild instability of emotions.

Although the setting is once more exotic, Hong Kong in 1919, we learn that the play may be an opium dream; all the slavery, mutilation, rape, and guilt is metaphoric of "the story of a family." The same characters, situations, and themes recur from play to play, including detectives, whores, incest, harsh family conflict, disguises, and ruined lives.

The investigation of power and evil is central to *Zastrozzi, The Master of Discipline*. A study in obsessive revenge and will to dominate, Zastrozzi appears a creature from the feudal past, with his whips, demand for slave-like obedience, and hatred (in 1896) of Impressionist art. He is driven by a code of honour and refuses introspection of his motives or examination of rights or wrongs. Underlying his brutality is a view of life as arbitrary, which he covers up through activity. Zastrozzi is opposed by Victor, the modern, liberal, rational man, who is unable to kill him even when he has the opportunity and, like many of Walker's voices of conscience, is bound to fail. *Zastrozzi* is more unified than the plays that preceded it. The characters are representative archetypes of western civilization. As Walker's work develops, narrative becomes increasingly important, as is the opposition between the power of evil and the weakness of good. *Zastrozzi* has the grotesque melodrama of Jacobean tragedy, and is visually powerful because of its whippings, sword displays, love-making, and murders.

Walker's aesthetics, based on parody, pastiche, and caricature of popular, exotic, and past art, is a product of postmodernism with its collapse of artistic distinctions. The problem is how to go beyond the limitations of junk art. In the three "Power plays"—*Gossip*, *Filthy Rich*, and *The Art of War*—Walker imitates the conventions of popular art forms for a trilogy meditating on the nature, use, and misuse of power. Tyrone M. Power (the name ironically alludes to the movie star, although this Tyrone Power is short and balding) is first an investigative reporter (allowing Walker to parody the hardboiled journalist films of the 1930's) and later a hard-drinking, cynical, but really soft-hearted private detective. *Gossip* and *Filthy Rich* have similarities to Raymond Chandler's stories of Los Angeles political corruption, and the moral corruption of the rich and their influential, attractive daughters. At first a loner, then in *Filthy Rich* joined by Jamie, a young working-class Sancho Panza with a more practical bent, Power quixotically takes on the local political establishment, uncovering their crimes, but earns nothing by it except to lose what friends he has and make himself more cynical. In *Gossip* he finds that he is being used by others, who for revenge want corruption exposed. The romantic individualism of the investigative reporter and private eye pays off neither financially nor emotionally. By the time of *The Art of War* Power has become a Sherlock Holmes fighting a losing battle against his Moriarty, an international master criminal who must win because Power, unwilling to rely on the police, is unwilling to shoot the arch-criminal when he has him at his mercy. While the criminal laughs at him and escapes, Power can only ponder, Hamlet-like, his inaction. The play was originally written for performance before an anti-war group.

The struggle between good and evil continues in *Science and Madness*, with its horror-film conventions, and becomes confused in *Theatre of the Film Noir*, which begins with a French police inspector—in a pastiche of cheap French detective fiction and grade-B film voice-overs—warning that as it is the first days of the liberation of Paris from German occupation all order has broken down and there is no clear standard of morality or absolute guilt. He investigates the recent killing of a young Resistance fighter. The suspects include the Communists who need a martyr, the young man's homosexual lover who is a dangerous psychopath, and the young man's sister, a collaborationist with whom he had incestuous relations and who fears exposure of her German-Nazi officer lover with whom her brother had a homosexual relationship. Walker is concerned with the breakdown of significance, the instability and unpredictability of character. Morality has become a question of circumstance. People make themselves through violence, dominance, and deception.

Walker's characters and situations, filled with insults, violence, surprises, and rapid action, are outrageous and require an unpolished acting style. Everything is stripped down, there is no waste. In *Criminals in Love* two innocent teenagers, trapped by their environment and lacking the will to break free, find themselves eventually transformed from unwilling accomplices of criminals to defiantly armed terrorists. Things always go wrong in Walker's plays for those who allow themselves to be manipulated by the strong and unscrupulous. The play is very funny and visually memorable. It opens in a schoolyard with a young man's head under a girl's sweater while he derives pleasure from her breasts; at the play's conclusion they return to the same posture, but now armed and surrounded by police.

—Bruce King

WALKER, Joseph A. American. Born in Washington, D.C., 23 February 1935. Educated at Howard University, Washington, D.C., B.A. in philosophy 1956; Catholic University, Washington, D.C., M.F.A. 1970. Served in the United States Air Force: 2nd lieutenant. Married 1) Barbara Brown (divorced 1965); 2) Dorothy A. Dinroe in 1970. Worked as taxi driver, salesman, and postal clerk; English teacher in Washington, D.C., and New York; actor with the Negro Ensemble Company, New York, from 1969; playwright-in-residence, Yale University, New Haven, Connecticut, 1970; taught at City College, New York, 1970's; currently member of the drama department, Howard University. Address: Department of Drama, Howard University, 2400 6th Street, N.W., Washington, D.C. 20059, U.S.A.

PUBLICATIONS

Plays

The Believers, with Josephine Jackson, music and lyrics by Benjamin Carter and others (produced New York, 1968).
The Harangues (produced New York, 1969). Shortened version, as *Tribal Harangue Two*, in *The Best Short Plays 1971*, edited by Stanley Richards, Philadelphia, Chilton, 1971.
Ododo (also director: produced New York, 1970). Published in *Black Drama Anthology*, edited by Ron Milner and Woodie King, New York, New American Library, 1971.
The River Niger (produced New York, 1972). New York, Hill and Wang, 1973.
Yin Yang, music by Dorothy A. Dinroe-Walker (also director: produced New York, 1973).
Antigone Africanus (produced New York, 1975).
The Lion Is a Soul Brother (also director: produced New York, 1976).
District Line (produced New York, 1984).

Screenplay: *The River Niger*, 1976.

*

Theatrical Activities:
Director: several of his own plays.
Actor: **Plays**—*The Believers*, New York, 1968; *Cities in Bezique* by Adrienne Kennedy, New York, 1969. **Films**—*April Fools*, 1969; *Bananas*, 1971. **Television**—*NYPD* series; *In Black America* (narrator).

* * *

The dramas of Joseph A. Walker explore various aspects of black life such as male-female relationships, interracial strife, and family and community bonds. However, the focus of most of his works is on the psyche of black American males. Cut off from their ancestral home and exploited by whites, these disoriented men are portrayed as lacking a sense of identity, purpose, and self-worth. Efforts by some of these men to obtain power and wealth are most often thwarted by white America's black sycophants. Whether or not one agrees with this simplistic ideology, frequently exhorted in the 1960's and 1970's, Walker's plays are still relevant because of their compelling depictions of those black males stagnated by feelings of impotence, frustration, and hopelessness.

While the black male characters are deftly drawn and complex, Walker's portraits of black women and whites rarely escape the limitations of stereotypes. Black women seldom have any personal goals, but instead function as either supporters or "castrators" of their men. White women serve as sexual playmates and status symbols for their black lovers. White men exploit blacks and destroy those who pose a threat to their way of life. Lacking depth and plausible motivations for their actions, these characters weaken the credibility of Walker's plays.

As its title suggests, *The Harangues* is used as a vehicle for the playwright to vent his opinions. Composed of two episodes and two one-act plays, the work portrays a despairing view of black life. In the first episode, a 15th-century West African man chooses to kill his son rather than subject him to life as a slave in the New World. The second episode mirrors the first by showing a contemporary black American revolutionary who kills his child rather than allow him to grow up in a despondent society. Black women plead for their children's lives in the episodes, but are conspicuously absent in the one-acts. The first one-act, set in Washington, D.C., concerns a black male and his pregnant white fiancée. Incredibly, with little hesitation, the white woman agrees to assist her lover in the murder of her father who will disinherit her if she marries. However, the plan backfires and results in the death of the scheming black man due to the actions of a traitorous black "friend." In the second one-act, unless they can convince him of their worthiness to live, a deranged black man threatens to kill his three captives: a white liberal and an assimilationist black man and his white lover. After exposing their perverted lives, only the white woman who endures several sexual indignities is deemed to be virtuous. However, as the death penalty is being carried out, the woman takes a bullet meant for her contemptible black lover. In an ensuing struggle, the assimilationist gains control of his captor's gun and kills him. As in the first one-act, a desperate black man dies at the hands of a black minion of the white race.

In sharp contrast to the pessimistic outlook which envelopes *The Harangues*, *The River Niger* celebrates the enduring qualities of the black man and offers a hopeful vision of the future. Johnny Williams, a middle-aged house painter and poet living in Harlem, uses liquor to escape the bleak reality of a life stagnated by unrealized dreams. Johnny places his hopes for the future in his son Jeff's career in the air force. But his son's homecoming brings another disappointment to Johnny's life. Jeff admits that he was dismissed from the military which he abhored. He contends his ouster was due to his refusal to be a "supernigger"—a black man who tries to prove he has capabilities comparable to whites. He further announces he will no longer be bound by familial and societal expectations but will instead seek only to fulfill his own needs and desires. Despite his intentions, Jeff soon finds himself involved in the self-destructive affairs of his former gang. When prison terms appear imminent for Jeff and the gang after they are betrayed by one of their members, Johnny has a shoot-out with the traitor which results in both of their deaths. But before Johnny dies, he demands to take the rap for the shooting and the gang's alleged offense. Johnny's wife Mattie admonishes her family and the gang not to fail to cooperate and carry out her husband's wishes. Johnny's heroic gesture provides Jeff and other gang members with a new lease on life and a powerful example of the unconditional selfless love that a father can have for his son.

The portraits of the men are well crafted and realistic. The characters function as representatives of differing moral values, abilities, aspirations, and perspectives within the black community. Johnny emerges as the most eloquent and convincing spokesman who, through his poem "The River Niger," speaks of the need to be cognizant of one's unbreakable link to all people of African descent.

Although the play's black women represent various age groups and cultures, they share similar attitudes toward their men. The women serve their men's needs with little concern for their own desires or ambitions. Mattie even accepts the fact that her husband chooses to confide in his West Indian friend instead of her. Incredibly, during a conversation between Mattie and Jeff's South African lover, Johnny's wife agrees with the younger woman that women are incapable of having a similar type of relationship because "women don't trust one another." Despite this and several other questionable remarks made by the women, their behavior as selfless and loyal supporters of their men foreshadows the concluding message of the play. As Johnny's final actions and his demand for cooperation demonstrate, survival of the race requires a communal effort with little thought of self-interest.

A Washington, D.C. taxi-stand serves as the setting for *District Line*. The play depicts a day in the lives of six cab drivers: two white and three black males and one black female. The drivers reveal their past experiences, present concerns, and aspirations as they interact with each other and their passengers. Black males continue to be Walker's most poignant characterizations. Of greatest interest are the scenes concerning two drivers—Doc, a moonlighting Howard University professor and Zilikazi, an exiled South African revolutionary. Women characters, whether black or white, appear to be gratuitous in the drama and remain stereotypes. However, the playwright does portray white men in roles other than the liberal or oppressor of blacks. Still, the work suffers in comparison to Walker's other plays because of a few fundamental flaws. Dramatic action is not adequately developed and sustained throughout the play and the work lacks a central theme to tie all the scenes together. Consequently, the drama fails to create the intense emotional impact characteristic of Walker's other plays.

—Addell Austin Anderson

WALTER, Nancy. American. Born in 1939. See 2nd edition, 1977.

WANDOR, Michelene (Dinah). British. Born in London, 20 April 1940. Educated at Chingford Secondary Modern School, 1954–56, and Chingford County High School, 1956–59, both Essex; Newnham College, Cambridge, 1959–62, B.A. (honours) in English 1962; University of Essex, Colchester, 1974–75, M.A. in sociology 1975. Married the literary agent Ed Victor in 1963 (divorced 1975); two sons. Poetry editor, *Time Out* magazine, London, 1971–82; regular contributor, *Spare Rib* magazine, London, 1972–77; reviewer, *Plays and Players*, *Listener*, and *New Statesman*, all London, and *Kaleidoscope* programme, BBC Radio. Playwright-in-residence, University of Kent, Canterbury, 1982–83. Currently student, performers' course in Renaissance and Baroque music, Trinity College of Music, London. Recipient: Arts Council bursary, 1974, 1983; Emmy award, 1987. Address: 71 Belsize Lane, London NW3 5AU, England.

PUBLICATIONS

Plays

You Too Can Be Ticklish (produced London, 1971).
Brag-a-Fruit (produced London, 1971).
The Day after Yesterday (produced London, 1972).
Spilt Milk, and Mal de Mère in *Point 101* (produced London, 1972). Published in *Play Nine*, edited Robin Rook, London, Arnold, 1981.
To Die among Friends (includes *Mal de Mère, Joey, Christmas, Pearls, Swallows*) (produced London, 1974). Included in *Sink Songs*, 1975.
Friends and Strangers (produced on tour, 1974).
Sink Songs, with Dinah Brooke. London, Playbooks, 1975.
Penthesilia, adaptation of the play by Heinrich von Kleist (produced London, 1977).
The Old Wives' Tale (produced London, 1977). Included in *Five Plays*, 1984.
Care and Control (produced London, 1977). Published in *Strike While the Iron Is Hot*, edited by Wandor, London, Journeyman Press, 1980.
Floorshow, with others (produced London, 1978).
Whores d'Oeuvres (produced London, 1978). Included in *Five Plays*, 1984.
Scissors (produced London, 1978). Included in *Five Plays*, 1984.
Aid Thy Neighbour (produced London, 1978). Included in *Five Plays*, 1984.
Correspondence (broadcast 1978; produced London, 1979).
Aurora Leigh, adaptation of the poem by Elizabeth Barrett Browning (produced London, 1979). Published in *Plays by Women 1*, edited by Wandor, London, Methuen, 1982.
Future Perfect, with Steve Gooch and Paul Thompson (produced on tour, 1980).
The Blind Goddess, adaptation of a play by Ernst Toller (produced on tour, 1981).
Five Plays (includes *To Die among Friends, The Old Wives' Tale, Whores d'Oeuvres, Scissors, Aid Thy Neighbour*).

London, Journeyman Press, 1984; New York, Riverrun Press, 1985.

The Wandering Jew, with Mike Alfreds, adaptation of a novel by Eugène Sue (produced London, 1987). London, Methuen, 1987.

Wanted (produced London, 1988). London, Playbooks, 1988.

Radio Plays and Serials: *Correspondence*, 1978; *The Unlit Lamp*, from the novel by Radclyffe Hall, 1980; *Precious Bane*, from the novel by Mary Webb, 1981; *Lolly Willowes*, from the novel by Sylvia Townsend Warner, 1983; *An Uncommon Love*, 1984; *Kipps*, from the novel by H.G. Wells, 1984; *Venus Smiles*, from the story by J.G. Ballard, 1985; *The Brothers Karamazov*, from a novel by Dostoevsky, 1986; *The Nine Tailors*, from the novel by Dorothy L. Sayers, 1986; *Persuasion*, from the novel by Jane Austen, 1986–87; *Helbeck of Bannisdale*, from the novel by Mrs. Humphry Ward, 1987; *Gardens of Eden*, 1987; *Whose Body?*, from the novel by Dorothy L. Sayers, 1987; *The Dwelling Place*, from the novel by Catherine Cookson, 1988; *Frenchman's Creek*, from the novel by Daphne du Maurier, 1989; *Ben Venga Maggio*, 1990; *The Courtier, the Prince and the Lady*, 1990; *The Mill on the Floss*, from the novel by George Eliot, 1991; *A Summer Wedding*, 1991; *Killing Orders*, from the novel by Sara Paretsky, 1991; *A Question of Courage*, from the novel by Marjorie Darke, 1992; *The King's General*, from the novel by Daphne du Maurier, 1992; *Deadlock*, from the novel by Sara Paretsky, 1993.

Television Plays: *The Belle of Amherst*, from the play by William Luce, 1987; *The Story of an Hour*, adaptation of a story by Kate Chopin, 1988.

Novel

Arky Types, with Sara Maitland. London, Methuen, 1987.

Short Stories

Tales I Tell My Mother, with others. London, Journeyman Press, 1978; Boston, South End Press, 1980.
Guests in the Body. London, Virago Press, 1986.
More Tales I Tell My Mother, with others. London, Journeyman Press, 1987.

Verse

Upbeat: Poems and Stories. London, Journeyman Press, 1982; New York, Riverrun Press, 1985.
Touch Papers, with Judith Kazantzis and Michèle Roberts. London, Allison and Busby, 1982.
Gardens of Eden: Poems for Eve and Lilith. London, Journeyman Press, 1984; New York, Riverrun Press, 1985.
Gardens of Eden: Selected Poems. London, Random Century, 1990.

Other

The Great Divide: The Sexual Division of Labour; or, Is It Art?, with others. Milton Keynes, Buckinghamshire, Open University Press, 1976.
Understudies: Theatre and Sexual Politics. London, Eyre Methuen, 1981; revised edition, as *Carry On, Understudies*, London, Routledge, 1986.
Look Back in Gender: Sexuality and the Family in Post-1956 British Drama. London, Methuen, 1987.

Wandor on Women Writers: Antonia White, Elizabeth Barrett Browning, Hannah Culwick, Dorothy Richardson, Jean Rhys. London, Journeyman Press, 1988.
Once a Feminist: Stories of a Generation. London, Virago, 1990.

Editor, *The Body Politic: Writings from the Women's Liberation Movement in Britain 1969–1972*. London, Stage 1, 1972.
Editor, with Michèle Roberts, *Cutlasses and Earrings* (poetry anthology). London, Playbooks, 1977.
Editor, *Strike While the Iron Is Hot: Three Plays on Sexual Politics*. London, Journeyman Press, 1980.
Editor, *Plays by Women 1–4*. London, Methuen, 4 vols., 1982–85.
Editor, *On Gender and Writing*. London, Pandora Press, 1983.

*

Critical Studies: "The Personal Is Political: Feminism and the Theatre" by Wandor, in *Dreams and Deconstructions* edited by Sandy Craig, Ambergate, Derbyshire, Amber Lane Press, 1980; *Feminist Theatre* by Helene Keyssar, London, Macmillan, 1984, New York, Grove Press, 1985.

Michelene Wandor comments:

I began writing plays in 1969, when the "fringe" began. I also was writing poetry and theatre reviews. For me the activities of fiction/non-fiction have always been complementary. At that time I became aware of, and developed, socialist and feminist convictions. For about ten years I wrote plays just for the stage, in a variety of forms—social realism, collage, surreal, comedy, abstract: whatever. Since 1979 I have written extensively for radio, a stimulating medium. I have dramatised/transposed a number of texts for radio—a way of working with the voices and styles of other writers that is both exciting and rewarding. I have absolutely no pre-conceived ideas about the appropriateness or otherwise of dramatic form. For me the appropriate form arrives as a combination of content and my approach to it. Having said that, I can also be lured by any subject. I have written a lot of female-centred work and male-centred work, and am always as aware as I can be of the way an inevitable (though variable) gender-bias operates in every drama.

*   *   *

Michelene Wandor is a playwright who is also known for her poetry and fiction, and for her writing about the theatre. In her theatre writing, Wandor established her reputation with two key texts: *Understudies: Theatre and Sexual Politics* and *Look Back in Gender: Sexuality and the Family in Post-1956 British Drama*. These books, and others to which she has contributed, have earned her a reputation as one of England's most flexible writers, adept at producing critical essays and overviews of the state of the theatre and at writing plays for theatre, radio, and television.

As a playwright, Wandor has worked in a wide variety of different contexts, from her early work with feminist collectives and fringe theatre companies, to her work for the Royal National Theatre and the BBC. Some of her plays have been published in anthologies with playwrights such as Howard Brenton and Frank Marcus, marking her as one of the most notable "political playwrights" of her generation. She is also one of the few women—along with more "mainstream" playwrights such as Caryl Churchill, Pam Gems, and Louise

Page—who was in on the watershed of women's alternative theatre in the 1970's. She has worked with and for Monstrous Regiment, Mrs. Worthington's Daughters, and Gay Sweatshop, as an independent playwright, and as a commissioned writer of radio and television drama.

Wandor is best known for a few early stage plays and for a number of highly successful radio dramas. She attributes the high profile of her radio plays to the fashion in contemporary theatre for "conservative" forms, styles, and themes, including the current popularity of dramatic adaptations. In her words:

> If theatre had not become so conservative so quickly, and if the theatre had retained its early 1970's openness, more of my work would be done in the theatre. Basically, to be successful in the theatre as a woman playwright, you need to have patrons who will bandwagon you. To work well in radio some similar things apply, but I genuinely believe that there are more radio producers whose commitment is to the work rather than to the fashion.

The comment reflects on the nature of Wandor's writing, which is always informed by politics; whether social, cultural, sexual, or personal. Thus, it has been Wandor's adaptations which, on the whole, have best suited the "conservative" trend of theatre production. Her best radio work includes *Ben Venga Maggio*, a dramatic poem in the voice of the popular character Columbina; it is a play which blends spoken language and Italian carnival music. Another notable radio play of the same period is *The Courtier, the Prince and the Lady*, which is set in Renaissance Italy and draws on Machiavelli and Castiglione as source material, while incorporating the music of Josquin and his contemporaries. In 1991, Wandor adapted George Eliot's *The Mill on the Floss* in a five-part serial dramatization. She has since adapted feminist detective stories by Sarah Paretsky and some of the writings of Marjorie Darke.

Wandor has also had considerable success in television drama. She won an Emmy award for her television adaptation of William Luce's play about the life of Emily Dickinson, *The Belle of Amherst*. In 1988, she wrote a short film adaptation of Kate Chopin's *The Story of an Hour*. *The Well Woman*, her television adaptation of Radclyffe Hall's *The Well of Loneliness*, has yet to be produced.

Yet Wandor's most characteristic work is found in her own original stage plays. One important contribution to British theatre was her scripting, from devised and group-researched material, of Gay Sweatshop's *Care and Control* in 1977. That play was among the first political theatre pieces to address the issue of the state and motherhood. It had a considerable social impact as well as theatrical and critical success, as did *Aid Thy Neighbour*, produced at London's New End Theatre in 1978. The latter play offered a frank treatment of the process of artificial insemination by donor, another crucial issue for contemporary women. In these and many of her other stage plays, Wandor combined her feminist politics and social activism in her writing for the stage. While some of her work could be described by labels such as "agitprop" or "social realism," Wandor herself would be the first to qualify and explain these terms. In fact, analysis of the influence of politics on the theatre of the 1970's and 1980's is one of the threads running through Wandor's critical writing about the theatre. For Wandor, playwriting and political involvement (real and representational) tend to go hand in hand.

Partly for reasons related to the politics (and "fashionability") of radio and theatre production, Wandor wrote more and more adaptations in the 1980's, including *Aurora*

Leigh—an adaptation of Elizabeth Barrett Browning's poem —produced by Mrs. Worthington's Daughters in 1979 and revived at the Royal National Theatre in 1981. Her major mainstage theatre success was also an adaptation: *The Wandering Jew*, co-written with Mike Alfreds and adapted from Eugène Sue's novel about the Jesuits, given a mainstage production at the Royal National Theatre in 1987.

Yet in the late 1980's and early 1990's, Wandor's stage plays have begun to convey more of her own distinct voice. In *Wanted*, for instance, she took an experimental tack in her depiction of a mixed bag of characters (an angel, an unborn being, and the biblical Sarah), all engaged in a witty and topical theatrical representation of the issue of surrogacy. Here, as in her earlier plays *Care and Control* and *Aid Thy Neighbour*, the concern for gender relations and family structure are central themes. Yet the style of *Wanted* reveals a developmental shift in Wandor's work, a move away from social realism and the structure of adaptations, to the refinement of a distinctive personal voice. That voice, fractured in *Wanted* into three, is still shifting too quickly to predict the next phase in Wandor's career as a playwright. Yet it does seem clear that her current work is developing in conjunction with (and sometimes in a challenging opposition to) current debates about post-modernist and post-structuralist theatres.

—Lizbeth Goodman

WARD, Douglas Turner. American. Born in Burnside, Louisiana, 5 May 1930. Educated at Xavier University Preparatory School, New Orleans, 1941–46; Wilberforce University, Ohio, 1946–47; University of Michigan, Ann Arbor, 1947–48; Paul Mann's Actors Workshop, New York, 1955–58. Married Diana Hoyt Powell in 1966; one son and one daughter. Co-founder, 1967, and artistic director, Negro Ensemble Company, New York. Recipient: Vernon Rice award, 1966; Obie award 1966, 1970, for acting, 1973; Drama Desk award, for acting, 1970; Boston Theatre Critics Circle award, for directing, 1986. Agent: William Morris Agency, 1350 Avenue of the Americas, New York, New York 10019. Address: Negro Ensemble Company, 165 West 46th Street, Suite 800, New York, New York 10036, U.S.A.

PUBLICATIONS

Plays

Happy Ending, and Day of Absence (produced New York, 1965; *Day of Absence* produced Edinburgh, 1987). New York, Dramatists Play Service, 1966; as *Two Plays*, New York, Third Press-Viking Press, 1971.
The Reckoning (produced New York, 1969). New York, Dramatists Play Service, 1970.
Brotherhood (also director: produced New York, 1970). New York, Dramatists Play Service, 1970.
Redeemer, in *Holidays* (produced Louisville, 1979; in *About Heaven and Earth*, also director: produced New York, 1983).

*

Critical Study: introduction by Sheila Rush to *Two Plays* by Ward, New York, Third Press-Viking Press, 1971.

Theatrical Activities:

Director: **Plays**—*Daddy Goodness* by Richard Wright and Louis Sapin, New York, 1968; *Man Better Man* by Errol Hill, New York, 1969; *Contribution* by Ted Shine, New York, 1969; *Brotherhood and Day of Absence*, New York, 1970; *Ride a Black Horse* by John Scott, New York, 1971; *Perry's Mission* by Clarence Young III, New York, 1971; *The River Niger* by Joseph A. Walker, New York, 1972; *A Ballet Behind the Bridge* by Lennox Brown, New York, 1972; *The Great MacDaddy* by Paul Carter Harrison, New York, 1974, 1977; *The First Breeze of Summer* by Leslie Lee, New York, 1975; *Waiting for Mongo* by Silas Jones, New York, 1975; *Livin' Fat* by Judi Ann Mason, New York, 1976; *The Offering* by Gus Edwards, New York, 1977; *The Twilight Dinner* by Lennox Brown, New York, 1978; *The Raft* by John Pepper Clark, New York, 1978; *Black Body Blues* by Gus Edwards, New York, 1978; *Zooman and the Sign* by Charles Fuller, New York, 1980, 1981; *Home* by Samm-Art Williams, New York, 1980; *Weep Not for Me* by Gus Edwards, New York, 1981; *A Soldier's Play* by Charles Fuller, New York, 1981; *The Isle Is Full of Noises* by Derek Walcott, Hartford, Connecticut, 1982; *About Heaven and Earth* by Ward, Julie Jensen, and Ali Wadad, New York, 1983; *Manhattan Made Me* by Gus Edwards, New York, 1983; *District Line* by Joseph A. Walker, 1984; *Ceremonies in Dark Old Men* by Lonne Elder III, New York, 1985; *The War Party* by Leslie Lee, New York, 1986; *Jonah and the Wonder Dog* by Judi Ann Mason, New York, 1986; *Louie and Ophelia* by Gus Edwards, New York, 1986; *We* (includes *Sally* and *Prince*) by Charles Fuller, New York, 1988; *Jonquil* by Charles Fuller, New York, 1990; *Lifetimes on the Streets* by Gus Edwards, New York, 1990.

Actor as Douglas Turner and Douglas Turner Ward: **Plays**—Joe Mott in *The Iceman Cometh* by O'Neill, New York, 1957; Matthew Kumalo in *Lost in the Stars* by Maxwell Anderson, New York; Moving Man, then Walter Younger, in *A Raisin in the Sun* by Lorraine Hansberry, New York, 1959, then tour, 1960–61; Archibald in *The Blacks* by Jean Genet, New York, 1961; Porter in *Pullman Car Hiawatha* by Thornton Wilder, New York, 1962; understudied Fredericks in *One Flew over the Cuckoo's Nest* by Dale Wasserman, New York, 1963; Zachariah Pieterson in *The Blood Knot* by Athol Fugard, New York, 1964 and tour; Fitzroy in *Rich Little Rich Girl* by Hugh Wheeler, Philadelphia, 1964; Roman Citizen in *Coriolanus*, New York, 1965; Arthur in *Happy Ending*, New York, 1965; Mayor and Clan in *Day of Absence*, New York, 1965; with the Negro Ensemble Company, New York—Oba Danlola in *Kongi's Harvest* by Wole Soyinka, 1968, in *Summer of the Seventeenth Doll* by Ray Lawler, 1968, Thomas in *Daddy Goodness* by Richard Wright and Louis Sapin, 1968, Russell B. Parker in *Ceremonies in Dark Old Men* by Lonne Elder III, 1969, 1985, Scar in *The Reckoning*, 1969, Black Man and Asura in *The Harangues* by Joseph A. Walker, 1969, in *Frederick Douglass Through His Own Words*, 1972, Johnny Williams in *The River Niger* by Joseph A. Walker, 1972, Harper Edwards in *The First Breeze of Summer* by Leslie Lee, 1975, Mingo Saunders in *The Brownsville Raid* by Charles Fuller, 1976, Bob Tyrone in *The Offering* by Gus Edwards, 1977, Fletcher in *Black Body Blues* by Gus Edwards, 1978, Flick in *The Michigan* by Dan Owens, 1979, Technical Sergeant Vernon C. Waters in *A Soldier's Play* by Charles Fuller, Edinburgh, 1984, Jonah Howard in *Jonah and the Wonder Dog* by Judi Ann Mason, 1986, and Louie in *Louie and Ophelia* by Gus Edwards, 1986; Papa in *This Isle Is Full of Noises* by Derek Walcott, New Haven, Connecticut, 1982; New Ice Age and New Ice Age II in *Lifetimes on the Streets* by Gus Edwards, New York, 1990.

Douglas Turner Ward comments:

I am a black playwright, of black sensibilities, primarily utilizing the devices of satire, exaggeration, and mordant humor to explore and express themes of contemporary life, particularly as they relate to black survival.

* * *

Douglas Turner Ward, a black American, is one of those rare individuals who have successfully combined careers as actor, writer, and director. He has twice won Obie awards for plays which he wrote and in which he performed: in 1966 for *Happy Ending* and *Day of Absence*, and in 1970 for *The Reckoning*. Since 1967 he has been artistic director of the Negro Ensemble Company, an important repertory company which he and actor-director Robert Hooks founded.

Despite his success as an actor, Ward is better known as a dramatist, particularly for his first two plays, *Happy Ending* and *Day of Absence*, which treat satirically the relationships between blacks and whites. The history of these award-winning one-acts is almost as ironic as their subject matter. Although both plays were completed by 1960, Ward could not find a producer until, five years later, Robert Hooks, operating on limited financing, arranged to have them produced at St. Mark's Theatre.

As *Happy Ending* opens, two black female domestics are lamenting their employer's decision to divorce his promiscuous wife. Their sorrow is interrupted by their dapper nephew, who rebukes them for pitying people who have overworked and underpaid them. This, he informs them, is their chance to escape from domestic labor. Then, they educate him to the ironies of life: as middle-aged black women, with limited formal education (four strikes against them), they can expect only low-paying jobs which will barely provide subsistence. In contrast, as domestic laborers, though they have received little money, they have provided their nephew with fashionable clothes not missed from the employer's wardrobe and with food smuggled from the employer's larder. As the nephew joins in their sorrows, they receive the happy news that the employers have become reconciled.

Day of Absence is a one-act satirical fantasy about the turmoil in a southern city on a day when all blacks disappear. White couples begin to argue as they discover that they have no experience tending the house or caring for their children. The Ku Klux Klan is bitter because, with black people gone, it no longer has a pretext for existence and victims for sadistic practices. Elected repeatedly on a campaign of keeping blacks in their places, the mayor proves incompetent to manage the affairs of the town. In the midst of the despair, the reappearance of one black reassures the whites that others will return. The play ends, however, with the question of whether the whites have fully learned how much they depend upon blacks.

Ward's first full-length play, *The Reckoning*, produced by the Negro Ensemble Company in 1969, focuses on a confrontation between a black pimp and a southern governor. Ward continued his satire in the one-act *Brotherhood*, in which a white husband and wife try to mask their anti-black sentiments from a middle-class black couple whom they have invited to their house. The blacks are not deceived. In 1966, in an article published in the Sunday *New York Times*, Ward adumbrated the need for a predominantly black audience "to readily understand, debate, confirm, or reject the truth or falsity" of the creations of the black playwright. Ward insisted that whenever a black playwright writes for a predominantly white audience—"least equipped to understand his intentions, woefully apathetic or anesthetized to his experience, often prone to distort his purpose"—that writer must restrict himself to the rudimentary re-education of that audience. Consequently, he has no opportunity to develop artistically. Although he admitted that a black playwright could gain the necessary "theatre of Negro identity" in a black community, Ward saw no possibility for such a theatre prior to massive reconstruction of the urban ghettos.

His hope of such a black-oriented theatre inspired the founding of the Negro Ensemble Company, whose notable successes include Lonne Elder III's *Ceremonies in Dark Old Men* and Charles Fuller's *A Soldier's Play*.

—Darwin T. Turner

WASSERSTEIN, Wendy. American. Born in Brooklyn, New York, 18 October 1950. Educated at Calhoun School, Manhattan; Mount Holyoke College, South Hadley, Massachusetts, B.A. 1971; City College, City University of New York, M.A. 1973; Yale University School of Drama, New Haven, Connecticut, M.F.A. 1976. Recipient: Pulitzer prize, 1989; New York Drama Critics Circle award, 1989; Susan Smith Blackburn award, 1989; Tony award, 1989; National Endowment for the Arts grant; Guggenheim grant. Lives in New York. Agent: International Creative Management, 40 West 57th Street, New York, New York 10019, U.S.A.

PUBLICATIONS

Plays

Any Woman Can't (produced New Haven, Connecticut, 1973).
Happy Birthday, Montpelier Pizz-zazz (produced New Haven, Connecticut, 1974).
When Dinah Shore Ruled the Earth, with Christopher Durang (produced New Haven, Connecticut, 1975).
Uncommon Women and Others (produced New Haven, Connecticut, 1975; New York, 1977; Edinburgh, 1985). New York, Avon, 1979.
Isn't It Romantic (produced New York, 1981; revised version produced New York, 1983). New York, Dramatists Play Service, 1985.
Tender Offer (produced New York, 1983).
The Man in a Case, adaptation of a story by Chekhov, in *Orchards* (produced Urbana, Illinois, 1985; New York, 1986). New York, Knopf, 1986.
Miami, music and lyrics by Bruce Sussman and Jack Feldman (produced New York, 1986).
Smart Women/Brilliant Choices in *Urban Blight* (musical revue), based on an idea by John Tillinger, music by David Shire, lyrics by Richard Maltby, Jr. (produced New York, 1988).
The Heidi Chronicles (produced Seattle, Washington and New York, 1988). New York, Dramatists Play Service, 1990.
The Heidi Chronicles and Other Plays (includes *Uncommon Women and Others*, *Isn't It Romantic*). San Diego, California, Harcourt Brace, 1990.
The Sisters Rosensweig (produced New York, 1992).

Television Play: *The Sorrows of Gin*, from the story by John Cheever, 1979.

Other

Bachelor Girls (essays). New York, Knopf, 1990.

*

Theatrical Activities:
Actress: **Play**—in *The Hotel Play* by Wallace Shawn, New York, 1981.

*   *   *

Identity is the theme in all of Wendy Wasserstein's plays, but is most fully integrated in her major works—*Uncommon Women and Others*, *Isn't It Romantic*, and *The Heidi Chronicles*. Wasserstein's commercial success with *The Heidi Chronicles*, which received both the Pulitzer prize and the Tony award for best play in 1989, has placed her in the slippery position of championing women's causes and feminist concerns. However, the playwright is more concerned with genetics than gender; and more likely to employ humor than humanism in creating her female characters. Her early works, which are not published, are precursory exercises exploring themes of sexuality, marriage, and relationships using episodic structure, music, and comic caricatures. Male characters are primarily used as foils and are rarely fully developed. Most of Wasserstein's female characters are not traditionally developed either, and are often representative of types. What unifies and sustains her dramaturgy is Wasserstein's coy sense of humor supported by keen observations of everyday life.

Wasserstein uses traditional American rituals as a means to exploit traditional roles. In two early plays, *When Dinah Shore Ruled the Earth* and *Any Woman Can't*, she uses a beauty pageant in the former and a dance audition in the latter to both exhort and extol the eclectic roles of ambitious females in a male-dominated society. In *Happy Birthday, Montpelier Pizz-zazz*, the college party scene is the backdrop for the exploitation of both stereotypical roles and stereotypical expectations of college students. The primary issues center around women's options but the play depends too much on caricature to be taken seriously. *Uncommon Women and Others*, Wasserstein's first major work, makes better use of college rituals as a means to explore both character and issue.

Uncommon Women and Others is not unique but it is risky in terms of subject matter. The reunion format of five women who meet in 1978 and then travel back six years to their final year at Mount Holyoke College provides the structure of the all-female play. What makes the play compelling are the concerns that each of the five women have regarding their role in society, in relation to each other, and to themselves. There is no real plot that unifies the play, and no real ending. A disembodied male voice is heard between each scene reciting extracts from a traditional graduation address. The technique serves to unify the play not only structurally but also thematically, since each excerpt raises issues that the women are trying to work through and choices that they are facing in the future.

Isn't It Romantic is similar to *Uncommon Women and Others* in terms of episodic structure, the use of music to create mood and exploit ritual, and in terms of the disembodied voice, which takes the form of telephone messages from various characters in the play and characters who are not physically present. *Isn't It Romantic* offers a better developed plot, characters with more dimension, and thematically the strongest philosophical bent of any Wasserstein work. The play, benefiting from some major rewrites after its initial New York première, contains the best linguistic foreplay of wit and wisdom stemming from Wasserstein's keen sense of irony and honest portrayal of the two major characters.

The central character, Janie Blumberg, is "a little kooky, a little sweet, a little unconfident." By contrast, her best friend Harriet Cornwall could be "the cover girl on the best working women's magazine." With Janie, her friends, and her parents along with Harriet and her mother, Wasserstein creates a Chekhovian *Cherry Orchard* where the plot is simple and the characters, each of whom is a bit eccentric and lives in his or her own world, discover that each must fulfill his or her own desires; that each must have his or her own dream. Janie grows by recognizing the discrepancies in everyone else's desires. The final tableau shows Janie as she begins to dance to "Isn't It Romantic" while the audience hears the voice of a friend leaving a desperate message on the telephone machine. Janie's dancing becomes more confident until she is "dancing beautifully," symbolizing her growth and celebrating an optimistic future.

The final tableau in Wasserstein's most celebrated work, that of Heidi sitting in a rocker singing softly to her adopted child, is in stark contrast to that of Janie's ebullient face and dancing silhouette. Unfortunately, *The Heidi Chronicles* overshadows the merits of *Isn't It Romantic*. The plays are similar, both dealing with a single woman looking for her place in society and in life. However, Heidi more closely resembles Harriet or Kate from *Uncommon Women and Others*. All are successful in their careers, but all have paid a price for success.

Wasserstein's most prize-winning play is not without merit, but it does not live up to its potential as a well-documented play that promises a comparison of "lost women painters" from the 16th century to the "lost feminists" of the 20th century.

Heidi, an art historian, opens the play in mid-lecture in front of a slide screen of a Sofonisba Anguissola painting. The painting and the lecture serve as both a literal and symbolic framing device. Scenes move back in time from 1965 to 1977, and from 1980 to 1989. The play explores Heidi's disillusionment with the women's movement, dramatizing its history at the same time. It raises serious and important issues only to undercut them with a loosely constructed plot and a contrived ending. Homosexuality, single parenting, politics, and art are all subjects that remain unexplored. As the heroine of the play, Heidi has an unusual role in that much of the time she is a spectator. And most of the action is that of encountering and re-encountering the various people in her life who have influenced her. The humor is closer to that of television sitcom and lacks the risqué verbiage of *Uncommon Women and Others* or the strong philosophical wit of *Isn't It Romantic*. Wasserstein's strengths lie in her ability to create characters who laugh at themselves while questioning others. She serves as a role model for women who wish to be successful in the New York theatre venue. All her plays are quirky and interesting and offer strong roles for women.

—Judy Lee Oliva

WATERHOUSE, Keith (Spencer). British. Born in Leeds, Yorkshire, 6 February 1929. Educated at Osmondthorpe Council Schools, Leeds. Served in the Royal Air Force. Married 1) Joan Foster in 1951 (divorced 1968), one son and two daughters; 2) Stella Bingham (divorced 1989). Since 1950 freelance journalist and writer in Leeds and London; columnist, *Daily Mirror*, 1970–86, and *Daily Mail* since 1986, both London. Member, Kingman Committee on Teaching of English Language, 1987–88. Recipient (for journalism): Granada award, 1970, and special award, 1982; IPC award, 1970, 1973; British Press award, 1978; *Evening Standard* award, for play, 1991. Honorary fellow, Leeds Polytechnic. Fellow, Royal Society of Literature. Agent: London Management, 235 Regent Street, London W1A 2JT. Address: 29 Kenway Road, London, S.W.5, England.

PUBLICATIONS

Plays

Billy Liar, with Willis Hall, adaptation of the novel by Waterhouse (produced London, 1960; Los Angeles and New York, 1963). London, Joseph, 1960; New York, Norton, 1961.
Celebration: The Wedding and The Funeral, with Willis Hall (produced Nottingham and London, 1961). London, Joseph, 1961.
England, Our England, with Willis Hall, music by Dudley Moore (produced London, 1962). London, Evans, 1964.
Squat Betty, with Willis Hall (produced London, 1962; New York, 1964). Included in *The Sponge Room, and Squat Betty*, 1963.
The Sponge Room, with Willis Hall (produced Nottingham and London, 1962; New York, 1964). Included in *The Sponge Room, and Squat Betty*, 1963; in *Modern Short Plays from Broadway and London*, edited by Stanley Richards, New York, Random House, 1969.
All Things Bright and Beautiful, with Willis Hall (produced Bristol and London, 1962). London, Joseph, 1963.
The Sponge Room, and Squat Betty, with Willis Hall. London, Evans, 1963.
Come Laughing Home, with Willis Hall (as *They Called the Bastard Stephen*, produced Bristol, 1964; as *Come Laughing Home*, produced Wimbledon, 1965). London, Evans, 1965.
Say Who You Are, with Willis Hall (produced Guildford, Surrey, and London, 1965). London, Evans, 1966; as *Help Stamp Out Marriage* (produced New York, 1966), New York, French, 1966.
Joey, Joey, with Willis Hall, music by Ron Moody (produced Manchester and London, 1966).
Whoops-a-Daisy, with Willis Hall (produced Nottingham, 1968). London, French, 1978.
Children's Day, with Willis Hall (produced Edinburgh and London, 1969). London, French, 1975.
Who's Who, with Willis Hall (produced Coventry, 1971; London, 1973). London, French, 1974.
Saturday, Sunday, Monday, with Willis Hall, adaptation of a play by Eduardo De Filippo (produced London, 1973; New York, 1974). London, Heinemann, 1974.
The Card, with Willis Hall, music and lyrics by Tony Hatch and Jackie Trent, adaptation of the novel by Arnold Bennett (produced Bristol and London, 1973).
Filumena, with Willis Hall, adaptation of a play by Eduardo De Filippo (produced London, 1977; New York, 1980). London, Heinemann, 1978.
Worzel Gummidge (for children), with Willis Hall, music by Denis King, adaptation of stories by Barbara Euphan Todd

(produced Birmingham, 1980; London, 1981). London, French, 1984.

Steafel Variations (songs and sketches), with Peter Tinniswood and Dick Vosburgh (produced London, 1982).

Lost Empires, with Willis Hall, music by Denis King, adaptation of the novel by J.B. Priestley (produced Darlington, County Durham, 1985).

Mr. and Mrs. Nobody, adaptation of *The Diary of a Nobody* by George and Weedon Grossmith (produced London, 1986).

Budgie, with Willis Hall, music by Mort Shuman, lyrics by Don Black (produced London, 1988).

Jeffrey Bernard Is Unwell (produced Brighton and London, 1989).

Bookends, adaptation of *The Marsh Marlowe Letters* by Craig Brown (produced London, 1990).

Our Song, adaptation of his novel (produced London, 1992).

Screenplays, with Willis Hall: *Whistle Down the Wind*, 1961; *The Valiant*, 1962; *A Kind of Loving*, 1963; *Billy Liar*, 1963; *West Eleven*, 1963; *Man in the Middle*, 1963; *Pretty Polly* (*A Matter of Innocence*), 1967; *Lock Up Your Daughters*, 1969.

Radio Plays: *The Town That Wouldn't Vote*, 1951; *There Is a Happy Land*, 1962; *The Woolen Bank Forgeries*, 1964; *The Last Phone-In*, 1976; *The Big Broadcast of 1922*, 1979.

Television Plays: *The Warmonger*, 1970; *The Upchat Line* series, 1977; *The Upchat Connection* series, 1978; *Charlie Muffin*, from novels by Brian Freemantle, 1979; *West End Tales* series, 1981; *The Happy Apple* series, from a play by Jack Pulman, 1983; *This Office Life*, from his own novel, 1984; *Charters and Caldicott*, 1985; *The Great Paper Chase*, from the book *Slip Up* by Anthony Delano, 1988; *Andy Capp* series, 1988; with Willis Hall—*Happy Moorings*, 1963; *How Many Angels*, 1964; *Inside George Webley* series, 1968; *Queenie's Castle* series, 1970; *Budgie* series, 1971–72; *The Upper Crusts* series, 1973; *Three's Company* series, 1973; *By Endeavour Alone*, 1973; *Briefer Encounter*, 1977; *Public Lives*, 1979; *Worzel Gummidge* series, from stories by Barbara Euphan Todd, 1979.

Novels

There Is a Happy Land. London, Joseph, 1957.

Billy Liar. London, Joseph, 1959; New York, Norton, 1960.

Jubb. London, Joseph, 1963; New York, Putnam, 1964.

The Bucket Shop. London, Joseph, 1968; as *Everything Must Go*, New York, Putnam, 1969.

Billy Liar on the Moon. London, Joseph, 1975; New York, Putnam, 1976.

Office Life. London, Joseph, 1978.

Maggie Muggins; or, Spring in Earl's Court. London, Joseph, 1981.

In the Mood. London, Joseph, 1983.

Thinks. London, Joseph, 1984.

Our Song. London, Hodder and Stoughton, 1988.

Bimbo. London, Hodder and Stoughton, 1990.

Other

The Café Royal: Ninety Years of Bohemia, with Guy Deghy. London, Hutchinson, 1955.

How to Avoid Matrimony: The Layman's Guide to the Laywoman, with Guy Deghy (as Herald Froy). London, Muller, 1957.

Britain's Voice Abroad, with Paul Cave. London, Daily Mirror Newspapers, 1957.

The Future of Television. London, Daily Mirror Newspapers, 1958.

How to Survive Matrimony, with Guy Deghy (as Herald Froy). London, Muller, 1958.

The Joneses: How to Keep Up with Them, with Guy Deghy (as Lee Gibb). London, Muller, 1959.

Can This Be Love?, with Guy Deghy (as Herald Froy). London, Muller, 1960.

Maybe You're Just Inferior: Head-Shrinking for Fun and Profit, with Guy Deghy (as Herald Froy). London, Muller, 1961.

The Higher Jones, with Guy Deghy (as Lee Gibb). London, Muller, 1961.

O Mistress Mine: or, How to Go Roaming, with Guy Deghy (as Herald Froy). London, Barker, 1962.

The Passing of the Third-Floor Buck (*Punch* sketches). London, Joseph, 1974.

Mondays, Thursdays (*Daily Mirror* columns). London, Joseph, 1976.

Rhubarb, Rhubarb, and Other Noises (*Daily Mirror* columns). London, Joseph, 1979.

The Television Adventures [and *More Television Adventures*] *of Worzel Gummidge* (for children), with Willis Hall. London, Penguin, 2 vols., 1979; complete edition, as *Worzel Gummidge's Television Adventures*, London, Kestrel, 1981.

Worzel Gummidge at the Fair (for children), with Willis Hall. London, Penguin, 1980.

Worzel Gummidge Goes to the Seaside (for children), with Willis Hall. London, Penguin, 1980.

The Trials of Worzel Gummidge (for children), with Willis Hall. London, Penguin, 1980.

Worzel's Birthday (for children), with Willis Hall. London, Penguin, 1981.

New Television Adventures of Worzel Gummidge and Aunt Sally (for children), with Willis Hall. London, Sparrow, 1981.

Daily Mirror Style. London, Mirror Books, 1981; revised, edition as *Waterhouse on Newspaper Style*, London, Viking, 1989.

Fanny Peculiar (*Punch* columns). London, Joseph, 1983.

Mrs. Pooter's Diary. London, Joseph, 1983.

The Irish Adventures of Worzel Gummidge (for children), with Willis Hall. London, Severn House, 1984.

Waterhouse at Large (journalism). London, Joseph, 1985.

The Collected Letters of a Nobody (Including Mr. Pooter's Advice to His Son). London, Joseph, 1986.

The Theory and Practice of Lunch. London, Joseph, 1986.

Worzel Gummidge Down Under (for children), with Willis Hall. London, Collins, 1987.

The Theory and Practice of Travel. London, Hodder and Stoughton, 1989.

English Our English (and How to Sing It). London, Viking, 1991.

Editor, with Willis Hall, *Writers' Theatre*. London, Heinemann, 1967.

* * *

See the essay on Willis Hall and Keith Waterhouse.

WATSON, Fred. British. Born in 1927.
See 1st edition, 1973.

WEBB, Leonard. British. Born in 1930.
See 3rd edition, 1982.

WEIDMAN, Jerome. American. Born in 1913.
See 2nd edition, 1977.

WEINSTEIN, Arnold. American. Born in New York City,
10 June 1927. Educated at Hunter College, New York, B.A.
in classics 1951 (Phi Beta Kappa); University of London,
1949–50; Harvard University, Cambridge, Massachusetts,
A.M. in comparative literature 1952; University of Florence
(Fulbright Fellow), 1958–60. Served in the United States
Navy, 1944–46. Married Suzanne Burgess in 1969. Visiting
lecturer, New York University, 1955–56, and University of
Southern California, Los Angeles; United States Information
Service Lecturer, Italy, 1958–60; director of Drama
Workshop, Wagner College, Staten Island, New York, sum-
mers 1964, 1965; visiting professor, Hollins College, Virginia,
1964–65; professor of dramatic literature, New School for
Social Research, New York, 1965–66; chair of the depart-
ment of playwriting, Yale University, New Haven,
Connecticut, 1966–69; visiting professor, University of
Colorado, Boulder, Summer 1969; chair of the department of
drama, Columbia College, Chicago, 1969–70; visiting professor, Southampton College, Southampton, New York,
1978–79, and Columbia University, New York, from 1979.
Co-director, with Paul Sills, Second City, and other improvisational groups; director, Free Theatre, Chicago, Actors
Studio, New York and Los Angeles, and Rock Theatre and
Guerilla Theatre, Los Angeles. Recipient: Guggenheim fellowship, 1965. Agent: Sam Cohn, International Creative
Management, 40 West 57th Street, New York, New York
10019. Address: Department of English and Comparative
Literature, Columbia University, New York, New York
10027, U.S.A.

PUBLICATIONS

Plays

Red Eye of Love (produced New York, 1958). New York,
Grove Press, 1962.
White Cap (produced New York, 1960).
Fortuna, music by Francis Thorne, adaptation of a play by
Eduardo De Filippo and Armando Curcio (produced New
York, 1962).

The Twenty Five Cent White Hat (in *3 x 3*, produced New
York, 1962).
Food for Thought: A Play about Food, with Jay and Fran
Landesman (produced St. Louis, 1962).
Dynamite Tonite, music by William Bolcom (produced New
York, 1963; revised version produced New York, 1964;
revised version produced New Haven, Connecticut, 1966).
New York, Trio Music, 1964.
Party (produced New York, 1964; revised version, music by
Laurence Rosenthal, produced New York, 1976).
They (produced Philadelphia, 1965).
Reg. U.S. Pat. Off., in *Pardon Me, Sir, But Is My Eye
Hurting Your Elbow*, edited by Bob Booker and George
Foster. New York, Geis, 1968.
Story Theatre (produced New Haven, Connecticut, 1968).
Greatshot, music by William Bolcom (produced New Haven,
Connecticut, 1969).
Ovid, music by The True Brethren, adaptation of
Metamorphoses by Ovid (produced Chicago, 1969; New
York, 1971).
Mahagonny, adaptation of the libretto by Brecht, music by
Kurt Weill (produced New York, 1970). Excerpts pub-
lished in *Yale/Theatre* (New Haven, Connecticut), 1969.
The American Revolution, with Paul Sills, music by Tony
Greco, lyrics by Weinstein (produced Washington, D.C.,
1973).
More Metamorphoses, adaptation of the work by Ovid (pro-
duced Spoleto, Italy, 1973).
Gypsy New York (produced New York, 1974).
Lady Liberty's Ice Cream Cone (produced New York, 1974).
Captain Jinks, adaptation of the play by Clyde Fitch, music
arranged by William Bolcom (produced New York, 1976).
America More or Less, music by Tony Greco (produced San
Francisco, 1976).
Monkey, with Paul Sills (produced New York, 1978).
Stories for Theatre (produced Southampton, New York,
1979).
Casino Paradise, with Thomas Babe, music by William
Bolcom (produced Philadelphia, 1990).

Improvisational Material: *Second City*, New York, 1963–64.

Television Plays: *Improvisation*; *The Last Ingredient*, music
by David Amram.

Verse

Different Poems by the Same Author. Rome, United States
Information Service, 1960.

Recording: lyrics for *Black Max: Cabaret Songs*, music by
William Bolcom, RCA, 1985.

*

Manuscript Collection: Yale University, New Haven,
Connecticut.

Critical Studies: *American Drama since World War II*, New
York, Harcourt Brace, 1962, and *The Jumping-Off Place*,
Harcourt Brace, 1969, both by Gerald Weales; *A Theatre
Divided*, Boston, Little Brown, 1967, and *Opening Nights*,
New York, Putnam, 1969, both by Martin Gottfried;
Common and Uncommon Masks by Richard Gilman, New
York, Random House, 1971.

Theatrical Activities:
Director: **Plays**—*Second City* (co-director, with Paul Sills), and other improvisational groups; his own and other plays at the Free Theatre, Chicago, Actors Studio, New York and Los Angeles, and the Rock Theatre and the Guerilla Theatre, Los Angeles; *A Memory of Two Mondays* by Arthur Miller, Southampton, New York, 1979; *The White House Murder Case* by Jules Feiffer, New York, 1980.

Arnold Weinstein comments:

I try to write the history and mythology of today. The schoolroom, the churchroom, the theatre are one, or all are lost. Drama and karma are one. Look them up. Look them up and down. The audience is half the action, the actors the other half; the author starts the fight. Power. The passing of power. It really is life there in the dark, here. The lightning of television terrifies most. Right in the word the intrusion of fear—fear of loss of control, loss of sale, loss of sorcery. Loss of power. Our fear sends us through the channels, puts us on our tracks. If the trinity does not control the power, what's left? Only everything. Everything running around in formless rampant ranks waiting for daring brutes to pick up the wire reins.

* * *

The generation of American playwrights that followed Arthur Miller and Tennessee Williams was a troubled one, reflecting a country that was emerging from a history of brute domination into a future of questions and complexities. These playwrights were similarly trapped between the theater styles and values of an outgoing past and the uncertainty of a fast-approaching future. Such writers as Jack Gelber and Jack Richardson have never fulfilled their early promise, but Arnold Weinstein's inability to find himself as a playwright is perhaps the most painful, for he is the most artistic, talented, and original of the lot. But he has been hurt by a combination of critical rejection and changing taste, and though the author of charming plays and libretti, his career seems frustrated.

His New York professional debut was a production by the Living Theatre of *Red Eye of Love*, which remains his best known full-length play. The Living Theatre at the time was in its Brecht stage and so was Weinstein, who was to prove too affected by changing fashion and too insecure in his own style. The play is a romantic fable about American capitalism. Its hero is a toy inventor in love with a girl who feels it her "duty to marry money." She turns to the owner of a 13-story meat market, which grows beyond 40 stories as the play progresses. This girl vacillates between the inventor (artist) and the butcher (capitalist) while the play does vaudeville turns to Joycean word games with a whimsicality that would prove a Weinstein signature. The author's stage energy, his antic humor, his feel for America, and his deep love of cheap sentiment are established as they would persist through his subsequent work, but the play is too often precious and almost blatantly Brechtian.

In 1962 he wrote the libretto for an off-Broadway musical of inspired zaniness—*Fortuna* (Weinstein was to become involved with many musical projects, one of America's rare artistic playwrights to appreciate their value, but though several were planned, none reached Broadway). *Fortuna*, adapted from an Italian comedy, told of the impoverished and luckless title character who inherits a fortune on the condition that he have no sons. After a series of farcical complications, Fortuna gets his fortune. Once again, Weinstein was dealing with a Schweikian hero-victim (expressionist and absurdist influences would for too long influence his work and keep him from self-discovery).

His one-act absurdist play, *The Twenty Five Cent White Hat*, opened and closed off-Broadway, unappreciated by New York's critics. Though the play was a trite plea for the importance of individuality, it was filled with Weinstein's lively and poetic comedy writing.

The turning point in the playwright's career came with *Dynamite Tonite*, his "comic opera for actors" written with composer William Bolcom. Though not without relation to Brecht, the work had a brisk originality of its own. For though it was a legitimate opera, it was indeed written for actors—that is, non-singers. Weinstein's libretto was intensely pacifist, yet romantic and comic, tender and suffused with affection for a vulnerable mankind. Its operetta-style hero and heroine sang hilarious Wagnerian parodies in counterpoint to flatfooted soldiers doing soft shoe dances, and set as the work was on the battleground of a neverneverland it had an odd mixture of expressionism and Americana that somehow worked.

Dynamite Tonite is a superb theater work, but it was so brutally criticized that it closed on its first night. Several attempts were made to revive it, first by the Repertory Theatre at Yale Drama School and once more off-Broadway, but it seemed doomed to rejection despite (or perhaps because of) its artistic superiority.

Greatshot, another musical work with Bolcom—also produced at Yale—was in the style of the then-popular self-creative companies (such as his friends at the Living Theatre had developed), but there was no soul to the work, nor clarity of intention. The structured, verbal theater to which the playwright naturally inclined did not mesh with physical, improvisational, anti-verbal theater he was emulating.

Meanwhile, Weinstein had been long preparing a new translation of the great Brecht-Weill opera, *Mahoganny*, and when it was finally produced after many years of effort, his work proved mediocre, though hardly showcased by the disastrous production.

Weinstein's history, then, is one of victimization by the American theater's commercialism, which leaves little room for so creative, artistic, and poetic a playwright; it is a victimization by British-American theater generally, with its overwhelming sense of trend (absurdism, once hailed as *the* style for moderns, was obsolete after no more than five years of fashion); and it is a victimization by rejection. His past shows some fulfillment and great promise; his present is in limbo; his future depends on his own resolve and his treatment at the hands of both the theater and circumstance.

—Martin Gottfried

WELLER, Michael. American. Born in New York City, 26 September 1942. Educated at Stockbridge School; Windham College; Brandeis University, Waltham, Massachusetts, B.A. in music 1965; Manchester University, Lancashire. Recipient: Creative Artists Public Service grant, 1976. Agent: Michael Imison Playwrights, 28 Almeida Street, London N1 1TD, England. Address: 215 East 5th Street, New York, New York 10003, U.S.A.

PUBLICATIONS

Plays

Cello Days at Dixon's Palace (produced Cambridge, Massachusetts, 1965).

Fred, music by Weller, adaptation of the novel *Malcolm* by James Purdy (produced Waltham, Massachusetts, 1965).

How Ho-Ho Rose and Fell in Seven Short Scenes, music by Weller (produced Manchester, 1966; London, 1972).

The Making of Theodore Thomas, Citizen, adaptation of the play *Johnny Johnson* by Paul Green (produced London, 1968).

Happy Valley (produced Edinburgh, 1969).

The Bodybuilders, and Now There's Just the Three of Us (produced London, 1969). With *Tira Tells Everything There Is to Know abour Herself*, 1972; in *Off-Broadway Plays 2*, London, Penguin, 1972.

Poison Come Poison (produced London, 1970).

Cancer (produced London, 1970). London, Faber, 1971; as *Moonchildren* (produced Washington, D.C., 1971; New York, 1972), New York, French, 1971.

Grant's Movie (produced London, 1971). With *Tira*, London, Faber, 1972.

Tira Tells Everything There Is to Know about Herself (produced London, 1971). With *The Bodybuilders*, 1972; as *Tira* (produced New York, 1975), with *Grant's Movie*, London, Faber, 1972.

The Bodybuilders, and Tira Tells Everything There Is to Know about Herself. New York, Dramatists Play Service, 1972.

More Than You Deserve, music by Jim Steinman, lyrics by Weller and Steinman (produced New York, 1973).

Twenty-Three Years Later (produced Los Angeles, 1973).

Fishing (produced New York, 1975; London, 1976). New York, French, 1975.

Alice, in *After Calcutta* (produced London, 1976).

Split (one-act version; produced London, 1977; New York, 1978). New York, French, 1979; *as Abroad* in *Split* (full-length version), 1981.

Loose Ends (produced Washington, D.C., and New York, 1979; London, 1981). New York, French, 1980.

Barbarians, with Kitty Hunter Blair and Jeremy Brooks, adaptation of a play by Gorky (produced New York, 1980). New York, French, 1982.

Dwarfman, Master of a Million Shapes (produced Chicago, 1981).

At Home (produced London, 1981). Included in *Split* (full-length version), 1981.

Split (full-length version; includes *At Home* [*Split*, part 1] and *Abroad* [*Split*, part 2]. New York, French, 1981.

Five Plays (includes *Moonchildren, Fishing, At Home, Abroad, Loose Ends*). New York, New American Library, 1982.

The Ballad of Soapy Smith (produced Seattle, 1983; New York, 1984). New York, French, 1985.

Ghost on Fire (produced La Jolla, California, 1985). New York, Grove Press, 1987.

A Dopey Fairy Tale, adaptation of a story by Chekhov, in *Orchards* (produced Urbana, Illinois, 1985; New York, 1986). New York, Knopf, 1986.

Spoils of War (produced New York, 1988). New York, French, and London, Faber, 1989.

Screenplays: *Hair*, 1979; *Ragtime*, 1982; *Lost Angels*, 1989; *God Bless You Mr. Rosewater*, 1991.

*

Theatrical Activities:
Actor: **Play**—Star-Man in *The Tooth of Crime* by Sam Shepard, London, 1972.

* * *

Chronicling his own generation, Michael Weller has sent interim reports from the front lines of bourgeois American youth as students moved from universities into communes, from the city to the country, and from idealism to Madison Avenue competitiveness. Whatever the surrounding environment, his basic concern has been with personal relationships and their vulnerability.

Many of his early plays were introduced to London by the American expatriate Charles Marowitz of the Open Space Theatre, and Weller had an English reputation before he had an American one, despite earning his first production while he was still a student at Brandeis University. His plays generally appeared in a kind of hyper-ventilating realism which matched the extremes of emotion that afflict his characters without detailing too completely their day-to-day existence.

His first play to have a genuine transatlantic impact was the very specifically American drama which was called *Cancer* when it had its premiere at London's Royal Court Theatre. Cancer is, of course, an astrological sign as well as a disease, and the play was retitled *Moonchildren* for its first American performance at Arena Stage in Washington D.C. Although written and first produced in 1970, there was something nostalgic and historical in its portrait of a group of college students sharing an apartment during the heady days of resistance to President Nixon and the war in Vietnam.

Perhaps Weller drew the battle lines too clearly, placing his young people in a sort of drug-armed camp opposing the adult society which was represented by police, landlords, and relatives. The sharp details of the young people's conversational exchanges spoke well for his dramatist's ear, however, and there was an optimism in his writing which suggested that goodwill, high spirits, and visionary certitude would break down the barriers between police and students, an idea which grew sour in the later plays where the broken barriers more often represented a capitulation of idealism. What balanced the comical anarchy in *Cancer* was finally the familial call across generations, the news given to one boy that his mother was dying of cancer—actually, painfully, and beyond the relief of metaphor.

Grant's Movie followed *Cancer* almost immediately, and drew harsher lines between the generations. Police and anti-war demonstrators have come to serious violence, and a policeman is kidnapped by three peace-seeking hippies who believe the man might have murdered the brother of a friend during a demonstration. The friend is Grant and the planned torment of the policeman is according to his script: everybody is in Grant's movie.

Weller's next leap was a review of the hippie alternative as it appeared in 1975: *Fishing*, a play that came to be seen as the second part of an extended trilogy that began with *Cancer*. Three drop-outs are discovered in a backwater of the Pacific Northwest, short on cannabis, short on cash, and exploring a new fantasy of beginning a commercial fishery—if they can raise $1,500 to buy a boat. In the course of the play, real death again enters the fable when the man who was selling the boat dies, and again when the chicken who was becoming a pet is killed, plucked for eating, and pulled apart in rage. Another death is flirted with, when one of the three plans suicide on his motorcycle before changing his mind in favour of the fishing: "Oh you're right, it's a dumb idea, no doubt about it. You and me. Two of the finest minds of our generation. But it's something to do. And, you know, if we approach it just the right way, after a while, if we manage to stick to it, and we don't get seasick and we do catch fish we might find there's a good reason for doing it."

Weller's ear for dialogue had become more acute by then, and the acid wit was refined, but the play that best represented his developing perspective was *Loose Ends*, his 1979 report on the progress of the alternative society of the 1960's. It was panoramic in intention, first evoking an accidental meeting on the hippie road to paradise when a young couple come together on a beach in Bali, he returning to America from a depressing tour in the Peace Corps, and she on her way to enlightenment in India. Weller's comedy and optimism survive his story of that relationship, which stretches forward from 1970 across the decade of Vietnam, Watergate, and disillusion.

With the panoramic structure of *Loose Ends*, Weller constructed a play consisting entirely of dramatic touchpoints: the form remained realistic but every meeting was a contrast to what had gone before and what would have been a gradual evolution of a drop-out into a hip property speculator becomes a comical commentary as the woodsman becomes a long-haired man in a business suit. Gurus and passing fashions are recorded for their worth, then brushed aside while the original couple fall into competition with each other, rejecting then courting financial success. Their path was to divorce instead of enlightenment and although their careers remain on the edge of art, in photography and filmmaking, the world is busy overcoming their ideals.

With *Cancer* and *Fishing* it forms a rounded trilogy of reportage, and the plays make a dramatic document of value. Weller remains a writer for the theatre, contributing new, short pieces such as *Split* and important longer works such as *Ghost on Fire* and *Spoils of War*. With such adaptations for the cinema as his screenplay for E.L. Doctorow's *Ragtime*, his reputation has also been growing elsewhere.

—Ned Chaillet

WELLMAN, Mac (John McDowell). American. Born in Cleveland, Ohio, 7 March 1945. Educated at University School, Shaker Heights, Ohio, graduated 1963; School of International Service, American University, Washington D.C., B.A. in international relations and organization 1967; University of Wisconsin, Madison, M.A. in English literature 1968. Associate professor of English, Montgomery College, Rockville, Maryland, 1969–72; playwright-in-residence, New York University, 1981–82, Yale University School of Drama, New Haven, Connecticut, 1992, and Princeton University, New Jersey, 1992–93; teacher of playwriting, Mentor Playwrights' Project at the Mark Taper Forum, Los Angeles, University of New Mexico, Albuquerque, New York University, Iowa Playwright's Lab, Iowa City, Brown University, Providence, Rhode Island, and New Dramatists, New Voices, Boston, Massachusetts, 1984–92; resident, Bellagio Study and Conference Centre, the Rockefeller Foundation, Bellagio, Italy, 1991; PNM distinguished chair in playwriting, University of New Mexico, Albuquerque, 1991; master artist, Atlantic Center for the Arts, New Smyrna, Florida, 1991. Recipient: New York Foundation for the Arts fellowship, 1986, 1990; McKnight fellowship, 1989; Rockefeller fellowship, 1989; Guggenheim fellowship, 1990; National Endowment for the Arts fellowship, 1990; Obie award, 1990 (three times), 1991; Outer Circle Critics award, 1990; Bessie award, 1992; American Theater Critics Association award, 1992. Lives in New York. Agent: Wiley Hausam, International Creative Management, 40 West 57th Street, New York, New York 10019, U.S.A.

PUBLICATIONS

Plays

Fama Combinatoria (broadcast 1973; produced Amsterdam, The Netherlands, 1975).
The Memory Theatre of Giordano Bruno (broadcast 1976; produced Washington, D.C., 1976).
Opera Brevis. San Francisco, Heron Press, 1977.
Starluster (produced New York, 1979). Published in *Wordplays 1*, edited by Bonnie Marranca, New York, Performing Arts Journal Publications, 1980.
Dog in the Manger, adaptation of a play by Lope de Vega (produced New York, 1982).
The Self-Begotten (produced New York, 1982).
Phantomnation, with Constance Congdon and Bennett Cohen, music by James Ragland (produced Mill Valley, California, 1983).
The Professional Frenchman (produced Minneapolis, 1984). Published in *Theatre of Wonders*, edited by Wellman, Los Angeles, Sun and Moon Press, 1985.
Harm's Way, music by Bob Jewett and Jack Maeby (broadcast 1984; produced New York, 1985). New York, Broadway Play Publishing, 1984.
Energumen (produced New York, 1985). Published in *Women with Guns*, edited by Christopher Gould, New York, Broadway Play Publishing, 1986.
The Bad Infinity (produced Minneapolis, 1985). Published in *7 Different Plays*, edited by Wellman, New York, Broadway Play Publishing, 1988.
1951, with Anne Bogart and Michael Roth (produced San Diego, California and New York, 1986).
The Nain Rouge, music by Michael Roth (produced New York, 1986).
The Distance to the Moon, music by Melissa Shiftlett (produced New York, 1986).
Cleveland (produced New York, 1986).
Dracula, adaptation of the novel by Bram Stoker (produced Woodstock, New York, 1987; New York, 1992).
Bodacious Flapdoodle. Auburn, California, Video Research Institute Library, 1987.
Albanian Softshoe (produced New York, 1988).
Peach Bottom Nuclear Reactor Full of Sleepers (produced New York, 1988).
Cellophane (produced New York, 1988). Hadley, Massachusetts, Playwrights Press, 1988.
Without Colors, adaptation of *Cosmicomics* by Italo Calvino, music by Melissa Shiftlett (produced Minneapolis, 1989).
Whirligig (produced New York, 1989). Published in *Plays in Process* (New York), vol.10, no.7, 1989.
Bad Penny (produced New York, 1989). Los Angeles, Sun and Moon Press, 1990.
The Ninth World (produced San Diego, California, 1989; New York, 1991).
Terminal Hip (also director: produced New York, 1989). Published in *Performing Arts Journal* (New York), no.40, 1992.
Crowbar (produced New York, 1990).

Sincerity Forever (produced Stockbridge, Massachusetts and New York, 1990).

7 Blowjobs (produced San Diego, California, 1991; New York, 1992). Published in *TheaterForum* (New York), no. 1, 1992.

A Murder of Crows (produced Dallas, Texas, 1991; New York, 1992). Published in *Plays in Process* (New York), 1992.

Tallahassee, adaptation of Ovid's *Metamorphoses*, with Len Jenkin, (produced New Smyrna Beach, Florida, 1991).

Coat Hanger (produced New Haven, Connecticut, 1992).

Strange Feet (produced Washington, D.C. and New York, 1993).

The Land of Fog and Whistles (produced New York, 1993).

Radio Plays (all broadcast in The Netherlands): *Nobody*, 1972; *Fama Combinatoria*, 1973; *Mantices*, 1973; *Two Natural Drummers*, 1973; *The Memory Theatre of Giordano Bruno*, 1976; *Harm's Way*, 1984.

Novel

The Fortuneteller. Los Angeles, Sun and Moon Press, 1991.

Verse

In Praise of Secrecy. Washington, D.C., Word Works, 1977.
Satires. Minneapolis, New Rivers Press, 1985.
A Shelf in Woop's Clothing. Los Angeles, Sun and Moon Press, 1990.

Other

Editor, *Breathing Space: An Anthology of Sound-Text Art*. Washington, D.C., Blackbox, 1977.

Editor, *Theatre of Wonders*. Los Angeles, Sun and Moon Press, 1985.

Editor, *7 Different Plays*. New York, Broadway Play Publishing, 1988.

Editor, *Slant Six*. Minneapolis, New Rivers Press, 1990.

*

Theatrical Activities:
Director: **Play**—*Terminal Hip*, New York, 1990.

*   *   *

Mac Wellman is one of the most original, daring, and important playwrights in America. His work is spiky, challenging, fiercely funny, radical in its formal strategies and in its politics, and in every line a rebuke to the timid, dull, stultifying, and sentimental naturalism that still dominates the American theatre. Consequently, his work has rarely been produced outside New York City, other than in small fringe theatres around the country, and rarely, if ever, performed on the strait-laced stages of the mainstream regional theatres. Artistic directors may admire Wellman's work, but few have the courage or recklessness to produce his plays and risk awakening and alienating their slumbering subscription audiences.

Wellman is also a poet and novelist, and is one of a handful of American playwrights who care about writing, who are investigating the possibilities of the American language, whose language is carefully wrought and poetically charged, and whose plays are always, in some part, whatever their other concerns, about the American language (and hence, about American culture and American politics). In his disdain for naturalism, his rejection of linear narrative, psychological subtext, and traditional notions of character, his deliberate subversion and mockery of mainstream theatrical convention, and his love of (in his words) "Gritty, dirty, slimy American language when spoken in the theatre," Wellman is colleague and kindred spirit to a group of playwrights who include Len Jenkin, Eric Overmyer, and Jeffrey Jones, writers who are, in Jones's words, "the Huck Finns" of the American theatre.

Wellman is also a critic, editor, and teacher, and has tried, along with the playwrights mentioned above, to generate a new movement in American playwriting, a movement based in American language, and in rebellion against mainstream American playwriting, against the kind of play characterized by the dramaturge James Magruder as "the talking about my problems in your living room kind of play." To this end, he has edited two influential anthologies, *Theatre of Wonders* and *7 Different Plays*, and published numerous articles.

Wellman was born and raised in Cleveland, Ohio, and his writing evinces the dry humor and flat twang of his Midwestern roots:

> *Lights up on a pair of boots protruding from a washtub.*
> Nella: That's not Andy. That's dad, and he's dead.
>
> Nella: When the kids were young the sea was normal. Of the logic of the sea my younger one, Susannah, said: It's lucky the shallow end is near the beach.
> —*A Murder of Crows*

His Cleveland background shows in recurring images of toxicity and pollution; the plays are full of poisoned landscapes and poisoned families. It is not surprising that a playwright from Cleveland should be concerned with blight, death, and decay. After all, the river which flows through the middle of the city is so polluted it once caught fire, a landmark event in the history of the American ecology movement. That image, a burning river of sludge, seems to inform Wellman's work in a pervasive, subterranean way, its smudgy fumes percolating up from the depths of his writing.

> Nella: Not to mention the county dump, where that hellacious grease pit is. The rivers in this part of the state all look like bubble baths, and the air's all mustardy. Even the local ocean's a little oily and waxy. Like a big bowl of custard, wiggly custard.
>
> Howard: Nella's alright. Only she's never been the same since the avalanche by the . . . grease pit. Landfill or whatever it was. Godawful sludge heap. That ghastly, wolfish slime.
> —*A Murder of Crows*

Wellman's concern with blight extends, of course, to the American language, "as she is spoke" in the theatre. He is attempting to dig himself out from under the avalanche of advertising hype, sentimental cliché, received ideas and politically correct jargon, and sheer mendacity which poison public discourse, tyrannize and terrorize the artist in America, and reduce most American theatre to ersatz television. Two of his newest plays, *7 Blowjobs* and *Sincerity Forever*, are direct responses to the right-wing attack on art and artists in America, and to the assault on the National Endowment for the Arts led by the conservative senator from North Carolina, Jesse Helms. *Sincerity Forever* is about, among other things, the Ku Klux Klan, and with typical puckish humor, Wellman dedicated the play to Senator Helms and sent him a copy. *7 Blowjobs* was inspired by the furore over Robert Mapplethorpe's homoerotic photographs. Both pieces generated considerable public controversy.

Ironically, the terrified bureaucrats at the NEA tried to disassociate themselves from *Sincerity Forever*, not wanting the unreliable Wellman as an ally.

Wellman has said he is interested in "bad language," a term which means non-standard American language, and which originates with H.L. Mencken. In an interview, Wellman said, "I think there are deep truths about the American psyche that you can understand better by a little of the downside, the dark side of American language. There is a powerful yearning that is present there, a powerful urge for transcendence. A very deep and spiritual side to all Americans that's most evident when we're not being correct grammatically or stylistically, in our use of language." (Interview with Allan Havis in *Theatre Forum* [San Diego], Spring 1992.)

A typical example of Wellman "bad language," in which he mines American folk talk and twists and forges it into his own idiom, occurs in *A Murder of Crows*:

> Raymond: . . . Crows jerk and juke about and the winds wind up a medley of talkative hacksaws. We edge near the pit, back off and think by baking apple pie we've got the key to the whole shitwagon and maybe we do. Maybe we don't. I'd love to know what the inside of a storm feels like to be one. I really do. But if it were up to me I'd skin the cat with a touch more care, seeing as how the consequences of what passes for luck at gin rummy, poker and horses has a strange way of barking up the wrong tree.

Another of Wellman's principal linguistic strategies is the use of free verse. His lines are broken in such a way, and with such care, that they acquire a terrific sprung rhythm, a tin-can tied to a tail-pipe sort of clatter, great energy, and unexpected humor. The use of verse also acts as a series of linguistic speed bumps, slowing the headlong hurtle of the actor and the audience as one speaks and the other listens, revitalizing the language, and subverting expectations and assumptions. Much of Wellman's recent work, like *Cellophane*, a long dramatic poem for an ensemble of actors, and *Terminal Hip*, a demented tour-de-force monologue, is pure language, without conventional narrative or action or character: tirades from the edge of darkness which harangue an American culture twisted and scarred and maimed by advertising and television and politics.

Mac Wellman's other major works include *The Bad Infinity*, *Harm's Way*, *Crowbar*, and *Bad Penny*. *Harm's Way*, a Western (or rather, a Midwestern), is a meditation upon violence, upon the language of violence, and upon the American culture of violence. Violence is America's original sin, the dark stain on the American psyche; it is a subject too little explored in serious non-exploitative endeavors in any medium, and almost never in the theatre. *Harm's Way* is a dark, brooding meditation on the conquest of the frontier and, by extension, on subsequent American foreign policy, an x-ray of American myth, and American history, both official and counter-cultural. Its hero is a gunfighter named Santouche, a glorified psychopath and serial killer, and the play probes the American penchant for making heroes of such monsters. (See the recent popularity of Dr. Hannibal Lecter in *The Silence of the Lambs*.) The play ends with Santouche murdering his woman, a whore named Isle of Mercy, while a crowd of children taunt the gunslinger: "You gonna kill everyone, Mister? You gonna kill everyone, Mister? You gonna kill everyone, Mister?", a haunting refrain which evokes the scorched-earth tragedy of Vietnam, as well as countless Hollywood movies, both Western and contemporary. *Harm's Way* is an American *Woyzcek*.

> You know the story of Rip
> Van Winkle? Well the true
> story of Rip Van Winkle
> runs as follows: there's
> this old fart who went
> to sleep for twenty years
> and woke up to find
> everything. THE SAME.
> (pause)
> Except him. He was twenty
> years older.
> Was he ever surprised.
> And horrified.
> EXACTLY THE SAME.
>
> —*The Bad Infinity*

A "Bad Infinity" is a flawed system which replicates itself forever—like most human systems. More correctly, the term is from Hegel, and means any series of logical operations which never reaches a final result or accelerates to another level, a dialectic which never achieves synthesis or transcends itself. In *The Bad Infinity* Wellman explores a number of such systems: geopolitics, fashion, economics, professional sports, crime, international banking, art, criticism, media, and the theatre itself. Or, rather, the shopworn conventions of the conventional theatre. The American theatre: a bad infinity if ever there was one.

Bad Penny and *Crowbar* are site-specific pieces, written for En Garde Arts, a New York-based producing organization run by Anne Hamburger which produces on-site theatrical events. *Crowbar* was written for and produced in the Victory Theatre, an old, *grande dame* of a Broadway house which was reclaimed and refurbished for the event. (It had fallen on hard times; long ago abandoned as a legit theatre, it had become, in recent years, a porno house, showing terrifying triple-bills at bargain basement prices.) *Crowbar* used the history of the Victory Theatre as inspiration for an evocative, ghostly, ultimately tender and sad piece about the decay of Broadway, the theatre, and the city itself, and its present crime-ridden, derelict, end-of-days condition as a great, hulking, once-magnificent, now dangerous, ruin.

Bad Penny is one of Wellman's best plays, playful, funny, and exhilarating. Produced at, and written for, Bow Bridge in Central Park, *Bad Penny* is a comic sonata of urban life, alienation, and insanity. A hapless motorist from Big Ugly, Montana, breaks down in the big city, and finds himself stranded in the middle of Central Park, surrounded by inspired New York lunacy. *Bad Penny* is spare and taut, and contains some of Wellman's most inspired writing. The following passage is the monologue which ends the play:

> First Woman: For all things beneath the sky are
> lovely, except those which
> are ugly; and these are odious
> and reprehensible and must be
> destroyed, must be torn limb from limb howling,
> to prepare the ritual banquet, the
> ritual of the Slaughter of Innocents.
> For the Way is ever difficult to discover
> in the wilderness of thorns and mirrors
> and the ways of the righteous are full
> strange and possess strange hats and
> feet. For the Way leads over from the
> Fountains of Bethesda, where the Lord
> performed certain acts, acts unknown to
> us, across the Bow Bridge of our human
> unknowability, pigheadedness, and the
> wisenheimer attitude problem of our

undeserving, slimeball cheesiness; and
scuttles into the Ramble, there, of
utterly craven, totally lost, desperate
and driven incomprehensibility—friend
neither to fin, to feather, nor tusk
of bat, bird, weasel, porcupine, nor gnat.
And we who are not who we are must forever
bury the toxic waste of our hidden hates
in the dark, plutonic abysm of our human
hearts, and be always blessed in the empty promise
of the sky that looks down upon us with
a smile, a divine smile, even as she
crushes us all beneath her silver foot.

Mac Wellman's plays are political in every line. They are not direct. They are oblique, ironic, and have multiple, even contradictory meanings. They are many-faceted. They are dense and extraordinary. In a word, they are poetic, theatrical. They are, to use an image from *The Bad Infinity*, like horizontal avalanches. An avalanche of images, language, and ideas, moving the viewer from his or her received ideas and assumptions as relentlessly and irresistibly as a wall of mud or a glacier grinding down a canyon. I understand Wellman's plays as I understand poetry, on a deep, cellular level that almost resists reason and explanation. There is much in life that is mysterious, that resists reduction and categorization and simple-minded explanation. Such are Wellman's plays. They are beautiful, subversive works, important works, and deserve to be more frequently produced and better known.

—Eric Overmyer

WERTENBAKER, (Lael Louisiana) Timberlake. British and American. Educated at schools near St. Jean-de-Luz, France; attended university in the United States. Journalist in London and New York; teacher of French in Greece, one year. Resident writer, Shared Experience, 1983, and Royal Court Theatre, 1985, both London. Recipient: Arts Council of Great Britain bursary, 1981, grant, 1983; Thames Television bursary, 1984, 1985; *Plays and Players* award, 1985; *Evening Standard* award, 1988; Olivier award, 1988; Whiting award, 1989; London Theatre Critics Circle award, 1991, 1992; Writers Guild Macallan award, 1992. Lives in London. Agent: Michael Imison Playwrights, 28 Almeida Street, London N1 1TD, England.

PUBLICATIONS

Plays

This Is No Place for Tallulah Bankhead (produced London, 1978).
The Third (produced London, 1980).
Second Sentence (produced Brighton, 1980).
Case to Answer (produced London, 1980; Ithaca, New York, 1981).
Breaking Through (produced London, 1980).
New Anatomies (produced London, 1981; New York, 1990).
    Published in *Plays Introduction*, London, Faber, 1984.
Inside Out (produced Stoke-on-Trent, 1982).

Home Leave (produced Ipswich, Suffolk, 1982).
False Admissions, adaptation of a play by Marivaux (produced London, 1983).
Successful Strategies, adaptation of a play by Marivaux (produced London, 1983).
Abel's Sister, based on material by Yolande Bourcier (produced London, 1984; New York, 1985).
The Grace of Mary Traverse (produced London, 1985). London, Faber, 1985.
Léocadia, adaptation of the play by Jean Anouilh (broadcast 1985). Published in *Five Plays*, by Anouilh, London, Methuen, 1987.
Mephisto, adaptation of the play by Ariane Mnouchkine, based on a novel by Klaus Mann (produced London, 1986).
Our Country's Good, adaptation of *The Playmaker* by Thomas Keneally (produced London, 1988; Los Angeles, 1989; New York, 1991). London, Methuen, 1988; revised edition, 1990.
The Love of the Nightingale (produced Stratford-on-Avon and London, 1988). With *The Grace of Mary Traverse*, London, Faber, 1989.
Pelléas and Mélisande, adaptation of the play by Maeterlinck (broadcast 1988; produced London, 1989).
Three Birds Alighting on a Field (produced London, 1991). London, Faber, 1991.
The Thebans, adaptation of three plays by Sophocles (includes *Oedipus Tyrannos*, *Oedipus at Colonus*, *Antigone*) (produced Stratford-on-Avon and London, 1992).

Radio Plays: *Léocadia*, 1985; *La Dispute*, from the play by Marivaux, 1987; *Pelléas and Mélisande*, from the play by Maeterlinck, 1988.

Television Plays: *Do Not Disturb*, 1991; *The Children*, adaptation of a novel by Edith Wharton, 1992.

*

Timberlake Wertenbaker comments:
    I like monologues. I think they are an unused and rather beautiful form of communication. I do not like naturalism. I find it boring. My plays are an attempt to get away from the smallness of naturalism, from enclosed rooms to open spaces, and also to get ideas away from the restraints of closed spaces to something wider. My plays often start with a very ordinary question: If women had power, would they behave the same way as men? Why do we seem to want to destroy ourselves? Is the personal more important than the political? If someone has behaved badly all of their lives, can they redeem themselves? Parallel to this will be some story I may have heard, some gossip about somebody, a sentence heard or read. A friend of mine once told me his mother had been taught how to be a good hostess by being made to talk to empty chairs. I used that as the opening scene of *The Grace of Mary Traverse*. I once heard about a young couple where the woman, for no apparant reason, had come out of the bath and shot herself. That became *Case to Answer*. Somebody showed me a print of the Japanese courtesan Ono No Komachi. I wrote a play about her. Everything gets collected and used at some point. I'm sure it's the same for all writers, but I haven't asked. Once I have the idea and the people, I do a lot of research. I think plays should be accurate, whatever their subject. Then the imagination can be let free, but only after a solid knowledge of the world, the people, the age, whatever is the world of the play.
    I don't think you can leave the theatre and go out and make a revolution. That's the naïvety of the 1970's. But I do think

you can make people change, just a little, by forcing them to question something, or by intriguing them, or giving them an image that remains with them. And that little change can lead to bigger changes. That's all you can hope for. Nor do I think playwrights should have the answers. A play is like a trial: it goes before the jury, the audience, and they decide—to like or not like the people, to agree or not to agree. If you really have the answers, you shouldn't be a writer but a politician. And if you're only interested in slice of life, then you should make documentaries. The theatre is a difficult place, it requires an audience to use its imagination. You must accept that and not try to make it easy for them. You must give them language, because it is best heard in the theatre and language is a potent manifestation of hope. In some theatres in ancient Greece, the number of seats corresponded to the number of adult males with voting rights. I think that is right: theatre is for people who take responsibility. There is no point in trying to attract idiots. Theatre should never be used to flatter, but to reveal, which is to disturb.

* * *

There is a wonderful continuity in the work of Timberlake Wertenbaker, which is none the less full of surprise, invention, and a delight in inversion. It is never possible to predict how she may wish to say something, though familiarity with her work shows themes and preoccupations which are part of her powerful personal identity as a writer. In form and setting, however, her dramas roam freely over historical periods and cultures: from antique Greece to a Japanese story which spans centuries; from an Australian penal colony to Islamic cross-dressing and the art world in London in the 1990's.

With the worldwide success of her major play, *Our Country's Good*, originally performed at London's Royal Court Theatre, Wertenbaker moved from the ranks of the much courted and professionally admired (for she is that rarity, a "writers' writer" who repeatedly demonstrates the potential of dramatic writing) to the genuinely popular. The play came about when the theatre's director, Max Stafford-Clark, brought her Thomas Keneally's novel, *The Playmaker*, an historical retelling of a production of Farquhar's *The Recruiting Officer* by prisoners at a penal settlement in Australia.

Although it springs from Keneally's novel, *Our Country's Good* is richly original theatre in its own right. A densely populated play, it maintains a constant focus on the individuals in the story and finds in the convict population a creative and positive energy which is lacking in the British officers who oppress them. As much as any of her plays, it demonstrates her sure instinct for the theatrical situation, for instance, her development of the character of a woman rehearsing her role despite a sentence of death which will mean her execution before the first performance.

Such skills did not come about overnight, although they seem to flower spectacularly in the collaborative creative atmosphere of the Royal Court. Before her first four major plays, *The Grace of Mary Traverse*, *Our Country's Good*, *The Love of the Nightingale*, and *Three Birds Alighting on a Field*, she had established an intriguing and peculiar body of work. There was individuality and dramatic inversion in even the most straightforward of her plays, such as *Home Leave*, which she wrote about women working in a factory at the end of World War II. Her opening stage directions present her leading character with calculated ambiguity: "She's in overalls, her hair hidden in a cloth cap and it should be impossible to tell she's a woman." Often the tilt of her writing explores a fluidity between the sexes that is far more revolutionary than

any declaration of equality, and she does not hesitate to subvert legend or history in her examinations of human nature.

Perhaps the most elaborate statements about the intentions of her early work appear in her play *Inside Out*, borrowed from the Japanese legend of Komachi, a famous beauty and poet who was doomed to suffer because of the task undertaken by one of her admirers which led to his death. Unable to match the poetic speech of Komachi in his declaration of love, he vowed to return from an arduous journey every night for 100 nights, but returned only 99 times. In Wertenbaker's version, Komachi first appears as an old woman who has survived into our present, and who has become interchangeable with Shosho, the lover. When the story of the love affair is retold, the old woman becomes Shosho and another actress plays the young Komachi who first rebuffs him and then, through desire, regrets the delay. Shosho remains steadfast in his promise.

As if that were not enough sexual ambiguity, it is by draping Shosho in her clothes and exchanging roles with him that Komachi extracts the promise of the 100 visits. Because it is by imagining himself as Komachi that Shosho has invented the idea of the poetic action, it is forever unclear who really suggested the task, but what remains equally unclear is the function of gender in Wertenbaker's version of the story.

The chorus reports: "They say a woman is a man turned inside out. Most evident in the genitals, his turned out, hers turned in, hers waiting for his, waiting for completion, that's what they say." But while that may be what "they say," it is obvious that Wertenbaker is not convinced. The chorus also asks: "Question: what is the anatomy of a woman?" and is answered by Komachi's companion Li: "Not what you imagine through your genitals."

Another of Wertenbaker's plays, *New Anatomies*, tackles that physical question more directly. It tells the story of Isabelle Eberhardt, a young woman who dresses as a male Arab to find acceptance among the Muslims and, ironically, is persecuted by the French. In her Arab persona as Si Mahmoud she seeks spiritual enlightenment and though the Arabs have more than a fair idea that she is actually a woman, they befriend her and accept her own determination of her sex. In the stage version, written for a women's theatrical troupe, all the roles, male and female, are taken by women. That ambiguity was not helpful as the issue of Isabelle's self-determined sexuality is profound, and the dressing-up of other women undermines both the spiritual search and the intended clash of western and oriental cultures. However, as a text it carefully and provocatively defines its arguments.

As a woman of American heritage, educated in France and resident in Britain, Wertenbaker herself juggles cultures and influences and in addition to her original work she has already made significant contributions to translation from the French, particularly with her translations from Marivaux. His stylish comic knowingness about sexuality and faithlessness has been well reflected in her English versions of *False Admissions*, *Successful Strategies*, and *La Dispute*, where she has maintained a cool ironical posture which admirably suggests the French originals. Although she has also provided convincing versions of Jean Anouilh's *Léocadia* and Ariane Mnouchkine's *Mephisto*, it is in Marivaux's writing that her own preoccupations are best reflected.

Ancient Greek is another of her languages, and her notable plain-spoken version of the Oedipus plays of Sophocles, *Oedipus Tyrannos*, *Oedipus at Colonus* and *Antigone*, were presented successfully by the Royal Shakespeare Company as *The Thebans*.

Possibly the most straightforward of her original plays is

Abel's Sister, written with material provided by Yolande Bourcier. It is none the less emotionally complex. Although set in the English countryside, it has some of the mythical aspirations of Sam Shepard's versions of the American family. Sandra, the spastic twin sister of Howard, has removed herself from the "centre" where she lives to move in on her brother and his girlfriend. When she announces that her favourite story is Cain and Abel, because it was right that Cain should at least kill the brother who suffocated him, she prepares the way for an attack on her brother by an American neighbour who has been led to believe that Howard is dangerously violent.

It is typical of Wertenbaker that she should turn to a basic biblical source, again inverting the sexes, to explain the motivation of her characters. In addition to the Japanese Nō theatre and investigations of Muslim culture, she has also explored the radicalization of Electra in her short (and relatively minor) reshaping of the *Oresteia*, *Agamemnon's Daughter* (as yet unproduced).

Her own most radical historical revision is her dramatic fantasia *The Grace of Mary Traverse*, in which she portrays Lord Gordon, the disaffected peer accused of treason after the destructive "Gordon Riots" of 1780, as a man who discovers power through the impulsive rape of a woman in the streets. In her version of events, he is a peripheral character and the dramatic catalyst is Mary Traverse, a young woman trained only in polite conversation by her father. After witnessing the rape by Gordon, she determines not to be a victim and decides to enter Georgian London as an equal of the rapacious men. She gambles with them, hires a male whore to deflower her, prostitutes herself to her father, and buys the sexual services of a woman for her own pleasure. She, too, finds power a seduction, and helps reignite the hatred for Catholics, though the horrors of mass violence finally chill her.

The classicism and cosmopolitan dramaturgy of Wertenbaker's writing seemed to mark her out from most of her contemporaries as a writer who dealt with the present only through metaphor. Her play for the Royal Shakespeare Company, *The Love of the Nightingale*, enforced that perception but when she returned to the Royal Court for *Three Birds Alighting on a Field* she was to provide one of the most articulate "de-constructions" of the 1980's to appear on stage.

Her central characters are Biddy, an English society woman who is ordered by her wealthy Greek husband to become interesting, and Stephen, a painter of English landscapes who has been exiled for a decade in the countryside for being unfashionable. In the original production the play included scenes that retold the parallel story of Philoctetes, the Greek hero abandoned on an island by Odysseus because of the smell of a wound. In order to win the Trojan War, Odysseus needed to trick Philoctetes back into his service, and in order for the gallery owner in Wertenbaker's play to survive the recession of the 1990's, he needs to lure Stephen back into his fold.

When the play was revived by the Royal Court a year after its first production, Wertenbaker dispensed with the enacted scenes of the Philoctetes story and allowed the modern story to stand on its own, secure in its parallels and confident of its own message. Events conspire to remove Biddy from her wealth and the limitations of her class while she becomes the agent who restores Stephen to the society of art. In the years covered by his exile, the world has changed. The ideological certainties of the left and the right have been vanquished by the collapse of Eastern Europe and western economies, and Wertenbaker's play is witty, knowing and eloquent in its depiction of the results.

Even in her most explicitly classical plays, Wertenbaker manages to wear her erudition lightly. What she demonstrates in *Three Birds Alighting on a Field* is the enduring strength of those classical values in the most topical of dramas. With her grasp of classical storytelling, her great gift of language and individuality of perception, she is likely to provide some of the most enduring drama of the late 20th century.

—Ned Chaillet

———————

WESKER, Arnold. English. Born in Stepney, London, 24 May 1932. Educated at Upton House Technical School, Hackney, London, 1943–48; London School of Film Technique, 1955–56. Served in the Royal Air Force, 1950–52. Married Doreen Bicker in 1958; two sons and two daughters. Furniture-maker's apprentice and carpenter's mate, 1948; bookseller's assistant, 1949 and 1952; plumber's mate, 1952; seed sorter on farm, 1953; kitchen porter, 1953–54; pastry cook, London and Paris, 1954–58; founder and director, Centre 42, 1961–70. Chair of the British Centre, 1978–83, and president of the Playwrights Permanent Committee, 1981–83, International Theatre Institute. Recipient: Arts Council grant, 1958; *Evening Standard* award, 1959; Encyclopaedia Britannica award, 1959; Marzotto prize, 1964; Best Foreign Play award (Spain), 1979; Goldie award, 1987. Fellow, Royal Society of Literature, 1985. Litt.D.: University of East Anglia, Norwich, 1989. Lives in London. Agent: Ian Amos, Duncan Heath Associates, Oxford House, 76 Oxford Street W1R 1RB, England.

PUBLICATIONS

Plays

The Wesker Trilogy. London, Cape, 1960; New York, Random House, 1961.
  Chicken Soup with Barley (produced Coventry and London, 1958; Cleveland, 1962). Published in *New English Dramatists 1*, London, Penguin, 1959.
  Roots (produced Coventry and London, 1959; New York, 1961). London, Penguin, 1959.
  I'm Talking about Jerusalem (produced Coventry 1960; revised version produced London, 1960). London, Penguin, 1960.
The Kitchen (produced London, 1959; New York, 1966). Published in *New English Dramatists 2*, London, Penguin, 1960; expanded version (produced Coventry and London, 1961; New York, 1966), London, Cape, 1961; New York, Random House, 1962.
Chips with Everything (produced London, 1962; New York, 1963). London, Cape, 1962; New York, Random House, 1963.
The Nottingham Captain: A Moral for Narrator, Voices and Orchestra, music by Wilfred Josephs and Dave Lee (produced Wellingborough, Northamptonshire, 1962). Included in *Six Sundays in January*, 1971.
Menace (televised 1963). Included in *Six Sundays in January*, 1971; in *The Plays of Arnold Wesker 2*, 1977.
Their Very Own and Golden City (produced Brussels, 1965; revised version produced London, 1966). London, Cape,

1966; revised version (also director: produced Aarhus, Denmark, 1974), in *The Plays of Arnold Wesker 2*, 1977.

The Four Seasons (produced Coventry and London, 1965; New York, 1968). London, Cape, 1966; in *The Plays of Arnold Wesker 2*, 1977; revised version in *The Plays of Arnold Wesker 2*, 1990.

The Friends (also director: produced Stockholm and London, 1970). London, Cape, 1970; in *The Plays of Arnold Wesker 2*, 1977.

The Old Ones (produced London, 1972; New York, 1974). London, Cape, 1973; revised version, edited by Michael Marland, London, Blackie, 1974; in *The Plays of Arnold Wesker 2*, 1977.

The Wedding Feast, adaptation of a story by Dostoevsky (produced Stockholm, 1974; Leeds, 1977; revised version produced Birmingham, 1980). Included in *The Plays of Arnold Wesker 4*, 1980.

The Journalists (produced Coventry, 1977; Los Angeles. 1979). London, Writers and Readers, 1975.

Love Letters on Blue Paper, adaptation of his own story (televised 1976; produced Syracuse, New York, 1977; also director: produced London, 1978; New York, 1984). London, TQ Publications-Writers and Readers, 1978.

The Plays of Arnold Wesker:
1. *The Kitchen, Chips with Everything, The Wesker Trilogy*. New York, Harper, 1976; revised edition as *The Wesker Trilogy* (includes *Chicken Soup with Barley, Roots, I'm Talking About Jerusalem*), London, Penguin, 1979.
2. *The Four Seasons, Their Very Own and Golden City, Menace, The Friends, The Old Ones*. New York, Harper, 1977; revised edition as *The Kitchen and Other Plays* (includes revised version of *The Four Seasons*; *The Kitchen*; *Their Very Own and Golden City*), London, Penguin, 1990.
3. *Chips with Everything, The Friends, The Old Ones, Love Letters on Blue Paper*. London, Penguin, 1980; revised edition as *Chips with Everything and Other Plays*, 1990.
4. *The Journalists, The Wedding Feast, The Merchant*. London, Penguin, 1980; revised edition as *Shylock and Other Plays* (includes *The Journalists, The Wedding Feast, The Merchant* as *Shylock*), 1990.
5. *One Woman Plays: Yardsale, Whatever Happened to Betty Lemon?, Four Portraits of Mothers, The Mistress, Annie Wobbler*. London, Penguin, 1989.
6. *Lady Othello and Other Plays: One More Ride on the Merry-Go-Round, Caritas, When God Wanted a Son, Lady Othello, Bluey*. London, Penguin, 1990.

The Merchant (produced Stockholm, 1976; revised version produced Philadelphia and New York, 1977; revised version produced Birmingham, 1978). Included in *The Plays of Arnold Wesker 4*, 1980; revised version published separately, London, Methuen, 1983; revised version as *Shylock* included in *The Plays of Arnold Wesker 4*, 1990.

Caritas (produced London, 1981). London, Cape, 1981.

Mothers: Four Portraits (produced Tokyo, 1982; as *Four Portraits of Mothers*, produced Edinburgh, 1984; Colorado, 1985; London, 1987). As *Four Portraits of Mothers*, included in *The Plays of Arnold Wesker 5*, 1989.

Annie, Anna, Annabella (broadcast 1983; as *Annie Wobbler*, also director: produced Birmingham and London, 1983; New York, 1986). As *Annie Wobbler*, included in *The Plays of Arnold Wesker 5*, 1989.

Sullied Hand (produced Edinburgh, 1984).

Yardsale (broadcast 1984; produced Edinburgh, 1985; also director: produced London, 1987; New York, 1988). Included in *The Plays of Arnold Wesker 5*, 1989.

Bluey (broadcast 1985). Included in *The Plays of Arnold Wesker 6*, 1990.

One More Ride on the Merry-Go-Round (produced Leicester, 1985). Included in *The Plays of Arnold Wesker 6*, 1990.

Whatever Happened to Betty Lemon? (produced Paris, 1986; also director: produced London, 1987; New York, 1988). Included in *The Plays of Arnold Wesker 5*, 1989.

Little Old Lady (for children) (produced Sigtuna, Sweden, 1988; Basildon, Essex, 1989). Published in *New Plays 1*, edited by Peter Terson, Oxford, Oxford University Press, 1988.

Beorhtel's Hill (produced Basildon, Essex, 1989).

Shoeshine (for children). Published in *New Plays 3*, edited by Peter Terson, Oxford, Oxford University Press, 1989.

The Mistress (also director: produced Arezzo, Italy, 1991). Included in *The Plays of Arnold Wesker 5*, 1989.

Three Woman Talking (produced Evanston, Illinois, 1992).

Letter to a Daughter (televised 1992; produced Seoul, South Korea, 1992).

Screenplay: *The Kitchen*, 1961.

Radio Plays: *Annie, Anna, Annabella*, 1983 (Germany); *Yardsale*, 1984; *Bluey*, 1985 (Germany).

Television Plays: *Menace*, 1963; *Love Letters on Blue Paper*, from his own story, 1976; *Diary of a Good Neighbour*, adaptation of Doris Lessing's *The Diary of Jane Somers*, 1989; *Letter to a Daughter*, 1992 (Norway).

Short Stories

Love Letters on Blue Paper. London, Cape, 1974; New York, Harper, 1975.

Said the Old Man to the Young Man: Three Stories. London, Cape, 1978.

Love Letters on Blue Paper and Other Stories. London, Penguin, 1980; revised edition, 1990.

Other

Labour and the Arts: II, or, What, Then, Is to be Done? Oxford, Gemini, 1960.

The Modern Playwright; or, "O Mother, Is It Worth It?" Oxford, Gemini, 1961.

Fears of Fragmentation (essays). London, Cape, 1970.

Six Sundays in January (miscellany). London, Cape, 1971.

Say Goodbye—You May Never See Them Again: Scenes from Two East-End Backgrounds, paintings by John Allin. London, Cape, 1974.

Words as Definitions of Experience. London, Writers and Readers, 1976.

Journey into Journalism. London, Writers and Readers, 1977.

Fatlips (for children). London, Writers and Readers, and New York, Harper, 1978.

The Journalists: A Triptych (includes the play *The Journalists*, *A Journal of the Writing of "The Journalists,"* and *Journey into Journalism*). London, Cape, 1979.

Distinctions (essays, lectures, journalism). London, Cape, 1985.

*

Critical Studies: *Mid-Century Drama* by Laurence Kitchin, London, Faber, 1960, revised edition, 1962; *The Writer and Commitment* by John Mander, London, Secker and Warburg,

1961; *Anger and After* by John Russell Taylor, London, Methuen, 1962, revised edition, 1969, as *The Angry Theatre*, New York, Hill and Wang, 1962, revised edition, 1969; "Two Romantics: Arnold Wesker and Harold Pinter" by Clifford Leech, in *Contemporary Theatre*, edited by John Russell Brown and Bernard Harris, London, Arnold, 1962, New York, St. Martin's Press, 1963; *Arnold Wesker* by Harold U. Ribalow, New York, Twayne, 1966; "Arnold Wesker, The Last Humanist?" by Michael Anderson, in *New Theatre Magazine* (Bristol), vol.8, no.3, 1968; *Arnold Wesker* edited by Michael Marland, London, Times Newspapers, 1970; *Arnold Wesker* by Ronald Hayman, London, Heinemann, 1970, revised edition, New York, Ungar, 1973, Heinemann, 1979; *The Plays of Arnold Wesker: An Assessment* by Glenda Leeming and Simon Trussler, London, Gollancz, 1971, and *Arnold Wesker*, London, Longman, 1972, and *Wesker the Playwright*, London, Methuen, 1983, both by Leeming, and *Wesker on File* edited by Leeming, Methuen, 1985; "Production Casebook 2: Arnold Wesker's *The Friends*" by Garry O'Connor, in *Theatre Quarterly* (London), April 1971; *Theatre Language: A Study of Arden, Osborne, Pinter, and Wesker* by John Russell Brown, London, Allen Lane, and New York, Taplinger, 1972; article by Margaret Drabble, in *New Review* (London), February 1975; *Stages in the Revolution* by Catherine Itzin, London, Eyre Methuen, 1980; *Understanding Arnold Wesker* by Robert Wilcher, Columbia, University of South Carolina Press, 1991.

Theatrical Activities:
Director: **Plays**—*The Four Seasons*, Havana, 1968; *The Friends*, Stockholm and London, 1970; *The Old Ones*, Munich, 1973; *Their Very Own and Golden City*, Aarhus, Denmark, 1974; *Love Letters on Blue Paper*, London, 1978, and Oslo, 1980; *Annie Wobbler*, Birmingham and London, 1983, London, 1984; *Yardsale*, Stratford-on-Avon, 1985, London, 1987; *Whatever Happened to Betty Lemon*, London, 1987; *The Merry Wives of Windsor* by Shakespeare, Oslo, Norway, 1990; *The Kitchen*, Madison, Wisconsin, 1990; *The Mistress*, Rome, 1991.

Arnold Wesker comments:

(1982) It is really for others to write about me. I try every so often to explain myself in lectures, articles, interviews. Never satisfactorily. Certain themes and relationships seem to pre-occupy me: the relationship between lovers, husband and wife, parent and child, friends, state and the individual; the themes of injustice, defiance, the power of knowledge.

I have no theories about the theatre writing through which I pursue these themes and relationships. Each play comes to me with its own metaphor, dictates its own form, creates its own atmosphere. All literature contains a mixture of poetry and journalism. Poetry in the theatre is that indefinable *sense* of truth which is communicated when two dissimilar or unrelated moments are placed side by side. "Sense" of truth, not *the* one and only truth. I would like to think my plays and stories have a larger proportion of poetry than journalism, and that if I have any talent it is for identifying the metaphors which life contains for the purpose of illuminating itself.

One day I hope someone may write as generously of me as Ruskin did of Turner:

This you will find is ultimately the case with every true and right master; at first, while we are tyros in art, or before we have earnestly studied the man in question, we shall see little in him; or perhaps see, as we think, deficiencies; we shall fancy he is inferior to this man in that, and to the other man in the other; but as we go on studying him we shall find that he has got both that and

the other; and both in a far higher sense than the man who seemed to possess those qualities in excess. Thus in Turner's lifetime, when people first looked at him, those who liked rainy weather said he was not equal to Copley Fielding; but those who looked at Turner long enough found that he could be much more wet than Copley Fielding when he chose. The people who liked force said that "Turner was not strong enough for them; he was effeminate; they liked De Wint,—nice strong tone;—or Cox—great, greeny, dark masses of colour—solemn feeling of the freshness and depth of nature; they liked Cox—Turner was too hot for them." Had they looked long enough they would have found that he had far more force than De Wint, far more freshness than Cox when he chose,—only united with other elements; and that he didn't choose to be cool, if nature had appointed the weather to be hot . . . And so throughout with all thoroughly great men, their strength is not seen at first, precisely because they united, in due place and measure, every great quality . . .

* * *

In an interview in the *Tribune* in 1978. Arnold Wesker characterised himself as "world-weary." "over-whelmed with a sense of frustration and impotence." "For reasons which I don't understand, I do seem to arouse hostilities and irritations." Nevertheless, Wesker continues to write and if he can find no place, or small room, in the British theatre, his plays enjoy a considerable success in other countries. The paradox of a major British writer continually premiering his work abroad, in translation, is heightened when one considers the obsessive concern, in the earlier plays, with the necessity of acting in community to transform and transcend the immediate environment in order to live authentically and fully.

Wesker's plays are plays of ideas, dramatising a debate, expressed in passionate terms, about the complexity and necessity of moral choices, when there is no clear precept to follow. In the earlier plays these moral dilemmas are often laid out in set pieces. In *Roots* Beatie tells the story of the girl in love with one man who deserts her, and loved by another who rejects her because she has given herself to the first. Idealism is seen very early to contain its own negative dialectic. "Tell me your dreams," says Peter, in *The Kitchen*, and unleashes the dream of the man who wants to drop a bomb on the CND marchers, because they hold up the buses.

Ironically, Wesker enjoyed much more success with the earlier plays, in which the dialectics between idealism and frustration were presented more simply, than with the later plays, where the issues are much more complex. Often values which had been seen positively in the earlier plays are revealed to be illusory. The search for "words" through which to apprehend the world, express one's thoughts and feelings, and build "bridges" fails to achieve those aims and becomes a way of obscuring or evading the issues. The realisation of self, through education and culture, which is to be the means of Beatie's liberation, becomes in *The Friends* a source of frustration, isolation, and contempt for others.

Wesker's stature in the theatre declined during the 1960's and 1970's. Until 1964 his battle against apathy and purely materialist values, for the individual's right to life, liberty, and the pursuit of happiness through the orderly and gradual reform of society, could be seen as a feasible, and socialist, course of action. The political and economic crises of the mid-1960's through the 1970's called for either a cynical withdrawal from these aims, a dropping out into anarchistic individualism, or a commitment to a programme, however vague, for mass revolution. Wesker's concern with values that surmount the material has embarrassed his opponents. His concern with the individual has led those who share his own passionate concern for the realisation of working-class potential to brand his work as elitist, subjective, and, ultimately, conformist.

It is very easy to select from Wesker's plays quotations which support a critique of counter-revolutionary idealism. After all, in *The Friends* Manfred has a speech in which he says, "The working class! Hate them! It's coming, Macey. Despise them! I can hear myself, it's coming. Hate them! The working class, my class, offend me. Their cowardly acquiescence, their rotten ordinariness—everything about them— Hate them! There!" Wesker leaves himself open to such criticisms, not because he necessarily agrees with such views but because, recognising that such thoughts and feelings are part of the dialectics of his own make-up, he allows his characters to express them with extreme feeling, without explicitly denying them by suppressing them or taking a committed authorial stance against them. Examined closely, Wesker's later plays present a complex dialectical discourse of contrasting and often contradictory views as to what the central issue involves. Friend and foe alike might condemn this as nit-picking over dead ground of a perverse adherence to idealism in the stern face of reality. Politicos may call for a sword to cut through the Gordian knots with which Wesker becomes enmeshed. He himself relentlessly pursues metaphysical values in an increasingly materialistic world, charting as he goes the deepening frustrations of compromise and the high price exacted for sticking to your beliefs.

What is clear from the line of development through his plays is the continual decrease of the spatial area in which the individual can act. The major shift in his work occurred in the mid-1960's and coincides with his withdrawal from public action, as expressed through his involvement with CND, the Committee of 100, and Centre 42. There are fewer scenes of concerted action in the later plays to mark the potential power of the working-class shown in the first act of *The Kitchen* or the coal-stealing scene in *Chips with Everything*. The size of the community participating in the ritual celebrations becomes smaller and more enclosed. In the first act of *Chicken Soup with Barley* the setting is a room, but there is constant reference to the world outside. The streets of the East End and the battlefields of Spain are arenas of political action. Education will make the world Beatie Bryant's oyster. In *The Old Ones* both the streets and the classroom are potential areas of mindless violence. In *The Merchant* Shylock's actions are confined within the space and rules of the ghetto. The line culminates in the walling up of the nun, Christine, in *Caritas* while she repeats "This is a wall, this is a wall. . . ." The area of the action shrinks and the concerns become more metaphysical.

Wesker's world-weariness and his sense of isolation and impotence are nihilistic only if he sees them subjectively. A move out into the world would reveal them as a common feature of the contemporary human condition. If it is harder to keep faith with Sarah Kahn's injunction to "care," her corollary still stands, "if you don't care you'll die." The struggle might be harder and the issues less clear-cut than they appeared before but the battle must still be waged. But to do this the ghetto has to be broken out of, and being walled up for your beliefs is too high a price to pay for integrity.

Since 1981 Wesker's work has marked time with no major play coming from him. However, there are signs that there is some resurgence of light-heartedness and fun if not optimism. *One More Ride on the Merry-Go-Round* is Wesker's attempt

at writing pure comedy but, not unexpectedly, serious themes intrude. The main action of the comedy is the revival of energy and purpose in a 50-year-old academic and his wife. Two further plays, *When God Wanted a Son* and *Lady Othello*, continue the theme of a middle-aged academic in affairs with younger women. Through these plays, Wesker explores further the process first encountered in *Roots*, the education and culturalization of women by an auto-didactic male. In these plays the issues become more complex. In *When God Wanted a Son*, the play centres on the wife, separated from her husband, who returns obsessively to exasperate and infuriate her. In *Lady Othello*, Wesker's finest play for some time, but so far unperformed, the couple in the relationship are incompatible in terms of age, colour, race, and his feelings of guilt. In both of these plays the destructive and divisive effects of education and learning are explored as well as the positive. Alongside these plays, Wesker has written a a series of one-woman plays, the best known and most often performed being *Annie Wobbler*. These serve to remind that Wesker is, above all, a great writer of character parts. His reputation internationally remains unabated but at home he remains bitter and alienated by the lack of respect and production for his plays.

—Clive Barker

WESLEY, Richard (Errol). American. Born in Newark, New Jersey, 11 July 1945. Educated at Howard University, Washington, D.C., 1963–67, B.F.A. 1967. Married Valerie Deane Wilson in 1972; three children. Passenger service agent, United Airlines, Newark, 1967–69; member of the New Lafayette Theatre Company and managing editor of *Black Theatre* magazine, New York, 1969–73; founding member, 1973, and member of the Board of Directors, 1976–80, Frank Silvera Writers Workshop, New York; teacher of black theatre history, Manhattanville College, Purchase, New York, Wesleyan University, Middletown, Connecticut, 1973–74, and Manhattan Community College, New York, 1980–83; member of the board of directors, Theatre of Universal Images, Newark, 1979–82; teacher, Rutgers University, New Brunswick, New Jersey, 1984. Recipient: Drama Desk award, 1972; Rockefeller grant, 1973; Audelco award, 1974, 1977; NAACP Image award, 1974, 1975. Agent: Jay C. Kramer, 135 East 55th Street, New York, New York 10022. Address: P.O. Box 43091, Upper Montclair, New Jersey 07043, U.S.A.

PUBLICATIONS

Plays

Put My Dignity on 307 (produced Washington, D.C., 1967).
The Street Corner (produced Seattle, 1970; New York, 1972).
Headline News (produced New York, 1970).
Knock Knock, Who Dat (produced New York, 1970).
The Black Terror (produced Washington, D.C., 1970; New York, 1971). Published in *The New Lafayette Theatre Presents*, edited by Ed Bullins, New York, Doubleday, 1974.
Gettin' It Together (produced Roxbury, Massachusetts, 1971;

New York, 1972). With *The Past Is the Past*, New York, Dramatists Play Service, 1979.

Strike Heaven on the Face! (produced New York, 1973).

Alicia (produced Waterford, Connecticut, 1973; as *Goin' Thru Changes*, produced New York, 1974).

Eight Ball (produced Waterford, Connecticut, 1973).

The Sirens (produced New York, 1974). New York, Dramatists Play Service, 1975.

The Mighty Gents (produced Waterford, Connecticut, 1974; as *The Last Street Play*, produced New York, 1978; as *The Mighty Gents*, produced New York, 1978). New York, Dramatists Play Service, 1979.

The Past Is the Past (produced Waterford, Connecticut, 1974; New York, 1975). With *Gettin' It Together*, New York, Dramatists Play Service, 1979.

On the Road to Babylon, music and lyrics by Peter Link, based on a concept by Brent Nicholson (produced Milwaukee, 1980).

Butterfly (produced Waterford, Connecticut, 1985).

The Talented Tenth (produced New York, 1989).

Screenplays: *Uptown Saturday Night*, 1974; *Let's Do It Again*, 1975; *Fast Forward*, 1985; *Native Son*, 1986.

Television Play: *The House of Dies Drear*, from the novel by Virginia Hamilton, 1974.

*

Manuscript Collection: Dramatists Play Service, New York.

*   *   *

Richard Wesley writes about the black community of America's urban ghettos. He charts the stoops, poolrooms, and tenements of the inner city and the ways of the people who live there: pimps, prostitutes, derelicts, street gangs. While his sensibility is lyrical, his intentions are political. Wesley questions the values that entrap his characters in aimless days and barren futures. He examines the rules by which they try to survive and the human and social costs when these rules prove inadequate.

While black playwrights such as Ed Bullins and Ron Milner really came from the ghettos they dramatize, Wesley grew up in a middle-class family in Newark, New Jersey. He was, he says, nearly a teenager before he discovered that college wasn't compulsory. At Howard University he not only came under the influence of the fabled Owen Dobson, mentor of many black theatre artists, but also embraced the black nationalist movement which took root on campuses in the 1960's. Upon graduation in 1967, he joined Bullins at the Black Playwrights Workshop of Harlem's New Lafayette Theatre, known for its activist posture and the cross-pollination it encouraged between the stage and the surrounding street culture.

His early play *The Black Terror* is a satire on the contradictions Wesley now detected in cultural nationalism. The playwright introduces us to members of a radical cadre pledged to revolutionary suicide in the service of urban guerrilla warfare. Through the character of Keusi, a pragmatic Vietnam veteran, Wesley debates the movement's tactics and its leaders' image of themselves as a kamikaze vanguard. "To die for the revolution is the greatest thing in life," says one of the militants. "But revolution is about life, I thought," Keusi

answers. "Our first duty as revolutionaries is to live. . . . Why we gotta fight a revolution with a value system directed toward death?"

Although its ideological emphasis is unique among his plays, *The Black Terror* incorporates many stylistic traits, blended impressionistically, that Wesley would refine in his increasingly humanistic later works. Raised more on television than live entertainment, he favors the stage equivalents of filmic crossfades, superimpositions, and jump cuts to shift locations rapidly, juxtapose moods, and suggest simultaneous action—an approach which subsequently brought him several Hollywood contracts. From the classics he borrows choral and ritualistic elements which he mingles with characters and scenes more typical of contemporary naturalistic drama. His dialogue, a pungent street argot, is expanded by poetic rhythms and refrains, while his monologues approach direct address soliloquies.

For the series of short plays he produced between 1972 and 1974, Wesley muted the stylistic exuberance of *The Black Terror* in favor of compassionate yet unsentimental character studies. In *Gettin' It Together* and *Goin' Thru Changes* polarized young couples struggle both against each other and against cheapening odds to piece together a future. *Strike Heaven on the Face!* brings a war hero home to peacetime defeat. *The Past Is the Past* is set in a poolhall, where a son in search of his heritage confronts the father who long ago abandoned him. Inspired in part by Fellini's *Nights of Cabiria*, a second reunion play, *The Sirens*, probes the life of a prostitute, eventually faced with a choice between her hard won but precarious independence and reconciliation with the husband who vanished a decade before to chase a dream now belatedly come true.

Individually, the plots of these five miniatures are casual, mere hooks on which Wesley's hangs family portraits. Taken as montage, however, they together gain a thematic solidarity which presents the scenography of a condition. A number of issues that played supporting roles in *The Black Terror* here become Wesley's preoccupations: the breakdown of family structures, leading to alienation among men and women, parents and children; connections between past and present, through which a legacy of defeat passes from generation to generation; thwarted efforts to wrench self-worth from deluded hopes and to stake out a little turf from which pride can be harvested. How, Wesley asks, can the quest for manhood succeed opposite frustrations that lead to inertia on one hand and savagery on the other?

His cinematic style refined, his ability to draw tenderly detailed characters matured, Wesley assembled his thematic concerns in a full-length drama about the important present and harsh destiny in store for the remnants of an expired Newark street gang. *The Last Street Play* opened to enthusiastic reviews, some of which compared Wesley's inner city tragedy to Kurosawa's *The Seven Samurai* and Fellini's *I vitelloni*, film classics concerning disoriented young toughs, now past their prime, who confront tomorrow with a gallows bravado as deluded as it is fatal. Under the title *The Mighty Gents*, the play transferred to Broadway, a commercial tribute that remains rare for legitimate dramas by black authors, and which italicizes the universality of Wesley's subject: the American dream, examined from a black perspective. Frankie Sojourner, onetime Gents leader, owes a debt to Studs Lonigan, the Irish Catholic title character of James T. Farrell's Depression novel of another squandered youth, another wasted generation. Among fellow playwrights who came of age in the 1970's, Wesley has most in common with David Mamet, whose *American Buffalo* in many ways resembles *The Mighty Gents*. In both plays, might-have-been men cling to a past in which, briefly, they were somebody. In both, desperation ignites violent schemes to regain self-esteem in the eyes of a world where, as Frankie puts it, "The census don't count us and welfare don't even know we alive." More largely, each evaluates American society in our times and the standards we use to govern it.

—C. Lee Jenner

———

WHEELER, Hugh (Callingham). American. 1912–1987. See 3rd edition, 1982.

———

WHELAN, Peter. British. Born in Newcastle-under-Lyme, 3 October 1931. Educated at Hanley High School, Stoke-on-Trent, 1941–49; Keele University, Staffordshire, 1951–55. National Service, 1950–51. Married Ffrangcon Price in 1958; two sons and one daughter. Assistant surveyor, Town Planning Office, Stoke-on-Trent, 1949–50; farm worker, Endon Farm, Staffordshire, 1950; manservant, Uffington Hall, Lincolnshire, and demolition worker, Staffordshire, both 1955; hall porter, English Speaking Union Hotel, London, 1956; advertising copywriter, A.S. Dixon Ltd., London, 1956–57; English teacher, Berlitz School, Bergen, Norway, 1957–58; teacher, West London College, London, 1958; advertising copywriter and director, various agencies in London, 1959–90. Recipient: Ford Foundation grant, 1964; Sony Radio award, 1990. Lives in London. Agent: Lemon, Unna, and Durbridge, 24 Pottery Lane, Holland Park, London W11 4LZ, England.

PUBLICATIONS

Plays

Lakota, with Don Kincaid (produced London, 1970).
Double Edge, with Les Darbon (produced London, 1975). London, French, 1976.
Captain Swing (produced Stratford-on-Avon, 1978; London, 1979). London, Collings, 1979.
The Accrington Pals (produced London, 1981; New York, 1984). London, Methuen, 1982.
Clay (produced London, 1982). London, Methuen, 1983.
A Cold Wind Blowing Up, with Les Darbon (produced Cologne, Germany, 1983).
World's Apart, adaptation of a work by Jose Triana (produced Stratford-on-Avon, 1986; London, 1987).
The Bright and Bold Design (produced London, 1991; Washington, D.C., 1992). London, Warner Chappell, 1991.
The School of Night (produced Stratford-on-Avon, 1992). London, Warner Chappell, 1992.

*

Peter Whelan comments:
I feel that any play I embark on must take me into the mysterious areas of human connection. The forces released must be beyond my absolute control. I must never know all the answers. The wastage of human conflict—often seen against a background of larger conflict—is, I suppose, my preoccupation.

I was a late starter, 40 before my first play, *Captain Swing*. I was drawn to it by wishing to counteract despairing visions of humanity as innately violent or socially brutalised. *The Accrington Pals*, *The Bright and Bold Design*, and *Clay* form almost a trilogy, drawing on my extended family background in the potteries and Salford. At the centre of it is the force of attraction and repulsion between people swept along by the times they live in and yearning for some peace in one another. I greatly regret that I have not so far been able to turn this into out-and-out comedy—but there is still time.

I am always impressed by Henry Moore's statement: "If I knew too clearly what I was doing I might not be able to do it." I am influenced by: Yeats, "Hammer your thoughts into a unity"; Tennessee Williams and Chekhov, for humanity; Miller, Brecht, and Ibsen, for structure; and Beckett, for defining where we are now.

*   *   *

Autumn 1830. Within sight of the harvest they have gathered, the farm labourers of Britain are starving while the gentry rejoice in their new threshing machines. Fires flare in Kent. In a small Sussex village, Mathew Hardness, wheelwright and committed democrat ("It's the people who keep the law . . . let those who govern break it. . . . No making revolution but restoring our natural right") encourages peaceful confrontation between labourers and landowners. Meanwhile, the gentry receive threatening letters from "Captain Swing, avenger of the people."

The gentry are engulfed by terror, their guilt sowing fear of anarchy in dynamic contrast to the reason and restraint of the local Swing rebels. However, the infiltration of an Irishman, O'Neil, professional revolutionary hot from the fires of France, greedy for power and violent rebellion, creates factions and confusion amongst the workers, and the arrival of a badly burned soldier, Farquare, on the run from the Dragoons and near death, inflames revolutionary zeal. Gemma, barmaid and town whore, in a passion for Farquare, embraces the revolution with fanatical fervour, vows celibacy, and proclaims Farquare to be Captain Swing.

Flails strike against the bare stage; tri-colour and black flags fly; the menacing presence of giant corn men provides a dark sense of historical and metaphysical necessity setting the immediate moment of history ringing with the energy of unresolved patterns of historical and imminent crisis.

Captain Swing is an impressive stage debut. The scope of the action, the impressive use of stage space, and the powerful construction of dramatic image herald an exciting new writer.

Peter Whelan gives even the most minor characters distinction by activating their personal demands in relation to the historical situation. From Mathew to Agnes, who seeks justice from the committee for her husband's murder of their child, each character is unmistakably both a private individual with personal needs and concerns and an active, unavoidable member of the social context.

On the one hand, this economic approach to character development creates the sensation that every possible attitude toward the immediate crisis and its implications has been argued for our assessment. On the other, it forms the very core of Whelan's structure and themes. The tension between the characters' individual and social identities and responsibilities provides the central dynamic of his work and arguably its most dramatically powerful element.

In *The Accrington Pals* the interdependence between the individual and the community is created by presenting World War I from the perspective of the Home Front. May, a fiercely independent woman who runs a fruit and vegetable stall, is unable to confess her love for Tom, an artist, partly because she knew him as a child, partly because she is older than he, but mainly because, against her deepest fears, he has enlisted. Whelan describes the play as "a story of a class-cum-love relationship between a strong-minded, rugged individualist woman and a dreamy, Utopian idealist young man." This relationship provides the framework for an intense discussion about personal will and success, community responsibility and, as in *Captain Swing*, the personal and social consequences of social and historical power struggles. Occasional letters from the Front and a remarkable scene where May meets Tom's corpse bring the war onto the stage, and when the town learns of the deaths of the Accrington Pals they turn on their own leaders. However, the relationship between the individual and the social context is, typically, ambiguous and complex. Despite its futile waste of human resources, the war affords May the chance to achieve her dream of owning a shop.

Whelan's plays are most successful when his overt question —"How shall we live?"—is set in the conundrum of incorporating private needs and expression with the recognition and responsibility of social demands. His attempt to explore these themes in the drawing-room through the discussion of personal experience is both less engaging and less revealing. *Clay* lacks the social context and social commitment of the first two plays and, hence, both their dramatic dynamism and their complexity. Micky and her husband Ben, Staffordshire potters, are visited by old friends, Win and Pat, recently returned from West Germany. A close foursome as teenagers, the middle-class, middle-aged couples struggle to recapture their relationships, both group and personal (Win and Pat's marriage has nearly failed). Although "How shall we live?" is still on the tip of Whelan's tongue, it is literally and simplistically stated here. The translation of the question to personal angst reduces the discussion to specific personal experience, the issues, like the characters, are limited and hypothetical. The four characters never take on the weight that would allow them to stand as analogous examples. Win doesn't come to "stand for all of us who have ever looked for a refuge from that future"; rather, her obsessive idealizing suggests a pathetic, private pathology. Whelan's occasional insistence on extended relevance—"(clay's) tough. You can't get rid of it. It looks fragile but in five thousand years they'll still be digging lots of it up. . . . When everyone's gone and the churchyard's empty. And that's the ultimate satisfaction of being a potter. Finally, you get buried in your work"—are self-conscious and literary. Separate from the necessities of social interaction and responsibility, the characters are credible but rather unengaging stage people whose personal problems may be viewed with detached sympathy and discarded when the curtain descends.

In *The Bright and Bold Design*, however, a return to historical context seems to re-inspire Whelan's courageous dramatization of unresolved complexities. In his introduction, Whelan implies that he intends to celebrate individualism, and in a manner unusual to his work, isolates Jessie, a talented freehand painter and designer working in a Staffordshire pottery in the 1930's, focusing on her personal experience and emotions. But the effect of the play is more complex. Jessie seeks recognition and self-expression through painting and eventually leaves the factory to stay with an aunt, help in the aunt's shop, and paint. She braves the pressures of Jack, the new design manager (who recognizes

her talent and promotes her designs but demands that she amend them to his ideas), and of the community, represented by the other painters and Jack's ideal of bringing beautiful tableware to the workers. However, Whelan's unwillingness to simplify the issues at stake make the intended celebration of individualism ambivalent and more dramatic, demanding further contemplation of the relationship between community and individual. Jack's ideals are tinged and distorted by his personal desires. Simultaneously. Jessie's isolation and the drabness of her "self-fulfilment" makes her apparent victory less glitteringly absolute, especially since she is still, willy-nilly, dependent on others for that independence. It is notable that we last see Jessie back in the community for Jack's funeral. The play asks whether individuality and talent cannot be better used by the community, or even, more pertinently, how we might organize our world so both society and the individual might benefit and grow.

Whelan is constantly exploring how the values in conflicting ideals might be synthesized to mutual advantage; given that we are both uniquely ourselves and inescapably members of our world and responsible to it: "How shall we live?"

—Elaine Turner

WHITE, Edgar Nkosi. American. Born in Montserrat, West Indies, 4 April 1947. Brought to the United States in 1952. Educated at the City College, City University of New York, 1964–65; New York University, 1966–69, B.A.; Yale University School of Drama, New Haven, Connecticut, 1971–73; since 1992, the New York Theological Seminary. Playwright-in-residence, Yale University School of Drama, New Haven, Connecticut, New York Shakespeare Festival Joseph Papp Public Theater, 1971–72, and Cafe La Mama, New York, 1992; artistic director, Yardbird Players Company, New York, 1974–77. Recipient: New York State Council on the Arts grant, 1975; O'Neill award, 1977; Rockefeller grant, 1989. Agent: Helen Merrill, 361 West 17th Street, New York, New York 10011, U.S.A; and, Marion Boyars, 24 Lacy Road, London SW15 1NL, England.

PUBLICATIONS

Plays

The Mummer's Play (produced New York, 1965).   Included in *Underground*, 1970.
The Wonderful Yeare (produced New York, 1969).   Included in *Underground*, 1970.
The Figures at Chartres (produced New York, 1969).
The Life and Times of J. Walter Smintheus (produced New York, 1971).   With *The Crucificado*, New York, Morrow, 1973.
The Burghers of Calais (produced Boston, 1971; New York, 1972).   Included in *Underground*, 1970.
Fun in Lethe; or, The Feast of Misrule (produced Providence, Rhode Island, 1974).   Included in *Underground*, 1970.
Underground: Four Plays. New York, Morrow, 1970.
Seigismundo's Tricycle: A Dialogue of Self and Soul (produced New York, 1971).
Lament for Rastafari (produced New York, 1971; London,

1978). Included in *Lament for Rastafari and Other Plays*, 1983.

Transformations: A Church Ritual (produced New York, 1972).

The Crucificado (produced New Haven, Connecticut, 1972; New York, 1972). With *The Life and Times of J. Walter Smintheus*, New York, Morrow, 1973.

La Gente (produced New York, 1973).

Ode to Charlie Parker (produced New York, 1973).

Offering for Nightworld (produced New York, 1973).

Les Femmes Noires (produced New York, 1974; London, 1981). Included in *Redemption Song and Other Plays*, 1985.

The Pygmies and the Pyramid (produced New York, 1976).

The Defense (produced Waterford, Connecticut and New York, 1976).

Trinity: The Long and Cheerful Road to Slavery (includes *Man and Soul*, *The Case of Dr. Kola*, *That Generation*) (produced London, 1982; New York, 1987). Included in *Lament for Rastafari and Other Plays*, 1983.

Lament for Rastafari and Other Plays. London, Boyars, 1983.

Like Them That Dream (produced New York, 1988). Included in *Lament for Rastafari and Other Plays*, 1983.

The Nine Night (produced London, 1983). With *Ritual by Water*, London, Methuen, 1984.

Ritual by Water (produced London, 1983). With *The Nine Night*, London, Methuen, 1984.

Redemption Song (produced London, 1984). Included in *Redemption Song and Other Plays*, 1985.

The Boot Dance (produced London, 1984). Included in *Redemption Song and Other Plays*, 1985.

Ritual (produced London, 1985).

Redemption Song and Other Plays. London, Boyars, 1985.

Moon Dance Night (produced London, 1987).

I Marcus Garvey (also director: produced Jamaica and New York, 1992).

Live from Galilee (produced New York, 1992).

Other

Sati, the Rastafarian (for children). New York, Lothrop, 1973.

Omar at Christmas (for children). New York, Lothrop, 1973.

The Yardbird Reader. Privately printed, 1973.

Children of Night (for children). New York, Lothrop, 1974.

The Rising. London, Boyars, 1988.

*

Critical Studies: *The Drama of Nommo* by Paul Carter Harrison, New York, Grove, 1972; *Drumbeats, Masks, and Metaphors: Contemporary Afro-American Theatre* by Genevieve Fabre, Cambridge, Massachusetts, Harvard University Press, 1983.

Edgar Nkosi White comments:

My work mainly has to do with ritual. The central theme of my work is the business between man and God. My interest in theatre began with the church (African, Caribbean, American). I am at present studying for my Masters in Divinity at the New York Theological Seminary.

I am a very slow writer. I have no control over what direction my work, my interest, my craft will lead me. I also find myself falling in love with film. I am still a black writer. After 20 years of writing I am beginning to learn the craft. My perspective is global.

* * *

Edgar Nkosi White's drama is concerned with the black predicament within a predominantly white universe. And for him a black is a black whether he comes from Africa or the Caribbean, and he is even more so to the white man. His plays highlight the deprivation and hardship of the developing nations and the usual dreams of a better life in the developed nations. It is hardly surprising that migration, exile, and alienation are the central focus as he follows black exiles through their humiliations and disappointments in the cities of Europe and North America.

White's first collection of plays, *Underground*, contains *The Burghers of Calais*, *Fun in Lethe*, *The Mummer's Play* and *The Wonderful Yeare*. *The Burghers of Calais* deals with the wrongful conviction of the Scottsboro boys for rape. The play centres around Bagatelle and his mates in prison as their fate is thrown from one court to another without much hope for a reprieve. White here shows his concern with the manifest injustice which black people face. Of the four plays in the collection, this is the one with the largest focal range and is the one in which White is closest to his fellow victims of racism. The play's structure is very complex, displaying the playwright's bold experiments with dramatic form. Of especial interest is his application of a highly developed cinematic sensibility to create plays that very often challenge the audience's ability to integrate diverse material. His scenes are as varied as the huge canvas on which his characters conduct their complex relationships.

Fun in Lethe explores the theme of migration, exile, and alienation by dramatizing the journey of a West Indian poet through Great Britain. Harmatia represents the numerous "citizens of Empire" who return to claim their own piece of the "motherland" and his experience typifies the problems and disillusionment of the black son who stakes his claim on mother England. It is even worse for the pretentious ones like Harmatia and like Legion in *Redemption Song* who are writers trying to eke out a living through their craft in a very hostile environment. This play is typically a mishmash of characters, events, and ideas that though amusing aren't always effective structurally.

The Mummer's Play returns to an America described as "one large unflushed toilet." A note of impatient anger creeps into White's writing, a note which he retains up to *Redemption Song*. The black victims, because they merely laze around and do nothing to help themselves, get sympathy neither from White nor from the audience. Here, as in other plays, White explores the various myths about West Indians and in the end he tries to explode some of them. When he looks at alienation in *Redemption Song*, *The Mummer's Play*, *The Wonderful Yeare*, and *The Boot Dance*, he does not simply blame America or Europe but also the victims who through an enervating anguish allow themselves to become alienated. And when he deals with migration and exile as he does in most of his plays, he seeks to expose the deeper structures of social inequality in Caribbean society which is responsible for the famed migratory consciousness of West Indians. And he does this well in *Redemption Song* as he follows Legion, the failed and alienated migrant who returns to his island only to face further alienation and subsequent death from the oppressors of Redemption City.

The Wonderful Yeare is set in a New York slum and deals with social deprivation among and petty racial jealousies between America's oppressed ethnic minorities. This deeply ironic play in which White shows his understanding of the *lazzis* and improvisation of the *commedia dell' arte* is about the "gift of life in the midst of death." Even as the plague rages, life goes on, and on a positive note, unlike White's other artists, Misserimus does something in the end—he marries Maria and goes to work.

White's second collection contains *Lament for Rastafari*, *Like Them That Dream*, and *Trinity*. *Lament for Rastafari* is structurally episodic and narrative continuity is maintained solely through characters. It is about the spiritual as well as physical journey of a West Indian family first to England and then to America. Lindsay, Barret, and Laputa, like White's other migrants and exiles, are driven by want and racial oppression to leave home and scour the cities of Europe and North America. In this play White begins his experiments with the West Indian dialect which we see in full flow in *Redemption Song*. *Like Them That Dream* is about Sparrow, a South African painter, who flees apartheid only to encounter it in other forms in America. In the end he has to make a choice, either to keep running or stand and confront apartheid head on. And it is only when he does the latter that he is able to appreciate the love and stability which Sharon offers him. The play is in many respects like *The Boot Dance*, which concerns Lazarus, another exile who in fleeing oppressive apartheid finds himself oppressed and powerless in an English mental asylum where only blacks are the inmates and the doctor is white. All in all, what emerges from this and other plays is White's extreme despairing vision of the black condition.

Trinity is a group of three plays—*Man and Soul*, which deals with the misunderstanding and antagonism between blacks from Africa and those from the West Indies, and also the racist law which lumps them together as criminals; *The Case of Dr. Kola*, which shows the idiocies of African governments and corrupt politicians, as well as the equally hopeless military men who replace them through coups; and finally, *That Generation*, which follows Wallace and Phyllis on the journey from a very comfortable life in the West Indies to one of penury and denigration in England. Again, a sense of despair pervades these plays since they are coloured by White's essential pessimism.

Les Femmes Noires displays all the characteristics of White's dramaturgy and, as he himself points out, it is "poly-scenic" and was conceived as representing the "viewpoint of a blind man perceiving sound." The action progresses as if seen through the roving lens of a movie camera or the playing-out of sounds and motion in a dream as it follows the dreary lives, individual anguish, and fading hopes of a group of black women in New York City. However, the play is rescued from White's usual pessimism by the sisterly striving and support which these women offer to each other, and it is their basic humanity which survives.

White's plays suggest that each is a personal journey, and the central characters—often black artists struggling to survive in the unfriendly cities of Europe and North America—are projections of his own psyche which he probes in order to come to terms with his exile and alienation. His central characters are thus one person seen in different situations, sometimes speaking the same lines as in *Fun in Lethe* and *Lament for Rastafari* but always the exile. The plays capture White's lonely and restless search for meaning through their cinematic structure. It is this dialectic between content and form which makes White an interesting dramatist.

—Osita Okagbue

WHITE, John (Sylvester). American. Born in Philadelphia, Pennsylvania, 31 October 1919. Educated at Gonzaga High School, Washington, D.C., 1933–37; University of Notre Dame, Indiana, 1937–41, A.B. in English 1941. Married Vasiliki Sarant in 1966. Actor for 25 years: charter member, Actors Studio, New York. Lives in Hawaii. Address: c/o Greenevine Agency, 9021 Melrose Avenue, Suite 304, Los Angeles, California 90069, U.S.A.

PUBLICATIONS

Plays

Twist (produced New York, 1963).
Bugs (produced New York, 1964). With *Veronica*, New York, Dramatists Play Service, 1966.
Sand (produced New York, 1964).
Veronica (produced New York, 1965). With *Bugs*, New York, Dramatists Play Service, 1966.
Bananas (produced New York, 1968).
The Dog School (produced New York, 1969).
Lady Laura Pritchett, American (produced Southampton, New York, 1969).
Mirage (produced Hanover, New Hampshire, 1969).
The Passing of Milldown Muldern (produced Los Angeles, 1974).
Ombres (produced Paris, 1975).
Les Punaises (produced Paris, 1975).

Screenplay: *Skyscraper*, 1959.

Other

Editor (American version), *Report from Palermo*, by Danilo Dolci. New York, Orion, 1958.

*

Manuscript Collection: Lincoln Center Library of the Performing Arts, New York.

Theatrical Activities:
Actor: **Plays**—as John Sylvester: roles in *Richard III*, New York, 1943; *Sundown Beach* by Bessie Brewer, New York, 1948; *Danny Larkin* by James V. McGee, New York, 1948; *All You Need Is One Good Break* by Arnold Manoff, New York, 1950. **Television**—Mr. Woodman in *Welcome Back, Kotter* series, 1975–79; roles in other television and radio plays.

John White comments:

(1973) Unless writing for hire, I write privately, from within, using for material the backwash of fifty years of existence, sometimes even living. I cannot work from the daily paper or the latest vogue. Indeed, I am turned off by the world. When I think about it, I can't write. I have been accused of being formless and have been applauded, on the other hand, for good form. I detest critics (in the main; there are a few splendid exceptions) and professional "knowers-how." Lonely is the word.

* * *

Though represented by professional productions of just one full-length and a few one-act plays, John White in the 1960's established himself as one of the freshest and most talented playwrights in America. Writing in a strikingly idiosyncratic style—the hallmark of any artist—he applied modern surrealism (less than absurdist, more than naturalist) to find a mythology in American roots. His small body of work is uneven—*Bugs* a good one-act play, *Veronica* a superlative one, and *Bananas* a prematurely produced full-length play that, with polishing, would have been a major work. But like too many playwrights producing in New York during this period, White was hurt by a powerful and ignorant fraternity of critics (it was an era when *Waiting for Godot*, *Entertaining Mr. Sloane*, and *The Homecoming* by Beckett, Orton, and Pinter were rejected). The playwright fled to Hollywood to seek a living wage at least. Ironically, the style that he plumbed has since become familiar (and therefore palatable) through the work of playwrights from Pinter to Sam Shepard.

Bugs (American vernacular for mad) is about a disturbed young man who has escaped from a hospital and returned to a home where things aren't much saner. His mother and girlfriend are respectively and insanely cheerful and stupid. His father, when not hidden behind a newspaper, is a ranting menace. Though the play might have been more, it gave clear promise of the author's specialness.

Veronica fulfilled the promise. Its central characters are a popular American songwriting team of the 1930's. They are holed up in a hotel room, trying desperately to repeat the huge success they had with a song called "Veronica." They are interrupted by a most peculiar burglar whose very philosophy of life, as it turns out, was inspired by the lyrics of that song.

These lyrics, in accurate satire of the period's popular music, spell out the passé, nostalgic, American dream as once advertised—a dream of beautiful blonds and money and trips to tropical islands. But has this sweet, silly dream now grown obsolete, only to be superseded by mundane social responsibility? One of the songwriters is too absorbed by war and disease to write again about June and moon. His partner is furious—"People haven't changed—a kiss is still a kiss, a sigh is still a sigh."

This yearning for a country once foolish and lovable—this choice of innocence over sophistication—was more deeply explored in the ambitious *Bananas*. The play is set in a period burlesque house during a rehearsal by three comics and an actress. A critic arrives. A series of sketches begins in which the author relates the techniques for burlesque to those of absurdism, suggesting that in a nostalgic, truthful-sardonic way, everything is bananas (another American slangword for madness, obviously White's view of existence). As the play continues, the metaphor of a show as life changes from the burlesque theater to a modern television studio, but everyday conversation remains as a replica of dialogue we have heard on some stage, somewhere.

The idea is excellent and much of the technique is virtuosic, but the play was produced prematurely, and is ultimately confusing, though its argument seems clear enough—a preference for the innocence of actors, entertaining, over the hopeless attempts by intellectuals to make sense of life. Without being repetitious, White—like most fine playwrights—had from the start a consistency to his style and content.

But sadly, a start seems to be all that his playwriting career will have. Like too many in the brutal, competitive, business controlled, and mindlessly commercial and anti-artistic American theater, his sensitivity as a playwright seems to have been beaten down by senseless rejection and unappreciation.

—Martin Gottfried

WHITE, Patrick (Victor Martindale). Australian. 1912–1990.
See 4th edition, 1988.

WHITEHEAD, Ted (Edward Anthony Whitehead). British. Born in Liverpool, Lancashire, 3 April 1933. Educated at St. Francis Xavier's Jesuit College; Christ's College, Cambridge, B.A. (honours) in English 1955, M.A. Served in the King's Regiment, 1955–57. Married 1) Kathleen Horton in 1958 (marriage dissolved 1976), two daughters; 2) Gwenda Bagshaw in 1976. Milkman, postman, bus conductor, sales promotion writer, salesman, and teacher, 1959–65; advertising copywriter and account executive, 1965–71; resident dramatist, Royal Court Theatre, London, 1971–72; fellow in creative writing, Bulmershe College, Reading, Berkshire, 1975–76. Recipient: George Devine award, 1971; *Evening Standard* award, 1971. Agent: Casarotto Ramsay Ltd., National House, 60–66 Wardour Street, London W1V 3HP, England.

PUBLICATIONS

Plays

The Foursome (produced London, 1971; Washington, D.C., 1972; New York, 1973). London, Faber, 1972.
Alpha Beta (produced London, 1972; New York, 1973). London, Faber, 1972.
The Punishment (televised 1972). Published in *Prompt Three*, edited by Alan Durband, London, Hutchinson, 1976.
The Sea Anchor (produced London, 1974; New York, 1982). London, Faber, 1975.
Old Flames (produced Bristol, 1975; London, 1976; New York, 1980). London, Faber, 1976.
Mecca (produced London, 1977; New York, 1980). London, Faber, 1977.
The Man Who Fell in Love with His Wife, adaptation of his television series *Sweet Nothings* (produced London, 1984). London, Faber, 1984.
Dance of Death, adaptation of a play by Strindberg (produced Oxford, 1984; London, 1985).

Radio Play: *The Old Goat Gone*, 1987.

Television Plays: *Under the Age*, 1972; *The Punishment*, 1972; *The Peddler*, 1976; *The Proofing Session*, 1977; *The Irish Connection* (*Crown Court* series), 1979; *Sweet Nothings* series, 1980; *World's End* series, 1981; *The Detective* serial, from the novel by Paul Ferris, 1985; *The Life and Loves of a She-Devil* serial, from the novel by Fay Weldon, 1986; *First Born*, from a novel by Maureen Duffy, 1988; *Jumping the Queue*, from the novel by Mary Wesley, 1989; *The Free Frenchman*, from the novel by Piers Paul Read, 1989; *Murder East Murder West*, 1990.

Novel

World's End (novelization of television series). London, BBC Publications, 1981.

* * *

Ted Whitehead's chosen dramatic territory is marriage and the impossible demands the institution makes on love and fidelity. His principal characters are most often drawn from the white-collar working class. They are witty and articulate but not intellectuals. His dialogue is a rapid verbal sparring, which frequently breaks down into hysteria or physical violence. His writing drives towards as plain a style as possible in the exposition of his emotional and sexual themes, although he is capable of occasional passages of lyrical beauty. "Escape" and "freedom" are key positives in his vocabulary, but they turn out to be chimeras for both men and women. His plays chart accurately the major debates around the family, sex, and marriage since the early 1960's and, while he has little interest in plot or character-development, his ear is very sharp for the changing discourses of male and female in this area.

A comparison between his first stage success, *Alpha Beta*, and his latest original play, *The Man Who Fell in Love with His Wife*, is immediately instructive. *Alpha Beta* has only two characters, Mr. and Mrs. Elliot, and covers the years 1962 to 1971. Mr. Elliot is a manager on the Liverpool docks and his wife is a housewife. When the play opens he is 29 and she is 26. They have two children who remain as an off-stage audience to the bickering, fighting, violence, and hysteria which make up the play. Mr. Elliot already has a mistress, Eileen, and wants a divorce. His wife won't give him one. Although marriage has turned into a bitter trap for both of them, Mrs. Elliot stands by the moral law of until death us do part. For Mr. Elliot they're dead already. He wants the freedom to "fuck a thousand women." He's no different, he claims, from all his male friends, except they sublimate their desires in blue movies and dirty jokes. "I'm sick of fantasy," he says, "I want reality." Elliot's view is that he married too young and too early for the permissive 1960's. Marriage is changing, he warns his wife, and even a woman like her, in the future, will "want a bit of what's going, for herself." A mutual enslavement like theirs shouldn't last. "Man and women are going to share free and equal unions that last because they want them to last. Not because they're forced!" Mrs. Elliot has only contempt for his "honesty" and his sociology. In her view he's retarded. He's never grown out of the role of working-class bucko, tomcatting around after eternal youth. She won't let him escape his duties as head of the household. Over the years of the play they evolve a kind of compromise. Mr. Elliot pays the bills and resides in the house but pursues his extra-marital affairs. His wife runs the house and just about hangs onto her sanity. The play ends with a suicide threat by Mrs. Elliot which her husband takes half seriously but which fires no buried love or affection in him. It's an unsatisfactory ending because there can be no ending to a war on these terms. As the title suggests, this couple must go down through the alphabet of their hatred and then start all over again.

The Man Who Fell in Love with His Wife begins with just that change in women's status that Mr. Elliot foresaw. Mary Fearon, in her late thirties, has got her first job, in the Civil Service. Her husband Tom, aged 41, is also employed as a dock manager in Liverpool. Mary's office life causes him extreme jealousy but also refuels his sexual passion for her. Suspender-belts and instamatic photos play their part in maintaining an ardour that Mary, who still loves him deeply, cannot match. Love in marriage can be as stifling as hatred. Tom wants to replay their adolescence and courtship. The Platters and Ike and Tina Turner are his favourite music. He drags his wife out to a freezing session on a favourite beach

near Liverpool. Mary wants to move on and eventually she moves out. By then Tom has given up his job to monitor his wife throughout the day. The roles and emotions of *Alpha Beta* have been reversed, and there is now a chance for the kind of freedom for both sexes that Mr. Elliot prophesied. For this is the 1980's, and between the Fearons and their daughter intervenes a new role-model, the divorcée in her thirties. She is Julia, an office friend of Mary's, who supports her bid for independence and counters Tom's arguments with reason and confidence. "Is it selfish for me to want my wife to love me?" he asks. "It's selfish to demand it regardless of what she wants," Julia replies. In the end they have to settle for separate lives, although old connections can't be broken. "I love you—even if I can't live with you," says Mary, and Tom, now a cab driver, has to become adult out of his own resources.

Glimpses of this comparative optimism can be seen in other Whitehead plays in the 1970's. In *The Sea Anchor* men and women friends wait, on Dublin Bay, for the arrival of daredevil Nick after his solo voyage across the Irish Sea for Liverpool in a ten-foot dinghy. The play is also about the other side of marriage, since all the characters are engaged in adulterous relationships. Nick is their hero since he "does exactly what he wants to do" while the others all cover up in various ways. Whitehead's theme of the trapped, randy male is complemented by that of the calculating, randy female and in the character of Jean we see a coarser precursor to Julia. The backchat is vulgar and witty, but Andy is given two lyrical passages, when he recalls a shoal of mackerel at night, "a giant ripple, V-shaped . . . it came hissing along beside the boat," and the time he and Nick heard black bodies barking in the silver sea and discovered they were porpoises, which sharply contrast with the brutality of the sexual relationships. Nick's boat comes in, empty. His sea anchor, "a kind of parachute, keeps you steady," hasn't saved him. A lost hero is useless and the sea is a false escape from domestic complexity.

Nor is abroad any solution. The group of English tourists in *Mecca* brings its marital conflicts and emotions intact to Morocco. Middle-aged Andrew sublimates his desire for the 20-year-old Sandy into a false fatherly protectiveness. His wife, Eunice, isn't fooled, but her verbal barbs have an articulacy which Mrs. Elliot lacked. Ian is young and fancy-free and Martin is the gay protector for the defensive bravado of Jill, 38, divorced, and feeling herself caught between the insouciance of Sandy and the certainties of Eunice. "She's not afraid of sex," says Jill to Eunice, "and neither is her generation. That's why they don't get used-up like us." But Sandy's innocence leads her, dressed only in a towel, outside the compound where the tourists live into the poor and violent world of Arab North Africa. She gets raped, a boy who hangs round the compound is suspected, and when he's cornered Andrew beats him to death. His menopausal desire is displaced into murderous aggression. The police and courts are finally bought off, and the tourists take off with relief for "civilization." But back home, as Whitehead's other plays show, the war goes on.

—Tony Dunn

———

WHITEMORE, Hugh (John). British. Born in Tunbridge Wells, Kent, 16 June 1936. Educated at Judd School,

Tunbridge Wells, 1945–51; King Edward VI School, Southampton, 1951–55; Royal Academy of Dramatic Art, London, 1956–57. Married 1) Jill Brooke in 1961 (marriage dissolved); 2) Sheila Lemon in 1976; one son. Freelance writer: drama critic, *Harpers and Queen*, London, 1970. Recipient: Emmy award, 1971, 1984; Writers Guild award, 1971, 1972; RAI prize, 1979; Italia prize, 1979; Neil Simon Jury award, 1984. Lives in London. Agent: Judy Daish Associates, 83 Eastbourne Mews, London W2 6LQ, England; or, Phyllis Wender, Rosenstone and Wender, 3 East 48th Street, 4th Floor, New York, New York 10017, U.S.A.

PUBLICATIONS

Plays

Horrible Conspiracies (televised 1971). Published in *Elizabeth R*, edited by J.C. Trewin, London, Elek, 1972.
Stevie: A Play from the Life and Work of Stevie Smith (produced Richmond, Surrey, and London, 1977; New York, 1979). London, French, 1977; New York, Limelight, 1984.
Pack of Lies (produced Brighton and London, 1983; New York, 1985). Oxford, Amber Lane Press, 1983; New York, Applause, 1986.
Breaking the Code, adaptation of the book *Alan Turing: The Enigma of Intelligence* by Andrew Hodges (produced London, 1986; New York, 1987). Oxford, Amber Lane Press, 1987.
The Best of Friends (produced London, 1987). Oxford, Amber Lane Press, 1988.
The Towers of Trebizond (produced Edinburgh, 1991).
It's Ralph (produced London, 1991).

Screenplays: *Decline and Fall . . . of a Birdwatcher!*, with Ivan Foxwell and Alan Hackney, 1968; *All Neat in Black Stockings*, with Jane Gaskell, 1968; *Man at the Top*, with John Junkin, 1973; *All Creatures Great and Small*, 1975; *The Blue Bird*, 1976; *Stevie*, 1978; *The Return of the Soldier*, 1983; *84 Charing Cross Road*, 1987.

Television Plays: *The Full Chatter*, 1963; *Dan, Dan the Charity Man*, 1965; *Angus Slowly Sinking*, 1965; *The Regulator*, 1965; *Application Form*, 1965; *Mrs. Bixby and the Colonel's Coat*, from a story by Roald Dahl, 1965; *Macready's Gala*, 1966; *Final Demand*, 1966; *Girl of My Dreams*, 1966; *Frankenstein Mark II*, 1966; *Amerika*, from the novel by Kafka, 1966; *What's Wrong with Humpty Dumpty?*, 1967; *Party Games*, 1968; *The Last of the Big Spenders*, 1968; *Hello, Good Evening, and Welcome*, 1968; *Mr. Guppy's Tale*, from a story by Dickens, 1969; *Unexpectedly Vacant*, 1970; *The King and His Keeper*, 1970; *Killing Time*, 1970; *Cider with Rosie*, from the book by Laurie Lee, 1971; *Horrible Conspiracies* (*Elizabeth R* series), 1971; *An Object of Affection*, 1971; *Act of Betrayal*, 1971; *Breeze Anstey* (*Country Matters* series), from the story by H.E. Bates, 1972; *The Strange Shapes of Reality*, 1972; *The Serpent and the Comforter*, 1972; *At the Villa Pandora*, 1972; *Eric*, 1972; *Disappearing Trick*, 1972; *Good at Games*, 1972; *Bedtime*, 1972; *Intruders*, 1972; *The Adventures of Don Quixote*, from a novel by Cervantes, 1973; *Deliver us from Evil*, 1973; *The Pearcross Girls*, 1973; *A Thinking Man as Hero*, 1973; *Death Waltz*, 1974; *Outrage*, 1974; *David Copperfield*, from the novel by Dickens, 1974; *Trilby*, from the novel by George du Maurier, 1975; *Goodbye*, 1975; *84*

Charing Cross Road, from the book by Helene Hanff, 1975; *Moll Flanders*, from the novel by Defoe, 1975; *The Eleventh Hour*, with Brian Clark and Clive Exton, 1975; *Censors*, with David Edgar and Robert Muller, 1975; *Brensham People*, from novels by John Moore, 1976; *William Wilson*, from the story by Poe, 1976; *Moths*, from the novel by Ouida, 1977; *Exiles*, from the book by Michael J. Arlen, 1977; *Dummy*, 1977; *Mrs. Ainsworth*, from a novel by E.F. Benson, 1978; *Losing Her*, 1978; *Rebecca*, from the novel by Daphne du Maurier, 1979; *Contract*, 1981; *A Dedicated Man*, from the story by Elizabeth Taylor, 1982; *I Remember Nelson*, 1982; *A Bit of Singing and Dancing*, from the story by Susan Hill, 1982; *Lovers of Their Time*, from the story by William Trevor, 1982; *My Cousin Rachel*, from the novel by Daphne du Maurier, 1983; *Office Romances*, from stories by William Trevor, 1983; *Down at the Hydro*, from a story by William Samsom, 1983; *Concealed Enemies*, 1984; *The Boy in the Bush*, from a story by D.H. Lawrence, 1984; *The Final Days*, from a novel by Bob Woodward and Carl Bernstein, 1989.

* * *

Hugh Whitemore is best known as a writer for television, and from 1963 he has had a long list of plays to his credit both as parts of series and as individual efforts. His adaptation of Laurie Lee's *Cider with Rosie* won him a Writers Guild award, as did his contribution to *Country Matters* in 1972; and *Elizabeth R*—a series of six plays, one of which, *Horrible Conspiracies*, was provided by Whitemore—received an Emmy award. *Horrible Conspiracies* deals with events surrounding the execution of Mary Queen of Scots, and its fascination with the world of spying and conspiracy was to become a recurrent theme in his work. Gloriana is presented as an aging ruler, ruled by superstition and fear, fixated on thoughts of death, and her court as far from magnificent.

The predominant style of *Horrible Conspiracies* is that of conventional television naturalism—although the play is prefaced by a grim masque portending death—and the piece jumps quickly through a series of locations which suggests the complexities of espionage and counter-espionage that lurk immediately beneath the outward display of power. Little interest is shown in the intricacies of psychological behaviour or in any larger political context, and the play seems very much a part of a larger series in which each individual writer is considerably restrained by the overall structure. Over the years, Whitemore has shown himself as adept at meeting the strictures of such demands, and as able to turn out a consistently well-crafted piece.

The influence of his work on television is evident in his belated stage entrance. *Stevie: A Play from the Life and Works of Stevie Smith* makes few bows in the direction of the stage. Information is given in the conventional format of recalled anecdotes raised in the course of a series of conversations between Stevie and the aunt she lived with for most of her life. The atmosphere of suburban London comes across well, as does Stevie's delight in the absurdity of her life there, but we gain little insight into her obsession with death and her failed attempt at suicide. It is a well-made play, offering the kind of "coffee-table" approach to biography so frequently to be found on television. Its chief virtue lies in Whitemore's success in creating in the central character a plausible human being, even if we learn little more than superficial things about her. That this was done in a beautifully realized suburban set does little to take the edge off a feeling that *Stevie* is essentially a television play put on stage.

His next stage play, *Pack of Lies*, was exactly this, having started life as the successful BBC television "Play for Today,"

Act of Betrayal. The play concerns the intrusion into a suburban family of the British Secret Service, intent on trapping as Russian spies their close friends and neighbours, the Krogers. The play, which is based on real events in 1960–61, again captures well the restrictions and niceties of suburban life and builds to a traditional theatrical climax as the host family become increasingly and ambivalently involved in the enquiry; but again it is difficult to see what exactly is added to the piece by its adaptation to the stage. The direct narrative asides to the audience apart, its predominant tone is still that of a safe naturalism. It asks no questions that cannot be contained within the confines of plot and set, and it is hard not to think that the chief reason for its appearance in London's West End is the latest bout of interest in Burgess, Philby, et al. One obvious attraction to theatrical managements is that it is a cheap production in a theatrical world currently dominated by excessively expensive musicals.

However, Whitemore's fourth stage-play, *Breaking the Code*, does succeed in making the break from the small screen to the stage. Far more ambitious than his two earlier efforts, it presents the story of Alan Turing, the man who broke the German Enigma code in World War II and pioneered the development of computers. Taking on board the difficult task of elucidating the theory behind Turing's work—and succeeding surprisingly well—the play blends the theme of scientific exploration with its depiction of an establishment England that could have the scientist's name obliterated from the record book because he was a practising homosexual—the two sets of broken codes in conflict. Whitemore has been fortunate in having Derek Jacobi play his protagonist, but it says much for the play's superiority to its predecessors that the actor is able to fill the part so well. *Breaking the Code* is, no less than all Whitemore's work, a classically well-made play, produced to a given West End formula, but the difference is that here, for the first time, the formula has been stretched to fit what the writer wants to say rather than acting as a straitjacket.

Although Whitemore has continued to work for television, the commercial success of his first stage plays has led to three further productions, *The Towers of Trebizond*, produced in Edinburgh, and two more products for London's West End—*The Best of Friends*, and *It's Ralph*. The latter fitted a familiar pattern of small-cast, single-set domestic dramas. The rural home of a successful journalist and his music-publisher wife is invaded by the unwelcome Ralph, an old friend of the husband—a guest whose presence, in the traditional manner, allows the even greater articulation of mid-life crisis and marital depression. With this play Whitemore was compared inevitably to Ayckbourn, although the sudden removal of the by now emotionally involved Ralph towards the end promises, without properly delivering, a new permutation of the theme.

—John Bull

WILDER, Thornton (Niven). American. 1897–1975. See 2nd edition, 1977.

WILKINSON, Christopher. British. Born 4 May 1941. Address: 33 Yates Lane, Milnsbridge, Huddersfield HD3 4NW, England.

PUBLICATIONS

Plays

Their First Evening Alone Together (produced Sheffield, 1969; London, 1971).
Wally, Molly and Polly (produced Sheffield, 1969).
Teasdale's Follies, with Frank Hatherly, music by Jeremy Barlow (produced Sheffield, 1970).
Strip Jack Naked (produced Sheffield, 1970; London, 1971).
Dynamo (produced London, 1971).
Plays for Rubber Go-Go Girls (produced London, 1971).
I Was Hitler's Maid (also director: produced Sheffield and London, 1971).
Sawn Off at the Knees, with Veronica Thirlaway (produced Sheffield, 1978).

*

Theatrical Activities:
Director: **Play**—*I Was Hitler's Maid*, Sheffield and London, 1971.

* * *

Christopher Wilkinson is best known for his work with two fringe companies—the touring Portable Theatre, and the Vanguard Theatre Club (now the Crucible Theatre-in-Education group), which is attached to Sheffield's main repertory theatre, the Crucible. These close associations have influenced his work. Wilkinson has written ordinary scripts, such as *Strip Jack Naked*, which revealed his wit, his ear for a good line of dialogue, and his delight in a Grand Guignol situation. But he later chose not to write formal scripts, but rather to suggest themes and games for the acting companies to explore—in improvisation and other ways. *I Was Hitler's Maid* is an example of this non-scripted play. Wilkinson offered the actors some stories taken from semi-pornographic men's magazines: blood, sex, and action. These magazines were of a type distributed to American troops in Vietnam, and were therefore considered to relate in some way to a real political situation. The stories were all exceptionally violent. Some were set in World War II—among SS officers and patriots of the French resistance—others in South America—among guerrilla bands and the forces of Law and Order. But the settings were almost irrelevant, for the situations were pointedly similar. A girl was tortured and repeatedly raped by the Enemy, before being rescued by the Hero. In the opening scene, she is whipped by "Hitler"; in a later scene, she becomes "Calamity Jane," the whipping Wild West heroine. The dialogue is based on the clichés of the genre: and the actors were encouraged to break up the story patterns, the snatches of rehearsed scenes, even the moments of violence, in order to emphasize the arbitrary lack of logic of the fantasies. The production progresses towards two main climaxes—an orgy scene (three men raping one girl) and a disembowelling scene, where three soldiers attack a lifelike (female) doll hanging in a cupboard.

Some critics thought that *I Was Hitler's Maid* was not so much a comment on pornography as pornography itself, while others deplored the deliberate lack of construction. But few productions could have achieved such a telling diatribe against sex-and-violence comics without seeming lofty and puritanical. Wilkinson, by presenting the stories on stage— where actors leapt up in astonishing health after being beaten senseless—and by denying the elementary logic which kept the stories credible, brought out the full sado-masochistic absurdity of the genre. A somewhat similar production, *Dynamo*, was less successful perhaps because Wilkinson's moral intentions had to be more overtly expressed. *Dynamo* is set in a strip club, and the first section consists of ordinary dull strip routines performed by gum-chewing, bored girls. We watch them preparing to go on stage, collecting their props and records, adjusting their hair: then we see the routines. But after a time the strip club becomes an interrogation cell, where a girl is tortured by a police chief, kicked around the floor, and finally hung up naked. Wilkinson wished to draw the parallel between ordinary pornographic fantasies and the political torture of an Algerian suspect by the French police: but the play failed because the association between the two events seemed at best clichéd and at worst tenuous and unconvincing. If Wilkinson meant to imply that in both cases women were treated like mere objects of male desire, the theme is convincing enough but rather obvious and could have been developed in many other ways. If he was suggesting that pornography leads to political violence, then the fact that there was no logical connecting link between the scenes damaged his argument.

Wilkinson's most successful work, however, is *Plays for Rubber Go-Go Girls*. These are sketch sequences, loosely linked by an attack on American imperialism and on the sexual fantasies supporting repression. The first half of the production consists of various sex-and-violence stories in the style of *I Was Hitler's Maid*: but the deliberate disorganization of the earlier plays is replaced by a solemn burlesque treatment—high camp. The stories could come from an outrageous adventure story, in the style of James Bond, with beautiful girls from Vietnam and Latin America, submitting with delight to Commie-hating G.I.s. The second half is an amusing skit on childhood training in America. A cop warns his daughter, Fuzz Child, against everything, from drugs to long hair, which might threaten the purity of American middle-class life. The juxtaposition of the repressed fantasies with the formal teaching are related to the Vietnam war, until the war itself is shown to be an effect of various cultural forces. Among these forces is perhaps Wilkinson's most typical preoccupation—the maltreatment of women by men. Women are presented as rubber girls who can be endlessly stabbed either with a phallus or a bayonet. This serious theme is treated with an immense satirical verve and accuracy: the fantasies are funny, familiar, and, shocked out of their usual contexts, have been presented to the public as grotesque art objects, as representative of our civilization as the pyramids were of ancient Egypt. Wilkinson's great achievement as a writer is to make us look afresh at the clichés surrounding our lives.

—John Elsom

WILLIAMS, (George) Emlyn. British. 1905–1987. See 3rd edition, 1982.

WILLIAMS, Heathcote. British. Born in Helsby, Cheshire, 15 November 1941. Associate editor, *Transatlantic Review*, London and New York; founding editor, *Suck*, Amsterdam. Recipient: *Evening Standard* award, 1970; George Devine award, 1970; John Whiting award, 1971; Obie award, 1971. Agent: Judy Daish Associates, 83 Eastbourne Mews, London W2 6LQ, England.

PUBLICATIONS

Plays

The Local Stigmatic (produced Edinburgh, and London, 1966; Boston, 1967; New York, 1969). Published in *Traverse Plays*, London, Penguin, 1965; with *AC/DC*, New York, Viking Press, 1973.
AC/DC (produced London, 1970; New York, 1971). London, Calder and Boyars, 1972; with *The Local Stigmatic*, New York, Viking Press, 1973.
Remember the Truth Dentist, music by Bob Flagg (produced London, 1974). With *The Speakers*, London, Calder, 1980.
The Speakers (produced Birmingham, 1974). With *Remember the Truth Dentist*, London, Calder, 1980.
Very Tasty—A Pantomine (produced London, 1975).
An Invitation to the Official Lynching of Michael Abdul Malik (produced Newcastle upon Tyne, 1975).
Anatomy of a Space Rat (produced London, 1976).
Hancock's Last Half-Hour (produced London, 1977; Huntington Station, New York, 1978). London, Polytantric Press, 1977.
Playpen (produced London, 1977).
The Immortalist (produced London, 1977). London, Calder, 1978.
At It, in *Breach of the Peace* (produced London, 1982; produced separately Edinburgh and London, 1983).
Whales (produced Liverpool and London, 1986).

Screenplay: *Malatesta*, 1969.

Television Play: *What the Dickens!*, 1983.

Verse

Whale Nation. London, Cape and New York, Crown, 1988.
Falling for a Dolphin. London, Cape, 1988; New York, Crown, 1989.
Sacred Elephant. London, Cape and New York, Crown, 1989.
Autogeddon. London, Cape and New York, Arcade, 1991.

Other

The Speakers. London, Hutchinson, 1964; New York, Grove Press, 1967.
Manifestoes, Manifesten. Rotterdam, Cold Turkey Press, 1975.
Severe Joy. London, Calder, 1979.
Elephants. London, Knockabout Comics, 1983.

*

Critical Study: "Heathcote Williams Issue" of *Gambit 18–19* (London), 1971.

Theatrical Activities:
Actor: **Films**—*The Tempest*, 1980; *Little Dorrit*, 1987; *Orlando*, 1993.

* * *

Often regarded as a one-play dramatist, Heathcote Williams merits praise not only for his acknowledged counter-culture classic of the 1960's, *AC/DC*, but also for plays that have received only cursory critical treatment. All his plays center on social misfits, who either hope for the reformation of a corrupt society or erect barriers against the void that threatens to engulf them.

The spectacular setting and visceral (and often unintelligible) dialogue of *AC/DC* dazzled audiences of the 1960's. In an amusement arcade, three hippies meet two schizophrenics, Maurice and Perowne; all are trying to shed media-induced personalities. Maurice helps Perowne achieve this goal by speaking long fantastic monologues. Maurice's monologues so intimidate two of the hippies, a couple, that, silenced, they drop out of the play altogether.

Such bludgeoning dialogues thread through *AC/DC*, though they are not of thematic importance. Sadie, the remaining hippie, competes with Maurice for control of Perowne. Like Maurice, she relies on long, unrelated fantasies to free Perowne from his enslavement to the video-screens, television, and radio, which are the environment for the second half of the play. Besides fantasizing to Perowne, she also trepans him, thus freeing him from media personalities. Sadie thereby overwhelms Maurice, and she dismisses him for being "into the same territory-sex-adrenalin-bullshit" as everyone else. Sadie looks for a revolution that will destroy such alienation.

Like *AC/DC*, *The Local Stigmatic*, an earlier play, dramatizes a Pinteresque struggle for dominance. Ray often contradicts and challenges Graham, but ultimately he accedes to the latter's game of assaulting strangers. These games lend form to their otherwise pointless existence.

Hancock's Last Half-Hour, like *The Local Stigmatic*, pits an individual against meaninglessness, but in this play the individual loses. Hancock, a former clown, desperately performs comedy to keep the silence from deafening him. He has locked himself in a hotel-room and there engages in the performance that is the play. The performer's fear of audience indifference drives Hancock and accounts for the desperation of his monologue that includes jokes, readings from encyclopedias, Freud's *Jokes*, and press clippings, and parodies of such set-pieces as Hamlet's soliloquy. This fear also accounts for his self-mockery and for his final suicide.

The Immortalist is not as compressed or exciting a play as *AC/DC*, nor does it question existence as do *The Local Stigmatic* and *Hancock's Last Half-Hour*. The play is essentially and atypically didactic. The Immortalist will not die of natural causes, but he *can* be killed. Consequently, he would preserve the earth and its inhabitants from human desecration. He argues against passivity: "Listen, people foul up because they stay in the same place. They've traded Utopia for reality . . . Consuming as a substitute for being . . . You have radio as a substitute for telepathy, television as a substitute for astral projection. Aeroplanes are a substitute for inner fire."

Williams's freaks indict a society that fosters passivity and consumerism through its mass media. As individuals, they can find no structures or values by which to order and give meaning to their lives.

—Frances Rademacher Anderson

WILLIAMS, Nigel. British. Born in Cheadle, Cheshire, 20 January 1948. Educated at Highgate School, London; Oriel College, Oxford. Married; three sons. Recipient: Somerset Maugham award, for fiction, 1978. Agent: Judy Daish Associates, 83 Eastbourne Mews, London W2 6LQ. Address: c/o Faber and Faber, 3 Queen Square, London WC1N 3AU, England.

PUBLICATIONS

Plays

Double Talk (produced London, 1976).
Snowwhite Washes Whiter, and Deadwood (produced Bristol, 1977).
Class Enemy (produced London, 1978; New York, 1979). London, Eyre Methuen, 1978.
Easy Street (produced Bristol, 1979).
Sugar and Spice (produced London, 1980). With *Trial Run*, London, Eyre Methuen, 1980.
Line 'em (produced London, 1980). London, Eyre Methuen, 1980.
Trial Run (produced Oxford and London, 1980). With *Sugar and Spice*, London, Eyre Methuen, 1980.
W.C.P.C. (produced London, 1982). London, Methuen, 1983.
The Adventures of Jasper Ridley (produced Hull, 1982; London, 1983).
My Brother's Keeper (produced London, 1985). London, Faber, 1985.
Deathwatch, adaptation of a play by Jean Genet (produced Birmingham and London, 1985).
Country Dancing (produced Stratford-on-Avon, 1986; London, 1987). London, Faber, 1987.
As It Was, adaptation of a book by Helen Thomas (produced Edinburgh, 1987).
Nativity (produced London, 1989).

Television Plays: *Talkin' Blues*, 1977; *Real Live Audience*, 1978; *Baby Talk*, 1981; *Let 'em Know We're Here*, 1981; *Johnny Jarvis* series, 1983; *George Orwell* (documentary), 1983; *Charlie*, 1984; *Breaking Up*, 1986; *Centrepoint*, 1990; *The Last Romantics*, 1991.

Novels

My Life Closed Twice. London, Secker and Warburg, 1977.
Jack Be Nimble. London, Secker and Warburg, 1980.
Charlie (novelization of television play). London, Methuen, 1984.
Star Turn. London, Faber, 1985.
Witchcraft. London, Faber, 1987.
Breaking Up (novelization of television play). London, Faber, 1988.
Black Magic. London, Hutchinson Books, 1988.
The Wimbledon Poisoner. London, Faber, 1990.
They Came from SW19. London, Faber, 1992.

Other

Johnny Jarvis (for children). London, Penguin, 1983.

*

Theatrical Activities:
Director: **Television**—*George Orwell*, 1983; *Cambodian Witness* (documentary) by James Fenton, 1987.

* * *

Each of Nigel Williams's early plays (1977–80) explores the interaction of and relations between a handful of sharply distinguished individuals who have been isolated by some circumstance, or who isolate themselves, to form a closed group. A convincing (and relishful) rendering of Cockney speech rhythms enables Williams to generate considerable claustrophobic intensity within this dramatic framework. The intensity, however, is largely negative. The plays are dominated by variations on one particular figure: an overbearingly voluble and physically aggressive embodiment of destructive energy. He (or she) stands outside every recognizable position, whether social, sexual, or political, and aims to discredit and destroy those positions (represented by the other characters) by violence both verbal and physical. Though the theme of each play, be it class, race, or sex, is at least *implicitly* political, the presence of this central figure ensures that the dramatic treatment is less political than psychological. The figure catalyzes and externalizes hidden tensions, sometimes with self-destructive consequences, tearing away "civilized" constraints in such a way as to lay bare not political or economic causes but atavistic, tribal impulses.

The tribal emerges clearly in *Class Enemy*. The growing tension and final conflict here take place not between groups but within a single group. Six fifth-formers in a London school fill up an unsupervised afternoon by each "teaching a lesson" on his pet subject. The friction between Iron, the voluble, violent representative of inner-city despair who cherishes his pessimism and seems to relish debasement, and Sky-Light (the nicknames are of course significant), who despite the social circumstances retains trust in the essential goodness of human nature and a radiant perception of the world, erupts into a fight for leadership of the group. Iron wins the fight but, as Sky-Light realizes, the self-directed violence of his moral nature and the frustration of his fevered demand for an indefinable "knowledge" reveal him as the real victim, the "loser."

Sky-Light stands against and illuminates the moral collapse of Iron, but in *Sugar and Spice*, which focuses on sex-hatred as *Class Enemy* focuses on class-hatred, neither the prostitute Suze nor the lovers Carol and Steve are strong enough to counter the disruptive force of the lesbian Sharon and her male counterpart, the Iron-like John. Each contrives the ritual sexual humiliation (by stripping) of a member of the other sex and each addresses a savage climactic speech to the naked victim's genitals. The hatred embodied in Sharon and John represents not just a critique of society's distortion of sexuality but a mutual revulsion of the sexes which seems to extend to a revulsion from sexuality itself.

Though they are no less bleak in tone than the previous plays, *Trial Run* and *Line 'em* both conclude more decisively. In *Trial Run* a young Sikh, Gange, and Billy who is of mixed parentage, stage a mock trial with hostages they have taken while holed up waiting for the police to surrender a Special Patrol Group man upon whom Gange wants revenge. But the disruptive Billy, with his hatred of society in general, wants more than *personal* revenge. After Gange has been killed by police marksmen Billy mysteriously (and unexpectedly) assumes that posture of inner stillness and blank patience of his Eastern ancestors. His abandonment of the social will makes itself felt as an affirmation, yet in *Line 'em* it is precisely this social will, represented by a solidarity that seems less political than tribal, which is finally affirmed. The anarchistic Foreman mocks and undermines the picket line organized by the old-style union man Sam, yet when soldiers arrive to break the picket he reunites his own ranks by

causing insubordination in those of the enemy, and by questioning the validity of the Commanding Officer's values. In the final tableau the two "armies" confront one another.

It will be apparent from these accounts that the power of Williams's drama is cumulative: each play concentrates on a single situation and builds up to an explosive climax. His two comic-satiric plays of the early 1980's, *W.C.P.C.* and *The Adventures of Jasper Ridley* (Williams's most explicitly political play), depart from this pattern in adopting a more obviously scenic form for the presentation of the experiences of their naïve-innocent central figures within their respective milieux. However *My Brother's Keeper* again focuses intensely on a single—but this time familial and significantly middle-class—situation. As an old actor lies dying in hospital after a severe stroke, he is visited by his immediate family. His will to live is insistently provoked by his playwright son Tony, whose own thwarted energy arises out of a sense of life wasted through the withholding of feelings, especially love, within this "ordinary" middle-class family. Though vehemently opposed by his brother Sam, a successful businessman with an enduring sense of exclusion from the aesthetic side of the family, Tony attempts to break the maternal domination which he sees as having crippled the family emotionally by encouraging a confrontation (between his parents especially) and a purgation, a speaking out. A point of resolution is reached only when the dying actor-father stumblingly articulates the necessity for mutual *acceptance* within a family of relationships as "states of conflict." Unusually for Williams—and this could be seen as a significant shift of emphasis in his drama—the energies of the play, and of its central figure Tony, make themselves felt as positive. Yet one does suspect here, more strongly than with Williams's previous work, that a great deal of dramatic heat is being expended in the generation of a rather ordinary light.

In *Country Dancing* Williams's work takes on an historical focus. Within a narrative framework provided by an encounter in 1914 between folk-song collector Cecil Sharp and an ancient village fiddler born in the year of Waterloo, the story of the fiddler's life and relationships is played out. It is a story of deprivation, love, betrayal, oppression, and abandonment, but one in which the fate of the individual is shown to be inextricably linked to—even determined by—the enormous social shifts occurring in the century between the two moments of "pointless slaughter." The experience and consequences of rural protest and depopulation, and of urbanization and mass industrialization, are suggested with point and ingenuity by the songs and dances which punctuate the action. Dance functions as invocation, provocation, counterpoint, and above all as a complex metaphor of social, personal, and labour relations—larger patterns shaping the lives of individuals. As life becomes a "business" and political economy triumphs, the cosmopolitan individualism of the waltz displaces the rooted community of country dance, and the uprooted fiddler loses both his wife and his musical gift. But music is "the only certain thing," and the gift revives, just at this moment of impending European holocaust. In its formal fluidity and lucid stylization—quite different from the dense naturalism with which Williams originally made his mark—*Country Dancing* seems to represent a significant shift in his writing for the stage.

—Paul Lawley

WILLIAMS, Tennessee (Thomas Lanier Williams). American. 1911–1983.
See 3rd edition, 1982.

WILLIAMSON, David (Keith). Australian. Born in Melbourne, Victoria, 24 February 1942. Educated at Monash University, Clayton, Victoria, B.E. in mechanical engineering 1964; Melbourne University. Married 1) Carol Anne Cranby in 1965 (divorced 1972), two children; 2) Kristin Ingrid Lofvén in 1974, two foster children. Design engineer, General Motors-Holden's, Melbourne, 1965; lecturer, Swinburne College of Technology, Melbourne, 1966–72. Visiting professor, University of Aarhus, Denmark, 1978. Commissioner, Australian Broadcasting Corporation, 1978–79; chair, Australian National Playwrights Conference, 1979–80; president, Australian Writers Guild, 1979–86. Recipient: George Devine award, 1971; Australian Writers Guild award, 1972, 1973, 1977, 1979, 1980; London *Evening Standard* award, 1974; Australian Film Institute award, 1975, 1977. Officer, Order of Australia, 1983. Agent: Anthony Williams Management, The Basement, 55 Victoria Street, Potts Point, New South Wales 2011, Australia.

PUBLICATIONS

Plays

The Coming of Stork (produced Melbourne, 1970). Included in *The Coming of Stork, Jugglers Three, What If You Died Tomorrow*, 1974.
The Removalists (produced Melbourne, 1971; London and Cleveland, 1973; New York, 1974). Sydney, Currency Press, 1972; London, Eyre Methuen, 1973.
Don's Party (produced Melbourne, 1971; London, 1975). Sydney, Currency Press, and London, Eyre Methuen, 1973.
Jugglers Three (produced Melbourne, 1972). Included in *The Coming of Stork, Jugglers Three, What If You Died Tomorrow*, 1974.
What If You Died Tomorrow (produced Melbourne, 1973; London, 1974). Included in *The Coming of Stork, Jugglers Three, What If You Died Tomorrow*, 1974.
The Coming of Stork, Jugglers Three, What If You Died Tomorrow. Sydney, Currency Press, and London, Eyre Methuen, 1974.
The Department (produced Adelaide, 1974). Sydney, Currency Press, 1975; London, Eyre Methuen, 1976.
A Handful of Friends (produced Adelaide, 1976). Sydney, Currency Press, 1976.
The Club (produced Melbourne, 1977; London, 1980; as *Players*, produced New York, 1978; as *The Team*, produced Toronto, 1981). Sydney, Currency Press, 1978.
Travelling North (produced Sydney, 1979; London, 1980). Sydney, Currency Press, 1980.
Celluloid Heroes (produced Sydney, 1980).
Gallipoli (screenplay), in *The Story of Gallipoli*, by Bill Gammage. Melbourne, Penguin, 1981.
The Perfectionist (produced Melbourne, 1982; London, 1983). Sydney, Currency Press, 1983.
Sons of Cain (also director: produced Melbourne, 1985; London, 1986). Sydney, Currency Press, 1985.

Collected Plays 1 (includes *The Coming of Stork, The Removalists, Don's Party, Jugglers Three, What If You Died Tomorrow*). Sydney, Currency Press, 1986.
Emerald City (produced Sydney, 1987; London and New York, 1988). Sydney, Currency Press, 1987.
Top Silk. Sydney, Currency Press, 1989.
Money and Friends (produced Los Angeles, 1992).

Screenplays: *Stork*, 1971; *The Family Man* (episode in *Libido*), 1972; *Petersen*, 1974; *The Removalists*, 1975; *Don's Party*, 1976; *Mrs. Eliza Fraser*, 1976; *The Club*, 1980; *Gallipoli*, 1981; *The Year of Living Dangerously*, with Peter Weir and C.J. Koch, 1983; *Phar Lap*, 1983; *Travelling North*, 1986.

Television Plays: *The Perfectionist*, 1985; *The Four-Minute Mile*, 1988 (U.K.).

Other

Counterpointforum: The Australian Image, with Geoffrey Bolton. Murdoch, Western Australia, Murdoch University, 1981.

*

Critical Studies: "Mask and Cage: Stereotype in Recent Drama" by Margaret Williams, in *Meanjin* (Melbourne), September 1972; in *Southerly* (Sydney), June 1973; "*The Removalists*: A Conjunction of Limitations" by Williamson, in *Meanjin* (Melbourne), no. 4, 1974; "Australian Bards and British Reviewers" by Arlene Sykes, in *Australian Literary Studies* (Hobart, Tasmania), May 1975; "The Games People Play: The Development of David Williamson," in *Contemporary Australian Drama* edited by Peter Holloway, Sydney, Currency Press, 1981, and "David Williamson's Plays since *The Department*," in *Southerly* (Sydney), March 1986, both by Brian Kiernan; *Modern Australian Styles* by Mark O'Connor, Townsville, Queensland, Foundation for Australian Literary Studies, 1982; "A New Map for Australia: The Plays of David Williamson" by John McCallum, in *Australian Literary Studies* (St. Lucia, Queensland), May 1984; interview with Paul Kavanagh and Peter Kuch, in *Southerly* (Sydney), June 1986; *David Williamson* edited by Ortrun Zuber-Skerritt, Amsterdam, Rodopi, 1988.

Theatrical Activities:
Director: **Play**—*Sons of Cain*, Melbourne, 1985.

David Williamson comments:
I would regard my early plays as mounting a satiric-ironic attack, albeit with a modicum of ambivalent affection, on the conformist philistine, materialist, sexist, and aggressive aspects of the Australian social ethos. In my later plays the personal as distinct from the sociological observations are accorded more weight but the ironic-satiric stance of the earlier plays is, I think, maintained.

* * *

David Williamson is Australia's most widely produced playwright at home and abroad as well as its busiest screenwriter. He communicates an accurate, often unflattering, view of Australia's urban middle-class. His dramas tend to be heightened naturalistic portraits with which audiences identify, while also making satiric comments on a culture which

Williamson describes as "the conformist, philistine, materialistic, sexist, and aggressive aspects of the Australian social ethos." Embodied in his work are serious thematic concerns arising from the tensions of group interaction, power struggles, violence, sexual insecurity, the failure to recognize one's potential, the search for self-discovery, and the struggle of pragmatism versus idealism.

Using aggressively honest language, Williamson's early plays focus with sharp-edged criticism on sociological observations and they adopt an implicit moral stance, without judgmental proscription, that underlies all of his work. Outstanding among his early plays is *The Removalists* (later a successful screenplay). The action centers on an idealistic rookie policeman so humiliated by his cynical superior that he angrily beats to death a feisty, working class wife-basher who has resisted the policeman's imperious involvement in the repossession of his estranged wife's furniture by an indifferent removalist (furniture-mover). The victim represents the very image of macho fighter and lover, but his fate nevertheless engages audience sympathy. *The Removalists* attacks not the police so much as authoritarianism, in a powerful portrayal of the lurking violence in humanity and in male-dominated Australian society in particular. Williamson questions whether violence's arousal and acceptance can be ended in any society which vicariously relishes it.

Other plays of the 1970's also establish Williamson's craftsmanship and satiric-ironic bent. He explores, with critical affection, patterns of social interaction within the darkly humorous rituals of a gathering, party, or meeting. The title character of *The Coming of Stork* (and of the film *Stork*) is a gauche, anti-establishment, "ocker" (proletarian) student who disrupts a Melbourne gathering, drunkenly protests a couple's contemplated marriage, and reveals his own hypocrisy. More notable than this somewhat uneven play's attack on middle-class propriety is its new prototype of the urban male. The disrupted ritual of a party also forms the center of the more successful *Don's Party*. Here the interaction of a group of university-educated men in their 30's reflects failed ambitions and hopes as they are caught up in a world of materialistic concerns. This effective social comedy presents well-realized characters and carries an undertone of indictment. *A Handful of Friends* compellingly if bleakly treats the betrayal of friendship, as a failed academic, a film-maker, and their wives conclude a reunion after having torn each other apart, revealing subtle threads that bind them all. In the somewhat autobiographical *What If You Died Tomorrow*, a novelist and his journalist wife find themselves playing hosts to an odd assortment of unexpected guests whose acidulous revelations underscore the play's thematic concern with loss of never-to-be-regained systems of definite values.

By 1977, Williamson admitted his plays were becoming less committed to social change, while maintaining their strong moral concern. This is apparent in three plays about institutional or professional environments. A popular success, *The Club* depicts a football club's infighting which results in two self-aggrandizing administrators holding onto power and winning out over coaches representing the true spirit of the game. Amidst comically-veined confrontations is a trenchant look at the failure of democracy within a sports club. Academic idealism foiled by institutional bureaucracy and personal interest is the outcome of an engineering faculty-staff meeting in *The Department*, a work drawing on its author's experience as a technical-college lecturer. The well-integrated play focuses on power struggles and relationships when a self-protective department head subverts a pragmatic solution to a pressing boiler problem and misdirects resources away from the department's ostensible goals. The comic absurdity of the situation is artfully emphasized, enhanced by strong characterizations. Williamson in *Sons of Cain* sardonically views the press through an aggressive newspaper editor's crusade which uncovers high-level corruption involving a government that nevertheless has achieved commendable social reform. The editor worriedly foresees his efforts leading to this government's being superseded by another equally corrupt but less progressive.

Returning to the exploration of moral duty as it clashes with claims of self, Williamson inaugurates his 1980's work with *Travelling North*. This excellent, bitter-sweet comedy traces the autumnal relationship between a widowed, retired construction engineer of socialistic opinions and prickly temperament and a conventional middle-aged divorcee ridden with guilt about her neglectful mothering of grown daughters with troubled marriages. Displaying Williamson's maturing theatrical craftsmanship, *Travelling North* presents multi-dimensional characters in an unsentimental voyage toward self-fulfilment, and it exceeds national bounds to examine questions more universal than peculiarly Australian. Less successful in its plumbing of relationships, *The Perfectionist* examines the need for give and take in a marriage between a self-absorbed perfectionist academic and a wife who wants attention and independence. Her attachment to a Danish student hired as house help results in a failed attempt toward freedom but initiates more respectful awareness from the husband.

Williamson's recent play *Emerald City* is effective comedy with autobiographical underpinnings, treating the issue of pragmatism versus idealism. A high-principled screenwriter and his book-editor wife move from Melbourne to Sydney to enlarge their careers. Trying to resist the city's magnetic pull toward commercialism, the screenwriter is the first to succumb, abandoning low-profit serious filmwriting, only to fail at writing trash, and ultimately returning to serious work. At the conclusion the couple have undergone disillusionment but remain in the Emerald City, Sydney, with a guarded acceptance. The play's American productions received mixed critical reviews, with merited praise for its depiction of the problems and possibilities of contemporary urban life.

Over two decades Williamson has drawn a societal map of urban Australia on which he has plotted with developing craftsmanship the personal issues which he and his characters confront. Whether or not he has been successful at transmitting his experience of Australian society to audiences outside his native land is less important than that his plays collectively encompass many vital issues faced by middle-class audiences of the 1970's and 1980's.

—Christian H. Moe

WILLIS, Ted (Edward Henry Willis; Baron Willis of Chislehurst). British. Born in Tottenham, Middlesex, 13 January 1918. Educated at state schools, including Tottenham Central School, 1923–33. Served in the Royal Fusiliers, 1940; writer for the War Office and Ministry of Information. Married Audrey Hale in 1944; one son and one daughter. Artistic director, Unity Theatre, London, 1945–48. Director, World Wide Pictures since 1967, and Vitalcall since 1983. Executive member, League of Dramatists, London, 1948–74; chair, 1958–63, president, 1963–68 and 1976–79, and since 1988 life president, Writers Guild of Great Britain; president, International Writers Guild, 1967–69. Since 1964 governor,

Churchill Theatre Trust, Bromley, Kent; member of the Board of Governors, National Film School, London, 1970–73. Recipient: Berlin Festival award, for screenplay, 1957; Edinburgh Festival award; Writers Guild award, 1964, 1967; Royal Society of Arts Silver medal, 1967; Variety Guild of Great Britain award, 1976; Willis Trophy, for television writing, 1983. Fellow, Royal Society of Arts; fellow, Royal Television Society. Life Peer, 1963. Agent: Elaine Greene Ltd., 31 Newington Green, London N16 9PU; and, Lemon, Unna, and Durbridge, 24 Pottery Lane, Holland Park, London W11 4LZ. Address: 5 Shepherds Green, Chislehurst, Kent BR7 6PB, England.

PUBLICATIONS

Plays

Sabotage (as John Bishop) (produced London, 1943).
Buster (produced London, 1943). London, Fore Publications, n.d.
All Change Here (produced London, 1944).
"God Bless the Guv'nor": A Moral Melodrama in Which the Twin Evils of Trades Unionism and Strong Drink are Exposed, "After Mrs. Henry Wood" (produced London, 1945). London, New Theatre Publications, 1945.
The Yellow Star (also director: produced London, 1945).
What Happened to Love? (produced London, 1947).
No Trees in the Street (produced London, 1948).
The Lady Purrs (produced London, 1950). London, Deane, and Boston, Baker, 1950.
The Magnificent Moodies (produced London, 1952).
The Blue Lamp, with Jan Read (produced London, 1952).
A Kiss for Adele, with Talbot Rothwell, adaptation of the play by Barillet and Grédy (produced London, 1952).
Kid Kenyon Rides Again, with Allan Mackinnon (produced Bromley, Kent, 1954).
George Comes Home. London, French, 1955.
Doctor in the House, adaptation of the novel by Richard Gordon (produced London, 1956). London, Evans, and New York, French, 1957.
Woman in a Dressing Gown (televised, 1956). Included in *Woman in a Dressing Gown and Other Television Plays*, 1959; (revised version, produced Bromley, Kent, 1963; London, 1964); London, Evans, 1964.
The Young and the Guilty (televised, 1956). Included in *Woman in a Dressing Gown and Other Television Plays*, 1959.
Look in Any Window (televised, 1958). Included in *Woman in a Dressing Gown and Other Television Plays*, 1959.
Hot Summer Night (produced Bournemouth and London, 1958). London, French, 1959.
Woman in a Dressing Gown and Other Television Plays (includes *The Young and the Guilty* and *Look in Any Window*). London, Barrie and Rockliff, 1959.
Brothers-in-Law, with Henry Cecil, adaptation of the novel by Cecil (produced Wimbledon, Surrey, 1959). London, French, 1959.
When in Rome, with Ken Ferry, music by Kramer, lyrics by Eric Shaw, adaptation of a play by Garinei and Giovannini (produced Oxford and London, 1959).
The Eyes of Youth, adaptation of the novel *A Dread of Burning* by Rosemary Timperley (as *Farewell Yesterday*, produced Worthing, Sussex, 1959; as *The Eyes of Youth*, produced Bournemouth, 1959). London, Evans, 1960.
Mother, adaptation of the novel by Gorky (produced Croydon, Surrey, 1961).
Doctor at Sea, adaptation of the novel by Richard Gordon

(produced Bromley, Kent, 1961; London, 1966). London, Evans, and New York, French, 1961.
The Little Goldmine. London, French, 1962.
A Slow Roll of Drums (produced Bromley, Kent, 1964).
A Murder of Crows (produced Bromley, Kent, 1966).
The Ballad of Queenie Swann (televised, 1966; revised version, music by Dick Manning and Marvin Laird, lyrics by Willis, produced Guildford, Surrey, 1967; as *Queenie*, produced London, 1967).
Dead on Saturday (produced Leatherhead, Surrey, 1972).
Mr. Polly, music by Michael Begg and Ivor Slaney, lyrics by Willis, adaptation of the novel by H.G. Wells (produced Bromley, Kent, 1977).
Stardust (produced Bromley, Kent, and London, 1983).
Tommy Boy (produced Richmond, Surrey, 1988).
Intent to Kill (produced Bromley, Kent, 1990).

Screenplays: *The Waves Roll On* (documentary), 1945; *Holiday Camp*, with others, 1947; *Good Time Girl*, with Muriel and Sydney Box, 1948; *A Boy, A Girl, and a Bike*, 1949; *The Huggetts Abroad*, with others, 1949; *The Undefeated* (documentary), 1950; *The Blue Lamp*, with others, 1950; *The Wallet*, 1952; *Top of the Form*, with John Paddy Carstairs and Patrick Kirwan, 1953; *Trouble in Store*, with John Paddy Carstairs and Maurice Cowan, 1953; *The Large Rope*, 1953; *One Good Turn*, with John Paddy Carstairs and Maurice Cowan, 1954; *Burnt Evidence*, 1954; *Up to His Neck*, with others, 1954; *It's Great to Be Young*, 1956; *The Skywalkers*, 1956; *Woman in a Dressing Gown*, 1957; *The Young and the Guilty*, 1958; *No Trees in the Street*, 1959; *Six Men and a Nightingale*, 1961; *Flame in the Streets*, 1961; *The Horsemasters*, 1961; *Bitter Harvest*, 1963; *Last Bus to Banjo Creek*, 1968; *Our Miss Fred*, with Hugh Leonard, 1972; and other documentaries.

Radio Plays: *Big Bertha*, 1962; *And No Birds Sing*, 1979; *The Buckingham Palace Connection*, from his own novel, 1981; *The Left-Handed Sleeper*, from his own novel, 1982; *Obsession*, 1983; *Death May Surprise Us*, from his own novel, 1984.

Television Plays: *The Handlebar*, *The Pattern of Marriage*, *Big City*, *Dial 999*, *The Sullavan Brothers*, *Lifeline*, and *Taxi* series; *Dixon of Dock Green* series, 1954, and later series; *The Young and the Guilty*, 1956; *Woman in a Dressing Gown*, 1956; *Look in Any Window*, 1958; *Strictly for the Sparrows*, 1958; *Scent of Fear*, 1959; *Days of Vengeance*, with Edward J. Mason, 1960; *Flowers of Evil* series, with Mason, 1961; *Outbreak of Murder*, with Mason; *Sergeant Cork* series, 1963; *The Four Seasons of Rosie Carr*, 1964; *Dream of a Summer Night*, 1965; *Mrs. Thursday* series, 1966; *The Ballad of Queenie Swann*, 1966; *Virgin of the Secret Service* series, 1968; *Crimes of Passion* series, 1970–72; *Copper's End* series, 1971; *Hunter's Walk* series, 1973, 1976; *Black Beauty* series, 1975; *Barney's Last Battle*, 1976; *Street Party*, 1977; *Man-Eater*, from his own novel, 1980; *Einetleim für Tiere*, series (from 1984, Germany); *Mrs. Harris, M.P.*, 1985; *Mrs. Harris Goes to New York*, 1987; *The Iron Man*, 1987; *Mrs. Harris Goes to Moscow*, 1987; *Racecourse* series, 1987; *The Valley of Dream*, 1987; *Mrs. Harris Goes to Monte Carlo*, 1988; *Vincent Vincent*, 1989; *Mrs. Harris Goes to Majorca*, 1990.

Novels

The Blue Lamp. London, Convoy, 1950.
Dixon of Dock Green: My Life, with Charles Hatton. London, Kimber, 1960.

Dixon of Dock Green: A Novel, with Paul Graham. London, Mayflower, 1961.

Black Beauty. London, Hamlyn, 1972.

Death May Surprise Us. London, Macmillan, 1974; as *Westminster One*, New York, Putnam, 1975.

The Left-Handed Sleeper. London, Macmillan, 1975; New York, Putnam, 1976.

Man-Eater. London, Macmillan, 1976; New York, Morrow, 1977.

The Churchill Commando. London, Macmillan, and New York, Morrow, 1977.

The Buckingham Palace Connection. London, Macmillan, and New York, Morrow, 1978.

The Lions of Judah. London, Macmillan, 1979; New York, Holt Rinehart, 1980.

The Naked Sun. London, Macmillan, 1980.

The Most Beautiful Girl in the World. London, Macmillan, 1982.

Spring at the Winged Horse: The First Season of Rosie Carr. London, Macmillan, and New York, Morrow, 1983.

The Green Leaves of Summer: The Second Season of Rosie Carr. London, Macmillan, 1988; New York, St. Martin's Press, 1989.

The Bells of Autumn: The Third Season of Rosie Carr. London, Macmillan, 1990; New York, St. Martin's Press, 1991.

Other

Fighting Youth of Russia. London, Russia Today Society, 1942.

The Devil's Churchyard (for children). London, Parrish, 1957.

Seven Gates to Nowhere (for children). London, Parrish, 1958.

Whatever Happened to Tom Mix? The Story of One of My Lives. London, Cassell, 1970.

A Problem for Mother Christmas (for children). London, Gollancz, 1986.

Evening All: Fifty Years over a Hot Typewriter. London, Macmillan, 1991.

*

Manuscript Collection: Boston University.

Theatrical Activities:
Director: **Plays**—Unity Theatre, London: *The Yellow Star*, 1945; *Boy Meets Girl* by Bella and Sam Spewack, 1946; *All God's Chillun Got Wings* by Eugene O'Neill, 1946; *Golden Boy* by Clifford Odets, 1947; *Anna Christie* by Eugene O'Neill.

Ted Willis comments:
I am a good example of what can be done by hard work. I've taken a small talent, honed and sharpened it into a good professional instrument. Might have been a better writer if I'd stuck to one area and kept out of politics (both writing and national) but that's the way I am.

*   *   *

There is no doubt in my mind that Ted Willis owes his success in life to his quite extraordinary power of concentration. At a very early age he decided that he was going to be a writer. When he left school finally at 15 and confided to the Headmaster his determination to write, the crisp comment was "Don't be a fool. You've no literary gift whatever. Much better learn a trade." But to waste time and energy in learning a trade was no part of the Willis plan. He was teaching himself one, and making progress. His intensive study of the cinema was encouraging him to try his hand at that medium, and television; so he took the kind of ill-paid jobs that were open to an unskilled man, and went on writing.

His pen was by now a very well-tempered instrument; but it was through his politics, not his fiction, that this first became publicly known. His views were of the extreme left-wing order, and he expressed them with a force and pungency that made him a valuable asset to the Labour Party. But it was during army service in World War II that he was given the chance to write his first screenplays. This decided his future—for when he went back into civil life in 1945 and was invited to stand for a safe Labour seat in Parliament, he refused. He was still a writer.

He is an inventive storyteller, and his high standard of craftsmanship and severe self-discipline have lead inevitably to success, especially in such compositions as his television series *Dixon of Dock Green* and *Mrs. Thursday*. What it does not necessarily lead to is artistry; and one gathers that Willis knows this very well himself, for he once said modestly to an interviewer, "There are hundreds of better writers with much greater talent than mine. But less ability to work hard."

That honest, if overstated, attempt at self-assessment has a modicum of truth in it, and it is remarkable that not one of his productions has ever induced West End audiences to show much enthusiasm. Even *Woman in a Dressing Gown* (by common consent his best play) caused little stir.

So evident an effect must have a definable cause; but to say simply that Willis has a better talent for screen and television plays than for stage plays is merely to define the matter without explaining it. There could be a dozen explanations but one is fundamental. The world of the living theatre was unknown to the boy who played truant from school to revel in the glories of the cinema. When Willis first encountered the stage in his mid-twenties it was in the spirit not of a lover but of an immensely industrious student. He learned much; but it is not thus that a dramatist acquires that mysterious sense of the theatre which enables him to serve the art of the actor. The hard-working student may well deserve success, but in the theatre he cannot command it.

—W.A. Darlington

———————

WILSON, August. American. Born in Pittsburgh, Pennsylvania, 27 April 1945. Educated at Gladstone High School, Pittsburgh, 1960–61. Married Judy Oliver in 1981; one daughter. Founder, Black Horizons Theatre Company, Pittsburgh, 1968. Member, New Dramatists, New York. Recipient: Jerome fellowship, 1980; Bush fellowship, 1982; Rockefeller fellowship, 1984; McKnight fellowship, 1985; New York Drama Critics Circle award, 1985, 1987, 1988; Guggenheim fellowship, 1986; Whiting Foundation award, 1986; American Theatre Critics award, 1986, 1989, 1991; Outer Circle award, 1987; Drama Desk award, 1987; John Gassner award, 1987; Tony award, 1987; Pulitzer prize, 1987, 1990; Helen Hayes award, 1988; Los Angeles Drama Critics Circle award, 1988. Member, American Academy of Arts and Sciences. Agent (attorney): John Breglio, Paul Weiss

Rifkind Wharton and Garrison, 1285 Avenue of the Americas, New York, New York 10019. Address: c/o Emily Kretschmer, Assistant, 1290 Grand Avenue, Suite 105, St. Paul, Minnesota 55101, U.S.A.

PUBLICATIONS

Plays

Black Bart and the Sacred Hills (produced St. Paul, 1981).
Jitney (produced Pittsburgh, 1982).
The Mill Hand's Lunch Bucket (produced New York, 1983).
Ma Rainey's Black Bottom (produced New Haven, Connecticut, and New York, 1984; London, 1989). New York, New American Library, 1985; with *Fences*, London, Penguin, 1988.
Fences (produced New Haven, Connecticut, 1985; New York, 1987; Liverpool, 1990). New York, New American Library, 1986; with *Ma Rainey's Black Bottom*, London, Penguin, 1988.
Joe Turner's Come and Gone (produced New Haven, Connecticut, 1986; New York, 1988; London, 1990). New York, New American Library, 1988.
The Piano Lesson (produced New Haven, Connecticut, 1987; revised version produced New York, 1990). New York, New American Library, 1990.
Two Trains Running (produced New Haven, Connecticut, 1990; New York, 1992).
Three Plays (includes *Ma Rainey's Black Bottom*, *Fences*, *Joe Turner's Come and Gone*). Pittsburgh, University of Pittsburgh Press, 1991.

*

August Wilson comments:
I write about the black experience in America and try to explore in terms of the life I know best those things which are common to all cultures. I see myself as answering James Baldwin's call for a profound articulation of the black experience, which he defined as "that field of manners and ritual of intercourse that can sustain a man once he has left his father's house." I try to concretize the values of the black American and place them on stage in loud action to demonstrate the existence of the above "field of manners" and point to some avenues of sustenance.

* * *

August Wilson is one of America's most significant playwrights. His acclaimed major works comprise his proposed cycle of dramas depicting African-American life in each decade of the 20th century. Cut off from their African roots due to the legacy of slavery, Wilson's black characters are often victims of racism and economic oppression. Feeling powerless to change their bleak condition, some even vent their frustrations on each other. Those able to reclaim their history and spirituality not only find a way to survive, but are inspired to challenge the injustices which plague their lives.

Set in a Pittsburgh boarding house in 1911, *Joe Turner's Come and Gone* portrays a man, Herald Loomis, in search of "his song"—that elusive element which would make his life meaningful. Seven years prior to his journey to Pittsburgh, Loomis lived in Tennessee with his wife and young daughter. Falsely jailed on a trumped-up charge, he was forced to work in one of the chain gangs run by the governor's brother. The years of hard labor broke Loomis's spirit. When released

from jail, he finds his wife has left his daughter in the care of her mother. Loomis and his daughter travel to Pittsburgh ostensibly in search of his wife. However, a "conjure" man named Bynum shows him it is not the loss of his wife, but a lack of direction in his life which has been plaguing him. Despite the painful hardships he has endured, Loomis learns to look within himself to find the unique and life-affirming quality which will serve as the source of inspiration and guidance throughout the remainder of his years.

One of Wilson's few plays set outside of Pittsburgh, *Ma Rainey's Black Bottom* examines the consequence of black rage which can find no other outlet for expression except through violence. Set in Chicago in 1927, the play has less to do with the famed blues singer Gertrude "Ma" Rainey, than her studio band. Most of the musicians trade retorts and stories about life, while accepting the exploitation of their talents by whites as an inherent part of the entertainment business. A cocky but gifted young trumpeter, Levee, mistakenly believes he can break through the racial barriers which have prohibited his peers from reaping their rightful rewards. However, when rebuffed by the establishment he sought to join, he does not lash out at his oppressors. Instead, his wrath results in the death of one of his black musician colleagues. Thus, the playwright suggests black-on-black crime to be a direct result of the prevailing inequitable socio-economic system.

Set in 1936 in Pittsburgh, *The Piano Lesson* concerns the trials and tribulations a family endures over the legacy of a piano. As slaves in the mid-19th century, two members of the Charles family were exchanged by their owners, the Sutter family, for a piano. When the Sutters order one of the remaining members of the Charles family to carve decorations into the piano, the sculptor instead creates a memorial not only to those recently sold, but to his ancestors who survived from the middle passage to the present time. Stolen for the Sutter family by the grandsons of the sculptor, 80 years later the piano is now in the possession of Berniece, whose father was killed in retaliation for the theft. Two of the Charles descendants, Berniece and her brother Boy Willie, fight over the piano, not fully understanding its symbolic and emotional worth. Obsessed with the anguish suffered by her mother over the piano, Berniece fails to recognize the more important connection it has with her family's legacy. Boy Willie sees more value in the piano as a commodity to sell in order to purchase land. At play's end, the family is reconciled as each member comes to realize that the piano must remain as a living symbol of the family's painful, yet proud heritage.

Set in Pittsburgh in 1957, *Fences* tells the story of a garbage man named Troy Maxson and his family. A former player in the Negro baseball leagues, Troy had developed into a fine batter. However, he became embittered when the major leagues finally opened its door to black athletes and Troy, being past his prime, could not compete with younger players. In Pittsburgh, he married a woman named Rose who bore him a son, Cory. Troy found himself in a seemingly endless routine revolving around his work and familial responsibilities. He also recognized bitterly that he could not have purchased his house or adequately supported his family if it were not for the income supplements from his brother's disability checks. Thus, Troy understands that poverty and racism have kept him from achieving the American dream. His dissatisfaction with his life consequently leads Troy to betray his family through infidelity and a misguided sense of what is best for them. His ill-fated actions threaten to tear the family apart, while leaving deep emotional scars on those he loved the most. Through the play, Wilson teaches that blacks cannot survive on bitterness or thoughts of what should have been. Instead, blacks must learn that adaptation is the key to their survival. Indeed, it is this ability to adjust to new situations which has allowed African-Americans to endure horrific experiences.

Though set in the volatile 1960's, the great political and social upheaval of the times seem to have little effect on the characters of Wilson's more recent play, *Two Trains Running*. Set in Pittsburgh, the characters who pass through a diner owned by Memphis Lee enjoy spinning tales and appear to have a passive view of life. A frustrated and embittered man, Memphis struggles with his own feelings of self-worth as exemplified by the conflict he has with white city officials over the price offered for his home for an urban development project. Ironically, it is a mentally impaired handyman who first illustrates that one does not have to accept the role of being a victim in a racist society. For nine years, each day he demands the agreed payment of a ham for the painting of a butcher's fence. His refusal to acquiesce to the butcher's offering of a chicken as compensation inspires others finally to take a stand for their rights. With the added encouragement and wisdom of an ancient sage, Memphis is motivated to demand and acquire his just rewards from those formerly thought to be immovable, omnipotent opponents.

—Addell Austin Anderson

WILSON, Doric. American. Born in Los Angeles, California, 24 February 1939. Studied with Lorraine Larson, Tri-Cities, Washington, 1955–58; apprenticed to Richland Players, Washington, 1952–58; attended University of Washington, Seattle, 1958–59. Founding member and playwright-in-residence, Barr/Wilder/Albee Playwrights Unit, New York, 1963–65; artistic director, Ensemble Project, New York, 1965–68; founding member and playwright-in-residence, Circle Repertory Company, New York, 1969–71; founding, artistic director, TOSOS Theatre Company, New York, 1973–77; playwright-in-residence, The Glines, New York, 1978–82, and Jerry West's Funtastic Shows, Portland, Oregon, 1983–84; director, New City Theatre Playwright's Workshop, Seattle, 1985. Since 1986 director and playwright-in-residence, Pioneer Square Theater, Seattle. Recipient: San Francisco Cable Car award, 1981; Chambers-Blackwell award, 1982; Villager award, 1983; Newsmaker award, 1984. Address: 506 9th Avenue, Apartment 3FN, New York, New York 10018, U.S.A.

PUBLICATIONS

Plays

And He Made a Her (produced New York, 1961).
Babel, Babel, Little Tower (produced New York, 1961).
Now She Dances! (produced New York, 1961; revised version produced New York, 1975).
Pretty People (produced New York, 1961).
In Absence (produced New York, 1968).
It Was a Very Good Year (produced New York, 1970).
Body Count (produced New York, 1971).
The West Street Gang (also director: produced New York, 1977). Included in *Two Plays*, New York, Sea Horse Press, 1979.

Ad Hoc Committee (produced New York, 1978).
Surprise (produced New York, 1978).
Turnabout (as Howard Aldon) (produced Richland, Washington, 1979).
A Perfect Relationship (produced New York, 1979). Included in *Two Plays*, New York, Sea Horse Press, 1979.
Forever After: A Vivisection of Gaymale Love, Without Intermission (also director: produced New York, 1980). New York, JH Press, 1980.
Street Theater: The Twenty-Seventh of June, 1969 (produced New York, 1981). New York, JH Press, 1983.

*

Manuscript Collection: Lincoln Center Library of the Performing Arts, New York.

Critical Studies: introduction by William M. Hoffman to *Gay Plays*, New York, Avon, 1979; *Lavender Culture* by Karla Jay and Allen Young, New York, Jove, 1979: "Caffe Cino" by Wilson, in *Other Stages* (New York), 8 March 1979; interview with Robert Chesley, in *Advocate* (San Francisco), 5 April 1979; "Gay Plays, Gay Theatre, Gay Performance" by Terry Helbing, in *Drama Review* (New York), March 1981.

Theatrical Activities:
Director: **Plays**—many productions in New York, most recently *The Madness of Lady Bright* by Lanford Wilson, 1974; *The Hostage* by Brendan Behan, 1975; *What the Butler Saw* by Joe Orton, 1975; *Now She Dances!*, 1976; *The West Street Gang*, 1977; *Forever After*, 1980.

* * *

Doric Wilson is a quintessentially urban dramatist who grew up in rural Washington State but lived in New York City for more than two decades. He specializes in stylish farce, ironic comedy of wit, and urbane satire. His combination of fantasy and whimsy and his intellectual dialectic may suggest the touch of a Giraudoux or a Shaw, a Wilder or a Wycherley. Yet underlying his often caustic comedy is a surprisingly romantic sensibility which finds him subtly rooting for happy ever afters.

And He Made a Her (1961) may have been the first play written specifically for Caffe Cino—and therefore for off-off-Broadway. Like many of the Cino writers, Wilson is gay, and, after stints as an original member of both the Barr/Wilder/Albee Playwrights Unit and the Circle Repertory Company, in 1973 he formed the first professional gay company, TOSOS (The Other Side of Silence), which he founded with his income as a bartender.

Wilson excels at accurate observation of life, particularly gay life, which he satirizes but with which he also sympathizes. He was the first to write openly about gay characters who are neither sick nor miserable. Although he dislikes the word "gay," this is a linguistic rather than a political stance. A pioneer in his efforts to write about gay subjects and produce for gay audiences, Wilson has been a leader among up-front homosexuals combating gay self-hatred, and his sharpest satire is reserved for homophobes, whether straight or gay. Wilson's plays speak particularly to gay spectators, but they promote tolerance, affection, honesty, and understanding among people of any sexuality.

Wilson's work is characterized by its playfulness, its fantasy, and its feminism. *And He Made a Her*, for example, dramatizes the displeasure among Adam and the angels caused by Eve's creation. The angelic host—including one described as "of liberal size and liberal party but not left winged enough to fly—or fall—with Lucifer"—worry about Eve, who's disturbing the natural animosity of the animals, domesticating the plants, and intent upon reproduction. Clearly superior to Adam, she provokes amazement "that woman is able to look up at someone shorter than she is." More surprising, perhaps, as early as 1961 is Wilson's substitution—for the response "Amen"—of "A Women." Other early Wilson one-acts which exemplify these characteristics are his satire of narcissism *Pretty People*, set in a museum displaying live people, and the political satire *Babel, Babel, Little Tower*, in which the narcissists are warmongers and religious freaks from several historical periods.

Although these early Wilson plays are not specifically gay in subject, another piece from that period which is concerned with homosexuality has been expanded into a full-length play. *Now She Dances!* comments upon both Oscar Wilde's imprisonment and contemporary America by dramatizing the Salome story according to the dramatic conventions of *The Importance of Being Earnest*. As Lane the butler ("with excellent references from another play") puts it, *Now She Dances!* gives us "farce fencing force over tea." In both versions, Lady Herodias's daughter, Miss Salome, demands and finally receives a man's head on a tray covered with a tea cozy; in the full-length version the word "head" is subject to double entendre which may go over the heads of some. In the original, Wilde is the prisoner, and he won't come out of the closet; in the rewrite, the prisoner is an unashamed and clever contemporary American homosexual whom Salome tries to seduce. The words she speaks as she unbuttons her bodice typify Wilson's simultaneous accomplishment of more than one objective: "In years to come, when you talk of this, and you will, be kind."

Those famous lines directed, in Robert Anderson's *Tea and Sympathy*, toward a boy who is sympathetic because he is *not* gay, serve as implicit critique of years of theatrical treatment of the homosexual, who, until recently, is usually ignored or despised or pitied. Wilson hardly misses an opportunity to mix in comments on the theatre with his wider political satire. Among jabs at animal symbols of women (seagull, wild duck), Actors Studio nonsense about an actress who plays a maid "identifying" with the soup she's serving, and tedious first scenes ("a lovely bouquet of blue expositions"), Wilson spoofs gay dramatists such as Genet and Wilde who do not give us a reasonable facsimile of the life thousands of homosexuals actually live.

In *Street Theater*, his play about the hours preceding the Stonewall riots (which gave birth to the gay rights movement), Wilson mocks the self-contemptuous pair from *The Boys in the Band* and a closet queen as well as the heterosexual mobster bar owner who exploits his "queer" customers and a couple of Vice Squad cops, one of whom arrests the other. Set on the street near the Stonewall gay bar, this comedy offers politically provocative wit plus an array of New York homosexuals deftly characterized and suggests what sort of homophobic treatment prompted them to turn on their tormentors in revolt.

Another treatment of the street-bar scene by one of its own aficionados is *The West Street Gang*, which likewise dramatizes the victimization of gays by homophobes, opportunists, and each other. Set in a downtown west-side leather bar, it was also performed in one (the Spike). It shows the bar's patrons threatened by a gang of teenage fag bashers of the type who regularly try to murder gays with baseball bats and tire chains. Their efforts at self-protection are led by a transvestite and are hampered by a so-called gay rights leader, by Arthur Klang (a thinly disguised Arthur Bell of the *Village Voice*), and Bonita Aryant (a still more thinly disguised Anita Bryant, then waging a nationwide anti-homosexuality crusade). *The West Street Gang* offers more than just appropriate politics. It's a hilarious treatment of some familiar New Yorkers, who turn out to be more than mere stereotypes. There's the hustler who gets rolled, the pacifist who urges violence, and, best of all, the drag queen who leads the fight against the marauding street gang. "She" initially follows the butch dress code on her entrance, then heads for the head and simpers back on in a dress. Whether hero or heroine, she stands up very well not only to the homophobic cops and bar owner and to Bonita (who mistakes the bar's patrons for longshoremen) but to her less than broadminded gay fellow bar patrons. Indeed, the varied characters lead us to conclude that tolerance, cooperation, and mutual respect are the qualities Wilson most admires.

Among his domestic love stories, *Turnabout* is one of several Wilson satires of straight relationships; *A Perfect Relationship* depicts the friendship of two men who don't recognize that they ought to be lovers; and *Forever After* is both a romantic comedy and a parody of same.

Written under the pseudonym "Howard Aldon" *Turnabout* is a suburban sit com in which a wife teaches her adulterous husband a lesson without actually sleeping with other men. A play in which non-stop one-liners compete with very funny situations as sources of humor, *Turnabout* devastates the complacent husband's double standard. It demonstrates Wilson's capacity for exactly the sort of heterosexual commercial comedy with which he could regale Broadway if he weren't more interested in a different kind of dramaturgy. He has, however, written several other satires of heterosexual relations, including *In Absence*, *It Was a Very Good Year*, *Body Count*, and *Surprise*.

In *A Perfect Relationship* the protagonists, Ward and Greg, are roommates whose lifestyle is built upon a commitment to non-commitment. Both thrive on cruising, which Greg practices at discos and Ward at backroom bars. Although they aren't lovers, they bicker as though they were—over who does the laundry, or cooks dinner, or takes the first shower. They even keep score, as though it were an organized sport, while denigrating each other's masculinity. They have a "perfect" relationship until both sleep with the same trick, a young opportunist who uses this one-night stand to acquire Ward and Greg's desirable Christopher Street apartment. Along the way to discovering that they ought to be lovers, Ward and Greg deal with the kooky heterosexual woman from whom they are subletting. She and her boyfriends behave as though they're at a zoo and the young men are the animals, yet her preconceptions about gays aren't much sillier than their own. Although she outdoes them in promiscuous non-involvement, she helps the roommates to recognize that they share a lot more than the rent.

The kind of love story which Wilson writes in *A Perfect Relationship* he sets out to parody in *Forever After*, yet he maintains an effective tension in the latter between amusement at romanticism and acceptance of long-term commitment between men. Tom and David's amorous remarks are jeered by two mocking muses in drag seated in proscenium boxes. Actually it's Melpomene, the tragic muse, who sets out to destroy the affair. It is her descent into the fray to coach the lovers in suspicion and disharmony which prompts the comic muse Thalia to follow and defend the playwright's prerogative to give the young men a happy-ever-after conclusion. Something of a descendant of Sheridan's *The Critic* or the Duke of Buckingham's *The Rehearsal*, *Forever After* mixes presentational and representational styles while lampooning such theatrical targets as Sam Shepard's *Buried*

Child, Martin Sherman's *Bent*, Edward Albee's *The Lady from Dubuque*, Robert Patrick's *T-Shirts*, general negativity in drama, and the claims made by performers in gay plays that they're straight. The particular object of Wilson's wrath—and wisecracks—however, is melodramas in which the homosexual is a tormented degenerate.

Wilson's ear for the varieties of gay attitudes, jargon, and quips is as good as ever in *Forever After*, and his penchant for punning is true to his best form. The dialogue is among his most raunchy and real. As to his appraisal of the dispute between the muses, Wilson shares Thalia's views; he sees the funny and playful side of everything, including love, but on the subjects of human relations and aesthetics he's no cynic. Although *Forever After* demonstrates it's easier to fight than to sustain a relationship, Wilson sets us to cheering those who succeed at commitment.

—Tish Dace

WILSON, Lanford (Eugene). American. Born in Lebanon, Missouri, 13 April 1937. Educated at Ozark High School, Missouri; Southwest Missouri State College, Springfield, 1955–56; San Diego State College, California, 1956–57; University of Chicago, 1957–58. Worked at various jobs, and in advertising, Chicago, 1957–62; director, actor, and designer for Caffe Cino and Cafe La Mama theatres, New York, and other theatres. Since 1969 co-founder and resident playwright, Circle Repertory Company, New York. Recipient: Rockefeller grant, 1967, 1974; Vernon Rice award, 1968; ABC-Yale University fellowship, 1969; New York Drama Critics Circle award, 1973, 1980; Obie award, 1973, 1975, 1983; Outer Circle award, 1973; American Academy award, 1974; Drama-Logue award, 1978, 1979; Pulitzer Prize 1980; Brandeis University Creative Arts award 1981. Agent: Bridget Aschenberg, International Creative Management, 40 West 57th Street, New York, New York 10019. Address: c/o Hill and Wang, 19 Union Square West, New York, New York 10003, U.S.A.

PUBLICATIONS

Plays

So Long at the Fair (produced New York, 1963).
No Trespassing (produced New York, 1964).
Home Free! (also director: produced New York, 1964; London, 1968). Included in *Balm in Gilead and Other Plays*, 1965; with *The Madness of Lady Bright*, London, Methuen, 1968.
Balm in Gilead (produced New York, 1964; Edinburgh, 1986). Included in *Balm in Gilead and Other Plays*, 1965.
The Madness of Lady Bright (also director: produced New York, 1964; London, 1968). Included in *The Rimers of Eldritch and Other Plays*, 1967; with *Home Free!*, London, Methuen, 1968.
Ludlow Fair (produced New York, 1965; Edinburgh, 1967; London, 1977). Included in *Balm in Gilead and Other Plays*, 1965.
Balm in Gilead and Other Plays. New York, Hill and Wang, 1965.

Sex Is Between Two People (produced New York, 1965).
The Rimers of Eldritch (also director: produced New York 1965). Included in *The Rimers of Eldritch and Other Plays*, 1967.
This is the Rill Speaking (also director: produced New York, 1965). Included in *The Rimers of Eldritch and Other Plays*, 1967.
Days Ahead (produced New York, 1965). Included in *The Rimers of Eldritch and Other Plays*, 1967.
The Sand Castle (produced New York, 1965). Included in *The Sand Castle and Three Other Plays*, 1970.
Wandering: A Turn (produced New York, 1966). Included in *The Rimers of Eldritch and Other Plays*, 1967.
The Rimers of Eldritch and Other Plays. New York, Hill and Wang, 1967.
Miss Williams: A Turn (produced New York, 1967).
Untitled Play, music by Al Carmines (produced New York, 1967).
The Gingham Dog (produced Washington, D.C., 1968; New York, 1969; Manchester, 1970). New York, Hill and Wang, 1969.
The Great Nebula in Orion (produced Manchester, 1970; New York, 1972; London, 1981). Included in *The Great Nebula in Orion and Three Other Plays*, 1973.
Lemon Sky (produced Buffalo and New York, 1970). New York, Hill and Wang, 1970.
Serenading Louie (produced Washington, D.C., 1970; New York, 1976). New York, Dramatists Play Service, 1976; revised version (produced New York, 1984), New York, Hill and Wang, 1984.
The Sand Castle and Three Other Plays (includes *Wandering*, *Stoop: A Turn*, *Sextet (Yes): A Play for Voices*). New York, Dramatists Play Service, 1970.
Sextet (Yes): A Play for Voices (produced New York, 1971). Included in *The Sand Castle and Three Other Plays*, 1970.
Summer and Smoke, music by Lee Hoiby, adaptation of the play by Tennessee Williams (produced St. Paul, 1971; New York, 1972). New York, Belwin Mills, 1972.
Ikke, Ikke, Nye, Nye, Nye (produced New Haven, Connecticut, 1971; New York, 1972; London, 1981). Included in *The Great Nebula in Orion and Three Other Plays*, 1973.
The Family Continues (produced New York, 1972). Included in *The Great Nebula in Orion and Three Other Plays*, 1973.
The Great Nebula in Orion and Three Other Plays (includes *Ikke, Ikke, Nye, Nye, Nye*; *The Family Continues*; *Victory on Mrs. Dandywine's Island*). New York, Dramatists Play Service, 1973.
The Hot l Baltimore (produced New York, 1973; London, 1976). New York, Hill and Wang, 1973.
The Mound Builders (produced New York, 1975). New York, Hill and Wang, 1976.
Brontosaurus (produced New York, 1977; London, 1982). New York, Dramatists Play Service, 1978.
5th of July (produced New York, 1978; Bristol, 1987). New York, Hill and Wang, 1979.
Talley's Folly (produced New York, 1979; London, 1982). New York, Hill and Wang, 1980.
Bar Play, in *Holidays* (produced Louisville, 1979).
Talley and Son (as *A Tale Told*, produced New York, 1981; revised version, as *Talley and Son*, produced New York, 1985). New York, Hill and Wang, 1986.
Angels Fall (produced New York, 1982). New York, Hill and Wang, 1983.
Thymus Vulgaris (produced New York, 1982). New York, Dramatists Play Service, 1982.

Three Sisters, adaptation of a play by Chekhov (produced Hartford, Connecticut, 1985; New York, 1986; revised version produced Hartford, Connecticut, 1992).
Say deKooning (produced Southampton, New York, 1985). Included in *Hall of North American Forests*, 1988.
Sa-Hurt? (produced New York, 1986).
A Betrothal (produced London, 1986; New York, 1987). Included in *Hall of North American Forests*, 1988.
Burn This (produced Los Angeles and New York, 1987; London, 1990). New York, Hill and Wang, 1988.
Dying Breed (produced New York, 1987).
A Poster of the Cosmos (produced New York, 1987; London, 1992).
Hall of North American Forests (includes *The Bottle Harp, Say deKooning, A Betrothal*) (produced New York, 1987). New York, Dramatists Play Service, 1988.
The Moonshot Tape (produced New York, 1990).
Redwood Curtain (produced Seattle, Washington, 1992; New York, 1993).

Screenplays: *One Arm*, 1970; *Burn This*, 1992; *Talley's Folly*, 1992.

Television Plays: *The Migrants*, from a story by Tennessee Williams, 1974; *Taxi!*, 1979.

*

Bibliography: *Ten Modern American Playwrights* by Kimball King, New York, Garland, 1982.

Theatrical Activities:
Director: **Plays**—many of his own plays, including *Home Free!*, New York, 1964; *The Madness of Lady Bright*, New York, 1964; *The Rimers of Eldritch*, New York, 1965; *This Is the Rill Speaking*, New York, 1965; *Indecent Exposure* by Robert Patrick, New York, 1968; *Not to Worry* by A.E. Santaniello, New York, 1975; *In Vienna* by Roy London, New York, 1980. Actor: **Plays**—in *The Clown*, New York, 1968; *Wandering*, New York, 1968; *Him* by E.E. Cummings, New York, 1974.

* * *

Lanford Wilson's plays are deeply concerned with the conflict between the traditional values of the past and the insidious pressures of modern life. While he has been only intermittently successful at resolving this conflict, it has provided him with dramatic material of great variety and interest. The eccentric characters of *Balm in Gilead* and *The Madness of Lady Bright* fight or flee convention, and their desperation is sharply and sympathetically drawn. *The Rimers of Eldritch* or *This Is the Rill Speaking* ridicule the hypocrisy, bigotry, and convention of a small town while they rejoice in the confused innocence and energy of its adolescents. These "collage" plays, in which different strands of dialogue interweave, scenes overlap, and actors double their roles, allowed Wilson deftly to juxtapose the rooted strengths and values of the old with the energy and explorations of the young.

Wilson's experiments with the collage style resolved themselves in *The Hot l Baltimore*, set in a deteriorating flophouse (whose sign has lost its "e") peopled by whores, retirees, outcasts, and deadbeats. At the Hotel Baltimore, however, it is the old who have rejected convention, and the young Girl who fights to recover the past. This callgirl is as dismayed that no one will fight to save the hotel—"That's why nothing gets done anymore. Nobody's got the conviction of their passions"

—as she is furious that a young stranger gives up the search for his grandfather too easily. More naturalistic than earlier plays, *The Hot l Baltimore* uses a clear and simple prose and the physical symbol of the hotel to focus on Wilson's basic concerns.

Wilson's trilogy about the Talley family again used buildings as the symbol of an emotional and social conflict between past and present. *5th of July*, set in the present, reunites the scattered Talleys: Aunt Sally Talley, her nephew Ken and his homosexual lover, and Sally's niece June and her illegitimate daughter. Since Ken (whose legs were paralyzed in Vietnam) and June are offering the house to two old friends who were fellow radicals in the 1960's, the play was frequently described as an evaluation of the decade's politics. However, the politics are not deeply felt, and quickly become secondary to the sale of the house, which comes to represent the rejection of the family's roots in favor of a future they don't want or like. *Talley and Son* (set in World War II but the last play to be written) hinges on the struggle between Sally Talley's father and grandfather over control of the family business. While this play was excessively (and clumsily) complex, *Talley's Folly* (whose action is concurrent with that of *Talley and Son*) concerns the elegantly compact and dramatically clear courtship of Sally Talley by a New York lawyer, Matt Friedmann. Described as "a valentine" by Matt (who frequently and non-naturalistically addresses the audience), the play unites tradition and progress through Matt's warm, obstinately honest, and ultimately successful wooing of Sally.

While *Talley's Folly* avoided topical issues to its benefit, *Angels Fall* used an accident at a nearby nuclear plant to trap characters in a small Catholic church (compare *Bus Stop*). Parallelling a young, intelligent Navaho's rejection of his responsibility to his community with an art historian's sudden and violent rejection of his life's work, the play's pretext seems gratuitous and its resolution of the characters' spiritual crises mechanical.

A talented craftsman of dialogue, Wilson often fails to weld his situations seamlessly to his deepest concerns. However, when his primary values—honesty and the love of friends, family, and home—are tied closely to his dramatic situations his plays enact crucial questions about how the fabric of society is woven and cared for over generations.

—Walter Bode

WILSON, Robert M. American. Born in Waco, Texas, 4 October 1941. Educated at the University of Texas, Austin, 1959–62; Pratt Institute, Brooklyn, New York, 1962–65, B.F.A. 1965; studied painting with George McNeil, Paris, 1962; apprentice in architecture to Paolo Soleri, Acrosanti community, Phoenix, Arizona, 1966. Since 1970 artistic director, Byrd Hoffman Foundation, New York; frequent lecturer at seminars and workshops from 1970. Artist: individual shows since 1971. Recipient: Best Foreign Play award (France), 1970; Guggenheim fellowship, 1971, 1980; Drama Desk award, for directing, 1971; Obie award, for directing, 1974, 1986; Rockefeller fellowship, 1975, and award, 1981; Maharam award, for design, 1975; BITEF, Belgrade Grand prize, 1977; Lumen award, for design, 1977; French Critics award, for musical theatre, 1977, for best foreign play, 1987; German Critics award, 1979; Der Rosenstrauss, Munich,

1982; Harvard University citation, 1982; San Sebastian Film Festival award, 1984; Berlin Theatre Festival award, 1984, 1987; Malaga Theatre Festival Picasso award, 1986; Boston Theatre Critics Circle award, 1986; Skowhegan medal, for drawing, 1986; Bessie award, 1987; American Theatre Wing Design award, for noteworthy unusual effects, 1987; Mondello award, Palermo, 1988; The American Institute of Architects honor, 1988; New York Public Library Lion of the Performing Arts, 1989; São Paulo great prize, for best event, 1989; Italian Theatre Critics award, 1989; Barcelona Festival of Cinema Art grand prize, for video, 1989; Paris Film Festival special mention, for video, 1989; German Theatre Critics award, 1990. Address: Byrd Hoffman Foundation, 131 Varick Street, Number 908, New York, New York 10013, U.S.A.

PUBLICATIONS

Plays

Dance Event (produced New York, 1965).
Solo Performance (produced New York, 1966).
Theater Activity (produced New York, 1967).
ByrdwoMAN (produced New York, 1968).
Alley Cats (produced New York, 1968).
Watermill (produced New York, 1969).
The King of Spain (produced New York, 1969). Published in *New American Plays 3*, edited by William M. Hoffman, New York, Hill and Wang, 1970.
The Life and Times of Sigmund Freud (produced New York, 1969).
Deafman Glance (produced Iowa City, 1970; New York, 1971).
Program Prologue Now, Overture for a Deafman (produced Paris, 1971; New York, 1972).
Overture (produced New York, 1972).
Ka Mountain and GUARDenia Terrace: A Story about a Family and some People Changing (produced Shiraz, Iran, 1972).
King Lyre and Lady in the Wasteland (produced New York, 1973).
The Life and Times of Joseph Stalin (produced Copenhagen and New York, 1973).
Dia Log/A Mad Man a Mad Giant a Mad Dog a Mad Urge a Mad Face (produced Rome and Washington, D.C., 1974).
The Life and Times of Dave Clark (produced São Paulo, 1974).
"Prologue" to A Letter for Queen Victoria (produced Spoleto, Italy, 1974).
A Letter for Queen Victoria (produced Spoleto, Italy, on tour, and New York, 1974). New York, Byrd Hoffman Foundation, 1974.
To Street (Bonn, 1975).
The $ Value of Man (produced New York, 1975).
Dia Log, with Christopher Knowles (produced New York, 1975).
Spaceman, with Ralph Hilton (produced New York, 1976).
Einstein on the Beach, music and lyrics by Philip Glass (produced Avignon, France and New York, 1976). New York, EOS Enterprises, 1976.
I Was Sitting on My Patio This Guy Appeared I Thought I Was Hallucinating (produced Ypsilanti, Michigan, and New York, 1977; London 1978). New York, Byrd Hoffman Foundation, 1978.
Dia Log/Network, with Christopher Knowles (produced Boston, 1978).

Overture to the Fourth Act of Deafman Glance (produced Purchase, New York, 1978; New York, 1987).
Death, Destruction, and Detroit (produced Berlin, 1979). New York, Gnome Baker, 1978.
Dia Log/Curious George, with Christopher Knowles (produced Brussels, 1979; New York, 1980).
Edison (produced Lyon, France, and New York, 1979).
The Man in the Raincoat (produced Cologne, 1981).
Medea, with Gavin Bryars (produced Washington, D.C., 1981; New York, 1982).
Great Day in the Morning, with Jessye Norman (produced Paris, 1982).
The Golden Windows (produced Munich, 1982; New York, 1985). Munich, Hanser, 1982.
the CIVIL warS: a tree is best measured when it is down (sections produced Rotterdam, 1983; with Heiner Müller, Cologne, 1984; with Maita di Niscemi, Rome, 1984; with *The Knee Plays*, music and lyrics by David Byrne, Minneapolis, 1984; Tokyo, 1984: Marseille, 1984; Cambridge, Massachusetts, 1985). Sections published Amsterdam, Meulenhoff Landshoff, 1983; Frankfurt, Suhrkamp, 1984; Rome, Edizioni del Teatro dell' Opera, 1984; Los Angeles, Otis Art Institute, 1984; with *The Knee Plays*, with David Byrne, Minneapolis, Walker Art Center, 1984; with Heiner Müller, Cambridge, Massachusetts, American Repertory Theater, 1985.
King Lear (produced Hollywood, 1985).
Readings (produced Dublin, 1985).
Alcestis, adaptation of the play by Euripides, with Heiner Müller (produced Cambridge, Massachusetts, 1986). Stuttgart, Staatstheater Stuttgart, 1987.
Death, Destruction, and Detroit II (produced Berlin, 1987).
Parzival, with Tankred Dorst (produced Hamburg, 1988). Hamburg, Thalia Theatre, 1987.
Cosmopolitan Greetings (book only), music by Rolf Liebermann and George Gruntz, text by Allen Ginsberg (produced Hamburg, 1988).
The Forest (book only), music by David Byrne, text by Heiner Müller and Darryl Pinckney (produced Berlin and New York, 1988). Berlin, Theater der Freien Volksbuhne, 1988.
De Materie, music by Louis Andriessen (produced Amsterdam, 1989).
Orlando, adaptation of the novel by Virginia Woolf, text by Darryl Pinckney (produced Berlin, 1989).
The Black Rider: The Casting of Magic Bullets, music and lyrics by Tom Waits, text by William S. Burroughs (produced Hamburg, 1990).

Screenplay: *Overture for a Deafman*, 1971.

Video: *Spaceman*, with Ralf Hilton, New York, 1976, Amsterdam, 1984; *Video 50*, Ecublens, Switzerland, 1978; *Deafman Glance*, 1981; *Stations*, 1982; *La Femme à la Cafetière*, Paris, 1989; *The Death of King Lear*, 1989.

Recordings: *The Life and Times of Joseph Stalin*, Byrd Hoffman Foundation, 1973; *Einstein on the Beach*, music and lyrics by Philip Glass, CBS, 1979; *the CIVIL warS: Knee Plays*, music and lyrics by David Byrne, Warner Brothers, 1985.

*

Manuscript Collection: Rare Book and Manuscript Library, Columbia University, New York.

Critical Studies (selection): *The Theatre of Visions: Robert Wilson* by Stefan Brecht, Frankfurt, Suhrkamp, 1979, London, Methuen, 1982; *Robert Wilson: The Theater of Images* edited by Craig Nelson, Cincinnati, Contemporary Arts Center, 1980, revised edition, New York, Harper, 1984; *Robert Wilson and His Collaborators* by Laurence Shyer, New York, Theatre Communications Group, 1990.

Theatrical Activities:
Director and Designer: **Plays**—all his own plays; *American Hurrah* by Jean-Claude van Itallie, New York, 1966 (design only); *A Letter to Queen Victoria*, Spoleto, Italy, on tour, and New York, 1974; *Hamletmachine* by Heiner Müller, New York, and Hamburg, 1986, London, Paris, on tour, Madrid, and Palermo, 1987; *Quartet* by Heiner Müller, Stuttgart, 1987, Cambridge, Massachusetts, 1988; *Swan Song* by Chekhov, Munich, 1989, Tokyo, 1990; *King Lear* by Shakespeare, Frankfurt, 1990; *When We Dead Awaken*, adaptation of the play by Ibsen, Cambridge, Massachusetts, 1991. **Opera**—*Medée* by Marc-Antoine Charpentier, Lyon, France, 1984; *Alceste* by C.W. Gluck, Stuttgart, 1986, Chicago, 1990; *Salome* by Richard Strauss, Milan, 1987; *Le Martyre de Saint Sebastian* by Claude Debussy (choreographed with Suzushi Hanayagi), Paris and New York, 1988; *Doktor Faustus*, adaptation of the novel by Thomas Mann, music by Giacomo Manzoni, Milan, 1989; *La Nuit d'avant le jour* (inauguration of the Opera Bastille), Paris, 1989; *Parsifal* by Richard Wagner, Hamburg, 1991. **Films**—*The House*, 1963; *Slant*, 1963; *Overture for a Deafman*, 1971.

* * *

Robert M. Wilson is an atypical dramatist in that he composes with pictures rather than words, and creates through directing his works (few of which have been published) on the stage. Early productions with his Byrd Hoffman School of Byrds (named after Wilson's dance therapist) had affinities with the 1930's surrealists. Drama therapy work with a deaf mute, and a man with severe brain damage, showed that one picked up sounds in the form of vibrations or "interior impressions," while the other created a "graphic" logic from the aural shape of words independent of conventional sense.

Wilson's "performance pieces" express this "autistic" perception of the world, from his first, relatively simple piece— *Deafman Glance* which formed part of the epic *Ka Mountain and GUARDenia Terrace*—through to recent collaborations with Heiner Müller. Their structure is an architectural arrangement of sounds, words, and movement, in which images are restated or varied to form thematic motifs. The presentation is designed to sensitize the spectator to the same subliminal range of nuances as a brain-damaged deaf mute. Seeing autism as an increasingly common psychological response to the pressures of contemporary life, Wilson's aim is therapeutic: to open the audience to "interior impressions." The result is an audio-visual collage of dream-like and seemingly disconnected images, deliberately presented with obsessive repetitiveness and painful slowness. This kind of temporal fourth dimension reached its fullest extension with *Ka Mountain* at the Shiraz festival, which spread over seven days, and moved from a picture-frame stage to cover a whole mountain-side.

At one point the only movement was that of a live turtle crossing the empty stage, which took almost an hour, while the mountain behind was dotted with unrelated two-dimensional cardboard cut-outs: Noah's ark, a dinosaur, flamingoes, the Acropolis surrounded by a ring of ICBM rockets, Jonah's whale, a graveyard, and the Manhattan sky-line on the summit. This last cut-out was burnt to the ground on the final day of the performance, and replaced by a Chinese pagoda with the Lamb of God inside. (The original plan, vetoed by the Iranian festival authorities, had been to blow up the mountain top or paint it entirely white.) There was no intellectual sense to be made out of this apocalyptic collage. The dialogue resembled automatic writing, or dadaist free association. Yet there were obvious mythical connotations: the creation of the world corresponding to the seven-day performance of the play, "ka" representing the soul, and a seasonal birth/death/resurrection pattern.

Wilson's "chamber" pieces tend to draw their dream-imagery from social rather than religious archetypes, as in *A Letter for Queen Victoria*. Queen Victoria listens while a long and totally meaningless letter is read out. Couples in white sit at café tables gesticulating frenetically and speaking the same lines—"chitter-chatter, chitter-chatter"—simultaneously. However, the effect is disorienting rather than satiric, with two ballet dancers slowly spinning either side of the stage throughout the performance, and somnambulistic characters talking in endless *non sequiturs*. Again, there are apocalyptic overtones: a sniper shoots the couples who collapse one by one across their tables; and the performance ends with a long-drawn-out scream. But the focus is on perception itself, instead of on what is perceived. Four aviators/Lindberghs stand with their backs to the audience, looking at a changing land/cloudscape through a huge window; a Chinese man stands behind another enormous window-frame staring out at the audience through a continually opening and closing Venetian blind.

Coexisting independently in their collaborative work, Müller's verbal poetry and Wilson's visual imagery—like the separated halves of metaphor—form overlapping layers of sign versus signifier, where the multiple possible meanings are more than the sum of the statements, making rational comprehension almost impossible. This surrealistic unrelatedness and conflict of opposites, the hallmark of Wilson's later drama, is represented by *the CIVIL warS: a tree is best measured when it is down*.

Originally intended for performance at the 1984 Olympics, this multilingual, multimedia epic has reached the stage only in fragmented segments. Texts by both Wilson and Müller—plus excerpts from letters by Frederick the Great and Kafka, and fragmented passages from Empedocles, Goethe, Hölderlin, Shakespeare, and Racine—accompanied a sequence of pictures drawn by Wilson (the initial step in any of his productions from which movements and tableaux are developed). The flow of images turned history into a multinational stream-of-consciousness; and a major theme was the way events get recorded in art. The starting point of Act III scene E—produced with Act IV, scene A, and the Epilogue, in Cologne and at the ART—was Mathew Brady's American Civil War photographs, with the anachronistic presence of Frederick the Great leading into other types of conflict: Frederick's invasion of neighbouring territories to unify Germany (which spread to North America, becoming a prototype for modern world wars); Frederick's battles with his father representing familial conflict; Frederick's schizoid combination of Enlightenment liberalism and militaristic brutality as the emblem of a single person at war with himself. The apocalyptic final section presented documentary film of New York high-rise buildings being demolished.

Although the material can be described in such linear terms, the effect was hallucinatory. Fantastical figures— elongated black scribes bearing huge black quills like swords; a white scribe, dressed in ornate folds of paper and transfixed by a massive pencil; a half-human dog; waltzing polar bears—

share the stage with historical characters. Frederick the Great was played by several different actors, both male and female. In the epilogue, Abraham Lincoln (a stick-like 20-foot top-hatted puppet, which topples like a felled tree) is juxtaposed with mythical Hopi Indian beings—Snow Owl, and Earth Mother—and with King Lear mourning the dead Cordelia (actually a pile of crumpled newspaper).

History as hallucination, time scales that distort conventional modes of perception, deconstructed reality as myth—these are the defining features of Wilson's drama.

—Christopher Innes

WILSON, Snoo (Andrew Wilson). British. Born in Reading, Berkshire, 2 August 1948. Educated at Bradfield College, Berkshire, 1962–66; University of East Anglia, Norwich, 1966–69, B.A. (upper second) in English and American studies 1969. Married Ann McFerran in 1976; two sons and one daughter. Founding director, Portable Theatre, Brighton and London, 1968–75; script editor, *Play for Today* series, BBC Television, 1972; dramaturge, Royal Shakespeare Company, 1975–76; director, Scarab Theatre, 1975–80. Henfield fellow, University of East Anglia, 1978. Recipient: John Whiting award, 1978; US Bicentennial fellowship, 1980; San Diego Theater Critics Circle award, 1988. Agent: Casarotto Ramsay Ltd., National House, 60–66 Wardour Street, London W1V 3HP. Address: 41 The Chase, London SW4 0NP, England.

PUBLICATIONS

Plays

Girl Mad as Pigs (produced Norwich, 1967).
Ella Daybellfesse's Machine (produced Norwich, 1967).
Between the Acts, adaptation of the novel by Virginia Woolf (produced Canterbury, 1969).
Charles the Martyr (produced Southampton, 1970).
Device of Angels (produced Edinburgh and London, 1970).
Pericles, The Mean Knight (also director: produced London, 1970).
Pignight (also director: produced Leeds and London, 1971). With *Blowjob*, London, Calder, 1975.
Blowjob (produced Edinburgh and London, 1971). With *Pignight*, London, Calder, 1975.
Lay By, with others (also director: produced Edinburgh and London, 1971). London, Calder and Boyars, 1972.
Reason (as *Reason the Sun King*, produced Edinburgh, 1972; as *Reason: Boswell and Johnson on the Shores of the Eternal Sea*, in *Point 101* produced London, 1972; as *Reason*, produced Chicago, 1975). Published in *Gambit* (London), vol. 8, no. 29, 1976.
England's Ireland, with others (also director: produced Amsterdam and London, 1972).
Vampire (produced London, 1973). Published in *Plays and Players* (London), July 1973; revised version (produced London, 1977; New York, 1979), Ashover, Derbyshire, Amber Lane Press, 1979.
The Pleasure Principle: The Politics of Love, The Capital of Emotion (produced London, 1973). London, Eyre Methuen, 1974.

The Beast (produced London, 1974; New York, 1977). Published in *Plays and Players* (London), December 1974 and January 1975; revised version, as *The Number of the Beast* (produced London, 1982), with *Flaming Bodies*, London, Calder, and New York, Riverrun Press, 1983.
The Everest Hotel (also director: produced London 1975). Published in *Plays and Players* (London), March 1976.
A Greenish Man (televised 1975; produced London, 1978). London, Pluto Press, 1979.
The Soul of the White Ant (produced London, 1976). London, TQ Publications, 1978; New York, French, 1983.
Elijah Disappearing (produced London, 1977).
England-England, music by Kevin Coyne (produced London, 1977).
The Glad Hand (produced London, 1978). London, Pluto Press, 1979.
In at the Death, with others (produced London, 1978).
The Language of the Dead Is Tongued with Fire (produced London, 1978).
Flaming Bodies (produced London, 1979). With *The Number of the Beast*, London, Calder, and New York, Riverrun Press, 1983.
Magic Rose (produced London, 1979).
Spaceache, music by Nick Bicât (produced Cheltenham and London, 1980).
Salvation Now (produced Seattle, 1981).
The Grass Widow (produced Seattle, 1982; London, 1983). London, Methuen, 1983.
Our Lord of Lynchville (produced New York, 1983; as *Lynchville* produced London, 1990).
Loving Reno (produced New York, 1983; also co-director: produced London, 1983).
La Colombe, music by Gounod, adaptation of the libretto by Barbier and Carré (produced Buxton, Derbyshire, 1983).
Hamlyn (produced Loughborough, Leicestershire, 1984).
Orpheus in the Underworld, with David Pountney, music by Offenbach, adaptation of the libretto by Crémieux and Halévy (produced London, 1985).
More Light (also co-director: produced London, 1987).
80 Days, music and lyrics by Ray Davies (produced La Jolla, California, 1988).
Walpurgis Night (produced London, 1992).

Screenplay: *Shadey*, 1986.

Television Plays: *The Good Life*, 1971; *Swamp Music*, 1972; *More about the Universe*, 1972; *The Barium Meal*, 1974; *The Trip to Jerusalem*, 1975; *A Greenish Man*, 1975; *Don't Make Waves* (*Eleventh Hour* series), with Trevor Griffiths, 1975.

Novels

Spaceache. London, Chatto and Windus, 1984.
Inside Babel. London, Chatto and Windus, 1985.

*

Critical Study: interview in *Theatre Quarterly* (London), Spring 1980.

Theatrical Activities:
Director: **Plays**—*Pericles, The Mean Knight*, London, 1970; *Pignight*, Leeds and London, 1971; *Lay By*, Edinburgh and London, 1971; *England's Ireland*, Amsterdam and London, 1972; *Bodywork* by Jennifer Phillips, London, 1974; *The Everest Hotel*, London, 1975; *Loving Reno* (co-director, with

Simon Callow), London, 1983; *More Light* (co-director, with Simon Stokes), London, 1987.
Actor: **Plays**—*Lay By*, London, 1971; The Porpoise in *Freshwater* by Virginia Woolf, London, 1983; Andy Warhol in *Warhola!*, London, 1990.

Snoo Wilson comments:

(1973) More than anything else the proscenium arch theatre suggests the success of drawing room conversation as a mirror for a mature civilization. In these mirrors, the even keel of the state slices through the waters of unconsciousness, and very few playwrights have managed to knock any holes in the boat, though a number have suggested that the ship was sinking without their assistance, and others, like the stewards on the *Titanic*, bicycle gaily round the first-class gym, declaring that there is no list to the ship. These last are the ones most likely to be rewarded by the first-class passengers for their élan vital, even while the bilge water is rising round the ankles of the steerage families. The bicycling stewards are most likely to be able to command support that is quite independent of anything except people's gratitude at being amused, and many of them die peacefully in their beds declaring that there was always a slight list to port anyhow, and their reward was plainly a just one since people came and gave willingly, and were briefly happy.

A different brand of steward feels considerable unease at the condition of the ship, and his actions are likely to be much less popular at first than the bicyclists, though as time passes and his costume becomes charmingly archaic his pieces will be revived as Art, safe now from the Life he tried to redirect, which will have moved on in a lateral, unexpected direction. Television in Britain created a brand of "responsible" playwrights whose reputations at first were large and abrasive but now have stabilised in characteristic and therefore unsurprising because recognisable positions of social dynamism, and there the matter rests, a compromise acceptable both to producers who would like to produce more radical plays but have taken "Grandmother's footsteps" as far as they think the head of drama will let them, and to an audience stunned by tedium and kept alive by a feeling they ought to watch plays, sustained by tiny whiffs of excellence that occur in the smog of apathy. Both television and the theatre with one or two exceptions had failed either to make any formal advances in technique or to investigate areas of emotion which would force advances on them: I say "failed" because I believe that there must always be a technical evolution in theatre if only to remind audiences that they are watching a particular genre: playwrights who are adept at naturalism can take the edge off the most workmanlike oeuvre by making its naturalism subliminal.

The small groups who started with very little assistance at first—sometimes none—from the Arts Council in the late 1960's had a different sort of audience, a different sort of motive, and were a growth outside the conventional structure of theatre in Britain largely because it was dull and extremely conservative and did not provide outlets for the sort of things they wanted to do, or, in the case of Portable Theatre, a writer's theatre first, to write. Since there was very little money anyway the opportunity to write what the writer wanted to write and put it on in the way he wanted was possible, and a series of one night stands provided continuous platforms for plays which in the beginning we were prepared to take anywhere.

Now, there are a large number of studio theatres, almost a circuit, round the country. The success of *Lay By*, a group play written round a newspaper story, at the Edinburgh Festival, suggested that it was desirable and possible to launch a play about contemporary events to tour large theatres round England and Scotland. After six months of extreme difficulty we managed to set up a tour of a play about Northern Ireland, called *England's Ireland*, which had its first three weeks in Holland because we were unable to find theatres in England in sufficiently large numbers prepared to take the risk of an unknown play by a previously, quote, experimental group.

When we did bring the play to England, sadly it was in Chalk Farm at the Roundhouse rather than in Glasgow where it drew a significant response, and Lancaster and Nottingham were the only large repertory companies which would have it.

This demonstrates, among other things, the self-stultifying conservatism of the control of British theatre boards who believe that their audiences should be fed what they are accustomed to consume, either the costume drama of Ibsen's *Choice*, or on plays which by ignoring all but the most trivial of human difficulties and miseries close minds rather than open them in a stuffy two hours at the theatre.

The title I would choose for this essay, *The Freudian Landscape and the Proscenium Mind*, suggests that the middle-class mind is firmly ensconced on stage; this is true only by its being a self-perpetuating situation: it is not true that if we want to widen the range of theatrical experience we have to abandon the theatre. The theatre has always been a whore to safe fashion, but at the moment there is a pressure for a particular sort of awareness and articulacy which hopefully may lead to the good lady opening her legs to a different position, and renewed and enlarged clientele being the result. The plangent cries of either the affronted audience or management should not be an invitation to a secondary dialogue, whose end is respectability. Nor should this secondary dialogue be mistaken for a play, for the theatre is not that self-sufficient, being old, and bloated with the worst vices of time serving and sycophancy: and these will show through shallow devices. It is ourselves, finally, rather than the civilisation, who we have to prove mature; so, paradoxically, the struggle for exposure which shapes the ideas must not dent them, any more than an achieved articulacy within theatrical convention supplants the need for further thought.

*   *   *

Snoo Wilson began his writing career in the late 1960's with Portable Theatre, of which he was a founding director along with two friends from Cambridge, David Hare and Tony Bicât—Wilson himself studied at the then new University of East Anglia. His earlier plays, particularly *Pignight* and *Blowjob*, are extremely clever and dark works which reflect a good many of Wilson's general preoccupations. Though never an overtly "political" dramatist Wilson has always been concerned with problems of individual psychology, in particular schizophrenia, with moral anarchy, and most specifically with the threat of pollution on a planet which, like the absurdists with whom he has so much in common, he shows to be in direct if often comic opposition to man's dreams and aspirations. In *Pignight* a Lincolnshire farm is taken over by a sinister gangster and turned into a machine for the organized butchering and processing of the animals in question. Underneath this surface violence runs a thread of eeriness—Smitty, a psychopathic farm labourer inherited by the new owners, is a running reminder of the war (he suffers from mysterious brain damage) and takes delight in committing acts of savagery (including the blowing up of the farm dog, Robby). *Blowjob* is an equally violent exercise in alienation, with two skinheads planning to blow up a safe in a factory, an act which they bungle. During their travels they meet up with a homosexual security guard who tries unsuccessfully to pick them up and with a girl student who, typically for the time of the play, is alienated from her academic environment—the whole play acting as a caustic comment on role-playing and its stultifying effect on personality.

Both *Vampire* and *The Pleasure Principle* are plays which further develop Wilson's preoccupation with external ethical codes and their effect on individual freedom. *Vampire*, which has been both revived and revised by Wilson, has a conventional three-act structure which moves from a late 19th-century Presbyterian parsonage and a scene of astral sex in an Edwardian cricket pavilion to a contemporary scene of youthful disquiet (the setting has been altered in a subsequent version from a secular funeral parlour to the pagoda in Kew Gardens), and finishes with Enoch Powell, risen vampire-like from the coffin and delivering his famous "Rivers of Blood" speech. The second act of *Vampire* is a neat example of Wilson's developing style.

In tune with a belief that the stage is the freest medium, he concentrates on sharp juxtapositions which transcend conventional unities of time and place, and—despite Wilson's often underestimated gift for composition—continually upstage the dialogue spoken by his characters. Sarah, an upper-class girl, is wooed by a handsome young cricketer called Henry, killed in World War I. He returns in his astral form to try and make love to Sarah who is frightened of being seen—Freud and Jung suddenly appear on stilts to discuss her hang-up in their own jargonistic fashion, while a talking ox grunts "Let's go to my place and fuck." *The Pleasure Principle* concentrates on the almost undefined relationship between two characters whose opposing ideas of pleasure prevent them from consummating their mutual attraction until the last act. Robert and Gale in fact make it after a seduction sequence played out in a cardboard swan, while the nervous breakdown of Robert, an aggressive businessman with a great belief in capitalism, is prefigured by the entrance of a pair of dancing gorillas bearing messages.

Wilson is by now something of grand old man of the British fringe but still refuses or is unable to be assimilated into the mainstream despite a belief on his own part that his plays are designed to be both popular and fun. Indeed he has developed an eclectic and mercurial interest in occult subjects and in trendy pseudo-science. In *The Beast* and *The Soul of the White Ant*, the latter a quite breathtaking short play, he has explored the worlds of two dead cult figures, the satanist Aleister Crowley and the South African naturalist Eugène Marais, whose reputation, part visionary's, part charlatan's, is tested by the methods of free association that characterise Wilson's work at its best. The title of the play derives from one of Marais's works about the corporate soul which Wilson employs as a metaphor for the collective insanity of his characters, a group of white South Africans who congregate in and around a bar run by a boozy eccentric, Mabel. In typical Wilsonian fashion, the bar is mud-caked and threatened by etymological disaster while Marais himself enters as a back-street abortionist, white-suited, visionary, and also corrupt, a combination of killer and life-giver, as symbolized by an act which he performs when Mabel goes mad and shoots her houseboy, whose carefully collected sperm is now filling her freezer. When the stuff is thrown into the local river two of Mabel's friends, Edith and June, are impregnated and it is Marais who saves them, but only after Mabel's bizarre act of racial and sexual mutilation.

Wilson's most ambitious and perfectly realised play to date is probably *The Glad Hand* which works on many levels both as a political thriller and as a bizarre and often whacky study in synchronisation. On the surface the piece concerns the attempt of one Ritsaat, a South African fascist, to locate and confront the anti-Christ whom Ritsaat claims to have been present on earth during a cowboy strike in Wyoming in 1886. Ritsaat's plan is simple: he will charter an oil tanker and by time-travel via the Bermuda Triangle confront the anti-Christ in person. In fact Ritsaat, through ingenuously offering "cowboy fun" in his recruiting advertisement, acquires two camp actors as part of the crew, along with a family of stock "Paddy" Irish, a portly American scriptwriter, a Cuban cook, a CIA agent, and a dubious psychic surgeon who performs an operation on board. Indeed the ship acts as setting for the recreated cowboy strike which includes passages of riveting documentary description of conditions prevailing at the time of the "real" incident (which did in fact happen). There's also the arrival on board of a raunchy American lesbian who sparks off several more of the play's coincidences until a final mutiny against Ritsaat's rule develops into an alliance of Cuban cook and chauvinist Irishman. Before dying Ritsaat manages to utter: "Between you and your perceptions is the mirror which you think reflects reality." It's a comment which sums up a good deal of Wilson's own intentions. Indeed in showing that "reality" is something which can be changed or at least rearranged he is making both a theatrical point about naturalism and a political point about the world as it exists, although how much real substance there is behind the technique is open to serious questioning.

In *A Greenish Man* Wilson employs his associative powers on the subject of Northern Ireland. Troy Phillips, a half-Irish Liverpudlian, is sent to Kilburn on an errand of revenge and encounters an IRA dinner being organized by the local Irish publican and a bedraggled factory owner who has perfected a formula for green paint made entirely from grass clippings, as well as a battered divorcée with a liberal conscience and a tax lawyer. It's a play which fell down in production because the knots with which Wilson tied up the different strands of his ideas didn't survive the tug of live performance.

Flaming Bodies is set in the smart and characterless office of a Los Angeles film producer, whose overweight, compulsively hungry script editor, Mercedes, has just been sacked but refuses to leave the office. Again, Wilson uses this Hockneyesque setting as a launching pad for a trip in which Mercedes rediscovers herself, but only after experiencing such events as a Chevy from another film crashing through the window of the office block, King Herod discovering his love of small boys (the film she's working on at the time of her sacking is a life of Christ), Mary and Joseph (both pregnant) turning up on an inflatable donkey, and her mother's ashes turning up in a film producer's lunch! Indeed Mercedes spends a good deal of the time on the phone, talking to her mother to whom she protests her lesbianism, and to her psychiatrist, to whom she protests her sanity. In the flip, weight-conscious world of California film production, Mercedes is attacked on all sides—even by her dead father who hovers in the air outside the office's huge picture window.

In the cartoon play *Spaceache* Wilson created an Orwellian world where the unwanted and unemployed are cryogenically freeze-dried and reduced to milk-bottle size before being sent into orbit until their time comes for resurrection. This play certainly does not exhibit Wilson's talents at their most representative, unlike those in which surface organization is being continually broken up and recreated and, in an often mundane theatrical terrain, supernatural forces or natural powers are often the real arbiters of the proceedings.

Unfortunately as he reaches maturity Wilson's refusal to compromise on his chosen artistic progression has continued to cause him problems. Though he has moved with some success into novels, films, and opera, his work refuses to find a home on the main stages of any of Britain's premier subsidised companies despite initial plans and interest from both the National and the Royal Shakespeare Company. His last play for the Royal Court, *The Grass Widow*, was a rather unsuccessful jumble of ideas and effects inspired by a year's sabbatical in California. *The Number of the Beast* was an effectively reworked version of *The Beast*. Wilson's obsession with Aleister Crowley still produces dividends, and the piece was an immensely entertaining essay on Crowley's bizarrely revolutionary life. Wilson's film, *Shadey*, with Antony Sher as the eponymous sexually confused character, was well reviewed. But his single most stunning recent success was the libretto for David Pountney's production of Offenbach's *Orpheus in the Underworld*, a much-seen version for the English National Opera. Here it seemed that Wilson's ability to challenge accepted notions of taste and presentation, his impressive grasp of theatrical metaphor, were welded to a firm base. Sadly, though his work is increasingly produced abroad, notably in America, he remains an exciting playwright still to realise his enormous potential at home.

—Steve Grant

WOLFE, George C. American. Born in Frankfort, Kentucky in 1954. Educated at Pomona College, Claremont, California, B.A.; New York University, M.F.A. in dramatic writing and musical theatre. Recipient: Hull-Warriner award, 1986; Playwrights U.S.A. award, 1988; Obie award, for direction, 1990; Tony award, 1992. Address: c/o Grove/Atlantic Monthly Press, 841 Broadway, New York, New York 10003, U.S.A.

PUBLICATIONS

Plays

Paradise!, music by Robert Forest (produced Cincinnati, 1985; New York, 1985).
The Colored Museum (produced New Brunswick, New Jersey and New York, 1986; London, 1987). London, Methuen, 1987; New York, Grove, 1988.
Queenie Pie, music by Duke Ellington (produced New York, 1987).
Over There in *Urban Blight* (musical revue), based on an idea by John Tillinger, music by David Shire, lyrics by Richard Maltby, Jr. (produced New York, 1988).
Spunk, adaptation of stories by Zora Neale Hurston, music by Chic Street Man (includes *Sweat*, *Story in Harlem Slang*, *The Gilded Six-Bits*) (also director: produced New Brunswick, New Jersey, 1989; New York, 1990).
Jelly's Last Jam (also director: produced New York, 1992).

* * *

Besides August Wilson, George C. Wolfe is probably the most prominent African-American dramatist writing at the present time. Wolfe's most popular play, *The Colored Museum*, presents 11 satirical skits, called "exhibits," which deftly portray modern-day African-American life. The first

exhibit, "Git on Board," depicts a gleeful stewardess on a "celebrity slaveship" who takes her passengers on a trip at warp speed through African-American history. In "Cookin' with Aunt Ethel," an earthy, black woman recalling an "Aunt Jemima" stereotype sings a biting blues song about the ingredients needed to make up a "batch of Negroes." "The Photo Session" lampoons blacks who are stylish in dress, but lack any substantive thoughts or feelings. "Soldier with a Secret" portrays a facet of black life characterized by a sense of hopelessness which drives people to seek desperate measures to eliminate the pain of their existence. In the skit, the ghost of a Vietnam soldier kills members of his platoon to spare them from enduring lives of anguish they are sure to experience once they return home. "The Gospel According to Miss Roj" depicts a "snap queen" who initially compels one to laugh at his outrageous attire, speech, and behavior. However, just as one becomes comfortable being amused by this self-styled "extraterrestrial" being, he forces us to examine our own smugness and disinterest in the wellbeing of others. "The Hairpiece" is a hilarious look at the preoccupation blacks have in reconciling their dual identities as Africans and Americans. "The Last Mama-on-the-Couch Play" parodies such dramas as Lorraine Hansberry's *A Raisin in the Sun* and Ntozake Shange's *For Colored Girls Who Have Considered Suicide*, while also satirizing classical training for blacks and the unrealistic portrayal of blacks in musicals. In "Symbiosis," a middle-class black man finds he cannot discard his ethnic past in order to better assimilate into the dominant white society of which he wants so desperately to be a part. "Lala's Opening" reveals an entertainer of international prominence who, like the man in the previous skit, tries unsuccessfully to ignore all traces of her African-American heritage. In "Permutations," a once-neglected and denigrated young woman creates a new image of self-worth through the experience of giving birth and nurturing her newborn. In the final exhibit, "The Party," a number of famous African-Americans gather to celebrate their cultural heritage. Through the character of Topsy Washington the play's theme is revealed. The survival of blacks as a people comes from an appreciation of one's past and a "madness" which allows one to adapt to and endure the absurdities and needless pain of African-American life.

Wolfe's next major work, *Spunk*, is based on three short stories concerning male-female relationships by the famed writer, folklorist, and anthropologist Zora Neale Hurston. Throughout the show, the songs of the Guitar Man and Blues Speak Woman complement the scenes. The first tale, *Sweat*, depicts a destructive relationship in rural Florida. The sole support of the household, Delia, leads an unpleasant life with her abusive and adulterous husband, Sykes. Although Delia has purchased and cared for their home, Sykes decides to drive her out of it so he can share the house with his lover, Bertha. Knowing his wife is greatly afraid of reptiles, Sykes attempts to terrorize her by bringing a rattlesnake into the home. Though frightened, Delia refuses to succumb to his act of intimidation. Growing impatient, Sykes decides to attack Delia in bed, but ironically meets his own doom when the snake gives him a fatal bite. In stark contrast to the preceding scene, *Story in Harlem Slang*, is a comical look at male-female relations told in the vernacular of the people of Harlem. Two gigolos, Jelly and Sweet Back, boast of their seductive talents and decide to test their appeal on a young woman. However, after sizing them up, the woman quickly deflates their egos as she belittles them both for believing her to be so naïve as to yield to their dubious charms. Perhaps the most poignant of the three tales is *The Gilded Six-Bits*. The wife in a once-happy marriage is seduced by the allure of gold possessed by a businessman. Catching his wife in an adulterous act, the husband proves her lover to be nothing more than a con artist deceiving people with his gilded coins. Although the couple remain married, their relationship changes drastically as the husband takes on an aloof posture toward his wife. However, after she gives birth to a son, the husband finds he can forgive her and begins to nurture their relationship once again. Thus, the power of love overcomes the deceptions of the past.

Wolfe wrote the book for a more recent work, the musical *Jelly's Last Jam*, based on the life of the first great jazz composer, Jelly Roll Morton. The play is unlike those musicals which are little more than an excuse for blacks to sing and dance or those historical dramas which only provide praise of its subject. Instead, the musical takes a critical look at Morton's accomplishments, as well as his ignoble traits. Set on the eve of his death, the play dramatizes events of his life and dares to question whether the Creole musician neglected to credit his African-American heritage for the uniqueness and appeal of the musical style he helped to make popular.

—Addell Austin Anderson

WOOD, Charles (Gerald). British. Born in St. Peter Port, Guernsey, Channel Islands, 6 August 1932. Educated at Chesterfield Grammar School, 1942–45; King Charles I School, Kidderminster, Worcestershire, 1945–48; Birmingham College of Art, 1948–50. Served in the 17/21st Lancers, 1950–55: corporal. Married Valerie Elizabeth Newman in 1954; one son and one daughter. Factory worker, 1955–57; designer, scenic artist, and stage manager, Theatre Workshop, London, 1957–59; staff member, Bristol *Evening Post*, 1959–62. Recipient: *Evening Standard* award, 1963, 1973; Screenwriters Guild award, 1965; prix Italia Rai, 1988; BAFTA award, 1988. Fellow, Royal Society of Literature, 1985. Agent: Jane Annakin, William Morris Agency, 31–32 Soho Square, London W1V 5DG. Address: Long Barn, Sibford Gower, Near Banbury, Oxfordshire OX15 5RT, England.

PUBLICATIONS

Plays

Prisoner and Escort (televised 1961; produced in *Cockade*, London, 1963).
Cockade (includes *Prisoner and Escort, John Thomas, Spare*) (produced London, 1963). Published in *New English Dramatists 8*, London, Penguin, 1965; published separately, New York, Grove Press, 1967.
Tie Up the Ballcock (produced Bristol, 1964; New York, 1986). Published in *Second Playbill 3*, edited by Alan Durband, London, Hutchinson, 1973.
Don't Make Me Laugh (produced London, 1965).
Meals on Wheels (produced London, 1965; shortened version produced Liverpool, 1971).
Fill the Stage with Happy Hours (produced Nottingham, 1966; London, 1967). Published in *New English Dramatists 11*, London, Penguin, 1967.
Dingo (produced Bristol and London, 1967). London, Penguin, and New York, Grove Press, 1969.

Labour (produced Bristol, 1968).
H, Being Monologues at Front of Burning Cities (produced London, 1969). London, Methuen, 1970.
Colliers Wood (produced Liverpool, 1970; London, 1971).
Welfare (includes *Tie Up the Ballcock, Meals on Wheels, Labour*) (produced Liverpool, 1971).
Veterans; or, Hair in the Gates of the Hellespont (produced Edinburgh and London, 1972). London, Eyre Methuen, 1972.
The Can Opener, adaptation of a play by Victor Lanoux (produced London, 1974).
Jingo (produced London, 1975).
The Script (produced London, 1976).
Has "Washington" Legs? (produced London, 1978; Cambridge, Massachusetts, 1981). With *Dingo*, London, Eyre Methuen, 1978.
The Garden (produced Sherborne, Dorset, 1982).
Red Star (produced London, 1984).
Across from the Garden of Allah (produced Guildford, Surrey, and London, 1986).
Tumbledown: A Screenplay (televised 1988). London, Penguin, 1987.
The Plantagenets, adaptation of Shakespeare's *Henry VI* plays (produced Stratford-on-Avon, 1988).
Man, Beast and Virtue, adaptation of a play by Pirandello (produced London, 1989).

Screenplays: *The Knack*, 1965; *Help!*, with Mark Behm, 1965; *Tie Up the Ballcock*, 1967; *How I Won the War*, 1967; *The Charge of the Light Brigade*, with John Osborne, 1968; *The Long Day's Dying*, 1968; *The Bed-Sitting Room*, with John Antrobus, 1969; *Fellini Satyricon* (English dialogue), 1969; *Cuba*, 1980; *Vile Bodies*, 1981.

Radio Plays: *Cowheel Jelly*, 1962; *Next to Being a Knight*, 1972.

Television Plays: *Prisoner and Escort*, 1961; *Traitor in a Steel Helmet*, 1961; *Not at All*, 1962; *Drill Pig*, 1964; *Drums along the Avon*, 1967; *A Bit of a Holiday*, 1969; *The Emergence of Anthony Purdy, Esq.*, 1970; *A Bit of Family Feeling*, 1971; *A Bit of Vision*, 1972; *Death or Glory Boy*, 1974; *Mützen ab*, 1974; *A Bit of an Adventure*, 1974; *Love Lies Bleeding*, 1976; *Do As I Say*, 1977; *Don't Forget to Write!* series, 1977, 1979; *Red Monarch*, from stories by Yuri Krotkov, 1983; *Wagner*, 1984; *Puccini*, 1984; *Dust to Dust* (*Time for Murder* series), 1985; *Company of Adventurers* series, 1986 (Canada); *My Family and Other Animals*, from the book by Gerald Durrell, 1987; *Tumbledown*, 1988; *The Setting of the Sun* (*Inspector Morse* series), 1989; *On the Third Day*, from the novel by Piers Paul Read, 1992.

*

Critical Studies: *The Second Wave* by John Russell Taylor, London, Methuen, and New York, Hill and Wang, 1971; *Revolutions in Modern English Drama* by Katharine J. Worth, London, Bell, 1973.

Theatrical Activities:
Director: **Film**—*Tie Up the Ballcock*, 1967.
Actor: **Film**—*The Knack*, 1965.

* * *

Charles Wood grew up in a theatrical family. He served five years as a regular soldier. In both theatre and war he sees a sordid reality sold to the public as glamorous. A line from one of his earliest plays, *Spare*, epitomizes his vision: "he . . . wet hisself grotesque at Waterloo." His most interesting works—and, perhaps, his most and least successful respectively—are those where the interest in theatre and war come together, *Dingo* and *H, Being Monologues at Front of Burning Cities*.

The two acts of *Dingo* give two equally desolate views of World War II. The first is in a desert emplacement during the North African campaign. various soldiers drop in on its two occupants, Dingo and Mogg, most notably a Comic who attempts to entertain the troops. Some of the same characters are in the internment camp of the second act, including the Comic. This time he functions as Master of Ceremonies for a camp entertainment that provides cover for an escape by the officers. The play ends with the liberation of the camp; even Churchill arrives, to "urinate on the West Wall of Hitler's Germany."

In *Dingo*, Wood protests against the glamorization of World War II and even suggests that its conduct was affected by how it could be sold to the public. Its grim reality is all the more horrific for being constantly counterpointed against culturally approved and sanitized images of war. For example, at the end of the play Tanky—whose screams as he burns to death in his tank have come right after the opening dialogue of the play, and whose charred, seated form has been carried around like a ventriloquist's dummy by his mate—keeps repeating "He killed me" through the camp's liberation and the beginning of the glorification of the now-finished war. While the stubborn fact of the phrase and the charred corpse are unchanging, "he" seems to shift reference from N.C.O. to officer to Churchill, so that the simple statement seems to become an indictment of a system. The phrase, thrice repeated, is the last line of the play. It is appropriate that the dead should have the last word.

H, in rough and often awkward verse, dramatizes the Indian Mutiny in spectacular Victorian style with set-piece battles, *tableaux vivants* with actors in the positions of Imperial paintings, painted backdrops, and front cloths which fall as charging officers stagger or slide beneath them. Extraordinary staging demands are made: sepoys advance from beneath an elephant, "five men are mutilated in a horrible manner," a rebel soldier is tied over the mouth of a cannon and blown to bits, raining pieces of flesh in the form of rose petals into the audience. But as that last stage direction suggests, all is subverted by Wood's mid-20th-century theatrical consciousness. The dramatic interest lies in the different characters of the commanders and officers, and in a captain's wife who is raped by an Indo-Irish rebel and bears his child at the end of the play. One can admire the play's ambitiousness and ingenuities, but there are too many assaults and at the end too long a deathbed scene.

The sense that we are watching theatrical "turns" is strong in all Wood's plays. Wood's characters often try out attitudes on each other, particularly in *Veterans*, or parody beliefs they do not share, as in *Dingo*, so the audience is more than usually aware of the transitions from one unit or "beat" to the next. In addition, Wood brings theatrical performance into the script itself. To take *Dingo* as an example, as well as the corpse who is treated as a ventriloquist's dummy, there is also the comedian who attempts to entertain the soldiers stuck in their desert emplacement, sits on a toilet with Churchill and Eisenhower glove-puppets arguing about Arnhem, and M.C.s a climactic POW camp concert with the men in drag. There is nothing so scabrous in *How I Won the War*, directed by Richard Lester with John Lennon in the lead role, for which Wood was scriptwriter in the same year that *Dingo* was

produced, but he brought to it a similar presentational style: as men are killed, each is dyed a different colour and continues marching with his platoon.

Wood has twice written plays about making films about war, *Veterans* and *Has "Washington" Legs?* The former was inspired by Wood's experience as scriptwriter for *The Charge of the Light Brigade*. We see the ageing stars engaging in sometimes bitchy banter and in reminiscence while waiting for their call. The overall tone is nostalgic, even elegiac. In contrast, *Has "Washington" Legs?* deals with the business of making movies, and shows the emptiness not of the performers' assumed or faked emotions but of American corporate happy talk, of manipulative psychobabble, as various financial or artistic claimants to a piece of the action jockey over a lamentably unclear project to film the American Revolution. Wood's fierceness is undiminished, and his mockery of the mythification of war continues, but his target has changed to the mediators and middle managers of a service-industry society.

Wood's one play directly about the theatre, *Fill the Stage with Happy Hours*, may be one of the sourest comedies ever written. The characters, especially Albert, the manager of a tatty rep company, and his wife Maggie, whose acting career has given way to managing the bar, try on various attitudes as though to see if they fit the situation. For example, at one point Albert affects moral indignation at the juvenile lead's supposed seduction of his son, at another offers his son a man-to-man chat about seizing career opportunities when the sexual interest of a visiting *grande dame* of the stage is evident. Genuine emotion is either no longer possible for them or, ironically, can only be shown through the adoption of an appropriate borrowed attitude. At the end of the play Maggie tells Albert what he has refused to recognize: that she is dying of cancer. The curtain falls slowly as she sings "Smiling Through" and he turns heroic: "By God, I'll do *Ghosts*, I'll show this bloody town . . . . Isn't she marvellous, your mother—that's what it's about, son—that's how to use it. . . . It's given us a good life, hasn't it Maggie . . .?" Her reply ends the play: "Shut up, dear—you're not very good at it are you?" In the original production the actors stopped the fall of the curtain to bow and blow kisses to the audience, game troupers all.

—Anthony Graham-White

WRIGHT, Nicholas. British. Born in Cape Town, South Africa, 5 July 1940. Educated at Rondebosch Boys' School, Cape Town; London Academy of Music and Dramatic Art. Director, Theatre Upstairs, Royal Court Theatre, London, 1970–75; joint artistic director, Royal Court Theatre, 1976–77; associate director of new writing 1984, literary manager, 1987, and since 1992 associate director, Royal National Theatre, London. Recipient: Arts Council bursary, 1981. Agent: Judy Daish Associates, 83 Eastbourne Mews, London W2 6LQ. Address: 33 Navarino Road, London E.8, England.

PUBLICATIONS

Plays

Changing Lines (also director: produced London, 1968).
Treetops (produced London, 1978).

The Gorky Brigade (produced London, 1979).

One Fine Day (produced London, 1980; New York, 1986).

The Crimes of Vautrin, adaptation of a novel by Balzac (produced Stockton-on-Tees, County Durham, and London, 1983). London, Joint Stock, 1983.

The Custom of the Country (produced London, 1983). London, Methuen, 1983.

The Desert Air (produced Stratford-on-Avon, 1984; London, 1985). London, Methuen, 1985.

Six Characters in Search of an Author, adaptation of a play by Pirandello (produced London, 1987).

Mrs. Klein (produced London, 1988; Washington D.C., 1992). London, Hern, 1988.

Thérèse Raquin, adaptation of the novel by Zola (produced Chichester, West Sussex, 1990).

Other

99 Plays (essays). London, Methuen, 1992.

* * *

Nicholas Wright's first play appeared as far back as 1968, but although he has spent most of his professional life in the theatre, he has not produced a large body of work. It is not yet possible to speak of a development in his writing, yet certain definite shifts of emphasis can be discerned within a drama which is notable for combining a careful eclecticism of form and mode with steady concentration on a large but well-defined thematic territory.

Wright's work focuses on periods of social and political change or transition and seeks to explore, in a wide range of ways, the relation of the individual, whether as agent or as victim, to the large historical movement. *Treetops*, his earliest success, is typical in its (South) African setting—Cape Town in the year of the death of George VI and of the accession of Elizabeth II, 1952. The action is basically naturalistic, but the sunstroke-induced hallucination which prompts the disillusioned English liberal "Rusty" Walker to leave home and family, secede from the reactionary Torch Commando organization for ex-servicemen, and make an illegal gesture is presented surrealistically: Rusty realizes that he is standing within the footprint of a giant, and a chimpanzee on a bicycle brings an enigmatic message from the dead king which nonetheless makes it clear that the giant is the British Empire, within whose soon-to-be-dismembered body Rusty has been living. Rusty's political activism is a matter of quasi-physical impulse rather than of "correct analysis," but his liberal gestures serve to awaken the hitherto dormant energies of the friend to whom he appeals for help and advice, Leo Skiba, an émigré Lithuanian socialist ideologue and organizer. The personal and political symbiosis which moves Leo finally to action and which affords Rusty "moments of the most intense joy" is throughout paralleled, indeed partly articulated, by the movingly realized relationship—one of affection and provocation, need and violence—between Rusty's son Rupert and Leo's son Mark.

The debt to Brecht evident in Wright's formal strategies throughout his work is most clearly felt in *The Gorky Brigade*, which again scrutinizes the relation between political organization, energy for action, and individual dissent at a time of historical change. In Year Three of the Soviet revolution (1920–21), the revolutionary teacher Ekaterina undertakes the supervision and instruction of a colony of teenage "bourgeois anarchists." In Act 1 her initial despair, her new "scientific" (dialectical) teaching methods, and her eventual success in enabling the colonists to form themselves into the

"Gorky Brigade" (under which banner they rob rich peasants in order to further their own revolutionary purposes), are presented in a series of scenes after the Brechtian epic model, some of them attached to rubrics taken from Gorky. However, the Gorky sentences are rotated ironically in Act 2 when Ekaterina's star student Minnie, who has been away at university for six years, returns to the colony. Gorky himself is at last to visit his admirers, and she has come to request his help and influence in the case of a professor of hers who is being condemned and persecuted for his work in genetics. The colony, once in the vanguard of the revolution but now isolated and out of touch by virtue of its very idealism, humiliates and rejects Minnie; and Gorky, feeling himself (after his sojourn in Italy) "europeanized" into doubt and non-commitment, can respond to her appeals, despite his climactic public reaffirmation of Soviet aims and thinking, only with gestures of impotence and bad faith. Yet Minnie will not *retreat* into individual dissent. She refuses to leave the colony again, and as the play ends she is trying to call a meeting of all the colonists in order to regalvanize revolutionary principles and action.

In both *Treetops* and *The Gorky Brigade*, different though they are formally and stylistically, the exploration of the role of individual dissent in the process of political change is clearly shaped and underwritten by a commitment to socialism. In his plays of the 1980's, however, Wright's dramatic attitude towards the individual as a motive force in history is firmly ironic, and his treatment less direct than in those of the late 1970's. The tendency, already apparent in the earlier plays, to make a character represent or embody an attitude or class or group emerges with increasing strength through a more obvious stylization of action. In reference to *The Desert Air*, "embody" is emphatically the word. The enormous central figure (memorably incarnated in the Royal Shakespeare Company production by Geoffrey Hutchings), a caricature on a heroic scale, is Colonel—later Brigadier—"Hippo" Gore, a "vulgar toad" in whose "swollen and distended" gut is embodied a whole social movement and moral attitude. Put in charge of a Secret Service unit in wartime Cairo (1942–43), the Hippo dedicates himself to "wangling" his way up through the class-determined hierarchy of the British army, a "stumpy" intent on toppling "those long, tall, *pointy* bastards." Thus the class war cuts across and usurps in importance the World War, and the transference of British support in occupied Yugoslavia from the royalist Chetniks to the communist-led Partisans is effected not by principle or decisive strategic thinking but by the Hippo's self-interested wangling. The physical state figures forth the moral one, often hilariously, sometimes painfully, in the Hippo and his agents, and although he is eventually disgraced, Gore is allowed a final "apotheosis" through a self-interested self-sacrifice, his distended body blown apart at last for the sake of glory in posterity as the man who had "the *guts* to change" British policy—literally.

Wright's handling of the ironic interaction of representative figures is even more impressive in *The Custom of the Country* —all the more so as it is negotiated within the strict generic framework of romantic comedy. Title and plot both derive from Fletcher and Massinger, and there is an authentically Jacobean relish of pace and event in the conduct of a narrative charged with the pathos of yearning and unfulfilment. Wright's decision to set the play in the cultural melting-pot of the southern Africa of the 1890's (mostly Johannesburg) serves to introduce a political dimension into the comedic action. It is the plot's several plotters, rather than the young-married lovers they manipulate, who are the central representative figures: the self-deluding "entrepreneuse," brothel-keeper Daisy Bone, who is persuaded to cast the missionary hero Paul as her "perfect love"; her business manager, the Eastern European Jewish intellectual Lazarus, who looks forward to a moral apocalypse and finds union in death with Daisy; the Afrikaner goldmine owner Henrietta van Es, whose hitherto frustrated femininity finds its sexual object in Paul's "gentleman of leisure" brother Roger, and its maternal project in the reclamation of her errant "zombie" son Willem; and Dr. Jamieson, the agent of British imperialist designs on the African interior whose ultimate success ensures the preparation and impending dispatch of a Pioneer Column to the territory which will eventually become Rhodesia. Happy ending and historical implication are thus posed in an ironic counterpoint which is emphasized by the innocently portentous curtain speech of Paul's African bride Tendai. Such precision of dramatic nuance is characteristic of this play, and indeed of Wright's work at its best.

The historical and political dimensions hitherto characteristic of Wright's work are effectively absent from *Mrs. Klein*. But although this play is not a satire, its dominating, egotistical central figure could be seen as a distant cousin of the Hippo. In *Mrs. Klein* an irony which is at once astringent and sympathetic operates within a tightly patterned and witty meditation upon the complexity of maternal-filial relationships. Set in London in 1934, it is an intimate trio which dramatizes an episode in the life of the emigrée psychoanalyst Melanie Klein. The journey through the "primitive jungle" of mourning for the death of her son triggers a crisis in the relationship of Mrs. Klein with her daughter Melitta—who is also an analyst. Their encounters play out in real terms the familiar categories of analysis. The confrontation turns on rival interpretations of the son's apparent suicide. But Mrs. Klein's assistant, Paula, extricates herself from this conflict, gathers the available facts, and constructs an alternative narrative. The truth of the son's death is a truth not of the suicidal energy of transference of feeling—as Mrs. Klein and Melitta, despite their conflict, both believe—but of freedom and contingency. The death was the result of an accident which befell a happy man. This truth forces a self-confrontation on Mrs. Klein, which in turn lifts the veil of mourning and enables a reaffirmation of her professional calling. The end is open, understated, and intriguingly poised.

—Paul Lawley

WYMARK, Olwen (Margaret, née Buck). American. Born in Oakland, California, 14 February 1932. Educated at Pomona College, Claremont, California, 1949–51; University College, London, 1951–52. Married the actor Patrick Wymark in 1950 (died 1970); two daughters and two sons. Writer-in-residence, Unicorn Theatre for Young People, London, 1974–75, and Kingston Polytechnic, Surrey, 1977; script consultant, Tricycle Theatre, London; lecturer in playwriting, New York University; part-time tutor in playwriting, University of Birmingham, 1989–91. Member, Arts Council of Great Britain Drama Panel, 1980–84. Recipient: Zagreb Drama Festival prize, 1967; Actors Theatre of Louisville Best New Play award, 1978. Lives in London. Agent: Lemon, Unna, and Durbridge, 24 Pottery Lane, Holland Park, London W11 4LZ, England.

PUBLICATIONS

Plays

Lunchtime Concert (produced Glasgow, 1966). Included in *Three Plays*, 1967; in *The Best Short Plays 1975*, edited by Stanley Richards, Radnor, Pennsylvania, Chilton, 1975.
Three Plays (as *Triple Image: Coda, Lunchtime Concert, The Inhabitants*, produced Glasgow, 1967; *The Inhabitants*, produced London, 1974). London, Calder and Boyars, 1967.
The Gymnasium (produced Edinburgh, 1967; London, 1971). Included in *The Gymnasium and Other Plays*, 1971.
The Technicians (produced Leicester, 1969; London, 1971). Included in *The Gymnasium and Other Plays*, 1971.
Stay Where You Are (produced Edinburgh, 1969; London, 1973). Included in *The Gymnasium and Other Plays*, 1971; in *The Best Short Plays 1972*, edited by Stanley Richards, Philadelphia, Chilton, 1972.
No Talking (for children; produced London, 1970).
Neither Here nor There (produced London, 1971). Included in *The Gymnasium and Other Plays*, 1971.
Speak Now (produced Edinburgh, 1971; revised version produced Leicester, 1975).
The Committee (produced London, 1971). Included in *Best Friends, The Committee, The Twenty-Second Day*, 1984.
The Gymnasium and Other Plays. London, Calder and Boyars, 1971.
Jack the Giant Killer (produced Sheffield, 1972). Included in *The Gymnasium and Other Plays*, 1971.
Tales from Whitechapel (produced London, 1972).
Daniel's Epic (for children), with Daniel Henry (produced London, 1972).
Chinigchinich (for children; produced London, 1973).
Watch the Woman, with Brian Phelan (produced London, 1973).
The Bolting Sisters (for children; produced London, 1974).
Southwark Originals (collaborative work for children; produced London, 1975).
The Twenty-Second Day (broadcast 1975; produced London, 1975). Included in *Best Friends, The Committee, The Twenty-Second Day*, 1984.
Starters (collaborative work for children; includes *The Giant and the Dancing Fairies, The Time Loop, The Spellbound Jellybaby, The Robbing of Elvis Parsley, I Spy*) (produced London, 1975; Wausau, Wisconsin, 1976).
Three For All (collaborative work for children; includes *Box Play, Family Business, Extended Play*) (produced London, 1976).
We Three, and After Nature, Art (produced London, 1977). Published in *Play Ten*, edited by Robin Rook, London, Arnold, 1977.
Find Me (produced Richmond, Surrey, 1977; Louisville, 1979). London, French, 1980.
The Winners, and Missing Persons (for children; produced London, 1978).
Loved (produced London, 1978; Syracuse, New York, 1979). London, French, 1980.
The Child (broadcast 1979). London, BBC Publications, 1979.
Please Shine Down on Me (produced London, 1980).
Female Parts: One Woman Plays (includes *Waking Up, A Woman Alone, The Same Old Story, Medea*), adaptations of plays by Dario Fo and Franca Rame, translated by Margaret Kunzle and Stuart Hood (produced London, 1981). London, Pluto Press, 1981.
Best Friends (produced Richmond, Surrey, 1981). Included

in *Best Friends, The Committee, The Twenty-Second Day*, 1984.

Buried Treasure (produced London, 1983).

Best Friends, The Committee, The Twenty-Second Day. London, Calder, and New York, Riverrun Press, 1984.

Lessons and Lovers (produced York, 1985). London, Faber, 1986.

Nana, adaptation of the novel by Zola (produced Winchester and London, 1987). London, Absolute Press, 1990.

Strike Up the Banns (produced Mold, Clwyd, 1988). London, French, 1988.

Brezhnev's Children (produced London, 1991). London, French, 1992.

Mirror Mirror (opera; produced London, 1992).

Radio Plays: *The Ransom*, 1957; *The Unexpected Country*, 1957; *California Here We Come*, 1958; *The Twenty-Second Day*, 1975; *You Come Too*, 1977; *The Child*, 1979; *Vivien the Blockbuster*, 1980; *Mothering Sunday*, 1980; *Sea Changes*, 1984; *A Wreath of Roses*, from the novel by Elizabeth Taylor, 1985; *Mothers and Shadows*, from a novel by Marta Traba, 1987; *Christopher Columbus*, from the novel by Elizabeth von Arnim, with Barbara Clegg, 1989; *Oroonoko*, from the novel by Aphra Behn, 1990.

Television Plays: *Mrs. Moresby's Scrapbook*, 1973, *Vermin*, 1974, *Marathon*, 1975, *Mother Love*, 1975, *Dead Drunk*, 1975, and *Her Father's Daughter*, 1984 (all in *Crown Court* series); *Oceans Apart*, 1984; *Not That Kind of People*, 1984.

*

Olwen Wymark comments:

I didn't start writing plays until my mid-thirties and for the first few years wrote only one-act, rather experimental plays; Harold Hobson called them "atonal." I also wrote about eight plays for children. Since 1977 I've written full-length plays in a more naturalistic form as well as some adaptations. I've recently written an opera which was performed in 1992 and hope I will write more. I'm currently concentrating on writing for television.

* * *

Olwen Wymark has written some three dozen plays for radio, television, and stage. These range from one-act plays through full-length ones, and her children's plays typify the playful side of her personality. Indeed smallness figures again and again in her work—though, like so much else, one has to unmask it from her work even as she herself relies on a series of unmasking for dramatic effect. *Find Me*, for example, is a documentary play about a mentally disturbed girl who had, in real life, died in a special hospital. Those expecting the play to concentrate sympathy on the little girl must have been disappointed: it is far easier to sympathize with the restaurant owners, friends, and family who have their peace and property destroyed by the girl's predilection for starting fires. Indeed, though she died in the hospital, viewers find themselves sympathizing with the desperate hospital authorities rather than with Verity. She is so small as to disappear in the maelstroms she creates. It is difficult to find her, let alone love her. For the play was sparked off by letters which the girl had written, and which her family had allowed Wymark to read; one began, "Dear Whoeveryouare. Please find me and have me as your beloved." Here, in Wymark's view, is everyman's dilemma: you feel unsure of yourself, and yet it is precisely that self-doubt which fuels creativity. At least it is so in her own case.

Her early plays are exteriorizations of internal anguish, games devised by the characters to reflect and exercise their griefs and dissatisfactions. In *The Gymnasium*, two friends begin a friendly boxing match, with the elderly and gentlemanly one requesting his pretty cockney partner not to talk. They have hardly commenced sparring when the boy turns on a stream of vitriolic abuse. There is plenty of time to attempt puzzling this through, before one realizes that this is a regular marriage therapy session, in which the cockney plays the gentleman's wife and incites his partner to beat him up instead of the wife who is protected by the fine walls of custom and civility.

Most of Wymark's plays are about boringly familiar situations, rooted as they are in the emotional hothouse of upper-middle-class life. What makes the plays dramatic is a lively sense of timing; she offers to her audience the pleasure of solving marvellously constructed puzzles. It is not always possible to sort out the stories, however; and, as in *Neither Here nor There*, "a series of false certainties recede in infinite perspective. Her characters fall through one trapdoor to the solid ground beneath, only to find that collapsing beneath them as well" (Irving Wardle's review in the *Times*). Is the play a comment on the nightmarish quality of experience? Hardly, because the schoolgirls are inventing the whole game themselves.

Situation and theme; anxieties, tensions, and emotional states; guilt, futility, and desperation—these come across in her bizarre and intense plays much more strongly than characters and situations, though these are presented starkly enough. Whenever it is possible to piece her stories together, one begins to care for her characters. Otherwise her plays remain merely ingenious. Witty, arresting at their best, their lack of shape reflects a deeper problem. *Stay Where You Are* shows us a girl at the mercy of two people who appear to be lunatics. Their lunacy turns out, however, to be designed to wake her from her complacency. Quasi-existentialism no longer brings the excitement it did in the 1960's, and this is Wymark's biggest problem: she needs to find something new or fresh or more substantial that she can say through the pressure and sparkle of her work.

What saves her work is that she is aware of this, and that she laughs at herself: *The Technicians* is a marvellous attack on technical cunning which operates in a moral vacuum. Modern experimental theatre is here hoist with its own petard, and what makes the attack poignant is that Wymark loves modern theatre; in it she lives and moves and has her being.

—Prabhu S. Guptara

Y

YANKOWITZ, Susan. American. Born in Newark, New Jersey, 20 February 1941. Educated at Sarah Lawrence College, Bronxville, New York, B.A. 1963; Yale University School of Drama, New Haven, Connecticut, M.F.A. 1968. Married Herbert Leibowitz in 1978; one son. Recipient: Vernon Rice award, 1970; MacDowell Colony fellowship, 1971, 1973; National Endowment for the Arts fellowship, 1972, 1979; Rockefeller grant, 1973; Guggenheim fellowship, 1974; Creative Artists Public Service grant, 1974; New York State Council on the Arts grant, 1984; Japan/US Friendship Commission grant, 1985. Agent: Flora Roberts, 157 West 57th Street, New York, New York 10019. Address: 205 West 89th Street, New York, New York 10024, U.S.A.

PUBLICATIONS

Plays

The Cage (produced New York, 1965).
Nightmare (produced New Haven, Connecticut, 1967; New York, 1968).
Terminal (produced New York, 1969). Published in *Three Works by the Open Theatre*, edited by Karen Malpede, New York, Drama Book Specialists, 1974.
The Ha-Ha Play (produced New York, 1970). Published in *Scripts 10* (New York), October 1972.
The Lamb (produced New York, 1970).
Slaughterhouse Play (produced New York, 1971). Published in *New American Plays 4*, edited by William M. Hoffman, New York, Hill and Wang, 1971.
Transplant (produced Omaha, 1971).
Basics, in *Tabula Rasa* (produced New York, 1972).
Positions, in *Up* (produced New York, 1972).
Boxes (produced New York, 1972). Published in *Playwrights for Tomorrow 11*, edited by Arthur H. Ballet, Minneapolis, University of Minnesota Press, 1973.
Acts of Love (produced Atlanta, 1973).
Monologues for *Wicked Women Revue* (produced New York, 1973).
Wooden Nickels (produced New York, 1973).
America Piece, with the Provisional Theatre (produced Los Angeles, 1974).
Still Life (produced New York, 1977).
True Romances, music by Elmer Bernstein (produced Los Angeles, 1977).
Qui Est Anna Marks? (Who Done It?) (produced Paris, 1978).
A Knife in the Heart (produced Williamstown, Massachusetts, 1983).
Baby (original story), book by Sybille Pearson, music by David Shire, lyrics by Richard Maltby, Jr. (produced New York, 1983).
Alarms (produced London, 1987).
Night Sky (produced New York, 1991). New York, French, 1992.

Screenplays: *Danny AWOL*, 1968; *The Land of Milk and Funny*, 1968; *Silent Witness*, 1979.

Radio Plays: *Rats' Alley*, 1969; *Kali*, 1969.

Television Writing: *The Prison Game (Visions* series), 1976; *The Forerunner: Charlotte Perkins Gilman*, 1979; *Arrow to the Sun: The Poetry of Sylvia Plath*, 1987.

Novel

Silent Witness. New York, Knopf, 1976.

*

Manuscript Collection: Kent State University, Kent, Ohio.

Critical Studies: interviews with Erika Munk in *Performance* (New York), December 1971, and Arthur Sainer in *The Radical Theatre Notebook* edited by Sainer, New York, Avon, 1975; *Interviews with Contemporary Women Playwrights* edited by Kathleen Betsko and Rachel Koenig, New York, Beech Tree, 1987.

Susan Yankowitz comments:

(1973) Most of my work for the theatre has been an attempt to explore what is intrinsically unique in the theatrical situation. That is, I've been interested in sound, gesture, and movement as a corollary to language; in the interaction between the visual and verbal elements of stage life; in the fact of live performers engaged with live audience members in an exchange; and in the development of a theatrical vocabulary. My work has been generally informed by the social and political realities which impinge on all our lives; these, to a large extent, influence and shape my plays. In addition, I have been interested in a collective or collaborative approach to evolving works for the theatre and in working improvisationally with actors and directors to "find" a play which is a creative expression of our shared concerns.

At present, I am growing more concerned with the question of language—its limits and possibilities—and am moving into the realm of fiction which I feel is a more appropriate medium for that adventure.

* * *

Susan Yankowitz enlivens non-realistic, highly theatrical images of sociological problems with music, dance, pantomime, patterned speech, bold sets and costumes. These devices reinforce her verbal attacks on such contemporary social sins as conformity, alienation, racism, and sexism. These devices also enable her to avoid didacticism. Yankowitz's emphasis on *theatre* was undoubtedly encouraged by the Open Theatre, whose ensemble work contributed to the several versions of the published text of *Terminal*. *Terminal* cannot be understood apart from the Open Theatre production; the text merely suggests the performance and may be altered by other groups.

Terminal achieves unity through ritual rather than through coherent plot. It argues that people must face their deaths, and satirizes people who do not. The dying in *Terminal* turn to "Team Members" who offer them a mass-produced panacea for death. The living conduct this impersonal ritual; they also embalm and touch up the dead to hide the fact of death. The dead pierce the subterfuge practiced by and upon the dying; they "come through" the dying to judge the living and themselves. The enactment of necrophilia or the graphic description of embalming involves the audience in this common human fate.

As ritual is the binding thread in *Terminal*, so the structure of a parable unifies *The Ha-Ha Play*. Like *Terminal*, this play exposes a general human failing, but emphasizes rectification rather than exposure. Children, abducted to a woods (in which the audience sits) by hyenas wearing masks, learn to communicate through laughter. Communication is thus not only possible between groups, but it also dissolves enmity between them.

In contrast to *Terminal* and *The Ha-Ha Play*, *Slaughterhouse Play* traces the growth of consciousness of a unifying character, the black slaughterhouse worker, Junius. *Slaughterhouse Play* attacks racism: its central symbol is the slaughterhouse, which whites run and in which blacks work, slaughtering black troublemakers and selling their "meat" to whites. As in *Terminal*, action and dialogue involve the audience. The most prized black meat is that of the male genitals, which a white butcher displays in his shop, and which Junius and other rebellious blacks steal to wear around their necks as symbols of their rebellion. *Slaughterhouse Play* ends with a sequence in which blacks stab whites and whites shoot blacks repeatedly.

Not only is *Boxes* in a much lighter vein than *Slaughterhouse Play*, but literal boxes function theatrically as a fictional slaughterhouse cannot. Characters carve windows in boxes, and from within those boxes define themselves according to type and speak in clichés. Yankowitz underlines this conformity by having the characters wear hats with boxes that match their box dwellings. People in their separate boxes perform their daily chores at the same time that others experience great pain or joy. Such caricature unifies *Boxes*. Ultimately the boxes become coffins.

Yankowitz dramatizes individual or social problems and involves her audience either by shock or mimicry. Once engaged, the audience is forced to admit its responsibility for such failures as avoiding death, alienation, conformity, and racism. And this is Yankowitz's aim.

—Frances Rademacher Anderson

———————

Z

ZINDEL, Paul. American. Born in Staten Island, New York, 15 May 1936. Educated at Port Richmond High School, Staten Island; Wagner College, New York, B.S. in chemistry 1958, M.Sc. 1959. Married Bonnie Hildebrand in 1973; one son and one daughter. Technical writer for chemical company, New York, 1959; chemistry teacher, Tottenville High School, New York, 1960–69; playwright-in-residence, Alley Theatre, Houston, 1967. Recipient: Ford grant, 1967; Obie award, 1970; Vernon Rice award, 1970; New York Drama Critics Circle award, 1970; Pulitzer prize, 1971. D.H.L.: Wagner College, 1971. Lives in New York City. Agent: Curtis Brown, 10 Astor Place, New York, New York 10003. Address: c/o Harper and Row, 10 East 53rd Street, New York, New York 10022, U.S.A.

PUBLICATIONS

Plays

Dimensions of Peacocks (produced New York, 1959).
Euthanasia and the Endless Hearts (produced New York, 1960).
A Dream of Swallows (produced New York, 1964).
The Effect of Gamma Rays on Man-in-the-Moon Marigolds (produced Houston, 1965; New York, 1970; Guildford, Surrey, and London, 1972). New York, Harper, 1971; in *Plays and Players* (London), December 1972.
And Miss Reardon Drinks a Little (produced Los Angeles, 1967; New York, 1971; London, 1976). New York, Random House, 1972.
Let Me Hear You Whisper (televised 1969). New York, Harper, 1974.
The Secret Affairs of Mildred Wild (produced New York, 1972). New York, Dramatists Play Service, 1973.
The Ladies Should Be in Bed (produced New York, 1978). With *Let Me Hear You Whisper*, New York, Dramatists Play Service, 1973.
Ladies at the Alamo (also director: produced New York, 1975).
A Destiny with Half Moon Street (produced Coconut Grove, Florida, 1983), revised version as *Amulets Against the Dragon Forces* (produced New York, 1989). New York, Dramatists Play Service, 1989.

Screenplays: *Up the Sandbox*, 1973; *Mame*, 1974; *Maria's Lovers*, with others, 1984; *Runaway Train*, with Djordje Milicevic and Edward Bunker, 1985.

Television Play: *Let Me Hear You Whisper*, 1969.

Novel

When a Darkness Falls. New York, Bantam, 1984.

Fiction (for children)

The Pigman. New York, Harper, 1968; London, Bodley Head, 1969.
My Darling, My Hamburger. New York, Harper, 1969; London, Bodley Head, 1970.
I Never Loved Your Mind. New York, Harper, 1970; London, Bodley Head, 1971.
I Love My Mother, illustrated by John Melo. New York, Harper, 1975.
Pardon Me, You're Stepping on My Eyeball! New York, Harper, and London, Bodley Head, 1976.
Confessions of a Teenage Baboon. New York, Harper, 1977; London, Bodley Head, 1978.
The Undertaker's Gone Bananas. New York, Harper, 1978; London, Bodley Head, 1979.
The Pigman's Legacy. New York, Harper, and London, Bodley Head, 1980.
A Star for the Latecomer, with Bonnie Zindel. New York, Harper, and London, Bodley Head, 1980.
The Girl Who Wanted a Boy. New York, Harper, and London, Bodley Head, 1981.
To Take a Dare, with Crescent Dragonwagon. New York, Harper, 1982.
Harry and Hortense at Hormone High. New York, Harper, 1984; London, Bodley Head, 1985.
The Amazing and Death-Defying Diary of Eugene Dingman. New York, Harper, and London, Bodley Head, 1987.
A Begonia for Miss Applebaum. New York, Harper, and London, Bodley Head, 1989.

*

Manuscript Collection: Boston University.

Critical Study: *Presenting Paul Zindel* by Jack Jacob Forman, Boston, Twayne, 1988.

Theatrical Activities:
Director: **Play**—*Ladies at the Alamo*, New York, 1975.

* * *

Most parts in most plays are male. In realist and humorist Paul Zindel's work, however, almost all the roles are for women. They aren't very nice women because they tend, like so many of Tennessee Williams's women, to be neurotic freaks. The tormented women who people his plays are dumpy and defensive, lonely and lacerating, bitter and—psychologically, at least—brutal. Yet Zindel stirs our compassion by imparting to them a vulnerability which guarantees that they must endure at least as much pain as they inflict.

Not all of Zindel's characters are adults. Perhaps because he was initially a high school chemistry teacher on his native Staten Island, he has taken an interest in the distress of young people, not only in his best known play, *The Effect of Gamma*

Rays on Man-in-the-Moon Marigolds, but also in such teen novels as *My Darling, My Hamburger*, *The Pigman*, and *The Pigman's Legacy*. He likewise introduces animals in his scripts with considerable frequency.

Regardless of who their victims may be, Zindel's characters damage those for whom they have reason to feel affection and to whom they are bound, either by blood or in other ways. Where the relationship is familial or a surrogate for the sibling, parental, or conjugal bond, the suffocating intimacies create a dramatic tension familiar from the work of such other American writers of domestic drama as Inge, Williams, O'Neill, and Miller. Most of Zindel's characters are sexually unfulfilled. Despite their tenacity in surviving, his creations are clinging to unlived lives or, in the nuclear terminology of *Marigolds*, half lives, which in some of the plays are shadowed by the dead and the doomed. Yet the terrible plight in which Zindel's characters find themselves is relieved by considerable humor.

The melodrama *Marigolds* has enjoyed far more success than any other of Zindel's plays. Its original New York production ran for over two years and won its author several prizes. This play takes its remarkable title from the project on this subject which withdrawn Tillie, a girl in her early teens, has prepared for her school science fair. Tillie finds solace in the perspective of her place in the whole history of evolution beginning with the creation of the universe. Understanding the continuity of life, of energy and matter, encourages her to look beyond her own squalid surroundings. Her attitude contrasts sharply to the narcissism shared by her crude older sister Ruth and cynical mother Beatrice.

Beatrice is at once eccentric, selfish, and pathetic. She forces Tillie to miss school and then lies about it to the teacher. When she's angry at the other kids' derision of Tillie, her resentment stems not from sympathy with her daughter but from a suspicion they're really ridiculing her. She flirts with the teacher on the phone but insults him behind his back, talks constantly of hairbrained get-rich-quick schemes, taunts and torments her helpless senile boarder and her emotionally crippled daughters. And she kills the girls' pet rabbit.

Yet we grow fond of Beatrice, and of Ruth too, in spite of her resemblance to her mother, with whom she shares lipstick, cigarettes, hostilities, and neuroses. We observe Ruth's dread of thunder and death and her mother's fear of failure and life, we watch them wound and comfort each other, and we find Zindel's craft compelling us to care for women who might well have seemed monsters. When Ruth destroys her mother's confidence and makes her miss the science fair in which Tillie's project wins first prize, we even appreciate the agony out of which she chloroforms Ruth's rabbit.

Marigolds dramatizes a recurrent Zindel subject, disturbed women, and a recurrent Zindel theme, the suffering friends and relatives inflict on their "loved ones." All three women are "crazies" whose behavior reflects that of more controlled but no less destructive "normal" people. Just as the marigolds have been exposed to gamma rays, these women have been subjected to high concentrations of anguish; Ruth and Beatrice correspond to the dwarfed plants and Tillie to the rare mutants made beautiful by more moderate radiation.

In *And Miss Reardon Drinks a Little*, another play which depicts women who both cause pain and suffer from it, Zindel sides with the vulnerable but abnormal against the ruthless or insensitive but normal. Each Miss Reardon—one alcoholic, the other depressive—is harmless compared to their executive sister and her unsupportive husband. In one respect, that couple resemble Mildred and her spouse in *The Secret Affairs of Mildred Wild*. The sexual repression which is mostly implicit in the earlier play, however, becomes an explicit issue in the latter. Mildred absorbs herself in movie magazines and cinematic fantasies instead of her marriage, and her husband in his turn fails to consummate an extra-marital affair because he's distracted by his sweet tooth. While Mildred watches movies day and night, her diabetic candy-store owner of a husband is swallowing all his merchandise. Naturally both the business and the relationship are bankrupt. Yet somehow the pair survive their eccentricities and—more importantly—their disillusionment with each other to subscribe to the further fantasy of reconciliation.

The farce of *Mildred Wild*—complete with a modernization of the screen scene from *The School for Scandal*—is less successful than the acerbic wit—replete with profanity and obscenity—of *Ladies at the Alamo*. More of a cat fight than a literal shoot-out, this play does take place in Texas, where control of a regional theatre constitutes the battle's stakes. Even though the Alamo is only a theatre, a massacre of sorts does occur, with devastating destruction wrought to each of the five women's egos. Funny, foul-mouthed insults fly amid women feuding over whether the Artistic Director, Dede, will continue to run the theatre she's built from a little box into an empire. The loyalties are complex, the betrayals still more so. Dede is far from admirable and probably wins because she's the biggest bully, but when the dust settles we're somehow glad she's survived. *Alamo* is another Zindel triumph in manipulation of audience sympathies.

The drunken neurotics of that play resemble the bridge players of a short work, *The Ladies Should Be in Bed*. The principal action in this play forms a minor incident as well in *Alamo*, when one of the women maliciously phones parents of teenagers and reports sexual activity with a "pervert." But it's the ladies themselves who are sex obsessed and therefore "should be in bed." Sexuality is likewise a subject of *Amulets Against the Dragon Forces* in which a boy unsure of his sexual preference is thrust temporarily, by his mother's employment as a nurse, into a gay male household. But, with alcoholic longshoreman Floyd and teenage Chris, Zindel especially depicts the products of dysfunctional families. This play rivals *Marigolds* in its dramatization of a youngster's effort at self-protection when threatened by tormented and tormenting adults. Unusual in Zindel's menagerie of female misfits, *Amulets*'s neurotics (or dragons) include both men and women.

—Tish Dace

TITLE INDEX

The following list includes the titles of all stage, screen, radio, and television plays cited in the entries. The name in parenthesis directs the reader to the appropriate entry where fuller information is given. The date is that of first production or publication. These abbreviations are used:

s   screenplay
r   radio play
t   television play

A (Fratti), 1959
"A" is for "Actor" (S. Sherman), 1987
A la Recherche du Temps Perdu (Pinter), 1977
A-A-America (E. Bond), 1976
Aare Akogun (Ogunyemi), 1968
A-B-C in Six Months (Tsegaye), 1974
Abelard and Heloise (Millar), 1970
Abel's Sister (Wertenbaker), 1984
Aber wie heisst das Wort für "Faharrad"? (S. Sherman), 1990
Abide with Me (Keeffe), 1976
Abide with Me (t J. Mitchell), 1976
Abigail's Party (Leigh), 1977
Abingdon Square (Fornés), 1984
Able's Will (t Hampton), 1977
Abortive (r Churchill), 1971
About Face (t Harris), 1989
About Heaven and Earth (Ward), 1983
About Time (Hailey), 1982
Above the Gods (Murdoch), 1986
Abracadabra (Moore), 1979
Abroad (Weller), 1981
Absence of Emily (t Cannan), 1982
Absent Forever (Hopkins), 1987
Absent Friends (Ayckbourn), 1974
Absolute Beginners (t Griffiths), 1974
Absolute Decline (r Jeffreys), 1984
Absolute Power over Movie Stars (R. Patrick), 1968
Absolute Strangers (r Anderson), 1991
Absolution (s A. Shaffer), 1981
Absurd Person Singular (Ayckbourn), 1972
Abugida Transform (Tsegaye), 1976
Abundance (Henley), 1989
Acada Campus (r Sowande), 1980
Academic Murders (Koch), 1966
Academy (Fratti), 1963
Academy Award Show (t Gelbart), 1985
Acapulco (Berkoff), 1986
Acastos (Murdoch), 1986
Access to the Children (t Trevor), 1973
Accident (s Pinter), 1967
Accidental Death of an Anarchist (Nelson), 1984
Accidental Poke (Romeril), 1977
According to the Book (Campton), 1979
Accrington Pals (Whelan), 1981
AC/DC (H. Williams), 1970
Aces High (s Barker), 1976
Aces Wild (Hendry), 1972
Achilles (Sunde), 1991

Achilles Heel (t B. Clark), 1973
Acid (Edgar), 1971
Acrobats (Horovitz), 1968
Across from the Garden of Allah (Wood), 1986
Across Oka (Holman), 1988
Across the River and into the Jungle (Kopit), 1958
Across the Water (t Rudkin), 1983
Act (Furth), 1977
Act of Betrayal (t Whitemore), 1971
Act of the Imagination (Slade), 1988
Action (R. Patrick), 1966
Action (Shepard), 1974
Action at a Distance (Foreman), 1977
Activists Papers (E. Bond), 1980
Actor (t Lawrence, Lee), 1978
Actor and the Alibi (t Leonard), 1974
Actor and the Invader (R. Patrick), 1969
Actors and Actresses (N. Simon), 1983
Actors' Delicatessen (Mednick), 1984
Actor's Nightmare (Durang), 1981
Actos (Valdez), 1971
Acts of Love (Yankowitz), 1973
Ad Hoc Committee (D. Wilson), 1978
Adam (Carter), 1966
Adam Adamant (t Frisby), 1966
Adam and Eve and Pinch Me (Laffan), 1974
Adam Redundant (Laffan), 1989
Adam Smith (t Griffiths), 1972
Adam Was a Gardener (Page), 1991
Adams County, Illinois (Mac Low), 1963
Adam's Rib (s Kanin), 1949
Adelaise (r Forsyth), 1951
Adella (Reckord), 1954
Adrian (Birimisa), 1974
Adrift (Mowat), 1970
Advances (Terry), 1980
Advantage of Dope (OyamO), 1971
Adventures of a Black Girl (Howarth), 1980
Adventures of Awful Knawful (Flannery), 1978
Adventures of Don Quixote (t Whitemore), 1973
Adventures of Frank (t J. McGrath), 1979
Adventures of Gervase Beckett (Terson), 1969
Adventures of Jasper Ridley (N. Williams), 1982
Adventures of Marco Polo (N. Simon), 1959
Adventures of Sasa and Esi (Owusu), 1968
Advice to Eastern Europe (r Nelson), 1990
Aesop's Fables (Terson), 1983
Afamako—the Workhorse (Sowande), 1978
Affair (Millar), 1961

Male of the Species (t Owen), 1969
Mama Malone series (t McNally), 1983
Mame (Lawrence, Lee), 1966
Mame (s Zindel), 1974
Mammals (McClure), 1972
Mamzell's Luck (Ebejer), 1982
Man about Hollywood (r Lawrence), 1940
Man above Men (t Hare), 1973
Man and Dog (Tabori), 1967
Man and His Mother-in-Law (t Leonard), 1968
Man and His Music (t Chin), 1967
Man and Soul (E. White), 1982
Man at the Top (s Whitemore), 1973
Man, Beast and Virtue (Wood), 1989
Man Behind the Gun (r Laurents), 1943
Man Better Man (Hill), 1960
Man Born to Be King (t Moore), 1961
Man Dangling (Schisgal), 1988
Man for All Seasons (r R. Bolt), 1954
Man Friday (t A. Mitchell), 1972
Man from Chicago (Romeril), 1969
Man from Clare (Keane), 1963
Man from Mukinupin (Hewett), 1979
Man Has His Pride (Holden), 1970
Man Has Two Fathers (J. McGrath), 1958
Man in a Case (Wasserstein), 1985
Man in a Side-Car (t Simon Gray), 1971
Man in a Suitcase (t Harris)
Man in a/the Chair (Greenspan), 1981
Man in Love (s Horovitz), 1988
Man in Room 2538 (S. Sherman), 1986
Man in the Green Muffler (Conn), 1970
Man in the Manhole (Abbott), 1912
Man in the Middle (s W. Hall, Waterhouse), 1963
Man in the Raincoat (Ustinov), 1949
Man in the Raincoat (R. Wilson), 1981
Man in Town (t Jack Gray), 1962
Man Inc. (Moore), 1970
Man Is Man (Gooch), 1971
Man Like Orpheus (t Hopkins), 1965
Man Like That (r Eveling), 1966
Man Loses His Dog More or Less (t Sainer), 1972
Man of Character (Henshaw), 1957
Man of Letters (t De Groen), 1985
Man of Many Parts (Hibberd), 1980
Man of the Moment (Ayckbourn), 1988
Man on Her Back (t Luke), 1966
Man Only Dines (Edgar), 1974
Man Who Bought a Battlefield (Marcus), 1963
Man Who Caught Bullets (t Moore), 1962
Man Who Changed His Mind (s R. Gow), 1928
Man Who Changed Places (Terson), 1969
Man Who Climbed the Pecan Trees (Foote), 1988
Man Who Dug Fish (Bullins), 1969
Man Who Fell in Love with His Wife (Whitehead), 1984
Man Who Had All the Luck (A. Miller), 1944
Man Who Had Three Arms (Albee), 1982
Man Who Married a Dumb Wife (r Seymour), 1956
Man Who Never Died (Stavis), 1954
Man Who Never Was (t J. Mitchell), 1972
Man Who Shot the Albatross (Lawler), 1972
Man Who Understood Women (t England), 1967
Man Who Would Be Perfect (r Hoar), 1986
Man with a Feather in His Hat (t Barnes), 1960
Man with a Hatchet (r Gallacher), 1976
Man with Bags (Horovitz), 1977
Man with the Twisted Lip (t Plater), 1986

Manchester Enthusiasts (r Arden), 1984
Manchester Tales (Crane), 1975
Manchurian Candidate (s Axelrod), 1962
Mandala (Cristofer), 1968
Mandela (t Harwood), 1987
Mandragola (Murrell), 1978
Mandragola (Shawn), 1984
Mandrake (Shawn), 1977
Man-Eater (t Willis), 1980
Manhattan at Midnight (r Laurents), 1939
Manipulator (r Campton), 1964
Manly Bit (Burrows, Harding), 1976
Manny and Jake (Fierstein), 1987
Man's a Man (Pomerance), 1975
Man's Best Friend (Saunders), 1969
Man's Estate (Linney), 1974
Manslaughter (s Abbott), 1930
Mantices (r Wellman), 1973
Manual of Trench Warfare (Gorman), 1978
Many Young Men of Twenty (Keane), 1961
Map of the World (Hare), 1982
Maple Sugaring (Mamet), 1985
Marae (Broughton), 1992
Marathon (t Wymark), 1975
Marat/Sade (A. Mitchell), 1964
Marble Arch (Mortimer), 1970
March On, Boys! (t Cross), 1975
March on Russia (Storey), 1989
Marco Polo Sings a Solo (Guare), 1976
Marcus Brutus (Foster), 1975
Marginal Farm (Buzo), 1983
Maria's Lovers (s Zindel), 1984
Marico Moonshine and Manpower (B. Simon), 1981
Marie and Bruce (Shawn), 1979
Marie Laveau (Walcott), 1979
Marigolds in August (s Fugard), 1980
Marjorie and the Preacher Man (t Bill), 1987
Mark Massey Is Dead (t Ransley), 1974
Mark of the Zebra (Ebejer), 1980
Mark of Zorro (Mednick), 1966
Marko's (Bernard), 1969
Marks (t Bennett), 1982
Marksman (t Hutchinson), 1987
Mark-2 Wife (t Trevor), 1969
Marquis of Keith (Gooch), 1990
Marranos (Mamet), 1972(?)
Marriage (r Musaphia), 1965
Marriage (Ustinov), 1981
Marriage Is Alive and Well (t Kalcheim), 1980
Marriage of Anansewa (Sutherland), 1971
Marriage of Bette and Boo (Durang), 1973
Marriage of Figaro (Enright), 1983
Marriage of Figaro (Holden), 1990
Marriage of Figaro (Nelson), 1982
Marriage of Figaro (Ridler), 1991
Marriages (Pinner), 1969
Marriages (Trevor), 1973
Married Alive (t Mortimer), 1970
Married Love (Luke), 1985
Marry Me a Little (Lucas), 1980
Marrying Kind (s Kanin), 1952
Marrying Maiden (Mac Low), 1960
Marrying Man (s N. Simon), 1991
Marrying Sort (R. Gow), 1935
Martello Towers (Buzo), 1976
Martha Goodwin (Hivnor), 1942
Martians (Johnstone), 1967

Marty Feldman Comedy Machine (t Gelbart), 1971
Marty Feldman Show (t Antrobus), 1972
Marvellous Melbourne (Hibberd, Romeril), 1970
Marvin Loves Johnny (R. Patrick), 1973
Mary (t Chin), 1969
Mary (Rayson), 1981
Mary, After the Queen (Hutchinson), 1985
Mary and Lizzie (McGuinness), 1989
Mary Barnes (Edgar), 1978
Mary Beth Goes to Calgary (r Pollock)
Mary Goldstein and the Author (OyamO), 1979
Mary Jane (Bernard), 1971
Mary of Scotland (t Moore), 1966
Mary Queen of Scots (s Hale), 1972
Mary Queen of Scots Got Her Head Chopped Off
    (Lochhead), 1987
Marya (Hampton), 1967
Mary's Name (Arden), 1977
Ma's Bit o' Brass (R. Gow), 1938
Ma's Flesh Is Grass (Daniels), 1981
Masada (s A. Shaffer), 1974
M*A*S*H (t Gelbart), 1972
Masha, Too (Sunde), 1991
Mask (Ridler), 1950
Mask of Moriarty (Leonard), 1985
Mask of Orpheus (Cross), 1976
Masked Choir (McClure), 1976
Masks of Childhood (Reaney), 1972
Masque (Reaney), 1972
Masque of Aesop (Davies), 1952
Masque of Mr. Punch (Davies), 1962
Masquerade (t Ayckbourn), 1974
Masquerade (J. Clark), 1964
Masquerade (J. Patrick), 1979
Mass Media Mash (A. Mitchell)
Massa (Gooch), 1989
Massachusetts Trust (Terry), 1968
Massage (Berkoff), 1987
Masses and Mainstream (Childress), 1950
Master (r R. Bolt), 1953
Master (Schevill), 1963
Master and the Frauds (Sowande), 1979
Master Class (Pownall), 1983
"Master Harold" and the Boys (Fugard), 1982
Mastergate (Gelbart), 1989
Masterpieces (Daniels), 1983
Masters (Millar), 1963
Mata Hari (Stott), 1965
Matau (Sinclair), 1984
Match Play (Kalcheim), 1964
Match Point (Gilroy), 1990
Match-Fit (t W. Hall), 1976
Matchmaker (Keane), 1975
Mates (Musaphia), 1986
Matilda's England (t Trevor), 1979
Mating Season (r Plater), 1962
Matter of Conscience (t McCabe), 1962
Matter of Faith (Fornés), 1986
Matter of Innocence (s W. Hall, Waterhouse), 1967
Matter of Life and Death (Drexler), 1986
Matter of Pride (t Gilroy), 1957
Matter of Scandal and Concern (t Osborne), 1960
Matter of Style (r Pownall), 1988
Matter of Timing (r Moore), 1971
Matter Permitted (r Dear), 1980
Mature Relationship (r Seabrook), 1979
Maurice (C. Bolt), 1973

Max (Cannan), 1949
Max and Maxie (McLure), 1989
Max Dugan Returns (s N. Simon), 1983
Mayakovsky (Kempinski), 1979
Maybury (t Pownall), 1983
Maydays (Edgar), 1983
Mayerling (s Cannan), 1968
Mayor of Casterbridge (t Potter), 1978
Mayor of Zalamea (A. Mitchell), 1981
Mayor's Charity (t Livings), 1977
Maze (t McClure), 1967
McCloud (t Elder), 1970
McClure on Toast (McClure), 1973
McGonagall and the Murderer (Spurling), 1974
McKinley and Sarah (t Morrison), 1973
McMillan and Wife (t Hailey), 1971
Me and My Brother (s Shepard), 1969
Me, I'm Afraid of Virginia Woolf (t Bennett), 1978
Me Mammy (t Leonard), 1970
Me, Myself, and I (Ayckbourn), 1981
Me Times Me Times Me (Ayckbourn), 1971
Meals on Wheels (Wood), 1965
Mean Man I (Schevill), 1981
Mean Man II (Schevill), 1982
Mean Man III (Schevill), 1985
Mean Tears (Gill), 1987
Mean Time (Crane), 1975
Meaning of the Statue (Howard), 1971
Meantime (t Leigh), 1983
Meanwhile, Backstage in the Old Front Room (Howarth),
    1975
Measure for Measure (Brenton), 1972
Meatball (McClure), 1969
Mecca (Whitehead), 1977
Mechanic (s Carlino), 1972
Medea (Harrison), 1985
Medea (Koutoukas), 1966
Medea (B. Simon), 1978
Medea (van Itallie), 1979
Medea (R. Wilson), 1981
Medea (Wymark), 1981
Medea of Euripides (r Mathew), 1954
Medicine for Love (Henshaw), 1964
Medicine Man (Forsyth), 1950
Meet Corliss Archer (r Lee), 1942
Meet My Father (Ayckbourn), 1965
Meet the Feebles (s Sinclair), 1992
Meetings (Matura), 1981
Meg (Vogel), 1977
(M)Ego and the Green Ball of Freedom (Milner), 1971
Mein Kampf (Tabori), 1989
Mekdem (Tsegaye), 1980
Melikte Proletarian (Tsegaye), 1979
Melinda (t Elder), 1972
Mellon (t Foster), 1980
Melodrama Play (Shepard), 1967
Melon (Simon Gray), 1987
Melons (Pomerance), 1985
Member of the Family (t Foote), 1957
Memed, My Hawk (s Ustinov), 1984
Memo (s Dear), 1980
Memoir (Murrell), 1977
Memoirs of a Carlton Bohemian (Hibberd), 1977
Memorial Day (Schisgal), 1965
Memorial of the Future (Howard), 1979
Memories (t Trevor), 1978
Memories in the Moonlight (Sofola), 1977

Moon over Miami (Guare), 1989
Moon Watcher (s Henley), 1983
Moonchildren (Weller), 1971
Moondog (T. McGrath), 1981
Mooney and His Caravans (t Terson), 1966
Moonlight on the Highway (t Potter), 1969
Moonshine (r Gee), 1977
Moonshine (Saunders), 1955
Moonshot Tape (L. Wilson), 1990
Moonstone (t Leonard), 1972
Moonstone (s A. Shaffer), 1975
Moonstruck (s Shanley), 1987
Moorcock (r Livings), 1981
Moorli and the Leprechaun (J. Davis), 1986
Moral Force (t Murphy)
Morality (O'Neill), 1971
Morality (Seabrook), 1971
More about the Universe (t S. Wilson), 1972
More Barnes' People (r Barnes), 1989
More Deadly Than the Sword (t Frisby), 1966
More Female Trouble (Lavery), 1982
More Fun Than Bowling (Dietz), 1986
More Greenroom (Dickins), 1986
More Light (S. Wilson), 1987
More Metamorphoses (Weinstein), 1973
More Milk Evette (s Tavel), 1966
More, More (Matura), 1978
More! More! I Want More! (Smith), 1966
More Out Than In (Kops), 1980
More Sketches (Campton), 1967
More Than a Touch of Zen (t Barnes), 1989
More Than You Deserve (Weller), 1973
More the Merrier (s Kanin), 1943
More the Merrier (Millar), 1960
More Things in Heaven and Earth (t Jenkin), 1976
More War in Store (Carter), 1970
Morecambe and Wise (r Speight), 1956
Moribundian Memorandum (r Cook), 1986
Morituri (Mowat), 1972
Morning (Horovitz), 1968
Morning after Optimism (Murphy), 1971
Morning, Noon, and Night (Horovitz, McNally, Melfi), 1968
Morning Place (t Mosel), 1957
Morocco (Havis), 1984
Morountodun (Osofisan), 1979
Morris and Joe (Mamet), 1985
Morru Sejhu lill-Werrieta (t Ebejer), 1979
Mortification (r Bermange), 1964
Mortimer's Patch (t McGee), 1984
Mortmain (t Mortimer), 1975
Moscow Gold (Brenton), 1990
Moscow Trials (Kempinski), 1972
Moses and Aaron (Rudkin), 1965
Moss (t Kops), 1975
Most Beautiful Fish (t Ribman), 1969
Most Beautiful Girl in the World (t Slade), 1958
Most Cheerful Man (Terson), 1973
Most Recent Least Recent (Mowat), 1970
Most Unfortunate Accident (t Bowen), 1968
Most Wonderful Thing (r Livings), 1976
Motel (van Itallie), 1966
Moth and the Star (r Cannan), 1950
Mothballs (Hibberd), 1981
Mother (Arden), 1984
Mother (Gooch), 1973
Mother (Willis), 1961
Mother Adam (Dyer), 1971

Mother Country (Hollingsworth), 1980
Mother Country (Kureishi), 1980
Mother Courage (Kureishi), 1984
Mother Courage (Tabori), 1970
Mother Courage (Tsegaye), 1975
Mother Courage and Her Children (Shange), 1980
Mother Earth (s Duberman), 1971
Mother Figure (Ayckbourn), 1973
Mother Goose (Congdon), 1990
Mother Goose (Darke), 1977
Mother in India (r Hollingsworth)
Mother Love (t Wymark), 1975
Mother O (Schevill), 1990
Mothering Sunday (r Wymark), 1980
Motherlode (Ferlinghetti), 1963
Mothers (Fornés), 1986
Mothers (Wesker), 1982
Mothers and Fathers (Musaphia), 1975
Mothers and Shadows (r Wymark), 1987
Mothers and Sons (Carter), 1987
Mother's Aria (Havis), 1986
Mother's Day (J. Patrick), 1984
Mother's Day (Storey), 1976
Mother's Hot Milk (r Dewhurst), 1979
Mother's Kisses (Friedman), 1968
Mother's Nine Faces (Tsegaye), 1961
Moths (t Whitemore), 1977
Motion of History (Baraka), 1977
Motivators (Gorman), 1981
Motocar (Pownall), 1977
Motor Show (Gooch), 1974
Motorbike (Ebejer), 1985
Motorcade (r Hutchinson), 1980
Mound Builders (L. Wilson), 1975
Mountain (Saunders), 1979
Mountain Language (Pinter), 1988
Mountain Men (t Pownall), 1987
Mountain Rites (Owens), 1978
Mountains and Electricity (Koch), 1973
Mouthful of Birds (Churchill, Lan), 1986
Mouthpieces (Evaristi), 1980
Mouths (Shange), 1981
Move after Checkmate (t England), 1966
Move Over Jehovah (A. Mitchell)
Move Over, Mrs. Markham (Cooney), 1969
Movie Movie (s Gelbart), 1978
Movie Star Has to Star in Black and White (Kennedy), 1976
Movie Starring Me (r Edgar), 1991
Moving (Fennario), 1983
Moving (Kalcheim), 1991
Moving (Leonard), 1992
Moving Clocks Go Slow (Churchill), 1975
Moving Pictures (Lowe), 1985
Moviola (t Hanley), 1980
Mowgli's Jungle (A. Mitchell), 1981
Mozamgola Caper (Holden), 1986
Ms. (t Osborne), 1974
Muck from Three Angles (Halliwell), 1970
Mud (Fornés), 1983
Mud (Holman), 1974
Mud Angel (Cloud), 1990
Mud Fair (A. Mitchell), 1976
Mug (Brenton), 1973
Mug's Game (t Leigh), 1973
Multiple Choice (R. Hall), 1983
Mum and Son (Mornin), 1981
Mummer's Play (E. White), 1965

Overture for a Deafman (s R. Wilson), 1971
Overture (R. Wilson), 1972
Overture to the Fourth Act of Deafman Glance (R. Wilson), 1978
Ovid (Weinstein), 1969
Ovonramwen Nogbaisi (Rotimi), 1971
Owl and the Pussycat (s Friedman), 1971
Owl Answers (Kennedy), 1965
Owl Killer (Dean), 1973
Owl on the Battlements (Cross), 1971
Owners (Churchill), 1972
Oy Vay Maria (t O'Malley), 1977
Ozidi (J. Clark), 1966
Ozidi of Atazi (s J. Clark)

P & O (t Leonard), 1969
Pack of Lies (Whitemore), 1983
Paddy Pedlar (Molloy), 1953
Page Miss Glory (Abbott), 1934
Pageant (Linney), 1988
Pageant of Labour History (Kempinski), 1973
Pain(t) (Foreman), 1974
Painted Veg and Parkinson (Russell), 1976
Painting a Wall (Lan), 1974
Painting Churches (Howe), 1983
Painting It Red (Dietz), 1986
Paisley Patterns (Byrne), 1987
Pajama Game (Abbott), 1954
Pal (t Owen), 1971
Pal Joey (Greenberg), 1992
Pals (T. McGrath), 1984
Pamela Stephenson One Woman Show (Lavery), 1981
Panchina del Venerdi (Fratti), 1970
Pandering to the Masses (Foreman), 1975
Pandora (t Leonard), 1971
Pandora's Cross (Hewett), 1978
Panel (Bernard), 1984
Pansy (McClure), 1969
Pantomime (Walcott), 1978
Paolo and Francesca (Walcott), 1951(?)
Paper Roses (t Potter), 1971
Parades (s Tabori), 1972
Parade's End (t Hopkins), 1964
Paradise (Lan), 1975
Paradise (Lowe), 1990
Paradise (r Keeffe), 1989
Paradise! (Wolfe)
Paradise Gardens East (Gagliano), 1966
Paradise Lost (Fry), 1978
Paradise Postponed (t Mortimer), 1986
Paradise Run (t Brenton), 1976
Paranormalist (J. Gems), 1982
Parcel (r Campton), 1968
Pardon Me, Sir, But Is My Eye Hurting Your Elbow? (Richardson, Weinstein), 1968
Pardon My Inquisition (Busch), 1986
Parents' Day (Millar), 1972
Paris by Night (s Hare), 1989
Paris Not So Gay (Ustinov), 1958
Paris, Texas (s Shepard), 1984
Paris Trip (t Harwood), 1966
Paris When It Sizzles (s Axelrod), 1963
Park People (t Owen), 1969
Park Your Car in Harvard Yard (Horovitz), 1980
Parnell and the Englishwoman (t Leonard), 1991
Parole (t B. Clark), 1976
Parole of Don Juan (Gallacher), 1981

Parson's Pleasure (t Harwood), 1986
Particle Theory (Foreman), 1973
Partisans (Howard), 1983
Partita (Fratti), 1960
Partners (Harris), 1969
Partridge Family (t Slade), 1964
Parts (r Halliwell), 1989
Party (Griffiths), 1973
Party (Matura), 1970
Party (Weinstein), 1964
Party for Divorce (Kalcheim), 1963
Party Games (t Whitemore), 1968
Party of the First Part (t Plater), 1978
Party Piece (Harris), 1990
Party Time (Pinter), 1991
Party's Over (Bleasdale), 1975
Parzival (R. Wilson), 1987
Pasionaria (P. Gems), 1985
Pass It On (Renée), 1986
Passing By (M. Sherman), 1974
Passing Game (Tesich), 1977
Passing of Milldown Muldern (J. White), 1974
Passing Scene (Ritter), 1982
Passing Through (t Owen), 1979
Passing Through from Exotic Places (Ribman), 1969
Passion (E. Bond), 1971
Passion (Harrison), 1977
Passion (Nichols), 1983
Passion Flower Hotel (Mankowitz), 1965
Passion in Six Days (Barker), 1983
Passion of Peter Ginty (Leonard), 1961
Passion Play (Nichols), 1981
Passione (Innaurato), 1980
Passport to Florence (Campton), 1967
Past Is Here (Lyssiotis), 1991
Past Is the Past (Wesley), 1974
Past Lives, Present Mind (r Hoar), 1990
Pastiche (Gallacher), 1972
Pat and Mike (s Kanin), 1952
Pat Boone Show (t Gelbart), 1954
Patchwork Girl of Oz (A. Mitchell), 1988
Pater Noster (Cregan), 1973
Paths of Glory (r Bermange), 1965
Patience of Maigret (t Plater), 1992
Patience on a Monument (r R. Gow), 1944
Patrice Munsel Show (t Gelbart), 1954
Patricia Neal Story (r Anderson), 1980
Patrick Pearse Motel (Leonard), 1971
Patrick's Day (Morrison), 1972
Patriot for Me (Osborne), 1965
Patriot Game (Murphy), 1991
Patter Merchant (Lochhead), 1989
Pattern of Marriage (t Willis)
Patty Hearst (Fratti), 1975
Paul Robeson (Dean), 1978
Pauline (C. Bolt), 1973
Pauline Meditation (Mac Low), 1982
Paul's Case (t Cowen), 1977
Pavane (van Itallie), 1965
Pax (Levy), 1984
Pax Americana (Elisha), 1984
Pay As You Go (r Saunders), 1965
Payments (Duberman), 1971
Peace in Our Time (Spurling), 1972
Peach Bottom Nuclear Reactor Full of Sleepers (Wellman), 1988
Peacock Feathers (r Campton), 1982

Roses round the Door (Campton), 1967
Rosetti's Apologetics (Melfi), 1983
Rosie (Gooch), 1977
Rosinda (Ridler), 1973
Rosmersholm (Jellicoe), 1952
Rosmersholm (McGuinness), 1987
Rosmersholm (r Rudkin), 1990
Rotten Teeth Show (Dickins), 1978
Rottingdean (t Crane), 1980
Rough and Ready Lot (r Owen), 1958
Rough and the Smooth (t Terson), 1975
Rough Crossing (Stoppard), 1984
Rough Trade (Lucie), 1977
Round and Round the Garden (Ayckbourn), 1973
Round the Bend (t Cooney), 1962
Round Trip (Hailey), 1984
Round Two (Bentley), 1990
Rousseau's Tale (Pownall), 1991
Route of All Evil (Crane), 1974
Route 66 (t Carlino), 1963
Routines (Ferlinghetti), 1964
Row of Potted Plants (t Simpson), 1967
Row over La Ronde (r Marcus), 1982
Roy Murphy Show (Buzo), 1971
Royal Borough (Horsfield), 1987
Royal Commission Review (Antrobus), 1964
Royal Hunt of the Sun (P. Shaffer), 1964
Royal Pardon (Arden), 1966
Royal Show (Nowra), 1982
Royal Suite (t Hendry), 1976
Royboys (Dickins), 1987
Royston's Day (Abbensetts), 1988
Ruby (Gibson), 1955
Rudi Dutschke Must Stay (Arden), 1971
Ruffians (t Owen), 1960
Rug Merchants of Chaos (Ribman), 1991
Rule Britannia (Barker), 1973
Rules of the Game (Hare), 1971
Rules That Jack Made (t Hale), 1965
Ruling Class (Barnes), 1968
Rum an' Coca Cola (Matura), 1976
Rum and Coke (Reddin), 1985
Rumors (N. Simon), 1988
Rumours of Our Death (G. Walker), 1980
Rumpole (r Mortimer), 1988
Rumpole of the Bailey (t Mortimer), 1975
Rumpole's Return (t Mortimer), 1980
Rumstick Road (Spalding Gray), 1977
Run for the Money (r W. Hall), 1956
Run for Your Wife (Cooney), 1983
Run, Run, Runaway (Morrison), 1986
Runaway (Ransley), 1974
Runaway Train (s Zindel), 1985
Rundle Gibbet (r Terson), 1981
Runner (t Owen), 1980
Runner (t Seymour), 1960
Runners (s Poliakoff), 1983
Running Away (r Trevor), 1988
Running Gag (Terry), 1979
Running Late (t Simon Gray), 1992
Running Man (s Mortimer), 1963
Running Milligan (Dewhurst), 1968
Running of the Deer (Sunde), 1978
Rupert Show (Edgar), 1972
Rust (t J. Mitchell), 1973
Rusty and Rico (Melfi), 1978
Ruth (t Owen), 1971

Ruzzante (Holden), 1968
Ryan's Daughter (s R. Bolt), 1970

S-1 (Baraka), 1976
Sabotage (Willis), 1943
Sack Judies (t Pownall), 1981
Sacktown Rag (G. Walker), 1972
Sad Lament of Pecos Bill on the Eve of Killing His Wife
  (Shepard), 1976
Sad Professor (t Greenberg), 1989
Saddest Barn Dance Ever Held (r Cook), 1985
Saddest Summer of Samuel S (Donleavy), 1972
Sad-Eyed Girls in the Park (s Horovitz), 1971
Safe House (Elisha), 1989
Safe House (t Morrison), 1990
Safe Sex (Fierstein), 1987
Sa-Hurt? (L. Wilson), 1986
Saigon (t Hare), 1983
Saigon Rose (Edgar), 1976
Sail (McClure), 1971
Sailing Under Water (r Hollingsworth)
Sailing with Homer (r Kops), 1992
Sailor Who Fell from Grace with the Sea (s Carlino), 1976
Sailor's Return (t Saunders), 1980
Saint (r Lee), 1945
Saint and the Football Players (Breuer), 1976
St. Elsewhere (t Overmyer), 1985
St. Hydro Clemency (Terry), 1973
St. James Infirmary (Enright), 1992
St. Martin's Summer (t Delaney), 1974
St. Nicholas Hotel (Reaney), 1974
Saints Go Cycling In (Leonard), 1965
Saki (t Leonard), 1962
Sakonnet Point (Spalding Gray), 1975
Salaam, Huey Newton, Salaam (Bullins), 1991
Salesman (Munro), 1982
Salesman (Speight), 1970
Saliva Milkshake (Brenton), 1975
Sally (Fuller), 1988
Sally Ann Hallelujah Band (Lowe), 1977
Salonika (Page), 1982
Salt Lake City Skyline (Babe), 1980
Salt Land (t P. Shaffer), 1955
Salt of the Earth (Godber), 1988
Salt-Water Moon (French), 1984
Salty Tears on a Hangnail Face (John Gray), 1974
Saluting Battery (Ebejer), 1980
Salvation Army (R. Patrick), 1968
Salvation Army (t Terson)
Salvation Now (S. Wilson), 1981
Sam, Grace, Doug, and the Dog (t G. Walker), 1976
Sam O'Shanker (Russell), 1972
Sam, Sam (Griffiths), 1972
Sam Slade Is Missing (r Morrison), 1971
Samaritan (Terson), 1971
Samba (Abbensetts), 1980
Same Old Story (Wymark), 1981
Same Time, Next Year (Slade), 1975
Sameness (Smith), 1990
Samizdat (Romeril), 1981
Sammy and Rosie Get Laid (s Kureishi), 1988
Sammy Going South (s Cannan), 1963
Samskara (s Karnad), 1969
Samson (Selbourne), 1970
Samson and Delilah (t Hale), 1966
Samson and Delilah (Mankowitz), 1978
Samson Riddle (Mankowitz), 1972

San Fran Scandals (Holden), 1973
San Salvador (Dewhurst), 1980
San Ysidro (Gagliano), 1985
Sanctions (r Caute), 1988
Sanctity of Marriage (Mamet), 1979
Sanctuary (t Edgar), 1973
Sanctuary (OyamO), 1992
Sanctuary Lamp (Murphy), 1975
Sanctus for Women (Sowande), 1979
Sand (Crane), 1981
Sand (Mednick), 1967
Sand (J. White), 1964
Sand Castle (L. Wilson), 1965
Sand Mountain (Linney), 1985
Sand Mountain Matchmaking (Linney), 1985
Sand Pebbles (s Anderson), 1966
Sandbox (Albee), 1960
Sandboy (Frayn), 1971
Sandra (P. Gems), 1979
Sane Scientist (R. Patrick), 1981
Sanibel and Captiva (r Terry), 1968
Santa Claus from Florida (t Hendry), 1976
Santiago (s Clifford), 1992
Santis (r Gooch), 1980
Sara Dane (t Seymour), 1981
Sarafina! (Ngema), 1987
Sarah and Abraham (Norman), 1988
Sarah and the Sax (Carlino), 1962
Sarah B. Divine! (P. Gems), 1973
Sarah's Laughter (t Mosel), 1959
Sarid's Summons (Ebejer), 1965
Sarita (Fornés), 1984
Sarrasine (Bartlett), 1990
Sasa and the King of the Forest (Owusu), 1968
Sasa and the Witch of the Forest (Owusu), 1968
Satan's Ball (Crane), 1977
Satie Day/Night (A. Mitchell), 1986
Saturday Adoption (t Cowen), 1968
Saturday at the Commodore (Munro), 1989
Saturday, Late September (r Page), 1978
Saturday Night at the Movies (Hoffman), 1966
Saturday Night at the War (Shanley), 1978
Saturday Night Kid (s Abbott), 1929
Saturday Night Out (t Maddy), 1980
Saturday Party (t B. Clark), 1975
Saturday, Sunday, Monday (W. Hall, Waterhouse), 1973
Satyricon (Foster), 1972
Satyricon (Hendry), 1969
Sausage (R. Gow), 1924
Savage Amusement (Flannery), 1978
Savage Dilemma (J. Patrick), 1972
Savage in Limbo (Shanley), 1985
Savage Parade (A. Shaffer), 1963
Savage/Love (Shepard), 1979
Savages (Hampton), 1973
Saved (E. Bond), 1965
Saving It for Albie (t Harris)
Savoury Meringue (Saunders), 1971
Sawn Off at the Knees (Wilkinson), 1978
Saxon Shore (Rudkin), 1986
Say deKooning (L. Wilson), 1985
Say It with Flowers (t Munro), 1990
Say Something Happened (t Bennett), 1982
Say Who You Are (W. Hall, Waterhouse), 1965
Say Your Prayers (Darke), 1981
Says I, Says He (Hutchinson), 1977
Scales (Spalding Gray), 1966

Scandal (t Kanin), 1980
Scandal Point (J. Patrick), 1967
Scapegoat (s Vidal), 1959
Scar (r Gallacher), 1973
Scar (Mednick), 1985
Scaramouche (s Millar), 1951
Scarborough (Howarth), 1972
Scarlet Pimpernel (r Anderson)
Scarlet Pimpernel (Cross), 1985
Scarlett O'Hara War (t Hanley), 1980
Scars of Welfare (Sinclair), 1983
Scenario (r Bermange), 1981
Scenario (Stott), 1976
Scene from a Balcony (t Hollingsworth), 1987
Scene One (Romeril), 1969
Scenes from a Marriage (Barnes), 1986
Scenes from American Life (Gurney), 1970
Scenes from an Album (r Trevor), 1975
Scenes from an Execution (r Barker), 1984
Scenes from Family Life (t Bermange), 1969
Scenes from Maps (Terry), 1980
Scent of Fear (t Willis), 1959
Scent of Flowers (Saunders), 1964
Schellenbrack (Gallacher), 1973
Scheme (Ogunyemi), 1967
Schism in England (Clifford), 1989
Schmoedipus (t Potter), 1974
Schneider (Schisgal), 1986
School for Scoundrels (s Ustinov), 1960
School for Secrets (s Ustinov), 1946
School for Wives (Bartlett), 1990
School of Night (Whelan), 1992
School Play (Howarth), 1969
Schoolroom (t Trevor), 1972
School's Out (Rhone), 1975
Schoolteacher (t O. Davis), 1963
Schreber's Nervous Illness (Churchill), 1972
Schrecks (Schisgal), 1960
Science and Madness (G. Walker), 1982
Scissors (Wandor), 1978
Sclerosis (Barnes), 1965
Scooping (Nelson), 1977
Score Me with Ages (B. Simon), 1989
Scorpions (Leonard), 1983
Scotia's Darlings (Evaristi), 1978
Scott of the Antarctic (Brenton), 1971
Scott of the Antarctic (r Hoar), 1989
Scotty Dog (s Koch), 1967
Scourge of Hyacinths (r Soyinka), 1990
Scout (t McGuinness), 1987
Scrap! (Morrison), 1982
Scream (Laurents), 1978
Screen Guild Theatre (r Lawrence, Lee), 1946
Screen Test (s Tavel), 1965
Screens (Brenton), 1973
Screwball (Pinner), 1982
Scribes (Keeffe), 1975
Script (Wood), 1976
Scuba Duba (Friedman), 1967
Scully (Bleasdale), 1975
Scully's New Year's Eve (t Bleasdale), 1978
Scum (C. Bond), 1976
Scuttleboom's Treasure (R. Gow), 1938
Sea (E. Bond), 1973
Sea Anchor (Whitehead), 1974
Sea and Sky (r Hendry)
Sea at Dauphin (Walcott), 1954

Strapless (s Hare), 1990
Strawberry Fields (Poliakoff), 1977
Strawberry Statement (s Horovitz), 1970
Stray Cats and Empty Bottles (Kops), 1961
Streamers (Rabe), 1976
Street Corner (Wesley), 1970
Street Party (Abbensetts), 1988
Street Party (t Willis), 1977
Street Play (Bullins), 1973
Street Sounds (Bullins), 1970
Street Theater (D. Wilson), 1981
Streetlight Sonata (Herlihy), 1950
Streets of Yesterday (t Lan), 1989
Streetwise (Reckord), 1982
Stretch of the Imagination (Hibberd), 1972
Strictly for the Sparrows (t Willis), 1958
Strictly Matrimony (Hill), 1959
Strike (t G. Walker), 1976
Strike Heaven on the Face! (Wesley), 1973
Strike Pay (t Hale), 1966
Strike Up the Banns (Wymark), 1988
Strike '26 (Gooch), 1975
Striker Schneiderman (Jack Gray), 1970
Strindberg (S. Sherman), 1986
String (Childress), 1969
String Game (Owens), 1965
Strings (t Renée), 1986
Strip Jack Naked (Wilkinson), 1970
Strip the Willow (Cross), 1960
Strippers (Terson), 1984
Strip-Tease Murder (Laffan), 1955
Stripwell (Barker), 1975
Strive (Lowe), 1983
Strong Breed (Soyinka), 1964
Strong Man Act (Campton), 1979
Strong Medicine (s Foreman), 1978
Stronger Than the Sun (t Poliakoff), 1977
Strongest Man in the World (Collins), 1978
Strong-Man's Weak Child (Horovitz), 1990
Strongroom (s Harris), 1965
Struck Dumb (van Itallie), 1989
Structures (Seymour), 1973
Strumpet City (t Leonard), 1980
Studies of the Nude (Marcus), 1967
Studio (t Minghella), 1983
Studio One (t Gilroy)
Study in Scarlet (t Leonard), 1968
Sty of the Blind Pig (Dean), 1971
Style of the Countess (t Simon Gray), 1970
Subject of Scandal and Concern (Osborne), 1961
Subject Was Roses (Gilroy), 1962
Substance of Fire (Baitz), 1992
Substitute (t Keeffe), 1972
Subterranean Homesick Blues Again (Reardon), 1983
Subtopians (Frisby), 1964
Suburb of Babylon (Leonard), 1983
Suburban Strains (Ayckbourn), 1980
Success and Succession (Tavel), 1983
Successful Life of Three (Fornés), 1965
Successful Strategies (Wertenbaker), 1983
Such Impossibilities (Griffiths), 1977
Sudden Return (Owusu), 1973
Suddenly It's Tomorrow (r Musaphia), 1963
Suddenly, Last Summer (s Vidal), 1959
Sufficient Carbohydrate (Potter), 1983
Sugar and Spice (Lavery), 1979
Sugar and Spice (N. Williams), 1980

Sugar and Spite (Evaristi), 1978
Sugar in the Morning (Howarth), 1959
Sugar Wolves (McClure), 1973
Suicide (Fratti), 1965
Suicide (Nelson), 1980
Suicide (s Tavel), 1965
Suicide, Anyone? (J. Patrick), 1976
Suicide in B Flat (Shepard), 1976
Suicidio (Fratti), 1962
Sullavan Brothers (t Willis)
Sullen Sisters (t Leonard), 1972
Sullied Hand (Wesker), 1984
Sullivan and Gilbert (Ludwig), 1983
Summer (E. Bond), 1982
Summer (Leonard), 1974
Summer and Smoke (r Anderson)
Summer and Smoke (L. Wilson), 1971
Summer Evening (Shawn), 1976
Summer Holidays (Ebejer), 1980
Summer of the Aliens (r Nowra), 1989
Summer of the Seventeenth Doll (Lawler), 1955
Summer Party (Poliakoff), 1980
Summer Passions (r Abbensetts), 1985
Summer Pavilion (t Vidal), 1955
Summer Rain (Enright), 1983
Summer Romance (Schisgal), 1984
Summer Sports (Edgar), 1975
Summer the Snows Came (s Noonan), 1972
Summer Trade (Darke), 1979
Summer Wedding (r Wandor), 1991
Summerland (Balodis), 1984
Summer's Lease (t Mortimer), 1989
Summer's Pride (t Foote), 1961
Summertree (Cowen), 1967
Sun (Kennedy), 1969
Sun and I (Stavis), 1933
Sun and the Moon (Reaney), 1962
Sun Gods (s Babe), 1978
Sunday Breakfast (Campton), 1979
Sunday Childhood Journeys to Nobody at Home (Sainer),
  1980
Sunday in Perspective (t Harris)
Sunday Judge (t Lan), 1985
Sunday on the Roof (Ebejer), 1971
Sunday Runners in the Rain (Horovitz), 1980
Sunglasses (Melfi), 1965
Sunny Side of the Street (r Abbensetts), 1977
Sunny-Side Up (McClure), 1976
Sunrise (Howard), 1973
Sunrise (Nowra), 1983
Sunset Across the Bay (t Bennett), 1975
Sunset and Evening Stance (Schevill), 1974
Sunset Freeway (van Itallie), 1983
Sunset Gang (t Ribman), 1991
Sunsets and Glories (Barnes), 1990
Sunshine (Mastrosimone), 1989
Sunshine Boys (N. Simon), 1972
Sunshine on the Righteous (Campton), 1952
Sunshine Town (Moore), 1956
Sunstroke (Ribman), 1969
Superannuated Man (Laffan), 1971
Supercoon (s Baraka), 1971
Superscum (O'Malley), 1972
Superstition Throu' the Ages (Pollock), 1973
Superstitions (Shepard), 1983
Supporting Cast (Furth), 1981
Surprise (D. Wilson), 1978

NOTES
ON
ADVISERS
AND
CONTRIBUTORS

ADAMS, Elizabeth. Freelance writer in Cleveland, Ohio. Author of fiction and essays in *The Massachusetts Review*, Yale *Theatre*, *The North American Review*, *The Chicago Review*, *The Alaska Quarterly Review*, and other journals. **Essay:** Mark Medoff.

ANDERSON, Addell Austin. Director, Black Theatre Program, Wayne State University, Detroit, Michigan; serves as an officer of the Black Theatre Network. Author of articles in *The Drama Review*, *College Language Association Journal*, *Theatre Survey*, and in other journals, and in books including *Masterplots II*, *The Feminist Director*, and the *African-American Encyclopedia*. Editor of *The Black Theatre Directory*. **Essays:** Alice Childress; Lonne Elder III; Loften Mitchell; OyamO; Joseph A. Walker; August Wilson; George C. Wolfe.

ANDERSON, Frances Rademacher. Freelance writer, Sacramento, California. **Essays:** Heathcote Williams; Susan Yankowitz.

ANDERSON, Gary. Co-founder and artistic director, Plowshares Theatre, Detroit, Michigan; publicist, Black Theatre Network; theatre instructor, Wayne State University, Detroit, Michigan. Author of articles in the *African-American Encyclopedia*. **Essay:** Ron Milner.

APPLE, Thomas. Lecturer in Renaissance and modern drama, University of Canterbury, Christchurch, New Zealand. Professional actor and former lecturer, Bryn Mawr College, Pennsylvania. **Essays:** Thomas Babe; Horton Foote; Garson Kanin.

BALLET, Arthur H. Professor Emeritus of theatre, University of Minnesota, Minneapolis. Continuing consultant to various funding organizations in the United States and advisory editor, *New Theatre Quarterly*. Formerly: program director (theatre), National Endowment for the Arts, Washington, D.C.; executive director, Office for Advanced Drama Research, Minneapolis; dramaturg at the Guthrie Theatre, Minneapolis, and at the American Conservatory Theatre, San Francisco. Editor of *Playwrights for Tomorrow*, volumes 1–13. **Essays:** Steven Dietz; Nick Enright; Lee Kalcheim; Terrence McNally; Barrie Stavis.

BANHAM, Martin. Professor of drama and theatre studies, University of Leeds. Author of *Osborne*, 1969, and *African Theatre Today*, 1976. Editor of *Plays by Tom Taylor*, 1985, and *The Cambridge Guide to World Theatre*, 1988, and 1992. Co-editor (with John Hodgson) of three volumes of *Drama in Education*, 1972, 1973, and 1975.

BANKS, Carol. Independent scholar and former dramaturg and high school English teacher. **Essay:** Christina Reid.

BARKER, Clive. Senior lecturer in theatre studies, University of Warwick, Coventry; joint editor of *New Theatre Quarterly*, Cambridge. Author of *Theatre Games*, 1977. **Essay:** Arnold Wesker.

BARLOW, Judith E. Associate professor of English and women's studies, State University of New York, Albany. Author of *Final Acts: The Creation of Three Late O'Neill Plays*, 1985, and many theatre reviews and articles on O'Neill, Crothers, Tina Howe, and American drama. Editor of *Plays by American Women (1900–30)*, 1981, and O'Neill centennial issue of *Theatre Survey*, 1988. **Essay:** Tina Howe.

BARNETT, Gene A. Professor of English, Department of English, Languages, and Philosophy, Fairleigh Dickinson University, Teaneck, New Jersey. Author of *Denis Johnston*, 1978, *Lanford Wilson*, 1987, and articles on modern drama and American literature. **Essay:** Thomas Kilroy.

BENEDIKT, Michael. Author of several books of poetry—the most recent being *Night Cries*, 1976, and *The Badminton at Great Barrington*, 1980—and three plays, *The Vaseline Photographer*, *The Orgy Bureau*, and *Clyde's Wife*. Editor (with G.E. Wellwarth) of anthologies of plays in translation: *Modern French Plays: From Jarry to Ionesco*, 1964, *Postwar German Theatre*, 1965, and *Modern Spanish Theatre*, 1967. Editor of *Theatre Experiment: American Plays*, 1967. Has also edited anthologies of poetry and has taught at several American universities.

BENNATHAN, Joss. Freelance writer and critic, drama teacher, actor, and community theatre worker. **Essays:** Harry Kondoleon; Doug Lucie.

BENSON, Eugene. Professor of English, University of Guelph, Ontario; editor of the journal *Canadian Drama*. Former chair of the Writers' Union of Canada, 1983–4. Author of the plays *Joan of Arc's Violin*, 1972, *The Gunners' Rope*, 1973; the novels *The Bulls of Ronda*, 1976, *Power Game*, 1980; and the critical monograph, *J.M. Synge*, 1980. Librettist of the operas *Heloise and Abelard*, 1973, *Everyman*, 1974, and *Psycho Red*, 1980. Co-editor (with L.W. Connolly) of *English-Canadian Theatre*, 1980, and *The Oxford Companion to Canadian Theatre*, 1989. **Essay:** James Reaney.

BENTLEY, Eric. See his own entry.

BEN-ZVI, Linda. Professor of English and theatre, Colorado State University, Fort Collins. Editor of *Samuel Beckett*, 1986, *Women in Beckett*, 1991, *Susan Glaspell: A Collection of Critical Essays*, 1993, and *Vital Voices: An Anthology of Contemporary American Women Playwrights*, 1993. **Essay:** Suzan-Lori Parks.

BERKOWITZ, Gerald M. Professor of English, Northern Illinois University, De Kalb. Author of *David Garrick: A Reference Guide*, 1980, *Sir John Vanbrugh and the End of Restoration Comedy*, 1981, *New Broadways: Theatre Across America 1950–1980*, 1982, and *American Drama of the Twentieth Century*, 1992. Editor of *The Plays of David Garrick*, 1981. **Essays:** Tom Kempinski; Anthony Shaffer.

BERTIN, Michael. Play reviewer, graduate of the Yale School of Drama, works for the Salvation Army at the Alexandria Community Shelter for the Homeless in Virginia. Editor of *The Play and Its Critic: Essays for Eric Bentley*, 1986. **Essay:** Eric Bentley.

BIGSBY, C.W.E. Professor of American studies, University of East Anglia, Norwich. Author of *Confrontation and Commitment: A Study of Contemporary American Drama*, 1967, *Edward Albee*, 1969, *Tom Stoppard*, 1976 (revised 1979), *The Second Black Renaissance*, 1980, *Contemporary English Drama*, 1981, *Joe Orton*, 1982, *A Critical Introduction to Twentieth-Century American Drama*, 3 vols., 1982–85, *David Mamet*, 1985, and a television play, *The After Dinner Game* (with Malcolm Bradbury), 1975. Editor of *Three Negro Plays*, 1969, *The Black American Writer*, 1970, *Dada and Surrealism*, 1972, *Superculture*, 1974,

Edward Albee: A Collection of Critical Essays, 1976, *Approaches to Popular Culture*, 1976, *The Radical Imagination and the Liberal Tradition* (with Heide Ziegler), 1982, *Cultural Change in the United States since World War II*, 1986, *The Plays of Susan Glaspell*, 1987, *Miller on File*, 1988, *Miller and Company*, 1990, and *American Drama 1945–1990*, 1992. **Essay:** Robert Anderson.

BILLINGTON, Michael.   Theatre critic for *The Guardian* since 1971, and London correspondent for New York *Times* since 1978; author and broadcaster. Formerly theatre, film, and television critic for *The Times*, 1965–71. Author of *The Modern Actor*, 1973, *How Tickled I Am*, 1977, *Alan Ayckbourn*, 1983, *Tom Stoppard: Playwright*, 1987, *Peggy Ashcroft*, 1988. Editor of *The Performing Arts*, 1980, *The Guinness Book of Theatre Facts and Feats*, 1982, and *Director's Shakespeare: "Twelfth Night"*, 1990. **Essays:** Denis Cannan; Jim Cartwright.

BLAU, Herbert.   Distinguished professor of English and comparative literature, University of Wisconsin, Milwaukee; formerly artistic director of Kraken, co-founding director of the Actors Workshop, San Francisco, and co-director of the Repertory Theater of Lincoln Center, New York. Director of the American premieres of *Mother Courage*, *Serjeant Musgrave's Dance*, and *The Condemned of Altona*. Author of *The Impossible Theater*, 1964, *Take Up the Bodies: Theater at the Vanishing Point*, 1982, *Blooded Thought*, 1982, *The Eye of Prey: Subversions of the Postmodern*, 1987, *The Audience*, 1990, *To All Appearances: Ideology and Performance*, 1992, *Telegraph Hill* and *A Gift of Fury* (plays), and texts for Kraken.

BODE, Walter.   Editor-in-chief, Grove Press, New York. Editor of *Audition Pieces: Monologues for Student Actors*. **Essays:** Richard Foreman; Michael McClure; Leonard Melfi; Arthur Sainer; Lanford Wilson.

BOWEN, John.   See his own entry. **Essays:** Stephen Bill; John Hale; David Lan.

BRADISH, Gaynor F.   Late adjunct associate professor, Union College, Schenectady, New York. Author of the introduction to Arthur Kopit's *Oh Dad, Poor Dad . . .*, 1960. Director of *Asylum* by Kopit, New York, 1963, and of many plays for drama workshops and university groups. Died 1988 or 1989. **Essays:** Michael Cristofer; Jack Gelber; Albert Innaurato; Jack Richardson.

BRISBANE, Katharine.   Founding managing editor of Currency Press Pty. Ltd., Sydney. Author of introductions to works by Alexander Buzo, Peter Kenna, Jim McNeil, Katharine Susannah Prichard, John Romeril, Patrick White, and David Williamson, the drama section of *The Literature of Australia*, 1976, a chapter in Allardyce Nicoll's revised version of *World Drama*, 1976, and articles in *Contemporary Australian Drama*, 1981. Editor of *Entertaining Australia*, 1991, a history of the performing arts in Australia. **Essays:** Janis Balodis; Alexander Buzo; Jack Davis; Dorothy Hewett.

BRISSENDEN, Constance.   Freelance writer and editor. Formerly: dramaturg, Playwrights Canada, editor of *Toronto Theatre Review*, and managing editor, EXPO 86, Vancouver. **Essay:** Carol Bolt (with Sandra Souchotte).

BROWN, John Russell.   Professor of theatre, University of Michigan, since 1985. Formerly: head of drama, University of

Birmingham, 1964–71; professor of English, University of Sussex, 1971–82; literary manager and associate of the National Theatre of Great Britain, 1973–88. Author of *Shakespeare and His Comedies*, 1957, *Shakespeare's "Macbeth"*, 1963, *Shakespeare's Plays in Performance*, 1966, *Effective Theatre*, 1969, *Shakespeare's "The Tempest"*, 1969, *Shakespeare's Dramatic Style*, 1970, *Theatre Language: A Study of Arden, Osborne, Pinter, Wesker*, 1972, *Free Shakespeare*, 1974, *Shakespeare in Performance*, 1976, *Discovering Shakespeare*, 1981, *Shakespeare and His Theatre*, 1982, *A Short Guide to Modern British Drama*, 1982, *Studying Shakespeare: A Casebook*, 1990, and *Shakespeares*, 1991. General editor of the Stratford-upon-Avon Studies, 1960–67, and Theatre Production Studies. Editor of Shakespeare's *The Merchant of Venice*, 1955, Webster's *The White Devil*, 1960, *The Duchess of Malfi*, 1965, and Shakespeare's *Henry V*, 1965. **Essay:** David Selbourne.

BRUCHAC, Joseph.   Editor of *Greenfield Review*, Greenfield Center, New York. Author of 14 collections of poetry, several novels, and five collections of retellings of Native American stories. Editor of numerous anthologies including *Breaking Silence: Asian American Poetry*, 1984, and of *Survival This Way: Interviews with American Indian Poets*, 1987. **Essays:** R. Sarif Easmon; Obi B. Egbuna; Lewis Nkosi.

BULL, John.   Lecturer in English literature and drama, University of Sheffield. Author of *New British Political Dramatists*, 1984, *Stage Right: The Recovery of the Mainstream*, 1988, and articles on modern British drama. Editor of *Howard Brenton: Three Plays*, 1988, and *The Penguin Book of Pastoral Verse*, 1988. **Essays:** Peter Barnes; John Godber; John McGrath; Julian Mitchell; Stephen Poliakoff; Hugh Whitemore.

BURIAN, Jarka M.   Professor Emeritus of theatre, State University of New York at Albany. Author of *The Scenography of Josef Svoboda*, 1971, *Svoboda: Wagner*, 1983, and many articles on scenography, design, and Czechoslovakian theatre for *Theatre Journal*, *Theater Crafts*, *Drama Review*, *Modern Drama*, *American Theater*, and other journals. Editor and translator of Josef Svoboda's *Secret of Theatrical Space*, 1993. **Essay:** Tad Mosel.

CAMERON, Alasdair.   Lecturer in theatre studies, University of Glasgow, Scotland. Theatre reviewer in Scotland for *The Times* and *The Sunday Times*. Author of *A Critical History of Twentieth-Century Scottish Theatre and Drama*, 1989, revised edition, 1993. Editor of *Scot-Free*, an anthology of new Scottish plays, 1989. **Essay:** Neil Bartlett.

CARLSON, Susan.   Professor of English, Iowa State University, Ames. Author of *Women of Grace: Henry James's Plays and the Comedy of Manners*, 1985, *Women and Comedy: Rewriting the British Theatrical Tradition*, 1991, and articles in *Modern Drama*, *New Theatre Quarterly*, *Themes in Drama*, *Theatre Research International*, *Journal of Dramatic Theory and Criticism*, and other journals. **Essay:** Sue Townsend.

CARRAGHER, Bernard.   Freelance writer. **Essays:** Lonnie Carter; Charles Dizenzo.

CHAILLET, Ned.   Producer, BBC Radio Drama, London. Formerly: with the *Washington Star* and the *Times Literary Supplement*; deputy drama critic, *The Times*; and London theatre critic, *The Wall Street Journal*, Europe. **Essays:** Jon

Robin Baitz; Steven Berkoff; Richard Crane; Nick Dear; Marcella Evaristi; Athol Fugard; Barrie Keeffe; Hugh Leonard; Tom McGrath; Richard Nelson; Caryl Phillips; Wallace Shawn; Michael Weller; Timberlake Wertenbaker.

CHAMBERS, D.D.C. Associate professor of English, Trinity College, Toronto. Author of *Thomas Traherne*, 1987. **Essays:** Jack Gray; John Herbert.

CHRISTIANSEN, Richard. Entertainment editor, Chicago *Tribune*.

CLURMAN, Harold. Critic and lecturer. Author of *The Fervent Years: The Story of the Group Theatre*, 1945, *Lies Like Truth: Theatre Essays and Reviews*, 1958, *All People Are Famous: Instead of an Autobiography*, 1974, *The Divine Pastime: Theatre Essays*, 1974, and *Ibsen*, 1977. Producer and director of many plays, starting in the 1920's. Died 1980.

COCO, Bill. Contributing editor of *Performing Arts Journal*, and member of the drama faculty, Columbia University, New York; dramaturg for Joseph Chaikin and the Living Theatre. Author of articles in *Theatre Journal*, *Performing Arts Journal*, *Drama Review*, and *Performance*. Currently editing the papers of Joseph Chaikin. **Essays:** Lee Breuer; Jean-Claude van Itallie.

COHN, Ruby. Professor of comparative drama, University of California, Davis; on the editorial board of *Modern Drama*, *Theatre Journal*, and *Cambridge Guide to World Drama*. Author of *Samuel Beckett: The Comic Gamut*, 1962, *Currents in Contemporary Drama*, 1969, *Edward Albee*, 1969, *Dialogue in American Drama*, 1971, *Back to Beckett*, 1971, *Modern Shakespeare Offshoots*, 1976, *Just Play: Beckett's Theatre*, 1980, *From Desire to Godot*, 1987, *Retreats from Realism in Recent English Drama*, 1990, and *New American Dramatists 1960–1990*, 1991. **Essays:** Edward Bond; Rick Cluchey; Lawrence Ferlinghetti; Christopher Hampton; Joan Holden; James Schevill; Sam Shepard.

COLOMBO, John Robert. Freelance writer, editor, and communications consultant. Author or editor of over 80 books including poetry, science fiction, lore, literature, cultural guides, and *The Dictionary of Canadian Quotations*, 1991. Translator of works by Robert Zend, Eva Lipska. Lyubomir Levchev, Ludwig Zeller, George Faludy, and others.

COLVIN, Clare. Freelance writer, reviewer, and critic for *The Times*, *Sunday Times*, *Sunday Express*, and other newspapers and magazines. **Essays:** Nell Dunn; Hanif Kureishi.

COOK, Albert. Professor of classics, English, and comparative literature, and Ford Foundation professor, Brown University, Providence, Rhode Island. Author of several plays, four books of poetry, and many critical works, including *Enactment: Greek Tragedy*, 1971, *Shakespeare's Enactment*, 1972, *Myth and Language*, 1980, *French Tragedy*, 1981, *Changing the Signs: The Fifteenth-Century Breakthrough*, 1985, *Thresholds: The Romantic Experience*, 1985, and *Soundings: On Shakespeare, Modern Poetry, Plato, and Other Subjects*, 1991.

COOKE, Judy. Editor of *Fiction Magazine*, London, and of the anthology *The Best of Fiction Magazine*, 1986. **Essay:** Wolf Mankowitz.

COOKE, Patricia. Theatre critic for the *Dominion Sunday Times*, Wellington. Formerly: teacher of English and drama; tutor, Victoria University of Wellington; and secretary of the Shakespeare Globe Centre, New Zealand. **Essays:** John Broughton; Stuart Hoar; Anthony McCarten; Renée; Stephen Sinclair.

CORBALLIS, Richard. Professor of English, Massey University, Palmerston North, New Zealand. Author of *Stoppard: The Mystery and the Clockwork*, 1984, and *Introducing Witi Ihimaera* (with Simon Garrett), 1984. Editor of *George Chapman's Minor Translations: A Critical Edition of His Renderings of Musaeus, Hesiod and Juvenal*, 1984. **Essay:** Vincent O'Sullivan.

CORRIGAN, Robert W. Dean, School of Arts and Humanities, University of Texas at Dallas. Author of *Theatre in Search of a Fix*, 1973, *The World of the Theatre*, 1979, 2nd edition, 1992, and *The Making of Theatre*, 1980. Editor of *Arthur Miller: A Collection of Critical Essays*, 1969, several anthologies of plays, and volumes on comedy and tragedy. Founding editor of *Tulane Drama Review* (later *Drama Review*).

DACE, Tish. Professor of English, Southeastern Massachusetts University, North Dartmouth; contributor to *Plays International*, *Plays and Players*, *Theater Week*, *Theatre Crafts*, *Other Stages*, *Village Voice*, New York *Times*, *American Theatre*, *Playbill*, and other periodicals. Author of *LeRoi Jones (Imamu Amiri Baraka): A Checklist of Works by and about Him*, 1971, *The Theatre Student: Modern Theatre and Drama*, 1973, and *Langston Hughes: Early Critical Responses*, 1991. **Essays:** Harvey Fierstein; Spalding Gray; John Guare; Wendy Kesselman; Bernard Kops; Susan Miller; James A. Saunders; Martin Sherman; Karen Sunde; Paula Vogel; Doric Wilson; Paul Zindel.

DARLINGTON, W.A. Member of the editorial staff, and chief drama critic, 1920–68, *Daily Telegraph*, London. Author of *Alf's Button*, 1919 (novel), 1924 (play); *I Do What I Like*, 1947; *The Actor and His Audience*, 1949; and *Six Thousand and One Nights*, 1960. C.B.E. 1963. Died 1979. **Essays:** Ronald Gow; Ronald Millar; Ted Willis.

DAWSON, Terence. Lecturer in English literature at the National University of Singapore since 1988. Has contributed articles on both English and French literature to numerous journals including the *Modern Language Review*. **Essay:** Peter Luke.

DIAMOND, Elin. Associate professor of English, Rutgers University, New Brunswick, New Jersey. Author of *Pinter's Comic Play*, 1985, and articles on Pinter, Beckett, Churchill, Benmussa, and Duras in *Theatre Journal*, *Modern Drama*, *Comparative Drama*, and other journals. **Essay:** Adrienne Kennedy.

DOUGLAS, Reid. University teacher and freelance writer; former editor of *Contemporary Theatre*. **Essay:** Ray Mathew.

DUNN, Tony. Senior lecturer in literary and cultural studies, Portsmouth University, Hampshire; editor of *Gambit*, London. Author of articles on Howard Barker, British theatre in the 1980's, and reviews, features, and interviews in *Gambit*, *Drama*, *Plays and Players*, and *Tribune*. **Essays:** Howard Barker; Alan Bleasdale; Deborah Levy; Willy Russell; Ted Whitehead.

EDINBOROUGH, Arnold. President of the Council for Business and the Arts in Canada; member of the Board of Governors of the Stratford Festival, Ontario. Author of *Canada*, 1962, *Some Camel . . . Some Needle*, 1974, *The Enduring Wood*, 1978, *The Festivals of Canada*, 1981, *Winston's: The Life and Times of a Great Restaurant*, 1988, and articles in the *Financial Post*, *Canadian Churchman*, and other periodicals. **Essay:** Mavor Moore.

EDWARDES, Jane. Theatre editor, *Time Out*, London. Contributor to Kaleidoscope, BBC Radio. **Essays:** Debbie Isitt; Clare McIntyre.

ELSOM, John. Senior lecturer, City University, London. Author of *Theatre Outside London*, 1972, *Post-War British Theatre*, 1976 (revised 1979), *The History of the National Theatre*, with Nicholas Tomalin, 1978, and *Post-War British Theatre Criticism*, 1981. Editor of *Is Shakespeare Still Our Contemporary?*, 1989. **Essays:** Barry Bermange; Chris Bond; J.P. Donleavy; John Grillo; Wilson John Haire; Willis Hall and Keith Waterhouse; Alan Plater; Peter Terson; Christopher Wilkinson.

ESTRIN, Mark W. Professor of English and director of film studies, Rhode Island College, Providence, since 1966. Editor of *Lillian Hellman: Plays, Films, Memoirs*, 1980, *Critical Essays on Lillian Hellman*, 1989, and *Conversations with Eugene O'Neill*, 1990. Essays and reviews in numerous publications including *Resources for American Literary Study*, *Modern Drama*, *Literature/Film Quarterly*, *The Journal of Narrative Technique*, and *Choice*. **Essays:** David Rabe; Ted Tally.

FALCONIERI, John V. President Emeritus, American University of Rome; editor of *Theatre Annual*; member of the editorial board, *International Drama*. Author of *A History of the Commedia dell'Arte in Spain*. **Essay:** Gore Vidal.

FEINGOLD, Michael. Drama critic, *Village Voice*, New York. Director: productions include plays by John Arden and Lanford Wilson. Translator of plays by Brecht, Ibsen, Molière, Prévert, Diderot, Bernhard, and others. Literary director of the Guthrie Theatre, Minneapolis, 1970–79. **Essay:** Kenneth Bernard.

FITZPATRICK, Peter. Senior lecturer in English, Monash University, Clayton, Victoria, and director of its Centre for Drama and Theatre Studies. Author of *After "The Doll": Australian Drama Since 1955*, 1979, books on the plays of David Williamson and Stephen Sewell, and a number of articles on Australian drama. **Essays:** Hannie Rayson; Stephen Sewell.

FLEISCHER, Leonard. Senior executive staff writer, RCA, New York; member of the New York Bar. Author of articles and reviews in *Saturday Review*, *London Jewish Quarterly*, *Congress Bi-Weekly*, and other publications. **Essay:** Oliver Hailey.

FOTHERINGHAM, Richard. Lecturer in drama, University of Queensland, St. Lucia, Brisbane. Author of *Sport in Australian Drama*, 1992. Editor (with Veronica Kelly) of *Australian Drama Studies* since 1982 and editor of *Community Theatre in Australia*, 1987. **Essay:** John Romeril.

FRANK, Leah D. Theatre critic, New York *Times* Long Island Supplement; theatre critic and feature writer for many newspapers and magazines, including New York *Times*, New York *Daily News*, *Elle*, *Other Stages* (founding editor), Stamford *Advocate*, Connecticut, and *New York Theater Review*. **Essays:** Frank D. Gilroy; Robert Patrick.

FRIEDMAN, Melvin J. Professor of comparative literature, University of Wisconsin, Milwaukee; advisory editor of *Journal of Popular Culture*, *Studies in the Novel*, *Renascence*, *Journal of American Culture*, *Studies in American Fiction*, *Fer de Lance*, *Contemporary Literature*, *Journal of Beckett Studies*, *International Fiction Review*, *Arete*, *Journal of Modern Literature*, and *Yiddish*. Author of *Stream of Consciousness: A Study in Literary Method*, 1955. Author or editor of works about Beckett, Flannery O'Connor, Styron, Catholic novelists, Ezra Pound, and Ionesco. **Essay:** Bruce Jay Friedman.

GILBERT, Helen. Lecturer, Monash University, Clayton, Victoria. Author (with Joanne Tompkins) of *Re-acting (to) Empire: Performance and Post-Colonial Drama*, 1993. **Essays:** Alma De Groen; Jill Shearer.

GILBERT, Reid. Professor of drama, Capilano College, North Vancouver, British Columbia. Author of the play *A Glass Darkly*, 1973, and numerous articles and reviews in *Canadian Drama*, *Canadian Theatre Review*, *Journal of Canadian Theatre History*, *Journal of the Association for Canadian Theatre Research*, *Capilano Review*, and other periodicals, and in the Profiles in Canadian Literature series. **Essays:** Michael Cook; David Fennario; David Freeman; John Gray; Tom Hendry; Sharon Pollock.

GILMAN, Richard. Professor of drama, Yale University, New Haven, Connecticut. Author of *The Confusion of Realms*, 1970, *Common and Uncommon Masks*, 1971, *The Making of Modern Drama*, 1975, *Decadence*, 1979, and *Faith, Sex, Mystery: A Memoir*, 1987. Former literary editor of *New Republic* and drama critic for *Commonweal* and *Newsweek*.

GOODMAN, Lizbeth. Lecturer in literature, The Open University, Milton Keynes; member of the editorial committee for *New Theatre Quarterly*. Author of *Contemporary Feminist Theatres: To Each Her Own*, 1993. Editor (with others) of *Imagining Women: Cultural Representations and Gender*, 1992. **Essays:** Sarah Daniels; Debbie Horsfield; Charlotte Keatley; Bryony Lavery; Rona Munro; Winsome Pinnock; Michelene Wandor.

GORDON, Lois. Professor, Department of English and Comparative Literature, Fairleigh Dickinson University, Teaneck, New Jersey. Author of *Stratagems to Uncover Nakedness: The Dramas of Harold Pinter*, 1969, *Donald Barthelme*, 1981, *Robert Coover: The Universal Fiction-making Process*, 1983, *American Chronicle: Six Decades in American Life 1920–1980*, 1987, *American Chronicle: Seven Decades in American Life 1920–1989*, 1990, *Harold Pinter: A Casebook*, 1990, and articles on Arthur Miller, Tennessee Williams, Samuel Beckett, T.S. Eliot, W.B. Yeats, William Faulkner, Randall Jarrell, Philip Roth, Elizabeth Bishop, William Gaddis, and other writers. **Essays:** Arthur Miller; Harold Pinter.

GOTTFRIED, Martin. Freelance writer, drama critic, and lecturer. Author of *A Theater Divided*, 1968, *Opening Nights*, 1970, *Broadway Musicals*, 1979, *Jed Harris: The Curse of Genius*, 1984, *In Person: The Great Entertainers*, 1986, *All His Jazz*, 1990, *More Broadway Musicals*, 1991, *Sondheim,*

1993, and a forthcoming biography of Danny Kaye. **Essays:** Lewis John Carlino; Arnold Weinstein; John White.

GRAHAM-WHITE, Anthony. Professor, Department of Communication and Theater, University of Illinois, Chicago. Author of *The Drama of Black Africa*, 1974, and articles in various journals. Former editor of *Educational Theatre Journal* (now *Theatre Journal*). **Essays:** Ama Ata Aidoo; David Campton; Frank Chin; John Pepper Clark; David Cregan; Philip Kan Gotanda; Len Jenkin; Ngugi wa Thiong'o; Efua Sutherland; Tsegaye Gabre-Medhin; Charles Wood.

GRANT, Steve. Assistant editor of *Time Out*, London. Author of five plays, essays on fringe theatre in *Dreams and Deconstructions*, 1980, and articles in *The Guardian*, *The Observer*, *The Times*, *The Sunday Times*, *Morning Star*, *Cosmopolitan*, and other periodicals. **Essays:** John Byrne; Snoo Wilson.

GRAY, Frances. Lecturer in drama, University of Sheffield. Author of *John Arden*, 1982, *Noël Coward*, 1987, radio plays including *Mary*, 1983, *Neverland*, 1985, and *Dawnhorse*, 1991, and articles on radio drama, modern theatre, and women in comedy. Editor of *Second Wave at the Albany*. **Essays:** Shirley Gee; Tony Marchant.

GUERNSEY, Otis L., Jr. Author and editor of the Applause-Best Plays series of theatre yearbooks, 1964 to the present, the *Dramatists Guild Quarterly*, 1964 to the present, *The Directory of the American Theater 1894–1971*, 1971, *Curtain Times: The New York Theater 1965–1987*, 1987, and the anthologies *Playwrights, Lyricists, Composers on Theater*, 1974, and *Broadway Song and Story*, 1986.

GUPTARA, Prabhu S. Professor, European Institute of Purchasing Management, France, and chair, Advance Management Training Ltd. Freelance writer, lecturer, and broadcaster. Author of two books of poetry, *Beginnings*, 1975, and *Continuations*, 1976, and articles in *Encyclopaedia Iranica*, *The Oxford Companion to English Literature*, 1985, and the *Times Literary Supplement* and other journals. **Essays:** Michael Abbensetts; John Antrobus; Michael Hastings; John Spurling; Olwen Wymark.

HADFIELD, Paul J.A. Senior lecturer in theatre studies, University of Ulster, Coleraine, Londonderry. Director of Theatre Ireland since 1982; member of the Association of International Theatre Critics since 1987 and of the Advisory Board for the Yeats International Festival since 1991. **Essays:** John B. Keane; Stephen Lowe; Daniel Mornin.

HAMMOND, Jonathan. Late vice-president, National Union of Journalists; former editor, Penguin Books, London. Author of articles in *Culture and Agitation* and *Plays and Players*. Died 1983. **Essays:** John Burrows and John Harding; Stewart Conn; Roger Howard; Alun Owen.

HANSFORD, James. Teacher of English, Royal Grammar School, Guildford; tutor in literature, Open University; tutor in literature, Surrey University Extra-Mural Department. Author of essays on Beckett for *The Journal of Beckett Studies* and *Studies in Short Fiction*, on Conrad for *The Conradian* and *Conradiana*, on Gabriel Josipovici and Alan Burns in *Prospice*, and a pamphlet on Post-War British drama for the English Association. **Essay:** Gregory Motton.

HAYMAN, Carole. Actress, writer, and director. Has

acted at the Bristol Old Vic, The Traverse Theatre Workshop, Edinburgh, with Joint Stock Theatre Group, and in more than 20 productions at the Royal Court Theatre, London. Since 1980 has directed plays by Sue Townsend, Jane Thornton, Andrea Dunbar, and Sarah Daniels at the Royal Court, Soho Poly, and for Joint Stock. Associate director at the Royal Court, 1986–87. Author of *Letters from Kim* (radio play), 1986, *All the Best Kim*, 1988, *Ladies of Letters*, 1991, *Rides* (television series), 1992–93. Editor, with Dale Spender, of *How the Vote Was Won and Other Suffragette Plays*, 1985.

HAYMAN, Ronald. Freelance writer and director. Author of *Techniques of Acting*, *The Set-Up: An Anatomy of British Theatre*, *British Theatre since 1955*, *Theatre and Anti-Theatre*, *Fassbinder*, *Film-maker*, studies of Beckett, Pinter, Osborne, Arden, Whiting, Robert Bolt, Wesker, Miller, Albee, Stoppard, Ionesco, Leavis, Artaud, Tolstoy, and Sylvia Plath, biographies of Kafka, Brecht, de Sade, Sartre, Nietzsche, John Gielgud, and Proust, and the radio series, *Such Rotten Luck*, 1989, 1991. Director of plays by Peter Handke, Martin Walser, Rainer Werner Fassbinder, and others. **Essays:** Ted Allan; David Caute; Nick Darke; Donald Howarth; Doris Lessing; David Pinner.

HERN, Nick. Publisher of Nick Hern Books since 1988. Lecturer in drama, University of Hull, 1967–72, University of Glasgow, 1972–74, and drama editor, Methuen, 1974–88.

HIGGINS, Dick. Freelance writer and publisher. Author of plays for stage, screen, and radio, and more than 40 books, including *Jefferson's Birthday/Postface*, 1964, *Die fabelhafte Geträume von Taifun-Willi*, 1969, *Le petit cirque au fin du monde*, 1973, *A Dialectic of Centuries: Notes Towards a Theory of the New Arts*, 1978, *Selected Early Works*, 1982, *Horizons: The Poetics and Theory of the Intermedia*, 1983, and *Pattern Poetry: Guide to an Unknown Literature*, 1988. Artist: individual exhibitions in Europe and the U.S.A. since 1973. **Essay:** Jackson Mac Low.

HILL, Errol. See his own entry. **Essay:** Amiri Baraka.

HIRSCH, Foster. Professor of film, Brooklyn College, New York. Author of *Harold Prince and the American Musical Theatre*, *Acting Hollywood Style*, and books on the Actors Studio, Laurence Olivier, Williams, Albee, O'Neill, film noir, George Kelly, Elizabeth Taylor, Edward G. Robinson, Woody Allen, Joseph Losey, and forthcoming studies of the Schuberts and American theatre in the 1920's. **Essay:** George Abbott.

HOBSON, Harold. Special writer for the *Sunday Times*, London. Author of *The First Three Years of the War*, 1942, *The Devil in Woodford Wells* (novel), 1946, *Theatre*, 1948, *Theatre II*, 1950, *Verdict at Midnight*, 1952, *The Theatre Now*, 1953, *The French Theatre of Today*, 1953, *Ralph Richardson*, 1958, *The French Theatre since 1830*, 1978, *Indirect Journey* (autobiography), 1978, and *Theatre in Britain: A Personal View*, 1984. Editor of five volumes of *International Theatre Annual*. Knighted 1977. **Essay:** Charles Dyer.

HOFFMAN, William M. See his own entry. **Essays:** Michael T. Smith; David Starkweather.

HUERTA, Jorge A. Professor of drama, University of California, San Diego. Author of *A Bibliography of Chicano and Mexican Dance, Drama, and Music*, 1971, *Chicano*

Theater: Themes and Forms, 1982, and many articles. Editor of *El Teatro de la Esperanza: An Anthology of Chicano Drama*, 1973, and *Necessary Theatre: Six Plays About the Chicano Experience*, 1989. Producer and director of several plays. **Essay:** Luis Valdez.

INNES, Christopher. Professor of English, York University, Toronto, Ontario. Author of *Erwin Piscator's Political Theatre*, 1972, *Modern German Drama*, 1979, *Holy Theatre: Ritual and the Avant Garde*, 1981, *Edward Gordon Craig*, 1983, *Modern British Drama: 1890–1990*, 1992, *Avant Garde Theatre: 1892–1992*, 1992, and articles on drama and theatre. General editor of the Directors in Perspective series for Cambridge University Press, co-editor of *Modern Drama*, and member of the editorial board of the *Cambridge Guide to World Theatre*. **Essays:** Michael Frayn; Pam Gems; Robert M. Wilson.

IROBI, Esiaba. Senior lecturer, School of Media, Critical and Creative Arts, Liverpool John Moores University. Author of articles and books including *Politics and Aesthetics in West African Cinema*, 1993. **Essays:** Matsemela Manaka; Maishe Maponya; Mbongeni Ngema; John Ruganda.

ISTEL, John. Freelance writer, editor and playwright. Has worked as assistant editor of *American Theatre* magazine and associate editor for Back Stage Books. Has contributed articles and reviews to the *Village Voice*, *American Theatre*, *Mother Jones*, and the *Brooklyn Free Press*. **Essays:** Darrah Cloud; Richard Greenberg; Joan M. Schenkar; John Steppling.

JENNER, C. Lee. Freelance writer, New York. **Essays:** William M. Hoffman (with Michael T. Smith); Richard Wesley.

KAUFFMANN, Stanley. Visiting professor of drama, City University of New York Graduate Center; film critic, *New Republic*. Author of several books of film criticism, including *A World of Film*, 1966, *Figures of Light*, 1971, *Living Images*, 1975, *Before My Eyes*, 1980, and *Field of View*, 1986, theatre criticism—*Persons of the Drama*, 1976, and *Theater Criticisms*, 1984—and *Albums of Early Life* (memoirs), 1980.

KELLY, Veronica. Senior lecturer in English, University of Queensland, Brisbane; editor (with Richard Fotheringham) of *Australasian Drama Studies* since 1982. Author of *Louis Nowra*, 1987, and articles on contemporary Australian drama for *Australasian Drama Studies*, *Kunapipi*, *Southerly*, and other periodicals. Editor of Garnet Walch's *Australia Felix; or, Harlequin, Laughing Jackass and the Magic Bat*, 1988. **Essays:** Michael Gow; Louis Nowra.

KEMP, David E. Head of the Drama Department, Queen's University, Kingston, Ontario; also actor, writer, and director. Author of the book, *A Different Drummer*, and the performance piece, *A Child Growing Up*. **Essay:** Ronald Harwood.

KENDLE, Burton S. Professor of English, Roosevelt University, Chicago. Author of articles on D.H. Lawrence, John Cheever, William March, Tennessee Williams, Paul Bowles, and other writers, and on screenwriting. **Essays:** Alan Bennett; James Leo Herlihy.

KERJAN, Liliane. Professor of American studies and vice-president, University of Rennes II. Author of *Albee*, 1971, *Le*

Théâtre d'Edward Albee, 1978, *L'Égalité aux États-Unis, Mythes et Réalités*, 1991, and numerous articles on American theatre and law. **Essay:** Edward Albee.

KEYSSAR, Helene. Associate professor of communications and drama, University of California, San Diego. Author of *The Curtain and the Veil: Strategies in Black Drama*, 1981, *Feminist Theatre*, 1985, (with Vladimir Pozner) *Remembering War: A U.S.-Soviet Dialogue*, 1990, *Robert Altman's America*, 1991, and articles in *Educational Theatre Journal*, *Prospects*, and other journals. Has directed and acted with the Eureka Ensemble and other groups. **Essays:** Charles Gordone; Murray Schisgal.

KHAN, Naseem. Freelance writer; member of the editorial board, *Drama*, London. Author of *The Arts Britain Ignores: The Arts of Ethnic Minorities in Britain*, 1976, and many articles and reviews.

KING, Bruce. Adjunct professor of English, University of Guelph, Ontario; general editor of the series "Modern Dramatists" and "English Dramatists". Formerly professor and visiting professor of English at universities in the United States, Canada, Scotland, France, Israel, Nigeria, and New Zealand. Author of *Dryden's Major Plays*, 1966, *Marvell's Allegorical Poetry*, 1977, *The New English Literatures: Cultural Nationalism in a Changing World*, 1980, *History of Seventeenth Century English Literature*, 1988, *Modern Indian Poetry in English*, 1987/1989, *Coriolanus*, 1989, *Three Indian Poets: Ezekiel, Ramanujan and Moraes*, 1991, and *V.S. Naipaul*, 1993. Editor of *Twentieth Century Interpretations of "All for Love"*, 1968, *Dryden's Mind and Art*, 1969, *Introduction to Nigerian Literature*, 1971, *Literatures of the World in English*, 1974, *A Celebration of Black and African Writing*, 1976, *West Indian Literature*, 1979, *Contemporary American Theatre*, 1991, *The Commonwealth Novel Since 1960*, 1991, and *The Later Fiction of Nadine Gordimer*, 1993. **Essays:** Francis Ebejer; Yulisa Amadu Maddy; Trevor D. Rhone; George F. Walker.

KITCHIN, Laurence. Former professor of liberal arts, City University of New York; has taught at Bristol, Tufts, Stanford, and Simon Fraser universities. Author of *Len Hutton*, 1953, *Three on Trial*, 1959, *Mid-Century Drama*, 1960 (revised 1962), *Drama in the Sixties*, 1966, and numerous radio scripts.

KLAUS, H. Gustav. Part-time professor of English, University of Osnabrück, Germany. Former visiting professor, University of Queensland and University of Edinburgh. Author of *Caldwell in Kontext*, 1978, and *The Literature of Labour*, 1985. Editor of *The Socialist Novel in Britain*, 1982, *The Rise of Socialist Fiction 1880–1914*, 1987, and *Tramps, Workmates and Revolutionaries*, 1991. **Essays:** Shelagh Delaney; Trevor Griffiths.

KOSTELANETZ, Richard. Writer and artist. Author of radio plays, several books of poetry (most recently *Arenas Fields Pitches Turfs*, 1982), collections of short stories (most recently *More Short Fictions*, 1980, and *Epiphanies*, 1983), volumes of experimental prose (*Aftertexts/Prose Pieces*, 1986), and critical works including *The Theatre of Mixed-Means*, 1968, *The End of Intelligent Writing*, 1974, *Twenties in the Sixties*, 1979, *The Old Poetries and the New*, 1981, *The Old Fictions and the New*, 1986, *On Innovative Music(ian)s*, 1989, *The New Poetries and Some Old*, 1991, *On Innovative Art(ist)s*, 1992, and *On Innovative Performance(s)*, 1993.

Editor of many collections and anthologies of experimental writing. Visual poetry and related language art exhibited at galleries and universities since 1975. **Essays:** Robert Hivnor; Kenneth Koch.

KUHN, John G.   Professor of English and theater, and director of theater, Rosemont College, Pennsylvania. **Essays:** María Irene Fornés; Milcha Sánchez-Scott.

LANGE, Bernd-Peter.   Professor of English, University of Oldenburg, Germany. Former editor of *Gulliver* and *German-English Yearbook.* Author of *Charles Dickens*, 1969, *George Orwell*, 1975, *The Theory of Genres*, 1979, *Orwell, "1984"*, 1982, *Cultural Studies*, 1984, *The Spanish Civil War in British and American Literature*, 1988, *Classics in Cultural Criticism 1: Britain*, 1990, and *Contemporaries in Cultural Criticism*, 1991. **Essay:** Steve Gooch.

LAWLEY, Paul.   Senior lecturer in English, University of Plymouth, Exmouth, Devon. Author of essays and reviews in *Journal of Beckett Studies, Modern Drama, Modern Fiction Studies, Theatre Journal, Modern Language Review,* and of chapters in *The Cambridge Companion to Beckett Studies* and *"Make Sense Who May": Essays on Samuel Beckett's Later Works.* **Essays:** Brian Clark; David Edgar; Ron Hutchinson; Terry Johnson; Frank McGuinness; Bill Morrison; Billy Roche; David Rudkin; Nigel Williams; Nicholas Wright.

LEECH, Michael T.   Freelance writer. Author of *Italy*, 1974 (revised 1987), *Amsterdam*, 1985, *Exploring Rural Italy*, 1988 and *Essential Kenya*, 1991. **Essay:** Jerome Lawrence and Robert E. Lee.

LLOYD, Matthew.   Associate director, Hampstead Theatre, London. Former literary manager, Hampstead and Bush theatres. Editor of *First Run 3*, 1991. **Essays:** John Clifford; Chris Hannan; Stephen Jeffreys.

LONDRÉ, Felicia Hardison.   Curators' professor of theatre, University of Missouri, Kansas City; dramaturg for Missouri Repertory Theatre. Author of *Tennessee Williams*, 1979, *Tom Stoppard*, 1981, *Federico García Lorca*, 1984, *The History of World Theatre, 2*, 1991, and articles on continental European and American theatre history for essay-collections, casebooks, and various journals including *Theatre Research International, Theatre History Studies, Theatre Journal, Theater Week, Slavic and East European Arts, Studies in Popular Culture,* and *Comparative Drama.* **Essays:** William Hauptman; Tom Stoppard.

LONEY, Glenn.   Professor Emeritus of theatre, City University of New York; secretary, New York Outer Critics Circle, American Theatre Critics Association, International Theatre Critics Association, and Music Critics Association; editor of *Art Deco News, The Modernist,* contributing editor, *Theatre Crafts International, Dramatics, Theatre Week, Western European Stages,* associate editor, *Opera Monthly,* founder-editor of *Arts Archive,* U.S. critic and representative, *New Theatre Quarterly.* Author or editor of many books, including *The Shakespeare Complex*, 1972, *Peter Brook's Royal Shakespeare Company Production of A Midsummer Night's Dream*, 1974, *The House of Mirth: The Play of the Novel*, 1980, *Your Future in the Performing Arts*, 1980, *Twentieth-Century Theatre* (chronology), 2 vols., 1983, *California Gold-Rush Plays*, 1983, *Musical Theatre in America*, 1984, *Unsung Genius: Jack Cole*, 1984, *Staging Shakespeare: Seminars on Production Problems*, 1990, and articles and

reviews in *Opera News, Dance, Stages, Theatre Crafts, Performing Arts Journal,* and other journals. **Essays:** William Alfred; William Mastrosimone; Neil Simon.

MacDONALD, James.   Fellow in drama, University of Exeter, and play-reader for Northcott Theatre, Exeter. Formerly associate editor of *The Freethinker.* Reviewer and author of articles on humanism and the arts for *The Freethinker*, 1977–81. **Essay:** David Storey.

MAGRUDER, James.   Resident dramaturg, Center Stage, Baltimore, Maryland. Former literary manager of the La Jolla Playhouse. Author of plays and adaptations including *Nesteggs for Armageddon, Turcaret, The Triumph of Love,* and *The Sinking of the Titanic,* and of articles and theatre criticism in *Theater, American Theatre,* and *The Village Voice.* **Essays:** Charles Busch; Eric Overmyer; Keith Reddin.

MARCUS, Frank.   See his own entry. **Essays:** Maureen Duffy; David Mowat.

MARKHAM, E.A.   Freelance writer. Author of several books of poetry—*The Lamp*, 1978, *Pierrot*, 1979, *Love Poems*, 1979, *Games and Penalties*, 1980, *Human Rites*, 1984, *Living in Disguise*, 1986, *Lambchops in Papua/New Guinea*, 1986, and *Towards the End of the Century*, 1989—*Love, Politics, and Food*, 1982, and *Something Unusual* (stories), 1986. Editor of *Hinterland*, 1989. **Essays:** Douglas Archibald; Barry Reckord.

MARKUS, Thomas B.   Artistic director, Theatre by the Sea, Portsmouth, New Hampshire. Author of *The Professional Actor: From Audition to Performance*, 1980, and essays on Genet and Albee. Has been a director and actor in New York and Hollywood. **Essays:** Ron Cowen; Martin Duberman.

MARRANCA, Bonnie.   Publisher and editor, with Gautam Dasgupta, *Performing Arts Journal* and Performing Arts Journal Publications, New York. Author of *American Playwrights: A Critical Survey,* with Dasgupta , 2 vols., 1981, *Theatre-writings*, 1984, and numerous essays. Editor of *The Theatre of Images*, 1977, *American Dreams: The Imagination of Sam Shepard*, 1981, *American Garden Writing*, 1988, *Hudson Valley Lives*, 1991, and *Interculturalism and Performance*, 1991.

MARTIN, John.   Artistic director, Pan Project, London. **Essay:** Girish Karnad.

McCALLUM, John.   Senior lecturer in theatre studies and director of the Australian Theatre Studies Centre, University of New South Wales, Kensington. Author of many articles on recent Australian drama. **Essay:** Ray Lawler.

McCORMACK, Thomas J.   Chair of St. Martin's Press, New York; director of Macmillan Publishers, London. Author of the play *American Roulette*, 1969, and *The Fiction Editor, the Novel, and the Novelist*, 1988. Editor of *Afterwords*, 1969. **Essay:** Jason Miller.

McGILLICK, Paul.   Lecturer in applied linguistics, University of Sydney; theatre critic for *Australian Financial Review.* Formerly editor of *New Theatre Australia.* Author of *Jack Hibberd*, 1988, and numerous monographs and articles on theatre and the visual arts. **Essay:** Jack Hibberd.

McGUINNESS, Arthur E.   Professor of English,

University of California, Davis. Author of *Henry Home, Lord Kames*, 1970, *George Fitzmaurice*, 1975, and articles in *Eire-Ireland*, *Irish University Review*, *Themes in Drama*, *Studies in Short Fiction*, *Texas Studies in Literature and Language*, and *Studies in Scottish Literature*. **Essay:** M.J. Molloy.

McNAUGHTON, Howard.   Reader in English, University of Canterbury, Christchurch, New Zealand. Author of *Bruce Mason*, 1976, *New Zealand Drama*, 1981, and the section on the novel in *The Oxford History of New Zealand Literature* (forthcoming). Editor of *Contemporary New Zealand Plays*, 1976, and *James K. Baxter: Collected Plays*, 1982. **Essays:** John Bowen; Barry Collins; Rosalyn Drexler; Ron Elisha; Paul Foster; Peter Gill; Clem Gorman; Roger Hall; Tony Harrison; David Mamet; Greg McGee; Percy Mtwa; Marsha Norman; Megan Terry.

MESERVE, Walter J.   Distinguished professor of theatre and English, Graduate School, City University of New York; co-editor of *Journal of American Drama and Theatre*. Formerly professor of theatre and drama and director of the Institute for American Studies, Indiana University, Bloomington. Author of *An Outline History of American Drama*, 1965, *Robert Sherwood: Reluctant Moralist*, 1970, *An Emerging Entertainment: The Drama of the American People to 1828*, 1977, *American Drama* (vol. 8 of the Revels History), with others, 1977, *American Drama to 1900: A Guide to Reference Sources*, 1980, *Heralds of Promise: The Drama of the American People During the Age of Jackson 1829–1849*, 1986. Editor of *The Complete Plays of William Dean Howells*, 1960, *Discussions of Modern American Drama*, 1966, *American Satiric Comedies*, 1969, *Modern Drama from Communist China*, 1970, *The Rise of Silas Lapham by Howells*, 1971, *Studies in Death of a Salesman*, 1972, and *Modern Literature from China*, 1974. Compiler of *Who's Where in the American Theatre*, 1990, and (with M.A. Meserve) *A Chronological Outline of World Theatre*, 1992. **Essays:** George Axelrod; Herb Gardner; William Hanley; Arthur Laurents; Dennis J. Reardon.

MILNE, Geoffrey.   Lecturer in drama, La Trobe University, Bundoora, Victoria, and drama critic for the Australian Broadcasting Corporation (radio). Author of numerous articles on Australian dramatists and theatre organisations, contributor to *The Australian Encyclopaedia*, 1988, and to the forthcoming *Companion to the Theatre and Dance in Australia*. **Essay:** Barry Dickins.

MITCHELL, Louis D.   Associate professor of English, University of Scranton, Pennsylvania. Author of songs and lyrics for *Star of the Morning*, 1971, and many articles in *Theatre Notebook*, *Eighteenth Century Studies*, *Crisis*, and other journals. **Essays:** Ossie Davis; Errol Hill.

MITCHELL, Tony.   Lecturer in performance studies, University of Technology, Sydney. Author of *Dario Fo: People's Court Jester*, 1986, *File on Brenton*, 1987, *File on Dario Fo*, 1989. **Essay:** Tes Lyssiotis.

MOE, Christian H.   Professor and chair of theater, Southern Illinois University at Carbondale; member of the advisory board, Institute of Outdoor Drama; member of the Dramatists Guild. Author or co-author of *Creating Historical Drama*, 1965, an essay on Nathaniel West, and several adult dramas and plays for youth. Co-editor of *Six New Plays for Children*, 1971, and *Eight Plays for Youth: Varied Theatrical

Experiences for Stage and Study, 1991. **Essays:** Christopher Durang; William Gibson; Dusty Hughes; Romulus Linney; James McLure; John Ford Noonan; John Patrick; John Pielmeier; Bernard Pomerance; David Williamson.

MURRAY, Christopher.   Statutory lecturer in English, University College, Dublin; member of the executive board, *Irish University Review*. Author of *Robert William Elliston, Manager*, 1975. Editor of *St. Stephen's Green* (an Irish Restoration comedy), 1980, *Selected Plays of Lennox Robinson*, 1982, and (with Masara Sepine), *Yeats and the Noh: A Comparative Study*, 1990. **Essays:** Brian Friel; Eugene McCabe; Tom Murphy.

NADLER, Paul.   Adjunct lecturer in theatre, Hunter College, New York. Author of essays in *Black Women in the United States: An Historical Encyclopedia*, 1991, *The Bloomsbury Theatre Guide*, 1991, and the play, *Scrambles Amongst the Alps*. **Essay:** Steve Tesich.

NIGHTINGALE, Benedict.   Freelance writer; drama critic, *New Statesman*, London, 1969–86; professor of English, University of Michigan, Ann Arbor, 1986–87. Author of *An Introduction to Fifty Modern British Plays*, 1982 (as *A Reader's Guide to Fifty Modern British Plays*, 1982), and *Fifth Row Center: A Critic's Year On and Off Broadway*, 1986. **Essays:** Paul Ableman; Beverley Cross; John Hopkins.

OBAFEMI, Olu.   Professor and head of the Modern European Languages Department, University of Ilorin, Nigeria. Author of *Revolutionary Aesthetics in Recent Nigerian Theatre*, 1982, *Political Perspectives and Popular Theatre*, 1982, *Nigerian Writers and Nigerian Civil War*, 1992, and the plays, *The New Dawn*, 1986, *Nights of a Mystical Beast*, 1986, and *Suicide Syndrome*, 1988. Editor of the *Ilorin Journal of Language and Literature* and on the editorial board of *African Theatre Review*. **Essays:** Wale Ogunyemi; Zulu Sofola; Bode Sowande.

O'CONNOR, Garry.   Playwright and biographer. Author of *French Theatre Today*, 1975, *The Pursuit of Perfection* (biography of Maggie Teyte), 1979, *Darlings of the Gods: One Year in the Lives of Laurence Olivier and Vivien Leigh*, 1984, *Ralph Richardson: An Actor's Life*, revised edition 1986, *Sean O'Casey: A Life*, 1988, *The Mahabharata*, 1989, *Party of the Gods* (novel), 1990, *William Shakespeare: A Life*, 1991, and seven stage and radio plays, including *The Musicians*, *Semmelweis*, and *The Kingdom of Allemonde*. Editor of *Laurence Olivier: In Celebration*, 1987. **Essays:** Robert Bolt; Peter Nichols; Michael O'Neill and Jeremy Seabrook; Mike Stott.

O'CONNOR, Marion.   Lecturer in English, University of Kent, Canterbury. Author of *William Poel and the Elizabethan Stage Society*, 1987. Editor (with Jean E. Howard), *Shakespeare Reproduced: The Text in History and Ideology*, 1987. **Essay:** Tom Gallacher.

OKAGBUE, Osita.   Lecturer in theatre studies, School of Humanities and Performance, University of Plymouth, Exmouth, Devon. Author of articles on theatre in *Maske Unikothurne*, *Okike*, and *New Literatures Review*. **Essays:** James Ene Henshaw; Martin Owusu; Barney Simon; Wole Soyinka; Edgar Nkosi White.

O'LEARY, John.   Freelance writer, London. **Essay:** Mike Leigh.

Editor of many collections and anthologies of experimental writing. Visual poetry and related language art exhibited at galleries and universities since 1975. **Essays:** Robert Hivnor; Kenneth Koch.

KUHN, John G. Professor of English and theater, and director of theater, Rosemont College, Pennsylvania. **Essays:** María Irene Fornés; Milcha Sánchez-Scott.

LANGE, Bernd-Peter. Professor of English, University of Oldenburg, Germany. Former editor of *Gulliver* and *German-English Yearbook.* Author of *Charles Dickens*, 1969, *George Orwell*, 1975, *The Theory of Genres*, 1979, *Orwell, "1984"*, 1982, *Cultural Studies*, 1984, *The Spanish Civil War in British and American Literature*, 1988, *Classics in Cultural Criticism 1: Britain*, 1990, and *Contemporaries in Cultural Criticism*, 1991. **Essay:** Steve Gooch.

LAWLEY, Paul. Senior lecturer in English, University of Plymouth, Exmouth, Devon. Author of essays and reviews in *Journal of Beckett Studies, Modern Drama, Modern Fiction Studies, Theatre Journal, Modern Language Review*, and of chapters in *The Cambridge Companion to Beckett Studies* and *"Make Sense Who May": Essays on Samuel Beckett's Later Works.* **Essays:** Brian Clark; David Edgar; Ron Hutchinson; Terry Johnson; Frank McGuinness; Bill Morrison; Billy Roche; David Rudkin; Nigel Williams; Nicholas Wright.

LEECH, Michael T. Freelance writer. Author of *Italy*, 1974 (revised 1987), *Amsterdam*, 1985, *Exploring Rural Italy*, 1988 and *Essential Kenya*, 1991. **Essay:** Jerome Lawrence and Robert E. Lee.

LLOYD, Matthew. Associate director, Hampstead Theatre, London. Former literary manager, Hampstead and Bush theatres. Editor of *First Run 3*, 1991. **Essays:** John Clifford; Chris Hannan; Stephen Jeffreys.

LONDRÉ, Felicia Hardison. Curators' professor of theatre, University of Missouri, Kansas City; dramaturg for Missouri Repertory Theatre. Author of *Tennessee Williams*, 1979, *Tom Stoppard*, 1981, *Federico García Lorca*, 1984, *The History of World Theatre, 2*, 1991, and articles on continental European and American theatre history for essay-collections, casebooks, and various journals including *Theatre Research International, Theatre History Studies, Theatre Journal, Theater Week, Slavic and East European Arts, Studies in Popular Culture*, and *Comparative Drama.* **Essays:** William Hauptman; Tom Stoppard.

LONEY, Glenn. Professor Emeritus of theatre, City University of New York; secretary, New York Outer Critics Circle, American Theatre Critics Association, International Theatre Critics Association, and Music Critics Association; editor of *Art Deco News, The Modernist*, contributing editor, *Theatre Crafts International, Dramatics, Theatre Week, Western European Stages*, associate editor, *Opera Monthly*, founder-editor of *Arts Archive*, U.S. critic and representative, *New Theatre Quarterly.* Author or editor of many books, including *The Shakespeare Complex*, 1972, *Peter Brook's Royal Shakespeare Company Production of A Midsummer Night's Dream*, 1974, *The House of Mirth: The Play of the Novel*, 1980, *Your Future in the Performing Arts*, 1980, *Twentieth-Century Theatre* (chronology), 2 vols., 1983, *California Gold-Rush Plays*, 1983, *Musical Theatre in America*, 1984, *Unsung Genius: Jack Cole*, 1984, *Staging Shakespeare: Seminars on Production Problems*, 1990, and articles and reviews in *Opera News, Dance, Stages, Theatre Crafts, Performing Arts Journal*, and other journals. **Essays:** William Alfred; William Mastrosimone; Neil Simon.

MacDONALD, James. Fellow in drama, University of Exeter, and play-reader for Northcott Theatre, Exeter. Formerly associate editor of *The Freethinker.* Reviewer and author of articles on humanism and the arts for *The Freethinker*, 1977–81. **Essay:** David Storey.

MAGRUDER, James. Resident dramaturg, Center Stage, Baltimore, Maryland. Former literary manager of the La Jolla Playhouse. Author of plays and adaptations including *Nesteggs for Armageddon, Turcaret, The Triumph of Love*, and *The Sinking of the Titanic*, and of articles and theatre criticism in *Theater, American Theatre*, and *The Village Voice.* **Essays:** Charles Busch; Eric Overmyer; Keith Reddin.

MARCUS, Frank. See his own entry. **Essays:** Maureen Duffy; David Mowat.

MARKHAM, E.A. Freelance writer. Author of several books of poetry—*The Lamp*, 1978, *Pierrot*, 1979, *Love Poems*, 1979, *Games and Penalties*, 1980, *Human Rites*, 1984, *Living in Disguise*, 1986, *Lambchops in Papua/New Guinea*, 1986, and *Towards the End of the Century*, 1989—*Love, Politics, and Food*, 1982, and *Something Unusual* (stories), 1986. Editor of *Hinterland*, 1989. **Essays:** Douglas Archibald; Barry Reckord.

MARKUS, Thomas B. Artistic director, Theatre by the Sea, Portsmouth, New Hampshire. Author of *The Professional Actor: From Audition to Performance*, 1980, and essays on Genet and Albee. Has been a director and actor in New York and Hollywood. **Essays:** Ron Cowen; Martin Duberman.

MARRANCA, Bonnie. Publisher and editor, with Gautam Dasgupta, *Performing Arts Journal* and Performing Arts Journal Publications, New York. Author of *American Playwrights: A Critical Survey*, with Dasgupta , 2 vols., 1981, *Theatre-writings*, 1984, and numerous essays. Editor of *The Theatre of Images*, 1977, *American Dreams: The Imagination of Sam Shepard*, 1981, *American Garden Writing*, 1988, *Hudson Valley Lives*, 1991, and *Interculturalism and Performance*, 1991.

MARTIN, John. Artistic director, Pan Project, London. **Essay:** Girish Karnad.

McCALLUM, John. Senior lecturer in theatre studies and director of the Australian Theatre Studies Centre, University of New South Wales, Kensington. Author of many articles on recent Australian drama. **Essay:** Ray Lawler.

McCORMACK, Thomas J. Chair of St. Martin's Press, New York; director of Macmillan Publishers, London. Author of the play *American Roulette*, 1969, and *The Fiction Editor, the Novel, and the Novelist*, 1988. Editor of *Afterwords*, 1969. **Essay:** Jason Miller.

McGILLICK, Paul. Lecturer in applied linguistics, University of Sydney; theatre critic for *Australian Financial Review.* Formerly editor of *New Theatre Australia.* Author of *Jack Hibberd*, 1988, and numerous monographs and articles on theatre and the visual arts. **Essay:** Jack Hibberd.

McGUINNESS, Arthur E. Professor of English,

British Theatre (with Kenneth Richards), 1971, *The Eighteenth-Century English Stage* (with Richards), 1973, *Lord Byron's Family* by Malcolm Elwin, 1975, and *Plays* by Dion Boucicault, 1984. **Essay:** Martin Crimp.

TOMPKINS, Joanne. Lecturer in drama, La Trobe University, Bundoora, Victoria. Author (with Helen Gilbert) *Re-acting (to) Empire: Performance and Post-Colonial Drama*, 1993. **Essay:** Judith Thompson.

TREWIN, J.C. Late drama critic, *Illustrated London News*, *The Lady*, and the Birmingham *Post*. Author of more than 40 books, including *Mr. Macready*, 1955, *Benson and the Bensonians*, 1960, *Shakespeare on the English Stage 1900–1964*, 1964, *Peter Brook: A Biography*, 1971, *Theatre Bedside Book*, 1974, *The Edwardian Theatre*, 1976, *Going to Shakespeare*, 1978, *Companion to Shakespeare*, 1981, and *Five and Eighty Hamlets*, 1987; co-devised *Farjeon Reviewed*, 1975. Editor of *Plays of the Year* series, 1949–81, and many other books. O.B.E. 1981. Died 1990.

TURNER, Darwin T. University of Iowa Foundation professor of English, and head of Afro-American world studies, University of Iowa, Iowa City, Author of *Katharsis* (poetry), 1964, *Nathaniel Hawthorne's The Scarlet Letter*, 1967, *Afro-American Writers*, 1970, *In a Minor Chord: Three Afro-American Writers*, 1971, and *The Teaching of Literature by Afro-American Writers*, 1972. Editor of several books, including *Images of the Negro in America*, 1965, *Black American Literature*, 3 vols., 1969, *Black Drama in America*, 1971, *Voices from the Black Experience*, 1972, *The Wayward and the Seeking: A Collection of Writings by Jean Toomer*, 1980, *The Art of Slave Narrative*, 1982, and *Cane: An Authoritative Text, Backgrounds, and Criticism*, 1988. **Essay:** Douglas Turner Ward.

TURNER, Elaine. Lecturer in drama, University of Warwick; also teaches at Central School of Speech and Drama and the British American Drama Academy; member of the editorial board of *New Theatre Quarterly*. **Essays:** John Arden; Henry Livings; Louise Page; Peter Whelan.

WANDOR, Michelene. See her own entry. **Essay:** Mary O'Malley.

WARDLE, Irving. Drama critic, *The Times*, London. Author of *The Houseboy* (play), 1974, and *The Theatres of George Devine*, 1978.

WATERMEIER, Daniel J. Professor of theatre and drama, University of Toledo, Ohio. Formerly, visiting professor of drama, University of Southern California, Los Angeles. Author of articles and reviews on 19th-century actors, American drama, and Shakespearian production for *Theatre History Studies*, *Theatre Research International*, *Shakespeare Quarterly*, and *The Cambridge Guide to World Theatre*, 1988. Editor of *Between Actor and Critic: Selected Letters of Edwin Booth to William Winter*, 1971, *Edwin Booth's Performances: The Mary Isabella Stone Commentaries*, 1990, and the forthcoming international guide to Shakespeare companies and festivals. Associate editor of *Shakespeare Around the Globe: A Guide to Notable Postwar Revivals*, 1986. **Essay:** Robertson Davies.

WEALES, Gerald. Professor Emeritus of English, University of Pennsylvania, Philadelphia; drama critic for the *Reporter* and *Commonweal*. Author of *Religion in Modern English Drama*, 1961, *American Drama since World War II*, 1962, *A Play and Its Parts*, 1964, *Tennessee Williams*, 1965, *The Jumping-Off Place: American Drama in the 1960's*, 1969, *Clifford Odets*, 1971 (revised 1985), and *Canned Goods as Caviar: American Film Comedy in the 1930's*, 1985. Editor of several collections of plays and essays and of *The Complete Plays of William Wycherley*, 1966. **Essays:** Phillip Hayes Dean; Jules Feiffer; David Henry Hwang; Arthur Kopit; Ronald Ribman.

WETZSTEON, Ross. Theater editor, *Village Voice*, New York. Editor of *The Obie Winners*, 1980, and *Fool for Love and Other Plays* by Sam Shepard, 1984.

YOUNG, B.A. Drama critic, *Financial Times*, London, 1964–1991. Author of several radio and television plays, and books including *Cabinet Pudding* (novel), 1967, *The Colonists from Space* (novel), 1979, *The Mirror Up to Nature: A Review of the Theatre 1964–1982*, 1982, and *The Rattigan Version* (biography), 1986. **Essay:** Frank Marcus.

SCHIFF, Ellen.   Professor Emeritus of French and comparative literature, North Adams State College, Massachusetts. Author of *From Stereotype to Metaphor: The Jew in Contemporary Drama*, 1982, and articles in the New York *Times*, *Massachusetts Review*, *Modern Drama*, and chapters in *Holocaust Studies Annual*, *Anti-Semitism in American History*, and *Handbook of American Jewish Literature*. **Essay:** Emily Mann.

SCHNEIDER, Alan.   Late professor of drama, University of California, San Diego. Director of Broadway and off-Broadway plays by Albee, Beckett, Edward Bond, Grass, Preston Jones, Pinter, Saroyan, Ted Whitehead, Tennessee Williams, Elie Wiesel, and Lanford Wilson. Died 1984.

SCULLION, Adrienne.   Lecturer in drama studies, the Samuel Beckett Centre, Trinity College, Dublin. **Essay:** Liz Lochhead.

SHRAGGE, Elaine.   Freelance writer, San Francisco. **Essay:** Rochelle Owens.

SIDNELL, Michael.   Professor, Graduate Centre for the Study of Drama, University of Toronto; actor and director. Co-author of *Druid Craft* (on Yeats), 1971, and *The Secret Rose*, 1981, and author of *Dances of Death: A History of the London Group Theatre*, 1984, *Mode Narratif et Mode Dramatique*, 1992, and articles on Irish and theatre subjects. **Essay:** Beverley Simons.

SMITH, Christopher.   Senior lecturer in French and comparative literature, University of East Anglia. Author of *Jean Anouilh: Life Work and Criticism*; *Alabaster, Bikinis and Calvados*, 1985; and numerous articles on drama and translation. Editor of Jean de Taille's *Dramatic Works*, Jacques de la Taille's *Alexandre*, A. Montchrestien's *Two Tragedies*, and of the journal *Seventeenth-Century French Studies*. **Essays:** Keith Dewhurst; John Mortimer; G.F. Newman; Dennis Potter; Anne Ridler.

SMITH, Michael T.   See his own entry. **Essays:** George Birimisa; William M. Hoffman (with C. Lee Jenner); H.M. Koutoukas; Murray Mednick; Ronald Tavel.

SOGLIUZZO, A. Richard.   Theatre critic, historian, and professor of drama; assistant editor, *Theatre Annual*. Author of *Luigi Pirandello, Director*, 1982, and articles on Italian theatre, Arthur Miller, and Eugene O'Neill, in *A Handbook of Modern Drama*, *A History of the Theatre*, and in periodicals. **Essays:** Mario Fratti; Frank Gagliano.

SOUCHOTTE, Sandra.   Freelance journalist and theatre critic, Yellowknife, Northwest Territories, Canada. **Essay:** (with Constance Brissenden): Carol Bolt.

SPURLING, John.   See his own entry. **Essays:** Barry England; Stanley Eveling; David Halliwell.

STERN, Carol Simpson.   Professor and chair, Department of Performance Studies, Northwestern University, Evanston, Illinois; immediate past president of the American Association of University Professors. Author of articles and theatre and book reviews in *Victorian Studies*, *Literature in Performance*, and *British Mystery and Thriller Writers Since 1940*. Author, with Bruce Henderson, of *Performance: Texts and Contexts*, 1993. **Essays:** Eric Bogosian; Kenneth H. Brown; Caryl Churchill; James Goldman; Simon Gray; Iris Murdoch; Peter Shaffer.

STRACHAN, Alan.   Artistic director, Theatre of Comedy, London. Productions in London include *The Watched Pot* by Saki, 1970; *John Bull's Other Island*, 1971, and *Misalliance*, 1973, by Shaw; *The Old Boys* by William Trevor, 1971; *A Family and a Fortune* by Julian Mitchell, 1975; *Just Between Ourselves* by Alan Ayckbourn, 1977; devised and co-directed *Cowardy Custard*, 1972, *Cole*, 1974, *Shakespeare's People*, 1975, and *Yahoo*, 1976; at Greenwich Theatre 1978–1988: many new plays, including *An Audience Called Édouard* by David Pownall, *The Paranormalist* by Jonathan Gems, and *One of Us* by Robin Chapman, and revivals including *Private Lives* and *Present Laughter* by Noël Coward, and *A Streetcar Named Desire* and *The Glass Menagerie* by Tennessee Williams. **Essays:** George Furth; Larry Gelbart; Jonathan Gems; A.R. Gurney, Jr.; Richard Harris; Keith Johnstone; Craig Lucas; Ken Ludwig; Sharman MacDonald; Anthony Minghella; Bernard Slade; William Trevor; Peter Ustinov.

STYAN, J.L.   Franklyn Bliss Snyder Professor of English Literature, and professor of theatre (Emeritus), Northwestern University, Evanston, Illinois. Author of *The Elements of Drama*, 1960, *The Dark Comedy*, 1962 (revised 1968), *The Dramatic Experience*, 1965, *Shakespeare's Stagecraft*, 1967, *Chekhov in Performance*, 1971, *The Challenge of the Theatre*, 1972, *Drama, Stage and Audience*, 1975, *The Shakespeare Revolution*, 1977, *Modern Drama in Theory and Practice*, 3 vols., 1981, *Max Reinhardt*, 1982, *The State of Drama Study*, 1984, *All's Well That Ends Well* (*Shakespeare in Performance* series), 1984, and *Restoration Comedy in Performance*, 1986. **Essay:** Christopher Fry.

SYKES, Alrene.   Late senior lecturer in English, University of Queensland, Brisbane. Formerly editor in the Drama Department, Australian Broadcasting Commission. Author of *Harold Pinter*, 1970, and articles on modern drama and Australian fiction. Editor of *Five Plays for Radio* and four other anthologies of Australian plays. Died 1990. **Essay:** Alan Seymour.

TAUBMAN, Howard.   Drama critic, 1960–66, and critic at large, 1966–75, New York *Times*. Adviser to the Exxon Corporation on its "Theatre in America" series and other arts programs. Author of *The Making of American Theatre*, 1965, and several books on music.

TAYLOR, John Russell.   Art critic, *The Times*, London. Author of many books, including *Anger and After*, 1962 (revised 1969, as *The Angry Theatre*, 1962, revised 1969), *The Second Wave*, 1971, *Directors and Directions*, 1975, *Hitch: The Life and Work of Alfred Hitchcock*, 1978, *Strangers in Paradise*, 1981, and *Impressionist Dreams: The Artists and the World They Painted*, 1990, and studies of Pinter, David Storey, Peter Shaffer, Ingrid Bergman, Alec Guinness, Vivien Leigh, Orson Welles, Edward Wolfe, the television play, and various aspects of film and art. Editor of *Look Back in Anger: A Casebook*, 1968, and the film criticism of Graham Greene.

THOMSON, John.   Senior lecturer in English, Victoria University, Wellington. Author of *New Zealand Drama 1930–1980*, 1984. **Essay:** Joseph Musaphia.

THOMSON, Peter.   Professor of drama, University of Exeter, Devon. Author of *Brecht* (with Jan Needle), 1981, *Shakespeare's Theatre*, 1983, and *The Everyman Companion to the Theatre* (with Gāmini Salgādo), 1985. Editor of *Julius Caesar* by Shakespeare, 1970, *Essays on Nineteenth-Century*

OLIVA, Judy Lee. Assistant professor of theatre, University of Tennessee, Knoxville, and chair of the Theatre History Focus Group of the Association for Theatre in Higher Education. Author of *David Hare: Theatricalizing Politics*, 1990, essays in *Casebook on Howard Brenton*, 1992, *Dictionary of Stage Directors*, 1993, and articles in *Theatre Journal*, *Theater Three*, *Theatre Studies*, and *Journal of Dramatic Theory and Criticism*. **Essays:** Lee Blessing; Beth Henley; Alfred Uhry; Wendy Wasserstein.

OSBORN, M. Elizabeth. Freelance writer, editor and dramaturg. Editor, *On New Ground: Contemporary Hispanic-American Plays*, 1987, and *The Way We Live Now: American Plays and the AIDS Crisis*, 1990. Formerly book editor, Theatre Communications Group, New York. **Essays:** Constance S. Congdon; David Greenspan; Allan Havis; Tony Kushner; Eduardo Machado.

OVERMYER, Eric. See his own entry. **Essay:** Mac Wellman.

PAGE, Malcolm. Professor of English, Simon Fraser University, Burnaby, British Columbia. Author of *John Arden*, 1984, *Richard II* (critical study), 1987, and *Howards End* (critical study), 1992. Editor of *File on Arden*, 1985, *File on Stoppard*, 1986, *File on Shaffer*, 1987, *File on Osborne*, 1988, *File on Ayckbourn*, 1989, *File on Hare*, 1990. Co-editor (with Simon Trussler) of *File on Edgar*, 1991. **Essays:** Alan Ayckbourn; Peter Flannery; David Hare; Margaret Hollingsworth; Ann Jellicoe; Mustapha Matura; John Murrell; John Osborne; David Pownall.

PARKER, Dorothy. Associate professor of English, Victoria College, University of Toronto. Editor of *Modern American Drama: Williams, Miller, Albee, and Shepard*, 1986, and *Modern Drama*. **Essays:** David French; Erika Ritter.

PETZOLD, Roxana. Editor, Grove Weidenfeld, New York. **Essay:** JoAnne Akalaitis.

POUNTNEY, Rosemary. Lecturer in English, Jesus College, University of Oxford, and senior lecturer in drama, King Alfred's College, Winchester. Formerly a professional actress. Author of *Notes on "Waiting for Godot"*, 1981, *Theatre of Shadows: Samuel Beckett's Drama, 1956–76*, 1988, and articles and reviews on Beckett and contemporary theatre. **Essays:** Howard Brenton; N.F. Simpson.

RAYNOR, Henry. Schoolmaster and freelance writer. Author of *Joseph Haydn*, 1962, *Wagner*, 1970, *Radio and Television*, 1970, *A Social History of Music from the Middle Ages to Beethoven*, 1972, *Mahler*, 1975, *Music and Society since 1815*, 1976, *The Orchestra*, 1978, *Mozart*, 1978, and *Music in England*, 1980. **Essays:** Terence Frisby; Kevin Laffan; Johnny Speight.

READ, Leslie du S. Lecturer in drama, University of Exeter, Devon. Contributor to *The Cambridge Guide to World Theatre*, 1988, *The Cambridge Encyclopaedia*, 1990, and to the *Encyclopaedia of Literature and Criticism*, 1990. **Essay:** Robert Holman.

REILLY, John M. Professor of English, State University of New York, Albany. Author of many articles on Afro-American literature, popular crime writing and social fiction, and bibliographical essays in *Black American Writers*, 1978,

and *American Literary Scholarship*. Editor of *Twentieth-Century Interpretations of Invisible Man*, 1970, *Richard Wright: The Critical Reception*, 1978, and the reference book *Twentieth Century Crime and Mystery Writers*, 1980 (2nd edition 1985). **Essay:** Ed Bullins.

RICHARDS, Sandra L. Assistant professor of drama, and director of the Committee on Black Performing Arts, Stanford University, California. Author of the introduction to *Center Stage: An Anthology of Twenty-one Black American Plays*, 1981, and articles on Amiri Baraka, the actor Bert Williams, and Nigerian playwrights in *Theatre Journal*, *Mime*, and *San Francisco Theatre*. **Essays:** Charles Fuller; Femi Osofisan; Ola Rotimi; Ntozake Shange.

ROOSE-EVANS, James. Director, author, and founder of the Hampstead Theatre, London. Author of plays including *84 Charing Cross Road*, *Re:Joyce!*, *Cider with Rosie*, *Augustus*, radio documentaries including *The Female Messiah*, *The Third Adam*, a saga of seven books for children, *The Adventures of Odd and Elsewhere*, and *Directing a Play*, 1968, *Experimental Theatre from Stanislavsky to Peter Brook*, 1970, revised 1984 and 1989, *London Theatre: From the Globe to the National*, 1977, and a novel, *Inner Journey: Outer Journey*, 1987. Director of many plays, most recently works by Hugh Whitemore, Václav Havel, Anthony Stevens, Sean Mathias, Christopher Fry, and Pam Gems. **Essays:** James Forsyth; Peter Ransley; Colin Spencer.

SADLER, Geoff. Assistant librarian, Local Studies, Chesterfield, Derbyshire. Author of 18 western novels (as Jeff Sadler and Wes Calhoun), including, most recently, *Ghost Town Guns*, 1990, and *Headed North*, 1992 (as Sadler), and *Texas Nighthawks*, 1990 (as Calhoun), as well as the *Justus* trilogy of plantation novels (as Geoffrey Sadler), 1982, *Journey to Freedom*, (war-time memoir, with Antoni Snarski), 1990, and *Shirebrook: Birth of a Colliery* (with Ernest I. Roberts), 1991. Co-author of *Tom's Times*, co-operatively written play by Shirebrook Writers' Group, 1991. Editor, *Twentieth Century Western Writers*, 1991. **Essays:** Dannie Abse; Ray Cooney; Adrian Mitchell; Derek Walcott.

SAINER, Arthur. See his own entry. **Essays:** Israel Horovitz; Ruth Krauss; John Patrick Shanley; Stuart Sherman; George Tabori.

SCHECHNER, Richard. Founding director, the Performance Group, New York; professor of performance studies, New York University. Author of *Public Domain*, 1968, *Environmental Theatre*, 1973, *Theatres, Spaces, and Environments* (with Jerry N. Rojo and Brooks McNamara), 1975, *Essays in Performance Theory*, 1977, revised 1988, *The End of Humanism*, 1982, *Performative Circumstances*, 1983, and *Between Theater and Anthropology*, 1986. Joint editor of *Free Southern Theatre*, 1969, *Ritual, Play, and Performance*, 1976, and *By Means of Performance: Intercultural Studies of Theatre and Ritual*, 1990. Director for the Wooster Group.

SCHECHTER, Joel. Chair of the Theatre Arts Department, San Francisco State University, California. Former dramaturg and professor of dramatic criticism, Yale School of Drama, New Haven, Connecticut, and literary adviser, American Place Theatre, New York. Author of *Durov's Pig: Clowns, Politics and Theatre*, 1985, contributor to *American Theatre*, *The Drama Review*, *In These Times*, *The Nation*, the New York *Times*, *The Partisan Review*, and other journals. Editor of *Theater* magazine at Yale from 1977–1992 and guest editor of *Teatr* in Moscow, 1989.